RANDOM HOUSE ROGET'S

THESAURUS

Published by Ballantine Books:

RANDOM HOUSE WEBSTER'S DICTIONARY
RANDOM HOUSE ROGET'S THESAURUS
RANDOM HOUSE GUIDE TO GOOD WRITING
RANDOM HOUSE WEBSTER'S POWER VOCABULARY BUILDER
RANDOM HOUSE WEBSTER'S WORD MENU™
RANDOM HOUSE LATIN-AMERICAN SPANISH DICTIONARY
RANDOM HOUSE SPANISH-ENGLISH ENGLISH-SPANISH DICTIONARY
RANDOM HOUSE JAPANESE-ENGLISH ENGLISH-JAPANESE DICTIONARY
RANDOM HOUSE GERMAN-ENGLISH ENGLISH-GERMAN DICTIONARY
RANDOM HOUSE FRENCH-ENGLISH ENGLISH-FRENCH DICTIONARY

RANDOM HOUSE ROGET'S

THESAURUS

Fourth Edition

BALLANTINE BOOKS • NEW YORK

A Ballantine Book
Published by The Random House Publishing Group

Published in the United States by Ballantine Books, an imprint of The Random House Publishing Group, a division of Random House, Inc., New York, and simultaneously in Canada by Random House of Canada Limited, Toronto.

Originally published by Ballantine Books in somewhat different form as the *Random House Thesaurus* in 1998.

www.ballantinebooks.com

ISBN 0-345-44726-3

This edition published by arrangement with Reference & Information Publishing, Random House, Inc.

Manufactured in the United States of America

First Ballantine Books Edition: August 1992
Second Ballantine Books Edition: August 1996
Third Ballantine Books Edition: August 1998
Fourth Ballantine Books Edition: August 2001

OPM 9 8

CONTENTS

STAFF

Editor: Joyce O'Connor
Project Editor: Enid Pearsons
Database Manager: Constance A. Baboukis
Database Applications Manager: Helen Langone
Systems Consultant: Paul Hayslett, CowBay Software
Assistant Managing Editor: Beth E. Levy

Director of Production: Patricia W. Ehresmann
Associate Production Manager: Lisa J. Abelman
Designers: Charlotte Staub
Jennifer L. Dowling, Seaside Press

Editorial Director Emeritus: Sol Steinmetz
Editorial Director: Wendalyn Nichols
Publisher Emeritas: Charles M. Levine
Publisher: Sheryl Stebbins

ABOUT THIS BOOK

This version of *Random House Roget's Concise Thesaurus* combines the essential features of a thesaurus with additional characteristics of both a dictionary and a usage guide. That is, while it is primarily a word finder, its entries are arranged in alphabetical order, like those in a dictionary. Like a dictionary, it contains further information about the entry words and synonyms. And like a usage guide, it offers brief studies that explore distinctions among words. The aim of this design is to help you with several important tasks, enabling you:

- to find the words you are looking for in an easy and logical way
- to examine the wealth of vocabulary choices to which a single word can lead you
- to select the most accurate or interesting word from words with similar meanings
- to understand the differences among words that share a basic sense but are not necessarily interchangeable
- to expand your vocabulary not only in writing but in speaking

The three language resources embraced by this one volume have distinct characteristics.

Thesaurus. A thesaurus is what you turn to when you are groping for a word or a particular turn of phrase, as when writing a business letter or report, doing a school assignment, or composing an article for a journal or magazine. Sometimes the word that initially comes to mind is almost, but not quite, right, or even if the word will do, you don't want to keep using the same one over and over. There, in your thesaurus, is the word you really needed, in all its preciseness, or a word that leads to other entries with even more accurate or illuminating synonyms. The satisfaction of augmenting your expressive powers in such an instance is enormous. But in addition, continued exposure to these words and to the relationships among them encourages both the enlargement of your general vocabulary and an appreciation for the enormous variety available in the English language.

A thesaurus also reveals that a great many "synonyms" are not exact substitutes for one another. Rather, they have a basic sense in common to which each individual word contributes a subtle shade of meaning. In fact, synonym lists often include both general and specific words, offering choices that are not interchangeable. For example, one synonym for the verb *cringe* is *shrink*. *Shrink* is usable in almost every context where *cringe* occurs, yet *cringe* can be substituted for *shrink* in only a limited sense.

Where it would be useful, this thesaurus also offers lists of antonyms, words that are opposite in meaning to the entry word. In this way, this book provides yet another means of finding the precise term you need.

Dictionary. *Random House Roget's Concise. Thesaurus* presents more than 11,000 entry words in straightforward A-to-Z order, as a dictionary does. Likewise, this book gives the part of speech for each entry—noun, adjective, verb, etc. When appropriate, it describes the form a word usually takes; (e.g., plural), or indicates whether it is usually used with *the* or with a capital letter. It includes important spelling variations for some entry words, and it provides several types of cross references. Labels identify, among other things, levels of usage (*Informal, Slang*), terms from other languages (*French, German*), sources (*Bible, Nautical*), and the status of a word (*Archaic, Regional*). In some entries, brief phrasal definitions clarify which meaning of a word is being addressed.

Usage Guide. An outstanding feature of *Random House Roget's Concise Thesaurus* is the Synonym Study, a paragraph explaining how certain clusters of similar words relate to or differ from one another. Synonym Sudies appear in more than 400 entries throughout the book. Each study first presents the meaning shared by the entry word and one or more of the synonyms given for it. Then each word is defined and its usage clarified in an example phrase or sentence. Occasionally, a Synonym Study deals with words that are not synonymous but are often confused. All the synonyms in a study have entries of their own, with cross references to the entry where the study appears.

It is important to understand that the Synonym Studies in *Random House Roget's Concise Thesaurus* focus on only one sense of a given word, the sense that it shares with a handful of other words. No Synonym Study in this book implies that a given word has only a single meaning. Fuller coverage of a word can be found in *Random House Webster's College Dictionary.*

For a guide to the contents of each thesaurus entry, see "Guide to the Thesaurus."

GUIDE TO THE THESAURUS

1. **Main entries.** Appears in boldface type. Words spelled alike but with different meanings, and sometimes different pronunciations, are followed by superscript numbers (see the entries for **last**). Some main entries consist only of a cross reference to another entry (see also item 7, below).

2. **Parts of speech.** Are shown as standard abbreviations: *n.* for noun, *v.* for verb, *adj.* for adjective, *adv.* for adverb, *prep.* for preposition, *conj.* for conjunction, and *interj.* for interjection. If an entry consists of more than one part of speech, each is listed separately. The label *pl.* is used for plural forms.

3. **Synonyms and senses.** When an entry word has multiple senses, each is preceded by a boldface number and has its own list of synonyms. Within the listing, synonyms are separated by commas. Groups of synonyms are sometimes separated by a semicolon to distinguish nuances of meaning and to show which synonyms are appropriate to those meanings. Senses of an entry, or word groupings within a synonym list, may be introduced by a brief definition in brackets (see the entry **abandon**).

4. **Labels.** Appear in italics and precede the term or terms to which they belong. Labels are self-explanatory and for the most part deal with level of usage, language of origin or use, specific fields of knowledge, or restrictions on usage. When given, a label applies to all words that follow it up to the next label, semicolon, or period. Two special labels are *variously* and *loosely.* The first indicates that the upcoming words, while synonymous with the entry word in some way, are not usually synonyms for each other (see the entry **dance**). The second indicates that the following words are synonyms for the entry word only in a very broad sense and must be used carefully or in limited contexts (see the entry **log**).

5. **Synonym Studies.** Are preceded by *Syn. Study* in boldface italic type. When the entry word at which such a study appears has multiple senses, the study includes the number of the sense(s) to which the discussion applies. If a study applies to all the senses of an entry, the number reference is omitted.

6. **Antonyms.** Are preceded by the word *Ant.* in boldface italics. Antonyms are keyed by number to the senses of multiple-sense entries. Semicolons generally separate clusters of antonyms in relation to the synonyms in the entry.

7. **Cross references.** Are preceded by *See* or *See also.* Cross references are found at all entry words treated in Synonym Studies. If an entry has multiple senses, the cross reference includes the relevant number(s). Some entries in the thesaurus contain only a cross reference, usually

because they are variant spellings of an entry word or because they are part of a Synonym Study in which their usage is made clear (see the entry **skilled**). Some entry words are discussed in more than one Synonym Study; in these cases a "See also" cross reference appears at each Synonym Study.

8. **Additional abbreviations.** Occur thoughout: *Usu.* (usually), *esp.* (especially), and *etc.*

abandon *v.* **1.** desert, forsake, depart from, leave behind, withdraw from, evacuate; [run out on] give up, quit, relinquish, jilt, let go, cast aside, turn one's back on, forswear, abdicate, renounce, repudiate. **2.** discontinue, give up, drop, stop, cease, forgo, waive, discard, junk, wash one's hands of, get rid of, relinquish, forfeit, surrender, scrap. —*n.* **3.** unrestraint, freedom; immoderation, intemperance; recklessness, wantonness, impulsiveness, impetuosity, spontaneity; enthusiasm, gusto, élan, exuberance, spirit, dash, verve, ardor, animation. **—Ant. 1** claim, take; keep, hold, possess. **2** continue, maintain. **3** restraint, control, caution, prudence; moderation, tameness, deliberation.

abandoned *adj.* **1.** deserted, forsaken, vacant, desolate, unoccupied; discarded, cast aside, cast away, relinquished, rejected, jilted, left behind, marooned, neglected. **2.** debauched, debased, dissipated, dissolute, licentious, degraded, profligate, reprobate, shameless, immoral, disreputable, sinful, wild, wicked, loose, wanton, unprincipled; impure, unchaste, lewd; irreformable, irreclaimable, incorrigible, unrepentant. **—Ant. 1** occupied; well-kept, kept, claimed. **2** virtuous, reputable, respectable, upright, high-principled, worthy, elevated, healthy, conscientious; moral, sinless, pure, chaste; reformed, redeemed, penitent, regenerate.

abase *v.* humble, bring low, cast down; *Informal* put down, badmouth, bring down a peg, cut down to size; humiliate, disgrace, dishonor, defame, discredit, belittle, malign, vilify, denigrate, vitiate; downgrade, degrade, demean, cheapen, devaluate, besmirch, debase; shame, mock, mortify. **—Ant.** elevate, raise, exalt, uplift, lift; dignify, honor, acclaim, praise, laud, extol; promote, upgrade, inflate.

abashed *adj.* embarrassed, ashamed, chagrined, mortified, humiliated, humbled, selfconscious, dismayed, taken aback, bewildered, confused, dumbfounded, nonplussed, disconcerted, disheartened, daunted, confounded, fazed; shy, bashful, cowed, overawed, subdued, crushed, intimidated. **—Ant.** proud, pleased, elated, exalted, buoyed; confident, poised, heartened, undaunted, emboldened, reassured.

abate *v.* decrease, diminish, reduce, lessen, subside, decline, fade, fade away, recede, dwindle, moderate, mitigate, weaken, wane, ebb, curtail, slack, slacken, go down, lower, fall off, fall away, taper off, lighten, soften, quiet, quell, slow, slow down, slake off, temper, cool, blunt; ease, relieve, alleviate, assuage, pacify, soothe, allay, mollify, palliate, dull; dampen, restrain, restrict. **—Ant.** increase, intensify, magnify, enhance, heighten, aggravate, amplify, grow; multiply, rise, come up, strengthen, sharpen, heat up; quicken, accelerate, hurry, speed, speed up; prolong, extend.

abbey *n.* monastery, friary, cloister, priory, hermitage, cenoby; convent, nunnery; seminary; church, cathedral, chapel.

abbreviate *v.* shorten, abridge, curtail, condense, compress, summarize, synopsize, contract, reduce, diminish; cut, cut down, cut short, boil down, trim, clip, truncate. **—Syn. Study.** See SHORTEN. **—Ant.** lengthen, extend, elongate, stretch, stretch out, draw out; expand, enlarge, amplify, increase, inflate, augment, add to, pad out; prolong, protract; write out, write in full.

abbreviation *n.* shortened form, short form, shortening, condensed form, reduced form, compressed form, contracted form, cut-down form; reduction, contraction, diminution, abridgment, condensation, compression, abstraction, digest, synopsis, summary, abstract, brief; lessening, trimming, curtailment, cutting, clipping, pruning. **—Ant.** full form, written-out form; lengthening, extending, extension, elongation, stretching, stretching out, drawing out; expansion, enlargement, amplification, increase, increasing, augmentation, prolongation.

abdicate *v.* renounce, resign, vacate the throne; relinquish, give up, abnegate, abandon, surrender, abjure, quit, forgo, cede, waive, yield. **—Ant.** accede to the throne; claim, possess, usurp, assume, seize; keep.

abdomen *n.* stomach, visceral cavity, venter, epigastrium; belly, tummy; gut, paunch, breadbasket, bay window, pot, pot belly.

abduct *v.* kidnap, carry off, make off with, run off with, steal, take away, bear off, seize. **—Ant.** return, bring back; free, set free; restore, relinquish, surrender.

aberration *n.* **1.** irregularity, deviation, exception, departure, abnormality, anomaly, incongruity, divergence, digression, aberrance, aberrancy; wandering, rambling, straying, lapse. **2.** minor mental disorder, mental lapse, abnormality, curiosity, quirk, peculiarity, idiosyncrasy, eccentricity, unconformity, nonconformity, oddity, singularity, strangeness, distortion, mutation; illusion, delusion, self-deception, hallucination; madness, insanity, lunacy, derangement. **—Ant. 1, 2** normality, regularity, uniformity, conformity. **2** sanity, soundness of mind.

abet *v.* encourage, support, endorse, sustain, back, give moral support to, sanction, advocate, promote, advance, uphold; urge, urge on, goad, spur, incite, instigate; lead on, egg on; assist, help, aid, second, join with. **—Ant.** discourage, talk out of, dissuade, expose, denounce; deter, stop, check, hinder, impede, undermine, thwart, obstruct, balk.

abeyance *n.* postponement, suspension, intermission, remission, deferral, adjournment, discontinuance, inaction, dormancy, latency; pause, delay, cessation, quiescence, recess, hiatus, waiting period, in a holding pattern; in cold storage, on ice, on a back burner. **—Ant.** continuance, continuation, continuity, ceaselessness.

abhor *v.* detest, hate, loathe, dislike, despise, disdain, scorn, shun, abominate, execrate; feel aversion toward, be revolted by, find repulsive, shudder at, recoil at, shrink from, regard with repugnance, view with horror, eschew, can't stand, can't stomach, be nauseated by. **—Syn. Study.** See HATE. **—Ant.** love, adore, like, delight in, dote on, cherish, relish, treasure, prize, value, enjoy, admire; desire, crave, covet.

abide *v.* **1.** bear, stand, tolerate, put up with, endure, last, stomach, brook; suffer, submit to, accept, stand for. **2.** stay, remain, tarry, linger, stop; live, reside, dwell; visit, sojourn, sit; *Slang* stick with, stick around. **—Ant. 2** go, leave, quit, depart; escape, flee, fly; abandon, shun, avoid; move, migrate, journey.

abiding *adj.* lasting, everlasting, enduring, eternal, unending, continuing, permanent, durable, firm, fast; changeless, unchanging, steadfast, constant, steady, unshakable, wholehearted, unquestioning, immutable, indissoluble. **—Ant.** temporary, passing, momentary, impermanent, ephemeral; weak, shaky, failing; changeable, fickle.

ability *n.* capability, capacity, power, facility, faculty, aptitude, potential, potentiality, proficiency, knack, competence, qualification; skill, talent, know-how, expertise, adeptness, adroitness, acumen; flair, genius, gift, mind for, bent. **—Syn. Study.** ABILITY, FACULTY, TALENT denote power or capacity to do something. ABILITY is the general word for a natural or acquired capacity to do things; it usu. implies doing them well: *a leader of great ability; ability in mathematics.* FACULTY denotes a natural or acquired ability for a particular kind of action: *a faculty for putting people at ease.* TALENT usu. denotes an exceptional natural ability or aptitude in a particular field: *a talent for music.* **—Ant.** inability, incapacity, incapability, inaptitude, incompetence, maladroitness; weakness, inadequacy, powerlessness, helplessness.

abject *adj.* **1.** hopeless, inescapable, complete, thorough; wretched, miserable, deplorable, terrible, horrible. **2.** lacking courage, spiritless, cringing, groveling; contemptible, despicable, vile, base, mean, low, ignoble, sordid. **—Ant. 1** hopeful; partial; dignified, honorable. **2** courageous, spirited, bold, staunch; manly, domineering, vain, arrogant, haughty, insolent; admirable, respected, esteemed, worthy.

abjure *v.* **1.** disclaim, disallow, repudiate, disavow, reject. **2.** renounce, abandon, relinquish, desert, give up, forswear, recant. **—Ant.** maintain, embrace, swear by, uphold.

ablaze *adj.* **1.** burning, blazing, on fire, afire, conflagrant, flaming, aflame, in flames; ignited, alight; fiery, glowing. **2.** eager, excited, fervent, fervid, zealous, impassioned; feverish, flushed, intoxicated; red-hot, passionate, ardent; turned-on, hopped-up, switched-on.

able *adj.* **1.** skillful, proficient, capable, competent, expert, good, talented, highly qualified, accomplished, masterful, effective, efficient, adroit, adept, apt; experienced, practiced, learned. **2.** capable, fit, fitted, competent, having the means; equal to, adequate, qualified. **—Ant. 1** unskillful, incapable, incompetent, inexpert, inept, inefficient, ineffective, amateurish; mediocre, indifferent, fair. **2** incapable, unfit, incompetent, inadequate, unqualified.

able-bodied *adj.* muscular, brawny, robust, strong, vigorous, well-built, athletic, thewy, beefy, herculean, strapping, rugged, hardy, sturdy, stalwart, hearty, lusty, broad-shouldered. **—Ant.** weak, puny, flabby, feeble, frail, infirm.

ablution *n.* **1.** ceremonial washing, ritualistic washing; bathing, cleansing, purification. **2.** washing, bathing, cleaning, lavation; wash, bath.

abnegation *n.* self-denial, sacrifice, renunciation, relinquishment, surrender, resignation, giving up, eschewal, forbearance, forbearing; abstinence, temperance, continence; rejection, refusal. **—Ant.** self-indulgence, indulgence, abandon; intemperance, incontinence; affirmation, concession.

abnormal *adj.* unnatural, atypical, unusual, irregular, aberrant, deviant, anomalous; uncommon, unconventional, exceptional, extraordinary, unexpected, unaccustomed, inordinate; strange, peculiar, rare, queer, odd, freakish, eccentric, bizarre, curious, outlandish, unheard of, grotesque, weird, monstrous, deformed. **—Ant.** normal, natural, typical, usual, ordinary, common; conventional, routine, regular, expected, customary, familiar, unexceptional.

abnormality *n.* deformity, malformation; irregularity, aberration, aberrance, anomaly, deviation, perversion; oddity, curiosity, peculiarity, idiosyncrasy, eccentricity, unconformity.

abode *n.* residence, place of residence, dwelling place, habitat, dwelling, habitation; house, home, living quarters, domicile, lodging, address, *Slang* pad, nest.

abolish *v.* eliminate, eradicate, erase, obliterate, extinguish, exterminate, annihilate, extirpate, terminate, end, put an end to, wipe out, stamp out, blot out, do away with, squelch, quash; repeal, revoke, annul, nullify, invalidate, declare null and void, rescind, cancel; abrogate, vitiate, set aside, repudiate. **—Ant.** establish, institute, introduce, create, inaugurate, build, found; support, promote, increase, sustain, continue; revive, reinstate, renew, repair, restore, reintroduce; authorize, legalize, enact.

abolition *n.* elimination, ending, termination, eradication, dissolution, extinction, abolishment, invalidation, vitiation; repeal, annulment, nullification, revocation, cancellation, recantation, retraction, rescinding, repudiation, abrogation. **—Ant.** establishment, institution, introduction, creation, inauguration, founding; authorization, legalization, enactment, passing; promotion; continuation; reinstatement, restoration, reintroduction.

abominable *adj.* **1.** detestable, despicable, contemptible, reprehensible, loathsome, hateful, abhorrent, execrable, disgusting, revolting, repulsive, repugnant, repellent, odious; vile, base, wretched, heinous, ignominious, villainous, infamous, atrocious, horrid, horrible, foul, hellish, damnable, evil, cursed, accursed. **2.** very unpleasant, disagreeable, miserable, terrible, deplorable, foul, extremely bad, unsuitable, awful, *Informal* lousy. **—Ant. 1** laudable, praiseworthy, commendable, admirable, respectable, desirable, applaudable; satisfactory, gratifying, charming, enchanting, likable. **2** pleasant, agreeable, enjoyable, pleasing, delightful, good, wonderful, charming, suitable, *Informal* beautiful.

abomination *n.* **1.** abhorrence, anathema, evil, obscenity, horror, disgrace, torment, defilement, plague, affliction, annoyance, bugbear, *French* bête noire. **2.** revulsion, loathing, repugnance, disgust, detestation, hate, hatred, abhorrence, antipathy, aversion. **—Ant. 1** delight, joy, pleasure, treat; benefit, blessing, boon, satisfaction, gratification. **2** love, liking, affection, fondness, relish, regard; admiration, appreciation, respect, approval, esteem.

aboriginal *adj.* native, indigenous, original, endemic, autochthonous; earliest, first, ancient, primordial, primeval, primitive, primary, prime. **—Ant.** alien, foreign, immigrant, imported, exotic; late, recent, subsequent, successive, modern.

aborigine *n.* original inhabitant, primitive inhabitant, indigenous person; native, aboriginal. **—Ant.** alien, foreigner, immigrant; newcomer, late arrival, Johnny-come-lately.

abort *v.* **1.** miscarry, terminate the pregnancy of. **2.** terminate, end, halt, stop, call off; fail, fail to develop fully. **—Ant. 1** give birth, bear, deliver. **2** carry through, see through, conclude, complete, finish; execute, perform, effect, achieve.

abortion *n.* **1.** miscarriage, termination of pregnancy. **2.** failure, unsuccessful attempt, fruitless attempt, fiasco, disaster; halting, calling off, ending, termination. **—Ant. 1** childbirth, parturition, giving birth, delivery. **2** success, successful completion, realization, achievement.

abortive *adj.* fruitless, useless, unsuccessful, unproductive, inefficacious, bootless, sterile, ineffective, profitless, unavailing, vain, ineffectual, futile, worthless, unfruitful, unprofitable, unrewarding, nonviable. **—Ant.** successful, fruitful, profitable, rewarding, productive.

abound *v.* teem, overflow, spill over, be flooded, be filled, have plenty of, luxuriate, be well supplied, be rich in, swarm, run wild, proliferate, superabound; exist in great numbers, be plentiful, flourish, thrive, be numerous; *Informal* gush. **—Ant.** lack, want, have too few, be deficient in, fall short, be scant; be in short supply.

about-face *n.* reversal, rightabout, turnaround, tergiversation, reverse, turnabout, switch, shift, *French* volte-face; change of heart, disavowal, recantation, retraction.

aboveboard *adj.* candid, open, honest, truthful, forthright, straightforward, sincere, frank, straight, square-dealing, plain-dealing, straight-shooting, undissembling, on the up and up, square, foursquare; guileless, ingenuous, artless;

blunt, direct, plain, unconcealed. —**Ant.** devious, roundabout, evasive, underhand.

abracadabra *n.* hocus-pocus, mumbo-jumbo, open sesame; witchcraft, sorcery, voodoo, magic, magic spell, incantation, invocation, spell, charm, exorcism.

abrasion *n.* **1.** scraped spot, scrape; scratch, lesion. **2.** scraping, grating, rubbing, friction, excoriation, scouring, chafing; erosion, wearing away, wearing down.

abrasive *n.* **1.** scraping material, grinding material, scouring material; smoothing substance. —*adj.* **2.** harsh, coarse, annoying, irritating, excoriating; rasping, grating, rough, caustic, sharp, cutting, biting, nasty, hurtful, galling, chafing. —**Ant.** mild, soothing, healing, comforting, gentle, pleasant, agreeable.

abreast *adv., adj.* side by side, in a line across, in rank, aligned, in alignment. —**Ant.** one behind another, one after another, in single file, Indian file.

abridge *v.* **1.** shorten, condense, reduce, compress, digest, abbreviate, cut, cut down, scale down, pare down, trim, telescope, truncate. **2.** restrict, limit, curtail, diminish, lessen, reduce, decrease; deprive one of, take away. —**Syn. Study. 1, 2** See SHORTEN. —**Ant. 1** expand, enlarge, lengthen, increase, extend, amplify; prolong; augment, add to, supplement. **2** increase, augment, add to.

abridgment *n.* **1.** shortened form, condensed form, condensation, abbreviation, digest, truncation. **2.** restriction, limitation, restraint, curtailment, reduction, lessening, decrease, diminishing, diminution. —**Ant. 1** lengthened version. **2** expansion, enlargement, amplification, increase, augmentation, extension, inflation.

abroad *adv.* **1.** overseas, out of the country. **2.** out of doors, outside, out, out of the house, forth, out in the open air. **3.** in circulation, at large, making the rounds, all around, round and about; spread far and wide, rife, astir. —**Ant. 1** nearby, near home; in one's native land, within the country. **2** indoors, inside, in, in the house, at home, within four walls; *French* chez soi, *German* zuhause.

abrogate *v.* abolish, cancel, terminate, put an end to, end, do away with, quash; repeal, revoke, rescind, annul, nullify, void, invalidate, set aside, override, reverse, undo, negate, dissolve, vitiate; retract, countermand, recall, withdraw, repudiate, renounce, abjure; *Informal* junk, throw out. —**Ant.** institute, establish, create, found; enact, ratify, fix; confirm, sustain, uphold, support, sanction; continue; revive, renew.

abrupt *adj.* **1.** sudden, unexpected, unforeseen, unanticipated, impulsive, unlooked for, unannounced; hasty, quick, rapid, swift, instantaneous, precipitate. **2.** curt, brusque, blunt, brisk, gruff, short, crisp; discourteous, impolite, uncivil, ungracious, unceremonious, rude, rough. **3.** steep, sheer, sharp, precipitous. —**Ant. 1** anticipated, expected, foreseen; gradual, leisurely, unhurried, deliberate, slow, easy. **2** courteous, polite, gracious, thoughtful, civil; gentle, easy. **3** gradual, smooth, easy, slow.

abscond *v.* flee, take flight, fly, vanish, disappear, depart hastily, leave suddenly; take off, make off, steal off, steal away; escape, run away, run off; *Informal* skip; *Slang* split.

absence *n.* **1.** not being present, nonattendance, nonpresence, nonappearance, absenteeism; truancy, cut. **2.** lack, unavailability, nonexistence; scarcity, deficiency, insufficiency, scantiness, want, dearth. —**Ant. 1** presence, attendance, appearance. **2** existence, supply; abundance, plenty, sufficiency, adequacy, surfeit, plethora.

absent *adj.* **1.** not present, nonpresent, nonattendant; away, gone, missing, out, truant. **2.** inattentive, unthinking, heedless, oblivious, unaware, unconscious, absent-minded, preoccupied, distracted; vacant, blank, faraway, removed, empty, vague, dreamy, musing; *Slang* out of it, tuned out, out to lunch. —*v.* **3.** cause to be not present, fail to attend, not appear, stay away, keep away, play truant, *Informal* not show up, cut. —**Ant. 1** present, in attendance, attendant. **2** attentive, thoughtful, meaningful, conscious, aware, alert; *Slang* with it, tuned in. **3** attend, appear at, show up.

absentee *n.* truant, deserter, runaway; apostate, renegade, backslider; slacker, shirker, malingerer, quitter.

absent-minded *adj.* forgetful, distracted, withdrawn, unheeding, unmindful, preoccupied, absent, faraway, woolgathering, oblivious, engrossed, absorbed, lost in thought, daydreaming, distrait; out of it, not with it. —**Ant.** attentive, alert, heedful, observant; with it, hip.

absolute *adj.* **1.** unrestricted, unrestrained, unlimited, unconditional, unqualified, unbounded; complete, supreme, pure, full, *Informal* out-and-out. **2.** complete, pure, total, definite, thorough, unqualified, unrestricted, unadulterated, unmitigated, utter, sheer, unlimited; perfect, consummate, outright; *Informal* out-and-out, through and through. **3.** positive, definite, conclusive, sheer, certain, sure, decisive; real, genuine, reliable, unqualified, unmitigated, unquestionable, undeniable, confirmed, infallible, unequivocal. **—Ant. 1** restricted, restrained, conditional, limited, provisional, qualified; constitutional. **2, 3** qualified, limited, partial, conditional, provisional, questionable, dubious, unconfirmed, equivocal; not complete, incomplete.

absolutely *adv.* **1.** entirely, completely, thoroughly, wholly, utterly, definitely, positively; unconditionally, without limitation. **2.** positively, certainly, utterly, definitely, decidedly, truly, really, indeed; undoubtedly, unquestionably, unequivocally, indubitably. **—Ant. 1** somewhat, fairly, reasonably, approximately. **2** probably, conditionally.

absolution *n.* pardon, amnesty, forgiveness, mercy, deliverance, vindication, quittance, exculpation, exoneration, remission, acquittal, clearance, dispensation, indulgence, liberation, release. **—Ant.** blame, censure, condemnation, conviction, prosecution.

absolve *v.* **1.** pardon, forgive, shrive, declare removed. **2.** acquit, find not guilty, judge innocent; exonerate, vindicate, exculpate, clear. **3.** release, free, set free, excuse, exempt, discharge, loose, deliver. **—Syn. Study. 2** ABSOLVE, ACQUIT, EXONERATE all mean to free from blame. ABSOLVE is a general word for this idea. To ACQUIT is to release from a specific and usu. formal accusation: *The court must acquit the accused if there is insufficient evidence of guilt.* To EXONERATE is to consider a person clear of blame or consequences for an act (even when the act is admitted), or to justify the person for having done it: *to be exonerated for a crime committed in self-defense.* **—Ant. 1** accuse, blame; condemn. **2** convict, charge, find guilty. **3** obligate, oblige, bind, hold to, be held responsible.

absorb *v.* **1.** soak up, take up, suck up, swallow up, drink in, sponge up. **2.** take in completely, assimilate, incorporate, digest, ingest; *Informal* drink in, make part of oneself. **3.** engross, immerse, occupy, preoccupy, consume, engage, enwrap; arrest, rivet, fix, fascinate. **—Ant. 1** exude, eject, cast off, cast out, disperse, dispel; drip. **2** give out, disperse, impart. **3** unoccupy; distract.

absorbent *adj.* permeable, spongy, penetrable, absorptive, porous, thirsty, pervious, bibulous, osmotic, assimilative. **—Ant.** moistureproof, waterproof, water-repellent, impermeable, watertight, impenetrable.

absorbing *adj.* fascinating, interesting, engrossing, captivating, intriguing, engaging; exciting, thrilling.

abstain *v.* refrain, desist, forbear, eschew, avoid, forgo, hold back, decline, refuse; deny oneself, resist. **—Ant.** partake of, indulge in, yield to, surrender, give in to; overdo, abandon oneself to, make a slave of oneself to.

abstemious *adj.* abstinent, ascetic, austere, temperate, continent, nonindulgent, teetotal, self-denying, sparing, self-disciplined, abstentious. **—Ant.** self-indulgent, abandoned, undisciplined, uncontrolled, hedonistic, profligate, licentious, unrestrained, immoderate.

abstention *n.* abstaining, nonindulgence, refraining, desisting, holding back, forbearance, eschewing, eschewal, avoidance, refusal; nonparticipation, denying oneself, resistance. **—Ant.** indulgence, abandon.

abstinence *n.* nonindulgence, self-denial, self-restraint, self-control, discipline, forbearance, abstention; (*variously*) temperance, sobriety; continence, chastity. **—Ant.** indulgence, self-indulgence, abandon, excess; (*variously*) intemperance, dissipation; wantonness; gorging, gluttony; greediness, covetousness, graspingness, acquisitiveness.

abstract *adj.* **1.** theoretical, theoretic, conceptual, unapplied, general, generalized, imaginary, visionary, intangible, hypothetical, indefinite, nonspecific, remote, impractical; subtle, profound, abstruse, obscure, esoteric, recondite, arcane, intellectual. *—n.* **2.** summary, synopsis, précis, résumé, brief, recapitulation; digest, extract, condensation, abridgment; outline. *—v.* **3.** extract, remove, withdraw, take out, take; separate, dissociate, isolate. **4.** summarize, synopsize; digest, condense, abridge, compress; outline. **—Ant. 1** concrete, obvious, specific, clear, uncomplicated, material; practical; factual, definite, real, actual. **2** amplification, enlargement, expansion. **3** add, inject; mix, unite, combine.

absurd *adj.* unreasonable, illogical, irrational, senseless; ridiculous, foolish, inane, silly, stupid, ludicrous, idiotic, nonsensical, preposterous, asinine, farcical; funny, comical, laughable; *Informal* crazy, wild; *Slang* screwy, kooky. **—Syn. Study.** ABSURD, RIDICULOUS, PREPOSTEROUS all mean inconsistent with reason or common sense. ABSURD means utterly opposed to truth or reason: *an absurd claim.* RIDICULOUS implies that something is fit only to be laughed at, perhaps contemptuously: *a ridiculous suggestion.* PREPOSTEROUS implies an extreme of foolishness: *a preposterous proposal.* **—Ant.** reasonable, logical, sensible, rational, sound; smart, intelligent, sagacious, judicious, prudent, wise.

absurdity *n.* nonsense, unreasonableness, unbelievability, idiocy, inanity, asininity, irrationality, ridiculousness, drivel; falsehood, fallacy, delusion; foolishness, buffoonery, comicalness, silliness. —**Ant.** truth; reasonableness, credibility; wisdom, sagacity.

abtruse *adj.* hard to understand, obscure, incomprehensible, unfathomable, complex, complicated, puzzling, perplexing, arcane, enigmatic; profound, deep, subtle, abstract, remote, esoteric, recondite. —**Ant.** simple, direct, easy, obvious, straightforward, clear, uncomplicated; superficial, light, amusing, entertaining.

abundance *n.* ample amount, great supply, full measure, profusion, sufficiency; excess, more than enough, plenty, surplus, glut, plenitude, repletion, plethora, surfeit, cornucopia, copiousness; heap, flood, bounty, wealth, richness. —**Ant.** scarcity, deficiency, lack, dearth, scantiness, sparseness, paucity.

abundant *adj.* ample, sufficient, enough, plenty, more than enough, profuse, copious, plentiful, prolific, bounteous, bountiful, abounding, lavish, rich, luxuriant, brimming, teeming; rife, replete, galore. —**Syn. Study.** See PLENTIFUL. —**Ant.** insufficient, scant, sparse, meager, uncommon, scarce, skimpy, sparing.

abuse *v.* **1.** misuse, use improperly, exploit, take advantage of, ill-use; mistreat, maltreat, ill-treat; harm, hurt, injure, torment, excoriate; impose upon. **2.** insult, speak ill of, scold, berate, carp at, rail at, revile, vilify, castigate; speak harshly to, reproach, criticize, censure, bawl out, upbraid; belittle, deride, malign, ridicule, slur, denigrate; curse, slander, denounce, defame, disparage, inveigh against, *Slang* badmouth. —*n.* **3.** misuse, unfair use, improper use, misapplication, misemployment; exploitation, imposition. **4.** mistreatment, maltreatment, oppression, ill-use, torment, cruelty; injury, harming, beating, assault. **5.** insulting language, insults, harsh language, torments; berating, railing, invective, tirade; reproach, criticism, tongue-lashing, censure, scolding, upbraiding, castigation, diatribe, carping; belittling, sneering, disparagement, slander, ridicule, derision, vilification; cursing, defamatory remarks, defamation. —**Syn. Study. 5** ABUSE, CENSURE, INVECTIVE all mean strongly expressed disapproval. ABUSE implies an outburst of harsh and scathing words, often against one who is defenseless: *abuse directed against an opponent.* CENSURE implies blame, adverse criticism, or condemnation: *severe censure of her bad judgment.* INVECTIVE applies to strong but formal denunciation in speech or print, often in the public interest: *invective against graft.* —**Ant. 1** respect, protect, care for. **2** praise, speak well of, compliment, extol, laud, flatter, sweet-talk, acclaim. **5** praise, compliment, acclaim; flattery.

abusive *adj.* **1.** insulting, harsh, vituperative, mean, railing, acrimonious; offensive, obscene, foulmouthed, vile, rude, gross; derogatory, disparaging, defamatory, scurrilous, deprecatory, castigating, critical, censorious, slanderous, reviling, maligning, vilifying, scornful. **2.** cruel, improper; harmful, hurtful, injurious. —**Ant. 1** laudatory, flattering, complimentary, praising, extolling, mild, courteous, respectful, polite. **2** kind; just.

abut *v.* meet end to end, meet, join, adjoin, touch; border, be contiguous, be adjacent to, be next to.

abysmal *adj.* thorough, endless, unending, complete; bottomless, boundless, incredible, unbelievable, unimaginable, unfathomable, deep, profound, enormous, extreme, vast, stupendous, immense.

abyss *n.* bottomless pit, vast chasm, crevasse, fissure, gorge, gully; void, depth, nadir, gulf. —**Ant.** elevation, height; mountain, hill, mount; summit, zenith.

academic *adj.* **1.** school, scholastic, educational; collegiate, university. **2.** scholarly, studious; learned, educated, erudite; pedantic, bookish. **3.** general, liberal-arts, scholastic, college-preparatory; nontechnical, nonvocational, nonspecialized. **4.** theoretical, hypothetical, abstract, moot, speculative, conjectural, suppositional, presumptive; not practical, remote, ivory-towered. —**Ant. 2** nonscholarly, nonstudious, unpedantic; uneducated, unschooled, untaught, unlettered, unlearned. **3** technical, vocational, trade, specialized. **4** practical, realistic, immediate, commonsense; everyday, functional, ordinary, matter-of-course, matter-of-fact.

accede *v.* **1.** consent to, approve, agree to, grant, assent to, accept, concur with; concede, permit, yield to, submit to, defer to, acquiesce, surrender to; subscribe to, abide by, comply with, conform to; admit, acknowledge, endorse. **2.** succeed to, inherit. —**Ant. 1** reject, refuse, disallow, spurn, decline, veto; oppose, object to, resist, protest, disapprove, demur; shy away from, balk at.

accelerate *v.* **1.** to go faster, to move faster, speed up, pick up speed, quicken pace. **2.** speed up, hurry, quicken, hasten, rush, step up, augment, spur; expedite, further, promote, advance, precipitate, facilitate, intensify, impel. —**Ant.** 1, 2 slow, slow down, decelerate, brake.

2 delay, retard, slacken, hinder, impede, hamper, obstruct.

accent *n.* **1.** stress, emphasis; primary accent, primary stress. **2.** pronunciation, enunciation, articulation, inflection, manner of speaking, twang, drawl; intonation, tone, modulation, tonality. **3.** hint, touch, embellishment, detail; ornament, adornment, trimming. —*v.* **4.** stress, emphasize, accentuate, punctuate, give prominence to; underline, underscore, feature, spotlight, highlight.

accept *v.* **1.** take something offered, receive willingly, receive with favor. **2.** agree to, consent to, grant as satisfactory, accede to, go along with, assent to, receive with approval, acknowledge; *Slang* swallow, buy, fall for. **3.** assume, undertake, bear, acknowledge, admit, avow. **—Ant. 1, 2** refuse, reject, decline, spurn, turn down, resist. **3** disown, repudiate; deny, disavow, disacknowledge.

acceptable *adj.* **1.** capable of being accepted, agreeable, proper, suitable, admissible, satisfactory; worthy, good. **2.** adequate, suitable, passable, tolerable, allowable, fair; barely satisfactory, *Informal* so-so. **—Ant. 1, 2** unacceptable, unsatisfactory, unsuitable, inadmissible, substandard.

acceptance *n.* **1.** accepting, taking, receiving; receipt, reception. **2.** approval, consent, agreement, permission, concession, acquiescence; *Informal* O.K., stamp of approval; sanction, endorsement, affirmation. **3.** approval, approbation, belief, recognition, acknowledgment; affirmation, confirmation. **—Ant. 1, 2** rejection, refusal, repudiation; disapproval. **3** rejection; disavowal.

accepted *adj.* agreed upon, approved, acceptable, confirmed, acknowledged, established; common, normal, usual, conventional, standard, regular, customary, universal, time-honored.

access *n.* **1.** admittance; entrance, entrée. **2.** a means of reaching, an approach, passage, passageway, gateway, entrance, entry; road, path, way, avenue, course.

accessible *adj.* **1.** available, ready, at hand, on hand, handy, within reach, nearby; obtainable, attainable, reachable, possible. **2.** available, approachable, reachable. **—Ant. 1** unavailable, far-off, unobtainable, impossible, beyond reach; hidden, hidden away, secreted. **2** unapproachable, unavailable, inaccessible, unreachable, standoffish, forbidding.

accession *n.* assumption, induction, installation, investment, inheritance, inauguration, taking over, arrogation; seizure, usurpation. **—Ant.** abdication, deposition, resignation, renunciation.

accessory *n.* **1.** addition, supplement, plus; adjunct, attachment, component, extension, auxiliary. **2.** accompaniment, adornment, decoration; complement, accent, detail. **3.** accomplice, confederate, partner; associate, cohort, colleague, assistant, contributor, auxiliary. **—Syn. Study. 1** See ADDITION.

accident *n.* **1.** chance, fluke, happenstance; luck, fate, good fortune, fortuity, serendipity. **2.** collision, crash, wreck, smashup; mishap, misadventure, mischance; bit of bad luck, misfortune. **—Ant. 1** plan, intention, intent, design, calculation, purpose.

accidental *adj.* unplanned, unintentional, unpremeditated, uncalculated, unwitting, unforeseen; unexpected, unanticipated, fortuitous, serendipitous; chance, haphazard, random, incidental, inadvertent. **—Ant.** planned, intentional, intended, premeditated, calculated; foreseen, expected; prepared, designed, projected.

acclaim *v.* **1.** praise, loudly approve, applaud, cheer, hail; laud, extol, commend, sing the praises of, exalt, cheer, compliment, eulogize; honor, celebrate, salute. **2.** name by acclamation. —*n.* **3.** great praise, loud approval, applause, plaudits, kudos, bravos, cheering, ovation, acclamation, endorsement, rejoicing, enthusiasm. **—Ant. 1** criticize, denounce, condemn, disapprove, *Informal* pan, boo, hiss, heckle, shout down, give the raspberry, give the Bronx cheer; *Slang* razz. **3** criticism, condemnation, disapproval, *Informal* panning, booing, hissing, heckling; *Slang* razzing.

acclamation *n.* ovation, burst of applause, cheering, shout of approval, salutation; acclaim, homage, tribute, approbation, plaudits, adulation; cheers, hurrahs, hosannas. **—Ant.** booing, hissing, Bronx cheers; disapproval, denunciation, censure, disapprobation, execration, excoriation.

acclimate *v.* get used to, accustom, adapt, adjust, reconcile, habituate, become seasoned to, accommodate, inure.

accolade *n.* award, honor, tribute, prize, trophy, decoration, citation, testimonial; praise, compliment, commendation, acclaim, recognition, admiration.

accommodate *v.* **1.** do a kindness for, do a favor for; oblige, help, aid, assist; supply, provide, furnish, lend a hand. **2.** have capacity for, furnish room for, house, billet, quarter, shelter, board, bed down; entertain; hold, contain; lodge, put up. **3.** adapt, adjust, fit, acclimate, accustom, bring into line; conform, modify, harmonize; reconcile, get used to. **—Syn. Study. 1** See OBLIGE. **2** See CONTAIN. **—Ant. 1** inconvenience, disoblige, trouble.

accommodating *adj.* obliging, helpful, considerate, kind, hospitable, *Informal* neighborly; polite, courteous, gracious; conciliatory, yielding. **—Ant.** disobliging, inconsiderate; rude, churlish.

accommodation *n.* **1.** rooms, quarters, lodgings, housing; arrangements. **2.** compromise, settlement, adjustment; agreement, concord, reconciliation.

accompany *v.* **1.** go in company with, go along with; conduct; attend, escort, chaperon, convoy, usher, guard, support, *Informal* back up. **2.** occur with, go together with, go hand in hand with, go hand in glove with, be connected with, coexist with, follow. **3.** play accompaniment for, supply music for, provide background or harmony for, back up. **—Syn. Study. 1** ACCOMPANY, ATTEND, CONVOY, ESCORT mean to go along with. To ACCOMPANY is to go as an associate or companion, usu. on equal terms: *My daughter accompanied me on the trip.* ATTEND usu. implies going along as a subordinate, as to render service: *to attend the queen.* To CONVOY is to accompany ships or other vehicles with an armed guard: *to convoy a fleet of merchant vessels.* To ESCORT is to accompany in order to protect, honor, or show courtesy: *to escort a visiting dignitary.*

accomplice *n.* confederate, accessory, partner, collaborator, co-conspirator, partner-in-crime, *Informal* crony; associate, cohort, colleague, ally, comrade, *Informal* henchman, sidekick; assistant, subordinate, aide, helper, supporter, abettor, *Slang* stooge; participant.

accomplish *v.* **1.** achieve, succeed at, carry out, do; perform, realize, execute, attain, fulfill; bring about, produce, expedite, *Slang* knock off. **2.** do, get done, finish, complete, achieve, realize, *Slang* knock off. **—Ant. 1** fail, fall short, miss the mark; give up, forsake. **2** leave undone.

accomplished *adj.* **1.** existing, realized, effected, completed, consummated; established, accepted, proven, proved, concluded. **2.** expert, able, proficient, capable, fine, skilled, skillful; masterly, practiced, well-trained, finished, experienced, seasoned, eminent, polished, cultivated; talented, gifted, brilliant, adroit, deft, apt, qualified. **—Ant. 1** nonexistent, unrealized, unestablished, unproven. **2** unskilled, poor, incompetent, incapable, inept, inexpert; inexperienced; unpolished, crude; untalented, amateurish, clumsy.

accomplishment *n.* **1.** achievement, realization, execution, attainment, triumph, victory, fulfillment, success, carrying out; culmination, consummation. **2.** achievement, feat, tour de force, success, attainment, exploit, triumph, victory; deed, act. **3.** achievement, feat, skill; talent, gift, proficiency, capability. **—Ant. 1** failure. **2** failure, blunder. **3** lack, deficiency, lacuna, incapacity.

accord *v.* **1.** agree, concur; conform, correspond, be in unison, match, comply with, tally, jibe, harmonize; *Informal* square, be in tune, go along with. **2.** grant, present, give, bestow, award, render, tender, bequeath, vouchsafe; concede, allow, cede. **—*n.* 3.** agreement, harmony, accordance, mutual understanding, concurrence, unison, concert, unanimity, uniformity, conformity, consonance; rapport, sympathy. **—Ant. 1** differ, disagree, conflict, clash, collide, contrast. **2** withhold, deny, refuse, hold back. **3** conflict, discord, disagreement, dissidence, dissension; variance, contention.

accordingly *adv.* **1.** in accordance with the fact, correspondingly, suitably, conformably. **2.** therefore, thus, so, hence, wherefore, whereupon, consequently, as a result, ergo; in which case, then, whence, thence, in due course. **—Ant. 1** conversely.

accost *v.* hail, call to, speak to suddenly, greet, salute, address; confront, approach, buttonhole, waylay, *Informal* nab, stop, halt; solicit, make an appeal to, proposition. **—Ant.** evade, avoid, ignore, overlook; slight, shun.

account *n.* **1.** description, report; story, history, record, chronicle, tale, narrative, narration, commentary; explanation, version, statement, enumeration, recital, *Slang* megillah. **2.** reason, cause, grounds, basis, sake, consideration, regard, *Informal* score. **3.** importance, import, worth, significance, consequence, note; value, use, merit; esteem, honor, repute, distinction, dignity, standing, rank. **4.** financial record, financial statement, bookkeeping, books, accounting. **—*v.* 5.** consider, regard, believe, look upon as, view as, think, judge, count, deem, hold, take to be; rate, estimate, calculate, reckon, value, appraise, weigh, gauge. **6.** explain, justify, clarify, illuminate, give a reason for, show cause.

accountable *adj.* liable, answerable, responsible, obligated, chargeable, to blame, guilty, at fault, culpable, blameworthy. **—Ant.** blameless, exempt, innocent, guiltless, excused, clear.

accountant *n.* certified public accountant, CPA; bookkeeper, auditor, actuary.

accredit *v.* **1.** furnish with credentials, certify, license, endorse, guarantee, commission, authorize, sanction, officially recognize; empower. **2.** attribute, ascribe, assign, credit.

accretion *n.* increase, addition, supplement, increment, augmentation, rise, accumulation, accrual, growth, extension, expansion, enlargement, amplification. **—Ant.** loss, decrease, diminution, shrinkage, reduction.

accrue *v.* accumulate, collect, build up, amass, pile up, add up; grow, increase. **—Ant.** dwindle, decrease, diminish, lessen, wane, dissipate, dribble away.

accumulate *v.* gather, gather together, pile up, heap up, amass, collect, accrue, assemble, aggregate; grow, congregate, cumulate, garner; save up, store up, hoard. **—Ant.** scatter, disperse, distribute; dissipate, waste, get rid of.

accumulation *n.* **1.** collection, assemblage, conglomeration; mass, heap, pile, stack, hoard, stockpile, store; stock, supply, pile-up, aggregation, accrual. **2.** collecting, amassing, gathering; acquiring, agglomerating, hoarding. **—Ant. 2** distribution, dispersing, dispersal, scattering.

accuracy *n.* accurateness, correctness, freedom from error; exactness, exactitude, precision; truth, truthfulness, verity, fidelity, faithfulness. **—Ant.** error, inaccuracy, incorrectness, carelessness, slovenliness; lies, lying, fallaciousness.

accurate *adj.* correct, without error, unerring, true, truthful, faithful, perfect, authentic, faultless, exact, right, precise, scrupulous, punctilious, meticulous, careful. **—Syn. Study.** See CORRECT. **—Ant.** incorrect, wrong, inaccurate, fallacious; inexact, defective, imperfect, faulty; careless, slipshod, slovenly, sloppy.

accusation *n.* charge, allegation, insinuation, complaint, imputation, incrimination, citation, indictment. **—Ant.** reply, answer, plea; denial, rebuttal; vindication, exoneration.

accuse *v.* **1.** charge, lodge a complaint against, arraign, indict, cite. **2.** charge, reproach, take to task, call to account, upbraid; blame. **—Ant. 1, 2** reply, answer, plea, rebut; deny, defend; acquit, absolve, vindicate, exonerate.

accustomed *adj.* **1.** usual, common, normal, regular, general, customary, habitual, established, conventional, set, routine, commonplace, ordinary, familiar, everyday, well-known, prevailing, prevalent, fixed, ingrained; hackneyed, trite, cliché, expected. **2.** used to, acclimated, seasoned, familiarized, acquainted with, inured, in the habit of, given to, habituated, hardened, wonted, prone. **—Ant. 1** unusual, uncommon, rare, strange, unfamiliar, foreign, exotic; singular, infrequent, occasional; peculiar, abnormal, unconventional, odd, queer, erratic. **2** unused, unaccustomed.

ace *n.* **1.** champion, winner, master, victor, star, headliner, medalist, expert. *—adj.* **2.** outstanding, top, top-rated, crack, front-ranking, excellent. **—Ant. 1** failure, disaster, fiasco, dud, klutz.

acerbity *n.* **1.** ill-tempered manner, brusqueness, sarcastic irritability, sarcasm, irascibility, acrimony, pointed rudeness, nastiness, sharpness. **2.** acidity, sourness, tartness, bitterness, astringency, pungency, acridity. **—Ant. 1** good nature, cordiality, good humor, affability, pleasantness, mellowness, complaisance. **2** blandness, tastelessness, lifelessness, indifference.

ache *n.* **1.** pain, throb, twinge, pang, hurt, discomfort, soreness. *—v.* **2.** hurt, feel pain, be sore, smart, throb. **3.** grieve, mourn, lament, suffer, sorrow, agonize, lament. **4.** desire, want, crave, need, hunger, yearn, hanker, covet, long for.

achieve *v.* **1.** accomplish, attain, realize, reach, complete, finish, arrive at, fulfill; bring to pass, bring about, carry out, effect, effectuate, succeed in, do, dispatch. **2.** attain, obtain, realize, reach, gain, get, earn, win, acquire, procure. **—Ant. 1** fail to, fall short of. **2** lose, be deprived of.

achievement *n.* **1.** accomplishment, attainment, realization, fulfillment; fear, coup, tour de force, exploit, effort, act, deed. **2.** accomplishment, attainment, acquirement; skill, mastery, expertise, command. **—Ant. 1** failure, defeat, frustration, fiasco.

acid *adj.* **1.** sour, tart, astringent, pungent, sharp, biting, harsh, vinegary, vinegarish. **2.** acerbic, acrimonious, acidulous, sharp, biting, stinging, cutting, scalding, harsh, scathing, bitter, acrid, caustic, nasty, vitriolic, crabbed; sarcastic, satirical, irascible, ironic. **—Ant. 1** sweet, succulent; alkaline; pleasant-tasting, mild, gentle, bland. **2** kindly, gentle, sweet, mild, soft; pleasant; friendly, warmhearted, benign, compassionate.

acknowledge *v.* **1.** accept, admit, own, own up to, confess; recognize, allow, grant, concede; accede, concur, yield, assent. **2.** recognize, extend cognizance to, take notice of; call upon, call upon to speak, call upon to vote. **3.** respond to, reply to, answer; express appreciation for, thank for. **—Syn. Study. 1** ACKNOWLEDGE, ADMIT, CONFESS agree in the idea of declaring something to be true. ACKNOWLEDGE implies making a statement reluctantly, often about something previously doubted or denied: *to acknowledge one's mistakes.* ADMIT esp. implies acknowledging under pressure: *to admit a* *charge.* CONFESS usu. means stating somewhat formally an admission of wrongdoing or shortcoming: *to confess guilt; to confess an inability to understand.* **—Ant. 1** disclaim, repudiate, reject, renounce, contradict; deny, disavow. **2, 3** ignore, disregard, disdain, slight, spurn, reject; deny.

acknowledgment *n.* **1.** recognition, recognizance, credit. **2.** affirmation, admission, confession, concession. **3.** thanks, gratitude, appreciation; response, answer, reply. **—Ant.** 1, 2 denial, disavowal, disclaimer, demurrer.

acme *n.* height, peak, pinnacle, zenith, high point, highest point, climax, summit; heyday, flowering; crown, crest, apex, culmination, apogee. **—Ant.** depth, low point, worst point, bottom, nadir, abyss.

acolyte *n.* **1.** altar boy; novice, ministerial assistant. **2.** follower, admirer, adherent, devotee, *Informal* fan, *Slang* groupie; assistant, helper, attendant.

acquaint *v.* **1.** introduce, make known socially, meet. **2.** familiarize, apprise, disclose, reveal, advise, tell, inform, notify, enlighten, make aware, divulge to. **—Ant. 2** hide, conceal, keep secret, keep private; withhold, reserve, retain, hold back.

acquaintance *n.* **1.** person slightly known, distant friend; associate. **2.** friendship, relationship, association, dealings. **3.** familiarity, awareness, knowledge, conversance, cognizance. **—Syn. Study.** See FRIEND. **—Ant. 1** stranger; good friend, intimate, bosom buddy. **3** unfamiliarity, ignorance.

acquiesce *v.* consent, agree, assent, accede, allow; bow to, yield, submit, capitulate, give in; admit, concede, grant, comply, concur, conform, fall in with; resign oneself, reconcile oneself. **—Ant.** resist, fight, contest, refuse, balk at, veto; protest, object, disagree, dissent, demur.

acquire *v.* get, obtain, attain, gain, secure, procure, capture; achieve, realize; earn, win, pick up; cultivate. **—Syn. Study.** See GET. **—Ant.** lose, be deprived of; relinquish, give up, forgo.

acquisition *n.* **1.** acquirement, procurement, possession, property, gain, purchase, prize. **2.** attainment, obtainment, achievement, acquirement, procurement, gain.

acquisitive *adj.* covetous, grasping, greedy, avaricious; possessive, materialistic, selfish. **—Ant.** self-denying, abstemious, nonpossessive; altruistic; generous.

acquit *v.* **1.** declare not guilty, declare innocent, clear; exonerate, vindicate, exculpate, absolve, let off, discharge, release, relieve, reprieve, deliver, liberate, pardon, set free; exempt, excuse. **2.** conduct, behave, comport, act. **—Syn. Study. 1** See ABSOLVE. **—Ant. 1** charge, indict, blame; convict, declare guilty; condemn, damn, doom.

acrid *adj.* **1.** caustic, harsh, sharp, bitter, burning, stinging, irritating, biting, pungent; smelly, foul-smelling, malodorous. **2.** harsh, sharp, biting, bitter, nasty, acrimonious, vitriolic, acid; sarcastic, ironic, satirical. **—Ant. 1** sweet, pleasing; fragrant, aromatic. **2** kindly, gentle, sweet, sweet-natured, good-natured; benign, compassionate.

acrimonious *adj.* sarcastic, spiteful, rancorous, bitter, peevish, testy, ill-natured, nasty, *Slang* bitchy; venomous, vitriolic, caustic, corrosive, sour, cutting, biting, splenetic, irascible. **—Ant.** forgiving, benign, benignant, pleasant, agreeable, good-humored, kindhearted, civil, polite.

acrimony *n.* ill will, hard feelings, rancor, anger, bitterness; animosity, hostility, derision, spitefulness, antagonism, asperity, malignity, spite, scorn, malignancy, spleen, animus. **—Ant.** good will, good feelings, love, liking, friendliness, politeness, civility.

act *n.* **1.** deed, action, performance, step, move; feat, exploit, accomplishment, achievement. **2.** action, process of doing. **3.** official decision, law, edict, decree, enactment, legislation, bill, resolution, statute, mandate, ordinance, measure, order. **4.** segment of a play, main division of a play; short performance, routine, *Informal* skit, bit, *Slang* gig. **5.** pretense, front, pose, posture, fake, pretension, insincere act, affectation, show, performance, *Informal* put-on, stance. **—*v.* 6.** do it, perform, do, function, go about, execute, carry out, operate, move; press on, put forth; commit oneself. **7.** behave, conduct oneself, comport oneself; work, operate, function. **8.** pretend to be, feign, fake, affect, simulate, counterfeit. **9.** perform, play, portray, enact; represent; impersonate. **—Ant. 1** inactivity, inaction. **6** stay, stop, rest, procrastinate, put off.

acting *adj.* **1.** temporary, substitute, surrogate, deputy, provisional, officiating, interim; simulated, ersatz. **—*n.* 2.** dramatics, thespianism, stage playing; theater, dramaturgy, stagecraft. **—Ant. 1** permanent; real, true.

action *n.* **1.** power, force, work, effort; effect, influence; movement, motion. **2.** operation, activity, functioning, performing, performance; process; production. **3.** act, deed, step, move, endeavor, enterprise; exploit, feat, achievement. **4.** activity, work, effort, exertion, movement, enterprise; committed attention, achievement, accomplishment, progress, execution. **5.** combat, battle, fighting, conflict, warfare. **6.** movement, excitement, adventure. **7.** legal proceedings, prosecution, suit, judicial redress. **—Ant. 2** inaction, inactivity, rest. **4** complacency. **6** dialogue, exposition.

activate *v.* start, turn on, actuate, put into action, set going, stimulate, propel, prompt; drive, impel, motivate, energize; vitalize, mobilize, *Informal* stir. **—Ant.** deactivate, immobilize, paralyze, deaden; stop, turn off, halt, check.

active *adj.* **1.** energetic, vigorous, lively, animated, frisky, peppy, spirited, indefatigable; busy, on the go, occupied, engaged, industrious, enterprising, ambitious, go-getting, forceful, assertive, aggressive, zealous. **2.** strenuous, energetic; vigorous; lively, animated. **3.** functioning, actively operative, working, acting, effectual, productive; in force, at work. **4.** alert, quick, vigorous, alive, lively; agile, spry, nimble, sprightly, animated, imaginative; industrious, diligent. **—Ant. 1–4** inactive. **1** unoccupied; torpid, sluggish, indolent, idle, lazy. **2** sedentary; dull. **3** nonfunctioning, inoperative; dormant. **4** sluggish, slow, dull; unimaginative.

activity *n.* **1.** action, movement; enterprise; commotion, hustle, bustle, tumult, agitation, flurry, stir, fuss, hurly-burly; sprightliness, vivacity, liveliness, animation, *Informal* goings on. **2.** exercise, exertion, movement. **3.** undertaking, pursuit, enterprise, function, venture, endeavor, project, avocation, occupation, assignment. **—Ant. 1** inactivity, immobility, torpor, dullness. **2** relaxation, rest, stillness, serenity.

actor *n.* **1.** performer, thespian, dramatic artist, trouper, player, *Slang* ham; *(variously)* star, feature actor, supporting actor, character actor, working actor, bit player, walk on; starlet. **2.** participant, doer, functionary, perpetrator.

actual *adj.* **1.** real, existing, *Informal* true-to-life, factual, true, genuine, bona fide, authentic, legitimate, confirmed. **2.** real, physical, corporeal, existent, existing, concrete, tangible, verifiable, certain, sure; current, present, prevailing. **—Ant. 1** fictional, fictitious, made-up; hypothetical, theoretical. **2** probable, supposed, projected, conjectured.

actuality *n.* reality, fact, truth, point of fact, plain fact, brutal fact, verity, substance. **—Ant.** pretense, falseness, make-believe, illusion.

actually *adv.* in fact, really, truly, verily, genuinely, literally, indeed.

actuate *v.* **1.** See ACTIVATE. **2.** motivate, prompt, cause, induce, stimulate, instigate, incite, bring about, move, drive, impel, trigger, arouse, rouse; influence, inspire, excite, stir, animate. **—Ant. 1** See ACTIVATE. **2** check, curb, restrain, hinder, deter, dampen, damper, inhibit, thwart.

acumen *n.* keenness, acuteness, smartness, astuteness, shrewdness, cleverness; discernment, intelligence, wisdom, sound judgment; perspicacity, clearheadedness, sagacity, insight, perception, ingenuity. **—Ant.** obtuseness, dullness, ignorance, stupidity, folly, bad judgment.

acute *adj.* **1.** sharply pointed, sharp, peaked, needle-shaped. **2.** severe, intense, fierce, powerful, very great, very bad, critical; excruciating, distressing, piercing, agonizing. **3.** keen, penetrating, piercing, sharp; discriminating, discerning, perceptive, intuitive, sensitive, clever, ingenious. **—Ant. 1** obtuse, dull, blunt, blunted. **2** mild, moderate, *Medical* chronic. **3** obtuse, dull, dense, stolid.

adage *n.* saying, proverb, maxim, axiom, motto, aphorism, epigram; dictum, truism, wise observation, precept, platitude, cliché, *Informal* saw, old saw, quip.

adamant *adj.* insistent, unyielding, inflexible, rigid, fixed, set, firm, tough, immovable, uncompromising, unbending, resolute, intransigent, determined, stubborn, *Informal* hard as rock, obdurate, inexorable, *Slang* uptight. **—Ant.** yielding, flexible, lax, undemanding, easygoing, indifferent, *Slang* loose; submissive, capitulating, pliant, compliant, compromising.

adapt *v.* **1.** adjust, conform, accommodate, acclimate, fit, suit, assimilate, acculturate, coordinate, harmonize, reconcile, attune to. **2.** reshape, shape, fashion, frame, transform, rework, convert, adjust, make suitable, make fit, recompose, remodel, modify, change, alter. **—Syn. Study. 2** See ADJUST.

adaptable *adj.* **1.** flexible, pliant, compliant, unrigid, open-minded, easygoing; obliging, accommodating, conformable, malleable, tractable, amenable. **2.** usable, serviceable, applicable, accommodative; changeable, adjustable, alterable. **—Ant. 1** inflexible, rigid, fixed, closed-minded, *Slang* uptight. **2** inflexible, nonadjustable, unalterable; unusable, unserviceable.

adaptation *n.* **1.** alteration, modification, remodeling, conversion, metamorphosis; refitting; adjustment, change, shift. **2.** altered version, modification, reworking, revision, reshaping.

add *v.* **1.** total, sum up, count up, figure up, compute, calculate, reckon; combine. **2.** include, attach, append, affix, join, join on, tack on; offer in addition, supplement, increase by, enlarge by. **—Ant. 1** subtract, deduct. **2** remove, exclude, eliminate, withdraw; take, take away, reduce.

addendum *n.* added section, supplement, addition, codicil, postscript; appendage, afterthought, attachment.

addict *n.* **1.** drug addict; *Slang* junkie, user, head, freak, dope fiend. **2.** devotee, fan, adherent, habitué, acolyte, votary; *Slang* nut, hound, buff. *—v.* **3.** give (oneself) habitually, yield obsessively, surrender, indulge in, submit; *Slang* hook, turn on. **—Ant. 3** withdraw, break the habit, *Slang* kick the habit; renounce, give up, eschew.

addiction *n.* addictedness, obsession, enslavement, fixation, enthrallment, mania, compulsion, craze, fetish, quirk, hangup, preoccupation; alcoholism, dipsomania, barbiturism, cocainism, morphinism.

addition *n.* **1.** mathematical summation, totaling, counting up, summing up, summation, reckoning, enumeration. **2.** adding, including, encompassing, embracing; joining, adjoining, annexing, appending, attaching; extending, increasing. **3.** increase, increment; extension, enlargement, extra, additive, augmentation, expansion. **4.** annex, wing, extension, appendage; adjunct, appurtenance, accessory, attachment; addendum, added contribution. **—Syn. Study. 4** ADDITION, ACCESSORY, ADJUNCT, ATTACHMENT refer to something joined to or used with something else. ADDITION is the general word for anything joined to something previously existing; it carries no implication of size, importance, or kind: *to build an addition to the town library.* An ACCESSORY is a nonessential part or object that makes something more complete, convenient, or attractive: *clothing accessories; camera accessories.* An ADJUNCT is a subordinate addition that aids or assists but is usu. separate: *a second machine as an adjunct to the first.* An ATTACHMENT is an supplementary part that may be easily connected and removed: *a sewing machine attachment for pleating.* **—Ant. 1–3** subtraction. **2** subtracting, removing, removal, detaching, detachment. **3** decrease, reduction, deduction, lessening, diminution.

additional *adj.* extra, spare, added, added on, supplementary, appended, over-and-above.

addled *adj.* confused, mixed-up, muddled, befuddled, nonplused; foolish, silly.

address *n.* **1.** street number, city, and state; mailing address, postal address, street address, street number; place of residence, dwelling, place of business; location, locality. **2.** speech, talk, statement, oration, discourse, harangue. *—v.* **3.** write for delivery to, put an address on. **4.** give a formal talk, talk to, speak to, orate, lecture, greet, salute in words; write to. **—Syn. Study. 2** See SPEECH.

adept *adj.* skilled, skillful, expert, proficient, accomplished, master, masterful, ingenious, practiced; good, apt, able, adroit, dexterous, gifted. **—Ant.** amateurish, beginning; unskilled, inept, unaccomplished, clumsy, awkward.

adequate *adj.* suitable, satisfactory, sufficient, equal to need, passable, tolerable, fitting, fit; enough, ample, *Informal* so-so. **—Ant.** inadequate, unsuitable, unsatisfactory, insufficient; imperfect, defective; too little, not enough.

adhere *v.* **1.** stick, stick fast, hold, cling, cleave, cohere; glue, glue on, paste, cement; fix, fasten. **2.** be faithful, be loyal, be constant, be true, keep, keep to, hold closely, maintain, cling, stick, cleave, stand by, abide by, remain fixed. **—Syn. Study. 1** See STICK. **—Ant. 1** come unstuck, come loose, come unglued; detach, unfasten. **2** break with, part from, separate from, leave, be disloyal, be untrue.

adherence *n.* **1.** adhesion, adhesiveness, stickiness. **2.** strict observance, attachment, keeping to, obedience; loyalty, fealty, faithfulness, fidelity, constancy, allegiance, devotion. **—Ant. 1** looseness; slickness. **2** breaking, disobedience, disloyalty, unfaithfulness, infidelity.

adherent *n.* **1.** follower, supporter, advocate, disciple, upholder; devotee, partisan, champion, ally, fan; acolyte, pupil. *—adj.* **2.** adhesive, sticky, sticking, gummy, viscous, viscid, clinging, adhering, holding fast. **—Syn. Study. 1** See FOLLOWER. **—Ant. 1** opponent, detractor. **2** slick; watery.

adhesive *adj.* **1.** adherent, adhering, sticky, sticking, clinging; gummy, mucilaginous; gummed. *—n.* **2.** sticky substance, adhering substance, gummy substance; glue, paste, rubber cement, cement, epoxy, solder, mortar, stickum. **—Ant. 2** solvent.

adieu *n.* **1.** goodby, so long, see you later, take it easy, godspeed, farewell, by-by, *Hawaiian* aloha, *Italian* ciao, *German* Auf Wiedersehen, *Spanish* adios; *French* au revoir, à demain, à bientôt; *Brit.* cheerio, ta-ta, good day, toodle-oo. **2.** goodby, leavetaking, farewell, valediction.

ad infinitum ceaselessly, continuously, endlessly, unendingly, unceasingly; interminably; infinitely, limitlessly, boundlessly. **—Ant.** occasionally, on occasion, sporadically, now and again, off and on; never, not at all, at no time; seldom, infrequently, rarely.

adjacent *adj.* next to, beside, right beside, next door to; abutting, touching, adjoining, bordering, tangential; contiguous with, conterminous, proximate, juxtaposed. **—Syn. Study.** ADJACENT, ADJOINING both mean near or close to something. ADJACENT implies being nearby or next to something else, with nothing of the same sort intervening: *a motel adjacent to the highway; the adjacent houses.* ADJOINING implies touching at a common point or line: *adjoining rooms.* **—Ant.** far from, remote from, distant from, separated from.

adjoining *adj.* joining, joined, touching, connected, interconnected, contiguous, next-door, adjacent. **—Syn. Study.** See ADJACENT. **—Ant.** separate, detached, individual.

adjourn *v.* **1.** recess, suspend, interrupt, discontinue, break off, put off, postpone; close, end, dismiss, dissolve. **2.** repair, remove, withdraw, move; depart for. **—Ant. 1** convene, be in session, call to order, open, reopen; assemble, gather, convoke, continue. **2** remain, stay, stay put.

adjudge *v.* decide, determine, consider, adjudicate, settle, rule, arbitrate, rule on, issue a decree; ordain, decree, pronounce; referee, umpire.

adjunct *n.* accessory, supplement, complement, auxiliary part, subsidiary, secondary feature, addition, attachment; incidental, appurtenance. **—Syn. Study.** See ADDITION.

adjust *v.* **1.** set, fix, move, regulate, change, order. **2.** accustom, acclimate, accommodate, adapt, attune, reconcile, conform; fix, alter, modify, regulate. **—Syn. Study. 1, 2** ADJUST, ADAPT, ALTER imply making necessary or desirable changes, as in position, shape, or the like. To ADJUST is to make a minor change, as to move into proper position for use: *to adjust the eyepiece of a telescope.* To ADAPT is to make a change in character, or to make something useful in a new way: *to adapt a method to a new task.* To ALTER is to change the appearance but not the use: *to alter a suit.* **—Ant. 1** leave as is, let remain as is, leave alone.

adjustment *n.* **1.** adjusting, alignment, straightening; fixing, regulation, regulating, modification, alteration; bringing into agreement, justification, reconciliation, rectification; focusing. **2.** control, regulator, adjusting device; setting. **3.** settling in, settlement, acclimation, adapting, *Informal* getting used to; orientation.

adjutant *n.* assisting staff officer, aide, assistant, right-hand man, right hand, aide-de-camp.

ad-lib *n.* **1.** extemporaneous wisecrack, improvisation. **—***v.* **2.** improvise, extemporize, speak extemporaneously, speak off the cuff, speak impromptu, make up. **—Ant. 2** follow the script, speak from notes.

administer *v.* **1.** manage, run, direct, *Informal* boss, administrate, govern, supervise, superintend, preside over, oversee. **2.** dispense, apply, give, tender.

administration *n.* **1.** administering, application, execution, management; dispensation, distribution, tendering. **2.** management, executive duty, superintendence, leadership, overseeing; governing, government. **3.** officers, executives, *Slang* brass; governing body, management, managerial organization, government.

administrative *adj.* executive, managerial, management, supervisory, organizational.

admirable *adj.* worthy of admiration, commendable, praiseworthy, laudable, estimable, venerable. **—Ant.** deplorable, reprehensible, censurable, disappointing; bad, untrustworthy, worthless, faulty.

admiration *n.* high regard, high opinion, esteem; veneration, honor, commendation, praise, approval, respect. **—Ant.** low regard, low opinion, disdain.

admire *v.* view with approval, hold in high regard, hold in esteem, think highly of, respect, esteem, praise, value, prize, take pleasure in. **—Ant.** hold in low regard, hold a low opinion of, view with disapproval, disdain, abhor.

admissible *adj.* capable of being admitted, permitted, allowed, allowable, permissible, acceptable, legitimate, admittable, tolerated, tolerable, passable. **—Ant.** inadmissible, unacceptable, disallowed, nonpermissible, intolerable.

admission *n.* **1.** admittance, permission to enter, entry, entrance, entreé, access. **2.** price of admission, entrance fee; ticket; fee, charge, tariff. **3.** acknowledgment, confession, profession, concession, declaration; assent, affirmation. **—Ant. 3** denial, disavowal; rejection, negation.

admit *v.* **1.** let in, allow to enter, let enter, give access to, grant entrance; appoint, induct, invest; receive, welcome. **2.** acknowledge, confess, concede, profess, declare, *Informal* own up. **3.** allow, permit, grant, let. **—Syn. Study. 2** See ACKNOWLEDGE. **—Ant. 1** exclude, keep out, debar; dismiss, reject. **2** deny, disavow, reject, negate. **3** prohibit, forbid, disallow.

admixture *n.* blend, amalgam, combination, compound, composite, amalgamation, mixture, intermixture, intermingling, mélange, medley, commingling, commixture; hodgepodge, confusion, conglomeration, jumble, mess, mishmash, potpourri, salmagundi, gallimaufry.

admonish *v.* **1.** warn, caution, put on guard, tip off; advise, counsel, enjoin. **2.** reprove, censure, reprimand, rebuke, reproach, remonstrate, chide, chasten, scold, upbraid, criticize, take to task, call to account, rap on the knuckles. **—Syn. Study. 1** See WARN. **2** See REPRIMAND. **—Ant. 2** praise, compliment, commend.

admonition *n.* reprimand, mild reproof, scolding, reproach, remonstrance, rebuke, rap on the knuckles; warning, chiding, cautionary reminder, advice. **—Ant.** compliment, commendation, bit of praise, pat on the back.

ado *n.* bustle, commotion, stir, bother, flurry, flutter, pother, fuss, trouble; to-do, turmoil, agitation, tumult, hurly-burly, hubbub, confusion, uproar, furore, racket, fracas. **—Ant.** tranquillity, serenity, calm, calmness, peace, peacefulness.

adolescent *n.* **1.** teenager, teen, young teen, young man or woman, minor, youth, schoolboy, schoolgirl, lad, lass, lassie; stripling, fledgling. *—adj.* **2.** for a teenager, befitting a teenager, not adult; immature, sophomoric, puerile, pubescent, juvenile; callow, undeveloped; youthful, boyish, girlish; childish, babyish. **—Ant. 1** adult; child. **2** adult, grownup, mature.

adopt *v.* **1.** become the legal parent of, take as one's own child. **2.** formally approve, accept, choose, appropriate, take up, follow, embrace, espouse; utilize, employ, assume, affect, use; acknowledge, conform to. **—Ant. 1** give up for adoption, place; disinherit. **2** give up, cast aside, cast off; spurn, forswear, repudiate, reject, disclaim; annul, abrogate.

adorable *adj.* lovable, delightful, precious, darling, likable, pleasing, divine; appealing, charming, winsome, captivating, engaging, fetching, irresistible. **—Ant.** hateful, unlovable, unlikable, hard to like, despicable; displeasing, unappealing.

adoration *n.* worship, worshiping, glorification, exaltation, veneration, reverence, adulation, devotion; honor, idolization, magnification. **—Ant.** blasphemy, denunciation, reviling, execration, belittling.

adore *v.* **1.** love, hold dear, cherish; *Informal* worship, revere, glorify; fancy, like, prize, dote on; admire. **2.** worship, glorify, exalt, revere, venerate, idolize. **—Ant. 1** hate, dislike, abhor, loathe, despise. **2** blaspheme, revile, denounce, execrate, belittle.

adorn *v.* ornament, decorate, embellish, array, bedeck, bejewel, *Informal* deck out; beautify, set off to advantage, furbish. **—Ant.** strip, bare; simplify.

adornment *n.* ornament, ornamentation, decoration, jewelry, embellishment; finery, attire.

adrift *adj.* **1.** drifting, afloat, unmoored, aweigh, unanchored. **2.** confused, lost, uncertain, bewildered, unstable, at sea, perplexed, irresolute, unsettled. **—Ant. 1** moored, fastened, secured, anchored. **2** stable, certain, resolute, sure, confident.

adroit *adj.* dexterous, nimble; deft, apt, proficient, skilled, skillful, expert, masterful; clever, artful, facile, cunning, slick. **—Syn. Study.** See DEXTEROUS. **—Ant.** clumsy, awkward, unhandy.

adulation *n.* flattery, adoration, fawning, fulsome praise. **—Ant.** condemnation, denunciation, defamation, aspersion, abuse, vituperation, censure, ridicule; hatred, dislike, loathing.

adult *n.* **1.** grownup, man, woman; father, mother, parent; elder, oldster, senior citizen; grandfather, grandpa, grandmother, grandma, granny. *—adj.* **2.** mature, big, of age, full-grown, grownup, senior; seasoned, experienced, developed. **—Ant. 1** child, baby, infant, adolescent. **2** immature, raw, green, inexperienced, callow.

adulterate *v.* contaminate, thin, water, water down; depreciate, *Informal* cut.

adultery *n.* unfaithfulness, fornication, marital infidelity, illicit intercourse, cuckoldry, carnality, unchastity, promiscuity, extramarital relations, violation of the marriage bed, criminal conversation. **—Ant.** fidelity, faithfulness, steadfastness, constancy.

advance *v.* **1.** go forward, come forward, bring forward, send forward, progress, bring up, move up, send up, move onward, press on, propel; put up front, promote. **2.** proffer, bring forward, offer, bring to notice, bring to attention, lay down, assign. **3.** bring forward, further, increase, improve, upgrade, promote, add to, multiply, further the growth of, take a step forward. **4.** pay beforehand, give beforehand; pay on account, pay now. *—n.* **5.** forward movement, progress, onward movement. **6.** improvement, advancement, progress, furthering, promotion, step, breakthrough, growth, gain. **7.** prepayment, down payment; binder. **8.** pass, amorous overture, overture; proposition.

—*adj.* **9.** forward, foremost, before all others, in front, up front. **10.** preliminary, previous, prior, before the fact, *Informal* pre. —**Ant. 1** retreat, go backward, regress, retrogress, move back, withdraw; demote, degrade. **2** hide, keep secret, withhold, suppress, hold back, keep under wraps; recall. **3** decrease, lessen, diminish, subtract from, set back, retard, weaken. **4** defer payment, withhold payment. **5** retreat, withdrawal, regression, retrogression. **6** worsening, regression, retrogression, setback. **7** deferred payment. **9** rear, hindmost, in back.

advantage *n.* **1.** asset, help, benefit, aid, service, profit; blessing, boon, support, comfort, convenience. **2.** edge, upper hand, initial supremacy, *Slang* clout, precedence, dominance; superiority, success. —**Syn. Study. 1** ADVANTAGE, BENEFIT, PROFIT all mean something that is of use or value. ADVANTAGE is anything that places a person in a favorable or superior position, esp. in coping with competition or difficulties: *It is to your advantage to have traveled widely.* BENEFIT is anything that promotes the welfare or improves the state of a person or group: *The new library will be a great benefit to our town.* PROFIT is any valuable or useful gain, usu. financial, moral, or educational: *profit from trade; profit from experience.* —**Ant. 1, 2** disadvantage. **1** hindrance, difficulty, drawback, deterrent, disservice, curse; discomfort, inconvenience. **2** handicap, *Slang* short end of the stick.

advantageous *adj.* **1.** helpful, beneficial, useful, valuable, profitable, of assistance, of service. **2.** superior, favorable, dominating, auspicious, enviable, fortunate; *Informal* win-win. —**Ant. 1** unhelpful, useless, detrimental; harmful, injurious. **2** inferior, unfavorable, unfortunate; *Informal* behind the eight ball, up the creek.

advent *n.* coming, arrival, onset, beginning, occurrence, commencement, start, appearance, bowing in, appearing, opening up. —**Ant.** end, conclusion, finish, demise, expiration.

adventure *n.* enterprise, undertaking, venture, quest, escapade, *Poetic* emprise.

adventurer *n.* daredevil, dragonslayer, vagabond, romantic, giant-killer, hero, heroine, soldier of fortune, buccaneer, swashbuckler.

adventurous *adj.* **1.** seeking excitement, eager for experience, daring, bold, venturesome, audacious; brave, courageous, valiant, intrepid. **2.** challenging, risky, hazardous, dangerous, perilous. —**Ant. 1** unadventurous, cautious, hesitant. **2** dull, boring, routine; completely safe.

adversary *n.* opponent, rival, competitor, foe, antagonist, enemy. —**Syn. Study.** ADVERSARY, ANTAGONIST refer to a person, group, or personified force contending against another. ADVERSARY suggests an enemy who fights determinedly, continuously, and relentlessly: *a formidable adversary.* ANTAGONIST suggests one who, in hostile spirit, opposes another, often in a particular contest or struggle: *a duel with an antagonist.* —**Ant.** ally, accomplice, colleague, teammate; friend.

adverse *adj.* unfavorable, contrary, opposing, unpropitious, detrimental, negative, difficult; hostile, antagonistic, unfriendly, inimical; pernicious, harmful, injurious. —**Ant.** favorable, helpful, beneficial, supporting, agreeable; auspicious.

adversity *n.* unfavorable circumstances, misfortune, calamity, disaster, ill-fortune, bad luck, catastrophe, hardship, suffering, mishap; affliction, trouble, distress, trial, tribulation, woe. —**Ant.** good fortune, success, blessings.

advertise *v.* publicize, call attention to, give public notice of, proclaim, broadcast, vaunt, tout, noise abroad; display, reveal, show. —**Ant.** hide, conceal, keep hidden, keep under cover, keep secret, keep under wraps.

advertisement *n.* want ad, classified ad, announcement, flier, handbill, poster, placard, public notice, leaflet, circular, broadside, throwaway, commercial, trailer.

advice *n.* **1.** recommendation, suggestion, opinion, view; counsel, advisement, guidance. **2.** information, intelligence, communication, word, tidings, news, report, notification, message, account. —**Syn. Study. 1** ADVICE, COUNSEL refer to opinions offered as worthy bases for thought, conduct, or action. ADVICE is a practical recommendation, generally from a person with relevant knowledge or experience: *Get a lawyer's advice about the purchase.* COUNSEL is weighty and serious advice, given after careful deliberation and consultation: *to seek counsel during a personal crisis.*

advisable *adj.* recommendable; prudent, judicious, wise, smart; suitable, seemly, expedient, sound, proper, fitting, fit; *Informal* best, a good bet. —**Ant.** unsuitable, unsound, improper; inexpedient, stupid, silly; unfitting.

advise *v.* **1.** counsel, recommend, recommend to, suggest, suggest to, offer an opinion, offer the opinion that; commend, urge, encourage, enjoin; caution, warn, admonish, exhort. **2.** inform, tell, notify, apprise, report, give notice, make known, communicate.

adviser, advisor *n.* **1.** consultant,

counselor, idea person, resource person; aide, surrogate, assistant. **2.** counselor, guide, mentor, preceptor, monitor, admonitor, director, coach; instructor, teacher, tutor.

advisory *adj.* informational, informative, consultatory, consultative, counseling, instructive, guiding; admonitory, cautionary, warning.

advocacy *n.* championship, campaigning for, pleading the case of, speaking out for, support, patronage, supporting, backing, espousal, pressing for, advancement, furthering, promotion, propagation; recommendation, endorsement, defense. **—Ant.** opposition; combatting, assault, attacking.

advocate *v.* **1.** recommend, advise, propose, prescribe; champion, urge, promote, campaign for, plead the cause of, argue for, speak out for, stand up for, push for; encourage, endorse, favor, support, back, press for, espouse; advance, further, propagate. *—n.* **2.** champion, backer, supporter, proponent, promoter, spokesman for; believer, upholder, apostle, patron; defender, pleader, apologist, propagandist. **3.** lawyer, attorney, legal adviser, counsel, counselor, attorney-at-law, barrister, solicitor, *Slang* mouthpiece. **—Ant. 1** oppose, combat, attack, assail, impugn. **2** opponent, adversary, enemy, antagonist, detractor; attacker, accuser.

aegis *n.* sponsorship, auspices, protection, patronage, guard, favor, wing, shelter, backing, support, guardianship, championship, guaranty, surety.

aerial *n.* **1.** antenna. *—adj.* **2.** air, in the air, from the air, by air, airborne; by aircraft, of aircraft, flying, capable of flight; atmospheric, airy, wind-created. **3.** dreamy, ethereal, ephemeral, airy, lofty, unsubstantial, unreal, fanciful, soaring, visionary, imaginary; elusive, tenuous, impractical. **—Ant. 2** land, on the ground; by land. **3** down to earth, real, realistic, practical, pragmatic.

affable *adj.* amiable, genial, congenial, agreeable, friendly, cordial, gracious, sociable, compatible; good-natured, good-humored, pleasant, warm, easygoing, open; courteous, civil, mannerly. **—Ant.** unfriendly, disagreeable, unsociable, unapproachable, inaccessible, distant, haughty, *Informal* standoffish; ill-humored, unpleasant, cold; discourteous, uncivil, ungracious, rude, brusque, curt, surly.

affair *n.* **1.** personal business, private matter, concern, business; personal problem, interest, pursuit. **2.** undertaking, activity, matter, business, operation, function, transaction, effort; incident, occurrence, episode, event, happening, proceeding, circumstance, adventure. **3.** celebration, festivity, party, social gathering, social function, occasion, *Slang* shindig. **4.** love affair, romance, relationship, liaison, intrigue, amour.

affect[1] *v.* **1.** influence, be of importance to, impinge on, act on, produce an effect on, alter, change, modify; concern, relate to, pertain to, interest, regard. **2.** have an emotional effect on, move, touch, stir, impress. **—Ant. 2** leave unmoved, *Informal* leave cold; bore.

affect[2] *v.* make a pretense of, pretend, pretend to, feign, fake, put on, assume, adopt, imitate, counterfeit, simulate; fancy, show a preference for, tend toward, embrace, be inclined toward. **—Syn. Study.** See PRETEND. **—Ant.** repudiate, scorn, reject, shed, cast aside, cast off.

affectation *n.* false mannerism, pretense, pretension, sham, façade; airs, false air, insincerity, artificiality, *Slang* put-on. **—Ant.** the genuine article; naturalness, sincerity, genuineness, artlessness, simplicity.

affected[1] *adj.* **1.** acted upon, concerned, pertinent, interested; influenced, changed. **2.** moved, touched, stirred, impressed; grieved, sorry, sorrowful, troubled, upset, distressed, afflicted. **3.** upset, harmed, injured, impaired. **—Ant. 1–3** unaffected. **1** unconcerned, uninterested. **2** unmoved, untouched, *Informal* cold. **3** healed, cured; unharmed, uninjured, untouched.

affected[2] *adj.* pretentious, pompous, conceited, vainglorious, vain; artificial, unnatural, mannered, unreal, not genuine, phony, assumed, contrived, studied. **—Ant.** natural, unpretentious, genuine, real; modest.

affection *n.* **1.** emotional attachment, love, fondness, tenderness, warmth; liking, kind disposition, proclivity. **2.** sickness, illness, disease, ailment, malady, disorder, physical complaint. **—Ant. 1** hate, loathing, antipathy, enmity; dislike, coldness, coolness. **2** healthiness, well-being, healthfulness, salubriousness.

affectionate *adj.* loving, demonstrative; warm, warmhearted, tender, tenderhearted, fond, doting, caring; ardent. **—Ant.** cold, cool, undemonstrative, impassive, stolid; apathetic, callous.

affiance *v.* engage to marry, betroth, pledge, solemnly promise.

affiliate *v.* **1.** associate, connect; join, unite, amalgamate, ally, incorporate, band together, merge; fraternize, consort. *—n.* **2.** close associate, legally connected associate, colleague; branch, chapter, part, arm, division, subdivision. **—Ant. 1** disassociate; leave, quit, resign from.

affiliation *n.* association, relationship, alliance, connection, union.

affinity *n.* **1.** natural liking, partiality, fancy, penchant, liking, fondness; leaning, bent, tendency, proclivity, propensity, inclination; sympathy, rapport. **2.** family resemblance, similarity, likeness, parallelism, homology; relation, connection, compatibility. **—Ant. 1** aversion, repulsion, antipathy, disliking. **2** dissimilarity.

affirm *v.* **1.** declare, assert, aver, avow, maintain, proclaim; profess, allege, hold, contend, claim. **2.** confirm, sustain, ratify, validate, endorse, approve, uphold, support, warrant. **—Syn. Study. 1** See DECLARE. **—Ant. 1** deny, refute, repudiate, disavow, renounce. **2** reject, deny, rescind, nullify, veto, disallow, contravene, forswear.

affirmation *n.* **1.** strong assertion, avowal, declaration. **2.** confirmation, ratification, approval, consent, endorsement, certification. **—Ant. 1** denial, refutation, repudiation, disavowal, renunciation. **2** rejection, nullification, veto.

affirmative *adj.* **1.** yes, assenting, positive, affirmatory; approving, concurring, confirmatory. **2.** positive, confirming, confirmatory, corroborative, ratifying, affirming, concurring; emphatic, conclusive, categorical. *—n.* **3.** side in favor of a question; positive side, optimistic side. *—adv.* **4.** yes. **—Ant. 1–4** negative. **1** negating, no. **2** nonconfirming; inconclusive, doubtful. **4** no.

affix *v.* attach, fasten, fix, add on, tack on, put on; set to, seal, stick, glue, paste, tag. **—Ant.** detach, unfasten, take off; unglue.

afflict *v.* distress, oppress, torment, plague, beset. **—Ant.** relieve, comfort, console, solace, assuage; bless, delight.

affliction *n.* distress, hardship, trouble, trial, tribulation, torment, oppression, adversity, misfortune, ordeal, calamity, pain, anguish, misery, wretchedness, curse. **—Ant.** relief, comfort, consolation, solace; blessing, joy, delight.

affluent *adj.* rich, wealthy, prosperous, well-to-do, moneyed, well-off, *Slang* loaded, well-heeled, well-fixed. **—Ant.** poor, impoverished, impecunious; destitute, indigent.

afford *v.* **1.** have the money for, meet the expense of, manage, bear, support. **2.** bear the consequences of, bear, sustain; risk, chance. **3.** give, provide, offer, supply, furnish, command, grant, yield, lend, impart.

affray *n.* fight, brawl, row, donnybrook, fracas, free-for-all, altercation, melee, scuffle, ruction, rumpus, scrap, set-to, battle royal, skirmish, tussle, wrangle, commotion, squabble.

affront *v.* **1.** offend, insult, provoke, cause umbrage to. *—n.* **2.** offense, insult, slur, slight, indignity; rudeness, discourtesy, insolence, impertinence, contemptuousness; outrage, dishonor, disgrace, ignominy, humiliation, mortification, *Informal* put-down; wrong, abuse, injury, ill-treatment. **—Syn. Study. 2** See INSULT. **—Ant. 1** pamper, flatter, humor, indulge, gratify; honor, please; appease, smooth the feathers of. **2** courtesy, deference, compliment, honor; apology.

afraid *adj.* **1.** scared, fearful, frightened, terrified, terror-stricken, alarmed, anxious, anxiety-ridden, apprehensive, timorous, panicky, panic-stricken; fainthearted, cowardly; *Informal* lily-livered, chicken-livered, chickenhearted; *Slang* chicken. **2.** regretful, sorry, apologetic, unhappy; disappointed. **—Ant. 1** fearless; bold, audacious, venturesome; indifferent. **2** happy, pleased.

afresh *adv.* anew, again, over, once more, another time; again and again, over and over.

aftermath *n.* consequence, outcome, result; sequel, follow-up, upshot, offshoot, byproduct, *Slang* payoff.

agape *adv.* **1.** wide open, gaping. **2.** wonderstruck, spellbound, dumbstruck, dumbfounded, stupefied, amazed, astonished, awestruck, flabbergasted, agog.

age *n.* **1.** period of existence, duration of life, life span; lifetime, generation. **2.** old age, advanced age, seniority; adulthood. **3.** era, epoch, period, phase, date; stage of time, stage of life. **4.** a long time, eon, millennium; forever. *—v.* **5.** advance in age, grow older, mature, develop; make old. **6.** mature, ripen, mellow, season, develop. **—Syn. Study. 3** AGE, EPOCH, ERA, PERIOD all refer to an extent of time. AGE usu. implies a considerable extent of time, esp. one associated with a dominant personality, influence, characteristic, or institution: *the age of chivalry.* EPOCH and ERA are often used interchangeably to refer to an extent of time characterized by changed conditions and new undertakings: *an era (or epoch) of invention.* EPOCH sometimes refers esp. to the beginning of an era: *The steam engine marked a new epoch in technology.* A PERIOD usu. has a marked condition or feature: *a period of industrial expansion; the Victorian period.* **—Ant. 2** youth, childhood, adolescence. **4** short time, instant, second.

aged *adj.* **1.** old, elderly, of advanced age, advanced in years, ancient. **2.** of the age of, as old as, having lived for. **3.** mature, ripe, ripened, mellow. **—Ant.**

1 young, youthful, juvenile. 3 unripe, immature.

agency *n.* 1. service organization, bureau, department. 2. power, action, activity, operation; intervention, mediation, force, influence, charge, means, instrument, instrumentality.

agenda *n.* list of things to be done, schedule, docket, program, timetable; items of business.

agent *n.* 1. representative; emissary, envoy, deputy, advocate; intermediary, negotiator, go-between. 2. force, power, agency, mover, effective principle; means, instrument, cause, author, vehicle. 3. doer, perpetrator, performer, practitioner, worker, mover, operator, executor. —**Ant.** 2 counteragent, counteractor, opponent, neutralizer.

agglomerate *v.* gather, assemble, amass, cluster, condense, collect, accumulate, conglomerate, heap together, lump together, pile up, heap up, bunch, clump, gather into a mass; rally, muster, mobilize. —**Ant.** disperse, scatter, unwind.

aggrandize *v.* enlarge, increase, amplify, magnify, extend, inflate, blow up, build up, expand, broaden, widen; strengthen, intensify, beef up; stretch, bloat, puff up, distend, dilate. —**Ant.** decrease, diminish, contract, constrict, deflate, collapse, crunch.

aggravate *v.* 1. make worse, worsen, make more severe; intensify, inflame, irritate, exacerbate, increase, heighten. 2. irritate, annoy, exasperate, anger, vex, rile, nettle, affront. —**Ant.** 1 improve; soothe, relieve, assuage, alleviate, ease; lessen, mitigate, pacify. 2 please; soothe, calm, placate, ease.

aggregate *n.* composite, compound, union, combination, gathering, accumulation, collection, amassing, bringing together, summation, mixture, mix, blend, mass, conglomeration, conglomerate.

aggression *n.* hostile behavior, hostility, fighting spirit, active anger, viciousness, pugnacity, belligerence, combativeness; act of war, hostile act, assault, invasion, raid, offense. —**Ant.** peacefulness, friendliness, submissiveness; peace, pacification.

aggressive *adj.* 1. hostile, belligerent, combative, assailant, pugnacious, vicious, tending to attack, contentious, take-no-prisoners, warring. 2. self-assertive, forceful, competitive, bold; enterprising, ambitious, energetic, zealous, take-no-prisoners. —**Ant.** 1 peaceful, friendly; submissive. 2 retiring, quiet, shy, bashful, mild; lazy.

aggrieved *adj.* sorrowful, saddened, troubled, pained, disturbed; sad, grieving, grief-stricken, tearful, mournful; offended, affronted, wronged, hurt, stung, wounded, injured, abused, ill-treated, maltreated, put upon, persecuted, distressed, imposed upon.

aghast *adj.* 1. astonished, amazed, stunned, astounded, thunderstruck. 2. filled with horror, horrified, terrified, horror-struck, shocked, appalled; fear-struck, frightened. —**Ant.** 1 expectant, expecting, confident; nonplussed. 2 pleased, calmed; indifferent, unmoved, unaffected, unexcited.

agile *adj.* nimble, spry, supple, limber, lithe, dexterous, athletic, graceful; quick, swift, fleet, clever, alert, keen, active. —**Ant.** clumsy, awkward, heavy, ponderous; slow, sluggish, lethargic, inactive, torpid.

agitate *v.* 1. stir, stir up, shake, shake up, churn, mix; beat, rock, jar. 2. upset, excite, work up, bring to a fever pitch; provoke, goad, disquiet, trouble, disturb, alarm, foment. —**Ant.** calm, calm down, soothe, pacify, quiet, compose, still.

agitator *n.* inciter, instigator, fomentor, provoker, troublemaker, provocateur, *French* agent provocateur, incendiary, rabble-rouser, mischief-maker, inflamer, firebrand, revolutionary.

agnostic *n.* nonbeliever, unbeliever; disbeliever, doubter, skeptic, secularist, doubting Thomas, free spirit, freethinker, empiricist; heathen, heretic, infidel, pagan, atheist. —**Syn. Study.** See ATHEIST.

agog *adj.* openmouthed, awestruck, enthralled, thrilled, excited, worked up, astir, eagerly expectant. —**Ant.** indifferent, uninterested; bored.

agonize *v.* feel pain, be in agony, suffer, anguish, be tormented, be tortured, be distressed; worry, strain, struggle, labor, wrestle, *Slang* sweat. —**Ant.** enjoy, exhilarate; relax.

agony *n.* 1. suffering, pain, torment, throes, torture; anguish, distress, misery, affliction, woe; sorrow, anxiety. 2. effort, striving, struggle, strain; trial, tribulation. —**Ant.** 1, 2 pleasure, joy, enjoyment; comfort, ease; relief, consolation.

agrarian *adj.* agricultural, farming, crop-raising, agronomical. —**Ant.** manufacturing, industrial.

agree *v.* 1. assent, consent, accede, go along with; think alike, be of one mind, side with, support, subscribe, come to the same conclusion, admit, grant, concede, accept, allow. 2. concur, accord, coincide, conform, correspond; jibe, match, square, harmonize, chime, tally. 3. settle, come to an understanding, see eye to eye. —**Ant.** 1–3 disagree, differ. 1 dissent, dispute, refute, deny, oppose. 2 contradict.

agreeable *adj.* **1.** pleasing, pleasant, gratifying, congenial; to one's liking, to one's taste, acceptable, suitable, appropriate, fitting. **2.** in accord, consenting, complying, amenable, going along with; approving, concurring. **—Ant. 1** disagreeable, unpleasant, displeasing, unlikable, offensive; unacceptable, unsuitable, inappropriate, unfitting. **2** disapproving.

agreement *n.* **1.** mutual understanding, accord; concord, concordance, alliance, harmony, concert, meeting of the minds. **2.** harmony, in keeping, compliance, conformance, conformity, compatibility, accordance, affinity; similarity, analogy, correspondence. **3.** promise, contract, compact, pact, arrangement, settlement, covenant, bargain, *Informal* deal. **—Syn. Study. 3** AGREEMENT, BARGAIN, COMPACT, CONTRACT all suggest an arrangement between two or more parties. AGREEMENT ranges in meaning from a mutual understanding to a binding obligation: *an agreement to meet next week; a tariff agreement.* BARGAIN applies particularly to agreements about buying and selling; it suggests haggling: *We made a bargain that I would do the work if they supplied the materials.* COMPACT applies to treaties or alliances between nations or to solemn personal pledges: *a compact to preserve the peace.* CONTRACT is used esp. in law and business for such agreements as are legally enforceable: *a contract to sell a house.* **—Ant. 1, 2** disagreement, discord. **1** dissension. **2** inconsistency, dissonance, difference, dissimilarity, discrepancy.

agriculture *n.* farming, husbandry, crop-raising, cultivation, tillage, market gardening; agronomy, agronomics, geoponics.

aground *adj., adv.* stranded, grounded, foundered, stuck, beached, ashore. **—Ant.** afloat.

aid *v.* **1.** help, assist, abet, lend assistance, give a helping hand; support, give support to, sustain, minister to, succor, serve, accommodate; contribute, give alms to. **2.** foster, further, promote, advance; facilitate, make easy, serve. *—n.* **3.** help, assistance, helping hand; support. **4.** relief, dole; charity, donation, contribution, assistance; subsidy, allowance. **5.** Usu. **aide.** assistant, right-hand man, associate, subordinate, adjutant, auxiliary, girl Friday, man Friday; helper, abettor; follower, adherent, retainer; *Religious* acolyte, *Military* aide-de-camp. **—Syn. Study. 1** See HELP. **—Ant. 1** hurt, harm, injure; oppose, hinder. **2** hinder, obstruct, block, *Informal* hold up; oppose, discourage, thwart, impede, detract from. **3** hindrance. **5** superior, boss; leader.

ail *v.* **1.** bother, annoy, trouble, distress, worry, upset; be the matter with, afflict, sicken, make ill; pain. **2.** be sick, be ill, be unwell, be indisposed; fail in health, be infirm; *Slang* be on the sick list. **—Ant. 1** make happy; comfort, solace, console. **2** be in good health, make well; be strong, thrive, flourish.

ailment *n.* disorder, complaint, malady, infirmity, discomfort, affliction, disability; illness, sickness, disease, infection; indisposition, weakness. **—Ant.** good health, healthy sign; fitness.

aim *v.* **1.** point, direct, level, slant, beam, train on; take aim, sight, focus. **2.** try, strive, aspire to, work toward, endeavor, seek, attempt, be after; intend, mean, want, wish, desire, essay, have in mind; have in view, have an eye to. *—n.* **3.** aiming, line of sighting; marksmanship. **4.** desire, wish, intention, intent; aspiration, goal, ambition, target, purpose, object, end; plan, scheme, design. **—Syn. Study. 4** AIM, END, OBJECT all imply something that is the goal of one's efforts. AIM implies a direct effort toward a goal, without diversion from it: *Her aim is to be an astronaut.* END emphasizes the goal as separate from the effort: *unscrupulous means to achieve noble ends.* OBJECT emphasizes the goal of a specific effort: *the object of my research.*

aimless *adj.* directionless, undirected, unorganized, erratic, unsystematic, unguided, rudderless; pointless, purposeless, unfocused; wayward, frivolous, chance, unpredictable, haphazard, accidental, random, indiscriminate, hit-or-miss, inconsistent. **—Ant.** well-organized, purposeful, systematic, methodical, discriminating, consistent.

air *n.* **1.** the air we breathe, *Slang* ozone. **2.** atmosphere, stratosphere, sky. **3.** wind, breeze, draft, air current, air flow, blast, puff, zephyr, whiff, waft, breath of air. **4.** atmosphere, aura, mood, spirit, feeling, tone, ambience; quality, manner, style, look, appearance. **5. airs.** affectations, affectedness, pretensions, pretense, artificial manners; haughtiness, hauteur, arrogance, superciliousness, swank. **6.** tune, ditty, melody, song, strain; ballad, lay, carol. *—v.* **7.** ventilate, expose to air, aerate. **8.** voice, express, declare, vent, tell, utter; proclaim, make public, reveal, disclose, divulge, display, exhibit, publicize, expose. **—Ant. 8** keep silent; suppress, repress, hide, conceal.

airplane *n.* plane, aircraft, heavier-than-air craft, *British* aeroplane; *(variously)* jet, prop-jet, propeller-driven plane; *Slang* bird, crate, flying jenny; *Obsolete* airship.

airport *n.* airfield, landing field, flying

field, field; airstrip, landing strip; airdrome, *British* aerodrome; air base, jet base.

airship *n.* lighter-than-air craft; *(variously)* dirigible, blimp, balloon.

airy *adj.* **1.** open to the air, well-ventilated, sunny, spacious; windy, breezy, drafty. **2.** jaunty, sprightly, lively, frolicsome; lighthearted, light, light-of-heart, merry, cheerful, cheery. **3.** imaginary, fanciful, dreamy, ethereal, gossamer, unsubstantial, immaterial, unrealistic, illusory, idealized. **—Ant. 1** airless, stifling; gloomy, dark, dank. **2** ponderous, heavy, sluggish, clumsy, slow; cheerless, doleful. **3** material, substantial, factual, realistic; solid, hard.

aisle *n.* passageway, passage; walkway, walk, path, way, corridor, avenue, lane, alley; ambulatory, cloister.

ajar *adv.* partly open; open, unclosed, agape, gaping.

akin *adj., adv.* **1.** related by blood, related, kin, kindred; of the same stock, having a common ancestor, consanguineous; connected, allied, affiliated. **2.** alike, like, identical, uniform; similar, resembling, parallel, comparable, corresponding, analogous; agreeing, congenial, correlative. **—Ant. 1, 2** unrelated, unconnected; foreign, alien. **2** unlike, different, divergent, dissimilar, disparate; disagreeing, noncongenial.

alacrity *n.* **1.** willingness, enthusiasm, eagerness, fervor, zeal, avidity; alertness, promptness, dispatch, readiness. **2.** liveliness, briskness, sprightliness; agility, nimbleness. **—Ant. 1** unwillingness, indifference, unconcern, apathy, impassiveness, reluctance, disinclination; languor, lethargy, dullness. **2** slowness, sluggishness.

alarm *n.* **1.** warning, danger signal, alert. **2.** call to arms, summons to arms, war cry; hue and cry, beat of drum. **3.** apprehension, trepidation, consternation, agitation, dismay, distress, perturbation, misgiving; fear, fright, affright, panic, terror. *—v.* **4.** unnerve, frighten, scare, terrify; panic; dismay, disturb, make uneasy, distress, trouble, make anxious, make nervous, agitate, appall. **—Ant. 1** all clear. **3** composure, self-possession, equanimity, sang-froid, calmness, coolness, serenity, tranquillity. **4** give courage; calm, assure, relieve, comfort.

album *n.* scrapbook, book, portfolio; register.

alcoholic *adj.* **1.** intoxicating, inebriating, inebriative, spirituous, hard, strong; fermented, distilled; *Slang* with a kick. *—n.* **2.** drunkard, drunk, dipsomaniac, inebriate; hard drinker, sot, rummy, guzzler, tippler, imbiber, toper; *Slang* lush, souse, barfly, soak, boozer, whiskey head. **—Ant. 1** nonalcoholic, nonintoxicating, soft. **2** teetotaler, abstainer.

alcoholism *n.* acute alcoholism, chronic alcoholism, dipsomania, pathological drunkenness, alcoholic psychosis, oenomania; delirium tremens, DT's, intemperance, chronic intoxication, chronic drunkenness.

alcove *n.* recess, niche, nook, bay; cubicle, compartment, corner, opening.

alert *adj.* **1.** aware, attentive, wide-awake, observant, perceptive, intelligent; active, quick, lively, sprightly, nimble. **2.** watchful, vigilant, diligent, attentive, keen-eyed, wary, on guard, careful, heedful. *—n.* **3.** alarm, siren; warning, signal. *—v.* **4.** warn, forewarn, make aware of, signal, notify, inform. **—Ant. 1** unaware, oblivious, half-asleep; slow, listless, sluggish, inactive, lethargic, languid. **2** unwary, off guard, careless, heedless, lackadaisical, unconcerned, dilatory. **3** all clear. **4** lull.

alias *n.* assumed name, pseudonym, nom de guerre.

alibi *n.* defense of being elsewhere; excuse, explanation, justification, pretext, *Slang* out.

alien *n.* **1.** resident foreigner, foreigner, outsider, outlander, stranger; immigrant, newcomer. *—adj.* **2.** foreign, not native, strange; remote, distant, outlandish, exotic. **3.** contrary, opposed, contradictory, inconsistent, incompatible, conflicting; unlike, different, dissimilar, unconnected, unrelated, incongruous; separated, estranged. **—Syn. Study. 1** See STRANGER. **—Ant. 1** citizen, natural, subject, countryman; native. **2** native, indigenous. **3** in accordance with, agreeable, compatible, consistent, congenial; like, related, relevant, congruous.

alienate *v.* estrange, separate, keep at a distance, come between, divorce, turn away, set against. **—Syn. Study.** See ESTRANGE. **—Ant.** make friendly, draw close, unite; reunite, reconcile, turn to.

alight *v.* come down, get down, dismount, descend, land, touch down, thump down, climb down, get off, disembark, detrain, deplane.

align *v.* **1.** arrange in line, line up; straighten, even, even up; make parallel, put in a row. **2.** join, ally, side, go along with, cast one's lot with; associate, affiliate.

alike *adj.* **1.** same, identical, uniform, equal, even, of a piece, akin, one and the same, kindred; parallel, corresponding, equivalent, synonymous, homogeneous, analogous. *—adv.* **2.** equally, in the same way, similarly, identically, evenly, uniformly. **—Ant. 1** different, unlike, dissimilar, distinct, separate, divergent, diverse. **2** differently, unequally, unevenly, distinctly, separately, disparately, diversely.

alive *adj.* **1.** living, among the living, animate, breathing, subsisting, *Archaic* quick, *Informal* alive and kicking, above ground. **2.** full of life, vital, lively, active, vivacious, animated, vigorous, energetic, spry; aware, eager, alert, spirited. **3.** in existence, extant, in force, operative, in operation; not dead, unextinguished, unquenched; possible, viable. **—Ant. 1** dead, deceased, expired, defunct, lifeless, departed, no more; inanimate. **2** lifeless, unanimated, dispirited, spiritless, apathetic; inactive, unaware. **3** extinct, inactive, inoperative, inoperable; gone, lost, down the drain.

all *adj.* **1.** the whole of, the total of; the entire contents of, every part of. **2.** every one of, each of, each and every one of, every single one of; any of, any one of; the whole number of, the total of, the sum of; to a man. **3.** complete, total, full, entire, perfect, utter, utmost, the greatest possible. *—adv.* **4.** completely, entirely, totally, utterly, wholly, altogether; very, exceedingly, in the highest degree, fully. *—n.* **5.** everything, every item; the whole quantity, the greatest number, the whole amount, the greatest amount, the total, the entirety, the utmost possible. **6.** everyone, each, every member. **—Ant. 1, 2** none of; some. **3** partial. **4** somewhat, partially, a little. **5** nothing, none; some. **6** no one, none; some.

all-around *adj.* versatile, many-sided, multifaceted, well-rounded, all-round; adaptable, gifted, flexible, adroit, ambidextrous.

allay *v.* **1.** calm, quiet, put to rest, soothe; subdue, cause to subside, quell, hush, smooth, appease, pacify, mollify. **2.** relieve, ease, alleviate; lessen, assuage, reduce, diminish, check; lighten, soften, mitigate, mollify; blunt, dull, moderate, slake, slacken, subdue, quiet, quench. **—Ant. 1** arouse, awake, kindle, stir, stir up, excite, provoke; stimulate, fan. **1, 2** make worse, aggravate, increase, intensify, heighten, enhance, magnify, multiply.

allegation *n.* assertion, declaration, claim, avowal, profession, contention, statement; charge, accusation, indictment. **—Ant.** retraction; denial, disavowal, refutation.

allege *v.* claim, declare, state, assert, maintain, say, avow, contend, affirm, aver, profess, impute; charge, accuse, impugn. **—Ant.** retract; disclaim, deny, disavow, refute.

allegiance *n.* loyalty, faithfulness, fidelity, fealty, adherence, constancy; deference, devotion, obedience, homage. **—Ant.** disloyalty, betrayal, treachery, perfidy, deceit, faithlessness; treason, traitorousness, sedition, rebellion; alienation.

allegory *n.* fable, parable. **—Ant.** true story, history.

alleviate *v.* relieve, ease, allay, assuage; lessen, reduce, abate, diminish, check, temper, lighten, soften, mitigate, mollify; blunt, dull, moderate, slake, slacken, subdue, quit, quench. **—Ant.** make worse, aggravate, increase, intensify, heighten, enhance, magnify, multiply.

alley *n.* narrow back street, byway; passageway, passage, pathway, lane.

alliance *n.* **1.** agreement, pact, compact, treaty, concordat, entente cordiale. **2.** association, partnership, affiliation, league, company; confederation, confederacy, federation, union, coalition, bloc. **—Syn. Study. 2** ALLIANCE, LEAGUE, CONFEDERATION, UNION refer to the joining of states for mutual benefit or for the joint exercise of functions. ALLIANCE refers to a combination of states for the promotion of common interests: *a trade alliance.* LEAGUE usu. suggests a closer, more formal combination or a more definite purpose: *The League of Nations was formed to promote world peace.* CONFEDERATION applies to a fairly permanent combination for the exercise in common of certain governmental functions: *a confederation of Canadian provinces.* UNION implies an alliance so close and permanent that the separate states become essentially one: *the union of England and Scotland to form Great Britain.* **—Ant. 2** separation, secession, disunion.

allied *adj.* **1.** joint, combined, united; associated; federated, affiliated; incorporated, corporate, amalgamated. **2.** related, kindred, akin, cognate; similar, resembling, alike, like. **—Ant. 1** unallied, uncombined, disunited; individual. **2** alien, foreign to each other, unrelated; different, dissimilar, unalike, disparate; divergent.

allocate *v.* set aside, designate, earmark, allot, assign, allow, apportion; budget, appropriate. **—Syn. Study.** See ASSIGN. **—Ant.** withhold, hold back, deny, refuse, veto.

allot *v.* assign, allocate, earmark, give out, appoint, consign, grant, allow, dispense; apportion, portion out, distribute, parcel out, dole out, divide up, mete out, provide. **—Syn. Study.** See ASSIGN. **—Ant.** withhold, retain, keep; deny, refuse.

allotment *n.* share, portion, quota, measure, apportionment, allocation, ration, consignment; allowance, appropriation, grant, dispensation.

all-out *adj.* full-out, unstinted, unreserved, full-scale, total, complete, maximum, thoroughgoing, intensive, exhaustive, unqualified, out-and-out, unremitting, unlimited. **—Ant.** half-hearted, indifferent, perfunctory, lukewarm.

allow *v.* **1.** permit, let, give permission to, give leave to; authorize, concede to, sanction, agree to, approve. **2.** allot, allocate, assign, grant, give, provide. **—Syn. Study. 1** ALLOW, PERMIT, LET imply granting or conceding the right of someone to do something. ALLOW suggests passivity or even oversight; it points to the absence of an attempt or intent to hinder: *The baby-sitter allowed the children to run around the house.* PERMIT implies a more positive or willing consent; it is often used of a formal authorization: *Bicycle riding is not permitted in this park.* LET is a familiar, conversational term used in a similar sense: *My parents let me stay up late.* **—Ant. 1** forbid, refuse, prohibit, disallow, deny.

allowance *n.* **1.** allotment, ration, subsidy, stipend, grant, payment, bounty; annuity, income, pension. **2.** discount, deduction, reduction, concession, subtraction. **—Ant. 2** increase, addition.

alloy *n.* **1.** fusion, compound, amalgam, mixture, admixture, synthesis, commixture, blend, composite. *—v.* **2.** mix, admix, commix, interblend, combine, conglomerate, intermix; impair, adulterate, dilute.

all right *adj., adv.* **1.** well, healthy, in good health, hale, hearty; safe, uninjured, unharmed, unimpaired, *Informal* O.K. **2.** satisfactorily, acceptably, fair, *Informal* O.K.; correctly, properly. **3.** yes, very well, *Informal* O.K.; certainly, absolutely. **—Ant. 1** bad, poorly, in bad health, incapacitated; injured, harmed. **2** badly, poorly, unsatisfactorily, unacceptably; incorrectly. **3** no, not at all; absolutely not.

allude *v.* mention, refer, speak of, touch upon; hint, suggest, intimate. **—Ant.** keep secret, keep quiet about, be close-mouthed about.

allure *v.* **1.** lure, attract, entice, tempt, lead on, bait, seduce; fascinate, beguile, charm, enchant, intrigue, captivate. *—n.* **2.** attraction, enticement, lure, temptation; fascination, enchantment, charm, glamour, intrigue. **—Ant. 1** repel, alienate, drive away, deter, damp one's enthusiasm, *Slang* turn off; bore, be indifferent to.

allusion *n.* reference, mention; hint, suggestion.

ally *n.* **1.** partner, associate, confederate, affiliate; collaborator, accomplice, accessory; colleague, confrere. *—v.* **2.** unite, join together, join forces, band together, combine, bind together; affiliate, confederate, league. **—Ant. 1** enemy, foe, adversary, opponent; rival, competitor, antagonist. **2** go separate ways; separate.

almighty *adj.* **1.** unlimited, absolute, sovereign, supreme, infinite, transcendent, invincible, omnipotent, all-powerful. *—n.* **2. The Almighty.** See GOD.

almost *adv.* nearly, very nearly, about, just about, practically, approximately, close to, all but, not quite, not far from, on the verge of, within an inch of, well-nigh. **—Ant.** exactly, definitely; certainly, surely.

alms *n.* donation, gift, contribution, offering, gratuity, present, handout, baksheesh, pittance; assistance, aid, charity, benefaction, dole, relief, mercy, subsidy, largess, beneficence, tribute.

aloft *adv.* in the air, above, overhead, in the sky, in the clouds, skyward, heavenward; up, high up, way up, on high; in a higher place. **—Ant.** down, low, low down; lower, below, beneath; earthward.

alone *adv., adj.* **1.** by oneself, without others, unaccompanied, separately, singly, solitarily; single, solitary, isolated; unescorted, unattended, unchaperoned. **2.** without help, unaided, unassisted, single-handedly, with one's own two hands; all by oneself, only, on one's own, solely, sole. **3.** unique, uniquely, singular, singularly; unsurpassed, unequalled, unrivaled, unmatched, matchless, peerless, without peers, unparalleled, nonpareil, incomparable. **4.** lonely, lonesome, friendless; forsaken, deserted, abandoned, isolated, separated; forlorn, desolate. **—Ant. 1** accompanied, with others, jointly; escorted, attended, chaperoned. **2** with assistance, assisted, with help, helped, aided; jointly, together, with others. **3** among others, equally, equalled; surpassed, overshadowed.

aloof *adj.* **1.** cool, cold, chilly, detached, indifferent, standoffish, distant, remote, unsociable, reserved, unapproachable, unsympathetic, uninterested, unconcerned, unresponsive, haughty, high-hat, formal. **2.** apart, at a distance, above. **—Ant. 1** warm, friendly, familiar, open, sociable, gregarious, neighborly; interested, sympathetic, compassionate.

aloud *adv.* not in a whisper; in a normal speaking voice, audibly. **—Ant.** whispered, in a whisper; inaudibly, silently.

alpine *adj.* mountainous, towering, lofty, elevated, aerial, alpen; alpestrine, subalpine; cloud-capped, snow-capped, snow-clad; heaven-touching, sky-kissing, cloud-touching, cloud-piercing.

alter *v.* change, transform, make different, amend, revise, remodel, convert; modify, adjust, vary, recast. **—Syn. Study.** See ADJUST, CHANGE. **—Ant.** keep, retain, *Informal* stick to.

alteration *n.* change, modification, remodeling; transformation, transmutation, conversion; adjustment. **—Ant.** permanence, changelessness, stability.

altercation *n.* dispute, argument, controversy, quarrel, spat, row, *Informal* scene, wrangling; discord, falling-out, disagreement; fight, bickering, scrape, fracas, scuffle, affray, rumpus, brawl, melee, *Slang* broil. **—Ant.** agreement, accord, concord, harmony; peace; making-up.

alter ego *n.* twin, other self, second self, *doppelgänger*, double, counterpart, other likeness, other image; simulacrum, semblable, duplicate, complement, match.

alternate *v.* **1.** take turns, perform by turns, rotate; interchange, intersperse; vary, change, alter. *—adj.* **2.** every other, every second; alternating, reciprocal, consecutive, successive. **3.** another, substitute, second, backup. *—n.* **4.** substitute, surrogate, sub, second, standby, backup, understudy, *Informal* stand-in, pinch hitter; deputy, proxy.

alternative *n.* choice, other choice, option, recourse, way out; selection, substitute. **—Syn. Study.** See CHOICE.

altitude *n.* height, elevation; tallness, loftiness; prominence, eminence, sublimity; apex, zenith, vertex. **—Syn. Study.** See HEIGHT. **—Ant.** depth, pit, abyss.

altogether *adv.* **1.** completely, entirely, utterly; absolutely, totally, wholly, thoroughly, perfectly, fully, out and out; in general, on the whole, quite. **2.** in all, as a whole, in toto, in sum total; collectively, all inclusive. **3.** all told, all in all, on the whole, in sum, *Informal* when all is said and done. **—Ant. 1** partially, partly, incompletely. **2** in part; separately, individually. **3** partially, partly; somewhat.

altruism *n.* selflessness, magnanimity, generosity, unselfishness, largeheartedness, beneficence, humanitarianism, philanthropy, benefaction, benevolence, liberality, humanity. **—Ant.** selfishness, misanthropy, self-centeredness, self-servingness.

altruistic *adj.* unselfish; generous, benevolent, largehearted; humanitarian, charitable, philanthropic, public-spirited. **—Ant.** selfish, self-seeking, covetous, greedy; egoistic, egocentric, self-centered; malevolent, mean, grudging.

alumnus *v.* male graduate, former student.

always *adv.* **1.** every time, on every occasion, without exception; regularly, invariably, consistently. **2.** forever, forever and ever, for all time, eternally, everlastingly, perpetually, evermore; continually, unceasingly, unremittingly, incessantly. **—Ant. 1** never; rarely.

amalgam *n.* mixture, blend, fusion, combination, amalgamation, union, merger, compound, admixture, commixture, composite, intermixture, alloy; assemblage, joining, alliance, league; *Slang* combo, mishmash.

amalgamate *v.* combine, blend, merge, fuse, mix, commingle; unite, unify, join together, consolidate, coalesce, incorporate, federate, integrate, synthesize. **—Ant.** separate, part, divide, disunite.

amass *v.* accumulate, gather, collect, acquire, assemble, compile, heap up, pile up, round up. **—Ant.** scatter, disperse, distribute, dispense.

amateur *n.* **1.** nonprofessional, dabbler, hobbyist, dilettante; beginner, novice, neophyte, greenhorn, tyro. *—adj.* **2.** nonprofessional; unprofessional, unpolished, inexperienced; unskilled, inexpert. **—Ant. 1, 2** professional, expert. **2** experienced, practiced, polished, finished; skilled.

amatory *adj.* amorous, passionate, ardent, impassioned, romantic, infatuated, doting, loverlike, loving, adoring, languishing, devoted, tender, fond, lovesick, fervent, rapturous, yearning; erotic, libidinal, lascivious, sensual, hot, steamy, sexy, sexual, sexed-up. **—Ant.** hateful, mean, spiteful, vindictive, contemptuous.

amaze *v.* surprise, astonish, astound; flabbergast, awe, daze, shock, dumbfound, stupefy, stun, stagger. **—Ant.** expect, anticipate.

amazement *n.* astonishment, surprise, shock, stupefaction; disbelief, incredulity, bewilderment; wonder, awe. **—Ant.** anticipation, expectation; calmness, composure, indifference.

ambassador *n.* ambassadress (fem.), diplomat, representative, minister, envoy, agent, deputy, emissary, consul, legate, nuncio, go-between, intermediary, courier, *Brit.* diplomatist, minister plenipotentiary, consul general, attaché, career diplomat.

ambience Also **ambiance** *n.* atmosphere, environment, surroundings, climate, milieu, setting; character, mood, temper, flavor, spirit, tenor. **—Syn. Study.** See ENVIRONMENT.

ambiguity *n.* equivocation, vagueness, abstruseness, uncertainty, doubtfulness, indefiniteness. **—Ant.** clarity, clearness, explicitness, definiteness, certainty.

ambiguous *adj.* vague, unclear, cryptic, enigmatic, puzzling, indefinite, uncertain, doubtful; equivocal, misleading, having a double meaning, deceptive. **—Syn. Study.** AMBIGUOUS, EQUIVOCAL both refer to words or expressions that are not clear in meaning. AMBIGUOUS describes that which is capable of two or more contradictory interpretations, usu. unintentionally so: *an ambiguous line in a poem; an ambiguous smile.* EQUIVOCAL also means susceptible of contradictory interpretations, but usu. by a deliberate intent to mislead or mystify: *an equivocal response to an embarrassing question.* **—Ant.** explicit, definite, specific, direct, conclusive; clear, plain, frank, unmistakable, obvious, simple, lucid; unquestionable, honest.

ambition *n.* **1.** drive, zeal, desire, push, striving. **2.** aspiration, goal, aim, intent, objective, purpose, plan, design; desire, dream, hope, longing, yearning. **—Ant. 1** indifference; indolence, sloth.

ambitious *adj.* **1.** aspiring; zealous, eager, intent, desirous, ardent, avid; enterprising, industrious, energetic, determined. **2.** grand, complicated; grandiose, pretentious, ostentatious. **3.** strenuous, difficult, arduous. **—Ant. 1** unambitious, unaspiring; apathetic, indolent, slothful, lazy. **2** modest, humble, lowly. **3** easy, simple. **—Syn. Study. 1** AMBITIOUS, ENTERPRISING describe a person who wishes to rise above his or her present position or condition. An AMBITIOUS person strives for worldly success; such efforts may be admired or frowned on by others: *an ambitious college graduate; an ambitious social climber.* An ENTERPRISING person is characterized by energy and daring in undertaking projects: *This company needs an enterprising new manager.*

ambivalent *adj.* contradictory, conflicting, opposing, clashing, warring; confused, undecided, unfocused, mixed, wavering, fluctuating, vacillating, *Informal* wishy-washy. **—Ant.** definite, positive; unwavering.

amble *v.* stroll, walk leisurely, wander aimlessly, ramble, meander, saunter. **—Ant.** rush, run, race.

ambulatory *adj.* up and about, not confined to bed; walking, moving, mobile, peripatetic. **—Ant.** bedridden; not walking, immobile.

ambush *n.* **1.** concealment, cover, hiding, ambuscade, hiding place, hideaway, blind, stalking-horse. **—***v.* **2.** waylay, surprise, trap, entrap, lay for, attack, assault.

ameliorate *v.* **1.** improve, better, help, heal, fix up, patch up, correct, rectify; amend, reform, revise, improve upon, make an improvement upon; advance, promote. **2.** improve, get better, grow better, perk up, pick up, progress, come along, mend, show improvement. **—Syn. Study. 1** See IMPROVE. **—Ant. 1** ruin, botch, queer, screw up, wreck, destroy. **2** deteriorate, go downhill, decline, weaken, worsen.

amen *interj.* so be it, it is so, let it be so, so shall it be, would that it were so; truly, verily; *Informal* hear hear, yes indeed.

amenable *adj.* agreeable, willing to agree, willing to listen, responsive, cooperative; favorably disposed, cordial, persuadable, tractable, open, open-minded, acquiescent, willing, obliging, complaisant, sympathetic, yielding, submissive. **—Ant.** closed-minded, obstinate, stubborn, headstrong, truculent, recalcitrant, autocratic, autonomous.

amend *v.* **1.** change, revise, modify, alter, emend. **2.** improve, better, perfect, develop, polish, enhance; emend, correct, rectify, reform, remedy, mend, fix. **—Syn. Study.** AMEND, EMEND both can mean to alter, improve, or correct something written. AMEND is the general term, used of any such correction or improvement in details; it may refer to adding, taking away, or changing a character, word, or phrase: *to amend spelling and punctuation in a report; to amend a contract.* EMEND applies specifically to the critical alteration of a text in the process of editing or preparing it for publication; it implies improvement in the direction of greater accuracy: *The scholar emended the text by restoring the original reading.* **—Ant. 2** corrupt, spoil, damage, harm, injure, hurt, impair, blemish; vitiate.

amendment *n.* **1.** addition, adjunct. **2.** revision, modification, change, alteration, emendation; improvement, correction, rectification, reform.

amends *n. pl.* apology, defense, justification, explanation, vindication; redress, restitution, recompense, retribution, compensation, reparation, indemnification, restoration, payment, requital, expiation, *Informal* peace offering; atonement, acknowledgment, satisfaction.

amenity *n.* **1. amenities.** good manners, politeness, courtesies, niceties, gallantries, bits of etiquette; refinement, gentility. **2.** geniality, amiability, affability, agreeableness, pleasantness, graciousness, friendliness, civility; gentleness, mildness. **—Ant. 1** bad manners, impoliteness, discourtesy, rudeness, boorishness. **2** unpleasantness, surliness, incivility.

amiable *adj.* friendly, agreeable, amicable, pleasant, congenial, good-natured, kindly, obliging, cordial, sociable, affable; pleasing, attractive, engaging, winning, charming; polite, genial, gracious.

—**Ant.** unfriendly, hostile, disagreeable, unpleasant, ill-humored, sullen, surly, sour; displeasing, unattractive, repellent, repugnant, loathsome, offensive.

amicable *adj.* friendly, peaceable, agreeable, amiable, amenable, harmonious, cordial, civil, polite, courteous, kind, kindly, kindhearted, benevolent; sociable, neighborly. —**Ant.** unfriendly, hostile, belligerent, antagonistic, contentious, pugnacious, bellicose, quarrelsome; disagreeable, nasty, unsociable, unkind, cold.

amiss *adj.* **1.** wrong, awry, askew, inappropriate, unsuitable, improper, out of order, *Slang* off base; faulty, mistaken, incorrect, erroneous; false, fallacious, mixed-up; untoward. —*adv.* **2.** wrongly, wrong, inappropriately, unsuitably, improperly, mistakenly, untowardly, out of order, *Informal* out of line; incorrectly, erroneously, falsely, faultily, inaccurately, awry, astray. —**Ant. 1** right, proper, appropriate, suitable, *Informal* perfect, O.K., in good shape; in order; correct, true. **2** rightly, properly, appropriately, suitably; correctly, truly.

amity *n.* friendship, harmony, good will, understanding, sympathy; cooperation, agreement, accord, concord; cordiality, fellowship, fraternity, brotherhood. —**Ant.** enmity, antagonism, hostility, animosity, conflict, contention, ill will; disagreement, dissension, discord, strife.

amnesty *n.* pardon, reprieve; forgiveness, absolution, reconciliation; immunity. —**Syn. Study.** See PARDON.

amorous *adj.* loving, enamored, lovesick; ardent, passionate, impassioned; fond, affectionate, tender, doting. —**Ant.** unloving, indifferent, uncaring, cold, frigid; hateful.

amorphous *adj.* shapeless, formless, undefined, undelineated, unshapen; vague, nondescript, indeterminate, characterless, anomalous.

amount *n.* **1.** total, sum, sum total, aggregate; extent, magnitude. **2.** quantity, measure; volume, bulk, mass.

amour *n.* love affair, affair, romance, intrigue, liaison.

ample *adj.* **1.** enough, sufficient, adequate, satisfactory; substantial, capacious, more than enough, plenty, abundant, plentiful, bountiful, profuse, copious, generous, liberal. **2.** large, big, immense, huge, vast; wide, broad, extensive, expansive, outspread, extended, roomy, spacious, voluminous, commodious. —**Syn. Study. 1** See PLENTIFUL. —**Ant. 1** insufficient, inadequate, unsatisfactory; limited, restricted; scant, scanty, sparse, meager, skimpy, scrimpy; niggardly, stingy. **2** small, little, minute, wee.

amplification *n.* **1.** enlargement, expansion, increasing, development, extension, aggrandizement; heightening, broadening, widening. **2.** elaboration, rounding out, developing, augmentation, added detail, fleshing out. —**Ant. 1** reduction, decreasing, curtailment, contraction, cutting down, paring down; narrowing. **2** simplification, simplifying; condensing, abridging, cutting, boiling down.

amplify *v.* **1.** increase, intensify, strengthen, heighten, raise; expand, broaden, extend, enlarge, widen, lengthen, deepen. **2.** elaborate on, illustrate, expatiate on; expand, develop, add to, augment, supplement, fill out, complete. —**Ant. 1** reduce, decrease, curtail, cut down, pare down. **2** simplify, condense, abbreviate, abridge; summarize, boil down.

amplitude *n.* **1.** magnitude, extent, size; vastness, largeness, bigness; spaciousness, capaciousness; dimension, breadth, width; bulk, volume, mass. **2.** range, scope, extent, compass, sweep, reach; expanse; completeness, fullness, richness; abundance, profusion, plenitude, copiousness, plethora. —**Ant. 1** smallness. **2** limitation, narrowness, restriction, circumscription.

amply *adv.* adequately, sufficiently, satisfactorily, thoroughly, completely, fully; more than enough, abundantly, plentifully, profusely, copiously, bountifully, generously, liberally, lavishly, richly, unstintingly. —**Ant.** inadequately, insufficiently; scantily, meagerly, skimpily.

amputate *v.* cut off, sever, dismember, excise, remove; *Informal* lop off.

amuck *adv.* amok, wildly, insanely, murderously, uncontrollably, maniacally, in a frenzy, ferociously, frenziedly, berserk; *Slang* nuts, crackers, bonkers.

amulet *n.* charm, talisman, fetish, lucky piece.

amuse *v.* divert, entertain, occupy; interest, engross, absorb, beguile; please, gladden, cheer, enliven. —**Syn. Study.** AMUSE, DIVERT, ENTERTAIN mean to occupy the attention with something pleasant. That which AMUSES is usu. playful or humorous and pleases the fancy. DIVERT implies turning the attention from serious thoughts or pursuits to something light, funny, or lively. That which ENTERTAINS usu. does so because of a plan or program that engages the attention by being pleasing and sometimes instructive. —**Ant.** bore; tire, weary; vex, annoy.

amusement *n.* **1.** pastime, diversion, pleasure, distraction; entertainment, recreation, avocation, hobby; fun, play, game, revel. **2.** merriment, pleasure, delight, enjoyment. **—Ant. 1** bore, boredom, tedium, monotony, ennui. **2** sadness; displeasure, disgust.

amusing *adj.* **1.** entertaining, diverting, interesting, beguiling, engrossing, absorbing; pleasant, delightful, pleasurable, pleasing, cheering. **2.** funny, comical, comic, humorous, witty, droll, farcical, waggish. **—Syn. Study. 2** AMUSING, COMICAL, DROLL describe that which causes mirth. That which is AMUSING is quietly humorous or funny in a gentle, good-humored way: *The baby's attempts to talk were amusing.* That which is COMICAL causes laughter by being incongruous, witty, or ludicrous: *His huge shoes made the clown look comical.* DROLL adds to COMICAL the idea of strangeness or peculiarity, and sometimes that of sly or waggish humor: *a droll imitation.* **—Ant. 1** boring, dull, tedious, monotonous. **2** sad, depressing.

analgesic *n.* painkiller, anodyne; *(variously)* anesthetic, narcotic, opiate, drug. **—Ant.** irritant.

analogous *adj.* similar, like, comparable, akin, equivalent, parallel, correlative, corresponding. **—Ant.** dissimilar, unlike; different, divergent.

analogy *n.* similarity, likeness, resemblance, similitude; comparison, correspondence, parallelism, correlation, equivalence; simile, metaphor. **—Ant.** dissimilarity, difference.

analysis *n.* **1.** separation, breakdown, breakup, reduction, dissection, resolution, partition, dissociation. **2.** examination, investigation, inquiry, observation, study, test, search. **3.** judgment, evaluation, diagnosis, reasoning, thinking, interpretation, speculation, estimation, assay, appraisal; summary, review, outline, synopsis, abstract, précis, digest, brief. **4.** psychoanalysis, psychotherapy, therapy. **—Ant. 1** synthesis, uniting, union, combining, combination.

analyst *n.* **1.** psychoanalyst; *Slang* headshrinker, shrink. **2.** judge, evaluator, estimator, appraiser; examiner, investigator, observer, tester.

analytic, analytical *adj.* logical, rational, systematic, organized, problem-solving; inquiring, studious, searching, testing, diagnostic. **—Ant.** illogical, disorganized, unsystematic, chaotic.

analyze *v.* **1.** separate and examine the parts of. **2.** examine, study, investigate, question, search, assay, appraise; evaluate, diagnose, consider, judge, think through, reason out. **—Ant. 2** ignore, overlook, pay no heed to, shut one's eyes to; neglect, slight, pass over, brush aside.

anarchist *n.* rebel, revolutionary, insurgent, terrorist, mutineer; syndicalist; nihilist. **—Ant.** loyalist, tory, conservative; disciplinarian.

anarchy *n.* **1.** absence of government, disorder, lawlessness, chaos. **2.** utopia, the millennium. **—Ant. 1** order, discipline, authority; government, organization, control; regimentation, subjection.

anathema *n.* **1.** abomination, taboo, unmentionable. **2.** curse, malediction; excommunication, ban, censure, proscription; denunciation, condemnation. **—Ant. 1** beloved; welcomed. **2** blessing, benediction.

anathematize *v.* excommunicate, maledict, damn; condemn, accurse, execrate, abominate, hold in abomination.

ancestor *n.* **1.** forefather, forebear; progenitor, procreator, begetter. **2.** forerunner, predecessor, antecedent, precursor, prototype. **—Ant. 1** descendant, inheritor; progeny, scion, issue, offspring. **2** successor.

ancestry *n.* **1.** descent, extraction, derivation; origin, stock, heredity, race. **2.** ancestors, lineage, progenitors; family, line, parentage, house; genealogy, pedigree, blood line, family tree. **—Ant. 1** posterity. **2** descendants, progeny, issue.

anchor *n.* **1.** *Informal* hook; ground tackle, mooring. **2.** mainstay, support, bulwark, strong point, basis, foundation; safeguard, security, defense. *—v.* **3.** secure by anchor, moor; drop anchor, cast anchor, ride at anchor. **4.** secure, fix, affix, fasten. **—Ant. 3** lift anchor, weigh anchor, break free.

anchorage *n.* harbor, roadstead, port, mooring, harborage, berth, seaport, dock, marina, quay, key, jetty, bund, dockage.

ancient *adj.* **1.** long past, remote, olden, old; early, primeval, primitive, prehistoric; *Historical use* Greco-Roman, classical, prior to A.D. 476. **2.** old, very old, aged, age-old; antique, timeworn, hoary. **3.** out-of-date, old-fashioned, out-of-fashion, outmoded, antiquated, passé, bygone, *Informal* old hat; obsolete, obsolescent, archaic, fossilized. **—Syn. Study.** ANCIENT, ANTIQUE, ANTIQUATED refer to something dating from the past. ANCIENT implies existence or first occurrence in the distant past: *an ancient custom.* ANTIQUE applies to what has survived intact beyond its own time and may thus have a curious or pleasing quality: *antique furniture.* ANTIQUATED connotes something that is outdated or no longer useful: *antiquated methods; antiquated ideas.* **—Ant. 1** recent, late. **2** new, brand new, spanking new, young. **3** modern, fresh, novel, modernistic; current, up-to-date, newfangled, new-fashioned, in vogue, modish, *Slang* with it.

ancillary *adj.* supplementary, auxiliary, accessory, contributory, adjunct; secondary, subordinate, subsidiary, additional; minor, dependent, subservient, inferior. **—Ant.** main, major, primary, prime; independent; counteractive, contrary, at odds with.

anecdote *n.* story, tale, yarn, short narrative, brief account, sketch, reminiscence.

anemic Also **anaemic** *adj.* **1.** deficient in hemoglobin, thin-blooded. **2.** pale, pallid, wan, dull, colorless, subdued, quiet; weak, feeble, characterless. **—Ant. 2** bright, colorful, florid, loud, flashy; strong, powerful.

anesthesia, anaesthesia, anesthesis *n.* insensibility to sensations, loss of feeling, insentience, numbness; unconsciousness, stupor.

anesthetic, anaesthetic *n.* painkiller, analgesic, narcotic, opiate, drug. **—Ant.** stimulant, analeptic.

anew *adv.* again, once more, over again; from scratch, in a new way, afresh, newly. **—Ant.** never again, nevermore.

angel *n.* **1.** messenger of God, heavenly spirit, celestial being; *(variously)* seraph, cherub, throne, domination, virtue, power, principality, archangel. **2.** angelic person, *Slang* doll, gem, jewel, treasure, saint. **3.** financial backer, patron, benefactor, sponsor, underwriter. **—Ant. 1** devil.

angelic *adj.* **1.** ethereal, celestial, heavenly, divine, spiritual, saintly, beatific; seraphic, cherubic. **2.** angellike, good, ideal, pure, innocent; beautiful, lovely, enrapturing, rapturous, entrancing, adorable. **—Ant. 1, 2** demonic. **1** hellish, netherworld. **2** diabolical, fiendish; ugly, ugly as sin, repulsive.

anger *n.* **1.** rage, outrage, fury, wrath, ire, temper, gall, bile, choler, spleen, pique, dander; indignation, resentment, exasperation, petulance, vexation, irritation, annoyance, displeasure, umbrage, disapprobation; antagonism, animosity, hostility, hatred, enmity, acrimony; ill temper, hot temper. *—v.* **2.** infuriate, enrage, outrage, madden, incense, inflame, pique, rile, gall, nettle, chafe, ruffle, exacerbate; provoke, exasperate, vex, irritate, rankle, annoy, displease; antagonize, embitter, cause ill feelings; *Informal* make bad blood, ruffle one's feathers, get one's dander up. **—Syn. Study. 1** ANGER, INDIGNATION, RAGE, FURY describe deep and strong feelings aroused by injury, injustice, etc. ANGER is the general term for sudden violent displeasure accompanied by an impulse to retaliate: *insults that provoked a burst of anger.* INDIGNATION, a more formal word, implies deep and justified anger, often directed at something unworthy: *The scandal aroused public indignation.* RAGE is vehement, uncontrolled anger: *rage at being fired from a job.* FURY is rage so great that it resembles insanity: *He smashed his fist against the wall in a drunken fury.* **—Ant. 1** love, liking, fondness; good will, peacefulness, mildness, amiability; approval, acceptance, condonation; calmness, equanimity; pleasure, gratification; forgiveness. **2** placate, appease, pacify, mollify, propitiate, calm, soothe; please, delight, gladden, gratify, *Informal* tickle.

angle *n.* **1.** *Geometry* space between two lines or planes that meet; divergence. **2.** bend, turn, corner, edge, cusp. **3.** point of view, viewpoint, standpoint, position, side, aspect, slant; outlook, focus, perspective.

angry *adj.* mad, furious, infuriated, enraged, outraged, raging, fuming, boiling, turbulent, incensed, inflamed, irate, indignant, exasperated, resentful, vexed, piqued, riled, nettled, galled, *Slang* burnt up; provoked, irritated, annoyed, displeased, offended, affronted; hostile, hateful, antagonistic, acrimonious, embittered; ill-tempered, petulant, irascible, splenetic, huffy. **—Ant.** loving, fond, friendly; calm, soothing, peaceful, mild, complaisant, agreeable, pleasant, amiable; happy, pleased, pleasing, gratified, gratifying; good-natured, even-tempered; apologetic, forgiving, unresentful, placating.

anguish *n.* distress, pain, agony, suffering, torment, despair, misery; anxiety, heartache, grief, woe; remorse, sorrow. **—Ant.** comfort, ease; relief, solace, consolation, alleviation.

angular *adj.* **1.** sharp-cornered, bent, crooked, jagged. **2.** bony, gaunt, spare, lean, rawboned, scrawny, lanky, lank. **—Ant. 1** straight; rounded. **2** chubby, fleshy, rotund, plump, stout, portly.

animal *n.* **1.** living being, creature, organism, biological system. **2.** nonhuman; *(variously)* wild animal, beast, farm animal, pet. **3.** mammal, quadruped. **4.** brute, beast. *—adj.* **5.** carnal, libidinous, sexual, sensual, erotic; fleshly. **—Syn. Study. 5** See CARNAL.

animate *v.* **1.** make alive, vivify, vitalize, quicken. **2.** make lively, enliven, invigorate, give energy to, add spirit to, energize; excite, fire, fire up, warm. **3.** stimulate, arouse, stir, inspire, spur on, move, impel, set on, incite, instigate, activate, actuate; goad, urge, prompt, provoke, work up. *—adj.* **4.** alive, having life; moving. **—Ant. 1** kill, deaden, make lifeless, devitalize. **2** depress, dishearten, cool, put a damper on, dull; bore. **3** discourage, dampen; deter, restrain, inhibit, curb, check. **4** inanimate, dead, lifeless.

animated *adj.* lively, spirited, active, vivacious, vigorous, zestful, invigorating, energetic, exciting, elated, vibrant, dynamic, vivid, bright, fervent, ebullient, ardent, zealous, passionate, hot, glowing, buoyant, airy, sprightly, quick, brisk, breezy, blithe, gay, sportive. **—Ant.** dull, deadly, lifeless, boring, monotonous; depressed, dejected; inactive, listless, spiritless, lethargic, torpid, slow, apathetic, passive; dispirited.

animation *n.* liveliness, life, spirit, high spirit, good spirit, animal spirit, blithe spirit, vivacity, vitality, vital power, zest, vigor, vim, verve, exhilaration, eagerness, enthusiasm, ebullience; excitement, ardor, elation, glow, vibrancy, fire, alertness, brightness, alacrity, sprightliness, buoyancy, briskness, gaiety, good cheer, sportiveness; action, activity. **—Ant.** lifelessness, dullness, spiritlessness; lethargy, apathy, passivity, inertness, stolidity, sluggishness, dejection, depression, low spirits.

animosity *n.* ill will, antagonism, bitterness, dislike, unfriendliness, malice, malevolence, malignity, hatred, hate, hostility, enmity, antipathy, anger, strife, resentment, rancor, acrimony. **—Ant.** good will, love, friendship, friendliness, harmony, congeniality, kindness, sympathy.

animus *n.* animosity, hatred, hostility, enmity, ill will, antagonism, dislike, bad blood, antipathy, ill feeling, rancor, venom. **—Ant.** friendliness, harmony, affection, good will, amicability, friendship.

annals *n.* yearly records, chronological records; chronicles, historical rolls, records, registers, archives; history, chronology; minutes.

annex *v.* **1.** attach, add, incorporate, acquire, appropriate, expropriate, seize, merge, connect, join, subjoin, adjoin, affix, append, tack on, *Informal* grab. —*n.* **2.** addition, attachment, appendage. **—Ant. 1** detach, separate, disconnect, remove, disengage. **2** separation, detachment.

annihilate *v.* wipe out, exterminate, liquidate, *Slang* waste; demolish, destroy completely, reduce to nothing, lay waste, decimate, obliterate, extinguish, end, abolish, eradicate, erase, extirpate. **—Ant.** let live; build, construct, create, make.

anniversary *n.* commemoration, fete, celebration, holiday, feast day; name day, birthday; centennial or centenary, sesquicentennial, bicentennial or bicentenary.

annotate *v.* explicate, commentate, elucidate, interpret, expound; construe, explain, comment, remark; gloss, footnote.

annotation *n.* note, footnote, gloss, marginalia; remark, comment, observation; commentary, elucidation, interpretation, explication, *explication de texte,* exegesis, *apparatus criticus.* **—Ant.** main text, text.

announce *v.* **1.** proclaim, declare, promulgate, publish; broadcast, advertise, disseminate, give out, sound abroad, trumpet; disclose, divulge, reveal. **2.** herald, harbinger, foretell, presage, augur, betoken, portend, signify, signal. **—Syn. Study. 1** ANNOUNCE, PROCLAIM, PUBLISH mean to communicate something in a formal or public way. To ANNOUNCE is to give out news, often of something expected in the future: *to announce a lecture series.* To PROCLAIM is to make a widespread and general announcement of something of public interest: *to proclaim a holiday.* To PUBLISH is to make public in an official way, now esp. by printing: *to publish a book.* **—Ant. 1, 2** suppress, secrete, hide, cover up, conceal, bury, withhold, hush, keep back, keep secret, repress; hold back, reserve.

annoy *v.* disturb, bother, pester, badger, harry, harass, nag, heckle, tax, hector, tease; trouble, worry, torment, plague, inconvenience, distract; irritate, provoke, exasperate, vex, gall, irk, ruffle, rile, nettle. **—Syn. Study.** See ANNOY. **—Ant.** calm, soothe, comfort, relieve, solace, console; please, gratify; appease, mollify.

annul *v.* render null and void, nullify, negate, invalidate, cancel, void; abrogate, revoke, rescind, retract, recall, repeal, reverse; abolish, dissolve, undo. **—Ant.** validate; enact, perform.

annulment *n.* nullification, invalidation, cancellation, voiding; abrogation, revocation, retraction, recall, repeal, reversal; dissolution, undoing, repudiation, abolition. **—Ant.** validation.

anoint *v.* **1.** put oil on, smear with oily liquid, pour oil on, oil. **2.** crown, ordain, consecrate by unction, make holy by anointing, sanctify by anointing.

anomalous *adj.* **1.** odd, strange, peculiar, incongruous, out of keeping, bizarre. **2.** irregular, abnormal, atypical; monstrous. **—Ant. 1** common, usual, standard, typical, familiar, unexceptional, ordinary, natural, normal, regular, conventional, customary. **2** normal, typical.

anomaly *n.* irregularity, exception to

the rule; oddity, rarity; abnormality, deviation, aberration; eccentricity, peculiarity, incongruity. —**Ant.** the norm, the rule, the common thing.

anonymous *adj.* nameless, unnamed, bearing no name, unsigned; unidentified, unacknowledged, of unknown authorship. —**Ant.** named, signed; identified, acknowledged, known.

answer *n.* **1.** reply, response, acknowledgment; rejoinder, retort, riposte, comeback. **2.** solution, explanation, resolution. —*v.* **3.** reply, respond, acknowledge, react to; write, say, rejoin, retort. **4.** give a solution to, solve, resolve. **5.** (usu. followed by **for**) be responsible, be accountable, be liable; pay for, suffer for, make amends for, atone for, expiate. **6.** meet, fill, fulfill, serve, suit; be sufficient, be adequate, be enough, pass muster, be satisfactory, do well enough; conform, correspond, be similar, be like, be equivalent, be the counterpart of, be correlated. —**Syn. Study. 1** ANSWER, REPLY, RESPONSE, REJOINDER, RETORT all refer to words used to meet a question, proposal, charge, etc. An ANSWER is something said or written in return: *an answer giving the desired information.* A REPLY is usu. somewhat more formal or detailed: *a courteous reply to a letter.* A RESPONSE is often a reaction to an appeal, suggestion, etc.: *an enthusiastic response to a plea for cooperation.* A REJOINDER is a quick, usu. clever answer to another person's reply or comment: *a rejoinder that silenced the opposition.* A RETORT is a keen, prompt answer, usu. to a charge or criticism: *The false accusation provoked a sharp retort.* —**Ant. 1** question, query, inquiry, interrogation; summoning, summons, call, challenge. **2** problem. **3** question, ask, query, inquire, interrogate; summon, call, challenge. **4** ask. **6** fail; differ.

answerable *adj.* accountable, responsible, liable. —**Ant.** excused, exempt, unaccountable, not responsible.

antagonism *n.* hostility, opposition, conflict, friction, clashing, discord, strife; animosity, enmity, antipathy, rivalry, dissension; animus, bitterness, rancor, spite, resentment; hatred, dislike, aversion, detestation. —**Ant.** love, friendship, friendliness, amity, liking; peacefulness, agreement, accord, concord, harmony; sympathy, understanding.

antagonist *n.* opponent, adversary, rival, competitor, opposer, contestant, disputant; enemy, foe, attacker, assailant. —**Syn. Study.** See ADVERSARY. —**Ant.** ally, partner, colleague, teammate; supporter, patron, defender; friend.

antagonize *v.* alienate, estrange, repel, offend. —**Ant.** conciliate, placate, pacify, appease, mollify, propitiate.

ante *n.* stake, bet, beginning bet, wager, pot.

antecedent *adj.* **1.** precursory, preexistent, anterior, precedent, previous, prior. —*n.* **2.** precursor, forerunner, predecessor, precedent, ancestor; harbinger, herald, pioneer. **3. antecedents.** ancestors, forefathers, forebears, family, predecessors, ancestry; family tree, lineage, pedigree, stock, house, extraction, progeniture. —**Ant. 1** subsequent, following, posterior; later, after. **2** successor, sequel; consequence, result, aftermath, upshot. **3** descendants, progeny, issue, offspring.

antedate *v.* precede, come first, be of older date than, occur earlier than, predate, go before, happen before, anticipate, antecede. —**Ant.** follow, succeed, come after, postdate.

antediluvian *adj.* antiquated, antique, archaic, obsolete.

anterior *adj.* **1.** front, in front, forward, placed before. **2.** previous, precedent, prior, antecedent. —**Ant. 1** posterior, rear, back. **2** subsequent, posterior.

anthology *n.* collection, compendium, compilation, choice; treasury, chapbook, garland, florilegium; digest, selections, extracts, miscellanea, scrapbook, commonplace book, miscellany, analects, gleanings, collectanea.

antic *n.* Usu. **antics.** pranks, tricks, monkeyshines, tomfoolery, clownishness, buffoonery, sport, practical jokes; playful behavior, fanciful acts, shenanigans, ridiculous acts, skylarking, larks, escapades. —**Ant.** seriousness, solemnity, gravity.

anticipate *v.* expect, look for, await; count on, prepare oneself for, look toward; look forward to, long for, pin hope on; foresee, forecast, predict, envision, foretell. —**Ant.** despair of, doubt; dread, fear; remember, recollect.

anticipation *n.* **1.** expectation, expectancy, hope. **2.** expectation, preparation.

anticlimax *n.* letdown, comedown, disappointment, dull ending. —**Ant.** exciting climax, lofty ending.

antidote *n.* **1.** antipoison, counterpoison, countervenom, antitoxin, counteragent. **2.** remedy, cure, countermeasure, corrective.

antipathy *n.* dislike, aversion, distaste; disgust, repulsion, loathing, repugnance, abhorrence; antagonism, animosity, ill will, enmity, rancor, hostility, unfriendliness. —**Ant.** affinity, fellow feeling, regard, sympathy, attraction, partiality; love, affection, attachment.

antiquated *adj.* antique, old-fashioned, outmoded, passé, dated, out-of-date, outdated, of the old school; ancient; obsolete, archaic, obsolescent. —**Syn.**

Study. See ANCIENT. **—Ant.** modern, new, young, current, recent, fresh, novel; up-to-date, new-fashioned, fashionable, newfangled, stylish, modish, smart.

antique *adj.* **1.** old, ancient. **2.** antiquated. *—n.* **3.** relic, rarity, curio, memorabile, objet d'art, bibelot, trinket. **—Syn. Study.** See ANCIENT. **—Ant. 1** modern, new. **2** fashionable, recent, current.

antiquity *n.* **1.** ancientness, great age, oldness. **2.** ancient times. **3. antiquities.** relics, monuments, artifacts. **—Ant. 1** modernity, newness. **2** modern times, the present, today.

antiseptic *n.* **1.** disinfectant, germicide, germ killer, bactericide, prophylactic. *—adj.* **2.** sterile, germ-free, aseptic.

antisocial *adj.* **1.** unfriendly, unsociable, retiring; unsocial, asocial, misanthropic. **2.** hostile, menacing, antagonistic, belligerent; alienated, disruptive, rebellious, sociopathic. **—Ant. 1** gregarious, friendly, sociable, genial, social. **2** cooperative, conformist, well-adjusted, normal.

antithesis *n.* **1.** direct opposite, reverse, inverse, converse, opposite extreme, contrary, contrast, antipode. **2.** opposition of one idea against another in the same sentence, stating opposites in one sentence, setting of one clause against another in a sentence.

antonym *n.* antithesis, opposite; *abbreviation* ant.

anxiety *n.* uneasiness, unease, worry, apprehension, misgiving, foreboding, distress, concern, tension, anguish, angst, suspense, fretfulness, disquiet, disquietude; dread, fear, alarm; solicitude. **—Ant.** relief; assurance, certainty, confidence; calmness, tranquility, serenity, composure, self-possession, aplomb.

anxious *adj.* **1.** uneasy, distressed, apprehensive, tense, *Slang* uptight, disturbed, worried, troubled, disquieted, concerned, fretful, fraught with anxiety, anguished, fearful, alarmed, overwrought. **2.** eager, impatient, desirous, wanting, itching, yearning, expectant; earnest, intent, keen, ardent, fervent, avid, zealous. **—Ant. 1** relieved, assured, sure, confident; calm, composed, cool, collected, unruffled, unperturbed, nonchalant. **2** reluctant, averse, hesitant, loath, disinclined, indisposed.

anyhow *adv.* See ANYWAY.

anyway *adv.* **1.** anyhow, nevertheless, nonetheless, just the same, regardless. **2.** in any case, in any event, at any rate, anyhow. **3.** carelessly, haphazardly, indifferently, anyhow, without concern, sloppily. **—Ant. 3** with care, carefully, perfectly, neatly.

apace *adv.* fast, quickly, rapidly, swiftly, hastily, precipitately, speedily, posthaste, *Mil.* on the double, expeditiously, at top speed, flat-out, lickety-split, double-quick, at a good clip, hell-bent for leather. **—Ant.** slow, slowly, dawdlingly, lackadaisically, listlessly.

apart *adv.* **1.** into pieces, into parts, asunder. **2.** distant, one from another, afar; separately. **3.** aside, to one side, by oneself, by itself, alone, aloof; isolated, separate, cut off, divorced. **—Ant. 1** together. **2** near; together, adjoining. **3** in the midst of, surrounded.

apartment *n.* **1.** set of rooms, suite, flat, *Slang* pad. **2.** apartment building, multiple-dwelling building.

apathetic *adj.* indifferent, unconcerned, uninterested, unresponsive, uncommitted, disengaged, impassive, impossible, unmoved; unemotional, emotionless, unfeeling, cold, passionless, phlegmatic, spiritless. **—Ant.** concerned, interested, responsive, committed, active; stirred, aroused, roused, excited; emotional, passionate, zealous, vehement, hot.

apathy *n.* indifference, unconcern, lack of interest, inattention, unresponsiveness, passiveness, lethargy, lassitude; lack of feeling, numbness, emotionlessness, coolness, impassibility, impassivity. **—Ant.** concern, interest, attention, responsiveness, action; emotion, feeling, excitement, passion, zeal, vehemence, enthusiasm, fervor.

ape *n.* **1.** tailless monkey, primate, *(loosely)* monkey. *—v.* **2.** mimic, imitate, copy, echo, parrot, mirror, emulate, follow; mock, parody, caricature, burlesque, travesty.

aperture *n.* opening, hole, orifice, slit, space, interstice, slot; rift, rent, cleft, gap; chink, fissure, breach. **—Ant.** closure.

apex *n.* summit, highest point, pinnacle, peak, height, tip, zenith, crest, vertex, crown, crowning point, cap; climax, acme, apogee, culmination, consummation. **—Ant.** bottom, base, foot; lowest point, low point, depth, nadir, perigee.

aphorism *n.* maxim, epigram, proverb, adage, axiom, slogan, apothegm, dictum, saying, truism, *Slang* old saw.

aphrodisiac *n.* **1.** love potion, philter, magic potion, cantharis, cantharides. *—adj.* **2.** erotic, sexually stimulating, prurient, sexy, fleshly, carnal, raunchy.

apiece *adv.* each, individually, severally, respectively. **—Ant.** together, all together, overall, collectively, en masse, as a group.

aplomb *n.* composure, poise, self-composure, self-possession, calmness, coolness, equanimity, level-headedness, stability, balance, imperturbability; self-assurance, self-confidence, confidence, intrepidity, savoir faire, sang-froid. —**Ant.** awkwardness, confusion; embarrassment.

apocalyptic *adj.* prophetical, prophetic, oracular, predictive, revelational, revealing, revelatory, far-seeing, prescient, disclosing, eye-opening, prognosticative.

apocryphal *adj.* probably untrue, doubtful, questionable, dubious, unauthentic; mythical, fictitious, fabricated, unauthenticated, unverified, unsubstantiated, disputed; unauthorized, unofficial, uncanonical, spurious. —**Ant.** undisputed, unquestionable, without a doubt, authentic, creditable, true, factual; verified, authenticated, substantiated, attested; authorized, approved, official, sanctioned, canonical.

apogee *n.* farthest point, highest point, most distant point; vertex, apex, zenith, meridian, acme; top, crest, pinnacle, summit, peak; climax, culmination. —**Ant.** nadir, bottom, lowest point, weakest point.

apologetic *adj.* **1.** regretful, sorry, contrite, remorseful, self-reproachful, penitent. **2.** making excuses, defensive, excusatory, extenuatory, vindicatory, justificatory, exonerative, mitigatory, apologetical. —**Ant. 2** proud.

apologize *v.* express regret, make apology, beg pardon, say one is sorry.

apology *n.* **1.** expression of regret, saying one is sorry, begging pardon; acknowledgment of error. **2.** explanation, justification, defense, vindication, excuse.

apostate *n.* heretic, dissenter, dissident, traitor, defector, deserter, backslider, renegade, seceder, tergiversator, recanter, turncoat, turnabout, recusant, bolter, nonconformist.

apostle *n.* **1.** missionary, evangelist, proselytizer, disciple, witness; envoy, emissary, messenger, zealot, preacher. **2.** advocate, pioneer, supporter, proponent, exponent, spokesperson, propagator, propagandist, activist, zealot. —**Ant.** opponent, detractor.

apotheosis *n.* immortalization, deification, exaltation, glorification, magnification, enshrinement, idealization, canonization, elevation, consecration, dignification; quintessence, embodiment, epitome, essence.

appall *v.* horrify, dismay, shock, offend, outrage; disgust, sicken, repel, revolt, nauseate; stun, terrify, alarm, unnerve, dishearten, abash, frighten. —**Ant.** please, gladden; attract; reassure, calm, comfort, console.

appalling *adj.* dreadful, horrible, horrifying, horrific, awful, terrible, dire, grim, dismaying, horrid, frightful, fearful, ghastly, shocking, outrageous, intolerable, insufferable, abominable; disgusting, sickening, revolting, nauseating, repulsive, repellent; alarming, disheartening, terrifying, frightening. —**Ant.** pleasing, pleasant; reassuring, comforting.

apparatus *n.* **1.** equipment, machinery, mechanism, machine, contraption, device, contrivance, appliance, gadget, *Informal* gismo; tools, implements, instruments, utensils, gear, paraphernalia, outfit, tackle; materials, material. **2.** system, organization, setup.

apparel *n.* clothing, clothes, garments, dress, attire, *Slang* duds, threads, togs; vestments, vesture, raiment, robes, habit, garb, costume; equipment, gear, array, trappings, accouterments.

apparent *adj.* **1.** evident, obvious, manifest, self-evident, plain, open, patent, marked, overt, blatant, conspicuous, clear, clear as day, clear-cut; understandable, unmistakable, unequivocal. **2.** probable, seeming, according to appearances, likely, presumable, ostensible. **3.** visible, discernible, perceivable, perceptible; conspicuous, distinct. —**Syn. Study.** APPARENT, EVIDENT, OBVIOUS all refer to something easily perceived. APPARENT applies to that which can readily be seen or perceived: *an apparent effort.* EVIDENT applies to that which facts or circumstances make plain: *Your innocence was evident.* OBVIOUS applies to that which is unquestionable, because of being completely manifest or noticeable: *an obvious change of method.* —**Ant. 1** unclear, uncertain, doubtful, ambiguous; hidden, covered up, veiled, disguised. **2** improbable, doubtful, unlikely, obscure. **3** invisible, hidden, concealed, indiscernible, imperceptible; dim, fuzzy.

apparition *n.* **1.** ghost, phantom, specter, spirit, phantasm, wraith, shade, revenant, spook; materialization, manifestation, presence. **2.** unusual sight, strange spectacle, phenomenon.

appeal *n.* **1.** plea, request, entreaty, petition, supplication, solicitation, adjuration, suit, *Informal* S.O.S. **2.** attraction, charm, fascination, interest, allure, charisma, *Informal* pull. —*v.* **3.** plead, entreat, implore, call upon, petition, apply, solicit, beseech, invoke, adjure, sue to, beg, supplicate. **4.** attract, interest, allure, entice, invite, tempt, fascinate, excite, charm, engage, *Slang* turn one on. —**Ant. 1** refusal, rejection, repudiation, denial. **2** repulsiveness, alienation. **3** refuse, reject, repudiate, deny, rebuff. **4** repel, repulse, alienate, revolt, disgust, sicken, *Slang* turn one off; bore.

appear *v.* **1.** come into view, become

visible, show, show up, turn up, crop up, loom up, come to light; materialize, emerge, arise, surface. **2.** look, seem, strike one as being. **3.** be evident, be apparent, be obvious, be clear, be plain, be manifest, be patent. **4.** be published, come out, be placed before the public; be on the stage, come before the public, perform. **—Syn. Study. 2** See SEEM. **—Ant. 1** disappear, disappear from sight, vanish. **3** be uncertain, be unclear, be unknown; be doubtful.

appearance *n.* **1.** appearing, coming into view, showing up, turning up; arrival, coming, advent, emergence, materialization, manifestation. **2.** look, aspect, image. **3.** outward show, pretense, guise, pretext, impression. **—Syn. Study. 2, 3** APPEARANCE, ASPECT, GUISE refer to the way in which something outwardly presents itself to view. APPEARANCE refers to the outward look: *the shabby appearance of the hotel.* ASPECT refers to the appearance at some particular time or in special circumstances; it often has emotional implications, either ascribed to the object itself or felt by the beholder: *In the dusk the forest had a terrifying aspect.* GUISE suggests a misleading appearance, assumed for an occasion or a purpose: *an enemy in friendly guise.* **—Ant. 1** disappearance, vanishing; departure, passing.

appease *v.* **1.** calm, make peaceful, pacify, quiet, soothe, solace, mollify, lull, compose, placate. **2.** satisfy, ease, allay, abate, assuage, alleviate, temper, mitigate, relieve; slake, quench, quell, blunt, still, quiet, dull. **3.** conciliate, accommodate, propitiate. **—Syn. Study. 3** APPEASE, CONCILIATE, PROPITIATE imply trying to overcome hostility or win favor. To APPEASE is to make anxious overtures and often undue concessions to satisfy someone's demands: *Chamberlain tried to appease Hitler at Munich.* To CONCILIATE is to win over an enemy or opponent by friendly gestures and a willingness to cooperate: *to conciliate an opposing faction.* To PROPITIATE is to soften the anger of a powerful superior who has been offended: *Offerings were made to propitiate the gods.* **—Ant. 1–3** aggravate, provoke, inflame, arouse. **1** disturb, upset, bother, annoy, dissatisfy, perturb. **3** anger, enrage, infuriate; antagonize, *Informal* cross.

appeasement *n.* **1.** acceding to demands, conciliation, propitiation, accommodation; submission, giving in. **2.** means of quieting, means of calming, pacification, easing; alleviation, allaying, abating, mollification, assuagement, assuasion, mitigation, abatement, dulling, blunting, quenching; satisfaction, gratification. **—Ant.** aggravation, provocation, arousal; disturbance, annoyance.

appellation *n.* name, title, designation, epithet, cognomen, sobriquet, nom de guerre, *Slang* handle, moniker, tag.

append *v.* add, affix, attach, join, subjoin, tack on, supplement; suspend, hang on. **—Ant.** remove, omit, leave out; subtract, take away, detach, disconnect, disengage, separate.

appendage *n.* **1.** addition, attachment, adjunct, extension; supplement, auxiliary, accessory. **2.** extremity, member, projecting part, offshoot; *(variously)* branch, limb, arm, leg, feeler, tentacle, tail. **—Ant. 1** main body. **2** body.

appendix *n.* supplement, codicil, back matter; addendum, addition, postscript. **—Ant.** front matter, introductory material; main body, body of the text.

appertain *v.* belong to, be part of, pertain to, be characteristic of, inhere in; relate to, apply to, concern, be proper to, refer to, touch upon, bear upon. **—Ant.** be unrelated, be irrelevant, have no bearing upon.

appetite *n.* **1.** hunger, thirst. **2.** desire, craving, yearning, passion, inclination, penchant, proclivity; relish, zest, gusto, fondness, liking, stomach. **—Ant. 2** surfeit, fill; distaste, aversion, dislike, detestation, disgust, loathing, revulsion, repugnance, repulsion.

appetizer *n.* cocktail; tidbit, savory, dainty, delicacy; *French* apéritif, canapé, bonne bouche, hors d'oeuvre; *Italian* antipasto.

appetizing *adj.* mouth-watering, appealing, tempting, inviting, enticing, alluring, tantalizing; attractive; savory, palatable, succulent, tasty. **—Syn. Study.** See TASTY. **—Ant.** unappetizing; nauseating, sickening, repulsive; unpalatable, unsavory, distasteful.

applaud *v.* **1.** clap. **2.** praise, laud, congratulate, commend, compliment; acclaim, hail, extol, sing the praises of, eulogize. **—Ant. 1** boo, hiss, *Slang* give the raspberry, give the Bronx cheer. **2** criticize, censure; disparage, deride, ridicule, decry, deprecate, belittle.

applause *n.* **1.** clapping, ovation. **2.** praise, accolades, acclaim, plaudits, compliments, kudos, approval. **—Ant. 1** booing, hissing, *Informal* raspberries, Bronx cheers. **2** criticism, condemnation, derision, ridicule.

appliance *n.* device, apparatus, fixture, machine, mechanism, contraption, contrivance, implement; equipment, gear.

applicable *adj.* relevant, pertinent, adaptable, germane, apt, useful, suitable, fit, befitting, fitting, apropos. **—Ant.** inapplicable, inappropriate, wrong, useless, unsuitable, unfit, irrelevant.

applicant *n.* candidate, aspirant, hopeful; job seeker, office seeker; petitioner, suppliant, claimant.

application *n.* **1.** spreading on, putting on. **2.** ointment, salve, unguent, lotion, balm, wash, solution, poultice, dressing, emollient. **3.** relevance, pertinence, germaneness, suitability, appositeness. **4.** request, requisition, form; petition, claim, appeal, suit, entreaty, solicitation. **5.** attention, attentiveness, diligence; perseverance, persistence, industry, effort, exertion; dedication, commitment, assiduity. **—Syn. Study. 5** See EFFORT. **—Ant. 5** inattention, *Slang* goofing off; laxness, indolence.

apply *v.* **1.** put on, lay on, spread on. **2.** use, utilize, employ, exercise, practice, implement, adapt, bring to bear. **3.** be applicable, refer, pertain, relate, have bearing upon, be appropriate, fit, suit. **4.** make application, request, petition. **5.** devote, dedicate, direct, address. **—Ant. 1** remove, take off. **3** be inapplicable, be irrelevant, be inappropriate, be unsuitable.

appoint *v.* **1.** name, designate, assign, deputize, commission, delegate; select, nominate, engage. **2.** designate, set, fix, determine, establish, prescribe; decide on, choose, settle, arrange. **3.** furnish, equip, fit out, provide, supply. **—Syn. Study. 3** See FURNISH. **—Ant. 1** dismiss, discharge, cashier, fire. **2** cancel; change, rearrange. **3** strip, divest, denude, dismantle.

appointment *n.* **1.** designation, assignment, placement, commissioning; naming, selection, choosing, nomination. **2.** assignment, position, office, situation, post, job, station, spot, place, berth. **3.** meeting, engagement, date, rendezvous; meeting time, meeting place. **4.** **appointments.** furnishings, furniture; accouterments, outfit, equipment, equipage, gear. **—Ant. 1** dismissal. **3** accidental meeting; cancellation.

apportion *v.* allocate, allot, distribute proportionally, prorate, portion out, parcel out, measure out, mete out, deal out, dole out, ration; divide, disperse, consign, partition, share. **—Ant.** collect, receive, gather, assemble; keep, retain; give all, dispense all at once.

apposite *adj.* appropriate, suitable, fitting, apropos, applicable, pertinent, apt, relevant, germane, material. **—Ant.** unsuitable, inappropriate, irrelevant, inapt.

appraisal *n.* **1.** evaluation, judgment, estimate, assessment. **2.** monetary evaluation, estimated value, valuation; assessment.

appraise *v.* **1.** value, estimate to be worth, assay; assess. **2.** evaluate, judge, examine, inspect, review, *Informal* size up, assess.

appreciable *adj.* noticeable, obvious, evident, definite, clear-cut, substantial, significant, pronounced; recognizable, perceptible, perceivable, discernible, detectable, ascertainable. **—Ant.** unnoticeable, imperceptible, immaterial, unsubstantial, indistinguishable, undetectable; minor, small.

appreciate *v.* **1.** be grateful for, be thankful for, feel indebted; acknowledge. **2.** realize the worth of, estimate justly; regard highly, rate highly, value, prize, hold in high regard, cherish, relish, treasure, savor; like, admire, respect, esteem. **3.** realize, understand, comprehend, recognize, perceive, sympathize, be conscious of, be aware of, be cognizant of; acknowledge. **4.** rise in value, improve; inflate, enhance. **—Syn. Study. 2** APPRECIATE, VALUE, PRIZE, ESTEEM imply holding a person or thing in high regard. To APPRECIATE is to exercise wise judgment, delicate perception, and keen insight in realizing worth: *to appreciate fine workmanship.* To VALUE is to attach importance because of worth or usefulness: *I value your opinion.* To PRIZE is to value highly and cherish: *to prize a collection of rare books.* To ESTEEM is to feel respect combined with a warm, kindly sensation: *to esteem one's former teacher.* **—Ant. 1** be ungrateful. **2** undervalue, underrate, underestimate; belittle, disparage, scorn, disdain, ignore. **3** be unaware, be insensitive to; misunderstand, misjudge, misconceive. **4** depreciate; devaluate, deflate.

appreciation *n.* **1.** gratitude, gratefulness, thankfulness, thanks, regard. **2.** awareness, understanding, comprehension, clear perception, cognizance, recognition of worth; admiration, relish, liking, sympathy. **3.** increase in value; growth, rise, elevation, advance. **—Ant. 1** ingratitude; disregard. **2** ignorance, incomprehension; dislike, antipathy, aversion. **3** depreciation, devaluation; fall, decline, drop.

apprehend *v.* **1.** arrest, take into custody, take prisoner; catch, seize, capture, *Informal* nab, bag, *Slang* collar. **2.** comprehend, understand, perceive, discern, see, grasp; realize, recognize, know, sense. **—Ant. 1** release, free, let go; discharge; liberate. **2** be unaware of, be unconscious of; misunderstand, misconceive, miss, lose.

apprehension *n.* **1.** foreboding, uneasiness, misgiving, dread, dismay, anxiety, alarm, suspicion, mistrust, disquiet, apprehensiveness; worry, concern, distress; presentiment of evil, premonition of trouble. **2.** arrest, capture, seizure. **3.**

comprehension, perception, understanding. **—Ant. 1** confidence, assurance; tranquillity, trust; unconcern, nonchalance, composure. **2** release, freeing; discharge; liberation. **3** incomprehension, lack of understanding.

apprehensive *adj.* uneasy, filled with misgiving, anxious, disquieted, distressed, alarmed, worried, concerned, fearful, afraid, *Informal* scared; nervous, jittery; suspicious, distrustful. **—Ant.** confident, assured, calm, at ease, cool, composed, unruffled, nonchalant; unafraid.

apprentice *n.* indentured assistant, learner, student, pupil; beginner, novice, tyro, neophyte. **—Ant.** expert, master, professional, *Informal* pro.

apprise *v.* inform, notify, advise, tell, make acquainted, make aware, make cognizant of, disclose, enlighten. **—Ant.** keep secret, keep quiet about.

approach *v.* **1.** come, near, come near, draw near, come nearer to, come close, move toward, gain upon. **2.** come close to, approximate; equal, match, compare, be like, resemble. **3.** make overtures to, broach a subject to, make advances to, solicit, make a proposal to, sound out. **4.** embark on, undertake, set about, enter upon, begin, begin work on, initiate. *—n.* **5.** drawing near, coming nearer, advance. **6.** access, way; road, avenue, passage, passageway. **7.** way of handling, method of attack, attitude; method, procedure, modus operandi, technique, system. **—Ant. 1** leave, go, draw away; retreat, withdraw, retire, go back. **2** be different, diverge. **3** ignore, overlook, pass over, pass by. **4** leave, finish, end. **5** departure, leaving, withdrawal. **6** exit.

approbation *n.* praise, congratulation, compliment, good word, applause, acclaim; approval, acceptance, support, endorsement, ratification, commendation, laudation, official sanction. **—Ant.** censure, condemnation, criticism; disapproval, dissatisfaction, protest, rejection, veto.

appropriate *adj.* **1.** suitable, proper, well-suited, congruous, fitting, befitting, correct, seemly, apt, apropos, well-chosen; characteristic, belonging, pertinent, relevant, germane, to the purpose, to the point, opportune. *—v.* **2.** allocate, set apart, allot, apportion, assign, earmark. **3.** take possession of, take, confiscate, expropriate. **—Ant. 1** inappropriate, improper, ill-suited, unsuitable, unsuited, unfitting, incongruous, unbefitting, unseemly, incorrect, wrong, inconsonant, incompatible, *outré;* uncharacteristic, out of place, inopportune, irrelevant. **2** withhold. **3** give, bestow, donate; relinquish, cede, dispose of.

appropriation *n.* **1.** allocation, money set aside, apportionment of funds, allotment. **2.** taking for one's own use, taking, misappropriation, expropriation, arrogation, confiscation, usurpation. **—Ant. 1** withholding of funds. **2** return, reimbursement, repayment, paying back, recompense.

approval *n.* **1.** good opinion, regard, admiration, acceptance, respect, esteem, acclaim, appreciation, approbation, acknowledgment, favor, liking. **2.** permission, consent, endorsement, concurrence, agreement, confirmation, compliance, acquiescence, leave, sanction, countenance, license; authorization, mandate. **—Ant. 1** disapproval, disfavor, dislike, dissatisfaction, displeasure, censure, criticism, rebuke, reproof, reproach, disparagement. **2** refusal, disapproval, objection; denial, refutation, veto.

approve *v.* **1.** consider favorably, judge as good, regard as worthy, think highly of, have a good opinion of, be pleased with, receive with favor; esteem, respect, appreciate, praise, like, accept; believe in. **2.** permit, allow, consent to, condone, countenance, assent to, concur in, accede to, advocate, uphold, go along with, subscribe to, defend, second. **3.** confirm, affirm, sustain, uphold, ratify, pass, authorize, endorse, sanction, rubber-stamp; permit, allow. **—Ant. 1** disapprove, dislike; criticize, disparage, condemn. **2** disallow, repudiate, reject, object to, refute. **3** reject, disapprove, veto.

approximate *adj.* **1.** rough, very near, estimated, relative; nearly accurate, almost exact, inexact. *—v.* **2.** almost match, approach, come close to, border on, verge on, nearly equal; look like, closely resemble. **3.** estimate, figure roughly; reckon, guess, make a stab at. **—Ant. 1** exact, precise, correct, accurate; definite, specific. **2** differ completely, be nowhere near.

approximately *adv.* just about, almost, around, more or less, very nearly, close to, not far from, in the vicinity of, in the neighborhood of, circa, generally. **—Ant.** exactly, precisely, on the dot; definitely, specifically.

apropos *adj.* appropriate, fitting, befitting, suitable, well-suited, opportune, just the thing, congruous, correct, seemly, apt; pertinent, relevant, germane, applicable, related, to the point. **—Ant.** inappropriate, unsuitable, ill-suited, unsuited, inapt, unfitting, unseemly, incorrect, wrong, incongruous, out of place, inopportune, irrelevant, untimely, unrelated.

apt *adj.* **1.** likely, liable; inclined, prone, given to, disposed to, predisposed. **2.**

bright, clever, intelligent, gifted. **3.** appropriate, suitable, well-suited, proper, fitting, befitting, congruous, seemly, apropos; pertinent, relevant, germane, opportune. **—Syn. Study. 3** APT, RELEVANT, PERTINENT all refer to something suitable or fitting. APT means to the point and particularly appropriate: *an apt comment.* RELEVANT means pertaining to the matter in hand: *a relevant question.* PERTINENT means directly related to and important to the subject: *pertinent information.* **—Ant. 1** unlikely; averse, disinclined. **2** slow to learn, slow, dull. **3** inappropriate, unsuitable, ill-suited, unsuited, improper, unfitting, incongruous, unseemly; irrelevant, inopportune.

aptitude *n.* ability, capacity, capability, talent, gift, faculty, genius, knack, flair, facility, proficiency, endowment, quickness, cleverness; inclination, tendency, predisposition, leaning, turn, bent, propensity, penchant, proclivity, proneness, predilection. **—Ant.** inaptitude, ineptitude; aversion, disinclination.

aquatic *adj.* **1.** at home in water, living in or near water, growing in water; marine *(salt water),* oceanic, pelagic *(open sea),* thalassic *(seagoing),* lacustrine *(lake-dwelling),* fluvial, fluviatile *(river and stream),* littoral, neritic *(offshore),* abyssal *(deepest parts of the ocean).* **2.** occurring on water, carried on in water. **—Ant. 1** land, terrestrial.

aqueduct *n.* conduit, channel, artificial waterway, watercourse, duct, race.

aqueous *adj.* watery, liquid, moist, waterish, lymphatic, hydrous, damp, serous.

arable *adj.* cultivable, farmable, plowable, tillable; productive, fruitful, fertile, fecund. **—Ant.** uncultivable, unfarmable, untillable; unproductive, barren, unfertile.

arbiter *n.* judge, referee, umpire, arbitrator; authority, connoisseur, pundit.

arbitrary *adj.* **1.** subjective, personal, willful, chance, random, summary; capricious, frivolous, whimsical, fanciful, inconsistent. **2.** absolute, unlimited, unrestrained, peremptory, uncontrolled, imperious, autocratic, despotic. **—Ant. 1** objective, impersonal. **2** constitutional, lawful.

arbitrate *v.* **1.** decide, settle, mediate, reconcile, bring to terms, sit in judgment; judge, adjudge, adjudicate; umpire, referee. **2.** submit to arbitration, allow to be decided by an arbitrator. **—Ant.** negotiate.

arbitrator *n.* mediator, arbiter, adjudicator, judge; referee, umpire; *(loosely)* negotiator, moderator, intermediary, go-between.

arbor *n.* vine-covered bower, shaded walk, pavilion, grotto, pergola; summerhouse, kiosk, gazebo, belvedere, *Brit.* folly.

arc *n.* curve, arch, semicircle, crescent, half-moon, bow.

arcade *n.* colonnade, archway, cloister, gallery, loggia, *Brit.* piazza, peristyle, covered passageway, vaulted passage; areaway, breezeway, underpass, overpass, skywalk.

arcane *adj.* mysterious, enigmatic, esoteric, occult, abstruse, recondite, obscure, hermetic, mystic, mystical. **—Ant.** clear, obvious, evident, understood, known, well-known, open, revealed.

arch[1] *n.* **1.** curved span, vault, dome. **2.** curvature, curve, arc, bow shape, bend. *—v.* **3.** span, curve, bend. **4.** curve, bend. **—Ant. 2** straightness. **4** straighten out, unbend.

arch[2] *adj.* **1.** chief, primary, principal, main, major. **2.** mischievous, sly, wily, roguish, saucy, designing, cunning. **—Ant. 1** minor, petty, lesser. **2** frank, open, forthright.

archaic *adj.* antiquated, obsolete, obsolescent, gone out of use, out-of-date, old-fashioned, bygone, passé, behind the times; ancient, antique. **—Ant.** modern, current; new, fresh, novel, up-to-date, fashionable, newfangled, modish, *Slang* trendy.

archenemy *n.* foe, adversary, archfoe, nemesis, antagonist, opponent; assailant, combatant, disputant; bugbear, *French* bête noire, scourge. **—Ant.** friend, companion, comrade, champion, defender, ally, supporter, benefactor.

archetype *n.* original, prototype, classic, model, exemplar, prime example.

architect *n.* **1.** building designer, master builder. **2.** engineer, originator, creator, author, designer, planner, draftsman, deviser, contriver, founder, artificer; instigator, prime mover, shaper, innovator.

architecture *n.* **1.** science of building, art of designing buildings; structural design, construction, architectonics. **2.** design, construction, structuring, style.

archives *n. pl.* **1.** depository, library, museum. **2.** documents, papers, records, annals, chronicles, memorabilia.

arctic *adj.* **1.** north of the Arctic Circle, near the North Pole; polar, far-northern; septentrional, hyperborean. **2.** bitter, icy, frigid, ice-cold, glacial, freezing, frostbound, icebound, frozen, gelid. *—n.* **3. Arctic.** region north of the Arctic Circle, North Pole, north polar region. **—Ant. 2** torrid, hot, warm, summery. **3** Antarctica, the Antarctic, South Pole.

ardent *adj.* impassioned, passionate, zealous, eager, fervent, fervid, fiery, tempestuous, vehement, emotional, enthusiastic, intense, fierce, keen, earnest; lusty, spirited, feverish. **—Ant.** indifferent, half-hearted, nonchalant, dispassionate, unenthusiastic, apathetic, impassive, phlegmatic, detached; unloving, unamorous, cold, cool, frigid.

ardor *n.* **1.** feeling, passion, fervor, intensity, gusto, zeal, vehemence, fierceness, warmth, excitement, eagerness, enthusiasm, spirit, feverishness, animation, vigor, verve. **2.** passion, rapture, amorousness, devotion, love, warmth. **—Ant. 1** indifference, unconcern, disinterestedness, apathy, detachment, dispassion, languor, languidness; coldness, coolness, frigidity.

arduous *adj.* difficult, hard, laborious, toilsome, wearisome, exhausting, fatiguing, tiring, burdensome, heavy, tough, troublesome, onerous, trying, full of hardships, formidable, severe, Herculean; vigorous, strenuous, energetic. **—Ant.** light, facile, easy, simple, effortless, smooth.

area *n.* **1.** expanse, extent, stretch, portion, zone, space. **2.** region, locality, terrain, territory, *Slang* turf, section, tract, range, district, precinct. **3.** field, sphere, realm, domain, province, arena, scope.

arena *n.* **1.** coliseum, stadium, amphitheater, bowl, gymnasium, field, hippodrome, circus; ring, stage, platform. **2.** field, realm, area, province, territory, domain, sphere, scene, theater, stage; battleground, battlefield, sector, lists, playing field, marketplace.

argot *n.* criminal jargon, cant; *(loosely)* lingo, vernacular, idiom, slang, patois.

argue *v.* **1.** reason, contend, maintain, assert, claim, hold, plead, expostulate, remonstrate. **2.** have an argument, quarrel, dispute, debate, bicker, quibble, wrangle. **3.** show, indicate, exhibit, display, manifest, demonstrate, evince; express, imply, denote, point to. **—Ant. 2** agree, concur. **3** hide, conceal; raise doubt, disprove.

argument *n.* **1.** quarrel, bickering, squabble, row, clash, altercation, fight, spat, tiff, imbroglio, embroilment; disagreement, dispute, debate, controversy, heated discussion, war of words. **2.** reason, line of reasoning, case, line of argument, argumentation. **3.** outline, abstract, summary, plot, synopsis, story, central idea, contents, gist. **—Syn. Study. 1** ARGUMENT, CONTROVERSY, DISPUTE imply the expression and discussion of differing opinions. An ARGUMENT usu. arises from a disagreement between two persons, each of whom advances facts supporting his or her point of view: *an argument over a debt.* A CONTROVERSY is usu. a public expression of contrary opinions; it may be dignified and of some duration: *a political controversy.* A DISPUTE is an oral contention, usu. brief, and often of an angry or undignified character: *a heated dispute between neighbors.* **—Ant. 1** agreement, accord, concord, concurrence, harmony. **2** rebuttal, refutation, retort, rejoinder, response, answer.

argumentative *adj.* quarrelsome, contentious, belligerent, combative, disputatious, litigious, scrappy; cantankerous, snappish, fractious, querulous, peevish, testy, petulant, contrary. **—Ant.** congenial, amenable, cordial, sympathetic.

aria *n.* solo, song, tune, melody, air; selection, number, section, excerpt; *Italian* arietta, canzonetta, aria cantabile.

arid *adj.* **1.** dry, dried-up, waterless, parched, drought-scourged, desertlike; barren. **2.** dull, tedious, lifeless, colorless, uninteresting, dreary, vapid, uninspired, unimaginative, jejune, dry as dust; pedantic. **—Syn. Study. 1** See DRY. **—Ant. 1** well-watered; lush, verdant. **2** lively, full of life, interesting, exciting, spirited, imaginative, pithy.

arise *v.* **1.** get out of bed, awake, wake, wake up; get up, rise, stand up. **2.** rise, move upward, ascend, go up, mount, climb. **3.** come into being, occur, spring up, crop up, set in, emanate, ensue; originate, stem from, start, begin, commence, dawn, result, appear, make its appearance, emerge, show itself, come to light. **—Ant. 1** retire, lie down, go to bed, recline; sit, sit down, kneel. **2** descend, come down, fall. **3** cease, stop, end, die; disappear, go away, fade away, be suppressed, be hidden.

aristocracy *n.* nobility, peerage, patricians; upper class, high society, society, beau monde, elite, *haut monde,* upper crust, gentry. **—Ant.** commons, common people, bourgeoisie, demos, plebs, commoners, populace, masses; lower classes, working class, proletariat, hoi polloi, riffraff, rabble, canaille.

aristocrat *n.* noble, nobleman, noblewoman, lord, peer, grandee; gentleman, gentlewoman, Brahmin, blue blood, silk stocking, patrician. **—Ant.** commoner, bourgeois, plebeian, proletarian, peasant.

aristocratic *adj.* noble, titled, lordly, royal, regal, courtly, blue-blooded; highborn, wellborn, highbred, of gentle blood, of high rank, patrician, gentlemanly, silk-stocking, upper-class; genteel, refined, dignified. **—Ant.** common; bourgeois, middle-class, lower-class, working-class, plebeian, lowbred; unrefined, crude.

arm *n.* **1.** *(of humans)* upper limb, forearm, upper arm; appendage, offshoot, branch, projection. **2.** branch, division, department, section, sector, detachment.

3. arms. firearms, guns, weapons; ordnance, weaponry, armament, matériel. **4.** coat of arms, heraldic emblem, insignia, crest, blazonry. —*v.* **5.** take up arms, obtain arms; furnish with weapons, prepare for war. **6.** prepare, make ready, prime, forearm; equip, outfit, fortify, strengthen, protect, brace. **—Ant. 5** disarm.

armada *n.* fleet, flotilla, squadron, escadrille, navy.

armament *n.* **1.** weapons, arms, guns, ordnance, equipment, outfitting, munitions. **2.** military might, war-making machine, weaponry.

armistice *n.* suspension of hostilities, cease-fire, truce; peace. **—Ant.** outbreak of war, attack; war, hostilities.

armor *n.* **1.** protective covering, protection, shield, bulwark. **2.** suit of armor, coat of mail, mail, chain.

armory *n.* arsenal, arms depot, ordnance depot.

army *n.* **1.** military force, military machine, military; land forces, land force, troops, soldiers, soldiery, fighting men, legions, legion, militia. **2.** host, horde, swarm, pack, multitude, legion, throng, congregation, force, crowd, mob, band, gang, crew, bevy; mass, aggregation. **—Ant. 1** civilians. **2** small number.

aroma *n.* good smell, pleasant odor, perfume, scent, fragrance, bouquet, redolence, savor. **—Syn. Study.** See PERFUME. **—Ant.** stench, stink.

aromatic *adj.* fragrant, sweet-smelling, sweet-scented, scented, perfumed, odoriferous, odorous, redolent; piquant, spicy, pungent. **—Ant.** nonaromatic, unscented; bad-smelling, stinking, malodorous, noisome, rank, putrid, fetid, acrid.

arouse *v.* **1.** awaken, wake up, waken, rouse, bestir. **2.** summon up, call forth, excite, stimulate, provoke, spur, incite, kindle, stir up, foster, foment, move, quicken; pique, sharpen, whet, goad, fan, heat up, warm. **—Ant. 1** put to sleep, lull. **2** end, kill, still, quench; damp, dampen, dull, calm, quell, quiet, allay, mitigate, assuage, alleviate, relieve, pacify, moderate, placate, mollify.

arraign *v.* **1.** indict, charge. **2.** accuse, charge, indict; call to account, take to task, denounce, censure, criticize, find fault with, impute. **—Ant. 2** withdraw charges, drop charges; exonerate, absolve, excuse, pardon, exculpate, overlook; defend, vindicate; condone, approve, support, praise, acclaim.

arrange *v.* **1.** group, array, set out, range, pose; order, set in order, organize, sort, assort, assign places to, file, classify, marshal, rank, line up, systematize, methodize. **2.** plan, schedule, map out, lay out, prepare, devise, contrive, plot, provide, design, fix up; settle, agree to. **3.** orchestrate, score, adapt. **—Ant. 1** disorganize, disarrange, jumble, disturb, mess up; scatter, disperse.

arrangement *n.* **1.** grouping, arraying, disposal, assortment, distribution, ordering; order, organization, systematization, classification, categorization, methodization. **2.** Often **arrangements.** plans, preparations, measures, provisions; settlement, agreement, terms, compact. **3.** orchestration, score, adaptation. **—Ant. 1** disorder, disorganization, disarray, topsy-turviness.

arrant *adj.* thorough, thoroughgoing, utter, confirmed, outright, downright, egregious, unmitigated, flagrant, out-and-out, rank, extreme, notorious; undisguised. **—Ant.** partial, sometimes, incomplete, inconsistent, modified.

array *n.* **1.** display, exhibition, arrangement, disposition, marshaling, order, show, parade, pageantry; collection, assortment, supply. **2.** finery, fine clothes, attire, clothing, apparel, raiment, garments, dress, garb, *Informal* glad rags, Sunday best. —*v.* **3.** arrange, group, order, organize, marshal, align, range, rank; set out, place, display, deploy, pose. **4.** clothe, attire, dress, adorn, bedeck, deck, fit out, outfit, robe, wrap. **—Ant. 1** disarray, hodgepodge, odds and ends. **2** rags. **3** disarrange, mix up, mess up.

arrears *n.* overdue debt, unpaid debt, outstanding debt; indebtedness, liability, obligation, debit, balance due. **—Ant.** prepayment, early payment.

arrest *v.* **1.** take into custody, apprehend, catch, seize, capture, take prisoner, collar; detain, hold, secure, *Slang* bust, nab, pinch. **2.** catch, attract; fix, hold, seize, capture, occupy, engage, rivet, absorb, engross. **3.** check, block, stay, halt, stop, end, bring to a standstill; delay, slow, retard, inhibit, hold back, restrain, hinder, stall, suppress, interrupt. —*n.* **4.** apprehension, capture, seizure, taking into custody, *Slang* bust, roust. **5.** stopping, stoppage, halt, blocking, checking, staying; slowing, inhibiting, holding back, retention. **—Syn. Study. 3** See STOP. **—Ant. 1** release, free, set free, let go. **2** be ignored, be passed over. **3** encourage, quicken, speed up. **4** releasing, freeing. **5** quickening.

arrival *n.* **1.** arriving, coming, advent, appearance, approach, entrance. **2.** comer, visitor, visitant, newcomer, entrant. **—Ant. 1** departure, leaving, going, withdrawal.

arrive *v.* **1.** come, reach, get to, appear, show up, turn up, reach a destination; approach, near, draw near, go toward.

2. come, occur, happen, befall, take place, come to pass, appear. 3. achieve recognition, succeed, make good, reach the top. **—Ant. 1, 2** depart, go, go away, leave, withdraw, retire, *Slang* scram, beat it, cut out, make tracks; set out, set forth, be off. **3** fail, fall.

arrogance *n.* overbearing pride, haughtiness, assurance, presumption, pretension, loftiness, imperiousness; vanity, conceit, egoism, bluster, swagger, vainglory, self-importance, braggadocio; insolence, disdain, contempt, scorn, lordliness. **—Ant.** humility, modesty, simplicity, politeness, self-deprecation, self-effacement, diffidence, bashfulness, meekness, shyness.

arrogant *adj.* overbearing, haughty, presumptuous, pretentious, imperious, overweening, high-and-mighty; vain, conceited, egoistical, vainglorious, self-important, self-assuming, swaggering; insolent, disdainful, contemptuous, scornful, lordly, pompous, supercilious. **—Ant.** unassuming, polite, considerate, modest, diffident, deferential; self-effacing, bashful, meek, shy.

arrogate *v.* take over, claim, appropriate, seize, preempt, usurp, commandeer, assume, adopt, help oneself to, make free with. **—Ant.** cede, relinquish, surrender, yield, resign, renounce.

arsenal *n.* **1.** armory, arms depot, ordnance depot, military storehouse; ammunition dump, magazine; arms factory, munitions factory. **2.** cache of weapons, weapon collection, weapons, military stores.

art *n.* **1.** artistic activity, creative work, artistry. **2.** works of art, objects of art. **3.** artistry, genius, mastery, expertise, skill, facility, virtuosity, dexterity. **4.** liberal arts, humanities. **5.** craft, technique, methods, principles, strategy; fine points, subtleties, finesse, knack. **—Ant. 1** science. **2** junk, worthless objects. **3** lack of skill, ineptitude, incompetence, inability.

artful *adj.* **1.** cunning, crafty, sly, wily, foxy, strategic, diplomatic, politic, scheming, designing, contriving, machinating, maneuvering; deceitful, deceptive, underhand, disingenuous, shifty, tricky. **2.** skillful, smart, clever, shrewd, sharp, astute, quick, adroit, deft, resourceful, ingenious, inventive, imaginative, nimble-minded, dexterous, knowing, subtle; able, apt, adept, masterly, proficient, gifted, talented. **—Ant. 1** artless; simple, natural, candid, open, frank, straightforward, unsophisticated, ingenuous, naïve. **2** dull, clumsy, plodding; ungifted, untalented, unadept, unskilled.

article *n.* **1.** piece, write-up, story, item, essay, paper, theme, sketch, commentary, review. **2.** item, thing, piece, object, product, commodity; substance, matter. **3.** item, piece, point, count, particular, matter, detail; clause, paragraph, part, division, portion; term, condition, stipulation, proposition, provision, proviso.

articulate *adj.* **1.** enunciated, intelligible, meaningful, speechlike, expressive. **2.** capable of speech. **3.** eloquent, expressive, fluent, facile; clearly expressed. *—v.* **4.** enunciate, utter, pronounce, enounce. **5.** express, convey, state, voice; formulate, organize. **6.** hinge, connect, join, fit together, hook up. **—Syn. Study. 3** See ELOQUENT. **—Ant. 1–3** inarticulate. **1** unintelligible, incomprehensible, indistinct. **2** dumb, mute, aphasic. **3** inexpressive, nonfluent. **4** mumble, murmur, swallow words.

articulation *n.* **1.** utterance, enunciation, pronunciation; diction, elocution. **2.** joint, juncture, connection, hinge.

artifice *n.* **1.** trick, device, tactic, stratagem, maneuver, contrivance; subterfuge, ruse, dodge, feint, wile; hoax, blind, trap. **2.** cunning, craftiness, guile, slyness, wiliness, artfulness, intrigue, trickery, machination, scheming, foxiness; deceit, deception, duplicity, imposture, falsehood; ingenuity, inventiveness, invention, cleverness. **—Syn. Study. 1** See TRICK. **—Ant. 2** frankness, candor, openness, artlessness, ingenuousness, sincerity; truthfulness, honesty.

artificial *adj.* **1.** manmade, manufactured, synthetic, nonnatural; imitation, simulated, fake, counterfeit, false, sham, phony, mock, spurious, specious, ersatz. **2.** insincere, feigned, pretended, phony, forced, labored, unnatural, affected, mannered, stilted, factitious, theatrical, stagy. **—Ant. 1** natural, real, genuine, authentic, bona fide, true, actual. **2** sincere, natural, honest, frank, candid, open; unaffected.

artillery *n.* cannon, big guns, mounted guns, ordnance.

artisan *n.* craftsman, handicraftsman; skilled worker, technician; master, master craftsman. **—Syn. Study.** See ARTIST.

artist *n.* **1.** practitioner of a fine art. **2.** master, expert, virtuoso. **—Syn. Study. 1, 2** ARTIST, ARTISAN both refer to a person having superior skill or ability, or one capable of superior workmanship or performance. An ARTIST is a creative person who is skilled in one of the fine or performing arts: *The concert featured a famous pianist and other noted artists.* An ARTISAN is one who is skilled in a craft or applied art that requires manual dexterity: *carpentry done by skilled artisans.* **—Ant. 2** amateur, beginner, tyro, novice.

artistic *adj.* **1.** aesthetic. **2.** befitting an artist, of an artist, of art, in art. **3.** elegant, exquisite, attractive, handsome, tasteful, aesthetic, stylish, graceful. **—Ant. 1** inartistic, unaesthetic. **3** tasteless, inelegant, unattractive; unpolished, uncultured, unrefined; unaccomplished, untalented, inexpert.

artistry *n.* artistic ability, mastery, talent, proficiency, sensibility, taste, touch; accomplishment, virtuosity.

artless *adj.* **1.** frank, candid, open, honest, true, guileless, innocent, naïve, simple, humble, straightforward; sincere, unpretentious, trusting, undesigning, open-hearted, ingenuous, unsophisticated, unaffected, unselfconscious. **2.** natural, pure, unadorned, plain, simple, primitive, crude. **3.** inartistic, lacking art; without artistic talent, untalented. **—Ant. 1** cunning, crafty, sly, wily, dishonest, deceitful, designing, artful, insincere, pretended, faked, phony, false, counterfeit; sophisticated, affected, self-conscious; suspicious, distrustful. **2** artificial, unnatural, synthetic. **3** artistic, aesthetic.

arty *adj.* precious, highbrow, affected, pretentious, overnice, overrefined, bluestocking, overblown, high-sounding; effeminate, foppish, dainty, dandified, fruity, faggy; artsy-craftsy.

ascend *v.* **1.** rise; climb, mount, scale. **2.** succeed to, inherit. **—Ant. 1** descend; fall.

ascendancy, ascendance *n.* power, control, domination, dominance, predominance, superiority, supremacy, preeminence, leadership, mastery, advantage, edge, sway, upper hand, whip hand; command, authority, influence, rule, reign, sovereignty. **—Ant.** inferiority, weakness, subordination, subjection, servility; disadvantage, defeat.

ascension *n.* ascent, ascendancy; rising, mounting, climbing, scaling.

ascent *n.* **1.** ascension, climb, climbing, scaling, mounting, rise, rising, upward movement. **2.** gradient, upgrade, grade, incline, slope. **3.** advancement, advance, rise, progression, climb, ascension. **—Ant.** descent. **3** fall, retrogression.

ascertain *v.* find out, establish, verify, determine, certify, learn, discover, detect, unearth, ferret out. **—Syn. Study.** See LEARN.

ascetic *n.* **1.** self-denier, abstainer, self-mortifier; hermit, recluse, solitary, eremite, anchorite, celibate, cenobite; religious, monk, nun, flagellant; yogi, fakir, dervish. *—adj.* **2.** austere, self-denying, abstemious, strict, stern, Spartan, rigorous, self-mortifying. **—Ant. 1** hedonist, sensualist, voluptuary, sybarite, bon vivant. **2** self-indulgent, indulgent, pampered, luxurious, comfortable; abandoned, dissolute, voluptuous, sensuous, sensual, sybaritic.

ascribe *v.* attribute, credit, accredit, charge to, assign, impute, trace to, relate. **—Syn. Study.** See ATTRIBUTE. **—Ant.** discredit, deny, discount; dissociate.

ashamed *adj.* feeling shame, put to shame, mortified, embarrassed, humiliated, chagrined, discomfited, disconcerted, abashed, distressed, crestfallen, chapfallen, shamefaced; shy, bashful, prudish, squeamish; guilt-stricken, conscience-stricken. **—Ant.** proud, honored; arrogant, vain; gratified, satisfied, pleased, comforted.

ashen *adj.* wan, pale, pallid, pasty, gray, leaden, blanched, livid, anemic. **—Ant.** bright, vivid, colorful, warm-hued; rosy, red-cheeked, blushing, robust.

ashore *adv.* to shore, onto the shore, on shore, on land, on dry land. **—Ant.** on board, at sea, sailing; to the sea, on the sea, in the sea.

asinine *adj.* stupid, foolish, silly, ridiculous, absurd, senseless, brainless, idiotic, moronic, imbecilic, feeble-minded, witless, half-witted, insane, lamebrained, simpleminded, irrational, muddleheaded, dunderheaded, thickheaded, thick-skulled, thick-witted. **—Ant.** smart, wise, intelligent, clever, sage; sensible, rational, reasonable, sane.

ask *v.* **1.** inquire, query, request an answer to; request information about, request information from, question, interrogate, quiz, pump, grill, sound out. **2.** invite, request, bid, summon, call, send for. **3.** express a desire for, seek, request, call, apply, petition, solicit, sue, appeal, plead, urge, implore, entreat, beseech, beg, supplicate, press. **4.** state as a price, charge, demand, claim; request, desire, seek, expect. **—Ant. 1** answer, inform, supply information. **2** ignore, pass over; blackball; accept; refuse, decline, reject. **3** grant, give; refuse, reject, deny, spurn. **4** declare not for sale; offer, pay, give, shell out.

askance *adv.* skeptically, distrustfully, mistrustfully, suspiciously; disdainfully, disapprovingly. **—Ant.** trustfully, unsuspiciously.

askew *adv., adj.,* crooked, crookedly, awry, lopsided, aslant, *Slang* cockeyed. **—Ant.** straight, centered, even, right, true, in line, in a line, aligned, plumb, *Informal* straight as an arrow.

asleep *adj., adv.* sleeping, slumbering; *(variously)* sound asleep, fast asleep, dead to the world, dozing, napping, taking a siesta. **—Ant.** awake, wide awake; up.

aspect *n.* **1.** look, air, appearance; guise. **2.** feature, point, side, facet, angle, consideration. **—Syn. Study. 1** See APPEARANCE.

asperity *n.* crossness, crankiness, acerbity, acrimony, churlishness, crabbedness, irritability, irascibility, sullenness, surliness, bitterness, harshness, tartness, waspiness, testiness, shirtiness, snappishness, captiousness. **—Ant.** affability, cheerfulness, geniality, amiability.

aspersion *n.* slur, abuse, smear, slander, deprecation, disparagement, detraction, defamation, reproach, censure, vilification, railing, reviling, calumny, obloquy. **—Ant.** praise, laudatory remark, plaudit, compliment, commendation, *Informal* pat on the back.

asphyxiate *v.* suffocate, smother, stifle, choke, strangulate. **—Ant.** breathe, inhale, take in oxygen.

aspiration *n.* ambition, object, objective, daydream, end, mark, endeavor, design, purpose, intent, intention, hope, desire, longing, wish, yearning, craving, hankering.

aspire *v.* desire, wish for, hope for, long for, yearn for, crave, covet, hanker after, thirst after, hunger over, pine for, pant after; seek, pursue, aim at.

ass *n.* **1.** donkey, male jackass; burro. **2.** jackass, fool, idiot, numskull, dolt, blockhead, bonehead, lamebrain, nitwit, nincompoop, ninny, *Slang* jerk, half-wit, moron, imbecile, dunce, dunderhead, lunkhead, booby, dum-dum. **—Ant. 2** sage; brain, genius.

assail *v.* attack, assault; set upon, lunge at, pitch into, fly at, descend upon. **—Syn. Study.** See ATTACK. **—Ant.** defend, support, champion; retreat, withdraw.

assailant *n.* attacker, mugger, assaulter, assailer, molester, aggressor.

assassin *n.* killer, murderer, slayer, executioner, *Slang* hit man.

assassinate *v.* kill, murder, slay, exterminate, liquidate, put to death, do to death, *Slang* bump off, rub out.

assault *n.* **1.** attack, onslaught, assailing, aggression; *(variously)* raid, strike, foray, charge, sally, lunge, thrust, drive, push, offense, invasion, storming, bombardment, siege. **—*v.* 2.** attack, assail, set upon, strike at, fall upon, lunge at, fly at, lash out at, *(variously)* raid, strike, charge, thrust at, invade, storm, bombard, besiege. **—Syn. Study. 2** See ATTACK. **—Ant. 1** defense, resistance, protection; retreat, withdrawal. **2** defend, protect, resist, withstand; retreat, withdraw.

assay *v.* **1.** try, attempt, endeavor, undertake, essay. **2.** analyze, assess, evaluate, appraise, rate, estimate; test, try, prove.

assemblage *n.* collection, gathering, assembly, aggregation, aggregate, congregation, amassment, accumulation; bunch, group, body, company, store, stock, throng, conclave, flock, herd, pack, cluster, clump, mass, pile, heap, batch.

assemble *v.* **1.** gather, convene, come together, congregate, meet, rally, convoke, flock; call together, summon. **2.** gather, collect, accumulate, round up, bring together, group together, amass, muster, marshal, compile, heap up, pile up. **3.** put together, fit together, construct, fabricate; join, connect. **—Syn. Study. 2** See GATHER. **—Ant. 1** disperse, scatter, go separate ways; disband, adjourn, dismiss. **2** disperse, scatter, distribute, divide, dispense. **3** disassemble, dismantle, take apart, *Informal* knock down.

assembly *n.* **1.** assemblage, gathering, company, congregation, convocation, convention, conference, conclave; group, body, crowd, throng, flock, herd, pack, troop; collection, aggregate, aggregation, cluster, mass. **2.** Usu. **Assembly.** lower house of a legislature, state house of representatives, chamber of deputies; legislature, congress, council. **—Syn. Study. 1** See CONVENTION. **—Ant. 1** dispersion, dismissal, disunion, disruption. **2** upper house, Senate.

assent *v.* **1.** agree, concur, accept, subscribe to, fall in with, concede, approve, allow, grant; acquiesce, defer to, consent, comply, yield, accord, permit. **—*n.* 2.** agreement, concurrence, acceptance, consent, approval, compliance, acquiescence, accord, concession, confirmation, approbation, admission, affirmation, ratification, endorsement, sanction, acknowledgment, recognition, corroboration, verification. **—Ant. 1** dissent, disagree, differ, disapprove, protest, object, reject, refuse, deny, negate, spurn, disallow. **2** disagreement, dissent, dissension, difference, disapproval, protest, objection; refusal, rejection, unacceptance; denial, negation, disavowal, disallowance, veto.

assert *v.* maintain, contend, insist, avow, claim, uphold, affirm, swear, declare, state, aver, profess, propound, advocate, argue, advance, put forward, set forth, avouch; stress, accent, emphasize. **—Syn. Study.** See DECLARE. **—Ant.** deny, disavow, disclaim, refute, negate, repudiate; laugh off, *Informal* put down; retract, take back.

assertion *n.* claim, contention, declaration, statement, dictum, upholding, maintaining, argument, protestation; avowal, averment, allegation. **—Ant.**

denial, disavowal, disclaimer, negation, repudiation; retraction.

assertive *adj.* positive, forceful, decisive, strong-willed, confident, self-assured, self-assertive, insistent, emphatic; aggressive, domineering, pushy, outspoken, cocksure. **—Ant.** retiring, reserved, shy, bashful, meek, timid, timorous, submissive; hesitant, uncertain, fearful.

assess *v.* **1.** value for taxation, estimate, appraise, value. **2.** levy a charge on, tax. **3.** judge, evaluate, appraise, look over, consider.

assessment *n.* **1.** value for taxation, rate; appraisal. **2.** tax, tariff, impost, fine, toll, charge, fee, dues. **3.** judgment, evaluation, appraisal, estimation.

asset *n.* **1.** benefit, advantage, help, aid, service, boon, plus. **2. assets.** financial resources, means, wealth; money and cashable possessions; *(loosely)* cash, property, effects, possessions, belongings, capital, money, reserves. **—Ant. 1** liability, handicap, disadvantage, disservice, drawback, hindrance. **2** liabilities, debts.

asseverate *v.* avow, state, avouch, assert, declare, aver, affirm, declare solemnly, attest, swear, contend, certify. **—Ant.** deny, disavow, repudiate, take back, retract.

assiduous *adj.* diligent, industrious, hardworking, laborious, unremitting, determined, persistent, persevering, earnest, steadfast, constant, tenacious, dogged, untiring, tireless, unflagging, indefatigable, sedulous. **—Ant.** indolent, lazy, idle; haphazard, casual, cavalier, lax, hit-or-miss, undetermined, inconstant, happy-go-lucky.

assign *v.* **1.** allocate, allot, consign, set apart, distribute, apportion, mete out; dispense, grant, give. **2.** designate, name, appoint, commission, delegate, choose; charge, entrust, invest. **3.** name, fix, set, appoint, specify, designate, stipulate, prescribe, determine. **—Syn. Study.** ASSIGN, ALLOCATE, ALLOT mean to apportion or measure out. To ASSIGN is to distribute available things, designating them to be given to or reserved for specific persons or purposes: *to assign duties.* To ALLOCATE is to earmark or set aside parts of things available or expected in the future, each for a specific purpose: *to allocate income to various types of expenses.* To ALLOT implies making restrictions as to amount, size, purpose, etc., and then apportioning or assigning: *to allot spaces for parking.* **—Ant. 2** dismiss, discharge, divest, relieve. **3** keep open, hold in abeyance.

assignation *n.* tryst, date, rendezvous, meeting, appointment.

assignment *n.* **1.** homework, lesson, exercise, chore, task, job, duty. **2.** post, appointment, designation, commission. **3.** distribution, apportionment, parceling out, dealing out, doling out, allotment, allocation. **—Syn. Study. 1** See TASK.

assimilate *v.* absorb, take in, digest, metabolize, incorporate, integrate, imbibe, ingest. **—Ant.** keep out, reject; keep apart, segregate, isolate.

assist *v.* **1.** help, aid, abet, serve, accommodate, work for, lend a hand, wait on; work with, collaborate, cooperate, support, benefit, sustain, succor, uphold, back up, reinforce. *—n.* **2.** helping hand, hand, aid, boost. **—Syn. Study. 1** See HELP. **—Ant. 1** hinder, hamper, impede, obstruct; oppose, counteract.

assistance *n.* **1.** help, aid, support, helping hand, service; collaboration, cooperation, reinforcement. **2.** financial support, contribution, charity, alms, relief, subsidy, sustenance, stipend. **—Ant. 1** hindrance, obstruction; opposition, resistance, counteraction.

assistant *n.* helper, subordinate, aide, second-in-command, subaltern, lieutenant, adjutant, associate, sidekick, auxiliary, apprentice, aid, aider, helping hand; colleague, co-worker, collaborator, partner, accessory, confederate, accomplice, cooperator, ally, supporter.

associate *v.* **1.** identify, relate, link, connect, affiliate, ally, league, couple; pair, bind, tie, yoke, combine, unite, merge, join, correlate. **2.** fraternize, be friends, consort, mix, mingle, club, run around, pal around, hobnob, hang out, rub elbows. *—n.* **3.** colleague, confrere, co-worker, peer, fellow, partner, collaborator, confederate, ally, accomplice. **4.** comrade, companion, fellow, friend, intimate, confidant, pal, buddy, chum, mate, crony, sidekick; acquaintance. *—adj.* **5.** subordinate; closely connected, affiliated, related, allied, fellow. **—Syn. Study. 4** See FRIEND. **—Ant. 1** separate, disconnect, dissociate, divorce; distinguish. **2** avoid, ignore; alienate, estrange. **4** stranger. **5** major, main, leading, chief; unaffiliated, unrelated, unallied.

association *n.* **1.** organization, federation, confederation, confederacy, alliance, league, union, combine, syndicate, coalition, fraternity, society, body, group, club, clique; company, corporation, partnership. **2.** affiliation, connection, alliance, participation, membership, relation, relationship, relations, collaboration; friendship, acquaintance, familiarity, intimacy, friendliness, fraternization, companionship, fellowship, camaraderie. **3.** identification, connection, relation, correlation, linkage, bond, tie, affiliation, alliance. **4.** combination, mixture, blend, meld, mingling, union, assemblage, community. **—Ant. 2** disassociation, dissociation, separation, independence; alienation, estrangement.

assorted *adj.* mixed, various, varied, diverse, diversified, sundry, miscellaneous, motley, different, heterogeneous. **—Ant.** identical, uniform, like, unvaried, all the same, homogeneous.

assortment *n.* **1.** variety, mixture, selection, conglomeration, diversity, miscellany, motley, medley, potpourri, hodgepodge, mélange; array, collection, stock, store, quantity. **2.** assorting, sorting, grouping, classifying, classification, arrangement, arranging, disposition. **—Ant. 1** uniformity, sameness, monotony. **2** mixing, heaping together, disarrangement.

assuage *v.* allay, ease, relieve, mitigate; lighten, lessen, soften; mollify, alleviate, soothe, calm, quiet, still, pacify, appease, temper, take the edge off, tone down. **—Ant.** intensify, aggravate, irritate, exacerbate, heighten, sharpen, increase, augment; provoke, excite, arouse, kindle, inflame.

assume *v.* **1.** take for granted, suppose, presume, suspect, believe, think, understand, guess, imagine, gather, fancy; infer, postulate, theorize, deduce, hypothesize, surmise, speculate, conjecture, judge. **2.** take on, take up, take over, become responsible for, take care of, shoulder, attend to, accept, enter upon, undertake, set about. **3.** seize, take, appropriate, usurp, arrogate, commandeer, expropriate. **4.** pretend, put on, affect, feign, fake, adopt, counterfeit, simulate. **—Syn. Study. 4** See PRETEND. **—Ant. 1** know, prove. **2, 3** relinquish, renounce, abandon, give up, give over, hand over, put aside, divest oneself of, leave. **4** shed, reject, repudiate, cast aside, cast off, scorn.

assumed *adj.* **1.** pseudonymous, pseudonymic, fictitious, make-believe, made-up, phony, bogus, falsified, fake, false. **2.** supposed, presupposed, presumed. **—Ant. 1** real, authentic, actual, true, original, natural. **2** stated, known, proved; positive, absolute.

assuming *adj.* presumptuous, forward, brazen, audacious, nervy, bold, cheeky, presuming; overbearing, pushy, self-assertive, haughty, arrogant, insolent. **—Ant.** meek, mild, retiring, reticent, modest, humble, soft-spoken.

assumption *n.* **1.** belief, supposition, presumption, presupposition, premise, theory, hypothesis, postulate, postulation. **2.** taking on, taking up, becoming responsible for, assuming, shouldering, accepting, acceptance, entering upon, undertaking. **3.** seizure, taking, appropriating, usurpation, arrogation.

assurance *n.* **1.** pledge, promise, word of honor, vow, oath, profession, averment, affirmation; guarantee, warranty, binder. **2.** self-assurance, assuredness, confidence, self-confidence, self-possession, certitude, certainty, sureness, poise, coolness; boldness, aggressiveness, self-reliance. **—Syn. Study. 2** See CONFIDENCE. **—Ant. 1** lie, fib, falsehood, fiction, tall story, cock-and-bull story, fish story, whopper; doubt, uncertainty, skepticism, suspicion, distrust, disbelief. **2** shyness, timidity, bashfulness; timorousness, self-doubt, uncertainty, hesitancy; nervousness, apprehension.

assure *v.* **1.** vow to, promise, pledge to, give one's word to, guarantee. **2.** make sure, make certain, guarantee, ensure; clinch, secure, confirm. **—Ant. 1** deny, refute, disavow, disclaim; lie, fib; doubt, express doubt, disbelieve. **2** be uncertain, be unsure, be up in the air; make doubtful.

assured *adj.* **1.** guaranteed, certain, sure, secure, dependable, settled, fixed, positive; undoubted, unquestionable, irrefutable, indisputable, indubitable. **2.** self-assured, self-confident, self-possessed, confident, secure, poised. **—Ant. 1** uncertain, unsure, insecure, unsettled; questionable, doubtful, disputable, dubious. **2** timid, timorous, shy, bashful; self-doubting, uncertain; nervous, apprehensive, fearful.

astern *adv.* to the stern, toward the stern, aft, abaft, to the rear, behind. **—Ant.** fore, afore, forward; ahead, before, in front.

astir *adj., adv.* awake, roused, out of bed, up, up and about, afoot, moving about, on the move, in motion, active, bustling about. **—Ant.** asleep, napping, in bed, lying down, reclining; quiet, still.

astonish *v.* surprise, astound, amaze, overwhelm, take aback; startle, stun, shock, electrify, stupefy, daze, dazzle, stagger, strike dumb, dumfound, flabbergast, make one's eyes pop, take one's breath away; perplex, bewilder, confound, confuse. **—Ant.** come as no surprise, be expected, anticipate, foresee, count upon; bore.

astonishing *adj.* surprising, astounding, amazing, overwhelming, overpowering; startling, breathtaking, staggering, striking, impressive, shocking, electrifying, stupefying, dazzling; perplexing, bewildering, confounding, confusing. **—Ant.** expected, anticipated, foreseen, looked for.

astonishment *n.* amazement, surprise, shock, wonder, wonderment, awe; bewilderment, perplexity, confusion, stupefaction. **—Ant.** calmness, indifference; boredom.

astound *v.* astonish, amaze, overwhelm, stun, startle, electrify, shock, stupefy, stagger, dazzle, daze, strike dumb, dumfound, flabbergast, surprise, take back, make one's eyes pop, take one's breath away.

astray *adj., adv.* off the right track, off the course, off the mark, amiss, afield, off, into error. **—Ant.** on the right track, on course.

astringent *adj.* **1.** tonic, invigorating, bracing, restorative, salutary, salubrious, curative; styptic, contracting. **2.** stern, severe, austere; incisive, sharp, penetrating, keen; biting, stabbing, piercing. **—Ant. 1** bland, mild. **2** noncommittal, unclear, ambiguous, indecisive, pussyfooting.

astute *adj.* shrewd, smart, sagacious, clever, keen, keen-minded, sharp, acute, bright, able, intelligent, perceptive, discerning, perspicacious, knowing, penetrating, subtle; cunning, sly, foxy, wily, crafty; adroit, Machiavellian, artful, politic, designing, calculating. **—Ant.** dull, slow, thick, unknowing, unintelligent, stupid, dumb, gullible, naïve.

asunder *adj., adv.* apart, into pieces, to shreds; in pieces, rent, torn apart, broken apart.

asylum *n.* **1.** institution, home; *(variously)* sanitarium, sanatorium, mental hospital, mental institution, state hospital, insane asylum, madhouse, poorhouse, almshouse, eleemosynary institution, orphanage, children's home. **2.** refuge, haven, harbor; shelter, home; place of immunity, retreat, sanctuary, preserve.

atheism *n.* disbelief, unbelief, godlessness, irreligion, apostasy. **—Ant.** religion, belief.

atheist *n.* disbeliever, unbeliever, nonbeliever, denier of God's existence, skeptic; godless person, infidel, pagan, agnostic, heathen. **—Syn. Study.** ATHEIST, AGNOSTIC, INFIDEL refer to persons not inclined toward religious belief or a particular religious faith. An ATHEIST denies the existence of a deity or of divine beings. An AGNOSTIC believes it is impossible to know whether there is a God without sufficient evidence. An INFIDEL is an unbeliever, esp. one who does not accept Christianity or Islam; the word is usu. applied pejoratively. **—Ant.** believer, religionist, God-fearing person.

athlete *n.* person active in physical exercise and sports, *Slang* jock, sportsman, game player; contestant, contender, champion.

athletic *adj.* **1.** strong, able-bodied, muscular, brawny, powerful, sturdy, strapping, hardy, robust, husky, stalwart, burly; manly, masculine, virile. **2.** physically active, vigorous, hardy. **—Ant. 1** frail, weak, puny, fragile, delicate, feeble, run down, out of shape, flabby, sickly. **2** sedentary, inactive.

athletics *n. pl.* exercise, exercises, sports, gymnastics, physical training.

athwart *adv., prep.* across, astride; crosswise, crossways, sidewise, sideways, transversely, from side to side of, at a right angle to. **—Ant.** parallel to, to the side of.

atmosphere *n.* **1.** gaseous envelope, air. **2.** mood, spirit, feeling, feel, ambience, aura, quality, tone, color; environment, surroundings.

atom *n.* **1.** smallest part of a chemical element; *(loosely)* indivisible particle. **2.** particle, scrap, shred, speck, grain, iota, *Informal* smidgen, bit, whit, jot, trace, mite, dot, morsel, crumb, fragment, scintilla, tittle, smithereen, mote. **—Ant. 1** compound; subatomic particle. **2** mass, load, quantity, heap.

atomic *adj.* **1.** nuclear, fission, fissionable, thermonuclear; uranium, plutonium, hydrogen, cobalt, neutron, superatomic. **2.** subatomic, microscopic, microcosmic, infinitesimal, molecular; imperceptible, impalpable, indiscernible, unseeable.

atone *v.* repent, do penance for, make amends for, make up for, make expiation, expiate, pay for, compensate, recompense, remunerate, make reparation for, render satisfaction for, redeem, shrive.

atonement *n.* repentance, penance, penitential act, amends, satisfaction, shrift, expiation, redress, reparation, compensation, recompense, redemption.

atrocious *adj.* **1.** cruel, brutal, inhuman, heinous, monstrous, horrible, terrible, villainous, outrageous, nefarious, enormous, infamous, grievous, pitiless, merciless, ruthless, flagrant, vile, evil, bad, savage, barbarous, vicious, fiendish, diabolical, hellish, infernal, black, dark. **2.** bad, dreadful, execrable, terrible, tasteless, uncouth, vulgar, tawdry, vile, rude, low. **—Ant. 1** humane, kind, benevolent, generous, merciful, gentle, tender, civilized; virtuous, honorable; admirable, wonderful. **2** good, fine, elegant, tasteful, high-class.

atrocity *n.* crime against humanity, savage deed, atrocious deed, outrage, horror, villainy, enormity; barbarity, barbarism, brutality, inhumanity, heinousness, savagery. **—Ant.** humaneness, kindness, benevolence, mercifulness, gentleness, tenderness; good deed, kind act.

atrophy *n.* wasting away, withering, degeneration, deterioration, emaciation, shriveling, drying up, decaying, decline; lack of development, lack of use.

—**Ant.** growth, development, strengthening; exercise, use.

attach *v.* **1.** fasten to, make fast, join, connect, couple; affix, fix, secure; append, annex. **2.** assign, allocate, allot, designate, detail, destine, earmark; associate, affiliate, connect. **3.** be fond of, be devoted to, be in love with; feel affection for, be bound by love of, feel regard for. —**Ant. 1** detach, unattach, unfasten, disconnect, unconnect, remove, release, separate, disengage. **2** withdraw, recall; disassociate, dissociate, separate, retire.

attaché *n.* diplomat, consul, envoy, emissary, minister, consul general, ambassador, ambassadress, vice consul, military attaché, *Brit.* diplomatist, Foreign Service officer; aide, assistant, adjutant, subordinate.

attachment *n.* **1.** attaching, fastening, coupling, connection; affixing, fixing, securing. **2.** love, devotion, affection, fondness, tenderness, bond, affinity, predilection; friendship, liking, regard, respect. **3.** accessory, fixture; supplement, addition, adjunct, appendage, addendum, appendix. —**Syn. Study. 3** See ADDITION. —**Ant. 1** separation, unfastening, detachment, parting. **2** aversion, antipathy, hatred, animosity, enmity, dislike; estrangement, alienation, indifference, coolness.

attack *v.* **1.** assail, assault, strike, take the offensive, begin hostilities against, set upon, fall upon, bear down upon, descend upon, charge, fly at, lunge at, pitch into. **2.** censure, denounce, disparage, damn, denigrate, impugn, blame, criticize, fault. **3.** set about, undertake, go to work on, go at, tackle. —*n.* **4.** offensive, offense, assault, invasion, onslaught, incursion, aggression, charge, onset. **5.** censure, impugnment, denigration, abuse, disparagement, criticism. **6.** seizure, stroke, fit, spasm, paroxysm, spell. —**Syn. Study. 1** ATTACK, ASSAIL, ASSAULT all mean to set upon someone forcibly, with hostile or violent intent. ATTACK is a general word that applies to the beginning of any planned aggressive action, physical or verbal: *to attack an enemy from ambush; to attack a candidate's record.* ASSAIL implies a vehement, sudden, and usu. repeated attack that aims to weaken an opponent: *assailed by gunfire; assailed by gossip.* ASSAULT implies a violent physical attack involving direct contact; it may also refer to a sudden and violent verbal attack: *an elderly couple assaulted by a mugger; a reputation assaulted by the press.* —**Ant. 1** withdraw, retreat; defend, guard, protect, resist. **2** defend, support, uphold, sustain, vindicate, excuse, whitewash. **4** retreat, withdrawal; defense, resistance. **5** defense, support, vindication, excuse, whitewash.

attain *v.* achieve, gain, procure, win, earn, obtain, secure; accomplish, effect, acquire, reach, realize, reap, bring off. —**Syn. Study.** See GAIN. —**Ant.** lose, let go, give up, forfeit; fail at, fall short of.

attainment *n.* **1.** attaining, obtaining, gaining, getting, winning, earning, securing, acquirement, acquiring, acquisition, procuring, procurement, realization, fulfillment. **2.** achievement, accomplishment, success, acquirement; proficiency, competence, mastery, skill, talent.

attempt *v.* **1.** try, strive, endeavor, venture, undertake, seek, essay, aim, work at, make an effort, have a go at, take a whack at, take a crack at, tackle, hazard. —*n.* **2.** effort, undertaking, try, endeavor, venture, essay, aim. **3.** assault, attack, onslaught. —**Syn. Study. 1** See TRY.

attend *v.* **1.** be present at, go to, appear at, show up, frequent; visit. **2.** take care of, tend to, look after, mind, serve, service, be attendant on, minister to, wait upon, care for, provide for. **3.** accompany, conduct, escort, convoy, squire, usher, watch over, oversee, superintend, have charge of. **4.** accompany, be associated with, be connected with, go hand-in-hand with; follow. **5.** heed, mind, listen to, harken to, give thought to, consider, pay attention to, note, observe, mark, take to heart. —**Syn. Study. 3** See ACCOMPANY. —**Ant. 1** absent oneself from, be absent, play truant, miss, *Informal* cut, skip. **2** ignore, disregard, neglect, slight. **4** disassociate, dissociate, be unrelated to. **5** ignore, disregard, turn a deaf ear to.

attendance *n.* **1.** presence, attending, being there, appearance. **2.** record of attendance. **3.** number present, audience, crowd, assemblage, house, gate. —**Ant. 1** absence, nonattendance.

attendant *n.* **1.** servant, underling, menial, lackey, flunky, aid, assistant, helper; companion, escort, chaperon; follower, adherent. —*adj.* **2.** accompanying, associated, related; accessory, consequent.

attention *n.* **1.** heed, regard, note, notice, mind, concern, consideration; observance, alertness, vigilance, wariness. **2.** concentration, diligence, alertness, thought, thoughtfulness, deliberation, contemplation. **3.** courtesy, civility, thoughtfulness, politeness, deference, respect; service, care, homage. **4.** devotion, suit, court, wooing; gallantries, compliments, assiduities. —**Ant. 1–4** inattention, disregard, neglect, negligence, indifference, unconcern. **2** distraction, thoughtlessness, carelessness. **3**

thoughtlessness, discourtesy, incivility, rudeness, impoliteness.

attentive *adj.* **1.** heedful, mindful, considerate, intent, awake, wide awake, alert, listening, observant. **2.** thoughtful, considerate, obliging, accommodating, courteous, respectful, deferential, polite; dedicated, devoted, diligent, painstaking, zealous. **—Ant. 1** inattentive, indifferent, unconcerned, heedless, neglectful. **2** thoughtless, inconsiderate, unaccommodating; discourteous, impolite, rude; negligent, remiss, careless.

attenuate *v.* **1.** draw out, make thin, make fine, make slender, spin out. **2.** weaken, reduce, diminish, lessen, decrease; dilute, water down, adulterate, impair, enervate, enfeeble. **—Ant. 1** broaden, make thick, make coarse, make fat, enlarge, expand. **2** increase, amplify, intensify, augment, strengthen, develop.

attest *v.* testify, swear to, verify, confirm, corroborate, vouch for, certify, warrant, affirm, assert, evince, assure, declare; prove, demonstrate, exhibit, show, display, support, substantiate, give evidence, bear witness, bear out. **—Ant.** refute, deny, disavow; controvert, contradict, disprove, gainsay, belie, cut the ground from under.

attic *n.* garret, loft, clerestory, cockloft, mansard, *French* grenier, *Spanish* guardilla, *German* Dachboden.

attire *v.* **1.** dress, clothe, garb, robe, gown, deck out, array, bedeck, costume, don, invest, fit out, turn out, rig out. *—n.* **2.** dress, garments, apparel, clothing, clothes, costume, outfit, garb, wardrobe, habiliments, raiment, vestments, *Slang* duds, togs; finery, array, glad rags. **—Ant. 1** undress, disrobe, unclothe, strip, bare, denude.

attitude *n.* **1.** disposition, frame of mind, outlook, point of view, perspective, manner, demeanor, air. **2.** posture, stance, pose, position. **—Syn. Study. 2** See POSITION.

attorney *n.* lawyer, counsel, counselor, legal adviser, attorney at law, member of the bar, *British* barrister, solicitor, advocate; *Slang* mouthpiece, beak, ambulance chaser.

attract *v.* **1.** draw, lure, allure, entice, invite, beckon, pull; interest, appeal to, fascinate; captivate, charm, enchant, bewitch. **2.** draw, induce, provoke, cause, bring about, precipitate, evoke. **—Ant. 1** repel, repulse; disgust, antagonize, affront, offend, outrage.

attraction *n.* appeal, fascination, allure, lure, enticement, inducement, magnetism, charisma, drawing power, pull, temptation, enchantment, captivation, tendency, affinity; charm, glamour, attractiveness. **—Ant.** repulsion, repugnance; aversion, disinclination, indifference, apathy.

attractive *adj.* appealing, pleasing, likable, agreeable, pleasant; charming, delightful, enchanting, engaging, charismatic, winning; lovely, beautiful, pretty, handsome, becoming, fetching, fair, sightly, chic, elegant, tasteful; inviting, tempting, enticing, fascinating, alluring, bewitching, captivating, seductive, drop-dead. **—Ant.** unappealing, displeasing, unlikable, unpleasant, unpleasing, offensive, repellent, repugnant, repulsive, revolting, obnoxious, distasteful; ugly, unbecoming, inelegant; uninviting.

attribute *v.* **1.** ascribe, credit, assign, allege to belong; charge to, set down to, lay to, account for, impute, trace to, blame on, bring home to, saddle with, lay at the door of; cause by, derive from. *—n.* **2.** characteristic, trait, quality, virtue, aspect, facet, feature, character, property; accomplishment, acquirement, attainment, faculty, ability, distinction, grace, gift, talent, endowment. **—Syn. Study. 1** ATTRIBUTE, ASCRIBE, IMPUTE mean to assign something to a definite cause or source. Possibly because of an association with *tribute*, ATTRIBUTE often has a complimentary connotation: *to attribute one's success to a friend's encouragement.* ASCRIBE is used in a similar sense, but has a neutral implication: *to ascribe an accident to carelessness.* IMPUTE usu. means to attribute something dishonest or discreditable to a person; it implies blame or accusation: *to impute an error to a new employee.* **2** See QUALITY.

attrition *n.* **1.** wearing down, wearing away, friction, abrasion, erosion, disintegration, grinding, scraping. **2.** decrease, reduction, decimation, loss.

attune *v.* adapt, accustom, adjust, acclimate, acclimatize, tailor. **—Ant.** resist, fight against; alienate.

atypical *adj.* unusual, uncommon, untypical, nontypical, anomalous, unrepresentative, out of keeping, unlooked for, contrary, abnormal, unnatural, irregular, uncustomary. **—Ant.** typical, representative; common, familiar, ordinary, usual, customary, in keeping, normal, natural, regular, expected.

auburn *adj.* **1.** reddish-brown, golden-brown, tawny, chestnut-colored, nut brown, cinnamon, russet, rust-colored, copper-colored, henna. *—n.* **2.** reddish-brown, golden-brown, nut brown, russet, henna.

audacious *adj.* **1.** bold, daring, adventurous, venturesome, enterprising; brave, courageous, fearless, unafraid, valiant, intrepid, dauntless, stouthearted, lionhearted, stalwart, valorous, plucky, *Slang* gutsy. **2.** bold, daring, reckless, rash, risky, daredevil, devil-may-care, death-defying, breakneck; heedless, foolhardy, injudicious, imprudent, desperate, hotheaded, self-willed, wild. **3.** impudent, impertinent, insolent, brazen, fresh, shameless, outrageous, defiant, unabashed, presumptuous, assuming, forward, saucy, cheeky, bossy, pert; disrespectful, rude, discourteous. **—Ant. 1** unadventurous, unenterprising; cowardly, fainthearted, craven, frightened, timid, pusillanimous, *Slang* yellow, chickenhearted, lily-livered. **2** careful, guarded, discreet; prudent, circumspect, cautious, judicious. **3** tactful, gracious, unassuming, cordial, amiable, ingratiating, deferential, reverential, obsequious, *Informal* kowtowing; polite, courteous, mannerly, well-mannered, gentlemanly, ladylike, refined, polished, formal.

audacity *n.* **1.** boldness, daring, nerve, spunk, grit, pluck, mettle, *Slang* guts, backbone; derring-do, venturesomeness; fearlessness, valor, bravery, courage; recklessness, temerity, rashness, foolhardiness. **2.** impudence, impertinence, insolence, brashness, effrontery, brazenness, brass, shamelessness, cheek, gall, *Slang* chutzpah, presumption, forwardness, bumptiousness. **—Ant.** discretion, prudence, caution, wariness, circumspection; cowardice, faintheartedness, timidity, timorousness.

audible *adj.* loud enough to be heard, heard, perceptible, discernible, clear, distinct. **—Ant.** inaudible, muffled, faint.

audience *n.* **1.** listeners, spectators, onlookers, assembly, congregation, house. **2.** public, following, readership, market; constituency. **3.** interview, personal meeting, hearing, audition, reception; conference, discussion, consultation, talk, parley.

audit *v.* **1.** examine, inspect, check, go over, investigate, scrutinize; verify, balance, review, take stock of. **—*n.* 2.** examination, inspection, investigation, scrutinizing; verification, review.

audition *n.* **1.** tryout, hearing, test performance. **—*v.* 2.** try out, give a test performance.

auditor *n.* **1.** financial examiner; *(loosely)* accountant, bookkeeper, comptroller. **2.** one who listens, listener.

auditorium *n.* assembly hall, lecture hall, concert hall, meeting hall, auditory; arena, theater, coliseum.

aught[1] *n.* zero, naught; a cipher (0); nothing, null, *Slang* goose egg, zip, horse collar; *Tennis* love.

aught[2] *pron.* all.

augment *v.* add to, increase, enlarge, expand, extend, raise, boost, swell, inflate, amplify, magnify, intensify, build up, flesh out; heighten, lengthen, widen, deepen. **—Ant.** decrease, reduce, diminish, lessen, lower; curtail, cut back, abridge, shorten, narrow, contract, shrink, moderate, subside.

augur *n.* **1.** oracle, prophet, seer; diviner, prognosticator, soothsayer. **—*v.* 2.** prophesy, predict, prognosticate, presage, bode, intimate, be an omen of; be a sign of, signify, portend, forecast, foretell, herald, forewarn, foreshadow, promise.

augury *n.* **1.** prophecy, divination, prognostication, soothsaying, fortunetelling; auspice, sortilege. **2.** omen, portent, sign, token, warning, forewarning, indication; herald, forerunner, precursor, promise, harbinger.

august *adj.* awe-inspiring, monumental, majestic, magnificent, impressive, imposing, sublime, grand, grandiose, noble, dignified, distinguished, eminent, illustrious, stately, solemn, venerable, exalted, estimable, glorious, supreme, superb, lofty, high-ranking, regal. **—Ant.** unawesome, unimpressive, unimposing, uninspiring; mean, common, commonplace, undistinguished, undignified, unstately, ignoble, unmajestic, unexalted; paltry, insignificant; ridiculous, comic.

aura *n.* atmosphere, ambience, mood, feeling, feel, character, quality, suggestion, air, essence, aroma, emanation.

auspice *n.* **1.** indication, sign, portent, omen, warning, augury, prognostication. **2. auspices.** sponsorship, patronage, support, advocacy, aegis, championship; care, charge, authority, control, countenance, guidance, influence, protection.

auspicious *adj.* **1.** being a good omen, encouraging, favorable, promising, propitious, heartening, reassuring, hopeful. **2.** happy, felicitous, benign, good, fortunate, successful, lucky, opportune, timely, red-letter. **—Ant.** inauspicious. **1** ill-omened, ominous, sinister, discouraging, unfavorable, unpromising, unpropitious, disheartening, adverse, unsatisfactory. **2** sad, unhappy, sorrowful, baleful, melancholy, cheerless, joyless, pathetic, dismal; unfortunate, unlucky, black.

austere *adj.* **1.** stern, strict, severe, forbidding, ascetic. **2.** rigorous, rigid, Spartan, ascetic, self-denying, abstemious, strict, simple, spare, stark, strait-laced, chaste. **—Ant. 1** permissive, lenient, indulgent, easy, flexible, lax; frivolous, gay, cheerful, joyful, merry, lighthearted, jovial, jolly, jaunty, nonchalant, lively, exuberant, vivacious, effervescent, high-spirited, playful, convivial; kindly, kind, sweet, genial. **2** luxurious, lush, comfortable, easy; sophisticated, cosmopolitan; loose, corrupt, dissolute, dissipated, debauched, degenerate, depraved, wanton, abandoned, self-gratifying, free-and-easy, immoral, wicked, evil, sinful, impure, lewd, licentious, lascivious.

authentic *adj.* **1.** genuine, real, true, actual, bona fide, legitimate, original. **2.** true, actual, real; factual, accurate, faithful, veritable, valid; verified, authenticated, attested, accredited, unquestioned, pure, unadulterated; reliable, dependable, trustworthy, authoritative. **—Ant. 1** imitation, counterfeit, simulated, synthetic, fake, sham, phony, bogus, mock, specious. **2** unreal, false, untrue, inaccurate, unfaithful; fictitious, pretended, make-believe, hypothetical, supposed, unverified, unreliable, untrustworthy, undependable; deceptive, misleading, fraudulent, corrupt, adulterated.

authenticate *v.* establish as genuine, document, verify, confirm, corroborate, attest, vouch for, avouch, validate, substantiate, certify, guarantee, warrant, endorse. **—Ant.** impugn, gainsay, invalidate, disprove, discredit, negate, contravene; repudiate, deny, refute, reject, spurn.

author *n.* **1.** writer; *(variously)* novelist, short-story writer, poet, essayist, playwright. **2.** creator, originator, maker, prime mover, innovator, initiator, inventor, father, framer; founder, producer, planner, organizer.

authoritarian *adj.* **1.** favoring authority, repressing individual freedom; strict, harsh, severe, unyielding, inflexible, uncompromising, austere, disciplinary, disciplinarian, dogmatic, doctrinaire; dictatorial, tyrannical, fascist; by the rule, by the book. *—n.* **2.** disciplinarian, rule follower; martinet, autocrat, tyrant, little dictator. **—Ant. 1** revolutionary, insurgent, mutinous, dissenting, nonconformist; lenient, permissive, flexible. **2** anarchist, rebel, revolutionary, insurgent, mutineer; malcontent, dissenter, nonconformist.

authoritative *adj.* **1.** official, sanctioned, commanding, commanding obedience; administrative, sovereign, ruling. **2.** showing authority, commanding, imperative, decisive, masterful, imposing, impressive, peremptory; arrogant, lordly, autocratic, dogmatic, dictatorial, tyrannical. **3.** trustworthy, reliable, dependable, sound, valid, authentic, definitive, factual, scholarly, learned. **—Ant. 1** unofficial, unsanctioned, unauthorized, without authority; facetious, frivolous. **2** subservient, servile; weak, indecisive, meek, timid, humble, modest. **3** untrustworthy, unreliable, undependable, invalid; deceptive, misleading.

authority *n.* **1.** command, control, power, sway, force, weight, rule, supremacy, domination, dominion, strength, might, influence, importance, respect, prestige, esteem, bully pulpit, *Slang* clout; jurisdiction, administration. **2. authorities.** powers that be, government administration; officialdom, police. **3.** expert, specialist, scholar, mastermind, pundit, connoisseur; accepted source, trustworthy source. **—Syn. Study. 1** AUTHORITY, CONTROL, INFLUENCE denote a power or right to direct the actions or thoughts of others. AUTHORITY is a power or right, usu. because of rank or office, to issue commands and to punish for violations: *to have authority over subordinates.* CONTROL is either power or influence applied to the complete and successful direction or manipulation of persons or things: *to be in control of a project.* INFLUENCE is a personal and unofficial power derived from deference of others to one's character, ability, or station; it may be exerted unconsciously or may operate through persuasion: *to have influence over one's friends.* **—Ant. 1** servility, servitude, weakness. **2** follower; public, masses.

authorize *v.* **1.** give authority to, empower, permit, allow, commission, license, entitle, invest, charter, enable, give leave. **2.** give authority for, approve, sanction, green-light, confirm; certify, accredit, warrant, vouch for. **—Ant. 1** enjoin, prohibit, forbid, proscribe, preclude, interdict; prevent, disallow.

autocracy *n.* dictatorship, monocracy, totalitarian regime, autarchy, absolute monarchy; despotism, absolutism, tyrannical rule, tyranny, totalitarianism, czarism, Hitlerism, Stalinism, Bonapartism, Caesarism, kaiserism.

autocrat *n.* absolute ruler, ruler, dictator, monarch, overlord; tyrant, despot.

autocratic *adj.* having absolute power, dictatorial, monarchical, czaristic; tyrannical, tyrannous, despotic, imperious, authoritarian, repressive, oppressive, iron-handed. **—Ant.** limited, constitutional, democratic, egalitarian; lenient, permissive, indulgent, forbearing, tolerant.

autograph *n.* signature, John Hancock, John Henry, X, mark, sign, endorsement, inscription, handwriting, countersignature.

automatic *adj.* **1.** self-operating, self-acting, self-moving, self-propelling, electric, mechanical, push-button, automated. **2.** occurring independently, involuntary, reflex, instinctive, unconscious, spontaneous, natural, nonvolitional, uncontrolled, unwilled, inherent; mechanical, routine, habitual. **—Ant. 1** manual. **2** voluntary, conscious, intentional, controlled, deliberate.

automation *n.* automatic machinery, machine-operated machinery, robotism.

automaton *n.* robot, machine, android; puppet, marionette, *Italian* fantoccino; pawn, cat's-paw, tool, stooge, patsy, fall guy.

automobile *n.* See CAR.

autonomous *adj.* self-governing, self-determined; self-sufficient, self-reliant, independent, sovereign, free. **—Ant.** governed, dependent, subject.

autonomy *n.* self-government, home rule, self-rule, self-determination; independence; sovereignty, freedom, liberation. **—Ant.** foreign rule, dependency; colonial status.

autumn *n.* fall, Indian summer, harvest time; autumnal equinox.

auxiliary *adj.* **1.** supplementary, ancillary, subordinate, secondary, subsidiary, accessory; reserve, emergency, backup. *—n.* **2.** supplement, subsidiary, accessory; partner, companion, accomplice, associate; helper, assistant, giver of aid, helping hand; reserve, backup. **—Ant. 1** main, chief, primary, first-line. **2** main body, major item; opponent, antagonist, hindrance, drawback.

avail *n.* **1.** use, usefulness, advantage, purpose, service, benefit, success, profit; help, aid. *—v.* **2.** use, utilize, profit from, take advantage of; benefit, help, aid, assist, serve, be of use, be of advantage, profit. **—Ant. 1** detriment, disadvantage, disservice, harm. **2** overlook, neglect, ignore, slight, pass up, spurn; hinder, harm, hurt, be useless.

available *adj.* ready for use, ready for service, free, open, obtainable, accessible, at one's disposal, convenient, on hand, in reserve, at hand, handy, at one's elbow, on tap, up for grabs. **—Ant.** unavailable, unobtainable, in use, occupied, spoken for, taken; inconvenient, inaccessible; unusable, unserviceable.

avalanche *n.* **1.** snowslide; earthslide, rockslide. **2.** overwhelming amount, barrage, bombardment, flood, deluge, inundation, cataclysm, torrent, cascade, blizzard, heap, pile, mass. **—Ant. 2** paucity, scantiness; dearth, lack, deficiency, insufficiency, shortage, drought, famine.

avant-garde *n.* artistic innovators, advance guard, vanguard, trailblazers, trendsetters, pioneers, tastemakers, leaders, forerunners, originators.

avarice *n.* lust for money, greed, greediness, money-grubbing, rapacity, venality, graspingness, covetousness, worship of the golden calf; miserliness, stinginess, parsimony, penury, niggardliness, penny-pinching, close-fistedness. **—Ant.** generosity, benevolence, magnanimity, munificence, charitableness, unselfishness; extravagance, liberality, open-handedness.

avaricious *adj.* **—Syn. Study.** See GREEDY.

avenge *v.* take vengeance for, wreak vengeance, revenge, retaliate, get even for, *Informal* get back at, repay, punish, exact satisfaction for, inflict injury for, injure, exact an eye for an eye. **—Ant.** excuse, forgive, pardon, overlook; accept, be resigned to, tolerate.

avenue *n.* **1.** boulevard, thoroughfare, broad street; parkway, tree-lined road, esplanade, concourse. **2.** way, route, road, course, path, pathway, passage, passageway, direction; opportunity, chance, means, access, approach, gate, gateway, outlet. **—Ant. 1** alley, lane.

aver *v.* assert, declare, affirm, state, avow, avouch, maintain, swear, insist, emphasize, contend, profess, represent, proclaim, pronounce, protest, asseverate; certify, verify, guarantee. **—Ant.** deny, disavow, disclaim, repudiate; doubt, be uncertain, gainsay.

average *n.* **1.** arithmetical mean, mean amount; *(loosely)* mean, median, ratio, medium, norm, midpoint, par; standing, accomplishment. **2.** the ordinary, the standard, the typical, the general, the usual, normal, the run of the mill, the rule. *—adj.* **3.** mean, par; *(loosely)* medium, median, medial. **4.** typical, ordinary, common, normal, usual, standard, moderate; fair, passable, so-so, tolerable, mediocre, indifferent, not bad, run-of-the-mill, betwixt and between, rank and file. **—Ant. 1, 3** maximum; minimum. **4** unusual, uncommon, different, special, remarkable, exceptional, extraordinary, extreme, abnormal; memorable, conspicuous, noticeable, prominent; outstanding, superlative, surpassing, excellent, wonderful, terrific, stupendous, tremendous, great, fine, good; awful, bad, dreadful, terrible, horrible, lousy.

averse *adj.* opposed, loath, disinclined, unwilling, reluctant, indisposed, ill-disposed, unfavorable, recalcitrant, antipathetic, unamenable, inimical. **—Syn. Study.** See RELUCTANT. **—Ant.** agreeable, amenable, willing, inclined, disposed, favorable; eager, avid, ardent, desirous, intent, keen.

aversion *n.* dislike, unwillingness, reluctance, antipathy, disinclination; distaste, repugnance, prejudice against, opposition; abhorrence, loathing, hatred, disgust, detestation, revulsion, repulsion, animosity, hostility, horror. **—Ant.** willingness, inclination; eagerness, desire, love, liking.

avert *v.* **1.** turn aside, turn away, turn, deflect, shift. **2.** prevent, forestall, deter, avoid, preclude, ward off, stave off, keep off, fend off, beat off, keep at bay, nip in the bud, frustrate, sidetrack. —**Ant.** **1** hold steady. **2** allow, permit, let.

aviation *n.* flying, flight, aeronautics, aerodynamics.

aviator Also (for a woman) **aviatrix** —*n.* pilot, flyer, airman, *Slang* birdman, bird, fly-boy.

avid *adj.* **1.** eager, greedy, avaricious, insatiable, hungry, desirous, keen, anxious; grasping, covetous, acquisitive, voracious, rapacious. **2.** devoted, enthusiastic, ardent, intense, zealous, rabid, fanatic. —**Ant.** indifferent, apathetic **1** unconcerned, disdainful; indisposed, disinclined, loath. **2** reluctant, recalcitrant, unwilling.

avocation *n.* sideline, secondary occupation; hobby, diversion, pastime, distraction, recreation, entertainment. —**Ant.** vocation, occupation, work, business, *Informal* line.

avoid *v.* evade, elude, dodge, escape, avert, sidestep, skirt, fight shy of; keep away from, shun, keep clear of, steer clear of, refrain from, eschew, forsake, forbear, boycott. —**Ant.** meet, face, confront, incur, contact; approach, find, seek out, invite, solicit; pursue, embrace.

avoidance *n.* keeping away from, shunning, evasion, eluding, shirking, skirting. —**Ant.** search, invitation, soliciting; pursuit, embrace; meeting, facing, confronting.

avouch *v.* declare, own, affirm, assert, aver, announce, asseverate, swear, certify, confirm; admit, confess, acknowledge. —**Ant.** deny, repudiate, recant, controvert, gainsay, disclaim, disavow.

avow *v.* declare, admit, announce, confess, own, disclose, reveal, proclaim, profess, affirm, acknowledge; assert, state, swear, aver. —**Ant.** disavow, disclaim, deny, repudiate; keep hidden, keep secret.

avowal *n.* admission, confession, profession, declaration, proclamation, acknowledgment; affirmation, assertion, statement, protestation, assurance, word, averment. —**Ant.** disavowal, disclaimer, repudiation; hiding, keeping secret.

avowed *adj.* self-declared, professed, self-proclaimed, confessed, sworn; acknowledged, declared, admitted. —**Ant.** secret, undisclosed, unrevealed, private, closet, clandestine, surreptitious, furtive.

await *v.* wait for, look for, look forward to, anticipate, expect; be in readiness for, be in waiting, attend.

awake *v.* **1.** wake, wake up, awaken, raise from sleep. **2.** make awake, arouse, incite, inspire, stimulate, spark, excite, provoke, bestir, alert, make aware, make heedful. —*adj.* **3.** not sleeping, wide-awake, open-eyed. **4.** alert, aware, attentive, watchful, vigilant, heedful, mindful, conscious, wide-awake, alive to. —**Ant.** **1** sleep, go to sleep; doze, nap. **2** put to sleep, make unaware; dull. **3** asleep, sleeping, dozing, napping; dormant, hibernating. **4** unaware, inattentive, unmindful, unconscious.

awaken *v.* **1.** wake, wake up, awake, rouse from sleep. **2.** arouse, kindle, call forth, make aware, stimulate, stir up, excite; revive, fan, fire, give new life to. —**Ant.** **1** go to sleep, put to sleep. **2** quiet, dampen, dull, subdue, check.

awakening *n.* **1.** awaking, waking, waking up; arising, getting up, rising from sleep. **2.** arousal, stimulation, stirring, sparking.

award *v.* **1.** grant, accord, confer on, bestow, give; assign, allot, allow, concede; decree, appoint. —*n.* **2.** prize, trophy; medal, decoration, laurels, honor, citation, tribute. —**Ant.** **1** withhold; refuse, disallow; deny. **2** booby prize.

aware *adj.* conscious, cognizant, familiar with, acquainted with, informed, apprised, enlightened on, knowledgeable, sensible, sentient, conversant, *au courant,* mindful, awake to, alert to, alive to, with it, in the know, *Slang* hip to, tuned in to, down. —**Syn. Study.** See CONSCIOUS. —**Ant.** unaware, unfamiliar with, unacquainted with, uninformed about, ignorant, unknowledgeable, nonconversant, unmindful, insensible, unconscious, oblivious, unenlightened on.

awareness *n.* realization, recognition, cognizance, familiarity, sensibility, understanding, mindfulness, acquaintance, appraisal, alertness, consciousness, perception, acuteness; knowledge, information. —**Ant.** unawareness, unfamiliarity, insensibility, obliviousness, ignorance, unenlightenment.

awe *n.* **1.** wonder, reverence, veneration, solemnity, exaltation, respect, adoration, amazement, astonishment, abashment. **2.** fright, fear, terror, dread, panic, dismay, alarm, apprehension, consternation, disquietude, perturbation, trepidation, shock, horror, trembling, quaking, quivering. —*v.* **3.** strike with wonder, amaze, astonish, abash, overawe, cow, intimidate, fill with reverence; frighten, beset by fear, terrify, fill with dread, panic, dismay, alarm, disquiet, perturb, shock. —**Ant.** **1** contempt, scorn, disdain; irreverence, disrespect, insolence, arrogance, superciliousness, levity. **2** scorn, disdain. **3** take in stride.

awesome *adj.* solemn, inspiring, majestic, magnificent, wondrous, formidable, astonishing, amazing, awe-inspiring, breathtaking, overwhelming, stupefying;

fearsome, fearful, frightening, terrifying, dreadful, alarming, disquieting, perturbing, intimidating.

awful *adj.* **1.** bad, dreadful, terrible, horrible, horrendous, deplorable, distressing, lousy, unpleasant, disagreeable, displeasing, appalling, frightful, ghastly, fearful, horrifying, hideous, ugly, gruesome, monstrous, shocking, revolting, reprehensible, despicable, contemptible, mean, low, base, heinous; dire, redoubtable, formidable, alarming. **2.** awe-inspiring, awesome; wondrous, solemn, majestic, amazing, stupefying; fearsome, terrifying, dreadful, disquieting. **—Ant. 1** good, fine, O.K., wonderful, terrific, tremendous, pleasant, pleasing; attractive, beautiful, pretty; admirable, likable.

awfully *adv.* very, extremely, quite, exceptionally, terribly, horribly, dreadfully, immensely, excessively. **—Ant.** somewhat.

awkward *adj.* **1.** clumsy, uncoordinated, without grace, graceless, ungainly; inexpert, unskillful, inept, bungling, blundering, gauche, maladroit. **2.** unwieldy, unhandy, cumbersome, inconvenient, troublesome, difficult, unmanageable. **3.** embarrassing, unpleasant, trying, difficult, uncomfortable, disconcerting, ticklish, touchy, delicate, troublesome, inconvenient. **—Ant. 1** graceful, well-coordinated, effortless, dexterous; skillful, adept. **2** handy, convenient. **3** proud; pleasing, pleasant, easy, comfortable.

awry *adj., adv.* **1.** askew, crooked, crookedly, unevenly, uneven, turned to one side, twisted, out of kilter, obliquely. **2.** wrong, amiss, askew, astray. **—Ant. 1** straight, even, evenly, in line, true; horizontally, vertically. **2** right, perfectly.

axiom *n.* basic, principle, postulate, assumption, precept, fundamental law. **—Ant.** contradiction, paradox; absurdity.

axiomatic *adj.* assumed, accepted, generally understood, demonstrable, apodictic, self-evident, incontestable, indisputable, manifest, unquestioned, given; platitudinous, aphoristic, epigrammatic; banal, cliché. **—Ant.** debatable, questionable, moot, controversial, arguable.

axis *n.* **1.** line around which a rotating body turns, line of rotation, line of symmetry, center line; shaft, spindle, stem; pivot, pivotal point. **2.** alliance, coalition, alignment, affiliation, confederation, compact, entente.

aye *n.* yes, yea; affirmative vote. **—Ant.** nay, no; negative vote.

azure *n.* **1.** sky blue, clear blue, cerulean, cobalt, lapis lazuli. *—adj.* **2.** clear blue, sky blue, cobalt, cerulean, lapis; cloudless.

babble *n.* **1.** gabble, drivel, twaddle, blabber, blab, gab, jabber, jabbering, prattle, chitchat, chitter-chatter. **2.** murmur, clamor, hubbub, hum, din. **3.** murmur, murmuring, babbling, burble, gurgle. —*v.* **4.** gurgle, murmur, gibber, coo. **5.** talk, talk incoherently, talk foolishly, prattle, jabber, chatter, chitchat, blabber, blather, blab, gab, gabble, prate, rattle on, run off at the mouth. **6.** murmur, gurgle. —**Ant. 2** silence, stillness, quietness. **4** articulate, enunciate.

babe *n.* baby, infant, child, tot.

babel Sometimes **Babel** *n.* tumult, confusion, turmoil, uproar, pandemonium, bedlam, hullabaloo, clamor, hubbub, din. —**Ant.** stillness, silence, quiet, quietness; calm, tranquillity.

baby *n.* **1.** infant, babe, babe in arms, newborn child, neonate. **2.** youngster; junior member, youngest member, newest member. **3.** sniveler, crybaby, coward. —*v.* **4.** pamper, indulge, overindulge, spoil, coddle, mollycoddle, humor. —*adj.* **5.** young; small, diminutive, miniature, tiny, little, minute, petite, wee, midget, pygmy, dwarf, dwarfish, bantam, pocket-sized. —**Ant. 1** adult; elder, oldster, old man, old woman, ancient. **2** oldest, oldster, senior member, oldest member. **3** adult; stoic, good sport. **4** mistreat, abuse. **5** adult, mature; giant, large, great, huge, enormous.

babyish *adj.* childish, infantile, immature, juvenile, puerile; babylike.

bacchanal *n.* drunken party, spree, orgy, debauch, debauchery, carouse, carousal, revel, wassail, revelry, Saturnalia; festival, carnival, frolic, merrymaking, feast.

bachelor *n.* unmarried man, single man. —**Ant.** husband; bridegroom, groom.

back *n.* **1.** rear part of the body; backbone, spine, spinal column, dorsum; hindquarters. **2.** rear, rear end, posterior, hind part, tail, far end, afterpart; reverse, reverse side, far side. —*v.* **3.** move backward; move away, retreat, retire, withdraw, pull back, fall back, draw back, back down, back off, turn tail, beat a retreat; reverse, retract, revert, retrogress, recede, ebb; return, rebound, recoil, spring back. **4.** help, assist, support, aid, abet, sustain, maintain; endorse, sponsor, vouch for, advocate, promote, encourage, sanction, uphold, countenance, second, reinforce, corroborate, substantiate, confirm, bear witness, attest, testify for, validate, certify, affirm, verify, bolster, hold up, take sides with; praise, protect, guard, succor; patronize, finance, subsidize, underwrite, warrant. —*adj.* **5.** rear, hindmost, hind, hinder, behind, after; posterior, dorsal, caudal, tail, tail end, tergal; furthermost, farthermost. **6.** minor, unimportant; secluded, unpopulated, untraveled, undeveloped, rural, countrified, countryside, backwoods, remote, distant. **7.** past, previous, former, earlier; out-of-date, obsolete, expired, elapsed, behind, bygone, gone. **8.** overdue, tardy, late, belated, delayed, past, elapsed; in arrears, not paid. —**Syn. Study. 5** BACK, REAR, HIND, POSTERIOR refer to something situated behind something else. BACK means the opposite of front: *a back window.* REAR is used of buildings, conveyances, etc., and in military language it is the opposite of fore: *the rear end of a truck; rear echelon.* HIND, and the more formal word POSTERIOR, refer to the rearmost of two or more, often similar objects: *hind wings; posterior lobe.* —**Ant. 1** front; face, stomach. **2** front, head, fore. **3** move forward, move ahead, move toward, approach, advance, progress; attack. **4** hinder, oppose, resist, combat, block; repudiate, invalidate, negate, weaken, undermine, subvert, *Slang* knock. **5** front, fore. **6** major, main, important; busy, urban, populated. **7** future, late. **8** advance.

backbiting *adj.* **1.** belittling, detracting, deprecating, abusive, maligning, slanderous, libeling, defamatory, calumnious, scandalous, disparaging, censuring, hurtful, injurious, derogating, denigrating, vilifying, malicious, catty, gossipy, scandal-mongering. —*n.* **2.** reviling, scurrility, vilification, traduction, vituperation, contumely, invective, calumny, calumniation, gossip, slander, defamation, aspersion, malice, maliciousness, traducement, abuse, obloquy, detraction, cattiness, belittling, disparagement, *Slang* badmouthing, backstabbing, bitchiness.

backbone *n.* **1.** spine, spinal column, vertebrae, vertebral column, back; chine, dorsum. **2.** strength of character, character, fortitude, resolve, resoluteness, resolution, strength, mettle, tenacity, spunk, pluck, nerve, firmness, spirit, grit, sand, guts, intrepidity, steadfastness; bravery, courage, dauntlessness, manliness. **3.** mainstay; basis, foundation, strength. —**Ant. 2** spinelessness; cowardliness, cowardice.

backer *n.* supporter, champion, advocate, promoter; adherent, ally, follower, well-wisher; sponsor, patron, guarantor, angel, underwriter, investor, financier. —**Ant.** detractor; hinderer, enemy, competitor, adversary, opponent.

backfire *v.* miscarry, go awry, come to naught, come to nothing, fall through, boomerang, ricochet, backlash, flop, fizzle, crash, lay an egg, bounce back, come to grief, miss, disappoint. —**Ant.** thrive, work out, succeed, come off, make it, *Slang* click.

background *n.* **1.** distance, rear, landscape, *Theater* mise-en-scène, backdrop, setting, set, flats. **2.** environment, circumstances, milieu, context, backstory; upbringing, rearing, family connections, antecedents, breeding, heritage, life story; training, experience, education, preparation, grounding, past, history, credentials. —**Ant. 1** foreground; fore, forefront. **2** future.

backing *n.* **1.** help, support, aid, assistance; endorsement, sanction, sponsorship, patronage, advocacy, championing, encouragement, prompting, aegis, sustenance, succor, cooperation, helping hand. **2.** back, interior, core, inner layer. —**Ant. 1** discouragement, hindrance, opposition, detraction, resistance; repudiation, subversion, ill will. **2** front, covering, cover, exterior, outer layer.

backlash *v.* **1.** boomerang, snap back, ricochet, backfire, rebound, bounce back, recoil, kick back, snag, ravel, come to nothing, come to naught, come to grief, miscarry, go away, fall through, fizzle, flop, crash. —*n.* **2.** negative reaction, resistance, recalcitrance, recoil, reversion, counteraction, antagonism, animosity, hostility, opposition. —**Ant. 2** agreement, sympathy, cooperation, support, concurrence.

backlog *n.* inventory, supply, reserve, stock, reserve supply, store, backlist, hoard, stockpile, accumulation, amassment, excess, abundance, superabundance, assets, savings, nest egg, reservoir. —**Ant.** shortage, dearth, lack, deficiency, shortfall, scarcity, want.

backside *n.* posterior, rump, buttocks, derriere, behind, rear, rear end, sitter; *Slang* setter, settee, tail, duff, fanny, prat, buns, keister; *Vulgar* butt.

back talk *n.* sass, lip, negative response, jaw, guff, impudence, sassiness, sauciness, cheek, insolence, pertness, impertinence. —**Ant.** concurrence, agreement, respect, diffidence.

backward Also **backwards** *adv.* **1.** toward the rear, rearward, to the rear, back, in reverse, back away from, in retreat. **2.** with the back first, back; *(variously)* upside down, inside out, wrong side out, topsy-turvy, wrong, improperly, disorderly, chaotically, messily. **3.** in reverse, toward the past, to the past. —*adj.* **4.** turned away from the front, turned toward the back, reversed, inverted. **5.** slow, slow-paced, retarded, behind, undeveloped, remiss, tardy, impeded, sluggish, laggard; slow-witted, dull, dense. **6.** shy, bashful, timid, withdrawn, reserved, reticent, uncommunicative. **7.** reverse, ebbing, receding, retreating, withdrawing, returning, retrograde, regressive, retrogressive. —**Ant. 1** forward, frontward. **2** right side up, right side out; properly, correctly. **3** forward. **5** advanced, ahead. **6** forward, bold, brazen, brash, precocious; eager, willing. **7** forward.

backwash *n.* **1.** aftermath, wake, consequence, aftereffect, outcome, upshot, result. **2.** hinterland, backwater, boondocks, *Slang* boonies, backcountry, provinces, upcountry, frontier; *Slang* sticks; tank town, burg.

backwoods *n.* remote area, unpopulated area, hinterland, country, rural area, wilds; woodland, countryside; *Slang* sticks, boondocks, boonies. —**Ant.** city, metropolis, metropolitan area, urban area, populated area.

bacteria *n.* germ, microbe, microorganism, virus, *Slang* bug; bacillus, pathogen.

bad *adj.* **1.** not good, poor, inferior, wretched, awful, terrible, dreadful, below standard, substandard, below par, second-rate, lousy; faulty, defective, imperfect, deficient, lacking, inadequate, valueless, useless, unproductive, unfit, baneful. **2.** immoral, unethical, sinful, evil, wicked, naughty, wrong, offensive, corrupt, unprincipled, opprobrious, villainous, false, disreputable, criminal, detestable, deplorable, perfidious, reprehensible, base, mean, vile, nefarious, beastly, rotten. **3.** erroneous, wrong, incorrect, not correct, imperfect, unsound, fallacious, faulty, questionable; inefficient, ineffective, poor. **4.** harmful, unhealthy, hurtful, injurious, detrimental, distractive; disadvantageous, troublesome, nonproductive; risky, dangerous, hazardous, menacing. **5.** unpleasant, unwelcome, disagreeable, disappointing, distressed, distressing, discouraged, sorry, discouraging, disturbing, regrettable, troubled, troubling; gloomy, glum, melancholy, joyless, grim, disheartening, unnerving, dreadful, obnoxious; cross, angry, short-tempered, offensive, irascible, irritable, touchy. **6.** sorry, sad, regretful, remorseful, contrite, guilty, conscience-stricken, terrible. **7.** spoiled, rotten, decayed, foul, decomposed, sour, rancid, turned, rank, putrescent, moldy, mildewed; contaminated, polluted, tainted. **8.** disagreeable, unpleasant, sickening, loathsome, odious, nasty, distasteful, foul, disgusting, nauseating, putrid, fetid, unpalatable, bitter, acrid, sour, revolting, repulsive, vile, repugnant, noxious. **9.** ill, sick, sickly, unwell, ailing, infirm, indisposed, unhealthy, under the weather. **10.** severe, harsh, terrible, serious, grave, disastrous, painful, acute, frightful, dreadful, calamitous, dire, tragic; agonizing, distressing, searing, excruciating, grievous, wretched, miserable. —*n.* **11.** harmful things, sad events, disappointment, misfortune. **12.** evil, wickedness, immorality, sin, offenses, wrongs, villainy, crimes. —**Ant. 1–9, 11, 12** good. **1** fine, excellent, above average, superior, first-rate. **2** virtuous, moral, ethical, right, righteous, exemplary, high-minded. **3** correct, right, perfect, sound, intelligent. **4** beneficial, healthful, salubrious; harmless, safe. **5** pleasant, welcome, heartening, encouraging, promising, hopeful, cheerful, cheering, happy, joyful, joyous, sweet, smiling, good-tempered, sweet-tempered. **7** fresh, sweet, uncontaminated. **8** agreeable, pleasant, fragrant, aromatic, sweet. **9** well, healthy, sound, fit. **10** mild, light, frivolous, trivial, unimportant, minor.

badge *n.* emblem, insignia, medallion, ensign, shield, seal, brand, device; symbol, sign, hallmark, mark, earmark, token, stamp.

badger *v.* goad, bully, provoke, bait, pester, nag, harass, hector, harry, hound, persecute, tease, annoy, vex, irritate, nettle, chafe, trouble, torment, plague, coerce, beset.

badly *adv.* **1.** poorly, improperly, incorrectly, not well, in an inferior way, wretchedly, shoddily, imperfectly, defectively, deficiently, inadequately, erroneously, wrong, wrongly, faultily, unsoundly, unsatisfactorily, incompetently, ineptly, carelessly, sloppily. **2.** immorally, unethically, sinfully, wickedly, wrongly, offensively, corruptly, without principle, villainously, disreputably, criminally, basely, vilely, nefariously. **3.** very much, greatly, exceedingly, extremely, desperately; intensely, severely, acutely, sorely, horribly, terribly, dreadfully, frightfully. —**Ant. 1** well, fine, excellently, superbly; properly, correctly, perfectly, competently, ably, splendidly, satisfactorily; right, rightly. **2** well, morally, ethically, virtuously, righteously.

baffle *v.* **1.** stop, restrain, inhibit, thwart, foil, bar, check; deaden, dull, minimize, reduce. **2.** confuse, bewilder, perplex, mystify, confound, befuddle, stump, puzzle, muddle, nonplus; daze, astonish, astound, disconcert, dumfound, amaze, surprise. —**Ant. 1** admit, allow; transmit. **2** clarify to, explain to, elucidate to, clear up for.

bag *n.* **1.** sack, paper bag; packet, bundle, pouch, receptacle. **2.** See SUITCASE. **3.** See PURSE. —*v.* **4.** sag, droop, hang loosely; bulge, swell out, protrude. **5.** kill in hunting, shoot; capture, catch, trap, entrap, snare, ensnare; get, take, collect, obtain, acquire.

baggage *n.* **1.** luggage, suitcases, bags, bundles, packages, traveling bags, valises, grips, trunks. **2.** equipment, movables, gear, paraphernalia, accouterments, trappings, apparatus, impedimenta; belongings, effects.

baggy *adj.* **1.** sagging, droopy, loose, loose-fitting, slack, limp; unshapely, unpressed. **2.** flabby, flaccid, paunchy, bulbous, swollen, bloated, puffed. —**Ant. 1** tight, tight-fitting, close-fitting; well-cut, shapely; neat, pressed.

bail[1] *n.* **1.** bond, surety, guarantee. —*v.* **2.** post bond for, post bail for.

bail[2] *v.* scoop, ladle, lade, dip, spoon.

bailiwick *n.* domain, province, realm, dominion, department, sphere; neighborhood, place, territory, area, beat, arena, *Slang* turf, orbit, compass.

bait *n.* **1.** lure. **2.** lure, allure, allurement, inducement, enticement, temptation, attraction, magnet, bribe, come-on. —*v.* **3.** put bait on. **4.** tease, torment, tantalize, antagonize, provoke, annoy, vex, harry, heckle, harass, hound, hector, badger, worry; *Slang* needle, ride.

bake *v.* cook, roast, oven-bake, toast, sauté, sear, braise, fry, grill, pan-fry, parboil, simmer, stew, boil; swelter, scorch, burn.

balance *n.* **1.** also **balances.** scales, scale. **2.** equilibrium, stability, equipoise, counterpoise, weight, equality, equalization; symmetry, parity. **3.** equilibrium, ratio, proportion, harmony; middle ground, mean. **4.** stability, steadiness, poise, aplomb, composure, *Slang* cool, equanimity, equilibrium, equipoise, self-possession, level-headedness, imperturbability, unflappability, coolness, presence, judgment, judiciousness. **5.** comparison, evaluation, consideration, appraisal, estimate, opinion. **6.** amount owed, amount credited, sum minus payment; remainder, rest, leftover, residue, remnant, outstanding portion. —*v.* **7.** steady, keep steady, hold equilibrium, stabilize, poise, counterpoise; make level, level off, parallel. **8.** offset, set off, counterbalance, equate, counteract, neutralize, compensate for. **9.** compare, contrast, juxtapose, evaluate, weigh; consider, estimate, deliberate, reflect, ponder, cogitate, sum up. **10.** compute, calculate, sum up, total, tally, reckon, tot up, square; pay. —**Syn. Study. 2**

See SYMMETRY. —**Ant. 3** imbalance, disproportion. **4** instability, flightiness, self-doubt, uncertainty, irrationality, incertitude, shakiness. **8** upset, overbalance, outweigh, underbalance.

balanced *adj.* fair, equitable, just, impartial, unprejudiced, disinterested. —**Ant.** one-sided, lopsided, prejudiced, biased, slanted, distorted, unfair.

balcony *n.* **1.** deck, veranda, upstairs porch, portico, loggia, terrace. **2.** mezzanine, loges, upper circle, boxes; upper floor, foyer.

bald *adj.* **1.** baldheaded, baldpated, hairless, depilated, smooth, glabrous. **2.** bare, without cover, treeless, denuded, naked, barren. **3.** open, bare, undisguised, flagrant, blunt, flat, obvious, unadorned, stark, naked, straightforward, plain, simple, unvarnished, unembellished; outright, out-and-out, categorical, unequivocable, unqualified, utter. —**Ant. 1** hairy, hirsute, coiffed. **2** overgrown, forested. **3** elaborate, complicated, embellished, fancy; hidden, disguised, devious, roundabout, underhanded, surreptitious.

balderdash *n.* nonsense, poppycock, tommyrot, tomfoolery, stuff and nonsense, drivel, trash, rot, claptrap, bunk, buncombe (or bunkum), bosh, twaddle, *Slang* bull, hot air, crock; gibberish, double-talk, obfuscation, flummery. —**Ant.** sense, good sense; truth, fact.

bale *n.* bound bundle, bundle, pack, packet, parcel, package, case; load.

baleful *adj.* sinister, ominous, threatening; evil, malignant, malign, malevolent, malicious, baneful, venomous, spiteful, dire, furious, cold, cold-hearted, icy; hurtful, deadly, harmful. —**Ant.** kindly, friendly, benevolent, beneficent, benign, salutary, warm; favorable.

balk *v.* **1.** shirk, refuse, resist, demur, recoil, draw back, hang back, shrink from, shun, evade, hesitate, eschew. **2.** thwart, stall, forestall, stymie, frustrate, prevent, hinder, defeat, check, baffle, foil, impede, block, obstruct, bar, spike, inhibit, derail. —**Ant. 1** accept willingly, do eagerly, submit; relent, yield, acquiesce. **2** aid, help, assist, abet; further, promote, advance, support, encourage, expedite, facilitate; allow, permit.

balky *adj.* contrary, stubborn, obstinate, recalcitrant, perverse, ornery; unmanageable, unruly, rebellious, restive, refractory, disobedient, willful, intractable, fractious, wayward, mulish, pigheaded. —**Ant.** obedient, submissive, willing, cooperative, amenable; tame, docile, subdued, tractable.

ball[1] *n.* **1.** round mass, sphere, spheroid, pellet, globe, globule, orb. **2.** game of ball, ball game. **3.** shot, bullets, projectiles. —**Ant. 1** cube.

ball[2] *n.* dance, dancing party, cotillion; promenade, prom, soiree, *Slang* hop.

ballad *n.* **1.** narrative poem, narrative verse, rhyming story. **2.** folk song, song, lay; ditty, chanty, carol.

ballast *n.* stabilizing material, counterweight, counterpoise, weight, dead weight; makeweight; balance, counterbalance, ballasting, control, equipoise, stabilizer.

balloon *n.* **1.** air-filled bag, gas-filled bag, inflatable bag. —*v.* **2.** billow, swell out, puff out, fill with air, inflate, fill out, blow up, distend, increase, expand, belly, bloat, enlarge, grow, dilate. —**Ant. 2** deflate, collapse, shrink, flatten.

ballot *n.* **1.** list of candidates to be voted on, ticket, slate. **2.** vote, round of voting, voting, poll, polling.

ballyhoo *n.* **1.** promotion, publicity, advertising, public relations, propaganda, hoopla, buildup, puffery, hullabaloo; *Slang* hype. —*v.* **2.** publicize, promote, advertise, tout, push, trumpet, proclaim, herald; *Slang* puff, hype. —**Ant. 2** keep secret, hide, obscure.

balm *n.* **1.** ointment, salve, unguent, emollient, lotion, cream, balsam. **2.** solace, comforter, comfort, restorative, curative, anodyne, palliative, narcotic, sedative, tranquilizer. —**Ant. 1** irritant, abrasive. **2** annoyance, nuisance, vexation, affliction, stimulant.

balmy *adj.* **1.** gentle, mild, soft, fair, clement, bland, temperate, summery, warm, pleasant, refreshing, agreeable; calm, calming, easing, soothing, salubrious. **2.** fragrant, sweet-smelling, aromatic, perfumed, ambrosial, refreshing, redolent. **3.** eccentric, weird, odd, *Slang* kooky. —**Ant. 1** harsh, raw, strong, intense, severe, inclement, rough, discomforting, irksome, vexing, annoying; stormy, unseasonable. **2** stinking, smelly, malodorous, foul, offensive, rank, fetid, putrid, putrescent.

baluster *n.* post, support, upright, rail, column, pillar, pilaster.

bamboozle *v.* dupe, deceive, trick, cheat, swindle, victimize, defraud, cozen, gull, rook, gyp; delude, mislead, hoodwink, fool, hoax; lure, beguile, coax, con, *Slang* take.

ban *v.* **1.** prohibit, bar, exclude, banish, debar, disallow, enjoin, forbid; proscribe, suppress, interdict. —*n.* **2.** prohibition, forbiddance, barring, proscription, taboo, interdiction, interdict, exclusion, restriction, restraint, censorship, embargo, banishment, stoppage. —**Ant. 1** allow, permit, let, approve, authorize, O.K., countenance, endorse, sanction. **2** approval, permission, allowance.

banal *adj.* stale, trite, unoriginal, hackneyed, ordinary, commonplace, prosaic, pedestrian, unexciting, unimaginative, everyday, stock, humdrum, dull, uninteresting, conventional, stereotyped, insipid, threadbare, shopworn, tired, corny, cliché-ridden, vapid, platitudinous, bromidic, jejune. **—Syn. Study.** See COMMONPLACE. **—Ant.** original, new, novel, unique, exciting, fresh, unusual, extraordinary, innovative, distinctive, stimulating, stimulative, gripping, provocative, challenging, imaginative, interesting.

band[1] *n.* **1.** group, company, party, body, troop, crowd, caucus, gang, junta, party, pack, bunch, throng, assembly, multitude; confederacy, confederation, association, society, clique, crew, fellowship, league, club, set, circle, brotherhood, sisterhood. **2.** orchestra, ensemble, group. *—v.* **3.** unite, join, consolidate, gather, group. **—Ant. 3** split up, divide, disperse.

band[2] *n.* strip, stripe, streak, ring, fillet, circlet, strap, hoop, binding; ribbon, sash, belt, collar, bandeau, thong, girdle, swath, surcingle, cincture.

bandage *n.* **1.** dressing, binding, compress, plaster. *—v.* **2.** cover with a bandage, dress, bind.

bandanna, bandana *n.* kerchief, neckerchief, silk square, handkerchief, scarf.

bandit *n.* outlaw, robber, desperado, highwayman, badman, thief, brigand, burglar, crook, thug, ladrone; blackleg, footpad, *Obsolete* road agent.

bandy *v.* toss back and forth, trade, swap, exchange, interchange, barter, shuffle, play with, toss about.

bane *n.* **1.** plague, curse, scourge, torment, nuisance; affliction, blight, burden, woe, canker, poison, ruin, ruination; pain in the neck, thorn in the side, fly in the ointment; disaster, calamity, tragedy, detriment, destroyer, downfall. **2.** poison, toxin, venom. **—Ant. 1** blessing, treasure, treat, prize, bright spot, joy, pleasure; comfort, consolation, solace, balm, apple of one's eye. **2** antitoxin.

bang *n.* **1.** loud sound, sudden noise, report, boom, pop, clap, burst, slam, crash, explosion. **2.** blow, hit, knock, smack, clout, rap, box, wallop, whack, tap, slap, cuff, thwack, thump, lick, buffet, *Slang* sock. **3.** *Slang.* thrill, excitement, pleasure, enjoyment, delight, good time, *Slang* charge, kick. *—v.* **4.** strike noisily, beat, close loudly, slam. *—adv.* **5.** headlong, suddenly, smack, slap, crashingly.

bangle *n.* fob, charm, ornament, bauble, trinket, knickknack, gewgaw, fribble, tinsel, gimcrack, bibelot; wristlet, bracelet, chain; costume jewelry, junk jewelry.

banish *v.* **1.** exile, expel, eject, evict, outlaw, deport, extradite, cast out, turn out, drive out, send away, dismiss, send to Coventry; excommunicate. **2.** ban, shut out, bar, dismiss, put away, exclude; cast out, drive out, eliminate, remove, get rid of, shake off, erase, cast away, send away, drop, dispel, dislodge, discharge, eradicate, evict, oust, discard, eject, reject. **—Ant. 1, 2** invite, admit, accept, receive, receive with open arms, welcome, entertain; harbor, shelter; foster, nourish, cherish.

bank[1] *n.* **1.** embankment, mound, heap, pile, mass; ridge, rise, hill, knoll, dune, dike, parapet, barrow, terrace. **2.** shore, side, edge, margin, strand, brink. **3.** shoal, reef, shallow, bar, shelf, sandbank, flat. *—v.* **4.** pile up, heap, stack, amass. **5.** have one side higher than the other, slope, slant, tilt, tip. **—Ant. 1** ditch, trench; valley, dip. **3** deep water, depths. **4, 5** level, plane, smooth out.

bank[2] *n.* row, tier, rank, line, file, string, lineup, series, array, keyboard, succession, train, chain.

bank[3] *n.* **1.** banking house, financial institution; trust company, savings bank, commercial bank; exchequer. **2.** repository, depository, storehouse; store, stockpile, supply, accumulation, fund, savings, reserve, reservoir. *—v.* **3.** transact business with a bank; deposit money in a bank, save, keep.

bankrupt *adj.* ruined, failed, without funds, unable to pay debts, insolvent, broke, wiped out; destitute, indigent, penniless, impoverished, depleted, exhausted, in the red, *Slang* busted. **—Ant.** solvent, sound; prosperous.

banner *n.* **1.** standard, flag, colors, ensign, pennant, pendant, streamer, burgee. *—adj.* **2.** outstanding, most successful, notable, leading, record, red-letter; profitable, winning.

banquet *n.* **1.** feast, repast, dinner, symposium. *—v.* **2.** feast, dine, eat one's fill, revel. **—Ant. 1** snack, light meal; fasting, starvation; abstinence. **2** fast, starve; abstain.

bantam *adj.* miniature, small, tiny, little, diminutive, minute, petite; stunted, dwarf, dwarfed, pocket-size, pocket-sized, runty, wee, weeny, teeny, teeny-weeny; Lilliputian. **—Ant.** large, enlarged, blown-up, overgrown, big, giant, colossal.

banter *n.* **1.** kidding, joking, ribbing, joshing, jesting, teasing, repartee, word play, waggery, raillery, ragging, badinage, chaff, chaffing. —*v.* **2.** kid, josh, rib, taunt, mock, jolly, twit, chaff, dish, ride, needle, tease.

baptism *n.* **1.** Christian sacrament of initiation; sprinkling, immersion; spiritual rebirth, purification. **2.** initiation, rite of passage; introduction, beginning. —**Ant. 2** last act; farewell.

baptize *v.* **1.** administer the Christian sacrament of baptism to. **2.** christen, name, dub.

bar *n.* **1.** pole, rod, stick, stake, rail, pale, paling, grating, rib; *(variously)* crosspiece, crossbar, lever, crowbar, jimmy, spar, sprit. **2.** block, ingot, cake. **3.** sandbar, reef, shoal, shallow, spit, bank, shelf, flat. **4.** tavern, saloon, taproom, cocktail lounge, lounge; public house, pub, alehouse, brewpub; speakeasy; serving counter, long table; canteen, lunchroom, sandwich bar. **5.** band, strip, stripe, ribbon, streak, stroke, beam, belt, slice, line. **6.** obstacle, barrier, obstruction, impediment, stumbling block, block, check, curb, barricade, snag, catch, hindrance, constraint, restraint, restriction, injunction, limitation, taboo. **7.** legal profession, legal fraternity, body of lawyers. **8.** court, tribunal, forum; judgment. **9.** measure. —*v.* **10.** put a bar across, lock, bolt, fasten, secure; block up, close up, barricade. **11.** ban, prohibit, enjoin, stay, stop, restrain, prevent, forbid, obstruct, block, blacklist, blackball, debar, disallow, restrict, limit, exclude, preclude, impede. **12.** exclude, shut out, lock out; banish, expel, evict, eject, exile, oust, cast out. —**Ant. 3** deep water, depths. **6** aid, help, advantage, boon, benefit, edge. **10** open, unlock, clear. **11, 12** allow, permit, let, accept; admit, invite, welcome, receive.

barb *n.* **1.** spur, backward point, point, spike, prong, tine, snag, bristle, nib, cusp, prickle, barbule, spicule. **2.** disagreeable remark, sarcasm, insult, complaint, criticism, affront, badmouthing, dig, jibe, cut, *Slang* putdown.

barbarian *n.* **1.** savage, alien, outlander. **2.** hoodlum, roughneck, ruffian, rowdy, tough, punk, hood, hooligan, delinquent, vandal, bully, lout. **3.** anti-intellectual, lowbrow, philistine, peasant, vulgarian, illiterate, ignoramus, know-nothing, troglodyte, yahoo, boor. —*adj.* **4.** savage, alien. **5.** uncultivated, uncultured, lowbrow, crude, philistine, unsophisticated, provincial, uncouth, boorish. —**Ant. 1** native, citizen. **3** highbrow, intellectual, connoisseur, sophisticate; *plural* literati, cognoscenti. **5** cultivated, cultured, highbrow, intellectual; refined, literate, humane, liberal.

barbaric *adj.* **1.** barbarian, uncivilized, untamed, barbarous, savage, wild. **2.** coarse, uncouth, crude, ill-mannered, vulgar, rude, unpolished, uncivilized, boorish. —**Ant.** civilized, cultivated, gentlemanly, gracious, polite.

barbarity *n.* savageness, cruelty, brutality, ruthlessness. —**Ant.** humaneness, gentleness, mildness.

barbarous *adj.* **1.** cruel, brutal, mean, inhuman, vicious, harsh, barbaric, outrageous. **2.** coarse, crude, rough, vulgar, crass, impolite. —**Ant. 1** humane, merciful, compassionate, lenient, humanitarian, benevolent, benign.

barber *n.* **1.** haircutter, hairdresser. —*v.* **2.** cut, trim, tonsure, shave; dress, arrange, style.

bard *n.* **1.** poet-singer, epic poet, poet. **2.** narrative poet, writer, versifier, rhymer, rhymester, poetaster, poetizer; minstrel, troubador.

bare *adj.* **1.** stripped, naked, nude, undressed, unclothed, unrobed, disrobed, uncovered, unclad, *Slang* in the raw, exposed, peeled. **2.** empty, without contents, void, vacant, blank; unadorned, unembellished, naked, undecorated, unornamented; austere, stark, plain. **3.** threadbare, bald, thin, hapless, worn. **4.** just sufficient, just enough, scant, mere, marginal, meager, supportable, endurable. **5.** plain, undisguised, stark, bald, simple, fundamental, basic, essential, elementary, unelaborated, straightforward, unadorned, unembellished, unvarnished, uncolored. —*v.* **6.** uncover, undress, strip, unveil, undrape; unsheathe, denude. **7.** open, reveal, uncover, show, expose, divest, unmask, offer. —**Ant. 1** clothed, dressed, clad, covered, attired, robed, appareled. **2** full, overflowing, well-stocked, crammed; adorned, embellished, ornamented, dressed up. **3** thick. **4** abundant, profuse, copious, plentiful, bounteous, ample. **6** cover, clothe, dress, veil, robe. **7** hide, conceal, mask; suppress.

barefaced *adj.* brazen, impudent, shameless; transparent, palpable, bald; bold, unabashed, insolent, brash, fresh, cheeky, sassy, forward, flippant, flip, *Slang* snotty. —**Ant.** modest, reticent, shy.

barefoot *adj.* barefooted, unshod, shoeless, unsandaled, discalced, discalceate.

barely *adv.* almost not, only just, just, scarcely, hardly, no more than, just about, almost, slightly, sparingly, scantly, meagerly, faintly; by the skin of one's teeth. —**Syn. Study.** See HARDLY. —**Ant.** fully, completely; abundantly, amply, copiously, profusely.

bargain *n.* **1.** agreement, compact, pact, promise, pledge, accord, understanding, settlement, arrangement, contract, transaction, covenant, treaty, entente. **2.**

good deal, good buy; *Slang* steal. —*v.* **3.** negotiate, haggle, dicker, barter, higgle, deal. —**Syn. Study. 1** See AGREEMENT. —**Ant. 2** extravagance, white elephant, swindle.

bark[1] *n.* **1.** yelp, yip, yap, howl, howling, bay, cry; woof, arf-arf, bow-wow. —*v.* **2.** yelp, yip, yap, howl, bay. **3.** shout, bellow, yell, roar, holler, cry out. —**Ant. 3** whisper, murmur, mutter.

bark[2] *n.* **1.** covering, husk, sheathing, skin, casing, rind, peel, crust, hide, hull, *Scientific* periderm. —*v.* **2.** scrape, skin, abrade, scale, rub, flay, strip.

baroque *adj.* extravagant, florid, ornate, flamboyant. —**Ant.** classical, simple.

barrage *n.* **1.** bombardment, shelling, salvo, volley, cannonade, fusillade, battery, curtain of fire, *Slang* ack-ack. **2.** volley, salvo, fusillade, deluge, torrent, outpouring; blast, burst, stream, shower, spray.

barrel *n.* **1.** cask, keg, tub, vat, hogshead, butt, drum, tun; the amount a barrel can hold, *(in technical use)* 31 gallons of liquid or 105 dry quarts. **2.** tube, tubular part (as of a gun or a pen).

barren *adj.* **1.** infertile, sterile, infecund, *(of cows)* farrow. **2.** infertile, unproductive, unfruitful, depleted, waste, desolate, austere; arid, dry. **3.** unproductive, unfruitful, fruitless, unrewarding, ineffectual, useless, futile; uninteresting, dull, prosaic, uninformative, lackluster, uninstructive, uninspiring, stale. —**Ant.** productive, fertile. **1** fecund, prolific. **2** lush, rich, luxuriant. **3** useful, worthwhile, fruitful, profitable, interesting, instructive.

barricade *n.* **1.** barrier, rampart, bulwark, blockade, obstruction, impediment, obstacle, fence. —*v.* **2.** block, obstruct, protect or shut in with a barrier.

barrier *n.* **1.** obstruction; *(variously)* obstacle, barricade, blockade, fortification, rampart, fence, wall, hedge; ditch, trench, moat. **2.** obstacle, obstruction, impediment, hindrance, handicap, bar, difficulty, restriction, limitation, stumbling block, hurdle. —**Ant. 1** entrance, opening, passage, passageway, way. **2** aid, help, advantage; encouragement, spur.

barter *v.* trade, swap, exchange, interchange.

basal *adj.* **1.** basic, fundamental, necessary, essential, intrinsic, prerequisite, indispensable, key, cardinal, vital. **2.** elementary, primary, lower-level, rudimentary, initial, beginning; easy, simple, simplified. —**Ant. 1** superfluous, ancillary, supplementary, extra, accessory.

base[1] *n.* **1.** support, pedestal, stand, bottom, foundation, underpinning, substructure, ground, groundwork, bed. **2.** foundation, basis, essence, principle, root, core, backbone, heart, key, rudiment, ground, source. **3.** essential ingredient, principal constituent. **4.** camp, station, post, billet, installation, garrison. —*v.* **5.** derive from, model on, found on. **6.** station, garrison, locate, situate, install, billet, ground, establish, place. —**Syn. Study. 1, 2** BASE, BASIS, FOUNDATION refer to anything upon which a structure is built and upon which it rests. BASE usu. refers to a physical supporting structure: *the base of a statue.* BASIS more often refers to a metaphorical support: *the basis of a report.* FOUNDATION implies a solid, secure understructure, literal or metaphorical: *the foundation of a skyscraper; the foundation of a theory.* —**Ant. 1** top, summit, apex, zenith, peak, pinnacle; superstructure. **2, 3** nonessentials, frills.

base[2] *adj.* **1.** inferior, poor quality; alloyed, impure, debased, adulterated, spurious. **2.** mean, vile, low, contemptible, despicable, ignoble, shameful, immoral, bad, scoundrelly, villainous, sinful, wicked, dishonorable, dastardly, scurvy, iniquitous, depraved, degenerate, vulgar, gross, cowardly, corrupt, sordid, craven, foul, faithless, nefarious, infamous, dissolute, debased, degraded, ignominious, unworthy, disgraceful, blackhearted, evil-minded, unprincipled, insidious, detestable, reprehensible, discreditable, disreputable, abject, petty, sneaky, dirty, scrubby, slimy. —**Syn. Study. 2** See MEAN. —**Ant. 1** precious, valuable, rare; pure, unadulterated, unalloyed. **2** virtuous, honorable, honest, just, aboveboard, righteous, upright, moral, ethical, lofty, good, admirable, heroic.

baseless *adj.* unfounded, groundless, ungrounded, without basis, unsupported, unsubstantiated, uncorroborated, unfactual, unjustified, unjustifiable, unsound. —**Ant.** well-founded, well-grounded, supported, substantiated, corroborated, factual, documented.

bashful *adj.* shy, timid, easily embarrassed, demure, retiring, unconfident, timorous, modest, overly modest, diffident, reticent, reserved, shrinking, constrained, uncertain, shamefaced, sheepish, skittish, blushing. —**Ant.** aggressive, brash, bold, brazen, impudent, immodest, forward, shameless, intrepid; conceited, egoistic, egotistic, confident, self-assured, fearless, arrogant.

basic *adj.* **1.** fundamental, elementary, vital, essential, intrinsic, rudimentary, key, core, base, prime, primary, foundational. —*n.* **2.** fundamental, prerequisite, essential, core, rudiment, base, foundation, underpinning, bedrock. **—Ant. 1** accompanying, supporting, supplementary, complementary, secondary; unimportant, trivial, minor. **2** unessential; frill, frivolity, triviality.

basin *n.* **1.** bowl, washbowl, pan, tub, washtub, vat, tureen, washbasin, lavatory, washstand, lavabo, sink, dishpan; finger bowl, porringer; font, stoup. **2.** valley, dale, dell, glen, gulch, gully, ravine, crater, hollow, sinkhole, depression, bowl.

basis pl. **bases** *n.* base, starting point, underpinning, root, ground, foundation, touchstone, bedrock, cornerstone, fundamental, essential, principle. **—Syn. Study.** See BASE.

bask *v.* **1.** warm oneself, toast oneself, soak up warmth; sunbathe. **2.** revel, wallow, luxuriate, delight, relish, savor.

bastard *n.* **1.** illegitimate child, natural child, love child. *—adj.* **2.** impure, irregular, imperfect, inferior, spurious.

bastion *n.* **1.** fortress, fort, citadel; rampart, breastwork, barbette. **2.** bulwark, stronghold, citadel, tower, pillar.

bat *n.* **1.** club, mallet, baton, stick; cane, staff, mace; cudgel, shillelagh, blackjack, truncheon, billy, bludgeon, rod. *—v.* **2.** hit, strike, smack, knock, cuff, clobber, wallop, whack, thwack, sock, slug, clip, buffet.

batch *n.* group, bunch, lot, amount, stock, collection, crowd, number, aggregate, quantity.

bath *n.* cleansing, ablution, shower, showerbath, wash, tub, douche, washing, sponge bath, sauna, Turkish bath, steam bath, sitz bath, hip bath, dip, lavement, irrigation, immersion.

bathe *v.* wash, cleanse, shower, soak, lave, dip, wet, douse, *Slang* douche, sponge, irrigate, *Brit.* tub.

bathos *n.* sentimentality, sentimentalism, mawkishness, false pathos, maudlinism, soppiness, slush, slushiness, mush, mushiness, corn, schmaltz.

bathroom *n.* washroom, men's room, ladies' room, *Brit.* lavatory, *Brit. Slang* loo, water closet, W.C., toilet, commode, facility, powder room, restroom, *Slang* john, *Slang* can, *Baby Talk* biffy, little girls' room, little boys' room, *Navy Slang* head, *Army* latrine.

baton *n.* staff, mace, crook, scepter, crosier, rod, wand; fasces, caduceus; stick, nightstick, cudgel, truncheon, shillelagh, war club, bludgeon, billy, billy club, bat.

batter *v.* **1.** beat, buffet, smash against, pound, pummel, smite, lash, *Slang* clobber. **2.** pound, smash, break, beat, shatter; crush. **3.** beat up, maul, mangle, knock out of shape.

battery *n.* **1.** group, pack, set, series, block, band, suite; troop, force, brigade, team, legion, company, army, convoy, spearhead, phalanx, lineup; cannon, cannonry, ordnance, armament; outfit, section, division, squadron, cadre. **2.** hitting, wounding, maiming, hurting, thrashing, beating, clubbing, caning, strapping, drubbing, flogging, whipping, cudgeling.

battle *n.* **1.** combat, clash, campaign, siege, war, warfare, skirmish, firefight, fight; contest, encounter, affray, fray, conflict, engagement, action; duel, bout. **2.** struggle, fight, contest; dispute, controversy, altercation, agitation, debate, confrontation, crusade. *—v.* **3.** war, fight, clash, skirmish, duel, meet, engage; struggle, contend, contest, combat, brawl, tussle, pitch into each other; quarrel, argue, feud, dispute, debate. **—Ant. 1** armistice, peace, truce; concord, agreement. **2** agreement, accord.

battlefield *n.* battleground, theater of war, field of battle, battle line, the front, front line, no man's land, theater of operations, scene of battle, war arena.

bawdy *adj.* earthy, lusty, risqué, ribald, indecent, coarse, gross, licentious, off-color, blue, suggestive, sexual, sexy, indecorous, immodest, improper, indelicate, vulgar, lewd, dirty, raunchy. **—Ant.** decent, modest, delicate, clean.

bawl *v.* **1.** cry, wail, howl, yowl, squall, blubber, weep. **2.** shout, bellow, yell, roar, cry out, howl, call, call out, clamor. **—Ant. 1** laugh. **2** whisper, murmur, mutter.

bay[1] *n.* cove, inlet, estuary, strait, narrows, arm of the sea, sound, gulf, bayou, basin, natural harbor; firth, fiord, bight, road, lagoon.

bay[2] *n.* alcove, nook, niche, recess, compartment.

bay[3] *n.* **1.** barking, howling, bellowing, cry, clamor, yelping, yapping, yelling. **2.** **at bay.** cornered, trapped, forced to stand and fight. *—v.* **3.** howl, bellow, bark, yelp, yap, cry.

bazaar, bazar *n.* **1.** market, marketplace, outdoor market, mart, shopping quarter, trade center, exchange. **2.** charity fair, charity sale; fair, carnival.

be *v.* **1.** exist, live, subsist. **2.** occur, happen, come to pass, take place, befall. **3.** be present, endure, last, continue, remain, stay, persist.

beach *n.* shore, seashore, strand, coast, littoral, water's edge.

beacon *n.* light, beam, signal; *(variously)* lighthouse, lighted buoy, landmark, seamark, watchtower, pharos; watch fire, bale-fire.

bead *n.* **1.** small pieces of glass, stones, wood, etc., used for ornament, as on a necklace. **2.** drop, droplet, globule, little ball, blob, pellet, spherule, bubble; speck, particle, dot, pill.

beam *n.* **1.** *(in technical use)* horizontal support; structural support, prop, girder, rafter, joist, brace, spar, stud, trestle, timber. **2.** ray, streak, stream, gleam, glimmer, glint, glow, radiation. **3.** widest part, width, expanse, breadth. —*v.* **4.** transmit, emit, radiate, broadcast; gleam, glimmer, glitter, glow, glare, shine. **5.** shine, gleam, glow, radiate.

bear *v.* **1.** support, sustain, maintain, carry, uphold, shoulder, take on, endure, hold up under, tolerate; underpin, brace, bolster. **2.** transport, carry, tote, convoy, bring, haul, take; accompany, lead, escort, conduct, go with, convey, deliver, transfer. **3.** give birth to, bring into being, bring forth, produce, deliver; reproduce, propagate, germinate, spawn, hatch, whelp, drop. **4.** produce, develop, bring forth, give, yield; engender, create, generate, render. **5.** maintain, carry, keep in mind, hold close, harbor, cherish, take. **6.** tolerate, abide, endure, stand, put up with, stomach, brook, take, undergo, submit to, suffer, brave. **7.** pertain, relate, apply, refer, appertain, concern, be pertinent to, affect, have bearing on, have respect to, touch upon. **8.** warrant, invite, admit, be susceptible to, permit, allow, encourage. **9.** exhibit, manifest, display, show, have, carry, contain, possess, be marked with, be equipped with, be furnished with, wear. **10.** press, push, bear down, force, drive. **11.** go in the direction of, aim for, turn, tend, bend, curve, diverge, deviate. **—Syn. Study. 6** BEAR, STAND, ENDURE refer to supporting the burden of something distressing, irksome, or painful. BEAR is the general word and suggests merely being able to put up with something: *She is bearing the disappointment quite well.* STAND is an informal equivalent, but with an implication of stout spirit: *I couldn't stand the pain.* ENDURE implies continued resistance and patience over a long period of time: *to endure torture.* **—Ant. 1** rest on; reject, cast off, throw off. **2** put down; leave. **4** shed, drop, loose. **5** put aside, forget; relinquish, abandon. **9** hide, conceal. **10** pull.

beard *n.* **1.** whiskers; bristles, stubble, five-o'clock shadow. —*v.* **2.** corner, bring to bay, trap, confront, face, defy, brave, dare.

bearded *adj.* bewhiskered, whiskered, unshaven, hairy, hirsute, shaggy, bushy, bristly. **—Ant.** clean-shaven, smooth-shaven.

bearing *n.* **1.** carriage, mien, manner, air, presence; demeanor, behavior, attitude, comportment, deportment, port. **2.** relevance, pertinence, significance, reference, application, applicability, connection, concern, relation, relationship, association; sense, meaning, meaningfulness, import, importance. **3.** reproducing, reproduction, giving birth, germination, procreation, propagation, producing, breeding, conception. **4.** **bearings.** sense of direction, orientation, direction, way, course, position. **—Ant. 2** irrelevance, insignificance.

beast *n.* **1.** animal, creature, mammal, quadruped, brute. **2.** brute, savage, barbarian, ogre, cad, swine, pig, cur, rat. **—Ant. 1** human being. **2** gentleman, lady; *Informal* angel, sweetheart, gem.

beastly *adj.* unpleasant, disgusting, disagreeable, nasty, vile, loathsome, abominable, contemptible; cruel, brutal, monstrous, inhuman, bestial, brutish, savage, barbarous, gross, coarse, degraded, swinish; bad, terrible, awful, dreadful, deplorable, *Slang* lousy. **—Ant.** pleasant, agreeable, appealing, admirable; humane, sweet, sensitive, gentlemanly, ladylike; good, fine, wonderful.

beat *v.* **1.** hit, strike, pound, wallop, whack, thwack, knock, smack, punch, slap, smite, clout, flail, bat, tap, rap, bang, hammer. **2.** thrash, pummel, batter, maul, trounce; whip, flog, flail, scourge, switch, strap, club, cane. **3.** defeat, be victorious over, triumph over, win over, overcome, overpower, vanquish, best; conquer, crush, rout, destroy, repel, repulse, quell, put down, master, subdue, whip, lick, clobber, shellac, trounce, drub. **4.** win out over, excel over, surpass, outdo, prevail over, predominate, eclipse, overcome, carry all before one. **5.** pulsate, pulse, throb, pound, palpitate, flutter, quiver, fluctuate, vibrate, quake, shake, twitch, go pit-a-pat; flap, flop. **6.** whip; stir vigorously, mix. —*n.* **7.** blow, stroke, strike, hit, whack, rap, slap. **8.** cadence, time, rhythm, meter, count, pulse, pulsation, stress, accent. **9.** route, rounds, circuit, path, course, way; area, zone, territory, domain, realm. **—Syn. Study. 1, 2** BEAT, HIT, POUND, STRIKE, THRASH refer to the giving of a blow or blows. BEAT implies the giving of repeated blows: *to beat a rug.* To HIT is usu. to give a single blow, definitely directed: *to hit a ball.* To POUND is to give heavy and repeated blows, often with the fist: *to pound the table.* To STRIKE is to give one or more forceful blows suddenly or swiftly: *to strike a gong.* To THRASH implies inflicting repeated blows as punishment, to show superior strength, or the like: *to thrash an opponent.* **—Ant. 1, 2** caress, stroke, pat, pet; soothe, comfort; shield, protect, guard. **3, 4** lose, suffer defeat, go down in defeat, surrender; fall, fail, get the worst of, go under.

beatific *adj.* blissful, serene, heavenly, divine, sublime, glorious, exalted, transcendental, angelic, saintly; enraptured, rapturous, rapt, ecstatic. **—Ant.** worldly, sophisticated; mundane, common, coarse, crude.

beatitude *n.* bliss, felicity, blessedness, saintliness; exaltation, exaltedness, transcendence, transfiguration; rapture, ecstasy, euphoria. **—Ant.** despair, hopelessness, dolor.

beau Plural **beaux** *n.* **1.** boyfriend, sweetheart, young man, steady, fellow, suitor, *Informal* guy, admirer, flame, gentleman caller or friend, squire, swain; fiancé, betrothed; love, beloved, lover. **2.** ladies' man, cavalier, dandy, fop, swell, playboy, gay blade, Romeo, Don Juan, blade; young blood, popinjay, coxcomb; nob, spark, dude, stud, buck, toff.

beautiful *adj.* **1.** handsome, pretty, lovely, good-looking, fine-looking, attractive, gorgeous, exquisite, ravishing, comely, fair, bonny, seemly, beauteous, radiant, pulchritudinous, resplendent; pleasing, enjoyable, captivating, alluring. **2.** very good, excellent, first-rate, superb, wonderful, fine, splendid, admirable, great, stupendous, commendable, estimable, worthy. **—Syn. Study.** BEAUTIFUL, HANDSOME, LOVELY, PRETTY refer to a pleasing appearance. BEAUTIFUL is used of a person or thing that gives intense pleasure to the senses; it may refer to a woman but rarely to a man: *a beautiful landscape; a beautiful actress.* HANDSOME often implies stateliness or pleasing proportions and symmetry; it is used of a man and sometimes a woman: *a handsome sofa; a handsome man.* That which is LOVELY is beautiful in a warm and endearing way: *a lovely smile.* PRETTY usu. suggests a moderate beauty in persons or things that are small or feminine: *a pretty blouse; a pretty child.* **—Ant. 1** ugly, unattractive, bad-looking, hideous, grotesque; unpleasant, bad, awful, disgusting, repulsive, repugnant, revolting. **2** bad, awful, terrible, lousy, second-rate.

beautify *v.* enhance, embellish, adorn, ornament, glamorize, improve, grace, dress up, smarten up, do up, *Slang* gussy up. **—Ant.** spoil, mar, disfigure, deface, besmirch.

beauty *n.* **1.** loveliness, handsomeness, good looks, pulchritude, attractiveness, splendor, resplendence, magnificence, radiance. **2.** beautiful woman, beautiful girl, belle, goddess, Venus; *Slang* knockout, beaut, doll, stunner, eyeful, good-looker, looker. **3.** advantage, asset, attraction, feature, good thing, excellence, benefit, grace, boon. **—Ant. 1** ugliness, repulsiveness, unpleasantness. **2** *Slang* witch, bag, dog, pig. **3** disadvantage, detraction, shortcoming, flaw.

beckon *v.* **1.** signal, motion, wave at, wave on, gesture, gesticulate, crook a finger at. **2.** entice, lure, allure, invite, attract, draw, pull, call, summon, coax. **—Ant. 2** repel, repulse, *Informal* put off.

becloud *v.* obscure, befog, confuse, obfuscate, hide, confound, muddle, cover up, camouflage, eclipse, screen, overcast, veil, shroud, overshadow.

become *v.* **1.** get, begin to be, grow, turn, come to be, get to be, turn out to be, commence to be; be converted into, be reduced to, settle into. **2.** suit, go with, flatter, complement, agree with, enhance; accord with, harmonize with, be proper to, be consistent with. **—Ant. 2** clash with, conflict with, disagree with, detract from.

becoming *adj.* **1.** suitable, appropriate, proper, seemly, fit, fitting, befitting, worthy, meet, congruous, consistent, in keeping. **2.** flattering, enhancing, attractive, pretty, good-looking; apt, harmonious, congenial, compatible. **—Ant.** unbecoming. **1** unsuitable, inappropriate, improper, unseemly, unfit, unfitting, unbefitting, unworthy, incongruous, inconsistent with, out of keeping, indecorous. **2** ugly, unattractive.

bed *n.* **1.** bedstead, place to sleep, bunk, pallet, berth, cot; *Slang* sack, hay; *(for infants)* cradle, crib. **2.** base, bottom, floor, foundation. **3.** layer, stratum, band, belt, zone; seam, deposit, lode. **4.** plot, patch, bank.

bedazzle *v.* **1.** daze, confuse, dumfound, bewilder, stupefy, nonplus, disconcert, befuddle, fluster. **2.** dazzle, confound, astound, stagger, flabbergast, overwhelm, overpower, enchant, captivate, sweep one off one's feet.

bedlam *n.* scene of wild confusion, uproar, pandemonium, chaos, madhouse, tumult, turmoil.

bedraggled *adj.* unkempt, untidy, sloppy, dirty, soiled, messy, disordered, dowdy, tattered, seedy, threadbare, down-at-the-heels, tacky, *Brit.* tatty, ragtag, out-at-the-elbows, draggletailed; frumpy, frumpish, sluttish, slatternly. **—Ant.** neat, dapper, well-groomed, immaculate.

bedroom *n.* sleeping room, bedchamber, boudoir.

beehive *n.* **1.** hive, apiary. **2.** busy place, powerhouse.

beer *n.* *(variously)* lager, ale, stout, porter, malt liquor, dark, bitter, light, near beer, bock beer; *Slang* brew, brewski, suds.

befall *v.* happen, occur, come to pass,

ensue, materialize, chance, fall, follow, betide.

befitting *adj.* suitable, appropriate, fitting, fit, proper, apt, seemly, right, decent, becoming; relevant. **—Ant.** unsuitable, inappropriate, unfit, unfitting, unbecoming, improper, unseemly, wrong; irrelevant, meaningless.

beforehand *adv.* earlier, sooner, before, before now, ahead of time, in advance, before the fact, in time. **—Ant.** afterwards, after.

befriend *v.* make friends with, get acquainted with, associate with, consort with, fraternize with; assist, help, help out, give aid to, succor, comfort, minister to, protect, defend, hold out a helping hand to, look after, sympathize with, embrace, welcome, support, sustain, stick by, stand by, side with, uphold, take under one's wing. **—Ant.** alienate, estrange.

befuddle *v.* **1.** confuse, perplex, bewilder, puzzle, baffle, confound, disorganize, daze, unsettle, rattle, fluster, muddle, mix up, knock off balance, disorient. **2.** addle, stupefy, make groggy, intoxicate, make drunk, make tipsy, inebriate. **—Ant. 1** make clear to, illuminate, bring into focus. **2** sober, clear one's head.

beg *v.* **1.** seek charity, solicit, panhandle, mooch, *Informal* cadge, sponge, bum, hustle, go from door to door, be on one's uppers. **2.** plead, entreat, implore, beseech, supplicate, sue, appeal to, petition, importune, pray. **3.** evade, avoid, dodge, shirk, shun, escape, avert, eschew, parry, fend off, sidestep, steer clear of, shy away from. **—Ant. 1** give, contribute, present, bestow, donate, confer. **2** demand, exact, insist, grant, give, accord.

beget *v.* **1.** father, sire, get, propagate, breed, engender, procreate, spawn. **2.** bring about, result in, cause, effect, occasion, lead to, produce, give rise to, call forth, engender, generate. **—Ant. 2** prevent, forestall, foil, block, ward off, deter, save.

beggar *n.* **1.** almsman, mendicant, panhandler, tramp; *Slang* sponger, bum, moocher. **2.** fellow, chap, guy, *Slang* devil. *—v.* **3.** make inadequate, be beyond, surpass; challenge, baffle. **—Ant. 1** giver, contributor, bestower, donor, donator, benefactor, philanthropist.

begin *v.* **1.** start, commence, initiate, set out, embark on, take the first step. **2.** come into existence, bring into existence, be born, start, commence, initiate, undertake; originate, establish, introduce, found, institute, launch, inaugurate; emerge, arise, burst forth, break out, crop up, set in motion. **—Syn. Study. 1** BEGIN, COMMENCE, INITIATE, START (when followed by noun or gerund) refer to setting into motion or progress something that continues for some time. BEGIN is the common term: *to begin knitting a sweater.* COMMENCE is a more formal word, often suggesting a more prolonged or elaborate beginning: *to commence proceedings in court.* INITIATE implies an active and often ingenious first act in a new field: *to initiate a new procedure.* START means to make a first move or to set out on a course of action: *to start paving a street.* **—Ant. 1, 2** end, finish, terminate, conclude, complete; stop, cease, quit.

beginner *n.* **1.** novice, neophyte, student, tyro, learner, fledgling, tenderfoot, greenhorn, rookie, freshman, apprentice, *Slang* babe, babe in the woods, newbie. **2.** founder, father, originator, initiator, creator, starter, inaugurator, prime mover, author, organizer. **—Ant. 1** expert, professional, master, authority, virtuoso, old hand.

beginning *n.* **1.** start, commencement, starting point, onset, outset, zero hour, *Slang* get-go. **2.** origin, source, foundation, fountainhead, wellspring, spring, springboard; embryo, inauguration, birth, inception, seed, germ, introduction, launching, kickoff. *—adj.* **3.** novice, neophyte, student, inexperienced, untried, new, preliminary, embryonic, incipient. **—Ant. 1, 2** end, ending, conclusion, finish, closing, termination, expiration. **3** experienced, accomplished, finished, skilled, learned, expert, master.

begone *v.* go away, away, be off, get out, out, depart, leave, *Slang* scram, vamoose, beat it, scat, shoo, get lost. **—Ant.** come here, come.

begrudge *v.* grudge, resent, hold against; envy, covet, be jealous of. **—Ant.** congratulate, wish well; be happy for.

beguile *v.* **1.** delude, lead astray, deceive, dupe, bamboozle, ensnare, lure, trick, cheat, hoodwink, hoax. **2.** lull, distract, enchant, charm, bewitch, captivate, please, cheer; entertain, divert, amuse, occupy. **—Ant. 1** enlighten, disabuse, make weary, *Informal* wise up. **2** alert, alarm, bring to one's senses, jar.

behave *v.* **1.** conduct oneself properly, comport oneself well, act correctly, control oneself. **2.** act, conduct oneself, comport oneself, deport oneself, acquit oneself. **—Ant. 1** misbehave.

behavior *n.* **1.** conduct, manner, attitude, control, self-control, comportment, deportment, bearing, demeanor. **2.** response, reaction, functioning, conduct, operation, action, performance. **3.** acts, deeds, actions, activity, conduct, practice, habits.

behead *v.* decapitate, send to the ax, bring to the block; guillotine, decollate.

behest *n.* order, direction, command, instruction, mandate, dictate, charge, say-so, injunction, bidding; decree, ruling, fiat, edict, ultimatum.

behold *v.* look, look at, look upon, observe, note, see, gaze at, stare at, view, discern, survey, regard, watch, examine, inspect, notice, scan, scrutinize, witness, *Slang* get a load of; attend, pay attention, heed, mark, contemplate. **—Ant.** overlook, disregard, ignore, miss.

beholden *adj.* under obligation, obligated, obliged, indebted, in one's debt, bound, liable; answerable, accountable, responsible.

behoove *v.* be advantageous, benefit, be advisable, be wise; be fitting, befit, become, suit, be proper, be necessary, be apt, be appropriate.

being *n.* **1.** existence, existing, occurrence, reality, actuality, life, living, subsistence. **2.** nature, soul, spirit, psyche, essence, true being, core, inner person, persona. **3.** living creature, creature, human being, human, person, fellow creature, mortal, individual. **—Ant. 1** nothingness, nonexistence, nullity.

belabor *v.* hammer away at, dwell on, go on (and on) about, repeat, rehash, reiterate, recapitulate, pound away at; beat a dead horse.

belated *adj.* late, tardy, past due, overdue, behind, behind time, slow, delayed, deferred, unpunctual, after the fact, behindhand. **—Ant.** early, ahead of time, beforehand, before the fact.

belch *v.* **1.** burp, eruct. **2.** emit, discharge, spew, spout, spurt, eject, issue, send forth, gush, roar forth, expel, erupt, disgorge, vomit, vent, cough up. **—*n.* 3.** burp, eructation. **4.** emission, discharge, spurt, spout, gush, ejection, issuing, eruption.

beleaguer *v.* **1.** besiege, surround, blockade, bombard, assail. **2.** harass, badger, pester, bother, annoy, assail, hector, vex, bombard, besiege, plague.

belfry *n.* bell tower, campanile; *(loosely)* steeple, spire, dome.

belie *v.* **1.** disprove, refute, contradict, controvert, repudiate, show to be false, give the lie to, invalidate, gainsay, negate, betray, deny, defy. **2.** misrepresent, falsify; disguise, camouflage, mask, conceal, cloak. **—Ant. 1** prove, verify, attest to, validate, support, confirm, corroborate. **2** represent, reveal, disclose, indicate.

belief *n.* **1.** conviction, firm notion, opinion, view, theory, persuasion; conclusion; assumption, supposition, presumption, feeling, expectation, judgment, impression, hypothesis, deduction, inference, guess. **2.** confidence, trust, faith, assurance, reliance, certitude. **3.** Often **beliefs.** conviction, persuasion, principle, way of thinking; morality, morals, teachings, ethics; faith, creed, dogma, doctrine, tenet, canon, gospel. **—Syn. Study. 1** BELIEF, CONVICTION refer to acceptance of or confidence in an alleged fact or body of facts as true or right without positive knowledge or proof. BELIEF is such acceptance in general: *belief in astrology.* CONVICTION is a settled, profound, or earnest belief that something is right: *a conviction that a decision is just.* **—Ant. 2** distrust, mistrust, doubt. **3** disbelief, unbelief, skepticism; denial, disavowal.

believable *adj.* plausible, credible, convincing, possible, imaginable, acceptable. **—Ant.** unbelievable, incredible, doubtful, dubious, unconvincing, implausible, questionable; unacceptable; fabulous.

believe *v.* **1.** trust, put faith in, place confidence in, be certain of, credit, rely on, depend on; presume true, accept as true, hold, be assured by, be convinced by, be persuaded by, judge accurate, count on, be sure of, swear by; swallow, fall for. **2.** presume, think, imagine, guess, surmise, suspect, judge, suppose, assume, consider, speculate, conjecture, presuppose; theorize, hypothesize, deduce, infer; maintain, hold. **—Ant. 1** doubt, question, distrust, mistrust, discredit, disbelieve. **2** know, know for sure.

belittle *v.* make light of, disparage, deride, scorn, disdain, sneer at, malign, cast aspersions on, deprecate, play down, minimize, mitigate, underrate, undervalue, underestimate, depreciate; *Slang* knock, run down, put down, pooh-pooh. **—Ant.** overpraise, praise, vaunt, glorify, elevate, exalt, play up, magnify; boast about, crow over, make a big fuss over.

bell *n.* tocsin, chime, carillon, gong; peal of bells, peal, ringing, tintinnabulation.

belle *n.* beautiful girl, beautiful woman, beauty; most beautiful woman, most beautiful girl, star, queen; charmer; *Slang* heart-stopper.

bellicose *adj.* See BELLIGERENT.

belligerence, belligerency *n.* warlike attitude, hostility, aggressiveness, combativeness, pugnacity, antagonism, unfriendliness, animosity. **—Ant.** peacefulness, friendliness.

belligerent *adj.* **1.** warlike, warring, hostile, antagonistic, aggressive, combative, martial, bellicose. **2.** unfriendly, hostile, antagonistic, bellicose, pugnacious, quarrelsome, contentious, irritable, bad-tempered, cantankerous, irascible, inimical, truculent. —*n.* **3.** warring country, nation at war, combatant, fighter, adversary; aggressor, attacker, antagonist. —**Ant. 1, 2** peaceful, peaceable. **1** pacific; neutral. **2** friendly, amicable, neighborly. **3** neutral, noncombatant; the attacked, defender.

bellow *v.* **1.** roar; shout, yell, bawl, holler, scream, shriek, whoop. —*n.* **2.** roar, shout, yell, shriek, scream, whoop. —**Ant. 1, 2** whisper. **1** murmur, mutter.

bellwether *n.* leader, guide, pilot, lead, doyen, pacesetter, standard-bearer; shepherd, conductor, director; precursor, forerunner, guidepost.

belly *n.* **1.** stomach, tummy, abdomen, paunch, vitals, *Slang* gut, guts, midriff, breadbasket. **2.** liking, desire, appetite, stomach, hunger, taste, yen. **3.** bowels, depths, recesses, interior, insides.

belong *v.* **1.** have as a proper place; be part of, attach to, go with; concern, pertain to, be connected with. **2.** be the property of, be owned by, be held by. **3.** be a member of, be included in; be associated with, be allied to.

belongings *n. pl.* possessions, effects, personal property, movables, goods; gear, paraphernalia, accouterments, things, stuff, *Slang* junk.

beloved *adj.* **1.** loved, cherished, dear, precious, treasured, adored, darling, endeared; respected, admired, highly valued, esteemed, revered. —*n.* **2.** sweetheart, loved one, love, dearest, precious; *(variously)* steady, lover, boyfriend, beau, girl friend, betrothed, fiancé, fiancée, spouse, husband, wife.

belt *n.* **1.** sash, band, cinch, waistband, cummerbund, girdle. **2.** circle, band, strip, stripe, layer. **3.** area, district, region, zone, country, land. —*v.* **4.** encircle by a belt, fasten with a belt, cinch, girdle, encircle.

bemoan *v.* grieve over, weep over, cry over, whine over, lament, bewail, mourn, regret, rue. —**Ant.** laugh at; celebrate, exult.

bemused *adj.* **1.** preoccupied, absent-minded, engrossed, thoughtful. **2.** confused, muddled, bewildered, fuzzy, dull-witted, stupefied, dazed, stunned. —**Ant. 1** angry, stern, unsympathetic. **2** clearheaded, perceptive, *Slang* sharp.

bench *n.* **1.** seat, settee, pew, rigid couch, backless couch, backless chair, stool. **2.** workbench, worktable, counter, trestle, board, table. **3.** court, tribunal, judiciary, seat of justice; judge's chair. **4.** substitute players, substitutes, second team, second string. —*v.* **5.** remove from active play, remove from the game, take out, sideline.

benchmark *n.* standard, yardstick, measure, gauge, criterion, touchstone, model, guide, exemplar, paradigm; reference, norm, principle, prototype, example.

bend *v.* **1.** twist, make crooked, become crooked, warp, buckle, contort; curve, arc, loop, turn, wind. **2.** flex; crouch, stoop, lean; bow, buckle, genuflect. **3.** bow down, submit, yield, give in, defer, accede, relent, succumb, be subjugated, surrender, capitulate, *Informal* knuckle under; force to submit, cause to yield, cause to give in, cause to defer, cause to relent, force to surrender, force, compel, coerce, control, shape, mold, influence, sway. **4.** apply oneself, attend, give oneself to, buckle down, put one's heart into. —*n.* **5.** curve, turn, crook, arc, hook, twist. —**Ant. 1, 2** straighten; stiffen.

benediction *n.* blessing, prayer, benison, consecration, invocation, closing prayer. —**Ant.** malediction, curse, imprecation, censure.

benefactor *n.* supporter, patron, donor, sponsor, upholder, backer, helper, friend, angel, fairy godmother; contributor.

beneficial *adj.* helpful, advantageous, propitious, useful, valuable, contributive, favorable, profitable, productive; healthful, healing, good for. —**Ant.** useless, detrimental, detractive, disadvantageous; unfavorable, harmful, pernicious, unwholesome.

beneficiary *n.* inheritor, legatee, heir, heiress; receiver, recipient, grantee.

benefit *n.* **1.** help, aid, service, use, avail, profit, value, gain, worth, advantage, asset, good, betterment, blessing; behalf, interest. **2.** charity affair, charity performance. —*v.* **3.** help, aid, assist, serve, be useful to, be an advantage to, do good for, advance, better, profit; be helped, be aided, be served, gain, profit from. —**Syn. Study. 1** See ADVANTAGE. —**Ant. 1** damage, harm, injury, impairment, privation; loss, disservice, disadvantage, drawback. **3** harm, injure, hurt, damage, impair, deprive; lose, detract from, be useless to, be bad for, worsen, hold back.

benevolence *n.* **1.** good will, kindliness, kindheartedness, kindness, compassion, benignity. **2.** generosity, charity, charitableness, humanitarianism, bountifulness, liberality. —**Ant. 1** ill will, unkindness, unkindliness, malevolence, malignity. **2** selfishness, greediness; stinginess, illiberality, niggardliness.

benevolent *adj.* **1.** kindhearted, warmhearted, kind, compassionate, tender, full of good will, benign, benignant, considerate, humane. **2.** unselfish, charitable, philanthropic, humanitarian; generous, liberal, considerable, bountiful, bounteous, bighearted. **—Ant. 1** unkind, cruel, malevolent, malicious, malignant. **2** selfish, greedy; stingy, miserly, niggardly, illiberal.

benighted *adj.* ignorant, backward, unenlightened, untutored, primitive, uncivilized, uncultivated, uncultured, illiterate, unlettered, crude, uneducated, unschooled, uninformed, untaught; know-nothing, empty-headed, dumb, *Slang* unhip. **—Ant.** cultured, educated, schooled, civilized, informed, cultivated.

benign *adj.* **1.** kind, kindly, genial, kindhearted, tender, tender-hearted, softhearted, soft, gentle, benevolent, humane; gracious, affable. **2.** good, favorable, salutary, auspicious, encouraging, propitious, lucky. **3.** temperate, mild, balmy, pleasant, nice; healthful, harmless, innocuous. **—Ant. 1** unkind, unkindly, hard-hearted, harsh, stern, malicious, malevolent, hateful, malign, inhumane, ungracious. **2** bad, unfavorable, discouraging, threatening, ominous, unlucky. **3** harsh, severe, extreme, unpleasant.

bent *adj.* **1.** angled, twisted, crooked, curved, arched, contorted, stooped, hunched, bowed. *—n.* **2.** leaning, tendency, inclination, propensity, penchant, proclivity, disposition, predisposition; mind, liking, fondness, bias, partiality, attraction, predilection; talent, gift, flair, knack, faculty, facility, ability, aptness, capacity, endowment, aptitude, genius. **—Ant. 1** unbent, straight, straight as an arrow, rigid, uncurved, unbowed. **2** aversion, disinclination, dislike, antipathy, hate, hatred, abhorrence.

bequeath *v.* will, leave, hand down, impart, consign, endow.

bequest *n.* legacy, inheritance, endowment, bestowal, settlement.

berate *v.* scold, upbraid, reprimand, rebuke, reprove, reproach, criticize, castigate, take to task, rail at, bawl out, chew out, tongue-lash. **—Ant.** praise, compliment, laud, thank, congratulate.

bereave *v.* deprive, rob, strip, dispossess, divest.

berserk *adj.* maniacal, frenzied, amok, wild, violent, out of control, frantic, wild-eyed; deranged, insane, demented, crazy; distracted, distraught, desperate. **—Ant.** calm, serene, tranquil, collected, pacific.

berth *n.* **1.** bunk, bed, sleeping place. **2.** dock, pier, slip, quay, anchorage, wharf; haven, resting place. **3.** job, position, situation, place, office, post, spot, niche, appointment, employ, billet.

beseech *v.* beg, plead with, implore, entreat, adjure, supplicate, pray.

beset *v.* **1.** attack on all sides, besiege, surround, hem in, assail, set upon; beleaguer, bedevil, plague, pester, badger, harass, hound, annoy, worry, dog. **2.** set, stud, array, deck, embellish, bead; set upon, place upon.

besiege *v.* **1.** lay siege to, surround and attack, beleaguer; assail, assault. **2.** beset, plague, pester, badger, harass, hound, bedevil, annoy, dog.

besmirch *v.* smear, taint, tarnish, corrupt, stain, sully, soil, defile, blacken; slander, dishonor, disgrace, degrade, discredit, defame, debauch. **—Ant.** respect, honor, do homage to, exalt, praise.

best *adj.* **1.** most excellent, superior, finest, choice, highest quality, topnotch, unrivaled, unsurpassed, unexcelled, unequaled; most helpful, most desirable. **2.** largest, greatest, most. *—adv.* **3.** most excellently, most successfully, beyond all others; in the highest degree; most, most of all, above all others; most profitably, most advantageously, to the greatest advantage. **4.** to the highest degree, most fully, most, most of all. *—n.* **5.** finest, most excellent, choice, elite, greatest, foremost, pick, cream, top. **6.** utmost, hardest, all that one can, the most that can be done, highest endeavor. **7.** most pleasant, nicest, loveliest, most competent, highest perfection. **8.** best wishes, kindest regards, greetings, compliments. **—Ant. 1, 3, 6, 7** worst. **2, 4, 6** least. **1** poorest. **3** most poorly.

bestial *adj.* brutal, cruel, beastly, ruthless, merciless, barbaric, barbarous, savage, depraved, inhumane. **—Ant.** tender, humane; kind, gentle, merciful.

bestow *v.* **1.** grant, confer, present, give, award, accord, render, impart, mete, dispense, *Slang* lay on; give away, donate, hand out, consign, turn over to, deliver, settle upon, apportion, deal out. **2.** apply, expend, devote, occupy; use, utilize, employ, spend, consume. **—Ant. 1** get, receive, acquire, procure, obtain, gain, earn, take, collect. **2** waste, lose, fritter away.

bet *v.* **1.** wager, gamble, make a bet, stake, risk, venture, speculate, chance, hazard, plunge. *—n.* **2.** wager, stake, speculation, gamble, ante.

betray *v.* **1.** be disloyal, be treacherous, be unfaithful, break faith with, sell out, inform against, play false with, double-cross, two-time, play Judas; deceive, trick, dupe; abandon, jilt. **2.** violate, let down; reveal, disclose, divulge, expose, uncover, show, tell, tell on, unmask, give away, lay bare, let slip, blurt out, *Slang* rat on, fink, squeal. **—Ant. 1** be loyal, be faithful, be true, keep the faith. **2** keep, guard, safeguard; preserve, hide, conceal, cover, mask.

betrayal *n.* **1.** treachery, treason, sedition, disloyalty, unfaithfulness, falseness, breach of faith, bad faith, perfidy, double-dealing, double-cross, two-timing; deception, chicanery, duplicity, trickery. **2.** revelation, disclosure, divulgence, telling, giving away, blurting out, violation. **—Ant. 1** loyalty, faithfulness. **2** keeping, guarding, safeguarding; preserving.

betroth *v.* engage, affiance, promise, pledge, espouse, contract, commit.

betrothal *n.* engagement, affiancing, troth, betrothing, espousal.

better *adj.* **1.** superior, finer, more excellent, of higher quality, greater; preferable, more useful, of greater value, more suitable, more desirable, more acceptable. **2.** greater, larger, longer, bigger. **3.** healthier, more healthy, stronger, fitter; improving, improved, mending, progressing, recovering. *—adv.* **4.** in a superior way, more completely, more thoroughly. **5.** more, greater; longer, farther. *—v.* **6.** improve, advance, further, forward, raise, upgrade, uplift, elevate, enhance, enrich, cultivate, refine, promote, increase, heighten, strengthen; ameliorate. **7.** surpass, exceed, outdo, outstrip, top. **—Syn. Study. 6** See IMPROVE. **—Ant. 1, 3, 4** worse, poorer. **1** inferior, lesser. **2** lesser, smaller; shorter. **3** sicker, weaker; failing, sinking. **5** less, under. **6** worsen, lessen, weaken; lower, downgrade, devaluate, depress, impoverish.

betterment *n.* improvement, advancement, amelioration, promotion, enrichment; correction, amendment, revision, regeneration, reform, reconstruction, rectification. **—Ant.** debasement, degeneration, decline, ruination, nemesis, destruction.

bevy *n.* **1.** flock, flight; group, coterie, covey, *(loosely)* brood, herd, pack, drove, swarm, clutch, gaggle, school, shoal. **2.** company, body, crowd, assemblage, gathering, collection, group, coterie, multitude, horde, band, party, host, throng.

bewail *v.* lament, mourn, grieve over, bemoan, moan over, cry over, weep over; regret, rue, deplore. **—Ant.** rejoice over, laugh over, celebrate, delight in.

beware *v.* look out, look out for, watch out for, take warning, guard against, take care, take precautions, be on the alert, be careful, be cautious, be wary, take heed, mind. **—Ant.** ignore, pay no attention to.

bewilder *v.* confuse, puzzle, perplex, bemuse, baffle, befuddle, mix up, muddle, addle, disconcert, nonplus, mystify, stupefy, fluster. **—Ant.** enlighten, inform, instruct, edify, educate, straighten out, advise, set straight, awaken.

bewilderment *n.* confusion, puzzlement, perplexity, mystification, frustration. **—Ant.** enlightenment, edification.

bewitch *v.* **1.** put under a spell, cast a spell on, *Informal* jinx, spook; bedevil. **2.** charm, enchant, entrance, captivate, fascinate, beguile, delight, enrapture, *Slang* turn on. **—Ant. 2** repulse; repel, disgust, displease, *Slang* turn off.

bias *n.* **1.** prejudice, leaning, inclination, bent, predilection, proneness, propensity, proclivity, tendency, feeling; fixed idea, preconceived idea, preconception, narrow view, slant, one-sidedness, unfairness, narrow-mindedness; bigotry, intolerance; partiality. **2.** angle, slant, diagonal line. *—v.* **3.** prejudice, predispose, sway. **—Syn. Study. 1** BIAS, PREJUDICE mean a strong inclination of the mind or a preconceived opinion about something or someone. A BIAS may be favorable or unfavorable: *bias in favor of or against an idea.* PREJUDICE implies a preformed judgment even more unreasoning than BIAS, and usu. implies an unfavorable opinion: *prejudice against a race.* **—Ant. 1** fairness, impartiality, dispassionateness, objectivity; open-mindedness, tolerance.

Bible *n.* **1.** the Holy Scriptures *(Hebrew and Christian)*; the Scriptures, Holy Writ, the Good Book, the Book, Gospel. **2. bible.** authority, guide; guidebook, reference book, handbook, manual.

bicker *v.* squabble, wrangle, quarrel, argue, spat, spar, dispute, haggle, disagree, fight. **—Ant.** agree, concur, accord, be of one mind; assent, consent, concede, acquiesce.

bicycle *n.* **1.** bike, two-wheeler, cycle, mountain bike, moped. *—v.* **2.** bike, cycle, ride.

bid *v.* **1.** command, order, direct, require, charge, call upon, enjoin, insist, instruct, demand, ordain; invite, summon, ask, request, call, beckon. **2.** tell, say, wish, greet. **3.** offer, proffer, tender, propose; submit an offer. *—n.* **4.** offer, offering, proposal, bidding; invitation. **5.** try, attempt, effort, endeavor. **—Ant. 1** forbid, prohibit, disallow, ban, bar.

bidding *n.* **1.** command, order, request, behest, demand, direction, charge, injunction, instruction, mandate, dictate; summons, summoning, invitation, bid, call, beck. **2.** offer, offering, offers, proffering, tendering, proposal.

bide *v.* **1.** remain, wait, stay, tarry, linger, abide, dwell. **2.** endure, put up with, suffer, tolerate, stand. —**Ant. 1** go, depart, leave. **2** resist, rebel against, abominate.

big *adj.* **1.** large, huge, enormous, vast, immense, gigantic, mammoth, great, colossal, monumental, grandiose; considerable, sizable, substantial, abundant, ample, prodigious; strapping, husky, bulky, hulking, heavy, massive. **2.** important, vital, major, consequential, significant, momentous, weighty; prominent, leading, eminent, notable, top, great, chief, main, prime, head, high. **3.** pretentious, arrogant, pompous, boastful, conceited, bragging, haughty. **4.** generous, magnanimous, benevolent, liberal, gracious, kind; noble, humane, honorable, just, princely, high-minded, chivalrous, heroic, great. **5.** mature, grown, grown-up, adult. —**Ant. 1** little, small, diminutive, microscopic, wee, tiny, petite, minute, miniature, bantam, pygmy, dwarf, pocket-sized, teeny, teeny-weeny, itsy-bitsy. **2** unimportant, insignificant, inconsequential, minor; low-ranking, subordinate, unknown. **3** ordinary, commonplace, modest, humble, unassuming, meek, unpretentious, mild, unpresuming, reserved, restrained, diffident. **4** stingy, cheap, petty, dishonorable, unjust, unchivalrous; ignoble, inhumane, unkind, cruel. **5** little, young, immature.

big-hearted *adj.* generous, unselfish, liberal, open-handed, free-handed, benevolent, unstinting, magnanimous, charitable, beneficent, open-hearted; bounteous, bountiful, lavish, prodigal, princely, handsome. —**Ant.** miserly, niggardly, stingy, tight-fisted, penny-pinching.

bigoted *adj.* prejudiced, intolerant, biased, narrow-minded, closed-minded. —**Ant.** unbigoted, unprejudiced, tolerant, unbiased, broad-minded, open-minded.

bigotry *n.* prejudice, intolerance, bias, narrow-mindedness, closed-mindedness; racism, discrimination, unfairness. —**Ant.** tolerance, open-mindedness, broad-mindedness.

big shot *n. Slang* wheel, big gun, big deal, wheeler-dealer, bigwig, big cheese, fat cat, VIP, high-muck-a-muck; mogul, nabob, magnate, dignitary, tycoon, somebody, name, personage. —**Ant.** nobody, nothing, cipher, nebbish, underling, minion, follower.

bilge *n.* nonsense, drivel, rubbish, stuff and nonsense, foolishness, gibberish, jabber; *Slang* bosh, bull, hogwash, twaddle, jabberwocky, balderdash, tosh, hooey, bunk, malarkey, piffle, humbug, baloney, rot, horsefeathers, tripe.

bilious *adj.* **1.** sick, queasy, nauseous, green at the gills, sickly, sickening; greenish, bilelike. **2.** irritable, peevish, ill-tempered, ill-humored, angry, grumpy, nasty, cranky, crabby, cross, grouchy, petulant, testy, touchy, snappish, short-tempered, cantankerous, huffy, out of sorts. —**Ant. 1** good, fine, healthy; attractive. **2** happy, pleasant, good-tempered, amicable, genial, cordial, gentle, mild, warm; agreeable, sympathetic, compliant, winsome.

bilk *v.* swindle, cheat, defraud, victimize, trick, dupe, deceive, bamboozle, hoodwink, fleece, gyp, rook, gull, cozen, *Slang* take, rip off.

bill *n.* **1.** statement, invoice, account, chit, charge, charges, fee, reckoning, tally. **2.** banknote, treasury note, treasury bill, greenback, silver certificate. **3.** piece of legislation, proposal; measure, act; law, statute, regulation, ordinance, decree. **4.** poster, placard, advertisement, bulletin; handbill, leaflet, circular, brochure. **5.** program, schedule, list, agenda, card, roster, calendar, catalog, inventory, ticket, register, docket.

billet *n.* **1.** quarters, lodging, lodgment, residence, dwelling, *Slang* digs. **2.** job, post, situation, berth, position, office, place, appointment. —*v.* **3.** lodge, house, quarter, put up, domicile.

billfold *n.* See WALLET.

billow *n.* **1.** wave, swell, breaker; surge, crest. **2.** wave, cloud, surge. —*v.* **3.** swell, puff up, balloon, belly; surge, roll. —**Ant. 1** trough. **3** deflate, collapse.

bind *v.* **1.** fasten, secure, tie, tie up, truss, gird, strap, rope, lash, hitch; join, attach, affix, stick, glue, paste. **2.** bandage, swathe; cover, encase, wrap. **3.** obligate, require, necessitate, oblige, compel, coerce, force, prescribe. **4.** border, edge, trim, rim, frame, fringe. **5.** confine, encumber, cramp; chafe. —**Ant. 1** untie, unbind, unfasten, unloose, loosen; free, set free, separate. **2** unbandage; unwrap, uncover. **3** free, release, exempt, absolve.

binge *n. Slang* drunken spree, spree, bender, blast, jag, fling, tear, bust, toot; carousal, orgy, bacchanalia.

birth *n.* **1.** being born; childbirth, bearing, delivery, parturition, confinement. **2.** descent, ancestry, family, parentage, extraction, lineage, derivation, breeding, genealogy, blood, stock, strain, origin, beginnings, background. **3.** start, beginning, commencement, origin, source, inception, genesis, emergence. —**Ant. 1** death; miscarriage, abortion. **3** conclusion, finale, end, finish, death.

bisect *v.* cut in two, cut in half, divide in two, split, split down the middle; intersect, cross.

bit *n.* **1.** small piece, piece, fragment, particle, smithereen, chip. **2.** small amount, trace, scrap, morsel, speck, dab, pinch, whit, iota, mite, smidgen, trifle, crumb, shred, snip, paring, shaving, grain, granule, drop, droplet, sprinkling, dollop. **3.** short while, little while, short time, spell, brief period, moment. **—Ant. 1** whole, entity, aggregation. **2** lot, mass, hunk, block, heap, the lion's share. **3** long time.

bitchy *adj.* spiteful, mean, vicious, malicious, malevolent, nasty, vindictive, cruel, wicked, heartless, hateful, backbiting, *Slang* catty.

bite *v.* **1.** seize with the teeth, eat into, nip, gnash, champ, gnaw, nibble; sting, pierce, prick. **2.** take hold, dig, grip. *—n.* **3.** small portion, small piece, mouthful, bit, speck, morsel, taste, scrap, crumb, shred, dab, snip. **4.** tooth wound, nip; sting, prick. **5.** sting, stinging, nip, smart.

biting *adj.* **1.** stinging, piercing, sharp, harsh, smarting, nipping, cutting, bitter. **2.** sarcastic, trenchant, mordant, sharp-tongued, cutting, stinging, piercing; caustic, withering, scathing. **—Ant. 1** mild. **2** pleasant, gentle, soothing, genial, flattering, complimentary.

bitter *adj.* **1.** sour, acid, acerbic, acrid, tart, sharp, caustic, biting, stinging, harsh, astringent. **2.** stinging, smarting, piercing, sharp, biting, severe. **3.** grievous, cruel, harsh, painful, wretched, distressing. **4.** resentful, sullen, morose, spiteful, crabbed, sour, rancorous, scornful, mean, angry. **—Ant. 1** sweet, sugary, saccharine, cloying; bland, mild, insipid, flat, dull. **2** mild, gentle, balmy. **3** happy, joyful, delightful, pleasant, gay; fortunate, lucky. **4** grateful, thankful, appreciative; friendly, amiable, genial, pleasant.

bizarre *adj.* strange, fantastic, weird, queer, freakish, grotesque, outlandish, odd, unusual, *Informal* way-out, *Slang* kooky, kinky, far-out. **—Syn. Study.** See FANTASTIC. **—Ant.** subdued, ordinary.

blabber *n.* **1.** chatter, jabber, prattle, drivel, palaver, babble, gab; *Slang* gabble, twaddle, blather, blah-blah, gobbledegook, mumbo-jumbo, gas, bull. *—v.* **2.** *Slang* gab, prattle, prate, blab, yak, blather, gibber, gabble.

blabbermouth *n.* gossip, gossiper, chatterbox, scandalmonger, gossipmonger, rumormonger, tattletale, busybody, talebearer, chatterer, informer, prattler, prater, jabberer, gabber, quidnunc; *Slang* blabber, bigmouth, liverlip.

black *adj.* **1.** coal-black, jet, raven, ebony, sable, inky, swarthy. **2.** dark, murky, lightless, stygian, sunless, moonless, unilluminated, unlighted. **3.** Often **Black.** Negro, colored, dark-skinned. **4.** gloomy, grim, dismal, somber, dim, calamitous. **5.** sullen, hostile, dark, furious, angry, threatening. **6.** evil, wicked, bad, nefarious. *—n.* **7.** ebony, jet, raven, sable. **8.** Often **Black.** Negro, Afro-American, black person. **—Ant. 1** white, snow-white, chalky, whitish. **2** bright, light, sunny, moonlit, illuminated, lighted, well-lighted, lit. **3** white, Caucasian. **4** optimistic, bright, happy, gay. **5** friendly, amiable, amicable, congenial, warm, pleased. **6** good, virtuous, wholesome, righteous, moral, honorable, upright, exemplary, pure. **7** white. **8** white, white person, Caucasian.

blackball *v.* ban, ostracize, banish, outlaw, proscribe, blacklist, boycott, exclude, debar, turn down, reject, vote against; snub, cut, cold-shoulder, send to Coventry. **—Ant.** welcome, invite, entice, ask, entreat, bid.

blacken *v.* **1.** make black, become black; darken, black. **2.** defame, dishonor, defile, disgrace, discredit, denigrate, stigmatize, tarnish, sully, stain, smear, befoul, besmirch, revile, slander, vilify, libel. **—Ant. 1** lighten, whiten; clear. **2** exalt, honor, credit, uplift, eulogize, praise.

blackguard *n.* villain, scoundrel, knave, rogue, rascal, cad, scamp, miscreant, rat, *Slang* louse, bastard, SOB. **—Ant.** hero; gentleman.

blacklist *v.* blackball, bar, debar, shut out, lock out, ban, preclude, exclude, reject, ostracize, shun. **—Ant.** welcome, accept, invite, meet with open arms.

blackmail *n.* **1.** hush money, extortion, shakedown, payoff, tribute. *—v.* **2.** extort, shake down, demand a payoff; threaten, force, coerce, *Slang* squeeze.

blade *n.* **1.** cutting edge, cutter; *(variously)* sword, knife, scalpel, razor; skate runner, sled runner. **2.** leaf, frond, needle, switch.

blah *n.* **1.** nonsense, bunkum, humbug, hooey, bosh, blather, eyewash, balderdash, twaddle, gibberish, hot air, guff, claptrap. *—adj.* **2.** lifeless, listless, nothing; tedious, dull, pedestrian, bland, dreary, characterless, uninteresting, unimaginative, humdrum, monotonous. **—Ant. 2** vivacious, energetic, alive; trenchant, gripping, dynamic.

blame *v.* **1.** hold responsible, accuse, charge; fault, find fault with, reproach, reprove, censure, condemn, rebuke, castigate, criticize, disapprove. *—n.* **2.** responsibility, accountability, liability, guilt, onus, fault, culpability, burden; accusation, charge, finger pointing, recrimination; reproach, censure, condemnation, reproof, rebuke, criticism, denunciation, castigation, remonstrance. **—Ant. 1** exonerate, vindicate, absolve, acquit, clear, exculpate; excuse, justify, forgive; praise, laud, acclaim, commend, compliment, approve of. **2** exoneration, vindication, absolution; excuse, alibi; praise, acclaim, commendation, compliment, congratulations, tribute, credit, honor, glory, distinction.

blameless *adj.* not responsible, not at fault, guiltless, not guilty, innocent, unblamable, clear, inculpable; irreproachable, spotless, unspotted, unsullied, untainted, unstained, unblemished, uncorrupted, unimpeachable. **—Ant.** responsible, at fault, guilty, implicated, culpable; sullied, tainted, censurable, reprovable.

blanch *v.* whiten, turn pale; bleach, fade, lighten. **—Ant.** darken, blacken; brighten, color, stain, dye.

bland *adj.* **1.** uninteresting, unexciting, dull, uninspiring, unstimulating, tedious, tiresome, monotonous, humdrum, flat, vapid, prosaic, *Slang* blah, nothing. **2.** mild, balmy, calm, calming, tranquil, quiet, moderate, temperate, unruffled, even, smooth, soothing, benign, peaceful, peaceable, untroubled, nonirritating. **—Ant. 1** interesting, exciting, electrifying, sensational, thrilling, astonishing, stimulating, inspiring, stirring, rousing, overpowering, moving. **2** turbulent, tempestuous, excited, volatile, explosive; harsh, severe, rough, irritating, annoying.

blandishment, Often **blandishments** *n.* flattery, cajolery, coaxing, wheedling, inveiglement, ingratiation, blarney, sweet talk. **—Ant.** intimidation, threats, scolding, insults, bullying, browbeating.

blank *adj.* **1.** not written on, clean, unmarked, unused, not filled out, not filled in; empty, vacant, clear, plain. **2.** vacant, empty, inexpressive, expressionless, unrecognizing, inane, uninterested, thoughtless, dull, vacuous, hollow, void. **3.** empty, idle, meaningless, futile, wasted, unrewarding, useless, worthless, valueless, inconsequential, insignificant, profitless, unprofitable, fruitless, unproductive. **—***n.* **4.** empty space, space, void, gap; emptiness, hollowness, vacuum, vacancy. **—Ant. 1** marked, filled out, filled in, full, completed. **2** thoughtful, interested, meaningful, expressive, intelligent, alert, sharp. **3** full, filled, busy; rewarding, valuable, worthwhile, useful, meaningful, significant, consequential, profitable, fruitful, productive.

blanket *n.* **1.** comforter, coverlet, quilt; throw, Afghan. **2.** covering, cover, coating, coat, mantle, carpet, overlay, film, veneer. **—***v.* **3.** cover, carpet, coat, overlay, cloak.

blare *v.* sound loudly, blast, resound, scream, bellow, roar; trumpet, make a fanfare, peal, honk. **—Ant.** mute, stifle; hum, murmur, whisper.

blarney *n.* flattery, fawning, overpraise, honeyed words, sweet words, line; cajolery, wheedling, inveigling, coaxing, blandishments; fanciful talk, exaggeration, overstatement, hyperbole, stories, fibs, *Slang* hot air, pitch, snow job, *Informal* spiel. **—Ant.** truth, frankness, candidness, guilelessness, directness.

blasé *adj.* bored, unexcited, unenthusiastic, unconcerned, uninterested, indifferent, insouciant, nonchalant, world-weary, spiritless, unmovable, apathetic; jaded, surfeited, gorged, full, glutted, saturated, satisfied. **—Ant.** enthusiastic, excited, interested, concerned, spirited.

blasphemous *adj.* irreverent, profane, sacrilegious, irreligious, impious, ungodly, godless. **—Ant.** reverent, religious, pious, godly.

blasphemy *n.* profanity, profanation, irreverence, sacrilege, impiety, impiousness; cursing, swearing. **—Ant.** prayer, praying; veneration, reverence, adoration; blessing, benediction, thanksgiving.

blast *n.* **1.** gust, gale, wind; surge, burst, rush, roar. **2.** loud noise, blare, scream, roar, bellow, bleat, shriek, toot, honk, peal. **3.** explosion, detonation, report, burst, boom, discharge, eruption. **—***v.* **4.** sound loudly, blare, resound, scream, shriek, roar, bellow, honk, peal, toot. **5.** explode, dynamite, torpedo, bomb, shell; burst, level, blow up, bore. **—Syn. Study. 1** See WIND.

blatant *adj.* **1.** obvious, unmistakable, clear, conspicuous, prominent, glaring, overt, flagrant. **2.** loud, obtrusive, offensive, crude, uncouth, gross, crass, coarse, vulgar, undignified, indelicate, cheap, tawdry, brazen, ill-mannered, unrefined, tasteless, unsubtle, ungenteel, unpolished; noisy, blaring, clamorous, harsh, ear-splitting, deafening, piercing. **—Ant.** inconspicuous, subtle. **1** unnoticeable, hidden. **2** unobtrusive, acquiescent, refined, genteel, dignified, delicate, well-mannered, tasteful, in good taste, cultured, polished, high-class, *Informal* classy; quiet, subdued, soft.

blaze *n.* **1.** fire, flame, flames, conflagration. **2.** glow, gleam, shimmer, glitter, flash, shine, glare, flare, beam, ray; radiance, brilliance, brightness, effulgence, resplendence. **3.** outburst, burst, blast, flash, rush; eruption, outbreak, torrent, explosion. **—***v.* **4.** burn brightly, burn, flame. **5.** glow, gleam, shine, glisten, glitter, shimmer, be resplendent, be bright, be brilliant; flash, beam, glare, flame, flare.

bleach *v.* whiten, blanch, lighten, fade,

make pale, wash out. —**Ant.** blacken, darken; color, stain, dye.

bleak *adj.* **1.** bare, barren, windswept, weather-beaten, desolate. **2.** gloomy, dreary, dismal, grim, depressing, cheerless; unpromising, distressing, somber, forbidding. **3.** bitter, raw, cold, icy, piercing, biting, nipping, frosty, chill, wintry. —**Ant. 1** covered with vegetation, wooded, forested; sheltered, protected, warm, cheerful, comfortable. **2** bright, cheerful, cheery, sunny; pleasant, genial; promising, encouraging. **3** mild, balmy, soft, warm, springlike.

blemish *n.* **1.** flaw, imperfection, defect, disfigurement; spot, blotch, blot, mark, stain, taint, *Slang* zit. —*v.* **2.** flaw, mar, spoil, tarnish, sully, taint, stain, smudge, smirch; spot, mark, blot, blotch, blur, disfigure. —**Syn. Study. 1** See DEFECT. —**Ant. 1** perfection, improvement; decoration, ornament, complement, refinement. **2** perfect, improve, complete, refine, enhance; purify, purge, reclaim, restore, rectify, correct.

blend *v.* **1.** mix, merge, combine, unite, mingle, intermingle; fuse, compound, melt together, incorporate, coalesce, amalgamate. **2.** harmonize, go well, complement. —*n.* **3.** mixture, mix, combination, merger, mergence, mingling, concoction; compound, amalgam, fusion. —**Syn. Study. 1** See MIX. —**Ant. 1** separate, divide. **2** clash. **3** separation, division.

bless *v.* **1.** make holy, consecrate, sanctify, hallow, dedicate, give benediction; anoint, baptize. **2.** favor, oblige, honor, benefit, endow, bestow, ordain, grace, give. **3.** guard, protect, watch over, support. —**Ant. 1** curse, anathematize. **2** curse, condemn, disfavor; handicap, harm, injure.

blessed *adj.* **1.** revered, holy, hallowed, sacred, sanctified, consecrated, adored, venerated. **2.** joyous, joyful, happy, felicitous, blissful, wonderful. **3.** fortunate, favored, lucky, endowed, graced. —**Ant. 1** cursed, accursed, anathematized. **2** unhappy, sad, unfortunate, grievous. **3** condemned, deprived.

blessing *n.* **1.** consecration, sanctification, dedication, hallowing, invocation, benediction; grace, prayer of thanks, thanksgiving. **2.** advantage, benefit, good, good fortune, favor, gift, bounty, gain, profit. **3.** approval, consent, concurrence, permission, leave, support, sanction, backing, good wishes, favor, regard. —**Ant.** curse. **1** imprecation, malediction, anathema. **2** deprivation, misfortune, disadvantage, detriment, drawback, harm, injury, damage. **3** disapproval, objection, disapprobation, condemnation, denunciation, censure, reproof; ill will, disfavor.

blight *n.* **1.** plant disease, pestilence; *(loosely)* dry rot, rot, rust, fungus, mildew, decay. **2.** affliction, cancer, curse, plague, scourge, pestilence, canker, contamination, corruption, *Slang* pox. —*v.* **3.** spoil, ruin, wreck, kill, destroy, smash, demolish, blast, crush; wither, shrivel, cripple, thwart, rot, injure, harm, frustrate. —**Ant. 2** blessing, good, favor, service, boon, bounty. **3** benefit, help, aid, improve, better, advance, further, foster, promote.

blind *adj.* **1.** sightless, unable to see, without vision, unseeing. **2.** ignorant, unaware, unknowing, unobserving, unobservant, incognizant, uncomprehending, unconscious of, unenlightened, unseeing, obtuse; unmindful, unfeeling, dull, insensitive, unperceptive or imperceptive, undiscerning, indifferent, neglectful, inattentive, heedless, unconcerned, uninterested, insouciant. **3.** uncontrolled, uncontrollable, unthinking, mindless, unreasonable, irrational, senseless, insane. **4.** hidden, concealed, obscure, unnoticeable, unnoticed. —*n.* **5.** shade, sun shield. **6.** cover, screen, front, subterfuge, disguise, masquerade, camouflage; dodge, ruse, pretext, deception, *Informal* smoke screen. —**Ant. 1** sighted, seeing. **2** aware, conscious, knowledgeable, observant, cognizant, alive to, awake to; mindful, sensitive, discerning, attentive, heedful, concerned. **3** controlled, controllable, rational. **4** in plain sight, obvious, noticeable, open.

blink *v.* **1.** wink, nictitate, squint, bat the eyes; waver, vacillate, falter, flinch. **2.** twinkle, flash, flicker, sparkle, glimmer, shine, shimmer.

bliss *n.* happiness, joy, ecstasy, delight, rapture, glee, gladness, luxury, heaven, paradise; exhilaration, exaltation, jubilation. —**Ant.** misery, agony, anguish, torment, distress; sorrow, sadness, grief, unhappiness; dejection, depression, gloom.

blithe *adj.* **1.** joyous, merry, happy, cheery, cheerful, gay, sunny, radiant, glad, gleeful, jolly, jovial, mirthful; carefree, light-hearted, frolicking, debonair, sprightly, jaunty, lively, ebullient, exaltant, airy, blithesome. **2.** heedless, careless, thoughtless, unmindful, insensitive, unconscious, uncaring, unfeeling, indifferent, unconcerned, blind, casual, inconsiderate. —**Ant. 1** sad, unhappy, sorrowful, dejected, depressed, gloomy, cheerless, glum, morose, dour, melancholy, heavy-hearted. **2** thoughtful, considerate, concerned, solicitous, obliging.

blizzard *n.* snowstorm, tempest, blow, squall, blast, gale, snow blast, snow squall, flurry, snowfall, winter storm.

bloat *v.* distend, swell, puff up, expand,

dilate, inflate, blow up, balloon, enlarge. —**Ant.** shrink, contract, shrivel.

bloc *n.* faction, group, wing, body, clique, ring, cabal; alliance, coalition, combination, combine, union.

block *n.* **1.** brick, bar, cube, square. **2.** obstruction, barrier, obstacle, blockade, bar, impediment; hindrance, interference, blockage. —*v.* **3.** obstruct, blockade, bar, choke, stop up, jam; hinder, impede, check, halt, prevent, thwart. **4.** shape, form, mold; reshape, reform. —**Ant. 3** clear, unblock, unbar, open, free; advance, further, forward, promote, foster, facilitate.

blockade *n.* block, blockage, roadblock, barrier, barricade, impediment, hindrance, obstruction, hurdle, stoppage, bar, restriction, check, *Mil.* checkpoint; dam, fortification, stockade, dike, earthworks, levee, parapet.

blockhead *n.* fool, dunce, nitwit, nincompoop, simpleton, booby, klutz, mushhead, noodlehead, *German* dummkopf, dum-dum, *Yiddish* yutz, featherbrain, dolt, dummy, harebrain, jackass, fathead; imbecile, moron.

blond, blonde *adj.* **1.** light-colored, yellowish, yellow, gold, golden, flaxen. **2.** fair, fair-skinned, light-complexioned, light, pale, fair-haired. —*n.* **3.** light tan, yellowish tan, whitish brown. **4.** blond-haired woman; person having fair skin and hair. —**Ant.** brunette, brunet. **1** dark, black. **2** dark, dark-skinned, olive-complexioned.

blood *n.* **1.** life fluid, vital fluid, gore. **2.** life-blood, source, vital principle, vital force, vitality. **3.** temper, passion, temperament, spirit. **4.** extraction, lineage, descent, ancestry, heritage, stock, family, family line, birth, consanguinity.

bloodshed *n.* carnage, killing, slaying, spilling of blood, slaughter, massacre, pogrom, bloodletting, butchery, manslaughter, murder, mass murder, blood feud, blood bath, gore.

bloodthirsty *adj.* murderous, homicidal, savage, inhuman, brutal, murdering, barbarous, ruthless, bestial, bloody, cutthroat, sanguinary, sanguineous.

bloom *n.* **1.** blossom, flower, bud; flowerage, blossoming, florescence. **2.** glow, flush, rosiness, radiance, luster, shine, beauty, vigor, zest, strength, prime, heyday; flowering, blossoming, flourishing. —*v.* **3.** flower, blossom, burgeon, sprout, bear fruit, fructify. **4.** flourish, thrive, fare well, prosper, succeed, bear fruit, germinate, burgeon; develop, grow, flare. —**Ant. 2** pallor, grayness, wanness, ashenness; decay, decadence, blight. **3** wither, die; be sterile. **4** wither, fade, fail, wane.

blooper *n.* mistake, error, blunder, lapse, slip, gaffe; *Informal* goof, *Slang* boo-boo, fluff, bobble, boner, screwup, botch.

blossom *n.* **1.** flower, bloom. —*v.* **2.** flower, bloom, burgeon. **3.** bloom, grow, develop; flourish, thrive, burgeon, progress. —**Ant. 2** wither, die, be sterile. **3** wither, fade, fail, diminish.

blot *n.* **1.** blotch, spot, splotch, smudge, smear, stain, mark, discoloration. **2.** blemish, flaw, blotch, taint, stain, stigma, bad mark, smirch. —*v.* **3.** smear, smudge, splotch, blotch; spot, stain, besmirch. **4.** soak up, absorb, take up; remove, dry. —**Ant. 2** credit, distinction, honor, feather in one's cap.

blotch *n.* spot, splotch, mark, blot.

blow *n.* **1.** hit, knock, punch, smack, whack, clout, thump, sock, wallop, box, jab, bash, crack, bang, belt, cuff. **2.** shock, jolt, upset, disappointment, rebuff, reversal, detriment; tragedy, disaster, calamity, misfortune, catastrophe, affliction. **3.** gale, squall, tempest, windstorm, storm, wind, gust of wind, blast. —*v.* **4.** move by wind; gust, puff. **5.** exhale, breathe, expel air, puff. **6.** sound, toot, honk, whistle, blast, play. **7.** burst, explode, blow out, pop, burn out. —**Ant. 1** caress, pat. **2** comfort, relief, blessing, consolation; achievement, victory. **3** calm. **4** still. **5** inhale.

blue *adj.* **1.** bluish, azure, cerulean, sky blue, cobalt blue, cobalt, Prussian blue, navy blue, navy, robin's-egg blue, powder blue, sapphire, lapis lazuli, indigo, aqua, aquamarine, ultramarine, turquoise. **2.** depressed, dejected, sad, gloomy, despondent, downcast, low, downhearted, disconsolate, morose, melancholy, doleful, down, down in the dumps, down in the mouth. —**Ant. 2** elated, exultant, excited, exhilarated, jubilant, happy, overjoyed, joyful, pleased, delighted, blithe, glad, gay, merry, jolly, up, up in the clouds, in high spirits.

bluff[1] *adj.* **1.** outspoken, plain-spoken, blunt, frank, open, unceremonious, candid, direct, straightforward, forthright, bold, headlong; abrupt, brusque, curt, rough, crusty. —*n.* **2.** promontory, cliff, palisade, headland, bank, ridge, precipice, escarpment, crag, peak. —**Ant. 1** retiring, reticent, repressed, hesitant, unsure, mealymouthed, shy; indirect, roundabout, deceptive; formal, ceremonious, mannered, tactful.

bluff[2] *v.* **1.** deceive, delude, humbug, mislead, fool, bamboozle, dupe, *Slang* fake out; fake, sham, lie, counterfeit, pretend, hoax. —*n.* **2.** pretense, fake, sham, fraud, lie, humbug, deception, subterfuge; idle boast, boast, bragging. **3.** bluffer, pretender, fraud, faker; liar, fast-talker, boaster, braggadocio, windbag. —**Ant. 2** truth, fact.

blunder *n.* **1.** mistake, error, slip; impropriety, indiscretion, gaucherie, gaffe, faux pas, boner, *Informal* goof, *Slang* boo-boo. **—***v.* **2.** make a mistake, be in error, be at fault, slip up, *Informal* goof, *Slang* make a boo-boo. **3.** flounder, bumble, bungle, stumble, stagger. **—Syn. Study. 1** See MISTAKE. **—Ant. 1** achievement, success. **2** be correct, be accurate, be exact. **3** go alertly, move purposely.

blunt *adj.* **1.** dull, dulled, unsharpened; thick, edgeless, unpointed. **2.** outspoken, candid, frank, straightforward, explicit, to the point; curt, abrupt, brusque, rough, tactless, insensitive. **—***v.* **3.** dull, numb, benumb, weaken, deaden, make insensitive, stupefy; moderate, mitigate, soften, lighten. **—Syn. Study. 2** BLUNT, BRUSQUE, CURT characterize manners and speech. BLUNT suggests unnecessary frankness and a lack of regard for the feelings of others: *blunt and tactless remarks.* BRUSQUE connotes a sharpness and abruptness that borders on rudeness: *a brusque denial.* CURT applies esp. to disconcertingly concise language: *a curt reply.* **—Ant. 1** sharp, keen, acute; edged, serrated, pointed. **2** tactful, subtle, diplomatic, politic, sensitive, polite, courteous, polished. **3** sharpen, hone, put an edge on, make keen; stimulate, excite, animate, vitalize.

blur *v.* **1.** cloud, becloud, fog, befog, make hazy, dim, bedim, darken, obscure, veil, make indistinct. **2.** smear, smudge, blotch, spread, run, blot. **—***n.* **3.** smudge, smear, blotch, splotch, blot. **4.** confusion, fog, haze, cloud, obscurity. **—Ant. 1** clear, brighten, outline, spotlight.

blush *v.* **1.** flush, redden, turn red, color, grow red. **—***n.* **2.** reddening, rosy tint, pinkish tinge. **—Ant. 1** blanch, turn pale, pale, turn ashen.

bluster *v.* **1.** boast, swagger, rant, brag, crow, gloat, bloviate; protest, threaten, storm, bully. **—***n.* **2.** bluff, swagger, swaggering, bravado, bombast, boasting, ranting, gloating, crowing, boisterousness, noisy talk, noise. **—Ant. 1** be retiring, be reticent, be shy. **2** shyness, meekness, mildness, reticence.

board *n.* **1.** plank, piece of lumber; slat, clapboard, panel, deal, batten. **2.** meals, daily meals, food. **3.** board of directors, directors, council, tribunal. **—***v.* **4.** lodge, house, quarter, put up; billet, bed; feed. **5.** enter, get on, go onto, embark. **—Ant. 5** leave, get off or out of, disembark, deplane, detrain.

boast *v.* **1.** brag, crow; vaunt, talk big, blow one's own horn. **2.** be proud of, speak proudly of, show off, exhibit, flaunt; have, contain, possess. **—***n.* **3.** brag, vaunt. **—Syn. Study. 1** BOAST, BRAG imply vocal self-praise or claims to superiority over others. BOAST usu. refers to a particular ability, possession, etc., that may justify a good deal of pride: *He boasts of his ability as a singer.* BRAG, a more informal term, usu. suggests a more ostentatious and exaggerated boasting but less well-founded: *He brags loudly about his golf game.* **—Ant. 1** disclaim, disavow, deprecate, depreciate. **2** be ashamed, cover up. **3** disclaimer, disavowal.

boastful *adj.* conceited, cocky, vainglorious, puffed up, full of swagger, pretentious, pompous, cocksure, bragging, braggadocio; vaunting, crowing, exaggerated, inflated, swollen. **—Ant.** modest, self-disparaging, deprecating, self-belittling.

boat *n.* vessel, craft, ship.

bob[1] *v.* move up and down; bounce, hop, leap, jump about, dance; duck, nod.

bob[2] *v.* crop, shorten, cut, clip, shear, trim; dock.

bodily *adj.* **—Syn. Study.** See PHYSICAL.

body *n.* **1.** person, being; thing, quantity, mass. **2.** physique, figure, build, form, shape; frame, main part, torso, trunk. **3.** corpse, remains, deceased, cadaver, carcass, *Slang* stiff. **4.** majority, bulk, mass, group, throng, mob, multitude. **5.** assembly, confederation, federation, congress, council, faction, bloc, coalition, combine, league, society, force, brotherhood. **6.** consistency, thickness, stiffness, cohesion. **—Syn. Study. 3** BODY, CARCASS, CORPSE, CADAVER all refer to a physical organism, usu. human or animal. BODY denotes the material substance of a human or animal, either living or dead: *the muscles in a horse's body; the body of an accident victim.* CARCASS means the dead body of an animal, unless applied humorously or contemptuously to the human body: *a sheep's carcass; Save your carcass.* CORPSE usu. refers to the dead body of a human being: *preparing a corpse for burial.* CADAVER refers to a dead body, usu. a human one used for scientific study: *dissection of cadavers in anatomy classes.* **—Ant. 2** soul, spirit; mind, intellect, intelligence, psyche; limb, wing, protuberance. **4** minority; handful, scattering, few.

bog *n.* **1.** marsh, marshland, swamp, swampland, wetlands, mire, fen, spongy ground, quagmire, morass. **—***v.* **2.** be stuck, mire, sink, be partially buried, be partially immersed. **—Ant. 1** dry ground, firm ground.

bogus *adj.* counterfeit, fraudulent, spurious, forged; artificial, synthetic, pseudo, fake, imitation, simulated, fake, phony, dummy, sham, false, feigned, make-believe, pretend, ersatz. **—Ant.** genuine, real, authentic, legitimate, true, bona fide, actual, natural.

Bohemian, Also **bohemian** *n.* **1.** nonconformist, hippie, beatnik. *—adj.* **2.** nonconformist, unconventional, unorthodox. **—Ant. 1** conformist, *Slang* square, straight. **2** conventional, conformist, *Slang* square, straight.

boil *v.* **1.** simmer, seethe, brew; parboil, stew. **2.** bubble, froth, foam, churn, well up, toss, simmer. **3.** rage, rave, storm, seethe, fume, burn, sizzle, smolder, simmer, stew; fulminate, rant, foam, blow one's cool, blow one's stack, blow one's top, *Slang* raise Cain; quiver, chafe, bristle. *—n.* **4.** sore, abscess, fester, pustule, carbuncle, furuncle. **—Syn. Study. 3** BOIL, SEETHE, SIMMER, STEW are used figuratively to refer to agitated states of emotion. To BOIL suggests being very hot with anger or rage: *He was boiling when the guests arrived late.* To SEETHE is to be deeply stirred, violently agitated, or greatly excited: *a mind seething with conflicting ideas.* To SIMMER means to be at the point of bursting out or boiling over: *to simmer with curiosity; to simmer with anger.* To STEW is an informal term that means to worry, or to be in a restless state of anxiety and excitement: *to stew over one's troubles.* **—Ant. 1** freeze; cool, gel. **2** subside, calm. **3** calm, appease, assuage, simmer down, *Slang* chill out.

boisterous *adj.* clamorous, uproarious, noisy, loud; disorderly, wild, rowdy, unruly, obstreperous, out-of-hand, unrestrained. **—Ant.** quiet, silent, still, calm, peaceful, tranquil, serene, sedate; well-behaved, restrained.

bold *adj.* **1.** brave, courageous, valiant, unafraid, fearless, heroic, valorous, stalwart, dauntless, indomitable, stouthearted, lionhearted, intrepid, unshrinking; daring, audacious, adventuresome, daredevil, imaginative, creative. **2.** rude, impudent, fresh, insolent; brazen, impertinent, defiant, cheeky, saucy, brash, forward, presumptuous; fiery, spirited. **3.** colorful, loud, eye-catching, hot, vivid, striking, flashy. **—Syn. Study.** BOLD, BRAZEN, FORWARD, PRESUMPTUOUS refer to behavior or manners that break the rules of propriety. BOLD suggests shamelessness and immodesty: *a bold stare.* BRAZEN suggests the same, together with a defiant manner: *a brazen liar.* FORWARD implies making oneself unduly prominent or bringing oneself to notice with too much assurance: *The forward young man challenged the speaker.* PRESUMPTUOUS implies overconfidence, or taking too much for granted: *It was presumptuous of her to think she could defeat the champion.* **—Ant. 1** cowardly, fainthearted, fearful, shrinking, flinching; *Slang* chicken, chickenhearted, yellow; mundane, ordinary, modest, unimaginative, uncreative or noncreative. **2** meek, timid, timorous, retiring, bashful, shy; courteous, polite, gracious, tactful. **3** pale, dull, soft, colorless, pastel, conservative, cold, cool.

bolster *v.* **1.** support, brace, prop up, hold up, buttress, reinforce, maintain, sustain, shore up, shoulder, cradle. **2.** support, uphold, sustain, strengthen, reinforce, add to, help, aid, assist. *—n.* **3.** cushion, pillow. **—Ant. 1** weigh down. **2** diminish, lessen, weaken, tear down.

bolt *n.* **1.** sliding bar, bar, catch, fastener, rod, latch, lock. **2.** fastening rod, pin, peg, dowel, rivet. **3.** dash, rush, run, scoot, sprint; spring, jump, leap. **4.** roll, length. **5.** thunderbolt, firebolt, shaft, dart, stroke, flash, brand. *—v.* **6.** bar, latch, lock, fasten, secure. **7.** dash, rush, run, fly, speed, hasten, hurry, scoot, flee, tear, hurtle, sprint; spring, jump, leap, bound. **8.** eat rapidly, gobble, gulp, swallow whole, wolf. **—Ant. 6** unbolt, unlatch, unbar, unlock, unfasten, open. **7** saunter, stroll, amble, creep, sneak.

bomb *n.* **1.** explosive device, explosive missile, grenade, mine, *Slang* egg. **2.** failure, fiasco, flop, dud, *Slang* lemon, bust, washout. *—v.* **3.** set off a bomb in, drop a bomb on, throw a bomb at, bombard. **4.** fail, flop, fizzle, *Slang* wash out.

bombard *v.* **1.** rain explosives upon, fire upon, batter, pepper, open fire on, shell, bomb, cannonade, strafe. **2.** barrage, besiege, beset, pepper, assail, assault, attack; harass, pester, hound, worry.

bombastic *adj.* grandiloquent, pompous, magniloquent, flowery, pretentious, windy, padded, inflated, tumid, turgid, verbose, wordy. **—Syn. Study.** BOMBASTIC, FLOWERY, PRETENTIOUS all describe a use of language more elaborate than is justified by or appropriate to the content being expressed. BOMBASTIC suggests language with a theatricality or staginess of style far too powerful or declamatory for the meaning or sentiment being expressed: *a bombastic sermon on the evils of gambling.* FLOWERY describes language filled with extravagant images and ornate expressions: *a flowery eulogy.* PRETENTIOUS refers specifically to language that is purposely inflated in an effort to impress: *a pretentious essay filled with obscure allusions.* **—Ant.** temperate, unpretentious, modest, natural, simple, unaffected, deflated, quiet.

bona fide *adj.* genuine, real, actual,

true, authentic, legitimate; honest, sincere, in good faith, honorable, lawful, legal. **—Ant.** counterfeit, fraudulent, spurious, forged; artificial, synthetic, imitation, simulated, fake, phony, sham, bogus, false, feigned, make-believe, pretended.

bonanza *n.* windfall, sudden profit, gold mine. **—Ant.** disaster, loss.

bond *n.* **1.** Usu. **bonds.** bindings, fastenings; *(variously)* rope, cord, chains, shackles, manacles, handcuffs, irons, fetters. **2.** tie, affinity, allegiance, union, connection, knot, link, attachment. **3.** guarantee, pledge, compact, agreement, obligation, stipulation, promise. **4.** promissory note, security, certificate; scrip.

bondage *n.* slavery, servitude, enslavement, vassalage, serfdom, captivity, yoke; bonds, shackles, chains, fetters. **—Syn. Study.** See SLAVERY. **—Ant.** freedom, liberty, emancipation, independence, liberation.

bonus *n.* gift, gratuity, premium, dividend, honorarium, prize, reward, benefit, bounty. **—Syn. Study.** BONUS, BOUNTY, PREMIUM refer to a gift or an additional payment. A BONUS is a gift to reward performance, paid either by an employer or by a government: *a bonus based on salary; a soldier's bonus.* A BOUNTY is a public reward offered to stimulate interest in a specific purpose or undertaking and to encourage performance: *a bounty for killing wolves.* A PREMIUM is usu. something additional given as an inducement to buy, produce, or the like: *a premium received with a magazine subscription.* **—Ant.** fine, penalty, withholding.

book *n.* **1.** volume, written work, bound work, tome, opus, treatise, publication, audiobook, eBook. **2.** notebook; album, tablet. **—*v.*** **3.** reserve, make reservations, arrange for, engage, procure, schedule, program, slate, line up, bill. **4.** register, list, record, enter, put down, write down, mark down, note, insert, post, enroll; file, catalog, index; charge, accuse, indict. **—Ant. 3** cancel, disengage.

boom¹ *n.* **1.** bang, roar, rumble, blast, thunder. **2.** prosperous period, successful period, good times; upsurge, upturn, boost, spurt, thrust, push, expansion, growth, development, increase, gain, improvement, advance. **—*v.*** **3.** bang, rumble, roar, blast, thunder. **4.** thrive, flourish, prosper, increase, grow, develop, spurt. **—Ant. 2** depression, recession, bad times, hard times, slump, downturn, decrease, bust, burst. **4** fail, slump.

boom² *n.* horizontal pole, spar; beam, shaft, bar.

boondocks *n.* backwater, backwoods, hinterland, backcountry, frontier, provinces; *Slang* boonies, bush, outback, veld, sticks, Podunk, squaresville, nowheresville.

boor *n.* lout, oaf, yokel, churl, bumpkin, clodhopper, guttersnipe, peasant, rube, hick, hayseed, rustic; vulgarian, brute, philistine. **—Ant.** sophisticate, cosmopolitan; gentleman, gallant, lady.

boorish *adj.* crude, rude, coarse, vulgar, unrefined, unpolished, uncouth, gauche, loutish, oafish, rustic, peasantlike. **—Ant.** genteel, polite, polished, cultured, refined, cultivated, gentlemanly, courtly, gallant, lady-like; sophisticated, urbane, cosmopolitan.

boost *v.* **1.** lift, raise, heave, hoist, elevate, push, shove, pitch, give a leg up. **2.** increase, raise, advance, raise upward, add to, enlarge, expand, advance, develop, improve. **3.** promote, advance, foster, further, forward, support, sustain, nurture; speak well of, propound, praise, extol, acclaim, laud, urge on, root for, put in a good word for, stick up for. **—*n.*** **4.** lift, heave, hoist, raise, shove, push. **5.** increase, raise, hike, addition, increment; growth, development, enlargement, expansion, advance, improvement, rise, pickup, upsurge, upswing, upturn, upward trend. **6.** favorable mention, good word, good review, free ad, *Informal* plug, promotion, praise, compliment, applause. **—Ant. 1, 2** lower, let down, push down, drop. **2** decrease, reduce, diminish, lessen, subtract from, deduct, cut, curtail, crop, pare, whittle down, scale down, moderate, ease. **3** hinder, hold back, condemn, criticize, *Informal* knock. **5** decrease, reduction, cutback, curtailment, lessening, decline, fall, falling off, diminution, dwindling, wane, ebb, deterioration. **6** condemnation, criticism, *Informal* knock.

booth *n.* **1.** compartment, enclosure, cubbyhole, nook; hutch, coop, pen. **2.** stall, stand, counter, table; tent.

booty *n.* loot, plunder, spoils, pillage, takings, pickings; prize, gain, winnings, *Slang* boodle. **—Ant.** fine, forfeiture.

border *n.* **1.** edge, rim, periphery, perimeter, circumference, extremity, verge, margin, brim, brink, curb, hem, skirt, frame, outskirt, fringe, pale, limit. **2.** frontier, boundary, line. **—*v.*** **3.** be next to, adjoin, join, flank, touch, neighbor on, abut, skirt, verge upon. **4.** edge, trim, fringe, befringe, frame, bind, rim, hem, skirt. **—Syn. Study. 2** See BOUNDARY. **—Ant. 1** interior, inside, middle, center.

borderline *adj.* marginal, halfway, problematic, open, indefinite, unclear, uncertain, ambivalent, indefinable, obscure, indeterminate, equivocal, inexact, undecided, vague, ambiguous, unsettled. —**Ant.** decisive, unambiguous, clear, precise, positive, definite.

bore[1] *v.* **1.** be tedious to, tire, weary, fatigue, exhaust, tax one's patience, wear out, *Slang* be a drag. —*n.* **2.** dull person, tiresome thing, *Slang* drag, drip, wet blanket. —**Ant. 1** excite, interest, amuse, stimulate, delight. **2** life of the party, *Slang* ball, gas.

bore[2] *v.* **1.** drill, tunnel, hollow out, gouge out, sink, pierce, burrow, drive. —*n.* **2.** inside diameter, caliber. —**Ant. 1** fill, plug.

boredom *n.* dullness, tedium, ennui, monotony, tediousness, doldrums, weariness. —**Ant.** excitement, interest, stimulation; amusement, entertainment, diversion.

boring *adj.* dull, unexciting, uninteresting, tiresome, monotonous, humdrum, repetitious, tedious, wearisome, flat, stale, insipid, tiring. —**Ant.** exciting, interesting, stimulating, exhilarating; amusing, entertaining.

born *adj.* **1.** given birth to, brought forth, delivered. **2.** natural, innate, intuitive; endowed from birth..

borrow *v.* **1.** use, take on loan, take and return. **2.** appropriate, take, get, obtain, acquire, copy, use, usurp; filch, pirate, plagiarize, pilfer, steal, commandeer. —**Ant.** lend. **1** return. **2** contribute, give, present.

bosom *n.* **1.** breast, bust, chest. **2.** heart, innermost being, inmost nature, soul, spirit, core, breast, center. **3.** midst, inner circle, heart, center, nucleus, core. —*adj.* **4.** close, intimate, cherished, dear, beloved. —**Ant. 4** distant, remote.

boss *n.* **1.** employer, supervisor, foreman, manager, superintendent, administrator, executive, chief, leader, head, master, *Slang* kingpin, big cheese. —*v.* **2.** order, command, *Informal* push. —**Ant. 1** employee, worker, man in the ranks, subordinate, underling; follower.

botch *v.* **1.** spoil, muff, bungle, make a mess of, ruin, do unskillfully, butcher, mar, mismanage; blunder, fail, err, fumble, flub, *Slang* louse up, foul up, goof, blow. —*n.* **2.** mess, bungle, blunder, failure, hash, fumble, butchery, flop. —**Ant. 1** master, perfect, do well at, do skillfully, make a success of, triumph at. **2** success, triumph, achievement, *Informal* hit.

bother *v.* **1.** annoy, trouble, distress, inconvenience, dismay, disquiet, worry, disturb, upset, pester, nag, harass, harry, aggravate, plague, fret, vex, irk, try, irritate, tax, strain. **2.** trouble, attempt, make an effort. —*n.* **3.** inconvenience, problem, trouble, difficulty, hardship, strain, stress, load, tax, onus, encumbrance, nuisance, trial, affliction, *Slang* drag; hindrance, impediment, worry, responsibility, care, aggravation, vexation, irritation, *Informal* headache, pain in the neck; fuss, disturbance, commotion, tumult, stir, ado, flurry, rumpus, racket. —**Syn. Study. 1** BOTHER, ANNOY, PLAGUE imply persistent interference with one's comfort or peace of mind. To BOTHER is to cause irritation or weariness, esp. by repeated interruptions in the midst of pressing duties: *Don't bother me while I'm working.* To ANNOY is to cause mild irritation or mental disturbance, as by repetition of an action that displeases: *The dog's constant barking annoyed the neighbors.* To PLAGUE is to trouble or bother, but usu. connotes severe mental distress: *The family was plagued by lack of money.* —**Ant. 1** help, aid, convenience, comfort, solace, console, calm, quiet, appease, placate, pacify, mollify. **2** neglect. **3** convenience, help, aid, solution, answer, cinch; pleasure, delight, comfort.

bothersome *adj.* troublesome, annoying, inconvenient, aggravating, vexing, taxing, distressing, disturbing, worrisome, disquieting. —**Ant.** convenient, helpful, comforting, consoling; pleasant, delightful, comfortable.

bottle *n.* glass container, vessel; *(variously)* phial, vial, jar, canteen, carafe, flask, flagon.

bottleneck *n.* block, barrier, bar, impediment, jam, gridlock, obstacle, obstruction, blockage, clog, congestion, detour, stop, stoppage; *Med.* thrombus, embolus, infarction, embolism; costiveness, constipation.

bottom *n.* **1.** base, foot, pedestal, foundation. **2.** lowest part, deepest part. **3.** underside, underpart, lower side, belly, sole. **4.** ocean floor, riverbed, depths. **5.** rump, backside, buttocks, seat, fundament; *Slang* fanny, can. **6.** basis, base, root, heart, core, center, substance, essence, principle; gist, quintessence, foundation, source, origin, beginning, cause, ground, rudiments, mainspring, spring, wellspring. —*adj.* **7.** lowest, lower; deepest, deeper. —**Ant. 1–4, 7** top. **1** crown, peak, summit, height, acme, apex; cover, lid. **4** surface. **7** highest, uppermost, higher, upper.

bough *n.* branch, limb.

boulevard *n.* avenue, wide street, tree-lined street, parkway, concourse. —**Ant.** alley, back street.

bounce *v.* **1.** rebound, ricochet, bound, recoil, bob, jounce, bump, thump. —*n.* **2.** rebound, bound, hop. **3.** vitality, liveliness, pep, animation, vivacity, vigor, verve, energy, life, dynamism, spirit. —**Ant. 3** staidness, calmness, calm, tranquillity, composure; weariness, tiredness.

bound[1] *adj.* **1.** tied, tied up, fastened, secured, tethered, trussed, lashed together; in bonds. **2.** encased, wrapped, covered. **3.** sure, certain, fated, destined, doomed. **4.** required, obliged, restrained, confined, limited, liable, beholden, forced; determined, resolved, resolute, committed. **—Ant. 1** unbound, untied, loose. **3** unsure, uncertain; avoidable, escapable. **4** free, unlimited, unrestrained; irresolute.

bound[2] *n.* **1.** limit, boundary, border, confine, demarcation, line; periphery, extremity, rim, pale. **2.** area, territory, region, compass, range, domain, province, district; realm, bailiwick, orb, orbit. *—v.* **3.** surround, enclose, encircle, circumscribe, border, edge, hedge, fringe; mark, define, limit, confine, demarcate.

bound[3] *v.* **1.** leap, jump, vault, spring; bounce, bob, prance, dance, gambol, romp, flounce. *—n.* **2.** leap, jump, vault, spring; bounce, rebound, flounce, bob. **—Ant. 1** crawl, creep, amble, hobble, limp.

bound[4] *adj.* going to, heading for, destined.

boundary *n.* border, dividing line, line, demarcation, frontier, barrier; landmark, rim, edge, margin, pale, periphery, extremity. **—Syn. Study.** BOUNDARY, BORDER, FRONTIER refer to that which divides one territory or political unit from another. BOUNDARY most often designates a line on a map; it may be a physical feature, such as a river: *Boundaries are shown in red.* BORDER refers to a political or geographic dividing line; it may also refer to the region adjoining the actual line: *crossing the Mexican border.* FRONTIER refers specifically to a border between two countries or the region adjoining this border: *Soldiers guarded the frontier.*

boundless *adj.* vast, immense; limitless, unlimited, unbounded, endless, inexhaustible, measureless, immeasurable, infinite, incalculable, without end, unending, everlasting, perpetual, unrestricted. **—Ant.** limited, restricted, bounded, circumscribed; small, little.

bounteous *adj.* **1.** abundant, plentiful, plenteous, bountiful, profuse, copious, ample, prolific, lavish, large, rich, full, teeming, overflowing, abounding. **2.** generous, bountiful, munificent, unstinting, unsparing, magnanimous, charitable, beneficent, liberal, free, large, philanthropic, benevolent. **—Ant. 1** sparse, spare, meager, scant, scanty, scrimpy, lean, slender, modest, small, limited, restricted, inadequate. **2** stingy, miserly, niggardly, sparing, stinting, close, penurious, uncharitable, frugal, parsimonious; greedy, covetous, avaricious.

bountiful *adj.* See PLENTIFUL.

bounty *n.* **1.** generosity, benevolence, munificence, charitableness, charity, philanthropy, assistance, aid, help, giving, liberality, openhandedness, almsgiving. **2.** grant, reward, recompense, bonus, tribute, bestowal, benefaction, endowment; gift, present, favor, gratuity, premium, donation, contribution. **—Syn. Study. 2** See BONUS. **—Ant. 1** stinginess, closeness, niggardliness, miserliness; greed, covetousness, avarice.

bouquet *n.* **1.** bunch of flowers, garland, spray, nosegay; boutonniere. **2.** aroma, scent, odor, fragrance, perfume, essence.

bourgeois *n.* **1.** member of the middle class, commoner, burgher, *(disparagingly)* Babbitt. *—adj.* **2.** middle-class, conventional, ordinary, unimaginative, *Slang* square.

bout *n.* **1.** fight, boxing match, match, battle, contest, tourney, conflict, struggle, fray, brush, tilt, skirmish, embroilment, scuffle, clash, encounter, engagement, contention, affair, *Informal* go-round, set-to. **2.** spell, session, turn, course, interval, period, term, siege, spree, series, cycle.

bow[1] *v.* **1.** bend, salaam, stoop, genuflect; *(of a female)* curtsy. **2.** yield, give in, submit, surrender, capitulate, succumb, defer, comply, relent, agree, acquiesce, concede, knuckle under, kowtow. *—n.* **3.** bend, salaam, genuflection; *(of a female)* curtsy. **—Ant. 2** fight, battle, contest, resist, stand fast.

bow[2] *n.* forward end, front, prow. **—Ant.** stern.

bowels *n.* **1.** guts, intestines, entrails, innards, stomach, vitals, viscera, vital organs. **2.** depths, innermost part, interior, abyss, insides, guts, innards, core, pit, hollow, heart, midst, bosom, womb.

bowl *n.* **1.** deep dish, vessel, container, receptacle; *(variously)* tureen, porringer, boat; bowlful, dishful, portion, helping. **2.** basin; hollow, depression, cavity, valley. **3.** stadium, amphitheater, coliseum, arena.

box[1] *n.* **1.** carton, cardboard container, container, receptacle; crate, chest, caddy; coffer. **2.** stall, compartment, booth.

box[2] *v.* **1.** cuff, slap, bat, hit, rap, belt, strike, punch, whack, thwack, buffet. **2.** fight, spar, exchange blows, engage in fisticuffs. *—n.* **3.** blow, cuff, slap, smack, whack, thwack, hit, rap; buffet, thumping.

boy *n.* male child, man child, lad, youth, stripling, youngster.

boycott *n.* **1.** refusal to buy, rejection,

spurning, exclusion, ostracism, blacklisting, blackballing. —*v.* **2.** refuse to have dealings with, reject, spurn, ostracize, exclude, blacklist, blackball. **—Ant. 1** mass patronage, group support, usage, acceptance. **2** patronize, support, welcome, use, accept.

boyfriend *n.* beau, fellow, young man, escort, cavalier, date, companion, gentleman caller, swain, admirer, suitor, wooer, steady; lover, beloved, truelove, sweetheart, paramour, inamorato, man, flame, Don Juan, Lothario, old man.

boyish *adj.* youthful, boylike, juvenile, innocent, fresh, tender; childish, childlike, immature, puerile; sophomoric, callow, boyey. **—Ant.** manly, rugged; adult, mature, grown-up, experienced, sophisticated, worldly.

brace *n.* **1.** reinforcement, support, bracket, prop, stanchion, stay, strut, truss, bracer. **2.** pair, couple, duo, twosome. —*v.* **3.** reinforce, strengthen, steady, prop, prop up, shore, shore up, bolster, fortify, buttress, support, sustain, hold up, prepare. **—Ant. 3** weaken, loosen; let fall.

bracelet *n.* armlet, bangle.

bracing *adj.* invigorating, stimulating, energizing, exhilarating, restorative, refreshing, arousing; strengthening, fortifying, reviving. **—Ant.** soporific, restful, dulling, depressing; weakening, debilitating, enervating.

bracket *n.* **1.** support, brace, stay, strut, prop, stanchion. **2.** group, grouping, class, classification, category, range, division, rank, designation, status. —*v.* **3.** support, brace; prop, prop up, shore, shore up, truss. **4.** class, classify, group, rank, categorize, designate.

brackish *adj.* salty, briny, saline, salt. **—Ant.** fresh, clear, sweet.

brag *v.* **1.** boast, extol oneself, vaunt, crow, talk big, puff oneself up, exaggerate, blow one's own horn, pat oneself on the back. —*n.* **2.** boast, boasting, boastfulness, bragging, self-praise, big talk, exaggeration, crowing. **—Syn. Study. 1** See BOAST. **—Ant. 1** be humble, be self-deprecating, deprecate, depreciate, disclaim, disavow; be ashamed, cover up. **2** humility, humbleness, modesty, self-deprecation, disclaimer, disavowal, self-criticism, shame.

braggart *n.* bragger, boaster, big talker, self-trumpeter, *Slang* blowhard. **—Ant.** humble person, self-effacing person, modest person.

braid *v.* plait, weave, intertwine, entwine, twine, interlace, twist, ravel, lace, knit, wreathe.

brain *n.* **—Syn. Study.** See MIND.

brake *n.* **1.** stopping device; curb, constraint, restraint, control, rein, check, drag. —*v.* **2.** stop, halt, arrest, stay, check; reduce speed, slow; curb, control. **—Ant. 1** starter, accelerator, gas pedal; acceleration, stimulus; freedom. **2** start; move, accelerate, speed up, hasten, quicken, expedite.

branch *n.* **1.** limb, bough, spray. **2.** leg, prong, channel, tributary, feeder; extension, offshoot, section, part. **3.** section, part, segment, component, arm, wing, member, extension, division, subdivision, chapter, offshoot; bureau, office, branch office, department, agency. —*v.* **4.** divide, diverge, radiate, separate, fork, shoot off, ramify, bifurcate. **—Ant. 1** trunk. **2** main channel. **3** complex, composite, mass, conglomerate, union, affiliation, alliance; main office, home office.

brand *n.* **1.** branding iron; mark made by branding; label, mark, emblem, stamp, sign, trademark. **2.** brand name, make, manufacture; type, kind, sort, variety, grade, class, quality. **3.** stigma, stain, mark, disgrace, smirch, smear, slur, taint, spot, blot, blemish. —*v.* **4.** mark with a branding iron, mark, sear, burn in. **5.** stigmatize, mark, stain, taint, besmirch, spot, blemish, disgrace, discredit. **—Ant. 3** trophy, laurel, honor. **5** bring honor to, commemorate.

brandish *v.* flourish, wave, shake, swing, wield, waggle; flaunt, display, exhibit, show off. **—Ant.** sheathe, put away; put down, lower.

brash *adj.* **1.** rash, reckless, incautious, foolhardy, imprudent, careless; unconsidered, impetuous, madcap, hasty, too quick, precipitous. **2.** impudent, impertinent, brazen, forward, rude, cheeky, sassy, *Slang* fresh; bold, heedless, overconfident, know-it-all, *Slang* smart-alecky. **—Ant. 1** cautious, prudent, careful, well-considered, thoughtful, circumspect. **2** respectful, deferential, polite, reserved; hesitant, uncertain, timid, timorous.

brassy *adj.* brazen, bold, impudent, saucy, insolent, sassy, forward, overbold, shameless, barefaced, unblushing, unabashed, brash, outspoken, impertinent, arrogant, cocky. **—Ant.** shy, modest, retiring, reticent, self-effacing.

brat *n.* spoiled child, rude child, hoyden, whelp, chit, rascal, imp, devil, little devil, scamp, little monster. **—Ant.** little angel, little darling, cherub.

bravado *n.* show of courage, swaggering, swagger, braggadocio, bravura, boasting, boastfulness, bragging, big talk, crowing, bombast, cockiness, bluster, puffery, blowing. **—Ant.** nervousness, trembling, quaking; shame.

brave *adj.* **1.** courageous, valiant, valorous, heroic, fearless, dauntless, undaunted, stouthearted, lionhearted, intrepid, unafraid, unflinching, unshrinking, bold, daring; plucky, spunky, gritty, game, doughty, stalwart, *Slang* gutsy. —*v.* **2.** dare, confront, challenge, face, defy, outbrazen, breast, stand up to, look in the eye; endure, bear, withstand, tolerate, take, put up with, suffer, sustain, stand, weather, brook, abide, stomach, undergo. **—Syn. Study. 1** BRAVE, COURAGEOUS, VALIANT, FEARLESS refer to facing danger or difficulties with moral strength and endurance. BRAVE is a general term that suggests fortitude, daring, and resolve: *a brave pioneer.* COURAGEOUS implies a higher or nobler kind of bravery, esp. as resulting from an inborn quality of mind or spirit: *courageous leaders.* VALIANT implies an inner strength manifested by brave deeds, often in battle: *a valiant knight.* FEARLESS implies unflinching spirit and coolness in the face of danger: *a fearless firefighter.* **—Ant. 1** cowardly, cringing, frightened, fearful, afraid, craven, fainthearted, *Slang* chicken, chickenhearted, yellow, yellow-livered; timid, timorous, shrinking. **2** retreat from, back away from, give in to, surrender to, give up in the face of, *Informal* turn tail.

bravery *n.* courage, valor, heroism, fearlessness, intrepidity, dauntlessness; boldness, daring, pluck, spunk, audacity, spirit, mettle, *Slang* grit. **—Ant.** cowardice, fright, fearfulness, faintheartedness, timidity, *Slang* chickenheartedness, yellowness.

brawl *n.* fight, scuffle, fracas, fray, melee, row, ruckus, scrap, broil, clash, set-to, battle, uproar, rumpus, embroilment, altercation, imbroglio; quarrel, squabble, tiff, dispute, wrangle.

brawn *n.* brawniness, muscles, muscular development, robustness, huskiness, beefiness, sturdiness, stamina, ruggedness; strength, might, power. **—Ant.** slightness, scrawniness, leanness, thinness, skinniness, slenderness; weakness, feebleness, fragility.

brawny *adj.* muscular, burly, robust, husky, rugged, sturdy, strapping, strong, powerful, mighty. **—Ant.** scrawny, gaunt, slender, slight, skinny, thin, slim, lean, lanky, lank; weak, feeble, fragile, delicate.

brazen *adj.* bold, impudent, shameless, boldfaced, barefaced, brash, unabashed, insolent, saucy, forward, immodest, audacious; open, arrogant, brassy, cheeky. **—Syn. Study.** See BOLD. **—Ant.** reserved, reticent, diffident, respectful, decorous, well-mannered, mannerly, polite; cautious, modest, timid, timorous, shy, bashful; underhand, secret, stealthy, surreptitious.

breach *n.* **1.** opening, break, hole, rift, gap, gash, rent, crack, split, chink, cleft, crevice, slit, rupture, fissure. **2.** violation, infraction, infringement, transgression, disobedience, trespass, defiance; nonobservance, noncompliance, disregard, neglect, dereliction, failure. **—Syn. Study. 2** BREACH, INFRACTION, VIOLATION all denote an act of breaking or disregarding a legal or moral code. BREACH is most often used of a legal offense, but it may refer to the breaking of any code of conduct: *breach of contract; breach of etiquette.* INFRACTION most often refers to the breaking of clearly formulated rules or laws: *an infraction of regulations.* VIOLATION often suggests a willful, forceful refusal to obey: *done in violation of instructions.* **—Ant. 1** closure; stoppage, blockage. **2** adherence to, observance, compliance with, obedience, fidelity to; attention, heed, regard.

breadth *n.* **1.** width, wideness, broadness, latitude. **2.** broadness, scope, range, reach, spread, compass, stretch, span, expanse, extent, extensiveness; size, area, dimensions, measure. **—Ant. 1** length, longness, longitude. **2** narrowness, confinement, circumscription, restrictedness, slightness, scantiness.

break *v.* **1.** shatter, fragment, burst, crack, fracture, rupture, snap, split, chip, splinter, *Slang* bust; smash, crush, pulverize, granulate, powder, disintegrate, demolish. **2.** Often **break off, break away.** detach, separate, pull off, tear off, wrench away, sever, divide, cleave, sunder, rive, rend, disjoint, disconnect, dismember. **3.** be inoperative, work improperly, become useless; ruin, destroy. **4.** Usu. **break off.** end, stop, cease, halt, suspend, shut down, interrupt, discontinue. **5.** disclose, reveal, divulge, announce, proclaim, tell, inform, make public, give out. **6.** erupt, burst out, come forth suddenly; happen, occur, appear. **7.** tame, train, master, discipline, control, subdue, overcome, bend to one's will. **8.** bankrupt, ruin, wipe out, cripple financially, strap for funds, impoverish, make insolvent, make impoverished, take all one's money, put on the rocks. **9.** take the force of, soften, diminish, cushion, weaken, lessen, lighten. **10.** surpass, exceed, better, top, outdo, outstrip, overcome, overshadow, beat, cap, excel, go beyond, transcend, eclipse. **11.** escape, get away from, make a getaway, slip away, take to one's heels, fly the coop; flee, run, run away, fly, dash, make a dash, take flight. **12.** violate, be guilty of infraction of, infringe on, transgress against, disobey, defy; disregard, ignore, pay no heed to, be derelict in, neglect, shirk, fall back on, renege on. —*n.* **13.** shattering, breaking, burst, snap, fracturing, cracking, splitting; breach, opening, rupture, fissure, hole, rent, crack, fracture, gap, gash, rift, tear, split, cleft, division, separation. **14.** interruption, interlude, recess, interval, intermission, hiatus, lapse, rest, respite, pause. **15.** stroke of luck, opportunity, chance, fortune, opening. —**Ant. 1** repair, fix, mend, heal. **2** connect, join, unite, fasten, secure, attach, bind, weld. **3** repair, fix. **4** start, begin, commence, open; continue, preserve, prolong. **5** keep quiet about, conceal, hide, secrete, cover up. **6** end, stop, cease, halt; die down, die away, diminish. **7** submit to, yield to, acquiesce; free. **8** make wealthy, make prosperous, enrich, fill one's pockets, feather one's nest, give one money to burn. **9** increase. **10** fall short of, be under, be lower than. **11** capture, catch. **12** obey, adhere to, comply with; heed, observe, regard. **13** mending, repair, fixing, healing; closing, stopping, blockage. **14** continuation, resumption.

breakable *adj.* fragile, delicate, brittle, crumbly, frail, flimsy, shaky. —**Ant.** unbreakable, sturdy, strong.

breakdown *n.* **1.** failure, collapse; disorder, mishap, deterioration, decline, *Slang* crackup. **2.** division, categorization, detailed list, item-by-item count, step-by-step instructions; analysis.

breakup *n.* separation, breaking, dispersal, split, splitting, disintegration, crackup.

breast *n.* **1.** chest, bust, bosom. **2.** heart, innermost self, very marrow, core.

breath *n.* **1.** air breathed in and out. **2.** breathing, respiration, wind, inhalation, exhalation. **3.** spirit, vital spirit, vital spark, divine spark, life force, lifeblood, animation, vitalization.

breathe *v.* **1.** draw breath, draw in air, inhale and exhale, respire; gasp, pant, puff, huff. **2.** whisper, murmur, impart, utter.

breathtaking *adj.* exciting, awesome, amazing, astonishing, startling, surprising.

breech *n.* **1.** buttocks, rump, seat, behind, posterior, fundament; hindquarters, hind part, haunches. **2. breeches.** knee breeches; *(loosely)* trousers, pants.

breed *v.* **1.** reproduce, propagate, beget, multiply, procreate, produce offspring, bear, spawn, bring forth, give forth; raise, grow, proliferate. **2.** foster, nurture, develop, cultivate, promote, mother, father; generate, produce, spawn, give rise to, cause, lead to, occasion, sire. —*n.* **3.** species, strain, race, stock, order, family, variety, type, sort, kind. —**Ant. 2** destroy, extinguish, kill, wipe out, eradicate, erase, demolish, extirpate; stifle, hinder, harm, injure, block, obstruct, stop, stay.

breeding *n.* **1.** raising, producing, production, growing; reproduction, propagation, begetting, multiplying, mating, procreation, generation, germination, bearing, spawning, hatching, bringing forth. **2.** lineage, bloodline, line, heredity, ancestry, parentage, extraction, pedigree, family tree, descent, genealogy. **3.** manners, refinement, polish, gentility, background, politeness, courtesy, grace, cultivation; upbringing, training, rearing.

breeze *n.* **1.** gentle wind, light wind, current of air, puff of wind, light gust, zephyr, waft. —*v.* **2.** move in a carefree manner, sweep, sail, glide, flit, float, coast, waft, pass. —**Syn. Study. 1** See WIND.

breezy *adj.* **1.** windy, windswept, gusty, blowy, blustery, squally. **2.** light, carefree, free and easy, casual, blithesome, buoyant, lively, animated, vivacious, gay, cheerful, sunny, merry, jaunty, pert, debonair, fresh, airy, brisk, peppy, spry, frisky, sprightly, spirited, energetic, bouncy, resilient. —**Ant. 1** calm, still, windless. **2** heavy, careworn, depressed, dull, sad, mournful, morose, lifeless, inanimate, unspirited; serious, pompous, heavy-handed.

brevity *n.* briefness, shortness, quickness, conciseness, pithiness, succinctness, terseness; impermanence, transience, ephemerality. —**Syn. Study.** BREVITY, CONCISENESS refer to the use of few words in speaking. BREVITY emphasizes the short duration of speech: *a commencement address noted for its brevity.* CONCISENESS emphasizes compactness of expression: *clear in spite of great conciseness.* —**Ant.** long-windedness, prolixity; lengthiness.

brew *v.* **1.** boil, steep, seethe, cook; ferment, soak. **2.** concoct, contrive, scheme, plot, devise, plan, think up, arrange, prepare, make, produce, foment, *Informal* cook up; originate, initiate, germinate, hatch, start, begin, form, formulate, gather, ripen. —*n.* **3.** beverage, drink, concoction, mixture; *(variously)* beer, ale, stout, porter, malt liquor. —**Ant. 1** chill; drain, distill. **2** cancel, disperse, break up, die away.

bribe *n.* **1.** payoff, hush money, illegal gift, graft, inducement, *Slang* payola, grease. —*v.* **2.** buy off, pay off, suborn, *Informal* grease the palm of, grease the hand of.

bric-a-brac *n.* baubles, trinkets, ornaments, bibelots, knickknacks, gimcracks, gewgaws, kickshaws.

bridal *adj.* bride's; wedding, marriage, matrimonial, nuptial.

bridge *n.* **1.** span, overpass, passageway; viaduct, catwalk. **2.** bond, link, tie, band, connection, union, association, alliance, liaison. **—***v.* **3.** span, cross, cross over, traverse, go over, extend across, reach across; link, connect, bind, band, unify. **—Ant. 2** separation, division, schism, split, break, disassociation. **3** widen, separate, divide, split, break.

bridle *n.* **1.** head harness; *(loosely)* bit and brace, restraint, muzzle, check, curb. **—***v.* **2.** put on the head harness; harness. **3.** curb, check, restrain, control, restrict, suppress, repress, constrain, inhibit, hinder, arrest, muzzle, gag; master, manage, harness, direct, rule. **4.** thrust up one's head, rear up, draw up; recoil, draw back, flinch. **—Ant. 2** unbridle, unharness. **3** express, voice, utter, air, vent, let out, let go, free. **4** cringe, cower, grovel.

brief *adj.* **1.** short, short-lived, momentary, temporary, quick, hasty, swift, fleeting, transient, transitory. **2.** short, concise, succinct, terse, pithy, compact, thumbnail; abbreviated, condensed, abridged, compressed, limited, shortened, curtailed, summarized, summary. **—***v.* **3.** inform, inform quickly, give the high spots, fill in on, give the details of, describe to, advise, instruct, prepare. **—***n.* **4.** legal summary, (*loosely*) argument, contention, case, defense; précis, abstract, capsule, abridgment, résumé, summary, digest, synopsis. **—Syn. Study. 1** See SHORT. **4** See SUMMARY. **—Ant. 1, 2** long, lengthy, extended, prolonged, protracted, extended, extensive. **3** keep uninformed, conceal, keep secret, hide, cover up.

brigade *n.* **1.** *(technically, two or more)* regiments, battalions, army groups, squadrons; *(loosely)* military unit, unit, legion, contingent, body of troops, detachment. **2.** company, corps, unit, force, squad, team, contingent, outfit, crew, group, organization.

brigand *n.* outlaw, bandit, desperado, ruffian, cutthroat, gunman, hoodlum; marauder, plunderer, looter, vandal, pillager, spoiler, despoiler, pilferer; *(variously)* highwayman, robber, thief, rustler, pirate, buccaneer, privateer, corsair.

bright *adj.* **1.** brilliant, blazing, dazzling, shimmering, vivid, intense, shining, glowing, gleaming, beaming, radiant, sparkling, glittering, resplendent; luminous, lustrous, lambent, effulgent; illuminated, light-filled, sunny, warm. **2.** intelligent, smart, brainy, brilliant; wise, profound, sage, sagacious, shrewd, keen, clever, inventive, resourceful, ingenious, perceptive, discerning, alert, wide-awake, clearheaded, aware, quick, quick-witted, sharp, acute, astute; talented, gifted, capable, competent, proficient, masterful, excellent, great, illustrious, grand, magnificent, outstanding, remarkable, splendid. **3.** merry, gay, blithe, happy, joyous, joyful, cheerful, glad; jolly, lively, exhilarating, sparkling. **4.** promising, favorable, auspicious, propitious, hopeful, optimistic, exciting, rosy; successful, prosperous, happy, healthy, sunny, excellent, grand, good. **—Ant.** dull. **1** dim, pale, subdued, dark, drab, gloomy, murky, obscure, dusky, cloudy, misty, cool. **2** dumb, stupid, muddleheaded, slow-witted, witless, brainless, simple-minded, simple, foolish, fool-headed, unwise, rattlebrained, featherbrained, doltish, oafish, dunderheaded, moronic, idiotic, imbecilic, half-witted, asinine, thick, slow, retarded, lethargic, sluggish, ignorant; untalented, ungifted, incapable, incompetent. **3** sad, glum, dreary, joyless, gloomy, forlorn, unhappy, dismal, cheerless, grim, depressed, dejected, doleful, melancholy, downcast, downhearted, heavy-hearted. **4** unpromising, inauspicious, hopeless, pessimistic, dim, grim; failing, unsuccessful, unhappy, cloudy, bad, awful, terrible, poor.

brighten *v.* **1.** make brighter, lighten, enliven, perk up; illuminate, light. **2.** gladden, cheer, make happy, perk up, buoy up, lift, lift up, boost, enliven, animate, stimulate. **—Ant. 1** darken, dull, blacken. **2** sadden, depress, make downcast.

brilliance, brilliancy *n.* **1.** brightness, radiance, sparkle, glitter, luster, gleam, glow, shine, sheen, shimmer, dazzle, blaze, resplendence, splendor, luminosity, effulgence, intensity, vividness. **2.** intelligence, smartness, braininess, wisdom, profundity, sagacity, shrewdness, keenness, cleverness, inventiveness, resourcefulness, ingenuity, perception, discernment, alertness, clearheadedness, awareness, quickness, sharpness, acuity; genius, talent, gift, capability, proficiency, masterfulness, excellence, greatness, illustriousness, magnificence, grandeur, distinction. **—Ant. 1** dullness, dimness, paleness, darkness, drabness, obscurity. **2** stupidity, dumbness, dullness, idiocy, asininity, imbecility, thickness, simple-mindedness, doltishness, oafishness, folly, silliness; inanity, ineptitude, incompetence, mediocrity.

brilliant *adj.* **1.** See BRIGHT, def. **1. 2.** See BRIGHT, def. **2. —Ant.** See BRIGHT, Antonym list **1** and **2.**

brim *n.* **1.** upper edge, brink, rim, ledge, border, margin, verge; projecting rim, lip. **—***v.* **2.** fill, fill up, well up, overflow, flood. **—Syn. Study. 1** See RIM.

brine *n.* salt water, salt solution, saline

solution, pickling solution; the sea, sea water. —**Ant.** fresh water, clear water.

bring *v.* **1.** carry, convey, bear, tote, fetch, deliver, transport, take; accompany. **2.** bring about, cause, induce, effect, institute, begin, start, initiate, usher in, result in; create, engender, generate, originate, produce. **3.** compel, force, make, persuade, convince. **4.** sell for; fetch. —**Ant. 1** take away, send, remove. **2** quash, kill, prevent, suppress, quell, crush, repress, extinguish, put down, squelch, squash, dispel, nullify, abolish, void, revoke.

brink *n.* edge, margin, rim, brim, verge, border, skirt, shore, bank; threshold, point.

brisk *adj.* **1.** quick, swift, lively, active, sprightly, spry, energetic, vigorous, snappy, peppy, alert, animated, spirited, vivacious, chipper, breezy, bustling, busy, dynamic. **2.** bracing, invigorating, refreshing, fresh, stimulating, stirring, rousing, exhilarating, vivifying. —**Ant. 1** sluggish, torpid, lethargic, lazy, indolent, slothful, inactive, unenergetic, heavy, dull. **2** tiring, exhausting, fatiguing, wearisome; boring, monotonous, dull.

brittle *adj.* breakable, fragile, frangible, crumbly, friable, frail. —**Syn. Study.** See FRAIL. —**Ant.** strong, sturdy, supple, elastic, resilient, flexible; unbreakable.

broach *v.* mention, suggest, introduce, bring up, touch on, pose, propose, advance, submit, institute, open up, launch. —**Ant.** repress, suppress, keep hidden, conceal, secrete; close, end.

broad *adj.* **1.** wide; outspread. **2.** expansive, extensive, extended, spacious, immense, capacious, roomy, rangy, large, ample, sizable, thick. **3.** extensive, comprehensive, sweeping, general, inclusive, far-reaching, encyclopedic, universal, wide, wide-ranging, all-embracing, immense, unlimited; nonspecific, undetailed. **4.** full, plain, open, clear, obvious. —**Ant.** narrow. **1** long, lengthy. **2, 3** limited, confined, circumscribed, restricted, small, slight, scant. **3** specific, detailed. **4** partial, veiled, obscure, hidden, enigmatical.

broadcast *v.* **1.** transmit, send out, beam, put on the air, radio, televise, relay, cable; distribute, disseminate. —*n.* **2.** program, show; announcement, talk, statement, (*on the Internet*) Webcast.

broaden *v.* widen, spread out, stretch, enlarge, expand, extend, distend, dilate, swell; increase, raise, boost, build up, amplify, augment, supplement, develop, advance, improve, strengthen, reinforce, intensify. —**Ant.** narrow, squeeze, contract, decrease; reduce, simplify, subtract from, diminish.

broad-minded *adj.* open-minded, tolerant, catholic, unprejudiced, unbiased, unbigoted, undogmatic, liberal, flexible, unprovincial, charitable, amenable, receptive, magnanimous. —**Ant.** narrow-minded, closed-minded, intolerant, prejudiced, biased, bigoted, inflexible, dogmatic, provincial, uncharitable.

brochure *n.* pamphlet, leaflet, circular, flier, handbill, throwaway, booklet, folder.

broil *v.* **1.** cook by direct heat. **2.** make very hot, burn, scorch, sear, cook, blister, bake, roast, fry, toast, parch.

broke *adj.* without funds, bankrupt, penniless, insolvent, wiped out, impoverished, strapped, strapped for funds. —**Ant.** wealthy, rich, prosperous, affluent, solvent.

broken-hearted *adj.* heartbroken, melancholy, gloomy, wretched, miserable, sad, woebegone, mournful, forlorn, dejected, depressed, despairing, crushed, long-faced, disconsolate. —**Ant.** cheerful, elated, light-hearted, merry, jolly, carefree.

bronze *adj.* reddish-brown, copper-colored, chestnut, reddish-tan, tan, brownish.

brooch *n.* pin, clasp.

brood *n.* **1.** hatchlings, chicks, young, offspring, litter, spawn, family, children. —*v.* **2.** sit upon, incubate, hatch, cover. **3.** worry, fret, agonize, mope, sulk, dwell, mull, chew.

brook[1] *n.* stream, streamlet, creek, rivulet, rill, run.

brook[2] *v.* take, stand, abide, allow, accept, tolerate, bear, put up with, suffer, endure, stomach. —**Ant.** reject, refuse, dismiss, forbear, forbid, prohibit, disallow, bar, banish, resist, repudiate, rebuff, renounce.

broth *n.* stock, clear soup, bouillon, consommé.

brothel *n.* whorehouse, house of prostitution, sporting house, fancy house, bawdy house, house of ill repute, house of ill fame, house, bordello, bordel, bagnio, stew, *Slang* cathouse; *French* maisòn de passe, maison close.

brother *n.* **1.** male sibling, blood brother. **2.** fellow member, kinsman, peer; fellowman, fellow citizen, countryman, landsman; comrade, companion; colleague, confrere, associate, partner, *Informal* pal, buddy, chum. **3.** monk, friar, monastic, cleric. —**Ant. 1** sister, female sibling. **2** nonmember, foreigner, stranger.

brow *n.* **1.** forehead. **2.** edge, brink, brim, rim, periphery, verge, margin, side, border, boundary.

browbeat *v.* bully, intimidate, cow, cower, domineer, tyrannize, abash, henpeck, *Slang* bulldoze; badger, harass, hector; threaten, terrorize, frighten. **—Ant.** coax, persuade, flatter, invite, charm, beguile, seduce.

brown *adj.* **1.** brownish, brunet, brunette, chocolate, cocoa, coffee, mahogany, walnut, nut brown, drab, khaki, greenish-brown, olive drab, dirt-colored, liver-colored, chestnut, tawny, sorrel, hazel, bay, purplish-brown, puce, umber, reddish-brown, terra-cotta, rust, russet, roan, bronze, yellow-brown, buff, golden-brown, copper, auburn, light brown, dun, sand-colored, cinnamon, toast, ginger, tan, camel, fawn, beige. *—v.* **2.** sauté, fry, cook.

browse *v.* **1.** graze, pasture, nibble, feed, eat. **2.** peruse, look through, look over, glance through, examine cursorily, check over, skim, scan, survey, dip into; wander through.

bruise *v.* **1.** discolor, mark, blacken, mar, blemish; injure, wound, hurt, damage. **2.** offend, wound, hurt, injure, abuse. *—n.* **3.** contusion, black mark, discoloration, mark, blemish; injury, wound.

brunet, brunette *adj.* **1.** dark-haired, brown-haired; brown-haired and brown-eyed, dark, olive-skinned. *—n.* **2.** a dark-haired woman or girl; a dark-haired man or boy. **—Ant.** blond, blonde. **1** fair, light, light-haired, light-skinned.

brunt *n.* full force, force, impact, thrust, main shock, violence, stress.

brush[1] *n.* **1.** bristled tool; *(variously)* paintbrush, whisk, whiskbroom, duster, clothes brush, hairbrush, nailbrush, scrub brush, wash brush, toothbrush, shoe brush. **2.** brushing, sweep, whisk, flick, grazing, dusting; touch, stroke. **3.** encounter, meeting, confrontation, skirmish, engagement, fracas, scuffle, battle, set-to, run-in. *—v.* **4.** use a brush on; *(variously)* wash, clean, cleanse, scrub, dust, groom, paint, polish, shine, varnish. **5.** sweep, whisk, flick; graze, touch, stroke, caress.

brush[2] *n.* underbrush, brushwood, undergrowth, bush, bushes, shrubbery, shrubs; thicket, bracken, fern, copse, sedge, scrub, forest, woodland, woodlands, bush country.

brush-off *n.* rejection, cold shoulder, rebuff, snub, repudiation, disregard, slight, squelch, cut; *Slang* brush, put-down.

brusque *adj.* abrupt, curt, short, gruff, bearish, crusty, blunt, bluff, harsh, rough, tart; rude, impolite, ungracious, unceremonious, discourteous, ungentle. **—Syn. Study.** See BLUNT. **—Ant.** civil, considerate, patient, gentle, courteous, polite, gracious, cordial, genial.

brutal *adj.* cruel, vicious, savage, inhuman, barbaric, barbarous, ruthless, hardhearted, heartless, pitiless, merciless, remorseless, unfeeling, bloody, brutish, fierce, demoniacal, bloodthirsty, atrocious, hellish; harsh, crude, coarse. **—Ant.** humane, gentle, sweet, kind, softhearted, merciful, sympathetic, sensitive; noble, civilized, refined.

brutality *n.* cruelty, viciousness, savagery, savageness, inhumanity, ruthlessness, barbarity, brutishness, ferocity, harshness. **—Ant.** humaneness, gentleness, kindness, tenderness.

brute *n.* **1.** savage, barbarian, cruel person, monster, demon, fiend, devil, swine. **2.** beast, wild animal, animal, dumb creature, beast of the field. **—Ant. 1** gentleman, angel. **2** angel; human, man.

bubble *n.* **1.** air ball, globule, droplet, blister, bleb. **2. bubbles.** foam, froth, fizz, effervescence. *—v.* **3.** boil, percolate, seethe; foam, froth, fizz, fizzle, effervesce, sparkle, gurgle, burble. **—Ant. 3** be flat.

buccaneer *n.* pirate, privateer, freebooter, corsair.

bucket *n.* pail, tub, can, cask, container, pitcher, receptacle, vessel; scoop, scuttle, hod; bucketful, pailful.

buckle *n.* **1.** clasp, hasp, fastener, catch, clip. *—v.* **2.** clasp, fasten, catch, secure, hook, couple. **3.** bend, belly out, bulge, sag, warp, curl, crinkle, wrinkle, contort, distort; collapse, cave in, crumple. **—Ant. 2** unbuckle, unfasten, unhook, uncouple, release, loosen. **3** straighten.

bud *n.* **1.** unopened flower; shoot, sprout. *—v.* **2.** put forth shoots, sprout, open; begin to grow, begin to bloom, blossom, flower, develop, burgeon.

buddy *n.* friend, pal, *Brit.* mate, chum, comrade, associate, companion, crony, sidekick, partner, fellow, intimate, colleague, confidant, *Spanish* amigo, confederate, confrere, brother. **—Ant.** foe, enemy, opponent, rival, adversary.

budge *v.* **1.** stir, move, shift, dislodge, dislocate, push, slide, roll. **2.** move, change, shift, influence, persuade, sway, convince. **—Ant. 1** stick, remain, stay.

budget *n.* **1.** financial plan, spending plan, financial statement; allowance, allotment, allocation, funds, moneys, resources, means, cost. *—v.* **2.** allocate, schedule, plan, apportion, portion out, arrange, ration.

buff *n.* **1.** leather, buffalo hide. **2.** nakedness, bare skin, *Informal* the raw. **3.** polisher; swab, dauber. **4.** devotee, admirer, fan, enthusiast, follower, connoisseur, mavin, *Slang* nut, bug, freak.

—*adj.* **5.** yellowish-brown, tan, tawny; straw, sandy, yellowish. —*v.* **6.** polish, rub, burnish, smooth.

buffer *n.* shield, cushion, protector, bumper.

buffet *v.* hit, strike, beat, box, jab, wallop, cuff, slap, knock, baste, pound, thump, bang, rap, thwack, pummel, thrash; push, bump, shove.

buffoon *n.* clown, jester, joker, prankster, trickster, funnyman, mimic, zany, silly-billy, comedian, comic, merry-andrew, madcap, wag; fool, harlequin, pantaloon, punchinello, Punch, Scaramouch, Pierrot.

bug *n.* **1.** insect, *(in technical use)* Hemiptera, Heteroptera. **2.** virus, germ. **3.** defect, drawback, flaw, fault, weakness. —*v.* **4.** bother, annoy, pester, nag, badger. **5.** wiretap, eavesdrop, listen in.

build *v.* **1.** construct, erect, make, put up, set up, put together, fabricate, fashion, manufacture, produce, forge. **2.** increase, enlarge, greaten, extend, develop, raise, enhance, build up, improve, intensify, multiply, augment, supplement, amplify, strengthen, renew, reinforce, harden, steel, brace; establish, found, originate, launch, institute, begin, start, initiate, inaugurate, set up, open, embark on, undertake. **3.** form, shape, mold, produce, create. —*n.* **4.** physique, form, figure, body, construction, structure, shape. —**Ant. 1–3** demolish, tear down, dismantle, destroy. **2** decrease, diminish, reduce, lessen; lower, contract, attenuate, curtail, shrink, scale down; weaken, dilute, deplete, decline, impair, sap, undermine, debilitate, cripple, harm, injure; end, stop, terminate, finish, conclude, wind up, close, discontinue, suspend, relinquish.

building *n.* structure, edifice, construction.

bulge *n.* **1.** lump, bump, protuberance, protrusion, projection, swelling, prominence, curve; sagging, bagginess, excess. —*v.* **2.** swell, swell out, puff out, protrude, distend, project, stand out, stick out, bag, sag. —**Ant. 1** hollow, cavity, hole, pocket. **2** shrink, cave in, collapse.

bulk *n.* **1.** mass, massiveness, largeness, bigness, amplitude, magnitude, size, volume, weight, dimensions, proportions, extent, quantity, measure, substance, greatness, hugeness, enormity. **2.** main part, major part, greater part, principal part, better part, lion's share, body, most, majority, preponderance, plurality. —**Ant. 2** lesser part, minor part, smaller part.

bulky *adj.* cumbersome, unwieldy, clumsy, awkward, unhandy, ungainly, unmanageable, lumpish; large, big, huge, massive, immense, voluminous, enormous, hulking, extensive, capacious, sizable. —**Ant.** manageable, wieldy, small, little, petite, diminutive, slim.

bull *n.* male; *(variously)* male bovine, ox, male elephant, male whale, male seal, male elk, male moose.

bulldoze *v.* **1.** drive, thrust, push, force, press, shoulder, bump, jostle, propel, shove; rage, fell, level, flatten. **2.** browbeat, intimidate, cow, *Slang* buffalo, bully, dragoon, hector, coerce, bludgeon, subdue.

bulletin *n.* brief announcement, news report, report, dispatch, release, account, communiqué, communication, statement, message, notification, note.

bully *n.* **1.** tormentor, intimidator, browbeater, petty tyrant, despot, oppressor, coercer; tough, ruffian. —*v.* **2.** intimidate, cow, browbeat, bulldoze, tyrannize, domineer, terrorize, frighten, coerce, harass, annoy, ride over, tread on. —*interj.* **3.** hurray, hurrah, cheers, good, well done, *Slang* swell, right on. —**Ant. 2** lure, entice, flatter, coax, cajole, urge, persuade.

bulwark *n.* **1.** defensive wall, earthwork, embankment, rampart, parapet; barrier, guard. **2.** support, mainstay. —**Ant. 2** weakness, weak link.

bum *n.* *(Informal)* **1.** tramp, hobo, derelict, vagrant, vagabond, bag lady; loafer, idler, drifter. —*v.* **2.** beg, borrow, cadge, *Slang* grub, mooch, sponge.

bump *v.* **1.** hit, strike, knock, slam, bang, smack, whack, crack, thump, rap; collide, crash into, crash, smash into, run into, butt, buffet, clash. **2.** bounce, jolt, jar, jounce, jostle; shake, rattle. —*n.* **3.** blow, rap, knock, impact, hit, whack, wallop, slam, smack, sock, smash, bang, crack, slap, punch, crash, jolt, collision; *Slang* poke. **4.** lump, swelling, node; hump, knob, protuberance, bulge, excrescence, gnarl, knot, nodule. —**Ant. 2** roll, glide, sail, flow, slide, slip, glissade, coast.

bumptious *adj.* overbearing, aggressive, pushy, self-assertive, impudent, insolent, cocky, cocksure, overconfident, impertinent, brazen, obtrusive, forward, presumptuous, *Dialect* bodacious; arrogant, haughty, conceited, swaggering, boastful. —**Ant.** shy, retiring, self-effacing, demure, timid, modest, bashful.

bun *n.* **1.** roll, soft roll, sweet roll. **2.** coil, knot.

bunch *n.* **1.** cluster, clump; bundle, batch, collection, assortment, accumulation, array, stack, heap, pile, quantity, lot, mass, number, amount; shock, knot. **2.** group, band, flock, bevy, troop, pack, multitude, crowd, host, company, gang, tribe, team, mob, string, gathering; assembly. —*v.* **3.** huddle, crowd, gather, cluster, group, mass, collect, draw together, congregate, assemble, pack, flock, herd, cram together. **—Ant. 3** separate, disperse, scatter, leave.

bundle *n.* **1.** package, parcel, packet; bale, sheaf, pack, stack, heap, pile, array, bunch, batch, collection, assortment, accumulation, multitude; mass, group, lot, amount, quantity. *—v.* **2.** tie together, wrap, package, bind, truss, bale, stack. **—Ant. 2** disperse, scatter.

bungle *v.* blunder, botch, miff, mismanage, do badly, spoil, ruin, mar, butcher, mess up, make a mess of, miscalculate, misreckon, misestimate, miscompute, misjudge; *Slang* foul up, louse up, goof, screw up, *Informal* flub. **—Ant.** succeed, accomplish, effect, carry off, carry out, triumph.

bunk[1] *n.* berth, built-in bed, platform bed, bed, pallet, cot.

bunk[2] *n. Informal* poppycock, baloney, hokum, tommyrot, rot, hogwash, claptrap, humbug, hooey, malarky, spinach, applesauce, hot air, stuff and nonsense, stuff, bull, bunkum, balderdash, blather; nonsense, foolishness, inanity, bombast, ridiculousness.

buoy *n.* **1.** floating marker, bellbuoy, float, beacon, bell. *—v.* **2.** keep afloat, keep from sinking. **3.** lift, uplift, raise, boost, elevate, lighten, cheer, cheer up, gladden, brighten. **—Ant. 2** sink, drown. **3** lower, crush, dash, cast down, depress, deject, deaden, sadden, dull, darken, chill, damp, dampen.

buoyancy, buoyance *n.* **1.** floatability, floatiness; lightness, weightlessness. **2.** good spirits, animation, vivacity, enthusiasm, exhilaration, good humor, cheerfulness, cheeriness, gladness, joyousness, sunniness, brightness, glee, gaiety, lightheartedness, joviality, jollity. **—Ant. 2** depression, dejection, low spirits, bad humor, cheerlessness, sadness, gloominess, melancholy, tears; dullness, lethargy.

buoyant *adj.* **1.** afloat, floating, floatable; light, weightless. **2.** animated, vivacious, enthusiastic, exhilarated, elated, cheerful, happy, glad, joyful, joyous, sunny, bright, gay, light, lighthearted, blithesome, merry, jolly; optimistic, hopeful, carefree, free and easy, breezy, sportive; energetic, peppy, lively, sprightly. **—Ant. 2** gloomy, glum, dour, sullen, moody, sad, joyless, cheerless, unhappy, tearful, depressed, dejected, morose, doleful, melancholy, despondent; pessimistic, careworn; forlorn, hopeless, despairing; dull, lethargic.

burden *n.* **1.** load, weight; cargo, freight, pack. **2.** weight, load, strain, stress, care, responsibility, onus, trouble, anxiety; encumbrance, hardship. *—v.* **3.** weigh down, load with, load, overload; make responsible for, obligate, saddle with, trouble, encumber, try, tax, vex, press down, afflict, handicap, oppress, hamper, strain, hinder. **—Ant. 2** freedom, ease. **3** lighten, free, ease.

bureau *n.* **1.** chest of drawers, dresser, chiffonier, cabinet, commode. **2.** agency, department, office, division, station, administration, branch, service.

bureaucrat *n.* civil servant, public servant, functionary, *Russian* apparatchik, officeholder, official, *Slang* penpusher, politician, politico, rubber stamp, mandarin.

burgeon *v.* thrive, flourish, expand, enlarge, grow, develop, mushroom, escalate, wax, increase, spring up, shoot up, proliferate, augment, spread; bloom, blossom, flower, blow, effloresce, open, fructify, bear fruit.

burglar *n.* housebreaker, prowler; robber, thief, pilferer, purloiner; second-story man, cracksman, *Slang* yegg.

burglary *n.* breaking and entering, break-in, theft, robbery, housebreaking, burglarizing, stealing, larceny, felony; filching, pilfering, purloining.

burial *n.* inhumation, interment, entombment; funeral, obsequies, rites. **—Ant.** exhumation, disinterment.

burlesque *n.* satire, parody, farce, takeoff, spoof, caricature, mockery, ridicule, travesty; comedy, slapstick comedy, buffoonery. **—Syn. Study.** BURLESQUE, CARICATURE, PARODY, TRAVESTY refer to literary or dramatic forms that imitate works or subjects to achieve a humorous or satiric purpose. The characteristic device of BURLESQUE is mockery of serious or trivial subjects through association with their opposites: *a burlesque of high and low life.* CARICATURE, usu. associated with visual arts or with visual effects in literary works, implies exaggeration of characteristic details: *The caricature emphasized his large nose.* PARODY achieves its humor through application of the style or technique of a well-known work or author to unaccustomed subjects: *a parody of Hemingway.* TRAVESTY takes a serious subject and uses a style or language that seems incongruous or absurd: *a travesty of a senator making a speech.* **—Ant.** factual representation, history, portrait; tragedy.

burly *adj.* sturdy, strapping, hefty, bulky, brawny, beefy, stocky, thickset, big, large, sizable, strong, ponderous, hulking. **—Ant.** puny, weak, thin, slim, skinny, scrawny, lean, spare, lanky, gaunt, angular, rawboned; small, diminutive.

burn *v.* **1.** be on fire, blaze, be ablaze,

flame, be in flames, smoke, smolder; incandesce, glow, flare, flash, flicker. **2.** ignite, kindle, fire; set on fire, set fire to, incinerate, consume with flames, reduce to ashes, cremate; char, scorch, sear, scald, singe, blister, oxidize, wither, shrivel, parch. **3.** use as fuel, consume. **4.** be feverish, be hot, swelter, be flushed. **5.** pain, hurt, smart, sting, tingle, prickle, prick, bite, nip; chafe, abrade, scrape, skin, blister, irritate, nettle. **6.** sunburn, tan, suntan, brown, bronze. —*n.* **7.** *(variously)* first-degree burn, reddening, second-degree burn, blistering, blister, third-degree burn, charring; smart, sting, tingle, pain, prickle, bite; abrasion, chafe, scrape, irritation. **8.** incineration, burning, fire, flames, smoke, smoldering, kindling. —**Ant. 1, 2** extinguish, put out, go out, burn out, smother. **4** be cold, shiver, have a chill, chill. **5** tickle, cool, assuage, soothe. **6** whiten, pale, fade.

burning *adj.* **1.** flaming, aflame, afire, blazing, fiery, ignited, kindled, smoldering, smoking, raging, sizzling, glowing, flaring, flickering, flashing. **2.** all-consuming, raging, fervent, fervid, passionate, impassioned, ardent, eager, fanatic, zealous, intense, frantic, frenzied, fiery, red-hot, glowing, boiling, hot, heated, aglow; resolute, compelling, sincere. **3.** stinging, smarting, piercing, irritating, prickling, tingling; painful, caustic, biting, sharp, astringent, acrid, corroding, pungent. —**Ant. 2** half-hearted, indifferent, lukewarm, mild, perfunctory, faint, passive, apathetic, lethargic, laconic, phlegmatic, lackadaisical. **3** soothing, cooling, numbing.

burnish *v.* polish, wax, buff, shine, smooth, rub up. —**Ant.** abrade, scratch, mar.

burrow *n.* **1.** hole, furrow, dugout, den, lair, tunnel, cave, covert. —*v.* **2.** dig, tunnel, excavate, scoop out, hollow out. —**Ant. 2** fill in, cover over.

bursar *n.* treasurer, purser, cashier, cashkeeper, paymaster.

burst *v.* **1.** break, break open, shatter, fly apart, fragment, disintegrate; explode, blow up, blast, detonate, discharge, pop; rupture, fracture, split, crack, splinter, pull apart, tear apart, separate, detach, divide, sunder, rend, disjoin, disconnect. **2.** erupt, break, break out, gush forth, spout; rush, run, spring forth, barge, fly, *Slang* bust. —*n.* **3.** explosion, detonation, discharge, blast, bang, pop; breaking, shattering, crashing, cracking, splitting. **4.** outburst, outpouring, outbreak, eruption, rush, torrent. —**Ant. 1** put together, hold together, connect, join, unite, fasten, secure, attach. **4** cessation, stopping; slowing down, deceleration.

bury *v.* **1.** inter, entomb, inhume, lay in the grave, consign to the grave, deposit in the earth. **2.** hide, conceal, secrete, cache, cover, cover up, submerge, submerse, immerse, engulf, enclose, encase. —**Ant. 1** exhume, disinter; resurrect. **2** unearth, uncover, discover, find, bring to light, reveal, expose, show, exhibit, display.

bush *n.* **1.** plant, shrub, shrubbery, hedge. **2.** woods, woodlands, veld, barrens, forest, jungle, brush.

business *n.* **1.** job, profession, vocation, occupation, career, calling, pursuit; work, employment, line, industry, trade, field, activity, specialty, specialization, function, duty, position, place, province, assignment, mission, livelihood, living, means of support, walk of life, bread and butter, *Slang* racket. **2.** commerce, industry, manufacturing, trade, buying and selling, merchandising, (*on the Internet*) e-tailing, e-business, e-commerce; dealing, transaction, negotiation, bargaining, affairs. **3.** firm, establishment, concern, store, shop, factory, office, enterprise, venture, undertaking; corporation, company, partnership, *Internet Slang* dot-com. **4.** concern, affair, problem, question, responsibility; matter, job, task, duty, chore, situation, procedure, case, subject, topic, point. —**Ant. 1** unemployment, inactivity; avocation, hobby, entertainment, relaxation.

businesslike *adj.* orderly, organized, systematic, methodical, regular, efficient, practical, professional, correct; serious, careful, thorough, diligent, industrious, sedulous, assiduous, painstaking. —**Ant.** disorderly, disorganized, unorganized, unsystematic, irregular, miscellaneous, catch-as-catch-can, frivolous; inefficient, unprofessional, impractical, careless, sloppy, messy, untidy, slipshod.

bust *n.* **1.** bosom, breast, chest. **2.** head, sculpture.

bustle *v.* **1.** scurry, hurry, rush, hustle, scamper, dash, scramble, tear, fly, flit, scuttle, flutter, fluster; stir, bestir, be active, press on, make haste, be quick, make the most of one's time, work against time, not let the grass grow under one's feet. —*n.* **2.** commotion, flurry, tumult, hustle, stir, agitation, hurly-burly, activity, fuss, hurry, excitement; pother, to-do, ado. —**Ant. 1** move slowly, crawl, creep, drag one's feet, procrastinate, waste time; loaf, relax, rest. **2** inactivity, quiet, peacefulness, tranquillity.

busy *adj.* **1.** occupied, active, engaged, employed, working, hard at work, laboring, toiling, industrious, slaving, on duty, in harness; engrossed, absorbed, intent. **2.** active, strenuous, full, bustling. **—*v.* 3.** occupy, keep occupied, engage, employ, work at, labor at, be engrossed in, be absorbed in. **—Ant. 1, 2** idle, inactive, unoccupied, unemployed, at leisure, off duty. **2** lazy, slothful, sluggish, indolent, relaxed, slack.

busybody *n.* meddler, snoop, pry, Paul Pry; gossip, scandalmonger, telltale, tattletale, blabbermouth, blabber, chatterbox, newsmonger, talebearer.

butcher *v.* **1.** massacre, murder, kill, assassinate, slaughter, exterminate, liquidate, slay, decimate, purge, annihilate. **2.** botch, ruin, spoil, mess up, bungle, manhandle, mishandle, fumble, boggle; *Slang* louse up, screw up, goof, muff. **—*n.* 3.** killer, murderer, mass-murderer, assassin, slaughterer, liquidator, exterminator, bloodshedder, homicide, hatchet man, hit man, homicidal maniac. **—Syn. Study. 1** See SLAUGHTER.

butt[1] *n.* **1.** end, blunt end, bottom, shank, stub, stump. **2.** *Slang* See BUTTOCKS. **—Ant.** front, top.

butt[2] *n.* target, victim, mark, object, laughingstock, dupe, *Slang* goat.

butt[3] *v. (with the head or horns)* push, shove, bump, knock, hit, strike, bunt, smack, thump, thwack, rap, ram, buck, thrust, buffet, jostle, jab, slap.

buttocks *n.* posterior, rump, seat, rear, rear end, backside, bottom, derrière, *Informal* fanny, keister, *Slang* behind, butt; fundament, hindquarters, haunches.

buttress *n.* **1.** support, brace, prop, stanchion, abutment, arch, stay, shoulder. **—*v.* 2.** prop, prop up, brace, shore, shore up, reinforce, strengthen, bolster, support, boost, steel.

buxom *adj. (of women)* plump, robust, well-developed, strapping, chesty, large-breasted, bosomy, voluptuous, *Yiddish* zaftig. **—Ant.** frail, delicate, thin, slender, skinny, lean; pale, wan; small-breasted, flat-chested.

buy *v.* **1.** purchase, put money into, pay for, invest in, acquire, procure, obtain, gain, get. **2.** bribe, buy off, corrupt, influence, suborn. **—*n.* 3.** bargain, worthy purchase. **—Ant. 1** sell, vend, retail, auction, hawk; rent, lease.

buzz *n.* **1.** murmur, whisper; buzzing, hum, humming sound. **—*v.* 2.** hum, drone, whir.

bygone *adj.* gone by, past, earlier, previous, former, departed, of yore, olden, ancient. **—Ant.** future, to come, coming, prospective, subsequent, succeeding, later, unborn.

bypass *v.* go around, go by, circumvent, detour around, avoid, dodge, avert. **—Ant.** go through, bisect, cross, meet, confront.

bypath *n.* back road, side road, secondary road, lane, trail, dirt road, byway, bypass, footway, footpath, alley, way, track, pathway, garden path, shortcut, walkway.

bystander *n.* on-looker, looker-on, spectator, witness, observer, beholder, viewer, watcher, attender; passerby. **—Ant.** participant, principal.

byword *n.* rule, dictum, principle, precept, law, truth; pet phrase, slogan, motto, saying, maxim, proverb, axiom, adage, watchword, aphorism, apothegm, catchword, shibboleth, saw.

cab *n.* taxi, taxicab, hack.

cabal *n.* **1.** junta, faction, combination, band, ring, league. **2.** intrigue, conspiracy, plot, design, scheme, plan, machination, connivance. **—Syn. Study. 2** See CONSPIRACY.

cabalistic *adj.* obscure, occult, mysterious, supernatural, abstruse, esoteric, arcane, secret, mystic; impenetrable, unknowable, inscrutable, unfathomable, incomprehensible. **—Ant.** obvious, apparent, unmistakable, self-evident, crystal-clear.

cabaret *n.* supper club, nightclub, bistro, café, *Informal* club.

cabin *n.* **1.** log cabin, hut, shack, shanty, hutch; lodge, cottage, bungalow. **2.** stateroom, quarters, room; compartment. **—Ant. 1** mansion, palace, castle.

cabinet *n.* **1.** council, group of counselors, official advisers, advisory board, ministry. **2.** cupboard, kitchen cabinet, china closet, china cabinet, breakfront, bureau; case, chest, chest of drawers, file, box, receptacle.

cable *n.* **1.** bundle of wires, electric wire, wires, wire line, line, wire rope; rope, cord, twisted strand; chain, mooring, hawser; fastening. **2.** cablegram, overseas telegram, wire.

cache *n.* **1.** store, stockpile, stock, secret repository, hoard, heap. **2.** hiding place, hide-away, secret place. **—Ant. 2** display, exhibition, show, array.

cacophonous *adj.* dissonant, inharmonious, harsh, raucous, discordant, unmusical, unmelodious, strident, screechy, jarring, grating, disharmonious, nonmelodious; out of tune, off-key, off-pitch.

cad *n.* dishonorable man, bounder, rotter, lout, churl, dastard, *Slang* cur, louse, heel, rat; villain, scoundrel, rascal, knave, rogue, caitiff. **—Ant.** gentleman, cavalier; hero, champion, worthy, *Informal* prince.

cadaver *n.* corpse, dead body, body, cadaver, remains, deceased, *Slang* stiff. **—Syn. Study.** See BODY.

cadaverous *adj.* corpselike, deathlike, deathly; ghastly, gaunt, pale, ashen, chalky, pallid, bloodless, blanched.

cadence *n.* rhythmic pattern, beat, tempo, swing, lilt, throb, pulse, accent, measure, meter, rhythm.

café *n.* restaurant, bistro, coffeehouse, inn, tavern, bar and grill, cafeteria, luncheonette, automat, diner, chophouse, lunchroom; *Slang* eatery, hash house, beanery; night club, supper club, discotheque, cabaret; *Slang* nitery.

cage *n.* **1.** barred enclosure, enclosure, pen, coop. **—*v.* 2.** lock up, shut in, pen, pen in, coop up, encage, impound, imprison; confine, restrict, restrain. **—Ant. 2** let out, free, liberate.

cagey *adj.* wary, cautious, chary, careful, prudent, alert, watchful, heedful, discreet, leery; wily, cunning, crafty, shifty, sly, foxy, artful, shrewd, sharp, keen. **—Ant.** unwary, careless, heedless, reckless, rash, unthinking, unguarded, trusting, imprudent, indiscreet; dense, dull, slow-witted, stolid.

cajolery *n.* wheedling, coaxing, inveigling, enticement, beguilement, promises, *Informal* sweet talk, *Slang* soft soap; persuasion; flattery, fawning, adulation, blandishment, blarney. **—Ant.** threats, extortion, coercion, force.

cake *n.* **1.** (*variously*) layer cake, loaf cake, cupcake, gateau; (*loosely*) pastry, sweet rolls, buns, tortes, éclairs, cookies. **2.** block, bar; mass, lump. **—*v.* 3.** harden, solidify, dry, coagulate, congeal, thicken, crust; mass, compress, consolidate.

calamitous *adj.* disastrous, catastrophic, fatal, ruinous, cataclysmic, adverse, destructive, detrimental, harmful, deleterious, pernicious, blighting; tragic, distressful, dreadful, woeful, baleful, unfortunate, unlucky. **—Ant.** beneficial, advantageous, favorable, helpful, valuable, fortunate, good, convenient.

calamity *n.* disaster, catastrophe, tragedy, cataclysm, adversity, affliction, hardship, misfortune, tribulation, trial, undoing, downfall, reverse, blow, failure, scourge, ruin; mishap, mischance, ill fortune, bad luck, stroke of ill luck; distress, misery, trouble, woe, sea of troubles, ill, ill wind. **—Syn. Study.** See DISASTER. **—Ant.** benefit, blessing, advantage, help, aid, boon, good fortune, good luck, piece of luck, windfall.

calculate *v.* **1.** compute, figure, reckon, determine, ascertain, work out; count, sum up, add up, measure. **2.** judge, estimate, figure, reckon, surmise, predict, conjecture. **3.** design, intend, plan, devise, project, mean, aim at.

calculating *adj.* scheming, designing, plotting, contriving, intriguing, Machiavellian, crafty, manipulative, devious, cunning, wily, tricky, artful; shrewd, foxy, sly. **—Ant.** open, candid, frank, direct, plain-spoken, sincere, aboveboard, honest; naïve, artless, guileless, ingenuous, undesigning.

calculation *n.* **1.** computation, figuring, reckoning; answer, result. **2.** judgment, estimation, reckoning.

calendar *n.* **1.** chart of days, weeks, and months. **2.** agenda, day book, diary, schedule, list, register, docket, program, table.

caliber *n.* **1.** bore, inside diameter. **2.** worth, merit, excellence, quality, ability, competence, capability, capacity, talent, gifts, skill, power, scope; stature, reputation, repute, importance, prominence, prestige, eminence, distinction, estimation, achievement, position, rank, place.

call *v.* **1.** call out, cry out, cry, shout, yell, bellow, scream, roar, clamor, bawl, speak loudly, holler, hail, halloo. **2.** summon, ask, bid, invite, order, command, demand, require, direct, instruct, charge; call together, convene, assemble, convoke, muster, collect, gather, rally. **3.** appeal to, ask, ask for, call upon, entreat, bid, request, petition, invoke, summon, invite, supplicate, pray to. **4.** visit, pay a visit, look in on, drop in, stop off, stop by. **5.** proclaim, announce, declare, decree, order, command, convoke. **6.** name, dub, christen, title, entitle, term, identify, designate, style, label, tag, characterize, describe as, know as, specify. **7.** telephone, phone, contact, *Informal* buzz, *Slang* get on the horn to, *Chiefly British* ring. —*n.* **8.** outcry, crying out, cry, shout, yell, scream, bellow, clamor; hail, halloo, *Informal* holler. **9.** summons, order, notice, command, demand, direction, instruction, charge; invitation, request, bid, appeal, entreaty, petition, supplication, plea; announcement, proclamation, declaration, decree. **10.** visit, stop. **11.** telephone call, phone call, telephone message. **12.** right, need, cause, reason, grounds, claim, occasion, justification, excuse, warrant. **—Ant. 1** be silent, be still, be quiet; whisper, murmur. **2** excuse, dismiss, release, disperse, scatter. **3** grant, give. **5** call off, cancel, renounce. **8** whisper, murmur. **9** excuse, dismissal, release.

calling *n.* **1.** calling out, crying out, outcry, crying, shouting, yelling, screaming, bellowing, hailing, hallooing. **2.** main interest, mission, first love, attachment, dedication, devotion, passion, enthusiasm, preferred pursuit, province, forte, specialty, specialization, métier; life's work, career, profession, vocation, occupation, employment, business, job, work, line, field, trade, craft, activity, function, assignment, livelihood, living, means of support, walk of life, bread and butter. **—Ant. 1** whispering, murmuring. **2** hobby, avocation; bane, nuisance, affliction, scourge, curse, plague, aversion, dislike, anathema, abomination, bane of one's existence, thorn in the flesh.

callous *adj.* **1.** callused, hard, hardened, horny, tough, thick-skinned, pachydermatous. **2.** unsympathetic, unfeeling, insensitive, uncaring, cold, hard, hardened, inured, hard-hearted, heartless, cruel, apathetic, dispassionate, unresponsive, indifferent. **—Ant. 1** tender, soft, thin-skinned. **2** compassionate, sympathetic, sensitive, soft, soft-hearted, warm-hearted, caring, responsive, gentle.

callow *adj.* immature, inexperienced, unseasoned, untried, green, raw, unschooled, uninitiated, uninformed, ignorant, shallow, awkward, unsophisticated, naïve, crude, artless; childish, juvenile, infantile, puerile, sophomoric. **—Ant.** mature, grown-up, adult, experienced, tried and true, finished; informed, sophisticated, polished.

calm *adj.* **1.** motionless, smooth, quiet, still, unruffled, undisturbed, placid, mild, balmy, bland, pacific, gentle, tranquil, serene, halcyon. **2.** unperturbed, unshaken, unruffled, unexcited, composed, self-possessed, unagitated, collected, cool, cool-headed, impassive, sedate; passionless, imperturbable, untroubled, relaxed, serene, placid, peaceful, tranquil; *Slang* unflappable. —*n.* **3.** calmness, quiet, quietness, peacefulness, tranquillity, serenity, restfulness, stillness, smoothness; windlessness, stormlessness; composure, self-control, placidity, repose, self-possession, impassivity, imperturbability, coolness, *Slang* cool. —*v.* **4.** calm down, compose, collect, quiet, pacify, cool off, becalm, simmer down, *Slang* chill out. **5.** allay, assuage, soothe, quell, mollify, mitigate, relieve, alleviate, moderate, subdue, cause to subside, placate, tranquilize, ease, lessen, diminish, reduce. **—Syn. Study. 2** CALM, COLLECTED, COMPOSED, COOL imply the absence of agitation. CALM implies an unruffled state in the midst of disturbance all around: *He remained calm throughout the crisis.* COLLECTED implies complete command of one's thoughts, feelings, and behavior, usu. as a result of effort: *The witness was remarkably collected during questioning.* COMPOSED implies inner peace and dignified self-possession: *pale but composed.* COOL implies clarity of judgment and absence of strong feeling or excitement: *cool in the face of danger.* **—Ant. 1, 2** agitated, disturbed, ruffled, violent, raging, fierce, wild. **1** turbulent, stormy, rough. **2** excited, aroused, hotheaded, heated, passionate; tense, troubled, perturbed, worried, upset, uncollected, discomposed, shaken, jolted, rocked, frantic, frenzied. **3** disturbance, agitation, violence, fierceness, wildness, tempestuousness. **4** excite, agitate, disturb, arouse, work up. **5** irritate, aggravate, intensify, inflame.

calumny *n.* slander, libel, defamation, backstabbing, vilification, depreciation, backbiting, deprecation, disparagement, derogation, animadversion, revilement, calumniation, malice, innuendo, denigration; slur, smear, insinuation, barb. **—Ant.** praise, acclaim, kudos, encomium, eulogy.

camaraderie *n.* conviviality, good-fellowship, sociability, good will, friendliness, affability, jollity, companionship, clubbiness, congeniality, brotherhood, comradeship, esprit de corps, bonhomie. **—Ant.** hostility, enmity, animosity, rancor, hatred.

camouflage *n.* **1.** deceptive markings, deceptive covering, disguise; mask, masquerade, subterfuge, false appearance, blind, front, cover, screen, cloak, concealment. *—v.* **2.** cover with a disguise, disguise, give a false appearance to; mask, screen, cloak, conceal, hide, cover up, veil, shroud. **—Ant. 2** show, expose, display, exhibit.

camp *n.* **1.** encampment, campground, temporary shelter, tents, tent, bivouac, lodging, quarters; army base, barracks. *—v.* **2.** lodge in temporary quarters, encamp, pitch a tent; bivouac; rough it.

campaign *n.* **1.** military operation, operation, offensive, regional battle, battle series, action. **2.** drive, effort, push, movement, endeavor, offensive, crusade, action. *—v.* **3.** electioneer, solicit votes, compete for office, run, stump, whistle-stop, beat the drums, stump the countryside.

canal *n.* **1.** artificial waterway, man-made waterway; channel, conduit, aqueduct; arm of the sea. **2.** duct, tube, passage, channel.

cancel *v.* **1.** call off, set aside, quash, do away with, dispense with, abolish, revoke, recall, call back, rescind, repeal, countermand, retract, recant, blue-pencil, vitiate; annul, nullify, invalidate, abrogate, repudiate, void, declare null and void, delete. **2.** offset, make up for, compensate for, counterbalance, balance out, neutralize, erase. **—Ant. 1, 2** confirm, affirm, reaffirm, ratify; implement, enact, enforce, uphold, sustain, maintain.

cancer *n.* **1.** malignant growth, malignancy, malignant tumor, carcinoma, sarcoma, neoplasm. **2.** malignancy, plague, sickness, rot, scourge.

candid *adj.* **1.** frank, open, honest, truthful, sincere, genuine, blunt, straightforward, forthright, plain-spoken, outspoken, direct, plain, outright, downright, free, unvarnished, tell-all, fair, just. **2.** impromptu, spontaneous, unposed, extemporaneous, informal, relaxed, natural. **—Syn. Study. 1** See FRANK. **—Ant. 1** diplomatic, flattering, fawning, honeyed, subtle, mealy-mouthed, complimentary, kind. **2** formal, posed.

candidate *n.* applicant, nominee, aspirant, eligible, possibility, hopeful, competitor, contender, contestant; office seeker, job seeker.

candle *n.* taper; *Archaic and Literary* tallow, light, rush light, wax, dip, bougie, *French* cierge.

candlestick *n.* candleholder, candelabrum, sconce, chandelier, girandole; *Eastern Orthodox Church* dikerion, trikerion; *Judaism* menorah.

candor *n.* frankness, openness, honesty, truthfulness, sincerity, bluntness, straightforwardness, forthrightness, plainspokenness, directness, artlessness, fairness, justness, impartiality, freedom from prejudice. **—Ant.** diplomacy, flattery, subtlety, evasiveness, deceit, artfulness, dishonesty, insincerity, hypocrisy, unfairness, partiality, bias, prejudice.

candy *n.* sugar candy, confection, confectionary, dainty, sweet, sweets, sweetmeat; *(variously)* hard candy, filled candy, chocolate, kiss, bonbon, fudge, cream, jelly, toffee, taffy, caramel, nougat, fondant, comfit, candy bar, lollipop, all-day sucker, candy cane, peanut brittle, brittle, praline, gumdrop, jellybean.

cane *n.* **1.** walking stick, stick, staff, rod. *—v.* **2.** *(with a cane)* flog, thrash, beat, whip, flail, trounce, baste, drub, tan, lash, switch; strike, hit, whack, wallop, rap, smite.

canker *n.* **1.** mouth sore; lesion, inflammation, ulcer, sore. **2.** source of corruption, cancer, blight.

canny *adj.* artful, skillful; knowing, wise, astute, shrewd, sharp, clever, subtle, convincing, cunning, crafty, foxy, wily, cagey; wary, careful, judicious, sagacious, intelligent, perspicacious, circumspect. **—Ant.** unskilled, inept, dumb, obtuse, blatant; bumbling, fumbling.

canon *n.* **1.** doctrine, dogma, decree, edict. **2.** rule, principle, precept, code, model, pattern, standard, yardstick, criterion, bench mark, touchstone; regulation; order, ordinance, law, decree, statute.

canonical *adj.* accepted, authorized,

sanctioned, orthodox, recognized, authoritative, approved, legitimate, authentic, proper, conventional, customary. **—Ant.** freakish, bizarre, outlandish, eccentric.

canopy *n.* awning, covering, cover, tester, hood.

cant *n.* **1.** hypocrisy, insincerity, humbug, pretentiousness, pretense, sham, sanctimoniousness, lip service. **2.** jargon, lingo, talk, parlance, slang, argot, vernacular.

cantankerous *adj.* quarrelsome, argumentative, contentious, contrary, testy, touchy, peevish, fretful, huffy, ill-tempered, ill-natured, ill-humored, disagreeable, grouchy, grumpy, irascible, irritable, cranky, cross, bearish, surly, churlish, snappish, waspish, crabbed, morose, sullen, sulky, short, crusty, mean, choleric, splenetic. **—Ant.** agreeable, good-humored, good-natured, pleasant; amiable, affable, genial, kindly; placid, calm, complaisant, mellow; merry, gay, happy, jolly, jaunty, breezy, vivacious, cheerful, lighthearted.

canteen *n.* **1.** flask, pocket flask, bottle. **2.** commissary, post exchange, PX, club.

canvas *n.* **1.** sailcloth, tent cloth, duck; tarpaulin. **2.** painting, picture (*on canvas*) .

canvass *v.* **1.** survey, analyze, examine, scrutinize, investigate, scan, explore, inquire into, take stock of, give thought to. *—n.* **2.** poll, investigation, survey, tally, evaluation, analysis, study, enumeration, inquiry, exploration, scrutiny.

canyon *n.* gorge, gully, pass, ravine, chasm, gap, col, valley, corridor, gulch, defile, coulee, draw, water gap, wash, crevasse, arroyo, *Arabic* wadi; cut, break, cleft, fissure, divide, crack, opening, notch.

cap *n.* **1.** brimless hat, visored hat, headdress, headgear. **2.** top, lid, cover, seal. *—v.* **3.** better, surpass, exceed, outdo, outstrip, top off.

capability *n.* ability, competency, competence, attainment, proficiency, facility, faculty, capacity, skill, art, know-how, qualification; power, efficacy, potential, potentiality, talent, gift, flair, knack. **—Ant.** incompetence, ineptitude, inadequacy, inability, inefficiency, impotency, powerlessness.

capable *adj.* able, competent, expert, skillful, skilled, masterly, accomplished, gifted, talented, proficient, adept, apt, deft, adroit, effective, efficacious; clever, intelligent, artful, ingenious. **—Ant.** incapable, incompetent, unaccomplished, unqualified, inexpert, unskilled, inept, ineffective, amateurish.

capacious *adj.* roomy, spacious, commodious, ample, extensive, expansive, broad, wide, expandable, amplitudinous, voluminous; big, large, vast, mammoth, gigantic, massive, huge, tremendous. **—Ant.** small, confined, narrow, cramped, restricted.

capacity *n.* **1.** maximum contents, limit, extent, volume, size, amplitude, room, space. **2.** ability, power, capability, faculty, facility, strength, might; scope, range. **3.** ability, endowment, talent, gifts, faculty, aptitude, potential; intelligence, intellect, sagacity, brain power, mind; perspicacity, discernment, judgment. **4.** role, function, position. **—Ant. 2, 3** inability, incapacity.

cape *n.* **1.** cloak, mantle, shawl, manta, pelisse, tabard, poncho, serape. **2.** peninsula, point, promontory, headland, tongue, spit.

caper *v.* **1.** prance, gambol, frisk, cavort, romp, frolic; leap, jump, hop, skip, bounce, bound. *—n.* **2.** lark, escapade, caprice, adventure, spree, fling, frolic; trick, prank, practical joke, antic, stunt, shenanigans, high jinks, carrying on, jape, monkey business.

capital *n.* **1.** seat of government; chief city, first city, center, headquarters. **2.** capital letter, uppercase letter, large letter, majuscule. **3.** investment funds, working capital, income-producing property, resources, available means, money, cash, cash on hand, wealth, riches, financing, principal, working assets, wherewithal. *—adj.* **4.** excellent, supreme, great, fine, super, superb, first-rate, first-class, matchless. **5.** major, principal, chief, primary, prime, leading, cardinal. **—Ant. 2** small letter, lowercase letter, minuscule. **3** debts, debits, red ink. **4** bad, poor, inferior, awful, lousy, second-rate.

capitalism *n.* free enterprise, private ownership. **—Ant.** socialism, communism, collectivism.

capitalist *n.* **1.** investor, businessperson. **2.** financier, tycoon, plutocrat, mogul. **—Ant.** worker, laborer, proletarian; socialist, communist, collectivist.

capitalize *v.* **1.** bankroll, finance, fund, back, stake, subsidize, support; foot the bill, put up the money. **2.** take advantage of, profit by, make capital of, exploit, utilize, cash in on, avail oneself of, trade on, put to advantage, make the most of, turn to account, make a good thing of; make hay while the sun shines, strike while the iron is hot, turn an honest penny.

capitol *n.* legislative building; statehouse, government house; seat of government.

capitulate *v.* surrender, submit, acknowledge defeat, give up, give in, yield, acquiesce, accede, succumb, lay down one's arms, relent, come to terms, sue for peace, cry quits, hoist the white flag. —**Ant.** defeat, win over, be victorious.

caprice *n.* whim, fancy, quirk, notion, impulse; eccentricity, idiosyncrasy, oddity, peculiarity, crotchet, erraticism, vagary; lark, escapade, caper, stunt, prank, antic, spree, fling; craze, fad.

capricious *adj.* changeable, fickle, variable, impulsive, erratic, flighty, skittish, mercurial, inconstant, fanciful, faddish; indecisive, undecided, irresolute, uncertain, wavering, vacillating, shilly-shallying; irresponsible, inconsistent, unsteady, unstable, fitful, uneven, eccentric, quirky. —**Syn. Study.** See FICKLE. —**Ant.** consistent, unchangeable, inflexible, unmovable, firm, fixed, unwavering, invariable, unswerving; resolute, determined, steadfast, certain, decided, decisive; serious, responsible, steady, stable, even.

capsize *v.* overturn, turn over, keel over, tip over, flip over, invert, upset, turn turtle. —**Ant.** right, upright.

captain *n.* **1.** commanding officer, commander, master, skipper, *Slang* old man; pilot. **2.** company commander, commanding officer, commandant, chief officer. **3.** leader, headman, chief, chieftain, head, boss. —**Ant. 1** able seaman, deckhand. **3** follower, member.

captious *adj.* carping, nitpicking, hypercritical, faultfinding, caviling, picayune, niggling, censorious, querulous, deprecating, picky, cutting, belittling; peevish, testy, snappish, petulant; perverse, contrary, ornery, fractious, mean, cantankerous. —**Ant.** flattering, laudatory, approving, appreciative, fawning.

captivate *v.* fascinate, charm, enchant, bewitch, dazzle, hypnotize, mesmerize, enthrall, delight, enrapture, transport, carry away, win over, lure, seduce, attract, infatuate, enamor, take the fancy of, turn the head of. —**Ant.** repulse, repel, alienate, turn away, disenchant, antagonize; disgust, nauseate, make sick.

captive *n.* **1.** prisoner, internee; hostage. —*adj.* **2.** imprisoned, incarcerated, confined, penned, caged, locked up; subjugated, enslaved, oppressed. —**Ant. 1** captor, guard; free person. **2** free, unconfined, at liberty; freed, liberated, independent, emancipated.

capture *v.* **1.** seize, take, grasp, grab, procure; take prisoner, take captive, catch, trap, ensnare, snare, bag, snag, lay hold of; arrest, apprehend, take into custody, *Slang* pinch, collar, nab, bust. —*n.* **2.** seizure, taking, capturing, taking prisoner, taking captive, catching, trapping, snaring, ensnaring, bagging, collaring, laying hold of; arrest, apprehension. —**Ant. 1** release, free, let go, liberate. **2** release, freeing, liberation; escape.

car *n.* **1.** automobile, auto, motorcar, motor, machine, vehicle, motor vehicle, *Slang* jalopy, heap, flivver, tin lizzie, wheels, buggy, hot rod (*variously*) sedan, van, minivan, convertible, sports car, SUV, sport-utility vehicle, four-door, two-door. **2.** railway car; (*variously*) coach, carriage, parlor car, sleeping car, Pullman car, sleeper, dining car, diner, baggage car, freight car, boxcar, cattle car, coal car; streetcar, cable car, horsecar.

caravan *n.* procession, parade, column, cortege, train, string, file, motorcade, wagon train, company, cavalcade, line, band, queue, convoy, retinue, entourage, troop; coffle, chain gang.

card *n.* **1.** playing card. **2.** postcard, (*variously*) picture postcard, greeting card, birthday card, Christmas card, anniversary card, New Year's card, Easter card, Valentine's Day card, Valentine, get-well card. **3.** (*variously*) business card, calling card. **4.** program, bill, ticket.

cardinal *n.* **1.** *Roman Catholic Church* member of the college of cardinals. —*adj.* **2.** first, foremost, basic, prime, primary, fundamental, elementary, chief, main, key, principal, central, leading, most important, paramount, highest, greatest, outstanding, dominant, predominant, preeminent, uppermost, top, head, underlying; vital, necessary, essential, indispensable, intrinsic. **3.** deep red, cherry, blood-red, carmine, wine-colored, claret, scarlet. —**Ant. 2** second, secondary, subordinate, insignificant, least important, unessential, unnecessary, irrelevant, immaterial, extraneous, dispensable; lowest, smallest.

care *n.* **1.** carefulness, caution, precaution, circumspection, diligence, attention, attentiveness, heed, watchfulness, vigilance, thought; regard, concern, effort, pains, consideration, discrimination, solicitude, conscientiousness, application, fastidiousness, meticulousness, exactness, scrupulousness. **2.** concern, worry, responsibility, load, anxiety, strain, stress, pressure; bother, annoyance, nuisance, vexation, tribulation, heartache, distress, trouble, hardship, affliction, sorrow, grief, misery, anguish, sadness, unhappiness. **3.** ministration, attention, supervision, custody, control, management, charge, keeping, responsibility, protection. —*v.* **4.** be concerned, be interested in, be worried, mind, regard, bother about, trouble about. **5.** want, wish, desire. —**Syn. Study. 2** See CONCERN. —**Ant. 1** carelessness, neglect, negligence, abandon, recklessness, unconcern, disregard, inattention, thoughtlessness, heedlessness, indifference. 2 relaxation; pleasure, delight, happiness. 4 disregard, forget about. 5 dislike, hate, detest, abhor, loathe; reject.

career *n.* profession, vocation, calling, occupation, employment, work, job, business, livelihood, lifework, activity, line, pursuit, walk of life. **—Ant.** hobby, avocation, sideline, diversion, entertainment, relaxation.

carefree *adj.* free of care, careless, without worry, without a worry in the world, untroubled, happy-go-lucky, lighthearted, relaxed, easygoing, free-and-easy; in high spirits, joyous, elated, jaunty, optimistic, buoyant, jubilant, breezy; happy, cheerful, sunny, glad, laughing, smiling, radiant, full of life, gleeful, jolly, gay. **—Ant.** careworn, heavy-hearted, worried; unhappy, sad, sorrowful, joyless, cheerless, melancholy, crestfallen, blue, gloomy, dismal, dreary, depressed, dejected, disconsolate, desolate, despondent.

careful *adj.* **1.** cautious, watchful, wary, guarded, chary, alert, observant, attentive, on guard, vigilant, diligent, concerned, thoughtful, mindful, regardful, heedful, prudent, painstaking, scrupulous; circumspect, discreet, tactful, judicious, solicitous. **2.** precise, punctilious, exact, fastidious, particular, meticulous, conscientious, fussy, painstaking, fine, nice, scrupulous, accurate, correct. **—Syn. Study.** CAREFUL, CAUTIOUS, DISCREET, WARY imply a watchful guarding against something. CAREFUL implies guarding against mistakes, harm, or bad consequences by paying close attention to details and by being concerned or solicitous: *He was careful not to wake the baby.* CAUTIOUS implies a fear of some unfavorable situation and an investigation before acting: *cautious about investments.* DISCREET implies being prudent in speech or action and being trustworthy: *discreet inquiries about his credit rating.* WARY implies a vigilant lookout for a danger suspected or feared: *wary of telephone calls from strangers.* **—Ant. 1** careless, reckless, rash, abandoned, slack, lax, neglectful, negligent, remiss, heedless, perfunctory, thoughtless, unthinking, inattentive, unconcerned, improvident. **2** careless, sloppy, slipshod, slovenly, slapdash, casual; inexact, imprecise, inaccurate; unrigorous, slack, indifferent.

careless *adj.* **1.** thoughtless, unthinking, heedless, mindless, unmindful, absent-minded, sloppy, slipshod, lax, slack, negligent, rash; inconsiderate. **2.** nonchalant, offhand, indifferent, heedless, thoughtless, unconcerned, devil-may-care, forgetful, negligent, neglectful, lackadaisical, carefree, untroubled, casual, lax, slack, slipshod, slapdash; untidy, slovenly, sloppy, messy, disorderly; inexact, imprecise, incorrect, inaccurate. **3.** See CAREFREE. **—Ant. 1** careful, cautious, wary, alert, attentive, diligent, watchful, mindful, concerned. **2** careful, fastidious, neat, tidy, meticulous, fussy, painstaking, orderly; scrupulous, correct, precise, exact, accurate.

caress *n.* **1.** gentle touch, stroking, pat, petting, fondling; embrace, hug. **—*v.* 2.** stroke, fondle, toy with, pet, pat, touch; embrace, hug, clasp; cuddle. **—Ant. 1** hit, blow, slap, cuff, box. **2** hit, beat, thrash, slap, cuff, box.

caretaker *n.* custodian, keeper, overseer, curator, concierge, steward, warden; superintendent, janitor, porter; watchman, gatekeeper.

cargo *n.* freight, shipment, consignment, load, lading, burden; goods, merchandise.

caricature *n.* **1.** lampoon, takeoff, burlesque, parody, satire, travesty, mockery; distortion, absurdity, exaggeration. **—*v.* 2.** lampoon, burlesque, parody, satirize, mock. **—Syn. Study. 1** See BURLESQUE.

carnage *n.* slaughter, butchery, blood bath, great bloodshed, mass killing, massacre.

carnal *adj.* sexual, sensual, erotic, voluptuous, sensuous, prurient, lustful, libidinous, fleshly, animal, unchaste, lewd, lascivious, lecherous, salacious, immoral, sinful, impure, venereal, wanton. **—Syn. Study.** CARNAL, SENSUAL, ANIMAL all refer to the physical rather than the rational or spiritual nature of human beings. CARNAL, although it may refer to any bodily need or urge, most often refers to sexuality: *carnal knowledge; the carnal sin of gluttony.* SENSUAL most often describes the arousal or gratification of erotic urges: *sensual eyes; sensual delights.* ANIMAL may describe any physical appetite, but is sometimes used of sexual appetite: *animal greediness; animal lust.* See also SENSUAL. **—Ant.** chaste, modest; virginal, pure, innocent.

carnival *n.* **1.** small circus, traveling sideshow. **2.** fair, festival, jamboree, celebration, jubilee, fete, gala; Mardi Gras; holiday.

carnivorous *adj.* meat-eating, flesh-eating, predatory, predaceous. **—Ant.** herbivorous; vegetarian.

carol *n.* Christmas carol, noel; hymn, canticle, paean, song of praise, song of joy. **—Ant.** dirge, lament.

carouse *v.* revel, make merry, *Informal* live it up, make whoopee, *Slang* party; drink, tipple, imbibe, guzzle, quaff, wassail, *Informal* go on a binge.

carp *v.* complain, find fault, fault-find, nag, cavil, criticize, disapprove, deride, belittle, knock, condemn, deprecate, disparage, chide, decry, reproach, censure, impugn, abuse, pick on, jibe at, pull to pieces. **—Ant.** compliment, praise, applaud, laud, approve.

carpet *n.* **1.** rug; matting, mat. **2.** blanket, layer, covering, sheet.

carriage *n.* **1.** coach, horse-drawn coach; wagon, buggy, rig; vehicle, conveyance. **2.** bearing, posture, comportment; demeanor, mien, attitude, appearance, air, poise, aspect; presence, manner, behavior, deportment.

carrion *n.* remains, bones, corpse, cadaver, dead body, carcass, putrefying flesh, *Slang* crowbait, *Law* corpus delicti; refuse, garbage, offal, waste, wastage, leavings.

carry *v.* **1.** take, bring, tote, bear, fetch, haul, lug, cart, lift; move, transport, transmit, convey, transfer, conduct, shift, displace, ship, deliver. **2.** support, sustain, maintain, bear, uphold, hold up, prop, brace, shoulder, lift. **3.** communicate, transmit, disseminate, publish, run, print, broadcast, release, offer. **4.** supply, stock, keep on hand, display, offer. **—Ant. 1** throw down, drop, let go. **3** withhold, reject, delete, censor; cover up, keep secret.

cart *n.* **1.** wagon, truck, tumbrel, dumpcart, curricle, trap; two-wheeler, dogcart, gig, dray, tipcart; go-cart, pushcart, handcart, barrow, wheelbarrow, handbarrow. *—v.* **2.** transport, haul, lug, tote, carry, truck; *Slang* schlepp; bear, move; take, bring, fetch, convey, transmit, transfer, transplant.

carte blanche *n.* a free hand, free reign, full authority, unconditional power, blank check, license, open sanction.

cartel *n.* monopoly, trust, syndicate, consortium, combine, chain, pool, corporation, federation.

carton *n.* box, cardboard box, container, cardboard container; packing case, case, packing crate, crate.

carve *v.* **1.** sculpture, sculpt, chisel, hew, block out; shape, mold, model, fashion, pattern, form, work, turn; engrave, etch, incise. **2.** slice, cut up, dissever, saw, hack, slash; cleve, rend, split, divide, quarter, apportion, allot.

Casanova *n.* ladies' man, Lothario, Don Juan, Romeo, lover boy; admirer, suitor, wooer, lover, swain, gallant, cavalier, beau, paramour; womanizer, lady-killer, philanderer, chaser, wolf, libertine, profligate, roué, lecher, *Slang* lech, bounder, cad, rounder, rip.

cascade *n.* **1.** waterfall, falls, cataract, Niagara; rapids, chute. *—v.* **2.** surge, pour, gush, plunge, rush, fall, tumble. **—Ant. 2** trickle, dribble, drip, drop, seep.

case[1] *n.* **1.** instance, incidence, incident, occurrence, situation, event, episode, happening, condition, example, illustration, circumstance; matter, business, affair, concern. **2.** lawsuit, suit, litigation, action; dispute, controversy, debate, argument, inquiry, hearing, proceeding; plea, appeal, cause. **3.** patient, sick person, invalid, victim, sufferer; disease, injury.

case[2] *n.* **1.** box, crate, carton, chest, container, receptacle; tray, cabinet, display case, bin. **2.** wrapper, cover, covering, sheath, sheathing, jacket, envelope, overlay, housing, protection.

cash *n.* **1.** money, currency, legal tender, paper money, bank notes, bills, coins, change; *Slang* bread, dough; coin of the realm, cash on the barrelhead. *—v.* **2.** turn into money, give cash for, obtain cash for; redeem, exchange, change. **—Ant. 1** check; charge, chit, promissory note, note, IOU.

cashier *n.* cash keeper; teller, bank teller; bursar, purser, treasurer, banker.

cask *n.* vat, barrel, keg, hogshead, tub, butt, tun, pipe.

casket *n.* **1.** coffin, sarcophagus, pall. **2.** jewel box, chest, coffer, case.

cast *v.* **1.** pitch, toss, fling, hurl, throw, let fly, sling, heave; propel, launch, fire, shoot, discharge, project, catapult. **2.** shed, spread, diffuse, direct, deposit, scatter, disseminate, disperse, distribute, circulate, broadcast, sow. **3.** assign, appoint, pick, choose, give parts to. **4.** mold, form, shape, model, set, sculpt; mint. *—n.* **5.** pitch, toss, throw; fling, hurl, heave, sling; propulsion, launch, launching. **6.** performers, actors, company, troupe, players; list of characters, dramatis personae. **7.** mold, form, shape, pattern, casting, casing, impression, stamp, set, model. **8.** look, appearance, semblance, mien, set, stamp.

castaway *n.* outcast, pariah, Ishmael, offscouring, unperson, leper, untouchable, nonperson; outlaw, exile, expatriate, renegade, deportee; vagrant, rover, wanderer, vagabond, nomad, hobo, knight-of-the-road, beachcomber, derelict, down-and-outer, stray, waif, foundling, *Slang* bum.

caste *n.* hereditary social class, lineage, rank, position, status, condition, station.

castigate *v.* chastise, upbraid, rebuke, censure, reprimand, reproach, chasten, reprove, berate, scold, admonish, criticize, chide, call on the carpet, bawl out, chew out, dress down, haul over the coals, take to task; punish, discipline, correct, penalize. **—Ant.** praise, laud, compliment, honor; reward, encourage.

castle *n.* palace, mansion, hall, manor, villa, chateau; fortified residence, stronghold, citadel, fortress, tower, keep.

casual *adj.* **1.** chance, unexpected, accidental, fortuitous, serendipitous, unplanned, unarranged, unforeseen, unpremeditated, unintentional, undesigned, unlooked for. **2.** incidental, informal, haphazard, random, undirected, offhand, vague, so-so, half-hearted, indiscriminate, passing, relaxed, cool, easygoing, lackadaisical, blasé, nonchalant, indifferent. **3.** informal, non-dressy, sporty; haphazard, random. **—Ant.** formal. **1** intentional, calculated, planned, fixed, arranged, designed, deliberate, intentional, premeditated, foreseen, expected; studied, considered, well-advised. **2** serious, committed, concerned, specific, direct, systematic, professional; all-consuming, wholehearted, fanatic, passionate, enthusiastic. **3** dressy, ceremonial.

casualty *n.* injured, victim, wounded or dead person; injury, fatality.

casuistry *n.* sophistry, sophism, speciousness, deceptiveness, equivocation, pettifoggery, sophistication, fallacy, Jesuitism; quibbling, nitpicking, hairsplitting, guile, subtlety, deceit.

cat *n.* **1.** feline, house cat, pussycat, pussy, puss, tabby, tabby cat, mouser; (*young*) kitten, kitty; (*male*) tomcat, tom. **2.** (*loosely*) lions and tigers; (*variously*) lion, tiger, leopard, panther, cougar, lynx, ocelot, wildcat, bobcat.

cataclysm *n.* catastrophe, calamity, disaster, debacle, upheaval, devastation, blow. **—Syn. Study.** See DISASTER. **—Ant.** triumph, victory, success; benefit, good fortune, boon.

catalog, catalogue *n.* **1.** list, listing, inventory, file, record, index, roll, roster, register, directory, syllabus, magalog. —*v.* **2.** list, inventory, classify, enumerate, tabulate, file, record, post, index, register. **—Syn. Study. 1** See LIST.

catapult *n.* **1.** hurling engine, sling, slingshot. —*v.* **2.** hurl, be hurled, hurtle, fling, throw, propel, heave, pitch, cast, toss, shoot.

cataract *n.* **1.** rapids, falls, waterfall, cascade. **2.** deluge, torrent, downpour; flood, inundation.

catastrophe *n.* disaster, calamity, misfortune, mishap, tragedy; affliction, scourge, cataclysm, devastation, havoc, debacle, ravage, blow. **—Syn. Study.** See DISASTER. **—Ant.** benefit, good fortune, boon.

catcall *n.* boo, hiss, hoot, whistle, jeer, gibe, heckling; *Slang* raspberry, Bronx cheer. **—Ant.** applause, cheering; hurrah, huzzah.

catch *v.* **1.** seize, seize and hold, capture, take captive, take, lay hold of, trap, snare, bag, grab, snag, hook, corner, corral; arrest, apprehend, take into custody, collar, snatch, nab; *Slang* bust. **2.** overtake, reach, get to, intercept, make. **3.** discover, detect, come upon, discern, expose, find out, spot, descry; surprise, take off guard, unmask. **4.** deceive, fool, trick, dupe, take in, delude, mislead, betray, play false, hoodwink, bamboozle; lure, trap, ensnare, bait. **5.** strike, hit, belt, bang, bump, bat, buffet, whack, smack, smite. **6.** contract, get, come down with, become infected with, break out with. **7.** captivate, attract, allure, charm, enchant, bewitch, enthrall, transport, carry away; delight, dazzle, enrapture; *Slang* turn on. **8.** sense, feel, discern, grasp, understand, perceive, recognize, comprehend, fathom. **9.** fasten, hook, latch, clasp, lock. —*n.* **10.** catching, seizure, snatch, snap, grab, grasp, snare, capture. **11.** take, haul, bag, capture, seizure, find, pickings, yield, prize, booty. **12.** fastening, latch, hook, clasp, hasp, closure, coupling, lock. **13.** hitch, snag, drawback, stumbling block, disadvantage, trick, hoax, deceit, *Informal* kicker, *Slang* gimmick. **14.** break, crack, rasping. **—Ant. 1** free, release, loose, let go, give up, liberate; drop, fumble. **2** miss. **3** to be undetected, to be undiscovered. **4** undeceive, untrick, undupe, undelude. **5** miss. **6** avoid, evade; be resistant to. **7** repel, alienate, turn away; *Slang* turn off. **9** unfasten, unhook, unlatch, unlock. **10** drop; fumble. **11** loss, losings. **13** advantage, benefit, boon, reward.

catching *adj.* contagious, communicable, infectious, transmittable. **—Ant.** noncatching, noncontagious, uncommunicable, noninfectious, nontransmittable.

catchword *n.* **1.** slogan, pet phrase, cliché, motto, byword, watchword, password, shibboleth; war cry, battle cry. **2.** guide word.

categorical *adj.* absolute, unconditional, unqualified, unequivocal, unmistakable, unreserved, express, flat, sure, certain, emphatic, explicit, pronounced, definite. **—Ant.** conditional, qualified, equivocal, ambiguous, vague, dubious, doubtful, questionable, indefinite, unsure, uncertain, hesitant, enigmatic.

category *n.* classification, class, grouping, division.

cater *v.* humor, pamper, indulge, pander; satisfy, gratify, please.

caterwaul *v.* howl, wail, cry, scream, shriek, screech, whine, yelp, squawk, squeal, bawl, clamor, rend the air.

catharsis *n.* purification, cleansing, purging, release, venting.

catholic *adj.* **1. Catholic.** Roman Catholic. **2.** universal, world-wide, all-inclusive, all-embracing. **3.** broad, comprehensive, universal, liberal. **—Ant. 1** non-Catholic. **2, 3** sectarian, parochial, provincial, narrow, exclusive, limited.

cattle *n.* livestock, stock, cows, *Archaic* kine; (*male*) bulls, bullocks, steers, beefs, beeves, oxen; (*female*) cows, milk cows, dairy cattle; (*young*) calves, dogies.

catty *adj.* **1.** spiteful, malicious, mean, malignant, malevolent. **2.** catlike.

caucus *n.* assembly, meeting, conclave, council, conference, parley, *Informal* powwow, session.

causation *n.* origin, genesis, cause, etiology, source, mainspring, root, reason, stimulus, antecedent, determinant, origination, conception, invention, inspiration; author, inventor, originator, generator, creator. **—Ant.** result, aftermath, effect, consequence, outcome, causatum.

cause *v.* **1.** bring about, lead to, give rise to, bring to pass, produce, generate, create, effect, make, provoke, incline, precipitate; motivate, incite, stimulate, stir up, impel, inspire. *—n.* **2.** reason, source, root, prime mover; provocation, inducement, motivation, motive, grounds, incentive, instigation, inspiration, initiation, occasion, stimulus, foundation, origin, mainspring, spring, genesis, etiology. **3.** goal, aspiration, object, purpose, principle, ideal, belief, conviction, tenet, persuasion, side. **—Syn. Study. 2** See REASON. **—Ant. 1** prevent, forestall, deter, inhibit, ward off, stop, foil. **2** effect, result, end result, consequence, fruit, outcome, final outgrowth, end.

caustic *adj.* **1.** burning, corrosive, corroding, erosive; astringent, stinging, biting, gnawing, sharp. **2.** sarcastic, biting, stinging, cutting, scathing, sharp, harsh, acrid, acrimonious, tart, bitter. **—Ant. 1** soothing, healing; bland, mild. **2** flattering, complimentary; sweet, kind, loving, pleasant, pleasing, gentle, gracious, agreeable, mild, bland.

caution *n.* **1.** care, carefulness, wariness, alertness, watchfulness, vigilance, prudence, precaution, heed, heedfulness, concern, thought, regard, discretion, restraint, circumspection, deliberation, guardedness, mindfulness. **2.** warning, forewarning, alarm, tip-off, admonition, caveat. *—v.* **3.** warn, forewarn, alert, put on one's guard, tip off, admonish, exhort, advise; alarm, notify. **—Syn. Study. 3** See WARN. **—Ant. 1** carelessness, recklessness, foolhardiness, rashness, heedlessness, imprudence, indiscretion, daring, daredevilry. **2** put off one's guard; dare.

cautious *adj.* careful, wary, cagey, alert, watchful, vigilant, attentive, guarded, prudent, circumspect, discreet, judicious. **—Syn. Study.** See CAREFUL. **—Ant.** careless, reckless, rash, foolhardy, heedless, inattentive; daring, impetuous, adventurous, venturous, venturesome.

cavalcade *n.* parade, procession, column, retinue, troop; caravan.

cavalier *n.* **1.** cavalryman, mounted soldier, horse soldier, horse trooper, horseman; lancer, dragoon, hussar. **2.** gallant, courtier, courtly man, fine gentleman, beau; dandy, swell, fop; man about town, playboy, gay blade, blade. *—adj.* **3.** disdainful, uncaring, offhand, thoughtless, cursory, indifferent, easygoing, nonchalant; arrogant, haughty, cocky. **—Ant. 1** infantryman, foot soldier. **2** bum, tramp. **3** conscientious, considerate, diligent, caring, thoughtful, sincere.

cavalry *n.* mounted troops, horse soldiers, horse troops, mounted men; lancers, dragoons, hussars. **—Ant.** infantry, foot soldiers.

cave *n.* underground chamber, cavern, grotto; dugout, hollow, den, cavity.

caveat *n.* warning, caution, forewarning, admonition, alarm, tip-off, alert, red light, red flag, aviso, admonishment, word to the wise, flea in the ear, handwriting on the wall, high sign, danger sign, yellow jack.

cavern *n.* large cave, large underground chamber.

cavernous *adj.* vast, huge, yawning, gaping, cavelike, chasmal, spacious, roomy, enormous, immense, tremendous. **—Ant.** small, cramped, crowded, confined, restricted.

cavil *v.* complain, find fault, faultfind, criticize, disparage, deprecate, belittle, discredit, deride, quibble, pick to pieces, *Informal* nitpick. **—Ant.** praise, applaud, compliment, flatter, approve.

cavity *n.* crater, concavity, depression, hole, excavation, basin, hollow, pit, sink, dent, pocket, dip, vacuity; tunnel, burrow, bore, orifice, aperture, opening, niche.

cavort *v.* caper, prance, frisk, frolic, gambol, bound, romp, play.

cease *v.* stop, halt, leave off, desist, quit, conclude, end, bring to an end, finish, terminate, forbear, break off, adjourn, discontinue, suspend, pause, refrain from, abstain from; die away, pass, surcease, abate, come to a standstill. **—Ant.** begin, commence, start, initiate, continue, persist.

ceaseless *adj.* endless, uninterrupted,

incessant, continuous, unending, unceasing, perpetual, interminable, everlasting, constant, enduring, protracted, never-ending, eternal, permanent, unremitting. —**Ant.** fitful, transitory, intermittent, spasmodic, fleeting.

cede *v.* yield, grant, deliver, deliver up, hand over, surrender, give, tender, relinquish, release, abandon, leave, transfer. —**Ant.** keep, retain, withhold, hold back, maintain.

celebrate *v.* **1.** commemorate, observe; engage in festivities, ceremonialize. **2.** proclaim, broadcast; acclaim, praise, extol, venerate, honor, exalt, applaud, laud, cheer, commend, revere. **3.** observe, solemnize, hallow, consecrate, honor, ritualize, bless, sanctify, glorify. —**Ant. 1** ignore, disregard, overlook. **2** condemn, despise, dishonor, profane. **3** desecrate, dishonor, profane.

celebrated *adj.* famous, famed, renowned, well-known, prominent, notorious; important, distinguished, acclaimed, noted, notable, outstanding, eminent, illustrious, respected, revered, venerable, honored, treasured, prized, lionized. —**Syn. Study.** See FAMOUS. —**Ant.** unknown, little-known, forgotten, undistinguished, unacclaimed, unnotable, insignificant, trivial, paltry; dishonored, degraded, unpopular.

celebration *n.* celebrating, party, festivity, festival, feast, gala, fete, jubilee, carnival, revelry; commemoration, ritual, observance, ceremony, ceremonial, solemnization, hallowing, memorialization, sanctification.

celebrity *n.* **1.** famous person, star, notable, luminary, personality, name; dignitary, personage, person of note; *Slang* big shot, bigwig, wheel. **2.** fame, stardom, renown, note, notoriety, notability, distinction, glory, prominence, eminence, popularity, a name for oneself. —**Ant. 1** unknown, nobody; has-been. **2** obscurity, oblivion.

celerity *n.* haste, swiftness, dispatch, briskness, quickness, speed, velocity, speediness, rapidity, expedition, expeditiousness, nimbleness, alacrity, legerity, hurry, hustle, precipitance, fastness, snappiness, lightning speed, fast clip. —**Syn. Study.** See SPEED. —**Ant.** slowness, laxness, sluggishness, languidness, torpor.

celestial *adj.* **1.** heavenly, divine, angelic, seraphic, blissful, hallowed, sublime, beatific, ethereal, elysian, otherworldly, un-earthly, empyrean, paradisiacal. **2.** astral, astronomical, solar, planetary, stellar; sky. —**Ant. 1** earthy, earthly, mundane, worldly, mortal; hellish, infernal, satanic. **2** earthly, terrestrial.

celibacy *n.* chastity, virginity, continence, abstinence; bachelorhood, spinsterhood.

celibate *adj.* unmarried, unwed, single, bachelor, spinster; chaste, virginal, continent, abstinent, pure. —**Ant.** married, wed, wedded; unchaste, incontinent, impure; promiscuous, loose, wanton.

cellar *n.* basement, downstairs; underground room, subterranean room; cave, den, dugout. —**Ant.** attic, garret; upstairs.

cement *n.* **1.** *(loosely)* concrete, mortar; glue, paste. —*v.* **2.** glue, paste, stick, fix, seal, weld, set; unite, join, bind, fuse, secure.

cemetery *n.* graveyard, burial ground, memorial park, churchyard, burying ground, necropolis, catacomb, ossuary, *(of paupers)* potter's field; *Slang* boneyard, Boot Hill.

censor *n.* **1.** inspector, custodian of morals, examiner, reviewer, investigator, judge, scrutinizer, guardian of the public morals, expurgator, amender, bowdlerizer. —*v.* **2.** expurgate, blue-pencil, amend, clean up, edit, bowdlerize, blip, purge, excise, black out, suppress.

censure *n.* **1.** reprimand, reproof, upbraiding, rebuke, reprobation, reproach, admonition, castigation, scolding, chiding, remonstrance, criticism, complaint, condemnation, disapproval, disapprobation, dressing-down, bawling-out, chewing-out, tongue-lashing, slap on the wrist. **2.** abuse, invective. —*v.* **3.** rebuke, reprimand, admonish, upbraid, reproach, castigate, denounce, condemn, chide, berate, disapprove, criticize, reprove, scold, reprehend; rake over the coals, haul over the coals, rap on the knuckles, pan, *Informal* bawl out, *Slang* chew out, rap. —**Syn. Study. 2** See ABUSE. **3** See REPRIMAND. —**Ant.** praise. **1** approval, eulogy, commendation, compliment, encouragement. **2** commend, applaud, compliment, eulogize, laud.

center Also *Chiefly British* **centre** *n.* **1.** middle point, dead center, hub; middle, mid, central part; core, heart, interior, pivot, axis, nucleus. **2.** focal point, focus, main point, main place, hub, heart, crux, essence. —*v.* **3.** concentrate, direct, address, fix, focus, converge, gather. —**Ant. 1** exterior, outside; perimeter, edge, rim, circumference. **3** diffuse, scatter, disperse.

central *adj.* **1.** in the center, middle, middlemost, midmost, interior, inner, inmost. **2.** major, main, principal, most important, chief, key, leading, primary, paramount, prime, dominant, predominant, foremost, focal, pivotal, basic, fundamental, essential. **—Ant. 1** outermost, outside, outer, exterior. **2** minor, subordinate, subsidiary, secondary.

centralize *v.* focus, concentrate, consolidate, coalesce, center, center on, converge, congregate, gather, collect, unify, compact, integrate. **—Ant.** disperse, scatter, dispel, spread, dissipate, disband.

ceremonial *adj.* **1.** formal, ceremonious, ritualistic. **2.** used in ceremonies, liturgical. *—n.* **3.** ritual, rite, service, ceremony, liturgy, sacrament; formality, celebration, observance. **—Ant. 1** informal, relaxed, casual, down-to-earth, plain, simple.

ceremonious *adj.* formal, stiff, correct, overly polite, proper, starched, rigid, meticulous, careful, precise, methodical, exact, punctilious, fussy; solemn, dignified, pompous. **—Ant.** unceremonious, informal, relaxed, casual, down-to-earth, plain, simple.

ceremony *n.* **1.** rite, ritual, service, observance, ceremonial, celebration, pageant, function, formalities, commemoration. **2.** formality, formal behavior, etiquette, politeness, decorum, protocol, propriety, custom, conventionality; nicety, amenity. **—Ant. 2** informality.

certain *adj.* **1.** sure, positive, confident, convinced, undoubting, undoubtful, satisfied, secure, assured, cocksure. **2.** definite, inevitable, positive, inescapable, bound to happen, settled, sure; conclusive, indubitable, unequivocal, unmistakable, unquestionable; unqualified, indisputable, undisputed, undeniable, incontrovertible, incontestable, irrefutable, reliable, absolute, unalterable, unchangeable, unshakable, well-grounded, valid. **3.** specific, particular, individual, special, express. **—Ant. 1** uncertain, doubtful, dubious, unconvinced. **2** doubtful, unlikely, questionable, unclear, unsure, unsettled, indefinite, inconclusive, undecided, disputable, unreliable, unfounded; equivocal, qualified, fallible.

certainty *n.* **1.** positiveness, confidence, certitude, assurance, surety, sureness, conclusiveness; conviction, belief, trust, faith, presumption, authoritativeness. **2.** fact, reality, actuality, inevitability, inescapability, sure thing, sure bet. **—Ant.** uncertainty. **1** indecision, inconclusiveness, unsureness; skepticism, disbelief, faithlessness, doubt.

certificate *n.* document, certification, credential, permit, license, deed, affidavit, voucher, authorization, authentication, warranty, testimonial, diploma.

certify *v.* confirm, corroborate, attest, substantiate, validate, verify, witness, testify to, vouch, swear, guarantee, warrant, endorse, authorize, ratify, underwrite, notarize, second, support, sanction, authenticate, assure, declare, aver, give one's word. **—Ant.** repudiate, disavow, deny, question, disprove.

cessation *n.* stopping, stop, ceasing, halting, halt, desisting, quitting, ending, end, concluding, termination, surcease, leaving off, breaking off; discontinuing, discontinuance, suspension, adjournment, stay, pause, respite, interruption, recess. **—Ant.** starting, start, beginning, commencement, initiation; continuance, continuation, persistence; resumption.

chafe *v.* **1.** rub, scratch, scrape, rasp, abrade. **2.** be irritated, be exasperated, be annoyed, rage, rankle, seethe, boil, burn, fume, foam. **—Ant. 1** soothe, cool, heal, protect. **2** pacify.

chaff *n.* **1.** husks, hulls, shells, pods, shucks, remnant, leavings, residue, sweepings; waste, rubbish, refuse, debris, trash, litter, rubble; dross, slag, junk, shoddy. *—v.* **2.** rib, kid, razz, josh, jolly, twit, rag, ride, bug, ridicule.

chagrin *n.* shame, humiliation, embarrassment, mortification, distress, dismay. **—Syn. Study.** See SHAME. **—Ant.** pride, glory, triumph, exultation.

chain *n.* **1.** linked cable, metal links; fob. **2.** Usually **chains.** shackles, fetters, bonds, irons; manacles, handcuffs, leg irons. **3. chains.** bondage, subjugation, enslavement, slavery, servitude, serfdom, thralldom. **4.** series, sequence, succession, string, train. *—v.* **5.** shackle, fetter, fasten, tie, tie up, secure, bind, lash, tether, moor; put in irons, manacle. **—Ant. 5** unchain, unfasten, untie, unshackle, unstrap; free, let go, let loose, liberate.

chairman *n.* presiding officer, head, administrator, executive, director, manager, supervisor, chairwoman, chairlady, chairperson; chair, moderator, master of ceremonies, *Slang* emcee, speaker, leader, toastmaster.

chalice *n.* goblet, cup, vessel.

challenge *n.* **1.** summons, dare, bid, hostile invitation, demand. **2.** test, trial, gage. *—v.* **3.** dare, summon, bid, invite to compete, defy, fling down the gauntlet. **4.** question, impute, dispute, take exception to, doubt. **5.** test, try, tax. **—Ant. 4** accept, believe, agree with; concede, yield, acquiesce.

chamber *n.* **1.** room, inner room, office; apartment; hall. **2.** bedroom, boudoir; sitting room, parlor, drawing room, salon. **3.** legislative body; council, assembly, congress, board, diet, house; court.

champion *n.* **1.** title holder, contest

winner; victor, winner, conqueror, vanquisher; master, laureate, paragon. **2.** upholder, advocate, protagonist, defender, supporter, protector, backer, promoter. **—*v.* 3.** fight for, battle for, uphold, support, back, defend, stand up for, promote, advocate, aid, abet, speak for, espouse. **—Ant. 1** loser; contender. **2** opponent, enemy, detractor. **3** oppose, combat; hinder.

chance *n.* **1.** accident, happenstance; fortune, luck, destiny, fate, providence. **2.** possibility, likelihood, likeliness, probability. **3.** opportunity, try, attempt, occasion, possibility. **4.** risk, danger, hazard; gamble, speculation, jeopardy. **—*v.* 5.** happen, occur, come to pass, come about, turn out, fall, befall, fall to one's lot. **6.** take a chance, risk, hazard, venture, gamble, try, attempt, rely on fortune. **—*adj.* 7.** accidental, unintentional, unexpected, unlooked for, unplanned, unforeseen, random, undesigned, unpremeditated, fortuitous, fortunate, lucky. **—Ant. 1** plan, design, intent, intention, premeditation. **2** unlikelihood, impossibility, improbability, certainty. **4** surety, certainty, sure thing. **7** intentional, planned, premeditated; designed, arranged, expected, foreseen, looked for.

chancy *adj.* risky, precarious, dubious, doubtful, uncertain, unpredictable, hazardous, problematical, speculative, venturesome, capricious, erratic, whimsical, touchy, unsound, tricky; *Slang* dicey, iffy. **—Ant.** sure, safe, infallible, predictable, certain, unmistakable.

change *v.* **1.** alter, modify, make different, adjust; shift, vary, recast, restyle, remodel, reorganize, reform, revolutionize; transfer, transmute, mutate, transform, turn, convert, metamorphose. **2.** exchange, replace, substitute, swap, trade, switch, shift, interchange, shuffle; remove and replace. **—*n.* 3.** difference, modification, switch, shift, variation, deviation, variety, fluctuation, veering; alteration, conversion, substitution, swapping, reform, reformation, revolution, reorganization, remodeling, restyling; metamorphosis, transformation, transposition, turn about, conversion, transmutation, transfiguration. **4.** novelty, something different, exception, switch; diversion, variety. **5.** coins, small coins, silver, pocket money, pin money, *Slang* chump change. **—Syn. Study. 1** CHANGE, ALTER both mean to make a difference in the state or condition of a thing. To CHANGE is to make a material or radical difference or to substitute one thing for another of the same kind: *to change a lock; to change one's plans.* To ALTER is to make some partial change, as in appearance, but usu. to preserve the identity: *to alter a garment; to alter a contract.* See also ADJUST. **—Ant. 1** hold, keep; bide, stay, remain. **2** keep. **3** uniformity, permanence, immutability, fixedness, constancy, stability, invariability, unchangeableness, monotony. **5** bills, paper money.

changeable *adj.* variable, varying, erratic, irregular, alternating, deviating, inconstant, fickle, flighty, volatile, fluctuating, mercurial, capricious, fitful, vacillating, unsteady, uncertain, unstable; mutable, reversible, transformable, modifiable, convertible. **—Ant.** unchangeable, invariable, regular, undeviating, constant, steady, certain, reliable, stable, immutable, irreversible, inconvertible.

channel *n.* **1.** strait, passage, watercourse, narrows. **2.** groove, furrow, trough, gash, cut, gutter. **3.** route, course, avenue of communication. **—*v.* 4.** route, direct, send, convey, guide, steer, lead.

chant *n.* **1.** song, hymn, melody, lied, strain, theme, chanson; psalm, doxology, plainsong, canticle, offertory, Gregorian chant, chorale, Gloria Patri, descant; dirge, threnody, elegy, ode, monody, monophony, homophony. **—*v.* 2.** sing, croon, intone, vocalize, carol, descant, troll, trill, chorus.

chaos *n.* turmoil, upheaval, confusion, agitation, tumult, uproar, furor, bedlam, pandemonium, turbulence, commotion; disorder, disarray, disorganization, disarrangement, mess, muddle, jumble, discomposure. **—Ant.** order, organization, routine, efficiency; calmness, calm; quiet, composure, peacefulness.

chaperon, chaperone *n.* **1.** adult overseer, adult attendant; guardian, protector, custodian, attendant, duenna. **—*v.* 2.** oversee, keep an eye on, shepherd; guard, safeguard, watch, accompany, escort.

chaplain *n.* priest, minister, rabbi, padre, father, reverend; *Military Slang* sky pilot, Holy Joe; cleric, churchman, ecclesiastic, curate, abbé, vicar, pastor, rector, parson, preacher.

chapter *n.* **1.** part, section, division, subdivision, portion; episode; clause, period, span, phase, era. **2.** branch, affiliate, group, division, subdivision; body, unit.

char *v.* singe, scorch, sear, burn; incinerate, reduce to charcoal, carbonize.

character *n.* **1.** qualities, traits, attributes; nature, self, being, makeup, individuality, distinctiveness, personality. **2.** honor, integrity, moral strength, morality, honesty, goodness, rectitude, uprightness; reputation, repute, name. **3.**

person, individual, specimen, being, personality. **4.** odd person, eccentric, original, one-of-a-kind; *Slang* weirdo, oddball. **5.** fictional person, person, persona; role, part; *(plural)* dramatis personae. **—Syn. Study. 1** CHARACTER, PERSONALITY refer to the sum of the characteristics possessed by a person. CHARACTER refers esp. to the moral qualities and ethical standards that make up the inner nature of a person: *It is not in his character to be unkind.* PERSONALITY refers particularly to outer characteristics, as wittiness or charm, that determine the impression that a person makes upon others: *a pleasing personality.* **2** See REPUTATION. **—Ant. 2** dishonor, dishonesty, moral weakness.

characteristic *adj.* **1.** typical, representative, indicative, symbolic, emblematic, distinctive, distinguishing. *—n.* **2.** attribute, trait, quality, aspect, feature, property, mark, earmark; mannerism, peculiarity, specialty, trademark. **—Syn. Study. 2** See FEATURE. **—Ant. 1** uncharacteristic, unusual, atypical, unrepresentative, rare.

characterization *n.* representing, representation, portrayal, portrait, picturing, depiction; delineation, description.

charge *v.* **1.** fix as a price, put a value on, ask, demand, require, exact, price; request payment, assess, levy. **2.** put on one's account, incur a debt, take credit, delay payment; debit. **3.** load, fill, lade, pack, stuff; pile, stack, heap. **4.** command, order, direct, instruct, bid, call upon, summon, enjoin. **5.** attribute, ascribe, fix responsibility for, lay the blame for, impute, assign; accuse, incriminate, blame, indict, lodge a complaint against, prefer charges against. **6.** rush, attack, storm, come at, make a dash at, beset, assail, assault, make an onslaught. *—n.* **7.** fee, cost, price, expense, assessment, rate, amount, payment; payment due, toll, duty. **8.** attack, onslaught, assault, storming, rush, onset, sortie. **9.** care, custody, keeping, safekeeping, guardianship, protection; jurisdiction, superintendence, supervision, administration, control, command, management. **10.** allegation, accusation, complaint; arraignment, indictment. **11.** direction, advice, instruction, injunction; order, command, bidding, dictate, enjoining; rule of conduct. **—Ant. 1** give away, give. **2** pay, pay cash. **3** empty, unload. **5** absolve, exculpate; vindicate, exonerate, pardon, acquit. **6** retreat, withdraw. **8** retreat, withdrawal. **10** absolution, vindication, exoneration; acquittal, pardon.

charisma *n.* charm, appeal, magnetism, presence, fascination, glamour, allure, bewitchery, enchantment, witchery, attractiveness, sex appeal.

charitable *adj.* **1.** generous, giving, bountiful, bounteous, munificent, openhanded, liberal; philanthropic, almsgiving, eleemosynary, benevolent. **2.** forgiving, understanding, sympathetic, sympathizing, kindly, kind, kindhearted, benevolent, warmhearted, gracious, considerate, magnanimous; lenient, liberal, tolerant, indulgent. **—Syn. Study. 1** See GENEROUS. **—Ant. 1** uncharitable, stingy, parsimonious, miserly, ungiving, ungenerous. **2** unforgiving, strict, rigid, unkind, malevolent, unsympathetic, hard-hearted, cold-hearted, inconsiderate.

charity *n.* **1.** philanthropy, contributions, donations, donating, alms, almsgiving, giving, financial help, help, aid, gift, assistance, offering, endowment, benefaction, fundraising, handout; generosity, munificence, open-handedness, bounty, benefaction; charitable institution, fund. **2.** good will, love of mankind, altruism, love, humanity, compassion, sympathy, kindness, goodness, benevolence, benignity, tolerance, graciousness. **—Ant. 1** uncharitableness, stinginess, parsimony. **2** malice, ill will, hate, hatred, selfishness, cruelty, intolerance.

charlatan *n.* fake, fraud, deceiver, quack, impostor, cheat, swindler, trickster, cozener, confidence artist, mountebank.

charm *n.* **1.** power to please, charisma, fascination, enchantment, allure, allurement, attraction, magnetism, lure, draw. **2.** spell, incantation, conjuration; sorcery, magic. **3.** lucky piece; amulet, talisman; trinket, bauble, ornament. *—v.* **4.** please, give pleasure, delight, gratify, make happy, enrapture, enthrall; fascinate, attract, allure, engage, entrance, enchant, grip, captivate, take, bewitch, *Slang* turn on. **5.** lure, seduce, cajole, win over, beguile, bewitch. **6.** change by magic, work magic on, cast a spell, conjure. **—Ant. 1** unattractiveness, repulsiveness. **4** repel, alienate, disgust, displease; *Slang* turn off.

charming *adj.* attractive, pleasing, charismatic, delightful, agreeable, lovely, graceful, winning, winsome, likable; entrancing, fascinating, captivating, engaging, enthralling, bewitching, enchanting, fetching, enticing, magnetic, irresistible, alluring. **—Ant.** unattractive, unpleasing, unpleasant, unlikable, repulsive, repellent, disgusting.

chart *n.* **1.** map, navigator's map, mariner's map; diagram, graph, table, tabulation; blueprint, scheme, plan, outline, sketch. *—v.* **2.** map, map out, draw up, diagram; plot, draft, plan, delineate, design, outline, sketch, tabulate, lay out.

charter *n.* **1.** permit, license, authority, franchise, agreement, contract, compact, covenant, deed, concession, sanction. —*v.* **2.** establish by charter, license, commission, grant, authorize. **3.** rent, hire, lease, let, engage, commission, employ. —**Syn. Study. 3** See HIRE.

chary *adj.* wary, suspicious, leery, cautious, circumspect, careful, prudent, watchful, vigilant, heedful, guarded, alert, distrustful, shy, *Slang* cagey. —**Ant.** reckless, rash, headstrong, daring, heedless, bold.

chase *v.* **1.** pursue, go in pursuit of, go after, run after, try to overtake, try to catch up with; hunt, stalk, trail, track, follow, tail, dog, hound, shadow. **2.** drive, put to flight; evict, oust, send away, drive away, rout, shoo, send packing, cast out; scatter, dispel, repulse. —*n.* **3.** hunt, hunting, quest, pursuit, pursuing, following, stalking, tracking. —**Ant. 1** let go, let escape, lose, lose track of; escape, flee, elude.

chasm *n.* abyss, fissure, rift, split, gorge, ravine, gap, crevasse, divide, gulch, gulf, break, cleft, crack, breach; pit, crater, hold, cavity.

chaste *adj.* **1.** virginal, pure, continent. **2.** clean-living, wholesome, decent, virtuous, sinless, clean, righteous, untainted, uncorrupted, unsullied, immaculate. **3.** pure, classic, restrained, modest, austere, severe, strict, precise; unadorned, unornamented, unembellished. —**Ant. 1** unchaste, incontinent, impure, lewd, obscene, wanton, promiscuous, licentious, ribald; married, wed. **2** corrupt, unwholesome, dishonorable, immoral, sinful, immodest; impure, unclean, tainted, sullied, soiled, dirty, blemished, tarnished. **3** ornate, flashy, gaudy, unrestrained, self-indulgent, vulgar.

chasten *v.* See CHASTISE.

chastise *v.* punish, discipline, penalize, beat, whip, spank, thrash, flog, strap; reprimand, scold, castigate, upbraid, rebuke, reproach, admonish, chasten, reprove, correct, censure, criticize, chide, call down, berate, scourge, roast, take to task, fulminate against, call on the carpet, give a tongue-lashing to, haul over the coals. —**Ant.** reward, honor, praise, compliment, applaud, commend, congratulate, give kudos to.

chastity *n.* celibacy, purity, virginity, innocence, continence, abstinence, abstemiousness; singleness, bachelorhood, spinsterhood. —**Ant.** incontinence; promiscuity, lewdness, wantonness, licentiousness; marriage.

chat *v.* **1.** talk, converse, chatter, gab, chitchat, prate, prattle, palaver, chew the rag, chew the fat, *Slang* rap. —*n.* **2.** talk, conversation; chitchat, palaver, confabulation, talk session, heart-to-heart talk, *Slang* rap session.

chattel *n.* **1.** bondman, bondwoman, slave, serf, servant; possession, personal property. **2. chattels** effects, personal effects, personal possessions, belongings, movable property, movables; paraphernalia, gear, things, trappings, accouterments. —**Syn. Study. 2** See PROPERTY.

chatter *v.* **1.** talk, talk idly, babble, jabber, prattle, prate, gabble, chitchat, palaver, confabulate, gossip, twaddle, blather, chitterchatter, blab, patter, *Slang* gas. **2.** clatter, click, clank. —*n.* **3.** jabber, gibber, babble, talk, talking, gossip, chit-chat, chitterchatter, gabble, palaver, twaddle, blather, blabbing, blabber, patter, idle talk.

chatterbox *n.* talker, jabberer, gabber, blatherskite, chatterer, chatterbasket, babbler, prattler; *Slang* windbag, gasbag, blabbermouth, hot-air artist; gossip, talebearer, tattletale, tattler, telltale.

chatty *adj.* talkative, talky, effusive, voluble, chatting; garrulous, gabby, gushing, gushy, babbling, long-winded, loquacious, prating, jabbering, verbose, windy, gassy; gossipy, blabbering, tongue-wagging, loose-tongued, loose-lipped. —**Ant.** quiet, close-mouthed, secretive, uncommunicative, taciturn.

chauvinism *n.* superpatriotism, ethnocentricity, blind patriotism, flag-waving, jingoism, militarism, nationalism.

cheap *adj.* **1.** inexpensive, low-priced, economical, reasonable. **2.** effortless, costless, easy. **3.** shoddy, shabby, inferior, worthless, poor, second-rate, trashy, meager, paltry, gimcrack; flashy, gaudy, in bad taste, tawdry, tacky, common, inelegant. **4.** contemptible, petty, despicable, sordid, ignoble, wretched, mean, base, *Slang* two-bit; vulgar, immoral, indecent. **5.** tight, stingy, miserly, penurious, tightfisted, close, near; thrifty. —**Syn. Study. 1** CHEAP, INEXPENSIVE agree in their suggestion of low cost. CHEAP now often suggests shoddiness, inferiority, showy imitation, unworthiness, and the like: *a cheap fabric.* INEXPENSIVE emphasizes lowness of price (although more expensive than CHEAP) and suggests that the value is fully equal to the cost: *an inexpensive dress.* It is often used as an evasion for the more pejorative CHEAP. —**Ant. 1** expensive, costly, high-priced, high, overpriced. **2** worthwhile, valuable; hard-won, difficult, troublesome. **3** superior, good, fine, first-rate, worthy; in good taste, tasteful, high-class, classy, elegant, chic, smart. **4** admirable, commendable; moral, decent. **5** generous, charitable, openhanded.

cheat *v.* **1.** swindle, defraud, trick, bilk, gyp, fleece, scam; *Slang* take, rook; deceive, dupe, victimize, betray, delude, hoodwink, bamboozle, humbug, cozen, hoax, gull; *Slang* con. **2.** practice fraud, practice trickery, break the rules, act unfairly. **3.** escape, thwart, foil, circumvent, outwit, frustrate, baffle, fool, shortchange, mislead, defeat. —*n.* **4.** swindler, trickster, con artist, shark, double-crosser, deceiver; fraud, charlatan, mountebank, crook; quack, fake, impostor, chiseler, dodger. —**Syn. Study. 1** CHEAT, DECEIVE, TRICK, VICTIMIZE refer to the use of fraud or artifice to obtain an unfair advantage or gain. CHEAT usu. means to be dishonest in order to make a profit for oneself: *to cheat customers by shortchanging them.* DECEIVE suggests misleading someone by false words or actions: *He deceived his parents about his whereabouts.* TRICK means to mislead by a ruse or stratagem, often of a crafty or dishonorable kind: *I was tricked into signing the note.* VICTIMIZE means to make a victim of; it connotes a particularly contemptible act: *to victimize a blind person.*

check *v.* **1.** stop, bring to a standstill, stay, halt, restrain, slow, hold back, curb, limit, brake, inhibit, arrest, constrain, rein in, rein, harness, bridle, stall; impede, obstruct, choke, prevent, suppress, block, muzzle, retard, smother, frustrate, thwart, circumvent, hold, gag. **2.** inspect, look at, test, examine; search, look into, peruse, explore. **3.** investigate, study, take stock of, review, probe, inspect, survey, look over, examine, scrutinize, explore. **4.** agree, correspond, fit, tally, conform, jibe, mesh, chime, harmonize, be uniform. —*n.* **5.** restraint, limit, limitation, restriction, control, curb, prevention, prohibition, constraint, hindrance, impediment, barrier, bar, block, obstacle, obstruction, repression, bridle; stop, stoppage, halt, end, stay, cessation. **6.** test, inspection, scrutiny, examination, survey, search, perusal, probe, investigation, exploration, study. —**Syn. Study. 1** CHECK, CURB, RESTRAIN refer to putting a control on movement, progress, action, etc. CHECK implies arresting suddenly, halting or causing to halt by means of drastic action: *to check a movement toward reform.* CURB implies slowing or stopping forward motion: *to curb inflation; to curb a horse.* RESTRAIN implies the use of force to put under control or hold back: *to restrain one's enthusiasm; to restrain unruly spectators.* See also STOP. —**Ant. 1** begin, initiate, start; accelerate, speed up, spur, let loose, give free rein, unleash, release; foster, encourage, further, urge on; help, abet, aid, support. **2, 3** ignore, overlook, disregard. **4** disagree, contradict, jar. **5** accelerator, spur, encouragement, fostering, furthering, help, aid; start, beginning.

checkered *adj.* **1.** checked, particolored, variegated, motley, mottled, dappled, piebald, pied. **2.** varied, uneven, motley, inconstant, irregular, fitful, fluctuating, vacillating, up-and-down, seesaw. —**Ant. 1** solid. **2** consistent, constant, unvarying, unvaried, unvariable, unchanging, steady, stable, even, smooth.

cheek *n.* **1.** jowl, side of the face. **2.** impudence, impertinence, nerve, insolence, arrogance, effrontery, audacity, brazenness, brass, boldness, forwardness, brashness, temerity. —**Ant. 2** reserve, reticence, shyness, bashfulness, timidity, timorousness, humility, self-effacement.

cheep *v.* **1.** peep, chirp, chirrup, tweet, twitter, chitter. —*n.* **2.** chirp, peep, chirrup, tweet, twitter, chitter.

cheer *n.* **1.** approving shout, encouraging cry, acclamation, acclaim, hooray, huzzah, bravo, yell, shriek. **2.** assurance, reassurance, encouragement, comfort, hopefulness, hope; optimism, buoyancy. **3.** gaiety, fun, merriment, animation, joy, joviality, liveliness, revelry, gladness, high spirits, vivacity, buoyance, joyfulness, delight, pleasure, glee, geniality, rejoicing, jubilation, merrymaking, festivity. —*v.* **4.** root, hail, encourage, hurrah, shout, yell, cry. **5.** brighten, enliven, gladden, animate; assure, reassure, encourage, comfort, hearten, warm, inspire, fortify, buoy up, uplift. —**Ant. 1** boo, catcall, hiss, Bronx cheer, raspberry. **2** gloom, discouragement, hopelessness, pessimism. **3** gloom, sadness, despair, depression, despondency. **4** deride, discourage, taunt, ridicule, boo, hiss. **5** darken, sadden; discourage, dispirit, depress, dishearten.

cheerful *adj.* **1.** cheery, gay, joyful, joyous, lighthearted, happy, glad, gladsome, merry, sunny, high-spirited, in high humor, jovial, buoyant, elated, gleeful, jolly, agreeable, pleasant; breezy, jaunty, blithe, optimistic, airy, lively, sprightly. **2.** bright, lively, cheery, gay, sparkling, sunny. —**Ant. 1** cheerless, glum, gloomy, sullen, dour, morose, dejected, depressed, depressing, downcast, downhearted, melancholy, sad, doleful, despondent, disconsolate, dismal, rueful, unhappy, joyless, miserable; dispiriting, unpleasant; lifeless, dull. **2** cheerless, dull, somber, lifeless, depressing.

cheerless *adj.* gloomy, downcast, dreary, glum, dispirited, despondent, dolorous, forlorn, downhearted, funereal, doleful, spiritless, dejected, joyless, desolate, heavy-hearted, solemn, austere, grim, saturnine, morose, sullen, sad, melancholy, miserable, mournful, lugubrious, woebegone, unhappy, disconsolate, rueful, woeful; bleak, gray, dull, sunless, somber, dismal, uninviting, depressing, comfortless. **—Ant.** cheerful, gay, joyful, light-hearted, happy, merry, jolly, gleeful, elated.

cherish *v.* **1.** love, hold dear, treasure, value, prize, dote on, appreciate; revere, venerate, honor, esteem, idolize. **2.** care for, take care of, sustain, succor, nurture, nurse, nourish, foster. **3.** foster, harbor, shelter; encourage, indulge, entertain. **—Syn. Study. 1, 2** CHERISH, FOSTER, HARBOR imply the giving of affection, care, or (literally or figuratively) shelter. CHERISH suggests regarding or treating something or someone as an object of affection or value: *to cherish a friendship.* FOSTER implies sustaining and nourishing something with care, esp. in order to promote, increase, or strengthen it: *to foster a hope.* HARBOR may suggest maintaining someone or something undesirable: *to harbor a criminal; to harbor a grudge.* **—Ant. 1** hate, dislike, scorn, despise, disdain. **2** desert, forsake, abandon, renounce, neglect, ignore. **3** neglect, abandon.

chew *v.* masticate; champ, gnaw, crunch, munch, nibble, grind, crush; ruminate.

chic *adj.* fashionable, stylish, smart, elegant; modish, voguish, natty, *Informal* swank, swanky, *Slang* classy, ritzy, snazzy. **—Ant.** unfashionable, unstylish, passé; dowdy, inelegant, shabby, shoddy.

chicanery *n.* deception, trickery, fraud, deceit, cozenage, gulling, guile, hocus-pocus, double-dealing, duplicity, duping, subterfuge, hoodwinking, pettifoggery, humbuggery; knavery, roguery, rascality, villainy.

chichi *adj.* **1.** showy, ostentatious, flashy, frilly, gimcrack, splashy, flamboyant, garish, vulgar; pompous, pretentious, grandiose, affected. **2.** precious, fussy, arty, arty-tarty, artsy-craftsy, finical, overnice, nasty-nice, overrefined; prissy, sissyish. **—Ant. 1** plain, simple, uncomplicated, natural, unaffected.

chide *v.* admonish, reprimand, scold, chasten, rebuke, reproach, reprove, upbraid, berate, take to task; find fault, criticize, censure, denounce. **—Ant.** praise, commend, laud, extol, applaud, compliment.

chief *n.* **1.** head, leader, director, chairman; boss, overseer, administrator, superintendent, supervisor; commander, captain; ring-leader, master; ruler, chieftain, monarch, overlord, lord, sovereign, potentate. *—adj.* **2.** major, main, prime, primary, first, number-one, foremost, cardinal, highest-ranking, greatest, dominant, predominant, paramount, uppermost, prevailing, highest, supreme, principal, preponderant, key, leading, outstanding; governing, ruling, crowning. **—Syn. Study. 2** CHIEF, MAJOR, PRINCIPAL apply to a main or leading representative of a kind. CHIEF often means highest in office or power; it may mean most important: *the chief clerk; the chief problem.* MAJOR refers to someone or something that is greater in number, quantity, or importance: *a major resource; a major poet.* PRINCIPAL refers to the most distinguished, influential, or foremost person or thing: *a principal stockholder; the principal reason.* **—Ant. 1** subordinate, underling, follower, hanger-on; subject. **2** minor, least, last, subordinate, secondary, subsidiary.

chiefly *adv.* primarily, principally, mainly, in the main, first, mostly, most of all, predominantly, particularly, above all, expressly, especially. **—Ant.** least, last, least of all, in a small way.

child *n.* youth, youngster, juvenile, kid, boy, lad, girl, lass, *Informal* tad; baby, infant, tot, little one, tyke, toddler, moppet; son, daughter, offspring. **—Ant.** adult, grownup, man, woman; parent.

childbirth *n.* childbearing, giving birth, delivery, parturition; confinement.

childhood *n.* youth, boyhood, girlhood; nursery days, school days, adolescence. **—Ant.** adulthood, maturity.

childish *adj.* immature, childlike, infantile, puerile, juvenile, callow, adolescent, babyish; silly, foolish, naïve, simple, asinine. **—Syn. Study.** CHILDISH, INFANTILE, CHILDLIKE refer to characteristics or qualities of childhood. CHILDISH refers to attitudes, actions, etc. that are undesirable and unpleasant: *childish greed.* INFANTILE usu. carries an even stronger idea of disapproval or scorn: *infantile temper tantrums.* CHILDLIKE refers to those characteristics that are desirable or merely neutral: *childlike innocence.* **—Ant.** mature, grown-up, adult, sophisticated; manly, manful, womanly, womanlike.

childlike *adj.* See CHILDISH.

chill *n.* **1.** chilliness, coolness, iciness, frostiness, frigidity; crispness, sharpness, nip, bite, rawness. **2.** cold; fever. *—adj.* also **chilly. 3.** chilling, cold, wintry, arctic, icy, frigid, frosty, penetrating, cool; brisk, biting, bitter, raw, keen, shivery, crisp, sharp, cutting, nippy. **4.** icy, frigid, cold, aloof, hostile, unfriendly, stony, callous, indifferent, uncaring, unresponsive, stiff, unfeeling, passionless, forbidding, harsh. **—Ant. 1** warmth, warmness. **3** warm, warming, hot, tropical, balmy, mild. **4** warm, friendly, cordial, congenial, emotional.

chime *n.* **1.** set of bells, carillon. **2.** peal, pealing, ring, ringing, toll, tollings, sound, knell, tinkling, jingle, ding-dong, gong, tintinnabulation. —*v.* **3.** peal, ring, sound, toll, knell, tintinnabulate, jingle, tinkle.

chimera *n.* delusion, illusion, dream, fantasy, fancy, idle whim, pipe dream, bubble, daydream, self-deception, self-deceit, figment of one's imagination, mirage, hallucination, castle in the air, castle in Spain, fool's paradise, will-o'-the-wisp.

china *n.* dishes, cups and saucers, plates, tableware, chinaware; pottery, crockery, earthenware, stoneware, porcelain, ceramic ware.

chink[1] *n.* crack, slit, rift, rent, crevice, cleft, fault, breach, fissure, cut, split, gap, gash, cut, break; hole, opening, aperture.

chink[2] *v.* clink, jingle, jangle, clank, tinkle, ring, rattle.

chintzy *adj.* **1.** shabby, sleazy, tacky, *Slang* schlocky, dowdy, *Brit.* tatty, frowzy, frumpy. **2.** stingy, cheap, tight, miserly, close, grudging, niggardly, closefisted, stinting, parsimonious, penny-pinching, penurious. —**Ant. 1** stylish, elegant, chic, classy, ritzy, fashionable.

chip *n.* **1.** small piece, fragment, scrap, sliver, chunk, shaving, splinter, shred, slice, paring, cutting; flake, crumb, morsel, bit, wafer. **2.** nick, gash. —*v.* **3.** nick, gash, split, splinter. **4.** hew, chop, cut, whittle, hack, chisel.

chipper *adj.* lively, animated, spirited, alive, sprightly, cheerful, jaunty, peppy, pert, spry, carefree, high-spirited, energetic, light-hearted, gay, easygoing, frisky, vivacious. —**Ant.** downhearted, sad, morose; sluggish, lethargic.

chirp *v.* **1.** chirrup, tweet, twitter, sing, chitter, cheep, peep. —*n.* **2.** chirrup, tweet, twitter, chitter, cheep, peeping, cheeping, chirr.

chivalrous *adj.* gallant, courtly; polite, mannerly. —**Ant.** ungallant, loutish, boorish, discourteous, rude, unmannerly, disloyal, untrustworthy, inconstant, dishonorable; cruel.

chivalry *n.* knighthood; gallantry, courtliness, politeness, courtesy. —**Ant.** loutishness, boorishness, rudeness, impoliteness, unmannerliness, discourtesy, disloyalty, inconstancy; cruelty, inhumanity.

choice *n.* **1.** choosing, decision, deciding, discretion, opting, determination; alternative, option, voice, vote, say. **2.** selection, preference, pick, appointment. **3.** selection, variety, pick, stock, supply, store, collection, assemblage, assortment, array, display. —*adj.* **4.** select, well-chosen, superior, first-rate, first-class, A-one, best, better, prime, prize, preferred, preferable, exclusive, special, excellent, fine; exceptional, superlative, elite, top drawer, tip-top, extraordinary, consummate. —**Syn. Study. 1** CHOICE, ALTERNATIVE, OPTION suggest the power of choosing between things. CHOICE implies the opportunity to choose freely: *Her choice for dessert was ice cream.* ALTERNATIVE suggests a chance to choose only one of a limited number of possibilities: *I had the alternative of going to the party or staying home alone.* OPTION emphasizes the right or privilege of choosing: *He had the option of taking the prize money or a gift.* —**Ant. 1** coercion, force; command, order. **4** poor, inferior, worse, second-rate, second-class, mediocre, fair, average, common, ordinary, indifferent.

choke *v.* **1.** strangle, garrote, throttle; smother, asphyxiate, suffocate, gag, stifle. **2.** stop up, clog, obstruct, constrict, blockade, block, congest, plug, plug up, dam, dam up, stuff; impede, retard, hold back, arrest, check, hinder, constrain, restrain, hamper, inhibit, bridle, suppress, repress. —**Ant. 2** clear, unclog, unstop, unblock, unplug; spur, speed, accelerate, aid, help, encourage.

choleric *adj.* cranky, dyspeptic, cantankerous, testy, *Brit.* shirty, snappish, peevish, irate, mad, angry, irascible, wrathful, indignant, hot-tempered, illtempered, touchy, quick-tempered, short-tempered, thin-skinned, infuriated, short-fused, sour-tempered, furious, vexed, waspish, enraged. —**Ant.** placid, cool, tranquil, easygoing, nonchalant, serene.

choose *v.* **1.** select, pick out, pick, take, decide on, settle on, fix upon, single out, opt for, call out, extract; make up one's mind, resolve, espouse, embrace, adopt. **2.** decide, determine, resolve, prefer, commit oneself, opt, elect, intend, see fit, desire, wish, be inclined, like. —**Ant. 1** reject, eschew, refuse, decline, spurn, repudiate, cast away, cast out, leave, throw aside, disclaim, dismiss; forgo, forbear.

choosy *adj.* fussy, finicky, particular, fastidious, picky, discriminating, selective.

chop *v.* **1.** cut, fell; sunder, hew, hack, split, cleave, slash, gash, lop, crop. **2.** cut up, dice, mince, chip, cube; pulverize, fragment. —*n.* **3.** stroke, whack, blow, hit, cut, hack, swipe. **4.** cutlet, rib slice, slice, cut, *French* côtelette.

chore *n.* **1.** household task, domestic work, farm task, small job, task, job, duty, responsibility, work, assignment, stint, errand. **2.** unpleasant task, difficult job, strain, burden, tedious job, exacting task. —**Syn. Study. 1** See TASK.

chortle *v.* **1.** chuckle, snort merrily, laugh. —*n.* **2.** chuckle, merry snort, laugh, gleeful whoop.

chorus *n.* **1.** refrain, antiphony, response. **2.** choir, singing group, glee club, choral society, vocal ensemble; line of dancers; group of speakers. **3.** concert, unison, unity, one voice; accord, concord, concordance, consensus, unanimity.

christen *v.* baptize, sprinkle, dip, immerse; name, designate, dub, dedicate, launch.

chronic *adj.* habitual, longstanding, continual, continuous, constant, persistent, persisting, enduring, lasting, abiding, confirmed, inveterate, perennial, ingrained, deep-seated, deep-rooted; recurring, recurrent, periodic, intermittent. **—Ant.** temporary, infrequent, once-in-a-lifetime, fleeting.

chronicle *n.* **1.** record, history, chronology, journal, diary, account, log, annals, archives; narrative, story, epic, saga. —*v.* **2.** record, set down, list, docket, log, note, post, enter; recount, relate, report, narrate.

chronological *adj.* consecutive, successive, ordered, progressive, serial, dated, time-ordered, sequent, succeeding, sequential, chronometric, chronoscopic, chronographic.

chubby *adj.* pudgy, stocky, podgy, plump, thickset, stout, portly, paunchy, tubby, fat, corpulent, flabby, overweight, fleshy, rotund, heavyset, buxom; *Slang* zaftig, roly-poly. **—Ant.** lean, skinny, gaunt, bony, thin, emaciated, underweight.

chuck *v.* **1.** poke lovingly, pat, tap, pet, tickle. **2.** toss, fling, sling, cast, throw, heave, pitch.

chum *n.* friend, close friend, pal, buddy, bosom buddy, companion, comrade, cohort, intimate, confidant, crony, *Slang* sidekick; playmate, playfellow. **—Ant.** stranger, casual acquaintance; enemy, antagonist.

chummy *adj.* friendly, close, intimate, familiar, congenial, affectionate, devoted; *Slang* palsy, palsy-walsy, buddy-buddy. **—Ant.** estranged, alienated, unfriendly, antagonistic, distant, aloof, cool.

chunk *n.* lump, hunk, piece, mass, batch, clod, block, square, wad, gob, nugget.

chunky *adj.* stocky, thickset, beefy, pudgy, stubby, squat, chubby, dumpy, thick-bodied, heavyset, stodgy, portly, squabby. **—Ant.** slim, slender, gangling, scrawny, lithe, lanky.

church *n.* **1.** house of worship, house of God, Lord's house, tabernacle, chapel, temple; cathedral, basilica, mosque, synagogue. **2.** religious service; service, divine worship, devotions. **3.** religion, denomination, faith, affiliation, persuasion, belief, sect, cult.

churlish *adj.* surly, grouchy, sullen, crabbed, bearish, brusque, crusty, quarrelsome, ill-tempered, irascible, petulant, testy, irritable, rancorous, bilious, choleric, splenetic, captious, waspish, sour, tart; uncivil, ill-mannered, unmannerly, rude, boorish, impolite, insulting, discourteous; ill-bred, crude, uncouth, dastardly, obnoxious, contemptible, arrogant, impudent, insolent. **—Ant.** pleasant, agreeable, amiable, easygoing, sweet, kind, good-humored, even-tempered; civil, polite, courteous, gallant, mannerly; well-bred, noble, admirable, cultivated, gentlemanly, humble.

churn *v.* beat, whisk, whip, shake, shake up, stir up, agitate, vibrate; toss, heave, swirl, roll, roil, foam, rage, convulse, disturb, pulsate, palpitate.

cinder *n.* ember, ash; piece of burned coal or wood or iron slag; (*also in plural*) embers, ashes, clinkers, scoria, slag, dross.

cinema *n.* motion pictures, moving pictures, movies, films, flicks.

cipher *n.* **1.** zero, naught, aught; nothing, nil; *Slang* goose egg, zip. **2.** nobody, nonentity, nullity, nothing, naught, obscurity. **3.** code, secret writing; cryptogram, cryptograph; anagram, acrostic. **—Ant. 1** infinity, something. **2** somebody, something, notable, personage, star.

circle *n.* **1.** ring, circuit; halo, corona, orb, hoop, belt, girdle, cordon, circlet, ringlet, girt, girth. **2.** group, set, coterie, clique, society, cabal, knot, crowd, company, club; sphere, orbit, field, realm, compass, circuit, bounds, region, domain, range, reach, arena, theater, sweep, swing, province, dominion, territory, bailiwick. **3.** cycle, round, revolution, turn, swing, circuit, course, sequence, progression. —*v.* **4.** encircle, surround, ring, ring around, border, enclose, hedge in, hem in, border, circuit, belt, gird, girdle, wind about, loop, bound, envelop, encompass, circumscribe. **5.** revolve around, curve around, move around, circumnavigate, circumrotate; revolve, pivot, reel, curve, curl, turn. **—Syn. Study. 2** CIRCLE, CLUB, COTERIE refer to restricted social groups. A CIRCLE is a little group; in the plural it often suggests a section of society interested in one mode of life, occupation, etc.: *a sewing circle; theatrical circles.* CLUB implies an organized association with fixed requirements for membership: *an athletic club.* COTERIE suggests a small and exclusive group intimately associated because of similar backgrounds and interests: *a literary coterie.* **—Ant. 1** square.

circuit *n.* **1.** circling, orbiting, revolving; revolution, course, pivoting. **2.** circumference, perimeter, sphere, compass, area, distance around; border, bounds, limit, confines, extremity, edge, margin, frontier. **3.** beat, route, round, course, run, territory, tour, lap; journey, jaunt, excursion, trek, walk.

circuitous *adj.* circular, winding, roundabout, circumlocutory, indirect, devious, meandering, rambling; tortuous, twisting, turning, serpentine, labyrinthine. **—Ant.** direct, straight, undeviating, as the crow flies.

circular *adj.* **1.** round, rounded, ring-shaped, curved, winding, circuitous. **2.** turning, rotary, revolving, spinning, twirling, winding, pivoting, spiraling, coiling, curling, swiveling, gyrating; rolling, rocking. *—n.* **3.** handbill, bill, flier, leaflet, throwaway, advertisement, bulletin, notice, announcement. **—Ant. 1** square, rectangular, straight. **2** linear.

circulate *v.* **1.** flow, circle, move around, pass through, course, radiate; go around, make the rounds, move about; travel, journey, get abroad, go forth, visit around. **2.** distribute, disperse, disseminate, pass around, issue, put forward, put about, give out; make public, spread, scatter, strew, publicize, announce, broadcast, make known, publish. **—Ant. 1** stop, stagnate. **2** keep, hold back; keep secret, hide, conceal, suppress.

circulation *n.* **1.** flow, flowing, circling, rotation, motion. **2.** distribution, dissemination, dispersion, diffusion, radiation, propagation, transmission, promulgation. **—Ant. 1** stagnation.

circumference *n.* distance around, periphery, perimeter, circuit; boundary, bounds, extremity, border, edge, margin, rim, girdle, girth, outline, compass, limits, fringe. **—Ant.** center, interior.

circumlocution *n.* roundaboutness, roundabout expression, wordiness, meandering, verbiage, garrulity, verbosity, discursiveness, long-windedness, rambling, digression. **—Ant.** directness; conciseness, terseness, succinctness, brevity, briefness.

circumscribe *v.* **1.** circle, encircle, outline, delineate, define; surround, enclose, encompass. **2.** limit, proscribe, restrict, restrain, confine, constrain, impede, hem in, check, curb, bridle, corset, fix. **—Ant. 2** expand, extend, enlarge, open, throw open, unfetter.

circumspect *adj.* careful, cautious, guarded, vigilant, alert, wide-awake; watchful, discreet, deliberate, wary, thoughtful, judicious, prudent, sagacious, sage, discriminating, contemplative, discerning, particular, perspicacious. **—Ant.** rash, reckless, foolhardy, heedless, careless; audacious, adventurous, venturous, daring, venturesome, bold.

circumstance *n.* **1.** fact, factor, occurrence, happenstance, event, incident, happening, phenomenon, condition, state of affairs, vicissitude, detail, particular, item, thing, point, element, matter. **2.** ceremony, pageantry, ritual, formality; splendor, resplendence, magnificence, brilliance.

circumstantial *adj.* **1.** presumed, inferred, inferential, conjectural, evidential, implied, deduced, hearsay; incidental, provisional, secondary; nonessential, extraneous. **2.** detailed, precise, accurate, explicit, exhaustive, full, complete, unabridged, thorough, blow-by-blow, particular, minute. **—Ant. 2** short, abridged; cursory, superficial; terse, pithy.

circumvent *v.* circle, circumnavigate, go around, bypass, skirt; escape, avoid, elude, evade, keep away from, shun, miss, dodge, thwart, outwit, frustrate. **—Ant.** face, confront, meet, meet head on, go through; follow, conform to.

citadel *n.* fortress, fort, stronghold, bastion, fortification, rampart.

citation *n.* **1.** quotation, quote, excerpt, passage, extract, cite; illustration, example, instance. **2.** commendation, official praise; medal, award, honor, kudos.

cite *v.* **1.** allude to, refer to, specify, quote, mention, note, bring forward, indicate, give as example, advance, present, exemplify, document, enumerate. **2.** commend, praise, honor, mention, name. **—Ant. 1** ignore, disregard; conceal, keep secret. **2** condemn, rebuke, chastise, chasten, criticize; dishonor.

citizen *n.* national, subject; inhabitant, resident, denizen, native. **—Ant.** alien, foreigner; nonresident, visitor, transient, tourist, out-of-towner.

city *n.* **1.** town, big town, metropolitan area, megalopolis, metropolis; incorporated town, municipality, township, *Slang* burg. **2.** population of a city, townspeople, inhabitants, residents, denizens.

civic *adj.* **1.** citizen's, public. **2.** communal, community, local, public.

civil *adj.* **1.** citizen, citizen's, individual. **2.** community, communal, state, city, municipal, civic, public. **3.** communal, secular, lay, civic, public; nonmilitary. **4.** courteous, polite, well-mannered, mannerly, respectful, gentlemanly; affable, gracious, cordial, neighborly, amiable, obliging, conciliatory, genial, decorous, civilized. **—Syn. Study.** CIVIL,

COURTEOUS, POLITE imply avoidance of rudeness toward others. CIVIL suggests only minimal observance of social amenities: *a civil reply*. COURTEOUS implies respectful, dignified, sincere, and thoughtful consideration for others: *a courteous thank-you note*. POLITE implies habitual courtesy, arising from a consciousness of one's training and the demands of good manners: *a polite young woman*. **—Ant. 1** state. **3** religious; military. **4** uncivil, impolite, rude, discourteous, ill-mannered, unmannerly; uncordial, ungracious.

civilian *n.* private citizen, nonmilitary person, nonuniformed person; lay person. **—Ant.** soldier, member of the military; uniformed fire fighter, uniformed police officer.

civility *n.* politeness, courtesy, courteousness, good manners, manners, respect, respectfulness, tact; graciousness, agreeableness, affability, amiability, cordiality, good temper, pleasantness. **—Ant.** impoliteness, discourtesy, discourteousness, bad manners, disrespect; unfriendliness, hostility, unpleasantness, disagreeableness, ungraciousness.

civilization *n.* **1.** civilized life or society. **2.** culture, cultivation, enlightenment, refinement, sophistication, worldliness. **—Ant. 1, 2** ignorance; barbarism, barbarity, barbarousness, savagery.

civilize *v.* refine, culture, educate, teach, train, instruct, inform, enlighten, cultivate, humanize, edify, polish, acculturate, elevate, develop, sophisticate.

clad *adj.* clothed, dressed, attired, outfitted, garbed, arrayed. **—Ant.** undressed, unclothed, naked.

claim *v.* **1.** assert, profess, declare, maintain, proclaim, avow, allege, affirm, charge. **2.** lay claim to, seek as due, demand, exact, command, insist on; call for, collect, pick up, ask, request, take. *—n.* **3.** assertion, avowal, affirmation, declaration, profession, protestation, postulation, statement, proclamation, plea, allegation. **4.** demand, call, requirement, exaction, request; right, title, ownership, access, pretension. **—Ant. 1** disavow, deny. **2** disclaim, renounce, disown, reject, repudiate, refuse, relinquish, forgo, abnegate, abjure, waive, cede. **3** disclaimer, disavowal, denial, repudiation.

clairvoyant *adj.* telepathic, psychic, extrasensory, prescient, precognitive, prophetic, divining, oracular, telekinetic, psychokinetic, psychometric, foreknowing, second-sighted.

clammy *adj.* cold and damp, damp, sticky, slimy, pasty; wet, sweaty, perspiring. **—Ant.** dry, cool.

clamor *n.* **1.** noise, uproar, din, blast, hubbub, brouhaha, hullabaloo, jangle, racket, clangor, tumult, rumpus, commotion, chaos, bedlam, shouting. **2.** cry, outcry, hue and cry, shout, call, bellow, yell, howl, wild chorus, storm, thunder. *—v.* **3.** shout, cry out, cry, call out, call, bellow, howl, yell, vociferate, bluster, make a racket. **—Syn. Study. 1** See NOISE. **—Ant. 1–3** whisper, murmur. **1** silence, quiet.

clamp *n.* **1.** clip, clasp, grip, vise, fastener, brace, bracket. *—v.* **2.** clinch, clench, clip, clasp, fasten, secure.

clan *n.* **1.** tribal family, family group, house, dynasty; line, lineage, lineal group, strain, stock, pedigree, breed. **2.** circle, group, gang, party, alliance, ring, knot, crowd, company; society, brotherhood, cabal, guild, fraternity, league, affiliation, association.

clandestine *adj.* secret, undercover, hidden, covert, cloaked, secretive, masked, underground, veiled, concealed; private, confidential, secluded, undisclosed, unrevealed; stealthy, sneaking, surreptitious, furtive, underhand, underhanded. **—Ant.** open, out in the open, public, aboveboard, disclosed, revealed, unconcealed; straightforward, forthright, frank, candid.

clang *v.* **1.** ring loudly, resound, peal, bong, gong, chime, toll, knell, jangle. *—n.* **2.** clash, clashing, din, clangor, clank; ringing, resounding, peal, tolling, knell, bong, gong, jangle, chime.

clank *n.* **1.** rattle, clang, clash, clashing, clink, clangor, chink, jangle. *—v.* **2.** rattle, clang, clink, chink, jangle, clash, clatter.

clannish *adj.* cliquish, exclusive, snobbish, unreceptive, cold, aloof, distant, unfriendly; sectarian, narrow, restricted, provincial, parochial, insular. **—Ant.** open, friendly, hospitable, receptive, warm.

clap *v.* **1.** applaud. **2.** slap, smack, rap, strike, whack, thump, swat, hit, smite, thwack; bump, buffet, bang, crack, clatter. **3.** set suddenly, cast, thrust, slam, hurl, rush, propel, pitch, fling, force, dash, toss, push, shove, drive, plunge. *—n.* **4.** slap, slam, rap, bat, tap, smack, swat, hit, whack, strike, cuff, thump, crack, wallop, thwack. **5.** peal, burst, roar, crack, bang, clack, clatter, slam, explosion. **—Ant. 1** boo, hiss, give a Bronx cheer, give the raspberry.

claptrap *n.* pretentiousness, humbug, sham, fustian, tomfoolery, staginess, tinsel, gaudiness, quackery, affectation, tawdriness, hokum, nonsense, blarney, twaddle; *Slang* bull, baloney, flapdoodle, bosh, tripe, bilge.

clarify *v.* **1.** clear, purify, refine, purge.

2. explain, clear up, make clear, resolve, solve, disentangle, illuminate, elucidate, explicate, lay open, make plain, make understandable, bring to light, shed light on. **—Ant. 1** cloud, muddy. **2** obscure, confuse, mix up, entangle, cloud, muddle.

clarion *adj.* clear, shrill, high-pitched, ringing, sharp, acute, piercing, blaring; resonant, sonorous; distinct, stirring, compelling, commanding, imperative. **—Ant.** dull, muted, muffled, soft; low.

clarity *n.* **1.** clearness, lucidity, intelligibility, comprehensibility, plainness, simplicity, directness; precision, exactness, explicitness. **2.** clearness, transparency, purity, translucence, lucidity; brightness, brilliance, glassiness, luminosity, radiance, effulgence. **—Ant. 1** obscurity, confusion; imprecision, complexity. **2** cloudiness, muddiness, murkiness; dullness, opaqueness.

clash *v.* **1.** crash, clang, clank, bang, rattle, clatter, crash. **2.** battle, fight, contest, contend, combat, grapple, skirmish, tussle, cross swords, exchange blows. **3.** argue, dispute, quarrel, wrangle, squabble, boil, altercate, tiff, feud, lock horns. *—n.* **4.** crash, crashing, clang, clank, rattle, clatter, clangor, jangle. **5.** battle, fight, combat, conflict, contest, fray, skirmish, encounter, struggle; fracas, set-to. **6.** conflict, disagreement, difference, opposition, discord, dissidence, disharmony, jarring, friction, antagonism. **—Ant. 2** make peace. **3** agree, concur; make up. **5** peace, truce. **6** concord, accord, harmony, agreement.

clasp *n.* **1.** fastening, fastener, catch, latch, grip, hook, coupler, hasp, link, clinch, bolt, clamp, buckle, lock, snap. **2.** hold, grip, embrace, hug, grasp, clutch, squeeze. *—v.* **3.** latch, catch, hook, clamp, lock, hasp, buckle, clinch, link, couple, secure, fasten, clip, snap. **4.** hold, grip, grasp, hug, embrace, clutch, grapple, press, squeeze. **—Ant. 3** unclasp, unfasten, open, unlock, unlatch, unhook, unbuckle, uncouple, unsnap. **4** let go, drop; release, give up.

class *n.* **1.** classification, category, group, type, kind, sort, order, variety, division, genre, breed, pedigree, species, genus. **2.** set of pupils, graduating group, grade, form, group, section. **3.** course, session, section; lesson. **4.** social stratum, social rank, station, status, position, caste, condition, sphere, state; circle, clique, set, group. *—v.* **5.** classify, group, categorize, designate, departmentalize, type, rank, codify, rate, brand, label, pigeonhole; catalog, arrange, index, order; grade, size, number.

classic, classical *adj.* **1.** definitive, authoritative, absolute, accepted, traditional, model, archetypal, prototypal, exemplary; excellent, outstanding, distinguished, distinguishing, first-class, first-rate, consummate, masterly, ageless, heroic, enduring, epic. **2.** ancient Greek or Roman; Greco-Roman. *—n.* **3.** masterpiece, standard work; prototype, archetype, model, first-class example, paragon. **—Ant. 1** bad, poor, inferior, awful, terrible, lousy, second-rate; unrepresentative, atypical. **2** modern. **3** piece of junk, trash.

classification *n.* **1.** grouping, categorization, categorizing, classing, arrangement, arranging, gradation, organization, organizing, ordering, codification, labeling, systematization, taxonomy, assortment, disposition. **2.** group, grouping, class, category, division, section, designation, order, rank, series, family, species, genus, kind, sort, type.

classify *v.* organize, class, grade, type, rank, rate, distinguish, categorize, group, assort, range, arrange, pigeonhole, segregate; label, catalog, index, brand, list, codify, tag, ticket; size, number, order.

classy *adj.* smart, elegant, fashionable, high-class, aristocratic, stylish, modish, chic, opulent, genteel, refined, ultrasmart; *Slang* posh, swell, ritzy, swank, tony, nifty, spiffy, dressy, swanky, *British* nobby. **—Ant.** shabby, wretched, miserable, tacky, *Slang* unclassy.

clatter *v.* **1.** clash, clack, rattle, bang, clump, crash, clang, clank, clink, jangle. *—n.* **2.** clattering, clack, clank, rattling, racket, jangle, crashing, clamor, chatter.

clause *n.* **1.** simple sentence or part of a sentence. **2.** provision, proviso, stipulation, specification, term, condition, article, covenant, proposition.

claw *n.* **1.** talon, animal nail. **2.** paw, foot; clawed hand, pincer. *—v.* **3.** tear, maul, lacerate, slash, scratch, scrape; clutch, seize, grip.

clean *adj.* **1.** unsoiled, spotless, immaculate, sanitary, unblemished, unstained, unspotted; cleaned, cleansed, washed, scrubbed, bathed, scoured, laundered, fresh; neat, tidy, orderly. **2.** perfect, flawless, faultless, neat, fine, trim, well-made. **3.** unpolluted, pure, clear, uncontaminated, unadulterated, untainted, uninfected, undefiled. **4.** wholesome, honorable, upright, virtuous, moral, decent, decorous, innocent, healthy, chaste, unsoiled, exemplary, untainted, stainless, unsullied, unblemished, unspotted. *—v.* **5.** cleanse, wash, scour, scrub, launder, bathe, shampoo; sweep, vacuum, mop, dust; tidy, tidy up, order, neaten. **—Ant. 1** dirty, filthy, soiled, stained, spotted; unwashed, unbathed; messy, untidy, disorderly. **2** flawed, imperfect, faulty, crude, ragged, awkward, sloppy, messy. **3** contaminated, polluted, impure, infected, tainted. **4** unwholesome, dishonorable, indecorous, immoral, indecent, stained, unhealthy, tainted, sullied, blemished; evil, wicked, depraved. **5** soil, dirty, stain; mess up, disorder.

cleanse *v.* **1.** clean, wash, bathe, launder, scrub, scour, shampoo. **2.** rid, free, expunge, expurgate, clear, flush, sweep out, erase, absolve; release, unburden, deliver. **—Ant. 1** soil, dirty, befoul, stain. **2** burden, weigh down, charge, fill, load.

clear *adj.* **1.** unclouded, cloudless, unobscured, fair, halcyon, serene, sunny; bright, brilliant, radiant, gleaming, dazzling, luminous, shining light, glistening, glowing, sparkling; lucid, transparent, translucent, crystalline, pellucid; gauzy, diaphanous. **2.** distinct, audible, intelligible, distinguishable, plain, recognizable, articulate. **3.** plain, obvious, unmistakable, evident, self-evident, manifest, comprehensible, clear-cut, undisguised, unambiguous, straightforward, explicit, inescapable, apparent, unhidden, unconcealed, positive, certain, definite, unequivocal, unqualified, undeniable, pronounced, patent, express. **4.** unconfused, unmuddled, unencumbered, alert, keen, wide-awake, sharp, discerning. **5.** open, free, unobstructed, unimpeded, unblocked. *—adv.* **6.** clearly, distinctly, plainly, audibly, articulately. **7.** entirely, wholly, completely, all the way. *—v.* **8.** become unclouded, brighten, lighten; become fair. **9.** unblock, unstop, empty, rid, clean, open; remove, free, remove obstacles from. **10.** pass over, fly over; vault over, leap over, skip over, hop over, bound over, *Informal* make. **11.** vindicate, exculpate, exonerate, free, absolve, acquit. **—Ant. 1** cloudy, clouded, obscured; hazy, stormy, murky, muddy, unclear, opaque. **2** inaudible, unclear, indistinguishable, indistinct, unrecognizable, unarticulate. **3** unclear, ambiguous, uncertain, hidden. **4** confused, muddled. **5** obstructed, blocked, barricaded, clogged, closed. **6** unclearly, indistinctly, inarticulately. **8** cloud, darken. **9** obstruct, block, clog, close. **11** convict; accuse, blame.

clear-cut *adj.* exact, precise, distinct, manifest, definite, well-defined, explicit, lucid, plain, express, detailed, unambiguous, crystal-clear, unequivocal, understandable, unmistakable, unconfused. **—Ant.** hazy, vague, muddled, indefinite, ambiguous, unclear, confused.

clearheaded *adj.* awake, alert, clear-sighted, clear-witted, sensible, realistic, astute, perspicacious, practical, discerning, rational; *Slang* on the ball, on the stick, on one's toes. **—Ant.** unrealistic, foolish, irrational, impractical, *Slang* dopey.

clearly *adv.* undoubtedly, beyond doubt, beyond question, unquestionably, decidedly, palpably, undeniably, certainly, plainly, evidently, unmistakably, assuredly, recognizably, patently, distinctly, noticeably, unequivocally, indubitably.

cleave[1] *v.* cling, stick, hold, hold fast, adhere, fuse, be joined, unite; be faithful, be constant, be true, stand by, abide by, uphold. **—Ant.** separate, come loose, slip off; let go, release, free; forsake, abandon, relinquish.

cleave[2] *v.* **1.** split, divide, bisect, halve, rend, slit, slice, part, crack, rive; cut, slash, chop, hack, hew, lay open, open, plow, furrow, tear. **2.** sever, cut off, disjoin, sunder, detach, separate, chop off, disengage, dismember, break off. **—Ant. 1, 2** unite, join. **2** attach, affix.

cleft *n.* **1.** split, crack, crevice, crevasse, rift, fissure, rent, cranny, opening, aperture, break, breach, divide, gap, cleavage, division, separation, notch, indentation, slit, furrow, trough, trench. *—adj.* **2.** divided, cloven, bisected, split, slotted, notched; forked, branched.

clemency *n.* **1.** mercy, mercifulness, charity, forbearance, forgivingness, magnanimity, tolerance, sympathy, compassion, humanity, benevolence, kindness, indulgence, leniency. **2.** mildness, moderation, softness, pleasantness, temperance. **—Ant. 1** sternness, strictness; cruelty, mercilessness, hard-heartedness. **2** harshness, severity.

clench *v.* **1.** close tightly, set, set firmly, tighten, stiffen, tense, strain tight. **2.** grasp firmly, clinch, clasp, clutch, fasten on, grip, hold fast. **—Ant. 1** unclench, loose, loosen, relax. **2** unclench, unclasp, release, let go.

clergy *n.* ministry, priesthood, pastorate, rabbinate, the cloth, the pulpit, the church, the first estate; clergymen, preachers, churchmen, ministers, pastors, prelates, clerics, clericals, priests, rabbis.

clergyman *n.* member of the clergy, minister, priest, reverend, rabbi, father; preacher, pastor, chaplain, parson, cleric, prelate, man of the cloth, churchman; *Slang* padre, sky pilot. **—Ant.** lay person.

clerical *adj.* **1.** of clerks, of general office work, clerkly, office; (*variously*) bookkeeping, accounting, recordkeeping, filing, typing. **2.** ecclesiastical, churchly, cleric, pastoral, ministerial, priestly, rabbinical. **—Ant. 2** lay, secular.

clerk *n.* **1.** clerical worker, office worker; (*variously*) file clerk, bookkeeper, typist. **2.** salesclerk, salesperson, salesman, saleswoman.

clever *adj.* **1.** smart, bright, intelligent,

sharp, keen, astute, quick, quick-witted, able, adroit. **2.** inventive, ingenious, imaginative, creative, original, deft, adroit, artful, crafty, shrewd, resourceful, expert; cute, humorous, witty, keen, acute, sharp, smart. **—Ant. 1** dull, stupid, witless, dim-witted, dense, obtuse, inept, incompetent, slow-witted, unaccomplished. **2** clumsy, awkward, maladroit, *Slang* klutzy; unimaginative, uninventive, unresourceful, boring, tedious, dull.

cleverly *adv.* ingeniously, inventively, imaginatively, creatively, craftily, artfully, adroitly, sharply, expertly, deftly, intelligently, smartly; wittily, humorously. **—Ant.** unimaginatively, inexpertly, stupidly, clumsily, awkwardly.

cliché *n.* hackneyed expression, saw, old saw, old story, stereotype, banality, platitude, trite phrase, bromide.

click *n.* **1.** sharp sound, clack, clink, snap. **—*v.* 2.** clack, clink, clap, crack, crackle, snap, tap, rattle.

client *n.* person represented, advisee; patron, customer, buyer, purchaser, shopper.

cliff *n.* bluff, palisade, precipice, promontory; ledge, crag, tor.

climate *n.* **1.** usual weather, weather pattern, weather; weather region, weather zone. **2.** general feeling, mood, atmosphere, disposition, condition, pulse, frame of mind, attitude, spirit, tone, character, temper, quality, air, ambience.

climax *n.* **1.** highest point, high point, culmination, supreme moment, crowning point, best part, height, acme, summit, peak, pinnacle, apex, crown. **2.** turning point, decisive point, critical point, crisis, moment of revelation, denouement, point of highest development. **—Ant. 1** nadir, bottom. **2** anticlimax.

climb *v.* **1.** ascend, mount, clamber up, scramble up, scale, rise hand over hand; rise, go up, come up. **—*n.* 2.** ascent, climbing. **—Ant. 1** descend, go down, come down, climb down. **2** descent.

clinch *v.* **1.** make sure of winning, win, ensure victory; make sure of obtaining, obtain, make sure, assure, settle, cinch, secure, decide; close, conclude, establish, fix, bind, verify, confirm, cap, crown, complete, culminate, wind up, finish off. **2.** nail, screw, clamp, bolt, couple, fasten, make fast. **3.** clasp, clutch, grab hold of, grasp, grip, grapple, hold firmly, seize and hold.

cling *v.* stick, hold, hold fast, adhere, cleave, fuse; stay close; grasp, grip, hang on to, hold on to, clasp, hug, clutch, grab hold of; be faithful, be constant, be true, stand by, maintain. **—Ant.** separate, come loose, slip off; let go, release, free; forsake, abandon, relinquish, give up.

clinic *n.* medical center, outpatients' ward, polyclinic; infirmary.

clink *n.* **1.** jangle, clank, jingle, tinkle, ring sharply; click, clack; rattle. **—*n.* 2.** tinkle, ting, jingle, jangle, sharp ring, clank, click, clack.

clip[1] *v.* **1.** cut off, cut short, cut out, shorten, trim, crop, bob, snip, shear. **—*n.* 2.** clipping, trim, crop, cropping, cut, bob, shearing, cutting, snipping, paring.

clip[2] *v.* **1.** clamp, staple, fasten, couple, attach, fix, secure, clinch. **—*n.* 2.** fastener, hook, grip, clasp, buckle, clinch. **—Ant. 1** unclip, unstaple, unfasten, uncouple, separate.

clique *n.* group, coterie, circle, set, faction, clan, crowd, gang.

cloak *n.* **1.** cape, mantle, robe, tunic, burnoose, pelisse. **2.** cover, screen, curtain, shield, concealment, camouflage, mantle, veil, curtain. **—*v.* 3.** robe, shroud, wrap. **4.** hide, mask, screen, veil, conceal, secrete, disguise, camouflage. **—Ant. 4** reveal, show, display, expose, bare, uncover.

clobber *v.* thrash, wallop, whip, batter, beat up, hit, punch, strike, whack, lick, clout, trim, smash, beat the tar out of; *Slang* belt, slug, sock, shellac, smear, lambaste.

clock *n.* timepiece, watch, horologe, chronometer.

clod *n.* **1.** lump, clump, chunk, wad, hunk, glob. **2.** boor, yokel, rube, bumpkin, lout; dolt, oaf, dope, blockhead, clown, dunce, moron, imbecile, ignoramus, numskull, simpleton, *Informal* dummy, fathead. **—Ant. 2** sophisticate, gentleman; genius, savant.

clodhopper *n.* hick, yokel, provincial, rube, rustic, bumpkin, plowboy, oaf, clod, lout, booby, hayseed, lubber, lummox, clown, galoot, lunkhead, slob, clodpoll, hillbilly, redneck.

clog *v.* **1.** stop up, stop, block, obstruct, choke, congest, close, dam up. **—*n.* 2.** stoppage, obstruction, block, blockage; obstacle, impediment, barrier, restraint, check. **—Ant. 1** unclog, unblock, clear, free, open.

cloister *n.* **1.** monastery, abbey, friary; *(female)* convent, nunnery. **2.** colonnade, gallery, arcade, portico, stoa, ambulatory, walkway, courtyard, promenade. **—*v.* 3.** confine, sequester, shut away, shut up, seclude, closet, embower, coop up, immure, wall up, hole up, conceal.

cloistered *adj.* secluded, sheltered, insulated, isolated, withdrawn, dissociated, aloof, recluse, sequestered, closeted, confined, immured, solitary, alone, separate, apart, detached; hidden, concealed, secreted. **—Ant.** public, social, gregarious.

close *v.* **1.** shut, secure; close up, stop up, stop, fill up, fill, fill in, stuff, clog, clog up, plug, plug up, shut off, blockade, block, obstruct, seal off; shut in, shut up, confine, pen in, enclose, pen, coop up. **2.** join, link, connect, couple, unite, fuse, bring together. **3.** end, finish, conclude, terminate, stop, halt, cease, bring to an end, wind up; adjourn, recess, suspend, discontinue, dismiss, leave off, break off, shut down. *—adj.* **4.** near, nearby, next to, neighboring, approximate, hard by; imminent, at hand, impending, forthcoming, nigh. **5.** tight, firm, secure, fast, fixed, solid; alert, intense, intent, watchful, careful, attentive, vigilant, keen, sharp, thorough. **6.** congested, crowded, teeming, swarming, populous; tight, cramped, confined, narrow, restricted, compact, compressed, pinched, stuffed, squeezed, jammed; dense, solid, impenetrable, impermeable. **7.** stuffy, suffocating, stagnant, unventilated; muggy, humid, stifling, sweltering, uncomfortable, hot, warm. **8.** attached, friendly, intimate, familiar, loving, warm, devoted; inseparable, allied, *Informal* thick as thieves, *Slang* tight. **9.** near, similar, akin, almost like, almost alike, much the same as, resembling, approaching; nearly even, nearly equal, well-matched, nip-and-tuck. **10.** stingy, miserly, tight, tight-fisted, close-fisted, penurious, parsimonious, niggardly, stinting, scrimping, penny-pinching, ungenerous, grudging. **11.** near to the skin, smooth, trim, neat, short. *—n.* **12.** end, finish, conclusion, termination, windup, completion; closing, ending, finale. *—adv.* **13.** near, nearby, in proximity. **—Ant. 1–3, 5, 6, 10** open. **1** unstop, unplug, unclog; free, release, let out. **2** widen, spread, expand; separate, part, divide, disunite. **3** begin, start, commence, inaugurate, initiate. **4** far, far off, distant, a long way off. **5** loose, weak, relaxed; careless, inattentive. **6** spacious, roomy, uncrowded, uncongested, vacant, empty; open wide, spread out, unrestricted, unconfined; loose, porous, lacy. **7** fresh, refreshing; cool, airy. **8** unfriendly, estranged, alienated, distant, detached, aloof, cold, cool, indifferent, hateful. **9** far, dissimilar; unequal, uneven, unmatched. **10** extravagant, generous, open-handed, free, liberal, unstinting, magnanimous, charitable, bountiful, lavish. **12** beginning, start, commencement, opening, initiation, inauguration, inception. **13** far, far away.

close-fisted *adj.* stingy, miserly, tight, niggardly, parsimonious, penurious, penny-pinching, mingy, close-handed, tight-fisted, ungenerous, grudging, mean. **—Ant.** generous, open-handed, prodigal, profligate, lavish.

closely *adv.* carefully, diligently, attentively, heedfully, alertly, intently, sharply, keenly, watchfully, vigilantly; intensely, vigorously. **—Ant.** carelessly, inattentively.

close-mouthed *adj.* tight-lipped, uncommunicative, diffident, cool, reticent, retiring, reserved, taciturn, secretive, terse; shy, distant, bashful, withdrawn. **—Ant.** open, frank, candid, forthright, talkative, outgoing.

closure *n.* **1.** plug, stopper, cork, bung; cover, lid; faucet, tap, spigot. **2.** shutting, sealing, securing, bringing together, locking, barring, bolting, stoppering. **3.** termination, conclusion, ending, cessation, stop, closing, finish, cloture, discontinuance, stoppage, discontinuation. **—Ant. 3** commencement, beginning, opening, start, onset, kickoff.

clot *n.* **1.** embolism, occlusion, coagulation, gob, mass, lump, thrombus. *—v.* **2.** coagulate, congeal, thicken, solidify.

cloth *n.* fabric, dry goods, piece goods, yard goods, goods, material, textile.

clothe *v.* **1.** dress, attire, robe, garb, array, drape, accouter, cloak, don; deck, deck out, bedeck, outfit, bedizen, rig out, costume. **2.** cover, envelop, wrap, enwrap, sheathe, shroud, encase, case, swaddle, cloak, coat, screen, cloud, veil. **—Ant. 1** undress, disrobe, strip, unclothe; divest, dismantle. **2** uncover, lay bare, denude, expose, exhibit.

clothes *n. pl.* clothing, wearing apparel, apparel, garments, wardrobe, wear, attire, habiliments, dress, raiment, garb, costume, ensemble, finery, regalia, *Slang* duds, togs, rags.

clothing *n.* See CLOTHES.

cloud *v.* **1.** grow cloudy, overcast, darken, dim; overshadow, shadow, shade, eclipse; obscure, blur, shroud, cover, veil, cloak, screen, conceal, hide, curtain. **2.** place under suspicion, call to question, cast doubt on, discredit, tarnish, sully. **3.** impair, distort, upset, mar, disturb; confuse, muddle, muddy, blind, make vague. **—Ant. 1** clear, uncloud; uncover, unveil, show, reveal, uncloak. **2** recommend, honor, confirm, second; clear, exonerate. **3** clear, clarify, purify; restore, cure.

cloudy *adj.* **1.** clouded, overclouded, overcast, dark, gray, leaden, dreary, gloomy, hazy, murky, sunless. **2.** unclear, vague, confused, confusing, nebulous, hazy, indefinite, undefined, mysterious, obscure, veiled. **—Ant. 1** uncloudy, clear, bright, fair, sunny, sunfilled. **2** clear, transparent, plain, obvious, straightforward, distinct, definite, well-defined.

clown *n.* **1.** buffoon, jester, harlequin, comic, comedian, comedienne, fool, mime, zany, funny person, joker, madcap; merry-andrew; wit, wag, card, humorist. —*v.* **2.** joke, jest, cut up, kid around, fool around.

cloy *v.* glut, satiate, surfeit, sate, pall, saturate, overdo; weary, bore, tire, benumb, tire, exhaust; nauseate, choke, gag.

club *n.* **1.** truncheon, bludgeon, stick, bat, billyclub, billy, shillelagh, cudgel. **2.** group, society, coterie; league, association, affiliation, union, alliance, guild; fraternity, sorority, brotherhood, sisterhood, lodge. **3.** clubhouse; country club. —*v.* **4.** beat, strike, hit, pommel, pummel, slug, bat, batter, bash, buffet, cudgel, bludgeon, flail, flog, lay on. —**Syn. Study. 2** See CIRCLE.

clue *n.* sign, hint, trace, cue, indication, evidence, mark, key, scent, glimmer, inkling; guide, indicator, pointer; intimation, inference, suggestion, insinuation.

clump *n.* **1.** cluster, group, mass, batch, shock, bunch, assemblage, collection, aggregate; thicket, grove, copse. **2.** lump, mass; bump, knot, knob, bulb. **3.** thump, thud, clunk, clomp, plunk, bump. —*v.* **4.** tramp, stomp, stamp, plunk, clunk; plod, lumber.

clumsy *adj.* **1.** blundering, bungling, maladroit, careless, butterfingered, heavy-handed, unhandy, like a bull in a china shop, inept, graceless, ungraceful, awkward, gawky, *Slang* klutzy. **2.** unhandy, cumbersome, bulky, unwieldy, unmanageable, ungainly; awkward, crude, rough, unskilled, inept, ill-contrived, makeshift, careless. —**Ant. 1** dexterous, deft, handy, adroit, careful; graceful, smooth. **2** handy; professional, expert, skillful.

cluster *n.* **1.** clump, bunch, sheaf, batch, shock, mass; group, crowd, block, knot, band, collection, assemblage, throng, aggregate, congregation, company, swarm, herd, pack, bevy, accumulation, agglomeration, conglomeration. —*v.* **2.** gather, group, crowd, bunch, collect, congregate, assemble, throng, swarm, muster, flock, herd, converge; mass, amass, heap, pile, accumulate, aggregate. —**Ant. 2** disperse, scatter, fan out.

clutch *v.* **1.** grasp, clasp, hold, grip, clench, hug, embrace, squeeze, hang on to, cling to. —*n.* **2.** grasp, hold, grip, clasp, hug, embrace. —**Ant. 1** let go, let loose, loose, free.

clutter *v.* **1.** strew, scatter, litter, fill, pile, heap. —*n.* **2.** pile, heap, mess, litter, hodgepodge, jumble, tangle, disorder, disarray, confusion, chaos. —**Ant. 1** straighten, straighten up, tidy, arrange, order, organize, clean. **2** neatness, tidiness, order, orderliness, organization.

coach *n.* **1.** carriage, four-wheeler, four-in-hand; stagecoach, stage. **2.** railroad passenger car; motor coach, bus, omnibus; automobile, sedan, limousine. **3.** second class, inexpensive accommodation, economy class. **4.** trainer, athletic director; tutor, private teacher, preceptor, mentor. —*v.* **5.** train, instruct, tutor, teach, drill; advise, guide, direct. —**Ant. 3** first class; Pullman, sleeping car. **4** player; student. **5** learn.

coagulate *v.* clot, congeal; solidify, set, gel, jell, jellify, harden, curdle; thicken. —**Ant.** liquefy, melt, dissolve, soften.

coalesce *v.* unite, unify, combine, integrate, fuse, meld, form, join, amalgamate, agglutinate, mix, blend; join forces, band together, come together, cohere, form an alliance, ally, consolidate, become one, merge. —**Ant.** separate, divide, disunite, part; split, disintegrate, dissolve.

coalition *n.* union, alliance, partnership, league, affiliation, federation, association, confederacy, combination, syndicate, society; fusion, consolidation, conglomeration, amalgamation, agglomeration.

coarse *adj.* **1.** coarse-grained, unrefined; rough, rough-textured, harsh, scratchy, prickly, nubbly, shaggy, bristly, bristling, *Slang* sandpaper. **2.** crude, crass, unrefined, lacking taste, rough, unpolished; ungentlemanly, unladylike, ill-bred, uncouth, boorish, loutish, inelegant, common, brutish, rude, impolite, ill-mannered; vulgar, indelicate, indecent, improper, indecorous, offensive, gross, foul-mouthed, obscene, dirty, lewd, licentious, lascivious, ribald; sordid, odious, repulsive, revolting, scurrilous, vile, disgusting. —**Ant. 1** fine-grained, fine, refined, smooth, soft, silky, satiny. **2** refined, gentlemanly, ladylike, genteel, well-bred, cultivated, cultured, civilized, polished, elegant; polite, well-mannered, mannerly; decent, delicate, proper, decorous, inoffensive, clean; pleasant, pleasing, appetizing.

coast *n.* **1.** seacoast, shore, littoral, strand, shoreline, seashore, seaside; seaboard. —*v.* **2.** glide, glissade, float, drift, waft, sweep, skim; slide, slip. —**Ant. 1** interior, midlands, hinterland.

coat *n.* **1.** topcoat, overcoat, wrap; raincoat, slicker, mackinaw, mackintosh; jacket, sports coat, blazer. **2.** hair, fur, hide, pelt. **3.** coating, covering; layer, overlay. —*v.* **4.** cover, spread, overlay, smear; envelop, encase, encrust; (*variously*) paint, enamel, lacquer, glaze, whitewash, plaster, laminate. **—Ant. 4** remove, uncover, clear; clean, wash, dust, scrape, dissolve.

coating *n.* coat, covering, layer, overlay, film, sheet, veneer, skin, envelope.

coax *v.* wheedle, cajole; inveigle, talk into; *Informal* soft-soap, butter up, sweet-talk. **—Ant.** intimidate, cow, threaten, menace, pressure, bully, bulldoze, browbeat; coerce, force, compel.

cobbler *n.* **1.** shoemaker, shoe repairer, bootmaker. **2.** deep-dish fruit pie, pie.

cock *n.* **1.** cockerel, chanticleer, rooster; male bird. **2.** valve, faucet, handle, knob. **—***v.* **3.** draw back the hammer, raise the hammer of. **4.** turn to one side, raise, tip, stand up, perk up; set erect, bristle up. **—Ant. 1** hen; chick. **3** uncock.

cockeyed *adj.* **1.** awry, aslant, askew, off-center, crooked, twisted, asymmetrical, tilted, lopsided, sideways, unbalanced, irregular, *Slang* out of whack. **2.** ridiculous, absurd, foolish, inane, preposterous, senseless, nonsensical; mad, insane, crazy; *Slang* nutty, goofy, cockamamie, wild, weird. **—Ant. 1** straight, symmetrical, centered, even. **2** plausible, sensible, reasonable, commendable.

cocksure *adj.* cocky, overconfident, conceited, arrogant, brash, vain, smug, bumptious, overbearing, swaggering, pert, swell-headed, self-assured; assertive, aggressive, audacious; *Slang* pushy, cheeky, snooty. **—Ant.** humble, shy, self-effacing, deferential, timid.

coddle *v.* **1.** pamper, spoil, indulge, baby, mollycoddle, humor, dote on. **2.** fondle, cuddle, caress, pet, pat. **—Ant. 1** neglect, ignore, deny.

code *n.* **1.** secret writing, secret language, cipher; cryptogram, cryptograph. **2.** laws, rules, regulations, guidelines, standards, principles, proprieties, precepts; statute, ordinance.

codicil *n.* added clause, addendum, rider; postscript, subscript; addition, supplement, extension, appendix.

codify *v.* classify, catalog, categorize, systematize, order, arrange, organize, tabulate, index, methodize, coordinate, group, regularize, grade, rank, rate.

coerce *v.* force, pressure, compel, constrain, drive, oblige, make, intimidate, cow, dragoon, bully, browbeat, bulldoze, threaten, strong-arm. **—Ant.** free, allow, permit; coax, cajole, flatter.

coercion *n.* force, pressure, compulsion, intimidation, constraint, threats, duress, bullying, browbeating. **—Ant.** by choice, by one's own free will, volition, desire, by preference, self-motivation.

coeval *adj.* **—Syn. Study.** See CONTEMPORARY.

coffer *n.* **1.** repository, depository, chest, treasure chest, box, strongbox, case. **2. coffers.** treasury, money supply, vaults, safes, cash boxes.

coffin *n.* casket, pall, box, catafalque, sarcophagus.

cogent *adj.* compelling, valid, persuasive, forceful, powerful, potent, trenchant, convincing, well-founded, incontrovertible, sound, meritorious, weighty, effective, undeniable, well-grounded. **—Ant.** unconvincing, unsound, dubious, implausible, improbable.

cogitate *v.* think, ponder, contemplate, deliberate, ruminate, meditate, reflect; think about, think over, reflect upon, deliberate on, mull over, consider thoroughly, study, concentrate upon, weigh.

cognate *adj.* **1.** related, akin, kindred, relative, consanguine, familial, affiliate. **2.** similar, like, alike, parallel, close. **—***n.* **3.** word that is related to another word or words by derivation, borrowing, or descent. **—Ant. 1, 2** unrelated. **2** unlike, unalike, dissimilar, different, opposite, contrary, contradicting, conflicting; unallied, unassociated, unaffiliated, diverse.

cognizance *n.* **1.** notice, note, heed, attention, recognition, cognition, awareness; regard, observation, scrutiny. **2.** knowledge, awareness, cognition, familiarity; apprehension, comprehension, grasp, perception, understanding; sensibility, consciousness. **—Ant. 1** inattention, disregard, nonobservance, neglect, oversight. **2** ignorance, unfamiliarity, unawareness, incomprehension; insensibility, unconsciousness.

cognizant *adj.* aware, informed, knowledgeable, knowing, familiar, acquainted, conversant, no stranger to, understanding, with it, in the know, *Slang* hip to, tuned in to; enlightened, versed in, instructed, posted, mindful, conscious. **—Syn. Study.** See CONSCIOUS. **—Ant.** unaware, uninformed, ignorant, unfamiliar, unknowledgeable, unknowing, unacquainted, unenlightened, unapprised, oblivious, unconscious, insensible.

cohere *v.* **1.** stick, stick together, hold together, unite, join, fuse, cling, bind, adhere, cement, glue, hold, combine, coalesce, consolidate; set, solidify, congeal, coagulate. **2.** agree, coincide, correspond, match, fit, tally, synchronize, harmonize, conform, concur, be consistent, jibe, square, dovetail; be related, be connected. **—Syn. Study. 1** See STICK. **—Ant. 1** separate, fall apart, come apart, unstick, detach, disjoin; scatter, disperse. **2** disagree, differ, diverge, be inconsistent, be at odds, be unlike; be disconnected, be unrelated.

coherence *n.* consistency, cohesion,

congruity, conformity, rationality, clarity, organization, logic, accordance; unity, harmony, concord, consonance. **—Ant.** confusion, chaos, incoherence, muddle, inconsistency.

coherent *adj.* logical, meaningful, intelligible, articulate, rational, clear, lucid, connected, comprehensible, understandable; organized, orderly, systematic; consistent, cohesive, harmonious, corresponding, congruous, in agreement, in keeping. **—Ant.** disjointed, disconnected, rambling, inconsistent, incongruous; irrational, illogical, meaningless, confusing, chaotic, vague, hazy, unintelligible, incomprehensible.

cohesive *adj.* coherent, cohering, viscous, sticky, sticking, agglutinative; inseparable, connected, consolidated, solid, cemented, indivisible, set.

cohort *n.* companion, friend, comrade, fellow, chum, pal, buddy, crony, associate; accomplice, follower, myrmidon.

coiffure *n.* hairdo, haircut, hairstyle, *Slang* coif; wave, permanent wave, cold wave, home permanent, perm, blowcut, shag, bob, comb-out, beehive, pompadour, upsweep, bun, pageboy, *Slang* Afro, cornrows; flattop, G.I. trim, ducktail, D.A.

coil *v.* **1.** wind, spiral, loop, twist, twine; entwine, circle, encircle, curl, writhe. *—n.* **2.** loop, spiral, ring, circle, curl, roll, braid.

coin *n.* **1.** metal piece of money, piece; change, silver. *—v.* **2.** mint, strike. **3.** create, make up, conceive, originate, fabricate, invent, devise, concoct, think up, dream up, hatch.

coincide *v.* **1.** meet, come together, converge, synchronize, cross; be concurrent, occur simultaneously. **2.** agree, concur, accord, harmonize, correspond, match, tally, fit, conform, jibe, square, dovetail. **—Ant. 1** diverge, separate, divide, part, split. **2** disagree, differ, contradict, counter, be unlike, be at odds, be inconsistent.

coincidence *n.* **1.** chance, accident, luck, fate, happenstance. **2.** simultaneous occurrence, concurrence, synchronism. **—Ant. 1** design, plan, premeditation, purpose.

coincident *adj.* **—Syn. Study.** See CONTEMPORARY.

coincidental *adj.* **1.** accidental, unplanned, chance, happenstance. **2.** simultaneous, synchronous, synchronal, contiguous, concomitant.

cold *adj.* **1.** cool, cooled, chilled, chilly, icy, ice-cold, gelid, frosty, frosted, frigid; unheated, unwarmed. **2.** wintry, freezing, chilling, chilly, chill, cool, icy, ice-cold, frigid, glacial, arctic, polar, brisk, crisp, snappy, nippy, nipping, bitter, sharp, harsh, severe, cutting, biting, penetrating, piercing, stinging, marrow-chilling, bone-chilling, teeth-chattering. **3.** chilled, chilly, cool, ice-cold, chilled to the bone, chilled to the marrow, freezing, frozen, frozen stiff, numbed. **4.** unemotional, passionless, frigid, unresponsive, unfeeling, undemonstrative, unmoved, unimpressionable, impervious, passive, impassive, unexcitable, stiff, unstirred; apathetic, antipathetic; unsympathetic, unconcerned, uninterested, indifferent, phlegmatic, uncaring, unloving; unfriendly, reserved, detached, distant, remote, aloof, haughty, supercilious, disdainful, reticent, uncommunicative, inaccessible, unapproachable, forbidding, steely, stony, heartless, cold-hearted, cold-blooded, cruel, hard, hardened, inured, harsh, callous. **5.** old, stale, flat, uninteresting; faint, faded, dead. **6.** unconscious, insensible, insensate. *—n.* **7.** coldness, coolness, chill. **—Ant. 1–5** hot, warm. **1** red-hot, steaming; heated, warmed. **2** sweltering, scorching, warming, balmy, mild, summery, sunny. **3** sweltering, roasting, perspiring, sweating. **4** emotional, passionate, ardent, fervent, responsive, demonstrative, alive, vital, animated, excitable, spirited, gay; sympathetic, compassionate, concerned, caring, interested; loving, friendly, open, unreserved, warm-hearted. **5** new, fresh; sharp, strong. **6** conscious; semiconscious. **7** heat, warmth.

cold-blooded *adj.* **1.** cold, unfeeling, unemotional, heartless, cold-hearted, hard-hearted, passionless, unimpassioned, unsympathetic, implacable, unfriendly, reserved, formal, stiff, unresponsive, insensitive; unconcerned, uninterested, detached, disinterested, indifferent, uncaring, unmoved, unimpressible, unimpressionable, impervious, passive, impassive, unexcitable, unstirred; contemptuous, disdainful; calculating, deliberate; steely, flinty, stony, hard, cruel, callous, hardened, inured, harsh. **2.** brutal, inhuman, inhumane, bloodthirsty, savage, barbarous, fiendish, ruthless, merciless, unmerciful, unpitying, pitiless, diabolical, demonic, satanic, evil, villainous. **—Ant. 1** warm, feeling, emotional, heartfelt, kindhearted, soft-hearted, passionate, excitable, impassioned, sympathetic, compassionate, friendly, open, responsive, sensitive, concerned, interested, involved, caring, loving, kind, gentle, humane. **2** humane, civilized, merciful, benevolent, charitable.

coliseum *n.* stadium, arena, amphitheater, bowl; hippodrome, theater, circus; exhibition hall.

collaborate *v.* **1.** work together, work

side by side, team up, join forces, create together, cooperate, unite. **2.** cooperate, collude, join, assist.

collaborator *n.* **1.** associate, colleague, confederate, coworker, teammate, co-partner, ally. **2.** collaborationist, puppet, quisling, traitor.

collapse *v.* **1.** cave in, fall, buckle, fall to pieces, give way, break apart, disintegrate, crumple. **2.** break down, disintegrate, fail, fall through, come to nothing, be in vain, flounder, run aground, *Slang* flop, fizzle, fold. **3.** fall prostrate, become unconscious, swoon, *Slang* keel over; take sick, be stricken, become ill, suffer a breakdown; fall helpless, give way, break up. —*n.* **4.** fall, falling apart, disintegration, downfall, breakdown, failure, cave-in, buckling, giving way. **5.** breakdown, sudden illness, crack-up, seizure, attack; fall, faint, swoon; coma. —**Ant. 1** stand. **2** succeed, triumph, flourish. **3** stand up; get well, recover. **5** good health.

collateral *n.* **1.** security, pledge, warranty, warrant, guarantee, insurance, bond, surety, endorsement. —*adj.* **2.** secondary, subordinate, incidental; auxiliary, supplementary, ancillary, accessory, additional, extra, supporting, supportive, contributory, parallel. —**Ant. 2** superior, overshadowing; primary, essential, fundamental, basic, chief, key.

colleague *n.* confrere, associate, fellow; partner, co-partner, coworker, fellow worker, confederate, teammate, collaborator, mate. —**Ant.** rival, competitor, opponent, adversary, antagonist.

collect *v.* **1.** gather, assemble, congregate, flock together, cluster around, herd together, rally, meet, come together, get together, draw together, convene; marshal, muster, bring together. **2.** accumulate, concentrate, amass, pile up, heap up, aggregate, compile. **3.** raise, obtain, receive, solicit, amass, get, scrape up, scrape together, marshal, muster, assemble. **4.** pick up, call for, gather up. **5.** compose, calm, control, get hold of, get together, pull together, summon; prepare, muster, rally, marshal. —**Syn. Study. 1** See GATHER. —**Ant. 1–4** disperse, scatter. **3, 4** distribute, disperse.

collected *adj.* self-controlled, self-assured, self-possessed, composed, confident, poised, calm, cool, cool-headed, restrained, level-headed, steady, even-tempered; quiet, serene, tranquil, peaceful, placid, unruffled, unperturbed, undisturbed, unemotional, unflappable. —**Syn. Study.** See CALM. —**Ant.** nervous, perturbed, disturbed, ruffled, unsteady, shaky, troubled, distressed; unpoised, uncontrolled, excitable, irritable, emotional.

collection *n.* **1.** group, gathering, assembly, assemblage, aggregation, crowd, bunch, pack, body, throng, mob, drove, swarm, hoard, flock, bevy; accumulation, assortment, array, jumble, clutter, miscellany, hodgepodge, variety, heap, pile, cluster, clump, mass. **2.** assemblage, aggregation, compilation, treasury, store, anthology, corpus. **3.** collecting, gathering, amassing, accumulating, muster, receiving, soliciting; gift, offertory, oblation.

collective *adj.* unified, united, joint, combined, cooperative, mutual, common, integrated; collected, gathered, aggregate, cumulative, accumulated, composite. —**Ant.** individual, separate, divided, uncombined, uncooperative, fragmented, piecemeal.

collide *v.* **1.** run into one another, crash, hit, smash, meet, meet head on, crack up; strike against, hurtle against, beat against, knock into, bump into. **2.** disagree, conflict, clash, diverge. —**Ant. 1** miss; avoid, evade. **2** agree, coincide, accord, harmonize, mesh, jibe, fit, square.

collision *n.* **1.** crash, smash-up, accident; impact, smash, clash, bump, striking together. **2.** conflict, clash of arms, battle, combat, fight, encounter, engagement, skirmish, struggle.

colloquial *adj.* folksy, homespun, homey, chatty, ordinary, vernacular, idiomatic, conversational, informal, casual, common, everyday, workaday, plain, unsophisticated, familiar. —**Syn. Study.** COLLOQUIAL, CONVERSATIONAL, INFORMAL refer to types of speech or to usages that are not on a formal level. COLLOQUIAL is often mistakenly used with a connotation of disapproval, as if it meant "vulgar" or "bad" or "incorrect" usage, whereas it merely describes a casual or familiar style used in speaking and writing: *colloquial expressions.* CONVERSATIONAL refers to a style used in the oral exchange of ideas, opinions, etc.: *The newsletter was written in an easy conversational style.* INFORMAL means without formality, without strict attention to set forms, unceremonious; it describes the ordinary, everyday language of cultivated speakers: *informal English.* —**Ant.** formal; sophisticated, literary, cultured, refined.

colloquy *n.* talk, conversation, dialogue, conference, seminar, discussion, parley, chat, discourse, commerce, council, caucus, converse, congress, intercourse, palaver, confabulation, communion, *Slang* rap session, interchange.

collusion *n.* secret agreement, conspiracy, collaboration, intrigue, guilty association, connivance, complicity; treason; fraud.

colony *n.* **1.** settlement, province, territory, dependency, dominion, protectorate, possession, mandate, satellite state. **2.** community, group, body, set, band, swarm, flock.

color *n.* **1.** coloring, coloration, tint, hue, shade, tone, tinge, cast; pigment, pigmentation, paint, dye, dyestuff. **2.** natural complexion, skin hue; bloom, rosiness, glow, blush, redness, flush. **3.** tone, feeling, spirit, mood, aspect, intent, intention, force, stress, effect, implication, insinuation, intimation, connotation, import, significance, sense, meaning, drift. —*v.* **4.** paint, stain, dye, tint, pigment, tinge, crayon, chalk, wash. **5.** prejudice, influence, affect, bias, distort, slant, warp, twist, pervert, taint. **6.** redden, blush, flame, burn, flush, glow, go crimson, become florid; change color. —**Ant. 2** paleness, pallor, wanness, sallowness, whiteness. **3** denotation. **6** blanch, go white.

colorful *adj.* **1.** brightly colored, bright, brilliant, vibrant, full-toned, gay, florid, loud, showy; multicolored, many-colored, particolored, variegated. **2.** picturesque, interesting; unusual, distinctive, unique; graphic, vivid, vivacious, animated, spirited, vigorous, zestful, dynamic, forceful, compelling. —**Ant. 1** dull, drab, dingy, dreary, monotonous, dark, gray, faded, washed out, pale. **2** dull, uninteresting, colorless, unexciting, lifeless, flat, boring.

colorless *adj.* **1.** without color, undyed, natural, neutral; white, whitened, grayed, pale, bleached, faded, washed out, dull, drab, dingy, dreary. **2.** pale, pallid, ashen, ashy, wan, blanched, white, sallow, pasty, anemic, bloodless, sickly, cadaverous, ghastly, ghostly. **3.** dull, unexciting, uninteresting, lifeless, monotonous, boring, dreary, drab, lackluster, flat, unanimated, spiritless, uninspired, ordinary, commonplace, prosaic, neutral, vapid, insipid, pale, anemic, bloodless. —**Ant. 1** bright, brilliant, lustrous, colorful. **2** ruddy, glowing, healthy, robust. **3** colorful, bright, exciting, interesting, lively, full of life, animated, spirited, vigorous, dynamic, forceful, compelling, strong; unusual, unique, distinctive.

colossal *adj.* huge, vast, immense, massive, enormous, gigantic, giant, titanic, mammoth, great, grand, mighty, extreme, exceeding, excessive, extravagant, tremendous, stupendous, spectacular, prodigious, inordinate, incredible, overwhelming, imposing, awe-inspiring, monumental, *Slang* humongous. —**Syn. Study.** See GIGANTIC. —**Ant.** small, little, tiny, minute, diminutive, miniature, *Baby Talk* teeny, teensy, teeny-weeny, teensy-weensy; slight, weak, feeble; ordinary, common, average, so-so.

column *n.* **1.** pillar, support, upright, post, shaft, pilaster, pylon. **2.** vertical row, vertical list; row, line. **3.** row, line, queue, file, string; procession, formation, parade, caravan, cavalcade, train, phalanx.

comatose *adj.* **1.** unconscious, insensible, cataleptic, catatonic; stuporous, drugged, narcotized. **2.** sluggish, leaden, dull, lifeless, torpid, languid, lethargic, listless, phlegmatic, spiritless, inactive, inert; apathetic, unconcerned, passive, indifferent, unresponsive; lazy, indolent, slothful, idle, lax. —**Ant. 2** brisk, energetic, active, lively, industrious.

comb *n.* **1.** hair comb, toilet comb, dressing comb, fine-tooth comb; card, currycomb. **2.** cockscomb, topknot, head tuft; tuft, plume, panache. —*v.* **3.** dress, groom, untangle; style, arrange; curry, card. **4.** search, hunt over, seek through, look through, rummage through, scour, ransack, cast about, explore.

combat *n.* **1.** military action, action, fighting, battle, engagement, clash, skirmish. **2.** conflict, battle, clash, struggle, fight, fighting, encounter, confrontation, contest, contention. —*v.* **3.** fight, battle, do battle with, war against, wage war, go to war, make warfare, attack, contest, march against, grapple with, come to blows, struggle; resist, oppose, work against, contest against, make a stand against. —**Ant. 1** peacetime, peace; armistice, truce; surrender, capitulation. **2** agreement, accord, concord, compliance, concurrence, acquiescence. **3** make peace, declare a truce; surrender, capitulate, give up; support, uphold, accept, comply, assent, concur, acquiesce, welcome.

combatant *n.* fighting man, soldier, serviceman, man-at-arms, warrior, fighter. —**Ant.** noncombatant, nonfighting man; civilian.

combination *n.* **1.** combining, mixture, mix, mixing, blend, blending, pooling, union, joining, composition, compound, composite, synthesis, amalgamation, amalgam, alloy, fusion; medley, variety, assortment. **2.** union, federation, confederation, confederacy, merger, alliance, association, coalition, league, joining, combining, coalescing. —**Ant. 1, 2** division, separation; dissolution, dissolving.

combine *v.* unite, unify, join, bring together, put together, merge, consolidate, couple, pool, lump together, league; mix, blend, mingle, commingle, commix, compound, amalgamate, incorporate, fuse, synthesize. —**Syn. Study.** See MIX. —**Ant.** separate, divide, part, sever, sunder, detach; dissolve, dissociate, disunite.

combustible *adj.* flammable, inflammable, incendiary, conflagrative, burnable, combustive, ignitable.

combustion *n.* burning, ignition, kindling, incineration, conflagration, flaming, firing.

come *v.* **1.** move toward, go toward, approach, draw near, advance; present oneself. **2.** arrive, reach a destination; appear, show up, turn up, drop in. **3.** take place, fall, occur, happen, come about, come to pass, rise, arise, emerge, appear, materialize, arrive, spring forth, rear its head; advance, approach, be imminent, impend, loom, be in the wind, be on the horizon, bear down upon. **4.** become; be, grow to be. **5.** be a resident, be a native; issue, spring, arise, descend, follow; bud, germinate; be a product of, originate in, emanate. **6.** reach, extend, go, stretch, range, spread. **7.** be made, be produced, be available, be offered. **—Ant. 1–3** go, go away, depart, leave, withdraw, retreat.

comedian *n.* comic, (*fem.*) comedienne, joker, jokester, humorist, wag; clown, funny person, jester, buffoon, fool, madcap, zany, prankster, cutup, practical joker; comic actor.

comedy *n.* **1.** play with a happy ending, farce, satire, light entertainment; travesty, burlesque. **2.** joking, jesting, humor, wit, drollery, banter, pleasantry, raillery; fun, silliness, pranks, foolery, tomfoolery, fooling around, cutting up, buffoonery, horseplay. **—Ant. 1** tragedy, tragic drama, high drama, serious play, melodrama; opera. **2** seriousness, solemnity, sobriety; tears, sadness, melancholy.

comely *adj.* **1.** pretty, fair, sightly, well-favored, attractive, bonny, winsome, fetching, pleasing, engaging, winning; wholesome, blooming. **2.** seemly, becoming, suitable, tasteful, proper, decorous, nice, correct, fitting; appealing, pleasing, pleasant, agreeable, engaging, winning, charming; natural, simple, unaffected. **—Ant. 1** ugly, homely, plain, unsightly, unlovely, unattractive, ill-favored, repulsive, disagreeable; jaded, faded. **2** unseemly, unbecoming, unsuitable, tasteless, distasteful, tactless, indecorous, inappropriate, unfitting, improper, scandalous; disagreeable, unappealing, unpleasant, repellent, repulsive; unnatural, affected, pretentious.

come-on *n.* lure, enticement, inveiglement, temptation, attraction, magnet, allurement, seducement, seduction, bewitchery, bait, decoy, snare, trap, hook.

comfort *v.* **1.** console, solace, soothe, quiet, calm, compose, ease, reassure, lighten one's burden, quiet one's fears; cheer, cheer up, hearten, encourage, bolster up, bolster one's spirits. —*n.* **2.** solace, succor, reassurance, consolation, serenity, composure, peace, calm, cheering up, encouragement, help, relief. **3.** consolation, solace, satisfaction, pleasure, source of serenity, source of encouragement, comforter. **4.** creature comforts, ease, satisfaction, pleasure, gratification, well-being, contentment, warmth, coziness, snugness, relaxation, freedom from distress; luxury, opulence. **—Syn. Study. 1** COMFORT, CONSOLE, SOOTHE imply assuaging sorrow, worry, discomfort, or pain. COMFORT means to lessen someone's grief or distress by giving strength and hope and restoring a cheerful outlook: *to comfort a despairing friend.* CONSOLE, a more formal word, means to make grief or distress seem lighter by means of kindness and thoughtful attentions: *to console a bereaved parent.* SOOTHE means to pacify or calm: *to soothe a crying child.* **—Ant. 1–4** discomfort, distress, torment, bother, burden, trouble. **1** aggravate, annoy, irk, rile, ruffle, stir up, excite; sadden, depress, dishearten, discourage. **2–4** aggravation, irritation, annoyance, sadness, discouragement, dissatisfaction, displeasure. **3** bane. **4** poverty, hardship, inconvenience.

comfortable *adj.* **1.** providing comfort, giving ease; pleasurable, pleasant, congenial, agreeable, gratifying; suitable, satisfactory, adequate. **2.** at ease, easy, at home, relaxed, contented, cozy, serene, untroubled, undisturbed; free from distress. **—Ant.** uncomfortable. **1** unsatisfactory, unsuitable, displeasing, unpleasant, disagreeable, uncongenial. **2** uneasy, nervous, tense, fretful, worried, troubled, disturbed, distressed, miserable, wretched, discontented.

comic Also **comical** *adj.* funny, humorous, laughable, amusing, ridiculous, ludicrous, silly, farcical, absurd, nonsensical, mirthful, merry, risible, whimsical, jocose, jocular, jovial, nimble-witted, droll, witty, rich, facetious. **—Ant.** tragic; serious, grave, solemn, sober; pathetic, touching, poignant, melancholy; sad, depressing, doleful, dolorous. **—Syn. Study.** See AMUSING.

coming *n.* **1.** arrival, arriving, approach, approaching, imminence, nearing, proximity; appearance, advent, occurrence, emergence, materializing. —*adj.* **2.** next, forthcoming, subsequent, arriving, advancing, approaching; future, imminent, impending, to come, prospective, on the way, in view, on the horizon, in the wind. **—Ant. 1** departure, withdrawal, disappearance. **2** departing; past, previous, prior.

command *v.* **1.** order, direct, bid, charge, require, adjure, call upon, instruct, decree; call for, summon, ordain, enjoin. **2.** direct, lead, head, have authority over, have charge of, be master of, rule, boss, govern; guide, conduct, manage, supervise, superintend, administer. **3.** call forth, elicit, receive, get, deserve, compel, draw, extract, evoke, induce, prompt, provoke, inspire, motivate, kindle, incite. —*n.* **4.** order, commandment, fiat, direction, directive, ordinance, injunction, demand, charge, ultimatum, summons, behest, bid, call, instruction, edict, decree. **5.** control, domination, rule, grip, grasp, hold, power, authority; direction, charge, conduct, governing, leadership, management, administration, supervision. **6.** mastery, comprehension, understanding, grasp, knowledge, familiarity. **—Syn. Study. 1** See DIRECT. **—Ant. 1** plead, beg, supplicate; obey. **2** follow. **3** repel; deter, discourage.

commandeer *v.* appropriate, expropriate, seize, take, usurp, shanghai.

commander *n.* commanding officer, commander-in-chief; chief, leader, head; ruler, director, conductor, manager, boss. **—Ant.** subordinate, follower; inferior.

commanding *adj.* **1.** authoritative, imposing, forceful, compelling, powerful, strong, dynamic, gripping, arresting; impressive, important, striking; distinguished, stately, grand, lofty. **2.** in command, directing, controlling, leading, governing; chief, head, ruling, ranking, senior. **3.** dominating, towering, imposing, prominent, significant, overshadowing. **—Ant. 1** shrinking, retiring, timid, shy, modest, weak; unimposing, unimpressive. **2** subordinate, subservient, junior.

commemorate *v.* **1.** memorialize, honor, pay homage to, pay tribute to, acclaim, hallow. **2.** celebrate, observe, salute, hail, mark, acknowledge, show respect for, glorify, extol, solemnize, revere, venerate. **—Ant. 1, 2** dishonor, shame, degrade. **2** overlook, ignore, pass over, forget.

commence *v.* begin, start, get started, get going; inaugurate, initiate, originate. **—Syn. Study.** See BEGIN. **—Ant.** end, conclude, finish, stop, halt, terminate.

commencement *n.* **1.** beginning, start, initiation, inauguration, outset, dawn, morning; onset, inception, genesis, birth, origination; first step. **2.** graduation, graduation day, graduation ceremonies, commencement exercises. **—Ant. 1** end, ending, close, conclusion, finish.

commend *v.* **1.** recommend, endorse, put in a good word for, support, back, stand by; speak highly of, laud, praise, extol, approve, acclaim, *Informal* O.K. **2.** entrust, give over, hand over, leave in the hands of, give, commit, consign, confer, convey, pass over, relegate, delegate, transfer. **—Ant. 1** denounce, renounce, condemn, blackball; criticize, censure, deride, attack. **2** withhold, keep; withdraw.

commendable *adj.* to be commended, worthy, praiseworthy, admirable, laudable, meritorious, honorable, creditable, notable, exemplary, deserving, estimable. **—Ant.** unworthy, dishonorable, discreditable, disreputable, undeserving.

commensurate Also **commensurable** *adj.* in accord, consistent, in agreement, suitable, fitting, appropriate, compatible, corresponding, proportionate, comparable, on a proper scale, relative, equal, equivalent, even, balanced, meet, parallel, relative, square. **—Ant.** inconsistent, unsuitable, inappropriate, unfitting, incompatible, disproportionate, dissimilar, incomparable, unequal, discordant.

comment *n.* **1.** commentary, criticism, remark, explanation, observation, reflection, elucidation, clarification, explication, exemplification; note, annotation. **2.** remark, statement, commentary, observation, reflection; word, utterance, expression, assertion. —*v.* **3.** explain, clarify, elucidate, expound, expand on, shed light, touch upon; discuss, talk about, remark, make a statement.

commentary *n.* **1.** series of comments, explanatory essay, critique, explanation, explication, exposition, interpretation, review, criticism; treatise, dissertation, scholium. **2.** See COMMENT (senses **1, 2**).

commentator *n.* newscaster, news analyst, columnist, critic, reviewer; reporter, explainer, interpreter, speaker, writer; panelist.

commerce *n.* business, trade, traffic, trading, buying and selling, exchange, barter, mercantilism, (*on the Internet*) e-tailing, e-business, e-commerce; industry.

commercial *adj.* **1.** business, trade, mercantile, buying-and-selling, sales, profit-making. —*n.* **2.** advertisement, ad, infomercial, *Informal* sales pitch. **—Ant. 1** artistic, professional; nonprofit-making, charitable, philanthropic, eleemosynary.

commiserate *v.* feel for, express sorrow, sympathize with, show pity, have compassion for, express fellow feeling, grieve with, lament with, send one's condolences, share one's sorrow.

commission *n.* **1.** committing, committal, carrying out, act, acting out, performing, performance, doing, perpetration, transacting, exercise, conduct. **2.**

authority, authorization, power, capacity, mandate, charge, duty, task, appointment, mission, assignment, office, function, role, deputation, warrant, license, proxy, commitment, entrusting, trust. **3.** officer's rank, rank, position, appointment, office; appointment papers, document, certificate, written orders. **4.** commissioners, board, agency, council, committee; delegation, representatives, deputation. **5.** percentage, cut, portion, piece, fee; allotment, allowance, dividend, stipend; *Slang* rake-off, piece of the action. **—*v.* 6.** authorize, empower, appoint, assign, name, delegate, charge, bid, order, direct, give the go-ahead, engage, employ, hire, contract, charter. **7.** grant officer's rank, appoint; give a document, certify. **—Ant. 1** noncommission, omission, noncommittal, nonperformance. **5** salary, straight salary. **6** release, fire, let go.

commit *v.* **1.** perform, carry out, do, act, enact, transact, practice, perpetrate, execute, effect, pursue, participate in; *Slang* pull, pull off. **2.** consign, put in the custody of, give over, put in the hands of, deliver, entrust, transfer, place, put, assign, deposit; confine, intern, institutionalize. **3.** obligate, bind, make liable, engage, decide, determine, resolve. **—Ant. 1** omit. **2** withhold, hold back, take from; receive, accept; release, free. **3** disavow, disregard; waver, vacillate, shilly-shally.

commitment *n.* **1.** consignment, assignment, delivery, dispatching, transfer, giving over; confinement, internment, institutionalizing, imprisonment, detention, incarceration, restraint. **2.** obligation, liability, responsibility; bond, guarantee, warranty, pledge, assurance, vow, word, promise; resolution, decision, determination, stand. **—Ant. 1** withholding; release, freeing, liberation. **2** negation, disavowal, reneging; indecisiveness, wavering, vacillation, shilly-shallying.

commodious *adj.* roomy, spacious, capacious, large, ample, unconfining, uncramped. **—Ant.** cramped, confining, small, narrow.

commodity *n.* **1.** article of trade, article of commerce, merchandise, product, ware, goods, stock, staple. **2.** asset, possession, property, chattel, belonging, holding, convenience, advantage. **—Ant. 2** liability, handicap, disadvantage, hindrance, burden.

common *adj.* **1.** public, general, joint, shared, collective, communal; widespread, universal. **2.** commonplace, ordinary, frequent, often met with, routine, regular; customary, conventional, standard, settled, established, familiar, everyday, well-known, widely known, popular, traditional, oft-repeated, pervasive; stock, garden-variety, household, homespun, prosaic, threadbare, moth-eaten, old-hat, worn-out, worn thin; informal, colloquial. **3.** ordinary, plain, simple, average, normal, middling, *Slang* workaday, garden-variety, dime-a-dozen; undistinguished, obscure, unknown, nameless, unnoticed, inglorious, ignoble, unexalted, middle-class, plebeian, bourgeois; without rank, unimportant, insignificant, lowly, low, vulgar, minor, lesser, subordinate, mediocre. **4.** coarse, crude, crass, uncouth, insensitive, callous, brutal, boorish, loutish, brash, brazen, shameless, shameful, unblushing, disagreeable, unrefined, uncultured, unpolished, tasteless, gross, base, mean, cheap, tawdry, bad, deficient; rude, impolite, ill-mannered, ill-bred, low-bred, ignoble; vulgar, despicable, obnoxious, offensive, contemptible, vile, disgraceful, low-minded, lewd, smutty, obscene, ribald. **—Syn. Study. 1, 2** See GENERAL. **3** COMMON, ORDINARY, VULGAR refer, often with derogatory connotations, to what is usual or most often experienced. COMMON applies to what is widespread or unexceptional; it often suggests inferiority or coarseness: *common servants; common cloth.* ORDINARY refers to what is to be expected in the usual order of things; it suggests being average or below average: *a high price for something of such ordinary quality.* VULGAR means belonging to the people or characteristic of common people; it suggests low taste, coarseness, or ill breeding: *vulgar manners; vulgar speech.* **—Ant. 1** private, personal, individual, separate, secret. **2** uncommon, unusual, rare, infrequent, strange, unique, odd, abnormal, exceptional, unfamiliar, extraordinary, unpopular, unorthodox, unconventional, unheard of, scarce, unknown, little-known; formal, sophisticated; literary. **3** superior, outstanding, exceptional, extraordinary, important; distinguished, famous, renowned, noble, ranking, noteworthy, glorious, exalted. **4** polished, refined, cultured, gentle, delicate, sensitive, gentlemanly, ladylike, gallant, noble; polite, well-mannered, well-bred, becoming, pleasing, modest, unassuming.

commonly *adv.* usually, ordinarily, generally, normally, customarily, of course, regularly, routinely, traditionally, conventionally, habitually, frequently, often, most often, repeatedly, in most instances, by and large, in general, as a rule, for the most part, generally speaking, as a matter of course, by force of habit, popularly, widely; familiarly, informally. —**Ant.** rarely, seldom, infrequently, scarcely; privately, secretly; formally, politely.

commonplace *adj.* **1.** common, ordinary, usual, routine, everyday, familiar, regular, standard, traditional, customary, general, widespread. **2.** common, dull, banal, run-of-the-mill, pedestrian, humdrum, uninteresting, unimaginative, unoriginal, trite, hackneyed, stereotyped, stale, old, old-hat, oft-repeated, worn-out, worn thin, threadbare, moth-eaten. —*n.* **3.** hackneyed expression, banality, platitude, cliché, adage, bromide, received idea, truism. —**Syn. Study. 2** COMMONPLACE, BANAL, TRITE, HACKNEYED describe words, remarks, and styles of expression that are lifeless and uninteresting. COMMONPLACE characterizes expression that is so ordinary, self-evident, or generally accepted as to be boring or pointless: *a commonplace affirmation of the obvious.* BANAL often suggests an inane or insipid quality: *banal conversation.* TRITE suggests that an expression has lost its force because of excessive repetition: *trite poetic imagery.* HACKNEYED is a stronger word implying that the expression has become meaningless from overuse: *hackneyed metaphors.* —**Ant. 1, 2** uncommon, unusual, unfamiliar, rare, strange, unique, odd, extraordinary, exceptional, infrequent. **2** exciting, interesting, imaginative; original, new, distinguished.

common sense *n.* native reason, good sense, good judgment, natural sagacity, basic intelligence, mother wit; *Slang* horse sense.

commotion *n.* hullabaloo, fuss, bustle, stir, ado, to-do; excitement, tumult, furor, uproar, turmoil, disturbance, agitation, perturbation, fussing and fuming, racket, clatter, *Informal* ruckus. —**Ant.** peace, tranquillity, calm, calmness, serenity; quiet, quietness.

communal *adj.* community, common, collective, mutual, joint, shared, public. —**Ant.** private, personal, individual.

commune *v.* communicate, talk, converse, confer, discourse, parley, chat, visit, chatter, palaver, confabulate, prattle, babble; *Slang* rap, chin, yak, gossip, gab, schmooze, chew the fat, chew the rag, shoot the breeze, powwow.

communicable *adj.* contagious, catching, infectious, transmittable, transmissible, transferable. —**Ant.** uncommunicable, uncontagious.

communicate *v.* **1.** make known, inform of, announce, apprise of, tell, notify, advise, pass on, convey, disclose, divulge, reveal, relate, bring word, proclaim, broadcast, publish, publicize; state, declare, say, mention; show, exhibit, signify. **2.** give, transmit, impart, pass on; convey. **3.** exchange information, express feelings; converse, speak together, talk, correspond, write. —**Ant. 1** keep secret, hush up, suppress, repress, withhold, hold back, cover up.

communication *n.* **1.** exchanging information, expressing feelings; rapport, liaison; conversation, speaking, correspondence, writing. **2.** notices, report, message, news, information; intelligence, communiqué, liaison; (*variously*) bulletin, directive, statement, declaration, proclamation; correspondence, letter, missive, missal, dispatch, document, note; telephone call, telegram, wire, cablegram, cable, radio message, broadcast, e-mail, fax.

communicative *adj.* talkative, free-spoken, unreserved, loquacious, voluble, chatty, outgoing, sociable, friendly, open, candid, frank, forthright; informative, expressive, revelatory, revealing. —**Ant.** uncommunicative, untalkative, quiet, reserved, introverted, unsociable, secretive, guarded; uninformative.

communion *n.* **1.** often **Communion.** Holy Communion, the Eucharist. **2.** sharing, harmony, concord, accord, agreement, affinity, sympathy. **3.** spiritual concentration, contemplation, rapport, communication. —**Ant. 2** alienation, disunion, division, separation; disharmony, discord, disagreement.

communiqué *n.* bulletin, dispatch, message, communication, announcement, missive, notice, statement, notification, letter, epistle, memorandum, note, report, aviso, flash; cable, telegram, wire.

community *n.* **1.** neighborhood, district, locale, area, vicinity, quarter, residential suburb, environs; environment, surroundings. **2.** group, social group, interest group; populace, population, citizenry, public, people, folk, society. **3.** area, sphere, field, range, realm, scope, province, arena, commonwealth; sameness, similarity, likeness, affinity, agreement. —**Ant. 3** difference, dissimilarity, disparity, disagreement, conflict.

commute *v.* change, reverse, exchange, substitute, adjust, alter, replace, switch, supersede; alleviate, soften, mitigate, diminish; transmute, transform, transpose, redeem, convert, metamorphose, transfigure, transmogrify.

compact[1] *adj.* **1.** compressed, pressed, tightly packed, dense, concentrated, clustered, crammed, stuffed. **2.** small, little, snug, close, tidy. —*v.* **3.** pack closely, compress, press, pack, stuff, cram, squeeze. —**Ant. 1** loosely packed, loose, spread-out, dispersed, scattered, sprawling. **2** spacious, rambling, roomy, large, big, huge. **3** disperse, loosen; separate.

compact[2] *n.* agreement, pact, treaty, covenant, contract, concordat, bond; understanding, arrangement, alliance, bargain, deal. **—Syn. Study.** See AGREEMENT.

companion *n.* **1.** associate, friend, comrade, crony, chum, pal, buddy, mate. **2.** attendant, helper, assistant, escort. **—Syn. Study. 1** See FRIEND. **—Ant. 1** stranger; enemy, foe.

companionate *adj.* harmonious, suitable, providing companionship, compatible, consonant, concordant, accordant; nonsexual, platonic, passionless, nonphysical, unfleshly, spiritual; companionable, friendly, easygoing, amicable, cordial, agreeable, warm, affectionate, genial, warm-hearted. **—Ant.** antagonistic, discordant, inharmonious, clashing, conflicting, incompatible.

companionship *n.* friendship, friendly relations, close acquaintance, fellowship, comradeship, camaraderie, sociability, familiarity; friends, companions, company, associates, comrades, chums, pals, buddies. **—Ant.** isolation, solitude, loneliness, aloneness.

company *n.* **1.** guest, guests, visitor, visitors, callers. **2.** presence, companionship, friendship, fellowship, comradeship, camaraderie, society, sociability; people, friends, comrades, companions. **3.** business concern, concern, firm, business corporation, syndicate, conglomerate, establishment; *Slang* outfit, *Internet Slang* dot-com. **4.** assembly, assemblage, congregation, gathering, group, band, mob, multitude, throng, bunch, party, gang. **—Ant. 1** host, hostess. **2** isolation, solitude, loneliness, aloneness.

comparable *adj.* similar, like, equal, equivalent, as good as, on a par with, akin to, roughly the same as, analogous, tantamount, commensurable, commensurate; parallel, approximate, approaching, close, a match for, in a class with, up to. **—Ant.** incomparable, different, unlike, dissimilar, incommensurable, incommensurate, unequal.

comparative *adj.* relative, by comparison; near, approximate.

compare *v.* **1.** note the similarities of, note the differences of, contrast, balance against. **2.** liken, equate, describe as similar, draw a parallel between, correlate, relate, identify with. **3.** be comparable, match, equal, compete with, approach, be as good as, bear comparison, hold a candle to, vie with, come near to, be in a class with, be on a par with, be up to. **—Ant. 3** bear no comparison, be unlike, be dissimilar, be incomparable, be unequal.

comparison *n.* **1.** comparative estimate, selective judgment, notation of similarities and differences, contrast. **2.** similarity, comparability, likeness, resemblance, equality, analogy, relation, correlation, parallel, kinship, connection. **—Ant. 2** difference, dissimilarity, inequality, discrepancy.

compartment *n.* cubicle, niche, alcove, hole, nook, pigeonhole, cubbyhole, cell, pew, section, booth, box, crib, crypt, stall, vault; berth, room, cabin, closet, anteroom, chamber, antechamber, roomette, bunker, hold, brig.

compass *n.* **—Syn. Study.** See RANGE.

compassion *n.* sympathy, empathy, commiseration, feeling, fellow feeling, pity, tenderness, tender-heartedness, heart, humanity. **—Syn. Study.** See SYMPATHY. **—Ant.** apathy, unconcern, indifference, detachment, disdain; coldheartedness, hard-heartedness.

compassionate *adj.* sympathetic, pitying, humane, merciful, kindhearted, kind, benevolent, tender-hearted, charitable. **—Ant.** uncompassionate, inhumane, unfeeling, unsympathetic, unpitying, pitiless.

compatibility *n.* affinity, harmony, rapport, agreement, accord, unanimity, like-mindedness, congeniality, concord. **—Ant.** incompatibility, disharmony, disagreement, disaccord, discord.

compatible *adj.* in harmony, like-minded, congenial, mutually sympathetic; fitting, fit, suitable, in accord, in keeping, seemly, apt, appropriate. **—Ant.** incompatible, unharmonious, uncongenial; contradictory, unfitting, unsuitable, out of keeping, unseemly, inapt, inappropriate, inconsistent, counter.

compel *v.* force, drive, impel, require, necessitate, oblige, make, give no choice but. **—Syn. Study.** COMPEL, IMPEL agree in the idea of forcing someone to be or do something. COMPEL implies an external force; it may be a persuasive urging from another person or a constraining reason or circumstance: *Bad health compelled him to resign.* IMPEL suggests an internal motivation deriving either from a moral constraint or personal feeling: *Guilt impelled him to offer money.* **—Ant.** stop, deter, thwart, hinder, prevent.

compensate *v.* **1.** recompense, reimburse, make restitution, pay back, repay, make up, cover, redress, redeem, make compensation, indemnify; pay, remunerate. **2.** make up, offset, balance, counterbalance, make amends, square.

—**Ant.** 2 emphasize, exaggerate, worsen, add insult to injury.

compensation *n.* **1.** recompense, reimbursement, restitution, repayment, redress, indemnity; benefits, settlement, satisfaction, consideration. **2.** pay, payment, salary, wages, fee, remuneration, income, earnings; reward, profit, gratuity, return, gain. —**Ant. 1, 2** loss, expenditure, time and trouble.

compete *v.* **1.** be rivals, contend, contest, vie, match strength, match wits, oppose. **2.** fight, combat, battle, lock horns, strive against. —**Syn. Study. 1** COMPETE, CONTEND, CONTEST mean to strive or struggle. COMPETE emphasizes a sense of rivalry and of striving to do one's best: *to compete for a prize.* CONTEND suggests striving in opposition or debate as well as competition: *to contend against obstacles; to contend about minor details.* CONTEST implies struggling to gain or hold something in a formal competition or battle: *to contest with the incumbent for the nomination.* —**Ant.** surrender, give up, yield.

competence *n.* ability, ableness, capability, competency, proficiency, skill, expertness, mastery, expertise, know-how; *Slang* the goods, what it takes. —**Ant.** incompetence, inability, incapacity, inadequacy.

competent *adj.* skilled, skillful, expert, proficient, efficient; qualified, fit, trained, practiced, experienced, versed, dependable, responsible, trustworthy. —**Ant.** incompetent, incapable, unskilled, unskillful, inexpert; unqualified, unfit, inexperienced, inadequate, undependable, irresponsible, untrustworthy.

competition *n.* **1.** competing, rivalry, contention, opposition, struggle, conflict. **2.** opposition, rival, opponent, contender. **3.** contest, event, match, tournament, tourney. —**Ant. 1** cooperation, collaboration, concert, joint effort, teamwork. **2** partner, helper, aider, abettor.

competitive *adj.* competing, opposing, contending; fighting, combative, striving, aggressive. —**Ant.** cooperative, mutual, joint; noncombative, unaggressive.

competitor *n.* rival, opposition, opponent, adversary, contestant, contender, fighter. —**Ant.** ally, partner, collaborator.

compilation *n.* **1.** compiling, collecting, gathering, accumulating, collating, mustering, marshaling, garnering, assembling, aggregating, drawing together. **2.** assemblage, group, collection, aggregation, body; assortment, compendium, accumulation. —**Ant. 1** distribution, dispersal, scattering, disbanding, dispelling, dissipation.

compile *v.* collect, accumulate, assemble, amass, collate, heap up, gather, muster, marshal, bring together, draw together, garner. —**Ant.** distribute, disperse, scatter.

complacent *adj.* self-secure, content, contented, self-satisfied, smug; untroubled, unbothered, at ease. —**Ant.** unsatisfied, insecure, discontent, discontented, troubled, uneasy, soul-searching, self-questioning.

complain *v.* criticize, carp, cavil, nag, whine, pick, gripe, kick, grouse, grouch, grumble, state a grievance, express dissatisfaction, find fault, *Slang* beef, bellyache, squawk. —**Syn. Study.** COMPLAIN, GRUMBLE, WHINE are terms for expressing dissatisfaction or discomfort. To COMPLAIN is to protest against or lament a condition or wrong: *to complain about high prices.* To GRUMBLE is to utter surly, ill-natured complaints half to oneself: *to grumble about the service.* To WHINE is to complain in a meanspirited, objectionable way, using a nasal tone; it often suggests persistence: *to whine like a spoiled child.* —**Ant.** compliment, praise, laud, commend; approve, appreciate.

complaint *n.* **1.** grievance, dissatisfaction, criticism, faultfinding, protest, objection, tirade; *Informal* beef, gripe, kick, squawk. **2.** disorder, malady, infirmity, debility, ailment, impairment, sickness, illness. —**Ant. 1** compliment, praise, commendation; approval, appreciation. **2** remedy, salve, balm, ointment.

complaisant *adj.* obliging, solicitous, pleasing, agreeable, compliant, cordial, congenial, affable, warm, gracious, friendly, pleasant, pleasing, amiable, good-natured, good-humored, easygoing. —**Ant.** unobliging, contrary, unsolicitous, uncooperative, indifferent; disagreeable, unpleasant, cold, unfriendly, ungracious.

complement *n.* **1.** completion, consummation, rounding-out; supplement, companion, counterpart, balance, parallel. **2.** full amount, full number, total, ensemble, aggregate; completion, whole, entirety; required number, necessary amount. —*v.* **3.** make complete, round out, perfect, crown, cap, consummate, *Informal* finish off; match, serve as a companion, supplement. —**Syn. Study. 3** COMPLEMENT, SUPPLEMENT both mean to make additions to something; a lack or deficiency is implied. To COMPLEMENT means to complete or perfect a whole; it often refers to putting together two things, each of which supplies what is lacking in the other: *Statements from different points of view may complement each other.* To SUPPLEMENT is to add something in order to enhance, extend, or improve a whole: *Some additional remarks supplemented the sales presentation.*

complementary *adj.* integral, corresponding, correspondent, interrelated, compatible, companion, matched, correlative. **—Ant.** uncomplementary, incompatible, incongruous, inconsistent; different, diverse; contradictory.

complete *adj.* **1.** entire, whole, full, plenary, unabridged, unbroken, intact, undivided. **2.** thorough, absolute, total, utter, conclusive, perfect, consummated, fully realized, accomplished, achieved, performed, executed, carried out, settled. **—***v.* **3.** make complete, make whole; finish, end, conclude, terminate, make an end of, accomplish, achieve, perform, execute, carry out, fulfill, discharge, settle, consummate; *Informal* polish off, wrap up. **4.** complement, round out, perfect, crown, cap. **—Syn. Study. 1** COMPLETE, ENTIRE, INTACT suggest that there is no lack or defect, nor has any part been removed. COMPLETE implies that a unit has all its parts, fully developed or perfected; it may also mean that a process or purpose has been carried to fulfillment: *a complete explanation; a complete assignment.* ENTIRE describes something having all its elements in an unbroken unity: *an entire book.* INTACT implies that something has remained in its original condition, complete and unimpaired: *a package delivered intact.* **—Ant. 1, 2** incomplete, partial. **2** inconclusive, imperfect, deficient, spoiled, marred, blemished, tainted, unfinished, unsettled, unachieved, unaccomplished, undone. **3** start, begin, commence, initiate; undo. **4** spoil, ruin, mar, taint.

completion *n.* **1.** completing, finishing; concluding, ending, closing, terminating, windup. **2.** conclusion, end, close, termination, finish, expiration, windup; fulfillment, consummation. **—Ant. 1** beginning, starting, initiating, commencing. **2** start, beginning, commencement, initiation.

complex *adj.* **1.** complicated, intricate, involved, difficult, perplexing, bewildering, puzzling, enigmatic; composite, compound, manifold, multiple, multifarious, variegated, mixed, tangled, knotty, labyrinthian, labyrinthine. **—***n.* **2.** system, network, aggregate, conglomerate, maze. **3.** subconscious idea, fixed idea, psychological feeling; obsession, preoccupation. **—Ant. 1** simple, uncomplicated, easy, uninvolved, clear, obvious, unconfused.

complexion *n.* **1.** skin coloring, coloring, pigmentation, coloration, color, hue, tone; skin texture. **2.** appearance, impression, aspect, look, outlook, guise, slant, image, countenance, character.

complexity *n.* complication, intricacy, elaboration, involution, crabbedness, involvement; perplexity, bafflement, entanglement, inextricability, puzzle; obscurity, incomprehensibility, unintelligibility. **—Ant.** simplicity, clearness, clarity, obviousness, unmistakability.

compliance *n.* conformity, conforming, obedience, yielding, giving in, submission, deference; assent, acquiescence, complaisance, pliancy, nonresistance, passivity, docility, meekness. **—Ant.** noncompliance, nonconformity, disobedience, resistance, rebelliousness, assertiveness, individuality, stubbornness; obstinacy.

complicate *v.* make complex, make intricate, make difficult, involve, confound, confuse, muddle, entangle, knot, snarl, ravel, tangle. **—Ant.** uncomplicate, simplify, clarify, unsnarl, untangle, disentangle, unknot, clear up.

complication *n.* problem, difficulty, aggravation, disadvantage, handicap, drawback, hitch, snag, obstacle, obstruction, stumbling block, hindrance, impediment, quandary, dilemma, predicament, perplexity. **—Ant.** answer, solution; boon, bonus, help, aid, asset, advantage, benefit, boost.

complicity *n.* connivance, conspiracy, collusion, intrigue, confederacy, scheming, finagling, contrivance, plotting, schemery, abetment; entanglement, involvement, implication.

compliment *n.* **1.** expression of praise, approving remark, commendation, praise, kudos, laudation, adulation, flattery, acclamation, tribute, honor, homage, congratulation. **2. compliments.** regards, respects, good wishes, best wishes, best, greetings, felicitations, salutations; congratulations, praise, homage; salute, toast. **—***v.* **3.** pay a compliment to, praise, pay tribute to, laud, applaud, salute, toast, commend; speak highly of, sing the praises of, extol, exalt. **—Ant. 1** insult, denunciation, condemnation, criticism, deprecation, disparagement, reproach, complaint; *Informal* beef, gripe, kick, squawk. **3** insult, criticize, denounce, decry, disparage, condemn, censure, reprehend, reproach.

complimentary *adj.* **1.** commendatory, praising, praiseful, admiring, laudatory, plauditory, extolling, panegyric; appreciative, congratulatory, flattering, adulatory. **2.** free, gratis, gratuitous, without charge. **—Ant. 1** uncomplimentary, disparaging, abusive, insulting, critical, disapproving, unflattering.

comply *v.* conform, accede, adhere, abide by, follow, obey, mind, observe, fulfill, meet, satisfy, be faithful to; surrender, submit, yield, give in, defer, consent, acquiesce, bow, bend. **—Ant.** disobey, break, reject, repudiate, spurn, disregard, ignore; resist, fight, oppose.

component *adj.* **1.** constituent, ingredient, modular, member, composing, material, fundamental, elementary, intrinsic, essential, elemental. *—n.* **2.** part, component part, constituent, module, member, element, ingredient, segment, piece, item; detail, particular. **—Ant. 1, 2** whole, complex, compound.

comport *v.* conduct, carry, deport, bear; behave, acquit.

compose *v.* **1.** create, make, conceive, form, formulate, frame, shape, fashion, devise, write. **2.** be part of, be a portion of, make up, form, comprise, constitute, belong to. **3.** calm, settle, collect, pull oneself together, get hold of oneself, quiet, relax, lull, soothe, pacify, placate, quell, modulate, smooth down one's feathers. **—Ant. 1** destroy, demolish, obliterate, tear up. **2** contain, include, embrace, enfold, encompass, comprise, embody. **3** excite, upset, agitate, rouse, stir up, antagonize, inflame, become nervous, fly off the handle, lose one's cool.

composed *adj.* calm, serene, at ease, placid, peaceful, tranquil, sedate, quiet, quiescent, cool, cool-headed, collected, poised, controlled, steady, level-headed, even-tempered, unflappable, imperturbable, unperturbed, unagitated, undisturbed, unexcited, unruffled, untroubled, unemotional, restrained, dispassionate, undemonstrative. **—Syn. Study.** See CALM. **—Ant.** hotheaded, unpoised, uncontrolled, perturbed, agitated, disturbed, anxious, upset, *Slang* uptight; distraught, nervous, uneasy, ruffled, excited, stirred up, steamed up, inflamed.

composite *adj.* combined, compound, compounded, blended, mosaic. **—Ant.** uncombined, single, uncompounded, unmixed, unblended.

composition *n.* **1.** work, opus, piece, creation; concoction, production, product, exercise, essay, etude. **2.** composing, forming, formulation, creating, creation, making, framing, shaping, fashioning, preparation, devising, compilation, organizing, organization. **3.** structure, design, configuration, arrangement, form, organization, framework, layout; make-up, constitution, combination.

composure *n.* poise, aplomb, calm, calmness, serenity, ease, cool, coolness, cool-headedness, sang-froid, control, self-control, self-possession, self-restraint, even-temperedness, self-assurance, equanimity, levelheadedness, patience, dignity, unexcitability, imperturbability, unflappability. **—Ant.** discomposure, nervousness, uneasiness, disquiet, impatience, excitability, agitation, hotheadedness, perturbation, unrestraint, instability.

compound *adj.* **1.** combined, complex, complicated, composite, conglomerate, mixed, blended. *—n.* **2.** combination, composition, composite, blend, mixture, union, fusion, amalgam, alloy, conglomeration. *—v.* **3.** put together; combine, blend, mix, mingle, unite, fuse, alloy, incorporate, formulate, prepare, devise, make, concoct, fabricate, synthesize. **4.** add to, augment, increase, heighten, enlarge, magnify, amplify, reinforce, boost. **—Ant. 1** single, simple, pure, unmixed, unblended, uncompounded. **2** element. **3** separate, part, divide, disunite, divorce, split; isolate, segregate, sift. **4** lessen, decrease, ameliorate, palliate, mitigate, modify, minimize, moderate.

comprehend *v.* **1.** understand, grasp, fathom, make out, perceive, conceive, penetrate, absorb, assimilate, digest, appreciate, know, savvy, get, catch, *Slang* dig. **2.** include, embrace, encompass, comprise, subsume. **—Syn. Study. 2** See INCLUDE. **—Ant.** misunderstand, mistake, misapprehend, misinterpret, misconceive, miss the point of.

comprehension *n.* understanding, conception, grasp, perception, insight, apprehension, realization, awareness, consciousness, appreciation, acquaintance. **—Ant.** misunderstanding, misconception, incomprehension, misapprehension, unawareness.

comprehensive *adj.* all-inclusive, all-embracing, overall, extensive, expansive, broad, sweeping, widespread, universal, general; exhaustive, complete, thorough, full, copious, compendious. **—Ant.** limited, restricted, narrow, specialized, specific; exclusive, incomplete.

compress *v.* press, squeeze, compact, cram, pack; condense, reduce, shrink, shorten, curtail, abbreviate, abridge. **—Ant.** stretch, spread, expand, enlarge, increase, lengthen.

comprise *v.* **1.** include, contain, be composed of, consist of, be made of; embrace, comprehend. **2.** constitute, make up, form, compose. **—Syn. Study. 1** See INCLUDE.

compromise *n.* **1.** mutual concession, accommodation, agreement, settlement, conciliation, adjustment, arrangement, rapprochement; balance, happy medium; truce, compact. *—v.* **2.** make mutual concessions, adjust differences, come to an understanding, strike a bargain, come to terms, make a deal, settle, agree, meet halfway; *Slang* split the difference. **3.** endanger, jeopardize, imperil, risk;

discredit, prejudice, undercut, make suspect, make vulnerable, implicate, embarrass. **—Ant. 1** difference, dispute, disagreement, contention, controversy, quarrel, strife. **2** differ, disagree, dispute, contest, argue, quarrel. **3** enhance, support, boost; establish, assure, save.

compulsion *n.* coercion, duress, force, pressure, domineering; obligation, necessity, requirement, demand; strong inducement, urging. **—Ant.** choice, free will, option.

compulsive *adj.* **1.** unable to resist, uncontrollable, obsessive, fanatic, compelled, compelling, driving, driven, addicted, habitual; *Slang* hooked. **2.** See COMPULSORY. **—Ant. 1** noncompulsive, resistible, controllable, uncompelling; weak, wishy-washy.

compulsory *adj.* mandatory, obligatory, required, imperative, requisite, demanded, prescriptive, binding, unavoidable; enforced, compulsive, coercive, forcible. **—Ant.** voluntary, optional, discretionary, nonobligatory, nonrequired, nonrequisite, unimperative, unnecessary, nonbinding.

compunction *n.* pang of conscience, qualm, demur, misgiving, regret, anxiety, shame, concern, contrition, unease, remorse, distress of mind, scruple. **—Ant.** pride, self-respect, righteousness; shamelessness.

compute *v.* add, add up, total, sum up, count up, tally; calculate, determine mathematically, reckon, ascertain, figure out, work out. **—Ant.** guess, suppose, conjecture, surmise, estimate, approximate, make a stab at.

comrade *n.* companion, boon companion, friend, crony, confrere, intimate, pal, chum, buddy, bosom buddy, confidant; colleague, fellow member, associate, helpmate, coworker, ally, partner, confederate, collaborator. **—Ant.** stranger; enemy, foe, antagonist.

concatenation *n.* joining, connection, union, junction, conjunction, link, hookup, coupling, linking, bracketing, confluence, reunion, intercommunication, interconnection, interlinking, interassociation.

concave *adj.* curving inward, sunken, hollow, depressed, indented. **—Ant.** convex, protuberant, rounded.

conceal *v.* hide, cover, cover up, keep out of sight, secrete, keep secret, disguise, mask, shield, screen, cloak, camouflage, obscure. **—Syn. Study.** See HIDE. **—Ant.** reveal, disclose, divulge, expose, exhibit, display, show, lay bare, uncover, unmask, uncloak, unveil, flash.

concealment *n.* **1.** concealing, hiding, covering, covering up, secreting, secretion, masking, screening. **2.** hiding, hiding place, hideaway, hideout, under cover, cover, secret place. **—Ant. 1** disclosure, developing, revealing, revelation, exposure, exhibition, displaying, display, showing, show, uncovering.

concede *v.* **1.** grant, agree, acknowledge, be persuaded, vouchsafe, acquiesce, accept, recognize, own, allow, confess, admit. **2.** surrender, give up, yield, abandon, relinquish, resign, cede, hand over, deliver, tender. **—Ant. 1** deny, refute, reject, repudiate, disclaim, disavow, dissent, contest, protest, contradict, controvert, debate, dispute, argue. **2** make a stand, fight to the last man; win, defeat, beat.

conceit *n.* vanity, pride, vainglory, egotism, self-love, self-esteem, self-importance, *Slang* ego trip; bragging, boastfulness. **—Syn. Study.** See PRIDE. **—Ant.** humility, modesty; self-deprecation.

conceited *adj.* vain, overproud, arrogant, egotistical, self-important, swellheaded, vainglorious, puffed up, *Informal* stuck-up; boasting, bragging, bombastic, strutting, smug. **—Ant.** humble, modest, unassuming, unaffected; self-effacing.

conceivable *adj.* imaginable, thinkable, possible, perceivable, knowable, believable, credible, supposable. **—Ant.** inconceivable, unthinkable, unimaginable, unbelievable, incredible.

conceive *v.* **1.** think up, produce, form, create, hatch, contrive, frame, concoct, invent, dream up; initiate, originate, start. **2.** imagine, envision, envisage, understand, comprehend; think of, consider.

concentrate *v.* **1.** focus, center, converge, bring to bear, direct toward, close in, hem in; give full attention to, pay attention to, fasten on, pay heed, consider closely, attend to, be engrossed in, put one's mind to. **2.** mass, amass, congregate, converge, accumulate, assemble, gather, cluster, bunch, heap up. **3.** reduce, condense, thicken. **—Ant. 1** spread out, deploy, dissipate; let one's mind wander, pay no attention. **2** scatter, spread, spread out, disperse, diffuse. **3** dilute, water down, thin.

concentration *n.* **1.** concentrating, close attention, fixed regard, mental application, deep thought, intentness, absorption, engrossment, diligence. **2.** mass, cluster, assemblage, collection, accumulation, aggregation, gathering; centralization, convergence, consolidation, focus; boiling down, reduction, thickening. **—Ant. 1** inattention, inattentiveness, disregard, distraction, absentmindedness. **2** scattering, spreading out, dispersion, diffusion, divergence; dilution, thinning.

concept *n.* idea, thought, conception, theory, hypothesis, postulate, notion, surmise, supposition, impression, image, view; opinion, belief, conviction.

conception *n.* **1.** conceiving, envisioning, imagining, forming, formation, formulation, concocting, devising, creating, originating; inception, genesis, birth, invention, initiation, start, beginning, hatching, launching. **2.** idea, image, picture, concept, thought, notion; perception, understanding, apprehension, notion, inkling. **3.** becoming pregnant, getting with child, fertilization, inception of pregnancy. **—Syn. Study. 2** See IDEA. **—Ant. 1** completion, finish, ending, termination; outcome, result, issue.

concern *v.* **1.** affect, touch, bear upon, involve, be relevant to, relate to, pertain to, appertain to, apply to, interest, occupy, be one's business. **2.** worry, trouble, disturb, make anxious, distress, disconcert. —*n.* **3.** consideration, business, interest, matter, affair, involvement, thing of moment; job, duty, chore, charge, mission. **4.** worry, anxiety, apprehension, trouble, care, distress, disturbance; thoughtfulness, regard, solicitude, consideration, heed, attention. **5.** firm, establishment, company, corporation, business, enterprise, undertaking; store, house. **—Syn. Study. 4** CONCERN, CARE, WORRY connote an uneasy and burdened state of mind. CONCERN implies an anxious sense of interest in or responsibility for something: *concern over a friend's misfortune.* CARE suggests a heaviness of spirit caused by dread, or by the constant pressure of burdensome demands: *Poverty weighed them down with care.* WORRY is a state of agitated uneasiness and restless apprehension: *distracted by worry over investments.* **—Ant. 1** be irrelevant to, be unrelated to, disinterest. **4** unconcern, indifference, disregard, inattention, heedlessness, carelessness.

concerned *adj.* **1.** involved, committed, engaged, participating, active; caring, interested, solicitous, attentive. **2.** worried, anxious, uneasy, disturbed, troubled, distressed, upset. **—Ant. 1** unconcerned, indifferent, aloof, detached, uninterested; neglectful, remiss. **2** undisturbed, untroubled, carefree, without a care.

concert *n.* unity, harmony, collaboration, accord, union, concord, agreement, teamwork, cooperation, association, complicity, unanimity, accordance, congruity, correspondence. **—Ant.** opposition, discord, disruption, disunity.

concerted *adj.* united, joint, cooperative, by assent; planned, predetermined, prearranged, premeditated, agreed upon. **—Ant.** disunited, separate, individual, uncooperative; unplanned, unpremeditated, uncontrived.

concession *n.* **1.** admission, acknowledgment, assent, acquiescence. **2.** compromise, adjustment, modification; yielding, giving in, indulgence. **3.** franchise, lease, privilege. **—Ant. 1** denial, disavowal, dissent.

conciliate *v.* appease, propitiate, accommodate; placate, soothe, pacify. **—Syn. Study.** See APPEASE.

conciliatory *adj.* peacemaking, reconciling, friendly, reassuring, placatory, pacifying, mollifying, accommodative, appeasing. **—Ant.** antagonistic, hostile, unfriendly, unforgiving.

concise *adj.* terse, to the point, succinct, pithy, condensed, compact, brief, short, abbreviated. **—Syn. Study.** CONCISE, SUCCINCT, TERSE refer to speech or writing that uses few words to say much. CONCISE implies that unnecessary details or verbiage have been eliminated: *a concise summary of a speech.* SUCCINCT suggests clarity of expression as well as brevity: *praised for her succinct statement of the problem.* TERSE suggests brevity combined with wit or polish to produce particularly effective expression; however, it may also suggest brusqueness: *a terse prose style; offended by a terse reply.* **—Ant.** rambling, discursive, wordy, verbose.

conciseness *n.* concision, succinctnesss, terseness, brevity, briefness. **—Syn. Study.** See BREVITY.

conclave *n.* private meeting, secret council, private gathering; meeting, convocation, assembly, council, conference, session, convention, parley, *Informal* powwow.

conclude *v.* **1.** close, draw to a close, finish, end, complete; discontinue, stop, terminate, halt, break off, ring down the curtain on. **2.** settle, decide, resolve, arrange; effect, accomplish, bring to pass, carry out. **3.** decide, determine, judge; deduce, reason, surmise, infer, gather. **—Ant. 1** begin, commence, start, initiate, inaugurate, open; prolong, protract, extend.

conclusion *n.* **1.** end, finish, close, completion, windup, termination, finale, final part, denouement, resolution. **2.** arrangement, settlement, resolution, agreement, working out, completion. **3.** finding, determination, decision, judgment, summation, deduction, inference, presumption; result, outcome, resolution, upshot. **—Ant. 1** beginning, commencement, start, initiation, inauguration, opening.

conclusive *adj.* decisive, determining,

compelling, convincing, definite, absolute, clinching, certain, categorical; undeniable, irrefutable, incontrovertible, unquestionable, incontestable, inescapable, unanswerable, unimpeachable; clear, demonstrable, manifest, obvious, patent, palpable. —**Ant.** inconclusive, indecisive, unconvincing, indefinite, uncertain; deniable, refutable, doubtful, dubious, questionable, disputable, contestable, impeachable; vague, obscured, confused.

concoct *v.* cook up, mix, brew, compound, formulate; make up, think up, create, invent, fabricate, frame, devise, contrive, hatch.

concoction *n.* mixture, brew, conglomeration, potpourri, blend, medley, compound, jumble, creation, invention, fabrication, contrivance.

concomitant *adj.* attendant, accompanying, contributing, additional, related, connected, corollary, secondary, accessory, complementary, supplemental. —**Ant.** unattendant, noncontributory, unconnected.

concord *n.* peace, harmony, agreement, cooperation, mutual understanding, goodwill, cordial relations, accord; amity, friendship, amicability. —**Ant.** discord, conflict, strife, disagreement, dissension, contention; animosity, ill will.

concourse *n.* flocking together, confluence, meeting, association, junction, conglomeration, flowing together, concursion, linkage, joining, assembling, congregation, convergence, focalization, conflux, aggregation, concentration, amassment. —**Ant.** separation, dispersal, spreading, division, disjunction, fragmentation.

concrete *n.* **1.** fused stones, alloyed rocks, (*loosely*) cement; (*technical use*) mixture of cement, sand, and water. —*adj.* **2.** real, material, tangible, solid, factual, substantial; definite, specific, precise, explicit, distinct, express, particular. —**Ant. 2** theoretical, abstract, immaterial, intangible, insubstantial; vague, indefinite, inexplicit, nonspecified.

concupiscence *n.* sexual desire, lechery, lustfulness, lust, randiness, lasciviousness, lewdness, libertinism, lecherousness, libidinousness, wantonness, prurience, lubricity, satyrism; *Slang* horniness, goatishness, hot pants, itch; passion, desire, craving, longing, appetite.

concur *v.* agree, be in accord, correspond, coincide, conform, be uniform, tally, square, match, go hand in hand, go along with, hold with. —**Ant.** disagree, differ, diverge, be at odds.

concurrence, concurrency *n.* **1.** agreement, accord, concord, harmony, unanimity, mutual consent, consensus, meeting of the minds; cooperation, collaboration, working together. **2.** simultaneous occurrence, happening at the same time, coincidence, correspondence, conformity, conjuncture, coexistence, synchronism. —**Ant. 1** disagreement, discord, difference, divergence, disharmony.

concurrent *adj.* **1.** agreeing, in agreement, in accordance, of the same mind, at one, harmonious; commensurate, consonant, correspondent, aligned; allied, congenial, sympathetic, compatible; matching, congruous, coincident. **2.** occurring at the same time, coinciding, simultaneous, synchronous, coexisting; contemporary, contemporaneous. —**Ant. 1** in disagreement, different, unsympathetic, incompatible.

condemn *v.* **1.** censure, disapprove, criticize, decry, denounce, reprehend, rebuke. **2.** sentence, doom, damn, proscribe. —**Ant. 1** praise, compliment, commend, applaud, acclaim, laud, extol, condone, approve. **2** free, liberate.

condemnation *n.* **1.** censure, disapproval, criticism, reprehension, reproach, reproof, rebuke, denunciation, disapprobation. **2.** pronouncement of guilt, conviction, judgment; punishment, sentence. —**Ant. 1** praise, compliment, commendation, approval, acclaim, lauding, extolling. **2** acquittal, exoneration, exculpation, vindication.

condensation *n.* abridgment, condensed version, digest, shortened form, reduction.

condense *v.* **1.** liquefy, precipitate. **2.** abridge, digest, shorten, abbreviate, reduce, cut, trim, pare down, boil down, blue-pencil. **3.** thicken, concentrate, reduce, boil down; compress, compact, consolidate, contract. —**Ant. 1** evaporate, vaporize. **2** expand, lengthen, enlarge, increase, round out, piece out, beef up. **3** dilute, water down; amplify.

condescend *v.* **1.** humble oneself, lower oneself, deign, stoop, submit, descend, *Informal* unbend, come down a peg, come down off one's high horse. **2.** patronize, talk down to, look down on, disdain, *Informal* get on one's high horse with. —**Ant. 1** scorn, spurn, disdain. **2** accept, treat as an equal, respect.

condescending *adj.* patronizing, superior, disdainful, overbearing, *Informal* high-hat.

condescension *n.* **1.** assumption of equality, self-effacement, humbleness, humility, modesty, self-abasement; graciousness, deference. **2.** haughtiness, loftiness, disdain, hauteur, patronizing attitude; *Informal* high-and-mighty attitude, airs. —**Ant. 1** arrogance, haughtiness, superiority, pride.

condign *adj.* fitting, appropriate, suitable, fair, just, right, merited, earned, due, proper, warranted, deserved, worthy, meet. —**Ant.** unjust, unwarranted, unmerited, inappropriate.

condition *n.* **1.** state, situation, circumstances, state of affairs, shape, standing, position, status. **2.** state of health, state, physical fitness, shape, fettle; ailment, malfunction, malady, complaint, problem. **3.** term, provision, proviso, stipulation, demand, arrangement, agreement; prerequisite, requisite, contingency; qualification, restriction, limitation, reservation. —*v.* **4.** prepare, ready, train, equip, fit, put in shape, tone up, accustom, adapt, make used to. —**Ant. 4** disqualify, incapacitate; unaccustom.

conditional *adj.* provisional, tentative, with reservations, qualified, limited, restricted, contingent, stipulative, dependent. —**Ant.** unconditional, absolute, unlimited, unrestricted, categorical.

condolence *n.* sympathy, commiseration, solace, comfort, compassion, consolation, pity. —**Ant.** congratulation, felicitation.

condone *v.* overlook, let pass, ignore, disregard, put up with, wink at; forgive, excuse, pardon, justify, absolve, forget. —**Ant.** condemn, denounce, censure, disapprove; punish, castigate.

conducive *adj.* contributive, contributory, favorable, instrumental, calculated to produce, helpful in bringing about, helpful, expeditious, promotive, beneficial; salutary. —**Ant.** harmful, hurtful, deleterious, damaging.

conduct *n.* **1.** behavior, comportment, deportment, ways, manner, action, deeds. **2.** management, administration, direction, guidance, supervision, leadership, control, government, generalship. —*v.* **3.** guide, lead, escort, usher, convey, convoy, pilot, steer, marshal, attend, accompany; preside over, chair. **4.** behave, comport, act, carry, bear. **5.** manage, administer, direct, guide, regulate, rule, control, govern, superintend, supervise; perform, transact, carry on, carry out, discharge, dispatch, execute, operate, enact, look after. —**Ant. 3** follow, trail.

conduit *n.* main, pipe, duct, tube, canal, channel, passage; (*variously*) watercourse, flume, aqueduct, sewer, gutter, trough, drain.

confederacy *n.* **1.** alliance, league, coalition, association, federation, confederation, union, combine, fusion; guild, society, band, bloc, syndicate. **2. the Confederacy.** the Confederate States of America, the C.S.A., the Southern Confederacy, the Southern states, the South, the secessionist states.

confederate *n.* ally, colleague, partner, associate, collaborator, accomplice, coworker, fellow-conspirator, cohort, accessory, helper, abettor, cooperator, comrade, companion, right hand, helping hand. —**Ant.** opponent, rival, enemy, foe.

confederation *n.* league, association, alliance, coalition, federation, confederacy, union, combine, fusion; society, band, guild, syndicate. —**Syn. Study.** See ALLIANCE.

confer *v.* **1.** present to, bestow upon, award, accord, give, grant. **2.** consult, discuss, hold a conference, deliberate together, parley, talk together, converse, compare notes, palaver. —**Syn. Study. 1** See GIVE. **2** See CONSULT. —**Ant. 1** withdraw, take away; withhold, deny.

conference *n.* discussion, talk, consultation, deliberation, parley; meeting, convention, convocation, symposium, seminar, conclave, council, assembly. —**Syn. Study.** See CONVENTION.

confess *v.* admit, acknowledge, reveal, disclose, divulge, make known, bring to light, expose, lay bare, declare, avow, blurt out, make a clean breast of, unbosom one's self, own up; *Slang* come clean, sing. —**Syn. Study.** See ADMIT. —**Ant.** disavow, repudiate, disown; deny, hide, conceal, cover; remain silent, keep mum, button one's lips.

confession *n.* **1.** admission, acknowledgment, revelation, disclosure, divulgence, declaration, avowal. **2.** priestly confession, confessional, acknowledgment of one's sins, *Archaic* shrift. —**Ant. 1** denial, disavowal, refutation, concealment, hiding.

confidant, (*fem.*) **confidante** —*n.* intimate, friend, trusty companion, crony, bosom buddy.

confide *v.* tell secretly, tell privately, reveal, disclose, make known, impart, divulge, let know, let in on; confess, lay bare, unbosom oneself. —**Ant.** keep one's own counsel, keep secret, remain silent, keep mum, button one's lips; deny, repudiate.

confidence *n.* **1.** trust, faith, conviction, belief, reliance, credence. **2.** self-confidence, assurance, self-assurance, faith in oneself, certainty, certitude; self-reliance, courage, intrepidity, mettle, spirit, nerve, boldness, daring, audacity; spunk, pluck, grit, guts. **3.** secret, intimacy, private matter, confidential matter, inside information. —**Syn. Study. 2** CONFIDENCE, ASSURANCE both imply a faith in oneself. CONFIDENCE usu. implies a firm belief in oneself without a display of arrogance or conceit: *His friends admired his confidence at the party.* ASSURANCE implies even more sureness of one's own abilities, often to the point of offensive boastfulness: *She spoke with assurance but lacked the qualifications for the job.* —**Ant. 1** distrust, mistrust, doubt, misgiving, apprehension, disbelief. **2** self-doubt, uncertainty, timidity, bashfulness, shyness.

confident *adj.* **1.** convinced, certain, sure, positive, secure, assured, optimistic, expectant. **2.** self-confident, self-assured, cocksure, sure of oneself, self-reliant, intrepid, dauntless, daring, bold, cocky. —**Ant. 1** unconfident, uncertain, unsure, distrustful, dubious, doubtful, apprehensive, fearful, pessimistic. **2** self-doubting, unsure of oneself, insecure, hesitant, nervous, jittery.

confidential *adj.* **1.** secret, private, not to be disclosed, privy, undisclosed, off-the-record, top-secret, classified, *Informal* hush-hush. **2.** familiar, intimate. —**Syn. Study. 2** See FAMILIAR. —**Ant. 1** public, open; published, publicized. **2** distant, unknown.

confidentially *adv.* in strict confidence, in secret, secretly, privately, behind closed doors, between ourselves, sub rosa, just between you and me. —**Ant.** openly, publicly.

confine *v.* **1.** limit, restrict, restrain, keep, regulate, govern. **2.** keep in, shut in, shut up, coop up, hold, fence in, cage, pen, tie, bind; imprison, jail, incarcerate, hold in custody, lock up, impound, sequester. —**Ant. 1** extend, expand, amplify. **2** release, free, liberate, loose, let out.

confinement *n.* **1.** lying in, accouchement, childbirth, parturition. **2.** restriction, limitation, restraint, circumscription. **3.** detention, constraint, custody, shutting in, cooping up, imprisonment, incarceration. —**Ant. 2, 3** release, freeing, liberation.

confines *n. pl.* limits, border, bounds, boundaries, precinct, edge, margins, circumference.

confirm *v.* **1.** corroborate, bear out, uphold, sustain, verify, validate, substantiate, authenticate, establish, prove, clinch. **2.** acknowledge, agree to, approve, accept; make firm, make certain, make binding; validate, authorize, certify, ratify. —**Ant. 1** contradict, refute, repudiate, deny, disavow, disprove, impugn, contravene, controvert. **2** cancel, reject, refuse; annul, abrogate, repeal.

confirmation *n.* **1.** substantiation, verification, corroboration, affirmation, authentication, validation, proof. **2.** acceptance, approval, endorsement, ratification, sanction; assent, agreement. —**Ant. 1** denial, repudiation, refutation, contradiction, disavowal, recantation. **2** rejection, refusal, disapproval, cancellation, annulment.

confirmed *adj.* **1.** corroborated, substantiated, authenticated, verified, proven true, validated, established. **2.** established, inveterate, ingrained, chronic, set, fixed, dyed-in-the-wool, deep-seated, deep-rooted, hardened. —**Ant. 1** unconfirmed, unsubstantiated, unverified, unproven; contradicted, refuted, repudiated, denied. **2** temporary, sometimes, occasional, on-and-off, now-and-then.

confiscate *v.* seize, commandeer, appropriate, possess, preempt, take, take over, impound, sequester, expropriate. —**Ant.** release, return, restore.

conflagration *n.* fire, blaze, wildfire, inferno, firestorm, holocaust, bonfire, wall of fire, sheet of flame, sea of flames, raging fire, brush fire, forest fire.

conflict *v.* **1.** disagree, oppose, be contrary, clash, collide, be inharmonious, be contradictory. —*n.* **2.** fight, combat, battle, struggle, clash, warfare, hostility, encounter, confrontation, action, skirmish, engagement, fray, scuffle, melee, set-to, fracas, tussle. **3.** disagreement, difference, discord, division, variance, dissent, dissension; antagonism, friction, strife. —**Ant. 1** agree, harmonize, coincide, reconcile. **2** peace; truce, treaty. **3** agreement, harmony, accord, concord.

confluence *n.* conflux, convergence, coming together, junction, concourse, union, meeting, linkage, gathering, juncture, flowing together, joining, concursion, assembling, concentration, association.

conform *v.* **1.** follow, comply with, obey, submit to, be guided by, adhere to, acquiesce in, fall in with, act in agreement with. **2.** correspond to, agree with, tally with, square with, fit, jibe with; reconcile, adjust, adapt. —**Ant. 1** disobey, oppose, diverge, differ. **2** differ, be dissimilar.

conformation *n.* form, shape, formation, configuration, build, figure, structure, framework, arrangement, anatomy.

conformity *n.* agreement, harmony, accord, compliance, observance, acquiescence, assent, obedience, submission; uniformity, conventionality, resemblance, likeness, correspondence, similarity. —**Ant.** disagreement, disharmony, discord, disobedience, opposition, rebellion; difference, dissimilitude, divergence.

confound *v.* perplex, confuse, baffle, bewilder, puzzle, mystify, mix up, disconcert, unsettle, nonplus, rattle, fluster, throw off the scent; amaze, astound, astonish, surprise, startle, dumfound, flabbergast, strike with wonder. —**Ant.** enlighten, explain, solve, clear up, clarify.

confront *v.* face, face up to, meet, encounter, cope with; withstand, challenge, dare, brave, defy. —**Ant.** avoid, evade, flee, turn tail; surrender to, yield to.

confrontation *n.* showdown, opposition, encounter, eyeball-to-eyeball encounter, contest, face-to-face meeting, face-off, conflict, battle, run-in, set-to, skirmish, clash, engagement.

confuse *v.* **1.** perplex, bewilder, baffle, puzzle, stump, mystify, fluster, rattle, muddle, addle, befuddle, mix up, confound, disconcert, unsettle, nonplus, discompose. **2.** mix up, mistake; confound, make perplexing, make baffling, make unclear, muddle, befog, throw into disorder. —**Ant. 1** enlighten. **2** differentiate, untangle; explain, solve, clarify, clear up.

confusion *n.* **1.** bewilderment, stupefaction, bafflement, perplexity, puzzlement, mystification; disconcertment, discomposure, abashment. **2.** chaos, disorder, disarrangement, disarray, disorganization, untidiness, shambles, upheaval, mess; muddle, clutter, jumble, hodgepodge, snarl, tangle; riot, tumult, madhouse, turmoil, pandemonium, hullabaloo, hubbub, commotion, ferment, disturbance, bedlam, uproar. —**Ant. 1** enlightenment, explanation, solution, clarification; composure, calm. **2** organization, order, orderliness, arrangement, tidiness, neatness.

congeal *v.* harden, set, stiffen, solidify, thicken, curdle, clot, coagulate, jell, gelatinize; freeze. —**Ant.** dissolve, soften, melt, thaw.

congenial *adj.* **1.** similar, compatible, kindred, harmonious, well-suited, consistent, like, agreeing, related, sympathetic, corresponding. **2.** agreeable, pleasing, pleasant, amenable, gracious, affable, genial, cordial, companionable, social, sociable, convivial. —**Ant. 1** dissimilar, different, incompatible, opposite, unrelated, unlike. **2** disagreeable, displeasing, unpleasant, ungracious.

congenital *adj.* innate, inherent, inborn, inbred, intrinsic, hereditary, inherited, ingrained; natural, native. —**Syn. Study.** See INNATE. —**Ant.** acquired, extrinsic, assumed, learned.

congested *adj.* crowded, overcrowded, filled, packed, jammed, gorged, saturated. —**Ant.** uncongested, empty, uncrowded, free.

congestion *n.* crowding, overcrowding, jam, mass, mob, pile-up, obstruction, bottleneck, snarl. —**Ant.** uncrowding, emptiness, desertedness.

conglomeration *n.* mixture, collection, assortment, combination, aggregate, aggregation, potpourri, medley, agglomeration; jumble, hodgepodge, mishmash.

congratulate *v.* give one's best wishes, wish one joy, salute, felicitate, hail, compliment, rejoice with, wish many happy returns of the day. —**Ant.** rebuke, reprove, censure, condemn, criticize, reprehend.

congratulations *n. pl.* best wishes, good wishes, greetings, well-wishing, salute, felicitations, blessings, many happy returns of the day. —**Ant.** rebuke, reproof, censure, condemnation, criticism, reprehension.

congregate *v.* assemble, gather, collect, cluster, come together, crowd together, mass, amass, throng, flock, swarm. —**Ant.** disperse, scatter, separate, part.

congregation *n.* **1.** audience, assembly, gathering, crowd, group, throng, multitude, horde, flock. **2.** church membership, religious assembly, parishioners, parish, brethren, laity.

congress *n.* **1.** conference, convention, assembly, council, gathering, caucus, discussion group; delegates, representatives. **2.** Usu. **Congress.** legislature, legislative body, national council, federal council; (*variously*) parliament, chamber of deputies, diet.

conjectural *adj.* theoretical, speculative, hypothetical, surmised, putative, suppositional, abstract, doubtful, supposed, inferential, reputed, supposititious. —**Ant.** factual, certain, actual, evidential, literal, proven.

conjecture *n.* **1.** guesswork, supposition, inference, deduction, surmise, guess, view, judgment, speculation, suspicion, opinion, notion, idea, theory, hypothesis, assumption, augury, *Informal* shot in the dark, *Slang* guesstimate. —*v.* **2.** guess, suppose, think, calculate, reckon, surmise, theorize, imagine, infer, forecast, speculate, hypothesize, presume, presuppose, judge, fancy. —**Syn. Study. 2** See GUESS. —**Ant. 1** fact, surety, certainty. **2** know.

conjugal *adj.* marital, wedded, married, matrimonial, nuptial, connubial, spousal. —**Ant.** single, unmarried, unwedded.

conjunction *n.* combination, union, joining, meeting, association, concurrence, coincidence.

conjure *v.* call forth, call upon, make appear, summon, raise, command, invoke; call away, make disappear, allay; practice sorcery, bewitch, charm, enchant, cast a spell.

connect *v.* **1.** join, attach, unite, fasten together; couple, tie, hinge, combine, merge. **2.** associate, relate, compare, correlate, combine. **—Syn. Study. 1** See JOIN. **—Ant. 1** disconnect, detach, unfasten, disjoin, sunder, separate, divide, part. **2** dissociate, separate.

connection *n.* **1.** coupling, coupler, fastening, link, bond, linkage, connector, attachment, nexus, tie, junction. **2.** relation, relationship, interrelation, association, correlation, affinity, attachment, alliance. **3.** relative, relation, family, kin, kinfolk, kinsfolk, kinsman, kith and kin, flesh and blood; friend, associate, acquaintance, contact. **—Ant. 1** disconnection, detachment. **2** detachment, dissociation. **3** stranger.

connive *v.* conspire, plan, plot, cooperate secretly, participate surreptitiously, collude, be a party to, be accessory to, be in collusion with, lend oneself to, aid, abet; allow, shut one's eyes to, wink at. **—Ant.** have no part, be innocent of, deter, resist; censure, deplore, condemn, expose.

connoisseur *n.* expert, judge, authority, mavin, person of good taste, cognoscente; epicure, gourmet.

connotation *n.* suggested meaning, suggestion, implication, undertone, insinuation, import, significance, coloring, intimation, spirit, drift, evocation. **—Ant.** denotation, basic meaning, literal meaning.

connote *v.* imply, suggest, hint at, intimate, insinuate, bring to mind.

connubial *adj.* conjugal, wedded, married, marital, matrimonial, nuptial. **—Ant.** single, unmarried, unwedded.

conquer *v.* **1.** defeat, vanquish, win over, overcome, overpower, triumph over, prevail over, beat, whip, thrash, drub, trim, rout, lick, best, floor, subdue, subjugate, humble; occupy, possess, rule. **2.** overcome, surmount, master, rise above, prevail over, get the better of, get the upper hand of, quell. **—Syn. Study. 1** See DEFEAT. **—Ant. 1** be defeated, be beaten, lose, surrender, capitulate, give up, bow to. **2** give in to, yield to, surrender to.

conqueror *n.* victor, vanquisher, conquistador, subjugator, subduer, winner; champion. **—Ant.** conquered, conquest, defeated, vanquished, subjugated, loser.

conquest *n.* **1.** conquering, defeat, vanquishment, mastery, overcoming, victory, triumph, winning, ascendancy, subjugation, domination, upper hand, sway, whip hand. **2.** captured territory, captive, acquisition; adherent, follower, fan, lover, adorer. **—Syn. Study. 1** See VICTORY. **—Ant. 1** failure, surrender, submission, loss.

conscience *n.* moral sense, sense of right and wrong, ethical feelings, scruples, principles.

conscientious *adj.* conscionable, high-principled, dutiful, upright, scrupulous, responsible, honest, ethical, trustworthy; painstaking, careful, exact, particular, meticulous, fastidious. **—Syn. Study.** See PAINSTAKING. **—Ant.** unconscientious, unprincipled, unscrupulous, unreliable, untrustworthy; careless, neglectful, remiss, negligent, heedless, thoughtless, slack, lax, feckless, irresponsible.

conscious *adj.* **1.** able to feel and think, sentient, sensible, having awareness. **2.** aware, cognizant, discerning, knowledgeable, perceiving, noticing, observing, apperceptive, awake to, alert to, alive to, in the know, with it, *Slang* hip to, tuned in to. **3.** deliberate, calculated, studied, premeditated. **—Syn. Study. 2** CONSCIOUS, AWARE, COGNIZANT refer to a realization or recognition of something about oneself or one's surroundings. CONSCIOUS usu. implies sensing or feeling certain facts, truths, conditions, etc.: *to be conscious of an extreme weariness; to be conscious of one's own inadequacy.* AWARE implies being mentally awake to something on a sensory level or through observation: *aware of the odor of tobacco; aware of gossip.* COGNIZANT, a more formal term, usu. implies having knowledge about some object or fact through reasoning or through outside sources of information: *to be cognizant of the drawbacks of a plan.* **—Ant. 1–3** unconscious. **2** unaware, ignorant, insensible, oblivious, *Informal* out of it.

consciousness *n.* **1.** awareness, sensibility, mental activity. **2.** awareness, cognizance, perception, mind, thoughts, senses, feelings, discernment. **—Ant. 1** unconsciousness; unawareness, insensibility.

conscript *v.* **1.** draft, induct, call up, impress, select, conscribe, mobilize, recruit, enlist, register, muster, enroll, levy, *Navy* shanghai; hire, engage, take on, employ. *—n.* **2.** draftee, inductee, rookie, recruit, selectee, enlistee; private, buck private, P.F.C., boot, seaman.

consecrate *v.* **1.** declare sacred, make sacred, sanctify, hallow, bless, glorify, immortalize. **2.** devote, dedicate. **—Syn. Study. 2** See DEVOTE. **—Ant. 1** desecrate, profane, defile.

consecutive *adj.* successive, following one another, progressive, sequential, serial, continuous, uninterrupted, unbroken, in turn. **—Ant.** nonconsecutive, random, haphazard, hit-or-miss, disordered.

consensus *n.* general agreement, majority opinion, general opinion; common consent, unanimity, concord, accord, concurrence. **—Ant.** minority opinion; disagreement, discord, difference.

consent *v.* **1.** agree, concur, assent, approve, accept, accede, acquiesce, concede; yield, submit, fall in with, permit, allow, sanction, confirm, ratify, endorse. —*n.* **2.** agreement, concurrence, assent, approval, acceptance, willingness, permission, sanction, confirmation, ratification, endorsement, accord, concord, acquiescence. **—Ant. 1** dissent, refuse, disallow, decline, resist, balk, demur, disagree, disapprove. **2** refusal, unacceptance, unwillingness, disapproval, dissent, disagreement, discount.

consequence *n.* **1.** result, outcome, development, upshot, outgrowth, issue, aftermath, end, sequel, fruit. **2.** importance, import, significance, note, moment, magnitude, distinction, prominence, notability, seriousness, gravity, influence, avail, worth, value, account, usefulness. **—Syn. Study. 1** See EFFECT. **2** See IMPORTANCE. **—Ant. 1** prelude, source, root, cause, determinant, reason. **2** insignificance, unimportance, paltriness, triviality.

conservation *n.* preservation, husbandry, care, careful use, safekeeping, protection, maintenance, upkeep. **—Ant.** waste, destruction, decay, loss, neglect.

conservative *adj.* **1.** nonliberal, unprogressive, traditional, right-wing, reactionary, unchanging; old-line, cautious, moderate, undaring, quiet, middle-of-the-road, *Slang* square. —*n.* **2.** opponent of change, champion of the status quo, middle-of-the-roader, moderate, right-winger, reactionary, *Slang* square. **—Ant. 1** radical, liberal, progressive, revolutionary; innovative, avant-garde, imaginative, speculative, faddish. **2** radical, innovator, changer, progressive.

conservatory *n.* **1.** greenhouse, hothouse, nursery, glasshouse; arboretum. **2.** music school, music academy, conservatoire.

conserve *v.* preserve, save, use less, use sparingly, husband, not waste, cut back; maintain, care for, safeguard, guard. **—Ant.** waste, squander.

consider *v.* **1.** think about, reflect on, envision, contemplate, regard, weigh, appraise, gauge, examine, review, mull over, ponder, turn over in one's mind, study, cogitate on, deliberate on, bear in mind, be aware of, note, pay heed; respect, honor, make allowances for. **2.** regard, hold to be, judge, deem, think, believe, hold, opine. **—Syn. Study. 1** See STUDY. **—Ant. 1** ignore, neglect, overlook, disregard.

considerable *adj.* sizable, substantial, large, great, goodly, tidy, of some size, ample, not small, a good deal of; of some importance, significant, notable, noticeable, estimable, noteworthy, remarkable, impressive. **—Ant.** insubstantial, meager, small, insignificant; ordinary, average, unimportant, workaday, unremarkable, inestimable.

considerably *adv.* substantially, significantly, noticeably, notably, sizably, largely, greatly, amply, abundantly, estimably, remarkably. **—Ant.** minimally, unnoticeably, insignificantly, little.

considerate *adj.* thoughtful, kind, kindly, solicitous, attentive, concerned, obliging, mindful. **—Ant.** inconsiderate, thoughtless, unfeeling, oblivious, heedless, selfish.

consideration *n.* **1.** thought, regard, attention, concern, heed, notice, deliberation, contemplation, meditation, cogitation, reflection, judgment, advisement, study, review, examination. **2.** thoughtfulness, regard, considerateness, respect, solicitude, tact, honor, kindliness. **3.** factor, point, concern, interest; inducement, motive, reason, cause, ground. **—Ant. 1** disregard, inattention. **2** thoughtlessness, heedlessness, selfishness.

consign *v.* hand over, transfer, deliver, entrust, commit, deposit with, convey, remit, remand, assign, relegate, delegate, commend to. **—Ant.** receive; keep, retain, withhold.

consignment *n.* **1.** transfer, delivery, committing, depositing, assignment, handing over, consigning, entrusting, relegation, delegation, committing. **2.** shipment, goods shipped, goods for sale, goods sent on approval. **—Ant. 1** reception, receiving; keeping, retention.

consist *v.* **1.** to be composed of, be made up of, be comprised of, contain, include. **2.** lie, to be found in, reside.

consistency, consistence *n.* **1.** texture, viscosity, density, thickness, firmness, stiffness, compactness; body, composition, construction, structure, makeup. **2.** constant performance, undeviating behavior, steady effort, uniform standards, persistence; steadfastness, faithfulness. **3.** harmony, congruity, unity, uniformity, conformity, agreement, accordance, coherence, correspondence, connection, compatibility. **—Ant. 2** inconsistency, erratic behavior, volatility. **3** inconsistency, disharmony, incongruity, disagreement, discordance, incompatibility.

consistent *adj.* **1.** constant, steady, regular, persistent, unchanging, undeviating, conforming to type. **2.** harmonious, consonant, in agreement, agreeing, of a piece, unified, compatible, congenial, meet, correspondent, congruous, suitable. **—Ant. 1** inconsistent, irregular, erratic, nonuniform, changing, deviating. **2** inconsistent, in disagreement, incompatible, noncongenial, incongruous, discordant, contradictory, contrary, unsuitable.

consolation *n.* solace, comfort, relief, succor, assuagement, help, alleviation, soothing, easement, support, encouragement, cheer; condolence, sympathy. **—Ant.** depression, discomfort, discouragement.

console *v.* soothe, comfort, calm, succor, cheer, ease, support, sustain; condole with, commiserate with, lament with, express sorrow, express sympathy for, sympathize. **—Syn. Study.** See COMFORT. **—Ant.** distress, trouble, discompose, upset, annoy, disturb, perturb, agitate, aggravate, grieve, sadden, hurt, wound, disquiet.

consolidate *v.* **1.** combine, unify, centralize, incorporate, unite, merge, bring together, band together, join, fuse, amalgamate, coalesce, league, integrate, federate, compress, condense, concentrate. **2.** strengthen, fortify, solidify, make solid, make sure, make firm. **—Ant. 1** separate, divide, part, sever, sunder; dissolve. **2** weaken, make uncertain, leave up in the air.

consonance *n.* harmony, agreement, accord, accordance, correspondence, compatibility, consistency, coherence, concord, concordance, congruity, congruence, consonancy, unison, conformity, unanimity, like-mindedness, homogeneity, one-ness. **—Ant.** conflict, disagreement, dissonance, disparity, inconsistency, discrepancy, discord.

consort *n.* **1.** spouse, mate, husband, wife, *Informal* other half; partner, companion, associate, *Slang* sidekick. *—v.* **2.** keep company, accompany, pal around, go around, fraternize, mingle, mix, pair off, club, hang out, rub elbows. **—Ant. 2** dissociate, separate, part, estrange.

conspicuous *adj.* **1.** standing out, easily seen, easily noticed, highly visible, obvious, striking; plain, clear, evident, manifest, patent, distinct, glaring, prominent, arresting, flagrant. **2.** outstanding, striking, notorious, remarkable, notable, illustrious, distinguished, glorious, memorable, celebrated, prominent, eminent, renowned, famous, well-known, splendid, brilliant, great. **—Ant. 1** inconspicuous, unnoticeable, concealed, hidden, unseen, invisible, imperceptible, unapparent, indiscernible. **2** inconspicuous, undistinguished, trifling, unmemorable, common, ordinary, modest, humble; mediocre, average, commonplace.

conspiracy *n.* criminal plan, treasonous plan, secret plan, plot, intrigue, cabal; collusion, connivance, machination; sedition, treason, treachery. **—Syn. Study.** CONSPIRACY, PLOT, INTRIGUE, CABAL refer to surreptitious or covert schemes to accomplish some end, most often an illegal or evil one. A CONSPIRACY usu. describes a treacherous or illicit plan formulated in secret by a group of persons: *a conspiracy to control prices.* A PLOT is a carefully planned secret scheme formulated by one or more persons: *a plot to seize control of a company.* An INTRIGUE usu. involves duplicity and deceit aimed at achieving personal advantage: *the petty intrigues of civil servants.* CABAL usu. refers to a scheme formulated by a small group of highly placed persons to gain control of a government: *The regime was overthrown by a cabal of generals.*

conspirator *n.* plotter, schemer, conniver, traitor, subversive, intriguer.

conspire *v.* **1.** scheme, intrigue, collude, connive, machinate, plot treason. **2.** contribute jointly, combine, unite, cooperate, concur, work together.

constant *adj.* **1.** fixed, uniform, steady, regular, even, unchanging, invariable, unalterable, unvaried, undeviating, permanent, stable, immutable, unswerving, unfailing. **2.** incessant, unceasing, ceaseless, unrelenting, continual, endless, never-ending, everlasting, eternal, interminable, perpetual, persistent, unbroken, uninterrupted, sustained; *Slang* 24/7. **3.** loyal, devoted, faithful, true, tried-and-true, trustworthy, trusty, steadfast, staunch, dependable, diligent, resolute, abiding, unflagging, unwavering, enduring, stalwart. **—Syn. Study. 3** See FAITHFUL. **—Ant. 1** variable, fluctuating, changing, changeable, erratic, irregular, uneven, unfixed, deviating, alterable, unstable. **2** occasional, intermittent, irregular, spasmodic, sporadic, fitful, random, unsustained. **3** inconstant, disloyal, unfaithful, faithless, false, perfidious; untrustworthy, undependable, irresolute, wavering, flagging, fickle.

constellation *n.* configuration, pattern, assemblage, cluster, group, gathering, collection; galaxy, nebula, spiral, spiral nebula, island universe; company, group, circle, rally, host, throng.

consternation *n.* paralyzing fear, panic, shock, terror, horror, fright, alarm; dismay, apprehension, trepidation. **—Ant.** composure, calmness, equanimity, aplomb, self-possession, sang-froid, presence of mind; fearlessness, boldness.

constitute *v.* **1.** form, compose, make up, make, produce, compound. **2.** establish, create, set up, institute, found; appoint, delegate, commission, authorize, empower, name, invest.

constitution *n.* **1.** composition,

makeup, construction, structure, configuration, figuration, formation, texture. **2.** physical condition, physique, figure, health, strength, mettle, stamina, vitality. **3.** governing charter, charter, fundamental principles, basic laws.

constitutional *adj.* **1.** organic, physical, internal, congenital, natural, inborn, inherent, intrinsic. **2.** of the Constitution, chartered, basic, fundamental, vested. —*n.* **3.** walk, stroll, ramble, turn. —**Ant. 1** inorganic, nonphysical, external, fortuitous; foreign, alien, extraneous, extrinsic, acquired, environmental, accidental. **2** unconstitutional, unlawful, illegal.

constrain *v.* **1.** force, compel, coerce, oblige, urge, drive, necessitate, strong-arm, enforce, pressure, *Slang* put the screws on. **2.** restrain, curb, fight down, suppress, repress, check, quash, put down, squelch, crush, subdue. —**Ant. 1** beg, implore, ask, request, plead. **2** free, loose, unleash, release, let go, liberate.

constraint *n.* **1.** force, obligation, coercion, pressure, compulsion, necessity, duress, enforcement. **2.** restraint, reserve, suppressed feelings, inhibition, diffidence. —**Ant. 1** free will; desire, wish. **2** naturalness, openness, frankness, boldness.

constrict *v.* squeeze, cramp, pinch, strangle, strangulate, choke, bind; contract, compress, shrink. —**Ant.** free, release, loosen, unbind, untie; distend, swell.

constriction *n.* tightness, compression, contraction, narrowing, stricture, constraint; squeezing, cramping, choking, pinching, binding, shrinking, strangling. —**Ant.** loosening, freeing, releasing, unbending; expansion, widening, dilation, distension, swelling.

construct *v.* build, erect, make, fabricate, set up; create, formulate, form, frame, design, devise, fashion, shape, organize, arrange. —**Ant.** demolish, destroy, raze, tear down, take apart.

construction *n.* **1.** constructing, building, putting together, erecting, rearing, raising, fabrication, fashioning, creation, production, manufacture. **2.** building, structure, edifice. **3.** style, form, configuration, build, conformation, composition, format, make. **4.** rendition, version, explanation, interpretation, explication, elucidation, reading. —**Ant. 1** demolition, razing, destruction, tearing down.

constructive *adj.* helpful, productive, practical, handy, useful, beneficial, advantageous, valuable. —**Ant.** destructive, unhelpful, useless.

construe *v.* interpret, understand, comprehend, take, read, decipher, translate, make out, figure out; explain, elucidate.

consul *n.* diplomatic agent, representative, foreign officer, minister, envoy, emissary.

consult *v.* **1.** refer to, inquire of, ask advice of, seek counsel from, seek the opinion of; take into account, consider, regard, have an eye to. **2.** confer, exchange views, deliberate together, talk over, discuss together, parley, compare notes. —**Syn. Study. 2** CONSULT, CONFER imply talking over a situation or a subject with someone. To CONSULT is to seek advice, opinions, or guidance from a presumably qualified person or source: *to consult with a financial analyst.* To CONFER is to exchange views, ideas, or information in a discussion: *The partners conferred about the decline in sales.* —**Ant. 1** ignore, disregard, bypass.

consultation *n.* meeting, conference, council, deliberation, hearing, discussion, palaver, interview.

consume *v.* **1.** use up, expend, spend, deplete, exhaust, drain; waste, squander, dissipate, fritter away. **2.** eat, devour, eat up, swallow up, gulp, guzzle, drink up. **3.** destroy, lay waste, ravage, devastate, demolish, annihilate. **4.** absorb, engross, eat up, devour. —**Ant. 1** conserve, preserve, save; provide, supply.

consumer *n.* **1.** user, customer, buyer, purchaser, patron, client. **2.** user, spender, drain; waster, dissipater, squanderer. —**Ant. 1** manufacturer, maker, seller. **2** saver, preserver, conserver; supplier, provider.

consummate *v.* **1.** complete, perfect, fulfill, execute, accomplish, achieve, realize, effect, finish, bring about, carry out, perform, do. —*adj.* **2.** finished, complete, accomplished, faultless, perfect; thorough, absolute, utter, unquestioned, unconditional, undisputed, supreme, unmitigated, sheer, total, through-and-through, 100 percent. —**Ant. 1** begin, start, initiate, conceive, inaugurate. **2** unfinished, incomplete, imperfect, deficient; crude, rough, raw; partial, conditional.

consummation *n.* achievement, realization, fulfillment, attainment, execution, accomplishment; completion, finish, conclusion, close, culmination, end. —**Ant.** beginning, inception, start, initiation; failure, breakdown.

consumption *n.* **1.** use, using up, consuming, utilization; expenditure, depletion, exhaustion, exploitation. **2.** tuberculosis, TB. —**Ant. 1** conservation, preservation, saving.

contact *n.* **1.** touch, connection; meeting, touching, junction, union, adjacency, abutment. **2.** communication, connection, association. —*v.* **3.** touch, meet, connect, join. **4.** communicate with, reach, get in touch with, get hold of.

contagious *adj.* catching, infectious, communicable, transmittable, spreading, spreadable. **—Syn. Study.** CONTAGIOUS, INFECTIOUS are usu. distinguished in technical medical use. CONTAGIOUS, literally "communicable by contact," describes a very easily transmitted disease, as influenza or the common cold. INFECTIOUS refers to a disease involving a microorganism that can be transmitted from one person to another only by a specific kind of contact; venereal diseases are usu. infectious. In nontechnical senses, CONTAGIOUS emphasizes the rapidity with which something spreads: *Contagious laughter ran through the hall.* INFECTIOUS suggests the pleasantly irresistible quality of something: *Her infectious good humor made her a popular guest.* **—Ant.** noncontagious, noncatching, noninfectious.

contain *v.* **1.** hold, include, enclose; accommodate, incorporate, embody, embrace, involve. **2.** control, hold back, hold in, suppress, repress, restrain, inhibit, keep within bounds, curb, check, keep back, *Slang* keep the lid on. **—Syn. Study. 1** CONTAIN, HOLD, ACCOMMODATE express the idea that something is so designed that something else can exist or be placed within it. CONTAIN refers to what is actually within a given container. HOLD emphasizes the idea of keeping within bounds; it refers also to the greatest amount or number that can be kept within a given container. ACCOMMODATE means to contain comfortably or conveniently, or to meet the needs of a certain number. A plane that ACCOMMODATES fifty passengers may be able to HOLD sixty, but at a given time may CONTAIN only thirty. **—Ant. 2** express, vent, release, let out.

container *n.* receptacle, holder; (*variously*) vessel, carton, box, bag, can, bucket, pail, bottle, jar, vat, barrel.

contaminate *v.* taint, pollute, dirty, soil, infect, foul, befoul, make impure, spoil, blight, poison, corrupt, defile, adulterate, debase, besmirch. **—Ant.** purify, clean, cleanse, purge.

contamination *n.* polluting, dirtying, soiling, fouling, poisoning, defilement, spoiling, adulteration; impurity, pollution, dirtiness, foulness, uncleanness, filth, putridity. **—Ant.** purity, cleanness.

contemplate *v.* **1.** regard, survey, examine, inspect, scan, note, look at fixedly, view attentively, stare at, gaze at, observe. **2.** ponder, mull over, reflect upon, think about, consider fully, deliberate on, cogitate on, weigh, meditate on, speculate about, muse about, ruminate. **3.** expect, anticipate, envision, imagine, project; plan, intend, look forward to, think of, aspire to, have in view. **—Ant. 1** disregard, overlook, ignore.

contemplation *n.* **1.** viewing, observation, inspection, examination, seeing, survey, scanning, looking, gazing. **2.** thought, thinking, reflection, cogitation, pondering, meditation, study, deliberation, consideration, musing, rumination, reverie.

contemplative *adj.* thoughtful, reflective, meditative, musing, ruminating, cogitative, pensive, speculative, introspective, studious, engrossed, lost in thought. **—Ant.** active, practical, pragmatic; thoughtless, impetuous, impulsive.

contemporaneous *adj.* **—Syn. Study.** See CONTEMPORARY.

contemporary *adj.* **1.** modern, up-to-date, up-to-the-minute, current, present-day, recent, late, new, newfangled, brand-new, ultra-modern, advanced, *Slang* with-it. **2.** of the same time, coexistent, concurrent, contemporaneous, coeval, coincident, simultaneous. **—Syn. Study. 2** CONTEMPORARY, CONTEMPORANEOUS, COEVAL, COINCIDENT mean happening or existing at the same time. CONTEMPORARY often refers to persons or their acts or achievements: *Hemingway and Fitzgerald, though contemporary, shared few values.* CONTEMPORANEOUS is applied chiefly to events: *the rise of industrialism, contemporaneous with the spread of steam power.* COEVAL refers either to very long periods of time, or to remote or distant times: *coeval stars, shining for millennia; coeval with the dawning of civilization.* COINCIDENT means occurring at the same time but without causal relationship: *World War II was coincident with the presidency of Franklin D. Roosevelt.* **—Ant. 1** antique, old-fashioned, old, early, out-of-date, archaic, obsolete.

contempt *n.* disdain, scorn, derision, ridicule, shame, humiliation, disgrace, dishonor, ignominy; disrepute, disfavor, disregard, disgust, distaste, repugnance, revulsion, aversion, detestation, loathing, hatred, hate, abhorrence, antipathy. **—Syn. Study.** CONTEMPT, DISDAIN, SCORN imply strong feelings of disapproval and aversion toward what seems base, mean, or worthless. CONTEMPT is disapproval tinged with disgust: *to feel contempt for a weakling.* DISDAIN is a feeling that a person or thing is beneath one's dignity and unworthy of one's notice, respect, or concern: *a disdain for crooked dealing.* SCORN denotes open or undisguised contempt often combined with derision: *He showed only scorn for those* *who were not as ambitious as himself.* **—Ant.** honor, respect, esteem, admiration, regard; liking, love.

contemptible *adj.* mean, vile, low, base, shameful, ignominious, miserable, wretched, unworthy, abject, cheap, shabby, paltry; disgusting, repugnant, revolting, despicable, detestable. **—Ant.** honorable, respectable, admirable, laudable, praiseworthy, worthy; pleasant, attractive, appealing.

contemptuous *adj.* scornful, disrespectful, insolent, disdainful, arrogant, snobbish, condescending, haughty, lordly, pompous, supercilious, derisive. **—Ant.** humble, awestruck; respectful, deferential, civil, obliging, gracious, amicable, admiring.

contend *v.* **1.** be a rival, fight, struggle, strive, contest, contest for, combat, battle, war, wrestle, grapple, tussle, jostle, spar, clash, skirmish; compete, compete for, vie. **2.** assert, declare, avow, aver, claim, insist, hold, maintain, put forward, allege, propound; argue, quarrel, debate, dispute, contest. **—Syn. Study. 1** See COMPETE. **—Ant. 1** concede, yield, surrender, give up. **2** deny, disavow, refute.

content[1] *n.* **1.** (*Often plural*) thing contained, insides, load; capacity, volume, area, size. **2.** substance, essence, heart, core, thoughts, ideas, matter, meaning, gist, thesis, text.

content[2] *adj.* **1.** satisfied, contented, gratified, wanting no more, pleased, happy, comfortable, complacent; untroubled, unconcerned, unmoved, at ease, serene, at rest. *—v.* **2.** satisfy, suffice, comfort, gratify, please, make easy, cheer, set at ease, appease. *—n.* **3.** satisfaction, contentment, gratification, comfort, peace of mind, peace, serenity, pleasure, happiness. **—Ant. 1–3** discontent. **1** dissatisfied, unsatisfied, unhappy, displeased, uncomfortable; troubled, concerned, worried, restless. **2** dissatisfy, displease, provoke, pique, upset, annoy. **3** dissatisfaction, discomfort, unhappiness, displeasure.

contented *adj.* satisfied, content, gratified, pleased, happy; comfortable, at ease, serene, at peace. **—Ant.** discontented, discontent, dissatisfied, displeased, uncomfortable, uneasy, worried, troubled, concerned, annoyed, piqued.

contentment *n.* satisfaction, content, contentedness, gratification, happiness, pleasure, peace, ease, serenity, comfort. **—Ant.** discontent, dissatisfaction, unhappiness, displeasure, discomfort.

contest *n.* **1.** conflict, struggle, fight, battle, combat, war, encounter, bout, engagement, dispute; competition, match, tournament, tourney, rivalry, game. *—v.* **2.** fight for, battle for, combat for, struggle for, compete for, contend for, contest for, vie for. **3.** dispute, call in question, argue against, challenge, debate, oppose, controvert, object to. **—Syn. Study. 2** See COMPETE. **—Ant. 1** agreement, accord, peace. **2** relinquish, surrender, yield, give up. **3** accept, agree to, approve, support, maintain.

context *n.* framework, setting, frame of reference, ambience, situation, environment, surroundings, circumstances, background, connection, relationship, conditions, precincts, milieu, climate, atmosphere, meaning.

contiguous *adj.* adjoining, bordering, abutting, adjacent, next-door, neighboring, tangent, touching, conterminous; nearby, close, close-by, handy. **—Ant.** remote, distant, far-off, faraway.

continence *n.* self-restraint, forbearance, abstinence, moderation; (*variously*) purity, chastity, sobriety, temperance. **—Ant.** incontinence, abandon, self-indulgence, excess; licentiousness, wantonness, drunkenness.

contingency *n.* emergency, unforeseen event, likelihood, possibility, accident; extremity, urgency, predicament.

contingent *adj.* dependent, subject to, controlled by, conditioned. **—Ant.** independent, uncontrolled, unrelated.

continual *adj.* **1.** ceaseless, unceasing, continuous, constant, incessant, unremitting, perpetual, perennial, never-ending, unending, endless, interminable, everlasting, eternal, unbroken, uninterrupted; *Slang* 24/7. **2.** frequent, habitual, constant, recurring, persistent, oft-repeated. **—Ant. 1** ceasing, terminable, broken, fitful, spasmodic, intermittent, irregular. **2** infrequent, rare, occasional, sporadic, spasmodic, exceptional.

continuance *n.* continuation, continuing, persistence, perseverance, lasting, permanence, stay, extension, protraction, prolongation. **—Ant.** end, cessation, stopping, termination.

continuation *n.* addition, continuance, continuing, extension, prolongation, protraction, sequence, sequel, supplement. **—Ant.** end, cessation, termination.

continue *v.* **1.** keep on, keep up, go on, proceed, endure, persist, persevere, last, extend, carry on, drag on; resume. **2.** remain, stay, stay on, keep on, carry on, abide. **—Syn. Study. 1** CONTINUE, ENDURE, PERSIST, LAST imply existing uninterruptedly for an appreciable length of time. CONTINUE implies duration or existence without break or interruption: *The rain continued for two days.* ENDURE, used of people or things, implies persistent continuance despite influences that tend to weaken, undermine, or destroy: *The temple has endured for centuries.* PERSIST implies steadfast and longer than expected existence in the face of opposition: *to persist in an unpopular belief.* LAST implies remaining in good condition or adequate supply: *I hope the liquor lasts until the end of the party.* **—Ant. 1** discontinue, stop, cease, desist, quit, pause, stay. **2** leave, resign, retire, quit, step down.

continuity *n.* flow, progression, succession, continuation, continuance, continuum, chain.

continuous *adj.* **1.** unbroken, successive, progressive, consecutive; linked, connected. **2.** unremitting, constant, uninterrupted, unceasing, incessant, interminable, continual, continuing, lasting, ceaseless, steady, endless, perpetual, everlasting, eternal, persistent, persevering, enduring, extensive, protracted, prolonged. **—Ant. 1** intermittent, broken, disconnected. **2** passing, spasmodic, sporadic, occasional; inconstant, interrupted, ending, ceasing.

contort *v.* twist, bend, distort, deform, warp, be misshapen. **—Ant.** straighten, unbend.

contour *n.* outline, profile, shape, form, silhouette, figure, lines, physiognomy.

contraband *n.* prohibited articles, illegal imports, illegal exports, smuggled goods, unlicensed goods, unlawful trafficking, bootlegging, black-marketeering.

contract *n.* **1.** agreement, written agreement, legal document, compact, pact, treaty, covenant, arrangement, bargain. **—***v.* **2.** draw together, become smaller, compress, tighten, constrict; shorten, narrow, shrink, dwindle, condense, reduce. **3.** acquire, incur, get, take, develop, assume, absorb, enter into, engender. **4.** sign an agreement, agree, pledge, promise, make a bargain, undertake, negotiate, come to terms. **—Syn. Study. 1** See AGREEMENT. **—Ant. 2** expand, stretch, distend, enlarge, dilate, swell, lengthen, widen, grow, increase. **3** avoid, evade, elude, escape, shun, eschew; avert, ward off. **4** disagree, refuse.

contraction *n.* drawing in, constriction, compression, tightening, shrinkage, shriveling, decrease, reduction, lessening, shortening, narrowing, condensation, abbreviation. **—Ant.** expansion, extension, increase, stretching, swelling, enlargement, lengthening, widening, broadening.

contradict *v.* refute, deny, confute, controvert, impugn, oppose, counter, dispute, be contrary to, disagree with, gainsay, rebut; disprove, belie. **—Ant.** corroborate, confirm, verify, substantiate, authenticate, agree with, affirm, sustain, support, endorse.

contradiction *n.* refutation, denial, confutation, disagreement, rebuttal, counter, negation. **—Ant.** corroboration, confirmation, verification, substantiation, affirmation, support, endorsement; agreement, accord.

contradictory *adj.* conflicting, opposing, dissenting, contrary, disagreeing, countervailing, antithetical, discrepant, irreconcilable, refutatory, inconsistent. **—Ant.** similar, like, parallel, agreeing.

contrary *adj.* **1.** opposed, opposite, contradictory, counter, at variance, at cross purposes, conflicting, incompatible, antithetical, inimical, converse, discordant, disparate. **2.** disagreeing, contradictory, unaccommodating, stubborn, obstinate, intractable, refractory, balky, recalcitrant, willful, headstrong, froward, wayward; hostile, antagonistic. **3.** unfavorable, adverse, disagreeable, unpropitious, untoward, inauspicious, unsuitable, unfitting. **—Ant. 1** consistent, parallel, accordant. **2** complaisant, compliant, obliging, accommodating, acquiescent, tractable, agreeing, unassuming, submissive; good-natured, agreeable, pleasant, peaceful. **3** favorable, propitious, auspicious, suitable, fitting.

contrast *v.* **1.** differentiate, set in opposition; differ, diverge, deviate, depart, disagree with. **—***n.* **2.** comparing differences, comparison, differentiation; difference, dissimilarity, unlikeness, variance, disparity, divergence, distinction. **—Ant. 1** liken, compare, resemble, parallel. **2** similarity, likeness, comparison, parallelism, sameness, similitude, agreement.

contravene *v.* **1.** infringe on, violate, transgress, trespass against, act against, breach, disobey, overreach, overstep, infract, offend, encroach upon. **2.** oppose, deny, contradict, gainsay, fight, combat, repudiate, spurn, reject, abjure, exclude, resist, disclaim, disown; nullify, abrogate, annul. **—Ant. 1** observe, respect, comply with, adhere to. **2** endorse, support, go along with, agree with, second.

contribute *v.* **1.** give, donate, bestow, grant, confer, hand out, present, endow. **2.** advance, influence, lead to, help bring about, forward, be conducive to, have a hand in, bear a part. **—Ant. 1** take, receive; withhold, deny. **2** curb, check, slow, impede, detract.

contribution *n.* donation, gift, bestowal, endowment, grant, benefaction, dispensation, subsidy, offering; charity, alms.

contrite *adj.* conscience-stricken, sorrowful, regretful, repentant, rueful, penitent, remorseful, apologetic, chastened, humbled. —**Ant.** proud, pleased, uncontrite, unrepentant, unapologetic.

contrition *n.* self-reproach, regret, remorse, qualms of conscience, compunction; repentance, penitence, penance, atonement.

contrivance *n.* **1.** device, contraption, gadget, instrument, apparatus, implement, tool, machine, mechanism, invention; *Slang* gizmo, doodad, thingamajig. **2.** plan, trick, stratagem, plot, artifice, intrigue, measure, design, machination.

contrive *v.* **1.** devise, create, concoct, improvise, invent, design. **2.** scheme, plot, plan, devise a plan; maneuver, manage, effect by stratagem.

control *v.* **1.** command, govern, rule, master, regulate, manipulate, manage, have charge of, superintend, supervise, steer; dominate, reign over. **2.** restrain, restrict, repress, subdue, contain, curb, master, bridle. —*n.* **3.** command, management, mastery, regulation, direction, sway, rule, dominion, domination, jurisdiction, authority, supervision, charge. **4.** curb, restraint, suppressant, brake. —**Syn. Study. 3** See AUTHORITY. —**Ant. 2** free, release, let loose, give vent.

controversial *adj.* widely discussed, causing debate; polemical, debatable, disputable, arguable, open to discussion, questionable, at issue. —**Ant.** noncontroversial, undebatable, indisputable, incontrovertible, unquestionable, proven, sure, certain.

controversy *n.* debate, discussion, dispute, contention, argument, quarrel, wrangle, squabble, altercation; disagreement, dissension. —**Syn. Study.** See ARGUMENT. —**Ant.** agreement, unanimity, accord.

controvert *v.* deny, disprove, contradict, oppose, refute, dispute, rebut, confute, confound, contravene, gainsay, disaffirm; challenge, question, protest. —**Ant.** corroborate, prove, affirm, demonstrate, uphold, verify.

contumacious *adj.* contrary, perverse, rebellious, froward, factious, disobedient, mutinous, seditious, refractory, fractious, unruly, disrespectful, ungovernable, unmanageable, insolent, insubordinate, intractable, headstrong. —**Ant.** compliant, acquiescent, obedient, submissive, amenable, tractable, docile.

contumely *n.* abuse, contempt, rudeness, insolence, scorn, disdain, brusqueness, obloquy, reproach, opprobrium, invective, vituperation, scurrility, billingsgate; arrogance, pomposity, overbearingness, haughtiness. —**Ant.** civility, politeness, regard, respect, consideration, esteem.

contusion *n.* bruise, discoloration, black-and-blue mark; abrasion, injury, hurt, sore, black eye; *Slang* mouse, shiner.

conundrum *n.* puzzle, riddle, enigma, mystery, poser, puzzler, paradox, arcanum, brain-teaser, stumper, stopper, Chinese puzzle, rebus, problem.

convalescence *n.* recovery, recuperation, restoration, return to health, *Archaic* recruit.

convene *v.* gather, come together, assemble, hold a session, bring together, summon, call together, convoke, muster, collect, round up. —**Ant.** adjourn, disperse, dissolve, dismiss, disband.

convenience *n.* **1.** usefulness, utility, service, benefit; handiness, accessibility, availability. **2.** comfort, accommodation, facility; appliance, work saver. **3.** accommodation, use, ease, enjoyment, pleasure, satisfaction. **4.** opportunity, chance, convenient time, suitable time. —**Ant. 1** inconvenience, nuisance, uselessness, hardship. **2** nuisance. **3** inconvenience, dissatisfaction, discomfort, annoyance.

convenient *adj.* **1.** suitable, suited, useful, helpful, adapted, easy to use, handy, serviceable, advantageous, beneficial. **2.** easily accessible, nearby, at hand. —**Ant. 1** inconvenient, unsuitable, awkward, unwieldy, useless, unhandy. **2** inconvenient, inaccessible, distant.

convent *n.* society of nuns, nunnery, cloister.

convention *n.* **1.** assembly, conference, congress, convocation, conclave, caucus, meeting, gathering. **2.** custom, social rule, standard, code, precept, practice, propriety, protocol, formality. —**Syn. Study. 1** CONVENTION, ASSEMBLY, CONFERENCE, CONVOCATION refer to meetings for particular purposes. CONVENTION usually suggests a formal meeting of members or delegates of a political, social, or professional group: *an annual medical convention.* ASSEMBLY usually implies a regular meeting for a customary purpose: *an assembly of legislators; a school assembly in the auditorium.* CONFERENCE suggests a meeting for consultation or discussion: *a sales conference.* CONVOCATION usually refers to an ecclesiastical or academic meeting whose participants were summoned: *a convocation of economic experts.*

conventional *adj.* traditional, customary, accepted, proper, orthodox; normal, standard, regular, common, routine, usual. —**Ant.** unconventional, unorthodox, extraordinary, uncommon, abnormal.

converge *v.* come together, meet, approach; focus, concentrate, bring together. **—Ant.** diverge, separate, part, scatter, disperse.

conversant *adj.* familiar, acquainted, knowledgeable of, well-informed, up on, proficient, tutored, erudite, skilled, practiced, privy to, on good terms with; *French* au fait, au courant. **—Ant.** ignorant, unversed, unfamiliar, uninformed.

conversation *n.* talk, discourse, dialogue, chat, chit-chat, tête-à-tête, palaver, confabulation; *Slang* gabfest, rap, bull session.

conversational *adj.* **—Syn. Study.** See COLLOQUIAL.

converse[1] *v.* talk, speak together, engage in conversation, chat, chitchat, confabulate, palaver; *Slang* gab, chin, jaw, chew the rag, chew the fat, shoot the breeze, rap.

converse[2] *n.* opposite, reverse, contrary, antithesis. **—Ant.** identical, same.

conversion *n.* **1.** change, transformation, modification, transfiguration, metamorphosis, transmutation. **2.** change, change of religion, changeover, change of heart, change in beliefs.

convert *v.* **1.** change, transform, modify, turn. **2.** change one's religion, change one's belief; cause a change of opinion, proselytize. *—n.* **3.** converted person; proselyte, neophyte, novice. **—Syn. Study. 1** See TRANSFORM.

convex *adj.* curved outward, rounded, protuberant, bulging. **—Ant.** concave, sunken, hollowed out.

convey *v.* **1.** carry, transport, bear, conduct, bring, move, transmit. **2.** communicate, make known, impart, transmit, dispatch, relate, give, tell, disclose, reveal, divulge, confide to. **3.** transfer, deliver over, cede, deed, consign, grant; will, bequeath, leave. **—Ant. 2** conceal, hide, receive, listen. **3** retain, keep, hold on to, cling to.

conveyance *n.* **1.** conveying, transport, transportation, carrying, transfer, carriage, movement, transmission. **2.** transportation, vehicle; (*variously*) bus, car, truck, rig, carriage, van, wagon, cart, buggy.

convict *v.* **1.** declare guilty, prove guilty, find guilty; condemn, doom. *—n.* **2.** prisoner, felon; *Slang* jailbird, yardbird, con. **—Ant. 1** acquit, find innocent.

conviction *n.* **1.** belief, view, viewpoint, opinion, judgment, principle, tenet, faith, persuasion, position, creed, doctrine, dogma. **2.** certainty, certitude, assurance, firm persuasion, steadfastness, intensity, ardor, earnestness, fervor, fever, zeal. **—Syn. Study. 1** See BELIEF. **—Ant. 2** doubt, uncertainty, misgiving, hesitation.

convince *v.* persuade, prevail upon, sway, win over, bring around, influence, assure, satisfy.

convivial *adj.* sociable, friendly, companionable, genial, affable, agreeable, fun-loving, merry, jovial, gregarious, festive. **—Ant.** unsociable, unfriendly, reserved, reticent, serious, sober, grave, sedate, solemn.

convocation *n.* convention, congress, conference, caucus, council, conclave, assembly, gathering, ingathering, meeting, roundup, roster, muster. **—Syn. Study.** See CONVENTION. **—Ant.** adjournment, dismissal, disbanding.

convolution *n.* coiling, coil, twisting, twist, winding, undulation, contortion; sinuosity, sinuousness, tortuousness; maze, labyrinth. **—Ant.** uncoiling, unwinding.

convoy *v.* **1.** escort, conduct, usher, accompany, go along with, attend. *—n.* **2.** escort, protection, safeguard, armed guard; (*variously*) column, fleet, formation. **—Syn. Study. 1** See ACCOMPANY.

convulsion *n.* **1.** spasm, fit, contortion, seizure, paroxysm. **2.** outburst, fit, spasm; commotion, disturbance, tumult, agitation.

cool *adj.* **1.** slightly cold, somewhat cold, chill, chilly, not warm. **2.** calm, unexcited, composed, unflappable, imperturbable, self-possessed, collected, deliberate, cool-headed, undisturbed, untroubled, unemotional, dispassionate, impassive, serene. **3.** unfriendly, uncordial, unsociable, distant, reserved, aloof, standoffish, offish, unresponsive, indifferent, nonchalant, cold, icy, frosty. *—v.* **4.** make cool, become cool, chill, lose heat. **—Syn. Study. 2** See CALM. **—Ant. 1** warm, *Informal* warmish. **2** excited, frenzied, frantic, wild, delirious, impassioned, high-strung, nervous, tense, wrought-up, overwrought, hysterical, agitated, perturbed, disturbed, troubled, upset. **3** friendly, cordial, warm, responsive. **4** warm, heat.

cooperate *v.* work together, participate, collaborate, unite, act jointly, join, join forces, take part, share in, pitch in, work side by side, go along, bear part in, stand shoulder to shoulder, join hands, pull together. **—Ant.** oppose, fight, conflict, rival; counteract, negate, neutralize, nullify.

cooperation *n.* cooperating, working together, participation, collaboration, joint action, teamwork, give and take, pulling together; concurrence, agreement, accordance, concert, détente.

—**Ant.** opposition, hindrance, conflicting, rivalry, dissension, infighting; disagreement, discord.

coordinate *v.* **1.** organize, order, arrange, systematize, correlate, relate, match, mesh, harmonize. *—adj.* **2.** equal, coequal, parallel, equally important, correlative. —**Ant. 1** disorganize, muddle. **2** unequal, disparate.

cope *v.* contend, spar, wrestle, face, strive, struggle, tussle, hold one's own; manage, hurdle.

copious *adj.* profuse, plentiful, abundant, bountiful, extensive, full, ample, liberal, generous, lavish, plenteous. —**Ant.** skimpy, sparse, meager, scanty, scant, spare.

copy *n.* **1.** reproduction, facsimile, likeness, duplicate, carbon copy, replica, clone, representation; imitation, counterfeit, forgery, fake, sham. **2.** text, story, written material, reportage, manuscript. *—v.* **3.** make a copy of, reproduce, duplicate, clone; photostat, Xerox. **4.** emulate, follow, imitate, mimic, ape, parody, mirror, repeat. —**Ant. 1** original, archetype, prototype, model, pattern. **3** originate, create.

coquette *n.* flirt, vamp, heart-breaker, *Slang* tease.

cord *n.* twine, thin rope, braid, heavy string.

cordial *adj.* friendly, gracious, genial, amiable, affable, warm, affectionate, sincere, heartfelt, wholehearted, hearty, good-natured. —**Ant.** unfriendly, ungracious, cool, cold, frigid, indifferent, distant, detached, reserved, aloof, formal, ceremonious.

cordiality *n.* friendliness, warmth, affability, amiability, geniality, agreeableness, heartiness, amicability, graciousness, earnestness, sincerity, goodwill, affection. —**Ant.** coldness, insincerity, disagreeableness, ill will.

core *n.* **1.** kernel, center, central part, innermost part, nucleus. **2.** essence, essential part, gist, heart, center, pith, substance, sum and substance, crux, nub, meat; *Slang* guts, brass tacks, nitty-gritty.

corner *v.* **1.** trap, grab, seize, back into a corner; *Slang* nail, pigeonhole, collar, nab. *—n.* **2.** angle, bend, nook. **3.** predicament, dilemma, plight, impasse, awkward position, dead end, blind alley; *Slang* fix, jam, pickle, spot, hole, scrape.

corny *adj.* hackneyed, trite, commonplace, banal, stale, insipid, stereotyped, platitudinous, ordinary, square, old-fashioned, bromidic, unsophisticated, inane, fatuous, *Slang* hokey. —**Ant.** original, fresh, unhackneyed, sophisticated, unique.

coronet *n.* small crown, diadem; chaplet, tiara, circlet.

corporal *adj.* bodily, physical, fleshly, *Obsolete* corporeal; personal. —**Syn. Study.** See PHYSICAL.

corporation *n.* incorporated group, corporate body, association, legal entity; *(loosely)* company, holding company, association, syndicate, combine, conglomeration.

corporeal *adj.* physical, bodily, fleshly; mortal, worldly, nonspiritual, material; perceptible, tangible. —**Syn. Study.** See PHYSICAL. —**Ant.** spiritual, heavenly, ethereal, religious; intellectual, mental.

corps *n.* **1.** military branch; organized body of troops, combat unit, squad, outfit. **2.** team, crew, force, troop, party, band.

corpse *n.* dead body, body, cadaver, remains, carcass, *Slang* stiff. —**Syn. Study.** See BODY.

corpulent *adj.* fat, obese, overweight, rotund, fleshy, portly, stout, plump, well-padded, chubby, pudgy, roly-poly, chunky; well-fed, hefty; dumpy, lumpish. —**Ant.** emaciated, thin, slender, slim, lean, gaunt, skinny, scrawny; rawboned, lanky.

correct *v.* **1.** make right, remove the errors of, amend, rectify, repair, remedy, improve; alter, change, adjust, modify; regulate, fix; rework, revamp, revise. **2.** chasten, reprimand, admonish, berate, scold, rebuke, censure, reprove, lecture, chide, dress down, take to task, haul over the coals, read the riot act to; punish, castigate, discipline, chastise. *—adj.* **3.** free from error, accurate, right, faultless, flawless, perfect; exact, precise, true, factual, unerring. **4.** proper, fitting, fit, appropriate, suitable, seemly, becoming; conventional, acceptable. —**Syn. Study. 3** CORRECT, ACCURATE, PRECISE imply conformity to fact, standard, or truth. A CORRECT statement is one free from error, mistakes, or faults: *The student gave a correct answer in class.* An ACCURATE statement is one that, as a result of an active effort to comprehend and verify, shows careful conformity to fact, truth, or spirit: *The two witnesses said her account of the accident was accurate.* A PRECISE statement shows scrupulously strict and detailed conformity to fact: *The chemist gave a precise explanation of the experiment.* —**Ant. 1** spoil, mar, ruin, damage, harm, hurt, injure, impair. **2** excuse, condone, praise, compliment, laud. **3** incorrect, wrong, inaccurate, false, untrue. **4** improper, inappropriate, unfitting, unsuitable, unseemly, unbecoming, unconventional.

correction *n.* **1.** rectification, improvement, emendation; alteration, change, revision, modification, adjustment. **2.** discipline, punishment, reformation, chastisement, castigation.

corrective *adj.* counter, counteractive, counterbalancing; reformatory, rectifying; improving, ameliorative, therapeutic, remedial, compensatory; restorative, palliative.

correlate *v.* relate, show relationship between, bring together, compare, connect, correspond, parallel. **—Ant.** disconnect, contradict, oppose.

correspond *v.* **1.** exchange letters, write letters, communicate, keep in touch, drop a line to. **2.** agree, conform, concur, coincide, accord, parallel, harmonize, equate, match, fit, suit, tally, dovetail, jibe, square; be similar, be like, be equivalent, be complementary. **—Ant. 2** differ, disagree, belie, diverge.

correspondence *n.* **1.** mail, letters, missives, epistles; dispatches, bulletins, communiqués. **2.** similarity, resemblance, relation, analogy, association.

corridor *n.* hallway, hall, passageway; passage, aisle; approach, way, road, artery.

corroborate *v.* prove, verify, confirm, uphold, support, sustain, substantiate, affirm, validate, bear out, vindicate, authenticate, certify, endorse, back, back up. **—Ant.** disprove, contradict, refute, nullify, negate, invalidate.

corrode *v.* eat away, wear away, erode, disintegrate; rust, oxidize.

corrugated *adj.* bent into folds, ridged, furrowed, crenelated, puckered, pleated, fluted, grooved, creased, wrinkled, crinkled.

corrupt *adj.* **1.** dishonest, dishonorable, crooked, shady, unscrupulous, fraudulent, unethical, unprincipled. **2.** wicked, immoral, depraved, debased, iniquitous, base, mean, low, sinful, evil. *—v.* **3.** make immoral, deprave, debase, subvert, lead astray, debauch; contaminate, poison; pervert, seduce. **—Ant. 1** honest, honorable, upright, ethical, principled, scrupulous, righteous, moral; *Slang* straight. **2** virtuous, moral, ethical, righteous, noble, high-minded. **3** reform, uplift.

corruption *n.* **1.** dishonest practices, dishonesty, graft, bribery, fraud, malfeasance, shady dealings. **2.** wickedness, depravity, evil ways, immorality, iniquity, sinfulness, debauchery, perversion, turpitude, vice, wrongdoing, degeneracy, decadence, looseness. **—Ant. 1** honesty, righteousness, scrupulousness, trustworthiness, integrity. **2** goodness, good, righteousness, morality, nobility, purity.

corsair *n.* pirate, privateer, buccaneer, sea rover, sea robber, picaroon, freebooter, marauder, plunderer, sea dog, sea wolf, viking, sea looter; Long John Silver, Blackbeard, Captain Kidd.

corset *n.* girdle, foundation garment, corselet, laces.

cortege *n.* funeral procession, train, entourage, escort, retinue, company, attendants, staff, suite, column, string, caravan, line, motorcade, parade, cavalcade, following.

cosmic *adj.* **1.** of the universe, (*especially*) extraterrestrial, of outer space, interplanetary, interstellar. **2.** vast, immense, enormous, widespread, colossal, stupendous, grandiose; infinite, universal. **—Ant. 2** minor, small, minute, infinitesimal, microscopic, minuscule.

cosmopolitan *adj.* **1.** sophisticated, broad-minded, worldly, worldly-wise, urbane, international, not provincial. *—n.* **2.** man of the world, sophisticate, cosmopolite, citizen of the world, world traveler, globe trotter. **—Ant. 1** provincial, insular, parochial, narrow-minded, bigoted, hidebound, rigid, isolated; rustic, countrified. **2** provincial, rustic, boor.

cosmos *n.* universe, interstellar system, macrocosm, earth and the heavens, the whole wide world; heavenly bodies, starry host, vault of heaven, stars.

cost *n.* **1.** price, charge, amount, outlay, expense, expenditure, market price, bill, tab, toll, fee; worth, value, face value, valuation. **2.** loss, sacrifice; expense, price, penalty; pain, distress, suffering, hurt, harm, injury, damage. *—v.* **3.** sell for, be priced at, go for, fetch, bring in, take, amount to, come to, *Informal* run, set back. **4.** harm, injure, hurt, damage, burden, weigh down; cause suffering to, cause to lose, make sacrifice.

costly *adj.* **1.** expensive, high-priced, extravagant, dear, precious, stiff, steep, exorbitant. **2.** causing much loss, disastrous, catastrophic; harmful, damaging, deleterious. **—Ant. 1** cheap, inexpensive; reasonable, fair.

costume *n.* national dress, indigenous garb, historical dress; outfit, attire, dress, garb, raiment, apparel, garments, clothing, clothes; uniform, livery.

coterie *n.* set, clique, faction, camp, circle, crowd, group, band, clan, crew, club, gang. **—Syn. Study.** See CIRCLE.

cottage *n.* simple house, rustic house, cot, bungalow; lodge, chalet; hut, shack. **—Ant.** palace, castle, château, mansion, manor house, town house.

couch *n.* **1.** sofa, divan, davenport, settee; (*variously*) lounge, chesterfield, love seat, daybed. *—v.* **2.** express, voice, word, utter, put, state, set forth, phrase, frame; draw up, draft.

council *n.* **1.** convention, conference, congress, conclave, assembly, convocation, colloquy, synod; gathering, congregation. **2.** legislative body, assembly, governing body, representatives; cabinet, privy council, chamber, ministry, board, panel, committee.

counsel *n.* **1.** advice, opinion, guidance, recommendation, suggestion; consultation, advisement. **2.** lawyer, legal adviser, counselor, counselor-at-law, attorney; *British* barrister, solicitor. **—*v.* 3.** advise, recommend, suggest, advocate, prompt, urge, charge, call for, instruct; warn, admonish, caution. **—Syn. Study. 1** See ADVICE.

counselor Also **counsellor** *n.* **1.** adviser, instructor, tutor, mentor; cabinet member, minister. **2.** legal adviser, lawyer, attorney, counsel, counselor-at-law, advocate; *British* barrister, solicitor.

count *v.* **1.** add one by one, number, enumerate, numerate, tick off; add up, total. **2.** include, take into account, consider; regard, look on, ascribe, attribute, impute. **3.** consider, regard, deem, hold, look upon, rate, reckon, estimate, judge. **4.** matter, be worthwhile, tell, be effective, carry weight, be important, enter into consideration, add to the number. **5.** total, tally, calculation, enumeration, computation, reckoning, numbering, numeration. **—Ant. 2** exclude, except, leave out, ignore.

countenance *n.* **1.** expression, look, mien, appearance, air, aspect, presence, visage, traits; profile, silhouette, face, features, contours, build, physiognomy. **2.** approval, sanction, approbation, moral support, advocacy, auspices, encouragement, championship; assistance, help, aid, promotion. **—*v.* 3.** permit, approve, sanction, endorse, condone; advocate, support, promote, further, advance, uphold, forward, favor, champion, back, work for. **—Syn. Study. 1** See FACE. **—Ant. 2** disapproval, discouragement, disapprobation, disfavor, opposition. **3** prohibit, disapprove, oppose, condemn; discourage, hinder, thwart, frustrate, block.

counter[1] *n.* **1.** table, stand, display case; bar, fountain, soda fountain, buffet. **2.** playing piece, piece, disk, man.

counter[2] *adv., adj.* **1.** contrary, contrary to, contra, contradictory, in the opposite way, at variance, in defiance of, opposite, opposed, against, conflicting, in conflict. **—*v.* 2.** retaliate, strike back, fight back, hit back, get even, pay back; oppose, offset, reverse, resist, defy. **—Ant. 1** in agreement, similar to, parallel to, in unison with, as planned, as expected, accordant with, coincident with, consonant with. **2** accept, take; yield, give in, give up, surrender.

counteract *v.* act against, nullify, negate, neutralize, undo, offset, counterbalance, contravene; fight, oppose, check, thwart, frustrate, hinder, restrain, repress, curb, resist; alleviate, assuage; clash with, conflict with, counterattack; overpower, overcome, defeat, annihilate. **—Ant.** aid, assist, abet, reinforce, support, help, cooperate with, promote, advance, forward, further, encourage.

counterbalance *v.* offset, compensate for, atone for, make up for, correct, amend, rectify, check, balance, equalize, neutralize, recompense, make good, make compensation, counteract, counterweigh, countervail, counterpoise, outweigh, outbalance, set off, redeem.

counterfeit *adj.* **1.** forged, fake, phony, not genuine, bogus, sham, fraudulent, imitation, simulated, false, artificial, ersatz, spurious, feigned, make-believe. **—*n.* 2.** forgery, fake, phony, fraud, sham, imitation, facsimile, substitute, copy. **—Syn. Study. 1** See FALSE. **—Ant. 1** genuine, authentic, real, good, original.

countermand *v.* revoke, rescind, cancel, abrogate, overrule, call back, abolish, recall, withdraw, retract, annul, void, quash, nullify, disestablish, repeal, disenact, do away with, write off, declare null and void, reverse, set aside, render null and void. **—Ant.** endorse, support, reinforce, second, reiterate.

counterpart *n.* equal, one comparable to another, correspondent, correlative, parallel; match, twin, double, fellow, duplicate, copy, mate, the spitting image, doppelgänger. **—Ant.** antithesis, opposite, contradiction, contrast.

countless *adj.* innumerable, numberless, infinite, endless, myriad, multitudinous, unlimited, limitless, untold, immeasurable, measureless, unnumbered, incalculable. **—Ant.** finite, limited, enumerable.

country *n.* **1.** terrain, land, area, region, district, territory; countryside, landscape, scenery. **2.** nation, state, kingdom, commonwealth, realm. **3.** nation, population, populace, inhabitants, citizens, people, natives, public, community, countrymen. **4.** native country, native land, mother country, homeland, fatherland, native soil; nationality. **5.** rural areas, countryside, hinterlands, farming area, wide open spaces; *Slang* sticks, boondocks, backwoods, boonies. **—*adj.* 6.** rural, farming, farm, provincial, rustic, back-country; unsophisticated, simple. **—Ant. 5** city, town, urban area, metropolis. **6** urban, cosmopolitan, city, urbane, sophisticated, citified.

countryman *n.* **1.** compatriot, fellow citizen, fellow countryman, landsman. **2.** rustic, farmer, peasant, provincial; *Slang* yokel, hick, hayseed, country bumpkin, rube, clodhopper. **—Ant. 1** alien, foreigner, stranger. **2** city dweller, townsman, urbanite, metropolitan, cosmopolitan, city slicker.

coup de grace *n.* deathblow, finishing stroke, mercy stroke, decisive blow.

coup d'état *n.* overthrow, rebellion, revolution, palace revolution; subversion, uprising, mutiny.

couple *n.* **1.** pair, two of a kind, combination of two, doublet. **2.** twosome, pair, duo; man and wife, husband and wife, married pair, engaged pair, dating pair, man and woman. *—v.* **3.** connect, join, link, fasten, hitch, tie, bind, yoke. **—Ant. 3** detach, separate, disconnect, part, unfasten, unhitch, untie.

courage *n.* bravery, valor, fearlessness, dauntlessness, stout-heartedness, intrepidity, daring, boldness, nerve, derring-do, fortitude; *Slang* guts, pluck, spunk, mettle, grit, sand. **—Ant.** cowardice, faintheartedness, pusillanimousness, timidity; terror, fear, dread.

courageous *adj.* brave, valiant, bold, fearless, dauntless, strong-hearted, intrepid, unafraid, chivalrous, manly, dashing, valorous, doughty, dogged, gallant, resolute, indomitable, stalwart, bold-spirited, heroic. **—Syn. Study.** See BRAVE. **—Ant.** cowardly, fainthearted, craven, timid, fearful, apprehensive.

courier *n.* messenger, emissary, runner, dispatch bearer, go-between, dispatch rider, postrider, pony-expressman; herald, Mercury, herald angel, harbinger, Gabriel; envoy, legate, internuncio; postman, letter carrier, mailman, mail carrier.

course *n.* **1.** route, direction, path, channel, passage, road, track, way; orbit, trajectory. **2.** progression, development, sequence, onward movement, unfolding, flow, march. **3.** procedure, action, conduct, method, mode, policy, behavior. **4.** classes, lessons, lectures; course of study, curriculum, study program, subject. **5.** circuit, circle, round, run; racecourse, track. *—v.* **6.** run, flow, race, pour, surge, gush, stream.

court *n.* **1.** royal household, staff, entourage, retinue, train, advisers, council, following, cortege, attendants. **2.** audience, hearing, assembly, session, meeting. **3.** royal residence, palace, castle, château, hall, manor. **4.** courtyard, yard, enclosed area, atrium, plaza, quadrangle, quad. **5.** courtship, homage, respects, courtesies, address, solicitations, flattering attention; suit, wooing. **6.** court of law, court of justice, bench, bar, judicial tribunal. *—v.* **7.** curry favor with, fawn upon, pander to, flatter, blandish; woo, pay suit to, pay one's addresses to; pursue, run after. **8.** invite, attract, induce, provoke, seek. **—Ant. 7** avoid, shun, ignore, refuse, repudiate, reject, turn down, turn away.

courteous *adj.* polite, well-mannered, mannerly, well-behaved, refined, well-bred, civil, respectful, tactful, diplomatic, kind, gracious, considerate; soft-spoken, mild. **—Syn. Study.** See CIVIL. **—Ant.** discourteous, impolite, rude, uncivil, curt, ill-mannered, unmannerly, insolent, disrespectful, unkind, ungracious.

courtesy *n.* **1.** politeness, courteousness, good manners, manners, good behavior, civility, respect, deference, kindly consideration, graciousness, gentility, gentle breeding, cultivation, refinement, courtliness, gallantry. **2.** courteous act, favor, considerate gesture, kindness, consideration, indulgence; regards, respects. **—Ant. 1, 2** discourtesy. **1** impoliteness, discourteousness, bad manners, unmannerliness, rudeness, incivility, disrespect, insolence; churlishness, boorishness.

courtly *adj.* refined, genteel, polished, elegant, decorous, civilized, gallant, chivalrous, suave, debonair, dignified, stately; aristocratic, blue-blooded, highbred, silk-stockinged; polite, courteous, mannerly, gentlemanly, ladylike. **—Ant.** unrefined, inelegant, ungentlemanly, unladylike, undignified, unpolished, impolite; coarse, vulgar, base, low, boorish, loutish, plebeian; ill-mannered, discourteous, rude, uncivil.

courtship *n.* wooing, courting, suit, engagement period, keeping company.

cove *n.* bay, inlet, lagoon, estuary.

covenant *n.* solemn agreement, pledge, vow, promise, oath, bond; pact, treaty, contract, bargain.

cover *v.* **1.** put on, put over, lay on, overlay, blanket, clothe, sheathe, shroud, envelop, wrap, enwrap. **2.** protect, shield, guard, shelter, defend. **3.** hide, conceal, obscure, secrete; cloak, veil, hood, screen; mask, disguise, camouflage. **4.** deal with, include, involve, contain; embrace, encompass, embody, comprise, take in, comprehend; report, tell of, describe, chronicle, write up. **5.** travel through, pass over, pass through, traverse, cross. *—n.* **6.** lid, top, cap, covering; wrapper, case, encasement, envelope, jacket, sheath, binding. **7.** blanket, comforter, quilt, coverlet, eiderdown. **8.** shelter, protection, shield, guard, defense; asylum, refuge, sanctuary, concealment, hiding place. **—Ant. 1** uncover, remove, take off; unclothe, unwrap, expose. **2** expose. **3** uncover, reveal, exhibit, show, unmask, expose. **4** exclude, omit, leave out. **6** base, bottom, stand. **8** exposure.

coverage *n.* **1.** protection, indemnity; payment, reimbursement. **2.** reporting, description, analysis; publishing, broadcasting.

covering *n.* **1.** cover, wrapper, wrapping, casing, envelope, sheath. *—adj.* **2.** descriptive, explanatory, introductory.

covert *adj.* secret, clandestine, hidden, concealed, sub rosa, surreptitious, unknown, veiled, disguised. **—Ant.** overt, known, open, public; candid, frank, plain, clear, evident, obvious.

covet *v.* desire, desire greedily, crave, lust after, yearn for, want, long for, aspire to, have an eye on, fancy, hanker after. **—Ant.** reject, forswear, decline, refuse, renounce, relinquish.

covetous *adj.* craving, desirous, lustful, yearning; greedy, avaricious, rapacious, grasping, mercenary, selfish; envious, jealous. **—Syn. Study.** See GREEDY. **—Ant.** self-denying, self-abnegating, forswearing, renouncing, abjuring; liberal, generous, bountiful, unselfish.

cow *v.* intimidate, frighten, threaten, make cringe, terrorize, terrify, scare, browbeat, bully, bulldoze; dishearten, dismay, abash, discourage, deter. **—Ant.** calm, soothe, quiet, encourage, support, embolden.

coward *n.* uncourageous person, dastard, sissy, cad, caitiff, craven, poltroon; *Slang* chicken, yellow-belly; milksop, mollycoddle, Milquetoast. **—Ant.** brave person, hero, champion, daredevil.

cowardly *adj.* uncourageous, fainthearted, timorous, timid, dastardly, craven, pusillanimous; showing the white feather; *Slang* chickenhearted, yellow, yellow-bellied, lily-livered, gutless; frightened, afraid, fearful, apprehensive, anxious, nervous, shaky, tremulous. **—Ant.** brave, courageous, valiant, valorous, dauntless, stout-hearted, lionhearted, plucky, spunky; bold, daring, audacious, intrepid, doughty.

cowboy *n.* cowpoke, broncobuster, cowpuncher, cowhand, buckaroo, roughrider, cattle-herder, drover, cowherd; *Spanish* gaucho, vaquero; *Brit.* cowman; *Fem.* cowgirl.

cower *v.* crouch in fear, cringe, draw back, shrink, recoil, flinch, quail, tremble; grovel, crawl, truckle, bootlick, toady. **—Ant.** swagger, strut, stand tall; intimidate, bully, terrorize, cow, browbeat.

coy *adj.* shy, modest, bashful, sheepish, shrinking, timid, diffident, timorous, skittish; overmodest, prudish, blushing, demure; pretending to be shy, coquettish, kittenish. **—Ant.** brash, brazen, bold, forward, impudent, impertinent, flippant, flip, pert, saucy, immodest.

cozy *adj.* snug, snugly warm, comfortable, comfy, relaxing, easy, restful, snug as a bug in a rug; homelike, homey, *Spanish* simpático, *German* gemütlich.

crack *v.* **1.** sound sharply, snap, pop, crackle, clap, thunder; strike sharply. **2.** split, fracture, cleave, chip, splinter, break partially. **3.** break, break down, give way, lose control, become irrational, go to pieces. *—n.* **4.** sharp sound, report, burst, snap, pop, clap, crackle. **5.** split, fissure, rift, rent, cleft, slit, gash, crevice, rupture. **6.** wisecrack, joke, quip, gag, jest, jab, gibe, funny remark, teasing remark, witticism; insult, critical remark, smart-alecky remark, taunt.

crackpot *n.* **1.** eccentric, fool, crackbrain, maniac, lunatic, madman, crank, character; *Slang* nut, screwball, kook, weirdo, freak, dingbat, loony, wacko, oddball. *—adj.* **2.** insane, crackbrained, foolish, odd, eccentric, impractical; *Slang* weirdo, wacko, kooky, nutty, balmy, kinky, freaky. **—Ant. 2** rational, sensible, sane, sound, clear-headed.

crackup *n.* **1.** collision, smashup, pileup, smash, wreck, accident; disaster, calamity, catastrophe, debacle, mishap. **2.** nervous breakdown, nervous collapse, prostration, battle fatigue, exhaustion, combat fatigue, *Archaic* shellshock.

cradle *n.* **1.** bed on rockers, baby's bed; *(loosely)* crib, bassinet. **2.** beginning place, birthplace, nursery, source, origin, fountain, fountainhead, font, wellspring, spring. *—v.* **3.** rock, cuddle, snuggle, enfold, hug, clasp tenderly.

craft *n.* **1.** skill, ability, adeptness, deftness, fineness, proficiency, adroitness, knack, competency, expertise, expertness, know-how, technique, mastery. **2.** trade, business, occupation, vocation, employment; industry, commerce, pursuit, calling; handicraft, art. **3.** craftiness, cunning, artifice, artfulness, ruse, wile, trickery, chicanery; deception, guile, duplicity, deceit, perfidy; intrigue, sharp practice. **4.** ship, boat, vessel; aircraft, airplane, plane. **—Ant. 1** inaptitude, unskillfulness, maladroitness, inaptness, ineptitude, ineptness, inability, incompetency, clumsiness. **2** manual labor; intellectual pursuit. **3** openness, candor, frankness, straightforwardness, sincerity, ingenuousness.

crafty *adj.* cunning, shrewd, sharp, wily, foxy, tricky, sly, guileful, artful, shifty, underhand, devious, deceptive, deceitful, perfidious, unethical, dishonest; intriguing, scheming, designing, calculating, plotting; astute, canny, suspicious. **—Ant.** honest, open, candid, frank, aboveboard, ethical; naive, innocent, simple, ingenuous.

craggy *adj.* rocky, stony, cragged, rugged, rough, rockbound, bouldery, scraggy, jagged, ragged, snaggy, rock-ribbed; steep, precipitous, sheer, abrupt. —**Ant.** smooth, even, regular, level, straight, flat.

cram *v.* **1.** jam, pack, stuff, fill, fill to overflowing, crowd, overcrowd, congest; force, press, compress, squeeze, ram. **2.** study hastily, study hard, grind. —**Ant. 1** empty, deplete, drain, exhaust, clear.

cramp *n.* **1.** muscular contraction, spasm, seizure, stitch, crick, charley horse; sharp pain, pang. —*v.* **2.** hamper, hold back, restrict, limit, check, prevent, hinder, thwart, restrain, frustrate, handicap, obstruct, block, stymie. —**Ant. 2** help, aid, advance, forward, expand, increase; free, release, loose.

cranky *adj.* grouchy, cross, bearish, crabby, crotchety, ill-tempered, ill-humored, out of sorts, irascible, captious, splenetic, cantankerous, peevish, waspish, testy, touchy, petulant. —**Ant.** good-natured, good-humored, even-tempered, cheerful, gay, happy, amiable, agreeable, complaisant; placid, calm, serene.

crash *v.* **1.** fall heavily, dash, strike noisily, smash, shatter, clatter; topple, hurtle, tumble, plunge. **2.** collide, strike together, dash together, hit together, smash, bump, bang. **3.** enter without invitation, come uninvited to, enter without a ticket, slip in, sneak in, invade, intrude. —*n.* **4.** clatter, bang, din, racket, clangor, crack, boom; noisy breaking, shattering, smashing; noisy striking, hitting, bumping; heavy falling, toppling, tumbling. **5.** collision, smashup, crackup, accident, wreck, pileup. **6.** financial collapse, financial disaster, failure, bankruptcy, ruin; (*loosely*) depression, recession, slump, decline, setback. —**Ant. 4** silence; murmur, whisper. **6** prosperity, upsurge, flourishing, success.

crass *adj.* coarse, crude, vulgar, gross, unrefined, unpolished, inelegant; uncaring, insensitive, boorish, oafish, unsympathetic, unfeeling, hard-hearted, cruel. —**Ant.** refined, polished, elegant; deferential, obliging, sympathetic, kind, warmhearted, soft-hearted.

crave *v.* pine for, sigh for, wish for, hope for, desire, want, long for, yearn for, hunger for, thirst for, hanker after, have a fancy for, have a yen for, lust after, covet; require, need. —**Ant.** reject, spurn, repudiate, renounce, scorn, refuse, decline; detest, abominate, loathe, hate, despise, abhor.

craven *adj.* cowardly, dastardly, pusillanimous; timid, timorous, fearful, frightened, scared; *Slang* yellow, lily-livered, chicken-hearted; mean-spirited, base, low, lowdown. —**Ant.** brave, courageous, heroic, fearless, valorous, valiant, dauntless; bold, daring, audacious.

craving *n.* —**Syn. Study.** See DESIRE.

crawl *v.* **1.** move by dragging the body, creep, slither, squirm, wiggle, wriggle, writhe, worm; move on hands and knees, go on all fours. **2.** go at a snail's pace, inch, drag, worm, poke, mosey. —**Ant. 1** walk; run. **2** race, rush, dash, dart, spurt, hurry, hasten, tear, fly, go like sixty, go lickety-split, go like the wind.

craze *v.* **1.** drive mad, make crazy, make insane, drive wild, make berserk, derange, dement, unhinge, cause to run amuck. —*n.* **2.** fad, rage, furor, polular whim, mania, passion, infatuation. —**Ant. 1** calm, soothe, ease.

crazy *adj.* **1.** insane, mad, demented, deranged, maniacal, daft, berserk, unbalanced, unhinged; *Slang* cracked, touched, nuts, nutty, out of one's head, mad as a hatter, mad as a March hare. **2.** bizarre, weird, odd, unusual, peculiar, strange, uncommon, silly, absurd, outrageous, laughable; *Slang* far-out. **3.** foolish, imprudent, unwise, foolhardy; senseless, stupid, silly, ridiculous, idiotic, absurd. **4.** mad, smitten with, taken with, fanatical, wild, keen, rabid, avid, zealous, frantic, hysterical, excited; very fond, infatuated, passionate, enthusiastic, gaga, *Slang* nuts. —**Ant. 1** sane, mentally sound, rational, reasonable, sensible, well-balanced. **2** sensible, practical; acceptable, conservative, common, average, usual, run-of-the-mill. **3** smart, wise, prudent, sensible. **4** unenthusiastic, uncaring, unexcited, cool, indifferent.

creak *v.* rasp, squeak, screech, screak, grate, grind, scrape.

crease *n.* **1.** fold, wrinkle, ridge, crinkle, rumple, pucker, corrugation, furrow. —*v.* **2.** wrinkle, pucker, crinkle, ruffle, rumple, crimple, corrugate, furrow; fold, pleat, crimp. —**Ant. 2** smooth, flatten, straighten out.

create *v.* **1.** originate, invent, develop, devise, formulate, make, concoct, contrive, fashion, fabricate, design, form, mold, erect, construct, conceive, bring into being, give birth to; cause, bring to pass. **2.** found, establish, set up, institute, form, organize, appoint. —**Ant. 1** destroy, demolish, annihilate. **2** close, shut down.

creation *n.* **1.** the world, the universe, nature; all things, all living things. **2.** creating, making, institution, origination, development, devising, establishment, founding, production, bringing into existence, formation; building, construction, fabrication, fashioning, erection. **3.**

original work, imaginative work, invention, conception, brainchild, concoction, production, handiwork. **—Ant. 2** destruction, demolition, annihilation.

creative *adj.* original, imaginative, ingenious, inventive, resourceful, fanciful, *Informal* edgy.

creator *n.* **1.** originator, author, framer, designer, producer, architect, maker, initiator, inventor, founder, father, generator, begetter. **2. the Creator.** See GOD.

creature *n.* living being, living thing, earthling; animal, lower animal, beast, critter, dumb animal; (*variously*) quadruped, vertebrate, invertebrate, mammal, bird, fish, reptile, insect; human being, human, mortal, man, person, individual.

credence *n.* belief, confidence, trust, reliance, credibility, creditability, faith, trustworthiness, credit; reliability, dependableness, acceptableness; certainty, certitude. **—Ant.** doubt, mistrust, disbelief, skepticism, distrust, incredulity.

credentials *n.* (*diplomatic*) letter of credence; official testimonials; (*general*) written proof of status or qualifications, certificate, diploma, reference, letter of recommendation, testimonial, authorization, voucher, permit, license.

credible *adj.* believable, plausible, reasonable, likely, possible, probable, tenable; conceivable, thinkable, imaginable; reliable, trustworthy, dependable. **—Ant.** incredible, unbelievable, implausible, unreasonable, unlikely, improbable, inconceivable; unreliable, untrustworthy, dubious, doubtful, questionable, unthinkable.

credit *n.* **1.** recognition, acknowledgment; honor, high regard, esteem, glory, acclaim, commendation. **2.** the installment plan, charge account, time. **3.** allowance, prepayment. *—v.* **4.** attribute, ascribe, assign, acknowledge, recognize; honor, acclaim. **5.** believe, trust, have faith in, put confidence in, rely on, accept; *Informal* swallow, fall for, buy. **—Ant. 1** disgrace, shame, censure, ignominy. **2** cash, cash on the barrelhead. **3** debit, charge. **5** doubt, disbelieve, distrust, question.

creditable *adj.* admirable, commendable, praiseworthy, meritorious, laudable; reputable, estimable, respectable, worthy. **—Ant.** blamable, censurable, discreditable; disreputable, dishonorable.

credo *n.* creed, set of beliefs, set of principles, doctrine, tenet, code, rule, maxim, motto, philosophy.

credulous *adj.* ready to believe, easily convinced, gullible, trusting, believing; naive, unsophisticated, too trustful, overtrustful, unsuspecting, unsuspicious, unquestioning. **—Ant.** incredulous, unbelieving; suspicious, suspecting, wary, cynical.

creed *n.* religious belief, belief, profession of faith, doctrine, dogma, set of principles, set of beliefs, credo, group of tenets, canons, gospel.

creek *n.* stream, brook, small river, rivulet, rill, freshet, branch, run, spring, millstream.

creep *v.* **1.** crawl, slither, writhe, worm, wriggle, squirm. **2.** advance secretly, walk stealthily, come unnoticed, sneak, steal. **3.** move slowly, inch, crawl, dawdle, poke along, go at a snail's pace. **—Ant. 1** run. **2** blunder, bluster, trample. **3** race, rush, fly, tear, hasten, hurry, sprint, dart, dash, go like sixty, go lickety-split, go like the wind.

cremate *v.* reduce to ashes, burn, incinerate; char, sear, burn to a cinder, scorch, consume by fire, conflagrate, roast; set fire to, ignite, set on fire, enkindle, fire, kindle.

crest *n.* **1.** tuft, topknot, comb, plume, crown. **2.** top, summit, pinnacle, highest point, peak, tip, apex, height. **3.** emblem, coat of arms, arms, armorial bearings, escutcheon. **—Ant. 2** bottom, base.

crestfallen *adj.* downhearted, downcast, dejected, depressed, disappointed; discouraged, disheartened, dispirited, low-spirited, despondent, woebegone. **—Ant.** elated, exuberant, happy, joyful, up in the clouds, on cloud nine, in seventh heaven; encouraged, heartened, uplifted.

crevice *n.* fissure, crack, cleft, split, fracture, rift, breach, rent, slit; chasm, crevasse.

crew *n.* **1.** work gang, squad, corps, force, team, company, party. **2.** work force, company of sailors, company, complement, hands, sailors, mariners, seafarers, seamen; air crew, plane crew. **3.** band, body, pack, group, mob, throng, troop, horde; assemblage, multitude, mass, herd. **—Ant. 2** officers.

crime *n.* **1.** unlawful act, violation of the law, lawbreaking, foul play, offense; (*variously*) capital crime, tort, felony, misdemeanor, malfeasance. **2.** wrong, wrongdoing, misdeed, blameworthy action, misconduct; senseless act, wasteful act, outrage, villainy, abomination; sin, transgression, iniquity. **—Syn. Study. 1, 2** CRIME, OFFENSE, SIN agree in referring to a breaking of law. CRIME usu. refers to any serious violation of a public law: *the crime of treason.* OFFENSE is used of a less serious violation of a public law, or of a violation of a social or moral rule: *a traffic offense; an offense against propriety.* SIN means a breaking of a moral or divine law: *the sin of envy.* **—Ant. 1**

lawful act; retribution, pardon. **2** good deed, right, virtue, virtuous act; benefit, boon.

criminal *adj.* **1.** illegal, unlawful, lawbreaking, lawless, indictable, felonious, illicit, crooked, guilty, culpable, delinquent. **2.** wrong, blameworthy; senseless, wasteful; disgraceful, outrageous, villainous, abominable. *—n.* **3.** guilty person, person convicted of a crime; culprit, lawbreaker, outlaw, felon; *Informal* hood, crook; wrongdoer, transgressor, malefactor, offender. **—Syn. Study. 1** See ILLEGAL. **—Ant. 1** lawful, legal, licit; honest, law-abiding; innocent. **2** right, just, commendable, admirable, meritorious, honorable, praiseworthy. **3** innocent person.

cringe *v.* cower, flinch, shrink, quail, blench, recoil, dodge, duck; grovel, be servile, toady, truckle. **—Ant.** strut, swagger.

crinkly *adj.* wrinkly, wrinkled, crimped, crimpy, crimpled, crimply, puckered, puckery, cockled, rumpled, shriveled; twisted, kinky, ruffled; curly, wavy; frizzy, frizzled. **—Ant.** smooth, straight, flat, even, unwrinkled.

cripple *n.* **1.** lame person, the disabled, the handicapped, the impaired; *Slang* gimp. *—v.* **2.** make lame, disable, incapacitate; impair, damage, harm, maim. **3.** impair, disable, incapacitate, render impotent, paralyze, debilitate, hamstring, inactivate; stop, halt, bring to a standstill. **—Ant. 3** help, aid, assist, ease, facilitate.

crisis *n.* turning point, climax; emergency, critical stage, *Informal* crunch time, nail-biter.

crisp *adj.* **1.** crispy, brittle, snappy, crunchy. **2.** brisk, sharp, pointed, snappy, incisive, candid, terse; vivacious, energetic, lively, sparkling, witty. **3.** brisk, pleasantly cool, chilly, nippy, bracing, refreshing, fresh, invigorating. **—Ant. 1** limp, soft, wilted. **2** dull, slow, cautious, insipid. **3** warm, balmy.

criterion *n.* standard, measure, gauge, yardstick, guidepost, rule, principle, law, norm; model, precedent, example, touchstone. **—Syn. Study.** See STANDARD.

critic *n.* **1.** judge, connoisseur, expert, authority, mavin, cognoscente, virtuoso; evaluator, analyst, arbiter; professional reviewer, commentator. **2.** detractor, antagonist, attacker, faultfinder, censor, criticizer; carper, scold, backbiter, reviler, vilifier; *Informal* knocker, rapper.

critical *adj.* **1.** censorious, faultfinding, disparaging, derogatory, picky, fussy, nagging, caviling, carping, nitpicking, disapproving, finicky, hairsplitting. **2.** judging, discriminating, analytical, diagnostic; perspicacious, judicious. **3.** decisive, crucial, grave, serious, sensitive, urgent, momentous, pressing, vital; dangerous, perilous, precarious, hazardous, harrowing, risky, *Slang* hairy. **—Ant. 1–3** uncritical. **1** complimentary, approving, laudatory; inexact, haphazard, permissive. **2** undiscriminating, unanalytical, shallow. **3** secure, settled, calm, tranquil; safe.

criticize *v.* find fault with, disapprove of, disparage, cast aspersions on, reprove, reproach, denounce, censure; nag at, fuss, carp, cavil, pick, nitpick. **—Ant.** compliment, praise, commend, laud, extol, applaud.

critique *n.* critical essay, criticism, critical commentary, critical examination, analysis; review.

crony *n.* friend, companion, pal, chum, associate, acquaintance, *Brit.* mate, comrade, buddy, sidekick, bosom buddy; shipmate, bunkmate, *Slang* bunkie; ally, cohort, confederate, accomplice, collaborator, *Law* accessory, coconspirator.

crook *n.* **1.** bend, curve, turn, twist, angle, curvature; hook, arc, bow. **2.** cheat, dishonest person, knave, criminal, robber, thief, bandit, swindler, embezzler; outlaw, thug, burglar, robber.

crooked *adj.* **1.** askew, awry, not straight; curved, twisted, twisting, winding, meandering, tortuous, sinuous, serpentine, zigzag, spiral; bent, bowed, hooked; distorted, deformed, warped, out of shape. **2.** dishonest, corrupt, unscrupulous, dishonorable, criminal, unlawful; deceptive, fraudulent, unethical, underhanded, deceitful, perfidious, nefarious; sneaky, shifty, shady, wily, crafty. **—Ant. 1** straight, straight as an arrow; flat. **2** honest, legal, lawful, ethical, scrupulous, honorable, fair, aboveboard, upright.

crop *n.* **1.** harvest, yield, production, growth, gleaning, gathering, reaping. *—v.* **2.** cut short, clip, shear, trim, lop, snip, cut, bob, prune.

cross *n.* **1.** crux, rood, crucifix. **2.** burden, misfortune; affliction, distress, suffering, ordeal, adversity, difficulty, trial, tribulation, trouble. **3.** crossbreed, hybrid, half-breed; blend, combination, amalgam. *—v.* **4.** delete, erase, strike out, cancel, cross out, obliterate. **5.** go across, traverse, cut across, go over, pass over, travel over, ford, travel through; intersect, meet, crisscross. **6.** crossbreed, interbreed, mix, intermix; hybridize, cross-pollinate, cross-fertilize. *—adj.* **7.** intersecting, lying crosswise; athwart, transverse, oblique. **8.** angry, mad, ill-tempered, annoyed, in a bad mood, cranky, petulant, surly, disagreeable, ill-humored, grouchy, peevish, touchy, snappish, shirty, churlish, gruff, out of sorts, irritable, waspish, irascible, testy, choleric, cantankerous, crotchety, captious, splenetic; contrary, querulous, intractable. **—Ant. 2** relief, respite; boon, benefit. **3** thoroughbred. **4** write down, add, include. **8** good-humored, good-natured, good-tempered; agreeable, amenable, sweet.

crotchet *n.* quirk, eccentricity, idiosyncrasy, whim, peculiarity, quiddity, vagary, caprice, whimsy, oddity, irregularity, bent; characteristic, mannerism, trait, habit, foible, *Slang* hang-up.

crotchety *adj.* cranky, contrary, fussy, grouchy; eccentric, odd, peculiar, erratic.

crouch *v.* bend, stoop, squat, scrunch down, hunker down, hunch over, *Slang* scrooch down; cower, cringe, shrink, recoil, duck.

crow *v.* **1.** utter the cry of a rooster, cackle, cock-a-doodle-doo. **2.** gloat, boast, brag, strut, swagger, vaunt; *Slang* blow; exult, rejoice, jubilate, triumph, trumpet.

crowd *n.* **1.** throng, multitude, horde, mob, swarm, crush, herd, flock, host, legion; gathering, assemblage, congregation. **2.** set, circle, circle of friends, clique, claque, group, gang, coterie. *—v.* **3.** congregate, flock, swarm, gather, assemble; cluster, mass, herd, throng, huddle, concentrate. **4.** shove, push, press, cram, jam, squeeze, swarm, surge, elbow in. **—Syn. Study. 1** CROWD, MULTITUDE, SWARM, THRONG refer to large numbers of people. CROWD suggests a jostling, uncomfortable, and possibly disorderly company: *A crowd gathered to listen to the speech.* MULTITUDE emphasizes the great number of persons or things but suggests that there is space enough for all: *a multitude of people at the market.* SWARM as used of people is usu. contemptuous, suggesting a moving, restless, often noisy crowd: *A swarm of dirty children played in the street.* THRONG suggests a company that presses together or forward, often with some common aim: *The throng pushed forward to see the cause of the excitement.* **—Ant. 3** disperse, scatter; draw back, draw away, retreat.

crowded *adj.* crammed, jammed, jam-packed, packed, full, filled, mobbed, congested, teeming, swarming, thronged, overflowing. **—Ant.** empty; half-full.

crown *n.* **1.** coronet, tiara, diadem, circlet. **2.** wreath, garland, circlet, chaplet. **3.** royalty, sovereignty, monarchy, royal dominion. **4.** highest part, top, summit, pinnacle, peak, crest, apex, zenith, acme. **5.** top of the head, pate, head; *Slang* noodle, noggin. *—v.* **6.** invest with a crown, give royal power to, put a crown upon. **7.** top, top off, bring to the highest point, climax, complete, cap, fulfill, perfect, round out, reach a peak. **—Ant. 4** bottom, base, foot. **6** dethrone, depose.

crucial *adj.* decisive, critical, determining, significant, momentous, weighty, important, essential, pressing, knotty, urgent; grave, serious.

crude *adj.* **1.** raw, unrefined, unprocessed, unprepared; coarse, rude, clumsy. **2.** uncompleted, incomplete, unfinished, rough, undeveloped, sketchy, imperfect. **3.** vulgar, obscene, unrefined, coarse, tasteless, crass, gross, uncouth, unpolished. **—Syn. Study. 1** See RAW. **—Ant. 1** refined, processed, prepared; fine, fine-grained. **2** final, finished, completed. **3** refined, polished, tasteful, subtle.

cruel *adj.* inhuman, inhumane, sadistic, brutal, vicious, savage, merciless, unmerciful; heartless, pitiless, uncompassionate, unfeeling, hardhearted, ruthless, remorseless, cold-blooded. **—Ant.** humane, benevolent, merciful, compassionate, kind, warmhearted, sympathetic, tender, gentle, mild.

cruise *v.* sail, navigate, float, glide, coast, drift, stream, sweep, skim, scud, travel the bounding main, sail the seas, go by ship, seafare, ply the seas, go down to the sea in ships, sail the ocean blue, voyage.

crumb *n.* scrap, shred, bit, morsel, sliver, minute portion, particle, fragment, speck, grain.

crumble *v.* **1.** break into crumbs, fragment, splinter; crush, grind, pulverize, powder, grate. **2.** decay, disintegrate, fall apart, break up, waste away, wear away, decompose, go to wrack and ruin.

crumple *v.* **1.** wrinkle, rumple, crease, crinkle, crush; pucker, corrugate, crimple. **2.** collapse, give way, cave in, fall, fall to pieces, break up.

crunch *v.* chew noisily, chomp, gnaw, gnash, grind, munch; chew, masticate.

crusade *n.* **1.** often **Crusade.** military expedition against non-Christians. **2.** reform movement, idealistic campaign, movement, drive; rally, mass meeting.

crush *v.* **1.** mash, squash, squeeze, press, compress; crumble, crumple, pulverize, break, shatter, granulate. **2.** hug tightly, hold closely, embrace, enfold, squeeze, press. **3.** subdue, suppress, quash, smash, squash, squelch, put down, quell; overcome, overpower, overwhelm; quench, extinguish.

crusty *adj.* peevish, gruff, shirty, testy, waspish, brusque, sullen, surly, short-tempered, ill-tempered, ill-natured, curt, abrupt, blunt, short, snappish, cranky, splenetic, choleric, irascible, crabby, snippy, snippety. **—Ant.** agreeable, sweet-tempered, good-natured, placid, patient, understanding.

crux *n.* main point, decisive point, essence, essential, basis, heart, core, nub, gist, central issue; *Slang* brass tacks, nitty-gritty.

cry *v.* **1.** weep, shed tears, sob, bawl, blubber, snivel, boohoo; keen, mourn, lament, whimper, moan, wail, howl, groan. **2.** cry out, call, call out, shout, yell, scream, roar, bellow, shriek, howl, screech, exclaim, utter; whoop, cheer; hurrah, huzzah. **3.** beg, plead, implore, importune; appeal, sue, petition. **4.** proclaim, make public, call out, blare, trumpet, hawk, blazon; advertise, promulgate. —*n.* **5.** call, shout, yell, scream, yelp, screech, roar, bellow, shriek, howl, exclamation; outcry, clamor, whoop, cheer, hurrah, huzzah. **6.** plea, entreaty, appeal, supplication, petition, prayer; request, solicitation, adjuration. —**Ant. 1** laugh, snicker, giggle. **2, 5** whisper, murmur, mutter.

crypt *n.* underground chamber, vault, tomb, sepulcher, mausoleum, catacomb.

cryptic *adj.* puzzling, perplexing, enigmatical, mysterious, obscure; ambiguous, vague; secret, hidden, mystical, strange, dark, cabalistic, arcane, occult, esoteric.

cuddle *v.* **1.** hug tenderly, embrace, hold warmly, snuggle, nuzzle, cling to, clasp; caress, fondle, pet. **2.** snuggle, nestle, huddle, lie snug, draw close, curl up.

cudgel *n.* club, bludgeon, shillelagh, truncheon, staff, stick, billy club, blackjack, quarterstaff, baton.

cue *n.* actor's signal; signal, sign, hint, clue, key, intimation, insinuation, suggestion, tip, inkling.

cull *v.* **1.** choose, select, pick out, gather, garner, collect, single out, take, extract, winnow, sift, glean, sort out, separate, divide, set apart, segregate. —*n.* **2.** scrap, reject, discard, castoff, scouring, leaving, second; jetsam, junk, trash, dross, waste.

culminate *v.* **1.** top, top off, climax, cap, crown, complete, consummate, provide the high point of. **2.** conclude, end, end up, result, wind up, terminate, finish.

culpable *adj.* guilty, at fault, liable, blameworthy, blamable, censurable, to blame. —**Ant.** innocent, blameless.

culprit *n.* guilty party, offender; lawbreaker, criminal, felon; malefactor, miscreant, evildoer, sinner, transgressor, wrongdoer.

cult *n.* **1.** religious rites, religious observances; sect, religious group, faction. **2.** devotion, admiration; devotees, admirers, zealots, followers, disciples.

cultivate *v.* **1.** till, farm, raise crops from, garden; plow, hoe, spade, dig, weed; sow, plant, grow. **2.** develop, improve, enrich, enhance, elevate, advance. **3.** acquire, develop, seek, court; ingratiate oneself with, run after. —**Ant. 1** be fallow. **2** impoverish, bankrupt.

cultivation *n.* **1.** agriculture, farming, agronomy, husbandry, gardening; tilling, planting, sowing. **2.** culture, refinement, polish, elevation, gentility, manners, grace, good breeding, good taste.

culture *n.* **1.** art, music, and literature; the arts; good taste, enrichment, enlightenment, learning, accomplishments, erudition, knowledge. **2.** civilization, state of refinement, level of progress.

cultured *adj.* **1.** well-educated, artistically knowledgeable, learned, well-read, erudite, enlightened. **2.** cultivated, sophisticated, refined, polished, accomplished, genteel, elegant, well-bred. —**Ant. 1** uncultured, uncultivated, unenlightened, uneducated. **2** uncultivated, unrefined, unpolished, inelegant, coarse, crass, low-bred, common, vulgar.

cumbersome *adj.* unwieldy, clumsy, cumbrous, unmanageable, awkward, ungainly, bulky, hefty; ponderous. —**Ant.** compact, manageable, wieldy.

cumulative *adj.* accumulative, collective, aggregate, conglomerate, amassed, additive, heaped up, *Informal* piled up.

cunning *n.* **1.** craftiness, slyness, shrewdness, guile, artifice, wiliness, foxiness, artfulness; deviousness, duplicity, deception, deceit, trickery, chicanery. **2.** cleverness, art, craft, skill, dexterity, adroitness, deftness, finesse, subtlety; ability, aptitude, expertness, knack, talent, genius. —*adj.* **3.** shrewd, crafty, sly, artful, canny, ingenious, guileful, wily, foxy, Machiavellian, deceptive, deceitful, devious, shifty, underhand, tricky. —**Ant. 1** sincerity, candor, ingenuousness. **2** clumsiness. **3** ingenuous, artless.

cupboard *n.* kitchen cabinet, cabinet, closet; buffet, sideboard, china closet, storeroom; bureau, chiffonier, armoire, clothespress.

cupidity *n.* greed, avarice, covetousness, graspingness, avidity, acquisitiveness, concupiscence, greediness, rapacity, insatiability, selfishness, rapaciousness, avariciousness.

cur *n.* **1.** mean dog, unfriendly dog; mongrel, mutt, varmint. **2.** blackguard, scoundrel, villain, varlet, rascal, cad, rogue, wretch.

curb *n.* **1.** edge of a sidewalk, curbstone; edge, rim, border, ledge, brink. **2.**

restraint, restriction, control, check, bridle, harness, halter, rein, hindrance, limitation, retardation. —*v.* **3.** restrain, restrict, check, control, bridle, harness; repress, suppress, inhibit, limit, moderate, retard, slow down, slow up, hold back; slacken, decelerate. **—Syn. Study. 3** See CHECK.

curdle *v.* clabber, clot, curd, thicken, coagulate, solidify, congeal; turn, go off, ferment, sour, spoil, go bad; putrefy, putresce, rot, decay, deteriorate.

cure *v.* **1.** restore to health, make well, heal, eradicate sickness from, rid of an illness. **2.** preserve, smoke, dry, salt. —*n.* **3.** remedy, corrective, curative treatment, means of healing, antidote.

curiosity *n.* **1.** inquisitiveness, interest, questioning; prying; *Slang* nosiness. **2.** rare object, rarity, curio, novelty; phenomenon, marvel, wonder, sight, oddity, freak. **—Ant. 1** indifference, apathy, disregard.

curious *adj.* **1.** inquisitive, interested in, eager to learn, anxious to know, inquiring, questioning, searching; nosy, snooping, prying. **2.** unusual, odd, peculiar, bizarre, strange, queer, weird, *Informal* funny; novel, quaint, singular, uncommon, unique, rare. **—Ant. 1** incurious, uninterested, unconcerned, indifferent, apathetic. **2** customary, commonplace, common, usual, familiar, average, everyday.

curl *v.* **1.** form into ringlets, coil, wave; twist, frizz, frizzle, crimp. **2.** coil, curve, swirl, wind, twist, twirl, spiral. —*n.* **3.** ringlet, coil of hair, lock. **4.** coil, spiral, twist, curlicue, wave, corkscrew, scallop.

curmudgeon *n.* grouch, grumbler, crank, gruff person, irritable person, irascible person; *Slang* grump, crab, sourball.

currency *n.* **1.** medium of exchange, legal tender, money; cash, bills, coin, coinage, bank notes, paper money, ready money. **2.** popularity, vogue, acceptance, prevalence, predominance, universality.

current *adj.* **1.** present, present-day, up-to-date, contemporary, modern, existing; popular, prevailing, prevalent, in vogue, in style, du jour; *Slang* now, with-it. —*n.* **2.** flow, stream, tide; draft, flux. **3.** undercurrent, tendency, inclination, drift, trend, *German* zeitgeist; feeling, mood, spirit, atmosphere. **—Ant. 1** past, out-of-date; old-fashioned, out-of-style, outmoded, obsolete, passé, archaic.

curse *n.* **1.** evil spell, evil eye; *Slang* whammy; damnation, execration, malediction, denunciation, anathema, imprecation. **2.** swearing, oath; expletive, profanity, blasphemy, obscenity, *Informal* cuss. **3.** burden, ordeal, affliction, misfortune, trouble, trial, tribulation, bane, annoyance, torment, vexation, plague, scourge, cross, crown of thorns. —*v.* **4.** swear at, swear, utter a profanity, utter a blasphemy, utter an obscenity, *Informal* cuss; damn, blast, denounce, condemn, execrate; invoke evil on, anathematize. **5.** afflict, trouble, burden, torment, vex, plague, scourge. **—Ant. 1, 2** blessing, benediction. **3** joy, boon, benefit; relief, respite. **4** compliment, praise, laud, extol; bless. **5** benefit, relieve, help, aid.

cursory *adj.* quick, hasty, hurried, swift, brief, passing, perfunctory, random, haphazard, casual, offhand, superficial, desultory, careless, inattentive. **—Ant.** slow, careful, painstaking, meticulous, scrupulous, searching, profound, elaborate, minute.

curt *adj.* abrupt, blunt, bluff, brusque, short, terse, summary, peremptory; petulant, snappy, gruff, crusty, rude. **—Syn. Study.** See BLUNT. **—Ant.** warm, friendly, courteous, polite.

curtail *v.* cut short, cut, shorten, pare down, clip, trim; reduce, decrease, diminish, abridge, abbreviate, condense, contract. **—Syn. Study.** See SHORTEN. **—Ant.** lengthen, extend, prolong, elongate, protract, expand.

curve *n.* **1.** bend, turn, crook, arc, arch, bow, curvature, loop. —*v.* **2.** turn, bend, hook, curl, wind, arch, twist, swerve, coil, spiral.

cushion *n.* **1.** pillow, pad, bolster, mat. —*v.* **2.** soften, suppress, damp, dampen, stifle; muffle, quiet, deaden.

custodian *n.* **1.** caretaker, janitor, superintendent, attendant, concierge, watchman. **2.** guardian, keeper, warden; chaperon, duenna.

custody *n.* **1.** guardianship, charge, care, trusteeship, safekeeping, protection, watch; preservation, conservation. **2.** detention, confinement; possession.

custom *n.* **1.** practice, convention, usage, fashion, mode, form, habit. **2.** **customs** duty, import tax, tariff, levy, excise; toll, assessment; national customs department, customhouse. **—Syn. Study.** CUSTOM, HABIT, PRACTICE mean an established way of doing things. CUSTOM, applied to a community or to an individual, implies a more or less permanent way of acting reinforced by tradition and social attitudes: *the custom of giving gifts at Christmas.* HABIT, applied particularly to an individual, implies such repetition of the same action as to develop a natural, spontaneous, or rooted tendency or inclination to perform it: *He has an annoying habit of interrupting the speaker.* PRACTICE applies to a regularly followed procedure or pattern in conducting activities: *It is his practice to verify all statements.* **—Ant. 1** rarity, phenomenon, curiosity.

customary *adj.* usual, habitual, normal, regular, routine, wonted, typical, accustomed, conventional, traditional, general, common, ordinary, everyday. **—Syn. Study.** See USUAL. **—Ant.** unusual, uncommon, rare, exceptional; occasional, infrequent, irregular, sporadic.

customer *n.* patron, shopper, buyer, purchaser; client, habitué.

cut *v.* **1.** lacerate, incise, pierce, gash, slash, hack, nick, lance, slit; slice, carve, saw, chop, dice, cube, mince; divide, section, split, dissect; sever, sunder, rive. **2.** trim, clip, shear; mow, prune, pare, crop, snip, shave. **3.** condense, abridge, contract, abbreviate, pare down, reduce, diminish, curtail, decrease; leave out, delete. **4.** snub, ignore, refuse to recognize, refuse to greet, turn one's back on, give one the cold shoulder. **5.** cross, intersect, bisect, divide, go through, go across, move, change direction. **—*n.* 6.** incision, wound, gash, nick; slit, rent, opening; hollow, furrow, indentation, trench, excavation, channel, passage, course. **7.** piece, portion, share, slice, section, segment, part. **8.** reduction, decrease, abatement, decline, fall, diminution, contraction, shortening, shrinkage, curtailment, lessening. **—Ant. 3** expand, enlarge, increase, lengthen. **4** welcome, greet. **8** increase, rise, surge; expansion, enlargement.

cute *adj.* pretty, dainty, adorable, darling, sweet, precious, beautiful, handsome, attractive, lovable.

cutting *adj.* **1.** piercing, sharp, harsh, stinging, nipping, biting, penetrating, smarting; cold, raw, bitter. **2.** harsh, sharp, caustic, stringent, stinging, scathing, searing, biting, bitter, sarcastic, disparaging, acrimonious, acerbic, derisive. **—Ant. 1** balmy, soothing, pleasant. **2** gratifying, flattering; soothing, consoling, kind, mild.

cycle *n.* series, connected group, progression, sequence, succession, run.

cynic *n.* skeptic, scoffer, misanthrope, faultfinder, misogynist; pessimist. **—Ant.** humanitarian; optimist.

cynical *adj.* misanthropic, misogynic, skeptical, sneering, sardonic, scornful, scoffing, derisive, sarcastic. **—Ant.** philanthropic, humanitarian; hopeful, optimistic; credulous, ingenuous.

czar Also **tsar** *n.* emperor, ruler, potentate, overlord; (*loosely*) monarch, sovereign, caesar, king; despot, tyrant, dictator.

dab *v.* **1.** pat, tap, apply gently. —*n.* **2.** pat, bit, small quantity, smidgen, soupçon; small lump, little chunk. **3.** pat, stroke, tap, light slap.

dabble *v.* **1.** splash, slosh, spatter, sprinkle; play in water; dip in and out of water. **2.** putter, do something superficially, work on something casually, fiddle, flirt with, toy with, *Informal* fool around.

daily *adj.* on each day, day in day out, day by day, from day to day, of each and every day, every weekday; diurnal, everyday, quotidian, circadian, per diem.

dainty *adj.* **1.** delicate, fine, refined, lovely, pretty, beautiful, exquisite; attractive, pleasing, elegant. **2.** fussy, choosy, fastidious, particular; picky. **3.** delicious, choice, tasty, savory. **—Syn. Study. 1** See DELICATE. **—Ant. 1** gross, coarse, vulgar. **2** easily satisfied. **3** bad tasting.

dally *v.* **1.** dawdle, dillydally, trifle, loiter, idle, waste time, fritter away time. **2.** flirt, toy, play, trifle, fool around. **—Syn. Study. 1** See LOITER. **—Ant. 1** hurry, hasten, speed.

dam[1] *n.* **1.** barrier, wall, obstruction, hindrance. —*v.* **2.** block, bar, stop, barricade, hinder, obstruct, impede, inhibit, check, stanch, hold back, confine, stop up, clog, hold in, bridle, restrain, repress, block up, blockade, stuff up, plug, congest, plug up, stopper. **—Ant.** free, loose, release, unleash, let go, let out.

dam[2] *n.* female parent of an animal. **—Ant.** sire.

damage *n.* **1.** injury, harm, hurt, impairment, destruction, despoliation, loss. **2.** cost, compensation for a loss. —*v.* **3.** injure, hurt, harm, mar, impair, ravage. **—Ant. 1** improvement, betterment; reparation. **3** improve, repair, mend, better.

damn *v.* **1.** condemn, blast, criticize, censure, disparage, denounce, bring condemnation on, inveigh against, rail at. **2.** doom, condemn, sentence to hell. **—Ant. 1** commend, praise, laud, applaud, speak well of, declare successful. **2** redeem, bless.

damp *adj.* **1.** moist, wet, wettish, soggy, clammy, sodden, soaked, sopping, dripping. **2.** humid, muggy, dank, wet, rainy, drizzly, foggy, misty, dewy. —*n.* **3.** moisture, humidity, mist; clamminess, mugginess, dankness. **4.** curb, check, discouragement, restraint. —*v.* **5.** check, curb, restrain, hinder, hamper, inhibit; spoil, dash, discourage, depress; reduce, diminish, dull, deaden. **—Ant. 1, 2** dry. **1** watertight. **2** arid, without rain. **3** dryness, aridity, aridness.

dampen *v.* **1.** moisten, wet, wet down; make damp. **2.** See DAMP, SENSE.

damsel *n.* young lady, girl, lass, maiden.

dance *v.* **1.** move the feet and body to music, perform; jig, jiggle, tap, sway, swing, shake, shuffle, wiggle, jerk, slither, slide, undulate, bump and grind. **2.** leap, skip, jump, cavort, bounce, prance, frolic, gambol. —*n.* **3.** rhythmical steps or motions, usu. to music; (*variously*) fox-trot, waltz, Charleston, jitterbug, lindy, two-step, cakewalk, peabody, bunny hop, polka, tango, merengue, samba, conga, mambo, cha-cha, twist, frug, swim, monkey, disco, lambada, quadrille, minuet, mazurka, square dance, Virginia reel, jig, Irish jig, fling, Highland fling, cancan; tap dance, ballet; number, routine; choreography. **4.** dance music, music to dance to. **5.** the art of dancing. **6.** ball, party, cotillion; prom, hop.

dandy *n.* **1.** fop, clotheshorse, beau, coxcomb, fashion plate, man of fashion, fashionista; dude, peacock; sharp dresser. **2.** beauty, beaut; fine thing, something first-rate. —*adj.* **3.** fine, great, excellent, superb; swell, terrific, super, sensational; first-rate, very good. **—Ant. 1** slob, sloppy person. **3** bad, terrible, awful.

danger *n.* peril, risk, hazard, threat, menace, jeopardy, endangerment; exposure to injury, state of being exposed to harm. **—Syn. Study.** DANGER, PERIL, HAZARD imply harm that one may encounter. DANGER is the general word for liability to injury or harm, either near at hand and certain, or remote and doubtful: *secret agents in danger of being killed.* PERIL usually denotes great and imminent danger: *The passengers on the disabled ship were in great peril.* HAZARD suggests a danger that one can often foresee but cannot avoid: *A mountain climber is exposed to many hazards.* **—Ant.** security, safety, immunity, exemption; safeguarding, safeguard, protection.

dangerous *adj.* risky, perilous, hazardous, chancy, unsafe, precarious, treacherous, menacing, threatening; apt to harm, full of risk, *Slang* hairy. **—Ant.** safe, steady, secure; shielded.

dangle *v.* hang, suspend, depend, swing, oscillate, sway, hang down, drag, droop, sag, draggle, trail, hang over, hang out.

dank *adj.* damp, moist, wet; humid, muggy, clammy, sticky, soggy, sodden; chilly, cold.

dapper *adj.* smart, neat, trim, spruce, modish, stylish, sporty, jaunty, natty, well-groomed, *Slang* spiffy.

dappled *adj.* spotted, mottled, flecked, variegated.

dare *v.* **1.** venture, have the courage or nerve. **2.** challenge, defy. —*n.* **3.** challenge, bet; provocation; taunt.

daring *n.* **1.** boldness, courage, bravery; audaciousness, audacity, adventurousness. —*adj.* **2.** bold, gallant, valiant, courageous, brave, adventurous, venturesome, dauntless, undaunted, intrepid; plucky, game; audacious. —**Ant. 1** cowardice, timidity, timorousness. **2** cowardly, uncourageous.

dark *adj.* **1.** black, obscure, opaque, dim, dusky, shadowy, shady; overcast, murky, inky, dingy; sunless; without light. **2.** deeply colored, not light, not pale. **3.** gloomy, dismal, bleak, dreary, joyless, sorrowful, somber; disheartening, discouraging, hopeless. **4.** evil, wicked, sinister. **5.** angry, sullen, somber, gloomy, frowning; forbidding, ominous, bleak, sinister, threatening. **6.** hidden, concealed, secret; obscure, dim, deep. —*n.* **7.** darkness; absence of light, partial absence of light. **8.** nightfall, night, nighttime; evening, twilight, eventide. —**Ant. 1–3, 5, 7, 8** light. **1–3, 5** bright. **1** luminous, lit, illumined, illuminated; dazzling, radiant. **2** pale, fair, white. **3** happy, joyful, hopeful. **5** happy, joyful, cheerful. **6** open, known; clear, lucid, plain, transparent; comprehensible. **7** lightness, brightness. **8** dawn, morning, daytime, daybreak, afternoon.

darken *v.* **1.** dim, blacken, obscure, make dark, make darker, make dim, exclude light from. **2.** color, dye, tint; make less pale or fair; color deeper, shade a deeper hue. **3.** cloud, dispirit, sadden; make despondent, make gloomy, fill with gloom, cast a pall over. —**Ant. 1–3** lighten, brighten. **3** make happy.

darkness *n.* **1.** nighttime, night, dark; evening, twilight, dusk, nightfall, eventide. **2.** dark, blackness, dimness, shade.

darling *n.* **1.** beloved, dear, dearest, sweetheart, love. —*adj.* **2.** beloved, dear, dearest; precious, loved, lovable, adored, cherished; sweet, charming, enchanting, lovely. **3.** cute, attractive; charming, enchanting, captivating; adorable.

dart *n.* **1.** missile, spear, javelin, projectile; small arrow. **2.** dash, rush, sprint, run; spurt, leap, jump, bound, fling; sudden movement. —*v.* **3.** dash, rush, bolt, tear, run, race, sprint; hurry, hasten; spring, leap, jump, bound; flit; fly quickly, move quickly.

dash *v.* **1.** hurl, throw, fling, thrust, slam, smash, shatter, crash, splinter. **2.** dart, bolt, zip, tear, race, rush, run, bound, speed, hurry, hasten. **3.** splash, splatter, spatter. **4.** ruin, spoil; thwart, frustrate, foil; discourage, disappoint, throw a damper on, dampen. —*n.* **5.** dart, bolt, race, rush, run, sprint. **6.** sprint, short race; trial of speed. **7.** pinch, bit, a drop, touch, small addition, slight amount, soupçon. **8.** verve, vigor, spirit, flair, panache, zeal, exuberance, animation, élan, vivacity, energy, *Slang* pizazz, oomph.

dashing *adj.* impetuous, daring, audacious, bold, swashbuckling, gallant, spirited; brave, courageous, fearless, plucky, unafraid.

dastardly *adj.* cowardly, mean, sneaky, base, vile, despicable, atrocious, shameful, low. —**Ant.** gallant, valiant, valorous, brave, courageous.

data *n.* information, facts, figures; documents, evidence, dossier, *Slang* info, dope.

date *n.* **1.** particular point or period of time, day, month, or year. **2.** period, age, era, stage, epoch, historical period. **3.** appointment, engagement, rendezvous, agreement to meet. **4.** escort, companion, partner, *Slang* arm candy. —*v.* **5.** originate, to exist from, bear a date. **6.** put a date on, affix a date to, mark with a date, ascertain the date of, fix the time of. **7.** escort, court, go out on dates with, take out, keep company with.

dated *adj.* **1.** old-fashioned, unfashionable, out-of-date, outmoded, passé, antiquated, obsolete, *Slang* old hat. **2.** showing a date, having a date.

daub *v.* **1.** coat, cover, smear, paint. **2.** smear, smudge, spot, soil, dirty, stain, smirch. —*n.* **3.** blot, blotch, spot, splotch, stain.

daunt *v.* intimidate, dismay, faze, discourage, dishearten, deject, depress, dash, unnerve, subdue, browbeat, cow, abash, menace, threaten; frighten, scare, alarm, affright. —**Ant.** embolden, encourage, cheer, animate, enliven.

dauntless *adj.* fearless, unafraid, bold, courageous, brave, valiant, valorous, heroic, gallant, daring, resolute, stouthearted, undaunted, *Slang* gutsy. —**Ant.** cowardly, fearful, afraid, apprehensive, fainthearted, irresolute.

dawdle *v.* dally, dillydally, idle, loiter, loaf, delay; procrastinate; putter around, loll around, fool around; kill time, waste time, fritter away time. —**Syn. Study.**

See LOITER. —**Ant.** hurry, hasten, speed.

dawn *n.* **1.** daybreak, sunrise, sunup, daylight, dawning. **2.** beginning, commencement, birth, rise, inception, origin, advent, start, emergence, unfolding; first appearance; early development. —*v.* **3.** begin to grow light in the morning. **4.** begin, appear, rise, commence; develop, unfold, emerge. **5.** occur, strike, come to one's mind, begin to see or understand, begin to make an impression.

day *n.* **1.** time between sunrise and sunset, from dawn to dusk; period of 12 daylight hours; period of 24 hours. **2.** date; particular day. **3.** heyday, period, time, epoch, age; period of ascendancy. **4.** workday, period of activity. **5.** day's journey, distance that can be traveled in a day. —**Ant. 1** night, nighttime.

daybreak *n.* dawn, break of day; sunrise, sunup.

daydream *v.* **1.** muse, imagine, fantasize, fancy; wool-gather, dream. —*n.* **2.** fantasy, dream, reverie, pipe dream, castle in the air.

daylight *n.* **1.** sunlight, sunshine; light of day. **2.** daytime, day; the period between sunrise and sunset, the period between dawn and dusk, the daylight hours, the period of 12 daylight hours. **3.** dawn, daybreak, crack of dawn, sunrise, sunup, morning; beginning of day. **4.** public attention, full view; openness.

daze *v.* **1.** stun, shock, stupefy; stagger, confuse, bewilder, disorient, discombobulate; numb, benumb. **2.** amaze, astound, astonish, surprise, dazzle, startle, stun, flabbergast, *Slang* blow one's mind; excite, electrify. —*n.* **3.** stupor, muddle, shock, bewilderment; astonishment, surprise.

dazzle *v.* **1.** daze, blind, confuse, blur; blind temporarily, as with strong light; dim the vision. **2.** awe, overawe, overwhelm, overpower; excite, electrify; impress greatly.

dead *adj.* **1.** deceased, expired, perished, lifeless; no longer living, having no life. **2.** lifeless, inorganic, inanimate; incapable of life; devoid of life, having no life. **3.** defunct, extinct; obsolete; no longer in use. **4.** inoperative, inactive; not working, not responsive; out of operation. **5.** dull, lackluster, unexciting, vapid, flat, insipid. **6.** exact, unerring, precise. **7.** unproductive, ineffectual, unused, useless; unemployed, unprofitable, stagnant. **8.** total, complete, utter, absolute, thorough, entire. **9.** exhausted, tired, spent; worn-out, *Slang* beat. —*n.* **10.** midst, depth, middle; period of greatest darkness, cold, quiet, or gloom. **11. the dead.** dead people; those who have died. —*adv.* **12.** abruptly, suddenly. **13.** absolutely; completely, entirely, utterly. —**Ant. 1** alive, living, live, animate; breathing. **2** living, animate. **3** existing, living, in use. **4** working, responsive, operative, operating, active, in motion; alive. **5** lively, vivacious, exciting. **6** inaccurate, inexact. **7** productive, effective, useful. **8** partial, incomplete. **9** active, energetic.

deaden *v.* blunt, dull, diminish, subdue, moderate, mitigate; abate, lessen, weaken; soothe, assuage, alleviate; numb, drug, anesthetize, dope; muffle, smother, mute.

deadlock *n.* standstill; standoff, impasse, stalemate.

deadly *adj.* **1.** fatal, lethal, mortal, death-dealing, deathly; malignant; destructive, baneful. **2.** dangerous enough to kill, destroy, or harm; relentless, unrelenting, implacable. **3.** deathlike, cadaverous, ghostly, ashen, pallid, wan. **4.** excessive, extreme, inordinate; very great; undue. **5.** boring, dull, tedious, wearisome, tiresome; terrible, awful, dreadful. —*adv.* **6.** completely, entirely, fully, thoroughly, totally; terribly, awfully, horribly. —**Syn. Study. 1** See FATAL. —**Ant. 1** vital, wholesome, life-giving, benign, harmless. **2** relenting, appeasable, conciliatory, placable. **3** healthy, glowing. **5** exciting.

deal *v.* **1.** treat, handle, oversee; attend to, see to, take care of, cope with, dispose of. **2.** concern, consider; have to do with, be occupied with. **3.** act, behave. **4.** trade, market, buy and sell; do business. **5.** give, deliver, administer. **6.** distribute, dispense, apportion, give out, mete out, parcel out, dole out. —*n.* **7.** distribution, apportionment, round, hand, single game. **8.** bargain, agreement, arrangement. —**Ant. 1** ignore, overlook, disregard; neglect, leave undone. **6** receive, gather, collect, take back.

dealing *n.* **1.** Usu. **dealings.** relations, transactions, traffic, trade; business. **2.** treatment, practice; method or manner of conduct.

dear *adj.* **1.** precious, beloved, loved, cherished, much loved, fondly regarded, favorite; esteemed, respected, highly regarded (used in a salutation: "Dear Dr. Jones"). **2.** expensive, costly, high-priced; at a premium. —*n.* **3.** darling, sweetheart, love, angel, good person, kind person, generous person. —**Ant. 1** hated, abhorred, disliked. **2** inexpensive, cheap, low-priced; common; worthless.

dearth *n.* scarcity, lack, shortage, paucity; deficiency; insufficient supply. —**Ant.** abundance, superabundance, plethora, plenty; adequate supply.

death *n.* **1.** dying, demise, passing, departure, decease, expiration; loss of life. **2. Death.** grim reaper, angel of death. **—Ant. 1** life; birth, beginning, rise, growth.

deathless *adj.* immortal, eternal, perpetual, everlasting, not subject to death. **—Ant.** mortal; perishable; transitory; passing.

deathly *adj.* **1.** deathlike, resembling death. **2.** extreme, terrible, intense, overwhelming. *—adv.* **3.** extremely, very. **—Ant. 1** lifelike, lively.

debacle *n.* disaster, catastrophe, devastation, ruination, collapse, overthrow, rout, vanquishment, cataclysm, havoc, ruin, downfall, bankruptcy, dissolution, disintegration, wreck, breakdown. **—Ant.** success, victory, conquest, achievement, triumph.

debase *v.* lower, degrade, defile, disgrace, dishonor; befoul, desecrate, corrupt, deteriorate; adulterate; impair the worth of, reduce the quality of. **—Ant.** enhance, elevate, uplift, improve, heighten.

debatable *adj.* questionable, doubtful, dubious, undecided, uncertain, unsure; problematical, arguable, disputable; *Informal* iffy. **—Ant.** certain, sure, settled, decided, beyond question.

debate *n.* **1.** argument, discussion, dispute; formal discussion of opposing points of view. **2.** deliberation, consideration, reflection, meditation, cogitation. *—v.* **3.** argue, dispute, discuss, *Slang* hash over. **4.** deliberate, consider, reflect, ponder, think about, meditate upon, cogitate.

debauched *adj.* depraved, corrupted, debased, perverted, licentious, lascivious, lewd, libidinous, lecherous, wanton, vitiated, led astray, dissipated, dissolute, immoral, profligate, degraded. **—Ant.** pure, moral, good, saintly, virtuous, high-minded.

debauchery *n.* excess, intemperance, immoderation, self-indulgence, dissipation.

debilitate *v.* weaken, devitalize, enervate; make feeble, deprive of strength, wear out. **—Ant.** strengthen, invigorate, energize, vitalize; rejuvenate, renew, restore.

debility *n.* weakness, infirmity, feebleness, asthenia, frailty, invalidism, prostration, decrepitude, sickliness, senility; lassitude, exhaustion, fatigue, enervation. **—Ant.** vigor, stamina, robustness, vitality, energy.

debonair *adj.* **1.** charming, urbane, gracious, suave; refined, elegant, well-bred, sophisticated, genteel. **2.** carefree, lighthearted, jaunty, dapper, buoyant, sprightly, free and easy. **—Ant. 1** awkward, rude, gauche, uncivil. **2** serious, gloomy.

debris *n.* rubble, trash, junk, rubbish, scrap, detritus, clutter, wreckage, litter, ruins, waste, dregs, garbage, dross, fragments, shards; *Slang* dreck, crap.

debt *n.* liability, obligation, debit, bill, arrears, deferred payment; that which is owed.

debunk *v.* expose, uncover, bare, uncloak, deflate, show up, strip, unmask, disparage, demystify, demythologize; ridicule, satirize, burlesque, lampoon; *Slang* send up, take off.

debut Also **début** *n.* **1.** first public appearance. **2.** coming out, presentation, formal introduction into society.

decadence *n.* decline, deterioration, decay, corruption, immorality, degeneration, degeneracy, debasement.

decadent *adj.* corrupt, immoral, decaying, degenerate, debased, depraved, debauched, perverse, perverted, dissolute.

decamp *v.* **1.** depart from camp, break camp; move off, march off. **2.** depart suddenly, leave quickly or secretly, make off quickly, run away, sneak off, take off.

decay *v.* **1.** decompose, disintegrate, rot, spoil, putrefy; corrode. *—n.* **2.** decomposition, rot, rotting, putrefaction; spoiling. **—Syn. Study.** DECAY, DECOMPOSE, DISINTEGRATE, ROT imply a deterioration or falling away from a sound condition. DECAY implies either entire or partial deterioration by progressive natural changes: *Teeth decay.* DECOMPOSE suggests the reducing of a substance to its component elements: *Moisture makes some chemical compounds decompose.* DISINTEGRATE emphasizes the breaking up, going to pieces, or wearing away of anything, so that its original wholeness is impaired: *Rocks disintegrate.* ROT is applied esp. to decaying vegetable matter, which may or may not emit offensive odors: *Potatoes rot.* **—Ant. 1** flourish, flower, expand, grow, increase.

deceased *adj.* See DEAD.

deceit *n.* deception, cheating, fraud, fraudulence, double-dealing; duplicity, dishonesty, deceitfulness, trickiness, trickery, guile, underhandedness; misrepresentation. **—Syn. Study.** DECEIT, FRAUD, DUPLICITY, GUILE refer either to practices designed to mislead or to the qualities in a person that prompt such behavior. DECEIT is intentional concealment or misrepresentation of the truth: *Consumers are often victims of deceit.* FRAUD refers to deceit or trickery by which one may derive benefit at another's expense; it often suggests illegal or dishonest practices: *an advertiser convicted of fraud.* DUPLICITY is doing the opposite of what one says or pretends to do; it suggests hypocrisy or pretense: *the duplicity of a friend who does not keep a secret.* GUILE is crafty or cunning deceit; it suggests subtle but treacherous tactics: *The agent used guile to gain access to the documents.* **—Ant.** honesty, frankness, sincerity, openness, candor, forthrightness; truthfulness; fair dealing.

deceitful *adj.* untrustworthy, insincere, hypocritical; underhanded, false, dishonest, deceptive, treacherous; sneaky, duplicitous, double-dealing; tricky, cunning, crafty.

deceive *v.* mislead, delude, trick, fool, *Slang* con, put on; cheat, swindle, defraud, victimize. **—Syn. Study.** See CHEAT. **—Ant.** enlighten; guide; tell the truth to, be true to, be honest to.

decency *n.* propriety, decorum; respectability, modesty, appropriateness; quality of being decent. **—Ant.** indecency.

decent *adj.* **1.** proper, suitable, fitting, appropriate; seemly, correct. **2.** fair; fairly attractive. **3.** adequate, satisfactory, acceptable; passable, fair; ample, sufficient, reasonably satisfying. **4.** courteous, accommodating, obliging, gracious, nice. **—Ant. 1** improper, unsuitable, inappropriate, unseemly, incorrect, unbecoming; immodest, indecent, obscene, lewd. **3** inadequate, unsatisfactory, unfair, intolerable. **4** awkward, gauche, inept, maladroit, clumsy, crude; discourteous.

deception *n.* **1.** deceit, deceitfulness, deceptiveness, fraud, fraudulence; trickery, trickiness; duplicity, insincerity, double-dealing, treachery; cunning. **2.** trick, artifice, illusion. **—Ant. 1** candor, honesty, sincerity, truthfulness.

deceptive *adj.* misleading, dishonest, deceitful, fraudulent, *Informal* phony. **—Ant.** truthful, honest, trustworthy.

decide *v.* **1.** determine, resolve, settle; choose, elect; make up one's mind. **2.** settle, decree, rule; judge; come to a decision, make a decision. **—Syn. Study. 1** DECIDE, DETERMINE, RESOLVE imply settling something in dispute or doubt. To DECIDE is to make up one's mind after consideration: *I decided to go to the party.* To DETERMINE is to settle after investigation or observation: *It is difficult to determine the best course of action.* To RESOLVE is to settle conclusively with firmness of purpose: *She resolved to ask for a promotion.* **—Ant. 1** vacillate, waver, hesitate, falter, fluctuate.

decided *adj.* **1.** clear-cut, certain, unquestionable, unmistakable, definite, indisputable; beyond all question. **2.** determined, decisive, definite, unhesitating, unwavering, resolute, deliberate, emphatic, assertive, firm, strong-willed. **—Ant. 1** dubious, doubtful, questionable, ambiguous. **2** undetermined, indecisive, hesitating, wavering, irresolute, weak, weak-willed.

decipher *v.* decode, decrypt, cryptanalyze, translate, construe, explain, render, interpret, deduce, puzzle out, figure out, unravel, untangle, solve, make out, *Slang* dope out.

decision *n.* **1.** conclusion, judgment, verdict; resolution; determination; result arrived at after consideration. **2.** ruling, verdict, finding, outcome, decree; pronouncement by a court. **3.** determination, decisiveness, decidedness, resolution, resoluteness, resolve, purpose, purposefulness. **—Ant. 3** indecision, uncertainty, vacillation, vagueness.

decisive *adj.* **1.** conclusive, undeniable, indisputable, final, convincing, definitive. **2.** resolute, determined, decided, positive, definite, absolute; firm. **—Ant. 1** inconclusive, disputable, dubious, moot. **2** indecisive, irresolute, wavering, fluctuating; hesitant, reluctant.

deck *v.* decorate, adorn, dress, clothe, garb, apparel, accouter, outfit, array, bedeck, ornament, trim, embellish, festoon, garnish, furbish, beautify, enrich, bedizen, deck out, prank, spruce up, gussy up, doll up, tog out. **—Ant.** strip, divest, denude, uncover, expose, lay bare.

declaim *v.* **1.** orate, recite, utter aloud in rhetorical manner, make a formal speech, sermonize, pontificate. **2.** rail, inveigh.

declaration *n.* **1.** statement, affirmation; attestation, testimony, deposition; avowal, acknowledgment, assertion. **2.** announcement, proclamation; notification, notice, publication, document. **—Ant. 1** denial; disavowal, retraction.

declare *v.* **1.** proclaim, pronounce, announce. **2.** state, utter; affirm, assert, aver, asseverate, profess. **3.** reveal, show, express, give evidence of. **—Syn. Study. 2** DECLARE, AFFIRM, ASSERT imply making something known emphatically, openly, or formally. To DECLARE is to make known, sometimes in the face of actual or potential contradiction: *to declare someone the winner of a contest.* TO AFFIRM is to make a statement based on one's reputation for knowledge or veracity, or so related to a generally recognized truth that denial is not likely: *to affirm the necessity of high standards.* To ASSERT is to state boldly, usu. without other proof than personal authority or conviction: *to assert that the climate is changing.* **—Ant. 1** suppress, withhold. **2** deny, controvert. **3** hide, conceal.

decline *v.* **1.** refuse, reject, eschew, spurn; fail to accept, turn down, balk at. **2.** slope downward, incline downward, slope down. **3.** weaken, fail, flag, sink, deteriorate, worsen, *Slang* tank, go south; ebb, wane, diminish, dwindle, decrease, lessen. —*n.* **4.** downgrade, declivity, drop; downward incline, downward slope. **5.** downfall, deterioration, decay. **6.** slump, downswing, downfall, downward tendency. **7.** last part, period close to the end. **—Syn. Study. 1** See REFUSE. **—Ant. 1** accept, consent. **2** rise. **3** improve, increase, strengthen. **5, 6** rise, advancement, improvement. **7** first part.

decompose *v.* **1.** rot, decay, putrefy, spoil; disintegrate, go to pieces. **2.** separate; break up, disintegrate, break down. **—Syn. Study.** See DECAY.

decontaminate *v.* purify, sterilize, disinfect. **—Ant.** contaminate, infect.

decor, décor *n.* decoration, ornamentation; style of decorating.

decorate *v.* **1.** ornament, adorn, beautify, bedeck, deck, array, trim, garnish, embellish, festoon. **2.** honor; award a decoration to, confer distinction upon.

decoration *n.* **1.** adornment, ornamentation, beautification, embellishment. **2.** ornament, ornamentation, trimming, trim, embellishment, adornment, garnish. **3.** medal, award, emblem, ribbon, badge.

decorous *adj.* proper, correct, suitable, dignified, becoming, seemly, fit, appropriate; decent, polite, mannerly, respectful. **—Ant.** improper, unfit, unbecoming, unsuitable, undignified.

decorum *n.* propriety, politeness; tact, gentility, respectability, dignity, taste; good form. **—Ant.** impropriety, inappropriate behavior, bad manners.

decoy *n.* **1.** enticement, bait, lure, snare, inducement; smoke screen, *Slang* plant, come-on; deceptive stratagem. —*v.* **2.** bait, entice, lure, snare, allure; attract by some deceptive device.

decrease *v.* **1.** diminish, lessen, reduce, dwindle, shrink, drop, subside, de-escalate; slacken, ease, abate, taper, decline. —*n.* **2.** reduction, lessening, loss, decline, abatement, diminution, dwindling, cutback, de-escalation; fall-off. **—Syn. Study. 1** DECREASE, DIMINISH, DWINDLE, SHRINK imply becoming smaller or less in amount. DECREASE commonly implies a sustained reduction in stages, esp. of bulk, size, volume, or quantity, often from some imperceptible cause or inherent process: *The swelling decreased daily.* DIMINISH usu. implies the action of some external cause that keeps taking away: *Disease caused the number of troops to diminish steadily.* DWINDLE implies an undesirable reduction by degrees, resulting in attenuation: *His followers dwindled to a mere handful.* SHRINK esp. implies contraction through an inherent property under specific conditions: *Many fabrics shrink in hot water.* **—Ant. 1** increase, augment, enlarge, extend, lengthen, expand. **2** growth, extension, expansion, swelling.

decree *n.* **1.** order, command, proclamation, dictum, statute, law, edict, ruling, mandate. —*v.* **2.** order, authorize, command, proclaim.

decrepit *adj.* broken-down, dilapidated, battered, rickety.

decry *v.* criticize, denounce, rail against, condemn; denigrate, disparage, deprecate, censure. **—Syn. Study.** DECRY, DENIGRATE, DEPRECATE involve the expression of censure or disapproval. DECRY means to denounce or to express public disapproval of: *to decry all forms of discrimination.* DENIGRATE means to defame or to sully the reputation or character of: *to denigrate the memory of a ruler.* DEPRECATE means to express regretful disapproval of or to plead against: *to deprecate a new policy.* **—Ant.** extol, acclaim, laud, commend, praise.

dedicate *v.* **1.** devote, commit, pledge; give completely, consecrate. **2.** launch, present; devote to a special use. **3.** inscribe, address. **—Syn. Study. 1** See DEVOTE.

dedication *n.* **1.** ceremony or act of dedicating for a specific use. **2.** devotion, devotedness, commitment. **3.** prefatory inscription or address.

deduce *v.* conclude, reason, gather, infer, comprehend, understand.

deduct *v.* subtract, remove, take, withdraw; decrease by, take from. **—Ant.** add, enlarge, amplify; add to.

deduction *n.* **1.** conclusion, inference, assumption, presumption, judgment, supposition, interpretation, analysis, calculation; understanding, comprehension, reflection, guess, speculation, consideration. **2.** reduction, discount, markdown, rebate, concession, abatement, rollback, allowance, exemption, subtraction, credit. **—Ant. 2** increase, addition, increment, raise, appreciation.

deed *n.* **1.** act, action, feat, achievement, accomplishment; effort. **2.** legal document showing ownership of property.

deem *v.* think, believe, judge, regard, consider, hold, view.

deep *adj.* **1.** of great depth, far below the surface, extending far downward. **2.** far in or back, extending inward from front to back. **3.** intense, profound, extreme. **4.** absorbed, involved, immersed, engrossed; lost. **5.** intelligent, astute, sagacious, discerning, wise, learned; profound, philosophical. **6.** dark, strong, intense; rich, vivid. **7.** resonant, sonorous; low in pitch, not high, not sharp. —*n.* **8.** ocean, sea. **9.** midst; inmost part, part of greatest intensity. —*adv.* **10.** deeply; far down. **11.** far, late. —**Ant. 1, 2** shallow. **3** light. **4** uninvolved. **5** superficial; slow. **6** light, pale, faded; dull. **7** high, sharp; light. **9** shallowest part.

deeply *adv.* **1.** deep; far below the surface, far down. **2.** greatly, profoundly, intensely; passionately; acutely; completely, thoroughly, entirely. **3.** far on in time or place. **4.** resonantly, sonorously; with a deep tone, at a low pitch. **5.** vividly, intensely, richly. **6.** seriously, gravely; over one's head. —**Ant. 1** shallowly. **2** hardly, very little. **4** with a high tone, at a high pitch. **5** lightly, dully. **6** not seriously.

deface *v.* mar, damage, disfigure, impair; spoil, injure, bruise, mark, scar. —**Ant.** beautify; improve the looks of.

de facto 1. actually, really; in fact. **2.** actual, real, in existence.

defamation *n.* slander, libel, disparagement, calumny, vilification.

defamatory *adj.* libelous, slanderous, disparaging, derogatory, calumnious, vilifying.

defame *v.* slander, libel, malign, disparage, discredit, denigrate, degrade, derogate, vilify, calumniate; speak ill of, attack the good reputation of. —**Ant.** praise, laud, applaud, extol.

default *n.* **1.** failure to appear or act. **2.** nonpayment; failure to pay.

defeat *v.* **1.** conquer, overcome, overthrow, rout, vanquish, overpower, overwhelm, subdue, quell, crush, trounce, *Slang* shellac, cream; gain a victory over an opponent, prevail over. **2.** confound, baffle, thwart, foil, frustrate; elude, get the better of. —*n.* **3.** setback, loss of a contest, failure to win. **4.** frustration, disappointment, thwarting; loss. —**Syn. Study. 1** DEFEAT, CONQUER, OVERCOME, SUBDUE imply gaining victory or control over an opponent. DEFEAT usu. means to beat or frustrate in a single contest or conflict: *Confederate forces were defeated at Gettysburg.* CONQUER means to finally gain control over by physical, moral, or mental force, usu. after long effort: *to conquer poverty; to conquer a nation.* OVERCOME emphasizes perseverance and the surmounting of difficulties: *to overcome opposition; to overcome a bad habit.* SUBDUE means to conquer so completely that resistance is broken: *to subdue a rebellious spirit.* —**Ant. 1** lose, succumb, fall; surrender, capitulate, bow, yield, submit, give in. **3** success, triumph, victory.

defect *n.* **1.** fault, flaw, imperfection; blemish, spot, blotch, stain; scar, crack, break. **2.** deficiency, omission, incompleteness, shortcoming, fault, default; weakness, fraility, failing; foible, weak point. —*v.* **3.** desert or forsake (one's country), leave or quit (one's land for another) without permission. —**Syn. Study. 1** DEFECT, FLAW, BLEMISH refer to faults, both literal and figurative, that detract from perfection. DEFECT is the general word for any kind of shortcoming, imperfection, or deficiency, whether hidden or visible: *a birth defect; a defect in a plan.* A FLAW is usu. a structural defect or weakness that mars the quality or effectiveness: *a flaw in a diamond.* A BLEMISH is usu. a surface defect that mars the appearance; it is also used of a moral fault: *a skin blemish; a blemish on his reputation.* —**Ant. 1** perfection, completeness. **2** strength, forte.

defective *adj.* **1.** faulty, imperfect, lacking, deficient, flawed, impaired, inadequate, insufficient, wanting, broken; out of order, inoperative. **2.** abnormal; subnormal; lacking in normal development. —**Ant. 1** perfect, adequate; intact, entire, whole. **2** normal.

defend *v.* **1.** protect, preserve; secure, shield, shelter, guard, safeguard; keep safe, watch over. **2.** uphold, sustain, support, maintain; endorse, advocate, champion; stand by.

defense *n.* **1.** protection, preservation, security, safeguard, guard; maintenance; care, safekeeping, custody. **2.** fortification, stronghold, barricade; means of defending. **3.** upholding, justification, support, advocacy. **4.** the defendant(s) and their counsel in a legal situation. **5.** the side of a team which tries to prevent the other team from scoring. —**Ant. 4** prosecution. **5** offense.

defensible *adj.* justifiable, warrantable, proper, valid, suitable, fit, tenable, sensible, vindicable, allowable, excusable, admissible, supportable, pardonable, forgivable, permissible, condonable. —**Ant.** unsound, senseless, unwarranted, unjustifiable, inexcusable.

defer[1] *v.* delay, postpone, table, shelve, suspend, put off. —**Syn. Study.** DEFER, DELAY, POSTPONE imply keeping something from occurring until a future time. To DEFER is to decide to do something at a more convenient time in the future; it often suggests avoidance: *to defer making a payment.* DELAY is sometimes equivalent to DEFER, but it usu. suggests a hindrance, obstacle, or dilatory tactic: *Completion of the building was delayed by bad weather.* To POSTPONE is to put off to a particular time in the future, often to wait for new information or developments: *to postpone a trial.* **—Ant.** expedite.

defer[2] *v.* yield, submit, obey, capitulate, accede; respect; give in; pay respect to. **—Ant.** disobey, disrespect.

deference *n.* consideration, respect, reverence, honor, esteem, regard; obedience, capitulation. **—Ant.** disrespect, contempt; defiance, disobedience.

deferential *adj.* considerate, respectful, courteous, civil, polite, reverential, reverent, regardful; dutiful, obedient, submissive, acquiescent.

deferment Also **deferral** *n.* postponement, delay, extension, stay.

defiance *n.* disobedience, rebelliousness, rebellion, obstinacy, hostility.

defiant *adj.* rebellious, disobedient, provocative; aggressive, bold; truculent. **—Ant.** meek, timid; obedient, yielding, submissive.

deficiency *n.* **1.** shortage, insufficiency, inadequacy. **2.** flaw, defect, imperfection, failing, frailty, shortcoming, weakness. **—Ant. 1** sufficiency, adequacy, abundance.

deficient *adj.* **1.** lacking, inadequate, challenged, insufficient, short on. **2.** flawed, defective, inferior, substandard, weak, unsatisfactory. **—Ant. 1** sufficient, adequate. **2** up to par.

deficit *n.* shortage, shortfall, deficiency.

defile *v.* **1.** dirty, soil, befoul, besmirch, spoil, stain, smear, taint, tarnish, dishonor, debase, disgrace, degrade. **2.** desecrate, profane; treat sacrilegiously. **—Ant. 1** honor. **2** hallow, consecrate, sanctify.

define *v.* **1.** state the meaning of. **2.** specify, describe, state, designate, delineate; spell out, explain, clarify. **3.** delineate. **—Ant. 3** obscure, hide, conceal, camouflage.

definite *adj.* **1.** precise, exact, fixed, set. **2.** sure, positive, certain; clear-cut. **—Ant. 1, 2** indefinite, undetermined, indeterminate, unclear, uncertain.

definitely *adv.* doubtless, indubitably, unquestionably, absolutely, undeniably, surely, certainly, unequivocally, assuredly, positively, inescapably, categorically, unavoidably, incontrovertibly, expressly, explicitly, decisively. **—Ant.** perhaps, maybe, possibly, potentially, plausibly.

definition *n.* **1.** statement of meaning. **2.** description, as of nature, purpose, limits, etc. **3.** clarity, distinctiveness.

definitive *adj.* complete, reliable, conclusive, decisive, perfect, consummate; exact, decided. **—Ant.** incomplete, unreliable, inconclusive; imperfect, inexact.

deflect *v.* divert, swerve; cause to run aside, alter the course.

deform *v.* mar, disfigure, distort, contort, twist; mangle, maim; make ugly.

deformity *n.* deformation, malformation.

defraud *v.* cheat, bilk, fleece, swindle, rook, scam, *Slang* con, rip off.

deft *adj.* skillful, expert; dexterous, adroit, able, apt; quick, sure. **—Syn. Study.** See DEXTEROUS. **—Ant.** unskillful, inexpert, maladroit, gauche, inept; slow, unsure.

defunct *adj.* extinct, dead; nonfunctioning, nonoperating. **—Ant.** alive, live, living; in force, in vigor; in use, operating, effective.

defy *v.* **1.** challenge, confront, resist, stand up to, oppose; disregard, disdain, spurn. **2.** resist, withstand; stand up under. **—Ant. 1, 2** encourage. **1** support, help.

degenerate *v.* **1.** deteriorate, disintegrate, worsen, decline, retrograde, backslide, revert, go downhill, sink, go to pot, decay, rot, hit the skids, hit rock bottom, fall on evil days, retrogress. *—adj.* **2.** debased, dissolute, depraved, decadent, perverted, base, profligate, debauched, immoral, corrupt, degraded. **—Ant. 1** improve, progress, flourish, advance, develop. **2** virtuous, moral, upright, ethical.

degradation *n.* humiliation, disgrace. **—Ant.** exaltation; honor, dignity, uprightness.

degrade *v.* **1.** demote, lower, downgrade, lower in rank. **2.** lower, shame, debase, dishonor, disgrace, humble, humiliate; corrupt; bring contempt upon. **—Syn. Study. 2** See HUMBLE. **—Ant. 1** promote, elevate, lift in rank. **2** dignify.

degree *n.* **1.** step, grade, mark, point; phase, stage. **2.** level, order, grade. **3.** division, interval, unit.

deign *v.* stoop, condescend, think fit, consent, deem; see fit.

deity *n.* god, God, supreme being, goddess, divinity, divine being, godhead, immortal, *Latin* deus, idol, pagan god, moon goddess, sun god, sea god, Olympian, Olympic god.

dejected *adj.* depressed, downhearted, low, disheartened, despondent, desolate, disconsolate, down; sorrowful, sad, unhappy, discouraged, doleful, dispirited, spiritless, low-spirited, blue. **—Ant.** happy, elated, joyous, lighthearted, carefree; encouraged, cheerful, blithe.

delay *v.* **1.** postpone, defer, suspend; retard; shelve, table, put off. **2.** detain; hinder, impede; slow, check, suspend; inhibit, hamper, obstruct; hold up, keep back. **3.** procrastinate, dawdle, tarry, linger. *—n.* **4.** loitering, tarrying, lingering, dawdling. **5.** postponement, deferment, suspension, prolongation, stay, reprieve. **6.** stoppage, slowing; hindrance to progress. **—Syn. Study. 1** See DEFER. **—Ant. 1–3** expedite, hasten, speed, hurry. **4** progress without hindrance.

delectable *adj.* delightful, enjoyable, pleasurable, pleasant, agreeable, gratifying; delicious. **—Ant.** offensive, repulsive, disagreeable, revolting; distasteful.

delegate *n.* **1.** representative, agent, deputy, envoy, proxy. *—v.* **2.** designate, name, authorize; appoint as a representative. **3.** entrust, assign, give, give over, charge, transfer; commit to the care of, commission.

delegation *n.* **1.** commissioning, entrustment, authorization; designation; act of delegating. **2.** body of delegates, legation.

delete *v.* remove; cut, cancel, erase; take out, strike out, omit, leave out.

deleterious *adj.* harmful, hurtful, detrimental; dangerous, destructive, ruinous, injurious. **—Ant.** beneficial; healthy, healthful, helpful, advantageous.

deliberate *adj.* **1.** intentional, premeditated, planned, prearranged, purposeful, express; willful, voluntary; calculated. **2.** careful, considered, circumspect, cautious, wary, prudent, thoughtful. **3.** leisurely, slow, easy, unhurried, slow-paced; measured, gradual. *—v.* **4.** examine, consider, weigh; meditate, contemplate, cogitate; mull over, reason out. **5.** confer, debate, discuss; talk over. **—Syn. Study. 1** DELIBERATE, INTENTIONAL, VOLUNTARY refer to something not happening by chance. DELIBERATE is applied to what is done not hastily but with full realization of what one is doing: *a deliberate attempt to evade justice.* INTENTIONAL is applied to what is definitely intended or done on purpose: *an intentional omission.* VOLUNTARY is applied to what is done by a definite exercise of the will and not because of outside pressures: *a voluntary enlistment.* **3** See SLOW. **—Ant. 1, 2** impulsive, rash, impetuous, sudden, hasty. **3** fast, hurried.

deliberation *n.* **1.** careful consideration before decision. **2.** discussion, conference, debate. **3.** care, carefulness, circumspection, steadiness. **4.** forethought, premeditation, calculation, distinct intention, conscious purpose.

delicacy *n.* **1.** fineness, exquisiteness, elegance, softness, smoothness, lightness. **2.** precision, perfection, accuracy; fine workmanship, savoir-faire. **3.** choice food, something pleasing to the palate. **4.** tact, taste, discrimination; consideration; sensitiveness, sensitivity, sensibility. **5.** weakness, frailness, frailty, fragility, unsoundness. **—Ant. 1, 2** coarseness, roughness, inelegance, grossness. **4** insensitiveness, insensibility, inconsideration, rudeness. **5** strength, vigor, vitality; energy.

delicate *adj.* **1.** fine, dainty, exquisite, elegant. **2.** breakable, fragile, frail, flimsy, perishable; dainty. **3.** frail, feeble, debilitated, weakened; infirm, unwell, sickly, ailing. **4.** palatable, savory, delicious, appetizing, luscious, toothsome. **5.** soft, muted, subdued. **6.** exquisite, minute, detailed. **7.** tactful, tasteful, diplomatic, careful, sensitive, fastidious, scrupulous, refined. **8.** touchy, ticklish, sensitive; difficult, precarious. **—Syn. Study. 1** DELICATE, DAINTY, EXQUISITE imply beauty or subtle refinement such as might belong in rich surroundings. DELICATE suggests something fragile, soft, light, or fine: *a delicate carving.* DAINTY suggests a smallness, gracefulness, and beauty that forbids rough handling: *a dainty handkerchief;* of persons, it refers to fastidious sensibilities: *a dainty eater.* EXQUISITE suggests an outstanding beauty and elegance that appeals to the most refined taste: *an exquisite diamond ring.* **—Ant. 1** coarse, crude, rough, inelegant, gross. **2** unbreakable, strong. **3** strong, healthy, well; good. **4** unappetizing; disagreeable. **5** harsh, bright, glaring. **6** careless; crude, rough. **7** insensitive, inconsiderate, careless, disregardful, unrefined, vulgar.

delicious *adj.* delectable, palatable, savory, tasty, luscious, mouth-watering, appetizing; pleasant, pleasurable, delightful, joyful, charming. **—Ant.** distasteful, unpleasant, disagreeable.

delight *n.* **1.** pleasure, happiness, rapture, enjoyment, joy, gratification. **2.** something that gives joy or pleasure. *—v.* **3.** please, gratify, cheer; charm, fascinate, enchant, amuse. **4.** revel; take great pleasure in, take delight in. **—Ant. 1** disappointment, discontent, pain; displeasure. **3** displease; irk, bother. **4** dislike; take no pleasure in.

delighted *adj.* pleased, captivated, enthralled, enraptured, enchanted; elated, ecstatic. **—Ant.** displeased, disgusted.

delightful *adj.* enjoyable, pleasing, pleasurable, pleasure-giving; agreeable, charming, engaging, entertaining, amusing, enchanting, *Informal* peachy; amiable, congenial. **—Ant.** displeasing, unpleasant, distressing; disagreeable, distasteful.

delinquency *n.* **1.** negligence, dereliction; neglect of obligation. **2.** misbehavior, misconduct, misdeed.

delinquent *adj.* **1.** neglectful, negligent, derelict, remiss. **2.** due, overdue, late; in arrears. *—n.* **3.** misdoer, miscreant, wrongdoer; hoodlum, juvenile delinquent. —**Ant. 1** dutiful, mindful. **2** paid.

delirious *adj.* **1.** incoherent; hallucinating, raving. **2.** frantic, frenzied, carried away, excited, ecstatic. —**Ant. 1** coherent, rational. **2** calm.

deliver *v.* **1.** carry, bear, bring, convey; surrender; give over, hand over, turn over. **2.** give, utter, say, proclaim. **3.** launch, aim, throw, direct, deal, strike. **4.** save, rescue, liberate, emancipate, free, release; set free. —**Ant. 1** keep, hold. **4** enslave, oppress.

deliverance *n.* liberation, release, emancipation; rescue, salvation.

delivery *n.* transfer, transmittal, transferral, transmission, handing over, giving over.

delude *v.* mislead, deceive, fool, trick, dupe, *Slang* con, put on.

deluge *n.* **1.** flood, inundation. **2.** inundation, flood, barrage, torrent, overwhelming amount, spate. —*v.* **3.** overwhelm with a flood of water, inundate, drown, submerge, engulf, flow over, overflow; bury, swamp, flood, glut. —**Ant. 1** drought, dearth, aridity, aridness; ebb, abatement. **3** dry out.

delusion *n.* illusion, misbelief, misconception.

deluxe *v.* elegant, grand, fine, luxurious, splendid, choice, *Informal* posh, *Slang* classy.

delve *v.* search, probe, examine, explore, look into.

demagogue *n.* rabble-rouser, agitator, soapbox orator, haranguer, fomenter, political opportunist, tub-thumper, spouter, ranter, hothead, incendiary, malcontent, firebrand, inflamer, troublemaker.

demand *v.* **1.** exact, order, require; insist upon, lay claim to. **2.** need, require, call for. —*n.* **3.** command, order; act of demanding, something that is demanded. **4.** need, requirement, want, call.

demean *v.* debase, lower, degrade, humble, humiliate, disgrace, shame. —**Ant.** dignify, honor; glorify, elevate.

demeanor *n.* conduct, behavior, deportment, manner, comportment, bearing, presence, appearance.

demented *adj.* insane, mad, lunatic, crazy, crazed, deranged, *Slang* cuckoo, nuts. —**Ant.** sane, rational.

demise *n.* **1.** death, decease, passing, expiration. **2.** end, fall, collapse, ruin. —**Ant. 1** birth.

democracy *n.* **1.** government by the people, representative government; state having government by the people. **2.** fairness, equality, political equality.

democratic *adj.* **1.** advocating democracy, characterized by principles of political equality. **2.** characterized by social equality, tending to level distinctions in rank. **3.** of the Democratic party. —**Ant. 1** autocratic, despotic, tyrannical. **2** socially unequal.

demolish *v.* **1.** wreck, destroy, level, raze; tear down, *Slang* total. **2.** ruin, devastate; put an end to. —**Syn. Study. 1** See DESTROY. —**Ant. 1** build, create; restore, repair. **2** strengthen.

demolition *n.* destruction, wrecking, razing, leveling.

demon *n.* **1.** devil; evil spirit, malignant spirit. **2.** fiend, monster. **3.** go-getter, energetic person. —**Ant. 1, 2** angel. **1** cherub; good spirit. **2** kind person, gentle person, good person. **3** lazy person.

demonic Also **demoniac, demoniacal** *adj.* fiendish, devilish; frantic, frenzied, hellish, hectic. —**Ant.** calm, cool.

demonstrate *v.* **1.** teach, show; describe, illustrate, explain. **2.** show, reveal, display, exhibit, manifest. **3.** prove, show, establish; make clear by reasoning, make evident. **4.** picket, parade, march, hold a protest meeting.

demonstration *n.* **1.** exhibition, display, presentation, illustration. **2.** expression, manifestation, exposition, display. **3.** parade, march, picketing; protest meeting, rally.

demonstrative *adj.* **1.** affectionate; effusive, gushing, openly expressive. **2.** serving to demonstrate, offering proof.

demoralize *v.* discourage, dishearten, dispirit, undermine, disorganize, disconcert; break down the morale of. —**Ant.** stimulate, encourage.

demote *v.* lower in rank, degrade; *Slang* bust.

demur *v.* **1.** object, disagree; take exception. —*n.* **2.** hesitation, scruple, qualm, compunction, misgiving, objection, protest.

demure *adj.* shy, modest, prim, reserved; prudish, overly modest, bashful. —**Ant.** brazen, brash, impudent, barefaced; shameless, immodest.

demurrer *n.* objection, challenge, dissent, doubt, demurral, protest, stricture, question, remonstrance, misgiving, compunction, scruple, qualm, exception, rebuttal. —**Ant.** consent, agreement, endorsement, acceptance, acquiescence.

den *n.* **1.** lair, shelter, retreat. **2.** haunt, hangout; hotbed. **3.** study, library, private room, sanctuary.

denial *n.* **1.** disowning, disavowal, disclaimer. **2.** rejection, refusal. —**Ant. 1** affirmation, avowal, acknowledgment, admission. **2** granting.

denigrate *v.* defame, malign, slander,

tear down; disparage, decry, deprecate; abuse, stigmatize, traduce, run down, besmirch, downgrade, blacken, call names, calumniate, backbite, smear, vilify, revile, asperse, soil, sully; *Slang* give a black eye to, drag through the mud, stab in the back, badmouth, dump on. **—Syn. Study.** See DECRY. **—Ant.** praise, commend, acclaim, exalt, boost, extol.

denizen *n.* inhabitant, resident, dweller.

denomination *n.* **1.** name, designation, category, class, grouping. **2.** sect, religious group, persuasion. **3.** value, size.

denote *v.* indicate, mark, signal, signify, mean, name.

denouement *n.* outcome, upshot, solution; finale, conclusion, termination, end.

denounce *v.* **1.** condemn, criticize, censure, vilify. **2.** accuse; inform against. **—Ant. 1** commend, praise, extol, laud. **2** vindicate, exonerate.

dense *adj.* **1.** crowded, compressed, compact, close, concentrated, thick, impenetrable, heavy, intense. **2.** dumb, stupid, dull, ignorant, dimwitted, thick, thickheaded, slow. **—Ant. 1** sparse, scattered, dispersed; thin, transparent, light. **2** alert, bright, intelligent, quick, quick-witted, clever.

dent *n.* depression, pit, nick, hollow, indentation.

denunciation *n.* condemnation, censure, denouncement; attack against. **—Ant.** defense, apology; acclamation, recommendation.

deny *v.* **1.** contradict, disavow, disaffirm, disclaim, refute. **2.** refuse, disallow; withhold from. **3.** refuse to acknowledge, not recognize; contradict, declare untrue. **—Ant. 1** confirm, concede, admit, affirm, assert. **2** grant. **3** acknowledge, recognize; believe in.

depart *v.* **1.** go, leave; exit, go away, set out, start out, set forth, go forth. **2.** digress, turn aside, deviate. **—Ant. 1** arrive; remain, stay.

department *n.* **1.** division, bureau, branch, section, unit. **2.** district, division, province, sector.

departure *n.* **1.** leaving, going, exit, exodus; going away. **2.** digression, divergence, deviation. **—Ant. 1** arrival, return.

depend *v.* **1.** rely, count, believe in. **2.** place trust, have faith. **3.** hinge, rest, be determined by, be contingent upon, hang on, be dependent on.

dependable *adj.* reliable, trustworthy, unfailing, trusty, trusted; loyal, faithful, steady, steadfast; sure, true. **—Ant.** untrustworthy, unreliable, doubtful, questionable, unsteady, fickle, unstable.

dependence *n.* **1.** dependency. **2.** reliance, trust, confidence.

dependency *n.* dependence.

dependent *adj.* **1.** needing help, needful of, reliant. **2.** determined by; contingent on; subject to. **—Ant. 1** self-reliant, independent.

depict *v.* **1.** paint, portray, draw, sketch, limn, delineate, picture, sculpt, carve, represent, diagram, draft, map out, chart. **2.** describe, dramatize, narrate, record, chronicle, relate, recount, detail, define, verbalize, recite.

deplete *v.* exhaust, use up, drain, impoverish; lessen, reduce, decrease, consume. **—Ant.** increase, augment.

deplorable *adj.* **1.** wretched, awful, miserable. **2.** deserving reproach, reprehensible, blameworthy. **—Ant. 1** acceptable, good.

deplore *v.* **1.** lament, mourn, bemoan, bewail, grieve for. **2.** censure, condemn; disapprove of.

deport *v.* **1.** oust, expel; banish, cast out, exile, expatriate. **2.** behave, act, carry; conduct oneself.

deportment *n.* conduct, behavior; comportment, demeanor.

depose *v.* dethrone; oust; remove from office, unseat.

deposit *v.* **1.** put, place; set down. **2.** accumulate, place; put down. **3.** give as security, give as partial payment; put down. **4.** place for safekeeping; put in the bank, give in trust, commit to custody. *—n.* **5.** accumulation, sediment, pile. **6.** down payment, partial payment, installment.

deposition *n.* **1.** the act of deposing. **2.** testimony, declaration, statement. **3.** deposit, accumulation.

depot *n.* **1.** terminal, terminus; railroad or bus station. **2.** military storage place, dump.

depraved *adj.* corrupt, perverted, wicked, debased, debauched, degenerate, vile, degraded. **—Ant.** moral, virtuous, wholesome.

deprecate *v.* **1.** protest, condemn, decry; object to, take exception to, express strong disapproval of; denigrate. **2.** belittle, play down, depreciate. **—Syn. Study. 1** See DECRY. **—Ant. 1** approve, favor, endorse, sanction.

depreciate *v.* **1.** reduce or lower the value of, diminish; lose value. **2.** belittle, disparage, downgrade, scorn, denigrate; run down. **—Ant. 1** appreciate. **2** appreciate, cherish, esteem, prize.

depredation *n.* sack, plunder, looting, pillage, rapine, spoiling, sacking, robbery, freebooting, desecration, devastation, laying waste, spoliation, marauding, ravishment, ravage, brigandage.

depress *v.* **1.** dispirit, sadden, dishearten, deject, lower in spirits. **2.** lessen, weaken, diminish, reduce, cut back. **3.** lower; press down. **—Ant. 1** elate, cheer, gladden, hearten. **2** heighten, increase, strengthen.

depression *n.* **1.** sadness, gloom, dejection, discouragement, downheartedness; melancholia, melancholy, despondency, desolation. **2.** indentation, hollow, dimple. **3.** economic decline, recession. **—Ant. 1** cheerfulness, gladness; lightheartedness, joyousness. **3** boom.

deprive *v.* dispossess, divest, strip, confiscate; take from.

depth *n.* **1.** downward measurement, perpendicular measurement. **2.** profundity, deepness. **3.** timbre, deepness. **—Ant. 1** height. **2** superficiality.

deputy *n.* agent, substitute, alternate, representative, surrogate, proxy, second, delegate, envoy, go-between, messenger, emissary, ambassador, spokesperson, minister, middleman, pinch hitter.

deranged *adj.* insane, irrational, unbalanced, demented; crazy. **—Ant.** sane, normal, rational.

derelict *adj.* **1.** negligent, neglectful, delinquent, remiss; careless. **2.** abandoned, deserted. *—n.* **3.** bum, vagrant, outcast, tramp, hobo, homeless person, bag lady.

deride *v.* ridicule, mock, scoff, scorn, sneer at; taunt. **—Syn. Study.** See RIDICULE.

derision *n.* ridicule, mockery, disdain, scorn, sneering.

derivation *n.* **1.** deriving, acquiring, obtaining, getting. **2.** origin, source. **3.** etymology; historical development.

derive *v.* **1.** gain, obtain, glean, enjoy. **2.** descend; originate, arise; stem from.

derogatory *adj.* belittling, disparaging, uncomplimentary, unfavorable, unflattering, injurious. **—Ant.** flattering, complimentary, favorable.

descend *v.* **1.** drop, come down, go down, move downward. **2.** incline, dip, slope, slant. **3.** be inherited, pass, be handed down. **4.** swoop, invade; come in force. **—Ant. 1** ascend, climb, go up.

descendant *n.* offspring, issue, progeny. **—Ant.** ancestor, progenitor, forefather.

descent *n.* **1.** fall, drop, coming down. **2.** slope, slant, decline, declivity. **3.** ancestry, origin, lineage. **4.** sudden visit, sneak attack, raid, assault, incursion. **—Ant. 1** ascent, rise; upward climb.

describe *v.* **1.** detail, narrate, relate, recount, speak of, recite, explain; illustrate, characterize, portray; depict. **2.** draw, trace, outline; delineate, mark out.

description *n.* **1.** account, depiction, portrayal, illustration, characterization; narration. **2.** kind, sort, type, ilk, variety; species, class, genus, nature, manner, brand.

desecrate *v.* defile, violate, profane, dishonor. **—Ant.** honor, esteem.

desert[1] *n.* **1.** wasteland; arid region, barren wilderness. *—adj.* **2.** barren, desolate; infertile, arid, waste, uncultivated, untilled, wild, uninhabited.

desert[2] *v.* abandon, forsake, leave; run away from.

deserts *n. pl.* worth; due, payment, reward.

deserve *v.* merit, rate, warrant; be worthy of, be entitled to, qualify for, earn as due, be deserving of.

design *v.* **1.** plan, conceive, fashion, devise; draw, draft, sketch; draw up plans for. **2.** intend, destine, set up. *—n.* **3.** sketch, drawing, outline, plan, blueprint, diagram. **4.** pattern, motif; form, arrangement. **5.** plan, project, blueprint, intention, purpose, goal, target, objective, end, aim. **6.** plan, scheme, plot; intrigue.

designate *v.* **1.** specify, indicate, name, signify, pinpoint; select. **2.** appoint, choose, elect, select, name, nominate, assign. **3.** name, call, term, label, identify.

designing *adj.* scheming, conniving, crafty, cunning, wily, artful, plotting. **—Ant.** candid, frank, honest, open, guileless, artless.

desirable *adj.* **1.** pleasing, fine; worth desiring, worth having, in demand. **2.** advisable, advantageous, beneficial. **—Ant. 1** undesirable, disagreeable. **2** harmful, inadvisable, improper.

desire *v.* **1.** crave, want, wish; long for; yearn for, hunger for, thirst for. **2.** request, urge; ask for. *—n.* **3.** craving, longing, need, wish, yearning; thirst, hunger, appetite. **—Syn. Study. 3** DESIRE, CRAVING, LONGING, YEARNING suggest feelings that impel a person to the attainment or possession of something. DESIRE is a strong wish, worthy or unworthy, for something that is or seems to be within reach: *a desire for success.* CRAVING implies a deep and compelling wish for something, arising from a feeling of (literal or figurative) hunger: *a craving for food; a craving for companionship.* LONGING is an intense wish, generally repeated or enduring, for something that is at the moment beyond reach but may be attainable in the future: *a longing to visit Europe.* YEARNING suggests persistent, uneasy, and sometimes wistful or tender longing: *a yearning for one's native land.* **—Ant. 1** spurn, reject, refuse, decline, repudiate. **3** distaste, aversion, dislike.

desist *v.* cease, stop; discontinue, suspend; refrain from, leave off, *Slang* lay off. —**Ant.** begin, persist, continue, persevere.

desolate *adj.* **1.** deserted, uninhabited, empty, bare, barren, bleak, forsaken, abandoned. **2.** despondent, dejected, forlorn, downcast, down-hearted, depressed, sad, melancholy; sorrowful, wretched, miserable. —*v.* **3.** ruin, ravage, devastate; destroy, demolish; lay waste. **4.** sadden, grieve, depress, distress, dishearten; discourage. —**Ant. 1** inhabited, populous. **2** cheerful, light-hearted, joyous, happy, glad. **3** develop, nourish, cultivate. **4** cheer, hearten, encourage.

desolation *n.* **1.** ruin, devastation, destruction. **2.** barrenness, emptiness, bleakness, dreariness, bareness, wilderness. **3.** loneliness, seclusion, solitariness, solitude. **4.** sadness, melancholy, unhappiness, sorrow, depression, dejection, distress, misery.

despair *n.* **1.** hopelessness, discouragement, despondency, gloom, depression; desperation. **2.** burden, ordeal, trial. —*v.* **3.** have no hope, lose heart, lose faith in. —**Syn. Study.** DESPAIR, DESPONDENCY, DESPERATION refer to a state of mind caused by circumstances that seem too much to cope with. DESPAIR suggests total loss of hope, usu. accompanied by apathy and low spirits: *He sank into despair after the bankruptcy.* DESPONDENCY is a state of deep gloom due to loss of hope and a sense of futility and resignation: *despondency after a serious illness.* DESPERATION is a state in which loss of hope drives a person to struggle against circumstances, with utter disregard of consequences: *In desperation, they knocked down the door.* —**Ant. 1** hopefulness, cheerfulness. **2** delight, joy, pride. **3** have faith in, have confidence in.

desperado *n.* bandit, outlaw, lawbreaker, brigand, terrorist, criminal, convict, fugitive, ruffian, hooligan, rowdy, thug, hoodlum, gunman.

desperate *adj.* **1.** reckless, dangerous, wild, frantic. **2.** daring, rash. **3.** grave, critical, dangerous, serious; hopeless, incurable. **4.** despairing, despondent, wretched; beyond hope. **5.** extreme, great, urgent, critical, dire. —**Ant. 1** cautious, careful. **2** sensible, safe. **3** hopeful, promising; curable. **4** elated, joyful, happy; hopeful, optimistic.

desperation *n.* **1.** despair, hopelessness, despondency. **2.** recklessness, rashness; frenzy. —**Syn. Study. 1** See DESPAIR.

despicable *adj.* contemptible, detestable, vile, mean, base, disgraceful, reprehensible, outrageous. —**Ant.** praiseworthy, laudable, worthy.

despise *v.* dislike, scorn, loathe, detest, abhor; contemn, disdain; look down on. —**Ant.** like, admire, appreciate, respect, esteem.

despoil *v.* rob, plunder, ravage, pillage, loot.

despondency *n.* despair, hopelessness, depression, desperation, desolation; deep sadness, dejection, discouragement. —**Syn. Study.** See DESPAIR.

despondent *adj.* discouraged, depressed, dejected, downhearted, disconsolate, downcast, hopeless, disheartened, low, blue, *Slang* down, down in the dumps, down in the mouth, bummed out. —**Ant.** encouraged, light-hearted, joyful, joyous, happy, glad.

despot *n.* tyrant, dictator, autocrat, oppressor.

dessert *n.* final course; (*variously*) pie, tart, cake, sweet, ice cream, fruit, nuts; treat.

destination *n.* journey's end, goal, plan, purpose, ambition, objective, aim, target, end, object.

destiny *n.* **1.** future, fate, fortune, lot. **2.** fate, necessity, fortune, karma, kismet, *Greek* moira. —**Syn. Study. 2** See FATE.

destitute *adj.* poor, poverty-stricken, needy, indigent, penniless, broke, *Slang* busted. —**Ant.** rich, affluent, opulent, wealthy.

destroy *v.* ruin, demolish, wreck, waste, ravage, devastate; (*variously*) bomb, blast away, level, pulverize, disintegrate, incinerate, *Informal* nuke, *Slang* total. —**Syn. Study.** DESTROY, DEMOLISH, RAZE imply completely ruining or doing away with something. To DESTROY is to reduce something to nothingness or to take away its powers and functions so that restoration is impossible: *Disease destroys tissues.* To DEMOLISH is to destroy something organized or structured by smashing it to bits or tearing it down: *The evidence demolished the attorney's case.* To RAZE is to level a building or other structure to the ground: *to raze a fortress.* —**Ant.** save, preserve, conserve; establish, found, institute; make, form.

destruct *v.* destroy, demolish, ruin, raze, gut, decimate, devastate, wreck, tear down, pull down, desolate, wipe out, despoil, lay in ruins. —**Ant.** erect, build, put up, create, originate.

destruction *n.* destroying; ruin, demolition, wrecking, wreckage, devastation, havoc. —**Ant.** preservation, conservation; institution, organization.

destructive *adj.* **1.** damaging, ruinous, detrimental, injurious, devastating;

harmful, hurtful. **2.** not constructive. **—Ant. 1** beneficial, constructive, creative, restorative, preservative. **2** constructive.

detach *v.* **1.** separate, disconnect, disengage, sever, unhitch, unfasten, disentangle, loosen. **2.** send on a special mission, assign to special service. **—Ant. 1** attach, fasten, connect, engage, tie, bind.

detached *adj.* **1.** separated, disconnected; unfastened, disengaged, unhitched, unconnected, uncoupled, severed. **2.** impartial, neutral, unbiased, unprejudiced, disinterested, objective, dispassionate, fair-minded, fair. **3.** aloof, distant, reserved, indifferent. **—Ant. 1** attached, joined, connected, fastened. **2** partial, biased, prejudiced. **3** concerned, involved; warm, close, inviting.

detachment *n.* **1.** separation, disconnection, disengagement, severing, severance, cutting off. **2.** impartiality, objectivity, fairness, neutrality. **3.** aloofness, indifference, coolness; isolation, preoccupation. **4.** unit, force, special task force.

detail *n.* **1.** particular, item, fact, component, iota, feature, aspect, respect. **2.** particulars or items seen as a group. **3.** special duty, particular assignment, detachment; special service. **—*v.*** **4.** itemize, enumerate, particularize, specify, delineate, designate; relate, recount. **5.** select for special duty; assign to a task, appoint. **—Ant. 1** whole, aggregate, total, sum. **4** generalize.

detain *v.* **1.** delay, stop; hinder, retard, slow, slow down, slow up. **2.** confine, hold, keep in custody; arrest.

detect *v.* discover, uncover, notice, note, observe, perceive, see, spot, espy, catch; learn, ascertain. **—Syn. Study.** See LEARN.

detective *n.* investigator; special investigator; sleuth, *Slang* gumshoe, private eye, shamus, dick.

detention *n.* **1.** detainment, holding, keeping in, holding back. **2.** custody, confinement; imprisonment, incarceration. **—Ant.** release, liberation.

deter *v.* discourage, hinder, prevent, dissuade, daunt, divert; stop, impede.

deteriorate *v.* worsen, degenerate, decline, wane, ebb, lapse, fade; disintegrate, decay, crumble, fall off. **—Ant.** improve, ameliorate, advance.

determination *n.* **1.** decision, resolution, resolve; judgment, solution, verdict, conclusion, finding. **2.** determining, settling, resolving, reasoning, fixing, act of deciding. **3.** resolution, resoluteness, perseverance, tenacity, persistence, steadfastness, stick-to-it-iveness; boldness, spunk, power, pluck, grit. **—Ant. 1, 2** irresolution, indecision, doubt. **3** instability, hesitancy, hesitation, weakness.

determine *v.* **1.** ascertain, discover, learn, establish, detect; find out, figure out. **2.** control, regulate, affect; decide, influence; give direction to. **3.** settle, decide, resolve, conclude; come to a decision. **—Syn. Study. 3** See DECIDE.

deterrent *n.* restraint, curb, hindrance, check, discouragement, chilling effect.

detest *v.* abhor, despise, loathe, hate; dislike intensely, recoil from. **—Syn. Study.** See HATE. **—Ant.** like, love, adore, relish, cherish.

detestable *adj.* hateful, obnoxious, abhorrent, loathsome, odious; unpleasant, disagreeable; repulsive, vile, revolting, disgusting, offensive. **—Ant.** likable, lovable, agreeable, attractive.

detonate *v.* explode, set off, touch off, discharge, fire, shoot, ignite, fulminate; burst, erupt, go off, blow up.

detract *v.* diminish, reduce, lower, lessen; take away from, subtract from. **—Ant.** increase, heighten, enhance; add to.

detriment *n.* injury, damage, harm, loss; impairment, disadvantage. **—Ant.** improvement, enhancement; aid, advantage.

devalue *v.* revalue, devaluate, depreciate, demonetize, remonetize; mark down, lower, write down, underrate; cheapen, adulterate, debase, corrupt, pervert, degenerate, degrade, contaminate, defile, taint, pollute, infect. **—Ant.** raise, elevate, overrate, overestimate, enhance.

devastate *v.* waste, destroy, ravage, desolate, despoil, spoil, ruin, wreck, demolish, level, lay waste. **—Ant.** create, erect, develop; build up.

devastation *n.* ruin, ruination, destruction, demolition.

develop *v.* **1.** expand, broaden, augment, improve, advance; mature, cultivate, grow, flower, ripen. **2.** expand, enlarge, amplify; elaborate on. **3.** acquire, contract, pick up, come to have. **4.** evolve, turn out, unfold, come to light. **5.** build up, convert, energize. **6.** process, finish, print.

development *n.* **1.** progress, growth, evolution, history. **2.** event, advance. **3.** event, result.

deviate *v.* part, stray, wander, depart, digress, diverge, vary; turn aside, swerve, veer, go astray, sidetrack. **—Syn. Study.** DEVIATE, DIGRESS, DIVERGE imply turning or going aside from a path. To DEVIATE is to stray from a usual or established standard, course of action, or route: *Fear caused him to deviate from the truth.* To DIGRESS is to wander from the main theme in speaking or writing:

The speaker digressed to relate an amusing anecdote. To DIVERGE is to differ or to move in different directions from a common point or course: *Their interests gradually diverged.* **—Ant.** continue, remain; stick to.

device *n.* **1.** invention, contrivance, apparatus, contraption, gadget, mechanism. **2.** plan, plot, scheme, trick, ploy, design, artifice; strategy, stratagem, wile, ruse, gimmick, angle.

devil *n.* **1.** [chief enemy of God] the Devil, Satan, Archfiend, prince of darkness, Lucifer, Beelzebub, Old Nick, spirit of evil. **2.** mischief-maker, hellion, scoundrel, rogue, villain, ruffian. **3.** wretch, creature, unfortunate, so-and-so, thing; *Informal* fellow, guy.

devious *adj.* dishonest, deceitful, sneaky, tricky, wily, sly, treacherous, dishonorable, crooked, double-dealing. **—Ant.** forthright, aboveboard, straightforward; open, frank, honest.

devise *v.* design, invent, conceive, concoct, contrive, think up, frame, prepare, formulate, map out, block out, plot, forge, construct.

devoid *adj.* lacking, barren, wanting, bereft of, destitute, empty, without, unblest with. **—Ant.** full, abounding, replete, flush, rich, abundant, overflowing.

devote *v.* dedicate, give over to, direct, apply, address, utilize, concentrate, center one's attentions on, give oneself up to; consecrate. **—Syn. Study.** DEVOTE, DEDICATE, CONSECRATE share the sense of assigning or committing someone or something to a particular activity, function, or end. DEVOTE is the most general of these terms, although it carries overtones of religious commitment: *He devoted his evenings to mastering the computer.* DEDICATE implies a more solemn or noble purpose and carries an ethical or moral tone: *We are dedicated to the achievement of equality for all.* CONSECRATE, even in nonreligious contexts, implies an intense and sacred commitment: *consecrated to the service of humanity.*

devoted *adj.* dedicated, earnest, strongly committed, staunch, zealous, steadfast, unwavering; ardent, fond, loving, passionate; faithful, true, loyal, adhering. **—Ant.** uncommitted, undedicated, indifferent, dispassionate, unimpassioned, inconstant, unloving; unfaithful, disloyal.

devotee *n.* **—Syn. Study.** See FANATIC.

devotion *n.* **1.** attentiveness, dedication, commitment, devotedness, earnest attachment; regard, reverence, love, fondness, concern for; loyalty, adherence, faithfulness, fealty, allegiance, zeal, ardor. **2.** devoutness, religious fervor, holiness, piety, reverence, godliness, spirituality; religiosity. **3.** act of religious worship, prayer service, religious observance, meditation. **—Ant. 1** indifference, unconcern, disinterest, disregard; irreverence, negligence, aversion; unfaithfulness, disloyalty, faithlessness, inconstancy, infidelity. **2** impiety, irreverence.

devour *v.* **1.** eat voraciously, consume greedily, take in ravenously, gobble up, wolf down, stuff in, bolt down, gulp down. **2.** read eagerly and swiftly, read widely or compulsively, knock off, go through; absorb oneself in, become engrossed in. **—Ant.** refuse, pass up, ignore, be indifferent to. **1** disgorge, vomit, regurgitate.

devout *adj.* **1.** religious, orthodox, pious, worshipful, reverent. **2.** ardent, fervent, earnest, intense, serious, passionate, zealous. **—Syn. Study. 1** See RELIGIOUS. **—Ant. 1** irreligious, impious, irreverent, sacrilegious. **2** passionless, insincere, passive, indifferent.

dew *n.* moisture; condensation, film of precipitation, night or morning wetness; droplets of moisture.

dexterity *n.* manual skill, deftness, adroitness, handiness, nimbleness with the fingers, proficiency, facility.

dexterous *adj.* skillful, nimble, agile, adroit, deft; ingenious, resourceful, active, quick, gifted, efficient, able. **—Syn. Study.** DEXTEROUS, ADROIT, DEFT imply facility and ease in performance. DEXTEROUS most often refers to physical, esp. manual, ability but can also refer to mental ability: *a dexterous woodcarver; dexterous handling of a delicate situation.* ADROIT usu. implies mental cleverness and ingenuity but can refer to physical ability: *an adroit politician; an adroit juggler.* DEFT suggests a light and assured touch in physical or mental activity: *a deft waitress; deft manipulation of public opinion.* **—Ant.** clumsy, awkward, maladroit, inept.

diabolic Also **diabolical** *adj.* devilish, satanic, fiendish, wicked, evil, malevolent, demonic, impious, villainous, nefarious, monstrous, heinous, vicious, foul, baleful. **—Ant.** angelic, good, saintly, pious.

diagnosis *n.* identification of a disease, specification of illness, determination from examination, summary or conclusion from symptoms, medical or scientific report; investigation, study, examination, analysis, scrutiny.

diagram *n.* outline, representation, plan, drawing, map, line drawing, sketch, illustration, chart, rough projection, breakdown.

dialect *n.* language, variety of a language, vernacular, localism, regionalism, colloquialism, provincialism, idiom, lingo, jargon, argot, patois. **—Syn. Study.** See LANGUAGE.

dialogue, dialog *n.* **1.** formal discussion, conference, talk, exchange of viewpoints, parley, conclave, personal meeting. **2.** direct or spoken discourse in literature, verbal exchange, conversation in a book or play, lines, speech; literary piece completely in the form of a conversation. **—Ant.** monologue, soliloquy.

diaphanous *adj.* translucent, transparent, sheer, filmy, gossamer, gauzy, flimsy, pellucid, lucid, limpid. **—Ant.** opaque, solid, thick, heavy.

diary *n.* daily journal, day-to-day record, journal, daybook; log, chronicle.

diatribe *n.* verbal or written castigation, bitter harangue, tirade, violent denunciation, stream of abuse, accusatory language, invective, vituperation, contumely.

dicker *v.* negotiate, bargain, haggle, wrangle, chaffer, quibble, drive a hard bargain, *Scot.* higgle; talk down, beat down, underbid, outbid.

dictate *v.* **1.** say to a person for writing down, utter for another to record, speak into a machine for recording, transmit a message through. **2.** lay down, set forth, ordain, determine, order, enjoin, direct, prescribe, impose, pronounce, decree, declare with directive authority. *—n.* **3.** requirement, mandate, stricture, rule, ruling, order, edict, decree, ordinance, dictum; bidding, urging, inclination, counsel, prompting, exhortation. **—Ant. 1** record, write down. **2** follow, submit to, obey.

dictator *n.* absolute ruler, despot, autocrat, tyrant; (*variously*) emperor, czar, kaiser, duce, führer, caesar.

dictatorial *adj.* **1.** absolute, authoritative, unlimited, unrestricted, categorical, arbitrary. **2.** domineering, imperious, inclined to command, tyrannical, despotic, autocratic, magisterial, peremptory, lordly, willful, supercilious, overbearing, haughty, arrogant. **—Ant. 1** democratic, constitutional, limited, restricted. **2** suppliant, agreeable, humble, considerate, tentative.

diction *n.* **1.** choice of words, command of language, verbal style, rhetoric, wording, manner of expression, turn of expression, use of idiom, vocabulary, phraseology, verbiage. **2.** enunciation, distinctness of speech sounds, articulation, pronunciation, elocution.

dictum *n.* **1.** dictate, edict, decree, fiat, pronouncement, commandment, authoritative statement, order, dogmatic bidding. **2.** saying, saw, adage, maxim, axiom, proverb, truism, precept.

didactic *adj.* **1.** instructive, prescriptive, educational, intended for instruction, expository, edifying, tutorial, doctrinal. **2.** lecturelike, preachy, inclined to lecture, pedantic, pedagogic, academic, donnish; moralizing, homiletic; dogmatically overbearing.

die *v.* **1.** perish, suffer death, expire, pass away, pass on, pass over, leave this world, depart, meet death, come to one's end, be heard of no more, draw the last breath, go the way of all flesh, go to one's glory, go to one's Maker, meet one's Maker, go from dust to dust, give up the ghost; *Slang* croak, kick the bucket, buy it, buy the farm. **2.** wane, ebb, decline, recede, fade away, subside, melt away, fade, gradually diminish, become fainter and fainter, slowly disappear, wither, pass, come to an end, die away. **3.** fail, expire, become inoperative or inactive, run out, lose power, stop, break down, degenerate, rot, wear away, go flat; go stale, lose force, run down. **4.** yearn, be eager, be anxious, long, desire greatly, pine with desire, want keenly, wish ardently, be consumed with desire, ache, be beside oneself with desire, lust. **—Syn. Study. 1** DIE, PERISH mean to relinquish life. To DIE is to cease to live from any cause or circumstance; it is used figuratively of anything that has once displayed activity: *He died of cancer. Her anger died.* PERISH, a more literary term, implies death under harsh circumstances such as hunger or violence; figuratively, it connotes permanent disappearance: *Hardship caused many pioneers to perish. Ancient Egyptian civilization has perished.* **—Ant. 1** live, be born, survive, breathe, exist, flourish, begin, be immortal. **2** increase, build, become strong.

diet[1] *n.* **1.** nutritional regimen, particular selection of food for health or other reasons, prescribed food and drink, limitation of fare. **2.** nutrition, nourishment, eating habits, eating regimen, nutriment, nurture, board, sustenance, subsistence, victuals, provisions, edibles, comestibles. *—v.* **3.** eat abstemiously, eat judiciously, take food according to a regimen, follow prescribed eating habits, regulate one's food, cut back on one's food intake, restrict one's intake; eat sparingly, eat restrictedly; abstain from overindulgence.

diet[2] *n.* lawmaking body, legislature, bicameral assembly, representative body for acting upon public affairs; congress, convention, convocation, general assembly, parliament, synod; assemblage.

differ *v.* **1.** contrast, stand apart from, deviate from, depart from, diverge from; be unlike, be dissimilar, be distinct, be disparate. **2.** disagree, take issue, be of a different opinion, be at variance, stand opposed to, fail to go along, demur, think differently; dissent, dispute. **—Ant. 1** ape, mimic, copy. **2** concur, coincide, agree.

difference *n.* **1.** distinction, contradistinction, lack of resemblance, dissimilarity, unlikeness, dissimilitude, contrast, variation, disagreement, contrariety, deviation, divergence, contradiction; distinguishing characteristic, point of dissimilarity. **2.** discrepancy, disparity. **3.** dispute, argument, disagreement, clash, falling out, contretemps, quarrel, squabble, spat, set-to. **—Ant. 1** resemblance, similarity, likeness, similitude, analogy, affinity, agreement, uniformity, unity, consonance, identity, harmony, sameness. **3** agreement, concurrence, harmony, compatibility.

different *adj.* **1.** unlike, dissimilar, not identical, not alike, distinct, disparate, other than, divergent, contrasting. **2.** separate, distinct, individual. **3.** several, various, sundry, divers; variegated, manifold, miscellaneous, diversified; unrelated, separate, diverse, distinct. **4.** unconventional, unusual, not ordinary, uncommon, rare, unique, singular, distinctive, atypical, aberrant; foreign, strange, peculiar, anomalous, bizarre. **—Syn. Study. 1–3** See VARIOUS. **—Ant. 1** identical, alike, same, similar, like. **4** ordinary, common, usual, typical, conventional.

differentiate *v.* **1.** discriminate, distinguish, see the difference in. **2.** distinguish, set off, set apart, constitute a difference between, make different; contrast, separate, draw the line. **—Syn. Study. 1** See DISTINGUISH.

difficult *adj.* **1.** hard, onerous, laborious, strenuous, demanding, extreme, requiring much effort, arduous, not easy, burdensome, exhausting, tedious, wearisome, toilsome, formidable, troublesome, exacting, trying, uphill, Herculean, Sisyphean, tough; complex, complicated, intricate, problematical, hard to solve, thorny, ticklish, knotty, *Slang* hairy; enigmatic, perplexing, bewildering, hard to understand. **2.** hard to please, hard to satisfy, hard to deal with; unpredictable, unaccommodating; hard to manage, unruly, froward, obstinate, stubborn, willful, perverse, unmanageable, rambunctious, recalcitrant, obstreperous, unyielding, intractable, fractious, inflexible; critical, fastidious. **3.** hard, grim, rough, extreme, full of hardship, not easy, tough, trying, troublesome. **—Ant. 1** simple, easy, facile, light; clear, uncomplicated, lucid; plain, manifest. **2** easy, pleasant, amenable, cooperative, accommodating, manageable, flexible, tractable. **3** easy, pleasant, halcyon.

difficulty *n.* **1.** trial, troublesomeness, arduousness, laboriousness, uphill work, rough going, tough job, hard sledding; obstacle, impediment, obstruction, barrier, snag, stumbling block, hindrance; problem, dilemma, puzzle, quandary, intricacy, perplexity. **2.** trouble, predicament, pickle, critical situation, crisis, straits, hot water, mess, jam, deep water, muddle. **—Ant. 1** ease.

diffidence *n.* timidity, timidness, timorousness, shyness, meekness, insecurity, retiring disposition, reserve, constraint, introversion; bashfulness, extreme modesty, humbleness, want of self-confidence, unassertiveness, sheepishness, lack of self-assurance; hesitancy, reluctance. **—Ant.** boldness, audaciousness, forwardness, assertiveness, aggressiveness; self-confidence, confidence.

diffuse *adj.* **1.** scattered, spread out, unconcentrated, dispersed, extended widely; vaguely defined. **2.** wordy, verbose, discursive, rambling, long-winded, lacking conciseness, disjointed, digressive, not concentrated, desultory, roundabout, wandering, meandering, maundering, circumlocutory. **—Ant. 1** concentrated. **2** succinct, concise, terse, pithy, compact; methodical, organized.

diffusion *n.* **1.** spread, dispersal, scattering. **2.** verbosity, diffuseness, wordiness, prolixity, verbiage, profuseness; circumlocution, indirection, roundaboutness, rambling, maundering, disjointedness, discursiveness. **—Ant. 1** concentration, centralization, congestion. **2** conciseness, succinctness, terseness, condensation, compactness.

dig *v.* **1.** excavate, scoop out, gouge, penetrate and loosen ground, hollow out; bring to the surface, disinter, unearth, exhume, retrieve from the soil. **2.** search and find, retrieve, extricate, find among, come up with, pinpoint, salvage, bring to view. **3.** poke, drive, jab, thrust, prod. *—n.* **4.** poke, thrust, punch, jab, prod. **5.** cutting remark, gibe, jeer, slur, verbal thrust, wry comment, taunt, aside, *Slang* put-down.

digest *v.* **1.** assimilate, convert into an absorbable form, transform for bodily use, dissolve. **2.** grasp, comprehend, absorb, assimilate mentally, understand, realize, take in mentally, appreciate, take in wholly, fathom, *Slang* dig. *—n.* **3.** condensation, abridgment, summary, synopsis, précis, résumé, abstract, brief. **—Syn. Study. 3** See SUMMARY.

dignified *adj.* full of dignity, decorous, self-respecting, circumspect, reserved, distinguished, proper, upright, honorable, upstanding, proud, august. **—Ant.** undignified, crass, vulgar.

dignity *n.* **1.** comportment, dignified behavior, respectful deportment, self-possession, solemnity, decorum; stateliness, lofty bearing, proud demeanor, impressiveness of character; majesty, augustness. **2.** loftiness, high position, honor, station, official prerogatives, importance.

digress *v.* depart from the subject, stray, go off on a tangent, wander, divagate, deviate, diverge, turn aside, back up. **—Syn. Study.** See DEVIATE. **—Ant.** proceed, advance, continue.

digression *n.* divergence, departure, deviation, detour, straying, wandering; diversion, obiter dictum, side remark, divagation.

dilapidated *adj.* run-down, decrepit, decaying, broken-down, tumbledown, falling to pieces, falling into decay, ruined, ramshackle, deteriorated, crumbling, in disrepair, shabby, rickety, falling apart, battered, worn-out; *Slang* shot, beat-up.

dilate *v.* expand, swell, enlarge, distend, inflate, puff out, extend; make wider, widen, broaden. **—Ant.** constrict, contract, shrink, compress, condense, narrow.

dilatory *adj.* inclined to delay, slow, procrastinating, remiss, tardy, sluggish, phlegmatic, reluctant; dawdling, lackadaisical, negligent; indolent, slothful, lazy. **—Ant.** diligent, assiduous, sedulous, industrious, conscientious; punctual, prompt.

dilemma *n.* plight, difficult choice, bind, problem, quandary, predicament; impasse, deadlock, stalemate; Hobson's choice, crunch. **—Syn. Study.** See PREDICAMENT.

dilettante *n.* one who pursues various arts, cultured hobbyist; dabbler, amateur, trifler, experimenter. **—Ant.** artist, expert, professional.

diligent *adj.* industrious, hardworking, zealous, persevering, active, sedulous, assiduous, persistent, earnest, pertinacious, untiring, plodding, studious, painstaking; careful, thorough, well-intentioned, patient, concerted. **—Ant.** dilatory, lazy, careless, laggard, indifferent, inconstant, erratic.

dilute *v.* **1.** thin, make thinner, thin out, make less concentrated, make weak, weaken, adulterate; thin with water, water down, add water to; make more fluid, make more liquid. **2.** diminish, mitigate, temper, lessen the force of, decrease, weaken, attenuate, reduce, diffuse. *—adj.* **3.** diluted, watered down, watery, weak, weakened, adulterated, thinned out, reduced in strength by admixture. **—Ant. 1** thicken, concentrate, strengthen. **2** strengthen, intensify.

dim *adj.* **1.** lacking light, not bright, lacking luminosity, unilluminated, obscure from lack of light, darkened, dusky, tenebrous, shadowy, murky, adumbrated, indistinct, obscured, clouded, ill-defined, faint, nebulous, hazy; blurry, blurred; muffled, low, soft, weak, muted, feeble. **2.** vague, intangible, faint, indefinite, indistinct, remote, foggy; gloomy. **—Ant. 1** bright, brilliant, radiant, luminous, effulgent. **2** distinct, plain, clear, palpable, definite, pronounced, well-defined.

dimension *n.* Often **dimensions. 1.** measurements, size, length, width, height, thickness; proportion, physical extent, mass, massiveness, bulk, volume. **2.** range, scope, magnitude, extent, importance, volume, amplitude, measure, weight, greatness, massiveness.

diminish *v.* **1.** reduce, lessen, shrink, abate, decrease, make smaller, shorten, lower. **2.** become smaller, lessen, decrease, shrink, dwindle, narrow, be reduced, shrivel, wane, decline, subside, fall off, ebb, peter out. **—Syn. Study. 2** See DECREASE. **—Ant.** enlarge, augment, increase, amplify, enhance, heighten, magnify; expand, grow, burgeon, increase.

diminutive *adj.* **1.** tiny, little, small, short, slight, stunted, undersized, miniature, petite, minute, lilliputian, pocket-size, vest-pocket, *Slang* half-pint; teeny, wee, elfin, dwarfish; on a small scale, insignificant, unimportant, inconsiderable. *—n.* **2.** short form, affectionate expression, nickname, pet name, hypocoristic term. **—Ant. 1** enormous, immense, gigantic, oversized, huge, vast, colossal, mammoth, monumental.

dimwit *n.* dummy, blockhead, dunce, simpleton, fool, nitwit, numskull, chowderhead, meathead, booby, dolt, dullard, dummkopf, dumbbell, knucklehead, pinhead, dingbat, yo-yo, ding-a-ling, jerk.

din *n.* clamor, uproar, noise, loud confused noise, hubbub, racket, hullabaloo, tumult, commotion, clangor, stir, to-do, babble, clattering, ruckus; *Archaic* bruit. **—Syn. Study.** See NOISE. **—Ant.** quiet, silence, calm, stillness, serenity, tranquillity.

dine *v.* eat, sup, feast, break bread, banquet, partake, take a little nourishment, take sustenance, fall to, gourmandize, feed, gluttonize; eat (or have) dinner, supper, lunch, breakfast; *Slang* eat high off the hog.

dingy *adj.* dirty and drab, dusty, murky, lacking brightness, shabby, tacky, grimy, dreary, gloomy, dismal. **—Ant.** bright, burnished, radiant, glittering, luminous, shining, lustrous; gay, cheerful.

dint *n.* force, effort, struggle, strain, labor, exertion, will, stress, endeavor, energy, power, might, strength, determination, push, insistence, drive, forcefulness, charge, relentlessness.

dip *v.* **1.** dunk, place momentarily in a liquid, submerge, immerse briefly, plunge. **2.** take out with a ladle, scoop, lift by scooping, dish, dish up, dish out, ladle, spoon, bail; shovel. **3.** droop, descend, slope, incline downward, turn down, decline, sink, drop down. **4.** dabble, try tentatively, involve oneself slightly; study slightly, read here and there in a book, peruse, skim, take a cursory view of, glance at, run over. **—Syn. Study. 1** DIP, IMMERSE, PLUNGE refer to putting something into liquid. To DIP is to put down into a liquid quickly or partially and lift out again: *to dip a finger into water to test the temperature.* IMMERSE denotes a lowering into a liquid until covered by it: *to immerse meat in salt water.* PLUNGE adds a suggestion of force or suddenness to the action of dipping: *to plunge a lobster into boiling water.* **—Ant. 3** rise, climb, ascend. **4** involve deeply, immerse.

diplomacy *n.* **1.** conduct of international relations, statesmanship, national spokesmanship, discourse between nations, foreign affairs, foreign negotiation, international politics. **2.** tact, finesse, discretion, prudence, savoir-faire; artful management, skill, subtlety, delicacy, maneuvering, craft, artfulness. **—Ant. 2** tactlessness, crassness, awkwardness, clumsiness, ineptness.

diplomat *n.* **1.** [government negotiator with foreign countries] statesman, national representative, international affairs expert, negotiator, interlocutor; ambassador, consul, minister, envoy, attaché, emissary. **2.** tactful person, one who is artful in coping with situations, artful handler of people.

diplomatic *adj.* **1.** involving diplomatic service, ambassadorial, foreign-service, state-department. **2.** tactful, discreet, politic; sensitive, prudent, urbane, suave, attuned, smoothly skillful in handling others, skillful at attaining one's ends, strategic, artful, adept. **—Syn. Study. 2** DIPLOMATIC, TACTFUL, POLITIC imply ability to avoid offending others, esp. in situations where this is important. DIPLOMATIC suggests a smoothness and skill in handling others, usually in such a way as to attain one's own ends and yet avoid any unpleasantness or opposition: *diplomatic inquiries about the stockbroker's finances.* TACTFUL suggests a nice touch in the handling of delicate matters or situations; it often involves a sincere desire not to hurt the feelings of others: *a tactful way of correcting someone.* POLITIC emphasizes expediency or prudence in looking out for one's own interests, thus knowing how to treat people of different types in delicate situations: *a truth which it is not politic to insist on.* **—Ant. 2** tactless, rude, unthinking, indiscreet, insensitive, indelicate, ham-handed, *British* ham-fisted; gauche, clumsy, awkward, inept, boorish.

dire *adj.* **1.** dreadful, awful, appalling, horrible, terrible, woeful, harrowing, grave; calamitous, catastrophic, ruinous, cataclysmic, disastrous; urgent, desperate, extreme, fearful, crucial, critical. **2.** ill-boding, grim, ominous, portentous, dreadful, ill-omened, apocalyptic, dismal, inauspicious. **—Ant. 1** happy, pleasing, good, favorable. **2** favorable, auspicious, promising.

direct *v.* **1.** supervise, manage, oversee, head, serve as director for, handle, conduct, control, superintend, administer, lead, preside over; advise, urge, instruct, order, command, enjoin, charge. **2.** point the way, show the way, usher, indicate, put on the right track, conduct to, lead, guide, pilot, navigate. **3.** level at, aim, focus, train at, point toward, address, intend for, earmark, designate. —*adj.* **4.** face-to-face, head-on, personal, firsthand, without intervening agent, without intercessor, unmediated. **5.** straightforward, without circumlocution, frank, candid, clear, explicit, plain-spoken, point-blank, going straight to the point; sincere, honest, pointed, forward, forthright, blunt. **—Ant. 4** indirect, meandering, roundabout, circuitous; mediated, by proxy. **5** indirect, devious, subtle, ambiguous, sly, oblique. **—Syn. Study. 1** DIRECT, ORDER, COMMAND mean to issue instructions. DIRECT suggests also giving explanations or advice; the emphasis is on steps necessary to accomplish a purpose: *He directed me to organize the files.* ORDER connotes a more personal relationship and instructions that leave no room for refusal: *She ordered him out of the class.* COMMAND suggests greater formality and a more fixed authority: *The officer commanded the troops to advance.*

direction *n.* **1.** management, superintendence, headship, supervision, surveillance, guidance, leadership, control, charge; administration, command, care. **2.** way, line along which anything moves or lies, path, track, route, line of march, alignment; point of compass, course, bearing. **3.** line of thought or action, inclination, aim, tendency, bent, course, trend, track, bearing, drift, current. **4.** instruction, order, regulation, prescription, guidelines, recipe.

directly *adv.* **1.** straight, in a straight line, on a straight course, not obliquely, unswervingly, as the crow flies, in a beeline, without deviation from course; exactly, precisely. **2.** soon, presently, momentarily; forthwith, at once, immediately, instantly, right away, promptly, as soon as possible. **3.** face to-face, in person, personally. **4.** openly, honestly, frankly, straightforwardly, candidly, without circumlocution, in plain terms, unambiguously, unequivocally. **—Syn. Study. 2** See INSTANTLY. **—Ant. 1** indirectly, circuitously, crookedly; imprecisely, obliquely, inexactly. **2** later, eventually. **3** indirectly. **4** ambiguously, equivocally, cryptically, deceitfully, dishonestly.

director *n.* supervisor, manager, controller, superintendent, conductor, head, leader, organizer, overseer, administrator, boss, governor, chief, curator, foreman, commander, chairman, master.

dirge *n.* funeral song, requiem, death song, death march, lament, burial hymn, threnody, mournful composition; mournful sound.

dirt *n.* **1.** mud, mire, dust, filth, filthy substance, impurity, foul matter, trash, sweepings, refuse, garbage, rubbish, muck, grime, soot, smudge, slime, scum, sludge, slop, leavings, dross, excrement, offal. **2.** soil, earth, loam, ground, humus. **3.** smut, filth, pornography, muck, obscenity, moral filth, vileness, squalidness, scurrility, scabrousness, salaciousness, indecency, profanity, unclean language. **4.** gossip, defamatory talk, rumor, scuttlebutt, scandal, slander, sensational exposé.

dirty *adj.* **1.** unclean, grimy, soiled, begrimed, muddied, grubby, filthy, foul, besmeared, messy, unwashed, untidy, smudgy, befouled, sullied, tarnished, polluted, unsterile. **2.** unscrupulous, illegal, illicit, base, mean, contemptible, despicable, low-down, devious, deceitful, vile, shabby, nasty, sordid, squalid, dishonest, fraudulent, crooked, dishonorable, corrupt, perfidious, villainous, treacherous. **3.** obscene, vulgar, scabrous, pornographic, morally unclean, indecent, prurient, immoral, smutty, coarse, lewd, filthy, licentious; off-color, risqué, blue. **4.** distasteful, unpleasant, disagreeable, rotten, foul; hard, difficult. *—v.* **5.** soil, make dirty, slop up, mess up, sully, smear, besmear, smudge, muddy, stain, spot, tarnish, begrime, blacken; pollute, muck up. **—Ant. 1** clean, washed, pure, spotless. **2** honest, respectable, aboveboard, honorable. **3** moral, respectable, decent, reputable. **4** easy, agreeable, pleasant. **5** clean, tidy up.

disability *n.* **1.** handicap, particular incapacity, disablement, unfitness, infirmity, impairment, defect, affliction, debilitation, impediment, weakness, inadequacy. **2.** disadvantage, disqualification, handicap, shortcoming, minus. **—Ant. 1** fitness, capability, ability, capacity, strength. **2** advantage, merit, qualification, plus.

disable *v.* incapacitate, render inoperable, damage, cripple, impair; deprive of strength, weaken, hinder, handicap.

disabuse *v.* enlighten about, free from error, clear the mind of, disillusion, disenchant, rid of deception, relieve of, set straight, set right, open the eyes of, free of a mistaken belief.

disadvantage *n.* **1.** weak position, unfavorable condition, handicap; in arrears. **2.** drawback, handicap, detriment, weakness, weak point, inconvenience, impediment, hindrance, fly in the ointment, trouble, hardship, nuisance, burden, flaw. **—Ant. 1** advantage. **2** advantage, convenience, merit, desirability, benefit, perquisite; gain, profit.

disadvantaged *adj.* underprivileged, underdeveloped, impoverished, struggling, emerging, emergent, deprived, handicapped, troubled. **—Ant.** advantaged, privileged, affluent.

disaffect *v.* **—Syn. Study.** See ESTRANGE.

disaffected *adj.* estranged, alienated, antipathetic, withdrawn, unfriendly, hostile, discontented, dissatisfied, disturbed, upset, agitated, disgruntled, discomposed, irreconcilable, quarrelsome, belligerent, inimical. **—Ant.** contented, serene, easygoing, satisfied, well-adjusted.

disagree *v.* **1.** differ, be unlike, fail to agree, not coincide, vary, be at variance, conflict, be discordant, deviate, be dissimilar, diverge, depart; be of different opinion, think differently, stand apart, oppose one another, be unreconciled, differ in opinion, entertain contradictory views; be at loggerheads, clash. **2.** be injurious, cause problems, disconcert, distress, discomfit, make ill, be unfavorable in effect, upset. **—Ant. 1** agree, coincide, correlate.

disagreeable *adj.* **1.** unpleasant, nasty, displeasing, distasteful, unpalatable, grating, repugnant, disgusting, harsh, repellent, repulsive, offensive; uninviting, uncomfortable, unwelcome. **2.** unpleasant, ill-natured, irritable, difficult, uncongenial, unamiable, ill-tempered, churlish, nasty, bad-tempered, grouchy, cross, peevish, surly, petulant, testy, acrimonious, obnoxious, irascible. **—Ant. 1** agreeable, pleasant, propitious, delightful, inviting, welcome. **2** agreeable, pleasant, congenial, amiable, personable.

disagreement *n.* **1.** difference, lack of

agreement, variance, discrepancy, unlikeness, disparity, failure to correspond, lack of harmony, deviation, divergence, diversity, dissimilarity, incongruity, dissimilitude, disaccord, incompatibility. **2.** quarrel, squabble, fight, argument, difference, falling-out, misunderstanding, discord, dispute, clash. **—Ant. 1** agreement, unity, likeness, similarity, correspondence, convergence, congruity, accord, harmony.

disappear *v.* **1.** vanish, vanish from sight, become obscured, cease to be seen, pass out of sight, be lost to view, cease to appear; withdraw, retire, go, be gone, depart, exit, flee, leave; fade, fade away. **2.** melt away, evaporate, vanish, die out; end, cease to exist, be no more, cease to be known, leave no trace. **—Syn. Study. 1** DISAPPEAR, VANISH, FADE mean that something or someone passes from sight or existence. DISAPPEAR is used of whatever suddenly or gradually goes away: *We watched them turn down a side street and disappear.* VANISH suggests complete, generally rapid disappearance: *The sun vanished behind clouds.* FADE suggests a complete or partial disappearance that proceeds gradually and often by means of a blending into something else: *Dusk faded into darkness.* **—Ant. 1** appear, emerge; enter, arrive. **2** appear, materialize.

disappearance *n.* act of disappearing, vanishing, evanescence, sudden or unexplained loss, passing from sight. **—Ant.** appearance, materialization, manifestation.

disappoint *v.* fail to live up to the expectations of, let down, sadden, disillusion, chagrin, dishearten; thwart, frustrate, hinder, foil, mislead. **—Ant.** satisfy, gratify, fulfill.

disappointment *n.* **1.** letdown, failure, dissatisfaction, something that disappoints, disillusionment, washout, dud, fiasco, disaster, fizzle, *Slang* bomb. **2.** thwarted expectation, miscarriage of plan, unrealization, unfulfillment, loss, frustration, setback, dissatisfaction, defeat, failure; *Slang* the knocks. **—Ant. 1, 2** satisfaction, fulfillment.

disapprove *v.* **1.** view with disfavor, frown upon, discountenance, object to, find unacceptable, condemn, regard as wrong, think ill of, dislike, take exception to, look askance at; censure, criticize, deprecate, denounce, disparage, deplore, decry. **2.** refuse, turn down, withhold approval from, disallow, refuse assent to, veto, reject. **—Ant. 1** approve, commend, recommend, applaud, compliment, endorse, sanction, like. **2** approve, allow, authorize, accept, assent to.

disarm *v.* persuade, win over, convince, sway, influence, prevail on, move, entice, bewitch, charm, captivate, attract, fascinate, enchant, take the wind out of one's sails. **—Ant.** alienate, estrange, vex, irritate, repel.

disarming *adj.* winning, winsome, magnetic, charming, ingratiating, ingenuous, beguiling, melting, irresistible, captivating, entrancing, appealing, bewitching, seductive. **—Ant.** irritating, annoying, exasperating, infuriating.

disarrange *v.* scramble, disorder, mix up, displace, put out of order, disarray, upset, jumble, scatter, disorganize, confuse, put askew, muddle, turn topsy-turvy, *Slang* mess up; rumple, dishevel, ruffle. **—Ant.** arrange, order, systematize, methodize.

disarray *n.* disorder, messiness, sloppiness, upset, disarrangement, dishevelment, untidiness, confusion, disharmony, disorganization, chaos, jumble, clutter, scramble, shambles, mix-up. **—Ant.** order, arrangement, organization.

disaster *n.* calamity, catastrophe, adverse happening, misfortune, great mishap, cataclysm, tragedy, trouble, scourge, crushing reverse, accident, adversity, ruination, blight, harm, misadventure, wreck, fiasco. **—Syn. Study.** DISASTER, CALAMITY, CATASTROPHE, CATACLYSM refer to adverse happenings usu. occurring suddenly and unexpectedly. DISASTER may be caused by negligence, bad judgment, or the like, or by natural forces, as a hurricane or flood: *a railroad disaster that claimed many lives.* CALAMITY suggests great affliction, either personal or general; the emphasis is on the grief or sorrow caused: *the calamity of losing a child.* CATASTROPHE refers esp. to the tragic outcome of a personal or public situation; the emphasis is on the destruction or irreplaceable loss: *the catastrophe of a defeat in battle.* CATACLYSM, physically a sudden and violent change in the earth's surface, also refers to a personal or public upheaval of unparalleled violence: *a cataclysm that turned our lives in a new direction.* **—Ant.** blessing, benefit, good fortune, profit, gain, boon, windfall.

disastrous *adj.* ruinous, catastrophic, calamitous, critically injurious, devastating, ill-fated, ill-starred, hapless, inauspicious, dire, harmful, destructive, fatal, dreadful, terrible, tragic, adverse, unfortunate, grievous, desolating, horrendous, harrowing.

disavow *v.* repudiate, deny, contradict, denounce, reject, abjure, retract, recant, gainsay; disclaim knowledge of, deny responsibility for, deny connection with, disown, divorce oneself from, refuse to acknowledge. —**Ant.** acknowledge, admit; claim, accept.

disbelief *n.* skepticism, lack of credence, doubt, doubtfulness, unbelief, dubiety, incredulity, distrust, mistrust. —**Ant.** belief, credulity, trust, faith, credence.

disburse *v.* pay out, lay out, allocate, give out in payment, distribute; *Slang* shell out, fork out.

discard *v.* eliminate, get rid of, throw away, throw out, weed out, thrust aside, cast aside, remove; abandon, shelve, have done with, relinquish, drop, shed, junk, dispose of, dispense with, dump, scrap, throw overboard, jettison. —**Ant.** retain, keep, preserve.

discern *v.* detect, make out, perceive, espy, catch sight of, descry, see, observe, behold, notice, pick out, ascertain. —**Syn. Study.** See NOTICE.

discerning *adj.* perceptive, acute, perspicacious, sharp, astute, penetrating, keen-sighted, sensitive, piercing, discriminating, shrewd, intelligent, wise, judicious, sage, sagacious, clear-sighted, sharp-sighted; showing discernment, quick to discern, having keen insight. —**Ant.** undiscerning, unperceptive, indiscriminate.

discharge *v.* **1.** set off, shoot, activate, touch off, fire off, detonate, trigger, explode; send forth a missile from, eject, launch, propel, let fly. **2.** emit, throw off, pour forth, send forth, project, expel, give forth, exude, gush. **3.** fire, dismiss, release, expel, oust, let go, terminate, sack, get rid of, give the gate to, can, axe, give one his walking papers, bounce, lay off, send packing, cashier, remove from office. **4.** release, allow to go, let go, free, set free, liberate. —*n.* **5.** firing, discharging, detonating, triggering, firing off, activating, exploding; detonation, explosion, blast, fusillade, shot, report, burst. **6.** release, release document, walking papers; demobilization. **7.** flow, suppuration, drainage, emission, ooze, issue, secretion, seepage. —**Syn. Study. 3, 4** See RELEASE.

disciple *n.* pupil, student, follower, devotee, aficionado, pursuer; adherent, believer, admirer, supporter, partisan; proselyte, neophyte, convert; *Informal* nut, freak. —**Ant.** master, teacher, leader, guru.

disciplinarian *n.* one who maintains discipline, enforcer of rules and order, stickler for rules, strict taskmaster, martinet, authoritarian, one who goes by the book.

discipline *n.* **1.** training, drill, drilling, schooling, indoctrination, enforcement of rules, rigor, diligent exercise, practice, preparation. **2.** method, regulated activity, prescribed habit, regimen, self-enforced practice, course of exercise. —*v.* **3.** train, instruct, teach by exercise, drill, prime, break in. **4.** punish, chastise, chasten.

disclaim *v.* disavow, disaffirm, deny, repudiate, renounce, decline, disown, forswear, abnegate, wash one's hands of. —**Ant.** claim, avow, affirm, acknowledge, accept, admit.

disclose *v.* **1.** tell, reveal, divulge, make known, lay bare, bare, uncover, unveil, leak, communicate, broadcast, publish, make public, impart. **2.** uncover, allow to be seen, reveal, show, expose, bring into view, cause to appear, bring to light. —**Ant. 1** conceal, hide, withhold. **2** cloak, mask, cover, veil.

discolor *v.* stain, spot, spoil the color of, change the color of, tarnish, streak, bleach, tinge.

discomfort *n.* **1.** ache, hurt, pain, soreness, irritation, affliction; hardship, absence of comfort, uncomfortableness, trouble, trial, disquietude; vexation, annoyance, nuisance, distress, malaise, misery. —*v.* **2.** make uneasy, embarrass, make uncomfortable, discomfit, distress, try, discompose, disquiet. —**Ant. 1** comfort, ease, pleasure.

discomposure *n.* perturbation, agitation, uneasiness, distraction, disturbed condition, confusion, disquietude, discomfiture, embarrassment, discomfort, flurry, anxiety, nervousness. —**Ant.** composure, poise, equanimity, impassiveness, easiness, quietude.

disconcerted *adj.* distracted, fazed, ruffled, nonplussed, agitated, unsettled, confused; upset, annoyed, disturbed, troubled, perturbed, thrown off, rattled. —**Ant.** unruffled, impassive, undistracted, stolid.

disconnected *adj.* confused, rambling, jumbled, disorganized, illogical, incoherent, mixed-up, disjointed, irrational. —**Ant.** connected, organized, logical, coherent.

disconsolate *adj.* depressed, downcast, unhappy, inconsolable, desolate, sad, dejected, crushed, despondent, miserable, forlorn, brokenhearted, pessimistic, heavyhearted, sorrowful, dispirited, woeful, woebegone, discouraged, doleful, low-spirited, melancholy, wretched, blue, *Slang* down, down in the dumps, down in the mouth, bummed out. —**Ant.** happy, joyous, cheerful, hopeful, optimistic, comforted.

discontented *adj.* unhappy, dissatisfied, regretful, displeased, bored, disgruntled, miserable, malcontent, fretful. —**Ant.** contented, satisfied, happy.

discontinue *v.* stop, break off, interrupt, terminate, suspend, drop, cease, desist, give up, quit, abstain, abandon, leave off, end, put an end to. **—Ant.** continue, further, extend.

discord *n.* **1.** dispute, disagreement, conflict, quarreling, contention, discordance, differences, dissension, disunity, division, lack of concord, being at odds, clashing, wrangling, friction, strife, incompatibility. **2.** discordance, dissonance, disharmony, harshness, grating noise, cacophony, unpleasant sounds. **—Ant. 1** harmony, consonance, accord, agreement, amity, unity, solidarity, compatibility. **2** harmony, consonance.

discount *n.* reduction, deduction, subtraction, concession, cut rate, cut, break, exemption, allowance, abatement; rebate.

discourage *v.* **1.** daunt, lessen the self-confidence of, dishearten, deject, unnerve, do in, dispirit, dismay, depress, prostrate; dash one's hopes, dampen one's spirits, disparage, decimate, destroy confidence in, unman, intimidate. **2.** dissuade, deter, divert from, restrain, keep back, disincline, advise against, express disapproval of, attempt to prevent; warn off, warn away. **—Syn. Study. 1** DISCOURAGE, DISMAY, INTIMIDATE mean to dishearten or frighten a person so as to prevent some action. To DISCOURAGE is to dishearten by expressing disapproval or by suggesting that a contemplated action will probably fail: *He was discouraged from going into business.* To DISMAY is to dishearten, shock, or bewilder by sudden difficulties or danger: *a prosecutor dismayed by disclosures of new evidence.* To INTIMIDATE is to deter by making timid: *The prospect of making a speech intimidates me.* **—Ant. 1** encourage, hearten, fortify, inspire, embolden. **2** encourage, urge, bid; welcome, support.

discouragement *n.* **1.** depression, dejection, melancholy, hopelessness, despair, despondency, low spirits, downheartedness, gloom, dismay, pessimism, moroseness, lack of spirit, heaviness of spirit. **2.** consternation, worry, damper, constraint, restraint, curb, hindrance, obstacle, impediment, chilling effect. **—Ant. 1** encouragement, hopefulness, high spirits, optimism, cheerfulness. **2** encouragement, boost, uplift.

discourse *n.* **1.** conversation, talk, intercourse, converse, discussion, colloquy, dialogue, chat, gab. **2.** lecture, address, speech, sermon, oration; dialogue, formal discussion of a subject; harangue, diatribe; essay, dissertation, treatise. **—***v.* **3.** talk, talk together, converse, confer, discuss.

discourteous *adj.* rude, impolite, ungracious, uncivil, uncourteous, unmannerly, ill-mannered, ungallant, cheeky, surly, boorish, disrespectful, impertinent, fresh, insolent, impudent; ill-bred, ill-behaved, ungentlemanly, uncourtly, unladylike, uncouth. **—Ant.** courteous, civil, polite, gracious, mannerly, respectful; well-bred, well-behaved, gentlemanly, ladylike.

discover *v.* **1.** find, come upon, stumble upon, chance upon, light upon, gain sight or knowledge of; learn, learn of, ascertain, detect, uncover, unearth, locate, bring to light, root out, ferret out, dig up. **2.** realize, perceive, discern, ascertain, detect, become cognizant of, recognize, notice, see, spot, determine, find. **—Syn. Study. 1, 2** See LEARN.

discredit *v.* **1.** defame, abuse, dishonor, impair the reputation of, disgrace, vilify, disparage, smirch, smear, debase, degrade, demean, vitiate, tarnish, taint, undermine, slur, sully, stigmatize, drag through the mud. **2.** prove false, deny, disallow, disprove, reject; destroy confidence in, shake one's faith in, undermine belief in; dispute, challenge, question. **—Ant. 1** credit, praise, laud. **2** credit, prove, support, accept, verify.

discreet *adj.* prudent, careful, tactful, sensitive, thoughtful, judicious, circumspect, diplomatic, polite, politic; cautious, wary. **—Syn. Study.** See CAREFUL. **—Ant.** indiscreet, rash, heedless, imprudent, careless, incautious, impetuous.

discrepancy *n.* difference, inconsistency, variance, disagreement, discordance, lack of correspondence, disparity, dissimilarity, divergence, incongruity, gap. **—Ant.** correspondence, accord.

discrete *adj.* separate, distinct, different, detached, disconnected, discontinuous, disjunctive, unattached, independent, unassociated; several, various. **—Ant.** merged, combined, interdependent, united, linked, connected.

discretion *n.* **1.** good judgment, power of choosing, preference, individual choice, predilection, inclination, volition, option. **2.** good sense, judgment, sound judgment, judiciousness, sagacity, acumen, discernment, prudence, discrimination, tact. **—Ant. 2** indiscretion, rashness, thoughtlessness, recklessness, irresponsibility, insensitivity, heedlessness, tactlessness, carelessness.

discriminate *v.* **1.** demonstrate bias, set apart as different, show disfavor toward, make a distinction against, disfranchise, disdain, treat as inferior. **2.** differentiate, draw a distinction, distinguish, separate. **—Syn. Study. 2** See DISTINGUISH.

discrimination *n.* **1.** bias, prejudice, differential treatment, bigotry, distinction, inequity, favoritism. **2.** discretion, discernment, judgment, distinction; taste, refinement; astuteness, acumen, shrewdness, sagacity, keenness, perspicacity.

discursive *adj.* digressive, rambling, roundabout, wandering, meandering, circuitous, diffuse, long-winded. **—Ant.** direct, methodical, coherent, succinct.

discuss *v.* talk about, talk over, speak of, discourse about, review, exchange views on, converse about, parley, debate, consider, examine, dissect.

discussion *n.* talk, dialogue, discourse, debate, parley, argument, disputation, review, consideration, deliberation; inquiry, colloquy, scrutiny, investigation, analysis; *Slang* hashing-out, powwow, rap.

disdain *v.* **1.** look down upon, frown upon, think unworthy of notice, spurn, despise, abhor, treat with contempt, loathe, detest, discountenance, snub, brush aside, deride; recoil from with pride, deem unbecoming, consider beneath oneself, deem unacceptable. **—*n.*** **2.** scorn, contempt, abhorrence, dislike, disrespect, distaste; feeling of superiority, haughty indifference, icy aloofness, intolerance. **—Syn. Study. 2** See CONTEMPT. **—Ant. 1** favor, admit, admire, like, love. **2** regard, admiration, respect, esteem, reverence, awe, fear.

disease *n.* illness, sickness, ill health, physical disorder, ailment, malady, infirmity, affliction, morbid condition. **—Ant.** health, salubriousness, healthiness.

disembark *v.* land, leave a ship, go ashore from a ship, get off a ship, debark; detrain, deplane; *Informal* pile out. **—Ant.** embark, go aboard; entrain, enplane.

disfavor *n.* **1.** disapproval, disapprobation, displeasure, disesteem, dislike, disregard, dissatisfaction, odium, disrespect; disgrace, unacceptableness, ignominy. **2.** disservice, harmful act, ill turn, discourtesy. **—Ant. 1** favor, approval, approbation, esteem, respect. **2** favor, service, kindness, courtesy.

disfigure *v.* mar the features of, deform, deface, cut up, injure the appearance of, render unsightly, maim, make ugly, scar, scarify, blemish; mutilate, damage, impair.

disgorge *v.* dislodge, throw up, discharge, regurgitate, throw out from the throat or stomach, spout, vomit forth, spew, eject, expel, cough up, spew up, cast up.

disgrace *n.* **1.** shame, dishonor, ignominy, infamy; discredit, reproach, embarrassment; blot, smirch, blemish, stain, tarnish; scandal, eyesore. **2.** disfavor, ill favor, contempt, disrepute, discredit; (be in) bad odor, *Slang* (be in) the doghouse. **—*v.*** **3.** embarrass, humiliate, dishonor, debase, bring reproach upon, shame, degrade, abase, bring shame upon, cause to lose favor, discredit; blot, smirch, taint, derogate, disparage. **—Syn. Study.** DISGRACE, DISHONOR, IGNOMINY, INFAMY imply a very low position in the opinion of others. DISGRACE implies being excluded and held in strong disfavor by others: *to bring disgrace to one's family by not paying debts.* DISHONOR suggests a loss of honor or honorable reputation; it usu. relates to one's own conduct: *He preferred death to dishonor.* IGNOMINY is disgrace that invites public contempt: *the ignominy of being caught cheating.* INFAMY is shameful notoriety, or baseness of action or character that is widely known and recognized: *The children never outlived the infamy of their father's crime.* **—Ant. 1** grace, honor, credit, glory. **2** grace, favor, esteem. **3** grace, honor, credit, distinguish.

disgraceful *adj.* shameful, dishonorable, scandalous, shocking, appalling, disreputable, discreditable, outrageous, ignominious; unworthy, unseemly, unbecoming; degrading, low, mean, inglorious, base, obnoxious, detestable, reprehensible, opprobrious, infamous, odious, despicable, vile. **—Ant.** honorable, reputable, creditable, worthy, seemly, becoming.

disgruntled *adj.* sulky, grumpy, vexed, peevish, displeased, irritated, discontented, malcontent, dissatisfied, sullen, petulant, grouchy, testy, shirty. **—Ant.** happy, contented, pleased, satisfied.

disguise *v.* **1.** assume a false identity, camouflage one's outward appearance, dress up, garb, mask, cloak, camouflage, veil; simulate, counterfeit, feign. **2.** conceal, hide, falsify, dissemble, cover up, muffle, mask, veil, shroud, misrepresent, gloss over. **—*n.*** **3.** cover, counterfeit appearance, masquerade, getup, deceptive covering, camouflage, concealment, guise, costuming, false appearance; veil, cover-up, mask, screen, blind, false front, veneer, façade, sham, pretense, pose.

disguised *adj.* camouflaged, in disguise, unrecognizable, undercover, incognito, masked; cloaked, dressed up, veiled.

disgust *v.* **1.** repel, revolt, be repulsive to, appall, put off, offend, fill with loathing, cause aversion; sicken, nauseate, turn one's stomach. **—*n.*** **2.** revulsion, repugnance, loathing, distaste, abhorrence, repulsion, aversion, contempt, hatred, detestation, antipathy, disaffection, displeasure, dislike, disrelish. **—Ant. 1** please, delight, impress. **2** liking, taste, relish, fondness, love, satisfaction, affection, pleasure.

dish *n.* **1.** plate, saucer, serving dish, platter, shallow bowl, flat receptacle, vessel. **2.** food, recipe, particular food, fare, article of food, victuals, edibles, comestible. **3.** dishful, portion, plateful, bowlful, serving, helping. —*v.* **4.** place, transfer, scoop, spoon, ladle; dole, portion, serve, dispense.

dishearten *v.* dispirit, dismay, discourage, faze, daunt, deject, depress, dash, abash, weaken the resolution of, crush, take the heart out of, sadden. —**Ant.** encourage, uplift, hearten, make determined.

disheveled *adj.* unkempt, ruffled, rumpled, disorderly, disarrayed, disarranged, mussed, messy, sloppy, untidy, in disorder, tousled, frowzy, blowsy, uncombed, bedraggled. —**Ant.** ordered, orderly, unruffled, neat, tidy; kempt, groomed.

dishonest *adj.* **1.** corrupt, not honest, untrustworthy, disposed to cheat, false, lacking integrity, perfidious, destitute of good faith, faithless, crooked, unscrupulous, deceitful, insincere, dishonorable, disingenuous, unprincipled, false-hearted, two-faced, fraudulent, underhanded. **2.** not honest, misleading, specious, deceptive, false, fraudulent, mendacious, untruthful, spurious. —**Ant. 1** honest, upright, honorable, forthright, aboveboard, law-abiding, principled, lawful. **2** honest, true, supportable, demonstrable.

dishonor *n.* **1.** shame, dishonorableness, disgrace, ill repute, discredit, ignominy, odium, disrepute, public disgrace, infamy, derogation, disfavor, humiliation, scandal; stigma, blot, blemish, stain. **2.** slight, affront, insult, offense, discourtesy. —*v.* **3.** disgrace, shame, bring shame on, bring reproach upon, defame, deprive of honor, discredit, abase, blacken, tarnish, stain the character of, sully, debase, stigmatize, disparage, degrade, humiliate, *Slang* dis. —**Syn. Study. 1** See DISGRACE. —**Ant. 1** honor, glory, renown, repute, fame; reverence, veneration; esteem, respect, regard, admiration. **2** honor, compliment, courtesy. **3** honor, credit.

disillusion *v.* undeceive, shatter one's illusions, free from illusion, open the eyes of, burst the bubble, clue in, disenchant, disenthrall, disabuse, bring one down to earth, break the spell. —**Ant.** deceive, lead on, beguile.

disintegrate *v.* fall apart, break up, break apart, go to pieces, shatter, crumble, crumble to fragments, reduce to particles, reduce to fragments, splinter, cause to fall to pieces; decay, decompose, rot. —**Syn. Study.** See DECAY. —**Ant.** blend, fuse, merge, coalesce; unite, combine, link up, join, connect.

disinterested *adj.* impartial, unbiased, neutral, free from bias, unprejudiced, fair, impersonal, outside, uninvolved, dispassionate, free from self-interest. —**Syn. Study.** See FAIR. —**Ant.** partial, biased, prejudiced, selfish, having an axe to grind.

disjointed *adj.* **1.** disconnected, detached, having the joints separated, unconnected, unattached, split, divided, apart, disarticulated, helter-skelter. **2.** rambling, mixed-up, confused, spasmodic, disconnected, disorganized, jumbled, tangled, chaotic, disharmonious, discontinuous, heterogeneous, incoherent, irrational, illogical. —**Ant. 1** jointed, connected, attached. **2** sensible, coherent, logical.

dislike *v.* **1.** regard with disfavor, not like, feel repugnance toward, hold as disagreeable, regard with displeasure, have no taste for, object to, look on with aversion, consider obnoxious; loathe, abhor, despise, hate, detest, abominate, scorn. —*n.* **2.** distaste, aversion, antipathy, disaffection; loathing, repugnance, hatred, repulsion, revulsion, abhorrence, abomination, detestation, disgust; antagonism, hostility, malice, animosity, disdain, animus, enmity, rancor. —**Ant. 1** like, esteem, favor. **2** liking, relish, delight, inclination, attraction, esteem, admiration.

dislocate *v.* put out of joint, disjoint, disconnect, disarticulate, unhinge, uproot, disengage, separate, disunite.

dislodge *v.* dig out, remove, displace, force out, eject, disturb, oust, uproot, extricate, disentangle, expel, dispel. —**Ant.** lodge, situate, bury, embed, root, plant, establish, seat.

disloyal *adj.* unfaithful, inconstant, untrue, false to one's obligations, recreant, dishonorable, undutiful; perfidious, seditious, treasonable, treacherous, traitorous, faithless, subversive. —**Ant.** loyal, faithful, constant, true, steadfast.

disloyalty *n.* faithlessness, unfaithfulness, apostasy, betrayal of trust, infidelity, lack of fidelity, breaking of faith, recreancy, perfidy, deceitfulness, falseness, falsity, breach of trust, inconstancy, double-dealing; treachery, treason, subversion, subversive activity. —**Ant.** loyalty, fealty, allegiance, fidelity, constancy.

dismal *adj.* **1.** gloomy, cheerless, somber, bleak, dreary, drab; doleful, mournful, dolorous, despondent, sad, joyless, dejected, pessimistic, hopeless, morbid, downcast, depressed, unhappy, lugubrious, sorrowful, disheartened, heavy-hearted, desolate, woeful, melancholy, in the dumps, disconsolate, rueful, down-in-the-mouth, woebegone, forlorn; grim-visaged, long-faced. **2.** poor, unmentionable, awful, terrible, abysmal, very bad, abominable, dreadful, horrible. **—Ant.** **1** cheerful, bright, inviting, gay, happy. **2** good, fine, excellent, admirable.

dismay *v.* **1.** fill with consternation, alarm, frighten, distress, appall, scare, unnerve, horrify; cow, daunt, dishearten, abash, intimidate, discourage; disillusion, disappoint, put off. *—n.* **2.** alarm, apprehension, anxiety, distress, concern, complete loss of courage, consternation, perturbation, trepidation; panic, terror, dread, fright, affright, horror, scare; utter disheartenment, discouragement, intimidation. **3.** disappointment, disillusionment, discouragement, exasperation. **—Syn. Study. 1** See DISCOURAGE. **—Ant. 1** cheer, reassure, relieve, encourage, hearten. **2** confidence, assurance, aplomb, self-possession, encouragement. **3** satisfaction, happiness, joy, reassurance, relief.

dismiss *v.* **1.** allow to leave, permit to go, release, excuse, send forth, let go, disperse, discharge; dissolve, adjourn, disband; free, liberate. **2.** fire, oust, discharge from office, put out of a job, sack, can, let go, terminate, remove from service, release, bounce, send packing, give one his walking papers, cashier, *Slang* pink-slip, give the heave-ho. **3.** put out of mind, reject, set aside, disregard, disclaim, discard, lay aside, repudiate, eliminate. **—Syn. Study. 1, 2** See RELEASE. **—Ant. 1** hold, detain, recall. **2** hire, employ, accept, admit. **3** welcome, accept.

disobedient *adj.* insubordinate, unsubmissive, rebellious, noncompliant, unmanageable, ungovernable, obstinate, recalcitrant, intractable, contrary, stubborn, refractory, fractious, froward, defiant, wayward, haughty, undutiful, perverse, unruly, disorderly, unyielding, seditious, insurgent, mutinous. **—Ant.** obedient, submissive, compliant, manageable, governable, dutiful, yielding, well-behaved.

disobey *v.* disregard, ignore, defy, break, go counter to, refuse to obey, rebel against, violate, overstep, transgress, resist, refuse to submit to, fail to comply with, infringe on. **—Ant.** obey, follow, abide by.

disorder *n.* **1.** disarray, mess, clutter, jumble, muddle, disorderliness, disarrangement, disorganization, chaos, disruption, confusion. **2.** ailment, illness, sickness, affliction, disease, organic disturbance, malady, indisposition, complaint. **3.** commotion, disturbance, public disturbance, fracas, turmoil, riot, ruckus, uproar, dissension, minor uprising, disturbance of peace, breach of order. **—Ant. 1** order, orderliness, organization, neatness.

disordered *adj.* disorganized, confused, disarranged, jumbled, haphazard, *Informal* messed up. **—Ant.** ordered, organized.

disorderly *adj.* **1.** disordered, out of order, unsystematized, disarranged, disorganized, unsystematic, pell-mell, unsorted, chaotic, jumbled, confused, topsy-turvy, helter-skelter; untidy, messy, sloppy, disheveled, slipshod, straggling, unkempt, careless, slovenly. **2.** unlawful, lawless, disruptive, unrestrained, rebellious, wayward, violating constituted order, constituting a nuisance; unruly, undisciplined, wild, boisterous, obstreperous, riotous, noisy, rowdy, rowdyish, rough-and-tumble, improper, bad, disreputable. **—Ant. 1** orderly, ordered, arranged, organized, methodical, neat, tidy.

disorganized *adj.* confused, disordered, jumbled, muddled, mixed-up, unsystematic, disordered, chaotic. **—Ant.** organized, ordered, systematic, systematized, methodized.

disoriented *adj.* not adjusted, confused, distracted, mixed-up, out of touch, out of joint; unstable.

disown *v.* disinherit, disclaim, disavow, repudiate, renounce, cast off, forsake, denounce, reject, refuse to acknowledge, refuse to recognize. **—Ant.** claim, accept, acknowledge, recognize.

disparage *v.* belittle, ridicule, discredit, run down, put down, mock, denigrate, demean, undervalue, underrate, depreciate, slight, detract from, derogate, *Slang* dis. **—Ant.** applaud, praise, laud, extol, acclaim, commend, compliment, appreciate.

disparate *adj.* dissimilar, different, unlike, contrasting, at odds, at variance, discrepant, discordant. **—Ant.** similar, like, homogeneous, parallel, accordant.

disparity *n.* inequality, imparity, discrepancy, gap, dissimilarity, disproportion, divergence, contrast, difference, dissemblance, dissimilitude, inconsistency; disagreement, contradiction. **—Ant.** accord, correspondence, parity, equality, unity.

dispassionate *adj.* unemotional, cool, unexcited, unimpassioned, undisturbed, imperturbable, unmoved, calm, serene, collected, composed, level-headed, unruffled, uninvolved, detached; impartial, unbiased, unprejudiced, fair, impersonal, disinterested, neutral. **—Ant.** passionate, impassioned, emotional, excited, apprehensive, concerned, disturbed, partial, biased, prejudiced, interested.

dispatch *v.* **1.** send off, send on the way, transmit rapidly, post, forward. **2.** finish, complete, conclude, execute quickly, wind up, carry out, dispose of rapidly, expedite, settle, discharge speedily, carry out speedily, make short work of. **3.** kill, finish off, execute, put to death, slay, put an end to; summarily shoot; murder, assassinate, bump off; slaughter, massacre. **—***n.* **4.** message, report, missive, bulletin, official communication, flash; letter, story, news account, item, piece, telegraphic message, communiqué. **5.** promptness, haste, quickness, expedition, swift execution, swiftness, rapidity, speed, celerity, alacrity.

dispel *v.* scatter, drive away, drive away by scattering, disseminate, diffuse, expel, repel, rout, drive off, disperse; put an end to, make disappear, dissipate, resolve, allay, eliminate, remove, dismiss, banish. **—Syn. Study.** See SCATTER.

dispensable *adj.* unnecessary, expendable, nonvital, disposable, unessential, nonessential, unimportant, of secondary importance, accessory, extrinsic, superfluous, extraneous. **—Ant.** indispensable, necessary, essential, needed, important.

dispensation *n.* **1.** distribution, dispensing, allocation, designation, dealing out, meting out, apportioning, dissemination, diffusion, consignment, allotment, bestowal, conferment, division; reparation, remuneration. **2.** permission, authorization, decree, credential, exemption, relaxation of a law, approval. **—Ant. 2** prohibition.

disperse *v.* drive off, scatter, disseminate, dissipate, send scurrying, send off, rout, dispel, disband; distribute, spread throughout, diffuse. **—Syn. Study.** See SCATTER. **—Ant.** assemble, gather, amass, call in, collect, pool, congregate, convene, summon, muster, concentrate, recall.

dispirited *adj.* dejected, down, downhearted, discouraged, downcast, disheartened, crestfallen, forlorn, glum, moody, unhappy, sad, cheerless, morose, melancholy, depressed; *Slang* down-in-the-mouth, down-in-the-dumps. **—Ant.** cheerful, light-hearted, up, elated, joyful.

displace *v.* **1.** supplant, supersede, replace, take the place of, unseat, oust, bump; crowd out, force out. **2.** dislocate, dislodge, move, shift; put out of the usual place, put in a wrong place. **3.** fill the space of, take the place of.

display *v.* **1.** exhibit, show, demonstrate, manifest, reveal, bring into view, make visible, put in plain sight. **—***n.* **2.** exhibition, exhibit, show; presentation, demonstration; manifestation. **—Syn. Study. 1** DISPLAY, EXHIBIT, MANIFEST mean to show or bring to the attention of another or others. To DISPLAY is literally to spread something out so that it may be most completely and favorably seen: *to display goods for sale.* To EXHIBIT is to display something to the public for inspection or appraisal: *to exhibit African violets at a flower show.* They may both refer to showing or revealing one's qualities or feelings: *to display wit; to exhibit surprise.* MANIFEST means to show feelings or qualities plainly or clearly: *He manifested his anger with a scowl.* **—Ant. 1** disguise, cloak, hide, conceal.

displease *v.* annoy, irritate, irk, pique, offend, disturb, provoke, incense. **—Ant.** please, gratify.

displeasure *n.* annoyance, vexation, irritation, wrath, indignation; dissatisfaction, dislike, disapproval. **—Ant.** pleasure, satisfaction, approval, endorsement.

disposal *n.* **1.** disposition, riddance, discarding, dumping, junking; clearance, settlement. **2.** command, control, direction, power, authority, management, supervision, government, administration, regulation. **3.** arrangement, array, grouping, placement, disposition, distribution, configuration, pattern, order, juxtaposition, organization. **—Ant. 2** acquisition, accumulation, collection, storage, accrual.

dispose *v.* **1.** incline, motivate; be willing. **2.** arrange, array, place; organize, order, rank, classify. **3.** distribute, deal out; get rid of. **—Ant. 2** disarray, disarrange, disorganize.

disposition *n.* **1.** spirit, nature, temperament, mental constitution, characteristic mood. **2.** tendency, inclination; predisposition. **3.** organization, arrangement, grouping, placement, distribution. **4.** control, disposal, power to dispose of a thing. **5.** bestowal; final settlement of a matter. **—Ant. 1** disaffection, unwillingness.

dispossess *v.* deprive of, take away, take back; evict, oust, expel.

disprove *v.* refute, discredit; controvert, prove to be false or wrong, prove to the contrary. **—Ant.** prove, demonstrate; show to be true.

disputable *adj.* questionable, debatable, controvertible, doubtful, uncertain, dubious.

dispute *v.* **1.** doubt, question, challenge, contradict; call in question, question the truth of, impugn. **2.** argue, quarrel, wrangle, squabble, clash. **—***n.* **3.** controversy, debate, argument; quarrel, disagreement, squabble, bickering, clash, altercation, feud, wrangle. **—Syn. Study. 3** See ARGUMENT. **—Ant. 1** agree to, concede, concur with.

disqualify *v.* **1.** disable, make unqualified, make unfit. **2.** pronounce unqualified, declare ineligible, deny participation.

disquieting *adj.* disturbing, upsetting,

vexing, troubling; disconcerting, unsettling, distressing, perturbing, annoying, irritating, bothersome.

disregard *v.* **1.** overlook, ignore, slight, neglect; pay no heed to, pay no attention to, take no notice of. **—***n.* **2.** lack of regard or respect, lack of attention, willful oversight. **—Syn. Study. 1** See SLIGHT. **—Ant. 1** heed; pay attention to, regard. **2** consideration, esteem, appreciation.

disreputable *adj.* **1.** shady, dishonorable, unprincipled; notorious, infamous, having a bad reputation, not reputable, of bad character. **2.** shameful, disgraceful, shocking, scandalous; not respectable. **—Ant. 1** reputable, honorable; principled. **2** respectable, admirable.

disrespect *n.* contempt, dishonor, irreverence, disregard, impoliteness, rudeness, discourtesy, lack of respect. **—Ant.** respect, esteem, regard, reverence.

disrespectful *adj.* rude, impolite, discourteous, impertinent, contemptuous. **—Ant.** respectful, courteous, polite.

disrupt *v.* **1.** interrupt, interfere with. **2.** upset; throw into disorder.

dissatisfied *adj.* displeased, unhappy, discontented; not satisfied. **—Ant.** satisfied, pleased, content.

dissect *v.* **1.** cut apart, anatomize, lay open, separate into pieces. **2.** analyze, study; examine part by part, break down.

dissemble *v.* hide, mask, disguise, camouflage, feign, conceal, dissimulate. **—Ant.** show, manifest, evidence, reveal.

disseminate *v.* scatter, spread, diffuse, disperse, circulate, broadcast.

dissension *n.* **—Syn. Study.** See QUARREL.

dissent *v.* **1.** disagree, protest, object, oppose; withhold assent, withhold approval. **—***n.* **2.** disagreement, difference, opposition, dissension, discord. **—Ant. 1** agree, concur; think in like manner. **2** agreement, concurrence, accord.

dissertation *n.* **1.** thesis. **2.** treatise, disquisition, tractate, monograph, memoir, discourse.

disservice *n.* hurt, wrong, injustice, injury, harm, bad turn. **—Ant.** service, favor; good turn.

dissident *adj.* **1.** disagreeing, differing, dissenting, opposing. **—***n.* **2.** dissenter, rebel, agitator. **—Ant. 1** agreeing, consenting, contented, satisfied. **2** conformist.

dissimilar *adj.* unlike, different, distinct, disparate; not similar. **—Ant.** alike, similar, corresponding, akin; identical.

dissimulate *v.* hide, conceal, dissemble, mask, disguise, camouflage.

dissipate *v.* **1.** squander, waste, misspend, fritter away, deplete, spend foolishly. **2.** disperse, dispel, scatter; break up and drive off. **3.** carouse, overindulge, live dissolutely, be intemperate. **—Syn. Study. 2** See SCATTER.

dissociate *v.* separate, disonnect, break off with.

dissolute *adj.* dissipated, corrupt, loose, debauched, immoral; unrestrained, abandoned. **—Ant.** moral, upright, temperate, sober, prudent, circumspect.

dissolve *v.* **1.** melt, liquefy, render, soften, deliquesce, thaw, run, thaw out. **2.** end, terminate, finish, conclude, abrogate, disband, sever, break up, annul, void. **3.** vanish, disappear, fade, dematerialize, evanesce, disintegrate, dissipate. **—Ant. 1** congeal, thicken, harden, solidify.

dissonant *adj.* **1.** harsh, discordant, inharmonious, grating, raucous, jangling, unmelodious, cacophonous. **2.** incompatible, incongruous, incongruent, inconsistent, hostile, irreconcilable, clashing, jarring, disagreeing, discrepant, contradictory, warring. **—Ant. 1** melodious, mellifluous, harmonious, pleasing, agreeable. **2** compatible, congenial, sympathetic, cooperative.

dissuade *v.* discourage; persuade not to, advise against, urge not to. **—Ant.** persuade to, advise in favor of, urge to.

distance *n.* **1.** span, gap, interval, intervening space, stretch. **2.** reservation, restraint, reserve, formality; coldness, coolness, aloofness, stiffness. **—Ant. 1** closeness, nearness. **2** warmth, friendliness, familiarity, closeness.

distant *adj.* **1.** far, far-off, remote, faraway, far-removed. **2.** remote; not closely related. **3.** unfriendly, cool, cold, aloof, stand-offish, detached, restrained, reserved. **—Ant. 1, 2** near, close. **2** close. **3** friendly, cordial, warm, affectionate.

distasteful *adj.* unpleasant, displeasing, disagreeable, repugnant, loathsome, disgusting. **—Ant.** pleasant, pleasing, delightful; tasty.

distend *v.* swell, bloat, swell out, expand, bulge, inflate, billow, puff out.

distill *v.* **1.** evaporate, condense, vaporize. **2.** separate by evaporation, produce by vaporization and condensation, purify by distillation; extract, draw out, draw forth.

distinct *adj.* **1.** separate, different, dissimilar, diverse, individual, not identical.

2. clear, lucid, plain; definite, well-defined, clear-cut, unmistakable. **3.** well-defined, unmitigated, explicit, unquestionable; extraordinary, supreme. **—Syn. Study. 1** See VARIOUS. **—Ant. 1–3** indistinct. **1** same, similar, identical; connected. **2** unclear, vague, obscure, indefinite, ambiguous, blurred. **3** usual, common.

distinction *n.* **1.** differentiation, separation, discernment, discrimination. **2.** difference, differential, contrast. **3.** excellence, superiority; eminence, notability, prominence, renown, importance, preeminence, greatness.

distinctive *adj.* unique, different, characteristic, uncommon, individual, original, singular, atypical, special, extraordinary. **—Ant.** typical, common, ordinary.

distinguish *v.* **1.** differentiate, set apart, single out, make distinctive, define, characterize. **2.** differentiate, discern, note differences; discriminate. **3.** make well known, make famous, make celebrated, make prominent. **—Syn. Study. 2** DISTINGUISH, DIFFERENTIATE, DISCRIMINATE mean to note the difference between two or more similar things. To DISTINGUISH is to recognize differences based on characteristic features or qualities: *to distinguish a light cruiser from a heavy cruiser.* To DIFFERENTIATE is to find and point out the exact differences in detail: *The symptoms of both diseases are so similar that it is hard to differentiate one from the other.* To DISCRIMINATE is to note fine or subtle distinctions and to judge their significance: *to discriminate prejudiced from unprejudiced testimony.*

distinguished *adj.* **1.** notable, renowned, famous, celebrated, acclaimed, illustrious, prominent, eminent; great. **2.** dignified, refined, elegant, distingué; grand, splendid, magnificent, superb. **—Ant. 1, 2** undistinguished. **1** unknown, uncelebrated. **2** inelegant, common, inferior.

distort *v.* **1.** misrepresent, misconstrue, twist the meaning of, give a one-sided meaning to. **2.** contort, disfigure, deform; misshape, twist out of shape.

distract *v.* **1.** divert, entertain, amuse; draw away the attention of. **2.** disturb, trouble, perplex, agitate, worry, disorder, confuse, bewilder; torment, madden, craze.

distraction *n.* **1.** diversion, amusement, entertainment, pastime, recreation. **2.** madness, desperation, frenzy, mental distress or upset.

distraught *adj.* distressed, agitated, anxious, distracted, frantic; beside oneself, extremely troubled; mad, seething, frenzied. **—Ant.** collected, calm, serene, cool, composed.

distress *n.* **1.** pain, torment, agony, anguish, torture; need, want, acute suffering; trouble, danger. **—*v.* 2.** grieve, trouble, upset, disturb, torment. **—Ant. 1** comfort, solace, relief; happiness; safety. **2** relieve, console, make happy.

distribute *v.* **1.** divide, apportion, disperse, parcel, allot; scatter, dispense, dole out, give out. **2.** deliver, circulate, disseminate. **3.** classify, class, separate, spread out, arrange, systematize, catalog, tabulate, methodize. **—Ant. 1, 2** collect, amass, accumulate, gather.

distribution *n.* **1.** dissemination, dispersion, scattering, spreading, circulation. **2.** arrangement, grouping, disposition, sorting, organization. **3.** apportionment, allotment, allocation, division.

district *n.* neighborhood, ward, parish, precinct; area, region.

distrust *v.* **1.** suspect, doubt, mistrust, question; feel distrust of, regard with suspicion. **—*n.* 2.** suspicion, doubt, mistrust, misgiving; lack of faith. **—Syn. Study. 2** See SUSPICION. **—Ant. 1** trust; depend on; have confidence in, have faith in, believe in. **2** confidence, trust, reliance.

disturb *v.* **1.** interrupt, bother, intrude on, annoy; destroy the quiet of. **2.** unsettle, disarrange, disrupt, dislocate, disorganize, put out of order. **3.** worry, distress, trouble, upset, unsettle, perturb. **—Ant. 2** establish, organize; put in order.

disturbance *n.* **1.** interruption, distraction, bother, annoyance. **2.** outbreak, rioting, disorder, uproar, turmoil, tumult, hubbub, ruckus. **3.** worry, upset, perturbation, distress. **—Ant. 1** calm, serenity, quiet. **2** order.

ditch *n.* **1.** pit, trench; hollow, excavation. **—*v.* 2.** abandon, get rid of, discard; scrap, junk.

dive *v.* **1.** fall, plunge, leap, jump. **—*n.* 2.** lunge, dash, plunge; jump, leap. **3.** shabby bar, sleazy nightclub, gin mill, honky-tonk.

diverge *v.* **1.** separate, deviate, split off, swerve, deflect; digress. **2.** differ, conflict, disagree, be at odds. **—Syn. Study. 1** See DEVIATE. **—Ant. 1** converge, agree, concur.

divergent *adj.* **1.** separate, splitting off, drawing apart. **2.** different, disagreeing, conflicting. **—Ant. 1** convergent. **2** agreeing, concurring, similar, like; identical.

diverse *adj.* **1.** different, differing, dissimilar, disparate, contradictory, conflicting, opposite. **2.** varied, of many kinds, sundry, various, different; eclectic, far-flung. **—Syn. Study. 2** See VARIOUS. **—Ant.** identical, same.

diversify *v.* vary; increase the variety of, variegate; diffuse, divide up, spread out.

diversion *n.* **1.** drawing away, turning aside, deflection. **2.** distraction, pastime, amusement; hobby, avocation.

diversity *n.* difference, variance, diversification, divergence; heterogeneity, variety, assortment. **—Ant.** likeness, similarity, sameness, homogeneity.

divert *v.* **1.** deflect, sidetrack, turn aside from a path, draw away from a course. **2.** distract, amuse, entertain; turn from serious thoughts, draw off to a different subject. **—Syn. Study. 2** See AMUSE.

divest *v.* **1.** strip or remove (clothing), disrobe; take off, get out of, peel off. **2.** deprive, dispossess; rid, strip, free. **—Ant. 1** clothe, dress, cover.

divide *v.* **1.** separate, split, subdivide, part, partition, *Slang* divvy up. **2.** distribute, share; allocate, apportion, deal out. **3.** disunite, cause to disagree, split, cause to take sides. **4.** classify, arrange, sort, separate, put in order. **—Ant. 1** connect, unite, join, attach. **3** unite, cause to agree.

divination *n.* **1.** augury, soothsaying, prophecy, prescience. **2.** guess, prediction, premonition, conjecture, foreboding.

divine *adj.* **1.** heavenly, holy, sacred, celestial. **2.** heavenly, excellent, wonderful, marvelous, admirable. **—***v.* **3.** foretell, prophesy, predict, forecast; fathom, surmise, guess, suspect.

divinity *n.* **1.** holiness, divine nature. **2.** religion, theology, science of divine things, theosophy, science of God. **3.** god, goddess, deity; divine being, celestial being.

division *n.* **1.** separation, splitting up. **2.** partition, divider, room separator, room divider. **3.** part, branch, department, section, unit, wing. **4.** split, difference, disagreement, divergence, variance, discord, disunion. **—Ant. 4** agreement, accord, union.

divorce *n.* **1.** separation, split, rupture, breach, rift. **—***v.* **2.** separate, segregate, disunite, dissociate, divide. **—Ant. 1** unity. **2** unite, join.

divulge *v.* disclose, reveal, tell, impart, relate, communicate; make known. **—Ant.** conceal, hide; keep secret.

dizzy *adj.* **1.** shaky, giddy, reeling, whirly, unsteady, light-headed, vertiginous. **2.** rapid, quick, fleet, swift. **—***v.* **3.** make unsteady, make giddy; confuse, bewilder. **—Ant. 1** steady, calm, composed.

do *v.* **1.** perform, execute, administer, carry out, bring about. **2.** accomplish, conclude, finish, fulfill, complete, achieve. **3.** clean, put in order, prepare, arrange, organize. **4.** behave, act, comport oneself, conduct oneself. **5.** conduct, proceed, carry on. **6.** suffice, serve; be satisfactory, be enough. **7.** fare, get on, make out. **8.** cover, travel through, visit, look at, stop in.

docile *adj.* manageable, tractable, compliant, tame, obedient, complaisant, agreeable, obliging, willing. **—Ant.** unruly, wild, ungovernable, disobedient, untrainable.

dock[1] *n.* **1.** wharf, pier, quay, waterfront, landing. **—***v.* **2.** berth, come into port, guide a ship into dock, go into dry dock for repairs. **3.** couple, hook up, link up, join, fasten together.

dock[2] *v.* **1.** crop, cut short; cut off. **2.** deduct a part from; deduct from the wages of, subject to loss.

docket *n.* agenda, program, schedule, calendar, timetable, card, bill, slate, roster, lineup, program of operation, order of business, things to be done.

doctor *n.* **1.** physician, medical practitioner, person licensed to practice medicine; (*variously*) internist, general practitioner, GP, dentist, osteopath, pediatrician, podiatrist, opthalmologist. **—***v.* **2.** treat, apply medication to, give medical treatment to. **3.** falsify, change, alter, tamper with.

doctrinaire *adj.* dogmatic, inflexible, dictatorial, rigid, arbitrary, absolute, opinionated, authoritarian, imperious, pontifical, overbearing; pigheaded, stubborn, bullheaded, mulish, stiff-necked, narrow-minded. **—Ant.** reasonable, temperate, moderate, mild, flexible.

doctrine *n.* principle, belief, gospel, conviction, philosophy, tenet, precept, teaching, dogma.

document *n.* **1.** official paper, record, instrument, legal form. **—***v.* **2.** support, back up, give weight to, verify, certify, substantiate.

doddering *adj.* shaking, trembling, tottering, weak, feeble, decrepit, senile. **—Ant.** spry, agile, nimble; healthy, strong.

dodge *v.* **1.** duck, swerve, sidestep, turn aside. **2.** evade, avoid, elude; equivocate, hedge, fend off. **—***n.* **3.** sidestep, duck, quick jump aside. **4.** *Informal* trick, stratagem, wile, device, machination.

doer *n.* active person, activist, go-getter, hustler, dynamo. **—Ant.** do-nothing, idler, loafer, good-for-nothing.

doff *v.* remove, take off, cast off, put off, shed, toss off; strip, undress, throw off, bare, disrobe, drop, step out of; scrap, junk, do away with, eliminate, discard, abandon, throw out. **—Ant.** keep, retain, save, maintain, conserve.

dog *n.* **1.** canine; pup, puppy, mutt, mongrel, cur. **2.** heel, scoundrel, villain, beast, blackguard.

dogged *adj.* **—Syn. Study.** See STUBBORN.

dogma *n.* doctrine, teachings, set of beliefs, principles, philosophy; convictions, credo, tenet.

dogmatic *adj.* **1.** opinionated, arbitrary, biased, prejudiced; imperious, dictatorial, domineering; stubborn, obstinate. **2.** doctrinal, expressing dogma. **—Ant. 1** diffident, vacillating, uncertain; docile, complaisant.

doldrums *n.* depression, melancholy, gloom, blues, dumps.

dole *n.* **1.** welfare, allotment, apportionment, allocation, share, handout; food or clothing distribution. *—v.* **2.** give, hand out, distribute as charity, deal, parcel.

doleful *adj.* sad, gloomy, sorrowful, woeful, unhappy, joyless, dreary, dismal. **—Ant.** happy, joyful, cheerful, lighthearted.

doll *n.* **1.** dolly, figurine, dummy; (*variously*) baby doll, rag doll, teddy bear, golliwog, puppet, marionette. **2.** pretty child, beauty; honey, sweetheart, darling.

dolorous *adj.* mournful, sorrowful, woeful, grievous, woebegone, miserable, anguished, wretched, pathetic, pitiable; calamitous, harrowing, distressing, lamentable, doleful, unhappy, mournful, rueful. **—Ant.** cheerful, happy, carefree, lighthearted, gay.

dolt *n.* idiot, jerk, clod, imbecile, fool, blockhead, bonehead, moron, nitwit, numskull, jackass, half-wit. **—Ant.** whiz, brain, genius.

domain *n.* **1.** estate, land, territory, property, fief. **2.** dominion, territory, province, kingdom, empire. **3.** sphere, area, field, region, province, bailiwick.

domestic *adj.* **1.** devoted to home life, hearth-loving, given to the concerns of home. **2.** domesticated, tame; housebroken. **3.** native, not foreign, not imported, indigenous, endemic, produced at home, native-grown, home-grown, homemade. *—n.* **4.** servant, attendant; household help; (*variously*) maid, cook, butler, houseboy. **—Ant. 2** wild, ferocious, untame. **3** foreign, imported.

domicile *n.* residence, legal residence, dwelling, home, house, place where one lives.

dominant *adj.* **1.** ruling, controlling, predominating, predominant, superior, commanding, authoritative; major, principal, chief, paramount. **2.** outstanding, most important, most prominent. **—Syn. Study. 1** DOMINANT, PREDOMINANT, PARAMOUNT describe something outstanding or supreme. DOMINANT applies to something that exerts control or influence: *the dominant powers at an international conference.* PREDOMINANT applies to something that is foremost at a specific time: *English is one of the world's predominant languages.* PARAMOUNT refers to something that is first in rank or order: *Safety is of paramount importance.*

dominate *v.* **1.** rule, govern, direct, control, domineer; preside over, be at the head of. **2.** occupy a commanding position, command visually; tower over, dwarf.

domination *n.* rule, control, authority, command, power, mastery, superiority. **—Ant.** subjection, inferiority, subordination.

domineering *adj.* tyrannical, oppressive, dictatorial, despotic, imperious, authoritative, commanding, dogmatic; overbearing, arrogant. **—Ant.** subservient, submissive; timid, shy.

dominion *n.* **1.** rule, sovereignty, jurisdiction, supremacy, authority, command, mastery. **2.** domain, empire, realm; territory, land, region.

don *v.* wear, put on, dress in, invest oneself with, get into, pull on.

donate *v.* contribute, give, present, bestow, bequeath; make a gift of.

donation *n.* present, gift, contribution.

done *adj.* ready; cooked sufficiently, cooked enough, prepared, finished, completed.

Don Juan lothario, Romeo, Casanova, Lochinvar, gallant, paramour, suitor, wooer, pursuer, courter, swain, admirer, squire, lady-killer; *Slang* wolf, lover boy, steady; boyfriend, fellow, man, young man, gentleman caller, beau.

donkey *n.* **1.** ass; (*variously*) mule, burro, jackass. **2.** fool, idiot, ass, jackass.

donnybrook *n.* brawl, fight, fray, affray, knock-down-and-drag-out, dustup, scuffle, free-for-all, fracas, melee, row, skirmish, set-to, ruckus, rumpus, ruction.

donor *n.* contributor, benefactor, giver; philanthropist, humanitarian.

doohickey *n.* thing, whatsis, whatchamacallit, doodad, object, device, gadget, gizmo, thingamajig, thingamabob, widget, thingummy, thingamadoodle, dingus, dojigger, dojiggy.

doom *n.* **1.** fate, lot, portion, destiny; end, destruction, ruin, death. **2.** pronouncement, judgment, verdict. **3.** the Last Judgment, Judgment Day, doomsday, end of the world, Armageddon, resurrection day. *—v.* **4.** mark for demolition, consign to ruin, consign to destruction. **5.** condemn, convict; pronounce judgment against. **—Ant. 2** acquittal, discharge, freedom.

doomsday *n.* Day of Judgment, end of the world, Judgment Day, the Last Judgment.

door *n.* doorway, entrance, portal, entranceway, entry, ingress, hallway; exit, egress.

dope *n.* **1.** preparation, substance, additive; medication, astringent, antiseptic, disinfectant. **2.** narcotics, drugs, opiates; uppers, downers. **3.** tip, news; inside information, scoop. **4.** dummy, fool, jerk, creep, nerd, drip, *Yiddish* klutz. **—*v.* 5.** drug, sedate, anesthetize, narcotize.

dopey *adj.* **1.** dumb, stupid, dull-witted, slow-witted, mindless, witless, simpleminded, block-headed, idiotic, asinine, thickheaded, brainless. **2.** sluggish, lethargic, slow-witted, torpid, slumberous, leaden, comatose. **—Ant. 2** brisk, energetic, peppy, vivacious, animated.

dormant *adj.* inactive, quiescent, idle, inert; sleeping, somnolent, torpid; hibernating. **—Syn. Study.** See INACTIVE. **—Ant.** active, operative, moving, awake.

dose *n.* measure, portion, share, ration, quota, allotment, daily dose, allowance, quantity; cut, division, percentage, segment, slice, section; shot, slug, nip, dram, injection, needle, pill, tablet, capsule; overdose, O.D.

dossier *n.* file, record, portfolio, brief, detailed report.

dot *n.* **1.** mark, speck, small spot, fleck; period, point. **—*v.* 2.** dab, dapple, spot.

dotage *n.* senility, feeblemindedness, second childhood. **—Ant.** youth, heyday, salad days.

dote *v.* **1.** bestow excessive love on, fuss over, lavish foolish fondness on. **2.** be in one's dotage, be senile.

double *adj.* **1.** multiplied by two, twice as much, twice as great, again as much. **2.** paired, twin, two-part. **3.** two-sided, dual, ambiguous; twofold in character. **4.** meant for two; accommodating two. **—*n.* 5.** twin, counterpart, duplicate, replica, clone; *Slang* spitting image, dead ringer. **—*v.* 6.** make twice as great, multiply by two, increase twofold.

double-cross *v.* betray, deceive, abandon, run out on, two-time, break faith with, sell out, let down, inform on, snitch on, tell on, turn in, denounce, sell down the river, rat on, do dirt, blow the whistle on.

double entendre *n.* double meaning, ambiguous statement, statement with two interpretations; risqué remark, off-color joke.

double-talk *n.* mumbo jumbo, gobbledygook, gibberish, nonsense, flimflam, balderdash, hokum, hocus-pocus, twaddle, blather, gabble, jabber, drivel, prattle, palaver, baloney, bunk, bunkum, *Slang* jazz.

doubt *v.* **1.** question, wonder; be skeptical concerning, have doubts about, be doubtful, feel uncertain, waver in opinion. **2.** distrust, mistrust, suspect; lack confidence in. **—*n.* 3.** uncertainty, indecision, question, lack of conviction. **4.** misgiving, mistrust, suspicion, apprehension, qualm. **—Ant. 1** believe, feel certain. **2** trust, believe, rely on. **3** resolve. **4** trust, belief, confidence, faith.

doubtful *adj.* **1.** undecided, uncertain, unconvinced, unsettled; hesitating, tentative, irresolute. **2.** dubious, suspicious, skeptical, incredulous; suspect, questionable. **3.** unclear, vague, obscure, uncertain, inconclusive. **—Syn. Study.** DOUBTFUL, DUBIOUS, SKEPTICAL, INCREDULOUS all involve one's reluctance to be convinced. DOUBTFUL implies a strong feeling of uncertainty or indecision about something or someone: *to be doubtful about the outcome of a contest.* DUBIOUS usu. implies vacillation or hesitation caused by mistrust or suspicion: *dubious about the statements of a witness.* SKEPTICAL implies a general disposition to doubt or question: *skeptical of human progress.* INCREDULOUS suggests an unwillingness or reluctance to believe: *incredulous at the good news.* **—Ant. 1** decided, certain, positive. **2** indubitable, incontrovertible; definite.

doughty *adj.* courageous, brave, bold, intrepid, fearless, unafraid, dauntless, stout-hearted; strong, confident, determined. **—Ant.** cowardly, timid.

dour *adj.* gloomy, sullen, morose, sour; cheerless, unfriendly, solemn, forbidding. **—Ant.** happy, bright, sweet, cheerful; soft.

douse *v.* drench, submerge, immerse, soak, plunge into water, souse, saturate.

dovetail *v.* **1.** unite, join, fit together, connect by interlocking. **2.** harmonize, coincide, match, tally, jibe.

dowdy *adj.* drab, shabby, sloppy, slovenly, frumpy, unattractive, tacky. **—Ant.** smart, well-dressed, fashionable, chic; neat, trim, tidy.

down *adj.* **1.** downcast, disheartened, dispirited, dejected, depressed, blue; down-and-out. **2.** sick, ill, ailing. **—*v.* 3.** fell, floor, drop, knock down, *Slang* deck. **4.** swallow, gulp; drink down, put away. **—Ant. 1** gladdened, glad, happy, spirited.

downcast *adj.* unhappy, sad, disconsolate, disheartened, cheerless, depressed, dejected, low, blue, discouraged. **—Ant.** happy, glad, encouraged, spirited.

downfall *n.* **1.** fall, ruin, ruination, destruction, collapse. **2.** downpour, shower, rainstorm, rain shower.

downhearted *adj.* unhappy, sorrowful, depressed, sad, disheartened, dispirited, dejected, discouraged, downcast. **—Ant.** happy, glad, encouraged, spirited.

downpour *n.* shower, cloudburst, rainstorm, rain shower.

downright *adj.* **1.** absolute, total, utter, thoroughgoing, complete, out-and-out. **2.** direct, straightforward, candid, open, frank, blunt; sincere, honest, aboveboard, straight-from-the-shoulder. *—adv.* **3.** completely, thoroughly, unmistakably, unequivocally; utterly, plainly; actually, really, in truth. **—Ant. 1** indefinite, unclear. **2** indirect, devious; insincere, dishonest.

down-to-earth *adj.* realistic, hardheaded, pragmatic, matter-of-fact, hardboiled, plain-spoken, sober, sensible, practical, unidealistic, no-nonsense, unsentimental; coarse, crass, earthy. **—Ant.** airy, romantic; pretentious, highfalutin, hoity-toity, snooty.

downtrodden *adj.* oppressed, tyrannized, subservient; harshly ruled; exploited.

downturn *n.* decline, downward trend, downtrend, dwindling, dip, drop, downfall, downslide, downswing, waning, diminution, degeneration, deterioration, slide, slip, skid, slump, sag, depression. **—Ant.** upturn, boom, growth, expansion, recovery.

doze *v.* **1.** nap, snooze; sleep lightly. *—n.* **2.** nap, snooze, light sleep, siesta, forty winks, catnap.

drab *adj.* **1.** dreary, gloomy, dull, dingy, dismal, cheerless, lackluster, somber, gray. **2.** dull brown, dull grayish brown. **—Ant. 1** bright, cheery, cheerful, colorful.

draft *n.* **1.** sketch, outline, rough sketch; preliminary version. **2.** wind, breeze; current of air. **3.** conscription, induction; military service. **4.** drag, pull, haul. **5.** postal order, money order. **6.** drawing from a cask; drink, gulp, swallow. *—v.* **7.** outline, diagram, sketch. **8.** induct, conscript, call for military service.

drag *v.* **1.** pull, haul, lug; draw with effort, pull forcibly; bring. **2.** trail; be drawn, be pulled along. **3.** crawl, creep along, inch along; move slowly. *—n.* **4.** *Slang* spoilsport, party-pooper, wet blanket, bore.

drain *v.* **1.** draw fluid from, pump off; remove by degrees, empty out. **2.** discharge, flow off gradually, flow out, debouch. **3.** sap, empty, deplete, impoverish; dissipate, use up. *—n.* **4.** tube, pipe, outlet; conduit, sewer, channel. **5.** sap, drag, strain; depletion, continuous strain. **—Ant. 3** fill, supply, replenish.

drama *n.* **1.** play, theatrical piece, dramatic composition. **2.** dramatic art, acting, direction, mise-en-scène, the stage, the theater. **3.** excitement, suspenseful events; dramatic quality, intense interest, vividness.

dramatic *adj.* **1.** theatrical; of the drama, for the theater. **2.** emotional, striking, sensational, climactic, melodramatic, suspenseful.

drape *v.* cover, wrap, swathe, enwrap, cloak, wrap up, swaddle, enswathe, veil, envelop, sheathe, shroud, enshroud; adorn, dress, garb, deck, attire, array, apparel, enrobe, bedeck, festoon, *Archaic* bedight.

drastic *adj.* extreme, radical, rash; bizarre, outlandish; dire, dreadful; dangerous, deleterious.

draw *v.* **1.** pull, drag, haul, tow, pull along. **2.** extract, pull out, take out, draw out, pick, pick out. **3.** attract, lure; allure, entice, charm; evoke, elicit, bring forth, make appear. **4.** sketch, etch, limn, picture with pencil or crayon, make a picture of. **5.** draft, write, make up, make out. **6.** get, take, deduce, infer. **7.** stretch, attenuate, elongate; extend, protract. **8.** drain, siphon; suck dry, pump out. *—n.* **9.** attraction, lure, enticement, inducement, *Slang* come-on. **10.** tie, stalemate; deadlock. **—Ant. 1** push, shove. **2** put in. **7** contract. **9** repellent. **10** victory; defeat.

drawback *n.* obstacle, hindrance, handicap, detriment, impediment, stumbling block, disadvantage.

drawing *n.* **1.** sketch, picture, study, illustration, delineation, depiction. **2.** selection of winners, lottery.

dread *v.* **1.** fear, be afraid of, anticipate with horror, shrink from, cringe at, cower at. *—n.* **2.** fear, fright, terror, fearfulness, apprehension, anguish, anxiety, trepidation. *—adj.* **3.** frightening, alarming, terrifying, fearful, awful, horrifying. **—Ant. 1** be unafraid. **2** confidence, courage, fearlessness, bravery.

dreadful *adj.* awful, terrible, horrible, tragic; fearful, frightful, alarming, shocking, distressing.

dream *n.* **1.** sleeping vision; nightmare, incubus. **2.** daydream, fantasy, reverie, vision. **3.** desire, wish, goal, hope; prospect, expectation. **4.** joy, pleasure, delight. *—v.* **5.** have a dream, have a sleeping vision. **6.** daydream, be lost in thought, pass time in reverie, muse. **7.** consider, think, give serious thought to. **8.** desire, wish, hope for, have as a goal, look forward to.

dreary *adj.* gloomy, depressing, cheerless, bleak, drab, sad, dismal, mournful, forlorn, melancholy. —**Ant.** cheerful, joyful, happy, bright.

dregs *n.* **1.** residue, sediment, settlings, grounds, deposit. **2.** the coarse part, lowest and worst part, lower depths; riffraff, rabble, canaille.

drench *v.* douse, saturate, wet, soak.

dress *n.* **1.** gown, frock, robe; costume. **2.** clothing, clothes, costume, attire, apparel, garb. —*v.* **3.** clothe oneself, attire, put on clothes. **4.** trim, adorn, ornament, decorate, deck, embellish, garnish. **5.** arrange, curl, groom; comb out, do up. **6.** treat, bandage, apply a dressing to, cleanse, disinfect.

dressmaker *n.* seamstress; couturier, (*fem.*) couturiere, *French* midinette.

dribble *v.* **1.** drip, drizzle, trickle, fall in drops, run bit by bit. **2.** bounce; kick.

drift *v.* **1.** be carried by a current, be borne along; wander, ramble, meander, amble, peregrinate. **2.** pile up, amass, gather, accumulate; scatter. —*n.* **3.** direction, course, current, flow, stream; movement. **4.** heap, pile, mass, accumulation. **5.** implication, meaning, gist, sense; object, objective, aim, direction, purpose, intention.

drill *n.* **1.** machine for drilling, boring tool. **2.** practice, training, repetition, repeated exercises. —*v.* **3.** punch, pierce, puncture, bore. **4.** instruct by repetition, train, exercise, work with.

drink *v.* **1.** [ingest] imbibe, absorb, take in, partake of, taste; (*variously*) quaff, drain, sip, swallow, gulp, guzzle, slug, swig, swill, *Slang* belt, chug-a-lug, chug, knock back. **2.** [consume alchoholic beverages] tipple, tope, *Informal* booze, booze it up, bend an elbow. **3.** toast, salute, drink in honor of. —*n.* **4.** beverage, liquid refreshment, libation. **5.** alcohol, alcoholic liquor; alcoholism, drunkenness, heavy drinking, *Informal* the bottle, booze, *Slang* the sauce. **6.** quaff, sip, taste, gulp, swallow, swig, slug, draft, *Slang* belt. —**Syn. Study. 1** DRINK, IMBIBE, SIP refer to taking liquids into the mouth. They are also used figuratively in the sense of taking in something through the mind or the senses. DRINK is the general word: *to drink coffee; to drink in the music.* IMBIBE is a more formal word, used most often in a figurative sense but also in reference to liquids, esp. alcohol: *to imbibe culture; to imbibe with discretion.* SIP implies drinking little by little: *to sip a soda; to sip the words of Shakespeare.*

drip *v.* **1.** trickle, dribble; splash, sprinkle, drizzle; let fall in drops. —*n.* **2.** trickle, dribble, dripping. **3.** ass, jerk, creep, nerd, bore, dummy, *Yiddish* klutz.

drive *v.* **1.** move, advance; lead, guide, conduct; push forward, spur, urge along. **2.** press, urge, prod, goad; incite, impel. **3.** advance, press forward; rush. **4.** go by car, ride, go driving, motor; guide, steer; operate. **5.** motivate; force, compel, coerce. **6.** suggest, intend, mean, insinuate. —*n.* **7.** ride, outing, excursion; trip by car. **8.** push, surge, advance, campaign, onward course. **9.** motivation, ambition, impulse, push.

drivel *v.* **1.** drool, dribble, slobber, slaver. **2.** ramble, babble, talk foolishly, talk nonsense. —*n.* **3.** gibberish, rambling, babbling, nonsense, senseless talk.

driver *n.* **1.** chauffeur. **2.** cowboy, drover, herdsman.

droll *adj.* humorous, whimsical, amusing, oddly amusing, funny, laughable, comic, comical; offbeat, eccentric, strange. —**Syn. Study.** See AMUSING. —**Ant.** ordinary, common; dull, boring.

drone[1] *n.* parasite, idler, loafer, lazy person.

drone[2] *v.* **1.** hum, buzz, whir, vibrate. —*n.* **2.** hum, buzz, whir, vibration, murmuring.

drool *v.* slobber, slaver, dribble, water at the mouth, salivate, drivel.

droop *v.* **1.** sag, hang down, hang listlessly, incline downward. **2.** weaken, wither, lower, dim; lose vigor, sink, flag, diminish. —**Ant. 1** rise. **2** revive, rally, flourish, perk up.

droopy *adj.* **1.** hanging down, limp, sagging, dangling, bowed, bent. **2.** downcast, depressed, dejected, downhearted, dispirited, cast down, spiritless, blue, doleful, down, subdued, dashed, down-in-the-mouth, world-weary, despondent, despairing, pining, languishing.

drop *n.* **1.** droplet, drip, driblet, globule, tear, bead. **2.** dash, dab, pinch, trace, smack, sprinkling, *Informal* smidgen, *French* soupçon. **3.** descent, fall; declivity, slope, plunge; precipice, abyss. **4.** decline, fall, lowering, decrease. —*v.* **5.** drip, dribble, trickle, fall in drops. **6.** fall, plunge, plummet, dive, descend. **7.** abandon, leave, forsake, give up; bring to an end, terminate, cease to consider. **8.** fall, lower, lessen, dwindle, decline, diminish, slacken, slide, sink. **9.** discharge, dismiss, fire, *Informal* can, sack. **10.** fell, floor, deck, knock down. **11.** leave out, omit, fail to include, fail to pronounce. —**Ant. 2** much, lots, loads, quantities. **3** rise. **4** rise, increase. **6** rise, soar, shoot up. **7** take up, discuss, consider, talk over. **8** rise, increase, go up. **9** hire, sign on, add. **11** include, pronounce.

drought also **drouth** *n.* **1.** aridity; period of dry weather, lack of rain. **2.** scarcity, paucity, lack, shortage, deficiency, want, dearth, need, insufficiency.

drown *v.* **1.** asphyxiate, suffocate; go to Davy Jones's locker, go down for the third time, meet a watery end. **2.** inundate, flood, deluge, immerse, submerge, drench, soak. **3.** overpower, overwhelm, overcome, engulf, swallow up. **—Ant. 2** dry, drain.

drowsy *adj.* **1.** sleepy, dozy, lethargic, languid, listless, sluggish, slow, lazy, tired. **2.** hypnotic, soporific, somnolent, soothing. **—Ant. 1** alert, lively.

drub *v.* beat, whip, bastinado, cane, thrash, flog, hit, whale.

drudge *n.* **1.** menial, lackey, toiler, hack, grubber, underling, subordinate, inferior. **—*v.* 2.** toil, hack, grub, plod, labor, struggle, slave.

drudgery *n.* distasteful work, menial labor, toil, hack work, travail, grind. **—Syn. Study.** See WORK.

drum *n.* **1.** barrel, keg, cask, tub. **—*v.* 2.** rap, tap, beat, beat rhythmically, tattoo. **3.** roll, roar, beat, rumble, reverberate, din, beat a tattoo; pulsate. **4.** expel, discharge, dismiss, drive out. **5.** repeat persistently, reiterate, drive home, force, hammer at, din, din in the ear, harp on.

drunk *adj.* **1.** intoxicated, inebriated, sodden, besotted, tipsy, under the influence of alcohol; *Slang* soused, plastered, smashed, stewed, looped, zonked, zapped, three sheets to the wind. **—*n.* 2.** drunkard, lush, sot, soak, rummy, souse, toper, barfly; alcoholic, dipsomaniac. **3.** drinking spree, binge, beer-bust, carousal, *Slang* bust, bender. **—Ant. 1** sober, abstemious, abstinent, temperate.

dry *adj.* **1.** arid, rainless, free from moisture. **2.** thirsty; desiring liquid, suffering for water, dehydrated, parched. **3.** uninteresting, dull, tedious, monotonous, boring, wearisome. **4.** deadpan, low-key; droll, quietly humorous. **—*v.* 5.** blot, wipe; remove the moisture from, make dry. **6.** become dry, shrivel up, desiccate, dehydrate. **—Syn. Study. 1** DRY, ARID both mean without moisture. DRY is the general word indicating absence of water or freedom from moisture, which may be favorable or unfavorable: *a dry well; a dry bath towel.* ARID suggests intense dryness in a region or climate, resulting in bareness or in barrenness: *arid tracts of desert.* **—Ant. 1** wet, damp, moist, humid, dank. **3** interesting, fascinating, lively, entertaining.

dual *adj.* two-fold, double, two-part. **—Ant.** single, singular.

dubious *adj.* **1.** doubtful, uncertain, unsure; skeptical, unconvinced, incredulous. **2.** questionable, suspicious, suspect, shady; unreliable, untrustworthy, undependable. **—Syn. Study. 1** See DOUBTFUL. **—Ant. 1** sure, positive, certain, definite. **2** reliable, trustworthy, dependable.

duck *v.* **1.** swerve, veer, dodge, sidestep; crouch, stoop. **2.** evade, avoid, elude, dodge, give the slip to.

ductile *adj.* **1.** flexible, pliable, plastic, formable, malleable, elastic, pliant, stretchable, bendable, tensile, moldable, supple, shapable, extensible. **2.** manipulable, tractable, swayable, susceptible, manageable; compliant, amenable, docile, adaptable, complaisant, submissive. **—Ant. 1** inflexible, rigid, set, fixed, firm, unbending.

dud *n.* failure, fiasco, debacle, disappointment, miscarriage, fizzle, botch; *Slang* flop, washout, dog, bust, bomb, bummer, lead balloon, lemon, clinker, loser, hash. **—Ant.** success, smash, sensation, triumph, winner.

due *adj.* **1.** unpaid, owing, owed, outstanding; in arrears. **2.** suitable, fitting, rightful, deserved, merited, appropriate, becoming, proper; sufficient, adequate. **3.** scheduled, expected to arrive. **4.** sufficient, adequate, enough, ample, plenty of. **—Ant. 2** inappropriate, unbecoming. **4** insufficient, inadequate, scanty, scant.

dulcet *adj.* pleasing, mellifluous, melodious, sonorous; lyrical, musical, tuneful.

dull *adj.* **1.** blunt; not sharp, not keen. **2.** slow, dense, thick, obtuse, dimwitted, stupid. **3.** slow, inactive, uneventful; not brisk. **4.** boring, uninteresting, vapid, vacuous, unimaginative, prosaic, trite. **5.** lackluster, muted, subdued, quiet. **6.** muffled, indistinct, subdued, deadened. **—Ant. 1** sharp. **2** intelligent, clever, bright. **3** active, lively, spirited. **4** interesting, imaginative, exciting. **5** bright. **6** distinct, clear, well-defined.

dullard *n.* dunce, dolt, nitwit, halfwit, imbecile, dumbbell, dummy.

duly *adj.* **1.** rightfully, properly, suitably, deservedly; correctly, appropriately. **2.** punctually; on time, at the proper time.

dumb *adj.* **1.** mute, aphasic, incapable of speech. **2.** silent, mute, mum, refusing to speak. **3.** stupid, unintelligent; foolish, dopey; dull, dense, dimwitted. **—Ant. 1** articulate; capable of speech. **3** smart, intelligent, clever, bright.

dumbbell *n.* dunce, ignoramus, fool, blockhead, oaf, clod, clown, dummy, numskull, simpleton, booby, nitwit, moron, imbecile, idiot, dimwit, *German* dummkopf; *Slang* dumb-dumb, meathead, lunkhead, noodlehead, lamebrain, birdbrain.

dumbfound Also **dumfound** *v.* stun, astonish, startle, amaze, flabbergast.

dummy *n.* **1.** mannequin, model, form, figure. **2.** blockhead, dolt, dumbbell, oaf, idiot, clown, simpleton, chowderhead, knucklehead, dunderhead, dumb-dumb, *Yiddish* klutz, *German* dummkopf.

dump *v.* **1.** toss, drop heavily, unload carelessly. **2.** unload, empty; dispose of, get rid of. **—***n.* **3.** dumping ground, rubbish heap, refuse pile, junkyard. **4.** hovel, hole; shack, shanty, hut.

dunce *n.* dummy, idiot, fool, moron, imbecile, simpleton, dimwit, nitwit, blockhead, numskull.

dunk *v.* douse, immerse, dip, plunge, submerge, souse, sop, duck, saturate, soak, steep, slosh, drench, bathe, drown, inundate, engulf, deluge, baptize.

duo *n.* pair, twosome, couple; combination, *Slang* combo.

dupe *n.* **1.** pawn, cat's paw, *Slang* patsy, fall guy, sucker. **—***v.* **2.** trick, fool, mislead, deceive, *Slang* put on; humbug, bamboozle, hoodwink, scam, *Slang* con.

duplicate *n.* **1.** facsimile, reproduction, replica, imitation; copy, carbon copy, photocopy, photostat. **—***v.* **2.** match, parallel, repeat, make again, copy, clone. **—Ant. 1** original.

duplicity *n.* deceit, deceitfulness, fraud, dishonesty, guile, cunning, falseness, deception. **—Syn. Study.** See DECEIT. **—Ant.** straightforwardness, forthrightness, candor.

durable *adj.* enduring, lasting, sound, substantial, sturdy, tough, strong, long-wearing. **—Ant.** fragile, frail, weak, flimsy.

duration *n.* continuance, extent, term, period, continuation.

duress *n.* force, constraint, threat, coercion; compulsion, pressure.

dusk *n.* twilight, sunset, sundown, nightfall.

dusky *adj.* **1.** dim, veiled, cloudy, gloomy, murky. **2.** dark, swarthy, dark-hued. **—Ant. 1** bright, clear. **2** fair, light.

dutiful *adj.* diligent, faithful, loyal; obedient, compliant, conscientious. **—Ant.** uncaring; disrespectful; disobedient; careless, remiss.

duty *n.* **1.** obligation, responsibility; onus; business, province. **2.** function, task, assignment, charge. **3.** tax, tariff, customs, excise, levy. **—Syn. Study. 1** DUTY, OBLIGATION refer to something a person feels bound to do. A DUTY often applies to what a person performs in fulfillment of the permanent dictates of conscience, piety, right, or law: *one's duty to tell the truth; a parent's duty to raise children properly.* An OBLIGATION is what is expected at a particular time in fulfillment of a specific and often personal promise, contract, or agreement: *social or financial obligations.*

dwarf *n.* **1.** fairy, pixie, sprite, elf, gnome, leprechaun, imp, goblin, troll. **2.** midget, pygmy. **—***adj.* **3.** diminutive, small, bantam, tiny, pygmy, miniature, petite, baby. **—***v.* **4.** overshadow, dim, diminish. **—Syn. Study. 2** DWARF, MIDGET, PYGMY are terms for a very small person. A DWARF is someone checked in growth or stunted, or in some way not normally formed. A MIDGET (not in technical use) is someone normally proportioned, but diminutive. A PYGMY is properly a member of one of certain small-sized peoples of Africa and Asia, but the word is often used imprecisely to mean dwarf or midget. **—Ant. 3** huge, gigantic.

dwell *v.* **1.** reside, live, inhabit, abide. **2.** linger over, continue for a time, harp on. **—Ant. 1** roam.

dwelling *n.* house, home, residence, abode, domicile, habitation, shelter, lodging, lodgings, *Informal* digs; apartment, flat, pied-à-terre, *Slang* pad; (*variously*) mansion, palace, homestead, hovel, hut, shack, shed, cottage, ranch, condominium, condo, co-op, nest, lair, den, burrow, cave. **—Syn. Study.** See HOUSE.

dwindle *v.* diminish, decrease, decline, lessen, shrink, become smaller; wane, fade. **—Syn. Study.** See DECREASE. **—Ant.** increase, grow; burgeon, flourish.

dye *n.* **1.** color, coloring, tint, shade, coloration, stain. **—***v.* **2.** color, tint, stain.

dynamic *adj.* active, vigorous, vital, energetic, forceful, driving, powerful.

dynamite *v.* destroy, demolish, blow up, wipe out, annihilate, devastate, raze, decimate, ruin, wreck, dismantle, shatter, obliterate, eradicate, extinguish, exterminate, *Slang* trash. **—Ant.** create, construct, erect, build, put up, make.

dynasty *n.* ruling house, line, regime, lineage, regnancy, regency, suzerainty, reign, monarchy, kingship, hegemony, crown; government, administration, dominion, authority, jurisdiction.

dyspeptic *adj.* bad-tempered, ill-natured, ill-humored, crotchety, hot-tempered, irritable, irascible, short-tempered, mean, choleric, touchy, sour-tempered, waspish, cantankerous, grouchy, crabby, grumpy, ornery, fractious, contentious, *Brit.* shirty. **—Ant.** good-natured, agreeable, imperturbable, even-tempered, calm, serene.

eager *adj.* **1.** excited, avid, keen, desirous, yearning, longing, impatient, raring, athirst, thirsting, hungering, agog. **2.** earnest, enthusiastic, intent, intense, fervent, fervid, ardent, impassioned, passionate, zealous, spirited; industrious, enterprising, hardworking, persevering, diligent, resolute; ambitious, aggressive. **—Ant. 1** indifferent, unconcerned, uninterested; opposed, adverse. **2** indifferent, uninterested, apathetic, impassive, heedless, unmindful, inattentive, irresolute, unambitious, unenterprising, unaggressive; lazy, negligent.

early *adv.* **1.** during the first part, near the beginning. **2.** ahead of time, in advance, beforehand; too soon, prematurely, before the usual time; betimes, in good time. *—adj.* **3.** first, initial. **4.** ahead of time, beforehand, premature. **5.** ancient, very old, primal, primitive, prehistoric, archaic, primeval, primordial. **—Ant. 1–5** late. **1** later, near the end. **2** late, tardily. **3** latter, later, last. **4** tardy. **5** modern.

earmark *n.* **1.** characteristic, feature, trait, quality, attribute, peculiarity, sign, token, identifying mark, singularity, label, tag, distinctive feature, stamp, band. *—v.* **2.** designate, tag, allocate, assign, reserve, set aside, put away, hold.

earn *v.* **1.** make, receive, gain, get, collect, draw, realize, reap, clear, net, pick up, bring home. **2.** deserve, merit, rate, warrant, be entitled to; attain, achieve, secure, gain, win. **—Syn. Study. 1, 2** See GAIN. **—Ant. 1** waste, lose, spend, forfeit, squander. **2** lose, forfeit.

earnest *adj.* **1.** resolute, serious, intent, eager, determined, purposeful, diligent, hard-working, persevering, industrious, assiduous, ambitious, devoted. **2.** sober, serious, thoughtful, grave, solemn, staid, sedate; stable, constant, fixed, steady, firm. **3.** sincere, honest, heartfelt, deeply felt, wholehearted; impassioned, passionate, intense, ardent, zealous, fervent, fervid, urgent, insistent, vehement; spirited, eager, enthusiastic. **—Syn. Study. 1, 3** EARNEST, RESOLUTE, SERIOUS, SINCERE imply having qualities of steady purposefulness. EARNEST implies having a purpose and being steadily and soberly eager in pursuing it: *an earnest student.* RESOLUTE adds a quality of determination: *resolute in defending the rights of others.* SERIOUS implies having depth and a soberness of attitude that contrasts with gaiety and frivolity; it may include the qualities of both earnestness and resolution: *serious and thoughtful.* SINCERE suggests genuineness, trustworthiness, and absence of superficiality: *a sincere interest in a person's welfare.* **—Ant. 1, 2** frivolous, capricious, trifling, irresolute, apathetic; sportive, jesting; unsteady, unstable; flippant, light. **3** insincere, indifferent, halfhearted, unimpassioned; unspirited, unenthusiastic.

earnings *n.* money earned, income, wages, salary, pay, payment, compensation, profits, receipts, proceeds. **—Ant.** costs, expenditures, outlay.

earth *n.* soil, dirt, ground, land, topsoil, sod, turf, loam, clay, dust.

earthly *adj.* **1.** worldly, mundane, terrestrial; secular, nonspiritual, humanistic, ungodly, temporal, material, materialistic; corporeal, physical, bodily. **2.** possible, practical; conceivable, imaginable, feasible. **—Syn. Study.** EARTHLY, WORLDLY, MUNDANE, TERRESTRIAL refer to that which is concerned with the earth literally or figuratively. EARTHLY now almost always implies a contrast to that which is heavenly: *earthly pleasures; our earthly home.* WORLDLY is commonly used in the sense of being devoted to the vanities, cares, advantages, or gains of physical existence to the exclusion of spiritual interests or the afterlife: *worldly success; worldly standards.* MUNDANE is a formal equivalent of WORLDLY and suggests that which is bound to the earth, is not exalted, and therefore is commonplace: *mundane pursuits.* TERRESTRIAL applies to the earth as a planet or to land as opposed to water: *the terrestrial globe; terrestrial areas.* **—Ant. 1** unearthly, celestial, heavenly, spiritual, divine, godly; nonmaterialistic.

earthquake *n.* quake, tremor, earth tremor, shock, seism, temblor, upheaval.

earthy *adj.* coarse, lusty, bawdy, ribald, crude, rough, unrefined, unblushing, robust, vulgar, primitive, uncultured, uncultivated, peasant; *Slang* raunchy, funky; smutty, dirty, filthy, obscene, indecent. **—Ant.** genteel, refined, dainty, elegant, polished.

ease *n.* **1.** comfort, relief, assuagement, solace, easement, freedom from pain. **2.** comfort, leisure, relaxation, restfulness, rest, quiet, repose, serenity, tranquillity, security, peace of mind, freedom from worry; prosperity, luxury, luxuriousness, abundance, plenty, affluence. **3.** easiness, effortlessness, facility, readiness. **4.** naturalness, relaxed manner, unaffectedness, unconstraint, aplomb, poise, composure, confidence. *—v.* **5.** relieve;

assuage, mitigate, abate, allay, alleviate, mollify, palliate, lessen, lighten, diminish; comfort, soothe, console, quiet, still, calm, pacify, disburden. **6.** move carefully, maneuver gently, handle with care, slip, slide. **—Ant. 1** pain, discomfort, misery, irritation. **2** hardship, difficulty, travail, misery, poverty, worry, concern, distortion; turmoil, disturbance, agitation, annoyance, toil, hard work, sweat. **3** difficulty, effort, exertion, great pains; clumsiness, awkwardness. **4** stiffness, formality, affectedness, tension, constraint; embarrassment, discomposure, self-consciousness, awkwardness. **5** worsen, irritate, aggravate, discomfort, make uneasy, make nervous, make tense.

easily *adv.* **1.** with ease, without difficulty, without trouble; with facility, handily, without a hitch; readily, effortlessly, facilely, lightly, freely, smoothly. **2.** beyond question, certainly, surely, far and away, by far, clearly, plainly, undoubtedly, undeniably, beyond doubt, beyond the shadow of a doubt. **—Ant. 1** with difficulty; awkwardly, clumsily. **2** by a hair, by the skin of one's teeth; questionably, doubtfully.

East, the *n.* the Orient, the Far East, Asia; the Near East; Eastern Hemisphere. **—Ant.** the West, Western Hemisphere, the Occident.

easy *adj.* **1.** not difficult, not hard, easily done, effortless, simple, not burdensome, light, painless. **2.** comfortable, untroubled, unworried, carefree; leisurely, relaxed, restful, serene, tranquil, peaceful, calm, composed, secure; wealthy, luxurious, well-to-do, affluent; *Slang* cushy. **3.** relaxed, unaffected, natural, easygoing, informal, friendly, outgoing, unconstrained, pleasant, gracious, open, candid, frank, unforced. **4.** not strict, lenient, permissive, not harsh, not oppressive, indulgent, accommodating, yielding, tractable, compliant, soft, gentle, benign, mild, docile; unsuspicious, gullible, overly trusting, naïve. *—adv.* **5.** easily, comfortably, without worry, without anxiety, without tension, serenely, peacefully, calmly, scarcely, leisurely. **—Ant. 1** difficult, hard, arduous, laborious, burdensome, exhausting. **2** hard, difficult, uncomfortable, impoverished, poor; troubled, worried, anxious, insecure. **3** stiff, rigid, formal, unnatural, affected, forced, tense, anxious; *Slang* uptight; introverted, constrained, self-conscious, embarrassed, secretive, mysterious. **4** hard, strict, harsh, rigid, difficult, demanding, exacting, authoritarian, dictatorial, oppressive, unyielding; suspicious, guarded. **5** uncomfortably, anxiously.

easygoing *adj.* calm, relaxed, carefree, happy-go-lucky, nonchalant, casual, offhand, unexcitable, insouciant, unruffled; even-tempered, mild-tempered, patient, unconcerned, unworried. **—Ant.** tense, worrying, compulsive, rigid, excitable, volatile, impatient, explosive; *Slang* uptight.

eat *v.* **1.** feed, take nourishment, take sustenance, take a meal, break bread; (*variously*) breakfast, lunch, dine, sup; feast, gormandize; consume, devour, take, ingest, dispatch, bolt, gulp, wolf down, gobble, nibble. **2.** corrode, waste away, dissolve, rust, wear away. **—Ant. 1** fast, abstain; starve, go hungry, famish.

eavesdrop *v.* listen surreptitiously, bend an ear, listen in, spy, overhear, attend, harken, pry, snoop, tap, monitor, wiretap, *Slang* bug; prick up one's ears, cock one's ear, strain one's ears, listen with both ears.

ebb *v.* **1.** recede, go out, flow away, flow back, fall away, move back, go down, retreat, withdraw. **2.** decline, fade away, abate, subside, dwindle, shrink, slacken, lessen, diminish, decrease, weaken, deteriorate, waste away, degenerate. **—Ant. 1** flood, rise, swell, ascend, flow. **2** increase, grow, mount, build, climb, advance, progress, improve, wax, flourish.

eccentric *adj.* **1.** off center, not circular, parabolic, elliptical. **2.** peculiar, odd, strange, queer, weird, bizarre, unusual, extraordinary, unique, singular, uncommon, offbeat, outlandish, freakish; quaint, whimsical, capricious, quixotic, rash; curious, unconventional, unorthodox, erratic, irregular; *Slang* funny, nutty, kooky, freaky, sick; abnormal, aberrant, unnatural; psychotic, insane. *—n.* **3.** character, peculiar person, odd person, unconventional person, crackpot; *Slang* curio, oddball, screwball, kook, nut, flake, weirdo, weirdie. **—Ant. 1** concentric; circular, round, centered. **2** common, ordinary, usual, conventional, customary, normal, natural, typical, regular. **3** normal person, conformist; *Slang* square.

eccentricity *n.* **—Syn. Study.** See IDIOSYNCRACY.

ecclesiastic *n.* **1.** clergyman, cleric, churchman, minister, priest, rabbi, preacher, pastor, parson, chaplain, curate, prelate, rector, vicar, deacon. *—adj.* **2.** See ECCLESIASTICAL.

ecclesiastical, ecclesiastic *adj.* religious, churchly, clerical, parochial, pastoral, episcopal. **—Ant.** secular, lay.

echelon *n.* level, rank, hierarchy, authority, position, grade, office; file, tier, line, rung.

echo *n.* **1.** reflection of sound, reverberation. —*v.* **2.** resound, reverberate, ring. **3.** match, follow, parallel, reflect, mirror, duplicate, reproduce, take after, simulate, imitate, copy, repeat; ape, parrot. —**Ant. 3** contradict, be at odds with, differ from, oppose, deny.

eclipse *n.* **1.** obscuration, darkening, veiling, cloaking, masking, covering, shadowing. **2.** diminishing, clouding, loss; blotting out, obliteration, overshadowing, annihilation, erasing, eradicating, wiping out. —*v.* **3.** cast a shadow upon, obscure, darken, cover, mask, cloak, conceal, hide. **4.** overshadow, outshine, dim, surpass, outdo, exceed, excel, transcend, tower above, outrival; wipe out, obliterate, blot out. —**Ant. 2** brightening, increase, enhancement. **3** illuminate, unveil, uncover, expose, display, show.

economic *adj.* **1.** material, monetary, productive, distributive. **2.** monetary, pecuniary, financial, fiscal, budgetary. **3.** See ECONOMICAL.

economical *adj.* thrifty, economizing, economic, saving, frugal, prudent, careful, not wasteful; tightfisted, closefisted, parsimonious, penurious, niggardly, chary, sparing, scrimping, spartan; low-priced, cheap, reasonable, modest. —**Syn. Study.** ECONOMICAL, THRIFTY, FRUGAL imply careful and efficient use of resources. ECONOMICAL implies prudent planning in the disposition of resources so as to avoid unnecessary waste or expense: *It is economical to buy in large quantities.* THRIFTY adds the idea of industry and successful management: *a thrifty shopper looking for bargains.* FRUGAL suggests saving by denying oneself luxuries: *so frugal that he never takes taxis.* —**Ant.** extravagant, spendthrift, uneconomical, wasteful, imprudent; generous, liberal, lavish; expensive, high-priced, exorbitant.

economize *v.* cut expenses, cut costs, be economical, practice economy, avoid waste, avoid extravagance, be prudent, be frugal, be parsimonious, tighten one's belt, save, conserve, skimp, scrimp, stint, pinch, use sparingly, husband. —**Ant.** be extravagant, squander, waste, dissipate, misuse.

economy *n.* **1.** thrifty management, thriftiness, thrift, frugality, prudence, providence. **2.** material well-being, financial status, monetary resources, productive power, financial management, resources management. —**Ant. 1** extravagance, lavishness, wastefulness, imprudence, improvidence.

ecstasy *n.* joy, bliss, rapture, transport, exaltation; delirium, trance; happiness, delight, elation. —**Syn. Study.** See RAPTURE.

ecstatic *adj.* full of ecstasy, joyful, joyous, overjoyed, happy, glad, delighted, rapturous, enraptured, rapt, transported, entranced, blissful, elated, exalted, ebullient, enthusiastic, excited, beside oneself, delirious. —**Ant.** unhappy, wretched, miserable, sorrowful, grief-stricken, downhearted, joyless, saddened, displeased; unexcited, unenthusiastic, indifferent, blasé.

ecumenical *adj.* universal, worldwide, global, international, catholic, cosmopolitan, general, comprehensive, all-inclusive, all-including, heavenwide, planetary, all-embracing, all-pervading; communalist, collectivist, communitarian, communist.

eddy *n.* countercurrent, whirling current, whirlpool, maelstrom, vortex. —**Ant.** flow, drift, course, stream.

edge *n.* **1.** boundary line, line, bound, border, outline, contour, periphery, margin, rim, fringe, side, extremity, limit; dividing line, brink, verge, threshold. —*v.* **2.** border, trim, rim, bind, fringe, outline, hem. **3.** steal, sneak, move sideways, sidle, inch, move little by little, advance slowly, creep, move with caution, move slyly, slink. —**Ant. 1** center, interior, middle. **3** rush, run, sprint, bound, leap, speed, hasten.

edible *adj.* eatable, fit to be eaten, suitable for eating, comestible, consumable; nonpoisonous, safe for eating; digestible. —**Ant.** inedible, uneatable; poisonous, dangerous, indigestible.

edict *n.* decree, proclamation, pronouncement, pronunciamento, fiat, ukase, dictate, command, order, ordinance, mandate, dictum, injunction, manifesto, public notice; law, statute, regulation, prescript, enactment, ruling; bull.

edification *n.* enlightenment, uplifting, moral improvement, advancement, elevation, teaching, education, educational benefit, indoctrination, instruction, guidance, direction; information.

edifice *n.* building, structure, construction.

edit *v.* revise, rewrite, correct, redact, annotate, polish, rephrase, adapt, emend, abridge, blue-pencil, copy-edit, condense, touch up, clean up; censor, bowdlerize, expunge, expurgate.

educate *v.* teach, instruct, train, school, develop, tutor, coach; enlighten, inform, edify, civilize. —**Syn. Study.** See TEACH.

education *n.* **1.** schooling, training, instruction, teaching, learning, academic learning, study; information, knowledge, enlightenment, edification, cultivation, culture, mental development, scholarship, erudition. **2.** art of teaching, teaching, pedagogics, pedagogy, tutelage, didactics.

eerie *adj.* inspiring fear, fearful, frightening, ominous, portentous, ghostly, spooky, creepy, weird, bizarre, mysterious, odd, queer, uncanny, strange, uneasy, apprehensive. **—Syn. Study.** See WEIRD. **—Ant.** soothing, comforting, consoling, relaxing; calm, tranquil, easy.

efface *v.* wipe out, obliterate, eradicate, erase, delete, blot out, rub out, expunge, excise, cancel, extirpate; destroy, annihilate, raze. **—Ant.** restore, replace, reinstate, renew, revive; keep, retain.

effect *n.* **1.** result, consequence, upshot, outcome, development, aftermath, aftereffect, outgrowth, sequel. **2.** influence, power, force, effectiveness, efficacy, impact, impression, weight, validity. **3.** operation, action, execution, force, enforcement; function, accomplishment. **4.** fact, actuality, reality, truth; significance, meaning, gist, general idea, purport, import, intent, intention; implication, essence, drift, tenor. **5.** Usu. **effects** personal property, possessions, things, goods, movables, furniture, trappings; personal estate, commodities, holdings, assets, chattels. *—v.* **6.** produce, accomplish, bring about, make, cause, achieve, carry out, execute, perform, create, realize, attain. **—Syn. Study. 1** EFFECT, CONSEQUENCE, RESULT refer to something produced by an action or a cause. An EFFECT is that which is produced, usu. more or less immediately and directly: *The drug had the effect of producing sleep.* A CONSEQUENCE, something that follows naturally or logically, as in a train of events or sequence of time, is less intimately connected with its cause than is an effect: *One consequence of a recession is a rise in unemployment.* A RESULT may be near or remote, and often is the sum of effects or consequences in making an end or final outcome: *The English language is the result of the fusion of many different elements.* **—Ant. 1** cause, occasion, inducement, incitement, foundation, source; beginning, origin. **6** prevent, hinder, deter, block, obviate, cancel out, frustrate.

effective *adj.* **1.** effectual, efficacious, efficient, productive, useful, serviceable, capable, competent, successful, forceful, forcible, dynamic, powerful, strong, influential, potent. **2.** operative, in operation, active, activated, in effect, a reality; actual, real; current. **3.** impressive, cogent, telling, convincing, compelling, persuasive; striking, forceful, powerful, successful, strong, incisive, moving, eloquent. **—Syn. Study. 1** EFFECTIVE, EFFECTUAL, EFFICACIOUS, EFFICIENT refer to that which produces or is able to produce an effect. EFFECTIVE is applied to something that produces a desired or expected effect, often a lasting one: *an effective speech.* EFFECTUAL usu. refers to something that produces a decisive outcome or result: *an effectual settlement.* EFFICACIOUS refers to something capable of achieving a certain end or purpose: *an efficacious remedy.* EFFICIENT, usu. used of a person, implies skillful accomplishment of a purpose with little waste of effort: *an efficient manager.* **—Ant. 1–3** ineffective. **1** ineffectual, inefficient, unproductive, bootless, inadequate, incompetent, useless, insufficient, impractical; forceless, powerless, impotent, weak. **2** inoperative, inactive. **3** weak, wishy-washy, tame, unimpressive, unconvincing; disappointing, unsatisfactory.

effects *n. pl.* **—Syn. Study.** See PROPERTY.

effectual *adj.* **—Syn. Study.** See EFFECTIVE.

effeminate *adj.* womanish, unmanly, sissyish, sissified. **—Ant.** manly, manlike, masculine, virile.

effervescence *n.* **1.** bubbliness, bubbling, bubbling up, fizz, fizzle, fizziness, froth, foaming. **2.** liveliness, ebullience, buoyancy, enthusiasm, life, vitality, vigor, vivacity, animation, spirit, zip, dash, gaiety. **—Ant. 1** flatness. **2** despondency, tiredness, lethargy; seriousness, gravity, sedateness.

effervescent *adj.* **1.** bubbling, bubbly, fizzy, fizzing, sparkling, foaming. **2.** lively, vivacious, ebullient, animated, exuberant, sparkling, bubbling, gay, merry, irrepressible. **—Ant. 1** flat. **2** subdued, sedate, sober, grave, staid.

effete *adj.* decadent, morally corrupt, depraved, degenerate; unproductive, unprolific, barren, sterile, enervated, worn-out, wasted, spent, exhausted. **—Ant.** healthy, wholesome, vital, productive, vigorous.

efficacious *adj.* **—Syn. Study.** See EFFECTIVE.

efficient *adj.* effective, productive, proficient, businesslike, workmanlike, capable, competent, skillful, apt, *Slang* crackerjack; work-saving, timesaving, unwasteful, effectual, efficacious. **—Syn. Study.** See EFFECTIVE. **—Ant.** inefficient, ineffectual, ineffective, unproductive, unworkmanlike, unbusinesslike; useless, wasteful.

effigy *n.* representation, image, likeness; (*variously*) statue, dummy, doll, mannequin, puppet, marionette, straw man, scarecrow, model.

effort *n.* **1.** exertion, power, force, energy, labor, work, industry, application, strain, struggle, toil, stress, pains, travail, trouble, elbow grease. **2.** endeavor, attempt, try. **—Syn. Study. 1, 2** EFFORT, EXERTION, APPLICATION, ENDEAVOR imply energetic activity and expenditure of energy. EFFORT is an expenditure of physical or mental energy to accomplish some objective: *He made an effort to control himself.* EXERTION is vigorous action or effort, frequently without an end in view: *out of breath from exertion.* APPLICATION is continuous effort plus careful attention and diligence: *application to one's studies.* ENDEAVOR means a continuous and sustained series of efforts to achieve some end, often worthy and difficult: *an endeavor to rescue survivors.*

effortless *adj.* easy, uncomplicated, simple, facile, smooth, graceful, not difficult, painless. **—Ant.** hard, difficult, complicated, tough.

effrontery *n.* shamelessness, brazenness, brashness, impertinence, insolence, impudence, presumption, arrogance; audacity, temerity, cheek, nerve, gall, brass, *Yiddish* chutzpah, *Slang* balls. **—Ant.** modesty, reserve, shyness, timidity, bashfulness; respect, diffidence.

effusive *adj.* lavish, unrestrained, profuse, gushy, gushing, unreserved, extravagant, expansive, copious, overflowing, free-flowing; ebullient, exuberant. **—Ant.** restrained, reserved, sparing, sparse.

egocentric *adj.* self-centered, egomaniacal, egoistic, egotistical, self-absorbed, self-concerned, self-involved, self-obsessed, self-serving, narcissistic, megalomaniacal, self-seeking; wrapped up in oneself, stuck on oneself, be on an ego trip. **—Ant.** altruistic, unselfish, modest, liberal, generous.

egoism *n.* self-centeredness, self-importance, self-absorption, self-love, egotism, narcissism, overweening pride, vanity. **—Syn. Study.** See EGOTISM. **—Ant.** humility, modesty; self-distrust, self-doubt.

egoist *n.* self-centered person, narcissist; selfish person.

egotism *n.* self-admiration, self-praise, bragging, boastfulness, braggadocio, immodesty, conceit, vanity, vainglory, smugness, arrogance, pride, hubris; egoism. **—Syn. Study.** EGOTISM, EGOISM refer to preoccupation with one's ego or self. EGOTISM is the common word for a tendency to speak or write about oneself too much; it suggests selfishness and an inordinate sense of one's own importance: *His egotism alienated most of his colleagues.* EGOISM, a less common word, emphasizes the moral justification of a concern for one's own welfare and interests, but carries less of an implication of boastful self-importance: *a healthy egoism that stood him well in times of trial.* See also PRIDE. **—Ant.** modesty, humility, bashfulness, self-criticism, self-abnegation.

egotist *n.* self-admirer, boaster, braggart, swaggerer, peacock, gascon, braggadocio, swellhead, show-off, *Slang* blowhard.

egregious *adj.* conspicuously bad, gross, flagrant, glaring, outrageous, shocking, notorious, extreme, monstrous, heinous, insufferable, intolerable, grievous. **—Ant.** tolerable, moderate, minor, unnoticeable.

egress *n.* **1.** exit, departure, withdrawal, escape; discharge, issue, outflow, seepage, leakage. **2.** way out, passage out, outlet, exit; aperture, vent. **—Ant. 1, 2** entrance.

eject *v.* **1.** discharge, emit, spew, spit out, spout, disgorge, exude, throw out, cast out. **2.** oust, evict, expel, remove, force out, turn out, kick out, drive out, *Slang* bounce; exile, banish, deport, dispossess. **—Ant. 1** take in, inject; retain, withhold, keep, house, store. **2** move in, bring in, receive, admit, introduce.

elaborate *adj.* **1.** complex, involved, complicated, intricate; painstaking, labored. **2.** fancy, elegant, ornate; ostentatious, showy, flashy, gaudy, garish, overdone. *—v.* **3.** expand, add details, particularize, specify, clarify, embellish. **—Ant. 1, 2** simple, plain. **3** digest, condense, abbreviate, summarize, sum up.

elapse *v.* pass, pass by, lapse, intervene, go by, slip by, slip away, glide by, roll by, slide by.

elastic *adj.* **1.** stretchable, flexible, resilient, supple, rubbery, recoiling, springy, rebounding. **2.** flexible, supple, pliant, pliable, tolerant, complaisant, yielding, accommodating, adaptable, responsive; recuperative, readily recovering. **—Ant. 1** stiff, inflexible, rigid. **2** inflexible, intolerant, unyielding, unaccommodating.

elated *adj.* overjoyed, jubilant, exalted, exhilarated, in high spirits, ecstatic, excited, animated; happy, delightful, joyful, joyous, pleased, glad, gleeful, rejoicing; proud, blissful, flushed with success. **—Ant.** dejected, depressed, dashed, dispirited, discouraged, blue, sad, unhappy; humbled, abashed, chagrined.

elder *adj.* **1.** older, firstborn, senior. *—n.* **2.** senior, older adult, *Informal* old-timer. **3.** patriarch, presbyter, head; church dignitary, church official. **—Ant. 1, 2** younger, junior. **3** neophyte; layman.

elderly *adj.* old, aged, venerable; old, past one's prime; *Slang* over the hill. **—Ant.** young, youthful.

elect *v.* **1.** select by vote, vote into office, choose by ballot; choose, pick, select. **2.** choose, select, decide on, opt for, adopt, resolve upon, fix upon, settle on, single out, pick out, espouse, embrace, take up, determine in favor of. **—Ant. 1** defeat, vote down, vote out. **2** reject, repudiate, decline, abjure, renounce, dismiss, turn one's back on.

election *n.* **1.** voting, choosing by vote, vote, balloting, poll. **2.** choice, selection, decision, option, alternative, determination, resolution, resolve.

elective *adj.* **1.** chosen by election, filled by election, passed by vote. **2.** optional, not required, not obligatory, voluntary, selective, discretionary, open to choice. **—Ant. 1** appointed, named; inherited. **2** required, obligatory, necessary.

electric, electrical *adj.* **1.** of electricity, for electricity, operated by electricity, power-driven. **2.** thrilling, stirring, exciting, dynamic, electrifying, spirited, stimulating, exalting, rousing, inspiring, soul-stirring, full of fire, galvanizing. **—Ant. 2** dull, flat, unexciting, spiritless, unmoving, uninspiring, tedious, boring, colorless, insipid, ordinary, prosaic.

electrify *v.* **1.** supply with electricity, equip for the use of electricity; pass an electric current through, charge with electricity. **2.** thrill, stir, excite, rouse, stimulate, galvanize, quicken, animate, fire up; fascinate, amaze, astound, astonish, startle, stun, daze, dazzle, surprise, take one's breath away.

eleemosynary *adj.* charitable, existing on donations; altruistic, benevolent, beneficent, philanthropic, nonprofitmaking. **—Ant.** profitmaking, business.

elegance *n.* luxuriousness, exquisiteness, sumptuousness, grandeur, richness; taste, refinement, delicacy, grace, gracefulness, *Slang* class; purity, balance, symmetry. **—Ant.** plainness; bad taste, crudeness; clumsiness, awkwardness.

elegant *adj.* **1.** exquisite, fine, grand, rich, sumptuous, luxurious, ornate, artistic; tasteful, delicate, refined, graceful, classic, symmetrical, well-proportioned; beautiful, handsome, lovely, attractive. **2.** refined, genteel, well-bred, polished, cultivated, dignified, gracious, charming, polite, courtly; *Slang* classy; fashionable, stylish, debonair, urbane, dapper. **—Ant. 1** plain, inelegant; tasteless, tawdry, crude, coarse, rough; ugly, hideous, misshapen; clumsy. **2** unrefined, coarse, low-bred, boorish, undignified, rude, ungraceful; unfashionable.

elegy *n.* poem of lamentation, lament for the dead, melancholy poem, sad poem; requiem, funeral song, song of lamentation, melancholy piece of music. **—Ant.** paean, jubilee, hallelujah, anthem.

element *n.* **1.** basic chemical substance, uncompounded substance, simple body; *Classical legend* earth, air, fire, water. **2.** basic part, basic unit, component part, component, constituent, ingredient, building block, member, subdivision. **3.** Usu. **elements.** principles, rudiments, foundations, basic ideas, origins, essence, features, factors; *Informal* basics. **4.** natural habitat, native state, natural medium, environment; milieu. **—Syn. Study. 2** ELEMENT, COMPONENT, CONSTITUENT, INGREDIENT refer to units that are parts of whole or complete substances, systems, compounds, or mixtures. ELEMENT denotes a fundamental, ultimate part: *the elements of matter; the elements of a problem.* COMPONENT refers to one of a number of separate parts: *Iron and carbon are components of steel.* CONSTITUENT refers to an active and necessary part: *The constituents of a molecule of water are two atoms of hydrogen and one of oxygen.* INGREDIENT is most frequently used in nonscientific contexts to denote any part that is combined into a mixture: *the ingredients of a cake; the ingredients of a successful marriage.* **—Ant. 1** compound, mixture, blend, amalgam. **2** whole, entity, total, sum, system. **3** advanced concept; frills, supplement.

elementary *adj.* basic, basal, fundamental, rudimentary, elemental; simple, plain, uncomplicated, easy, primitive, primary, original, first, undeveloped, crude. **—Ant.** advanced, higher, complex, complicated.

elevate *v.* **1.** raise, upraise, raise aloft, lift up, uplift, move up, hoist, heave, boost, place high, heighten, increase. **2.** raise, move up, promote, advance; dignify, ennoble, exalt; improve, better, refine, enhance, heighten, intensify. **3.** elate, boost, lift, raise, uplift, cheer, exhilarate, animate, excite, inspire, perk up. **—Syn. Study.** ELEVATE, EXALT, ENHANCE, HEIGHTEN mean to raise or make higher in some respect. To ELEVATE is to raise up to a higher level, position, or state: *to elevate the living standards of a group.* To EXALT is to raise very high in rank, character, estimation, mood, etc.: *A king is exalted above his subjects.* To ENHANCE is to add to the attractions or desirability of something: *Landscaping enhances the beauty of the grounds.* To HEIGHTEN is to increase the strength or intensity of: *to heighten one's powers of concentration.* **—Ant. 1–3** lower. **1** lower, drop. **2** demote, degrade; *Slang* kick downstairs, bust; humble, demean. **3** depress, sadden, deject; deaden, numb.

elevation *n.* **1.** height, altitude, height above sea level; prominence, lift. **2.** elevated place, high place, rising ground, acclivity, ascent, rise, hill, mountain. **3.** rise, promotion, advancement, boost; improvement, bettering, refinement, cultivation. **—Syn. Study. 1** See HEIGHT. **—Ant. 1** depth. **2** low ground, valley, depression, dip. **3** demotion.

elf *n.* pixie, puck, brownie, fairy, sprite, leprechaun, troll, gnome; gremlin, goblin, hobgoblin.

elicit *v.* bring forth, draw forth, draw out, call forth, evoke, extract, exact, extort, derive, wrest, fetch, cause, educe, bring to light. **—Ant.** repress, discourage.

eligible *adj.* qualified, able to be chosen, acceptable, authorized, appropriate, proper, suitable, fitting, applicable; desirable, worthwhile. **—Ant.** ineligible, unacceptable, inappropriate, unsuitable.

eliminate *v.* get rid of, do away with, banish, abolish, eradicate, erase, exterminate, cut out, annihilate, weed out, stamp out, rub out; remove, throw out, exclude, reject, drop, delete, except, leave out, omit; eject, expel, cast out, exile, dismiss, oust. **—Ant.** obtain, get, invite, establish; add, include, inject, accept, admit, incorporate.

elite *n.* best, choice, best group, choice class, select body, the pick, top, cream, flower; crème-de-la-crème, upper class, wealthy, society, high society, aristocracy, blue bloods, *French* haut monde; notables, celebrities, personages; *Slang* bigwigs, big shots. **—Ant.** worst, dregs, scum; lower class, working class; rabble, hoi polloi, riffraff.

elocution *n.* **1.** manner of speaking, articulation, pronunciation, intonation, diction. **2.** public speaking, oratory, speech, diction, articulation, enunciation, pronunciation.

elongate *v.* lengthen, extend, make longer, draw out, stretch out, prolong, protract. **—Ant.** shorten, curtail, contract, abbreviate, abridge.

eloquent *adj.* persuasive, forceful, striking, stirring, moving, spirited, emphatic, articulate, passionate, impassioned, vivid, poetic. **—Syn. Study.** ELOQUENT, ARTICULATE both refer to effective language or an effective user of language. ELOQUENT implies vivid, moving, and convincing expression: *an eloquent plea for disarmament.* ARTICULATE suggests fluent, clear, and coherent expression: *an articulate speaker.* **—Ant.** routine, ordinary, commonplace, pedestrian, unimpressive, weak, dull, prosaic, bland.

elucidate *v.* clarify, explain, explicate, make plain, clear up, throw light upon, illuminate, illustrate, describe, expound, detail, interpret, spell out, delineate, comment upon. **—Syn. Study.** See EXPLAIN. **—Ant.** confuse, obscure, becloud, muddle.

elude *v.* evade, avoid, escape, escape the notice of, dodge, circumvent, shun, fight shy of, keep clear of, slip by, get away from. **—Syn. Study.** See ESCAPE. **—Ant.** confront, meet, encounter; challenge.

elusive *adj.* **1.** hard to catch, evasive; tricky, slippery, shifty, wily, crafty, foxy. **2.** hard to grasp, difficult to comprehend; baffling, puzzling, hard to express.

emaciated *adj.* undernourished, starving, underfed, sickly, thin, wasted, gaunt, haggard, skinny, lean, scrawny, lank, wizened, skeletal, cadaverous. **—Ant.** robust, hardy, stout, fat, plump, chubby, beefy.

emanate *v.* **1.** come from, originate, stem, proceed, rise, spring; flow, issue, come forth, emerge, well. **2.** exude, give off, send forth. **—Syn. Study. 1** See EMERGE. **—Ant. 1** end, terminate, culminate.

emancipate *v.* free, set free, liberate, set at liberty, release, manumit; unfetter, unchain, unshackle. **—Ant.** enslave, subjugate; chain, manacle, shackle.

emasculate *v.* **1.** castrate, geld, alter. **2.** weaken, make less forceful, undermine, devitalize, soften, render impotent. **—Ant. 2** strengthen, reinforce, vitalize.

embargo *n.* ban, prohibition, restriction, interdiction, injunction, stoppage, impediment, proscription, restraint of trade, shutdown, inhibition, quarantine, standstill.

embark *v.* **1.** board ship, go aboard; board, put on board, entrain, enplane. **2.** start, begin, commence, undertake, launch, enter upon, set out. **—Ant. 1** disembark, go ashore; land, arrive. **2** conclude, finish, end, terminate.

embarrass *v.* make self-conscious, make ill at ease, mortify, shame, abash, chagrin, discomfit, disconcert, agitate, upset, distress, discompose, discountenance; fluster, rattle, confuse, faze, nonplus. **—Ant.** put at ease, be self-confident.

embarrassment *n.* **—Syn. Study.** See SHAME.

embattled *adj.* engaged in battle, hard-pressed, fighting, embroiled; equipped for battle, battle-ready, arrayed in battle order, prepared for battle, fortified.

embellish *v.* enhance, elaborate, exaggerate, ornament, decorate, adorn, beautify, garnish, gild, color, embroider, dress up, fancy up, set off, *Slang* gussy up. **—Ant.** simplify, strip bare.

ember *n.* live coal, smoldering remains; cinder, ash, clinker, slag.

embezzle *v.* misappropriate, defalcate; defraud, swindle, cheat; *Slang* fleece, filch, bilk, rook.

embitter *v.* envenom, make bitter, make resentful, make rancorous, rankle, sour, make cynical, make pessimistic. **—Ant.** comfort, please; gladden, delight.

emblem *n.* insignia, badge, symbol, hallmark, device, sign, design, representative figure, colophon.

embody *v.* **1.** express, represent, personify, exemplify, symbolize, realize, typify, manifest, substantiate. **2.** include, incorporate, consolidate, collect, contain, organize, bring together, embrace; assimilate, blend, merge, fuse. **—Ant. 1** disembody. **2** exclude, except; scatter, disperse.

embrace *v.* **1.** hug, clasp in the arms; grasp, clasp. **2.** accept, espouse, adopt. **3.** include, involve, contain, embody, comprise, incorporate, cover, encompass, comprehend. **—Syn. Study. 3** See CONTAIN. **—Ant. 2** spurn, reject, refuse, decline, repudiate, scorn, disdain, rule out. **3** omit, delete, exclude, except; ignore, disregard.

embroider *v.* **1.** decorate with stitches, make of decorative stitches. **2.** embellish, elaborate, adorn with fictitious details, exaggerate, fabricate, color, dress up; romanticize.

embryonic *adj.* undeveloped, beginning, rudimentary, incipient, immature; unfinished, imperfect, incomplete, rough.

emend *v.* correct, rectify, amend, revise, improve, change. **—Syn. Study.** See AMEND.

emerge *v.* **1.** rise, surface, emanate, issue, come up, come forth, come into view; discharge, emit, stream, gush, run, escape, flow, pour. **2.** develop, arise, dawn, become apparent, surface, appear, become visible, loom, become manifest, come to light, come out of hiding, crop up, turn up. **—Syn. Study. 1** EMERGE, EMANATE, ISSUE mean to come forth from a place or source. EMERGE is used of coming forth from concealment, obscurity, or something that envelops: *The sun emerged from behind the clouds.* EMANATE is used of intangible or immaterial things, as light or ideas, spreading from a source: *Rumors often emanate from irresponsible persons.* ISSUE is most often used of a number of persons, a mass of matter, or a volume of smoke, sound, or the like, coming forth through any outlet or outlets: *The crowd issued from the building.* **—Ant. 1** submerge, sink, fall, recede. **2** disappear, hide, fade away; retreat, depart, withdraw.

emergency *n.* unforeseen danger, pressing necessity, contingency, exigency, crisis, urgency, pinch, predicament.

emigrant *n.* émigré, expatriate; (*loosely*) wanderer, wayfarer. **—Ant.** immigrant.

emigrate *v.* move, migrate, remove; leave, depart, quit. **—Ant.** immigrate.

émigré *n.* exile, emigrant, expatriate, refugee, political refugee, expellee, evacuee, defector, immigrant, alien, fugitive, displaced person, DP.

eminence *n.* **1.** high position, elevated rank, repute, public esteem, preeminence, importance, standing, prominence, distinction, note, notability, fame, celebrity, conspicuousness, reputation, glory, greatness, excellence. **2.** elevation, high place, height, high point, prominence, promontory, hill, hillock, summit, rise, upland, ridge, mountain, peak, bluff, cliff, knoll, hummock. **—Ant. 1** lowliness, unimportance, lack of distinction; disrepute, dishonor, infamy, notoriety. **2** lowland, declivity, valley.

eminent *adj.* **1.** illustrious, preeminent, high-ranking, top, important, elevated, esteemed, distinguished, famous, renowned, prominent, exalted, laureate, celebrated, well-known, outstanding, noted, notable, signal, great, glorious, grand, imposing, paramount. **2.** extraordinary, remarkable, outstanding, notable, noted, noteworthy, unusual, utmost, memorable. **—Ant. 1** lowly, unimportant, undistinguished; little-known, unknown; infamous, notorious. **2** unremarkable, ordinary; inconspicuous.

emissary *n.* delegate, ambassador, envoy, legate, representative, deputy, agent; go-between, messenger, courier, herald.

emission *n.* **1.** discharge, ejection, emanation, voidance, expulsion, extrusion, excretion; (*variously*) smoke, fumes, pollutant, impurity, waste. **2.** sending out, emitting, transmission, issuance; throwing out, ejection, expulsion. **—Ant. 2** injection, reception.

emit *v.* send out, give forth, give, discharge, issue, secrete, transmit, pour forth, shed, dispatch, expel, excrete, throw out, cast out, vent, beam. **—Ant.** inject; receive, retain, withhold.

emollient *adj.* **1.** soothing, relieving, palliative, alleviative, healing, restorative, easeful, allaying, assuasive, lenitive, calming, relaxing, balmy. *—n.* **2.** balm, salve, lotion, lenitive, ointment, lubricant, oil. **—Ant. 1** irritating, painful, exacerbating, chafing, aggravating.

emotion *n.* **1.** feeling, strong feeling,

fullness of heart, excitement, agitation, passion, sentiment, zeal, ardor, vehemence, fervor, heat, warmth. **2.** concern, strong feeling; (*variously*) love, hate, anger, jealousy, sorrow, sadness, fear, despair, happiness, satisfaction, pride, regret, remorse, embarrassment, hope, eagerness, loyalty. **—Syn. Study. 1** See FEELING. **—Ant. 1** indifference, impassiveness, apathy.

emotional *adj.* **1.** appealing to the emotions, hot button, sentimental, warm, moving, touching, stirring, soul-stirring, heartwarming, thrilling, heart-rending, *Slang* tear-jerking. **2.** easily affected by emotion, temperamental, hypersensitive, vulnerable, responsive, demonstrative, sentimental; passionate, impassioned, fervent, fiery, ardent, zealous, enthusiastic, impetuous; excitable, hysterical, wrought-up, high-strung. **—Ant. 1, 2** unemotional, cold, dull. **2** insensitive, unfeeling, indifferent, apathetic, dispassionate, undemonstrative, unsentimental, unresponsive, unexcitable.

emotionalism *n.* show of emotion, demonstrativeness, sentimentality, mawkishness, gushiness, hysteria, hysterics; theatrics, melodramatics, melodrama. **—Ant.** impassivity, impassiveness, detachment, matter-of-factness.

empathy *n.* **—Syn. Study.** See SYMPATHY.

emperor Fem. **empress** *n.* ruler, monarch, sovereign; (*variously*) caesar, czar, mikado, sultan, kaiser, shah; (*fem.*) czarina, sultana, dowager empress.

emphasis *n.* **1.** stress, prominent point, focal point, feature, weight, underscoring. **2.** stress, accent, accentuation.

emphasize *v.* stress, accent, feature, dwell on, press home, iterate, underscore, underline, punctuate, accentuate, point up, bring into relief. **—Ant.** deemphasize, play down, underplay; equalize, balance.

emphatic *adj.* **1.** strong, vigorous, forceful, assertive, decisive, flat, unqualified, absolute, unequivocal, unyielding, insistent, unwavering, categorical. **2.** definite, unmistakable, undeniable, striking, certain, distinct, decided, telling, momentous, marked, express, pronounced, conspicuous, significant. **—Ant. 1** hesitant, unsure, uncertain, weak, wishy-washy, irresolute, qualified, equivocal. **2** uncertain, indistinct, insignificant, unremarkable, commonplace, average.

empire *n.* sovereignty, rule, dominion, realm, domain, commonwealth, imperium.

empirical *adj.* practical, experiential, pragmatic; experimental, firsthand. **—Ant.** theoretical, secondhand.

employ *v.* **1.** hire, use, engage, commission, retain, take on. **2.** use, utilize, make use of, put to use, apply, engage, keep busy, occupy, devote, exercise. *—n.* **3.** service, employment; hire, retainership. **—Ant. 1** discharge, dismiss, fire, let go, *Slang* can, sack. **2** waste, fritter away; misuse, misapply.

employee *n.* worker, wage earner, job holder, staff member, member; underling, hireling. **—Ant.** employer, boss.

employer *n.* boss; proprietor, business owner; business, firm, company, establishment, organization, outfit. **—Ant.** employee, worker, wage earner, job holder, staff member; underling, hireling.

employment *n.* **1.** work, job, employ, service; occupation, business, profession, vocation, calling, pursuit, trade, field, line; task, chore, preoccupation. **2.** utilization, exertion, using, use, employing, application, exercise, service, engagement. **—Ant. 1** unemployment, leisure, inactivity; avocation, hobby, sideline. **2** disuse, disregard, neglect, forgetting, putting aside.

emporium *n.* large store, department store, general store, store; market, bazaar, warehouse.

empower *v.* authorize, sanction, invest, vest, license, endow; permit, allow, enable; commission, delegate. **—Ant.** restrain, disbar, divest of power; disallow, forbid, enjoin.

empty *adj.* **1.** vacant, unoccupied, uninhabited, bare, void. **2.** aimless, meaningless, without substance, vacuous, insignificant, worthless, purposeless, futile, unfulfilled, idle, hollow; shallow, banal, trivial, inane, insipid, frivolous. *—v.* **3.** pour out, drain, dump, void, evacuate; discharge, flow, debouch. **—Ant. 1** full, stuffed, crammed, packed, jammed; occupied, inhabited. **2** meaningful, significant, substantial, useful, valuable, worthwhile, purposeful, fulfilled, busy, full, rich, vital, interesting, serious. **3** fill, pack, put in, stuff, cram, jam; receive.

emulate *v.* take as a model, follow the example of, pattern oneself after, follow, copy, imitate; try to equal, rival; mimic, ape.

enable *v.* make able, empower, qualify, capacitate, make possible for, allow, permit; aid, assist, support, facilitate, benefit. **—Ant.** prevent, bar, disqualify, prohibit, incapacitate; hinder, thwart, frustrate, block, keep back, hold back.

enact *v.* pass into law, pass, legislate, vote to accept, authorize, ratify; institute, proclaim, decree; sanction, approve. **—Ant.** reject, turn down, vote down, fail to pass, veto; abolish, annul, repeal, rescind, cancel.

enamor *v.* inflame with love, affect with fondness, enrapture, infatuate, allure, draw to, attach; enthrall, charm, enchant, entrance, captivate, bewitch, fascinate, excite, take a fancy to. **—Ant.** repel, repulse, revolt, disgust, disenchant, put off, *Slang* turn off.

enchant *v.* **1.** cast a spell over, place under a spell, bewitch, charm; hypnotize, mesmerize. **2.** charm, delight, entrance, enthrall, captivate, enrapture, fascinate, bewitch, transport. **—Ant. 1** release, free, exorcise. **2** repel, repulse, revolt, disgust, sicken, *Slang* turn off.

enchantress *n.* **1.** sorceress, witch, vampire, siren. **2.** seductress, temptress, vamp, charmer, femme fatale.

encircle *v.* circle, ring, surround, wreathe, girdle, gird, circumscribe, encompass; enclose, fence, wall, hem in.

enclose Also **inclose** *v.* **1.** surround, ring, circle, encircle, girdle, encompass, circumscribe, fence in, wall in, close in. **2.** include, insert, send along, put in the same envelope, put in the same package.

encompass *v.* **1.** surround, circumscribe, encircle, circle, enclose, ring, girdle, fence in, wall in, hem in. **2.** include, cover, embrace, contain, comprise, incorporate, embody, hold, involve, take in, touch on. **—Ant. 2** exclude, leave out, omit; ignore.

encounter *v.* **1.** meet, meet with, chance upon; sustain, confront, run into, experience, come upon; endure, undergo, suffer. **2.** clash with, meet and fight, do battle with, contend against, confront, engage in combat, grapple with, skirmish with, measure swords with, face, come face to face with. *—n.* **3.** battle, combat, fight, confrontation, hostile meeting, bout, affray, engagement, fracas, skirmish, clash, brush. **—Ant. 1** escape, shun, miss, elude, avoid. **3** retreat, withdrawal.

encourage *v.* **1.** inspire, give confidence to, inspirit, embolden, induce, give hope to, hearten, rally, egg on; spur, exhort, impel, sway; reassure, hearten, cheer. **2.** foster, promote, favor, advance, further, boost, forward, assist, help, prompt, aid. **—Ant. 1** discourage, dissuade, deter, depress, deject, dishearten, dispirit. **2** retard, hinder, prevent, inhibit, hamper.

encouragement *n.* encouraging, approbation, praise, backing, support, reinforcement, reassurance; boost, lift, *Slang* shot in the arm. **—Ant.** discouragement, criticism; disparagement, ridicule.

encroach *v.* intrude, infringe, invade, impinge, make inroads on, overrun, overstep, violate, break into, trespass, transgress, interfere. **—Syn. Study.** See TRESPASS. **—Ant.** respect, honor, recognize, observe; safeguard, protect.

encumber *v.* burden, weigh down, load, load down, lade, saddle; tax, inconvenience, hinder, handicap, impede, slow down, obstruct. **—Ant.** unload, unburden, unencumber.

encyclopedic *adj.* comprehensive, all-encompassing, exhaustive, universal, wide-ranging, broad, scholarly, erudite.

end *n.* **1.** extremity, terminus; edge, limit, boundary, border. **2.** conclusion, ending, termination, close, finish, expiration, cessation, completion, finale, windup, culmination, consummation, denouement. **3.** outcome, upshot, result, consequence, effect, issue, fulfillment, settlement. **4.** aim, goal, purpose, object, objective, result, intention, design. **5.** extinction, extermination, destruction, annihilation, termination, ruin; death, demise. **6.** remnant, leftover, fragment, scrap. *—v.* **7.** conclude, halt, draw to a close, terminate, cease, finish, stop, leave off, put an end to, run out, wind up, close, bring down the curtain. **8.** destroy, eradicate, kill, annihilate, exterminate, extinguish, finish off. **—Syn. Study. 4** See AIM. **—Ant. 1–3, 5** beginning, start, commencement, inauguration; inception, birth. **7, 8** begin, start, commence.

endanger *v.* threaten, put in danger, imperil, jeopardize, hazard, risk, expose, compromise. **—Ant.** protect, safeguard, preserve, defend, shield, save.

endear *v.* make beloved, make dear; create goodwill among, ingratiate with, make attractive. **—Ant.** alienate, estrange.

endearment *n.* loving word, fond utterance, sweet talk; pet name, affectionate term. **—Ant.** curse, malediction.

endeavor *v.* **1.** try, attempt, make an effort, strive, work at, undertake, take pains, labor, struggle, do one's best; aspire, aim, seek. *—n.* **2.** attempt, aim, effort, try, essay, exertion, striving, struggle. **3.** undertaking, enterprise, work, preoccupation, interest; occupation, vocation, job, career. **—Syn. Study. 1** See TRY. **2** See EFFORT. **—Ant. 1** neglect, ignore, pass up, overlook; abandon, dismiss.

ending *n.* conclusion, end, close, finish, windup, finale, termination, cessation, expiration, completion, culmination, consummation. **—Ant.** beginning, start, opening, inception.

endless *adj.* without end, unending, uninterrupted, unbroken, interminable, boundless, infinite, measureless, unlimited; perpetual, everlasting, never-ending, eternal, constant, continuous, continual, persistent. **—Syn. Study.** See ETERNAL. **—Ant.** finite, limited, bounded, circumscribed; temporary, short-lived, brief, passing, transitory, transient.

endorse Also **indorse** *v.* **1.** support, back, champion, approve, sanction, advocate, recommend, vouch for, subscribe to, stand behind, affirm, ratify, OK, second, lend one's name to. **2.** sign, countersign; authorize, validate, certify. **—Ant. 1** disapprove, denounce, condemn, discredit, disavow, reject, repudiate, spurn.

endow *v.* **1.** bestow a fund upon, provide with an income; bequeath, settle on, leave, will; award, confer, grant, bestow. **2.** supply, equip, provide, accord, invest, bestow, grant, furnish; bless, grace, favor. **—Ant. 2** divest, deprive, take.

endowment *n.* **1.** legacy, bequest, bestowed fund, willed income; benefaction, grant, gift, donation, award. **2.** natural gift, talent, flair, ability, capability, aptitude, faculty, attribute.

endurance *n.* **1.** stamina, hardihood, durability, strength; fortitude, perseverance, tenacity, tenaciousness, persistence, staying power, resolution, stick-to-itiveness. **2.** permanence, durableness; immutability, changelessness, stability. **—Ant. 1, 2** frailty, weakness.

endure *v.* **1.** sustain, bear, withstand, stand, experience, undergo, cope with, go through, weather, suffer, bear up under, brave; tolerate, countenance, brook. **2.** last, persist, prevail, live, live on, continue, remain. **—Syn. Study. 1** See BEAR. **2** See CONTINUE. **—Ant. 1** escape, evade, avoid, bypass, sidestep; lose to, be defeated by, surrender to. **2** perish, die, fail, succumb, subside, crumble, decay, end, wither away.

enemy *n.* **1.** antagonist, detractor, opponent, adversary, nemesis, foe, rival, competitor. **2.** opposing military force, armed foe; hostile nation, belligerent state; assailant, attacker. **—Ant. 1** friend, supporter, well-wisher. **2** ally, confederate.

energetic *adj.* full of energy, active, vigorous, lively, peppy, zippy, animated, restless, spirited; *Slang* jiggy; forceful, dynamic, brisk, robust, go-getting, high-powered, hard-working, industrious; alert, enthusiastic, quick-witted. **—Ant.** enervated, languid, inactive, lethargic, sluggish, listless; phlegmatic.

energy *n.* **1.** power, force; (*variously*) hydroelectric power, electric power, atomic energy, nuclear energy. **2.** vitality, vim, vigor, verve, zip, élan, pep, go, vivacity, dynamism, liveliness, animation, zest, zeal, enterprise, drive, hustle. **—Ant. 2** inertia, lassitude, listlessness, sluggishness.

enervate *v.* exhaust, weary, weaken, debilitate, devitalize, enfeeble, disable, sap one's energy, deplete, wash out, fatigue, tire, prostrate, *Slang* bush, fag, tucker. **—Ant.** energize, invigorate, strengthen, vitalize, stimulate, quicken.

enforce *v.* carry out, administer, keep in force, compel obedience to, insist on, impose, implement, execute, apply, exact; support, defend. **—Ant.** ignore, disregard; waive, forgo.

engage *v.* **1.** involve, occupy, engross, absorb; take part, participate, partake, busy oneself; undertake, set about, enter into, embark on. **2.** employ, hire, take on, retain, secure, take into service, commission. **3.** betroth, affiance, pledge, promise. **4.** begin conflict with, encounter in battle, fight with, give battle to, war with, combat. **—Ant. 2** fire, lay off, let go, *Slang* can. **4** flee, retreat, withdraw.

engagement *n.* **1.** appointment, date, commitment, meeting, arrangement; obligation, duty. **2.** betrothal, troth, banns, plighted faith, affiancing. **3.** employment, job, position, situation, *Slang* gig; post, berth, billet. **4.** battle, fight, encounter, combat, conflict, action, skirmish, brush, bout, contest, scuffle, fray.

engaging *adj.* winning, attractive, disarming, winsome, enchanting, charming, fetching, captivating, pleasing, likable, lovable, agreeable, appealing, ingratiating. **—Ant.** offensive, disagreeable, displeasing, unattractive, unpleasant, unlikable, unlovable; repulsive, repellent.

engender *v.* give rise to, cause, bring about, beget, breed, generate, produce, occasion, precipitate. **—Ant.** kill, end, crush.

engross *v.* absorb, occupy, preoccupy, involve, immerse, engage, hold, arrest, take up. **—Ant.** bore, tire, weary; vex, annoy, irritate.

engulf *v.* swallow up, envelop, bury, swamp, overrun, inundate, submerge, immerse, deluge.

enhance *v.* intensify, heighten, magnify, make more attractive, make more appealing; elevate, lift, raise, boost; redouble, embellish, augment, add to, complement. **—Syn. Study.** See ELEVATE. **—Ant.** diminish, reduce, lessen, decrease, minimize, depreciate, detract from.

enigma *n.* puzzle, riddle, question, perplexity, conundrum, mystery, secret, hidden meaning.

enigmatic, enigmatical *adj.* mysterious, secretive, puzzling, indecipherable, unfathomable, cryptic, baffling, perplexing, inscrutable, elusive, ambiguous, equivocal, paradoxical. **—Ant.** candid, frank, open, straightforward, self-explanatory, intelligible, lucid; explicit, expressive, express, definite, clear, manifest.

enjoin *v.* **1.** advise, counsel, warn, admonish, command, bid, charge, direct, instruct, call upon; beg, entreat, ask, urge. **2.** prohibit, forbid, restrain, place an injunction on, restrict, ban, bar, proscribe, interdict. **—Ant. 2** permit, allow, let.

enjoy *v.* **1.** like, appreciate, admire, think well of, take pleasure in, be pleased with, rejoice in, delight in, fancy, relish; savor; *Slang* eat up, get a kick out of. **2.** have the benefit of, be blessed with, have, possess, own. **—Ant. 1** dislike, hate, detest, loathe, abhor, abominate, despise.

enjoyable *adj.* pleasant, pleasing, providing enjoyment, pleasurable, agreeable, fun-filled, delightful, satisfying, rewarding, gratifying, *Slang* jiggy. **—Ant.** unpleasant, disagreeable, unenjoyable, unpleasurable, unsatisfying; hateful, detestable, loathsome, abominable, despicable.

enjoyment *n.* **1.** pleasure, delight, satisfaction, happiness, gratification, joy, zest, gusto, relish; fun, entertainment, amusement, diversion, recreation, good time. **2.** benefit, advantage, blessing, privilege, right, prerogative, exercise, possession. **—Ant. 1** displeasure, dissatisfaction, detestation, loathing, abhorrence, aversion, repugnance, hatred, dislike. **2** disadvantage, handicap.

enlarge *v.* **1.** make larger, increase, expand, swell, extend, inflate; augment, add to, multiply; magnify, amplify, lengthen, widen, broaden, elongate; become bigger, grow, develop. **2.** expand, amplify, elaborate, expound, expatiate, discourse. **—Ant. 1** decrease, shorten, curtail, shrink, contract, reduce, diminish, lessen. **2** condense, abridge, abbreviate, narrow.

enlighten *v.* inform, instruct, educate, edify, clarify, make aware, illuminate, cause to understand, apprise, advise; civilize, sophisticate, *Slang* wise up. **—Ant.** mystify, perplex, puzzle, bewilder, mislead, confound, confuse.

enlist *v.* **1.** join, join up, enroll, register, sign up, volunteer. **2.** recruit, engage, obtain, secure, procure, gain the assistance of. **—Ant. 1** withdraw, resign, retire, leave. **2** reject, refuse, dismiss.

enliven *v.* make lively, animate, pep up, cheer up, brighten, excite, quicken, vitalize, vivify, wake up, fire; *Informal* jump-start; renew, rejuvenate. **—Ant.** dampen, chill, cast a pall over, deaden, make dull, make boring, subdue, depress, weigh down.

en masse *adv.* in a group, in a body, together, all together, as a whole, as a group. **—Ant.** individually, separately, one by one.

enmity *n.* hostility, ill will, hatred, rancor, acrimony, animosity, animus, bitterness, antipathy, strife, malice, bad blood. **—Ant.** goodwill, amity, friendliness, friendship, amicability, love, affection, cordiality.

ennui *n.* weariness, boredom, tedium, languor, listlessness, lassitude; apathy, indifference. **—Ant.** excitement, eagerness, interest, curiosity, commitment.

enormity *n.* **1.** monstrousness, atrociousness, outrageousness, offensiveness, vileness, villainy, depravity, viciousness, wickedness, evilness, malignity, heinousness, baseness. **2.** immensity, hugeness, vastness, largeness, enormousness. **—Ant. 1** inoffensiveness, innocuousness, harmlessness, innocence. **2** smallness, insignificance, meagerness.

enormous *adj.* huge, vast, immense, tremendous, colossal, gigantic, mammoth, gargantuan, Brobdingnagian, titanic, elephantine, *Slang* humongous; massive, prodigious. **—Syn. Study.** See HUGE. **—Ant.** small, little, tiny, minute, miniscule, Lilliputian, diminutive, trivial, insignificant, meager, midget, dwarf, peewee, itty-bitty, teeny, (*fem.*) petite.

enough *adj.* **1.** adequate, sufficient, ample, plenty, abundant, copious. *—pron.* **2.** sufficient amount, sufficiency, ample supply, competence, plenty, plentitude, full measure. *—adv.* **3.** adequately, sufficiently, satisfactorily, amply, abundantly; passably, tolerably, reasonably. **—Ant. 1** inadequate, insufficient; skimpy, scant, meager. **2** insufficiency, inadequacy, paucity, scarcity. **3** inadequately, insufficiently.

enrage *v.* infuriate, incense, make furious, anger, madden, inflame, aggravate, provoke the wrath of, throw into a rage, make one's blood boil, *Informal* burn one up, get one's goat, make one see red. **—Syn. Study.** ENRAGE, INFURIATE, INCENSE imply stirring to violent anger. To ENRAGE or to INFURIATE is to provoke wrath: *They enrage/infuriate her by their deliberate and continual harassment.* To INCENSE is to inflame with indignation or anger: *to incense a person by making insulting remarks.* **—Ant.** placate, pacify, appease, mollify, conciliate, soothe, calm, allay, quiet, assuage.

enrapture *v.* enthrall, hold rapt, transport, entrance, enchant, captivate, beguile, charm, bewitch, delight, thrill. **—Ant.** bore, disinterest, put off.

enrich *v.* **1.** make rich, make wealthy, *Slang* feather the nest of. **2.** elevate, improve, enhance, upgrade, ameliorate, fortify, endow, refine; adorn, embellish. **—Ant. 1** impoverish. **2** degrade, downgrade, bastardize, weaken, divest, strip.

enroll *v.* register, sign up, enter, take on; admit, accept, engage; enlist, join, join up, recruit. **—Ant.** withdraw, drop out, retire; dismiss, expel.

enrollment *n.* **1.** enrolling, registration, matriculation, signing up; enlistment, recruiting, admittance. **2.** total number enrolled, registration, roster; enlistment. **—Ant. 1** withdrawing, dropping out.

en route *adv.* in transit, on the way, on the road.

ensemble *n.* **1.** totality, entirety, general appearance, overall effect; grouping, assembly, aggregate. **2.** outfit, costume, attire, *Slang* getup. **3.** group of performers, company, troupe.

ensign *n.* **1.** flag, banner, standard, pennant, pennon, colors, jack. **2.** insignia, badge, emblem, sign, mark; identifying device, symbol.

enslave *v.* make a slave of, hold in bondage, enthrall, indenture, enchain, shackle, put in shackles; subjugate, subdue, capture, control, dominate; addict. **—Ant.** free, emancipate, release, liberate.

ensue *v.* follow, result, come afterward, come to pass, derive, succeed. **—Syn. Study.** See FOLLOW. **—Ant.** herald, precede, introduce.

ensure Also **insure** *v.* **1.** assure, be sure of, make sure, make certain of, clinch; guarantee, warrant, secure. **2.** protect, guard, safeguard, make safe, secure.

entail *v.* require, necessitate, demand, call for; include, involve, incorporate, occasion. **—Ant.** eliminate, cut out; exclude, leave out.

entangle *v.* **1.** tangle, enmesh, ensnare, snare, enravel, snarl, encumber, intertwine, twist up. **2.** tangle, catch, trap, ensnare, involve, embroil; complicate, mix up, confuse, muddle, foul up; implicate, compromise, embarrass. **—Ant. 1** disentangle, free, extricate, extirpate, unravel.

entente *n.* understanding, rapprochement, agreement, accord, conciliation, *French* entente cordiale, cordial understanding, mutual understanding, consortium, unanimity, likemindedness, general agreement, consensus, confluence of minds, pact, treaty, covenant. **—Ant.** disagreement, misunderstanding, conflict, dispute, discord, rift, split.

enter *v.* **1.** come in, go in, pass into, proceed into, make an entrance, arrive, penetrate, intrude into, trespass. **2.** join, commit oneself to, embark upon, set out on, bind oneself, become a member of, participate in, take part in. **3.** enroll in, sign up for, register for, enlist in, join; list, record, post, inscribe. **—Ant. 1** exit, leave, depart, go out, go. **2, 3** leave, withdraw from, drop out of, take out of, resign from, retire from.

enterprise *n.* **1.** undertaking, venture, endeavor, project, campaign, program, operation, effort, attempt, task. **2.** initiative, drive, aggressiveness, push, ingenuity, ambition, industry, energy, enthusiasm, eagerness, zeal, willingness, spirit, vigor, alertness, daring, boldness, adventurousness. **—Ant.** laziness, spiritlessness, indolence.

enterprising *adj.* ambitious, industrious, hardworking, active, energetic, venturesome, inventive, intrepid, self-reliant, eager, up-and-coming, enthusiastic, zealous, earnest, alert, keen, wide-awake. **—Syn. Study.** See AMBITIOUS. **—Ant.** lazy, indolent, timid, cautious, wary, conservative.

entertain *v.* **1.** amuse, divert, give enjoyment to, beguile, please, regale, delight, enthrall, charm, engage pleasantly, interest, absorb, engross. **2.** have guests, give a party, play host, keep open house, offer hospitality. **3.** consider, admit, contemplate, imagine, harbor, foster, support, nurture, think about, keep in mind, heed, muse over, dwell on, ponder, cogitate on. **—Syn. Study. 1** See AMUSE. **—Ant. 1** bore, weary, tire; displease, disgust. **3** reject, ignore, disregard.

entertainment *n.* amusement, diversion, distraction, recreation, divertissement, fun, play, good time, pastime, novelty; pleasure, enjoyment, satisfaction. **—Ant.** work, job, preoccupation.

enthrall, enthral *v.* **1.** intrigue, spellbind, fascinate, enchant, captivate, charm, transport, transfix, rivet, enrapture, entrance, thrill, bewitch, beguile, hypnotize, seduce. **2.** enslave, put into slavery, keep in bondage, subjugate, overpower. **—Ant. 1** bore, disinterest. **2** free, emancipate, liberate.

enthusiasm *n.* **1.** eagerness, keenness, anticipation, excitement, fervor, zest, ardor, relish, zeal, exuberance, elation. **2.** interest, passion, love, devotion, craze, mania, rage, pet activity; hobby, hobbyhorse, diversion, distraction. **—Ant. 1** apathy, indifference, unconcern, detachment, aloofness, calmness, coldness, coolness.

enthusiast *n.* fan, buff, devotee, aficionado, fanatic, addict, *Slang* bug, nut, freak.

enthusiastic *adj.* wholehearted, ardent, fervent, fervid, eager, zealous, passionate, spirited, exuberant; unqualified, unstinting. **—Ant.** blasé, dispassionate, cool, lukewarm, unenthusiastic, disinterested, halfhearted, faint, feeble.

entice *v.* induce, tempt, beguile, lure, allure, incite, attract, seduce; persuade, coax, inveigle, wheedle. **—Ant.** repel, discourage, dissuade.

entire *adj.* **1.** whole, total, full, gross; complete, all-inclusive, thorough, absolute, *Latin* in toto. **2.** intact, unbroken, undamaged, unimpaired, in perfect condition. **—Syn. Study. 1, 2** See COMPLETE. **—Ant. 1** partial, incomplete. **2** broken, fragmented, defective, damaged, impaired.

entirely *adv.* completely, wholly, fully, totally, thoroughly, altogether, utterly, absolutely, unreservedly, unqualifiedly. **—Ant.** partially, somewhat, slightly, moderately, partly, tolerably.

entitle *v.* **1.** give the right to, authorize, qualify, make eligible, allow, permit, enable. **2.** title, name, designate, call, style, dub, label, tag. **—Ant. 1** disable, disqualify.

entity *n.* real thing, thing, object, article, structure, body, matter, substance, quantity; creature, being, individual, presence. **—Ant.** nonentity, fantasy, hallucination, illusion, mirage, delusion, chimera, phantom.

entourage *n.* retinue, attendants, train, cortege, escort, following, convoy, staff, court, suite; companions, followers, associates.

entrails *n. pl.* viscera, intestines, insides, innards, guts, bowels.

entrance[1] *n.* **1.** entry, entranceway, way in, access, approach, ingress; (*loosely*) door, doorway, gate, gateway, portal, passageway, opening. **2.** permission to enter, entry, admittance, access, ingress, entrée. **3.** entry, coming in, approach, ingress; appearance, introduction. **—Ant.** exit, departure, egress.

entrance[2] *v.* **1.** delight, gladden, enrapture, fill with wonder, spellbind, fascinate, transport, captivate, enthrall, charm, bewitch, beguile. **2.** put into a trance, hypnotize, mesmerize. **—Ant. 1** bore, disinterest.

entrap *v.* tempt, entice, allure, inveigle, beguile, seduce; capture, snare, catch, ensnare, draw in, drag in; *Slang* hook, bag, nail, rope in, land, suck in, nab, collar.

entreat *v.* ask earnestly, beseech, implore, plead with, appeal to, exhort, request, beg, supplicate, adjure, enjoin, petition, importune. **—Ant.** command, direct, demand.

entreaty *n.* earnest request, plea, appeal, supplication, prayer, petition, importunity. **—Ant.** demand, ultimatum.

entrée, entree *n.* **1.** admittance, admission, entry, entrance, ingress, access, *Slang* pull; acceptance, acknowledgment. **2.** main course, main dish, principal dish.

entrench Also **intrench** *v.* establish solidly, fix, set, install; embed, implant, ingrain, anchor, dig in, ensconce, plant, root; put in a strong position.

entre nous *adv.* between us, between you and me, between ourselves, confidentially, privately, in strict confidence, between me and thee.

entrepreneur *n.* impresario, manager, organizer, coordinator, director.

entrust Also **intrust** *v.* trust, put in trust of, charge with, authorize, give the custody of, hand over, turn over, commit, consign, assign, delegate.

entry *n.* **1.** entranceway, way, way in, approach, ingress, access; (*loosely*) door, doorway, gate, gateway, portal, passageway. **2.** entrance hall, foyer, doorway, vestibule. **3.** approach, introduction, appearance; entrance, entrée, admission, admittance, ingress. **4.** record, account, registration; note, memo, memorandum, minute, item, jotting. **5.** thing entered, person entered, contestant, competitor. **—Ant. 1** exit, egress. **3** exit, departure, leaving, leave-taking, withdrawal.

enumerate *v.* **1.** specify, numerate, cite, relate, detail, recount, spell out. **2.** count, count up, add, add up, sum up, total, tally, tabulate, number, list, tick off.

enunciate *v.* pronounce clearly, utter distinctly; articulate, sound, speak, voice, vocalize. **—Ant.** mutter, mumble, stammer, stutter.

envelop *v.* wrap, enwrap, cover, encase, sheathe, enfold, enclose, engulf, encircle, blanket, cloak, shroud, veil, contain, swathe, swaddle, surround, encompass; hide, conceal, obscure. **—Ant.** unwrap, uncover, expose, reveal, lay bare.

envelope *n.* letter covering, paper wrapper, gummed wrapper; wrapping, jacket, cover, covering.

enviable *adj.* worthy of envy, covetable; desirable, advantageous, agreeable, excellent, beneficial, salutary, fortunate, lucky.

envious *adj.* jealous, filled with envy, green with envy, covetous; grudging, jaundiced, resentful, spiteful.

environment *n.* medium, habitat, element; surroundings, setting, locale, scene, milieu, atmosphere, ambience, situation, background; circumstances, living conditions, climate. **—Syn. Study.** ENVIRONMENT, MILIEU, SETTING, AMBIENCE refer to the objects, conditions, or circumstances that influence the life of an individual or community. ENVIRONMENT may refer to physical or to social and cultural surroundings: *an environment of grinding poverty.* MILIEU, encountered most often in literary writing, refers to intangible surroundings: *a milieu of artistic innovation.* SETTING tends to highlight the person or thing surrounded by or set against a background: *a lovely setting for a wedding.* AMBIENCE applies to the mood or tone of the surroundings: *an ambience of ease and elegance.*

environs *n. pl.* outskirts, suburbs, surrounding area, exurbs, outlying area, outer limits, vicinity, adjacent district, precincts, metropolitan area. **—Ant.** central city, core city, inner city; downtown.

envisage *v.* picture, imagine, visualize, conjure up, conceive, envision, conceptualize, fancy, view in the mind's eye, contemplate, form a mental picture of, dream of, picture to oneself, dream up, have a picture of.

envoy *n.* representative, delegate, emissary, ambassador, agent, deputy, minister, attaché, legate, intermediary, middleman; courier, messenger.

envy *n.* **1.** jealousy, enviousness, resentfulness, resentment, grudging, greed, covetousness, spite, malevolence, the green-eyed monster. *—v.* **2.** feel envious toward, be jealous of, resent, be spiteful toward, begrudge. **—Syn. Study. 1** ENVY and JEALOUSY are very close in meaning. ENVY denotes a longing to possess something awarded to or achieved by another: *to feel envy when a friend inherits a fortune.* JEALOUSY, on the other hand, denotes a feeling of resentment that another has gained something that one more rightfully deserves: *to feel jealousy when a coworker receives a promotion.* JEALOUSY also refers to anguish caused by fear of losing someone or something to a rival: *a husband's jealousy of other men.*

ephemeral *adj.* brief, temporary, transient, short-lived, temporal, transitory, fleeting, impermanent, evanescent, momentary, passing, fugitive, unenduring, nondurable, inconstant, fly-by-night, flitting, fugacious. **—Ant.** permanent, lasting, enduring, everlasting, perpetual, abiding.

epic *n.* **1.** epic poem, historic poem, heroic poem, saga; heroic adventure, drama. *—adj.* **2.** heroic, great, majestic, imposing, superhuman, noble, exalted; legendary, fabled, storied, fabulous.

epicure *n.* gourmet, gastronome, *Slang* foodie; fastidious connoisseur, bon vivant; gourmand, glutton; sybarite, hedonist.

epicurean *adj.* **1.** devoted to luxury, pleasure-seeking, voluptuous, sensual, libertine, hedonistic, sybaritic, self-indulgent, intemperate. **2.** fit for an epicure, gourmet, luxurious, lavish, rich, sybaritic, Lucullan. *—n.* **3.** voluptuary, sensualist, libertine, hedonist, sybarite. **—Ant. 1–3** Spartan. austere, simple, plain, humble, modest. **3** Spartan; puritan, ascetic.

epidemic *n.* **1.** outbreak, contagion, infection; plague, pestilence, scourge. *—adj.* **2.** dangerously contagious, pandemic, rampant, widespread, far-reaching, rife, prevalent, pervasive, prevailing; catching, infectious.

epigram *n.* witty saying, clever comment, bon mot, witticism, quip; maxim, apothegm, aphorism, adage.

epilogue *n.* final section, concluding addition, addendum, rider, codicil, supplement, afterword, *Music* coda; concluding speech. **—Ant.** preface, prologue, introduction, *Music* overture.

episode *n.* **1.** milestone, event, occurrence, happening, period; incident, affair, experience, adventure. **2.** scene, passage, part, section, chapter; installment. **—Syn. Study. 1** See EVENT.

episodic *adj.* rambling, wandering, loosely connected, meandering, digressive, discursive, halting, segmented, discontinuous.

epistle *n.* letter, formal letter, missive, encyclical, written communication, message; text in letter form.

epithet *n.* **1.** appellation, designation, ascription, sobriquet, nickname. **2.** curse, abusive word, insult, expletive, obscenity, blasphemy.

epitome *n.* embodiment, exemplification, model, typification, representation, essence, summation, summary, sum and substance; ideal, peak, height.

epoch *n.* period, age, era, time, interval. **—Syn. Study.** See AGE.

equable *adj.* **1.** eventempered, easygoing, calm, tranquil, serene, placid, unexcitable, unruffled, imperturbable, *Slang* unflappable; good-natured, agreeable, pleasant, sunny. **2.** uniform, constant, unvaried, unchanging, even, steady, regular, consistent, dependable, stable, predictable. **—Ant. 1** fitful, nervous, tense, excitable, temperamental; disagreeable, unpleasant, harsh, gruff. **2** variable, fluctuating, changeable, uneven, varied, irregular, inconsistent, unstable, unpredictable.

equal *adj.* **1.** the same, even, like, uniform; identical, one and the same, matched, evenly matched, of a piece;

equivalent, proportional, corresponding, correlative, symmetrical, balanced, evenly balanced, tantamount, comparable, commensurate. —*n.* **2.** peer, match; equivalent, counterpart, parallel, opposite number. —*v.* **3.** be the same as, be even to, equate with, be identical to, accord with, agree with, tally with, match, square with, balance with, correspond to, parallel, *Slang* jibe with; equalize. **—Ant. 1** unequal, different, uneven, unlike, dissimilar, varied, diverse, disparate, disproportionate, incommensurate, irregular, unbalanced. **3** be unequal, be uneven, be different, disagree, diverge.

equality *n.* **1.** equal opportunity, justice, fairness, impartiality, fair treatment, fair play. **2.** parity, coequality, evenness, sameness, uniformity, equivalency, correspondence; balance, similarity. **—Ant. 1** inequality, injustice, unfairness, bias, prejudice. **2** inequality, dissimilarity, difference.

equanimity *n.* calmness, composure, self-possession, steadiness, poise, aplomb, coolness, imperturbability, presence of mind, self-control, tranquillity, sangfroid, *Informal* cool. **—Ant.** panic, hysteria, disquiet, perturbation, agitation, discomposure.

equate *v.* **1.** equal out, even out, match, be equivalent to, be proportionate to, be commensurate, equalize, average, balance. **2.** think of as, consider as, draw a parallel between, compare, liken.

equilibrium *n.* balance, stability, equipoise, symmetry; sense of balance.

equip *v.* furnish, supply, outfit, fit out, appoint, prepare, provide, provision, stock, accoutre; rig, caparison. **—Syn. Study.** See FURNISH. **—Ant.** divest, denude, strip.

equipment *n.* apparatus, gear, material, paraphernalia, outfittings, matériel, supplies, furnishings, accoutrements, equipage, tackle, stuff.

equitable *adj.* fair, just, evenhanded, impartial, unbiased, unprejudiced, reasonable, proper, due. **—Ant.** inequitable, unfair, unjust, unreasonable.

equity *n.* **1.** impartiality, fairmindedness, fairness, justness, evenhandedness, reasonableness; fair dealings, justice. **2.** assets over liabilities, assets after mortgage, cash value; (*loosely*) cash, value, profit, assets, investment. **—Ant. 1** unfairness, partiality, bias, prejudice, unreasonableness; injustice.

equivalent *adj.* **1.** equal, the same as, comparable, commensurate with, tantamount, corresponding, correspondent, correlative; even, one and the same, of a piece. —*n.* **2.** equal amount, comparable sum; correspondent, peer, counterpart, parallel, match. **—Ant. 1** unequal, dissimilar, incomparable, incommensurate, different.

equivocal *adj.* ambiguous, indefinite, imprecise, vague, nonspecific, indeterminate, uncertain, hazy, doubtful, enigmatic; misleading, having a double meaning. **—Syn. Study.** See AMBIGUOUS. **—Ant.** precise, definite, specific, clear-cut, explicit, certain.

equivocate *v.* evade, avoid the issue, hedge, stall, dodge, beat around the bush, fudge, pussyfoot, be ambiguous, mince words, prevaricate, straddle the fence.

era *n.* period, age, epoch, time, interval. **—Syn. Study.** See AGE.

eradicate *v.* eliminate, annihilate, exterminate, erase, expunge, extinguish, extirpate, destroy, wipe out, get rid of, do away with, abolish, remove, blot out, obliterate, liquidate. **—Ant.** establish, originate, implant, engender, create, breed.

erase *v.* wipe away, rub out, eradicate, expunge, remove, eliminate, delete, strike out, scratch. **—Ant.** write, draw, print, stamp, mark, record.

erect *adj.* **1.** upright, vertical, straight, unstooped, unbent; stiff, rigid. —*v.* **2.** construct, build, put up, raise. **3.** place upright, stand up, put in a vertical position, set right side up. **—Ant. 1** horizontal, supine, leaning, stooped, bent; limp, relaxed, flaccid. **2** raze, demolish, tear down, destroy.

erode *v.* corrode, eat away; wear away, waste, ravage, spoil, disintegrate, despoil. **—Ant.** build up, strengthen, reinforce.

erotic *adj.* unchaste, immodest, ribald, wanton, impure, suggestive, risqué; obscene, indecent, lascivious, lewd, bawdy, lusty, salacious, *Slang* raunchy; sexual, sexy, sexually stimulating, carnal, *Slang* hot, amorous, passionate, ardent, amatory, impassioned.

err *v.* **1.** make a mistake, slip up, be incorrect, be in error, be inaccurate, miscalculate, mess up, blunder. **2.** lapse from virtue, transgress, sin, slip from grace, go astray, misbehave, do wrong, do a bad thing.

errand *n.* mission, task, assignment, undertaking, duty, office, minor chore.

erratic *adj.* inconsistent, unpredictable, unstable, shifting, vacillating, changeable, variable, fitful, capricious, odd, eccentric, queer, strange, peculiar, unusual, unnatural, aberrant, wayward, abnormal. **—Ant.** consistent, unvariable, regular, undeviating, unchanging, stable, steady, certain, sure, reliable, predictable, dependable; typical, normal, customary, natural.

erroneous *adj.* inaccurate, incorrect,

untrue, wrong, false, fallacious, faulty, mistaken, unsound, unfounded, unsupportable, off base, spurious, *Slang* full of hot air, all wet. **—Ant.** correct, accurate, true, factual, wellfounded.

error *n.* mistake, inaccuracy, miscalculation, fault, flaw, boner, blooper, botch, bungle, howler, *Slang* boo-boo; misconception, misunderstanding, misapprehension, misinterpretation, fallacy, oversight. **—Syn. Study.** See MISTAKE. **—Ant.** accuracy, flawlessness, correctness.

ersatz *adj.* synthetic, artificial, imitation, not genuine, counterfeit, sham, fake, phony, bogus, pretended. **—Ant.** real, genuine, authentic, natural, the real McCoy.

erstwhile *adj.* former, past, bygone, previous, *Informal* ex. **—Ant.** current, present.

erudite *adj.* learned, well-informed, well-educated, well-versed, literate, well-read, cultured, cultivated, scholarly, thoughtful, intelligent, well-reasoned, wise, sapient. **—Ant.** uninformed, uneducated, illiterate, unscholarly; shallow, unthinking; rash, ill-advised.

erudition *n.* learning, formal education, knowledge, learnedness, culture, scholarship, literacy, skill, expertise, cultivation, refinement, education, schooling, book learning, enlightenment. **—Syn. Study.** See LEARNING. **—Ant.** illiteracy, ignorance, unenlightenment, dullness, dumbness.

erupt *v.* burst forth, break out, explode, blow up, pour forth, belch forth, eruct, discharge, be ejected, throw off, emit, vent, flow forth, gush. **—Ant.** retain, contain, hold, hold back; be dormant, subside.

eruption *n.* **1.** discharge, emission, ejection, venting, bursting forth, outburst, outbreak, pouring forth, flare-up, outpouring, belching forth, flowing forth, gushing, explosion, blowing up. **2.** rash, inflammation, flare-up, breaking out; dermatitis, eczema, festering. **—Ant. 1** retention, repression; dormancy, quiescence; inactivity, subsidence.

escalate *v.* **1.** rise, increase, advance, ascend, elevate, mount, accelerate, boost, swell. **2.** intensify, step up, accelerate, expand, extend, enlarge, amplify, magnify, broaden, aggrandize. **—Ant. 1** lower, decrease, fall, subside, descend, retreat. **2** deescalate, lessen, limit, narrow, contract, minimize.

escapade *n.* prank, caper, antic, trick, caprice, mischief; lark, fling, spree, adventure, revel, high old time.

escape *v.* **1.** break free, break loose, get away, make a getaway, make off, slip away, run away, flee, skip, bolt, cut and run, abscond, steal off, *Slang* fly the coop; avoid capture. **2.** avoid danger, get away safely, avert; avoid, elude, evade, dodge, skirt, shun, eschew. **3.** issue, emerge, emanate, be emitted, be discharged, leak, seep, pour forth, flow, stream, gush. **4.** elude, be forgotten by, slip from the memory of. **—*n.* 5.** breakout, exodus, gain of freedom, flight, decampment, getaway. **6.** avoidance of danger, safe getaway, extrication, deliverance; means of fleeing danger, exit, egress. **7.** diversion, distraction, evasion of worry, avoidance of problems, way of getting away from it all. **8.** discharge, emission, outflow, leakage, seepage, outpour, issuing forth, pouring forth, outburst, egress, efflux, effluence. **—Syn. Study. 2** ESCAPE, ELUDE, EVADE mean to keep free of something. To ESCAPE is to succeed in keeping away from danger, pursuit, observation, etc.: *to escape punishment.* To ELUDE is to slip through an apparently tight net, thus avoiding, often by a narrow margin, whatever threatens; it implies using adroitness or slyness to baffle or foil: *The fox eluded the hounds.* To EVADE is to turn aside from or go out of reach of a person or thing, usu. by using artifice to direct attention elsewhere: *to evade the police.* **—Ant. 1** capture, recapture, apprehend; stay. **2** meet, encounter, face; seek, hunt, chase; trap, catch. **3** retain, hold, contain; inject, pour in. **4** come to mind, be on the tip of one's tongue; remember, recollect. **5** capture, recapture, apprehension. **8** retention, containment; injection, influx.

eschew *v.* abstain from, forgo, give up, forbear, avoid, shun, steer clear of, keep shy of. **—Ant.** seek, chase after, hunt out; indulge in, welcome, embrace.

escort *n.* **1.** accompanying guard, guard, protective screen; attendant body, retinue, cortege, entourage, attendants, company, train. **2.** date, squire, *Slang* arm candy; companion, conductor, chaperon. **—*v.* 3.** conduct, guide, lead the way, take, convoy, usher; accompany, attend, squire, chaperon. **—Syn. Study. 3** See ACCOMPANY.

esoteric *adj.* **1.** incomprehensible, abstruse, recondite, arcane, cryptic, enigmatic, inscrutable, mysterious, obscure. **2.** secret, undisclosed, private, confidential, inviolable, hidden, concealed, covert, veiled, cloaked; mystical, occult. **—Ant. 1** obvious, clear, plain, simple. **2** public, open, exoteric.

especial *adj.* See SPECIAL.

especially *adv.* **1.** expressly, specifically, exclusively; principally, particularly, primarily. **2.** exceptionally, outstandingly, particularly, uncommonly, extraordinarily, unusually, singularly, notably, really, intensely.

espouse *v.* **1.** adopt, take up, embrace; support, champion, back, advocate, promote, further, side with, stand up for, express belief in, boost, tout. **2.** marry, become married, wed, unite in marriage. **—Ant. 1** reject, renounce, abjure; denounce, hinder, obstruct, block, thwart.

esprit de corps *n.* team spirit, group unity, fellowship, camaraderie, group enthusiasm, group pride, high morale, solidarity.

essay *n.* **1.** short composition, theme, paper; dissertation, treatise, tract, editorial, article, commentary, critique. **2.** attempt, effort, try, venture, endeavor, undertaking, experiment. **—*v.*** **3.** try, attempt, take on, undertake, venture, make an effort at, take a crack at, take a fling at, make a stab at.

essence *n.* **1.** basic quality, essential character, quintessence, nature, principle, substance, life-blood, spirit, heart, core, germ, soul; meaning, significance, gist, point, pith, sum and substance. **2.** concentrate, tincture, elixir, spirits, extract. **3.** perfume, scent, cologne, fragrance, toilet water.

essential *adj.* **1.** indispensable, requisite, necessary, needed, crucial, vital. **2.** basic, fundamental; main, key, principal, cardinal, leading, important, inherent, intrinsic, ingrained. **—*n.*** **3.** (*sometimes pl.*) basic need, requisite, necessity, indispensable element, key element, vital part, primary constituent; basics, fundamentals, rudiments, principles, *Slang* nitty-gritty. **—Syn. Study. 1** See NECESSARY. **2** ESSENTIAL, INHERENT, INTRINSIC refer to that which is in the natural composition of a thing. ESSENTIAL suggests that which is in the very essence or constitution of a thing: *Quiet is essential in a public library.* INHERENT means inborn or fixed from the beginning as a permanent quality or constituent of a thing: *properties inherent in iron.* INTRINSIC implies belonging to the nature of a thing itself and existing within it, without regard to external considerations or accidentally added properties: *the intrinsic value of diamonds.* **—Ant. 1, 2** dispensable, superfluous, peripheral, unimportant, incidental, unnecessary, immaterial, secondary, minor, lesser, minimal, trivial. **3** accessory, extra, option.

establish *v.* **1.** institute, found, set up, bring about, bring into existence, form, organize, create, begin, start, inaugurate, open, initiate. **2.** gain recognition for, win acceptance for, make secure, install, settle, sustain, situate, fix, implant. **3.** prove, show, confirm, verify, corroborate, authenticate, demonstrate, sustain, uphold, validate, put to rest any doubts about; justify, warrant. **—Ant. 1** close, disband, dissolve, liquidate, eradicate, destroy. **2** uproot, unsettle, dethrone. **3** refute, invalidate, deny, cast doubt on, bring into question, throw suspicion upon.

establishment *n.* **1.** establishing, setting up, instituting, founding, bringing about, formation, institution, foundation, development, organization, creation, building. **2.** business, company, concern, firm, corporation, outfit, organization, institution, building, plant, factory, office. **3. Establishment.** traditional leaders, entrenched leaders, ruling class; established order, entrenched social order, system, powers that be. **—Ant. 1** closing, dissolution, disbanding, liquidation, eradication, destruction. **2** revolutionaries, rebels, activists, young Turks, radicals, upstarts.

estate *n.* **1.** country estate, large residential property, landed property, manor, country place, compound, plantation. **2.** assets at death, assets, fortune, wealth, money, property, material possessions, belongings, holdings, effects, goods, chattels; inheritance, legacy, bequest, will. **3.** state, station, condition, status, situation, period of life; rank, grade, class, order. **—Syn. Study. 2** See PROPERTY.

esteem *v.* **1.** venerate, revere, honor, hold in high regard, think highly of, appreciate, admire, value, prize, treasure, cherish, attach importance to, set store by; respect, look up to. **2.** consider, regard, believe, think, hold, deem, judge, reckon, calculate. **—*n.*** **3.** regard, respect, favorable opinion, estimate, approval, admiration, veneration, appreciation, reverence. **—Syn. Study. 1** See APPRECIATE. **3** See RESPECT. **—Ant. 1** disdain, scorn, disparage, deprecate, discredit, *Slang* put down; decry, detest, despise, dislike, abominate, abhor, loathe; undervalue, belittle, underrate; devaluate, degrade. **3** disrespect, contempt, disdain, scorn, depreciation; aversion, dislike, detestation, abhorrence, repugnance, loathing.

esthetic, aesthetic *adj.* appreciative of beauty, appealing to artistic taste, having artistic tastes, artistic; sensitive, discriminating, cultivated, refined, fastidious. **—Ant.** unesthetic, unappreciative; insensitive, undiscriminating.

estimable *adj.* highly regarded, worthy of esteem, worthwhile, important, admired, reputable, treasured, prized, respected, revered, praiseworthy, commendable, laudable, honorable, admirable, good. **—Ant.** scorned, ridiculous, disdained, disparaged, deprecated, despised, disliked; unworthy, disreputable, undeserving, inferior, bad.

estimate *v.* **1.** evaluate, judge, reckon, calculate, appraise, value, assess, assay, figure. **2.** think, consider, believe, surmise, guess, conjecture, opine, conclude. —*n.* **3.** evaluation, estimation, assessment, appraisal, calculation, assay; opinion, judgment, reckoning, thinking, surmise, view, belief.

estimation *n.* **1.** opinion, judgment, appraisal, estimate, view, belief, consideration, evaluation, reckoning. **2.** esteem, respect, regard, favorable opinion, admiration, approval. **—Ant. 2** contempt, scorn, disrespect, disapproval.

estrange *v.* alienate, drive apart, disaffect, dissociate, part, destroy the affection of; antagonize, make hostile. **—Syn. Study.** ESTRANGE, ALIENATE, DISAFFECT share the sense of turning away from a state of affection, comradeship, or allegiance. ESTRANGE refers to the replacement of affection by apathy or hostility; it often involves physical separation: *lovers estranged by a misunderstanding.* ALIENATE often emphasizes the cause of antagonism: *His inconsiderate behavior alienated his friends.* DISAFFECT usu. refers to relationships involving allegiance or loyalty rather than love or affection: *disaffected workers ready to strike.* **—Ant.** unite, join, link, bind; reconcile; conciliate.

estuary *n.* tidal basin, inlet, arm of the sea; river mouth, firth.

etc., &c. and others, and the rest, and so forth, et cetera, and so on, et al., *Informal* whatnot, whatever, blah-blah-blah, yada-yada-yada.

eternal *adj.* **1.** lasting forever, everlasting, infinite, timeless, endless, perpetual, immortal, without end, imperishable. **2.** continual, unending, never-ending, perpetual, ceaseless, endless, persistent, relentless, uninterrupted, interminable; constant, abiding, undying. **—Syn. Study. 1** ETERNAL, EVERLASTING, ENDLESS, PERPETUAL imply lasting or going on without ceasing. That which is ETERNAL is, by its nature, without beginning or end: *God, the eternal Father.* That which is EVERLASTING will endure through all future time: *a promise of everlasting life.* That which is ENDLESS never stops but goes on continuously as if in a circle: *an endless succession of years.* PERPETUAL implies continuous renewal far into the future: *perpetual strife between nations.* **—Ant. 1** transient, transitory, fleeting, perishable, finite, evanescent, ephemeral, mortal, temporal. **2** occasional, infrequent, rare, spasmodic, irregular, scattered, random, temporary, spotty, on-and-off, haphazard, hit-or-miss.

eternity *n.* **1.** forever, infinity, time without end, endlessness, ages and ages, eons and eons. **2.** everlasting life, immortality, the hereafter, the next world, the afterworld, the world to come; Heaven, paradise, nirvana, Zion, New Jerusalem. **—Ant. 1** instant, moment, a second, a split second. **2** the here and now, life on earth, mortality.

ethereal *adj.* sublime, refined, celestial, exquisite, aerial, airy, unearthly, unworldly, delicate; elusive, rare, rarefied. **—Ant.** earthly, mundane, worldly; statuesque, monumental, solid.

ethical *adj.* moral, decent, virtuous, honorable, upright, right, proper, fitting, correct, just, fair, aboveboard, straightforward, open and aboveboard, scrupulous, *Slang* kosher. **—Ant.** unethical, underhanded, shady, improper, unfair, low-down, nefarious, crooked, unscrupulous, unbecoming, unseemly, indecorous, immoral, indecent.

ethics *n. pl.* (*Sometimes sing.*) moral code, moral standards, rules of conduct, moral principle, principles, moral values, morality, integrity, moral philosophy, sense of right and wrong, sense of duty, conscience.

ethnic *adj.* native, national, indigenous; racial, cultural; original, unique.

etiquette *n.* rules of behavior, amenities, protocol, conventions, behavior, proprieties, civilities, manners, usage, decorum, politeness, courtesy; gentility, good form, good taste. **—Ant.** impropriety, boorishness, rudeness, impoliteness, vulgarity, indecorum.

Eucharist *n.* Communion, Holy Communion, Sacrament of the Lord's Supper; consecrated wafer, consecrated elements of bread and wine; (*when given to a person in danger of dying*) viaticum.

eulogize *v.* praise highly, laud, panegyrize, extol, glorify, acclaim, hail, exalt, celebrate, magnify; compliment, tout, boost, commend, pay tribute to. **—Ant.** malign, defame, vilify, slander, libel, criticize, condemn.

eulogy *n.* oration of praise, praise of the dead, encomium, panegyric; high praise, tribute, homage, hosanna, acclamation, laudation, citation, paean, plaudit. **—Ant.** condemnation, criticism; vilification, defamation, aspersion, calumny, slander, libel.

euphemism *n.* mild expression, restrained expression, inoffensive expression, delicate term, refined term; prudish phrase, overdelicacy, overrefinement, prudishness.

evacuate *v.* **1.** leave, withdraw from, quit, vacate; abandon, desert, forsake. **2.** remove, move out, take out, order out. **—Ant. 1** enter, go in, occupy. **2** take in, move in.

evade *v.* avoid, dodge, elude, steer clear of, duck, parry, shun, escape, eschew, sidestep, circumvent, fend off, hedge; equivocate. **—Syn. Study.** See ESCAPE.

—**Ant.** face, face up to, meet eye to eye, confront; encounter, meet, meet head-on.

evaluate *v.* appraise, rate, assess, weigh, judge, estimate, gauge, size up, value, assay.

evangelist *n.* religious crusader, preacher, revivalist, missionary, soulsaver, minister of the Gospel, Bible Thumper, reformer, proselytizer, propagandist, missioner, apostolic.

evaporate *v.* **1.** dry up, vaporize, melt away; dehydrate, desiccate. **2.** disappear, vanish, fade away, melt away, dissolve, evanesce; scatter, dispel, dissipate. —**Ant. 1** condense, concentrate; reconstitute, reconstruct. **2** appear, materialize, emerge, gather, collect, converge.

evasion *n.* avoidance, dodging, eluding, attempt to escape, ducking, shrinking from, shunning, sidestepping, circumventing. —**Ant.** confronting, facing up to, meeting head-on; frankness, candor.

evasive *adj.* elusive, elusory, ambiguous, equivocal, equivocating, dodging, hedging, devious, dissembling, shifty, deceptive, misleading, deceitful. —**Ant.** candid, straightforward, frank, direct, open, honest, truthful, guileless.

even *adj.* **1.** level, smooth, flat, plane; plumb, straight, parallel, flush, true, uniform. **2.** constant, regular, steady, uniform, unvarying, unwavering. **3.** equal, identical, the same, uniform; equitable, matching, balanced, square. **4.** even-tempered, calm, steady, placid, equable, unruffled, unexcitable; balanced, fair, just, dispassionate, impartial, unbiased. —*v.* **5.** straighten, make parallel, make flush, make uniform; smooth, level, flatten; equal, equalize, balance. —**Ant. 1–4** uneven. **1** wavy, undulating, rough, bumpy; crooked, curving, twisting, turning; slanted, awry, irregular. **2** variable, changing, fluctuating, nonuniform, irregular. **3** unequal, different, unidentical, nonuniform, inequitable, unbalanced. **4** emotional, hot-tempered, quick-tempered, excitable, easily ruffled, biased, unfair, unjust, prejudiced.

evening *n.* sundown, sunset, twilight, dusk, gloaming; day's end, close of day; eve, even, eventide, nightfall. —**Ant.** dawn, dawning, sunrise, sunup, daylight, morning.

event *n.* **1.** occurrence, momentous occurrence, milestone; occasion, episode, happening, experience, incident. **2.** contest, competition, tournament, game, bout. —**Syn. Study. 1** EVENT, EPISODE, INCIDENT refer to a happening. An EVENT is usu. an important happening, esp. one that comes out of and is connected with previous happenings: *historical events.* An EPISODE is one of a series of happenings, frequently distinct from the main course of events but arising from them and having an interest of its own: *an episode in her life.* An INCIDENT is usu. a minor happening that is connected with an event or series of events of greater importance: *an amusing incident in a play.*

eventful *adj.* noteworthy, notable, memorable, thrilling, exciting, unforgettable; momentous, historic, epochal, important, significant, weighty, consequential; critical, crucial, fateful. —**Ant.** ordinary, dull, unexciting, uninteresting, trivial, trifling, unimportant, insignificant, inconsequential, irrelevant.

eventual *adj.* future, prospective, coming, later; impending, imminent, upcoming, ultimate, final; following, subsequent, consequent, resulting, ensuing. —**Ant.** past, previous, prior.

eventually *adv.* in the course of time, sometime, one day, ultimately, sooner or later, finally, in the end, in the long run, when all is said and done. —**Ant.** never; immediately, at once.

everlasting *adj.* **1.** eternal, immortal, perpetual, lasting, never-ending, infinite, endless. **2.** long-lasting, ever-living, timeless, imperishable, durable, indestructible, undying, continual. **3.** constant, endless, ceaseless, unceasing, incessant, perpetual, continuous, interminable, wearisome, tiresome, tedious. —**Syn. Study. 1** See ETERNAL. —**Ant. 1, 2** transitory, temporary, passing, fleeting, ephemeral, momentary, short-lived, transient. **3** intermittent, occasional.

everyday *adj.* **1.** daily, day after day, quotidian. **2.** routine, ordinary, common, commonplace, workaday, usual, customary, familiar, established, regular; conventional, stock, run-of-the-mill, dull, mundane, unimaginative; trite, hackneyed, stereotyped; *Slang* square. —**Ant. 1** occasional, infrequent, irregular, now and then, incidental, periodic, sporadic. **2** original, imaginative, extraordinary, uncommon, unusual, unique, individual, exciting, interesting, fantastic, outlandish; *Slang* far-out.

everywhere *adv.* every place, in all places, far and wide, far and near; extensively, ubiquitously; universally, all over, the world over; throughout, to the four winds. —**Ant.** nowhere, here and there.

evict *v.* turn out, remove, dispossess, dislodge, expel, eject, oust, kick out, throw out, get rid of.

evidence *n.* proof, grounds, material

proof, fact; substantiation, documentation, corroboration, confirmation, affirmation, authentication; exhibit, testimony, indication, sign, token; illustration, exemplification.

evident *adj.* clear, plain, obvious, apparent, manifest, perceptible, visible, demonstrable, noticeable, conspicuous, *Informal* plain as the nose on one's face; certain, patent, unmistakable, unquestionable, undeniable. **—Syn. Study.** See APPARENT. **—Ant.** unclear, obscure, imperceptible, inconspicuous; doubtful, uncertain, vague, questionable, dubious; secret, covert, undisclosed, unknown, hidden, concealed, undiscovered.

evidently *adv.* apparently, assumedly, to all appearances; obviously, clearly, plainly, certainly, unquestionably, unmistakably, undeniably, doubtless, doubtlessly.

evil *adj.* **1.** bad, wicked, iniquitous, immoral, sinful, base, unprincipled, sinister, malevolent, malicious, malignant, vile, villainous, vicious, nefarious, heinous, black-hearted, unscrupulous, pernicious, venal. *—n.* **2.** sin, wickedness, immorality, wrongdoing, vice, baseness, iniquity, depravity, turpitude, corruption. **—Ant. 1** good, honorable, worthy, moral, exemplary; wholesome, upright, virtuous, benevolent, kind, good, human, humane, merciful, sympathetic, benign. **2** good, goodness, virtue, morality, righteousness.

evoke *v.* bring forth, call forth, call up, summon, invoke, conjure up, elicit, invite, induce, produce, suggest, stimulate, provoke, excite, stir, arouse, rouse, waken, awaken. **—Ant.** repress, suppress, restrain, hold back, inhibit, stifle, curb, check, crush; prevent, subdue, silence, stop, extinguish.

evolution *n.* growth, development, unfolding, progression, rise, increase, expansion, enlargement; maturation, fruition; change, metamorphosis. **—Ant.** deterioration, withering, contraction, shrinking, decrease, diminution, falling off.

evolve *v.* develop, grow, expand, enlarge, increase, unfold, unroll, mature, ripen. **—Ant.** deteriorate, wither, contract, shrink, decrease.

exacerbate *v.* aggravate, exaggerate, intensify, inflame, heighten, worsen, magnify, sharpen, deepen, fan the flames, pour oil on the fire, add fuel to the flames, rub salt into the wound, add insult to injury. **—Ant.** relieve, soothe, comfort, alleviate, assuage, mollify.

exact *adj.* **1.** correct, accurate, specific, explicit, precise, right, true; clear-cut, unequivocal, on the head, on the nose, to the letter, literal. **2.** meticulous, painstaking, exacting, strict; careful, punctilious, scrupulous, systematic, methodical. *—v.* **3.** demand, claim, extract, take, wrest, force, require, compel, squeeze, mulct, extort. **—Ant. 1** approximate, imprecise, inaccurate, incorrect. **2** sloppy, careless, slovenly, devil-may-care.

exacting *adj.* **1.** demanding, meticulous, unsparing, critical, strict, rigid, unbending, stern, severe, harsh, hard, hard-headed, hard-nosed, no-nonsense. **2.** demanding, hard, arduous, difficult, tough, trying, strenuous. **—Ant. 1** easy, easygoing, carefree, nonchalant, devil-may-care, soft, softhearted, lenient, permissive. **2** easy, effortless, undemanding.

exactly *adv.* **1.** precisely, specifically, explicitly; accurately, correctly, truly, literally. **2.** just, entirely, absolutely, fully, wholly, precisely, quite, strictly. **3.** quite so, that's right, indeed, of course, certainly, definitely, assuredly, just so. **—Ant. 1** approximately, loosely, more or less; inaccurately, incorrectly.

exaggerate *v.* overstate, magnify, amplify, hyperbolize, enlarge on, stretch, embroider, embellish, overdo, boast, lay it on. **—Ant.** understate, minimize, disparage, qualify.

exalt *v.* **1.** laud, extol, praise, pay tribute to, honor, applaud, acclaim, cheer, celebrate, commend, make much of; glorify, venerate, magnify, worship. **2.** uplift, elevate, inspire, ennoble; elate, stimulate, exhilarate; intensify. **—Syn. Study. 2** See ELEVATE. **—Ant. 1** damn, condemn, disgrace, degrade, dishonor, shame, debase, demean, lower, humble, humiliate, disparage, depreciate, belittle, *Slang* put down. **2** depress, dispirit, dishearten, weary; dismay, appall.

exaltation *n.* **1.** tribute, praise, celebration, praising, eulogizing, panegyric, honor, dignity, glory; grandeur, nobility; worship, veneration, deification. **2.** elation, exultation, ecstasy, rapture, transport, exhilaration, happiness, bliss; high, rush. **—Syn. Study. 2** See RAPTURE. **—Ant. 1** damnation, condemnation, depreciation, debasement, belittling, degradation, dishonoring, humiliation, *Informal* put-down. **2** depression, dejection, melancholia, gloom, despondency, blues; sorrow, sadness, misery.

exalted *adj.* **1.** high-ranking, noble, lordly, august, lofty, illustrious; magnificent, glorious, grand, elevated, dignified, venerable, honorable, notable. **2.** ecstatic, rapturous, inspired, excited, happy, elated, blissful, heightened, lofty, uplifted, *Slang* up. **—Ant. 1** lowly, vulgar, common, ignoble, base, modest, unassuming; lowborn, lowbred, plebeian, servile. **2** depressed, dejected, glum, gloomy, despondent, blue; sorrowful, sad, low, miserable.

examination *n.* **1.** inspection, scrutiny, survey, perusal, looking over, probe, analysis, investigation, review, study, assay, audit; physical checkup. **2.** exam, test, review, quiz; midterm, final. **—Syn. Study. 1** EXAMINATION, INSPECTION, SCRUTINY refer to a looking at something. An EXAMINATION is an orderly attempt to test or to obtain information about something, often something presented for observation: *an examination of merchandise for sale.* An INSPECTION is usu. a formal and official examination: *An inspection of the plumbing revealed a defective pipe.* SCRUTINY implies a critical and minutely detailed examination: *His testimony was given close scrutiny.*

examine *v.* **1.** look over, inspect, scrutinize, view, survey, observe, peruse, scan. **2.** study, probe, look into, inquire into, consider, investigate, explore, ponder, review; audit, take stock of. **3.** test, quiz; question, query, interrogate, *Slang* pump, grill. **—Ant. 1** ignore, overlook. **2** accept at face value.

example *n.* sample, illustration, representation, exemplification, specimen, case in point, archetype, prototype, pattern, model, ideal, standard, exemplar, paragon. **—Ant.** anomaly, paradox; abnormality, aberration, contradiction, incongruity.

exasperate *v.* irritate, annoy, rile, irk, anger, madden, incense, infuriate, enrage; rankle, aggravate, provoke, try the patience of; offend, ruffle, chafe, harass, vex, pique, bother; *Slang* bug, turn off. **—Ant.** mollify, pacify, placate, appease, propitiate, conciliate; calm, assuage, tranquilize.

excavate *v.* make a hole in, hollow out, tunnel, dig, dig out, scoop out; gouge, mine, quarry, cut out; burrow, furrow, groove; unearth, uncover, dig up. **—Ant.** fill, fill in, fill up, bury, cover up.

exceed *v.* **1.** go beyond, go over, pass, overdo, outreach, outrun, outpace, outstrip, overshoot, transcend, surmount. **2.** excel, predominate, surpass, come first, be superior, outrival, outrank. **—Ant. 1** stay within, keep in, keep under. **2** fail, be inferior.

exceedingly *adv.* very, extremely, greatly, especially, notably, very highly; vastly, enormously, outstandingly, impressively, eminently, preeminently, supremely, surpassingly, immeasurably, excessively, superlatively, extraordinarily, unwontedly, unusually, inordinately, amazingly, astonishingly.

excel *v.* exceed, surpass, prevail, predominate, rank first, tower above, outstrip, outrival, outdo, walk off with the honors, *Slang* take the cake. **—Ant.** fail, fall behind, fall short, be inadequate, be inferior to.

excellence *n.* high quality, quality, superiority, perfection, greatness, merit, eminence, preeminence, transcendence, distinction. **—Ant.** inferiority, poor quality, imperfection, deficiency; fault, blemish, defect, flaw, shortcoming, inadequacy, failing, frailty.

excellent *adj.* outstanding, superior, superlative, exceptional, superb, classic, choice, capital, sterling, great, tremendous, terrific, wonderful, fine, superfine, topnotch, first-rate, first-class; admirable, notable; matchless, peerless, preeminent, exemplary; *Informal* prime, super, swell, aces, tops, grade A, A-1, *Slang* nifty, bang-up, def, down. **—Ant.** bad, poor, imperfect, inferior, terrible, awful, substandard, second-rate, second-class, below par, incompetent, inexpert, unskilled, faulty, *Slang* lousy.

except *prep.* **1.** excepting, excluding, exclusive of, but, save, saving, other than, barring, besides. **—*v.* 2.** exempt, excuse, exclude, omit, eliminate; bar, ban, shut out, enjoin, remove, pass over, count out, disallow, reject. **—Ant. 1** including. **2** include, reckon, count.

exception **1.** exclusion, exemption, omission, elimination, removal, debarment; separation, segregation, seclusion, isolation; leaving out, shutting out, disallowment; rejection, renunciation, repudiation. **2.** deviation, special case, anomaly, rarity, inconsistency, irregularity, oddity, peculiarity, difference. **—Ant. 1** inclusion, taking in, counting in. **2** consistency, regularity, conformity.

exceptional *adj.* **1.** unusual, extraordinary, unique, uncommon, rare, singular, irregular, atypical, anomalous, abnormal, peculiar, unwonted, unnatural, queer, strange, odd, aberrant, unprecedented, unheard of, phenomenal, freakish. **2.** better than average, outstanding, superior, excellent, noteworthy, first-class; wonderful, terrific, great, marvelous, special, extraordinary, remarkable, incomparable, inimitable, *Slang* out-of-sight. **—Ant. 1** common, ordinary, usual, normal, typical, regular, natural, expected, customary, familiar. **2** average, mediocre, so-so, bad, terrible, awful, second-rate; *Slang* lousy, crummy.

excerpt *n.* extract, selection, portion, fragment, section, piece, part, abstract, quotation, quoted passage.

excess *n.* **1.** surplus, overabundance, superabundance, undue amount, too much, oversupply, surfeit, plethora; profusion, fullness, lavishness, avalanche, flood, inundation, overflow; glut, repletion. —*adj.* **2.** surplus, extra, excessive, overflow; remainder, residue, spare. —**Ant. 1** deficiency, lack, shortage, scarcity, dearth, paucity, inadequacy, insufficiency, scantness. **2** insufficient, inadequate, scanty, scarce.

excessive *adj.* excess, overabundant, undue, too much, profuse; extreme, superfluous, extravagant, immoderate, inordinate, exaggerated, unreasonable, needless, unnecessary, disproportionate, senseless. —**Ant.** insufficient, deficient, inadequate, lacking, wanting, scarce, meager, scanty, scant, skimpy, sparse.

exchange *v.* **1.** trade, swap, barter, trade off, convert into. **2.** swap, interchange, give and take, reciprocate. —*n.* **3.** interchange, reciprocity, give-and-take; trade, swap, switch, bandying, tit for tat, *Latin* quid pro quo. —**Ant. 1** keep, hold on to.

excise[1] *v.* tax, duty, surcharge, impost.

excise[2] *v.* remove, cut out, cut off, eradicate, extract, pluck out.

excite *v.* **1.** thrill, electrify, galvanize, rouse, arouse, spur on, stir up, agitate, move, stimulate, energize, kindle, fire, inflame, provoke, animate, incite, foment, instigate; titillate, get a kick out of. **2.** evoke, elicit, waken, awaken, stimulate, whet, pique. —**Ant. 1** dull, lull, bore, soothe, quiet, calm, pacify. **2** allay, appease, mollify, diminish; deaden, kill, quench.

excitement *n.* thrill, adventure, *Slang* kicks; stimulation, interest, animation, enthusiasm, elation, action, activity, furor, ferment, commotion, ado, brouhaha, turmoil, tumult, agitation, flurry, flutter, frenzy, stir, *Informal* fireworks, *Slang* flap, to-do, hoopla. —**Ant.** serenity, peace; inactivity, lethargy, sluggishness; dullness, boredom.

exciting *adj.* thrilling, electrifying, breathtaking, hair-raising, spine-tingling, rousing, sensational, stirring, impelling, provocative, stimulating, moving, affecting, inspiring, dazzling, zestful; *Slang* jiggy; titillating, spicy, risqué. —**Ant.** unexciting, uninteresting, dull, quiet, stodgy, boring, monotonous, wearisome, humdrum, drab, dreary, soporific.

exclaim *v.* cry out, call out, ejaculate, shout, yell, bellow, howl, proclaim, vociferate.

exclamation *n.* ejaculation, vociferation, outcry, cry, shout, yell, shriek, bellow, howl, squeal, screech, yelp; interjection, expletive. —**Ant.** whisper, mutter, murmur, mumble; statement, question.

exclude *v.* **1.** keep out, bar, ban, shut the door on, shut out, prevent entrance of, blackball, boycott, reject, prohibit, forbid, disallow, refuse; evict, remove, banish, expel, oust, eject, throw out. **2.** rule out, omit, except, set aside, leave out; repudiate. —**Ant. 1** invite, welcome; admit, include, accept, allow.

exclusion *n.* keeping out, barring, nonadmission, debarment, rejection, prohibition, refusal; restraint, prevention, preclusion; eviction, removal, banishment, dismissal, expelling, ouster, ejection, expulsion, throwing out. —**Ant.** admittance, inclusion, acceptance.

exclusive *adj.* **1.** select, elect, high-class, *Slang* posh; restricted, restrictive; closed, private; clannish, cliquish; aloof, snobbish. **2.** sole, single, private, unshared, undivided; complete, entire, total, absolute, full. —**Ant. 1** open, unrestricted; popular, common. **2** nonexclusive, shared, divided; partial, incomplete.

excommunicate *v.* remove, exclude from sacraments, anathematize, divest of membership, unchurch; expel, eject, banish, ban, oust. —**Ant.** admit, enroll; readmit, reinstate.

excruciating *adj.* extremely painful, unbearable, insufferable, unendurable, agonizing, torturous, racking, tormenting; acute, severe, extreme, fierce, intense, violent, cutting, lacerating. —**Ant.** bearable, tolerable, endurable; mild, slight, gentle, trivial.

excursion *n.* outing, junket, trip, pleasure trip, short journey, tour, jaunt, sally, expedition, sortie; *(variously)* ride, drive, voyage, cruise, flight, walk, stroll, hike, tramp, ramble, trek.

excuse *v.* **1.** forgive, pardon, make allowance for, pass over, bear with, indulge, accept one's apology. **2.** apologize for, justify, explain, defend, vindicate, ask forgiveness for, condone, pardon, let one off, absolve, acquit, exonerate, exculpate, clear; mitigate, palliate, extenuate, disregard, gloss over, overlook, whitewash. **3.** release, exempt, free, spare, let off, relieve of. —*n.* **4.** justification, defense, vindication, acceptable explanation, absolution, exoneration, exemption, reason, alibi, argument, plea for forgiveness. —**Syn. Study. 1** EXCUSE, FORGIVE, PARDON imply being lenient or giving up the wish to punish. EXCUSE means to overlook some (usu.) slight offense, because of circumstance, realization that it was unintentional, or the like: *to excuse rudeness.* FORGIVE is applied to excusing more serious offenses; the person wronged not only overlooks the offense but harbors no ill feeling against the offender: *to forgive and forget.* PARDON often applies to an act of leniency or mercy by an official or superior; it usu. involves a serious offense or crime: *The governor was asked to pardon* *the condemned criminal.* **—Ant. 1, 2** censure, blame, criticize; chastise, castigate, discipline, chasten, correct, punish, charge, accuse, condemn, convict, sentence. **3** hold liable for, hold responsible for, subject to; compel, obligate, oblige, force into. **4** accusation, charge.

execute *v.* **1.** carry out, effect, put into effect, discharge, administer, accomplish, fulfill, achieve, complete, effectuate, consummate, realize, carry through, perpetrate, enforce. **2.** put to death, inflict capital punishment on; kill, slay; murder, assassinate, massacre. **3.** perform, render, play, do; act, enact, sustain.

execution *n.* **1.** carrying out, effecting, accomplishment, administration, performance, discharge, implementation, transaction, realization, fulfillment, achievement, completion. **2.** putting to death, infliction of capital punishment; killing, slaying. **3.** performance, doing, rendition, interpretation.

executive *n.* **1.** administrator, administrative head, director, manager; (*variously*) president, chairman, superintendent, supervisor, overseer. *—adj.* **2.** administrative, managerial, directorial, supervisory, leadership. **—Ant. 1** laborer, worker, subordinate, hired hand, flunky, menial, underling.

exemplary *adj.* **1.** worthy of imitation, emulative, model; admirable, praiseworthy, commendable, laudable, noteworthy, estimable, sterling, nonpareil, ideal, meritorious. **2.** typical, characteristic, model, illustrative, representative, sample. **—Ant. 1** objectionable, blameworthy, punishable. **2** atypical, unusual, uncommon, unique, peculiar.

exemplify *v.* typify, epitomize, characterize, illustrate, depict, represent, demonstrate, instance, embody, personify. **—Ant.** misrepresent, falsify.

exempt *v.* **1.** except, excuse, pardon, relieve, free, release, spare, absolve, clear, privilege, grant immunity to. *—adj.* **2.** not subject to, immune, excepted, excused, relieved, freed, absolved, spared, cleared, not liable to, released from; privileged. **—Ant. 1** subject, oblige, liable, expose. **2** liable, subject; responsible, chargeable, answerable.

exemption *n.* **1.** release, immunity, freedom, absolution, dispensation, exception, excuse; impunity. **2.** deduction, allowance; expense. **—Syn. Study. 1** EXEMPTION, IMMUNITY, IMPUNITY imply special privilege or freedom from requirements imposed on others. EXEMPTION implies release or privileged freedom from sharing with others some duty or legal requirement: *exemption from military service.* IMMUNITY implies freedom from a penalty or from some natural or common liability, esp. one that is disagreeable or threatening: *immunity from prosecution; immunity from disease.* IMPUNITY (limited mainly to the expression *with impunity*) suggests freedom from punishment: *The police force was so inadequate that crimes could be committed with impunity.* **—Ant. 1** responsibility, obligation, liability.

exercise *n.* **1.** workout, warm-up, movement, physical activity; calisthenics, aerobics, isometrics, gymnastics, a daily dozen. **2.** practice, training, schooling, drill. **3.** use, practice, employment, utilization, application, discharge; ceremony, performance, program. *—v.* **4.** work out, be physically active, do calisthenics; train, drill, follow a training regimen, discipline, school, break in, give lessons, tutor, teach, develop, prepare, inculcate, accustom. **5.** carry out, perform, execute, discharge, employ, utilize, wield; apply, practice, exert, display, demonstrate, show, exhibit. **—Ant. 1** inactivity, idleness. **3** avoidance, evasion, ignoring, overlooking. **4** be sedentary, be inactive. **5** avoid, evade, ignore, overlook, eschew.

exert *v.* put forth, put in action, set in motion, exercise, employ, wield, use, utilize, make use of, apply, expend, discharge, resort to, avail oneself of.

exertion *n.* effort, energy, strength, labor, toil, work, pains, trouble, struggle, travail, endeavor, industry, application, activity, elbow grease. **—Syn. Study.** See EFFORT. **—Ant.** idleness, inertia; rest, repose, ease, leisure.

exhale *v.* breathe out, respire, expire, emit breath, breathe; pant, puff, huff. **—Ant.** inhale, breathe in.

exhaust *v.* **1.** use up, run through, expend, deplete, dissipate, spend, consume, finish. **2.** wear out, tire, overtire, fatigue, drain, enervate, devitalize, sap one's energy; *Slang* poop, fag, bush; tax, strain, weaken, debilitate, disable. **3.** empty, draw out, draw off, drain. **—Ant. 1** amass, obtain, get, restock, replenish; save, conserve, preserve, keep, store, hoard. **2** invigorate, refresh, renew, revive, vivify, animate, enliven, innerve, strengthen.

exhausted *adj.* **1.** tired out, dead tired, fatigued, worn out, played out, all in, done in, devitalized, enervated, drained, spent, wearied; *Slang* beat, bushed, pooped. **2.** used up, finished, spent, gone, depleted, consumed, drained, expended, emptied; bankrupt, impoverished. **—Ant. 1** full of pep, ready to go, full of vim and vigor; invigorated, refreshed, revived, vivified, animated, enlivened. **2** replenished, restored, saved, conserved, preserved, kept.

exhaustion *n.* **1.** fatigue, weariness,

tiredness, enervation. **2.** using up, spending, consumption; depletion, draining. **—Ant. 1** energy, pep, vim, vigor, new strength. **2** replenishment; conservation, preservation.

exhaustive *adj.* comprehensive, profound, all-inclusive, thorough, intensive, complete, sweeping, in-depth, all-out, all-embracing. **—Ant.** hit-or-miss, catch-as-catch-can, incomplete, cursory, superficial.

exhibit *v.* **1.** display, show, put on view, present for inspection, make public, unveil, bring to light, air, flaunt, parade, brandish; demonstrate, reveal, manifest, evince, evidence. *—n.* **2.** exhibition, display, exposition, show, public showing. **—Syn. Study. 1** See DISPLAY. **—Ant.** hide, conceal, suppress, repress, mask, secret, bury.

exhibition *n.* exhibit, show, showing, public showing, display, exposition, public presentation, demonstration, unveiling, array.

exhilarate *v.* fill with high spirits, excite, stimulate, invigorate, hearten, lift, perk up, enliven, animate, quicken, elate, gladden, delight, cheer. **—Ant.** depress, dispirit, sadden, deject.

exhilaration *n.* high spirits, exaltation, elation, liveliness, animation, excitement, vivacity, delight, gladness, joyousness, lightheartedness, gaiety. **—Ant.** dejection, depression, sadness, gloom.

exhort *v.* encourage, spur, goad, press, prod, give a pep talk to; *Slang* egg on; urge, plead with, beseech, enjoin, implore, appeal to, persuade; advise, advocate, recommend, admonish, bid. **—Ant.** dissuade, discourage; forbid, prohibit, enjoin.

exigency *n.* **1.** emergency, contingency, crisis, circumstance, predicament, quandary, plight, strait, extremity, difficulty, hardship; *Slang* pickle, pinch, scrape, fix, jam. **2.** requirements, necessities, demands, needs, constraints, urgencies.

exile *v.* **1.** banish, deport, expel, eject, oust, expatriate, drive out, strip of citizenship. *—n.* **2.** banishment, expulsion, expatriation. **3.** exiled person, banished person, refugee, expellee, displaced person, D.P., émigré; outcast, pariah, expatriate. **—Ant. 1** grant refuge, grant citizenship; welcome, accept, embrace.

exist *v.* **1.** be in existence, survive, endure, last, remain, stay, abide. **2.** live, survive, maintain life, breathe. **3.** occur, have existence, prevail, happen, ensue, obtain. **—Ant. 1** pass away, disappear, vanish. **2** die, perish.

existence *n.* **1.** actuality, reality, presence, animation; tangibility, materiality. **2.** life, being, survival; subsistence, continuance, endurance. **—Ant. 1** nonexistence, nothingness. **2** death, passing away.

exit *n.* **1.** way out, egress, doorway out, passage out. **2.** departure, withdrawal, retreat, exodus, escape. *—v.* **3.** leave, depart, go out, withdraw, escape; *Slang* take a powder, blow, cut out, split. **—Ant. 1, 2** entrance. **3** enter, come in.

exodus *n.* departure, going forth, exit, flight, hegira, migration; emigration, exile.

exonerate *v.* clear, free, absolve, vindicate, exculpate; find innocent, acquit. **—Syn. Study.** See ABSOLVE. **—Ant.** prove guilty, condemn, blame; find guilty.

exorbitant *adj.* excessive, enormous, unreasonable, preposterous, outrageous, extreme, undue, out-of-line, inordinate, extortionate; overpriced, high-priced, expensive, extravagant, costly, dear. **—Ant.** fair, equitable; cheap, reasonable, inexpensive, dirt cheap.

exotic *adj.* **1.** foreign, not native, not indigenous, from abroad, alien. **2.** unusual, different, unique, intriguing, striking, exceptional, quaint, colorful, peculiar, strange, unfamiliar, outlandish. **—Ant. 1** native. **2** commonplace, run-of-the-mill, ordinary.

expand *v.* **1.** grow, increase, enlarge, magnify, multiply, amplify, develop, evolve, heighten, aggrandize, augment; widen, dilate, swell, distend, fatten, inflate. **2.** stretch, spread, spread out, outspread, extend, open, unfold, unfurl, unroll, unravel. **—Ant. 1** decrease, fall off, shrink, contract, curtail, condense. **2** close, fold, furl, roll up.

expanse *n.* extent, area, space, range, sweep, field, stretch, reach, breadth, magnitude, compass. **—Ant.** limit, confine, enclosure.

expansion *n.* enlargement, enlarging, increase, augmentation, growth, development, magnifying, amplification, multiplying, amplifying; extension, spreading, lengthening, widening, stretching; swelling, distention, dilation. **—Ant.** decrease, shrinkage, contraction, reduction, shortening, curtailment, cutback.

expansive *adj.* **1.** open, free, effusive, exuberant, extroverted, outgoing, unrestrained, liberal, genial, amiable, affable, uninhibited, unrepressed; generous, bountiful, bounteous. **2.** extensive, broad, vast, comprehensive, wide-ranging, wide, far-reaching, general, voluminous, capacious. **—Ant. 1** reserved, restrained, repressed, stiff, inhibited, introverted, shy, antisocial; taciturn, silent, reticent. **2** narrow, limited, restricted, circumscribed.

expatriate *n.* exile, émigré, refugee, displaced person, D.P., political refugee, banished person, deported person, outcast, pariah.

expect *v.* **1.** look forward to, plan on, look for, envision, anticipate, foresee, contemplate, reckon on, bargain for. **2.** demand, look for, require, trust, rely upon, reckon upon, count on, hope for. **3.** assume, presume, guess, suppose, believe, surmise, imagine, calculate, contemplate, conjecture, *Informal* reckon. **—Ant. 1** despair of, lose faith in; dread, fear.

expectation *n.* expectancy, anticipation, likelihood, prospect, chance, presumption, assurance, confidence, hope, trust, reliance, belief, contemplation. **—Ant.** memory, recollection; unlikelihood, despair, discouragement, hopelessness.

expedient *adj.* **1.** useful, helpful, worthwhile, advantageous, profitable, beneficial, practical, effective; desirable, advisable, wise, judicious. **2.** self-serving, self-seeking, conniving, calculating, selfish, self-interested; opportune, politic. *—n.* **3.** practical aid, help, advantage, benefit, profitable practice, strategem, tactic, resort, means, measure; makeshift device, instrument, stopgap. **—Ant. 1** inexpedient, impractical, ineffective, detrimental, disadvantageous, harmful, undesirable, inadvisable, unadvisable, futile, vain, fruitless. **2** unselfish, altruistic; just, ethical.

expedite *v.* hasten, speed up, accelerate, quicken, promote, further, facilitate, forward, advance, precipitate, dispatch, push through, rush, hurry. **—Ant.** slow, slow down, retard, impede, hinder, block, obstruct.

expedition *n.* **1.** trip, scientific trip, exploration; journey, voyage, trek; pilgrimage, mission, enterprise, campaign. **2.** travelers, voyagers, wayfarers, adventurers, explorers. **—Syn. Study. 1** See TRIP.

expeditious *adj.* prompt, speedy, hasty, ready, quick, fast, swift, rapid, immediate, instant, punctual; alert, awake, ready, snappy, bright-eyed, effective, efficacious. **—Ant.** slow, dilatory, sluggish, leisurely, deliberate, inefficient, ineffective, ineffectual.

expel *v.* **1.** force out, drive out, cast out, eject, discharge, excrete, evacuate, eliminate, void, dislodge, spew. **2.** eject, oust, remove, throw out; discharge, fire, dismiss, cashier, drum out; *Slang* bounce, sack; banish, exile, evict. **—Ant. 1** take in, ingest, inhale. **2** admit, accept, invite, welcome; hire, engage.

expend *v.* **1.** use up, spend, consume, go through; dissipate, drain, exhaust, empty, wear out, squander. **2.** spend, pay out, pay, disburse, dispense, give, donate, contribute; *Informal* fork out, shell out, lay out. **—Ant. 1, 2** conserve, save, preserve, hoard. **2** earn, receive, collect.

expendable *adj.* **1.** spendable, available, disbursable, payable. **2.** able to be sacrificed, relinquishable, consumable, forgoable, replaceable; dispensable, superfluous, extraneous, nonessential.

expenditure *n.* **1.** expenses, money spent, spending, disbursement, outlay, paying out; payment, cost, price, charge. **2.** spending, expending, exertion, application, output, use, employment, consumption. **—Ant. 1** receivables, receipts, income, profit. **2** conservation, saving, preservation, hoarding.

expense *n.* cost, price, charge, outlay; amount, quotation, rate, figure; source of expenditure, item paid for; drain, depletion; financial burden. **—Ant.** income, proceeds, return, profit, receipts, gain.

expensive *adj.* costly, high-priced, dear; overpriced, exorbitant, extravagant, excessive, unreasonable, immoderate, uneconomical, beyond one's means. **—Ant.** cheap, inexpensive, economical, reasonable, bargain-basement.

experience *n.* **1.** personal knowledge, personal involvement, firsthand knowledge, observation, doing, practice, training, seasoning, familiarity, exposure. **2.** event, episode, incident, adventure, happening, encounter, occurrence, affair. *—v.* **3.** know, undergo, live through, go through, encounter, meet, endure, suffer, sustain, bear; feel, sense, perceive, see, behold, view, observe; withstand. **—Ant.** inexperience; theory. **3** escape, miss.

experienced *adj.* accomplished, practical, trained, seasoned, qualified, well-versed, knowing, veteran, skilled, expert, able, capable, competent, efficient, master; sophisticated, wise, worldly-wise. **—Ant.** inexperienced, impractical, untrained, unqualified, untried, green, apprentice, unskilled; inept, incompetent.

experiment *n.* **1.** test, trial, tentative procedure, tryout, venture; *Informal* flier, feeler; research, investigation, examination, analysis, verification, assay, experimentation. *—v.* **2.** test, tryout, explore, *Slang* mess around with; research, investigate, analyze, examine, assay, seek proof for.

experimental *adj.* tentative, speculative, conjectural, conceptual, developmental, trial, test, trial-and-error, rough, first-draft, new, radical, fresh. **—Ant.** traditional, proven, tried-and-true; hackneyed, commonplace, routine.

expert *n.* **1.** authority, specialist, master, professional, virtuoso, connoisseur, mavin, ace, veteran, wizard, alpha male *Informal* whiz, *Slang* shark, geek, nerd. —*adj.* **2.** skilled, skillful, masterful, masterly, professional, experienced, master, accomplished, trained, practiced, knowledgeable, qualified, proficient, able, apt, adept, deft, adroit, competent, capable, first-class; *Informal* ace, crackerjack, A-1. **—Syn. Study. 2** See SKILLFUL. **—Ant. 1** amateur, tyro, novice; dabbler, dilettante. **2** unskilled, amateurish, inexperienced, untrained, unqualified, inept, incompetent.

expertise *n.* special skill, skill, know-how, expertness, specialization, professionalism, *Informal* savvy.

expiate *v.* atone for, do penance, rectify, make up for, make amends, redeem, compensate, redress, make reparation, make good, pay the penalty, pay the piper, wash away one's sins, shrive, square things, set one's house in order.

expire *v.* **1.** come to an end, run out, lapse, cease, discontinue, end, terminate, conclude, finish. **2.** die, pass away, perish, decease, succumb, *Informal* give up the ghost, *Slang* kick off, kick the bucket. **—Ant. 1** continue, renew, begin, start, commence. **2** live; be born.

explain *v.* **1.** describe, demonstrate, make clear, make plain, spell out, explicate, illustrate, illuminate. **2.** clarify, clear up, resolve, elucidate, expound, interpret, account for, give a reason for, fathom, justify, rationalize, give an explanation for. **—Syn. Study. 2** EXPLAIN, ELUCIDATE, EXPOUND, INTERPRET imply making the meaning of something clear or understandable. To EXPLAIN is to make plain, clear, or intelligible something that is not known or understood: *to explain a theory.* To ELUCIDATE is to throw light on what before was dark and obscure, usu. by illustration and commentary and sometimes by elaborate explanation: *They asked her to elucidate her statement.* To EXPOUND is to give a methodical, detailed, scholarly explanation of something, usu. scriptures, doctrines, or philosophy: *to expound the doctrine of free will.* To INTERPRET is to give the meaning of something by paraphrase, by translation, or by an explanation based on personal opinion: *to interpret a poem.* **—Ant. 2** confuse, obscure, misinterpret, muddle, ball up.

explanation *n.* **1.** explication, account, description, elucidation, clarification. **2.** reason, warrant, accounting, answer, cause, motive, motivation; justification, rationale, alibi, excuse.

explicit *adj.* specific, definite, precise, exact, express, certain, distinct, absolute, categorical, unequivocal, unqualified, clear, clearly expressed, straightforward; candid, frank, plain, direct, outspoken, blunt, pointed, unreserved. **—Ant.** vague, general, indefinite, inexact, ambiguous, equivocal, uncertain, enigmatic, cryptic, obscure; implicit, implied, indirect, oblique; suggested, hinted.

explode *v.* **1.** blow up, burst loudly, burst violently, go off; erupt, blast, discharge violently; set off, detonate. **2.** burst out emotionally, erupt, utter noisily, express noisily. **3.** disprove, prove wrong, prove false, belie, refute, expose, discredit, repudiate, invalidate, burst, destroy. **—Ant. 1** implode; fizzle.

exploit *n.* **1.** achievement, feat, accomplishment, heroic act, brave deed, adventure, daring deed. —*v.* **2.** use to advantage, turn to practical account, utilize, make use of, put to use, capitalize on, profit by. **3.** take advantage of, make selfish use of, abuse, misuse, take unfair advantage of. **—Ant. 1** failure, defeat. **2** pass up, ignore. **3** pamper, coddle, spoil.

explore *v.* **1.** scout, range over, travel over, travel to observe, survey, reconnoiter, travel and map, traverse, penetrate. **2.** look into, examine, research, scrutinize, investigate, search into, delve into, plumb, analyze, probe, pry into, inquire into, feel out, try, try out, experiment with.

explosion *n.* **1.** blowing up, detonation, blast; violent bursting, eruption, discharge, fulmination; report, crack, clap. **2.** burst, outburst, outbreak, eruption, paroxysm, fit, tantrum.

explosive *n.* **1.** blasting material; ammunition; pyrotechnics. —*adj.* **2.** liable to explode, capable of exploding, unstable, volatile. **3.** dangerous, tense, volatile, perilous, critical, precarious, strained, touchy, ticklish, shaky; emotional, keyed up.

exponent *n.* advocate, supporter, champion, proponent, backer, promoter, expounder, spokesman, defender, propagandist. **—Ant.** opponent, foe, enemy, detractor, critic.

export *v.* **1.** sell abroad, ship overseas, send out, dispatch. —*n.* **2.** foreign sale, selling abroad, marketing abroad, shipping overseas. **3.** exported commodity, trade commodity, shipped wares, material sent abroad, article of foreign trade.

expose *v.* **1.** subject, force to endure, leave unprotected, submit; endanger, imperil, jeopardize, hazard, risk. **2.** bare, uncover, show, display, exhibit, lay open to view; strip, denude, divest, exhibit nakedness. **3.** disclose, reveal, divulge, let out, let slip, uncover, bring to light, unearth. **4.** familiarize with, put in contact with, acquaint with, make conversant with, offer. **5.** disclose to be, reveal to be, show in one's real light; denounce, brand, betray. **—Ant. 1, 2** hide, conceal, mask, cover, shield. **1** protect, guard. **3** conceal, keep secret.

exposé *n.* exposure, scandalous disclosure, sensational report, divulgence, revelation, baring. **—Ant.** cover-up, whitewash.

exposition *n.* **1.** exhibition, display, exhibit, bazaar, mart, market, trade show, show; fair, trade fair, world's fair, *Informal* expo. **2.** explanation, explication, elucidation, clarification, account, interpretation, exegesis, commentary; presentation, demonstration, description, illustration, picture.

expostulate *v.* protest, object, remonstrate, inveigh against, cry out against, raise one's voice against, enjoin, plead with, exhort, forewarn, counsel, caution, reason against.

exposure *n.* **1.** disclosure, divulging, divulgence, revelation, laying open, bringing to light, bringing out in the open, exposé, public notice, unmasking, uncovering. **2.** subjection, submission, laying bare, laying open, making vulnerable. **3.** outlook, vista, frontage, prospect, perspective, view. **—Ant. 1** hiding, concealment, cover-up. **2** cover, covering, shelter, refuge, protection, shield.

expound *v.* state in detail, give a full account of, hold forth, explain, describe, elucidate, make clear, explicate, interpret; defend, uphold. **—Syn. Study.** See EXPLAIN.

express *v.* **1.** put into words, articulate, phrase, word, couch, relate, communicate, state, say, speak, utter, declare, describe, verbalize, voice, vocalize. **2.** reveal, divulge, disclose, show, exhibit, evidence, evince, convey, communicate, make known. *—adj.* **3.** explicit, definite, specific, unequivocal, categorical, exact, clear, lucid, precise, direct, plain, certain, particular; vivid, forceful. **4.** nonstop, stopping infrequently; fast, high-speed, quick, swift, rapid. **—Ant. 1** remain silent, be quiet, be still. **2** hide, conceal, cover, veil, mask, cloak; suppress, repress. **3** implicit, implied, indirect, oblique, hinted, suggested, vague, general, indefinite, obscure, enigmatic, ambiguous, equivocal.

expression *n.* **1.** wording, phraseology, style, language; stating, saying, speaking, voicing, airing, venting, telling, uttering, declaration, assertion, setting forth, relating, communication. **2.** term, word, phrase, turn of phrase, phrasing, phraseology, idiom, locution. **3.** look, appearance, aspect, mien, countenance. **4.** eloquence, emotion, meaning; modulation, enunciation, articulation, tone. **—Ant. 1** suppression, restraint, repression.

expressive *adj.* eloquent, moving, meaningful, effective, telling, significant, poignant, thoughtful, indicative, forceful, vivid, powerful, compelling, striking.

expressly *adv.* **1.** explicitly, definitely, pointedly, unequivocally, categorically, decidedly, clearly, distinctly, plainly, in no uncertain terms. **2.** specifically, particularly, specially, precisely. **—Ant. 1** implicitly, indirectly, obliquely; vaguely, indefinitely, equivocally.

expropriate *v.* confiscate, appropriate, take, take over; seize, commandeer.

expulsion *n.* expelling, ejection, ousting, removal; exile, banishment, eviction, exclusion, debarment, prohibition, proscription; discharge, elimination. **—Ant.** acceptance, entering, entrance, welcoming, inclusion; injection.

expurgate *v.* cut, cut out, remove, delete, excise, censor, remove as offensive, bowdlerize, purge, blue-pencil, edit, *Television* blip, bleep out.

exquisite *adj.* **1.** delicate, fine, elegant; particularly beautiful, beautifully dainty, lovely, precious. **2.** superb, superlative, consummate, matchless, peerless, flawless, incomparable, excellent, fine, choice, admirable, splendid. **3.** discriminating, admirable, impeccable, faultless, perfect, fastidious, meticulous. **—Syn. Study. 1** See DELICATE. **—Ant. 1** clumsy, bulky, ugly, hideous, *Slang* klutzy. **2** sloppy, clumsy; mediocre, ordinary; inferior, bad. **3** common, unrefined, indiscriminate, careless, slovenly.

extant *adj.* in existence, existing, existent, surviving, to be found; present, living.

extemporaneous *adj.* impromptu, spontaneous, improvised, extemporary, ad-lib, without notice, extempore, unprepared, unpremeditated, unrehearsed, off the top of one's head, spur-of-the-moment, offhand, without notes, *Informal* off the cuff. **—Syn. Study.** EXTEMPORANEOUS, IMPROMPTU are used of expression that is not planned. EXTEMPORANEOUS may refer to a speech given without any advance preparation: *extemporaneous remarks.* IMPROMPTU is also used of a speech, but often refers to a poem, song, etc., delivered without preparation and at a moment's notice: *She entertained the guests with some impromptu rhymes.* **—Ant.** well-rehearsed, prepared, planned; premeditated.

extend *v.* **1.** stretch out, draw out, lengthen, make longer, elongate; continue, protract, prolong. **2.** advance, submit, put out, stretch forth, reach out;

offer, give, hold out, proffer, bestow, impart, grant. **3.** broaden, widen, expand, enlarge, increase, spread, stretch, amplify, augment. **—Syn. Study. 1** See LENGTHEN. **—Ant. 1** shorten, curtail, abbreviate, abridge, contract, shrink, condense. **2** withdraw, take back. **3** narrow, decrease, restrict, limit, reduce.

extended *adj.* **1.** spread out, stretched out, unfolded, unfurled. **2.** prolonged, long, continued, protracted, lengthened, drawn out. **3.** wide-spread, extensive, comprehensive, thorough; widened, broadened, expanded, enlarged. **—Ant. 1** folded, furled, contracted. **2** short, shortened, curtailed, abbreviated, abridged. **3** narrow, limited, restricted.

extension *n.* **1.** lengthening, continuation, increase, prolongation; delay, postponement. **2.** wing, branch, appendage, arm, annex, adjunct, addition, appendix, enlargement, expansion, continuation. **—Ant. 1** shortening, curtailment, decrease.

extensive *adj.* **1.** wide, broad, large, vast, huge, extended, voluminous, enormous, great; lengthy, long, protracted. **2.** wide, broad, comprehensive, considerable, all-inclusive, far-flung, thorough, universal, capacious. **—Ant. 1, 2** narrow. **1** small, little, tiny; short. **2** restricted, specialized.

extent *n.* expanse, stretch, area; scope, range, compass, breadth, magnitude, size, sweep, dimensions, amplitude, reach, amount, degree; duration, time, length. **—Ant.** limitation, limits.

extenuating *adj.* justifiable, serving as an excuse, explanatory; mitigating, attenuating, qualifying, tempering, moderating, lessening, diminishing. **—Ant.** unjustifiable, inexcusable; aggravating, intensifying.

exterior *adj.* **1.** outside, outer, outermost, external, superficial, outward. **2.** external, foreign, alien, exotic, extrinsic, extraneous. *—n.* **3.** outside, outer side, surface; façade, face, coating, covering, finish, shell, skin. **4.** outward appearance, manner, demeanor, bearing. **—Ant. 1** inside, internal, inner. **2** internal, domestic, native; intrinsic, inherent, ingrained. **3** interior, inside, core.

exterminate *v.* destroy, wipe out, kill, slaughter, massacre, annihilate, eliminate, *Slang* waste, zap; eradicate, abolish, root out, erase, expunge; extinguish, demolish. **—Ant.** increase, develop, foster, build up; create, generate, originate, beget; replenish, restore.

external *adj.* **1.** outside, outer, outermost, exterior, surface, superficial, outward. **2.** from the outside, extraneous, extrinsic; foreign, alien. **—Ant. 1** internal, inner, innermost, interior, inward, inside. **2** internal; intrinsic, inherent.

extinct *adj.* **1.** defunct, dead, vanished, lost, gone, no longer in existence, died out, no longer surviving. **2.** no longer burning, quenched, extinguished, put out, gone out. **—Ant. 1** extant, surviving, living; flourishing, thriving. **2** burning; active.

extinguish *v.* **1.** put out, douse, quench, smother, suffocate; blow out, snuff out. **2.** wipe out, destroy, end, abolish, eliminate, kill, demolish, dispel, eradicate, cancel, crush, quash, stifle, dash, *Slang* zap, do in. **—Ant. 1** ignite, light, fire. **2** increase, foster, promote, forward, build up; secure, establish, confirm, maintain, support.

extol *v.* praise, laud, commend, compliment, acclaim, celebrate, glorify, applaud, eulogize, sing the praises of. **—Ant.** decry, denounce, damn, curse, condemn, censure, criticize, belittle, denigrate.

extortion *n.* blackmail, shakedown; threats, force, coercion; forced payments, hush money, graft, *Informal* payola; ransom, tribute.

extra *adj.* **1.** additional, supplemental, further, more, spare, auxiliary, accessory; superfluous, surplus, redundant, unnecessary. *—n.* **2.** accessory, additional feature, special accompaniment, adjunct, appurtenance, attachment, complement. *—adv.* **3.** unusually, uncommonly, exceptionally, especially, particularly, additionally, remarkably, extraordinarily. **—Ant. 1** fewer. **2** basic necessity. **3** less.

extract *v.* **1.** pull out, take out, draw out, pry out, remove, extricate, pluck out, root out, extirpate. **2.** get, glean, obtain, derive, exact, wrest, evoke, bring out, elicit, deduce, educe. **3.** process chemically, separate, take out, draw out, squeeze out, press out, distill. **4.** excerpt, choose, select, cull, abstract, copy out; cite, quote. *—n.* **5.** concentrate, essence, distillate, juice. **6.** excerpt, selection, passage, abstract; quotation, citation. **—Ant. 1, 2** insert, embed, implant, inject, infuse.

extraneous *adj.* **1.** irrelevant, unrelated, not germane, not pertinent, inappropriate, nonessential, immaterial, incidental, superfluous, inadmissible. **2.** foreign, alien, exotic, extrinsic, strange, adventitious. **—Ant. 1** relevant, pertinent, germane, appropriate, material, connected, related, essential. **2** native, intrinsic, inherent.

extraordinary *adj.* unusual, uncommon, remarkable, phenomenal, unique, rare, out of the ordinary, exceptional, notable; amazing, fantastic, incredible, unbelievable, inconceivable, unheard of; strange, odd, queer, monstrous. **—Ant.** usual, common, average, ordinary, unremarkable, run-of-the-mill, everyday, familiar, customary.

extravagance *n.* **1.** excessive spending, overspending, squandering, inordinate outlay; waste, wastefulness, improvidence, prodigality. **2.** excess, excessiveness, unrestraint, immoderation; unreasonableness, absurdity, folly, caprice, capriciousness, recklessness, profligacy. **—Ant. 1** economy, frugality, saving, stinginess, tightfistedness, miserliness. **2** moderation, restraint, reasonableness.

extravagant *adj.* **1.** expensive, high-priced, costly, overpriced, exorbitant. **2.** profligate, spending readily, prodigal, overspending, lavishly spending, openhanded, spendthrift; wasteful, squandering, imprudent, improvident. **3.** excessive, immoderate, unrestrained, inordinate, unreasonable, outlandish, preposterous, outrageous, absurd, fantastic, fabulous, unreal, high-flown, foolish, wild. **—Ant. 1** cheap, reasonable, economical, lowpriced. **2** thrifty, economical; frugal, stingy, tightfisted, miserly, close; conservative, saving, prudent. **3** moderate, restrained, reasonable, sensible, serious, realistic, sober, down-to-earth; careful, cautious.

extravaganza *n.* spectacle, pageant, spectacular, phantasmagoria; stage show, vaudeville, wild west show, opera, ballet, carnival, Broadway show, opéra bouffe, operetta, opéra comique, sound and light show, *French* son et lumière, fair, exposition.

extreme *adj.* **1.** severe, intense, very great, excessive, immoderate, extraordinary, unusual, uncommon; inordinate, exaggerated. **2.** radical, advanced, avant-garde; outrageous, extravagant. **3.** most distant, farthest, outermost, farthest removed. **—*n.* 4.** ultimate limit, extremity, boundary, height, depth, end; excess, excessive degree, *Informal* nth degree. **—Ant. 1** moderate, mild, reasonable, common, average, ordinary. **2** traditional, conservative. **3** near, nearest.

extremely *adv.* very, quite, unusually, exceptionally, especially, extraordinarily, uncommonly, exceedingly, excessively, immoderately, intensely, singularly, surprisingly, remarkably, terribly, awfully; unnaturally, abnormally, freakishly, peculiarly, curiously.

extremity *n.* **1.** end, farthest end, terminus, extreme, edge, outer edge, tip, brink, margin; most distant point, reach, limit, boundary, bound, border, periphery, confine. **2.** hand, foot; limb, arm, leg; finger, toe. **—Ant. 1** beginning, start, commencement; nearest point.

extricate *v.* free, release, get out, loose, rescue, liberate, deliver; untangle, disentangle, disengage, disencumber, wriggle out of. **—Ant.** catch, trap, snare, ensnare, tangle, entangle, trip up, tie, tie up.

extrovert *n.* outgoing person, gregarious person, sociable person, hail-fellow-well-met; exhibitionist, show-off, *Informal* life of the party. **—Ant.** introvert; loner.

exuberance *n.* enthusiasm, energy, vitality, liveliness, spirit, zeal, vigor, buoyancy, sprightliness, vivacity, animation, élan, life, eagerness, excitement, *Informal* zip; effervescence. **—Ant.** despair, dejection; lethargy.

exuberant *adj.* **1.** enthusiastic, lively, spirited, sprightly, animated, eager, excited, energetic, zealous, vigorous. **2.** growing thickly, lavish, profuse, copious, abundant, plentiful, superabundant, luxuriant, rich, lush, plenteous, bounteous. **—Ant. 1** despairing, dejected, unenthusiastic, dispirited, dull, lethargic. **2** thin, sparse, scant, scanty, meager, sporadic.

exult *v.* rejoice, be jubilant, be elated, be delighted, be exhilarated, be in high spirits, glory; *Informal* jump for joy; crow, gloat. **—Ant.** be downcast, be gloomy, be blue, feel sad.

eye *n.* **1.** (*variously*) eyeball, iris, pupil; *Informal* orb, peeper. **2.** eyesight, vision, sight; perception, discrimination, taste. **—*v.* 3.** glance at, look at, gaze at, view, scan, take in, observe, regard, study, inspect, scrutinize, survey, stare at, watch, behold.

eyewitness *n.* spectator, looker-on, bystander, passerby, onlooker, viewer, observer, beholder, witness, informer, gazer, testifier, attester or attestor, gawker, gaper, rubberneck.

fable *n.* **1.** parable, tale, fairy tale, legend, romance, allegory, myth. **2.** tall story, untruth, fiction, fabrication, falsehood, invention, fib, hoax, lie; *Slang* whopper, yarn, leg-pull. **—Syn. Study. 1** FABLE, LEGEND, MYTH refer to stories handed down from earlier times, often by word of mouth. A FABLE is a fictitious story intended to teach a moral lesson; the characters are usu. animals: *the fable about the fox and the grapes.* A LEGEND is a story associated with a people or a nation; it is usu. concerned with a real person, place, or event and is popularly believed to have some basis in fact: *the legend of King Arthur.* A MYTH is one of a class of purportedly historical stories that attempt to explain some belief, practice, or natural phenomenon; the characters are usu. gods or heroes: *the Greek myth about Demeter.*

fabled *adj.* fanciful, imaginary, unreal, fictitious; legendary, mythical, mythological, fabulous, storied. **—Ant.** real, authentic, historical, factual, honest-to-goodness.

fabric *n.* **1.** cloth, textile, material, dry goods, yard goods, stuff. **2.** framework, structure, frame, makeup, superstructure, organization, substance; texture; foundation, substructure, infrastructure.

fabricate *v.* **1.** build, form, construct, assemble, frame, manufacture, produce, erect, fashion, shape, compose. **2.** invent, concoct, make up, hatch, devise, design, contrive, formulate, *Slang* fake; embroider, counterfeit, falsify, simulate, forge, feign, *Informal* trump up. **—Ant. 1** destroy, raze, demolish, dismember.

fabrication *n.* **1.** building, construction, constructing, manufacture, assemblage, production, erection, composition, makeup, fashioning, creation. **2.** falsehood, invention, lie, untruth, fiction, fib, concoction, fable, prevarication, myth, forgery, cock-and-bull story, yarn, fairy tale. **—Ant. 1** destruction, razing, breakdown. **2** truth, fact, actuality.

fabulous *adj.* **1.** amazing, marvelous, extraordinary, astonishing, astounding, incredible, unbelievable. **2.** marvelous, wonderful, fantastic, superb, great, spectacular, stupendous, *Informal* smashing. **3.** fabled, legendary, mythical, mythological, storied, fanciful, imaginary, apocryphal, fictitious, invented, fantastic. **—Ant. 1** credible, ordinary, routine. **2** ordinary, common, fair, commonplace. **3** genuine, authentic, real, natural, historical, actual, true.

façade *n.* **1.** building front, frontage, front view, face. **2.** false appearance, pretense, superficial manner, false front, mask, veneer.

face *n.* **1.** countenance, visage, features, facial features, physiognomy; *Slang* mug, pan, puss, kisser. **2.** expression, aspect, look, countenance, air; grimace, facial contortion, pout, look of annoyance. **3.** appearance, look, semblance, external aspect. **4.** reputation, good name, dignity, repute, image, prestige, self-respect. **5.** front surface, obverse side, principal side, finished side, façade, frontage, forepart. **6.** nerve, boldness, daring, pluck, self-assurance, mettle, spunk, confidence, bravado, grit, hardihood; cheek, front, sand, brass, gall, effrontery, impudence. **—*v.* 7.** encounter, confront, meet face to face, turn toward, look toward. **8.** front on, give toward, overlook. **9.** surface, cover, coat, overlay. **—Syn. Study. 1** FACE, COUNTENANCE, VISAGE refer to the front of the (usu. human) head. FACE is used when referring to physical features: *a pretty face with high cheekbones.* COUNTENANCE, a more formal word, denotes the face as it is affected by or reveals a person's state of mind; hence, it often signifies the look or expression on the face: *a thoughtful countenance.* VISAGE, still more formal, refers to the face as seen in a certain aspect, esp. as revealing a person's character: *a stern visage.* **—Ant. 5** back, underside, reverse, side. **6** shyness, timidity.

facet *n.* **1.** surface, polished surface, plane, cut. **2.** aspect, side, phase, part, angle.

facetious *adj.* humorous, funny, amusing, jocular, joking, jovial, jesting, witty, clever, jocose, droll, comic, comical, playful, wisecracking. **—Ant.** solemn, serious, sober, lugubrious, grave, sedate, staid, sad, dull.

facile *adj.* **1.** skillful, adroit, handy, quick, artful, clever, apt, adept, proficient; fluent, effortless, smooth. **2.** glib, slick, careless, casual, superficial, shallow, cursory. **—Ant. 1** clumsy, awkward, plodding, halting, maladroit, unskillful, slow. **2** determined, serious, careful, thoughtful, penetrating.

facilitate *v.* expedite, speed up, accelerate, ease, simplify, help in, make less difficult, make easier, assist the progress of, lessen the labor of, lighten, smooth; forward, help to advance, promote, further, advance, aid, foster. **—Ant.** hinder, hamper, complicate, encumber, slow down.

facility *n.* **1.** ease, fluency, expertness, skill, proficiency, efficiency, readiness, effortlessness, adroitness, aptness, dexterity, knack, deftness, smoothness, bent, capability, competence. **2.** ease, practicability, effortlessness, easiness, smoothness. **3.** appliance, convenience, aid, advantage, resource, means. **—Ant. 1** ineptness, clumsiness, awkwardness, maladroitness; rigidity, woodenness, effort, exertion, pains. **2** difficulty, hardship, labor.

facsimile *n.* copy, reproduction, replica, imitation, duplicate, reprint, likeness, clone, transcript; photostat.

fact *n.* happening, deed, occurrence, event, act, circumstance, incident, thing done, particular, specific; reality, actuality, truth, certainty, verity. **—Ant.** fiction, supposition, fancy, opinion, unreality, falsehood, lie, delusion, invention.

faction *n.* **1.** group, side, subdivision, section, unit, clique, combine, ring, set, circle, coterie, gang, cabal, bloc, sect, minority, splinter group. **2.** discord, dissension, conflict, disagreement, dissidence, division, contention, strife, rebellion, insurgency, schism, split, incompatibility, breach, quarreling, sedition, rupture, clash, disruption. **—Ant. 2** agreement, accord, harmony, concord.

factious *adj.* contentious, divisive, quarrelsome, bickering, disputatious, disagreeing, dissentious, insubordinate, rebellious, mutinous, combative, belligerent, insurrectionary, contending, warring, fighting, at sixes and sevens, at loggerheads; alienated, estranged, disaffected. **—Ant.** consenting, agreeing, harmonious, assenting, acquiescing.

factor *n.* consideration, reason, circumstance, element, part, component, constituent, influence, cause.

factotum *n.* handyman, jack-of-all-trades, right-hand man, man Friday, girl Friday; *Informal* guy Friday, gal Friday.

factual *adj.* full of facts, matter-of-fact, plain, circumstantial, literal; genuine, actual, authentic, real, correct, exact, faithful, true, scrupulous, accurate; unadorned, unembroidered. **—Ant.** fanciful, imaginary, embellished, figurative.

faculty *n.* **1.** teaching staff, teaching body, professors, teachers. **2.** knack, capacity, capability, ability, special ability, skill, gift, talent, genius, quality, bent, penchant, power, skillfulness, aptitude, adeptness, flair. **3.** power, capability of the mind, inherent physical capability, function, endowment. **4. faculties.** wits, reason, normal intelligence, mental powers. **—Syn. Study. 2** See ABILITY. **—Ant. 2** inability, incapacity, unskillfulness, weakness, failing.

fad *n.* craze, rage, fashion, mania, latest word, latest thing, vogue, mode, *French* dernier cri; whim, whimsy, fancy.

fade *v.* **1.** pale, dim, dull, bleach, lose luster, lose color, lose brightness, make pale, become colorless, make colorless, grow dim, become dull, lose clarity, whiten. **2.** decline, dwindle, flag, fail, diminish, wither, fall off, lessen, taper, ebb, shrivel, languish, crumble, droop, wane, blur, slowly disappear, vanish; dissolve, evanesce, evaporate, recede, melt away, dissipate; die gradually, pass away. **—Syn. Study. 2** See DISAPPEAR. **—Ant. 1, 2** brighten. **2** flourish; rise, increase, bloom, grow; endure, abide, last, stand.

fail *v.* **1.** not succeed, stop short of, be unsuccessful, miss the mark, fall short of; come to nothing, come to naught, abort, fall through, turn out badly, miscarry, founder, be defeated, run aground, meet one's Waterloo, collapse, misfire, meet with disaster, be in vain, prove of no use; *Informal* come to grief, fizzle out, go up in smoke, end in smoke, be stillborn, slip up; *Slang* lay an egg, bomb, flop. **2.** flunk, get less than a passing grade; give less than a passing grade. **3.** disappoint, let down, forsake, desert. **4.** decline, dwindle, fade away, waste away, die, wane, become weaker, languish, deteriorate, flag, droop, perish gradually, disappear, give out, ebb, lose vigor, collapse; stop working, stop operating. **5.** go bankrupt, go under, become insolvent, go out of business, crash, *Informal* fold. **—Ant. 1** succeed. **2** pass. **4** grow, bloom, strengthen, flourish, prosper, gain.

failing *n.* **—Syn. Study.** See FAULT.

failure *n.* **1.** failing, proving unsuccessful; lack of success, vain attempt, ill success, labor in vain; nonfulfillment, washout, botch. **2.** neglecting, dereliction, negligence, nonperformance, remissness, delinquency, default, nonobservance. **3.** bankruptcy, crash, financial disaster, insolvency, ruin, ruination, folding, collapse, downfall. **4.** nonsuccess, disappointment, washout, botch, muddle, mess, miscarriage, misfire, mishap, fizzle; *Slang* flop, dud, bomb; ne'er-do-well, loser. **5.** decline, loss of strength, failing, deterioration, deteriorating, breakdown. **—Ant. 1** success; fulfillment. **2** observance, care. **3** success, prosperity. **4** success, effectiveness, adequacy. **5** strength, strengthening, improvement.

faint *adj.* **1.** soft, inaudible, remote, low, dulcet, indistinct, weak, muffled, whispered, muted; dim, pale, almost imperceptible, faded, subtle, delicate, obscure, inconspicuous. **2.** feeble, weak, slight, small, inconsiderable, meager, thin, frail, fragile, little. **3.** dizzy, lightheaded, vertiginous, about to swoon, giddy; feeble, weak, exhausted, lacking strength, drooping, torpid, lethargic, fatigued, languid, worn out. **4.** timorous, timid, fainthearted, lacking spirit, fearful, lacking courage, cowardly, lily-livered. —*v.* **5.** swoon, black out, pass out, lose consciousness, collapse. **—Ant. 1** bright, brilliant, clear, conspicuous, fresh, hearty, vigorous, loud, blaring, distinct, glaring. **2** strong, considerable, vigorous. **3** strong, steady, sturdy, hearty. **4** strong, brave, bold, courageous.

fainthearted *adj.* weak, feeble, irresolute, halfhearted, indifferent; lacking courage, cowardly, lily-livered, timid. **—Ant.** stronghearted, brave, courageous, bold.

fair *adj.* **1.** unprejudiced, impartial, equitable, evenhanded, treating all sides alike, just, unbiased, affording no undue advantage, dispassionate, objective, legitimate, disinterested; honest, reasonable, square, upright, honorable, aboveboard; according to the rules, proper, justified, *Slang* kosher, on the up and up. **2.** average, moderate, pretty good, middling, so-so, mediocre, passable, adequate, reasonable, satisfactory, decent, tolerable, respectable, medium, ordinary, indifferent, run-of-the-mill. **3.** cloudless, unclouded, rainless, sunny, sunshiny, pleasant, fine, bright. **4.** light-colored, not dark, pale, blond, creamy; fair-skinned, light-skinned. **5.** attractive, lovely, good-looking, pretty, comely, well-favored, beautiful, bonny. —*adv.* **6.** justly, truthfully, honestly, honorably, legally, ethically, squarely, forthrightly, candidly. **—Syn. Study. 1** FAIR, IMPARTIAL, DISINTERESTED refer to lack of bias in opinions, judgments, etc. FAIR implies the treating of all sides alike, justly and equitably: *a fair solution.* IMPARTIAL also implies showing no more favor to one side than another, but suggests particularly a judicial consideration of a case: *an impartial judge.* DISINTERESTED implies a fairness arising from lack of desire to obtain a selfish advantage: *a disinterested concern that the best person win.* **—Ant. 1** unfair, prejudiced, partial, inequitable, biased; dishonest, dishonorable, improper. **2** exceptional, poor, bad. **3** cloudy, stormy, dark, foul, threatening. **4** dark. **5** ugly, homely. **6** unfairly, dishonestly.

fairly *adv.* **1.** justly, honorably, honestly, squarely, equitably, in a fair manner, evenhandedly, in a just way, rightly, impartially, dispassionately, objectively, legitimately, properly. **2.** rather, tolerably, passably, moderately, reasonably, somewhat. **3.** actually, really, fully, completely, absolutely, positively; so to speak, in a manner of speaking. **—Ant. 1** unfairly, unjustly, inequitably, wrongly, partially, dishonestly, improperly. **2** extremely, very, immoderately, exceptionally.

faith *n.* **1.** belief, confidence, trust, security, certitude, reliance, assurance, certainty, credence, conviction. **2.** religion, creed, persuasion, denomination, sect, church. **3.** obligation, verbal pledge, word of honor, promise; fidelity, constancy, loyalty, fealty. **—Ant. 1** doubt, uncertainty, skepticism, dubiety; unbelief, disbelief; mistrust, suspicion; misgiving, apprehension, denial, dissent, distrust, incredulity, discredit, infidelity, rejection, agnosticism.

faithful *adj.* **1.** loyal, devoted, constant, steadfast, steady in the performance of duty, conscientious, staunch, true, true blue, reliable, unwavering, trustworthy, dependable, worthy of confidence, incorruptible, unswerving, resolute, trusty; scrupulous, honest, upright, truthful. **2.** exact, strict, truthful, factual, precise, accurate, verifiable; true-to-life, lifelike; close, similar. **—Syn. Study. 1** FAITHFUL, CONSTANT, LOYAL imply qualities of stability, dependability, and devotion. FAITHFUL implies enduring fidelity to what one is bound to by a pledge, duty, or obligation: *a faithful friend.* CONSTANT suggests lack of change in affections or loyalties: *a constant companion through thick and thin.* LOYAL implies firm support and defense of a person, cause, institution, or idea considered to be worthy: *a loyal citizen.* **—Ant. 1** faithless; disloyal, false, perfidious, traitorous, treacherous; fickle, inconstant, unstable, unfaithful, untrue, untrustworthy, wavering. **2** inexact, imprecise, inaccurate, dissimilar.

fake *v.* **1.** pretend, feign, simulate, fabricate, put on, dissemble, dissimulate, hoax, sham. **2.** counterfeit, fabricate, contrive, forge, trump up, falsify. —*n.* **3.** counterfeit, imitation, forgery, fraud, sham, dummy, make-believe; contrivance, trick, hoax, fabrication, put-on, imposture, delusion, deceit, deception, artifice, ruse, dodge. **4.** imposter, poseur, fraud, pretender, faker, quack, phony, charlatan, deceiver, humbug. —*adj.* **5.** not real, false, bogus, counterfeit, phony, pseudo, spurious, sham, fabricated, put-on, contrived, forged, simulated, specious, artificial, invented, concocted, make-believe, fictitious. **—Ant. 5** real, authentic, actual.

fall *v.* **1.** drop, drop down, tumble, plunge, topple, plop, crumple, come down suddenly, collapse, crash down. **2.** decline, come down, become less, decrease, diminish, become lower, cheapen, depreciate. **3.** extend down, hang down, slope, droop, cascade; descend, drop. **4.** surrender, be captured, be overthrown, be defeated, be taken, pass into enemy hands, collapse, topple, capitulate, succumb; be destroyed, come to destruction; be wounded, be slain, perish, die. **5.** transgress, give in to temptation, succumb, go astray, lapse, sin, depart from rectitude, err. **6.** occur, come to pass, happen, take place, come off, crop up, come around. —*n.* **7.** plunge, descent, drop, falling, dropping, spill, tumble, slip, plummet. **8.** drop, decline, lowering, sinking, diminution, decrease, reduction, slump, depreciation; ebb, subsidence, wane. **9. falls.** waterfall, cascade, cataract. **10.** autumn, Indian summer, harvest time. **11.** corruption, ruin, loss of innocence, deviation from virtue, slip, going astray, lapse into sin, surrender to temptation, subversion; disgrace, downfall, comedown, loss of eminence, debasement. **12.** surrender, capitulation, overthrow, capture, downfall, collapse, defeat. **—Ant. 1, 2** rise, climb, ascend, mount, soar, increase. **4** triumph, prevail, endure, hold out, survive. **7** rise, ascent. **8** rise, climb, increase, advance, appreciation.

fallacy *n.* **1.** misconception, error, false notion, misleading notion, mistake, false belief, misbelief, delusion, illusion, misapprehension. **2.** fault, faultiness, flaw, inconsistency, erroneous reasoning, mistake, pitfall, catch. **—Ant. 1** truism, surety, verity, sureness, fact, certainty. **2** logic, proof, soundness, verity, truth, surety, certainty, consistency.

fallen *adj.* **1.** overthrown, deposed; ousted, discharged, turned out. **2.** tumbled, sprawled, toppled, dropped, spilled. **3.** immoral, sinful, loose, disgraced, ruined, debased. **4.** dead, slain; massacred, slaughtered, butchered.

fallible *adj.* imperfect, frail, liable to error; human, mortal; faulty, unsure, unreliable. **—Ant.** infallible, perfect; divine, superhuman.

fallow *adj.* idle, inactive, inert, dormant, unproductive, untilled, unplanted, unused, unsowed, unfruitful, uncultivated; worn out, depleted, barren, arid, exhausted. **—Ant.** fecund, prolific, productive, fruitful, fertile.

false *adj.* **1.** faulty, incorrect, untrue, wrong, fallacious, apocryphal, not correct, erroneous, mistaken, inaccurate, invalid, unsound, inexact, unfounded; delusive, misleading, deceptive, deceiving, spurious, factitious. **2.** disloyal, faithless, unfaithful, false-hearted, two-faced, untruthful, double-dealing, devious, hypocritical, dishonest, treacherous, perfidious, traitorous, inconstant, deceitful, tricky. **3.** artificial, bogus, fake, make-believe, imitation, ersatz, spurious, feigned, pseudo, sham, phony, unreal, forged, counterfeit. **—Syn. Study. 3** FALSE, SHAM, COUNTERFEIT agree in referring to something that is not genuine. FALSE is used mainly of imitations of concrete objects; it sometimes implies an intent to deceive: *false teeth; false hair.* SHAM is rarely used of concrete objects and usu. has the suggestion of intent to deceive: *a sham title; sham tears.* COUNTERFEIT always has the implication of cheating; it is used particularly of spurious imitation of coins and paper money. **—Ant. 1** true, correct, right, accurate, valid, sound, exact. **2** loyal, true, faithful, constant, sincere, steadfast, honest. **3** real, genuine, authentic, bona fide.

falsehood *n.* **1.** lie, untruth, false statement, fabrication, falsification, canard, invention, fiction, story, figment; *Informal* fib, whopper; white lie. **2.** lying, untruthfulness, falseness, dishonesty, falsity, falsification, deceptiveness, deception, misrepresentation, inaccuracy, deceit, distortion, mendacity, perjury, misstatement, dissimulation, double-dealing, dissembling; perfidy, hypocrisy, duplicity, bad faith, two-facedness, insincerity. **—Ant. 1** truth, verity, fact. **2** veracity, genuineness, honesty, honor.

falsify *v.* **1.** alter fraudulently, misrepresent, fake, distort, doctor, represent falsely, tamper with, pervert, misuse. **2.** disprove, belie, rebut, show to be false, prove unsound, refute, confute. **—Ant. 2** verify, confirm, certify, justify.

falter *v.* **1.** hesitate, be undecided, waver, vacillate, fluctuate, demur, be irresolute, show weakness, shrink, lag; *Informal* dillydally, blow hot and cold. **2.** stammer, speak haltingly, pause nervously, stutter, mumble, halt. **3.** stumble, move unsteadily, teeter, stagger, totter, reel; shamble, shuffle, dodder. **—Ant. 1** persevere, persist, proceed.

fame *n.* eminence, prominence, repute, renown, reputation, celebrity, public esteem, glory, popularity, illustriousness, prestige, notoriety, notability, preeminence, distinction, note, laurels. **—Ant.** obscurity, oblivion; disgrace, dishonor, disrepute, discredit, infamy, ignominy.

familiar *adj.* **1.** often encountered, well-known, known, seen frequently, generally seen; frequent, habitual, commonplace, ordinary, everyday, common, proverbial, customary, accustomed, usual, general; conventional, accepted, stock, traditional. **2.** acquainted, cognizant of, conversant, informed about, versed in, abreast of, no stranger to, apprised of, experienced at, at home in; skilled in, proficient at, seasoned. **3.** friendly, amicable, close, intimate, confidential, unreserved, informal, cozy, snug, chummy, hand and glove, brotherly, fraternal, accessible, companionable, *Spanish* simpático, *German* gemütlich; forward, unduly intimate, free, bold, impertinent, taking liberties, disrespectful, intrusive. —*n.* **4.** friend, close acquaintance, crony, buddy, intimate, chum, pal, confidant, boon companion. **—Syn. Study. 3** FAMILIAR, CONFIDENTIAL, INTIMATE suggest a friendly relationship between persons, based on frequent association, common interests, etc. FAMILIAR suggests an easygoing and unconstrained relationship between persons who are well-acquainted: *on familiar terms with one's neighbors.* CONFIDENTIAL implies a sense of mutual trust that extends to the sharing of confidences and secrets: *a confidential adviser.* INTIMATE connotes a very close and warm relationship characterized by empathy and sharing of private thoughts: *intimate letters to a friend.* **—Ant. 1** unfamiliar, unknown, uncommon, new, unusual, unconventional, infrequent, rare, unaccustomed, extraordinary. **2** unfamiliar, ignorant, unversed, unacquainted, uninformed; unskilled, unseasoned. **3** distant, detached, indifferent, formal, aloof, cold.

familiarity *n.* **1.** knowledge, acquaintance, cognizance, acquaintanceship, intimacy, comprehension, understanding, skill, know-how, proficiency, mastery, conversance, experience. **2.** closeness, intimacy, friendship, association, close acquaintance; fellowship, brotherhood, amity, fraternity, brotherliness; *Informal* coziness, chumminess. **3.** informality, ease, absence of ceremony, casualness, naturalness, unconstraint, unreserve. **4.** impertinence, disrespect, impudence, forwardness, presumption, undue intimacy, overfamiliarity, undue liberty, intrusiveness, impropriety, unseemliness, indecorum. **—Ant. 1** unfamiliarity, ignorance, inexperience. **2** unfamiliarity, distance. **3** formality, constraint, reserve. **4** propriety, properness, respect, decorum.

familiarize *v.* acquaint, make familiar, accustom, make conversant, instruct, educate, edify, inculcate, teach, wean on, school, inform, tutor, enlighten; make used to, acclimatize, habituate, season.

family *n.* **1.** parents and children; children of two parents, issue, offspring, progeny, brood. **2.** relatives, kin, kinsmen, kith and kin, kinfolk, kinsfolk, relations. **3.** house, lineage, ancestry, line, dynasty, clan, tribe, breed; genealogy, race, stock, blood, extraction; forebears, parentage, forefathers. **4.** group, division, class, classification, kind, order, set, category.

famine *n.* **1.** general scarcity of food, half rations, starvation, famishment, extreme hunger. **2.** acute shortage, want, deficiency, paucity, dearth, lack, scarcity, scantiness, insufficiency, exhaustion, meagerness, depletion, destitution, poverty, short supply. **—Ant. 1, 2** abundance, surfeit, sufficiency, feast, bounty, glut.

famish *v.* be eager for food, be ravenous, suffer extreme hunger, distress with hunger, deprive of nutriment.

famous *adj.* well-known, noted, celebrated, prominent, renowned, far-famed; eminent, illustrious, notable, distinguished; conspicuous, notorious. **—Syn. Study.** FAMOUS, CELEBRATED, RENOWNED, NOTORIOUS refer to someone or something widely known. FAMOUS is the general word for a person or thing that receives wide public notice, usu. favorable: *a famous lighthouse.* CELEBRATED refers to a famous person or thing that enjoys wide public praise or honor for merit, services, etc.: *a celebrated poet.* RENOWNED usu. implies wider, greater, and more enduring fame and glory: *a renowned hospital.* NOTORIOUS means widely known and discussed because of some bad or evil quality or action: *a notorious criminal.* **—Ant.** obscure, unknown, undistinguished, unsung, inglorious, obscure, forgotten, uncelebrated.

fan *n.* enthusiast, aficionado, follower, supporter, rooter, partisan, booster, zealot, fanatic, addict, buff; *Informal* fiend, *Slang* nut, freak, bug.

fanatic *n.* zealot, extremist, maniac, hothead, member of the lunatic fringe, *Slang* freak, nut, crazy; activist, radical, militant; enthusiast, devotee. **—Syn. Study.** FANATIC, ZEALOT, DEVOTEE refer to persons showing more than ordinary enthusiasm or support for a cause, belief, or activity. FANATIC and ZEALOT both suggest extreme or excessive devotion. FANATIC further implies unbalanced or obsessive behavior: *a wild-eyed fanatic.* ZEALOT, slightly less unfavorable in implication, implies single-minded partisanship: *a tireless zealot for tax reform.* DEVOTEE is a milder term, suggesting enthusiasm but not to the exclusion of other interests or possible points of view: *a devotee of baseball.* **—Ant.** unbeliever, cynic; passivist.

fanaticism *n.* zealotry, enthusiasm, extreme zeal, fervor, intemperance, ruling passion, obsession, monomania, extremism, wild and extravagant notions; activism, militantism, radicalism; opinionatedness, dogmatism. **—Ant.** cynicism, skepticism, indifference, passivism; latitudinarianism.

fanciful *adj.* **1.** whimsical, flighty, imaginative, capricious, humorous, inventive, quixotic, romantic, fantastic, bizarre, odd, eccentric, curious, unusual, unpredictable. **2.** unreal, imaginary, visionary, fictitious, fabulous, based on fancy, fantastic, chimerical, apocryphal, illusory, mythical, legendary. **—Ant. 1** unimaginative, conventional, conservative, sensible, sober, ordinary; prosaic, predictable. **2** real, realistic, true.

fancy *n.* **1.** imagination, whimsy, caprice, fantasy. **2.** illusion, fantasy, figment, daydream, reverie, conceit, vagary, crotchet, vision, notion, idea, dream, caprice. **3.** leaning, liking, longing, fondness, predilection, inclination, relish, penchant, partiality, capricious preference, taste, desire, *Informal* hankering, yen; weakness. *—adj.* **4.** showy, not plain, unusual, ornamental, decorative, ornate, intricately wrought, elegant, elaborate; florid, rococo, gingerbread, baroque; fine, special, distinctive, superior, superfine, custom, exceptional, specially selected, deluxe, epicurean, gourmet; expensive, high-priced, extravagant. *—v.* **5.** imagine, dream of, picture, conceive of. **6.** suspect, suppose, think, assume, opine, conjecture, imagine, surmise, presume, be inclined to think, suspect, take it. **7.** like, have a mind to, take a liking to, be bent upon, take to, have an eye for, want, long for, favor, be fond of, be pleased with, crave, yearn for, *Informal* hanker after; relish, enjoy. **—Ant. 2** conviction, certainty. **3** dislike, distaste, aversion. **4** plain, ordinary, undecorated; common, inferior; low-priced, cheap, modest, inexpensive.

fantastic *adj.* **1.** weird, odd, queer, freakish, antic, bizarre, amazing, wild, extravagant, absurd, crazy, mad, ridiculous, preposterous, outlandish, grotesque, implausible, unbelievable, incredible, strange, irrational, extreme, farfetched, *Informal* way-out, *Slang* far-out; romantic, visionary, imaginary, chimerical, fanciful, quixotic, illusory. **2.** great, extravagant, extreme, huge, enormous, tremendous. **3.** *Informal* marvelous, extremely good, wonderful, sensational, fabulous, terrific, great, superb, *Slang* awesome. **—Syn. Study. 1** FANTASTIC, BIZARRE, GROTESQUE share a sense of deviation from what is normal or expected. FANTASTIC suggests a wild lack of restraint and a fancifulness so extreme as to lose touch with reality: *a fantastic new space vehicle.* BIZARRE implies striking or odd elements that surprise and captivate the observer: *bizarre costumes for Mardi Gras.* GROTESQUE implies shocking distortion or incongruity, sometimes ludicrous, but more often pitiful or tragic: *the grotesque gestures of a mime.* **—Ant. 1** reasonable, sensible, credible, ordinary, rational, common. **2** ordinary, moderate, limited. **3** common, ordinary, poor, *Informal* lousy, *Slang* crummy.

fantasy *n.* **1.** fancy, imagination, realm of dreams, mind, make-believe, unreality. **2.** fancy, illusion, daydream, imagining, dream, reverie, invention, fabrication, visionary idea, notion, fiction, figment, supposition, caprice, whimsy; nightmare, vision, chimera, apparition, mirage, phantasm, phantom, hallucination. **—Ant. 1, 2** reality, actuality, fact.

far *adv.* **1.** a long way, at a great distance, distantly, deeply, to a remote point, to a distant point, yonder, afar, beyond range. **2.** very much, much, incomparably, to a great degree, immeasurably, greatly, transcendently, a great deal, considerably. *—adj.* **3.** distant, faroff, far-away, remote, way-off, yonder, out-of-the-way, far-removed. **—Ant. 1** close, near, nigh. **2** less, little. **3** near, nearby, close.

farce *n.* **1.** satirical comedy, broad comedy, burlesque, harlequinade, parody, low comedy. **2.** buffoonery, horseplay, tomfoolery, ridiculousness, absurdity, nonsense, drollery. **3.** sham, mockery, travesty, pretense, make-believe, absurdity, parody. **—Ant. 1** tragedy. **2** seriousness. **3** reality.

fare *n.* **1.** charge, passage money, ticket price, fee, cost of transportation. **2.** paying passenger, rider, customer, client. **3.** food, food and drink, provisions, victuals, diet, table, comestibles, menu, regimen, board. *—v.* **4.** manage, get on, get along, experience good or bad fortune, go through an experience, turn out, do, make out, perform.

farewell *interj.* **1.** good-bye, so long, Godspeed; *French* adieu, au revoir, *Spanish* adios, *Italian* arrivederci, ciao, *German* auf Wiedersehen, *Japanese* sayonara. *—n.* **2.** good-bye, parting wish, parting compliment, valediction. **3.** leave-taking, departure, departing, parting, adieu. **—Ant. 1** hello, greetings. **2** salutation, welcome, greetings. **3** meeting, arrival.

far-fetched *adj.* improbable, unlikely, implausible, doubtful, dubious, preposterous, unconvincing, strained, *Slang* cockamamie. **—Ant.** likely, probable, plausible.

farm *n.* **1.** tract, spread, truck farm, ranch, grange, plantation, country place. *—v.* **2.** cultivate, have under cultivation, use for raising crops, produce crops, till the soil, plant, engage in agronomy, practice husbandry; (*variously*) plow, harvest, reap, sow.

farmer *n.* grower, raiser, planter, cultivator of land, agriculturist, person who runs a farm, agrarian, agronomist, tiller of the soil, agricultural laborer, husbandman, harvester, rancher, granger, reaper, sharecropper, truck gardener, truck farmer.

farsighted *adj.* **1.** long-sighted, hyperopic. **2.** foresighted, forehanded, farseeing, long-sighted, foreseeing, prescient, clairvoyant, provident, wise, judicious, prudent, levelheaded, commonsensical, acute, shrewd; wisely planned. **—Ant. 1** nearsighted, myopic, shortsighted. **2** shortsighted, improvident, injudicious.

farther *adv.* **1.** further, to a greater distance, past the point that, at a greater distance; beyond, at or to a more advanced point; to a greater degree or extent, deeper. *—adj.* **2.** more distant, more remote, remoter, further, more removed. **3.** longer, lengthier. **—Ant. 2** closer, nearer. **3** shorter.

fascinate *v.* charm, captivate, bewitch, attract and hold, beguile, entrance, enchant, allure, grip the attention of, engross, delight, enthrall, enrapture, allure, spellbind, absorb, interest greatly, enravish; transfix, hold motionless, rivet, overpower, spellbind, hold spellbound. **—Ant.** bore, repel.

fascinating *adj.* gripping, engrossing, enthralling, absorbing, riveting, overpowering, charming, captivating, enchanting, bewitching, beguiling, entrancing, alluring, interesting, delightful, spellbinding. **—Ant.** boring, uninteresting, dull; repellent.

fascism *n.* right-wing dictatorship, corporate state, corporatism, corporativism; (*variously*) national socialism, Nazism; totalitarianism, police state; autocracy, plutocracy, oligarchy. **—Ant.** socialism, democracy.

fashion *n.* **1.** style, custom, mode, trend, general practice, usage, habit, prevailing taste, vogue, craze, fad, rage; conventionality, convention, form. **2.** way, manner, demeanor, air, mode of action, attitude; tenor, behavior. *—v.* **3.** shape, create, make, form, contrive, design, frame, devise, forge, pattern, fabricate, hew, mold, construct; compose, produce, manufacture, carve.

fashionable *adj.* in fashion, stylish, in style, modish, smart, in vogue, voguish, all the rage, chic, current, du jour, prevailing, popular; *Slang* in, with-it, hip. **—Ant.** unfashionable, old-fashioned, out-of-date, dated, unstylish, passé; *Slang* old hat.

fast[1] *adj.* **1.** swift, quick, fleet, moving quickly, winged, able to move rapidly, rapid; brisk, hasty, flying, hurried; accelerated; taking only a short time, done in little time, speedy, expeditious, *Slang* lickety-split; ahead, in advance. **2.** wild, reckless, pleasure-mad, immodest, extravagant, dissipated, profligate, intemperate, wanton, dissolute, self-indulgent, rakish, free in behavior and morals, immoral, loose, lustful, debauched, lascivious, licentious. **3.** steadfast, firm, constant, unwavering, abiding, enduring, resolute, durable, steady, unswerving; loyal, devoted, staunch, stable, true, lasting, faithful. **4.** secure, fastened, firm, steady, immovable, rigid, firmly fixed in place, firmly tied, resistant, securely attached, stationary, taut, tight. **5.** permanent, ineradicable, lasting, durable, unfading. *—adv.* **6.** firmly, fixedly, tightly, securely, tenaciously, immovably, solidly. **7.**. soundly, fully, completely. **8.** swiftly, rapidly, speedily, quickly, hastily, hurriedly. **9.** ahead, in advance. **—Syn. Study. 1** See QUICK. **—Ant. 1** slow. **2** upright, respectable, moral, steady, sober, virtuous, *Slang* square. **3** unsteady, wavering, inconstant, irresolute, unstable, disloyal, unfaithful. **4** loose, weak, movable, insecure, unsteady. **6** loosely, insecurely. **8** slowly, slow, dawdlingly. **9** slow, behind, late.

fast[2] *v.* **1.** forbear eating, deny oneself food, go without food, abstain from food, go hungry; starve, famish. *—n.* **2.** fasting, starvation, doing without food, abstinence from food, hunger strike; fast day, period of fasting. **—Ant. 1** eat. **2** eating, feast.

fasten *v.* **1.** attach, tie, fix firmly in position, make fast, hold fixed, hold immovable, secure, make secure, anchor, affix; (*variously*) lash, hitch, tether, moor, truss, pin, bolt, screw, rivet, weld, pinion, bind, stick, yoke, clamp, cement, solder, fuse; unite, join, wed, connect, adhere, put together, hold together, (*variously*) close, bar, hook, lock, latch, button, couple, clasp, clip, snap, dovetail, link, dowel. **2.** fix, direct, focus, rivet, hold. **—Ant. 1** unfasten; loosen, loose; separate, untie, part, sever, sunder, divorce, divide, undo, relax, remove, detach, unbolt, unhitch, disunite, uncouple, disconnect.

fastidious *adj.* fussy, particular, excessively critical, hard to please, persnickety, picky, difficult, finicky, meticulous, proper, hypercritical, choosy, exacting, overprecise; overdelicate, dainty, overrefined, precious; squeamish, queasy. **—Ant.** remiss, neglectful, slack, casual, lax; uncritical, indulgent, easy; indelicate, unrefined, coarse.

fat *n.* **1.** grease, greasy substance, animal fat, adipose tissue. *—adj.* **2.** stout, heavy, plump, chubby, overweight, obese, thickset, fleshy, pudgy, rotund, paunchy, portly, beefy, potbellied, lumpish, corpulent. **3.** fatty, greasy, oily, containing fat, unctuous, suety, blubbery. **4.** *Informal* lucrative, rewarding, remunerative; fortunate, palmy, productive, fruitful, fertile. **5.** well-stocked, full, replete, plentiful, plenteous, flush, abundant, copious, well-furnished, chockful, stuffed.

—**Ant.** **2** lean, spare, lank, lanky, skinny, gaunt, scrawny, rawboned, angular; thin, slender, slim, slight, cadaverous. **3** lean. **4** lean, unprofitable, unlucrative, poor, scarce, scanty, unrewarding, unremunerative, unfruitful, unproductive. **5** barren, empty, lean.

fatal *adj.* **1.** terminal, deadly, lethal, mortal, causing death; virulent. **2.** ruinous, lethal, destructive, calamitous, disastrous, catastrophic. —**Syn. Study. 1** FATAL, DEADLY, LETHAL, MORTAL apply to something that has caused or is capable of causing death or dire misfortune. FATAL may refer to the future or the past; in either case, it emphasizes inevitability or inescapable consequences: *a fatal illness; fatal errors.* DEADLY refers to the future, and suggests something that causes death by its very nature, or has death as its purpose: *a deadly disease; a deadly poison.* LETHAL is usu. used in technical contexts: *Carbon monoxide is a lethal gas.* MORTAL usu. refers to death that has actually occurred: *He received a mortal blow.* —**Ant. 1** harmless, slight, minor, nonlethal. **2** lifegiving, constructive, beneficial, vitalizing, restorative, helpful.

fatalism *n.* submission to fate, passive acceptance, acquiescence, resignation, stoicism, predestination; helplessness, powerlessness.

fatality *n.* **1.** deadliness, mortality, lethality, malignancy, perniciousness, banefulness. **2.** death, casualty, violent death, fatal accident.

fate *n.* **1.** destiny, predestination, predetermination; providence, will of heaven. **2.** fortune, lot, destiny, karma, portion, doom, kismet, *Greek* moira. **3.** future, outcome, upshot, prospect, ultimate fortune, chances; consequence, effect. —**Syn. Study. 2** FATE, DESTINY refer to a predetermined and usu. inescapable course or outcome of events. The two words are frequently interchangeable. FATE stresses the irrationality and impersonal character of events: *It was Napoleon's fate to be exiled.* The word is often used lightly: *It was my fate to meet her that very afternoon.* DESTINY is often used of a favorable or exalted lot in life: *It was her destiny to save her people.* —**Ant. 1** will, choice, decision, independence, freedom, chance.

fateful *adj.* momentous, decisively important, critical, decisive, determinative, crucial, significant; ominous, threatening, portentous; fatal, disastrous. —**Syn. Study.** See OMINOUS. —**Ant.** unimportant, ordinary, insignificant.

father *n.* **1.** male parent, sire, (*variously*) dad, daddy, papa, pater, pop, *Slang* old man. **2.** forefather, ancestor, forebear, progenitor. **3.** inventor, creator, architect, designer, begetter, originator, founder, author, maker. **4.** priest, padre, abbé, pastor, curé, parson, preacher, dignitary of the church, confessor; (*variously*) pope, cardinal, archbishop, bishop, monsignor. —*v.* **5.** sire, act as the father of, beget, engender, procreate. **6.** found, originate, create, begin, hatch, author, design.

fatherland *n.* homeland, native land, native soil, native country, mother country, motherland, birthplace; *Latin* patria, *French* patrie, *German* Heimat.

fatherly *adj.* paternal, fatherlike, parental; benevolent, beneficent, benign, tender, kindly, affectionate, demonstrative, sympathetic, forbearing, indulgent, protective.

fathom *v.* penetrate, figure out, comprehend, understand, follow, hunt out, probe, divine, discover, get to the bottom of, ferret out, unravel, uncover, root out.

fatigue *n.* **1.** tiredness, exhaustion, weariness, debilitation, lassitude, enervation, heaviness, listlessness, languor, drowsiness, tedium, overtiredness. —*v.* **2.** exhaust, tire, overtire, weary, wear out, enervate, debilitate, drain, weaken; *Informal* bush, fag, tucker. —**Ant. 1** energy, alertness, vigor, indefatigability. **2** rest, refresh, restore, rejuvenate, renew, relieve.

fatty *adj.* greasy, containing fat, shortened, buttery, oily, suety, lardy, blubbery.

fatuous *adj.* foolish, inane, silly, vacant in mind, simple, stupid, brainless, witless, vapid, vacuous, asinine, imbecile, idiotic, puerile, obtuse, besotted, senseless, moronic, ridiculous. —**Syn. Study.** See FOOLISH. —**Ant.** sensible, prudent, judicious, wise, sage, sapient, clever, bright, intelligent, smart, witty.

fault *n.* **1.** shortcoming, defect, deficiency, insufficiency, imperfection, impediment, snag, flaw, failing, foible, infirmity, frailty, weakness, weak point, drawback, vice, *Informal* bug, *Slang* glitch; taint, stain, blemish. **2.** error, blunder, wrong, mistake, misdeed, mistake of judgment, transgression, sin, oversight, offense, wrongdoing, dereliction, indiscretion, slip, cause for blame, peccadillo, misdemeanor, crime. **3.** responsibility, guilt, answerability, accountability, culpability, blame, negligence, mistake of judgment. —*v.* **4.** find fault with, blame, impugn, censure, criticize, reprove. —**Syn. Study. 1** FAULT, FOIBLE, WEAKNESS, FAILING, VICE refer to human shortcomings or imperfections. FAULT refers to any ordinary shortcoming; condemnation is not necessarily implied: *Of his many faults the greatest is vanity.* FOIBLE suggests a weak point that is slight and often amusing, manifesting itself in eccentricity rather than in wrongdoing: *the foibles of an artist.* WEAKNESS suggests that a person is unable to control a particular impulse or response, and gives way to it: *a weakness for ice cream.* FAILING is particularly applied to humanity at large, suggesting common, often venial, shortcomings: *Procrastination is a common failing.* VICE is the strongest term and designates a habit that is detrimental, immoral, or evil: *to succumb to the vice of compulsive gambling.* —**Ant. 1** merit, excellence, virtue, perfection, strength, sufficiency. **3** credit. **4** credit, praise.

faultfinder *n.* critic, quibbler, carper, complainer, censor, caviler, fussbudget, derogator, detractor, Mrs. Grundy, nitpicker, bear, sorehead, crab, grouch, crank, grouser, curmudgeon; *Slang* bellyacher, fuddy-duddy.

faultless *adj.* perfect, without blemish, free from imperfection, flawless, without fault, ideal, exemplary, irreproachable, immaculate, unblemished, impeccable, unimpeachable; correct, accurate. —**Ant.** faulty, incomplete, imperfect, incorrect, defective, inaccurate, erroneous.

faulty *adj.* unsound, defective, impaired, imperfect, injured, awry, out of order, amiss, inadequate, deficient, inferior; incorrect, mistaken, erroneous, unsatisfactory, bad, unreliable, wrong, false. —**Ant.** sound, perfect, complete, adequate, blameless, faultless, correct, accurate.

faux pas *n.* breach of etiquette, mistake, blunder, gaffe, indiscretion, false step, error, impropriety, lapse; *Informal* slip-up, *Slang* goof, boo-boo, howler, boner.

favor *n.* **1.** good turn, kind act, good deed, service, accommodation; benefaction, largesse, courtesy, dispensation, act of grace. **2.** approval, goodwill, friendly disposition, esteem, kindly regard, good opinion, approbation; support, patronage, commendation, countenance; championship, advocacy, espousal. **3.** gift, present, goodwill token, memento, souvenir. —*v.* **4.** approve, be in favor of, support, endorse, back, be for, go in for, like, commend, sanction, esteem, countenance, encourage, smile upon, side with, uphold. **5.** prefer, have a preference for, fancy, side with, patronize, be partial to; pamper, deal gently with, humor, indulge, use lightly, use gently. **6.** support, aid, help, assist, oblige, succor, foster, accommodate, abet, show favor to, do a kindness for. **7.** look like, resemble, take after, be the image of. —**Ant. 1** injury, disservice, harm, hurt. **2** ill will, disfavor, malice, malevolence, antipathy, prohibition, animosity, enmity, hostility, disapproval, oppose, be against, disapprove, dislike. **5** dislike, object to. **6** hurt, harm, inconvenience, thwart, foil.

favorable *adj.* **1.** advantageous, good, giving help, affording aid, helpful, beneficial, serviceable, convenient, timely, fair. **2.** approving, showing favor, commendatory, salutary, good, showing approval, well-disposed; friendly, kind, benign, amicable, sympathetic. **3.** promising, propitious, opportune, auspicious, good, hopeful, conducive, predisposed. —**Ant. 1–3** unfavorable. **1** disadvantageous, unhelpful. **2** disapproving, ill-disposed, unfriendly, unsympathetic. **3** unpromising, inauspicious.

favorite *n.* **1.** preferred one, choice, pet, fancy, jewel, darling, fair-haired one, apple of one's eye. **2.** probable winner, one favored to win, front-runner. —*adj.* **3.** best-liked, preferred, pet, choice, most popular, special.

favoritism *n.* partiality, bias, favoring of one over others, one-sidedness, partisanship.

fawn *v.* be servile, be obsequious, ingratiate oneself, truckle, toady, pander, seek favor, bow and scrape, flatter, pay court. —**Ant.** be insulting, ignore.

faze *v.* disconcert, fret, rattle, daunt, worry, disturb, upset, bother, discompose, perturb, discomfit, embarrass, abash, confound, fluster, flurry.

fear *n.* **1.** dread, fright, foreboding, terror, panic, threat, horror, affright, apprehension, alarm, dismay, trepidation, consternation, disquietude, quaking, perturbation, qualm, anxiety, worry, concern, fearfulness, cowardice. **2.** qualm, phobia, apprehension, source of anxiety, dread; nightmare, bugaboo, bugbear, specter, bogey; worry, concern, care. **3.** reverence, awe, reverential regard, wonder, veneration, esteem, deep respect. —*v.* **4.** be afraid of, dread, be frightened of, regard with fear, be apprehensive of, take fright, be scared of, tremble at, shudder at. **5.** feel awe for, revere, respect deeply, honor humbly, venerate, reverence, esteem. —**Ant. 1** fearlessness, bravery, intrepidity, courage, confidence, security, calm, assurance, aplomb; backbone, endurance, grit, guts, heroism, pluck.

fearful *adj.* **1.** frightening, frightful, dreadful, causing fear, terrible, dread, alarming, formidable, appalling, macabre, ominous, ghastly, terrifying, distressing, shocking, portentous, horrible, sinister, dire, horrid, eerie, lurid, awful. **2.** afraid, frightened, apprehensive, alarmed, aghast, panicky, haunted with fear, anxious, worried, scared, full of fear, uneasy, concerned, nervous. **3.** frightened, tremulous, nervous, showing fear, intimidated, diffident, timid, timorous, anxious, skittish, panic-stricken, panicky, scared, fainthearted, chickenhearted, apprehensive. **—Ant. 1** reassuring, encouraging, pleasant, benign. **2** fearless, unafraid, confident. **3** fearless, audacious, brave, courageous, bold, dauntless, valiant, intrepid.

fearless *adj.* dauntless, bold, undaunted, unafraid, confident, intrepid, brave, courageous, undismayed, without fear, unflinching, unshrinking, gallant, daring, venturesome, adventurous, unabashed, valiant, indomitable, valorous, heroic, audacious, stout-hearted, doughty, lionhearted, plucky, gritty. **—Syn. Study.** See BRAVE. **—Ant.** fearful, cowardly, timorous, daunted, afraid, dismayed, apprehensive, flinching, shrinking, terrified.

feasible *adj.* practicable, possible, conceivable, workable, achievable, attainable; desirable, advisable, appropriate, viable, reasonable, fitting, suitable, politic. **—Syn. Study.** See POSSIBLE. **—Ant.** unfeasible, infeasible, unworkable, unachievable, impractical, impossible, unsuitable, impracticable.

feast *n.* **1.** banquet, sumptuous repast, festive board, large dinner, elegant meal, large spread, bacchanal; rich supply, surplus, bounty. **2.** holiday, festival, feast day, celebration, festal day, fete, jubilee, saint's day, *Italian* festa. *—v.* **3.** eat richly, dine, have a feast, fare sumptuously, wine and dine, banquet, gorge, gluttonize, eat one's fill, gormandize. **4.** feed luxuriously, entertain expensively, wine and dine, entertain with a feast. **—Ant. 1** fast, famine, fasting. **2** fast, fast day, fasting.

feat *n.* deed, act, action, task, achievement, accomplishment, exploit, performance, attainment; maneuver, stroke; adventure, enterprise, triumph, tour de force.

feature *n.* **1. features.** parts of the face, visage, aspect, lineaments, physiognomy. **2.** attribute, quality, hallmark, trait, characteristic, peculiarity; mark, property, earmark, character, important part. **3.** highlight, main item, special attraction, specialty, drawing card. *—v.* **4.** represent prominently, play up, display, spotlight, headline, highlight, star, present. **5.** *Informal* imagine, see, picture, conceive of, envision, fancy. **—Syn. Study. 2** FEATURE, CHARACTERISTIC, PECULIARITY refer to a distinctive trait of an individual or of a class. FEATURE suggests an outstanding or marked property that attracts attention: *A large art exhibit was a feature of the convention.* CHARACTERISTIC means a distinguishing mark or quality always associated in one's mind with a particular person or thing: *A fine sense of humor is one of his characteristics.* PECULIARITY means a distinctive and often unusual property exclusive to one individual, group, or thing: *A blue-black tongue is a peculiarity of the chow chow.*

federation *n.* union, united group, league, confederation, confederacy, alliance, association, coalition, combine, syndicate, amalgamation, brotherhood, sisterhood.

fee *n.* charge, consideration, payment for professional services, compensation, price, commission, honorarium, stipend, emolument, remuneration, salary, wage, hire; toll, fare, tariff.

feeble *adj.* **1.** enfeebled, weak, weakened, infirm, sickly, disabled, not strong, ailing, fragile, debilitated, delicate, frail, decrepit, enervated, powerless, impotent, puny, forceless, senile, doddering, declining. **2.** ineffective, poor, flat, spiritless, thin, frail, lacking force, tame, meager, vapid, faint, weak, flimsy, flabby, slight, insipid, lame, ineffectual, paltry, wishy-washy, colorless, inadequate. **—Ant. 1** robust, strong, sturdy, stout, stalwart, vigorous, lusty, energetic, hale, healthy. **2** effective, effectual, successful; forceful, cogent, vehement, ardent; hearty, strong, spirited.

feebleminded *adj.* mentally slow, retarded, backward, subnormal, halfwitted, moronic, imbecilic; senile; weakminded, stupid, dull, childish, senseless. **—Ant.** bright, intelligent, smart.

feed *v.* **1.** supply with nourishment, provide food for; feast, cater, wine and dine; give as food. **2.** eat, take nourishment, consume, take food, devour, fare; graze, pasture. **3.** nourish, nurture, support, fuel, augment, encourage, maintain, strengthen, bolster, sustain, foster; gratify, satisfy, minister to. *—n.* **4.** foodstuff, nourishment, food for animals, provisions, fodder, victuals, provender, viands, comestibles, forage, mash, pasture. **—Syn. Study. 4** FEED, FODDER, FORAGE, PROVENDER mean food for animals. FEED is the general word; however, it most often applies to grain: *chicken feed.* FODDER is applied to coarse feed that is fed to livestock: *Cornstalks are good fodder.* FORAGE is feed that an animal obtains (usu. grass, leaves, etc.) by grazing or searching about for it: *Lost cattle can usually live on forage.* PROVENDER denotes dry feed for livestock, such as hay, oats, or corn: *a supply of provender in the haymow.* **—Ant. 1** starve. **3** starve, thwart, deny, stifle.

feel *v.* **1.** perceive by touch, sense, touch, examine by touching, have the feeling of; palpate, paw, handle, finger, manipulate, press. **2.** have a sensation of, experience, sense, perceive, suffer from, be aware of; understand, comprehend, know, see, discern, observe, notice. **3.** grope, find by touching, fumble, search with the hands; reach, probe. **4.** be of the opinion that, believe, think, be convinced, sense, have an impression. **5.** have sympathy, sympathize with, share the feelings of, have compassion, be moved by, be touched by, be stirred by. **—***n.* **6.** feeling, sensation, touch, texture, composition, character, makeup.

feeling *n.* **1.** sense of touch, sensation, tactile sense, perception by touch, sensibility, awareness, consciousness. **2.** emotion, sense, sensation, thrill, reaction, impression, response, sentiment; aura, atmosphere. **3.** emotion, passion, sentiment; ardor, fervor, vehemence, zeal, earnestness, verve, enthusiasm, affection, warmth, gusto, spirit; sympathy, compassion, concern, sensitivity, susceptibility, pity. **4.** opinion, view, point of view, attitude, impression, instinct, intuition, inclination, sentiment. **—Syn. Study. 3** FEELING, EMOTION, PASSION, SENTIMENT refer to pleasurable or painful sensations experienced when one is stirred to sympathy, anger, fear, love, grief, etc. FEELING is a general term for a subjective point of view as well as for specific sensations: *to be guided by feeling rather than by facts; a feeling of pride, of dismay.* EMOTION is applied to an intensified feeling: *agitated by emotion.* PASSION is strong or violent emotion, often so overpowering that it masters the mind or judgment: *stirred to a passion of anger.* SENTIMENT is a mixture of thought and feeling, esp. refined or tender feeling: *Recollections are often colored by sentiment.* **—Ant. 1** numbness, insensibility, insensateness. **3** insensitivity, unconcern, imperturbability, coldness, apathy. **4** unfeeling, unemotional, dispassionate, cold.

feelings *n. pl.* sensibilities, susceptibilities, emotions, passions, sensitivities; pride, ego, self-esteem.

feign *v.* **1.** simulate, affect, assume, pretend, fake, make believe, sham, imitate deceptively, put on, make a show of. **2.** make up, invent, forge, concoct, counterfeit, devise deceptively, fabricate, fake, *Informal* cook up. **—Syn. Study. 1** See PRETEND.

feint *n.* feigned attack, pass, bluff, deceptive movement, move; artifice, stratagem, pretense, maneuver, ruse, ploy, trick, gambit, hoax, subterfuge, wile, dodge, pretext; mask, blind.

felicitation *n.* congratulations, compliments, best wishes, good wishes, blessings, joy; greetings, salutations, cheers, pat on the back, wishes for happiness.

felicitous *adj.* **1.** happy, joyful, joyous, fortunate, propitious. **2.** apt, appropriate, suitable, relevant, pertinent, germane, fitting, well-chosen, well-put, well-said, pleasing, happy, inspired; effective. **—Ant. 1** infelicitous, solemn, inappropriate. **2** infelicitous, awkward, clumsy, unfortunate.

felicity *n.* **1.** happiness, blissfulness, bliss, ecstatic joy, delight, delectation, paradise, heavenly contentment, heaven, beatitude, ecstasy. **2.** aptness, charm, grace, nicety, fitness, effectiveness, suitability, relevancy, appropriateness; skill, knack, ingenuity. **—Ant. 1** sorrow, misery, sadness, unhappiness. **2** inappropriateness, clumsiness, awkwardness.

fell *v.* knock down, cut down, cause to fall, hew down, level, prostrate; demolish, destroy, raze.

fellow *n.* **1.** boy, man, chap, *Slang* guy, dude. **2.** companion, associate, friend, comrade, consort, chum, co-worker, compatriot, colleague, pal; *British* mate; peer, equal. **—Ant. 1** girl, woman, gal. **2** foe, opponent, antagonist, stranger.

fellowship *n.* companionship, comradeship, friendliness, cordiality, friendship, sociability, amicability, intimacy, familiarity, amity, affability; society, association, fraternity, brotherhood. **—Ant.** unfriendliness, unsociability; antagonism, hostility.

female *adj.* **1.** girl, woman; offspring-bearing, childbearing. **2.** feminine, womanly, ladylike, womanlike, distaff; womanish. **—***n.* **3.** woman, girl, lady. **4.** female animal, offspring-bearing animal; (*variously*) mare, dam, sow, heifer, cow, bitch, tabby, hen. **—Syn. Study. 2** FEMALE, FEMININE describe women and girls or whatever is culturally attributed to them. FEMALE classifies individuals on the basis of their genetic makeup or their ability to produce offspring in sexual reproduction. It contrasts with MALE in all uses: *her oldest female relative; the female skeleton.* FEMININE refers to qualities and behavior deemed especially appropriate to, or ideally associated with, women and girls; these have traditionally included such features as charm, gentleness, and patience: *to dance with feminine grace; a feminine sensitivity to moods.* FEMININE is sometimes used of physical features too: *small, feminine hands.* See also WOMANLY. **3** See WOMAN. **—Ant. 1** male. **2** male, masculine, manly, virile. **3** male, man, boy. **4** male.

feminine *adj.* **1.** womanly, female, femalelike, like a woman, girlish, ladylike, gentle, soft; dainty, delicate. **2.** female, of the female sex, woman, distaff. **—Syn. Study. 1** See WOMANLY, FEMALE. **—Ant. 1** masculine, male, manly, virile; indelicate, rough, mannish, unfeminine. **2** male.

femininity *n.* womanliness, female

quality, girlishness, femaleness, feminineness; softness, gentleness. **—Ant.** masculinity, manliness, virility; toughness, mannishness.

fence *n.* **1.** barrier, protective enclosure, palings, palisade, rail, barricade, stockade. *—v.* **2.** enclose with a fence, surround, secure, encompass, gird, corral, hedge, pen, encircle, hem in, wall in, coop, confine. **3.** duel, cross swords, engage in swordplay.

fend *v.* **1.** ward off, avert, push away, keep off, avoid, repel, repulse, parry. **2.** manage, provide, shift, do, make out; survive, take care of, support.

ferment *v.* **1.** turn partly into alcohol, undergo fermentation, turn; sour, seethe, bubble up, foam, froth, effervesce. **2.** seethe, be turbulent, smolder, fester, agitate, inflame. *—n.* **3.** fermentation, fermentation agent; yeast, mold, enzyme, leaven, leavening. **4.** unrest, disquiet, disruption, agitation, inflammation, fomentation, turmoil, turbulence, tumult, commotion, uproar. **—Ant. 4** calmness, quiet.

ferocious *adj.* savage, bestial, rapacious, brutish, ravening, predatory, fierce, violent; relentless, merciless, barbarous, ruthless, atrocious, murderous, maddened, enraged, bloodthirsty, fiendish, brutal, truculent, cold-blooded, deadly. **—Syn. Study.** See FIERCE. **—Ant.** tame, domesticated, subdued, submissive, mild, calm.

fertile *adj.* **1.** productive, fruitful, fructuous, fecund, vegetative, plenteous, luxuriant, loamy, rich; generative, reproductive, capable of bearing offspring, prolific; capable of developing, fertilized, fecundated, fructified. **2.** imaginative, productive, prolific, resourceful, inventive, creative; original, ingenious. **—Syn. Study. 1** See PRODUCTIVE. **—Ant. 1** infertile, barren, unproductive, unfertilized, poor, dry, unfruitful; impotent, sterile. **2** unproductive, uninventive, unimaginative, uncreative.

fertilize *v.* make fertile, render productive, impregnate, make fruitful, fructify, furnish with pollen, fecundate, pollinate, inseminate; enrich, feed with nutrients, manure.

fervent *adj.* earnest, impassioned, fervid, warmhearted, passionate, ardent, devout, zealous, intense, keen, eager, vehement, spirited, fierce, heartfelt, wholehearted, hearty, fiery, heated, burning, enthusiastic. **—Ant.** cool, cold, chilly, frigid; apathetic, impassive, phlegmatic, unfeeling, unimpassioned.

fervor *n.* ardor, passion, intensity, earnestness, vehemence, verve, zeal, animation, gusto, fire, enthusiasm, heartiness, eagerness, zest, warmth; piety, devoutness, seriousness, purposefulness. **—Ant.** boredom, ennui, apathy, detachment, dispassion.

fester *v.* **1.** form pus, suppurate, become infected, inflame, ulcerate, blister; rot, putrefy. **2.** rankle, torment, smolder, intensify, grow, grow virulent, plague; gall, irritate, chafe, fret, nettle, pique, rile, vex.

festival *n.* feast, celebration, holiday, carnival, fete, festivities, jubilee, gala day, gala, jamboree, fiesta.

festive *adj.* festal, joyous, gala, merry, jolly, gay, convivial, lighthearted, celebratory; larkish, playful, sportive, frolicsome. **—Ant.** funereal, gloomy; sad, lugubrious, glum, drab, dreary.

fetch *v.* **1.** get and bring back, go for, retrieve, get, obtain, bring. **2.** sell for, bring, procure, yield, realize, get; cost, afford, amount to, *Informal* go for.

fete *n.* **1.** party, feast, celebration, gala, garden party, banquet, carnival; *French* bal masqué, fête champêtre; festival, holiday. *—v.* **2.** wine and dine, give a party for, feast, banquet; treat, regale.

fetid *adj.* stinking, malodorous, rank, foul, ill-smelling, noisome, stenchful, stenchy, mephitic; rotten, putrid; gamy, nasty, tainted, rank, rancid; musty, fusty, moldy; suffocating, stifling. **—Ant.** fragrant, odorous, odoriferous, aromatic, redolent, balmy; perfumed, scented; clean, fresh, pure.

fetish *n.* **1.** charm, talisman, magic object; superstition; idol, image, golden calf, totem, amulet, scarab, joss, phylactery. **2.** preoccupation, obsession, craze, mania, passion, idée fixe.

fetter *n.* **1.** foot shackle, ankle irons, bond, chain, tether, yoke, manacle, handcuff, *Slang* bracelet. **2.** hindrance, obstruction, curb, restraint; confinement, imprisonment, durance, duress. *—v.* **3.** shackle, hobble, put into bilbos, confine, tether, trammel, pin down, tie down, tie up, truss up, bind hand and foot; manacle, handcuff, chain. **4.** hamper, hinder, hold back, impede, restrain, bind, encumber; confine, cage, shut in. **—Ant. 3, 4** free, unfetter, liberate, release; extricate, disencumber. **4** encourage, promote.

feud *n.* **1.** bad blood, vendetta, dispute, quarrel, strife; conflict, altercation, disagreement, bickering, falling out, argument; hostility, animosity, ill will, enmity, hard feelings, bad blood, discord, controversy; schism, faction; breach, rupture; fracas, affray, clashing, brawl, wrangle; *Informal* spat, fuss, tiff, set-to, squabble. *—v.* **2.** quarrel, dispute, be at odds, disagree, argue, bicker; clash, brawl, wrangle; *Informal* squabble, spat, row.

feverish *adj.* **1.** fevered, hot, febrile, flushed, pyretic; fiery, red-hot, inflamed, burning, parched. **2.** ardent, fanatic, impatient, overeager, passionate, fervent, zealous, impassioned; frenzied, excited, restless, wrought-up, high-strung. **—Ant. 2** composed, collected, cool; calm, unruffled, serene, tranquil; offhand, nonchalant.

few *adj.* **1.** not many, scarcely any, hardly any; scant, scanty, thin, sparse, skimpy, rare, exiguous, scarce; occasional, sporadic, infrequent, few and far between; limited, piddling, paltry, meager, inconsiderable, infinitesimal, insignificant, unusual, uncommon, unique. *—n.* **2.** small number, some, several, handful. **—Ant. 1** many, abundant, numerous, abounding, plentiful, bounteous; unstinted, inexhaustible.

fiasco *n.* complete failure, disaster; nonsuccess, debacle, labor in vain, miscarriage; *Slang* flop, botch, washout, bomb, fizzle. **—Ant.** success, triumph, smash, coup.

fiat *n.* command, decree, law, act, rule, ukase, edict, commandment, mandate, order, ruling, dictum.

fib *n.* **1.** harmless lie, half-truth, white lie; untruth, prevarication, misrepresentation, falsification, fiction, fabrication, invention. *—v.* **2.** lie, tell a white lie, tell a half-truth, stretch the truth, prevaricate, equivocate, hedge.

fickle *adj.* changeable, unpredictable, vacillating, inconstant, irresolute, inconsistent, mercurial; whimsical, capricious, volatile; giddy, feather-brained, frivolous, light-headed, flighty, erratic, fitful, spasmodic, feather-headed, wavering, fluctuating, unstable, unsteady, variable, shifting; unreliable, untrustworthy. **—Syn. Study.** FICKLE, INCONSTANT, CAPRICIOUS describe persons or things that are not firm or steady in affection, behavior, opinion, or loyalty. FICKLE implies an underlying perversity as a cause for the lack of stability: *once idolized, now rejected by a fickle public.* INCONSTANT suggests an innate disposition to change: *an inconstant lover, flitting from affair to affair.* CAPRICIOUS implies unpredictable changeability arising from sudden whim: *a capricious reversal of policy.* **—Ant.** constant, true, faithful, loyal, staunch, steadfast, firm, resolute, changeless, invariable; settled, stable, steady, sure, reliable, trustworthy.

fiction *n.* **1.** imaginative literary work, prose narration, romance; (*variously*) narrative, novel, novella, short story, short novel, tale, play; invention, imagination, fantasy, storytelling. **2.** falsehood, fabrication, prevarication, made-up story, factoid, fable, fib, tall tale, concoction, lie, forgery; *Slang* whopper, yarn, cock-and-bull story. **—Ant. 1** nonfiction, journalism. **2** certainty, fact, history; reality, truth, verity.

fictitious *adj.* unreal, false, untrue, assumed, feigned, invented, fanciful, imaginary, unfounded, counterfeit, forged, fabricated, bogus, fraudulent, spurious, supposititious, not genuine; artificial, sham, fake, phony, made-up, trumped-up, simulated; legendary, mythical, apocryphal. **—Ant.** real, true, actual; genuine, authentic, veritable; veracious, truthful.

fidelity *n.* **1.** devotion, loyalty, faithfulness, adherence, constancy, truehearted-ness, fealty; trustworthiness, integrity, honesty, truthfulness, probity; honor, allegiance, staunchness; sincerity, good faith, earnestness. **2.** accuracy, exactness, exactitude, faithfulness, correspondency, adherence to fact; closeness, precision; reliability. **—Ant.** faithlessness, unfaithfulness, perfidy, perfidiousness, falseness, falsity, disloyalty, treacherousness, treachery, traitorousness, untruthfulness; disaffection, infidelity; inexactness, inaccuracy.

fidgety *adj.* restless, restive, impatient; unquiet, jumpy, jittery, jerky, twitchy, squirmy, *Slang* antsy; nervous, uneasy, fussy, apprehensive; irritable; tremulous.

field *n.* **1.** meadow, grassland, pasture, grazing land, lea, mead, sward; lawn, green, common, yard, acreage; heath, clearing. **2.** playing field; arena, turf, court, course, diamond; lists. **3.** battlefield, battleground, theater of war, front, front lines. **4.** realm, domain, province, territory, region, area, sphere, department, bailiwick; occupation, profession, calling, line. **5.** scope, range, area, extent, reach, expanse, sweep, stretch, orbit, circle, spectrum. *—v.* **6.** catch, pick up, run down, grab, retrieve, glove.

fiend *n.* **1.** evil spirit, demon, dybbuk, incubus, succubus; devil, Satan, hellhound, prince of darkness. **2.** wicked person, villain, scoundrel, demon, monster, brute, beast, devil incarnate; barbarian.

fierce *adj.* **1.** wild, savage, ferocious, menacing, fearful, threatening, bloodthirsty, violent, brutal, cruel, fell, feral, barbarous, merciless; enraged, raging, furious, tigerish, leonine; truculent, bellicose; voracious, ravenous, ravening; horrible, terrible. **2.** powerful, strong, violent, vehement, intense, overpowering, extreme, inordinate, immoderate, overwhelming; unrestrained, unbridled, uncurbed, untamed; passionate, fiery, fervent, fervid, intensely eager, impetuous. **—Syn. Study. 1** FIERCE, FEROCIOUS, TRUCULENT suggest vehement hostility and unrestrained violence. FIERCE implies an aggressive, savage, or wild temperament and appearance: *the fiercest of foes; a fierce tribe.* FEROCIOUS implies merciless cruelty or brutality, esp. of a bloodthirsty kind: *a ferocious tiger.* TRUCULENT implies an intimidating or menacing fierceness: *a truculent bully.* **—Ant. 1** tame, docile, gentle, harmless, domesticated; cool, civilized; kind, patient; submissive, affectionate, sweet. **2** mild, peaceful, temperate, calm.

fiery *adj.* **1.** full of fire, flaming, burning; intensely hot, sweltering, torrid, blazing, alight, ablaze, afire; glowing, glaring, red-hot, flashing. **2.** feverish, fevered, burning, febrile, inflamed, flaming, pyretic. **3.** ardent, passionate, fervent, fervid, violent, impassioned; high-strung, impulsive, fierce, impetuous, demonstrative, temperamental; spirited, mettlesome, enthusiastic; zealous, vehement. **4.** hotheaded, hot-tempered, easily angered, excitable, headlong, readily provoked, impetuous, precipitate, choleric, peppery, irascible; angry, irate, violent, wrathful, irritable. **—Ant. 1** extinguished, quenched. **2** cool, chilly, cold, icy, frigid. **3** indifferent, passionless, phlegmatic, unimpassioned; dispassionate; mild, tame.

fiesta *n.* festival, party, gala, festive occasion, carnival, jamboree, fete; feast, picnic, street fair, fun-fair, block party; feast day, saint's day; celebration, commemoration, observance.

fight *n.* **1.** skirmish, struggle, fray, melee, strife, encounter, confrontation, contest, duel, tussle, scuffle, scrimmage, quarrel, fracas, brush, bout, dogfight; battle, combat, armed action, clash of arms, war, armed conflict, pitched battle, battle royal. **2.** spirit, pluck, grit, toughness, combativeness, disposition to struggle, mettle, gameness; belligerency, pugnacity, bellicosity. **3.** dispute, altercation, discord, contention, encounter, confrontation, quarrel, feud, difference, controversy, wrangling, set-to, tussle, bickering, dissension; *Informal* squabble, brawl, scrap, row, brush, spat, tiff. **4.** bout, match, prizefight, event, tournament, tourney, round; joust, tilt. **—*v.* 5.** battle, do battle with, join battle with, take up arms against, cross swords with, come to grips with, combat, struggle with, encounter, confront, engage, battle; rise up in arms, go to war, wage war, exchange blows, take up the cudgels, scuffle, brawl, skirmish, tussle, scrap, box, spar, duel; joust, tilt. **6.** resist, contend against, strive with, struggle against, oppose, repulse. **7.** wage, conduct, carry on. **8.** argue, dispute, clash, feud, wrangle, bicker, squabble. **—Ant. 1** pacification, reconciliation, reconcilement; appeasement, compromise.

fighter *n.* **1.** boxer, pugilist, prizefighter; sparrer. **2.** person with spirit, scrapper. **3.** warrior, soldier, military man, combatant, fighting man; belligerent, militarist.

figment *n.* product, fabrication, creation, fancy, fantasy, fiction, invention, concoction; story, fable, canard; falsehood. **—Ant.** fact, reality, actuality, certainty.

figurative *adj.* metaphorical, not literal, symbolic, involving a figure of speech; ironic, satirical, humorous; hyperbolical; allegorical; flowery, florid, ornate. **—Ant.** literal, precise, verbatim, faithful, exact; prosaic, unpoetical, plain.

figure *n.* **1.** numerical symbol, digit, number, cipher, numeral. **2.** price, amount, rate, cost, quotation, sum, value. **3. figures.** arithmetic, sums, calculations, computations. **4.** form, shape, outline, silhouette, body, physique, build; contour, cut, cast; configuration, frame, anatomy. **5.** personage, character, person, notable, eminence, force, leader, factor, presence, man, woman. **6.** pattern, design, device, motif, emblem; sign, symbol, plan, schema; diagram, illustration, drawing. **—*v.* 7.** calculate, compute, count up, add up, sum, reckon, cast, find the amount of, total, tot up, foot; assess, appraise, estimate. **8.** embellish, adorn, ornament, mark, pattern, variegate, diversify. **9.** calculate, reckon, think, suppose, conjecture; presume, believe, judge, imagine, guess. **10.** have a part, play a part, be mentioned, appear; be conspicuous, be prominent, be placed, count, shine forth, appear.

figurehead *n.* authority in name only, token, ornament, puppet, dummy, front; cipher, nonentity, tool.

filch *v.* **1.** steal, rob, purloin, pilfer, swipe, lift; *Slang* boost, heist, cop, hook. **2.** appropriate, pirate, copy, lift, expropriate, plagiarize, crib, arrogate, use as one's own.

file *n.* **1.** collection of papers or documents, information for reference, data; records, archives, stacks; filing cabinet, folder, drawer, dossier. **2.** line, queue, rank, row; string, chain, tier. **—*v.* 3.** store, put away, arrange for later reference, classify, catalog, index, place on file; record, list, chronicle, make an entry of. **4.** apply, submit a claim, petition, put in, request. **5.** walk in line, march in a file, follow the leader, walk Indian fashion, move forward in a line, advance in a queue.

filial *adj.* befitting one's child, sonlike or daughterly; respectful, dutiful.

fill *v.* **1.** make full, fill up; pervade, permeate, overspread, charge; saturate, impregnate, infuse, suffuse; load, lade, pack; crowd, cram, glut; feed fully, gorge, sate, satisfy, satiate. **2.** occupy, take up, assign, fulfill, supply; function, serve, act; preside, do duty; execute, discharge, carry out. **3.** make up, furnish, replenish, supply, provide; provision, outfit, stock; lay in, lay by, store. **4.** satisfy, meet, supply, answer, take care of. **5.** expand, inflate, dilate, distend; blow up, puff. —*n.* **6.** full amount, sufficiency, surfeit. —**Ant.** drain; empty, evaporate, shrink, diminish, ebb, subside; exhaust, vacate.

film *n.* **1.** thin layer, coat, coating, membrane, skin, sheet; veil, cloud, haze, mist. **2.** motion picture, movie, moving pictures, *Slang* flick. **3. films.** the film industry, cinema, movies, screen, motion pictures, moving pictures, *Slang* flicks. —*v.* **4.** haze, veil, mist. **5.** make a movie of, shoot.

filter *n.* **1.** strainer, sieve, screen, purifying device. —*v.* **2.** strain, pass through a filter, cleanse, refine, purify, clarify, filtrate. **3.** seep, dribble, leak, trickle; ooze, drain, well out, exude, effuse. —**Ant. 2** muddle, disturb, befoul; thicken; mix, merge, combine.

filth *n.* **1.** foul matter, dirt, trash, ordure, sewage, muck, slime; contamination, squalidness, squalor, nastiness, filthiness, pollution, defilement, impurity; dung, excrement, feces, excreta, manure; slop, refuse, garbage, offal, carrion, putridness; mud, mire, sludge, slush. **2.** pornography, obscenity, smut; grossness, indecency, immorality, lewdness; foul language, dirty-mindedness, vileness, corruption; suggestiveness, indelicacy; ribaldry.

final *adj.* **1.** last, closing, concluding, drop dead; rear, rearmost, hindmost, hindermost; ending, terminating, terminal; latest, last-minute; extreme, ultimate. **2.** decisive, conclusive, definitive, determinative; complete, thorough, finished, exhaustive; irrevocable, unchangeable, unappealable. —**Ant. 1** opening, first, initial. **2** preliminary; inconclusive, incomplete, changeable.

finale *n.* last part, conclusion, close, end, epilogue, curtain, finish, finis, windup, termination, culmination, swan song, crowning glory.

finally *adv.* **1.** in the end, lastly, at the last, in conclusion, ultimately; eventually, at length. **2.** conclusively, definitively, once and for all; inescapably, inexorably, incontrovertibly.

finance *n.* **1.** money management, banking, investment banking, investment counseling, fiscal matters, economics, accounts. —*v.* **2.** pay for, raise money for, supply money for, underwrite.

financial *adj.* —**Syn. Study.** See MONETARY.

financier *n.* expert in money matters, broker, banker, large-scale investor, underwriter, backer, angel; rich man, man of means, man of substance, moneyed man, millionaire, capitalist.

find *v.* **1.** discover, come upon, light upon, stumble upon, come across, chance upon; meet with, encounter, bump into. **2.** uncover, discover, hit upon, come by; unearth, dig up, disinter; track down, ferret out; detect, expose, learn, ascertain, determine. **3.** discern, catch sight of, espy, spot, see, meet. **4.** regain, recover, get back, retrieve, repossess, locate. **5.** acquire, gain, attain, achieve, get, procure, win, earn. **6.** declare a verdict, determine, pronounce; decide, rule, decree, judge, adjudge, adjudicate, award. —*n.* **7.** bargain, good buy, discovery; bonanza, windfall; catch, acquisition; godsend, lucky hit. —**Ant. 1** lose, miss, overlook; mislay, misplace.

fine[1] *adj.* **1.** high-quality, choice, top-grade, exceptional, first-class, superior, superb, splendid, admirable, excellent, flawless, exquisite, magnificent; tasteful, smart; rare; *Slang* dandy, nifty, neat, swell, spiffy. **2.** thin, slender; silky, silken, delicate; lightweight, flimsy, gossamer, cobwebby, diaphanous, sheer, transparent; airy, ethereal. **3.** powdery, pulverized, powdered, ground, refined. **4.** keen, sharp; precise, perfect; skillful, polished, brilliant, highly skilled, accomplished, consummate. **5.** delicate, fragile, exquisite, dainty, ethereal, gauzy. **6.** elegant, refined, fastidious, well-bred, exquisite; smart, chic, stylish, modish. **7.** clear, bright; pleasant, sunny, rainless, cloudless, fair. **8.** subtle, hard to discern, minute, small, nice, hairsplitting; slight, tenuous, thin, unsubstantial. **9.** handsome, attractive, comely, good-looking, well-favored, fair; beautiful, pretty, bonny, lovely. —*adv.* **10.** very well, excellently, swimmingly. —**Ant. 1** coarse, rough, unfinished, plain, crude. **2, 3** thick, coarse, rough, heavy, stout. **4** dull, blunt. **5** poor, inferior. **6** rough, crude, clumsy. **7** cloudy, dark, foul. **8** broad, clear, obvious. **9** ill-favored, disagreeable. **10** poorly, badly.

fine[2] *n.* **1.** penalty, sum demanded as punishment, assessment, charge, damages, forfeit, mulct. —*v.* **2.** punish by a fine, penalize, assess, charge, mulct.

finery *n.* showy dress, elegant clothing, fine things, frippery, frills; trimmings, gaudery, paraphernalia, trappings; gewgaws, tinsel, spangles, trinkets, baubles.

finesse *n.* **1.** delicacy, tact, discretion, artful management, savoir-faire, artfulness, craft, savvy. **2.** wile, ruse, subterfuge, artifice, stratagem, dodge; trickery, cunning, guile; intrigue, deception.

finger *n.* **1.** organ of touch, digit; (*variously*) thumb, forefinger, middle finger, ring finger, little finger; pointer; *Slang* feeler. —*v.* **2.** handle, touch, feel, caress, toy with, manipulate, play with, meddle with; poke, punch, squeeze; *Informal* paw, twiddle.

finicky *adj.* overparticular, fussy, meticulous, overprecise, overexacting, hairsplitting, nit-picking, picky, niggling, fastidious, pernickety, persnickety. —**Ant.** sloppy, slapdash, careless, slovenly, messy, slipshod.

finish *v.* **1.** end, conclude, bring to a close, complete, wind up, bring to an end; terminate, discontinue; stop, cease; seal, clinch; draw to a close; get done, accomplish, carry out, carry through, achieve, fulfill, consummate, make good; close, put an end to; get out of the way, dispose of, *Informal* knock off; realize, discharge, do thoroughly, settle. **2.** use up, dispatch; consume, devour. **3.** eradicate, exterminate, destroy, kill, get rid of, put out of the way; defeat, overcome completely. **4.** surface, veneer, face, glaze, gild; lacquer, varnish, coat. —*n.* **5.** conclusion, end, close, termination, completion; finale, finis, fall of the curtain, ending, curtain; epilogue, denouement; final event, windup, closing period, last, last stage; goal, objective. **6.** surface, exterior, coating, veneer, lacquer; polishing, finishing touches, last touch. —**Ant. 1** begin, start, undertake, commence; originate, create. **5** beginning, commencement, genesis; inauguration, inception; birth, conception.

finished *adj.* **1.** completed, concluded, ended; complete, final; consummated, perfect; entire, full, whole. **2.** faultless, flawless, consummate, accomplished, skilled, impeccable; elegant, refined; beautiful, shapely, well-set; classic, ideal; cultivated, urbane, exquisite, well-bred, trained, polished, well-mannered. —**Ant. 1** unfinished, incomplete, imperfect; begun. **2** green, callow, raw; inexperienced, unskilled; unrefined, inelegant, inartistic; rough, rude, coarse, crude.

finite *adj.* measurable, limited, bounded, countable, circumscribed, terminable, subject to limitations, confined, restricted; not everlasting, temporal, short-lived. —**Ant.** infinite, unlimited, unbounded, boundless, measureless; endless, perpetual.

fire *n.* **1.** conflagration, blaze, flame, bonfire; flash, spark, flare; inferno, holocaust. **2.** ardor, vigor; power, intensity, force, genius, inspiration, imaginativeness, vehemence, spirit, burning passion, fervor, fervency; enthusiasm, eagerness, vivacity, gusto, earnestness; dash, élan, punch, verve, vim; splendor, brilliance, effulgence, luster, radiance. **3.** discharge of firearms, firing; salvo, fusillade, bombardment, volley, cannonade, broadside, enfilade; sniping, sharpshooting. —*v.* **4.** shoot, discharge, project a missile, open fire, bombard, shell, fusillade, enfilade; fire off, make go off, hurl, project, eject. **5.** ignite, kindle, light, set on fire, set fire to, set burning, inflame; burn, catch fire. **6.** arouse, stimulate, rouse, vivify, spark, inspire, animate, excite, inspirit; fill with ardor, inflame, incite, stir, stir up, quicken, instigate, foment, galvanize, trigger. **7.** bake, cook. **8.** dismiss, let go, oust, remove from service, cashier; *Slang* sack, boot, dump, bounce, can, give one his walking papers; depose.

firearm *n.* gun, small arm, sidearm, *Informal* shooting iron; (*variously*) pistol, rifle, shotgun, revolver, machine gun, submachine gun, *Slang* rod, piece, Saturday-night special.

firm[1] *adj.* **1.** stiff, hard, rigid; unbending, unyielding; solid, compressed, dense, compact; rocky, stony, adamantine; steely, flinty. **2.** settled, fixed, definite, established, confirmed; unalterable, indissoluble. **3.** steady, not shaking, stable, fast, secure; rooted, moored, anchored; immovable; close, taut, tight, rigid, inflexible. **4.** resolute, steadfast, determined, unwavering, resolved, staunch, persistent, unflinching, unshaken, unfaltering; earnest, serious, decided, intent, constant, definite, steady; strong-willed, strong-minded, dogged, dead set; tough, obstinate, bent, inflexible, inexorable, *Slang* hard-nosed; grim, tenacious, obdurate; fearless, invincible. —**Ant.** loose, flabby; soft, flaccid, limp, loppy; flimsy, sleazy; shaky, unsteady, unstable; wavering, irresolute, inconstant, unreliable.

firm[2] *n.* company, concern, organization, business, establishment, house; commercial house, partnership, corporation, conglomerate, *Internet Slang* dot-com.

firmament *n.* sky, heavens, vault, welkin, the blue, air, ether, canopy, canopy of heaven; space, outer space, the void, interstellar space, intergalactic space.

first *adj.* **1.** foremost, leading, chief among others, principal, main, prime, head, first-string, ranking, highest; superior, preeminent, supreme, paramount; vital, essential. **2.** earliest, original, premier, eldest; primitive, primal, primeval, primordial, aboriginal; beginning, maiden. **3.** basic, fundamental, elementary, rudimentary, primary, introductory, beginning. —*n.* **4.** beginning, introduction, commencement, start, outset, inception, starting point. —*adv.* **5.** before anything else, to begin with, at the outset, initially; first and foremost. **6.** by preference, by choice, before; rather, sooner, preferably. —**Ant. 1** secondary, subordinate, lesser. **2** later, subsequent.

first-rate *adj.* best, choice, excellent, very good, first-class, prime, finest, superior, ace, elite, outstanding, select, A-one, top-drawer, topflight, topnotch, incomparable, distinguished, exclusive, nonpareil; *Slang* tops, crack; *Brit. Slang* top-hole. —**Ant.** run-of-the-mill, mediocre, ordinary, so-so, indifferent.

fiscal *adj.* financial, monetary, pecuniary, budgetary, economic. —**Syn. Study.** See MONETARY.

fish *v.* **1.** attempt to catch fish, angle, cast; hook, net, troll, trawl, seine. **2.** search, hunt, grope, rummage, ferret, look about, cast about.

fishy *adj. Informal* **1.** doubtful, dubious, improbable; suspicious, suspect, unreliable, questionable; peculiar, strange, odd, weird, queer; extravagant, exaggerated, farfetched; slippery, shady, dishonest, unscrupulous. **2.** glassy-eyed, dull, vacant, expressionless, blank.

fit[1] *adj.* **1.** suitable, good, adapted, appropriate; right, proper, meet, correct; seemly, fitting, becoming, befitting, decorous; pertinent, relevant, applicable, consonant; timely, seasonable; opportune, convenient; apposite, apropos. **2.** qualified, competent, trained, able; capable, capacitated, efficient; prepared, primed, initiated; mature, ripe; ready, eligible. **3.** healthy, hale, hardy, sound, well, in good physical condition, strong, robust, toned up, in trim. **4.** worthy, deserving, suitable, acceptable; good enough, sufficiently virtuous. —*v.* **5.** be suitable for, be adapted to; agree, harmonize, accord; conform, be adapted to; be the right size or shape for, correspond; become, befit; match, equal; coincide, concur. **6.** try on for size, adjust, make suitable, suit, adapt; shape, alter, fashion; graduate, calibrate; correct, rectify. **7.** equip, outfit; prepare, ready, make qualified, qualify, make competent; enable, empower, capacitate, train. —**Ant. 1** unfit, ill-suited, unsuitable, inappropriate; unprepared, ill-fitted, inadequate, improper, unseemly; inexpedient, ill-timed, untimely, amiss.

fit[2] *n.* **1.** epileptic seizure, convulsion, spell; (*variously*) grand mal, petit mal. **2.** spell, sudden acute attack, spasm, paroxysm, seizure, outbreak. **3.** outburst, explosion, burst, access; passing mood, whim, caprice, crotchet, whimsical notion.

fitful *adj.* irregular, intermittent, periodic, sporadic, spasmodic, now-and-then, now-and-again; unsteady, changeable, erratic, fluctuating, uneven, random, variable, convulsive; weak, listless. —**Ant.** constant, steady, incessant; even, equable, regular, uniform; orderly, systematic, methodical; predictable, calculable; changeless, unchanging, immutable.

fitting *adj.* suitable, proper, decorous, seemly, appropriate, apt, befitting, meet, fit, congruous. —**Ant.** unfitting, unsuitable, improper, unseemly, ill-suited.

fix *v.* **1.** secure, fasten, attach, affix, moor, make fast, implant, rivet, anchor, place permanently, connect. **2.** set, settle, determine definitely, decide, establish, stabilize, prescribe. **3.** harden, solidify, make rigid, make firm, become stable, become set; congeal, consolidate. **4.** place, put, impose, affix. **5.** repair, mend, patch up, correct, set right, put to rights, adjust, renovate, put in good condition, rebuild; adjust, regulate. **6.** prepare, make, put together, assemble. **7.** get even with, get revenge on, get back at; *Slang* fix one's wagon, settle one's hash, cook one's goose; retaliate, take action against. —*n.* **8.** predicament, embarrassing situation, plight, difficulty, dilemma, awkward spot, quandary, impasse, ticklish situation; *Slang* spot, jam, pickle, bind, scrape, hot water; muddle, mess, entanglement, involvement.

fixation *n.* obsession, preoccupation, fixed idea; delusion, complex, monomania; quirk, crotchet, fetish.

fixed *adj.* **1.** stationary, immovable, fast, firmly implanted; firm, stable, fastened, set, rooted, motionless, still, rigid. **2.** not varying, not fluctuating, constant, steady; intent, steadily directed, persistent, determined, resolute; unbending, unpliant, inflexible, firm, unwavering. —**Ant.** moving, mobile, wavering, unstable, unsteady, inconstant; bending, pliant; varying.

fixture *n.* **1.** apparatus, appliance, equipment; attachment, appendage, appurtenance, appointment, equipage, paraphernalia. **2.** regular; devotee, habitué; *Informal* familiar sight, old reliable, *Slang* addict.

fizzle *v.* **1.** sputter, hiss; bubble, gurgle, fizz. **2.** *Informal* come to nothing, fail, abort, misfire, fall through, miscarry, come to grief, fall short, miss the mark; *Slang* flop, fizzle out; break down, collapse, founder. —*n.* **3.** hiss, sputter. **4.** failure, washout, disaster, fiasco; *Informal* botch, muddle, mess, flop; *Slang* turkey, bomb, dud, dog.

flabbergast *v.* amaze, confound, astound, astonish, shock, stun, stupefy, *Slang* knock for a loop, stagger, dumbfound, overcome, puzzle, bewilder, render speechless, bowl over, strike dumb.

flabby *adj.* **1.** limp, flaccid, soft, yielding, inelastic; feeble, weak, hanging loosely, slack, floppy, drooping limply; doughy, baggy, spongy. **2.** feeble, enervated; adulterated, emasculated, spiritless, effete, impotent, listless, lame, flimsy. **—Ant. 1** firm, hard, solid; tight, taut, tense; tough, sturdy, strong. **2** plucky, gritty, tenacious.

flag *n.* **1.** banner, emblem, standard, ensign, streamer, pennant, colors; (*in the U.S.*) stars and stripes, Old Glory, stars and bars; (*in Great Britain*) Union Jack. *—v.* **2.** signal, warn, wave. **3.** decline, grow weak, wilt, give way, languish; grow spiritless, fall off in vigor, abate, slump, succumb, subside, sag, pall; fade, grow weary, tire, totter, dodder; faint, sink, ebb, wane, fail. **—Ant. 3** freshen, recover, brace up.

flagrant *adj.* shockingly bad, shameless, brazen, blatant, flaunting, audacious, immodest; glaring, gross, sheer, obvious, crying, arrant, barefaced; notorious, scandalous, conspicuous, outrageous, heinous, monstrous. **—Syn. Study.** FLAGRANT, GLARING, GROSS suggest something offensive that cannot be overlooked. FLAGRANT implies a conspicuous offense so far beyond the limits of decency as to be insupportable: *a flagrant violation of the law.* GLARING emphasizes conspicuousness but lacks the imputation of evil or immorality: *a glaring error by a bank teller.* GROSS suggests a mistake or impropriety of major proportions: *a gross miscarriage of justice.* **—Ant.** minor, venial, mild, insignificant, unimportant, trivial, petty, minimal, forgiveable; inconspicuous, unnoticeable.

flair *n.* bent, knack, talent, aptitude, gift, genius; keen perception, discernment, feel, feeling, touch, ingenuity, faculty, capacity; style, taste; verve, dash, panache.

flake *n.* **1.** flat thin piece, scale, sheet, bit, fleck, shaving, patch. *—v.* **2.** peel off, peel, layer, strip, come off in flakes, scale off, chip off, chip, crumble.

flamboyant *adj.* **1.** ornate, gaudy, garish, florid; baroque, rococo; showy, flashy, ostentatious, *Slang* jazzy. **2.** dashing, colorful, exciting, sensational, theatrical, wild, *Slang* jazzy.

flame *n.* **1.** flare, blaze, fire, burning vapor, light, conflagration; spark, glare, gleam, glow, flash. **2.** ardor, passion, fervor, intensity, fervency, glow, excitement, burning zeal; enthusiasm, warmth, affection. **3.** sweetheart, heartthrob, passion, lover, *Slang* squeeze, main squeeze; girlfriend, lady love, inamorata; boyfriend, beau, swain, suitor, inamorato. **4.** burst into flames, fire, flare, kindle, light, ignite, blaze, burn with a flame; glare, shine brilliantly, flash; flush, redden, blush.

flaming *adj.* **1.** blazing, burning, fiery, afire, ablaze, alight; igneous, inflammable, smoldering, glowing; bright, brilliant, shining. **2.** violent, stormy, ardent, intense, vehement, fervid, fervent, passionate; conspicuous, flagrant, glaring, egregious.

flammable *adj.* inflammable, combustible, igneous, combustive, incendiary. **—Ant.** nonflammable, fireproof.

flank *adj.* **1.** side, haunch, loin, hip. **2.** side, wing, edge, border. *—v.* **3.** line, border, skirt; edge, fringe; lie along, wing; screen, shield, cover.

flap *v.* **1.** wave about, swing loosely, flop, flutter; shake, beat, vibrate, oscillate, agitate, bat, move to and fro, bang. *—n.* **2.** flop, flapping, bang, banging, flutter. **3.** hanging piece, lap, lappet, fly, tab; skirt, apron.

flare *v.* **1.** flame, blaze, burn, gleam, coruscate, glare, glow, incandesce, ignite, flash. **2.** erupt, explode, break out, burst forth, blow up, boil over. **3.** widen, broaden, spread, expand, distend, stretch, dilate.

flash *n.* **1.** burst, streak, blaze, glare, gleam, flare, flame; radiance, coruscation, incandescence, fulmination. **2.** outburst, instance, occurrence, spark, glimmer, touch. **3.** instant, moment, minute, second, split second, trice, twinkling of an eye, blink, shake, wink, *Informal* jif, jiffy. *—v.* **4.** blink, go on and off, flicker, sparkle, glitter; shine, blaze, glare, flame, glow, gleam; scintillate, coruscate; glisten, glimmer.

flashy *adj.* dazzling, flamboyant, showy; smart, sporty; pretentious, gaudy, garish, loud, tawdry, ostentatious, *Slang* jazzy; bedizened, tricked out, tinsel, raffish, vulgar, in bad taste. **—Ant.** plain, modest, simple, natural, unaffected.

flat *adj.* **1.** level, horizontal, smooth; plane, planar, regular, equal, unbroken, flush. **2.** recumbent, prostrate, prone, lying at full length, flush, low, reclining, supine; leveled, laid low. **3.** unqualified, unequivocal, thorough, out-and-out, positive, definite, downright, absolute, complete, total, peremptory; clear, direct, plain, unmistakable. **4.** lacking effervescence; stale, tasteless, insipid, flavorless; dull, vapid, dead, unpalatable. *—n.* **5.** Often **flats.** level land, flat ground, lowlands; open country, prairie, plain;

shallow, shoal, marsh. **6.** blowout, deflated tire, blown-out tire, puncture. —*adv.* **7.** horizontally, levelly, prostrate. **8.** exactly, precisely. —**Ant. 1** uneven, rough, rugged, broken, irregular, scabrous, hilly, rolling; slanting, sloping; vertical, upright, perpendicular. **4** bubbly, effervescent, sparkling, fizzy; flavorful, flavorsome, tasty, savory; palatable.

flatten *v.* **1.** make flat, smooth, level; plane, even; press down, compress; deflate. **2.** knock down, floor, fell, ground, prostrate, *Slang* deck; crush, defeat, overwhelm, overcome.

flatter *v.* **1.** overpraise, compliment, praise lavishly, gratify by praise; eulogize, adulate, laud, extol, panegyrize, honor; court, cajole, blandish, beguile, wheedle; curry favor with, cotton up to, truckle to, toady; *Informal* sweet-talk, *Slang* butter up, soft-soap, bootlick, brown-nose. **2.** represent too favorably, become, show off well. **3.** delude, deceive, mislead, fool.

flatterer *n.* yes man, fawner, sycophant, wheedler, truckler, toady, eulogist; *Slang* apple-polisher, bootlicker; lickspittle.

flattery *n.* excessive compliment, false praise, *Slang* snow job; sycophancy, toadyism, toadying, obsequiousness, fawning, wheedling, servility; cajolery, blandishment, soft soap, truckling, jollying, blarney; adulation, eulogy, panegyric, encomium.

flaunt *v.* **1.** show off, parade, exhibit, brandish, vaunt, air, make a show of, advertise, broadcast, strut; boast, brag. **2.** flourish, brandish, wave, sport, blazon, dangle. —**Ant.** conceal, hide, screen; cloak, mask, disguise, dissemble.

flavor *n.* **1.** characteristic taste, savor; tang, piquancy; relish, gusto; seasoning, flavoring; lacing. **2.** subtle quality, distinctive character, attribute, essence, soul, spirit; aspect, style, tenor, aura, ambience, tone. —*v.* **3.** give flavor to, season, spice, lace; imbue, infuse, instill. —**Ant. 1** tastelessness, flatness; odorlessness, scentlessness; insipidity, vapidity, mawkishness.

flaw *n.* **1.** defect, blemish, fault, imperfection, marring feature, weakness, weak spot, fallacy, shortcoming, frailty; error, mistake; deformity, injury, defacement, disfigurement; spot, speck; blot, smudge, stain, blotch; failing, foible, vice. —*v.* **2.** mar, impair, harm; weaken, compromise, detract from, make defective, blemish, deface, injure, disfigure. —**Syn. Study. 1** See DEFECT, FAULT.

flawless *adj.* faultless, errorless, impeccable, perfect; sound, without blemish, immaculate. —**Ant.** defective, flawed, marred, impaired.

flay *v.* **1.** skin, scalp, peel, decorticate, pare, bark; strip, fleece, plunder. **2.** chastise severely, castigate, excoriate, censure harshly; assail, scold, rebuke, upbraid, punish.

fleck *n.* **1.** spot, patch of color, mark, speck, flake, freckle, dot, speckle; mole, blemish; small bit, drop, jot, tittle, particle. —*v.* **2.** speckle, mark with flecks, spot, flake, spatter, dapple, bespeckle, bespot, dot, besprinkle; streak, stipple, mottle.

fledgling *n.* inexperienced person, novice, beginner, tyro, freshman, apprentice; *Informal* greenhorn, tenderfoot.

flee *v.* **1.** escape from, run away from, get away from, hasten away from, make one's escape from; make a getaway, take to one's heels, take flight, abscond, skip, fly the coop, cut and run, *Slang* split; decamp, desert, make off, hasten off, speed off, fly away; vanish, disappear. **2.** evade, avoid, shun, wriggle out of; elude, dodge.

fleet *n.* **1.** naval force, navy, naval division, group of warships, *Archaic* armada; flotilla, squadron. **2.** large group, number, array, band, squadron. —*adj.* **3.** swift, rapid, speedy, fast, swift-footed, fast of foot, light-footed, nimble-footed, nimble; hurried, quick, expeditious, hasty, cursory; transient, brief, evanescent; sudden, instantaneous, momentary; short, transitory. —**Ant. 3** deliberate, slow, laggard, tardy.

fleeting *adj.* swiftly passing, brief, flitting, passing, momentary, evanescent, short-lived, quick; fugitive, transitory, transient, fugacious, ephemeral, temporary, temporal; perishable, impermanent; precarious, unenduring. —**Ant.** lasting, permanent, enduring, imperishable, durable, long-lived.

flesh *n.* **1.** muscular tissue, soft tissue of a body, muscle and fat, brawn; meat, animal food; fat, fatness. **2.** body, physical nature, physique, flesh and blood, materiality; strength, vigor, power, muscular energy, animal force; carnality, sensuality, bodily desire. **3.** mankind, humanity, human race, man, people, living creatures. **4.** pulp, substance, meat, edible part. —*v.* **5.** fatten, fill out, make plump, become plump. **6.** fill out, characterize fully, realize, individualize, particularize, give depth to, embody.

fleshy *adj.* plump, corpulent, obese, fat, beefy, overweight, stout, chubby, stocky, portly, thickset, paunchy, potbellied, well-padded, tubby, roly-poly. —**Ant.** thin, skinny, underweight, scrawny, lean.

flexible *adj.* **1.** easily bent, elastic, resilient, springy, extensible, bendable, ductile, plastic, malleable, tractable, pliable, pliant; supple, limber, lithe, soft. **2.** adaptable, changeable, yielding, responsive, manageable, malleable, compliant, complaisant; docile, submissive, easily managed; amiable, genial; mild, gentle. **—Ant. 1** inflexible, stiff, rigid, inelastic. **2** intractable, unyielding, inexorable; absolute, dogmatic.

flicker *v.* **1.** flutter; glow, glisten, glitter, glimmer, shimmer; flare, blaze, flash; sparkle, coruscate, wave to and fro, quiver, flit, vibrate; waver, quaver, wriggle, tremble; undulate, oscillate; shake, waggle; throb, pulsate; sway; fluctuate, vacillate. **—***n.* **2.** unsteady light, glitter, flare, gleam, spark, flash. **3.** small amount, vestige, modicum, scintilla, flame, spark, glimmer, glint, trace.

flight *n.* **1.** air travel, flying, winging, soaring; aeronautics, plane trip; space travel. **2.** flock, flying group, squadron, wing. **3.** rush, swift movement, quick passage. **4.** hasty departure, running away, rout, fleeing, retreat, escape, withdrawal; exodus, hegira.

flighty *adj.* unstable, frivolous, irresponsible, fickle, impractical, whimsical, capricious, changeable, mercurial, inconstant, volatile, quixotic; scatterbrained, harebrained, dizzy, reckless, thoughtless, light-headed, giddy; irresolute, indecisive.

flimsy *adj.* **1.** unsubstantial, thin, slight, frail, fragile, delicate; diaphanous, sheer, filmy, gossamer, gauzy, cobwebby; shoddy, ill-made, jerry-built; ramshackle, shabby, sleazy, dilapidated, cheap, trashy. **2.** feeble, weak, inadequate; poor, worthless, foolish; trivial, trifling, petty, frivolous; shallow, superficial. **—Ant. 1** stout, sturdy, strong; heavy, weighty. **2** sound, cogent; substantial, solid.

flinch *v.* **1.** wince, draw back, jerk back, shrink, recoil, start, cringe, blench, shy, shudder, falter, shiver, quiver, quake, quaver, cower, quail; grimace, contort; retreat, fly, give ground. **—***n.* **2.** start, blench, wince, jerk, shiver, grimace.

fling *v.* **1.** throw with force, hurl, heave, pitch, toss, cast, dash, let fly, precipitate, propel, sling; eject, emit, expel. **—***n.* **2.** spree, bit of fun; *Slang* ball, bash, lark. **3.** attempt, trial, go, try.

flip *v.* **1.** toss, flick, throw, spin. **2.** turn, thumb, turn over. **—***n.* **3.** tap, flick, fillip; toss, throw, spin.

flippant *adj.* impudent, brash, impertinent, disrespectful, saucy, insolent, pert, rude; *Informal* cheeky, flip, lippy; trifling, frivolous; presumptuous, bumptious. **—Ant.** respectful, considerate.

flirt *v.* **1.** toy, play at love, dally, trifle in love, tease, *Slang* make eyes at. **2.** toy, play, trifle; entertain an idea. **—***n.* **3.** flirter, tease, heartbreaker; (*fem.*) coquette, vamp.

flit *v.* dart, skim, move lightly and swiftly, flicker, flitter, flutter; fly rapidly, wing, hasten, speed, scurry, scud.

float *v.* **1.** rest on water; be poised in air; drift, hover, waft, slide, move gently, bob, be buoyant, be buoyed up; levitate. **2.** make buoyant, buoy up, bear up, hold up, keep afloat, give support to; launch. **—Ant. 1, 2** sink, settle, go to the bottom, submerge.

flock *n.* **1.** herd, pack, bunch, group, clique, troop, drove, multitude; band, company, bevy, coterie, collection, aggregation; brood (of young birds), school (of fish), swarm (of insects), pride (of lions), pod (of seals or whales), covey (of game birds), gaggle (of geese). **2.** crowd, mob, gang, throng, crush, large number; gathering, assemblage; congregation. **—***v.* **3.** go, run, gather, assemble, muster, converge, swarm, cluster, congregate, herd; crowd, surge, mass, throng, huddle, stream, rush.

flog *v.* whip, lash, thrash, beat, horsewhip, scourge, flail, flagellate, drub; strike, smite, lambaste, cuff; club, maul, cudgel; cane, birch, paddle, switch; strap, hide.

flood *n.* **1.** inundation, great overflowing of water, overflow; deluge, cloudburst, downpour. **2.** torrent, stream, flow, outpouring, tide, cascade, downpour, deluge, current, gush. **—***v.* **3.** inundate, deluge, submerge, cover with a flood, wash over, fill to overflowing, flow over. **4.** oversupply, overwhelm, glut, saturate, inundate, deluge; shower, drench. **—Ant. 1** drought, scarcity, lack, shortage, subsidence, stoppage.

floor *n.* **1.** bottom surface, bottom, flooring, base, ground; pavement, parquet. **2.** story, stage, level; tier, deck. **3.** base rate, base, minimum, bottom. **—***v.* **4.** knock down, ground, fell, level, prostrate, *Slang* deck.

flop *v.* **1.** move clumsily or heavily; fall heavily, tumble, topple, drop, plop, flap awkwardly. **2.** *Informal* fail, close, close down, go under, shutter, fold, wash out, *Slang* bomb, lay an egg. **—***n.* **3.** failure, fiasco, disaster, disappointment, labor in vain, washout; *Slang* fizzle, bust, bomb, turkey. **—Ant. 2** succeed, triumph, make a hit; flourish, prosper. **3** success, triumph, hit.

floral *adj.* of flowers, flowery, blossomy, bloomy; botanical, herbaceous; verdant.

florid *adj.* **1.** ruddy, rosy, reddish, high-colored, rubicund; ruddy-faced, red-faced, flushed, sanguine, red-complexioned; inflamed, blowsy, hectic.

2. flowery, showy, ornamented, elaborate, ornate, ostentatious, gaudy, highly embellished, flamboyant, high-flown, grandiloquent; rococo, baroque. **—Ant. 1** pallid, anemic, bloodless. **2** unadorned, bare, prosaic, matter-of-fact.

flotsam *n.* floating wreckage, floating goods, debris; castoffs, odds and ends, refuse, garbage, junk.

flounce[1] *v.* **1.** sashay, strut, hurl oneself, fling oneself, storm, stamp, stomp; bounce, spring, bound; trip, skip, prance, caper, gambol. *—n.* **2.** flouncing movement, bound, spring, leap.

flounce[2] *n.* **1.** ruffle, frill, ornament, furbelow; valance, fringe, trimming; hem, edging, skirting. *—v.* **2.** trim, ruffle, frill, ornament, fringe, hem, edge.

flounder *v.* **1.** struggle, move unsteadily, proceed clumsily, stumble, stagger; toss about, plunge clumsily; wallow, welter; lurch, totter, flop, shamble, tumble; limp, hobble. **2.** falter, waver, hesitate, be uncertain, halt; lose oneself, miss one's way, blunder, muddle, wander aimlessly.

flourish *v.* **1.** prosper, thrive, grow, succeed, turn out well, fare well, be successful; get ahead, get on, rise in the world, go up in the world, *Informal* make one's pile; have a run of luck, feather one's nest; bloom, blossom, flower, burgeon. **2.** *—n.* **3.** waving, shaking, brandishing, agitation, wielding, twist, swinging, thrashing; ostentatious display, show, parade, ostentation; swagger, strut, swashbuckling; pomp, glitter, splash, dash. **4.** embellishment, decorative figure, curl, curlicue, decoration; musical ornament, turn, grace note, appoggiatura, cadenza. **5.** bravado, bluff, braggadocio, boasting, vaunting; rant, fustian, hot air, grandiloquence, magniloquence. **6.** trumpet call, fanfare, fanfaronade. **—Syn. Study. 1** See SUCCEED. **—Ant. 1** decline, fail, fade.

flout *v.* scorn, show contempt for, scoff at, spurn, laugh at, jeer at, gibe at, sneer at, defy, treat with disdain, mock, poke fun at; twit, taunt, chaff, rag, insult. **—Ant.** revere; regard, respect, esteem.

flow *v.* **1.** course, roll along, move in a stream, run, pour, stream, cascade; rush, gush, well out, issue, effuse; discharge, debouch, drain; surge, deluge, swirl; filter, seep; move gracefully, glide, sweep, pass, drift, float. **2.** abound, be full of, overflow, run, be copious. *—n.* **3.** stream, course, torrent, flood; current, tide; rapids, millrace. **4.** outpouring, stream, cascade, effusion, outflow, flux, tide, discharge; efflux, effluence, emanation, debouchment; spurt, spout, gush, jet; train, succession, sequence, progression; abundance, plenty, plethora.

flower *n.* **1.** blossom, bloom, posy; floret, floweret, bud; nosegay, bouquet, floral tribute. **2.** best, pick, choicest part, finest part, cream; elite, aristocracy. *—v.* **3.** bloom, produce blossoms, produce flowers, blossom, open, be in flower, blow; burgeon; bud; develop fully, mature, ripen, flourish, prosper. **—Ant. 2** dregs, residue.

flowery *adj.* **1.** covered with blossoms, flowering, burgeoning, blooming, blossoming; florescent, efflorescent; decorated with flowers, floral. **2.** ornate, ornamented, embellished, fancy, florid; euphuistic, rhetorical, figurative, grandiloquent, magniloquent, bombastic, pretentious. **—Syn. Study. 2** See BOMBASTIC.

fluctuate *v.* **1.** rise and fall, change often, vary irregularly, shift, bob up and down, wobble, veer; come and go, ebb and flow. **2.** waver, vacillate, sway, oscillate, undulate, swing, be irresolute, be unsettled, hesitate, be undetermined, falter, shift, alternate, vary, be inconstant; dawdle, dillydally. **—Ant.** hold fast, persist, stand fast, stand firm, remain steady.

fluent *adj.* able to speak readily, ready in speech; glib, smooth-spoken, vocal, voluble, eloquent, articulate, smooth-tongued, silver-tongued; effortless, facile; effusive, garrulous, talkative; self-assured, well-versed. **—Syn. Study.** FLUENT, GLIB, VOLUBLE may refer to an easy flow of words or to a person able to communicate with ease. FLUENT suggests the easy and ready flow of an accomplished speaker or writer; it is usually a term of commendation: *a fluent orator.* GLIB implies an excessive fluency and lack of sincerity or profundity; it suggests talking smoothly and hurriedly to cover up or deceive: *a glib salesperson.* VOLUBLE implies the copious and often rapid flow of words characteristic of a person who loves to talk and will spare the audience no details: *a voluble gossip.* **—Ant.** hesitant, stammering, halting, tongue-tied.

fluffy *adj.* soft and light as fluff, feathery, downy; fuzzy, fleecy, woolly, nappy; light and airy.

fluid *n.* **1.** liquid, solution. *—adj.* **2.** liquid, liquefied, of fluids, watery. **3.** flexible, adaptable, adjustable; changeable, indefinite; unstable, unfixed, unsettled, shifting; floating, liquid, flowing, fluent. **—Ant. 1** solid. **2** solid, hard, firm. **3** fixed, settled, definite.

fluke *n.* accident, unlikely event, quirk of fate, chance, mischance, hap, vicissitude, freak; stroke of luck, piece of luck, windfall, miracle.

flurry *n.* **1.** sudden wind, gust, windy blast, breeze, puff, squall; shower, light snowfall. **2.** bustle, sudden excitement, commotion, fuss, ado, fluster, flutter, stir, pother; nervous hurry, agitation, turbulence, tumult, disturbance, perturbation, discomposure, restlessness, fidgets, confusion, trepidation; fever, heat, flush; haste, hurry-scurry. —*v.* **3.** make nervous, put into a flurry, fluster, agitate, disquiet, disturb, perturb; rattle, confuse, discompose, disconcert, flutter, confound; panic, alarm.

flush[1] *n.* **1.** blush, rosiness, rosy glow; bloom, tinge of color, high color, tint; redness, ruddiness. **2.** cleansing flow, watery gush, wash, rinse, swab, spray, douche, deluge. **3.** rush of emotion, impulse, access; tremor, flutter, quiver; thrill, shock; jubilation, exultation. **4.** bloom, glow, glowing, strength, freshness. —*v.* **5.** blush, redden, color, grow crimson, glow. **6.** cleanse by flooding, wash out, flood, douche; rinse, scour, scrub, sponge, swab; drench, dampen, moisten. **7.** animate, elate, make proud, puff up; thrill, excite.

flush[2] *adj.* **1.** even, level, on the same plane. —*adv.* **2.** squarely, in contact with, so as to touch.

fluster *v.* **1.** disconcert, ruffle, make nervous, disturb, perturb, upset, agitate, shake, startle, discompose, discomfit, befuddle, muddle, discombobulate, confuse; perplex, daze, bewilder, throw off balance. —*n.* **2.** nervous excitement, confusion, flutter, agitation, turmoil, commotion, hubbub, flurry, dither, discomposure, discomfiture, bewilderment.

flutter *v.* **1.** wave, toss about, flap, flitter, flit; throb, tremble, shake, pulsate; bob, wobble, quiver; palpitate. **2.** flit, flitter; wing, soar. —*n.* **3.** agitation, vibration, flapping, beating; quiver, tremble, tremor. **4.** twitter, fluster; confusion, flurry, perturbation; hurry, hurry-scurry, commotion; thrill, sensation, tingling; ripple, stir.

flux *n.* **1.** flow, current, course, flood, stream, tide; motion. **2.** continuous change, fluctuation, alteration, modification; motion, unrest; shifting, transition, mutation, transformation.

fly *v.* **1.** travel through the air; pilot a plane; wing, take wing, take the air, take off, soar, glide, sail, coast, swoop. **2.** wave, flutter, float, undulate, flap, vibrate, hover, display in the air, hoist in the air. **3.** move quickly, pass rapidly, go suddenly. **4.** flee, run away, hasten away, make one's escape, make one's getaway, take flight, take to one's heels, hasten, hustle, hurry, *Informal* skip, *Slang* split.

fly-by-night *adj.* undependable, untrustworthy, untrusty, unreliable, irresponsible, unstable, disreputable; shady, shifty, crooked, dishonest. —**Ant.** honest, reliable, dependable, trustworthy, honorable, responsible.

foam *n.* mass of tiny bubbles, froth, head, fizz, sparkle, effervescence, bubbling; scum, spume; suds, lather.

foamy *adj.* frothy, bubbling, effervescent, sparkling, fizzy; lathery.

focus *n.* **1.** focal length, focal point, point of concentration, converging point. **2.** center, hub, middle; meeting place, gathering place, headquarters, rallying point; spotlight, limelight; rendezvous, trysting place; haunt, retreat, resort; heart, core, nucleus. —*v.* **3.** bring into focus, adjust, center; converge, bring to a point, concentrate; fix, center, direct, aim, bring to bear.

fodder *n.* feed, food, silage, forage, provender, rations. —**Syn. Study.** See FEED.

foe *n.* enemy, adversary, opponent, foeman, antagonist; attacker, assailant; rival, competitor, contender, disputant, combatant. —**Ant.** friend, comrade, companion; ally, confederate.

fog *n.* **1.** thick mist, haze, smog, murkiness, cloudiness, brume; *Slang* soup, pea soup. **2.** daze, haze, stupor, trance, bewilderment. —*v.* **3.** cover with fog, enclose in mist or fog. **4.** bewilder, muddle, daze, confuse, perplex, obscure, dim, cloud, darken. —**Ant. 2** clarity, comprehension, perspicuity. **3** clear, brighten, clarify, purge, purify.

foggy *adj.* **1.** misty, hazy, brumous; clouded, cloudy, beclouded, filmy, overcast, murky, smoggy, *Slang* soupy; vaporous, nebulous. **2.** unclear, confused, vague, fuzzy, musty, cloudy, dim, obscure, indistinct, *Slang* spacey; resembling fog, shadowy, dusky, dark. —**Ant. 2** lucid, distinct, decisive, accurate, clear, bright; shrewd, sharp; alert, alive, awake.

foible *n.* fault, minor fault, weakness, shortcoming, frailty, failing, minor vice, imperfection, weak point, weak side, infirmity, defect, deficiency; quirk, kink, whimsy, crotchet. —**Syn. Study.** See FAULT. —**Ant.** strength, forte, virtue, perfection; crime, atrocity; sin, enormity, abomination.

foil[1] *v.* frustrate, balk, thwart; hinder, prevent, check, nip. —**Ant.** advance, further, forward; endorse, promote, abet, sustain, foment, incite, instigate.

foil[2] *n.* **1.** leaf, flake, lamina, sheet, film, wafer. **2.** contrast, antithesis, complement, supplement, match, counterpart, correlative, backdrop, setoff. —*v.* **3.** set off, enhance.

foist *v.* pass off, palm off, impose, unload, get rid of.

fold[1] *v.* **1.** double, crease, pleat, corrugate, lap; gather, tuck, dog-ear, pucker;

wrinkle, rumple, crumple; crinkle, crimp, curl. **2.** wrap, wrap up, envelop, enfold, encase. **3.** embrace, embosom, clasp, enfold, entwine, hug. —*n.* **4.** gather, tuck, pleat, layer, crimp, crinkle, pucker, ruffle, flounce, furrow, overlap. **5.** crease, folding, doubling, bend. —**Ant. 1, 2** unfold, unwrap, uncover; expose, exhibit, disclose, reveal.

fold[2] *n.* **1.** pen, enclosure, corral, close, yard, sty; barnyard, stockade, compound. **2.** religious life, straight and narrow; the church, congregation, flock, parish, sect, group, community.

foliage *n.* leaves, foliation, leafage, verdure.

folklore *n.* legends, lore, traditions, folk tales, fables, myths.

folks *n. pl.* **1.** people, the public, everyone. **2.** parents, family, family members, relatives, kinsfolk, kinfolk, kith and kin, kinsmen, blood relations.

follow *v.* **1.** come after, go behind, tread on the heels of, walk in the steps of, tread in the rear of, proceed in the wake of; bring up the rear. **2.** succeed, come next, come after, ensue, result; replace, supplant, take the place of, step into the shoes of. **3.** accept as an authority, give allegiance to; follow the example of, emulate, imitate, copy, take after. **4.** obey, heed, act in accordance with, comply with, observe, mind, conform to, be guided by; notice, watch, regard, note. **5.** pursue, chase, go after, run after; track, stalk, trail, trace, hunt; *Informal* shadow, tail, dog, hound; attend, accompany. **6.** emulate, cherish, strive after, aim at; cultivate. **7.** take up, engage in, practice, carry on; be concerned with, attend to, prosecute. **8.** understand, grasp, comprehend, catch on; keep up with. —**Syn. Study. 2** FOLLOW, ENSUE, RESULT, SUCCEED imply coming after something else, in a natural sequence. FOLLOW is the general word: *We must wait to see what follows. A detailed account follows.* ENSUE implies a logical sequence, what might be expected normally to come after a given act, cause, etc.: *When the power lines were cut, a paralysis of transportation ensued.* RESULT emphasizes the connection between an effect, consequence, or outcome and a given cause or event: *confusion resulting from unclear instructions.* SUCCEED implies coming after in time, particularly coming into a title, office, etc.: *The oldest son succeeded his father as head of the company.* —**Ant. 1** precede, lead, guide; pilot, steer. **3** forsake, desert, abandon. **4** disobey, ignore, flout. **5** elude, evade, escape. **7** avoid, shun; quit, abandon, renounce, give up.

follower *n.* **1.** pursuer, stalker, chaser; *Slang* tail, shadow; hunter. **2.** disciple, adherent, apostle, proselyte, convert; devotee, admirer, fan, partisan, supporter, advocate; pupil, protégé. **3.** attendant, servant, servitor, retainer, dependent; henchman, accessory, satellite, stooge; hanger-on, parasite, toady, sycophant. —**Syn. Study. 2** FOLLOWER, ADHERENT, PARTISAN refer to someone who demonstrates allegiance to a person, doctrine, cause, or the like. FOLLOWER often has an implication of personal relationship or of deep devotion to authority or to a leader: *a follower of Gandhi.* ADHERENT, a more formal word, suggests active championship of a person or point of view: *an adherent of monetarism.* PARTISAN suggests firm loyalty, as to a party, cause, or person, that is based on emotions rather than on reasoning: *a partisan of the conservatives.* —**Ant. 2** leader, teacher, guru; enemy, foe, antagonist, dissenter; rival, opponent, contender, detractor.

following *n.* **1.** audience, public, patronage, body of followers, attendance, clientele; partisans, adherents; suite, retinue, train, entourage. —*adj.* **2.** next, succeeding, subsequent, ensuing; successive, consecutive; consequent, sequential. **3.** ensuing, subsequent, below, now to be mentioned, coming next.

folly *n.* **1.** foolishness, senselessness, idiocy, brainlessness, imbecility, inanity, asininity; fatuousness, silliness, doltishness, irrationality. **2.** imprudence, mistake, indiscretion; foolishness, frivolity, absurdity, tomfoolery, nonsense, giddiness, levity, trifling. —**Ant. 1** wisdom, prudence, sound judgment, good sense; sobriety, sober-mindedness, levelheadedness; sanity, rationality, lucidity.

foment *v.* stir up, incite, foster, promote, instigate, provoke, urge, excite, stimulate, galvanize, foster; rouse, arouse, kindle, inflame, spur, goad, agitate; irritate, aggravate, exacerbate, quicken, fan the fire, fan into flame, blow the coals. —**Ant.** quell, suppress, repress, quench; check, curb, restrain; allay, discourage, destroy, extinguish, extirpate.

fond *adj.* **1.** having a liking for, enamored, addicted to, crazy about. **2.** loving, tender, affectionate, amorous, devoted, passionate, impassioned, ardent, enamored, infatuated, sentimental, desirous; doting, indulgent, overaffectionate, foolishly loving, overfond. **3.** cherished, held dear, preserved, harbored, sustained; naive, somewhat foolish. —**Ant. 1** averse, indifferent. **2** unconcerned, aloof; unloving, unaffectionate, undemonstrative; strong-minded, rational, austere.

fondle *v.* caress, stroke, pet, touch fondly; cuddle, hug, embrace, nestle, fold in one's arms, clasp to one's bosom; nuzzle, spoon, bill and coo, *Slang* smooch, make out. **—Ant.** worry, annoy, chafe, irritate; ruffle, tease, heckle, badger, bait; torment, aggravate.

fondness *n.* **1.** tenderness, affection, attachment, devotion, care; love, amorousness, desire, passion, ardor. **2.** partiality, predilection, penchant, preference, inclination, propensity, bent, desire, fancy, liking; weakness, susceptibility. **—Ant. 1** antagonism, hostility, antipathy; hatred, contempt, loathing; harshness, brutality. **2** dislike, aversion, repulsion, revulsion.

food *n.* **1.** foodstuffs, provisions, rations, comestibles, victuals, viands, provender, eatables, edibles, nourishment, nurture, nutrition, sustenance, subsistence; *Slang* grub, chow; board. **2.** fodder, forage, feed, silage, provender; pasture, pasturage.

fool *n.* **1.** stupid person, idiot, dolt, blockhead, bonehead, simpleton, lunkhead, nitwit, half-wit, dummy, imbecile, moron, nincompoop, dunderhead, numskull, ignoramus, ass, dunce, ninny, oaf, clod, chump, goose, *Slang* airhead, meathead; *German* dummkopf, jester, clown, buffoon, dunce, merry-andrew, stooge; harlequin, Punchinello, Pierrot, Scaramouch. *—v.* **2.** trick, deceive, make a fool of, dupe, flimflam, hoodwink, cheat, defraud, hoax, bilk, fleece, gull, *Slang* con, rip off; beguile, bamboozle, cozen, humbug, diddle. **3.** joke, jest, play the fool, cut capers, play the monkey, frolic, cut up; pretend, feign, make believe, tease. **—Ant. 1** genius, wise man, savant, sage, pundit, guru; adept, expert, scholar, master.

foolhardy *adj.* rash, reckless, incautious, impulsive, impetuous, imprudent, daredevil, madcap, hotheaded, harebrained, headstrong, brash, hasty; heedless, careless, thoughtless. **—Ant.** wary, cautious, circumspect; prudent, careful, heedful, mindful, watchful, alert; calculating, shrewd, farsighted, judicious.

foolish *adj.* unwise, imprudent, ill-considered, indiscreet, ill-advised, incautious, short-sighted, irresponsible; unintelligent, absurd, fatuous, inane, witless, senseless; stupid, half-witted, brainless, boneheaded, silly, simple-minded; moronic, asinine, idiotic, imbecilic; preposterous, ridiculous, ludicrous. **—Syn. Study.** FOOLISH, FATUOUS, INANE imply weakness of intellect and lack of judgment. FOOLISH implies lack of common sense or good judgment or, sometimes, weakness of mind: *a foolish decision; a foolish child.* FATUOUS implies being not only foolish, dull, and vacant in mind, but complacent and highly self-satisfied as well: *a fatuous grin.* INANE suggests a lack of content, meaning, or purpose: *inane conversation about the weather.* **—Ant.** intelligent, bright, smart; quick-witted, brilliant, sane, rational, sensible; wise, sage, sagacious, sapient; judicious, prudent, circumspect, cautious; clear-sighted, perspicacious, strong-minded, sound; clever, calculating, sharp.

foolishness *n.* imprudence, folly, extravagance, irresponsibility, indiscretion; absurdity, preposterousness, ridiculousness, asininity; injudiciousness, senselessness, witlessness, brainlessness, unwisdom; childishness, silliness, puerility; stupidity, fatuousness, idiocy, lunacy, imbecility.

foot *n.* **1.** terminal part of the leg, lower extremity; *Slang* tootsy, dog; (of animals) hoof, paw, trotter, pad. **2.** foot soldiers, infantry. **3.** base, lower part, bottom, foundation.

foothold *n.* footing, grip, hold, purchase, toehold; firm place, stable position, firm footing, support.

foot-loose *adj.* free, unattached, uncommitted, unencumbered, fancy-free, carefree.

fop *n.* dandy, coxcomb, dude, popinjay, beau, Beau Brummel, swell, prettyboy, fashion plate, silk stocking.

foppish *adj.* dandyish, foplike, showy, ostentatious, dandified; gaudy, ornate, overelaborate; vain, affected, finical. **—Ant.** unassuming, modest, unostentatious, unpretentious, unaffected; dowdy, seedy, slovenly, tacky; clownish, gauche, yokelish, rustic, provincial, hayseed, cornball.

forage *n.* **1.** fodder, feed, provender, silage; food, provisions; pasture, pasturage. **2.** search for provisions, foray. *—v.* **3.** search, rummage, seek, hunt, explore, look about, cast about; scavenge, scrounge, come up with; raid, strip of supplies, plunder, despoil, ravage. **—Syn. Study. 1** See FEED.

foray *n.* **1.** raid, sudden attack, invasion, depredation, incursion, inroad; sally, thrust; expedition, venture. *—v.* **2.** plunder, pillage, ravage, raid; invade, attack, make an incursion.

forbear *v.* **1.** refrain, desist, abstain, do without, hold back, give up; eschew, renounce, forgo, abnegate, discontinue, leave off, stop, cease, quit, break off. **2.** restrain oneself, hold back, show self-control, be patient, be tolerant, tolerate, show indulgence; suffer, endure, bear.

forbearance *n.* patience, leniency, resignation, tolerance, indulgence, self-restraint, command of temper, endurance, longanimity; mildness, meekness, submission; mercy, mercifulness, clemency, pity, pardon; moderation, abstinence, temperance. —**Ant.** anger, impatience, intolerance.

forbid *v.* prohibit, not allow, command not to, order not to, interdict, enjoin, proscribe; ban, veto, taboo, bar, exclude, disallow; hinder, prevent, render impossible, preclude, obviate, obstruct, inhibit, impede; oppose, gainsay; refuse, restrain, reject. —**Ant.** permit, allow, let, suffer; authorize, bid, license; approve, sanction, endorse; order, command.

forbidding *adj.* disagreeable, unpleasant, dour, inhospitable, unapproachable, unfriendly; dangerous-looking, sinister, ominous, grim, threatening, prohibitive, prohibitory; ugly, repellent, odious, offensive, horrible, repulsive, abhorrent, hideous. —**Ant.** attractive, alluring, inviting.

force *n.* **1.** energy, power, potency, vigor, strength; vim, vitality, animation; effectiveness, efficacy; attraction, magnetism, charisma. **2.** significance, meaning, value, import, weight, weightiness, signification; effect, impact, clout; cogency, validity, emphasis. **3.** power, might, strength, potency, pressure, energy, momentum, stress, impact, puissance, stamina. **4.** coercion, constraint, duress, compulsion, enforcement; violence. **5.** group, body, team, unit, division, squad, gang, crew; army, corps, detachment, squadron, battalion. —*v.* **6.** oblige, compel, push, make necessary, necessitate, require, constrain, enjoin, make, impel, drive, overpower; persuade, induce. **7.** thrust, propel, push, press, drive, coerce, urge, impel; impose, intrude, obtrude. **8.** obtain by force, pull, wrest, squeeze, pry, wrench, drag; coerce, extort; coax, elicit. **9.** break, break open, use violence on. —**Ant. 1** weakness, frailty; ineffectiveness, inefficiency, inefficacy.

forced *adj.* **1.** enforced, compelled, coerced, involuntary, unwilling, obliged, obligatory, required, constrained, compulsory, binding, mandatory; slave, enslaved, impressed. **2.** strained, labored, grudging, not natural; artificial, insincere, mannered, affected. —**Ant.. 2** easy, natural, simple, unforced, unpretending.

forceful *adj.* powerful, strong, full of force, puissant, dynamic, intense, vigorous, potent, energetic, emphatic; impressive, effective, vivid, pithy, valid, cogent; robust, virile. —**Ant.** feeble, weak, spent, exhausted.

fore *adj.* front, forward, frontal, headmost, anterior. —**Ant.** rear, aft, posterior, back, hindmost.

forebear Also **forbear** *n.* ancestor, forefather, progenitor, antecedent, forerunner; procreator, begetter.

foreboding *n.* premonition, presentiment, prescience, apprehension; omen, prognostic, forewarning, foreshadowing, intuition, augury, portent; dread, boding; misgiving.

forecast *v.* **1.** predict, prognosticate, project; prophesy, augur, foresee; expect, anticipate, calculate, extrapolate; envision, envisage, divine; foretell, presage, portend, foreknow. —*n.* **2.** prediction, prognostication, prophecy, prognosis, outlook; projection, foreknowledge, precognition, prevision, prescience, presentiment; presage, augury; anticipation, conjecture. —**Syn. Study. 1** See PREDICT.

forefather *n.* ancestor, forebear, progenitor, primogenitor, antecedent; patriarch, forerunner, precursor; originator, begetter, procreator, author, father. —**Ant.** descendant, progeny, issue, child.

forefront *n.* lead, head, vanguard, position of prominence, fore; public attention, widespread acceptance, fame, celebrity.

foreign *adj.* **1.** from another land, alien, not domestic, not native; imported, introduced; strange, exotic, outlandish; distant, remote; unfamiliar, unknown; heathenish, barbarous. **2.** extraneous, extrinsic, unconnected, unrelated; irregular, unusual, uncharacteristic, inappropriate, antipathetic, inconsistent, incongruous, incompatible, inconsonant; not pertinent, irrelevant, inapplicable, beside the point, inadmissible. —**Ant. 1** domestic, native. **2** relevant, pertinent, applicable; intrinsic, characteristic; congenial, agreeable, suited.

foreigner *n.* alien, outlander, nonnative; immigrant, newcomer, émigré, outsider, stranger; barbarian, pagan. —**Syn. Study.** See STRANGER. —**Ant.** native, citizen, aborigine.

foreknowledge *n.* prior knowledge, advance notice; foresight, foresightedness; clairvoyance, second sight, precognition, prescience, intuition, prevision; presentiment, anticipation, apprehension, premonition.

foreman *n.* manager, overseer, supervisor, crew leader, chief workman, boss, coordinator, superintendent, (*fem.*) forewoman; spokesman, chairman, president, presiding juryman.

foremost *adj.* principal, leading, main, preeminent, chief, head; paramount, supreme, capital, cardinal; vital, essential.

forerunner *n.* **1.** precursor, predecessor, prototype; ancestor, forebear, forefather, progenitor; trial balloon, stalking-horse. **2.** herald, harbinger, foretoken, omen, portent, sign, presage, precursor, prognostic, token, augury, premonition, forewarning.

foresee *v.* anticipate, expect, look forward to, envision, look ahead to; prophesy, foretell, predict, prognosticate, forecast; be clairvoyant, be prescient, foreknow, have second sight; augur, presage; divine, forebode. **—Syn. Study.** See PREDICT.

foresight *n.* **1.** clairvoyance, foreknowledge, prescience, power of foreseeing, second sight, prevision, precognition. **2.** preparedness, prudence, farsightedness, forethought, anticipation, provision for the future, planning, forehandedness, provident care, providence, longsightedness; shrewdness, perspicacity, sagacity; discretion, precaution, wisdom; premeditation. **—Ant. 1** hindsight, retrospection. **2** unpreparedness, carelessness, neglect, improvidence.

forest *n.* woods, wood, thick growth of trees and underbrush, timberland, wooded area, woodland, bush, wildwood; stand, grove, thicket, copse; wilderness, jungle.

forestall *v.* prevent, thwart, ward off, avert, deter, avoid, head off, circumvent; counteract, block, preclude, obviate; anticipate, guard against; *Informal* steal a march on, beat to the punch.

foretell *v.* predict, prophesy, foresee, prognosticate, divine, augur, forecast; apprehend, foreknow; presage, forebode, portend; tell fortunes, cast a horoscope, soothsay, act the seer.

forethought *n.* **1.** careful planning, prudence, carefulness, foresight, providence, farsightedness, sagacity, shrewdness; caution, heed, wariness, circumspection. **2.** deliberation, prior thought, discretion, consideration, premeditation; precaution, prudence, anticipation. **—Ant. 1** unpreparedness, carelessness, neglect, improvidence. **2** impulsiveness, spontaneity.

forever *adv.* **1.** eternally, for all time, always, everlastingly, to the end of time, ever, perpetually, undyingly, for aye, till the crack of doom, till doomsday. **2.** continually, perpetually, unremittingly, constantly, always, interminably, ceaselessly, unceasingly, incessantly. **—Ant.** never, at no time, sporadically, occasionally.

forewarn *v.* caution, alert, put on guard, give warning, tip off, prewarn, give advance notice, *Slang* put a flea (or bug) in someone's ear, sound the alarm, cry havoc.

foreword *n.* preface, introduction, introductory statement, preliminary remarks, preamble, prologue; prelude. **—Syn. Study.** See INTRODUCTION.

forfeit *n.* **1.** penalty, fine, damages, assessment, forfeiture, waiver. **—*v.* 2.** lose because of some offense, surrender, yield, default, waive; squander, waste, let slip, miss, allow to slip through the fingers.

forge *n.* **1.** furnace, hearth; blacksmith's shop, smithy, ironworks. **—*v.* 2.** hammer out, beat into shape, shape, form, fabricate, make, manufacture, fashion, produce, turn out; devise, contrive. **3.** sign falsely, imitate fraudulently, counterfeit, falsify, fabricate; copy, imitate, simulate, clone.

forgery *n.* **1.** fraudulent imitations; falsification, counterfeiting, cloning, misrepresentation; deception, fraudulence. **2.** counterfeit, imitation, copy, clone, fraud, fake, sham; make-believe, hoax.

forget *v.* **1.** fail to recollect, not remember, have escape the memory, be forgetful of, be unable to recall, let slip from the memory, lose sight of, lose the memory of; neglect, slight, disregard. **2.** leave behind, overlook, fail to take, omit unintentionally; think no more of, pass over, dispense with, be done with, consign to oblivion, let bygones be bygones. **—Ant. 1** remember, recollect, recall; reminisce, think back on, bring to mind, acquire, learn, retain; treasure, mind.

forgetful *adj.* apt to forget, absent-minded; heedless, neglectful, inattentive, oblivious, unmindful, negligent, mindless, careless, remiss, *Slang* out of it; amnesiac. **—Ant.** retentive, unforgetting, unforgetful, attentive, careful, mindful.

forgive *v.* pardon, excuse, absolve, reprieve, cease to feel resentment against, make allowances for, bear with; think no more of, allow for; bury the hatchet, pocket the affront; remit the penalty of; acquit, clear, exonerate, exculpate, condone, pass over, overlook; discharge, set free, release; *Informal* wipe the slate clean, let bygones be bygones. **—Syn. Study.** See EXCUSE. **—Ant.** blame, condemn, censure, charge.

forgo Also **forego** *v.* give up, do without, relinquish, renounce; surrender, yield, waive; abstain from, refrain from, eschew, skip, abnegate; sacrifice.

fork *n.* **1.** pronged implement, eating utensil; pitchfork; trident. **2.** division, branching, branch, bifurcation, divergence, separation, intersection; crotch, angle, bend, elbow; turning point. **—*v.* 3.** pierce, take hold of with a fork, stab, skewer, impale. **4.** diverge, divide, bifurcate, branch, branch out, split, ramify.

forlorn *adj.* **1.** unhappy, depressed, dejected, despondent, dispirited; brokenhearted, woebegone, bereft, bereaved, disconsolate, miserable, comfortless, hopeless, despairing, desperate, inconsolable; abject, pitiable, wretched, pathetic. 2. forsaken, deserted, solitary; desolate, dreary, dismal; friendless, lonesome, lonely, lone; destitute, abandoned, helpless, forgotten. —**Ant.** 1 happy, cheerful, elated, hopeful. 2 thriving, bustling.

form *n.* 1. shape, outline, figure, pattern, contour; figuration, configuration; formation, conformation; structure, format, design, style, plan. 2. body, figure, shape, anatomy, build, physique, person; being, presence. 3. mold, cast, frame, framework, matrix. 4. appearance, phase, aspect, manifestation, arrangement, image, likeness, semblance, guise; incarnation. 5. type, variety, kind, sort; genus, species, genre, class; description, denomination; model, brand, character, stamp. 6. order, system, structure, orderliness, harmony, arrangement, regularity; shapeliness, proportion, symmetry. 7. prescribed method, order, format, rule, habit, proceeding, practice, liturgy, formality, ceremony, rite, ritual; formula, style, mode; way, manner. 8. social behavior, manners, deportment, practice, conduct, custom, usage, propriety, decorum; etiquette, conventionality. 9. trim, fettle, fitness, shape, top condition, healthy condition. —*v.* 10. fashion, shape, mold; carve, sculpt, cut, sculpture, chisel, model; rough-hew, hew, block out; cast, stamp, pattern; construct, structure, fabricate, forge, build; produce, make, create, devise, put together, manufacture; found, set up, establish. 11. compose, comprise, make up, constitute; serve to make up. 12. develop, acquire, contract, pick up.

formal *adj.* 1. ceremonial, official, conventional, ritualistic, prescribed, regular, customary, *Latin* pro forma; external, outward, perfunctory. 2. definite, settled, fixed; explicit, positive; proper, in due form, authoritative; legal, lawful. 3. reserved, decorous, proper, strict, cool, aloof, distant, standoffish, prim, straitlaced, prudish; stiff, starched, stilted; rigid, inflexible, uncompromising; solemn, pompous; ceremonious, punctilious. 4. dressy, stylish, grand, smart; solemn, fancy, full-dress, *Informal* highfalutin. —**Ant.** informal, casual, spontaneous, folksy, easygoing, unceremonious.

formality *n.* 1. observance of form, conventionality, propriety, decorum, etiquette, punctilio; reserve, coolness. 2. ritual, rite, custom, convention, rule of procedure, ceremony, ceremonial, mere form, motion. —**Ant.** informality, ease, casualness.

formation *n.* 1. ordered group, configuration, arrangement, constellation, set; structure, composition, makeup. 2. creation, establishment, development, organization, genesis, generation; production, manufacture, fabrication, building.

formative *adj.* impressionable, susceptible, accessible, sensitive; plastic, shaping, determinative.

former *adj.* 1. past, prior, bygone, gone by; elapsed, lapsed, gone, passed away; ancient, olden, old-time, of yore. 2. first-mentioned, before-mentioned, first-named; aforementioned, aforesaid. 3. previous, earlier, anterior, preceding, prior; antecedent, foregoing; erstwhile, quondam; *Informal* ex; *Archaic* whilom. —**Ant.** 1 modern, coming, future. 2 latter, succeeding, following. 3 ensuing, subsequent; present.

formerly *adv.* once, at one time, in times past, originally, previously; long ago, of old, of yore, anciently, hitherto, lately, ere now; *Archaic* whilom.

formidable *adj.* awesome, imposing, impressive; fearful, terrifying, alarming, dreadful, portentous, menacing, threatening, forbidding; overwhelming, terrific, overpowering; difficult, demanding, dangerous; taxing, onerous, mammoth.

formula *n.* 1. prescription, recipe, blueprint, plan, guideline, rule, principle, precept. 2. incantation, rigmarole, set phrase, slogan, saying, verbal form, chant; cliché, platitude, pleasantry, cant.

formulate *v.* express clearly, state, define, systematize; frame, draft, compose; specify, particularize, itemize; devise, invent.

forsake *v.* 1. desert, abandon, leave, quit, vacate, cast off; abdicate, resign, lay down; fling away, part with, jettison, dispose of; flee, depart. 2. renounce, forswear, abjure, give up, have done with, repudiate, spurn, abandon; relinquish, yield, surrender; waive, drop; reject, discard; disclaim, disavow; deny, go back on.

forswear *v.* retract, repudiate, recant, abjure, gainsay, take back, deny, disavow, disclaim, disown, reject, renounce, revoke, contravene. —**Ant.** reaffirm, uphold, confirm, support, champion.

fort *n.* fortress, fortification, stronghold; bulwark, bastion, castle, citadel, fastness; garrison, base, station, camp.

forte *n.* strong point, special gift, specialty, particular talent, strength, chief excellence; natural turn, unusual aptitude, bent, knack, skill, proficiency.

forth *adv.* 1. forward, onward, ahead, outward, on to the end. 2. into consideration, to notice, into view, before one's attention; out from concealment, from retirement, from confinement.

forthcoming *adj.* 1. about to appear,

upcoming, coming, approaching; prospective, imminent, impending. **2.** ready as needed, available, obtainable, accessible, at hand, handy, on tap; openhanded, cooperative, helpful.

forthright *adj.* **1.** frank, open, blunt, outspoken, candid, direct, plain-spoken, straightforward, *Informal* up-front; painfully truthful, not mincing matters, downright; *Informal* calling a spade a spade. —*adv.* **2.** straightforwardly, straight, straight out, directly, frankly, openly, bluntly, outspokenly, candidly, truthfully. **—Ant. 1** furtive, secret, underhand; dishonest, untruthful, deceitful.

forthwith *adv.* immediately, without delay, at once, directly, instantly, right off, straightaway, quickly, promptly, in a jiffy, *Slang* pronto.

fortification *n.* fortress, fort, citadel, garrison, bastion, tower, bulwark, rampart, stronghold; breastwork, earthwork.

fortify *v.* **1.** strengthen against attack, defend with fortifications, protect, secure, shield; fortress, bulwark, garrison. **2.** make strong, strengthen, reinforce, add strength to, brace, shore up, buttress; harden, stiffen. **3.** sustain, make strong, build up, support, strengthen, buoy up, boost, brace, hearten, cheer, reassure; encourage, embolden, urge on; stimulate, invigorate. **4.** enrich, add nutrients to; add alcohol to, lace. **—Ant. 2** weaken, undermine, debilitate, impair. **3** demoralize, dishearten, unnerve, discomfit.

fortitude *n.* endurance, courage, strength of mind, moral strength, resoluteness, mettle; *Informal* guts, grit, sand, spunk, backbone; spirit, firmness, resolution, determination, prowess, pluck, tenacity; hardihood, dauntlessness, fearlessness, intrepidity, heroism; valor, bravery, boldness; nerve, dash, daring. **—Ant.** cowardice, weakness, faintheartedness.

fortress *n.* large fortified place, fort, citadel, stronghold, fortification, acropolis; bastion, rampart, bulwark, buttress.

fortuitous *adj.* chance, accidental, random, casual, unexpected; undesigned, unpremeditated, unpurposed, unintentional, inadvertent, unintended; stray, hit-or-miss, haphazard, incidental; not meant, never thought of, adventitious; serendipitous, lucky, happy, fortunate. **—Ant.** prearranged, planned, purposed, intentional, premeditated.

fortunate *adj.* **1.** lucky, having good fortune, blessed, favored; successful, booming, flourishing, happy, felicitous; rich, prosperous, well-to-do, well-off; *Informal* on easy street, sitting pretty. **2.** bringing good luck, auspicious, propitious, favorable, advantageous, profitable, resulting favorably; well-timed, timely, opportune, convenient; promising, encouraging, providential; palmy, bright, rosy, fair, benign, halcyon. **—Syn. Study. 1** FORTUNATE, LUCKY, HAPPY refer to persons who enjoy, or events that produce, good fortune. FORTUNATE implies that the success is obtained by the operation of favorable circumstances more than by direct effort: *fortunate in one's choice of a wife; a fortunate investment.* LUCKY, a more colloquial word, is applied to situations that turn out well by chance: *lucky at cards; my lucky day.* HAPPY emphasizes a pleasant ending or something that happens at just the right moment: *By a happy accident I received the package on time.* **—Ant. 1** unlucky, unfortunate. **2** ill-starred, baleful, unhappy, miserable, disastrous, calamitous.

fortune *n.* **1.** immense amount of money, wealth, riches, ample stock of wealth; affluence, prosperity, opulence, easy circumstances; bonanza, windfall, godsend; substance, property, capital, estate, means; revenue, income; treasure, mint, gold mine, pile. **2.** fate, destiny, luck, chance, providence, accident, fortuity, haphazard; good luck, lady luck; kismet. **3.** Usu. **fortunes** lot, portion, destiny, fate, luck, condition in life, circumstances; star; doom, fatality. **—Ant. 1** poverty, destitution, indigence. **2** design, intent, intention, purpose.

fortuneteller *n.* clairvoyant, seer, crystal gazer, palmist, medium, magician, chiromancer, Gypsy; soothsayer, oracle, prophet, sibyl, augur.

forum *n.* **1.** public meeting place, public arena, assembly place; platform, rostrum, outlet, medium, lecture room. **2.** open discussion, symposium, seminar, colloquium.

forward Also **forwards** *adv.* **1.** ahead, onward, in advance, in front, toward the front, forth, frontward; before; toward the future. **2.** forth, into consideration, into discussion, into prominence; out, into view. —*adj.* **3.** moving ahead, advancing, onward; frontal, fore; anterior; progressive, go-ahead, forward-looking, up-to-date; enterprising. **4.** bold, brash, impudent, presumptuous, immodest, self-assertive, presuming, overconfident; fresh, impertinent, cheeky, sassy, insolent, unmannerly; brazen, shameless, offensive, barefaced; intrusive. —*v.* **5.** send forward, readdress, send on, pass on, relay, reroute. **6.** advance, help to progress, promote, further; assist, back, champion, accelerate, hasten, spread, quicken. **—Syn. Study. 4** See BOLD. **—Ant. 1** backward, to the rear. **3** backward, regressive. **4** retiring, modest. **6** hinder, impede, obstruct, bar, block.

foster *v.* **1.** encourage, promote, further,

forward, advance, accommodate, aid, nurture, help forward, help onward; advocate, support, back, take up the cause of, befriend, patronize; side with, favor, countenance, sanction; foment, stimulate. **2.** rear, bring up, raise, rear up; nurse, mother, care for, tend, take in, feed; nourish, nurture, support, sustain; cherish, treasure, hold dear, harbor, protect. **—Syn. Study. 1, 2** See CHERISH. **—Ant. 1** oppose, combat, resist, withstand; curb, restrain, inhibit.

foul *adj.* **1.** disgusting, loathsome, obnoxious, putrid, putrescent, stinking, smelly, malodorous; hateful, odious, revolting, repulsive. **2.** dirty, soiled, filthy, nasty, unclean; begrimed, besmeared, bedraggled; smeared, stained, sullied; muddy, grimy, grubby; squalid, sordid. **3.** stormy, squally, blustery, gusty; wet, rainy, drizzly, misty; foggy, murky, cloudy; muddy, turbid. **4.** coarse, vulgar, lewd, smutty, indecent, obscene; profane, scurrilous, blasphemous; risqué, indelicate, immodest, unseemly, gross; abusive, insulting. **5.** heinous, abominable, infamous, notorious; disgraceful, contemptible, detestable; vile, wicked, evil, monstrous, base, scurvy, nefarious, villainous, atrocious, flagitious. **6.** tangled, entangled, ensnared, befouled, encumbered, impeded, choked. *—v.* **7.** make foul, dirty, befoul, defile, sully, soil, begrime, besmirch, pollute, taint. **8.** tangle, clog, entangle, befoul, ensnare. **—Ant. 1** fair, fragrant, pleasing. **2** clean, spotless, stainless. **3** fair, clear. **4** mild, modest, seemly, pure. **5** admirable, exemplary; pleasant; honorable. **7** cleanse, purify; honor. **8** clear, untangle.

found *v.* **1.** establish, institute, organize, bring about, set up, originate, create, develop, give rise to, start, set going; settle, colonize. **2.** base, rest, sustain, locate, ground. **3.** build, construct, erect, raise, rear.

foundation *n.* **1.** base, substructure, understructure, underpinning, ground, groundwork, bed, bottom, lowest layer, support, foot, pedestal; basement, cellar; rock. **2.** basis, base, justification, cause, reason, rationale; root, ground, groundwork, source, origin, commencement; purpose, motive; premise, assumption, underlying principle, infrastructure. **3.** founding, establishment, institution, setting up, installation, creation; settlement. **4.** institution; charity, fund; philanthropy, benefaction, endowment. **—Syn. Study. 1** See BASE.

founder[1] *v.* **1.** sink, go down, go under, go to the bottom, swamp; capsize, shipwreck; run aground. **2.** fail utterly, come to grief, collapse, abort, miscarry, perish, succumb, drown, sink; disintegrate, break up, fall apart, topple, go under; come to nothing, end in smoke; hit rock bottom, turn out badly. **3.** go lame, stagger, limp, hobble, reel; trip, stumble, tumble, fall, lurch, topple, plunge, sprawl; break down; *Informal* come a cropper.

founder[2] *n.* originator, creator, builder, organizer, planner, architect, strategist; author, father.

fountain *n.* **1.** jet, stream of water; gush, flow, spout, upwelling. **2.** source of stream, fountainhead, wellspring, head of a stream, well, spring, fount; reservoir. **3.** origin, source; genesis, beginning, cradle; birth, derivation, first principles; reason, cause; supplier, purveyor, feeder.

foxy *adj.* cunning, crafty, clever, artful, wily, tricky, slick, guileful, sharp, canny, shrewd, shifty, astute; sly, stealthy, insidious, devious, oblique, sneaky, underhand; deceitful, deceptive; designing, intriguing, conniving, scheming. **—Ant.** straightforward, aboveboard, forthright; candid, open, plain, frank; artless, guileless, ingenuous, naive.

foyer *n.* antechamber, vestibule, anteroom, waiting room, hall; lobby; entrance porch, loggia.

fraction *n.* **1.** part of a whole, fractional part; section, segment, piece, portion, subdivision; ratio, quotient, proportion. **2.** small part, bit, few; particle, fragment, trifle, morsel; shaving, cutting, chip; scrap, crumb.

fractious *adj.* cross, irritable, peevish, ill-tempered, grouchy, snappish, fretful, querulous, irascible; touchy, huffy, shirty, waspish, petulant, shrewish, pettish; quarrelsome, unruly, refractory, rebellious, wayward, perverse, contrary, disputatious; recalcitrant, willful, unmanageable. **—Ant.** complaisant, amiable, good-humored, genial, agreeable, good-natured.

fracture *n.* **1.** break, severance, rupture, cleavage; breach, separation, division; split, rift, fault, crack. *—v.* **2.** break, crack, split, sever, shatter; disrupt, breach, rend, cleave.

fragile *adj.* **1.** easily broken, frangible, breakable; delicate, dainty, flimsy, brittle, shivery, splintery; crumbly, friable, crisp; ephemeral, evanescent. **2.** frail, infirm, delicate, feeble, weak, slight, decrepit; tender, soft; flimsy, rickety, sleazy, dilapidated, tumbledown, unsubstantial. **—Syn. Study. 1, 2** See FRAIL. **—Ant.** tough, strong, stout, sturdy; elastic, resilient, flexible; hardy, tenacious; durable, lasting.

fragment *n.* **1.** part broken off, piece, segment, factoid, section, remnant, fraction, portion; chip, shard, bit, snip, morsel, crumb, shred, scrap; trace, vestige, survival. —*v.* **2.** disunite, break apart, break up, splinter, shatter; divide, separate; chop up, cut up; crumble, chip, disintegrate. —**Ant. 2** unite, bring together, combine.

fragmentary *adj.* incomplete, unfinished, scrappy, piecemeal, disconnected; choppy, broken, segmented, disjointed, fractional, detached, not entire, scattered.

fragrance *n.* fragrant odor, perfume, scent, aroma; bouquet, sweetness, aura, redolence, incense, balm. —**Syn. Study.** See PERFUME. —**Ant.** stench, stink, effluvium, miasma, offensive odor.

fragrant *adj.* sweet-scented, sweet-smelling, redolent, odorous, odoriferous, aromatic, perfumed; balmy, spicy. —**Ant.** fetid, malodorous, stinking.

frail *adj.* **1.** fragile, frangible, brittle, breakable, shivery, splintery, crumbly, easily broken or destroyed; rickety, dilapidated; sleazy, flimsy, unsubstantial, puny; perishable, delicate; vulnerable, fallible. **2.** slight, weak, delicate, feeble, not robust, fragile, weakly; infirm, decrepit. —**Syn. Study. 1** FRAIL, FRAGILE, BRITTLE imply a delicacy or weakness of substance, condition, or construction. FRAIL applies particularly to health and immaterial things: *a frail constitution; frail hopes.* FRAGILE implies that something must be handled carefully to avoid breakage or damage; it is sometimes applied to a person's mental or psychic state: *fragile bric-a-brac; fragile self-confidence.* BRITTLE implies a hard material that snaps or breaks to pieces easily: *brittle as glass.* —**Ant. 1** strong, stout, sturdy, stalwart, tough. **2** healthy, sound, hale, robust, vigorous.

frailty *n.* weakness of character, moral weakness, fault, sin, vice, failing, defect, blemish, flaw, weak point, fallibility, imperfection, weak side, foible, susceptibility. —**Ant.** strength, virtue.

frame *n.* **1.** mounting, case, housing; border, setting, backing, edging, rim. **2.** framework, skeleton, structure, form, framing, scaffolding, casing, mold, body, chassis. **3.** physique, build, figure, shape, anatomy; system, scheme, constitution, make, construction; cast; outline, contour, set. **4.** attitude, state, mood, humor, nature, temperament, disposition, temper. —*v.* **5.** devise, conceive, contrive, invent, plan; draft, sketch, indite; concoct, scheme, hatch; formulate, map out, design; organize, systematize. **6.** incriminate unjustly, give false evidence against, *Slang* set up.

franchise *n.* **1.** right to vote, voting power, ballot, suffrage, enfranchisement. **2.** right, privilege, authorization, license, permission, official sanction; grant, charter; prerogative; freedom, immunity.

frank *adj.* candid, plain-spoken, direct, open, outspoken, straightforward, free, downright, forthright, straight from the shoulder, *Informal* up-front; bold, round, plain, unreserved, sincere, genuine, natural, honest, openhearted, aboveboard; ingenuous, artless; undisguised, transparent, evident, clear, apparent, unmistakable, unambiguous, unequivocal; manifest, distinct, patent, explicit. —**Syn. Study.** FRANK, CANDID, OPEN, OUTSPOKEN imply a freedom and boldness in speaking. FRANK implies a straightforward, almost tactless expression of one's real opinions or sentiments: *He was frank in his rejection of the proposal.* CANDID suggests sincerity, truthfulness, and impartiality: *a candid appraisal of her work.* OPEN implies a lack of reserve or of concealment: *open criticism.* OUTSPOKEN suggests free and bold expression, even when inappropriate: *an outspoken and unnecessary show of disapproval.* —**Ant.** reticent, evasive, indirect, reserved, close, covert, secretive; dissembling, underhand, crafty, disingenuous.

frantic *adj.* excited, agitated, hectic; frenzied, frenetic, distracted, overwrought, beside oneself, distraught, nervous; raging, impassioned, rabid, raving, furious, infuriated; wild, violent, ungovernable; crazy, mad, insane, deranged, delirious, berserk. —**Ant.** calm, collected, cool, unruffled, composed.

fraternal *adj.* brotherly, kindred, friendly, amicable, social; hearty, warmhearted; loving, devoted, affectionate; related, consanguineous. —**Ant.** hostile, antipathetic, inimical.

fraternity *n.* **1.** brotherliness, brotherhood, brotherly relation, kinship, interrelation; consanguinity, ties of blood, blood connection; propinquity. **2.** club, society, circle; league, alliance, federation, confederacy, coalition, united body; clique, coterie, clan, brotherhood; company, union, association.

fraternize *v.* mingle, keep company, associate, socialize, mix, hobnob, consort, band together, cooperate, combine, unite, coalesce, *Slang* hang around, pal around; confederate; sympathize, harmonize, concur. —**Ant.** shun, avoid, keep away from.

fraud *n.* **1.** fraudulence, swindling, cheating, trickery, deceit, deception, dishonesty, misrepresentation, sharp practice, duplicity, guile, cozenage, double-dealing, chicanery, treachery, *Slang* monkey business, hype; craft, artifice, subterfuge, dissimulation, machination, imposture, stratagem; sham, hoax, ruse, trick, swindle, humbug. **2.** impostor, charlatan, mountebank, sham, fake, counterfeit, pretender; knave, rascal, rogue; quack, swindler, cheat, four-flusher, con artist. —**Syn. Study. 1** See DECEIT. —**Ant. 1** fairness, good faith, honesty, integrity.

fraudulent *adj.* deceitful, dishonest, deceptive, treacherous, underhanded, guileful, crafty, wily, tricky, unprincipled, dishonorable, cunning, knavish; crooked, cheating; spurious, sham, bogus, false, counterfeit.

fraught *adj.* filled, full, laden, charged, abounding, loaded, teeming, replete, pregnant, heavy; attended, accompanied. —**Ant.** devoid, lacking, wanting, empty.

fray[1] *n.* **1.** quarrel, fight, dispute, disagreement, tiff, spat, controversy, squabble, bickering, fuss, set-to, altercation, contention, dissension; fracas, commotion, tussle, rumpus, scuffle; wrangle, brawl, riot, melee, tumult, *Slang* rumble. **2.** battle, conflict, contest, fight, combat, warfare; affray, skirmish, engagement.

fray[2] *v.* ravel, frazzle, tatter, wear out, become threadbare; strain, chafe, fret, rub.

freak *n.* **1.** monstrosity, monster, oddity, curiosity, deviation, aberration, mutation, abnormality, marvel, wonder; abnormal organism, sport, freak of nature. **2.** twist, quirk, vagary, irregularity, anomaly; kink, whim, caprice, crotchet, turn; fancy, humor, whimsy; craze, fad. —*adj.* **3.** odd, strange, queer, unusual, erratic, freaky, freakish, peculiar, bizarre.

free *adj.* **1.** self-governing, autonomous, self-directing, independent. **2.** emancipated, freed, liberated, enfranchised, at liberty, manumitted, delivered, released; unshackled, unfettered, unbound, unconfined, unconstrained, unbridled, unhampered, unmuzzled, unrestrained; bondless, unchained, unattached; fancy-free, uncommitted, footloose. **3.** exempted from; exempt from, not liable to, immune to, excused from, released from, absolved of; unaffected by, devoid of, lacking in. **4.** allowed, permitted, able, at liberty. **5.** complimentary, without cost, gratis, for nothing, on the house, costless, gratuitous, chargeless. **6.** loose, unattached; not in use, spare, extra; idle, unoccupied, available. **7.** open, abandoned, uninhibited, unrepressed, unrestrained, uncontrolled, familiar, informal, easy, expansive, unceremonious; forward, unreserved, bold, audacious, overfamiliar, daring; confident, assured, fearless; lax, careless; licentious, wanton, dissolute. **8.** generous, freehanded, liberal, openhanded, giving, lavish, prodigal, bounteous, big, big-hearted, handsome, bountiful, munificent. **9.** clear, devoid, not littered, unobstructed, uncluttered, unencumbered, unimpeded, unblocked, unclogged. —*adv.* **10.** without restriction, freely, loosely; leisurely, idly, carelessly. **11.** without charge, at no cost, gratis. —*v.* **12.** set free, liberate, make free, set at liberty, release, let loose, let go, emancipate, manumit, enfranchise, exempt; parole, discharge; redeem, save, ransom; unchain, uncage, unleash, unshackle, unfasten. **13.** release, disengage, extricate, rid of. —**Ant. 1** occupied, dependent. **2** subservient. **6** bound, engaged, busy, preoccupied. **7** reserved, restrained, restricted. **8** stingy, niggardly, close. **9** clogged, obstructed, cluttered. **12** imprison, jail, intern, incarcerate, confine, restrain, inhibit, restrict, limit.

freedom *n.* **1.** political independence, autonomy, self-determination, sovereignty, self-government; civil liberty, enfranchisement, emancipation, manumission; liberation, release, exemption from control. **2.** ease of movement, elbow room; latitude, scope, sweep, margin, range, play, swing; unrestricted use, wide berth. **3.** openness, frankness, unrestraint, abandon, abandonment, absence of reserve, unreservedness, candor, unconstraint; informality, naturalness; bluntness, directness, forwardness, downrightness. **4.** boldness, impudence, license, disrespect, rudeness, impertinence; impropriety, indecorum. —**Ant. 1** dependence, restriction; bondage, servitude, slavery, serfdom; imprisonment, captivity. **3** restraint, caution, reluctance, respectfulness, decorum.

free-for-all *n.* brawl, fight, affray, fray, melee, fracas, wrangle, ruckus, ruction, row, scrap, donnybrook, brannigan, *Slang* rhubarb, rough-and-tumble, knock-down-and-drag-out, tussle.

freeze *v.* **1.** become solid, solidify, turn to ice, harden; chill, cool, refrigerate; glaciate, congeal; frost. **2.** benumb, chill, stiffen with cold; nip, bite, sting, pierce; anesthetize. **3.** become immobile, become paralyzed, stop; halt, arrest; chill with fear, terrify. —*n.* **4.** frost, chill, below-freezing temperature. **5.** lawful control, ceiling, restriction.

freight *n.* **1.** transportation of goods, shipment of merchandise, truckage, cartage, portage, conveyance, transshipment. **2.** goods, lading, cargo, load, charge, burden; luggage, baggage. —*v.* **3.** load, lade, charge, burden; weigh down. **4.** send by freight, transport, ship, convey, transmit; carry, haul.

frenzy *n.* **1.** fit, seizure, transport, outburst, access, furor, delirium; madness, fury, distraction, hysteria; obsession, craze, mania. **2.** mental agitation, turmoil, state; mad rush, great haste. —**Ant. 2** calm, composure, collectedness, coolness, equanimity; sobriety, sanity, judgment.

frequency *n.* frequent occurrence, regularity, repetition, recurrence, reiteration, iteration, persistence.

frequent *adj.* **1.** occurring often, oft-repeated, at short intervals, numerous; continual, recurrent, habitual, reiterative; incessant, perpetual. **2.** regular, constant, habitual; daily, everyday; ordinary, common, familiar; wonted, customary; usual, accustomed. **—*v.* 3.** haunt, go to frequently, attend regularly, go often to, resort to, visit repeatedly, be seen at regularly, *Slang* hang out at, hang around in. **—Ant. 1** rare, occasional; few, scanty. **3** shun, avoid, eschew, steer clear of, keep away from, spurn.

frequently *adv.* often, ofttimes, many times, repeatedly; recurrently, constantly, continually, incessantly, perpetually, over and over again; usually, habitually, customarily, generally, ordinarily. **—Syn. Study.** See OFTEN. **—Ant.** rarely, seldom, hardly ever, infrequently.

fresh *adj.* **1.** newly made, not stale, recent; well-preserved, unfaded, unspoiled, in good condition, unwithered, unwilted, not deteriorated, undecayed; (*variously*) green, hot, sweet; unworn, unused; undimmed, untarnished. **2.** new, original, creative, inventive, not used before, novel, brand-new; unusual, unfamiliar, untried, unaccustomed; rare, strange, unique; modern, modernistic, new-fashioned, new-fangled; recent, late, just out, up-to-date. **3.** not salted, unsalted; not preserved, unpickled, unsmoked, undried, uncured. **4.** fit, alert, keen, lively, ready, active, energetic, unworn, not fatigued, unwearied; refreshed, freshened, rested, invigorated; unimpaired, unabated. **5.** wholesome, clear, youthful-looking; rosy, ruddy; blooming, gleaming, sparkling, glowing; fair, bright, flourishing. **6.** pure, refreshing, cool; chill, nipping, bracing, stinging, cutting, biting; stiff, brisk, keen. **7.** impudent, rude, cheeky, pert, saucy, sassy, brazen, insolent, *Informal* snotty; forward, presumptuous, flippant, nervy, *Informal* smart-alecky; bold, brassy, assuming; obtrusive, meddlesome. **—Syn. Study. 2** See NEW. **—Ant. 1** stale, old. **2** trite, ordinary, hackneyed, stereotyped, shopworn; secondhand. **3** salted, preserved, canned. **4** weary, fatigued, exhausted; dull. **5** sickly, wan, pallid, faded. **6** stale, impure, polluted, musty. **7** sweet, amiable, charming, well-mannered, courteous, respectful.

fret *v.* **1.** worry, brood, agonize, fume, stew, chafe; be peevish, be angry, be vexed, be irritated, be fretful; mope, lament, pout, pine, sulk; distress, gall, vex, ruffle, irritate. **2.** wear away, abrade, erode, corrode, rub, irritate, excoriate, gnaw, eat; tatter, fray. **—*n.* 3.** vexation, annoyance, displeasure, irritation, peevishness, fretfulness; disquiet, discomposure, fidgets, sulks.

fretful *adj.* peevish, irritable, touchy, cranky, grouchy, crotchety, sulky, cross, ill-natured, ill-tempered, pettish, querulous, complaining, contrary, petulant, waspish, snappish, *Brit.* shirty, huffy. **—Ant.** good-natured, cheerful, easygoing, agreeable, congenial; patient, forbearing.

friction *n.* **1.** rubbing, abrasion, grating, fretting, chafing; attrition; resistance, counteraction. **2.** conflict, opposition, discord, dissidence, disagreement, clash of opinion, dissension, antagonism, animosity, hostility, resentment, bad feeling, bad blood; strife, quarrel, contention.

friend *n.* **1.** acquaintance, comrade, companion, chum, confidant; partner, buddy, pal, amigo, sidekick, crony, mate; playmate, cohort, playfellow; consort; bedfellow, intimate, soul mate, *French* intime; boyfriend, girl friend, escort, beau, date; lover, mistress, favorite, paramour. **2.** patron, supporter, backer, benefactor; well-wisher, encourager; advocate, defender, partisan, adherent. **3.** ally, colleague, fellow, associate; copartner, partner, coworker; confrere, brother, follower, retainer, minion; henchman, myrmidon. **—Syn. Study. 1, 3** FRIEND, ACQUAINTANCE, COMPANION, ASSOCIATE refer to a person with whom one is in contact. A FRIEND is a person with whom one is on intimate terms and for whom one feels a warm affection: *a trusted friend.* An ACQUAINTANCE is a person one knows, though not intimately: *a casual acquaintance at school.* A COMPANION is a person who shares one's activities or fortunes; the term usu. suggests a familiar relationship: *a traveling companion; a companion in despair.* An ASSOCIATE is a person who is often in one's company, usu. because of some work or pursuit in common: *a business associate.* **—Ant. 1** foe, enemy. **2** antagonist, opponent, adversary. **3** rival, competitor.

friendly *adj.* **1.** kindly, kind, helpful, well-disposed; amiable, neighborly, amicable; loving, familiar, affectionate, kind-hearted, cordial, genial, warmhearted; ardent, devoted, intimate; sympathetic, gracious, generous, chummy, companionable, clubby, convivial. **2.** allied, not hostile, on good terms, being friends, fraternal, brotherly; hospitable, social, accessible, affable. **3.** favorable, helpful, auspicious, propitious, salutary, advantageous, beneficial, benign, fortunate, oportune. **—Ant. 2** belligerent, hostile, contentious. **3** unfavorable, sinister, inauspicious.

friendship *n.* **1.** acquaintanceship, fellowship, association as friends, relationship of friends, companionship, comradeship, brotherhood, friendly relations, fraternity; close tie, intimacy, familiarity. **2.** good feeling, friendliness, harmony, accord, concord, amity, comity, amicableness, consonance, understanding, sympathy, good fellowship, cordiality, neighborliness, goodwill. **—Ant. 1** enmity, animosity, hostility, antipathy, antagonism. **2** strife, conflict, combat.

fright *n.* fear, alarm, terror, panic, fear of danger, consternation; scare, perturbation; dread, apprehension, dismay, trepidation; affright, horror; concern, anxiety, misgiving; cold feet, funk; fear and trembling, the jitters, intimidation, reign of terror, disquietude, *Slang* the creeps, the willies; quaking, tremor, flutter, quivering, palpitation. **—Ant.** bravery, boldness, courage, fortitude, stoutheartedness.

frighten *v.* alarm, scare, make afraid, throw into a fright, terrify, terrorize, shock, horrify, disturb with fear, petrify, affright, frighten, startle; *Archaic* affray; intimidate, daunt; excite, agitate, disquiet. **—Ant.** calm, soothe, comfort, reassure.

frightful *adj.* **1.** horrible, horrendous, horrid, terrible, awful, fearful, shocking, appalling, dreadful, alarming; terrific, horrific, fearsome; lurid, grisly, ghastly, macabre, gruesome, sinister, baleful. **2.** offensive, loathsome, nasty, insufferable, hideous, disgusting, detestable; revolting, repulsive, repellent, abominable; monstrous, freakish, ogreish. **3.** very great, terrific, terrible, extreme, awful, dreadful, insufferable. **—Ant. 1** calming, soothing. **2** beautiful, attractive. **3** slight, partial, moderate.

frigid *adj.* **1.** cold, freezing cold, bitter cold, freezing, icy; gelid, glacial; cool, chilly; bleak, raw, bitter, nipping, piercing, biting, cutting. **2.** stiff, unresponsive, distant, forbidding, aloof; prim, formal, rigid, austere, frosty, cold, cool, chilly, icy, straitlaced. **—Ant. 1** hot, burning, sweltering, stifling. **2** cordial, friendly, warm, hospitable; ardent, passionate, impassioned.

frill *n.* **1.** ruffle, gathering, flounce, fringe, edging, furbelow. **2.** ornament, decoration, added touch, frippery, embellishment; affectation, superfluity, falderal; air, mannerism.

fringe *n.* **1.** edging, trimming, ornamental bordering, border, tassel, skirting, hem, margin, selvage; mane; edge, periphery, limit, frontier. *—v.* **2.** border, edge, skirt; surround, rim, outline, enclose; decorate, embellish.

frisk *v.* **1.** romp, frolic, caper, gambol, cavort, lark, prance, dance, bound, bounce, cut capers; disport, cut up, trip, sport, jump about; skip, leap, jump, spring, hop. **2.** search, examine, inspect; check quickly, look over; ransack, rummage through.

frisky *adj.* lively, animated, spirited, agile, vivacious, nimble, light-heeled, active; spry, sportive, playful, frolicsome, in high spirits, peppy, rollicking; waggish, prankish, mirthful, jocular; *Informal* feeling one's oats. **—Ant.** demure, sedate; pensive, meditative; stodgy, stolid.

fritter *v.* squander, waste, spend foolishly, use up, dissipate, deplete, run through, frivol away, trifle away, fool away, *Slang* blow, dribble away, diddle away, idle away, fribble away. **—Ant.** conserve, save, skimp, economize, budget.

frivolity *n.* giddiness, flightiness, levity, lightness, emptiness, folly; triviality, frippery, fickleness, flippancy, airiness; wantonness, thoughtlessness, abandon; dallying, play, whimsy, sport, jest, fun. **—Ant.** seriousness, staidness, sedateness; gravity, solemnity; soberness, earnestness.

frivolous *adj.* **1.** impractical, trifling, trivial, worthless, imprudent, improvident, ill-considered, unimportant, insignificant, pointless, silly, petty, paltry; slight, piddling, flimsy, niggling, minor; empty, airy, light, frothy, light-headed, flighty, careless; vain, self-indulgent, extravagant. **2.** flighty, superficial, unserious, silly, harebrained, light-minded; flippant, insouciant; rattlebrained, dizzy, shallowbrained; careless, heedless; foolish, senseless, fatuous; brainless, barmy, witless, stupid; inane, silly, nonsensical. **—Ant. 1** important, vital. **2** mature, adult; sensible, serious, earnest; intense, grave, solemn.

frock *n.* **1.** dress, gown, suit, coat, cloak, robe, smock, blouse. **2.** clerical garb, canonicals, clericals, vestment, monk's robe; cassock, soutane, surplice, chasuble.

frolic *n.* **1.** fun, gaiety, merriment, merrymaking, mirth, recreation, amusement; sport, play, festivity, entertainment; tomfoolery, buffoonery; jollity, joviality, pleasantry; antic, gambol, spree, romp, caper, lark, escapade, skylarking, prank. *—v.* **2.** romp, frisk, skip, caper, gambol, cavort, sport, disport, play merrily, amuse oneself, make merry; cut capers, act up, play pranks; *Informal* have a ball, live it up, make hay.

front *n.* **1.** face, forward part; façade, frontage. **2.** head, lead, top, beginning; fore; advanced guard, trenches, front rank, vanguard, front lines. **3.** external appearance, semblance, demeanor, carriage, mien, air, bearing, presence;

mask, pretense, façade. —*adj.* **4.** located in front, fore, anterior; first, beginning, initial. —*v.* **5.** face, look out, look forward, stand opposite to, give on, regard. —**Ant. 1, 2, 4** back, rear.

frontier *n.* **1.** border, boundary, boundary line; limits, verge, edge, perimeter, extreme, confines; march. **2.** outlying area, remote districts, hinterland, far country, backlands, backwoods, outskirts, outposts; territories; marches. —**Syn. Study. 1** See BOUNDARY. —**Ant.** interior, settled region.

frost *n.* **1.** below-freezing weather, cold spell, chill; frozen moisture, covering of ice, ice crystals; hoarfrost, rime. **2.** frigidity, iciness, chill, chilliness, coldness of manner, glaciality; unfriendliness, aloofness, distance, want of cordiality, inhospitality, coolness.

froth *n.* **1.** foam, spume, scum, head, fume, fizz, bubbles; lather, suds, yeast; whitecap, surf. **2.** trivia, frippery, trumpery, flummery, frivolity, triviality, nonsense; *Informal* bosh, fiddle-faddle, balderdash; trash, rubbish.

frown *v.* **1.** wrinkle the forehead, scowl, knit the brow, glower, look displeased, glare, look stern; mope, sulk, pout, fret; ponder, muse. **2.** disapprove of, view with disfavor, look disapprovingly on, take a dim view of, discountenance, look askance at; show disapproval of, show displeasure at, look down on. —*n.* **3.** frowning look, scowl, glower, black look, glare. —**Ant. 1** smile, show pleasure, express satisfaction, show kindliness. **2** approve, support, advocate, foster, cherish; favor, countenance.

frozen *adj.* **1.** icebound, obstructed, clogged, immobilized; stymied, stalemated; refrigerated, chilled, cooled, iced, gelid, solidified by cold. **2.** benumbed, numb, cold; chill, chilly; gelid, icy, glacial; frostbitten; wintry, hibernal; arctic, polar. —**Ant. 1** thawed, melted. **2** warm, hot; torrid.

frugal *adj.* **1.** economical, thrifty, unwasteful, prudent with money, sparing, economy-minded, penny-wise; parsimonious, tight, penny-pinching, stingy, niggardly; ascetic, abstemious. **2.** scant, not abundant, slim, sparing, skimpy. —**Syn. Study. 1** See ECONOMICAL. —**Ant. 1** extravagant, wasteful, imprudent, spendthrift. **2** luxurious, lavish, profuse.

fruit *n.* **1.** produce, product, crop, yield, production, harvest; young, offspring, progeny, issue. **2.** result, product, consequence, outgrowth, upshot, issue, effect, outcome; return, profit, benefit, advantage; revenue, remuneration, emolument, earnings; award, reward.

fruitful *adj.* **1.** productive, fecund, prolific, fructiferous; blooming, yielding, fertile, abounding in fruit; fruit-bearing. **2.** profitable, productive, advantageous, effective, successful, efficacious. —**Syn. Study. 1** See PRODUCTIVE. —**Ant. 1** unfruitful, barren, sterile, infertile, unproductive. **2** fruitless, pointless, useless, vain, futile, abortive, ineffectual; scarce, scanty.

fruition *n.* fulfillment, achievement, realization, attainment; satisfaction, gratification, actualization, materialization, consummation; maturity, ripeness.

fruitless *adj.* **1.** unfruitful, pointless, purposeless, useless, bootless, unsuccessful, unavailing, empty, hollow, vain, futile; ineffective, ineffectual, inefficacious; unrewarding, unprofitable, profitless, nugatory; worthless; abortive, inoperative; inept, incompetent. **2.** unfruitful, barren, infertile, arid, sterile; unproductive, unprolific. —**Ant. 1** useful, profitable, rewarding, fruitful; effective, worthwhile, productive. **2** fertile, fecund; abundant, prolific, fructiferous.

frustrate *v.* **1.** hinder, defeat, thwart, baffle, foil, circumvent, prohibit, inhibit, bring to naught, nullify, cancel, make of no avail, render invalid, make null and void, check, impede, block, bar; suppress; undermine, cut the ground from under; forestall, balk, obstruct, prevent, counter. **2.** discourage, fluster, upset, dispirit, disappoint, disconcert, dishearten; cripple, hamstring, clip the wings of. —**Ant. 1** foster, promote, further, forward, advance; incite, instigate, abet, foment. **2** encourage, hearten, cheer; satisfy, gratify.

frustration *n.* defeat, failure, futility, nonsuccess, nonfulfillment, foiling, thwarting, hindrance, balking, inhibition, interference, bafflement; contravention, counteraction, obstruction; disappointment, dissatisfaction, letdown, chagrin, discomfiture.

fry *v.* cook, sauté, brown, grill, frizzle, fricassee; pan-fry, French fry, deep fry.

fuel *n.* **1.** combustible material; (*variously*) wood, coal, oil, natural gas; gas, gasoline, petroleum. **2.** material, fodder, ammunition, inspiration; sustenance, means, wherewithal, impetus, motivation, stimulus. —*v.* **3.** provide with fuel, replenish with fuel, fill up, charge, recharge, stoke, kindle, fire, ignite, light, feed; activate, energize, stimulate, incite, fan, inflame; sustain.

fugitive *n.* **1.** runaway, deserter, outlaw; refugee, escapee; exile, expatriate; renegade, apostate; rover, wanderer, itinerant, straggler; vagrant, vagabond, nomad; tramp, loafer, hobo. —*adj.* **2.** escaping, escaped, fleeing, running away, flying. **3.** *Poetic.* fleeting, short-lived, transitory, evanescent, transient, fugacious, ephemeral; brief, momentary, passing, impermanent; unstable, errant, erratic, elusive, volatile, flitting, uncertain; hurried, hasty, cursory, summary; short, temporary; fading, shifting. **—Ant. 3** lasting, permanent, durable; changeless, immutable; endless, eternal.

fulfill *v.* **1.** carry out, accomplish, achieve, realize, effect, implement, effectuate, bring to pass, bring about; establish, execute, consummate; perfect, bring to perfection. **2.** obey, perform, do, abide by, keep, discharge, comply with, adhere to, be faithful to, live up to; keep faith with; redeem; observe, follow, heed. **3.** satisfy, suit, meet, fill out, make good, answer. **—Ant. 1** neglect, ignore, slight, overlook, disregard; fail in. **3** fall short of, fail to meet; disappoint, dissatisfy.

fulfillment Also **fulfilment** *n.* **1.** realization, accomplishment, effectuation, implementation, attainment, achievement; execution, establishment, completion, crowning, pinnacle, culmination; finishing touch. **2.** satisfaction, contentment, gratification; pleasure, delight, happiness, contentedness.

full *adj.* **1.** filled, heaping, brimming, brimful, flush; replete, abounding, fraught, crammed, bursting, packed, laden, loaded, chock-full; teeming, swarming, saturated; filled up, well-supplied, well-stocked; sated, surfeited, stuffed, gorged, glutted. **2.** complete, entire, whole, thorough, maximum, total; intact, unabridged, plenary; mature, perfect, up to the mark. **3.** ample, capacious, wide, broad, voluminous; comprehensive, all-inclusive; large, big; round, rotund, shapely, plump; rich, resonant. *—adv.* **4.** very, quite, perfectly; exactly, precisely. **—Ant. 1** empty, void; vacant, devoid, blank, exhausted. **2** partial, incomplete, qualified; altered, abridged. **3** tight, restricted; limited, exclusive; thin, meager, angular, faint.

full-fledged *adj.* complete, mature, full-blown, full-grown; trained, qualified, experienced, schooled, adept, proficient, skilled, expert, topflight, authoritative, masterly. **—Ant.** untrained, unschooled, green, inept, untried.

fully *adv.* **1.** completely, entirely, wholly, totally, altogether, quite; perfectly, in all respects, in every respect; from first to last, throughout, from top to toe, from head to foot; positively, utterly, at all points; substantially, on the whole; every inch, heart and soul. **2.** sufficiently, amply; abundantly, plentifully, copiously; richly.

fumble *v.* mishandle, bungle, botch, butcher, mess up, spoil, mar, muff, bumble, muddle, boggle, bollix, bobble; *Slang* blow, louse up, goof up, screw up.

fume *n.* **1.** smoke, haze, exhalation; vapor, gas, billow, waft; unpleasant odor, reek, stench; scent; miasma. *—v.* **2.** smoke, send forth fumes, puff, smolder, emit, exude, belch forth; exhale; smell, reek, stink, stench. **3.** display anger, rage, seethe, lose one's temper, get steamed up, burn, rant, rave, fly off the handle, explode, flare up, foam, boil, flame up, *Informal* carry on, *Slang* blow one's top, blow one's stack.

fun *n.* enjoyment, gaiety, pleasure, amusement, merriment, diversion; entertainment, recreation, distraction, relaxation; joking, jest, playfulness, waggishness, jollity, mirth, good humor, joviality; cheer, frolic, whoopee, skylarking, tomfoolery, buffoonery; game, sport, play, horseplay, romp, antic, prank, lark, spree, escapade, revelry, high jinks, good time; *Slang* ball, blast, trip, gas. **—Ant.** misery, melancholy, woe, gloom, tedium.

function *n.* **1.** purpose, role, activity, operation, job, business, task, duty; capacity, power, faculty; province, sphere, office, niche, place, scope, range, field; concern, objective, raison d'être. **2.** social gathering, fete, gala, affair, festivity, party, entertainment, reception, soiree; dinner party, feast, banquet; ceremony, occasion. *—v.* **3.** serve, act, perform, do duty; operate, behave, work, answer a purpose, help, benefit, render a service, serve one's turn.

functional *adj.* working, operative, operable, functioning; useful, serviceable, practical, utilitarian.

fund *n.* **1.** sum of money, accumulated amount, savings, accumulation, bank; nest egg; *Slang* kitty; pool, pot; foundation, endowment, investment. **2.** store, supply, stock; repository, reservoir, well, fount, spring; treasure, storehouse, hoard, reserve; mine, lode, vein. *—v.* **3.** finance, pay for, underwrite, foot, float; support, endow, patronize. **—Ant. 1** expenditure, outlay, outgo, disbursement; payment, remuneration.

fundamental *adj.* **1.** basic, underlying, essential, necessary, requisite, first, primary, elementary; key, crucial, vital, central; major, principal, main, chief; cardinal, indispensable, integral. *—n.* **2.** principle, basic, primary rule, ABC's, essential, requisite, axiom, element, component; base, basis, foundation, cornerstone; groundwork. **—Ant. 1** advanced; superfluous, accidental; secondary, subordinate, lesser.

funds *n. pl.* money, cash, cash on hand, wherewithal, means, resources, assets, capital, property, wealth, finances, income; *Slang* jack, lucre, dough, green stuff, pelf, wampum, bread, scratch, moola.

funeral *n.* rites, obsequies, requiem, memorial service, interment, burial, entombment, inhumation; cremation; wake.

funereal *adj.* sad, mournful, gloomy, dismal, doleful, woeful, grieving, solemn, dirgeful, somber, dreary, depressing; weepy, woebegone, lachrymose, lugubrious, cheerless, long-faced, grim, grim-faced; desolate, brokenhearted. **—Ant.** happy, gay, cheery, merry, lively, joyous, festive.

funnel *n.* **1.** cone-shaped utensil; channel, conduit, duct, shaft. **2.** smokestack; chimney, smoke pipe, stovepipe, ventilator, flue, air shaft. **—***v.* **3.** pour, concentrate, channel, focus, direct; siphon, pipe, filter.

funny *adj.* **1.** comical, amusing, humorous, diverting, laughable, hilarious, absurd, ridiculous, ludicrous; witty, droll, comic, facetious, waggish, jocular, jocose, sporting, jesting, antic, mirthful, merry; farcical. **2.** odd, strange, unusual, uncommon, weird, curious, bizarre, outlandish, queer, peculiar, offbeat. **—Ant. 1** serious, sober, humorless; solemn, grave; mournful, melancholy.

fur *n.* pelt, animal skin; hair, fleece, down.

furious *adj.* **1.** enraged, irate, angry, mad, irascible, hot under the collar, up in arms, on the warpath, infuriated, maddened, provoked, raging, wrathful, fuming; rabid, frenzied, wild, fanatical; unbalanced, frenetic. **2.** tempestuous, turbulent, fierce, intense, violent, vehement, stormy, raging, tumultuous, rampant; fiery, savage, passionate; ungovernable, unrestrained; reckless, heedless, wild. **—Ant. 1** calm, serene, pleased, placated. **2** mild, calm, tame.

furnace *n.* heater, heating system; oven, stove, incinerator; forge, boiler, kiln.

furnish *v.* **1.** provide, equip, supply, stock, accommodate; endow, vest; purvey, render; favor, indulge; provision; give, grant, bestow on. **2.** appoint, equip, outfit, fit out, array, fit up; rig; accoutre, dress; gird, arm, prepare. **—Syn. Study. 2** FURNISH, APPOINT, EQUIP refer to providing something necessary or useful. FURNISH often refers to providing necessary or customary objects or services that increase living comfort: *to furnish a bedroom with a bed, desk, and chair.* APPOINT, a more formal word, now usu. used in the past participle, means to supply completely with all requisites or accessories, often in an elegant style: *a well-appointed hotel; a fully appointed suite.* EQUIP means to supply with necessary materials or apparatus for a particular action, service, or undertaking; it emphasizes preparation: *to equip a vessel; to equip a soldier.*

furniture *n.* household goods, house fittings, movables, appointments, chattels, possessions, property, furnishings, effects.

furor *n.* **1.** commotion, uproar, excitement, to-do, reaction, noise; rage, fury, fit of anger, passion, frenzy, madness, brouhaha, agitation, raving, *Slang* hoopla, flap; lunacy, insanity; transport, fervor, fanaticism. **2.** craze, vogue, fad, rage, mania, obsession, enthusiasm, fashion, *French* dernier cri, *Slang* thing, word.

furrow *n.* **1.** trench, channel, depression, cut, rut, groove, corrugation, trough, ditch, track; rift, crevice, crack, fissure, cleft. **2.** wrinkle, crease, deep line, crow's foot, ridge. **—***v.* **3.** plow, trench, dig. **4.** wrinkle, line, seam, pucker, knit.

further *adv.* **1.** farther, yonder, at a greater distance, more remotely, farther on, more in advance; beyond, abroad, afar off, out of range. **2.** more, additionally; again, yet, too, likewise, also; besides, furthermore, moreover; over and above, to boot. **—***adj.* **3.** more distant, yonder, farther, farther on. **4.** additional, supplementary, more, extra, supplemental; spare, other, auxiliary, ancillary; new, fresh; contributory, accessory. **—***v.* **5.** forward, aid, assist, help, advance, encourage; foster, back, back up, champion, promote, propagate, work for, favor, stand by; lend a hand, contribute to, strengthen; hasten, quicken, expedite, speed, accelerate, oblige, accommodate. **—Ant. 1, 3** nearer, closer. **5** slow, retard; hinder, frustrate, thwart, impede, obstruct.

furtherance *n.* advancement, advance, promotion, support, aid, succor, help, assistance, lift; patronage, favor, interest; advocacy, championship, defense; countenance, cooperation. **—Ant.** opposition, hindrance, restraint; defeat, destruction.

furthermore *adv.* also, moreover, besides, in addition, too, additionally, as well, likewise; *Informal* to boot, into the bargain; over and above.

furtive *adj.* secret, secretive, surreptitious, stealthy, hidden, clandestine, covert; masked, veiled, shrouded, cloaked, private, secluded, unrevealed, unseen; confidential, mysterious, undercover; collusive, conspiratorial; sly, shifty, wily, crafty, underhand, sneaking, sneaky, skulking, shady, elusive, evasive. **—Ant.** forthright, straightforward, aboveboard; unconcealed, unreserved; public, undisguised, brazen, barefaced.

fury *n.* **1.** rage, anger, unrestrained anger, frenzy, furor, wrath, ire, choler; outburst, fit, tantrum, pet, snit, huff, dudgeon; acerbity, acrimony, virulence, gall, spleen; indignation. **2.** might, force, violence, fierceness, vehemence, ferocity, intensity, severity, turbulence; assault, attack; impetuosity, headlong rush; bluster, excitement. **3.** spitfire, she-devil, violent person, hellcat, hag, shrew, termagant, virago, vixen, she-dragon. **—Syn. Study. 1** See ANGER. **—Ant. 1** calm, serenity, tranquillity, quietude, peacefulness, composure, placidity, equanimity. **3** angel.

fuse[1] *v.* **1.** smelt, run together, meld, blend by melting together, liquefy by heat, weld, solder, melt. **2.** consolidate, merge, blend, mingle, intermingle, meld, join, link, weld, combine, incorporate; solidify, federate, amalgamate, league, band together, confederate; assimilate, coalesce, associate. **—Ant. 2** separate, disunite, disperse, diffuse.

fuse[2] *n.* detonator, igniting tube, ignition, firing material, wick, torch.

fusillade *n.* barrage, broadside, salvo, volley, bombardment, cannonade, enfilade; drumfire, raking fire, mortar barrage; shower, spray, hail.

fusion *n.* **1.** smelting, melting, liquefaction; dissolving. **2.** combination, blending, blend, union, merging, amalgamation, synthesis, unification; commixture, commingling, intermixture; federation, confederacy, confederation, league, alliance, association, coalescence, coalition, combine.

fuss *n.* **1.** bustle, ado, anxious activity, stir, to-do, flutter, flurry, pother, bother; commotion, hurly-burly, disturbance, hubbub, confusion, turmoil, turbulence, perturbation; ceremony, ceremoniousness, pomp, superfluity; fret, stew, fidget; worry, agitation; much ado about nothing, tempest in a teapot; fluster, hustle, scurry. **2.** quarrel, minor argument, dispute, set-to, spat, tiff. *—v.* **3.** stir about, bustle, busy oneself, potter, putter, pother; tinker, fool, fidget, flutter about. **4.** fume, fret, worry; nitpick, nag; carp, cavil, quibble, niggle; trouble, take pains, labor. **5.** fluster, disconcert, rattle, confuse, flurry; annoy, bother, pester, put into a fuss, trouble, perturb; excite, agitate. **—Ant. 1** inactivity, peace, tranquillity, simplicity.

fussy *adj.* particular, hard to please, exacting, demanding, compulsive, meticulous, nitpicking, finicky, finical; painstaking, assiduous, fastidious, squeamish, scrupulous; critical, persnickety, old-maidish, crotchety; bustling, busy, nervous; cluttered, ornate.

futile *adj.* useless, fruitless, vain, profitless, idle, worthless, valueless, bootless, unprofitable; ineffective, ineffectual, unsuccessful, unavailing, abortive, nugatory; trifling, trivial, insignificant, empty, petty, frivolous, unimportant. **—Syn. Study.** See USELESS. **—Ant.** effective, fruitful, successful; profitable, useful, worthy; important, significant.

future *n.* **1.** time to come, time from now on, futurity; hereafter, tomorrow, *Spanish* mañana, morrow, by-and-by, offing. **2.** outlook, prospect, chance for advancement, opportunity; anticipation, expectation; hope. *—adj.* **3.** from now on, in prospect, coming, to come, impending, prospective, eventual, projected, ultimate, anticipated, hereafter; following, subsequent, ensuing, succeeding; later, latter, after. **—Ant. 1** past, time gone by, antiquity. **3** past, gone, bygone, former, previous.

fuzz *n.* fluff, lint, bits of thread, down, downy fibers.

fuzzy *adj.* **1.** downy, linty, fluffy; frizzy, woolly; pubescent. **2.** blurred, indistinct, unclear, vague, ill-defined, out of focus, not clear, indefinite; shadowy, dim, obscure; misty, hazy, murky, foggy; confused. **—Ant. 1** smooth, slick. **2** clear, sharp, in focus.

gab *v.* **1.** chat, chatter, talk idly, jaw, babble, jabber, gibber, chitchat, blather, blab, patter, prattle, prate, gossip; *Informal* shoot the breeze, chew the fat, chew the rag; *Slang* rap. —*n.* **2.** *Informal* small talk, glib speech, chatter; conversation; blarney, baloney, balderdash; gossip, chitchat; idle talk, patter, prattle.

gabble *v.* **1.** chatter, gab, jabber, chitchat, gossip, babble, blather, prate, blab; *Slang* rap. —*n.* **2.** chatter, babbling, jabbering, gibbering, prattle, blathering, chattering, chitchat.

gadget *n.* contrivance, device, tool, contraption, mechanical invention; newfangled object, novelty, gimmick; attachment; accessory; *Slang* doohickey, doodad, jigger, thingamajig, thingamabob.

gag *v.* **1.** stop up the mouth of, silence, muffle, hush; suppress, smother, stifle, muzzle, choke; bottle up, close off, stop. **2.** retch, be sick, be nauseated, choke, heave. —*n.* **3.** restraint on mouth to prevent outcry, stoppage, block; cloture. **4.** *Slang* joke, practical joke, hoax, jest, horseplay, foolery, facetiousness.

gaiety Also **gayety** *n.* **1.** gay spirits, cheerfulness, vivacity, joyousness, jollity, high enthusiasm, good humor, mirth, high spirits, liveliness, animation; jauntiness, effervescence, sprightliness, sportiveness, festive spirits, airiness; elation, exhilaration; frolic, amusement, celebration, merrymaking, merriment, fun. **2.** brightness, colorfulness, showiness, brilliance; gaudiness, garishness; frippery, frumpery; tinsel, glitter, show, brummagem. —**Ant. 1** sadness, melancholy, misery, despair, gloom; gloominess, despondency.

gain *v.* **1.** acquire, obtain, secure, achieve, attain, get; gather, collect, get possession of, capture, bag, net; earn, reap, win, glean; pick up, procure. **2.** acquire, put on, add, build up. **3.** attain, reach, arrive at, hit, come to; fetch, overtake, close with. **4.** improve, recover, make progress; thrive, prosper, flourish; bloom, blossom. —*n.* **5.** Often **gains** earnings, winnings, profit, compensation, wages, salary, bonus, income, revenue, remuneration, dividend; proceeds, produce, yield; plus, favorable balance, black ink. **6.** increase, return, accretion, increment, addition, accumulation; advantage, improvement, attainment, plus; leap, jump. —**Syn. Study. 1** GAIN, ATTAIN, EARN, WIN imply obtaining a reward or something advantageous. GAIN suggests the expenditure of effort to get or reach something desired: *After battling the blizzard, we finally gained our destination.* ATTAIN suggests a sense of personal satisfaction in having reached a lofty goal: *to attain stardom.* EARN emphasizes a deserved reward for labor or services: *to earn a promotion.* WIN stresses attainment in spite of competition or opposition: *to win support in a campaign.* —**Ant. 1** lose, forfeit. **4** fail, decline, worsen. **5** loss, forfeiture, detriment; damage, injury; privation, deprivation.

gainfully *adv.* profitably, lucratively, productively, remuneratively; usefully.

gait *n.* walk, stride, step, pace, tread; carriage, bearing, deportment.

gala *adj.* **1.** festive, celebratory, glittering, ceremonial, gay; splendid, sumptuous, opulent, grand, spectacular, magnificent, majestic; glamorous, fancy-dress, star-studded. —*n.* **2.** celebration, festive occasion, festival, party, festivity, fete, benefit.

gale *n.* **1.** strong wind, windstorm, blow; gust, squall, tempest, cyclone. **2.** uproar, outburst, outbreak, eruption, gust, flurry; stir, commotion, fit, agitation, tumult.

gall[1] *n.* **1.** impudence, effrontery, boldness, audacity, temerity, assurance, brazenness; brass, nerve, cheek; insolence, rudeness, presumption, sauciness, highhandedness. **2.** bitterness, bile, rancor, spleen, venom, animosity, virulence, malignity, acrimony.

gall[2] *v.* **1.** chafe, make sore, rub sore, abrade, bruise; flay, score, excoriate. **2.** annoy, irritate, irk, provoke, gripe, vex, miff, exasperate, fret, displease, exacerbate, harass, rile, anger, ruffle, enrage, nettle; incense, affront, offend; sting, injure; *Slang* bug. —**Ant. 2** delight, please highly, amuse.

gallant *adj.* **1.** brave, valiant, heroic, noble, chivalrous, courageous, dauntless, fearless, intrepid, daring, bold, high-spirited, valorous; lionhearted, stalwart, stouthearted; high-spirited, plucky, *Slang* gutsy, game, resolute. **2.** chivalrous, cavalier, courtly, attentive, dashing, mannerly, courteous, polite, gentlemanly, suave, urbane, well-bred; considerate, thoughtful, kindly, obliging. —*n.* **3.** cavalier, dandy, dashing young man, blood, gay blade; *Slang* swell, dude, stud; fop, Beau Brummel. —**Ant. 1** cowardly, craven, fearful, afraid, ignoble. **2** impolite, discourteous, ill-mannered, rude, churlish, boring.

gallantry *n.* **1.** bravery, heroism, valor,

dashing, courage, courageousness, fortitude, fearlessness, dauntlessness, intrepidity, daring, mettle, derring-do; spirit, pluck, mettle, nerve, prowess, determination, resoluteness; *Slang* grit, sand. **2.** courtly attention, attentiveness, courtliness, chivalry, good manners, politeness, courtesy; good breeding, gentility, suavity, urbanity. **—Ant. 1** cowardliness, cowardice; irresolution. **2** boorishness, loutishness, churlishness; discourteousness, discourtesy, rudeness, ungraciousness, unattentiveness.

gallery *n.* **1.** covered walk, roofed promenade, arcade, portico, colonnade, cloister, passage, passageway, corridor, piazza, loggia, stoa; triforium, ambulatory. **2.** balcony, mezzanine; *Slang* peanut gallery, grandstand, bleachers. **3.** art gallery, picture gallery, exhibition hall, salon; art museum.

gallop *n.* **1.** fast gait; rapid ride, run, fast clip, mad dash; jog, trot, sprint. *—v.* **2.** go at a full gait, run, race; ride at a fast gait, ride at full speed. **3.** race, run, rush, hurry, hasten, make haste, hie, dash, speed, tear along, tear off, bowl along; bolt, bound, spring, fly, scurry, dart; *Informal* flit, scamper, whisk, scoot, skedaddle, whiz, skim, scuttle, scud, sprint, shoot. **—Ant. 1** slow gait. **2** amble, walk. **3** crawl, creep, walk, saunter, amble.

gallows *n.* scaffold, gibbet; (*loosely*) noose, rope, halter, Tyburn tree.

galore *adv.* in abundance, in great quantity, aplenty, to spare, as much as desired, *French* à gogo. **—Ant.** in short supply.

galvanize *v.* **1.** electrify, charge, energize, activate, stimulate, treat. **2.** arouse, rouse, excite, stimulate, stir, move, electrify, bring to vitality, quicken; infuse new life into, vitalize, fire, inspire, thrill, wake, awaken, spur on, rally, foment, provoke. **—Ant. 2** lull, soothe, pacify; dull, deaden.

gambit *n.* maneuver, ploy, stratagem, scheme, trick, feint, ruse, artifice; opening move, initial play; voluntary sacrifice.

gamble *v.* **1.** bet, wager, play for money; take a flyer, try one's luck, tempt fortune. **2.** take a chance, risk, hazard, speculate, chance; back, trust in, have blind faith in. *—n.* **3.** risk, hazard, uncertainty, speculation, venture, flyer; leap in the dark, random shot, tossup, blind bargain. **—Ant. 2** be conservative, conserve; play it safe, *Informal* play it close to one's vest. **3** surety, sure thing, safe bet, cinch.

gambol *v.* romp playfully, skip about, dance about, frolic, frisk, sport, caper, cut capers, cavort, disport, prance, jump about, rollick; leap, bound, spring, bounce, hop, vault.

game *n.* **1.** play, amusement, diversion, pastime, sport, entertainment, recreation, distraction; fun, merriment, frolic, merrymaking, gaiety, festivity; lark, romp, antic, gambol, spree. **2.** match, contest, athletic contest, competition, tournament, tourney. **3.** wild animals, wild fowl, game fish; hunted meat; prey, quarry. *—adj.* **4.** resolute, determined, plucky, unflinching, willing, dauntless, intrepid, courageous, brave, fearless, spunky, spirited, heroic, valiant, valorous, gallant; daring, cocky. **5.** disabled, incapacitated, lame, crippled, halt, limping, bad, *Informal* gimpy; deformed, crooked, hobbling. **—Ant. 1** work, toil, labor; duty; job, chore, business. **4** irresolute; fearful, afraid, cowardly. **5** healthy, strong, well.

gamut *n.* full range, complete scale, entire sequence, compass, sweep, scope, reach, ken, extent, purview, complete series; series of gradations, graded series.

gang *n.* **1.** crowd, group, band, flock, outfit, pack; clique, circle of friends, coterie; friends, comrades, chums, companions; *Informal* buddies, pals, cronies; associates, neighbors; fellow members; schoolmates, classmates; coworkers, fellow workers, crew. **2.** band, mob, company, troop, party, pack, contingent, body; ring. **3.** crew, squad, shift, team, relay; troop, company, detachment, phalanx.

gangster *n.* gunman, mobster, hoodlum, bandit, racketeer; syndicate member, mafioso; criminal, crook, felon, thug, ruffian; *Informal* hooligan, tough, hood, *Slang* goon.

gap *n.* **1.** opening, breach, empty space, hole, gape, aperture; crack, crevice, fissure, cleft, chink, break, slit, slot, cut, fracture, divide; puncture, rent, rift, gash, notch, cavity. **2.** blank space, interval, pause, void, vacuum, interim, lacuna, hiatus; break, interruption, intermission, recess, interlude. **3.** mountain pass; valley, canyon, ravine, gulch, gully; chasm, crevasse, abyss. **4.** difference, disparity, divergence.

gape *v.* **1.** stare open-mouthed, stare in wonder, stare stupidly, show astonishment, regard with awe, gawk, stare, look excitedly, peer, ogle, gaze; *Slang* rubberneck. **2.** open the mouth wide, gasp; yawn. **3.** part, separate, split, fly open, cleave, expand, open wide, spread out.

garb *n.* uniform, outfit, apparel, attire, dress, costume, clothing, clothes, garments, togs, get-up, rig; raiment, habiliments, habit, vesture, vestment;

gown, robe, suit, wardrobe, finery, gear, livery, trappings.

garbage *n.* **1.** refuse, kitchen scraps; rubbish, trash, dirt, sweepings, waste; swill, offal, carrion. **2.** junk, useless things, odds and ends; rubbish, litter, debris. **—Ant. 2** valuables, treasure.

garble *v.* confuse, jumble, mix up, be unclear, misunderstand; distort; fragment. **—Ant.** make clear, clarify, straighten out.

garden *n.* **1.** garden plot; (*variously*) flower garden, vegetable garden, kitchen garden, herb garden, truck garden, rock garden, yard, lawn, plot. **2.** small park, botanical garden, zoological park, natural park. **3.** fertile region, agricultural region; paradise, Eden, Arcadia, green oasis. **—***v.* **4.** cultivate a garden, plant a garden, tend a garden, work in a garden, work the soil, use one's green thumb.

gargantuan *adj.* gigantic, enormous, immense, huge, great, unbelievably big; vast, colossal, tremendous, mammoth, massive, stupendous, monstrous; titanic, herculean, elephantine, prodigious, amplitudinous; overgrown, lubberly, hulking, towering. **—Ant.** small, little, tiny, diminutive, miniature; dwarfish, puny, minuscule, pint-sized; compact, meager, scant, paltry, trivial, niggling.

garish *adj.* gaudy, loud, flashy, glaring, showy, blatant, bright; overelaborate, too colorful, extremely ornate, tastelessly showy, ostentatious, pretentious, cheap, brassy, obtrusive; tawdry, vulgar, flaunting, tinsel. **—Ant.** sedate, conservative, unobtrusive, modest; plain, simple, somber; refined, tasteful, elegant.

garland *n.* wreath, lei, festoon, diadem, crown, chaplet, circlet, coronet, headband, fillet, halo, corona, bay, laurel.

garment Often **garments** *n.* article of clothing; apparel, attire, garb, dress, gear, costume, raiment, togs, outfit, habit, vestment, habiliment.

garnish *v.* **1.** embellish, decorate, adorn, ornament, trim, beautify, deck, bedeck, array, spruce up, furbish, festoon, set off, smarten, gild, embroider, emblazon; *Informal* trick out, dress up, doll up, deck out. **—***n.* **2.** decoration, embellishment, adornment, ornament, trim, trimming, festoon. **—Ant. 1** strip, make bare, denude, deprive, divest.

garret *n.* attic, loft; topmost floor, floor under the eaves. **—Ant.** basement, cellar.

garrison *n.* **1.** soldiers stationed at a fort, detachment; (*variously*) division, brigade, regiment, squadron, platoon, battery, escadrille. **2.** fort, fortification; military camp, military base. **—***v.* **3.** place on duty, station, assign to, bivouac, put on duty in a garrison. **4.** occupy with troops, provide with a garrison; guard, watch over, secure, patrol.

garrulous *adj.* talkative, effusive, loquacious; wordy, windy, verbose, long-winded; gabby, voluble, chattery, chatty, prattling, prating, babbling; gossipy. **—Syn. Study.** See TALKATIVE. **—Ant.** reticent, taciturn, quiet, reserved, close-mouthed; terse, concise.

gas *n.* **1.** gaseous mixture; vapor, fume. **2.** gasoline, fuel, *British* petrol, *French* essence.

gash *n.* **1.** long cut, slash, gaping wound, incision; split, cleft, slit, crack, fissure, rent. **—***v.* **2.** make a long cut in, cut deeply, slash, make an incision in, incise, lance, pierce, wound, lacerate, slice; split, slit, cleave, rend, tear, hack; carve, quarter, dissect.

gasp *v.* **1.** struggle (*for breath*) with open mouth, inhale frantically, labor for breath; suck in (*air*), breathe convulsively; have trouble breathing, respire laboriously; gulp, pant, wheeze, puff, catch the breath. **2.** utter with gasps, exclaim in short breaths, speak breathlessly, blurt, vociferate, cry hurriedly. **—***n.* **3.** sudden short breath, convulsive breathing, sharp inhalation, gulp.

gastronomy *n.* **1.** art of good eating, epicurism, pleasures of food and drink. **2.** culinary practices; style of cooking and serving.

gate *n.* **1.** enclosure door, entrance to a pen, opening through a fence; portal, gateway, hatchway, doorway. **2.** entrance door; box office, ticket seller's booth; turnstile. **3.** sluice; tap, valve, spigot.

gather *v.* **1.** assemble, get together, bring together, collect, muster, marshal, accumulate, amass, mass, group, convene, cluster, come together, bunch together, concentrate, congregate; pile up, stack, heap up, lump together, stockpile. **2.** infer, deduce, assume, be led to believe, conclude; learn, understand, observe. **—***n.* **3.** fold, pucker; pleat, ruffle, shirr. **—Syn. Study. 1** GATHER, ASSEMBLE, COLLECT, MUSTER, MARSHAL imply bringing or drawing together. GATHER expresses the general idea usu. with no implication of arrangement: *to gather seashells.* ASSEMBLE is used of persons, objects, or facts brought together in a specific place or for a specific purpose: *to assemble data for a report.* COLLECT implies purposeful accumulation to form an ordered whole: *to collect evidence.* MUSTER, primarily a military term, suggests thoroughness in the process of collection: *to muster all one's resources.* MARSHAL, another chiefly military term, suggests rigorously ordered, purposeful arrangement: *to marshal facts for effective presentation.* **—Ant. 1** disperse, dissipate; separate.

gathering *n.* assembly, meeting, party, conference, conclave, convocation, concourse, convention; company, crowd, throng, assemblage, accumulation, congregation, aggregation, multitude, turnout; *Informal* gang, pack, mob, bunch, drove, flock, horde, crush, press, roundup; collection, concentration, convergence.

gauche *adj.* ill-mannered, uncouth, socially awkward, unpolished, lacking in social graces, inelegant, overly informal, tasteless, ungentlemanly, unmannerly, unrefined, uncultured, boorish, oafish, ill-bred; proletarian, plebeian; ungraceful, inept, blundering, clumsy, awkward, heavy-handed, bungling, maladroit. **—Ant.** polite, well-mannered, well-bred, elegant, polished, suave, urbane, smooth, gracious, formal, tasteful, refined; graceful.

gaudy *adj.* **1.** garish, flashy, loud, showy, overly fancy; cheap, vulgar, worthless, tasteless, tawdry, flimsy, sham, bespangled, tinsel. **2.** colorful, showy, eye-catching, striking, ostentatious, glaring, pretentious; brilliant, dazzling, glittering, vivid, intense; sparkling, lustrous. **—Ant. 1** sedate, conservative, quiet; modest, tasteful, refined, elegant, unpretentious, subtle. **2** dull, lackluster, colorless.

gauge, Also **gage** *v.* **1.** estimate, judge, appraise, ascertain, guess; evaluate, calculate, adjudge, rate, assess. *—n.* **2.** measuring instrument, measuring device, measure, meter; standard, criterion, yardstick. **3.** size, measurement, internal diameter, inner measurement, inner dimension.

gaunt *adj.* **1.** very thin, emaciated, scrawny, haggard; lanky, skinny, bony, lean, lank, slender, slim, scraggy, spindly, spare, meager, raw-boned, spindle-shanked; starved, cadaverous, wasted, withered, pinched, skeletal, shriveled. **2.** bleak, forsaken, desolate, deserted, barren; grim, forbidding. **—Ant. 1** plump, fat, chubby, stout, portly, corpulent, obese, rotund, well-fed; sleek. **2** lush, luxurious, blooming, inviting; bustling, active.

gawk *v.* stare stupidly, gape, look with astonishment; gaze, peer; rubberneck.

gawky *adj.* awkward, ungainly, clumsy, lubberly, *Slang* klutzy, bungling, fumbling, blundering, ham-handed, ham-fisted, all thumbs, graceless, gawkish, unwieldy, maladroit, lumpish. **—Ant.** graceful, polished, comely, attractive, urbane, suave.

gay *adj.* **1.** cheerful, cheery, happy, lighthearted, merry, joyous, joyful; jolly, sunny, lively, vivacious, sparkling, sprightly, gleeful, in good spirits, buoyant, dashing, sportive, insouciant, effervescent, frolicsome, jovial, jocular, jocose, hilarious, humorous, waggish; festive, convivial, social, jubilant, frivolous, playful, rejoicing, elated, exultant, glad, gladsome, blithe, genial, smiling, airy, bright; jaunty, skittish, chipper, frisky, animated, spirited, coltish, volatile, *Slang* fun. **2.** bright, colorful, showy, brilliant, vivid, intense, glowing, lustrous; parti-colored, multicolored, variegated; eye-catching, sumptuous, splendid; glittering, flamboyant, theatrical. **3.** homosexual; (of a female) lesbian, Sapphic. *—n.* **4.** homosexual; (of a female) lesbian. **—Ant. 1** grave, serious, somber, sedate, staid, solemn, sober; cheerless, joyless; quiet, still, silent; unhappy, morose, grim, miserable; heavy, sad, melancholy. **2** dull, somber, colorless, drab, lackluster; sedate, conservative.

gaze *v.* **1.** look steadily, look intently, look fixedly, contemplate, stare, watch, eye, keep one's look fixed, rivet the eyes, look long, look earnestly, strain one's eyes; study, peruse; look with wonder, gape, ogle, peer, scrutinize, survey, inspect, examine, pore over, witness, observe; glance, scan, behold, regard, peek; glare, glower, lower; *Slang* rubberneck. *—n.* **2.** intent look, stare, steady look, scrutiny.

gear *n.* **1.** toothed wheel, cogwheel; flywheel, cam. **2.** equipment, paraphernalia, outfit, things, accessories, apparatus, material, rigging, trappings; implements, instruments, tackle, rig, tools, contrivances; personal effects, belongings, property; apparel, clothing, clothes, attire, dress, garments, garb; *Informal* duds, togs; accoutrements.

gem *n.* **1.** jewel, precious stone; semiprecious stone, bijou; *Slang* rock. **2.** jewel, prize, treasure, wonder, marvel, one in a thousand; *Slang* beaut, peach, dear, doll, sweetheart.

genealogy *n.* family tree, ancestry, lineage, list of forebears, family descent, parentage, extraction, derivation, pedigree; stock; line, house, birth. **—Syn. Study.** See PEDIGREE.

general *adj.* **1.** comprehensive, collective, overall, generic, basic, taken as a whole; sweeping, blanket, extensive, panoramic; vague, nontechnical, imprecise, inexact; not special, not particular, not specific, not limited, nonexclusive; unspecified, miscellaneous, not partial. **2.** common, widespread, popular, prevalent, prevailing, universal, broad, public, pandemic; worldwide, ecumenical. **3.** usual, customary, regular, habitual, normal, natural, typical, accustomed, wonted; ordinary, everyday, conventional, frequent; current, prevalent, prevailing, most common. **—Syn. Study. 2** GENERAL, COMMON, POPULAR, UNIVERSAL agree in the idea of being nonexclusive and widespread. GENERAL means pertaining to or true of all or most of a particular class or body, irrespective of individuals: *a general belief.* COMMON means shared or experienced frequently or by a majority of group members: *a common problem.* POPULAR means belonging to or favored by the people or the public generally, rather than a particular class: *a popular misconception.* UNIVERSAL means found everywhere with no exception: *a universal need.* **—Ant. 1, 2** specific, concrete, definite, particular, individual; exact, precise, special, distinctive. **3** exceptional, rare, singular, uncommon, unusual, extraordinary, infrequent; peculiar, odd.

generality *n.* **1.** general statement, sweeping statement, generalization; abstract thought, vague notion, imprecise thinking, unorganized idea; undetailed plan, inexact presentation. **2.** universality, all-encompassing reach, far-flung scale; collectiveness, miscellaneousness; indiscriminateness. **3.** general rule, generalization, widespread principle, universal thing; obvious statement, truism, cliché, platitude. **—Ant. 1** specific, detail. **2** specialization; limit.

generalize *v.* infer, conclude, judge, form an opinion; speak in generalities, make a sweeping statement, make a generalization.

generally *adv.* **1.** usually, ordinarily, in general, as a rule, for the most part, in most cases, typically, mainly, in the usual course of things, habitually; often, frequently, repeatedly, currently; always, universally; extensively. **2.** without reference to particular persons or things, without particularizing, without noting the individual exceptions; for the most part, in the main, on the whole, largely, mainly, chiefly, principally, mostly. **—Syn. Study. 1** See OFTEN. **—Ant. 1** rarely, as an exception, occasionally, infrequently, in a few cases, unusually, especially, particularly. **2** specifically, individually.

generate *v.* **1.** produce, cause, make, form, bring about, engender, effectuate, induce, institute, bring into existence; construct, fabricate, invent, frame, fashion, contrive, coin, originate; develop, evolve, occasion. **2.** beget, father, sire, spawn; procreate, create; breed, reproduce, engender, propagate; proliferate, fructify, fecundate; impregnate, fertilize, bear, yield. **—Ant. 1** extinguish, end, terminate, annihilate, kill, stifle, crush, squelch, quash.

generation *n.* **1.** progeny, issue, offspring; family, tribe, race, clan, house, line, lineage, breed, strain, stock; kin. **2.** process of generating, reproduction, propagation, procreation, engendering, begetting, breeding; fertilization, impregnation; proliferation. **3.** creation, origination, production, formation, genesis; causation; development, growth, evolution.

generic *adj.* general, common, universal, nonexclusive, nonrestrictive, generalized, comprehensive, all-inclusive, sweeping, unspecified, collective. **—Ant.** specific, restricted, proprietary, exclusive, distinctive, explicit.

generous *adj.* **1.** openhanded, willing to give, freehanded, bighearted, ungrudging; charitable, beneficent, philanthropic, free-giving, hospitable; lavish, liberal, munificent, princely, bountiful, bounteous, unrestricted, unstinting, unstinted, spare-no-expense; extravagant, prodigal, effusive. **2.** plentiful, ample, bounteous, large, copious, plenteous, abundant, liberal; overflowing, plethoric. **3.** unselfish, humane, humanitarian, considerate, benevolent, noble, altruistic; accommodating, obliging; bighearted, largehearted, magnanimous; high-minded, lofty; honorable. **—Syn. Study. 1** GENEROUS, CHARITABLE, LIBERAL, MUNIFICENT all describe giving or sharing something of value. GENEROUS stresses the warm and sympathetic nature of the giver: *a retired executive, generous with her time.* CHARITABLE stresses the goodness and kindness of the giver and the indigence or need of the receiver: *a charitable contribution to a nursing home.* LIBERAL emphasizes the large size of the gift and the openhandedness of the giver: *a liberal bequest to the university.* MUNIFICENT refers to a gift or award so strikingly large as to evoke amazement or admiration: *a lifetime income, a truly munificent reward for his loyalty.* **—Ant. 1** stingy, tight, tightfisted, closefisted, cheap, niggardly, miserly, parsimonious, illiberal, penurious; avaricious, covetous, selfish. **2** small, little, tiny; scarce, picayune, scanty, minimal. **3** mean, ignoble, small, petty, churlish, rapacious, greedy.

genesis *n.* origin, beginning, commencement, creation, birth, inception, rise, root, generation, begetting, engendering. **—Ant.** end, termination, conclusion, finish.

genial *adj.* cordial, friendly, good-natured, congenial, amiable, gracious, affable, agreeable, pleasant, convivial, neighborly, companionable, sociable, social, courteous, civil, warm, happy, glad, hearty, expansive, kind, kindly, well-disposed, cheerful, sunny, vivacious, merry, cheery, jovial, jolly, jocund, gay, in good spirits, sparkling, mirthful, bright, lighthearted, festive, joyous, joyful; jaunty, lively, chipper. **—Ant.** unfriendly, unpleasant, uncongenial, ungracious, unsympathetic, cool, cold; rude, discourteous, uncivil; harsh, sullen, morose; cutting, sarcastic, sardonic, ironical, cheerless, caustic.

genius *n.* **1.** mental giant, mastermind, brilliant intellect, prodigy; child prodigy; *Slang* brain, mind, whiz, ace; master, expert, mine of information, walking encyclopedia. **2.** natural talent, creative power, faculty, gift, knack, natural endowment, aptitude, penchant, wizardry, proclivity, bent, propensity, flair, predilection, turn of mind; insight, perception, percipience, intuition; imagination, invention, ingenuity; wisdom, intelligence, sagacity, understanding, judgment, wit. **—Ant. 1** idiot, imbecile, half-wit, moron; oaf, fool, simpleton, dunce, dullard, dolt; numskull, blockhead, booby, nitwit, ninny, nincompoop, *Slang* stupe. **2** ineptitude.

genre *n.* style, category, kind, class, sort, type, classification, variety, genus, species; fashion, description; school.

genteel *adj.* **1.** refined, well-bred, courteous, mannerly, polite, civil, well-spoken, ladylike, gentlemanly, courtly, decorous, poised; polished, cultured, cultivated, urbane; aristocratic, thoroughbred, patrician, of gentle blood. **2.** elegant, stylish, fashionable, modish, suited to high society, elite; silk-stocking; *Slang* high-class, hoity-toity, highfalutin, high-hat, swank, ritzy, high-toned, swell, tony; overrefined, pretentious. **—Ant. 1** unrefined, uncultured, inelegant, unpolished; impolite, discourteous, unmannerly, uncivil, rude; boorish, plebeian, low-class, low-bred, ill-bred. **2** unaffected, natural, simple, plain, unsophisticated, unfashionable, inelegant.

gentility *n.* refinement, polish, savoir-faire, breeding, mannerliness, polished behavior, chivalry, gallantry, decorum, propriety, punctilio, suavity, urbanity, cultivation, civility. **—Ant.** grossness, coarseness, vulgarity, boorishness, indelicacy.

gentle *adj.* **1.** gentle-hearted, kindly, kind, peaceful, compassionate, tenderhearted, tender, sympathetic, mild, meek; tolerant, benign, lenient, indulgent, merciful; thoughtful, considerate. **2.** mild, soft, light, easy, slight; quiet, calm, serene, tranquil, placid; balmy, moderate, temperate, not violent, not rough, not severe; bland, smooth, untroubled, low. **3.** docile, tame, manageable, easily handled, tractable; domesticated, broken, harmless, subdued, pacific, peaceful, calm. **—Ant. 1** hard; cruel, unkind, heartless, hard-hearted, rough, harsh, offensive, aggressive. **2** rough, harsh, hard, intense, powerful, strong, sharp, violent, immoderate; sudden, abrupt. **3** wild, fierce, savage, intractable; unmanageable.

gentleman *n.* **1.** well-mannered man, honorable man, refined man, civilized man, polished man; man of social position, man of good family, man of gentle birth, man of good breeding, aristocrat, patrician, silk-stocking, *Informal* gent, swell; (*variously*) cavalier, caballero, don, hidalgo, chevalier, squire, esquire. **2.** man, young man, fellow, chap, guy; (*of a male*) person, individual, one. **—Syn. Study. 1, 2** See MAN. **—Ant. 1** brute, lout, churl, boor, scoundrel, dastard, bum, low-life.

gentry *n.* aristocrats, aristocracy, upper class, nobility, blue bloods, society, gentlefolk, elite, country gentlemen. **—Ant.** lower class, working class, bourgeoisie, plebeians, commoners, *Slang* hoi polloi.

genuine *adj.* **1.** real, authentic, true, bona-fide, proven, veritable, actual, honest, legitimate, true-blue, solid, pure, simon-pure, sterling, unalloyed, unadulterated, 100 percent. **2.** sincere, true, unaffected, earnest; frank, candid, open, straightforward, honest, heartfelt, natural; ingenuous, naive, artless, guileless, unsophisticated, simple, plain. **—Ant. 1** fake, false; artificial, phony, bogus, counterfeit, imitation, ersatz, fraudulent, simulated, feigned, sham, spurious. **2** insincere, affected, hypocritical, pretended, fake, false, phony, artificial.

germ *n.* **1.** microbe, virus, microorganism, bacterium, bacillus, *Informal* bug. **2.** beginning, first stage, spark, rudiment; origin, source, root, fountainhead, seed, embryo. **3.** bud, sprout, seed bud, offshoot; seed, ovule, ovum; egg, embryo; nucleus, germ cell, spore. **—Ant. 2** outcome, upshot, result; end, termination, consummation.

germane *adj.* pertinent, relevant, appropriate, applicable, connected, relative, material, related, native, proper, intrinsic; apropos, appertaining, suitable, fitting, fit, to the point, to the purpose, apt. **—Ant.** irrelevant, inappropriate, unrelated, immaterial, unconnected, extraneous, incompatible, extrinsic, incongruous, inconsonant; incidental; foreign, alien.

germinate *v.* sprout, put out shoots, push up, vegetate, spring up, generate, develop, burgeon, shoot; bud, flower, bloom, blow, burst forth, blossom, open. **—Ant.** wither, die, perish; stagnate.

gestation *n.* full term of a pregnancy, life from conception to birth, pregnancy, maturation; development, evolution, incubation, propagation, generation, epigenesis.

gesticulate *v.* gesture; signal, motion, wave the hand, make a sign, beckon, pantomime, indicate; (*variously*) shrug, nod, nudge, wink.

gesture *n.* **1.** bodily movement, hand and arm movement, gesticulation, pantomime; signal, sign, motion, dumb show; (*variously*) shrug, nod, wave, nudge, touch, wink, body English, high sign. **2.** polite action, empty offer, formality, courtesy, flourish, demonstration. **—*v.* 3.** gesticulate, signal, motion, wave, beckon.

get *v.* **1.** obtain, acquire, attain, receive, procure, fetch, pick up, come by, go after, secure, come into possession of, glean, meet with; achieve, win, gain, earn, realize, net, bag, reap, take; inherit, succeed to, pocket. **2.** become, come to be, get to be, change to, be changed to, grow, turn, turn to, turn into, be converted into, wax. **3.** have done, cause to be done, have, make ready, fix, prepare. **4.** reach, communicate with, contact; arrive, come to, get in to; meet with, transport. **5.** understand, comprehend, grasp, learn, perceive, hear, catch; take in, fathom, figure out, follow, sense. **6.** baffle, bewilder, perplex, puzzle, confound, confuse, mystify; upset, annoy, irritate, disconcert, *Slang* beat. **7.** persuade, induce, influence, prevail upon, enlist, dispose, incline; coax, wheedle, bring round, sway, win over, talk around, suborn; predispose, move, prompt. **8.** seize, grab, capture, lay hold of, take, snatch, grasp, collar, grip; ensnare, entrap. **9.** catch, contract, be afflicted with, suffer from, come down with. **—Syn. Study. 1** GET, OBTAIN, ACQUIRE, PROCURE, SECURE imply gaining possession of something. GET suggests gaining possession in any manner, either voluntarily or without effort: *to get a copy of a book.* OBTAIN suggests putting forth effort to gain possession of something wanted: *to obtain information.* ACQUIRE often suggests possessing something after a prolonged effort: *to acquire a fortune in the oil business.* PROCURE stresses the use of special means or measures to get something: *to procure a rare etching from an art dealer.* SECURE suggests obtaining something and making possession safe and sure: *to secure benefits for striking workers.* **—Ant. 1** give, give up; dish out, mete out; avoid, forgo, eschew, forswear; lose, relinquish, abjure, quit. **2** stay, remain. **4** leave, separate from; avoid. **5** misunderstand. **6** make sense, be logical to; please, comfort, calm. **7** dissuade. **8** let go, give up, release, free. **9** cure, heal, mend.

ghastly *adj.* **1.** ghostlike, ghostly, deathlike, corpselike, spectral, cadaverous; deathly pale, pallid, ashen, colorless, wan, pasty, blanched; lackluster, glassy, haggard, bluish-white. **2.** hideous, revolting, gruesome, grisly, repellent, repulsive, loathsome, ugly, dreadful, horrible, horrendous, horrid, odious, terrifying, frightful, terrible, shocking, appalling, grim, forbidding, dismal; uncanny, weird, fearful. **—Ant. 1** ruddy, robust, healthy, fresh, blooming. **2** attractive, appealing, beautiful, lovely, charming, enticing.

ghost *n.* **1.** spirit of a dead person, disembodied spirit, departed spirit; phantom, apparition, phantasm, wraith, specter, supernatural being, shadow, shade, *Slang* spook; manifestation, materialization; banshee, sprite, demon, chimera, goblin, hobgoblin; phantasma, *German* doppelgänger. **2.** trace, suggestion, hint, semblance; shadow.

ghostly *adj.* ghostlike, spectral, wraithlike, phantom, phantasmal, phantomlike, unearthly, supernatural; *Slang* spooky; shadowy, illusive; weird, eerie, uncanny, unreal; ghastly, pale. **—Ant.** earthly, natural.

ghoulish *adj.* macabre, weird, eerie, scary, sinister, diabolic, hellish, infernal, satanic, fiendish, monstrous, demonic, horrifying, gruesome, hair-raising, zombielike, ogreish, necrophilic.

giant *n.* **1.** imaginary being of huge stature, colossus, titan, Brobdingnagian, Gargantua, Goliath. **2.** tall person, tall thing, colossus, behemoth, titan; *Slang* whopper, spanker, thumper, strapper. **—Ant. 1** dwarf, pigmy, midget. **2** *Slang* shorty, half-pint, shrimp.

gibberish *n.* meaningless talk, senseless writing, nonsense, unintelligible language, babble, gobbledygook, drivel, gabble, inarticulate talk, meaningless words, foolish talk; *Informal* balderdash, stuff and nonsense, bosh, twaddle, fiddle-faddle, flapdoodle, hocus-pocus, double-talk, doublespeak, blab, mumbo-jumbo, blather.

gibe, Also **jibe** *n.* **1.** taunt, taunting, jeer, criticism, sarcastic remark, sarcasm, cutting remark, scoff, sneer, ridicule, mockery, derision; quip, wisecrack; *Informal* slings and arrows; *Slang* knock, brickbat. **—*v.* 2.** jeer, taunt, poke fun, make fun of, scoff, mock, ridicule, laugh at, deride, sneer, twit, chaff, flout, rail at; *Slang* rag, roast, razz, needle. **—Ant. 1, 2** compliment, praise. **2** applaud; salute.

giddy *adj.* **1.** dizzy, lightheaded; feeling

faint, faint, fainting, affected with vertigo, vertiginous, reeling, whirling, swimming. **2.** causing dizziness, dizzying, awesome, overpowering. **3.** flighty, frivolous, capricious, erratic, fickle, changeable, impulsive, fitful, volatile, unsteady, inconsistent; careless, thoughtless, reckless, irresponsible, silly, mercurial, inconstant, fanciful, whimsical, vacillating, harum-scarum, hare-brained, rattlebrained, muddled, befuddled. **—Ant. 1** steady, stationary, steady on one's feet. **2** steadfast, determined, resolute, single-minded; serious, earnest; calm, serene.

gift *n.* **1.** present, something given; award, donation, favor, tip, gratuity, boon, benefaction; bonus, prize, grant, fee, consideration, premium; handout, largess, alms, dole, contribution, offering, aid, help; bribe, sop, graft, tribute; legacy, bequest, dot, dowry, dower, endowment. **2.** special ability, talent, capacity, natural endowment, aptitude, flair, genius, knack, faculty, capability, facility; qualification, attribute, quality, power, forte, aptness, virtue, property, turn, bent; skill, expertise, ingenuity, adroitness, proficiency, competency, craft, power. **—Ant. 1** penalty, fine, forfeiture.

gifted *adj.* **1.** talented, naturally endowed, well-endowed, fitted for, cut out for, at home as; ingenious, clever, inventive, able, adroit, adept, resourceful; facile, proficient, accomplished, skilled, capable, qualified, expert, master, superior, masterly, polished, practiced, finished, experienced; deft, quick, handy, slick; *Slang* crack, crackerjack, wizard. **2.** especially intelligent, unusually smart, bright, brilliant, having a high IQ. **—Ant. 1** talentless; amateur, unskilled, inept. **2** retarded; dumb, dull, slow, slow-witted, slow-learning.

gigantic *adj.* very large, huge, vast, enormous, immense, giant, colossal, mammoth, massive, monstrous, tremendous, stupendous, jumbo, elephantine; mighty, unwieldy, ponderous, hulking, strapping, bulky, lumpish, lubberly, towering, voluminous; large-scale, prodigious; gargantuan, herculean, titanic. **—Syn. Study.** GIGANTIC, COLOSSAL, MAMMOTH are used of whatever is physically or metaphorically of great magnitude. GIGANTIC refers to the size of a giant, or to anything that is of unusu. large size: *a gigantic country.* COLOSSAL refers to the awesome effect and extraordinary size or power of a colossus or of something of similar size, scope, or effect: *a colossal mistake.* MAMMOTH refers to the size of the animal of that name and is used esp. of anything large and heavy: *a mammoth battleship.* **—Ant.** small, little, tiny, miniature, compact; *Slang* teeny-weeny, itty-bitty; infinitesimal, microscopic; feeble, puny, weak; petty, insignificant; dwarfish, pigmy.

giggle *v.* **1.** laugh in a silly way, laugh nervously, chuckle, cackle, titter, twitter, simper, snicker, snigger. *—n.* **2.** silly laugh, titter, snigger, snicker, simper, chuckle, cackle; tee-hee, hee-hee.

gild *v.* **1.** coat with goldleaf, paint gold, gold-plate. **2.** embellish with minor lies, exaggerate, twist; gloss over, touch up, cover up, slant, stretch, bend.

gimcrack *n.* knickknack, bauble, gewgaw, trinket, ornament, curio, bagatelle, trifle, kickshaw, bijou, whatnot; thingamabob, thingamajig, contrivance, plaything.

gimmick *n.* scheme, stunt, plan, stratagem, ruse, wile, design, subterfuge, ploy; *Slang* angle, wrinkle, dodge; device, contrivance, gadget.

gingerly *adv.* very carefully, cautiously, warily, carefully, guardedly, charily, watchfully, circumspectly, vigilantly, prudently, discreetly, heedfully; suspiciously, hesitantly, timidly, daintily, delicately, fastidiously, mincingly, finically, squeamishly. **—Ant.** boldly, confidently; rashly, brashly, carelessly, heedlessly.

gird *v.* **1.** encircle with a belt, bind with a girdle, girdle, strap, belt, lace round; secure, tie, girt; hitch, truss, tighten, fasten. **2.** surround, encircle, ring, encompass, hem in, circumscribe, circle, loop; enclose, confine, wall in, hedge in, pen; besiege, lay siege, blockade. **3.** brace, steel, strengthen, fortify, sustain, prepare; harden, stiffen, buttress.

girdle *n.* **1.** corselet, corset, foundation garment, waist cincher, bodice; stays. **2.** waistband, sash, cummerbund; circlet, girth, cincture; surcingle, baldric. **3.** ring, belt, circle, band, hedge, boundary, hem, contour.

girl *n.* **1.** young female, schoolgirl, miss, lass, lassie, colleen, ingenue; daughter, female child; unmarried woman, maiden, maid, virgin, damsel, demoiselle; *Informal* nymph, wench, minx, baggage, nymphette, soubrette; *Slang* chick, bird, pigeon, kitten, doll. **2.** maid, maidservant, domestic, female servant, hired woman, hired girl, cleaning woman, cleaning lady, female employee, help, maid-of-all-work; cook, scullion; lady's maid, handmaid. **3.** girlfriend, sweetheart; fiancée, betrothed, affianced; lady love, lover, flame, passion, darling, angel, inamorata; mistress, concubine, courtesan; prostitute, whore, streetwalker.

girlish *adj.* girl-like, maidenlike, maidenly, youthful. **—Ant.** matronly, mature, womanly.

girth *n.* **1.** circumference, perimeter, length around. **2.** saddle girth, saddle band, cinch.

gist *n.* essence, main idea, main point, essential part, sense, force, significance, substance, sum and substance, implication, theme, burden, effect, drift; core, crux, heart, center, pith, kernel, marrow, meat, spirit, tenor, import, purport.

give *v.* **1.** present, present to, make a gift, make a gift of, bestow, offer, donate; grant, accord, deliver freely, hand over; award, confer; commit, entrust. **2.** contribute, donate, make a gift, bestow, consign, apportion, allot, dispense, distribute, subscribe, assign, settle money upon, transfer money or property to, entrust, vouchsafe, make over, vest in, enrich; endow, bequeath, leave; *Slang* hand out, shell out, fork out. **3.** place in someone's care, give over, hand over, entrust; present, accord. **4.** put forth, show, provide, present, issue, convey, afford; utter, emit, offer, give vent to, voice, articulate, pronounce. **5.** hand to, accommodate with, provide with, supply with, equip with, present, furnish, deliver, hand over, indulge with, favor with, proffer, tender, offer. **6.** pay, compensate, recompense, remunerate, allow, exchange, dispose of, requite; tip, bribe, grease the palm of; hire, buy; grant, accord, confer, hand over, dispense, distribute, present; *Slang* shell out, fork over. **7.** notify, announce, let know, communicate, impart; present, issue, render. **8.** permit, allow, grant, enable; present, offer, accord, provide, supply, furnish, proffer, afford, confer, impart, vouchsafe, deign, concede; admit, yield. **9.** apply, devote; surrender, attach, lose oneself in, lend, offer; addict. **10.** give way, break down, collapse; slacken, loosen, unbend, ease, relax, relent, bend; retreat, move back, recede; shrink, become soft, sink, deliquesce. **11.** open on; lead on to, afford an entrance; look out on, provide a vista. —*n.* **12.** flexibility, resilience; bounce, springiness. **—Syn. Study. 1** GIVE, CONFER, GRANT, PRESENT mean that something concrete or abstract is bestowed on one person by another. GIVE is the general word: *to give someone a book.* CONFER usu. means to give as an honor or as a favor; it implies courteous and gracious giving: *to confer a medal.* GRANT is usu. limited to the idea of acceding to a request or fulfilling an expressed wish; it often involves a formal act or legal procedure: *to grant a prayer; to grant immunity.* PRESENT, a more formal word than GIVE, usu. implies a certain ceremony in the giving: *to present an award.* **—Ant. 1–8** receive, get, take, accept, keep, retain, withhold, hold; take back, withdraw, recall. **11** shut off, block, hide, screen, mask, conceal, obscure.

glacial *adj.* cold, chill, freezing, frigid, bone-chilling, polar, arctic, icy, frozen, congealed, frosty, wintry, gelid; raw, bitter, piercing, biting; hostile, unfriendly, inimical, antagonistic, disdainful, contemptuous. **—Ant.** hot, warm, mild, balmy; friendly, cheery, cordial.

glad *adj.* **1.** happy, delighted, pleased, elated, joyful, joyous, gleeful, cheerful, exhilarated, contented, rejoiced; *Slang* tickled, tickled pink. **2.** happy, delightful, pleasing, elating, joyous, joyful, joy-giving, exhilarating, cheerful, blissful, gratifying, entrancing, cheering. **—Ant. 1** sad, unhappy, melancholy, sorry, sorrowful, depressed, displeased, dejected, miserable; disappointed, discontented. **2** depressing, sad, unhappy, unpleasant, displeasing.

gladden *v.* cheer, cheer up, please, hearten, elate, delight, gratify, pleasure, exhilarate, make happy, rejoice, inspirit, animate, raise the spirits of, enliven. **—Ant.** disappoint, depress, sadden, grieve.

glamorous Also **glamourous** *adj.* fascinating, charming, bewitching, enchanting, dazzling, captivating, alluring; attractive; exciting, magnetic, charismatic. **—Ant.** unglamorous, unexciting, colorless, unattractive, dull, drab.

glamour Also **glamor** *n.* fascination, excitement, adventure, romance, challenge; attractiveness, allure, charm, enchantment, magnetism, *Informal* glam; magic, illusion, glitter.

glance *v.* **1.** look quickly, see briefly, view momentarily, observe quickly, scan, cast a brief look, snatch a glance, catch a glimpse of, glimpse, regard hastily; peek, peep. **2.** rebound, ricochet, careen, bounce; graze, brush, shave, skim, slip, touch, kiss. —*n.* **3.** quick look, brief look, quick view, glimpse; peek, peep, squint. **—Ant. 1** study, contemplate, scrutinize, peruse, inspect fully. **3** long look, perusal, thorough examination, close scrutiny, full inspection.

glare *n.* **1.** harsh light, gleam, glint, flash, flare, glitter, glisten, blaze, flame; brightness, luminosity, radiance, glow, resplendence; gloss, sheen, shimmer, sparkle. **2.** angry look, reproving look, black look, dirty look, threatening look, piercing stare, glower, scowl. —*v.* **3.** shine harshly, reflect brightly, glitter, flare, gleam, glimmer, dazzle; sparkle, glisten, shimmer, glow, flash, blaze; radiate, twinkle, flicker. **4.** stare angrily, look fiercely, scowl, look blackly, glower, lower.

glaring *adj.* **1.** harsh, bright, strong, brilliant, intense, blinding, dazzling, flaring, piercing, penetrating; glittering, shimmering; vivid, resplendent. **2.** conspicuous, obvious, blatant, flagrant, arrant, unconcealed, unmistakable, egregious, undisguised; outrageous, audacious, gross, rank. **—Syn. Study. 2** See FLAGRANT. **—Ant. 1** soft, subdued. **2** hidden, concealed, inconspicuous; subtle, discreet.

glass *n.* **1.** drinking glass, tumbler, goblet; beaker, chalice. **2.** glassful, tumblerful.

glaze *v.* **1.** glass over, fit with glass, cover with glass; put a glassy finish on, enamel, coat with a glaze. **2.** become glassy, film over, blur, grow dim. **—***n.* **3.** glossy coating, glazing, vitreous surface, gloss, finish, enamel, varnish.

gleam *n.* **1.** beam, ray, streak, glow, glitter, glimmer; spark, sparkle, flash. **2.** sheen, luster, gloss, brightness, gleaming, radiance, effulgence, brilliance, coruscation, glitter. **3.** trace, ray, inkling, glimpse, bit, drop, jot, iota, speck, grain, hint, least bit, tiny bit, glimmer, flicker. **—***v.* **4.** shine, glow, flash, glare, flare, shimmer, glitter, glisten, glimmer, sparkle, glint, scintillate, coruscate; blink, flicker, twinkle. **—Ant. 1** darkness. **2** dullness, tarnish.

glean *v.* gather piecemeal, discover gradually, collect little by little, pick up, cull, accumulate, amass, gather, piece together, scrape together, harvest.

glee *n.* merriment, gaiety, joy, joyfulness, joyousness, exhilaration, exultation, rapture, delight, gladness, ecstasy; jollity, hilarity, mirth, laughter, verve, jollification, cheerfulness, joviality, jocularity; playfulness, liveliness, sprightliness, sportiveness. **—Ant.** sadness, gloom, dejection, depression, melancholy, sorrow, misery; *Slang* the blues, the dumps.

gleeful *adj.* happy, elated, glad, delighted, merry, gay, joyful, joyous, jolly, blissful, exultant, cheerful, exhilarated, mirthful, jovial, jocund, lighthearted, lively, festive. **—Ant.** sad, gloomy, dejected, melancholy.

glen *n.* narrow valley, dell, dale, vale, hollow, bottom. **—Ant.** height, peak, summit, mountain, hill.

glib *adj.* facile, flippant, quick, ready, smooth, smooth-tongued, suave, fluent, talkative, gabby, voluble, nimble of speech, ready of tongue, easy of manner; insincere, devious; slippery, oily, unctuous. **—Syn. Study.** See FACILE. **—Ant.** well-considered, sincere, deliberate, artless, guileless; hesitant, hesitating; halting, silent, quiet, taciturn.

glide *v.* **1.** soar, float, coast, sail, drift, flow. **2.** move smoothly, move effortlessly, slide, float, flow, skim, slip; skate, glissade; roll, drift, stream. **3.** slip, pass quickly, go unnoticed, roll, steal, drift, run; elapse, proceed, issue. **—Ant. 1** fall, plummet, sink. **2, 3** lurch, stagger, flounder, stumble, trip, hobble, shuffle.

glimmer *n.* **1.** faint gleam, small glow, flickering light, shimmer, glimmering, twinkle; ray, scintilla. **2.** trace, gleam, flickering, drop, speck, grain, bit, hint, glimpse, intimation, fleeting view. **—***v.* **3.** shine, shine faintly, flicker, twinkle, flash, blink; gleam, sparkle, glitter, glisten, shimmer, scintillate, coruscate; glare, glow, flare, beam. **—Ant. 1** glare, flash, flare, blaze.

glimpse *n.* **1.** fleeting look, quick look, brief look, brief sight, momentary view, quick view, glance; peep, peek, squint. **—***v.* **2.** see fleetingly, see briefly, catch sight of, catch a glimpse of, spy, see, spot, espy, sight briefly, view momentarily; peep at, peek at. **—Ant. 1** long look, survey, observation, scrutiny, inspection. **2** survey, observe closely, scrutinize, study, inspect; drink in.

glisten *v.* shine, sparkle, glitter, glister, flash, scintillate, coruscate, shimmer, glow, glimmer, gleam, glint, twinkle, flicker, radiate.

glitter *v.* **1.** sparkle, shine, glisten, gleam, glow, glimmer, flash, glint, radiate, flare, twinkle. **—***n.* **2.** luster, shine, sheen, gleam, glow, sparkle, fire, radiance, brilliance, splendor; beaming, refulgence. **3.** glamour, splendor, grandeur, pomp, show, showiness, pageantry, display, tinsel; excitement, thrill, electricity. **—Ant. 2** dullness. **3** drabness, dullness, dreariness, monotony.

gloat *v.* crow over, vaunt, brag, revel in, triumph, bask, glory over, exult, preen oneself, rejoice selfishly, relish maliciously, be overly pleased; strut, swagger. **—Ant.** regret, deplore; belittle, disparage, deprecate, slight, detract from, deride, scoff at, sneer at; *Slang* run down, knock, put down.

global *adj.* worldwide, world, universal, planetary, intercontinental, international; general, widespread, comprehensive, all-encompassing, unlimited, unbounded, all-out. **—Ant.** local, neighborhood, regional, sectional, provincial, parochial; limited, restricted, confined, circumscribed.

globe *n.* **1.** sphere, spherical body, spheroid, spherule, ball, orb, globule. **2.** planet, celestial body, world, Earth, biosphere.

gloom *n.* **1.** darkness, dark, blackness, dimness, dinginess, murkiness, murk, gloominess; shadows, shade, cloudiness, dusk, duskiness, obscurity. **2.** depression, low spirits, despondency, dejection, sadness, melancholy, cheerlessness, unhappiness, moroseness, heavyheartedness, heaviness of mind; doldrums, blues, mopishness, disconsolateness, despair, hopelessness, forlornness, distress; woe, misery, oppression, sorrow, grief, dolor. **—Ant. 1** light, brightness; daylight, sunlight, radiance. **2** joy, glee, delight, happiness, gladness, cheerfulness, high spirits, merriment, mirth, jollity, smiles.

gloomy *adj.* **1.** dark, dim, dull, dismal, dreary, murky, shaded, shady, shadowy, somber, cloudy, overcast, sunless, dusky. **2.** sad, unhappy, downcast, dejected, melancholy, despondent, depressed, cheerless, glum, doleful, dispirited, low-spirited, disheartened, heavyhearted, downhearted, moody, morose, crestfallen, chapfallen, woebegone, mopy, dismal, dreary, grim, desolate, somber, morbid, funereal, in the doldrums; *Slang* down in the mouth, down in the dumps, down; discouraged, pessimistic, miserable, sorrowful, heartsick, forlorn, disconsolate, comfortless; frowning, dour, sour, ill-humored. **—Ant. 1** bright, light, sunny; radiant, brilliant, dazzling. **2** happy, glad, cheerful, joyful, jolly, joyous, gleeful, merry, jovial, jocund, blithe, gay, high-spirited, lighthearted, smiling, delighted; *Slang* on top of the world.

glorify *v.* give glory to, pay homage to, exalt, venerate, revere; deify, apotheosize, idolize, canonize, adore, worship, bow down and worship, enshrine, consecrate, sanctify, beatify, elevate, ennoble, dignify, immortalize, burn incense to, light candles before; praise, laud, extol, honor, celebrate, make more splendid, add luster to, sing the praises of; glamorize, romanticize. **—Ant.** desecrate, profane, blaspheme, defile, dishonor, debase, defame, degrade; condemn, mock.

glorious *adj.* **1.** gorgeous, beautiful, wonderful, marvelous, splendid, fine, great, grand, excellent, superb, delightful, divine; sparkling, brilliant, dazzling, shining, radiant, resplendent, glowing, lustrous. **2.** sublime, noble, magnificent, grand, supreme, majestic, august, imposing, impressive, stately, dignified, distinguished, famous, eminent, noted, celebrated, honored, preeminent, renowned, illustrious, notable, praiseworthy. **—Ant. 1** awful, horrible, horrid, ugly, unpleasant, *Slang* lousy; dull, drab, dreary, gloomy. **2** minor, unimportant, unimpressive, trivial, trifling; undistinguished, unknown.

glory *n.* **1.** adoration, worship, homage, veneration, praise, thanksgiving, gratitude, benediction, blessing, admiration. **2.** honor, renown, fame, eminence, preeminence, illustriousness, esteem, repute, distinction, celebrity, notability, prestige, mark, name. **3.** grandeur, splendor, magnificence, majesty, gloriousness, resplendence, impressiveness, sublimity, stateliness, nobility, dignity, solemnity, excellence. *—v.* **4.** take pride, rejoice proudly, revel, take delight; be boastful, pat oneself on the back, preen oneself, plume oneself, boast, vaunt. **—Ant. 1** blasphemy, profanity. **2** dishonor, disgrace, shame, infamy, ignominy, disrepute; condemnation, malediction, curse. **3** ugliness, meanness, triviality, paltriness.

gloss *n.* **1.** luster, shine, sheen, polish, glow, glaze, gleam, radiance, brightness, glossiness, brilliance, shimmer, luminousness. *—v.* **2.** shine, polish, give a sheen to; glaze, varnish, enamel, lacquer, japan, veneer. **3.** smooth over, treat lightly, mitigate; explain away, rationalize, excuse, whitewash, cover up, disguise, color, veil, mask, cloak. **—Syn. Study. 1** See POLISH. **—Ant. 1** dullness, dull film. **3** exaggerate, overemphasize, blow up; accept, recognize, face.

glow *n.* **1.** soft light, gleam, afterglow, glimmer, shimmer, flicker, radiation; low flame, soft heat, heat, warmth. **2.** color, warmth, brightness, intensity, vividness, reddening; flush, bloom, blush. **3.** warmth, radiance; enthusiasm, fervor, ardor, earnestness, eagerness, gusto. *—v.* **4.** burn softly, smolder; shine, gleam, glitter, shimmer, be incandescent, be fluorescent, glisten, twinkle, flicker. **5.** radiate, fill, flush, blush, thrill, tingle; feel intensely, be enthusiastic about, be eager, be animated. **—Ant. 2** paleness, pallor, whiteness, wanness, ashenness, grayness, dullness, drabness. **3** coldness, chill, coolness, iciness; indifference, dispassionateness, halfheartedness.

glower *v.* scowl, look angrily, look fierce, glare, stare, frown, lower, look black, stare sullenly; pout, sulk. **—Ant.** smile, grin; laugh, snicker, smirk.

glowing *adj.* **1.** ruddy, flushed, red; bright, vivid, luminescent, florid, hot, flaming. **2.** enthusiastic, rave, raving, fervent, ardent, ecstatic; thrilling, sensational, exciting, stimulating, passionate, rhapsodic. **—Ant. 1** pale, pallid, white, wan, ashen, gray, colorless, dull, drab. **2** unenthusiastic, cool, dispassionate, halfhearted, so-so; dull, boring; scathing, cruel, brutal, venomous, stinging, vitriolic.

glue *n.* **1.** mucilage, paste, library paste, cement, *Slang* stickum, epoxy, fixative; putty, mortar, concrete, plaster. *—v.* **2.**

paste, gum, stick, cement, fix, affix, plaster, agglutinate, fasten.

glum *adj.* morose, gloomy, dejected, depressed, dispirited, sad, melancholy, somber, lugubrious; low, blue, down in the mouth, down in the dumps; sullen, sulky, sour, dour. **—Syn. Study.** GLUM, MOROSE, SULLEN describe a gloomy, unsociable attitude. GLUM suggests a depressed, spiritless disposition or manner, usu. temporary: *The runner had a glum expression after losing the race.* MOROSE, which adds a sense of bitterness and peevishness, implies a habitual and pervasive gloominess: *His chronic illness put him in a morose mood.* SULLEN usu. implies a reluctance or refusal to speak, accompanied by a glowering look expressing anger or a sense of injury: *The child had a sullen look after being scolded.*

glut *v.* **1.** stuff, gorge, cram, fill, overfeed, eat to excess, overeat, satiate, eat one's fill, eat out of house and home, gluttonize, gormandize; devour, gulp, gobble, gobble up, bolt. **2.** oversupply, flood, deluge, overload, saturate, supersaturate, sate, surfeit, jade; choke, clog, congest, obstruct. **—***n.* **3.** oversupply, over-abundance, superabundance, saturation, supersaturation, surplus, excess, superfluity, surfeit, drug, burden, load, overdose, plethora, clog, obstruction. **—Ant. 1** starve; nibble. **2** undersupply, empty. **3** shortage, paucity, dearth, want, lack, scarcity.

glutton *n.* voracious eater, overeater, trencherman, gourmand, gormandizer, gorger, stuffer; *Slang* pig, hog, belly-slave, chowhound. **—Ant.** small eater, fussy eater, dainty eater, finicky eater; dieter.

gluttony *n.* excessive eating, overeating, voracity, voraciousness, ravenousness, gormandizing, gourmandism; intemperance, rapacity; *Slang* hoggishness, piggishness, eating like a pig. **—Ant.** dainty eating, eating like a bird; dieting.

gnarled *adj.* knotty, knotted, full of knots, nodular, covered with gnarls, snaggy, leathery, wrinkled, weather-beaten, rugged; contorted, twisted, distorted, crooked. **—Ant.** smooth, sleek, unblemished; unwrinkled, silky; straight.

gnash *v.* grind together, hit together, bite and grind, strike together, chomp, gnaw.

gnaw *v.* **1.** munch, eat away at, chew, nibble, nibble at, chomp, crunch, bite, masticate; graze, browse, ruminate. **2.** trouble, worry, torment, rankle, distress, chafe, fret, grate, gall, harrow, eat at.

gnome *n.* dwarf, troll, shriveled little old man; elf, goblin, gremlin; sprite, pixy, leprechaun. **—Syn. Study.** See GOBLIN.

go *v.* **1.** move toward, set out for, start for, begin, proceed, progress, be off, advance, make headway, go on, get on, wend, repair, stir; press onward, forge ahead, gain ground, sally forth. **2.** leave, depart, go away, take one's departure, withdraw, retire, decamp, move out, move away, quit; *Slang* scram, beat it, take off, vamoose, blow, split; steal away, steal off, slip off, sneak off, take French leave, flee, fly, take flight. **3.** lead, extend, reach, stretch to, spread to. **4.** work, operate, function, run, be operative, act, perform; be in motion. **5.** pass, pass by, go by, elapse, lapse, expire, flow, slide, glide by, slip away. **6.** be used, be applied on, be given, be awarded, be contributed. **7.** turn out, work out, fare, take place, come to pass, transpire; result, end, terminate, fall out. **8.** fit, have a place, belong; be compatible, be suited to, agree, harmonize, jibe, accord, blend; conform with, comport, tally. **9.** be known, be considered, be reckoned; be stated, be phrased, be expressed. **—***n.* **10.** ambition, drive, energy, vigor, vim, vim and vigor, vitality, force, initiative, steam, spirit, animation, vivacity, verve, pep, dash, élan, life, mettle, enterprise; *Slang* get up and go. **11.** try, attempt, turn, chance, whirl; effort, trial, endeavor, experiment. **—Ant. 1** stay, remain; arrive, finish, end. **2** arrive, come, move in. **4** be inoperative, be broken; stop. **5** stand still. **6** be unused; keep, retain. **8** mismatch, be incompatible, be unsuited, disagree. **10** laziness, lifelessness, lethargy.

goad *n.* **1.** prod, cattle prod, prick, pointed stick. **2.** incentive, stimulus, stimulant, motive, motivation, driving motive, pressure, spur; inducement, encouragement, instigation, whet, fillip. **—***v.* **3.** prod, urge, exhort, constrain, incite, spur, push, pressure, drive, stir up, arouse, *Slang* egg on; stimulate, impel, propel, move, press, set on. **—Ant. 2** detriment, curb. **3** deter, keep back, hold back.

goal *n.* **1.** aim, objective, ambition, purpose, object, intent, intention, design, end, target. **2.** goal line, end line, finish line, wire, home, mark, terminus. **3.** score, point, mark, tally.

goat *n.* **1.** (*variously*) billy goat, nanny goat, nanny, buck, kid. **2.** scapegoat, victim, fall guy, whipping boy, butt, laughingstock. **—Ant. 2** hero; victimizer, instigator.

gobble *v.* **1.** gabble, cackle, gaggle, caw. **2.** gulp, gulp down, bolt, bolt down, swallow quickly, eat quickly, devour, stuff, cram down, raven, wolf.

gobbledygook *n.* jargon, gibberish,

cant, balderdash, double-talk, bosh, nonsense, foolishness, buncombe, moonshine, bunk, rubbish, tommyrot, hocus-pocus, fiddle-faddle, mumbo jumbo, *Brit.* tosh, twaddle.

go-between *n.* intermediary, agent, middleman, representative, emissary, messenger, arbiter, arbitrator, fixer, mediator, interceder, intermediator, deputy, delegate, envoy, proxy, second.

goblin *n.* wicked elf, evil sprite, bogeyman, bogey, demon, ogre, gnome, gremlin, troll. **—Syn. Study.** GOBLIN, GNOME, GREMLIN refer to supernatural beings thought to be malevolent to people. GOBLINS are demons of any size, usu. in human or animal form, that are supposed to assail, afflict, and even torture human beings. GNOMES are small ugly creatures that live in the earth, guarding mines, treasures, etc. They are mysteriously malevolent and terrify human beings by causing dreadful mishaps to occur. GREMLINS are thought to disrupt machinery and are active in modern folklore.

God *n.* **1.** Lord, Our Father, God Almighty, the Almighty, the Supreme Being, the Deity, the Creator; the Godhead, the Omnipotent, the Omniscient, the All-Merciful; *Slang* the Man Upstairs. **2.** Usu. **god.** deity, divine being, ruling spirit, divinity. **—Ant. 1** the Devil, Prince of Darkness, Spirit of Evil, the Foul Fiend; Satan, Mephistopheles, Lucifer, Beelzebub; *Slang* Old Nick, Old Scratch, Old Harry. **1, 2** mortal, human, human being, flesh and blood.

godforsaken *adj.* desolate, deserted, remote; neglected, abandoned; bleak, wretched, lonely.

godless *adj.* evil, wicked, depraved; blasphemous, atheistic, agnostic, irreligious, sacrilegious, ungodly, impious, profane, heathen, unhallowed, unsanctified, unrepentant, unrighteous. **—Ant.** godly, God-fearing, pious, religious, devout, holy; sacred, hallowed, consecrated, sanctified; inspired.

godly *adj.* devout, pious, reverent, reverential, religious, righteous, devoted, God-loving, God-fearing, pietistic, believing, faithful, pure in heart, saintly, holy, divine, moral, good, spiritual; sacred, hallowed, consecrated, sanctified. **—Ant.** ungodly, godless, atheistic, irreligious, sacrilegious, impious, unrepentant, profane, heathen; evil, wicked, depraved.

gold *n.* **1.** (*variously*) gold dust, nugget, bullion, ingot, bar, *Chemistry* aurum. **2.** bright yellow, yellow, gilt. **3.** goodness, kindness, beauty, purity; goodwill, beneficence, humanity.

golden *adj.* **1.** bright-yellow, gold-colored, gold, aureate, blond; gilt, gilded; bright, shining, resplendent. **2.** advantageous, opportune, favorable, timely, promising, auspicious, propitious, seasonable, well-disposed, *Slang* rosy. **3.** joyous, most joyous, happy, happiest, great, splendid, glorious, most glorious, best, blest, delightful, beatific; flourishing, halcyon, palmy; most precious, most valuable, priceless, richest, extraordinary, exceptional. **—Ant. 1** black, dark, brunet; dull. **2** unfavorable, inauspicious, untimely, unpromising. **3** worst, sad, saddest, wretched, most wretched; lean, poorest.

good *adj.* **1.** virtuous, worthy, honorable, morally excellent, righteous, upright; honest, reliable, conscientious; moral, wholesome, praiseworthy, exemplary; religious, pious, devout, pure, innocent, unsullied, untainted; humane, considerate, benevolent, kindhearted, kind, kindly, gracious, sympathetic, well-disposed, altruistic, beneficent, obliging. **2.** dutiful, obedient, proper, seemly, well-mannered, decorous, well-behaved, orderly. **3.** satisfactory, excellent, fine, great, wonderful, splendid, first-rate, choice, select, sound, capital, tiptop; worthy, worthwhile; valuable, precious, priceless; admirable, commendable, *Slang* crack. **4.** skilled, skillful, capable, efficient, proficient, adroit, thorough; topnotch, first-rate, excellent, first-class, ace. **5.** beneficial, healthful, healthy, salutary, advantageous; suitable, appropriate, favorable, right, proper, fitting, fit, qualified, useful, adequate, becoming, adapted, deserving. **6.** enjoyable, pleasant, agreeable; cheerful, lively, sunny, genial, convivial, sociable, companionable. **7.** best; new, newest, smartest, most dressy, most stylish, expensive, valuable, precious, priceless. **8.** valid, bona fide, sound, real, genuine, authentic, honest, legitimate, proper; worthwhile, valuable. **9.** full, complete, solid, entire; considerable, large, fairly great, substantial, sizable, ample; adequate, sufficient. *—n.* **10.** goodness, virtue, merit, worth, value, excellence, kindness, righteousness, moral qualities; righteous acts, moral acts. **11.** benefit, advantage, gain, profit, prosperity, good fortune, success, welfare, interest, well-being, improvement; service, favor, good turn, boon; enjoyment, happiness, wealth; blessing, godsend, prize, windfall. **—Ant. 1–8, 10, 11** bad. **1** evil, wicked, sinful, dishonorable, immoral, dishonest, unreliable; unworthy, unwholesome, blamable; sullied, fallen, corrupt, corrupted, tainted; mean, cruel, unkind, ill-disposed, selfish. **2** improper, unseemly, ill-mannered, indecorous, naughty, mischievous. **3** unsatisfactory, unsatisfying, awful, second-rate, unsound, valueless, worthless. **4** unskilled, incompetent, inefficient, amateurish, awful, horrible, *Slang* lousy. **5** disadvantageous; wrong, improper, unfitting, unseemly, unsuitable, inappropriate, unqualified, useless, inadequate; unbecoming, undeserving. **6** awful, *Slang* lousy; unpleasant, disagreeable; dull, boring, cheerless, drab. **7** worst, valueless, worthless; informal, sporty, old, oldest. **8** phony, counterfeit, sham, fraudulent, bogus; false, invalid, unsound, dishonest, worthless. **9** scant, short, incomplete; small, insubstantial; inadequate, insufficient. **10** evil, wickedness, badness, sinfulness, meanness, baseness; immorality, dishonesty, corruption, cruelty. **11** detriment, loss; failure, ill fortune; decline.

good-by Also **good-bye** *interj.* **1.** farewell, so long, bye, bye-bye, bye-now, adieu, God be with you, Godspeed; till we meet again, be seeing you, see you later; *French* au revoir; *Spanish* adios, *Italian* ciao, arrivederci; *German* auf Wiedersehen; *Japanese* sayonara. —*n.* **2.** farewell, adieu, parting, leave-taking, departure, separation, send-off. **—Ant. 1** hello, hi, hi there. **2** meeting, greeting, welcoming; reunion.

good-humored *adj.* cheery, amiable, good-natured, cheerful, genial, complaisant, pleasant, kindly, congenial, affable, gentle, mild, easygoing. **—Ant.** irritable, cranky, crotchety, morose, surly.

good-looking *adj.* handsome, clean-cut, nice-looking, well-favored, attractive; beautiful, lovely, pretty, comely, fair, bonny, pulchritudinous, beauteous, eye-filling, eye-catching, sexy, ravishing, alluring, captivating, bewitching, enchanting, *Slang* foxy. **—Ant.** homely, ugly, plain, unattractive, unsightly.

good-natured *adj.* amiable, affable, friendly, pleasant, cheerful, congenial, agreeable, easygoing, genial, good-humored, good-tempered, obliging, complaisant, accommodating, warm-hearted. **—Ant.** cranky, cantankerous, cross, peevish, ill-natured, irritable.

goodness *n.* **1.** moral excellence, worth, honor, righteousness, honesty, integrity, merit, wholesomeness, probity; morality, virtue, virtuousness, rectitude, purity, innocence, benevolence, kindness, kindliness, generosity; piety, devotion; propriety, decorum. **2.** benefit, advantage, value, worth, usefulness, profit; service, favor; nutrition, nourishment. —*interj.* **3.** gracious, goodness gracious, mercy, heavens, good heavens, my stars, heavens to Betsy, sakes alive, landsakes, land alive; *Slang* wow, wowee, gee, gee whiz, golly, boy, boy-oh-boy, say, hey. **—Syn. Study. 1** GOODNESS, MORALITY, VIRTUE refer to qualities of character or conduct that entitle the possessor to approval and esteem. GOODNESS is the simple word for a general quality recognized as an inherent part of one's character: *Many could tell of her goodness and honesty.* MORALITY implies conformity to the recognized standards of right conduct: *a citizen of unquestioned morality.* VIRTUE is a rather formal word, and usu. suggests GOODNESS that is consciously or steadily maintained, often in spite of temptations or evil influences: *a man of unassailable virtue.* **—Ant. 1** badness, evil, wickedness, sinfulness, immorality, dishonesty, unwholesomeness, corruption, worthlessness. **2** detriment, disadvantage, drawback.

goods *n. pl.* **1.** possessions, property, effects, worldly goods, movables, movable effects, chattels, estate; paraphernalia, trappings, appurtenances, furnishings, things, gear, trappings. **2.** merchandise, stock, inventory, wares, articles of trade, commodities. **3.** cloth, fabric, material, woven goods; textiles, dry goods, piece goods, fabrics. **—Syn. Study. 1** See PROPERTY.

gore *n.* bloodshed, butchery, slaughter, carnage; blood, dried blood, clotted blood.

gorge *n.* **1.** steep valley, canyon, chasm, ravine, cleft, gully, gulch, defile; hollow, abyss, crevasse, gap; glen, dell, dale, vale; pass. **2.** throat, gullet, craw, esophagus; mouth, muzzle. **3.** disgust, revulsion, repugnance, repulsion, nausea; anger, wrath, blood, ire, animosity, hatred. —*v.* **4.** stuff, fill, glut, sate, fill, cram, satiate; overeat, overindulge, eat greedily, indulge, gormandize, gluttonize; swallow greedily, devour, gulp, gobble, bolt.

gorgeous *adj.* beautiful, attractive, good-looking, glorious, lovely, exquisite, stunning, ravishing, splendid, elegant, magnificent, grand, fine, sumptuous, rich, rich-looking, imposing, impressive, splendorous, splendiferous, opulent, luxurious, costly; shining, brilliant, dazzling, bright, glittering, resplendent. **—Ant.** ugly, hideous, unsightly, unattractive, repulsive, plain, homely, cheap, tawdry, shabby, trashy, shoddy, scrubby, sorry; drab, dull; dreary, gloomy, murky, dismal, somber, bleak, gray.

gory *adj.* **1.** bloody, bloodstained, bloodsoaked, stained with gore, covered with gore, ensanguined; bloodthirsty, murderous, sanguinary. **2.** bloody, scary, bloodcurdling, frightening, terrifying, horrifying, *Slang* creepy.

gospel *n.* **1.** Often **Gospel** the tidings of salvation proclaimed by Jesus Christ, the good news; any of the first four books of the New Testament: Matthew, Mark, Luke, or John. **2.** the whole truth, ultimate truth, the final word, the last word; doctrine, creed, credo.

gossip *n.* **1.** groundless rumor, hearsay, whispering behind one's back, backbiting, newsmongering, scandal, *Slang* dish; idle talk, prattle, twaddle, babble, tattle, tittle-tattle; comment, report, news. **2.** Also **gossiper** idle tattler, talebearer, idle talker, rumormonger, scandalmonger, gossipmonger, newsmonger, tattletale, blabbermouth, tattler, chatterbox, busybody, babbler, chatterer; snoop, snooper, meddler, magpie; *Yiddish* yenta. **—***v.* **3.** spread rumors, go about tattling, talk idly, tattle, prattle, prate, gabble, blab, talk one's arm off, give one an earful, *Slang* dish; snoop, pry, meddle, stick one's nose in other people's business. **—Ant. 3** keep quiet, keep mum, keep a secret, keep one's lips sealed, keep one's counsel.

gourmand *n.* trencherman, bon vivant, gormandizer, glutton, big eater; *Slang* chowhound. **—Ant.** small eater, nibbler, dainty eater, picky eater, fussy eater; dieter.

gourmet *n.* epicure, gastronome, gastronomer, gastronomist, *Slang* foodie; connoisseur, bon vivant.

govern *v.* **1.** administer, manage, rule, direct, head, lead, control, guide, steer, run, pilot, supervise, superintend, oversee, exercise authority over, be at the helm of; *Informal* be in the driver's seat, pull the strings. **2.** control, restrain, check, hold in check, curb, bridle, tame, inhibit, hold in hand, keep under control; discipline, command, rule, dominate, boss. **3.** guide, influence, sway, lead, steer, incline, form, rule. **—Ant. 1** be subject; follow, comply, obey, submit. **2** let loose, give free rein to; encourage.

government *n.* **1.** governing system, rule, administration, authority, law, management, control, domination, regulation, command, direction, guidance, supervision; state, dominion, statesmanship, reins of government. **2.** governing body, administration, regime.

gown *n.* **1.** formal dress, long dress, fancy dress, party dress; dress, frock; nightgown, nightdress. **2.** academic garb, robe, academic dress, academic attire.

grab *v.* **1.** seize, snatch, grasp, pluck, lay hold of; clutch, grip, hold, clasp; capture, catch, nab, collar, bag. **—***n.* **2.** sudden grasp, snatch, lunge, pass. **—Ant. 1** let loose, let go of, release, free; drop, put down, set.

grace *n.* **1.** gracefulness, elegance, supple ease, lissomeness, willowiness, fluidity; beauty, comeliness, pulchritude, good looks. **2.** charming quality, endowment, accomplishment, skill; charm, refinement, culture, cultivation, polish, urbanity, suavity, elegance, mannerliness, manners, savoir faire, decorum, etiquette, propriety, tact, taste. **3.** God's favor, God's love, divine goodness, divine influence; holiness, sanctity, saintliness, devoutness, moral strength; virtue, piety, excellence, merit, love, felicity. **4.** mercy, pardon, clemency, lenience, forgiveness, charity, reprieve, indulgence, mercifulness. **5.** extra time, exemption, reprieve, dispensation, indulgence. **—***v.* **6.** adorn, decorate, beautify, ornament, trim, embellish, set off, garnish, deck, bedeck; spruce up, smarten, dress up, enhance, enrich. **7.** dignify, honor, glorify, elevate, aggrandize, exalt, favor, endow. **—Ant. 1** clumsiness, awkwardness, inelegance, gawkiness, stiffness; ugliness. **2** bad habit, inelegance, boorishness, coarseness, bad manners, tactlessness, tastelessness. **4** disfavor, ill will, enmity, animosity; sternness, harshness, cruelty. **6** desecrate, ruin. **7** insult, dishonor, shame.

graceful *adj.* easy-moving, naturally supple, limber, lithe, willowy, shapely, sinuous, lithesome, lissome, light-footed; attractive, comely, lovely, beautiful; delicate, elegant, sylphlike. **—Ant.** clumsy, awkward, ungainly, ungraceful, graceless, inelegant, gawky, lumbering, ponderous, stiff; ugly, homely, plain.

gracious *adj.* **1.** kindly, courteous, cordial, amiable, affable, good-natured, hospitable, obliging, civil; polite, chivalrous, courtly, pleasant; kind, friendly, kindhearted, charitable, humane, tender, compassionate, benevolent, benign, benignant, merciful, lenient, clement. **—***interj.* **2.** good heavens, heavens to Betsy, mercy, goodness, goodness gracious, landsakes, my stars, ye gods, my; *Slang* wow, gee, gee whiz, boy, oh boy. **—Ant. 1** ungracious, uncordial, unpleasant, ill-natured, haughty, unfriendly, cold, cool, remote, stiff, unkind, discourteous, rude, impolite, brusque, curt, gruff, surly, sullen; cruel, mean.

grade *n.* **1.** incline, slope, gradient, ramp, inclined plane, acclivity, declivity; hill, bank. **2.** rank, degree, level, standing, place; order, class, status, station, position; estate, condition, caste; stage, step, sphere; quality, value, intensity, brand, pitch. **3.** mark; rating, standing. **—***v.* **4.** classify, sort; rank, order, gradate, value, rate, brand. **5.** mark, give a grade to, rate. **6.** level, even, make horizontal, smooth, flatten.

gradual *adj.* slow-but-steady, progressive, measured, regular, continuous, successive, graduated, incremental, slow, gentle, leisurely, steady, imperceptible, deliberate; piecemeal, step-by-step, little-by-little, inch-by-inch, drop-by-drop. **—Syn. Study.** See SLOW. **—Ant.** sudden, abrupt, precipitate, instantaneous, overnight.

graduate *n.* **1.** alumnus, alumna, recipient of a diploma, holder of a degree. —*v.* **2.** receive a diploma, receive a degree, complete one's studies, award a diploma to, confer a degree on, grant a degree to. **3.** mark with gradations, mark off, divide into degrees, calibrate, grade, measure out. —*adj.* **4.** postgraduate, postbaccalaureate. **—Ant. 1** dropout. **2** drop out of, flunk out of. **4** undergraduate.

graft[1] *n.* **1.** inserted shoot, implant, implantation, transplant, splice; slip, sprout, scion. —*v.* **2.** implant, transplant, ingraft; inset, infix, join; plant, bud.

graft[2] *n.* corruption, bribery, plunder, booty, loot; payoffs, bribes, hush money, rake-off, kick-back, spoils; *Slang* payola, swag.

grain *n.* **1.** edible seed plants, cereal; (*variously*) wheat, rye, barley, oats, corn, maize, millet. **2.** kernel, seed, ovule; cereal, grist; (*variously*) wheat, rye, barley, oats, corn, maize, millet. **3.** particle, granule; bit, pellet. **4.** bit, speck, particle, trace, spark, iota, jot, dot, scintilla, whit, tittle, atom, crumb, molecule, mite, morsel, fragment, granule; trifle, touch, pinch, dash, modicum. **—Ant. 2** chaff, stalks.

grand *adj.* **1.** magnificent, majestic, stately, monumental, august, imposing, elegant, impressive, distinguished, striking, splendid, superb, glorious, noble, sublime, lofty, imperial, palatial, royal, luxurious, sumptuous, opulent; fancy, dashing, showy; pretentious, ostentatious; large, big, huge, mammoth. **2.** stately, majestic, regal, noble, august, exalted, lofty, dignified, elevated, lordly, royal, kingly, queenly, princely; grandiose, arrogant, pompous, haughty, *Slang* highfalutin. **3.** good, splendid, excellent, wonderful, fine, great, terrific, marvelous, fabulous, superb, sensational, smashing, admirable, first-rate, choice; *Slang* A-1, swell, keen, super, out-of-this-world, out-of-sight, real cool, groovy, real gone. **4.** main, chief, head, principal, supreme, highest-ranking. **5.** complete, full, all-embracing, all-inclusive, comprehensive. **—Ant. 1** petty, paltry, trivial, trifling, measly, puny, small, little, meager, unimposing, insignificant; unimportant, secondary, incidental, inferior. **2** undignified, common, low-class, boorish; base, mean, contemptible, small. **3** bad, poor, unsound, wretched, worthless, inferior, second-rate; *Slang* rotten, terrible, awful, lousy.

grandeur *n.* magnificence, majesty, splendor, stateliness, impressiveness, resplendence, nobility, glory, sublimity; pomp, state, augustness, solemnity, dignity; importance, celebrity, eminence, fame, distinction; excellence, luster, loftiness. **—Ant.** paltriness, triviality, pettiness, smallness; insignificance, unimportance, degradation, inferiority, commonness, meanness.

grandiloquent *adj.* high-flown, high-sounding, flowery, florid, grandiose, pompous, pretentious, bombastic, inflated, turgid, swollen, stilted; magniloquent, lofty, rhetorical; *Slang* highfalutin. **—Ant.** simple, direct, unaffected, plain-spoken, matter-of-fact, low-keyed; base, lowly.

grandiose *adj.* grand, high-flown, flamboyant, splashy, theatrical, ostentatious, pretentious, pompous, affected, extravagant, *Slang* highfalutin. **—Syn. Study.** GRANDIOSE, OSTENTATIOUS, PRETENTIOUS, POMPOUS refer to a conspicuous outward display designed to attract attention. GRANDIOSE may suggest impressiveness that is not objectionable; however, it most often implies exaggeration or affectation to the point of absurdity: *the grandiose sweep of an arch; a grandiose idea to take a limousine to work.* OSTENTATIOUS has the negative connotation of trying to impress or outdo others: *ostentatious furnishings.* PRETENTIOUS is always derogatory, suggesting falseness or exaggeration in claims made or implied: *pretentious language that masked the absence of real content.* POMPOUS implies a display of exaggerated dignity or importance: *a pompous bureaucrat.*

grant *v.* **1.** give, allow, consent to, permit, bestow, accord, confer, vouchsafe, agree to; allot, allocate, present, donate, cede, assign, award, endow; dispense, deal out, apportion. **2.** concede, admit, accede to, allow, consent, vouchsafe, yield. —*n.* **3.** allotment, appropriation, present, presentation, gift, donation, award, endowment, benefaction, contribution, bestowal, largess; bequest, subsidy, offering, allowance, assignment, gratuity, tribute; concession, indulgence, favor, boon. **—Syn. Study. 1** See GIVE. **—Ant. 1** refuse, deny, withhold, withdraw. **2** refute, disagree.

graphic *adj.* **1.** vivid, realistic, lifelike, illustrative, pictorial, picturesque, well-drawn, well-delineated, forcible, striking, trenchant, explicit, clear, lucid, distinct, expressive, descriptive. **2.** visual, visible, seen; written, drawn, pictured, painted, printed. —**Ant.** **1** unrealistic, unpicturesque, hazy, obscure, vague, dull, indefinite; impressionistic, expressionistic. **2** abstract; performing.

grapple *n.* **1.** grappling hook, grapnel, large hook. —*v.* **2.** hold, hold tightly, clasp, fasten, make fast, grasp, grip, clutch, seize, catch, lay hold of. **3.** struggle, contend, combat, fight, wrestle, take on, do battle, encounter, engage, face, tackle, meet, confront, breast, deal with, try to overcome, *Slang* sink one's teeth into. —**Ant.** **2** free, let loose, let go, release. **3** avoid, evade, sidestep, run away from.

grasp *v.* **1.** seize, seize upon, grab, snatch, catch, catch at, take, take hold of, lay hold of; hold, clutch, clasp, grip, clinch; grapple. **2.** comprehend, understand, catch on to, get, take in, perceive, fathom, follow, master, *Slang* savvy; sense, infer, deduce. —*n.* **3.** grip, hold, clasp, clutch; clutches, embrace, handclasp; seizure, seizing, gripping. **4.** reach, power, control, compass, scope, range, sweep, sway. **5.** comprehension, understanding, perception, ken, knowledge, edge, mastery, talent, skill, sense. —**Ant.** **1** drop, release, free, let go, let loose, relinquish, surrender. **2** misunderstand.

grasping *adj.* greedy, avaricious, rapacious, predatory, covetous, selfish, miserly, acquisitive, mercenary, venal, wolfish, hoggish. —**Ant.** unselfish, altruistic, generous, large-hearted, public-spirited.

grate[1] *n.* **1.** fireplace, hearth, firebox, firebed, firebasket. **2.** grating, grill, screen, bars, lattice, latticework.

grate[2] *v.* **1.** scrape, rasp, grind, rub, scratch, abrade; screech, scream, jangle, buzz, burr, clack. **2.** shred, mince, pulverize. **3.** chafe, jar, gnaw at, irritate, annoy, rankle, gall, irk, vex, exasperate, go against the grain. —**Ant.** **1** slip, slide, glide. **3** calm, soothe, pacify, quiet, settle.

grateful *adj.* thankful, full of gratitude, deeply appreciative, gratified; obliged, obligated, under obligation, beholden, indebted. —**Ant.** ungrateful, unappreciative, disobliged.

gratification *n.* **1.** satisfaction, pleasure, enjoyment, comfort, solace; happiness, contentment, delight, joy, relish, gladness, elation, exhilaration, glee, jubilation, thrill, kick, bliss, rapture, transport, enchantment, ecstasy. **2.** gratifying, satisfying, indulgence, humoring, soothing, pleasing. —**Ant.** **1** frustration, disappointment, dissatisfaction; sorrow, sadness, gloom, pain. **2** control, discipline, curbing, restraint; denial, abnegation.

gratify *v.* **1.** give satisfaction to, satisfy, give pleasure to, please, delight, make glad; regale, gladden, exhilarate; divert, entertain, refresh, recreate; thrill, interest, take one's fancy, amuse, tickle, tickle one's fancy, suit, entrance, transport, enrapture, enthrall, enchant. **2.** satisfy, indulge, humor, pamper, coddle, favor; give in to, appease, soothe, flatter, compliment. —**Ant.** **1** frustrate, disappoint, dissatisfy, displease, offend; sadden, pain. **2** control, discipline, curb, restrict, deny.

grating[1] *n.* framework of bars, gate of bars, grate, grille, grid, gridiron; open latticework, trellis, lattice; tracery, fretwork, fret, filigree.

grating[2] *adj.* **1.** rasping, scraping, raspy, creaky, squeaky, harsh, shrill, jangling, piercing, high-pitched, strident, raucous, discordant, jarring, cacophonous. **2.** annoying, irritating, abrasive, disagreeable, unpleasant, displeasing, offensive; exasperating, vexatious, exacerbating. —**Ant.** **1** musical, melodic, dulcet, mellifluous, soft. **2** pleasing, pleasant, agreeable; calming, soothing.

gratitude *n.* gratefulness, appreciation, thankfulness, thanks, acknowledgment, recognition, obligation, beholdenness; giving thanks, thanksgiving. —**Ant.** ingratitude, ungratefulness, thanklessness, unthankfulness.

gratuitous *adj.* **1.** uncalled for, unprovoked, unwarranted, unjustified, groundless, unfounded; unproven, baseless, conjectural, presumptive; wanton, impertinent, irrelevant. **2.** free, free of cost, gratis, given without charge, obtained without payment, donated, complimentary, unrecompensed, without compensation; voluntary, unasked for, freely bestowed, spontaneous, willing. —**Ant.** **1** justified, warranted, provoked; well-founded, well-grounded, proven, real, relevant. **2** paid, compensated; compulsory, involuntary.

grave[1] *n.* excavation for burial, burial place, place of interment, last resting place; tomb, sepulcher, mausoleum, vault, crypt, catacomb, cenotaph, mound, ossuary.

grave[2] *adj.* **1.** solemn, sedate, serious, earnest, thoughtful, subdued, quiet, dignified, sober, staid; somber, gloomy, dour, frowning, grim-visaged, long-faced; sage, philosophical. **2.** serious, critical, crucial, urgent, pressing, acute, important, vital, momentous, of great consequence, consequential, significant, weighty, life-and-death. —**Syn. Study.** **1** GRAVE, SOLEMN, SOBER refer to the condition of being serious in demeanor or appearance. GRAVE indicates a dignified seriousness due to heavy responsibilities or cares: *The jury looked grave while* *pondering the evidence.* SOLEMN suggests an impressive and earnest seriousness marked by the absence of gaiety or mirth: *The minister's voice was solemn as he announced the text.* SOBER implies a determined but sedate and restrained manner: *a wise and sober judge.* **—Ant. 1** carefree, gay, joyous, happy, sunny, smiling, merry, boisterous; frivolous, facetious, flippant, flip, trifling, undignified; devil-may-care, dashing, exciting. **2** frivolous, trivial, unimportant, uncritical, inconsequential, insignificant, petty; mild.

graveyard *n.* cemetery, burying ground, memorial park, churchyard, necropolis, charnel, ossuary; potter's field, boot hill; *Slang* boneyard.

gravitate *v.* **1.** settle, settle down, sink, descend, fall. **2.** be drawn, be attracted, have a natural tendency, have a proclivity for, be prone to, incline; lean toward, converge, tend, move, head, point toward, zero in on.

gravity *n.* **1.** gravitation, gravitational attraction, attraction, mutual attraction of objects, pull, pull of the earth. **2.** seriousness, solemnity, solemnness, earnestness, thoughtfulness, dignity, sobriety, sedateness, staidness, gloominess, somberness, grimness, calmness, serenity, tranquillity. **3.** seriousness, urgency, concern, critical nature, crucial nature, danger, emergency; importance, import, moment, significance, consequence, consideration, magnitude, enormity. **—Ant. 1** antigravity; escape velocity, momentum. **2** frivolousness, frivolity, facetiousness, flippancy, thoughtlessness; gaiety, merriment, glee, joy, happiness. **3** inconsequentiality, unimportance, insignificance, pettiness.

gray Also **grey** *adj.* **1.** neutral, pearl-gray, grayish, silver, silvery, slate, dun, drab, dove-colored, mouse-colored; ashen, ashy, pale, hoary. **2.** gloomy, dismal, somber, cheerless, depressing, dark, murky, overcast, sunless, cloudy, clouded, foggy, misty. **3.** gray-haired, gray-headed, silver-haired, hoary-headed, grizzly, pepper-and-salt. **—Ant. 2** bright, clear, sunny.

graze[1] *v.* eat grass, feed on herbage, browse, crop; turn out to pasture, pasture.

graze[2] *v.* **1.** scrape, scratch, skin, abrade, bruise, rasp, rub, grind; touch lightly, brush, skim, glance, swipe. *—n.* **2.** scrape, scratch, abrasion.

grease *n.* **1.** fat, drippings, lard, tallow; oil, lubricant; ointment, salve, unguent, balm. *—v.* **2.** lubricate, oil, apply grease to, smear with grease, lard; anoint.

greasy *adj.* **1.** grease-covered, oily, lardaceous, buttery, waxy, oleaginous; slippery, slick, slithery. **2.** lardy, fat, fatty, grease-filled. **—Ant. 2** lean.

great *adj.* **1.** vast, immense, enormous, huge, large, big, tremendous, gigantic, colossal, stupendous, mammoth, prodigious, voluminous, gross, monstrous, cyclopean, titanic, gargantuan; many, countless, multitudinous, abundant, unlimited, boundless, inexhaustible, manifold. **2.** extreme, pronounced, decided, considerable, strong, high, extravagant, inordinate, prodigious. **3.** important, of much consequence, consequential, significant, weighty, heavy, momentous, grave, serious, critical, crucial. **4.** outstanding, remarkable, superb, superior, superlative, magnificent, notable, prominent, distinguished, glorious, leading, famous, noted, renowned, chief, illustrious, eminent, celebrated, esteemed; fine, good, excellent, marvelous; grand, splendid, wonderful, fabulous, fantastic, terrific, sensational, smashing, choice, first-rate; *Slang* A-1, swell, super, marvy, out of this world, out-of-sight, way out, groovy, real gone, real cool, fresh; expert, proficient, skillful, crack, able, apt, adroit; *Informal* crackerjack. **5.** fine, noble, high-minded, of lofty character, magnanimous, altruistic, humane, loving, generous, kind, gracious. *—adv.* **6.** *Informal* very well, well, fine, excellently, superbly, magnificently, grandly, splendidly, wonderfully. **—Ant. 1–4** small, little, tiny, diminutive, puny; insignificant, petty, paltry, trivial, trifling, measly, mean. **2** mild, weak, some. **3** unimportant, inconsequential, inconsiderable, insignificant, secondary, incidental. **4** poor, bad, worse, inferior, wretched, worthless, *Informal* rotten, terrible, awful, *Slang* lousy; second-rate, unnotable, undistinguished, average, inexpert, unskilled, inept. **5** mean, base, ignoble, low-minded; inhumane, wicked, hateful, unkind. **6** badly, poorly, terribly; *Slang* awful, lousy.

greatly *adv.* very much, tremendously, immensely, enormously, vastly, largely, immeasurably, infinitely, mightily, powerfully, abundantly, considerably, remarkably, markedly, notably. **—Ant.** little, insignificantly, mildly, somewhat.

greed *n.* greediness, money-hunger, avarice, avariciousness, covetousness, selfishness, avidity, craving, cupidity, rapacity, rapaciousness, piggishness, inordinate desire; itching palm. **—Ant.** generosity, munificence, liberality, altruism, unselfishness, benevolence.

greedy *adj.* **1.** money-hungry, avaricious, grasping, acquisitive, covetous, rapacious, predatory, selfish, mercenary, *Informal* hoggish. **2.** ravenous, gluttonous, voracious, insatiable, famished, hungry; devouring, gormandizing; *Informal* hoggish, piggish, swinish, wolfish. **3.** eager, avid, full of desire, keenly desirous, ardent, fervent, burning, thirsting, hungry, craving, impatient, anxious. **—Syn. Study. 1** GREEDY, AVARICIOUS, COVETOUS suggest a desire to possess more of something than one needs or is entitled to. GREEDY, the most general of these terms, suggests an uncontrolled desire for almost anything: *greedy for knowledge; greedy for power.* AVARICIOUS often implies a pathological, driven greediness for money or other valuables and usually suggests a concomitant miserliness: *an avaricious usurer.* COVETOUS implies a powerful and often illicit desire for the property or possessions of another: *The book collector was covetous of my rare first edition.* **—Ant. 1** generous, munificent, liberal, altruistic, unselfish, benevolent. **2** sated, full. **3** uncaring, apathetic, indifferent.

green *adj.* **1.** green-colored, (*variously*) yellow-green, chartreuse, lime, lime-green, olive, olive-green, greenish, grass-green, verdant, pea-green, forest-green, kelly-green, cobalt-green, jade, emerald, sea-green, aquamarine, blue-green. **2.** unripe, immature, not fully aged, underdeveloped, undeveloped; young, tender, unfledged, crude; raw, unseasoned, not dried, not cured; untanned, unsmoked, unmellowed. **3.** inexperienced, callow, raw, untrained, rough, undisciplined, crude, awkward; unpolished, unsophisticated, unversed, immature; unskilled, inexpert, ignorant, uninformed; gullible, easily fooled, credulous. *—n.* **4.** village green, common, heath, lawn, grassplot, turf, sward, greensward, verdure; campus; putting green, golf course. **—Ant. 2** ripe, mature, matured, aged, developed, seasoned, finished. **3** experienced, mature, sophisticated, seasoned, skilled, expert, trained.

greet *v.* **1.** welcome, bid welcome, salute, hail, receive, admit, meet, accost; recognize, tip one's hat to, doff the cap to, speak to, smile upon. **2.** meet, receive, welcome, accept. **—Ant. 1** ignore, shun, give the cold shoulder to; bid farewell, wave good-by.

greeting *n.* **1.** welcoming, welcome, saluting, salutation, salute, reception; introduction, presentation. **2.** Often **greetings** salutation, hello, regards, respects, remembrance, friendly message, felicitations, well-wishing, compliments, best, best wishes, good wishes.

gregarious *adj.* sociable, social, genial, outgoing, convivial, extroverted, companionable, affable, friendly; vivacious, lively, talkative. **—Ant.** unsociable, solitary, reclusive, introverted, retiring, shy.

gremlin *n.* **—Syn. Study.** See GOBLIN.

grief *n.* **1.** grieving, sorrow, sadness, heartbreak, heartache, misery, agony, woe, wretchedness, suffering, anguish, distress, despondency, despair, desolation; affliction, tribulation. **2.** grievance, hardship, trouble, burden, ordeal, worry, anxiety, care, concern, vexation, inconvenience, nuisance; remorse, discomfort. **—Ant. 1** consolation, comfort, solace; joy, happiness, bliss, cheer, delight, enjoyment, gaiety, gladness, glee, rejoicing. **2** joy, comfort.

grievance *n.* complaint, *Slang* beef; injustice, wrong, disservice, hurt, affliction, iniquity, outrage, hardship, injury; *Informal* bone to pick. **—Ant.** benefit, privilege, boon; compliment.

grieve *v.* **1.** feel grief, mourn, weep, lament, sorrow, be sad, be anguished, be heavy-hearted, rue, wail, shed tears, cry, cry one's eyes out, sob, moan, bemoan. **2.** sadden, make sorrowful, make unhappy, distress, agonize; pain, break the heart, make the heart bleed, wound the feelings of, cut to the quick; torture, harass, discomfort, oppress, deject, depress, disquiet, afflict. **—Ant. 1, 2** console, comfort, solace, soothe, ease. **1** rejoice, delight in, enjoy, be happy about, be glad of. **2** delight, please, gratify, gladden, cheer, amuse, entertain.

grievous *adj.* **1.** tragic, sorrowful, sad, heartbreaking, woeful, agonizing, distressing, painful, lamentable. **2.** very bad, grave, severe, serious, heavy, harsh, acute, critical, crucial, significant; appalling, atrocious, heinous, iniquitous, shocking, outrageous, monstrous, nefarious, shameful, deplorable, glaring; intolerable, insufferable, unbearable, harmful, distressing, lamentable, burdensome, destructive, calamitous. **—Ant. 1** delightful, pleasant, pleasing, welcome, joyous, happy, glad; laughable, amusing, entertaining. **2** trivial, trifling, facetious, frivolous, unimportant, inconsequential, insignificant, mild, light.

grill *n.* **1.** griddle, gridiron, grid, grating, crossbars; broiler. *—v.* **2.** broil, fry, griddle, sear, cook. **3.** interrogate, question, pump, quiz, query, give the third degree to; cross-examine.

grim *adj.* **1.** somber, gloomy, austere; sullen, grumpy, sulky, scowling, morose, cantankerous; stern, severe, harsh, fierce, ferocious, unyielding, unrelenting, hard, relentless, merciless, cruel, brutal, heartless, vicious, inhuman, fiendish; obstinate, implacable, determined, resolute, inexorable. **2.** horrible, ghastly, sinister, grisly, frightful, horrid, hideous, gruesome, macabre, lurid, dreadful; repellent, repulsive, repugnant, forbidding, loathsome, appalling, foul, odious, revolting, shocking, squalid, ugly. **—Ant.**

1 happy, cheerful, joyful, gay, merry; lenient, benign, merciful, sympathetic, soft, easy, kind, kindly, amiable, amenable, congenial, genial. **2** pleasant, pleasing; attractive.

grimace *n.* **1.** face, wry face, ugly expression, expression of distaste, smirk, contemptuous face, sneer. **—***v.* **2.** make a face, scowl, smirk, glower, lower.

grime *n.* oily grit, dirt, dust, soil, soot, smut, filth, smudge.

grin *n.* **1.** smile, beam, rictus, gleaming smile, broad grin, toothy grin, idiotic grin; simper, smirk. **—***v.* **2.** smile, beam, crack a smile, grin from ear to ear, grin like a chessy-cat; smirk, simper.

grind *v.* **1.** pulverize, powder, granulate, crush, triturate, mill. **2.** sharpen, whet, file, rasp; polish, scrape, abrade. **3.** grate, rasp, gnash, grit. **—***n.* **4.** chore, drudgery, dull task, laborious work, slavery, hard job. **5.** drudge, bookworm, crammer, plodder, burner of the midnight oil, *Slang* wonk. **—Ant. 2** dull, take the edge off. **4** easy job, enjoyable task, pleasure, joy, *Slang* piece of cake. **5** playboy, *Slang* goof-off.

grip *n.* **1.** grasp, clutch, clasp, hold. **2.** handclasp, handshake; gripping power. **3.** grasp, control, hold, retention, clutches, mastery, domination; understanding, comprehension, perception. **4.** handle, hilt. **5.** valise, suitcase, bag, traveling bag, satchel, gladstone. **—***v.* **6.** grasp, seize firmly, clutch, clench, hold fast, hold tight; seize hold of, catch hold of, seize, grab, snatch. **7.** hold, retain, take hold on, spellbind, rivet, attract, impress.

gripe *n.* **1.** Often **gripes.** stomachache, bellyache, colic, cramps, spasm; affliction, distress, twinge, pang, pain, twitch. **2.** grievance, protest, complaint, faultfinding, whining, grousing, grumbling; *Slang* beef, kick, squawk. **—***v.* **3.** complain, grumble, mutter, whine, find fault, grouse, grouch, fret, cavil, carp, rail, protest, *Slang* beef, kick, squawk, bellyache, *Yiddish* kvetch. **—Ant. 2** complaint, flattery. **3** thank, express appreciation; compliment on.

grisly *adj.* gruesome, horrible, horrid, horrendous, hideous, ghastly, macabre, lurid, frightful, dreadful, shocking, gory, abominable, grim; abhorrent, repugnant, repellent, forbidding, revolting, repulsive, loathsome, foul, odious, sinister, appalling. **—Ant.** pleasant, pleasing, innocuous, attractive, charming, nice.

grit *n.* **1.** soot, dirt, dust, filth, muck. **2.** spunk, pluck, fortitude, courage, nerve, guts, sand; mettle, backbone; determination, tenacity, doggedness, perseverance, resolution, indomitable spirit, stamina. **—***v.* **3.** grind together, rub, grate, scrape, rasp, gnash, crunch. **—Ant. 2** faintheartedness, cowardice, timidity; faltering, wavering, hesitation, vacillation.

groan *v.* **1.** moan, whimper; grumble, complain, murmur, wail, lament; roar, howl, bellow, bleat; bemoan. **2.** creak, resound harshly; squeak, screech. **—***n.* **3.** moan, whimper, whine, sorrowful murmur, wail, lament. **4.** moan, creak, crack, squeak.

groggy *adj.* lethargic, punchy, dopey, sluggish, befuddled, bewildered, perplexed, dazed, unsteady, stunned, dizzy, punch-drunk, staggering, reeling, shaky, *Slang* woozy, stupefied, addled, muddled, confused. **—Ant.** alert, on the ball, sharp, aware, on one's toes.

groom *n.* **1.** valet, manservant, servant, lackey, flunky; livery servant, *British* boots. **2.** stableboy, hostler; footman. **3.** bridegroom; newly married man, husband, spouse, consort. **—***v.* **4.** curry, currycomb, brush, comb, rub down. **5.** clean up, wash, make tidy, make neat, spruce up, primp, preen, comb, freshen, refresh; dress. **6.** prepare, prime, make ready; train, educate, develop, indoctrinate, familiarize with; initiate, drill, exercise, practice.

groove *n.* **1.** rut, furrow, gutter, channel, trench, flute, hollow; cut, cutting, scoring, score, corrugation. **2.** rut, habit, fixed routine, set way of doing things, beaten path, matter of course; convention, second nature, usage, procedure, rule, practice, custom, use. **—Ant. 1** ridge, bump.

grope *v.* **1.** feel about, fumble, probe; fish for, paw, finger; move blindly, feel one's way, move stumblingly. **2.** search blindly, fumble, probe; venture, try one's luck, see how the land lies, send up a trial balloon, throw out a feeler.

gross *adj.* **1.** total, whole, entire, aggregate; total before deductions, before expenses, before taxes. **2.** flagrant, downright, sheer, utter, complete, total, plain, glaring, obvious, manifest; rank, egregious, heinous, outrageous, unmitigated, unqualified, unequivocal. **3.** coarse, crude, unrefined, vulgar, indelicate, improper, uncouth, offensive, unseemly; lewd, lascivious, lecherous, carnal, smutty, foul-mouthed, earthy, ribald, indecent, obscene, licentious, sordid. **4.** fat, obese, overweight, heavy; big, large, bulky, unwieldy, huge, great, vast, immense, enormous, monstrous, gigantic, massive, stupendous, colossal, prodigious, titanic, gargantuan. **—***n.* **5.** sum total, total, total amount, whole, aggregate, lump sum; bulk, mass, main body; total before deductions. **—***v.* **6.** earn, take in, make a gross profit of, pick up, reap; *Slang,* bag, bring home. **—Syn. Study. 2** See FLAGRANT. **—Ant.**

1, 5 net; total after deductions, total after expenses. **2** partial, mitigated, qualified. **3** delicate, dainty, graceful; refined, cultivated, elegant; decent, proper, inoffensive, chaste. **4** thin, slim, svelte; small, little, tiny, petite. **6** net, clear; loose.

grotesque *adj.* **1.** distorted, deformed, odd-shaped, misshapen, contorted, unnatural, fantastic, weird, bizarre, fanciful, strange, outlandish, odd, peculiar, eccentric, incongruous; wild, extravagant, exotic, rococo, baroque. **2.** outlandish, absurd, odd, distorted, fantastic, antic, wild, extravagant, weird, bizarre, preposterous, *Informal* way-out, *Slang* far-out. **—Syn. Study. 2** See FANTASTIC. **—Ant. 1** well-proportioned, graceful, classic; realistic, natural, naturalistic; familiar. **2** routine, average, standard, normal, typical, unimaginative; down-to-earth.

grotto *n.* **1.** cavelike shrine, grot; catacomb. **2.** cavern, cave, recess, hollow; tunnel, burrow.

grouch *n.* **1.** complainer, grumbler, curmudgeon, sulky person, pouter, ill-humored person, sullen person, moper, mope, crab, crank; *Slang* wet blanket, killjoy, spoilsport. *—v.* **2.** complain, find fault, gripe, grumble, mutter, whine, cry, growl, grouse, cavil, carp, rail, protest; *Slang* beef, kick, bellyache; sulk, fret, pout, mope. **—Ant. 1** charmer, flatterer, prince charming; life of the party. **2** compliment, flatter.

ground *n.* **1.** the earth, firm land, terra firma; dry land. **2.** earth, soil, dirt, sod, turf, loam. **3.** Sometimes **grounds** tract of land, land, terrain; region, habitat, area, territory, realm, province, district, bailiwick, domain, sphere; property, premises, real estate, estate, lawns, gardens; yard, campus; farm, field, acres. **4.** Usu. **grounds** basis, cause, reason, motive, excuse; purpose, rationale, object, account, principle, occasion, considerations, arguments, inducement, call; reason why, pros and cons, the whys and wherefores. **5. grounds** sediment, dregs; settlings, deposit. *—v.* **6.** run aground, beach, strand, founder. **7.** base, establish, fix firmly, support, settle, found, set, secure, confirm, organize, institute. **8.** instruct, train, teach, familiarize with, educate, indoctrinate, inform, initiate; drill, exercise, practice, discipline, prepare. **—Ant. 1** the air, the sky; the sea, the ocean, water. **6** float; launch.

groundless *adj.* without basis, baseless, unjustified, unjustifiable, unwarranted, unfounded, unsupported, without reason, without cause, without foundation, uncalled for, needless, idle, gratuitous, illogical, not following, imaginary, chimerical, unreal, flimsy, empty; unproved, false, fallacious, faulty, erroneous, untrue. **—Ant.** well-founded, reasonable, justified, logical, true, proven, provable, supported, real, substantial.

groundwork *n.* **1.** foundation, basis, base, ground, grounds, underpinning, footing, bedrock, cornerstone, keystone, root, taproot, spring, cradle, origin, source; first principle, fundamental, fundamentals. **2.** preparation, planning, spadework, preliminary steps; apprenticeship, learning, training, practice, indoctrination.

group *n.* **1.** assemblage, aggregation, gathering, collection, congregation, representation; crowd, band, throng, party, company, cluster, bunch, pack, gang, troop, detachment; hoard, swarm, herd, flock. **2.** class, classification, variety, species, branch, division, subdivision, section; set, faction, clique, circle, coterie, association, league, brotherhood, fraternity; family, tribe, clan. *—v.* **3.** sort, organize, range, marshal, line up, align, arrange, combine, cluster, coordinate, classify, class, assign, sift, catalog, place, file, register, alphabetize, index, size; grade, graduate. **4.** associate, fraternize, mingle, cluster, marshal, hobnob, keep company, consort. **—Ant. 1, 2** individual. **3** separate, disperse, scatter.

grouse *v.* complain, grumble, fret, gripe, fuss, fume, grouch, mutter; *Slang* bellyache, crab, kick, beef, put up a squawk, take on, carry on. **—Ant.** praise, extol, laud, commend, acclaim.

grove *n.* **1.** thicket, copse, coppice, woodland, cluster of trees, small wood, bosk, wood lot, wildwood, brake; shrubbery, pinery; forest, timber. **2.** orchard, cluster of fruit trees, plantation.

grovel *v.* humble oneself, demean oneself, be servile, behave abjectly, cower, cringe; fawn, toady, crawl, kowtow, stoop, snivel, truckle, flatter, lick the boots of, bow and scrape. **—Ant.** be proud, be haughty, act superior; domineer, intimidate, browbeat.

grow *v.* **1.** become larger, grow taller, spring up, shoot up, fill out; expand, increase, swell, widen, stretch, spread, extend; magnify, amplify, aggrandize. **2.** develop, mature, come to fruition, ripen; germinate, vegetate, sprout, bud, fructify, blossom, flower, bloom. **3.** cultivate, raise, produce, propagate, breed; sow, plant, till, farm, garden. **4.** thrive, flourish, progress, develop, prosper, succeed, advance, improve, enlarge, increase, expand, rise, surge, wax, boom, mushroom, skyrocket. **5.** become, get to be, come to be. **6.** mature, develop; obtain experience, get practice, have training; become worldly, become sophisticated. **—Ant. 1, 4** shrink, decrease, diminish, lessen, dwindle. **2** die, fail, decline, decay. **4** decline, slacken, subside, wane.

growl *v.* **1.** snarl, bark menacingly. **2.** snap, speak harshly, reply gruffly, complain, grumble, grouse, gripe, fret; mutter, murmur, rumble, groan, grunt, whine, croak. **3.** rumble, whine, croak, grind; *Informal* talk back.

grownup *n.* **1.** adult, mature person, man, woman, gentleman, lady, grown man, grown woman. *—adj.* **2.** adult, mature, full-grown, of age, big, senior, ripe, full-fledged, full-blown, at the age of consent. **—Ant. 2** little, small, juvenile; childish, immature.

growth *n.* **1.** natural development, development; advancement, advance, progress, improvement; maturity, matureness, prime. **2.** expansion, increase, development, extension, increment, enlargement, burgeoning, surge, spread, swell, amplification, augmentation; progress, improvement, advancement, advance, prospering, flourishing, rise, success. **3.** crop, harvest, production, cultivation, produce, flowering, planting, sowing, propagation. **4.** mass of tissue, lump, gnarl, hump, tumor; excrescence. **—Ant. 2** decrease, decline, lessening, dwindling, shrinking, shrinkage, slackening, subsiding, retreat, backsliding, failure; stagnation.

grubby *adj.* dirty, grimy, sloppy, slovenly, unkempt, messy, seedy, frowzy, filthy, nasty, squalid, foul, shoddy, shabby, tacky, frumpy, bedraggled, sordid, *Slang* beat-up. **—Ant.** neat, well-groomed, well-pressed, clean, tidy, spick-and-span.

grudge *n.* **1.** ill will, resentment, hard feelings, malice, spite, malevolence, rancor, pique, aversion, dislike, animosity, animus, hatred. *—v.* **2.** begrudge, envy, resent, be provoked at, be indignant at, cast a jaundiced eye at. **—Ant. 1** appreciation, thankfulness, goodwill, benevolence, friendliness, liking. **2** celebrate, be pleased for.

grueling *adj.* tiring, exhausting, fatiguing; hard, punishing, racking, torturous, brutal. **—Ant.** easy, soft, *Slang* cushy; enjoyable, pleasant; exhilarating, exciting.

gruesome *adj.* horrible, horrifying, hideous, horrid, horrendous, grisly, gory, ghastly, frightful, spine-chilling, bloodcurdling; revolting, repulsive, loathsome, repellent; grim, forbidding, shocking, fearful, terrible, awful, macabre. **—Ant.** pleasing, pleasant, cheery, cheerful, delightful, lovely, appealing, benign, sweet, sentimental.

gruff *adj.* **1.** surly, brusque, curt, blunt, short, abrupt, stern, bluff; uncivil, rude, impolite, discourteous, ungracious, insulting; snarling, grumpy, grouchy, bearish, sour, crabbed, churlish; caustic, tart, sharp, waspish, ill-humored, ill-natured, ill-tempered, sulky, sullen, peevish, bristling, crusty. **2.** hoarse, husky, rough, harsh, throaty, raspy, gutteral; cracked, croaky, ragged, strident. **—Ant. 1** pleasant, kind, sweet, good-humored; courteous, polite, civil, gracious. **2** smooth, mellifluous, rich.

grumble *v.* grouse, fret, murmur discontentedly, mutter, complain, whine, grouch, gripe, growl, chafe, find fault. **—Syn. Study.** See COMPLAIN.

grumpy *adj.* surly, ill-tempered, crabby, cranky, grouchy, sullen, sulky, irritable, disgruntled, ill-humored, cantankerous, peevish, pettish, out of sorts, testy, out of humor, in a bad temper, in a bad mood, sour; churlish, ill-disposed, moody, splenetic, crusty. **—Ant.** in a good mood, in good humor, pleasant, cheerful, sweet, kindly disposed.

guarantee *n.* **1.** warranty, written promise of quality, written assurance of durability; surety, endorsement, guaranty, affirmation, pledge, assurance, avowal, word, word of honor, security, testimony; bond, bail. **2.** assurance, promise. *—v.* **3.** give a guarantee on, warrant, vouch for; assure, endorse, insure, underwrite, sponsor; avow, testify. **4.** promise, pledge, give one's word, vouch for, assure, affirm, allege, avow, attest, swear, stand behind; be responsible for, make oneself answerable for, make certain, answer for, become surety for, bind oneself, contract.

guaranty *n.* **1.** warrant, warranty, pledge, guarantee, formal assurance, security, surety, insurance, endorsement, covenant, promise; contract, agreement, voucher. **2.** collateral, security, pledge, pawn; bail, bond; deposit.

guard *v.* **1.** protect, safeguard, shield, shelter, defend; watch over, keep safe, preserve, secure; save; attend, tend, mind, escort, conduct, convoy. **2.** keep under surveillance, keep watch over, keep under close watch, keep from escaping. *—n.* **3.** sentinel, sentry, watchman, guardsman, warder, *Slang* watchdog; body of defenders, garrison, patrol, picket, watch, convoy, escort; protector, bodyguard, defender; guardian, custodian, gatekeeper, doorkeeper, concierge. **4.** shield, screen, safeguard; defense, protection, security, preservation. **—Ant. 1** expose to danger, endanger, threaten; menace, imperil.

guarded *adj.* cautious, chary, wary,

careful, restrained, discreet, circumspect, prudent, cagey, leery, mindful, heedful, on one's guard; hesitant, tentative. **—Ant.** reckless, careless, daring, frank, rash, foolhardy.

guardian *n.* **1.** protector, preserver, keeper, custodian, defender, guard, trustee, caretaker, shepherd, curator, conservator, watchdog, vigilante, warden, warder, wardsman; guard, escort, bodyguard, sentry, picket, sentinel, patrol, convoy, champion, safeguard, attendant, conductor. **2.** legal custodian, protector, patron, benefactor; guardian angel, champion, advocate, friend at court. **—Ant. 1** enemy, foe, opponent, attacker; traitor. **2** ward, protégé.

guess *v.* **1.** judge correctly, estimate correctly, correctly answer, answer with the facts; divine, figure out; speculate, conjecture, risk an opinion on, hazard a supposition, hypothesize, make a stab at. **2.** think, suppose, believe, assume, suspect, daresay, venture, conclude, gather, deduce, surmise, opine, fancy, imagine; judge, deem, reckon, estimate, predict, theorize, regard. —*n.* **3.** estimate, supposition, assumption, speculation, opinion, belief, view, hypothesis, conjecture, presumption, surmise, prediction, suspicion, feeling, divination, theory, guesswork, postulation, postulate. **—Syn. Study. 1, 2** GUESS, CONJECTURE, SURMISE imply attempting to form an opinion as to the probable. To GUESS is to risk an opinion regarding something one does not know about, or, wholly or partly by chance, to arrive at the correct answer to a question: *to guess the outcome of a game.* To CONJECTURE is to make inferences in the absence of sufficient evidence to establish certainty: *to conjecture the circumstances of the crime.* SURMISE implies making an intuitive conjecture that may or may not be correct: *to surmise the motives that led to the crime.* **—Ant. 1** know, prove. **3** certainty, fact.

guest *n.* **1.** invitee, visitor, caller, friend; company. **2.** (*variously*) roomer, boarder, lodger, sojourner, diner; patron, customer, client, paying customer, habitué, frequenter; patient, inmate. **—Ant. 1** host, hostess.

guffaw *n.* burst of laughter, peal of laughter, hearty laugh, boisterous laugh, roar of mirth, howl, scream, shout of merriment; *Slang* horse laugh, belly laugh.

guidance *n.* **1.** counsel, advice, help; information, instruction, intelligence, enlightenment, pointer, tip, suggestion, clue, hint. **2.** direction, leadership, management, conduct, supervision, auspices; escort, protection, lead.

guide *v.* **1.** lead, pilot, steer, show the way to, direct, conduct; escort, usher, accompany, convoy, shepherd. **2.** maneuver, manipulate, manage, handle, direct, conduct, control, command, engineer, steer, lead, pilot, regulate; rule, govern, preside over, oversee, superintend, have charge of. —*n.* **3.** pilot, escort, convoy; conductor, leader, helmsman, steerer, director, cicerone, usher; marshal, shepherd, attendant, chaperon. **4.** counselor, adviser, monitor, mentor, teacher, master; model, example, rule, pattern; landmark, signpost, marker, beacon, guiding light, polestar, lodestar. **—Ant. 1** misguide, mislead. **3** follower. **4** disciple, imitator, pupil.

guild *n.* professional organization, association, society, league, fraternity, brotherhood, sisterhood, alliance, company, corporation, federation, confederacy, order, coalition; union, trade union, labor union, craft union.

guile *n.* slyness, trickery, trickiness, cunning, craft, craftiness, artifice, chicanery, wiliness, artfulness, strategy, sharp practice; deceit, treachery, duplicity, fraud, fraudulence, deception, dishonesty, *Slang* hanky-panky; tricks, stratagems. **—Syn. Study.** See DECEIT. **—Ant.** candor, frankness, honesty, sincerity, naiveté, veracity, truthfulness.

guileless *adj.* straightforward, candid, frank, open, natural, honest, sincere, truthful, aboveboard; artless, undesigning; ingenuous, naive, unsophisticated, innocent, simple, unaffected, unselfconscious; harmless, innocuous, unoffending. **—Ant.** sly, cunning, deceitful, crafty, tricky, deceptive, artful; treacherous, fraudulent.

guilt *n.* **1.** guiltiness, guilty conduct, criminality, culpability; wrongdoing, misconduct, misdoing, misdeed, misbehavior, wrong, turpitude, transgression; sinfulness, sin, vice; trespass, delinquency, dereliction. **2.** guilty feeling, shame, disgrace, self-disgust, humiliation, degradation, dishonor, infamy; stigma, blot, black mark. **—Ant. 1** innocence, blamelessness, righteousness, sinlessness, good deed, virtue. **2** pride, honor, self-respect.

guilty *adj.* **1.** justly charged, having committed a crime, culpable, blamable, blameworthy, responsible for a wrongdoing. **2.** criminal; immoral, sinful, wrong, corrupt, erring, offensive. **3.** sheepish, hangdog; contrite, sorry, regretful, ashamed, conscience-stricken, penitent, repentant. **—Ant. 1–3** innocent. **1** blameless. **2** moral, righteous, virtuous. **3** proud, noble.

guise *n.* **1.** dress, attire, garb, costume, disguise, habit, clothing, apparel, clothes, mode, fashion. **2.** appearance, outward show; disguise, masquerade, pretense, pretext. —**Syn. Study. 2** See APPEARANCE.

gulf *n.* **1.** large bay, estuary, arm of the sea, firth, fjord, inlet, cove, lagoon. **2.** chasm, abyss, crevasse, canyon, gully, opening, rent, cleft, rift, split, separation.

gullible *adj.* easily fooled, easily deceived, easily cheated, easily duped; overtrusting, unsuspicious, credulous, trusting, trustful; naive, innocent, unsophisticated, inexperienced, green, simple. —**Ant.** cynical, suspicious, untrusting, hard to convince; sophisticated, worldly.

gully *n.* **1.** ravine, gulch, gap, small valley, defile, gorge, small canyon; watercourse, channel. **2.** ditch, drainage ditch, gutter; furrow, trench.

gulp *v.* **1.** swallow in large mouthfuls, swallow eagerly, swallow greedily, swill, guzzle, swig, quaff, wolf, toss off; bolt, devour. —*n.* **2.** mouthful, swallow, swig, large draft. —**Ant. 1** sip, drink daintily; nibble, eat daintily.

gumption *n.* initiative, spirit, drive, energy, resourcefulness, enterprise, courage, forcefulness, hustle, aggressiveness, verve, dash, spunk, push; *Slang* get up and go, pizazz, zip.

gun *n.* **1.** firearm; (*variously*) revolver, pistol, automatic, .45, .38, .22, six-shooter, Colt, derringer; rifle, shotgun, carbine, Winchester, musket, fowling piece, muzzle loader, blunderbuss, flintlock, Kentucky rifle, machine gun; *Slang* gat, shooting iron, iron, trusty-rusty, rod, piece, equalizer. **2.** cannon, fieldpiece, artillery piece, big gun, piece of ordnance; (*variously*) mortar, howitzer, Big Bertha, Long Tom. —*v.* **3.** hunt, go after, shoot, expect to shoot; try, attempt, aim.

gurgle *v.* **1.** flow noisily, bubble, burble, babble, plash, sputter, ripple. —*n.* **2.** gurgling, bubbling, babble, burble, murmur, plash, sputter.

gush *v.* **1.** flow forth, pour out, spurt, spout, stream, jet, well, burst forth, rush forth, issue, run, splash, squirt. **2.** talk effusively, be overenthusiastic, chatter, babble, burble, gab, prattle, blather, blabber, prate, rattle on, run off at the mouth; flatter excessively. —*n.* **3.** sudden outflow, outpouring, spurt, torrent, stream, jet, spout, squirt, splash, rush, outburst. **4.** foolish talk, boring talk, mawkishness, sentimentalism, emotionalism; nonsense, stuff and nonsense, twaddle, blabber, drivel, rubbish, chatter, blab; *Slang* hot air, gas, baloney, bull. —**Ant. 1** drip, trickle, dribble, ooze. **2** be closemouthed, be uncommunicative. **3** drip, trickle.

gust *n.* **1.** puff, blast, draft, breeze, wind; zephyr, squall, flurry, blow. **2.** burst, outburst, outbreak, sudden rush, explosion, paroxysm, fit. —*v.* **3.** blow in bursts, blow intermittently, puff, blast. —**Syn. Study. 1** See WIND.

gusto *n.* hearty enjoyment, relish, zest, enthusiasm, fervor, joy, exhilaration, zeal, delight, pleasure, appreciation, savor, satisfaction, appetite; personal liking, individual taste.

gut *v.* **1.** eviscerate, clean, disembowel. **2.** destroy the interior of; lay in ashes, level, ravage, raze, consume, lay waste, lay in ruins. —*n.* **3.** intestines, entrails, viscera; lower alimentary canal, bowels, *Slang* breadbasket. **4.** stomach, abdomen; paunch, belly; bay window, beer belly, spare tire. **5. guts** courage, bravery, boldness, mettle, spunk; daring, bravado, spirit, nerve, backbone, audacity, dash.

guttural *adj.* throaty, husky, deep, low; hoarse, harsh, raspy, croaking, gruff; thick, inarticulate. —**Ant.** nasal, high-pitched, high, squeaky.

guzzle *v.* drink greedily, gulp down; swill, swig, toss off, quaff, imbibe, tipple; eat greedily, bolt, devour. —**Ant.** sip, drink daintily; nibble, eat daintily.

gyp *v.* **1.** cheat, swindle, defraud, take advantage of, cozen, bamboozle, hoodwink, bilk, diddle, rook, soak; *Slang* rip off, burn. —*n.* **2.** fraud, flimflam, trick, deception, hoax, cheat, con game, fake, phony, humbug; *Slang* ripoff, con, scam.

gyrate *v.* spin around, rotate, revolve, circle, twirl, whirl, turn around, wheel, spiral, swirl, pirouette.

habit *n.* **1.** practice, behavior pattern, habitude, custom, convention, matter of course, routine, beaten path, rut, groove; characteristic tendency, trait, proclivity, peculiarity, inclination, wont, second nature; rule, observance, manner, mannerism. **2.** way, practice, acquired mode of behavior, habitual action, fixed practice, confirmed way; leaning, inclination, predisposition, predilection, partiality, fondness, propensity, prevailing tendency. **3.** dress, attire, costume, garment, garb, apparel, raiment, clothes, clothing, outfit, uniform, robe, vesture, livery; gear, trappings, accoutrements, habiliments. **—Syn. Study. 1** See CUSTOM.

habitat *n.* **1.** native environment, natural home, natural locality, area of distribution; terrain, territory, range, domain, realm, milieu, environment, haunt, place, spot, locale, setting, region, zone, precinct; *Slang* stamping ground, home base. **2.** dwelling, dwelling place, place of abode, abode, domicile, habitation; home, housing, lodging, lodgment, quarters; *Slang* digs, roost, pad.

habitation *n.* **1.** occupancy, tenancy, occupation, dwelling, lodging, lodgment, residence; abode, temporary stay. **2.** abode, place of residence, dwelling, dwelling place, home, habitat, place of abode, domicile, haunt, residence, house; housing, lodging, shelter, quarters; *Slang* digs, roost, pad. **3.** settlement, community, colony.

habitual *adj.* **1.** customary, usual, accustomed, regular, normal, natural, common, fixed, established, traditional, typical, wonted, familiar, expected, conventional; routine, recurrent, inveterate, confirmed; continual, incessant; by force of habit, second nature. **2.** chronic, confirmed, inveterate, constant, addicted, continual, frequent, repeated, periodic, recurrent, established, ingrained, deep-seated, deep-rooted, perpetual, systematic, methodical. **—Syn. Study. 1** See USUAL. **—Ant. 1** rare, uncommon, unusual, exceptional, abnormal, extraordinary, strange, unexpected, occasional. **2** infrequent, sporadic, irregular, unconfirmed.

habituate *v.* accustom, make used to, indoctrinate, inculcate; break in, inure, harden, instill, imbue, adapt, discipline, initiate, season, train, school, drill.

habitué *n.* frequenter, regular patron, frequent visitor, constant customer; *Informal* regular.

hack[1] *v.* **1.** cut roughly, cut, cut up, chop, hew, chip, mangle, mutilate, lacerate, notch, gash, slit, slice, cleave, slash; *Slang* whack. **2.** cough repeatedly, cough drily, emit short coughs, rasp; *Slang* bark.

hack[2] *n.* **1.** taxicab, taxi, cab. **2.** hackney coach, horse-drawn carriage, coach; horse-drawn carriage for hire. **3.** medium-sized horse, common horse, carriage horse, hackney; *Slang* nag, plug; worn-out horse; hired horse, horse for common hire; cart horse, shaft horse, dray horse, draft horse, workhorse. **4.** scribbler, penny-a-liner, grubstreet writer. **—Ant. 3** thoroughbred; pony.

hackneyed *adj.* commonplace, routine, common, stale, trite, banal, inane, insipid, vapid, stereotyped, clichéd, threadbare, pedestrian, stock, worn-out, worn, well-worn, shopworn, platitudinous, conventional, bromidic, ordinary, moth-eaten, humdrum, uninspired, unimaginative; dull, jejune. **—Syn. Study.** See COMMONPLACE. **—Ant.** original, new, fresh, novel, imaginative, creative, unusual, uncommon; striking.

hag *n.* harridan, crone, harpy, ogress, virago, shrew, hellcat, gorgon, witch, nag, beldam, vixen, termagant, biddy, frump, drab, fury; *Slang* bat, battle-ax.

haggard *adj.* **1.** tired-looking, hollow-eyed, gaunt, careworn, woebegone; exhausted, spent, weary, fatigued, tired, debilitated, drooping, fagged, toilworn, worn, wasted, overwearied, flagging; *Slang* tuckered out, beat, bushed, pooped. **2.** wild-eyed, wild-looking, wild, frenzied, overcome, overwrought, upset, raging, ranting, harassed, harrowed. **—Ant. 1** full of pep, energetic, vigorous, jaunty, bright-eyed and bushy-tailed, well-rested; hale, hale and hearty, glowing with health, robust, sleek. **2** calm, serene, tranquil.

haggle *v.* **1.** dicker, bargain, barter, higgle, beat down. **2.** squabble, quibble, bicker, wrangle, quarrel, dispute.

hail *v.* **1.** call to, shout at, cry out to, address, greet, accost, salute; welcome, receive, usher in, shake hands with, make welcome, bid one welcome. **2.** acclaim, cheer, applaud, exalt, honor, glorify, eulogize, extol, panegyrize, esteem, compliment, commend. *—n.* **3.** shout, call, accosting, calling out, hello, salutation, greeting, salute. **—Ant. 1** ignore, avoid, shun, cut. **2** condemn, rebuff, insult, criticize, boo, hiss.

hair *n.* **1.** head of hair, tresses, locks, curls, ringlets, bangs; *Slang* mop, mane;

(*of animal*) coat, fur, pelt, fleece; wool, down, mane. **2.** narrow margin, iota, hair's-breadth.

hairsplitting *adj.* hairline, minute, subtle, delicate, fine, minuscule; unapparent, imperceptible, inappreciable, inconsequential, infinitesimal; carping, quibbling, niggling, caviling, nitpicking, faultfinding, overcritical.

hairy *adj.* hirsute, pilose, shaggy, bushy, woolly, furry, fleecy.

halcyon *adj.* calm, peaceful, serene, pacific, quiet, placid, hushed, untroubled, reposeful, tranquil, unruffled, unagitated; carefree, contented, happy, blithe, cheerful, joyous. **—Ant.** tempestuous, stormy, blustery, tumultuous; troubled, agitated.

hale *adj.* healthy, hearty, hardy, well, robust, able-bodied, sound, vigorous, energetic, sturdy, fit, strapping, rugged, robustious, in fine fettle, in the pink, in shape, full of vim and vigor. **—Ant.** weak, sickly, infirm, frail, debilitated.

half *n.* **1.** one half, one of two equal parts, fifty percent; part, fraction, portion, section, some. *—adj.* **2.** one-half, halved; partial, fractional, incomplete, divided; inadequate, imperfect, limited, insufficient, deficient, meager, slight, scanty, skimpy; moderate, middling, tolerable, passable. *—adv.* **3.** partially, partly, in part, after a fashion, inadequately, insufficiently, slightly, barely, feebly, weakly, faintly; relatively, fairly, moderately, passably, tolerably, comparatively, rather; pretty nearly, all but. **—Ant. 1** whole, total, sum total, all, aggregate, entirety. **2** whole, complete, entire, full. **3** wholly, completely, entirely, fully, totally; strongly, adequately, sufficiently.

half-hearted *adj.* unenthusiastic, indifferent, lackluster, perfunctory, cool, cold, blasé, spiritless, faint, tame, lukewarm, passive, unaspiring, irresolute, neither hot nor cold, ambivalent, neither one thing nor the other; listless, lackadaisical, lethargic, apathetic, languid, phlegmatic. **—Ant.** wholehearted, enthusiastic, eager, spirited, zealous, avid, animated, warm, emotional, concerned, moved, excited; ambitious, aspiring, energetic, red-hot.

halfway *adv.* **1.** midway, half the distance, in the middle. **2.** partially, partly, in part, to a degree, in some measure, to some extent, nearly, pretty nearly, almost; somewhat, rather, moderately. *—adj.* **3.** middle, midway, intermediate, medium, medial, midmost, middlemost, equidistant, between two extremes.

half-wit *n.* fool, dunce, dummy, blockhead, dolt, ninny, nitwit, numskull, nincompoop, dimwit, dope, dumb-dumb; feeble-minded person, moron, imbecile, idiot, simpleton, mental defective, mental deficient, dullard.

hall *n.* **1.** hallway, corridor, passageway, passage; gallery, arcade. **2.** entrance hall, entry, lobby, foyer, vestibule; waiting room, reception room, anteroom, antechamber. **3.** concert hall, auditorium, assembly room, meeting place, amphitheater, chamber, club room; dining hall, banquet hall.

hallowed *adj.* sacred, consecrated, dedicated, honored; holy, blessed, sanctified, beatified, sacrosanct. **—Syn. Study.** See HOLY. **—Ant.** profane, unsanctified.

hallucination *n.* delusion, fantasy, illusion, mirage, apparition, phantasmagoria, chimera, figment, aberration, vision, dream, nightmare.

halo *n.* **1.** ring of light, aureole, nimbus, corona, radiance. **2.** aurora, chromosphere. **3.** atmosphere of glory, magnificence, splendor, resplendence, radiance, luminousness, luster, illustriousness, majesty, dignity, grandeur, holiness, sanctity, sublimity, spiritual aura, solemnity.

halt *v.* **1.** stop, come to a stop, come to a standstill, pull up, draw up, wait, rest, pause, tarry, linger, suspend, interrupt; terminate, quit, cease, discontinue, leave off; shut down, close up shop, hang fire, knock off, break off, call it a day, wind up; arrest, brake, check, rein in, throttle down, heave to. **2.** stop, end, arrest, bring to a standstill, defeat, choke off, prohibit, extinguish, prevent, cut off, vanquish, suppress, overthrow, overturn, put down, subdue, rout, quell, quash, crush, scotch; curb, check, hinder, impede, repress, restrict, restrain, balk, thwart, stem, stall, stay, delay, abate, frustrate, foil, hamper, hold in check, bridle, block, inhibit; *Slang* squelch, throw a wrench in the works, spike one's guns, cut the ground from under. *—n.* **3.** stop, cessation, standstill, discontinuance, suspension, termination, close, end; intermission, recess, respite, interval, pause, rest, interruption, delay, interlude; *Slang* breather, breathing spell, break, time out. *—interj.* **4.** stop, stand still, don't move, come to a halt. **—Syn. Study. 1, 2** See STOP. **—Ant. 1, 2** continue, go ahead, proceed; begin, start, resume. **2** support, encourage, forward, maintain, aid, abet, bolster, boost. **3** beginning, start; resumption, continuation. **4** proceed, move on.

halve *v.* cut in half, split in two, divide equally, bisect; lessen by one half, reduce 50 percent. **—Ant.** double, increase 100 percent.

hamlet *n.* small village, village, crossroads; *Slang* burg, one-horse town, jerkwater town, whistle-stop, hick town, tank town. —**Ant.** metropolis, city, megalopolis.

hammer *n.* **1.** (*variously*) claw hammer, ballpeen hammer, tack hammer; mallet, sledge hammer, sledge, steam hammer, pile driver, rammer; gavel. —*v.* **2.** nail; hit, pound, knock, strike, pummel, whack, tap, punch, bang, drive. **3.** forge, form with a hammer, beat out; fashion, shape, make.

hamper *v.* hinder, impede, interfere with, hold up, handicap, encumber, inhibit, thwart, prevent, frustrate, balk, stall, restrain, restrict, retard, curb, check, stem, block, obstruct, fetter, shackle, muzzle, gag, hog-tie. —**Syn. Study.** See PREVENT. —**Ant.** help, aid, assist, further, promote, forward, facilitate, expedite, speed, accelerate, hasten, encourage, bolster, boost.

hand *n.* **1.** manual extremity; palm, fist; *Slang* paw, mitt, meat-hook. **2.** laborer, hired hand, hired man, man, worker, workman, workingman, employee, aide, assistant, associate, helper, menial, handyman; member of a crew. **3.** help, assistance, aid, support, lift. **4.** Usu. **hands.** care, keeping, charge, custody, control, possession, power, hold, authority, command, management, guidance, dominion, jurisdiction, supervision, domination, auspices. **5.** handwriting, penmanship, script, calligraphy, longhand. **6.** round of applause, burst of applause; ovation. —*v.* **7.** give, pass, hand over, present, deliver, convey, turn over to, furnish with, *Informal* reach. **8.** give a hand to, hold out a helping hand to, help, assist, guide, aid, do a good turn for, minister to, come to the aid of. —**Ant. 2** employer, boss, foreman, overseer, supervisor.

handful *n.* small number, smattering, sprinkling, scattering; small quantity, tiny amount, minimum, scant amount, modicum, thimbleful. —**Ant.** horde, mob, crowd, throng, a large amount, a lot.

handicap *n.* **1.** drawback, disadvantage, detriment, impediment, restriction, limitation, shortcoming, defect, obstacle, barrier, stumbling block, difficulty, inhibition, burden, encumbrance, inconvenience. **2.** physical disability; (*variously*) lameness, loss of a limb, blindness, deafness, speech disability. —*v.* **3.** hinder, hold back, hamper, impede, encumber, shackle, retard, burden, restrict, limit, place at a disadvantage, inhibit, thwart, suppress, repress; restrain, curb. —**Ant. 1** advantage, benefit, asset, edge, boost, boon. **3** help, benefit, give an advantage to, assist, aid, forward, promote, further, boost.

handle *n.* **1.** shaft, shank, hilt; hold, grasp, pull, knob, grip. —*v.* **2.** take in the hands, pick up, hold; finger, knead, pinch, poke, touch, feel; stroke, caress, fondle, massage; *Slang* paw, paw over. **3.** control, steer, guide, maneuver, pilot; operate, run, work, manipulate, ply, use, utilize, employ, bring into play, manage, command. **4.** manage, deal with, *Slang* swing; take care of, care for; command, control, manipulate, conduct, treat. **5.** sell, offer for sale, carry, deal in, trade in, traffic in, market, merchandise.

handsome *adj.* **1.** good-looking, attractive, fine-looking, sightly, comely, easy on the eyes, easy to look at, lovely, exquisite, stunning, beauteous, beautiful, pretty, comely, bonny, fair; splendid, tasteful, elegant, stately, impressive, imposing, well-formed, well-proportioned, well-arranged. **2.** generous, magnanimous, liberal, bountiful; ample, considerable, sizable, sufficient, abundant, moderately large. **3.** gracious, generous, bountiful, unselfish, noble, magnanimous, big-hearted, princely; humanitarian, benevolent, merciful, benign, compassionate. —**Syn. Study. 1** See BEAUTIFUL. —**Ant. 1** ugly, unattractive, homely, bad-looking, repulsive, unsightly; tasteless, inelegant; ill-proportioned, unshapely. **2** ungenerous, illiberal, stingy, niggardly, miserly, cheap; small, meager, skimpy, scant. **3** mean, base, selfish, ignoble.

handy *adj.* **1.** accessible, close at hand, ready to hand, at hand, on hand, at one's elbow, within easy reach, easily accessible, available, obtainable, near, convenient, nigh, on call, in readiness, on tap, at one's beck and call. **2.** skillful, skilled, expert, adroit, dexterous, deft, nimble-fingered, competent, proficient, capable, adept, accomplished, clever, efficient. **3.** easy to use, convenient to handle, manageable, wieldy, useful, practical, serviceable, helpful. —**Ant. 1** out of the way, hard to get, inaccessible, unavailable, inconvenient, remote, far. **2** clumsy, awkward, inept, unskilled, all thumbs. **3** clumsy, awkward, unwieldy, cumbersome, inconvenient; useless, impractical.

hang *v.* **1.** suspend, fasten from above, append, attach, affix; dangle, swing freely, be pendent, depend. **2.** lynch, execute by hanging, send to the gallows, die on the gallows, *Slang* string up. **3.** depend, be dependent, be contingent, rest, turn upon, hinge, be subject to, lie in, revolve around, repose in. **4.** let droop, dangle, bow, lower, drop, incline, bend forward, bend downward, sag; lean over, trail. —*n.* **5.** knack; gist, point, meaning, thought. —**Ant. 1** take down, detach. **4** lift, raise.

hangdog *adj.* abject, defeated, intimidated, humiliated, browbeaten, wretched, degraded, hopeless, miserable, resigned, hopeless; ashamed, embarrassed, guilty-looking, crestfallen, shamefaced, chapfallen. **—Ant.** confident, assured, undaunted, bold, cocksure.

hanker *v.* **—Syn. Study.** See YEARN.

hankering *n.* longing, craving, desire, yearning, yen, hunger, thirst, urge, itch, aching, pining.

haphazard *adj.* unmethodical, disorganized, unsystematic, chaotic, unorganized, disordered, disorderly, random, arbitrary; careless, unthinking, indiscriminate, casual, chance, slapdash, fitful, sporadic, catch-as-catch-can, hit-or-miss, on-and-off; aimless, purposeless, fortuitous, undesigned, undirected, unpremeditated, accidental. **—Ant.** organized, methodical, systematic, orderly, ordered; careful, thoughtful, designed, planned, arranged, premeditated, purposeful, intentional, considered, deliberate.

hapless *adj.* unlucky, unfortunate, jinxed, ill-starred, ill-fated, star-crossed, unhappy, luckless, forlorn, hopeless, miserable, wretched, woeful, cursed, accursed; *Slang* rotten, lousy, no-good. **—Ant.** happy, fortunate, lucky, blessed, charmed.

happen *v.* **1.** take place, occur, come about, come to pass, ensue, transpire, result, betide, befall, eventuate; arise, spring up, crop up, come into existence, present itself, appear. **2.** have the fortune to be, have the luck to be; be the case, turn out. **3.** become of, befall, be one's fate, fall to one's lot, be one's fortune; be experienced by, be borne by, be endured by, be suffered by.

happening *n.* event, occurrence, incident, incidence, episode, affair, experience, matter, proceeding, occasion, circumstance, happenstance, adventure, advent, case; accident, vicissitude, just one of those things.

happiness *n.* **1.** gladness, joy, delight, felicity, contentment, content, sense of well-being, pleasure, enjoyment, satisfaction, lightheartedness, rejoicing, elation, jubilation, high spirits, bliss, beatitude, blessedness, rapture, ecstasy, gaiety, exultation, transport, exuberance; merriment, cheer, cheerfulness, cheeriness, glee, jollity, mirth. **2.** pleasure, satisfaction, gratification, blessing, comfort. **—Ant. 1** unhappiness, sadness, sorrow, grief, woe; depression, despondency, low spirits, misery, anguish, distress, discomfort. **2** bane, annoyance; calamity, misfortune, thorn in one's side, cross to bear.

happy *adj.* **1.** glad, pleased, delighted, content, contented, gratified, tickled, tickled pink; gay, cheerful, in high spirits, elated, joyous, overjoyed, exhilarated, blissful, rapturous, ecstatic, exultant, gleeful, transported, rhapsodic, jubilant, flushed with pleasure, exuberant, in seventh heaven; pleasant, pleasing, delightful, gratifying, cheering, joyful. **2.** fortunate, lucky, auspicious, favorable, felicitous, propitious; convenient, opportune, meet, timely, seasonable, fitting, fit, advantageous, agreeable. **—Syn. Study. 2** See FORTUNATE. **—Ant. 1** sad, unhappy, sorry, sorrowful, displeased, discontent; despondent, forlorn, miserable, gloomy, glum, melancholy, depressed, downcast, joyless, mournful, somber; down in the mouth, down in the dumps. **2** unfortunate, unlucky, luckless, inauspicious; unfitting, unseasonable.

happy-go-lucky *adj.* carefree, easygoing, untroubled, devil-may-care, unconcerned, heedless, insouciant, free and easy, unworried, light-hearted, nonchalant, blithe; feckless, irresponsible; flighty, skittish, scatterbrained. **—Ant.** cautious, circumspect, prudent, careful, discreet.

harangue *n.* **—Syn. Study.** See SPEECH.

harass *v.* **1.** attack repeatedly, raid frequently, assault continually, beset, besiege. **2.** torment, pester, badger, harry, worry, disturb, annoy, irritate, distress, bother, irk, vex, bedevil, plague, hound, discommode, exasperate, tease, bait, heckle, hector, ride, persecute, browbeat, bully, intimidate, cow.

harbinger *n.* herald, precursor, forerunner, indication, announcer, signaler, proclaimer; first sign, omen, portent, token, clue, symbol.

harbor *n.* **1.** port, protected anchorage, haven; (*variously*) dock, pier, wharf, quay, cove, bay, lagoon, inlet, basin; destination, goal, terminus, terminal point. **2.** haven, refuge, asylum, retreat, shelter, sanctuary, hideaway, concealment, hiding place. **—*v.* 3.** give refuge to, shelter, hide, conceal, give hiding place to, shield, protect, care for, keep safe; quarter, house, lodge, billet, take in, keep. **4.** nurture, foster, bear in the mind, hold, maintain, retain, feel, cling to; brood over, muse over. **—Syn. Study. 1** HARBOR, PORT, HAVEN refer to a shelter for ships. A HARBOR is a natural or an artificially constructed shelter and anchorage for ships: *a fine harbor on the eastern coast.* A PORT is a harbor viewed esp. with reference to its commercial activities and facilities: *a thriving port.* HAVEN is a literary word meaning refuge, although occasionally referring to a natural harbor that can be utilized by ships as a place of safety: *to seek a haven in a storm.* 3, 4 See CHERISH.

hard *adj.* **1.** firm, solid, hardened, rocklike, stony, steely; rigid, stiff, unmalleable, inflexible, unpliable. **2.** strong, powerful, forceful, heavy, intense, fierce, severe, violent. **3.** difficult, arduous, laborious, strenuous, tough, exacting, formidable, Herculean, troublesome, burdensome, wearisome; baffling, confusing, puzzling, perplexing, bewildering, unfathomable, cryptic; complex, complicated, involved, intricate, impenetrable, thorny, knotty. **4.** industrious, energetic, vigorous, enterprising, relentless, assiduous, diligent, persevering, persistent, unremitting, indefatigable, untiring, unflagging; earnest, zealous, eager, conscientious, willing, spirited, animated. **5.** strict, stern, severe, unyielding, stubborn, uncompromising, stringent, oppressive, unbending; hardhearted, cruel, cold, implacable, unrelenting, merciless, pitiless, inexorable, unremitting, callous, impervious, unsparing, ruthless, thick-skinned, hardened, insensitive; inhuman, brutal. **6.** severe, harsh, rough, difficult; unpleasant, disagreeable, distressing, oppressive, disheartening, burdensome, onerous, intolerable, unbearable, tormenting; harmful, hurtful, lamentable, sad, melancholy. **7.** hostile, belligerent, unfriendly, antagonistic, bellicose; mean, ugly, bitter, vicious, rancorous, venomous, malicious, acrimonious, vindictive, spiteful, sullen, cantankerous, unkind, critical, insulting. *—adv.* **8.** solidly, firm, firmly, tight, tightly, rigid, stiff, closely. **9.** forcefully, forcibly, powerfully, strongly, heavily, fiercely, severely, violently, intensely, sharply, vigorously. **10.** industriously, vigorously, rigorously, energetically, arduously, laboriously, furiously, intently, intensely, with all one's might, relentlessly, unsparingly, unceasingly, steadily, diligently, persistently, untiringly, determinedly, assiduously, unflaggingly, conscientiously, resolutely, earnestly, eagerly, keenly, seriously, closely. **11.** emotionally, to heart, with strong feelings, with much sorrow, distressfully, severely, painfully, agonizingly; with much anger, angrily. **—Ant. 1–3, 5, 6, 8** soft. **3, 5, 6** easy. **1** mushy; flexible, pliant, pliable, malleable. **2** weak, light, mild. **3** light, simple, uncomplicated, straightforward, clear, direct; easy as pie. **4** lazy, lethargic; lax, careless. **5** softhearted, lenient, permissive, yielding, kind, kindhearted, warmhearted, merciful, sensitive, humane, gentle. **6** mild, pleasant, agreeable, enjoyable, good, salubrious. **7** friendly, loving, amiable, warm, kind, sweet, good; complimentary. **8** loose, loosely, lightly. **9** softly, weakly, gently, mildly, lightly, faintly. **10** easily, effortlessly; lazily, lethargically. **11** calmly, unemotionally, mildly, placidly, serenely.

hard-and-fast *adj.* set, strict, inflexible, irrevocable, unyielding, exacting, binding, obligatory, compulsory, uncompromising, rigorous, unremitting, compelling, mandatory, unalterable, unbending; indisputable, incontestable, undeniable. **—Ant.** flexible, lax, elastic, yielding, lenient, debatable.

hardheaded *adj.* **1.** practical, objective, shrewd, astute, pragmatic, realistic; down-to-earth; unemotional, unfeeling, impersonal, sensible, tough-minded; not easily deceived, not easily ruffled, cool, coolheaded, self-controlled, poised, *Slang* unflappable. **2.** stubborn, obstinate, self-willed, willful, contrary, intractable, balky, unbending, inflexible, immovable, unyielding, refractory, mulish, pigheaded. **—Ant. 1** softhearted, idealistic, impractical, theoretical, philosophical; emotional, volatile, hotheaded, excitable. **2** flexible, yielding, receptive; agreeable, amenable.

hardhearted *adj.* cruel, cruelhearted, unfeeling, mean, heartless, merciless, remorseless, unsparing, unforgiving, uncaring, insensitive, indifferent, unsympathetic, coldblooded, ruthless, unpitying, pitiless, cold, stony, hard, callous, thick-skinned, inhuman, brutal. **—Ant.** kind, loving, sweet, compassionate, sympathetic, softhearted, warmhearted, understanding, sensitive, warm, gentle, humane, tender, merciful, forgiving.

hardly *adv.* **1.** barely, scarcely, only, just, not quite, almost not, faintly; rarely, uncommonly, infrequently, not often. **2.** by no means, not by any means, certainly not, in no manner, in no way, not by a great deal. **—Syn. Study. 1** HARDLY, BARELY, SCARCELY imply a narrow margin of sufficiency. HARDLY usu. emphasizes the difficulty or sacrifice involved: *We could hardly endure the winter.* BARELY implies no more than the minimum, as in performance or quantity: *We barely succeeded.* SCARCELY implies an even narrower margin, usu. below a satisfactory level: *He can scarcely read.* **—Ant. 1** fully, easily, amply, more than, well over, abundantly; often, frequently, commonly, usually. **2** by all means, certainly, really, truly, indubitably.

hard-nosed *adj.* stubborn, hardheaded, intractable, unyielding, inflexible, uncompromising, rigid, hard-line, unbending; tough, businesslike, unsentimental; shrewd, calculating, *Slang* one-way. **—Ant.** open-minded, flexible, amenable, reasonable, tractable.

hardship *n.* **1.** suffering, affliction, trouble, misfortune, adversity, ordeal, tribulation, misery, unhappiness, grief, sorrow, travail, woe, wretchedness, agony. **2.** privation, burden, handicap, encumbrance, difficulty, load, problem, millstone round one's neck, load, cross to bear. **—Ant. 1** comfort, ease, happiness; good fortune, benefit. **2** help, aid, blessing, boon, relief, load off one's back.

hardy *adj.* robust, rugged, sturdy, hearty, strapping, able-bodied, strong, tough, vigorous, mighty; healthy, fit, physically fit, stalwart, hale, in good condition, in fine fettle. **—Ant.** delicate, frail, fragile, dainty, soft, weak, feeble, sickly, debilitated.

harebrained *adj.* foolish, flighty, dimwitted, rattlebrained, skittish, scatterbrained, simple-minded, half-witted, silly, asinine, senseless, empty-headed, featherbrained, wacky, *Slang* wacko. **—Ant.** prudent, intelligent, sensible, wise, well-advised.

harlot *n.* prostitute, whore, strumpet, trollop, bawd, slut, doxy, tart, jade, chippy, wanton, streetwalker, scarlet woman, painted woman, fallen woman, jezebel, call girl; *Slang* pros, pro; mistress, courtesan, kept woman.

harm *n.* **1.** injury, hurt, damage, suffering, pain, agony, trauma; impairment, detriment, mischief, adversity, hardship, misfortune, ill, destruction, abuse, defacement, deterioration, scourge, calamity, havoc, devastation. **2.** wrong, wickedness, evil, sin, sinfulness, iniquity, immorality, vice, villainy; malice, malevolence, maliciousness. *—v.* **3.** impair, injure, hurt, wound, maim, ruin, cripple, pain, abuse, maltreat, do violence to, misuse, ill-use; damage, blemish, mar, spoil, deface, disfigure; debase, degrade, undermine; wrong, aggrieve. **—Ant. 1** good, benefit, help, aid, assistance; boon, blessing. **2** goodness, righteousness, blessing. **3** benefit, help, aid, assist; improve, better, ameliorate; cure, heal.

harmful *adj.* injurious, dangerous, deleterious, hurtful, destructive, ruinous, damaging, counterproductive, unwholesome, unhealthy, unhealthful, detrimental, adverse, bad, pernicious, baneful. **—Ant.** beneficial, good, helpful, favorable, wholesome, healthful, healthy; harmless, safe.

harmless *adj.* safe, not dangerous, not hurtful, benign, nontoxic, inoffensive, gentle, peaceable, mild, sinless, blameless, innocent, incorrupt, guiltless, innocuous, unobjectionable. **—Ant.** harmful, dangerous, unsafe, destructive, unhealthy, injurious, wholesome.

harmonious *adj.* **1.** melodious, sweet-sounding, mellifluous, euphonious, sweet, dulcet, agreeable, agreeably combined, matching, compatible, harmonizing, coordinated, consistent, unified, synchronized. **2.** likeminded, in agreement, in harmony, cordial, in accord, compatible, congenial, agreeable, amiable, amicable, sympathetic, friendly. **—Ant. 1** harsh, grating, unmelodious, cacophonous; clashing, incompatible, contrasting, uncoordinated, inconsistent. **2** incompatible, unalike, different, discordant, dissident, unfriendly.

harmony *n.* **1.** pleasing consistency, coordination, compatibility, agreement, concord, correlation, parallelism, matching, mutual fitness, balance, symmetry, order, proportion, unity, organic totality. **2.** agreement, accord, concord, unanimity, like-mindedness, conformity, unity, amicability, amity, congeniality, sympathy, compatibility, fellowship, friendship, cooperation, mutual regard, peace; good understanding, harmonious relations, concurrence in opinions. **—Syn. Study. 1** See SYMMETRY. **—Ant. 1** incongruity, inconsistency; conflict, disproportion. **2** disagreement, enmity, opposition, conflict, contention, discord, dissension, antagonism, hostility.

harness *n.* **1.** tackle, trappings; (*variously*) halter, bridle, reins, straps, traces, caparison, lines, tugs. *—v.* **2.** put in harness, hitch up, yoke, collar, rig up. **3.** control and use, direct to a useful purpose, utilize, employ, exploit, render useful, make productive, turn to account; restrain, curb, muzzle, bridle, rein.

harridan *n.* mean old woman, crone, old crone, shrew, hag, virago; *Slang* battle-ax, witch.

harrowing *adj.* distressing, disturbing, tormenting, traumatic, painful, upsetting; frightening, fearful, alarming, chilling, bloodcurdling, terrifying, threatening, dangerous.

harry *v.* **1.** attack repeatedly, raid frequently, beset; raid, plunder, sack, pillage, terrorize. **2.** trouble, torment, distress, haunt, disturb, bother, worry; harass, pester, gall, badger, annoy, irritate, irk, vex, plague, hound, exasperate, distract; tease, bait, hector, heckle, ride, intimidate, bully. **—Ant. 2** soothe, quiet, comfort, console, solace; support, help, aid, encourage.

harsh *adj.* **1.** unpleasant, piercing, jarring, grating, shrill, rasping, raspy, hoarse, strident, scratchy, discordant, raucous, unmusical, unharmonious, cacophonous, squawky, glaring, overbright, too bright. **2.** cruel, pitiless, ruthless, merciless, mean, unsparing, severe, stern, ungentle, unkind, abusive, vindictive, heartless, draconian, hardhearted, brutal; bitter, caustic, hard, rough, sharp, uncharitable. **—Syn. Study. 2** See STERN. **—Ant. 1** soft, gentle, mild, smooth, pleasant, pleasing, agreeable, soothing; harmonious, melodious, mellifluous. **2** kind, gentle, sweet, loving, merciful, charitable, lenient.

harum-scarum *adj.* **1.** disorganized, undependable, unreliable, inconsistent, erratic, careless, unsettled; foolish, giddy, scatterbrained, rattlebrained, featherbrained, harebrained, flighty, impulsive, impetuous, absent-minded, confused, bewildered; unplanned, haphazard. *—adv.* **2.** haphazardly, impulsively, recklessly, wildly, aimlessly, capriciously. **—Ant. 1** organized, well-planned, careful, efficient, consistent, settled, serious, methodical, responsible, conscientious. **2** thoughtfully, efficiently, carefully, wisely.

harvest *n.* **1.** harvesting, reaping, crop gathering; (*variously*) mowing, cutting, picking, haying. **2.** crop, yield, season's growth, produce; gathering, collection, accumulation, amassment. **3.** result, product, fruit, fruition, reward, benefit, proceeds, gain, return, yield, gleaning, reaping; aftermath, outgrowth, output. *—v.* **4.** gather, reap, pick, pluck, mow, cut; collect, amass, accumulate. **—Ant. 4** plant, sow, seed.

hassle *n.* **1.** squabble, quarrel, dispute, row, argument; fight, struggle, tussle, set-to, scrap, battle, conflict, contest. *—v.* **2.** harass, harry, persecute, vex, hound, bother, badger, annoy; *Slang* bug.

haste *n.* **1.** speed, speediness, hurry, rush, swiftness, quickness, celerity, hurriedness, rapidity, fleetness; expedition, dispatch. **2.** undue speed, careless hurry, precipitateness; recklessness, rashness, impetuousness, impulsiveness. **—Ant. 1** slowness, delay, procrastination, plodding, sluggishness, leisureliness, lagging, hanging back. **2** deliberation, care, carefulness, sureness, reflection, calmness.

hasten *v.* **1.** hurry, rush, speed, make haste, race, run, hustle, dash, scurry, fly, whisk, jump, sprint, bolt, dart, scuttle, flit, scamper, hurry up, lose no time, make time, go on the double, go like lightning; *Slang* go hell-bent for leather, go full blast, step on the gas, step right along; work against time, make short work of. **2.** accelerate, speed up, expedite, quicken, push forward, precipitate, advance, promote; hurry on, urge on, drive on, incite, impel, *Slang* egg on. **—Ant. 1** move slowly, creep, crawl; plod, shuffle; lag, procrastinate, dally, dawdle. **2** slow, slow down, delay, decelerate, slacken, retard, impede, inhibit, check, arrest, curb, hold back.

hastily *adv.* **1.** quickly, speedily, fast, hurriedly, promptly, straightaway, posthaste, apace; *Slang* pronto, on the double, like a shot, like greased lightning, lickety-split, hell-bent for leather, before one can say Jack Robinson. **2.** too quickly, rashly, recklessly, impetuously, impulsively, precipitately, thoughtlessly, summarily, carelessly, heedlessly, on the spur of the moment. **—Ant. 1** slowly, at a snail's pace. **2** deliberately, carefully, thoughtfully, calmly.

hasty *adj.* **1.** fast, quick, hurried, rapid, speedy, swift, prompt, fleet, quick as a wink; cursory, brief, rushed, fleeting, passing, momentary, breathless, superficial. **2.** unduly quick, rash, impetuous, impulsive, reckless, hurried, headlong, heedless, abrupt, precipitate, without deliberation. **—Ant. 1** slow, leisurely, plodding; long, protracted, detailed, meticulous, thorough, exhaustive. **2** deliberate, careful, considered, studied, thoughtful, premeditated.

hatch *v.* think up, devise, concoct, plot, plan, contrive, make up, formulate, conceive, design, evolve, create, frame, invent, fabricate, improvise, originate, construct, fashion, dream up, *Slang* cook up; manufacture, bring forth, produce, give birth to.

hate *v.* **1.** dislike, despise, abhor, detest, loathe, abominate, execrate, hold in contempt, bear malice toward, be hostile to, not be able to bear, have no use for, recoil from, shrink from, be repelled by, be sick of, be tired of, give one a pain, give one a pain in the neck. **2.** be sorry, be reluctant, be unwilling, feel disinclined to, be averse to, shrink from, not care to, would rather not, not have the heart to, dread, wish to avoid, feel sick at, have no taste for, have no stomach for, wince at, regard as distasteful. *—n.* **3.** hatred, dislike, distaste, disliking, aversion, loathing, repugnance, abomination, abhorrence; enmity, hostility, detestation, rancor, malice, antipathy, animosity, animus, venom, malevolence, resentment, vindictiveness, revengefulness, acrimony. **—Syn. Study. 1** HATE, ABHOR, DETEST imply feeling intense dislike or aversion toward something. HATE, the simple and general word, suggests passionate dislike and a feeling of enmity: *to hate autocracy.* ABHOR expresses a deep-rooted horror and a sense of repugnance or complete rejection: *to abhor cruelty.* DETEST implies intense, even vehement, dislike and antipathy, besides a sense of disdain: *to detest a combination of ignorance and arrogance.* **—Ant. 1–3** love, like. **1** be fond of, delight in, regard highly, esteem, treasure, prize, cherish, dote on, be attracted by. **2** be pleased, enjoy, relish, fancy, prefer, be inclined; wish, hope. **3** liking, fondness, affection, devotion, amity, goodwill.

hateful *adj.* **1.** offensive, disgusting, detestable, repugnant, repellent, loathsome, despicable, revolting, contemptible, deplorable, abhorrent, odious, obnoxious, foul, abominable, monstrous, ugly, nasty, vile, unpleasant, distasteful, sickening; mean, villainous, infamous, heinous, atrocious, insufferable, wicked, sinful; irritating, objectionable, intolerable, unbearable, unendurable. **2.** full of hate, expressing hate, evil, forbidding, scornful, contemptuous, disdainful. **—Syn. Study. 1** HATEFUL, OFFENSIVE, ODIOUS, OBNOXIOUS refer to something that provokes strong dislike or aversion. HATEFUL implies causing dislike along with hostility and ill will: *a hateful task.* OFFENSIVE is a general term that stresses the resentment or displeasure aroused by something that is insulting or unpleasant: *an offensive remark; an offensive odor.* ODIOUS emphasizes a disgusting or repugnant quality: *odious crimes.* OBNOXIOUS implies causing annoyance or discomfort by objectionable qualities: *His constant bragging is obnoxious.* **—Ant. 1** commendable, likable, desirable; pleasing, pleasant, charming, attractive, wonderful, lovable, good, sweet, kind, beautiful. **2** friendly, loving, affectionate, devoted, kind, sweet, pleasant.

hatred *n.* **1.** dislike, disgust, aversion, hate, loathing, abomination, abhorrence, distaste, detestation, repugnance, revulsion. **2.** hostility, enmity, malice, rancor, animosity, antagonism, antipathy, animus, malevolence, ill will, venom, resentment, vindictiveness, revengefulness, acrimony, bitterness, bad blood. **—Ant.** 1, 2 love, affection, fondness, devotion, liking, attachment, affinity, attraction. **2** friendliness, amiability, affection, amity, goodwill, kindness.

haughty *adj.* arrogant, overly proud, scornful, disdainful, contemptuous, overbearing, high and mighty, high-handed, lordly, aloof, officious; snobbish, conceited, condescending, patronizing, hoity-toity, swell-headed; *Slang* stuck-up, snooty, uppity, uppish, high-hat, highfalutin. **—Ant.** humble, modest; *Slang* regular, hail-fellow-well-met, one of the boys; servile, subservient, obsequious, self-effacing.

haul *v.* **1.** pull, drag, draw, heave, yank, jerk, wrench, lug, tug; carry, transport, move, convey, tote, cart, tow, fetch, bring, take, truck, remove. *—n.* **2.** pull, tug, yank, jerk, heave, wrench. **3.** take, catch, yield, gain, takings; profit, capture, reward, booty, spoils, swag, bag.

haunt *v.* **1.** frequent, visit often, go to repeatedly, beat a path to; hover about, loiter near, linger around; *Slang* hang around, hang out at, live in. **2.** obsess, weigh on, prey on, beset, obsess, preoccupy, trouble, torment, vex, distress, disturb, worry, plague; frighten, terrify, terrorize. *—n.* **3.** Often **haunts** hangout, gathering place, meeting place, rendezvous, stamping grounds, hideaway; (*of animals*) lair, den, burrow, hole, cave, nest, waterhole.

haven *n.* shelter, refuge, retreat, sanctuary, asylum, cover, hideaway, hideout; harbor, port. **—Syn. Study.** See HARBOR.

havoc *n.* widespread damage, destruction, devastation, ruin, wrack and ruin, disaster, catastrophe, cataclysm, ruination, chaos, disorder, calamity, upheaval.

hazard *n.* **1.** danger, risk, peril, threat, menace, endangerment, imperilment, pitfall, jeopardy. **2.** chance, accident, fluke, luck, stroke of luck, happenstance; mishap, mischance, misfortune, coincidence. *—v.* **3.** venture, chance, dare, risk, submit, throw out, advance, volunteer, offer, proffer; presume, daresay, suppose, guess, theorize, speculate, conjecture, hypothesize; gamble, bet, wager, stake, take a chance, chance it, tempt fate, trust to luck. **4.** endanger, risk, imperil, jeopardize, threaten, expose. **—Syn. Study. 1** See DANGER. **—Ant. 1** protection, safeguard, safety. **2** design, plan, calculation, premeditation. **4** protect, safeguard, make safe, preserve.

hazardous *adj.* **1.** dangerous, unsafe, perilous, precarious, risky, threatening. **2.** chancy, precarious, unsure, uncertain, unreliable, insecure, speculative, dubious, doubtful, shaky, iffy, untrustworthy; unsound, unstable. **—Ant. 1** safe, secure. **2** sure, certain, reliable, sound, stable.

haze *n.* **1.** mist, fog, smoke, pall; cloud, vapor, film, veil, screen, cloak, mantle. **2.** state of confusion, daze; befuddlement, muddle, bewilderment, fogginess.

hazy *adj.* **1.** misty, foggy, smoggy, smoky; overcast, cloudy, dim, murky, veiled; dusky, bleared, bleary, blurry, filmy, faint. **2.** vague, general, indefinite, ill-defined, uncertain, unclear, nebulous, faint, obscure, ambiguous, dim; confused, foggy, muddled. **—Ant. 1** clear, bright; light, sunny; cloudless. **2** clear, certain, sure, detailed, well-defined, explicit.

head *n.* **1.** mind, brain, mentality, intellect, I.Q., *Slang* gray matter; talent, gift, bent, genius, aptitude, capacity, ability, perception, understanding, apprehension, discernment, judgment, cleverness, acuteness, quickness of mind. **2.** leader, chief, director, boss, administrator, guiding light; master, overseer, supervisor, manager, foreman, forewoman, foreperson; *Slang* honcho, big cheese, top banana; (*variously in business*) chairman of the board, chairman, chief executive officer, chief executive, president, manager, superintendent, foreman, supervisor; (*variously in government*) dictator, king, queen, monarch, sovereign, ruler, czar, potentate, suzerain, president, prime minister, premier; (*variously in the military*) commander-in-chief, commanding general, general, captain, commandant, commander, admiral, commodore, field marshal, marshal. **3.** front, first place, forward part, front rank, forefront, lead, highest rank, place of honor. **4.** source, origin, beginning, birthplace, rise, fountainhead, spring, wellspring, fountain, font, well. **5.** climax, turning point, crisis, peak, extremity, utmost extent, conclusion, termination, culmination, inevitable result, end, fruition. **6.** upper end, top, peak, tip, apex, crown, crest, vertex, acme, zenith, summit, pinnacle. **—*adj.*** **7.** chief, highest ranking, ranking, managing, principal, main, foremost, first, highest, leading, dominant, supreme, superior, prime, premier, preeminent, paramount; governing, commanding, ruling, controlling. **8.** first, lead, leading, front, fore, foremost, headmost, highest, top, topmost, uppermost, primary, most prominent. **—*v.*** **9.** lead, go at the head of, go first, precede, lead the way, take the lead, be in the vanguard; start, begin, initiate, inaugurate, launch, introduce. **10.** be head of, direct, supervise, manage, take charge of, administer, superintend, lead, conduct, boss, command, govern, control, rule, be master of, have authority over, officiate at, preside over, be at the helm, take the reins, be in the driver's seat. **11.** steer, aim, turn, drive, pilot, guide, direct; move toward, direct one's course, go in the direction of, go, proceed, make for, hie, start off, make a beeline for. **—Ant. 2** follower, subordinate; (*variously*) cog, menial, drone, underling, worker, hired hand, laborer, working man, enlisted man. **3** end, foot, bottom, tail, last place, lowest rank. **4** mouth; end, foot. **6** bottom, foot; shaft. **7** lowest, inferior, subordinate. **8** last, end, trailing, hindmost; bottom, bottommost. **9** follow, go behind, be last, bring up the rear; end, finish, terminate, conclude. **10** follow, be subordinate to, be inferior to. **11** move away, retreat, withdraw.

headstrong *adj.* willful, bent on having one's own way, impulsive, rash, reckless, incautious, imprudent, hotheaded, intractable, ungovernable, froward, refractory, uncontrollable, contrary, defiant, unmanageable, incorrigible, unruly, wayward, recalcitrant; stubborn, obstinate, bullheaded, pigheaded, mulish, dogged, obdurate, perverse. **—Syn. Study.** See WILLFUL. **—Ant.** subservient, obedient, pliant, docile, submissive, impressionable, manageable; cautious, deliberate, methodical; cooperative, flexible, congenial, adaptable, easygoing, relaxed.

heady *adj.* **1.** intoxicating, potent, strong, hard, *Slang* high-voltage, high-octane. **2.** exciting, exhilarating, intoxicating, thrilling, stirring; tempting, inviting, alluring, seductive, tantalizing. **—Ant. 1** nonintoxicating, nonalcoholic, weak, soft. **2** depressing, disappointing, melancholy.

heal *v.* **1.** cure, remedy, make well, get well, treat, make whole, heal over, heal up, knit, mend; return to health, recover, recuperate, improve, convalesce. **2.** reconcile, conciliate, settle, compose, rectify, right, set to rights, make harmonious, restore good relations; alleviate, soothe, relieve, salve. **—Ant. 1** wound, hurt, injure, harm; reopen, break; make worse, get worse.

health *n.* **1.** physical condition, general condition. **2.** good health, healthfulness, freedom from disease, fitness, clean bill of health; well-being, hardiness, robustness, vigor, strength, vitality, stamina, hardihood. **—Ant. 2** sickness, illness, disease, ailment; weakness, debility, infirmity, frailty.

healthful *adj.* healthy, good for one's health, wholesome, conducive to health, healthgiving, salubrious, salutary, invigorating, nutritious, beneficial, nourishing; hygienic. **—Syn. Study.** See HEALTHY. **—Ant.** unhealthy, unwholesome; detrimental, deleterious, dangerous.

healthy *adj.* **1.** in good health, enjoying good health, able-bodied; hale, hearty, sound, strong, sturdy, robust, hardy, vigorous, sound of mind and limb, fit, in fine fettle, in the pink. **2.** healthful, healthgiving, wholesome, conducive to health, salutary, beneficial, nutritious. **—Syn. Study.** 1, 2 HEALTHY, HEALTHFUL, WHOLESOME refer to physical, mental, or moral health and well-being. HEALTHY most often applies to what possesses health, but may apply to what promotes health: *a healthy child; a healthy climate.* HEALTHFUL is usu. applied to something conducive to physical health: *a healthful diet.* WHOLESOME, connoting freshness and purity, applies to something that is physically or morally beneficial: *wholesome food; wholesome entertainment.* **—Ant.** sick, sickly, ill, infirm, diseased, unhealthy, ailing; feeble, frail, weak, delicate, fragile, unsound, debilitated.

heap *n.* **1.** pile, stack, mass, mound, cluster, bundle, batch, bunch; accumulation, collection, gathering, assemblage, agglomeration, aggregation; jumble, mess. **2.** large amount, lot, lots, good deal, great deal, load, abundance, profusion, great number, multitude, plenty, considerable amount, ocean, oceans, world, worlds, barrels, store, pack; *Informal* hunk, slew, slews; *Slang* gob, gobs, oodles. —*v.* **3.** pile, pile up, group, bunch, bundle, amass, mass, lump; collect, gather, concentrate. **4.** load, load up, pile, supply abundantly, give in profusion, mete out, shower upon, pour upon; fill, inundate, flood, deluge, engulf; accord, assign, award, present. —**Ant. 2** little, drop, dab, touch, tiny bit. **3** scatter, disperse, dissipate, dispel.

hear *v.* **1.** listen to, be among the listeners at, be present at, be a spectator at, appear at, attend, witness, look on, be an auditor at. **2.** understand, find out, be informed, be told, receive news, be led to believe, be made aware of, receive information, learn, gather, discover, ascertain; receive a letter; receive a phone call; *Slang* hear tell, get an earful. **3.** listen to, heed, favor, approve, receive, hearken to, accede to, hold with, grant, admit, acknowledge; concede, acquiesce, give assent, be favorably disposed to. **4.** judge, try; officially investigate, examine, inquire into. —**Ant. 3** ignore, reject, disapprove, disagree with.

hearing *n.* **1.** opportunity to be heard, interview, conference, audience, consultation, council; official investigation, inquiry, examination, review, probe; questioning, interrogation. **2.** earshot, hearing distance; range of hearing, carrying distance, reach of one's voice, sound.

hearsay *n.* rumor, gossip, report, grapevine, talk, idle talk; *Slang* scuttlebutt.

heart *n.* **1.** feelings, emotion, sentiment, nature, temperament, mood, disposition, humor; innermost feelings, true nature, soul. **2.** sympathy, compassion, tenderness, gentleness, softheartedness; tenderness, affection, fondness, love; tolerance, indulgence, forgiveness, charity, clemency. **3.** courage, enthusiasm, desire, spirit, firmness, resoluteness, fortitude, pluck, spunk, gameness, resolution; bravery, valor, fearlessness, stoutheartedness, daring, boldness, audacity, audaciousness, gallantry, manfulness; *Slang* guts, backbone, stomach. **4.** essence, core, root, source, base, main part, crux, nub, soul, nucleus, center, kernel, pith, meat, quintessence; essentials, fundamentals, rudiments, principles, foundation; *Slang* nitty-gritty, brass tacks, guts. **5.** center, central part, middle, hub, busiest part, inner part, interior. —**Ant. 2** dislike, hatred, hate, enmity; hardheartedness, cruelty. **3** timidity, cowardice, fear, yellow streak; shyness. **4** minor part, supplement, accessory; side issue, irrelevancy. **5** outskirts, periphery, environs.

heartfelt *adj.* sincere, honest, profound, fervent, ardent, genuine, devout, earnest, deep, keenly felt, wholehearted, intense; complete, total, all-inclusive, thorough, entire, full. —**Ant.** feigned, superficial, shallow, insincere.

hearth *n.* **1.** fireplace, fireside, chimney corner. **2.** home, abode, household, house, family life, family circle.

heartless *adj.* cruel, cruelhearted, coldhearted, hardhearted, callous, unfeeling, insensitive, unkind, unmoved, unstirred, cold, uncaring, unresponsive, unsympathetic, pitiless, unpitying, unmerciful; brutal, savage, mean, ruthless, inhuman, cold-blooded. —**Ant.** kind, generous, humane, compassionate, sympathetic, sensitive, merciful, sweet, soft-hearted, warmhearted.

hearty *adj.* **1.** sincere, genuine, wholehearted, cordial, warm; profuse, ample, effusive, generous, thorough, complete, unrestrained, unbounded, unreserved; vigorous, enthusiastic, zestful, heartfelt, lively. **2.** healthy, well, physically fit, hale, sound, vigorous, hardy, strong, robust. —**Ant. 1** halfhearted, lukewarm, mild, cool, cold, reserved, stiff. **2** sickly, ill, unhealthy, delicate, frail, weak, puny; feeble, debilitated.

heat *n.* **1.** hotness, warmness, warmth, high temperature; hot weather, warm weather; hot spell, swelter, oppressive heat. **2.** stress, passion, fervor, fervency, excitement, intensity; height, climax; enthusiasm, eagerness, thrill, zeal, ardor; rapture, transport. —*v.* **3.** make hot, warm, bring to a boil, warm up, heat up; (*variously*) cook, reheat, simmer, stew, roast, braise, steam, bake, fry, broil, boil, sear. —**Ant. 1** cold, coldness, coolness, cold temperature; cold wave, cold spell. **2** composure, calmness, coolness. **3** cool, let cool, cool off, chill; freeze.

heated *adj.* vehement, impassioned, passionate, fervent, excited, frenzied, fierce, emotional, intense; stormy, tempestuous, raging, hot, fiery, violent, furious, angry, inflamed, irate, infuriated, bitter. —**Ant.** dispassionate, calm, mild, peaceful, quiet; friendly, sociable.

heathen *n.* **1.** (*variously*) non-Christian, infidel; non-Jew, idolator, gentile, goy; non-Muslim, non-believer, unbeliever; any uncivilized denier of the God of the Old Testament; (*loosely*) pagan, savage, polytheist, barbarian, uncivilized native; atheist, agnostic. **2.** ignoramus, boor, troglodyte. —**Syn. Study. 1** HEATHEN,

PAGAN are both applied to peoples who are not Christian, Jewish, or Muslim; these terms may also refer to irreligious peoples. HEATHEN is often used of those whose religion is unfamiliar and therefore regarded as primitive, unenlightened, or uncivilized: *heathen idols; heathen rites.* PAGAN is most frequently used of the ancient Greeks and Romans who worshiped many deities: *a pagan civilization.* **—Ant. 1** (*variously*) Christian, true believer; Jew, adherent of Judaism, Israelite, Hebrew; Muslim, adherent of Islam, believer. **2** civilized person, intellectual, sophisticate.

heave *v.* **1.** hoist, haul up, pull up, drag up, draw up, yank up, lift, raise, elevate, boost; pry, lever. **2.** throw, pitch, fling, hurl, cast, toss, chuck, sling, let fly, propel, fire, peg, launch. **3.** utter wearily, breathe heavily, emit, exhale, eject, discharge, blow, puff; groan, moan, sob; *Informal* retch, vomit, regurgitate, puke. **4.** expand and contract, palpitate, surge; expand, swell, dilate, thrust up, bulge, be thrown upward, tilt up, arch; draw a deep breath, pant. **—Ant. 1** lower, take down, put down, pull down.

heaven *n.* **1.** Often **Heaven** paradise, abode of God and the angels, dwelling place of the righteous after death, our external home, afterworld, afterlife, next world, world to come, world beyond; life everlasting, eternal bliss, life beyond; the kingdom of Heaven, the heavenly kingdom, the City of God, the heavenly city, the Holy City, the Celestial City, our Father's house, the abode of saints, Elysium, Elysian fields, Island of the Blessed, Isle of the Blessed, Zion, New Jerusalem, Beulah Land, Abraham's bosom; Valhalla; Olympus; the happy hunting ground. **2. the heavens** the sky, the firmament, the starry heavens, the vault of heaven, the celestial expanse, the celestial sphere; space, outer space, *Slang* the wild blue yonder. **3.** complete happiness, bliss, sheer bliss, seventh heaven, heaven on earth, supreme happiness, paradise, nirvana, ecstasy, perfection, rapture, Shangri-la, utopia, dreamland, enchantment, glory, delight. *—interj.* **4.** heavens to Betsy, goodness, goodness gracious, good gracious, mercy, my stars, land sake, my oh my; *Slang* wow, boy oh boy. **—Ant. 1** hell, hades, the infernal regions, purgatory, the underworld, the nether world, the abyss, eternal agony, eternal fire; limbo. **3** hell, pure hell, agony, misery, torment.

heavy *adj.* **1.** weighty; cumbersome, cumbrous, burdensome, bulky, unwieldy, big, large, hefty. **2.** abundant, profuse, copious, extensive, excessive, intemperate, unrestrained, immoderate, inordinate, unstinting, extravagant, full, large, considerable; violent, strong, fierce, savage, forceful, raging, tempestuous, turbulent, rampaging, furious, seething, unrelenting, unremitting, roaring; hard, intense. **3.** burdensome, oppressive, hard to endure, onerous, harrowing, grievous, harsh, distressing, unbearable, intolerable, unendurable; damaging, injurious, detrimental, ruinous, calamitous, destructive, deadly, crushing, pernicious, deleterious. **4.** sorrowful, sad, gloomy, melancholy, full of care, pained, distressed, depressed, woeful, agonized, miserable, doleful, burdened; cheerless, joyless, downcast, dejected, forlorn, desolate, disconsolate, mournful, grieving, crestfallen, laden with sorrows, grief-stricken, tearful, stricken. **5.** serious, weighty, grave, solemn, momentous, important, overwhelming, of great import, of great consequence, consequential, impressive, awesome, imposing, notable, significant, noteworthy; profound, deep, difficult, complex; tedious, laborious, tiresome, wearisome; dreary, dull, monotonous, pedantic. **6.** ponderous, lumbering, clumsy, lumpish, leaden, slow, sluggish, lethargic; listless, torpid, lazy, lifeless, apathetic, languid, phlegmatic. **7.** fat, obese, stout, portly, plump, corpulent, overweight, hefty; thick, bulky, broad, massive; coarse, gross, dense, rough; rugged, sturdy. **—Ant.** light. **1** lightweight; compact, handy. **2** moderate, mild, soft, gentle, calm, weak; small, scant, sparse, slight, thin, little, skimpy, trifling, trivial. **3** easy, light, bearable, acceptable. **4** happy, gay, cheerful, exuberant, joyful, buoyant. **5** trivial, trifling; frivolous, gay; unimportant, insignificant, inconsequential; entertaining, exciting. **6** agile, brisk, spry, quick, rapid, buoyant, active. **7** thin, skinny.

heckle *v.* jeer at, harass, harry, harrow, badger, bait, provoke, needle, molest, bully, mock, hector, twit, taunt, annoy, ride, hound, chivy, hoot, shout down, boo, hiss.

hectic *adj.* frenetic, frantic, tumultuous, turbulent, furious, feverish, frenzied, wild, mad, stormy, headlong, breakneck; chaotic. **—Ant.** calm, serene, tranquil, relaxing, restful, orderly, peaceful.

hedge *n.* **1.** fence of shrubs, hedgerow, row of bushes; fence, wall, barrier, border, ring, bound, margin, circumference, delineation. **2.** protection, guard, insurance; compensation, counterbalance. *—v.* **3.** enclose, surround, border, bound, edge, encircle, outline, fence, wall, ring, shut in, hem, hem in; limit, delineate, demarcate, mark off. **4.** equivocate, evade, be evasive, temporize, duck, dodge, beg the question; *Informal* waffle, pussyfoot, give the runaround, beat around the bush.

hedonist *n.* pleasure seeker, libertine, profligate, voluptuary, dissipater, debauchee, sensualist, sybarite. **—Ant.** puritan; moralist.

heed *v.* **1.** follow, be guided by, mind, obey, accede to, defer to, yield to, concur, comply with, hold to, be ruled by, bow to, submit to, observe, respect; take notice of, listen to, consider, bear in mind, pay attention to, take note of, give ear to, give a thought to, take to heart. *—n.* **2.** attention, notice, regard, mind, mindfulness, care, observation, attentiveness, heedfulness, carefulness, prudence, precaution, pains; conscientiousness, scrupulousness, meticulousness, fastidiousness; perusal, study, examination, scrutiny. **—Ant. 1** ignore, disregard, slight, neglect, overlook; reject, refuse, turn a deaf ear to, be inattentive to, treat frivolously. **2** inattention, disregard, mindlessness; carelessness, neglect, thoughtlessness.

heedless *adj.* careless, thoughtless, mindless, unmindful, negligent, neglectful, uncaring, unthinking, inattentive, oblivious, unobserving, unobservant, unwatchful, unwary, unconcerned, unaware, unheeding; remiss, slack, lax, improvident, imprudent, incautious, rash, impetuous, foolhardy, reckless; harebrained, scatterbrained, foolish, witless; frivolous, happy-go-lucky. **—Ant.** careful, cautious, wary, prudent, circumspect, mindful, attentive, heedful, thinking, thoughtful, observant, watchful, vigilant; concerned, aware, alert.

hefty *adj.* husky, heavy, beefy, strapping, stout, strong, weighty, sturdy, bulky, substantial, burly, rugged, robust, powerful, massive, strong, hearty, muscular, stalwart. **—Ant.** small, puny, skinny, weak, feeble, fragile.

height *n.* **1.** altitude, elevation, upward extent; tallness, highness, loftiness. **2.** hilltop, vantage point, promontory, eminence; mountain, hill, highland, palisade, cliff, bluff, mound, rise, knoll, plateau; pinnacle, summit, peak. **3.** extremity, utmost degree, limit, ultimate, maximum, peak; pinnacle, tower, high point, crest, summit, zenith, acme, apex, apogee, culmination; supremacy, perfection, consummation, flowering, heyday. **—Syn. Study. 1** HEIGHT, ALTITUDE, ELEVATION refer to distance above a level. HEIGHT denotes extent upward (as from foot to head) as well as any measurable distance above a given level: *The tree grew to a height of ten feet. They looked down from a great height.* ALTITUDE usu. refers to the distance, determined by instruments, above a given level, commonly mean sea level: *The airplane flew at an altitude of 30,000 feet.* ELEVATION implies a distance to which something has been raised or uplifted above a level: *a hill's elevation above the surrounding country.* **—Ant. 1** depth, lowness. **2** valley, canyon, gulch, ravine, abyss; lowland. **3** depth, low point, nadir; minimum.

heighten *v.* **—Syn. Study.** See ELEVATE.

heinous *adj.* atrocious, abominable, abhorrent, repugnant, repulsive, reprehensible, despicable, deplorable, horrid, shocking, monstrous, inhuman, gross, detestable, loathsome, foul, hideous, contemptible, distasteful, objectionable, outrageous; disgusting, revolting, vile, sickening, nasty, beastly; infamous, villainous, iniquitous, nefarious, vicious, terrible, odious, grisly, ghastly, offensive; scandalous, outrageous, disgraceful; sinful, wicked, evil. **—Ant.** good, beneficial, worthwhile, attractive, charming, admirable, laudable, praiseworthy, meritorious; lovable, pleasing, pleasant.

heir, Fem. **heiress** *n.* beneficiary, inheritor, (*fem.*) inheritress, inheritrix; heir apparent, heir presumptive.

hell *n.* **1.** Often **Hell** abode of the damned, infernal regions, lake of fire, bottomless pit, the pit, the abyss, the lower world, the underworld, the nether world, the shades below, place of the lost, home of lost souls, Satan's kingdom, the Devil's house; everlasting fire, hell fire; (*variously*) hades, inferno, perdition. **2.** torment, anguish, agony, wretchedness, suffering, misery; despair, hopelessness, grief, martyrdom, remorse. **—Ant. 1, 2** heaven, paradise. **2** bliss, joy, felicity, rapture, enchantment, happiness, ecstasy.

help *v.* **1.** aid, assist, give assistance to, lend a hand, give a helping hand, cooperate with, collaborate with, contribute to, serve; support, back, champion, advance, uphold, further, promote, side with, endorse, encourage, advocate, take the part of, stand by, give moral support to, maintain, intercede for, stick up for, *Informal* go to bat for; befriend, guide, advise, minister to, succor, console, nurture; be of advantage; give to, contribute to, chip in for. **2.** save, rescue, aid, come to the aid of, snatch from danger, extricate, retrieve. **3.** relieve, alleviate, cure, soothe, calm, mitigate, ease, remedy, improve, lift, put at ease, ameliorate, allay, correct, make healthy, make whole, bring through, bring round, do a world of good for; rectify, emend. *—n.* **4.** assistance, aid, helping hand, cooperation, collaboration, service; support, backing, advancement, promotion, furtherance, endorsement, encouragement, contribution, gift, protection, friendship, support; benevolence, guidance, advice, care, welfare, good offices, kind regard. **5.** employees, workers, workmen, laborers, hands, hired hands, workhands, assistants, helpers, hired helpers; (*variously*) farmhand, domestic, servant, apprentice, underling, menial, retainer, factotum; staff, crew, work force, force. **6.** cure, remedy, corrective, preventive, restorative, aid, relief, balm, salve. **—Syn. Study.** HELP, AID, ASSIST, SUCCOR agree in the idea of furnishing someone with something that is needed. HELP implies furnishing anything that furthers one's efforts or satisfies one's needs: *I helped her plan the party.* AID and ASSIST, somewhat more formal, imply a furthering or seconding of another's efforts. AID suggests an active helping; ASSIST suggests less need and less help: *to aid the poor; to assist a teacher in the classroom.* To SUCCOR, still more formal and literary, is to give timely help and relief to someone in difficulty or distress: *Succor him in his hour of need.* **—Ant. 1** hinder, impede, obstruct, hold back, block, bar, frustrate, thwart, foil, balk; oppose, fight, side against, discourage, *Informal* put down. **2** harm, hurt, injure, attack; kill, let die. **3** make worse, aggravate, irritate, discomfit. **4** hindrance, obstruction, block, bar, opposition, discouragement. **6** bane, aggravation, irritant.

helper *n.* **1.** assistant, aid, aide, second, aide-de-camp, adjunct, right-hand man, right hand, man Friday, girl Friday, helping hand; auxiliary, deputy, subordinate; apprentice. **2.** partner, colleague, associate, accomplice, confederate, collaborator, coworker, confrere. **3.** backer, supporter, patron, benefactor, angel, good samaritan, fairy godmother; advocate, champion.

helpful *adj.* beneficial, useful, constructive, advantageous, favorable, usable, practical, serviceable; valuable, profitable; fine, good, nice, excellent, splendid. **—Ant.** pointless, useless, worthless; harmful, destructive, injurious.

henchman *n.* right-hand man, lieutenant, retainer; bodyguard, strong-arm man, hatchet man, attendant; hireling, minion, flunky, lackey, yes-man, hanger-on; *Slang* stooge, gorilla, goon, thug.

henpecked *adj.* wife-ridden, under the thumb of one's wife; submissive, meek, timid, docile, unassertive, browbeaten, obedient. **—Ant.** manly, dominating, *Spanish* macho; forceful, aggressive, assertive.

herald *n.* **1.** messenger, crier, proclaimer, courier. **2.** forerunner, harbinger, precursor, envoy, predecessor, foregoer, usher; omen, sign, augury, warning, token, indication, indicator, symbol, clue; forecast, portent. *—v.* **3.** announce, proclaim, report, foretell, prefigure, presage, make known, give tidings of, divulge, reveal, usher in; inform, communicate, publish, publicize, advertise, bruit abroad, give voice to.

herculean Sometimes **Herculean** *—adj.* **1.** strong, powerful, mighty, muscular, strong as Hercules, strapping, rugged, burly, brawny, sturdy, robust, hefty; hard, tough. **2.** strenuous, laborious, backbreaking, arduous, exhausting, wearying, fatiguing, toilsome, burdensome, difficult, onerous, prodigious, formidable. **—Ant. 1** weak, feeble, frail, delicate. **2** easy, effortless, relaxing, restful.

herd *n.* **1.** pack, drove, flock, bunch, group, cluster, gathering. **2.** crowd, mob, throng, horde, swarm, drove, bunch, gang, band, pack, press, mass, host, tribe, swarm, flock, cluster, army, troop, legion; gathering, group, assemblage, assembly, company, body, multitude, number, lot, congregation, convocation, conclave, collection, array, party. *—v.* **3.** drive, guide, force, goad, spur, lead. **4.** bring together, collect, muster, round up, assemble, gather, call together; crowd, cluster, huddle, bunch, come together, flock together, rally, group, convene.

hereafter *adj.* **1.** after this, from now on, in the future, henceforth, henceforward, subsequently, from this time forth; at a later date, at a later time, one of these days, ultimately. *—n.* **2.** afterlife, afterworld, next world, life after death, future life, life beyond, world to come, heaven, heavenly kingdom, paradise. **—Ant. 1** heretofore, before this, before now, before, in the past. **2** mortal life, here, here and now.

hereditary *adj.* **1.** inherited, inheritable, heritable; inbred, inborn, congenital, innate. **2.** inherited, handed-down, ancestral; traditional, established. **—Syn. Study. 1** See INNATE. **—Ant. 1, 2** acquired. **2** earned, saved.

heresy *n.* heretical beliefs, apostasy, heterodoxy, unorthodoxy, unsound doctrine, fallacy, unorthodox belief, unorthodox opinion, nonconformity, irreligion, dissension, iconoclasm, dissent. **—Ant.** orthodoxy, catholicity; convention, conformity, traditionalism.

heretic *n.* dissenter, apostate, skeptic, misbeliever; nonconformist, recusant, deviationist, freethinker, renegade; backslider, recreant. **—Ant.** orthodox believer, true believer, adherent.

heretical *adj.* unorthodox, contrary to accepted standards; unconventional, iconoclastic, nonconforming, nonconformist, dissident, radical. **—Ant.** orthodox; conventional, conforming.

heritage *n.* tradition, birthright, inheritance, portion, patrimony; estate, family possession, legacy.

hermit *n.* recluse, solitudinarian, solitary; religious recluse, eremite, anchorite, desert saint, cenobite, monastic.

hero *Fem.* **heroine** *n.* **1.** brave man, valorous man, man of courage, champion, fearless fighter, intrepid warrior; great man, noble man, chivalrous man, gallant; daredevil, adventurer, daring man; legendary person, idealized person, popular figure, idol, star, man of the hour. **2.** leading man, principal male character, protagonist, male lead, main actor, male star. **—Ant.** villain. **1** coward, dastard, poltroon. **2** antagonist; heavy.

heroic *adj.* **1.** brave, courageous, valiant, valorous, dauntless, undaunted, fearless, lionhearted, stouthearted, intrepid, resolute, unflinching, bold, daring; noble, gallant, chivalrous; legendary, mythological, mythical, Homeric. **2.** classic, grand, epic, elevated, dignified, exalted; highbrow, extravagant, grandiose, high-flown; ostentatious, pretentious; exaggerated, inflated, bombastic. **—Ant. 1** cowardly, fainthearted, afraid, timid, fearful, timorous, irresolute, wavering; ignoble, mean, base, craven, pusillanimous. **2** simple, straightforward, unadorned; earthy, lowbrow.

heroism *n.* bravery, courage, courageousness, prowess, valor, dauntlessness, fearlessness, lionheartedness, boldness, daring, intrepidity, fortitude; gallantry, nobility, chivalry. **—Ant.** cowardice, timidity; meanness, baseness.

hesitant *adj.* hesitating, reluctant, halfhearted, faltering, lacking confidence, hanging back; undecided, doubtful, indecisive, uncertain, halting, unsure, tentative, diffident, loath, irresolute, wavering, vacillating, shilly-shallying, sitting on the fence. **—Ant.** eager, willing, avid, keen; resolute, determined, steadfast, staunch, firm, certain, sure, confident, decisive, decided.

hesitate *v.* **1.** pause, delay, stop briefly, halt, falter; be undecided, be uncertain, be unsure, be irresolute, waver, vacillate, shilly-shally, dillydally, straddle the fence. **2.** shy at, be unwilling, stick at, stickle at; hang back, be reluctant, balk, shrink from; think twice, scruple. **—Ant. 1** go pell-mell, go headlong, continue; be decisive, decide, be firm, be certain, be sure, be confident. **2** welcome, do willingly, embrace, be determined, resolve.

heterogeneous *adj.* mixed, varied, diversified, diverse, assorted, jumbled, miscellaneous, motley, variegated, composite; dissimilar, unlike, unrelated, disparate, divergent. **—Ant.** homogeneous, uniform, matched; same, like, alike, identical, similar.

hew *v.* chop, hack, cut, cut down, ax, chop down, sever, lop, prune; carve, chisel, cut out, sculpture, whittle, form, shape, fashion, mold, devise, model.

hiatus *n.* lapse, interval, interim, break, space, gap, void, blank, interruption, disruption, vacuum, lacuna.

hide *v.* **1.** conceal, secrete, keep out of sight, prevent from being seen, prevent from being discovered, put in concealment, cache, seclude. **2.** lie concealed, be hidden, hide out, conceal oneself, remain in a hiding place, keep oneself out of sight, lie low, go into hiding, go underground. **3.** conceal, obscure, cover, veil, screen, cloak, curtain, shroud, cloud; repress, suppress; mask, disguise. **—Syn. Study. 1** HIDE, CONCEAL, SECRETE mean to keep something from being seen or discovered. HIDE is the general word: *A rock hid them from view.* CONCEAL, somewhat more formal, usu. means to intentionally cover up something: *He concealed the evidence of the crime.* SECRETE means to put away carefully, in order to keep secret: *The spy secreted the important papers.* **—Ant. 1, 3** reveal, show, expose, display, exhibit, parade, flaunt; find, discover, uncover. **2** find. **3** divulge, disclose, bare, unmask, unveil; admit, confess, avow, lay open, expose.

hideous *adj.* ugly, grotesque, dreadful, horrid, repulsive, repugnant, awful, abhorrent, abominable, frightful, ghastly, revolting, appalling, shocking, repellent, macabre, gruesome, grim, horrendous, horrible; monstrous, loathsome, detestable, disgusting, sickening, vile, odious. **—Ant.** beautiful, lovely, attractive, pleasant, pleasing, charming, captivating, entrancing, appealing.

high *adj.* **1.** tall, lofty, towering, soaring, high-reaching, sky-scraping, alpine, cloud-capped. **2.** great, extreme, excessive, inordinate, unreasonable, undue, intemperate, immoderate; extravagant, exorbitant, exaggerated, unrestrained, uncurbed, unbridled. **3.** important, serious, elevated, lofty, top, eminent, exalted, consequential, significant, notable, distinguished, prominent, preeminent, illustrious, august, superior, imposing, leading; prime, primary, foremost, chief, main, principal, capital, predominant, uppermost; peerless, ascendant, grand, excellent, noble. **4.** high-pitched, soprano, in the upper register; shrill, sharp, strident, piercing, earsplitting. **5.** excited, elated, exuberant, exhilarated, exultant; merry, joyful, joyous, gay, cheerful, lighthearted, playful, jubilant, overjoyed, jolly, gleeful, jovial, mirthful. *—adv.* **6.** at great altitude, at great height, way up, far up, aloft. **—Ant.** low. **1** short, stunted, dwarfed. **2** moderate, mild, average, reasonable, routine, reduced; subdued, suppressed, restrained. **3** low-ranking, lowly, unimportant, inconsequential, insignificant, undistinguished; secondary, common, routine, average; menial; debased, degraded, ignoble. **4** low-pitched, base, alto; deep, husky, gruff, hoarse. **5** sad, cheerless, gloomy, joyless, depressed, dejected, melancholy; angry, mad, irritable.

highbrow *n.* **1.** intellectual, scholar, mastermind, thinker, Brahmin, mandarin; elitist, snob; *Slang* egghead, brain, double-dome. *—adj.* **2.** intellectual, scholarly, erudite, cultured, cultivated, bookish, knowledgeable; snobbish, elitist. **—Ant. 1** lowbrow, hard-hat, redneck, ignoramus, Philistine. **2** unschooled, illiterate, untutored, uncultivated.

high-flown *adj.* lofty, elevated, grandiose; proud, self-important, lordly, presumptuous; pretentious, extravagant, inflated, high-flying, pompous, florid, flowery, high-sounding, sententious, exaggerated, flamboyant; bombastic, magniloquent, turgid, orotund, grandiloquent; *Slang* highfalutin. **—Ant.** down-to-earth, practical, realistic, pragmatic; straightforward, simple, to the point; terse, concise.

highland *n.* Often **Highlands** uplands, hill country, tableland, plateau, mountainous region, heights, headland; rise, promontory. **—Ant.** lowlands; valley.

highlight *n.* **1.** spot of intense light, strong illumination; focal point, prominent detail. **2.** climax, outstanding part, main feature, memorable part, high point, peak, most interesting aspect. *—v.* **3.** emphasize, stress, accent, feature, accentuate, give prominence to, point up, underline, focus attention on; make light, make bright. **—Ant. 1** shadow. **2** low point; disappointment. **3** de-emphasize, play down, gloss over, slight, neglect, overlook.

high-minded *adj.* honorable, honest, fair, ethical, principled, sincere, truthful, just, scrupulous, conscientious, upright, worthy, virtuous, reputable, uncorrupt, square-dealing; noble, idealistic, lofty, magnanimous. **—Syn. Study.** See NOBLE. **—Ant.** unprincipled, unworthy, dishonorable, dishonest, unfair, unethical, corrupt, unscrupulous, ignoble, mean, base, low.

high-strung *adj.* nervous, excitable, easily agitated, tense, uneasy, skittish, temperamental, jumpy, edgy, wrought-up, restless, impatient; *Slang* jittery, uptight; neurotic, oversensitive, moody. **—Ant.** phlegmatic, calm, collected, placid, stolid, even-tempered, *Slang* cool.

highway *n.* main road, thruway, expressway, freeway, speedway, turnpike; (*variously*) interstate, state highway, parkway, main artery, divided highway, four-lane road, thoroughfare, highroad; hard road, paved road; *British* royal road, coach road, King's Highway, Queen's Highway. **—Ant.** byway, back road, county road, side road.

hike *v.* **1.** march, tramp, journey on foot, trek, walk; trudge, roam, wander, rove, ramble; *Informal* hoof it, leg it, go by shank's mare, put on one's hiking shoes. **2.** pull up, hitch up, draw up, raise up, jerk up. *—n.* **3.** march, tramp, journey by foot, walk. **4.** increase, rise, raise, escalation, upward movement; expansion, addition, augmentation.

hilarious *adj.* **1.** very funny, laugh-provoking, comical, uproarious, hysterical, riotous, highly amusing, laughable, rollicking. **2.** lively, jubilant, jovial, jolly, gay, gleeful, joyous, mirthful, high-spirited, exuberant, exhilarated, jocund, joyful, merry, rollicking; boisterous, noisy, vociferous. **—Ant. 1** sad, serious. **2** dull, gloomy, depressed; quiet, sedate.

hill *n.* **1.** hilltop, knoll, foothill, rise, hillock, hummock, mount, promontory, dune, butte, bluff, cliff, highland, height, elevation, prominence, eminence; slope, incline, acclivity, hillside, climb, grade, upgrade, ramp, bank; downgrade, declivity. **2.** mound of earth, mound; heap, pile. **—Ant. 1** low ground, valley, canyon, gorge, gully, ravine, bottom, basin, hollow, dale, glen, dell, vale.

hind *adj.* **—Syn. Study.** See BACK.

hinder *v.* delay, slow down, hold up, hold back, detain, stop, stay, arrest, stall, check, curb, hamper, retard, encumber, obstruct, block, prevent, deter, impede, bar, restrain, handicap, inhibit, frustrate, interfere with, make difficult; stifle, stymie, thwart, foil, hobble, fetter, spike, hamstring, hog-tie, put a spoke in one's wheels. **—Syn. Study.** See PREVENT. **—Ant.** help, aid, support, further, advance, promote, benefit, encourage; expedite, facilitate, accelerate, speed, hurry, hasten, quicken.

hindrance *n.* impediment, stumbling block, obstacle, obstruction, blockage, handicap, encumbrance, restriction, limitation, interference, constraint, restraint, retardant, difficulty, bar, snag, catch, curb; barrier, blockade, barricade, clog, fetter, shackle. **—Syn. Study.** See OBSTACLE. **—Ant.** help, aid, benefit, assistance, support, furtherance, advancement, spur, boon.

hinge *n.* **1.** hinged joint, pivot. *—v.* **2.**

depend, hang, revolve around, be subject to, rest, turn, pivot, swing; be due to, result from, arise from, emanate from.

hint *n.* **1.** clue, inkling, notion, idea, tip, tip-off, pointer; suggestion, indication, insinuation, implication, innuendo, allusion, intimation, impression, whisper, indirection, slight knowledge; *Informal* flea in the ear, word to the wise. **2.** trace, little, slight amount, touch, tinge, whisper, smattering, bit, pinch, grain, whiff, iota, jot, suspicion, *French* soupçon. —*v.* **3.** intimate, imply, signify, insinuate, indicate, suggest, tip off. **—Syn. Study.** HINT, INTIMATE, INSINUATE, SUGGEST denote the conveying of an idea to the mind indirectly or without full or explicit statement. To HINT is to convey an idea covertly or indirectly, but in a way that can be understood: *She hinted that she would like a bicycle for her birthday.* To INTIMATE is to give a barely perceptible hint, often with the purpose of influencing action: *He intimated that a reconciliation was possible.* To INSINUATE is to hint artfully, often at what one would not dare to say directly: *Someone insinuated that the defendant was guilty.* SUGGEST denotes recalling something to the mind or starting a new train of thought by means of association of ideas: *Her restlessness suggested that she wanted to leave.* **—Ant. 2** abundance, profusion, plethora, amplitude; excess, surplus. **3** assert, declare, announce, state in no uncertain terms.

hire *v.* **1.** employ, engage, give employment to, take on, retain, appoint, secure, obtain, get, procure. **2.** rent, charter, lease, let, engage. —*n.* **3.** salary, wages, pay, compensation, remuneration, stipend, fee, emolument, recompense, income, receipts, payment, profit, reward, gain, earnings; cost, charge, rent. **—Syn. Study. 2** HIRE, CHARTER, RENT refer to paying money for the use of something. HIRE is most commonly applied to paying money for a person's services, but is also used in reference to paying for the temporary use of something: *to hire a gardener; to hire a convention hall.* CHARTER is applied to hiring a vehicle for the exclusive use of a group or individual: *to charter a boat.* RENT, although used in the above senses, is most often applied to paying a set sum at regular intervals for the use of a dwelling or other property: *to rent an apartment.* **—Ant. 1** fire, discharge, dismiss, let go, cashier; *Slang* sack, can, give the boot, kiss off.

hireling *n.* menial, minion, flunky, lackey, retainer; henchman, stooge, gorilla, thug, goon, hatchet man, strong-arm.

hirsute *adj.* hairy; unshaven, unshorn, bearded, bewhiskered, whiskered; bushy, woolly, shaggy, downy, nappy, bristled, bristly, prickly. **—Ant.** hairless, smooth-shaven; bald, closecropped.

hiss *v.* boo; give a Bronx cheer, give the raspberry, *Informal* hoot, razz; heckle, catcall, jeer, scoff, deride, shout down, mock, sneer at, revile. **—Ant.** applaud, clap, cheer, shout, approval.

historic *adj.* important in history, famed, well-known, notable, outstanding, renowned, memorable, celebrated. **—Ant.** unimportant, unknown, uncelebrated, trivial.

historical *adj.* in history, of history, grounded in history; authentic, actual, real, true, documented, factual, attested, recorded, chronicled, supported by historical evidence; bygone, ancient, belonging to the past, past, former. **—Ant.** present-day, current, contemporary; fictional, fictitious, legendary, mythical, fabulous.

history *n.* **1.** important events, major events, world events, national events, local events; political change, military action, human progress, development, growth, change; an interesting past, an unusual past; actual events, unalterable facts. **2.** narration of past events, factual story of the past, chronicle, account, record, saga, epic, annals; portrayal, recapitulation, review, résumé; narration, narrative, story, tale. **3.** the past, former times, bygone days, bygone times, olden times, old times, the old days, days of old, days of yore, yesteryear, yesterday; tradition. **—Ant. 1** current events. **1, 2** fiction, fantasy, legend, myth, fable. **3** the present, today, now; the future, time to come.

histrionics *n.* dramatics, dramaturgy, theatrics, staginess, melodramatics; temper tantrum, ranting and raving, tirade, outburst, fuss, bluster, bombast, rodomontade, *Slang* hamminess; performance, acting, playacting, theatricality.

hit *v.* **1.** strike, deal a stroke, deal a blow, sock, smash, slug, knock, jab, wallop, clip, punch, smack, slam, poke; *Slang* paste, clout, clobber, belt, slap, whack, thwack, baste, lambaste, bash; trounce, pommel, drub, pound, beat, flog, thrash, batter, pelt, punch, flail; smite, club, bat, cudgel. **2.** collide with, smash into, bump, butt, bang into; strike together. **3.** strike, succeed in striking, go straight to, make a bull's-eye, send to the mark; attain, connect with, reach, achieve, realize, arrive at; effect, execute, bring off. **4.** affect, touch, move, impress; overwhelm, overcome, crush, upset, hurt, devastate, shatter, abash; arouse, rouse, incite, provoke, quicken, stir, inflame. **5.** attack, strike, strike out at, assault, assail, mount an offensive;

denounce, damn, criticize, censure, condemn, revile, lash out at, reproach; *Slang* rap. —*n.* **6.** blow, impact, bump, knock, strike, rap, tap, whack, thwack, cuff, bang, thump; *Slang* clip, wallop, lob, bat, swat, clout, smash, crack, belt, sock; smash, paste, jab, punch, smack, slap. **7.** success, popular success, sensation, triumph, winner, *Slang* smash; victory, boon, find, coup, blessing, godsend. —**Syn. Study. 1** See BEAT. —**Ant. 1** caress, pat; block, parry, deflect, counterpunch. **2** miss. **3** miss, miss the mark; fail. **5** retreat, withdraw, surrender, give up; defend, support, champion, praise, acclaim, applaud, compliment. **7** flop, failure; *Slang* bomb, dog.

hitch *v.* **1.** tie, tether, loop, loop together, make fast, couple, attach, fasten, connect, bracket, yoke, clamp, secure; put in harness, harness. **2.** pull, tug, yank, hike, raise, haul, draw, jerk. —*n.* **3.** knot, loop; attaching, joining, coupling, connection, fastening, tying. **4.** pull, tug, yank, jerk. **5.** mishap, mischance, mistake, difficulty, complication, problem, catch, snag; trouble, delay, halt, obstacle, impediment, stumbling block, restraint, hindrance, restriction, curb, stop, check, interruption; handicap, limitation. —**Ant. 1** untie, unfasten, uncouple, free, release, loose, loosen. **2** pull down.

hither *adv.* here, over here, to this place, to the speaker, forward, onward, on, near, nearer, close, closer, close by, nearby. —**Ant.** thither, yon, there; away, farther, farther away.

hitherto *adv.* till now, until now, up to now, thus far, up to this time, before this, heretofore, hereto, ere now, to the present time. —**Ant.** henceforth, henceforward, hereafter, in future, after this, subsequently.

hive *n.* swarm of bees, colony, cluster; busy place, hub, center, heart.

hoard *n.* **1.** stockpile, cache, store, supply, reserve, fund; gathering, accumulation, collection, pile, heap, mass, amassment, quantity. —*v.* **2.** stockpile, store away, lay away, lay up, cache, save up, store, amass, accumulate, collect, buy up, acquire. —**Ant. 2** distribute, dispense, scatter, disperse; waste, squander, dissipate.

hoarse *adj.* husky, harsh, rasping, raspy, raucous, scratchy, croaky, rough, gruff, cracked, throaty, gravelly, guttural. —**Ant.** full, rich, sweet, clear, mellow, melodious, mellifluous.

hoary *adj.* **1.** gray with age, white with age; white, whitened, grizzled, grizzly, hoar, gray, grayed. **2.** old, ancient, aged; antique, out-of-date, dated, passé, *Slang* old hat. —**Ant. 2** brand-new, new, modern, up-to-date, recent, *Slang* with-it.

hoax *n.* **1.** mischievous deception, humorous deception, absurd story, exaggerated tale, false alarm, yarn, fish story, fiction; spoof, trick, prank, chicanery, deception, fake, fraud, cheat, humbug, canard, hocus-pocus. —*v.* **2.** hoodwink, deceive, delude, take in, fool, trick, mislead, bluff; defraud, swindle, cheat, bilk, dupe, victimize, gyp, cozen, gull; *Slang* bamboozle. —**Ant. 1** truth, true story, fact, factual account. **2** undeceive, enlighten.

hobble *v.* **1.** fetter, shackle, bind, manacle. **2.** limp, halt, walk lamely; shuffle, lumber, stumble, shamble, stagger, toddle. **3.** hold back, hinder, restrict, encumber, interfere with, inhibit, frustrate, hamper, thwart, impede, handicap, cramp, shackle, constrain, restrain, check, hamstring, hog-tie, block, obstruct, stymie. —*n.* **4.** fetter, shackle, manacle. **5.** limp, gimp, lame gait, uneven gait, jerking motion, stumbling motion, shuffle, stagger. —**Ant. 2** run, prance, walk briskly. **3** help, aid, assist, benefit, advance, further. **5** jaunty step, even gait.

hobby *n.* diversion, pastime, leisure-time activity, relaxation, sideline, amusement, entertainment, pursuit, avocation, divertissement. —**Ant.** work, job, vocation.

hocus-pocus *n.* **1.** magic formula, magic words, chant, incantation, mumbo jumbo; magic spell, charm, spell, bewitchment; magic tricks, magic, sleight of hand, legerdemain, prestidigitation. **2.** deception, trickery, deceit, dishonesty, humbug, hoax, delusion, sham, rubbish, bunkum, fakery; cheat, swindle, subterfuge, confidence game; *Informal* con game; *Slang* hanky-panky, flimflam, bosh, hogwash, poppycock, fiddle-faddle, flapdoodle, moonshine, tommyrot, stuff and nonsense, bull.

hodgepodge Also **hotchpotch** *n.* jumble, mess, confusion, mixture, muddle, miscellany, conglomeration, medley, mélange, hash, patchwork, mix, composite, potpourri; *Yiddish* mishmash.

hoi polloi *n.* the common people, the plebs, the proletariat, the proles, the working class; the lower orders, the masses, the crowd, the mob, the herd, the multitude, the lower classes, the vulgar, the rank and file, commonalty, populace, every Tom, Dick, and Harry; riffraff, rabble, *French* canaille. —**Ant.** aristocrats, blue bloods, the upper class, high society, the ruling class; the intelligentsia, the illuminati, The Beautiful People.

hoist *v.* raise, raise up, pull up, run up, upraise, uplift, lift, elevate, heave, take up, bear up, bear aloft. —**Ant.** lower, pull down, drag down.

hold *v.* **1.** keep in the hand, have in the hand, grasp, clutch, grip, clasp; keep in the arms, embrace, enfold; carry, bear, take; support, uphold, brace, prop, shore. **2.** stick, stick fast, cling, adhere, cleave; remain tied, remain bound, stay fixed; lock, unite, clinch, stay, resist breaking. **3.** have a capacity of, contain, accommodate, take in, include, enclose. **4.** restrain, contain, control, defer, postpone, repress, suppress, suspend, withhold, desist from, hold back, hold off, hold up, hold in check, hold down, forestall, stall, hinder, inhibit, frustrate, thwart, check, curb, stay, keep, halt, block, prevent, limit, restrict; detain, confine. **5.** keep, retain, reserve, set aside; watch, protect, guard; keep valid, be in force. **6.** keep, maintain, hold down; have, possess, occupy. **7.** conduct, carry on, have, execute, engage in, join in; preside over, direct, manage. **8.** maintain, assert, affirm, declare, profess, deem, consider, regard, think, believe, conceive, count, reckon, suppose, presume, assume, understand, surmise, conclude, deduct; propose, submit, offer, put forth, put forward, advance, present, tender, venture, advocate, urge; bind, obligate, enforce. —*n.* **9.** grasp, grip, clasp, clutch; embrace. **10.** handle, knob, strap, grasp, hilt, shaft; foothold, toehold, handhold, stand, anchorage, advantage; leverage, purchase. **11.** influence, controlling force, control, authority, sway, domination, dominance, mastery, rule, command, power, ascendancy; bond, attachment; possession, ownership. —**Syn. Study. 3** See CONTAIN. —**Ant. 1** let go, let loose, put down, let drop, droop; hand over, give over, give. **2** come undone, come unstuck, let go; come untied, loosen, let loose, break, give way. **4** give, bestow, accord, grant, tender, offer, release, let loose, free, let go. **5, 6** give over, turn over, give up. **5** cancel, let lapse. **7** cancel, call off; postpone. **8** disavow, disclaim, deny, refute, repudiate, controvert, reject, abjure, forswear, gainsay.

hole *n.* **1.** opening, aperture, breach, open space; break, gap, rent, slit, crack, slot; puncture, perforation. **2.** hollow place, depression, cavity, concavity, indentation, excavation, pocket, orifice; cave, cavern, tunnel, pit, shaft, dugout, crater; den, lair, burrow. **3.** fault, defect, fallacy, flaw, discrepancy, inconsistency. **4.** prison, keep, *Navy* brig; dungeon, dark cell, solitary confinement cell; *Slang* cage, slammer, lockup. —**Ant. 1** cover, plug, stopper, closure. **2** projection, protuberance, prominence, convexity, mound.

holiday *n.* **1.** holy day; feast day. **2.** celebration, jubilee, fiesta, festival, fete; vacation, vacation day, day of rest; *Canadian, British* vacation trip, outing, junket. —*adj.* **3.** festive, celebrating, gala, merrymaking, gay, joyous, joyful, cheery, cheerful. —**Ant. 2** workday. **3** serious, somber, sad, gloomy.

holiness *n.* sanctity, sacredness, blessedness, godliness, saintliness. —**Ant.** worldliness, secularity.

hollow *adj.* **1.** empty inside, empty, unfilled, not solid, vacant. **2.** concave, rounded inward, curving inward, sunken, cavernous, depressed, indented. **3.** dull, expressionless, unresonant, nonresonant, muted, sepulchral; deep, low, rumbling, reverberating. **4.** meaningless, unavailing, empty, vain, pointless, false, specious, deceptive, fruitless, profitless, useless, futile, unprofitable, worthless, valueless, unsatisfactory, disappointing, nugatory, inconsequential. —*n.* **5.** depression, concavity, cavity, hole, indentation, pocket, ditch, furrow, rut, dip, sink; dent, dimple; void, vacuum; cave, cavern, crater, crevasse. **6.** valley, dale, dell, vale, glen. —*v.* **7.** gouge out, scoop out, dig out, empty out, excavate; groove, channel. —**Ant. 1** solid, full, filled, occupied. **2** convex, protruding, rounded, raised. **3** vibrant, resonant; expressive. **4** worthwhile, profitable, useful, valuable, meaningful, significant; satisfying, gratifying, pleasing. **5** protuberance, projection, bump, hump, mound, knob. **6** hill, hillock, mountain, rise, hummock, knoll, bluff, height.

holocaust *n.* **1.** conflagration, deadly fire; devastating blaze; inferno; bonfire. **2.** devastation, ruin, havoc, ravage; vast slaughter, massacre, carnage, killing, annihilation, genocide, mass murder, butchery.

holy *adj.* **1.** of divine character, of divine origin, divine, divinely inspired, pertaining to God, from God, sacred, heavenly, spiritual, religious, from above, heaven-sent. **2.** saintly, godly, dedicated to God, devoted to God, spiritual, pure, pure in heart, sinless, angelic, immaculate, unstained, profoundly good, moral, righteous, guileless, uncorrupted, undefiled, unspotted, faithful, virtuous, unworldly; devout, pious, religious, reverent. **3.** consecrated, sacred, hallowed, blessed, sanctified; sacrosanct, inviolable, religious, solemn; worshiped, adored, venerated, revered. —**Syn. Study. 3** HOLY, SACRED, HALLOWED refer to something that is the object of worship or veneration. HOLY refers to the divine, that which has its sanctity directly from God or is connected with Him: *Remember the Sabbath day to keep it holy.*

Something that is SACRED is usu. dedicated to a religious purpose by human authority: *a sacred shrine*. Something that is HALLOWED has been made holy by being worshiped or venerated: *The church graveyard is hallowed ground.* **—Ant.** unholy. **1, 2** secular, worldly, earthly, human; profane, sacrilegious, unreligious, blasphemous, impious; sinful, wicked, evil, corrupt, immoral, impure. **3** unconsecrated, unsanctified, unhallowed, desecrated, impure.

Holy Spirit, Holy Ghost *n.* presence of God, third person of the Trinity, Paraclete; *Latin* spiritus sanctus, *Greek* hagion pneuma.

homage *n.* honor, respect, reverence, regard, veneration; praise, tribute, exaltation, glorification, esteem, devotion, deference, obeisance; worship, adoration, adulation. **—Ant.** dishonor, disrespect, irreverence; condemnation, blame, criticism.

home *n.* **1.** house, residence, place of residence, dwelling, dwelling place, domicile, abode, place of abode; place where one hangs one's hat, home sweet home. **2.** habitat, haunt, abode, habitation, native land, native region, natural environment; cradle, fountainhead; stamping ground, *Informal* hangout. **3.** institution, residence; (*variously*) nursing home, sanatorium, hospital, orphanage, asylum, poorhouse; refuge, haven. **—Syn. Study. 1** See HOUSE.

homely *adj.* **1.** plain-looking, plain, not good-looking, ordinary, drab, unattractive, ill-favored, uncomely, unhandsome, graceless, ungraceful; rather ugly. **2.** plain, simple, unassuming, unpretentious, unaffected, modest, ordinary, everyday, familiar, natural, artless, unsophisticated, rustic, provincial, homespun; homelike, homey, snug, cozy, comfy, comfortable. **—Ant. 1** beautiful, gorgeous, pretty, handsome, comely, lovely, attractive, good-looking, striking, eye-catching. **2** elegant, grand, splendid, regal, courtly, refined; pretentious, affected, ostentatious, showy, sophisticated.

homespun *adj.* homemade, handloomed, hand-woven, hand-crafted, hand-wrought; simple, plain, unpretentious, unaffected, artless, modest, natural, homely, folksy, native, down-home.

homicide *n.* **1.** murder, manslaughter, slaying, bloodshed, foul play; (*variously*) parricide (*killing one's parent or close relative*), matricide (*killing one's mother*), patricide (*killing one's father*), fratricide (*killing one's brother*), feticide or aborticide (*abortion*), infanticide (*killing an infant*), uxoricide (*killing a wife*), regicide (*killing a king*), vaticide (*killing a prophet*). **2.** murderer, slayer, killer, manslayer, man killer.

homogeneous *adj.* of the same kind, all alike, of a piece; uniform, unmixed, unvarying, unadulterated; consistent, constant, pure; akin, kindred, similar, identical. **—Ant.** heterogeneous, mixed, varied, varying, variegated, different, diverse, divers, various, divergent.

honest *adj.* **1.** law-abiding, ethical, truthful, decent, upright, fair, just, righteous, honorable, virtuous, principled, conscientious, scrupulous, blameless, proper, reasonable, faithful, true-blue, tried and true, reputable, fair and square, square, straight, straight-shooting, aboveboard, open and aboveboard, on the level, on the up-and-up, as good as one's word, honest as the day is long; legal, legitimate, lawful. **2.** true, truthful, frank, straightforward, candid, blunt, plainspoken, forthright, clear-cut, trustworthy, dependable, reliable, solid; valid, genuine, real, authentic, bona fide. **3.** sincere, open, frank, candid, plain, guileless, ingenuous, unaffected, innocent, artless, unsophisticated; unreserved, undisguised. **—Ant.** dishonest. **1** unethical, untruthful, unfair, unrighteous, dishonorable, bad, immoral, unprincipled, unscrupulous, improper, unfaithful; illegal, illegitimate, unlawful, corrupt, fraudulent; crooked, base, low, vile. **2** false, lying, untruthful, deceitful, unreliable, untrustworthy, undependable, treacherous, invalid, fake, counterfeit. **3** guilty, insincere, artful, deceitful, hypocritical, disguised, secretive.

honesty *n.* truthfulness, integrity, trustworthiness, probity, veracity, word, sincerity, uprightness, rectitude, incorruptibility, honor, faithfulness, morality, scruples, principles; fairness, just dealing, square dealing, straight shooting; reputability, good name; innocence, guiltlessness. **—Syn. Study.** See HONOR. **—Ant.** dishonesty, crookedness, corruption, deceitfulness, deception, unfairness, untruthfulness, falseness, falsity, lying, mendacity, trickery, fraud, chicanery, duplicity, insincerity, deceit, guile.

honor *n.* **1.** honesty, high-mindedness, principle, honorableness, probity, decency, uprightness, nobleness of mind, scrupulousness, trustworthiness, conscientiousness, faithfulness; honesty, integrity, virtue, fairness, justness, truthfulness, truth, veracity, sincerity, rectitude, goodness, constancy. **2.** respect, esteem, regard, deference, reverence, homage, veneration, admiration, approbation, tribute, adoration, worship, glorification, exaltation; fame, glory, acclaim, renown, greatness, importance, high standing, distinction, prestige, repute, commendation, praise, recognition, note, notability, celebrity, credit, eminence, prominence, illustriousness, good report, good name, a feather in one's cap. **3.** privilege, compliment, pleasure, favor; grant, authorization, permission, sanction, power, right, leave, liberty. —*v.* **4.** esteem, revere, venerate, respect, value, regard, admire, praise, laud, extol, commend, exalt, glorify, worship, have regard for, look up to, think much of, show deference to, pay homage to, pay tribute to, bow down before; venerate, adore. **5.** confer honor upon, give one the privilege of, favor, compliment, grant, dignify, glorify. **6.** take, accept, credit, acknowledge; (*of a check or draft*) make payment on, pay, redeem, cash, credit, make good. **—Syn. Study. 1** HONOR, HONESTY, INTEGRITY, SINCERITY refer to the highest moral principles. HONOR denotes a fine sense of, and a strict conformity to, what is considered morally right or due: *The soldier conducted himself with honor.* HONESTY denotes moral virtue and particularly the absence of deceit or fraud: *known for her honesty in business dealings.* INTEGRITY indicates a soundness of moral principle that no power or influence can impair: *a judge of unquestioned integrity.* SINCERITY particularly implies the absence of dissimulation or deceit and a strong adherence to the truth: *Your sincerity was evident in every word.* **—Ant. 1–5** dishonor. **1** bad character, meanness, lowness, baseness, dishonesty, unscrupulousness, insincerity. **2** low regard, disrespect, contempt, disdain, scorn, shame, disgrace, disrepute, condemnation, infamy, ignominy, degradation, debasement, bad name. **3** insult, disfavor. **4** condemn, hold in contempt, disrespect, disdain, scorn, insult, defame, shame, degrade, debase, discredit, slight, disobey. **5** insult, offend, affront. **6** refuse, reject; (*of a check or draft*) refuse payment on, bounce.

hoodlum *n.* gangster, mobster, gunman, crook, criminal, desperado; *Slang* gorilla, hood, strong arm, thug, plug-ugly; tough, hooligan, bruiser, ruffian, rowdy, juvenile delinquent; *Informal* punk.

hoodwink *v.* deceive, trick, dupe, cheat, swindle, mislead, inveigle, defraud, gyp, victimize, cozen, gull; *Slang* rook, bamboozle; fool, hoax.

hook *n.* **1.** grapple, grapnel, gaff, crook, bill, pothook, fluke, crampon, (*in lumbering*) peavey. **2.** bend, curve, crook, angle, arc, crescent, horseshoe, arch, loop, bow, curl, elbow. —*v.* **3.** fasten, latch, secure, make fast, make secure; buckle, hitch. **4.** bend, curve, wind, crook, angle, arc, arch, loop, curl. **5.** catch, take, bag, nab, seize, grab; (*variously*) net, snare, ensnare, trap, capture, *Informal* collar. **—Ant. 2** straight line, beeline, perpendicular. **3** unhook, unfasten, unlatch. **4** go straight, run straight, make a straight line, go straight as an arrow, make a beeline. **5** let go, loose; throw back.

hoot *v.* **1.** screech, shriek, scream, howl, wail, shrill, whoop, ululate; moan, whistle, blow, honk. **2.** howl, shout, cry out, sing out, bellow, proclaim, bawl, wail, screech, scream, roar, yelp, whoop, yowl, din, chorus; boo, jeer, hiss, scoff at, mock, cry down, sneer at, snicker at, taunt, deride, give a catcall, give a raspberry, give a Bronx cheer, *Informal* razz. —*n.* **3.** boo, jeer, hiss, catcall, sneer, snicker, taunt, cry of disapproval, caterwaul, *Slang* Bronx cheer, raspberry; shout, shouting, wail, wailing, screech, screeching, scream, screaming, yelp, whoop, yowl, outcry; uproar, tumult, commotion, racket. **—Ant. 2** hail, cheer, applaud, clap for, give a standing ovation; encourage, yell bravo, *Slang* root for; welcome, salute, acclaim. **3** cheer, applause, clapping, standing ovation; encouragement, shout of bravo, hurray, hurrah, huzzah; welcome, acclamation.

hop *v.* **1.** jump, spring, leap, bound, vault, bounce, skip; prance, gambol, frisk, bob, caper, romp, trip; jump over, leap over, spring over, vault over, bound over, skip over. —*n.* **2.** jump, spring, leap, bound, step, vault, skip, bounce.

hope *n.* **1.** faith, confidence, belief, assurance, reassurance, encouragement, trust, reliance, conviction, optimism, expectation, great expectations, expectancy, anticipation, assumption, presumption. **2.** desire, wish, aspiration, ambition, longing, craving, yearning, hunger, yen, *Informal* hankering; dream, daydream, fancy, heart's desire. **3.** chance, possibility, prospect; chance for survival, possible way out, help, rescue, salvation, saving grace. —*v.* **4.** trust, feel sure, be confident, desire, wish, aspire, look forward to, count on, expect, believe, contemplate, anticipate, reckon on, long for, crave, yearn for, hunger for, dream of, daydream, have one's heart set on, be bent upon, have an eye to, have a fancy for, *Informal* have a hankering, *Slang* yen for. **5.** be hopeful, have faith, hope for the best, trust in the Lord, trust; look on the bright side, take heart, be optimistic. **—Ant. 1** dread, despair, despondency, hopelessness, distrust, doubt, disbelief. **4** doubt, deem unlikely, despair of. **5** despair, dread, expect the worst.

hopeful *adj.* **1.** full of hope, in hopes,

expectant, anticipative, optimistic, confident, assured, trusting. **2.** promising, favorable, propitious, auspicious, heartening, sanguine, reassuring, cheering, encouraging, fortunate, of good omen. **—Ant. 1, 2** hopeless. **1** despairing, dejected, despondent, pessimistic, down in the mouth. **2** discouraging, depressing, unpromising, unfavorable, inauspicious, disheartening, unencouraging, adverse, unfortunate.

hopeless *adj.* **1.** without hope, past remedy, incurable, beyond recall, irrevocable, irreversible, irreparable, irredeemable, irretrievable, impossible, beyond help, lost, futile, vain, useless, pointless. **2.** without hope, pessimistic, despairing, dejected, abject, despondent, disconsolate, downcast, depressed, downhearted; sad, forlorn, heartbroken, heavyhearted, sick at heart, sorrow-stricken, grief-stricken; down in the mouth, melancholy. **—Ant. 1, 2** hopeful. **1** promising, encouraging, optimistic, favorable, propitious, auspicious, promising, heartening, reassuring, rosy; remediable, curable, redeemable, retrievable. **2** full of hope, confident, assured, encouraged, heartened, expectant, gay, cheerful, happy, uplifted, lighthearted, joyful.

horde *n.* multitude, host, pack, crowd, throng, mob, bunch, crush, drove, swarm, assemblage, assembly, gang, party, congregation, company, gathering; tribe, legion, band, troop.

horizon *n.* limit of experience, limit of knowledge, frontier, world, domain, area, range, vista, purview, scope, outlook, sphere, expanse, compass, perspective, stretch, field, realm, bounds, prospect.

horizontal *adj.* **1.** parallel to a base line, parallel to the horizon, level, parallel to the ground, level with the ground; flat, plane, even, plumb, flush. **2.** recumbent, prone, supine, reclining, prostrate, lying down, *Informal* flat on one's back. **—Ant. 1** vertical, up and down; inclined, uneven. **2** upright, on one's feet, standing.

horn *n.* **1.** antler, cornu; tusk; excrescence, spike, point. **2.** (*brass instrument: variously*) cornet, trumpet, trombone, tuba, bugle, baritone, sousaphone, euphonium, mellophone, French horn, alto horn; (*woodwind instrument: variously*) saxophone, clarinet, oboe, English horn, bassoon.

horrendous *adj.* horrible, horrid, awful, terrible, dreadful, appalling, frightful; revolting, repulsive, hideous, shocking, repellent, horrifying, ghastly, gory. **—Ant.** pleasing, pleasant, attractive, agreeable.

horrible *adj.* gruesome, harrowing, revolting, repulsive, sickening, awful, disgusting, loathsome, terrible, vile, repellent, hideous, grisly, nauseating, distasteful, detestable, disagreeable, unpleasant, unsavory, foul, rank, nasty, bad, horrid, abhorrent, odious, obnoxious, abominable, unbearable, insufferable, appalling, dreadful, atrocious, monstrous, ghastly, shocking, frightful, forbidding, unspeakable, disquieting, despicable. **—Ant.** pleasing, pleasant, agreeable, attractive, enchanting, appealing, delightful, wonderful, good, charming, enchanting, fetching, lovely.

horrify *v.* shock, terrify, frighten, affright, petrify, make one's flesh creep, make one's hair stand on end; disgust, sicken, repel, revolt, appall, nauseate, make one sick, make one turn pale; daunt, dishearten, disconcert, disquiet, dismay. **—Ant.** charm, enchant, please, attract, delight; gladden, reassure, calm, soothe.

horror *n.* **1.** fear, terror, dread, panic, apprehension, alarm, trepidation, dismay; aversion, loathing, abhorrence, detestation, abomination, hatred, distaste, disgust, dislike, antipathy, repugnance, revulsion, repulsion. **2.** cruelty, outrage, inhumanity, crime, atrocity; awfulness, hideousness, terribleness, misery, woe, distress, wretchedness, hardship, suffering, anguish, torment, discomfort, privation, affliction. **—Ant. 1** liking, affinity, delight, love, attraction. **2** pleasure, delight, gratification, happiness, joy, wonder, reward, goodness, benefit, boon.

hors d'oeuvre *n.* appetizer, canapé, tidbit; (*variously*) little sandwich, finger sandwich, dip, relish tray; *Slang* finger food; *Italian* antipasto.

horse *n.* **1.** (*young*) foal, yearling, pony; (*female*) filly, mare, broodmare; (*male*) colt, stallion, sire, stud, gelding; (*variously*) steed, charger, mount, equine, galloper, racehorse, trotter, pacer, mustang, cow pony, pinto, quarter horse, bronco, bronc, thoroughbred, draft horse, palfrey, dobbin, hackney, hack, jade; *Slang* plug. **2.** horse cavalry, cavalry, cavalrymen, soldiers on horseback, horse soldiers, mounted troops, troopers, mounted troopers, mounted warriors, dragoons, horse marines, lancers, hussars, cossacks. **—Ant. 2** infantry, foot soldiers.

horseman *n.* **1.** rider, horseback rider, equestrian, (*fem.*) equestrienne; jockey, postilion; (*variously*) horse breeder, trainer, groom, stable owner, stable keeper, stableman, stableboy, hostler, ostler. **2.** cavalry soldier, cavalryman, horse soldier, mounted trooper, trooper, roughrider, dragoon, horse marine, lancer, hussar, cossack.

hose *n.* stockings, hosiery; socks.

hospitable *adj.* **1.** gracious, cordial, sociable, gregarious, genial, friendly, warm, amicable, welcoming, convivial, neighborly, openhanded. **2.** receptive, accessible, open, open-minded, approachable, agreeable, responsive, amenable, tolerant. **—Ant. 1, 2** inhospitable, antisocial, reserved. **2** close-minded, unreceptive, unapproachable.

hospital *n.* **1.** medical center, clinic, polyclinic, medical pavilion; infirmary, sick bay. **2.** sanatorium; (*variously*) asylum, nursing home, home, rest home, state hospital.

hospitality *n.* welcome, hospitableness, friendliness, congeniality, amicability, cordiality, conviviality, heartiness, warmth, cheer, geniality, sociability, neighborliness, warmheartedness, kindliness, openness, *German* Gemütlichkeit.

host,[1] Fem. **hostess** *n.* **1.** master of ceremonies, mistress of ceremonies; party giver, welcomer. **2.** hotel manager, hotel keeper, innkeeper, hotelier, hosteler, proprietor, (*fem.*) proprietress, landlord; restaurant manager, receptionist, maitre d', headwaiter, head waitress. **—Ant. 1, 2** guest. **2** lodger, boarder, traveler; diner; customer, patron.

host[2] *n.* multitude, horde, swarm, troop, legion, army, drove, array, throng, *Informal* lot; band, group, party, gathering, body, convention, meeting, congress, confluence, conclave, company, convocation, congregation; mess, mob, crowd, gang, crew. **—Ant.** handful, sprinkling, small group, scattering.

hostile *adj.* **1.** enemy, belligerent, bellicose, opposing, opposed, fighting, battling, contending, clashing, warring, at war; dissident, on bad terms, at odds, at outs, at loggerheads, with crossed swords. **2.** belligerent, angry, antagonistic, contrary, contentious, quarrelsome, bristling, disputatious, argumentative, disagreeing; malicious, vicious, malevolent, venomous, spiteful, bitter, malignant, malign, mean, ugly; unfriendly, unkind, unsympathetic, ill-disposed, ill-natured, disagreeable, incompatible, cranky, cantankerous, snappish, truculent, testy, touchy; cold, chilly, icy. **—Ant. 1** friendly, peaceful. **2** friendly, approving, agreeable, amiable, amicable, cordial, congenial, sweet, kind, kindly, warm, sympathetic.

hostility *n.* **1.** Usu. **hostilities** war, warfare, act of war, state of war, warring, fighting, fight, conflict, combat, military operation, battle, battling, clash; contest, fray, fracas, scuffle, feud, duel, dispute, contention, argument, altercation, dissidence, disagreement, bickering. **2.** belligerence, animosity, antagonism, antipathy, enmity, opposition, contrariness; anger, malice, viciousness, malevolence, bitterness, spleen, unfriendliness, ill will, rancor, hatred, hate, vindictiveness, venom. **—Ant. 1** peace; truce, treaty, alliance. **2** agreement, approval, sympathy, good will, amity, fellow feeling; love, friendship, amiability, cordiality, congeniality.

hot *adj.* **1.** very warm, uncomfortably warm, warm, sweltering, sultry, torrid; at high temperature, highly heated, heated; simmering, steaming, burning, boiling, broiling, scalding, scorching, blistering, searing, baking, roasting, sizzling, piping hot, fiery, smoldering; melting, molten, red-hot, white-hot, incandescent. **2.** piquant, peppery, highly seasoned, sharp, nippy, biting, pungent. **3.** intense, violent, furious, raging, vehement, agitated, fierce, fiery, ardent, passionate, fervid, frenzied, feverish, stormy, tempestuous, hectic, excited, emotional, animated, earnest, wroughtup, fast and furious. **4.** very close, following very closely, in close pursuit, near. **5.** late, latest, new, recent, fresh. **6.** popular, most popular, successful, sought after, fast-selling; attractive, good, top, excellent. **7.** live, carrying current, electrified; radioactive. **—Ant. 1** cold, chilly, chilled, cool, cooled, frigid, freezing, icy, frosty. **2, 3** mild, bland, insipid. **3** peaceful; unemotional, objective, dispassionate. **4** cold. **5** old, out-of-date, old hat, stale.

hotel *n.* inn, lodging, hostel, hostelry, lodge, hospice; motel, motor inn.

hound *n.* **1.** hunting dog; dog, canine; *Slang* pooch, mutt, poochie, doggy; (*young*) pup, puppy, whelp. **—*v.* 2.** chase, pursue, track, trail, stalk, dog, follow, hunt, tail; nag, keep after, keep at, hector, bait, harass, pester, harry, bedevil, badger, worry, annoy, needle. **—Ant. 2** run from, flee, escape, evade, elude.

hour *n.* **1.** time, particular time, fixed time. **2.** period, interval, span, space. **3.** present time, current moment, day.

house *n.* **1.** home, residence, dwelling, dwelling place, abode, domicile, shelter, habitation; (*variously*) apartment, flat, coop, condominium, condo, pied-à-terre, hut, shack, shed, lean-to, cabin, lodge, palace, manor, mansion, castle, cave, pueblo, den, lair, nest; *Informal* digs, *Slang* pad. **2.** household, family. **3.** royal family, noble family, line, dynasty, clan; lineage, ancestry, descent, family tree, ancestors, strain. **4.** building, meeting place, gathering place; (*variously*) church, temple, theater, opera house, concert hall, auditorium, hippodrome, hall. **5.** audience, spectators. **6.** Often **House** congress, lower chamber, legislature, assembly, council; *U.S.* House of Representatives; *British, Canadian* House of Commons, Commons. **7.** business firm, company, concern, firm, business, organization, establishment, corporation, partnership; store, shop. —*v.* **8.** lodge, shelter, harbor, quarter, board, billet, put up, accommodate; furnish with a house. **9.** store, garage, shelter, keep, contain, accommodate. —**Syn. Study. 1** HOUSE, HOME, RESIDENCE, DWELLING are terms applied to a place in which people live. HOUSE is generally applied to a structure built for one or two families or social units: *a ranch house in the suburbs.* HOME may be used of an apartment or a private house; it retains connotations of domestic comfort and family ties: *Their home is full of charm and character.* RESIDENCE is characteristic of formal usage and often implies spaciousness and elegance: *the private residence of the prime minister.* DWELLING is a general and neutral word (*a houseboat is a floating dwelling*) and therefore commonly used in legal, scientific, and other technical contexts, as in a lease or in the phrases *multiple dwelling, single-family dwelling.* —**Ant. 6** upper chamber; *U.S., Canadian* Senate; *British* House of Lords. **8** evict, eject, oust, expel. **9** discard, throw away.

household *n.* **1.** family, family circle, house; home, domestic establishment, hearth. —*adj.* **2.** for a family, housekeeping; of a house, for a house, for home use.

housewife *n.* homemaker, wife; housekeeper, family manager, home economist.

housing *n.* **1.** house, home, dwelling, domicile; abode, shelter, lodging, lodgment, quarters, accommodations, residence, habitation. **2.** case, covering, casing, enclosure, shield, sheath, jacket, envelope.

hovel *n.* wretched dwelling, broken-down residence, cramped shelter, cabin, hut, ramshackle building; *Slang* dump, hole; shanty, shack. —**Ant.** mansion, palace, showplace, villa, castle, manor.

hover *v.* **1.** pause in flight, hang suspended, hang, poise, float; flutter, flit, flitter. **2.** linger about, hang about, hang around, wait near at hand, attend, haunt. **3.** waver, hang, pause, falter, hang in doubt, seesaw, fluctuate, vacillate. —**Ant. 1** fall, sink, drop. **2** leave alone; depart, go away, withdraw, retreat.

howl *v.* **1.** yelp, bay, cry, bark. **2.** cry out, yell, shout, bellow, roar, clamor, ululate, shriek, scream, hoot, yowl, yelp, wail. —*n.* **3.** cry, bay, yelp, bark, whine; outcry, clamor, uproar, yell, shout, bellow, roar, shriek, scream, yowl, hoot, wail, groan. —**Ant. 2, 3** whisper, murmur, mutter.

hub *n.* center, axis, pivot, core, focal point, heart, focus, nub, middle.

hubbub *n.* uproar, pandemonium, tumult, ruckus, fuss, bustle, to-do, hullabaloo, disturbance, stir, commotion, hue and cry, disorder, confusion, turmoil, bedlam, ferment, fuss, perturbation, agitation, pother; racket, noise, clamor, din, hurly-burly, babble. —**Syn. Study.** See NOISE. —**Ant.** quiet, quietness, serenity, calm, calmness, tranquillity, peacefulness, repose, equanimity, stillness, hush.

huddle *v.* **1.** crowd together, throng, cluster, gather closely, flock together, press together, converge, collect, bunch, herd. **2.** curl up, snuggle, nestle, cuddle, make oneself small. —*n.* **3.** gathering, conference, meeting, discussion, think session, putting together of heads. **4.** heap, jumble, mass, mess, muddle, medley, hodge-podge; crowd, group, bunch; confusion, disarray, disorder. —**Ant. 1** disperse, scatter. **2** stretch out, stand tall.

hue *n.* color, coloration, shade, tint, tincture, tone; cast, tinge.

hue and cry *n.* clamor, hullabaloo, uproar, outcry, bellow, roar, yell, shout, yowl, shriek; cry of alarm, alarm; howl of protest, dissenting shout.

huff *n.* bad mood, ill humor, fit of anger, fit of pique, fury, rage, resentment, outrage, vexation, annoyance, petulance, dudgeon; *Slang* pet, snit.

huffy *adj.* easily offended, touchy, sensitive, hypersensitive, angry, irate, waspish, quarrelsome, ill-humored, resentful, querulous, cranky, petulant, churlish, snappish, shirty, testy, thin-skinned, irritable, peevish, grumpy, cross, curt, rancorous, hard to live with, out of sorts, sulky, surly, sullen, resentful, offended, wounded, hurt, moping, glowering, disgruntled, discontented, moody, morose; *Informal* in a pucker, in a snit, in a lather. —**Ant.** calm, soothed; good-humored, cheerful, sunny, gay, friendly, pleasant, easy to live with.

hug *v.* **1.** embrace, hold, clasp, press to the bosom, hold close, clutch, squeeze, cuddle, snuggle, nestle; cling together. **2.** keep close to, cling to, follow closely, parallel closely, hover near.

huge *adj.* extremely large, enormous, tremendous, immense, vast, extensive, colossal, giant, gigantic, titanic, mammoth, monstrous, elephantine, jumbo, gargantuan, leviathan, herculean, cyclopean, Brobdingnagian, *Slang* humongous; massive, great, overwhelming, staggering, stupendous, imposing, mighty, spectacular, monumental, extravagant, prodigious. —**Syn. Study.** HUGE, ENORMOUS, TREMENDOUS, IMMENSE imply great magnitude. HUGE, when used of concrete objects, usu. adds the idea of massiveness, bulkiness, or even lack of shape: *a huge mass of rock.* ENORMOUS applies to what exceeds a norm or standard in extent, magnitude, or degree: *an enormous iceberg.* TREMENDOUS suggests something so large as to be astonishing or to inspire awe: *a tremendous amount of equipment.* IMMENSE, literally "not measurable," is particularly applicable to what is exceedingly great, without reference to a standard: *immense buildings.* All of these terms are used figuratively: *a huge success; enormous curiosity; tremendous effort; immense joy.* **—Ant.** small, little, tiny, dwarfish, Lilliputian, minute; *Informal* wee, itty-bitty, itsy-bitsy; microscopic, infinitesimal; petty, puny, insignificant.

hulking *adj.* bulky, heavy, massive, powerful, big, husky, oversized, massive, unwieldy, cumbersome, ponderous.

hull *n.* **1.** husk, shell, skin, pod, coating, shuck, peel, rind, case; epidermis, carapace, integument, tegmentum; body of a ship. *—v.* **2.** shell, husk, shuck.

hum *v.* **1.** croon, drone, intone. **2.** whir, purr, drone, thrum, murmur, vibrate; buzz. **3.** be busy, be active, bustle, thrive, be in full swing. *—n.* **4.** whirring, whir, drone, droning, purring, purr, vibration; buzzing, buzz; murmur, faint sound.

human *adj.* **1.** characteristic of mankind, like man; of man, of men, mortal, manlike, hominid, anthropoid. **2.** sympathetic, compassionate, humane, gentle, merciful, kindly; personal, individual; humanitarian. *—n.* **3.** human being, person; man, Homo sapiens. **—Ant. 1** nonhuman; god; animal. **2** inhuman, beastly, brutish, unsympathetic, cruel; impersonal.

humane *adj.* kind, kindly, compassionate, sympathetic, tender, goodwilled, benevolent, warmhearted, merciful, pitying, human, humanitarian, bighearted, philanthropic, charitable, magnanimous, unselfish. **—Ant.** inhumane, cruel, inhuman, harsh, brutal, barbarous, uncivilized, merciless, unmerciful, pitiless, ruthless; unkind, unsympathetic.

humanity *n.* **1.** the human race, mankind, man, humankind, Homo sapiens; mortals, human beings, people. **2.** humanness, human nature, mortality. **3.** kindness, kindliness, compassion, sympathy, gentleness, tenderness, benevolence, warmheartedness, charity, fraternal feeling, fellow feeling, brotherly love, goodwill, humaneness, magnanimity, mercy, love. **—Ant. 1–3** inhumanity. **3** unkindness, cruelty, brutality, ruthlessness.

humble *adj.* **1.** modest, unassuming, unpretentious, unpresuming, self-effacing, without arrogance, unostentatious; demure, gentle, meek; subservient, obsequious, deferential, respectful. **2.** poor, low, lowly, modest, wretched, shabby, miserable, inferior; plain, simple, common, ordinary, undistinguished, obscure, inglorious, insignificant, inconsequential, unimportant; low-ranking, plebeian. *—v.* **3.** bring down, put down, subdue, chasten, make humble, bring low, degrade, humiliate, abash, put to shame, embarrass, disgrace, mortify, shame, take down a peg; conquer, crush, pull down, trample underfoot, dishonor, demean, abase, lower, debase, make lowly, cast dishonor upon; derogate, disparage, *Informal* put down. **—Syn. Study. 3** HUMBLE, DEGRADE, HUMILIATE suggest a lowering in self-respect or in the estimation of others. HUMBLE most often refers to a lowering of pride or arrogance, but may refer to a lessening of power or importance: *humbled by failure; to humble an enemy.* DEGRADE literally means to demote in rank or standing, but commonly refers to a bringing into dishonor or contempt: *You degrade yourself by cheating.* To HUMILIATE is to make another feel inadequate or unworthy, esp. in a public setting: *humiliated by criticism.* **—Ant. 1** proud, arrogant, haughty, immodest, pretentious, vain, vainglorious, pompous, lordly, overbearing, snobbish, conceited, superior, boastful, assuming, ostentatious, presuming, presumptuous. **2** rich, wealthy, sumptuous, elegant; superior, out of the ordinary, distinguished, glorious, famous, illustrious, important, significant, consequential, high, high-ranking, aristocratic. **3** exalt, raise, elevate, magnify, aggrandize; extol, glorify.

humbug *n.* **1.** deception, deceit, trick, trickery, fraud, cheat, flimflam, swindle, gyp, artifice, double-dealing, forgery, fake, counterfeit, imposture, dodge; pretense, pretension, sham, make-believe, spoof, hoax, fiction. **2.** pretense, pretentiousness, pretension, sham, hypocrisy, flummery, equivocation, mendacity, lying, lies, falsification, falsehood; nonsense, poppycock; *Informal* bunk, bunkum, balderdash, blather, claptrap, hocus-pocus; *Slang* hokum, bull. **3.** fraud, quack, fake, faker, impostor, charlatan, mountebank; swindler, cheat, cheater, confidence man, con man, sharper, trickster; liar, fibber, perjurer, hypocrite. *—v.* **4.** deceive, trick, fool, hoax, bamboozle, mislead, beguile, hoodwink, dupe, cheat, swindle, cozen, gull, take in; lie, fib; falsify, fabricate, misrepresent. *—interj.* **5.** nonsense, rubbish, balderdash, *Slang* phooey. **—Ant. 2** truth, truthfulness; the real McCoy. **4** undeceive, disabuse.

humdrum *adj.* dull, boring, monotonous, run-of-the-mill, uninteresting, routine, everyday, mundane, dreary, tiresome, tedious, wearisome, wearying, lifeless, flat, insipid, trite, trivial, banal, commonplace, hackneyed, mediocre, pedestrian, uninspired, uninspiring, indifferent, unexciting, uneventful, unvarying, common, ordinary, conventional, unexceptional; *Slang* blah, dumb. **—Ant.** stimulating, exciting, provocative, entertaining, interesting, lively, gay, animated, exceptional, extraordinary.

humid *adj.* muggy, sticky, sultry, steamy, damp, moist, dank, clammy, soppy. **—Ant.** arid, dry, moistureless, parched.

humiliate *v.* embarrass, make ashamed, shame, mortify, chagrin, abash, humble, disgrace, dishonor, discomfit, chasten, crush, subdue, debase, degrade, belittle, bring low, take down a peg; derogate, disparage, *Informal* put down. **—Syn. Study.** See HUMBLE. **—Ant.** honor, make proud, elevate, exalt, elate, please.

humiliation *n.* embarrassment, shame, mortification, chagrin, discomfiture; disgrace, dishonor, degradation, abasement, debasement. **—Syn. Study.** See SHAME. **—Ant.** pride, honor, exaltation, elevation.

humility *n.* modesty, humbleness, lowliness, unpretentiousness, lack of proudness, self-abasement, diffidence, demureness; meekness, shyness, timidity, bashfulness. **—Ant.** pride, arrogance, haughtiness, pretentiousness, vanity, vainglory, pomposity, disdain, snobbishness, conceit, superiority, boastfulness, presumption, superciliousness.

humor *n.* **1.** funniness, comedy, comicality, ridiculousness, ludicrousness, drollery, nonsense, jocularity, jocoseness, jocosity. **2.** jokes, joking, wit, wittiness, witticisms, gags, wisecracks, jests, jesting, foolery, fooling, foolishness, tomfoolery, raillery, ridicule, buffoonery, waggery, monkeyshines, comedy, high comedy, low comedy, broad comedy, slapstick, low humor, broad humor, burlesque, farce, caricature, parody, travesty, satire, whimsy, wordplay, puns. **3.** mood, temper, disposition, spirits, frame of mind. **—*v.* 4.** indulge, pamper, flatter, spoil, baby, go along with, comply with, give in to, appease, soothe, placate, mollify, cajole; put up with, suffer, tolerate. **—Syn. Study. 2** HUMOR, WIT refer to an ability to perceive and express a sense of the clever or amusing. HUMOR consists principally in the recognition and expression of incongruities or peculiarities present in a situation or character. It is frequently used to illustrate some fundamental absurdity in human nature or conduct, and is generally thought of as a kindly trait: *a genial and mellow type of humor.* WIT is a purely intellectual, often spontaneous, manifestation of cleverness and quickness in discovering analogies between things really unlike, and expressing them in brief, diverting, and often sharp observations or remarks: *known for her quick and biting wit.* **4** See SPOIL. **—Ant. 1, 2** seriousness, gravity, solemnity, sobriety; sadness, grief, sorrow, melancholy. **4** stand up to, oppose, fight; aggravate, rouse, arouse, excite.

humorous *adj.* funny, comic, comical, full of humor, witty, droll, mirthful, laughable, amusing, sidesplitting, ribtickling, facetious, waggish, whimsical, sportive, jocular, jocose, farcical, satirical; ludicrous, ridiculous, nonsensical. **—Ant.** unfunny, grave, serious, solemn, sober; sad, melancholy; earnest, matter-of-fact.

hump *n.* **1.** protuberance on the back, hunch; bulge, lump, bump, mound, prominence, rise, swelling, convexity, projection, excrescence; knob, knurl. **—*v.* 2.** arch, hunch, raise in a hump, lift, bend, put up; tense.

hunch *n.* **1.** intuition, feeling, foreboding, premonition, presentiment; idea, good idea, suspicion, inkling, clue, glimmer. **—*v.* 2.** bend, hump, arch, tense.

hunger *n.* **1.** desire for food, hungriness, appetite, ravenousness, voracity; famine, starvation, malnutrition, lack of food. **2.** craving, greed, greediness, desire, lust, itch, yearning, yen, appetite, thirst, *Informal* hankering; fondness, liking, love, relish. **—*v.* 3.** long for, desire, crave, burn for, have an appetite for, wish, want, thirst after, lust after, yearn for; *Informal* itch for, pant for, have a yen for, hanker. **—Ant. 1** satiety, fullness; overeating. **2** repulsion, revulsion, disgust, repugnance, loathing, abhorrence, aversion, detestation, disgust, hatred.

hunk *n.* chunk, piece, block, gobbet, clod, lump; *Informal* wad, gob, glob; quantity, portion, mass.

hunt *v.* **1.** shoot, go after, chase, track, stalk, trail, seek; drive out, ferret out. **2.** pursue, chase, track, trail, trace, follow the trail of, stalk, follow the scent of, look for, search for, seek, try to find, look high and low for, go in quest of, follow; turn everything upside down, leave no stone unturned, peer into every corner; explore, probe, inquire into. **—*n.* 3.** chase, hunting; fox hunt, riding to hounds, course, coursing.

hurdle *n.* **1.** barrier, obstacle; (*in steeplechase racing*) fence, hedge, wall. **2.** obstacle, barrier, difficulty, hindrance, impediment, obstruction, roadblock, hazard, stumbling block, snag, interference. —*v.* **3.** jump, leap, vault, bound, surmount, spring over, clear.

hurl *v.* throw, fling, cast, sling, pitch, heave, chuck, toss, project, let fly; propel, launch, discharge, fire off. —**Ant.** catch, capture, seize; grasp, clutch, grab; take, receive.

hurrah Also **hurray, hooray** *interj.* **1.** good, fine, wonderful, excellent, great, bravo, heaven be praised, hallelujah, hosanna. —*n.* **2.** shout of joy, cry of acclaim, cheer, bravo, exaltation; acclaim, congratulation, salute; *Archaic* huzza, huzzah.

hurricane *n.* violent tropical storm, (*in the western Pacific*) typhoon; tempest, windstorm, cyclone, monsoon.

hurried *adj.* hasty, fast, speedy, rushed, pressed for time; impulsive, precipitate, headlong; frantic, frenetic, feverish, hectic, breakneck; cursory, superficial, slapdash, haphazard, slipshod, careless. —**Ant.** leisurely, slow, studied, thorough, deliberate.

hurry *v.* **1.** go quickly, come quickly, move fast, move hastily, hasten, make haste, speed, speed up, accelerate, rush, hustle, get a move on; bolt, dart, dash, scurry, scuttle, scramble, whiz, zip, make time, make tracks, step along, step on it, step on the gas, push on, press on, get hopping, get cracking, cover the ground, go like the wind, go like a shot, go like sixty, lose no time. **2.** urge on, goad, prod, drive on, push on, pressure, *Informal* egg on; rush, speed up, accelerate. —*n.* **3.** rush, haste, scurry; hustle and bustle, fuss, flurry, flutter, stew, hurry-scurry, tumult, turmoil, commotion, ado. —**Ant. 1** delay, slow down, slacken; procrastinate, dawdle, dally; move slowly, creep, crawl. **2** delay, slow, slow down, retard, detain. **3** slowness; composure, calmness.

hurt *v.* **1.** pain, ache, smart, sting, burn; torment, distress, agonize, torture. **2.** injure, harm, disable, maim, cripple, lame, mangle, mutilate, impair, damage, maul; bruise, cut, scratch, scar, mar, mark, disfigure, deface. **3.** hamper, impair, hinder, hold back, encumber, impede, retard, restrain, limit, frustrate, inhibit, weaken, obstruct, oppose, spike, check, thwart, foil, block, preclude, exclude, balk, forestall; decrease, lessen, reduce, diminish, lower, narrow, minimize. **4.** offend, sting, wound one's feelings, aggrieve, grieve, distress, trouble, cut to the quick. —*adj.* **5.** injured, bruised, cut, scratched; scarred, marked; disabled, crippled, lame; mangled, mutilated, damaged; painful, aching, smarting. **6.** offended, resentful, indignant, pained, wounded, injured, stung, piqued, miffed, crushed; distressed, crestfallen, dismayed, disheartened, aggrieved, mortified, chagrined; morose, melancholy, heartbroken, miserable, wretched, heartsick, dejected. —*n.* **7.** pain, soreness, ache, pang, sting, discomfort. **8.** pain, discomfort, sting, pique, resentment, mortification, embarrassment, chagrin, aggravation, annoyance; distress, suffering, misery, dismay, dejection, grief, heartbreak, wretchedness, torment, agony. —**Ant. 1** relieve, alleviate, assuage, soothe. **2** heal, cure; repair, fix, restore. **3** help, aid, abet, benefit, forward, promote, advance, expedite; increase, multiply, heighten, widen. **4** console, calm, soothe; please, compliment, compensate. **5** relieved, alleviated, assuaged, soothed; healed, cured; repaired, fixed, restored. **6** consoled, calmed, soothed, placated, complimented. **8** happiness, pleasure, joy, delight, ecstasy; pride, gratification, satisfaction.

hurtle *v.* speed, fly, race, plunge, charge, rush, spurt, shoot, tear, scoot, whiz, zip; run, hie, whisk, gallop, lunge, scamper, scurry, scuttle, bolt, dash, dart, bound; go like the wind, go like a shot, go lickety-split. —**Ant.** crawl, creep, inch, drag, go at a snail's pace.

husband *n.* **1.** spouse, hubby, mate, man, consort, *Slang* old man; groom, bridegroom; married man. —*v.* **2.** conserve, preserve, use sparingly, manage wisely; save, set aside, retain, store, save up, keep, maintain; hoard, accumulate, amass. —**Ant. 1** bachelor. **2** waste, squander, spend.

hush *interj.* **1.** be quiet, be still, be silent, quiet down, silence, quiet; *Informal* shut up, shush, pipe down, keep mum, *Slang* knock it off, sit on it. —*v.* **2.** quiet, shush, quell, silence, still; soothe, calm, mollify. —*n.* **3.** silence, stillness; quiet, quietude, quietness, peacefulness, tranquillity. —**Ant. 3** racket, din, noise, clamor.

husky *adj.* **1.** big, strong, robust, muscular, brawny, sturdy, strapping, stocky, burly, hefty, thickset, solid, broad-shouldered, powerful, athletic, strong as an ox; stout, beefy, overweight, plump. **2.** hoarse, harsh, rough, coarse, gruff, rasping, grating, guttural, throaty, raucous, croaking, cracked, thick. —**Ant. 1** small, puny, weak; thin, slim, underweight. **2** shrill.

hussy *n.* strumpet, brazen woman, brash girl, saucy miss, wench, minx; loose woman, jade, bawd, woman of easy virtue, adulteress, trollop, baggage, wanton; prostitute, harlot, tart, whore, lewd woman, fallen woman, scarlet woman.

hustle *v.* **1.** hurry, hasten, make haste, rush, speed up, move quickly, bolt, dart, dash, scurry, scuttle, scoot, scramble, make time, step on it, step along, fly, lose no time. **2.** be aggressive, work energetically, *Slang* be an eager beaver, be on the ball. **3.** push, shove, nudge, elbow, prod, jostle, shoulder, bounce, throw, toss. —*n.* **4.** energetic action, bustle, stir, hurry, scurry, rush, flutter, flurry, fuss, tumult, turmoil, commotion, scramble, hubbub, ado, hurry-scurry. **—Ant. 1** procrastinate, dawdle, dally. **2** relax, take it easy. **4** calmness, composure; peace, quiet, tranquillity.

hut *n.* shack, shanty, shelter, hutch, shed, lean-to, log cabin, cabin, cottage. **—Ant.** mansion, palace, castle, manor.

hutch *n.* pen, coop, cage, enclosure, shed, sty, cote, stall, crib.

hybrid *n.* crossbreed, cross, half-breed; mixture, composite, amalgam; six of one and half a dozen of the other, neither one nor the other. **—Ant.** thoroughbred.

hygienic *adj.* clean, sanitary, germ-free, prophylactic, sterile, disinfected, pure, unpolluted, uncontaminated, disease-free, aseptic; healthful, healthy, salutary, salubrious, wholesome; harmless, uninjurious. **—Ant.** unsanitary, contaminated, infected, dirty, impure, polluted; unhealthy, harmful.

hymn *n.* song in praise of God, anthem, psalm, paean, devotional song; song of praise.

hyperbole *n.* overstatement, exaggeration, enlargement, magnification, extravagant statement, figurative statement, stretch of the imagination; figure of speech, metaphor. **—Ant.** understatement.

hypocrisy *n.* insincerity, falsity, two-facedness, fakery, dissembling, duplicity, *Slang* phoniness; dishonesty, deceit, mendacity. **—Ant.** sincerity, truthfulness, honesty, frankness, candor, forthrightness.

hypocrite *n.* insincere person, false person, two-faced person, pretender, *Slang* phony; deceiver, dissembler.

hypocritical *adj.* insincere, false, two-faced, dishonest, deceitful, deceptive, truthless, feigning, feigned, counterfeit, false, *Slang* phony. **—Ant.** sincere, heartfelt, unfeigned, genuine, honest; forthright, plainspoken.

hypothesis *n.* theory, thesis, theorem, premise, assumption, postulate, proposition, assertion, presumption, proposal, conjecture, speculation, supposition, explanation, conclusion, guesstimate. **—Syn. Study.** See THEORY.

hypothetical *adj.* supposed, assumed, presumptive, theoretical, speculative, conjectural, possible, imaginary, suppositional, contingent, postulated; conditional, uncertain, questionable, dubious. **—Ant.** real, actual, true; certain, proved, proven, demonstrated, tested, tried, confirmed, established, substantiated, verified.

hysteria *n.* emotional outburst, hysterics, delirium, fit, frenzy; uncontrolled fear, panic, uncontrolled weeping.

hysterical *adj.* **1.** overcome with fear, distraught, beside oneself, distracted, uncontrollable, frenzied, crazed, raving, worked-up, wrought-up, overwrought; *Informal* carried away, crazy, out of one's wits. **2.** wildly funny, uproarious, comical, laughable, farcical, ridiculous, absurd, ludicrous, amusing, droll. **—Ant. 1** calm, composed, poised, self-possessed. **2** sad, somber, serious, grave, melancholy.

ice-cold *adj.* icy, freezing, frigid, glacial, icelike, frosty, supercold, supercooled, gelid, freezing cold, cold as ice, stone-cold; subzero, arctic, hyperborean, Siberian, polar. **—Ant.** hot, sultry, torrid, blistering, scorching, white-hot.

icky *adj.* **1.** sticky, gummy, gooey, gucky, tacky, gluey; viscid, glutinous, mucilaginous, viscous, syrupy. **2.** repulsive, nasty, offensive, disgusting, revolting, *Slang* gross; maudlin, mushy, pathetic, weepy.

iconoclast *n.* dissenter, rebel, nonconformist, upstart, radical, revolutionary. **—Ant.** conformist, assenter.

icy *adj.* **1.** frozen over, glazed, slippery, sleety; cold, frigid, frozen, freezing, bitterly chilly, wintry, brumal, glacial, arctic, raw, bitingly cold, frosty, gelid. **2.** hostile, unfriendly, cold, forbidding, without warmth or feeling, frigid, frosty, distant, impassive, aloof, haughty, cool, unemotional, coldhearted, glacial, chilly, chilling. **—Ant. 2** warm, friendly, gracious, sympathetic, cordial.

idea *n.* **1.** concept, mental picture, thought, conception, insight, interpretation, apperception, appreciation, conception, notion, belief. **2.** hint, inkling, clue, indication, intimation, impression, approximation, suggestion, notion. **3.** proposal, suggestion, approach, solution, recommendation. **4.** view, feeling, understanding, sentiment, opinion, impression, conclusion, outlook, conviction, belief. **—Syn. Study. 1** IDEA, THOUGHT, CONCEPTION, NOTION refer to a product of mental activity. IDEA refers to a mental representation that is the product of understanding or creative imagination: *She had an excellent idea for the party.* THOUGHT emphasizes the intellectual processes of reasoning, contemplating, reflecting, or recollecting: *I welcomed his thoughts on the subject.* CONCEPTION suggests imaginative, creative, and somewhat intricate mental activity: *The architect's conception of the building was a glass skyscraper.* NOTION suggests a fleeting, vague, or imperfect thought: *I had only a bare notion of how to proceed.*

ideal *n.* **1.** aim, objective, ultimate aim, optimal goal, ultimate end, highest goal; level of perfection, highest attainment. **2.** model, hero, idol, inspiration, standard, perfect model, epitome, standard of excellence; exemplar, last word, ultimate, criterion, paradigm, pattern, model, archetype; primary aim, objective, dream, chief hope, target of one's efforts. *—adj.* **3.** perfect, absolutely suitable, meeting every need or desire, exemplary, optimal, excellent, faultless, impeccable, matchless.

idealism *n.* belief in noble goals, persistent hopefulness, optimism, meliorism; wishful thinking, romanticism, utopianism. **—Ant.** realism, pragmatism, cynicism.

idealist *n.* **1.** persistent optimist, perfectionist. **2.** utopian, visionary, romantic, romanticist, dreamer, Pollyanna, stargazer. **—Ant. 1, 2** pragmatist, materialist, realist, skeptic, cynic.

identical *adj.* twin, duplicate, exactly alike, uniform, perfectly matched, indistinguishable, precisely corresponding, interchangeable, alike feature for feature; very same, one and the same, self-same; exactly as before, none other than. **—Ant.** diverse, different, disparate, contrary, divergent; distinct, separate, unlike, dissimilar.

identification *n.* **1.** establishment of identity; recognition, verification, confirmation, ascertainment; pinpointing, detection, revelation. **2.** assumed relationship, connection, association, affiliation. **3.** certificate of identity, credentials; (*variously*) proper papers, passport, identity book, identifying badge, label, or button; item or means of recognition.

identify *v.* **1.** recognize, know, distinguish, determine, place, designate, pick out, single out, tell the identity of, be sure of, verify, specify. **2.** associate, combine, attach by association, think of in connection, mention in the same breath, put in the same category; consider the same, consider to be intimately connected, regard as representative of. **3.** put oneself in the place of, feel empathy for, respond sympathetically to, take the point of view of. **—Ant. 1** mistake, confuse, overlook. **2** confuse, dissociate.

identity *n.* **1.** name, individuality, unique personal nature, delineation, social specificity. **2.** exact similarity, exact likeness, duplication, precise correspondence; oneness, accord, harmony, rapport, unanimity. **3.** individuality, distinctness of character, self, personality, self-perspective, distinctiveness, differentiation, personal uniqueness, social role. **—Ant. 2** difference, separateness, distinctness, contrariety.

ideology *n.* set of beliefs, body of concepts, principles, ideals, doctrine, theory, dogma, program, rationale, ethos, political philosophy.

idiocy *n.* **1.** cretinism, mongolism. **2.**

folly, senselessness, stupidity, absurdity, foolishness, foolhardiness, fatuity, abject silliness, inanity, asininity, insanity, madness, lunacy, utter rashness, suicide. —**Ant.** common sense, sense, sanity, wisdom, sagacity, judiciousness.

idiom *n.* **1.** phrase, characteristic expression, unique grammatical or semantic construction. **2.** language, mode of expression, characteristic style, parlance, speech; colloquialism, localism, dialect, argot, patois, vernacular, jargon, slang; lingo, brogue.

idiosyncrasy *n.* peculiar trait, peculiarity, eccentricity, quirk, unusual characteristic, unusual habit, anomaly, oddity, mannerism, distinction; personal mark. —**Syn. Study.** IDIOSYNCRASY, PECULIARITY, ECCENTRICITY, QUIRK all refer to some noticeable deviation in behavior, style, or manner from what is normal or expected. PECULIARITY is the most general of these words, referring to almost any perceptible oddity or departure from any norm: *a peculiarity of the language.* IDIOSYNCRASY refers to a variation in behavior or manner exclusive to or characteristic of a single individual: *idiosyncrasies of style that irritated editors but often delighted readers.* ECCENTRICITY usu. suggests a mildly amusing but harmless characteristic or style: *a whimsical eccentricity of dress.* QUIRK often refers to a minor, unimportant kind of oddity: *Her one quirk was a habit of writing long, rambling letters.* Sometimes QUIRK has overtones of strangeness: *sexual quirks.*

idiot *n.* **1.** helplessly feebleminded person, mental defective, cretin. **2.** foolish person, fool, simpleton, halfwit, dope, moron, dolt, ninny, ass, blockhead, damn fool, nitwit, dimwit, nincompoop, jerk, dummy, dumbbell, boob, dunce, numskull; *Slang* cluck. —**Ant. 1** genius, mastermind, prodigy.

idiotic *adj.* stupid, emptyheaded, absurd, asinine, moronic, feebleminded, imbecilic, stupidly clumsy or careless, ridiculous, rattlebrained, addled, doltish, halfwitted, foolish, foolhardy, irrational, senseless; *Informal* dopey, nutty, crazy. —**Ant.** intelligent, sensible, thoughtful, clever, sage, wise, brilliant, commonsensical.

idle *adj.* **1.** unemployed, lacking work, inactive, doing nothing, not working, unoccupied, out of work, jobless. **2.** not in operation, not being used, unused, not operating, doing nothing, gathering dust, inactive; fallow. **3.** indolent, sluggish, slothful, lazy, languid, somnolent, enervated, lethargic, inert, torpid, drowsy, listless, otiose; at leisure. **4.** baseless, worthless, empty, vapid, unsubstantiated, petty, trifling, trivial, valueless, vain, useless, unproductive; fruitless, futile, bootless, pointless, aimless, unimportant, good-for-nothing. —*v.* **5.** fritter, spend in idleness, pass lazily, while, wait out, putter, loaf, fool away, laze, waste, loiter, dally, dawdle. —**Syn. Study. 3** IDLE, INDOLENT, LAZY, SLOTHFUL apply to a person who is not active. IDLE means to be inactive or not working at a job; it is not necessarily derogatory: *pleasantly idle on a vacation.* INDOLENT means naturally disposed to avoid exertion: *an indolent and contented fisherman.* LAZY means averse to exertion or work, and esp. to continued application; the word is usu. derogatory: *too lazy to earn a living.* SLOTHFUL denotes a reprehensible unwillingness to do one's share; it describes a person who is slow-moving and lacking in energy: *The heat made the workers slothful.* **5** See LOITER. —**Ant. 1** active, employed, working, occupied, busy. **2** operative, operating, functioning, actuated, working, active. **3** energetic, industrious, busy, wide-awake, active. **4** important, meaningful, profitable, worthwhile, significant, advantageous, productive, beneficial, useful, purposeful, effective, fruitful.

idol *n.* **1.** religious effigy, icon, graven image, statue, effigy, simulacrum; artifact, relic. **2.** popular hero, popular figure, darling, public favorite; inspiration, adored person, hero, guiding light; person toward whom one directs one's aspirations; godlike figure.

idolatry *n.* **1.** worship of an object, image-worship, reverence of idols, idolization. **2.** inordinate love, worship, adoration, obsession, preoccupation, excessive fondness, passion, devotion, veneration, single-minded attention, infatuation, senseless attachment, madness, mania.

idolize *v.* **1.** worship, adore, venerate, revere, reverence, bow down before, deify, apotheosize. **2.** adore, love to excess, admire, honor, worship, dote loyally upon, treasure, give up one's heart to, prize; *Slang* go bananas over, be nuts about. —**Ant. 2** despise, scorn, disdain.

idyllic *adj.* peaceful, rustic, pastoral, arcadian, sylvan, bucolic, charmingly simple, unspoiled, romantic.

iffy *adj.* doubtful, unsettled, uncertain, dubious, unresolved, speculative, problematical, moot, conjectural, unsure, questionable, chancy, risky; capricious, erratic, whimsical, unpredictable. —**Ant.** certain, sure, sure-fire, settled, decided.

ignite *v.* **1.** set on fire, set fire to, fire, kindle, light, inflame, touch off; explode, blow up. **2.** catch fire, catch on fire, burn, take fire, blaze, flame. —**Syn.**

Study. 1 See KINDLE. —Ant. 1 stifle, extinguish, quench, douse.

ignoble *adj.* despicable, infamous, heinous, shameful, dishonorable, base, contemptible, nefarious, vile, dastardly, low, unconscionable, foul, degraded, mean, depraved, cowardly, pusillanimous, craven, degenerate, disgraceful, debased, inferior, discreditable, unworthy, indecent. —Ant. admirable, commendable, laudable, meritorious, lofty, sublime, glorious, splendid, distinguished, honorable, superior, exalted, grand, notable, fine, worthy, praiseworthy.

ignominious *adj.* humiliating, shameful, inglorious, disgraceful, wretched, degrading, abject, sorry, low, dishonorable, causing dishonor, discreditable, disreputable, despicable, grievous, unbearable. —Ant. creditable, honorable, reputable, admirable, estimable, worthy.

ignominy *n.* —Syn. Study. See DISGRACE.

ignoramus *n.* simpleton, fool, dunce, know-nothing, low-brow, numskull, nitwit, illiterate.

ignorance *n.* illiteracy, lack of knowledge or education, lack of learning, backwardness, mental darkness; unawareness, obliviousness, unenlightenment, confusion, lack of perception, unacquaintance, unfamiliarity. —Ant. knowledge, education, wisdom, sense, learning, erudition; comprehension, insight, perception, empathy, understanding.

ignorant *adj.* **1.** uneducated, unlearned, illiterate, lacking knowledge, unschooled, unlettered, unenlightened, untaught, untrained, untutored; naive, unworldly. **2.** uninformed, unknowing, innocent, unaware, unperceptive, insensitive, unknowledgeable, blind to, uncognizant, in the dark about. **3.** unintelligent, shallow, irresponsible, insensitive, foolishly uninformed; fatuous, asinine, dumb, stupid. —Syn. Study. 1 IGNORANT, UNEDUCATED, ILLITERATE mean lacking in knowledge or training. IGNORANT may mean knowing little or nothing, or it may mean uninformed about a particular subject: *An ignorant person can be dangerous. I confess I'm ignorant of higher mathematics.* UNEDUCATED particularly refers to lack of schooling: *an intelligent but uneducated clerk.* ILLITERATE most often means unable to read or write; however, it sometimes means not well-read or not well versed in literature: *classes for illiterate soldiers; an illiterate mathematician.* —Ant. 1 educated, instructed, learned, well-informed, wise, lettered, literate, cultured, cultivated. 2 aware, conscious, informed, briefed, knowledgeable, knowing. 3 sagacious, perceptive, astute, knowledgeable, wise, brilliant, sage.

ignore *v.* take no notice of, refrain from noticing, disregard, be oblivious to, pay no attention to, turn one's back on, pay no heed to, shut one's eyes to, brush aside, scorn, neglect, slight, eschew, give the cold shoulder to, snub; pass over, skip, omit, overlook. —Ant. heed, acknowledge, notice, note, regard, recognize, mark, attend.

ill *adj.* **1.** sick, sickly, unwell, ailing, unsound, poorly, afflicted, diseased, unhealthy, indisposed; failing, invalid, laid up, under the weather. **2.** evil, harmful, wicked, vile, foul, peevish, surly, cross; malicious, unkind, vengeful, acrimonious. **3.** unfavorable, boding bad luck, sinister, disturbing, unpropitious, unlucky, inauspicious, threatening, foreboding, ominous. —*n.* **4. ills.** affliction, ailment, disease, plague, complaint, malady, infirmity; woe, trouble, sorrow, slings and arrows, misfortune, trial. **5.** wickedness, malice, evil, mischief, abomination, cruelty, abuse, outrage, ill-treatment, ill-usage, harm, injury, damage, malefaction. —*adv.* **6.** not well, scarcely, hardly; by no means, nowise, noway. —Syn. Study. 1 ILL, SICK mean being in bad health, not being well. ILL is the more formal word. In American English the two words are used practically interchangeably except that SICK is always used when the word modifies a noun that follows it: *He looks sick* (*ill*); *a sick person.* In British English SICK is not interchangeable with ILL, but usu. has the connotation of nauseous: *She got sick and threw up.* SICK, however, is used before nouns just as in American English: *a sick man.* —Ant. 1 well, hale, healthy, strong, vigorous, robust. 2 kind, generous, selfless; favorable, complimentary, flattering. 5 good, beneficence, decency, honor, kindness. 6 well, easily, effortlessly, handily.

ill-advised *adj.* ill-considered, imprudent, unwise, injudicious, shortsighted, indiscreet, impolitic, ill-judged, myopic, unthinking, misguided; foolish, irresponsible, senseless, dumb, stupid, silly. —Ant. wise, prudent, sensible, smart, judicious.

ill-at-ease *adj.* uneasy, uncomfortable, disquieted, bothered, nervous, troubled, perturbed, disturbed, discomfited, on edge, discomposed, edgy; shy, selfconscious, embarrassed, nonplused, abashed, disconcerted, discountenanced. —Ant. self-assured, self-confident, positive, poised.

illegal *adj.* unlawful, against the law, not legal, prohibited, unsanctioned, proscribed, forbidden, banned, illicit, unauthorized; illegitimate, criminal, felonious, actionable, outlawed; against the rules, wrong. —**Syn. Study.** ILLEGAL, UNLAWFUL, ILLICIT, CRIMINAL describe actions not in accord with law. ILLEGAL refers to violation of statutes or, in games, codified rules: *an illegal seizure of property; an illegal block in football.* UNLAWFUL is a broader term that may refer to lack of conformity with any set of laws or precepts, whether natural, moral, or traditional: *an unlawful transaction.* ILLICIT most often applies to matters regulated by law, with emphasis on the way things are carried out: *the illicit sale of narcotics.* CRIMINAL refers to violation of a public law that is punishable by a fine or imprisonment: *Robbery is a criminal act.* —**Ant.** legal, licit, lawful, authorized, permissible, sanctioned.

illegible *adj.* unreadable, impossible to read, indecipherable, undecipherable, scribbled, unintelligible; obscured, hard to make out, unclear. —**Ant.** legible, readable, clear, intelligible.

illegitimate *adj.* **1.** illegal, improper, not legitimate, unwarranted, unlawful, illicit, unauthorized, lawless, unsanctioned, prohibited. **2.** bastard, natural, baseborn, misbegotten. —**Ant. 1** legitimate, lawful, legal. **2** legitimate.

ill-fated *adj.* unfortunate, doomed to disaster, ill-omened, ill-starred, doomed, luckless, blighted, unlucky, hapless, destined to end unhappily; jinxed.

illiberal *adj.* intolerant, narrow-minded, biased, prejudiced, hidebound, brassbound, small-minded, bigoted, shortsighted, small, narrow, opinionated, petty, ungenerous. —**Ant.** broadminded, liberal, tolerant, unprejudiced.

illicit *adj.* unlawful, not legal, illegal, against the law, illegitimate, impermissible, not permitted, criminal, felonious, lawless, prohibited, improper, unauthorized; clandestine; under-the-counter, black-market. —**Syn. Study.** See ILLEGAL. —**Ant.** licit, lawful, legal, legalized, legitimate, permissible, authorized; aboveboard, out in the open.

illiterate *adj.* **1.** unable to read and write, unlettered, ignorant, uneducated, unlearned, not educated, unschooled. **2.** badly written, ungrammatical, childish, amateurish, ludicrously bad, unscholarly, unreliable, witless, incoherent. **3.** ignorant, unknowledgeable, uninstructed, untutored, uninitiated, unversed, uninformed, unenlightened. —**Syn. Study. 1** See IGNORANT. —**Ant.** literate, taught, instructed, educated, schooled, informed, knowledgeable, expert.

ill-mannered *adj.* rude, impolite, discourteous, disrespectful, uncivil, ungracious, ungallant, ill-bred, ill-behaved; boorish, coarse, offensive, loutish, crude. —**Ant.** gracious, well-bred, well-mannered, courteous, respectful.

ill-natured *adj.* ill-humored, unfriendly, quarrelsome, antagonistic, cross, peevish, captious, contentious, grouchy, cranky, irritable, cantankerous, crotchety, surly, churlish. —**Ant.** congenial, agreeable, amiable, likable, cordial.

illness *n.* sickness, malady, disorder, disease, indisposition, ailment, infirmity, disability, affliction; complaint, malfunction; ill health, poor health. —**Ant.** health, robustness, wholesomeness, salubriousness, salubrity, hardiness.

illogical *adj.* inconsistent, unreasonable, fallacious, contradictory, erroneous, incongruent, incongruous; unsound, preposterous, absurd; *Slang* nutty, screwy, dopey, wacky, far-out. —**Ant.** orderly, coherent, logical, reasonable.

ill-suited *adj.* inappropriate, unsuitable, unsuited, malapropos, inapt, ill-matched, mismatched, misjoined, mismated, unbecoming, unbefitting, ill-adapted, uncongenial, inconsistent, incompatible. —**Ant.** apt, becoming, suitable, appropriate, congenial.

ill-tempered *adj.* peevish, cross, petulant, waspish, cantankerous, crotchety, ill-humored, ill-natured, *Brit.* shirty, cranky, testy, irritable, grouchy. —**Ant.** amiable, agreeable, amenable, pleasant.

illuminate *v.* **1.** light up, fill or supply with light, light, illumine, irradiate, brighten, cast light upon. **2.** clarify, explain, make understandable or lucid, make clear, throw light on, elucidate, enhance, spell out; give insight into; edify, enlighten, instruct; exemplify. —**Ant. 1** darken, obliterate, becloud, benight, cloud, obscure.

illumination *n.* **1.** illuminating, irradiation, illumining, lighting up. **2.** lights, lighting, light fixtures, lighting equipment; source of light. **3.** enlightenment, knowledge, perception, revelation, insight, wisdom, comprehension; information, instruction, edification, education. —**Ant. 1** darkening, adumbration, dimming, obscuring.

illusion *n.* **1.** semblance, misleading visual impression, optical illusion, unreality, deceiving appearance; impression, vision, false image, mirage; chimera, hallucination, apparition, phantasm, delusion, deception; hocus-pocus, humbuggery. **2.** false belief, false idea, erroneous impression, mistaken idea, delusion, misconception, misimpression, fallacy, misbelief, error, misapprehension, fancy, caprice, vagary. —**Ant. 1** reality, substantiation, actuality, truth.

illusory *adj.* unreal, illusive, deceptive, delusive, false, fallacious, spurious, erroneous, misleading, imaginary, fanciful, unrealistic, hallucinatory, sham, counterfeit; ostensible, apparent, seeming. —**Ant.** substantial, real, true.

illustrate *v.* **1.** make clear, explain, make intelligible, elucidate, throw light on, illuminate, define, clarify; emphasize, bring home, point up; demonstrate, show. **2.** ornament, provide with illustrations, decorate, adorn with pictures, pictorialize, portray, delineate; paint or draw illustrations for; represent, picture.

illustration *n.* **1.** picture, photograph, portrayal, drawing, figure, representation, image; plate. **2.** example, instance, typical occurrence, pertinent case, representative sample, specimen, exemplification.

illustrious *adj.* **1.** highly notable, famous, famed, eminent, renowned, celebrated, prominent, widely admired; of the first rank, distinguished, honored, acclaimed. **2.** distinguished, brilliant, splendid, lustrous, great, glorious, magnificent; exemplary, matchless, peerless.

ill-will *n.* malice, antipathy, hostility, enmity, aversion, dislike, animosity, rancor, spleen, antagonism, gall, abhorrence, animus, malevolence, hatred, loathing, bad blood. —**Ant.** goodwill, cordiality, friendliness, benevolence.

image *n.* **1.** representation, likeness, facsimile, copy, picture, pictorialization; effigy, portrait, figure, delineation, depiction; artistic or mechanical reproduction, photograph, semblance, simulacrum. **2.** reflection, mirroring, reflected appearance, likeness, semblance, countenance, visage. **3.** memory, recollection, concept, idea, mental picture. **4.** copy, duplicate, reproduction, replica, double, facsimile, incarnation. **5.** literary comparison; figure of speech; simile; metaphor; symbol. **6.** idol, fetish, icon, statue, effigy, graven image.

imaginary *adj.* **1.** unreal, invented, made-up, fictitious, fancied, fanciful; illusory, fantastic, fabulous, mythical, legendary, figmental, factitious, dreamed up; sham, counterfeit; *Slang* phony. —*n.* **2.** fanciful, romantic; fiction, fancy, illusion, delusion, figment, make-believe. —**Ant. 1** real, actual, corporeal, true, factual.

imagination *n.* **1.** inventiveness, fancy, invention; creativity, creative thought; power to picture mentally. **2.** resourcefulness, thought, ingenuity, inventiveness, thoughtfulness, creativeness, enterprise, creative use of resources; cunning, astuteness.

imaginative *adj.* original, creative, innovative, inventive; inspired, clever, ingenious; off the beaten path; unusual, out of the ordinary; enterprising, resourceful. —**Ant.** unimaginative, unromantic, literal, uninventive, ordinary, pedestrian, commonplace, unoriginal, uncreative, uninspired, prosaic, mundane, run-of-the-mill.

imagine *v.* **1.** envision, picture, pretend, conceive, project, visualize, envisage, dream up, fantasize. **2.** presume, gather, assume, suppose, should think, believe, guess, conjecture, infer, judge, surmise; take for granted; suspect, fancy.

imbecile *n.* **1.** fool, foolish person, idiot, nitwit, ass, jerk, dumbbell, dummy, dope, simpleton, moron, dunce, nincompoop, ninny, blockhead, dolt; *Slang* dingbat. —*adj.* **2.** Also **imbecilic.** foolish, dumb, stupid, asinine, silly, absurd, inane; careless, mindless, thoughtless.

imbibe *v.* consume, drink, quaff, ingest, swallow; tope, tipple, partake; (*variously*) guzzle, sip, swig, slug, swill, drain, toss down, wash down, *Slang* chug-a-lug, chug, belt. —**Syn. Study.** See DRINK.

imbue *v.* **1.** inspire, fill, endow, impress, instill, inculcate, infuse, ingrain; fire, arouse, animate. **2.** tinge, tint, color, tincture, bathe, steep, suffuse, permeate, pervade.

imitate *v.* **1.** follow the pattern of, copy in manner, fashion oneself after, mirror, take as a model, simulate, follow in the steps of, emulate, reproduce the image of. **2.** mimic, impersonate, do a takeoff on, act in imitation of, ape, parrot, represent, mime, parody, caricature. **3.** simulate, have the appearance of, copy, reproduce closely, duplicate, pass for, look like, counterfeit.

imitation *n.* **1.** simulation, copy of an original, counterfeit, fake, semblance, reproduction, facsimile, similarity; duplication. **2.** impersonation, impression, burlesque, mimicry, parody, takeoff, travesty, caricature, representation, adaptation, aping. —*adj.* **3.** simulated, fake, ersatz, phony, make-believe, mock, sham; synthetic, artificial, man-made. —**Ant. 3** real, actual, true, genuine.

immaculate *adj.* **1.** spotless, spic and span, impeccably clean and neat; unstained, unsoiled, stainless, untarnished, unsullied, shipshape. **2.** above reproach, faultless, morally blameless, pure, clean, virtuous, guiltless, perfect, ideal, unexceptionable, unimpeachable, intact, flawless, irreproachable, unsullied; innocent, sinless, saintly, chaste, virgin, virginal. —**Ant. 1** dirty, filthy, spotted, unclean, stained, sullied. **2** impure, corrupt, sinful, contaminated, defiled, polluted, tainted, spotted, filthy, tarnished, sullied, impeachable, blameworthy.

immanent *adj.* inherent, natural, inbred, innate, inborn, indigenous, intrinsic; ingrained, deep-rooted, congenital, instinctive, instinctual, deep-seated, indwelling. **—Ant.** extrinsic, alien, extraneous, acquired, superimposed.

immaterial *adj.* **1.** of no importance, not relevant, irrelevant, inconsequential, insignificant, extraneous, unimportant, of minor importance, trifling, trivial, matter of indifference, of no moment, having no bearing, of little account. **2.** spiritual, incorporeal, noumenal, bodiless, insubstantial, unsubstantial, impalpable, intangible, unbodied, unearthly, extramundane, ghostly, ethereal, evanescent, spectral, disembodied, shadowy, extrasensory, mystical. **—Ant. 1** relevant, significant, germane, important, essential, vital, crucial. **2** material, physical, real, tangible, corporeal, palpable, earthly.

immature *adj.* **1.** embryonic, unripe, young, youthful, rudimentary, infantile, pubescent, unformed, half-grown, not mature, undeveloped, unfinished; unmellowed, out of season, green. **2.** childish, juvenile, callow, puerile, infantile, babyish; *Informal* wet behind the ears, kiddish. **—Ant. 1** mature, adult, ripe, mellow, developed, full-fledged. **2** adult, mature, grown-up, responsible.

immeasurable *adj.* beyond measure, limitless, inestimable, incalculable, measureless, fathomless, immense, unlimited, illimitable, infinite, unbounded, boundless, unfathomable; interminable, endless, never-ending, inexhaustible. **—Ant.** measurable, finite, limited, circumscribed, restricted, bounded, specific; exact.

immediate *adj.* **1.** prompt, undelayed, instant, instantaneous, express, done without delay, sudden, abrupt, swift, speedy, hasty, punctual. **2.** next, near, adjacent, close, local, nearby, nearest, proximate, contiguous, nigh, not distant; recent. **—Ant. 1** delayed, postponed, leisurely, unhurried, slow, relaxed, late, tardy. **2** distant, peripheral, far, remote.

immediately *adv.* instantly, directly, promptly, quickly, instantaneously, without delay, posthaste, here and now. **—Syn. Study.** See INSTANTLY.

immemorial *adj.* ancient, timeless, dateless, olden, time-honored, ancestral, venerable, ageless, mythological, legendary, long-established, hallowed, longstanding.

immense *adj.* vast, enormous, monstrous, stupendous, extensive, measureless, great, tremendous, huge, massive, gigantic, prodigious, mammoth, colossal, Brobdingnagian, *Slang* humongous. **—Syn. Study.** See HUGE. **—Ant.** small, tiny, minute, wee, diminutive, petite, sparse, spare.

immerse *v.* **1.** submerge, dip, lower, dunk, duck, douse, drench, steep, soak, bathe, sink, plunge. **2.** involve deeply, absorb, occupy, be caught up in, engage, engross, preoccupy with, concentrate on. **—Syn. Study. 1** See DIP.

immigrate *v.* migrate, move to, relocate in; settle, colonize. **—Ant.** emigrate; leave, depart from.

imminent *adj.* impending, approaching, close at hand, near, immediate, near at hand; threatening, perilous, looming, menacing. **—Ant.** distant, future; delayed.

immobile *adj.* **1.** immovable, fixed, stationary, fast, secure, steadfast, riveted, rooted, unbudgeable, stable; rigid, stiff. **2.** incapacitated, laid up, motionless, not moving, still, quiet, quiescent, static, at rest, stock-still, immobilized. **—Ant. 1** mobile, portable, movable, transportable. **2** active, vigorous, up and about, on the move.

immoderate *adj.* excessive, extravagant, prodigious, unreasonable, unbridled, inordinate, uncalled-for, intemperate, extreme, exorbitant, unconscionable, undue, unrestrained, gargantuan, whopping, mind-boggling. **—Ant.** moderate; temperate; restrained, curbed, checked, inhibited; reasonable, rational, prudent, cautious, judicious, sensible.

immodest *adj.* **1.** indecorous, overly revealing, indecent, indelicate, shameless; lewd, loose, suggestive, indecent, risqué; coarse, gross, wanton, unchaste. **2.** vain, exaggerated, inflated, pompous, conceited, high-sounding, brazen, self-centered, self-aggrandizing, braggart, bombastic, boastful, pretentious, peacockish. **—Ant. 1** modest, decent, delicate, decorous, pure, chaste. **2** modest, humble, genteel, restrained.

immoral *adj.* unethical, unprincipled, corrupt, evil, wrong, vicious, wicked, profoundly bad, iniquitous, sinful, infamous, nefarious, heinous, profligate, dissipated, dissolute; sexually arousing, lewd, prurient, debauched, depraved, obscene, licentious, salacious, indecent; pornographic; *Informal* dirty, raunchy. **—Ant.** moral, upright, virtuous, law-abiding, conscientious, good, honorable, ethical, chaste, pure, clean, inoffensive.

immortal *adj.* **1.** undying, not mortal, eternal, everlasting, divine, deathless, imperishable, lasting through all time, enduring, abiding. *—n.* **2. Immortals** the gods, (*specifically*) the members of the Greek and Roman pantheon. **3.** monumental figure, titan, giant, all-time great; demigod, great, illustrious name. **—Ant. 1** mortal; transitory, fleeting, fugitive, ephemeral, evanescent, transient, short-lived, passing; fly-by-night.

immovable *adj.* **1.** unmovable, fixed,

set, settled, fast, secure, immobile, stationary, unbudgeable, fastened. **2.** unyielding in purpose, unchangeable, stubborn, obdurate, not to be put off, fixed, inflexible, stolid, inexorable, unbendable, adamant, resolute, dogged; unfeeling, impassive, unimpressionable, heartless, steely, coldhearted, icy, cold, unsympathetic, unimpressible, detached. **—Ant. 1** movable, portable, transportable, yielding. **2** flexible, persuadable, swayable, open-minded, reasonable, irresolute, changeable.

immune *adj.* **1.** resistant, unsusceptible, protected, safe, invulnerable, unthreatened by, not in danger of. **2.** exempt, free, not affected by, not liable to, not subject to, at liberty, clear, not vulnerable. **—Ant. 1** subject, vulnerable, exposed, susceptible; unprotected, unsafe. **2** subject, liable.

immunity *n.* **—Syn. Study.** See EXEMPTION.

immutable *adj.* unchanging, unchangeable, changeless, unvarying, unaltered, unalterable, incontrovertible, unmodifiable, intransmutable; permanent, lasting, enduring, stable; firm, fixed, solid, constant, inflexible. **—Ant.** changeable, unstable, alterable, flexible, variable.

imp *n.* **1.** small demon, evil spirit, sprite, elf, pixie, gnome, hobgoblin, little goblin, little devil, leprechaun. **2.** mischievous child, harmlessly naughty child, brat, scamp, devil, rascal, urchin, hoyden, upstart.

impact *n.* **1.** collision, crash, smash, violent blow, force, concussion, contact, jolt. **2.** effect, brunt, influence, burden, shock, thrust; implication, repercussion.

impair *v.* hinder, damage, mar, hurt, vitiate, harm, cripple, subvert, injure, lessen, weaken, enfeeble, decrease, undercut, detract from, reduce; enervate, debilitate, worsen. **—Syn. Study.** See INJURE. **—Ant.** improve, amend; repair; better, ameliorate, enhance, facilitate, increase.

impale *v.* **1.** fix on a stake, stick, run through. **2.** transfix, affix, tack, pin, stick.

impart *v.* **1.** make known, tell, pass on, communicate, relate, report, confide, mention, reveal, disclose, divulge, share. **2.** confer on, bestow on, give, lend, grant, render, contribute, deliver, offer, dispense, consign, accord, afford.

impartial *adj.* unbiased, fair, just, objective, equitable, nonpartisan, disinterested, dispassionate, detached, open-minded, evenhanded, neutral, unprejudiced, fair-minded. **—Syn. Study.** See FAIR. **—Ant.** partial, prejudiced, influenced, swayed, affected, biased, slanted, swayable, bigoted, unfair, unjust.

impasse *n.* deadlock, stalemate, blind alley, bottleneck, cul-de-sac, dead end; snag; dilemma, predicament, quandary, standstill, standoff.

impassioned *adj.* ardent, animated, intense, fervent, excited, inspired, passionate, heated, earnest, eager, zealous, fiery, stirring, rousing, forceful. **—Ant.** dispassionate, objective, cool, impassive, apathetic, indifferent, detached.

impassive *adj.* emotionless, unemotional, unmoved, imperturbable, dispassionate, aloof, stoical, untouched, stony, calm, cool, sedate, reserved, unperturbed, unimpressible, inscrutable, impervious, stolid, apathetic, phlegmatic, unimpressionable, insensible, indifferent. **—Ant.** responsive, emotional, passionate, excited, perturbed.

impatient *adj.* restless, nervous, edgy, tense, irritated, agitated, excitable, fussy, restive; enthusiastic, eagerly desirous, feverish, high-strung, rabid, passionate, hurried, hasty, ardent, itchy, anxious; peevish, irritable, irascible, testy, brusque, annoyed, touchy, intolerant. **—Ant.** patient; composed, imperturbable, unruffled, cool; calm, serene, tranquil, placid, restful, quiet; gradual, slow; unperturbed.

impeach *v.* **1.** accuse, indict, arraign, inculpate, charge, incriminate, prefer charges against, lodge a complaint against. **2.** question, call into question, challenge, assail, attack, belittle, impugn, disparage, discredit, slur, slander, *Slang* badmouth.

impeccable *adj.* flawless, faultless, immaculate, free from imperfection, unblemished, perfect, irreproachable, excellent, irreprovable, unassailable, blameless, above criticism, unexceptionable, unimpeachable. **—Ant.** deficient, defective; superficial, shallow, uncritical, cursory; culpable, blameworthy; faulty, tarnished, stained, corrupt, flawed.

impecunious *adj.* poor, penniless, indigent, destitute, needy, down-and-out, impoverished, poverty-stricken, broke; bankrupt, insolvent, straitened, pinched, *Informal* hard-up. **—Syn. Study.** See POOR. **—Ant.** affluent, well-off, well-heeled, prosperous, flush, well-to-do.

impede *v.* delay, slow down, block, interfere with, interrupt, check, retard, obstruct, hinder, prevent, thwart, frustrate, inhibit, arrest, sidetrack, stall, stymie, deter, hamper, hold back, halter, disrupt. **—Syn. Study.** See PREVENT. **—Ant.** assist, promote, advance, further, forward; help, aid.

impediment *n.* delay, slowing down, block, blockage, barrier, stumbling block, interference, obstruction, hindrance, interference, handicap, obstacle, drawback, detraction; defect, flaw, deformity. **—Syn. Study.** See OBSTACLE. **—Ant.** advantage, bolster, help, aid.

impel *v.* force, require, drive, push, compel, urge, necessitate, prompt, prod, induce, constrain, spur, stimulate, motivate, goad, incite. **—Syn. Study.** See COMPEL. **—Ant.** restrain, curb, check, inhibit, withhold, hinder.

impending *adj.* approaching, immediate, coming, due momentarily, imminent, near, oncoming, forthcoming, in prospect, brewing, looming; threatening, menacing.

impenetrable *adj.* **1.** impervious, inviolable, unenterable, impassable, invulnerable, inaccessible; solid, thick, dense, sealed. **2.** incomprehensible, defying interpretation or understanding, insensible, elusive, mysterious, unfathomable, inscrutable, inaccessible, insoluble, unpalpable, inexplicable, intangible, obscure, puzzling. **—Ant. 1** pierceable, penetrable, vulnerable, enterable, accessible, passable. **2** understandable, fathomable, soluble, explicable, clear, obvious, lucid.

impenitent *adj.* remorseless, unrepenting, unashamed, unrepentant, uncontrite, unapologetic; defiant, obdurate; hardened, callous, inured, incorrigible; lost, irreclaimable. **—Ant.** regretful, contrite, ashamed, remorseful, apologetic, penitent.

imperative *adj.* urgent, vitally important, essential, of the utmost necessity, requisite, necessary, needful, mandatory, compulsory, obligatory, pressing, unavoidable, crucial, critical. **—Ant.** unnecessary, unimportant, nonessential, avoidable; nonobligatory.

imperceptible *adj.* undetectable, unnoticeable, not readily apparent, inconsiderable, subtle, minimal, unappreciable, minute, small, scant, insignificant, hidden, indistinct, unperceivable; academic, slight, minor; infinitesimal. **—Ant.** manifest, obvious, clear, perceptible, palpable, noticeable, distinct.

imperfection *n.* **1.** defect, flaw, blemish, fault, impairment, faulty detail, deformity, shortcoming, weakness. **2.** faultiness, imperfectness, falling short, inadequacy, insufficiency, fallibility, incompleteness. **—Ant. 2** perfection, perfectness, completeness, faultlessness.

imperial *adj.* high-handed, imperious, dictatorial, despotic, authoritarian, domineering, lordly, feudal, magisterial, overbearing, *Slang* bossy, tyrannical, autocratic, arbitrary, peremptory, repressive.

imperil *v.* endanger, risk, jeopardize, hazard, chance, gamble, expose, compromise, expose to danger, put in jeopardy; *Slang* put on the spot. **—Ant.** protect, defend, shield, guard, preserve, safeguard.

imperious *adj.* domineering, overbearing, dictatorial, lordly, despotic, imperial, autocratic, commanding, tyrannical, *Slang* bossy; peremptory, arrogant, haughty. **—Ant.** servile, humble, obsequious, submissive; kindly, gentle.

impermanent *adj.* fleeting, temporary, transitory, unenduring, evanescent, ephemeral, fugitive, unstable, passing, not fixed, transient. **—Ant.** permanent, immortal, stable, fixed.

impersonal *adj.* **1.** general, all-encompassing, applicable to all; impartial, objective, dispassionate, neutral, detached, disinterested; perfunctory, remote, impassive. **2.** inanimate, inorganic; inhuman, soulless, spiritless, lifeless, dead. **—Ant. 1** personal, specific. **2** personal, animate; human, alive, vital.

impersonate *v.* **1.** pretend to be, pose as, dress up as, get oneself up as, take the role of, represent oneself as, act the part of, masquerade as, pass oneself off as. **2.** portray, play the part of, imitate, represent, personify, mimic, mime, copy, take off on, ape.

impertinent *adj.* **1.** rude, unmannerly, disrespectful, insolent, impudent, presumptuous, arrogant, uncivil, surly, brazen, peremptory, brassy, insulting, discourteous; *Informal* fresh, sassy. **2.** irrelevant, extraneous, unimportant, immaterial, not pertinent, extrinsic, not germane, beside the point, unrelated, inappropriate. **—Syn. Study. 1** See INSOLENT. **—Ant. 1** polite, respectful, mannerly, deferential. **2** pertinent, relevant, germane, related; important, vital, crucial.

imperturbable *adj.* unexcitable, calm, collected, cool, serene, undisturbed, unruffled, dispassionate, unflustered, levelheaded, sedate, composed; unsusceptible, impervious, impassive, unanxious, unfazable; *Slang* unflappable. **—Ant.** perturbable, choleric, touchy.

impervious *adj.* **1.** impenetrable, impermeable, inaccessible, allowing no passage to, unapproachable; sealed or closed against; invulnerable. **2.** immune to, protected against; untouched by, unmarked by. **3.** unmoved by, unaffected by, untouched by, invulnerable, closed. **—Ant. 1** susceptible, vulnerable. **2** open, exposed, susceptible, sensitive, liable, prone.

impetuous *adj.* **1.** rash, impulsive, hasty, headlong, precipitate; abrupt, unpremeditated, capricious, unexpected. **2.** headlong, violent, precipitate, forcible, rampant, stormy, vehement; relentless, inexorable. **—Syn. Study. 1** IMPETUOUS,

IMPULSIVE both refer to persons who are hasty and precipitate in action, or to actions not preceded by thought. IMPETUOUS suggests great energy, overeagerness, and impatience: *an impetuous lover; impetuous words.* IMPULSIVE emphasizes spontaneity and lack of reflection: *an impulsive act of generosity.* —**Ant. 1** cautious, wary. **2** moderate, leisurely, slow, mild.

impetus *n.* stimulus, stimulation, spur, moving force, motive, impulse, impulsion, propulsion, boost, drive, momentum, force, start, push, prod; incentive, motivation.

impinge *v.* encroach, intrude, infringe, trespass, transgress, violate, obtrude.

impious *adj.* disrespectful, sacrilegious, blasphemous, irreverent, ungodly, profane, irreligious, godless, iniquitous, iconoclastic, renegade, apostate, immoral, perverted. —**Ant.** devout, reverent, pious, godly.

impish *adj.* implike, mischievous, puckish, elfin, playfully naughty, sportive, roguish, rascally, prankish.

implacable *adj.* irreconcilable, unappeasable, inexorable, unamenable, inflexible, intractable, unpacifiable, uncompromising, relentless, unrelenting. —**Ant.** reconcilable, appeasable, yielding, lenient, relenting, forbearing, indulgent, tolerant, flexible.

implausible *adj.* unlikely, improbable, incredible, unbelievable, illogical, unreasonable, doubtful, inconceivable, barely conceivable, preposterous, senseless, ridiculous, outrageous, far-fetched. —**Ant.** plausible, credible, believable, reasonable, likely, conceivable, sensible.

implement *n.* **1.** tool, utensil, instrument, device, apparatus, appliance, article, piece; equipment, materials. —*v.* **2.** put into effect, begin, activate, enact, start, set in motion, carry out, bring about, fulfill, achieve, accomplish, realize. —**Syn. Study. 1** See TOOL.

implicate *v.* involve, associate, connect, entangle, ensnare, embroil, entangle; incriminate, inculpate. —**Ant.** dissociate; exclude, eliminate, rule out; extricate, disentangle, untangle, disconnect; acquit, exculpate.

implication *n.* **1.** ramification, suggestion, outcome, effect, overtone, intimation, insinuation, inference, consequence, significance, connotation, innuendo. **2.** association, connection, involvement, entanglement.

implicit *adj.* **1.** implied, hinted, suggested, tacitly expressed; inferred, deducible, understood. **2.** innate, inherent, unquestioning, absolute, complete, profound, certain, resolute, unshakable, unreserved, total, unshakable, steadfast, staunch.

implore *v.* beg, beseech, entreat, urge, plead with, importune, obtest, supplicate, go to on bended knee. —**Ant.** order, demand, command.

imply *v.* **1.** indicate, suggest, hint, insinuate, intimate, connote. **2.** presuppose, indicate, bespeak, betoken, presume; signify, mean, denote, evidence.

impolite *adj.* discourteous, ill-bred, ungenteel, unmannerly, rude, unrefined, undecorous, unfitting, uncivil, inconsiderate, not polite, disrespectful, impolitic. —**Ant.** polite, courteous, mannerly, civil, respectful, considerate.

import *n.* significance, importance, meaning, burden, implication, connotation, thrust, moment, ramification, overtones.

importance *n.* **1.** value, consequence, significance, import, weightiness, weight, momentousness, relevance, essentialness, worth, seriousness, moment. **2.** rank, position, influence, esteem, repute, stature, eminence. —**Syn. Study.** IMPORTANCE, CONSEQUENCE, SIGNIFICANCE, MOMENT refer to something valuable, influential, or worthy of note. IMPORTANCE is the most general of these terms, assigning exceptional value or influence to a person or thing: *the importance of Einstein's discoveries.* CONSEQUENCE may suggest personal distinction, or may suggest importance based on results to be produced: *a woman of consequence in world affairs; an event of great consequence for our future.* SIGNIFICANCE carries the implication of importance not readily or immediately recognized: *The significance of the discovery became clear many years later.* MOMENT, on the other hand, usu. refers to immediately apparent, self-evident importance: *an international treaty of great moment.* —**Ant. 1** unimportance, pettiness, triviality, paltriness, insignificance; nothingness, immateriality. **2** unimportance, insignificance.

important *adj.* **1.** meaningful, consequential, significant, weighty, momentous, great, influential, serious, imperative, distinctive, notable. **2.** leading, foremost, major, preeminent, remarkable, prominent, influential, esteemed; distinctive, original, creative, seminal. —**Ant. 1** unimportant, inconsequential, inconsiderable, indifferent, insignificant, slight, minor, unnecessary, needless, negligible, nonessential, secondary, trivial. **2** unimportant, insignificant, undistinctive, minor.

impose *v.* **1.** institute, lay on, introduce, place on, set, levy; *Slang* slap on. **2.** force, inflict, enact, establish, prescribe, dictate, command, apply, peddle, foist, thrust upon; *Informal* palm off. **—Ant.** lift, remove.

imposing *adj.* impressive, majestic, grand, outstanding, striking, massive, monumental, lofty, towering, awe-inspiring, commanding, stately. **—Ant.** unimposing, unimpressive, ordinary, insignificant.

impossible *adj.* **1.** out of the question, not possible, unable to bring about, unachievable, unattainable; beyond belief, beyond reason, unimaginable, inconceivable. **2.** intractable, stubborn, unyielding, intransigent, unmanageable; intolerable, insufferable, unbearable; unsolvable, insoluble, unanswerable. **—Ant. 1** possible, likely, probable, feasible.

impostor *n.* pretender, deceiver, trickster, impersonator, dissembler, mountebank, fraud, cheat, masquerader, defrauder, duper, bluffer, pettifogger, charlatan, counterfeit, sham, shammer; phony, quack, con man, *Informal* flimflam man.

impotence *n.* weakness, powerlessness, ineffectiveness, ineffectuality, inefficacy, helplessness, incapacity, disability, paralysis. **—Ant.** capacity, vigor, ability, power, potency, strength, effectiveness, efficacy.

impotent *adj.* unable to function; ineffective, powerless, frail, feeble, weak, disabled, helpless, paralyzed; feckless, hapless. **—Ant.** potent, powerful, puissant, forceful, vigorous.

impoverished *adj.* **1.** poor, destitute, abject, sorely wanting, without material resources, impecunious, indigent, without means, down-and-out, marked by extreme poverty, pauperized, wiped out, penniless, broke. **2.** exhausted, worn out, used up, wanting, depleted, bereft, sterile, effete, barren, drained, unproductive. **—Syn. Study. 1** See POOR. **—Ant. 1** rich, affluent, wealthy, well-to-do, well-off. **2** fertile, fecund, fructuous, rich, productive.

impractical *adj.* unrealistic, unwise, unintelligent, lacking foresight, disorganized, loose-ended, helter-skelter; starry-eyed, romantic, quixotic; sloppy, careless. **—Ant.** sound, sensible, down-to-earth, practical, pragmatic, clear-eyed, realistic, systematic.

impregnable *adj.* invincible, unattackable, unconquerable, invulnerable, unassailable, indomitable; powerful, strong, sturdy, mighty, potent. **—Syn. Study.** See INVINCIBLE. **—Ant.** vulnerable, frail, flimsy, assailable, weak, defenseless.

impregnate *v.* **1.** make pregnant, cause to conceive, get with young, cause to bear offspring; fructify, fecundate, inseminate, fertilize. **2.** saturate, wet, moisten, soak, imbrue, permeate, drench, steep, infuse, dampen, suffuse, inundate.

impress *v.* affect, influence, sway, move, reach, stir, touch, excite, strike, capture one's imagination, fix in the mind, seize one's mind or imagination; *Slang* grab, sink in; overwhelm, electrify, bedazzle, overpower.

impression *n.* **1.** effect, impact, sensation, feeling; reception, influence, imprint. **2.** feeling, opinion, belief, understanding, idea, notion, view, hunch, surmise, conviction. **3.** imprint, impress, mark, outline, track, indentation, stamp, mold, trace, contour.

impressionable *adj.* easily influenced, receptive, susceptible to impressions, sentient, passible, affective, emotionally affected; suggestible, gullible, vulnerable.

impressive *adj.* imposing, thrilling, awe-inspiring, magnificent, moving, soul-stirring, exciting, grand, majestic, striking, august, overpowering, outstanding, memorable, unforgettable. **—Ant.** unimpressive, unimposing, tame, ordinary, unmoving, uninspiring, unmemorable.

imprison *v.* place in prison, confine, incarcerate, jail, place in confinement, shackle, hold captive, restrain, engage, coop up, fence in, impound, lock up, constrain, pen, entomb, immure. **—Ant.** free, release, liberate.

improbable *adj.* not probable, unlikely, doubtful, unforeseeable; unreasonable, implausible, illogical. **—Ant.** probable, likely; reasonable, plausible, logical.

impromptu *adj.* **1.** improvised, unprepared, extemporaneous, unrehearsed, spur-of-the-moment, unexpected, sudden, offhand, unpremeditated, makeshift, spontaneous, impulsive, off the top of one's head, *Informal* off the cuff. *—adv.* **2.** without warning, without advance notice, on the spot, with no preparation, extemporaneously, on a moment's notice, right then and there, *Informal* off the cuff. **—Syn. Study. 1** See EXTEMPORANEOUS. **—Ant. 1** considered, planned, prepared, rehearsed, premeditated, deliberate.

improper *adj.* not suitable, unsuitable, inappropriate, unfit, unbefitting, malapropos, irregular, out of place, inapt, unseemly, unbecoming, indecorous, unconformable, contrary to accepted standards; out of tune, inharmonious, ill-suited, being at odds; indecent, lewd, suggestive, off-color. **—Syn. Study.** IMPROPER, UNSEEMLY, UNBECOMING, INDECENT are applied to that which is inappropriate or not in accordance with propriety. IMPROPER has a wide range, being applied to whatever is not suitable or fitting, and often specifically to what does not conform to the standards of conventional morality: *an improper diet; improper clothes; improper behavior in church.* UNSEEMLY is applied to whatever is unfitting or improper under the circumstances: *unseemly mirth.* UNBECOMING is applied to what is especially unfitting in the person concerned: *conduct unbecoming a minister.* INDECENT, a strong word, is applied to what is offensively contrary to standards of propriety and esp. of modesty: *indecent photographs.* **—Ant.** proper, right, correct, decorous, decent, fitting, apropos; *French* comme il faut, de rigueur.

improve *v.* **1.** make better, help, make more desirable or attractive, better, correct, repair, enhance, ameliorate, make improvements on; develop beneficially, recuperate, come around, take a turn for the better, gain ground, rally. **2.** enrich, enhance, put to good use, employ to a good or useful end, turn to account, make productive, cultivate, increase the resources of, develop. **—Syn. Study. 1** IMPROVE, AMELIORATE, BETTER imply bringing to a more desirable state. IMPROVE usu. implies remedying a lack or a felt need: *to improve a process.* AMELIORATE, a formal word, implies improving oppressive, unjust, or difficult conditions: *to ameliorate working conditions.* BETTER implies improving conditions that are adequate but could be more satisfactory: *to better a previous attempt; to better oneself by study.* **—Ant. 1, 2** impair; worsen; injure, harm, damage, mar.

improvement *n.* **1.** betterment, amelioration, beneficial development, progress, upswing, gain. **2.** enhancement, repair, reconstruction, reclamation, additive, amendment, emendation, reform. **3.** refinement, betterment, advance, advancement, step forward.

improvident *adj.* thriftless, spendthrift, unparsimonious, unthrifty, extravagant, wasteful, prodigal, lavish; imprudent, shortsighted, reckless, negligent. **—Ant.** provident, cautious, thrifty, penny-wise; prudent, farsighted, foresighted, forehanded.

improvise *v.* perform without preparation; invent offhand, make up, extemporize, come up with, do a makeshift job, throw together, ad-lib; create off the top of one's head; *Slang* wing it.

improvised *adj.* impromptu, ad-lib, offhand, extemporaneous, extempore, unrehearsed, improvisational, off-the-cuff, spontaneous, devised, contrived, concocted, hatched-up, dreamed-up, originated, invented, spur-of-the-moment, extemporized. **—Ant.** rehearsed, prepared, perfected, polished, memorized.

imprudent *adj.* incautious, unwise, rash, inadvisable, indiscreet, ill-advised, ill-considered, thoughtless, injudicious; heedless, untoward, foolish, foolishly impulsive, foolhardy; unthinking, mindless, crazy, *Informal* dopey. **—Ant.** prudent, wise, thoughtful, judicious, cautious, careful, discreet.

impudent *adj.* rude, brash, disrespectful, insolent, discourteous, impolite, shameless, saucy, bold, brazen, impertinent, upstart, forward, bumptious, cheeky, nervy; *Informal* fresh, smart-alecky, wise acreish. **—Syn. Study.** See INSOLENT. **—Ant.** respectful, courteous, polite, deferential.

impugn *v.* attack, assail, oppose, call in question, challenge, question, deny, contradict, negate, asperse, criticize, berate, denounce, *Slang* knock; libel, slander. **—Ant.** defend, support, uphold; back, advocate.

impulsive *adj.* **1.** pushing forward; propelling, propellant, impelling, driving; forceful, forcible. **2.** rash, capricious, whimsical, notional, devil-may-care, unpredictable; spur-of-the-moment, impromptu, offhand, unpremeditated, unplanned, involuntary, spontaneous, impetuous, incautious, extemporaneous. **—Syn. Study. 2** See IMPETUOUS. **—Ant. 1** curbing, arresting, halting. **2** deliberate, premeditated, considered, cautious, prudent, circumspect, calculating, planned, rehearsed, contrived.

impunity *n.* freedom from punishment, freedom from harm; immunity, clearance; absolution, dispensation; privilege, prerogative, exemption. **—Syn. Study.** See EXEMPTION. **—Ant.** blame, retribution, hazard; culpability, punishment, loss, harm, danger, risk.

impure *adj.* **1.** dirty, unclean, defiled, polluted; filthy, foul, sullied, vitiated, tainted, contaminated, noxious, noisome, unwholesome. **2.** adulterated, degraded, debased, devalued, depreciated; unrefined. **3.** immoral, improper, indecorous, indelicate, coarse, smutty, unchaste, immodest, licentious; smutty, dirty, lustful, lecherous, libidinous, prurient, salacious, obscene, lewd, indecent. **—Ant. 1–3** pure. **1** clean, unpolluted, untainted, uncontaminated, wholesome. **2** unmixed, unadulterated, unalloyed; perfect. **3** chaste, wholesome, moral, decent, decorous, clean, proper.

impurity *n.* **1.** taintedness, pollution, uncleanness, foulness, contamination, unwholesomeness, defilement, corruption, dirtiness, filth. **2.** adulterant, contaminant, pollutant, foreign matter; adulteration, alloy, taint, dross. **—Ant. 1** purity, cleanness, wholesomeness.

impute *v.* charge, ascribe, refer, credit, attribute, assign, set down to, lay at the door of, relate, see as a result. **—Syn. Study.** See ATTRIBUTE.

inaccessible *adj.* unapproachable, unreachable; beyond access, hopelessly remote, unattainable, unobtainable, not at hand. **—Ant.** accessible, reachable; approachable; attainable, obtainable.

inaccuracy *n.* **1.** inexactness, faultiness, incorrectness, fallaciousness, unreliability, imprecision, unclarity. **2.** error, mistake, slip, fault, fallacy, blunder; erratum, wrong; *Slang* boo-boo, goof. **—Ant. 1** accuracy, correctness, reliability, faultlessness, exactness, precision, preciseness.

inaccurate *adj.* incorrect, faulty, erroneous, full of errors, wrong, false, fallacious, unreliable, imprecise, inexact; wide of the mark; mistaken; not on target, off the track, off, off target. **—Ant.** accurate, correct, true, faithful, flawless, exact.

inactive *adj.* **1.** idle, inoperative, inert, quiet, still, dormant, on the shelf, out of service, unused, static. **2.** dormant, quiet, inert; sluggish, idle, torpid, languid, somnolent, low-intensity, low-key, easygoing, indolent, lazy, slothful, sedentary, dull, leisurely, otiose, do-nothing. **—Syn. Study. 2** INACTIVE, DORMANT, INERT, TORPID suggest lack of activity. INACTIVE describes a person or thing that is not acting, moving, functioning, or operating: *an inactive board member; inactive laws.* DORMANT suggests the quiescence or inactivity of that which sleeps or seems to sleep, but may be roused to action: *a dormant geyser.* INERT suggests something with no inherent power of motion or action; it may also refer to a person disinclined to move or act: *the inert body of an accident victim.* TORPID suggests a state of suspended activity, esp. of animals that hibernate: *Snakes are torpid in cold weather.* **—Ant. 1** active, operative, operating, functional. **2** active, bustling, dynamic, busy, industrious, vigorous.

inadequate *adj.* **1.** not adequate, deficient, insufficient, less than necessary or required, lacking, meager, wanting, below par, short, scanty. **2.** incompetent, incapable, unqualified, unfit, too raw, inept, not up to, imperfect, unfitted. **—Ant. 1** adequate, sufficient, abundant, enough. **2** adequate, qualified, equal, experienced.

inadvertent *adj.* unintentional, unintended, not on purpose, accidental, fortuitous, unmeant, unthinking, involuntary, unpremeditated. **—Ant.** deliberate, premeditated, intentional, studied, considered, conscious, aware.

inadvisable *adj.* unwise, injudicious, imprudent, ill-advised, not advisable, impolitic, inopportune, risky, chancy, inexpedient. **—Ant.** advisable, wise, prudent, politic, judicious, opportune, expedient.

inalienable *adj.* inviolable, unassailable, absolute, unimpeachable, unforfeitable, sacred, sacrosanct, inherent; protected, defended.

inane *adj.* foolish, senseless, vapid, silly, absurd, vacuous, void of intelligence, shallow, pointless, asinine, insipid, nonsensical, empty, ridiculous; unthinking, unintelligent; dumb, stupid, idiotic, meaningless, fatuous, *Informal* dopey. **—Syn. Study.** See FOOLISH. **—Ant.** meaningful, sensible, sound, thoughtful, significant, intelligent, wise, sage, deep, profound.

inapplicable *adj.* not applicable, irrelevant, unsuited, unsuitable, not pertinent, not apt, inappropriate, unfit, incompatible, not germane, inapposite. **—Ant.** applicable, suitable, suited, relevant, germane, pertinent, appropriate, apposite.

inappropriate *adj.* unsuitable, unsuited, improper, out of place, ill-timed, incongruous, unfitting, inapt, incompatible, in bad taste, indecorous, infelicitous, unbecoming, out of fashion. **—Ant.** appropriate, fitting, proper, felicitous, suitable, meet, fit, decorous, becoming.

inarticulate *adj.* **1.** incoherent, unintelligible, mumbled, babbled; blurred, garbled, indistinct, confused. **2.** incapable of speech, mute, dumb, tongue-tied, speechless, wordless; paralyzed. **3.** hesitant in speech, uncommunicative, poorly spoken, inexpressive. **—Ant. 1** articulate, clear, intelligible, coherent, distinct. **2** articulate. **3** expressive, glib, verbal, voluble.

inattentive *adj.* showing no interest; not attentive, careless, negligent, thoughtless, unmindful, unobservant, heedless, absentminded, distracted, forgetful, unaware, daydreaming. **—Ant.** attentive, heedful; mindful, careful, aware.

inaugurate *v.* **1.** begin formally, launch, set in action, undertake, initiate, institute, embark upon, usher in, set up, start, *Informal* kick off. **2.** induct formally into office, invest with office; induct, instate, install ceremoniously. **—Ant. 1** terminate, end, conclude, finish.

inauspicious *adj.* ill-chosen, badly timed, ill-omened, unpropitious, unfavorable, unlucky, unpromising, unfortunate, infelicitous, disastrous. **—Ant.** auspicious, favorable, propitious, fortunate, lucky, happy, providential, well-timed, hopeful, promising.

inborn *adj.* inherent, innate, inbred, congenital, constitutional, natural, native, intuitive, instinctive, inherited, intrinsic; basic, fundamental. **—Syn. Study.** See INNATE. **—Ant.** acquired, nurtured, learned, conditioned, taught, inculcated.

inbred *adj.* innate, natural, ingrained, inherent, congenital, hereditary, deep-seated, deep-rooted, inborn, intrinsic, indwelling, constitutional; instinctive, instinctual, primal. **—Ant.** superimposed, acquired, learned, extraneous.

incalculable *adj.* **1.** beyond counting or calculation, too great to be calculated, too numerous to count, inestimable, countless, measureless, immeasurable, uncountable, incomputable, innumerable, infinite. **2.** unknowable in advance, unforeseeable, uncertain, dubious, unpredictable. **—Ant. 1** calculable, estimable, measurable, countable, computable; limited, finite. **2** calculable, predictable, certain, foreseeable, knowable.

incandescent *adj.* **1.** glowingly hot, luminously hot, white-hot; brilliant, blindingly bright. **2.** brilliant, electrifying, galvanic, electric; dynamic, magnetic, scintillating, high-powered, glowing, radiant.

incantation *n.* charm, spell, sorcery, magic, witchcraft, voodoo, black magic, wizardry, necromancy; invocation, chant, conjuration; *Slang* hocus-pocus, mumbo-jumbo, abracadabra; hex, jinx.

incapable *adj.* **1.** unskilled, inept, incompetent, inferior, unfit, unqualified, untrained, inadequate, inefficient, ineffective. **2.** lacking the mettle for, unable, powerless, helpless, impotent. **—Syn. Study. 1** INCAPABLE, INCOMPETENT are applied to a person or thing lacking in ability, preparation, or power for whatever is to be done. INCAPABLE usu. means inherently lacking in ability or power to meet and fill ordinary requirements: *a bridge incapable of carrying heavy loads; a worker described as clumsy and incapable.* INCOMPETENT, generally used only of persons, means unfit or unqualified for a particular task: *incompetent as an administrator.* **—Ant. 1, 2** capable, able. **1** competent, qualified; efficient, effective, skilled.

incapacitate *v.* disable, render incapable, undo, make powerless, make unfit; cripple, maim, handicap, paralyze, enfeeble, lay up, put out of action; disqualify; *Informal* sideline.

incarcerate *v.* imprison, jail, confine, lock up, impound, immure, intern, commit; pen, restrain, *Slang* coop up. **—Ant.** free, release, liberate.

incautious *adj.* rash, brash, reckless, headstrong, impetuous, hotheaded; imprudent, thoughtless, unwary, injudicious, unthinking, careless, heedless, over-hasty. **—Ant.** calm, cool; wary, cautious; prudent, careful.

incense *v.* enrage, inflame, anger, make angry, infuriate, madden, make indignant, provoke, *Informal* burn one up, make one see red. **—Syn. Study.** See ENRAGE.

incentive *n.* motivation, spur, motive, encouragement, stimulus, inducement, lure, enticement, *Informal* come-on; inspiration. **—Syn. Study.** See MOTIVE. **—Ant.** deterrent, prohibition, warning, dissuasion.

inception *n.* commencement, beginning, origin, start, birth, onset, arrival, inauguration; outset, debut. **—Ant.** termination, end, ending, completion, finish, finishing, conclusion.

incessant *adj.* constant, ceaseless, continuous, continual, unceasing, unremitting, unending, perpetual, everlasting, persistent, interminable, unbroken, unrelenting, uninterrupted. **—Ant.** intermittent, periodic, sporadic, occasional; rare, infrequent.

inchoate *adj.* beginning, budding, incipient, commencing, embryonic, nascent; shapeless, formless, unformed, unshaped, amorphous; unorganized, uncohesive, disjointed, disconnected. **—Ant.** formed, shaped; finished, completed.

incidence *n.* frequency, rate, occurrence, commonness, routineness; scope, range, extent; occasion, happening, phenomenon.

incident *n.* **1.** event, particular event, episode, affair, occasion, occurrence, happening; small disturbance, scene, contretemps, clash. *—adj.* **2.** occurring naturally, related, arising from, happening in the course of, going along with, incidental, connected with, likely to happen. **—Syn. Study. 1** See EVENT.

incidental *adj.* **1.** secondary, extraneous, accessory, minor, subordinate; unexpected, unlooked-for. *—n.* **2.** **incidentals.** minor items; accessories, appurtenances, extras; odds and ends, minutiae. **—Ant. 1** essential, fundamental, basic.

incidentally *adv.* by the way; in passing, connected with that, by the by, apart from the main subject, apropos, speaking of that, parenthetically, while we're on the subject.

incipient *adj.* beginning, becoming apparent; nascent, inchoate, half-formed, rudimentary, developing; barely starting; promising, budding, embryonic, fledgling. **—Ant.** realized, achieved, finished, full-blown; accomplished.

incisive *adj.* **1.** keen, sharp, biting, crisp, brisk, curt, cutting, piercing, acute, mordant, trenchant, express, summary. **2.** penetrating, analytic, acute, sharp, precise; shrewd, well-aimed, perceptive, probing, penetrating, trenchant, intelligent, sharp.

incite *v.* rouse, activate, stimulate, actuate, induce, prod, arouse, urge on, inflame, provoke, foment, instigate, excite, agitate, egg on; stir, stir up, fire up, drive, impel, goad, prompt. **—Syn. Study.** INCITE, ROUSE, PROVOKE mean to goad or inspire an individual or group to take some action or express some feeling. INCITE means to induce activity of any kind, although it often refers to violent or uncontrolled behavior: *incited to greater effort; incited to rebellion.* ROUSE is used in a similar way, but has an underlying sense of awakening from sleep or inactivity: *to rouse an apathetic team.* PROVOKE means to stir to sudden, strong feeling or vigorous action: *Kicking the animal provoked it to attack.*

incivility *n.* rudeness, disrespect, discourtesy, impoliteness, misbehavior; coarseness, impudence, indecorum, boorishness, uncouthness, tactlessness, vulgarity, barbarism. **—Ant.** decorum, propriety, seemliness, mannerliness.

inclement *adj.* stormy, violent, rough, harsh, bitter, raw, severe, tempestuous, foul, nasty. **—Ant.** clement, mild.

inclination *n.* **1.** tendency, propensity, penchant, leaning, proneness, predilection, proclivity, preference, disposition, predisposition; fondness, bent, liking. **2.** nod, bow, bend, bending, lowering, inclining. **3.** slant, rise, dip, slope, acclivity, sloping, rake, pitch, hill, grade. **—Ant. 1** dislike, antipathy, disinclination.

incline *v.* **1.** tend, have a mind to, have a preference, prefer, enjoy, like, lean toward. **2.** tend, be apt, be likely, have a propensity, seem, wont. **3.** slope, slant, tilt, rake, decline, cant, pitch, lean. **4.** bend forward, lean, bend, tilt, bow. *—n.* **5.** slope, hill, gradient, pitch, cant, inclined plane, acclivity. **—Ant. 1** dislike, hate, abhor, be disinclined.

include *v.* contain, comprehend, comprise, embrace, enfold, cover, take in, incorporate, encompass, involve, entail, subsume. **—Syn. Study.** INCLUDE, COMPREHEND, COMPRISE, EMBRACE imply containing parts of a whole. INCLUDE means to contain as a part or member of a larger whole; it may indicate one, several, or all parts: *This anthology includes works by Sartre and Camus. The price includes appetizer, main course, and dessert.* COMPREHEND means to have within the limits or scope of a larger whole: *The plan comprehends several projects.* COMPRISE means to consist of; it usu. indicates all of the various parts serving to make up the whole: *This genus comprises 50 species.* EMBRACE emphasizes the extent or assortment of that which is included: *The report embraces a great variety of subjects.* **—Ant.** exclude, preclude; eliminate, rule out, omit, leave out, forget.

inclusive *adj.* including, comprising, incorporating, embracing, comprehending, taking in, encircling, surrounding; comprehensive, overall, general, sweeping, encyclopedic, all-encompassing.

incognito *adj.* unidentified, unnamed, disguised, concealed, unrevealed, undisclosed, unacknowledged, nameless, unknown, uncredited; protected. **—Ant.** well-known, famous; attributed, credited.

incoherent *adj.* disjointed, unintelligible, rambling, confused, bewildering, irrational, illogical, inconsistent, unclear, nonsensical, muddled. **—Ant.** coherent, intelligible, logical, connected, rational, consistent.

income *n.* revenue, earnings, livelihood, means, wages, salary, emolument. **—Ant.** expense, disbursement, outlay.

incomparable *adj.* peerless, matchless, unequaled, unrivaled, unapproachable, inimitable, superlative, transcendent, beyond compare. **—Ant.** ordinary, fair, mediocre, second-rate, average, inferior, run-of-the-mill.

incompatible *adj.* **1.** inharmonious, uncongenial, antagonistic, lacking rapport, at variance, at odds, mismatched, clashing, disagreeing. **2.** inconsistent, contrary, incongruous, jarring, discordant, at odds, contradictory, unsuited, not going well together, inappropriate. **—Ant.** compatible, accordant, consonant, consistent, congenial; harmonizing, harmonious, agreeing, appropriate.

incompetent *adj.* inept, untrained, unskilled, lacking ability, ineffectual, ineffective, inefficient, unfit, incapable, inexpert, unqualified. **—Syn. Study.** See INCAPABLE. **—Ant.** competent, apt, expert, efficient.

incomplete *adj.* unfinished, lacking a part, partial, not total, containing omissions, broken, fragmentary; wanting, defective, deficient. **—Ant.** complete, finished, whole, unbroken.

incomprehensible *adj.* baffling, bewildering, beyond understanding, ungraspable, beyond comprehension, befuddling, unintelligible, confusing, inscrutable, obscure, unfathomable, abstruse, impenetrable. **—Ant.** comprehensible, understandable, clear, plain, intelligible.

inconceivable *adj.* unthinkable, unbelievable, incredible, beyond belief, contrary to reason or belief; highly unlikely, unimaginable, strange, improbable, unlikely, impossible to comprehend. **—Ant.** conceivable, believable, credible, plausible, reasonable, likely, imaginable, probable, comprehensible.

inconclusive *adj.* undetermined, indeterminate, unresolved, unsettled, indefinite, open, up in the air, eluding settlement, indecisive, not definite, still doubtful, unconvincing. **—Ant.** conclusive, decisive, definite.

incongruous *adj.* **1.** inappropriate, odd, outlandish, out of keeping, out of place, unsuitable, not harmonious, *Slang* far-out. **2.** conflicting, contrary, at variance, incompatible, contradictory, inconsistent, irreconcilable, discrepant, disagreeing. **—Ant. 1** congruous, fitting, suitable, appropriate, consonant, consistent, accordant, agreeing, harmonious, becoming.

inconsequential *adj.* trivial, trifling, of no moment, valueless, slight, unimportant, of no consequence, insignificant, negligible, nugatory, meaningless, piddling, petty, picayune. **—Ant.** consequential, important, momentous, significant, meaningful, crucial.

inconsiderate *adj.* thoughtless, rude, uncivil, impolite, insensitive, uncaring, unkind, uncharitable, disregardful, ungracious; rash, unthinking, remiss, negligent, careless, tactless, lacking regard. **—Ant.** considerate, thoughtful; kind; polite.

inconsistent *adj.* **1.** incompatible, dissonant, inharmonious, inaccordant, inconsonant, discrepant, contrary, contradictory, not in agreement, incongruous, irreconcilable. **2.** erratic, unstable, constantly changing, wayward, inconstant, changeable; fickle, notional, unpredictable, irresolute, variable, vacillating, changeful. **—Ant. 1** consistent, consonant, coherent, compatible, congruous; according or accordant, agreeing, tallying, jibing, corresponding or correspondent, suitable. **2** consistent, unchangeable; stable, reliable; constant, steady.

inconspicuous *adj.* unnoticed, unnoticeable, unobtrusive, unostentatious, attracting little attention, not outstanding, not egregious; unassuming, modest; unapparent, dim, muted, faint. **—Ant.** conspicuous, noticeable; striking, prominent, egregious.

inconstant *adj.* **—Syn. Study.** See FICKLE.

incontrovertible *adj.* undeniable, indisputable, irrefutable, apodictic, beyond question, unquestionable, established, past dispute, unarguable. **—Ant.** disputable, questionable, debatable.

inconvenient *adj.* unhandy, inopportune, untimely, bothersome, troublesome, tiresome, awkward, annoying; burdensome, distressing. **—Ant.** convenient, opportune, timely; advantageous, helpful.

incorporate *v.* include, embody, work in, consolidate, fuse, amalgamate, introduce into, assimilate.

incorporeal *adj.* bodiless, unfleshly, spiritual, insubstantial, immaterial; unworldly, unearthly; ghostly, phantom, unreal, intangible, supernatural, occult, disembodied. **—Ant.** corporeal, bodied, solid, tangible, material.

incorrect *adj.* wrong, inexact, erroneous, untrue, false, mistaken, false, fallacious, inaccurate. **—Ant.** correct, right, accurate, true.

incorrigible *adj.* uncontrollable, unmanageable, unruly, beyond saving, hopeless, past changing, beyond help, intractable; delinquent, hardened, hardcore, thoroughly bad. **—Ant.** correctable, manageable, tractable, amenable.

incorruptible *adj.* pure, righteous, upright, honest, reliable, beyond corruption, irreproachable, above temptation, faultless, trustworthy, unbribable. **—Ant.** corruptible, bribable, dishonest, unreliable.

increase *v.* **1.** make greater or larger, enlarge, expand, enrich, add to, augment, advance, enhance. **2.** enlarge, become larger, swell, expand, burgeon, grow, wax, become more numerous, multiply. **—Ant.** decrease, diminish, lessen, reduce, abate, dwindle; shorten, abridge, abbreviate, curtail, retrench; contract, condense, shrink, deflate, decline, lower.

incredible *adj.* unbelievable, remarkable, unimaginable, awesome, hardly credible, inconceivable, preposterous, absurd, farfetched, amazing, astounding, astonishing, extraordinary. **—Ant.** credible, believable, unremarkable; ordinary, usual, common.

incredulous *adj.* dubious, skeptical, unwilling to believe, not believing, disbelieving, distrustful, doubtful, suspicious; showing disbelief. **—Syn. Study.** See DOUBTFUL. **—Ant.** credulous, gullible, believing, trustful, trusting.

increment *n.* increase, gain, benefit, profit, addition, augmentation, growth, rise, supplement, accumulation, enlargement, accretion, raise, appreciation, proliferation.

inculcate *v.* instill, impart, infuse, implant, infix, impress, imbue, teach, instruct, indoctrinate, enlighten; impress upon the mind, hammer into one's head, inscribe in the memory, etch indelibly in the mind; condition, brainwash.

incur *v.* contract, become liable for, bring into being, assume, bring on, acquire, fall into, become subject to; arouse, incite, stir up, involve, provoke, bring out, bring on oneself.

incurable *adj.* beyond cure, having no remedy, irremediable, cureless, uncorrectable; incorrigible, relentless, ceaseless, unflagging, inveterate, dyed-in-the-wool, hopeless. **—Ant.** curable, correctable, remediable.

incursion *n.* invasion, foray, sortie, attack; assault, encroachment, impingement, infiltration, raid; forcible entering, inroad, push; advance forward or into.

indebted *adj.* **1.** under obligation, in debt, burdened with debt; financially burdened; chargeable, accountable. **2.** obligated, bound, beholden, bounden; deeply appreciative, grateful, full of thanks, thankful. **—Ant. 1** unobligated, free and clear. **2** unobligated, unbeholden, ungrateful, unthankful.

indecent *adj.* **1.** unseemly, improper, lacking common decency, indiscreet, unbecoming, rude, ignoble, ill-bred, uncivil, offensive, vulgar, in bad taste. **2.** immoral, immodest, indecorous, obscene, pornographic, lewd, licentious, bawdy, salacious; arousing lust, prurient, unwholesome, dirty, filthy, blue, smutty. **—Syn. Study. 1, 2** See IMPROPER. **—Ant. 1, 2** decent. **1** proper, seemly, becoming, tasteful, appropriate; polite, civil. **2** chaste, pure, modest, virtuous, moral, ethical; high-toned, elegant, decorous, tasteful.

indecisive *adj.* **1.** not decisive, inconclusive, unsettled, indeterminate, doubtful, dubious, disputable, debatable; unclear, confusing. **2.** irresolute, vacillating, hesitant, hesitating, wavering, weak, mercurial, halfhearted, uncertain, blowing hot and cold, wishy-washy. **—Ant. 1** decisive, conclusive, firm, clear; indisputable, undebatable, certain. **2** decisive, resolute, certain.

indecorous *adj.* immodest, unbecoming, unseemly, unfitting, improper, unsuitable, inappropriate, not in good taste; ill-bred, low-class, gross; wicked, sinful; reprehensible, blameworthy. **—Ant.** decorous, decent, nice, demure; ceremonious, formal, conventional, standard, proper, suitable.

indeed *adv.* in fact, truly, in reality, without question, certainly, for sure, veritably, in truth, undeniably, really, to be sure, with certainty, positively, strictly speaking, joking apart, as a matter of fact, to tell the truth, to be honest, in point of fact, actually, coming right down to it.

indefatigable *adj.* tireless, inexhaustible, persevering, persistent, diligent, dogged, energetic, sedulous, unfaltering, unflagging, untiring, unwearying, staunch.

indefensible *adj.* **1.** unable to withstand attack, vulnerable, defenseless; open to attack, unprotected, pregnable, vincible. **2.** inexcusable, beyond justification, unjustifiable, unspeakable, unpardonable, without reason or rationale; open to criticism, improper, untenable. **—Ant. 1** defensible, invincible, invulnerable, protected. **2** defensible, justifiable, excusable, pardonable, reasonable, rational, tenable.

indefinite *adj.* **1.** unspecified, having no fixed limit, undetermined, indeterminate, unknown, inexact, inexplicit; illimitable, measureless, limitless. **2.** unsettled, uncertain, indistinct, vague; not clearly defined, dim, ill-defined, amorphous, indecisive, doubtful, tentative, obscure, ambiguous, unsure. **—Ant. 1** definite, clear-cut, certain, limited, known, specific. **2** definite, certain, settled, sure, unambiguous.

indelible *adj.* vivid, permanent, unforgettable, lasting, memorable; permanently fixed, fast, ineradicable, unerasable, unremovable, incapable of being deleted or wiped out, ingrained, deep-dyed.

indelicate *adj.* **1.** coarse, crude, rude, unrefined, unbecoming; clumsy, awkward. **2.** offensive, lacking good taste, indiscreet, unseemly, unrefined; off-color, immodest, crude, indecent, vulgar, suggestive, indecorous, lewd, risqué, broad, obscene, coarse, gross, improper. **—Ant. 1** delicate, refined, seemly, decorous, smooth, polite, polished. **2** decent, chaste, refined, discreet, proper.

indemnify *v.* reimburse, repay, pay back, compensate, requite, remunerate, recompense, make right, make restitution, make up for, make good, rectify, make amends, satisfy, atone.

indentation *n.* **1.** cut, notch, incision, cavity, furrow, score; recess, concavity, niche, pocket, bay, inset. **2.** dent, pit, gouge, depression, nick. **—Ant.** bump, protruberance, projection, prominence.

independence *n.* emancipation, liberty, freedom, self-determination, self-government, freedom from control, sovereignty, self-reliance, liberation, autonomy. **—Ant.** dependence; subordination, subjection; servitude, slavery, bondage; reliance, dependency.

independent *adj.* **1.** self-reliant, uncontrolled, on one's own, autonomous, free, self-directing, individualistic, uncoerced; unconstrained, free from the control or influence of others. **2.** free, self-governing, autonomous; self-determining, sovereign. **3.** separate, not joined to or associated with, unattached to, distinct from, exclusive, apart from, unconnected with, unallied. **4.** solvent, well-to-do, well-off, in easy circumstances, well-fixed, affluent, *Informal* well-heeled. **—Ant. 1** dependent; influenced, controlled, directed; subordinate, subject, tributary, subservient, servile, slavish, subject, attached, interrelated. **4** dependent, reliant, beholden, attached.

indescribable *adj.* beyond description, inexpressible, beyond words, ineffable, beggaring description; indefinable; overwhelming, unutterable.

indestructible *adj.* unbreakable, damage-resistant, infrangible, enduring, permanent, everlasting, imperishable, incapable of being destroyed. **—Ant.** destructible, perishable, breakable, unenduring, fragile, frangible.

indeterminate *adj.* unspecified, undetermined, unstipulated, uncertain, unfixed in extent or amount, unclear, obscure, not clear, unresolved, vague, undefined; ambiguous, problematic, perplexing, indefinite. **—Ant.** specified, precise, definite, clear, certain, determined, fixed, defined.

index *n.* **1.** alphabetical list, catalog, register, glossary. **2.** sign, token, indication, indicator, symptom, clue, evidence, manifestation, proof, mark.

indicate *v.* **1.** be a sign of, be symptomatic of, show, designate, denote, imply, point to, suggest; evince, bespeak, reveal, symbolize, signify, stand for, mean, represent. **2.** point out, point to, specify, direct attention to. **3.** show, make known, register, reveal, tell, establish, record.

indication *n.* sign, hint, intimation, signal, manifestation, token, warning, evidence, mark, clue, suggestion, foretoken, hint, symptom, gesture, demonstration; portent, augury, omen, boding, foreboding, premonition, presage; signifying, telling, indicating, designation, mention, showing, pointing.

indicative *adj.* suggestive, indicatory, characteristic, evidential, symptomatical, symptomatic, expressive, significant, emblematic, symbolic, representative, denotative, connotative, designative.

indict *v.* arraign, accuse, charge, inculpate, criminate, impute, bring to justice, cite, impeach, prosecute; find an indictment against, prefer charges, have up, pull up, bring up.

indifference *n.* **1.** unconcern, absence of feeling, lack of interest, disinterest, neglect, inattention, impassiveness, impassivity, nonchalance, aloofness, carelessness, negligence, insensibility, insensitivity, disdain, insouciance, apathy, coldness. **2.** unimportance, triviality, no import, insignificance, paltriness, inconsiderableness. **—Ant. 1** concern, warmth, sensibility; attention, interest, eagerness, caring. **2** importance, magnitude, significance, greatness.

indifferent *adj.* **1.** unconcerned, not caring, insensible, without interest, impervious, uninterested, insusceptible, detached, unmindful, impassive, unmoved, insouciant, apathetic, nonchalant, cool, aloof. **2.** perfunctory, mediocre, not very good, undistinguished, uninspired, ordinary, so-so, rote, commonplace, neither good nor bad, medium, middling, fair, modest, moderate, passable, average, betwixt and between; falling short of any standard of excellence, second-rate, rather poor. **—Ant. 1** avid, eager, keen, agog; interested, sensitive, susceptible, caring, sympathetic, responsive, compassionate, enthusiastic. **2** choice, notable, remarkable, exceptional, rare, first-class, superior, excellent, fine.

indigenous *adj.* native, growing naturally, aboriginal, originating in, characteristic of, endemic, homebred, homegrown, domestic, autochthonous. **—Ant.** naturalized; exotic; foreign, alien, extraneous, imported.

indigent *adj.* needy, destitute, in want, lacking the necessities of life, poor, in need, pinched, poverty-stricken, impoverished, penniless, without resources, badly off, moneyless, without food and clothing; *Informal* unable to keep the wolf from the door, hard-up. **—Ant.** wealthy, moneyed, rich, affluent, comfortable, solvent, flush.

indignant *adj.* incensed, offended, angry, mad, infuriated, displeased, piqued, peeved, resentful, irate, provoked, riled, wrathful, fuming; *Informal* miffed, huffy, put off, put out, worked up, sore, on one's high horse, steaming, wrought up. **—Ant.** pleased, delighted.

indignation *n.* **1.** resentment, displeasure, righteous anger, annoyance, vexation, dismay, irritation, pique, umbrage, exasperation. **2.** anger, rage, wrath, fury, ire, uproar, choler, huff, animus. **—Syn. Study. 2** See ANGER. **—Ant. 1, 2** calm, pleasure, serenity, composure, complacency, approval.

indignity *n.* abuse, insult, mistreatment, injury to dignity, outrage, affront, insult to one's self-respect, humiliation, injustice, contemptuous treatment, offense, dishonor, discourtesy, rudeness, slur, slight, *Informal* slap in the face. **—Syn. Study.** See INSULT. **—Ant.** dignity, honor, respect, deference, compliment, courtesy.

indirect *adj.* **1.** devious, roundabout,

winding, rambling, circuitous, meandering, oblique, zigzag, digressive, crooked, tortuous. **2.** incidental, unintentional, unintended; ancillary, secondary, derivative; distant, remote. **3.** evasive, not straightforward, discursive, oblique, rambling, digressive, circuitous, roundabout, vague, hedging. **—Ant. 1** direct, straight. **2** direct, connected, primary. **3** direct, forthright, straightforward.

indiscreet *adj.* imprudent, incautious, injudicious, uncalled-for, improvident, unseemly, uncircumspect, unbefitting, foolhardy, foolish, impolitic, tasteless, ill-judged, thoughtless, inconsiderate, unwise, careless, tactless, untactful, undiplomatic. **—Ant.** discreet, judicious, prudent, circumspect, cautious, politic, tactful.

indiscriminate *adj.* **1.** promiscuous, undiscriminating, unchoosy, random, unselective, undistinguishing, choosing at random, haphazard, hit-or-miss, without rhyme or reason. **2.** haphazard, random, unsystematic, disorganized, slapdash, jumbled, thrown together, motley, mongrel, confused, aimless, chaotic; *Informal* higgledy-piggledy, hodgepodge.

indispensable *adj.* essential, crucial, vital, imperative, necessary, absolutely necessary, needed, required, requisite, not dispensable, needful, obligatory, mandatory, compulsory; fundamental, basic. **—Syn. Study.** See NECESSARY. **—Ant.** dispensable, expendable, disposable, unnecessary, nonessential.

indisposed *adj.* **1.** ailing, sickly, ill, laid up, slightly sick, taken ill, not oneself, unwell, bedridden, *Informal* under the weather. **2.** averse, not disposed, reluctant, hesitant, disinclined, unwilling, not predisposed, loath, not in favor of, opposed. **—Ant. 1** healthy, hardy, hale, well, hearty, sound. **2** disposed, eager, avid, keen, anxious, willing, desirous, inclined.

indisputable *adj.* undeniable, irrefutable, incontestable, indubitable, incontrovertible, unassailable, unquestionable, evident, obvious, unmistakable, apparent, definite, conclusive, assured, beyond a shadow of doubt. **—Ant.** dubious, uncertain, questionable, doubtful, iffy.

indistinct *adj.* muffled, vague, not distinct, unintelligible, unclear, inaudible, weak, faint, not clearly defined, not clearly perceptible; obscure, ill-defined, indefinite, cloudy, murky, shadowy, clouded, out of focus, dim, nebulous, blurred, muddy; indecipherable, illegible; uncertain, mysterious, enigmatic, puzzling, hidden, indeterminate, ambiguous; incomprehensible, incoherent, confused. **—Ant.** distinct, intelligible, comprehensible, clear, audible, articulate, well-defined, perceptible, definite.

indistinguishable *adj.* not differentiable, identical with, not distinguishable; a carbon copy of, the perfect likeness of, *Informal* the spitting image of; indiscernible, unclear, imperceptible, unobservable, unnoticeable, inconspicuous, not capable of being made out, invisible, unapparent, indistinct, obscure. **—Ant.** distinguishable, differentiable; separate, unidentical, different; discernible, perceptible, observable, noticeable, visible, apparent, distinct, clear.

individual *adj.* **1.** special, especial, separate, particular, exclusive, personal, private, independent, singular, one's own, specific, exclusive, personalized. **2.** special, distinctive, unusual, original, personal, different, uncommon, unconventional, singular, characteristic, distinct, unique. **—*n.* 3.** person, somebody, single human being, self-determined being, distinct person, unique entity, autonomous being. **—Ant. 1** general, universal, group, collective, common. **2** conventional, ordinary, common, indistinct.

individuality *n.* independent nature, uniqueness, distinction, distinctiveness, particularity, singularity; unique character, specialness, cachet.

indoctrinate *v.* teach, inculcate, instruct in a doctrine, propagandize, brainwash, initiate, train, school, educate, tutor, brief, familiarize with, drill, give instruction to, infuse, instill, implant.

indolent *adj.* lazy, slothful, habitually idle, inactive, easygoing, shiftless, slack, sluggish, inert, lethargic, do-nothing, listless, lumpish, lackadaisical, dawdling, dilatory. **—Syn. Study.** See IDLE. **—Ant.** industrious; busy, diligent, conscientious, assiduous, sedulous; energetic, strenuous, vigorous, active.

indomitable *adj.* invincible, indefatigable, unconquerable, invulnerable, impregnable, unyielding, insuperable, unassailable; staunch, steadfast, formidable, unwavering, irrepressible, resolute, stubborn, dogged, unflinching, fearless, dauntless, unshrinking, intrepid, stalwart, courageous, undaunted, persevering, doughty, valiant, cast-iron. **—Syn. Study.** See INVINCIBLE. **—Ant.** yielding, weak, feeble, languid, wavering, faltering, flinching, shrinking, cowardly.

indorse *v.* See ENDORSE.

induce *v.* **1.** coax, persuade, influence, prompt, dispose, incline, impel, spur, prevail upon, bring round, encourage, get, sway, win over, prevail on. **2.** bring on, give rise to, lead to, occasion, prompt, cause, bring about, produce, motivate, inspire, sow the seeds of, set in motion, effect, instigate, incite, activate, actuate, provoke, arouse. **—Syn. Study. 1** See PERSUADE. **—Ant. 1** dissuade, prevent, disincline, deter, hinder, restrain. **2** deter, hinder, stop, squelch, curb, suppress.

inducement *n.* incentive, enticement, allurement, incitement, goad, spur, bait, stimulus, inspiration, motive, ground, cause, reason, provocation, temptation, persuasion, instigation, attraction. **—Syn. Study.** See MOTIVE. **—Ant.** deterrent, discouragement.

induct *v.* initiate, instate, install, introduce, inaugurate, establish, invest, lead in, usher in, bring in; frock, ordain, consecrate; crown, enthrone; conscript, enlist, draft, sign up, register.

indulge *v.* cater to, serve, go along with, oblige, gratify, accommodate, give way to, yield to, give loose rein to, treat, appease, yield to the desires of, pamper the whims of, coddle, pander to, baby, favor, humor, mollycoddle, humor to excess, spoil, cosset. **—Syn. Study.** See SPOIL. **—Ant.** deny, forbid, thwart, disappoint, discipline, abstain from.

indulgence *n.* **1.** luxury, something indulged in, self-indulgence, extravagance, excess, self-gratification, intemperance, immoderation; dissipation, profligacy, debauchery. **2.** sufferance, understanding, tolerance, forgiveness, forbearance, patience, lenience, compassion, permissiveness, allowance, kindness, graciousness, benignity. **—Ant. 1** abstinence, self-sacrifice, repression, restraint. **2** condemnation, castigation, reprehension.

indulgent *adj.* lenient, tolerant, understanding, forbearing, humoring, forgiving, permissive, easygoing, complaisant, clement, pampering, sparing, patient, yielding, obliging, benign, kind, tender, conciliatory. **—Ant.** strict, stern, severe, rigorous, stringent, harsh, rough, austere, intolerant, unmerciful, unforgiving, demanding.

industrious *adj.* hardworking, zealous, diligent, sedulous, assiduous, productive, purposeful; busy, occupied; active, energetic, indefatigable, unremitting, tireless, unflagging. **—Ant.** idle, lazy, shiftless, indolent, lethargic.

industry *n.* **1.** business, commerce, field, manufacture, trade. **2.** hard work, zeal, diligence, industriousness, sedulousness, application, go, labor, assiduity, bustle, hustle, enterprise, energy, perseverance, toil, patient plodding, indefatigability, activity, assiduousness.

inebriated *adj.* drunk, under the influence, intoxicated, besotted, befuddled, tipsy, drunken, drunk as a lord; *Slang* plastered, in one's cups, oiled, sozzled, tight, high, loaded, three sheets to the wind, potted, bombed, stoned, smashed, wrecked, zonked. **—Ant.** sober.

ineffable *adj.* indescribable, inexpressible, unspeakable, indefinite, indefinable, incommunicable; unutterable, untellable, unspeakable; ideal, transcendental, transcendent; divine, sacred, spiritual.

ineffective *adj.* of little use, not much good, futile, vain, not producing results, fruitless; inefficient, unproductive, weak, powerless, inadequate, useless, impotent, inoperative; incapable, worthless. **—Ant.** effective; effectual, efficacious, efficient; useful, profitable, capable, productive, adequate.

ineffectual *adj.* inept, incompetent, ineffective, inefficient, unsatisfactory, inefficacious, unprofitable, useless, unavailing, not up to par, unsuccessful, unproductive, profitless, vain, futile; weak, impotent, hapless, feckless, feeble, inadequate, lame. **—Ant.** effectual, efficacious, effective, profitable, fruitful, useful, successful, productive, gainful; efficient, satisfactory, competent, adequate.

inefficient *adj.* ineffective, incompetent, slipshod, ineffectual, slack, unproductive, inadequate, not efficient, wasteful of time or energy, inefficacious, inept, unskilled, good-for-nothing, indifferent; futile, pointless. **—Ant.** efficient, competent, able, capable, qualified; skillful, skilled, proficient, expert, adept; effectual, efficacious; *Slang* crackerjack.

ineligible *adj.* unqualified, disqualified, not eligible, unentitled, unfit, unacceptable, unsuitable. **—Ant.** eligible, qualified, suitable, fit.

ineluctable *adj.* inevitable, inescapable, unavoidable, ineludible, irrevocable, unevadable, inevasible, unpreventable, unstoppable, inexorable; certain, sure, fated, sure as fate. **—Ant.** dubious, doubtful, improbable, questionable.

inept *adj.* **1.** inefficient, incompetent, unskilled, untrained, unqualified, without dexterity, bungling, ineffective, inefficacious, ineffectual, awkward, clumsy, maladroit. **2.** out of place, unapt, pointless, empty, inane, inappropriate, unsuitable, unfitting, foolish, senseless, asinine, silly, fatuous, nonsensical. **—Ant. 1** efficient, skillful, apt, qualified, dexterous, competent, talented, effectual, effective, adroit, efficacious, able. **2** apt, germane, appropriate, pointed; sensible.

inequality *n.* unfairness, inequity, lack of equality, imparity, favoritism, prejudice; irregularity, difference, diversity, variableness, changeableness, dissimilarity, unequalness, dissimilitude, disparity, disproportion, inconstancy, divergence, unlikeness. **—Ant.** equality, fairness, impartiality, regularity, sameness, similarity, similitude, constancy, likeness.

inert *adj.* motionless, static, immobile, stationary, inactive, dormant, quiescent, still, passive, inanimate, impassive; listless, phlegmatic, sluggish, dull, numb, leaden, supine, slack, torpid, languid. **—Syn. Study.** See INACTIVE. **—Ant.** dynamic; animated; active, alert, kinetic, brisk, lively, energetic, vigorous.

inertia *n.* inertness, listlessness, sluggishness, languor, disinclination to move, passiveness, inactivity, laziness, inaction, lethargy, lassitude, torpidity, apathy, indolence, supineness, passivity, torpor, dullness, stupor, weariness. **—Ant.** activity, action, liveliness, energy, vigor, vitality, animation.

inevitable *adj.* inescapable, unavoidable, unpreventable, ineluctable, destined, predetermined, certain, written in the book of fate, fated, predestined, sure, sure to happen, ineludible. **—Ant.** escapable, avoidable, eludible, evadable, preventable; uncertain, indeterminate.

inexcusable *adj.* unpardonable, unforgivable, indefensible, unjustifiable, unallowable, intolerable, unbearable. **—Ant.** excusable, pardonable, forgivable, justifiable, defensible.

inexorable *adj.* unyielding, relentless, firm, inflexible, stiff, unbending, immovable, irresistible, intractable, adamant, adamantive, determined, obdurate, dogged, uncompromising, inescapable; cruel, pitiless, merciless, ruthless. **—Ant.** sympathetic, tender, indulgent, compassionate.

inexpensive *adj.* low-priced, not expensive, popular-priced, costing little, nominal-priced; reasonable, moderate, cheap, economical, good at the price; *Informal* light on the pocketbook. **—Syn. Study.** See CHEAP. **—Ant.** expensive, costly, high-priced.

inexperienced *adj.* unseasoned, unskilled, inexpert, unpracticed, untrained, unschooled, uninitiated, untutored; untried, unfledged, green, callow, fresh; unfamiliar, unversed, unaccustomed, unconversant, unacquainted; unsophisticated, naive. **—Ant.** experienced, skilled, practiced, seasoned, trained, expert, schooled, aged, versed, accustomed, conversant; sophisticated, worldly, worldly-wise.

inexplicable *adj.* unexplainable, unfathomable, inscrutable, insolvable, incomprehensible, unaccountable, insoluble, undecipherable; mysterious, mystifying, abstruse, baffling, puzzling, perplexing, enigmatical. **—Ant.** explicable, explainable, fathomable, solvable, comprehensible, accountable, soluble; reasonable, understandable, obvious, clear.

infallible *adj.* faultless, flawless, free from error, unerring, incapable of error, unfailing, not liable to err, free from mistake, unimpeachable, apodictic, absolutely trustworthy, impeccable, perfect, inerrant, irrefutable, incontrovertible; dependable, foolproof, sure, certain, reliable, assured, positive, perfect, surefire. **—Ant.** fallible, questionable, dubious, contestable, refutable, untrustworthy, controvertible, doubtful, unreliable, uncertain, unsure, undependable.

infamous *adj.* notorious, disreputable, having a bad reputation, villainous, of evil fame, of ill repute, nefarious, outrageous, dishonorable, vile, scandalous, shameful, ignoble, foul, heinous, monstrous, evil, wicked, opprobrious, disgraceful, base, damnable, odious, perfidious, detestable, abhorrent, sordid, recreant, abominable, low, iniquitous, treacherous, shamefully bad, corrupt, scurrilous, immoral, sinful, knavish, profligate. **—Ant.** illustrious; glorious, splendid, sublime, reputable, honorable, noble, good.

infamy *n.* dishonor, shame, disgrace, ignominy, disrepute, opprobrium, disesteem, discredit, scandal; evil, wickedness, villainy, corruption, abomination; notoriety, notoriousness. **—Syn. Study.** See DISGRACE. **—Ant.** integrity, honor, virtue, probity, nobility.

infant *n.* baby, babe, child, kid, newborn, toddler, nursling, neonate, suckling.

infantile *adj.* babyish, suitable to an infant, characteristic of an infant, childish, childlike, juvenile, infantlike, infantine, sophomoric. **—Syn. Study.** See CHILDISH. **—Ant.** mature, adult, manly, womanly, grown-up.

infatuated *adj.* enamored, enchanted, bewitched by, inspired with blind love for, inflamed by, beguiled by, spellbound by, carried away by, having a crush on, intoxicated by, smitten by, deprived of common sense by, obsessed by, entranced by, captivated by, charmed by, enraptured by, enthralled by.

infect *v.* **1.** contaminate, taint, poison, blight; afflict, indispose. **2.** touch, influence, spread among, affect adversely, work upon, have an effect on, spread through, leave a mark on; damage, corrupt, spoil, ruin.

infectious *adj.* **1.** contagious, catching, communicable, inoculable, virulent, epidemic, spreading, infective, *Informal* catchable. **2.** catching, contagious, tending to affect others, irresistible, compelling, captivating. **—Syn. Study. 1, 2**

See CONTAGIOUS. —**Ant.** 1 noncontagious, noncommunicable, incommunicable.

infer *v.* conclude, deduce, reckon, reason, judge; opine, guess, conjecture, speculate, gather, consider probable, glean, suppose, surmise, form an opinion, deem, presume.

inferior *adj.* **1.** worth less than, of lower quality than, less valuable than; lower in rank than, of less importance than, subordinate, subservient, secondary, junior, subsidiary. **2.** poor, substandard, low-quality, low-grade, second-rate, less valuable, of less excellence, indifferent, mediocre, *Informal* not up to snuff. —**Ant.** 1 superior, higher, senior, greater. 2 superior, first-rate, first-class, top, prime, fine, excellent.

infernal *adj.* **1.** hellish, Hadean, Plutonian, Stygian, lower, nether. **2.** damnable, hellish, devilish, horrible, fiendish, diabolical, demoniacal, awful, terrible, heinous, black, cursed, execrable, flagitious, vicious, accursed, malicious, nefarious, atrocious, vile, abominable, monstrous, iniquitous, horrendous. —**Ant.** 1 supernal, angelic, cherubic, heavenly.

inferno *n.* **1.** hell, Hades, netherworld, nether regions, the pit, lower world, underworld, abyss, perdition, *Bible* Tophet, the bottomless pit, infernal regions; hellfire, fire and brimstone. **2.** oven, hellhole, hotbox, furnace, fiery furnace; sizzler, roaster, scorcher. —**Ant.** 1 heaven, paradise, Eden; bliss, nirvana.

infertile *adj.* barren, unfruitful, sterile, unproductive, nonproductive, arid, bare, fallow, desolate, fruitless, impotent, unprolific, effete, infecund; depleted, exhausted, drained. —**Ant.** fertile, fruitful, productive, fecund.

infidel *n.* unbeliever, heathen, pagan, idolater, nonbeliever in God, atheist, agnostic, skeptic, apostate, heretic; savage, barbarian. —**Syn. Study.** See ATHEIST. —**Ant.** believer.

infidelity *n.* **1.** adultery, breaking of the marriage vows, marital faithlessness, unfaithfulness, violation of the marriage bed, betrayal, perfidy, disloyalty. **2.** nonobservance, nonadherence, breach, falsity, disregard, transgression, violation, infraction. —**Ant.** 1 fidelity, faithfulness, loyalty.

infinite *adj.* **1.** enormous, great, immense, tremendous; immeasurable, vast, measureless. **2.** boundless, interminable, limitless, uncircumscribed, unlimited; illimitable, unbounded, endless, knowing no limit, without end, inexhaustible; incalculable, measureless. —**Ant.** 1 small, little, limited. 2 finite; circumscribed, definitive, restricted, limited, bounded, measurable.

infinitesimal *adj.* tiny, inconsiderable, insignificant, microscopic, imperceptible, immeasurably small, diminutive, puny, minute, extremely small, undiscernible, *Informal* wee; inappreciable, negligible. —**Ant.** enormous, vast, infinite, huge, immeasurable, large, great.

infinity *n.* boundless time, eternity, eternal time, infinitude, endlessness, boundlessness, illimitability, limitlessness; immeasurability, measurelessness, inexhaustibility; incalculability, incomprehensibility; forever, perpetuity, everlastingness, sempiternity. —**Ant.** finiteness, transitoriness, limitedness, temporariness.

infirm *adj.* weak, feeble, frail, weakened, unsound, ailing, decrepit, enfeebled, doddering, shaky, unstable, anile, poorly, worn, helpless, failing, ailing, sickly, fragile, ill, debilitated, strengthless, powerless, enervated, disabled, emaciated. —**Ant.** hale; strong, sturdy, stalwart, stout; healthy, robust, sound.

infirmity *n.* **1.** disability, ailment, debility, infirmness, debilitation, malady, illness, disorder, indisposition, physical weakness, frailness, sickness, loss of health, lack of strength, handicap, fragility. **2.** failing, moral weakness, deficiency, flaw, defect, fault, frailty, vulnerability, imperfection; instability, unstableness. —**Ant.** 1 strength, vigor, healthfulness, soundness. 2 strength, perfection; stability.

inflame *v.* excite, electrify, intoxicate, arouse, provoke, rouse, ignite, kindle, fire, excite the passions of, incite, stir up, stimulate, agitate, work up, heat up, enkindle, craze; rile, incense, enrage, madden. —**Syn. Study.** See KINDLE. —**Ant.** extinguish (a passion), quench, allay, cool, calm, pacify, quiet, squelch, suppress.

inflammable *adj.* **1.** flammable, easily set on fire, capable of being set on fire, combustible, ignitable, incendiary. **2.** fiery, volatile, excitable, sensitive, inflammatory, easily roused, incendiary, high-strung, choleric, impetuous, precipitate, overhasty. —**Ant.** 1 nonflammable, uninflammable. 2 placid, calm, easy, passive, even, cool.

inflammatory *adj.* provocative, fiery, incendiary, rabble-rousing, enraging, inciting, rabid, arousing, tending to stir up strong feelings, intemperate, rebellious, insurgent, revolutionary, mutinous, demagogic; combustible, inflammable, explosive, fulminating, volcanic. —**Ant.** soothing, calming, pacifying.

inflate *v.* fill up, puff out, blow up, be blown up, swell, expand, bloat, pump up, fill with gas, distend, dilate. **—Ant.** deflate, empty, flatten.

inflexible *adj.* **1.** unbending, unyielding, rigid, hard, firm, solid, not flexible, fixed, taut, stiff, unplastic, unmalleable. **2.** unchangeable, rigid, unyielding, unbending, hidebound, obstinate, obdurate, intractable, stubborn, tenacious, pigheaded, mulish, dogged, headstrong, determined, adamant, adamantine, resolute, uncompromising, inexorable, implacable, unwavering, immovable; impervious, ironbound, stringent, hard and fast, firm, immutable. **—Ant. 1** flexible, elastic, resilient, supple, springy; pliable, pliant, yielding, plastic, malleable, ductile; fluid, liquid; expansive, buoyant, soft. **2** amenable, tractable, docile, biddable, flexible, yielding, changeable, compromising, irresolute, undetermined.

inflict *v.* lay on, visit upon, put upon, impose, administer, cause to suffer, bring to bear, perpetrate, wreak; *Slang* unload, dump. **—Ant.** spare, remove, alleviate, withdraw, suspend.

influence *n.* **1.** weight, sway, power, pull, effect, pressure, hold, potency, mastery, ascendancy, authority, domination, dominion, control, leverage, advantage, prestige; *Slang* clout. **—*v.* 2.** induce, persuade, impel, act upon, work upon, move, prompt, provoke, stir, inspire, incite, arouse, actuate, sway, exercise influence on, have a bearing on, play a decisive role in, incline, dispose, predispose, guide, be guided; bring pressure to bear on. **—Syn. Study. 1** See AUTHORITY. **—Ant. 1** ineffectiveness, impotency. **2** dissuade, restrain, hinder, impede.

influential *adj.* effective, instrumental, having influence, consequential, effectual, forceful, powerful, efficacious, important, significant, momentous, potent, puissant, strong, weighty; leading, moving, inspiring, activating. **—Ant.** uninfluential, weak, ineffective, ineffectual, unefficacious, inoperative, inconsiderable, unpersuasive, ineffectual, powerless, impotent, unimportant.

influx *n.* inflow, inundation, flowing in, indraft, infiltration, inpouring, ingress, entry, incursion, arrival, converging. **—Ant.** outflow, outpouring, exit, egress, exodus.

inform *v.* **1.** tell, apprise, notify, let know, give notice to, advise, make known to, report to, give knowledge of, give information, acquaint, familiarize, send word to, disclose to, forewarn, communicate to, declare to, mention to, enlighten, edify, serve notice on, signify to, announce to, indicate to, tip off, *Slang* clue in. **2.** denounce, give damaging evidence, furnish incriminating evidence, report an offense, tell on, tattle; *Slang* snitch, squeal, fink, rat, blow the whistle.

informal *adj.* **1.** casual, simple, without formality, unceremonious, unconventional, familiar, unofficial, easy, unconstrained, natural, not formal, easygoing, offhand, spontaneous, come-as-you-are. **2.** (*of speech*) colloquial, conversational, casual, everyday, vernacular, workaday, idiomatic, plain, ordinary, chatty. **—Syn. Study. 2** See COLLOQUIAL. **—Ant.** ceremonious, formal, official.

informant *n.* informer, adviser, appriser, respondent, enlightener, notifier, source, tipster; reporter, announcer, spokesman, spokeswoman, *Slang* horse's mouth.

information *n.* data, material, news, knowledge, report, facts, evidence, bulletin, communiqué, tidings, account, factfinding; (*variously*) documents, papers, notes, materials; announcement, notice, intelligence, enlightenment; briefing, notification.

informer *n.* police informant, betrayer, tattler, *Slang* stool pigeon, squealer, blabber, snitcher, fink, stoolie, rat, canary; traitor, Judas; *French* mouchard.

infraction *n.* violation, breaking of a law, lawbreaking, infringement, breach, transgression, trespass, encroachment; disobedience, unobservance, nonobservance; insubordination; peccadillo. **—Syn. Study.** See BREACH.

infrastructure *n.* basis, groundwork, foundation, base, support; underpinning, bottom, bedrock, substructure, understructure, footing, substratum, *Geology* substrate, ground, root.

infrequent *adj.* occasional, rare, seldom, not regular, few and far between, sporadic, uncommon, unusual, unique, few, not habitual, happening at long intervals, spasmodic, fitful, seldom happening. **—Ant.** frequent, usual, customary, ordinary, common, habitual.

infringe *v.* **1.** violate, transgress, break, commit an infraction of, act contrary to, disobey, commit a breach of, infract, contravene. **2.** trespass, encroach, intrude, invade, impinge, overstep; interfere with, butt in. **—Syn. Study. 2** See TRESPASS.

infuriate *v.* anger, make angry, inflame, madden, enrage, rile, kindle wrath, incense, provoke, make furious, outrage, vex, gall, offend, aggravate, irritate, lash into a fury, chafe, try one's temper, exasperate, *Informal* burn one up, raise one's dander, make one see red. **—Syn. Study.** See ENRAGE.

infuse *v.* instill, inspire, imbue, fortify; pour into, impart to, insinuate, introduce into, cause to penetrate, implant, inculcate, introject, breathe into.

ingenious *adj.* clever, cunning, artful, skillful, inventive, masterful, stunning, deft, adroit, dexterous, masterly, expert, exhibiting ingenuity, brilliant, shrewd, crafty, resourceful, original. **—Ant.** unoriginal, pedestrian, unimaginative, artless, unskillful, uninventive, unresourceful; clumsy, maladroit.

ingenuity *n.* cleverness, skill, skillfulness, inventiveness, resourcefulness, imagination, aptitude, good thinking, adroitness, ingeniousness, imaginativeness, adeptness, flair, mastery, expertise, know-how, sharpness, dexterity, deftness, cunning, shrewdness, facility, astuteness. **—Ant.** awkwardness, clumsiness, dullness, stupidity, unskillfulness, inability, ineptitude, maladroitness.

ingenuous *adj.* natural, artless, guileless, unaffected, genuine, simplehearted, openhearted, honest, open, unsophisticated, frank, direct, trusting, straightforward; *Slang* up front, straight-shooting. **—Ant.** worldly-wise, jaded, disingenuous; wily, devious, tricky.

inglorious *adj.* disgraceful, dishonorable, shameful, ignominious, infamous, ignoble, despicable, contemptible, heinous, depraved, corrupt, atrocious, nefarious, evil, base; scandalous, shocking, outrageous, flagrant. **—Ant.** admirable, commendable, praiseworthy, exemplary, worthy.

ingrained *adj.* fixed, inborn, inbred, inherent, innate, deep, deep-seated, deep-rooted, constitutional, implanted, rooted, indelible, thorough, intrinsic, inveterate, confirmed, firm.

ingratiating *adj.* **1.** winning, engaging, captivating, personable, likable, magnetic, attractive, appealing, enchanting, congenial, winsome, persuasive, charming, amiable, genial, pleasing, cordial, affable, sweet, lovable, gracious, friendly, good-humored. **2.** unctuous, gushing, oily, oleaginous, fulsome, smarmy, obsequious; self-serving, falsely disarming; presumptuous. **—Ant. 1** forbidding, austere, unattractive, unappealing, displeasing, unpleasant, abrasive, unlovable, charmless.

ingredient *n.* element, part, component, constituent, integral part; feature, factor, aspect, essential, contributor, principle.

inhabit *v.* reside in, live in, dwell in, occupy, tenant, lodge, take up one's abode in; people, populate, settle.

inhabitant *n.* resident, native, dweller, occupant, inhabiter, denizen, inmate, tenant, renter, lessee, occupier; boarder, lodger; citizen, villager, settler.

inhale *v.* breathe in, inbreathe, suck in, draw into the lungs, snuff, sniff, respire. **—Ant.** exhale, expire.

inherent *adj.* essential, innate, inseparable, hereditary, native, intrinsic, inborn, deep-rooted, inveterate, natural, inbred, ingrained, constitutional, inalienable. **—Syn. Study.** See ESSENTIAL. **—Ant.** foreign, alien, extrinsic, adventitious; subsidiary, superficial, supplemental.

inherit *v.* fall heir to, come into, come in for, be bequeathed, be willed, be left, get, come by, acquire, become heir to, have fall into one's hands, accrue to, have fall to one's lot, have fall to one's share.

inheritance *n.* legacy, bequest, bequeathal, estate, devise, bestowal, heritage, endowment; birthright, patrimony.

inhibit *v.* prevent, hold back, arrest, hinder, impede, restrain, suppress, check, stop, repress, smother, muzzle, harness, block, control, obstruct, curb, constrain, gag, restrict, hold in leash; forbid, prohibit, enjoin, bar. **—Ant.** allow, let, permit, suffer, further, encourage, support, abet.

inhibition Often **inhibitions** *n.* mental reservation, guardedness, self-consciousness, mental block, holding back of an action or thought, misgiving, inhibiting or restraining influence, reserve, restriction, constraint, restraint of action; impediment, obstruction, blockage, stricture, constriction, check.

inhospitable *adj.* aloof, unfriendly, unsociable, cool, distant, standoffish; rude, impolite, unkind, uncongenial, ungracious, discourteous, inconsiderate, unneighborly, unobliging, unaccommodating. **—Ant.** cordial, sociable, genial, congenial, obliging, accommodating.

inhuman *adj.* cruel, unfeeling, merciless, pitiless, heartless, coldhearted, brutal, ruthless, barbarous, barbaric, monstrous, cold-blooded, savage, malevolent, vicious, satanic, hardhearted, brutish, demoniac, diabolical, malignant, venomous, fiendish. **—Ant.** human, humane; benevolent, kind, humanitarian, charitable, altruistic, sympathetic, compassionate, tender.

inhumanity *n.* cruelty, savagery, brutality, bloodthirstiness, ruthlessness, barbarity, fiendishness, viciousness, brutishness, malevolence, coldbloodedness, heartlessness, sadism, mercilessness. **—Ant.** humaneness, consideration, altruism, kindness.

inimical *adj.* **1.** harmful, detrimental, injurious, dangerous, deleterious, destructive, hurtful, ruinous; toxic, virulent, venomous, poisonous. **2.** hostile, antagonistic, unfriendly, ill-disposed, acrimonious, antipathetic, rancorous, ill-willed, hateful. **—Ant. 1** helpful, beneficial, salutary, propitious. **2** friendly, amiable, congenial, well-disposed.

inimitable *adj.* matchless, unmatched, incomparable, unique, incapable of being imitated, peerless, preeminent, unparalleled, rare, unequaled, unsurpassed, nonpareil, beyond compare, unrivaled, unexcelled; consummate, superlative, supreme. **—Ant.** common, ordinary, imitable.

iniquity *n.* **1.** unfairness, gross injustice, dishonesty, violation of one's rights, immorality, unrighteousness, inequity, unjustness. **2.** wickedness, wrong, wrongdoing, evil, evildoing, sin, transgression, infamy, miscreancy, knavery, roguery, villainy, flagrancy; abomination, sinfulness, depravity, corruption, outrage, immorality, vice, profligacy, turpitude. **—Ant. 1** justice, fairness, integrity, virtue, rectitude, probity, honesty, uprightness, goodness, morality.

initial *adj.* first, starting, beginning, opening, commencing, primary, introductory, incipient, initiatory, inaugural, maiden; original, germinal, primal. **—Ant.** last, ultimate, ending, final, closing, concluding, terminal.

initiate *v.* **1.** begin, set afoot, start, be started, set going, get going, open, be opened, get under way, enter upon, commence, launch, be launched, originate, institute, found, start the ball rolling, kick off, inaugurate, take the lead, set up, break ground, lay the foundation, establish, lead the way, lay the first stone, blaze the trail. **2.** induct, usher in, receive, admit with special rites, inaugurate, install, give entrance to, take in, bring in, introduce, invest; haze. **3.** introduce, familiarize with, acquaint with; accustom to, habituate to. **—Syn. Study. 1** See BEGIN. **—Ant. 1** consummate; fulfill, execute, accomplish, achieve, terminate, conclude, finish, end, complete. **2** refuse, reject, expel.

initiation *n.* **1.** initiating, formal admission, introduction, induction, ushering in, admittance, entrance. **2.** introduction, indoctrination, inculcation, guidance. **3.** commencement, opening, beginning, genesis, inception, outset, onset, start, starting, beginning, introduction, inauguration, outbreak. **—Ant. 1** expulsion, rejection, exit. **3** end, finish, completion, finalization, termination, closure.

initiative *n.* **1.** lead, first step, first move, leading action, beginning step, introductory act. **2.** enterprise, leadership, forcefulness, dynamism, ability in initiating action, originality, creativity, power to begin, aggressiveness, *Slang* get-up-and-go.

inject *v.* insert, put, interject, throw in, interpolate, introduce, infuse, imbue, infix, instill, intromit; force; *Slang* pump.

injure *v.* harm, do injury to, wound, damage, do harm to, cause harm to, afflict, hurt, mar, impair; bruise, deface, disfigure, mangle, lacerate, maim, deform, mutilate, lame; wrong, violate, abuse, ill-treat, maltreat, affront, offend, misuse, sting, sully, stain, vitiate, malign, debase, spoil, blemish, scathe. **—Syn. Study.** INJURE, IMPAIR mean to harm or damage something. INJURE is a general term referring to any kind or degree of damage: *to injure one's spine; to injure one's reputation.* To IMPAIR is to make imperfect in any way, often with a suggestion of progressive deterioration: *One's health can be impaired by overwork.* **—Ant.** soothe, heal, pacify; aid, help, assist, benefit.

injurious *adj.* hurtful, damaging, harmful, causing injury, detrimental, destructive, deleterious, noxious, abusive, ruinous, calamitous, pernicious, disastrous, corrosive; inimical, adverse. **—Ant.** beneficial, helpful, advantageous, salutary; profitable.

injury *n.* hurt, harm, wound, damage, bruise, mutilation, cut, lesion, gash, contusion, stab, blow, affliction, scratch, laceration; abuse, blow, injustice, outrage, indignity, affront; defamation, vilification, detraction, impairment, aspersion, disservice.

injustice *n.* unjustness, unjust character, unfairness, inequality, bias, prejudice, partiality, inequity, bigotry, favoritism, partisanship; unjust act, wrong, disservice, infraction, injury, iniquity, wrongdoing, infringement, sin, persecution, unfair treatment, encroachment, tyranny, transgression, offense, foul play, evil, malpractice. **—Ant.** justice, equity, fairness, fair play, impartiality, lawfulness, rectitude, right, righteousness, equality.

inkling *n.* idea, vague idea, hint, suspicion, indication, tip, clue, suggestion, glimmer, glimmering, notion; cue, intimation, conception, supposition; whisper, insinuation, innuendo.

inlet *n.* cove, harbor, bay, gulf, estuary; narrows, waterway, strait, bight, fjord, firth.

inn *n.* public house, lodge, hotel, motel, lodging house, roadhouse, country hotel, hostel, pension, hospice, hostelry, tavern; caravansary.

innate *adj.* native, natural, inborn, inherent, inbred, instinctive, intuitive, natural, ingrained, intrinsic, essential, congenital, constitutional, inherited, hereditary, indigenous. —**Syn. Study.** INNATE, INBORN, CONGENITAL, HEREDITARY describe qualities, characteristics, or possessions acquired before or at the time of birth. INNATE, of Latin origin, and INBORN, a native English word, share the literal basic sense "existing at the time of birth," and they are interchangeable in most contexts: *innate/inborn stodginess/strength/abilities.* CONGENITAL refers most often to characteristics acquired during fetal development, esp. defects or undesirable conditions: *a congenital deformity; congenital blindness.* HEREDITARY describes qualities or things passed on from ancestors, either through the genes or by social or legal means: *Hemophilia is a hereditary condition; a hereditary title.* —**Ant.** acquired, learned; accidental, adventitious, incidental, fortuitous; assumed, affected, cultivated, fostered, nurtured; unnatural.

inner *adj.* **1.** interior, inward, inside, internal, central, middle. **2.** more secret, more intimate, unobvious, concealed, hidden, private, esoteric. **3.** spiritual, psychological, mental, psychic, emotional. —**Ant. 1** outer, outward, outside, exterior, external, outermost, open. **2** outer, external, open, public, obvious, exterior, exoteric.

innermost *adj.* most personal, most intimate, most private, deep-rooted, farthest inward, secret, deepest, inmost, deep-seated. —**Ant.** surface, superficial.

innocence *n.* **1.** guiltlessness, freedom from moral wrong, inculpability, blamelessness, impeccability, sinlessness, incorruption, clean hands, stainlessness; chastity, purity, spotlessness, immaculateness. **2.** simplicity, artlessness, ingenuousness, guilelessness, freshness, freedom from cunning or trickery, naiveté, purity, chastity. —**Ant. 1** guilt; offensiveness, contamination, sinfulness, impurity, corruption, wrongness. **2** artfulness, guile, cunning, trickery, wiliness, disingenuousness, worldliness.

innocent *adj.* **1.** guiltless, inculpable, blameless, faultless, free from moral wrong, above suspicion; sinless, irreproachable, upright, unimpeachable. **2.** guileless, open, unsuspicious, naive, unworldly, unsophisticated, simple, artless, ingenuous, childlike, honest, uncorrupt, uncorrupted, spotless, unblemished, clean, impeccable, undefiled, stainless, spotless, pristine, unstained, unsullied, virtuous, pure, immaculate, virginal, chaste. **3.** well-meant, meaning no harm, harmless, intending no damage, unmalicious, innocuous, inoffensive, unoffending. —*n.* **4.** young child, baby, little one, tot. **5.** naïf, unsophisticated person, artless one, (*fem.*) ingénue. **6.** tenderfoot, greenhorn, novice, tyro. —**Ant. 1** guilty, culpable, blameworthy, responsible; immoral, iniquitous, nefarious, sinful, unlawful, vicious, vile, wicked, evil, wrong; impure, tainted. **2** worldly, sophisticated, disingenuous, dishonest, artful, scheming; corrupt, sullied. **3** harmful, malicious, offensive.

innocuous *adj.* **1.** harmless, not damaging, painless, not injurious, innocent, mild, inoffensive. **2.** meaningless, vapid, insipid, dull, pointless, empty, barren; trite, banal, commonplace. —**Ant. 1** hurtful, deleterious, harmful, insidious, obnoxious, damaging, injurious, offensive, malicious. **2** powerful, trenchant, compelling, impressive.

innovation *n.* introduction, institution, establishment, inauguration, commencement; departure from the old, introduction of new methods, modernization, shift, drastic change, breaking of precedent; new measure, novelty, alteration, latest thing, latest fashion; *French* dernier cri.

innuendo *n.* insinuation, intimation, whisper, oblique hint, veiled allusion, sly suggestion, implication, inference, imputation, hint, indirect reference, overtone.

innumerable *adj.* countless, incalculable, myriad, numberless, incapable of being counted, numerous, multitudinous, manifold, many, too many to be counted, unnumbered. —**Syn. Study.** See MANY. —**Ant.** numerable, countable, computable; few, sporadic.

inoculation *n.* injection, vaccination, immunization, hypodermic, shot, booster shot, booster, needle, hypodermic injection.

inoffensive *adj.* harmless, unobjectionable, unoffending, tolerable, innocuous, endurable, sufferable; innocent, bland, mild, neutral; safe. —**Ant.** offensive, harmful, objectionable, offending, obnoxious; noxious.

inopportune *adj.* inconvenient, untimely, ill-timed, incommodious, badly timed, inappropriate, unpropitious, unsuitable, unseasonable; awkward, troublesome; undesirable, unfavorable, disadvantageous, inauspicious, unfortunate, ill-advised. —**Ant.** opportune, timely, convenient, appropriate, propitious, suitable, commodious; favorable, auspicious, fortunate.

inordinate *adj.* excessive, immoderate, extravagant, disproportionate, lavish, undue, unreasonable, unconscionable, superabundant, exorbitant, superfluous, overmuch, extreme, intemperate, unnecessary, profuse, unrestrained, wanton, overflowing, supersaturated, surplus, needless, uncalled-for, irrational; outrageous, scandalous, disgraceful, deplorable, shocking. **—Ant.** temperate, moderate; restrained, inhibited; rightful, equitable, reasonable, sensible.

inquest *n.* post mortem, autopsy, necropsy, coroner's inquest, ex post facto examination; inquiry, hearing, probe, investigation, probing, delving, inquisition.

inquire *v.* **1.** ask, query, seek information, question, make inquiry. **2.** investigate, probe, explore, study, look into, look deeper, inspect, examine, search, look behind the scenes of, scrutinize, look over, track down, *Informal* check out. **—Ant. 1** reply, answer, respond, rejoin, retort; inform.

inquiry Also **enquiry** *n.* **1.** investigation, seeking for truth, examination, questioning, inquisition, hunt, scrutiny, search, probe, interview, study, reconnaissance, inquest, quest, exploration, research, analysis, inspection, survey. **2.** query, question, interrogation, quiz.

inquisitive *adj.* **1.** eager for knowledge, searching, intellectually curious, inquiring, fond of investigation, investigative, questioning. **2.** prying, interfering, meddling, overcurious, unduly curious, intrusive, too curious, meddlesome, snooping; *Informal* snoopy, nosy. **—Ant. 1** indifferent, unconcerned, incurious, uninterested, apathetic, inattentive.

insane *adj.* **1.** mentally deranged, not sane, not of sound mind, mad, crazed, crazy, lunatic, unsound, demented, maniacal, out of one's mind, bereft of reason, not in touch with reality, mentally disordered, unbalanced; (*variously*) psychotic, manic, schizophrenic, paranoiac; *Informal* out of one's wits, out of one's head, touched, mad as a hatter, mad as a March hare, stark staring mad, unhinged; *Slang* loco, teched, bats, batty, nuts, bats in the belfry, nutty, nutty as a fruitcake, balmy, loony, off one's rocker, cracked, zany; *British* daft, round the bend, off one's chump, potty, bonkers; raving, frenzied, wild, berserk. **2.** idiotic, senseless, unreasonable, foolish, dumb, imbecilic, mad, crazy; imprudent, injudicious; absurd, ridiculous, insensate; bizarre, eccentric. **—Ant. 1, 2** sane; sensible, judicious, wise, sapient, prudent, sound, reasonable.

insanity *n.* **1.** mental illness, madness, mental disorder, derangement, raving, loss of reason, unsoundness, aberrance, aberration, craziness, lunacy, (*variously*) dementia, mania, psychosis, paranoia, schizophrenia, monomania, hallucination. **2.** idiocy, senselessness, foolishness, absurdity, stupidity, madness, craziness, folly, unreasonableness. **—Ant. 1** sanity, good sense, rationality, lucidity, reason, intelligence, soundness.

insatiable *adj.* unappeasable, voracious, ravenous, gluttonous, incapable of being satisfied, unquenchable, unsatisfiable, insatiate, bottomless, limitless, implacable; omnivorous. **—Ant.** satiable, appeasable, satisfiable, quenchable.

inscribe *v.* write, sign, autograph, scribble, scrawl; imprint, engrave, incise, carve, chisel, impress, mark, pen, letter, etch, brand, seal, blaze.

inscrutable *adj.* unknowable, incomprehensible, indecipherable, not easily understood, impenetrable to understanding, unfathomable, mysterious, mystifying, arcane, past comprehension, beyond interpretation, puzzling, perplexing, baffling, inexplicable, unsearchable, enigmatic, elusive, unintelligible, unreadable, unrevealed, mystical, obscure; hidden, concealed, veiled, masked; *Informal* pokerfaced, deadpan. **—Syn. Study.** See MYSTERIOUS. **—Ant.** obvious, palpable, plain, clear, manifest, open, evident, patent; penetrable, comprehensible, understandable; intelligible, explainable, self-evident, familiar, explicable, readable, knowable, revealing, transparent, lucid.

insecure *adj.* **1.** unsafe, endangered, exposed to danger, in danger, vulnerable, defenseless, exposed, ill-protected, unshielded, unprotected, unsheltered, risky, perilous, precarious, hazardous, on slippery ground, not out of the woods, under fire, dangerous, critical. **2.** not firm, unsteady, weak, shaky, unstable, dilapidated, wobbly, frail, unreliable, rickety, unsound, infirm, ramshackle, tottering, built upon sand, hanging by a thread, in a bad way, dangerous. **3.** uncertain, doubtful, beset by doubt, diffident, dubious, not confident, unsure, not sure, unassured, in a state of uncertainty, full of misgivings. **—Ant. 1** secure, safe, invulnerable, protected, shielded, sheltered, steady, trustworthy. **2** stable, sound, reliable, firm. **3** secure, confident, sure, certain, assured.

insecurity *n.* **1.** insecureness, instability, precariousness, shakiness, unsteadiness, vulnerability, defenselessness, unsafeness, endangerment. **2.** lack of assurance, lack of confidence, uncertainty, lack of sureness, lack of self-reliance, self-doubt, doubt, dubiousness, doubtfulness, diffidence, incertitude, apprehensiveness. **3.** Often **insecurities.** peril, hazard, danger, cause for alarm, risk, jeopardy, pitfall, contingency. **—Ant. 1** security, secureness, stability, invulnerability, safeness. **2** security, assurance, sureness, confidence, certitude. **3** security, safeness, sureness, certainty.

insensitive *adj.* unaware of, not sensitive, indifferent, unconcerned, apathetic, uncompassionate; hardened, unfeeling, callous, thick-skinned, blasé, cold; unaware of feeling, not capable of feeling, impervious, insensible, insensate, impassive, dead, numb. **—Ant.** sensitive, compassionate, tender; susceptible, subject, prone, open, exposed, hypersensitive, thin-skinned.

inseparable *adj.* constantly together, always in each other's company, attached, extremely intimate; not to be separated, incapable of being parted, indivisible, unseverable, indissoluble. **—Ant.** separable, unattached, divisible, sunderable, severable, soluble.

insert *v.* place in, put in, infix, set in, imbed, inject, inlay, inset, implant, put between, wedge in, push in, intersperse, slide in, infuse, interlard, press in, thrust in, stick in, stuff in, tuck in, drive in, *Informal* pop in; introduce, interpolate, interpose, interject, intrude, enter, add. **—Ant.** extract, disengage, detach, withdraw, remove, draw.

inside *n.* **1.** interior, inner part, inner space, interior part, inner surface, inner side. *—adj.* **2.** inner, innermost, inmost, inward; internal, interior. **3.** private, confidential, cliquish, for the elect or knowledgeable, secret, esoteric, intimate, internal, *Slang* in. **—Ant. 1** outside, exterior. **2** outside, outer, exterior, outermost, external, outward. **3** outside, public, open, exoteric.

insidious *adj.* **1.** devious, treacherous, deceitful, guileful, intending to entrap, crafty, tricky, stealthy, sly, wily, cunning, foxy, artful, contriving, underhanded, perfidious, crooked, slippery, shady, designing; surreptitious, subtle, Machiavellian, sneaky; falsehearted, disingenuous. **2.** secretive, stealthy, surreptitious, underhand, undercover, furtive, sneaking, clandestine, covert, undetected, concealed, disguised; pernicious, deleterious. **—Ant. 1** upright, forthright, artless, ingenuous, straightforward, sincere, open, honest, frank, candid. **2** open, conspicuous, innocuous, obvious; harmless.

insight *n.* perception, spontaneous understanding, apprehension, acumen, innate knowledge, penetration, discernment, intuition, penetrating judgment, immediate cognition, perspicacity, perspicaciousness, perceptiveness, perceptivity, instinctive knowledge, intuitiveness, clear understanding, comprehension. **—Ant.** obtuseness, blindness.

insignia *n.* emblem, badge, badge of office, mark, distinguishing mark of honor, decoration, patch, sign, mark of authority, ensign of royalty, symbol; (*variously*) bar, star, oak leaf, medal, epaulet, chevron, stripe.

insignificant *adj.* unimportant, inconsiderable, petty, negligible, trivial, of little account, of no consequence, inconsequential, having little meaning, paltry, nugatory, of no moment, small, minute, minuscule, trifling, picayune, meaningless, meager, irrelevant, not vital, worthless, immaterial, flimsy, puny, nonessential, indifferent, niggling, not worth the pains, beneath consideration, second-rate, piddling, not worth mentioning, *Informal* small potatoes. **—Ant.** significant, considerable, important, momentous, large, meaningful, essential, vital, appreciable; relevant, material.

insincere *adj.* hypocritical, dishonest, dissembling, deceitful, disingenuous, emotionally dishonest, two-faced, uncandid, untruthful, untrue, false, guileful, disingenuous, dissimulating, fraudulent, perfidious, mealymouthed, devious, lying, evasive, equivocal, double-dealing. **—Ant.** sincere, honest, candid, truthful, true.

insinuate *v.* **1.** imply, suggest, hint slyly, allude remotely to, intimate, asperse, whisper, let fall. **2.** ingratiate, push artfully, worm one's way, gently incorporate, introduce subtly, wheedle, inject, insert. **—Syn. Study. 1** See HINT. **—Ant. 1** deny. **2** withdraw, remove, retreat; alienate.

insipid *adj.* **1.** uninteresting, pointless, stupid, dull, characterless, banal, wearisome, bland, boring, trite, vapid, inane, barren, drab, prosaic, jejune, lifeless, zestless, arid, monotonous, lean, empty, commonplace; *Slang* blah, wishy-washy, namby-pamby. **2.** flat, tasteless, savorless, stale, vapid, unappetizing. **—Ant. 1** interesting, zestful, pungent, spirited, spunky, provocative, engaging, lively, stimulating, exciting, piquant, colorful. **2** pungent, piquant, spicy; fiery, peppery, gingery; savory, flavorful, tasty, palatable, appetizing; gusty.

insist *v.* **1.** maintain, state firmly, asseverate, assert positively, vouch, contend, claim, hold, assert, aver, take a firm stand, stress, stick to one's colors, repeat, reiterate, stand one's ground, be pertinacious, persist, be determined; protest, remonstrate. **2.** demand, advise firmly, urge, lay down the law, require, exhort, command, be emphatic, be firm about, press earnestly; warn, caution, admonish. **—Ant. 1** deny. **2** beg, plead, ask, request.

insolence *n.* insulting rudeness, impertinence, unmannerliness, disrespect, disobedience, overbearing contempt, overweening pride, lordliness, audacity, hauteur, arrogance, disdain, haughtiness, imperiousness, superciliousness, presumption, incivility, impoliteness, brazenness, bumptiousness, effrontery, gall, impudence, insulting disobedience.

—**Ant.** deference, modesty, respect, politeness, bashfulness, humility, mannerliness, civility.

insolent *adj.* disrespectful, insulting, impertinent, rude, discourteous, impolite, impudent, unmannerly, audacious, brazen, bumptious, outrageous, nervy, cheeky, arrogant, presumptuous, defiant, overbearing, haughty, supercilious, disdainful, contemptuous, galling, *Informal* fresh, smart-alecky, wise acreish. —**Syn. Study.** INSOLENT, IMPERTINENT, IMPUDENT refer to bold and rude persons or behavior. INSOLENT suggests the insulting or contemptuous behavior of an arrogant person: *The boss fired the insolent employee.* IMPERTINENT, from its primary meaning of not pertinent and hence inappropriate or out of place, has come to imply an unseemly intrusion into the affairs of others; it may also refer to a presumptuous rudeness toward persons entitled to respect: *impertinent questions; an impertinent interruption.* IMPUDENT suggests a bold and shameless rudeness: *an impudent young rascal.* —**Ant.** respectful, deferential; submissive, courteous, polite, civil, complimentary, mannerly.

insolvent *adj.* incapable of discharging liabilities, penniless, impecunious, unable to satisfy creditors, unable to pay one's bills, short of money, destitute, ruined, out of money, bankrupt, overextended, impoverished, moneyless; *Informal* broke, wiped out, unable to make ends meet, down-and-out. —**Ant.** solvent, wealthy, flourishing, thriving, sound, moneyed, rich, *Informal* flush.

insomnia *n.* sleeplessness, wakefulness, insomnolence, tossing and turning, *Latin* pervigilium, *French* nuit blanche.

insouciant *adj.* lighthearted, happy-go-lucky, carefree, easygoing, buoyant, unconcerned, untroubled, jaunty, debonair, free and easy, airy, breezy, perky, devil-may-care, *French* sans souci; flippant, mercurial, whimsical, capricious. —**Ant.** troubled, careworn, agitated, perturbed, uneasy.

inspect *v.* **1.** examine, scrutinize, look over carefully, look carefully at, look intently at, regard carefully, view closely and critically; investigate, reconnoiter, peruse, observe, contemplate, peer at, eye; explore, pore over, scan, study, survey, probe. **2.** review, view formally, survey formally, examine officially. —**Ant. 1, 2** ignore, overlook.

inspection *n.* —**Syn. Study.** See EXAMINATION.

inspiration *n.* **1.** incentive, stimulus, influence, inspiring action, incitement, motivation, motive, prompting, compulsion, spur, encouragement, impulse, creative impulse. **2.** flash, creative thought, idea, afflatus, divine afflatus, fancy, flight of fancy, revelation. —**Ant. 1** depressant, discouragement, disenchantment, deterrent.

inspire *v.* **1.** stimulate to creation, be an ideal for, fill with life or strength, infuse with inspiration, influence, exalt, illumine, illuminate, impel, motivate, prompt, occasion, galvanize, encourage, embolden, animate, vivify, fire, inspirit, hearten, enliven, quicken; cause, be responsible for. **2.** arouse, rouse, enkindle, engender, encourage, stimulate, prompt, induce, stir, excite, promote, inspirit, give rise to, provoke, cause, produce, occasion. —**Ant. 1** stifle, squelch, dispirit, dishearten, discourage. **2** stifle, kill, squelch, discourage, suppress.

instability *n.* unstableness, lack of stability, insecurity, lack of firmness, fluctuation, inconstancy, vacillation, unsteadiness, irresolution, indecision, wavering, changeability, capriciousness, flightiness, fitfulness, changeableness, inconsistency, mercurialness, vulnerability, weakness. —**Ant.** stability, security, constancy, strength, steadiness, equilibrium, resolution, consistency.

install Also **instal** *v.* **1.** place in service, lodge, establish, station, set in place, emplace, locate, position, plant, arrange, situate, move in, make operative; embed, lay. **2.** introduce into office, establish in an office or position, induct, invest, instate, receive, usher in, initiate, inaugurate, seat, crown, coronate, ordain. —**Ant. 1** remove, dislodge. **2** fire; retire.

installment *n.* **1.** payment, successive portion, amount due, money payable; section, fragment, part, unit, division, chapter, segment, issue. **2.** installing, installation, establishing in office or position; establishment, stationing, placing in service, locating, laying, connecting, hooking up. —**Ant.** removal, detachment.

instance *n.* example, illustration, case, case in point, circumstance, time, occasion, exemplification; sample, antecedent, object lesson, specimen, prototype, precedent.

instant *n.* **1.** split second, very short time, moment, minute; twinkling, jiffy, flash, trice. **2.** specific moment, particular time, point in time, very minute, second. —*adj.* **3.** immediate, quick, prompt, instantaneous; sudden, abrupt, unhesitating; on the spot, split-second. **4.** premixed, precooked; ready-to-use. —**Ant. 1** eon, age, eternity. **3** delayed, hesitant, slow.

instantaneous *adj.* immediate, sudden, extremely fast, happening in an instant, imperceptibly fast, unhesitatingly quick, prompt, abrupt, direct; quick as a flash, speedy, swift, rapid. **—Ant.** delayed, slow, gradual.

instantly *adv.* immediately, at once; without delay, instantaneously, without hesitation, promptly, directly, quickly, posthaste, ASAP; right now, here and now, instanter, in a flash, quick as a wink, on the spot. **—Syn. Study.** INSTANTLY, IMMEDIATELY, DIRECTLY, PRESENTLY were once close synonyms, all denoting complete absence of delay or any lapse of time. IMMEDIATELY and INSTANTLY still almost always have that sense and usu. mean at once: *He got up immediately. She responded instantly to the request.* DIRECTLY is usu. equivalent to soon, in a little while rather than at once: *You go ahead, we'll join you directly.* PRESENTLY changes sense according to the tense of the verb with which it is used. With a present tense verb it usu. means now, at the present time: *The author presently lives in San Francisco. She is presently working on a new novel.* In some contexts, esp. those involving a contrast between the present and the near future, PRESENTLY can mean soon or in a little while: *She is at the office now but will be home presently.* **—Ant.** later, in the future, in time, whenever; at one's leisure.

instead *adv.* as a substitute or equivalent, as a replacement, as an alternative, rather, in its place, in lieu of that.

instigate *v.* provoke, urge; bring about, incite, start, begin, initiate, spur, goad, rouse, prompt, stimulate; foment, stir up, kindle, set in motion. **—Ant.** repress, quell, quash, check, restrain, discourage, stop, suppress.

instill Also **instil** *v.* **1.** impart, introduce gradually, inculcate, teach, implant, inspire, induce; sow the seeds of, engender. **2.** add drop by drop, pour, mix in. **—Ant. 1, 2** remove, eliminate, eradicate, drain, extirpate.

instinct *n.* **1.** natural or inbred behavior, natural tendency, nature, native aptitude, inborn drive; blind knowledge, blood knowledge, intuition, mother wit. **2.** aptitude, gift, genius, natural sense, faculty, intuition, knack, natural inclination, proclivity, predisposition, capacity, tendency. **—Ant. 1** learned behavior, experience, reason, deliberation, judgment.

instinctive *adj.* innate, inherent, inborn, inbred, instinctual, resulting from instinct, intuitive, inspired, natural, native, unlearned, unacquired; involuntary, spontaneous, automatic, impulsive; deep-seated, ineradicable. **—Ant.** learned, acquired, voluntary, deliberate, willful.

institute *v.* **1.** establish, inaugurate, begin, found, originate, set up, bring into being, organize, constitute. **2.** start, initiate, inaugurate, introduce, put into effect, prescribe, pass, enact, ordain; undertake, get under way, get going, commence. **—*n.* 3.** institution, school, college, academy, professional school, graduate school, establishment; association, organization, society, foundation. **—Ant. 1** abolish, end, terminate, conclude, close, finish, complete. **2** squelch, stop, close, finish, wind up, terminate, end.

institution *n.* **1.** custom, established practice, convention, unwritten law, rite, ritual, habit, usage, fixture. **2.** company, organization, establishment, association, organized society, foundation. **3.** institute, school, academy, college, university, seminary. **4.** lunatic asylum, madhouse, mental hospital, *Slang* nuthouse, crazy house, bughouse; prison.

instruct *v.* **1.** teach, tutor, educate, school, train, drill, indoctrinate, guide, coach, catechize. **2.** give information to, notify, apprise, brief, advise, acquaint, inform, enlighten. **3.** command, direct, order, enjoin authoritatively, bid. **—Syn. Study. 1** See TEACH. **—Ant. 1, 2** misinform, mislead, deceive, neglect.

instruction *n.* **1.** instructing, teaching; education, guidance, coaching, training, tutoring, tutelage, indoctrination; pedagogy. **2.** Usu. **instructions** direction, information, guideline, prescription, recommendation, explanation, specification, advice, rule; lesson, maxim, precept, motto, moral, homily. **—Ant. 2** misinformation, misdirection.

instructor *n.* teacher, pedagogue, coach, professor, tutor, trainer, *British* don, lecturer, schoolteacher, schoolmaster, educator, mentor, preceptor, counsel, maestro, guide, guru; schoolmistress, governess, schoolmarm.

instrument *n.* **1.** implement, tool, device, utensil, appliance, apparatus, equipment, contrivance, machine, mechanism; gadget. **2.** agency, agent, means, medium, vehicle, tool; instrumentality; expedient. **3.** legal document; contract, deed, charter, paper, grant. **—Syn. Study. 1, 2** See TOOL. **—Ant. 2** obstruction, bar, stop, preventive; counteragent, opponent, neutralizer.

instrumental *adj.* helpful, serving as a means, useful, effective, effectual, active, contributory, functional, valuable, conducive, assisting; decisive, crucial, vital, essential. **—Ant.** ineffectual, useless; insignificant, negligible.

insubordinate *adj.* disobedient, refractory, insolent, defiant, intractable, recalcitrant, uncompliant, unsubmissive, unruly, rebellious, fractious, mutinous; disorderly, ungovernable. **—Ant.** obedient, docile, submissive, subdued; servile, obsequious.

insubstantial *adj.* **1.** unreal, immaterial, intangible, bodiless, impalpable; baseless, groundless; imaginary, visionary, apparitional; airy, gossamer, ethereal. **2.** slight, frail, flimsy, weak, delicate, fragile; shaky, unsound, unstable. **3.** modest, trifling, paltry, small, inconsiderable, trivial, piddling. **—Ant. 1–3** substantial. **1** real, material, tangible, palpable. **2** sturdy, hardy, sound, strong, stable. **3** large, great, considerable.

insufferable *adj.* unendurable, intolerable, unbearable; dreadful, insupportable, unspeakable; detestable, disgusting, hateful, outrageous, abominable. **—Ant.** tolerable, bearable; pleasant, pleasing, attractive, charming, appealing, disarming, ingratiating.

insufficient *adj.* inadequate, scanty, deficient, wanting, sparse, skimpy, lacking, not enough; unsatisfactory; impotent, incompetent. **—Ant.** sufficient, adequate, competent, enough; satisfactory.

insular *adj.* narrow, narrow-minded, bigoted, biased, illiberal, prejudiced, intolerant, limited; provincial, parochial, isolated, petty, insulated. **—Ant.** broad-minded, liberal, catholic, cosmopolitan, sophisticated, worldly.

insult *v.* **1.** treat with contempt, be rude to, slight, offend, treat insolently, abuse, scorn, deride, be discourteous to; cut, affront, disparage, belittle. **—*n.* 2.** affront, offense, indignity; rudeness, discourtesy, slight, outrage, slap; cheek, impudence; lese majesty. **—Syn. Study. 2** INSULT, AFFRONT, INDIGNITY, SLIGHT refer to acts or words that offend or demean. INSULT refers to a deliberately discourteous or rude remark or act that humiliates, wounds the feelings, and arouses anger: *an insult about her foreign accent.* AFFRONT implies open offense or disrespect, esp. to one's face: *Criticism of my book was a personal affront.* INDIGNITY refers to an injury to one's dignity or self-respect: *The prisoners suffered many indignities.* SLIGHT implies inadvertent indifference or disregard, but may also indicate ill-concealed contempt: *Not inviting me was an unforgivable slight.* **—Ant. 1** please, flatter, commend, praise. **2** compliment, flattery, honor, homage.

insulting *adj.* rude, discourteous, impolite, disrespectful, uncivil, insolent, offensive, nasty, abusive; derogatory, invidious, defamatory, disparaging, vicious.

insuperable *adj.* insurmountable, overwhelming, impossible, unconquerable, invincible, inexpugnable, unbeatable, unyielding, impassable, overpowering, overmastering, crushing, defeating. **—Ant.** possible, doable, reachable, conquerable, attainable.

insurance *n.* financial protection against loss, assurance; indemnity, coverage, policy; security, warranty, guarantee.

insure *v.* obtain insurance for, cover by insurance; guarantee against loss or risk; secure, underwrite. **—Ant.** imperil, jeopardize.

insurgent *n.* **1.** rebel, resister, mutineer, insurrectionist, dissident, renegade, revolter, revolutionist; guerrilla, partisan. **—*adj.* 2.** revolutionary, rebellious, mutinous, breakaway, dissident; lawless, insubordinate, disobedient, disorderly. **—Ant. 1** patriot, loyalist. **2** obedient, loyal, patriotic, subordinate.

insurmountable *adj.* incapable of being overcome, beyond reach, too great, insuperable, hopeless; unconquerable, unbeatable. **—Ant.** surmountable, beatable.

insurrection *n.* revolt, rebellion, revolution, insurgence, mutiny, riot, rising, uprising, outbreak. **—Ant.** obedience, submission, subsidence, acquiescence.

intact *adj.* undamaged, in one piece, whole, unbroken, integral, complete, entire, perfect; in good shape, untouched, without a scratch, unimpaired, unharmed, unhurt, uninjured, sound, safe. **—Syn. Study.** See COMPLETE. **—Ant.** impaired, damaged, injured, marred, broken, shattered.

intangible *adj.* **1.** incapable of being touched, untouchable, immaterial, abstract, ethereal, insubstantial, impalpable, imperceptible. **2.** vague, elusive, fleeting, evanescent, transient, fugitive, imperceptible, shadowy. **—*n.* 3.** abstraction, imponderable, accidental, unpredictable happening, unforeseen turn of events. **—Ant. 1, 2** tangible, palpable, perceptible; material, concrete, physical.

integral *adj.* **1.** essential, necessary, indispensable, component, constituent, inherent, basic, requisite. **2.** fulfilled, fulfilling, lacking nothing, whole, entire, full, complete, integrated, total, intact, perfect, finished, rounded, well-rounded. **—Ant. 1** peripheral, unessential, unimportant, unnecessary. **2** lacking, incomplete, imperfect, deficient.

integrate *v.* **1.** blend, combine, amalgamate, mix, mingle, merge, bring together, unify, fuse, intermix, unite. **2.** make available to every race; open for use by all; desegregate. **—Ant. 1** disperse, scatter, separate, divide. **2** segregate, separate.

integration *n.* **1.** combination, combining, mixing, blending, fusion, synthesis, union. **2.** desegregation, assimilation.

—**Ant. 1** separation, dispersion. **2** segregation, separation, apartheid.

integrity *n.* **1.** honesty, probity, uprightness, moral soundness, moral stature, principle, character, virtue, purity, rectitude, decency, self-respect, straightforwardness, morality, honor, sincerity. **2.** structural soundness; unimpaired condition, reliability, completeness; wholeness, strength, unity, coherence, cohesion. —**Syn. Study. 1** See HONOR. —**Ant. 1** duplicity; deceit, venality, corruption, dishonesty, immorality. **2** flimsiness, shakiness, fragility, faultiness, uncertainty, unsoundness.

intellect *n.* **1.** intelligence, mentality, mental power, power of comprehension, power of thinking, understanding, reasoning faculty, cognition, cognitive power, brain, brains, *Informal* smarts; sense, mind, rationality, consciousness, perception; wisdom. **2.** thinker, intellectual, *Informal* brain, egghead, *Slang* brains; wit. —**Syn. Study. 1** See MIND. —**Ant. 1** emotion, instinct; muscle. **2** idiot, moron.

intellectual *adj.* **1.** cerebral, of the mind, using the intellect, mental, abstract; academic, scholarly. **2.** intelligent, scholarly, studious; *Informal* bookish, brainy; reasoning, thoughtful, rational. —*n.* **3.** intellect, person interested in ideas; thinker, academic, scholar; pundit, sage, savant; mandarin, highbrow; *Informal* brain, longhair, egghead, rocket scientist, *Slang* geek. —**Ant. 1** physical, material, fleshly. **2** unintellectual, illiterate, unlearned, ignorant, stupid. **3** lowbrow, idiot, moron.

intelligence *n.* **1.** intellect, mental power, comprehension, understanding, mental skill, power of reasoning, wisdom, acumen, sagacity, shrewdness, perspicacity, *Informal* brains. **2.** information, news, knowledge, advice, notice, report, notification, advisement, *Slang* dope; tidings. —**Ant. 1** ignorance, stupidity, misapprehension, dullness. **2** concealment, suppression; misinformation.

intelligent *adj.* thoughtful, thinking, bright, alert, smart, clearheaded, sensible, informed, well-informed, sage, wise, perspicacious, perceptive, brilliant, keen, quick, knowing, sagacious, quick-witted, sharp-witted, clever, prudent, astute, canny, sharp, shrewd, *Informal* brainy. —**Syn. Study.** See SHARP. —**Ant.** unintelligent; foolish, idiotic, stupid, ignorant, dumb; irrational, unreasonable.

intelligentsia *n.* educated class, intellectual leaders, intellectual elite; thinkers, intellectuals, academe, ivory tower, academic community. —**Ant.** masses, hoi polloi; bourgeoisie.

intelligible *adj.* understandable, clear, distinct, comprehensible, coherent, lucid, well-defined, clear-cut, apparent, evident, obvious, definite, unmistakable, unambiguous. —**Ant.** vague, confused, unclear, muddled, incomprehensible.

intend *v.* plan, aim, contemplate, have in mind, mean, determine, propose, design, set as a goal, aspire, expect, wish, project, resolve, calculate.

intense *adj.* **1.** extreme, very great, concentrated, acute, sharp, strong, powerful, forceful, considerable, forcible, potent, violent, keen. **2.** fervent, earnest, passionate, ardent, strong, powerful, extreme, deep, vehement, burning, deeply felt, emphatic. —**Ant. 1** weak, mild, moderate, gentle. **2** subdued, relaxed, easy, moderate, casual, indifferent, cool, weak, mild.

intensify *v.* increase, heighten, quicken, aggravate, escalate, make more intense, sharpen, reinforce, strengthen, magnify, accelerate, boost, deepen, worsen, redouble. —**Ant.** reduce, lessen, diminish, mitigate, allay; abate; moderate, qualify; alleviate, lighten, relieve.

intensity *n.* **1.** magnitude, power, strength, depth, severity. **2.** passion, emotion, ardor, fervor, vehemence, energy, vigor, strength, power, force, potency, earnestness, zeal, forcefulness. —**Ant. 2** relaxation, languor, coolness, indifference, weakness.

intent *n.* **1.** intention, design, purpose, plan, determination, premeditation, aim, end. **2.** meaning, significance, purport, import, burden, drift; gist, substance. —*adj.* **3.** steady, steadfast, intense, fixed, highly attentive, undistracted, piercing; concentrated, preoccupied, engrossed, absorbed. **4.** set, bent, insistent, earnest, tenacious, resolved, determined, unbending, unwavering. —**Ant. 1** accident; chance, luck, fortune. **3** unsteady, wavering, wandering; casual, indifferent.

intention *n.* plan, aim, intent, objective, design, purpose, goal, resolution, target, object, resolve, end, determination.

intentional *adj.* deliberate, intended, willed, done on purpose, planned, purposeful, designed, premeditated, contemplated, voluntary, calculated. —**Syn. Study.** See DELIBERATE. —**Ant.** accidental, fortuitous, inadvertent, unintentional, unplanned, unpremeditated.

inter *v.* bury, entomb, lay away, inhume, lay to rest, inurn, ensepulcher, *Archaic* inearth, *Slang* put six feet under. —**Ant.** exhume, dig up, disinter.

interact *v.* interreact, interwork, engage, mesh, dovetail, interplay, intermesh, interlace, coact; cooperate, coordinate, join, conjoin, combine, unite.

intercede *v.* **1.** offer support or help,

lend a helping hand, put in a good word for, use one's influence; speak up, plead. **2.** arbitrate, mediate, play intermediary, serve as go-between, intervene, interpose, step in. **—Ant. 1, 2** withdraw, remain aloof, remain neutral.

intercept *v.* seize, get hold of, arrest, stay, detain, stop, block the passage of, catch, nab, take, grab, deflect, reroute, cut off; ambush. **—Ant.** transmit, relay; hasten, expedite; admit, permit.

interchangeable *adj.* switchable, tradable, exchangeable, transposable; equivalent, closely similar, synonymous, corresponding, parallel, analogous. **—Ant.** unswitchable; unlike, opposite.

intercourse *n.* **1.** communications, dealings, trade, traffic, relations, connection, exchange, correspondence, commerce; conversation, discourse, talk, communion, colloquy, parley. **2.** sexual relations, congress, copulation, coitus; coupling, pairing.

interest *n.* **1.** Often **interests** preferred activity, absorption, engrossment, pursuit, avocation, preoccupation; pastime, hobby. **2.** notice, attention, concern, curiosity, regard; suspicion. **3.** Sometimes **interests** behalf, benefit, service, weal, advantage, good. **4.** share, portion, stake, part, investment, holding, partial ownership. **5.** profit, bonus, yield, dividend, gain. **—***v.* **6.** absorb, engage the attention of, preoccupy, excite the curiosity of, divert, attract; touch, affect. **7.** concern, involve, engage. **—Ant. 2** unconcern, indifference. **3** disadvantage, detriment. **6** bore, *Slang* turn off.

interesting *adj.* absorbing, stimulating, arresting, striking; attractive, appealing, entertaining, engaging, pleasing; fascinating, magnetic, riveting; curious, suspicious. **—Ant.** uninteresting, dull, boring, flat, tedious, tiresome.

interfere *v.* **1.** conflict, be a hindrance to, be inconsistent, not be conducive to, counter, get in the way, be an obstacle to, frustrate, jar. **2.** mix, meddle, intervene, interpose, step in, rush in, intrude, intercede; *Slang* butt in, horn in, stick in one's oar. **—Ant. 1** aid, help, assist.

interim *n.* **1.** intervening time, interval, interlude, meantime. **—***adj.* **2.** temporary, provisional, temporal, tentative, stopgap, *Latin* pro tempore. **—Ant. 2** permanent.

interior *adj.* **1.** internal, inmost, inner, innermost, inside, located within, inward. **—***n.* **2.** internal part, inside, inner space. **3.** remote regions, inland parts, upcountry, bush, hinterland, heartland, backwoods. **—Ant. 1** exterior; outer, outward, outside, external. **2** exterior, outside. **3** coast, borderland.

interject *v.* insert, throw in, put in, interrupt with, interpose, interpolate, inject, force in, introduce, slip in, sneak in. **—Ant.** extract, remove, withdraw.

interloper *n.* intruder, outsider, trespasser; gatecrasher, unwanted presence, meddler, interferer, invader, persona non grata.

interlude *n.* interval, intervening period, respite, intermission, recess, pause, break, breathing spell, letup; episode, event, incident.

intermediary *adj.* **1.** intermediate, in-between, bridging, midway. **2.** mediating, acting as mediary, arbitrating, serving as mediator. **—***n.* **3.** mediator, arbitrator, middleman, intermediate, go-between; referee, umpire, adjudicator.

intermediate *adj.* **1.** middle, midway, intermediary, halfway, mid, mean, midmost, median, mediate, transitional, intervening. **2.** medium, moderate, average, middling, so-so; fair, mediocre. **—Ant. 1** first; last. **2** beginning; advanced.

interment *n.* burial, burial ceremony, entombment, inhumation; funeral. **—Ant.** exhumation.

interminable *adj.* endless, unending, ceaseless, boundless, without a stopping point, tediously long, long-drawn-out, prolix, long-winded, limitless, unlimited, illimitable, infinite, perpetual, continuous, incessant. **—Ant.** brief, short, fleeting.

intermingle *v.* mix, combine, commingle, blend, amalgamate, intermix, fuse, commix, unite, merge, interfuse, interlace, interblend, mix up, emulsify, mix together, conglomerate, homogenize. **—Ant.** disperse, scatter, break up, disband, separate.

intermission *n.* interim, period of respite, pause, stoppage, suspension, halt, interlude, stop, rest, break, recess; *British* interval; hiatus, gap. **—Ant.** continuance, prolongation, uninterruptedness.

intermittent *adj.* recurrent, spasmodic, occasional, periodic, starting and stopping, discontinuous, sporadic, on and off, on-again-off-again, fitful, irregular. **—Ant.** steady, unceasing, continuous.

internal *adj.* **1.** interior, located inside, inner, inmost. **2.** domestic; governmental, administrative, state, executive, sovereign, political. **—Ant. 1** outer, exterior, external, outside. **2** foreign.

international *adj.* between nations, involving two or more nations, cosmopolitan; worldwide, universal. **—Ant.** national, domestic.

interpolate *v.* insert, inject, put in, work in, stick in, throw in, add, introduce, interlard, intercalate, interline, interject, insinuate, intervene, intersperse, sandwich, implant, intrude, wedge in, *Slang* drag in by the heels.

interpret *v.* **1.** explain, make clear, clarify, explicate, explain the meaning of, assign a meaning to, decipher, define, elucidate, throw light upon, expound; unravel, puzzle out, figure out, piece together. **2.** understand, construe, take, accept, make out, decipher, see, read, account for. **3.** translate, rephrase in one's native language; restate, paraphrase, reword, render. **—Syn. Study. 1** See EXPLAIN. **—Ant. 2** mistake, confuse, confound, misconceive, misunderstand.

interrogate *v.* question, probe, examine, cross-examine; investigate, test, catechize, ask, query; *Informal* grill, give the third degree. **—Ant.** answer, retort, respond.

interrupt *v.* **1.** stop, break off, halt temporarily, cause to stop, break in on, discontinue, cut in on, disturb, interfere with, obstruct the course of. **2.** block partially, interfere with, break the continuity of, disconnect, intersect, sever, disjoin, punctuate. **—Ant. 1** continue, resume.

interruption *n.* halt, pause, stop, discontinuity, obstruction, hindrance, disconnection, interference; break, gap, hiatus, lacuna, intermission, rift, interlude. **—Ant.** continuance, resumption.

intersect *v.* **1.** cut across, cross, traverse, crosscut, pass through, pass across, bisect, divide, transect. **2.** cross, interconnect, crisscross, meet and cross, have a common point; meet, come together, overlap.

intersection *n.* junction, meeting point, crossroads, crossing, interchange, corner.

intersperse *v.* interpose, interpolate, intercalate, interlard, interfuse, interject, wedge in; strew, scatter, sprinkle, pepper, bestrew, broadcast, dot, disperse.

interval *n.* **1.** intervening period, interim, pause, rest, recess, break, interlude, intermission; season, spell, hiatus, interruption. **2.** space, opening, gap, interspace, separation, rift, cleft; gulf, breach.

intervene *v.* **1.** occur between times, pass, take place, come to pass, befall. **2.** step in, break in, interpose, intrude, interfere, mediate, arbitrate, intercede, come between, interrupt, *Slang* butt in.

intervention *n.* stepping in, breaking in, mediation, intermediation, interposition, arbitration, intercession; interference, intrusion, *Slang* butting in.

interview *n.* **1.** conversation, talk, chat; round table, conference, question-and-answer session, questioning. **2.** professional examination, evaluation, in-person appraisal, consultation; conference, meeting, parley; audience.

intestines *n.* alimentary canal; insides, entrails, viscera, bowels, *Informal* guts.

intimacy *n.* closeness, familiarity, caring, tenderness, fondness, dearness, affection, warmth, endearment; lovemaking, sexual relations, sexual intercourse; friendliness, amity, chumminess, brotherhood, camaraderie, fraternity. **—Ant.** separation, aloofness, alienation, estrangement, indifference.

intimate[1] *adj.* **1.** close, bosom, cherished, dear, familiar, confidential, personal, near and dear. **2.** deeply personal, innermost, confidential, private, guarded. **3.** detailed, deep, thorough, special, profound, personal, direct, experienced, first-hand, close. **—*n.* 4.** close friend, close associate, confidant, familiar; *Informal* chum, crony, pal, buddy. **—Syn. Study. 1** See FAMILIAR. **—Ant. 1** distant, formal, remote. **2** open, public, known. **3** superficial, limited, slight. **4** stranger, outsider; enemy, foe.

intimate[2] *v.* hint, suggest, imply, indicate, insinuate, allude, refer to indirectly, rumor. **—Syn. Study.** See SUGGEST. **—Ant.** state, declare, assert, proclaim.

intimation *n.* hint, suggestion, inkling, clue, innuendo, indication, veiled comment, rumor, allusion, insinuation, sign, portent.

intimidate *v.* terrorize, terrify, scare, cow, menace, make afraid, make timid, make fearful, frighten, fill with fear, alarm, subdue, bully, daunt, browbeat, buffalo; compel by threats, coerce; discourage, dismay. **—Syn. Study.** See DISCOURAGE. **—Ant.** encourage, inspire, embolden; reassure.

intolerable *adj.* unendurable, unbearable, insupportable, insufferable; excruciating, racking, torturous, agonizing; abominable, hateful, loathsome, abhorrent; unreasonable, excessive, outrageous. **—Ant.** tolerable, bearable, endurable, comfortable; reasonable.

intolerance *n.* **1.** bigotry, bias, prejudice, narrow-mindedness, lack of forbearance; xenophobia, chauvinism, racism. **2.** low tolerance, inability to bear, hypersensitivity; weak spot; *Informal* no stomach. **—Ant. 1** tolerance, compassion, forbearance, liberality. **2** tolerance, endurance.

intolerant *adj.* not tolerant, bigoted, prejudiced, narrow-minded, fanatical, closed-minded, parochial, sectarian, hostile, resentful, jealous, mistrustful; xenophobic, chauvinistic. **—Ant.** tolerant, liberal, forbearing, large-minded.

intone *v.* chant, drawl, singsong, hum,

croon, vocalize, intonate; say, speak, utter, voice, mouth, murmur, pronounce, enunciate, articulate.

in toto *adv.* as a whole, entire, uncondensed, uncut, unabridged, entirely, outright, completely, totally, in all, all together. **—Ant.** abridged, condensed, cut, in part, incompletely.

intoxicated *adj.* **1.** drunk, inebriated, drunken, *Informal* in one's cups, high, tight, tipsy, *Slang* wrecked, smashed, loaded, bombed, oiled, stoned, plastered, zonked, stinko, stewed. **2.** transported, rapt, enthralled, infatuated, delighted, elated, exalted, entranced, enchanted, exhilarated. **—Ant. 1** sober. **2** bored, indifferent.

intractable *adj.* stubborn, perverse, headstrong, ornery, hard to cope with, obstinate, willful, unmanageable, obdurate, incorrigible, mulish, unruly, fractious, froward, refractory, recalcitrant, ungovernable, uncontrollable, contumacious, unmalleable, inflexible. **—Syn. Study.** See UNRULY. **—Ant.** tractable, obedient, docile, submissive, subdued; compliant, acquiescent, amiable.

intransigent *adj.* uncompromising, stubborn, intractable, obdurate, ironwilled, steadfast, diehard, unyielding, unmovable, unbudgeable, inflexible. **—Ant.** compromising, yielding, flexible, open-minded, acquiescent, compliant.

intrepid *adj.* fearless, bold, valiant, brave, courageous, audacious, heroic, valorous, dauntless, resolute, doughty, daring, adventurous, undismayed. **—Ant.** cowardly, timid, fearful, cautious, prudent.

intricate *adj.* complicated, complex, sophisticated, involved, difficult to understand; *Informal* tricky, knotty; full of detail or difficulties, tangled, entangled; devious. **—Ant.** easy, simple, straightforward, effortless; obvious, plain, clear, patent.

intrigue *v.* **1.** interest greatly, fascinate, appeal strongly to, arrest, attract, absorb, enthrall, arouse the curiosity of, capture the imagination of, fire, tickle one's fancy, titillate. **2.** plot, conspire, machinate, maneuver craftily, scheme, collude, spy. *—n.* **3.** scheming, machination, secret plotting; underhanded or secret dealings; knavery, double-dealing, sharp practice, behind-the-scenes manipulation, plot, scheme, conspiracy, cabal. **4.** love affair, romance, amour. **—Syn. Study. 3** See CONSPIRACY. **—Ant. 1** bore. **3** sincerity, candor, honesty, openness, straightforwardness.

intrinsic *adj.* essential, innate, inherent, basic, fundamental, underlying, inborn, inbred, native, natural, ingrained, indigenous, per se. **—Syn. Study.** See ESSENTIAL. **—Ant.** extrinsic, accidental, incidental; added, appended; extraneous, alien, acquired.

introduce *v.* **1.** give an introduction, make acquainted, make known, present. **2.** bring knowledge to, acquaint, inform, expose, familiarize, make familiar, initiate. **3.** propose, advance, offer, put forward, present, originate, create, bring into notice; urge, sponsor, recommend. **4.** start, begin, lead off, lead into, *Informal* kick off. **5.** bring in, show, make familiar, import, bring into practice, institute, establish. **6.** put in, insert, interpolate, infuse, add, interject, interpose, *Informal* throw in. **—Syn. Study. 1** INTRODUCE, PRESENT mean to bring persons into personal acquaintance with each other, as by announcement of names. INTRODUCE is the ordinary term, referring to making persons acquainted who are ostensibly equals: *to introduce a friend to one's sister.* PRESENT, a more formal term, suggests a degree of ceremony in the process, and implies (if only as a matter of compliment) superior dignity, rank, or importance in the person to whom another is presented: *to present a visitor to the president.* **—Ant. 3** withdraw, remove, eliminate, exclude, delete, excise.

introduction *n.* **1.** introducing, instituting, institution, bringing in; conducting, ushering in; presentation; insertion. **2.** presentation, acquaintanceship, meeting of strangers. **3.** innovation, change, novelty. **4.** preface, prefatory material, preamble, foreword, opening part, opening; prelude, precursor; preliminary speech, opening remarks, prologue. **—Syn. Study. 4** INTRODUCTION, FOREWORD, PREFACE refer to material in the front of a book that introduces and explains it to the reader. An INTRODUCTION is a formal preliminary statement, often extensive, that serves as a guide to the book. It is written by the author and usu. printed as part of the text: *The introduction outlined the subjects covered in the book.* A FOREWORD is a short introductory statement that precedes the text proper. It is usu. written by someone other than the author, often an authority on the subject of the book: *The writer of the foreword praised the book and its author.* A PREFACE, also separate from the text proper, is the author's informal statement about the purpose, preparation, etc., of the book; it usu. includes acknowledgments: *The author thanked her family in the preface.* A PREFACE usu. follows a FOREWORD, if there is one. **—Ant. 1** extraction, elimination, removal, withdrawal; completion, end, termination. **4** epilogue, afterword.

introductory *adj.* serving to introduce,

preliminary, acquainting, initial, beginning, initiatory, prefatory, precursory, *Informal* get-acquainted. **—Syn. Study.** See PRELIMINARY. **—Ant.** final, concluding, last, conclusive, terminal.

introspection *n.* self-analysis, self-examination, reflection, soul-searching, heart-searching, self-consultation, self-contemplation, self-observation, meditation, brooding, self-questioning, deliberation, rumination, self-scrutiny.

introvert *n.* private person, withdrawn person; self-contained person; introspective person, inner-directed person; loner, thinker, contemplative, brooder. **—Ant.** extrovert, outgoing person.

intrude *v.* **1.** thrust, interject improperly, interpose, push, impose. **2.** enter uninvited, thrust oneself in, obtrude, interfere, intervene, interlope, come uninvited, trespass, encroach, meddle, *Slang* butt in.

intruder *n.* unlawful entrant, interloper, interferer, intervener; gate-crasher, trespasser, encroacher. **—Ant.** guest.

intuition *n.* innate knowledge, immediate cognition, instinct, instinctive feeling; extrasensory perception; telepathy, clairvoyance, precognition, second sight; insight, guesswork, surmise, sixth sense; *Informal* hunch, flash. **—Ant.** ratiocination, reasoning, deduction.

intuitive *adj.* innate, instinctive, intuitional, natural, native, constitutional, inborn, inbred; resulting from intuition, based on a hunch; nonrational, extrasensory, telepathic, psychic, clairvoyant. **—Ant.** acquired, learned, rational.

inundate *v.* **1.** engulf, overflow, fill with water, overspread, drench, submerge, flood, deluge, drown. **2.** swamp, glut, flood, saturate, overcome; load down, overburden, overwhelm. **—Ant. 1** drain dry, reclaim, desiccate, parch, empty.

inure *v.* accustom, habituate, familiarize, make used to, naturalize, custom; harden, strengthen, toughen, season, temper, desensitize, discipline, train, adapt, acclimatize, acclimate, get used to.

invade *v.* **1.** overrun, enter forcefully, swarm over, infest, enter as a conquering power, aggress upon, enter as an enemy, march into, strike at, assault, assail, attack. **2.** enter massively, overrun, engulf, flood, descend upon. **3.** overspread, spread throughout, permeate, penetrate, infect, infest. **4.** intrude on, infringe upon, encroach on, trespass, violate, restrict, limit; *Informal* chip away at. **—Ant. 1, 2** abandon, relinquish, vacate, evacuate. **3** bypass. **4** respect, honor.

invalid[1] *n.* **1.** chronically ill person, disabled person, enfeebled person, stricken person, valetudinarian; (*variously*) cripple, paraplegic, paralytic, amputee. *—adj.* **2.** infirm, enfeebled, unable to care for oneself, debilitated, disabled, sick, sickly, ailing, unwell, valetudinarian, incapacitated, powerless, weak, weakened. **—Ant. 2** strong, well, healthy, vigorous.

invalid[2] *adj.* not valid, void, null, nugatory, useless, forceless, ineffective, good-for-nothing, worthless; inoperative; dead letter; unconvincing, illogical, fallacious, unsupported, unsupportable, unsound, false. **—Ant.** valid, sound, legal, legitimate; correct, forceful, logical.

invalidate *v.* make invalid or worthless, make void, nullify, vitiate, annul, abrogate, repeal, countermand, cancel, deprive of legal force; weaken, discredit, undercut, undermine, refute. **—Ant.** validate, certify, authorize; strengthen, enhance.

invaluable *adj.* priceless, beyond price, very precious, of great worth, very valuable, extremely expensive, inestimable; rare, choice. **—Ant.** worthless, valueless.

invariable *adj.* constant, unfailing, uniform, unwavering, unvarying, unalterable, immutable, unchanging, changeless, undeviating, unchangeable, always the same, consistent. **—Ant.** variable, changing, changeable, varying.

invasion *n.* **1.** infiltration, penetration, incursion, aggression, assault, attack, raid, foray, sortie, inroad; onslaught, juggernaut. **2.** encroachment, breach, intrusion, infringement; trespass, overstepping, usurpation. **—Ant. 1** evacuation, retreat. **2** respect, honoring.

invective *n.* bitter language, harsh words, verbal abuse, venom, vilification, insult, contumely, diatribe, execration, sarcasm; vituperation, denunciation, revilement, censure, rant, railing, billingsgate. **—Syn. Study.** See ABUSE. **—Ant.** praise, honor, commendation.

inveigh *v.* denounce, criticize, castigate, rail, abuse, belittle, rebuke, harangue, reproach, upbraid, revile, scold, censure, dress down, vituperate; *Slang* put down, run down, slam, knock. **—Ant.** commend, praise, acclaim, approve.

inveigle *v.* entice, ensnare, beguile, trick, tempt, allure, seduce, mislead, bamboozle, wheedle, coax, flatter, cajole; *Slang* rope in, suck in, sweet-talk, soft-soap.

invent *v.* **1.** originate, create, develop, contrive, conceive, devise, put together, fabricate, fashion, formulate; *Informal* think up, come up with. **2.** make up, concoct, conceive, fabricate, contrive, conjure up, coin; *Informal* cook up, trump up. **—Ant. 1** copy, imitate, reproduce.

invention *n.* **1.** inventing, creation, fabrication, origination, discovery; production, development. **2.** contrivance, gadget; implement, device, apparatus, machine, contraption; design. **3.** inventiveness, resourcefulness, originality, imagination, ingenuity, creativity, fertility. **4.** fabrication, sham, fake, dissimulation, forgery, concoction, fiction, lie, prevarication, trumpery. **—Ant. 3** uninventiveness. **4** truth, fact.

inventory *n.* **1.** list, listing, catalog, roster, roll, record, schedule, register; [objects or items on a list] stock, merchandise, goods, supply. **2.** survey, accounting, stock-taking. **—Syn. Study. 1** See LIST.

inverse *adj.* reversed, back to front, converse, backward, right-to-left, bottom-to-top, inverted, opposite, indirect, contrary. **—Ant.** forward; direct.

inverted *adj.* turned upside-down, reversed in position, inverse, bottom up. **—Ant.** upright, right side up.

invest *v.* **1.** devote, give, allot, apportion, set aside, appoint. **2.** endow, supply, license, enable. **3.** endow, infuse, imbue, color, clothe, fill, enrich. **4.** clothe, garb, dress, cover, array, adorn. **—Ant. 1, 2** withhold, deny. **2** withdraw.

investigate *v.* inquire into, explore, examine closely, study, scrutinize, research, probe, look into, search into, delve into; question, query, ask about; sift, pore over, dissect, analyze, inspect, anatomize; survey. **—Ant.** conjecture, guess; ignore.

investigation *n.* inquiry, investigating, thorough examination, search, study, scrutiny, probe, survey, review, research, fact-finding; analysis, inspection, dissection, anatomy.

investment *n.* **1.** investing, allotment of funds, capital spending, stock acquisition; financial transaction. **2.** money invested, contribution, offering, share; risk, venture, stake, ante.

inveterate *adj.* **1.** confirmed, steadfast, constant, habitual, established, inured, hardened, ingrained, deep-rooted, deep-seated, diehard, adamant; incurable, unregenerate, unreconstructed. **2.** established, continuous, recurrent, chronic, long-standing. **—Ant. 1** undeveloped, incipient; reformed. **2** superficial, passing.

invidious *adj.* insulting, causing envy or hard feelings, inciting ill will, offensive, slighting; malevolent, resentful, malicious, vicious, rancorous, spiteful. **—Ant.** fair, just, placating; flattering.

invigorating *adj.* refreshing, restorative, enlivening, animating, strengthening, energizing, bracing, healthful, stimulating, rejuvenating, vitalizing, quickening. **—Ant.** tiring, weakening.

invincible *adj.* unconquerable, impregnable, insurmountable, insuperable, invulnerable, totally secure; indomitable, irrepressible, unbeatable, undefeatable. **—Syn. Study.** INVINCIBLE, IMPREGNABLE, INDOMITABLE suggest that which cannot be overcome or mastered. INVINCIBLE is applied to that which cannot be conquered in combat or war, or overcome or subdued in any manner: *an invincible army; invincible courage.* IMPREGNABLE is applied to a place or position that cannot be taken by assault or siege, and hence to whatever is proof against attack: *an impregnable fortress; impregnable virtue.* INDOMITABLE implies having an unyielding spirit, or stubborn persistence in the face of opposition or difficulty: *indomitable will.* **—Ant.** conquerable, vulnerable.

invisible *adj.* not visible, not perceptible to the eye, imperceptible, undiscernible, unapparent, unseeable, unseen; covert, concealed, veiled, obscure, hidden. **—Ant.** visible, apparent, plain.

invitation *n.* **1.** request for someone's presence, summons, solicitation, offer, call, bid, bidding. **2.** inducement, lure, enticement, allurement, temptation, open door; bid, bidding, call, summons; challenge. **—Ant. 1** rebuff, repulse, response.

invite *v.* **1.** request the presence of, summon courteously, urge, call, bid. **2.** request politely, ask formally; encourage, welcome, solicit. **3.** tempt, induce, attract, entice, lure, encourage, welcome; act so as to cause. **—Ant. 2, 3** repel, forbid, discourage.

inviting *adj.* tempting, attractive, appealing, magnetic, intriguing, alluring, engaging, enticing, charming, warm, welcoming. **—Ant.** uninviting, unattractive, forbidding, repellent.

invocation *n.* entreaty to a supernatural power, prayer, appeal, supplication, orison, petition, plea, summoning.

invoke *v.* **1.** entreat, call upon, petition, implore, appeal for, supplicate, pray for; beg, beseech, importune, ask for. **2.** put into effect, have recourse to, resort to, use, implement, employ, apply, introduce. **3.** summon by incantation, call forth, conjure.

involuntary *adj.* **1.** forced, coerced, unwilling, done without choice, unchosen, reluctant; compulsory, against one's will. **2.** spontaneous, reflex, unintentional, unconscious, instinctive, unwilled, automatic, inadvertent. **—Ant.** willing, voluntary, intentional.

involve *v.* **1.** include, contain, be a matter of, comprise; entail, depend on, imply. **2.** cause to be associated, implicate, embroil, entangle, mix up. **3.** absorb fully, preoccupy, commit, engage, wrap up. **—Ant. 2** extricate, disentangle, liberate, release. **3** disengage.

invulnerable *adj.* unconquerable, unassailable, invincible, insuperable, unbeatable, undefeatable, inexpugnable, impregnable, formidable, indomitable, undestroyable, imperishable. **—Ant.** weak, vulnerable, fallible, defenseless, unprotected.

inward Also **inwards** *adv.* **1.** toward the inside, toward the interior, interiorly. **2.** toward one's private thoughts, into the mind or soul, inwardly. *—adj.* **3.** directed toward the inside, ingoing, incoming, leading inside, going in, inner-directed, interior; personal, private, mental, spiritual, inner. **—Ant. 1, 2** outward, outside. **3** outer, exterior, superficial.

iota *n.* faint degree, small amount, particle, jot, smidgin, tiniest quantity, whit, shred, atom, scintilla, spark, bit, spot, speck. **—Ant.** mass, lot.

irascible *adj.* easily angered, touchy, cantankerous, choleric, waspish, bad-tempered, ill-humored, hot-tempered, irritable, intractable, ornery, splenetic, cross, testy, cranky, grumpy, grouchy, peevish. **—Syn. Study.** See IRRITABLE. **—Ant.** good-natured, amiable, gentle, mild, placid, serene, tranquil, easygoing.

irate *adj.* angry, angered, furious, rabid, enraged, infuriated; burned up, irritated, annoyed, livid, vexed, riled, galled, indignant, *Informal* mad. **—Ant.** good-humored, tolerant, pleased, tranquil.

ire *n.* anger, rage, outrage, fury, umbrage, wrath, vexation, indignation, resentment, choler. **—Ant.** goodwill, patience, forbearance, forgiveness.

iridescent *adj.* changeable in color, colorful, glowing, shiny, reflecting many hues, rainbowlike, opalescent, prismatic. **—Ant.** blanched, neutral, colorless, dingy, dull, lusterless.

irk *v.* annoy, irritate, vex, gall, ruffle, bother, pester, provoke, *Slang* bug. **—Ant.** please, delight, cheer; overjoy.

ironclad *adj.* inflexible, unalterable, irrevocable, irreversible, unchangeable, immutable, fixed, unchanging, permanent, unmodifiable, strict, inexorable, rigoristic. **—Ant.** variable, changeable, impermanent, revocable.

ironic Also **ironical** *adj.* **1.** mocking, sarcastic, expressing or filled with irony, sardonic, facetious; insincere, pretended; derisive, biting, cutting, stinging, sneering, caustic, abusive. **2.** incongruous, inconsistent, contradictory, surprising, unexpected, implausible; curious, strange, odd, weird; *Informal* funny. **—Ant. 1** sincere, straightforward, direct. **2** natural, predictable, expected.

irony *n.* **1.** indirection, double meaning; facetiousness, mockery, ridicule, derision, scorn; satire, sarcasm. **2.** incongruity, contrariness, absurdity, implausibility, reverse state of affairs, unexpected outcome. **—Syn. Study. 1** IRONY, SATIRE, SARCASM indicate mockery of a person or thing. IRONY is exhibited in the organization or structure of either language or literary material. It indirectly presents a contradiction between an action or expression and the context in which it occurs. One thing is said and its opposite implied, as in "Beautiful weather, isn't it?" said when it is raining. Ironic literature exploits the contrast between an ideal and an actual condition, as when events turn out contrary to expectations. SATIRE, also a literary and rhetorical form, is the use of ridicule in exposing human vice and folly. Jonathan Swift wrote social and political satires. SARCASM is a harsh and cutting type of humor. Its distinctive quality is present in the spoken word; it is manifested chiefly by vocal inflection. Sarcastic language may have the form of irony, as in "What a fine musician you turned out to be!", or it may be a direct statement, as in "You couldn't play one piece correctly if you had two assistants!" **—Ant. 1** sincerity, straightforwardness, directness.

irrational *adj.* **1.** incapable of logical thought, unthinking, unreasoning. **2.** unsound, illogical, unreasonable, not based in reality, unfounded, baseless, nonsensical, absurd, foolish, ill-advised. **—Ant. 1, 2** rational. **2** reasonable, wise, sensible, logical.

irreconcilable *adj.* beyond reconciliation, unadjustable, unbridgeable, intransigent, implacably hostile, unappeasable; inconsistent, incompatible, opposed. **—Ant.** reconcilable, appeasable.

irrefutable *adj.* undeniable, not refutable, incontrovertible, indisputable; proof positive, unquestionable. **—Ant.** refutable, disputable, moot.

irregular *adj.* **1.** uneven, crooked, out of line, unaligned; not smooth, rough, broken, bumpy; asymmetrical. **2.** nonconforming, unconventional, unusual, uncharacteristic, unexpected; improper, unsuitable, inappropriate, unfitting, indecorous; eccentric, peculiar, queer, odd, singular; abnormal, aberrant, anomalous; unsystematic, unmethodical, haphazard, desultory. **—Ant. 1** regular, even, smooth, uniform. **2** regular, normal, typical; usual, customary; legitimate, proper, common, established; methodical, orderly, systematic, uniform.

irrelevant *adj.* unconnected, unrelated, beside the point, inapt, unfitting, immaterial, nonpertinent, impertinent, malapropos, not apropos, extraneous, foreign, neither here nor there, not germane; *Informal* off base, out in left field. **—Ant.** relevant, pertinent, germane, apropos, related.

irreligious *adj.* not religious, not holding religious beliefs, unbelieving, godless, atheistic, agnostic, impious, profane, sacrilegious, unholy, ungodly. **—Ant.** religious, pious, devout.

irreparable *adj.* beyond repair or salvage, uncorrectable, irreversible, beyond redress, uncompensable, irremediable, remediless, unfixable. **—Ant.** reparable, salvageable, reversible, remediable.

irrepressible *adj.* unrestrainable, uncontrollable, unsquelchable, unquenchable, undamped; bubbling, ebullient, vibrant, galvanic, boisterous, tempestuous, full of life. **—Ant.** repressible, restrainable; depressed, damped, squelched.

irreproachable *adj.* beyond reproach or criticism, above reproof, without fault, flawless, blameless, faultless, inculpable, impeccable; unblemished, stainless, unspotted, unimpeachable. **—Ant.** reproachable, flawed, blameworthy, faulty.

irresistible *adj.* **1.** overwhelming, not resistible, not withstandable, overpowering, overmastering, superhuman. **2.** extremely tempting, enticing, alluring, not to be resisted, tantalizing, seductive, enchanting, beckoning, highly desirable. **—Ant. 1** resistible, withstandable, weak. **2** resistible, unattractive.

irresolute *adj.* indecisive, wavering, hesitating, hesitant, faltering, unsettled, doubtful, undecided, uncertain, unsure, changeable, vacillating, fickle, weak, unsteady, unresolved. **—Ant.** resolute, determined, unwavering, decisive; decided, certain.

irresponsible *adj.* careless, not responsible, undependable, unreliable, indifferent, immature, untrustworthy, thoughtless; imprudent, incautious, reckless, rash, ill-considered, capricious, injudicious, overhasty; foolish, scatterbrained, harebrained. **—Ant.** responsible, careful, thoughtful, trustworthy, dependable.

irreverent *adj.* disrespectful, lacking reverence, impious, irreligious, profane, blasphemous; impudent, brazen, shameless, saucy, sneering, nose-thumbing; disparaging, slighting, critical, skeptical, debunking.

irrevocable *adj.* final, conclusive, not subject to reversal, unchangeable, not commutable, irreversible, unalterable. **—Ant.** reversible, changeable, alterable.

irritable *adj.* ill-humored, easily irritated, easily annoyed, ill-tempered, easily angered, irascible, easily vexed, touchy, oversensitive, testy, peevish, grouchy, grumpy, waspish, impatient, snappish, pettish, fretful. **—Syn. Study.** IRRITABLE, IRASCIBLE, TOUCHY, TESTY mean easily excited, provoked, or disturbed. IRRITABLE means easily annoyed or bothered; it implies cross and snappish behavior, often of short duration: *The irritable clerk had no patience for my questions.* IRASCIBLE is a stronger term that means habitually angry or easily angered: *an irascible boss, roaring at employees for the slightest error.* TOUCHY stresses oversensitivity and readiness to take offense, even though none is intended: *touchy about any reference to shyness.* TESTY describes the same kind of response, particularly to minor annoyances: *Too little sleep put her in a testy mood.* **—Ant.** easygoing, amiable, good-natured, agreeable, genial, affable.

irritate *v.* **1.** annoy, vex, anger, make angry, make impatient, peeve, provoke, nettle, exasperate, irk. **2.** make painful, aggravate, worsen, make sensitive, inflame, make sore, make swollen, rub against, chafe. **—Ant. 1** appease, mollify, placate, pacify; gratify, please, delight. **2** soothe, balm, ease.

island *n.* **1.** isle, islet, atoll. **2.** sanctuary, refuge, shelter, retreat, haven, place of tranquil isolation, isolated spot, oasis, enclave.

isolate *v.* separate, segregate, place apart, set apart, insulate, quarantine, seclude, banish, sequester; disconnect, detach. **—Ant.** join, unite, combine, mix.

issue *n.* **1.** giving out, granting; sending out, putting forth, issuance, distributing, dispensation; number, publication. **2.** problem, question, dispute, matter for discussion, point of debate, matter to be settled, matter in dispute. **3.** result, consequence, outcome; yield, product. **4.** offspring, progeny, children, descendants, heirs, heritors, posterity. **5.** outpouring, gush, discharge, outflow, effluence, drainage, eruption. *—v.* **6.** pour forth, go out, emanate, flow out, spout, gush, erupt, pass out, emerge. **7.** put in circulation, circulate, distribute. **8.** give out, distribute, dispense, allot. **9.** result, proceed, follow, ensue, grow out of, rise, arise, emerge, stem, spring. **—Syn. Study. 6** See EMERGE. **—Ant. 3** start, beginning, inception, cause. **4** parent, sire. **7** withdraw, revoke, repeal. **8** withhold, withdraw. **9** cause; start, begin, initiate.

itch *v.* **1.** have an itch, feel the need to scratch, prickle, tickle, crawl, creep. **2.** long, yearn, hanker, have a yen, crave, desire, pine, ache. *—n.* **3.** prickling sensation, tingling, itchiness, prickliness, pruritis. **4.** strong wish, desire, yearning, restless urge, yen, appetite, hankering, craving, hunger, thirst.

item *n.* **1.** separate listing, article, notation, entry, detail, particular, unit, thing, matter, subject, point. **2.** report, news article, notice, piece, story, account, dispatch, paragraph, feature.

itemize *v.* list individually, individualize, state one by one, particularize, detail, state by item, enumerate, spell out, specify. **—Ant.** combine, group, *Informal* lump together.

itinerant *adj.* **1.** wandering, wayfaring, peripatetic, roving, roaming, migrant, traveling, nomadic, footloose, vagabond, vagrant, transient. **—*n.* 2.** person on the move; homeless traveler, transient, wayfarer, wanderer, roamer, rover, nomad, vagabond. **—Ant. 1** stationary, settled, resident. **2** resident, stay-at-home.

itinerary *n.* **1.** travel plan, schedule, detailed plan for a trip, list of places to be visited, timetable, course, route, circuit. **2.** log, record of a journey, travel record, journal, account, diary, day book.

jab *v.* **1.** poke, nudge, tap, bump, prod, dig, stab, strike, rap, hit, goad, elbow. —*n.* **2.** poke, short punch, quick thrust, pelt, cut, stroke, stab, dig, swing; hit, blow; *Slang* belt, sock, plug, clip, paste, lick, swat.

jabber *v.* **1.** babble, chatter, talk aimlessly, talk idly, maunder, prattle, prate, blather, drivel, gab, blab, talk nonsense, utter drivel, clack, ramble, gibber, rattle. —*n.* **2.** jabbering talk, gibberish, nonsense, drivel, idle talk, maundering, ranting, prattle, chatter, blabber, babble, prating, patter, blather, gab, chitter-chatter, twattle, clack, palaver, raving, gossip, chitchat, gushing, twaddle, cackle; *Slang* gas, hot air.

jacket *n.* **1.** short coat, (*variously*) sport coat, blazer, smoking jacket, dinner coat or jacket, mackinaw, pea jacket, Windbreaker. **2.** outer covering, wrapper, container, wrapping, cover, envelope, casing, case, coat, enclosure, folder, sheath.

jaded *adj.* **1.** shop-worn, worn-out, tired, played out, overused, stale; fatigued, exhausted, weary, wearied, dog-tired, fagged, spent, overwearied, tired out. **2.** blasé, bored, surfeited, spoiled, cloyed, dulled, satiate, satiated, sated, glutted, overindulged.

jagged *adj.* rough, snaggy, irregular, having uneven notches or points, indented, crenulated, ragged on the edges, jaggy, uneven, broken; knifelike, serrated, notched, sharp-toothed, saw-toothed, nicked, ridged, zigzag; angular, craggy, rugged, cragged, pointed; spiny, spinous, bristly, thorny; studded, spiked, barbed. —**Ant.** smooth, even, regular; level, straight.

jail Also *British* **gaol** *n.* **1.** prison, penal institution, penitentiary, prison house, house of correction; *Slang* pen, big house, hoosegow, lockup, jug, can, clink, cooler, slammer, stir, calaboose; reform school, reformatory, workhouse; station house, police station, detention house, halfway house, pound; *Military* guardhouse, guardroom, stockade, black hole, *Naval* brig; dungeon, keep, cell, bastille. —*v.* **2.** imprison, incarcerate, confine, lock up; hold in custody, take or make prisoner, take in, bring in, arrest, put under arrest, capture, seize, apprehend, arraign, book; *Informal* nab; *Slang* run in, pinch, collar, bust, bag. —**Ant. 2** release, liberate, free, parole.

jam *v.* **1.** press, cram, crowd, stuff, pack, overcrowd; squeeze, insert forcefully, ram, sandwich, wedge; work in, force in, edge in, worm in, foist in; put between. **2.** hit suddenly, push, thrust, press, bear down on. **3.** block, obstruct, congest, stick, suspend, stall, arrest, stop, interrupt, cease; become unworkable, become stuck, malfunction, break down momentarily. —*n.* **4.** impassable mass of objects or persons, crowd, tie-up, multitude, throng, sea, agglomeration, mob, horde, pack, flock, herd, swarm, host, drove, army; crush, shove, push, press. **5.** *Informal* fix, trouble, mess, predicament, strait, plight, dilemma, quandary; *Slang* pickle, scrape, pinch, hot water.

jamboree *n.* festival, fete, carnival, celebration, jubilee, frolic, festivity, gala, spree, party, carousal, *Spanish* fiesta, *French* fête champêtre, festive occasion, revel; *Slang* blowout, bash, do, shindig.

jangle *v.* **1.** rattle, clang, clatter, clank; tintinnabulate, chime, jingle, ring, reverberate; sound harshly, sound discordantly, make a racket, clash, crash. **2.** upset, jar, irritate, annoy, grate on. —*n.* **3.** rattle, clang, clatter, clank, racket, clangor, wild pealing, harsh ringing, din, reverberation; cacophony, jumble of sound, confusion of noise. —**Ant. 3** silence, quiet.

janitor *n.* custodian, cleaning man, cleaning woman, cleaning lady, janitress, handyman, superintendent, *Slang* super, caretaker, porter.

jar[1] *n.* container, receptacle, crock, pot, jug, bottle, canister, flask, decanter, beaker, urn, demijohn.

jar[2] *v.* **1.** disquiet, disturb, perturb, unsettle, upset, trouble, disconcert, distract, discompose, startle, shock, astound, stupefy, stun, take aback, shake up, confuse, fluster, bewilder, daze, befuddle; *Informal* give one a turn, throw, faze, floor. **2.** shake, vibrate harshly, rock, cause to quake, jiggle, jolt, cause to quiver, agitate, make tremble, convulse, joggle, stir, upheave. —*n.* **3.** rattle, clang, clatter, clank, racket, clashing, crash, clangor, din, reverberation; cacophony, discordance, jangle, bray, brawl, blare, blast, bong, buzz, bleating. **4.** concussion, reverberation, shake, jolt, agitation, impact, crash, shock, quake. —**Ant. 2** soothe, calm, quiet.

jargon *n.* **1.** specialized or professional language, idiom, parlance, phraseology, vocabulary, usage, vernacular, argot, lingo, cant, shibboleths. **2.** meaningless writing or talk, nonsense, gibberish, verbiage, grandiloquence, stuff and nonsense, prattle, drivel, prate, blather, twaddle, blabber, babble, jabberwocky, rigmarole, rubbish, fustian, tommyrot; *Slang* bunk, balderdash, hogwash, bosh, flapdoodle, folderol, hocus-pocus, abracadabra, poppycock, fudge, moonshine, gobbledygook, bull, hooey, baloney, malarkey, piffle. **3.** simplified language, vernacular, lingo, dialect, patois, brogue, pidgin, lingua franca. **—Syn. Study. 1** See LANGUAGE.

jaundiced *adj.* **1.** skeptical, cynical, doubting; blasé, bored, satiated. **2.** jealous, envious, covetous, green-eyed; resentful, hostile, bitter, embittered, feeling ill will, mistrustful, suspicious, doubting. **—Ant. 1** credulous, believing, trusting.

jaunt *n.* short trip, excursion, junket, trip, tour, outing, expedition, ramble, adventure, flight; *Informal* spin, stroll, promenade, airing.

jaunty *adj.* lighthearted, high-spirited, buoyant, bouncy, perky, lively, sprightly, vivacious, airy, breezy, blithe, free and easy, carefree; sporty, debonair, dapper, high stepping, spruce, neat, trim; *Informal* natty. **—Ant.** staid, sober, sedate, dignified; dull, lifeless, pessimistic.

jealous *adj.* **1.** envious, resentful, covetous, green-eyed, grudging. **2.** possessive, suspicious, mistrustful, mistrusting, wary, anxious, concerned, regardful, protective, watchful, apprehensive; conscious of, obsessed with, unduly proud of, zealous in maintaining or guarding something, mindful. **—Ant. 1** trusting, trustful. **2** indifferent, uncaring.

jealousy *n.* **—Syn. Study.** See ENVY.

jeer *v.* **1.** deride, sneer, mock, revile, laugh at, taunt, hoot, ridicule, scorn, harass, hound, make game or sport of, poke fun at, heckle, hector, gibe rudely, scoff, flout; hiss, boo, whistle at, whoop, catcall, give the raspberry, give the Bronx cheer, razz, *Informal* knock. **—*n.* 2.** jeering utterance, derision, taunt, mockery, contumely, slur, barb, yell of contempt, hoot, insult, aspersion, abuse, obloquy, scoff, scoffing, slam, dig, *Informal* knock, *Slang* rap. **—Syn. Study. 1** See SCOFF. **—Ant. 1** applaud, cheer. **2** encouragement, adulation, applause.

jeopardy *n.* danger, peril, openness to danger, imperilment, exposure, vulnerability, hazard, endangerment, unsafety, liability, risk, precariousness, insecurity. **—Ant.** security, safety.

jerk *n.* **1.** pull, snap, tug, yank; shake, twitch, quiver, spasm, reflex, start, trembling, tic. **2.** idiot, fool, dupe, dope, dunce, ass, dummy, klutz. **—*v.* 3.** pull, tug, twist, thrust, pluck, yank, wrench; shake, convulse, twitch, quiver, tremble.

jerry-built *adj.* flimsy, rickety, gimcrack, shoddy, unsubstantial, defective, faulty, weak, frail, shaky, thrown-together, thrown-up, run-up, unstable, ramshackle, slipshod, unsound; *Slang* tacky, sleazy, cheap-jack. **—Ant.** sound, sturdy, well-built, durable, substantial.

jest *n.* **1.** facetious remark, joke, jape, gibe, quip, wisecrack, crack, pleasantry, pun; *Informal* gag, trick, prank, game; witticism, bon mot. **—*v.* 2.** crack jokes, joke, quip, banter, fool, tease, act up, play the fool, laugh; *Slang* josh, wisecrack, horse around.

jester *n.* clown, fool, zany, buffoon, joker, wag, motley fool, madcap, funnyman, merry-andrew, punchinello, *Informal* card; harlequin, wearer of the cap and bells; (*variously*) mime, pantomimist, mimic, mimer, mummer, comedian, comic, wit, humorist, quipster.

jet *n.* **1.** stream, stream of liquid, fountain, spurt, spray, spout, squirt, swash, shoot, flush, gush, *German* Spritze. **2.** spout, nozzle, sprayer, sparger, sprinkler; atomizer, syringe, *German* Spritzer. **—*v.* 3.** spout, spurt, stream, shoot, shoot out, spray, squirt, issue, discharge, break or burst forth, gush, fountain, rush up, surge, effuse, vomit forth.

jettison *v.* throw overboard, pitch over, throw over, cast off, throw off ballast; eliminate, discard, throw out, dump, scrap, unload, eject, discharge.

jewel *n.* **1.** precious stone, cut and polished stone, gem, stone. **2.** ornament, piece of jewelry, bangle, bauble, bead, trinket, (*variously*) necklace, bracelet, earring, ring, tiara, lavaliere, locket, pendant, brooch. **3.** treasure, prize, gem, one in a thousand, one in a million, first-rater, ace; *Informal* topnotcher, pearl, pearl of great price, pure gold, find, honey, dear, apple of one's eye, salt of the earth; *Slang* crackerjack, whiz, humdinger, pip, winner, knockout; work of art, masterpiece.

jewelry *n.* jewels, gems, precious stones, adornments, personal ornaments, regalia; articles of gold, silver, or gems; trinkets, gewgaws, bangles, costume jewelry.

jibe *v.* agree, conform, accord, fit, harmonize, tally, correspond, match, square, coincide, concur, mesh, go together, fit together, dovetail, fit in, go. **—Ant.** conflict, contradict, oppose, differ, disagree.

jiffy *n.* moment, minute, instant, trice, flash, second, twinkling, split second, wink of the eye, twinkling of an eye; *Slang* jiff, shake, two shakes of a lamb's tail; millisecond, microsecond, nanosecond; *British Slang* half a mo.

jiggle *v.* shake, wiggle, joggle, agitate, jostle; wriggle, fidget, bounce, twitch, jerk.

jilt *v.* cast off a lover or sweetheart, break an engagement, break off with, break one's word or promise; forsake, leave, leave in the lurch, desert; betray, let down, break one's heart.

jingle *v.* **1.** jangle, ring, clank, clink, clatter, tinkle. *—n.* **2.** ringing, clang, tinkle, tintinnabulation, jangle, reverberation. **3.** a catchy poem or song, singing commercial, commercial tune, ditty, product theme; facetiae, burlesque poem or verse, trivial verse, doggerel, limerick.

jingoism *n.* chauvinism, nationalism, superpatriotism, flag-waving, blind patriotism, spread-eagleism, overpatriotism, patriotics, ultranationalism, wrapping oneself in the flag.

jinx *n.* evil spell, evil eye, hex, curse, plague, ill wind, *Slang* whammy; nemesis, bête noire, bugbear, bugaboo.

jitters *n.* nervousness, shakes, shivers, fidgets, anxiety, tenseness, jumpiness, shakiness, uneasiness, quivering, fidgetiness, skittishness; *Informal* butterflies, *Slang* willies, heebie-jeebies, whim-whams, jim-jams, the creeps, screaming-meemies. **—Ant.** calm, repose, ease, composure, serenity, poise.

job *n.* **1.** work, task, responsibility, charge, assignment, duty, business, affair; commission, mission, chore, errand, undertaking, function, role, part, stint, concern, care, trust; enterprise, activity, exercise, performance, accomplishment, achievement. **2.** position, situation, engagement, appointment, place, spot, opening; means of support, occupation, career, living, livelihood, business, line of business; capacity, role, part, function, office; profession, vocation, field, province, calling, pursuit, métier, trade, craft, kind of work. **3.** unit of work, assignment, contract, commission; completed effort, piecework, lot, allotment, quota, portion, share, output, product. **—Syn. Study. 1** See TASK.

jocose *adj.* jocular, joking, teasing, playful, humorous, jesting, roguish, arch, facetious, witty, comic, comical, waggish, jovial, jolly, droll, quick-witted, nimble-witted, sportive, prankish, *Slang* fun. **—Ant.** serious, earnest, solemn, staid, humorless.

jocular *adj.* humorous, lighthearted, given to joking or jesting, sportive, witty, jocose, joking, jesting, facetious, jolly, jocund, jovial, merry, gay, mirthful, laughter-loving, full of fun, funny, playful, rompish, prankish, roguish, frolicsome, waggish; entertaining, amusing, droll. **—Syn. Study.** See JOVIAL. **—Ant.** grave, earnest, sober, solemn; morose, gloomy, glum, melancholy, dour, sour.

jocund *adj.* cheerful, merry, pleasant, jovial, jolly, breezy, lively, lighthearted, elated, debonair, cheery, happy-go-lucky, easygoing, untroubled. **—Ant.** sober, serious, grave, sad, troubled.

jog *v.* **1.** trot, bounce, jar, rock, jiggle, jounce, shake, jostle, joggle, bob, jerk. **2.** nudge, stir, activate, energize, actuate, stimulate, prompt, animate, set going. *—n.* **3.** jerk, pull, twist, wrench, shake, twitch; *Informal* yank, tug.

join *v.* **1.** bring together, connect, conjoin, fasten, tie together, marry, couple, bind, fuse, unite, piece together; splice, merge, mix, band, combine, pool; chain, link, bridge. **2.** cement, glue, stick together, stick, hold fast, attach, paste; cohere, bind, connect, unify, unite, solder, affix. **3.** unite, ally, combine, merge, bring together, consolidate; federate, amalgamate, conglomerate, associate, confederate, syndicate; hold together, get together, meet, fraternize, cooperate. **4.** become a member of, associate oneself with, sign up with, enroll in, enlist in, enter, subscribe to. **5.** adjoin, border on, verge on, be adjacent to, conjoin, be contiguous with; connect with, meet, reach, touch, abut; hug, skirt, scrape, brush, graze. **—Syn. Study. 1** JOIN, CONNECT, UNITE imply bringing two or more things together more or less closely. JOIN may refer to a connection or association of any degree of closeness, but often implies direct contact: *to join pieces of wood to form a corner.* CONNECT implies a joining as by a tie, link, or wire: *to connect two batteries.* UNITE implies a close joining of two or more things, so as to form one: *to unite layers of veneer sheets to form plywood.* **—Ant. 1, 2** disjoin; part, separate, sever, sunder; detach, disengage; disentangle, untangle, divide, disconnect. **4** leave, resign, quit.

joint *n.* **1.** part where joining occurs, place of joining, connection, articulation, juncture, junction, coupling, hinge; nexus, link, knot; (*variously*) hock, knuckle, knee, elbow. *—adj.* **2.** mutual, common, shared, sharing or acting in common, community, communal, hand-in-hand, collaborative, collective, cooperative, coalitional, conjoined, conjunctive; combined, allied, united, corporate, unified, associated, associate, consolidated; like-minded, unanimous. **—Ant. 2** individual, solitary, lone.

jointly *adv.* together, in common, by combined action, conjointly, mutually, by mutual consent, collectively, in conjunction, in association, unitedly, in unison; *Informal* arm in arm, hand-in-hand, side by side. **—Ant.** separately, individually, on one's own.

joke *n.* **1.** jest, pleasantry, diversion, playful or mischievous trick or remark, play of wit, horseplay, facetiousness, whimsy, frolic; practical joke, gag, jape, monkeyshine, prank, caper, frolic, antic, lark; funny story, anecdote, shaggy-dog story, bon mot, wit, witticism, pun, quip, badinage, repartee, wisecrack, banter, satire, parody, lampoon, farce, travesty, burlesque, *Informal* put-on. **2.** object of joking or ridicule, butt, target, laughing stock; simpleton, fool, buffoon, clown, town fool, village idiot, bumpkin. **3.** cinch, pushover, trifle, nothing, mere nothing, snap of the fingers, child's play, lark, farce, no great matter, a little thing, nothing to speak of, nothing worth mentioning. *—v.* **4.** jest, clown, crack jokes, banter, play the fool, frolic, gambol; *Slang* josh, goof, gibe, horse around, wisecrack. **5.** poke fun at, make jokes about, mock, ridicule, make merry with, laugh to scorn, make game of, gibe at, laugh at, smile at, chortle, laugh up one's sleeve, snicker, deride, pooh-pooh, scoff at, jeer at; play a practical joke upon, send on a fool's errand, put on, dupe, gull, take in, fool, tease; *Slang* roast.

joker *n.* **1.** clown, jester, comedian, funnyman, wit, wag, jokester, life of the party, madcap, zany, humorist, punster, mimic, *Slang* wisecracker. **2.** hidden danger, pitfall, trap, obscure factor, catch, subterfuge, trick, hitch, snag, snare; fine print, escape clause, rider, codicil, addendum.

jolly *adj.* happy, merry, gay, mirthful, cheerful, sportive, funny, gleeful, delightful, rollicking, jocund, jocular, fun-loving, jovial, merry, droll, high-spirited, playful. **—Syn. Study.** See JOVIAL. **—Ant.** solemn, grave, serious; lugubrious, morose, dour, saturnine, gloomy, glum, sour.

jolt *v.* **1.** startle, disturb, perturb, upset, take aback; shake, jar, shake up, shock, stun, *Informal* throw; jerk, jog, bump, bounce, convulse, joggle, jump, bob, jiggle, jostle, bobble. *—n.* **2.** shock, jar, start, thunderbolt, trauma; setback, reversal, shaking, bounce, jounce, twitch, jerk, joggle, jostle, jog, bump, lurch, agitation; jiggle, quiver, quake.

josh *v.* tease, jolly, ridicule, twit, poke fun at, guy, sport with, chaff, haze; *Slang* rib, jive, kid, razz, put on, rag, roast. **—Ant.** praise, flatter, compliment, adulate.

jostle *v.* shove, bump, crowd, push roughly, hit against, collide, run against, shoulder, elbow, butt, push, knock against, prod, jab, poke.

jot *v.* **1.** write quickly, put down, take down, set down, make a note of, make a memorandum of, note, scribble; list, record, register, enter. *—n.* **2.** the least bit, one little bit, one iota, speck, whit, bit, dot, mite, trace, smidgen, trifle, particle, snip; modicum, scintilla, snippet.

journal *n.* **1.** daily record, diary, register, chronology, almanac, record, daybook, notebook, calendar, chronicle, memorandum, record book, memory book, yearbook, history, scrapbook, album; memoir, autobiography, confession; *Naval* log, logbook; *Bookkeeping* ledger, account book. **2.** newspaper, paper, gazette, chronicle, tabloid, sheet, daily, weekly; (*variously*) publication, periodical, magazine, monthly, quarterly, annual.

journalist newpaperman, newspaperwoman, commentator, news editor, anchor person; *Slang* bigfoot.

journey *n.* **1.** trip, tour, junket, expedition, trek, excursion, outing, jaunt, wandering, divagation, peregrination, roving, odyssey, pilgrimage, quest; flight, voyage, course of travel, cruise; route, itinerary, transit, circuit, passage, way. *—v.* **2.** travel, tour, take a trip, divagate, peregrinate, trek, sightsee, voyage, sail, navigate, cruise, fly, course, ramble, roam, rove, wander, pilgrimage, wend, meander, vagabond, tramp. **—Syn. Study. 1** See TRIP.

jovial *adj.* cheerful, merry, gay, mirthful, gleeful, cheery, blithe, zestful, jocund, jocular, jolly, jocose, sunny, buoyant, delightful, sportive, playful, frolicsome, fun-loving, convivial, laughing, humorous, hilarious, rollicking, hearty. **—Syn. Study.** JOVIAL, JOCULAR, JOLLY refer to someone who is in good spirits. JOVIAL suggests a sociable and friendly person, full of hearty good humor: *The jovial professor enlivened the party.* JOCULAR refers to an amusing person, given to joking or jesting in a playful way: *His jocular sister teased him about his haircut.* JOLLY suggests a cheerful person, full of fun and laughter: *a jolly Santa Claus.* **—Ant.** saturnine, dour, morose, gloomy, lugubrious, melancholy, glum.

jowl *n.* jaw, cheek, chops, mandible, muzzle (*of an animal*).

joy *n.* **1.** delight, happiness, gladness, exultation, satisfaction, rapture, fullness of heart, ecstasy, elation, excitement, cheerfulness, glee, gaiety, exhilaration, delectation, jubilation, enjoyment, pleasure, contentment. **2.** cause of gladness, source of pride or satisfaction, treasure, prize, pride, precious possession, gem, jewel. **—Ant. 1** sorrow, misery, despair, unhappiness, grief. **2** bane, trouble, affliction, trial, tribulation.

joyful *adj.* **1.** delighted, jubilant, happy, glad, pleased, exultant, cheerful, elated, full of joy, ecstatic, overjoyed, enraptured, transported, beside oneself with joy, gladsome. **2.** happy, gladsome, pleasing, heartwarming, causing or bringing joy, delightful, blessed, rosy, cheerful, bright, pleasurable, heartening, gratifying.

joyous *adj.* happy, glad, gladsome, joyful, festive, wonderful, rapturous, gay, mirthful, merry, cheerful, gleeful, lighthearted, gratifying, pleasurable, heartening, heartwarming, delightful. **—Ant.** sad, unhappy, joyless.

jubilant *adj.* joyful, overjoyed, ecstatic, flushed with excitement or pleasure, in good or high spirits, exultant, rejoicing, rapturous, delirious, radiant, enraptured, exuberant, elated, exhilarated; cheerful, joyous, merry, mirthful, gay, gladdened, glad, gladsome, delighted, smiling, laughing, happy, gleeful, pleased, gratified, jolly, lighthearted, cheery; blithe, blithesome, buoyant, rhapsodic, enrapt, charmed, captivated, intoxicated; *Informal* happy as a lark, merry as a cricket, floating on cloud nine, tickled pink, happy as the day is long. **—Ant.** doleful, sorrowful, despondent, sad, melancholy, *Informal* down in the dumps.

jubilee *n.* festival, fete, gala, revelry, frolic, celebration, observance, festivity, revels, holiday, anniversary, commemoration, jubilation, party, conviviality, merrymaking; *Slang* bash, wing-ding, blast, do, blowout, shindig.

judge *n.* **1.** justice, magistrate; official, arbitrator, arbiter, moderator, juror, adjudicator; critic, reviewer, censor; referee, umpire. **2.** critic, assessor, appraiser, evaluator, connoisseur; expert, authority. *—v.* **3.** rule on, settle, pass sentence, pronounce judgment on, administer justice, adjudge, adjudicate, arbitrate, sit in judgment on, determine, decide, find, announce a verdict; conduct, try, review, hear; referee, umpire. **4.** decide, ascertain, find, resolve, determine, discern, distinguish; estimate, surmise, guess, conjecture, suppose, believe, assume, imagine, fancy; consider, regard, deem, conclude; infer, deduce; *Informal* reckon. **5.** appraise, rate, rank, assess, value, weigh, gauge, size up, analyze. **—Syn. Study. 1** JUDGE, REFEREE, UMPIRE indicate a person who is entrusted with decisions affecting others. JUDGE, in its legal and other uses, implies that the person has qualifications and authority for rendering decisions in matters at issue: *a judge appointed to the Supreme Court; a judge in a baking contest.* REFEREE refers to an officer who examines and reports on the merits of a case as an aid to a court; it is also used of a person who settles disputes, esp. in a game or sport: *a referee in bankruptcy; a basketball referee.* UMPIRE refers to a person who gives the final ruling when arbitrators of a case disagree; it is also used of a person who enforces the rules in a game: *an umpire to settle the labor dispute; a baseball umpire.*

judgment Also *chiefly British* **judgement** *n.* **1.** decision, finding, ruling, verdict; decree, sentence; adjudication, arbitration. **2.** discretion, taste, judiciousness, discernment, discrimination; perceptiveness, perception, sense, shrewdness, acumen, percipience. **3.** opinion, appraisal, belief, conviction, conclusion, deduction, persuasion, estimate, valuation, assessment, view.

judicial *adj.* **1.** judiciary, jurisdictional, juristic, legal, official. **2.** befitting a judge, judgelike, magistral, magisterial, majestic, imposing, distinguished.

judicious *adj.* sensible, wise, sagacious, sage, perspicacious, sound of judgment, just, discriminating, discerning, astute, knowing, sound, levelheaded, practical, reasonable, clear-sighted, acute, shrewd, sober, percipient; diplomatic, politic, tactful, thoughtful, reflective, prudent, well-advised. **—Syn. Study.** See PRACTICAL. **—Ant.** injudicious, imprudent, unsound; thoughtless, unreasonable.

jug *n.* vessel, pitcher, ewer, jar, urn, crock, decanter, bottle, flagon, carafe, demijohn, tankard, stein, container.

juggle *v.* **1.** practice jugglery, keep aloft, keep objects in play. **2.** manipulate, falsify, alter, misrepresent, modify, disguise, tamper with, fool with, redo, reorganize, meddle with, tinker with.

juicy *adj.* **1.** juice-filled, fluid, moist, succulent, liquid, watery, wet, sappy, luscious, pulpy, lush, runny, flowing, fluent, dripping. **2.** vivid, intriguing, exciting, picturesque, colorful, thrilling, racy, spicy, risqué, sensational, graphic, lurid, tantalizing, captivating, fascinating, provocative. **—Ant. 1** dry, desiccated, arid, moistureless. **2** dull, vapid, colorless, lackluster, unimaginative.

jumble *v.* **1.** mix confusedly, mix up, throw together, toss at random, pitch, strew about, turn topsy-turvy, scatter, pile up, ball up, heap, bunch. *—n.* **2.** confusion, mixture, disarray, snarl, tangle, muddle, medley, conglomeration, mix, accumulation, aggregate, mélange, miscellany; mess, chaos, clutter, tumble, hodgepodge, gallimaufry, farrago, potpourri, stew, salmagundi, mishmash, patchwork, olio; *Informal* what the cat brought in, everything but the kitchen sink. —**Ant. 1** separate, isolate; order. **2** order, system, arrangement.

jumbo *adj.* huge, immense, gigantic, oversized, mammoth, colossal, stupendous, giant, elephantine, cyclopean, enormous, monumental, titanic, monstrous, mountainous, towering, mighty, vast. —**Ant.** small, tiny, minute, minuscule, wee.

jump *v.* **1.** leap, hop, skip, vault, spring, bounce, pitch, bound; buck, prance, gambol. **2.** skip, go over, hurdle, overrun, not be held back. **3.** start, flinch, blench, wince, recoil. **4.** attack, ambush, spring upon, pounce upon, fall upon. **5.** skip, pass, digress, maunder, switch, change abruptly, move quickly. **6.** increase or rise suddenly, climb rapidly, skyrocket, zoom up. —*n.* **7.** bound, leap, vault, skip, hop, spring. **8.** obstacle, obstruction, barrier, barricade, impediment, hurdle. **9.** sudden rise, increased volume, upturn; surge, swift increase, upsurge, advance, boost, increment, augmentation.

jumpy *adj.* jittery, nervous, skittish, fidgety, agitated, shaky, nervy, fluttery, trembling, twitching, twitchy, aflutter; fretful, apprehensive, anxious, uneasy; *Slang* uptight, goosey; alarmed, panicky, frightened. —**Ant.** calm, unruffled, composed, serene, sedate.

junction *n.* juncture, convergence, linkup, joining place, concurrence, confluence, conflux, joining, connecting point, crossroads, intersection, interchange. —**Syn. Study.** JUNCTION, JUNCTURE refer to a place, line, or point at which two or more things join. A JUNCTION is also a place where things come together: *the junction of two rivers.* A JUNCTURE is a line or point at which two bodies are joined, or a point of exigency or crisis in time: *the juncture of the head and neck; a critical juncture in a struggle.*

juncture *n.* **1.** point of time, occasion, moment, interval, pass; critical point, crisis. **2.** junction, joining, joint, connection, seam, mutual edge, closure, point of contact, meeting, intersection. **3.** intersection, convergence, confluence, joining place, joining, junction, linkup, connection. —**Syn. Study. 1, 2** See JUNCTION.

jungle *n.* rain forest, wilderness, wild impenetrable land, unexplored territory, virgin forest, bush, wild, woods, swampy forest; undergrowth, dense vegetation; uncivilized territory, lawless region, savage environment. —**Ant.** civilization, civilized territory.

junior *adj.* **1.** younger, minor. **2.** lesser, subordinate, lower, secondary, inferior, minor, second-string; more recent, newer, later. —**Ant. 1, 2** senior, elder, older; superior.

junk *n.* **1.** rubbish, litter, discarded material, clutter, trash, debris, refuse, waste, odds and ends, castoffs, oddments, rummage, scrap, garbage. —*v.* **2.** discard, throw away, dispose of, scrap, dump, throw out, pitch out.

jurisdiction *n.* **1.** judicial right, lawful power, authority, prerogative, legal right, say, control, dominion, command, sway, rule. **2.** extent of authority, scope of power, precinct, bailiwick, province, dominion, hegemony, domain, district, circuit, sphere, compass, zone, range, reach, scope, bounds, beat, quarter, area, latitude, field.

jurist *n.* justice, judge, magistrate, legal authority; lawyer, attorney-at-law, attorney, counselor, counsel, advocate, legal adviser; *British* barrister, solicitor.

just *adj.* **1.** fair, equitable, evenhanded, fair-minded, impartial, unbiased, unbigoted, unprejudiced; trustworthy, honest, moral, upright, uncorrupt, good, decent, blameless, ethical, principled, scrupulous, upstanding, high-minded, righteous, honorable, conscientious, aboveboard, open to reason; disinterested, dispassionate, objective. **2.** reasonable, sensible, sane, sound, balanced, logical, based on knowledge and understanding, ethical, reputable, conscionable; well-grounded, well-founded, firm, solid, strong. **3.** deserved, fair, justified, equitable, justifiable, worthy, merited, due, condign; suitable, appropriate, fitting, proper, befitting; logical, reasonable, adequate, acceptable. —*adv.* **4.** a brief time ago, a moment ago, but a moment before, a little while ago; a short time ago, not long ago, recently, lately, only now. **5.** exactly, precisely, in all respects, completely, fully, entirely, perfectly, absolutely, quite. **6.** by a narrow margin, narrowly, by a hair's breadth, barely, by a little, only just, no more than, hardly, scarcely. **7.** only, nothing but, merely, but, no more than, simply, at most. —**Ant. 1–3** unjust. **1, 2** crooked, devious, corrupt; untrue, dishonest, prejudiced, unfair, unreasonable, partial, unlawful, inequitable. **3** undeserved, unfit, inappropriate.

justice *n.* **1.** righteousness, goodness, probity, right, uprightness, fairness, fair play, rightness, justness, equity, equitability, equitableness, honor, truth, honesty, integrity, probity, virtue. **2.** legality, right, proper cause, legitimacy, lawfulness, the law, constitutionality; justification. **3.** due punishment, reparation, penalty, chastisement, correction, atonement, amends, redress, satisfaction, just deserts, compensation, payment, remuneration. **—Ant. 1–3** dishonesty, favoritism, inequity, injustice, partiality, unfairness, unlawfulness, unreasonableness, untruth, wrong.

justify *v.* vindicate, excuse, prove right, show to be just, warrant, support, validate, uphold, sanction, confirm, sustain, bear out, back up, defend, account for, explain, make explanation for.

jut *v.* extend, protrude, stand out, project, beetle, thrust forward, stick out, poke out, bulge, overhang, shoot out.

juvenile *adj.* **1.** young, youthful, adolescent, junior; immature, childish, childlike, pubescent, infantile, puerile, callow, boyish, girlish, sophomoric, unsophisticated. *—n.* **2.** minor, youth, youngster, stripling, teenager, child, infant. **—Ant. 1** adult, mature, matured, grownup, full-fledged; senile; manly, womanly. **2** adult, older person.

kaleidoscopic *adj.* many-colored, motley, rainbowlike, variegated, variable, changeable, fluctuating, ever-changing, checkered, protean, unstable, vacillating, shifting, mobile. **—Ant.** stable, constant, fixed, steady, uniform.

keen *adj.* **1.** sharp, fine, finely honed, sharp as a razor, razorlike, paper-thin. **2.** sharp, shrewd, astute, acute, penetrating, incisive, alert, intelligent, quick, quick-witted, clever, discerning, perspicacious, discriminating. **3.** eager, enthusiastic, impatient, excited; intense, fervid, ardent, earnest, fervent, avid, zealous, impassioned, fierce. **—Syn. Study. 2** See SHARP. **—Ant. 1, 2** blunt, dull, flat, obtuse. **2** dull, dull-witted, dense, thick, thickheaded, obtuse, slow, ignorant, stupid, dumb. **3** apathetic, indifferent, unexcited.

keep *v.* **1.** retain, hold, possess, preserve, maintain, conserve, reserve, withhold, hang on to. **2.** hold, store, place, deposit, accumulate, heap, stack, pile; have, lay in, furnish, carry, stock. **3.** care for, take care of, look after, mind; extend hospitality to, have as a guest; guard, watch over, safeguard, keep an eye on. **4.** support, provide for, supply with the necessities of life, sustain, pay for, maintain. **5.** hold, hold back, keep back, restrain; encumber, stall, retard, impede, inhibit, arrest, constrain, prevent; obstruct, block, hinder, bar, hamper, hamstring, cramp, clog, hobble, tie up, shackle; detain, delay, hold up, deter. **6.** continue, carry on, keep up, persist in; stay, abide, stick, remain, stand, maintain, be constant, persevere, endure, be steadfast. **7.** observe, hold, pay heed to, celebrate, solemnize, honor, ritualize, commemorate, memorialize. **—*n.* 8.** room and board, food and lodgings, sustenance, daily bread; subsistence, support, living, livelihood, maintenance. **9.** fortress, stronghold, donjon, fortification, fort, citadel, castle, tower. **—Ant. 1** discard, abandon, give up, lose. **5** release, liberate, free; speed, expedite, hurry. **7** ignore, disregard. **—Syn. Study. 1** KEEP, RETAIN, RESERVE, WITHHOLD refer to having or holding in one's possession, care, or control. KEEP means to continue to have or hold, as opposed to losing, parting with, or giving up: *to keep a book for a week.* RETAIN, a more formal word, often stresses keeping something in spite of resistance or opposition: *The dictator managed to retain power.* To RESERVE is to keep for some future use, occasion, or recipient, or to hold back for a time: *to reserve a seat; to reserve judgment.* To WITHHOLD is generally to hold back altogether: *to withhold evidence.*

keeper *n.* **1.** gamekeeper, attendant, guard. **2.** curator, caretaker, guardian, warden, custodian, retainer, conservator; governess, chaperon, duenna, nurse, nurserymaid, nursemaid, wet nurse; protector, bodyguard, guardian angel; guard, sentinel, sentry, escort; jailer.

keepsake *n.* memento, memory, token of remembrance, souvenir, remembrance, token, reminder, memorial, relic; symbol, emblem.

keg *n.* barrel, cask, drum, butt, vat, tank, rundlet, container, tun, tub, puncheon, hogshead, kilderkin.

kerchief *n.* scarf, muffler, cloth, handkerchief, neckerchief, neckcloth, neckwear, headpiece, babushka.

kernel *n.* seed, grain, germ, pit, stone, pip, nut; core, center, nub, gist; marrow, pith, nucleus, center, quintessence.

kettle *n.* teakettle, teapot, pot, pan, saucepan, cauldron, crucible, tub, vat, tureen, boiler.

key *n.* **1.** opening device, opener; (*variously*) latchkey, master key, passkey, skeleton key, house key. **2.** crucial determinant, solution, explanation, answer, meaning, translation, interpretation, elucidation, resolution, finding, explication, light, exposition; cue, clue, indicator, indication, indicant; point, pointer. **3.** tonality; scale, mode. **—*v.* 4.** adjust, fit, suit, adapt; address, direct, gear.

keynote *n.* theme, essence, main idea, gist, core, heart, substance, nub, nucleus, central point, sum and substance, salient idea, pattern, pith, marrow, quiddity, *Slang* nitty-gritty.

keystone *n.* basis, base, principle, cornerstone, root, foundation, mainspring, linchpin, crux, central idea, cardinal point, main thing, gravamen; *Slang* bottom line; name of the game.

kibitzer *n.* meddler, snoop, snooper, busybody, butt-in, prier, watcher, pry; *Slang* buttinsky, backseat driver.

kick *v.* **1.** strike with the foot, punt, boot, hit, strike. **2.** recoil, spring back, jump back, fly back, rebound. **3. kick out.** eject, throw out, cast out, turn out, remove, send packing, show the door, give the heave, give the gate, send about one's business; *Slang* give the boot to, boot out, give the bum's rush. **4.** *Informal* complain, fuss, make a fuss, protest, grouch, object, remonstrate, grumble, find fault, grouse, fret, fume, growl, gripe, beef. **—*n.* 5.** a hit with the foot, boot, stroke; act of kicking. **6.** recoil, kickback, springing back, rebound, return, reaction, backlash. **7.** thrill, pleasure, excitement, amusement, fun, enjoyment, *Slang* blast, trip, turnon; great satisfaction, gratification. **8.** flavor, pungency, high seasoning, tang, intensity, punch, sparkle, snap, dash, piquancy; pep, verve, zest, vigor, vim, power, force, vitality, life, animation. **9.** complaint, protestation, grievance, objection, remonstration, protest, gripe, beef.

kickback *n.* bribe, cut, share, commission, percentage, protection, compensation, remuneration, recompense, protection money, graft, payoff; *Slang* payola, boodle, hush money.

kid *n.* **1.** young goat, yearling; *Informal* billy goat, nanny goat. **2.** goatskin, goat hide, goat leather. **3.** child, little one, youngster, tot, moppet, shaver, tyke, little shaver, *Slang* squirt; juvenile, adolescent, teenager; baby, infant. **—*v.* 4.** tease, plague, harry, make fun of, mock, laugh at, make sport of, jest, josh, make game of, rag, rib, ride; ridicule, fool, mislead, delude, trick, deceive, hoodwink, gull, bamboozle, cozen, beguile, bluff, *Slang* put on. **—Ant. 3** adult, grown-up.

kidnap *v.* hold for ransom, abduct, carry off, capture, seize, impress, shanghai, bear away, lay hold of; hijack, skyjack; *Slang* snatch, put the snatch on, make off with.

kill *v.* **1.** murder, slay, slaughter, cut down, put to death, assassinate, butcher, massacre, shoot down, shoot, mortally wound, injure fatally, end the life of, take the life of, dispatch, put an end to, get rid of, do in, silence, stop the breath of, wipe out, exterminate, deal out death, shed blood, spill blood, execute; *Slang* knock off, bump off, rub out, blow away, finish off, erase, waste, take for a ride; (*variously*) strangle, garrote, smother, asphyxiate, suffocate, drown, poison, electrocute, hang, lynch, string up, bring to the gallows, behead, guillotine, bring to the block, decapitate, cut the throat of, burn to death, put to the stake, put to the sword, put to the knife, run through, dismember, hack or chop to pieces, tear limb from limb, draw and quarter, disembowel. **2.** extinguish, defeat, destroy, ruin, break, check, put a stop to, halt, stay, quell, stifle, smother, squelch. **—Ant. 1, 2** enliven, bring to life, revitalize.

killing *n.* **1.** murder, slaying, slaughter, homicide, manslaughter, massacre, violent death, death by violence, annihilation, elimination, extermination, decimation, butchery, bloodshed, capital punishment, execution; electrocution, fatality; (*variously*) shooting, stabbing, strangulation, strangling, garroting, guillotining, decapitation, lynching, hanging, poisoning, impalement, flogging to death, beating to death, stoning to death, burning to death; patricide, matricide, regicide, fratricide, sororicide, uxoricide, infanticide, suicide; crucifixion, martyrdom, immolation. **2.** stroke of luck, master stroke, success, coup, windfall, bonanza; *Slang* big hit, smash hit; cleaning up, cleanup. **—*adj.* 3.** lethal, mortal, deadly, causing death, deathly, fatal, death-dealing. **4.** extremely painful, excruciating, murderous, devastating.

killjoy *n.* spoilsport, sourpuss, grouch, malcontent, crapehanger, worrywart, Cassandra, complainer, grumbler; *Slang* party-pooper, wet blanket, dog in the manger, sourball, gloomy Gus.

kin *n.* family, relatives, kinfolk, relations, folks, people, kith and kin, tribe, clan, flesh and blood, race, kinsmen, connections, next of kin, tribesmen, clansmen; distaff side, spindle side.

kind[1] *adj.* kindly, benign, generous, good-hearted, tenderhearted, softhearted, tender, gentle, compassionate, merciful, good-natured, affectionate, charitable, warmhearted, bighearted, sympathetic, understanding, well-meaning, considerate, thoughtful; amiable, obliging, cordial, gracious, accommodating, amicable, friendly, neighborly, good-humored, well-disposed, gentle, polite, courteous, civil. **—Ant.** unkind, cruel, harsh, merciless, severe.

kind[2] *n.* sort, type, class, brand, make, variety, style, description; cast, mold, nature, genus, genre, designation, breed, ilk, strain, caste, kidney.

kindhearted *adj.* kind, kindly, benign, good-hearted, tenderhearted, compassionate, kindly disposed, charitable, philanthropic, good, warmhearted, softhearted, good-natured, sympathetic, generous, humanitarian, humane, loving, affectionate, gentle, gracious, warm, merciful, accommodating, helpful; understanding, thoughtful, considerate, well-meaning, well-intentioned, altruistic, amicable. **—Ant.** hardhearted, coldhearted, heartless, cold, selfish, unkind, cruel, harsh, severe, unsympathetic.

kindheartedness *n.* kindness, kindliness, benefaction, goodness, goodness of heart, tenderness, compassion, kindly nature, good nature, unselfishness, sympathy, understanding, benevolence, magnanimity, charitableness, philanthropy, altruism, humanitarianism, humaneness, love for mankind, goodwill, goodwill to man, humanity, mercy; graciousness, consideration. **—Ant.** unkindness, cruelty, meanness, selfishness, indifference, coldheartedness.

kindle *v.* **1.** enkindle, ignite, inflame, set on fire, set fire to, cause to start burning, light, apply a match to, *Informal* stick a match to. **2.** stir, arouse, rouse, stir up, inspire, call forth, waken, awake; enkindle, fire, ignite, inflame, stimulate, agitate, intensify, provoke, induce, incite, excite, invigorate, quicken, animate; sharpen, whet, foment, urge, prod, goad. **—Syn. Study. 1, 2** KINDLE, IGNITE, INFLAME literally mean to set something on fire. To KINDLE is to cause something gradually to begin burning; it is often used figuratively: *to kindle logs; to kindle someone's interest.* To IGNITE is to set something on fire with a sudden burst of flame; it also has figurative senses: *to ignite straw; to ignite dangerous hatreds.* INFLAME is most often used figuratively, meaning to intensify, excite, or rouse: *to inflame passions.* **—Ant. 1, 2** smother, stifle, extinguish, quench, dampen.

kindling *n.* **1.** tinder, firewood, material that burns easily, fuel; (*variously*) brush, brushwood, twigs, small branches, paper, shavings. **2.** setting fire to, igniting, ignition, enkindling, burning, flaming, lighting, firing, combustion.

kindly *adj.* **1.** kind, benign, good, generous, warmhearted, softhearted, affectionate, devoted, tender, warm, compassionate, gentle, charitable, merciful, sympathetic, philanthropic, benevolent, magnanimous, humanitarian, bighearted, humane, friendly, understanding, patient, considerate, tenderhearted, goodnatured, well-meaning, neighborly; amiable, gracious, cordial, goodhumored, courteous, amicable. *—adv.* **2.** benignly, generously, warmheartedly, warmly, softheartedly, affectionately, tenderly, compassionately, gently, charitably, mercifully, sympathetically, philanthropically, benevolently, magnanimously, humanely, bigheartedly, understandingly, considerately, tenderheartedly, goodnaturedly, well-meaningly, neighborly, amiably, cordially, graciously, goodhumoredly, amicably, well-manneredly, civilly. **—Ant. 1** unkindly, malevolent, malign, malicious, spiteful, unsympathetic; mean, cruel, harsh, severe. **2** unkindly, malevolently, malignly, maliciously; spitefully, unsympathetically, meanly, cruelly, harshly, severely.

kindness *n.* **1.** kindliness, benevolence, generosity, benefaction, beneficence, mercy, charity, charitableness, philanthropy, humanity, humanitarianism, humaneness, magnanimity, goodness, goodness of heart, sympathy, compassion, unselfishness, consideration, understanding, patience, toleration, tolerance, grace, graciousness; goodwill, goodwill to men, brotherly love, friendly feelings, warm feelings. **2.** kind act, humane gesture, kindly gesture, good deed, act of charity, act of generosity, good turn, act of grace, generosity, benefaction, bounty, gift, favor, kind office, help, aid, assistance, good treatment. **—Ant. 1** unkindness, malevolence, harshness, cruelty, severity, sternness, roughness, austerity. **2** cruel or unkind act, evil deed.

kindred *adj.* like, allied, closely related, similar, corresponding, alike, matching, resembling, analogous; united, harmonious, agreeing, accordant, congenial, sympathetic, *Spanish* simpático; consanguine, related, intimately related, akin, familial. **—Ant.** alien, unrelated, uncongenial, different.

king *n.* monarch, ruler, sovereign, liege, His Majesty, suzerain, crowned head, anointed ruler, royal personage, the anointed, royal person, potentate, protector, defender of the faith.

kingdom *n.* realm, nation, country, dominion, domain, land, territory, state, principality, duchy, dukedom, empire, monarchy; sphere, field.

kingly *adj.* majestic, kinglike, imperial, royal, regal, monarchal, sovereign, noble, princely, queenly; splendid, grand, magnificent, glorious, stately, aweinspiring, august, patrician; autocratic, absolute, imperious, lordly, commanding, mighty; despotic, tyrannical.

kink *n.* **1.** twist, tangle, gnarl, coil, crimp, crinkle, frizz, knot, frizzle. **2.** local pain, pang, twinge, spasm, stiffness, knot, cramp; *Informal* crick, charley horse. **3.** complication, hitch, defect, rough spot, difficulty, flaw, imperfection, loose end, tangle, snarl, knot, *Slang* glitch. **4.** peculiarity, eccentricity, oddity, crotchet, mental twist, twist, idiosyncrasy, quirk, queerness, weirdness, foible; freakishness, singularity, vagary.

kinky *adj.* **1.** knotted, tangled, twisted, matted, frizzled, wiry, crinkled, frizzly, twisty, frizzy. **2.** odd, eccentric, unusual, unorthodox, peculiar, bizarre, strange, queer, perverse, quirky, idiosyncratic; freakish, abnormal, aberrant, deviant, unnatural, *Slang* sick, kooky. **—Ant. 2** standard, usual, orthodox, normal, ordinary, *Slang* square.

kinsman *n.* relative, blood relative, relation, blood relation, kin, sib, countryman, landsman, fellow citizen; (*variously*) father, mother, sister, brother, aunt, uncle, grandmother, grandfather, cousin, child, offspring, son, daughter, heir, parent.

kismet *n.* destiny, fate, fortune, portion, lot, circumstance, Providence, predestination, one's lot in life *Greek* moira; end, doom, God's will, will of Allah, inevitability.

kiss *v.* touch with the lips, greet with a kiss, kiss the cheek, kiss the hand, osculate; *Slang* buss.

kit *n.* set of tools, instruments, implements, utensils; equipment, tools, supplies, devices, gear, tackle, outfit, necessaries, provisions; things, paraphernalia, accoutrements, trappings, impediments, furnishings, rig; *Slang* the whole kit and caboodle.

kitchen *n.* room equipped for cooking, cookroom, scullery, galley, cookhouse, *French* cuisine, *Spanish* cocina; bakery, bakehouse.

knack *n.* skill, talent, facility, gift, ability, aptitude, adroitness, dexterity, dexterousness, finesse, expertise, genius, faculty, flair, natural endowment, cleverness, ingenuity, quickness, readiness, proficiency, efficiency, competence, capability, capacity, forte, bent, inclination, propensity, turn. **—Ant.** ineptitude, clumsiness, awkwardness; disability.

knave *n.* rascal, rogue, scoundrel, blackguard, charlatan, swindler, reprobate, culprit, scalawag, scamp, rapscallion, cad, rotter, bounder, cur, dog, wretch, good-for-nothing, con man, con artist, phony, *Slang* rat, *Archaic* varlet. **—Syn. Study.** KNAVE, RASCAL, ROGUE, SCOUNDREL are disparaging terms applied to persons considered base, dishonest, or unprincipled. KNAVE, which formerly meant a male servant, in modern use emphasizes baseness of nature and intention: *a swindling knave.* RASCAL suggests a certain shrewdness and trickery: *The rascal ran off with my money.* ROGUE often refers to a worthless person who preys on the community: *pictures of criminals in a rogues' gallery.* SCOUNDREL, a stronger term, suggests a base, immoral, even wicked person: *Those scoundrels finally went to jail.* RASCAL and ROGUE are often used affectionately or humorously to describe a mischievous person: *I'll bet that rascal hid my slippers. The little rogues ate all the cookies.* **—Ant.** hero, gentleman.

kneel *v.* bow, bend the knee, bow down, genuflect, fall on one's knees, curtsy; make obeisance, prostrate oneself; kowtow, salaam, fall at the feet of.

knickknack Also **nicknack** *n.* small object, trifle, bagatelle, bauble, trinket, toy, plaything, gewgaw, gimcrack, thingamajig, frippery, bric-a-brac, bibelot.

knife *n.* **1.** cutting tool, blade, cutter, cutlery; *(variously)* pocketknife, penknife, jackknife, paring knife, switchblade knife, bowie knife, skinning knife, hunting knife, bread knife, butcher knife, table knife, carving knife, surgical knife, scalpel, palette knife, putty knife, pruning knife, machete, stiletto, dirk, dagger, *Slang* shiv. *—v.* **2.** cut, stab, wound, lacerate, cut apart, slash, mutilate, cut down, run through, pierce.

knight *n.* soldier, man-at-arms, warrior, fighter, fighting man, arms bearer, horseman, equestrian, Templar; defender, protector, guardian, champion, paladin, Lancelot, hero, vindicator, brave person, gallant, cavalier; gentleman, man of rank.

knit *v.* **1.** weave, do needlework, interweave, twist, intertwine, stitch, tat, plait, braid, crochet. **2.** draw, draw together, ally, join, attach, fasten, connect, unite, unify, bind, link. **3.** wrinkle, knot, crease, furrow.

knob *n.* **1.** rounded handle, handle, handhold, hold, grip; lever, latch. **2.** lump, hump, bump, knot, knurl, knur, snag, gnarl, bulb, tubercle, nub, nubbin, node, convexity, protuberance, protuberancy, protrusion, bulge, swell, swelling, projection, prominence.

knock *v.* **1.** rap, tap, hit, strike, bang, thump, thud. **2.** pound, pummel, smash, batter, hammer, strike. **3.** hit, strike, smite, slam, slap, pummel, pound, beat, thwack, kick, push, jostle, dash, cuff, swat; *Informal* belt, bat, crack, smack, clout, wallop, sock. **4.** criticize, find fault with, belittle, disparage, deprecate, peck at, cavil, carp at, abuse, lambaste, cry out against, decry, reprehend, inveigh against, censure, cut to pieces, condemn; *Slang* rap, bomb, murder. *—n.* **5.** stroke, hit, thump, thwack, bang, tap, rap, pat, slap; blow, smack, whack, punch, cuff, smash, bump, glancing blow, crash, crack; *Informal* sock, clip, clout, bat, lick. **6.** criticism, faultfinding, setback, failure, defeat; reprehension, censure, condemnation.

knot *n.* **1.** interlacement, twist, loop, braid, plait, intertwist; *(variously)* slipknot, square knot, half hitch, hitch, hawser fastening, slide knot, running knot, surgeon's knot, figure-eight knot, flat knot, single knot, double knot, overhand knot, midshipman's knot, hangman's knot, bowknot, cat's-paw. **2.** ornament, rosette, loop, braid, frog, star; shoulder knot, epaulet. **3.** cluster, bunch, clump; gathering, circle, group, assemblage, collection; bundle, pack, lump, heap, pile, mass; hump, bump, knurl. **4.** bun, chignon, braid, plait, topknot, tuft.

knotty *adj.* **1.** knobby, full of knots,

gnarled, nodular, unsmooth, rough, uneven, rough-grained, coarse, coarse-grained, rugged, bumpy, knurly, knurled; flawed, blemished, snaggy. **2.** difficult, thorny, tricky, complex, problematical, complicated, hard, tough, perplexing, puzzling, involved, intricate, baffling, ticklish, troublesome. **—Ant. 1** smooth. **2** plain, simple, obvious, easy.

know *v.* **1.** be certain, be sure, be positive, be confident, have no doubt, feel certain, be assured, have knowledge, have information about, be informed; discern, recognize, perceive, notice, see; comprehend, understand, apprehend, realize, be cognizant of, make out, be aware of, *Slang* be wise to, get wise to; be intelligent, be smart, be wise, be sagacious. **2.** have knowledge of, have in one's head, be acquainted with, be familiar with, have at one's fingertips; *Informal* have down pat, have down cold; know inside out, know backwards and forwards, know by rote, know by heart, know full well. **3.** be acquainted with, be familiar with, enjoy the friendship of, be on good terms with, be close to, be on intimate terms with; *Informal* be thick with, rub elbows with, have the ear of, be on a good footing with; have dealings with. **4.** identify, distinguish, be able to distinguish, discern, discriminate, make out, perceive; perceive differences, recognize differences, tell one from the other. **—Syn. Study. 1** KNOW, COMPREHEND, UNDERSTAND refer to perceiving or grasping facts and ideas. To KNOW is to be aware of, sure of, or familiar with something through observation, study, or experience: *She knows the basic facts of the subject. I know that he agrees with me.* To COMPREHEND is to grasp something mentally and to perceive its relationships to certain other facts or ideas: *to comprehend a difficult text.* To UNDERSTAND is to be fully aware not only of the meaning or nature of something but also of its implications: *I could comprehend everything you said, but did not understand that you were joking.* **—Ant. 1** be ignorant or illiterate, overlook, misunderstand, misconstrue. **3** be unacquainted with, be unfamiliar with.

know-how *n.* technique, expertise, skill, ability, proficiency, expertness, *French* savoir-faire, competence, *Slang* savvy, art, craft, mastery, capability, adeptness, skillfulness, adroitness, deftness, knowledge, experience. **—Ant.** incompetence, inexperience, ignorance, unfamiliarity.

knowing *adj.* **1.** sagacious, wise, sapient, erudite, intelligent, intellectual, knowledgeable, enlightened, bright, brainy, widely read, literary, scholastic, academic, educated, schooled, learned, well-informed, clever, astute, shrewd, canny, smart, sharp, aware, conscious, perceptive, percipient, perspicacious, sophisticated; profound, deep, philosophical, *Slang* highbrow; understanding, comprehending, discerning, sound, sensible, judicious. **2.** meaningful, significant, expressive, revealing, eloquent, fraught; conscious, aware, perceptive. **—Ant. 1** unknowing, unwise, unintelligent, uncomprehending. **2** blank, dull, empty.

knowledge *n.* **1.** learning, scholarship, erudition, education, wisdom, intelligence, ken, schooling, cultivation, enlightenment, information, *Informal* book learning. **2.** communication, information, data, news, tidings, intelligence; pronouncement, declaration, statement, report, announcement, notice, notification; tip, hint, divulging revelation, intimation, mention. **3.** awareness, realization, consciousness, perception, sense, cognizance, recognition, familiarity, memory, inkling, comprehension. **—Ant. 1** ignorance, illiteracy, inexperience, misunderstanding, unfamiliarity, unawareness.

knowledgeable *adj.* well-informed, abreast of, conversant with, acquainted with, no stranger to, versed in, at home in, familiar with, au courant, *Slang* hip.

known *adj.* recognized, acknowledged, familiar, popular, celebrated, famous, prominent, notorious, well-known, noted; apparent, obvious, evident, palpable, manifest, self-evident, plain, distinct, patent, definite, common. **—Ant.** unknown, unfamiliar, unrecognized; secret, unpublished, unrevealed.

knurled *adj.* knotted, gnarled, bumpy, lumpy, knurly, ridged, bulging, knobby, nodular, knotty, nubbly, gnarly.

kook *n.* crackpot, eccentric, crackbrain, harebrain, *Informal* cuckoo, loony, dingaling, dingbat, *Slang* nut, screwball, crazy, weirdo, wacko, flake, fruitcake.

kowtow *v.* stoop, bend, genuflect, curtsy, bow low, salaam, bow and scrape, grovel, toady, truckle; *Slang* soft-soap, butter up, apple-polish, bootlick; cringe, cower, fall on one's knees, prostrate oneself, bend the knee.

kudo *n.* award, prize, honor, plaudit, decoration, citation.

kudos *n.* praise, laudation, admiration, honor, acclaim, commendation, high regard, esteem, glory, prestige, celebratedness, fame, celebrity, repute, renown, distinctive mark.

label *n.* **1.** tag, ticket, sticker, slip, sign, stamp, mark, name, seal, docket, brand, tally; identification, designation, classification, appellation, characterization, specification, inscription; earmark. —*v.* **2.** mark, note, tag, ticket, docket, mark off; name, classify, describe, designate, title, define, denominate, characterize, put a mark on, earmark, brand.

labor Also *British* **labour** *n.* **1.** exertion, effort, industriousness, plodding, toil, menial work, manual labor, travail, drudgery, struggle, sweat of one's brow. **2.** manpower, employees, workers, work force, laborers, blue-collar workers. **3.** birth pangs, birth throes; parturition, childbirth, travail, accouchement. —*v.* **4.** work, drudge, toil, travail, plod, sweat, slave, work like a slave, struggle, work day and night; *Informal* work one's fingers to the bone, grind away, plug away; occupy oneself with, busy oneself with, employ one's time. **5.** smart under, suffer, agonize, be the victim of, be affected by, be troubled by, be burdened by. **—Syn. Study. 1** See WORK. **—Ant. 1** rest, repose, relaxation, leisure, respite, ease. **4** rest, relax.

labored *adj.* **1.** ponderous, heavy, stiff, wooden; difficult, strained, forced, laborious, cramped, halting; awkward, maladroit, clumsy. **2.** strained, studied, forced, contrived, unnatural, overdone, unspontaneous, drawnout, heavy, ponderous; self-conscious. **—Ant. 1, 2** easy, natural, simple, light.

laborer *n.* workman, worker, blue-collar worker, workhand, toiler, manual worker, proletarian, wage earner; hand, menial, hired hand, hireling, drudge, plodder, roustabout, handyman, coolie.

laborious *adj.* strenuous, burdensome, onerous, labored, toilsome, wearisome, arduous, difficult, hard, effortful, uphill, herculean; tiresome, irksome, troublesome, oppressive; severe, rigorous, demanding, brutal; fatiguing, wearying, wearing. **—Ant.** simple, light, easy, effortless, undemanding.

labyrinth *n.* maze, complex, network, convolution, perplexity, complexity, intricacy; snarl, tangle, web, knot, morass, jungle, wilderness, mare's nest, riddle.

lace *v.* **1.** tie, fasten, secure, bind, close, tie up, tighten, make fast; make taut, cinch, strap, truss, tether, lash, braid. **2.** punish, chastise; spank, give a whipping, whip, give a beating, beat, thrash, switch, cane, flail, lash. **3.** add liquor to, flavor, make more tasty, spice up, suffuse, infuse, fortify, strengthen, add spirits to, *Informal* spike; *Slang* dope, dope up. **—Ant. 1** unlace, untie, unfasten.

lacerate *v.* slash, cut, lance, gash, puncture, wound, stab, slice, tear, rip, sever, scratch, scar, deface; hurt, inflict pain, give pain, pain, torment, distress, torture, agonize, excruciate.

lack *n.* **1.** want, absence, deficiency, need; neediness, privation, deprivation; scarcity, scantness, dearth, shortage, exhaustion, depletion; omission. —*v.* **2.** miss, want, be short of, fall short of, come short of, be found wanting, be deficient in, be inadequate, be insufficient, be missing, fail to reach the mark, be caught short; need, require. **—Syn. Study. 2** LACK, WANT, NEED, REQUIRE indicate the absence of something desirable, important, or necessary. LACK means to be without or to have less than a desirable quantity of something: *to lack courage; to lack sufficient money.* WANT stresses the urgency of fulfilling a desire or providing what is lacking: *The room wants some final touch to make it homey.* NEED suggests even more urgency, stressing the necessity of supplying something essential: *to need an operation.* REQUIRE has a similar sense, although it is used in formal or serious contexts: *The report requires some editing.* **—Ant. 1** sufficiency, adequacy, competence; abundance, copiousness, plentifulness; excess, superfluity, surplus, plethora. **2** have, hold, possess, own, enjoy.

lackadaisical *adj.* indifferent, mindless, listless, lifeless, inanimate, spiritless, unexcited, unexcitable, uninspired, unambitious, unaspiring, unmotivated, idle, loafing, dillydallying; languid, languishing, lethargic, phlegmatic, apathetic; uninterested, indifferent, unconcerned. **—Ant.** animated, spirited, excited, inspired, ambitious, intense, diligent.

lackey *n.* attendant, servant, assistant, helper, retainer, employee, hireling, minion, hanger-on, toady, underling, inferior, slave, menial, flunky; follower, mercenary; (*variously*) waiter, usher, page, squire, steward, butler, valet, cupbearer.

lackluster *adj.* drab, dull, lifeless, pallid, lusterless, leaden, dreary, somber, colorless, bland, uninteresting, prosaic, commonplace, ordinary, humdrum, run-of-the-mill, boring; *Slang* blah, nothing. **—Ant.** vivid, exciting, vivacious, brilliant, scintillating, radiant.

laconic *adj.* short, concise, brief, succinct, terse, compact, condensed, pithy, concentrated, sparing of words, pointed, to the point, summary; curt, blunt. **—Ant.** voluble, wordy, loquacious, garrulous, verbose.

lacuna *n.* gap, hiatus, break, interstice, interval, interruption, interim, void, omission, cavity, hole, fissure, space, opening, gulf, breach, caesura, discontinuity, pause, suspension.

lacy *adj.* lacelike, gossamer, filigree, webby, filigreed, netlike, retiform, reticulate, latticelike, gridded, barred, meshy; cobwebby, diaphanous, gauzy, netty, fine, delicate, sheer.

lad *n.* boy, youth, juvenile, youngster, young man, schoolboy; stripling, shaver, sprig, kid, sprout; young fellow, young chap.

lady *n.* **1.** well-bred woman, respectable woman, woman of refinement, woman of good family, gentlewoman; wife, spouse. **2.** woman, matron, female. **3.** woman of rank, noblewoman, peeress, aristocrat; (*variously*) duchess, countess, viscountess, marchioness, baroness. **—Syn. Study. 1, 2** See WOMAN.

ladylike *adj.* (*of a woman*) well-bred, well-mannered, courtly, polite, courteous, mannerly, genteel, decorous, modest, refined, dignified, well brought up; cultured, polished, cultivated, elegant, proper, respectable, civil. **—Ant.** unladylike, ill-bred, ill-mannered, impolite, discourteous, unmannerly, unrefined, uncultured.

lag *v.* **1.** trail, drag behind, drag, be behind, linger, loiter, dawdle, tarry, delay, be slow, slacken, hang back, inch, inch along, limp, trudge, falter, stagger, halt; procrastinate, dally, take one's time, bide one's time, be idle, be late, be tardy, be overdue. *—n.* **2.** delay, slackening, falling behind, slowing down, slowdown, drag, hold up, setback; *Informal* snag, hitch. **—Ant. 1** lead, go ahead, hurry along. **2** speeding up, step up, advance.

laggard *n.* straggler, lingerer, loiterer, dallier, dawdler, idler, sluggard, do-nothing, mope, lounger, poke, loafer, slug, dilly-dallier, potterer, snail, slowfoot; *Informal* slowpoke; *Slang* stick-in-the-mud. **—Ant.** go-getter, live wire, self-starter, dynamo.

laic *adj.* secular, lay, secularistic, laical, worldly, civil, temporal, nonpastoral, nonecclesiastical, nonclerical, profane, popular; amateur, nonprofessional, inexperienced. **—Ant.** pastoral, clerical, spiritual; unworldly, nonsecular.

lair *n.* den, nest, retreat, resting place, sanctuary, cover, hideout, hideaway, mew, lie, haunt, covert; hole, burrow, cavern.

laissez-faire Also **laisser-faire** *n.* nonintervention, noninterference, let-alone policy; unconcern, indifference; live and let live, leave well enough alone, let them be.

lambaste *v.* **1.** beat, thrash, trounce, whip, pummel, lick, pelt, defeat, subdue, vanquish, overwhelm, wallop, bludgeon, smear, drub; *Informal* shellac; *Slang* clobber. **2.** scold, berate, castigate, censure, reprimand, dress down, rebuke, cuss out, give one what for, denounce; *Informal* bawl out; *Slang* light into, chew out. **—Ant. 2** praise, commend, extol, laud, approve, applaud.

lame *adj.* **1.** crippled, disabled, limping, halt, maimed, infirm, hobbled; game, unsound, deformed; feeble, faltering, weak, halting. **2.** weak, feeble, inadequate, sorry, clumsy, insufficient, deficient, flimsy, wanting, failing, unconvincing, unpersuasive, ineffectual, unsatisfactory. **—Ant. 2** bold, convincing, persuasive, effectual, effective.

lament *v.* **1.** mourn, weep, bewail; deplore, show concern for, complain about, express pity for, regret, sympathize with, commiserate with, condole with. *—n.* **2.** lamentation, sob, plaint, cry, moan, wail, outcry, keening, wail, whimper; mourning. **3.** dirge, song of lamentation, death song, funeral music, requiem.

lamentable *adj.* **1.** deplorable, dreadful, terrible, regrettable, woeful, grievous, unfortunate, distressing, shameful, disheartening. **2.** heartbreaking, distressing, dire, wretched, miserable, pitiable, piteous, pathetic. **—Ant. 1** encouraging, heartwarming, satisfying. **2** happy, fortunate, cheering, blessed, felicitous.

lamp *n.* light; (*variously*) electric lamp, battery lamp, gas lamp, oil lamp, lantern, reading light, headlight, ceiling light, ceiling fixture, floor lamp, table lamp, night light, chandelier, wall lamp; spotlight, klieg light, floodlight, searchlight, beacon, blinker, sunlamp, heat lamp; bulb; torch.

lampoon *n.* **1.** satire, burlesque, broadside, parody, mockery, spoof, travesty, farce, pasquinade, diatribe, squib, caricature; *Informal* takeoff, put-on, *British* send up. *—v.* **2.** satirize, parody, ridicule, burlesque, caricature.

lance *n.* spear, javelin, assegai, pike, halberd, shaft, harpoon, gaff.

land *n.* **1.** ground, earth, dry land, mainland, terra firma. **2.** ground, soil, earth, subsoil, dirt, loam, humus; terrain; real estate, realty, property, real property, grounds, acres. **3.** country, nation, commonwealth, state, republic, dominion, realm, empire, domain, kingdom, colony, settlement; region, territory, terrain, zone, area, district, section, vicinity, location; fatherland, motherland, homeland, native land, native soil, the old country. **4.** country, county, district, countryside, region, province, shire, canton, precinct, parish, ward, acreage, acres, fields, tract, terrain, grassland, cornfield, wheat field, farmland, meadow, lea, pasture, grass, park, lawn, green, village green. —*v.* **5.** come in for a landing, descend, come down, alight, light, settle down; *Informal* set down; make a three-point landing. **6.** dock, come to land, put into port, make port, arrive at land, anchor, reach land, put into the harbor, put in, drop anchor, moor, tie up; put into shore, set foot on dry land, make land, debark, disembark, lay anchor. **7.** lead one to, carry one to, bring one to; lay hold of, catch, gain, secure, get, win over, clinch, seize, grab, capture, *Informal* nab; take, snare, net.

landlord *n.* landholder, landowner, landlady, property owner, owner, proprietor, possessor, holder, freeholder; lord of the manor; squire. **—Ant.** tenant, lessee, renter.

landmark *n.* milestone, keystone, high point, turning point, cornerstone, highlight, watershed, signpost, guidepost, benchmark; monument, historic building.

landscape *n.* **1.** natural scenery, scenery, scenic view, scene, aspect, view, prospect, vista, spectacle, panorama, sight. **2.** painting or drawing of countryside, scenic representation, rural scene.

lane *n.* narrow thoroughfare, path, passageway, footpath, way, road, avenue, roadway, drive, alley, alleyway, passage, pass, bypath, course, route, trail, track, access, approach, byway.

language *n.* **1.** speech, tongue, vocabulary, idiom, mother tongue, native tongue, *Informal* lingo; dialect, patois, jargon; vernacular, slang, colloquialism, cant, argot, *Slang* jive. **2.** oral communication, self-expression, reading and writing, verbal intercourse, discourse, spoken language, elocution, public speaking; words, vocabulary. **3.** vocabulary, wording, phraseology, speech, prose, parlance, verbiage, expression, idiom, rhetoric, use of words; manner of speaking or writing, diction, idiom, mode of expression. **4.** profanity, cursing, swearing, imprecation, profane talk, *Informal* cussing. **—Syn. Study. 1** LANGUAGE, DIALECT, VERNACULAR, JARGON refer to patterns of vocabulary, syntax, and usage characteristic of communities of various sizes and types. LANGUAGE is applied to the general pattern of a people or nation: *the English language.* DIALECT is applied to regionally or socially distinct forms or varieties of a language, often forms used by provincial communities that differ from the standard variety: *the Scottish dialect.* JARGON is applied to the specialized language, esp. the vocabulary, used by a particular (usu. occupational) group within a community or to language considered unintelligible or obscure: *technical jargon.* The VERNACULAR is the natural, everyday pattern of speech, usu. on an informal level, used by people indigenous to a community.

languid *adj.* **1.** faint, feeble, weak, weary, drooping, sickly, declining, indisposed, debilitated, unhealthy, unsound, unstable, doddering, infirm, on the decline, fatigued, exhausted, enervated, worn-out, spent; rickety, shaky, trembling; lackadaisical, languorous, sluggish, torpid, apathetic, inert, inactive, supine. **2.** sluggish, listless, inanimate, inert, apathetic, lifeless, lethargic, languorous, spiritless, dull, heavy, torpid, slow, leaden. **—Ant. 1** strong, tireless, active, energetic, robust.

languish *v.* **1.** go into decline, droop, flag, faint, diminish, fade, wilt, wither, deteriorate, give away, break down, wane, ebb, waste away, become ill, take sick, sicken, go downhill, dwindle, fail. **2.** pine for, sigh for, be desirous of, yearn for, hunger for, hunger after, long for, thirst for; *Informal* have a yen for, hanker for; desire, covet, hunger, thirst. **—Ant. 1** luxuriate, thrive, prosper, flourish, bloom.

languor *n.* listlessness, torpor, lassitude, inertia, sluggishness, torpidity, weariness, dullness, lethargy, hebetude, lifelessness, languidness, leisureness. **—Ant.** vitality, enthusiasm, vigor, verve, gusto, zest.

lanky *adj.* lank, tall and thin, rangy, lean, bony, scrawny, weedy, skinny, rawboned, angular, gaunt, spare, gangling, gawky. **—Ant.** burly, husky, brawny, muscular, sinewy; plump, portly, rotund, chubby, fleshy, stocky, stout, fat, short, full, rounded.

lap *v.* **1.** lick, lick up, tongue, drink, sip. **2.** ripple, slosh, wash, awash, splash, plash, babble, murmur, bubble, gurgle.

lapse *n.* **1.** breach, disregard, dereliction, error, slight mistake, omission, slip, peccadillo, oversight, fault, flaw, negligence, delinquency, laxity, infraction, blunder, faux pas, *Informal* boner; loss, failure, failing, shortcoming, fall, forfeiture. **2.** decline, descent, downfall, drop, backsliding, relapse, regression, wane, slump, deterioration, degeneration, falling off. **3.** elapsing, period, interval, process of time, interim, interlude; intermission, interruption, passage, respite, pause, recess, *Informal* break; hiatus, gap. —*v.* **4.** fall, slip, decline, subside, sink, collapse; worsen, backslide, relapse, recede, deteriorate, degenerate, wither, sag, droop; drop, slump down. **5.** expire, become obsolete, run out, terminate, stop, cease, lose validity, fall into disuse. **6.** pass by, elapse, slip by, run out, slip away, go by, expire.

larceny *n.* stealing, theft, robbery, burglary; pilferage, pilfering, purloining, misappropriation, appropriation, looting, sacking, depredation, absconding, embezzlement, peculation, extortion, bilking, cheating, swindling, defalcation, fleecing, fraud, forgery, plagiarism; housebreaking, safecracking; petty larceny, petit larceny, grand larceny.

larder *n.* pantry, food room, buttery, supply room, storage room, storeroom, cuddy; *British* spence, stillroom.

large *adj.* big, huge, great, grand, massive, immense, enormous, gigantic, spacious, capacious, vast, roomy, expansive, sizable, imposing, Brobdingnagian; substantial, considerable, ample, goodly, liberal, unstinted, copious, extravagant, exorbitant; comprehensive, extensive, wide, broad, sweeping, far-reaching, unlimited, limitless, boundless, high; mighty, towering, hulky, strapping, heavy, rotund, obese, fat, portly, plump, overgrown, outsized, ponderous, monstrous, giantlike, colossal, gargantuan; magnificent, stupendous; *Informal* king-sized, man-sized. **—Ant.** small, little, tiny, diminutive, minute; brief, inconsiderable, infinitesimal; narrow, paltry, petty, mean, scanty, sparse, short, trifling, trivial, slight, slender, slim, thin.

largely *adv.* mostly, mainly, chiefly, for the most part, by and large, on the whole, primarily, principally, generally, predominantly, to a great extent, greatly, substantially, considerably; extensively, widely.

large-scale *adj.* extensive, far-reaching, wide-ranging, broad, wide, far-flung, all-out, all-encompassing; big, huge, great, mighty, vast, gargantuan, colossal, gigantic, stupendous, monstrous, tremendous. **—Ant.** small-scale, limited, local, restricted.

largess Also **largesse** *n.* generosity, benefaction, kindness, benevolence, bounty, philanthropy; donation, gift, offering, bestowal, boon, favor, assistance, aid, help, charity, mercy, benignity; reward, payment, remuneration, gratuity.

lark *n.* escapade, frolic, fling, spree, caprice, whim; *Informal* gag, high old time; trick, prank, antic, romp, gambol, caper, game, sportiveness, jape.

lascivious *adj.* indecent, obscene, lewd, immoral, improper, lustful, ribald, bawdy, prurient; filthy, vulgar, gross, coarse, indelicate, salacious, squalid, foul, dirty, dirty-minded, impure, unwholesome, immodest, lecherous, sordid, lurid; shameless, wanton, unblushing, licentious, depraved, ruttish.

lash[1] *v.* tie, bind, tie up, fasten, secure, leash, rope, make fast, truss, pinion, strap; tether, brace, moor, attach, fix, hitch.

lash[2] *n.* **1.** whip, scourge, cat-o'-nine-tails; strap, thong. **2.** whip, blow, stroke, hit. —*v.* **3.** whip, whip up, flog, thrash, lambaste, flail; horsewhip. **4.** beat, strike, smack, hit, knock, buffet, pound, hammer. **5.** tongue-lash, berate, castigate, rail against, revile, curse, upbraid, scold, lecture, take to task. **—Ant. 5** praise, compliment, commend, laud.

lass *n.* girl, young woman, damsel, schoolgirl, maiden, maid, female, miss, virgin; wench, colleen, lassie, lovely, pretty.

lassitude *n.* weariness, weakness, debility, sluggishness, fatigue, tiredness, exhaustion, fatigue, lack of energy, enervation, lethargy, listlessness, inertia, feebleness, indolence, faintness, torpor, torpidity, drowsiness, languor, languidness, prostration, dullness, droopiness; apathy, indifference, ennui, doldrums, boredom; malaise. **—Ant.** vigor, energy, strength, robustness, freshness; verve, spirit, vitality; *Informal* get-up-and-go, vim, pep.

last[1] *adj.* **1.** final, conclusive, closing, concluding, terminal, ultimate, extreme, farthest, furthest, utmost; rearmost, hindmost, behind, at the end, tailing, tagging along, bringing up the rear. —*adv.* **2.** after all others, after, behind, in back of, in the rear, trailing, in last place. **3.** finally, in conclusion, ultimately, eventually, once and for all, terminally. —*n.* **4.** final one, concluding person or thing; rearmost one. **5.** end, conclusion, crucial time, closing, ending, finish, terminus, finale; crack of doom, end of the world, doomsday, Day of Judgment, Armageddon. **—Ant. 1** first, initial, foremost, opening, introductory, initiatory; best, highest. **2** first, ahead of all others, in front. **4** first.

last[2] *v.* continue, go on, persist, extend, hold good, exist, survive, endure, stay, stand, remain, carry on, hold out, hold on, maintain, keep, persevere, abide, subsist, live; wear, stand up, hold up; outwear, outlive. **—Syn. Study.** See CONTINUE. **—Ant.** fail, die; end, stop, terminate, expire, depart, fade, cease; wear out, *Informal* give out.

lasting *adj.* enduring, abiding, continuing, durable, long-term, permanent, never-ending, lifelong, perdurable, long-lived, protracted; continuing a long time, of long duration, firm, steadfast, constant, incessant, perpetual, unceasing, indissoluble, indestructible; deep-rooted, deep-seated, established, fixed, firmly established, solid; persistent, lingering, chronic; eternal, immortal. **—Ant.** fleeting, fugitive, passing, transitory, transient, short-lived, ephemeral, momentary.

lastly *adv.* finally, in conclusion, in the end, at last, after all; all things considered, on the whole, taking everything into consideration, to sum up. **—Ant.** firstly, at the outset, in starting, in the beginning, at the first.

latch *n.* **1.** lock, catch, bolt, bar; fastening; hasp, clamp, hook, snap, loop, buckle, button, clip, clinch. *—v.* **2.** lock, bolt, fasten, hook, secure, make fast, close, shut. **—Ant. 2** unlock, unlatch, unfasten, loose.

late *adj.* **1.** tardy, overdue, unpunctual, dilatory, behind time; slow, delayed, detained, postponed, put off, held up. **2.** recent, new, fresh, newborn, modern. **3.** lately dead, recently deceased; departed, passed on, gone. *—adv.* **4.** behind time, after time, behindhand, tardily, dilatorily. **—Syn. Study. 2** See MODERN. **—Ant. 1** early, punctual, prompt, timely, ahead of time. **2** old, seasoned. **3** alive, still living, existing, extant. **4** early, ahead of time, in advance, beforehand.

lately *adv.* recently, latterly, of late, not long ago, yesterday, a short time ago; just now, right now, presently, currently. **—Ant.** at first, originally.

latent *adj.* dormant, sleeping, quiescent, inactive, passive, suspended, in abeyance, abeyant, potential, undeveloped, unrealized, not manifest, hidden, concealed, covert, lurking, intangible, unapparent, unexposed, inconspicuous, unexpressed. **—Ant.** activated, realized, developed; manifest, expressed, apparent, evident, obvious, conspicuous.

later *adv.* **1.** afterward, at a subsequent time, in a while, thereafter, in time, presently, subsequently, tardily, thereupon, after a while, in sequel, successively, since, next, behind, from that moment, in the course of time. *—adj.* **2.** subsequent, ensuing, successive, following, succeeding, consequent, consecutive. **3.** occurring late in time, mature; more recent, most recent; toward the end, latter. **—Ant. 2** earlier, antecedent, prior, beforehand.

lateral *adj.* side, sideways, sidewise, sideward, sided, sidelong; flanking, flanked; slanting, sloping, oblique; edgewise, edgeways; skirting.

lather *n.* **1.** foam, shaving foam, froth, head, suds, soapsuds; spume, scum. **2.** sweat, foam, froth. *—v.* **3.** soap, soap up; make froth, make foam.

latitude *n.* scope, opportunity, freedom of action, freedom of choice, free play, amplitude, range, compass, full swing, sweep, margin, leeway, elbowroom; liberality, independence, unrestrictedness, unrestraint, license, indulgence. **—Syn. Study.** See RANGE.

latter *adj.* **1.** second-mentioned, most recent, latest, later; ensuing, successive, succeeding, subsequent; last-mentioned, last; modern. **2.** later, final, last, end, ending, terminal. **—Ant. 1** former, previous; early, first, beginning. **2** first, initial, beginning, opening, commencing.

lattice *n.* trellis, openwork, latticework, network, grille, fretwork, webwork, reticulum, grating, framework, grid, screen, grate, fret, frame, framing, reticulation, trelliswork.

laudable *adj.* praiseworthy, estimable, admirable, commendable, worthy of admiration, deserving of esteem, meritorious, exemplary, model, unimpeachable, creditable, noble, sterling, excellent. **—Ant.** contemptible, lowly, base, unworthy, execrable, blameworthy, ignoble, reprehensible.

laudatory *adj.* praising, adulatory, complimentary, approving, favorable, approbatory, commendatory, eulogizing, eulogistic, encomiastic, panegyrical, flattering, acclamatory, celebratory, glorifying, admiring. **—Ant.** critical, censorious, denigratory, scornful, abusive.

laugh *v.* **1.** chuckle, giggle, express mirth, roar with laughter, roar, chortle, guffaw, snicker, titter, snigger, cackle, break up, split one's sides, roll in the aisle, howl. *—n.* **2.** guffaw, giggle, chortle, burst of laughter, roar, cackle, peal of laughter, mirth, glee, snicker, snigger, horselaugh, bellylaugh, ha-ha, ho-ho. **—Ant. 1** scowl, glower, frown; cry, mourn. **2** scowl, glower, frown; cry.

laughable *adj.* hilarious, funny, amusing, arousing laughter, worthy of laughter, risible, droll, merry, diverting, witty, comic, comical, farcical, sidesplitting, rib-tickling, tickling; worthy of scorn or derision, ludicrous, ridiculous, silly, stupid, asinine, inane, preposterous, outlandish, outrageous, dopey, grotesque, foolish, absurd. **—Ant.** solemn, serious, grave, somber, morose, sad, melancholy.

laughingstock *n.* joke, butt, fool, ass, figure of fun, dupe, fair game.

laughter *n.* mirth, conviviality, merriment, joy, jollity, hilarity, glee, gaiety, jollity, exhilaration, revelry, merry-making. **—Ant.** sorrow, lamentation, solemnity, gravity.

launch *v.* **1.** float, set afloat, send down the skids, put to sea, slide from the stocks, set into the water. **2.** inaugurate, begin, initiate, start, introduce, unveil, premiere; embark upon, set forth on, venture upon; institute, found, establish. **3.** shoot, discharge, let fly, thrust forward, hurl, propel, project, cast forth, catapult, throw, eject, set in motion, impel, send off, fire off, fire. **—Ant. 1** beach, ground; dock. **2** terminate, stop, withdraw, scrap. **3** withhold, retain, hold back.

launder *v.* wash, clean, cleanse, scrub, soak, rinse, scour, wash and iron, wash out.

laurels *n.* glory, fame, renown, honor, award, reward, praise, kudos, acclaim, distinction, illustriousness, tribute, commendation, recognition, celebrity, applause, credit, accolade, citation, acclamation, popularity.

lavish *adj.* **1.** free, profuse, plenteous, plentiful, abundant, extravagant, generous, effusive, prodigal, bounteous, bountiful, copious, without limit, overwhelming, intemperate, sumptuous, opulent, luxuriant, lush, plush, over-liberal, excessive, profligate, immoderate, unsparing, unstinting, munificent, greathearted; impetuous, wild, exuberant, unrestrained. *—v.* **2.** squander, spend freely, waste, dissipate, give overmuch, bestow generously, give in profusion, overindulge, pour out, shower, play Croesus with, fritter away. **—Syn. Study. 1** LAVISH, PRODIGAL, PROFUSE refer to that which exists in abundance and is poured out in great amounts. LAVISH suggests an unlimited, sometimes excessive generosity and openhandedness: *lavish hospitality.* PROFUSE emphasizes abundance, but may suggest exaggeration, emotionalism, or the like: *profuse thanks; profuse apologies.* PRODIGAL suggests wastefulness, improvidence, and reckless impatience: *He has lost his inheritance because of his prodigal ways.* **—Ant. 1** meager, parsimonious, sparing, scanty, frugal, cheap, thrifty, provident, stingy, niggardly, tightfisted, miserly. **2** withhold, stint, retain; begrudge.

law *n.* **1.** rule, governing principle, regulation, mandate, commandment, established dictate, decree, legal form, enactment, precept, edict, standing order, statute, ordinance, canon, bylaw, act, bill. **2.** system of laws, collection of rules, rules of conduct, code; lawful behavior, conformity to rules, civil peace, orderliness, legal process and provision, justice, due process of law, legality, writ. **3.** principle, standard, criterion, axiom, postulate, dogma, precept, fundamental, convention, working rule, generalization, model, formulation, theorem, truth, absolute, invariable. **4.** jurisprudence, the practice or profession of a lawyer, legal profession. **5.** police, law-enforcing agency; *Slang* fuzz, gendarmes. **—Ant. 2** chaos, anarchy, caprice, disorder.

lawbreaker *n.* transgressor, outlaw, criminal, offender, delinquent, miscreant, culprit, perpetrator, malefactor, scofflaw, crook, felon, wrongdoer, convict, recidivist; *Slang* jailbird, con, thug, hood.

lawful *adj.* **1.** legal, sanctioned by law, legally permitted, authorized, legitimate, legalized, legitimized, within the law, statutory, licit, allowed, warranted, permissible. **2.** rightful, proper, acknowledged by law, authorized, legally entitled, legitimate, prescribed, legally recognized, granted, titled, due. **—Ant. 1** unauthorized, unlawful, illegal, illicit, prohibited, forbidden. **2** pretended, disputed, illegitimate.

lawless *adj.* **1.** unlawful, contrary to law, indifferent to law, anarchic, lawbreaking, illegal, illegitimate, transgressive; insubordinate, disobedient, defiant, noncompliant. **2.** disorderly, rebellious, mutinous, unruly, uncontrollable, ungoverned, chaotic, insurgent, disorganized, terroristic, refractory, riotous. **3.** having no laws, heedless of law, ungoverned, chaotic, unrestrained, unbridled, wayward, freewheeling, wide open, out of hand, wanton, licentious. **—Ant. 1** obedient, lawful, law-abiding, orderly, compliant, licit, legitimate. **2** civilized, docile, restrained, disciplined, regimented, orderly. **3** well-governed, law-abiding, tightly run.

lawn *n.* grass, yard, greensward, grassy ground, sward, glade, grassy plot, turf, grounds, park, meadowland, green field, terrace.

lawyer *n.* attorney, attorney-at-law, counselor, counsel, advocate, legal advisor, jurist, counselor-at-law, prosecutor, legist, special pleader, pettifogger; *Slang* ambulance chaser, mouthpiece, shyster; *British* solicitor, barrister. **—Ant.** client; accused, defendant.

lax *adj.* **1.** negligent, neglectful, irresponsible, slack, loose, heedless, careless, unheeding, slipshod, remiss, derelict, yielding, indifferent, unconscientious, undutiful, unmindful, indifferent, casual, uncaring, unconcerned, thoughtless, oblivious; permissive, lenient. **2.** careless, vague, hazy, nebulous, unstructured, slack, negligent, ill-defined, imprecise, incoherent, inexact, cryptic, confusing. **3.** slack, drooping, hanging open, not firm, weak, relaxed, flaccid, loose, agape, loose-muscled, limp, floppy, flabby. —**Ant. 1** firm, scrupulous, strict, rigid, conscientious, unyielding, disciplined, severe, stern, austere, stringent. **2** exact, precise, careful, concise, specific. **3** tense, taut, rigid, firm, strong.

lay[1] *v.* **1.** put, place, set down, set, rest, repose, deposit, cause to lie. **2.** prostrate, knock down, level, fell, beat down, knock over, floor, ground, raze, throw to the ground. **3.** forward, present, offer, proffer, enunciate, elucidate, make a presentation of, place, put. **4.** wager, bet, gamble, hazard; give odds. **5.** produce, bear, deposit, oviposit. **6.** place, arrange, set, align, lay out, dispose, assemble. **7.** place, put, assign, allot, allocate, give, lend, apply; attribute, impute. **8.** set, locate, place, depict, seat, situate, stage, station. **9.** arrange, formulate, form, make, devise, concoct, organize, plan, hatch, put together. **10.** levy, charge, impose, exact, assess, demand, fine. —*n.* **11.** position, situation, arrangement, disposition, orientation, topography, configuration, contour, conformation. —**Ant. 1** elevate, raise, lift. **2** pick up, set standing, erect, raise, lift. **3** withhold, withdraw, hide, keep secret. **6** disarrange, confuse, muddle.

lay[2] *adj.* **1.** nonecclesiastical, profane, secular, nonclerical, laic, laical. **2.** nonprofessional, unprofessional, amateur, inexpert, inexperienced, partly informed, nonspecialist. —**Ant. 1** ecclesiastical, clerical, church. **2** professional, expert, specialized.

layer *n.* thickness, fold, lap, plate, leaf, sheet, coat, stratum, seam, tier, slab, stage, zone, level, story, bed; ply, lamina, scale.

layman *n.* nonprofessional, laic, lay person, parishioner, member of the flock, catechumen, churchman, communicant, churchwoman, brother, sister, lay brother, lay sister; outsider, amateur. —**Ant.** professional, insider, specialist; cleric, clergyman.

layoff *n.* dismissal, ouster, discharge, firing, termination, cashiering, sacking, furloughing; *Slang* the boot, the heave-ho, the gate, the axe, the bounce, walking papers, pink slip, *British* the sack; unemployment, disemployment, idling, shutdown, closedown; depression, hard times.

layout *n.* design, plan, model, blueprint, outline, diagram, sketch, drawing; arrangement, pattern, structure, form, motif.

lazy *adj.* **1.** idle, unwilling to work, shiftless, indolent, inert, inactive, slothful, slack, listless, lax, unindustrious. **2.** sluggish, lethargic, torpid, languid, laggard, apathetic, languorous, slow, slow-moving; easygoing, sleepy, drowsy. —**Syn. Study. 1** See IDLE. —**Ant. 1** industrious, quick, energetic, active, assiduous, diligent. **2** active, brisk, stimulated.

lead *v.* **1.** guide, show the way, steer, draw, direct, head, command, conduct, pilot, convey, shepherd, marshal, precede, go before. **2.** influence, persuade, attract, incline, induce, allure, lure, charm, tempt, seduce, draw, entice. **3.** proceed, direct, guide, advance, go, stretch, extend, aim. **4.** direct, moderate, conduct, manage, preside over, control, head, command, domineer. **5.** excel, rank first, outstrip, outdo, surpass, come first, set the pace; pioneer. **6.** go first, head, be in advance, top. **7.** pass, conduct, pursue, experience, live, have, undergo, go through. **8.** result in, produce, branch into, tend toward, issue in, bring on. —*n.* **9.** precedence, precedency, advance, first place, foremost position, antecedence, priority; edge, margin, advantage; plurality. **10.** clue, hint, guide. **11.** guidance, model, example, direction, indication, leadership. **12.** leading role, star part; protagonist, hero, principal performer, headliner; leading man, leading woman. —**Ant. 1** tail, trail. **2** disincline. **5** lag, trail.

leaden *adj.* **1.** numbed, deadened, dull, torpid, languid, sluggish, listless, unwieldy, cumbersome, hard to move, inanimate, inert; burdened, careworn, depressed, gloomy, glum, dreary. **2.** dark, gray, grayish, darkened, somber, murky, gloomy. —**Ant. 1** light, feathery; active, energetic; strong, vital. **2** light, bright, clear.

leader *n.* head, director, conductor, chief, chieftain, supervisor, superior, commander, manager, captain, foreman, boss; forerunner, frontrunner, pacesetter, pacemaker, pioneer, torchbearer, guide, pathfinder, trailblazer; *Slang* bigwig, kingpin; magnate, mogul, tycoon; patriarch, godfather; master, prophet, mentor, guru; *Informal* honcho. —**Ant.** follower, adherent, henchman, partisan, disciple.

leadership *n.* **1.** administration, directorship, managership, governorship, domination, hegemony, sway, stewardship, guardianship, superintendency, guidance, lead, supremacy, primacy, mastership, captaincy, headship; helm, wheel, reins. **2.** ability to lead, managerial skill, authoritativeness, command, supremacy, preeminence, charisma; self-assurance, self-reliance.

leading *adj.* **1.** foremost, most influential, most important, most significant, head, supreme, chief, prominent, notable, nonpareil, great, ranking, sovereign, prime, preeminent, unrivaled, unparalleled, unchallenged, principal, dominant, main, top, topmost, paramount, outstanding, stellar. **2.** leadoff, foremost in position, advance, first, prime, initial, pacesetting, advanced. **3.** principal, primary, guiding, directing, controlling, governing, ruling, motivating, prime, underlying, basic, essential, quintessential. **—Ant. 1–3** secondary. **1** subordinate, inferior, supernumerary, minor, lesser, rank and file. **2** following, hindmost. **3** incidental, superficial.

leaf *n.* **1.** frond, cotyledon, blade, needle, bract, foliole; petal. **2.** page, sheet, leaflet, folio. **3.** foil, lamination, sheet of metal, lamella. **4.** insert, inset, extension. **—***v.* **5.** produce leaves, green, turn green. **6.** turn pages quickly, flip, thumb, glance, browse, skim.

leaflet *n.* pamphlet, handbill, flyer, folder, brochure, booklet; advertisement, ad, circular; broadside, tract; handout, throwaway, broadsheet.

league *n.* **1.** alliance, association, group, collaboration, confraternity, partnership, guild, confederacy, confederation, federation, company, coalition, compact, cartel, union, fraternity, society, cooperative; conspiracy, cabal. **2.** alliance, association, network, cooperative, group of competing teams. **—***v.* **3.** combine, merge, unite in a league, band, consolidate, ally, confederate, join forces. **—Syn. Study. 1** See ALLIANCE. **—Ant. 1** disunion, separation, secession. **3** divide, separate, part, secede.

leak *n.* **1.** opening, gash, hole, aperture, puncture, fissure, crevice, cleft, crack, interstice, perforation, rupture, chink, break, breach, rent, fault, rift, rip. **2.** leaking, leakage, draining, drain, outflow, efflux, seepage, escape, ebb. **—***v.* **3.** admit leakage, be permeable, exude, seep, take in; discharge, vent, ooze, filter, percolate, dribble, let enter or escape. **4.** divulge, reveal, disclose, let out, make public, give away, let slip, confide, allow to become known; *Slang* blab, spill. **—Ant. 4** conceal, hide, suppress.

lean¹ *v.* **1.** rest, rest one's weight, support oneself, prop oneself, recline. **2.** bend, incline, tilt, slant, tip, list, bow, cant, slope; lurch. **3.** rely, depend, have faith in, seek solace in, resort to, take assurance from, set store by, trust in, count on. **4.** tend, incline, aim, have a propensity for, suggest a preference for; be partial to, prefer. **—Ant. 1, 2** stand erect, straighten up. **3** reject, withdraw from.

lean² *adj.* **1.** thin, spare, skinny, slender, willowy, svelte, slim, nonfat, skeletal, angular, spindly, lank, lanky, rawboned, scraggy; emaciated, gaunt, weedy, scrawny. **2.** meager, scant, scanty, inadequate, small, poor, spare, sparse, insufficient, exiguous, barren, thin, modest, slender. **—Ant. 1** fatty, brawny, fleshy, burly, plump, portly. **2** full, rich, abundant, plentiful, ample, profuse.

leap *v.* **1.** jump, spring, bound, hop, hurtle, bounce, gambol, prance, caper, frisk, frolic, skip, romp, cavort. **2.** jump over, jump across, spring over, overleap, vault, bound over, hop over, hurtle over. **3.** rush, hasten, jump, arrive prematurely, make unjustified assumptions, come hastily. **—***n.* **4.** bound, jump, spring, hurtle, hop, vault, saltation; *French* jeté. **—Ant. 1** walk, run, crawl.

learn *v.* **1.** master, pick up, acquire knowledge of; receive instructions in, become able. **2.** find out, determine, ascertain, discover, detect, unearth, uncover; *Informal* ferret out. **3.** hear, find out about, become apprised, become familiar with, become informed. **4.** memorize, commit to memory, con. **—Syn. Study. 2** LEARN, ASCERTAIN, DISCOVER, DETECT imply adding to one's store of knowledge or information. To LEARN is to come to know by chance, or by study or other application: *to learn of a friend's death; to learn to ski.* To ASCERTAIN is to find out and verify information through inquiry or analysis: *to ascertain the truth about the incident.* To DISCOVER is to find out something previously unseen or unknown; it suggests that the new information is surprising to the learner: *I discovered that they were selling their house.* To DETECT is to become aware of something obscure, secret, or concealed: *to detect a flaw in reasoning.* **—Ant. 1** forget; teach, instruct. **4** forget.

learned *adj.* wise, informed, educated, schooled, accomplished, erudite; profound, deep, scholarly, intellectual, well-educated, cultivated, cultured, literate, lettered, well-read, knowledgeable. **—Ant.** illiterate, unlettered, uneducated, unlearned, ignorant, *Informal* lowbrow.

learner *n.* student, pupil, schoolchild, schoolboy, schoolgirl, apprentice, trainee, disciple, follower, proselyte, scholar; novice, tyro, tenderfoot, rookie, recruit, draftee, enlistee, freshman, neophyte, novitiate.

learning *n.* education, scholarship, knowledge, schooling, culture, wisdom, erudition, enlightenment, information, understanding, comprehension, cultivation, edification, book learning. **—Syn. Study.** LEARNING, SCHOLARSHIP, ERUDITION refer to facts or ideas acquired through systematic study. LEARNING usu. refers to knowledge gained from extensive reading and formal instruction: *Her vast learning is reflected in her many books.* SCHOLARSHIP suggests a high degree of mastery in a specialized field, along with an analytical or innovative ability suited to the academic world: *The author is renowned for several works of classical scholarship.* ERUDITION suggests a thorough and profound knowledge of a difficult subject: *His erudition in languages is legendary.* **—Ant.** ignorance, unenlightenment, uncomprehension, benightedness.

leash *n.* **1.** strap, thong, lead, harness, curb, rein, bridle, line, string, tether, choker. *—v.* **2.** restrain, fasten, control, ruin, curb, harness, tether; hold in, suppress, contain, stifle. **—Ant. 2** unleash; unharness, release, vent.

leave *v.* **1.** go away from, separate from, quit, retire from, be off, depart, set out, go, exit, bid farewell, move on, start away from, embark from, decamp, fly, flee, abscond, venture away from, absent oneself; *Slang* shove off, push off, hotfoot it, bug out, take off, split. **2.** let stay, let remain, keep, maintain, retain, sustain. **3.** abandon, forsake, depart from, surrender, relinquish, desert, leave behind, yield, give up. **4.** yield, entrust, allot, consign, give over, resign, cede, waive, eschew, forgo, release, surrender, commit, assign. **5.** result in, produce, deposit, generate, cause. **6.** leave behind, be survived by. **7.** bequeath, bequest, legate, will, commit, assign, consign, allot, apportion, endow. *—n.* **8.** permission, consent, allowance, indulgence, sanction, approval, endorsement, understanding, tolerance, sufferance, concession. **9.** parting, departure, farewell, going, retreat, leave-taking, withdrawal. **10.** furlough, sabbatical, respite, liberty, recess, time off, vacation; *British* holiday. **—Ant. 1** arrive, come, appear, emerge. **3** persist, gain, hold, retain, stay, continue. **4** assume, take over. **5** remove, erase, eradicate. **8** rejection, refusal, denial, forbiddance, prohibition, interdiction. **9** stay, continuance, persistence; arrival. **10** duty.

leave-taking *n.* farewell, parting, adieu, au revoir, send-off, good-bye.

lecherous *adj.* lustful, lewd, libidinous, oversexed, lascivious, salacious, prurient, satyrlike, randy, erotic, licentious, carnal, lubricious, ruttish, goatish. **—Ant.** prudish, straitlaced, puritanical.

lechery *n.* hypersexuality, carnality, lust, lustfulness, promiscuity, nymphomania, excessive sexual desire, satyriasis, salaciousness, lewdness, prurience, lasciviousness. **—Ant.** purity, chasteness, celibacy.

lecture *n.* **1.** talk, address, speech, discourse, oral presentation, disquisition, oration; sermon, preachment, homily, reading, narration. **2.** rebuke, reprimand, admonitory speech, harangue, chastisement, admonishment, moralizing talk, cautionary speech, warning, remonstrance, censure, talking-to, dressing down, reproof, reproach, chiding. *—v.* **3.** talk, give a talk, speak, expound, discourse. **4.** reprove, rebuke, call down, take to task, harangue, rail at, scold, admonish, criticize at length, censure, chide, upbraid, moralize, preach, sermonize, hold forth. **—Ant. 4** praise, compliment, applaud, laud.

ledge *n.* **1.** shelf, projection, offset, ridge, outcropping, sill, step, foothold, shoulder. **2.** shelf, sill, mantel, mantelshelf, mantelpiece.

leer *n.* **1.** lewd look, lustful look, lascivious stare, ogle, goggle, sly glance, evil look, impolite gaze, insulting stare. *—v.* **2.** stare suggestively, give the eye to, look knowingly, look with insulting familiarity, ogle, glance wantonly, look with a leer; smirk, fleer.

leery *adj.* wary, suspicious, distrustful, circumspect, cautious, doubtful, unsure, skeptical, chary, guarded, mistrustful; hesitant, unsure, undecided, *Slang* cagey. **—Ant.** trusting, confident, credulous, gullible, unsuspecting.

leeway *n.* flexibility, extra time or resource, latitude, scope, margin, margin for error, allowance, cushion, reserve, elbowroom, room for choice or maneuverability; headroom, headway, clearance, play, slack, tolerance.

leftover *n.* **1.** residue, excess, remainder, surplus, residual, legacy, oddments, overage, survivor, carry-over; remaining food, remaining odds and ends, leavings. *—adj.* **2.** remaining, residual, surplus, excess; unused, uneaten.

leg *n.* **1.** lower extremity, limb, member; underpinning, shank, *Informal* stump, pin, *Slang* gam; (*bones*) femur, fibula, tibia. **2.** prop, support, upright, brace; post, column, pillar. **3.** portion, segment, part, stage, section, lap, stretch.

legacy *n.* **1.** bequest, devise, gift; inheritance, estate. **2.** heritage, tradition; leftover, remaining portion, survivor, vestige, carry-over, throwback, transmission; heirloom, birthright; hand-me-down.

legal *adj.* **1.** of law; juridical, jurisprudential, juristic; forensic, judicial, adjudicatory; courtroom. **2.** permitted by law, lawful, permissible, rightful, sanctioned, constitutional, valid, licit, legitimate; fair, within bounds; *Slang* cricket, kosher. **—Ant. 2** illegal, unlawful, illegitimate, illicit.

legality *n.* lawfulness, legitimacy, accordance with law; validity, licitness, constitutionality. **—Ant.** illegality, unlawfulness, illegitimacy, illicitness.

legation *n.* diplomatic mission, consulate, delegation, ministry, embassy, chancellery, mission.

legend *n.* —**Syn. Study.** See FABLE.

legendary *adj.* **1.** famous, familiar to all, famed, known by tradition, storied, proverbial, worthy of legend, celebrated. **2.** fabled, mythic, mythical, figuring in legends, fanciful, imaginary, unverifiable, fabulous, apocryphal, fictitious, unsubstantiated, unauthenticated. —**Ant. 1** unknown. **2** historical, authenticated, genuine.

legerdemain *n.* **1.** sleight of hand, prestidigitation, deftness, adroitness; juggling, jugglery. **2.** deception, trickery, artfulness, cunning, adroit manipulation, maneuvering.

legible *adj.* readable, easily read, plain, visible, decipherable, understandable, comprehensible, distinct, clear, clear-cut, neat. —**Ant.** illegible, undecipherable, unreadable, unclear, indistinct.

legion *n.* **1.** military force, army, division, brigade, troops, corps. **2.** multitude, mass, great number, throng, sea, swarm, spate, mob, drove, myriad, host, horde.

legislation *n.* **1.** lawmaking, making law, passage of law; government. **2.** legislative law, ordinance, enactment, regulation, bill, statute, amendment, act, measure, ruling.

legislator *n.* lawmaker, lawgiver, member of a legislature, representative, delegate, senator, representative, congressman, congresswoman, parliamentarian, councilman, assemblyman, alderman.

legislature *n.* lawmaking body; senate, parliament, congress, assembly, council, diet; house, chamber.

legitimacy *n.* legality, validity, lawfulness, rightfulness, correctness, appropriateness, genuineness, authenticity. —**Ant.** illegitimacy, illegality, unlawfulness.

legitimate *adj.* **1.** lawful, rightful, true, legal, licit. **2.** genuine, justified, authentic, believable, plausible, logical, sound, well-founded, just, tenable, valid, reasonable, fair; proper, correct, appropriate. —**Ant. 1** unlawful, illegal; fraudulent, sham, false. **2** unfounded, unjustified, unsound, unfair.

leisure *n.* free time, spare time, time off, holiday, idle hours, periods of relaxation, ease, relaxation, recreation, respite, rest, vacation, recess, repose, diversion. —**Ant.** duty, work, occupation, employment, labor, business; obligation, responsibility, burden.

leisurely *adj.* **1.** relaxed, restful, unhurried, without haste, slow-moving, slow, idle, casual; languid, lackadaisical. —*adv.* **2.** unhurriedly, slowly, lingeringly, without haste. —**Ant. 1** hasty, rushed, rapid, fast. **2** hurriedly, quickly, rapidly, fast.

lend *v.* **1.** loan, allow to use temporarily, make a loan of; *Informal* let one have, trust one for; advance. **2.** impart, furnish, give, invest, supply, contribute. **3.** contribute, give freely, put at another's disposal. —**Ant. 1** borrow. **2** deprive. **3** refuse, withhold, keep.

length *n.* **1.** reach, span, distance, end to end, extent, measure, longitude, range, compass, measurement. **2.** longer dimension, longer side, lengthiest part; *Informal* the long way. **3.** duration, extent, time; magnitude, period, stretch, term, elapsed time. **4.** piece, portion, segment, section, run, stretch. —**Ant. 2** width, breadth, depth.

lengthen *v.* extend, elongate, stretch, prolong, protract, draw out, drag out, expand, spin out, string out, increase; fill out, flesh out, add to, pad. —**Syn. Study.** LENGTHEN, EXTEND, PROLONG, PROTRACT agree in the idea of making longer. To LENGTHEN is to make longer, either in a material or immaterial sense: *to lengthen a dress; to lengthen human life.* To EXTEND is to lengthen beyond some original point or so as to reach a certain point: *to extend a railway line another fifty miles.* Both PROLONG and PROTRACT mean esp. to lengthen in time. To PROLONG is to continue beyond the desired, estimated, or allotted time: *to prolong an interview.* To PROTRACT is to draw out to undue length or to be slow in coming to a conclusion: *to protract a discussion.* —**Ant.** shorten, curtail, abbreviate, abridge, decrease.

lengthy *adj.* very long, overlong, of great length, extended, prolonged, protracted, elongated, long-drawn, extensive; discursive, long-winded, windy, garrulous, wordy, rambling, prolix, drawn out, padded, digressive; interminable, endless. —**Ant.** short, brief, limited; condensed, succinct, terse, to the point.

lenient *adj.* merciful, kind, clement, gentle, sparing, tenderhearted, indulgent, tolerant, forbearing, mild, soft, easygoing, kindhearted, soft-hearted, moderate, charitable, compassionate, sympathetic, benevolent, liberal, permissive, patient, forgiving. —**Ant.** harsh, stern, exacting, rigid, rigorous, stringent, strict, severe, cruel, merciless.

less *adv.* **1.** to a smaller extent, more limited way; little, meagerly, barely. —*adj.* **2.** smaller, not as great, more limited, slighter, not so significant. —*n.* **3.** a smaller amount, lesser action, less serious offense. —**Ant. 1–3** more. **2** greater, larger.

lessen *v.* decrease, decline, diminish, abate, dwindle, sink, reduce, subside, shrink, contract, lower, depreciate, slacken, wind down, ease, wane, ebb, abridge; alleviate, lighten, mitigate; dilute, thin. —**Ant.** increase, raise, lengthen, enlarge, extend, heighten, multiply, mount, build.

lesser *adj.* **1.** smaller, less important, secondary, slighter, humbler, inferior, minor. —*adv.* **2.** to a smaller degree, less, secondarily. —**Ant. 1** major, larger, primary, superior. **2** greater, primarily.

lesson *n.* **1.** exercise, segment, assignment, matter to be learned, student's task, study, instruction, homework. **2.** class, instruction, drill, learning session. **3.** example, model, exemplar, advisement, notice, instruction, study, guide, moral, message, warning, admonition, deterrent, example, caveat, remonstrance, caution, rebuke, punishment. **4.** reading, recitation, Scriptures. —**Ant. 3** misguidance, deception, bad example.

let *v.* **1.** permit, allow, authorize, warrant, license, approve, give assent to; sanction, endorse; suffer, leave, tolerate; admit, concede. **2.** rent, lease, hire out, charter, sublease, sublet. **3.** cause, make, enable, allow, permit, grant, empower. —**Syn. Study. 1** See ALLOW. —**Ant. 1** forbid, prohibit. **2** buy; sell.

letdown *n.* disappointment, anticlimax, disenchantment, discontent, dissatisfaction, comedown, disillusionment, mortification, discomfiture, disgruntlement, bafflement, frustration, balk, chagrin, regret, setback, rue, bitter pill; blighted hope, dashed hope, blow. —**Ant.** gratification, satisfaction, fulfillment, contentment.

lethal *adj.* deadly, fatal, mortal, killing, mortally toxic; dangerous, destructive; virulent, baneful, poisonous, venomous, malignant. —**Syn. Study.** See FATAL. —**Ant.** harmless, wholesome, healthful.

lethargic *adj.* lazy, drowsy, sleepy, soporific, languid, indolent, idle, dull, somnolent, comatose, enervated, debilitated, dispirited, unspirited, torpid, lackluster, sluggish, slothful, indifferent, passive, inert, listless, apathetic. —**Ant.** energetic, vigorous, alert, active, responsive, bright, spirited; energized, animated, stimulated.

lethargy *n.* languor, lassitude, apathy, indifference, drowsiness, sluggishness, dullness, inactivity, inertia, torpor, torpidity, stupor, laziness, indolence, listlessness, sloth, slothfulness. —**Ant.** vigor, alertness, liveliness, activity, eagerness.

letter *n.* **1.** orthographic character, alphabetic character, written symbol. **2.** epistle, dispatch, missive, note, message, e-mail, fax; memorandum, document, certificate; love letter, billet-doux. **3.** actual terms, specific details, literal wording, strict meaning, substance, exact sense, literalness, preciseness. **4. letters** literary accomplishment, learning, erudition, scholarly attainment; literature, belles lettres. —**Ant. 3** spirit, tenor, heart.

letup *n.* stopping, slackening, relief, cessation, surcease, pause, slowdown, retardation, lessening, remission, abatement, decrease, respite, lull; interlude, interval, vacation. —**Ant.** increase, speedup, intensification, acceleration.

level *adj.* **1.** flat, even, horizontal, flush, plane; uniform, consistent; lacking roughness or unevenness, smooth, unwrinkled; on an even keel; parallel to the horizon, in line with the horizon. **2.** even, on a line, aligned; equivalent to, comparable to, on a par with; together, tied, neck and neck. —*n.* **3.** height, elevation, vertical position, plane. **4.** stage, station, rank, position, achievement. **5.** floor, story, landing, elevation; layer, bed, stratum, zone, vein. —*v.* **6.** grade, make even, even out, make horizontal, align, plane, flatten, smooth, equalize. **7.** flatten, raze, knock down, topple, lay low, wreck, tear down, reduce, devastate. **8.** aim, direct, point. —**Ant. 1** slanted, tilted, uneven, warped, bumpy, hilly; vertical. **2** below, above. **6** roughen, furrow. **7** raise, erect; build, construct.

level-headed *adj.* sensible, prudent, cautious, circumspect, steady, judicious, sage, dependable, practical, sound; composed, cool-headed, unruffled, self-controlled, balanced, poised, even-tempered. —**Ant.** foolish, skittish, flighty, thoughtless, senseless.

levity *n.* frivolity, lightness, lightheartedness, whimsy, lack of earnestness or seriousness, triviality, hilarity, foolishness, silliness, joking, mirth, jocularity, trifling, flippancy, flightiness; pleasantry, fun. —**Ant.** gravity, seriousness, sobriety, earnestness, solemnity, dignity.

levy *n.* **1.** duty, excise, tax, assessment, fee, toll, imposition, tariff. **2.** conscription, calling up, draft, muster. —*v.* **3.** impose, demand, exact, assess, charge; collect. **4.** conscript, draft, call up, enlist. **5.** wage, start, carry on, make, prosecute, pursue.

lewd *adj.* obscene, indecent, vulgar, lustful, lecherous, goatish, bawdy, Rabelaisian, ribald, risqué, pornographic, lascivious, excessively erotic, lubricious, libidinous, wanton, licentious, libertine, immoral, salacious, prurient. —**Ant.** chaste, decent, modest; proper, prim, pure, moral.

lexicon *n.* wordbook, vocabulary, dictionary, thesaurus, glossary, index, gloss, code book, wordlist, concordance, synonymy, wordstock, onomasticon.

liability *n.* **1.** debt, obligation, indebtedness, debit, arrear, burden, duty, responsibility. **2.** disadvantage, drawback, onus, burden, obstacle, handicap, minus, impediment, hindrance, shortcoming, stumbling block, encumbrance, inconvenience, *Slang* drag. **—Ant. 1, 2** asset. **2** bonus, plus, advantage, head start, boon.

liable *adj.* **1.** vulnerable, susceptible, open, exposed, subject, prone, inclined, disposed, sensitive, ripe for. **2.** legally responsible, answerable, accountable, chargeable, obligated. **3.** likely, apt, inclined, prone. **—Ant. 1** exempt, immune. **2** unaccountable, exempt. **3** unlikely, disinclined.

liaison *n.* **1.** contact, connection, association, communication, intercommunication; alliance, bond, link, coordination, union, cooperation, interchange; mediator, go-between. **2.** love affair, illicit romance, amour, entanglement, dalliance, flirtation, intrigue; *French* aventure.

liar *n.* falsifier, prevaricator, fabricator, perjurer; fibber, storyteller.

libel *n.* **1.** printed slander, defamation, malicious falsehood, calumny, smear, aspersion, slur, vilification, obloquy; unjust accusation. **—*v.* 2.** vilify, malign unjustly, slur, derogate, discredit, slander, defame, revile, disparage, blacken, calumniate, asperse. **—Ant. 1** vindication, apology. **2** vindicate, apologize, retract. **2** set the record straight.

liberal *adj.* **1.** progressive, reformist, advanced, freethinking; civil libertarian, latitudinarian; left-wing. **2.** fair-minded, open-minded, broad-minded, tolerant, forbearing, magnanimous, unbigoted, unprejudiced, unbiased, impartial; enlightened, humanitarian. **3.** abundant, generous, lavish, bounteous, bountiful, handsome, extravagant, munificent, prodigal, plenteous, ample; unstinting, unsparing, openhanded, charitable. **4.** lenient, broad, unrigorous, not strict, casual, flexible, tolerant, open to reason, not literal. **—*n.* 5.** progressive, reformer, latitudinarian, libertarian; left-winger, leftist. **—Syn. Study. 3** See GENEROUS. **—Ant. 1** conservative, reactionary, right-wing. **2** intolerant, narrow, bigoted, biased, prejudiced, provincial, limited. **3** skimpy, inadequate, small, cheap. **4** strict, unbending, fixed, inflexible, rigid, literal. **5** conservative, reactionary, right-winger.

liberate *v.* set free, deliver, release, discharge, dismiss, disencumber, disengage, emancipate, manumit, redeem, absolve; rescue, extricate, let loose, let go, unshackle, let out; *Slang* spring. **—Syn. Study.** See RELEASE. **—Ant.** imprison, intern, confine, restrict, limit; entrap, enthrall, enslave.

libertine *n.* **1.** profligate, debauchee, rake, voluptuary, reprobate, lecher, roué, sensualist, seducer; immoralist, moral iconoclast, immoral person; satyr, womanizer, goat. **—*adj.* 2.** immoral, dissolute, loose, unchaste, licentious, lewd, lustful, wanton, lascivious, libidinous, lecherous, morally unrestrained, profligate. **—Ant. 1** prude, puritan. **2** straitlaced, moral, virtuous, chaste.

liberty *n.* **1.** freedom, self-determination, independence, autonomy; right, privilege. **2.** freedom, manumission, emancipation, liberation, delivery; citizenship, enfranchisement. **3.** leave, furlough, vacation, free time, shore leave. **4.** freedom, permission, leave, sanction, license, dispensation; carte blanche. **5. liberties** familiarity, license, impropriety, undue intimacy; distortion, misrepresentation, violation, misuse, falsification. **—Ant. 1** tyranny, despotism; restraint, constraint, compulsion, duress, coercion. **2** slavery, subjugation, captivity, imprisonment, restraint, enslavement. **3** duty. **5** propriety, judiciousness, rigorousness.

license *n.* **1.** authorization, charter, leave, liberty, permit, right, allowance, sanction, warrant, privilege, carte blanche, grant, admission, free passage, freedom, dispensation, franchise. **2.** permit, certificate, pass, passport, visa, safe-conduct. **3.** liberty, latitude, departure from rule, deviation from custom, nonconformity, privilege; laxity, looseness, slackness; audacity, brazenness, presumptuousness. **4.** abused freedom, too much liberty, indifference to others' rights, irresponsibility, recklessness, licentiousness, temerity, presumption, arrogant self-indulgence, debauchery, libertinism, anarchy, lawlessness, unruliness, disorder. **—*v.* 5.** authorize, issue a license to, certify, warrant, empower, enable, allow, let, sanction, accredit, commission; approve, endorse. **—Ant. 1** forbiddance, denial, restriction. **3** strictness, restraint. **4** restraint, constraint, restriction, moderation, sobriety, submission. **5** prohibit, forbid; restrain, curb, check; disallow.

licentious *adj.* **1.** irresponsible, unrestrained, amoral, unconstrained, excessive, lawless, unprincipled, unscrupulous, prodigal, ungoverned. **2.** lewd, libertine, lustful, lecherous, lascivious, immoral, libidinous, lubricious, debauched, wanton, abandoned, loose, promiscuous, salacious; goatish, profligate, dissolute, depraved, dissipated, ruttish, brutish; *Informal* dirty, sleazy, raunchy. **—Ant. 1** law-abiding, lawful, responsible, principled, scrupulous. **2** chaste, pure, puritanical, proper, moral, prudish.

licit *adj.* legal, lawful, authorized, allowable, acceptable, permissible, legitimate, admissible, constitutional, sanctioned, sanctionable, statutory, authorizable, valid; *Slang* legit, kosher. **—Ant.** forbidden, illegal, unlawful, illicit, banned, prohibited.

lick *v.* **1.** pass the tongue over, touch with the tongue, tongue, lap, collect with the tongue. **2.** pass lightly over, lap, touch; ignite, fire, kindle. **3.** defeat, beat, conquer, vanquish, overcome, overthrow, overpower, drub, subdue, subjugate, rout, outmatch, master; *Informal* trounce, clobber. **4.** spank, beat, whip, thrash, hit, wallop. **—*n.*** **5.** taste, sample; lap, suck. **6.** slap, blow, punch, hit, sock; verbal blow, denunciation, sally, crack. **7.** bit, speck, particle, modicum, touch, dab, jot, shred, snip, iota, hint, stroke, smattering, smidgen, trace, scintilla. **—Ant. 4, 6** caress, pet. **7** lot, pile.

lid *n.* top, cover, cap, stopper, plug, stopple, cork, operculum; curb, restraint; limit, ceiling, maximum.

lie[1] *n.* **1.** falsehood, prevarication, falsification, untruth, fib, fiction, invention, fabrication, story, false story, perjury, deception, deceit, misrepresentation, equivocation. **—*v.*** **2.** perjure oneself, prevaricate, falsify, speak falsely, fabricate, tell untruths, forswear oneself; fib, embellish, embroider, romance, stretch the truth, equivocate, misstate. **—Ant. 1** truth, veracity, fact, gospel.

lie[2] *v.* **1.** recline, rest, repose, be supine, be flat, be prone, sprawl, loll, lounge, stretch out. **2.** be buried, be interred, repose. **3.** be placed, be located, be found, exist, remain, abide, rest, stay, inhere, belong, be present, be established, obtain; range, extend. **—Ant. 1** rise, arise, stand; be active, go, change, run.

life *n.* **1.** living thing, living being, creature, organism, animal, plant; animate existence, being, substantiality, subsistence. **2.** human, human being, person, individual, soul. **3.** lifetime, term of existence, life span, life expectancy; survival, longevity, duration; career. **4.** career, lifework, path, course; existence, mode of living. **5.** biography, autobiography, story, life story, memoir. **6.** liveliness, vitality, animation, spirit, energy, zest, vivacity, vigor, verve. **—Ant. 1** death, lifelessness, nothingness. **6** lifelessness, spiritlessness, dullness, flatness.

lifeless *adj.* **1.** dead, without life, defunct; deceased, departed, late; inert, inactive; inanimate. **2.** static, lacking vitality, dull, spiritless, lifeless, torpid, vapid, sluggish, colorless, boring; stiff, wooden, flat, hollow, lackluster. **—Ant. 1** living, alive; animate. **2** animated, vital; active, dynamic, live, spirited.

lift *v.* **1.** hoist, heave, move upward, raise, elevate, raise up, rear, upraise, uplift, boost. **2.** cancel, revoke, rescind, put an end to, remove, banish, countermand. **3.** elevate, uplift, exalt, raise, give a boost to. **4.** rise, disperse, dissipate, scatter, vanish, disappear, float away, become dispelled; ascend, soar, move upward. **5.** steal, take, thieve, pilfer, pinch, purloin, filch, swipe, snatch, make off with, pick, palm, pocket; appropriate; pirate, plagiarize. **—*n.*** **6.** heave, hoist, boost, uplift, raising; ascent, gain in elevation, upward movement, climb, rise, ascendance. **7.** sense of well-being, rising of spirits; encouragement, enheartenment, reassurance, boost, inspiration, elation, uplift; *Slang* shot in the arm, high. **—Ant. 1** lower, drop. **2** establish, impose. **3** lower, disappoint, depress, crush, dash. **4** hang, descend, fall. **6** drop. **7** letdown, blow.

light[1] *n.* **1.** radiance, illumination, shine, luminosity, brightness, blaze, glare, glow, luster, sparkle, brilliance, effulgence; beam, sunbeam, moonbeam. **2.** source of light; (*variously*) lamp, lantern, beacon, torch, candle. **3.** approach, aspect, manner of understanding, viewpoint, attitude, slant, side, vantage point, direction, angle, frame of reference. **4.** elucidation, understanding, information, enlightenment, insight, illumination. **5.** means of ignition; match, lucifer, lighter; flame. **6.** model, exemplar, guide, paragon, paradigm, shining example, guiding light, beacon. **—*adj.*** **7.** bright, well lighted, having light, illuminated, luminous, radiant, brilliant, sunny, aglow. **8.** pale, light-toned, not deep or dark, light-hued, fair, bleached; blond, blondish. **—*v.*** **9.** ignite, set burning, set fire to, fire, catch fire, conflagrate, flame, spark, kindle. **10.** illuminate, illumine, give light to, irradiate, flood with light, brighten, floodlight; clarify. **11.** brighten, make cheerful, lighten, radiate, make radiant, cause to shine. **12.** turn on, switch on, put on. **—Ant. 1** dark, darkness; shadow, shade, gloom, dusk, dimness. **4** obscurity, mystery, cloud, shadow. **7** dark, dim, gloomy, shadowy, dusky. **8** dark, deep. **9** extinguish, put out, damp, douse, turn off, quench. **11** darken, cloud, dull.

light[2] *adj.* **1.** lightweight, underweight, not heavy, burdenless, weightless; gossamer, buoyant, ethereal. **2.** small, inconsequential, barely perceptible, inconsiderable, moderate, slight, puny, faint. **3.** lighthearted, amusing, funny, gay, carefree, frivolous, sprightly, blithe, nonintellectual, trifling; trivial, paltry, superficial, petty, inconsiderable, slight. **4.** soft, moderate, slight, faint, gentle. **5.** light-footed, airy, graceful, sylphlike. **6.** small, spare, frugal, modest in quality, not rich, slight, meager, scanty, restricted, not heavy, abstemious. **7.** high-spirited, gleeful, jolly, sportive, jaunty, jubilant, happy, chipper, bright, cheerful, gay, buoyant. **8.** easy, simple, manageable, effortless, moderate, untaxing, undemanding. **—Ant. 1, 2, 4–6** heavy. **1** burdensome, weighty. **2** strong, substantial. **3** serious, intense, deep, profound. **4** forceful. **5** clumsy. **6** rich, gluttonous. **7** serious, despondent, somber. **8** hard, strenuous, taxing.

light³ *v.* **1.** alight, descend, get down, get off, come off, step down, dismount. **2.** come to rest, alight, stop, land, perch, fall, settle, roost. **3.** chance, discover, meet with, stumble on, encounter, come across, come upon, happen upon, find. **—Ant. 1** ascend, mount, climb, get on, go aboard.

lighten¹ *v.* brighten, cause to become lighter, light up, irradiate, illuminate, make bright, become light; scintillate, shine, blaze, flare, flash, gleam, corruscate. **—Ant.** darken.

lighten² *v.* **1.** make lighter, make less burdensome, reduce in load, unload, ease, buoy up, unburden, disburden. **2.** ease, lessen, reduce, make less harsh, mitigate, disencumber, alleviate, relieve, assuage, allay, abate, moderate, temper. **3.** lift, gladden, elate, inspire, revive, enliven, buoy, uplift. **—Ant. 1** weight. **2** increase, heighten, intensify, aggravate. **3** depress, sadden, oppress, weigh down.

lighthearted *adj.* cheerful, cheered, cheery, gay, carefree, merry, joyous, jolly, joyful, glad, sunny, airy, free and easy, untroubled, blithe, chipper, buoyant, effervescent, insouciant, sprightly, lively, sanguine. **—Ant.** heavyhearted, cheerless, sad, depressed, dejected, despondent, melancholy, morose, glum, gloomy.

lightly *adv.* **1.** gently, hesitantly, weakly, faintly, timidly, softly. **2.** thinly, slightly, meagerly, sparingly, sparsely, moderately. **3.** easily, facilely, readily, without effort. **4.** nimbly, gingerly, airily; quickly, swiftly, buoyantly. **5.** carelessly, thoughtlessly, without concern, unconcernedly, frivolously, indifferently, slightingly, blithely, blandly, flippantly. **—Ant. 1** heavily, firmly, forcefully. **2** heavily, thickly, abundantly. **3** difficultly, arduously. **4** heavily, awkwardly, ploddingly, slowly, ponderously. **5** carefully, seriously, earnestly.

likable Also **likeable** *adj.* pleasing, genial, attractive, easily liked, charming, winsome, lovable, pleasant, amiable, agreeable, engaging, appealing, complaisant; nice, sympathetic; *Spanish* simpático. **—Ant.** unlikable, displeasing, unpleasant, hateful, odious, repellent, repulsive.

like¹ *adj.* identical, similar, akin, same, much the same, comparable, corresponding; congruent, matched, analogous, homologous, cognate, equivalent, equal, uniform, parallel; selfsame; allied, related, resembling. **—Ant.** unlike, dissimilar, different, diverse, divergent.

like² *v.* **1.** enjoy, take pleasure in, find agreeable, relish, fancy, be partial to, dote, savor, relish. **2.** esteem, admire, find agreeable, have a friendly feeling for, be partial to, be fond of, fancy, approve, endorse; favor, support; *Informal* take a shine to, have a crush on. **3.** care, think fit, feel inclined, wish, have a mind, choose. *—n.* **4. likes** partialities, favorites, inclinations, prejudices, preferences. **—Ant. 1–3** dislike. **1, 2** hate, abhor, detest, loathe, abominate.

likelihood *n.* prospect, probability, strong possibility, good chance, reasonableness, potentiality, possibility. **—Ant.** improbability, unlikelihood.

likely *adj.* **1.** inclined, apt, probable, liable, destined. **2.** plausible, credible, reliable, believable, reasonable, rational, seemingly truthful, verisimilar. **3.** suitable, fit, proper, befitting, appropriate, qualified. **4.** promising, able, apt. *—adv.* **5.** probably, presumably, in all probability. **—Ant. 1** unlikely. **2, 3** doubtful, dubious, questionable, problematic. **4** unpromising.

likeness *n.* **1.** portrait, picture, representation, image, study, model, delineation, depiction, rendition, portrayal; replica, facsimile, effigy. **2.** resemblance, similarity, similitude, semblance, agreement; correspondence, analogy, affinity. **—Ant. 2** dissimilarity, difference, divergence, disparity.

liking *n.* affinity, preference, taste, appetite, inclination, proclivity, partiality, affection, fancy, fondness, penchant, appetite, leaning, predilection, soft spot, propensity, bent, weakness. **—Ant.** dislike, disinclination; hatred, abhorrence, loathing, repugnance, aversion.

lily-white *adj.* **1.** blameless, guiltless, good, decent, exemplary, upstanding, inculpable, innocent, pure, virtuous, uncorrupted, righteous, irreproachable, faultless, proper, unimpeachable, upright, honorable, impeccable. **2.** all-white, segregated, discriminatory, bigoted, biased, exclusive, prejudiced, racist, unintegrated. **—Ant. 1** corrupt, depraved, wicked, degenerate, evil, immoral.

limb *n.* appendage, member, part, extension; branch, projection, bough, sprig, spur, twig, shoot, outgrowth; wing, arm, leg; *Slang* gam, pin; prosthesis.

limber *adj.* **1.** flexible, pliant, bending,

pliable, malleable, lithe, agile, lithesome, supple, lissome, elastic, loose-jointed. —*v.* **2.** make limber, loosen, relax. —**Ant. 1** stiff, rigid, unbending, inflexible, wooden. **2** stiffen.

limit *n.* **1.** end, furthest bound, greatest extent, end point, breaking point, ultimate. **2.** Often **limits** edge, border, boundary, rim, fringe, frontier, margin, confines, periphery, perimeter. **3.** limitation, restriction, maximum, greatest number allowed, ceiling, top; restraint, check, curb; quota. —*v.* **4.** restrict, restrain, confine, delimit, curb, check, bound, keep within bounds, narrow, inhibit; define, prescribe, circumscribe, qualify.

limited *adj.* defined, delimited, confined, special, bounded, restrained, controlled, circumscribed, specified, fixed, finite; narrow, cramped, restricted, minimal. —**Ant.** unlimited, unbounded, unrestricted, limitless.

limitless *adj.* endless, unlimited, unending, unbound, boundless, without measure, measureless, immeasurable, infinite, eternal, without limit. —**Ant.** limited, circumscribed, bounded, restricted, restrained, measured.

limp[1] *n.* **1.** lameness, halting walk, gimp, jerky step, halt, lame movement, falter, hobble. —*v.* **2.** hobble, falter, halt; crawl, skulk.

limp[2] *adj.* slack, loose, flabby, droopy, drooping, floppy, flaccid, yielding, lax, lacking vitality, lacking firmness, soft, dead tired, weak, lethargic, enervated, exhausted. —**Ant.** stiff, rigid, strong, hardy, robust.

limpid *adj.* lucid, clear, transparent, translucent, pure, pellucid; vitreous, crystalline; perspicuous, unambiguous, straightforward, clear-cut. —**Ant.** muddy, murky, cloudy, dark, dim, opaque.

line *n.* **1.** underscore, long thin mark, score, long stroke, stripe, dash, streak, slash; demarcation, border, outline, contour. **2.** wrinkle, mark, crease, furrow, crow's foot. **3.** queue, file, rank, tier, series, column, range, procession. **4.** note, brief message, letter, postcard, card, report, word. **5.** policy, stance, position, ideology, doctrine, idea, intention, scheme, system; course of action, belief, method; purpose, direction. **6.** lineage, stock, genealogy, race, family, house, strain, ancestry, breed. **7.** transit company, transportation service or company, transit route. **8.** occupation, business, profession, vocation, calling, pursuit, métier, trade, means of living, livelihood, craft. **9.** cord, strand, thread, cordage; fishline; cable, rope; towline. **10.** circuit, conductor, conduit, power supply, electrical system. **11. lines** pattern, habitual or fixed idea, convention, principle, model, example, general form or notion, routine. **12.** front line, firing line, fighting front, front, vanguard; trenches, barricades; defensive perimeter. —*v.* **13.** rule, mark or rule with lines: score, draw, inscribe. **14.** queue up, arrange in a line, align, array, form in a line, rank, marshal, file.

lineage *n.* extraction, derivation, line, stock, pedigree, blood, descent, heredity, genealogy, ancestry, parentage.

linger *v.* **1.** stay, remain, tarry, persist, delay, delay departure, wait, dawdle, dillydally, procrastinate, dally; loiter, idle, lag, trail, *Informal* hang around. **2.** last, persist in living, survive, hang on, die slowly, cling to life. —**Ant. 1** leave hastily, rush, hasten, depart, disappear.

linguist *n.* **1.** multilingual person, polyglot; interpreter, translator. **2.** linguistics expert, language scholar; (*variously*) philologist, etymologist, lexicographer, semanticist, morphologist, grammarian, phonetician, phonologist.

liniment *n.* ointment, medicated lotion, soothing liquid preparation, balm, unguent, emollient, salve.

link *n.* **1.** section of a chain, connective, bond, ring, loop, joint. **2.** tie, bond, connecting part, connection, interconnection, junction, splice, association, relation, liaison, relationship. —*v.* **3.** connect, conjoin, interconnect, tie, tie in, couple, combine, bind, fuse, unite; group, bracket, associate, relate, implicate, involve. —**Ant. 3** separate, sever, divorce, split, part, divide; clear, vindicate.

lionize *v.* acclaim, admire, exalt, praise, glorify, flatter, adulate, revere, celebrate, deify, eulogize, glamorize, aggrandize, ennoble, enshrine, immortalize. —**Ant.** belittle, deprecate, criticize, disparage, ridicule, deride.

liquid *adj.* **1.** fluid, melted, thawed; molten, liquefied; flowing, free-flowing, fluent. —*n.* **2.** drink, beverage, liquid substance, potable; fluid, solution. —**Syn. Study. 2** LIQUID, FLUID agree in referring to matter that is not solid. LIQUID commonly refers to substances, as water, oil, alcohol, and the like, that are neither solids nor gases: *Water ceases to be a liquid when it is frozen or turned to steam.* FLUID is applied to anything that flows, whether liquid or gaseous: *Pipes can carry fluids from place to place.* —**Ant. 1** solid, gaseous; hard, frozen, congealed; stiff, rigid, unyielding. **2** solid; vapor, gas.

liquidate *v.* **1.** settle, pay, discharge, dispose of, clear, pay off, wipe out, account for, put to rest, abolish, erase, cancel. **2.** close out, settle the affairs of, wind up, conclude, terminate. **3.** assassinate, kill, murder, eradicate, demolish, destroy, abolish, do away with, break up; *Slang* rub out, hit, waste.

liquor *n.* **1.** alcoholic beverage, alcoholic drink, spirits, intoxicants, inebriants, distilled spirits; (*variously*) whiskey, Scotch, bourbon, rye, gin, rum, vodka, brandy; *Slang* booze, hooch, sauce. **2.** liquid, juice, drippings, broth, extract.

lissome *adj.* lithe, limber, supple, flexible, pliant, lithesome, quick, nimble, agile, sprightly, lively, slender, graceful, light-footed. **—Ant.** rigid, stiff, wooden, inflexible; clumsy, awkward.

list[1] *n.* **1.** written series, register, roster, roll, muster, record, slate, catalog, inventory; index, schedule, enumeration, table. —*v.* **2.** write in a series, record, write down, catalog, tabulate. **—Syn. Study. 1** LIST, ROLL, CATALOG, INVENTORY imply a meaningful arrangement of items. LIST denotes a series of names, figures, or other items arranged in a row or rows: *a grocery list.* A ROLL is a list of names of members of a group, often used to check attendance: *The teacher called the roll.* CATALOG adds the idea of an alphabetical or other orderly arranged list of goods or services, usu. with descriptive details: *a mail-order catalog.* INVENTORY refers to a detailed, descriptive list of goods or property, made for legal or business purposes: *The company's inventory consists of 2,000 items.*

list[2] *n.* **1.** tilt, leaning, lean, inclination, slant, slope. —*v.* **2.** tilt, lean, incline, slope, slant, heel, tip, careen, bend.

listen *v.* attend, hark, list, heed, hearken, hear, make an effort to hear, pay attention, give heed, take notice, keep one's ears open, give ear, note carefully, prick up the ears, strain one's ears, *Informal* be all ears, bend an ear; eavesdrop, listen in, overhear. **—Ant.** be deaf to, turn a deaf ear to; ignore, neglect, disregard, pay no heed to, take no notice of.

listless *adj.* sluggish, lifeless, lazy, indolent, lacking zest, inactive, dull, spiritless, down, lethargic, lackadaisical, phlegmatic, leaden, soporific, torpid, enervated, sluggish; apathetic, uninterested, indifferent, unconcerned, mopish, languid, dreamy, drowsy. **—Ant.** lively, energetic, active, wide-awake, spirited; alert, interested, attentive.

litany *n.* **1.** ceremonial prayer, prescribed prayer, formal prayer, invocation with responses, prayer of supplication. **2.** recital, recitation, account, catalog, list, repetition, enumeration, rendition, description, narration, recapitulation.

literacy *n.* learning, erudition, eruditeness, scholarship, learnedness, intelligence, enlightenment, edification, culture, intellectuality; store of knowledge, acquisition of knowledge, liberal education. **—Ant.** illiteracy, ignorance, unenlightenment, benightedness.

literal *adj.* **1.** faithful, exact, precise, word-for-word, as close as possible to the original, verbatim, strict, accurate, direct, true, undeviating, *Latin* ad litteram. **2.** accurate, precise, factual, truthful, categorically true, without exaggeration, exact, correct, reliable, unimpeachable, trustworthy, honest, dependable, authoritative, undisputed, meticulous, scrupulous, conscientious, authentic, actual, real. **3.** matter-of-fact, prosaic, unimaginative, taking everything at face value. **—Ant. 1** free, liberal, general, figurative. **2** inaccurate, incorrect, wrong, erroneous, false, nonfactual, untruthful, unreliable, untrustworthy; careless, hazy, inexact, sloppy. **3** figurative; imaginative.

literary *adj.* **1.** of literature, of writings, of belles lettres, of books; fond of books, addicted to reading, bookish; artistic, poetic. **2.** bookish, intellectual, literate, lettered, belonging to the literati. **—Ant. 2** uneducated, unlettered, untutored, untaught, unschooled, unenlightened.

literate *adj.* **1.** able to read and write, proficient in reading and writing. **2.** educated, learned, schooled, well-informed, well-read, cultured, literary, lettered, knowledgeable.

literature *n.* **1.** literary work of lasting value, artistic writing, belles lettres, letters, classics. **2.** writings, works, books, publications, papers, treatises, dissertations, theses; scholarship, lore.

lithe *adj.* limber, supple, bendable, flexible, pliable, pliant, lissome, agile, nimble, graceful. **—Ant.** rigid, stiff, wooden, inflexible; clumsy, awkward.

litigation *n.* lawsuit, legal proceedings, suit, prosecution, contention, legal action, filing of charges, disputation, day in court, judicial process; dispute, contest, controversy.

litter *n.* **1.** scattered rubbish, rubbish, trash, refuse, debris; leavings, junk, mess, heap, jumble, pile. **2.** group of animals born at one birth; offspring, young, issue, progeny. **3.** stretcher, portable bed, portable couch. **4.** bed, nest, lair; bedding, pallet. —*v.* **5.** strew with rubbish, clutter with trash, strew, clutter, scatter; heap, pile, jumble. **—Ant. 5** clean up, pick up; organize, order, arrange, tidy, tidy up, neaten up.

little *adj.* **1.** small, diminutive, petite, bantam, pint-sized, pocket-sized, miniature, wee, tiny, minute, *Slang* itty-bitty, itsy-bitsy; undersized, dwarfish, stunted;

pygmy, elfin, Lilliputian; microscopic, infinitesimal. **2.** small, scant, meager; skimpy, hardly any, not much, scarcely any, short, insufficient, deficient; few and far between, to be counted on one's fingers. **3.** brief, short, hasty, quick, fleet, passing; short-lived, momentary. **4.** trivial, mild, slight, inconsequential, negligible, insignificant, unimportant, trifling, faint, piddling, paltry, of no account. **5.** narrow, petty, mean, shortsighted, opinionated, inflexible; worthless, unworthy, inferior, third-rate, mediocre, commonplace, run-of-the-mill. —*adv.* **6.** not at all, never, by no means, not in a thousand years; in only a small amount, in a small degree, not much, slightly, scarcely, hardly, somewhat; rarely, not often, seldom. —*n.* **7.** small amount, small quantity; pittance, next to nothing, minimum, drop, crumb, iota, jot, dot, whit, bit, speck, fragment, particle, dash, pinch, trifle, modicum, drop in the bucket, trace, hint, suggestion. **—Ant. 1, 2, 4** big, large, great, immense, huge, monstrous, enormous, colossal, giant, giant-sized. **2, 3** much, more than enough, abundant, ample, plentiful. **3** long. **4** major, important, momentous, grave, serious, considerable, significant, consequential. **5** broadminded, farsighted. **6** always, certainly, surely, assuredly; much. **7** lot, much, many.

liturgy *n.* ritual, ceremony, religious ceremony, form of public worship, collection of formularies for public worship, rite, particular arrangement of services; services, worship, service, mass, communion, prayer meeting, sacrament.

livable Also **liveable** *adj.* **1.** suitable for living in, habitable; homey, snug, cozy, comfortable, *Informal* comfy. **2.** worth living, worthwhile, agreeable, comfortable, convenient, enjoyable, pleasant, satisfying, gratifying; bearable, tolerable, endurable, acceptable, passable. **—Ant. 1** uninhabitable, unfit, unsuitable. **2** unpleasant, unsatisfactory; unbearable, intolerable, unendurable, painful, disagreeable.

live[1] *v.* **1.** be alive, have life, draw breath, breathe, have being; exist, be, be animate; see the light of day, come into existence, walk the earth. **2.** remain alive, survive, endure, prevail; cling to life, persist, hold on, abide; stand, obtain, escape destruction, be permanent. **3.** subsist, support oneself, provide for one's needs, maintain life, get along, make ends meet, make one's living; acquire a livelihood, earn money, follow a particular occupation, get ahead. **4.** subsist, feed, be nourished, survive, get along, be supported; thrive, flourish; increase, multiply. **5.** reside, be in residence, dwell, abide, make one's abode, make one's home, occupy, lodge, stay, bunk, billet; settle, remain, take root, pass one's life. **—Ant. 1, 2** die, pass away, decease, expire, perish, demise. **2** wither, fade, languish, decline, decay; depart, vanish. **3** be destitute, be indigent. **4** starve to death, starve.

live[2] *adj.* **1.** alive, living, quick, animate, breathing, existent; vital, physical, corporeal, incarnate, bodily, fleshly. **2.** pertinent, of present interest, active, pressing, prevalent, prevailing; current, present-day, up-to-date, still in use, happening, going on, at hand, at issue, in question. **3.** burning, afire, fiery, blazing, ablaze, aflame, flaming, aglow, glowing, alight, ignited; hot, red-hot, white-hot. **—Ant. 1** dead, defunct, deceased, departed. **2** inactive, dormant, out-of-date, old hat.

livelihood *n.* living, adequate income, support, maintenance, subsistence, sustenance, source of income; occupation, vocation, calling, business, line of work, trade, profession, career, métier; job, situation, position; venture, undertaking, enterprise. **—Ant.** destitution, indigence; avocation, hobby, entertainment, recreation, fun.

lively *adj.* spirited, brisk, sprightly, vivacious, animated, bouncy, energetic, full of life, full of spirit, eager, excited, enthusiastic, buoyant; active, vigorous, alert, peppy, perky; ardent, intense, fervent, vivid, excitable. **—Ant.** lifeless, inactive, dull, slow, sluggish, phlegmatic, leaden, listless, apathetic; decrepit, disabled, debilitated.

liven *v.* quicken, enliven, vivify, animate, invigorate, inspirit, energize, buoy; hearten, strengthen, embolden, fortify; *Slang* perk up, pep up, punch up; cheer, gladden, brighten, elate, delight, exhilarate. **—Ant.** delay, slow down; depress, dispirit, devitalize.

livery *n.* uniform, costume, servant's uniform, vestments, regalia, garb, attire, dress, clothing, raiment, suit.

livid *adj.* **1.** black-and-blue, discolored, purple; bruised, contused. **2.** enraged, irate, incensed, inflamed, furious, infuriated, raging, fuming, mad, angry, wrathful, indignant, *Slang* steamed up, ticked off; outraged, exasperated, vexed, riled, galled, provoked. **—Ant. 2** mollified, assuaged, forgiving; delighted, enchanted, enraptured, blissful, overjoyed, happy, content, pleased.

living *adj.* **1.** alive, live, existing, existent, quick, breathing, this side of the grave; animate, in the flesh, fleshly, bodily, embodied, incarnate, material, corporeal, organic; on the face of the earth, under the sun. **2.** presently in use, alive, live, active, operative, existent, extant, of present interest, up-to-date, going on; surviving, enduring, prevailing, persisting, remaining, permanent. —*n.* **3.** existing, existence, life, being, having life, drawing breath, subsisting, subsistence, animation. **4.** way of life, mode of living, life-style. **5.** income, subsistence, sustenance, livelihood, means of support, maintenance; occupation, vocation, calling, business, trade, profession, career, line of work, job, work, employment; venture, undertaking, enterprise. —**Ant. 1, 2** dead, deceased, expired, defunct, lifeless. **1** inanimate, inorganic. **2** vanishing, perishing, obsolescent; out-of-date, inactive. **3** dying, expiring. **5** destitution, indigence; avocation, hobby, entertainment, recreation, fun.

load *n.* **1.** quantity carried; (*variously*) wagonload, truckload, carload, planeload, shipload; cargo, shipment, freight, lading, haul; capacity, contents. **2.** quantity supported, burden, weight, deadweight, encumbrance, pressure; care, trouble, worry, oppression, misery, depression, affliction, tribulation; misfortune, unhappiness, unhappy lot. —*v.* **3.** fill, lade, pile, pack, heap, stack, stuff; weight, burden. **4.** weigh down, burden, overwhelm, crush, oppress, afflict, trouble, worry, vex, try; hamper, encumber, strain, handicap, hinder. —**Ant. 2** support; solace, consolation. **3** unload, discharge, empty, lighten, unpack. **4** free, liberate.

loaf *v.* waste time, idle, do nothing, kill time, fritter away time, take it easy, laze about, dally, loll, lounge around, twiddle one's thumbs, be lazy, malinger, *Slang* goldbrick, goof off. —**Ant.** work, toil, labor, slave.

loafer *n.* lazy person, idler, loiterer, malingerer, ne'er-do-well, laggard, shirker, wastrel, sluggard, lazybones, *Informal* couch potato, mouse potato; *Slang* deadbeat, bum, no-good, goldbrick, lounge lizard, drugstore cowboy; *Informal* sponger. —**Ant.** hard worker, worker, workingman, workingwoman, laborer.

loan *n.* **1.** permission to borrow, lending; advance, advancing, giving credit, accommodation. **2.** sum of money lent, thing lent, thing borrowed; credit, mortgage, advance. —*v.* **3.** lend, permit to borrow, advance, allow; mortgage, credit. —**Ant. 3** pay back, give back, return.

loath *adj.* unwilling, averse, loth, reluctant, disinclined, indisposed, opposed, counter, resisting, set against, against, hostile, inimical. —**Syn. Study.** See RELUCTANT. —**Ant.** willing, anxious, eager, keen, avid, enthusiastic, desirous, wanting.

loathe *v.* detest, hate, despise, dislike, find disgusting, abominate, abhor, deplore, be unable to bear, have a strong aversion to, have no stomach for; scorn, disdain, eschew, keep clear of, shrink from, recoil from, draw back from, blench from, flinch from, shy away from, view with horror. —**Ant.** love, adore; like, admire, relish, fancy, dote on, enjoy; desire, crave, hanker after, long for.

loathsome *adj.* detestable, hateful, despicable, disgusting, repulsive, abominable, abhorrent, unbearable, revolting, repugnant, nasty, vile, obnoxious, offensive, sickening, odious, nauseating, rank, mean, invidious, distasteful, foul. —**Ant.** lovable, adorable, likable, engaging, attractive, alluring, charming, delightful.

lobby *n.* **1.** vestibule, entrance hall, foyer, reception hall, anteroom, waiting room, reception room, antechamber. —*v.* **2.** politick, urge legislative action, solicit legislative votes, seek to influence legislators, exert influence, bring pressure to bear, *Informal* pull strings.

local *adj.* citywide, regional, sectional, provincial, neighborhood, territorial, native, homegrown; geographically restricted, limited, circumscribed, confined, narrow, insular, parochial; nearby, adjoining. —**Ant.** international, worldwide, national, nationwide; foreign, exotic.

locale *n.* setting, place where events occur, location, locality, site, spot, area, quarter, zone, vicinity, region, neighborhood, section, province, precinct.

locality *n.* neighborhood, area, district, section, province, precinct, zone, quarter, vicinity, region, territory, location; locale, place, site, spot.

locate *v.* **1.** find, discover the whereabouts of, track down, ferret out, search out, unearth, uncover, pinpoint, discern, detect, hit upon, come upon, light upon, stumble on, meet with, lay one's hands on. **2.** situate, place, establish, set down, seat, deposit, put, fix, station, post. **3.** settle, settle down, reside, take up residence, dwell, live, stay, establish one's home, put down roots, set up housekeeping; move to. —**Ant. 1** lose, shake; hide, conceal. **2** dislodge, displace. **3** leave, quit, forsake, abandon, desert, vacate.

location *n.* whereabouts, position, site, spot, place, situation, locale; neighborhood, district.

lock[1] *n.* **1.** fastening device, securing device, fastening; (*variously*) bolt, padlock, safety catch, latch; clasp, hook, clamp, catch. **2.** canal gate, dock gate, floodgate, sluice gate, dam. —*v.* **3.** fasten, secure, (*variously*) bolt, padlock, bar. **4.** secure, lock up, keep under lock and key; shut in, confine, jail, imprison, incarcerate, cage, pen, coop up, impound, put behind bars. **5.** join, entwine, link, interlink, unite, intertwine; clinch, grip, hold, grasp, clasp, grapple, seize, hold, grab, embrace. **—Ant. 3** unlock, unbolt, unbar, unfasten; open. **4, 5** free, release, let go.

lock² *n.* tress, ringlet, curl, hank, tuft, coil, skein, bang.

lockup *n.* jail, prison, penitentiary, reformatory, house of detention, house of correction; *Slang* slammer, jug, cooler, big house, pen, stir, clink, hoosegow.

locution *n.* expression, regionalism, term, idiom, saying, wording, verbalism, phrase, phrasing, usage, utterance, turn of phrase, turn of expression, set phrase, trope, figure of speech, phraseology, idiolect.

lodge *n.* **1.** cabin, cottage; hut, shelter; hotel, motel, resort, camp; country house. **—***v.* **2.** stay, put up, obtain lodgings, sojourn, room, furnish with lodgings, house, billet, bed, quarter, shelter, harbor. **3.** catch, become fixed, be positioned. **4.** submit, file, register, enter formally, place on record, make known.

lodging *n.* temporary quarters, place to stay, overnight accommodation, a room, bed for the night, temporary sleeping accommodations.

loft *n.* **1.** attic room, attic, garret, mansard; top floor, balcony, clerestory, gallery; belfry. **—***v.* **2.** throw high, lob, pop up, hit high, strike in a high arc. **—Ant. 1** basement, cellar. **2** ground.

lofty *adj.* **1.** soaring, towering, tall, high, elevated, high-reaching. **2.** exalted, imposing, stately, elevated, dignified, majestic, sublime, noble; high, high ranking, mighty, important, superior, distinguished, leading, illustrious, eminent, preeminent, glorious, grand, great. **3.** proud, haughty, arrogant, lordly, disdainful, scornful, insolent, aloof, distant, remote, cold, high-and-mighty, *Slang* hoity-toity; snobbish, imperious, patronizing, condescending, self-important, conceited; *Informal* puffed-up, stuck-up, snooty. **—Ant. 1** low, short, stunted, dwarfed. **2** lowly, undignified, debased, mean, ignoble, degraded, cheap; low, low ranking. **3** modest, unassuming, humble; friendly, cordial, hospitable, warm, receptive, open.

log *n.* **1.** length of tree trunk, timber, part of tree limb; block, stump. **2.** logbook; (*loosely*) daybook, journal, calendar, diary, docket, schedule, account, record. **—***v.* **3.** cut timber, fell trees, work as a lumberjack, lumber.

logic *n.* **1.** science of reasoning, syllogistic reasoning, inductive reasoning, organized thinking, argument, dialectics, deduction, induction, analysis. **2.** good sense, sound judgment, organized reasoning, reason, chain of thought, sense, coherence, cogency.

logical *adj.* **1.** consistent, well-organized, cogent, coherent, clear, rational, sound, reasonable, intelligent; relevant, pertinent, germane; valid, deducible; analytical. **2.** reasonable, likely, most likely, plausible, intelligent, enlightened, sensible. **—Ant. 1** illogical, inconsistent, unorganized, incoherent, irrational, unreasonable; intuitive, instinctive. **2** illogical, unlikely, implausible.

logy *adj.* drowsy, lethargic, sleepy, tired, dull, torpid, sluggish, groggy, weary, inert, enervated, phlegmatic, drowsy, listless, lifeless, inanimate, hebetudinous, comatose. **—Ant.** active, energetic, lively, animated, spirited, vigorous.

loiter *v.* linger idly about, hang around, hover around; skulk, lurk, slink; loll, laze, idle, loaf; tarry, dillydally, dally, dawdle, shilly-shally, procrastinate. **—Syn. Study.** LOITER, IDLE, DALLY, DAWDLE imply moving or acting slowly, stopping for unimportant reasons, and in general wasting time. To LOITER is to linger aimlessly: *to loiter outside a building.* To IDLE is to move slowly and aimlessly, or to spend a great deal of time doing nothing: *to idle away the hours.* To DALLY is to loiter indecisively or to delay as if free from care or responsibility: *to dally on the way home.* To DAWDLE is to saunter, stopping often and taking a great deal of time, or to fritter away time working in a halfhearted way: *to dawdle over a task.* **—Ant.** hasten, hurry, scurry, scuttle, scamper.

loll *v.* **1.** lounge, loaf, idle, dawdle, languish, take it easy, repose, relax; *Slang* goof off; recline, lean, slouch, slump, sprawl, flop over. **2.** dangle, droop, hang loosely; flop, flap, sag, drop, drag.

lone *adj.* sole, single, solitary, individual, alone, only, unattended, unescorted, unaccompanied, unpaired, unabetted, companionless, isolated, unique, singular.

lonely *adj.* **1.** by oneself, solitary, without company, unaccompanied, unattended, companionless; secluded, withdrawn, reclusive, hermitic, unsocial. **2.** lonesome, depressed by solitude, lacking companionship, friendless, forlorn, forsaken. **3.** isolated, secluded, remote, desolate, deserted, lonesome, unpopulated, uninhabited, unfrequented. **—Ant. 1** accompanied, together. **2** popular, befriended. **3** crowded, mobbed, populous, frequented, teeming, swarming, bustling.

lonesome *adj.* lonely, companionless,

unfriended, alone, friendless, forlorn, desolate, forsaken, alienated; aloof, detached, withdrawn, insular. **—Ant.** sociable, gregarious, friendly, popular.

long[1] *adj.* **1.** lengthy, extended, prolonged, protracted, drawn-out, spun out; interminable, unending. **2.** lengthy, extended, extensive, elongated, protracted, far-reaching, outstretched. *—n.* **3.** a long time, an extended period. *—adv.* **4.** throughout a period of time; over an extended period; during the time, throughout the period. **5.** in length, from end to end. **—Ant. 1, 2** short, brief; little, small. **1** momentary, fleeting, short-lived, quick. **2** abridged, abbreviated, curtailed, compressed.

long[2] *v.* yearn, crave, hunger, thirst, lust, hanker, sigh, pine, have a desire, have a yen for, hope, want, wish, aspire, have one's heart set on, covet, be bent upon. **—Syn. Study.** See YEARN. **—Ant.** despise, detest, loathe, abhor, abominate, hate, deplore, be repelled by; spurn, scorn, disdain, eschew, reject, renounce, forsake, refuse.

longing *n.* **1.** desire, strong desire, yearning, craving, hungering, thirst, wish; aspiration; *Informal* hankering, yen. *—adj.* **2.** desirous, yearning, craving, hankering, hungering, wishful, pining, languishing, ardent. **—Syn. Study. 1** See DESIRE. **—Ant. 1** disinterest, indifference, unconcern, apathy; loathing, disgust, hatred, abhorrence, antipathy, repulsion, revulsion. **2** disinterested, indifferent, unconcerned, apathetic, cold, cool; loathsome, disgusting, hateful, scornful.

longstanding *adj.* long-lived, long-lasting, enduring, long, lasting, durable, perennial, long-established, abiding, persisting, perpetual, ancient, rooted; hallowed, time-honored, venerable, hoary, unfading, hardy. **—Ant.** short, transient, passing, short-lived, transitory.

look *v.* **1.** see, watch, turn the eyes upon, fix the eyes on, regard, contemplate, stare, gape, glance, peep, scan, peek, behold, give attention to, study, scrutinize, survey, examine. **2.** appear, seem, show, present evidence, exhibit, manifest, strike one as being, have the expression, cut a figure, carry the appearance. **3.** face, front, have a view of, be directed, be situated opposite. *—n.* **4.** glance, glimpse, peek, peep, visual examination, once-over, contemplation, survey, scrutiny, visual search, reconnaissance, stare, view, observation, sight, gaze, ogle, glare. **5.** appearance, general aspect, countenance, presence, mien, expression, demeanor, air, guise, cast, bearing. **—Syn. Study. 2** See SEEM. **—Ant. 1** be blind, be unseeing; close one's eyes to, overlook, miss, pass over, neglect, ignore, disregard.

lookout *n.* **1.** alertness, watchfulness, readiness, vigilance, surveillance, guardedness, vigil, awareness, attention, mindfulness, heed, precaution. **2.** sentinel, watchman, guard, sentry, watchdog, observer, spotter, patrol, scout, watchkeeper, forward observer.

loom *v.* tower, soar, ascend; come into view suddenly, emerge, rise, appear; stand forth, stand out, hulk, take shape. **—Ant.** vanish, disappear, melt away, fade away, dissolve from view.

loop *n.* **1.** circle, spiral, whorl, convolution, twirl, coil; eye, eyelet, ring, ringlet, noose, opening, loophole, aperture; bend, twist, curve. *—v.* **2.** wind around, bend, twist, twirl, turn, curve around, encircle, circle, coil, curl, roll, furl; plait, braid.

loose *adj., adv.* **1.** unbound, untied, unfastened, free, freed, freely, liberated; untethered, unchained, unfettered, unyoked, unleashed, uncaged, unimprisoned; unattached, unconnected, unjoined. **2.** slack, free, not fitting tightly, not binding, not tight, not fastened; loosely. *—adj.* **3.** wanton, profligate, abandoned, dissipated, debauched, wild, fast, dissolute, licentious, immoral, libertine, lewd, unbridled, unconstrained, unchaste, rakehell. **4.** inexact, unexacting, imprecise, inaccurate, vague, careless, slack, heedless. *—v.* **5.** untie, untether, unbind, unfasten, loosen, unloose, undo; free, set free, release, let go, liberate; unbridle, unshackle, unchain, unleash, unmanacle, unhandcuff; slacken. **—Ant. 1** tied, bound, secured, fastened, tethered, fettered, chained; restrained, leashed, curbed. **2** tight. **3** moral, abstemious, virtuous, chaste, disciplined, puritanical, Spartan. **4** precise, exact, accurate, clear, meticulous. **5** tie, bind, fasten, tether, fetter, chain, manacle, handcuff; capture, cage, imprison.

loot *n.* **1.** spoils, plunder, booty, prize, take, stolen goods; *Slang* boodle, haul, swag. *—v.* **2.** plunder, pillage, ravage, sack, ransack, raid, rob, fleece, strip, pilfer.

lopsided *adj.* off-balance, askew, unequal, asymmetric, unbalanced, disproportional, irregular, uneven, disproportionate, crooked, *Slang* cockeyed, leaning, inclined, slanting, listing, tipped, tilting, slanted. **—Ant.** symmetrical, balanced, even, well-proportioned, straight.

loquacious *adj.* talkative, talky, prolix, garrulous, wordy, verbose, voluble, windy, long-winded; prating, chatty, chattery, chattering, babbling, prattling; *Informal* gabby, blabby. **—Syn. Study.** See TALKATIVE. **—Ant.** silent, reserved, taciturn, closemouthed, uncommunicative, reticent.

lord *n.* king, ruler, sovereign, monarch, crown; master, superior, chief, overlord, leader, commander; feudal superior, seignior, landowner, landholder, proprietor.

lordly *adj.* **1.** fit for a lord, grand, majestic, regal, magnificent, elegant, sumptuous, stately, princely; lofty, imposing, magisterial, noble; eminent, august, exalted, dignified. **2.** haughty, arrogant, lofty, proud, disdainful, scornful, aloof, distant, remote, cold, high-and-mighty, hoity-toity, snobbish, imperious, patronizing, condescending, conceited, self-important, *Informal* stuck-up, puffed-up, snooty; tyrannical, despotic, domineering, dictatorial, bossy. **—Ant. 1** lowly, plebeian, humble, modest, mean, abject. **2** modest, unassuming, humble; servile, submissive, gentle, mild.

lore *n.* popular knowledge, traditional knowledge, anecdotal knowledge; practical knowledge; traditions, beliefs, legends.

lose *v.* **1.** suffer loss of, incur the loss of, be deprived of, misplace, mislay; miss, be thrown off. **2.** stray from, miss, confuse; forget, ignore, fail to heed. **3.** be defeated in, be the loser, fail to win, suffer defeat in, fail, have the worst of it, forfeit, take a licking, come out second best. **—Ant. 1** keep, retain, hold; save, preserve; find, recover, get back. **2** find. **3** win, have the best of it.

loss *n.* **1.** wreck, wrecking, destruction, demolition, ruin, annihilation; extermination, extirpation, extinction, eradication; abolition, dissolution, removal. **2.** forfeiture, deprivation, privation, bereavement, expenditure, riddance; amount lost, number lost. **3.** losing, failure to win, defeat, undoing, overturn, vanquishment; *Slang* licking. **4.** losing, misplacing, mislaying, being without. **—Ant. 1** saving, preservation. **2** gain, acquisition; restoration, recovery, reimbursement. **3** winning, win. **4** finding, recovery.

lost *adj.* **1.** missing, mislaid, misplaced, gone out of one's possession; vanished, strayed, stray, astray, absent, lacking. **2.** gone astray, unable to find one's way, off-course. **3.** destroyed, wrecked, demolished, ruined, wiped out, abolished, obliterated, annihilated, exterminated, eradicated, extirpated; killed, murdered, perished. **4.** wasted, misapplied, squandered, misdirected, misused. **5.** absorbed, preoccupied, engrossed. **—Ant. 1** found, recovered, reclaimed, returned. **3** saved, preserved.

lot *n.* **1.** straw, counter. **2.** fate, allotted portion, share; apportionment, allowance, ration, measure, quota, proportion, allotment. **3.** parcel of land, plot, property, tract, piece of ground, portion of land; field, patch. **4.** great deal, much, many, *Informal* lots, lots and lots, oceans, oodles, gazillion; *French* beaucoup.

lothario *n.* lover, rake, Don Juan, Romeo, Casanova, seducer, roué, debauchee, debaucher, lecher, libertine, philanderer, sensualist, womanizer, sheik, lady-killer, skirt-chaser, profligate; *Slang* wolf, rip, lover-boy, swinger.

lotion *n.* ointment, cosmetic, balm, liniment, unction, wash, conditioner, unguent, salve, conditioner, skin cream, freshener, demulcent, emollient, moisturizer, embrocation, astringent, aftershave.

loud *adj.* **1.** noisy, earsplitting, earpiercing, deafening, clamorous, resounding, sonorous, stentorian, booming, thundering, blatant, intense; vociferous, loudmouthed. **2.** garish, gaudy, splashy, flashy; bright, vivid, colorful; showy, ostentatious. **—Ant. 1** soft, subdued; quiet, silent, inaudible. **2** sedate, somber, dull, colorless, conservative.

lounge *v.* **1.** loaf, idle, take it easy, do nothing, relax, lie around, pass time idly, fritter away time, kill time, dawdle, dally, dillydally; recline, repose, stretch out, laze, languish, flop, loll, sprawl, slump, slouch; rest, sleep, slumber. **—*n.*** **2.** (*loosely*) sofa, couch, divan, davenport; daybed. **3.** lobby, reception room, reception hall, vestibule; sitting room, reading room.

lousy *adj.* **1.** pediculous, infested with lice. **2.** *Slang* mean, shabby, nasty, crummy, unethical, unkind, hateful, vicious, contemptible, dreadful, unpleasant; inferior, bad, terrible, rotten, awful, second-rate, worthless.

lout *n.* boor, churl, clod, oaf, dunce, clown, lummox, ape, booby, dullard, dummy, yokel, rustic, bumpkin; *Slang* klutz. **—Ant.** gentleman, sophisticate, dandy, swell.

lovable Also **loveable** *adj.* adorable, winsome, endearing, engaging, winning, enchanting, captivating, lovely, charming, taking, fetching, delightful, cute, sweet, cuddly, darling. **—Ant.** hateful, detestable, odious, obnoxious, abominable, abhorrent, loathsome, repugnant, revolting, repellent, offensive.

love *n.* **1.** passion, passionate affection, the tender passion, rapture, amorousness, ardor, amour, infatuation; devotion, adoration, fondness, tenderness, affection, affectionate regard, warm personal attachment, warm feeling, sentiment, emotion, esteem, admiration; friendship, amity, brotherhood, fellow feeling, compatibility, affinity, sympathy, concord, congeniality, cordiality; charity, goodwill, benevolence, solicitude. **2.** strong liking, fondness, devotion, relish, taste, predilection, attachment, penchant, leaning, partiality, inclination, proclivity, weakness, turn, bent, mind. **3.** beloved, loved one, inamorata, truelove, paramour, lover, mistress, flame, light of one's life; sweetheart, darling, dear, dearest, precious, angel, sweetie, sweetie pie, honey; boyfriend, beau, fellow, man; girlfriend, girl, woman; fondness, attachment, penchant, choice. —*v.* **4.** have a passionate affection for, be filled with rapture by, feel amorous toward, be infatuated with, be enamored of, be devoted to, adore, be fond of, feel tenderness toward, lose one's heart to, hold dear, regard affectionately, feel warmly toward, admire, esteem, treasure, cherish; sympathize with, feel goodwill toward, feel solicitude for. **5.** like immensely, be fond of, be devoted to, relish, delight in, fancy, take pleasure in, enjoy, appreciate, savor, bask in, rejoice in, revel in, luxuriate in; *Slang* get a kick out of; have a penchant for, have a leaning toward, have a partiality for, have an inclination toward, be drawn to, have a weakness for. **—Ant. 1–3** hate, hatred, dislike, distaste, aversion, abhorrence, repugnance, repulsion, disgust, loathing, abomination, detestation, contempt, scorn. **1** animosity, antipathy, antagonism, acrimony, animus, bitterness, resentment, hostility, opposition, malice, ill will, incompatibility, uncongeniality. **3** enemy, foe, rival. **4, 5** hate, dislike, abhor, be disgusted by, loathe, abominate, detest, scorn. **5** find distasteful, be averse to, find repugnant.

lovely *adj.* attractive, handsome, comely, beautiful, adorable, exquisite, elegant, pretty; delightful, charming, enchanting, fascinating, enjoyable, agreeable, pleasing, pleasant; winsome, winning, lovable, cute, sweet, captivating, alluring, engaging, endearing, irresistible, fetching; good, fine. **—Syn. Study.** See BEAUTIFUL. **—Ant.** ugly, hideous, unattractive, tasteless; hateful, detestable, odious, obnoxious, offensive, distasteful, abominable, abhorrent, loathsome, repugnant, revolting, repelling, awful, bad.

lover *n.* **1.** paramour, mistress, *Informal* significant other; beloved, loved one, inamorata, truelove, love, sweetheart; dear, darling, sweetie, honey; boyfriend, beau, fellow, swain, lover boy, suitor, wooer, admirer, man; girlfriend, girl, woman. **2.** devotee, enthusiast, aficionado, follower; fan, buff, fanatic; *Slang* nut, freak.

loving *adj.* affectionate, fond, tender, amorous, erotic, ardent, passionate, enamored, amatory, devoted, doting; warm, sympathetic, caring, kind, friendly, warmhearted, solicitous, benevolent. **—Ant.** unloving, hateful, distasteful, disgusting, contemptuous, scornful, angry, hostile; indifferent, unconcerned, aloof, detached, cold, chilly, frigid, mean, cruel.

low *adj.* **1.** near the ground, not far above the horizon, low-lying; unelevated; near the floor, low-slung; lower. **2.** short, of less than average height, having little elevation, squat, stumpy, stubby, dumpy, snubbed, sawed-off, truncated; small, little. **3.** low-lying, below sea level, near sea level, unelevated, coastal; concave, sunken, depressed; underwater, submerged, deep, undersea, submarine; underground. **4.** unhappy, depressed, dejected, disheartened, despondent, doleful, downcast, down, melancholy, gloomy, dispirited, glum, lethargic; in the doldrums, blue, down in the dumps, down in the mouth. **5.** small, little; lowly, humble, insignificant, inconsequential, unimportant, low ranking, paltry, trifling, common, mediocre, inferior. **6.** mean, base, vile, awful, terrible, scurvy, despicable, ignominious, dishonorable, unworthy, contemptible, abominable, repulsive, repugnant, heinous, cruel, brutal, outrageous, scandalous, disrespectful, nefarious, scoundrelly, corrupt, unethical, wicked, evil, cowardly, dastardly; degraded, depraved, sordid, squalid, gross, coarse, vulgar, obscene, dirty; *Slang* crummy, cruddy. **7.** subdued, hushed, muffled, muted, quiet; whispered, murmured, faint, feeble; soft, gentle, soothing; low-pitched, of a low tone. —*adv.* **8.** in or to a low position, prone, prostrate; to a low degree; in a low tone, quietly, softly; deep. **—Syn. Study. 6** See MEAN. **—Ant. 1–5, 7, 8** high. **2** tall, lofty, soaring, towering. **3** elevated. **4** happy, elated, cheerful, gay, enthusiastic, peppy, full of pep, energetic, alert, bright-eyed and bushy-tailed. **5** superior, grand, lofty, elevated, exalted, eminent, consequential, significant, important, illustrious, high ranking, above average. **6** wonderful, fine, admirable, commendable, praiseworthy, laudable, meritorious, creditable, honorable, worthy, uplifted, angelic; courteous; brave. **7** loud, noisy, strong, raucous; high-pitched.

lower[1] *v.* **1.** make lower, decrease the height of, drop, pull down, let down, take down, put down, depress; submerge, immerse, duck, sink. **2.** decrease, reduce, diminish, make less, curtail, pare, pare down, cut, shorten, abbreviate, prune, lop off, render less, subtract from, detract from, deduct. **3.** tone down, soften, subdue, make less intense, dim, damp, muffle, mute, repress. —*adj.* **4.** reduced, decreased, diminished, lessened, curtailed, pared, pared down. —**Ant. 1–3** raise. **1** elevate, lift up, pull up, hoist. **2** increase, enlarge, inflate, boost, magnify, amplify, augment, aggrandize; extend, protract, prolong. **4** higher, increased, enlarged.

lower² *v.* **1.** scowl, glare, look sullen, give a dark look, frown, sulk, glower. **2.** grow dark, become threatening.

low-key *adj.* subdued, toned-down, restrained, modulated, subtle, understated, relaxed, low-pressure, muted, low-pitched, gentle, soft, muffled, softened; *Slang* laid-back, loose, soft-sell. —**Ant.** shrill, blatant, obvious, high-pitched, bold, obtrusive.

lowly *adj.* **1.** humble, simple, modest, unassuming, unpretentious, obscure, lowbred, lowborn, baseborn, plebeian, proletarian, ignoble. —*adv.* **2.** low, in or to a low position, to a low degree; in a low tone, softly. —**Ant. 1** exalted, elevated, lofty; proud, conceited.

low-priced *adj.* cheap, inexpensive, reasonable, cut-rate, moderate, dirt-cheap, reduced, economical, budget, token, marked-down, closeout, bargain-basement, low-cost, nominal. —**Ant.** expensive, high-priced, costly, dear, exorbitant.

low-spirited *adj.* depressed, sad, dejected, heartsore, dispirited, melancholy, glum, gloomy, unhappy, crestfallen, blue, down, forlorn, downhearted, downcast, morose, down-in-the-mouth, woebegone. —**Ant.** happy, cheerful, upbeat, high-spirited.

loyal *adj.* faithful, steadfast, true, constant, reliable, trusty, trustworthy, devoted, dependable, resolute, unwavering, unswerving, staunch, firm, dutiful, scrupulous, true-blue, tried and true. —**Syn. Study.** See FAITHFUL. —**Ant.** disloyal, false, faithless, unfaithful, perfidious, treacherous, untrustworthy; rebellious, traitorous, treasonous.

loyalty *n.* faithfulness, fidelity, steadfastness, constancy, trustworthiness, reliability, devotion, dependability, staunchness, firmness, allegiance, adherence, fealty. —**Ant.** disloyalty, falsity, falseness, faithlessness, inconstancy, perfidiousness, perfidy, treachery; sedition, rebellion, insurrection.

lozenge *n.* pastille, small confection, drop, troche; cough drop, small medicated confection, tablet, pill.

lucid *adj.* **1.** shining, bright, clear, transparent, crystalline, brilliant, resplendent, radiant, lustrous, luminous, scintillating, sparkling, dazzling; pellucid; illuminated. **2.** clear, easily understood, crystal clear, intelligible, understandable, articulate, comprehensible; precise, direct, straightforward, accurate, specific, well-organized, to the point, apposite, positive, certain. **3.** clearheaded, clear thinking, normal, rational; responsive, perceptive. —**Ant. 1** dark, darkling, gloomy, dusky, obscure, opaque, turgid, muddy, murky; overcast. **2** unintelligible, incomprehensible, vague, indistinct, unclear, ambiguous, equivocal, garbled, mystifying. **3** confused, muddled, irrational; unresponsive, unperceptive.

luck *n.* **1.** fortune, fate, lot, destiny, karma, kismet; chance, fortuity, happenstance, accident, Lady Luck, wheel of fortune. **2.** good luck, good fortune, happy accident, piece of luck, smile of fortune; success, victory, triumph. —**Ant. 1** design, cause and effect. **2** bad luck; failure, defeat.

lucky *adj.* **1.** fortunate, blest with good luck, in luck, favored, blessed, born under a lucky star. **2.** fortunate, opportune, timely, beneficial, good, happy, felicitous, providential, auspicious, propitious, favorable, bringing good luck, of good omen, promising. —**Syn. Study. 1, 2** See FORTUNATE. —**Ant. 1, 2** unlucky, luckless, unfortunate, ill-starred, ill-favored. **2** untimely, detrimental, bad, unhappy; inauspicious, unfavorable, unpromising, sinister, ominous.

lucrative *adj.* profitable, moneymaking, remunerative, high-paying, gainful, high-income; beneficial, fruitful. —**Ant.** unprofitable, low-paying, unremunerative.

ludicrous *adj.* ridiculous, absurd, crazy, outlandish, preposterous, nonsensical; amusing, laughable, comic, comical, funny, farcical; *Slang* wild, far-out. —**Ant.** sensible, logical; tragic, grave, solemn, serious, sad, sorry, doleful, dolorous, melancholy.

lug *v.* drag, tote, carry, carry with difficulty, heave, transport; pull, bear, tow, draw, haul, tug.

luggage *n.* baggage, bags, suitcases, valises, trunks; effects, gear, accouterments.

lugubrious *adj.* melancholy, dolorous, mournful, sorrowful, downcast, rueful, woeful, dour, glum, gloomy, depressing, miserable, woebegone, funereal, somber, elegiac. —**Ant.** joyous, lighthearted, cheerful, ebullient, happy.

lukewarm *adj.* **1.** tepid, warm, mild, room-temperature, body-temperature, temperate. **2.** halfhearted, unenthusiastic, aloof, cool, unconcerned, detached, indifferent, uninterested, apathetic, uncaring, perfunctory, lackadaisical. —**Ant. 2** impassioned, enthusiastic, wholehearted, caring.

lull *v.* **1.** soothe, quiet, calm, pacify,

hush, still, quell, subdue, compose, assuage, mollify, ease. —*n.* **2.** hush, quiet, temporary stillness, brief silence, quiet interval, pause, break, interlude, interruption, halt, hiatus, gap, caesura, lacuna, short rest, respite, recess, breather, breathing spell; calm, calmness, tranquillity. **—Ant. 1** excite, arouse, rouse, aggravate, provoke, incite. **2** continuation, resumption; flow, gush, spurt; excitement, tumult, turbulence, violence.

lumber[1] *n.* **1.** wood, construction wood, building wood, boards, planks. —*v.* **2.** log, work as a lumberjack, fell trees; cut timber into boards, prepare logs for market, operate a sawmill.

lumber[2] *v.* waddle, trudge, move clumsily, barge, move heavily, plod, clump, stamp, shamble, shuffle, flounder.

luminary *n.* **1.** light, luminosity, body that gives off light; source of light, illuminator. **2.** celebrity, famous person, eminent person, personage, dignitary, notable, *Slang* bigwig, big shot, wheel, somebody.

luminescent *adj.* glowing, aglow, luminous, gleaming, glimmering, shimmering; glistening, twinkling, flickering; fluorescent, phosphorescent, not incandescent, glowing without heat. **—Ant.** incandescent, caused by heat, hot.

luminous *adj.* reflecting light, luminescent, radiant, irradiated, glowing, lustrous, illuminated, shining; shining in the dark; bright, brilliant.

lump *n.* **1.** mass, gob, chunk, clod, clump, cake, hunk. **2.** bump, swelling, protuberance, knot, knob, node, nodule, knurl, protrusion, excrescence; tumor, tumescence, growth. —*v.* **3.** heap, pile, unite, mass, amass, gather, bunch, batch, group, compile, assemble, aggregate, collect; combine, merge, pool, fuse, mix, blend. **—Ant. 1** granule, grain, particle, bit. **2** depression, cavity, concavity, hollow, indentation, dent, pit, dip, dimple. **3** scatter, disperse; separate, divide.

lunacy *n.* **1.** insanity, insaneness, madness, mental derangement, dementia, mania, psychopathic condition. **2.** folly, foolishness, foolhardiness, imprudence, absurdity, silliness, senselessness, craziness; imbecility, idiocy, stupidity, asininity. **—Ant. 1** sanity, reason. **2** good sense, prudence.

lunatic *n.* **1.** madman, maniac, insane person, deranged person, crazy person; psychopath, demoniac; *Slang* nut, cuckoo, loony. —*adj.* **2.** insane, crazy, mad, deranged, demented, maniacal, unhinged, unbalanced, daft, irrational, non compos mentis, of unsound mind, mentally ill, senseless, reasonless; *Slang* nutty, cracked, crackbrained, batty, screwy, loony, cuckoo, touched, loco, off one's rocker, touched in the head, out of one's mind, not all there, not right in the head, not in one's right mind; psychotic, psychopathic; *British* round the bend, crackers, bonkers, potty. **—Ant. 2** sane, sound, rational, reasonable; *Slang* all there.

luncheonette *n.* café, diner, coffee shop, sandwich shop, lunchroom, beanery, eating house, snack bar, lunch counter, hash house.

lunge *n.* **1.** charge, rush, plunge, lurch, dash, dive, thrust; lightning attack, jab, stab, pass, swing, swipe, cut. —*v.* **2.** thrust, jab, stab, strike at, hit at; attack, charge, pounce, make a pass, set upon, fall upon. **—Ant. 2** recoil, step back; parry.

lurch *v.* roll, pitch, list, tilt, incline, cant, keel, slant, toss, swerve; jerk forward, lunge, plunge; stagger, stumble, sway, careen, reel, totter, teeter.

lure *n.* **1.** bait, decoy; trap, snare. **2.** enticement, allurement, inducement, allure, attraction, temptation; blandishment, cajolery, bribe; *Slang* come-on, drawing card. —*v.* **3.** entice, allure, attract, tempt, tantalize, fascinate, beguile, seduce; coax, cajole, persuade, induce. **—Ant. 1** repellent. **3** revolt, repel, deter.

lurid *adj.* **1.** fiery, bright-red, flaming, bloody, sanguine, scarlet, carmine, rubicund; glaring, glowing, shining. **2.** sensational, graphic, dramatic, vivid, melodramatic, wildly emotional; appalling, shocking, grim, ghastly, eerie, gory, bloodcurdling. **—Ant. 1** pale, watery, pastel. **2** mild, lighthearted, gay, sunny, breezy, jaunty, carefree.

lurk *v.* skulk, slink, sneak, prowl, lie in wait, lie concealed, hide, lie in ambush; go furtively. **—Syn. Study.** LURK, SKULK, SNEAK, PROWL suggest avoiding observation, often because of a sinister purpose. To LURK is to lie in wait for someone or to move stealthily: *The thief lurked in the shadows.* SKULK has a similar sense, but usu. suggests cowardice or fear: *The dog skulked about the house.* SNEAK emphasizes the attempt to avoid being seen or discovered; it suggests a villainous intent or the desire to avoid punishment: *The children sneaked out the back way.* PROWL usu. implies seeking prey or loot; it suggests quiet and watchful roaming: *The cat was prowling in search of mice.*

luscious *adj.* delicious, mouth-watering, succulent, sweet and juicy, delectable, appetizing, flavorful, tasty, savory, toothsome; fragrant, scented, perfumed, aromatic. **—Ant.** sour, acid, vinegary, tart, bitter; bland, flavorless, tasteless.

lush *adj.* **1.** luxuriant, profuse, flourishing, dense, prolific, abundant, rich. **2.** luxurious, grand, sumptuous, elegant, magnificent, elaborate, ornate, splendid, fancy; *Slang* posh. **—Ant. 1** sparse, thin, meager, scanty; barren, arid. **2** plain, simple, crude, Spartan.

lust *n.* **1.** passion, strong desire, craving; bodily appetite, fleshly desire, sexuality, libidinousness, lasciviousness, lewdness, salaciousness, satyriasis, nymphomania, carnality, lechery. *—v.* **2.** desire intensely, crave, have a passion for, covet, hunger for; seek sexually, be lascivious, be libidinous, be lewd, be lecherous. **—Ant. 1** unconcern, apathy. **2** be indifferent; spurn, disdain, scorn.

luster *n.* **1.** shine, gleam, sheen, gloss, polish, burnish, brightness, brilliance, resplendence, sparkle, radiance, refulgence, glow, glimmer, glitter, dazzle; radiation, luminosity, luminousness. **2.** glory, distinction, illustriousness, fame, prestige, honor, merit, notability. **—Syn. Study. 1** See POLISH. **—Ant. 1** dullness; tarnish. **2** ignominy, dishonor, shame, infamy, disrepute.

lustrous *adj.* bright, luminous, radiant, glistening, illuminated, burnished, effulgent, incandescent, dazzling, coruscating, glossy, shining, gleaming, polished, glowing. **—Ant.** dim, drab, dull, dingy, lusterless.

lusty *adj.* hearty, hale, full of life, vigorous, robust, virile, husky, brawny, rugged, sturdy, strapping, healthy, sound; exuberant, wholehearted, unrestrained, uninhibited, irrepressible. **—Ant.** lifeless, dull, lethargic, listless; effete, exhausted, feeble, weak, infirm, decrepit, frail, sickly.

luxuriant *adj.* **1.** lush, flourishing, dense, profuse, exuberant, abundant, overgrown, rank, teeming. **2.** elaborate, ornate, fancy, elegant, magnificent, splendid, extravagant, luxurious, grand, sumptuous; florid, flamboyant, flowery. **—Ant. 1** sparse, thin, meager, scanty; barren, arid. **2** plain, simple, unadorned.

luxuriate *v.* bask, delight, indulge in, relish, rejoice in, wallow in, live in luxury.

luxurious *adj.* **1.** expensive, costly, rich, grand, elegant, sumptuous; enjoyable, comfortable, pleasurable, gratifying, pleasure-giving. **2.** costly, extremely comfortable, wealthy, given to luxury; loving luxury, indulgent, overindulged, pampered; effete, decadent. **—Ant. 2** ascetic, austere, Spartan, deprived; frugal, thrifty, economical, sparing, temperate; poor, squalid.

luxury *n.* **1.** luxuriousness, material abundance, extreme comfort; high standard of living, wealth, riches; *Slang* high living. **2.** delight, enjoyment, pleasure, satisfaction, gratification, bliss, heaven, paradise. **3.** extravagance, indulgence, nonnecessity, nonessential. **—Ant. 1** poverty, penury, destitution, straitened circumstances; deprivation, austerity, need, want, difficulty, distress. **2** deprivation, privation, hardship, affliction, burden, trial, infliction, misery. **3** necessity.

lynch *v.* hang, gibbet, execute without due process of law; *Informal* string up.

lyric Also **lyrical** *adj.* **1.** songlike, melodious, euphonious, musical, tuneful, melodic, lilting, sweet-sounding, mellifluous, singing, mellifluent; poetic. *—n.* **2.** Often **lyrics** words of a song; poem.

macabre *adj.* gruesome, grisly, grim, ghastly, horrible, frightful, frightening, horrid, dreadful, horrific; eerie, weird, unearthly, ghostly, ghostlike. **—Ant.** pleasant, beautiful, lovely, appealing, inviting, delightful.

macerate *v.* **1.** liquefy, dissolve, liquidize, fluidize, soften, mash, squash, pulp; soak, steep, souse, saturate, permeate. **2.** become emaciated, waste away, shrink, shrivel, wither, lose weight; fade, decline, emaciate.

Machiavellian *adj.* scheming, designing, self-serving, underhanded, amoral, treacherous, perfidious, unscrupulous, cunning, crafty, devious, deceitful, false-hearted. **—Ant.** naive, ingenuous, open, candid, frank, straightforward.

machination *n.* scheme, intrigue, design, crafty plan, rule, conspiracy, plot, artifice, device, stratagem, maneuver, contrivance, ruse, dodge.

machine *n.* **1.** apparatus, appliance, device, mechanism, mechanical contrivance. **2.** organization, establishment, body, force, association, combine, union, society, pool, trust, faction, group, gang, crowd, ring, club, set, camp, coterie, army, corps; structure, machinery, system, setup.

machinery *n.* **1.** mechanical equipment, mechanism, apparatus, gear, contrivances; tools, tackle. **2.** system, organization, structure, setup, makeup; *Slang* wheels; instrumentality, agency, resources.

macrocosm *n.* cosmos, universe, the great world, creation, nature; heavens, firmament. **—Ant.** microcosm.

mad *adj.* **1.** angry, furious, irate, enraged, infuriated, incensed, wrathful, exasperated, provoked, miffed, fuming, foaming at the mouth, boiling over, seeing red, flushed with anger, in high dudgeon, wrought up, worked up, riled up, in a huff, up in arms; *Slang* teed off, ticked off, ticked. **2.** insane, crazy, demented, lunatic, crazed, deranged, maniacal, unbalanced, irrational, unhinged, bereft of reason, daft, balmy, not quite right, not all there, out of one's mind, not right in one's upper story; *Slang* nuts, nutty, nutty as a fruitcake, cuckoo, cracked, screwy, have a screw loose, off one's rocker, not have twelve cookies to the dozen, touched, loco; *British* crackers, round the bend; non compos mentis, *Informal* non compos. **3.** enthusiastic, wild, excited, fanatic, avid, devoted to, frenzied, impassioned, ardent; infatuated, in love with, beside oneself, distracted, distraught. **—Ant. 1** appeased, mollified. **2** sane, sound, rational. **3** calm, cool, collected, composed, unexcited, uncaring, nonchalant; disdainful.

madam *n.* lady, madame; matron, dowager, Mrs., *French* madame, *Spanish* señora, *Italian* signora, *German* Frau; *Archaic* dame, mistress.

madcap *adj.* wild, unruly, undisciplined, flighty, erratic, reckless, brash, thoughtless, inconsiderate, giddy, impulsive, hotheaded, rash, incautious, impractical, foolish, senseless. **—Ant.** cautious, prudent, careful, circumspect, practical.

madden *v.* enrage, anger, vex, pique, infuriate, provoke, upset, exasperate, frenzy, provoke, incense, outrage, inflame, aggravate, gall, craze, derange, unbalance, unhinge. **—Ant.** calm, soothe, appease, placate, mollify.

made *adj.* manufactured, fabricated, produced, constructed, built, assembled, formed; created, composed, developed.

madhouse *n.* **1.** insane asylum, lunatic asylum, mental hospital, mental institution, psychopathic hospital, state hospital; *Slang* loony bin, nuthouse. **2.** bedlam, scene of pandemonium, uproar, turmoil, wild confusion.

madman *n.* lunatic, insane person, maniac, deranged person, crazy person, demoniac, psychopath, psychotic, *Slang* loony, nut.

maelstrom *n.* **1.** whirlpool, rapids, vortex, swirl, eddy, white water, undertow, riptide, torrent, shoot. **2.** confusion, disorder, upheaval, tumult, uproar, pandemonium, bedlam, madhouse.

magazine *n.* **1.** periodical, journal; (*variously*) weekly, monthly, quarterly, zine, fanzine. **2.** powder magazine, powder room, munitions room; arsenal, military storehouse, military depot.

magenta *n.* reddish purple, purplish rose, fuchsia; maroon, vermilion; crimson, carmine.

maggot *n.* larva, grub, worm, mealworm.

magic *n.* **1.** black magic, voodoo, voodooism, hoodoo, sorcery, occultism, the black art, wizardry; witchcraft, witchery, demonology; spell, conjuration, divination. **2.** prestidigitation, legerdemain, sleight of hand, hocus-pocus, jugglery. **3.** animal magnetism, fascination, captivation, charisma, charm, enchantment, lure, allurement, entrancement. **—Ant.** **1** science, facts and figures.

magician *n.* **1.** wizard, sorcerer, necromancer, magus, shaman, warlock; witch doctor, medicine man; alchemist. **2.** prestidigitator, sleight-of-hand artist, expert in legerdemain, illusionist, escape artist; conjurer, juggler.

magistrate *n.* justice of the peace, *Informal* j.p.; minor judge, judicial officer, civil officer, prefect, police judge.

magnanimous *adj.* forgiving, free of vindictiveness, generous, largehearted, liberal; charitable, beneficent, philanthropic, altruistic, unselfish, princely, noble, high-minded. **—Syn. Study.** See NOBLE. **—Ant.** unforgiving, vindictive, resentful, small, petty, selfish; parsimonious, miserly.

magnate *n.* leader, dominant person, great man, empire builder, important person, VIP, giant, mogul, influential person, notable, celebrity, *Slang* bigwig, big shot, big wheel, big gun; nabob, tycoon, industrialist, giant of industry.

magnetic *adj.* **1.** of a magnet, of magnetism. **2.** attractive, fascinating, persuasive; captivating, charismatic, enchanting, alluring, entrancing, charming, irresistible, inviting, seductive. **—Ant.** **1** antimagnetic. **2** repellent, repulsive.

magnetism *n.* **1.** magnetic force, magnetic attraction. **2.** attraction, fascination, captivation, charisma, hypnotic appeal, enchantment, charm, enticement, allure, allurement, animal magnetism, lure, mesmerism, seduction. **—Ant.** **1** repulsion. **2** repulsiveness, repellency.

magnificent *adj.* splendid, superb, sublime, grand, glorious, extraordinary, wonderful, fine, elegant, exquisite, noble, majestic, exalted, imposing, commanding, impressive, stately, august, transcendent, brilliant, resplendent. **—Ant.** modest, ordinary, undistinguished, unimposing, unassuming, humble, mean, lowly, ignoble, poor, tawdry, trifling, trivial, petty, paltry, bad; *Slang* awful, lousy.

magnify *v.* **1.** enlarge optically, increase the apparent size of, *Informal* blow up. **2.** enlarge, expand, amplify, inflate, greaten, heighten, stretch, maximize, boost, double; *Informal* blow up, puff up; exaggerate, depict extravagantly, overstate, enlarge upon, overrate, embroider. **3.** laud, praise, acclaim, exalt, extol, glorify, revere, adore, worship, reverence. **—Ant. 1, 2** reduce. **2** diminish, decrease, deflate, lessen, lower, minimize, constrict, shrink; understate, underplay; belittle, deprecate.

magniloquence *n.* bombast, pomposity, pretentiousness, grandiloquence, fustian, euphuism, turgidity, grandiosity, orotundity, tumidity, fanfaronade, high-soundingness.

magnitude *n.* **1.** size, extent, expanse, dimensions, proportions, mass, bulk, amplitude, volume, measure; bigness, hugeness, enormity, largeness, vastness, immensity; brightness. **2.** eminence, distinction, renown, repute, fame, celebrity, importance, consequence, significance, greatness. **—Ant. 1** smallness, diminutiveness, meanness. **2** insignificance, unimportance, paltriness, triviality, triflingness.

maid *n.* housemaid, maidservant, female servant, domestic, hired girl, (*variously*) nursemaid, parlor maid, lady's maid, upstairs maid, *British Slang* tweeny.

maiden *n.* **1.** girl, lass, maid, virgin, miss, lassie, colleen, damsel, demoiselle, soubrette, ingenue, *Slang* chick. *—adj.* **2.** Also **maidenly** girlish, youthful, chaste, virginal; unmarried. **3.** first, initial, inaugural, untried, virgin, original, introductory, initiatory. **—Ant. 1** matron, dowager, lady, madam, grande dame. **2** matronly; unchaste; married, wedded, espoused.

mail[1] *n.* **1.** post; (*variously*) letters, postcards, e-mails, faxes, packages. **2.** mail delivery, postal service, post-office service; airmail, surface mail. *—v.* **3.** put in the mail, post, get out, dispatch, drop in a mailbox; send by mail, send by post.

mail[2] *n.* armor, arms, suit of mail, panoply, flexible armor of interlinked rings, defensive armor, harness.

maim *v.* mangle, mutilate, cut, slash, lacerate, wound, injure, rend, tear, rip, gash, disable, maul, dismember, cripple, incapacitate, lame, deface, disfigure, savage, hobble, hamstring.

main *adj.* leading, principal, central, chief, head, primary, foremost, prime, capital, predominant, paramount, outstanding, preeminent, supreme; vital, essential, necessary, indispensable, requisite, important, critical, crucial, urgent, pressing, consequential; special, particular. **—Ant.** subordinate, secondary, dependent, collateral, auxiliary, ancillary; unimportant, insignificant, trivial, minor, lesser, least, nonessential.

mainly *adv.* chiefly, principally, mostly, primarily, predominantly, for the most part, most of all, above all, in the main, on the whole, in great measure, first and foremost. **—Ant.** secondarily, subordinately; partially, slightly, least of all, minimally.

mainstay *n.* chief support, backbone, principal reliance; pillar, pillar of strength, bulwark, buttress, prop, anchor.

maintain *v.* **1.** keep, keep up, keep

alive, keep going, continue, sustain, preserve, conserve, uphold. **2.** take care of, support, provide for, keep, keep up, care for, finance; stand by, defend, uphold. **3.** declare, affirm, assert, state, insist, contend; hold, swear, avow, aver, profess, allege, claim. **—Ant. 1** end, terminate, conclude, discontinue, drop, finish, abolish, dissolve, suspend, break off. **2** give up, relinquish; abandon, desert. **3** retract, disavow.

maintenance *n.* **1.** preservation, conservation, keeping, safekeeping, safeguarding, protection; upkeep, repair. **2.** support, upkeep, subsistence, sustainment, sustenance, living, livelihood, keep. **—Ant. 1** destruction, dissolution, eradication, abolition, termination, discontinuance, suspension.

majestic Also **majestical** *adj.* stately, august, grand, imposing, impressive, magnificent, splendid, glorious, superb, sublime, noble, lofty, elegant; regal, imperial, royal, princely; distinguished, famous, esteemed, illustrious, eminent, renowned. **—Ant.** modest, ordinary, unimposing, unassuming, humble, lowly, mean, ignoble, tawdry, paltry, undistinguished.

majesty *n.* grandeur, splendor, magnificence, dignity, distinction, augustness, elevation, loftiness, eminence, stateliness, glory, pomp, gloriousness, impressiveness, illustriousness, elegance, mobility, luster, solemnity, sublimity. **—Ant.** meanness, shabbiness, paltriness, lowness; degradation, disgrace, shame, debasement.

major *adj.* **1.** greater, larger, main, principal, chief. **2.** leading, primary, foremost, predominant, principal, chief, main, capital, prime, paramount, outstanding, preeminent, ranking, supreme, most important, important, serious, significant, consequential; essential, vital, necessary, indispensable, requisite, critical, crucial, urgent, pressing. **—Syn. Study. 2** See CAPITAL. **—Ant. 1** lesser, smaller. **2** minor, lesser, subordinate, secondary, collateral, auxiliary, ancillary, insignificant, unimportant, trivial, trifling, inconsequential, nonessential.

majority *n.* **1.** mass, bulk, best part, greater part, preponderance, lion's share, greater than half the total, greater number, more than half. **2.** legal age, seniority, maturity, adulthood, womanhood. **—Ant. 1** minority, lesser part. **2** childhood, infancy.

make *v.* **1.** manufacture, construct, produce, fashion, form, fabricate, assemble, create, compose, devise, shape, frame, build, erect. **2.** cause, produce, bring about, effect, engender, foment, beget; cause to be; deliver, utter, speak, pronounce. **3.** compel, force, oblige, constrain, require, impel, dragoon, press. **4.** establish, put into effect, draw up, pass, enact, legislate; render, fix, appoint. **5.** reach, attain, arrive at; meet, arrive in time for, catch. *—n.* **6.** kind, brand, mark; structure, construction, composition, form, formation, makeup, fashioning. **—Ant. 1** destroy, demolish, wreck, ruin, raze. **2** end, conclude; terminate, abolish, dissolve. **3** ask, beg, plead, entreat. **4** repeal, revoke, nullify, abolish, cancel, set aside. **5** leave, depart, withdraw from; be late for, miss.

make-believe *adj.* **1.** imagined, imaginary, unreal, fantastic, simulated, pretended, invented, fictitious, artificial, made-up, assumed, feigned; phony, false, fake, spurious, counterfeit, sham. *—n.* **2.** pretense, fantasy, invention, fabrication, creation, fiction; fake, counterfeit, sham, falsification, charade.

makeshift *adj.* stopgap, temporary, provisional, expedient, make-do, alternate, standby, tentative, substitute; slapdash.

malady *n.* ailment, sickness, illness, disorder, disability, disease, complaint, affliction, affection, indisposition, infirmity, unhealthiness. **—Ant.** health, healthfulness, haleness.

malaise *n.* vague discomfort, minor complaint, twinge, throb, pang; discomposure, nervousness, uneasiness, lassitude, disquiet, anxiety.

malcontent *adj.* **1.** habitually unsatisfied, dissatisfied, discontented, hard to please, faultfinding, restive, restless, uneasy; glum, morose, sullen, grumpy, grouchy, sour, irritable, dejected, downcast, despondent. *—n.* **2.** complainer, fault-finder, grumbler, grouch, growler, repiner; insurgent, rebel. **—Ant. 1** contented, content, satisfied, happy, cheerful; complacent, easygoing, untroubled, unconcerned, unworried. **2** optimist.

male *adj.* **1.** masculine, of the sex that fathers young; manly, manlike, virile. *—n.* **2.** a male person or animal; man, youth, boy; (*variously*) stallion, tomcat, billy goat, bull, rooster, ram, stud. **—Syn. Study. 1** MALE, MASCULINE, VIRILE describe men and boys or whatever is culturally attributed to them. MALE classifies individuals on the basis of their genetic makeup or their ability to fertilize an ovum in bisexual reproduction. It contrasts with FEMALE in all uses: *his oldest male relative; the male parts of the flower.* MASCULINE refers to qualities or behavior deemed especially appropriate to or ideally associated with men and boys; this has traditionally included such traits as strength, aggressiveness, and courage: *a firm, masculine handshake; masculine impatience at indecision.* VIRILE implies the muscularity, vigor, and sexual potency of mature manhood: *a swaggering, virile walk. See also* MANLY. **2** See MAN. **—Ant. 1, 2** female, woman. **1** feminine.

malediction *n.* curse, damnation, imprecation, execration, evil spell, anathema; denunciation, diatribe, fulmination, proscription. **—Ant.** benediction, blessing; eulogy, praise, compliment.

malevolent *adj.* malicious, showing ill will, ill-disposed, spiteful, ill-intentioned, malignant, baleful, sinister, acrimonious, venomous, resentful, vicious, rancorous, revengeful, invidious, pernicious, malign; surly, sullen, ill-natured. **—Ant.** benevolent, benign, magnanimous, kind, gracious, friendly, amiable, warmhearted.

malformed *adj.* misshapen, deformed, not straight, distorted, contorted, twisted, irregular, grotesque.

malice *n.* ill will, evil intent, malevolence, maliciousness, malignity, hatred, spitefulness, spite, grudge, rancor, resentment, animosity, antagonism, acrimony, enmity, hate, venom, bitterness; evil disposition, uncharitableness, hardheartedness. **—Ant.** benevolence, goodwill, charity, friendliness, amiability, kindness, graciousness.

malicious *adj.* vicious, spiteful, malevolent, malignant, ill-disposed, baleful, harmful, vindictive, revengeful, resentful, rancorous, hateful, invidious, acrimonious. **—Ant.** benevolent, benign, friendly, amiable, amicable, kind, kindhearted, well-disposed.

malign *v.* **1.** slander, defame, speak ill of, revile, abuse, belittle, disparage, derogate, denigrate, deprecate, vilify, inveigh against, backbite, blacken the reputation of; *Informal* run down, put down; *Slang* bad mouth. *—adj.* **2.** evil, bad, harmful, injurious, detrimental, deleterious, pernicious, baneful, noxious; ominous, sinister, black, malignant, malevolent, threatening, menacing, malicious, hateful. **—Ant. 1** praise, extol, eulogize, compliment, commend. **2** benign, benevolent, good; kind, friendly, amiable, warmhearted.

malignant *adj.* **1.** deadly, pernicious, virulent; fatal, toxic, poisonous. **2.** malicious, malevolent, ill-disposed, vindictive, resentful, revengeful, spiteful, rancorous, hateful, vicious, invidious, acrimonious, bitter, venomous, hostile, fiendish, diabolical, evil, evil-minded. **—Ant. 1** nonmalignant. **2** benevolent, benign, friendly, amiable, amicable, kind, kindhearted, well-disposed.

malinger *v.* slack, shirk, procrastinate, loaf, dodge, evade, duck one's duty, lie down on the job; *Slang* goldbrick, goof off.

mall *n.* promenade, tree-lined walk, esplanade; square, plaza, piazza, court, quadrangle, yard, parade ground, circus; arcade, colonnade, cloister.

malleable *adj.* **1.** workable, easily shaped, easily wrought; ductile, tractable, plastic, pliant, flexible. **2.** impressionable, easily influenced, moldable, tractable, teachable, manageable, governable, docile; adaptable, flexible, pliable, compliant. **—Ant. 1** rigid, stiff, hard, firm; unyielding, inflexible, unbending, inelastic. **2** refractory, intractable, recalcitrant, ungovernable.

malnutrition *n.* undernourishment, lack of proper nutrition; starvation, emaciation.

malpractice *n.* professional negligence, improper professional practice, professional dereliction.

mammon *n.* wealth, riches, possessions, money, gold, profit, material goods, affluence, gain, the god of money.

mammoth *adj.* enormous, huge, immense, massive, monstrous, gigantic, colossal, very large, mighty, great, whopping, monumental, mountainous, prodigious, gargantuan, elephantine, herculean, cyclopean, stupendous, tremendous, ponderous. **—Syn. Study.** See GIGANTIC. **—Ant.** small, little, tiny, miniature, minute, dwarfish; *Informal* wee, peewee; *Slang* itty-bitty, itsy-bitsy.

man *n.* **1.** mankind, the human race, men and women, human beings, humankind, people, humanity, Homo sapiens. **2.** individual, person, human being, human, living being, living soul, soul, one; anyone, somebody, someone. **3.** male, masculine person; gentleman, chap, fellow, guy, gent. **4.** husband, spouse, married man, *Informal* hubby; boyfriend, lover, paramour, sweetheart, beau, steady, companion. **5.** handyman, workman, hired hand, hand, laborer, day laborer; employee, worker; manservant, male servant, valet, boy, waiter, footman, butler, male retainer; assistant, helper, right-hand man; male follower, subject, liegeman, henchman; crewman, soldier, trooper. *—v.* **6.** attend, staff, take up one's position in, take one's place at, get to one's post; supply with hands, furnish with men, people; equip, fit out, outfit; garrison. **—Syn. Study. 3** MAN, MALE, GENTLEMAN refer to adult humans of the sex that produces sperm for procreation. MAN, the most commonly used of the three, can be neutral: *a man of deep faith.* It can also signify possession of typical or desirable masculine qualities: *to take one's punishment like a man.* MALE emphasizes physical or sexual characteristics and can also apply to an animal or a plant: *two males and* *three females in the pack.* GENTLEMAN, once used only of men of high social rank, now also specifies a man of courtesy and consideration: *to behave like a gentleman.* It is used too as a polite term of reference (*This gentleman is next*) or, only in the plural, of address (*Are we ready, gentlemen?*). **—Ant. 3** woman, female. **4** bachelor.

manacle *n.* **1.** Usu. **manacles** handcuffs, hand-fetters, irons, shackles, chains, bonds, *Slang* bracelets. **—*v.* 2.** handcuff, fetter, tie one's hands, put in chains, put in irons,shackle, *Slang* put bracelets on. **—Ant. 2** unbind, unfetter, unchain; set free, free, liberate, turn loose, let go.

manage *v.* **1.** run, direct, oversee, superintend, have charge of, take care of, look after, watch over, supervise, head, administer, conduct, preside over, rule, govern, control, command, order, dominate, guide, steer, pilot, be at the helm, hold the reins. **2.** manipulate, maneuver, handle, control, work, operate, make go, run; guide, steer; use, wield, ply. **3.** survive, get along, get on, fare, shift, keep one's head above water, weather the storm. **4.** succeed, accomplish, deal with, cope with, cope, work out, bring about. **—Ant. 1** be under the care of, follow. **3** be destitute, starve. **4** fail, botch, bungle, spoil, make a mess of, muff, make a hash of.

management *n.* **1.** administration, supervision, direction, overseeing, superintendence, generalship; operation, guidance, regulation, conduct, conducting, command, control, ordering, charge, running, handling, care, rule; planning, organization; strategy, tactics, manipulation; dealing, negotiation, transaction. **2.** executives, executive board, executive committee, administrators, the administration, supervisors, supervisory board, board of directors, directors, bosses; *Slang* bigwigs, big shots, wheels, top brass. **—Ant. 2** labor; staff, employees, workers.

manager *n.* **1.** head, boss, supervisor, foreman, superintendent, overseer, executive director, administrator, majordomo, chief; agent, impresario. **2.** planner, organizer, budgeteer; tactician, manipulator, negotiator. **—Ant. 1** employee, worker, laborer, *Slang* flunky.

mandate *n.* **1.** protectorate, dependency, mandated territory, subject territory. **2.** order, edict, decree, command, dictate, bidding, behest, directive, direction, instruction, authorization, authority, approval, sanction, charge, requisition, commission. **—Ant. 2** petition, request, entreaty, supplication, appeal, solicitation, suit.

mandatory *adj.* compulsory, required, requisite, obligatory, incumbent on, not optional, binding, called for; essential, imperative, peremptory, necessary, needful, exigent.

maneuver *n.* **1.** troop movement, troop deployment; movement of warships, planes, armored vehicles, etc.; training exercise. **2.** scheme, stratagem, gambit, move, ploy, tactic; plot, artifice, device, contrivance, machination, trick, dodge, intrigue. **—*v.* 3.** deploy, move; manipulate, steer, pilot, guide. **4.** contrive, work surreptitiously, bring about in an underhand way, pull strings; scheme, plot, plan artfully, devise a way, intrigue, *Informal* finagle.

manful *adj.* **—Syn. Study.** See MANLY.

mangle *v.* mutilate, maim, disfigure, maul, press, crush, flatten; cut, lacerate, tear, slash; injure, damage, harm, hurt, lame, impair, ruin.

manhood *n.* **1.** adulthood, maturity, prime, legal age, majority, mature age. **2.** virility, manliness, manfulness, masculinity, machismo, maleness.

mania *n.* **1.** madness, violent derangement, insanity, lunacy, fanaticism, dementia; frenzy, delirium, raving, rage, hysteria, delusion, hallucination, aberration. **2.** passion, craze, craving, enthusiasm, exaggerated love, infatuation; obsession, fascination, monomania, compulsion, fixation. **—Ant. 1** sanity, rationality; self-control, equanimity, stability, levelheadedness, coolness, coolheadedness, calmness.

maniac *n.* madman, lunatic, psychotic, crazy person, insane person, deranged person; *Slang* nut, screwball, crackbrain, loony, cuckoo; psychopath; reckless person, fool, simpleton, ass, nitwit, half-wit.

manic *adj.* frenzied, excited, agitated, hyperactive, worked up, frantic, wrought up; *Slang* up, high, hyped up, freaked out, switched on. **—Ant.** low, sluggish, down, depressed.

manifest *adj.* **1.** obvious, clear, evident, self-evident, plain, apparent, patent, visible, noticeable, palpable, unmistakable, transparent, unconcealed, undisguised; open, frank, candid. **—*v.* 2.** indicate, show, exhibit, reveal, express, disclose, make known, demonstrate, evince, evidence, display, divulge, make visible, unveil, uncover, hold up to view, bare, expose. **—Syn. Study. 2** See DISPLAY. **—Ant. 1** hidden, concealed, suppressed, masked, obscured, vague, cryptic, inconspicuous, unseen. **2** hide, conceal, cover up, mask, cloak, bury, obscure, camouflage.

manifestation *n.* indication, symptom,

evidence, proclamation, revelation; demonstration, example, instance, show, display, exhibition, illustration, expression, presentation.

manifesto *n.* proclamation, declaration, pronouncement, edict, ukase, announcement, communiqué, statement, pronunciamento, annunciation, notice, notification, broadside, position paper; *Cath. Church* bull, encyclical.

manifold *adj.* many, numerous, multitudinous, multiple, myriad, innumerable; varied, variegated, diversified, many-sided, diverse, complex, multiform, multifarious. **—Syn. Study.** See MANY. **—Ant.** few, scant, limited; simple, uncomplicated, uniform.

manipulate *v.* **1.** handle, finger; feel, pinch, stroke, pat, massage, squeeze. **2.** operate, work, use, employ, handle, manage, control; wield, ply, drive. **3.** tamper with, change fraudulently, manage by crafty means, influence deviously, control illegally, direct unethically; deceive, defraud.

mankind *n.* the human race, humankind, Homo sapiens, the human species, man, men and women, humanity, mortals, people, persons, society.

manly *adj.* **1.** masculine, male, malelike, virile, manful. **2.** vigorous, hardy, strong, robust, husky, sturdy, muscular, athletic, brawny, strapping, powerful, stalwart; brave, courageous, daring, bold, resolute, stouthearted, valiant, fearless, staunch, indomitable, plucky, self-reliant; noble, heroic, chivalrous, gallant, gentlemanly. **—Syn. Study.** MANLY, MANFUL, MANNISH mean having traits or qualities considered typical of or appropriate to adult males. MANLY, a term of approval, suggests such admirable traits as maturity and steadiness: *a manly acceptance of responsibility.* MANFUL, also an approving term, stresses such qualities as courage and strength: *a manful effort to overcome great odds.* MANNISH is most often used, esp. derogatorily, in referring to the qualities or accouterments of a woman considered more appropriate to a man: *the mannish abruptness of her speech; She wore a severely mannish suit.* See also MALE. **—Ant. 1** unmanly, effeminate, womanish, boyish, juvenile, youthful, puerile, childlike, childish, babyish. **2** weak, frail, feeble; cowardly, faint-hearted, irresolute; villainous, dastardly.

man-made *adj.* artificial, manufactured, fabricated, synthetic, factitious, created, fashioned, formed, crafted, constructed, handcrafted, ready-made, originated, produced; mock, sham, simulated.

manna *n.* miraculous food, spiritual nourishment, divine sustenance; boon, bonanza, sudden gain, unexpected gift, award, reward.

manner *n.* **1.** way, style, mode, fashion, method, custom, practice, habit; guise, aspect, appearance, character. **2.** behavior, conduct; bearing, carriage, air, presence, deportment, demeanor. **3.** kind, type, sort, variety; classification, genre, species, category, breed, race, strain, stamp, brand, caste, make, form, mold; grade, rank.

mannerism *n.* peculiar action, habit, habitual gesture, distinctive way, characteristic style, eccentricity, idiosyncrasy, singularity; affectation, pose, affected gesture, mannered style, artificiality, pretense, pretension; airs.

mannerly *adj.* polite, well-mannered, civil, courteous, well-behaved; refined, well-bred, genteel, courtly, gentlemanly, gallant, chivalrous. **—Ant.** unmannerly, discourteous, rude, impolite, ill-mannered, gauche, boorish.

manners *n. pl.* **1.** social behavior, behavior, decorum, deportment. **2.** good manners, politeness, etiquette, courtesy, deference; refinement, breeding, polish, gentility, gallantry, courtliness, politesse, propriety, amenities. **—Ant. 2** rudeness, impoliteness, bad manners, discourtesy, boorishness.

mannish *adj.* **—Syn. Study.** See MANLY.

mansion *n.* stately residence, impressive house, imposing dwelling; manor, manor house, villa, château, castle, palace; estate. **—Ant.** hovel, shack, hut, cabin, cottage, *Slang* hole.

manslaughter *n.* accidental murder, unpremeditated killing, killing without malice aforethought; (*loosely*) murder, killing, homicide, spilling of blood.

mantle *n.* **1.** cloak, cape, tunic, wrapper; scarf for the head and shoulders, mantilla. **2.** covering, cover, veil, cloak, mask, envelope, curtain, blanket, canopy, screen, cloud, film, shroud, pall.

manual *adj.* **1.** hand-operated, nonautomatic. **2.** physical, done by hand, requiring physical strength. **—*n.* 3.** handbook, guidebook, instruction book; textbook, primer, workbook. **—Ant. 1** automatic; machine-operated, electric. **2** mental, intellectual.

manufacture *v.* **1.** produce, mass-produce, make, fabricate, mold, form, fashion, devise, frame; assemble, put together, construct, build. **2.** invent, fabricate, trump up, make up, concoct, create, think up, *Informal* cook up. **—Ant. 1** destroy, demolish.

manure *n.* dung, animal excrement, animal droppings, feces, ordure, excreta; fertilizer; compost, dressing.

manuscript *n.* typescript, script, written document; (*motion pictures, television*) shooting script.

many *adj.* **1.** numerous, innumerable, numberless, countless, myriad, multitudinous, manifold; several, various, divers, sundry. —*n.* **2.** a considerable number, a lot, lots, a heap, heaps, piles, scores, dozens, numbers; a liberal quantity, a profusion, an abundance. **—Syn. Study.** MANY, NUMEROUS, INNUMERABLE, MANIFOLD imply the presence of a large number of units. MANY is a general word that refers to a large but indefinite number of units or individuals: *many years ago; many friends and supporters.* NUMEROUS, a more formal word, stresses the individual and separate quality of the units: *to receive numerous letters.* INNUMERABLE denotes a number that is too large to be counted or, more loosely, that is very difficult to count: *the innumerable stars.* MANIFOLD implies that the number is large, but also varied or complex: *manifold responsibilities.* **—Ant. 1** few; sparse, scarce, rare, infrequent; once or twice, occasional. **2** few, hardly any, a handful; none, none at all.

map *n.* **1.** topographical chart, chart, graph, projection, elevation; plot, diagram, plan, representation. —*v.* **2.** make a map of, chart. **3.** plan, project, prepare, devise, design, contrive, arrange, plot, lay out, organize, ready.

mar *v.* **1.** disfigure, blemish, deface, mutilate, maim, damage, hurt, scar, mark, nick, scratch, stain; ruin, destroy. **2.** spoil, taint, blemish, impair, hurt, botch, detract from, make imperfect, diminish; defile, blight. **—Ant. 1** beautify, embellish, adorn, decorate, ornament; restore. **2** improve, enhance, restore.

marauder *n.* plunderer, pillager, depradator, ravager, looter, despoiler, spoiler; pirate, buccaneer, privateer, corsair, freebooter; roving outlaw band; guerrilla, ranger.

march *v.* **1.** parade, walk with measured steps, walk in step, walk in a procession, file by; go, go directly, walk, step, tramp, proceed. —*n.* **2.** hike, tramp, trek, group walk; parade, procession. **3.** progress, progression, development, advance, advancement, rise, growth. **4.** piece of music in march time; martial music, military tune; funeral march.

mare *n.* female horse, broodmare.

margin *n.* **1.** border, boundary, edge, side, rim, verge, confine, bound, hem, fringe, skirt. **2.** leeway, safeguard, extra amount, added quantity, extra room, allowance. **—Ant. 1** center, middle, interior.

marginal *adj.* **1.** in the margin, on the edge, along the border. **2.** barely profitable; barely useful.

marine *adj.* **1.** oceanic, sea, salt-water; of the sea, aquatic, oceanographic, pelagic. **2.** maritime, of ships, naval, nautical; seagoing, oceangoing, seafaring. **—Ant. 1** terrestrial, land, dry-land; fresh-water.

mariner *n.* sailor, deck hand, seaman, seafarer, seafaring man, able-bodied seaman, boatman; salt, tar, sea dog, bluejacket, *Slang* gob; navigator, pilot, helmsman; yachtsman. **—Syn. Study.** See SAILOR. **—Ant.** landlubber.

marionette *n.* puppet, articulated puppet, puppet on strings, *Italian* fantoccino.

marital *adj.* wedded, married, of marriage, matrimonial, conjugal, spousal, nuptial, connubial; husbandly, wifely. **—Ant.** single, unmarried, unwed, unwedded.

maritime *adj.* **1.** marine, naval, nautical, of ships, of the sea, of sea trade, seagoing, seafaring; oceanic, aquatic. **2.** coastal, bordering on the sea; engaged in sea trade, making a living from the sea. **—Ant. 1** land, terrestrial, dry-land; fresh-water. **2** inland.

mark *n.* **1.** spot, streak, line, stain; scratch, scar, cut, nick, dent, impression; pock, pit, notch, score; bruise, blemish. **2.** hallmark, sign, symbol, stamp, label, badge, emblem, brand, colophon, imprint; token, symbol, indication, evidence, measure, symptom, proof. **3.** grade; rating. **4.** target, goal, objective, intent, point, track, bull's-eye; standard, criterion, yardstick, touchstone. —*v.* **5.** spot, streak, stain; scratch, scar, cut, nick, dent, leave an impression on, pock, pit, notch, score; bruise, blemish; mar, deface, disfigure, harm, injure; make a line on, write on, write in. **6.** grade, correct, judge, rate. **7.** indicate, reveal, disclose, show, point out, designate, denote, signify, stand for; characterize, typify, symbolize, evidence, evince, suggest, betoken, manifest, be a sign of, distinguish, differentiate; label, stamp, brand. **8.** heed, attend, pay attention to, mind, note, regard. **—Ant. 5** clean, remove, obliterate, erase; repair. **7** hide, conceal, mask, veil, cover, screen, disguise, camouflage. **8** ignore, overlook, disregard.

marked *adj.* outstanding, distinct, conspicuous, striking, noticeable, obvious, prominent; exceptional, uncommon, noteworthy, extraordinary, unique, signal, singular, special, remarkable, particular, definite, decided. **—Ant.** ordinary, commonplace, everyday, undistinguished, routine, run-of-the-mill, mediocre.

market *n.* **1.** marketplace, wholesale market; stand; grocer's shop, grocery; meat market, butcher shop. **2.** stock market, stock exchange, curb market, *French* bourse; financial center; commodity market. —*v.* **3.** sell, vend, merchandise, retail, *Informal* peddle, hawk; put up for sale, dispose of. —**Ant. 3** buy.

marksman *n.* sharpshooter, good shot, good target-shooter, crack shot, dead shot, sure shot.

maroon¹ *v.* strand, cast ashore, leave behind, put ashore, cast away, abandon, desert, forsake, jettison, *Informal* leave high and dry.

maroon² *adj.* brownish red, wine, magenta, plum, terra cotta.

marriage *n.* **1.** matrimony, marital state, wedlock, holy wedlock, conjugal union, connubial state, nuptial state. **2.** wedding, marriage ceremony, nuptials, nuptial rites, tying the knot, leading to the altar, ringing of wedding bells. —**Ant. 1** divorce, annulment; single life, bachelorhood, spinsterhood.

marry *v.* **1.** wed, get married to, take in marriage, espouse, exchange wedding vows with, lead to the altar, bestow one's hand upon, take for a husband, take for a wife, take for better or for worse; *Slang* get spliced, tie the knot. **2.** wed, join in marriage, join in wedlock, unite in holy wedlock, make one. —**Ant. 1** divorce, get an annulment from.

marsh *n.* swamp, bog, fen, bottoms, slough; marshland, wetland, quagmire, quicksand, everglade, morass.

marshal *n.* **1.** law officer; sheriff, police chief; fire chief. **2.** master of ceremonies, honorary leader, ceremonial head; chief, leader, director, supervisor, manager. **3.** field marshal, commander in chief, generalissimo, chief officer, *French* maréchal. —*v.* **4.** arrange, order, organize, group, deploy, array, align, line up, draw up; gather, collect, muster, assemble, mobilize. —**Syn. Study. 4** See GATHER. —**Ant. 4** disorganize, jumble, jumble up, clump, bunch up; scatter, disperse.

mart *n.* trade center, trading center, exchange; marketplace, market; trade fair, trade show, exposition, show.

martial *adj.* **1.** military; soldierly, soldierlike. **2.** warlike, belligerent, Spartan, disposed to war, hostile, militant, combative, bellicose, pugnacious, contentious; military-minded. —**Ant. 1** civilian, civil. **2** peaceful, conciliatory.

martinet *n.* taskmaster, severe disciplinarian, authoritarian, hard master, tyrant, despot, dictator, drill-sergeant, drill master, Simon Legree, *Informal* control freak, *Slang* little Caesar.

martyr *n.* person willing to die or suffer for a cause; person killed for his beliefs; one who undergoes great suffering; one venerated for dying or suffering.

martyrdom *n.* the suffering of a martyr, death of a martyr; suffering, agony, anguish, torment, torture, ordeal, affliction; (*literary*) crown of thorns, bitter cup, cup of sorrow. —**Ant.** ecstasy, bliss, joy, pleasure, happiness, delight, gratification.

marvel *n.* **1.** miracle, wonder, phenomenon, wonderful thing, supreme example; rarity, spectacle. —*v.* **2.** be awed, be overwhelmed, be struck with wonder, be staggered, be amazed, be astonished, be stupefied, gape. —**Ant. 1** commonplace. **2** be bored; take in stride.

marvelous Also **marvellous** *adj.* wonderful, splendid, lovely, superb, outstanding, great, grand, fine, first-rate, fabulous, heavenly, divine, fantastic, extraordinary, stupendous, sensational, colossal, phenomenal, magnificent, remarkable, astonishing, amazing, *Slang* super, A-1, smashing. —**Ant.** terrible, awful, lousy, bad; ordinary, commonplace, routine, everyday, run-of-the-mill.

masculine *adj.* manly, male, manful, virile, macho; strong, vigorous, robust, sturdy, hardy, husky, powerful, muscular, strapping, brawny, athletic; brave, courageous, resolute, daring, bold, stouthearted, fearless, valiant, staunch, indomitable, plucky, intrepid, self-reliant, forceful. —**Syn. Study.** See MALE. —**Ant.** weak, unmanly, effeminate, womanish, girlish; female, feminine, womanly, ladylike, womanlike.

mash *v.* **1.** puree, reduce to pulp, crush, pulverize, squash, smash. —*n.* **2.** pulpy mass, soft mixture, paste, mishmash, mush.

mask *n.* **1.** false face; face covering, domino; face guard. **2.** cover, cover-up, screen, cloak, shroud, veil, curtain, blind; disguise, camouflage. —*v.* **3.** cover, put a mask over, obscure, hide, disguise. **4.** hide, conceal, shield from view, cover, screen, veil, cloak, shroud, curtain, keep secret; camouflage, disguise. —**Ant. 2** revelation, disclosure, display, manifestation, demonstration, show, exhibition. **3** unmask. **4** reveal, disclose, divulge, expose, show, display, exhibit.

masquerade *n.* **1.** masked party, costume party, masked ball, masque, mask, *French* bal masqué; harlequinade. **2.** cover, cover-up, mask, screen, veil, cloak, shroud; camouflage, pretense, pretext, subterfuge, guise, trick, artifice, ruse. —*v.* **3.** go under the guise of, pass oneself off as, pretend to be, pose as, impersonate, falsely claim to be; go disguised as. **—Ant. 2** revelation, disclosure, display, manifestation, demonstration, show, exhibition. **3** unmask, find out; expose, reveal to be.

mass[1] *n.* **1.** the quantity of matter in a body; (*loosely*) matter, material; weight. **2.** block, lump, chunk, hunk, knot, clot, cake, concretion. **3.** pile, heap, stack, pyramid, batch, lot, clump, bundle, pack, bunch; accumulation, cumulation, collection, assemblage, gathering, group, body, aggregate, aggregation, assortment, conglomeration; crowd, throng, mob, congregation, host, horde, corps, troop, crush, press, jam. **4.** greater part, preponderance, majority, plurality, bulk, main body, best part, lion's share. *—v.* **5.** collect, amass, gather, assemble, consolidate, congregate, accumulate; pile, heap, stack, bunch. **—Ant. 2** fragment, bit, chip, piece, portion, morsel. **3** scattering. **4** minority. **5** disperse, scatter, spread.

mass[2] *n.* Often **Mass** celebration of the sacrament, Communion service, Holy Communion, holy sacrament, celebration of the Lord's Supper, Eucharist; offering of bread and wine, consecration of the elements.

massacre *n.* **1.** mass slaughter, mass murder, indiscriminate killing, butchery, carnage, bloodletting, bloodbath. *—v.* **2.** slaughter en masse, kill at random, butcher, decimate; put large groups to death, perpetrate genocide. **—Syn. Study. 2** See SLAUGHTER.

massage *n.* **1.** rubdown; rubbing, kneading, stroking, manipulation. *—v.* **2.** rub, rub down, knead, chafe, stroke, manipulate, flex, handle, finger, stretch.

masses *n. pl.* the common people, the crowd, the mob, the multitude, the populace, the many, hoi polloi, the common herd, the great unwashed; the working class, the proletariat, the lower classes, proles, plebeians, plebes, the riffraff, rabble, the man in the street, the rank and file, every Tom, Dick, and Harry. **—Ant.** the élite, the aristocracy, the gentry, the upper class, bluebloods, silk stockings, society, high society, the crème de la crème, the Beautiful People, the intelligentsia, the cognoscenti, the illuminati; the middle class, the bourgeoisie.

massive *adj.* immense, huge, gigantic, monstrous, enormous, mammoth, colossal, great, stupendous, cyclopean, titanic, gargantuan, elephantine, whopping; monumental, impressive, imposing, vast, extensive, towering; hulking, heavy, hefty, ponderous, weighty, bulky, solid, massy, substantial, ample. **—Ant.** small, little, tiny, diminutive, minute; petty, trivial; flimsy, slight, frail, slender, light.

master *n.* **1.** owner, lord, conqueror, ruler. **2.** head, head man, boss, chief, leader, dominant person, controller, authority, overlord, governor, director, supervisor, manager, overseer, superintendent. **3.** ship's captain, skipper, commanding officer. **4.** expert, master hand, skilled artist, craftsman, wizard, genius, virtuoso, *Slang* ace, whiz. *—adj.* **5.** main, chief, principal, primary, prime, paramount, most important, predominant, supreme, choice, best. **6.** expert, skilled, masterly, proficient, first-rate, deft, able, practiced, accomplished, finished, talented, gifted, *Slang* ace, crack, A-1. *—v.* **7.** conquer, subdue, overcome, triumph over, control, regulate, govern, manage, dominate, tame, curb, suppress, check, bridle. **8.** grasp, learn thoroughly, be adept in, be skilled at, be proficient in, excel at, get the hang of. **—Ant. 1** slave; subject, vassal, servant. **3** crew; able-bodied seaman. **4, 6** amateur, novice, tyro. **5** minor, lesser, unimportant. **6** amateurish, incompetent, inept, unskilled, untalented, unaccomplished; bungling, clumsy. **7** surrender to, yield to, capitulate to, give in to, give way to.

masterful *adj.* **1.** masterly, skillful, skilled, expert, virtuoso, deft, able, accomplished, finished, superb, excellent. **2.** strong-willed, self-confident, self-reliant, resolute, dynamic, forceful; commanding, domineering, bossy, authoritarian. **—Ant. 1** amateurish, incompetent, inept, unskilled, untalented, unaccomplished, bungling, clumsy. **2** weak, wishy-washy, irresolute, meek, spineless.

mastermind *v.* **1.** plan, organize, conceive, engineer, direct. *—n.* **2.** planner, organizer, engineer, initiator, moving force, director. **3.** genius, mental giant, brilliant intellect, sage, wizard, pundit; expert, specialist, virtuoso, master, master hand, authority, past master, old hand. **—Ant. 3** idiot, moron, imbecile, simpleton, fool; amateur, incompetent, novice, tyro.

masterpiece *n.* great work of art, masterwork, classic, old master, monument, prize, jewel, treasure, prizewinner, paragon, nonpareil, brainchild, *Latin* ne plus ultra, *French* chef d'oeuvre.

mastery *n.* **1.** control, command, domination, dominance, leadership, supremacy, superiority, sway, rule, upper hand, whip hand. **2.** expert knowledge, expert skill, proficiency, ability, adroitness, deftness, grasp, acquirement, attainment, achievement, accomplishment. **—Ant. 1** subservience, submission, obedience. **2** incompetence, ineptness.

masticate *v.* chew; champ, munch,

gnaw, nibble. **—Ant.** swallow whole, gulp, bolt.

match *n.* **1.** matching pair, corresponding twosome; mate, one of a pair, duplicate, double, twin, companion. **2.** equal, equivalent, peer; parallel, counterpart. **3.** game, contest, competition, tournament, meet, event. *—v.* **4.** harmonize, correspond, be alike, suit, fit, go well with; combine, fit together, pair, couple, connect, join, unite, yoke, link together; agree, be equal, adapt. **5.** pit against, oppose, set against, put in competition with; contend; enter the lists with, vie with. **—Ant. 1** mismatch. **2** unequal, superior; inferior. **4** clash with, differ from; be unequal, be a mismatch.

matchless *adj.* incomparable, supreme, unmatched, unparalleled, unequaled, unrivaled; peerless, unsurpassed, unexcelled, unbeatable, crowning, superior, superlative, first rate, paramount, preeminent, foremost; rare, priceless, invaluable, inestimable, sterling, exemplary. **—Ant.** comparable, equaled, surpassed, excelled; average, mediocre, common, commonplace, ordinary, everyday; inferior, lesser, lower, cheaper, second-class.

mate *n.* **1.** one of a pair, duplicate, match, twin, counterpart, companion, equivalent. **2.** one of a pair of mated animals; spouse, partner, consort, helpmate; husband, *Informal* hubby; wife, better half. **3.** *British Informal* chum, pal, crony, buddy, friend, companion, comrade, sidekick; coworker, fellow worker, associate, confederate, colleague, partner; classmate; roommate; messmate. **4.** first mate, second mate; ship's officer below the rank of captain, master mariner. *—v.* **5.** pair off; couple, copulate, cohabit.

material *n.* **1.** matter, substance, stuff; constituents, elements. **2.** Often **materials** supplies, stores, stocks; timber, bricks and mortar; equipment, machinery, tools. **3.** fabric, textile, drygoods; piece goods, yard goods, cloth. **4.** facts, figures, data, observations, impressions, quotations, notes; references, citations. *—adj.* **5.** physical, formed of matter, tangible, substantial, substantive, essential, materialistic, concrete; bodily, corporeal. **6.** significant, important, substantial, consequential, essential, vital, indispensable; relevant, pertinent, germane, direct; grave, serious, weighty, momentous. **—Syn. Study. 1** See MATERIAL. **—Ant. 1** spirit, soul; mind, intellect. **5** nonmaterial, intangible; spiritual. **6** insignificant, unimportant, unsubstantial, inconsequential, trifling, piddling, unessential, dispensable, superficial; irrelevant, facetious, cavalier.

materialism *n.* love of possessions, love of material things, concern for comfort, pursuit of wealth; acquisitiveness, covetousness. **—Ant.** asceticism; idealism.

materialize *v.* appear, emerge, show, become visible, turn up, come into view, rise, come to light, issue, come forth, burst forth, loom, issue, spring forth, put in an appearance, manifest oneself, expose oneself; *Slang* pop up, bob up. **—Ant.** disappear, vanish, evaporate, dissolve, fade away.

materially *adv.* **1.** significantly, substantially, essentially, vitally, emphatically, considerably, to an important degree, seriously, in the main, for the most part. **2.** financially, monetarily, concerning material things, with regard to material comforts; in substance, tangibly, palpably, corporeally. **—Ant. 1** insignificantly, unsubstantially, on the surface, superficially; hardly, scarcely, barely, little. **2** spiritually; intellectually.

matériel *n.* military supplies, gear, equipment, materials; supplies, stores, provisions.

maternal *adj.* **1.** motherly, of a mother, motherlike; doting, fond; shielding, sheltering, protective. **2.** related through one's mother, on one's mother's side of the family. **—Ant. 2** paternal.

maternity *n.* motherhood, being a mother; child-bearing, childbirth, delivery, parturition, labor, accouchement; pregnancy.

mathematical Also **mathematic** *adj.* **1.** of mathematics, of higher mathematics; computational. **2.** precise, exact, accurate, unerring, scientific, well-defined, meticulous, scrupulous, strict, punctilious, rigid, rigorous. **—Ant. 2** careless, heedless, thoughtless, sloppy, inaccurate, inexact, loose, lax.

matinee *n.* afternoon performance; early performance, early show.

matriarch *n.* female head, female chieftain, female ruler, female leader, materfamilias, grande dame.

matriculate *v.* enroll, register, sign up, enlist, enter, join, check in.

matrimonial *adj.* married, wedded, bridal, nuptial, conjugal, marital, connubial, hymeneal, spousal, epithalamic, affianced, husbandly, wifely.

matrimony *n.* marriage, marital state, sacrament of wedlock, holy wedlock, conjugal union, connubial state, nuptial state. **—Ant.** divorce, annulment; single life, bachelorhood, spinsterhood.

matrix *n.* mold, cast, form, frame; die, punch, stamp.

matron *n.* **1.** married woman, middle-aged woman, stately woman, dowager, madam, dame. **2.** female supervisor, overseer, superintendent; directress, mistress, forelady, forewoman, housekeeper.

—**Ant.** **1** girl, maid, maiden, miss, lass, young woman.

matter *n.* **1.** material, stuff, substance, elements; object, thing. **2.** subject matter, text, subject, content, theme, topic, thesis, gist, sense, purport, drift, argument, essence, sum and substance; printed matter, written matter. **3.** affair, business, situation, transaction, thing, proceeding, episode, occurrence, experience, adventure, scrape, circumstance, event, happening. **4.** importance, consequence, significance, import, moment, difference. **5.** trouble, difficulty, cause of distress; predicament, emergency, crisis, exigency, dilemma, quandary, perplexity, strait; obstacle, impediment, *Informal* fix, snag. —*v.* **6.** be of importance, be of consequence, count, be of concern, be noteworthy; import, signify, carry weight, have influence. —**Syn. Study.** **1** MATTER, MATERIAL, STUFF, SUBSTANCE refer to that of which physical objects are composed. MATTER applies to anything occupying space and perceptible to the senses; it may denote a particular kind: *solid matter; vegetable matter.* MATERIAL refers to a definite kind of matter, esp. that used to manufacture or construct something: *woolen material; building materials.* STUFF is an informal term that applies to the basic material of which something is made; it may also denote an unspecified kind of material: *Do you have the stuff to make the rug?* SUBSTANCE is usu. a definite kind of matter thought of in relation to its characteristic properties: *a sticky substance.* These terms are also used abstractly, esp. with reference to thought or expression: *controversial matter; material for a novel; the stuff of dreams; the substance of a speech.* —**Ant.** **1** spirit, soul; mind, intellect. **4** insignificance, unimportance, meaninglessness. **5** solution, answer, resolution. **6** be unimportant, inconsequential, be of no concern.

matter-of-fact *adj.* practical, straightforward, realistic, factual, literal, down-to-earth, unaffected, real, natural, sensible, prosaic, hardheaded, unsentimental, mundane, pragmatic, commonplace, ordinary; straight-out, blunt, candid, outspoken, frank, direct. —**Ant.** speculative, vague, impractical, theoretical, impassioned, emotional.

mature *adj.* **1.** grown, matured, fully developed, completely grown, grownup, fullgrown, of age, adult, middle-aged, in one's prime; experienced, practiced, seasoned; marriageable, nubile, womanly; manly, virile; ripe, full-blown. **2.** completed, perfected, ready, finished, fullfledged. —*v.* **3.** maturate, reach maturity, come of age, become adult, grow up, develop; ripen, bloom, blossom, flower; mellow. —**Ant.** **1** immature, unripe, undeveloped, half-grown, underaged, young, juvenile, adolescent, childish, childlike, youthful, boyish, girlish; green, *Slang* wet behind the ears; callow, unfledged; unripe. **2** incomplete, unperfected, unfinished.

maturity *n.* **1.** adulthood, maturation, manhood, womanhood, full growth, full development; legal age, age of consent, majority; ripeness, full bloom; completion, perfection, readiness, fulfillment, culmination. **2.** experience, practice, seasoning; levelheadedness, composure, mature judgment, matureness, responsibility. —**Ant.** **1** immaturity, youthfulness, boyishness, girlishness, childishness, juvenility, puerility, callowness; incompletion, imperfection, crudeness. **2** irresponsibility, faulty judgment; excitability, hot-headedness.

maudlin *adj.* emotional, overemotional, sentimental, weakly sentimental, mawkish, bathetic, teary, lachrymose, gushing, tearful, *Informal* gushy, mushy, slushy. —**Ant.** realistic, matter-of-fact, unemotional, unsentimental.

maul *v.* manhandle, batter, beat, beat up, rough up, pummel, thrash, bruise, mangle, stomp, knock about.

maunder *v.* **1.** wander, ramble, drift, saunter, meander, stray, straggle, flounder, dawdle, loaf, dillydally. **2.** babble, blather, ramble on, prattle, run on, hem and haw, gibber, go on and on, gabble.

mausoleum *n.* stately tomb, family tomb, sepulchral monument.

mauve *adj.* light purple, bluish purple, lilac, lavender, puce, plum, violet.

maverick *n.* **1.** unbranded calf, yearling; unbranded cow; motherless calf. **2.** nonconformist, eccentric, independent, individualist, loner, independent thinker, one's own man; dissenter, dissident.

maw *n.* **1.** gullet, throat, esophagus, mouth; jaws, muzzle. **2.** crop, craw, first stomach of a bird.

mawkish *adj.* sentimental, oversentimental, maudlin, emotional, nostalgic, lachrymose, tearful, teary, *Informal* mushy, gushy, schmaltzy. —**Ant.** unsentimental, unemotional, matter-of-fact.

maxim *n.* adage, aphorism, axiom, proverb, apothegm, platitude, truism, saw, saying, old saw; motto, guiding principle, rule. —**Syn. Study.** See PROVERB.

maximum *adj.* greatest possible, optimum, greatest, utmost, top, highest, maximal; supreme, unsurpassed, paramount, foremost; most, largest. —**Ant.** minimum, minimal, least possible, least, lowest, bottom.

maybe *adv.* possibly, perhaps, perchance, peradventure, mayhap; feasibly, conceivably, imaginably; God willing, wind and weather permitting.

maze *n.* labyrinth, complex, network, meander, tangle, snarl, convolution, complex puzzle; jungle.

meadow *n.* grazing land, grassland, pasture, lea, savanna, pasturage, green, mead, meadowland, field, park; forage, herbage.

meager *adj.* scanty, scant, slight, paltry, little, skimpy, scrimpy, sparse, bare, slender, slim, token, thin, lean; inadequate, insubstantial, insufficient, deficient, wanting, short, stinted, spare, scarce. **—Syn. Study.** See SCANTY. **—Ant.** ample, abundant, plentiful, copious; adequate, sufficient, substantial.

meal[1] *n.* repast, spread, feast, banquet, refreshment, nourishment; food, cuisine, cooking, fare, victuals, bill of fare, menu, diet, *Slang* eats, grub, chow.

meal[2] *n.* ground grain, flour; (*variously*) cornmeal, oatmeal, groats, bran, grits, farina.

mean[1] *v.* **1.** intend, have in mind; propose, plan, purpose, aspire to, want, wish, dream of, think of, resolve, determine upon, aim at, drive at, have in view. **2.** denote, signify, express, stand for, symbolize, say, tell of; indicate, point to, imply, suggest, intimate, hint at, betoken. **3.** say truly, speak sincerely, feel honestly, express genuinely. **—Ant. 2** hide, conceal, mask. **3** lie, pretend, feign, counterfeit.

mean[2] *adj.* **1.** low, low-grade, poor, inferior, cheap, second-rate, flimsy, sleazy, gimcrack, jerry-built, trashy, rubbishy, squalid, wretched, miserable, sordid; menial, low-ranking, low-paying, trifling, petty, unimportant, trivial, paltry, piddling, insignificant, inconsequential, small, picayune. **2.** malicious, vicious, malign, malevolent, evil, villainous, low, base, petty, small-minded, shameful, contemptible, despicable, disgraceful, dishonorable, vile, nasty, disagreeable, rude, cruel, hardhearted, merciless, pitiless, inhumane, inhuman, unfeeling, unsympathetic, uncaring, unfair. **3.** stingy, miserly, pinchpenny, closefisted, tightfisted, niggardly, penurious; ungenerous, illiberal, tight, close, cheap; greedy, grasping, avaricious, venal, hoggish, selfish, self-seeking, mercenary. **—Syn. Study. 2** MEAN, LOW, BASE refer to characteristics worthy of dislike, contempt, or disgust. MEAN suggests a petty selfishness or lack of generosity, and may describe spiteful, unkind, or even vicious behavior: *mean rumors; a mean bully.* LOW means dishonorable in purpose or character; it describes that which is morally reprehensible or vulgar: *low deeds; low company.* BASE suggests moral depravity, greed, and cowardice; it describes dishonorable or exploitative behavior: *base motives.* **—Ant. 1** high, good, superior, excellent, superb, splendid, first-rate, choice, premium, deluxe; high-ranking, important, consequential, significant, big. **2** kind, goodhearted, warm, good, sweet, gentle, humane, sympathetic, compassionate; noble, honorable, praiseworthy, pleasing, attractive, agreeable, wonderful. **3** generous, liberal, openhanded, bountiful, munificent, princely; unselfish, altruistic.

mean[3] *n.* **1.** average, norm, par, median, rule; happy medium, golden mean, balance, compromise, midway point. —*adj.* **2.** average; normal, standard, medium, regular; commonplace, run-of-the-mill. **—Ant. 2** extreme, ultimate; best, highest, greatest, most; worst, lowest, smallest, least.

meander *v.* wind, circle, loop, zigzag, corkscrew, twist, snake, convolute, undulate, spiral; wander, ramble, go aimlessly, stray, rove. **—Ant.** go straight, go directly, make a bee line.

meaning *n.* denotation, sense, signification; significance, substance, sum and substance, content, subject matter, essence, gist, pith, meat, upshot; implication, drift, suggestion, intimation, indication, hint, pointer; intention, intent, purpose, purport, thrust, force, burden, goal, aim, point, object; value, worth, end; view, design, scheme, plan. **—Syn. Study.** MEANING, SENSE, SIGNIFICANCE, PURPORT denote that which is expressed or indicated by language or action. MEANING is a general word describing that which is intended to be, or actually is, expressed: *the meaning of a statement.* SENSE often refers to a particular meaning of a word or phrase: *The word "run" has many senses.* SENSE may also be used of meaning that is intelligible or reasonable: *There's no sense in what you say.* SIGNIFICANCE refers to a meaning that is implied rather than expressed: *the significance of a glance.* It may also refer to a meaning the importance of which is not immediately perceived: *We did not grasp the significance of the event until years later.* PURPORT usu. refers to the gist or essential meaning of something fairly complicated: *the purport of a theory.* **—Ant.** meaninglessness, insignificance, irrationality, absurdity.

meaningful *adj.* **1.** pointed, significant, having meaning, purposeful, eloquent, expressive, deep, portentous, pregnant, designing, suggestive, explicit, pithy. **2.** worthwhile, useful, substantial, significant, consequential, important, serious, meaty; gratifying, emotionally satisfying. **—Ant. 1, 2** meaningless, superficial, senseless, facetious. **2** worthless, useless, unsubstantial, insignificant, inconsequential, unimportant, pithy, trifling, trivial, paltry.

meaningless *adj.* **1.** unintelligible, incomprehensible, incoherent, impenetrable, inexpressive, undecipherable, illegible; puzzling, baffling, inscrutable, inexplicable, mystifying, perplexing, bewildering, enigmatic. **2.** without meaning, without purpose, purposeless, worthless, valueless, useless, unsubstantial, aimless, insignificant, inconsequential, unimportant, unessential, trivial, trite, paltry, piddling, shallow, senseless, frivolous, facetious, foolish, fatuous, absurd, stupid, nonsensical, idiotic, preposterous. **—Ant. 1, 2** meaningful. **1** intelligible, comprehensible, understandable, coherent, expressive, clear, obvious, evident, manifest, pithy, trenchant; legible, decipherable. **2** purposeful, worthwhile, valuable, useful, substantial, significant, momentous, consequential, important, deep, sensible.

means *n. pl.* **1.** money, resources, wherewithal, funds, dollars, income, revenue, *Slang* jack, long green, dough, bread; wealth, riches, substance, capital, property, affluence, easy circumstances. **2.** way, method, mode; resort, avenue, course, alternative; measure, process, modus operandi.

meantime *n.* interim, interval, the period between, the intervening time.

meanwhile *adv.* at the same time, simultaneously, concurrently; during the intervening period, in the interim, meantime, for the time being.

measurable *adj.* computable, reckonable, capable of being measured, mensurable, determinable, appraisable, assessable. **—Ant.** immeasurable, indeterminate.

measure *v.* **1.** ascertain the dimensions of, find the size of, size, pace off, step off, plumb, sound; time, clock; to be the size of, be long, be wide. **2.** evaluate, value, assess, appraise, gauge, survey, judge. *—n.* **3.** measurement, unit of measurement; (*variously*) gauge, rule, scale, yardstick. **4.** share, allotment, quantity, amount, portion, quota, allowance, extent, degree, range, scope; necessary amount, required amount. **5.** limit, limitation, bound, restraint, moderation, temperance. **6.** act, bill, proposal, law, enactment; plan, scheme, design, project, proposition. **7.** course, means, step, method, resort, proceeding, procedure.

measured *adj.* **1.** predetermined; precise, exact, verified. **2.** uniform, steady, regular, equal. **3.** studied, deliberate, premeditated, intentional, calculated, well-planned, carefully thought-out, cold-blooded. **—Ant. 2** haphazard, irregular, random. **3** spontaneous, rash, reckless, emotional, on the spur of the moment, unplanned.

measurement *n.* **1.** measuring, mensuration, surveying, sounding, plumbing; evaluation, assessment, appraisal, gauging, estimation, reckoning. **2.** dimension, size, breadth, depth, length, height, width, area; capacity, volume, content; mass, weight; magnitude, amplitude, extent.

meat *n.* **1.** edible animal flesh, animal tissue or organs. **2.** food, nourishment, victuals, sustenance, edibles, comestibles, fare, provisions, grub, provender. **3.** gist, point, essence, substance, core, heart, kernel, nut, nucleus.

mechanical *adj.* **1.** run by machinery, having to do with machinery; machine-driven, automatic, self-acting. **2.** perfunctory, routine, unfeeling, impersonal, cold, machinelike; automatic, instinctive, involuntary, unconscious, unthinking. **—Ant. 1** manual. **2** genuine, sincere, heartfelt, wholehearted, personal, warm; voluntary, conscious, thinking.

mechanism *n.* apparatus, tool, instrument, implement, utensil, contrivance, appliance, machine; works, machinery, motor.

medal *n.* citation, decoration, medallion, ribbon, award of honor; trophy, prize, award; honor, laurel, reward.

meddle *v.* interfere, intervene, intermeddle, intrude, concern oneself unasked, interlope, mix in, pry into, *Informal* butt in, horn in, stick one's nose in; tamper with; *Informal* kibitz. **—Ant.** keep out, *Informal* butt out.

meddlesome *adj.* intrusive, officious, impertinent, presumptuous, obtrusive, meddling, prying, pushing, interfering, snooping; *Slang* nosy, snoopy, pushy. **—Ant.** restrained, reserved; aloof, indifferent, standoffish.

mediate *v.* arbitrate, negotiate, moderate, intervene, intercede, interpose, settle a dispute, bring to terms, effect an agreement, bring about an agreement; make peace between, pacify, conciliate, reconcile, propitiate, restore harmony, step in, umpire, referee.

mediation *n.* arbitration, compromise, adjustment, conciliation, reconciliation, give-and-take, settlement of difficulties, coming to terms; negotiation, discussion, parley, intervention, intercession; pacification, peacemaking.

mediator *n.* arbitrator, negotiator, moderator, reconciler, go-between, intermediary, referee, umpire, peacemaker.

medical *adj.* relating to medicine, medicinal, medicative, curative, healing, therapeutic, remedial, restorative, sanative, health-bringing, salutary. **—Ant.** unhealthy, unhealthful, toxic, poisonous, virulent.

medication *n.* remedy, medicine, medicament, healing application, curative substance; tonic, restorative, palliative, balm; panacea, nostrum, elixir.

medicine *n.* **1.** curative agent, medication; drug, pill, remedy, nostrum, tonic, restorative; balm, salve. **2.** science of medicine, practice of medicine, healing art, medical treatment, therapeutics, materia medica. **—Ant. 1** poison, toxin, bane.

medieval *adj.* of the Middle Ages (the period between A.D. 476 and approximately 1450), pre-Renaissance.

mediocre *adj.* ordinary, run-of-the-mill, undistinguished, commonplace, pedestrian, indifferent, passable, tolerable, so-so, fair-to-middling, betwixt and between, average, medium, normal, common; unimportant, inconsequential, insignificant, negligible, inconsiderable, inappreciable, petty, slight, trifling, paltry, meager; inferior, rather poor, second-rate. **—Ant.** extraordinary, uncommon, distinctive, distinguished, unique, unexcelled, unsurpassed, unrivaled, incomparable; superior, fine, excellent, superb; important, significant.

mediocrity *n.* commonplaceness, indifference, ordinariness, unimportance, insignificance, pettiness, paltriness, meagerness, triviality; low-quality, inferiority, poorness. **—Ant.** distinction, uniqueness; importance, significance, consequence; excellence, superiority, greatness, brilliance.

meditate *v.* **1.** think, reflect, think quietly, think seriously, ruminate, muse, contemplate, ponder, study, cogitate, deliberate, collect one's thoughts, dwell upon, turn over in the mind, mull over. **2.** plan, devise, concoct, contrive, consider, propose, have in view, aim at, dream of, aspire to. **—Ant. 1** act, do.

meditative *adj.* **—Syn. Study.** See PENSIVE.

medium *n.* **1.** environment, surroundings, atmosphere; setting, milieu; material, technique. **2.** middle ground, midcourse, middle way; compromise, moderation, happy medium, mean, golden mean, balance. **3.** agency, means, way, mode, form, channel, instrument, vehicle, tool, avenue, instrumentality, organ; [means of mass communication] (*variously*) newspaper, newsletter, journal, magazine, quarterly, pamphlet, bulletin, broadside, circular, poster, flyer, radio, radio broadcast, television, television broadcast, newscast. **4.** spiritualist, psychic, clairvoyant, fortuneteller, diviner, crystal gazer, seer, prophet, channeler; go-between, intermediary, intermediate. *—adj.* **5.** average, common, normal, ordinary, middling, moderate. **—Ant. 2** extreme limit. **5** extreme, utmost, extraordinary, uncommon, distinctive, unique, unusual, undue, unreasonable.

medley *n.* miscellany, olio, mixture, assortment, potpourri, mélange, pastiche, mosaic, patchwork; jumble, gallimaufry, hodgepodge, farrago, *Informal* mishmash, hash, mess.

meek *adj.* submissive, deferential, complaisant, docile, yielding, tractable, acquiescent, unresisting, compliant, long-suffering, spineless, spiritless, weak-kneed, lamblike; humble, mild, gentle, modest, unassuming, unassertive, unpretentious, retiring, tolerant, tender-hearted. **—Ant.** domineering, bossy, willful, overbearing, self-assertive, bold, forward, presumptuous; spirited, *Informal* spunky; rebellious, insubordinate, unyielding; arrogant, lordly, proud, immodest, pretentious.

meet[1] *v.* **1.** be introduced to, be presented to, become acquainted with; welcome, greet. **2.** come across, encounter, run into, bump into, come into contact with, light upon; confront, face, come into the presence of, speak with. **3.** assemble, convene, gather, collect, congregate, rally, muster, come together. **4.** fulfill, comply with, satisfy, observe, abide by, adhere to, observe, execute, carry out, perform, discharge, heed, obey, be faithful to, follow, acknowledge, respect, keep one's pledge; equal, come up to, answer, match. **5.** cross, intersect, unite with, converge with; adjoin, abut, border. **—Ant. 1** become estranged. **2** avoid, elude, escape, miss. **3** adjourn; disperse, scatter, dispel. **4** fail, fall short of; renege. **5** diverge.

meet[2] *adj.* proper, appropriate, apposite, fitting, fit, befitting, suitable, seemly, right, apt, good, felicitous, decorous, becoming; allowable, admissible, permitted, permissible, pertinent, relevant, compatible, agreeable, congruous. **—Ant.** improper, unfitting, inappropriate, unsuitable, unseemly, wrong, unbecoming; incongruous, incompatible.

meeting *n.* **1.** introduction, presentation; encounter, confrontation; date, engagement, rendezvous, tryst, assignation. **2.** gathering, assembly, group, convocation, conclave, council, congress, caucus; conference, convention, get-together.

melancholy *n.* **1.** melancholia; depression, gloom, gloominess, dejection, despondency, disconsolateness, despair, forlornness, moodiness, low spirits, doldrums; *Slang* blues, dumps. *—adj.* **2.** suffering from melancholia; depressed, gloomy, dejected, despondent, disconsolate, forlorn, glum, moody, mopish, doleful, downhearted, heavyhearted, discouraged, dispirited, downcast, cheerless, heartsick, sick at heart, unhappy, morose, languishing, *Slang* down in the dumps, down in the mouth, blue. **3.** depressing, gloomy, dreary, somber, dismal, desolate, joyless, plaintive, mournful, funereal; dolorous, doleful; unfortunate, calamitous. **—Ant. 1** exhilaration, joy, delight, pleasure, cheer, happiness, gladness. **2** exhilarated, joyous, joyful, cheerful, lighthearted, happy, glad, vivacious, gay, lively, sprightly, merry. **3** exhilarating, joyous, delightful, cheerful, happy.

mélange *n.* mixture, mix, medley, potpourri, pastiche, miscellany, jumble, hodgepodge, mishmash, gallimaufry, assortment, patchwork, pasticcio, assemblage, compound.

meld *v.* merge, mix, blend, fuse, combine, consolidate, coalesce, unite, amalgamate, incorporate, mingle, join, commingle, intermingle, interweave, intertwine, intermix, jumble, scramble. **—Ant.** separate, dissociate, split, divide.

melee *n.* fistfight, brawl, row, free-for-all, fracas, fray, set to, scuffle, scrap, tussle, dogfight, altercation, commotion, rumpus, disorder, riot, pandemonium.

mellifluous *adj.* sweet-sounding, sweet-toned, euphonious, mellifluent, musical, harmonious, sweet, dulcet, melodious, mellow, soft, smooth; resonant, full-toned. **—Ant.** harsh, discordant, grating, jarring, raucous, hoarse, unmusical.

mellow *adj.* **1.** ripe, mature, matured; full-flavored, full-bodied, luscious, sweet, delicious; soft, rich. **—*v.* 2.** mature, season; make more understanding, make sympathetic, make compassionate, make more tolerant, soften, smooth the rough edges. **—Ant. 1** unripe, immature, green; raw, sour, biting, harsh. **2** harden, brutalize, make callous, make unfeeling, make stubborn.

melodic *adj.* of melody, creating melody, full of melody; melodious, tuneful, lyric. **—Ant.** unmelodic.

melodious *adj.* **1.** sweet-toned, mellifluous, mellifluent, euphonious, musical, sweet, dulcet, mellow, soft, smooth; clear, rich, full-toned, resonant, ringing. **2.** tuneful, full of melody, melodic, lyric. **—Ant. 1** harsh, discordant, grating, jarring, raucous. **2** unmelodic, untuneful, cacophonous, unharmonious.

melodramatic *adj.* exaggerated, flamboyant, overly theatrical, sensational, stagy, sentimental, overemotional, overwrought, frenzied, mawkish, maudlin, histrionic, spectacular, *Slang* hammy, corny, cornball, hokey. **—Ant.** realistic, matter-of-fact; understated, low-key, deadpan.

melody *n.* **1.** tune, air, strain, theme; song, aria, ballad, ditty. **2.** tunefulness, melodiousness, musicality, musical invention, melodic gift, melodic invention; euphony, harmoniousness, mellifluence, mellifluousness, concord, sweetness of sound, timbre. **—Ant. 1** harmony; rhythm. **2** dissonance; harshness, discordance, clashing, jarring.

melt *v.* **1.** dissolve, liquefy, thaw. **2.** dissipate, scatter, dispel, dwindle, fade, dissolve, disappear, evaporate, vanish; waste away. **3.** blend, fuse, merge, pass, shade, fade, dissolve. **4.** touch, soften, disarm, make gentle, affect, arouse pity; appease, conciliate, mollify, propitiate. **—Ant. 1** freeze, solidify; congeal, jell, set, harden. **2** accrue, gather, grow. **4** harden, make callous.

member *n.* **1.** extremity, appendage; (*variously*) limb, leg, foot, toe, arm, hand, finger, digit; (*animals*) wing, pinion, tail; part, organ; (*plants*) shoot, bough, branch. **2.** constituent, person who belongs to a group; component, element, part, piece, section, segment, portion, fragment, ingredient.

membership *n.* **1.** fellowship, affiliation, league, fraternal union, connection. **2.** roster, personnel, body of members, number of members; community, company, association; society, fraternity, brotherhood, club, fellowship.

membrane *n.* web, covering tissue; film, thin sheet, coating, thin skin, sheath, lining, envelope; integument, pellicle.

memento *n.* souvenir, token, keepsake, reminder, favor, remembrance, record, trophy, memorabilia, remembrancer, memorial, relic, commemoration.

memoir *n.* autobiography, diary, journal, recollections, reminiscences, reflections, experiences, adventures, confessions, biography, intimate biography, life, life story.

memorable *adj.* unforgettable, notable, noteworthy, impressive, illustrious, famous, celebrated, distinguished, eminent, prominent, important, significant, momentous, historic, outstanding, salient, remarkable, extraordinary, striking, stirring, red-letter. **—Ant.** unmemorable, forgettable, unimpressive, undistinguished, unimportant, insignificant, mediocre, commonplace, ordinary, pedestrian, prosaic, banal, trite, trivial, run-of-the-mill.

memorandum *n.* memo, reminder, minute, note, brief report, record, brief, jotting; list of items, agenda.

memorial *n.* **1.** monument, testimonial. **2.** tribute, homage, commemorative service, memorial service. —*adj.* **3.** commemorative, monumental, testimonial.

memory *n.* **1.** recall, ability to remember, power of recollection, mental retention, remembrance, remembering. **2.** recollection, mental impression, reminiscence, remembrancer, memento, souvenir, keepsake, reminder, token, memorial, commemoration, testimonial. **3.** fame, renown, eminence, reputation, repute, glory, prestige, distinction, esteem, honor, estimation, name, note, mark, regard, respect. —**Ant. 1** forgetfulness. **2** amnesia; a total blank. **3** oblivion, nothingness, void, nonexistence.

menace *n.* **1.** threat, danger, peril, hazard, jeopardy, risk, endangerment, imperilment, pitfall, cause for alarm. —*v.* **2.** endanger, imperil, be a hazard to, jeopardize, risk; terrify, intimidate, threaten, terrorize, bully, browbeat, cow, daunt; forebode, portend, presage. —**Ant. 1** blessing, benefit, boon, advantage. **2** benefit, help, aid, promote, further, advance; protect, guard, safeguard; soothe, console, calm.

mend *v.* **1.** repair, fix, put in order, restore, renovate, overhaul, recondition, touch up, retouch, patch, darn; heal, knit, cure, remedy. **2.** correct, reform, improve, better, ameliorate, meliorate, amend, rectify, revise. —**Ant. 1** damage, harm, mar, injure, lacerate, tear, break, split; spoil, ruin, destroy.

mendacity *n.* lying, falsehood, falsity, untruthfulness, falsification, prevarication, misrepresentation; deceit, deception, duplicity, dishonesty, hypocrisy, perfidy, double-dealing, fraud, chicanery, insincerity. —**Ant.** truth, truthfulness, veracity, frankness, openness, forthrightness; honesty, trustworthiness, uprightness, sincerity.

mendicant *n.* begging monk, begging friar; beggar, street beggar, alms-seeker, panhandler.

menial *adj.* **1.** lowly, degrading, low, humble, ignoble, mean, abject; servile, subservient, slavish, obsequious, fawning, groveling, truckling, cringing, sycophantic, *Informal* apple-polishing, bootlicking. —*n.* **2.** servant, flunky, lackey, underling, subordinate; employee, apprentice, helper; slave, drudge, drone; sycophant, toady. —**Ant. 1** noble, dignified, autocratic, aristocratic, high, elevated; overbearing, domineering, bossy, proud, haughty, conceited. **2** master, lord, overseer, superior, chief, commander, boss.

mental *adj.* **1.** of the mind, in the mind, done with the mind, intellectual, intelligent, cerebral, rational; psychic, psychological; abstract, metaphysical, subjective. **2.** mentally ill, mentally disturbed, psychotic, neurotic; insane, crazy, lunatic, disordered, disturbed, unbalanced, *Slang* nutty, cracked, psycho.

mentality *n.* intellect, mental ability, intelligence, mental power, mental endowment, mind, brains, gray matter; perception, judgment, understanding, discernment, perspicacity, acumen, wisdom, sagacity.

mention *v.* **1.** allude to, speak of briefly, refer to, touch upon; name, specify, cite, disclose, make known, divulge; hint at, intimate, imply, insinuate; state, observe, remark, tell, say, tell of, report, recount, narrate. —*n.* **2.** allusion, suggestion, indication, hint, insinuation, inkling, reference, remark, statement, utterance, comment, communication, advisement, announcement, notice, notification, report, specification, observation, designation, acquaintance, enlightenment. —**Ant. 1** omit, be silent about; forget, neglect, disregard, slight, ignore, drop, suppress. **2** omission, avoidance, neglect, silence, suppression.

mentor *n.* adviser, counselor, preceptor; teacher, instructor, professor, tutor; monitor, proctor; master, guru, guide, *Informal* significant other.

mercenary *adj.* **1.** selfish, greedy, venal; monetary, money-motivated, for gain, for pay; acquisitive, grasping, avaricious, covetous. —*n.* **2.** hired soldier, paid soldier in a foreign army, soldier fighting for spoils; hireling. —**Ant. 1** idealistic, selfless, unselfish, altruistic; generous, liberal, philanthropic, benevolent, munificent.

merchandise *n.* **1.** manufactured goods, goods, wares, stock, stock in trade; commodities, staples; effects, belongings. —*v.* **2.** sell, market, distribute; trade, deal in, buy and sell, carry on commerce in, do business in, traffic in; advertise, publicize, *Slang* huckster.

merchant *n.* salesman, saleswoman, dealer, wholesaler, purchaser, broker, jobber, trader; shopkeeper, retailer, tradesman, tradeswoman, vendor, storekeeper, peddler, hawker, chandler, monger, street vendor.

merciful *adj.* compassionate, humane, exercising mercy, kind, lenient, clement, sparing, sympathetic, forgiving, pitying, kindhearted, soft-hearted, understanding, feeling, benign, gracious, tender, beneficent. —**Ant.** merciless, unfeeling, uncompassionate, cruel, inhumane, hardhearted, pitiless.

merciless *adj.* pitiless, ruthless, unmerciful, inhumane, hardhearted, cold-blooded, inhuman, unrelenting, relentless, remorseless, cruel, fell; harsh, severe, fierce, unsparing, heartless, unpitying, callous, ferocious. —**Ant.** merciful, humane, forgiving, kind-hearted, clement, lenient.

mercurial *adj.* flighty, impulsive, changeable, inconstant, erratic, fickle, unstable, unpredictable, capricious, volatile, mobile, kinetic, fluctuating, variable, protean, impetuous, lively, electric, spirited, irrepressible. —**Ant.** unchanging, stable, fixed, phlegmatic.

mercy *n.* **1.** compassion, kindness, forbearance, benevolence, pity, clemency, sympathy, humaneness, soft-heartedness, humanity, tolerance, charity, commiseration, grace, fellow feeling, tenderheartedness, forgiveness, lenity, leniency, lenience. **2.** good thing, piece of luck, lucky break, blessing. —**Ant. 1** pitilessness, cruelty, harshness, rigor, severity, sternness, implacability, inhumanity, brutality.

mere *adj.* common, ordinary, inconsiderable, insignificant, trifling, commonplace, mundane, nugatory, paltry, negligible, unappreciable, uneventful; nothing else but, nothing more than, pure and simple, utter, plain, bare; sheer, scant, unmitigated, bald, sole.

meretricious *adj.* spurious, specious, bogus, sham, false, tawdry, fraudulent, counterfeit, deceptive, misleading, mock, pseudo, delusive, *Slang* phony, shoddy. —**Ant.** genuine, authentic, bona fide, legitimate.

merge *v.* combine, amalgamate, consolidate, fuse, become one, converge, blend, integrate, join, intermix, coalesce, weld, synthesize, unite, interfuse, interconnect, interlock, confederate, associate, band together, unify, link up. —**Ant.** separate, diverge, sever, part, disjoin, disband.

meridian *n.* zenith, acme, peak, summit, pinnacle, apex, top, tip, crest, vertex, apogee, climax, culmination, heights, brow, ridge, crown, point. —**Ant.** nadir, low, depths, bottom.

merit *n.* **1.** value, worth, worthiness, desert, virtue, advantage, benefit, justification; efficacy, credit, quality, stature, ability, worthiness, excellence, talent, distinction. —*v.* **2.** deserve, be entitled to, rate, be worthy of, have a right to, warrant, invite, prompt, have claim to, earn. —**Ant. 1** fault, defect, worthlessness, weakness, imperfection, discredit.

meritorious *adj.* commendable, laudable, praiseworthy, noteworthy, exceptional, deserving of reward or commendation, worthy, creditable, well carried out, estimable, excellent, fine, exemplary, admirable. —**Ant.** unexceptional, unpraiseworthy, unworthy, discreditable, undeserving, dishonest, dishonorable, ignoble, unchivalrous, ungenerous.

merriment *n.* mirth, laughter, gaiety, jollity, hilarity, frolic, fun, good fun, good spirits, revelry, glee, sportiveness, amusement, cheer, gleefulness, celebration, joviality, jocularity, lightheartedness, liveliness, jocundity, festivity, merrymaking, levity, good humor, jubilation, skylarking, exhilaration, conviviality, *Informal* whoopee, hoopla. —**Ant.** cheerlessness, joylessness, distress, misery, mourning.

merry *adj.* gay, jolly, cheerful, happy, cheery, gladsome, blithe, gleeful, jovial, joyous, sportive, carefree, mirthful, jocular, frolicsome, fun-loving, lighthearted, jocund, jolly, lively, high-spirited, partying, laughing, skylarking, festive, convivial, rollicking, animated, vivacious, reveling, sprightly. —**Ant.** sad, unhappy, gloomy, disconsolate, dismal, dejected.

merrymaking *n.* gaiety, festivity, revelry, jollity, merriment, revels, conviviality, sport, fun-making, celebration; carousal, bacchanalia, saturnalia; *Slang* whoopee, high jinks, hoopla, whoop-de-doo. —**Ant.** gloom, sorrow, melancholy, woe, sadness.

mesh *n.* **1.** web, netting, network, grille, reticulation, openwork, screen, sieve, plexus, webwork, meshwork, grid, webbing, wickerwork, latticework, grillwork, lacework. —*v.* **2.** engage, interlock, interweave, enmesh, intermesh, connect, dovetail, fit together, coordinate, interact.

mesmerize *v.* spellbind, bewitch, fascinate, magnetize, entrance, transport, charm, enthrall; hypnotize, put in a trance, control another's mind.

mess *n.* **1.** clutter, unsightly accumulation, jumble, litter, hodgepodge, confused mass, hash, mishmash, conglomeration; untidy condition, dirty state, disorder, disarray. **2.** predicament, difficulty, plight, muddle, mix-up, confusion, pickle, situation, quandary, fix, strait, stew, scrape, pinch, trouble, *Informal* hot water, pretty kettle of fish; dilemma, imbroglio, crisis. **3.** messhall, dining room, refectory, dining hall, commissary, cafeteria.

message *n.* **1.** notice, report, word, statement, news, communication, memorandum, communiqué, intelligence, tidings; dispatch, missive, note, letter, bulletin, e-mail, fax. **2.** point, theme, central idea, meaning, purport, moral.

messenger *n.* carrier, bearer, runner, deliverer, delivery boy, delivery man, courier, go-between, intermediary, emissary, envoy, delegate.

messy *adj.* **1.** disordered, cluttered, untidy, littered, sloppy, chaotic, disarranged, confused, jumbled, topsy-turvy;

bedraggled, sloppy, disheveled, unkempt, slatternly, frowsy, blowsy, grubby. **2.** awkward, difficult, unpleasant, embarrassing, tangled, inextricable, unenviable, ugly, uncomfortable, tricky. **—Ant. 1** ordered, neat, tidy, clean. **2** pleasant, comfortable, enviable.

metamorphosis *n.* **1.** transformation, change of form, mutation, transmutation, structural evolution, transfiguration, series of changes, modification, conversion, transmogrification. **2.** change in appearance or behavior, personality change, transformation, alteration, radical change, startling change, permutation.

metaphor *n.* image, representation, figurative expression, poetic equivalent, sensory symbol, figure of speech, simile, trope, metonymy, analogy, parallel, equivalence.

metaphysical *adj.* **1.** philosophical, speculative, abstract, unanswerable, intellectual; ultimate, essential, universal, eternal, fundamental, basic; ontological, cosmological, epistemological, existential; esoteric, mystical. **2.** abstract, intangible, vague, impalpable, lofty, highflown, abstruse, oversubtle, recondite, jesuitical, *Slang* far-out. **—Ant. 1** physical, material, mundane. **2** concrete, tangible, clear, comprehensible, down-to-earth.

mete *v.* Usu. **mete out** allocate, disburse, distribute, dispense, measure out, apportion, administer, deal out, dole out, parcel out, allot, divide, assign.

meteoric *adj.* flaming, fleetingly bright, transiently brilliant, fiery, flashing, blazing; rapid, speedy, fast, swift, unabated, sudden, instant; unstoppable, inexorable, ineluctable. **—Ant.** slow, sluggish, gradual, inconspicuous, obscure.

method *n.* **1.** system, technique, procedure, approach, process, way, course, means, scheme, form, routine, usage, program, tack, formula, fashion, modus operandi; style, mode, manner. **2.** purpose, plan, design, order, scheme, system, efficacy, viability. **—Syn. Study. 1** METHOD, WAY, MODE refer to the manner in which something is done. METHOD implies a fixed procedure, usu. following a logical and systematic plan: *the open-hearth method of making steel.* WAY is a general word that may often be substituted for more specific words: *the best way to solve a problem; an attractive way of wearing the hair.* MODE, a more formal word, implies a customary or characteristic manner: *Kangaroos have an unusual mode of carrying their young.*

methodical Also **methodic** *adj.* systematic, deliberate, precise, orderly, well-regulated, exact, tidy, uniform, regular, neat, careful, meticulous; logical, analytical; businesslike. **—Syn. Study.** See ORDERLY. **—Ant.** unmethodical, desultory, random, haphazard, casual, hit-or-miss, confused, disordered, chaotic, jumbled.

meticulous *adj.* fastidious, scrupulous, exact, exacting, minutely careful, solicitous about details, painstaking, precise, nice, finical, finicky, fussy, particular; punctilious, perfectionist. **—Syn. Study.** See PAINSTAKING. **—Ant.** careless, inexact, imprecise, sloppy, negligent.

métier *n.* vocation, calling, occupation, employment, profession, trade, work, livelihood, job, lifework, craft, specialty, pursuit, business, field, line, area, activity.

mettle *n.* courage, hardy temperament, nerve, spirit, gameness, grit, pluck, valor, backbone, intrepidity, spunk, fearlessness, audacity, fortitude, vigor, bravery, gallantry, vim, enthusiasm, determination, resolution, heroism, derring-do, boldness, temerity, manliness, *Informal* guts.

microbe *n.* germ, virus, microscopic organism, microorganism, bacillus, bacterium; (*variously*) parasite, spirochete, streptococcus, staphylococcus, zygote, gamete.

microscopic Also **microscopical** *adj.* **1.** so small as to be invisible without a microscope, infinitesimal, immeasurably small, atomic; of a microscope. **2.** very little, tiny, minute, diminutive, imperceptible, extremely small, *Informal* teeny. **—Ant. 1, 2** large, huge, immense; perceptible; macroscopic.

middle *adj.* **1.** central, mid, midway, halfway, midmost, medial, middlemost, median; intermediate, not extreme, main. *—n.* **2.** center, midpoint, central part, midst, main part; core, heartland, heart, hub, nucleus. **3.** waist, midriff, midsection, stomach, belly, *Slang* gut. **4.** midst, course, process, act, throes. **—Ant. 1** beginning, end, initial, final, extreme. **2** edge, periphery, outskirts.

middleman *n.* intermediary, agent, broker, go-between, dealer, jobber, distributor, wholesaler, entrepreneur, intercessor, mediator, liaison.

middling *adj.* average, ordinary, mediocre, fairish, passable, moderate, moderately good, so-so, fair, unremarkable, medium, just satisfactory, pretty good, tolerable, indifferent, run-of-the-mill; second-rate, minimal.

midget *n.* dwarf, Lilliputian, pygmy, manikin, munchkin, Tom Thumb, hop-o'-my-thumb, homunculus; shrimp, runt, small fry, fingerling, *Informal* squirt, pipsqueak, peewee, *Slang* half pint; puppet, doll. —**Syn. Study.** See DWARF. —**Ant.** giant, colossus, monster, titan.

midst *n.* **1.** heart, middle, center, interior, middle part, hub, bosom, thick, depths, deepest part, core, eye. **2.** heart, thick, most critical time, most important part, core, nucleus; halfway through, midway in.

mien *n.* bearing, air, demeanor, manner, behavior, carriage, presence, deportment, attitude, style, appearance, aspect, countenance, visage, look, feature, semblance, guise, expression.

miff *v.* annoy, provoke, irritate, vex, offend, irk, exasperate, anger, affront, rub the wrong way, rankle, nettle, rile, pique, make one sore, put one off, chafe, raise one's dander. —**Ant.** pacify, soothe, mollify, placate.

might *n.* power, force, strength, potency, prowess, vigor, puissance, robustness, durability, forcefulness, energy, competence, brawn, toughness, sturdiness, capability, capableness, lustihood, muscle; influence, *Slang* clout. —**Ant.** weakness, inability, feebleness.

mighty *adj.* **1.** powerful, strong, hardy, vigorous, robust, stout, lusty, indomitable, stalwart, sturdy, potent, puissant, overpowering, invincible, forceful, able; courageous, brave, bold, valorous, valiant; strapping, brawny, husky, manful. **2.** huge, enormous, of great size, immense, massive, extremely large, titanic, colossal, gigantic, vast, monstrous, majestic, monumental, imposing, prodigious, monolithic, gargantuan, stupendous, towering, Brobdingnagian, elephantine. —*adv.* **3.** *Informal* very, exceedingly, particularly, exceptionally; really, truly. —**Ant. 1** feeble, weak, impotent. **2** small, tiny, unimposing, negligible, unimpressive.

migrate *v.* **1.** emigrate, immigrate, trek, journey, transplant oneself, relocate, resettle. **2.** move, move periodically or seasonally, travel, go elsewhere, depart with others.

mild *adj.* **1.** gentle, calm, serene, placid, smooth, easygoing, good-tempered, docile, bland, easy, tranquil, moderate, pacific, pleasant, complaisant, forbearing. **2.** temperate, moderate, warm, balmy, not extreme, not severe, springlike, summery, pleasant. **3.** not strong, not sharp, soothing, soft, delicate, uninjurious, emollient, not severe, not astringent. —**Ant. 1–3** harsh, severe. **1** fierce, unkind, unpleasant; stormy, turbulent; piquant, biting, bitter, savage, rough, wild, violent. **2** stormy, intemperate, cold. **3** strong, sharp, astringent, powerful.

milestone *n.* **1.** road marker, signpost, milepost. **2.** significant event, crucial occurrence, turning point; decisive achievement, memorable moment, jubilee, red-letter day; anniversary.

milieu *n.* environment, culture, ambience, setting, background, backdrop, surroundings, mise-en-scène, element, scene, preferred company. —**Syn. Study.** See ENVIRONMENT.

militant *adj.* combative, combatant, aggressive, belligerent, contentious, uncompromising, assertive, extreme, defiant, pugnacious, disputatious; engaged in or favoring warfare, warlike, warring, military, paramilitary, fighting, warmongering, bellicose, martial. —**Ant.** moderate, concessive; peaceable, pacific, pacifist, noncombative, nonmilitant.

military *adj.* **1.** armed, martial, warmaking, combative; defensive. **2.** soldierlike, soldierly, strict, well-disciplined, crisp, Spartan, martial; belligerent, warlike. **3.** regimented, regulated, systematized. —*n.* **4.** army, armed forces, soldiers, standing army, militia, troops; generals, military establishment.

milksop *n.* coward, weakling, mollycoddle, sissy, softy, milquetoast, namby-pamby, pansy, pantywaist, poltroon, mama's boy, baby, mouse, crybaby; wimp, scaredy-cat, fraidy-cat. —**Ant.** he-man, brute, Tarzan, Superman, Rambo.

mill *v.* **1.** grind, pulverize, crush, reduce to powder, granulate; shape, finish, groove, or polish with a milling tool. **2.** roam, meander, wander or converge en masse, move around aimlessly, swarm, teem.

mimic *v.* **1.** ape, imitate, take off, impersonate, parrot; mirror, echo, simulate, counterfeit, copy, reproduce. —*n.* **2.** imitator, mime, impressionist, aper, copyist, copycat, burlesquer, feigner.

mince *v.* **1.** dice, chop fine, cut into tiny particles, cut into small pieces, shred, grate. **2.** pose, posture, put on airs, give oneself airs, attitudinize; affect daintiness, affect delicacy, affect primness. **3.** soften, moderate, mitigate, refine, palliate, whitewash, soften one's speech, qualify, be mealymouthed about, hold back, gloss over.

mind *n.* **1.** brain, intellect, mental capacity, apprehension, intellectual faculties, brains, thinking instrumentality, gray matter, *Informal* smarts; reason, judgment, reflection, comprehension, understanding, sense, intelligence, rationality, ratiocination, cognition, awareness, perception, percipience. **2.** sanity, reason, faculties, rationality, understanding, judgment, sense, common sense, wits, mental balance, *Slang* marbles. **3.**

judgment, opinion, point of view, outlook, reaction, response, way of thinking. **4.** opinion, conclusion, consideration, judgment, intent, intention, thought, notion, impression, sentiment, conception, liking, will, propensity, choice, inclination. **5.** remembrance, memory, consciousness, recall, inward attention, recollection, retrospection, reminiscence, contemplation. **6.** attention, concentration, thought, thinking, focus, preoccupation. —*v.* **7.** obey, heed, pay attention to, observe, follow, comply with, submit to, bow to, acquiesce to, adhere to, be careful concerning, be wary of, regard, note, be conscious of, take cognizance of, watch, notice, take notice of. **8.** tend, attend to, look after, take care of, take charge of. **9.** be cautious, be careful, take care, be wary about, watch. **10.** dislike, object to, resent, feel offended about, disapprove of, feel inconvenienced by, eschew, look askance at; shrink from, recoil from, turn up the nose at, have an aversion to, abhor, detest, hate. **—Syn. Study. 1** MIND, INTELLECT, BRAIN refer to that part of a conscious being that thinks, feels, wills, perceives, or judges. MIND is a philosophical, psychological, and general term for the center of all mental activity, as contrasted with the body and the spirit: *His mind grasped the complex issue.* INTELLECT refers to reasoning power, as distinguished from the faculties of feeling: *a book that appeals to the intellect, rather than the emotions.* BRAIN is a physiological term for the organic structure that makes mental activity possible, but is often applied to mental ability or capacity: *a fertile brain.* All of these words may also refer to a person of great mental ability or capacity: *a great mind of our age; a fine scholar and intellect; the brain in the family.* **—Ant. 1** body, spirit, soul. **2** insanity, irrationality. **7, 8** neglect, overlook, ignore, disregard, dismiss.

mindful *adj.* attentive to, alert to, regardful, cognizant, heedful, conscious, thoughtful, careful, watchful, aware, cautious, observant, alive to, open-eyed to, sensible, wary; taken up with, occupied with, engrossed in, absorbed in, preoccupied with. **—Ant.** mindless, heedless, inattentive, oblivious, unaware, incautious, unobservant, thoughtless.

mindless *adj.* **1.** witless, asinine, stupid, unintelligent, unthinking, nonsensical, obtuse, disregardful, unreasoning, sophomoric, simple-minded, doltish, cretinous, imbecilic, idiotic, insane. **2.** insensitive to, careless, regardless, thoughtless, unattuned, oblivious, heedless, indifferent, apathetic, inconsiderate, indiscriminate, unaware, inattentive, unheeding, neglectful, unobservant. **—Ant. 1** intelligent, reasoning, thinking, reasonable, sane. **2** mindful, sensitive, considerate, aware, attentive, observant.

mine *n.* **1.** pit, excavation, tunnel, shaft, quarry. **2.** supply, reserve, stock, store, fund, hoard, accumulation, cache, treasure, wealth, abundance. **3.** underground or underwater explosive, booby trap, land mine. —*v.* **4.** excavate, extract, take from the earth, remove from a mine, scoop out; dig for. **5.** burrow under, tunnel under, dig under; lay explosives under, booby-trap.

mingle *v.* **1.** blend, mix, intermix, combine, intermingle, merge, commingle, commix, interfuse, coalesce, fuse, unite, interweave, amalgamate, intertwine, intersperse, interlard. **2.** socialize, join, mix, associate, circulate, consort, intermix, fraternize, hobnob, rub shoulders with. **—Syn. Study. 1** See MIX. **—Ant. 1** separate, part, divide, dissolve, break apart. **2** stay aloof, stay separate, hold back, withdraw; avoid.

miniature *adj.* small-scale, petite, diminutive, tiny, little, bantam, elfin, pocket-size, Lilliputian, pygmy, minuscule, microcosmic, microscopic. **—Ant.** large, big, gigantic, full-size; oversize, outsize, enlarged, blown-up.

minimal *adj.* minimum, least possible, lowest acceptable, smallest permissible, scarcely satisfactory, nominal, unappreciable, token. **—Ant.** maximal, maximum.

minimum *n.* **1.** least possible amount, smallest amount possible, least possible degree, modicum, lowest quantity. —*adj.* **2.** lowest amount allowed; least, smallest, least possible; basic, base. **—Ant. 1, 2** maximum, largest, greatest.

minister *n.* **1.** clergyman, preacher, pastor, chaplain, cleric, priest, parson, ecclesiastic, padre, father, vicar, reverend, rabbi, abbé, evangelist, revivalist. **2.** chief government administrator, secretary, cabinet member. —*v.* **3.** attend to, be solicitous of, serve, answer, oblige, tend, take care of, accommodate, care for; pander to, cater to. **—Ant. 1** layman, congregant.

minor *adj.* **1.** small, insignificant, slight, light, unimportant, petty, inconsiderable, trivial, paltry, nugatory, trifling, piddling, picayune, inconsequential, lesser, secondary, subordinate. —*n.* **2.** child, youngster, teenager, youth, adolescent, *Legal* infant. **—Ant. 1** major, greater, main, important, significant. **2** adult, elder; grownup.

minority *n.* **1.** smaller portion, less, lesser, smaller amount. **2.** immaturity, adolescence, childhood, boyhood, girlhood, juniority, nonage, youth, *Legal* infancy.

minor-league *adj.* bush-league, small-time, insignificant, secondary, second-rate, dinky, lesser, small-fry; inferior, shabby, seedy, common; *Slang* punk, cheesy, tacky. **—Ant.** major-league, topdrawer, first-rate, choice.

minstrel *n.* **1.** troubadour, singer, songster, itinerant musician, bard, poet, player, serenader, entertainer, lyrist; versifier, poetaster. **2.** vaudevillian, comedian, singer, dancer, song-and-dance man, end man, blackface, interlocutor.

minute[1] *n.* **1.** sixty seconds, sixtieth part of an hour. **2.** moment, second, instant, flash, shake, jiffy, twinkling, wink, trice, a short time, breath. **—Ant. 2** forever, ages, eons.

minute[2] *adj.* **1.** little, extremely small, imperceptible, tiny, diminutive, infinitesimal, miniature, Lilliputian, fine, scant, microscopic, minikin, petite, *Informal* teeny, wee; slight, negligible, inappreciable, trifling, puny, inconsiderable, insignificant, petty. **2.** exhaustive, meticulous, close, detailed, scrupulous, itemized, precise, conscientious, careful, strict, exact. **—Ant. 1** tremendous, huge, vast, monstrous, great, enormous, grand. **2** general, quick, tentative, rough, superficial.

minutiae *n. pl.* trivia, trivialities, minor details, trifles, niceties, bagatelles, odds and ends, subtleties, particulars, particularities, pedantries.

miracle *n.* **1.** divine act, supernatural happening; wonder, marvel, prodigy, mystery; portent, sign, omen. **2.** marvel, wonder, phenomenon, prodigy, sensation, spectacle, masterpiece.

miraculous *adj.* **1.** divine, supernatural, visionary, wonderful, phenomenal, prodigious, preternatural, supernormal; wonderworking, thaumaturgical, magical; mysterious, inexplicable. **2.** extraordinary, exceptional, remarkable, wonderful, marvelous, spectacular; amazing, astonishing, astounding; unbelievable, incredible; phenomenal, preternatural. **—Syn. Study. 1** MIRACULOUS, SUPERNATURAL, PRETERNATURAL refer to that which seems to transcend the laws of nature. MIRACULOUS refers to something that apparently contravenes known laws governing the universe: *a miraculous recovery.* SUPERNATURAL suggests divine or superhuman properties: *supernatural aid in battle.* PRETERNATURAL suggests the possession of supernormal qualities: *Dogs have a preternatural sense of smell.* It may also mean *supernatural: Elves are preternatural beings.* **—Ant. 1, 2** ordinary, normal. **1** human, natural, mundane, of this world. **2** routine, unexceptional, predictable, run-of-the-mill.

mirage *n.* optical illusion, illusion, phantasm, unreality, imagined image, fancy, hallucination, delusion, wishful thinking, misconception, fantasy, will-o'-the-wisp, castle in the air.

mire *n.* **1.** mud, muck, ooze, slime, slush, sludge; quagmire, bog, marsh, fen. *—v.* **2.** bog down, ensnare, enmesh, lock into mud, entangle, halt the progress of. **3.** spatter, soil, begrime, besmirch, cake, smear, muddy.

mirror *n.* **1.** reflecting glass, looking glass, glass, cheval glass. **2.** model, example, exemplar, paragon, pattern for imitation, standard, epitome, paradigm, image, reflection, copy. *—v.* **3.** reflect, show, manifest, image.

mirth *n.* merriment, amusement, jollity, hilarity, gaiety, joviality, glee, laughter, cheerfulness, good spirits, levity, happiness, jocundity, jocularity, festivity, drollery, merrymaking, playfulness. **—Ant.** sadness, dejection, depression, melancholy, misery, moroseness.

misadventure *n.* mishap, misfortune, reverse, failure, disaster, calamity, catastrophe, unfortunate accident, contretemps, slip, adversity, casualty, debacle, setback, mischance, stroke of ill luck, bad break, infelicity, ill.

misanthropic *adj.* antisocial, unfriendly, unsociable, distrustful, unneighborly, inhospitable, morose, unpersonable, cynical, surly, discourteous, unaccommodating, unapproachable, unresponsive, cold, distant. **—Ant.** personable, amiable, amicable, loving, sociable, cordial; humanitarian; philanthropic, charitable.

misapprehension *n.* misunderstanding, misconception, miscalculation, misinterpretation, false impression, communication breakdown, misjudgment, mixup, misconstruction, mistake.

misappropriate *v.* misuse, embezzle, defraud, steal, peculate, misapply, channel selfishly, put to a wrong use, abuse, misemploy, bilk, mulct, defalcate, swindle, cheat, purloin, *Informal* dip one's hand into the till.

misbehave *v.* act up, disobey, behave improperly, deport oneself badly, do wrong, transgress, show poor manners, be rebellious, be defiant. **—Ant.** behave, toe the line.

misbehavior *n.* bad behavior, bad conduct, misconduct, impropriety, delinquency, disrespect, acting up; misdemeanor, offense, dereliction, lapse, transgression, trespass, misdeed, indiscretion, bad manners, impudence; unmanageableness, obstreperousness.

—**Ant.** good conduct, discretion, mannerliness.

miscarriage *n.* **1.** failure, undoing, misfire, failing, unrealization, collapse, nonsuccess, default, nonfulfillment, *Informal* fizzle, botch; washout, frustration, casualty, shipwreck, slip, short-circuiting, going awry. **2.** premature stillbirth, spontaneous abortion, disruption of pregnancy.

miscellaneous *adj.* varied, manifold, assorted, mixed, mingled, of mixed character, various, different, heterogeneous, motley, of many categories, diversified, diverse, divers, of every description, sundry. —**Ant.** homogeneous, uniform, identical.

miscellany *n.* collection, mixture, blend, medley, compilation, anthology, potpourri, mélange, pastiche, omnium-gatherum, gallimaufry, salmagundi, assortment; conglomeration, jumble, hodgepodge, mishmash.

mischance *n.* misfortune, bad luck, unfortunate occurrence, ill luck, ill lot, mishap, adversity, accident, misadventure, infelicity, ill wind.

mischief *n.* **1.** naughtiness, rascality, devilment, sportiveness, tendency to tease, devilry, deviltry, devilment, prankishness, playfulness, orneriness, roguery, roguishness, shenanigans; capriciousness, willfulness. **2.** wrongdoing, knavery, scheming, plotting, malice, villainy, wrong, foul play, injury, evil, depravity.

mischievous *adj.* **1.** naughty, impish, prankish, teasing, playfully annoying, elfin, elfish, playful, frolicsome, sly, roguish, devilish, sportive, waggish. **2.** wicked, vicious, spiteful, malicious, malign, malignant, gratuitous, uninvited, uncalled for, annoying, vexing, injurious, destructive, harmful, pernicious, wicked, noxious, exacerbating, deleterious, detrimental.

misconception *n.* misapprehension, erroneous idea, mistaken notion, misinterpretation, fallacious notion, error, misunderstanding, delusion, misconstruction, misjudgment, misinformation, misrepresentation.

misconduct *n.* transgression, wrongdoing, misbehavior, dereliction, malefaction, misprision, impropriety, peccadillo, delinquency, misdeed, misstep, malfeasance, misdemeanor. —**Ant.** uprightness, morality, probity, propriety.

misconstrue *v.* misinterpret, take in a wrong sense, construe wrongly, misreckon, misrender, misapprehend, mistranslate, distort, mistake, misunderstand, misjudge, miscalculate. —**Ant.** understand, apprehend.

miscreant *n.* villain, rascal, knave, scoundrel, blackguard, evildoer, sinner, wretch, malefactor, reprobate, lost soul, scamp, scalawag, black sheep; *Slang* heel, bad egg, bum.

misdeed *n.* transgression, misdemeanor, sin, offense, misconduct, faux pas, peccadillo, indiscretion, misbehavior, lapse, slip, wrong, trespass, violation, infringement, malfeasance, crime, felony, atrocity, outrage.

miser *n.* pennypincher, stingy person, Scrooge, skinflint, tightwad, skimper, pinchpenny, niggard, hoarder, *Informal* piker, *Slang* cheapskate. —**Ant.** spendthrift, profligate, spender.

miserable *adj.* **1.** wretched, impoverished, very poor, deplorable, lamentable, sorry, pathetic, unbearable, sordid, mean, shabby, degraded, desperate, scurvy, pitiable, second-rate, beggarly, rubbishy, needy, hapless, feckless, unfortunate, inferior; contemptible, despicable. **2.** forlorn, unhappy, heartbroken, woeful, crestfallen, disconsolate, wretched in mind, doleful, dolorous, brokenhearted, sorrowful, desolate, crushed, woebegone, despondent, dejected, heartsick, down in the mouth, grieved, mournful, depressed, cheerless, chapfallen, heavy-laden, sad. **3.** sorry, deplorable, inept, abysmal, far from satisfactory, atrocious, appalling, abject; contemptible, despicable. —**Syn. Study. 1, 3** MISERABLE, WRETCHED, SORRY mean in a state of, causing, or characterized by mental or physical distress. MISERABLE implies unhappiness, discomfort, or suffering, as from poverty, pain, or grief: *The peasants led a miserable life. He was miserable after his dog died.* WRETCHED implies a more severe or profound distress that arouses pity: *wretched hovels; the wretched homeless.* SORRY describes something that inspires sorrow but has connotations of contempt or scorn: *The prisoner was a sorry sight.* —**Ant. 1** comfortable, good, respectable. **2** happy, gay, joyous, cheerful. **3** admirable, laudable.

miserly *adj.* parsimonious, stingy, selfish, avaricious, mean, tight, tight-fisted, grasping, scrimping, penurious, pinching, penny-pinching, frugal, illiberal, closehanded, close-fisted, selfish, ungenerous, greedy, niggardly, near, meager, grudging, mean, cheap. —**Syn. Study.** See STINGY. —**Ant.** generous, unselfish, charitable, extravagant, prodigal, profligate.

misery *n.* **1.** sorrow, affliction, distress, trouble, suffering, woe, wretchedness, hardship, exaction, ordeal, trial, tribulation, privation, misfortune, catastrophe, disaster, calamity. **2.** wretchedness, heartache, desolation, extreme unhappiness, sorrow, sadness, grief, suffering, agony, woe, melancholy, distress, anguish, despair, torment, depression, dejection, despondency. **3.** sorrow, chagrin, regret, blow, curse, *Informal* bitter pill, bad deal, bad scene, bad news. —**Ant. 1** luxury, ease, comfort. **2** happiness, joy, contentment, pleasure, enjoyment. **3** boon, comfort, benefit.

misfortune *n.* **1.** trouble, bad luck, hard luck, ill fortune, hard times, calamity, adversity, hardship. **2.** blow, calamity, mishap, catastrophe, disaster, unfortunate accident, tribulation, trouble, reverse, affliction, setback, downfall, tragedy, loss, misery, ruination, casualty, misadventure, piece of bad luck. —**Ant. 1** good luck, good fortune. **2** stroke of luck, relief.

misgiving *n.* Usu. **misgivings** anxiety, fear, doubt, mental reservations, apprehension, foreboding, presentiment, lack of confidence, worry, suspicion, disquiet, qualm, skepticism, uncertainty, dread, alarm, mistrust, dubiousness, dubiety, doubtfulness, second thoughts. —**Ant.** confidence, trust, assurance, certainty.

misguided *adj.* mistaken, misled, in error, faulty, misdirected, misadvised, ill-advised, erroneous, led astray, injudicious, adrift, misinformed, *Informal* on the wrong scent, on the wrong track, wide of the mark, in the woods, at sea, off course, indiscreet, unwise, imprudent.

mishap *n.* misadventure, mischance, unfortunate accident, disaster, reverse, casualty, setback, miscarriage, difficulty, misfortune, slip, slipup, botch, snag, fiasco.

mishmash *n.* hodgepodge, mélange, patchwork, medley, pastiche, miscellany, assemblage, conglomeration, crazy quilt, jumble, mix, muddle, scramble, hash, salmagundi, stew, salad, mixed bag, omnium-gatherum.

misinform *v.* mislead, misdirect, misrepresent, give incorrect information to, apprise inaccurately, misguide, deceive, lead astray.

misjudge *v.* miscalculate, estimate incorrectly, judge wrongly, fail to anticipate, misconceive, misapprehend, underestimate, overestimate, misconstrue, misinterpret, exaggerate, understate, misunderstand; judge unfairly, show poor intuition about, mistake, err about.

mislead *v.* **1.** misguide, deceive, misinform, lead into error, misdirect, lead astray. **2.** delude, deceive, seduce, beguile, entice, inveigle, take in, take advantage of, victimize, play false, gull, dupe, hoodwink, betray, bamboozle, fool, double-cross, *Informal* lead down the garden path, string along.

mismanage *v.* botch, mishandle, bungle, spoil, ruin, mess up, mar, make a mess of, make a hash of, monkey-wrench; *Slang* foul up, louse up, screw up, bollix, muff, flub.

misnomer *n.* unsuitable term, misapplied name, inapplicable title, wrong designation, misusage, solecism, misnaming, wrong nomenclature, malapropism, bastardization, barbarism.

misplace *v.* **1.** mislay, lose, lose track of. **2.** place unwisely, entrust wrongly, abuse.

misrepresentation *n.* **1.** misstatement, distortion, falsification, falsifying, doctoring, adulteration, altering, incorrect picture, twisting, exaggeration. **2.** bad likeness, wrong impression, poor likeness, incorrect picture, mockery, travesty; burlesque, caricature.

miss[1] *v.* **1.** fail to hit, fail to reach, fail to strike; fall short, fail to attain, miss the mark, fly wide, fail to light upon; fail to receive, fail to obtain. **2.** fail to catch, fail to be present at, fail to meet, fail to get; be distracted from, be late for, be absent from. **3.** let slip, let pass, let go, skip, fail to take advantage of, forego, go without, disregard, pass over, overlook, neglect, surrender, *Informal* blow, muff. **4.** fail to perform, fail to meet, fail to accomplish. **5.** notice the loss of, note the absence of. **6.** want, long for, pine for, lack, feel the loss of, feel the absence of, yearn for. **7.** avoid, avert, escape. **8.** fail to perceive, fail to hear, fail to understand, fail to get, fail to see, lose. **9.** overlook, pass by, leave out, disregard, neglect, slip up on, pass over, gloss over; bypass, overrun, overshoot. —*n.* **10.** failure, failure to hit, failure to reach, false step, default, error, slip, miscue, blunder; omission, neglect, oversight, delinquency, mistake, loss. —**Ant. 1** hit, reach, strike, attain, obtain. **2** catch, meet, get, make. **3** seize, grasp, accept. **4** meet, fulfill, accomplish, make. **8** catch, hear, overhear. **10** hit, success.

miss[2] *n.* unmarried woman, maid, maiden, girl, young lady, mademoiselle, señorita, demoiselle, lass, colleen, lassie, schoolgirl, damsel; woman, lady; old maid, spinster.

missile *n.* projectile, shell, object or weapon that is thrown or shot; (*variously*) stone, spear, javelin, lance, harpoon, arrow, dart, bullet, ball, shaft; guided missile, rocket.

mission *n.* **1.** charge, assignment, undertaking, enterprise, quest, task, commission, mandate, job, purposive military operation. **2.** delegation, legation, diplomatic representative, missionary post, ministry. **3.** calling, pursuit, life's object, objective, end, principal task; raison d'être.

misspent *adj.* misapplied, wasted, spent foolishly, thrown away, idled away, profitless, squandered; depraved, dissolute, debauched. **—Ant.** productive, fruitful, unwasted, profitable.

misstate *v.* state wrongly, state falsely, misreport, state misleadingly, falsify, misrepresent, misquote, alter, distort, pervert, give a false impression of; garble, confuse, bollix.

misstep *n.* error, delinquency, shortcoming, fault, transgression, sin, vice, offense, defect, faux pas, gaffe, indiscretion, lapse, dereliction, breach of etiquette, slip; *Slang* blooper, boo-boo, goof, foul-up, screw-up, boner.

mistake *n.* **1.** error, misstep, wrong action, boner, blunder, miscalculation, slip, slip of the pen, slip of the tongue, slip-up, gaffe, oversight, faux pas, blooper, *Informal* goof, *Slang* boo-boo. **—***v.* **2.** confuse, identify incorrectly, take one for another, wrongly accept, confound, mix up,misidentify. **3.** misunderstand, miscalculate, misinterpret, misconstrue, misapprehend, misreckon, misjudge. **—Syn. Study. 1** MISTAKE, ERROR, BLUNDER, SLIP refer to an inadvertent deviation from accuracy, correctness, truth, or right conduct. MISTAKE refers to a wrong action, belief, or judgment; it may also suggest an incorrect understanding, perception, or interpretation: *a mistake in arithmetic; It was a mistake to trust them.* ERROR is similar in sense, but may mean a deviation from a moral standard: *I finally saw the error of my ways.* BLUNDER suggests a careless, clumsy, or stupid mistake, often serious: *a tactical blunder.* SLIP refers to a small mistake in speech or writing, or to a minor indiscretion: *I misspelled his name by a slip of the pen.*

mistaken *adj.* **1.** wrong, erroneous, in error, false, fallacious, incorrect, inaccurate, faulty, at fault, unfounded, unsound, unjustified, untrue, groundless, ungrounded, illogical. **2.** in error, making a mistake or misjudgment, deceived, *Informal* at sea, off course, on the wrong scent. **—Ant. 1** wise, accurate, true, well-advised, sound, logical. **2** correct, accurate, right, logical.

mistreat *v.* maltreat, ill-treat, ill-use, abuse, oppress, persecute, misuse, treat unjustly, harm, harass, wrong, hound, manhandle, mishandle, outrage, brutalize, bully, torment, molest, pervert, violate, assault, injure, harass.

mistress *n.* **1.** female head, matron, lady, headwoman, housewife, female owner. **2.** lover, paramour, concubine, doxy, kept woman, inamorata, girlfriend, sweetheart, ladylove. **3.** Madam, Miss, Mrs.

mistrust *n.* **1.** distrust, skepticism, misgiving, qualm, suspicion, doubt, dubiety, presentiment, leeriness, wariness, chariness, uncertainty, apprehension. **—***v.* **2.** distrust, suspect, disbelieve, doubt, have doubts about, question, challenge. **—Ant. 1** reliance, faith, confidence, trust. **2** trust, rely on, accept, believe, have confidence in.

misty *adj.* hazy, clouded by mist, vaporous, dewy, foggy, steamy; overcast, murky, cloudy, nebulous, indistinct; filmy, opaque. **—Ant.** clear, unclouded.

misunderstand *v.* misconstrue, misinterpret, understand wrongly, take in a wrong sense, misjudge, misconceive, misapprehend, mistake, misreckon, miscalculate, miss the point of, put a false construction on, misread, confuse. **—Ant.** understand, apprehend, perceive.

misunderstanding *n.* **1.** misreading, mistake as to meaning, failure to understand, misapprehension, misinterpretation, misconception, false impression, misjudgment, miscomprehension. **2.** quarrel, disagreement, dispute, difference, rift, spat, discord, dissension, contretemps, conflict, squabble, altercation, wrangle, *Informal* set-to.

misuse *n.* **1.** misemployment, wrong use, misappropriation, misapplication, waste, improper utilization, ill use; prostitution, perversion, squandering, abuse, desecration, corruption; ill treatment, maltreatment, mistreatment, profanation. **—***v.* **2.** use improperly, misapply, use wrongly, misemploy; profane, prostitute, pervert, corrupt, put to wrong use. **3.** ill-treat, ill-use, abuse, wrong, mistreat, hurt, harm, take advantage of, exploit, injure, outrage, debase, maltreat. **—Ant. 3** respect, esteem, honor, cherish, treasure, prize, appreciate.

mitigate *v.* lessen, relieve, moderate, moderate in severity, alleviate, abate in intensity, palliate, soften, assuage, allay, soothe, placate, weaken, mollify, ameliorate, ease, blunt, reduce, lighten, diminish, temper, extenuate. **—Ant.** increase, augment, heighten, enhance, strengthen.

mix *v.* **1.** combine, commix, join, put together, blend, unite, incorporate, interfuse, mingle, intermingle, commingle, compound, fuse, intermix, interlard, interweave, intersperse, intertwine, alloy, amalgamate; merge, coalesce. **2.** add, admix, put in, include, introduce, incorporate; fold, stir, whip, beat. **3.** fraternize, associate, consort, socialize, hobnob, club, be on intimate terms with, join. —*n.* **4.** mixture, combination of ingredients; mingling, fusion, assembly. **—Syn. Study. 1** MIX, COMBINE, BLEND, MINGLE concern the bringing of two or more things into more or less intimate association. MIX means to join elements or ingredients into one mass, generally with a loss of distinction between them: *to mix fruit juices.* COMBINE means to bring similar or related things into close union, usu. for a particular purpose: *to combine forces.* BLEND suggests a smooth and harmonious joining, often a joining of different varieties to obtain a product of a desired quality: *to blend whiskeys.* MINGLE usu. suggests a joining in which the identity of the separate elements is retained: *voices mingling at a party.*

mixed *adj.* **1.** mingled, alloyed, composite, combined, put together, fused, blended, inmixed, interwoven; hybrid, mongrel, adulterated, half and half. **2.** diversified, variegated, of various kinds, not pure, motley, heterogeneous, miscellaneous, hybrid, conglomerate, made up of different kinds. **3.** male-and-female, co-ed, heterogeneous. **4.** indecisive, ambivalent, tending both ways, inconclusive, neither here nor there, uncertain, positive and negative. **—Ant. 1** unmixed, pure, isolated, straight, unblended. **2** unmixed, homogeneous. **3** male, female, homogeneous.

mixture *n.* intermixture, combination, blend, admixture, union, fusion, amalgamation, adulteration; association, mix, alloy, amalgam, composite, compound, medley, stew, hodgepodge, jumble, hash, salmagundi, mélange, commixture, pastiche, potpourri, mishmash.

mixup *n.* **1.** misunderstanding, mistake, miscomprehension, misjudgment, miscalculation, failure in communication; muddle, tangle, confusion. **2.** *Informal* fight, melee, riot; disorder, fracas, imbroglio, mess.

moan *n.* **1.** groan, wail, lament, plaint, sob, lamentation. —*v.* **2.** groan, grumble; bemoan, lament, wail, bewail, keen.

mob *n.* **1.** riotous throng, disorderly crowd, rabble, horde, crush of people, gathering, assembly. **2.** common people, masses, rank and file, hoi polloi, populace, proletariat, plebeians, lower classes, rabble, multitude, *Informal* the great unwashed, herd. **3.** band or gang of criminals, organized crime, underworld network, syndicate, Mafia. —*v.* **4.** surround noisily, swarm around, flock to, converge on, crowd around excitedly.

mobile *adj.* **1.** movable, portable, transportable, traveling, ambulatory, locomotive, not permanent. **2.** moving readily, moving easily, motile, active, kinetic; rootless, wandering, nomadic, footloose. **—Ant. 2** immobile, immovable, firm, set, steady, permanent.

mobilize *v.* muster, call up, summon, activate, assemble for action, make operative, organize, marshal, call to arms, put in motion, tap in emergency. **—Ant.** immobilize, disband, disarm, disorganize, retire.

mock *v.* **1.** ridicule, make fun of, scorn, treat with contempt, be contemptuous of, deride, revile, jeer at, taunt, assail with ridicule, spurn, make sport of, laugh at, make game of, scoff at, sneer at, poke fun at; imitate, ape, copy, burlesque, parody, caricature, mimic. **2.** disappoint, frustrate, let down, show up, belie, insult, profane. **—Syn. Study. 1** See RIDICULE. **—Ant. 1** praise, honor, laud. **2** fulfill.

mockery *n.* **1.** ridicule, ridiculing, sarcasm, derision, scoffing, jeering, scorn, contumely, disrespect, raillery; mimicry, contemptuous imitation, burlesque, travesty. **2.** sham, joke, laughingstock, farce; burlesque, travesty.

mode *n.* **1.** manner, way, fashion, course, method, practice, means, system, rule, approach, procedure, form, process, style, technique. **2.** style, custom, fashion, manner, cut, appearance, taste, way, trend, vogue; rage, fad, craze. **—Syn. Study. 1** See METHOD.

model *n.* **1.** replica, miniature representation, prototype, representation, pattern, facsimile, simulacrum, copy, dummy, mock-up. **2.** archetype, paragon, standard, ideal, paradigm, example, exemplar, poster child, mirror, pattern, criterion. **3.** source, subject, real-life version, prototype; mannequin. **4.** design, style, version, type, variety. —*adj.* **5.** demonstrational, representative, simulated. **6.** perfect, worthy of imitation, ideal, exemplary, peerless. —*v.* **7.** fashion, form according to a model, create in emulation, mold, give shape to, design, shape, cast, build, outline. **8.** form, shape, build, fashion, cast, mold, give form to. **9.** display, show, wear as a demonstration, sport. **—Ant. 6** imperfect, flawed, unworthy.

moderate *adj.* **1.** average, medium, middling, modest, of medium quantity or extent, ordinary, mediocre, passable, fair; inexpensive, medium-priced. **2.** reasonable, temperate, mild, judicious, rational, not violent, dispassionate, unruffled, gentle, calm, cool, sober, peaceable, measured, careful. —*n.* **3.** middle-of-the-roader, mainstreamer. —*v.* **4.** temper, control, soften, tone down, curb, make less severe, lessen, subdue, tame, abate, diminish, hush, restrain. **5.** act as moderator, preside over, act as chairman; regulate, direct, manage, oversee, conduct. **—Syn. Study. 2** MODERATE, REASONABLE, TEMPERATE imply the avoidance of excess, as in action, thought, or feeling. MODERATE describes something that is within reasonable or proper limits: *a moderate amount of exercise.* REASONABLE suggests a limit imposed by reason or good sense: *a reasonable request.* TEMPERATE stresses the idea of caution, control, or self-restraint, esp. with reference to the appetites or emotions: *a temperate discussion.* **—Ant. 1** immoderate, excessive, extreme, inordinate, unusual; expensive. **2** unreasonable, extreme, intemperate, hysterical, violent, ruffled, radical, wild. **3** extremist, radical. **4** intensify, heighten, increase.

moderation *n.* temperance, abstemiousness, restraint, avoidance of extremes, forbearance, continence, economy, temperateness, frugality, self-control, moderateness; abatement, lessening, abating, allaying, alleviation, diminution, relaxation, mitigation, palliation, remission. **—Ant.** excess, intemperance; increase.

modern *adj.* new, contemporary, present-day, up-to-date, modernized, modernistic, 20th-century, streamlined, of our time, au courant; recent, current, late, contemporaneous; in vogue, modish, fashionable, (of a person) with-it, *Slang* hip. **—Syn. Study.** MODERN, RECENT, LATE apply to that which is near to or characteristic of the present as contrasted with any other time. MODERN, which is applied to those things that exist in the present age, sometimes has the connotation of up-to-date and, thus, good: *modern ideas.* That which is RECENT is separated from the present or the time of action by only a short interval; it is new, fresh, and novel: *recent developments.* LATE may mean nearest to the present moment: *the late reports on the battle.* **—Ant.** antique, ancient, old, archaic, obsolete, past, antiquated, former, old-fashioned.

modernity *n.* up-to-dateness, recentness, modernism, contemporaneity, *French* dernier cri, last word, latest trend, latest fad, new look, new fashionedness, novelty, newfangledness, vogue, fashion; *Slang* the rage, the in thing, latest wrinkle. **—Ant.** oldness, obsolescence, staleness, fustiness.

modernize *v.* renovate, rejuvenate, refurbish, revamp, regenerate, update, streamline, renew, recondition, do over, redo, redesign, restore, bring up to date, make modern, move with the times. **—Ant.** age, wear, outdate, antique, date.

modest *adj.* **1.** unassuming, humble, meek, not boastful, unassertive, self-effacing, unpretentious, free from vanity, devoid of egotism, unpretending. **2.** simple, plain, unpretentious, unshowy, limited, unostentatious, quiet, unobtrusive. **3.** moderate, nominal, not excessive, not extravagant; medium-priced, inexpensive. **4.** reserved, discreet, bashful, shy, self-conscious, constrained, quiet, timid, demure, coy, diffident, blushing, shrinking, timorous, proper, straitlaced, prim, circumspect, prudish, puritanical. **—Syn. Study. 4** MODEST, DEMURE, PRUDISH suggest conformity to the recognized standards of propriety and good taste, as in speech, manner, dress, or attitude. MODEST implies a becoming humility and reserve, and a taste for things that are simple and refined: *a successful, yet modest, executive.* DEMURE describes a subdued and proper manner, but often one that seems affected or insincere: *a demure glance.* PRUDISH suggests an exaggerated propriety and a self-righteous air that often irritates others: *a prudish objection to an off-color remark.* **—Ant. 1** immodest, vain, boastful, ambitious; showy, pretentious, egotistic, ostentatious, fancy. **3** generous, magnanimous. **4** shameless, brazen, barefaced, impudent; immodest, indecent, indelicate, indecorous, unseemly, improper.

modesty *n.* **1.** humility, humbleness, freedom from vanity, reserve, self-effacement, lack of self-importance, lack of boastfulness, restrained behavior, restraint, freedom from presumption, constraint. **2.** simplicity, unpretentiousness, plainness, naturalness, lack of ostentation, inexpensiveness, reasonableness. **3.** reserve, bashfulness, shyness, constraint, timidity, demureness, coyness, diffidence, timorousness, reticence, propriety, decency or reserve in dress; prudery. **—Ant. 1** immodesty, boastfulness, self-conceit, pride, sauciness, arrogance, vanity, confidence, egotism, presumption, vainness, assurance, boldness, haughtiness. **2** extravagance, pretentiousness, showiness, ostentation. **3** immodesty, indecency, forwardness, impropriety.

modicum *n.* minimum, drop, jot, fragment, sliver, smidgen, small quantity, mite, bit, pinch, trifle, small amount, dash, little bit, particle, dab, tinge, sprinkling, touch, speck, snatch, fraction, grain, iota, handful, crumb, morsel, whit, atom, scrap, inch.

modify *v.* **1.** alter, vary, change, make different, adjust, give a new form to, transform, transmute, convert, refashion, rework, redo, reshape, remold, remodel, reorganize, revise, adapt, transmogrify. **2.** reduce, moderate, modulate, temper, restrain, tone down, narrow, lower, remit, soften; qualify, limit, restrict, condition, control, adjust.

modish *adj.* fashionable, chic, stylish, faddish, voguish, smart, current, high-style, a la mode, up-to-the-minute, all the rage; *Slang* with it, now, trendy, today, in, sharp, nifty, snazzy, spiffy, hot stuff. **—Ant.** passé, old-fashioned, dated, *Slang* out.

modulate *v.* **1.** reduce, regulate, turn down, adjust to lesser intensity, tone down, moderate, lower, soften, temper. **2.** change, temper, vary in tune and accentuation, vary the inflection, inflect the voice. **3.** shift gradually, pass, progress, shift harmonically, change; attune, accord, harmonize.

mogul *n.* magnate, tycoon, important person, power, powerful figure, notable, czar, potentate, lord, baron, personage, man of distinction, influential person, *Slang* big shot, bigwig, big wheel, wheel, VIP.

moist *adj.* damp, watery, wettish, slightly wet, wet; muggy, humid, dewy, dank, clammy, rainy, drizzly, drippy, dripping, vaporous; tearful, aqueous, misty, lachrymose, wet-eyed. **—Ant.** dry, arid.

moisten *v.* wet, dampen, moisturize, damp, vaporize, dew, mist, saturate, soak, humidify, water, spray, splash, hose, sponge, irrigate, douche.

moisture *n.* dampness, moistness, wetness, damp, wet, wateriness; humidity, mugginess, dankness, dew, evaporation, vapor; perspiration, sweat, exudate; mist, drizzle.

mold[1] *n.* **1.** cast, form, shaper; matrix, die. **2.** shape, contour, line, formation, form, structure, frame, construction, cut, conformation, outline, turn, configuration. **3.** quality, type, ilk, sort, kind, character, stamp, kidney, make, brand. **—*v.*** **4.** model, shape, form, cast, fashion, create, knead, sculpt, figure, construct, pattern. **5.** form, fashion, remodel, turn, render, convert, transform, transmute, develop, bring along, train, make, transfigure.

mold[2] *n.* fungus, mildew, blight, rust, lichen.

molest *v.* bother, harass, vex, annoy, pester, disturb, harry, torment, plague, hector, beset, distress, trouble, fret, irritate, irk, worry, abuse, harm, attack, ill-treat, hurt, assault, injure, maltreat; sexually abuse.

mollify *v.* appease, calm, moderate, placate, quell, still, lessen, mitigate, allay, reduce, palliate, conciliate, make less violent, decrease, soften, pacify, soothe, tone down, quiet, lighten, temper, abate, ease, assuage, curb, check, dull, lull, blunt. **—Ant.** exasperate, exacerbate, agitate, stir, increase.

mollycoddle *v.* **1.** spoil, pamper, overindulge, baby, cater to, cosset, give in to, pet, indulge. **—*n.*** **2.** milquetoast, milksop, sissy, coward, weakling, mama's boy, crybaby; *Slang* cream puff.

molten *adj.* liquefied, melted, smelted, fusible, igneous, magmatic; red-hot.

moment *n.* **1.** minute, instant, twinkling, short period of time, second, jiffy, flash, split second, trice. **2.** point of time, the present time, instant, particular time, juncture. **3.** consequence, import, importance, worth, significance, weight, gravity, value, concern, interest, weightiness. **—Syn. Study. 3** See IMPORTANCE. **—Ant. 3** insignificance, unimportance, triviality, inconsequence, unconcern.

momentary *adj.* **1.** temporary, transitory, passing, fleeting, flashing, brief, short, hasty, quick, short-lived, transient, ephemeral, fugitive. **2.** sudden, imminent, instant, expected at any moment, instantaneous, immediate. **—Ant. 1** permanent, lengthy, lasting, long-lived.

momentous *adj.* important, of great portent, significant, of great consequence, essential, critical, decisive, crucial, influential, eventful, fateful, earth-shaking, far-reaching, consequential, salient; grave, serious, substantial, ponderous, weighty. **—Ant.** unimportant, insignificant, trivial, trifling, inconsequential.

momentum *n.* force, impetus, impelling force, energy, moment, property of a body that keeps it in motion, impulse, thrust, push, go, drive, headway, propulsion, velocity, dash, vigor, speed.

monarch *n.* hereditary sovereign, crowned head, majesty, prince; (*variously*) king, H.R.H., potentate, ruler, emperor, czar, kaiser; pharaoh, shah, khan, chieftain, doge, emir, rajah, (*fem.*) queen, princess; empress, czarina, kaiserin, rani.

monastery *n.* place of contemplation, retreat, cloister, convent, abbey, nunnery, priory, friary; community of monks, community of nuns.

monastic *adj.* of monks, of monasteries; contemplative, solitary, monkish, secluded, cloistral, cloistered, unworldly, hermitic, hermitlike, sequestered, celibate, ascetic, recluse, reclusive.

monetary *adj.* financial, pecuniary, budgetary, fiscal, in money, measured or valued in terms of money; sumptuary, economic, economical. **—Syn. Study.** MONETARY, FINANCIAL, PECUNIARY, FISCAL refer to matters concerned with money. MONETARY relates esp. to money as such: *The dollar is a monetary unit.* FINANCIAL usu. refers to money matters or transactions of some size or importance: *a lucrative financial deal.* PECUNIARY refers to money as used in making ordinary payments: *a pecuniary obligation; pecuniary rewards.* FISCAL is used esp. in connection with government funds, or funds of any organization: *the end of the fiscal year.*

money *n.* **1.** currency, cash, funds, revenue, paper money, coin, coinage, specie, hard cash, collateral, proceeds, assets, capital; *Informal* wherewithal, *Slang* dough, bread, scratch, greenbacks, long green, bucks; medium of exchange, measure of value, buying power, legal tender, payment. **2.** wealth, affluence, financial independence, hereditary wealth, riches, lucrative investments, great income, no financial problems.

moneyed Also **monied** *adj.* wealthy, affluent, rich, prosperous, solvent, well-to-do, well-off, well-heeled, opulent, flush, elegant, *Informal* flashy, swell, *Slang* loaded.

mongrel *adj.* **1.** mixed, of mixed breed, half-breed, crossbred, hybrid; bastard, anomalous. —*n.* **2.** mutt, cur, an animal of mixed breed, hybrid, half-breed, offshoot, crossbreed. —**Ant. 1, 2** purebred, thoroughbred. **1** pedigreed.

moniker *n.* name, appellation, designation, given name, surname, nickname, sobriquet, cognomen, title, epithet, denomination, eponym, taxonomy; *Slang* tag, label, handle.

monitor *n.* **1.** proctor, disciplinarian, overseer, stand-in, *Informal* watchdog. **2.** television set, studio television receiver, TV set, TV, scanner, pickup, screen; warning device, sensor. —*v.* **3.** watch attentively, observe critically; censor. **4.** supervise, oversee, tend, take charge of, teach, guide, direct; police.

monk *n.* brother, holy man, religious recluse, friar, abbé, abbot, monastic; hermit, recluse, anchorite, cenobite.

monkey *n.* **1.** primate, ape, simian, baboon. **2.** fool, dupe, ass, laughingstock, butt, clown, buffoon, *Slang* jerk. —*v.* **3.** meddle, toy, tamper, trifle, fool, fiddle, play around, dicker around; tinker, jimmy.

monologue Also **monolog** *n.* soliloquy, speech, oration, discourse, holding forth, address, lecture, expatiation, disquisition; sermon, screed. —**Ant.** dialogue, conversation.

monopolize *v.* **1.** control, regulate, dominate, manage, have a monopoly of, obtain exclusive possession of, corner, cartelize, appropriate, own, absorb, take over, consume. **2.** appropriate, dominate, arrogate, take up, take advantage of, preempt. —**Ant. 2** share, divide.

monopoly *n.* exclusive possession, dominion, corner, trust, cartel, consortium, syndicate, ownership, copyright, proprietorship, control, domination, jurisdiction, combine, bloc, sovereignty.

monotonous *adj.* **1.** unvaried, boring, dull, dreary, humdrum, repetitious, flat, colorless, tedious, tiresome, wearisome, prosaic, pedestrian, routine, one-note, mundane, uninteresting, banal, dry, stodgy, routine, jejune, plodding, insipid. **2.** without inflection, with a narrow range, droning, singsong, toneless, flat, soporific, somniferous, dull, torpid. —**Ant. 1** varied, diversified, interesting.

monotony *n.* tedium, humdrum, monotonousness, dullness, ennui, boredom, predictability, flatness, sameness, dreariness, tediousness, rut, wearisomeness, redundancy, iteration, reiteration, prosaism. —**Ant.** variety, innovation, excitement, diversity, stimulation.

monster *n.* **1.** deviant, variant, freak, freak of nature, *Latin* lusus naturae; phenomenon, anomaly, curiosity, oddity, wonder, marvel; miscreation, abnormality, monstrosity. **2.** mythical or legendary being, semihuman creature; (*variously*) Chimera, Gorgon, dragon, gargoyle, Hydra, incubus, succubus, mermaid, satyr, Harpy, Fury, centaur; bogeyman, zombie, vampire, Frankenstein, werewolf, Jekyll and Hyde, golem, ghoul. **3.** dangerous creation, destructive force, uncontrollable force, threat. **4.** fiend, demon, devil, beast, brute, wretch, villain, scoundrel, cutthroat, savage, barbarian, blackguard, caitiff. **5.** giant, mammoth, titan, colossus. —**Ant. 1** commonplace, everyday thing, routine thing. **3** boon, blessing. **4** paragon, saint. **5** dwarf, midget, pygmy, shrimp, runt, pipsqueak.

monstrous *adj.* **1.** huge, enormous, immense, gigantic, mighty, gargantuan, giant, titanic, tremendous, colossal, mammoth, hulking, stupendous, prodigious, Brobdingnagian; ghastly, revolting, gruesome, grisly, hideous, horrible. **2.** outrageous, cruel, vicious, flagrant, egregious, fiendish, heinous, evil, harried, obscene, villainous, nefarious, odious, atrocious, satanic, diabolical, shocking, scandalous; outright, obvious, bald.

monument *n.* **1.** memorial, testament, testimonial, remembrance, memento, witness, token, commemoration, reminder. **2.** memorial, shrine; tombstone, gravestone, obelisk, cenotaph, monolith, slab.

monumental *adj.* **1.** monolithic, cyclopean; statuary; gigantic, colossal, massive, heavy, huge, larger than life. **2.**

historic, epoch-making, classic, immortal, enduring, memorable, lasting, epochal, awesome, stupendous, unprecedented. **3.** egregious, colossal, immense, decisive, inestimable; fatal, horrendous, catastrophic, shattering, mind-boggling. **—Ant. 1** small, tiny, delicate, dainty, light, miniature. **2** unimportant, insignificant, petty, worthless; everyday, ephemeral.

mood *n.* humor, disposition, state of mind, temper, temperament, frame of mind, mental state, feeling, condition, spirit, emotional state, predisposition; state of dejection, depression, melancholia, melancholy, gloominess, bad spirits, doldrums, *Informal* dumps, blues; state of irritation, vexation, hypersensitivity.

moody *adj.* **1.** melancholy, dejected, gloomy, pessimistic, lugubrious, despondent, saturnine, morose, morbid, dismal, brooding, mopish, unhappy, *Slang* down-in-the-mouth; mean, irritable, irascible, sulky, ill-humored, sullen, testy, surly, peevish, crabby, temperamental. **2.** changeable, fickle, variable, unpredictable, inconstant, inconsistent, flighty, notional, mercurial, temperamental, capricious, volatile, erratic, whimsical, impetuous, impulsive. **—Ant. 1** happy, joyful, cheerful; amiable, personable, compatible. **2** stable, constant, consistent, steady.

moor[1] *v.* tie up, dock, anchor, berth, secure; fix firmly, affix, fasten, tether, chain, anchor, tie down, attach, make fast, lash. **—Ant.** untie, unfasten, cast off, set adrift.

moor[2] moorland, wasteland, heath, wold, down, fell, upland, tundra, steppe, savanna; marsh, fen.

moot *adj.* debatable, questionable, unsettled, subject to argument, disputed, disputable, arguable, problematical, undecided, unresolved, open, controvertible, conjectural, controversial, eristic. **—Ant.** indisputable, self-evident, axiomatic.

mope *v.* sulk, languish, be dejected, fret, worry, be gloomy, brood, pine, repine, lament, grieve, be downcast, pout, wear a long face, grouse, grumble.

moral *adj.* **1.** ethical, of right and wrong, of proper conduct, personal. **2.** ethical, right, proper, virtuous, honorable, noble, estimable, meritorious, principled, just, fair, aboveboard; pure, honest, high-minded, saintly. **3.** ethical, able to distinguish between right and wrong, conscionable. **4.** of morals, didactic, sermonizing, homiletic, preaching, moralizing, tendentious. *—n.* **5.** lesson, message, tag, moral teaching; saying, proverb, maxim, adage, epigram, aphorism, motto. **—Ant. 2** immoral, unmoral, amoral, wrong, sinful, unjust, unfair, dishonest, unethical, improper, dishonorable, unprincipled.

morale *n.* spirit, disposition, mental attitude, mood, temper, level of optimism, moral strength, confidence, self-confidence, self-assurance, resolution, esprit de corps.

morality *n.* **1.** ethical values, ethics, right or wrong. **2.** goodness, righteousness, virtue, rectitude, honor, uprightness, fairness, probity, integrity; code of ethics, ethical philosophy, set of values. **3.** sexual behavior, habits, chasteness, modesty, tastes. **—Syn. Study. 2** See GOODNESS. **—Ant. 2** immorality, wickedness, dishonor.

morass *n.* marsh, wetlands, slough, bog, quicksand, quagmire, swamp, mire, fen.

morbid *adj.* depressed, gloomy, glum, sad, morose, brooding, self-absorbed, dour, saturnine, moody, melancholic, lugubrious, despondent, somber, grim, pessimistic; unwholesome, preoccupied with death, suggesting an unhealthy mental state. **—Ant.** cheerful, optimistic, vital, life-centered.

mordant *adj.* cutting, stinging, biting, incisive, sarcastic, acerbic, bitter, caustic, waspish, venomous, acrimonious, scornful, trenchant, scathing, piercing, virulent, malicious, acidulous. **—Ant.** soothing, pacifying, charitable; bland, innocuous.

more *adj.* **1.** extra, additional, other, added, supplemental, supplementary, further; spare, reserve. *—adv.* **2.** to a greater extent or degree. **3.** further, longer, additionally. **—Ant. 1, 2** less. **1** fewer.

moreover *adv.* further, besides, also, more than that, what's more, furthermore, too, in addition.

mores *n.* customs, conventions, practices, standards, traditions, observances, code, usages, rules, rituals, forms, ethos, morals, etiquette, morality, proprieties.

moribund *adj.* dying, doomed, waning, stagnating, dying out, near death, fading out, phasing out, on its last legs.

morning *n.* **1.** morn, daybreak, dawn, sunrise, break of day, daylight, sunup, crack of dawn. **2.** forenoon, before 12 m. *—adj.* **3.** matutinal, early, of the morning, forenoon. **—Ant. 1, 2** afternoon, evening; dusk, sunset.

moron *n.* fool, dope, ass, simpleton, nit-wit, ninny, dunce, dumbhead, dummy, loony, dolt, nut, oaf, numskull, idiot, dimwit, imbecile, half-wit, muttonhead, bonehead, blockhead, dumbbell, nincompoop, boob, sap, jackass. **—Ant.** genius, brain, mastermind, wizard, whiz.

morose *adj.* depressed, low, crestfallen, sad, melancholy, downcast, moody, glum, dour, blue, down in the dumps, down in the mouth; saturnine, mopish, gloomy, despondent, mournful, solemn; sullen, sulky, cross, surly, testy, waspish, sour, churlish, grumpy, cranky, ill-tempered, irascible. **—Syn. Study.** See GLUM. **—Ant.** cheerful, blithe, buoyant, ebullient, happy, good-natured, pleasant, genial, amiable, friendly.

morsel *n.* nibble, tidbit, taste, bite, swallow, crumb, snack, sliver, sip, piece, nip, drop, small amount, dollop, mouthful; bit, scrap, touch, speck, little piece, segment, scintilla, trace, whit, modicum, fragment, iota, particle, fraction, grain, drop.

mortal *adj.* **1.** human, earthly, corporeal, mundane; fleeting, ephemeral, temporal, transitory. **2.** fatal, lethal, deadly, causing death. **3.** extreme, severe, intense, enormous, deep, grave, unimaginable; living. **—*n.* 4.** human being, person, creature, individual, *Informal* type, character. **—Syn. Study. 2** See FATAL. **—Ant. 1** immortal, undying, everlasting, eternal, divine, deathless, perennial.

mortality *n.* **1.** transience, impermanence, evanescence, ephemeral, transitoriness. **2.** human loss, loss of life, slaughter, fatality, extermination, carnage, bloodshed, death toll. **—Ant. 1** immortality, permanence; divinity.

mortify *v.* **1.** shame, horrify, embarrass, appall, chagrin, discomfit, abash, disconcert, make red-faced. **2.** deny, discipline, self-discipline, be abstinent, practice continence, practice rigorous austerities; fast, do penance. **3.** become gangrenous, fester, rot, decay, putrefy; make rotten, cause to decay. **—Ant. 1** gratify, satisfy, make confident, make proud. **2** indulge, satisfy.

most *adj.* **1.** the greatest in number, degree, or quantity; maximum; in the majority. **—*n.* 2.** largest amount, maximum; the majority. **—*adv.* 3.** in the greatest degree, extremely, to the greatest extent, very, in the highest degree, best.

mostly *adv.* primarily, chiefly, for the most part, predominantly, largely, mainly; especially, above all, specially, particularly, principally; as a rule, most often, generally, more or less, greatly.

mother *n.* **1.** female parent, *Informal* mom, mama, momma, mommy, mum, mummy, mums, old lady, *British* mater. **2.** origin, source, wellspring, stimulus, inspiration. **—*v.* 3.** bear, give birth to, bring forth, beget, produce, conceive, breed. **4.** care for, rear, raise, tend, mind, nurse, nurture, protect, indulge.

motherly *adj.* maternal, parental, tender, kind, loving, gentle, sheltering, protective, indulgent, devoted. **—Ant.** unmaternal, unkind, unloving.

motif *n.* style, theme, artistic theme, topic, subject, treatment, idea, shape, form, design, pattern, figure; refrain, thread.

motion *n.* **1.** movement, mobility, motility, act of moving, kinesis; drift, passage, stir, flow, stream, flux, progress, action. **2.** gesture, signal, sign, move, action, bodily movement, gesticulation, indication, cue. **3.** formal proposal, suggestion, request, proposition, recommendation. **—*v.* 4.** signal, beckon, nod, gesture, gesticulate. **—Ant. 1** rest, repose, stillness, immobility; quiet, quiescence, stasis.

motionless *adj.* still, stationary, inert, without motion, immobile, immovable, immobilized, unmoving, quiescent, calm, at rest, fixed, at a standstill, stable, tranquil, inactive, static; transfixed, riveted to the spot, frozen; lifeless, unresponsive, idle, dead. **—Ant.** mobile, active, alive.

motivate *v.* impel, induce, stimulate, stir, activate, move, arouse, provoke, influence, goad, prompt, persuade, actuate, stir up; *Slang* egg on, turn on, light a fire under. **—Ant.** discourage, dissuade, daunt, disincline.

motivation *n.* motive, reason, impulse, impetus, cause, driving force, impulsion, incentive, causation, provocation, inducement.

motive *n.* reason, purpose, object, cause, motivation, intention, occasion, design, thinking, grounds, rationale; inducement, incentive, provocation, enticement, stimulus, prompting, instigation, spur, incitement, inspiration; goal, aim, end. **—Syn. Study.** MOTIVE, INDUCEMENT, INCENTIVE apply to something that moves or prompts a person to action. MOTIVE is usu. applied to an inner urge that moves a person; it may also apply to a contemplated goal, the desire for which moves the person: *Her motive was a wish to be helpful. Money was the motive for the crime.* INDUCEMENT is used mainly of opportunities offered by another person or by situational factors: *The salary they offered me was a great inducement.* INCENTIVE is usu. applied to something offered as a reward or to stimulate competitive activity: *Profit sharing is a good incentive for employees.* See also REASON.

motley *adj.* **1.** varied, different, heterogeneous, disparate, composite, mixed, assorted, miscellaneous, variegated, sundry, diversified, unlike, incongruous, dissimilar, divergent, hybrid. **2.** of different colors, varicolored, checkered, multicolored, polychrome, dappled, pied, piebald, particolored, speckled, watered, tabby, brindled, kaleidoscopic, mottled, iridescent, harlequin. —*n.* **3.** varied colors, patchwork, rainbow pattern; clown's costume, jester or buffoon's garish apparel, clownish trappings. —**Ant. 1** uniform, homogeneous, identical, like, similar. **2** monochromatic, solid, plain. **3** monochrome.

mottled *adj.* motley, particolored, variegated, multicolor, piebald, polychromatic, iridescent, kaleidoscopic, pied, varicolored, flecked, brindled, blotchy, specked, speckled, stippled, tabby.

motto *n.* slogan, watchword, maxim, proverb, precept, byword, rule, principle, saw, aphorism, saying, adage, catchword, dictum, axiom, mot, epigram, truism.

mound *n.* **1.** pile, rampart, ridge, entrenchment, embankment, bulwark, earthwork; rick, stack, heap. **2.** knoll, hillock, hill, dune, mount, hummock, mogul, bump. —**Ant. 2** dip, valley, dell, sinkhole.

mount *v.* **1.** ascend, climb, go up, climb up, scale, get over, climb over. **2.** rise, ascend, go up, increase, intensify, grow, soar, swell, surge, wax, multiply, augment. **3.** climb up on, get astride, get upon, straddle. **4.** install, fit, equip, outfit, rig, fit out; put in position on, set into, affix, frame, fix, set, set off. —*n.* **5.** riding animal; horse, saddle horse, steed, charger; (*variously*) pony, elephant, camel. —**Ant. 1** drop, descend. **2** fall, decline, lessen, decrease, diminish. **3** dismount.

mountain *n.* peak, massif, natural elevation of the earth's surface, eminence, very high hill, elevation, height, range, highland, butte, bluff, ridge, mount, alp; volcano.

mountebank *n.* **1.** quack, quacksalver, medicine man, huckster. **2.** confidence man, charlatan, fraud, swindler, cheat, humbug, sharper, con artist, con man, hustler, operator, flimflam man, *Informal* phony.

mourn *v.* **1.** grieve, grieve for, express grief, lament, weep over, despair, sorrow, be sorrowful, bewail, wail, pine, languish, cry, wail, sob, weep, keen. **2.** regret, rue, deplore, bemoan. —**Ant. 1** rejoice, exult, laugh, triumph.

mourning *n.* **1.** grief, woe, grieving, lamentation, lamenting, dolor, bereavement, sorrow, sorrowing, anguish, despair; period of mourning. **2.** weeds, crape, black, black apparel. —**Ant. 1** rejoicing, celebration, merrymaking.

mousy *adj.* timid, shy, fearful, bashful, timorous, withdrawn, self-effacing, self-conscious; dull, colorless, drab; unobtrusive, inconspicuous, unnoticed; *Slang* wimpy. —**Ant.** brazen, brassy, conspicuous, flamboyant, self-assertive.

mouth *n.* **1.** oral opening, jaws, oral cavity, facial orifice. **2.** opening, aperture, lips, bell. **3.** inlet, bay, estuary, place where a river flows into another body of water, outlet, portal, wide opening, jaws. —*v.* **4.** pronounce, speak, declare, say, voice, propound; feign speech, feign singing, shape words, lip-synchronize.

move *v.* **1.** shift, stir, budge, change position, locomote, change place, proceed, advance, go; transpose, carry, pass, remove, transport, switch, bear, convey, transmit. **2.** transfer, relocate, change residence, change one's abode, shift, transplant. **3.** go, have motion, function, operate. **4.** cause, influence, induce, lead, impel, get, prompt, incite, drive, inspire, provoke, persuade, stimulate, motivate. **5.** touch, affect; arouse, rouse, excite, stir, sway, interest, impress, impassion, fire, strike. **6.** propose, suggest, recommend, request, ask, urge, exhort, plead. **7.** get started, start off, go, go ahead, begin; strike, attack. —*n.* **8.** movement, motion, gesture, stirring, budging. **9.** action, deed, act, maneuver, ploy, measure, stroke, step. **10.** turn, opportunity, *Informal* go. —**Ant. 1** stop, stay, arrest. **4** prevent. **5** untouched, unmoved, unimpressed.

movement *n.* **1.** motion, change of position, locomotion, stirring, progress, agitation, action. **2.** bodily rhythm, motion, steps, gestures, execution. **3.** activity, operation, maneuver. **4.** drive, crusade, undertaking, program, measure, effort. **5.** section, part, division. **6.** mechanism, action, works. —**Ant. 1** inertia, stasis, quiescence.

movie *n.* motion picture, film, cinema, screening, moving picture, show, showing, picture show, picture, feature, *Slang* flick; (*variously*) epic, horror flick, docudrama, biopic.

moving *adj.* **1.** movable, capable of moving, mobile, motile, interacting; motor, locomotive. **2.** motivating, spurring, inspiring, stimulating. **3.** touching, heart-rending, exciting, affecting, stirring, impressive, poignant. —**Ant. 1** stationary, immobile, unmoving, still. **3** unaffecting, unexciting, unimpressive.

moxie *n.* guts, spunk, grit, sand, pluck, courage, dauntlessness, nerve, spirit, mettle, backbone, stamina, hardihood, pluckiness, toughness, audacity. —**Ant.** timidity, cowardliness, faintheartedness.

much *adj.* **1.** abundant, ample, plenteous, sufficient, considerable, appreciable, copious, plentiful, plenty of, a lot of. **2.**

important, impressive, worthwhile, consequential, noteworthy, striking, satisfying. —*n.* **3.** appreciable amount, great deal, good deal, sufficiency, quantity; lots, loads, heaps, scores. —*adv.* **4.** greatly, decidedly, indeed, to a great degree, far; excessively, overly, exceedingly. **5.** somewhat, rather, nearly, approximately, about, almost. **6.** often, frequently, regularly, many times, oftentimes, a lot. —**Ant. 1** little, small, scarce, few. **1, 3** little. **2** unimportant, inconsequential, trifling, unsatisfying.

muck *n.* mud, dirt, filth, dung, sewage, slop, garbage, slime, sludge, mire, ooze, compost, *Informal* guck, gunk.

muddle *v.* **1.** confuse, mix up, ruin, botch, bungle, blunder, mess up, spoil, fumble, *Informal* muff; *Slang* blow, goof up. **2.** stupefy, mentally confuse, mix up, nonplus, daze, throw, confound, rattle, bewilder, boggle; act confusedly. —*n.* **3.** confused state, disconcertion, pother, haze, fog, daze; jumble, mess, disorder, disarray, chaos, disarrangement, clutter.

muffle *v.* **1.** wrap, cloak, swaddle, swathe, cover, enclose, conceal, mask, veil, envelop, shroud, gag. **2.** suppress, stifle, cut off, silence, block off, blot out, quiet, hush, still, mute, quell, dull, deaden, dampen, soften.

mug *n.* **1.** cup, tankard, tumbler, toby, toby jug, chalice, beaker, stoup, stein, goblet, flagon. **2.** *Slang* face, visage, countenance, kisser, puss.

muggy *adj.* humid, clammy, sultry, vaporous, steaming, steamy, oppressive, stuffy, sweaty, sticky, close, sweltering.

mule *n.* half donkey-half mare; (*loosely*) ass, burro, donkey, jackass.

mull *v.* Usu. **mull over** ponder, pore over, consider, reflect on, deliberate, think about for a while, give thought to, study, meditate, weigh, ruminate.

multifarious *adj.* varied, diverse, different, diversified, various, divers, variegated, manifold, multiform, motley, miscellaneous, multiplex, protean, sundry, heterogeneous, of many kinds, mixed, numerous, many, several.

multiply *v.* **1.** procreate, propagate, reproduce, proliferate, breed, increase, beget, generate. **2.** increase, enlarge, magnify, intensify, augment; add to, enhance, raise, extend, spread, heighten. —**Ant. 2** decrease, diminish, lessen, wane, reduce, abate, shrink; divide.

multitude *n.* crowd, throng, mob, legion, horde, scores, mass, array, conflux, host, myriad, troop, flock, slew, flood, crush, drove, army, pack, herd, swarm, large amount, great number. —**Syn. Study.** See CROWD.

mum *adj.* silent, still, quiet, wordless, closemouthed, taciturn, secretive, mute, tight-lipped, uncommunicative, tacit.

mumble *v.* **1.** mutter, murmur, utter indistinctly, speak inarticulately, speak incoherently, stammer, hem and haw, mouth. —*n.* **2.** indistinct utterance, mutter, rumble, murmur, inarticulate sound, growl, grunt. —**Ant. 1** articulate, enunciate.

mumbo jumbo *n.* hocus pocus, humbug, double-speak, gobbledygook, flummery, gibberish, double talk; cant, sophistry, obfuscation, obscurantism; *Slang* hot air, hokum, blah, Jabberwocky, tripe, rot, bosh, bilge, baloney, hooey, fiddlefaddle, *British* tosh.

mundane *adj.* ordinary, prosaic, commonplace, worldly, terrestrial, earthly, down-to-earth, day-to-day, routine, humdrum, everyday, practical, pedestrian, petty. —**Syn. Study.** See EARTHLY. —**Ant.** heavenly, celestial, ethereal, empyrean, unearthly, unworldly, spiritual.

municipal *adj.* civic, community, city, administrative, public.

municipality *n.* self-governing district, town, city, township, bailiwick, parish, village.

munificence *n.* generosity, bountifulness, liberality, benevolence, beneficence, benefaction, largesse, bounty, bounteousness, humanitarianism, philanthropy, charity, charitableness, patronage. —**Ant.** parsimoniousness, stinginess, pennypinching, niggardliness, miserliness.

munificent *adj.* generous, liberal, freehanded, open-handed, free, benevolent, beneficent, bountiful, magnanimous, bounteous, altruistic, kindly, philanthropic, humanitarian, charitable, eleemosynary; lavish, profuse, extravagant, princely. —**Syn. Study.** See GENEROUS. —**Ant.** stingy, penurious, mean, niggardly, parsimonious.

murder *n.* **1.** homicide, assassination, manslaughter, killing. —*adj.* **2.** *Informal* unbearable, intolerable, oppressive, agonizing; very difficult, impossible, formidable. —*v.* **3.** kill, slay, assassinate, commit homicide, butcher, slaughter, cut down, *Slang* knock off, waste. **4.** use incorrectly, abuse, mangle, misuse, bastardize, corrupt.

murderer *n.* killer, assassin, slayer, homicide; butcher, cutthroat.

murky *adj.* dark, dim, gloomy; hazy, misty, foggy, cloudy, vaporous, dusky, gray, overcast, sunless, obscure, lowering; dreary, somber, dismal, cheerless. —**Ant.** bright, clear, unobscured.

murmur *n.* purl, low sound, susurrus, rumble, soft utterance, whisper, undertone, rustle, swish, purr, hum, lapping, drone, buzz, sough, mumble; mutter, complaint, grumble, lament, whimper, sigh.

muscle *n.* **1.** bicep, flexor, sinew, tendon, thew, *Informal (pl.)* abs, glutes, lats, pecs, quads, traps. **2.** power, brawn, muscular strength, prowess, potency, might, thew, force, grit, puissance, energy, vigor, stamina, sturdiness, virility.

muscular *adj.* strong, husky, powerful, burly, brawny, tough, strapping, well-developed, fit, athletic, sinewy, *Slang* buff.

muse *v.* meditate, consider, ponder, deliberate, mull, speculate, ruminate, contemplate, cogitate, reflect, review; think reflectively, say reflectively.

mushroom *v.* grow, expand quickly, spread, flourish, proliferate, burgeon, increase, shoot up, spring up, sprout.

music *n.* **1.** harmonious sound, euphony, harmony, minstrelsy, song, tune, melody; melodiousness, tunefulness, lyricism. **2.** printed music, score, sheet music.

musical *adj.* melodious, melodic, euphonious, harmonious, tuneful, dulcet, sweet, mellifluent, pleasant-sounding, lilting, lyric, lyrical. **—Ant.** unmusical, discordant, inharmonious, unmelodious, cacophonous.

muss *v.* rumple, disturb, crumple, tousle, disorder, disarrange, ruffle, jumble, dishevel, mess, bedraggle, tangle, *Slang* foul up. **—Ant.** straighten, arrange, untangle, tidy.

muster *n.* **1.** assemblage, gathering, assembly, aggregation, company, agglomeration, meeting, rally, turnout, confluence. **—***v.* **2.** summon, assemble, mobilize, round up, convene, call, call together, line up, convocate, rally, marshal, collect, gather, raise. **—Syn. Study. 2** See GATHER.

musty *adj.* **1.** mildewed, moldy, stale, dusty, fusty, damp, dank, dirty, stuffy, *British* frowsty. **2.** hackneyed, stale, worn, worn-out, staled by time, old, threadbare, banal, antiquated, commonplace, trite, familiar, *Informal* tired, old hat. **—Ant. 2** new, novel, fresh, original.

mutable *adj.* changeable, transformable, adaptable, convertible, variable, versatile, flexible, pliable, adjustable, metamorphic, modifiable, permutable; mercurial, volatile.

mutation *n.* change, alteration, permutation, variation, metamorphosis, transformation, transmogrification, deviation, transfiguration, modification; anomaly, mutant.

mute *adj.* **1.** dumb, speechless, voiceless, aphasic. **2.** noncommittal, silent, nonvocal, unwilling to speak, mum, reticent, close-mouthed, tight-lipped, uncommunicative; reserved, tacit, quiet, speechless, inarticulate. **3.** unsounded, silent, unarticulated, unuttered, unpronounced. **—Ant. 2** expansive, informative, loquacious. **3** audible, pronounced, articulated.

mutilate *v.* butcher, maim, mangle, cut to pieces, lacerate, cripple, deform, disfigure, lame; deprive of bodily part, cut off, amputate, truncate, excise, dismember.

mutiny *n.* **1.** uprising, revolt, insurrection, rebellion, insurgency, takeover, overthrow, coup, upheaval. **—***v.* **2.** revolt, rebel, rise up, defy authority.

mutter *v.* mumble, grumble, murmur, grouse, grouch, grunt, rumble, growl, whisper; carp, complain, gripe; *Slang* kvetch.

mutual *adj.* **1.** shared by two parties, interchangeable, common, coincident, correlative, joint, communal, interactive, related. **2.** reciprocated, reciprocal, shared, interchanged, returned. **—Ant. 1** distinct, uncommon. **2** unreciprocated, unshared, disparate.

muzzle *v.* **1.** harness, gag, bridle; curb, bind, check, rein in. **2.** silence, quiet, still, suppress, throttle, stifle, strangle, gag.

myriad *adj.* innumerable, multitudinous, countless, boundless, measureless, infinite, incalculable, immeasurable, untold, limitless, manifold, uncounted, endless. **—Ant.** few.

mysterious *adj.* strange, puzzling, enigmatic, cryptic, secret, inscrutable, obscure, hidden, covert, clandestine, baffling, impenetrable, perplexing, secretive, undercover, sphinxlike, cloudy, inexplicable, surreptitious, unfathomable, dark, unknown, mystical, supernatural, undecipherable. **—Syn. Study.** MYSTERIOUS, INSCRUTABLE, OBSCURE, MYSTICAL refer to that which is not easily comprehended or explained. That which is MYSTERIOUS, by being unknown or puzzling, excites curiosity, amazement, or awe: *a mysterious disease.* INSCRUTABLE applies to that which is impenetrable, so enigmatic that one cannot interpret its significance: *an inscrutable smile.* That which is OBSCURE is discovered or comprehended dimly or with difficulty: *obscure motives.* That which is MYSTICAL has a secret significance, such as that attaching to certain rites or signs: *mystical symbols.* **—Ant.** clear, plain, apparent, manifest, palpable.

mystery *n.* **1.** sacred rites, things unexplainable, mysticism, occult, sacramental rite, symbolism, ineffability, holy of holies. **2.** puzzle, problem, secret, riddle, conundrum, enigma, obscurity. **3.** enigmatic manner, ineffability, ineffableness, mysterious quality, elusiveness, mystification, secrecy, ambivalence, quizzicality, vagueness.

mystical Also **mystic** *adj.* mysterious, inscrutable, obscure, unknowable, enigmatic, abstruse, esoteric, cabalistic, symbolic, symbolical, secretive, hidden, occult, cryptic; otherworldly, transcendental, ethereal, metaphysical, nonrational, inner. **—Syn. Study.** See MYSTERIOUS.

mystify *v.* bewilder, fool, deceive, mislead, elude, confound, perplex, puzzle, baffle, confuse, *Slang* bamboozle.

myth *n.* **1.** story, legend, tale, fairy tale, fable, allegory, parable. **2.** fiction, made-up story, fantasy; falsehood, lie, fib, tall tale, prevarication, canard, story, yarn; hearsay, rumor. **3.** illusion, delusion, falsehood, error, shibboleth. **—Syn. Study. 1** See FABLE. **—Ant. 1** historical fact, real-life occurrence. **2** truth, fact, actuality, reality; lowdown, *Slang* skinny.

mythical Also **mythic** *adj.* **1.** legendary, fabled, about myths, mythological. **2.** imaginary, fantasized, fictitious, fabricated, unsubstantial, illusory, unreal, pretended, conjured-up. **—Ant. 2** real, actual, real-life.

mythological Also **mythologic** *adj.* drawn from mythology; legendary, mythical, mythic, unreal, unfactual, fabulous, imaginary, fictitious, fantastic, imagined, illusory.

nab *v.* arrest, capture, apprehend, catch, seize, grab, snare, snag, lay hold of, take into custody, detain, pick up, pull in; *Slang* pinch, collar, snatch, nail, haul in, bust. **—Ant.** release, let go, liberate, loose, set free.

nadir *n.* lowest point, low point, apogee, zero, nothing, bottom, rock bottom, floor, base. **—Ant.** peak, apex, zenith, high point.

nag *v.* **1.** pester, harass, badger, harp, hector, upbraid, scold, nettle, irritate, annoy, plague, importune, bedevil, pick at, pick on, heckle, devil, goad, rail at, peck at, bicker, *Slang* hassle. *—n.* **2.** scold, shrew, virago, termagant, harpy, tartar, battle-ax, Xanthippe; vixen, fury.

nail *v.* hammer, pin, fasten, fix, secure.

naive Also **naïve** *adj.* **1.** innocent, unaffected, unsophisticated, childlike, unspoiled, simple, artless, unjaded, plain, ingenuous, guileless, unassuming, natural, candid, open, unworldly. **2.** gullible, foolish, simple, credulous, unsuspecting, unsuspicious, unwise, green, immature, unwary, susceptible. **—Ant. 1** sophisticated, disingenuous, jaded, blasé. **2** artful, sly, suspicious.

naiveté Also **naïveté, naivety** *n.* innocence, artlessness, ingenuousness, candor, openness, simplicity, naturalness, frankness, sincerity, unaffectedness, modesty; credulity; inexperience, callowness; foolishness, simplemindedness, childishness. **—Ant.** sophistication, worldliness, experience.

naked *adj.* **1.** nude, unclad, undressed, unappareled, unclothed, undraped, disrobed, bared, *Informal* in the buff, in one's birthday suit, in the altogether. **2.** uncovered, bare, laid bare, exposed, wide-open. **3.** plain, simple, unvarnished, frank, blatant, sheer, bald, patent, pure, palpable, manifest, perceptible, unqualified. **—Ant. 1** dressed, clothed, clad, covered. **3** euphemized, embellished, exaggerated.

namby-pamby *adj.* wishy-washy, indecisive, weak, insipid, colorless, vapid, dull, banal, inane, sapless, innocuous, characterless; prim, prissy, mincing, simpering, coy. **—Ant.** decisive, definite, forceful, dynamic.

name *n.* **1.** appellation, cognomen, title, designation; signature, denomination; taxonomy, nomenclature, term. **2.** nickname, chief characteristic, sobriquet, epithet, label. *—v.* **3.** call, christen, baptize, designate, *Informal* tag, label. **4.** choose, delegate, appoint, nominate, deputize, commission, ordain, authorize, select, specify.

nameless *adj.* **1.** unnamed, having no name, undesignated, without a name, untitled. **2.** unknown, anonymous; obscure, unheard-of, minor. **—Ant. 2** famous, well-known, renowned.

nap *v.* **1.** doze, take a short sleep, drowse, slumber, have a catnap, doze off, drift off, drop off, nod, rest, *Informal* snooze, catch forty winks; not pay attention, be off guard, be unaware, *Slang* goof off. *—n.* **2.** short sleep, catnap, slumber, rest, doze, siesta, *Informal* shut-eye, forty winks, snooze.

narcissistic *adj.* self-centered, egoistical, egocentric, conceited, egomaniacal, vain, self-absorbed, smug, self-satisfied, selfish, swelled-headed, self-admiring; *Slang* puffed-up, stuck on oneself.

narcotic *n.* drug, opiate, pharmaceutical, medicine, medication, medicament, soporific, painkiller, sedative, tranquilizer, medicinal drug.

narrate *v.* tell a story, retell, repeat, set forth, recount, relate, chronicle, detail, give an account of, describe, portray, recite, render.

narration *n.* storytelling, relating, speaking, telling, recounting, description, recitation, recital, voice-over.

narrative *n.* **1.** story, tale, chronicle, statement, account, report, recital. **2.** storytelling, technique of writing, fictional style; dialogue. *—adj.* **3.** telling a story, involving storytelling, anecdotal, having a plot, episodic, historical.

narrow *adj.* **1.** slim, not wide, slender, fine, attenuated, tapered. **2.** small, pinched, incapacious, close, scant, cramped, tight, scanty, restricted, confined, squeezed, compressed, constricted. **3.** bigoted, biased, opinionated, provincial, isolated, narrow-minded, illiberal, dogmatic, parochial, shallow, intolerant, set, hidebound; conservative, reactionary. **—Ant. 1** broad, wide. **2** spacious, ample, big. **3** open, liberal, receptive; radical.

narrow-minded *adj.* provincial, bigoted, straitlaced, prudish, opinionated, narrow, small-minded, parochial, conservative, hidebound, reactionary, one-sided, petty; unworldly, unsophisticated. **—Ant.** broad-minded, inquisitive, tolerant.

narrows *n.* strait, narrow part of a body of water, passage, neck, channel, canal, pass, isthmus; ravine.

nasty *adj.* **1.** foul, odious, awful, nauseating, repellent. **2.** vicious, beastly, mean, abominable, hateful, vile, horrible. **3.** unpleasant, distasteful, disagreeable, disgusting, awful, revolting. **—Ant.** 1, 3 pleasant, enjoyable, nice. **2** kind, sweet, admirable, honorable.

native *adj.* **1.** of one's place of birth, of one's homeland, natal, home, paternal. **2.** inherent, inborn, innate, inbred, inherited, hereditary, intrinsic, basic, congenital, elemental, natural, endemic, ingrained, instinctive. **3.** local, national, indigenous, autochthonous, domestic, homegrown. **—*n.*** **4.** aborigine, original inhabitant; primitive, savage. **5.** one born in a specific place, lifelong inhabitant, long-time resident, citizen, countryman, countrywoman. **—Ant. 1** adopted. **2** acquired, learned. **3** imported, foreign. **5** foreigner, alien.

natural *adj.* **1.** of nature, earthly, terrestrial. **2.** naturally occurring, formed naturally, native, formed over time, made by nature. **3.** instinctive, inborn, inherent, native, god-given, intuitive; normal, characteristic, essential, to be expected, regular. **4.** unaffected, spontaneous, genuine, straightforward, plain, unstudied, unmannered, unpretentious. **—Ant. 2** unnatural, artificial. **4** affected, assumed, counterfeited, feigned, calculated.

nature *n.* **1.** the natural world, world apart from man, created world, physical world, creation, earth, globe; cosmos, universe. **2.** instinct, constitution, disposition, bent, humor, mood; birth, character, spirit, essence; trait, characteristic, property, peculiarity, feature. **3.** kind, variety, sort, type, category, style, stamp, particularity.

naughty *adj.* **1.** bad, devilish, disobedient, misbehaving, mischievous, willful, wayward, perverse, bad, obstinate, recalcitrant, fractious, unmanageable, disrespectful. **2.** off-color, bawdy, vulgar, dirty, pornographic, blue, ribald, risqué.

nausea *n.* **1.** sickness, upset stomach, queasiness, biliousness; (*variously*) travel sickness, motion sickness, car sickness, seasickness, airsickness; retching, vomiting, heaving. **2.** disgust, revulsion, repulsion, contempt, loathing.

nauseate *v.* sicken, make sick, upset, make bilious, turn one's stomach, make sick to the stomach; disgust, repulse, revolt, offend, repel.

nauseated *adj.* sick to the stomach, sick, queasy, ill; disgusted, revolted, repelled, upset.

nauseous *adj.* **1.** sickening, nauseating, disgusting, unappetizing, repulsive, revolting, repellent, offensive, abhorrent, upsetting. **2.** sick, nauseated, upset, queasy, sick at one's stomach.

nautical *adj.* seagoing, of the sea, marine, oceanic, maritime, boating, aquatic, yachting, naval.

navigate *v.* **1.** cross, sail across, cover the body of water, sail, cruise, ride, voyage, ship, sail over, fly. **2.** chart a course, plot a course; sail, maneuver.

navigation *n.* art of sailing, seamanship, piloting, sailing, navigating, traveling, boating, cruising, voyaging.

navy *n.* warships, naval forces, fleet, armada, flotilla, task force, convoy.

near *adv.* **1.** close, close by, proximately, in propinquity, hereabouts, at close quarters, alongside, next door, close to home. **2.** nearly, almost, about, practically, all but, just about, nigh. **—*adj.*** **3.** close, imminent, impending, looming, approaching, threatening. **—*prep.*** **4.** close to, proximate to, in the vicinity of, not far from, in range of, in sight of. **—*v.*** **5.** approach, come close to, move toward, come up to, draw near, advance toward, close with. **—Ant. 1** distant, remote, far.

nearly *adv.* about, almost, near, nigh, approximately, all but, roughly, just about, close to, for the most part, practically.

nearness *n.* closeness, proximity, propinquity, contiguity, adjacency, immediacy; handiness, availability, accessibility; intimacy; neighborhood, vicinity, approximation. **—Ant.** remoteness, distance.

neat *adj.* **1.** orderly, straight, tidy, shipshape, organized, uncluttered; immaculate, clean. **2.** efficient, competent, purposive, intelligent, controlled, dexterous, methodical, systematic, succinct, concise, correct, accurate. **3.** great, exciting, striking, imaginative, ingenious, original, *Slang* groovy. **—Ant. 1** messy, disorderly, untidy, disorganized, cluttered. **2** inefficient, uncontrolled, incompetent. **3** bad, awful, terrible, lousy.

nebulous *adj.* vague, hazy, unclear, murky, obscure, cloudy, dark, dim, indistinct, confused, ambiguous, intangible, impalpable, indefinite, indeterminate, uncertain. **—Ant.** distinct, definite, precise.

necessarily *adv.* automatically, naturally, inexorably, inevitably, axiomatically, accordingly, compulsorily, by necessity, of course, perforce, unqualifiedly, incontrovertibly.

necessary *adj.* required, obligatory, needed, needful, requisite, compulsory, indispensable, essential, called for, fitting, desired, wanted; imperative, urgent, exigent, crucial. **—Syn. Study.** NECESSARY, REQUISITE, INDISPENSABLE, ESSENTIAL indicate something that cannot be done without. NECESSARY refers to something needed for existence, for proper functioning, or for a particular purpose: *Food is necessary for life. Sugar is a necessary ingredient in this recipe.* REQUISITE refers to something required for a particular purpose or by particular circumstances: *She has the requisite qualifications for the job.* INDISPENSABLE means absolutely necessary to achieve a particular purpose or to complete or perfect a unit: *He made himself indispensable in the laboratory.* ESSENTIAL refers to something that is part of the basic nature or character of a thing and is vital to its existence or functioning: *Water is essential to life.* **—Ant.** unnecessary, dispensable, nonessential, optional.

necessitate *v.* require, make necessary, enforce, cause, oblige, demand, impel, force, constrain, create a need for, compel; prescribe, call for.

necessity *n.* **1.** Often **necessities** something needed, necessary, essential, *sine qua non,* indispensable, requirement, requisite, exigency, must. **2.** urgency, demand, pressure, need.

necromancer *n.* magician, wizard, sorcerer, witch, warlock, black magician, conjurer, exorcist, magus, enchanter, hexer, occultist, voodooist, thaumaturgist, soothsayer, charmer.

need *n.* **1.** want, requisite, requirement, necessity, demand, exigency; essential, desideratum. **2.** poverty, want, neediness, penury, indigence, impecuniosity, destitution, pennilessness; reduced circumstances, extremity, distress, straits, hard times; insolvency, bankruptcy. *—v.* **3.** require, lack, want, demand, find necessary, find indispensable; have use for, have need of, call for, have occasion for; exact, necessitate, make a demand of; crave, yearn for. **—Syn. Study. 3** See LACK. **—Ant. 2** wealth, affluence; superfluity, excess, overabundance.

needless *adj.* unnecessary, unneeded, unessential, uncalled-for, superfluous, dispensable, gratuitous; useless, purposeless, unavailing, pointless, redundant, pleonastic; excessive, overabundant. **—Ant.** essential, obligatory, required, needful; useful, beneficial.

needy *adj.* poor, penniless, moneyless, destitute, indigent, impoverished, poverty-stricken, badly off, in want, *Informal* strapped, *Slang* broke, hard-up, down-and-out. **—Ant.** rich, affluent, wealthy, well-to-do, well-off.

ne'er-do-well *n.* idler, loafer, good-for-nothing, wastrel, bum, layabout, black sheep; *Slang* no-account, no-good, sad sack, do-nothing, goof-off, loser.

nefarious *adj.* evil, vile, infamous, atrocious, wicked, bad, foul, abominable, base, low, odious, iniquitous, execrable, despicable, detestable; vicious, depraved; unspeakable, unmentionable; hellish, devilish, infernal, ungodly; ghastly, beastly; scandalous, villainous, heinous; shameful, disgraceful, opprobrious, dishonorable. **—Ant.** good, honest, honorable, just; exalted, noble; admirable, praiseworthy, laudable.

negate *v.* nullify, invalidate, void, reverse; quash, squash, quell, squelch; vanquish, defeat, overthrow, overwhelm, destroy, wipe out, blot out; deny, abrogate, revoke, gainsay, retract, disavow; rebut, refute, contradict; disallow, set aside; veto, repeal; disown, disclaim, repudiate. **—Ant.** affirm, confirm, attest to, ratify, endorse, corroborate, reinforce, support.

negative *adj.* **1.** indicating "no," disapproving, refusing, declining, rejecting, opposing, opposed; disagreeing, objecting, dissenting, demurring. **2.** antagonistic, uncooperative, opposed, contrary, inimical, at odds, dissident; doubtful, dubious, skeptical; reluctant, unwilling, unenthusiastic; gloomy, bleak, dark, pessimistic, fatalistic, jaundiced, *Informal* downbeat, blue. **—Ant. 1** affirmative, positive, assenting; agreeing, approving; concurring. **2** positive, optimistic, cheerful.

neglect *v.* **1.** ignore, disregard, overlook, take no notice of, take no note of; let ride, let slide, let slip, slight, pass over, pass up, let pass, omit, let go; forget, fail, lose sight of, be remiss, be inattentive; pass by, shirk; abandon, shake off. *—n.* **2.** inattention, disregard, nonpreparation; neglectfulness, laxity, laxness, negligence, remissness, idleness, dereliction, slackness, noncompliance; indifference, carelessness, fecklessness, passivity; inaccuracy, slovenliness, inexactness; slight, omission, default, oversight; unfulfillment, underachievement. **—Syn. Study. 1** See SLIGHT. **—Ant. 1** attend to, take care of, perform, notice, appreciate, regard, value, prize. **2** attention, care, notice; regard, esteem, consideration, respect.

neglectful *adj.* negligent, careless, thoughtless, remiss, heedless, forgetful, unmindful, unthinking, unheeding, inattentive, unobservant, unwatchful, oblivious, disregardant; lazy, slack, procrastinating; derelict, happy-go-lucky, devil-may-care, indifferent; inconstant, untrue, unfaithful; improvident, thriftless. **—Ant.** attentive, thoughtful, considerate, regardful, careful.

negligee Also **negligé** *n.* dressing gown, robe, wrapper, kimono, peignoir; bathrobe, housecoat, duster.

negligent *adj.* neglectful, careless, indifferent, forgetful; inconsiderate, thoughtless; unthinking, unmindful, unheeding, heedless, remiss, slack, lax; inattentive, unobservant, unwatchful, untidy, slovenly. **—Ant.** careful, strict, rigorous; thoughtful, considerate, attentive, mindful, heedful.

negligible *adj.* unimportant, trifling, slight, inconsequential, insignificant, trivial, petty, minor, piddling, paltry, small, minute.

negotiate *v.* **1.** confer over, discuss, transact, arrange, bargain for, contract; agree to arbitration, come to terms, settle, meet halfway, adjust differences; haggle, barter, dicker. **2.** cope with, get over, handle, deal with, manage, make. **3.** sign over, transfer, convey, make over, transmit; pass, deliver, turn over, pass over; hand over, consign; redeem, cash, cash in.

neigh *v.* whinny, nicker, *Archaic* hinny.

neighbor *n.* **1.** person who lives nearby; adjoining country, borderer; friend, acquaintance, associate. **—*v.* 2.** border, border on, adjoin, conjoin, abut; touch, meet, be near, verge upon; come into contact with, connect with.

neighborhood *n.* **1.** district, quarter, place, area, locale, vicinity, region, community, part, section, purlieus, side, ward, confines, environs, precinct, parish. **2.** range, approximate amount, area, sphere, environs.

neighboring *adj.* nearby, adjacent, adjoining, close by; contiguous, abutting, bordering, lying close, close, near, next, at hand, near at hand; surrounding, circumjacent. **—Ant.** distant, faraway, far-off, remote.

neighborly *adj.* friendly, courteous, polite, amiable, kindly, kind, civil, hospitable, warmhearted, affable, considerate, helpful, cordial, well-disposed, gracious, obliging, amicable, *Informal* chummy. **—Ant.** antagonistic, uncivil, unfriendly, remote, hostile.

nemesis *n.* undoing, destruction, overthrow, ruin, downfall, *Informal* Waterloo; justice, vengeance, retaliation, retribution, punishment, revenge, an eye for an eye; avenger, punisher, instrument of fate; rival, match.

neologism Also **neology** *n.* nonce word, coinage.

neophyte *n.* beginner, tyro, apprentice, trainee, novice, probationer, newcomer, recruit, learner; tenderfoot, rookie, greenhorn, student, pupil; convert, proselyte, entrant, disciple, novitiate. **—Ant.** veteran, old hand, expert.

nerve *n.* **1.** courage, boldness, fearlessness, pluck, grit, mettle, endurance, determination, fortitude, hardihood, stoutheartedness, coolness, hardiness, steadiness, tenacity, dash, intrepidity, bravery, strength, resoluteness, *Informal* spunk, guts, backbone; gameness, spirit, confidence, self-assurance, self-reliance; valor, gallantry, derring-do. **2.** gall, insolence, presumption, arrogance, impertinence, impudence, effrontery, *Slang* brass, crust, sass, cheek; assurance, assumption; sauciness, flippancy, brazenness. **—Ant. 1** cowardice, faintheartedness, weakness, frailty, feebleness.

nervous *adj.* excitable, jumpy, jittery, shaky, high-strung, sensitive, touchy; *Slang* jiggy; ruffled, disturbed, uneasy, excited, tremulous, skittish, fidgety, neurotic, unsettled, trembling, unstrung, tense; anxious, hysterical, wild, delirious, fearful, apprehensive, timorous, feverish; alarmed, startled; peevish, irritable, impatient. **—Ant.** steady, calm, tranquil, peaceful; constant, even, equable, uniform; confident, bold; serene.

nervousness *n.* excitability, flutter, shaking, hysteria, quivering, trembling, twitching; hypersensitivity, touchiness, timorousness, timidity; perturbation, disturbance, agitation, irritability, irascibility; tension, tremor, fidgetiness; stage fright, apprehension, anxiety, *Informal* the shakes, the creeps, the fidgets. **—Ant.** calm, composure, coolness, equanimity.

nestle *v.* lie snug, snug, snuggle, lie, lie close, dwell, stay, remain, settle, settle down; embrace, clasp, enfold, fondle, nuzzle, cuddle, huddle, bundle, caress, coddle, pet, cosset; live, lodge, inhabit, occupy.

net[1] *n.* **1.** mesh, netting, meshwork, web, network, latticework, lattice; screen, screening; grid, gridiron; grate, grating; grillwork, grille; snare, trap. **—*v.* 2.** ensnare, snare, enmesh, trap, entangle; apprehend, seize, take, catch, lay hold of, get hold of, take captive, take prisoner, capture; snag, snap up, clasp, clutch, grab, grip.

net[2] *v.* realize in profit, gain, earn, clear a profit of, clear above expenses; accumulate, gather, pick up, collect, gather in, bring in, acquire, obtain, take in.

nether *adj.* lower, lowest, below, under, inferior, subjacent, downward; basal, bottom, bottommost, nethermost. **—Ant.** upper, higher, above.

nettle *v.* annoy, irritate, exasperate, vex, gall, provoke, bother, perturb, beset, bait; chafe, sting, harry, harass, prickle; *Slang* get one's goat, burn one up, get on one's nerves, give one a pain, miff, get in one's hair, put one off.

network *n.* complex, system,

connections, net, chain, grid, interconnections, mesh, nexus, web, wiring, circuitry; Internet, intranet, extranet, World Wide Web, the Web.

neurotic *adj.* unhealthy, nervous, anxious; psychoneurotic, sick, disturbed, abnormal, unstable, distraught, overwrought, emotionally disordered; obsessive, intense, immoderate.

neuter *adj.* asexual, sexless, neutral; barren, fallow, sterile, infertile, impotent; spayed, gelded, fixed.

neutral *adj.* **1.** nonbelligerent, noncombatant, nonparticipating, noninterventionist, nonpartisan, noninterfering. **2.** impartial, disinterested, unbiased; indifferent, unconcerned, uninvolved; withdrawn, dispassionate, remote, aloof, unaffected; of two minds, fence-sitting; pacifist, peaceful, peaceable. **3.** indefinite, in-between, middle, medium, intermediate, half-and-half; mean, normal, average; without hue, achromatic. **—Ant. 1** belligerent, active, participating, interfering. **2** partial, interested, biased, predisposed; decided, decisive. **3** positive, affirmative.

neutralize *v.* render ineffective, frustrate, balance, counterbalance, counterpoise, counteract, nullify, negate, offset, check, block, stymie; annul, cancel, stop, halt, impede, prevent; defeat, overcome, suppress, overpower; disable, incapacitate.

never *adv.* at no time, nevermore, not ever, under no circumstances, on no occasion, not at all, *Poetic* ne'er. **—Ant.** always, forever, eternally, evermore.

never-ending *adj.* everlasting, unceasing, incessant, interminable, nonstop, continual, continuous, unremitting, relentless, unbroken, persistent, repeated, recurring; constant, enduring, undiminished, steady.

never-failing *adj.* sure, steadfast, abiding, firm, unfaltering, enduring, reliable, dependable, proven, undeviating, unhesitating, trustworthy, trusty, unfailing, tried-and-true. **—Ant.** precarious, chancy, iffy, unreliable, faltering.

nevertheless *adv.* nonetheless, on the other hand, in spite of that, yet, but, regardless, anyhow, anyway, however, notwithstanding, though, although, in any event, even so, just the same, after all, for all that, contrarily, contrariwise, be that as it may, when all is said and done, at all events.

new *adj.* **1.** recently acquired, of recent make, brand-new, just out, spanking new, up-to-date, modern, current, up-to-the-minute, newly or lately issued, *Informal* newfangled; novel, original, late, fresh, recent. **2.** untried, unseasoned, unessayed, unaccustomed, unfamiliar; unused, unexercised, unventured; uncharted, unexplored; remote, out-of-the-way; untouched, ungathered, uncollected, *Informal* green, wet behind the ears. **3.** restored, reinvigorated, renewed, renovated, revivified, reborn, recreated, regenerated, refreshed; rebuilt, reconstructed, remodeled; resumed, reopened; changed, altered. **—Syn. Study. 1** NEW, NOVEL, FRESH describe things that have not existed or have not been known or seen before. NEW refers to something recently made, grown, or built, or recently found, invented, or discovered: *a new car; new species of insects.* NOVEL refers to something new that has an unexpected, strange, or striking quality, generally pleasing: *a novel experience.* FRESH refers to something that has been untouched or unspoiled by time or use, or that brings a welcome change from what has become boringly familiar: *fresh strawberries; fresh linens; fresh ideas.* **—Ant. 1** old, ancient, antique; stale, hackneyed, trite, passé, outmoded, old-fashioned; aged, elderly. **2** used, experienced, tried; familiar.

newcomer *n.* recent arrival, stranger, outsider; entrant, comer; foreigner, outlander, immigrant, alien; novice, tyro, neophyte, *Slang* newbie; intruder, trespasser, interloper.

newly *adv.* freshly, recently, lately, anew, afresh, of late, not long ago, just now.

news *n. pl.* information, intelligence, tidings, bulletin, communiqué, announcement, disclosure, account; report, release, story, dispatch, article, piece; dope, lowdown, exposé, revelation, divulgence, exposure; statement, *Informal* flash; message, word, rumor, talk, gossip, hearsay, chatter, mention, babble; scandal, libel, slander, dirt.

nib *n.* point, tip, peak, end; apex, vertex, top, pinnacle, tiptop; upper end, height; extreme, extremity.

nibble *v.* **1.** eat sparingly, bite, eat in small bites, gnaw; munch, crunch, chew; nip, peck, peck at. *—n.* **2.** bite, taste, small piece, morsel, tidbit; crumb, speck, particle, fragment.

nice *adj.* **1.** good, fine, pleasant, agreeable, excellent, pleasurable; amusing, marvelous, divine, fantastic, lovely, enchanting, wonderful, entrancing, *Informal* great, swell, dandy, jim-dandy. **2.** friendly, sympathetic, warmhearted, good, kind, agreeable, amiable, cordial, genial, congenial, pleasant; charming, attractive, interesting, delightful, gracious; understanding, compassionate; winning, pleasing; cheerful, likable. **3.** proper, refined, well brought up, virtuous, respectable, genteel, well-bred, correct, ladylike, seemly. **4.** careful, painstaking, scrupulous, precise, meticulous, skillful, sensitive, exact; correct, accurate, methodical, unerring; strict, rigorous; subtle, delicate, deft; fastidious, finicky, fussy, punctilious, overconscientious. **—Ant. 1** dreadful, miserable, awful; unpleasant, disagreeable. **2** unfriendly, unkind, mean. **3** coarse, vulgar, ill-bred, vicious. **4** sloppy, crude, rough, careless, haphazard, undiscriminating, inaccurate.

nicely *adv.* carefully, accurately, faultlessly, exactly, precisely, unerringly; happily, fortunately, opportunely; critically, fussily; fastidiously; attractively, neatly; pleasantly. **—Ant.** carelessly, haphazardly, sloppily; unfortunately; unattractively, unpleasantly.

nicety *n.* **1.** subtlety, delicacy, fine point, subtle detail, small distinction, particularity; good taste, tastefulness, flair; cultivated taste, culture, cultivation, refinement, refined feeling, fine feeling; polish, finesse, fastidiousness, grace, elegance, tact. **2.** meticulousness, attention to detail, delicacy, exactness, precision, preciseness, care, accuracy, attention; subtlety, minute attention, elaborateness, sensitivity; insight, penetration, acumen, perspicacity, discrimination. **—Ant. 2** coarseness, roughness, crudeness, inaccuracy, sloppiness, slovenliness, haphazardness.

niche *n.* **1.** recess, alcove, nook, cranny, cubbyhole, depression, hole in the wall; snug place, dugout, cove, cavity; corner, hollow. **2.** proper place, calling, suitable occupation, congenial job, vocation, trade, métier, slot, position, pigeonhole, *Slang* berth.

nick *n.* **1.** score, notch, cut, scratch, mar, scoring, mark, chip, dent, indentation, jag; wound, injury, incision, scar; cleft, depression, gash, gouge; marking. —*v.* **2.** cut, notch, scratch, lacerate, scarify, score, gash, injure, scar, damage, dent, indent; mar, deface, mark.

nickname *n.* sobriquet, agnomen, familiar name, cognomen, diminutive, *Slang* moniker, handle; appellation, designation, pseudonym, epithet; childhood name, pet name, baby name, school name.

niggardly *adj.* **1.** stingy, miserly, parsimonious, closefisted, tight, mean, cheap, stinting, ungenerous, illiberal, grudging, sparing, hardfisted, close, penurious; frugal, saving, thrifty; grubbing, mercenary. **2.** wretched, mean, insufficient, paltry, poor, sorry, beggarly, second-rate, meager, scanty, scrubby, measly; cheap, flimsy, tawdry, miserable, contemptible, shabby. **—Ant. 1, 2** bountiful, liberal, generous, munificent, handsome; profuse, lavish, prodigal, copious, ample, abundant, bounteous, plentiful.

niggling *adj.* small, trifling, petty, picayune, minor, piddling; quibbling, nitpicking, fussy, finicky, pettifogging, caviling, insignificant, inconsequential, negligible, nugatory. **—Ant.** important, considerable, sizable, consequential.

nigh *adv.* **1.** near, close, within sight, within view. **2.** almost, nearly, practically, verging on, on the brink of. —*adj.* **3.** close, close at hand, at hand, near; close by, handy; in the vicinity, adjacent, neighboring, bordering. **—Ant. 3** far, distant, remote, removed.

night *n.* nighttime, dark, darkness, tenebrousness; hours of sleep, bedtime; evening, eventide, nightfall, sundown, dusk; small hours, early morning; murkiness, obscurity.

nightfall *n.* twilight, dusk, day's end, evening, evenfall, eventide, sunset, sundown, moonrise, crepuscule, gloaming, dark, darkness. **—Ant.** daytime, dawn, daybreak, daylight.

nightly *adj.* **1.** night, evening, night after night; nocturnal, night-cloaked, night-mantled, night-veiled; dark, obscure. —*adv.* **2.** every night, nights, night after night; at night, by night, nocturnally, through the night. **—Ant. 1, 2** daily, during the day, every day. **1** diurnal. **2** diurnally.

nightmare *n.* bad dream; frightening vision, hallucination; incubus, succubus.

nightstick *n.* baton, cudgel, billy club, truncheon, shillelagh, bludgeon, mace; rod, staff, wand, scepter.

nihilism *n.* disbelief in anything, skepticism, universal doubt, agnosticism, amorality; nothingness, emptiness, nonexistence; anarchism, radicalism, iconoclasm; lawlessness, irresponsibility, license, chaos; terrorism; alienation, anomie.

nil *n.* nonexistent, none, naught, null, nullity, nothing, nothing whatever, none whatever, zero, cipher.

nimble *adj.* agile, light-footed, nimble-footed, spry, supple; animated, spirited, swift, quick, mercurial, fleet-footed, speedy, lively, sprightly, active, quick as lightning, fleet, rapid, light-legged, quick moving; light, deft, skillful, dexterous; expert, proficient; prompt, ready. **—Ant.** clumsy, slow, plodding, awkward, dull, heavy, inert, inactive; lethargic, lazy, indolent.

nincompoop *n.* ninny, dunce, harebrain, featherbrain, scatterbrain, simpleton, blockhead, jackass, bonehead, rattlebrain, knucklehead, noodlehead, muddlehead, fool, dumb bunny, dunderhead, dunderpate, numskull; dimwit, lummox, dolt, pumpkin head, nitwit, half-wit; moron, idiot, imbecile; dope, dummy, lunkhead, klutz, *German* dummkopf, *Slang* boob, jerk.

nip *v.* **1.** pinch, tweak, squeeze; clutch,

seize, snag, grab, snare, grasp, clasp, clamp, grip, snatch; snap, compress. **2.** cut off, lop, snip, cut, clip, dock, crop; cut short, abbreviate, curtail, shorten; snap, crack, shear, sever, sunder. **3.** check, cut off, curtail, put an end to, demolish, finish off, quash, deal a knockout blow to, destroy, ruin, crush; blast, thwart, frustrate. **4.** freeze, chill, frost; pierce, bite, cut; chill, benumb, make one shiver.

nitwit *n.* fool, blockhead, dummy, dolt, clod, dunce, dimwit, nincompoop, booby, lamebrain; *Slang* meathead, chowderhead, bonehead, klutz, pinhead, birdbrain, numskull, noodlehead, peabrain.

nobility *n.* **1.** noble classes, upper classes, aristocracy, ruling classes, elite, peerage, lords, patricians, patriciate; royalty; high society, *Informal* Beautiful People, upper crust, the four hundred, blue bloods, *French* noblesse. **2.** greatness, superiority, sublimity, exaltedness, dignity, loftiness, stateliness, mightiness; distinction, eminence, grandness, grandeur, prestige; preeminence, supremacy, primacy; majesty, splendor, magnificence. **3.** nobleness, aristocracy, gentility, exalted condition, high rank, high station, distinction, breeding, high breeding. **—Ant. 1** lower classes, peasantry, plebeians, obscurity, insignificance, meanness. **2** lowness, meanness, baseness, ignobility.

noble *adj.* **1.** exalted, highborn, patrician, gentle, high, high ranking, aristocratic, distinguished, pureblooded, blueblooded, thoroughbred, superior; princely, royal. **2.** great, lofty, selfless, superior, high-minded, magnanimous, excellent, exemplary, elevated, eminent; moral, virtuous, upright, meritorious, incorruptible, just, trustworthy, honorable, estimable, worthy, reputable, high-principled, honest, ethical. **3.** stately, grand, majestic, lordly, baronial, imposing, impressive, splendid, magnificent, superb, handsome; awesome, awe-inspiring; glorious, supreme, sublime; famed, renowned, famous, preeminent; dignified, courtly, lordlike, distinguished; lofty, regal, imperial. **—*n.* 4.** aristocrat, nobleman, don, patrician, grandee, peer, lord, thoroughbred; gentleman, chevalier, knight, cavalier, squire; great man, man of distinction, personage. **—Syn. Study. 2** NOBLE, HIGH-MINDED, MAGNANIMOUS suggest moral excellence and high ideals. NOBLE implies superior moral qualities and an exalted mind, character, or spirit that scorns the petty, base, or dishonorable: *a noble sacrifice.* HIGH-MINDED suggests exalted moral principles, thoughts, or sentiments: *a high-minded speech on social reform.* MAGNANIMOUS adds the idea of generosity, shown by a willingness to forgive injuries or overlook insults: *The magnanimous ruler granted amnesty to the rebels.* **—Ant. 1** lowborn, lowly, humble, plebeian, peasant, mean. **2** ignoble, base, selfish, despicable, contemptible, vulgar, doubtful, dishonest. **3** insignificant, modest, drab, mean, paltry, plain. **4** peasant, commoner, serf; scoundrel.

nocturnal *adj.* night, nighttime, of the night, nightly; night-cloaked, night-veiled, night-hidden; dark, obscure, darkling. **—Ant.** diurnal, daily, by day.

nod *v.* **1.** incline the head, bow one's head, bend the neck, make obeisance; shake up and down, lower and raise, bob; acknowledge, recognize, give salutation, greet, salute, hail, say hello, bid hello. **2.** express with a nod, indicate by nodding, reveal, show, signify, signal, beckon, motion, sign, gesture; agree, consent, assent, concur. **3.** doze, fall asleep, go to sleep; drop off, fall off; drowse, be torpid or languid, be inactive; be forgetful, be negligent, lapse, let up. **—*n.* 4.** quick bowing of the head; signal, sign, gesture.

node *n.* **1.** knot, woody formation, burl, joint, bud. **2.** lump, bump, nodule, prominence, protuberance, swelling, knob, bulge, button, hump; tumescence, excrescence.

nodule *n.* knob, outgrowth, protuberance, growth, bump, lump, node, wen, cyst, stud, knot, sac; projection, protrusion, prominence; swelling, tumescence, bulge; excrescence.

noise *n.* **1.** sound, din, racket, clamor, uproar, pandemonium, clatter, bedlam, tumult, babel, hullabaloo, blare, wail, boom, blast, bang, rumble, rumbling; barrage, thunder, cannonade; hubbub, commotion, stir, ado; discharge, report, reverberation, echo; dissonance, cacophony; roar, vociferation; bluster, caterwauling; shouting, brawling, gabbling. **—*v.* 2.** spread as news, circulate, repeat, pass, voice, rumor, bruit, broadcast, *Slang* blab. **—Syn. Study. 1** NOISE, DIN, RACKET, CLAMOR, HUBBUB refer to nonmusical or confused sounds. NOISE is a general word that usu. refers to loud, harsh, or discordant sounds: *noise from the street.* DIN is a very loud, continuous noise that greatly disturbs or distresses: *the din of a factory.* RACKET refers to a rattling sound or clatter: *to make a racket when doing the dishes.* CLAMOR refers to loud noise, as from shouting or cries, that expresses feelings, desires, or complaints: *the clamor of an angry crowd.* HUBBUB refers to a confused mingling of sounds, usu. voices; it may also mean tumult or confused activity: *the* *hubbub on the floor of the stock exchange.* **—Ant. 1** quiet, silence, hush, stillness; peace, serenity, calm; harmony, melody.

noisome *adj.* **1.** smelly, foul, malodorous, stinking, fetid, reeking, rank, rotten, nauseating, putrid, mephitic. **2.** harmful, noxious, injurious, hurtful, detrimental, unhealthy, deleterious, pernicious, toxic, baneful, poisonous. **—Ant. 2** wholesome, beneficial, healthful, salubrious.

noisy *adj.* loud, rackety, clamorous, deafening, earsplitting, uproarious, turbulent, blaring, strident, boisterous, thunderous, thundering, tumultuous, tempestuous, raging, stormy, resounding; alive, animated, lively; furious, rampageous; grating, jarring, harsh-sounding; dissonant, discordant; blatant, clangorous; shrill, piercing, cacophonous. **—Ant.** quiet, noiseless, silent, subdued, hushed, still; melodious, tuneful.

nomad *n.* wanderer, itinerant, mover, rambler, roamer, strayer, migrator, migrant, traveler, rover, vagabond, tramp, bohemian, gypsy, knight of the road, vagrant, hobo, stray, straggler; refugee, runaway, renegade; immigrant, emigrant.

nomadic *adj.* traveling, wandering, roaming, roving, drifting, migratory, migrant, itinerant, strolling, peregrinating; vagabond, peripatetic, footloose, vagrant.

nom de plume *n.* pen name; pseudonym, assumed name; false name, alias.

nomenclature *n.* terminology, phraseology, vocabulary, terms; naming, nomination, appellation, designation, taxonomy; language, jargon, lingo.

nominal *adj.* **1.** titular, ostensible, in name only, so-called, theoretical, official; purported, professed; pretended, suggested; baseless, groundless; puppet. **2.** small, low, minimum, moderate, reasonable, inexpensive, low-priced, cheap; unsubstantial, insignificant. **—Ant. 1** veritable, actual, real, true. **2** considerable, substantial.

nominate *v.* **1.** name as a candidate, propose, suggest, recommend, put forward; label, tag, call, term, style. **2.** name, pick, choose; authorize, place in authority, elevate, elect, install, select, invest.

nomination *n.* choice of a candidate, selection, election, designation; submission of a name, suggestion; appointment, installation; accession, inauguration, investiture.

nonbeliever *n.* doubter, unbeliever, skeptic, cynic, freethinker, doubting Thomas, backslider, questioner, empiricist, agnostic, atheist; heathen, pagan, infidel. **—Ant.** follower, devotee, disciple, convert, fanatic.

nonchalant *adj.* unconcerned, blasé, unheeding, imperturbable, unexcited, unemotional, unmoved, unaffected, unstirred, unruffled, cool, collected; offhand, casual, easygoing; indifferent, apathetic, uninterested, insouciant; withdrawn, dispassionate, unmindful, heedless, insensible; languid, phlegmatic, listless, lethargic, lazy, indolent, idle, careless; slack, lax. **—Ant.** concerned, moved, affected, stirred; anxious, agitated.

noncommittal *adj.* indefinite, equivocal, indecisive, vague, evasive; reserved, guarded, cautious, wary, careful, circumspect; tentative, ambiguous, neutral, temporizing; safe, cool, politic, prudent, discreet; mute, mum, unspeaking. **—Ant.** definite, decisive, positive, conclusive.

noncompliant *adj.* nonconforming, unorthodox, unconventional, iconoclastic, dissenting, disagreeing, noncooperating, differing, objecting, dissident; obstinate, rebellious, resistive, ungovernable, unruly. **—Ant.** agreeable, complaisant, obliging, obedient, compliant.

nonconformist *n.* dissenter, dissident, individualist, loner, free spirit, liberated person, protester, reformer, heretic, schismatic, rebel, revolutionary, radical, iconoclast; eccentric, exception, original, oddity; insurgent, maverick, deserter, renegade; freethinker, bohemian, vagabond, beat, hippy, *Informal* character, *Slang* oddball, crackpot, screwball, weirdo, freak, nut, card.

nondescript *adj.* undistinctive, usual, ordinary, vague, unexceptional, characterless, unimpressive, colorless, amorphous, undistinguished, stereotyped. **—Ant.** distinctive, unusual, extraordinary, vivid, unique.

nonentity *n.* nobody, unimportant person, unperson, mediocrity, small-fry, nothing, zero, cipher, nullity, *Informal* small potato, no-count. **—Ant.** celebrity, somebody, VIP.

nonessential *adj.* **1.** unessential, unnecessary, unimportant; extraneous, irrelevant, subsidiary, incidental, accidental, extrinsic, peripheral, secondary; dispensable, disallowable, unconnected, beside the point, impertinent, inappropriate; insignificant, trivial, inconsequential, inconsiderable. *—n.* **2.** unessential thing, unnecessary item, incidental; luxury, (*pl.*) trimmings, trivia. **—Ant. 1** vital, essential, important; apt, appropriate; significant.

no-nonsense *adj.* earnest, ardent, diligent, resolute, purposeful, determined, intent, dedicated, committed, grave, sober, solemn, sobersided, serious-minded, severe, grim. **—Ant.** frivolous, giddy, slapdash, scatterbrained, offhand.

nonpareil *adj.* **1.** unequaled, unique, unsurpassed, unmatched, unrivaled, one-of-a-kind; exceptional, supreme, extraordinary, elite, *Slang* super. *—n.* **2.** paragon, epitome, apotheosis, symbol, exemplar, ideal, pattern, model, representative, one of a kind, *Latin* ne plus ultra, *French* crème de la crème.

nonpartisan *adj.* unaffiliated, nonpolitical, politically independent; unbiased, unprejudiced; impartial; unswayed, uninfluenced; equitable, fair, just; uninvolved, disinterested, unimplicated; impersonal, objective; freethinking, unbigoted. **—Ant.** partisan, political; biased, prejudiced; unfair, unjust, inequitable.

nonplus *v.* confuse, confound, muddle, baffle, bother, abash, disconcert, discountenance, disturb, upset, dismay, embarrass, faze; perplex, puzzle, bewilder, stump, mystify; flabbergast, astound, dumbfound, put at a loss, astonish; stop, halt, bring to a standstill, stymie, deadlock, balk, foil.

nonsectarian *adj.* interdenominational, interchurch, undenominational, nondenominational, ecumenical; all-embracing, all-inclusive, all-encompassing. **—Ant.** sectarian, schismatic, denominational.

nonsense *n.* foolishness, folly, ridiculousness, absurdity, stupidity, inanity, senselessness, silliness, childishness; fooling, tomfoolery, joking, shenanigans, monkey business, horseplay, high jinks, antics; ludicrousness, meaninglessness, facetiousness; triviality, frivolity, extravagance, flummery, trifles; prattle, babble, chatter, blather, drivel, gibberish, *Informal* twaddle, bunk, trash, garbage, rubbish, hogwash, moonshine, rot, fiddle-faddle, piffle, flapdoodle; bombast, claptrap, balderdash, bosh, *Slang* baloney. **—Ant.** sense, common sense, wisdom; fact, reality, truth; gravity, seriousness, reason.

nonstop *adj.* continuous, endless, uninterrupted, unrelieved, unbroken, unremitting, constant, incessant, neverending, interminable, round-the-clock. **—Ant.** sporadic, periodic, interrupted.

nook *n.* recess, niche, alcove, cranny, corner; depression, cubbyhole, cavity, dugout; cove, snug place, retreat, refuge, shelter, haven, lair; hiding place, den, hideaway.

noon *n.* midday, twelve o'clock, twelve noon, 12 M.; noonday, high noon, noontime, lunchtime; zenith, meridian, highest point.

norm *n.* standard, average, rule, type; pattern, model, par; yardstick, gauge, barometer, criterion, measure, measuring rod.

normal *adj.* standard, average, usual, ordinary, expected, natural, regular; conformable, conforming, consistent; typical, par, representative, conventional; constant, steady, unchanging; steadfast, reliable, dependable; in good order, well-regulated, fit, sound, healthy; continuous, uninterrupted; incessant, unceasing, unremitting, unchanging, uniform; sane, reasonable, rational, right-minded; middling. **—Ant.** abnormal, unusual, exceptional, irregular; peculiar, rare, singular, uncommon; unprecedented, remarkable; monstrous, unnatural.

north *adj.* **1.** coming from the north, northerly; moving toward the north, northward; northern; polar, arctic; northernmost; upper. *—adv.* **2.** toward the north, northward; northerly.

nostalgia *n.* longing for the past, bittersweet memory; remembrance; homesickness, longing for home; pining, languishing; regret, remorse, regretfulness.

nostrum *n.* remedy, medicine, formula, medicament; physic, balm, elixir, drug, potion; treatment, cure, cure-all, panacea; dose, draft, prescription; patent medicine.

nosy Also **nosey** *adj.* inquisitive, all ears, curious, overcurious, prying, intrusive, snooping, eavesdropping, *Informal* snoopy.

notable *adj.* **1.** conspicuous, marked, pronounced, noticeable, salient, outstanding, remarkable, striking. **2.** renowned, reputable, distinguished, famed, famous, celebrated, prominent, eminent, well-known. *—n.* **3.** celebrity, dignitary, luminary, personage, name, personality, *Informal* VIP, bigwig, *Slang* wheel, biggie. **—Ant. 1** vague, ill-defined; imperceptible, concealed, hidden. **2** unknown, anonymous, obscure, little known.

notably *adv.* strikingly, markedly, noticeably, outstandingly, prominently, conspicuously, visibly; distinctly, unmistakably.

notation *n.* note, memorandum, entry.

notch *n.* **1.** nick, cut, dent, indentation, score, scoring. **2.** degree, level, grade, *Slang* cut. *—v.* **3.** nick, score, cut, mark, scratch.

note *n.* **1.** memorandum, notation. **2.** brief letter, message, epistle, missive, communication; dispatch, communiqué; memorandum, *Informal* line. **3.** bank note, bill, paper money; legal tender, money, currency; voucher, certificate, silver or gold certificate; draft, sight draft, bank draft; promissory note, mortgage note, *Informal* greenback, *Slang* folding money, green, scratch, bread, lettuce. **4.** regard, notice. **5.** importance, consequence, distinction, prominence, eminence, notability, reputation, fame, renown, celebrity. **—***v.* **6.** make a note of, mark down, set down, put down, enter, write, write down, jot down, make a memorandum of, make an entry of. **7.** notice, mark, perceive, take cognizance of, give attention to, take notice of, be aware of, be conscious of. **—Ant. 4** inattention, indifference, heedlessness, aloofness, unconcern. **5** obscurity, insignificance. **7** ignore, disregard, overlook.

noted *adj.* famous, renowned, eminent, celebrated, well-known, distinguished, prominent, illustrious, reputable; remarkable, notable, noteworthy, outstanding. **—Ant.** unknown, obscure, undistinguished; notorious, infamous.

noteworthy *adj.* distinguished, outstanding, significant, important, remarkable, notable; substantial, considerable; unusual, singular. **—Ant.** negligible, trivial, inconsequential.

nothing *n.* **1.** naught, no thing, nullity; insignificance, obscurity; trash, stuff, rubbish; bubble, air; bauble, bagatelle, trifle, gewgaw, trinket; trivia, inconsequentials. **2.** zero, naught, none, cipher, nix, *Slang* zilch, zip.

notice *n.* **1.** attention, regard, cognizance, heed. **2.** information, mention, notification, specification; intelligence, knowledge, *Slang* goods, dope, info; statement, declaration, communication, disclosure; poster, handbill, flyer, circular, leaflet; pamphlet, brochure; advertisement, announcement. **3.** warning, advisement, notification. **4.** review, critique, appraisal, rating. **—***v.* **5.** see, catch sight of, observe, eye, take in, take notice of, mark, remark, pay attention to, *Slang* get a load of; perceive, discern, note, become aware of. **—Syn. Study. 5** NOTICE, PERCEIVE, DISCERN imply becoming aware of something through the senses or the intellect. NOTICE means to pay attention to something one sees, hears, or senses: *to notice a newspaper ad; to notice someone's absence; to notice one's lack of enthusiasm.* PERCEIVE is a more formal word meaning to detect by means of the senses; with reference to the mind, it implies realization, understanding, and insight: *to perceive the sound of hoofbeats; to perceive the significance of an event.* DISCERN means to detect something that is obscure or concealed; it implies keen senses or insight: *to discern the outlines of a distant ship; to discern the truth.* **—Ant. 1** oversight, disregard, neglect, slight, connivance, omission, heedlessness; misinformation, ignorance. **5** ignore, slight, overlook, disregard, neglect; misjudge.

noticeable *adj.* definite, clear, plain, distinct, evident, obvious, conspicuous, unmistakable; striking, noteworthy, perceivable, perceptible, appreciable, observable, manifest, palpable.

notify *v.* inform, acquaint, let know, send word, advise, tell, enlighten, apprise; warn, serve notice on.

notion *n.* **1.** idea, côncept, suspicion, intimation, conception, thought. **2.** belief, view, opinion; whim, quirk, caprice, fancy; whimsy, conceit, humor, vagary, crotchet, eccentricity. **—Syn. Study. 1** See IDEA.

notoriety *n.* disrepute, ill repute, shame, disgrace, discredit, dishonor, infamy, ignominy, scandal, degradation, stigma, stain, blot. **—Ant.** honor, nobility, esteem, goodness, standing.

notorious *adj.* infamous, egregious, blatant, outrageous, glaring, arrant; widely known, renowned, famous, notable, celebrated, outstanding. **—Syn. Study.** See FAMOUS.

nourish *v.* nurture, feed, sustain; breast-feed, nurse, suckle. **—Ant.** starve, undernourish.

nourishment *n.* food, sustenance, nutriment, nutrition, viands, victuals, comestibles, food and drink, meat, bread, *Slang* eats, chow, grub.

novel *adj.* unusual, original, new, different, fresh, innovative, out of the ordinary, uncommon, unorthodox, unconventional, singular, unique. **—Syn. Study.** See NEW. **—Ant.** usual, customary, run-of-the-mill, habitual, ordinary, common, familiar; venerable, ancient, old-fashioned, time-honored, traditional.

novelty *n.* **1.** originality, newness, uniqueness, variation, innovation, surprise, change. **2.** trinket, gewgaw, gimcrack, bagatelle, bauble, knick-knack; token, souvenir, memento.

novice *n.* beginner, tyro, learner, apprentice, newcomer, *Slang* newbie; greenhorn, tenderfoot, amateur; pupil, student, disciple. **—Ant.** master, old hand, past master, professional, *Informal* pro.

noxious *adj.* harmful, poisonous, deleterious, injurious, baneful, damaging, pernicious, hurtful; lethal, deadly, virulent; putrid, putrescent, noisome, foul, foul-smelling, abominable, beastly, revolting, loathsome, disgusting. **—Ant.** wholesome, beneficial; sanitary, salutary, salubrious.

nuance *n.* subtle change, variation, nice distinction, delicate distinction; nicety, touch, shade, subtlety, refinement, modulation, delicacy, fineness, finesse; keenness, sharpness, discernment.

nub *n.* **1.** hump, knot, lump, knob,

node; bulge, swelling, tumescence, protuberance, prominence, projection. **2.** essence, crux, heart, core, gist, kernel, *Slang* nitty-gritty.

nucleus *n.* core, seed, nub, heart, kernel, center, pith. **—Ant.** exterior, face, integument; outer shell; appearance, features.

nude *adj.* naked, stark naked, bare, bared, unclad, mother-naked, undressed, stripped, exposed, unclothed, wearing nothing, unarrayed, unadorned, uncovered, *Informal* stripped to the buff, without a stitch; *Slang* raw, in the raw, in one's birthday suit. **—Ant.** clothed, covered, dressed, appareled, clad.

nudge *v.* elbow, poke, jab, punch; bump, jostle, jolt, jog; push, prod, touch, shove, press; motion, signal, indicate; nod.

nugatory *adj.* inconsequential, trifling, trivial, piddling, paltry, worthless, useless, valueless, meritless, profitless; empty, idle, hollow, functionless, otiose, ineffectual. **—Ant.** valuable, useful; efficacious, profitable.

nuisance *n.* annoyance, bother, pest, bore, irritation, thorn, aggravation; inconvenience, botheration; worry, fret; scourge, affliction; handicap, misfortune; grievance, vexation; plague, pestilence, blight, curse; trouble, hurt, pain, torment, burden. **—Ant.** pleasure, delight, satisfaction, benefit, blessing, gratification, happiness, joy.

null *adj.* invalid, inoperative, void, nonexistent, null and void; worthless, unimportant, insignificant, valueless, no good, immaterial, *Slang* NG. **—Ant.** valid, lawful, binding.

nullify *v.* repeal, abrogate, void, make void, cancel, annul, declare null and void, abolish; set aside, retract, revoke, rescind, veto, invalidate, override. **—Ant.** enact, decree, legislate, ratify, confirm; establish, institute.

numb *adj.* unfeeling, insensate, benumbed, insensible, dead, deadened, anesthetized, frozen, narcotized.

number *n.* **1.** numeral, figure, character, symbol, integer, cipher, digit; round number, even or odd number; amount, quantity, sum, aggregate, tally, total. **2.** quantity, multitude, company, assemblage, group, crowd, *Informal* mob, mass, bunch, herd, swarm; abundance, preponderance; indefinite number, indeterminate number; a good many, a great number; scores, quantities; host, army; bevy, array. **3.** issue, edition; book, magazine, quarterly; chapter, section, part, division; paragraph, passage. **—*v.*** **4.** give a number to, enumerate; figure, cipher; paginate, foliate, numerate; tally, figure up, tot, reckon, count, total; compute, calculate; estimate, make an estimate of. **—Ant. 2** scarcity, fewness, scantiness, paucity; want, lack; shortage, insufficiency. **4** guess, hazard, hypothesize, theorize, conjecture; lump, mass.

numberless *adj.* countless, innumerable, numerous, multitudinous, myriad, uncountable, uncounted, unnumbered, immeasurable, plenteous, illimitable, copious, unbounded, unending; *Slang* umpteen, zillions. **—Ant.** few, scarcely any, a handful of, a couple of.

numeral *n.* number, symbol, character, figure, cipher, digit, integer; cardinal number, Arabic or Roman numeral.

numerous *adj.* many, profuse, in profusion, copious, abundant, myriad, plentiful, a multitude of, multitudinous, manifold, innumerable, numberless. **—Syn. Study.** See MANY. **—Ant.** few, scarcely any, not many.

numskull Also **numbskull** *n. Slang* dunce, ninny, scatterbrain, blockhead, bonehead, dolt, half-wit, knucklehead, dummy, dunderhead, silly ass, dimwit, dullard, nitwit, idiot, imbecile, chowderhead, muttonhead, noodlehead, fool, simpleton, jerk, dope, klutz, sap, lunkhead, dummkopf, nincompoop.

nuptial *adj.* matrimonial, marital; conjugal, connubial, hymeneal.

nuptials *n.pl.* wedding, marriage, marriage ceremony, matrimonials, espousals, hymeneals, exchange of vows.

nurse *n.* **1.** (*variously*) trained nurse, practical nurse, registered nurse, private nurse, *British* sister; district nurse, public health nurse; governess, nanny, nursemaid; nurserymaid, nurse girl; dry nurse, wet nurse; guardian, attendant, caregiver, caretaker. **—*v.* 2.** attend, care for, minister to, attend to; doctor, treat, remedy. **3.** suckle, feed at the breast, wet-nurse, give suck to; succor, nourish, feed; foster, nurture, cultivate. **4.** keep in mind, bear in mind, have in mind; harbor, nurture, encourage, foster, promote. **—Ant.** neglect, disregard, slight; starve, kill, destroy.

nursery *n.* **1.** nursery school, day nursery, preschool; kindergarten, day school, infant school; children's room, schoolroom. **2.** greenhouse, botanical garden; cold frame, conservatory, forcing house; breeding place, hotbed, incubator.

nurture *v.* **1.** feed, nourish, foster, tend, sustain, maintain, strengthen; provision, victual, mess. **2.** train, discipline, develop, prepare, cultivate, tutor, school, educate, teach, instruct; bring up, rear, breed, raise. **—Ant. 2** neglect, overlook, slight; disregard, ignore; deprive, dispossess.

nut *n.* **1.** edible kernel, nutmeat; seed, stone, pit. **2.** *Slang* enthusiast, fanatic, devotee, zealot, fan, buff, aficionado. **3.** eccentric, crackpot, screwball, oddball, freak; madman, lunatic, maniac, loony; idiot; psychopath.

nutriment *n.* food, nourishment, foodstuff, *Slang* eats, chow; nutrition, nutrient, sustenance, subsistence, provisions, aliment; provender, feed, forage, mess, fodder, fare; groceries, victuals, edibles, eatables, board, daily bread, meat.

nutrition *n.* food, nourishment, nutriment, foodstuffs, eatables, edibles, sustenance; groceries, provisions, rations, subsistence, *Slang* chow, grub; provender, pasturage, forage, fodder; silage, feed.

nutritious *adj.* nourishing, nutritive, body-building, wholesome, sustaining.

nuts *adj.* crazy, wacky, bats, insane; *British* daft, potty; mad, unbalanced, cracked, demented; *Slang* wacko, round the bend, bonkers, dotty, balmy, loony, bananas.

nutty *adj.* foolish, senseless, crack-brained, inane, addlepated, lunatic, *British* daft, balmy, harebrained, silly; *Slang* goofy, wacky, screwy, cuckoo, dippy, wacko, squirrelly, meshuga, loony, bughouse, dotty, weirdo.

nuzzle *v.* cuddle, coddle, snuggle, nestle, caress, embrace, fondle; pet, cosset, pat; kiss, *Slang* buss, smack.

nymph *n.* female nature spirit, naiad, dryad, sylph, wood nymph; belle, charmer, beauty.

oaf *n.* dolt, lout, boob, booby, dunderhead, fool, numskull, bonehead, blockhead, dunce, dullard, simpleton, lummox, boor, ninny, nitwit, clod, ignoramus, nincompoop, moron, idiot, imbecile, half-wit, *Slang* jerk, sap, dope, dummy, klutz. **—Ant.** genius, intellectual, pundit, sage, guru, *Slang* egghead.

oasis *n.* **1.** watering place, water hole; fertile area, green spot. **2.** haven, refuge, harbor, sanctum, sanctuary, asylum, ivory tower, retreat, shelter. **—Ant. 1** desert, arid region.

oath *n.* **1.** vow, avowal, pledge, adjuration, affirmation, attestation; declaration, deposition, affidavit. **2.** curse, curse word, profanity, blasphemy, obscenity, expletive, *Informal* cuss word, swear word; swearing, imprecation, malediction. **—Ant. 2** benediction, blessing; prayer, invocation.

obdurate *adj.* **1.** stubborn, obstinate, intractable, unyielding, inflexible, adamant, immovable, willful, headstrong, pigheaded, mulish, bullheaded; unmanageable, uncontrollable, ungovernable. **2.** unmoved, uncaring, unfeeling, harsh, merciless, unmerciful, unpitying, pitiless, unsympathetic, uncompassionate, unsparing, untouched; hardened, callous, cruel, cold-blooded, hardhearted. **—Ant. 1** obedient, agreeable, compliant, flexible, amenable; manageable, docile, tractable. **2** compassionate, sympathetic, caring, feeling, merciful, relenting, softhearted, kind, gentle, tender.

obedience *n.* compliance, dutifulness, submissiveness, submission, subservience, docility, acquiescence, obeisance, deference, tractability, willingness, yielding, ductility, subjection; allegiance; conformance, conformability, compliance, accordance.

obedient *adj.* obeying, dutiful, compliant, amenable, submissive, subservient, yielding, docile, acquiescent, faithful, loyal, law-abiding, devoted, deferential, respectful, obeisant, governable, tractable. **—Ant.** disobedient, disobeying, insubordinate, rebellious; contrary, perverse, wayward, recalcitrant, refractory, intractable, unruly, contumacious, disrespectful, undutiful, arrogant, unyielding, obstinate, obdurate, stubborn, ungovernable, unmanageable.

obeisance *n.* bow, curtsy, kneeling, genuflection, submission, subjection, prostration; homage, courtesy, deference, respect, veneration, esteem, regard, reverence, honor, obedience, humility, humbleness, self-abasement; loyalty, fidelity, fealty, allegiance. **—Ant.** disrespect, disregard, dishonor, irreverence; disloyalty, treachery.

obese *adj.* fat, overweight, gross, corpulent, heavy, stout, tubby, pudgy, plump, porky, fleshy, chubby, portly; paunchy, rotund, potbellied, big bellied. **—Ant.** skinny, thin, slim, slender, scrawny, lean, spare, angular, rawboned, lank, lanky, gaunt.

obey *v.* comply with, be ruled by, follow orders, submit to, respect, observe, be regulated by, abide by, conform to, be governed by, mind, heed; acquiesce, serve, assent, concur, toe the line, submit to, bow to, yield to, succumb to, accede to. **—Ant.** disobey, defy, revolt, rebel, mutiny, resist, refuse, be insubordinate.

obfuscate *v.* confuse, obscure, blur, muddle, garble, scramble, mess up, befog, complicate, distort, becloud, confound, fluster, stupefy. **—Ant.** clear up, clarify, simplify, elucidate.

object *v.* **1.** be averse, take exception, disapprove of, oppose, protest, be at odds with, balk at, look askance at, frown on, demur from, shudder at, revolt at; dislike, loathe, shrink from, abhor, abominate, criticize, condemn, denounce, remonstrate against, cavil at, carp at, find fault with, *Slang* knock. **—*n.* 2.** thing, article, body, form, phenomenon; device, gadget, contrivance, *Slang* thingamajig, thingamabob, dingus, doohickey. **3.** subject, target, recipient, cynosure; victim, butt, dupe, prey, quarry. **4.** aim, goal, purpose, point, intent, intention, objective, design, end, target, mission, use; significance, reason, sense, meaning, explanation, substance, principle, essence, gist, pith, cause, motive, incentive, inducement, basis. **—Syn. Study. 4** See AIM. **—Ant. 1** approve, agree, welcome, admit, greet with open arms, accept, comply, concur, assert, consent, acquiesce, accede; like, love, fancy, praise, applaud, laud, admire, compliment.

objection *n.* **1.** complaint, criticism, opposing reason, contradiction, counter argument, rebuttal, protest, challenge, exception, demurral, cavil, *Slang* kick, beef. **2.** disapproval, opposition, disagreement, dissension, reservation, disapprobation. **—Ant. 2** approval, consent, agreement, endorsement, support, countenance, approbation.

objectionable *adj.* unacceptable, intolerable, unbearable, unendurable, disagreeable, unpleasant, displeasing, inappropriate, unseemly; offensive, obnoxious, nasty, foul, abominable, vile, odious, revolting, disgusting, abhorrent, loathsome, despicable, distasteful. **—Ant.** acceptable, agreeable, likable, pleasant, pleasing, appropriate, seemly, fit, meet.

objective *adj.* **1.** impartial, unprejudiced, detached, dispassionate, impersonal, unbiased, fair, just, uncolored, open-minded, disinterested, unswayed, uninfluenced; real, actual. *—n.* **2.** aim, goal, purpose, object, intent, intention, design, end, mission; destination, target, mark. **—Ant. 1** subjective, personal, biased, prejudiced, warped, unjust, unfair; abstract, theoretical.

obligation *n.* **1.** duty, responsibility, a favor owed, debt, indebtedness, liability, onus, charge, care, constraint, accountability, answerability. **2.** agreement, contract, compact, bond, commitment, pledge, promise, oath, word, understanding; warranty, guaranty. **—Syn. Study. 1** See DUTY. **—Ant. 1** choice, freedom.

obligatory *adj.* compulsory, mandatory, coercive, binding, required, enforced, requisite, imperative, peremptory, necessary, unavoidable. **—Ant.** noncompulsory, voluntary.

oblige *v.* **1.** obligate, to be duty bound, require, demand of, necessitate, make, impel, constrain, bind, compel, force, coerce. **2.** accommodate, favor, do a favor for, do a service for, put oneself out for; help, aid, assist, support, serve. **—Syn. Study. 2** OBLIGE, ACCOMMODATE imply making a gracious and welcome gesture of some kind. OBLIGE emphasizes the idea of doing a favor (and often of taking some trouble to do it): *to oblige someone with a loan.* ACCOMMODATE emphasizes providing a service or convenience: *to accommodate someone with lodgings and meals.* **—Ant. 1** free, unfetter, liberate, release, acquit; persuade, induce. **2** disoblige, inconvenience, trouble, discomfort; ignore, neglect, turn one's back on.

obliging *adj.* accommodating, helpful, cooperative, solicitous, kind, considerate, well-disposed; sympathetic, friendly, amiable, agreeable, good-natured, cheerful, complaisant, courteous, gracious, polite. **—Ant.** disobliging, unaccommodating, uncooperative, unhelpful, ill-disposed, inconsiderate; rude, discourteous, curt, surly, sullen.

oblique *adj.* **1.** diagonal, slanting, slanted, inclined, sloping, tilted, aslant; askew, awry. **2.** indirect, masked, covert, veiled, cloaked, sly, devious, underhand, furtive, sneaking, implied, hinted, suggested, allusive. **—Ant. 1** vertical; horizontal. **2** direct, frank, open, straightforward, forthright, candid, blunt, obvious, unveiled.

obliterate *v.* **1.** annihilate, eradicate, destroy, raze, level, wipe out. **2.** erase, expunge, wipe out, rub out, efface, delete, remove, abolish; write over, strike over, cancel, blot out. **—Ant. 1** construct, create, raise up; reconstruct, restore, rehabilitate. **2** write; add, keep.

oblivion *n.* **1.** obscurity, limbo, a forgotten state, disregard, insignificance. **2.** nothingness, nonexistence, the void, blankness; forgetfulness, obliviousness, unconcern, unconsciousness, insensibility, blotting out. **—Ant. 1** fame, popularity, celebrity, immortality. **2** being, existence, life; memory, remembrance, reminiscence, recollection, reminder.

oblivious *adj.* unaware of, unconscious of, undiscerning, insensible, unobservant; unmindful, disregardful, heedless of, unconcerned, forgetful, inattentive, careless. **—Ant.** aware, conscious, cognizant; heedful, concerned, troubled, worried, annoyed.

obloquy *n.* **1.** censure, rebuke, denunciation, verbal abuse, vilification, calumny, dressing-down, opprobrium, defamation, billingsgate, scurrility, invective. **2.** shame, disgrace, bad repute, ignominy, odium, infamy, humiliation, degradation, contempt, disfavor, discredit, opprobrium.

obnoxious *adj.* offensive, objectionable, disagreeable, unpleasant, displeasing, nasty, nauseating, repugnant, foul, vile, odious, revolting, disgusting, abominable, loathsome, despicable, abhorrent, repellent, hateful, detestable; unseemly, inappropriate, unbearable, unendurable, intolerable, insufferable. **—Syn. Study.** See HATEFUL. **—Ant.** agreeable, pleasant, pleasing, delightful, charming, engaging, likable, alluring, enchanting; acceptable, appropriate, seemly, fit, meet, in good taste.

obscene *adj.* indecent, foul, morally offensive, pornographic, prurient, lewd, lascivious, lubricious, salacious, vulgar, scatological, dirty, filthy, *Slang* smutty, blue. **—Ant.** decent, modest, chaste, innocent, clean.

obscenity *n.* **1.** indecency, pornography, lewdness, prurience, lasciviousness, salaciousness, vulgarity, dirtiness, smuttiness, filthiness. **2.** vulgarity, profanity, obscene expression, taboo word, *Slang* cuss word, swear word, four-letter word. **—Ant. 1** decency, modesty, chastity, innocence.

obscure *adj.* **1.** unclear, not easily understood, hidden, vague, uncertain, indefinite, indefinable, inscrutable, unfathomable, puzzling, perplexing, enigmatic, cryptic, confusing, confused; mystical, mysterious. **2.** unknown, little known, nameless, unheard of, unsung, forgotten, unrenowned, unnoted, insignificant, inconsequential, unimportant, out-of-the-way, inconspicuous. **3.** indistinct, faint, dim, shadowy, murky, cloudy, dusky; dark, lightless, unlighted, unilluminated, somber, dingy. —*v.* **4.** hide, conceal, cover, block, eclipse; veil, blur, bedim, cloud, becloud; fog, befog; shroud, curtain, cloak, screen; mask, disguise; overshadow, shadow, darken. **5.** confuse, obfuscate, muddle, befuddle, make hard to understand. **—Syn. Study. 1** See MYSTERIOUS. **—Ant. 1** clear, lucid, plain, transparent, obvious, evident, manifest, apparent, explicit, intelligible; straightforward, unmistakable. **2** well-known, famous, renowned, prominent, eminent, celebrated; important, major, significant. **3** distinct, conspicuous, prominent, well-defined; bright, light. **4** reveal, disclose, show, expose, exhibit. **5** clarify, explain.

obsequious *adj.* servile, fawning, toadying, sycophantic, subservient, menial, ingratiating, deferential, slavish, cringing, cowering, mealymouthed, truckling, *Slang* bootlicking, kowtowing, apple-polishing. **—Syn. Study.** See SERVILE. **—Ant.** domineering, overbearing, swaggering, lordly, imperious, proud, haughty, arrogant, impudent, brash, bold, assertive, forceful, aggressive.

observance *n.* **1.** obeying, following, compliance, adherence, attending, attention, heeding, keeping, regard, observation. **2.** ceremonial, commemoration, celebration, memorialization, solemnity; ceremony, ritual, rite, custom, practice, formality. **—Ant. 1** nonobservance, disobeying, noncompliance, inattention, disregard, omission.

observant *adj.* watchful, vigilant, alert, on the lookout, awake, careful; mindful, attentive, aware, heedful, regardful, perceptive, wide-awake, conscious. **—Ant.** unobservant, inattentive, oblivious; unmindful, heedless, indifferent, unconcerned.

observation *n.* **1.** observing, watching, viewing, seeing, beholding, eyeing, glimpsing, spotting, inspection, detection, examination, surveillance, scrutiny, survey, probe, search; notice, attention, interest, heed, watchfulness, heedfulness, cognizance. **2.** finding, firsthand information, discovery, description, diagnosis; remark, comment, statement, reflection, view, idea, opinion, theory, judgment, pronouncement, assertion, commentary.

observe *v.* **1.** see, watch, view, behold, peer at, catch sight of, stare at, make out, inspect, survey, glimpse, espy, spot, ogle, eye; notice, note, discover, detect, perceive, mark, heed, regard, pay attention to, size up, take stock of. **2.** remark, comment, state, say, mention, announce, assert, declare; opine, reflect, theorize. **3.** obey, comply with, conform to, follow, heed, abide by, adhere to, fulfill, keep, be guided by, acquiesce to, defer to, carry out, execute, perform, respect. **4.** celebrate, commemorate, honor; sanctify, consecrate, solemnize; recognize, acknowledge. **—Ant. 3** disobey, disregard, neglect. **4** profane.

obsessed *adj.* possessed, beset, dominated, controlled, having a fixation, maniacal, haunted, overwhelmingly desirous, overwhelmingly fearful, *Slang* hung up on.

obsession *n.* overwhelming fear, all-encompassing desire, fixation, fixed idea, mania, phobia, quirk, neurotic conviction, ruling passion, monomania; preoccupation, infatuation, craze.

obsolescent *adj.* becoming obsolete, becoming out-of-date, disappearing, declining, passing out of use, dying out, on the way out. **—Ant.** new, novel, modern, late, latest; up-to-date, current, fresh, new-fashioned, fashionable, in vogue, newfangled; in, mod, with-it.

obsolete *adj.* out, out-of-date, out of fashion, out of use, old-fashioned, outdated, passé, outmoded, antiquated, antique, archaic, bygone, dated, extinct.

obstacle *n.* barrier, barricade, hurdle, blockade; obstruction, hindrance, impediment, interference, stumbling block, limitation, restriction, stoppage, check, bar, block, roadblock, curb, snag, catch, problem, difficulty. **—Syn. Study.** OBSTACLE, OBSTRUCTION, HINDRANCE, IMPEDIMENT refer to something that interferes with or prevents action or progress and must be removed, overcome, or bypassed. An OBSTACLE is something, material or nonmaterial, that stands in the way of progress: *an obstacle in a steeplechase; an obstacle to success.* An OBSTRUCTION is something that more or less completely blocks passage: *an obstruction in a drainpipe.* A HINDRANCE interferes and causes delay or difficulty: *Interruptions are a hindrance to my work.* An IMPEDIMENT slows down proper functioning or interferes with free movement: *Heavy rain was an impediment to our departure.* **—Ant.** help, aid, benefit, boon, spur, expedient, furtherance, support, encouragement.

obstinate *adj.* stubborn, obdurate, unyielding, unbending, inflexible, willful, self-willed, headstrong, mulish, unreasonably stubborn, pigheaded; resolute, steadfast, staunch, dogged, persistent, tenacious; intractable, unmanageable, uncontrollable, ungovernable, refractory, recalcitrant. **—Syn. Study.** See STUBBORN. **—Ant.** compliant, complaisant, yielding, pliant, amenable, flexible; irresolute, undecided, wavering, wishy-washy; tractable, manageable, docile, obedient, submissive.

obstreperous *adj.* disorderly, unruly, refractory, uncontrolled, unrestrained, disobedient, perverse, unmanageable, ungovernable, uncontrollable; rampaging, uproarious, roistering, noisy, loud, boisterous, clamorous, vociferous. **—Ant.** orderly, restrained, obedient, well-behaved, manageable, tractable, docile; quiet, calm.

obstruct *v.* **1.** barricade, block, blockade, bar, debar, shut off, stop, dam up, choke off, close, close off, plug up; hide, eclipse, cover, shroud, mask, cloak. **2.** delay, hinder, impede, curb, inhibit, stall, retard, check, hobble, restrict, limit; stop, block, arrest, halt, frustrate, thwart, stifle, throttle, suppress, bring to a standstill. **—Ant. 1** unblock, clear, open. **2** help, aid, benefit, further, promote, advance, support, encourage, spur, expedite, facilitate, accelerate.

obstruction *n.* obstacle, encumbrance, barrier, blockage, block, stoppage, stop, barricade, hurdle, impediment, hindrance, hitch, check, curb, bar, snag, bottleneck. **—Syn. Study.** See OBSTACLE. **—Ant.** clearing, opening, freeing, unblocking; help, aid, assistance.

obtain *v.* **1.** acquire, get, attain, secure, procure, come by, pick up, get hold of; receive, earn, gain, glean, gather, achieve, get one's hands on, gain possession of, take, pick up. **2.** be in force, hold, stand, prevail, exist, be the case. **—Syn. Study. 1** See GET. **—Ant. 1** lose, be deprived, forgo, relinquish, forfeit, surrender; give, grant, bestow, present, offer, proffer, confer, dispense, distribute, deliver, assign.

obtrusive *adj.* **1.** interfering, intruding, intrusive, meddlesome, meddling, prying, *Informal* snoopy, nosy; interrupting; trespassing; forward, aggressive, brash, presumptuous, impertinent, familiar. **2.** prominent, conspicuous, salient, outstanding, sticking out; jutting out, protruding, projecting, bulging, protuberant. **—Ant. 1, 2** unobtrusive. **1** reserved, reticent, modest, unassuming, diffident, demure, timid, shy. **2** inconspicuous; concave, hollow.

obtuse *adj.* **1.** not sharp, not pointed; blunt, blunted, dull, unpointed, unsharpened. **2.** dull, dense, slow, slow-witted, thick, stupid, ignorant, simple; uncomprehending, insensitive, insensible, imperceptive, thick-skinned. **—Ant. 1** acute, sharp, pointed. **2** intelligent, bright, smart, clever, quick-witted, keen, sharp, alert, sensitive.

obviate *v.* avert, avoid, make unnecessary, circumvent, remove, do away with, preclude, prevent; forestall, divert, parry, sidetrack, ward off, turn aside, stave off, fend off, *Informal* nip in the bud. **—Ant.** necessitate, require, make essential, oblige, impel, cause, make unavoidable.

obvious *adj.* evident, self-evident, clear, plain, unmistakable, discernible, distinct, palpable, conspicuous, apparent, patent, manifest, undeniable, glaring, striking, *Informal* plain as the nose on your face; visible, perceptible, unconcealed, unhidden, unmasked, unveiled, undisguised, in plain sight. **—Syn. Study.** See APPARENT. **—Ant.** concealed, hidden, obscure, unclear, indistinct, inconspicuous, unapparent, imperceptible, invisible.

occasion *n.* **1.** event, special event, important event, occurrence, happening, episode, situation, incident, advent, experience, adventure, venture; affair, celebration, time. **2.** particular time, opportune time, opportunity, suitable time, convenient time, instance, circumstance, chance, opening. **3.** reason, cause, justification, provocation, motive, motivation, ground, grounds, base, basis, explanation, rationale. **—*v.* 4.** cause, elicit, bring about, prompt, lead to, provoke, inspire.

occasional *adj.* taking place from time to time, recurring, now and then, sporadic, fitful, spasmodic, intermittent, random, irregular, scattered, infrequent, incidental, uncommon, rare; unreliable, uncertain. **—Ant.** constant, continual, continuous, incessant; customary, habitual, usual, regular, routine.

occasionally *adv.* at times, sometimes, from time to time, now and then, every now and then, once in a while, infrequently, seldom, hardly ever, rarely, once in a blue moon; intermittently, sporadically, irregularly, periodically, fitfully. **—Ant.** always, constantly, continually, continuously, incessantly; often, frequently, regularly, again and again, over and over, habitually, customarily, generally, ordinarily, usually.

occlude *v.* obstruct, block, clog, shut off, shut up, choke, choke off, plug, close, barricade, congest, stopper, stop up, constrict, strangulate. **—Ant.** clear, unclog, open, unplug.

occult *adj.* supernatural, magic, mystic, mystical, secret, mysterious, dark, arcane, cabalistic, esoteric, private, revealed only to the initiated, unrevealed, undisclosed, hidden, concealed, obscure, veiled, shrouded.

occupancy *n.* tenancy, occupation, lodgment, habitation, habitancy, inhabitancy, possession, use, enjoyment, tenure, engagement. **—Ant.** eviction, dispossession, dislodgment; vacancy.

occupant *n.* dweller, householder, owner, resident, tenant, inhabitant, occupier; lessee, renter, roomer, lodger; addressee; settler, colonist, native.

occupation *n.* **1.** job, trade, business, line of work, line, profession, work, capacity, vocation, craft; employment, livelihood, living; calling, pursuit, walk of life, lifework, career, sphere, activity; forte, specialty, specialization, métier. **2.** military occupation, military control, foreign rule, subjugation, subjection, control, seizure, conquest, possession.

occupy *v.* **1.** fill, fill up, engage, take up, employ, busy, engross, absorb, monopolize, saturate, permeate, pervade, overrun, concern, amuse, entertain. **2.** take possession of, have control, hold in thrall, conquer, subjugate, enslave. **3.** dwell in, reside in, be the tenants of, inhabit, lodge in, room in; sit in, use, hold, possess, be in, be on, be situated in. **—Ant. 2** liberate, free. **3** vacate, quit, leave, evacuate; relinquish, give up, hand over.

occur *v.* **1.** happen, take place, come about, come to pass, come off, befall, transpire, ensue, result, eventuate. **2.** appear, arise, rise, turn up, crop up, spring up, emerge, develop, materialize, show itself, manifest itself, be found, be met with. **3.** enter one's mind, cross one's mind, suggest itself, *Slang* hit, strike. **—Ant. 1** be avoided, be evaded, be thwarted, be nipped in the bud. **2** disappear, vanish, fade away, be suppressed.

occurrence *n.* happening, event, incident, instance, episode, experience, business, proceeding, transaction, situation, venture, adventure, affair, occasion; appearance, circumstance, emergence, unfolding, development, manifestation, materialization.

ocean *n.* sea, high sea, deep, briny deep, main, water, flood, *Slang* pond, big pond.

odd *adj.* **1.** not divisible by two, not even. **2.** unusual, strange, queer, uncommon, unique, out of the ordinary, rare, peculiar, singular, curious, bizarre, freakish, outlandish, quaint, funny, weird, *Slang* far-out. **3.** being one of a pair, having no mate, unmatched, single; leftover, surplus, remaining. **4.** various, sundry, miscellaneous; occasional, casual, irregular, sporadic, spasmodic, periodic, spare, extra. **—Ant. 1** even. **2** common, ordinary, usual, familiar, customary, habitual, regular, typical, normal, natural, unexceptional. **3** matched, paired, mated. **4** regular, constant, steady, permanent, full time.

oddity *n.* rarity, phenomenon, curiosity, wonder, marvel, sight, freak, rara avis; strangeness, singularity, peculiarity, individuality, uniqueness, unusualness, outlandishness, freakishness; bizarreness, queerness, eccentricity, unnaturalness, abnormality.

odious *adj.* evil, vile, abominable, hateful, hated, despicable, contemptible, detestable, invidious, heinous, repulsive, repugnant, revolting, disgusting, loathsome, obnoxious, infamous, offensive, nasty, foul, nauseating, rotten, sickening, monstrous, hideous, objectionable, intolerable, unendurable, unbearable. **—Syn. Study.** See HATEFUL. **—Ant.** likable, attractive, lovable, delightful, charming, pleasing, pleasant, agreeable, acceptable.

odium *n.* **1.** discredit, disgrace, dishonor, infamy, disrepute, shame, opprobrium. **2.** hatred, antipathy, abhorrence, disgust, contempt, repugnance. **—Ant. 1** honor, repute, esteem. **2** love, affection, tenderness, fondness.

odor *n.* smell, aroma; scent, fragrance, perfume, essence, bouquet, redolence; atmosphere, aura, flavor; stench, stink, effluvium, reek. **—Syn. Study.** ODOR, SMELL, SCENT, STENCH all refer to a sensation perceived by means of the olfactory nerves. ODOR refers to a relatively strong sensation that may be agreeable or disagreeable, actually or figuratively: *the odor of freshly roasted coffee; the odor of duplicity.* SMELL is used in similar contexts, although it is a more general word: *cooking smells; the sweet smell of success.* SCENT may refer to a distinctive smell, usu. delicate and pleasing, or to a smell left in passing: *the scent of lilacs; the scent of an antelope.* STENCH refers to a foul, sickening, or repulsive smell: *the stench of rotting flesh.*

offal *n.* remains, carrion, carcass; garbage, refuse, junk, waste, rubbish, trash, debris, leavings, dregs, grounds, slag, residue.

off-color *adj.* risqué, racy, spicy, indelicate, salty, earthy, blue, suggestive, naughty, wicked, improper, offensive, indiscreet, *Slang* raunchy, obscene, scabrous, indecent.

offend *v.* **1.** affront, displease, insult, wound, disgust, antagonize, anger, incense, inflame, madden, annoy, vex, aggravate, irritate, exasperate, rankle, nettle, rile, miff, fret, gall, chafe, pique, disgruntle. **2.** sin, err, transgress, misbehave, lapse, stray from the straight and narrow, fall from grace. **—Ant. 1**

please, delight, beguile, captivate, charm, enchant, win over; soothe, calm, conciliate.

offense *n.* **1.** crime, misdeed, misdemeanor, felony, breach of conduct, infraction, violation, malfeasance, delinquency; sin, transgression, wickedness, peccadillo, lapse, slip, shortcoming; outrage, enormity, atrocity, evil deed. **2.** insult, affront, disrespect, insolence, impudence, rudeness, umbrage, harm, abuse, embarrassment, humiliation, indignity, outrage, slap, snub, twit, taunt, gibe, abuse. **3.** offensive, attack, assault, aggression, charge; offensive unit. **—Syn. Study. 1** See CRIME. **—Ant. 1** innocence, guiltlessness. **2** pleasure, delight, gratification, satisfaction. **3** defense, resistance, safeguard, guard, security.

offensive *adj.* **1.** insulting, disrespectful, insolent, impudent, rude, abusive, embarrassing, unmannerly, uncivil, ungallant; objectionable, rank, obnoxious, disgusting, unpleasant, disagreeable, distasteful, abominable, revolting, hateful, odious, nasty, foul, horrid, hideous, repulsive, ugly, loathsome, repugnant, abhorrent, detestable, sickening, nauseating, intolerable, insufferable. **2.** attacking, attack, assault, assaulting, assailing, belligerent, aggressive, charging, storming, bombarding. *—n.* **3.** offense, attack, assault, onslaught, onset, aggression. **—Syn. Study. 1** See HATEFUL. **—Ant. 1** polite, courteous, respectful, deferential, diffident, civil, conciliatory; pleasing, pleasant, delightful, charming, agreeable, attractive, captivating, winning. **2** defensive, defending, resisting. **3** defense, defensive.

offer *v.* **1.** proffer, tender, present, place at one's disposal. **2.** propose, submit, render, advance, suggest, put forth, put forward, propound, volunteer, hold out, extend, make a motion, bring forward, be willing. **3.** put on the market, put up. *—n.* **4.** proposition, proposal, offering, bid, invitation, submission, overture, suggestion. **—Syn. Study. 1** OFFER, PROFFER, TENDER mean to put something forward for acceptance or rejection. OFFER is the general word for presenting anything for acceptance, sale, consideration, or the like: *to offer help; to offer a cold drink.* PROFFER, chiefly a literary word, implies presenting something freely and unselfishly: *to proffer one's services.* TENDER is used in formal, legal, business, and polite social contexts: *to tender one's resignation; to tender payment.* **—Ant. 1, 2** retain, retract, withdraw, withhold, deny; accept, take, receive; reject, refuse, decline. **4** withdrawal, retraction, revocation; acceptance, reception; refusal, denial.

offhand Also **offhanded** *adj.* **1.** impromptu, extemporaneous, ad-lib, off-the-cuff, off the record, off the top of one's head, improvised, unpremeditated, unstudied, unprepared, unplanned, unrehearsed, spontaneous, chance, casual, random. **2.** casual, careless, thoughtless, heedless, haphazard, nonchalant, unconcerned, hasty; facetious, cavalier, relaxed. **—Ant. 1** prepared, planned, premeditated, studied. **2** serious, intent, sober, grave, responsible, careful, thoughtful.

office *n.* **1.** position, post, job, capacity, function, occupation, role, commission, appointment. **2.** Usu. **offices** favor, service, help, assistance; duty, charge, trust, function, task; province.

officer *n.* **1.** official, executive, manager, bureaucrat, head, administrator, officeholder, director, commissioner. **2.** policeman, police officer, officer of the law, law officer, patrolman, constable, detective, cop, *French* gendarme.

official *n.* **1.** officeholder, officer, executive, director, manager, administrator, supervisor; functionary, dignitary, agent; chairman, administrative head. *—adj.* **2.** formal, administrative, vested; authorized, approved, sanctioned, authoritative, certified, accredited, authentic, warranted, licensed. **—Ant. 1** underling, hireling; employee. **2** unofficial, unauthorized; informal, casual.

officiate *v.* preside, administer, oversee, direct, manage, run, head, superintend, be in charge of, moderate, emcee, chair, lead, handle, *Slang* call the shots for, regulate, supervise.

officious *adj.* obtrusive, intrusive, interfering, meddlesome, meddling, prying, poking one's nose in, offering gratuitous advice or services, *Informal* kibitzing; overbearing, domineering, self-important, self-assertive, high-handed, high and mighty; pompous, patronizing. **—Ant.** unobtrusive, in the background.

offset *v.* compensate for, make up for, counteract, countervail, counterweight, counterbalance, balance; cancel out, nullify, neutralize, equalize, redeem, *Informal* knock out.

offspring *n.* children, progeny, descendants, posterity, succession, issue, increase; child, descendant, heir, scion; young, brood, family, litter, fry, spawn, seed.

often *adv.* frequently, regularly, repeatedly, habitually, periodically, recurrently, over and over, much, time and again, again and again, generally, usually, customarily, commonly, as a common thing, continually, constantly, oft, oftentimes, ofttimes. **—Syn. Study.** OFTEN, FREQUENTLY, GENERALLY, USUALLY refer to experiences that are habitual or customary. OFTEN and FREQUENTLY are used interchangeably in most cases, but OFTEN implies numerous repetitions: *We often go there;* whereas FREQUENTLY suggests repetition at comparatively short intervals: *It happens frequently.* GENERALLY emphasizes a broad or nearly universal quality: *It is generally understood. He is generally liked.* USUALLY emphasizes time, and means in numerous instances: *We usually have hot summers.* **—Ant.** never; rarely, seldom, infrequently, occasionally, irregularly, now and then, once in a great while, once in a blue moon, hardly ever.

ogle *v.* stare at greedily, gaze at with desire; stare at, gape at, gawk at, goggle at, scrutinize, eye, give the eye, give the once-over, leer at, cast sheep's eyes at, goggle.

ogre *Fem.* **ogress** *n.* **1.** man-eating giant, monster, fiend, brute; bugbear, bogeyman; ghoul, harpy, demon. **2.** tyrant, martinet, dictator, despot, slave driver.

oil *n.* **1.** petroleum; (*variously*) mineral oil, fuel oil, whale oil, vegetable oil, cooking oil, motor oil, lubricant; melted grease, melted fat; liniment, ointment, unguent, balm, salve; pomade, hair oil. —*v.* **2.** lubricate; cream, grease, anoint, salve, cream, lard.

oily *adj.* **1.** greasy, slick, slippery, fatty, sebaceous, oleaginous, unctuous, slithery, buttery, lardy, lubricious. **2.** unctuous, smarmy, lubricious, oleaginous; ingratiating, subservient, servile, fawning, groveling, bootlicking, toadying.

ointment *n.* unguent, balm, pomade, spikenard, pomatum, salve, emollient, liniment, lotion.

old *adj.* **1.** of age. **2.** elderly, aged, hoary, grizzled, gray-headed, gray with age, white with age, venerable; antiquated, ancient, vintage, timeworn, age-old, antique, old-fashioned, out-of-date, outdated, archaic, obsolete, obsolescent. **3.** of long standing, long established, time-honored, traditional, age-old, of the past, from the past, of yore, bygone. **4.** worn-out, outworn, decrepit, dilapidated, used, much-used, timeworn, weathered, *Slang* beat-up; weather-beaten, deteriorated, battered, ramshackle, crumbling, tumbledown, rundown, broken-down; familiar, hackneyed. **—Ant. 2–4** new, recent, current, late. **4** young, immature; brand-new, spanking new, modern, novel, up-to-date, modish, newfangled, new-fashioned, fashionable; mod, with-it.

old-fashioned *adj.* **1.** out-of-date, out of fashion, outmoded, unfashionable, behind the times, out of style, passé, from time gone by, antiquated, antique, outdated, obsolete, *Slang* corny. **2.** having time-honored values, traditional; time-honored, old-time, long-standing. **—Ant. 1** modern, up-to-date, current, new-fangled, new-fashioned, in style, fashionable, in vogue, up-to-the-minute, chic, a la mode, avant-garde; *Slang* modish, mod, with-it.

old hat *adj.* out-of-date, antiquated, outmoded, outdated, old-fashioned, unfashionable, superseded, passé, stale, archaic, obsolete, obsolescent, outworn, *French* démodé, behind the times. **—Ant.** up-to-date, in, new, current, fashionable.

old-world *adj.* European, continental; traditional, conservative, old-fashioned; formal, ceremonial, ceremonious, conventional, established, prescribed, orthodox, old-line; courtly, chivalrous, gallant.

omen *n.* augury, sign, token, portent, auspice; indication, harbinger, herald, precursor, presage, foretaste, straw in the wind, handwriting on the wall; foreboding, warning. **—Syn. Study.** See SIGN.

ominous *adj.* threatening, minatory, menacing, foreboding, sinister, dismaying, disquieting, unpromising, unpropitious, unfavorable, inauspicious, ill-starred, portending evil, unlucky, ill-omened, monitory; portentous, fateful. **—Syn. Study.** OMINOUS, THREATENING, PORTENTOUS, FATEFUL describe something that foretells a serious and significant outcome or consequence. OMINOUS suggests an evil or harmful consequence: *ominous storm clouds.* THREATENING may point to calamity or mere unpleasantness, but usu. suggests that the outcome is imminent: *a threatening rumble from a volcano.* PORTENTOUS, although it may point to evil or disaster, more often describes something momentous or important: *a portentous change in foreign policy.* FATEFUL also stresses the great or decisive importance of what it describes: *a fateful encounter between two influential leaders.* **—Ant.** encouraging, promising, favorable, propitious, auspicious.

omission *n.* **1.** leaving out, exclusion, noninclusion, elimination, exception; neglect, negligence, delinquency, oversight. **2.** something omitted, exclusion, neglected item, thing overlooked, gap, hole. **—Ant. 1, 2** inclusion; addition, supplement.

omit *v.* **1.** leave out, exclude, except, miss, skip, pass over, forget about, preclude, jump, ignore, elide, delete, drop, excerpt, cut, set aside. **2.** neglect, fail, forget, overlook, let slip, ignore, avoid, shun, slight, bypass, leave undone. **—Ant. 1** include, put in, add. **2** remember, recollect, recall.

omnipotent *adj.* all-powerful, almighty, supreme; puissant, powerful, mighty. **—Ant.** powerless, helpless, impotent.

omniscient *adj.* all-knowing, all-seeing, having infinite knowledge, all-wise; supreme, preeminent, infinite. **—Ant.** ignorant, unknowing, unaware, fallible, deceivable.

omnivorous *adj.* all-devouring, pantophagous, polyphagic, gluttonous, predacious, rapacious, voracious, ravenous, edacious, crapulous, hoggish.

once *adv.* **1.** formerly, at one time, previously, some time back, some time ago, in times past, long ago, once upon a time, in other days, in the old days, in the good old days, years ago, ages ago; heretofore, hitherto. **2.** a single time, one time, on one occasion; once and for all, for the nonce. **—Ant. 1** in future, in time to come, after this, hereafter. **2** never, not at all, at no time; repeatedly, frequently, numerously, regularly, incessantly, continually.

oncoming *adj.* approaching, advancing, looming, onrushing, imminent, impending, nearing, coming, bearing down, close. **—Ant.** receding, retiring, retreating, withdrawing.

one *adj.* **1.** single, individual, a, an, sole, lone, solitary, only, singular, unique, unrepeated; entire, whole, complete. *—pron.* **2.** a person, an individual, a man, a human being, a creature, somebody, someone, you, a body, a soul, a mortal, a thing.

onerous *adj.* oppressive, burdensome, hard to endure, arduous, not easy to bear, distressing, painful, wearisome, taxing, exhausting, crushing, heavy, weighty, demanding, grievous. **—Ant.** easy, light, simple, effortless, trivial, trifling.

one-time *adj.* former, previous, earlier, erstwhile, *French* ci-devant, quondam, past, recent, prior, early, old. **—Ant.** current, present, presentday, latest.

ongoing *adj.* continuing, proceeding, forward-moving, uninterrupted, unbroken, unremitting, unending, endless, never-ending, lasting, enduring. **—Ant.** temporary, stopgap, sporadic, provisional.

onlooker *n.* spectator, observer, eyewitness, sidewalk viewer, watcher, bystander, *Slang* sidewalk superintendent, kibitzer, rubberneck, gazer, ogler.

only *adv.* **1.** alone, by oneself, by itself, solely, exclusively, individually, singly, without others, as the only one, without anything further. **2.** no more than, merely, just, simply, purely; barely, nothing but, at least, to such an extent. *—adj.* **3.** lone, sole, solitary, individual, single, singular, exclusive, unique, alone, one and only; unparalleled, unrepeated, unmatched. **—Ant. 1** together, collectively, among, amongst. **3** many, several, numerous, innumerable, multitudinous, myriad, manifold.

onrush *n.* onset, torrent, deluge, attack, assault, flood, flux, charge, storm, avalanche, cascade, wave, tide, stream, flow, current, spring, surge, gush.

onset *n.* **1.** start, beginning, outset, commencement, inauguration, initiation, outbreak; inception, genesis, birth, infancy, founding, incipience. **2.** attack, assault, onslaught, offensive, offense, raid, thrust, push, sally, charge, onrush, incursion, invasion, storming. **—Ant. 1** end, close, conclusion, termination; old age, death. **2** defense, resistance, counterattack.

onslaught *n.* attack, assault, coup, charge, thrust, push, raid, foray, sally, onset, onrush, putsch, blitz, blitzkrieg; offensive, offense, invasion, incursion, aggression. **—Ant.** defense, resistance; counterattack.

onus *n.* burden, burden of proof, responsibility, obligation, weight, load, strain, encumbrance, liability, duty, cross.

onward *adv.* Also **onwards 1.** forward, ahead, toward the front, frontward, toward one's goal, along, en route, on the way. *—adj.* **2.** forward, moving ahead, frontward, advancing, progressive, ongoing. **—Ant. 1, 2** backward. **1** backwards; aback, to the rear. **2** retreating, regressive.

ooze *v.* **1.** seep, percolate, exude, trickle, dribble, drip, leak, transpire, discharge, drain, filter; bleed, sweat. *—n.* **2.** soft mud, slime, sludge, silt, muck, mire, alluvium; secretion, exudation; seepage, leakage. **—Ant. 1** gush, stream, flood, cascade, pour, flow, effuse.

opaque *adj.* **1.** nontransparent, nontranslucent, impenetrable to light; dark, dull, murky, clouded, hazy, muddy, muddied. **2.** hard to understand, unclear, impenetrable, incomprehensible, difficult, obscure, abstruse, unintelligible, unfathomable. **—Ant. 1, 2** clear. **1** transparent, translucent, pellucid; shiny, bright, sparkling, gleaming. **2** lucid, intelligible, comprehensible.

open *adj.* **1.** not shut, unshut, not closed, unclosed, ajar, agape, gaping, yawning; not covered, uncovered, coverless, unenclosed, unsealed, unfastened, unlocked; extended, unfolded; welcoming. **2.** expansive, wide, unbounded, unfenced, unobstructed, uncluttered, exposed, clear; uncrowded, uninhabited, not built up. **3.** doing business, open for business, open to the public, available, accessible. **4.** openhearted, forthright, straightforward, sincere, natural, plain, artless, honest; outgoing, extroverted; candid, frank, direct, outspoken. **5.** impartial, objective, unprejudiced, unbiased, unbigoted, disinterested, impersonal, fair, just; receptive, responsive. —*v.* **6.** unclose, throw open, set ajar, move aside, swing aside; unlock, unfasten, unbar, unseal; unfold, expand, lay open, *Slang* crack; clear, unblock. **7.** begin, commence, start, initiate, inaugurate, originate, launch, embark upon, set in motion, get the ball rolling; institute, found, create, undertake, establish. **8.** open to the public, become available for use, permit access, afford entrance, receive customers, start business. **—Syn. Study. 4** See FRANK. **—Ant. 1–3** closed. **6–8** close. **1** shut; covered, enclosed, sealed, fastened, locked; folded. **2** restricted, shut in, bounded, protected, narrow; obstructed, crowded, cluttered. **3** unavailable, inaccessible, out of bounds, off limits. **4** introverted, reticent, reserved. **5** prejudiced, biased, bigoted, subjective; unfair, unjust; stubborn, obdurate. **6** shut; lock, fasten, bar, seal; fold; block, obstruct. **7** end, conclude, finish, terminate, shut down.

open-handed *adj.* generous, magnanimous, bountiful, bounteous, benevolent, liberal, beneficent, prodigal, lavish, unstinting, altruistic, ungrudging. **—Ant.** stingy, closefisted, niggardly, miserly.

opening *n.* **1.** hole, break, breach, gap, aperture, rent, rift, slit, cleft, crack, fissure, gash, slot, tear, vent, chink. **2.** inauguration, initiation, launching, installation; beginning, start, commencement, first part, preface, prelude, overture, introduction, *Slang* kickoff, send-off. **3.** job opening, vacancy, place, space, opportunity, possibility, chance, occasion; situation, position, job, *Informal* spot. **—Ant. 1** obstruction, blockage. **2** closing, close, termination, end, ending, conclusion, finish, finale, finis, postscript.

open-mouthed *adj.* dumbfounded, wide-eyed, astonished, amazed, flabbergasted, marveling, agape, aghast, surprised, confounded, staggered, thunderstruck, spellbound, awed, awestruck, bewitched, stupefied, wonderstruck. **—Ant.** bored, indifferent, apathetic, unmoved, unconcerned.

operate *v.* **1.** work, go, function, run, behave, perform; manage, superintend, oversee, be in charge of. **2.** perform surgery, perform an operation, *Informal* go in, open up, do an exploratory.

operation *n.* **1.** action, performance, operating, running, working, conduct, procedure, activity, pursuit; supervision, management, superintendence, overseeing. **2.** action, effect, force, influence, exertion; agency, instrumentality. **3.** surgery, *Informal* exploratory.

opiate *n.* sedative, hypnotic, narcotic, soporific, tranquilizer, somnifacient, anodyne, nepenthe, depressant, stupefacient, painkiller, calmative, palliative; *Slang* dope, downer. **—Ant.** stimulant, tonic; *Slang* upper, pep pill, pick-me-up.

opine *v.* think, say, state, suggest, volunteer, conjecture, surmise, allow, reckon, consider, offer, guess, imagine, speculate, deem, assume, conclude, presume, believe, *Slang* have a hunch.

opinion *n.* belief, estimate, estimation, assessment, evaluation, sentiment, judgment, view, impression, conviction, persuasion, notion, conclusion, idea, surmise, suspicion, conception, assumption, thinking, conjecture, speculation, theory. **—Syn. Study.** OPINION, SENTIMENT, VIEW are terms for one's conclusion about something. An OPINION is a belief or judgment that falls short of absolute conviction, certainty, or positive knowledge: *an opinion about modern art.* SENTIMENT refers to a rather fixed opinion, usu. based on feeling or emotion rather than reasoning: *sentiments on the subject of divorce.* A VIEW is an intellectual or critical judgment based on one's particular circumstances or standpoint; it often concerns a public issue: *views on government spending.* **—Ant.** fact, reality, actuality, certainty; act, deed, event, occurrence, happening.

opinionated *adj.* closed-minded, stubborn, bullheaded, obstinate, obdurate, headstrong, inflexible, unyielding, pigheaded, unbending, dogmatic, uncompromising. **—Ant.** open-minded, broadminded, unprejudiced, receptive, responsive, persuadable.

opponent *n.* opposition, rival, competitor, adversary, contender, challenger, antagonist, foe, enemy, assailant; disputant, resister. **—Ant.** ally, colleague, coworker, teammate, helper, accomplice, cohort; friend, supporter, promoter, backer.

opportune *adj.* timely, well-timed, advantageous, favorable, appropriate, suitable, fitting, apt, seasonable, proper, propitious, auspicious, expedient, convenient, profitable, fortunate, lucky, happy, felicitous. **—Ant.** inopportune, unfavorable, inappropriate, unsuitable, improper, unseasonable, unfortunate, inconvenient, untimely.

opportunity *n.* chance, good chance, favorable time, time, occasion, contingency, moment, means, situation, turn, opening.

oppose *v.* act in opposition to, speak against, fight, combat, battle, contest, contend against, struggle against, resist, withstand, defy, be set against, take a stand against, *Slang* buck; obstruct, thwart. **—Syn. Study.** OPPOSE, RESIST, WITHSTAND imply holding out or acting against something. OPPOSE implies offensive action against the opposite side in a conflict or contest; it may also refer to attempts to thwart displeasing ideas, methods, or the like: *to oppose an enemy; to oppose the passage of a bill.* RESIST suggests defensive action against a threatening force or possibility; it may also refer to an inner struggle in which the will is divided: *to resist an enemy onslaught; hard to resist chocolate.* WITHSTAND generally implies successful resistance; it stresses the determination and endurance necessary to emerge unharmed: *to withstand public criticism; to withstand a siege.* **—Ant.** support, aid, help, abet, champion, defend, advance, promote, advocate, foster, back.

opposite *adj.* **1.** facing, opposed, other; reverse, converse. **2.** opposing, opposed, conflicting, differing, contradictory, contrary, antithetical, antagonistic, adverse; counteractive, counter. **—Ant. 1** same. **2** alike, like, identical, uniform, similar, analogous, synonymous, agreeing, consistent, corresponding, parallel.

opposition *n.* **1.** resistance, contention against, disagreement, disapproval, rejection, aversion, negativism, defiance, contrariety, antagonism, hostility, enmity. **2.** opponent, competitor, rival, adversary, contender, antagonist, foe, enemy, other side. **—Ant. 1** support, backing, approval, aid, help, assistance, advancement, promotion. **2** supporter, backer, promoter; ally, cohort, colleague, helper.

oppress *v.* **1.** trouble, vex, worry, burden, weigh down, tax, try; depress, dispirit, cast down, dishearten, deject, discourage, sadden, pain, grieve, sorrow. **2.** tyrannize, despotize, persecute, treat harshly, abuse, maltreat. **—Ant. 1** unburden, relieve, ease; gladden, cheer, cheer up, hearten, encourage.

oppressive *adj.* **1.** tyrannical, despotic, repressive; cruel, brutal, harsh, severe, hardhearted. **2.** burdensome, onerous, wearing, trying, troublesome, worrisome, vexing, pressing; depressing, discouraging; painful, grievous; uncomfortable, distressing, unbearable. **—Ant. 1** humane, kind, gentle, compassionate, benevolent, tender, lenient, merciful, just. **2** soothing, relieving, gladdening, joyful, pleasant, pleasing, encouraging, comforting; comfortable.

opprobrious *adj.* **1.** damning, denunciatory, condemnatory, hypercritical, censorious, faultfinding; abusive, scurrilous, acrimonious, malicious, malevolent, maligning, vilifying, vitriolic, fulminating, reviling. **2.** disgraceful, dishonorable, shameful, disreputable, objectionable, unbecoming, deplorable, reprehensible, base, outrageous, shocking, scandalous, infamous, nefarious, despicable, corrupt, wicked. **—Ant. 1** complimentary, flattering, approving, praising, laudatory, uncritical. **2** honorable, noble, meritorious, upright, ethical, principled, virtuous, moral; becoming, praiseworthy, worthy, laudable, noteworthy, estimable.

opt *v.* choose, select, pick, decide on, go for, elect, vote for, single out, prefer, take, settle on, fix on, incline toward, tend toward. **—Ant.** reject, turn down, decide against, overrule.

optimism *n.* confidence, sanguineness, hopeful outlook, hoping for the best, hopefulness, bright outlook, seeing the good side of things, encouragement, cheerfulness, trust in the future, happy expectancy. **—Ant.** pessimism, cynicism; gloom, gloominess, glumness, depression, despondency.

optimistic *adj.* **1.** confident, sanguine, cheerful, disposed to take a favorable view, viewed favorably, hopeful, heartened, enthusiastic, encouraged, happily expectant, buoyed up. **2.** promising, auspicious, propitious, favorable, encouraging, bright, heartening, full of promise, roseate, rose-colored. **—Ant. 1, 2** pessimistic. **1** cynical; despairing, depressed, despondent, discouraged, glum, gloomy. **2** unpromising, inauspicious, unfavorable, discouraging, disheartening.

optimum *n.* **1.** ideal, peak, height, best point, most desirable, perfect degree, crest, zenith, perfection, quintessence, acme. *—adj.* **2.** ideal, best, perfect, most favorable, prime, choice, select, first-rate, first-class, flawless, faultless, unexcelled, superlative, supreme, capital, *Slang* A 1.

option *n.* **1.** franchise, free will, right of choosing, freedom of choice, will, self-determination, voice, decision, discretion. **2.** choice, alternative, selection, election; preference, partiality, liking, predilection, pleasure, will. **3.** first claim, right to buy, first choice to buy, right of first refusal, privilege. **—Syn. Study. 2** See CHOICE. **—Ant. 1** compulsion, coercion. **1, 2** requirement, obligation, necessity, must.

optional *adj.* left to one's choice, individually decided, elective, voluntary, nonobligatory, not required, volitional, unforced, discretionary, discretional; available at additional cost; open-ended, open; allowable. **—Ant.** mandatory, obligatory, required, compulsory.

opulence *n.* **1.** great wealth, riches, affluence, fortune, prosperity, ample means; luxuries, lavishness. **2.** abundance, profusion, copiousness, plenty, plentitude, amplitude, bounty, overflowing quantity, wealth, cornucopia; elegance, lavishness, richness, sumptuousness. **—Ant. 1** poverty, indigence, want, privation, impecuniousness, impecuniosity. **2** scarcity, scarceness, paucity, scantiness, dearth, lack, want, insufficiency.

opus *n.* work, *oeuvre,* piece, production, product, composition, creation, handiwork, brainchild, invention, effort, attempt.

oracle *n.* prophet, seer, augur, soothsayer, sage, clairvoyant, wizard, sibyl, diviner; predictor, forecaster, adviser.

oral *adj.* **1.** spoken, vocal, uttered, articulated, voiced, verbalized, using speech, viva voce, (*loosely*) verbal. **2.** treating the mouth, of the mouth; swallowed, ingested, taken into the body through the mouth. **—Ant. 1** written; unspoken, silent, tacit.

oration *n.* address, speech, formal speech, eulogy, talk; discourse, disquisition, peroration, recital, declamation, monologue, sermon, lecture, panegyric, harangue, *Informal* spiel. **—Syn. Study.** See SPEECH.

orator *n.* speaker, talker, elocutionist, rhetorician, declaimer, *Informal* spellbinder; public speaker, speechmaker, lecturer; preacher, sermonizer.

oratory *n.* rhetoric, eloquence, delivery, declamation; grandiloquence, bombast, grandeur of style; art of public speaking, speech, speechmaking, speechifying; elocution; preaching.

orb *n.* sphere, spheroid, ball, globe, globule, moon. **—Ant.** cube; square.

orbit *n.* **1.** course, track, trajectory, path, pathway, circuit, cycle, way, route, channel. **—***v.* **2.** circle, revolve around, travel around, circumnavigate.

orchestra *n.* **1.** company of musicians, ensemble, band, chamber orchestra, symphony orchestra, Philharmonic. **2.** main floor of a theater, parquet, parterre, pit, *British* stalls; orchestra pit.

ordain *v.* **1.** confer holy orders upon, name, invest, frock, consecrate; appoint, commission, delegate, deputize, elect. **2.** decree, rule, pronounce, will, prescribe, instruct, determine, adjudge, order, dictate, command, pass judgment; enact, legislate. **—Ant. 1** unfrock, defrock; discharge, dismiss, relieve of one's duties, impeach. **2** countermand, revoke, rescind, reverse, annul, void, invalidate, cancel; repeal, nullify, overrule.

ordeal *n.* nightmare, trial, harsh experience, trying experience, oppression, worry, vexation, trouble, burden, care, concern, pressure, strain, stress, tribulation, misery, torment, distress, agony, suffering, anguish, wretchedness, affliction, pain; unhappiness, sorrow, grief, heartache, tragedy, calamity. **—Ant.** delight, joy, happiness, elation, gladness, jubilation, ecstasy, rapture, bliss; relief, ease.

order *n.* **1.** command, dictate, decree, rule, pronouncement, instruction, bidding, law, commandment, demand, dictum, imperative, ultimatum, ukase, fiat. **2.** arrangement, organization, classification, system, categorization, tabulation, designation, codification, grouping, neatness, tidiness, orderliness; form, structure, pattern, framework. **3.** quiet, calm, law and order, peace and quiet, silence, peacefulness, harmony, tranquillity; control, discipline. **4.** classification, class, category, division, kind, species, family, caste, station, breed, sort, type, stripe; quality, caliber, position, standing, rank, status, degree, grade. **5.** society, sisterhood, brotherhood, organization, fraternity, sorority, guild, house, body, society, association, alliance, group, club, lodge, confederacy, company, federation. **—***v.* **6.** command, bid, direct, instruct, charge, decree, dictate, adjure, enjoin, ordain, call for. **7.** request, call for, ask for, book, engage, reserve, contract for, agree to, purchase, authorize the purchase of. **—Syn. Study. 6** See DIRECT. **—Ant. 1** request, plea, entreaty; supplication. **2, 3** disorder, confusion. **3** anarchy. **6** plead, entreat, supplicate, beg.

orderly *adj.* **1.** neat, tidy, spruce, shipshape, uncluttered; systematic, organized, methodical; classified, in a regular sequence. **2.** disciplined, restrained, controlled, well-behaved, civil, quiet, well-mannered, proper, peaceable, peaceful, tractable, law-abiding. **—Syn. Study. 1** ORDERLY, SYSTEMATIC, METHODICAL characterize that which is efficient, thorough, and carefully planned. ORDERLY emphasizes neatness, harmony, and logical sequence or arrangement: *an orderly library.* SYSTEMATIC emphasizes an extensive, detailed plan and a relatively complex procedure designed to achieve some purpose: *a systematic search.* METHODICAL is similar in meaning, but stresses a carefully developed plan and rigid adherence to a fixed procedure: *methodical examination of the evidence.* **—Ant. 1, 2** disorderly. **1** messy, sloppy, unsystematic, disorganized, cluttered, haphazard. **2** undisciplined, chaotic, uncontrolled, unregulated, riotous.

ordinance *n.* law, rule, ruling, regulation, statute; command, decree, edict, canon, fiat, dictum, order, enactment, act, writ, mandate, commandment, bull.

ordinarily *adv.* usually, generally, normally, customarily, commonly, as a rule, by and large, as a matter of course, routinely, in most instances, on the average, conventionally, habitually, regularly. **—Ant.** rarely, infrequently, as an exception, sporadically.

ordinary *adj.* **1.** common, commonplace, usual, average, customary, standard, normal, everyday, routine, familiar, typical, conventional, traditional, habitual, unexceptional, stereotyped, run-of-the-mill. **2.** undistinguished, commonplace, mediocre, indifferent, unimpressive, uninspired, unimaginative, pedestrian, run-of-the-mill, so-so; uninteresting, dull, humdrum; unimportant, inconsequential, insignificant, trivial, vulgar. **—Syn. Study. 1, 2** See COMMON. **—Ant. 1, 2** extraordinary, exceptional, outstanding, distinguished, unusual, uncommon, rare, unique, unfamiliar, novel, atypical, unconventional. **2** superior, impressive, imaginative, inspired; important, consequential, significant, exciting.

ordnance *n.* artillery, cannon, field pieces; military weapons and equipment, arms, munitions, war matériel, armaments.

organ *n.* **1.** pipe organ, reed organ, harmonium; hand organ, barrel organ, hurdy-gurdy. **2.** functional part, bodily part, bodily structure. **3.** publication, journal, trade journal, group publication, special interest publication; instrument, vehicle, agency.

organic *adj.* **1.** containing carbon; of living things, living, alive, animate, quick; natural, nonsynthetic. **2.** of an organ, physiological, physical, anatomical, constitutional. **3.** unified, ordered, harmonious, well-organized, patterned; systematic, planned, methodical, designed. **—Ant. 1, 2** inorganic. **3** haphazard, chaotic.

organism *n.* **1.** living thing, creature, animal, physiological unit; plant, organic structure; bacterium, microorganism, cell. **2.** organized body, organization, system, network, whole, entity, complex; institution, corporation, federation, association, society.

organization *n.* **1.** formulation, forming, formation, assembly, incorporation, coordination, arranging, structuring, constitution, making. **2.** arrangement, organization, design, pattern, composition, grouping, ordering, harmony. **3.** association, society, fraternity, federation, union, club, fellowship, order, league, group, alliance, corps, party; business organization, business, establishment, firm, company, corporation, outfit; sect. **—Ant. 1** dissolution, disbanding, breakup. **2** disorganization, confusion, chaos.

organize *v.* **1.** form, formulate, establish, originate, found, create, set up, put together, lay the foundation of, develop. **2.** arrange, systematize, make orderly, order, neaten, tidy, tidy up; classify, catalog, coordinate, categorize, group, codify, tabulate, index, file. **—Ant. 1** dissolve, disband, dismember, break up. **2** disorganize, disorder, confuse, mess up.

orgiastic *adj.* abandoned, bacchanalian, wanton, licentious, libertine, debauched, riotous, drunken, wild, Dionysian, undisciplined, dissolute, overindulgent, dissipated, unrestrained. **—Ant.** temperate, ascetic, moderate, restrained, disciplined.

orgy *n.* wild revelry, wild party, wanton celebration, drunken festivities, wassail, debauch, carousal, saturnalia, bacchanalia, bacchanal.

orient *n.* **1. the Orient** Asia; eastern Asia, the Eastern Hemisphere, the Far East. *—v.* **2.** accustom, familiarize, relate, acclimate, reconcile, make feel at home. **3.** locate, situate, set, fix, square, find, place with reference to the points of the compass, determine one's direction. **—Ant. 1** the Occident; Europe, the Americas, the Western Hemisphere. **2** estrange, alienate. **3** disorient, lose, confuse.

orientation *n.* **1.** familiarization, acclimatization, acclimation, adjustment. **2.** sense of direction, direction; alignment, location, situation. **—Ant. 1** estrangement, alienation; confusion, bewilderment, perplexity.

orifice *n.* opening, hole, cavity, aperture, slot, slit, gap, cleft, vent, entrance, passage, inlet, cranny, fissure, crevice, lacuna, mouth, oral cavity, hollow, pocket, pit, socket, alveolus.

origin *n.* **1.** source, cause, basis, base, foundation, derivation, reason, principle, agent, generator; originator, creator, father, mother, author, producer, prime mover, spring, fountainhead, taproot, root, ground. **2.** beginning, birth, genesis, inception, commencement; emergence, evolution, early development, growth, rise, derivation. **3.** extraction, descent, ancestry, parentage, family, lineage, house, stock, race, strain, breed, line; birth, nativity. **—Ant. 1** end, finish, termination, conclusion. **2** death, fall, extinction, finis. **3** posterity, issue, progeny, offspring.

original *adj.* **1.** first, initial, earliest, inaugural, introductory; basic, fundamental, essential, underlying, formative, germinal, seminal; aboriginal, primordial, primeval, primary, primal. **2.** having originality, imaginative, creative, inventive, ingenious, fresh, novel, new, new-fashioned, unique, unusual, different, bold, daring, out of the ordinary, extraordinary, singular; uncommon, unfamiliar, strange, atypical, unconventional, unorthodox, *Informal* newfangled. —*n.* **3.** prototype, first or earliest model, pattern, example, basis, first form, first copy. **—Ant. 1** last, latest, final; superficial. **2** unoriginal, common, commonplace, usual, typical, conventional, traditional, ordinary, average, standard, normal, familiar, banal, trite, stale; old, old-fashioned, antiquated, *Slang* old hat; derivative, borrowed, copied. **3** copy, reproduction.

originality *n.* imagination, creativity, inventiveness, ingenuity, cleverness, individuality, freshness, newness, novelty, uniqueness, boldness, daring, unconventionality, unorthodoxy, singularity. **—Ant.** unoriginality, routineness, commonness, conventionality, averageness, familiarity, banality, triteness, predictability; derivativeness.

originally *adv.* **1.** by origin; by derivation, by birth. **2.** at first, initially, at the outset, in the beginning. **3.** imaginatively, creatively, inventively, uniquely, differently, unusually, in an original way, unconventionally. **—Ant. 2** finally, in the end. **3** conventionally, traditionally, typically, routinely, unimaginatively, predictably, tritely.

originate *v.* **1.** begin, start, commence, proceed, emanate; arise, rise, derive, come, germinate, flow, issue, spring up, crop up, sprout, emerge, stem; be based in. **2.** create, invent, devise, initiate, inaugurate, formulate, fabricate, father, conceive, envision, design, draft; found, establish, organize, develop, evolve. **—Ant. 1** end, conclude, terminate, finish, stop, cease. **2** copy, imitate, follow.

ornament *n.* **1.** decoration, adornment, trimming, accessory, embellishment, trim, furbelow, frills, garnish; ornamentation, finery, beautification, enrichment, elaboration. —*v.* **2.** adorn, decorate, bedeck, festoon, trim, furbish, deck, trick out, garnish, gild; embellish, beautify, enrich.

ornate *adj.* elaborate, lavish, fancy, sumptuous, showy, flowery, florid, flashy, flamboyant, ostentatious, pretentious; decorated, adorned, embellished, baroque, rococo. **—Ant.** simple, plain, bare, unadorned, unembellished, undecorated.

ornery *adj.* mean, ill-tempered, ill-natured, irascible, surly, cantankerous, grouchy, quarrelsome, grumpy, snappish, crabby, dyspeptic, irritable, testy, peevish, curt, waspish, *Brit.* shirty.

orthodox *adj.* **1.** traditional, established, following established doctrine, accepted, authoritative, official, approved, *Slang* hard-shell; religious, pious, devout. **2.** conventional, traditional, customary, conformable, commonplace, usual, routine, standard, fixed, established, regular, ordinary; narrow, circumscribed, limited. **—Ant. 1, 2** unorthodox. **1** heretical, radical, liberal, heterodox, unconformable. **2** unconventional, unusual, uncommon, unique, original, novel; eccentric, nonconformist, independent.

oscillate *v.* **1.** swing, alternate, librate; pulsate, vibrate, pulse, move back and forth, seesaw, come and go, ebb and flow. **2.** waver, vacillate, hesitate, fluctuate, vary, hem and haw, shilly-shally, change, equivocate.

ossify *v.* harden into bone, fossilize; (*loosely*) harden, stiffen, become rigid, become fixed.

ostensible *adj.* titular, nominal, apparent, implied, presumable, outward, surface, seeming, alleged, avowed, declared, professed, manifest, perceivable, visible; pretended, assumed, feigned, specious, illusory. **—Ant.** real, true, actual, genuine, de facto.

ostentatious *adj.* flaunting wealth, fond of display, showing off, pompous, immodest, grandiose, affected, high-flown; conspicuous, pretentious, flamboyant, flashy, showy, gaudy, garish, loud, florid, overdone, exaggerated, obtrusive. **—Syn. Study.** See GRANDIOSE. **—Ant.** modest, reserved, conservative, somber, sedate; inconspicuous, simple, plain.

ostracize *v.* shun, snub, avoid, refuse to associate with, reject, exclude, shut out, banish, expel, oust, disown, blacklist, blackball, give one the cold shoulder, turn one's back on, *Slang* cut. **—Ant.** welcome, embrace, accept, acknowledge.

other *adj.* **1.** additional, more, further, added, extra, spare, supplementary, auxiliary. **2.** different, additional, more, dissimilar, unlike, contrasted, differentiated; opposite, reverse, contrasting, contradictory, contrary, alternate, remaining.

otherwise *adv.* **1.** if not, or else; under other circumstances, on the other hand. **2.** differently, in another manner; in opposition, in disagreement, in defiance, contrarily, contrariwise, inversely, in reverse. **3.** in other respects, excluding this, barring this, excepting this, apart from this. **—Ant. 2** similarly, alike, correspondingly.

otiose *adj.* **1.** lazy, slothful, idle, indolent, sluggish, resting, inactive, somnolent, lethargic, listless, laggard. **2.** useless, ineffective, impotent, unavailing, worn-out, inoperative, incompetent, futile, fruitless, abortive, unproductive, unrewarding, powerless. **—Ant. 1** energetic, active, dynamic. **2** effective, useful, rewarding.

oust *v.* expel, eject, evict, remove, banish, put out, cast out, throw out, kick out; dismiss, discharge, cashier, fire, unseat, *Slang* bounce, sack, give the gate, give the ax, send packing, boot out. **—Ant.** admit, invite, ask in, welcome; hire, engage, employ, appoint.

ouster *n.* ejection, overthrow, expulsion, dismissal, firing, discharge, dispossession, eviction, removal, banishment, dislodgment; *Slang* sacking, cashiering, drumming out, bouncing.

out-and-out *adj.* thorough, complete, absolute, utter, sheer, total, unconditional, unqualified, outright, straight-out; confirmed, inveterate, hardened, unregenerate, dyed-in-the-wool.

outbreak *n.* outburst, burst, eruption, explosion, outpouring, display, demonstration; sudden appearance, rapid spread, invasion, epidemic. **—Ant.** waning, ebbing, recession, decrease, decline, subsidence.

outburst *n.* burst, eruption, outbreak, explosion, outpouring, display, demonstration; fulmination, blast, thunder. **—Ant.** suppression, repression, control, restraint, stifling.

outcast *n.* **1.** exile, deportee, refugee, expatriate, displaced person, man without a country; pariah, castaway; outlaw, fugitive, runaway; lonely wanderer, roamer, rover, homeless man, vagabond, derelict, destitute person. **—*adj.* 2.** rejected, discarded, expelled, castaway, ousted, banished.

outcome *n.* result, consequence, effect, upshot, issue, end, fruit, *Slang* payoff; aftereffect, aftermath, outgrowth.

outcry *n.* crying out, cry, cry of alarm, cry of distress, cry of protest, shout, scream, shriek, caterwauling, screech, howl, yell, roar, bellow, whoop, yowl, yelp; clamor, uproar, commotion, noise, clangor, hubbub, hue and cry, hullabaloo; protest, complaint, objection, remonstrance. **—Ant.** whisper, murmur; quiet, stillness, silence, calm, tranquillity; assent, concurrence, ratification.

outdo *v.* excel, surpass, best, outshine, exceed, better, outclass, top, beat, eclipse, transcend, outstrip, outrank, outplay, defeat, overcome, worst, outfox, outwit, get the better of, steal a march on.

outer *adj.* exterior, external, outward, outside, distal, without; farther, farther out, extreme, remote, outlying, outermost, peripheral. **—Ant.** inner, interior, internal, inward, inside, within; central, close-by, close-in, nearby, adjacent.

outfit *n.* **1.** ensemble, costume, set of clothing, getup, wardrobe, habit; equipment, gear, paraphernalia, trappings, accoutrements, *Slang* rig. **—*v.* 2.** equip, provision, supply, furnish, appoint, fit, accouter, *Slang* rig up; dress, clothe, costume, array.

outgoing *adj.* **1.** outbound, going out, outward bound, leaving, departing, exiting. **2.** friendly, amiable, gregarious, convivial, genial, social, sociable, extroverted, sympathetic, cordial, warm, warmhearted. **—Ant. 1** incoming, inbound, arriving, entering. **2** austere, indifferent, distant, reserved, withdrawn.

outgrowth *n.* **1.** result, consequence, upshot, natural development, product, issue, fruit; end, conclusion, culmination, sequel, aftereffect, aftermath, offshoot. **2.** shoot, sprout, offshoot, outcropping, excrescence; protuberance, projection, bulge, node, knob, knot.

outing *n.* excursion, expedition, trip, pleasure trip, holiday, junket; hike, tramp, ramble, walk; drive, ride, tour, spin, jaunt, airing.

outlander *n.* stranger, alien, foreigner, *German* Ausländer; immigrant, settler, newcomer; wanderer, exile, displaced person, *French* émigré; barbarian, tramontane, ultramontane; intruder, invader.

outlandish *adj.* preposterous, incredible, outrageous, odd, bizarre, fantastic, freakish, ridiculous, eccentric, queer, weird, grotesque, strange, curious, peculiar, unusual, unconventional, unimaginable, unbelievable, inconceivable, unheard-of, unparalleled, *Slang* far-out, kooky. **—Ant.** commonplace, ordinary, everyday, routine, normal, familiar, standard, usual, run-of-the-mill.

outlast *v.* outwear, outstay, survive, endure, perdure, prevail, persist, stay on, keep on, hold on, carry on, continue, remain, hold out, persist, defy time.

outlaw *n.* **1.** criminal, fugitive, felon, bandit, desperado, highwayman, miscreant; outcast, pariah. **—*v.* 2.** make unlawful, forbid, prohibit, ban, bar, proscribe, exclude, deny, disallow, suppress, stop, interdict. **—Ant. 2** legalize, permit, allow; encourage, foster, welcome.

outlay *n.* expenditure, spending; amount spent, payment, disbursement, outgo, cost, expense, charge, fee; price. **—Ant.** profit, gain, yield, income.

outlet *n.* **1.** opening, egress, passage, channel, path, way, avenue; exit, gateway, gate, portal, door; duct, conduit; means. **2.** vent, means of expression, means of satisfying, way of getting rid of, escape. —**Ant. 1** entrance, ingress, entry.

outline *n.* **1.** profile, silhouette, contour, delineation, lineation; boundary line, limits, tracing, perimeter, periphery. **2.** synopsis, summary, résumé, brief report, brief, general sketch, thumbnail sketch, condensation, digest, abridgment, abstract, review, recapitulation. —*v.* **3.** draw a line around, trace, delineate; diagram, write a synopsis, sketch out, blueprint, plot. —**Ant. 1** bulk, mass, substance, volume; center, core, heart.

outlive *v.* —**Syn. Study.** See SURVIVE.

outlook *n.* **1.** view, vista, prospect, sight, aspect, panorama, spectacle, scene, picture. **2.** attitude, frame of mind, point of view, viewpoint, view, perspective. **3.** prospect, expectation, anticipation, forecast, assumption, presumption; probability, chance, promise. —**Ant. 3** hindsight; recapitulation.

outlying *adj.* outer, exterior, peripheral; remote, distant, far-off, rural, suburban, exurban. —**Ant.** central, inner, internal, core; nearby, near, neighboring, close-by, adjacent.

outmoded *adj.* out-of-date, dated, old-fashioned, old-timey, démodé, passé, archaic, antique, vintage, antiquated, out-of-fashion, outdated, behind the times; *Slang* old hat, corny, tired. —**Ant.** up-to-date, stylish, modish; *Slang* with it, hip, cool.

output *n.* production, yield, productivity, achievement, produce, product, harvest, crop, accomplishment, turnout, profit, proceeds, take, gain, reaping, gathering, gleaning.

outrage *n.* **1.** atrocity, inhumane act, act of brutality, wanton violence, barbarity, barbarousness, iniquity, enormity, monstrosity, gross offense, gross crime; evil, wrong, transgression, gross indecency; desecration, profanation. **2.** insult, affront, indignity, expression of contempt, disrespect, slap in the face. —*v.* **3.** anger, incense, enrage, infuriate, madden, provoke, arouse, exasperate, gall, rile, ruffle, make one's blood boil, make one see red, steam up, get one's back up; insult, affront, make indignant, offend, shock, scandalize, disquiet, discompose. —**Ant. 3** calm, soothe, quiet, pacify.

outrageous *adj.* **1.** atrocious, vile, base, heinous, grossly offensive, iniquitous, monstrous, barbarous, inhumane, inhuman, brutal, foul, despicable, contemptible, wicked, nefarious, horrifying, odious, reprehensible, unspeakable. **2.** offensive, abusive, shameless, shocking, scandalous, disgraceful, insulting, insolent, rude, disrespectful, contemptuous, scornful; infuriating, maddening, galling, exasperating. **3.** monstrous, extreme, unreasonable, preposterous, flagrant, unwarranted, unconscionable, gross, rank, exorbitant, immoderate, immense, excessive, enormous. —**Ant. 3** reasonable, moderate, mild, minor, trivial, paltry; equitable, fair, just; tolerable.

outright *adj.* **1.** utter, complete, total, downright, entire, full, unmitigated, unqualified, undiminished, unreserved, unconditional, absolute, sheer, thorough, thoroughgoing, out-and-out. —*adv.* **2.** utterly, altogether, completely, absolutely, downright, thoroughly, entirely; openly, visibly, patently, manifestly, demonstrably. **3.** instantly, immediately, at once, on the spot, promptly, forthwith. —**Ant. 1** partial, incomplete; qualified, conditional. **2** somewhat, partially. **3** later, eventually, ultimately, finally, in due course.

outside *n.* **1.** exterior, surface, outer side, façade, face; covering, case, sheath, skin, coating. —*adj.* **2.** outer, exterior, external, outward, outermost, outdoor. **3.** extraneous, foreign, alien, nonnative, nondomestic, unfamiliar, strange. **4.** remote, distant, faint, obscure, slight. —*adv.* **5.** outdoors, out-of-doors, on or to the outside. —*prep.* **6.** beyond the bounds of, distant from, beyond the confines of. —**Ant. 1, 2** inside, interior. **1** center. **2** inner, inmost, innermost, inward, internal. **3** native, domestic; familiar, known. **5** indoors. **6** inside.

outspoken *adj.* plainspoken, blunt, frank, honest, direct, straightforward, forthright, open, unreserved, opinionated, candid, unsparing; artless, ingenuous, guileless, undissembling, undissimulating. —**Syn. Study.** See FRANK. —**Ant.** tactful, diplomatic, gracious, judicious, reticent, guarded.

outstanding *adj.* **1.** foremost, eminent, prominent, famed, celebrated, distinguished, famous, renowned, best known, remarkable, memorable, unforgettable, striking, notable, noteworthy; exemplary, exceptional, extraordinary, marvelous, most impressive, magnificent, great, phenomenal. **2.** unpaid, unsettled, due, in arrears, uncollected, payable, owing. —**Ant. 1** commonplace, routine, ordinary, usual, everyday, run-of-the-mill; trite, banal. **2** paid, settled, collected.

outward *adj.* **1.** external, exterior, outer, outside, surface, superficial, visible, perceivable, perceptible, apparent, ostensible; evident, manifest, observable. —*adv.* **2.** Also **outwards.** out, toward the outside, away, from here. —**Ant. 1,**

2 inward. **1** internal, interior, inner, inside, inmost, innermost; invisible, imperceptible, unobservable. **2** in; toward the inside.

outwardly *adv.* to all appearances, apparently, evidently, seemingly, ostensibly, on the face of it, manifestly, visibly, clearly. **—Ant.** inwardly, secretly.

outweigh *v.* **1.** weigh more than, be heavier than, exceed the weight of. **2.** exceed, surpass, predominate, overshadow, eclipse, override, rise above, be more important than, prevail over, take precedence over.

outwit *v.* outsmart, outfox, outmaneuver, take in, trick, fool, dupe, foil, thwart, baffle, circumvent, get around; trap, ensnare.

outworn *adj.* out-of-date, obsolete, passé, unfashionable, superseded, disused, extinct, antiquated, old-fashioned, dated; defunct, discarded, abandoned, rejected, bygone, forgotten. **—Ant.** current, fashionable, new, up-to-date, in.

oval *adj.* egg-shaped, ovoid, ovate, elliptical, ellipsoidal, ovular, curved, rounded, oviform, *Botany* obovate, almond-shaped.

ovation *n.* enthusiastic applause, cheers, cheering, acclamation, adulation, homage, acclaim, tribute; hurrah, hurray, huzzah; fanfare. **—Ant.** jeering, taunts, catcalls, hoots, booing.

over *adv.* **1.** from beginning to end, from top to bottom, all through, all over; from head to foot, from cover to cover; from stem to stern, from end to end; along the course of. **2.** again, a second time, once more, anew, afresh; repeatedly, time and again, often, in repetition. **3.** remaining, in addition, in excess, on top of the rest, beyond a certain amount, into the bargain, to boot; too, else, also; extra, over and above. *—adj.* **4.** at an end, finished, ended, concluded, done, terminated, completed, settled; lapsed, elapsed, expired, passed away, no more, gone, past, bygone. **5.** in excess, in addition, above, extra, additional, excessive, surplus, too great, superfluous. **—Ant. 2** once, only once. **3, 5** under, below, short, deficient, wanting, lacking, shy. **4** begun, started, commenced; in progress.

overabundance *n.* abundance, superabundance, excess, surplus, oversupply, superfluity, profusion, plethora, supersaturation, surfeit, glut, embarrassment of riches. **—Ant.** shortage, scarcity, dearth, scantiness, insufficiency, lack, want.

overall *adj.* total, general, complete, entire, comprehensive, exhaustive, all-inclusive, all-embracing, sweeping, panoramic, extensive, thoroughgoing, widespread; long-range, long-term.

overbearing *adj.* arrogant, high-handed, self-assertive, self-important, cocky, lordly, high-and-mighty, know-it-all, disdainful, imperious, domineering, dictatorial, autocratic, tyrannical, despotic; egotistical, haughty, pompous, conceited, *Informal* stuck-up, snooty, high-hat. **—Ant.** modest, unassuming, humble, demure, meek, shy, timid, subdued, deferential, subservient; receptive, sympathetic, compassionate, gracious.

overcast *adj.* cloudy, overclouded, sunless, gray, dull, dreary, gloomy, dark, leaden, threatening, lowering, murky; misty, foggy, hazy. **—Ant.** cloudless, unclouded, clear, sunny, brilliant, bright.

overcome *v.* conquer, best, get the better of, master, surmount, vanquish, defeat, beat, lick, suppress, overthrow, put down, overwhelm, overpower, subdue, crush, quell, prevail over, triumph over, win over, transcend; survive. **—Syn. Study.** See DEFEAT. **—Ant.** surrender to, give in to, capitulate to, submit to; give up, admit defeat.

overconfident *adj.* too confident, overly sure of succeeding, self-assured, egotistical, cocksure; impudent, arrogant, presumptuous, brash, immodest, conceited, cheeky. **—Ant.** self-effacing, fearful, modest, sheepish, shamefaced.

overdo *v.* **1.** do to excess, carry too far, not know when to stop, be intemperate in; overtax oneself by; indulge oneself in. **2.** exaggerate, overstate, hyperbolize, stretch a point, *Informal* lay it on thick; magnify, expand, amplify, embroider, gild, overact, overplay, *Slang* ham it up. **—Ant. 2** understate, minimize, slight, neglect.

overdue *adj.* past due, belated, late, tardy, unpunctual, behind time, behindhand, delayed, slow, dilatory, long delayed. **—Ant.** early, ahead of time, beforehand, premature.

overflow *v.* **1.** flow over, run over, be filled to overflowing, overspill, slop over; overspread, inundate, flood. *—n.* **2.** overabundance, superabundance, surplus, excess, superfluity, profusion, oversupply, plethora, copiousness, flood, glut. **—Ant. 2** lack, want, scarcity, shortage, dearth, paucity, deficiency, insufficiency, inadequacy.

overhaul *v.* **1.** overtake, pass, catch up with, catch, beat. **2.** renovate, revamp, rebuild, reconstruct, remodel, recondition, take apart and put back together, inspect and repair, service, restore.

overhead *adv.* **1.** over one's head, above one's head; upward, up above,

above; aloft, atop, on top. —*adj.* **2.** ceiling, roof; overlying, overhanging; uppermost, upper, superior, topmost. —*n.* **3.** operating expenses, general expenses, *Slang* nut.

overjoyed *adj.* delighted, deliriously happy, jubilant, elated, joyous, gratified, enthralled, enraptured, exultant, thrilled, euphoric, exuberant, enchanted, ecstatic, transported, *Informal* carried away, tickled pink, happy as the day is long, happy as a lark. —**Ant.** disappointed, unhappy, sad, depressed, dejected, downcast, sorrowful, despondent, blue.

overlook *v.* **1.** forget, neglect, leave undone, not trouble oneself about, omit, leave out, miss, slight, pass over, pass up, disregard, skip. **2.** ignore, disregard, regard indulgently, pass over, blink at, wink at; excuse, forgive, shrug off, forget about, think no more of, let bygones be bygones, let ride. **3.** have a view of, look over, give on, look out on, survey; tower above, command. —**Syn. Study. 1** See SLIGHT. —**Ant. 1** remember, pay attention to, concentrate on, keep in mind. **2** complain, carp, nag, cavil, criticize, censure, find fault with, view with disfavor.

overly *adv.* excessively, needlessly, exceedingly, too, immoderately, inordinately, unreasonably, unfairly, unduly, exorbitantly, disproportionately, overmuch, too much, to a fault; extremely, very, acutely, highly, severely, intensely. —**Ant.** insufficiently, inadequately, too little; moderately, reasonably, mildly.

overpower *v.* **1.** overcome, overwhelm, affect strongly, move, sway, influence. **2.** subdue, overcome, get the better of, best, get the upper hand over, master, overwhelm, conquer, vanquish, defeat, worst, beat, triumph over, crush, quell. —**Ant. 2** surrender, give up, give in, capitulate.

overrate *v.* overpraise, overestimate, overesteem, rate too highly, overvalue, overprize, praise undeservedly, make too much of, attach too much importance to. —**Ant.** underrate, underestimate, undervalue; belittle, minimize.

overrule *v.* **1.** disallow, rule against, reject, override, dismiss, preclude, set aside, waive, eject, throw out, deny, veto, refuse, repudiate, invalidate, countermand, overturn, repel, revoke, cancel, annul, nullify, make null and void. **2.** prevail over, outvote, outweigh, bend to one's will. —**Ant. 1** accept, allow, permit, approve, grant, authorize, favor; sustain, support, promote, champion, back.

overrun *v.* **1.** swarm over, infest, surge over, rove over, run riot over, overspread, pour in on, overwhelm, invade; raid, invade, swoop down on; sack, pillage, plunder, loot, despoil; engulf, inundate, deluge; overgrow, choke, flourish in. —*n.* **2.** overproduction, surplus; additional cost, extra charge, higher price.

overseas Also **oversea** *adv.* **1.** abroad, in foreign lands, across the sea, beyond the sea; in foreign service. —*adj.* **2.** foreign, external, alien, exotic; transoceanic, ultramarine. —**Ant. 1** at home, on native soil. **2** domestic, internal, native, indigenous.

oversee *v.* supervise, superintend, overlook, have charge of, handle, attend to, see to, keep an eye on; administer, manage, direct, run, boss, command, govern, rule, guide, watch, preside over, carry on, pilot, steer, be at the helm of, regulate.

overseer *n.* supervisor, chief, head, boss, manager, director, foreman, superintendent, captain, taskmaster, governor, slave driver.

overshadow *v.* **1.** cast a shadow over, eclipse, shade, darken; obscure, hide, conceal, cover, screen, mask, shroud, veil, fog. **2.** outshine, eclipse, dwarf, tower over, render insignificant by comparison, diminish the importance of, steal the limelight from.

oversight *n.* omission, mistake, blunder, heedless mistake, inadvertence, careless error, slight; negligence, neglect, neglectfulness, carelessness, laxity, inattention, thoughtlessness, heedlessness, disregard, absent-mindedness. —**Ant.** care, attention, heed, heedfulness, diligence, alertness, vigilance, meticulousness, scrupulousness.

overstate *v.* exaggerate, overstress, overdo, embellish, embroider, oversell, enlarge, overdraw, overpaint, increase, inflate, magnify, stretch, enlarge on; *Slang* touch up, play up, lay it on, spread it on thick. —**Ant.** understate, minimize, undervalue, underplay.

overt *adj.* apparent, obvious, noticeable, visible, observable, ostensible, plain, public, open, easily seen, unconcealed, perceptible, perceivable, palpable, evident, revealed, manifest, undisguised. —**Ant.** covert, unrevealed, unnoticeable, invisible, hidden, concealed, covered, masked, secret, undisclosed, disguised; private, personal.

overtake *v.* **1.** come abreast of, catch up with, catch, come up beside, gain on, reach, approach, run down; pass, overhaul, go by. **2.** take by surprise, come upon suddenly, befall, catch unprepared, catch off guard. —**Ant. 1** fall back from, lose ground to.

overthrow *v.* **1.** overturn, topple, bring down, cast down from power, put an end to by force, overcome, overpower, defeat, abolish, undo, crush, do away with. —*n.* 2. toppling, bringing down, casting out of power, undoing, downfall, defeat, overturn, abolition; revolution, rebellion, insurrection, mutiny. —**Ant.** 1 preserve, conserve, maintain, uphold, support, keep, perpetuate; defend, protect, guard. 2 preservation, perpetuation; defense, protection.

overtone *n.* suggestion, intimation, insinuation, hint, implication, connotation, slight indication, innuendo, drift, coloring, hue.

overture *n.* 1. prelude, introduction, prologue; foreword, preface, preamble; beginning. 2. opening move, preliminary offer, receptive sign, invitation, approach, bid, offering, advance, tender, motion, signal, gesture, suggestion, proposal, proposition. —**Ant.** 1 finale, close; epilogue, afterword, coda. 2 rejection, spurning, repudiation, rebuke.

overturn *v.* 1. capsize, knock over, upset, knock down, upend, push over, topple, turn upside down, turn topsy-turvy. 2. defeat, vanquish, overthrow, conquer, overcome, overpower, overwhelm, depose, turn out, crush, beat, thrash, oust.

overweening *adj.* overbearing, haughty, disdainful, arrogant, pompous, highhanded, patronizing, egotistical, overconfident, domineering, imperious, presumptuous, cocky, brassy, bigheaded, bossy, self-important, *Slang* pushy. —**Ant.** modest, shy, unassuming, self-effacing.

overweight *adj.* obese, fat, corpulent, pudgy, chubby, plump, chunky, well-padded, fleshy, overstuffed, fatty, fattish, potbellied, roly-poly, portly, tubby; *Slang* piggy, beer-bellied, gross. —**Ant.** underweight, skinny, bony, gaunt, emaciated, anorexic.

overwhelm *v.* 1. overrun, overpower, overcome, overthrow, defeat, vanquish, subjugate, conquer, beat; quash, crush, quell, bury, swamp, engulf, inundate. 2. overcome, overpower, devastate, crush, stagger, confound, bowl over. —**Ant.** 1 surrender, capitulate, give up, give in; rescue, deliver, save. 2 unaffect, leave indifferent; encourage, lift.

overwrought *adj.* overexcited, excited, agitated, wrought up, worked up, carried away, near hysteria, riled, greatly disturbed, distracted, inflamed, wild, frenzied, wild-eyed, uneasy, perturbed, ruffled; nervous, high-strung, oversensitive, touchy. —**Ant.** calm, tranquil, placid, unruffled, serene, unexcited, untroubled, cool, composed, *Slang* unflappable.

owe *v.* be in debt, be indebted to, be obligated, have a loan from; be under obligation to, be bound in gratitude, be beholden to. —**Ant.** repay, pay back, reimburse, liquidate, amortize, compensate.

own *adj.* 1. belonging to oneself, belonging to itself; personal, private, individual, particular. —*v.* 2. possess, have possession of, be in receipt of, be the owner of, have, retain, keep, maintain, hold. 3. admit, acknowledge, confess to, concede, disclose, tell; grant, allow, yield, consent to, recognize; avow, assent, concur, acquiesce. —**Ant.** 1 someone else's, another's. 3 deny, disown, disclaim, repudiate, abjure; deprive, divest, disallow, refuse, withhold.

owner *n.* possessor, landlord, landlady, proprietor, proprietress, holder, landholder, partner, copartner, landowner, master, mistress, titleholder, householder.

pace *n.* **1.** step, stride, gait, tread, slow gait, walk, amble, saunter. **2.** rate, speed, velocity, clip, motion, momentum, flow, gait. —*v.* **3.** walk nervously back and forth across; walk, go, go at a slow gait, amble, stroll, saunter; plod, trudge. —**Syn. Study. 3** PACE, PLOD, TRUDGE refer to a steady and monotonous kind of walking. PACE suggests steady, measured steps, as of someone lost in thought or impelled by some distraction: *to pace up and down the hall.* PLOD implies a slow, heavy, laborious walk: *The mail carriers plod their weary way.* TRUDGE implies a spiritless but usu. steady and doggedly persistent walk: *The farmer trudged to the village to buy supplies.* —**Ant. 1, 2** trot, canter, run.

pacific *adj.* calm, serene, placid, peaceful, tranquil, quiet, restful, reposeful, smooth, undisturbed, untroubled, still, halcyon, unruffled, harmonious, peaceable; conciliatory, pacifying, gentle, dovelike, inoffensive. —**Ant.** agitated, troubled, overwrought; quarrelsome, belligerent, violent.

pacify *v.* appease, calm, quiet, allay, bring to a state of peace, soothe, placate, propitiate, assuage, compose, mollify; restore to peace, restore harmony, conciliate, reconcile, settle differences, bring to terms, heal the breach. —**Ant.** make hostile, anger, enrage, madden, inflame, agitate, aggravate, provoke; begin hostilities, start a fight.

pack *n.* **1.** package, packet, parcel, bundle, kit, box, container; batch, bunch, set, lot, heap, mass, cluster, clump; accumulation, collection, assortment, miscellany. **2.** crowd, throng, group, horde, mob, multitude, swarm, flock, herd, drove, covey, passel, bevy, gaggle. —*v.* **3.** fill, load, jam, cram, stuff; bundle, bunch, batch, group, gather, assemble, tie, bind, truss. —**Ant. 3** unpack, empty; unwrap, untie, unload.

package *n.* **1.** pack, parcel, packet; bundle, box, carton, case, container, kit, wrappings. —*v.* **2.** wrap, wrap up, pack, encase; display in a container.

packet *n.* parcel, package, pack, bundle, pouch, bag, box, sheaf, bale, roll, quiver.

pact *n.* treaty, international agreement, agreement, compact, contract, convention, concordance, concordat; bond, covenant, alliance, understanding.

pad *n.* **1.** cushion, cushioning, padding; mattress, mat, bolster. **2.** tablet, writing tablet, notebook; desk pad, memorandum book, memo pad. —*v.* **3.** cushion, protect; upholster; stuff, fill. **4.** fill out unnecessarily, expand needlessly, enlarge excessively, amplify freely, stretch out, inflate, fatten, blow up, puff out.

padding *n.* **1.** wadding, stuffing, filler, filling, lining, packing, wrapping. **2.** wordiness, prolixity, verbiage, verboseness, verbosity, redundancy, superabundance, surplus, surfeit, extravagance. —**Ant. 2** shortage, lack, dearth, want, scarcity.

pagan *n.* **1.** one who is not a Christian or Jew or Muslim; heathen, infidel, idolator, idol worshiper, polytheist; nonbeliever, unbeliever, atheist. —*adj.* **2.** heathen, heathenish, idolatrous, polytheistic; barbarian. —**Syn. Study. 1** See HEATHEN. —**Ant. 1** Christian, Jew, Muslim; true believer, believer. **2** Christian, Jewish, Muslim, monotheistic, Christianized, civilized, enlightened.

pageant *n.* spectacle, elaborate performance, show, exhibition, display, extravaganza; ceremony, ritual, pomp, rite; procession, parade.

pageantry *n.* display, pomp, pageant, ceremony, spectacle, drama, ritual, rite; grandeur, magnificence, splendor, glitter, show, theatrics, showiness, extravagance, ostentation, flashiness, flair, *Slang* splash.

pain *n.* **1.** ache, aching, soreness, hurt, hurting, smarting, pang, throb, twinge, pinch, stitch, discomfort, malaise. **2.** suffering, distress, anguish, agony, torment, torture, ordeal, hell, misery, grief, woe, heartache, heartbreak, sorrow, sadness, affliction, wretchedness, unhappiness. —*v.* **3.** hurt, ache, smart, throb, sting, discomfort. **4.** distress, agonize, torment, torture, make miserable, trouble, worry, disturb, grieve, sadden; displease, annoy, vex, gall, harass, rile, chafe, pique, exasperate, try one's patience. —**Ant. 1** comfort, relief. **2** delight, joy, pleasure, sweetness, satisfaction, gladness, enjoyment, ecstasy, happiness, rapture, comfort, peace, solace. **3** relieve, ease, comfort. **4** delight, please, gladden, enchant, enrapture, captivate, charm, satisfy, gratify; comfort, solace.

painful *adj.* **1.** aching, very sore, agonizing, excruciating, throbbing, smarting, stinging, sharp, piercing, hurtful, torturous, racking, distressful; hurtful, afflictive. **2.** unpleasant, distressing, disagreeable, distasteful, difficult, trying, arduous, grueling, disturbing, disquieting;

grievous, lamentable, sad, sorrowful, pathetic, dire, dismal, dreary. **—Ant. 1** painless; soothing, comforting, alleviating, relieving. **2** pleasant, pleasurable, delightful, enjoyable, agreeable, happy, gratifying, satisfying.

painstaking *adj.* careful, thorough, thoroughgoing, scrupulous, meticulous, conscientious, punctilious, precise, exacting, fussy, finicky, diligent, persevering, assiduous, earnest, industrious, energetic, strenuous. **—Syn. Study.** PAINSTAKING, METICULOUS, CONSCIENTIOUS mean extremely careful or precise about details. PAINSTAKING stresses laborious effort and diligent attention to detail in achieving a desired objective: *the painstaking editing of a manuscript.* METICULOUS suggests a more extreme attention to minute details: *to be meticulous about matching shoes and clothing.* CONSCIENTIOUS stresses scrupulous effort to obey one's sense of moral obligation to perform tasks well: *a conscientious description of the facts.* **—Ant.** careless, haphazard, slapdash, *Informal* catch-as-catch-can; neglectful, negligent, feckless, heedless, thoughtless; halfhearted, lazy, frivolous.

painter *n.* artist, illustrator, old master, portrait painter, oil painter, watercolorist, drawer, sketcher, delineator, landscapist, miniaturist; house painter.

pair *n.* **1.** two matched items, set of two, team, brace, yoke, span. **2.** couple, duo, twosome, doublet, dyad; match, combination. **—*v.* 3.** match, match up, mate, pair off, couple, combine, unite.

pal *n.* buddy, bosom buddy, chum, comrade, companion, boon companion, crony, friend, intimate, intimate friend, confidant, *British* mate; sidekick, partner, alter ego, *Informal* pard; cohort, accomplice, associate, colleague.

palace *n.* royal residence, castle; (*variously*) mansion, stately residence, manor house, château, villa, hacienda.

palatable *adj.* **—Syn. Study.** See TASTY.

palatial *adj.* luxurious, opulent, sumptuous, stately, plush, noble, splendid, rich, regal, monumental, magnificent, imposing, grand, grandiose, elegant, showy; *Slang* posh, swanky, ritzy. **—Ant.** simple, humble, unpretentious, modest.

pale[1] *adj.* **1.** colorless, white, pasty, ashen, ash-colored, pallid, wan, sallow, drained of blood, bloodless, anemic, cadaverous, deathly, deathlike, ghostlike, ghastly. **2.** light, light-colored, light-toned, bleached, whitish. **—*v.* 3.** become pale, blanch, whiten. **—Syn. Study. 1** PALE, PALLID, WAN imply an absence of color, esp. from the human countenance. PALE implies a faintness or absence of color, which may be natural when applied to things (*the pale blue of a violet*), but when used to refer to the human face usu. means an unnatural and often temporary absence of color, as arising from sickness or sudden emotion: *pale cheeks.* PALLID, limited mainly to the human countenance, implies an excessive paleness induced by intense emotion, disease, or death: *the pallid lips of the dying man.* WAN implies a sickly paleness, as after a long illness: *wan and thin;* or it may suggest weakness: *a wan smile.* **—Ant. 1** ruddy, rosy-cheeked, rosy, rubicund, high-colored, florid, flushed. **2** dark, deep, vivid. **3** flush, blush.

pale[2] *n.* **1.** stake, post, picket, paling, upright, palisade. **2.** enclosure, pen, fold, confine, close, closure, fenced-in area.

palisade *n.* **1.** fence of stakes, fence of pales, enclosure, fence, close, stockade, bulwark, rampart. **2. palisades** line of cliffs, cliffs, bluffs; escarpment, ledge, crag, promontory.

pall[1] *n.* dark covering, darkness, shadow, haze, dimness; gloom, melancholy, depression, moroseness, cheerlessness, oppression, desolation. **—Ant.** light, brightness; joviality, gaiety, joy, cheer, merriment, exuberance, exhilaration, high spirits.

pall[2] *v.* become boring, become dull, be tiresome, weary, sicken, cloy; sate, satiate. **—Ant.** interest, excite, animate, create enthusiasm, delight.

palliate *v.* relieve, sooth, ease, lessen, alleviate, mitigate, assuage, soften, moderate, temper, reduce, cushion; tame, check, curb, subdue; quiet, still, calm, hush, lull. **—Ant.** arouse, increase, intensify, exacerbate.

pallid *adj.* **1.** pale, anemic looking, sallow, wan, ashen, ghostly, peaked, pasty, colorless, ashy, waxen. **2.** dull, insipid, unimaginative, uninteresting, lifeless, boring, tedious, humdrum, monotonous, bland, vapid, *Slang* blah. **—Syn. Study. 1** See PALE. **—Ant. 1** rosy, hale, rubicund, glowing. **2** lively, exciting, imaginative, vivacious.

pallor *n.* paleness, pallidness, colorlessness, whiteness, pastiness, ashen color, wanness, bloodless coloring, bloodlessness, cadaverous color, ghostliness, gray complexion. **—Ant.** ruddy complexion, ruddiness, flush.

palmy *adj.* prosperous, bounteous, thriving, flourishing, successful, booming, blooming, golden, halcyon, balmy, sunny, rosy; agreeable, pleasant, pleasurable, congenial. **—Ant.** failing, dwindling, fading, waning.

palpable *adj.* tangible, obvious, plain, clear, noticeable, visible, discernible, manifest, apparent, perceivable, perceptible, recognizable, definite, distinct, evident, unmistakable; feelable, tactile, touchable. **—Ant.** intangible, unnoticeable, undiscernible, imperceptible, indistinct.

palpitate *v.* throb, pound, pulsate rapidly, beat, beat quickly, pulse rapidly, flutter, quiver, quaver, go pit-a-pat; vibrate, shake, tremble, shiver.

palsied *adj.* palsy-stricken, spastic; shaking, trembling, quaking, uncontrollable.

paltry *adj.* petty, trifling, trivial, of little value, piddling, puny, measly, picayune, shabby, scrubby, sorry; unimportant, insignificant, inconsequential, inconsiderable, wretched, inferior, poor, not worth mentioning. **—Syn. Study.** See PETTY. **—Ant.** important, significant, consequential, essential, major, valuable, worthy, considerable, grand, magnificent.

pamper *v.* spoil, indulge, cater to, cater to one's every whim, humor, give in to, cosset, coddle, mollycoddle. **—Ant.** be stern with, lay down the law; mistreat; maltreat, abuse, tyrannize, domineer, oppress, intimidate, bully.

pamphlet *n.* booklet, brochure; leaflet, circular, folder, bulletin, throwaway; tract, monograph.

panacea *n.* cure-all, universal cure, nostrum, elixir, sovereign remedy; easy solution, simplistic solution, final answer.

pandemonium *n.* tumult, turmoil, chaos, bedlam, disorder, wild confusion, rumpus, commotion; uproar, clamor, racket, din, hubbub, disturbance, hullabaloo. **—Ant.** order, peace, quiet, calm, tranquillity.

pander Also **panderer** *n.* procurer, flesh-peddler, pimp; *Slang* hustler, cadet, mack; *French* souteneur, maquereau.

panegyric *n.* eulogy, laudation, praise, homage, tribute, extolment, citation, commendation, compliment, encomium, testimonial, good word. **—Ant.** condemnation, denunciation, censure, reproach, vituperation, diatribe.

panel *n.* **1.** surface section; compartment, partition, piece, pane, insert, divider, bulkhead. **2.** committee, board, group, expert group, advisory group, select group, jury; discussion group, round table.

pang *n.* twinge, brief sensation; ache, pain, throb, smart, pinch, stick, stitch, sting, distress, discomfort; agony, anguish, suffering. **—Ant.** pleasure, delight, gratification, satisfaction, enjoyment, joy, happiness, comfort, solace, relief.

panic *n.* **1.** terror, overwhelming fear, fear and trembling, alarm, hysteria, scare, fright, affright, cold sweat; horror, dread, apprehension, anxiety, trepidation, nervousness, perturbation, consternation, confusion. **—*v.*** **2.** give way to panic, succumb to fear, become hysterical, be overwhelmed by dread; *Slang* fall apart, go to pieces, go ape.

panorama *n.* sweeping view, scenic view, scene, scenery, vista, prospect, tableau, picture, perspective, survey, overview, bird's-eye view, diorama; overall picture, long view.

panoramic *adj.* sweeping, extensive, all-embracing, all-encompassing, wide, far-ranging, far-reaching, extended, all-inclusive, bird's-eye, overall.

pant *v.* **1.** breathe hard, gasp for breath, gasp, huff, puff, blow, wheeze. **2.** long for, yearn for, lust after, hunger for, crave, desire, covet, want, have a yen for, hope for, wish for, aspire to, sigh for; *Informal* itch for, set one's heart on, lick one's chops for. **—*n.*** **3.** gasp, short intake of breath, puff, huff, wheeze.

pants *n. pl.* **1.** trousers, pair of trousers, slacks, dungarees, knickers, denims, breeches; *Informal* britches, bluejeans, jeans. **2.** underpants, drawers, underdrawers, undershorts, shorts, panties, *British* knickers.

pantywaist *n.* weakling, milksop, sissy, Milquetoast, mama's boy, namby-pamby, weak sister, softy, crybaby, mollycoddle; *Slang* wimp, sissy-pants, sissy-britches.

pap *n.* **1.** mush, mash, gruel, cereal, soft food, paste, pulp, Pablum. **2.** childish nonsense, drivel, triviality, trivia, rubbish, rot, twaddle, junk, tosh, bosh, balderdash, *Slang* flapdoodle.

papal *adj.* of the pope, pontifical, apostolic.

paper *n.* **1.** (*variously*) writing paper,notepaper, stationery, letter paper, bond, carbon paper, onionskin; cardboard, paperboard, construction paper; tissue paper, tissue, tracing paper; wrapping paper, gift wrap; printing paper, newsprint, stock, pulp; wallpaper. **2.** document, instrument, certificate, deed, record, writing. **3.** newspaper, journal, gazette, tabloid, news, chronicle; daily, weekly, monthly; publication, periodical, trade paper. **4.** composition, essay, article, theme, report, work, opus; manuscript, typescript, draft; white paper. **—*v.*** **5.** wallpaper; line with paper, cover with paper.

par *n.* **1.** equal footing, parity, equality, evenness, equilibrium, equivalency; balance, stability, level, identity, sameness, identicalness. **2.** average, normal, usual, standard, the norm.

parable *n.* allegory, story, tale, morality tale, fable, allegorical story, myth, legend, homily, apologue, folk story, folk tale.

parade *n.* **1.** procession, march, march past, review; cavalcade, caravan, motorcade, cortege, column, line, progression, train, string. **2.** show, display, array, exposition, demonstration, spectacle, flaunting, vaunting, ostentatious display; pageantry, pomp. **—*v.*** **3.** march in a procession, march; go in a column, defile. **4.** show off, make a show of, display, make a display of, vaunt, flaunt, strut, be ostentatious with; *Slang* grandstand, put on the ritz, put on airs, put on the dog. **—Ant. 2** suppression, hiding, concealing, masking, cloaking. **4** suppress, secrete, hide, conceal, mask, cloak, veil.

paradigm *n.* model, ideal, paragon, example, exemplar, pattern, matrix, standard, criterion, yardstick; prototype, archetype, original, sample.

paradise *n.* **1.** Eden, Garden of Eden; utopia, Shangri-la; happy valley, Land of Cockaigne; nirvana, heaven. **2.** delight, bliss, joy, enjoyment, ecstasy, rapture, transport, heaven, pleasure, happiness, satisfaction, gratification, seventh heaven. **—Ant. 2** misery, torment, hell, agony, torture, pain.

paradox *n.* self-contradiction, self-contradictory statement; seeming contradiction, incongruity, anomaly, inconsistency, oddity; enigma, puzzle, riddle, poser, seeming absurdity. **—Ant.** rule, axiom, maxim, truism, aphorism, proverb.

paragon *n.* model, example, exemplar, prototype, archetype, paradigm, apotheosis, idea, symbol, pattern, standard, norm, criterion, yardstick.

parallel *adj.* **1.** running side by side, coextensive, lying side by side, equidistant, concurrent, alongside, abreast. **2.** similar, like, alike, analogous, comparative, comparable, collateral, corresponding, akin, correlative; twin, equivalent. **—*n.*** **3.** comparison, analogy, likeness, correlation, identification, relation, connection, parallelism, correspondence, resemblance, similarity, coincidence. **4.** counterpart, equivalent, equal, corollary, match, correspondent, correlative, analogue, same, twin. **—*v.*** **5.** run parallel to, follow; run abreast of, keep pace with. **6.** be equivalent to, be similar to, be alike, compare with, be comparable to, correspond to, be analogous to, amount to the same thing, duplicate, equal, match. **—Ant. 1** nonparallel. **2** dissimilar, unlike, distinct, different, divergent, disparate. **3** dissimilarity, difference, divergence, unlikeness, disparity. **4** opposite, reverse, counter. **6** be dissimilar, be unlike, differ, diverge.

paralyze *v.* stun, immobilize, benumb, incapacitate, stupefy, petrify, disable, debilitate, cripple, disarm, weaken, enfeeble, freeze, deaden; destroy, demolish, wipe out, neutralize, bring to a halt.

paramount *adj.* main, chief, foremost, utmost, greatest, preeminent, highest, predominant, dominant, preponderant, supreme, leading, premier, principal, capital, essential, superior, peerless, leading, cardinal, outstanding, unmatched, incomparable, transcendent. **—Syn. Study.** See DOMINANT. **—Ant.** secondary, subordinate, least, smallest, negligible, insignificant, inconsequential, unimportant, slight, trifling, minor.

paramour *n.* lover; mistress, kept woman, girl friend, doxy, lady friend, inamorata, courtesan, concubine; boyfriend, man, fancy man, lover boy, gigolo, inamorato, sugar daddy, lothario, Romeo, Don Juan, Casanova.

paranoid *adj.* paranoiac, affected by paranoia; having a persecution complex, having delusions of grandeur; oversuspicious, excessively wary, unreasonably distrustful.

parapet *n.* defensive wall, breastwork, earthwork; rampart, bulwark, barricade, palisade, battlement, abutment.

paraphernalia *n.* equipment, gear, outfit, implements, accoutrements, rig, stuff, regalia, apparatus, supplies, things, provisions, trappings, accessories, utensils, tackle, harness, fittings, material; personal effects, effects, properties, belongings, furnishings.

paraphrase *v.* restate, reword, rephrase, state in other words, state in one's own words; recapitulate; *Slang* recap, rehash. **—Ant.** quote, state verbatim.

parasite *n.* **1.** living thing that nourishes itself on another organism. **2.** beggar, cadger, sponger, scrounger, freeloader, leech, bloodsucker; loafer, slacker, shirker, deadbeat, *Slang* goldbrick, moocher.

parcel *n.* **1.** package, packet, bundle, pack, bale. **2.** lot, tract, plot, piece of land, property. **3.** piece, part, portion, section, segment, division, fragment, fraction, allowance, allotment. **—*v.*** **4.** apportion, distribute, divide, allot, allocate, disperse, dispense, dole out, deal out, partition, carve up, split up. **—Ant. 3** entirety, whole. **4** collect, gather, amass, accumulate; combine, merge, pool.

parch *v.* dry out, dry up, desiccate, shrivel, sun-dry, evaporate, dehydrate; wither, scorch, char, burn, blister, sear, singe, bake. **—Ant.** wet, moisten, water, flood, inundate.

parchment *n.* sheepskin, goatskin, papyrus, vellum; scroll, polished brown paper, parchment paper.

pardon *n.* **1.** forgiveness, forbearance, indulgence; absolution, mercy, remission, deliverance, grace; release, exculpation, amnesty. *—v.* **2.** forgive, excuse, forbear, indulge; overlook, disregard, blink at, wink at, shrug off, forgive and forget, let bygones be bygones. **3.** absolve, vindicate, exonerate, exculpate, grant amnesty; remit the penalty of, reprieve, set free, release, discharge. **—Syn. Study. 1** PARDON, AMNESTY refer to the remission of a penalty or punishment for an offense; these terms do not imply absolution from guilt. A PARDON is often granted by a government official; it releases the individual from any punishment due: *The governor granted a pardon to the prisoner.* AMNESTY is usu. a general pardon granted to a group of persons for offenses against a government; it often includes an assurance of no further prosecution: *to grant amnesty to the rebels.* **2** See EXCUSE. **—Ant. 1** punishment, penalty, retaliation, retribution, vengeance, revenge, redress, reparation, condemnation, guilt. **2** punish; penalize, fine, discipline, correct. **3** condemn, doom, censure, blame, chasten, castigate, chastise, rebuke, admonish.

pare *v.* **1.** peel, skin, strip, trim, shuck, shell, hull, husk, decorticate. **2.** cut, cut down on, cut back, slash, shave, trim, prune, reduce, decrease, lessen, diminish, lower, curtail, shrink; crop, lop, dock, clip, shear. **—Ant. 2** increase, inflate, enlarge, advance, raise, elevate, boost, step up.

parent *n.* mother, father; dam, sire, begetter, procreator; creator, originator, producer; ancestor, progenitor, predecessor, precursor, forerunner, antecedent; prototype, original, model, exemplar.

parentage *n.* ancestry, antecedents, forbears, genealogy, ancestors; lineage, descent, heredity, origin, background, birth, extraction, strain, pedigree, derivation, family tree, roots.

parenthetical *adj.* in parentheses, bracketed, braced; incidental, interposed, inserted, intervening, aside, casual, extraneous, impertinent, irrelevant, immaterial, superfluous.

pariah *n.* outcast, undesirable, untouchable, exile, expatriate, man without a country, stray, vagabond, rover, roamer, wanderer; outlaw.

parish *n.* **1.** church district, archdiocese, diocese, shire, canton; district, precinct, section, county, province, department; community, neighborhood. **2.** congregation, parishioners, pastorate, fold, flock, church members, brethren.

park *n.* green, parkland, common, public park, sanctuary, woodland, grove, preserve, reserve, grassland, woods, picnic grounds; field, meadow, lawn, grounds, square, quadrangle.

parley *n.* discussion, conference, conclave, summit, meeting, council, exchange of views, talk, conversation, palaver, discourse, diplomatic consultation, *Slang* confab, powwow; peace talk, negotiation, arbitration, mediation.

parlor *n.* sitting room, front room, living room, drawing room, salon, reception room, saloon, best room.

parochial *adj.* **1.** parish, church, religious. **2.** local, regional, sectional, provincial, insular, countrified, small-town; narrow-minded, limited, narrow, restricted, petty, small, little, illiberal, hidebound. **—Ant. 1** public; lay. **2** international, worldwide, universal, national; sophisticated, cosmopolitan; broad-minded, open-minded, liberal.

parody *n.* **1.** burlesque, takeoff, ludicrous imitation, caricature, lampoon, satire, travesty. *—v.* **2.** burlesque, caricature, mimic, lampoon, satirize, travesty, *Informal* take off on. **—Syn. Study. 1** See BURLESQUE.

parrot *n.* **1.** tropical bird of the *Psittaciformes* order; (*variously*) macaw, cockatoo, lory, parakeet. **2.** mimic, mimer, imitator, *Slang* copycat; monkey, ape. *—v.* **3.** repeat mindlessly, echo, reiterate, chorus; imitate, mimic, ape.

parry *v.* fend off, ward off, repulse, stave off, repel, beat off; dodge, shun, avoid, elude, avert, sidestep, duck, circumvent, fight shy of, keep at a distance. **—Ant.** receive, take, welcome, face, confront, meet.

parsimonious *adj.* frugal, saving, thrifty, economical, sparing, penny-pinching; miserly, penurious, tight, tight-fisted, close, closefisted, niggardly, ungenerous, stingy, money-grubbing. **—Syn. Study.** See STINGY. **—Ant.** extravagant, spendthrift, wasteful; lavish, liberal, munificent, generous, open-handed.

part *n.* **1.** section, portion, division, subdivision, sector, branch, department, unit, component, element, member, constituent, ingredient, region; piece, segment, fragment, fraction, scrap, shred, bit, sliver, chip, shard, sherd, snippet, cutting, slice, crumb, morsel, *Slang* hunk; item, detail. **2.** role, character; impersonation, personification, guise, disguise. **3.** role, function, capacity, share, concern, charge, care, place, business, assignment, job, chore, task, duty. *—v.* **4.** separate, disengage, open, disunite, divide; detach, disconnect, disjoin, break apart, split, slit, sunder, sever, rend, tear, tear assunder; cleave, break. **5.** depart, go, go away, leave, take one's leave, go one's way, set forth, set out, start out, take one's farewell, say goodbye, tear oneself away, get up and go, be on one's way; *Slang* mosey along, push off; end a relationship, break off, call it quits. **—Ant. 1** whole, entirety, totality; mass, bulk, quantity. **4** unite, combine, join, close; hold, cling, stick, adhere. **5** arrive, come, appear; stay, remain, abide, tarry, linger.

partake *v.* share, take part, share in, enjoy, savor, sample; participate, engage in, join in, play a part in. **—Ant.** be excluded; abstain, forswear, forbear, forgo, refrain from, refuse, decline, eschew, relinquish, set out, pass up.

partial *adj.* **1.** incomplete, fractional, limited, fragmentary, unfinished, uncompleted, inconclusive. **2.** partisan, factional, biased, prejudiced, predisposed, slanted, prepossessed, subjective, one-sided, unbalanced, interested; unjust, unfair, inequitable. **—Ant. 1** complete, entire, whole, total, full, final, finished. **2** impartial, unbiased, objective, balanced, disinterested, unprejudiced, equitable.

partiality *n.* **1.** bias, prejudice, tilt, predisposition, slant, predilection, one-sidedness, partisanship, favoritism. **2.** fondness, liking, inclination, predisposition, predilection, weakness, love, taste, affinity, propensity, penchant, fancy, bent, leaning, tendency, attraction, proclivity; choice, preference. **—Ant. 1** impartiality, evenhandedness, objectivity, disinterest; justice, fairness. **2** dislike, disinclination, distaste, disgust, abhorrence, aversion, loathing, revulsion, detestation, antipathy.

partially *adv.* partly, in part, partway, incompletely, fractionally, piecemeal, somewhat. **—Ant.** all, completely, entirely, wholly, totally.

participant *n.* participator, partaker, member, partner, party, sharer, helper, worker, contributor, shareholder, colleague, fellow, associate, confrere; accomplice, accessory.

participate *v.* take part, engage in, join in, be a participant, perform, play a part, partake, share, form a part of, *Slang* have a finger in. **—Ant.** be excluded; abstain, forswear, forgo, forbear, refrain from, eschew, sit out, pass up.

particle *n.* small piece, small fragment, bit, speck, grain, shred, scrap, crumb, smidgen, morsel, granule, jot, iota, atom; trifle, trace, snippet, snip, whit, tittle, scintilla, modicum, mite.

particular *adj.* **1.** specific, exact, explicit, express, special, especial, fixed, concrete, individual; definite, well-defined, distinct, single, personal, separate, sole, particularized, itemized, detailed. **2.** hard to please, critical, demanding, exacting, picky, fussy, finicky, *Slang* persnickety; strict, fastidious, meticulous, painstaking, scrupulous, punctilious. **—*n.* 3.** Usu. **particulars.** detail, specific, item, fact, circumstance, event. **—Ant. 1** general, universal; vague, unspecified, indefinite, undefined, impersonal. **2** easy to please, uncritical, undemanding, indifferent, heedless, inattentive; careless, slipshod, slapdash, haphazard, sloppy, inexact, carefree.

particularly *adv.* **1.** especially, exceptionally, unusually, extraordinarily, strikingly, markedly, notably, eminently, supremely, prominently; mainly, principally. **2.** in particular, explicitly, expressly, especially, specially, definitely, distinctly.

partisan *n.* **1.** supporter, follower, adherent, sympathizer, champion, advocate, ally, backer, upholder, enthusiast, fan, zealot, devotee, rooter, booster. **2.** freedom fighter, guerrilla, irregular, insurgent; (*U.S. Civil War*) bushwhacker, jayhawker. **—*adj.* 3.** favoring one political party, predisposed toward one group, favoring a cause, partial, biased, prejudiced, one-sided, slanted, unbalanced, subjective. **—Syn. Study. 1** See FOLLOWER. **—Ant. 1** detractor, defamer, censor, critic, backbiter, knocker; opponent, foe, adversary, rival, contender. **3** nonpartisan, bipartisan, unbiased, impartial, unprejudiced, disinterested, objective, broad-minded, open-minded.

partition *n.* **1.** division, dividing, separation, severance, splitting, parting; distribution, apportionment, allotment, allocation, assignment, demarcation, segregation. **2.** dividing wall, nonsupporting wall, wall, divider, separator, panel, screen, barrier, fence, *Nautical* bulkhead. **—*v.* 3.** divide, subdivide, separate, split up; distribute, disperse, dispense, apportion, allot, allocate, assign, parcel out, deal out, mete out.

partly *adv.* partially, in part, part way, fractionally, to a degree, in some measure, somewhat, incompletely, not wholly, to a limited extent; comparatively, relatively, in a manner of speaking, after a fashion. **—Ant.** fully, wholly, completely, entirely, totally.

partner *n.* **1.** joint owner, co-owner, copartner; associate, colleague, fellow worker, confrere, collaborator, accomplice, confederate, teammate, assistant, helper, aid, aider; accessory; friend, fellow, comrade, ally, confrere, companion, buddy, chum, sidekick, pal, mate; sharer, partaker, participant. **2.** spouse, mate, helpmate; husband; wife, better half.

party *n.* **1.** social function, social gathering, gathering of friends, gathering, celebration, festivity, fete, get-together, affair, reception, at-home, soiree, *Slang* bash, blowout, do, wing-ding. **2.** alliance, federation, confederacy, league, coalition, conclave, faction, wing, coterie; group, crew, team, band, body, company, squad, corps, unit, force, gang. **3.** participant, participator, perpetrator, (*legal use*) participant in a lawsuit, (*variously*) contestant, litigant, petitioner, plaintiff, claimant, accused, defendant, appellant, respondent.

pass *v.* **1.** go by, go on, go past, go beyond, go ahead, go onward, move onward, progress, proceed. **2.** go, go by, go away, elapse, glide by, slide by, slip by, flow, proceed, progress; pass away, be over, end, terminate, expire, die away, die, fade away, melt away, blow over, peter out, run its course, vanish, disappear, dissolve, evaporate, depart, leave. **3.** spend, expend, use, consume, employ, engage, busy, occupy, fill, take up, devote. **4.** surpass, exceed, go by, go beyond, go ahead, best, excel, outshine, eclipse, overshadow, outstrip, outdo, top, cap. **5.** receive a satisfactory grade in, complete successfully, satisfy, qualify, meet, get through, achieve, accomplish, finish, come up to scratch, stand the test, meet the standard of. **6.** exact, legislate, establish by law, vote approval on, approve, ratify, authorize, sanction, decree, ordain, legalize, accept; affirm, confirm. **7.** hand, hand over, hand along, give, present, turn over, let have, convey, transfer, transmit, deliver, throw, toss, hit, kick. —*n.* **8.** mountain pass, gap, gorge, canyon, ravine, gulch; passageway, pathway, trail, way, lane, course, route, avenue; channel, narrows, canal. **9.** permission to be absent, permission to leave, furlough; free ticket, complimentary ticket, *Slang* freebie, Annie Oakley; right of passage, permit, authorization. **10.** state of affairs, situation, juncture, predicament, complication, difficulty, exigency, plight, juncture, strait, extremity, quandary, *Slang* pickle. **—Ant. 1, 2** stop, halt, cease, standstill, pause, wait; withdraw, retreat. **2** begin, start, commence; continue. **3** waste, squander. **4** fall behind, falter, drag, pull back. **5** fail, flunk. **6** vote down, defeat, reject, veto; disapprove. **7** hold, keep, retain. **8** peak, summit; barrier, obstacle.

passable *adj.* **1.** traversable, fit for travel, clear, open, unobstructed; crossable, navigable, fordable. **2.** presentable, respectable, allowable, acceptable, pretty good, adequate, not bad, so-so, better than nothing, fair, admissible, middling, mediocre, tolerable. **—Ant. 1** impassable, impenetrable, closed, blocked, obstructed. **2** inadequate, unacceptable, insufficient; exceptional, extraordinary, unusual, uncommon.

passage *n.* **1.** section, portion, piece, selection; clause, paragraph, sentence, column, verse, chapter. **2.** progression, passing, movement; trip, journey, voyage, excursion, expedition, tour, junket, trek, transit; right to pass; cost of ship transportation, ship's fare. **3.** passing into law, enactment, legislation, ratification, approval, authorization, ordainment, legalization, sanction, endorsement, acceptance; affirmation, confirmation. **4.** pass, passageway, way, course, route, path, road, corridor, hallway, hall, aisle, tunnel, canal, channel; access, approach, right of access. **—Ant. 3** veto, defeat, rejection, voting down. **4** barrier, obstacle, obstruction.

passageway *n.* corridor, hallway, hall, arcade, passage, aisle, tunnel; access, entrance, entryway, exit, doorway, gateway; path, walk, sidewalk, lane, *Nautical* gangway, companionway.

passé *adj.* out of fashion, old-fashioned, out-of-date, outdated, outmoded, démodé, antiquated, antediluvian, superannuated, quaint; ancient, antique, archaic, obsolete, stale, hoary, *Slang* prehistoric; lapsed, disused, retired, outworn, faded, past. **—Ant.** modern, new, novel, current, up-to-date, newfashioned, newfangled, *Slang* mod, hip, with-it, *French* au courant, á la page, dans le vent.

passion *n.* **1.** emotion, feeling, warmth, heart, ardor, fervor, fire, intensity, sentiment, rapture, transport, ecstasy, intoxication, enthusiasm, earnestness, gusto, eagerness, vehemence. **2.** lust, sexual desire, sexual appetite, carnality, carnal love, fleshly desire; amorousness, love. **3.** obsession, craze, mania, fancy, rage, craving, urge, desire, hunger, thirst; idol, beloved, loved one, infatuation, flame, inamorata. **—Syn. Study. 1** See FEELING. **—Ant. 1** apathy, indifference, coldness, coolness, frigidity, unconcern.

passionate *adj.* impassioned, fervent, fervid, ardent, emotional, earnest, intense, fiery, fierce, furious, raging, tempestuous, excited, wrought-up, inflamed, feeling, heartfelt, enthusiastic, hot, heated, vehement, intoxicating, ecstatic; loving, amorous, desirous, lustful, sensuous, carnal, erotic, *Slang* sexy. **—Ant.** dispassionate, cold, cool, apathetic, passive, lethargic, indifferent; calm, soothing.

passive *adj.* submissive, inactive, unassertive, apathetic, impassive, compliant, acquiescent, yielding, inert, quiescent, docile, pliable, tractable, lifeless, spiritless, listless, dormant, nonresistant, unresisting; patient, resigned, enduring. —**Ant.** active, domineering, dominant, forceful, aggressive, assertive, dynamic, energetic, alive, alert.

password *n.* watchword, keyword, shibboleth, *French* passe-parole, word, countersign; key, tessera, open sesame, catchword.

past *adj.* **1.** gone by, passed away; elapsed, expired, ended, finished, gone, departed, dead and gone; belonging to the past, bygone, ancient, historical, former, previous, earlier, prior. —*n.* **2.** days gone by, days of yore, days of old, yesteryear, former times, previous times, times gone by, long ago, ancient times, olden times, antiquity, ancient history, history, events gone by. —*adv.* **3.** by, across one's field of vision; beyond, through. —**Ant. 1** future, coming, later; present, now, begun, started, arrived. **2** future, time to come, days to come, tomorrow; present, today, now, this day and age.

pastel *n.* **1.** coloring stick; (*loosely*) coloring pencil, chalk, crayon. —*adj.* **2.** pale, faint, soft, light, muted, dim, washed-out, faded. —**Ant. 2** bright, deep, dark, strong, vibrant.

pastime *n.* diversion, hobby, avocation, spare-time activity, relaxation, distraction, amusement, divertissement, entertainment, fun, play, sport, game. —**Ant.** business, work, occupation, calling, employment, profession, job, chore, labor.

pastor *n.* minister, priest, cleric, preacher, parson, rector, clergyman, vicar, dean, curé; padre, father, chaplain.

pastoral *adj.* **1.** bucolic, rustic, rural, portraying country life, depicting the life of shepherds; arcadian, idyllic. **2.** ministerial, ecclesiastical, clerical; priestly, episcopal, sacerdotal. —**Ant. 1** worldly, sophisticated, cosmopolitan; urban, urbanized, city, citified, metropolitan. **2** secular, lay.

pasty *adj.* **1.** like paste, gluey, mucilaginous, gummy, sticky, doughy; starchy, glutinous, *Slang* gooey. **2.** pale, ashen, ashy, wan, sallow, colorless, pallid, chalky, white, peaked, anemic, bloodless, ghostlike, deathly, gray. —**Ant. 1** dry, powdery. **2** ruddy, rosy, florid, rosy-cheeked, rubicund.

pat *v.* **1.** pet, stroke, caress, fondle. —*n.* **2.** light blow, gentle stroke, tap, small spank; hit, thwack, slap, thump, rap. **3.** little slab, small square, cake, dab, daub. —*adj.* **4.** contrived, rehearsed, glib, facile, ready, easy, slick, smooth, flippant. **5.** perfect, ideal, exact, precise; appropriate, relevant, fitting, pertinent, suitable, apt, apropos, easy, simple; satisfactory. —**Ant. 4** impromptu, spontaneous; sincere, well-considered, thoughtful, serious. **5** imperfect, inexact; irrelevant, unsuitable; difficult; unsatisfactory.

patch *n.* **1.** mend, repair, small piece of material sewn on, reinforcement; insignia. **2.** plot, garden, tract, lot, field, clearing; area, spot, stretch, expanse, zone. —*v.* **3.** mend, cover with a patch, repair, fix, darn, stitch, sew up, reinforce.

patchwork *n.* jumble, medley, potpourri, pastiche, mélange, miscellany, omnium-gatherum, scramble, hodgepodge, conglomeration, mixture, muddle, tangle, hash, mess, gallimaufry, salmagundi, confusion, mishmash; *Slang* grab bag, mixed bag.

patent *n.* **1.** government registration of an invention, certificate of invention, inventor's exclusive rights; registry, license, permit. —*adj.* **2.** protected by patent, trademarked, copyrighted, copyright; nonprescription, needing no prescription. **3.** obvious, manifest, evident, self-evident, apparent, open, plain, overt, transparent, express, palpable, decided, indubitable, downright, unreserved, glaring, unmistakable, pronounced, conspicuous, striking, rank, flagrant, bold, glaring, gross, prominent, clear, distinct, bald, undisguised, unconcealed, *Informal* plain as the nose on one's face. —*v.* **4.** obtain a patent for, register as an original invention, obtain an inventor's exclusive rights to. —**Ant. 2** unpatented. **3** imperceptible, subtle, hidden, concealed, disguised, questionable, dubious, equivocal, ambiguous, vague.

paternal *adj.* fatherly, fatherlike, of a father, from the father's side of the family, patriarchal; of a parent, parental, tender, kind, indulgent, benevolent, solicitous; concerned, interested, watchful, vigilant.

path *n.* walk, lane, pathway, trail, walkway, footpath, bypath; course, route, track, way, process, plan, approach, means.

pathetic *adj.* pitiful, moving, affecting, touching, poignant, plaintive, distressing, arousing sympathy, calling forth compassion; to be pitied, piteous, pitiable, lamentable, sorrowful, rueful, sad, doleful, dolorous, miserable, woeful, wretched, deplorable, grievous. —**Ant.** amusing, funny, laughable, comical, humorous, ludicrous, ridiculous, droll, entertaining.

pathos *n.* pathetic quality, power to affect, ability to touch, ability to arouse sympathy, poignancy, plaintiveness, sadness, feeling, sentiment, sentimentalism, sentimentality, pitiableness, anguish, heartache, agony, misery, distress, woe, desolation. **—Ant.** comicality, amusement, humor, fun.

patience *n.* **1.** calm endurance, forbearance, uncomplaining nature, sufferance, tolerance, restraint, long-suffering, imperturbability, equanimity, longanimity, fortitude; composure, self-control, poise. **2.** persistence, perseverance, diligence, application, tenacity, determination, resolution, indefatigableness, tirelessness, stamina, industry, stick-to-itiveness. **—Ant. 1, 2** impatience. **1** restlessness, exasperation, fretfulness, agitation, irritation, nervousness, peevishness, passion, frenzy. **2** vacillation, irresolution.

patient *n.* **1.** person under medical care, case; sick person. *—adj.* **2.** persevering, enduring, long-suffering, uncomplaining, forbearing, unperturbed, serene, composed; persistent; persevering, diligent, determined, tenacious, resolute, tireless, indefatigable, industrious, unflagging, unfaltering, unwavering, unswerving, undaunted, dogged, dauntless.

patio *n.* terrace, porch, veranda, piazza, deck, *Hawaiian* lanai.

patrician *n.* **1.** aristocrat, noble, nobleman, peer, lord, silk-stocking, blueblood, gentleman. *—adj.* **2.** aristocratic, noble, lordly, princely, imposing, stately, dignified, genteel, well-bred, upper-class, highborn. **—Ant. 1** peasant, commoner, working man, member of the proletariat, hoi polloi. **2** peasant, plebeian, common, vulgar, ignoble, proletarian, working-class, lower-class, lowborn; bourgeois, middle-class, lowbrow, philistine.

patrimony *n.* inheritance, estate, legacy, endowment, bequeathal; *Law* devise, jointure, dower, hereditament; birthright, portion, share, lot; legacy, bestowal, heritage.

patron *n.* **1.** customer, client, buyer, shopper; frequenter, habitué, visitor; spectator, attender. **2.** sponsor, supporter, backer, benefactor, (*fem.*) benefactress, financer, promoter, philanthropist, *Slang* angel; protector, defender, advocate, champion, upholder, encourager, helper, sympathizer, well-wisher, friend. **—Ant. 1** employee. **2** protégé, (*fem.*) protégée, ward.

patronage *n.* **1.** business, trade, buying, purchasing, commerce, custom, dealing; clientele, customers, patrons, clients. **2.** financial support, support, sponsorship, charity, benefaction, philanthropy, backing, help, aid, assistance, favor; auspices, protection, advocacy, encouragement, fosterage, friendship. **3.** political favors, political appointments, spoils, government contracts, *Slang* pork barrel, plums.

patronize *v.* **1.** do business with, trade with, deal with, shop at, buy from, frequent, be a habitué of, be a client of. **2.** treat in a condescending way, condescend, act superior toward, assume a lofty attitude toward, act disdainfully toward, indulge unnecessarily, humor. **—Ant. 2** flatter, toady to, be subservient to.

patter *v.* **1.** pat, beat, pound, tap, rap, drum, thrum, pad, go pitter-patter; tattoo, spatter, sprinkle. *—n.* **2.** pattering, pitter-patter, rat-a-tat, tattoo, pad, pat, tap, tapping, drumming; beat, palpitation.

pattern *n.* **1.** design, decorative design, motif; form, shape. **2.** guide, design, plan, draft, model; original, archetype, prototype, stereotype; standard, criterion, example, paradigm, exemplar, sample, specimen, illustration, ideal, apotheosis, paragon. *—v.* **3.** model, fashion, shape, mold, make resemble, form; imitate, emulate, copy, mimic, follow, simulate, parallel, duplicate.

paucity *n.* scarcity, dearth, lack, shortage, scarceness, scantiness, deficiency, poverty, sparsity, meagerness, puniness, thinness, poorness, insufficiency. **—Ant.** surfeit, overflow, excess, surplus, superabundance.

paunch *n.* **1.** stomach, abdomen, midsection, *Informal* tummy. **2.** potbelly, belly, bay window, breadbasket, gut, pot, corporation, spare tire, beer belly.

pauper *n.* poor person, indigent, down-and-outer, bankrupt, insolvent; charity case, beggar, starveling, almsman, mendicant. **—Ant.** rich man, millionaire, magnate, tycoon, Midas.

pause *n.* **1.** stop, halt, rest, break, cessation, interval, hiatus, time out, letup, gap, suspension, discontinuance, interlude, intermission, interim, interruption. *—v.* **2.** stop briefly, halt, cease, rest, let up, take time out, break off; hesitate, wait, delay, deliberate. **—Ant. 1** continuity, continuation, progress, progression, advancement. **2** continue, proceed, progress, advance.

pave *v.* surface, resurface, face; cement, tar, asphalt, black top, macadamize.

pavilion *n.* **1.** tent, tentlike building, light open structure, temporary building; exhibition hall, exposition building; (*variously*) summerhouse, gazebo, pergola, arbor, kiosk, bandshell. **2.** hospital building, hospital section, ward, wing.

pawn[1] *v.* **1.** give as security, pledge, raise money on, borrow on, *Slang* hock. *—n.* **2.** security, pledge, assurance, bond, guarantee, guaranty. **—Ant. 1** redeem, take out of hock.

pawn[2] *n.* instrument, agent, puppet, tool, creature, dupe, cat's-paw; lackey, flunky, underling, hireling, henchman; *Slang* patsy. **—Ant.** leader, chief, head, boss, *Slang* kingpin.

pay *v.* **1.** give money owed to, give money for; pay in full, remit, settle, square accounts, foot, honor, meet, liquidate, make good on, *Informal* plunk down one's money for; *Slang* shell out, come across, cough up, ante up, chip in. **2.** be advantageous, be worthwhile, be useful, benefit, compensate, repay, serve, bear fruit, be a good investment, stand one in good stead. **3.** offer as remuneration, offer as compensation, offer as wages, bring in, reimburse; profit, yield, return, be a good investment. **4.** give, grant, render, extend, proffer, present. **—*n.*** **5.** wages, salary, earnings, paycheck, income; compensation, recompense, fee, payment, reimbursement, stipend. **—Ant. 1** collect, receive; owe, be in debt. **2** be disadvantageous, be worthless, be useless, be futile. **3** charge, cost. **4** withhold, retain, suppress, repress; receive.

payable *adj.* due, owed, owing, unpaid, outstanding, mature, demandable, receivable, in arrears.

payment *n.* **1.** paying, remittance, settlement, liquidation, defrayal, discharge, outlay, expenditure, disbursement, debt, spending. **2.** installment, partial payment, remittance, premium; remuneration, compensation, recompense, reimbursement, fee, pay, salary, allowance, contribution. **—Ant. 1** nonpayment, nonremittance; income, profit, return, credit.

payoff *n.* **1.** clincher, outcome, climax, windup, upshot, result, finish, end, culmination, denouement, finale, resolution, conclusion; *Slang* crunch, bottom line. **2.** bribe, protection, hush money, graft; *Slang* payola, grease, soap.

peace *n.* **1.** harmony, accord, concord, amity, entente, agreement, pacification, reconciliation, armistice, truce. **2.** calm, serenity, tranquillity, ease, repose, placidity, content, composure. **—Ant. 1** conflict, war, hostilities, belligerence. **2** turmoil, agitation, tumult, disorder, chaos.

peaceful *adj.* **1.** free from war, nonwarring, peacetime; peaceable, peace-loving, inclined toward peace, pacific, pacifistic, nonbelligerent. **2.** amicable, friendly, without violence, nonviolent, without hostility, free from strife, harmonious, agreeable. **3.** quiet, still, silent, placid, serene, tranquil, restful, calm, undisturbed, untroubled. **—Syn. Study. 3** PEACEFUL, PLACID, SERENE, TRANQUIL refer to what is characterized by lack of strife or agitation. PEACEFUL, although it can be applied to persons, generally refers to situations, scenes, and activities free of disturbances or, occasionally, of warfare: *a peaceful afternoon; a peaceful protest.* PLACID, SERENE, TRANQUIL are used mainly of persons; when used of things (usu. elements of nature) there is a touch of personification. PLACID suggests an unruffled calm that verges on complacency: *a placid disposition; a placid stream.* SERENE is a somewhat nobler word; when used of persons it suggests dignity, composure, and graciousness; when applied to nature there is a suggestion of mellowness: *a serene summer landscape.* TRANQUIL implies a command of emotions that keeps one unagitated even in the midst of excitement or danger: *She remained tranquil despite the chaos around her.* **—Ant. 1** warring, wartime; belligerent, bellicose, hostile, warlike. **2** violent, hostile, strife-torn, bitter, antagonistic, angry, unfriendly. **3** noisy, loud, raucous, tumultuous; disturbed, perturbed, disquieted, agitated, upset.

peacemaker *n.* conciliator, intermediary, diplomat, ambassador, negotiator, mediator, go-between, pacificator, placater, arbitrator, adjudicator; peacekeeper, peacemonger.

peak *n.* **1.** summit, pinnacle, tip, top, apex, crown, crest; apogee. **2.** culmination, climax, maximum point, highest degree, acme, prime, zenith, crest, flood. **—*v.*** **3.** reach a maximum, crest, climax, culminate. **—Ant. 1** base, bottom, foot, foundation. **2** nadir.

peaked[1] *adj.* with a peak, pointed, pointy, spiked, tapered; spiny, spiky.

peaked[2] *adj.* pale, pallid, wan, sallow, ashen, white; sickly, ailing, ill, weak, infirm, debilitated, wizened; thin, lean, spare, skinny, scrawny, gaunt, emaciated, shriveled, pinched, haggard, drawn. **—Ant.** hearty, hale, hale and hearty, healthy; robust, hardy, sturdy, husky, strapping, brawny; ruddy, rosy-cheeked, florid, flushed, blushing.

peal *n.* **1.** ringing, ring, reverberation, resounding, clang, clangor, toll, knell, din, tintinnabulation; clap, crash, crack, roar, blare, boom, blast, rumble, roll. **—*v.*** **2.** ring, reverberate, resound, clang, toll, knell, tintinnabulate; crash, crack, roar, blare, boom, blast, rumble, roll.

peccadillo *n.* misdemeanor, misdeed, lapse, slip, misconduct, misstep, petty sin, transgression, wrongdoing, trespass, wrong step, false move; faux pas, blunder, *Slang* boo-boo.

peck[1] *v.* **1.** strike with the beak, bore with the beak, pick up with the beak; tap, strike, thump, pat. **2.** pick at, nibble, snack. **—*n.*** **3.** light kiss, absent-minded kiss, *Slang* buss, smack; tap, rap, stroke, light jab. **—Ant. 2** devour, gobble, wolf down, gulp, bolt.

peck² *n.* **1.** a quarter of a bushel, the amount of eight quarts. **2.** a great deal, a considerable quantity, lots, heaps, worlds, a slew, stack, scads, gobs, oodles, mess, bunch, batch, abundance. **—Ant. 2** little, drop, crumb, grain.

peculiar *adj.* **1.** particular, individual, distinctive, distinct, distinguishing, characteristic, typical, representative, unique, singular, exclusive, private, personal, special, specific. **2.** odd, queer, strange, unusual, abnormal, curious, quaint, outlandish, unconventional, freakish, weird; eccentric, bizarre, idiosyncratic, erratic, capricious, whimsical, *Slang* far-out. **—Ant. 1** common, general, unspecific, universal, indistinctive. **2** commonplace, usual, ordinary, expected, conventional, familiar, everyday.

peculiarity *n.* **1.** feature, trait, distinguishing quality, attribute, uniqueness, characteristic, quality, singularity, particularity, distinction, mark, badge, stamp. **2.** eccentricity, idiosyncrasy, quirk, odd trait, oddity; freakishness, strangeness, unnaturalness, weirdness, queerness, bizarreness, erraticism; abnormality. **—Syn. Study. 1** See FEATURE. **2** See IDIOSYNCRASY. **—Ant. 1** universality, common quality, general thing. **2** conventionality, normalcy.

pecuniary *adj.* **—Syn. Study.** See MONETARY.

pedagogic *adj.* educational, tutorial, professorial, scholarly, instructional, academic; bookish, pedantic, didactic, donnish.

pedagogue Also **pedagog** *n.* teacher, schoolteacher, schoolmaster, schoolmistress, schoolmarm, educator, educationist, tutor, instructor, professor, academic.

pedant *n.* ostentatious man of learning; bookworm, plodding scholar, doctrinaire scholar; methodologist, purist, dogmatist.

pedantic *adj.* ostentatiously learned, pompous, academic, scholastic, didactic, doctrinaire, bookish, stilted, dogmatic, punctilious, hairsplitting, nitpicking, overly meticulous, fussy, finicky, overparticular. **—Ant.** succinct, pithy, straightforward; vague; general, comprehensive.

peddle *v.* hawk, vend, sell, retail, carry about for sale; dispense, deal out, dispose of. **—Ant.** buy, purchase, get, obtain, acquire.

pedestrian *n.* **1.** walker, traveler afoot, foot-traveler, stroller, *Informal* trekker. *—adj.* **2.** for pedestrians, for walking; ambulatory, perambulatory, perambulating; peripatetic, itinerant. **3.** unimaginative, mediocre, commonplace, ordinary, prosaic, mundane, run-of-the-mill, tedious, unexciting, unimportant, inconsequential, insignificant, mediocre. **—Ant. 1** driver, vehicle. **2** vehicular, for vehicles. **3** imaginative, exciting, interesting, intriguing, fascinating, compelling; important, significant, consequential, outstanding, remarkable, noteworthy.

pedigree *n.* record of ancestry, official record of descent, family tree, genealogy, genealogical table; line of descent, descent, lineage, ancestry, family, parentage, line, bloodline, derivation, extraction, strain. **—Syn. Study.** PEDIGREE, GENEALOGY refer to an account of ancestry. A PEDIGREE is a table or chart recording a line of ancestors, either of persons or (more commonly) of animals, as horses, cattle, and dogs; in the case of animals, such a table is used as proof of superior qualities: *a detailed pedigree.* A GENEALOGY is an account of the descent of a person or family traced through a series of generations, usu. from the first known ancestor: *a genealogy that includes a king.*

peep¹ *v.* **1.** peek, look surreptitiously, steal a look, look from hiding; peer, give a quick look, give a cursory look, glimpse, skim. **2.** peer out, come partially into view, begin to appear, emerge, come forth. *—n.* **3.** quick look, glimpse, glance, peek. **—Ant. 1** scrutinize, inspect, examine, observe, contemplate; stare. **2** disappear, submerge, hide. **3** good look, examination, inspection.

peep² *n.* **1.** peeping, cheep, chirp, tweet, twitter, chirrup, squeak; word, whisper, mutter, whimper, murmur. *—v.* **2.** cheep, chirp, chirrup, tweet, twitter, squeak.

peer¹ *v.* **1.** look, gaze, stare, gape, peep, peek, squint. **2.** appear, come into view, emerge, become visible.

peer² *n.* **1.** equal, compeer; fellow citizen. **2.** nobleman, noble, lord; aristocrat, gentleman, patrician, blue blood.

peerless *adj.* unsurpassed, matchless, unmatched, unexcelled, unequaled, incomparable, unrivaled, inimitable; superlative, surpassing, supreme, consummate, preeminent, transcendent; faultless, flawless. **—Ant.** commonplace, ordinary, mediocre, routine, indifferent, pedestrian; inferior, poor, second-rate.

peeve *v.* **1.** annoy, provoke, gall, irritate, chafe, exasperate, irk, vex, nettle, aggravate, rile, fret, perturb, *Slang* eat at, eat, gnaw at, gripe, bug, frost, give one a pain, give one a pain in the neck. *—n.* **2.** dislike, aggravation, annoyance, irritation, vexation, exasperation, provocation, complaint, grievance, gripe, *Informal* thorn in the side, pain in the neck. **—Ant. 1** please, delight, charm, enchant, captivate, enrapture. **2** pleasure, delight, like.

peevish *adj.* cross, irritable, testy, grumpy, grouchy, ill-humored, sulky, petulant, surly, snappish, fractious, cantankerous, cranky, crabby, churlish, huffy, pettish; mean, ill-natured, ill-tempered, bad-tempered, splenetic, quarrelsome, querulous. **—Ant.** agreeable, easygoing, good-natured, affable, pleasant, genial, amiable.

peg *n.* pin, spike, skewer, nail, toggle; cleat, fastener, thole, dowel, tholepin.

pejorative *adj.* belittling, disparaging, uncomplimentary, deprecatory, detracting, derogatory, scornful, negative, depreciatory, slighting, demeaning, unpleasant, downgrading, mocking, degrading, debasing, ridiculing, disdainful, contemptuous, disapproving. **—Ant.** complimentary, approving, praising, favorable, commendatory.

pellet *n.* ball, drop, bead, sphere, pearl, globule, marble, pea, pill; pebble, stone.

pell-mell *adv.* helter-skelter, slapdash, recklessly, posthaste, impetuously, rashly, hastily, precipitately, hurry-scurry, hurriedly, heedlessly, thoughtlessly, carelessly, incautiously, imprudently, *Slang* at half cock. **—Ant.** orderly, neatly, methodically; calmly, serenely.

pelt[1] *v.* hit, strike, batter, pummel, pound, punch, buffet, whack, thwack, thrash, rap, pepper; *Slang* clobber, sock, belt.

pelt[2] *n.* animal skin, skin, hide, fur; coat, fleece.

pen[1] *n.* enclosure, fold, pound, corral, paddock, compound, stockade; cage, coop, sty, crib, hutch, stall.

pen[2] *n.* **1.** fountain pen, quill; ballpoint pen. *—v.* **2.** write, write in ink, write by hand, scribble, scrawl, pencil; compose, draft.

penal *adj.* of punishment, disciplinary, punitive, corrective, penalizing, punishing, castigatory, retributive; of jails, of prisoners.

penalty *n.* punishment, forfeiture, retribution, infliction, assessment, suffering; fine, forfeit, handicap, disadvantage. **—Ant.** reward, prize.

penance *n.* repentance, expiation, atonement, contrition, mortification, penitence, propitiation; self-flagellation, sackcloth and ashes, hair shirt.

penchant *n.* fondness, partiality, liking, strong inclination, fancy, preference, predilection, proclivity, propensity, leaning, attraction, taste, relish, tendency, affinity, predisposition, disposition, proneness, prejudice, bias; flair, bent, readiness, turn, knack, gift. **—Ant.** hatred, dislike, loathing, aversion, abhorrence, disinclination, repulsion.

pendent Also **pendant** *adj.* **1.** hanging, suspended, dangling, pendulous, pensile, swinging. **2.** jutting, overhanging, protruding, extending, protuberant, sticking out, projecting.

pending *adj.* awaiting decision, awaiting settlement, undetermined, undecided, unsettled, unresolved, unfinished, up in the air, in suspense; imminent, in the offing.

pendulous *adj.* hanging, suspended, dangling, pendent, swinging, pensile; drooping, sagging.

penetrate *v.* **1.** pierce, puncture, cut into, bore, prick, perforate; cut through, pass through, traverse. **2.** pervade, permeate, saturate, impregnate, seep in; enter, invade, infiltrate. **3.** understand, comprehend, perceive, discern, fathom, get, get to the bottom of, figure out, unravel, see through, catch; decode, decipher. **—Syn. Study. 1** See PIERCE. **—Ant. 1** ricochet, carom, rebound, glance off.

penetrating *adj.* **1.** piercing, sharp, stinging, caustic, biting, acrid, strong, pungent, harsh, reeking; heady, redolent; pervading, pervasive, permeating, saturating. **2.** keen, sharp, sharp-witted, perceptive, discerning, thoughtful, perspicacious, shrewd, astute, intelligent, smart, clever, percipient, trenchant; alive, alert, aware. **—Ant. 1** mild, sweet. **2** obtuse, unperceptive, uncomprehending, thoughtless, shallow, dull, stupid, dumb; indifferent, apathetic.

penetration *n.* **1.** power of penetrating, foray, passage, invasion, intrusion, infusion, access; perforation, piercing, boring, puncturing. **2.** insight, keenness, sharpness, perception, discernment, perspicacity, shrewdness, astuteness, intelligence, cleverness, quickness, grasp. **—Ant. 2** obtuseness, stupidity, shallowness, dullness.

penitence *n.* repentance, remorse, self-reproach, compunction, regret, sorrow, humiliation, contrition; penance, attrition, expiation, atonement. **—Ant.** impenitence, unrepentance, obduracy; hardness, callousness.

penitent *adj.* **1.** penitential, repentant, contrite, atoning, remorseful, self-reproaching, compunctious, sorry, conscience-stricken, rueful, regretful. *—n.* **2.** a penitent person, one who is remorseful for sin or fault; devotee, pilgrim. **—Ant. 1** impenitent, unrepentant, obdurate; remorseless, callous.

penitentiary *n.* federal prison, state

prison; (*loosely*) prison, jail, penal institution, house of correction, house of detention, workhouse, reformatory; *Slang* pen, joint, slammer, stir, big house.

pennant *n.* flag, banner, streamer, banderole, ensign, standard, colors, jack, pennon, burgee, bunting, ensignia, oriflamme.

penniless *adj.* moneyless, destitute, strapped, poverty-stricken, impoverished, indigent, poor, needy, pauperized, impecunious; insolvent, ruined, bankrupt, down-and-out, wiped out; broke, flat broke, *Informal* busted. **—Syn. Study.** See POOR. **—Ant.** rich, wealthy, affluent, moneyed, well-heeled, *Slang* in the chips.

pensive *adj.* sadly thoughtful, meditative, contemplative, reflective, introspective, musing, dreaming, daydreaming, dreamy; sad, wistful, melancholy, solemn, serious, somber, grave. **—Syn. Study.** PENSIVE, MEDITATIVE, REFLECTIVE suggest quiet modes of apparent or real thought. PENSIVE suggests dreaminess or wistfulness, and may involve little or no thought to any purpose: *a pensive, faraway look.* MEDITATIVE involves thinking of certain facts or phenomena, perhaps in the religious sense of "contemplation," without necessarily having a goal of complete understanding or of action: *a slow, meditative reply.* REFLECTIVE has a strong implication of orderly, perhaps analytic, processes of thought, usu. with a definite goal of understanding: *a reflective critic.* **—Ant.** frivolous, joyous, happy, cheerful, gay, jovial, carefree, lighthearted.

pent-up *adj.* repressed, suppressed, restrained, stifled, checked, penned-up, penned-in, hedged-in, boxed-up, bottled-up, stored-up, held back, reined in.

penury *n.* poverty, impoverishment, want, indigence, need, privation, destitution, straitened circumstances, dire necessity; financial ruin, insolvency, bankruptcy. **—Ant.** wealth, prosperity, opulence, luxury, elegance, abundance, affluence.

people *n. pl.* **1.** human beings, humans, mortals, men and women, individuals, humankind, homo sapiens, mankind, humanity. **2.** citizens, citizenry, inhabitants, population, populace; family, ancestors, relatives, kin, kinfolk, *Informal* folks. **3.** the public, the common people, the little people, the rank and file, the masses, the multitude, the millions, the man in the street, John Q. Public; commoners, the common run; the lower classes, the lower orders, the working class, the working man, the mob, the rabble, the herd, the crowd, the great unwashed, the hoi polloi. **—Ant. 3** nobility, aristocracy, gentry, upper classes, blue bloods, silk-stockings.

pep *n.* vigor, vim, vitality, verve, energy, snap, zip, dash; *Informal* go, get-up-and-go; animation, vivacity, spirit, enthusiasm, life, ginger, gusto, liveliness.

peppery *adj.* highly seasoned, spicy, hot, piquant, fiery, burning, pungent, sharp. **—Ant.** bland, mild, tasteless, insipid.

peppy *adj.* brisk, lively, spirited, energetic, vigorous, dynamic, animated, vivacious, sparkling, snappy, enthusiastic, perky, active. **—Ant.** listless, spiritless, lethargic, sluggish, slow, leaden, somber, dull.

perambulate *v.* walk, stroll, saunter, promenade, amble, mosey, ramble, meander, pace, tour.

perceive *v.* **1.** notice, be aware of, detect, note, discern, make out, recognize, distinguish, apprehend, discover; observe, see, hear, smell, taste, feel, sense. **2.** understand, comprehend, apprehend, grasp, gather, realize, know, conclude, deduce, gain insight into, savvy, get. **—Syn. Study. 1** See NOTICE. **—Ant. 1** overlook, ignore, miss, pass over.

perceptible *adj.* perceivable, discernible, noticeable, apparent, detectable, observable, visible, discoverable, ascertainable; obvious, evident, manifest, distinct, conspicuous, clear, plain, palpable, tangible, prominent, notable, unmistakable, well-defined; unconcealed, unhidden. **—Ant.** imperceptible, indiscernible, unnoticeable, unapparent, undetectable, inconspicuous; concealed, hidden, obscured.

perception *n.* discernment, awareness, sense, faculty, apprehension, conception, recognition, cognizance, comprehension, consciousness, detection, discrimination, judgment, understanding, grasp.

perceptive *adj.* understanding, full of insight, sensitive, responsive, aware, discerning, penetrating; intelligent, keen, sharp, shrewd, astute, acute, sensible, quick, quick-witted. **—Ant.** insensitive, obtuse, callous, indifferent; stupid, thick, slow-witted, dull, dumb.

perch *n.* **1.** roost, roosting place, eyrie; resting place, rest, seat. **—*v.* 2.** sit, roost, rest, settle; light, alight, land.

perdition *n.* damnation, condemnation, destruction, ruin, ruination, loss of heavenly salvation, loss of one's soul; everlasting punishment, hellfire, Hell.

peregrination *n.* journey, travel, wandering, trip, expedition, trekking, excursion, roaming, rambling, roving, hiking, jaunt, sally, junket, globe-trotting.

peremptory *adj.* **1.** absolute, final, irrevocable, irreversible, incontrovertible, undeniable, unquestionable, decisive, unequivocal; unavoidable, obligatory, imperative. **2.** domineering, overbearing, authoritative, dictatorial, assertive, aggressive, lordly, imperious, high-handed; opinionated, closed-minded, dogmatic, biased. **—Ant. 1, 2** indecisive. **2** submissive, unassertive, passive, docile, tractable, compliant, meek; cooperative, open-minded.

perennial *adj.* perpetual, everlasting, permanent, constant, incessant, unceasing, ceaseless, continual, continuous, unremitting, persistent; fixed, changeless, unchanging, immutable, durable, imperishable, indestructible, lasting, enduring, long-lasting, undying, timeless, unfailing, long-lived. **—Ant.** temporary, occasional, sporadic, intermittent, periodic, evanescent; perishable, transient, fleeting, ephemeral, temporal.

perfect *adj.* **1.** exact, accurate, precise, true, pure, correct in every detail, flawless, unerring, strict, scrupulous, faithful. **2.** faultless, flawless, without defect, unblemished, unimpaired, undamaged; complete, whole, entire, unbroken, finished, absolute, thorough, pure, consummate, unqualified, unmitigated, impeccable, matchless, unequaled, unrivaled, ideal, supreme, peerless, superlative, sublime; blameless, untainted, immaculate. **—*v.* 3.** bring to perfection, develop, complete, achieve, accomplish, effect, realize, evolve, fulfill, consummate. **—Ant. 1, 2** imperfect. **2** faulty, flawed, defective, blemished, impaired, ruined, spoiled, damaged, incomplete, deficient, unfinished; partial, mixed, impure, qualified; inferior, poor, bad, worthless, *Informal* awful, *Slang* lousy.

perfection *n.* **1.** perfectness, excellence, faultlessness, flawlessness, impeccability, superiority, sublimity, ideal state; exactness, accurateness, precision, purity. **2.** development, completion, achieving, accomplishment, realization, evolution, fulfillment, consummation.

perfectly *adv.* **1.** to perfection, superbly, wonderfully, flawlessly, faultlessly, without fault, without defect, without blemish, impeccably, consummately. **2.** entirely, thoroughly, completely, totally, fully, wholly, altogether, quite, utterly, absolutely, supremely, infinitely, preeminently, consummately, to the nth degree; downright, positively, purely. **—Ant. 1** imperfectly, faultily, defectively, poorly, badly. **2** not; incompletely, partially; mistakenly, erroneously, inaccurately.

perfidious *adj.* treacherous, traitorous, treasonous, deceitful, false, disloyal, unfaithful, faithless, treasonable, dishonorable, untrustworthy, unscrupulous; dishonest, corrupt, untruthful, undependable, lying, cheating; *Informal* sneaky, double-dealing, shifty, two-faced.

perforate *v.* pierce, prick, puncture, stab, bore, penetrate, punch, lancinate, drill, hole, stick; slit, gash, slash, split.

perform *v.* **1.** do, accomplish, carry out, execute, perpetrate, achieve, effect, realize, attain, fulfill, bring to pass, bring about, finish, consummate, discharge, dispose of, meet; *Slang* knock off, pull off, polish off. **2.** play, present, render; act, enact, take part in; tread the boards, troupe; portray, represent, depict. **—Ant. 1** fail, founder, neglect, forsake.

performance *n.* **1.** discharge, accomplishment, execution, performing, doing, acquittal, exercise, transaction, fulfillment, realization, attainment, conduct, achievement, dispatch, perpetration, effectuation; completion, consummation. **2.** show, presentation, rendering, production, exhibition; (*variously*) play, concert, opera, ballet, recital, entertainment, spectacle, ceremony.

perfume *n.* **1.** fragrance, scent, extract, essence, cologne; aroma, smell, odor, bouquet. **—*v.* 2.** imbue with odor, give fragrance to, aromatize, scent, sweeten. **—Syn. Study. 1** PERFUME, FRAGRANCE, AROMA all refer to agreeable odors. PERFUME often indicates a strong, rich smell: *the perfume of flowers.* FRAGRANCE is usu. applied to a sweet, delicate, and fresh smell, esp. from growing things: *the fragrance of new-mown hay.* AROMA is usu. restricted to a distinctive, pervasive, somewhat spicy smell: *the aroma of coffee.* **—Ant. 1** stench, stink, smell.

perfunctory *adj.* indifferent, casual, disinterested, offhand, careless, unconcerned, unthinking, cursory, inattentive, lax, hasty, superficial, routine, mechanical, halfhearted, lukewarm, apathetic, spiritless, listless, passionless; negligent. **—Ant.** careful, thorough, thoughtful, diligent, assiduous, attentive, warmhearted, effusive, spirited, ardent, keen, zealous.

perhaps *adv.* maybe, mayhap, possibly, God willing, conceivably, perchance, as the case may be, imaginably, for all one knows, *Archaic* peradventure, wind and weather permitting, *French* peut-être. **—Ant.** definitely, certainly, unquestionably, surely.

peril *n.* risk, danger, hazard, jeopardy, pitfall, threat, menace, cause for alarm; vulnerability, exposure to danger, openness to attack, defenselessness, insecurity, uncertainty, unsafety. **—Syn. Study.** See DANGER. **—Ant.** safety, security, secureness, certainty, surety; invulnerability, unassailability, impregnability.

perilous *adj.* risky, hazardous, dangerous, fraught with danger, unsafe, ominous, threatening; uncertain, unsure, chancy, venturesome, insecure, vulnerable, shaky, slippery, precarious, ticklish.

perimeter *n.* periphery, border, borderline, circumference, bounds, confines; margin, edge. **—Ant.** center, middle, hub, heart, core, kernel, nucleus.

period *n.* **1.** time, span of time, interval, interlude, duration, term, season; era, epoch, age, eon. **2.** end, stop, close, finish, termination, limit, discontinuance, halt, cessation, finale, *Slang* curtain. **—Syn. Study.** See AGE.

periodic Also **periodical** *adj.* repeated, recurring, recurrent, frequent, intermittent, regular, routine, at fixed intervals, cyclic, seasonal.

periodical *n.* publication; (*variously*) newspaper, paper, magazine, newsmagazine, newsletter, journal, bulletin, review, daily, weekly, monthly, quarterly, annual.

periodically *adv.* regularly, routinely, at fixed intervals, repeatedly, often, frequently; occasionally.

peripatetic *adj.* wandering, itinerant, traveling, roving, migrant, rambling, walking, ambulating, tramping, peregrinating, roaming, gallivanting; migratory, nomadic.

periphery *n.* outskirts, fringes; boundary, edge, perimeter, circumference, border, bound. **—Ant.** center, middle, hub, heart, core, nucleus.

perish *v.* die, expire, pass away; become extinct, cease to exist, vanish, disappear, wither away, decay, come to ruin, crumble, be destroyed. **—Syn. Study.** See DIE. **—Ant.** be born, come into being, arise, appear; thrive, flourish, proliferate, prosper, fructify.

perishable *adj.* subject to decay, subject to spoiling, decomposable, unstable; short-lived, fleeting, transitory, ephemeral, evanescent. **—Ant.** nonperishable, stable, durable, long-lasting, long-lived, lasting.

perjury *n.* giving false testimony, lying under oath, false swearing.

perky *adj.* jaunty, pert, lively, gay, vivacious, animated, sprightly, spirited, full of spirit, alert, saucy, brisk; cheerful, happy, sunny, smiling, lighthearted, free and easy. **—Ant.** passive, lethargic, spiritless, sluggish, phlegmatic; somber, grave, serious, dour, sullen, gloomy, glum, sour, morose, sad, cheerless.

permanent *adj.* **1.** lasting forever, lasting, perpetual, everlasting, eternal, infinite, endless, undying, never-ending, unending, immortal, deathless, abiding, indestructible, imperishable, unyielding, unalterable, unfailing, changeless, immutable; long-lasting, long-lived, durable, enduring, unfading, constant, stable. *—n.* **2.** permanent wave, set, wave, perm. **—Ant. 1** impermanent, temporary, brief, fleeting, momentary, finite, mortal, passing, short, short-lived, transitory, fugitive, unstable, variable, changing, inconstant, ephemeral, evanescent.

permeate *v.* penetrate, pass through, soak through, seep through; pervade, saturate, diffuse throughout, infuse, fill, imbue. **—Ant.** bounce off, ricochet, glance off, slide off.

permissible *adj.* permitted, allowed, allowable, unprohibited, tolerated, admissible, granted; sanctioned, authorized, licensed, lawful, legal, legitimate, licit. **—Ant.** forbidden, prohibited, banned, disallowed, proscribed; unauthorized, unlawful, illegal, illicit.

permission *n.* leave, consent, assent, approval, acquiescence, concession, agreement, compliance, approbation; authorization, sanction, allowance, dispensation, indulgence, endorsement, grant, license, permit. **—Ant.** refusal, denial, prohibition, ban, prevention, interdiction.

permissive *adj.* indulgent, lenient, lax, assenting, consenting, acquiescent, tolerant, easygoing, forbearing; allowing, permitting, granting; unproscriptive, unprohibitive. **—Ant.** strict, rigid, authoritarian, domineering, proscriptive; refusing, denying, forbidding, withholding, grudging.

permit *v.* **1.** allow, let, give permission, give leave to, give assent to, agree to, consent to; tolerate, suffer, endure, bear with, put up with, let pass, approve, condone, OK; authorize, sanction, endorse, license. *—n.* **2.** license, official permission, authorization, warrant, authority, sanction. **—Syn. Study. 1** See ALLOW.

pernicious *adj.* harmful, injurious, serious, destructive, damaging, deleterious, detrimental, dangerous, disastrous, baneful, lethal, deadly, fatal, mortal, toxic, venomous, poisonous, noxious, malignant. **—Ant.** harmless, innocuous; beneficial, advantageous, helpful; healthful, healthy, wholesome, salutary, salubrious.

peroration *n.* speech, oration, declamation, discourse, address, sermon, lecture; tirade, exhortation, harangue, diatribe, jeremiad, filibuster, philippic.

perpetrate *v.* commit, perform, carry out, execute, do, enact, transact, bring about, pursue, inflict, *Slang* pull off.

perpetual *adj.* lasting forever, lasting, permanent, everlasting, eternal, abiding, enduring, constant, sustained, endless, never-ending, unending; continuous, ceaseless, incessant, unceasing, interminable, uninterrupted, unremitting, inexhaustible, repeated, continual. **—Syn. Study.** See ETERNAL. **—Ant.** temporary, impermanent, brief, fleeting, momentary, passing, short-lived, transitory, transient, ephemeral.

perpetuate *v.* cause to endure, make last, immortalize, make perpetual, make everlasting, eternalize, memorialize; preserve, save, sustain, maintain, continue. **—Ant.** destroy, obliterate, annihilate, exterminate, abolish, stamp out, snuff out; forget, ignore; avoid, eschew.

perpetuity *n.* eternity, forever, permanence, time without end, infinity, all time, end of time, endlessness, timelessness, everlastingness, perpetuation, neverendingness, perdurability, perennialness. **—Ant.** transience, impermanence, ephemerality, transitoriness.

perplex *v.* puzzle, baffle, confuse, bewilder, mix up, confound, dumbfound, muddle, befuddle, boggle, nonplus, stump, mystify; rattle, throw into confusion, *Informal* make one's head spin.

perquisite *n.* benefit, emolument, privilege, advantage, right, due, fringe benefit, *Slang* perk, gift, present, reward, inducement, recompense, honorarium.

persecute *v.* harass, harry, annoy cruelly, pursue continually, oppress, tyrannize, victimize, plague, harrow, hector, hound, bully, badger, bait; torment, vex, annoy, maltreat, abuse. **—Ant.** pamper, indulge, humor; favor, accommodate; support, uphold, champion, back.

perseverance *n.* **—Syn. Study.** See TENACITY.

persevere *v.* persist, be steadfast, be determined, be resolved, be resolute, be obstinate, work unflaggingly, not give up, keep on, maintain one's efforts, work hard, keep at it; *Informal* plug away, hammer away, stick to it, stick to one's guns, hang on, hang in there. **—Ant.** be irresolute, waver, vacillate, shilly-shally, falter, let down; give up, give in.

persist *v.* **1.** persevere, work unflaggingly, maintain one's efforts, pursue relentlessly, be tenacious, not give up, stop at nothing, be obstinate, hold steadfast, stand fast, be determined, be resolute, keep at it, not yield, work day and night; *Informal* stick to it, stick to one's guns, hang on, hang in there, move heaven and earth, leave no stone unturned, not take "no" for an answer, never say die. **2.** last, endure, survive, remain, stay, continue, hold on, hold out, go on. **—Syn. Study. 2** See CONTINUE. **—Ant. 1** be irresolute, waver, vacillate, shilly-shally; falter, quit, give up, surrender, stop, cease, end, leave off. **2** die, expire, wither away, fade, shrivel up.

persistence *n.* **—Syn. Study.** See TENACITY.

persistent *adj.* **1.** stubborn, determined, obstinate, tenacious, relentless, persisting, obdurate, dogged, persevering, steadfast, resolute, unfailing, unswerving. **2.** constant, unrelenting, unceasing, incessant, continual, continuous, endless, perpetual, eternal, sustained, interminable, inexhaustible, unremitting, unshakable; lasting, enduring, abiding. **—Syn. Study. 1** See STUBBORN.

persnickety *adj.* fussy, particular, nitpicking, finicky, overprecise, fastidious, meticulous, pernickety, punctilious, finical, choosy, overdemanding, fuddy-duddy, picayune. **—Ant.** sloppy, careless, indifferent, haphazard.

person *n.* individual, human being, human, being, creature, mortal, living soul, soul, living body, body; earthling.

personable *adj.* agreeable, affable, having a pleasing personality, likable, friendly, outgoing, sociable, amiable, warm, cordial, charming, attractive, pleasant, cordial, well-mannered, complaisant, tactful, diplomatic, amicable, sympathetic, well-disposed. **—Ant.** unpleasant, surly, ill-natured, sullen, rude, discourteous.

personage *n.* luminary, dignitary, VIP, notable, nabob, celebrity, public figure, leading light, popular hero; *Slang* bigwig, big shot, big name, somebody, heavyweight, high-muck-a-muck. **—Ant.** nothing, nobody, cipher, lightweight.

personal *adj.* **1.** private, own, individual, intimate, exclusive, confidential, secret, special, particular, privy; inward, inwardly felt, subjective. **2.** bodily, physical, corporeal.

personality *n.* **1.** outward character, disposition, temperament, makeup, nature; identity, individuality, distinctiveness. **2.** charm, personal attraction, friendliness, agreeableness, amiability, affability, magnetism, charisma. **—Syn. Study. 1** See CHARACTER.

personify *v.* embody, represent, exemplify, incorporate, characterize, express, symbolize; externalize, incarnate, personalize.

personnel *n.* employees, workers, staff, staff members, members, work force, crew, manpower, associates, human resources.

perspective *n.* **1.** the art of conveying distance, sense of depth. **2.** panoramic view, bird's-eye view, overview, vista, scene, scape, view, outlook, prospect. **3.** broad view, overview, comprehensive point of view, viewpoint, sense of proportion.

perspicacious *adj.* discerning, perceptive, astute, shrewd, penetrating, acute, keen, sharp, sharp-witted, keen-sighted, clearheaded, clear-sighted, clear-eyed, alert, awake, sagacious. **—Ant.** undiscerning, dull, dull-witted, stupid, thickheaded; dense, doltish, vacuous.

persuade *v.* induce, influence, move, get, prevail upon, motivate, convince, win over, bring around, talk into, sway, prompt, coax, wheedle, cajole, inveigle; lure, tempt, entice. **—Syn. Study.** PERSUADE, INDUCE imply influencing someone's thoughts or actions. They are used mainly in the sense of winning over a person to a certain course of action: *I persuaded her to call a doctor. I induced her to join the club.* They differ in that PERSUADE suggests appealing more to the reason and understanding: *I persuaded him to go back to work;* INDUCE emphasizes only the idea of successful influence, whether achieved by argument or promise of reward: *What can I say that will induce you to stay at your job?* Owing to this idea of compensation, INDUCE may be used in reference to the influence of factors as well as of persons: *The prospect of a raise in salary induced me to stay.* **—Ant.** dissuade, discourage, deter, repel, inhibit; forbid, prohibit.

persuasive *adj.* convincing, compelling, cogent, forceful, believable, plausible, logical, credible; effective, influential, winning, seductive, inviting, alluring, coaxing.

pert *adj.* **1.** impudent, impertinent, insolent, brash, flippant, flip, fresh, saucy, nervy, cheeky, brazen, brassy, audacious, smart-alecky, impolite, discourteous, insulting. **2.** lively, sprightly, brisk, perky, nimble, spry, chipper, alert, wide-awake, quick, energetic. **—Ant. 1** shy, bashful, meek, retiring, demure, modest, reserved; respectful, diffident, polite, courteous.

pertinacity *n.* persistence, obstinacy, determination, stubbornness, bullheadedness; pigheadedness, mulishness, obdurateness, inflexibility, intransigence, contrariness, perverseness, willfulness, intractability. **—Ant.** tractability, submissiveness, compliance, flexibility.

pertinent *adj.* relevant, to the point, germane, material, appropriate, fitting, concerning the matter at hand, befitting, apt, applicable, suitable, apropos, apposite, meet; related, congruent, concerned, connected, corresponding, consistent. **—Syn. Study.** See APT. **—Ant.** irrelevant, immaterial, inappropriate, unfitting, unsuited, unsuitable; unrelated, incongruous, unconnected, foreign, alien, discordant.

perturb *v.* disturb, trouble, worry, distress, disquiet, upset, bother, fluster, discompose, disconcert.

perusal *n.* reading, examination, scrutiny, review, run-through, inspection, study, scanning, *Slang* look-through, contemplation, scrutinizing.

pervade *v.* permeate, spread through, diffuse throughout, saturate, suffuse, fill, infuse, imbue, penetrate.

perverse *adj.* contrary, stubborn, obstinate, obdurate, inflexible, balky, hardheaded, wrongheaded, mulish, ornery, dogged, pigheaded; headstrong, willful, wayward, intractable, disobedient, rebellious. **—Syn. Study.** See WILLFUL. **—Ant.** cooperative, complaisant, pliant, flexible; agreeable, good-natured, accommodating, obliging, amiable.

pervert *v.* distort, warp, contort, abuse, misuse, corrupt, misrepresent, misapply, put a false interpretation on, falsify; desecrate, corrupt, subvert, degrade, debase, deprave.

perverted *adj.* distorted, twisted, warped, contorted, unbalanced, misconstrued, misconceived, misunderstood; false, faulty, untrue, fallacious, erroneous, imperfect, unsound; degraded, depraved, debased, corrupt, unnatural, abnormal, aberrant, deviant. **—Ant.** sound, true, valid, balanced, correct, natural, normal; good, straight, worthy, commendable.

pesky *adj.* annoying, exasperating, irksome, bothersome, vexatious, troublesome, galling, pestiferous, nettlesome, chafing, aggravating, infuriating, maddening, disturbing; offensive, objectionable, disagreeable, distasteful, obnoxious. **—Ant.** agreeable, soothing, comforting, delightful.

pessimism *n.* gloomy outlook, seeing only the gloomy side, belief that bad prevails; despair, hopelessness, discouragement, downheartedness, gloom, gloominess. **—Ant.** optimism, hopefulness, courage, dauntlessness, enthusiasm, cheerfulness.

pessimist *n.* defeatist, one who sees only the bad side, one who believes that bad prevails; *Slang* prophet of doom, Cassandra, crepehanger, gloomy Gus, sourpuss, kill-joy, spoilsport, wet blanket. **—Ant.** optimist, utopian, incurable romantic, Pollyanna.

pest *n.* troublesome insect, troublesome animal, destructive plant; annoying person, nuisance, bother, scourge, blight, bane, annoyance, irritation, vexation, curse, *Informal* thorn in one's side, *Slang* pain in the neck.

pester *v.* bother, annoy, torment,

badger, plague, provoke, harass, harry, hector, taunt, nag, vex, irritate, irk, fret, nettle, disturb, trouble, worry, bait; try one's patience, get on one's nerves.

pet *n.* **1.** household animal, house pet. **2.** favorite, darling, baby, *Slang* apple of one's eye; dear, beloved, loved one, sweetheart. —*adj.* **3.** favorite, choice, favored, preferred, cherished, dearest, dear to one's heart. —*v.* **4.** pat, stroke, caress, fondle.

petition *n.* **1.** formal request, appeal, entreaty, plea; proposal, suit, solicitation; application, requisition; prayer, supplication, invocation, beseechment, orison; imploring. —*v.* **2.** ask, beg, sue, beseech, entreat, call upon, appeal to, apply to, request of, plead with, urge, press, seek; pray, supplicate, invoke.

petrified *adj.* **1.** stony, rocklike, hard as a rock, solidified, turned to stone; hard, hardened, dense, solid. **2.** paralyzed, frozen, immobilized, transfixed, stupefied, dumbstruck, dumbfounded, numb, numbed, benumbed, dazed, shocked, terror-stricken, spellbound, *Informal* scared stiff.

petty *adj.* **1.** trivial, trifling, insignificant, unimportant, inconsequential, minor, paltry, slight, small, picayune, piddling, niggling, flimsy, inconsiderable. **2.** small-minded, narrow-minded, mean, ignoble, shabby, ungenerous. **—Syn. Study.** PETTY, TRIVIAL, TRIFLING, PALTRY apply to something that is so insignificant as to be almost unworthy of notice. PETTY implies lack of significance or worth: *petty quarrels.* TRIVIAL applies to something that is slight or insignificant, often being in contrast to something that is important: *a trivial task.* TRIFLING is often interchangeable with TRIVIAL; however, TRIFLING implies an even lesser, almost negligible, importance or worth: *to ignore a trifling error.* PALTRY applies to something that is contemptibly small or worthless: *I was paid a paltry sum.* **—Ant. 1** important, major, consequential, significant, momentous, considerable. **2** broad-minded, large-hearted, magnanimous, generous, tolerant.

petulant *adj.* peevish, fretful, irritable, cross, snappish, sullen, sulky, surly, grumpy, grouchy, testy, huffy, pettish, irascible, fractious, gruff, cantankerous, sour, crotchety, crabbed, bearish, ungracious, ill-natured, ill-tempered, out of sorts, thin-skinned, touchy, tetchy, uncivil; faultfinding, complaining, contentious, quarrelsome. **—Ant.** agreeable, pleasant, good-natured, cheerful, happy, smiling, complaisant, cooperative, content, gracious, amenable.

phantasm *n.* phantom, ghost, apparition, vision, specter, spirit, shade, incubus, succubus; figment, illusion, fantasy; delusion, mirage.

phantom *n.* apparition, specter, spirit, ghost, wraith, phantasm, phantasmagoria, dream, mirage, chimera, figment of the imagination, hallucination, illusion, vision.

phase *n.* **1.** stage, condition, period, degree, level, step, development, point of development, juncture. **2.** aspect, facet, feature, side, angle, slant, circumstance, view, viewpoint, attitude, guise, appearance.

phenomenal *adj.* extraordinary, exceptional, outstanding, remarkable, superior, super, surpassing, uncommon, unusual, unprecedented, unparalleled, stupendous, prodigious, unique, singular, unheard-of, incredible, miraculous, marvelous, spectacular, fantastic, sensational, astonishing, amazing, overwhelming. **—Ant.** ordinary, common, unexceptional, usual, everyday, routine, normal, standard, average, familiar, customary, accustomed.

phenomenon *n.* **1.** occurrence, happening, visible fact, natural event, part of existence, contingency, thing, actuality, fact of life, proceeding, occasion, incident, episode. **2.** rarity, marvel, miracle, wonder, remarkable person, exceptional thing, exception, singularity, sensation, nonpareil, curiosity.

philanderer *n.* trifler, Don Juan, flirt, gallant, rake, libertine, womanizer, lothario, adulterer, lady-killer, rakehell, lecher, dallier, woman-chaser, wanton; *Slang* swinger, rip, wolf, lover boy, tomcat.

philanthropic Also **philanthropical** *adj.* charitable, almsgiving, eleemosynary, benevolent, humanitarian, generous, liberal, bounteous, magnanimous, munificent, beneficent. **—Ant.** misanthropic; miserly, niggardly.

philanthropist *n.* benefactor of charities, contributor, donor, giver, almsgiver, humanitarian, Good Samaritan, *Slang* do-gooder. **—Ant.** misanthrope; miser, niggard, pinchpenny.

philanthropy *n.* charity, charitableness, humanitarianism, almsgiving, benevolence, beneficence, largeheartedness, generosity, munificence, unselfishness, public-spiritedness, goodness, openhandedness, liberality, bounty.

philistine *n.* **1.** lowbrow, cultural ignoramus, barbarian, savage, yahoo; bourgeois, conformist, conventionalist, Babbitt. —*adj.* **2.** uncultured, uncultivated, unrefined, uneducated, unenlightened, untutored, unlettered, uninformed, ignorant; lowbrow, bourgeois, conventional, conformist, commonplace, prosaic; anti-intellectual. —**Ant. 1** intellectual, highbrow; *Slang* egghead.

philosopher *n.* student of basic truths, seeker of universal laws; seeker of wisdom, truth seeker, wise man, sage, savant; logician, rationalist, reasoner, philosophizer, metaphysician, thinker, dialectician, theorizer.

philosophic, philosophical *adj.* **1.** reasonable, logical, rational, judicious, thoughtful, sagacious; theorizing, theoretical, abstract, learned, erudite. **2.** stoic, stoical, resigned, complacent, fatalistic, patient, impassive, unemotional, self-restrained, composed, calm, serene, tranquil, imperturbed, unruffled, unexcited, quiet. —**Ant. 1** illogical, irrational, thoughtless, careless, ill-considered; scientific, practical, factual, pragmatic. **2** emotional, excited, impulsive, hotheaded, rash, reckless, unrestrained; upset, perturbed, distraught.

philosophy *n.* **1.** study of basic truths, search for universal laws, seeking after wisdom, love of wisdom; logic, rationalism, reason, reasoning, thought, thinking, philosophizing, theorizing, ideas; esthetics, metaphysics. **2.** system of beliefs, beliefs, convictions, conception, doctrine, basic idea, principle; opinion, view, viewpoint. **3.** stoicism, resignation, fatalism, patience, complacency, forbearance, restraint, impassivity, composure, calm, serenity, imperturbability, tranquillity.

phlegmatic *adj.* indifferent, apathetic, nonchalant, unemotional, unimpassioned, undemonstrative, unresponsive, imperturbable, unconcerned, unexcitable, cool, calm, serene, tranquil, impassive, stoical; spiritless, listless, languid, lethargic, sluggish, dull, passive, unfeeling, insensitive. —**Ant.** emotional, passionate, excited; active, demonstrative, alert, lively, animated, energetic, interested.

phobia *n.* unreasonable fear, terror, horror, dread, aversion, loathing, apprehension, overwhelming anxiety; *Slang* bugbear, bugaboo. —**Ant.** love, liking, fondness, fancy, bent, relish, penchant, inclination, predilection.

phonograph *n.* record player, hifi, *Informal* phono, *British* gramophone; (*variously*) stereo, hifi; (*trademark*) Victrola.

phony Also **phoney** *adj.* **1.** not genuine, fake, counterfeit, forged, sham, spurious, bogus, specious, mock, pretended; artificial, imitation, synthetic, false, fraudulent, deceptive, trick, unreal, pseudo, unauthentic, untrue. —*n.* **2.** fake, sham, fraud, counterfeit, imitation, make-believe, synthetic, fraud, hoax, forgery. —**Ant. 1** real, authentic, genuine, original, bona fide, true. **2** the genuine article, *Slang* the real McCoy.

phrase *n.* **1.** expression, words, turn of phrase, word group, construction, utterance, remark, locution. **2.** figure of speech, saying, expression, truism, proverb, maxim, aphorism, cliché, platitude, banality, colloquialism, dictum; idiom, locution. —*v.* **3.** express, word, put into words, find words, couch, put, state, declare, impart; say, voice, utter, enunciate, communicate, verbalize, articulate.

physical *adj.* **1.** material, existing, existent, natural, tangible, substantive, palpable, solid, concrete, real, actual, apparent, external, essential. **2.** of the body, bodily, corporeal, corporal, human, living, fleshly, animal, carnal, sensual. —**Syn. Study. 2** PHYSICAL, BODILY, CORPOREAL, CORPORAL agree in pertaining to the body. PHYSICAL means connected with or pertaining to the animal or human body as a material organism: *physical strength.* BODILY means belonging to or concerned with the human body as distinct from the mind or spirit: *bodily sensations.* CORPOREAL, a more poetic and philosophical word, refers esp. to the mortal substance of which the body is composed, as opposed to spirit: *our corporeal existence.* CORPORAL is usu. reserved for reference to suffering inflicted on the human body: *corporal punishment.* —**Ant. 1** nonmaterial, intangible. **2** spiritual, moral; mental, intellectual.

physician *n.* doctor, M.D., medical doctor; medical examiner, GP, general practitioner, surgeon, specialist; *Slang* medic, medico, medicine man, doc, pill peddler, sawbones.

physiognomy *n.* features, outward appearance, countenance, visage, face; shape, profile, outline, contour, silhouette, configuration, façade.

picaresque *adj.* roguish, waggish, prankish, rascally, scampish, devilish, roistering, raffish, mischief-loving; adventuresome, daring, foolhardy.

picayune Also **picayunish** *adj.* trifling, trivial, petty, paltry, insignificant, unimportant, inconsequential, inconsiderable, slight, measly, piddling, niggling, small, little, dinky, nugatory, flimsy.

pick *v.* **1.** select, choose, decide upon, settle upon, single out, fix upon, elect, opt for. **2.** pluck, pull off, pull out, detach, crop, cut; gather, collect, harvest. —*n.* **3.** choice, the best, prize, preference, favored one, elect, elite, flower, cream, *French* crème de la crème. —**Ant. 1** reject, refuse, decline, spurn, scorn, disclaim, repudiate. **3** the worst, the booby prize.

picket *n.* **1.** stake, palisade, pale,

pointed stick, paling; post, upright, stanchion; tether, restraint. **2.** forward lookout, lookout, sentinel, watch, sentry, guard, patrol. **3.** striker, protester, boycotter, blockader. —*v.* **4.** enclose, fence, corral, pen in, shut in, wall in, hedge in, hem in; restrict, restrain. **5.** demonstrate against; (*loosely*) strike, walk out, go out, boycott, blockade.

pickle *n.* **1.** pickled cucumber, cucumber pickle; (*variously*) sweet pickle, dill pickle, gherkin, sour pickle, kosher dill, mixed pickle, bread-and-butter pickle, mustard pickle. **2.** *Informal* predicament, difficulty, tight spot, plight, jam, quandary, fix, mess, difficult position, extremity, emergency, crisis, dilemma, scrape; *Slang* hot water, pretty pickle, pretty pass, fine kettle of fish. —*v.* **3.** preserve in brine, preserve in vinegar, corn; treat with diluted acid.

picture *n.* **1.** representation, delineation, portrayal, illustration; drawing, painting, sketch, study, etching; photograph, photo, snapshot; tintype, daguerreotype. **2.** motion picture, moving picture, film, *Informal* movie, *Slang* flick, *British* cinema. **3.** likeness, image, duplicate, copy, facsimile, double; *Slang* dead ringer, spitting image, carbon copy. **4.** perfect example, model, paragon, mirror, exemplification, personification, essence, embodiment. —*v.* **5.** portray, represent, depict, illustrate, feature, delineate; paint, draw, sketch; photograph. **6.** imagine, see, envision, call to mind, see in the mind, conceive of, fancy, believe.

picturesque *adj.* quaint, exotic, colorful, striking, distinctive, unusual, interesting, imaginative, pictorial; attractive, charming, beautiful, artistic. **—Ant.** everyday, usual, commonplace, uninteresting, drab, dull, flat, tame, insipid; unattractive, inartistic.

piddling *adj.* trifling, trivial, insignificant, inconsequential, unimportant, picayune, paltry, skimpy, slight, measly, modest, niggardly, small, little, petty, puny, flimsy.

piebald *adj.* dappled, mottled, spotted, speckled, flecked; variegated, many-colored, particolored, motley, multicolored, varicolored, many-hued.

piece *n.* **1.** portion, quantity, amount, share, slice, cut, chunk, hunk, lump; pat, blob, bit, fraction, scrap; fragment, shard, part, shred, sliver; swatch, length, cutting, paring; component, member, section, segment, division. **2.** instance, example, case, specimen, sample; unit, item, article, member, thing, entity. **3.** selection, composition, work, creation, study; play, drama, sketch; story, article, essay, review, item. —*v.* **4.** piece together; patch, patch up, mend, repair, restore, fix. **—Ant. 1** all, everything, total, sum total, entire amount, entirety, the whole; nothing, none, zero, naught, nullity. **4** tear, break, pierce, crack, shred.

pierce *v.* **1.** perforate, puncture, penetrate, make a hole in, bore through, cut through, run through, drill, pass through; stick, prick, stab, spear, spike, lance, impale. **2.** sting, hurt, pain; cut, wound; affront, grieve, distress. **—Syn. Study. 1** PIERCE, PENETRATE suggest the action of one object passing through another or making a way through and into another. These terms are used both concretely and figuratively. To PIERCE is to perforate quickly, as by stabbing; it suggests the use of a sharp, pointed instrument impelled by force: *to pierce the flesh with a knife; a scream that pierced my ears.* PENETRATE suggests a slow or difficult movement: *No ordinary bullet can penetrate an elephant's hide; to penetrate the depths of one's ignorance.* **—Ant. 1** glance off; patch, block, stop up. **2** soothe, calm, quiet; please, delight, gladden, cheer, gratify.

piercing *adj.* **1.** shrill, grating, screeching, shrieking, strident; loud, earsplitting, ear-shattering, deafening. **2.** sharp, keen, penetrating, searching, probing; biting, cutting, intense, fierce, furious, raw, bitter, cruel, caustic; angry, painful, hurtful, agonizing, torturous, excruciating. **—Ant. 1, 2** calm, soothing. **1** mellifluous, melodic; quiet, low. **2** vague, easy; pleasant, delightful, cheering, gratifying.

piety *n.* piousness, religiousness, devoutness, devotion, godliness; reverence, respect, loyalty, dutifulness, humility; religiosity. **—Ant.** impiety, sacrilege, ungodliness, blasphemy, irreverence; disrespect, disloyalty, infidelity.

pig *n.* **1.** small hog, swine, porker, (*male*) boar, (*female*) sow; (*young*) shoat, piglet, suckling pig, *Informal* piggy. **2.** glutton, ravenous eater, large eater, guzzler, gourmand, gormandizer; *Slang* hog, chowhound.

pigheaded *adj.* stubborn, obstinate, wrongheaded, bullheaded, unyielding, unbending, inflexible, opinionated, obdurate, deaf to advice, blind to reason, mulish, dogged; willful, insistent, contrary, perverse, recalcitrant, refractory. **—Ant.** complaisant, flexible, open-minded, agreeable, tractable, docile, amiable, cooperative, obliging.

pigment *n.* color, coloring, coloring matter, tint, dye, dyestuff.

pike[1] *n.* lance, bill, halberd, poleax, spear, spike, assegai; javelin; harpoon.

pike[2] *n.* turnpike, toll road; superhighway, throughway, thruway, expressway, speedway, freeway, parkway, highway, hard road, interstate, *British* King's (or Queen's) highway, *German* autobahn. **—Ant.** secondary road, back road, country road.

piker *n.* cheapskate, pinchpenny, penny pincher, tightwad, skinflint, miser; trifler, petty person, niggard. **—Ant.** big spender, spendthrift, squanderer.

pile[1] *n.* **1.** heap, stack, mass, batch, pyramid, mound; accumulation, collection, assortment, amassment, aggregation, hoard, store; large amount, quantity, profusion, abundance. *—v.* **2.** heap, mass, amass, stack, assemble; accumulate, collect, gather, agglomerate. **—Ant. 2** scatter, disperse, strew, spread, broadcast.

pile[2] *n.* nap, shag, fluff; surface, plush, fleece, grain, warp, fibrousness.

pile[3] *n.* piling, support, post, upright, pier, pillar, stanchion; foundation.

pilfer *v.* steal, rob, thieve, purloin; plagiarize, pirate; *Slang* boost, hook, lift, pinch, heist, swipe, cop, snitch, finger.

pilgrimage *n.* **1.** religious journey to a shrine, religious journey, devotional trip, *Islam* hadj, penitential sojourn. **2.** journey, excursion, trek, trip, long trip, sojourn, voyage, expedition; ramble, wandering, roving, roaming, peregrination. **—Syn. Study. 2** See TRIP.

pillage *v.* **1.** plunder, raid, sack, loot, rifle, rob, despoil, strip, fleece, ravage, maraud. *—n.* **2.** plunder, loot, booty, spoils, stolen goods, filchings; looting, robbery, plundering, sack, piracy.

pillar *n.* **1.** column, post, colonnade, upright, support, pile, piling, shaft, stanchion; pilaster, obelisk. **2.** mainstay, tower of strength, important person, ranking personage, leading light, rock, support, champion; *Slang* VIP, somebody, wheel.

pilot *n.* **1.** flyer, aviator, airman, aeronaut; *Slang* birdman, sky jockey, fly-boy. **2.** helmsman, wheelman, steersman, coxswain; guide, leader. *—v.* **3.** steer, be at the helm of, be at the wheel of, handle the tiller of, keep on course, control, manage, handle, navigate; direct, lead, conduct, escort, guide, accompany.

pin *n.* **1.** (*variously*) straight pin, common pin; safety pin, diaper pin; hatpin; pushpin; tine, skewer, prong; tholepin, dowel. **2.** brooch, clasp, clip, stickpin, breast pin; medal, badge, decoration. *—v.* **3.** attach with a pin, affix, secure, fasten, clasp. **4.** pinion; hold fast, hold down; restrain, bind, fasten.

pinch *v.* **1.** tweak, squeeze, nip; cramp, crimp, compress, tighten, crush. **2.** *Slang* arrest, take into custody, apprehend, run in, *Informal* collar, *Slang* bust; nab, catch, grab, capture. **3.** *Slang* steal, snatch, swipe, snitch, lift, crib, purloin, cop, filch. *—n.* **4.** tweak, nip, squeeze. **5.** bit, speck, mite, jot, iota, spot, snip, trace, tittle. **6.** pain, discomfort, hardship, ordeal, trial, affliction, misery, strait, plight; emergency, crisis, predicament, difficulty, exigency, squeeze, clutch, jam, pickle. **7.** *Slang* arrest, collar, capture, *Slang* bust.

pine *v.* **1.** yearn, long, hanker, sigh, languish; crave, hunger for, thirst after, desire, covet; pant for, have a yen for. **2.** fail in health, decline, weaken, ebb, waste away, languish, wither, wilt, droop, dwindle, flag; die, expire. **—Syn. Study. 1** See YEARN.

pinnacle *n.* **1.** highest point, peak, summit, apex, crest, vertex, zenith, height, top, tiptop, acme, crown, cap. **2.** spire, steeple, tower; belfry, bell tower, campanile.

pinpoint *n.* **1.** dot, spot, speck, jot, iota. *—v.* **2.** locate exactly, localize, detect precisely, zero in on, home in on; describe precisely, detail, characterize.

pioneer *n.* **1.** first settler, early immigrant, colonist; frontiersman, explorer. **2.** leader, trailblazer, forerunner, pathfinder, innovator, developer, founder, founding father, father, establisher; predecessor, antecedent, precursor; herald, harbinger. *—v.* **3.** be a leader, blaze the trail, lead the way, show the way, start, establish, found, discover, invent, create, develop.

pious *adj.* **1.** devout, religious, dedicated, faithful, reverent, reverential, worshipful; godly, spiritual, holy, divine, saintly, sainted. **2.** sanctimonious, holier-than-thou, unctuous, pietistic, self-righteous, rationalizing; hypocritical, insincere. **—Syn. Study. 1** See RELIGIOUS. **—Ant. 1** impious, irreverent, irreligious, ungodly, godless, unholy. **2** humble, meek; sincere, genuine.

pipe *n.* **1.** tube, conduit; conveyor; main, duct, conductor. *—v.* **2.** whistle, sing, cheep, peep, trill, warble, twitter, chirp, tweet; play a flute, play a bagpipe.

piquant *adj.* **1.** pungent, spicy, sharp, tangy, zesty, savory, highly seasoned, hot, peppery, strong-flavored; bitter, acid, biting, stinging, piercing, mordant. **2.** lively, peppy, sharp, zesty, vigorous, spirited, scintillating, sparkling, clever, bright, stimulating, animated, rousing, interesting, provocative, trenchant, incisive; racy, salty, spicy, peppery. **—Ant. 1** bland, mild. **2** banal, inane, insipid, tame, jejune, uninteresting, boring, dull.

pique *v.* **1.** displease, offend, affront, hurt one's feelings, annoy, irritate, vex, irk, gall, nettle, incense, provoke, exasperate, disquiet, perturb; *Informal* put one's back up, miff, peeve, put one's nose out of joint. **2.** arouse, kindle, stimulate, rouse, provoke, excite, stir, quicken, spur, goad. —*n.* **3.** resentment, hurt feelings, displeasure, annoyance, irritation, vexation, exasperation, indignation, ire, umbrage, discomfort; grudge, snit, spite, malice, vindictiveness, ill feelings; embarrassment, humiliation, mortification. **—Ant. 1** please, delight, gratify, satisfy, compliment. **2** deaden, dull, kill, quench.

pit[1] *n.* **1.** hole, hollow, hole in the ground, cavity, crater, depression; gully, trough; indentation, gouge, concavity, furrow, dent, dimple, notch, dip, pock; scar, pockmark. —*v.* **2.** gouge, dent, indent, nick, notch, pock, scratch, scar. **3.** match, set against, oppose, put in competition; contrast, juxtapose. **—Ant. 1** mound, lump, bump, protuberance.

pit[2] *n.* seed, stone, kernel, nut.

pitch *v.* **1.** set up, raise, erect; set, place, fix, settle, plant, establish, locate, station. **2.** throw, hurl, heave, fling, cast, toss, lob, chuck, sling, fire, propel, shy, let fly. **3.** fall headlong, fall headfirst, fall, topple, tumble. **4.** rock from front to back, toss, plunge, lurch, bob, shake, jolt, jerk, oscillate, undulate. —*n.* **5.** slant, slope, incline, declivity, grade, cant, angle. **6.** throw, delivery, heave, toss, lob, cast, fling, chuck. **7.** tone, sound; harmonic, speed of vibration. **8.** level, degree, point; height, peak, apex, summit, zenith, pinnacle, crown, top. **9.** forward plunge, headlong fall, dip, rocking, lurch, lurching, bobbing, oscillation, undulation.

piteous *adj.* pitiable, pitiful, sad, poignant, moving, heartrending, deplorable, heartbreaking, distressing, woeful, pathetic, touching, affecting. **—Syn. Study.** See PITIFUL. **—Ant.** cheering, heartwarming, delightful, joyous.

pitfall *n.* hazard, risk, danger, peril, snare, quagmire, quicksand, stumbling block, trap, springe, booby trap, ambush.

pithy *adj.* to the point, meaningful, cogent, forceful, effective, expressive, trenchant; concise, terse, succinct, concentrated. **—Ant.** diffuse, vague; wordy, verbose, rambling, turgid.

pitiable *adj.* **—Syn. Study.** See PITIFUL.

pitiful *adj.* **1.** pitiable, piteous, arousing pity, deserving pity, heartrending, heartbreaking, moving, touching, poignant, pathetic; sad, lamentable, distressing, mournful, plaintive, miserable, forlorn, doleful. **2.** contemptible, deserving of scorn, miserable, despicable, pitiable, wretched, worthless, shabby, poor, sorry, abject, measly, insignificant, paltry, dreadful, abominable, god-awful. **—Syn. Study. 1, 2** PITIFUL, PITIABLE, PITEOUS apply to that which arouses pity (with compassion or with contempt). That which is PITIFUL is touching and excites pity or is mean and contemptible: *a pitiful leper; a pitiful exhibition of cowardice.* PITIABLE may mean lamentable, or wretched and paltry: *a pitiable hovel.* PITEOUS refers only to that which exhibits suffering and misery, and is therefore heartrending: *piteous poverty.* **—Ant. 1** happy, cheerful, merry, glad, joyous, joyful. **2** commendable, praiseworthy, laudable; noble, lofty, sublime, exalted, dignified, great, grand, glorious; delightful, endearing, lovable, charming.

pitiless *adj.* merciless, heartless, without pity, inhuman, unmerciful, unpitying, unsparing, hard-hearted, cold-blooded, relentless, unrelenting, ruthless, cruel, brutal; unmoved, unresponsive, indifferent, untouched, insensitive, uncaring, implacable. **—Ant.** merciful, sparing, relenting, softhearted, compassionate, benign, kind; concerned, caring, responsive, touched.

pittance *n.* small amount, trifle, modicum, minimum, little, smidgen, crumb, mite; trifling sum, small allowance, minimal wage.

pity *n.* **1.** sympathy, compassion, empathy, commiseration, condolence; cause for sorrow, regret, sad thing, shame, crying shame. **2.** mercy, charity, clemency, leniency, kindliness, humanity, tenderness, softheartedness, indulgence, forbearance, lenity, magnanimity. —*v.* **3.** feel sorry for, have compassion for, commiserate with, sympathize with, lament, feel for, bleed for, weep for. **—Syn. Study. 1** See SYMPATHY. **—Ant. 1** anger, rage, wrath, fury; scorn, disdain, indifference, apathy, disinterest. **2** cruelty, brutality, hardheartedness, harshness, inhumanity, mercilessness, pitilessness, ruthlessness; severity.

pivot *n.* **1.** pin or shaft about which something turns; (*loosely*) axis, axle, swivel, hinge, fulcrum. —*v.* **2.** rotate, revolve, wheel, swivel, circle, spin, twirl, turn, swing around, whirl, pirouette. **3.** depend, hang, rely, be contingent on, hinge on, revolve around, turn, focus, center, be in the hands of.

pivotal *adj.* decisive, crucial, critical, vital, determining, climactic.

placate *v.* calm, soothe, pacify, quiet, lull, mollify, assuage, alleviate; appease, propitiate, win over, conciliate.

place *n.* **1.** space, spot, niche, point; site, location, position, whereabouts, *Law* venue. **2.** establishment, concern, business, store, shop, company, firm. **3.** position, situation, post, appointment, job, office, niche, berth, station, commission; function, standing, duty, rank. **4.** residence, home, abode, house, dwelling, domicile, habitation, lodgings, quarters, premises, office, building, *Informal* digs; farm, ranch, plot, land, property. **5.** city, town, village; state, county, township, borough, district, neighborhood, vicinity, area, province, region, locality, locale, zone, quarter; country, territory. —*v.* **6.** put, set, rest, stand, situate, position, plant, deposit, settle, array, locate, ensconce, install; fix, affix, attach; house, lodge, harbor, shelter. **7.** get a job for, find hire, find work for, appoint, assign, install, commission, invest. **8.** identify, remember, recognize, classify. **—Ant. 6** remove, take away, dislodge, dislocate; detach, take off.

placid *adj.* calm, quiet, tranquil, peaceful, pacific, serene, restful; untroubled, unruffled, smooth, undisturbed, collected, composed, self-possessed, poised, undemonstrative, unexcited, unexcitable, imperturbable; gentle, mild. **—Syn. Study.** See PEACEFUL. **—Ant.** turbulent, agitated, rough; excitable, excited, tempestuous, emotional, passionate, impassioned, impulsive, disturbed, perturbed, rattled, distracted.

plague *n.* **1.** bubonic plague, Black Death; widespread epidemic, pandemic, fatal epidemic, pestilence; contagious disease, epidemic disease, *French* peste. **2.** affliction, scourge, visitation, calamity, hardship, misery, agony, suffering, woe, trouble, burden; evil, curse, bane, blight, cancer. —*v.* **3.** torment, trouble, distress, worry, disquiet, perturb, persecute, harass, disturb, bother, vex, irk, peeve, nettle, gall, harry, chafe, fret, badger, annoy; pain, aggrieve, afflict, embarrass, haunt, prey on one's mind; try the patience of, get on one's nerves, go against the grain. **—Syn. Study. 3** See BOTHER.

plain *adj.* **1.** clear, distinct, legible, discernible, conspicuous, obvious, prominent, visible, apparent, glaring, pronounced, striking, outstanding, vivid, clear-cut, well-defined, well-marked, manifest, palpable. **2.** easily understood, simple, clear, straightforward, direct, explicit, specific, unambiguous, unmistakable, understandable, comprehensible, unequivocal. **3.** honest, frank, blunt, candid, open, sincere, forthright, straight, undisguised, undiluted, naked, bald, bare, unembellished, unvarnished, unadorned; plain-spoken, outspoken, unreserved. **4.** simple, unaffected, unpretentious, unassuming; modest, everyday, ordinary, average, common, matter-of-fact; obscure, undistinguished, commonplace; unadorned, undecorated, unornamented, ungarnished, without frills. **5.** homely, not beautiful, unhandsome, unattractive, unlovely, uncomely, having plain features, not striking. —*n.* **6.** prairie, grassland, tableland, plateau, open country. **—Ant. 1** indistinct, vague, blurred, illegible, indiscernible, inconspicuous; hidden, concealed. **2** obscure, abstruse, complex, difficult, indirect, ambiguous, incomprehensible; affected, pretentious. **3** deceptive, evasive, disguised, veiled, indirect. **4** affected, pretentious, assuming, snobbish; sophisticated, worldly, distinguished; decorated, ornamented, adorned, fancy, frilly. **5** beautiful, gorgeous, good-looking, attractive, comely, handsome.

plainly *adv.* **1.** simply, unpretentiously, unaffectedly, unassumingly, modestly, ordinarily; without adornment, without ornamentation. **2.** clearly, obviously, conspicuously, prominently, markedly, visibly, strikingly, vividly, discernibly, manifestly, apparently, undeniably, unquestionably, undoubtedly, doubtless, definitely, without doubt, beyond doubt. **3.** clearly, distinctly, explicitly, directly, unmistakably, unambiguously, comprehensibly, unequivocally, honestly, frankly, bluntly, candidly, openly, baldly, positively.

plain-spoken *adj.* frank, direct, open, forthright, genuine, sincere, candid, plain, honest, straight, open-faced, aboveboard, straight-out.

plaint *n.* complaint, grievance, resentment, grudge, objection, gripe, grouse, grumble, regret, *Slang* beef, squawk; reproach, accusation, charge, reproof, remonstrance; lament, cry, wail, moan, sob.

plaintive *adj.* sad, mournful, sorrowful, lamenting, moaning, melancholy; doleful, dolorous, grievous, woebegone, tearful, wretched, heartrending, rueful, lugubrious, pathetic, piteous, pitiful.

plan *n.* **1.** scheme, program, proposal, suggestion, idea, conception, proposition, procedure, method, way, strategy, stratagem; design, blueprint, sketch, map, diagram. —*v.* **2.** organize, devise, make arrangements, make preparations, conceive, think out, plot, contrive, prepare, fabricate, design; form, frame, outline, shape; block out, lay out, project, map out, diagram. **3.** intend, aim, purpose, propose.

plane *n.* **1.** flat surface, level surface. **2.** level, elevation, standing, condition, position, status, station, degree. **3.** airplane, aircraft; jet, *Slang* bird. —*adj.* **4.** flat, level, regular, plumb.

plant *n.* **1.** vegetation, flora, herbage; (*variously*) tree, flower, bush, shrub, vine, herb, weed, wort, grass, moss, algae, fungi; seedling, slip, vegetable. **2.**

factory, shop, works, yard, mill, foundry; business, establishment. —*v.* **3.** put in the ground, sow seed, broadcast, scatter, set in, set out; transplant. **4.** implant, instill, engender, inculcate, infuse, inspire, propagate, establish, cultivate, foster, sow the seeds of.

plaster *n.* **1.** pasty mixture of gypsum or lime, sand, and water; calcined gypsum, grout, stucco, spackle, powdered gypsum; plaster of paris. —*v.* **2.** cover with plaster; coat, smear, spread thickly, overlay, lather, daub, bedaub.

plastic *adj.* **1.** capable of being molded, easily molded, shapable, formable, pliable, pliant, ductile, malleable, flexible, tractable, yielding, elastic, supple, soft. —*n.* **2.** moldable substance; synthetic organic compound. **—Ant. 1** hard, rigid, stiff, inflexible, inelastic.

plate *n.* **1.** dish; serving dish, platter, saucer. **2.** serving, helping, platter, platterful, portion, dish.

plateau *n.* elevated plain, tableland, table, mesa; highland, upland. **—Ant.** valley, ravine; gulch, gully, savanna, swamp, lowland.

platform *n.* **1.** speaker's platform, stage, stand, rostrum, dais, pulpit, podium. **2.** program, policy, plan, plank, set of principles, tenets, creed, goal; campaign promises.

platitude *n.* trite remark, stereotyped expression, cliché, banality, commonplace, truism, hackneyed saying, old saw, saw, threadbare phrase, *Slang* chestnut, bromide, old familiar tune, same old thing.

platoon *n.* two or more squads; (*loosely*) unit, detachment, group, force, team, crew, corps, band, body.

plaudit *n.* Usu. **plaudits** praise, approval, acclaim, commendation, approbation, kudos, compliment, rave, bouquet; applause, ovation, cheer, cheering, hurrah, hallelujah, huzzah. **—Ant.** condemnation, jeer, taunt, hoot, *Slang* brickbat, rap, knock, slam, dig; boo, hiss, raspberry, Bronx cheer.

plausible *adj.* believable, probable, credible, convincing, likely, persuasive, reasonable, rational, tenable, feasible, conceivable, possible, justifiable, acceptable, logical, sound, sensible, valid. **—Ant.** unbelievable, improbable, incredible, unlikely, implausible, unreasonable, inconceivable, impossible, illogical.

play *n.* **1.** drama, stage play, dramatic piece, dramatic performance; (*variously*) comedy, tragedy, farce, melodrama; show, spectacle, extravaganza, pageant, entertainment. **2.** amusement, recreation, entertainment, diversion, fun, merrymaking, pleasure, enjoyment; caper, romp, lark, gambol, frolic, jest, sport. **3.** free motion, freedom of movement, swing, sweep; room, space, elbowroom, leeway. —*v.* **4.** engage in games, amuse oneself, entertain oneself, divert oneself, have fun, make merry, enjoy oneself, gambol, romp, revel, frisk, frolic, sport, cavort, caper, skylark, antic, disport, while away the time; trifle, toy. **5.** contend against, compete with, vie with, perform in a game; participate in a sport, take part, be on a team. **6.** perform on, perform; act, act out, act the part of, take the part of, impersonate, personify, enact, represent.

playboy *n.* pleasure seeker, nightclub habitué, party goer, party boy, good-time Charlie, profligate, hedonist, jet-setter; rake, lecher, womanizer, lady-killer, ladies' man, Romeo, Lothario, Casanova, Don Juan, *Slang* wolf, swinger, sheik. **—Ant.** ascetic, monk, puritan; hermit, recluse.

player *n.* **1.** team member, performer, athlete, jock; participant, contender, competitor, contestant, opponent, antagonist, adversary, gamester. **2.** actor, actress, thespian, trouper, mummer, mime, performer, entertainer.

playful *adj.* full of play, frolicsome, frisky, lively, rollicking, coltish, sprightly, sportive; not serious, amusing, jesting, humorous, mirthful, capricious, waggish, impish, prankish, fun-loving, lighthearted. **—Ant.** sedate, serious, somber, grave, morose, despondent, gloomy, glum.

playwright *n.* dramatist, dramaturgist, author, dramaturge, dramatic poet, dramatizer, melodramatist; librettist, play doctor; scriptwriter, scenarist.

plea *n.* **1.** appeal, entreaty, prayer, suit, petition, supplication, solicitation, beseeching, begging, adjuration, request. **2.** excuse, defense, explanation, argument, justification, vindication, apology, extenuation; pretext; alibi.

plead *v.* beg, beseech, implore, entreat, appeal to; petition, ask, request, importune, solicit, enjoin, supplicate, adjure.

pleasant *adj.* **1.** agreeable, pleasing, pleasurable, enjoyable, gratifying, satisfying, lovely, charming, attractive, inviting, felicitous, good, fine, nice; mild, gentle, soft. **2.** likable, congenial, genial, friendly, affable, amiable, cheerful, good-humored, good-natured, companionable, sociable, gregarious, cordial, warm, amicable, tactful, polite. **—Ant. 1** unpleasant, displeasing, disagreeable, distasteful, wretched, distressing, miserable, horrible, bad, awful. **2** unlikable, unfriendly, cold, offensive, repulsive, ill-humored, ill-natured, rude, impolite, ill-mannered.

pleasantry *n.* polite remark, good-natured remark, greeting, salutation; quip, jest, witticism, sally, bon mot, humorous remark, joke, jape, *Slang* wisecrack.

please *v.* **1.** gladden, delight, give pleasure to, make happy, gratify, satisfy, suit, content, elate, charm, fascinate, enthrall, entrance, enrapture, thrill; tickle; amuse, divert, entertain. **2.** like, wish, choose, desire, want, will, be inclined, elect, prefer, opt. **—Ant. 1** displease, dissatisfy, repel, disgust, offend; sadden, depress, grieve; anger, madden, incense, annoy, provoke, pique, vex, nettle, chafe.

pleasing *adj.* pleasurable, gratifying, satisfying, enjoyable, gladdening, delightful, amusing, diverting, entertaining; attractive, agreeable, inviting, likable, winning, captivating, charming, fascinating; friendly, affable, amiable, congenial, genial, cheerful, good-natured, good-humored, polite, mannerly, well-mannered. **—Ant.** displeasing, unpleasant, unpleasurable, unattractive, disagreeable, distasteful, disgusting, unlikable.

pleasure *n.* **1.** enjoyment, happiness, joy, delight, gratification, cheer, bliss, elation, exultation, rapture; gaiety, mirth, lightheartedness, merriment, jubilation, high spirits. **2.** amusement, fun, gratification, diversion, entertainment, recreation, festivity, gaiety, beer and skittles. **3.** desire, choice, like, wish, will, inclination, preference, selection, option. **—Ant. 1** displeasure, unhappiness, sorrow, sadness, suffering, pain, affliction, misery, anger, vexation. **2** work, labor, toil; self-denial, abstinence. **3** necessity, duty, obligation, compulsion; coercion.

plebeian *adj.* **1.** vulgar, coarse, common, lowbrow, low-class, unrefined, uncultivated, uncultured, commonplace, popular, banal, ordinary, low, mean, base; of the common people, lowborn, proletarian, bourgeois. *—n.* **2.** common man, commoner, average man, average citizen, everyman, one of the masses; proletarian, bourgeoisie. **—Ant. 1** highbrow, refined, cultivated, cultured, educated; upper class, aristocratic, royal, elevated. **2** aristocrat, blue blood, silk stocking, patrician, noble, nobleman, peer, lord; intellectual, highbrow.

pledge *n.* **1.** vow, solemn promise, oath, word, assurance, adjuration, avowal, troth; agreement, pact, compact, covenant, contract. **2.** security, warranty, guaranty, collateral, surety; pawn, bond, bail. *—v.* **3.** promise solemnly, promise, vow, swear, bind by an oath, assert, guarantee, warrant, give one's word.

plenitude *n.* **1.** fullness, completeness, repletion, wholeness, entireness, amplitude, totality. **2.** abundance, bounty, mass, volume, profusion, quantities, quantity, cornucopia. **—Ant. 1** scantiness, meagerness, paucity. **2** shortage, insufficiency, scarcity, inadequacy.

plentiful *adj.* abundant, bountiful, profuse, copious, bounteous, prolific, lavish, ample, abounding, plenteous, overflowing, lush, liberal, generous, large, unsparing, unstinted, infinite, inexhaustible. **—Syn. Study.** PLENTIFUL, ABUNDANT, BOUNTIFUL, AMPLE describe a more than adequate supply of something. PLENTIFUL suggests a large or full quantity: *a plentiful supply of fuel.* ABUNDANT and BOUNTIFUL both imply a greater degree of plenty: *an abundant rainfall; a bountiful harvest.* AMPLE suggests a quantity that is sufficient for a particular need or purpose: *an auditorium with ample seating for students.* **—Ant.** scant, scanty, sparse, inadequate, insufficient, deficient, scarce, skimpy, sparing, small, meager.

plenty *n.* **1.** an abundant supply, ample amount, a full measure, abundance, sufficiency, profusion, plenitude, good deal, great deal, a wealth, enough and to spare, slew, *Slang* lots, oceans, worlds, oodles, gobs, scads. **2.** prosperity, good times, affluence, well-being, good fortune, riches, wealth, luxury, opulence. **—Ant. 1** scarcity, sparsity, dearth, lack, shortage, scantiness, insufficiency, paucity, inadequacy, deficiency. **2** poverty, indigence, hard times.

plethora *n.* excess, surplus, superfluity, surplusage, surfeit, overabundance, superabundance, glut, overage, redundancy. **—Ant.** shortage, lack, scarcity, deficiency.

pliable *adj.* **1.** flexible, easily bendable, pliant, plastic, resilient, elastic, springy; supple, lithe, limber. **2.** impressionable, pliant, compliant, receptive, willing, responsive, flexible, easily influenced; accommodating, manageable, adaptable, submissive, yielding, acquiescent, tractable. **—Ant. 1** stiff, rigid, unbending. **2** stubborn, obstinate, inflexible, unyielding, willful, headstrong, dogged, intractable, dogmatic.

plight *n.* condition, situation, circumstance, state; poor condition, distressing situation, dangerous circumstances, predicament, dilemma, quandary, extremity, distress, trouble, difficulty, vicissitude, trial, tribulation; crisis, impasse, emergency, exigency, scrape, pinch, *Slang* pickle, straits, fix, muddle, jam. **—Syn. Study.** See PREDICAMENT.

plod *v.* **1.** trudge, walk heavily, drag, slog, tramp, lumber, shuffle, waddle; pace. **2.** work slowly, drudge, toil, moil, sweat, grind, struggle; persevere, be resolute, stick with it, peg away, *Slang* plug, grub. **—Syn. Study. 1** See PACE.

plot¹ *n.* **1.** conspiracy, intrigue, cabal, secret plan, evil plan, scheme, machination, maneuver, design, stratagem. **2.** story, story line, tale, narrative, incidents, yarn, plan, action, design. *—v.* **3.** conspire, scheme, intrigue, design, plan, contrive, maneuver, collude, be in collusion. **4.** chart, map, compute, calculate, determine; mark, draw, sketch, outline, diagram, blueprint, draft. **—Syn. Study. 1** See CONSPIRACY.

plot² *n.* area, space, section, area of ground, patch; lot, tract, field, clearing.

plow Also **plough** *v.* **1.** dig up, turn up, spade, dig, till, break, break up, loosen, work; furrow, harrow, cultivate. **2.** push, press, plunge, drive, cut, shove, forge, *Slang* bulldoze.

ploy *n.* stratagem, subterfuge, ruse, trick, artifice, game, maneuver, strategy, tactic, gambit, wile, scheme, game, design, *Slang* gimmick.

pluck *v.* **1.** pick, pull out, pull off, pull at, draw; jerk, grab, yank, snatch; uproot, extirpate. *—n.* **2.** spirit, mettle, courage, bravery, valor, boldness, daring, *Slang* spunk, grit, sand, guts; resolution, temerity, determination, resolve, fortitude, doggedness, perseverance, persistence, tenacity.

plug *n.* **1.** stopper, stopple, bung, cork. *—v.* **2.** stop up, close, shut off, stanch, cork, fill up, stuff.

plumb *n.* **1.** plumb line, plummet, lead; plumb bob, level. *—v.* **2.** take soundings, sound, fathom, measure, test, cast the lead; probe, penetrate, gauge, examine. *—adj.* **3.** vertical, straight up and down; straight, true, sheer. **—Ant. 3** horizontal; crooked, awry, askew, off-center, aslant.

plummet *v.* plunge, fall, fall headlong, drop straight down, dive, tumble, descend abruptly, nosedive. **—Ant.** rise, ascend, shoot upward, soar.

plump¹ *adj.* chubby, pudgy, somewhat fat, fleshy, corpulent, obese, stout, portly, stocky, rotund; rounded, buxom. **—Ant.** slender, slim, lean; thin, skinny, scrawny, lanky, skeletal, cadaverous.

plump² *v.* **1.** drop, plop, flop, plunk, sink, sprawl, collapse; spill, fall heavily, tumble. *—adj.* **2.** direct, straightforward, forthright, outright, downright, blunt, abrupt; unswerving, undeviating, firm, solid.

plunder *v.* **1.** sack, pillage, loot, ransack, raid, rifle, rob, pilfer, ravage, maraud, despoil, fleece, strip. *—n.* **2.** loot, booty, pillage, takings, spoils, pilferings, filchings, prize, *Slang* swag, haul, take.

plunge *v.* **1.** dip, thrust, cast, douse, immerse, duck; submerge, submerse, descend, sink; dive, jump, leap, throw oneself, fall headlong, tumble, pitch. **2.** rush, dash, run, dart, charge, speed, hurtle, bolt, sprint, scramble, lunge, hasten, scurry, scuttle, hustle, whisk, tear, shoot, fly, streak, scuttle; surge, push, press, drive, swarm. **3.** pitch, toss, lurch, heave, reel, rock, jerk, roll, sway, tumble about, prance about. *—n.* **4.** drop, fall, dive, headlong rush, jump, leap. **—Syn. Study. 1** See DIP. **—Ant. 1** emerge, rise, withdraw, take out. **2** stroll, amble, crawl.

plus *adj.* additional, extra, added, supplementary; supplemental, other, spare, auxiliary; helpful, desirable, useful, beneficial, advantageous.

plush *adj.* sumptuous, elegant, luxurious, opulent, deluxe, lavish, palatial, fancy, extravagant, grand, rich; *Slang* posh, classy, ritzy, lush, swank, swanky, snazzy. **—Ant.** spare, simple, Spartan, bare, austere.

ply¹ *n.* layer, stratum, thickness, sheet, plate, leaf, sheath, lamina, slice; strand, twist, plait.

ply² *v.* **1.** employ, wield, put to use, utilize, manipulate, operate, work, handle. **2.** practice, carry on, exercise, follow, labor at, pursue, occupy oneself with, persevere at, bend one's efforts to, devote oneself to. **3.** besiege, press, thrust upon, urge upon, prevail upon, supply persistently, offer repeatedly. **4.** travel regularly, make repeated trips, go back and forth; sail, navigate, run, fly.

pocket *n.* **1.** pouchlike part of a garment; compartment, envelope, receptacle, *Archaic* placket; chamber, cavity, hollow; pouch, bag, sack; purse, handbag, pocketbook. **2.** isolated mass; vein, lode, pit, strip, streak, strain. *—v.* **3.** steal, pilfer, put into one's pocket, appropriate, arrogate, usurp, help oneself to, take possession of; attain, get, obtain, come by, gain, receive. *—adj.* **4.** pocket-size, for carrying in the pocket, small, compact, little, miniature, diminutive, vest-pocket, bantam, pygmy; portable; for the pocket.

pocketbook *n.* purse, handbag, bag, shoulder bag, clutch; wallet, pocket secretary, notecase, money purse, coin purse, moneybag, pouch, satchel.

pod *n.* husk, jacket, hull, shell, sheath, case, seed case, seed vessel, pericarp.

poem *n.* verse, rhyme, verse composition, jingle, doggerel; (*variously*) ballad, ode, sonnet, elegy, epic, madrigal, lyric, idyll, song, ballad, lay, limerick.

poet *n.* maker, singer; (*variously*) lyricist, lyrist, lyric writer, song-writer, librettist, improviser, reciter, minstrel, balladeer, balladist, sonneteer, verseman, versifier, rhymer, rhymester, poetaster, poet laureate, bard.

poetic Also **poetical** *adj.* lyric, lyrical, imaginative, rhythmic, metrical, musical, melodic, songlike, lilting, melodious. **—Ant.** unpoetical, prosaic, routine, realistic, commonplace, matter-of-fact, unimaginative.

poetry *n.* verse, metrical composition, poesy, rhyme; versification.

poignant *adj.* moving, affecting, touching, heartrending, pitiful, pitiable, piteous, distressing, pathetic, woeful, grievous, lamentable, sad, sorrowful, tearful, rueful, doleful; biting, trenchant, cutting, piercing, penetrating, sharp, pungent, piquant. **—Ant.** unaffecting, unmoving, cold, blunt, unfeeling; insipid, trite, vapid, banal, superficial.

point *n.* **1.** sharp end, tapered end, tip, nib; spike, pike, apex, prong; projection, protuberance, prominence, extension, offshoot, promontory, outgrowth, spur. **2.** degree, stage, position, condition, place; limit, mark. **3.** instant, moment, time, very minute, juncture. **4.** main idea, purpose, object, end, reason; gist, essence, heart, kernel, pith, core, meat, marrow, sum and substance. **5.** sense, reason, cause, object, objective, aim, intention, purpose, end, value, use. **6.** detail, item, particular, aspect, feature, quality. **7.** score, tally; unit, number; (*variously*) hit, basket, run, goal, game. *—v.* **8.** aim, train, direct; steer, guide, turn, bend, slant, level. **9.** indicate, suggest, imply, signify, intimate, hint at; portend, foreshadow, presage, bode, argue; testify; demonstrate, manifest, prove.

pointed *adj.* **1.** peaked, sharp, pointy, acute, acuminate, cuspidate, aciculate. **2.** pertinent, incisive, fitting, telling, penetrating, trenchant, appropriate, accurate, piercing, cutting, biting; insinuating, hinting. **—Ant. 1** blunt, dull, rounded. **2** pointless, irrelevant, inappropriate.

pointer *n.* **1.** indicator, arrow, guide, stick; hand, arm, needle. **2.** piece of advice, bit of information, hint, suggestion, tip, advisement, recommendation; admonition, caution, warning.

pointless *adj.* **1.** without a point, unpointed, rounded, obtuse; blunt, dull, worn down, unedged, unsharpened. **2.** useless, purposeless, unproductive, unprofitable, bootless, unavailing, meaningless, fruitless, futile, worthless, aimless, invalid, ineffectual; unreasonable, irrational, illogical, absurd, preposterous, ridiculous, stupid, irrelevant, senseless, inapplicable, beside the point. **—Ant. 1** pointed, sharp. **2** useful, profitable, meaningful, fruitful, productive, beneficial, worthwhile, valid, invaluable; appropriate, fitting, proper, to the point; reasonable, logical, sensible; desirable, advisable.

poise *n.* **1.** assurance, self-assurance, self-confidence, self-command, self-control, presence of mind, presence, aplomb, equanimity, calm, composure, *French* savoir faire, sangfroid. *—v.* **2.** balance, be in equilibrium; hold aloft, raise, elevate.

poison *n.* **1.** toxic chemical, harmful chemical, bane; (*loosely*) toxin, venom, harmful drug. **2.** evil, harm, curse, bane, disease, cancer, malignancy, malignity, canker, plague, pestilence; outrage, enormity, abomination, corruption. *—v.* **3.** kill with poison, harm with poison, give poison to; infect, contaminate, disease, make sick, impair, weaken, debilitate. **4.** contaminate, pollute, taint, adulterate; corrupt, defile, debase, degrade, corrode. **—Syn. Study. 1** POISON, TOXIN, VENOM are terms for any substance that injures the health or destroys life when absorbed into the system. POISON is the general word: *a poison for insects.* A TOXIN is a poison produced by an organism; it is esp. used in medicine in reference to disease-causing bacterial secretions: *A toxin produces diphtheria.* VENOM is esp. used of the poisons injected by bite, sting, etc.: *snake venom; bee venom.* **—Ant. 1** antidote. **2** good, benefit, salve, balm.

poisonous *adj.* lethal, fatal, toxic, venomous, noxious, deadly, pernicious, baneful, virulent, mortal, pestilential, deleterious. **—Ant.** beneficial, healthful, healthy, salubrious; harmless, innocuous.

poke *n.* **1.** jab, thrust, punch, hit, push, prod, nudge, jolt, dig, thump. *—v.* **2.** prod, jab, dig, nudge, jolt, thrust, push, butt, hit, punch, stick, stab, gore. **3.** dawdle, idle, dally, dillydally, shilly-shally, fiddle, delay, potter; drag, shuffle, crawl, hang back, saunter, meander, shamble, *Slang* mosey.

police *n.* **1.** law-enforcement organization, police force, sheriff's office; law-enforcement officers, policemen, troopers, constabulary, *Informal* cops, gendarmes, men in blue, *Slang* fuzz. *—v.* **2.** patrol, guard, protect, go on one's beat; maintain law and order, keep in order, regulate, control. **3.** clean, clean up, tidy, tidy up, pick up trash from, neaten, spruce up.

policeman *Fem.* **policewoman** *n.* police officer, officer, officer of the law, law-enforcement officer, bluecoat, *Informal* arm of the law, gendarme, *Slang* cop, dick, flatfoot; (*variously*) patrolman, cop on the beat, motorcycle policeman, traffic cop; sheriff, marshal, constable.

policy *n.* practice, procedure, course of

action, mode of management, line of conduct, system, program, routine, habit, custom, rule, behavior, way, method, platform, principle, style; plan, scheme, strategy, tactics, design.

polish *v.* **1.** shine, buff, rub up, burnish, smooth, sand, pumice; wax, gloss, varnish, glaze. **2.** perfect, refine, improve, enhance, round out, touch up, emend, correct. **—***n.* **3.** wax, shining substance, gloss, varnish, glaze, oil; abrasive, sandpaper, pumice, rouge. **4.** gloss, luster, sheen, shine, glaze, gleam, shimmer, glow; brightness, brilliance. **5.** grace, culture, cultivation, refinement, elegance, finesse, suavity, urbanity; good manners, politeness, politesse, courtesy, gentility, *Slang* class. **—Syn. Study.** POLISH, GLOSS, LUSTER, SHEEN refer to a smooth, shining, or bright surface from which light is reflected. POLISH suggests the smooth, bright reflection often produced by friction: *a lamp rubbed to a high polish.* GLOSS suggests a superficial, hard smoothness characteristic of lacquered, varnished, or enameled surfaces: *a gloss on oilcloth.* LUSTER denotes the characteristic quality of the light reflected from the surfaces of certain materials, as pearls or freshly cut metals: *a pearly luster.* SHEEN sometimes suggests a glistening brightness such as that reflected from the surface of silk: *the sheen of a satin gown.* **—Ant. 1** tarnish, oxidize, discolor, dull, corrode, erode. **3** remover. **4** dullness, lusterlessness, film, filminess, haziness; matte finish. **5** boorishness, clumsiness, awkwardness; indecorum, gaucheness, uncouthness.

polite *adj.* **1.** courteous, well-mannered, mannerly, well-behaved, cultivated, proper, civil, respectful, diffident, ladylike, gentlemanly, courtly, gallant, ceremonious. **2.** refined, cultured, polished, genteel, well-bred, civilized, elegant, fashionable, high, elite, patrician. **—Syn. Study. 1** See CIVIL. **—Ant. 1** rude, impolite, discourteous, ill-mannered, unmannerly, uncouth; insulting, impudent, impertinent. **2** unrefined, uncultured, ill-bred, unpolished, crude, boorish.

politic *adj.* tactful, judicious, wise, prudent, circumspect, discreet, shrewd, diplomatic, artful, cautious, chary, perspicacious, mindful. **—Syn. Study.** See DIPLOMATIC. **—Ant.** rude, tactless, blundering, rash.

politician *n.* professional in party politics, politico, political careerist; office seeker, campaigner, officeholder, incumbent, public servant, legislator, statesman. **—Syn. Study.** POLITICIAN, STATESMAN refer to one skilled in politics. POLITICIAN is more often derogatory, and STATESMAN laudatory. POLITICIAN suggests the scheming of a person who engages in politics for party ends or personal advantage: *a dishonest politician.* STATESMAN suggests the eminent ability, foresight, and patriotic devotion of a person dealing with important affairs of state: *a distinguished statesman.*

politics *n. pl.* **1.** political science, art of government, administration of public affairs, practice of government; affairs of state, government policy, statecraft, statesmanship. **2.** political views, political matters, party policy, party leadership, political maneuvers.

poll *n.* **1.** voting place; voting list; voting, vote, returns, tally, figures. **2.** public opinion poll, public survey, sampling, census, canvass, nose count, count; public opinion. **—***v.* **3.** take the vote of, register the vote of, solicit the vote of, canvass, survey, interview, sample the opinion of, count noses. **4.** receive a vote; register, tally.

pollute *v.* contaminate, befoul, foul, dirty, soil, adulterate, sully, make filthy; defile, profane, desecrate, debase, deprave. **—Ant.** purify, clean, cleanse, clarify, purge.

pollution *n.* contamination, contaminating, befouling, fouling, dirtying, soiling, defiling; uncleanness, foulness, adulteration; pollutant, impurity.

pomp *n.* stately display, ceremony, solemnity, pageantry, spectacle, splendor, grandeur, magnificence, brilliance, glory; flourish, style, show, display; pompousness, ostentation, pretentiousness, showiness, grandiosity, affectation, *Informal* front.

pompous *adj.* self-important, ostentatious, pretentious, haughty, arrogant, patronizing, snobbish, condescending, overbearing, presumptuous, *Informal* uppish, puffed-up; vain, conceited, egotistic, supercilious, vainglorious, proud, imperious, blustering, swaggering, grandiose, lordly, high and mighty, affected, mannered, overdone. **—Syn. Study.** See GRANDIOSE. **—Ant.** simple, modest, inglorious; dull.

pond *n.* small lake, lagoon, pool, tarn; water hole; basin.

ponder *v.* consider, meditate on, reflect on, contemplate, think over, give thought to; cogitate, cerebrate, ruminate, deliberate, study, concentrate upon, puzzle over, rack one's brain, examine, *Informal* put on one's thinking cap; mull over, muse, reflect, speculate, wonder, brood over.

ponderous *adj.* **1.** heavy, weighty, burdensome, awkward, cumbrous, cumbersome, unwieldy; massive, bulky, enormous, big, large, *Informal* hefty. **2.** heavy, awkward, ungraceful, lumpish, hulking, graceless, lumbering, bovine, corpulent. **3.** dull, heavy, heavy-handed, labored, lusterless, boring, unexciting, dreary, unlively, sluggish; long-winded, wordy, tedious, droning, monotonous, wearisome. **—Ant. 1** light, weightless; small, tiny, dainty. **2** graceful, light on the feet; dainty. **3** exciting, absorbing, lively; short, terse, brief, concise, succinct, to the point.

pontifical *adj.* **1.** churchly, priestly, ecclesiastical, clerical, episcopal, apostolic. **2.** pompous, pretentious, condescending, patronizing; imperious, overbearing, opinionated, dogmatic, authoritarian.

pool *n.* **1.** pond, lake, tarn, mere, (*variously*) fishpond, millpool, swimming pool; puddle, splash. **2.** group, association, combine, coalition, confederation, cooperative, collective, alliance, union. **3.** stakes, kitty, pot, bank. *—v.* **4.** combine, merge, amalgamate, share, consolidate, band together, unite, ally.

poor *adj.* **1.** poverty-stricken, indigent, insolvent, destitute, impoverished, penniless, moneyless, pauperized, bankrupt, impecunious, broke; needy, in need, in want, in straits, strapped, badly off, *Informal* hard up, on the rocks. **2.** unfertile, infertile, barren, sterile; desolate, forlorn, meager, bare, exhausted, depleted, empty; uncultivable, fallow, unproductive, dead, wasted, worn. **3.** inferior, inadequate, deficient, defective, imperfect, wanting, faulty, lacking something, devoid of; paltry, wretched, sorry, meager, beggarly, indifferent, worthless, fruitless, vain, futile, unprofitable, unworthy. **4.** pitiable, unfortunate, unlucky, pathetic, miserable, wretched, sorry; distressed, unhappy, sad, grieving. *—n.* **5.** the unfortunate, the needy, the penniless, the destitute, the indigent, the impoverished. **—Syn. Study. 1** POOR, IMPOVERISHED, PENNILESS, IMPECUNIOUS refer to those lacking money. POOR is the simple word for the condition of lacking the means to obtain the comforts of life: *a very poor family.* IMPOVERISHED often implies a former state of greater plenty: *the impoverished aristocracy.* PENNILESS refers to extreme poverty; it means entirely without money: *The widow was left penniless.* IMPECUNIOUS often suggests that the poverty is a consequence of unwise habits: *an impecunious actor.* **—Ant. 1, 2** rich. **1** affluent, wealthy, moneyed; fortunate, lucky, *Informal* well-off, *Slang* in the chips, on easy street; comfortable. **2** fertile, productive, fecund, cultivable, fruitful, fructiferous. **3** worthy, superior, excellent. **5** the rich, the affluent, the wealthy.

pop *v.* **1.** explode, burst; boom, bang, discharge, detonate, crack, snap. **2.** appear, materialize, issue forth suddenly, burst, arise, come. *—n.* **3.** explosion, detonation, boom, shot, discharge, bang, blast, report, crack, burst. **4.** soda, soda pop, soft drink.

poppycock *n.* *Informal* balderdash, bunk, bosh, tosh, nonsense, stuff, rubbish, trash, garbage, hogwash, rot, falderal, gibberish, *Slang* jive; jabberwocky, twaddle, blather, blabber, prattle, fustian, tommyrot, wish-wash, fiddlefaddle, flapdoodle, rigmarole, *Slang* gobbledygook; absurdity, drivel, inanity, froth, flummery, abracadabra, hocus-pocus, mumbo-jumbo, moonshine, hooey, fudge, baloney, applesauce.

popular *adj.* **1.** sought-after, well-received, in favor, in demand, accepted; preferred, approved, well-liked, favorite, admired; well-known, celebrated, famous. **2.** public, of the people, general, common, universal; communal, community, civic, democratic, social, sociological, civil, national; inexpensive, affordable, cheap. **3.** current, prevalent, fashionable; accepted, approved, familiar, stock, conventional, established, orthodox. **—Syn. Study. 2** See GENERAL. **—Ant. 1–3** unpopular. **1** in disfavor, unaccepted; unliked, odious, displeasing. **3** uncommon, unusual, rare, unconventional, unorthodox.

popularity *n.* favor, acceptance, approval, acclaim, vogue, fashion, fame, reputation, celebrity, repute, renown, note, notability; glory, *Informal* kudos; acclamation, esteem, regard, admiration; notoriety.

population *n.* inhabitants, residents, habitancy; citizenry, public, citizens, body politic, commonality; people, folk, populace.

populous *adj.* full of people, full of inhabitants, populated, peopled, crowded, teeming, jammed, swarming, thronged, thickly settled, dense.

pore[1] *v.* read, study, ponder, examine, scrutinize, peruse, inspect, scan, run the eye over; study, consider, search, probe, delve into, dig into, explore, survey, review.

pore[2] *n.* tiny opening, hole, orifice, aperture, outlet.

pornographic *adj.* obscene, indecent, lewd, gross, salacious, dirty, prurient, lascivious, smutty, filthy, off-color, blue, coarse, vulgar, bawdy, licentious.

porous *adj.* absorbent, permeable, penetrable, pervious; honeycombed, sievelike, cellular, riddled, lacy; spongy.

port *n.* seaport, harbor, dock, pier, wharf, quay, landing, harborage, anchorage, mooring, dry dock; shelter, refuge, haven; destination. **—Syn. Study.** See HARBOR.

portable *adj.* transportable, movable,

haulable, conveyable, transferable, cartable, liftable; compact, folding, pocket, pocket-sized, vest-pocket, small, bantam; light, manageable, ready-to-go, handy, convenient.

portal *n.* Usu. **portals** entrance, entranceway, door, gate, gateway, adit, doorway, wicket, approach, entry, threshold, arch, portcullis, vestibule, portico.

portend *v.* foretell, forecast, augur, bode, prophesy, predict, prognosticate; herald, signify, point to, warn of, forewarn, give token of, presage, prefigure, betoken, denote, suggest, forebode, foreshadow, foretoken, bespeak.

portent *n.* warning, sign, forewarning, boding, foreboding, threat, dire prospect; omen, sign, token, augury, presage, harbinger. **—Syn. Study.** See SIGN.

portentous *adj.* **1.** foreboding, threatening, intimidating, ominous, menacing, alarming, frightening; significant, fateful, prophetic; unpropitious, inauspicious. **2.** prodigious, stupendous, amazing, astonishing, surprising, remarkable, extraordinary, incredible, superlative, exceptional, superb. **3.** pompous, self-important, pretentious, grandiose; bombastic, grandiloquent. **—Syn. Study. 1** See OMINOUS.

porter *n.* baggage carrier, redcap, skycap, carrier, transporter, bearer, conveyer, conductor; (*in the Far East*) coolie.

portion *n.* **1.** part, section, division, segment, sector; piece, fraction, fragment; measure, quantity, amount, sum. **2.** part, division, allowance, allotment, share, apportionment, allocation; serving, helping, ration, percentage, *Slang* cut. **3.** fortune, lot, destiny, fate, doom, luck, kismet, *Greek* moira; God's will. **—***v.* **4.** divide, distribute, deal out, disperse; cut up, slice, carve, separate, sever, split, segment, partition, demarcate; apportion, allocate, dole; parcel, break up.

portly *adj.* large, substantial, heavy, fat, big, corpulent, obese, fleshy, plump, pudgy, full-figured, rotund, stout, round, full, stocky, burly, chubby, beefy, brawny, tubby, endomorphic. **—Ant.** thin, slender, trim.

portrait *n.* **1.** painting, sketch, drawing, photograph, picture, likeness. **2.** description, verbal picture, word painting, personal report, thumbnail sketch, impression, picturization, graphic account, depiction, representation, vignette, cameo.

portray *v.* **1.** depict, describe, picture, delineate, model; sketch, draw, illustrate, paint, carve, sculpture, photograph. **2.** enact, play, represent, characterize, impersonate, pose as, simulate; imitate, mimic, ape. **3.** describe, depict, characterize, represent, detail; figure, set forth, narrate, delineate, picture.

pose *v.* **1.** position, arrange, group, order, set, line up. **2.** posture, act self-consciously, act affectedly, show off, give oneself airs. **3.** pretend to be, pass oneself off as, impersonate. **4.** state, put forward, submit, set forth, postulate, advance, throw out, present, propose, propound, bring up, suggest. **—***n.* **5.** attitude, posture, position, stance, bearing, carriage; mien, cast, air, mannerism, style. **—Syn. Study. 5** See POSITION.

posh *adj.* elegant, fancy, refined, high-class, deluxe, classy, chic, swell, smart, stylish, extravagant, lavish, luxurious, opulent, swanky, ritzy, chi-chi. **—Ant.** plain, simple, modest, unpretentious, austere.

position *n.* **1.** place, location, placement, locus, situation, disposition; locality, site, station, spot. **2.** posture, stance, attitude, pose. **3.** one's station, usual or proper place, work station, spot, space. **4.** situation, predicament, condition, state, circumstances, plight; standing, place. **5.** standing, status, station, elevation, prominence, eminence, distinction, importance, prestige, consequence, notability, class, caste, place, order. **6.** job, place, career, post, capacity, function, role, charge, appointment, assignment, responsibility, duty, commission, office. **7.** opinion, viewpoint, outlook, point of view, stand, frame of mind. **8.** location, vantage, ground, field position. **—***v.* **9.** put, place, arrange, array, set; pose, establish, stand, fix, situate, locate, lodge, deposit. **—Syn. Study.** POSITION, POSTURE, ATTITUDE, POSE refer to an arrangement or disposal of the body or its parts. POSITION is the general word for the arrangement of the body: *in a reclining position.* POSTURE is usu. an assumed arrangement of the body, esp. when standing: *a relaxed posture.* ATTITUDE is often a posture assumed for imitative effect or the like, but may be one adopted for a purpose (as that of a fencer or a tightrope walker): *an attitude of prayer.* A POSE is an attitude assumed, in most cases, for artistic effect: *an attractive pose.*

positive *adj.* **1.** conclusive, firm, absolute, decisive, unqualified, definite, definitive, leaving no doubt, unequivocal, explicit, corroborative, confirmatory, undisputed, irrefutable, incontrovertible. **2.** sure, certain, undoubting, confident, satisfied, assured, cocksure, dead certain, convinced. **3.** practical, practicable, effective, constructive, useful, helpful, serviceable, applicable; beneficial, gainful, good, salutary, contributory. **4.** forward-looking, optimistic, progressive, affirmative, cooperative. **5.** real, honest-to-goodness, absolute, complete, veritable, total, thoroughgoing. **6.** dogmatic, opinionated, narrow, autocratic, overbearing, dictatorial; obdurate, unchangeable, immovable; assertive, self-assured, *Informal* cocksure. **—Ant. 1** inconclusive, qualified, indefinite, disputable. **2** unsure, tentative, doubting, uncertain. **3** negative; impractical, speculative; wild, foolish, useless. **4** pessimistic; conservative, reactionary; neutral, indifferent; vain, idle. **6** amenable, tractable, self-effacing.

positively *adv.* **1.** absolutely, unhesitatingly, unquestionably, indisputably, decidedly, definitely, unmistakably, indubitably; emphatically, categorically, unqualifiedly, affirmatively, assuredly, confidently, certainly. **2.** definitely, literally, unquestionably, beyond question, without doubt, assuredly, absolutely.

possess *v.* **1.** own, have, have title to, hold, occupy, maintain. **2.** have, be endowed with, be blest with, boast; command; enjoy. **3.** conquer, vanquish, overrun, grab, control, occupy, absorb, take over, acquire. **4.** dominate, control, influence, obsess, consume; fascinate, fixate, mesmerize, enchant, be eaten up, hypnotize, bedevil, bewitch; dominate, make insane, drive crazy.

possession *n.* **1.** possessing, owning, ownership, proprietorship, vested interest; occupation, occupancy, control, custody, hold, title, tenancy. **2.** belonging, asset, material thing, effect, resource, accoutrement. **3.** dominion, territory, province, protectorate. **4.** self-possession, presence of mind, self-control, composure, even temper, calmness, unexcitability, coolness, placidity, sangfroid, poise, equanimity, equilibrium; control, command.

possibility *n.* **1.** chance, likelihood, prospect, probability, hope, odds. **2.** chance, eventuality, risk, hazard, gamble, contingency. **3.** potentiality, promise, prospects; feasibility, practicability, workability.

possible *adj.* **1.** potential, contingent, conceivable, thinkable, imaginable, hypothetical; credible, thinkable, worth consideration, reasonable, compatible; admissible, cognizable. **2.** capable of being done, within reach, attainable, obtainable, achievable, feasible, practicable, workable, performable, manageable, conceivable; capable of happening. **—Syn. Study. 2** POSSIBLE, FEASIBLE, PRACTICABLE refer to that which may come about or take place without prevention by serious obstacles. That which is POSSIBLE is naturally able or even likely to happen, other circumstances being equal: *He offered a possible compromise.* FEASIBLE refers to the ease with which something can be done and implies a high degree of desirability for doing it: *Which plan is the most feasible?* PRACTICABLE applies to that which can be done with the means at hand and with conditions as they are: *We ascended the slope as far as was practicable.* **—Ant. 1, 2** impossible. **1** inconceivable, unimaginable, improbable; incredible, unthinkable, unreasonable, incompatible; unlikely. **2** unobtainable, inaccessible; unfeasible.

possibly *adv.* **1.** perhaps, maybe, could be, may be, conceivably, as luck may have it, perchance, mayhap, God willing. **2.** conceivably, normally, at the most. **3.** by any means, in any way, at all, by the remotest chance.

post[1] *n.* **1.** stake, picket, upright, pale, support, column, shaft, pole, mainstay, brace, splint, pile. **—*v.* 2.** put up, fasten up, tack up, publish, place in public view; make known, announce, broadcast, circulate, declare, disclose, report, advertise; proclaim; inform, notify, instruct, advise, acquaint, apprise, enlighten.

post[2] *n.* **1.** place of duty, station, round, beat, routine. **2.** job, position, office, situation, place, spot, station, seat; capacity, role, function, work, part; assignment, mission, appointment. **3.** military camp, base, headquarters; settlement; trading post, post exchange, PX, exchange. **—*v.* 4.** station, situate, install, place, put, fix, set, establish; quarter, lodge, house, camp, settle; locate.

posterior *adj.* **1.** rear, back, hindmost, aftermost, tail, hind, hinder, rearward; dorsal, caudal. **—*n.* 2.** rump, buttocks, backside, behind, seat, bottom, stern, *Informal* fanny, *Slang* butt, can, keister, prat, tail, tush, tushy, *French* derrière, *British* bum. **—Syn. Study. 1** See BACK.

posterity *n.* future generations, succeeding ages, history; offspring, descendants, heirs, issue, successors, progeny; family, young, children; descent, lineage, succession.

postpone *v.* defer, delay, put off, waive, lay over, adjourn, hold in abeyance, reserve, remand, suspend; stay, keep back, table, shelve. **—Syn. Study.** See DEFER.

postulate *v.* **1.** propose, put forth, submit; assume, take as an axiom, presume, take for granted, presuppose; conjecture, guess, hazard, surmise, theorize, hypothesize, speculate. **—*n.* 2.** premise, assumption, fundamental principle, presumption, presupposition, axiom, theorem, theory, hypothesis.

posture *n.* **1.** stance, carriage, bearing, pose, shape, contour; position, set, attitude, mien. **2.** position, station, situation, status, standing, condition, post, place. **3.** mood, tone, tenor, aspect, air, attitude, state, case, phase; situation, circumstance, predicament. **—Syn. Study. 1** See POSITION.

potent *adj.* **1.** powerful, strong, mighty, forceful, vigorous, overpowering, formidable, solid, tough. **2.** influential, convincing, persuasive, compelling, impressive; forceful, powerful, forcible, dynamic. **3.** effective, efficacious, operative. **—Ant. 1, 2** impotent, weak; ineffectual, inefficient. **1** weak, frail, puny. **2** unconvincing, ineffective, unimpressive.

potentate *n.* ruler, sovereign, sultan, suzerain, monarch, chieftain, mogul, satrap, lord, emperor, prince, head of state, crowned head.

potential *adj.* **1.** possible, conceivable, latent, concealed, hidden, lurking, covert, unapparent; unrealized, dormant, quiescent, passive; unexerted, unexpressed, implicit, undisclosed. *—n.* **2.** Also **potentiality** ability, possibilities, capability. **—Ant. 1** actual, real, manifest.

potion *n.* elixir, brew, concoction, dram, tonic, philter, draft, mixture, draft, potation, libation.

potpourri *n.* medley, mixture, mélange, pastiche, miscellany, olla podrida; hodgepodge, confused mass, mishmash, gallimaufry, olio, goulash, stew, hash, jumble, mess, farrago; mosaic, patchwork; salmagundi, motley.

pouch *n.* bag, sack, satchel, receptacle, container; (*variously*) pocket, wallet, purse, pocketbook, handbag, carryall, reticule; rucksack, kit, ditty bag.

pounce *v.* **1.** swoop down on, fall upon, drop from the sky, plunge, strike at, spring upon, fly at, dash at, jump at, snatch; surprise, take unawares, ambush. *—n.* **2.** swoop, downrush, spring, leap, jump.

pound *v.* **1.** beat, hit, strike, hammer, drum, batter, bang, *Informal* clobber; pummel, maul, trounce, thump, thwack, clout, cudgel, smack, wallop; drub, lambaste, thrash, paste, fustigate, bruise, beat black and blue. **2.** throb, beat, pulsate, palpitate. **3.** pulverize, crush, crumble, grind. **4.** stomp, thunder, march, tramp, clomp. **—Syn. Study. 1** See BEAT.

pour *v.* **1.** let flow, decant; tap, draw off; spill, squirt, effuse, slop; lade out. **2.** stream, issue, flow, gush, spout, cascade; seep, ooze, dribble, drop, drip; drain. **3.** rain heavily, rain hard, rain in torrents, *Informal* rain cats and dogs, come down in buckets, come down in sheets; flood, deluge, drench.

pout *v.* sulk, look sullen, grimace petulantly, have a hangdog look, make a long face, scowl, crab, fume, brood, brood over, fret, mope; be out of humor, frown, glower, lower.

poverty *n.* **1.** privation, need, neediness, destitution, indigence, penury, impoverishment, pennilessness, insolvency, bankruptcy, pauperism; want, lack; beggary, mendicancy. **2.** lack, deficiency, insufficiency, shortage, dearth, paucity, scarcity, deficit, meagerness. **—Ant. 1** affluence, luxury, opulence, comfort; richness. **2** abundance, sufficiency, overabundance, plethora.

powdery *adj.* pulverized, ground, pestled, milled, floury, mealy, chalky, dusty, triturated, comminuted, crushed; shredded, grated.

power *n.* **1.** faculty, capability, capacity, competence, aptitude, talent, skill, genius, attribute, qualification, gift, endowment, property, quality. **2.** strength, force, might, potency, energy, puissance, powerfulness, pressure, muscle, brawn, iron grip; vigor, vitality. **3.** right, prerogative, status, influence, sway, prestige, authority, license. **4.** authority, ruler; dominant state, superpower, major nation. **5.** electricity, hydroelectric power, nuclear energy, solar energy, thermal energy. *—v.* **6.** energize, activate, operate, supply with power, give energy to. **—Ant. 1** incapability, incapacity. **2** weakness, impotence, feebleness; enervation, listlessness.

powerful *adj.* **1.** strong, able-bodied, mighty, potent, indomitable, unconquerable, invincible; vigorous, robust, sturdy, hardy, brawny, husky, athletic, muscular, strapping, stalwart, stout, herculean. **2.** commanding, authoritative, cogent, forceful, high-powered, energetic, rousing, moving, exciting, emphatic, incisive, intense, effective.

powerless *adj.* **1.** helpless, without strength, impotent, feeble, incapable, impuissant, feckless, weak, debilitated, incapacitated, disabled, prostrate, immobilized, crippled, infirm. **2.** defenseless, unarmed, weaponless, pregnable, vulnerable.

powwow *n.* **1.** meeting, conference, parley, talk, consultation, interview, palaver, discussion, huddle, discourse; forum, colloquy, round table, colloquium; council, congress, conclave, assembly, convention, summit conference. *—v.* **2.** confer, consult, discuss, talk, parley, palaver, huddle, convene, caucus, meet.

practicable *adj.* practical, feasible, workable, attainable, doable, possible, achievable, functional, viable, performable, accomplishable, within one's powers, within the realm of possibility. —**Syn. Study.** See POSSIBLE. —**Ant.** impracticable, impractical, unworkable, unfeasible, impossible.

practical *adj.* **1.** useful, sound, sensible, realistic, functional, solid, down-to-earth, serviceable, utilitarian, pragmatic, pragmatical, systematic, efficient, businesslike, judicious; hardheaded, unsentimental, unromantic, matter-of-fact. **2.** working, practiced, seasoned, veteran, experienced, versed, accomplished, proficient, skilled, skillful, qualified, able, expert; trained, instructed. —**Syn. Study. 1** PRACTICAL, SENSIBLE, JUDICIOUS refer to good judgment in action, conduct, and the handling of everyday matters. PRACTICAL suggests the ability to adopt means to an end or to turn what is at hand to account: *to adopt practical measures for settling problems.* SENSIBLE implies the possession and use of reason and shrewd common sense: *a sensible suggestion.* JUDICIOUS implies the possession and use of discreet judgment, discrimination, and balance: *a judicious use of one's time.* —**Ant. 1, 2** impractical, unpractical. **1** theoretical, speculative, unsound, injudicious. **2** inexperienced, unversed, unqualified.

practically *adv.* virtually, in effect, actually, essentially, nearly, in the main, almost, just about, all but, substantially; fundamentally, basically, to all intents and purposes.

practice *n.* **1.** training, drill, repetition, discipline, preparation, seasoning, exercise, rehearsal. **2.** operation, action, use, usage, effect, execution, performance, exercise, application, play. **3.** custom, wont, habit, procedure, rule, routine, process, method, manner, fashion, mode, way, ritual, ways, conduct, observance, tendency, modus operandi. **4.** method, action, deed, maneuver, trick, ruse, dodge, device. —*v.* **5.** rehearse, drill, discipline, train; familiarize with, become proficient at, prepare for, qualify. **6.** perform, do, carry out, follow, put into practice, put into action, apply, use, utilize, live up to, turn to use, bring into play, set to work. **7.** perform in, work at, engage in, pursue, be engaged in. —**Syn. Study. 3** See CUSTOM.

pragmatic *adj.* down-to-earth, matter-of-fact, practical, utilitarian, hardheaded, sober, businesslike, hard-boiled, sensible, realistic, unidealistic, hard-nosed, materialistic, unsentimental. —**Ant.** idealistic, theoretical; romantic, dreamy, sentimental.

praise *n.* **1.** good words, compliments; approval, appreciation, approbation, acclaim, congratulation, commendation, laudation; admiration, regard, esteem, respect; applause, accolade, plaudit, cheer, hurrah; eulogy, panegyric, encomium, tribute, testimonial. **2.** worship by hymn-singing, adoration. —*v.* **3.** commend, laud, approve, acclaim, extol, congratulate, compliment, applaud, cheer, root for; panegyrize, eulogize, exalt, *Slang* tout, build up. **4.** worship, celebrate, glorify, exalt; revere, venerate, honor.

praiseworthy *adj.* worthy, estimable, excellent, fine, exemplary, commendable, admirable, laudable, meritorious.

prance *v.* dance, skip, cavort, caper, gambol, romp, frolic; leap, spring, jump, vault; bounce, bound, frisk; strut, swagger.

prank *n.* trick, caper, joke, escapade, antic, shenanigan, horseplay, lark, mischief, gambol, practical joke, stunt, spoof, tomfoolery.

prattle *n.* **1.** gab, babble, blab, prate, twaddle, chitchat; *Slang* hot air, yak; cackling, gibbering, jabbering, gabbling. —*v.* **2.** jabber, chatter, babble, blather, gabble, blab, chitchat.

pray *v.* **1.** make devout petition to God, commune with God, address the Lord, offer a prayer, say one's prayers, invocate; fall on bended knee. **2.** beg, beseech, entreat, implore, plead, supplicate, make an entreaty for, importune, cry to; ask earnestly, request, solicit, call upon, petition, urge, sue, bid.

prayer *n.* **1.** litany, orison, praise, thanksgiving, adoration, worship, glorification. **2.** Often **prayers** hope, dream, aspiration; request, appeal, plea, petition, solicitation; supplication, invocation; entreaty, suit, beseechment.

prayerful *adj.* pious, devout, godly, religious, holy, pietistic, worshipful, reverent, solemn, spiritual, reverential. —**Ant.** blasphemous, impious, irreverent; disdainful, contemptuous.

preach *v.* **1.** sermonize, proclaim, discourse, evangelize, homilize, preachify. **2.** advocate, urge, advise, counsel, profess, press urgently, exhort, propagate, stand for, hold forth, declare, pronounce, expound, admonish, promulgate, prescribe.

preacher *n.* clergyman, minister, churchman, ecclesiastic, evangelist, reverend, pastor, man of the cloth, prebendary, parson, vicar, curate, chaplain, *Informal* sky pilot; sermonizer, homilist.

precarious *adj.* **1.** vulnerable, uncertain, problematical, ticklish, uncontrolled, critical, insecure, touch-and-go, not to be depended upon, unreliable, undependable, doubtful, dubious, questionable. **2.** hazardous, risky, perilous, unsafe, chancy, unsteady, unstable, shaky;

alarming, sinister. **—Ant. 1** certain, sure, secure, dependable, reliable, unquestionable. **2** safe, steady, stable.

precaution *n.* safety measure, caution, care, safeguard, defense; protection, security; forethought, provision, prudence, foresight, anticipation, carefulness, heedfulness, circumspection, wariness.

precede *v.* go before, go ahead of, come before, take place before, go on before; antedate, antecede.

precedence Also **precedency** *n.* **1.** antecedence, priority in time, preexistence. **2.** importance, preeminence, predominance, preference, prevalence; priority.

precedent *n.* example, pattern, model, guideline, standard, criterion.

preceding *adj.* previous, earlier, prior, foregoing, preliminary, precursory, antecedent, anterior; preexistent, former, first-named or -mentioned, aforesaid, aforementioned, abovementioned.

precept *n.* maxim, principle, axiom, rule, teaching, motto, dictate, declaration, commandment; law, edict, dictum, decree, statute, regulation, canon, ordinance, bull, ukase.

precious *adj.* **1.** costly, dear, expensive, high-priced, valuable, priceless, invaluable, inestimable, beyond price, not to be had for love or money; rare, uncommon, choice, exquisite. **2.** valuable, highly esteemed, cherished, choice, treasured, prized, valued, beloved, adored; sweet, darling, adorable, lovable. **3.** excessively nice, dainty, affected, pretentious, overrefined, fastidious, prissy, finicky, fussy, particular, meticulous, finical.

precipice *n.* cliff, cliff edge, ledge, escarpment, bluff, headland, palisade, crag, declivity.

precipitate *v.* **1.** hasten, bring on, quicken, expedite, speed up, accelerate, advance, spur. **2.** throw, hurl, thrust, cast, fling, propel, drive, launch, catapult, discharge, let fly. *—adj.* **3.** hurried, hasty, abrupt, rushed, proceeding rapidly, speedy; headlong, reckless, rash, incautious, foolhardy, imprudent, thoughtless, impetuous, impulsive.

précis *n.* summary, synopsis, brief, digest, condensation, abstract, résumé, compendium, abridgment, epitome, rundown, outline, sketch, recapitulation, *French* aperçu.

precise *adj.* **1.** exact, specific, strict, true, clear-cut, express, definite, explicit, accurate, correct, incisive, unequivocal, to the point, distinct, literal; careful, painstaking, meticulous, fastidious. **2.** exact, particular, unbending, inflexible, meticulous, distinct, rigid, strict, finicky, fussy. **—Syn. Study. 1** See CORRECT. **—Ant. 1** inexact, implicit, indefinite, ambiguous, equivocal, indistinct, vague, indeterminate, nebulous; careless, heedless, loose, lax, incautious. **2** flexible, changing, haphazard.

precision *n.* exactness, preciseness, accuracy, meticulousness, scrupulous care, rigor, attention; authenticity, factualness, truthfulness, fidelity.

preclude *v.* prevent, foil, thwart, hamper, hinder, stop, check, inhibit, curb, forestall, head off, stave off, deter, nip in the bud, debar. **—Ant.** encourage, help, facilitate, enable.

precocious *adj.* uncommonly smart, mature, advanced, smart, bright, brilliant, gifted, quick, clever, apt. **—Ant.** slow, backward, retarded, stupid.

preconception *n.* prejudgment, predisposition, fixed idea, notion, presumption; bias, prejudice.

precursor *n.* vanguard, advance guard, forerunner; harbinger, messenger; usher, herald; predecessor, antecedent; sign, token, mark, omen, portent, warning; symptom.

predatory *adj.* rapacious, raptorial, predacious, vulturine, plunderous, piratical, thievish, marauding, pillaging, larcenous.

predestination *n.* fate, fortune, kismet, destiny, providence, what must be, God's will, inevitability, force of circumstances; preordination, predetermination. **—Ant.** accident, chance.

predetermined *adj.* already settled, foreordained, preplanned, decided, predestined, calculated, premeditated, prearranged, deliberate, intentional, planned, destined, fated.

predicament *n.* plight, dilemma, dangerous condition, trouble, crisis, difficulty, imbroglio, perplexity, straits, sad strait, corner, quandary, scrape, fix, bind, mess, hornet's nest, pinch, pickle, trying situation, *Informal* hot water, jam. **—Syn. Study.** PREDICAMENT, PLIGHT, DILEMMA, QUANDARY refer to unpleasant or puzzling situations. PREDICAMENT and PLIGHT stress more the unpleasant nature, DILEMMA and QUANDARY the puzzling nature, of a situation. PREDICAMENT, though often used lightly, may also refer to a crucial situation: *Stranded in a strange city without money, he was in a predicament.* PLIGHT, however, though originally meaning peril or danger, is most often used lightly: *When her suit wasn't ready at the cleaners, she was in a terrible plight.* DILEMMA means a position of doubt or perplexity in which a person is faced by two equally undesirable alternatives: *the dilemma of a person who must support one of two friends in an election.* QUANDARY is the state of mental perplexity of one faced with a difficult situation: *There seemed to be no way out of the quandary.*

predict *v.* prophesy, foresee, forecast, foretell, prognosticate, divine, read the signs, anticipate, envision; betoken, presage, augur, omen. **—Syn. Study.** PREDICT, PROPHESY, FORESEE, FORECAST mean to know or tell beforehand what will happen. To PREDICT is usu. to foretell with precision of calculation, knowledge, or shrewd inference from facts or experience: *Astronomers can predict an eclipse;* it may, however, be used without the implication of knowledge or expertise: *I predict it will be a successful party.* To PROPHESY is usu. to predict future events by the aid of divine or supernatural inspiration: *Merlin prophesied that two knights would meet in conflict;* this verb, too, may be used in a less specific sense: *I prophesy she'll be back in the old job.* FORESEE refers specifically not to the uttering of predictions but to the mental act of seeing ahead; there is often a practical implication of preparing for what will happen: *He was able to foresee their objections.* FORECAST means to predict by observation or study; however, it is most often used of phenomena that cannot be accurately predicted: *Rain is forecast for tonight.*

prediction *n.* prophecy, soothsaying, forecast, foretelling, prognostication, crystal gazing, augury, portent, divination; anticipation, announcement, proclamation, declaration.

predilection *n.* preference, predisposition, partiality, proneness, proclivity, propensity, leaning, penchant, bent, inclination, tendency; attraction, love, liking, fondness, fancy, desire, taste, hunger, appetite, relish; prepossession, prejudice, bias, favor. **—Ant.** aversion, disinclination, dislike, hatred.

predispose *v.* incline, dispose, make of a mind to, bias, prejudice, sway, influence, prevail upon, prompt, induce, persuade, urge, encourage; seduce, win over, entice, lure, tempt.

predominant *adj.* dominant, important, major, reigning, sovereign, chief, main, leading, supreme, paramount; controlling, authoritative, ruling, influential, ascendant, powerful, strong, forceful, potent, vigorous. **—Syn. Study.** See DOMINANT. **—Ant.** subordinate, secondary; minor, unimportant, lesser, inferior; uninfluential, weak.

preeminent *adj.* foremost, superior, supreme, paramount, second to none, unequaled, consummate, unrivaled, unparalleled, unsurpassed, matchless, peerless, incomparable, best, greatest, dominant, predominant; eminent, renowned, illustrious, famous, famed, celebrated, honored, distinguished.

preempt *v.* appropriate, expropriate, arrogate, take, seize, usurp, confiscate, take over, commandeer, help oneself to. **—Ant.** give up, renounce, surrender, acquiesce.

preface *n.* **1.** foreword, prologue, preamble, introduction, prelude, overture, proem. *—v.* **2.** begin, introduce, lead into, open, start, commence, initiate, launch, usher into. **—Syn. Study. 1** See INTRODUCTION. **—Ant. 1** epilogue, postscript, appendix. **2** close, end, conclude, wind up.

prefer *v.* **1.** choose rather, like better, fancy, single out, adopt, pick out, elect, make a choice of, select, have rather, favor, pick and choose, opt, make one's choice, think better, take to, fix upon. **2.** file, lodge, put forward, set forth, present, bring forward, offer, proffer, tender. **3.** promote, raise in office, advance in rank, graduate, elevate; aggrandize, exalt, dignify, ennoble. **—Ant. 1** dislike, reject, eschew; hate, loathe, detest, abhor.

preference *n.* **1.** partiality, first choice, liking, fancy, predilection, inclination, bent, leaning, predisposition, bias, prejudice, proclivity, proneness, propensity; option, selection, pick. **2.** favoring, precedence, advantage, favored treatment, priority; ascendancy, predomination, supremacy. **—Ant. 1** dislike, aversion, eschewal; hatred, abhorrence.

pregnant *adj.* **1.** with young, parturient, gravid, gestating, with child, having a baby, *Informal* expecting, in a family way; about to become a mother. **2.** full, replete, filled, fraught, abounding, teeming, plenteous, rich; fruitful, fertile, prolific, luxuriant, fecund, copious; productive, proliferous, fructiferous; life-giving. **3.** meaningful, important, provocative, significant, weighty, seminal, momentous; suggestive, full of possibilities, impressive, forceful, potential.

prejudice *n.* **1.** bias, preconception, slant, prejudgment, predisposition, onesidedness, narrow-mindedness, bigotry; intolerance, unfairness, discrimination, partiality, predilection, favoritism. **2.** impairment, injury, detriment, damage, harm, hurt, ill; loss, disadvantage. *—v.* **3.** affect with a prejudice, influence against, sway, bias; predispose, jaundice, poison, infect, taint, contaminate. **4.** damage, harm, hurt, injure, mar, impair, spoil. **—Syn. Study. 1** See BIAS.

preliminary *adj.* preparatory, initiatory, preparative, introductory, prefatory, prelusive, prelusory, precursory. **—Syn. Study.** PRELIMINARY, INTRODUCTORY both refer to that which comes before the principal subject of consideration. That which is PRELIMINARY is in the nature of preparation or of clearing away details that would encumber the main subject or problem; it often deals with arrangements and the like that have to do only incidentally with the principal subject: *preliminary negotiations.* That which is INTRODUCTORY leads with natural, logical, or close connection directly into the main subject of consideration: *introductory steps.* **—Ant.** final, concluding; subsequent, following.

prelude *n.* **1.** preliminary, introduction, preparation; opening, beginning, preamble, preface, prologue. **2.** short instrumental piece, brief musical selection; overture, introductory movement.

premature *adj.* **1.** too soon, too early, hasty, abortive, overhasty, previous, too advanced, precipitate; untimely, ill-timed, inopportune, unseasonable. **2.** unripe, undeveloped, immature, raw, green; unfledged, unprepared, unready, callow; incomplete, embryonic, unhatched, vestigial; rudimentary. **—Ant.** **1** on time, well-timed, timely, opportune; too late, overdue. **2** mature, ripe; overripe.

premeditated *adj.* prearranged, predesigned, plotted, predetermined, predevised, studied, planned; deliberate, conscious, intended, intentional, purposeful, calculated, considered, contrived, willful, voluntary; in cold blood, with malice aforethought.

premise *n.* **1.** hypothesis, basis for reasoning, proposition, argument, postulate, principle, theory; assumption, presumption, supposition, presupposition. **2.** **premises** buildings and grounds, property, site; immediate area, vicinity, environs, precincts.

premium *n.* **1.** prize, gift, reward, bonus, award, bounty, gain, return; remuneration, reparation, recompense, compensation, payment; incentive, encouragement; benefit, consideration. **2.** inflated rate, overpayment, increased value, appreciation. **3.** high value, great stock, priority. **—Syn. Study.** **1** See BONUS.

premonition *n.* forewarning, foreboding, prediction, omen, portent, presage, sign, augury, auspice, token, foretoken; indication, presentiment, feeling, inkling, *Informal* hunch.

preoccupy *v.* engross, occupy wholly, absorb, immerse, arrest, engage the attention, take up, make uppermost in the mind, wrap up; fascinate, obsess.

preparation *n.* **1.** anticipation, precaution, prior measure, safeguard, provision, timely care; prudence, foresight, forethought, expectation. **2.** readying, preparing. **3.** Usu. **preparations** plan, arrangement, measure, preliminary. **4.** concoction, composition, prescription, mixture, elixir, tincture, dressing; confection, prepared food. **5.** experience, qualification, training, apprenticeship, instruction, direction, education, guidance, tutelage, teaching, seasoning.

prepare *v.* **1.** ready, make ready, get ready, fix, adapt, arrange, prearrange. **2.** ready, prime, be resolved, make provision for, provide, be prepared, be ready; take steps, clear for action, put things in order, make all snug, set one's house in order.

preponderance Also **preponderancy** *n.* predominance, prevalence, profusion, domination, majority, greater numbers, dominance, mass, bulk, lion's share, plurality; excess, superabundance, glut, surplus, oversupply, surfeit, plethora, redundance.

prepossessing *adj.* attractive, striking, charming, pleasant, engaging, nice, personable, winsome; alluring, fascinating, bewitching, captivating, inviting, tantalizing, enchanting, entrancing, beguiling. **—Ant.** unprepossessing, unpleasant; uninviting.

preposterous *adj.* outrageous, ridiculous, ludicrous, absurd, unthinkable, fatuous, foolish, silly, imbecilic, asinine, idiotic, stupid, inane, nonsensical, laughable, irrational, unreasonable, bizarre, *French* outré. **—Syn. Study.** See ABSURD.

prerequisite *adj.* **1.** required beforehand; required, mandatory, called for, necessary, imperative, essential; indispensable, demanded, *French* de rigueur. *—n.* **2.** requirement, something needed beforehand, qualification, postulate, necessity, need, requisite, condition, exigency, stipulation, demand, *Latin* sine qua non.

prerogative *n.* privilege, warrant, right, license, claim; liberty, freedom, advantage, exemption; birthright, rightful power, authorization, legal power; grant, due, franchise; choice, option. **—Syn. Study.** See PRIVILEGE.

prescribe *v.* legislate, enact, rule, direct, specify, stipulate, dictate, order, enjoin, command, decree, ordain, proclaim, require, impose, demand; institute, appoint, establish, settle, authorize, set, fix, assign; recommend, advocate, urge, require.

presence *n.* **1.** attendance; existence, being, substantiality, subsistence; hypostatization, reification; entity, life. **2.** company, midst; neighborhood, immediate circle, group. **3.** personal appearance, features, lineaments, aspect, favor, look, figure; charisma, compellingness, character, vitality; air, manner, bearing, carriage, deportment, demeanor, mien, expression. **4.** spirit, shadow, ghost, curse, manifestation, specter, incorporeality, phantasm, wraith, apparition, revenant, vision, phantom, eidolon.

present[1] *adj.* **1.** current, existent, existing, contemporary, at the moment, contemporaneous, now, prevalent, immediate, instant, coeval; now under consideration. **2.** here, attending, in attendance, not absent, not away, accounted for; in, at hand, near, nearby, near, about, in the room, *Informal* on-the-spot, on hand; nigh, vicinal; existing in a place or thing, embedded, unremoved, implanted, rooted, ensconced. —*n.* **3.** now, nowadays, here and now, today, this day and age, the time being, the moment. **—Ant. 1** past; future. **2** absent. **3** the past, the future.

present[2] *v.* **1.** give, give a gift to, confer, bestow, award, grant, accord, hand over; make a present of, donate, place at one's disposal, provide, supply; proffer, offer, propose, submit, put forward, advance, tender; give away, give out, mete out, dole out, render; contribute, *Informal* chip in. **2.** summon, call up, introduce, show, exhibit, display, produce, bring on; offer, proffer, tender, bring forward, draw forth. **3.** state, assert, declare, apprise of, tell, impart, make known, give by way of information, give notice of, communicate; propound, asseverate, frame, allege, profess, cite, pronounce, aver, hold forth; recount, relate, recite, deliver, read, *Informal* come up with; advance, offer, proffer, tender, propose, put forth, expound. **4.** submit, hand in, give over, turn in, surrender. —*n.* **5.** gift, offering, thing presented; donation, endowment, bequest, legacy, benefaction, boon, largess, gratuity, perquisite, tip, grant, oblation, fee; alms, liberality, bounty. **—Syn. Study. 1** See GIVE. **2** See INTRODUCE.

presentable *adj.* **1.** becoming, proper, fit to be seen, suitable, appropriate, acceptable, decent; fashionable, stylish, modish, chic. **2.** good enough, passable, respectable, not bad, suitable, decent, unobjectionable, so-so, tolerable, acceptable, better than nothing, fair-to-middling.

presentation *n.* **1.** offering, proposal, proposition, proffering, submission, offer, proffer; overture, advance. **2.** show, exhibition, exposition, production, demonstration, exhibit, display; materialization, appearance, unfoldment, unfolding, exposure, disclosure. **3.** gift, present, bestowal, largess, grant, boon, oblation; benefaction, favor, gratuity, tip, compliment; fee; liberality, bounty.

presently *adv.* **1.** soon, pretty soon, shortly, anon, forthwith, directly, before long, in a while, after a while, in no time now, any time now, in a short time. **2.** now, at present, at the present time, at the moment, currently, contemporaneously; (*variously*) this week, this month, this semester, this year. **—Syn. Study. 1** See INSTANTLY.

preservation *n.* conservation, saving, salvation; safeguarding, safekeeping, protection, defense, maintenance. **—Ant.** abandonment, decay, ruin, destruction.

preserve *v.* **1.** keep safe, guard, protect, watch over, care for, shield, shelter, conserve, save, defend, safeguard, maintain, keep intact, perpetuate, secure, keep sound, nurse, foster. **2.** (*variously*) can, conserve, *Informal* put up; seal, insulate; freeze, refrigerate; cure, smoke, salt, season, marinate, corn, pickle; dehydrate, dry; embalm, mummify. —*n.* **3.** Often **preserves** jelly, jam, conserve, confection, compote, marmalade, comfit, sweetmeat, sweet. **4.** wildlife enclosure, sanctuary, haven, reservation, reserve, shelter, refuge, park, game preserve.

preside *v.* be in authority, hold the chair, be at the head of, hold authority; wield authority, chair, chairman, preside at the board, preside at a meeting; direct, conduct, control, govern, administrate, administer, rule, command, *Informal* boss; supervise, manage, superintend, keep order, regulate; watch, overlook, oversee; host, hostess.

president *n.* **1.** Usu. **President** executive officer, chief executive, chief of state, head of the nation, head of government, commander in chief, chief magistrate, first citizen. **2.** chief officer, chief official, head, executive head, chairman, ruler.

press *v.* **1.** push; depress, push down, force down, thrust down, push in, flick; condense, compress, mash, crush, reduce, squeeze, cram, jam, stuff, force, strain. **2.** iron, smooth, steam, flatten, hot-press; calender, mangle. **3.** hold closely, hug, squeeze, fold in one's arms, embrace, clasp; fondle, caress, pet, snuggle. **4.** trouble, oppress, burden, bear upon, weigh heavily upon, bear down upon. **5.** beg, implore, importune, urge repeatedly, entreat, plead, enjoin, supplicate, appeal, exhort; dun, tax; beset, *Informal* bug, hit, tap; urge insistently, prod, urge with force, compel, constrain, insist on, put the screws on; exact, extort, force from, hound, pressure, bear down on, set on. **6.** crowd, press in upon, surge, swarm, throng, mill, assemble, congregate, come together, gather, flock together, collect, cluster, herd, huddle. **7.** push, rush, hurry, be in short supply of, constrict, be hard put. —*n.* **8.** the Fourth Estate, reporters, journalists, newsmen, public press, newspapermen; media, newspapers, periodicals, radio, TV, television, broadcasting, news services. **9.** printing press, letter press, printing machine; machine for compressing; printing, publication, final form. **10.** crowd, throng, mob, multitude, swarm, bunch, host, horde, pack, drove, legion, army, body, heap, crush. **11.** pressure, duress, stress, obligation, duty, compulsion; annoyance, bother.

pressing *adj.* urgent, imperative, necessary, vital, critical, crucial, essential, indispensable, needed, needful, exigent, important; insistent, crying, clamoring, importunate, demanding. **—Ant.** unnecessary, nonessential, dispensable, unimportant, trivial; regular, customary, routine.

pressure *n.* **1.** air pressure, compression, compaction, squeeze; weight, heaviness, gravity, density. **2.** stress, strain, tension, difficulty, adversity, straits, trouble, trial, grievance, load, care, oppression, burden, affliction, anxiety, distress. **3.** influence, sway, pull, weight; power, potency, force, bias, interest. **4.** press, urgency, exigency, hurry; stress, strain, pinch; compulsion, coercion; need, necessity, want; demand, requirement.

prestige *n.* fame, celebrity, glory, renown, reputation, prominence, note, repute, mark, notability, distinction, significance, authority, account, import, importance, consequence, preeminence, eminence, honor, respect, esteem, regard, report.

prestigious *adj.* distinguished, illustrious, esteemed, honored, respected, reputable, notable, famed, prominent, renowned, eminent, acclaimed, famous, celebrated, well-known, important, outstanding. **—Ant.** inconsequential, unknown, insignificant, unimportant.

presumably *adv.* doubtless, probably, assumably, likely, presumptively, in all probability, all things considered, in all likelihood, ostensibly, to all appearances, apparently, unquestionably, to all intents and purposes.

presume *v.* **1.** assume, guess, take for granted, take it, believe, postulate, posit, think likely, suspect, imagine, conceive, fancy; suppose, hypothesize, surmise, gather, deduce, have it. **2.** dare, take leave, take a liberty, make free, venture, make bold, be so bold, act presumptuously, have the audacity. **3.** rely too much, take undue advantage of, impose.

presumption *n.* **1.** assumption, premise, belief, supposition, postulate; speculation, guess, surmise, conjecture; preconceived opinion, presupposition, prejudgment, preconception. **2.** audacity, brass, effrontery, arrogance, gall; *Informal* cheek, nerve; *Slang* lip, chutzpah; impertinence, impudence, insolence, rudeness, flippancy, presumptuousness, pride, haughtiness, egotism; boldness, daring, forwardness. **—Ant. 2** respect, deference, politeness.

presumptuous *adj.* **1.** bold, audacious, daring, overconfident, overfamiliar, forward, nervy, shameless, brash, brazen, brassy, fresh, cocky. **2.** haughty, proud, snobbish, assuming, overbearing, lofty, patronizing, pompous, lordly, imperious; disdainful, contemptuous, domineering, dictatorial, arrogant. **—Syn. Study. 1** See BOLD.

pretend *v.* **1.** make believe, take a part, fill a role, imagine, fancy, suppose; mimic, impersonate, masquerade, playact. **2.** fake, affect, put on, assume, feign, simulate, imitate, make a show of; counterfeit, sham, dissimulate, dissemble, put on a false front. **3.** affect, claim, purport. **—Syn. Study. 2** PRETEND, AFFECT, ASSUME, FEIGN imply an attempt to create a false appearance. To PRETEND is to create an imaginary characteristic or to play a part: *to pretend sorrow.* To AFFECT is to make a consciously artificial show of having qualities that one thinks would look well and impress others: *to affect shyness.* To ASSUME is to take on or put on a specific outward appearance, often with intent to deceive: *to assume an air of indifference.* To FEIGN implies using ingenuity in pretense, and some degree of imitation of appearance or characteristics: *to feign surprise.*

pretense *n.* **1.** make-believe, pretension, fake, hoax, invention, fabrication, imposture, sham, counterfeit; trick, trickery, deceit, deception. **2.** deception, subterfuge, guile, feint, camouflage, pretext, disguise, mask, cloak, cover. **3.** show, pretentiousness, showing off, ostentation, display, fanfaronade, ostentatiousness, affectedness, affectation, false show, airs; boasting, bragging, vaunt, bombast, bluster, pomposity. **—Ant. 1** reality, actuality, fact. **2** truthfulness, honesty. **3** simplicity, sincerity, candor, frankness, ingenuousness, openness.

pretension *n.* **1.** claim, right, title, pretense; aspiration, ambition. **2.** ostentation, affectation, snobbery, hypocrisy, pretense, airs, showing off, ostentatiousness, grandioseness, display, show, showiness, pretentiousness; pomp, bombast, self-importance, pomposity.

pretentious *adj.* showy, ostentatious, pompous, fatuous, bombastic, pedantic, boastful, flaunting, overbearing, affected, unnatural, insincere, presuming, assuming; lofty, airy, snobbish, *Informal* high-and-mighty, hoity-toity, stuck-up; puffed-up, blown-up, inflated, exaggerated, theatrical, grandiose, stagy; flashy, tawdry, ornate, gaudy, garish, florid, flowery, extravagant, overdone; self-glorifying, self-important, self-praising, smug. **—Syn. Study.** See BOMBASTIC, GRANDIOSE. **—Ant.** unpretentious, modest, unaffected, natural, unassuming; plain, simple.

preternatural *adj.* supernatural, superhuman, supranatural, supernormal, miraculous, hypernormal, preterhuman; extramundane, unearthly, unworldly; metaphysical, transcendental; occult, mystical; esoteric, mysterious, arcane; bizarre, weird, strange, eerie, uncanny. **—Syn. Study.** See MIRACULOUS. **—Ant.** mundane, worldly, everyday, commonplace.

pretext *n.* excuse, alleged reason, professed purpose, basis, ground, pretense, subterfuge, semblance, bluff, feint, pretension; justification, vindication.

pretty *adj.* **1.** attractive, beautiful, pleasing to the eye, lovely, comely, bonny, handsome, good-looking, beauteous, sightly, pulchritudinous, well-favored, fair, goodly; delicate, dainty, graceful; captivating, alluring, fetching, charming, engaging; well-proportioned, symmetrical, shapely, well-set, well-made. *—adv.* **2.** moderately, adequately, reasonably, satisfactorily, fairly, rather, somewhat. **—Syn. Study. 1** See BEAUTIFUL. **—Ant. 1** unattractive, ugly, plain, unsightly, clumsy, graceless, unseemly; unshapely, unsymmetrical.

prevail *v.* **1.** abound, exist generally, be current, be widespread, obtain, exist, be prevalent. **2.** predominate, be prevalent, preponderate, abound; have sway, hold sway, rule, reign. **3.** triumph, be victorious, win, win out, be a winner, be the victor, gain the palm, win the laurels; prove superior, succeed, conquer, overcome, carry the day, *Informal* bring home the bacon.

prevailing *adj.* **1.** current, popular, in style; widespread, prevalent, general, usual, customary, normal, conventional, accustomed; definite, fixed, established, set. **2.** principal, main, prevalent, dominant, predominant, preponderant. **—Ant. 1** dated, out-of-date, old-fashioned; unusual, rare, uncommon. **2** infrequent, uncommon; minor, subordinate, lesser, inferior.

prevalent *adj.* numerous, common, frequent, frequently occurring, prevailing, general, widespread, rife, pervasive, universal, abundant, extensive, rampant, ubiquitous, habitual, usual, normal, conventional, everyday, commonplace, familiar, customary, popular. **—Ant.** infrequent, rare, unusual, uncommon.

prevaricate *v.* lie, fib, stretch the truth, dissemble, perjure, deceive, palter, be untruthful, tell a story, tell a tall story, be evasive; falsify, misstate, fake, hoodwink, counterfeit, misrepresent, mislead, distort.

prevent *v.* keep from occurring, defend against, counteract, fend off, hold back, stave off, ward off; block, bar, dam, deter, thwart, frustrate, hamper, hinder, impede, foil, anticipate, balk, arrest, nip in the bud, forestall, avoid, preclude, avert; stop, halt, obviate, veto, prohibit, forbid, rule out; intercept, sidetrack, turn aside, deflect, draw off, turn away. **—Syn. Study.** PREVENT, HAMPER, HINDER, IMPEDE refer to different degrees of stoppage of action or progress. To PREVENT is to stop something effectually by forestalling action and rendering it impossible: *to prevent the sending of a message.* To HAMPER is to clog or entangle or put an embarrassing restraint upon: *to hamper preparations for a trip.* To HINDER is to keep back by delaying or stopping progress or action: *to hinder the progress of an expedition.* To IMPEDE is to make difficult the movement or progress of anything by interfering with its proper functioning: *to impede a discussion by repeatedly demanding explanations.* **—Ant.** permit, allow, encourage, urge, incite.

prevention *n.* avoidance, stoppage, hindrance, inhibition, restraint, preclusion; obviation, deterrence, elimination, defeat; frustration, thwarting, forestallment, interception.

previous *adj.* prior, preceding, earlier, early; foregoing, foregone, antecedent, former, erstwhile, before, aforesaid, aforementioned. **—Ant.** subsequent, consequent, ensuing, succeeding, following, later.

previously *adv.* before, earlier, at one time, once, a while back, a while ago, formerly, in times past, long ago, heretofore, earlier on, sometime back, back when.

prey *n.* **1.** quarry, game, kill, food; victim; quest, prize. **2.** victim, dupe, target, gull; *Slang* pigeon, fall guy, cat's-paw, sucker, patsy. *—v.* **3.** feed upon, devour, consume, eat, feast upon, fatten upon, gorge oneself upon; live off; fasten upon, fasten oneself to, parasitize, infest; suck the blood of.

price *n.* **1.** cost, face value, amount, charge, fee, rate, expenditure, expense, outlay; selling price, current price, market value, list price, retail price, wholesale price; value, worth, exchange value, par value; penalty, punishment, fine, forfeiture. *—v.* **2.** assess, evaluate, set a price on, appraise, value.

priceless *adj.* without price, beyond price, invaluable, valuable, precious, dear, high-priced, costly, expensive, worth a king's ransom; irreplaceable, rare; incomparable, peerless; cherished, prized, treasured, valued. **—Ant.** worthless, cheap, inexpensive; common.

pride *n.* **1.** satisfaction, pleasure, enjoyment, delight, joy, happiness; gratification, comfort. **2.** self-esteem, dignity, self-respect, honor. **3.** self-importance, conceit, egoism, egotism, vanity, self-love, self-glorification, vainglory; immodesty, smugness, self-satisfaction; show, display, ostentation, parade, pomp, airs, pretension; swagger, arrogance, hubris, haughtiness, superciliousness, pomposity, imperiousness. **—***v.* **4.** be proud of, be pleased with, have a feeling of pride in oneself, be satisfied with, be delighted at, be gratified at. **—Syn. Study. 3** PRIDE, CONCEIT, EGOTISM, VANITY imply a favorable view of one's own appearance, advantages, achievements, etc., and often apply to offensive characteristics. PRIDE is a lofty and often arrogant assumption of superiority in some respect: *Pride must have a fall.* CONCEIT implies an exaggerated estimate of one's own abilities or attainments, together with pride: *blinded by conceit.* EGOTISM implies an excessive preoccupation with oneself or with one's own concerns, usu. but not always accompanied by pride or conceit: *Her egotism blinded her to others' difficulties.* VANITY implies self-admiration and an excessive desire to be admired by others: *His vanity was easily flattered.* See also EGOTISM. **—Ant. 3** humility, modesty, meekness.

prig *n.* prude, puritan, bluenose, fuddy-duddy, bluestocking, *Informal* stuffed shirt; hypocrite, bigot; pretender; pedant, precisionist, formalist, attitudinarian; faultfinder, nitpicker.

prim *adj.* particular, fussy, overprecise, strict, proper, tidy, fastidious, straitlaced, puritanical, prudish, squeamish; priggish, prissy, fuddy-duddy, starched, unbending, inflexible, stiff-necked, starched, no-nonsense, stuffy, haughty, smug. **—Ant.** careless, loose, untidy; informal, casual, easygoing, relaxed, carefree.

primarily *adv.* chiefly, mainly, principally, mostly, largely, predominantly, first and foremost, essentially, fundamentally, for the most part, basically, in the main, generally.

primary *adj.* **1.** first, introductory, beginning, initial, elementary, preparatory; rudimentary, nascent. **2.** chief, main, principal, fundamental, basic, key, cardinal; prominent, predominant, dominant, ruling, star, leading, greatest, highest, utmost; important, necessary, vital, essential. **3.** primitive, primordial, primal, primeval; initial, original, prime, beginning, first; basic, fundamental, elementary, elemental, rudimental, rudimentary, key, basal; native, indigenous, aboriginal, natural, inherent, innate; oldest, earliest. **—Ant. 1** secondary, following, subsequent, succeeding, ensuing, later. **2** lesser, unimportant, subordinate, inferior; indirect, supplemental.

prime *adj.* **1.** primary, chief, main, principal, cardinal, most important, leading, predominant; ruling, preeminent; greatest, highest, maximal, crowning, paramount, superlative, supreme, utmost; unsurpassed, unmatched, matchless, best, without peer, peerless; important, necessary, essential, vital. **2.** superior, quality, of the best quality, Grade A, choice, specially selected, select, first-class, unparalleled; *Slang* A1, top-drawer, top-flight, ace, top-hole. **3.** basic, fundamental, elementary, rudimentary, elemental, basal, essential; intrinsic, inherent, innate, congenital; native, indigenous, natural; primal, oldest, earliest, first, original. **4.** best, preferred, most advantageous, most favored, choice; timely, in good time, opportune, convenient; fit, seemly, suitable, fitting, propitious, befitting, expedient, well-timed, provident, auspicious, lucky; in good season, seasonable, early, bright and early. **—***n.* **5.** peak, perfection, ideal level, excellence; full strength, greatest strength; height, zenith, heyday, best days; maturity, full flowering, blossoming, bloom, flower, full beauty, pink. **—***v.* **6.** prepare, ready, fit, make ready, put into readiness, get ready, adapt, adjust; groom, coach, train, instruct, breed, raise, educate, school, tutor; inform, fill in, guide, prompt, brief. **—Ant. 1** secondary, lowest, least important. **2** the worst, second-class, third-rate. **4** untimely, inconvenient, unfit, unsuitable, inauspicious; unseasonable.

primeval *adj.* prehistoric, primordial, ancient, primitive, antediluvian, early, aboriginal, ancestral; legendary, mythological.

primitive *adj.* **1.** early, earliest, original, first, primary; beginning, elementary, introductory; undeveloped, unrefined, crude, rudimentary. **2.** uncivilized, native, aboriginal, backward; antique, archaic. **3.** unsophisticated, simple, uncomplicated; artless, uncultivated, undeveloped, unskilled, unlearned. **4.** uncomfortable, inconvenient, crude; bare, Spartan, austere, ascetic. **—Ant. 1** advanced, later; developed, sophisticated, refined. **2** civilized, modern. **3** sophisticated, artful, fashionable. **4** comfortable, elaborate.

primp *v.* groom oneself, dress carefully, dress fastidiously, preen, groom, plume, prettify, spruce up; make up, gussy up, doll up.

principal *adj.* **1.** chief, leading, foremost, most important, supreme, superior, capital, main, preeminent, dominant, prominent, predominant, outstanding, major, controlling, most considerable, cardinal; primary, prime, first; fundamental, essential, basic; greatest, ultimate, paramount. —*n.* **2.** star, leading man, leading lady, protagonist, featured player, *Informal* first fiddle. **3.** head of a school, headmaster, master, dean, preceptor; person in authority, chief person, chief authority, superior. **4.** original sum, original investment, capital sum, invested sum, fund; money. —**Syn. Study. 1** See CHIEF. —**Ant. 1** least important, inferior, minor, least powerful, weakest, inconsiderable; secondary, auxiliary, subsidiary, supplemental.

principally *adv.* mostly, primarily, chiefly, mainly, largely, predominantly, for the most part, basically, fundamentally, first and foremost, particularly, especially, above all.

principle *n.* **1.** rule, truth, law, assumption, precept, fact, basis, fundamental, rudiment, proposition, element, formula; regulation, canon, code, direction, dictum; theorem, axiom, maxim. **2.** belief, article of faith, credo, tenet, theory, creed; dogma, doctrine, religious belief, scruple, way of thinking, system of belief; teaching, view, attitude, position. **3.** morality, standards, ethics, uprightness, honesty, probity, scruples; honor, integrity, incorruptibility, sense of honor; righteousness, rectitude, respectability; goodness, virtue, morals; conscientiousness. —**Ant. 3** immorality, dishonesty; dishonor.

prior *adj.* previous, preceding in time, preexisting, preexistent, antecedent, anterior, earlier, former; precursory, erstwhile, going before, foregoing, prefatory, preparatory; aforementioned, aforesaid. —**Ant.** subsequent, following, later.

priority *n.* precedence, greater importance, preference, urgency, immediacy, the lead, precedency, preeminence; antecedence, seniority, superiority, ascendancy.

prison *n.* jail, jailhouse, *British* gaol; house of detention, penitentiary, penal institution, reformatory, house of reform, house of correction, internment center; dungeon, tower, bastille, penal colony, *Navy* brig, *Slang* jug, clink, slammer, tank, brig, stir, can, cooler, pokey, calaboose, pen, big house, joint.

pristine *adj.* undefiled, unsullied, untouched, unspoiled, untarnished, virginal; uncontaminated, unpolluted, pure, unmarred. —**Ant.** sullied, defiled, contaminated, polluted, spoiled, tarnished.

privacy *n.* **1.** privateness, seclusion, security, integrity; solitude, solitariness, sequestration; isolation, dissociation; retirement, withdrawal, retreat. **2.** secrecy, privity, secret, clandestineness.

private *adj.* **1.** privately owned, personal, special, exclusive, express, restricted, closed, limited, confined, fixed; not public, nonpublic. **2.** confidential, clandestine, privy, secret, inviolate; unofficial, nonofficial; undercover, covert, classified, undisclosed, off-the-record, concealed, unrevealed, hidden, underground, buried, invisible; *Informal* under wraps, hush-hush; mysterious, cryptic, obscure, esoteric, indistinct, dark. **3.** secluded, isolated, remote, desolate, reclusive, privy, sequestered, lonely, solitary, lonesome, unfrequented. —**Ant. 1, 2** public. **1** unrestricted, open, general, unlimited, unconfined. **2** known; official; disclosed, unconcealed, revealed; *Informal* out in the open. **3** unsecluded, frequented, visited.

privation *n.* need, neediness, want, lack; poverty, impoverishment, indigence, penury, impecuniousness, pauperism, exigency, mendicancy, destitution, beggary, bankruptcy, reduced circumstances; distress, misery, hardship, straits, pinch. —**Ant.** ease, wealth, riches, affluence, success, good luck; sufficiency, gain, acquisition.

privilege *n.* **1.** right, due, entitlement, prerogative, prerequisite, birthright, freedom, liberty; license, power, authority, franchise, title, charter, patent; advantage, favor, boon, benefit; honor, pleasure. —*v.* **2.** grant, permit, empower, allow, entitle. —**Syn. Study. 1** PRIVILEGE, PREROGATIVE refer to a special advantage or right possessed by an individual or group. A PRIVILEGE is a right or advantage gained by birth, social position, effort, or concession. It can have either legal or personal sanction: *the privilege of paying half fare; the privilege of calling whenever one wishes.* PREROGATIVE refers to an exclusive right claimed and granted, often officially or legally, on the basis of social status, heritage, sex, etc.: *the prerogatives of a king; the prerogatives of management.*

privileged *adj.* limited, special; exempt, free, immune, excused; allowed, granted, permitted, licensed, sanctioned, warranted, empowered, entitled, authorized; unaccountable, not liable.

prize *n.* **1.** award, trophy, medal, medallion, cup; reward, citation, guerdon, premium; ribbon, decoration, blue ribbon, laurels, honors, accolade, crown. **2.** jewel, pearl, gem, diamond, pure gold, treasure, masterpiece, choice bit, champion; *French* crème de la crème; *Slang* honey, catch, humdinger, dandy, crackerjack, lulu, pip, peach. —*adj.* **3.**

honored, winning, award-winning, blue-ribbon. —*v.* **4.** value, set store by; admire, respect, look up to, honor, esteem, regard, like, hold in esteem, appreciate; hold in affection, hold dear, treasure, cherish. **—Syn. Study. 4** See APPRECIATE.

probable *adj.* likely, possible, promising, presumable, presumptive, presumed, expected, supposed; encouraging, assuring, seeming, ostensible, apparent; *Informal* in the cards; credible, logical, reasonable, plausible, tenable, thinkable, conceivable, believable.

probably *adv.* in all probability, most likely, in all likelihood, as like as not, presumably, supposedly.

probe *v.* **1.** investigate, look into, inspect, pry into, delve into; scrutinize, study, examine, test; question, inquire, interrogate, quiz, query; hunt, pursue, follow up, seek after. **2.** look for, seek, explore with a probe, search; *Informal* fish for, rummage; penetrate. —*n.* **3.** investigation, inspection, exploration, examination, inquiry, inquest, study, search, research, survey, analysis, trial, test, review.

probity *n.* integrity, uprightness, honesty, virtue, high-mindedness, morality, character, principle, honor, trustworthiness, incorruptibility, straightness, decency, goodness, righteousness. **—Ant.** dishonesty, duplicity, unscrupulousness, corruption.

problem *n.* **1.** question, query, poser, puzzle, riddle, conundrum; difficulty, disagreement, disputed point. —*adj.* **2.** unruly, difficult, hard to manage, uncontrollable, unmanageable; intractable, incorrigible, stubborn. **—Ant. 2** perfect, model, manageable.

problematic *adj.* uncertain, doubtful, questionable, dubious, unsettled, undetermined, enigmatic, unknown; perplexing, paradoxical, puzzling; difficult, troublesome, worrisome. **—Ant.** certain, settled, known, undisputed, unquestionable.

procedure *n.* method, way, manner, course, process, strategy, modus operandi, M.O., technique, approach, mode, methodology, routine.

proceed *v.* **1.** go, go forward, move ahead, move forward, go ahead, move on, go on, continue, carry on, progress, advance, make one's way; press on, push on, keep moving. **2.** undertake, set out, begin, commence, start; take action, act, move, operate, function, work. **3.** result, arise, issue, take rise, come, follow, ensue, succeed, be caused, spring, flow, emanate, start, derive, be derived, be produced, originate, grow, stem. **—Ant. 1** retreat, go backward, get behind; discontinue, stop; regress, lose ground; stop moving.

proceedings *n. pl.* **1.** activity, happenings, occurrences, transactions, events, incidents, operations, affairs, matters, actions, goings on, doings. **2.** legal action, legal process, lawsuit, suit, action at law; litigation, trial, case, cause. **3.** minutes, records, account, report, returns, description, memoranda, archives.

proceeds *n. pl.* profit, gain, receipts, gross, net, gate, box office, yield, income, revenue, earnings, assets; reward, remuneration, returns; money, lucre, pelf, winnings, take, pickings.

process *n.* **1.** method, system, manner, practice, procedure, mode; course of action, plan, scheme, project, line of action, policy, ways and means; measure, step; usage, function. **2.** procedure, set of changes, proceeding, passage, course, movement, motion, transformation; unfolding; flux, flow, change, progress, progression. **3.** summons, court order, writ, subpoena. —*v.* **4.** prepare, treat, convert, alter, transform; (*variously*) freeze, preserve, freeze-dry, smoke, dehydrate, dry, candy, can. **5.** take care of, fill, ship, handle, deal with, dispose of.

procession *n.* parade, march, caravan, pageant, cavalcade, motorcade, cortege, train, file, rank, column, array, line; sequence; course; passage, progression, progress, succession.

proclaim *v.* declare, announce, herald, make known, make manifest, make public, broadcast, give out; promulgate, assert, affirm, set forth, state, profess; publish, advertise, circulate, blaze abroad, publicize, trumpet, blazon, call out, blare, cry, sing out, hawk about; tell, voice; report, enunciate, communicate; release, disclose, divulge, reveal. **—Syn. Study.** See ANNOUNCE. **—Ant.** retract, recall; suppress, repress, conceal, secrete.

proclivity *n.* propensity, leaning, inclination, disposition, affection, liking, proneness, affinity, tendency, predilection, penchant, bent, bias, prejudice, partiality, predisposition, turn of the mind; appetite, taste, desire, impulse; *Informal* yen, soft spot. **—Ant.** dislike, aversion, hatred, loathing, disinclination.

procrastinate *v.* delay, stall, play for time, temporize, kill time, dally, tarry, loiter, dillydally, dawdle, waste time, twiddle one's thumbs, linger, drag one's feet; put off action, defer, postpone, adjourn, put on ice, wait till tomorrow; hesitate, hold back, hang back, lag, be dilatory. **—Ant.** expedite, hasten, hurry, speed, speed up.

procreate *v.* beget, breed, engender,

propagate, father, mother, sire, bear, reproduce, generate, spawn, give birth to, create, get, conceive, bring forth, produce; multiply, proliferate.

procure *v.* obtain, acquire, get, secure, get into one's hands, lay hands on, attain, achieve, come by; take possession of, receive, pick up; take, appropriate, help oneself to, seize, commandeer; win, earn, gain; get together, accumulate, gather; buy, purchase; cause to occur, effect, bring about, contrive, elicit, induce, evoke, incite. **—Syn. Study.** See GET.

prod *v.* **1.** poke, jab, prick, flog, whip, lash, needle; shove, push; accelerate, quicken, speed, propel. **2.** impel, stir, incite, excite, stimulate, instigate, prompt; actuate, rouse, stir up, set in motion, move, animate, encourage, motivate; urge, exhort, goad, provoke, egg on, nag, spur, bear down upon, pressure.

prodigal *adj.* **1.** wasteful, spendthrift, unthrifty, thriftless, overliberal, profligate, extravagant, exorbitant, lavish, excessive, gluttonous; improvident, dissipating, inordinate, intemperate, immoderate, reckless, impetuous, precipitate, wanton. **2.** bountiful, profuse, abounding, abundant, plentiful, bounteous, ample; lush, luxuriant, lavish, exuberant, generous; numerous, countless, numberless, innumerable, multitudinous; teeming, swarming, myriad, replete, copious. *—n.* **3.** spendthrift, squanderer, spender, wastrel, profligate. **—Syn. Study. 1, 2** See LAVISH. **—Ant. 1** thrifty, frugal, economical, cautious, miserly, stingy; provident, temperate, moderate. **2** scarce, scanty, deficient, scant, meager, sparse, few, limited.

prodigious *adj.* exceptional, rare, singular, extraordinary, uncommon, unique, impressive, striking, noteworthy, renowned; surprising, startling, amazing, astounding, astonishing, dumbfounding, overwhelming, wonderful, remarkable, marvelous, wondrous, miraculous; enormous, vast, huge, immense, far-reaching, large, terrific, big, grand, great, monumental, mighty, stupendous, tremendous, gigantic, colossal, monstrous; inconceivable, unimaginable, unthinkable; uncustomary, unwonted, unprecedented. **—Ant.** unexceptional, ordinary, common, usual; unimpressive, unremarkable; small, negligible.

prodigy *n.* gifted child, great talent, child genius, young genius, wonder child, *German* Wunderkind; genius, wizard, master, mastermind, expert, whiz, whiz kid; marvel, wonder, sensation, phenomenon, *Informal* stunner; rare occurrence, rarity, *Latin* rara avis.

produce *v.* **1.** make, create, manufacture, construct, fashion, shape, compose, devise, fabricate, turn out, frame, evolve, form, concoct, conceive, develop; originate, institute, found, give birth to, beget, generate, invent, procreate, give life to, hatch, bring into being, give origin to, bring into existence, bring into the world. **2.** provide, supply, furnish, give, bear, yield, afford; flower, sprout, bloom, bear fruit. **3.** show, exhibit, present, show forth, present for inspection, bring into view, advance, cause to appear, put on view, hold up to view, manifest, bring forward, bring in, adduce, evince, set forth, bring out, bring to light, display, put on display; materialize, reveal, divulge, uncover, disclose, unveil, discover, unmask, make plain, *Informal* come up with. **4.** cause, effect, give rise to, set up, put into effect, put in force, effectuate, bring about, bring off; achieve, accomplish, bring to pass, carry into execution. *—n.* **5.** agricultural products, staple commodities, fruits, vegetables, greens, staples, greengrocery, foodstuffs. **—Ant. 3** conceal, hide, withhold. **4** prevent.

production *n.* **1.** making, producing, manufacture, manufacturing; building, construction, formation, origination, creation, fabrication; execution, effectuation, performance, fulfillment. **2.** presentation, theatrical offering, show, drama, play, stage show, entertainment, musical; motion picture, film, cinema, movie; carnival, circus. **3.** introduction, appearance, showing, exhibit, display, materialization, show, presentation, manifestation, demonstration; disclosure, revelation.

productive *adj.* **1.** producing, creating, creative, accomplishing much, prolific, effectual, efficacious; active, busy, vigorous, dynamic. **2.** fertile, fruitful, fecund, proliferous, prolific, fructiferous; luxuriant, rich, plentiful, plenteous, copious, teeming, producing in abundance, yielding. **3.** profitable, remunerative, gainful, worthwhile, paying, moneymaking. **4.** responsible for, bringing about, causing, bringing to pass. **5.** useful, contributing, valuable, invaluable. **—Syn. Study. 2** PRODUCTIVE, FERTILE, FRUITFUL, PROLIFIC apply to the generative aspect of something. PRODUCTIVE refers to a generative source of continuing activity: *productive soil; a productive influence.* FERTILE applies to that in which seeds, literal or figurative, take root: *fertile soil; a fertile imagination.* FRUITFUL refers to that which has already produced and is capable of further production: *fruitful species; fruitful discussions.* PROLIFIC means highly productive: *a prolific farm; a prolific writer.* **—Ant. 1–3, 5** unproductive. **1** inactive; ineffectual. **2** unfertile, barren, sterile, unfruitful; poor, unyielding. **3** unprofitable, ungainful. **5** useless.

profane *adj.* **1.** irreverent, blasphemous, ungodly, godless, atheistic, agnostic, unbelieving, sacrilegious, irreligious, undevout, heretical, impious, unholy, unsaintly; foul, filthy, nasty, vile, abusive; wicked, evil, sinful, hellbound, diabolic, satanic, shameless, unchaste, unseemly, impure; crude, coarse, vulgar, obscene, lewd, bawdy, ribald, off-color. **2.** secular, nonreligious, lay, temporal, worldly, earthly, terrestrial. —*v.* **3.** desecrate, debase, abuse, commit sacrilege, blaspheme; offend, outrage; misuse, misemploy, ill-use, waste; pollute, pervert, contaminate, prostitute, violate; mock, revile, scorn. **—Ant. 1, 2** sacred, religious, spiritual. **1** holy, reverent, divine; decorous, proper, clean; delicate, seemly.

profanity *n.* swearing, cursing, cussing, curse words, dirty words, expletives, four-letter words, obscenities, swearwords, oaths; scurrility, billingsgate, blue language, bad language, dirty talk; filth, scatology; obscenity, execration; blasphemy, irreverence, impiety, ungodliness.

profess *v.* **1.** claim, allege, lay claim, assume, purport; dissimulate, dissemble, sail under false colors, make a pretense of, pass oneself off, make out as if; simulate, act, pretend, put on, sham, feign, counterfeit, fake. **2.** confess, admit, own, acknowledge, affirm, confirm, certify, avow, vouch, aver, asseverate, depose; declare, state, proclaim, propound, announce; allege, assert, put forward, offer, advance; tell, say, enunciate; hold forth, contend, maintain. **3.** declare one's faith in, embrace, believe in, practice.

profession *n.* **1.** occupation, line of work, line, business, job, field, specialty, employment, work, vocation, walk of life, career, calling, métier, pursuit, undertaking, endeavor; office, position, situation, post, field, sphere; practice, service, industry, trade, craft. **2.** branch of learning, higher discipline; (*variously*) law, medicine, teaching. **3.** declaration, statement, announcement, pronouncement; acknowledgment, confession, affirmation, confirmation, deposition, testimony, attestation; avowal, averment, promise, word, word of honor, troth, plight, pledge, vow, guarantee, assurance; assertion, claim, allegation. **—Ant. 1** avocation, hobby. **3** denial, refutation, recantation.

professional *adj.* **1.** paid, receiving pay, in business as. **2.** highly skilled, competent, knowledgeable, practiced, expert, experienced, adept, well-trained, well-informed. —*n.* **3.** expert, specialist, authority, adept. **—Ant. 1, 3** amateur. **2** incompetent, inept.

professorial *adj.* academic, bookish, donnish, pedantic, teachery, schoolmasterish, schoolmarmish, schoolteacherish, pedagoguish, preachy, didactic, *Slang* teachy.

proffer *v.* **—Syn. Study.** See OFFER.

proficient *adj.* skilled, skillful, capable, competent, able, good, adroit, deft, apt, adept, dexterous; expert, clever, sharp, masterly, masterful, efficient, effective, ready, quick, handy; trained, practiced, polished, accomplished, experienced, qualified, professional; talented, gifted, versatile. **—Ant.** unskilled, incapable, inept, incompetent, bad, maladroit, unaccomplished.

profile *n.* **1.** outline, contour, delineation, lineaments, configuration, form, shape, figure; side view, side, half face, silhouette; skyline; picture, portrait, sketch, drawing. **2.** biography, short biography, tale, character sketch, portrait, vignette.

profit *n.* **1.** gain, return, realization; (*variously*) gross profit, net profit, clear profit, marginal profit; money, remuneration, income, revenue, pay, earnings; proceeds, receipts; consideration, compensation, financial reward. **2.** advantage, benefit, interest, advancement, gain, improvement; good, benefaction, boon, favor; service, utility, use, avail, account, value. —*v.* **3.** benefit, help, serve, avail, stand in good stead. **4.** make good use of, make the most of, be better for, be improved by, learn a lesson from, reap the benefit of, make use of, utilize, use, put to use. **5.** make money, earn, gain, come out ahead. **—Syn. Study. 2** See ADVANTAGE.

profitable *adj.* **1.** gainful, rewarding, yielding profit, paying, moneymaking, remunerative, lucrative, well-paying; fruitful. **2.** worthwhile, rewarding, productive, favorable, beneficial, advantageous, salutary, serviceable, useful; valuable, invaluable.

profligate *adj.* **1.** dissolute, debauched, depraved, libertine, dissipated, degenerate, degraded, immoral, wicked, iniquitous; wanton, loose, abandoned, erotic, sybaritic, corrupt, evil, sinful, immoral, promiscuous, wild, fast, unprincipled, unbridled, unrestrained, licentious, lascivious, satyric. **2.** wasteful, prodigal, extravagant, lavish, unthrifty, spendthrift, improvident; unrestrained, unbridled, reckless. —*n.* **3.** reprobate, profligate person, rake, satyr, debauchee, degenerate, dissipater, *French* roué; libertine, pervert, sinner, wrongdoer; spendthrift, wastrel, prodigal. **—Ant. 1**

moral, decent, upright; kind, good, virtuous, chaste.

profound *adj.* **1.** deep, thoughtful, wise, sagacious, sage, penetrating, piercing, learned, erudite, intellectual, scholarly, educated; knowledgeable, comprehensive, recondite, omniscient, all-knowing; philosophical, reflective, thoughtful, well-considered, sober, serious, sober-minded; informed, well-informed, knowing, enlightened. **2.** deep, severe, abject, extreme; thorough, thoroughgoing, far-reaching, radical, utter, out-and-out, complete, consummate; penetrating, piercing, pronounced, decided, positive. **3.** deeply felt, heartfelt, keenly felt, sincere, heart-stirring, strongly felt, deep-seated, soul-stirring, moving; hearty, intense, keen, acute, abject. **—Ant. 1** shallow, superficial, unwise, stupid, unlearned, uneducated, unknowledgeable, thoughtless, inconsiderate; uninformed, unenlightened; imprudent. **2** slight, su perficial, shallow, surface, external. **3** insincere, shallow, hollow.

profundity *n.* deepness, profoundness, reconditeness; erudition, wisdom, sagacity, learnedness; abstruseness, impenetrableness, abstractness. **—Ant.** superficiality, shallowness, frivolousness, triviality.

profuse *adj.* **1.** generous, munificent, abundant, bountiful, bounteous, copious, ample, rich, lavish. **2.** wasteful, unthrifty, prodigal, improvident, spendthrift, intemperate, inordinate, immoderate, excessive, lavish, extravagant. **3.** prolix, wordy, verbose, long-winded, garrulous, discursive, digressive, rambling, loquacious, diffuse. **—Syn. Study. 1, 2** See LAVISH. **—Ant. 1** meager, scanty, inadequate, exiguous, sparse, cheap, stinting, skimpy, illiberal, close-fisted. **2** thrifty, penny-pinching, provident, temperate, moderate. **3** short, terse, pithy, brief, to the point.

profusion *n.* great amount, great quantity, multiplicity, abundance, oversupply, plethora, multitude; superfluity, extravagance, excess, waste, surfeit, surplus, glut.

progeny *n.* descendant, offspring, young, child, children, issue, seed, offshoot; heir, heirs, scion, son, family, kin, kindred, blood, clan; posterity, race, stock, lineage, breed, line.

program *n.* **1.** schedule, order of events, things to be done, agenda, plan, order of business, curriculum, syllabus; timetable; card, bill, prospectus; book, slate, calendar, bulletin. **2.** playbill, list of players, list of selections; notice, sketch, outline. **3.** show, presentation, production; series. **—*v.* 4.** schedule, arrange, book, slate, bill, calendar, docket, register, list; design, intend, expect; *Informal* line up.

progress *n.* **1.** headway, advance, forward movement, advancement, furtherance; accomplishment, achievement; development, betterment, improvement, success. **2.** development, growth, rise, promotion; enrichment, enhancement, improvement; forward motion. **3.** process, development, course, unfolding, action, movement, stride. **—*v.* 4.** advance, proceed, move ahead, continue ahead, shoot ahead, go forward, get ahead, make headway, gain, make strides, gain ground, get on. **5.** advance, improve, become better, get better, make a turn for the better, grow better, make progress, make strides, make headway; increase, climb, mount; develop, grow, mature, grow up, ripen. **—Ant. 1** regression; loss, failure, decline, retrogression, relapse, recession. **4** move backward, regress, retrogress, recede, go backward; lose ground, lose, get behind. **5** become worse, grow worse.

progression *n.* sequence, succession, consecutiveness, continuance, order, series, continuation, continuousness; string, chain, strain; course, run; progress, advancement, furtherance, advance, ascent, climb, forward movement.

progressive *adj.* **1.** concerned with progress, supporting change; dynamic, forward-going, forward-looking, going ahead; advancing, advanced; enterprising; up-to-date; liberal, reformist. **2.** advancing step-by-step, gradual, increasingly severe, steadily going on, enlarging, incremental; traveling, spreading, ongoing. **—*n.* 3.** liberal, reformist; ameliorist, activist; populist. **—Ant. 1, 3** reactionary, conservative.

prohibit *v.* **1.** forbid, disallow, proscribe, say no to, negate, disqualify, deny, veto. **2.** prevent, inhibit, check, obstruct, impede, limit, hinder, block, curb, hamper, bar, interfere with; delay, stay, stop, preclude, obviate; ban, suppress, repress, withhold; restrict, enjoin, restrain. **—Ant. 1, 2** permit, let, allow, suffer, tolerate; authorize, order. **1** endure, bear; command, consent to, give permission, license. **2** direct, empower, give consent, give leave; further.

prohibitive Also **prohibitory** *adj.* inhibitive, restrictive, circumscriptive, enjoining, restraining, forbidding; suppressive, repressive; preventive, injunctive; hindering, obstructive, disallowing, disqualifying, inadmissible, unacceptable.

project *n.* **1.** undertaking, job, task, work, activity, assignment; plan, design, scheme, intention, ambition, aim, objective, goal. **—*v.* 2.** plan, design, draft, outline, propose, devise, frame, contrive, concoct, invent, map out. **3.** extend, jut out, stand out, stick out, protrude, overhang, beetle, bend over. **4.** transmit, throw, throw out, cast, fling; eject, ejaculate, emit, expel, discharge, send; shoot, propel, hurtle, launch, fire. **5.** forecast, describe future conditions, calculate; predetermine. **6.** forecast, plan ahead, predetermine, extrapolate.

projection *n.* **1.** ledge, shelf, extension, jutty, overhang, eave, brow, extrusion, protrusion, protuberance, bulge, ridge, bump. **2.** estimate, estimation, approximation, guess, *Slang* guesstimate, prediction, prospectus, forecast, extrapolation.

proletariat *n.* working class, laboring classes, laborers, rank and file, wage earners, the common people, the masses, the people, populace, the crowd; the multitude; commonalty, commoners, commonage; *Greek* hoi polloi; *Latin* plebs, populus, vulgus mobile; *Disparaging* lower classes, lower orders, the herd, the horde, the mob, rabble, the great unwashed, *French* canaille. **—Ant.** upper class, aristocracy, blue bloods, upper crust, gentry, nobility.

proliferate *v.* multiply, increase, reproduce rapidly, breed quickly, overproduce, procreate, regenerate, propagate, pullulate, teem, swarm; hatch, breed, spawn.

prolific *adj.* **1.** reproductive, proliferous, proliferative, breeding, propagating; fertile, fruitful, productive, yielding, fecund, procreative, multiplying, progenitive, germinative; luxuriant, copious, abundant, profuse, lush. **2.** very productive, creative. **—Syn. Study. 1** See PRODUCTIVE. **—Ant. 1** barren, unfruitful, unyielding, unproductive, unfertile, sterile. **2** unproductive.

prolix *adj.* **—Syn. Study.** See WORDY.

prolong *v.* lengthen, extend, make longer, stretch, elongate, attenuate, protract, draw out; maintain, sustain, continue, perpetuate, spin out, drag out; slow down, hold back, delay, retard. **—Syn. Study.** See LENGTHEN. **—Ant.** curtail, shorten, abridge, abbreviate, limit, lessen; expedite, hurry, speed up.

prominence *n.* **1.** eminence, distinction, importance, preeminence, fame, renown, prestige, celebrity, notability, reputation, name; conspicuousness, salience, noticeability, significance; brilliance, greatness, illustriousness; grandeur, nobility, majesty, splendor; respectability, honor, dignity; mark, credit, popularity, notoriety; weight, influence, significance, might, superiority. **2.** projection, extrusion, protuberance, bulge, convexity, process, excurvature, excrescence, tumescence, rising, swelling, protrusion, hump, knurl, bump, knob, lump, node. **3.** high point, height, promontory, precipice, pinnacle, summit, crest, cliff; elevation, high place, peak, mountain, hill, knoll, rise, hillock, rising ground, mound, mesa, tor, dune; overhang, bluff, extension, jutty, outshoot, spur.

prominent *adj.* **1.** conspicuous, evident, noticeable, apparent, easily seen, salient, obvious, definite, well-marked, pronounced, remarkable; discernible, recognizable; glaring, staring, arresting, striking. **2.** jutting out, extended, jutting, protruding, protrusive, standing out, protuberant, bulging, projecting, convex, excurved, swelling, swollen. **3.** important, prestigious, preeminent, illustrious, distinguished, honored, respected, well-known, leading, eminent, outstanding, renowned, celebrated, notable, famous. **—Ant. 1** inconspicuous, unnoticeable, indefinite; unrecognizable; secondary, insignificant, minor, indistinguishable, indistinct, unimportant. **2** receding, concave, indented. **3** unimportant, undistinguished, unknown.

promiscuous *adj.* **1.** indiscriminate, uncritical, indiscriminative, undiscriminating, undiscerning, unselective, indifferent, uncritical, undirected, helter-skelter, haphazard, desultory, casual, careless, aimless. **2.** mixed, heterogeneous, intermixed, mixed together, mixed-up, mingled, commingled, medley, composite, miscellaneous, variegated, motley; diverse; sweeping, wholesale; jumbled, scrambled, disorderly, disordered, disorganized, disarranged; chaotic, perplexed, confused. **3.** wanton, loose, lax, fast, rakish, wild, immoral, unchaste, unvirtuous, impure; licentious, lewd, lascivious, dissipated, satyric, dissolute, of easy virtue, intemperate, immodest, immoral, morally loose, incontinent. **—Ant. 1** discriminating, discerning, selective, critical, distinguishing; careful, prudent. **2** unmixed, unmingled; orderly, neat, ordered, organized, arranged. **3** moral, upright, temperate, modest, chaste, virtuous, pure.

promise *n.* **1.** word, pledge, word of honor, parole, vow, oath, troth, plight, avowal, covenant, agreement, stipulation; assurance, guarantee, warrant, warranty; declaration, profession. **2.** potential, capability, good prospects, cause for hope. **—*v.* 3.** give a promise, take an oath, give one's word of honor, pledge, vow, plight, aver, avow, vouch, guarantee, assure, warrant; covenant, agree, undertake, be bound, commit oneself, plight one's honor, make an avowal, swear, swear an oath, assert under oath. **4.** indicate, give hope of, make one expect, lead one to expect, hint of, suggest, betoken, augur, imply; hold a probability, be probable.

promising *adj.* giving promise, full of promise; favorable, hopeful, reassuring, assuring, encouraging; rising, advancing, up-and-coming; inspiriting, bright, cheerful, cheering, rosy, optimistic, happy; propitious, auspicious, of good omen, lucky, fortunate, looking up. **—Ant.** unfavorable, unpromising, discouraging.

promontory *n.* headland, hill, high point of land, point, neck of land, spur, ness, cape, peninsula, embankment; projection, overhang, precipice, jutty; cliff, bluff, height.

promote *v.* **1.** publicize, advertise, help the progress of, forward, help forward, further, advance, urge forward, *Slang* push, plug; work for, render a service to, work toward, clear the way for, ease, expedite; speak for, advocate, foster, encourage, support; cultivate, refine, develop, improve upon, enhance; aid, help, assist, abet. **2.** advance in rank, raise, elevate, upgrade, graduate; prefer. **—Ant. 1** impede; hinder, obstruct, prevent.

promotion *n.* **1.** advancement in position or rank, elevation, raise, upgrading, preferment. **2.** advertising, advertisement, publicity, fanfare, puffery, *Slang* ballyhoo; hype, advancement, furtherance, promulgation, advance, progress, encouragement, boosting. **—Ant. 1** demotion, degradation. **2** denigration, depreciation, discouragement.

prompt *adj.* **1.** instant, immediate, quick, instantaneous, unhesitating; punctual, timely, on time. **2.** fast to react, ready, quick to act; *Informal* Johnny-on-the-spot; alert, sharp, bright, on one's toes, on guard, attentive, open-eyed, open-eared, eager, zealous, observant, wide-awake, vigilant, watchful; active, animate, lively, alive; efficient, intent, keen. *—v.* **3.** spur, impel, induce, inspire, stimulate, actuate, stir, excite, inspirit, activate, incite, move, motivate, instigate, goad, provoke, cause, occasion; push, thrust, press, propel, drive, force; incline, dispose, influence, determine, persuade. **4.** cue, assist one's memory, supply with a cue; remind, jog the memory, prod, set back on the track; assist, help out, put words in one's mouth. **—Ant. 1, 2** remiss, lax, slack; dilatory, hesitating, slow, late, tardy. **2** inactive, sluggish, unready, inattentive, unobservant; inanimate; inefficient; unresponsive. **3** discourage, dissuade, deter.

promulgate *v.* set forth, expound, present, communicate, enunciate, elucidate; teach publicly, instruct, explain, interpret; sponsor, foster, promote.

prone *adj.* **1.** inclined, susceptible, liable, tending, disposed, predisposed, apt, likely, subject, accustomed, habituated. **2.** flat, face-down, recumbent, reclining, level, prostrate, horizontal. **—Ant. 1** averse, disinclined. **2** erect, upright, vertical, face-up, supine.

prong *n.* tine, point, projection; hook, tooth, horn, branch; spur, spike, barb.

pronounce *v.* **1.** articulate, speak, say, enunciate, enounce, vocalize, sound; give forth, utter, emit; frame, form. **2.** declare, proclaim, decree, rule, announce, state, voice, orate; judge, pass judgment.

pronounced *adj.* decided, distinct, unmistakable, broad, definite, well-defined, clear-cut, unquestionable, positive, clearly indicated, clear, plain, noticeable, obvious, conspicuous; apparent, strongly marked, outstanding, arresting, vivid, bold; patent, evident, recognizable, unhidden, visible, manifest, undisguised.

pronouncement *n.* official statement, formal statement, announcement, declaration, proclamation, decree.

proof *n.* **1.** conclusive evidence, corroboration, verification, certification, documentation, ratification, substantiation, confirmation, attestation. **2.** trial, test, probation, essay, assessment, scrutiny, examination, ordeal, weighing. **3.** *(in printing)* trial impression, proof, sheet, galley proof, galley.

prop *n.* **1.** support, mainstay, pillar, buttress, reinforcement, stanchion, sustainer, supporter, stay, brace. *—v.* **2.** support, shore up, hold up, brace, bolster, shoulder, buttress, underpin. **3.** rest, lean, set, stand.

propagate *v.* **1.** multiply, reproduce, proliferate, breed, progenerate, procreate, increase, generate, engender, bear, bring forth, beget, give birth, hatch, spawn. **2.** spread, disseminate, make known, promulgate; publish, publicize, issue, give to the world, broadcast, noise abroad, trumpet, blazon; circulate; make public, give currency to, bring into the open, put forth, purvey, report, notify, proclaim, preach, give out; tell, repeat, enunciate, air, communicate, impart, herald; whisper about, rumor, hint abroad; scatter, disperse, bestrew, sow, spray; instill, implant, inculcate. **—Ant. 1** reduce, diminish, decrease; extinguish. **2** hush up, silence, suppress, repress, stifle.

propagation *n.* **1.** reproduction, procreation, breeding; siring, begetting; giving birth, pregnancy, gestation, bearing, yielding; hatching, laying, spawning; generation, engendering. **2.** spreading, dispersion, diffusion, dissemination, circulation, distribution; transmission, publication, issuance.

propel *v.* shoot, catapult, eject, set in motion, impel, drive forward, drive, force, push forward, push, prod, shove, goad, poke; start, launch, send, thrust, precipitate; send, discharge, project, toss, cast, hurl, pitch, heave, sling.

propensity *n.* inclination, leaning, proclivity, predilection, liking, partiality, weakness, preference, penchant; attraction, liking, affinity, sympathy, favor, pleasure, taste, fancy; turn, bent, tendency, predisposition, bias, prejudice, disposition. **—Ant.** disinclination, aversion, loathing, dislike, hatred, antipathy, displeasure.

proper *adj.* **1.** right, correct, appropriate, suitable, fitting, applicable, pertinent, germane, relevant; apropos, fit, apt, meet, conformable; conventional, orthodox. **2.** decorous, decent, becoming, seemly, befitting, fitting, suitable, fit, acceptable; polite, courteous; modest, nice. **3.** individual, own, assigned, respective, particular, specific; distinguishing, peculiar, distinctive, characteristic, typical, appropriate, marked, representative. **4.** strictly defined, in the limited sense, within legal limits, officially bounded, per se; express, particular, precise, correct, true. **—Ant. 1** wrong, inappropriate, irrelevant, unfit, unsuitable, inapt, malapropos. **2** unseemly, unbecoming, impolite, discourteous, objectionable, rude, indecent, vulgar.

properly *adv.* **1.** in a proper manner, appropriately, suitably, aptly, acceptably; decently, decorously, politely, tastefully; conventionally. **2.** correctly, exactly, right, without error, accurately, precisely, perfectly.

property *n.* **1.** belongings, effects, possessions, goods, chattels; estate, wealth, assets, resources, holdings; appointments; funds, means, investments, stock, treasure, capital, moneys; right of possession, ownership, hold, title, proprietorship. **2.** land, real estate, realty, acres, acreage, grounds, estates, territory. **3.** quality, aspect, characteristic, trait, feature, particularity, attribute; peculiarity, idiosyncrasy, singularity, individuality; mark, point, badge, earmark. **—Syn. Study. 1** PROPERTY, EFFECTS, GOODS, CHATTELS, ESTATE refer to what is owned. PROPERTY is the general word: *She owns a great deal of property. He said that the umbrella was his property.* EFFECTS is a term for any form of personal property, including even things of the least value: *All my effects were insured against fire.* GOODS refers to household possessions or other movable property, esp. the stock in trade of a business: *The store arranged its goods on shelves.* CHATTELS is a term for pieces of personal property or movable possessions; it may be applied to livestock, automobiles, etc.: *a mortgage on chattels.* ESTATE refers to property of any kind that has been, or is capable of being, handed down to descendants or otherwise disposed of in a will: *He left most of his estate to his niece.* It may consist of personal estate (money, valuables, securities, chattels, etc.) or real estate (land and buildings). **3** See QUALITY.

prophecy *n.* **1.** foretelling the future, prediction, forecasting, soothsaying, forecast, divination, prognostication. **2.** prediction, forecast, prognostication; augury, portent; revelation, sign from God.

prophesy *v.* predict, foretell, presage, forecast, divine, soothsay, prognosticate, premonish, warn, forewarn, foresee, augur, portend, apprehend, forbode. **—Syn. Study.** See PREDICT.

prophet *Fem.* **prophetess** *n.* **1.** revealer of the word of God, proclaimer of holy truth; evangelist, inspired spokesman, guide, intercessor, interpreter, preacher. **2.** predictor, foreteller, forecaster, prognosticator, prophesier, Cassandra, sibyl, soothsayer, oracle, clairvoyant, seer, seeress, diviner, divinator, augur; crystal gazer, palmist, fortune-teller, geomancer; sorcerer.

propitiate *v.* appease, placate, pacify, calm, assuage, mollify, conciliate, accommodate, soothe, allay. **—Syn. Study.** See APPEASE. **—Ant.** anger, madden, infuriate, roil, pique, provoke.

propitious *adj.* favorable, fortunate, auspicious, opportune, well-timed; beneficial, fit, suitable, advantageous, promising, lucky; golden, happy, bonny, providential, benign. **—Ant.** adverse, harmful, deleterious, unlucky, pernicious.

proponent *n.* advocate, supporter, exponent, endorser, champion, espouser, spokesman, enthusiast, apologist, representative; defender, vindicator, backer, booster, partisan, upholder, votary, patron, friend.

proportion *n.* **1.** relative amount, relationship, ratio, balance, distribution, correlation, correspondence. **2.** proper relation, balance, symmetry, perspective, proportionality, ideal distribution, evenness, consistency, commensuration, correspondence; harmony, agreement. **3. proportions** dimensions, size, extent, measurements, area, scope, expanse, range, span, spread, width, breadth; amplitude, magnitude, volume, capacity, greatness, bulk, mass. **4.** part, amount; division, segment, fraction, share, portion; ratio, quota, percentage, measure, lot, degree. **—*v.* 5.** adapt, adjust in size, adjust in relation, fit, form, shape, gauge, gear, measure, apportion, put in proportion; modulate, regulate, order, accommodate; equalize, equate, conform, match; poise, balance, harmonize, balance the parts of; rectify, correct, grade, graduate. **—Syn. Study. 2** See SYMMETRY. **—Ant. 2** disproportion, unevenness, inconsistency, disparity; disagreement, contrast, disharmony.

proposal *n.* **1.** recommendation, proposition, plan, program, project, course, scheme, resolution, line of action; plot, design, conception, idea, stratagem; prospectus, prospect, presentation, outline, draft, sketch, theory. **2.** invitation, proposition, offer, suggestion, motion, appeal, proffer, bid, nomination, presentation, overture; marriage proposition, suit.

propose *v.* **1.** recommend, suggest, present, submit, tender, proffer, come up with, offer for consideration, introduce, bring forward, put forward, put forth, advance, propound, set forth. **2.** plan, intend, set about, mean, design, plot, scheme, undertake, venture, purpose, determine, expect, aspire, aim, hope, contemplate, have in mind, have in view, have a mind. **3.** press one's suit, woo, make one's suit; ask for one's hand, affiance; *Informal* pop the question.

proposition *n.* **1.** offer, proposal, offer of terms, deal, bargain; negotiation, agreement, stipulation, contract, guarantee, assurance. **2.** proposal, suggestion, recommendation, scheme, resolution, plan, undertaking; subject, topic, issue, question, matter, point.

proprietor *n.* landlord, owner, proprietress, landowner, titleholder, landholder; master, lord of the manor; manager; possessor, holder.

propriety *n.* correctness; courtesy, decorum, good behavior, decorousness, dignity, good manners, etiquette, formality, gentlemanly or ladylike behavior, respectability; savoir faire, appropriateness, becomingness, applicability, fitness, suitableness, seemliness, aptness, rightness. **—Ant.** impropriety, incorrectness, discourtesy, misbehavior, misconduct, bad manners, faux pas, inappropriateness, unsuitability, unseemliness, inaptness, wrongness.

prosaic *adj.* dull, flat, tiresome, dry, stale, unimaginative, vapid, pedestrian, plebeian, hackneyed, platitudinous, uninteresting, unentertaining, tedious, monotonous, dull, spiritless, jejune, trite, common, matter-of-fact, humdrum, usual, routine, ordinary; *Slang* blah; prosy, wordy, unpoetical. **—Ant.** exciting, imaginative, fascinating, interesting, entertaining, spirited; uncommon, unusual, extraordinary; poetical.

proscribe *v.* denounce, condemn, censure, disapprove, repudiate; curse, damn, anathematize; outlaw, prohibit, forbid, interdict, ban, excommunicate; banish, exile; boycott. **—Ant.** allow, permit, encourage, aid.

prosecute *v.* **1.** try, put on trial, arraign, indict, bring before a court, bring to justice, bring to trial; sue, bring action against, bring suit against, prefer charges against, go to law, take to court. **2.** persevere in, be resolute in, stick to, keep at or on, persist in, continue, prolong, maintain, sustain; follow up, pursue, go with, carry on, wage, see through. **3.** carry on, conduct, perform, discharge, execute, administer, direct, deal with, manage, handle.

prospect *n.* **1.** Usu. **prospects** chances, outlook, probability of success, likelihood, probability; anticipation, foretaste, expectation, hope, promise. **2.** expectation, contemplation, anticipation, expectancy, hope, intention, ambition; plan, design, proposal. **3.** view, vision, picture; scene, scenery, landscape, vista, panorama; outlook, aspect. **4.** potential client, potential customer, candidate, possibility. **—***v.* **5.** explore, seek, search; go after, look for; work a mine. **—Syn. Study. 3** See VIEW.

prospective *adj.* **1.** future, coming, impending, approaching, to come, close to hand, to be, forthcoming, about to be, eventual, destined; in prospect, in view, foreseen, on the horizon, expected, looked-for, intended, hoped-for, in expectation; in the wind, looming, threatening. **2.** likely, possible, potential, promising.

prosper *v.* thrive, gain, get on, get ahead, make good, be fortunate, fare well, come off well, run smoothly; be successful, flourish, succeed; advance, increase, progress, flower, bear fruit, fructify; make one's fortune, grow rich. **—Syn. Study.** See SUCCEED. **—Ant.** fail, lose, be unfortunate, be unsuccessful; decrease, be fruitless; grow poor.

prosperity *n.* success, well-being, affluence, thriving condition, material comfort, ease, prosperousness; good fortune, run of luck, good luck, advantage; profit, gain, advance, progress, advancement; affluence, wealth, bounty, opulence, luxury, abundance, plenty; blessings, welfare; palmy days, halcyon days, golden age, good times. **—Ant.** want, poverty, indigence, destitution, misfortune, bad luck, disadvantage; failure, reverses, adversity; shortage, depression.

prosperous *adj.* **1.** successful, thriving, flourishing; fortunate, lucky; rich, opulent, wealthy, affluent, moneyed; well-to-do, comfortable, well-off, in easy circumstances; *Slang* on easy street. **2.** auspicious, propitious, providential, fortunate, of good omen, lucky, timely, opportune; good, favorable, promising, well-disposed, heartening, hopeful, encouraging, cheering, reassuring, pleasing; bright, rosy, golden, smiling, sunny, fair, happy. **—Ant. 1** unsuccessful, unfortunate, unlucky; failing; poor, impoverished; defeated, beaten. **2** unpropitious, unfortunate, inauspicious, unlucky, untimely, inopportune; bad, unfavorable, unpromising.

prostitute *n.* **1.** whore, harlot, slut, hooker, hustler, streetwalker, lady of the night, lewd woman, loose woman, fallen woman, jade, bawd, tart, hussy, strumpet, trollop, call girl; courtesan; *Informal* floozy, tart, chippy. **—***v.* **2.** debase, cheapen, sell out, degrade, demean, lower, corrupt, pervert, spoil, defile, debauch; abuse, misuse, misemploy, misdirect, misapply; profane, desecrate.

prostrate *v.* **1.** bow down, kneel down, abase, kowtow, fall to one's knees. **2.** throw flat, flatten; overthrow, overcome, *Informal* floor, *Slang* deck. **—***adj.* **3.** lying flat, lying full length, lying face down, stretched out, laid out, prone, horizontal, recumbent, flat; bowed low, supplicating, beseeching, crouching, on bended knee, on one's knees. **4.** overcome, worn out, bone weary, dead tired, exhausted, prostrated, spent, *Informal* fagged, on one's last legs.

prostration *n.* **1.** act of prostrating; bow, genuflection, kneeling; submission, subjection, lowliness, abasement. **2.** exhaustion, weakness, weariness, enervation, dejection, depression; paralysis, impotence, helplessness, depth of misery, desolation, despondency, desperation, despair, anguish, woe, distress, wretchedness, heartache, sorrow, misery, grief.

protagonist *n.* hero, heroine, main character, central character, title role, principal, lead, leading man, leading lady, star, headliner, superstar; diva, prima donna; danseur noble, prima ballerina; *French* jeune premier, jeune première.

protect *v.* guard, shield, defend, watch over, safeguard, secure, take care of, care for, tend, look after; shelter, cover, hide, veil, harbor, screen; keep, maintain, sustain, conserve, save, preserve. **—Ant.** attack, assault, assail; expose.

protection *n.* **1.** protecting, guarding, safeguard, defense, championship, preservation, safekeeping, guardianship, custody, charge, care, keep, conservation, saving; support, aid, assistance; immunity, safety, security. **2.** protector, shield, guard, defense, preserver, safeguard, security; barrier, buffer, fence, wall; cover, shade, screen, shelter; asylum, refuge, haven, harbor, preserve, sanctuary.

protective *adj.* **1.** protecting, guarding, safeguarding, safekeeping, preventive, shielding, defensive. **2.** sheltering, shielding; watchful, vigilant, heedful, careful, solicitous; fatherly, motherly, paternal, maternal, sisterly, brotherly, big-brotherly, avuncular, grandfatherly, grandmotherly.

protest *n.* **1.** demonstration, march, picketing, boycott, sit-in, strike; opposition, dissent, contradiction; dispute, disagreement, dissidence, resistance, disaffection, difference of opinion, demurral, discountenance, remonstrance, remonstration, deprecation, renunciation, formal complaint, disclaimer; objection, protestation; *Informal* kick, beef, gripe. **—***v.* **2.** complain, express disapproval, cry out, object, take exception; oppose, disapprove, dissent, beg to differ, disagree, differ in opinion, contradict, deny, controvert. **3.** assert, vow, avow, declare, contend, insist, announce, put or set forth, put forward, propound, hold out, maintain, offer; profess, speak, state, enunciate, pronounce; testify, attest, affirm, asseverate, aver, assure, allege, avouch. **—Ant. 1** endorsement, agreement, sanction; acquiescence, approval. **2** approve, agree, sanction, endorse, acclaim, subscribe to.

protocol *n.* diplomatic code, diplomatic or court etiquette; proprieties, amenities, code of behavior, good form, decorum, formality, manners, usage, customs, standards, conventions, dictates of society.

protract *v.* prolong, extend, lengthen, draw out, stretch out, drag out, spin out, keep going, keep up. **—Syn. Study.** See LENGTHEN. **—Ant.** shorten, curtail, abbreviate, condense, abridge.

protrude *v.* jut out, project, stand out, stick out; bulge, swell, belly, push forward.

protuberance *n.* bulge, swelling, prominence, projection, excrescence, *Archaic* protuberancy; knob, bump, hump, knot, lump, node, gnarl; convexity, excurvature, roundness, bow; elevation, rising, ridge, welt, weal.

proud *adj.* **1.** independent, self-sufficient, dignified, scrupulous, honorable, self-respecting; strict, punctilious, principled, high-minded; lofty, elevated, reserved, distinguished; fine, admirable, august. **2.** filled with pride, pleased, satisfied, gratified, contented, delighted, happy. **3.** conceited, vain, smug, self-satisfied, self-important; prideful, self-praising, bragging, boastful, braggart, egotistical, swollen, vainglorious, know-it-all, complacent; pompous, overbearing; assuming, affected, puffed up, inflated, bloated; arrogant, insolent, flaunting; patronizing, condescending, supercilious, disdainful, contemptuous, intolerant; haughty, aloof, snobbish, lordly, high-and-mighty, imperious; *Informal* uppish, uppity, snooty, cocky, stuck-up; *Slang* high-hat, snotty. **4.** glorious, exalted, elevated, euphoric. **5.** stately, noble, majestic, magnificent, great, lordly, grand, august; revered, venerable, storied, cherished. **—Ant. 1** humble, lowly, submissive; ignoble, dishonorable, undignified, servile, cringing, abject. **2** ashamed, displeased, dissatisfied, discontented. **3** humble, unassuming, modest, unobtrusive, meek, unpresuming, deferential. **4** ignominious, humiliating. **5** base, ignoble.

prove *v.* **1.** verify, establish, substantiate, bear out, uphold, support, sustain, corroborate, document, witness, authenticate, confirm, affirm, attest, certify, warrant, testify to; justify, make good, validate, ascertain, show clearly, demonstrate, manifest, evidence. **2.** test, try, try out, put to the test, verify, make trial of, subject to trial; check, analyze, examine, probe, look into. **3.** result in, turn out to be, be found to be, end up, wind up, eventuate, result. **—Ant. 1** disprove, refute, negate, contradict, contravert, rebut, discredit, rule out.

provender *n.* **—Syn. Study.** See FEED.

proverb *n.* saying, popular saying, adage, maxim, aphorism, truism, accepted truth; epigram, precept, apothegm, saw, axiom, moral; dictum, mot, byword, motto; cliché, bromide, platitude, commonplace. **—Syn. Study.** PROVERB, MAXIM are terms for short, pithy sayings. A PROVERB is such a saying popularly known and repeated, usu. expressing simply and concretely, though often metaphorically, a truth based on common sense or practical human experience: *"A stitch in time saves nine."* A MAXIM is a brief statement of a general and practical truth, esp. one that serves as a rule of conduct: *"It is wise to risk no more than one can afford to lose."*

provide *v.* **1.** furnish, give, place at one's disposal, offer, submit, present, tender, impart, render; yield, produce, grant, confer, bestow, donate, contribute, afford, pay, allow, accord, award, deliver, dispense; arm, equip, fit, outfit, supply. **2.** prepare, make plans, take measures, anticipate needs; get ready, arrange, plan, accumulate, save up; make arrangements, make provision, cater. **3.** state, stipulate, postulate, specify, require. **—Ant. 1** deprive, withhold, refuse, disallow. **2** neglect, overlook.

providence *n.* prudence, farsightedness, foresight, forethought, provision, forehandedness, circumspection, husbandry. **—Ant.** short-sightedness, improvidence, imprudence, heedlessness.

provident *adj.* foresighted, well-prepared, farseeing, foreseeing, farsighted, forehanded, thoughtful, discreet, judicious, circumspect, discerning; cautious, wary, precautious, vigilant, careful; ready, equipped; prudent, frugal, thrifty, economical, saving, parsimonious, chary. **—Ant.** improvident, unprepared, shortsighted; injudicious, undiscerning; incautious, unwary, reckless, heedless; imprudent, wasteful, uneconomical.

province *n.* **1.** administrative division, state, territory, subdivision, department, zone, canton, county, arrondissement, region, area, section, part. **2.** area, field, sphere, bailiwick, territory, capacity, function, office, jurisdiction, domain, job, authority; responsibility, charge, business, duty, assignment, station, place, role, scope of duties.

provincial *adj.* **1.** of a province, regional, territorial, local. **2.** rural, country, countrified, rustic, bucolic, small-town, backwoods; unsophisticated; homespun, homely, rude, rough; *Disparaging* crude; gauche; unpolished, unrefined, clumsy, loutish, boorish, oafish; clownish, awkward, cloddish, yokelish, clodhopping, hayseed, down-home, gawky. **3.** narrow, parochial, insular. **—Ant. 1** standard, national. **2** big-city, citified, urban, fashionable, polished, refined, smooth. **3** cosmopolitan.

provision *n.* **1.** providing, supplying, furnishing, giving, endowment, donation. **2. provisions** supplies, food, eatables, edibles, comestibles, sustenance, stores, commons, groceries, victuals, viands, provender; feed, forage, fodder. **3.** arrangement, anticipation, forehandedness, provident measures or steps, prearrangement, forethought, wherewithal; provident care, precaution, preparation, readiness. **4.** proviso, requisite, requirement, obligation, stipulation, condition, term, article, clause; restriction, limitation, reservation, modification, qualification; *Informal* string.

proviso *n.* condition, restriction, limitation, qualification, modification, stipulation, requirement; clause, amendment, addition, rider; *Informal* string.

provocation *n.* cause, motivation, incitement, instigation, fomentation, goad, spur, prodding, stimulation, actuation, stimulus, vexation, irritation, pique, annoyance, perturbation, aggravation; excitation, slight, insult, affront, offense.

provocative *adj.* **1.** provoking, annoying, aggravating, irritating, vexing, vexatious, irksome, *Slang* in-your-face. **2.** seductive, tempting, tantalizing, captivating, intriguing, entrancing, enchanting, fascinating, beguiling, bewitching, alluring, attractive, sexy; exciting, intoxicating, thrilling, stimulating, arousing, ravishing, irresistible, inviting.

provoke *v.* **1.** anger, enrage, incense, outrage, infuriate, madden, irritate, vex, agitate, annoy, gall, aggravate, irk, exasperate, rile, try one's patience, chafe, grate, move to anger, work into a passion, make one's blood boil, put out of humor, put out; *Slang* get one's goat, get under one's skin, get to one. **2.** cause, prompt, excite, incite, inspire, impel, instigate, induce, compel, arouse, stimulate, rouse, stir, animate, move, motivate. **3.** arouse, stimulate, bring on, give rise to, cause, produce, bring about, effect, actuate, motivate, prompt, pique, put in motion, galvanize, foment, incite, generate, create, establish; stir, stir up, rouse, awaken, call forth, elicit, fire, inflame, kindle, quicken, excite, evoke. **—Syn. Study. 2** See INCITE. **—Ant. 1** gratify, assuage, calm, soothe, mollify, ease, propitiate, please.

prowess *n.* **1.** bravery, valor, courageous deeds, heroism, fearlessness, intrepidity, gallantry, courage, grit, nerve, daring, boldness, derring-do, dauntlessness; strength, might, power, vigor, fortitude, stamina, endurance, mettle, spirit, hardihood, *Informal* spunk, *Slang* guts. **2.** ability, skill, skillfulness, competence, aptitude, know-how, knack, talent, faculty, genius, accomplishment, adeptness, expertness, proficiency. **—Ant. 1** cowardice, cowardliness, fear, timidity, meekness. **2** incompetence, ineptness.

prowl *v.* stalk, hunt, scavenge, roam, slink, steal, sneak, range, lurk, skulk, creep. **—Syn. Study.** See LURK.

prudent *adj.* wise, sensible, careful, showing good judgment, judicious, expedient, discerning, sagacious, sage, politic, sapient, levelheaded, well-advised, rational, sane, self-possessed; thoughtful, considerate, reflecting, prudential, provident, heedful, vigilant, wide-awake, cautious, wary, circumspect, shrewd, guarded, chary; prepared, foresighted, discreet, farsighted, precautious; frugal, thrifty, saving, economical, sparing. **—Ant.** imprudent, indiscreet, unwise, irrational; thoughtless, inconsiderate, improvident, careless, heedless, reckless, rash, incautious, wasteful, extravagant, uneconomical.

prudish *adj.* prim, extremely proper and modest, Victorian, overmodest, priggish, puritanical, prissy, old-maidish, straitlaced; precise, fastidious, finical, particular; timid, shy, demure, skittish, queasy, squeamish; smug, sanctimonious, self-righteous, punctilious, pedantic, mincing; stilted, starched, stuffy. **—Syn. Study.** See MODEST.

prune *v.* **1.** trim, clip, snip, thin, thin out, shear, pull, crop, lop. **2.** reduce, curtail, trim, shorten, cut; abridge, condense, abbreviate; simplify, clarify.

prurient *adj.* lustful, sexy, libidinous, concupiscent, hot-blooded, passionate, goatish, lascivious, licentious, lecherous, salacious, carnal, lubricious, lewd, obscene, priapic, satyric.

pry[1] *v.* snoop, poke, butt, nose, stick one's nose in, sniff, peek, peer; probe, explore, delve, inquire, search; meddle, interfere, mix in, butt in, intrude, intervene, *Slang* horn in.

pry[2] *v.* **1.** force, break, prize, work, lever, crack, jimmy. **2.** force, wring, squeeze; wrench, tear, wrest, extract; worm, winkle, ferret, smoke.

pseudo *adj.* false, spurious, mock, pretended, feigned, simulated, make-believe, fictitious, counterfeit, forged, sham, bogus, fraudulent, fake, phony; self-described, self-styled, *French* soi-disant. **—Ant.** genuine, real, authentic.

pseudonym *n.* alias, assumed name, false name, nickname, sobriquet; *French* nom de guerre, nom de plume, nom de théâtre; cognomen, anonym, pen name, professional name, stage name.

psyche *n.* soul, mind, spirit, makeup, personality, self; ego, superego, id; subconscious, unconscious, anima; *Archaic* bowels, penetralia.

psychic *adj.* **1.** mental, psychological; cerebral, intellectual; spiritual. **2.** extrasensory, preternatural, telekinetic, supernatural, occult, mystic; supersensory, telepathic, clairvoyant. *—n.* **3.** clairvoyant, sensitive, telepathist; prophet, soothsayer, diviner, augur; medium, paragnost, spiritualist; *French* voyant, (*fem.*) voyante.

psychology *n.* mental processes, mind, makeup, attitude, feeling, head.

psychotic *adj.* **1.** insane, psychopathic, lunatic; mad, disturbed, demented, deranged, non compos mentis; *Slang* loony, crazy, nutty, kooky. *—n.* **2.** insane person, psychopath, madman, maniac, lunatic; *Slang* nut, kook, loony, loon.

pub *n. Brit.* public house, tavern, barroom, bar, taproom, inn, saloon, grogshop, pothouse, rummery, rumship, bistro, *Slang* ginmill, alehouse, beer parlor, *Archaic* speakeasy.

public *adj.* **1.** common, general, popular, societal, social; political, civic, civil; state, statewide, national, nationwide, countrywide. **2.** open to all persons, free to all, used by all, shared, not private or exclusive; unrestricted, available, accessible, passable, unbarred, unenclosed, unfenced, unbounded, not circumscribed, unobstructed; communal, community-owned. **3.** widely known, familiar to many people, notorious, recognized, acknowledged, disclosed, divulged, open, overt, outward, unabashed, unashamed, plain, frank, obvious, conspicuous, evident, visible, unconcealed, exposed, apparent, undisguised, revealed, patent, manifest, observable, discernible, perceivable, in sight or view, in broad daylight. —*n.* **4.** people, everyone, populace, community, nation, population, citizenry, commonality, society, body politic, proletariat, folk, bourgeoisie, multitude, masses, hoi polloi, rank and file, mob. **5.** following, attendance, audience, followers, those interested; buyers, purchasers, clientele, trade, patrons; constituency, supporters. —**Ant. 1** private, personal, individual. **2** private, proprietary, exclusive, restricted, unavailable, inaccessible, barred, secluded, closed. **3** secret, unknown, unrecognized, hidden, unrevealed, mum.

publicity *n.* public notice, attention, currency, publicness, notoriety; circulation, promulgation, advertising, salesmanship, promotion; information, propaganda; build-up, puffery, write-up; *Informal* ballyhoo, plug, hype, flack, puff, blurb.

publicize *v.* promote, make known, make public, bring into public notice, give currency, spread word of, advertise, sell, circularize, propagandize, proclaim, acclaim, announce, broadcast, herald, emblazon, propagate, promulgate; *Informal* ballyhoo, push, plug, puff, hype. —**Ant.** keep secret, suppress, cover up, hush up, conceal, hide.

publish *v.* **1.** print for sale, put to press, issue, bring out, put out. **2.** print, make generally known, announce, make public, publicize, give publicity to, promote; disclose, release, give out, vent, air, broadcast, give to the world, tell, communicate, utter, impart, divulge, diffuse, disseminate, spread, propagate, promulgate, circulate; proclaim, declare, trumpet, herald, advertise, placard. —**Syn. Study. 2** See ANNOUNCE. —**Ant. 2** conceal, hide, secrete; muffle, smother; bury, suppress; withhold, keep secret.

pucker *v.* **1.** draw together, contract, shrink; pinch, crease, purse, compress, squeeze; wrinkle, crinkle; gather, fold, tuck, pleat, make a pleat. —*n.* **2.** fold, tuck, gather, pinch, pleat, crease, wrinkle, crinkle, crumble, rumple, ruffle.

pudgy Also **podgy** *adj.* fat, obese, stout, chunky, chubby, stocky, fleshy, paunchy, plump, buxom, rotund, thickset, tubby, roly-poly, squat, stubby, short and fat, dumpy.

puerile *adj.* childish, foolish, silly, immature, babyish, infantile, simple, childlike, callow, sophomoric, raw, green, juvenile; irrational, senseless, inane, nonsensical, ridiculous, frivolous, vapid, harebrained; trivial, piddling, petty, unimportant, worthless. —**Ant.** adult, mature; rational; intelligent.

puff *n.* **1.** short blast, abrupt emission, sudden gust, whiff, breath, exhalation, flurry, small cloud, wisp. **2.** swelling, rising, bulge, elevation, node, inflammation, distention, inflation, dilation, excurvature, bow, convexity, hump, protuberance, extension, protrusion, protuberancy, excrescence, tuberosity. **3.** exaggeration, overcommendation, sales talk, euphemism, overpraise, overlaudation, flattery, encomium, flummery, puffery, panegyric, much ado about nothing, misrepresentation, blurb, publicity; bluster, bombast; *Informal* plug, ballyhoo. —*v.* **4.** breathe hard, be out of breath, pant, heave, wheeze, gasp, exhale, blow, be winded. **5.** blow in puffs, send forth, emit, discharge. **6.** draw, suck, inhale; smoke. **7.** be inflated, be distended, swell, blow up, inflate, expand, extend, distend, dilate, stretch, bloat.

puffy *adj.* swollen, inflated, puffed up, bloated, bulging, inflamed, distended, enlarged, expanded; round, corpulent, fat, fleshy.

pugnacious *adj.* quarrelsome, given to fighting, antagonistic, unfriendly; aggressive, combative, defiant, warlike, hostile, menacing, militant; contentious, belligerent, bellicose, fractious, disputatious, argumentative; threatening, with teeth bared; with a chip on one's shoulder. —**Ant.** peaceful, calm, friendly, conciliatory, accommodating.

pulchritude *n.* beauty, prettiness, comeliness, beauteousness, loveliness, fairness, *Scot.* bonniness, personableness, attractiveness, exquisiteness. —**Ant.** homeliness, plainness, drabness, ugliness.

pull *v.* **1.** haul, drag, lug, tug, draw; take in tow, tow; troll, trawl. **2.** tug, jerk, grab, yank. **3.** draw out, remove, detach, withdraw; extract, wrest, wring; uproot, extirpate, dig out, weed out. **4.** rip, tear, rend, split, sever, rive. **5.** go, move, drive. **6.** strain, stretch, twist, wrench, sprain. **7.** draw, attract; lure, entice. —*n.* **8.** tug, jerk, yank, shake. **9.** pulling power, drawing power; lure, allure, attraction, attractiveness, influence, enticement, fascination, appeal, allurement; gravity, magnetism. —**Ant. 1, 2, 8** push, shove. **3** insert, plant. **7** repel.

pulsate *v.* expand and contract rhythmically, throb, beat, palpitate, vibrate, reverberate, thump, pound, pulse, undulate, oscillate, tick, quiver, flutter, shake, shiver, quaver, shudder, tremble; wave, waver; come and go, alternate, ebb and flow.

pulse *n.* **1.** throb, regular beat, rhythm, cadence, pulsation, palpitation, recurrence, stroke, undulation, vibration, oscillation. **—***v.* **2.** beat, throb, palpitate, pulsate, thump, vibrate; quiver, shudder, tremble, oscillate.

pulverize *v.* reduce to powder or dust, grind, pound, granulate, comminate, triturate, powder, atomize, mince, crush, crumble, crumb, mill, mash.

punch *n.* **1.** blow, hit, jab, thrust, clout, stroke, cuff, slam, thump, box, poke, knock; *Informal* chop, sock; *Slang* roundhouse, haymaker. **—***v.* **2.** hit with the fist, strike, smite, box, thwack, whack, jab, poke, pelt, wallop, clobber, clout, swat, cuff, slam, clip; *Informal* sock, conk, plug, paste; baste, pummel, pound, beat.

punctilious *adj.* exact, precise, correct, meticulous, painstaking, proper, scrupulous; exacting, rigid, strict, fussy, particular, demanding, finicky, picky, rigorous. **—Syn. Study.** See SCRUPULOUS. **—Ant.** casual, indifferent, negligent, careless, slipshod.

punctual *adj.* on time, not late, early, in good time, well-timed, prompt, ready, regular, steady, constant; quick, expeditious, instant, immediate, instantaneous; seasonable, timely; *Informal* on the dot. **—Ant.** unpunctual, late, tardy; irregular, unsteady.

punctuate *v.* **1.** mark with punctuation marks; insert the stops, separate, break. **2.** interrupt, break, intersperse, pepper, sprinkle, scatter, lace.

puncture *n.* **1.** hole, break, rupture, opening, perforation, nick, cut; wound, bite, sting. **—***v.* **2.** pierce, make a hole in, prick, pink, stick; wound, cut, nick. **3.** deflate, depreciate; let down, knock down, shoot down, bring back to earth.

pundit *n.* sage, expert, authority, savant, guru, wizard, master, guide, mentor, thinker, learned person.

pungent *adj.* **1.** sharp-tasting, highly flavored, savory, spicy, flavorful, piquant, flavorsome, palatable, tasty, highly seasoned, salty, peppery, hot; nippy, tangy, strong, stimulating, sharp; sharp-smelling, acrid, sour, acid, tart, astringent, vinegary, caustic, bitter, acetous, biting, stinging, smarting, penetrating. **2.** sharp, piercing, pointed, acute, trenchant, keen, poignant; stinging, biting, mordant, caustic, invidious, cutting, incisive, penetrating, sarcastic, smart, wounding, tart, acrimonious, bitter; stimulating, stirring, provocative, tantalizing, racy, spicy, scintillating; sparkling, brilliant, clever, snappy, keen-witted, witty. **—Ant. 1** bland, mild; unsavory, unpalatable, flavorless, tasteless; weak, unstimulating. **2** dull, mild, moderate, inane, vapid; pointless.

punish *v.* subject to a penalty, penalize, chastise, correct, discipline; sentence, imprison, fine; give one his deserts; rebuke, reprove, admonish, castigate, chasten, take to task, dress down; avenge, take revenge, take vengeance on, bring to account, get even with, retaliate, settle accounts with; whip, flog, beat. **—Ant.** excuse, pardon, forgive; exonerate, absolve, vindicate; praise, laud, reward.

punishment *n.* penalty, punition; penance, penal retribution, price, penalization, payment, retribution, deserts; fine, forfeit, damages, reparation, redress; discipline, correction, chastisement, castigation, chastening, (*variously*) spanking, whipping, flogging, flaying, crucifying, hanging.

puny *adj.* **1.** small and weak, undersized, underdeveloped, slight, pint-sized, runty, sawed-off, little, bantam, mite-sized, miniature, diminutive, tiny; weakly, sickly, poor, feeble; thin, fragile, emaciated, delicate, frail, runtlike, infirm. **2.** feeble, poor, weak, inadequate, insignificant, slight, impotent, light, inconsiderable, insufficient, meager; unimportant, picayune, picayunish, petty, trivial, worthless, trifling, paltry, piddling, shallow, flimsy, tenuous, measly. **—Ant. 1** large, great, robust, healthy, strong, vigorous; colossal, gigantic. **2** significant, potent, strong, forceful, considerable, important; adequate, sufficient.

pupil *n.* student learner, schoolgirl, schoolboy, coed; undergraduate, scholar; beginner, novice, tyro, initiate, probationer, apprentice, trainee, disciple. **—Ant.** teacher, master.

puppet *n.* **1.** animated doll, marionette, manikin; hand puppet; doll, toy. **2.** tool, creature, pawn, cat's paw, dupe, instrument; lay figure, figurehead; man of straw, jackstraw; hireling, underling, subordinate, flunky, servant, lackey, henchman.

purchase *v.* **1.** buy, pay for, pick up. **—***n.* **2.** acquisition, buying, acquirement; buy. **3.** advantage, hold, leverage; footing, foothold, toehold, support; power-exerting means, influence, edge. **—Ant. 1** sell, dispose of, liquidate, divest, convert into cash. **2** sale, selling; disposal; liquidation.

pure *adj.* **1.** unmixed, full-strength, unadulterated, unmodified, unalloyed, unmingled, neat, straight; perfect, faultless, flawless, undefiled, uncorrupted, untainted, unblemished, unmarred; clean, fresh, immaculate, uncontaminated, uninfected, unpolluted, disinfected, antiseptic, germfree, sterilized, sterile, sanitary, healthful, wholesome, fit for consumption; purebred, of unmixed descent, thoroughbred, pedigreed, pure-blooded. **2.** mere, sheer, stark; absolute, complete, whole, entire, full, utter, downright, out-and-out, positive, perfect; unqualified, thorough. **3.** innocent, guiltless, sinless, decent, uncorrupted, moral, righteous, ethical, upright; virtuous, chaste, undefiled, virgin, virginal, unsullied, unspoiled, spotless, immaculate, untainted, untarnished, unblemished, inviolable, inviolate; blameless, above suspicion, unimpeachable, true, sincere, guileless, angelic. **4.** theoretical, abstract, hypothetical, conjectural, speculative, fundamental, basic, higher. **—Ant. 1–3** impure. **1** adulterated, mixed, alloyed, mingled; imperfect, flawed, corrupted, tainted, blemished; unclean, dirty, contaminated; infected, polluted, unsterilized, unhealthful; mixed. **2** qualified. **3** guilty, culpable, sinful, corrupt, corrupted, immoral; unvirtuous, unchaste, defiled, sullied, spoiled, spotted, tarnished, blemished, contaminated; impeachable, untrue, insincere; immodest, indecent, filthy, gross, lewd, obscene. **4** applied, practical.

purely *adv.* **1.** only, solely, merely, simply, essentially; completely, entirely, totally, absolutely, fully, wholly. **2.** virtuously, chastely, virginally, incorruptibly, morally, innocently, cleanly, admirably, worthily, in all honor; piously, devoutly. **3.** without admixture, cleanly, flawlessly, faultlessly. **—Ant. 2** immorally, dishonorably, unwholesomely, impiously. **3** impurely, faultily.

purge *v.* **1.** clean up, cleanse, purify, clean out, sweep out, shake up. **2.** remove, get rid of, do away with, oust, dismiss, kill, liquidate, eliminate, expel, uproot, discharge, banish, crush, rout out; eradicate, exterminate. **3.** wash away, expiate, atone for; obtain absolution, pardon, forgiveness, or remission from. **—***n.* **4.** purging, purgation, cleanup, shake-up, purification. **5.** laxative, purgative, cathartic, aperient; clyster, physic, emetic.

purify *v.* make pure, disinfect, decontaminate, sanitize, clear, clarify, (*variously*) boil, chlorinate, filter, distill, sterilize, pasteurize. **—Ant.** contaminate, pollute, dirty, infect.

puritanical *adj.* strict, severe, ascetic, austere, puritan, prim, prissy, prudish, priggish, straitlaced, stiff-necked, bluenosed, stilted, stiff, stuffy, rigid, dogmatic, fanatical, narrow, sanctimonious, bigoted. **—Ant.** permissive, broad-minded, latitudinarian.

purity *n.* **1.** pureness, clearness, clarity, lucidity, limpidity; cleanliness, cleanness, immaculateness, immaculacy, brilliance; excellence, fineness; homogeneity, uniformity. **2.** guiltlessness, guilelessness, innocence, clear conscience; modesty, temperance, chastity, virginity, chasteness, virtuousness, virtue, decency, uprightness, morality, rectitude; piety, holiness, saintliness, sanctity; integrity, honesty, incorruptibility, honor; simplicity, plainness, directness. **—Ant. 1, 2** impurity, impureness. **1** contamination, cloudiness; diversity. **2** vice, immodesty, unchasteness, immorality.

purport *v.* **1.** claim, profess; declare, allege, or assert oneself. **—***n.* **2.** meaning, import, significance, signification, implication, sense, reason, rationale, bearing; intention, purpose, design, end, aim, object, objective, intent, burden, point; gist, substance, drift, tenor, trend. **—Syn. Study. 2** See MEANING.

purpose *n.* **1.** object, objective, function, point, rationale, intention, intent, raison d'être; meaning, reason, sense, aim, design. **2.** goal, aim, ambition, aspiration, object, objective, mission, intent, intention, target, resolution, plan, motive, design, scheme, project, proposal; disposition, desire, wish, expectation, hope. **3.** resolve, determination, resolution, motivation, will, fixed intent. **—***v.* **4.** intend, mean, resolve, aim, aspire, drive at, persist, persevere; design, propose, plan, determine, conclude; endeavor, take upon oneself, set about, undertake, elect, choose; commit oneself, decide, make up one's mind; think to, contemplate, have a mind to. **—Ant. 3** purposelessness, aimlessness; inconstancy.

purposeful *adj.* deliberate, intentional, calculated, conscious, considered, studied, premeditated; resolute, strong-willed, committed, decided, resolved, determined upon. **—Ant.** aimless, purposeless, vacillating, irresolute, faltering, wavering; undecided, unresolved, undetermined.

purposely *adv.* deliberately, on purpose, intentionally, consciously, with intent, calculatedly, expressly, willfully, designedly, by design; knowingly, wittingly, advisedly, voluntarily, consciously. **—Ant.** accidentally, unintentionally, inadvertently, unknowingly, unconsciously, unthinkingly, unwittingly, by chance.

purse *n.* **1.** handbag, pocketbook, shoulder bag, clutch, bag; moneybag, wallet, pouch, sporran. **2.** winnings, prize, award, stake; proceeds, fund, treasury, coffer. —*v.* **3.** pucker, wrinkle, knit; pleat, pinch, gather, fold; bunch, contract.

pursue *v.* **1.** chase, follow in hot pursuit, go after, give chase to, race after, run after; chase after, track, trail. **2.** seek, try for, try to accomplish, aspire to, aim for or at, contrive to gain, be determined upon; push toward, strive for, labor for, be intent upon, set one's heart upon, be after. **3.** engage in, carry on, perform.

purview *n.* **1.** range, scope, sweep, responsibility, compass, extent; dominion, realm, domain, reach, commission, territory, field, area. **2.** ken, understanding, overview, experience, comprehension, viewpoint, outlook, horizon, *Slang* savvy, mental grasp.

push *v.* **1.** press, exert force on, move. **2.** make one's way, work, drive, press, struggle, force one's way; shove, elbow, squeeze, worm, wiggle, wedge, shoulder, nudge; ram, butt, hustle, jostle, fight, forge. **3.** urge, encourage, egg on, goad, incite, prod, spur, instigate, rouse, inspire, induce, arouse, animate, motivate, impel, prompt, stimulate, provoke, move, propel, sway, persuade, importune, exhort; hound, dun, bear down hard upon, harass, browbeat, heckle, badger, harry, coerce, constrain, compel, force, drive, prevail upon; *Informal* put the screws on, strong-arm; *Slang* buffalo. **4.** promote, publicize, propagandize, advertise, make known, boost; *Informal* hustle, plug. **5.** stick, thrust, drive, shove, stuff, plunge. —*n.* **6.** shove, nudge, prod, jolt. **7.** *Informal* energy, vitality, drive, go, get-up-and-go, vigor, vim and vigor, ambition, determination. **8.** thrust, advance, incursion, inroad, foray. **—Ant. 1** pull, drag, haul, tow, lug, yank; pluck, withdraw, remove.

pusillanimous *adj.* cowardly, lily-livered, fainthearted, mean-spirited; timorous, fearful, apprehensive; spiritless. **—Ant.** courageous, brave, valorous; bold, daring, spirited.

pussyfoot *v.* hedge, dodge, weasel, evade, sidestep, straddle the fence, evade the issue, beg the question; tread warily, tiptoe, walk on eggshells; sneak.

put *v.* **1.** place, set, rest, lay, position, deposit. **2.** assign, set, employ. **3.** place, bring. **4.** drive, force, throw. **5.** assign, place, fix, set, lay, attribute, ascribe, impute. **6.** express, phrase, word, state; articulate, enunciate. **7.** propose, submit, offer, bring forward, present; throw out, pose. **8.** throw, heave, pitch, cast. **—Ant. 1** remove, raise, withdraw, displace, misplace, transpose, transfer, change.

putrefy *v.* rot, decay, decompose, putresce, molder, deteriorate, disintegrate, biodegrade; spoil, taint, turn, stagnate.

putrid *adj.* spoiled, rotten, decomposing, decaying, bad, purulent, putrefied, putrefactive, putrescent, polluted, contaminated, tainted, rancid, fetid, rank, foul, stinking. **—Ant.** pure, clean, wholesome, uncontaminated, fresh, untainted, good.

putter *v.* fiddle, fool, dillydally, tinker, potter, piddle; loiter, dawdle, diddle, dally, drift, loaf, idle, lounge, lallygag, loll, laze.

puzzle *v.* **1.** perplex, nonplus, bewilder, confuse, confound, baffle, mystify, stump; outwit, foil, hoodwink. **2.** wonder, mull, brood, ponder. —*n.* **3.** mystery, problem, dilemma, bewilderment, bafflement, mystification, perplexity, complication, difficulty, enigma, conundrum, riddle.

pygmy *n.* **1.** midget, dwarf, homunculus, manikin, Lilliputian, Tom Thumb; shrimp, runt, pipsqueak, half-pint, bantam, mite, peewee, elf. —*adj.* **2.** dwarf, dwarfish, miniature, diminutive, short, tiny, small, wee, midget, toy, bantam, undersized, elfin. **—Syn. Study. 1** See DWARF.

quack *n.* **1.** ignorant pretender, medical impostor, fake doctor, charlatan, quacksalver. *—adj.* **2.** fake, fraudulent, phony, pseudo, sham, counterfeit.

quaff *v.* drink, swallow, gulp, guzzle, swig, toss off, down, swill, lap up, drink deeply, imbibe; *Slang* chug-a-lug, belt down, knock back.

quagmire *n.* **1.** soft muddy ground, marsh, bog, swamp, fen, morass, mire, quag, slough, sludge, ooze, sump. **2.** predicament, difficulty, critical situation, crisis, dilemma, perplexity, Gordian knot, quandary, plight, involvement, intricacy, entanglement, strait, imbroglio, scrape, fix, mess, muddle, morass, mire, quicksand, pickle, pinch, *Informal* hot water, jam.

quail *v.* shrink, shrink with fear, blanch, lose courage, be cowardly, take fright, show a yellow streak, have cold feet, lose heart, lose spirit; recoil, flinch, wince; run away, turn tail, shy, fight shy, cower; quake, shudder, tremble, shake, shiver in one's shoes, shake in one's boots. **—Syn. Study.** See WINCE.

quaint *adj.* charmingly old-fashioned, out-of-the-way, picturesque, old-timey, antique, antiquated; unusual, strange, odd, bizarre, queer, eccentric, outlandish, peculiar, singular, curious, unique, original, unconventional, uncommon, rare, singular, extraordinary; droll, fanciful, whimsical. **—Ant.** modern, current, new, newfangled, modish, up-to-date, fashionable.

quake *v.* **1.** shake, shudder, quaver, stand aghast, tremble, shiver, blanch, quail, quiver. *—n.* **2.** earthquake, tremor, seismic disturbance. **3.** quiver, shiver, thrill, shudder, trembling, wave, ripple, spasm, throb.

qualification *n.* **1.** requisite, prerequisite, requirement; eligibility, fitness, suitableness; competency, capability, ability, capacity, faculty, endowment, talent, accomplishment, achievement, aptitude, gift, skill, property; attribute, forte; standard; credential, bona fide, certification. **2.** limitation, restriction, reservation, stipulation, condition, postulate, provision, proviso; exception, exemption, escape clause; objection; modification, arrangement.

qualified *adj.* **1.** experienced, trained, competent, practiced, versed, knowing; eligible, fit, fitted, equipped, suited, meet, equal; capable, adept, able, talented, skilled, skillful, accomplished, expert; certified, licensed, authorized; efficacious, proficient, efficient. **2.** limited, indefinite, conditional, provisional, reserved, guarded; restricted, limited, hedging, equivocal, ambiguous. **—Ant. 1** inexperienced, untrained, unpracticed.

qualify *v.* **1.** make fit, make eligible, fit, train, ground, prepare, adapt, ready, condition, equip, make competent or capable, enable, endow; license, sanction, permit; empower, entitle, authorize, give power, commission; certify, legitimate; be eligible, measure up, be accepted; *Informal* have what it takes. **2.** limit, restrict, restrain, circumscribe, narrow; modify, moderate, alter, adapt, adjust, accommodate; temper, soften, assuage, mitigate, abate, ease, diminish, reduce. **3.** describe, characterize, modify.

quality *n.* **1.** characteristic, attribute, trait, mark, feature, aspect, property; character, nature, constitution, disposition, temperament; qualification, capacity, faculty. **2.** value, worth, caliber, degree of excellence, grade, rank, class, merit. **3.** social status, rank, family, position, high station, standing, blood; eminence, distinction, dignity. **—Syn. Study. 1** QUALITY, ATTRIBUTE, PROPERTY refer to a distinguishing feature or characteristic of a person, thing, or group. A QUALITY is an innate or acquired characteristic that, in some particular, determines the nature and behavior of a person or thing: *the qualities of patience and perseverance.* An ATTRIBUTE is a quality that we assign or ascribe to a person or to something personified; it may also mean a fundamental or innate characteristic: *an attribute of God; attributes of a logical mind.* PROPERTY is applied only to a thing; it refers to a principal characteristic that is part of the constitution of a thing and serves to define or describe it: *the physical properties of limestone.* **—Ant. 3** inferiority, low rank, low station.

qualm *n.* **1.** scruple, misgiving, uneasiness, compunction, twinge of conscience, reservation; hesitation, reluctance, unwillingness, indisposition, disinclination. **2.** queasiness, faintness, dizzy spell, giddiness, vertigo, nausea, turn, sick feeling. **—Ant. 1** willingness, inclination.

quandary *n.* dilemma, difficulty, predicament, strait, impasse, crisis, pinch, fix, entanglement, plight, imbroglio, involvement, morass, mire, quagmire, kettle of fish, pickle, scrape, *Informal* hot water, jam. **—Syn. Study.** See PREDICAMENT.

quantity *n.* amount, sum, number; measurement, measure, size, extent, extension; abundance, aggregate, multitude; volume, mass, magnitude, bulk, greatness, amplitude, area, vastness, expanse, length; dosage, dose, portion, share, proportion, quota, apportionment, allotment.

quarantine *n.* **1.** isolation, sequestration, medical segregation, *French* cordon sanitaire. *—v.* **2.** isolate, confine, segregate, sequester.

quarrel *n.* **1.** dispute, squabble, bickering, argument, conflict, spat, scrap, tiff, fuss, row, misunderstanding, falling out, open variance, difference; disagreement, breach of peace, dissension, strife, contention, discord, dissidence, controversy. **2.** dispute, disagreement, cause for complaint, complaint, objection, bone of contention, apple of discord. *—v.* **3.** disagree angrily, argue, bicker, wrangle, fuss, have words, raise one's voice, squabble, spat, be at odds, dispute, be at variance, be at loggerheads, differ, dissent; altercate, brawl, contend, fight, row, be at each other's throats; fall out, misunderstand; clash, jar, feud, conflict; cavil, nag, carp, raise a complaint, find fault, pick a fight. **—Syn. Study. 1** QUARREL, DISSENSION refer to disagreement and conflict. QUARREL applies chiefly to a verbal disagreement between individuals or groups and is used with reference to a large variety of situations, from a slight and petty difference of opinion to a violent altercation: *It was little more than a domestic quarrel. Their quarrel led to an actual fight.* DISSENSION usu. implies a profound disagreement and bitter conflict. It also applies chiefly to conflict within a group or between members of the same group: *dissension within the union; dissension among the Republicans.* **—Ant. 1** agreement, accord, accordance, concurrence, concord, amity, concordance, harmony; understanding; peacefulness, congeniality. **3** agree, accord, concur, coincide, consent, assent.

quarrelsome *adj.* belligerent, contentious, truculent, pugnacious, combative, militant, bellicose, disputatious, argumentative; antagonistic, fractious, captious, churlish, disagreeable, contrary, cantankerous, irascible, petulant, peevish, querulous. **—Ant.** friendly, easygoing, amiable, agreeable.

quarter *n.* **1.** one of four equal parts, fourth part, one-fourth, fourth, 25 percent; 25 cents, quarter dollar; three months. **2.** area, place, part, location, locality, locale, district, region, province, precinct, zone, territory, terrain; specific place, spot, station, position, situation; sphere, domain, realm; direction, point of the compass, side. **3.** Usually quarters lodging, lodgings, housing, place to stay, place to live, board, shelter, billet. **4.** mercy, pity, clemency; leniency, compassion, humanity, sympathy, indulgence. *—v.* **5.** cut into quarters, slice four ways, quadrisect. **6.** furnish with quarters, billet, lodge, house, install, put up; place, station, post.

quash *v.* **1.** suppress, put down, crush, smash, quell, squelch, squash, quench, subdue, repress; stop, put an end to, extinguish, exterminate, obliterate, annihilate, ruin, destroy, wreck, devastate, strike out, blot out, delete, cancel, expunge, erase, efface, dissolve, eradicate, dispel, extirpate; undo, overturn, overthrow, overwhelm. **2.** set aside, annul, nullify, void, abrogate, declare null and void, invalidate, vacate; overrule, override, countermand; retract, rescind, recall, revoke, reverse, repudiate.

quasi *adj.* almost, near, virtual; somewhat, part, halfway, semi; apparent, seeming, resembling; imitation, so-called, synthetic, ersatz.

quaver *v.* **1.** shake, quiver, shiver, tremble, shudder, quake; wave, wobble, totter, teeter, falter, waver; wriggle, writhe; oscillate, sway, vibrate, pulsate, throb, beat; trill. *—n.* **2.** tremulous shake, quavering tone, tremor, trembling, quiver, throb, vibration; trill, vibrato, tremolo.

quay *n.* landing, wharf, pier, dock, levee, mole, jetty; waterfront, basin, marina.

queasy *adj.* sick to the stomach, sickish, nauseous, nauseated, giddy, disposed to vomit; nauseating, sickening, bilious; qualmish, uneasy, uncomfortable, uncertain, troubled, upset.

queen *n.* female monarch, empress, *Latin* regina, *French* reine, *Spanish* reina, *German* Königin; (*variously*) princess, czarina, ranee.

queer *adj.* **1.** strange, odd, funny, unusual, uncommon, peculiar; bohemian, unconventional, nonconforming, unorthodox, eccentric, erratic, *French* outré; extraordinary, exceptional, original, unique, rare; irrational, unbalanced, crazy, unhinged, touched, daft; unparalleled, unprecedented, unexampled; abnormal, unnatural, outlandish, freakish, bizarre, weird, grotesque, exotic; fantastic, preposterous, absurd, ludicrous, laughable, ridiculous, comical, droll, fanciful, capricious; curious, quaint, off the beaten track, out of the way; astonishing, remarkable. **2.** suspicious, doubtful, questionable, irregular, farfetched; *Informal* shady, fishy. **3.** queasy, slightly ill, qualmy, faint, dizzy, giddy, light-headed, reeling, vertiginous, woozy. *—v.* **4.** *Informal* ruin, wreck, spoil, thwart, damage, harm, hurt, impair, injure, disrupt, compromise. —**Ant. 1** common, regular, conventional, customary, orthodox, ordinary, unexceptional, unoriginal; normal, natural; rational, sane. **2** straight, believable. **4** help, aid, boost, enhance.

quell *v.* **1.** crush, put down, put an end to, squelch, quench, quash, extinguish, ruin, destroy, stamp out; vanquish, wreck, conquer, defeat, beat down, worst, rout; overcome, overpower, overthrow, overwhelm; subdue, subjugate, suppress; reduce, scatter, disperse. **2.** quiet, still, silence, hush, stay, calm, lull, becalm, compose, tranquilize; pacify, appease; mitigate, mollify, palliate, allay, alleviate, assuage, ease, soothe; deaden, dull, blunt, soften; stem, abate. —**Ant. 1** encourage, foster, foment, defend; enlarge. **2** agitate, disturb, perturb, stir; annoy, bother.

quench *v.* **1.** satisfy, allay, satiate, sate, appease, slake. **2.** extinguish, put out, blow or stamp out, stifle, smother; dampen, cool suddenly, douse; crush, quell, put down, suppress, annihilate.

querulous *adj.* complaining, grumbling, peevish, fretful, disagreeable, faultfinding, finicky, fussy, finical, exacting, difficult, obstinate; dissatisfied, discontented, resentful, long-faced, sour; whining, whiny, shrewish, petulant, pettish, crabbed, grouchy, disputatious, captious, splenetic, irascible, quarrelsome, nettlesome, irritable, cross, cranky, touchy, testy, waspish. —**Ant.** uncomplaining, agreeable, good-tempered, complacent; contented, satisfied, pleased; genial, cheerful, easy, calm, equable.

query *n.* **1.** question, inquiry; matter in dispute, problem, issue, question at issue; request, demand; inquisition, investigation, inquest; examination, interrogation; search, quest. —*v.* **2.** ask, question, put a query to, inquire of, make inquiry, quiz, interrogate, seek by asking, sound out; investigate, subject to examination, examine, look into, inspect; catechize. **3.** consider questionable, question, doubt, have doubts about, suspect, harbor suspicions, distrust, mistrust, impugn; dispute, controvert, challenge, impeach.

quest *n.* **1.** search, pursuit, exploration, hunt, seeking, crusade, pilgrimage, mission, voyage, journey, enterprise, adventure. —*v.* **2.** seek, search; pursue, hunt.

question *n.* **1.** something asked, request for information, query. **2.** matter of discussion, issue, point in dispute, moot point, question at issue, subject of investigation, proposal, proposition, motion, subject; bone of contention; uncertainty, doubt, dubiety, misgiving, objection; dispute, controversy. **3.** problem, difficulty, consideration, matter, *Informal* rub. —*v.* **4.** ask, inquire of, query, quiz, interrogate, put questions to, sound out, *Informal* pump; grill, put through the third degree, examine, cross-examine, bombard with questions, subject to examination, investigate, look into; test, drill, catechize. **5.** consider questionable, be uncertain of, lack confidence in, doubt, have one's doubts about, call in question; hesitate to believe, harbor suspicions about, suspect; distrust, mistrust, impugn; refuse to believe, disbelieve; take exception to, challenge, oppose, dispute. —**Ant. 1, 4** answer, reply. **1** response. **3** solution, explanation. **4** respond. **5** trust, be certain of, have confidence in, have no doubts about; believe.

questionable *adj.* **1.** doubtful, debatable, moot, unsure, undecided, ambiguous, unproven, controversial, arguable, hypothetical, disputable. **2.** dubious, puzzling, mysterious, perplexing, confusing, mystifying, enigmatic; suspicious, shady, *Slang* fishy, suspect, equivocal. —**Ant. 1** certain, definite, assured, proven. **2** unimpeachable, aboveboard, proper, legitimate.

queue *n.* line, column, file, row, train, chain, rank, string.

quibble *v.* **1.** argue, bicker, squabble, hassle; raise trivial objections, carp, nag, cavil, nitpick, haggle, niggle; pick a fight, spar, fence; be evasive, dodge the issue, equivocate, waffle, fudge. —*n.* **2.** trivial objection, cavil, petty distinction, nicety; evasion, equivocation, dodge, shift, shuffle, distraction, delaying tactic; subtlety, subterfuge; white lie, prevarication, pretense, artifice, duplicity.

quick *adj.* **1.** brief, fast, swift, rapid, sudden, precipitate, headlong; fleet, whirlwind, hasty, expeditious, accelerated; abrupt, hurried. **2.** swift, fleet, flying, nimble-footed, light-footed, winged; brisk, spirited, lively, sprightly, agile, spry, nimble, frisky, animated, active, energetic, vigorous, vivacious. **3.** quick-witted, bright, apt, intelligent, discerning, perspicacious; smart, clever, acute, keen, astute, sharp, alert, wide-awake, vigilant; sagacious, *Informal* brainy; prompt, eager, shrewd, penetrating; expert, skillful, facile, able, dexterous, adroit, deft, adept. **4.** excitable, impetuous, impulsive, high-strung, impatient; irritable, sharp, keen, snappish, fiery, peppery, hot-blooded, hot-tempered, irascible, choleric, splenetic; waspish, petulant; testy, touchy, temperamental. —**Syn. Study. 1** QUICK, FAST, SWIFT, RAPID describe a speedy rate of motion or progress. QUICK applies particularly to an action or reaction that is almost instantaneous, or of brief duration: *to take a quick look around.* FAST refers to a person or thing that acts or moves speedily;

when used of communication or transportation, it suggests a definite goal and continuous movement: *a fast swimmer; a fast train.* SWIFT, a more formal word, suggests great speed as well as graceful movement: *The panther is a swift animal.* RAPID applies to one or a series of actions or movements; it stresses the rate of speed: *to perform rapid calculations.* **3** See SHARP. **—Ant. 1–3** slow. **1** long, lingering, gradual. **2** deliberate; sluggish, lazy, lethargic; heavy; inert, inactive; dull, wearisome. **3** dull, unintelligent, stupid, unresponsive, slow-witted; inexpert, unskillful, maladroit; sluggish, lazy. **4** calm, patient; restrained, temperate.

quicken *v.* **1.** make more rapid, speed, accelerate, expedite, hasten, hurry, hurry on, precipitate, hustle; further, advance, propel, drive, rush, dispatch; press, urge, egg on, impel. **2.** excite, stimulate, activate, stir, pique, provoke, spur, goad, rouse, arouse, affect, instigate, galvanize, kindle, incite, enkindle, inspire, inspirit, fire; actuate, vitalize, vivify, animate, enliven, energize, revive, invigorate, move, sharpen, refresh. **—Ant. 1** slow down, slacken, check, delay, hinder, impede, obstruct, retard. **2** deaden, put to sleep, enervate, dull.

quick-tempered *adj.* bad-tempered, cantankerous, quarrelsome, peevish, testy, ill-humored, touchy, *Brit.* shirty, waspish, churlish, choleric, temperamental, snappish, shrewish; cross, cranky, grouchy, irascible, irritable. **—Ant.** even-tempered, placid, serene.

quick-witted *adj.* keen, perceptive, witty, smart, clever, brilliant, alert, bright, penetrating, shrewd, ready, intelligent, sharp, incisive, perspicacious. **—Ant.** slow-witted, stupid, dull, plodding.

quiet *adj.* **1.** making no sound, silent, noiseless, soundless, hushed, soft, low, still, calm, not busy or active; reticent, saying little, taciturn, reserved, uncommunicative, mum, speechless, inarticulate, voiceless, mute. **2.** restful, untroubled, unruffled; calm, mild, halcyon, serene, tranquil, peaceful, peaceable, pacific, placid. **3.** inactive, inert, passive, undisturbed, becalmed, at rest; dormant, sleeping, slumbering, dozing, comatose, lethargic; still, motionless, immobile, at a standstill, stock-still; unmoved, fixed, stable, stationary, immovable, stagnant. **4.** gentle, clement, mild, meek, docile, not rough or turbulent, retiring, easygoing, contented; sedate, composed, coolheaded, phlegmatic, collected, steady, unexcitable, imperturbable, unperturbed, patient; humble, modest, moderate, temperate; unobtrusive, undemonstrative, unimpassioned, dispassionate, even-tempered. **5.** not showy or loud, plain, simple, unostentatious, unassuming, unpresumptuous, unpretentious; not bright, soft, mellow, subdued. **—*v.* 6.** make quiet, silence, still, hush, mute; stifle, muffle, smother; bridle one's tongue. **7.** relieve, allay, mitigate, palliate, comfort, soothe, soften, alleviate, mollify, assuage, settle, set at ease, compose, calm, pacify, tranquilize; dull, blunt, deaden; lessen, decrease, weaken; still, abate, lull, quell, subdue, bring to a standstill; stay, stop, curb, check, arrest, put a stop to, suspend, discontinue, terminate, bring to an end. **—*n.* 8.** quietness, silence, still, stillness, hush, lull, quietude, soundlessness, noiselessness, muteness; calm, calmness, tranquillity, serenity, peace, peacefulness, placidity, rest, repose, relaxation; ease, gentleness. **—Ant. 1** noisy, talky, verbose, loquacious. **2** excited, troubled, ruffled, agitated, upset, perturbed, turbulent. **3** active, busy, disturbed, restless, agitated, disquieted; awake, alert. **4** turbulent, violent, mercurial, excitable, perturbable, impatient; immoderate, intemperate, passionate, high-spirited. **5** obtrusive, demonstrative, conspicuous, showy, blatant, loud, ostentatious, pretentious; bright, harsh, glaring. **6** stir, agitate, disturb, perturb. **7** worsen, heighten, enlarge, strengthen, intensify, increase. **8** noise, din, activity, disturbance, commotion.

quietly *adv.* **1.** silently, soundlessly, noiselessly, mutely, softly; speechlessly, inaudibly. **2.** patiently, calmly, serenely, contentedly; composedly, collectedly, unexcitedly, unperturbedly, placidly, tranquilly, peacefully, pacifically; tamely, meekly, mildly; moderately, temperately; undemonstratively, dispassionately. **3.** unobtrusively, unpretentiously, unostentatiously, unassumingly, without ceremony; modestly, humbly, unboastfully, diffidently, bashfully; coyly, demurely.

quintessence *n.* essence, elixir, heart, core, pith, soul, gist, marrow, sum total, quiddity, distillation, sum and substance; embodiment, exemplar, personification.

quip *n.* clever remark, witty saying, witticism, retort, repartee, wisecrack, *French* bon mot; banter, badinage, sally, spoof, riposte; play on words, wordplay, pun, epigram, double entendre; cutting remark, crack, barb, putdown, sarcasm, jest, taunt, gibe, jeer, raillery, jape, joke, gag.

quirk *n.* **1.** peculiarity, oddity, eccentricity, idiosyncrasy, mannerism, affectation, crotchet; odd fancy, foible, caprice, vagary, whimsical notion, whimsy, whim; aberration, abnormality; kink, fetish. **2.**

sudden twist, turn, freak accident. **—Syn. Study. 1** See IDIOSYNCRASY.

quit *v.* **1.** stop, desist, cease, cease from, forswear, make an end of, discontinue, end, terminate; give up, relinquish, yield, surrender; part with, let go; forgo, waive, set aside; lose interest in. **2.** leave, go away from, take off, depart, get away from, withdraw, drop out, retire from; take wing or flight, skip or flee the coop from. **3.** resign, leave a job, have done with, renounce, reject, disavow, disown, relinquish, let go, part with, give up, abdicate; abandon, forsake. *—adj.* **4.** released from obligation, clear, free, rid, exempt, absolved, discharged; exculpated, exonerated, acquitted, all straight; clear of debt, owing nothing. **—Ant. 1** start, begin, continue, persist, keep on. **2** arrive at, come to; remain, stay. **3** keep, maintain.

quite *adv.* **1.** totally, completely, entirely, wholly, *Latin* in toto; fully, at all points, altogether; perfectly, utterly, positively; exactly, precisely; outright, out-and-out, in all respects, throughout. **2.** actually, in fact, really, surely, in reality, indeed, truly, verily, in truth, veritably; certainly, assuredly; absolutely. **3.** to a considerable extent, exceedingly, extremely, remarkably, very, excessively, considerably, in a great degree, to a high degree, highly; vastly, hugely, enormously, exceptionally, unusually.

quiver *v.* **1.** shake slightly, shudder, tremble, shiver, quake, quaver, vibrate, convulse, twitch, jump, jerk, jolt; palpitate, throb, pulsate; oscillate, fluctuate; wriggle, wobble, totter; be agitated, pant. *—n.* **2.** quivering, tremulous motion, vibration, tremble, shiver, shudder, shake, tremor, flutter, flicker; quaver, convulsion, seizure; throb, pulsation, palpitation; tic, spasm, twitching.

quixotic *adj.* extravagantly chivalrous, absurdly romantic, starry-eyed, fanciful, impulsive, whimsical; chimerical, dreamy, sentimental, poetic, head-in-the-clouds, utopian, idealistic, unrealistic, visionary, impractical; ineffective, inefficacious; fantastic, wild, madcap, preposterous, absurd, ridiculous. **—Ant.** realistic, down-to-earth, practical, serious.

quiz *v.* **1.** question, examine, subject to examination, test; query, ask, inquire of, sound out, put to the proof; interrogate, investigate, cross-examine, *Informal* pump. *—n.* **2.** test, examination, exam; investigation, interrogation, questioning, inquest, inquisition, inquiry; cross-examination; catechism.

quizzical *adj.* **1.** inquisitive, questioning, puzzled, inquiring, perplexed, searching, curious, baffled. **2.** mocking, teasing, joking, impudent, bantering, arch, coy, derisive, insolent. **—Ant. 1** comprehending, understanding, assenting. **2** serious, straight-faced, sincere.

quota *n.* portion, part, share, proportion; allotment, apportionment, distribution, allocation, assignment; quantity, measure, ration, percentage; minimum.

quotation *n.* quote, excerpt, citation, extract, passage, selection, reference; cutting, clipping, illustration.

quote *v.* cite, refer to, repeat, extract, retell, excerpt; name, adduce, exemplify, paraphrase, instance; recall, reproduce, recollect.

rabble *n.* **1.** mob, swarm, disorderly crowd. **2.** commoners, proletariat, lower classes, the masses, rank and file, populace, the great unwashed, riff-raff, hoi polloi, *German* Lumpenproletariat, the herd, *French* canaille. **—Ant. 2** aristocracy, upper classes, nobility, elite, high society.

rabid *adj.* **1.** suffering from rabies, hydrophobic, foaming at the mouth. **2.** fanatical, wild, wild-eyed, violent, raging, frenzied, frantic; maniacal, berserk, deranged, crazed. **3.** zealous, fervent, ardent.

race *n.* **1.** competitive trial of speed, contest, competition, heat. **2.** campaign, contest. *—v.* **3.** run a race, enter in a race, engage in a contest of speed, compete in a race; operate. **4.** hasten, hurry, run, run like mad, hie oneself, rush, hustle, make a mad dash, hotfoot it, dart, fly, dash. **—Ant. 4** go slowly, crawl, creep.

racism *n.* racial discrimination, racial bias, bigotry, racial prejudice, race hatred, segregation, color bar, color line.

racket *n.* **1.** noise, loud noise, din, shouting, caterwauling, babel, clamor, clangor, commotion, clatter, uproar, vociferation, roar; hubbub, tumult, hullabaloo, hurly-burly, rumpus; pandemonium, disturbance, stir, turmoil, thrashing, crashing, banging around, turbulence. **2.** illegitimate enterprise or occupation, underworld business undertaking, *Informal* game. **3.** business, occupation, line, profession, work, trade, *Informal* game. **—Syn. Study. 1** See NOISE. **—Ant. 1** quiet, silence, tranquillity, serenity, calm, peace.

raconteur *n.* skilled storyteller, anecdotist, narrator, spinner of yarns, teller of tales, fabulist, romancer.

racy *adj.* **1.** vigorous, exhilarating, heady, zesty, zestful, keen, energetic, spirited, fast-paced, lively, animated, exciting, stimulating, buoyant, sparkling, glowing. **2.** suggestive, lurid, risqué, bawdy, ribald, off-color, salacious, indecent, immodest, prurient, erotic, obscene, pornographic, vulgar, crude, smutty. **—Ant.** unexciting, dull, flat, bland, insipid, flat, stale, jejune.

radiance Also **radiancy** *n.* **1.** luster, sparkle, glitter, dazzle, iridescence, lambency, gleam, sheen, splendor, resplendence, brightness, brilliancy, brilliance, luminosity, effulgence, refulgence, luminousness, coruscation, incandescence. **2.** animation, joy, happiness, rapture. **—Ant. 1** dullness, dimness, murkiness, darkness. **2** sadness, glumness, dourness.

radiant *adj.* **1.** shining, bright, sunny, giving off rays of light, luminous, effulgent, refulgent, lustrous, glowing, aglow, incandescent; glittering, gleaming, dazzling, brilliant, sparkling, scintillating, flashing. **2.** bright with joy, beaming, glowing, happy, elated, ecstatic, overjoyed, joyous, blissful, rapturous, pleased, delighted, gladsome. **—Ant. 1** dull, dark, somber, dismal, murky, lusterless, sunless, shadowy, cloudy, gloomy, overcast, black. **2** sad, sorrowful, unhappy, disconsolate, gloomy, somber, joyless, cheerless; displeased, unpleased.

radiate *v.* **1.** emit heat, light, or other radiation; give out, circulate, give off, beam, shed, transmit; diffuse, scatter, disperse, spread, disseminate, shed, pour, spread, spread out, carry. **2.** branch out, spread, diverge, go in all directions. **—Ant. 1** absorb, soak up. **2** converge, come together, move together, meet, focus, center, concentrate, close in, zero in.

radical *adj.* **1.** basic, fundamental. **2.** severe, extreme, immoderate, drastic, precipitate, rash, inordinate. **3.** favoring drastic reforms, extreme, extremist, militant, revolutionary. *—n.* **4.** revolutionary, extremist, left-wing militant; rebel, firebrand, freethinker, antiestablishmentarian. **—Ant. 1** superficial, negligible, inessential, trivial. **2, 3** conservative, moderate, middle-of-the-road. **4** right-winger, rightist, reactionary, conservative, ultraconservative.

ragamuffin *n.* urchin, waif, guttersnipe, street arab, hoyden, *French* gamin, (*fem.*) gamine; tatterdemalion, sloven, wretch; beggar, tramp, bum, derelict, itinerant, hobo, vagabond, ragpicker, vagrant; panhandler.

rage *n.* **1.** violent anger, wrath, extreme agitation, frenzy, indignation; fury, choler, vehemence, temper, furor, excitement; resentment, animosity, bitterness, spleen, madness, perturbation, ire, umbrage, high dudgeon, displeasure, irritation, pique; passion, violent emotional state, rampage, storm, frenzy, temper tantrum, ferment, paroxysm. **2.** object of widespread enthusiasm, prevailing taste, current style, fashion, vogue, mode, craze, mania, fad, the latest thing, the thing, the "in" thing, the last word, *French* le dernier cri. *—v.* **3.** speak with anger, act with fury, storm, throw a fit, flare up, fly off the handle, lose one's temper, show violent anger, be violently agitated, be furious, vent one's spleen, blow one's top, explode, blow up, fulminate, rant, roar, raise cain, fume, seethe, boil, rave, froth at the mouth, blow one's stack, lose one's cool. **4.** continue violently, go at full blast. **—Syn. Study. 1** See ANGER. **—Ant. 1** calm, calmness, coolness, equanimity; pleasure, gratification, joy, delight. **3** be pleased, be gratified; remain unruffled, keep one's cool.

ragged *adj.* **1.** clothed in tatters, wearing worn clothes, dressed in rags, seedy. **2.** worn to rags, worn-out, worn, tattered, shaggy, shabby, torn, rent, threadbare, frayed, tacky, battered, shredded, the worse for wear, patched, shoddy, *Slang* beat up. **3.** overtaxed, strained, exacerbated, aggravated, at the breaking point, run down.

raid *n.* **1.** surprise attack, sudden assault, razzia, onset, predatory incursion, invasion, inroad, sortie, sally, foray. **2.** authorized police break-in, roundup, *Slang* bust. **—***v.* **3.** attack, assault, swoop down on, pounce upon, invade, storm, enter suddenly, make a raid on, *Slang* bust.

rail[1] *n.* **1.** horizontal support, bar, railing, barrier, fence, banister. **2.** railway, railroad, train, *Archaic U.S.* the cars.

rail[2] *v.* vociferate, inveigh, fulminate, speak harshly, declaim, scold, talk angrily, raise one's voice, vituperate, rant, rant and rave, rage; shout abuse, take on, carry on; scream, gnash one's teeth, foam at the mouth, raise a hue and cry, *Slang* pitch a bitch, blow up, blow one's stack.

raillery *n.* jesting, joking, kidding, banter, teasing, fooling, japing, badinage, sport, persiflage, pleasantry; satire, lampoonery; *Slang* razzing, roasting, ribbing, ragging.

rain *n.* **1.** precipitation, rainfall, (*variously*) drizzle, mist, sprinkle, cloudburst, thundershower, rainstorm, shower, downpour, drencher, squall, hurricane, deluge, torrent. **2. rains** the rainy season, monsoon. **3.** shower, deluge, spate, plethora. **—***v.* **4.** (*variously*) pour, shower, drizzle, sprinkle, *Slang* come down in buckets, rain cats and dogs, come down in sheets. **5.** shower, drop, send down, down. **6.** lavish, shower.

raise *v.* **1.** erect, put up, elevate, lift. **2.** build, set up, construct, erect, put up. **3.** grow, breed, produce, cultivate, develop, nurse, nurture, foster; rear, bring up. **4.** excite, stimulate, pique, sharpen, rouse, arouse, awaken, summon up, stir up, spark, urge, spur, inspire, boost, kindle, inflame. **5.** put forward, bring up, advance. **6.** increase, make higher, inflate, *Informal* hike up, hike, jack up. **7.** collect, solicit, canvass, obtain, bring in, procure, amass. **8.** lift, end, terminate. **—***n.* **9.** increase, elevation, promotion, advancement. **—Ant. 1** lower, let down, drop; sink, depress. **2** destroy, ruin, raze, demolish, wreck, smash, tumble, level. **4** quell, quash, put to sleep, calm, soothe. **5** suppress, keep quiet, pass over in silence. **6** decrease, lessen, cut, reduce, diminish. **8** start, begin, initiate, establish, effect; reinstate. **9** decrease, cut, slash, demotion.

rake[1] *v.* **1.** comb, scour, ransack, go over with a fine-tooth comb. **2.** sweep with gunfire, enfilade, pepper.

rake[2] *n.* dissipated man of fashion, playboy, voluptuary, sensualist, libertine, roué; lecher, satyr, goat, seducer, womanizer, Don Juan, Lothario, Casanova, immoralist, debauchee, rakehell, prodigal, profligate; rascal, rogue, *Informal* sport, swinger.

rakish *adj.* **1.** loose living, profligate, depraved, lascivious, lecherous, lustful, libertine, dissolute, dissipated, immoral, debauched. **2.** jaunty, sporting, breezy, sauntering, airy, dashing, dapper, sporty, cavalier, debonair, gallant, bumptious, swaggering.

rally *v.* **1.** reassemble, bring together again, reconvene, reunite, call together, unite, assemble, collect, gather, muster. **2.** come to the aid or support of a person or cause, rush, be at beck and call. **3.** recover strength, revive, get well, get better, recuperate, improve, convalesce, *Archaic* recruit; take a turn for the better, pick up, pull through, come round, get one's second wind, catch up, score. **—***n.* **4.** gathering, caucus, meet, mass meeting, convention, assembly, assemblage, congregation, convocation, *Slang* powwow. **5.** recovery, revival, recuperation, renewal of strength, restoration, convalescence, improvement. **—Ant. 1** disband, dissolve, dismiss, muster out, discharge, release, disperse. **2** desert, abandon, forsake. **3** lose strength, become weaker, get worse, take a turn for the worse, sink, fail. **5** relapse, loss of strength, collapse.

ram *v.* **1.** drive, force, jam, thrust, push firmly; strike, hit, beat, hammer. **2.** slam, crash, smash, run into, hurtle; dash, batter, butt, bump.

ramble *v.* **1.** wander, stroll, amble, saunter, meander, perambulate, peregrinate, traipse, rove, drift, roam, gad, gad about, range, gallivant. **2.** meander, zigzag, snake, wind, twist, go here and there. **—***n.* **3.** idle walk, stroll, saunter, traipse, roam, hike.

rambling *adj.* digressive, discursive,

circuitous, prolix, diffuse, disjointed, uneven. —**Ant.** concise, to the point, direct.

rampage *n.* **1.** violent spree, jag of violence. —*v.* **2.** move or behave violently, storm, rage; go berserk, run riot, run amok.

rampant *adj.* **1.** widespread, rife, prevalent, universal, unchecked, unrestrained, raging, ungovernable, uncontrollable; epidemic, pandemic. **2.** (of a four-legged animal) standing on the hind legs, standing up, erect. —**Ant. 1** restrained, curbed, checked.

rampart *n.* protective barrier, defensive wall; fortification, barrier, barricade, protective wall, bulwark, earthwork, breastwork, parapet, bastion.

ramshackle *adj.* shabby, deteriorating, dilapidated, falling to pieces, tumbledown, decrepit, run-down, crumbling; shaky, rickety, flimsy, unsteady, unstable, tottering. —**Ant.** well built, solid, substantial; steady.

rancid *adj.* rank tasting, rank smelling, malodorous, stinking, putrid, foul, mephitic, gamy; old, strong, high. —**Ant.** fresh, pure.

rancor *n.* resentment, bitterness, ill feeling, ill will, hostility, antagonism, malevolence, spleen, acrimony; hatred, animosity, spite, spitefulness, animus, antipathy, malice, enmity, hate. —**Ant.** amity, goodwill, friendship, friendliness, amicability.

random *adj.* occasional, chance, unintentional, unplanned, undesigned, unpremeditated, unintended, unexpected, fortuitous, accidental, hit-or-miss, offhand, casual, haphazard, aimless, adventitious, stray. —**Ant.** deliberate, planned, designed, intentional, intended, premeditated.

range *n.* **1.** extent, reach, limit, radius, bounds, purview, compass, latitude, scope; sphere, field, orbit, domain, province. **2.** variety, gamut, selection, assortment. **3.** chain of mountains, ridge, sierra, massif. **4.** grazing land, pasture, plains. —*v.* **5.** extend, run, stretch, reach. **6.** rove, wander, roam, explore. —**Syn. Study. 1** RANGE, COMPASS, LATITUDE, SCOPE refer to extent or breadth. RANGE emphasizes extent and diversity: *the range of one's interests.* COMPASS suggests definite limits: *within the compass of one's mind.* LATITUDE emphasizes the idea of freedom from narrow confines, thus breadth or extent: *granted latitude of action.* SCOPE suggests great freedom but a proper limit: *the scope of one's obligations.*

rank[1] *n.* **1.** grade, quality, class, order, type, sort. **2.** social standing, position, class, standing, status, estate; echelon, professional grade, level, classification. **3.** line, row, file, column. —*v.* **4.** have rank, take rank, be ranked, have place, be classed, stand, rate, come out. **5.** hold the highest rank, have supremacy, be number one, come first.

rank[2] *adj.* **1.** overgrown, overabundant, luxuriant, lush, lavish, dense, profuse, tall, high-growing, jungly, tropical, wild. **2.** strong smelling, ill smelling; rancid, foul; stale. **3.** utter, absolute, total, complete, sheer, bald, unmitigated, downright, flagrant, arrant, rampant, glaring; gross, crass, coarse, filthy, nasty, scurrilous; outrageous, monstrous, atrocious. —**Ant. 1** spare, scanty, sparse. **2** fresh, sweet smelling, unspoiled.

rankle *v.* irritate, gall, chafe, gripe, rile, pique, fester, not sit well. —**Ant.** please; soothe.

ransack *v.* **1.** rummage through, rake, comb, search, turn upside down, scour. **2.** pillage, sack, vandalize, plunder, loot, rifle, raid, devastate, despoil, ravage, gut, strip, lay waste.

rant *v.* **1.** harangue, rave, orate, rage, bluster, storm, spout, bellow, yell, explode, scold, fume; *Slang* blow one's top, blow one's stack, shoot off one's mouth. —*n.* **2.** bombast, declamation, bluster, exaggeration, bravado. —**Ant. 1** whisper, mutter, mumble, murmur.

rap *v.* **1.** tap, thump, drum, knock. **2.** *Slang* talk, speak, chat, converse, communicate; shoot the breeze, jaw. **3.** *Informal* criticize, knock, come down on, *Slang* pan, roast, clobber, dump on. —*n.* **4.** light quick blow, knock, tap, bang. **5.** *Informal* blame, responsibility, adverse consequences. —**Ant. 3** praise, eulogize, laud, flatter, rave about.

rapacious *adj.* plundering, marauding, ransacking, thievish, pillaging, looting, predatory; greedy, avaricious, covetous, grasping, mercenary; insatiable, voracious, wolfish, ravenous.

rapid *adj.* quick, fast, fleet, express, swift, speedy, instant; hasty, hurried, precipitate; brisk, active; expeditious, prompt; feverish, agitated, rushing, galloping, flying; accelerated, unchecked. —**Syn. Study.** See QUICK. —**Ant.** slow, leisurely, gradual; deliberate; lazy, sluggish, dilatory.

rapidly *adv.* swiftly, fast, speedily, expeditiously, with rapid strides, apace, quickly, at a great rate, by leaps and bounds, overnight, at full speed; briskly, hurriedly, hastily, pell-mell, helter-skelter, as fast as one's legs will carry one, like a house on fire, like a shot, in high gear. —**Ant.** slowly, gradually.

rapport *n.* relationship, camaraderie, understanding, affiliation, fellowship; connection, link, tie, interrelationship.

rapprochement *n.* reconciliation, reconcilement, understanding, accord, entente, détente, agreement, conciliation, settlement, harmonization, appeasement, accommodation, pacification.

rapt *adj.* **1.** engrossed, enthralled, absorbed, interested, attentive, intent. **2.** transported, ecstatic, rapturous, enrapt, enraptured, spellbound, enchanted, charmed, bewitched, captivated, moonstruck, entranced, fascinated, delighted; bemused, dreamy. **—Ant. 1** uninterested, disinterested, detached, indifferent, incurious; bored.

rapture *n.* ecstasy, joy, elation, thrill, felicity, delight, euphoria, transport, exaltation, bliss, beatitude. **—Syn. Study.** ECSTASY, RAPTURE, TRANSPORT, EXALTATION share a sense of being taken out of oneself or one's normal state and entering a state of heightened feeling. ECSTASY suggests an emotion so overpowering and engrossing as to produce a trancelike state: *religious ecstasy; an ecstasy of grief.* RAPTURE most often refers to an elevated sensation of bliss or delight, either carnal or spiritual: *the rapture of first love.* TRANSPORT suggests a strength of feeling that often results in expression of some kind: *They jumped up and down in a transport of delight.* EXALTATION refers to a heady sense of personal well-being so powerful that one is lifted above normal emotional levels: *wild exaltation at having finally broken the record.* **—Ant.** unhappiness, sorrow, woe, misery, sadness, dejection, depression, despair.

rare *adj.* seldom found, seldom to be met with, hard to find; scarce, few, few and far between, infrequent, uncommon, unusual, exceptional, out of the common run, unique. **—Ant.** plentiful, many, bountiful, abundant; ubiquitous, profuse, manifold, often found, easy to find; frequent, habitual, regular.

rarely *adv.* seldom, not often, hardly ever, uncommonly, scarcely ever, infrequently, on rare occasions, only occasionally; hardly; once in a great while, once in a blue moon. **—Ant.** often, frequently, always, continually, ordinarily, usually.

rascal *n.* **1.** mischievous person, trickster, prankster, scamp, imp, devil, scalawag, rapscallion. **2.** rake, rogue, devil, delinquent, reprobate, rakehell, scoundrel, knave, villain, cad, blackguard. **—Syn. Study. 2** See KNAVE.

rash *adj.* precipitate, brash, abrupt, hasty, premature, imprudent, injudicious, indiscreet, incautious; irresponsible, reckless, headlong, impulsive, impetuous, adventurous, ungoverned, uncontrolled, unchecked, unadvised; careless, heedless, thoughtless, unthinking; harebrained, devil-may-care; foolhardy, foolish.

rate *n.* **1.** speed, pace, tempo. **2.** price, charge, figure, fee, dues; cost, expense, levy, tariff, toll; assessment. **—*v.* 3.** classify, class, rank, count, measure; regard, deem, look on.

rather *adv.* to a certain extent, quite, very, pretty; somewhat, a bit, slightly, in some degree, comparatively, relatively, fairly, in some measure, moderately, *Informal* sort of, kind of; after a fashion, more or less.

ratify *v.* confirm, validate, approve, uphold, affirm, make valid, authenticate, make good, endorse, support, acknowledge, sanction; settle firmly, authorize, certify, *Informal* okay; consent to, agree to, accede to. **—Ant.** veto, disapprove, refute, disagree to; invalidate, disavow, repudiate.

ratio *n.* proportional relation, interrelationship, proportion, proportionality, equation, fixed relation; arrangement, distribution, apportionment.

ration *n.* **1.** food share, allotment, apportionment, provision; measure, dole, due. **2. rations** provisions, stores, food, provender. **—*v.* 3.** distribute by restricted allotments, apportion, allocate, allot, mete out.

rational *adj.* **1.** based on reason, sound, reasonable, logical; solid, wise, sage, sagacious; judicious, advisable, perspicacious; credible, feasible, plausible. **2.** sane, compos mentis, in one's right mind, lucid, clearheaded, balanced, normal, sound, responsible, *Slang* all there. **—Ant. 1, 2** irrational, unreasonable, unsound, insane.

rationale *n.* basis, underlying reason, explanation, logic, foundations, grounds; reasoning, philosophy, key concept.

rationalize *v.* **1.** justify, account for, make allowance for, make excuses for, excuse, explain away, put a gloss upon, palliate, whitewash. **2.** explain, interpret rationally; account for objectively.

rattle *v.* **1.** clatter, clink, clank, roll loosely, jar, shake, bounce. **2.** chatter, maunder, gab, prate, blather. **3.** shake, upset, disturb, perturb, agitate, jangle, faze, discomfit, fluster, flurry, discompose, disconcert, distract, throw; nonplus, bewilder, confuse. **—*n.* 4.** clacking, clatter, clang, clank. **—Ant. 3** calm, compose, soothe, settle, relax.

raucous *adj.* harsh, rough, jarring, grating, raspy, hoarse, grinding, jangling; discordant, strident, cacophonous, inharmonious, dissonant, stertorous, blaring, loud, earsplitting; shrill; piercing. **—Ant.** soft, dulcet, mellow, mellifluous, soothing, pleasant.

ravage *v.* cause widespread damage to,

ruin, lay in ruins, raze, gut, lay waste, waste, wreck, desolate, destroy, demolish, devastate, rape, spoliate, despoil, shatter; pillage, plunder, maraud, sack, loot, strip, ransack, raid, overrun.

rave *v.* **1.** rant, rage; babble, ramble; make delirious utterances. **2.** storm, fume, be furious, be mad, go on, be angry, lose one's temper, flare up, explode, thunder; sputter, bluster, run or go amok, *Slang* fly off the handle, blow one's top. **3.** speak glowingly, gush, effervesce, bubble, wax, go on and on, expatiate, rhapsodize; rant, carry on. —*n.* **4.** an extravagantly good review, an extremely favorable criticism, *Informal* kudos, good press, compliments, words of praise, high praise, flattery. —*adj.* **5.** laudatory, highly favorable. **—Ant. 3** cavil at, deplore, score. **4** condemnation, disapproval, *Slang* knock. **5** condemning, faultfinding; bad, disparaging.

ravenous *adj.* predatory, ravening, rapacious, covetous, greedy, avaricious, grasping, insatiable, insatiate; hungry, voracious, starved, starving, famished; gluttonous, piggish.

ravine *n.* valley, gulch, gorge, *Spanish* arroyo, chasm, gap, cleft, canyon, pass, *Brit.* clough, wadi, gully.

ravish *v.* **1.** seize and carry away by force, make off with, snatch. **2.** rape; outrage, violate, abuse, deflower, defile. **3.** transport, enrapture, enthrall, overjoy, delight, gladden, cheer, captivate, enchant, charm, entrance, fascinate; tickle, *Slang* knock out. **—Ant. 3** displease, disgust, provoke, rile, pique.

ravishing *adj.* enchanting, alluring, charming, fascinating entrancing, captivating, bewitching; very pleasing, delightful, gorgeous, splendid, striking, beautiful, sensational, *Slang* smashing. **—Ant.** terrible, awful, disgusting, repulsive.

raw *adj.* **1.** uncooked, unprepared, unbaked; underdone, undercooked, rare. **2.** natural, crude, unrefined, unprocessed, rough, not manufactured, not finished, basic, rude, coarse. **3.** untrained, unskilled, undisciplined, unpracticed, unexercised, undrilled, unprepared, inexperienced, inexpert, amateurish, uninitiated, unseasoned, untried, untested, undeveloped, crude, unrefined; untaught, ignorant; fresh, green, unfledged, *Slang* rookie; immature, unripe, callow, young. **4.** frank, plain, brutal, unembellished, unvarnished, bare. **5.** chilly, damp, bleak; cold, harsh, nipping, pinching, biting, piercing, cutting, bitter, numbing, freezing; inclement, blustery, windswept. **—Syn. Study. 2** RAW, CRUDE, RUDE refer to something not in a finished or highly refined state. RAW applies particularly to material not yet changed by a process, by manufacture, or by preparation for consumption: *raw leather.* CRUDE refers to that which still needs refining: *crude petroleum.* RUDE refers to what is still in a condition of rough simplicity or in a roughly made form: *rude agricultural implements.* **—Ant. 1** cooked, prepared; baked; done, well-done, well cooked. **2** refined, manufactured, wrought, finished. **3** trained, skilled, disciplined, practiced, experienced, professional. **4** embellished, gilded, smoothed over, edulcorated. **5** warm, balmy, fair, sunny, mild.

raze *v.* tear down, pull down, level, fell, flatten, knock down, topple, break down, dismantle, reduce; wreck, smash, demolish, destroy, ruin, wipe out, obliterate, remove. **—Syn. Study.** See DESTROY.

reach *v.* **1.** arrive at, get to, come to, make, get as far as, set foot in or on, land at, enter, *Slang* make, *Nautical* put in or into; succeed in touching, contact, touch, go to, attain, get hold of, seize, grasp, secure, get to, come to. **2.** stretch, stretch out, extend, outstretch; strain after something, grab at; make an effort. **3.** contact, get, find, get in touch with, communicate with. **4.** extend, climb, spread; approach, move, amount to, go to, hit. —*n.* **5.** act of reaching, stretch; grab, grasp, clutch.

reaction *n.* **1.** chemical change, chemical transformation; nuclear change in an atom, change in the nucleus of an atom. **2.** response, reply, answer, counteraction, reflex. **3.** (*variously*) resurgent conservatism, right-wing comeback, counterrevolution, restoration, backlash.

reactionary *adj.* **1.** reversionary, regressive, counterrevolutionary, diehard, right-wing, ultraconservative. —*n.* **2.** ultraconservative, right-winger, counterrevolutionary, diehard, rightist, mossback. **—Ant. 2** radical, liberal, revolutionary, left-winger, leftist.

read *v.* **1.** apprehend, understand, construe, comprehend, discern, perceive; make out the meaning or significance of, translate, interpret, explain; study, pore over, scan, analyze, decipher. **2.** peruse, scan, glance or run the eye over, note, study; pore over. **3.** utter, render in speech, speak aloud something written, recite; give a public reading or recital; deliver, present. **4.** adduce, extrapolate, construe. **5.** have a certain wording, be worded, say, go; show, indicate.

readily *adv.* **1.** promptly, immediately, at once, straightway, instantly, quickly, expressly, in no time, without delay, speedily, pronto; easily, without difficulty, effortlessly, smoothly, with no effort, with one hand tied behind one's back, hands down; on the spur of the moment, at short notice, at the drop of a hat. **2.** willingly, without reluctance or demur, in ready manner, freely, graciously, with good grace, with goodwill, ungrudgingly. **—Ant. 1, 2** unreadily. **1** slowly, with difficulty. **2** unwillingly, reluctantly, grudgingly.

ready *adj.* **1.** completely prepared, in readiness, set, all set, duly equipped, fitted out, furnished; in condition for immediate action or use, fit, serviceable, in working order; immediately available for use, accessible, present, at hand, handy, on hand, on tap, in harness, primed; punctual, speedy, expeditious, prompt; equal to, up to; mature, ripe. **2.** willing, eager, disposed, inclined, prone, predisposed, apt. **3.** prompt in understanding or comprehending, acquisitive, perceptive, discerning, quick in perceiving, attentive, alert, wide-awake, bright, astute, sharp, acute, keen, cunning, shrewd, showing quickness, quick-witted, clever, ingenious, resourceful; skillful, artful, masterly, expert, dexterous, apt, adroit, deft, facile, versatile. **4.** likely at any time or moment, liable; tending; on the verge of, on the brink of, at the point of, set, just about. **—***v.* **5.** prepare, put in order, make ready, equip, fit out. **—Ant. 1–4** unready. **1** unprepared, unequipped, unfurnished; unfit, out of order; unavailable, inaccessible, unhandy; tardy, late, slow, inexpeditious; immature. **2** unwilling, loath, disinclined, indisposed, reluctant, hesitant. **3** slow, plodding, pedestrian, unexceptional.

ready-made *adj.* ready-to-wear, off-the-rack, store manufactured; *Slang* store-bought. **—Ant.** custom-made, handmade, tailor-made, made-to-order.

real *adj.* **1.** genuine, actual, authentic, bona fide. **2.** true, factual, valid, veritable, unquestionable, veracious, truthful; actual, well-grounded, solid, substantial, substantive, tangible; rightful, legitimate; absolute, positive, certain, unadulterated, unalloyed, unvarnished. **3.** sincere, not affected, unaffected, genuine, unfeigned; true, honest, pure, unadulterated. **—Ant. 1–3** unreal, fake, false. **1** imitation, counterfeit, factitious. **2** imagined, imaginary. **3** insincere, affected, feigned, faked.

realistic *adj.* pragmatic, down-to-earth; true-to-life, natural, naturalistic, objective, lifelike, graphic, representational, descriptive, depictive; real, authentic, genuine, truthful, faithful, precise. **—Ant.** unrealistic, impractical, idealistic, romantic, fanciful.

reality *n.* actuality, fact, truth, verity; materiality, substantiality, physical existence, corporeality, tangibility. **—Ant.** unreality, pretense, illusion, myth.

realize *v.* **1.** comprehend, apprehend, understand, gather, grasp, get, fathom, appreciate, absorb, feel strongly; perceive, see into, penetrate, make out, discern; be cognizant of, recognize, cognize; conceive, imagine. **2.** actualize, fulfill, complete, consummate, bring to pass, bring about, effectuate, carry out, execute, carry through, work out, discharge, do, produce, perform; attain, get, achieve, accomplish, make good. **3.** get as profit, gain, acquire, profit, clear, net, obtain a return, make money, make capital of, accomplish.

really *adv.* actually, in fact, truly, truthfully, genuinely; literally, indeed; surely, certainly, veritably, verily, positively, unquestionably, absolutely, categorically.

realm *n.* **1.** dominion, kingdom, domain, empire, royal domain, monarchy, demesne, land, country; nation, state. **2.** sphere, province, orbit, region, field.

reap *v.* gather, glean, harvest, take in, bring in; earn, gain, obtain, acquire, procure, realize, derive, profit, get, win, secure, score. **—Ant.** waste, dissipate, lose, spend.

rear[1] *n.* **1.** back, end, tail end, heel, stern, hind part, back part, postern, posterior; after part, area or position behind. **2.** last or back part of an armed force, rear guard. **—***adj.* **3.** at, of, in, or near the back; back, hind, hindmost, aftermost, after, posterior, rearmost; dorsal; aft. **—Syn. Study. 3** See BACK. **—Ant. 1** front, fore, forefront, forepart; foreground; frontage. **2** front rank, front lines, advanced guard, vanguard. **3** front, frontmost, forward, foremost, leading.

rear[2] *v.* bring up, raise, care for; train, educate, cultivate, develop, nurture, nurse, foster, cherish.

reason *n.* **1.** cause, occasion, motive, grounds, justification, explanation, rationale. **2.** brains, head, faculties, wit, comprehension, apprehension, understanding, perception, intelligence, intellect, perspicacity, acumen, sense, penetration, awareness, discernment, insight. **3.** common sense, logic, reasoning, appeal to reason, argumentation, exhortation. **4.** rationality, soundness of mind, reasonableness, mental balance, sanity, normality, sense, lucidity, clearheadedness. **—***v.* **5.** think through, figure, solve; ratiocinate. **—Syn. Study. 1** REASON, CAUSE, MOTIVE are terms for a circumstance (or circumstances) that brings about or explains certain results. A REASON is an explanation of a situation or circumstance that made certain results seem possible or appropriate: *The reason for the robbery was the victim's careless display of money.* The CAUSE is the way in which the circumstances produce the effect; that is, make a specific action seem necessary or desirable: *The cause was the robber's immediate need of money.* A MOTIVE is the hope, desire, or other force that starts the action (or an action) in an attempt to produce specific results: *The motive was to use the stolen money to gamble.* See also MOTIVE. **—Ant. 4** irrationality, unsoundness, mental unbalance, insanity, abnormality, incoherence.

reasonable *adj.* **1.** judicious, wise, sensible, intelligent; logical, rational; sane, sound, credible, plausible, probable, possible, likely; well-grounded, well-founded, admissible, justifiable, understandable; legitimate, proper, suitable, fitting, equitable, fair, just. **2.** of good sense or sound judgment, exercising reason, rational, logical, thinking, understanding, thoughtful, reflective; just, fair, impartial, objective, judicious, level-headed, patient, coolheaded; moderate, prudent, circumspect, temperate; intelligent, sensible, wise, knowing, sage. **3.** not exceeding a reasonable limit, not unlikely, not excessive, not extreme, natural, predictable, moderate, lenient, temperate, fair, just, tolerable, equitable. **—Syn. Study. 2** See MODERATE. **—Ant. 1–3** unreasonable, irrational, unintelligent, unsound, impossible; unjust, unfair, outrageous.

reasoning *n.* **1.** ratiocination, logic, thought, cogitation, thinking; deduction, inference, analysis, penetration. **2.** argument, train of thought, rationale, analysis, interpretation, reflection, ground, basis.

reassure *v.* personally assure, bolster, inspire hope in, encourage, inspirit, uplift, buoy up, cheer; comfort, set one's mind at rest. **—Ant.** dishearten, discourage, unnerve, disconcert.

rebel *n.* **1.** insurgent, insurrectionist, traitor, turncoat, deserter; secessionist, seceder, separatist, anarchist; revolutionist, revolutionary, resister; iconoclast, nonconformist, dissenter, malcontent, maverick, upstart. *—v.* **2.** resist lawful authority, defy authority, rise up, take arms against an established order, oppose by force, revolt, mutiny, riot. **3.** be repelled by, turn away from, pull or draw back from, flinch, wince, quail, react, shrink, shy, recoil, be unwilling, avoid.

rebellion *n.* insurrection, revolt, insurgency, sedition, revolution, mutiny, uprising, upheaval, defiance; putsch, coup d'état. **—Ant.** resignation, submission.

rebellious *adj.* defiant, disobedient, insubordinate, intractable, refractory, contrary, recalcitrant, pugnacious, fractious, contumacious, quarrelsome; up in arms, mutinous, seditious, insurgent, insurrectionary, revolutionary, turbulent, truculent, unruly, unmanageable, ungovernable, uncontrollable, disorderly, alienated. **—Ant.** patriotic, loyal, dutiful, deferential; obedient, unresistant, subordinate, subservient.

rebuff *n.* **1.** rejection, refusal, putting off; repulse, snub, slight, cold shoulder, *Slang* put-down, slap in the face. *—v.* **2.** snub, slight, reject, spurn, ignore, disregard, cold-shoulder, refuse, repel, repulse, deny, decline, *Slang* turn down; check, keep at a distance, put off. **—Ant. 1** welcome, acceptance, encouragement, come-on, come hither; spur, aid. **2** welcome, encourage.

rebuke *v.* **1.** scold, upbraid, reproach, admonish, take to task, reprimand, reprove, chide, remonstrate with, lecture; censure, berate, call down, dress down, *Slang* chew out, take down a peg; find fault with, blame, score. *—n.* **2.** scolding, reprimand, remonstrance, admonishment, upbraiding, admonition, reprehension, reproach, reproof, reproval, tongue-lashing; disapproval, censure, castigation, chiding, berating, *Slang* chewing out, dressing down. **—Ant. 1, 2** praise. **1** laud, applaud, congratulate; commend, compliment, approve. **2** laudation, commendation, compliments, approval; *Informal* pat on the back, congratulation.

rebuttal *n.* refutation, rejoinder, confutation, contradiction, disagreement, disproof, denial, retort, riposte, counterargument, counterreply, disproval, negation, *Law* surrejoinder. **—Ant.** validation, corroboration, substantiation, verification.

recalcitrant *adj.* stubborn, obstinate, unwilling, unsubmissive, headstrong, refractory, mulish, pigheaded, bullheaded, willful, contrary, balky, unruly, disobedient, intractable. **—Syn. Study.** See UNRULY. **—Ant.** obedient, compliant, amenable, submissive, yielding; controllable, manageable, governable.

recall *v.* **1.** recollect, remember; recognize, place. **2.** reactivate, remobilize, call back; reinstitute, revive, reanimate. *—n.* **3.** recollection, memory, remembrance; faculty of memory, ability to remember.

recant *v.* retract, take back, deny, abjure, withdraw, unsay, repudiate, disavow, renege, recall, revoke, renounce, rescind, disclaim, disown, forswear, repeal, eat one's words, apostatize, change one's mind. **—Ant.** reaffirm, confirm, repeat, validate.

recapitulate *v.* summarize, recap, repeat in essence, sum up; reiterate, recount, repeat, relate, restate, reword, rephrase, epitomize. **—Syn. Study.** See REPEAT.

recede *v.* retreat, go back, back up, regress, abate, ebb, subside; retire, retreat, retrogress. **—Ant.** advance, proceed, move forward, progress.

receipt *n.* **1.** arrival, receiving, reception, recipience, admission, admittance, acceptance, acquisition, possession. **2.** written acknowledgment of payment or goods received, voucher, release, discharge, transferral. **3. receipts** amount or quantity received, profits, net profits, return, returns, gain, proceeds, share, *Slang* take, split, gate; revenue, income, earnings; pay, wages, payment, reimbursement, remuneration, emolument. **4.** recipe, formula.

receive *v.* **1.** get, acquire, secure, come by, be in receipt of, obtain, be given. **2.** accommodate, take in; admit, put up. **3.** encounter, meet with, experience, go or pass through, have inflicted on one, submit to, be subjected to, undergo, sustain, suffer. **4.** be at home to, entertain, admit; welcome, greet, meet. **5.** regard, accept, approve, react to, adjudge.

recent *adj.* new, modern, up-to-the-minute, contemporary, up-to-date, lately made, late; novel, fresh; not long past, of yesterday, latter-day. **—Syn. Study.** See MODERN. **—Ant.** old-fashioned, dated, old, long past, remote, long ago.

receptacle *n.* holder, container, vessel, depository, repository, receiver, carrier; (*variously*) box, bin, basket, hopper, hamper, compartment, bottle, jar, can, bag, file, tray.

reception *n.* **1.** act of receiving one, welcome, greeting, recognition. **2.** affair, social gathering; party, fete, soiree, *Informal* do.

receptive *adj.* favorably disposed, openminded, accessible, approachable, amenable, hospitable, friendly, responsive, interested, susceptible. **—Ant.** unreceptive, illiberal, unresponsive, closed-minded, narrow-minded, prejudiced, biased.

recess *n.* **1.** suspension of business, intermission, break, coffee break, time out, respite, rest, breathing spell, hiatus, pause, lull, *Informal* letup; interim, interlude, interval; holiday, vacation. **2.** receding part of space, indentation, hollow, break, fold; alcove, cell, nook, niche, slot, pigeonhole, corner, bend; inlet, bay, cove, harbor, gulf; cleft, gorge, gap, pass. **3. recesses** inmost part, depths, penetralia.

recherché *adj.* rare, exotic, unique, choice, select, special, uncommon, original, unusual, different, exceptional, superior, valuable, priceless, prize, scarce, one of a kind. **—Ant.** ordinary, commonplace, run-of-the-mill, routine.

reciprocal *adj.* mutual, common; shared; interdependent, returned, given in return, exchanged, equivalent, give-and-take, one for one; complementary, bilateral, corresponding, interrelated, interchangeable, interchanged, linked. **—Ant.** one-way, unilateral.

reciprocate *v.* return, feel, give in return, give or take mutually, requite, interchange; respond, return the compliment, act likewise, make return, retaliate.

recital *n.* **1.** solo musical performance, concert. **2.** recapitulation, narration, recitation, rendition, delivery, performance, reciting; narrative, telling, talk, discourse, dissertation; report, description, detailed statement, particulars, graphic account; public reading, oral exercise.

recite *v.* declaim, perform, speak, narrate, recount, tell, deliver, repeat, relate, say by heart, quote, communicate, do one's number, give a recitation. **—Syn. Study.** See RELATE.

reckless *adj.* incautious, heedless, unheeding, unmindful, careless, irresponsible, thoughtless, regardless, inconsiderate, mindless, unthinking, neglectful, negligent, unwatchful, unwary, unaware, oblivious, inattentive, unconcerned; wild, daring, cavalier, daredevil, devil-may-care, volatile; precipitate, rash, unsolicitous, indiscreet, imprudent, uncircumspect, hasty, impulsive, fickle, unsteady; foolhardy, foolish, insensible; flighty, madcap, scatterbrained, harebrained, giddy. **—Ant.** cautious, heedful, mindful, careful, wary, aware, observant, thoughtful, regardful, responsible, deliberate.

reckon *v.* **1.** count, add, add up, total, tally, balance, figure, calculate, compute, estimate. **2.** regard, esteem, consider, deem, think, judge, adjudge, estimate; count, account, class, rank, rate, appraise, assess, value; determine, surmise, estimate, come to or arrive at a conclusion regarding, figure, decide, guess, speculate. **3.** *Informal* guess, fancy, expect, presume, surmise, suppose, imagine, figure. **4.** count, figure, bank, plan, bargain. **5.** deal, cope, handle.

reckoning *n.* **1.** count, total, tally, adding, summation, calculation, computation; appraisal, estimate, estimation, evaluation, statement of an amount due, bill, account, charge, tab; settling of an account. **2.** judgment, final judgment, doom.

recline *v.* lie back, lie down, rest, rest in a recumbent position, repose; lean, take one's ease, lounge, loll, sprawl.

recognition *n.* **1.** identification, act of being recognized, discovery. **2.** acceptance, acknowledgment, understanding, comprehension, notice; act by which one government recognizes the existence of another, validation, diplomatic relations.

recognize *v.* **1.** know, identify, place, make out, discern, pick out, sight, spot. **2.** be aware of, appreciate, understand, comprehend, respect, acknowledge, realize, see, discern, make out; admit, know. **3.** acknowledge as entitled to speak, give the floor to, yield or submit to, concede to. **4.** establish diplomatic relations with, acknowledge. **—Ant. 2, 3** ignore, overlook, turn one's back on, close one's eyes to.

recoil *v.* **1.** draw back, hang back, start, shrink back, jump back, retreat, blench, quail, revolt; wince, flinch, demur, falter, shirk, blink, fail; cower, cringe. **2.** fly back, spring back, rebound, bound back, jump back, kick. **—Syn. Study. 1** See WINCE.

recollect *v.* recall, call to mind, remember, place.

recommend *v.* **1.** put forward, present as worthy of, mention favorably, speak well of, favor, endorse, advocate, vouch for. **2.** urge, suggest, encourage, propose, advise, prescribe, order, counsel. **—Ant. 1** mention unfavorably, disapprove. **2** forbid, discourage.

recommendation *n.* praise, commendation, good word, behest, approval, endorsement, reference, *Slang* plug. **—Ant.** condemnation, criticism, disapproval, rejection.

recompense *v.* **1.** compensate, remunerate, pay, reimburse, repay, reward. *—n.* **2.** compensation, remuneration, payment, reparation, repayment, return, reward, indemnification.

reconcile *v.* **1.** conciliate, propitiate, restore to friendship, reunite. **2.** conciliate, win over, persuade, resign. **3.** settle, set straight, make up, square; harmonize, fix up, patch up, rectify, adjust, correct.

reconnaissance *n.* inspection, survey, scrutiny, viewing, observation, reconnoitering, scouting, investigation, exploration; surveillance.

reconsider *v.* rethink, review, reexamine, reevaluate, modify, reassess, think over, mull over, ponder, think better of, sleep on, revise, amend, correct, take under advisement, think twice about.

record *v.* **1.** write down, set down in writing, put or place on record, make an entry of, register, transcribe, take down, note, copy, inscribe for posterity, jot down, make a memorandum of; enter, catalog, list, enroll, post, admit, introduce, log; chronicle; register, tape. **2.** register, show, indicate. *—n.* **3.** account, report, document, register; docket, file; journal, annals, chronicle, archive, history, proceedings; note, memorandum, memo, jotting. **4.** facts known about a person or thing, history, report of actions, account; background, experiences, adventures; conduct, performance, career. **5.** best performance known, top performance, greatest achievement of its kind to date, unbeaten mark, ultimate example, best rate attained. **—Ant. 1** erase, obliterate, expunge, cancel, delete; disregard, omit.

recount *v.* **—Syn. Study.** See RELATE.

recoup *v.* regain, reacquire, retrieve, redeem, recover, replace; make up for, make good, make amends for, atone; provide an equivalent for.

recover *v.* **1.** get back, retrieve, recoup, regain, reacquire, repossess, reclaim, redeem, recapture, reconquer, retake, win back; make up for, make good, restore, offset, balance, compensate. **2.** return to good condition, regain strength, be restored to health, get well, recuperate, convalesce, return to health, take a turn for the better, improve, heal, mend; rally, come around, pull through; regain control of oneself, be oneself again, revive, revivify, resuscitate, rejuvenate, restore, pick up. **—Ant. 2** relapse, fail, grow worse, worsen.

recreation *n.* diversion, leisure activity, pastime, play, hobby, sport, entertainment, amusement, avocation; diversion, relaxation.

rectify *v.* right, set right, put right, make right, correct, adjust, regulate, straighten, square; focus, attune; mend, amend, emend, fix, repair, revise; remedy, redress, cure, reform.

rectitude *n.* integrity, probity, uprightness, righteousness, principle, decency, incorruptibility, honor, high-mindedness, morality, trustworthiness, virtuousness, irreproachability. **—Ant.** immorality, corruption, laxity, crookedness.

recumbent *adj.* lying down, prone, prostrate, supine, flat, couchant, stretched out, horizontal; reclining, leaning. **—Ant.** upright, erect, standing, standing up, vertical; sitting.

recuperate *v.* recover, get well, get better, come around, come back, heal, mend, pull through, improve, convalesce, return to health, regain one's strength, be on the mend. **—Ant.** fail, sink, worsen, succumb.

recur *v.* **1.** occur again, repeat; return, come again, reappear; resume, persist, continue. **2.** come back, return to mind, flash across the memory, be remembered, haunt one's thoughts.

recurrent *adj.* recurring, frequent, periodic, intermittent, regular, appearing again, reappearing, repeating, repetitive.

red *adj.* **1.** blood-colored; (*variously*) maroon, wine, ruby, vermilion, crimson, cardinal, scarlet, cherry, rosy, rose; auburn; pink, coral, flame. **2.** blushing, reddened, ruddy, flushed, rosy, florid, blooming, rubicund, rubescent, aglow, glowing, inflamed, flaming, burning.

red-blooded *adj.* vigorous, sturdy, robust, strong, vital, energetic, intense, dynamic, forceful, powerful, peppy, spirited; passionate, lusty, ardent, hot-blooded.

redeem *v.* **1.** buy back, repurchase; ransom; reclaim, recover, retrieve, regain, repossess, recoup. **2.** keep, fulfill, make good; discharge. **3.** make up for, cover, defray, compensate for, make good, settle; make amends for, atone for, satisfy, recover, regain, retrieve. **4.** rescue, save, deliver from sin and its consequences, evangelize, turn from sin, set straight again; convert, reform. **—Ant.** **1** lose, forfeit, yield, give up. **2** break; shun, disregard, violate.

redolent *adj.* **1.** fragrant, aromatic, balmy, perfumed, spicy, savory, odorous, odoriferous; smelly, stinking, reeking. **2.** reminiscent, suggestive, indicative, expressive, evocative, mindful.

redress *n.* **1.** reparation, compensation, recompense, payment, indemnification, restitution, rectification, amends, satisfaction, easement, relief. **—***v.* **2.** correct, right, set right, rectify, make reparation for, compensate for, make retribution for, amend, make up for; reform; remedy, ease, relieve. **—Syn. Study.** **1** REDRESS, REPARATION, RESTITUTION suggest making amends or giving compensation for a wrong. REDRESS may refer either to the act of setting right an unjust situation or to satisfaction sought or gained for a wrong suffered: *the redress of grievances.* REPARATION refers to compensation or satisfaction for a wrong or loss inflicted. The word may have the moral idea of amends, but more frequently it refers to financial compensation: *to make reparation for one's neglect; the reparations demanded of the aggressor nations.* RESTITUTION means literally the giving back of what has been taken from the lawful owner, but may refer to restoring the equivalent of what has been taken: *The servant convicted of robbery made restitution to his employer.*

reduce *v.* **1.** lessen, diminish, discount, mark down, slash, cut. **2.** lose weight by dieting, slim down, diet, trim down, slenderize. **3.** lower in rank, demote, *Slang* bust, break; force, lower. **4.** bring down, leave in; damage, bring to destruction. **5.** minimize, lessen, lower, cut down, dilute, thin, water, blunt the edge of, dull; modulate, tone down, moderate, temper, ease, abate, mitigate, assuage, soften; checkmate, retard, slow down, curb, check; debilitate, atrophy, weaken, devitalize, enfeeble, cripple, incapacitate, undermine. **—Ant.** **1, 3** increase. **1** add to, augment, enlarge, extend, mark up. **2** gain weight, put on pounds. **3** promote, elevate. **5** heighten, enhance, strengthen.

redundant *adj.* **1.** repetitious, tautological, pleonastic; (of speech or writing) wordy, verbose, prolix. **2.** superfluous, unnecessary, inessential, dispensable, overflowing, extra, excess, surplus, superabundant. **—Syn. Study.** **1** See WORDY. **—Ant.** **2** necessary, essential, indispensable.

reek *n.* **1.** unpleasant smell or odor, stink, stench, effluvium. **2.** fume, emanation, cloud of smoke. **—***v.* **3.** smell strongly, give off, smell, be malodorous, stink, smell to high heaven. **4.** smoke, fume, steam.

reel *v.* **1.** rock, move uncertainly, stagger, totter, teeter, wobble, sway, stumble, lurch, pitch, roll. **2.** turn round and round, rotate, whirl, swirl, spin, revolve, sway, waver. **3.** feel dizzy, be giddy, be in a vertiginous state.

refer *v.* **1.** direct, send. **2.** hand over, submit, deliver, transmit, transfer, pass along. **3.** advert, make reference; allude, mention, cite. **4.** go, turn; consult.

referee *n.* **1.** judge, umpire, arbitrator, arbiter, adjudicator, moderator, mediator, intermediary, intercessor. **—***v.* **2.** umpire, arbitrate, settle, determine, judge, adjudicate, decree, pronounce judgment; mediate, moderate, intervene, intercede. **—Syn. Study.** **1** See JUDGE.

reference *n.* **1.** mention, allusion, suggestion, hint, intimation, innuendo, inkling, implication. **2.** recommendation, testimonial, credentials, endorsement, certification, deposition, affirmation, *Slang* good word.

refine *v.* **1.** strain, filter, process, free from impurities, purify, cleanse. **2.** develop, improve, cultivate, perfect. **—Ant.** **1** contaminate, adulterate. **2** coarsen.

refined *adj.* **1.** purified, cleansed, clean, clarified. **2.** well-bred, free from coarseness, genteel, gentlemanly, ladylike, courtly, polite, courteous, mannerly; discriminating, fastidious, elegant, cultured, cultivated, civilized, polished, suave, finished; urbane, gentle, graceful, delicate. **—Ant.** **1, 2** unrefined. **1** impure, unpurified. **2** ill-bred, coarse, crude, vulgar, boorish, common, philistine, ungenteel, ungentlemanly, unladylike, unmannerly; undiscriminating; inelegant.

refinement *n.* **1.** fine sensibilities, fineness, cultivation, urbanity, culture, finish, finesse, elegance, grace, polish, tastefulness, discrimination, discernment, fastidiousness; dignity, gentility, breeding; suavity, urbanity, *French* savoir faire; graciousness, gentleness, delicacy; politeness, civility, courtesy, good manners, courteousness, propriety; nicety, example of refined manners. **2.** purification, cleaning, cleansing, filtration, distillation. **3.** improvement, revision, rectification, amendment; development, amelioration, enhancement, betterment; advance, progression, advancement, step up, step forward. **—Ant. 1** vulgarity, crudeness, coarseness, boorishness, tastelessness, gracelessness, discourtesy.

reflect *v.* **1.** mirror, cast back from a surface, cause to return or rebound, send back, throw back, return, give back or show an image of, image, copy, imitate, reproduce. **2.** cast, throw, bring upon, bring as a result of one's actions. **3.** show, display, express, exhibit, bring to light, reveal, disclose, indicate, evince, uncover, expose, manifest, set forth, present, demonstrate, register, represent, mirror. **4.** bring discredit, undo, undermine, betray, cast or bring reproach, condemn. **5.** think, think carefully, deliberate, reason, ponder, weigh, consider, study, muse, meditate, contemplate, speculate, revolve in the mind, mull over, cogitate, ruminate, cerebrate, dwell upon, concentrate. **—Syn. Study. 5** See STUDY. **—Ant. 1** absorb, keep, retain. **3** conceal, mask, hide, cover.

reflection *n.* **1.** image, mirror image, optical counterpart. **2.** serious thought, deliberation, thought, consideration, attention, thinking, pondering, meditation, musing, pensiveness, study, concentration, rumination, cogitation, cerebration. **3.** thought, notion, idea, sentiment, conviction, opinion, impression, view. **4.** statement or action that brings doubt or blame, derogation, insinuation, imputation, insult, blot, unfavorable observation or remark, slur, reproof, reproach, disparagement.

reflective *adj.* **—Syn. Study.** See PENSIVE.

reform *n.* **1.** correction, rectification, reformation, amendment. *—v.* **2.** change for the better, better, improve, correct, rectify, set straight again, restore, rehabilitate, remodel, rebuild, remedy, repair; revise, convert, be converted, progress; mend, amend, repent, atone, abandon evil conduct, mend one's ways, turn over a new leaf, set one's house in order.

refractory *adj.* **—Syn. Study.** See UNRULY.

refrain *v.* abstain, restrain oneself, keep oneself, hold off, desist, stay one's hand, curb oneself; forbear, forgo, renounce, eschew, avoid, refuse, resist, leave off. **—Ant.** indulge in, be intemperate; continue, persist, go ahead.

refresh *v.* **1.** freshen, invigorate, brace, vivify, restore, recruit, strengthen, revive, renew, energize, rejuvenate, cool off, recreate, reanimate. **2.** prompt, prod, jog, arouse, rouse, stimulate, stir up, activate, quicken; revive, renew, awaken. **—Ant. 1** weaken, tire, weary, fatigue.

refreshment *n.* **1.** food and drink, nourishment, snack, appetizer, hors d'oeuvre, *Informal* pick-me-up, bite, eats; beverage, drink, thirst quencher, bracer, restorative, refresher, cocktail, drinkable, potable, potation. **2.** invigoration, restoration, reinvigoration, recreation, relaxation, rejuvenation.

refrigerate *v.* cool, chill, freeze, congeal, keep cool, keep cold, store in the refrigerator, put on ice, keep on ice. **—Ant.** warm, heat, cook, simmer.

refuge *n.* **1.** shelter, sanctuary, protection. **2.** place of shelter, haven, retreat, safehold, sanctuary, asylum, resort; harbor, harborage, anchorage, home, port in a storm. **3.** resort, hideout, means of self-defense, technique for escaping, help in distress. **—Ant. 1** exposure, peril, danger, threat, menace; insecurity.

refugee *n.* fugitive, exile, emigrant, émigré, expatriate, escapee, DP, displaced person, evacuee; absconder, runaway, eloper, bolter.

refund *v.* **1.** give back (money), return, reimburse, pay back, repay, recompense, make compensation for, remunerate, remit, rebate, make restitution for. *—n.* **2.** rebate, repayment, reimbursement, remittance; amount repaid. **—Ant. 1** withhold.

refurbish *v.* renovate, fix up, spruce up, remodel, improve, renew, redo, restore, recondition, overhaul, repair, mend; clean, tidy up, freshen.

refusal *n.* rejection, denial, turndown, declination, declining, nonacceptance, nonconsent, disapproval, noncompliance, unwillingness, regrets; veto.

refuse[1] *v.* not accept, say no to, reject, veto, turn down, spurn, decline; forbid, prohibit, disallow, withhold, deny. **—Syn. Study.** REFUSE, REJECT, SPURN, DECLINE imply nonacceptance of something. REFUSE is direct and emphatic in expressing a determination not to accept what is offered or proposed: *to refuse an offer of help.* REJECT is even more forceful and definite: *to reject an author's manuscript.* To SPURN is to reject with scorn: *to spurn a bribe.* DECLINE is a milder and more courteous term: *to decline an invitation.* **—Ant.** approve, accept, consent to, permit, allow, agree to, give.

refuse² *n.* rubbish, trash, garbage, waste, junk, litter, offal; debris, rubble.

refute *v.* disprove, confute, give the lie to, invalidate, counter, rebut, answer, challenge, contradict, deny. **—Ant.** prove, vindicate, support, confirm, corroborate, substantiate.

regain *v.* recover, retrieve, repossess, get again, gain anew, get back, retake, reclaim, recapture, recoup, redeem, win back.

regal *adj.* royal, kingly, queenly, noble, princely, lordly, proud, kinglike, princelike, queenlike; stately, majestic, splendid, magnificent, grand, imposing, august, splendiferous.

regale *v.* **1.** amuse, entertain, divert; delight, please; enthrall. **2.** feed sumptuously, feast, serve nobly, wine and dine, fete, ply, banquet; lionize.

regard *v.* **1.** consider, look upon, view, see, think, judge, account, believe, hold, set down, put down, reckon, estimate, rate. **2.** heed, follow, accept, respect, esteem, show consideration for, consider, mind, note well, pay attention to, listen to, hearken to. **3.** value, esteem, think highly of, think well of, respect, look up to, admire, hold a high opinion of. **4.** gaze at, look at, view, look upon, contemplate, behold, eye, turn one's eyes toward, cast the eyes on; scan, survey, watch, scrutinize, take the measure of, take in. *—n.* **5.** thought, consideration, concern, attention, notice, note, observation, heed, mind, care, meditation, reflection. **6.** respect, esteem, admiration, estimation, appreciation. **7.** respect, matter, point, subject, aspect, detail; reference, relation, connection. **—Ant. 1–6** disregard. **2, 3** reject, repudiate, despise, scorn, disrespect, spurn, ignore, think badly of, look down on, disparage, detest, loathe, dislike. **4** look away from, shun, ignore. **5** heedlessness, indifference, contempt.

regardless *adv.* nevertheless, nonetheless, notwithstanding, anyway, anyhow, for all that, in spite of everything.

regenerate *v.* **1.** reform, rejuvenate, redeem, uplift, make a new man of, enlighten. **2.** generate anew, give new life to, revive, renew, reawaken, resuscitate, resurrect, revivify; inspirit, restore, retrieve. **3.** grow back an injured or lost part; revivify.

regime *n.* government, rule, reign, administration, dynasty, power, leadership, command, direction, control, jurisdiction, dominion, management.

regimentation *n.* discipline, order, uniformity, control, regulation, system, method, rigor, rigorousness, orthodoxy, regimen, methodization, doctrinaire approach.

region *n.* **1.** area, territory, space, expanse, tract, range, country, land, district, neighborhood, zone, province; locality, vicinity. **2.** area, field, province, sphere, domain, realm.

register *n.* **1.** record book; ledger, daybook, diary, log, logbook, roll, registry. **2.** dial, meter, indicator, gauge; recorder, calculator, counter. **3.** range, scale, compass. **4.** heat vent, heat outlet, hot-air vent, heater, heat duct, radiator. *—v.* **5.** write down, record, put in writing, put on the record, make a record of, note down, set down, take down. **6.** enroll, sign up, check in, enlist. **7.** show, indicate, exhibit, disclose, manifest, mark, point to, record; portray, express, betray, betoken.

regress *v.* **1.** go back, ebb, move backward, lose ground, withdraw, reverse, retrogress, revert, retreat, backslide, recede, back, fall, fall back, pass back; relapse, deteriorate. *—n.* **2.** return, exit. **—Ant. 1** progress, advance; climb, rise, ascend. **2** ingress, entrance.

regret *v.* **1.** be sorry for, feel sorrow for, feel remorse for, be ashamed of, be remorseful, rue, be rueful, rue the day, repent, bemoan, deplore, bewail, moan, mourn, grieve at, lament, weep over, feel distress over, reproach oneself for, have second thoughts about, *Informal* eat humble pie, eat one's words, eat crow. *—n.* **2.** sorrow, grief, remorse, remorsefulness, regretfulness, rue, ruefulness, compunction, contrition, apology, apologies, repentance, grievance, lamentation; disappointment, dissatisfaction, anguish, woe, qualm, reservation, scruple, pang of conscience, twinge, second thought; self-condemnation, self-reproach; heartache. **—Syn. Study. 2** REGRET, REMORSE imply a sense of sorrow about events in the past, usu. wrongs committed or errors made. REGRET is a feeling of sorrow or disappointment for what has been done or not been done: *I remembered our bitter quarrel with regret.* REMORSE is a deep sense of guilt and mental anguish for having done wrong: *The killer seemed to have no remorse.* **—Ant. 1** feel happy for, rejoice, laugh at; feel satisfaction over. **2** remorselessness, impenitence, satisfaction, pleasure, contentment.

regrettable *adj.* lamentable, pitiable, unhappy, grievous, woeful, unfortunate, deplorable, calamitous. **—Ant.** happy, joyous; fortunate, successful, lucky, fortuitous.

regular *adj.* **1.** usual, normal, customary, standard, typical, ordinary, common, commonplace, familiar, daily, steady, constant, habitual, undeviating, invariable, unvarying, unchanging, set, fixed, established. **2.** consistent, habitual, frequent, recurrent, recurring, periodic, periodical. **3.** orthodox, correct, proper, classic, established, accepted. **4.** *Informal* genuine, real, down-to-earth, plain, natural, typical, everyday; thorough, real, absolute, complete. **5.** uniform, even, smooth, well-proportioned, fine, symmetrical, well-balanced. —*n.* **6.** regular customer, regular client, habitué, faithful, old reliable, dependable; loyalist, true blue, stalwart, trusty. **—Ant. 1–3, 5** irregular. **1** unusual, abnormal, unconventional, exceptional, rare, uncommon, variable, inconsistent, inconstant, varied, deviating, varying; sloppy, disorderly, unmethodical. **2** occasional, infrequent, rare. **3** erratic, unorthodox. **4** phony, fake. **5** uneven, variable.

regulate *v.* **1.** control, govern, handle, manage, superintend, supervise, oversee, monitor, guide, organize, direct. **2.** adjust, fix, regularize, rectify, moderate, balance, modulate. **—Ant. 1** confuse, disrupt, disorganize; neglect, set free, decontrol.

regulation *n.* **1.** adjusting, adjustment, handling, control. **2.** rule, ordinance, decree, standing order, direction, statute, dictate, order, command, edict, commandment.

rehabilitate *v.* **1.** restore to society, resocialize, straighten out, reeducate, set straight; redeem, save. **2.** salvage, renovate, make over, remake, reconstruct, restore, fix, readjust, refurbish, recondition. **3.** restore, reinstate.

rehearsal *n.* practice, reading, walk-through, run-through, dress rehearsal, drill, exercise, repetition, recapitulation; reiteration, preparation, polishing, perfecting. *Slang* recap; trial run, tryout, audition, test run, hearing.

rehearse *v.* **1.** prepare, practice, ready, drill, polish, train, go over, run through; read one's lines, study one's lines. **2.** repeat, recite, give a recital of, recount, relate, narrate; reiterate, retell.

reign *n.* **1.** regnancy, rule, tenure, regnum, incumbency, government, regime, dominion, sovereignty. **2.** influence, dominance, tutelage, supervision. —*v.* **3.** have royal power, wear the crown, occupy the throne, sit on the throne, exercise sovereignty; rule, govern, hold authority, exercise authority, hold sway, command.

reimburse *v.* pay back, rebate, refund, repay, remunerate, indemnify, square up, pay up, remit, compensate, recompense, make restitution.

rein *n.* **1.** Usu. **reins** bridle. **2.** restraint, check, hold, bridle, harness. —*v.* **3.** control, check, curb, hold back, bridle, harness; restrict, limit, suppress; watch, keep an eye on.

reinforce *v.* make stronger, strengthen, support, buttress, prop, bolster, brace up, fortify, steel. **—Ant.** weaken, debilitate; diminish, lessen, harm, hurt.

reiterate *v.* repeat, resay, reprise, iterate, retell, reword, rephrase, restate, recapitulate; stress, hammer, go over and over, pound away at, pound into someone's head. **—Syn. Study.** See REPEAT.

reject *v.* **1.** refuse, say no to, decline, turn down; shrug off, dismiss, turn from, repudiate, repel, repulse, rebuff, disdain, spurn, disallow, deny. —*n.* **2.** castoff, castaway, discard; flotsam. **—Syn. Study. 1** See REFUSE. **—Ant. 1** accept, say yes to, pay attention to, receive willingly, approve, countenance, be in favor of, agree with; allow, permit; select. **2** treasure, prize.

rejection *n.* refusal, rejecting, declining, rebuffing, scorning, spurning, disdain, dismissal, rebuff, ruling out. **—Ant.** acceptance, approval, selection, espousal, affirmation.

rejoice *v.* be glad, be happy, be pleased, be transported, be delighted, be overjoyed, exult, jubilate, glory, delight, sing for joy, be elated, make merry, revel, celebrate, exhilarate. **—Ant.** be sad, be unhappy, mourn, lament, grieve.

rejoicing *n.* celebration, festivity, revelry, reveling, merrymaking, mirth, merriment, liveliness, gaiety, jubilee, jollity, good cheer; happiness, gladness, jubilation, jubilance, joyfulness, delight, pleasure; exultation, elation, ecstasy; triumph, cheering.

rejoinder *n.* answer, reply, response, retort, rebuttal, return, comeback, back talk, riposte, remonstrance, refutation, repartee, counterblast, countercharge, counterstatement; *Law* surrebuttal, surrejoinder. **—Syn. Study.** See ANSWER.

rejuvenate *v.* make youthful again, restore, put new life into, reinvigorate, revive, revivify, revitalize, reanimate, restore. **—Ant.** age, make older; tire, weary, fatigue; weaken, debilitate.

relapse *v.* **1.** fall back, slip back, sink back, turn back, revert, backslide, degenerate, regress, retrogress, lapse, worsen. —*n.* **2.** lapse, fall, reversion, return to illness, turn for the worse, falling back, retrogression, reverse, regression, backsliding, deterioration, decline, recurrence, worsening.

relate *v.* **1.** tell, recount, recapitulate, give an account of, report, detail, particularize, describe, make known, reveal, disclose, divulge, impart, convey, communicate, state, say, utter, speak, narrate, recite. **2.** connect, associate, attach, link, refer, have reference, pertain, concern, be relevant, appertain, apply, belong. **3.** feel close, have rapport, interact well, communicate, be sympathetic, be responsive, feel empathy with. **—Syn. Study. 1** RELATE, RECOUNT, RECITE mean to tell, report, or describe in some detail an occurrence or circumstance. To RELATE is to give an account of happenings, events, circumstances, etc.: *to relate one's adventures.* To RECOUNT is usu. to set forth consecutively the details of an occurrence, argument, experience, etc., to give an account in detail: *to recount an unpleasant experience.* To RECITE may mean to give details consecutively, but more often applies to the repetition from memory of something learned with verbal exactness: *to recite a poem.* **—Ant. 1** keep to oneself, keep secret. **2** dissociate, disconnect, separate, divorce, detach; be unconnected, be irrelevant.

relation *n.* **1.** Also **relationship** connection, tie-in, tie, link, bond, interrelationship, association, affiliation. **2.** relative, kin, kinsman. **3.** regard, connection, reference, bearing, relevance, concern, pertinence, correlation, application, applicability. **4.** narrating, narration, telling, recital, recitation; narrative, account, report, description, version, retelling, communication. **—Ant. 1** disconnection, dissociation, independence.

relative *n.* **1.** relation, cognate, kinsman, kinswoman, kinfolk, kin, kith, kith and kin, people, family, folks, blood relative, cousin, flesh and blood, connection, clan, tribe. *—adj.* **2.** comparative, comparable, dependent, not absolute, relational. **3.** related, correlated, correlative, connective, connected, associated, affiliated, allied, interrelated, interconnected. **4.** pertinent, appropriate, pertaining, having reference or regard, relevant, referable, respective, applicable, germane. **—Ant. 1** stranger, alien, foreigner. **2** absolute. **3** unconnected, unrelated. **4** irrelevant, remote, inappropriate.

relax *v.* **1.** make less tense, loosen up, calm, soothe; cool off, unwind, unbend, ease up, let up. **2.** make less severe, make less strict, slack, slacken, loosen, soften, make lax, bend, unbend, ease, decrease. **3.** rest, take it easy, enjoy oneself, vacation, holiday; be idle, idle, be lazy, laze, loaf, lie around, unbend. **—Ant. 1** tense, tighten, alarm, alert, bear down. **2** tighten, intensify, heighten, increase. **3** work, be busy, be active.

relaxation *n.* **1.** remission, loosening, bending, abatement, slackening. **2.** recreation, enjoyment, fun, amusement, entertainment, diversion, pleasure, refreshment; pastime, avocation, hobby, sport, games; rest from work, repose, leisure. **—Ant. 1** tightening, stiffening. **2** work, toil, labor, strain.

release *v.* **1.** free, set free, let out, let go, dismiss, discharge, liberate, set at liberty. **2.** relieve; set loose, loose, untie, unloose, unfasten, unbind; disengage, detach, extricate. **3.** distribute, circulate, present, communicate. *—n.* **4.** releasing, liberating, freeing, liberation, setting free, emancipation, setting loose, letting go, extrication, dismissal. **5.** distribution, publication, circulation. **—Syn. Study. 1** RELEASE, FREE, DISMISS, DISCHARGE, LIBERATE all mean to let loose or let go. RELEASE and FREE both suggest a helpful action; they may be used of delivering a person from confinement or obligation: *to release prisoners; to free a student from certain course requirements.* DISMISS usu. means to force to go unwillingly; however, it may also refer to giving permission to go: *to dismiss an employee; to dismiss a class.* DISCHARGE usu. means to relieve of an obligation, office, etc.; it may also mean to permit to go: *The soldier was discharged. The hospital discharged the patient.* LIBERATE suggests particularly the deliverance from unjust punishment, oppression, or the like, and often means to set free through forcible or military action: *to liberate occupied territories.* **—Ant. 1** imprison, incarcerate; detain, hold, keep. **2** fasten, engage. **3** withhold, conceal, hide. **4** imprisonment, incarceration, internment, detention, holding.

relent *v.* grow lenient, grow less severe, become milder, weaken, melt, soften, unbend, relax, bend, yield, give in, let up, give way, capitulate, have pity, be merciful, give quarter, come around.

relentless *adj.* unrelenting, remorseless, implacable, inexorable, unyielding, inflexible, uncompromising, undeviating, adamant, harsh, hard, stern, severe, stiff, rigid, rigorous, ruthless, pitiless, merciless. **—Ant.** relenting, remorseful, yielding, flexible, pliant, compromising; kind, sparing, gentle, compassionate, feeling, pitying, merciful, lenient, softhearted, sympathetic, forgiving.

relevant *adj.* related, pertinent, referring, bearing, concerning, connected, cognate, intrinsic, tied in, allied, associated; germane, material, significant, appropriate, apposite, applicable, apropos; apt, suitable, suited, fit, fitting, to the point, to the purpose, on the subject. **—Syn. Study.** See APT. **—Ant.** irrelevant, unrelated, unconnected; inappropriate, inapplicable, immaterial, extraneous, extrinsic, foreign, alien, beside the point.

reliable *adj.* dependable, unfailing,

faithful, trustworthy, trusty, responsible, solid, sound, conscientious, true, tried and true. —**Ant.** unreliable, capricious, undependable, untrustworthy, irresponsible, questionable.

reliance *n.* trust, confidence, dependence, faith, credence, credit, belief, assurance. —**Ant.** distrust; uncertainty.

relic *n.* remembrance, keepsake, token, memento, souvenir, records, reminder, fragment, remnant, scrap, vestige, trace; antique, heirloom, artifact.

relief *n.* **1.** easement, alleviation, assuagement, palliation, abatement, amelioration, mitigation, reduction, remedy, cure, panacea, balm, anodyne, antidote, palliative, lenitive. **2.** peace of mind, release from anxiety, cheer, encouragement, elation. **3.** dole, welfare assistance, welfare, public assistance. **4.** respite, rest, break. —**Ant. 1** discomfort, aggravation, intensification; oppression. **2** anxiety, upset, depression, mental suffering, discouragement. **4** hardship, burden.

relieve *v.* **1.** ease, lighten, abate, alleviate, assuage, solace, palliate, mitigate, appease, pacify, mollify, temper, allay, subdue, soothe. **2.** reassure, free from fear, comfort, calm, console, solace, cheer, encourage. **3.** bring help to, aid, help, succor, assist, support. **4.** break up, punctuate, mark, interrupt; set off, put in relief, contrast. **5.** remove, take out, release, let out, replace, free; spell, take the place of. —**Ant. 1** increase, intensify, heighten, aggravate. **2** alarm, discourage, concern. **3** burden, oppress.

religion *n.* **1.** belief in God or gods, faith, belief, religious faith, worship, adoration, devotion, reverence, veneration, homage; piety, devoutness, godliness, religiousness, spirituality; theology, dogma, cult, creed, canon. **2.** system of faith, system of worship; creed, denomination, sect, cult, persuasion, affiliation, church. —**Ant. 1** atheism, godlessness, impiety, irreligion, irreverence, sacrilege, unbelief.

religious *adj.* **1.** spiritual, holy, sacred, theological, divine, denominational, devotional. **2.** religious-minded, devout, spiritual-minded, godly, god-fearing, pious. **3.** conscientious, unswerving, constant, staunch, steadfast, undeviating, unerring, faithful, devout, devoted, scrupulous, exact, rigid, fastidious, meticulous, punctilious; ardent, wholehearted. —**Syn. Study. 2** RELIGIOUS, DEVOUT, PIOUS indicate a spirit of reverence toward God. RELIGIOUS is a general word, indicating adherence to a particular set of beliefs and practices: *a religious family.* DEVOUT indicates a fervent spirit, usu. genuine and often independent of outward observance: *a deeply devout though unorthodox church member.* PIOUS implies constant attention to, and extreme conformity with, outward observances; it can also suggest sham or hypocrisy: *a pious hypocrite.* —**Ant. 1, 2** irreligious. **1** secular. **2** impious, unfaithful, irreverent, profane, unbelieving, godless; atheistic, agnostic, freethinking. **3** unconscientious, feckless, unreliable, inconstant.

relinquish *v.* **1.** renounce, repudiate, deny, disclaim, dismiss, lay aside, shed, cast off, discard, put aside; surrender, cede, give up, deliver up, hand over, yield; forgo, forbear, waive, sign away; resign, abdicate, quit, withdraw from, leave, vacate, forsake, abandon, turn one's back on, wash one's hands of, rid oneself of, drop. **2.** release, let go, give up, break off. —**Ant.** keep, retain, hold, cling to; sustain, maintain.

relish *n.* **1.** liking, partiality, fondness, love, appreciation; enjoyment, zest, want, desire, wish, longing, penchant, propensity, predilection, hankering, fancy, taste, palate, stomach, appetite. **2.** pleasure, delight, satisfaction, gratification, enjoyment, ebullience, exuberance, enthusiasm; pleasing quality, zest, gusto, savor, tang, spice, taste, flavor, accent, piquancy. **3.** condiment, *(variously)* sweet relish, pickle relish, tomato relish, chili sauce, corn relish, beef relish, chutney, piccalilli, horseradish. —*v.* **4.** like, have a liking for, love, fancy, look forward to, dote on, take pleasure in, delight in, rejoice in, enjoy, be pleased with, appreciate, luxuriate in, *Informal* be crazy about, get a kick out of, *Slang* dig, groove on. —**Ant. 1** dislike, hatred, distaste, antipathy. **2** displeasure, dissatisfaction; distaste. **4** dislike, hate, loathe.

reluctant *adj.* unwilling, loath, averse, disinclined, indisposed; hesitant, diffident, slow, shy, laggard. —**Syn. Study.** RELUCTANT, LOATH, AVERSE describe disinclination toward something. RELUCTANT implies some sort of mental struggle, as between disinclination and sense of duty: *reluctant to expel students.* LOATH describes extreme disinclination: *loath to part from a friend.* AVERSE describes a long-held dislike or unwillingness, though not a particularly strong feeling: *averse to an idea; averse to getting up early.* —**Ant.** eager, enthusiastic, keen, willing, desirous, inclined.

rely *v.* depend, be dependent, feel sure of, rest, lean, count, bank, reckon, give credence, credit, believe, swear, bet, place one's trust in.

remain *v.* **1.** stay, continue, persist, go on, linger, hang on, hold up, endure, abide, last, survive, subsist, prevail, remain alive. **2.** stay, stay behind, stay in the same place, not move, not stir, wait, *Informal* stay put, stand, stand pat; be left, be left behind, be left over. **—Ant. 1** leave, die, pass, disappear. **2** go, leave, depart.

remainder *n.* balance, rest, remains, residuum, excess, residue, residual, surplus, overage, leftovers, leavings, remaining part, remnant, superfluity, surplusage; waste, refuse, scourings, wastage.

remark *v.* **1.** observe, say, say in passing, mention, comment. **2.** mark, note, notice, take notice of, take note of, make note of, perceive, see, look at, behold, observe, espy, regard, survey, view; pay heed, give heed to, mind, pay attention to, fix the mind on, contemplate. **—***n.* **3.** commentary, reflection, comment, observation, word. **4.** consideration, note, notice, attention.

remarkable *adj.* noteworthy, notable, conspicuous, unusual, singular, phenomenal, signal, extraordinary, exceptional, memorable, unforgettable, outstanding; distinguished, striking, impressive. **—Ant.** ordinary, usual, common, commonplace, everyday, unsurprising; mediocre, unexceptional; undistinguished, insignificant, inconspicuous, unimpressive.

remedial *adj.* corrective, helpful, beneficial, correctional, advantageous; curative, reformative, therapeutic, restorative, prophylactic, healing, meliorative, mending, sanative, salutary. **—Ant.** harmful, baneful, pernicious, destructive.

remedy *n.* **1.** cure, medicine, relief, nostrum, medicament, medication, treatment, corrective. **2.** corrective, preventive, panacea, cure-all, help, aid, assistance, relief, redress, rectification. **—***v.* **3.** cure, heal, effect a remedy, relieve, ease, calm, alleviate, palliate, assuage, ameliorate, soothe, make easy, mitigate, mollify; restore to health, make sound, put into condition, set right, fix, regulate, improve, make better, help, aid, repair, mend; correct, rectify, restore, redress, right, amend, emend. **—Ant. 1** toxin, poison; disease. **3** aggravate, exacerbate, heighten, intensify, worsen, make worse.

remember *v.* **1.** recall, recall to the mind, call to mind, bring to mind, recollect; keep in mind, have in mind, retain the thought of, not forget, bear in memory, bear in mind. **2.** take note of, appreciate, recognize, take care of, do something for; reward, tip. **—Ant.** forget, disregard, ignore, neglect, overlook, *U.S. Regional* disremember; *Slang* draw a blank.

remembrance *n.* **1.** memory, recall, remembering, recollection, reminiscence, retention in the mind; recognition, recognizance; nostalgia. **2.** reminder, souvenir, favor, keepsake, relic, memento, token; memorial, commemoration. **—Ant. 1** forgetfulness, obscurity, oblivion.

remind *v.* bring to mind, bring back to, suggest to, bring to recollection, awaken memories of, put in memory, put in mind.

reminisce *v.* remember, recollect, hark back, think back, look back, exchange memories, swap remembrances, tell old tales; reflect, ponder, muse, mull.

reminiscent *adj.* remindful, similar to, analogous to; remembering, recollecting, retrospective, nostalgic. **—Ant.** forgetful, oblivious, unremembering.

remiss *adj.* careless, negligent, lax, undutiful, unmindful, unthinking, thoughtless, derelict, delinquent; sloppy, slipshod, slack, loose; slow, dilatory, indolent, slothful, lazy, laggard, do-nothing, shiftless, loafing, idle, inactive; neglectful, forgetful, inattentive, indifferent, uncaring, oblivious, unwatchful. **—Ant.** careful, dutiful, heedful, attentive, diligent; neat, meticulous, scrupulous, blameless.

remit *v.* **1.** send in payment, pay; make good, reimburse, compensate, put to rights; discharge, send, forward, dispatch, ship, transmit. **2.** forgive, pardon, excuse, overlook, pass over, absolve, clear. **3.** free, release, set free, let go, let out, liberate. **4.** diminish, decrease, moderate, reduce; slacken, slack, relax. **—Ant. 1** withhold. **2** condemn, accuse, punish. **3** retain, hold, keep, imprison. **4** increase, strengthen, maximize, heighten.

remnant *n.* remainder, relic, shred, token, leftover, trace, monument, vestige; piece, bit, scrap, fragment; remains, odds and ends; leavings, discard, residue, residuum, survival.

remonstrate *v.* protest, dispute, object, complain, argue, dissent, demur, contend, differ, expostulate; reproach, chide, admonish, rebuke, reprove, scold. **—Ant.** agree, assent, accept, comply.

remorse *n.* regret, regretfulness, rue, ruefulness, guilt, feelings of guilt, self-reproach, self-reproof, compunction, qualm, pangs of conscience, second thoughts; contrition, repentance, penitence; sorrow, grief, lamentation, anguish. **—Syn. Study.** See REGRET. **—Ant.** satisfaction, guiltlessness, pride.

remote *adj.* **1.** far, far-off, faraway, distant, far-removed, a long way off, out of the way; exotic, alien, strange, foreign. **2.** secluded, set apart, isolated, God-forsaken, solitary, sequestered, segregated, separate; out-of-the-way; lonely, alone, quiet. **3.** distant, slight, faint, slim, meager; unlikely, doubtful, dubious, implausible. **4.** removed, distant, standoffish, aloof, withdrawn, detached, faraway, far-off. **—Ant. 1** close, near, nearby; familiar. **2** prominent; busy. **3** immediate, imminent; accessible, approachable, attainable. **4** attentive, interested, involved, alert.

remove *v.* **1.** take off, doff; take away, take out, dislodge, expel, oust, eject, evacuate, cart off, take away, sweep out, carry off. **2.** amputate, cut away, chop off, cut off, lop off. **3.** move, transfer, transport, transplant; displace, change, shift; depart, leave, go away, take leave, quit, vacate, withdraw, make an exit, retreat, retire. **4.** wipe out, get rid of, take out, erase, extract, eliminate, cancel, delete, blot out, drop. **5.** dismiss, discharge, unseat, oust, eject, fire, *Slang* kick out, boot out. **—Ant. 1** put on, don, put back; join, unite, combine; keep, retain, detain, hold. **3** keep, sustain, maintain, hold, retain; hang on, stay, remain. **4** install, establish, set, put in.

remunerate *v.* pay, recompense, reimburse, compensate, repay, reward, requite, indemnify, satisfy, grant, award, vouchsafe. **—Ant.** charge, tax, assess, fine.

renaissance *n.* rebirth, renewal, renascence, revival, resurrection, reestablishment, rejuvenation, revivification, resurgence, reawakening, reemergence, revitalization, regeneration, restoration, *Italian* risorgimento, rekindling.

rend *v.* **1.** rip, tear, split, rive, divide, rupture, cleave, sunder, sever, dissever, splinter, fracture, break, crack, break into pieces, shatter, fall to pieces. **2.** lacerate, afflict, sear, pain, tear, rip, cut, hurt, wound. **3.** split, pierce with sound. **4.** tear, disintegrate; divide, polarize, split, splinter. **—Ant. 1** join, reunite, unite, bind, secure; mend, heal, join.

render *v.* **1.** cause to be, make, cause to become. **2.** do, perform, play, execute, interpret. **3.** give, present, make available, tender, accord, grant, donate; supply, dispense, deal out, dole out, hand out, allot, *Informal* come across with, shell out, fork over. **4.** pay as due; make restitution of, remit, make payment of, make requital, pay back, give in return, requite. **5.** give up, yield, surrender, cede, turn over, relinquish, hand over. **6.** translate, construe, interpret. **—Ant. 3** withhold, refuse, keep, retain. **4** hold, keep, hang on to.

rendezvous *n.* **1.** agreement to meet, prearranged meeting, date, appointment, engagement, encounter, assignation, tryst, tête-à-tête. **2.** meeting place, gathering place, stamping ground, retreat, haunt, focal point, focus, mecca; *Informal* watering hole. *—v.* **3.** meet by appointment, get together; tryst; assemble, gather, muster.

rendition *n.* rendering, translation, interpretation, arrangement, version, edition, reading, performance, portrayal, depiction.

renegade *n.* **1.** traitor, deserter, slacker, betrayer, defector, turncoat; recreant, apostate, heretic, forsaker, rebel, dissenter, insurgent, quisling, treasonist, mutineer; backslider; runaway, fugitive, outlaw. *—adj.* **2.** traitorous, mutinous, apostate, recreant, unfaithful. **—Ant. 1** adherent, follower, loyalist.

renege *v.* break a promise, break one's word, go back on one's word, fall back, back out, back down, weasel out, turn one's back, repudiate, withdraw, pull out, *Informal* fink out, get cold feet. **—Ant.** fulfill, carry out.

renew *v.* **1.** begin again, resume, continue, take up again, pick up; reestablish, reinstate. **2.** extend, continue, prolong, sign again, offer again, maintain, retain. **3.** revive, rejuvenate, regenerate, reinvigorate, revitalize, refresh, save, salvage, redeem. **4.** renovate, repair, restore, rejuvenate, revitalize, make sound, put back into shape. **—Syn. Study. 4** RENEW, RENOVATE, REPAIR, RESTORE suggest making something the way it formerly was. RENEW means to bring back to an original condition of freshness and vigor: *to renew one's faith.* RENOVATE means to bring back to a good condition, or to make as good as new: *to renovate an old house.* To REPAIR is to put into good or sound condition after damage, wear and tear, etc.: *to repair the roof of a house.* To RESTORE is to bring back to a former, original, or normal condition or position: *to restore a painting.* **—Ant. 1** forget, discontinue, end. **2** discontinue, cancel, let lapse, drop. **4** age, depreciate, wear out.

renounce *v.* give up, relinquish, resign, abdicate, give up claim to, cede, part with, quit, forgo, eschew, waive; abandon, abnegate, wash one's hands of, cast aside, put aside, lay aside, dismiss; repudiate, abjure, forswear, recant, abrogate, deny, disavow, disclaim, reject, disown, cast off, write off, turn from, discard. **—Ant.** avow, assert, proclaim, maintain, uphold, defend, claim; keep, retain, hold, accept, approve, acknowledge.

renovate *v.* repair, mend, fix, improve; make over, remake, revamp, modernize, redecorate, remodel, restore, refurbish, renew. **—Syn. Study.** See RENEW.

renown *n.* fame, acclaim, repute, reputation, popularity, prominence, note, notoriety, celebrity; eminence, status, distinction, mark. **—Ant.** obscurity, unpopularity; disrepute, infamy, shame, disgrace.

renowned *adj.* celebrated, well-known, popular, famous, famed, notable, noteworthy, noted, prominent, outstanding, acclaimed, eminent, distinguished. **—Syn. Study.** See FAMOUS. **—Ant.** obscure, unknown, forgotten, unpopular, insignificant, undistinguished.

rent[1] *n.* **1.** rental, payment; dues, fee. *—v.* **2.** sell the use of, let, rent out, lease; buy the use of, hire, charter, lease. **—Syn. Study. 2** See HIRE.

rent[2] *n.* **1.** opening, rip, tear, tatter, rift, hole, rupture, fissure, cleft, chink, breach, crack, slit; chasm, gash, gap, hiatus, crevasse; split, fracture. **2.** breach, break, rift, split, wrench, division, schism, cleavage.

renunciation *n.* renouncing, rejection, repulsion, spurning, refusal, repudiation; denial, disavowal, disclaiming, eschewing, forgoing, abandonment, relinquishment, forswearing, abjuration. **—Ant.** acceptance, retention.

repair[1] *v.* **1.** fix, restore, mend, set right, make good, recondition, refurbish, renovate, renew, rebuild, patch. **2.** make up for, remedy, redress, rectify, patch up, mend, amend, emend, correct. *—n.* **3.** repairing, fixing, mending, patching, reconditioning, rebuilding; refurbishing, overhaul. **4.** general condition, state, shape. **—Syn. Study. 1** See RENEW. **—Ant. 1** break, destroy, ruin. **2** aggravate, exacerbate, worsen, deepen. **3** destruction, breaking.

repair[2] *v.* withdraw, retire, remove, move, betake oneself, go.

reparation *n.* amends, redress, restitution, compensation, damages, requital, recompense, return, quittance, satisfaction, peace offering. **—Syn. Study.** See REDRESS.

repartee *n.* witty reply, witty retort, bon mot, clever rejoinder, snappy comeback, riposte; badinage, persiflage, word play, pleasantries, bandying of words, banter, chit-chat.

repast *n.* meal, table, board, banquet, feast, spread; food, provision, victuals, nourishment, refreshment, snack.

repay *v.* pay back, reimburse, make restitution, recompense, remunerate, indemnify, refund, requite, reward, make requital, make retribution, give in exchange, return, return the compliment, match; make a return for, pay in kind, reciprocate; get back at, get even with.

repeal *v.* **1.** cancel, abrogate, abolish, annul, nullify, void, declare null and void, invalidate, set aside, revoke, rescind. *—n.* **2.** abrogation, cancellation, abolition, termination, annulment, nullification, voiding, invalidation, revocation. **—Ant. 1** confirm, reestablish; validate. **2** confirmation, reestablishment; validation.

repeat *v.* **1.** restate, reiterate, say again, say over, recapitulate; echo, imitate, mimic. **2.** tell, relate, recite, retell, recount, quote, pass on. **3.** duplicate, redo, perform again, reproduce, replicate. *—n.* **4.** repetition, reiteration, duplication, rerun, *Slang* retread. **—Syn. Study. 1** REPEAT, REITERATE, RECAPITULATE refer to saying or doing a thing more than once. To REPEAT is to say or do something over again: *to repeat an order.* To REITERATE is to say (or, sometimes, to do) something over and over again, often for emphasis: *to reiterate a refusal.* To RECAPITULATE is to restate in brief form often by repeating the principal points in a discourse: *to recapitulate a news broadcast.*

repel *v.* **1.** push back, force back, drive back, rout, beat back, repulse, rebuff; dispel, scatter, disperse, chase away, put to flight, drive away; *Informal* send packing; keep off, hold off, ward off, fend off, forfend, stave off, throw off, resist, be proof against, foil, frustrate, deflect, withstand, oppose; keep at bay, keep at arm's length, check, keep out. **2.** disgust, repulse, revolt, be offensive to, be repugnant to, put off, go against one's grain; sicken, nauseate, turn one's stomach, make one's flesh crawl, set one's teeth on edge, make one shudder; offend, alienate, *Slang* turn off. **—Ant. 1, 2** attract, draw. **2** please, delight, captivate, invite, fascinate, entrance, enchant.

repellent *adj.* **1.** repelling, resisting; impermeable, proof. **2.** repugnant, repulsive, disgusting, nauseating, sickening, distasteful, abhorrent, offensive, revolting, loathsome.

repent *v.* regret, deplore, be grieved for, lament, bewail, weep over, bemoan; feel remorse, be ashamed, be regretful, repine, reproach oneself, rue; be penitent, be contrite.

repentance *n.* remorse, regret, grief, sorrow; self-reproach, self-condemnation, compunction, guilt, pangs of conscience; penitence, contrition. **—Ant.** contentment, complacency, impenitence.

repercussion *n.* **1.** result, effect, consequence, side effect, aftereffect, reaction, reverberation, backlash, boomerang effect. **2.** reverberation, concussion, echo.

repetition *n.* repeat, retelling, recapitulation, restatement, iteration, reiteration.

repetitious *adj.* redundant, repetitive, repeated, wordy, prolix. **—Ant.** concise, pithy, succinct, terse.

replace *v.* **1.** take the place of, fill the

place of, succeed, supersede, supplant, displace, take over for, substitute for, spell. **2.** put back, put back in place, return, restore. **—Syn. Study. 1** REPLACE, SUPERSEDE, SUPPLANT refer to putting one thing or person in place of another. To REPLACE is to take the place of, to succeed: *Ms. Jones will replace Mr. Smith as president.* SUPERSEDE implies that that which is replacing another is an improvement: *The typewriter has superseded the pen.* SUPPLANT implies that that which takes the other's place has ousted the former holder and usurped the position or function, esp. by art or fraud: *to supplant a former favorite.*

replenish *v.* fill up again, refill, restock, reload, replace, renew, refresh, restore, reorder. **—Ant.** dissipate, empty, drain.

replete *adj.* abundantly filled, filled to repletion, abounding, teeming, fraught, well-stocked, loaded, crammed, jam-packed, full to bursting, brimming; stuffed, full, gorged, sated, satiated, surfeited. **—Ant.** empty, bare, barren; hungry, starved, ravenous, famished.

replica *n.* duplicate, copy, close copy, carbon copy, imitation, likeness, double, facsimile, replication, reproduction, model.

reply *v.* **1.** answer, respond, rejoin, make rejoinder, retort, come back with, counter, react. **—***n.* **2.** response, answer, retort, rejoinder, counter, reaction; acknowledgment. **—Syn. Study. 1** See ANSWER. **—Ant. 1** question, demand, ask. **2** request, question; invitation.

report *n.* **1.** account, description, version, relation, narration, story, write-up, summary, record, article, news story, press release. **2.** dispatch, message, communiqué, note, memorandum, missive. **3.** information, word, gossip, hearsay, rumor, talk. **4.** noise, sound, boom, discharge, detonation, bang, crack. **—***v.* **5.** announce, communicate, relate, tell, divulge, disclose, reveal, state, recount, recite, put in writing, write down, put on the record, describe, detail. **6.** denounce, inform against, expose, tell on, complain about. **7.** present oneself, appear; *Informal* show up, check in. **—Ant. 5** keep secret, withhold, conceal.

reporter *n.* journalist, newsman, newspaperman, gentleman of the press, newswoman, newspaperwoman; *Slang* newshawk, newshound, newshen; member of the press, investigative reporter, roving reporter, correspondent, foreign correspondent, columnist; announcer, commentator, newscaster, anchorman, news analyst.

repose *n.* **1.** rest, respite, ease, tranquillity, calm, quiet, quietude, quiescence, peacefulness, relaxation, leisure, inactivity. **—***v.* **2.** rest, be at rest, lie, lie at rest, recline; relax, be calm, settle.

repository *n.* storage place, depository, depot, magazine, storehouse, warehouse, treasure-house.

reprehensible *adj.* condemnable, unworthy, objectionable, shameful, disgraceful; heinous, villainous, opprobrious, nefarious, foul, infamous, despicable, ignoble, base, vile, wicked, evil, bad; unpardonable, inexcusable, unjustifiable; deserving of blame, deserving censure, censurable, blamable, blameworthy, culpable, guilty. **—Ant.** admirable, laudable, commendable, praiseworthy, blameless, guiltless, unobjectionable, irreproachable, pardonable, forgivable.

represent *v.* **1.** stand for, symbolize, designate, denote, be the equivalent of, express, indicate, be, mean, equal, serve as; typify, characterize, emblematize, betoken. **2.** act in place of, stand in the place of, act as a substitute for, be proxy for, be an agent for, agent, be deputy for, be in the position of; speak and act for. **3.** portray, depict, show, show a likeness of, picture, illustrate, sketch, outline, delineate, describe; state, present. **4.** describe, depict, give an account of, portray, delineate. **5.** portray, impersonate, appear as, appear in the character of, enact, act the part of; pose as.

representative *n.* **1.** agent, deputy, emissary, envoy, proxy, delegate, substitute, proctor, surrogate, spokesman, *Informal* mouthpiece. **2.** member of a legislature, legislator, delegate; congressman, congresswoman, assemblyman, assemblywoman, member of parliament, M.P. **—***adj.* **3.** serving to represent, typifying, symbolic, symbolical; exemplary, exemplifying, typical, characteristic, illustrative, descriptive, emblematic, delineative, denotative. **4.** representational, republican, democratic, elected, elective; delegated, delegatory, deputed. **5.** representing the whole, balanced, varied, cross-sectional.

repress *v.* **1.** hold back, keep in check, control, keep down, curb, check, restrain, inhibit, hold in, hold back, suppress, hide, conceal, mask, cloak, cover, veil, stifle, muffle, smother, squelch, strangle; pen up, bottle up, shut up, box up. **2.** crush, quash, quell, subdue, put down, squash, silence. **—Ant. 1** let out, release, express. **2** encourage, incite, foment.

reprieve *n.* respite, delay, postponement, remission, adjournment, suspension, stay, moratorium; *Slang* breather, breathing spell; lull, pause.

reprimand *n.* **1.** sharp reproof, reproval, rebuke, reproach, admonition, admonishment, upbraiding, scolding, remonstrance, castigation, chiding, dressing down, berating, trimming, censure, criticism, obloquy, opprobrium, rebuff, denunciation, disparagement, rap on the knuckles, *Informal* bawling out, *Slang* chewing out. —*v.* **2.** reprove severely, rebuke, reproach, upbraid, rail at, chastise, castigate, scold, chide, admonish, berate, trim, dress down, call to account, take down, tell off, tongue-lash, give a tongue-lashing to, take to task, lecture, rap on the knuckles, *Informal* bawl out, *Slang* chew out; raise one's voice against, denounce, dispraise, disparage; reprehend, reprobate, revile, criticize, censure, *Slang* rap. —**Syn. Study. 2** REPRIMAND, UPBRAID, ADMONISH, CENSURE mean to criticize or find fault with someone for behavior deemed reprehensible. REPRIMAND implies a formal criticism, as by an official or person in authority: *The lawyer was reprimanded by the judge.* UPBRAID suggests relatively severe criticism, but of a less formal kind: *The minister upbraided the parishioners for their poor church attendance.* ADMONISH refers to a more gentle warning or expression of disapproval, often including suggestions for improvement: *I admonished the children to make less noise.* CENSURE suggests harsh, vehement criticism, often from an authoritative source: *The legislators voted to censure their fellow senator.* —**Ant. 1** commendation, compliment, praise, applause, approval. **2** commend, compliment, praise, applaud, approve, endorse.

reprisal *n.* retaliatory act, retaliation, revenge, redress, counterattack, counterblow, counteroffensive, retribution, vengeance, requital, tit for tat, blow for blow, *Latin* quid pro quo. —**Syn. Study.** See REVENGE.

reproach *v.* **1.** find fault with, chide, admonish, reprimand, rebuke, reprove; criticize, censure, condemn, stigmatize, malign, vilify, revile, blame; scold, upbraid, rail at, castigate, charge, tongue-lash, call to account, take to task; disparage, denounce, asperse; shame, disgrace. —*n.* **2.** blame, rebuke, reproof; upbraiding, scolding, remonstrance, criticism, censure, hard words, tirade, diatribe. **3.** cause of blame, badge of infamy, stigma, taint, blemish, stain, blot, spot, tarnish, slur; indignity, insult, offense; shame, humiliation, degradation, embarrassment, scandal, disgrace, dishonor, discredit. —**Ant. 1** praise, commend, applaud, compliment. **2** commendation, compliment, praise, applause, honor. **3** honor, credit.

reprobate *n.* **1.** wicked person, degenerate, profligate, roué, prodigal, rake, rakehell, immoralist, voluptuary, wanton, abandoned person; rascal, scamp, black sheep, rapscallion, rotter; miscreant, sinner, transgressor, evildoer, wrongdoer, outcast, castaway, pariah, derelict, untouchable. —*adj.* **2.** corrupt, incorrigible, depraved, profligate, degenerate, dissolute, abandoned, shameless; wicked, evil, evil-minded, low, base, bad, vile. —**Ant. 1** angel, paragon, saint. **2** pure, virtuous, righteous, saintly, angelic.

reproduce *v.* **1.** make a duplicate of, duplicate, replicate, copy, match, represent, redo; repeat, re-echo, mirror, reflect; imitate, counterfeit. **2.** produce young, produce offspring, procreate, propagate, generate, proliferate, give birth, beget, sire, bring forth, multiply, breed, spawn.

reproduction *n.* **1.** copy, carbon copy, likeness, duplicate, replica, facsimile, representation; imitation, simulation. **2.** generation, propagation, procreation, proliferation, progeneration, multiplication, breeding. —**Ant. 1** original, prototype.

reproof *n.* rebuke, reproach, remonstrance, scolding, dressing-down, reprimand, admonition, chiding, criticism, censure, blame, condemnation. —**Ant.** approval, commendation, praise, reward.

reprove *v.* reproach, rebuke, chide, admonish, reprimand; censure, castigate, chasten, scold. —**Ant.** praise, applaud, encourage.

republic *n.* republican nation, representative government, popular government, democracy, constitutional government.

repudiate *v.* **1.** reject, disavow, deny, disclaim, protest; rescind, reverse, revoke, repeal, retract, void, nullify, annul, declare null and void, abrogate, cancel, abolish, dissolve. **2.** disown, disavow, reject, cast off, discard, wash one's hands of, abandon, desert, forsake, renounce. —**Ant. 1** accept, approve; adopt, espouse. **2** acknowledge, accept, embrace, welcome.

repugnant *adj.* **1.** repellent, offensive, causing disgust, disgusting, nauseating, sickening, repulsive, foul, nasty, vile, obnoxious, revolting, objectionable, unacceptable, undesirable, disagreeable, unpleasant; distasteful, unpalatable, unsavory, unappetizing; odious, hateful, loathsome, detestable, abhorrent, abominable, insufferable. **2.** contrary, opposed, adverse, counter, antipathetic, uncongenial. —**Ant. 1** attractive, pleasant, tasteful, unobjectionable, desirable, agreeable, favorable. **2** consistent, harmonious, compatible.

repulse *v.* **1.** repel, throw back, drive back, beat back. **2.** reject, refuse, rebuff, turn one's back on, be deaf to, ignore, be cold to, spurn, stand aloof from, avoid, shun, shrink from, recoil from; *Informal* cold-shoulder. —*n.* **3.** refusal, rebuff, rejection, spurning, shunning. —**Ant. 2** welcome, accept, encourage. **3** encouragement, acceptance, welcome.

repulsion *n.* revulsion, repugnance, disgust, distaste, indisposition, disinclination; dislike, antipathy, detestation, aversion, loathing, hatred, abomination, abhorrence.

repulsive *adj.* repugnant, repellent, offensive, abhorrent, disgusting, obnoxious, nauseating, nasty, vile, revolting, objectionable, disagreeable, distasteful, loathsome, hateful, detestable, abominable, odious. —**Ant.** attractive, agreeable, pleasant, tasteful.

reputable *adj.* respectable, respected, creditable, trustworthy, held in good repute, esteemed, honored, reliable, of good name. —**Ant.** disreputable, untrustworthy, shady.

reputation *n.* standing, stature, repute, name, character. —**Syn. Study.** REPUTATION, CHARACTER apply to the personal history one has acquired or the distinguishing qualities one possesses. REPUTATION refers to the position one occupies or the standing that one has in the opinion of others, in respect to attainments, integrity, and the like: *a fine reputation; a reputation for honesty.* CHARACTER is the combination of moral and other traits that make one the kind of person one actually is (as contrasted with what others think of one): *Honesty is an outstanding trait of her character.* It can sometimes be used interchangeably with REPUTATION: *a public assault on the governor's character.*

repute *n.* **1.** respectability; standing, reputation, renown, prominence, fame, regard, esteem, celebrity, notoriety. —*v.* **2.** consider, regard, hold, esteem, estimate, judge, deem; believe, think, suppose, account, reckon, view, say.

request *n.* **1.** application, solicitation, petition. —*v.* **2.** ask, ask for, apply for, call for; solicit, bid for, seek, sue for, make suit for, petition for, make entreaty for, entreat, desire, importune.

require *v.* **1.** need, stand in need of, have need of; want, lack, miss; desire, hope for, wish for, long for, crave. **2.** command, charge, enjoin, order, oblige, constrain, compel, direct, dictate, bid. **3.** necessitate, make imperative, entail, imply. —**Syn. Study. 1** See LACK. —**Ant. 1** dispense with, forgo.

requirement *n.* **1.** prerequisite, essential, requisite, must, desideratum, *Latin* sine qua non. **2.** guideline, specification, standard, criterion. —**Syn. Study. 1** REQUIREMENT, REQUISITE refer to that which is necessary. A REQUIREMENT is some quality or performance demanded of a person in accordance with certain fixed regulations: *requirements for admission to college.* A REQUISITE is not imposed from outside; it is a factor that is judged necessary according to the nature of things, or to the circumstances of the case: *Efficiency is a requisite for success in business.* REQUISITE may also refer to a concrete object judged necessary: *the requisites for perfect grooming.*

requisite *adj.* **1.** required, mandatory, compulsory, obligatory, prerequisite, necessary, essential, imperative, needed, indispensable. —*n.* **2.** prerequisite, requirement, need, necessity, essential, must, desideratum, *Latin* sine qua non. —**Syn. Study. 1** See NECESSARY. **2** See REQUIREMENT. —**Ant. 1** unnecessary, superfluous, unessential, unneeded, optional, dispensable, discretionary. **2** superfluity, luxury, nonessential, option.

rescind *v.* revoke, reverse, retract, repeal, recall, take back, invalidate, countermand, overrule, counterorder, override, set aside, discard, get rid of, sweep aside; void, annul, abrogate, abolish, declare null and void, nullify, cancel, quash, dissolve. —**Ant.** uphold, support; validate.

rescue *v.* **1.** save, recover, salvage, extricate, deliver, liberate, ransom. —*n.* **2.** rescuing, saving, recovery, liberation, deliverance, freeing, extrication, release. —**Ant. 1** abandon. **2** loss, abandonment.

research *n.* **1.** inquiry, investigation, search, factfinding, analysis, scrutiny, study, inspection, examination, probe, exploration, scholarship, delving. —*v.* **2.** do research on, study, investigate, conduct an examination on, probe.

resemblance *n.* likeness, similarity, closeness in appearance, affinity, similitude, semblance, analogy, correspondence, parallel, congruence. —**Ant.** unlikeness, dissimilarity, difference.

resemble *v.* bear a resemblance to, look like, appear like, favor, take after, be like, be similar to, correspond to, be akin to, parallel.

resent *v.* feel bitter anger at, be indignant at, be provoked at, be in a huff about, be piqued at, view with dissatisfaction; dislike, feel displeasure at, be offended at, take exception to, take amiss, take offense at, take umbrage at, be insulted by, be jealous of, bear a grudge against. —**Ant.** like, approve; welcome.

resentment *n.* indignation, bad feelings, anger, outraged spirit, ire, crossness, bad temper, dudgeon, huff, asperity, ill will, rancor; acrimony, bitterness, acerbity, sourness, soreness, irritation, irritability; pique, wounded pride, umbrage, offense, hurt feelings, displeasure; animosity, animus, malice, vindictiveness, vengefulness, spite; jealousy.

reservation *n.* **1.** reluctance, doubt, hesitancy, uncertainty; compunction, scruple; qualification, strings, condition, stipulation, provision, proviso. **2.** reserved land, reserve; preserve, encampment, installation, establishment, settlement. **3.** accommodation, booking, prearrangement, appointment, date, reserved place.

reserve *v.* **1.** keep, keep back, withhold, retain, hold, keep as one's own; preserve, spare, conserve, save, husband, lay up, store up, salt away, hoard up, amass, stock, stockpile, put by for a rainy day; postpone, delay, put aside, shelve, table. **2.** set apart, prearrange, provide for, engage, book; schedule. —*n.* **3.** emergency fund, contingency fund, reservoir, savings, nestegg, hoard, stockpile. **4.** reticence, reservedness, aloofness, retiring disposition. —*adj.* **5.** stored up, unused, extra, spare, additional; second-string, backup. **—Syn. Study. 1** See KEEP. **—Ant. 1** give, grant; squander, splurge, spend; throw away, waste. **4** sociability, warmth, affability, conviviality, openness, frankness.

reserved *adj.* **1.** kept in reserve, retained, booked, taken, engaged, spoken for, bespoken. **2.** reticent, aloof, self-contained, undemonstrative, inhibited, restrained, constrained, formal, ceremonious, strained, distant, standoffish, unsocial, unsociable, unresponsive, uncommunicative. **—Ant. 1, 2** unreserved. **2** demonstrative, open, uninhibited; sociable, warm, affable.

reservoir *n.* **1.** water reserve; basin, millpond, well, fount, cistern. **2.** tank, receptacle, container, repository, depository. **3.** supply, store, reserve, fund, stock, accumulation, pool, stockpile, hoard, backlog.

reside *v.* **1.** dwell, live, occupy, inhabit, domicile, have residence, have one's abode, keep house, lodge, room, sojourn. **2.** lie, rest, exist, belong, be present, be inherent, be ingrained, be intrinsic.

residence *n.* home, house, homestead, household, lodging, quarters, dwelling, dwelling place, habitation, domicile, abode, address, place, apartment, flat, pied-à-terre, room, *Informal* digs, *Slang* pad; stay, sojourn. **—Syn. Study.** See HOUSE.

resident *n.* inhabitant, resider, sojourner, dweller, housekeeper, citizen, denizen, townsman, local; tenant, occupant, lodger.

residual *adj.* remaining, continuing, abiding, lasting, enduring, lingering; extra, leftover, surplus, supplementary.

residue *n.* remainder, remains, leavings, scraps, dregs, residuum, remnant, rest, balance.

resign *v.* **1.** give up, step down from, quit, relinquish, leave, abdicate, renounce, disclaim. **2.** submit, reconcile.

resignation *n.* **1.** quitting, retirement, withdrawal, departure. **2.** submission, submissiveness, passiveness, nonresistance, acquiescence, equanimity, stoicism, fatalism, patience. **—Ant. 1** retention. **2** rebellion, resistance, protest, impatience.

resilient *adj.* rebounding, elastic, flexible, springy, supple, rubbery; expansive, rapidly recovering, responsive, buoyant, resistant, irrepressible; hardy, tenacious, adaptable. **—Ant.** inflexible, stiff, rigid, tense; flaccid.

resist *v.* **1.** fight against, oppose, strike back, beat back, fight, combat, contest, withstand, make a stand against, hold out against, bear up against, stand up to, weather, repel, counter, counteract, stop, stem, thwart, baffle, balk, foil, frustrate. **2.** not give in to, abstain from, refrain from, say no to, refuse, reject; turn down. **—Syn. Study. 1, 2** See OPPOSE. **—Ant. 1, 2** give in to, surrender to, submit to. **1** yield, comply with, succumb to, capitulate, acquiesce. **2** indulge in, enjoy.

resistance *n.* opposition, contention, noncompliance, obstinacy, defiance, recalcitrance, intransigence; rejection, rebuff, refusal, obstruction; struggle, armed struggle, insurgency, national liberation movement; insurrection, mutiny, rebellion.

resolute *adj.* determined, purposive, set in purpose, deliberate, serious, steadfast, staunch, steady, tenacious, pertinacious, earnest, zealous, industrious, assiduous, diligent, vigorous; persevering, relentless, persistent, dogged, untiring, unflagging, indefatigable; unyielding, unwavering, unfaltering, unflinching, inflexible, uncompromising, undeviating, unswerving, unbending, strong-minded, strong-willed, decisive, stern, stubborn, obstinate, intrepid. **—Syn. Study.** See EARNEST. **—Ant.** irresolute, unresolved, doubtful, undecided, undetermined, unsteady, vacillating, weak.

resolution *n.* **1.** motion, formal proposition, proposal. **2.** resolve, promise, intent, intention, purpose, plan, design, ambition; objective, object, aim, goal. **3.** resoluteness, firmness of purpose, fixed purpose, persistence, determination, tenacity, resolve, will power, perseverance, resilience, steadfastness, stability, steadiness, constancy; zeal, earnestness, energy, indefatigability, mettle, spirit, aggressiveness, follow-through. **4.** solution, resolving, clearing up, working-out.

resolve *v.* **1.** make up one's mind, dedicate oneself to, determine, decide, form a resolution, purpose, plan, intend, design, set out. **2.** clear up, settle, solve, find the solution to, explain, answer, elucidate. **3.** determine, settle, vote on, decide, adjudge, make up one's mind. —*n.* **4.** determination, resolution, decision, fixed intention, commitment, purpose. **5.** resoluteness, resolution, steadfast purpose, firmness of purpose. **—Syn. Study. 3** See DECIDE.

resonant *adj.* full, rich, vibrant, sonorous, ringing; stentorian, bellowing, resounding, reverberant, booming, orotund, thunderous.

resort *v.* **1.** have recourse to, bring into play, avail oneself of, apply, take up, exercise, make use of, employ, use, utilize. —*n.* **2.** holiday retreat, vacation place, tourist spot. **3.** recourse, expedient; avail, hope, chance.

resound *v.* peal, ring, sound, reverberate, resonate, tintinnabulate, clang, fill the air, echo, reecho, vibrate.

resource *n.* **1.** source, recourse, expedient, wherewithal, means of supplying. **2.** Usu. **resources** collective wealth, capital, funds, assets, means, money, revenue, income, collateral, wherewithal; belongings, effects, possessions.

resourceful *adj.* inventive, creative, talented, imaginative, innovative, original, ingenious, smart, bright, sharp, cunning, shrewd, artful; adroit, skillful, able, competent, capable, effectual, proficient, ready, enterprising. **—Ant.** unresourceful, uninventive, uncreative, artless; unskillful, incompetent, incapable.

respect *n.* **1.** detail, point, particular, matter, circumstance, feature, point of view, aspect, regard, sense. **2.** relation, regard, reference, connection, bearing. **3.** regard, esteem, appreciation, affection; deference, veneration, reverence; praise, laudation, admiration, approval; notice, recognition; consideration. **4.** **respects** expressions of friendship or esteem, compliments, personal observance, consideration, tribute, fealty, regards, greetings, remembrances. —*v.* **5.** honor, esteem, do honor to, revere, venerate, pay deference to, defer to, pay respect to, regard, pay attention to; look up to, be appreciative of, understand, set store by, admire, value, cherish, prize. **6.** consider, treat with consideration, treat with forbearance, refrain from interfering with, show consideration for, appreciate, regard, honor, comply with, obey, heed, follow, abide by, observe, adhere to, be faithful to, acknowledge. **—Syn. Study. 3** RESPECT, ESTEEM, VENERATION imply recognition of a person's worth, or of a personal quality, trait, or ability. RESPECT is commonly the result of admiration and approbation, together with deference: *to feel respect for a great scholar.* ESTEEM is deference combined with admiration and often with affection: *to hold a friend in great esteem.* VENERATION is an almost religious attitude of reverence and love, such as one feels for persons or things of outstanding superiority, endeared by long association: *veneration for noble traditions.* **—Ant. 2, 3, 5** disrespect, disregard. **3** irreverence, contempt, scorn, disdain. **5** pay no attention to; think lowly of, have a low opinion of, scorn, hold in contempt, disdain. **6** neglect, ignore, disregard, disdain, abuse.

respectable *adj.* **1.** worthy of respect, admirable, worthy, praiseworthy, reputable, estimable, honorable, noble, dignified, upright, honest, aboveboard; proper, decent, decorous, correct; becoming, presentable; refined, polished, courtly, civil, polite. **2.** ample, sufficient, fairly good, fairly large, considerable, fair, moderate, proper, passing, satisfactory, admissible, decent, worthy. **—Ant. 1** unworthy, disreputable, dishonorable, ignoble, improper, indecent, indecorous, unbecoming, unpresentable; unrefined, impolite. **2** small, poor, paltry, inadequate, demeaning.

respectful *adj.* deferential, polite, courteous, civil, showing politeness, mannerly, solicitous, regardful, gracious; decorous, reverent, reverential; ceremonious, formal, attentive, admiring, obliging, accommodating, genial, winning, amiable, personable. **—Ant.** disrespectful, impolite, discourteous, rude, uncivil, unmannerly, unrefined, ungracious, irreverent, indecorous; heedless, hostile, antagonistic.

respiration *n.* breathing, respiratory action.

respite *n.* rest period, recess, break, breathing spell, intermission, pause, lull, letup; reprieve, postponement of execution, delay, extension, temporary suspension.

resplendent *adj.* refulgent, brilliant, bright, sparkling, dazzling, splendid; gleaming, coruscating, glittering, glowing, radiant, beaming, blazing; luminous, lustrous, lambent. **—Ant.** dull, lusterless, lackluster, gray, somber, dimmed, flat, mat.

respond *v.* **1.** reply, answer, give answer, speak up; rejoin. **2.** react, act in response, reply; recognize, acknowledge.

response *n.* **1.** answer, reply; rebuttal, counterstatement, countercharge; retort, return, rejoinder, riposte, comeback. **2.**

reaction, impression, acknowledgment, feedback. —**Syn. Study. 1** See ANSWER. —**Ant. 1** query, question. **2** proposal, proposition.

responsibility *n.* **1.** liability; accountability, answerability, blame, burden, culpability. **2.** charge, trust, function, task, burden, obligation, duty, order. **3.** dependability, reliability, trustworthiness, ability to come through. —**Ant. 3** unreliability, undependability, untrustworthiness.

responsible *adj.* **1.** accountable, duty-bound, liable, answerable, under obligation. **2.** requiring maturity and ability, important, challenging, demanding; administrative, executive. **3.** liable to be called to account, culpable, guilty, at fault. **4.** conscientious, reliable, dependable, trustworthy, creditable; capable, mature, self-assured, adult, of age. —**Ant. 1, 2, 4** irresponsible. **1** unaccountable, under no obligation. **4** unconscientious, immature, unreliable, undependable, untrustworthy.

responsive *adj.* reactive, retaliative, retaliatory, sharp, quick to answer, alive, awake; susceptible, impressionable, sensitive, sympathetic, compassionate, understanding, receptive, aware of. —**Ant.** unresponsive, apathetic, silent; slow to respond; impassive, dead, insensitive, unsympathetic.

rest[1] *n.* **1.** relief from work or exertion, respite, break, recess, pause, lull, intermission, interruption, suspension, quiet spell, breathing spell; *Informal* breather; vacation, holiday; ease, relaxation, leisure; peace, quiet, stillness; sleep, slumber, hibernation; bed rest, nap, siesta, *Slang* snooze, forty winks. **2.** death, one's final peace, repose, the grave, demise, end, departure, decease, cessation. **3.** state of motionlessness, standstill, halt, stop. **4.** supporting device, holder, support, prop, base, stand, platform, trivet. —*v.* **5.** relax, take one's ease, be at ease, take time out, take a breather, pause, let up; settle down, be quiet, be at peace; lie down; *Informal* cool one's feet, recline, loll, repose; sleep; give rest to, ease, laze, lounge, loaf. **6.** come to a standstill; stand, lie, be, remain. **7.** set down, deposit, set, place, lay; lean, prop. **8.** be founded, be based, depend, rely, hang, hinge; be found, reside, be, exist, lie. —**Ant. 1** unrest, restlessness; work, toil, activity, bustle, exertion, stir, excitement, disquiet.

rest[2] *n.* **1.** remains, remainder, remaining part, complement, that which is left, balance, that which remains, remnant, residue, residuum, the others; scraps, leftovers. —*v.* **2.** remain, go on being, continue to be, keep, stay.

restaurant *n.* café, dining room, lunchroom, luncheonette, cafeteria, diner, brasserie, bistro, steak house, chop house, coffeehouse, grillroom, tearoom; *Slang* beanery, hashhouse, eatery; *German* Rathskeller.

restful *adj.* relaxed, comfortable, giving rest, soothing, full of rest; unagitated, undisturbed, peaceful, tranquil, serene, calm, placid, quiet, pacific. —**Ant.** unrestful, unrelaxed, uncomfortable; agitated, disturbing, busy.

restitution *n.* redress, satisfaction, atonement, amends, reparation, remuneration, compensation, recompense, indemnification, indemnity, reimbursement, requital, repayment, paying back, restoral, restoration, reinstatement; *Law* replevin, replevy. —**Syn. Study.** See REDRESS.

restless *adj.* **1.** restive, wakeful, sleepless, insomniac, fitful, awake, unquiet; agitated, uneasy, disquieted, ill at ease, uncomfortable; nervous, jittery, jumpy, fidgety, worried, fretful, anxious, high-strung, hyperactive, excitable, impatient, *Slang* jiggy. **2.** always in motion, never at rest, on the go, on the move, transient, incessant, unsettled. —**Ant. 1** restful, quiet, undisturbed, easy, comfortable, relaxed, carefree.

restore *v.* **1.** bring back, get back, recoup, recover, retrieve, rescue, reclaim; reinstate, reestablish, reinstall; recreate. **2.** reconstruct, rebuild, recondition, rehabilitate, refurbish, convert, renew, renovate, remodel, make over, do over, fix, mend, repair, patch up, retouch, touch up. **3.** bring back to health, bring round, rally, pull through, make well, rehabilitate, set on one's feet; strengthen, energize, stimulate, exhilarate, reinvigorate, revitalize, reanimate, revive, revivify, resuscitate, refresh; cure, remedy, heal, treat, medicate, dose. **4.** put back, reinstate, reinstitute, reestablish, reinstall; return, bring back, give back. —**Syn. Study. 2** See RENEW.

restrain *v.* keep under control, suppress, contain, withhold, hold back, inhibit, temper, chasten, restrict, limit, check, curb, bridle, arrest, muzzle, gag, constrain, hold, prevent, curtail, stop; bind, shackle, fetter, trammel, pinion, harness, tether, leash; handicap. —**Syn. Study.** See CHECK.

restrict *v.* confine, constrain, restrain, suppress, hold back, check, curb, impede, frustrate, thwart, squelch, crimp, cramp, hamper, obstruct, inhibit, prevent; keep within limits, limit, hem in, hold, circumscribe; narrow, constrict, straiten.

restriction *n.* **1.** curbing, limitation, control, restraint, regulation. **2.** rule, regulation, provision, proviso, condition, stipulation, qualification, reservation, consideration, requirement.

result *v.* **1.** arise, ensue, follow; eventuate, happen, stem, owe to, derive, originate, turn out, issue, spring. **2.** culminate, wind up, end up, pan out. —*n.* **3.** finding, decision, verdict, opinion, judgment, determination, resolution, solution, report; consequence, outcome, effect, upshot, eventuality, reaction, development, product, aftereffect, aftermath, outgrowth, sequel, fruit, issue. **—Syn. Study. 1** See FOLLOW. **3** See EFFECT. **—Ant. 1** originate, prompt. **3** cause, determinant; antecedent, origin, source, seed, root.

resume *v.* take up again, begin again, go on, go on with, proceed, continue, recommence, reembark, reestablish.

résumé *n.* **1.** summary, summation, epitome, summing-up, abstract, synopsis, digest, abridgment, condensation, précis, brief. **2.** work history, curriculum vitae, CV, biography, *Informal* bio.

resurgence *n.* revival, appearing again, rising again, rebirth, renaissance, renewal, rejuvenation, recrudescence, return, renascence, reemergence. **—Ant.** passing away, decline, fading.

retain *v.* keep, hold, hold on to, hang on to, maintain, keep possession of, possess, grasp, absorb, reserve, withhold; keep in mind, bear in mind, commit to memory, memorize, fix in the mind, remember, recall, recollect, call to mind; have at one's fingertips. **—Syn. Study.** See KEEP. **—Ant.** discard, lose, surrender, relinquish, abandon.

retaliate *v.* counter, reciprocate, take retribution, return like for like, repay in the same coin, give measure for measure, give one a dose of his own medicine, exact one's pound of flesh; return, repay, requite, return the compliment; pay back, pay off, avenge, revenge, take revenge, take vengeance.

retard *v.* slow up, slow down, impede, delay the progress of, detain, check, block, obstruct, clog, fetter, hamper, hinder, baffle, inhibit, arrest, prevent; delay, hold up, hold back, prolong, draw out, drag, slacken, decelerate, brake. **—Ant.** speed, speed up, accelerate, expedite, quicken, hasten, rush; advance, further.

retarded *adj.* backward, disabled, dull, unsound, handicapped, simpleminded, slow, simple, subnormal, mentally defective, slow-witted; moronic, imbecilic, idiotic, mongoloid.

reticent *adj.* taciturn, quiet, uncommunicative, silent, sparing of words, closemouthed, tight-lipped; reserved, retiring, shy, withdrawn, diffident, self-contained, restrained, subdued, closed. **—Ant.** voluble, talkative, communicative, unreserved, expansive, inclined to speak freely, candid, frank, open, plain.

retinue *n.* entourage, train, suite, following, convoy, attendance, court; attendants, retainers, followers, associates, courtiers; employees, personnel, staff, hired help.

retire *v.* **1.** go away, betake oneself, depart, retreat, withdraw, remove, resort. **2.** go to bed, turn in, go to sleep, lie down to rest, call it a day; *Informal* hit the sack, hit the hay, flake out. **3.** withdraw from public life or business, give up office, resign, remove from active service, secede, abdicate, drop out. **—Ant. 2** get up, arise, stay up; wake up, awaken. **3** join, sign on, enlist.

retiring *adj.* withdrawn, self-effacing, uncommunicative, unsocial, reticent, quiet; shy, diffident, bashful, modest, demure, shrinking, meek, sheepish, timid, timorous; unassuming, inconspicuous, unassertive, humble, unpretentious; reserved, self-contained. **—Ant.** outgoing, gregarious, sociable, bold, brazen, brassy, forward, audacious, *Informal* pushy.

retort *v.* **1.** reply sharply, counter, return, rejoin, rebut; give answer, say, respond, reply, answer, come back with, fire back. —*n.* **2.** sharp reply, pointed answer, counterblast, rebuttal, quip, rejoinder, witty reply, riposte, quick response, comeback. **—Syn. Study. 2** See ANSWER.

retract *v.* **1.** withdraw, take back, recant, recall, rescind, revoke, repeal, reverse, abnegate, abrogate, repudiate, disavow, disown, disclaim, deny, abjure, renounce, forswear. **2.** draw back, pull back, peel back, draw in, recede, retreat, withdraw, recoil; reel in. **—Ant. 1** offer, proffer. **2** poke out, protrude.

retreat *n.* **1.** strategic withdrawal, falling back, pulling back, backing out, retirement, evacuation, flight, departure, getaway, escape. **2.** withdrawal, retirement, seclusion, solitude, isolation, immurement, reclusion; hibernation, rustication. **3.** place of seclusion, privacy, or refuge; resort, haunt, refuge, hideaway, asylum, sanctum, sanctuary, den, haven, shelter, harbor, port. —*v.* **4.** withdraw, retire, fall back, move back, fall to the rear, draw back, back away, recoil, shy away, shrink, make a retreat, depart, go, leave, make a getaway, escape, turn tail, make oneself scarce; flee, abscond, bolt, take flight. **—Ant. 1** advance, charge. **2** entrance; participation. **4** advance, move forward, rush to, meet head on, engage.

retrench *v.* cut back, cut down, economize, cut costs, conserve, tighten one's belt, scrimp, scrape, reduce, curtail, slash, reduce expenses, pinch pennies,

Slang put the squeeze on. **—Ant.** fritter away, run through, squander, waste.

retribution *n.* requital, retaliation, justice, satisfaction, redress, amends, restitution, return, reparation, reciprocation, recrimination, reprisal, penalty, punishment, reward; recompense, vengeance, revenge, an eye for an eye and a tooth for a tooth, measure for measure, vindication, just deserts. **—Syn. Study.** See REVENGE.

retrieve *v.* recover, regain, get again, get back, get back again, find again, recoup, reclaim, repossess, redeem, ransom, recapture, rescue, salvage; fetch, go and get, snag, find and fetch; *Hunting* find and bring back game.

retrospect *n.* contemplation of time past, review, retrospection, remembrance, reminiscence, flashback, looking backward; second thought, reconsideration, afterthought, hindsight.

return *v.* **1.** come back, go back, reappear, recur. **2.** send back, bring back, put back, restore; reinstate, reinstall, reestablish, reseat. **3.** give back, repay, give in recompense, give in turn, requite, reciprocate. **4.** repay, yield, provide, earn, produce, be profitable, give interest, render. **5.** announce, hand down, come to, render. **—***n.* **6.** returning, coming back, homecoming, arrival, advent; reinstatement, restoral, reestablishment, restoration, recovery, retrieval; putting back. **7.** returning, recurrence, reappearance, reversion, happening again. **8.** profit, income, revenue, earnings, proceeds, yield, interest, gain, reward, advantage, benefit, compensation, gross, net. **—Ant. 1** depart, leave, go away, disappear. **2** retain, keep, hold, withhold; remove. **4** lose, be unprofitable. **6** departure, leaving, removal.

reveal *v.* make known, divulge, give out, disclose, impart, unearth, bare, lay bare, bring to light, unmask, unveil, expose, uncover, make public; publish, come out with, let out, betray, give the lowdown, give inside information, point out; lay open to view, display, show, exhibit; manifest, evidence, unfold. **—Ant.** conceal, hide, keep secret, veil, mask, cover.

revel *v.* **1.** take great pleasure, derive pleasure from, rejoice, take delight, delight, enjoy, relish; indulge, wallow in, bask in, be in seventh heaven. **2.** make merry, indulge in festivities, celebrate, take one's pleasure, *Informal* paint the town red; carouse, roister, have one's fling, go on a spree; frolic, gambol, romp, caper, skylark.

revelation *n.* **1.** disclosure, divulgation, divulgence, divulgement; confession, admission; bombshell, shocker, eyeopener, exposure, exposé; discovery, unveiling. **2.** vision, apocalypse, prophecy, revelatory writing. **—Ant. 1** coverup, concealment, veiling, smoke-screen.

revelry *n.* boisterousness, boisterous festivity, reveling, merrymaking, merriment, celebrating, rejoicing, celebration, jollity, jollification, conviviality, exultation, festival, carnival, jamboree; celebrating; carousal, roistering, high jinks, spree.

revenge *v.* **1.** inflict punishment in return for a wrong done, exact expiation, take vengeance for, take revenge, avenge; wreak one's vengeance, have one's revenge, make reprisal for, vindicate, take an eye for an eye, give tit for tat, return like for like, undertake a vendetta, demand one's pound of flesh; reciprocate, retaliate, requite, repay, pay back, recompense. **—***n.* **2.** vengeance, paying back, retaliation, reprisal, satisfaction, retribution, requital, repayment, eye for an eye, tooth for a tooth. **—Syn. Study.** REVENGE, VENGEANCE, REPRISAL, RETRIBUTION suggest a punishment or injury inflicted in return for one received. REVENGE is the carrying out of a bitter desire to injure another for a wrong done to oneself or to those who are close to oneself: *to plot revenge for a friend's betrayal.* VENGEANCE is usu. vindictive, furious revenge: *He swore vengeance against his enemies.* REPRISAL is used specifically in the context of warfare; it means retaliation against an enemy: *The guerrillas expected reprisals for the raid.* RETRIBUTION usu. suggests deserved punishment for some evil done: *a just retribution for wickedness.*

revenue *n.* income, salary, earnings, pay, wages, compensation, emolument, profit, return, proceeds, gains, yield, receipts, interest, remuneration; pension, allowance, annuity, subsidy; *Slang* take, pickings.

reverberate *v.* carry, echo, resound, ring, vibrate, be reflected, boom, rumble, thunder.

revere *v.* honor, treat with veneration, venerate, esteem, defer to, show honor and devotion to, reverence, look up to, show deep regard for, respectfully cherish, respect, deeply respect. **—Ant.** disrespect, dishonor; despise, scorn, disparage, mock, contemn, snap one's fingers at.

reverence *n.* deep respect, esteem, regard, honor, homage, deference, veneration, admiration, adoration, devotion, worship; awe, fear; devoutness, piety, gesture indicative of deep respect, observance; genuflection, prostration, religiosity. **—Ant.** irreverence, disrespect, disregard, scorn, contempt, dishonor; hatred.

reverie *n.* **1.** daydream, brown study,

dreamy spell. **2.** fantasy, flight of fancy, musing, daydream, dream. **3.** meditation, abstracted preoccupation, woolgathering, musing, dreamland. **4.** fantasy, fancy, extravagance, castle-building, castles in the air, castles in Spain, woolgathering, wishful thinking, quixotism, fantasticality.

reverse *adj.* **1.** turned backward, reversed, opposite, backward, converse, inverse, inverted, back, rear. —*n.* **2.** contrary, opposite, antithesis, counter, counterpart, converse, inverse. **3.** back, rear, other side, posterior, tail. **4.** reversal, change for the worse, adversity, setback, upset, disappointment, mischance, misfortune, mishap, hardship, trouble, hard times; frustration, failure, defeat. —*v.* **5.** turn around, turn over, turn upside down, turn end for end, upend, upturn, turn topsy-turvy; turn inside out, invert, transpose. **6.** change, undo, unmake, revoke, rescind, repeal, retract, recall, recant, withdraw; overrule, override, set aside, countermand, invalidate, nullify, annul, declare null and void, void, negate, cancel, abrogate. —**Ant.** **3** obverse, front. **4** advance, benefit. **6** ratify, uphold, stick to.

revert *v.* go back, return, reverse, turn back, regress, recidivate, repeat, retrogress, backslide, lapse, relapse, fall back on.

review *n.* **1.** critique, criticism, critical piece, notice, commentary, evaluation. **2.** magazine, journal. **3.** examination, reevaluation, reassessment, reconsideration, recapitulation, study, scrutiny, rehash, contemplation of past events, retrospection, reflection, survey. **4.** military inspection, presentation, formal examination, military display; parade, procession; show, exhibition, exposition, demonstration. —*v.* **5.** look at again, go over again, look over again, reevaluate, reexamine, reassess, reconsider, retrace, hash over, scrutinize, study; reiterate, run over, recapitulate; restate briefly, summarize, sum up. **6.** write a critique of, criticize, evaluate, report on, comment upon, discuss in a critical review, pass judgment on, analyze.

revile *v.* scold, berate, tongue-lash, upbraid, bawl out, castigate, vilify, denounce, disparage, deride, scorn, abuse, lash out at, reproach, rebuke; *Slang* dress down, sail into, chew out. —**Ant.** praise, extol, laud, commend.

revise *v.* correct, change, alter, modify, edit, redact, rewrite, redo, amend, blue-pencil, rectify, emend, emendate, doctor, overhaul, recast, review, tinker with, fix up, revamp; bring up to date, make an up-to-date version of, update.

revision *n.* change, alteration, modification, correction, improvement, emendation, amendment; revised version, recension, edition.

revive *v.* **1.** restore to consciousness, bring back to life, resuscitate. **2.** bring back to life, reanimate, rouse again, reawaken, infuse new life into, give new life to, refresh, freshen, renew *Informal* jump-start. **3.** present again, bring back into use, produce again, set going again, bring back into notice, make operative again, resurrect; *Slang* dig up, drag up; restage, reproduce, repeat.

revoke *v.* withdraw, take back; negate, annul, nullify, invalidate, vacate, void, declare null and void, cancel, abrogate, abolish, expunge, erase, quash, do away with; repeal, rescind, reverse, recall, call back, retract; override, overrule, countermand, set aside, disallow, dismiss, abjure, renounce, disclaim, repudiate. —**Ant.** restore, give, maintain, grant; authorize, validate.

revolt *v.* **1.** rise, rebel, rise up, mutiny. **2.** disgust, repel, repulse, offend, go against, sicken, make one sick, nauseate, turn the stomach; make the flesh crawl, horrify, appall, shock, distress, *Slang* turn one off. —*n.* **3.** rebellion, active resistance against authority, insurrection, insurgency, uprising, coup, putsch, revolution, opposition, disorder, mutiny, sedition, dissent, factiousness. —**Ant.** **1** give allegiance to, give loyalty to, support, obey, bow, submit to. **2** attract, lure; delight, amuse, please, fascinate.

revolting *adj.* disgusting, repulsive, repellent, repugnant, disagreeable, offensive, objectionable, distasteful, obnoxious, nasty, vile, foul, odious, invidious, horrid, shocking, appalling, horrible, horrific, grim, frightful, dreadful, sickening, nauseating, abhorrent, abominable, loathsome, hateful; malodorous, noxious, noisome, stinking. —**Ant.** pleasant, agreeable, attractive, delightful, charming, unobjectionable; sweet-smelling, fragrant.

revolution *n.* **1.** complete change, radical new departure, basic reformation, big shift. **2.** overthrow of an established regime, replacement of an old regime, coup d'état, coup, putsch. **3.** (*variously*) revolutionary war, armed struggle, war of national liberation, insurrection, uprising, rising, rebellion, revolt, mutiny. **4.** revolving, circling, movement in an orbit, circumvolution, circumrotation. **5.** single turn, rotation, gyration. —**Ant.** **1** reaction, retrogression, regression. **2, 3** counterrevolution, countercoup, reaction, restoration, backlash.

revolutionary *adj.* **1.** opposed to the established order, revolutionist, radical, extremist, insurrectionary, insurgent, rebellious, mutinous, subversive, seditious, dissenting. **2.** radically innovative, fundamentally novel, unprecedented, superadvanced. **—Ant. 1** reactionary, counterrevolutionary; loyalist, conservative. **2** old, usual.

revolve *v.* move in orbit, go around, circle, rotate, circumrotate, turn, gyrate, wheel, twist, spin. **—Syn. Study.** See TURN.

revulsion *n.* strong disgust, loathing, repugnance, aversion, distaste, abhorrence, detestation. **—Ant.** attraction, fascination, relish, taste.

reward *n.* **1.** prize, compensation, recompense, payment, bounty, guerdon, remuneration, quid pro quo, award, consideration, premium, bonus; token of appreciation, deserts, wages, due, reckoning, what is coming to one. *—v.* **2.** repay, requite, recompense, compensate, remunerate, take care of. **—Ant. 1** penalty, fine, damages, punishment. **2** punish, penalize.

rhapsodic *adj.* ecstatic, elated, thrilled, transported, rapturous, overjoyed, excited, walking on air, blissful, in seventh heaven, exhilarated, on cloud nine, beside oneself, beaming, delirious. **—Ant.** sad, morose, depressed, disenchanted.

rhetoric *n.* **1.** art of speaking or writing, rules of composition, classic style. **2.** effective use of formal language, verbal communication, elocution, discourse, oratory, eloquence, high style, mannered language. **3.** eloquence, magniloquence, grandiloquence, flamboyance, figures of speech, hyperbole, euphuism, empty phrases, fustian, *Slang* hot air, wind, hocus-pocus, hokum, hooey, bunkum, bunk.

rhetorical *adj.* **1.** flamboyant, high-flown, bombastic, grandiloquent, oratorical, eloquent, showy, inflated, windy, grandiose, magniloquent, silver-tongued, extravagant, high-sounding, ornate, aureate, florid, purple, flowery, embellished, euphuistic. **2.** used for stylistic effect, expressive, decorative, ornamental. **3.** stylistic, elocutionary. **4.** verbal, linguistic, discursive; disputative, disputatious, argumentative.

rhythm *n.* fluctuation, recurrence, natural flow, recurrent alternation, flow pattern, time, movement, meter, measure, accent, beat, pulse, pulsation, throb, stress, cadence, number, rhythmic pattern, accentuation, emphasis, swing, lilt, syncopation.

ribald *adj.* bawdy, lewd, risqué, vulgar, off-color, indecent, improper, crude, rude, coarse, uncouth, earthy, unrefined, gross, shocking, lascivious, licentious, libidinous, salacious, racy, wanton, rakish, raffish, prurient, suggestive.

rich *adj.* **1.** well-off, well-to-do, wealthy, affluent, flush, moneyed, on easy street, propertied, prosperous, well-heeled, *Informal* in clover. **2.** valuable, estimable, highly valued, precious, opulent, luxurious, sumptuous, splendid, prodigal, lavish, expensive, costly, fine, priceless. **3.** heavy, filling, full-bodied; sweet. **4.** intense, lush, dark, deep, bright, vivid; resonant, deep-toned, sonorous, euphonious, mellow, mellifluous. **5.** abundant, abounding. **6.** productive, fruitful, fertile, fecund, loamy, luxuriant, lush. **—Ant. 1, 5, 6** poor. **1** impoverished, destitute, penniless, indigent, impecunious, penurious, needy, poverty-stricken. **2** worthless, valueless, inexpensive, cheap. **3** bland, dull, flat. **4** weak, flat, dull; high-pitched, tinny. **5** wanting, lacking, scarce, rare, scanty, meager. **6** unproductive, unfertile, unfruitful, barren, sterile, dry.

rickety *adj.* **1.** tumbledown, shaky, unsteady, wobbly, tottering, flimsy, brokendown, deteriorated, dilapidated, decrepit. **2.** decrepit, weakjointed, feeble, frail, fragile, infirm, debilitated, weak, weakly, tottering, withered, wasted. **—Ant. 1** sturdy, durable, steady, solid, sound.

rid *v.* free, purge, clear, eliminate, remove, unburden, disburden, disencumber, disabuse, liberate. **—Ant.** burden, encumber, take on, adopt.

riddance *n.* clearing out, clearance, removal, ejection, expulsion, ouster, dislodgment; relief, deliverance, freeing. **—Ant.** encumbrance, adoption.

riddle *n.* mystery, enigma, secret; puzzle, poser, conundrum, puzzler, problem, brain twister, rebus, *Slang* stumper.

ride *v.* **1.** manage, control, handle. **2.** move, move along, travel, progress, journey; transport, drive, carry, support; move along, be supported, be carried.

rider *n.* additional clause, addition, amendment, codicil, supplement, appendage, suffix, affix, adjunct, addendum, appendix, attachment.

ridge *n.* **1.** hill, rise, crest, hillock, mound, spine, knoll, hump, bank, bluff, promontory. **2.** rib, ripple, crinkle, crimp, wrinkle, corrugation, rim, fret, bar, weal, welt, wale.

ridicule *n.* **1.** mockery, sneering, derision, derogation, disparagement, aspersion, scorn, sarcasm, taunt, jeer, gibe, snicker, ribbing, teasing, caricature, burlesque, travesty, lampoonery. *—v.* **2.** make fun of, make sport of, poke fun at, mock, mimic, imitate insultingly, laugh at, laugh to scorn, sneer at, scoff at, belittle, treat with disrespect, deride, ride, disparage, humiliate, taunt, jeer, gibe at, twit, razz, josh, guy, rib, tease, make a butt of, make sport of, play tricks on, make a monkey of, caricature, burlesque, lampoon, parody. —**Syn. Study. 2** RIDICULE, MOCK, DERIDE, TAUNT mean to make fun of a person. To RIDICULE is to make fun of, either playfully or with the intention of humiliating: *to ridicule a pretentious person.* To MOCK is to make fun of by imitating the appearance or actions of another: *She mocked the seriousness of his expression.* To DERIDE is to laugh at scornfully: *a student derided for acting silly.* To TAUNT is to call attention to something annoying or humiliating, usu. maliciously and in the presence of others: *The bully taunted the smaller boy.* —**Ant. 1, 2** praise, honor; respect. **1** homage, veneration, deference.

ridiculous *adj.* absurd, ludicrous, preposterous, asinine, nonsensical, foolish, silly, idiotic, fatuous, inane, irrational, destitute of reason, unreasonable, senseless, frivolous; incredible, astonishing, fantastic, outlandish, queer, odd, grotesque, bizarre, laughable, comical, funny, droll, amusing; hysterical, farcical, crazy, *Slang* nutty, screwy, screwball. —**Syn. Study.** See ABSURD.

rife *adj.* **1.** teeming, swarming, alive with, thick, populous, crowded, packed, chockfull, *Informal* plumbfull; dense, close, solid, studded. **2.** prevalent, general, prevailing, predominant; extensive, universal, widespread, common, far-reaching; epidemic, pandemic.

riffraff *n.* mob, herd, masses, rabble, *French* canaille, crowd, peasantry, rank and file, proletariat, *Slang* proles, commonalty, lumpen proletariat; trash, scum, dregs, vermin, *Slang* the great unwashed. —**Ant.** gentry, upper crust, swells, bigwigs, high muck-a-mucks.

rifle *v.* search and rob, rob, plunder, go through, pillage, ransack, ravage, burglarize, sack, loot, despoil, spoliate.

rift *n.* **1.** cleft, split, crack, fissure, fracture, break, chink, breach, rent, cut, slit, aperture, gash, rupture; chasm, crevice, gap, cranny, fault, crevasse, abyss, gulch, gully, gulf, gorge, ravine. **2.** division, breach, rupture, break, breakup, misunderstanding, disagreement, quarrel, falling out.

right *adj.* **1.** good, exemplary, proper, decent, morally excellent, virtuous, nice, fitting, seemly, rightminded, moral, upright, righteous, honest, aboveboard, ethical, scrupulous, honorable, unimpeachable, correct, punctilious, meet, square, fair and square, even-handed; equitable, just, fair. **2.** valid, allowable, admissible, satisfactory; correct, accurate, free from error, unmistaken, perfect, infallible, exact, precise, true, factual, veracious, veridical, truthful. **3.** rational, normal, regular, sane, sound, reasonable. **4.** most appropriate, suitable, seemly, fitting, proper, becoming; desirable, favorable, preferable, convenient, opportune, advantageous, ideal. **5.** actual, genuine, real, authentic; definite, clear-cut, certain; unquestionable, irrefutable, undisputed, incontestable; rightful, lawful, legal, licit, legitimate, valid. —*n.* **6.** just claim, legal title, legal claim, due, moral claim, justification, birthright, inheritance; privilege, prerogative, liberty, power, license, freedom, grant, permission, sanction; authority, legal power, authorization, jurisdiction. **7.** good, virtue, goodness, righteousness, moral excellence, good behavior, good actions, morality, morals; integrity, honor, nobleness, uprightness, propriety, rectitude, probity; what ought to be, what should be. **8.** Often **rights** ownership, deed, proprietorship, authorization, warrant, interest in property. —*adv.* **9.** directly, promptly, straight, straightaway, completely. **10.** correctly, appropriately, suitably, properly, accurately, perfectly; exactly, precisely, just. **11.** well, favorably, satisfactorily, *Informal* O.K. **12.** immediately, at once, directly, presently, in a moment. —*v.* **13.** set upright, stand up, restore to the proper position. **14.** correct, put right, amend, solve, remedy, put in order; vindicate, redress, recompense, make up for, make restitution for. —**Ant. 1, 2, 4, 5, 7, 10, 11** wrong. **1** bad, foul, sinful, iniquitous, nefarious, improper, indecent, unvirtuous, immoral; dishonest, unethical, unscrupulous, dishonorable; unjust, unfair, false, illegitimate. **2** unsatisfactory; incorrect, inaccurate, mistaken, invalid, erroneous, erring, imperfect, inexact, fallacious, untrue, unfactual, false, untruthful. **3** irrational, abnormal, insane, unsound. **4** inappropriate, unsuitable, unseemly, unfitting, unbecoming; undesirable, unfavorable, inconvenient, disadvantageous. **5** false, fake, phony, sham, counterfeit, fraudulent; indefinite, uncertain, questionable, contestable, unlawful, illegal, illicit, illegitimate. **7** evil, badness, venality, villainy, sinfulness, corruption, transgression, iniquity, bad behavior, immorality; dishonor, impropriety. **9** indirectly, circuitously, slowly; incompletely. **10** incorrectly, improperly; inaccurately, imperfectly. **11** badly, unfavorably, poorly. **13** set down, put down; make crooked, topple.

righteous *adj.* moral, honorable, ethical, honest, upright, elevated, just, fair, equitable, good; godly, pious, devout, God-fearing, religious, reverent, holy, spiritual, pure in heart; virtuous, chaste, incorrupt, unsullied, blameless, innocent. —**Ant.** unrighteous, immoral, bad, evil, wicked, sinful, villainous, dishonorable, disreputable, dishonest, corrupt, unscrupulous, unprincipled, false, iniquitous, unjust, unfair; ungodly, irreligious, unholy, irreverent, unvirtuous.

rightful *adj.* having a right, having a just claim, deserving, right, true, proper, correct, legitimate, legal, lawful, held by a just or legal claim, allowed, sanctioned, authorized, valid, constitutional, designated, prescribed, inalienable, deserved, appropriate, fitting, condign. **—Ant.** unrightful, untrue, improper, unjust, incorrect, illegitimate, illegal, unlawful, usurping.

rigid *adj.* **1.** stiff, unyielding, inflexible, unpliant, unbending, inelastic, fixed, hard, set, firm, tense, taut; wooden. **2.** strict, stringent, hard, stern, severe, harsh, austere, sharp, rigorous, exacting; stubborn, unrelenting, obdurate, uncompromising, inflexible, unbending, unyielding, strong, firm, fixed, set, cut and dried, clear-cut; strait-laced, formal, puritanical. **—Syn. Study. 2** See STRICT. **—Ant. 1, 2** flexible, yielding. **1** pliant, supple, limber, bending, mobile, elastic, plastic. **2** lenient, soft, tolerant, indulgent, merciful, lax; informal.

rigorous *adj.* **1.** demanding, challenging, trying, stern, austere, harsh, exacting, tough, very harsh, severe, strict, stringent, rigid. **2.** exact, accurate, correct, precise, scrupulous, meticulous, punctilious. **—Syn. Study. 1** See STRICT.

rile *v.* irritate, pique, vex, annoy, irk, provoke, gall, chafe, miff, nettle, gripe, plague, aggravate, bother, roil, peeve; *Slang* give someone a pain, get someone's goat, get in someone's hair, rub one the wrong way. **—Ant.** soothe, calm, cool, pacify, placate.

rim *n.* edge, outer edge, border, margin, side; brim, verge, brink, ledge, lip. **—Syn. Study.** RIM, BRIM refer to the boundary of a circular or curved area. A RIM is a line or surface bounding such an area, an edge or border: *the rim of a glass.* BRIM usu. means the inside of the rim, at the top of a hollow object (except of a hat), and is used particularly when the object contains something: *The cup was filled to the brim.* **—Ant.** core, center, hub, inside.

ring[1] *n.* **1.** circle, perimeter, circumference, loop, circuit, hoop; cordon. **2.** gang, band, party, cabal, syndicate, combine, league, cartel, federation, bloc. *—v.* **3.** draw a ring around, circle, circumscribe. **4.** surround, encircle, encompass; enclose, seal off; blockade, besiege.

ring[2] *v.* **1.** sound, resound, reverberate, vibrate, fill the air, tintinnabulate, chime, peal, clang, knell, toll, jingle, jangle, tinkle; strike. **2.** announce, make known, broadcast, proclaim, herald; call, summon, signal, buzz. **3.** reverberate, resound, echo. *—n.* **4.** ringing sound, resonance, reverberation, tintinnabulation, chime, peal, clang, ringing, striking, vibration, toll, knell, tinkle, ting-a-ling. **5.** quality, sound, tone, aura.

riot *n.* **1.** public disturbance, disorder, violence, breach of the peace, lawlessness; tumult, strife, turbulence, outburst, turmoil, trouble, Donnybrook, rumpus, melee, fracas, commotion, uproar, pandemonium, confusion; revolt, rebellion, insurrection, uprising. *—v.* **2.** break the peace, raise an uproar, be violent, kick up a row, act up, run amok, run riot, rage, rampage, take the law into one's own hands, rebel, resist, revolt, mutiny, rise in arms, arise.

rip *v.* **1.** tear, rend, slash, rive, cleave, rupture, shred, cut apart. **2.** tear open, split, burst, sever. *—n.* **3.** tear, rent, rent made by ripping, split, cut, slash, laceration, rift, incision, cleavage, fracture, fissure, slit, gap.

ripe *adj.* **1.** fully grown, fully developed, mature, maturated; mellow, seasoned. **2.** come, due; timely; ideal, perfect; consummate, complete, accomplished, finished; fully prepared, fit, primed, ready. **—Ant. 1** unripe, unready, underdeveloped, undeveloped, immature, green, raw, unseasoned. **2** incomplete, unaccomplished, unprepared, unfit, untimely, unready.

rise *v.* **1.** get up, stand, arise; get out of bed, meet the day. **2.** arise in opposition, rebel, revolt, resist, mutiny; go to war, take up arms; take the law into one's own hands; disobey, defy; strike, stand up, meet, face. **3.** go up, move upward, ascend, climb; mount, soar, spire, tower; extend directly upward, slope upward. **4.** increase, become greater, rocket, spire, surge, become larger, swell, burgeon, become louder. **5.** reach a higher level or rank, rise in the world, work one's way up, be successful; climb, go up, succeed, prosper, thrive, flourish. **6.** soar, surge, mount, grow, improve, lift, elevate, balloon. *—n.* **7.** rising, advance; progress, advancement, headway; growth, increase in rank, climb. **8.** increase, upswing, march; addition, gain, augmentation, enlargement, expansion, extension. **—Ant. 1, 3–7** fall. **1** sit, sit down; lie down, retire. **3–6** sink, descend, drop, plunge. **4** decrease, decline, shrink, lessen, abate. **6** descent. **8** decrease, drop, plunge, decline, lessening, contraction, downturn.

risk *n.* **1.** hazard, peril, danger, imperilment, endangerment, jeopardy; chance, venture, speculation, gamble, uncertainty. —*v.* **2.** endanger, jeopardize, put in jeopardy, imperil, put in peril. **3.** take the chance of, run the chance of; venture, hazard, speculate, dare, try one's luck, tempt Providence, have a fling at.

risky *adj.* hazardous, perilous, dangerous, fraught with danger, unsafe, unprotected, precarious, insecure, daring, venturesome, adventurous, daredevil; uncertain, ticklish, chancy, hit or miss, haphazard. **—Ant.** safe, sure, secure, certain.

risqué *adj.* off-color, improper, ribald, bawdy, indecorous, indecent; indelicate, immodest, immoral; racy, spicy, suggestive, daring, salacious, lascivious, lewd, licentious, offensive, vulgar, coarse, gross, dirty, obscene, smutty, pornographic, blue.

rite *n.* formal act or procedure, formality, ceremony, ceremonial, liturgy, ritual, service; solemnity, observance.

ritzy *adj.* chic, elegant, stylish, luxurious, sumptuous; *Slang* classy, swank, high-class, posh, high-toned, tony, snazzy, spiffy, sharp. **—Ant.** *Slang* crummy, dumpy, schlocky, tatty.

rival *n.* **1.** competitor, contestant, disputant, contender, opponent, adversary, antagonist, foe, enemy. —*adj.* **2.** contending, competing, adversary, opposing. —*v.* **3.** compete with, contend with, try to win from, clash with, do battle with, fight, strive. **4.** be an equal of, equal, be a match for, match, touch, approach; excel, surpass, outdo, eclipse, outshine. **—Ant. 1** ally, friend; associate, helper, assistant, supporter, champion, abettor, backer. **2** allied, noncompeting. **3** aid, assist, help, support, back.

road *n.* way, thoroughfare, boulevard, avenue, street, route, roadway, parkway, expressway, highway, turnpike, freeway, throughway, byway, trail, lane, path.

roam *v.* travel, ramble, rove, range, meander, jaunt, gad, stray, gallivant, wander, stroll, traipse, tramp, peregrinate, divagate, drift.

roar *v.* **1.** howl, bellow, bay, growl, cry; thunder, boom, resound; shout, scream, bawl, cry aloud, yell, vociferate, bluster, clamor. **2.** laugh loudly, guffaw; howl. —*n.* **3.** cry, howl, bellow, bay, growl, grunt, snort; yell, outcry, bawl, shout, shriek, scream, bluster, clamor, rumble, boom, uproar, outburst, thunder, roll, racket, blare, din, noise.

rob *v.* hold up, stick up, raid; (*loosely*) steal from, thieve, burgle, burglarize, ransack, pillage, pilfer, sack, forage, despoil, plunder, loot, *Slang* heist; filch, steal, seize, purloin, rifle, lift, carry off, appropriate, help oneself to; skin, swindle, cheat, bamboozle, bilk, fleece, embezzle.

robber *n.* thief, bandit, outlaw, crook, brigand; (*variously*) burglar, stickup-man, second-story man, yegg, embezzler, con man, sharper, swindler, larcenist, plunderer, highwayman, marauder, raider, pirate, buccaneer, despoiler, forager, pickpocket, rustler. **—Syn. Study.** See THIEF.

robe *n.* gown; (*loosely*) dress, garment, costume, vestment, habit; (*variously*) dressing gown, bathrobe, housecoat, negligee, smock, kimono, duster, lounging robe.

robust *adj.* hale, hardy, strong, tough, powerful, mighty, potent, forceful, puissant; healthy, well, wholesome, sound, healthful, hearty, fit, in fine fettle, able-bodied, rugged, sturdy, firm, athletic; virile, muscular, brawny, sinewy, wiry, husky, strapping; vigorous, lusty, stalwart, stout, staunch, energetic, active. **—Ant.** weak, unhealthy, infirm, unsound, unfit, sickly, frail, feeble, delicate, fragile, puny, anemic, slender, thin, emaciated.

rock[1] *v.* **1.** sway to and fro, move backward and forward, move from side to side; swing, toss, roll, pitch, flounder; wobble, totter, bob, quake, shake, convulse, agitate; undulate, oscillate. **2.** shake, jar, convulse; disturb, upset, stun. —*n.* **3.** rocking, undulation, sway; wobbling, tottering, bobbing; shaking; convulsion.

rock[2] *n.* stone, boulder; (*variously*) crag, cliff, reef; pebble, flint; gravel, limestone, marble.

rod *n.* **1.** stick, staff; (*variously*) wand, baton, scepter, mace, cane, crook, alpenstock, caduceus, stanchion, stake, pale, pole, swagger stick. **2.** stick, cudgel; (*variously*) switch, birch, cane, rattan, lash, whip, scourge; (*loosely*) punishment, penalty, retribution.

rogue *n.* dishonest person, deceiver, fraud, mountebank, rotter, rascal, scoundrel, rapscallion, cur, good-for-nothing, wretch, knave, blackguard, villain, snake in the grass, bad man, bounder, evildoer, malefactor, miscreant, reprobate, *Archaic* varlet; hellion, mischief-maker; scalawag, scamp, scapegrace, devil. **—Syn. Study.** See KNAVE.

role *n.* **1.** character, part, characterization, impersonation, portrayal, representation, persona, personification; pose, posture, guise. **2.** capacity, function, duty, service, chore, task, assignment, post; job, work.

roll *v.* **1.** turn over and over; turn, revolve, rotate, gyrate; spin, go round, swirl, whirl; wheel, swing, flip, turn. **2.** wheel, coast; flow, swell, billow, surge.

3. boom, crack, rumble, thunder, roar, sound, resound, reverberate, echo. **4.** wind, curl, coil, loop, twist, twirl, furl, knot, entwine; form into a ball. **5.** rock, undulate, toss, tumble, tumble about; lurch, pitch, reel, sway. *—n.* **6.** rolling, turning, tumble, toss, throw; rocking, tumbling, tossing, undulation. **7.** scroll, tube, cylinder, spool, reel. **8.** list, catalog, inventory, roster, muster, schedule. **9.** rumble, rumbling, boom, booming, thunder, drumming, drumbeat, reverberation. **—Syn. Study. 8** See LIST.

rollicking *adj.* joyous, happy, gay, merry, cheerful, lighthearted, gleeful, mirthful, hearty, rip-roaring, jolly, jovial, jocular, jocund, hysterical, devil-may-care; lively, spirited, free and easy, exuberant, full of play, frolicsome, frolicking, playful, romping, gamboling, sprightly, bright, sparkling, sunny. **—Ant.** joyless, unhappy, sad, sorrowful, sorry, distressing, depressing, cheerless, mirthless; dull, somber, gloomy.

romance *n.* **1.** love story; novel, *Slang* bodice ripper; fiction, melodrama, made-up fanciful story, fairy tale, fantasy. **2.** love affair, affair of the heart, relationship, affair, attachment; amour, idyll, tender passion; courtship, flirtation. **3.** invention, wishful thinking, self-delusion, imagination, illusion, flight of fancy; exaggeration, concoction, fiction, fabrication; *Informal* tall story, fish story, cock-and-bull story, moonshine, bosh. **4.** romantic quality, exoticism, appealing quality, allure, pull, fascination, call.

romantic *adj.* **1.** concerning romance, conducive to romance, idyllic, sentimental; melodramatic. **2.** loving, amorous, ardent, enamored, passionate, impassioned, warmhearted, fond, devoted; sentimental, tender, sensitive; ardent, fervent; *Informal* mushy, soppy. **3.** high-flown, idealized, impractical, improbable, rhapsodical; unreal, unrealistic, idealistic, utopian, flighty, whimsical, extravagant, fanciful, imaginary, dreamy, visionary; fantastic, preposterous, quixotic. **—Ant. 1–3** unromantic. **1** realistic, prosaic, uninspiring. **2** unloving, unimpassioned, dispassionate, coldhearted; unsentimental, insensitive; unaffectionate.

Romeo *n.* lover, Lothario, Lochinvar, Don Juan, Casanova, paramour, beau, boyfriend, wooer, swain, gallant, inamorato, cavalier, sheik.

romp *v.* play in a lively manner, frolic, run around, frisk, rollick, caper, gambol, disport, disport oneself, sport, jump about, skip, hop, cut up.

room *n.* **1.** chamber, cubicle, compartment; lodging, lodging place. **2.** space, extent, range, scope, expanse, territory, area, volume, elbow room. **3.** chance, provision, leeway, allowance, margin.

roomy *adj.* spacious, capacious, generous, commodious, sizable, ample, expansive; wide, long, lengthy, broad, extensive, large, vast, immense, big, huge, boundless, unlimited. **—Ant.** small, tiny, uncomfortable, closed-in, cramped; short; bounded, limited, confined.

root[1] *n.* **1.** underground part, stem, embedded part, bulb, tubes; radicle, radix; hidden base; lower part, bottom. **2.** basic part, basic element, fundamental, essential element, most important part, base, foundation. **3.** origin, source, spring, derivation, fount, fountain, fountainhead, foundation, basis, ground; starting point, motive, prime mover, determining condition, reason, rationale; rise, mainspring, occasion, inception, beginning, commencement, start. *—v.* **4.** fix, set, establish; fasten, stick, nail, bind.

root[2] *v.* cheer on, cheer, encourage, shout for, stick up for, bolster, boost, pull for, applaud, hail, acclaim, clap; support, back, second.

roster *n.* muster, roll, list, register, listing, slate, panel, catalog, record, schedule, posting, agenda, docket, cadre.

rostrum *n.* stage, platform, dais, stand, pulpit, lectern, podium, soapbox, stump.

rosy *adj.* **1.** pink, blushing, reddish, reddening, flushed, flushing, blooming, ruddy, rubicund, rubescent, florid, glowing, inflamed, high-colored. **2.** rose-colored, hopeful, cheerful, cheering, inspiriting, encouraging, promising, full of promise, reassuring, hopeful, optimistic, looking up, bright, auspicious, favorable, of good omen, propitious, felicitous; confident. **—Ant. 1** pale, pallid, ashen, gray, whitish; sickly. **2** cheerless, discouraging, unpromising, hopeless, pessimistic, inauspicious; insecure, unsure.

rot *v.* **1.** spoil, go bad, decay, decompose, putrefy, putresce, disintegrate, wither up, molder; go to pieces, fall into decay, deteriorate, degenerate, break down, crumble. **2.** pervert, debase, defile, warp, deprave; infect, poison; corrupt, pollute, contaminate, tamper with; taint, stain; mar, impair, damage, injure, harm, hurt. *—n.* **3.** rotting, decay, rottenness, dry rot, decomposition, deterioration, disintegration; putrescence, putrefaction, putridity, purulence; contamination, corruption. **4.** nonsense, tommyrot, bosh, bunk, bull, balderdash, poppycock, gobbledygook, twaddle, stuff and nonsense, moonshine, flapdoodle, inanity, absurdity, flummery, fiddle-faddle, trash, rubbish, gibberish, jabber, drivel, blather, folderol. **—Syn. Study. 1** See DECAY.

rotate *v.* **1.** move about a center, turn around on an axis, go round, turn, revolve, spin, roll, circle, reel, circulate, whirl, gyrate, twirl, twist, swirl, wheel, eddy, pirouette, pivot, swivel. **2.** alternate, change, take turns, interchange, act interchangeably; go from one to the other. **—Syn. Study. 1** See TURN.

rotten *adj.* **1.** decomposing, decomposed, decaying, decayed, putrid, putrefied, putrescent, purulent, tainted, moldering, worm-eaten, bad, rancid, fetid, reeky, foul, rank. **2.** dishonest, corrupt, deceitful, insincere, faithless, unscrupulous, dishonorable, disgraceful, contemptible, treacherous, untrustworthy, double-dealing, two-faced, devious, villainous, iniquitous, scurvy, crooked, criminal, vicious, venal, mercenary; immoral, indecent, dissolute. **3.** *Informal* very bad, base, contemptible; unpleasant, nasty, dirty, filthy, scurrilous, unforgivable. **—Ant. 1** wholesome, untainted, fresh, pure, unspoiled, good. **2** honest, scrupulous, honorable, trustworthy; moral, decent, incorruptible.

rotund *adj.* **1.** round, globular, bulbous, rounded, spherical, ball-like, circular, ring-like; ovoid, egg-shaped, ovate, curved. **2.** plump, fat, obese, full-fleshed, corpulent, fleshy, chubby, tubby, pudgy, lumpish, stout, portly, potbellied. **—Ant. 1** angular, square, edged. **2** thin, slender, slim, trim, lean, lank, lanky, skinny, gaunt, scrawny, rawboned, emaciated, angular.

roué *n.* rake, libertine, lecher, cad, bounder, profligate, seducer, debauchee, womanizer, rakehell, wanton, rip, playboy, philanderer, dallier, trifler, Don Juan, Lothario, Casanova; *Slang* wolf, skirt-chaser.

rough *adj.* **1.** coarse, unsmooth, uneven, jagged, ragged, rough-hewn, irregular, broken, craggy, unlevel, bumpy, rocky, scraggy; (*variously*) rugged, scratchy, knotty, stubbly, scaly, scabrous, chapped, gnarled. **2.** violent, rigorous, rugged; tough, violently disturbed, agitated, choppy, turbulent, turbid, roiled, tumultuous, tempestuous, stormy, raging; untamed, wild, savage, ferocious. **3.** sharp, harsh, tough, austere, stringent, severe, ungentle, hard, unfeeling, cruel, brutal; inconsiderate; extreme, drastic. **4.** boorish, rude, ill-mannered, unmannerly, ungentlemanly, uncourtly, ungenteel; unpolished, unrefined, raw, inelegant, ill-bred, ungracious, uncouth; bearish, loutish, churlish, crusty, gruff, bluff, surly, gauche, awkward, clumsy; blunt, brusque, abrupt; coarse, vulgar, indelicate, crude; callow, green. **5.** without ordinary comforts, uncomfortable, unluxurious; difficult, unpleasant, tough, rugged, hard, austere. **6.** not elaborated, unfinished, incomplete, not perfected, imperfect, crude, hastily done; quick, hasty; vague, sketchy, general, rudimentary, preliminary, approximate, not exact, inexact, imprecise. **7.** gruff, husky, raspy, rasping, hoarse, grating, jarring, raucous, strident, harsh; inharmonious, discordant, cacophonous, unmusical. *—v.* **8.** roughen, make rough, coarsen. **9.** treat violently, manhandle, push around, physically intimidate, brutalize, beat, thrash; *Slang* beat on, do a number on, knock on. **10.** indicate in rough form, prepare hastily, do roughly, draft, outline, sketch out. **—Ant. 1, 2, 4, 5, 8** smooth. **1** smooth-surfaced, regular, unbroken, level, plain, flat; soft, silky, satiny, velvety. **2** calm, easy, gentle, tender; tranquil, quiet; tamed, mild, halcyon. **3** soft, mild, kind, lenient, just, considerate. **4** polite, courteous, civil, well-mannered, mannerly, gentlemanly, courtly, genteel; polished, refined, urbane, elegant, well-bred; gracious, gentle; graceful, delicate, cultivated, sophisticated. **5** comfortable, luxurious, velvety, easy, cushy, pleasant, plush, nice. **6** elaborated, finished, well-made, complete, perfected, perfect, detailed, specific, exact, precise. **8** make smooth, smoothen, make soft, mollify, soften.

round *adj.* **1.** circular, globular, globoid, cylindrical, orbed, spherical, spheroid, ball-shaped; elliptical, oval, ovate, ovoid, egg-shaped, pear-shaped; rounded, curved. **2.** rotund, full-fleshed, obese, corpulent, fat, full-formed, plump, chubby, tubby, pudgy, stout, portly. **3.** entire, full, whole, complete, perfect; unbroken, intact, undivided; thorough, total. **4.** full and rich, sonorous, resonant, smooth, flowing, fluent; harmonious, mellifluent. *—n.* **5.** complete course, circle, series, succession, procession, progression, cycle. **6.** Often **rounds** circuit, beat, route, watch. *—v.* **7.** travel around, go around, make a circuit, skirt. **—Ant. 1** angular, rectangular, square, many-sided, polygonal. **2** slim, thin, trim, slender, skinny, lean, lank, gaunt, angular, rawboned, emaciated. **3** incomplete, broken, imperfect, divided. **4** rough, gruff, harsh, hoarse, grating, jarring, shrill, strident; inharmonious.

roundabout *adj.* indirect, meandering, labyrinthine, circuitous, sinuous, twisting, rambling, erratic, discursive, tortuous, devious, oblique, zigzag, winding, serpentine; circumlocutory, wordy; random, desultory. **—Ant.** straight, direct.

rouse *v.* **1.** awaken, wake, awake, wake up, get up, arouse, activate, call, summon; arise, stir. **2.** excite, animate, incite, prod, stir up, provoke, arouse, inflame, move, goad, stimulate, pique, instigate, foment, galvanize, spur, *Slang* turn on. —**Syn. Study. 2** See INCITE. —**Ant. 2** soothe, pacify, quell, restrain, curb.

rout *n.* **1.** disastrous defeat, total repulse, ruin, beating, drubbing, licking, disorderly retreat, disorderly flight, complete dispersal; panic, chaos, disorganization. —*v.* **2.** put to flight, scatter, throw into confusion; repel, drive off, repulse, chase away, drive away; defeat, vanquish, worst, overpower, overthrow, overcome, crush, subdue, conquer, quell; drub, lambaste, beat, thrash; *Informal* lick, trim, cream, clobber.

route *n.* **1.** course, way for passage, itinerary; pass, road for travel, passage; (*variously*) parkway, highway, thoroughfare, road, roadway, turnpike, throughway, artery, boulevard, path, track, run, tack. **2.** fixed course or territory, beat, round, circuit. —*v.* **3.** send by a particular route, forward by a specific route; direct, ship, dispatch, remit, transmit; detour.

routine *n.* **1.** regular procedure, practice, established usage, custom, ordinary way; method, system, arrangement, order, operation, formula, technique. —*adj.* **2.** customary, conventional, usual; regular, typical, normal. **3.** predictable, unexceptional, dull, habitual, boring, periodic, tedious, ordinary, run-of-the-mill. —**Ant. 2, 3** special, uncustomary, unusual, irregular, abnormal, different, exceptional, extraordinary.

rove *v.* wander, wander about, roam, ramble, travel, meander, gad about, range, drift, stroll, gallivant, traipse; prowl.

row[1] *n.* line; file, tier, queue, string; echelon; series, sequence, succession, rank, range, chain, column; train.

row[2] *n.* noisy dispute, quarrel, spat, tiff, set-to, difference, squabble, altercation, argument, words, wrangle, wrangling, scrape, scrap, brawl; fracas, melee, imbroglio, disorder, contretemps.

rowdy *adj.* boisterous, disorderly, roughneck, unruly, obstreperous, rowdyish, raffish, mischievous; lawless. —**Ant.** peaceful, law-abiding, orderly, gentle; refined, mannerly, decorous.

royal *adj.* **1.** regal, sovereign, monarchal. **2.** fit for a king, regal; majestic, august, stately, imposing, magnificent, grand, splendid, resplendent, superb; lavish, munificent.

royalty *n.* sovereignty, majesty, regality, kingship, queenship, dominion, supremacy, divine right, hegemony, command, sway.

rub *v.* **1.** polish, buff, burnish, smooth, wipe; scrub, braze, scour, clean, swab; smear, spread, slather. **2.** massage, knead, stroke; handle, touch, finger, pass the fingers over; manipulate, move with pressure against something, abrade, chafe. —*n.* **3.** rubbing, rubdown, massage, kneading, handling, manipulation, stroke, stroking. **4.** annoying circumstance, hitch, catch, problem, obstacle, secret, trick, thing, impediment, difficulty, trouble, strait, dilemma, hardship; pinch, setback.

rubbish *n.* **1.** refuse, trash, garbage, waste; waste matter, junk, rubble, debris, litter, worthless material, dross, offal, jetsam. **2.** *Informal* nonsense, gibberish, inanity, balderdash, rot, rigmarole, drivel, bosh, flapdoodle, twaddle, babble, blather, silliness, idiocy, folderol.

ruddy *adj.* rosy, rosy-cheeked, red, reddish, florid, flushed, blushing, scarlet; of a red color, rubicund, roseate, sanguine. —**Ant.** pale, pallid, wan, colorless, ashen, gray, sallow.

rude *adj.* **1.** discourteous, inconsiderate, uncourteous, uncivil, disrespectful, impolite, impudent, insulting, abusive, impertinent, peremptory, insolent, saucy, fresh; unmannerly, bad-mannered, ungentlemanly, unladylike, uncourtly, ungallant, ungracious, undignified, ill-bred; indelicate, indecorous, indecent, profane; brusque, blunt, abrupt, gruff, surly, sullen, sulky, crusty; callow, green, uncouth. **2.** roughly made, crude, roughly built, roughhewn, slapdash, makeshift, uneven, rough, rugged, scraggy, raw. **3.** blunt, without refinement, coarse, unrefined, inelegant, unpolished, artless, without culture, uncultured, ungraceful, awkward, gauche, clumsy; gross, uncouth, vulgar, boorish, loutish, churlish; uneducated, untaught, unlearned, untutored, untrained, ignorant, illiterate; primitive, rustic, provincial, countrified, homely, homebred, wild, uncivilized, brutish. —**Syn. Study. 2** See RAW. —**Ant. 1** courteous, polite, civil, respectful, considerate; mannerly, well-mannered, gentlemanly, ladylike, courtly, urbane, suave, gallant, gracious, dignified, well-bred; decorous, decent, affable, sociable, cordial, amiable. **2** well-made, well-built, well-formed; wrought, fashioned, formed, shapely, finished, even, smooth, slick. **3** refined, elegant, polished, artful, cultured, graceful; educated, taught, learned, tutored, trained, literate; urbane, civilized.

rudimentary *adj.* **1.** elementary, basic, elemental, concerning first rules or steps, initial, primary, primitive, formative. **2.** incompletely developed, undeveloped, prototypal, incomplete, imperfect, premature, simple; immature, vestigial, primitive. —**Ant. 1** advanced. **2** completely developed, developed, finished, complete, perfect, mature.

rue *v.* feel sorrow over, be sorry for, reproach oneself for, regret, repine, repent, wish undone, lament, mourn, bemoan; deplore.

ruffian *n.* brute, bully, tough, rough, roughneck, villain, scoundrel, rogue, knave, blackguard, ugly customer, cutthroat; rowdy, roisterer, hooligan, hoodlum; *Informal* hood; mugger, thug, gangster, crook.

ruffle *v.* **1.** muss, muss up, dishevel, disorder, disarrange, wrinkle, rumple, roughen, ripple. **2.** gather into folds, fold, pleat, rimple, flounce, furbelow, crinkle, ruff, plait, pucker, corrugate. **3.** disturb, trouble, upset, disquiet; perturb, disconcert, discompose, unsettle, confuse; agitate, excite, aggravate. *—n.* **4.** disturbance, agitation, commotion, wave, ripple. **5.** pleat, flounce, frill, ruche, ruff, edging. **—Ant. 1** arrange, order; smooth. **3** compose, calm, settle.

rugged *adj.* **1.** rough, uneven, irregular, craggy, cragged, ridged, jagged, rocky, rock-strewn, bumpy, scraggy. **2.** wrinkled, furrowed, lined, worn, weathered, weather-beaten, hard-featured, roughhewn, coarse. **3.** hardy, hale, robust, vigorous, sturdy, stalwart, able-bodied, tough; husky, brawny, wiry, muscular, well-knit, sinewy, athletic; virile, masculine. **4.** harsh, tough, difficult, hard, severe, stern, trying, taxing, strenuous, arduous, onerous, laborious; rude, unrefined, uncultivated, graceless, uncouth. **—Ant. 1** even, smooth, regular, level; easy, soft. **2** smooth, unmarked, delicate, youthful, refined, pretty. **3** weak, frail, fragile, sickly, puny, skinny, slim; effeminate. **4** gentle, tender; refined, graceful, elegant, cultivated.

ruin *n.* **1. ruins** remains, remnants, wreckage; fallen structure, shell. **2.** disintegration, decay, disrepair, wreckage; pot, seed. **3.** downfall, fall, undoing, breakdown, ruination, crack-up, failure, defeat, overthrow; decay, disintegration, dissolution, destruction, devastation, doom. *—v.* **4.** bring to ruin, reduce to wreckage, demolish, destroy, wreck, shatter, pull to pieces, devastate, lay waste, gut, ravage, raze, level, fell, cut down, pull down, upset, overthrow, overturn, defeat, crush, quell, quash, squash, spoil, harm, put an end to. **5.** make poor, reduce to poverty, bankrupt, impoverish, bring to want, beggar, pauperize, break. **—Ant. 3** construction, creation, building up; success. **4** construct, build, build up; improve, help, enhance. **5** enrich, profit.

ruinous *adj.* calamitous, disastrous, catastrophic, ravaging, devastating, damaging, destructive, deleterious, cataclysmic; baneful, pernicious; fatal, deadly.

rule *n.* **1.** law, regulation, order, ordinance, decree, canon, precept, principle; maxim, axiom, adage, golden rule, rule of thumb, doctrine. **2.** practice, method, system, routine, custom, policy, normal condition. **3.** guide, guideline, precedent, criterion, model, precept, form, formula, prescription; standard, convention. **4.** reign, regnancy, sovereignty, suzerainty, regime, dominion, empire; control, command, authority, direction, administration, leadership, domination, supremacy, sway, influence, jurisdiction, government. *—v.* **5.** control, command, govern, regulate, direct, administer, manage, run; exercise dominion over, have authority over, reign, lead, preside over, be at the head of, head; sway, influence, dominate, domineer, prevail, predominate, have the upper hand. **6.** decide, determine, conclude, settle, resolve, establish, find, judge, adjudicate, adjudge, pass upon; declare, pronounce, decree.

ruler *n.* **1.** leader, commander, head of state, (*variously*) president, sovereign, monarch, crowned head, emperor, king, queen, prince, czar; lord, viceroy, suzerain; potentate, dynast, sultan, satrap, emir, shah, pharaoh, sheik, chieftain, rajah, khan, shogun; chairman, governor, manager, director, administrator, supervisor, controller, coordinator; chief, head, boss; judge, arbiter, referee. **2.** rule, yardstick, straightedge, measure, tape measure; slide rule.

rumble *v.* **1.** boom, reverberate, resound, roar, thunder, roll. *—n.* **2.** roar, thunder, boom, booming, drumming, resonance, reverberation, roll; clap, bang.

ruminate *v.* ponder, mull, mull over, brood, think, reflect, think about, meditate, cogitate, deliberate, weigh, contemplate, think over, bring up again for consideration, consider, study, muse, speculate.

rummage *v.* search thoroughly, look through, root, examine, explore, poke around, delve into, probe, sift through; disarrange, ransack, turn over.

rumor *n.* **1.** unverified information, report, story, supposition, babble, gossip, whisper, hearsay, insinuation, innuendo, talk, *Slang* scuttlebutt. *—v.* **2.** whisper, gossip, breathe about, buzz about, intimate, insinuate; circulate, spread abroad, bruit about, put into circulation, report.

rump *n.* hindquarters, rear, posterior, rear end, haunches, buttocks, backside, bottom, croup, seat, behind, stern, dorsum, breech, *Informal* fanny, *French* derrière.

rumple *v.* **1.** wrinkle, crumple, crease, crinkle, rimple, crush, pucker, corrugate, ruffle; disarrange, disorder, dishevel, muss, tousle. —*n.* **2.** wrinkle, fold, crease, crumple, pucker, ruffle, crinkle, crimp.

rumpus *n.* fuss, ado, to-do, disturbance, pother, stir; uproar, tumult, agitation, upheaval, fracas, confusion, noise, tempest; *Slang* ruckus, brouhaha, rhubarb.

run *v.* **1.** go quickly, step quickly, make off rapidly, move swiftly, race, dart, sprint, jog, trot, dash; hustle, hasten, hurry, hie, scamper, scurry, rush, scramble; speed, tear along, fly, bound. **2.** leave, take flight, flee, fly, bolt; steal away, escape, decamp, abscond, take to one's heels, beat a retreat; *Informal* skedaddle, take off; *Slang* vamoose, hightail it, split. **3.** go, ply. **4.** compete, enter the lists, stand, campaign, make a bid. **5.** flow, pour, stream, course, roll, glide, sweep along; surge, issue; wander, meander. **6.** cause to move, drive, propel, thrust, push, impel; direct, navigate, maneuver, pilot. **7.** operate, manage, direct, supervise, oversee, coordinate; head, preside over, boss. **8.** pass, glide. **9.** get past, get through, sweep past, break through, penetrate, pierce; defy. **10.** extend in time, go by, pass, elapse, last, endure; proceed, move on, go, continue, advance. **11.** become, get. **12.** cost, amount to, total, add up to. **13.** bleed, lose color, mingle colors. **14.** come unraveled, separate, tear, ladder. **15.** vary, extend, be, go. **16.** print, publish; display; make copies of. **17.** incur, bring on, court, invite; be liable to, be exposed to; encounter, meet, meet with; fall into. **18.** dissolve, melt, become fluid, liquefy; vanish, disappear, evanesce. —*n.* **19.** running, trot, canter, gallop, jog, sprint, dash. **20.** trip, excursion, journey, pilgrimage, voyage, tour, drive, outing. **21.** unraveled place, *Informal* ladder. **22.** course, passage, tendency, direction, drift, flow, progress, onward movement. **23.** freedom, unrestricted use. **24.** continuous performance; series, course, continuance, continuation, perpetuation, duration; period, stretch, streak, spell, while. **25.** enclosure, pen. **26.** class, kind, sort, genre, type. **27.** flow, flowing movement, stream, race, course, current, motion. **28.** point in baseball, score, tally, circuit of the bases. —**Ant. 1** walk, crawl. **2** remain, stay. **10** stop, halt, cease. **18** solidify, congeal, harden. **19** walk, saunter. **24** discontinuance, stoppage.

runaround *n.* slip, dodge, evasion, shunting off, evasiveness, avoidance, shunning, side step, bypass, elusiveness, equivocation.

runaway *n.* **1.** fugitive, deserter, escapee, refugee, bolter, *Slang* skedaddler. —*adj.* **2.** absolute, unqualified, complete, out-and-out, pure, perfect, unmitigated, unalloyed.

rundown[1] *n.* outline, summary, résumé, synopsis, abstract, précis, brief, review, condensation, digest, sketch, capitulation.

run-down[2] *adj.* **1.** broken-down, seedy, tacky, shabby, dilapidated, tired, deteriorated, tattered, rickety, tumbledown, *Slang* beat-up. **2.** ailing, weary, exhausted, frail, feeble, fatigued, sickly. —**Ant. 1** renovated, rebuilt, renewed, refurbished. **2** fit, robust, sturdy, able-bodied, stalwart.

run-of-the-mill *adj.* ordinary, commonplace, routine, everyday, mediocre, passable, banal, so-so, unimpressive, undistinguished, humdrum, middling, indifferent, modest, second-rate. —**Ant.** superior, superlative, prime, preeminent.

runt *n.* peewee, half-pint, chit, shrimp; dwarf, midget, Tom Thumb, Lilliputian, pygmy, homunculus, elf. —**Ant.** giant, colossus, behemoth, titan, monster.

rupture *n.* **1.** breaking, bursting, break, burst, split, fracture, crack, fissure, rent, severance, cleavage, cleft. **2.** break, rift, split, breach, schism, separation, dissociation, disunion, disagreement, dissension, falling out, discord; friction, clash. —*v.* **3.** break, burst, break up, sunder, crack, puncture, dissever, come apart, part, snap, pop, divide. **4.** cause a break in, cause a breach in, disrupt, disunite, divide, break up. —**Ant. 2** union; understanding, agreement; continuity. **4** unite, heal, knit.

rural *adj.* country, up-country, pastoral, bucolic, rustic, countrified, provincial, *Informal* hick. —**Syn. Study.** RURAL and RUSTIC are terms that refer to the country. RURAL is the neutral term: *rural education.* It is also used subjectively, usu. in a favorable sense: *the charm of rural life.* RUSTIC, however, may have either favorable or unfavorable connotations. In a derogatory sense, it means provincial, boorish, or crude; in a favorable sense, it may suggest a homelike simplicity and lack of sophistication: *rustic manners.* —**Ant.** urban, city, citified, cosmopolitan, urbane.

ruse *n.* stratagem, machination, maneuver, device, shift, scheme, crafty device, contrivance, artifice, subterfuge, trick, hoax, deception, deceit, dodge, blind, feint. —**Syn. Study.** See TRICK.

rush *v.* **1.** speed, race, hasten, hie, hurry, run, dash, tear, scramble, dart, hustle, scurry, scamper. **2.** speed up, accelerate, dispatch, expedite, perform hastily, finish with speed; work against time, hurry. **3.** spur, whip, urge, goad, drive; pressure, push, press, keep at. **4.**

go carelessly, go headlong, act thoughtlessly, leap, plunge, precipitate oneself. **5.** attack suddenly, storm, charge, descend upon, have at. —*n.* **6.** run, dash, sprint. **7.** haste, speed, dispatch, urgency. —*adj.* **8.** urgent, emergency, top priority. —**Ant. 1** walk, crawl. **2** slow. **7** leisure; dawdling, idling.

rust *n.* **1.** corrosion, oxidation; stain, blight, rot, decay. **2.** reddish-yellow, reddish-brown, russet, auburn. —*v.* **3.** corrode, oxidize; decay, weaken with disuse, decline, deteriorate, crumble.

rustic *adj.* **1.** country, rural, provincial, pastoral, agrarian, bucolic. **2.** simple, plain, unsophisticated; rough, countrified, rude, unpolished, unrefined, inelegant, uncouth, uncultured, crude, loutish, coarse, churlish, boorish; awkward, gauche, cloddish. —*n.* **3.** country person, countryman, provincial, peasant, bumpkin, hayseed, yokel, clodhopper, rube. —**Syn. Study. 1** See RURAL. —**Ant. 1** urban, cosmopolitan. **2** sophisticated, fancy, polished, refined, elegant, courtly, urbane, citified. **3** sophisticate, cosmopolitan.

rustle *v.* **1.** move with soft sounds, swish, rustle, riffle, hiss, whish, stir, rub. —*n.* **2.** rustling, whispering sound, swish, hiss.

rusty *adj.* **1.** covered with rust, rusted, corroded; rotten, moldy, tainted. **2.** reddish, rust-colored. **3.** out of practice, stiff, no longer agile, sluggish, inept through neglect.

rut *n.* **1.** deep track, depression, furrow, hollow, ditch, gutter, cut, trench, channel, trough, tread, groove. **2.** fixed way of life, dull routine, monotonous round, narrow orbit, pattern, habit. —*v.* **3.** dig into, furrow, depress, hollow, groove, mark, channel, score.

ruthless *adj.* without pity, unmerciful, merciless, pitiless, unpitying, unforgiving, without compassion, unfeeling, heartless, callous, hardhearted, harsh, cruel, unsparing, remorseless, relentless, unrelenting; inhuman, vicious, barbarous, savage, ferocious, brutal, brutish, bestial, cold-blooded, murderous, deadly, bloodthirsty, sanguinary. —**Ant.** merciful, pitying, compassionate, forgiving, kind, tender, tenderhearted, gentle, sparing, lenient, remorseful, humane.

Sabbath *n.* Sabbath day, day of rest, day of worship, (*Christian Church*) Lord's Day.

sabotage *n.* **1.** undermining of a cause, subversion; malicious destruction, malicious disruption. —*v.* **2.** undermine, sap, conspire against, subvert, damage from within; disable, vandalize, paralyze, cripple, retard, incapacitate, destroy, disrupt.

saccharine *adj.* oversweet, cloying, syrupy, sugary, honeyed, sugared, candied; maudlin, sentimental, mawkish; *Slang* mushy, soppy, gooey; nauseating, sickening; offensive, revolting, disgusting. —**Ant.** sharp, sour, biting, acid, corrosive.

sack[1] *n.* **1.** bag, (*variously*) pouch, knapsack, rucksack, haversack, gunnysack, duffel bag. —*v.* **2.** put into a sack, bag; pack, store.

sack[2] *v.* **1.** pillage, plunder, loot, ransack, tear up, pull apart, lay waste, despoil, spoil, ravage, spoliate, prey upon, raid, maraud, depredate; steal from, rob. —*n.* **2.** plundering, pillage, rapine, ravishment, ravage, devastation, depredation, waste, lay waste, despoliation; raid, marauding.

sacrament *n.* rite, ceremony, liturgy, solemnity, observance, ceremonial, ministration; pledge, promise, vow, covenant, troth, obligation, contract, plight, affirmation.

sacred *adj.* **1.** consecrated, hallowed, blessed, sanctified, holy. **2.** venerable, awe-inspiring, revered. **3.** religious, ecclesiastical, hieratic, church; scriptural, holy, Biblical; hallowed, divinely inspired. —**Syn. Study. 1** See HOLY. —**Ant. 1** unconsecrated, profane. **3** profane, secular, lay, temporal.

sacrifice *n.* **1.** offering, oblation, homage; ritual slaughter, immolation, lustration. **2.** relinquishment, cession, concession, renunciation, surrender. **3.** loss. —*v.* **4.** make a sacrifice of, offer up, make an offering of; immolate. **5.** give up, relinquish, forgo, forfeit, waive, renounce, surrender, cede. **6.** sell at a loss. —**Ant. 3** profit, gain.

sacrilege *n.* profanation, desecration, misuse of sacred things; blasphemy, profanity, profaneness, impiousness, impiety, irreligion, irreverence, mockery; sin, wickedness, sinfulness, violation, outrage, iniquity.

sacrosanct *adj.* sacred, consecrated, hallowed, sanctified, solemn, holy, godly, religious, spiritual, divine, heavenly, celestial; inviolable, inviolate, immune from attack; unexamined, unquestioned, blindly accepted.

sad *adj.* **1.** unhappy, cheerless, joyless, grieved, griefstricken; dispirited, downcast, low, crestfallen, heavyhearted, chapfallen, disconsolate, desolate, despondent, melancholy, inconsolable, depressed, dejected; *Informal* down in the mouth, down in the dumps, blue; distressed, miserable, pessimistic, troubled, full of care, despairing, brokenhearted, hurt, crushed; wretched, forlorn, sorrowful, doleful, mournful. **2.** pitiful, touching, pathetic, lamentable, dismal; lachrymose, maudlin. **3.** unfortunate, grievous, serious, grave, calamitous, grim, dismal, solemn; lamentable, heartbreaking, heartrending, woeful, mournful, distressing; trying, taxing, difficult, hard, adverse, troublesome; tragic. —**Ant. 1** happy, cheerful, smiling, joyful, glad, spirited, lighthearted, pleased, merry, optimistic. **2** happy, amusing, cheery, bright. **3** easy, fortunate, lucky, prosperous, flourishing, successful.

sadden *v.* grieve, depress, dishearten, discourage, crush, deject, dispirit, sorrow, subdue, damp, dash, burden, aggrieve. —**Ant.** delight, cheer, gladden, please, encourage.

sadistic *adj.* deliberately cruel, brutal, vicious, fiendish, perverse, perverted, bloodthirsty.

safe *adj.* **1.** secure, out of danger, safe and sound, impregnable, out of harm's way; unharmed, unhurt, undamaged, unscathed, unscratched, unbroken, intact, whole. **2.** secure, protecting, protected, guarded, defended, invulnerable, unexposed. **3.** cautious, prudent, circumspect, conservative, modest, discreet, noncommittal, wary; sure, certain. **4.** not dangerous, dependable, reliable, trustworthy, to be trusted; sure, steady, firm, stable, sound, tried and true; harmless, innocuous. —*n.* **5.** locked box, storage box, safe-deposit box; vault. —**Ant. 1** harmed, damaged; imperiled; jeopardized, at risk. **2** unsafe, risky, hazardous, perilous. **3** wild, risky, extravagant; impetuous; speculative. **4** unsafe, undependable, unreliable; harmful, risky, pathogenic; lethal, toxic.

safeguard *n.* **1.** defense, protection, shield, armor, bulwark, guard, security, ward, buffer, screen, precaution; charm, amulet, talisman. —*v.* **2.** guard, shield, defend, fortify, protect, screen, conserve, preserve, shelter, harbor, secure, armor, garrison. —**Ant. 1** danger, hazard, peril, threat. **2** imperil, jeopardize, risk.

sag *v.* **1.** bend downward, droop, slump, bow, sink, drop, descend, decline, plunge, give way, settle; sway, keel, list, dip, lean, pitch, tilt. **2.** droop, flop, flap, hang loosely, billow. **3.** weaken, diminish, decline, lose strength, break down; flag, weary, tire; fail, fizzle out.

saga *n.* narrative, long narrative, tale, heroic tale, epic, legend, myth, adventure; chronicle, history; yarn, romance.

sagacious *adj.* wise, shrewd, knowing, astute, intelligent, judicious, discriminating, sage, sapient, perspicacious, discerning, perceptive, practical, prudent; smart, clever, brainy, nimble-witted, sharp, acute, canny, cunning, calculating, foxy; sensible, sound, rational, tactful, discreet, diplomatic. —**Ant.** stupid, ignorant, dumb, obtuse, foolish, fatuous, silly.

sage *n.* **1.** wise man, magus, pundit, mage, philosopher, savant, scholar, guru, mandarin, solon, *Slang* egghead. —*adj.* **2.** wise, sapient, shrewd, prudent; sensible, sound, sagacious, knowing, astute, intelligent. —**Ant. 1** fool, idiot. **2** stupid, foolish, senseless.

sail *n.* **1.** sailing trip, cruise, voyage, boat ride; journey by water, excursion. —*v.* **2.** cruise, go by water, navigate, ride the waves, boat, course, skim, scud, steam; set sail, set out on a voyage, put to sea, shove off, get under way. **3.** float, fly, drift, glide, soar.

sailor *n.* seaman, mariner, yachtsman, deck hand, seafarer, seafaring man, navigator, voyager; tar, salt, sea dog, *Slang* gob. —**Syn. Study.** SAILOR, SEAMAN, MARINER, SALT are terms for a person who leads a seafaring life. A SAILOR or SEAMAN is one whose occupation is on board a ship at sea, esp. a member of a ship's crew below the rank of petty officer: *a sailor before the mast; an able-bodied seaman.* MARINER is a term found in certain technical expressions: *mariner's compass* (ordinary compass as used on ships); the word now seems elevated or quaint: *"The Rime of the Ancient Mariner."* SALT is a casual term for an experienced sailor: *an old salt.*

saintly *adj.* sainted, godly, holy, blessed, devout, pious, beatific, reverent, religious, spiritual, faithful, believing; virtuous, good, upright, moral, righteous, benevolent. —**Ant.** wicked, sinful, immoral, ungodly; corruptible, frail, flawed.

sake *n.* **1.** good, benefit, consideration, well-being, welfare, care, interest, concern, cause, behalf, regard, account, respect; advantage, profit, gain, enhancement. **2.** end, purpose, object.

salary *n.* compensation for work, wages, pay, earnings, income; stipend, allowance; remuneration, recompense, emolument.

sale *n.* **1.** selling, transfer, exchange. **2.** disposal of goods at reduced prices, markdown, reduction, discount, cut; bargain, special, *Informal* blowout. —**Ant. 1** purchase, acquisition.

salient *adj.* prominent, protruding, obvious, conspicuous, standing out, jutting up, striking, noticeable, easily noticed, palpable, outstanding, manifest, flagrant, egregious, arrant, glaring, marked, pronounced, important, remarkable, notable, noteworthy; considerable, substantial. —**Ant.** low-lying, depressed; inconspicuous, minor, trifling.

sallow *adj.* yellowish, yellow, jaundiced, sickly, tallow-faced, anemic, bilious; pale, wan, ashen, livid, pallid, washed-out, gray, gray complected, green at the gills. —**Ant.** ruddy, rosy, flushed, blooming.

sally *n.* **1.** sortie, thrust, counterattack, bursting forth, foray, raid, attack. **2.** excursion, journey, expedition, trip, outing. **3.** clever remark, mot, ready reply, flash of wit, witticism, repartee, badinage, banter, retort, quip, wisecrack. —*v.* **4.** erupt, rush out, break out, issue suddenly, debouch, pour, surge, flow, spring; attack, charge, take the offensive, seize the initiative.

salon *n.* **1.** large room, drawing room, hall, gallery. **2.** stylish shop, beauty parlor, establishment.

saloon *n.* bar, tavern, pub, barroom, bistro, taproom, beer parlor, alehouse, cocktail lounge, inn, roadhouse, speakeasy, *Slang* ginmill.

salt *n.* **1.** wit, humor, pungency, piquancy; seasoning, smack, savor, flavor. **2.** best, quintessence, choice, pick, select, elect, cream. **3.** sailor, seaman, mariner, tar, sea dog, *Slang* gob. —*adj.* **4.** saline, salty, salted, brackish, briny. —*v.* **5.** season, flavor, savor, spice. **6.** cure, brine, marinate, pickle, corn, souse. **7. salt away** save, store up, put away, lay away, set aside. —**Syn. Study. 3** See SAILOR.

salubrious *adj.* healthful, healthy, health-promoting, therapeutic, good for one, salutary, bracing, beneficial, wholesome, lifegiving, invigorating. —**Ant.** unhealthful, unhealthy, harmful, unwholesome, insalubrious, deleterious.

salute *v.* **1.** address, greet, hail, welcome; make obeisance to, bow to, nod to, wave to. **2.** applaud, cheer, praise, honor, respect, pay tribute to, take one's hat off to. —*n.* **3.** expression of goodwill, salutation, greeting, recognition, honor, homage, reverence; applause, accolade, laudation, acclamation.

salvage *n.* **1.** recovery, reclamation, retrieval. **2.** property saved from destruction, reclaimed materials, remains, scrap, junk, debris; flotsam and jetsam. —*v.* **3.** save, rescue, retrieve, recover, rehabilitate, restore.

salvation *n.* **1.** saving of the soul from sin, redemption, deliverance; election, grace. **2.** means of surviving, protection, lifeline, mainstay, rock. **3.** saving, rescue, preservation, salvage, retrieval, reclamation, recovery, survival. **—Ant. 1** perdition, damnation, condemnation. **2** downfall. **3** destruction, loss.

salve *n.* **1.** unguent, ointment, balm, emollient, lotion, liniment, dressing, healing agent, alleviative, anodyne. —*v.* **2.** ease, assuage, alleviate, mitigate, relieve, temper, moderate, mollify, lessen, reduce, calm, pacify. **—Ant. 2** irritate, exacerbate, inflame, aggravate.

same *adj.* **1.** identical, selfsame, one and the same, very, alike, twin, like, of like kind, similar. **2.** corresponding, equivalent, parallel; equal, on a par, on even terms. **3.** unchanged, invariable, consistent, uniform. **—Ant. 1–3** different. **1** dissimilar, other. **3** changed, variable, inconsistent.

sample *n.* **1.** representative, specimen, example, illustration, instance, cross section, portion, segment, exemplification, pattern, model, paradigm. —*v.* **2.** judge by a sample, test, examine; partake of, taste, try, dip into, experience.

sanctify *v.* bless, consecrate, hallow, anoint, make holy, enshrine, exalt, beatify, dedicate; purify, cleanse, absolve; sanction, legitimize, legitimate, legitimatize, uphold. **—Ant.** profane, desecrate, pollute, defile.

sanctimonious *adj.* making a show of sanctity, affectedly holy, belligerently pious, pietistic, aggressively devout, self-righteous, holier-than-thou, unctuous, pharisaical; solemn, overblown, pretentious, pompous, canting, preachy.

sanction *n.* **1.** approval, commendation, endorsement, assent, consent, permission, authorization; leave, liberty, license, authority; ratification, confirmation, support. **2.** penalty, pressure, punitive measure, coercion. —*v.* **3.** approve, endorse, authorize, legitimate, allow, permit, countenance, accept, agree to, favor, ratify, support. **—Ant. 1** disapproval, forbiddance, refusal, ban, prohibition. **2** incentive, encouragement. **3** disapprove, reject, ban, prohibit.

sanctuary *n.* **1.** holy place, consecrated place, house of worship, house of prayer, house of God, church, temple, chapel, shrine; sanctum, sanctum sanctorum. **2.** refuge, haven, retreat, safe place; safety, protection, asylum, shelter, immunity from pursuers; hiding place, cover. **3.** protected area, reserve, preserve, park.

sane *adj.* **1.** of sound mind, reasonable, in possession of one's faculties, compos mentis, clearheaded, sober, balanced, responsible, rational, lucid; *Slang* all there. **2.** reasonable, well-founded, sensible, judicious, sagacious, logical, farsighted; credible, plausible. **—Ant. 1** insane, unsound, mentally ill, non compos mentis, deranged, mad, irrational. **2** insane, senseless, stupid, foolish, injudicious, unreasonable, incredible, implausible.

sanguine *adj.* **1.** optimistic, hopeful, confident, happy, cheerful, sunny, bright; lighthearted, elated, buoyant, in good spirits. **2.** red, reddish, ruddy, crimson, scarlet; florid, rubicund, flushed, rosy, inflamed, glowing, blooming. **—Ant. 1** pessimistic, doubtful, gloomy, depressed, despairing, heavy-hearted, dispirited, morose. **2** pale, ashen, pallid, white.

sanitary *adj.* health-promoting, healthful, salubrious, healthy, wholesome; sterile, sterilized, clean, germ-free, disease-free, hygienic, disinfected, aseptic, uninfected, prophylactic, unpolluted. **—Ant.** unhealthy, unwholesome; unsterile, dirty.

sanity *n.* mental health, soundness of mind, saneness, mental balance, normality; soundness of judgment, reason, rationality, sensibleness, sense, lucidity, reasonableness, clearheadedness, coherence. **—Ant.** insanity, insaneness, madness, derangement; irrationality, incoherence.

sap *v.* deplete, reduce, rob; weaken, undermine, tax, wear, enervate, enfeeble, exhaust, debilitate, devitalize; break down, impair, cripple, disable, afflict; subvert, destroy, ruin, devastate; bleed, drain.

sarcasm *n.* ridicule, irony, derision, contempt, scorn, mockery, scoffing, disparagement; cutting remark, sneer, taunt, gibe, jeer, rub, jest. **—Ant.** compliment, praise, enthusiasm, appreciation. **—Syn. Study.** See IRONY.

sarcastic *adj.* ironic, contemptuous, mocking, derisive, taunting; biting, cutting, piercing, stinging, bitter, caustic, mordant, acerb, sardonic, scornful, sneering, disparaging.

sardonic *adj.* sarcastic, satiric, cynical, sneering, mocking, contemptuous, derisive, scornful, disparaging; caustic, mordant, biting, taunting, jeering.

Satan *n.* the Devil, the Prince of Darkness, the Evil One, the Old Serpent, the

Tempter, Beelzebub, Lucifer, Mephistopheles, the Foul Fiend, Old Nick, Old Scratch, Moloch, Belial, Apollyon.

satanic *adj.* befitting Satan, hellish, diabolical, demoniacal, demonic, infernal, devilish, fiendish, fiend-like; malicious, malignant, malevolent, bad, wicked, evil, infamous, inhuman, heinous, vicious, cruel, vile, sadistic. **—Ant.** angelic, heavenly, benevolent, good, humane, kind.

sate *v.* satisfy fully, satiate, fill; glut, stuff, surfeit, cloy, gorge.

satellite *n.* **1.** moon. **2.** attendant, assistant, follower, disciple; companion, crony, retainer, servant; vassal, menial, underling, puppet, hanger-on, parasite, toady, sycophant. **3.** client state, vassal, tributary, puppet.

satiate *v.* satisfy, fill, gratify, suffice, content; slake, quench; glut, stuff, sate, surfeit, overfill, overdo, cloy, saturate; sicken, disgust, nauseate; jade, bore, weary.

satire *n.* comic criticism, parody, take-off, send up, burlesque, lampoon, travesty, caricature; mockery, ridicule, derision; pointed wit, sarcasm, irony, acrimony; raillery, banter, persiflage. **—Syn. Study.** See IRONY.

satirical *adj.* ironically critical, sardonic, sarcastic, mordant, ironical; derisive, mocking, sneering, biting, malicious, scornful, bitter, caustic; comic, humorous, tongue-in-cheek.

satisfaction *n.* **1.** pleasure, comfort, gratification, happiness, fulfillment, pride, content, contentment. **2.** reimbursement, repayment, compensation, recompense, restitution, remuneration, payment, remittance; settlement, quittance, damages, deserts; requital, redress, rectification, justice, amends, atonement, correction, reckoning, answering, measure for measure. **—Ant.** **1** dissatisfaction, grief, shame, unhappiness, discontent.

satisfactory *adj.* good enough, competent, adequate, suitable, sufficient, all right, acceptable, passable, up to standard, up to the mark, OK. **—Ant.** unsatisfactory, inadequate, bad.

satisfy *v.* **1.** make content, content, please, mollify, pacify, gratify, delight; meet, fill, fulfill, serve, suffice, be adequate to, answer; sate, satiate, slake, quench, appease, remove, put an end to. **2.** pay off, settle, discharge, clear, annul; pay, remit, repay, reimburse, recompense, compensate, requite. **3.** convince, free of doubt, persuade, assure, reassure. **—Ant.** **1** dissatisfy, displease, annoy; intensify, worsen. **3** dissatisfy, dissuade.

saturate *v.* **1.** soak thoroughly, drench, souse, douse; immerse, submerge. **2.** fill, infiltrate, cover, permeate, infuse, suffuse, pervade, impregnate, imbue. **—Ant.** **1** drain, dry.

saturnine *adj.* gloomy, sullen, glum, morose, moping, sulky, dour; downcast, downhearted, dejected; solemn, somber, grave, serious, staid, reserved, stern, taciturn, withdrawn, uncommunicative, apathetic. **—Ant.** genial, amiable, cheerful, cheery, happy.

saucy *adj.* **1.** impudent, insolent, impertinent, forward, audacious, bold, brash, brazen, unabashed, barefaced, flippant, cheeky, fresh, smart-alecky, cocky; rude, impolite, discourteous, disrespectful. **2.** pert, lively; high-spirited. **3.** jaunty, trim, smart, natty, spruce.

saunter *v.* **1.** walk casually, amble, stroll, traipse, promenade; wander, ramble, roam, stray, meander; straggle, loiter, *Slang* mosey. **—*n.*** **2.** stroll, leisurely walk, amble, ramble, promenade.

savage *adj.* **1.** ferocious, fierce, brutal, barbaric, brutish, cruel, unkind, merciless, unmerciful, pitiless, sadistic, ruthless, relentless, bloody, murderous. **2.** untamed, wild, undomesticated, feral. **3.** uncivilized, primitive, uncultivated, uncultured, heathenish, barbaric, barbarous. **4.** violent, harsh, rough, rugged. **—*n.*** **5.** primitive, aborigine, aboriginal, native, barbarian. **6.** fierce person, brute, fiend, maniac, barbarian, *Informal* animal; hoodlum, hooligan, ruffian; boor, yahoo. **—Ant.** **1** kind, merciful, lenient, gentle, tender. **2** tame, domesticated. **3** civilized, cultivated, cultured. **4** mild, soft, calm. **5** civilized person.

save *v.* **1.** rescue, recover, free, deliver, preserve, protect, safeguard, spare, salvage, redeem, help. **2.** conserve, preserve, husband, spare. **3.** set aside, store, reserve, set apart, withhold, hold, keep, conserve, preserve, put away, put aside. **4.** treat carefully, keep safe, protect, take care of, look after, safeguard, shield, defend, watch over, guard. **5.** be thrifty, avoid spending, curtail expenses, economize, retrench; provide for a rainy day, lay up, lay by, put by, hoard, amass, accumulate, husband, deposit, bank, heap up, garner, stock. **—Ant.** **1** endanger, imperil, risk, hazard. **2** use, consume, waste. **3** use, spend. **4** expose, risk, endanger. **5** spend, be extravagant.

saving *adj.* **1.** redeeming, redemptory, reclaiming, restoring, compensating, reparative. **2.** frugal, thrifty, penny-wise, careful, prudent, conservative, economical, sparing, provident; stingy, miserly, stinting, niggardly, close, illiberal; *Informal* tight. **—*n.*** **3.** amount saved, reduction in cost, price-cut, markdown. **4.** **savings** money laid aside, store of money, financial reserve, funds, bank deposit; nest egg.

savior *n.* **1.** protector, champion, defender, preserver, guardian; rescuer, deliverer, salvation, liberator, emancipator, freer; redeemer, guiding light. **2.** **Saviour** Christ, the Messiah, Redeemer, Prince of Peace, the Son of God.

savoir faire *n.* social grace, social skill, tact, aplomb, graciousness, finesse, smoothness, adroitness, discretion; poise, complaisance; presence, assurance, composure, self-possession; polish, suavity, urbanity, worldliness. **—Ant.** awkwardness, clumsiness, ineptness, maladroitness.

savor *n.* **1.** taste, flavor, tang, spice, piquancy, pungency; smell, aroma, odor, scent, fragrance; smack, relish, zest. **2.** character, nature, particular quality, characteristic, property, particularity, distinctive feature, peculiarity, trait, aura, quality; substance, essence, gist, spirit, soul. **—***v.* **3.** taste, smell, smack, have a touch, show traces, have the earmarks, be suggestive. **4.** spice, season, flavor. **5.** enjoy, relish, like; take pleasure in, delight in, luxuriate in, rejoice in, appreciate. **6.** experience, taste, sample, try.

savory *adj.* **1.** tasty, appetizing, mouthwatering, aromatic, fragrant, odorous; pungent, piquant, tangy, delectable, delicious, luscious, tasty, tasteful, palatable, toothsome, full-flavored, flavorous, scrumptious, yummy. **2.** reputable, respectable, edifying, in good odor, inoffensive, honest; attractive, alluring, charming. **—Syn. Study. 1** See TASTY. **—Ant. 1** ill-tasting, tasteless, insipid, malodorous, smelly. **2** unsavory, disreputable, shady.

say *v.* **1.** speak, tell, utter, give utterance to, voice, verbalize, vocalize, articulate; express, word, mouth, phrase; state, declare, pronounce, announce; remark, comment, mention; communicate, convey; come out with, let out, divulge, repeat, reveal, make known, disclose. **2.** recite, read, speak, deliver, render, pronounce, mouth, repeat, rehearse, perform, do. **3.** guess, suppose, surmise, assume, hazard a guess, conjecture, imagine; judge, reason; daresay; be sure, be certain, feel convinced. **4.** report, rumor, spread, circulate, bruit, noise abroad, put forth; allege, hold, claim, assert, maintain; contend, hint, imply, intimate, suggest, insinuate. **—***n.* **5.** right to speak, voice, participation; vote, franchise. **6.** opportunity to speak, chance, day in court; comment, expressed opinion; *Slang* two cents worth. **—Ant. 1** be quiet about, suppress.

saying *n.* expression, proverb, saw, adage, maxim, truism, aphorism, dictum, motto, precept, apothegm, epigram, byword, moral.

scale¹ *n.* **1.** thin piece, flake, chip; plate. **2.** coating, film, thin covering, skin, peel, lamina, membrane, layer, lamella, crust, shell. **—***v.* **3.** scrape, scour. **4.** chip off, flake, shave, rub off; delaminate; shell, peel, husk.

scale² *n.* **1.** Often **scales** weighing machine, balance. **—***v.* **2.** have a weight of, weigh.

scale³ *n.* **1.** gradation, graduation, calibration, rule; measure. **2.** classification, range, series, progression; spread, spectrum, continuum, order, ladder. **3.** proportion, ratio. **4.** register, range, octave; key. **—***v.* **5.** climb up, climb over, clamber, go up, ascend, mount, surmount, escalade, rise, progress upward, work upward. **6.** adjust, regulate, set; vary according to a scale.

scamp *n.* rascal, scalawag, rogue, scoundrel, rapscallion, knave, scapegrace, villain, miscreant, imp, mischief-maker, tease, prankster; *Slang* cut-up, rip; *British* bounder, rotter, blighter.

scamper *v.* **1.** run, rush, hasten, fly, hurry, race, sprint, dart, dash, scuttle, scud, flit, zip, scurry; *Informal* scoot, skedaddle. **—***n.* **2.** quick run, dash, sprint, hasty run; scurry, zip. **3.** frolic, running about playfully, gambol, frisk, romp.

scan *v.* **1.** examine, peruse, pore over, scour, probe, scrutinize, inspect, study, size up, take stock of; search, explore, sweep, survey, check. **2.** read hastily, glance at, browse through, skim. **3.** divide into feet, show the metrical structure of; analyze.

scandal *n.* **1.** public disgrace, revelation of misconduct, exposure of wrongdoing, embarrassment, sensation, exposé. **2.** dishonor, disgrace, disesteem, embarrassment, discredit; shame, outrage; smirch, stain, stigma, blot, debasement, odium, ignominy, opprobrium. **3.** malicious gossip, slander, libel, aspersion, defamatory talk, obloquy, calumny, detraction, disparagement, revilement, vituperation, abuse, evil-speaking. **—Ant. 2** honor, esteem, credit, praise.

scandalous *adj.* **1.** disgraceful, shameful, disreputable, highly improper, offensive, shocking, outrageous, reprehensible. **2.** slanderous, libelous, scurrilous, defamatory, gossiping. **—Ant. 1** proper, reputable, decent. **2** kind, praising, laudatory, sweet.

scant *adj.* **1.** limited, meager, exiguous, deficient, insufficient, inadequate; small, short, paltry, sparse. **2.** not full, bare, incomplete. **3.** ill-supplied, in need, short. **—***v.* **4.** limit, stint, hold back, skimp on, reduce, cut. **—Ant. 1** plentiful, profuse, copious, abundant, ample, adequate. **2** full, overflowing. **3** well-supplied. **4** lavish.

scanty *adj.* inadequate, scant, insufficient; meager, deficient; thin, slender, sparse, skimpy, small, modest, short, stunted, undersized, paltry. **—Syn. Study.** SCANTY, MEAGER, SPARSE refer to insufficiency or deficiency in quantity, number, etc. SCANTY denotes smallness or insufficiency of quantity, number, supply, etc.: *a scanty supply of food.* MEAGER indicates that something is poor, stinted, or inadequate: *meager fare; a meager income.* SPARSE applies particularly to that which grows thinly or is thinly distributed: *sparse vegetation; a sparse population.*

scapegoat *n.* victim, dupe, gull, whipping boy, laughingstock; *Slang* butt, fall guy, patsy, goat.

scar *n.* **1.** mark left by an old wound, cicatrix, wound, seam, stitch mark, pit, pock; dent, gash; defect, flaw, blemish. —*v.* **2.** leave a scar on, wound, cut, scratch, gash, lacerate, mutilate, mangle; mark, bruise, brand, deface, disfigure; hurt, impair, damage; influence, affect.

scarce *adj.* **1.** in short supply, hard to find, scanty, sparse, hard to obtain; wanting, insufficient, deficient, not abundant, not plentiful. **2.** rare, rarely seen, unusual, uncommon, exceptional. **—Ant. 1** abundant, plentiful. **2** numerous, common.

scarcely *adv.* **1.** hardly, barely, slightly, faintly, just, but just, at most, no more than, not easily. **2.** definitely not, certainly not, in no manner, in no way, by no means, not at all, not in the least, hardly, on no account. **—Syn. Study. 1** See HARDLY.

scarcity *n.* **1.** insufficient supply, insufficiency, shortage, scantiness, lack, dearth, deficiency, want, paucity, stint, thinness. **2.** rarity, infrequency of occurrence, rareness, scarceness, sparsity, uncommonness, sparseness, fewness.

scare *v.* **1.** fill with fear, strike terror into, make afraid, frighten, terrify, startle, terrorize, horrify, make one's flesh crawl, make apprehensive, panic, alarm, intimidate, harrow, daunt, disquiet, give a turn, disconcert, dishearten; become frightened. —*n.* **2.** sudden fright, start, sudden terror, alarm, shock, panic; shake, palpitation, shiver, turn, nervousness, consternation; *Slang* jitters, the willies. **—Ant. 1** reassure, calm, soothe, comfort. **2** calm, reassurance.

scary *adj.* frightening, terrifying, creepy, hair-raising, shocking, goosepimply, disturbing, discomfiting, menacing, alarming, threatening, fearful, *Slang* hairy; bad, awful, difficult. **—Ant.** cheering, reassuring, comforting, pleasant, pleasing.

scathing *adj.* brutal, cutting, scorching, lacerating, searing, mordant, stinging, caustic, vitriolic, biting, acrimonious, excoriating; savage, ferocious, rancorous, hostile, virulent; trenchant, sharp, tart, pointed, keen, incisive. **—Ant.** kind, gentle, considerate, mild.

scatter *v.* **1.** spread loosely, distribute, disperse, throw, strew, sprinkle, spatter, cast, sow; circulate, broadcast, disseminate. **2.** disperse, separate; dispel, dissipate, rout, chase away. **—Syn. Study. 2** SCATTER, DISPERSE, DISPEL, DISSIPATE imply separating and driving something away so that its original form disappears. To SCATTER is to separate something tangible into parts at random and drive these in different directions: *The wind scattered leaves all over the lawn.* To DISPERSE is usu. to cause a compact or organized tangible body to separate or scatter in different directions, to be reassembled if desired: *Tear gas dispersed the mob.* To DISPEL is to drive away or scatter usu. intangible things so that they vanish: *Your explanation has dispelled my doubts.* To DISSIPATE is usu. to scatter by dissolving or reducing to atoms or small parts that cannot be reunited: *He dissipated his money and his energy in useless activities.* **—Ant.** gather, assemble, collect.

scatterbrained *adj.* hare-brained, muddleheaded, rattlebrained, birdbrained, featherbrained, light-minded, empty-headed, flighty, madcap, giddy, silly, zany, dizzy, stupid; absentminded, forgetful; foolish, foolhardy, wild, reckless, rash, heedless, careless, imprudent, frivolous, devil-may-care; irresponsible, unsteady, unstable; *Informal* crazy, nutty. **—Ant.** serious, intense, intelligent; careful, prudent; responsible, reliable, steady, stable.

scavenger *n.* **1.** carrion eater. **2.** trash picker, garbage picker; salvager; collector, magpie.

scenario *n.* **1.** screenplay, teleplay, working script, shooting script; manuscript, book. **2.** master plan, game plan, conception, scheme, plan, idea, concept; outline, summary, abstract, synopsis, précis.

scene *n.* **1.** setting, site, location, locale, locality, whereabouts; place, spot, position, region. **2.** vista, view, vision, sight, panorama, prospect, picture, show, display, spectacle; survey. **3.** display of temper, embarrassing spectacle, fuss, to-do, commotion. **4.** setting, locale, milieu; backdrop, background, scenery. **5.** episode, part, division, sequence, act. **—Syn. Study. 2** See VIEW.

scenery *n.* **1.** landscape, terrain; general

appearance, view, spectacle, vista. **2.** stage setting, backdrops, backgrounds, scenes, sets.

scent *n.* **1.** smell, odor, aroma, fragrance, bouquet, essence, perfume. **2.** odor left in passing; trail, track, course, path, wake, wind, pursuit, spoor. **—*v.* 3.** smell, sniff, breathe, inhale; get wind of, get a hint of, detect, distinguish, recognize, discern, suspect; trace, trail, track. **4.** fill with an odor, give odor to, perfume, aromatize. **—Syn. Study. 1** See ODOR.

schedule *n.* **1.** list of events, agenda, calendar, program; roll; inventory. **2.** list, table; timetable. **—*v.* 3.** set the time for, slate, fix, plan, book; appoint, set down, fit in, put down.

scheme *n.* **1.** plan, design, program, project, course; method, means, system, way, device, procedure, policy; strategy, tactics. **2.** secret plan, conspiracy, plot, maneuver, ruse, shift; contrivance, connivance; intrigue, cabal, stratagem, machination. **3.** arrangement, system, grouping, organization, network, disposition. **4.** schematic diagram, outline, delineation, layout, sketch, design, drawing; chart, map. **—*v.* 5.** plan secretly, plot, conspire, connive; contrive, devise, concoct, study, design; frame, organize, maneuver, machinate, cabal, intrigue; *Archaic* complot.

scheming *adj.* conniving, designing, contriving, calculating; Machiavellian, crafty, arch, sly, wily, artful, slippery, insidious, cunning, shrewd, tricky, intriguing. **—Ant.** naive, artless, ingenuous.

scholar *n.* **1.** learned person, erudite person, sage, wise man, man of letters, pundit, savant, mandarin; academic specialist, humanist, intellectual; *Slang* egghead, brain. **2.** pupil, student, learner, studier, matriculant; schoolboy, schoolgirl, undergraduate, collegian; *Informal* coed; *Slang* bookworm, grind. **—Ant. 1** dunce, dolt; ignoramus, illiterate.

scholarly *adj.* erudite, learned, informed, educated, well-read, academic, intellectual, lettered, literate, liberal, humane.

scholarship *n.* **1.** academic attainments, knowledge gained by study, learning, erudition, education, enlightenment, intelligence; thoroughness, accurate research, sound academic practice. **2.** aid granted a student, grant, endowment, maintenance for a student, stipend; assistantship, fellowship. **—Syn. Study. 1** See LEARNING. **—Ant. 1** ignorance, stupidity, idiocy, foolishness.

scholastic *adj.* of schools, educational, academic; scholarly, instructional, pedagogic, professorial, pedantic.

school *n.* **1.** place for instruction; academy, lyceum, institute; (*variously*) kindergarten, grade school, high school, college, university, seminary. **2.** group of people who think alike, order, faction, denomination, way of thinking, thought, ism, system, method, style, view; persuasion, doctrine, theory, faith, belief; *Informal* bunch, crowd. **—*v.* 3.** teach, train, instruct, educate.

science *n.* **1.** natural phenomena, empirical knowledge, organized knowledge, systematic knowledge; field of systematic inquiry. **2.** art, technique, method, discipline; finished execution, skill, aptitude, acquirement, finesse, facility.

scintillating *adj.* sparkling, lively, animated, ebullient, effervescent, exuberant, brilliant, dazzling, stimulating, glittering; charming, bright, witty. **—Ant.** dull, boring, lackluster.

scion *n.* offspring, child, heir, successor, descendant, son, daughter, heiress, offshoot; progeny, issue, seed, progeniture, posterity.

scoff *v.* mock, ridicule, deride, poke fun at, laugh at; deride, make sport of, make light of, belittle, make game of; flout, taunt, jeer, sneer; revile, contemn, rail at, run down, razz, put down, *Informal* knock. **—Syn. Study.** SCOFF, JEER, SNEER imply behaving with scornful disapproval toward someone or about something. To SCOFF is to express insolent doubt or derision, openly and emphatically: *to scoff at a new invention.* To JEER suggests expressing disapproval and scorn more loudly, coarsely, and unintelligently than in scoffing: *The crowd jeered at the pitcher.* To SNEER is to show by facial expression or tone of voice ill-natured contempt or disparagement: *He sneered unpleasantly in referring to his opponent's misfortunes.* **—Ant.** praise, compliment, exalt; applaud, cheer.

scold *v.* **1.** rebuke, upbraid, reprove, reprehend, remonstrate with, reprimand, chide, dress down, set down, take to task, bring to book, rake over the coals, put on the carpet, criticize, castigate, censure, blame angrily, berate, lash out at; find fault, nag, carp at, rail at, complain about. **—*n.* 2.** constant faultfinder, complainer, nagger, *Slang* kvetch; shrew, virago, termagant. **—Ant. 1** praise, honor, compliment, applaud.

scoop *n.* **1.** hand shovel; ladle, dipper, spoon, trowel. **2.** exclusive news story, *Slang* beat. **—*v.* 3.** dish out; lade out, ladle, lift out, shovel, spoon; empty with a scoop, bail, clear, clean. **4.** hollow, dig out, excavate, burrow, shovel, render concave, gouge.

scope *n.* **1.** range or extent of view, vision; application, bearing; effect, force, influence, competence, breadth of knowledge, reach, grasp; aim, purpose, goal, motive, intention, ambition, destination, determination. **2.** extent in space, area, span, stretch, spread, extension, compass, bounds, reach, confines. **3.** space for movement or activity, opportunity for operation; free course, rein, latitude, compass, margin, range, field, room, elbow room, vent; freedom, liberty. **—Syn. Study. 3** See RANGE.

scorch *v.* burn the surface of, singe, sear; shrivel with heat, wither, parch, scathe, char; dry, dry out, dehydrate; blacken, discolor.

score *n.* **1.** record of points made, tally, count; (*variously*) point, goal, run, basket. **2.** grade, test result, mark. **3.** notch, incision, nick, scratch, mark, groove, cut, slash, gash, slit. **4.** set of twenty. **5. scores** large numbers, multitudes, throngs, hosts, lots, masses, legions, droves, swarms. **6.** amount owed, amount due, account, bill, obligation, charge, debt, tab; grievance, grudge, difference. **7.** *Informal* facts, reality, truth, true situation. **8.** music (for a play, motion picture, etc.); written form of a musical composition. *—v.* **9.** make, gain, tally, register; pile up, amass. **10.** grade, mark, evaluate, judge; keep a tally, keep track of points. **11.** notch, scratch, cut, groove; mar, damage, deface. **12.** achieve, win, strike, register. **13.** orchestrate, arrange.

scorn *n.* **1.** contempt, scornfulness, disdain, haughtiness, arrogance; opprobrium, derision, contumely; scoffing, sarcasm, mockery, ridicule. *—v.* **2.** look down on, esteem lightly, contemn, be contemptuous of, despise, curl one's lip at, hold in contempt, disdain, treat with disdain, refuse to recognize, not countenance, care nothing for; spurn, refuse, rebuff, reject, repulse; ignore, disregard, refuse to deal with, have nothing to do with, refuse to listen to, turn a deaf ear to, slight; ostracize, spit upon. **—Syn. Study. 1** See CONTEMPT. **—Ant. 1** affection, deference, respect, esteem. **2** esteem, revere, look up to, admire; accept.

scotch *v.* suppress, stop, kill, destroy, put down, thwart, quash, crush, stamp out, confound, foil, put to rest, undermine, obstruct, sabotage; *Slang* nip in the bud, short-circuit. **—Ant.** encourage, spur, stimulate, boost, promote.

scoundrel *n.* villain, miscreant, rogue, cur, snake in the grass, weasel, ruffian, blackguard, knave, cad, bounder, rotter, *Archaic* varlet; mountebank, good-for-nothing, ne'er-do-well; thief, crook, swindler, sharper, shark, trickster, four-flusher; rascal, scamp, rapscallion, scalawag; turncoat, copperhead, carpetbagger, varmint. **—Syn. Study.** See KNAVE.

scour[1] *v.* clean by rubbing, scrub, scrape, cleanse, wash vigorously; abrade, polish, burnish, buff; shine, brighten.

scour[2] *v.* search through, comb, scan, rake, rummage, ransack; range over, pass over, traverse; move swiftly over, race through.

scourge *n.* **1.** whip, lash, flail, cat-o'-nine-tails, strap; switch, birch, rod, cane. **2.** cause of plague, bane, curse, terror; affliction, troublement, vexation. *—v.* **3.** flog, whip, lash, flail, thrash, beat; punish, discipline, flagellate; cane, switch, strap, birch, give the stick. **4.** criticize severely, castigate, chastise, chasten, take to task, excoriate, rake over the coals, censure, *Slang* blast.

scout *n.* **1.** person sent ahead, reconnoiterer, vanguard, advance guard, advance man, point man, outrider, lookout; guide, pilot, escort. **2.** person employed to discover new talent, talent scout, recruiter. *—v.* **3.** make reconnaissance, reconnoiter, survey, observe, put under surveillance, *Slang* case; spy, spy out.

scowl *v.* frown, glower, lower, glare, look daggers, grimace, look sullen, pout, *Slang* give a dirty look.

scramble *v.* **1.** scurry, rush, race, run. **2.** scuffle, struggle, vie, fight, strive, engage, scrimmage, combat, battle, come to blows, scrap, tussle, jostle, collide, clash. **3.** stir together; mix together, mix up, jumble, garble, disarrange, shuffle, disorganize, confuse, disorder; mess up, bring into disorder, upset, throw into confusion, unsettle, disturb, scatter. *—n.* **4.** rush, race, run. **5.** scuffle, struggle, tussle, free-for-all, competition, scrimmage.

scrap[1] *n.* **1.** small piece, small quantity, fragment, snippet, fraction, trace, sliver, particle; minimum, modicum, glimmer, smattering, sprinkling; bit, morsel, speck, dab, drop; atom, molecule, jot, iota, grain, crumb. **2.** discarded material, reclaimable material, junk; trash, refuse. *—v.* **3.** put in the scrap heap, sell as scrap; discard as worthless, junk, abandon, jettison. **—Ant. 3** keep, repair, maintain.

scrap[2] *Informal n.* **1.** fight, brawl, squabble, row; free-for-all, melee, fracas, brouhaha, *Slang* ruckus. *—v.* **2.** fight, quarrel, spat, brawl, row, come to blows.

scrape *v.* **1.** rub hard, abrade, scour; clean, smooth, plane, buff, burnish. **2.** graze, bruise, abrade, grate; scuff, skin. **3.** collect with difficulty, dig, forage, get by hook or crook; secure, procure, acquire, obtain, pick up, glean, gather, amass. **4.** grate, rasp, grind, scratch. **5.** economize, be frugal, save, scrimp, stint, pinch pennies. —*n.* **6.** skin injury, abrasion, bruise; mark, score, gash, gouge, groove. **7.** troublesome situation, predicament, difficulty, tough spot, tight spot, dilemma, pretty pickle, plight, straits; fight, scuffle, tussle, confrontation, run-in.

scratch *v.* **1.** make a mark on, graze, score, scrape, streak; cut, gash, lacerate; mar, blemish; damage slightly. **2.** scrape, rub, dig at; claw; relieve the itching of. **3.** draw along a rough surface, rub, scrape; strike. **4.** strike out, cancel, cross out, delete, draw the pen through, withdraw, eliminate, remove, rule out, blot out, expunge, exclude, omit, erase, rub out. **5.** draw crudely, scrawl, scribble; incise, cut, etch. **6.** sound harshly, scrape, grate, rasp, grind. —*n.* **7.** slight flesh wound, laceration, abrasion, nick, cut, gash.

scrawny *adj.* extremely thin, spindly, skinny, spare, lean, sinewy, lank, lanky; bony, gaunt, angular, rawboned; scraggy; puny, undersized, underweight, stunted, runty; fleshless, skeletal, emaciated, drawn, wasted, attenuated. —**Ant.** fat, plump, chubby, brawny, muscular.

scream *v.* **1.** shriek, howl, cry out, wail; screech, squawk, yowl, yelp, squeal, bellow, roar. **2.** shout, yell, call out loudly, cry out, holler. —*n.* **3.** loud, shrill cry; shriek, outcry, shout, yell, holler; screech, squeal, whine, wail, yelp, squawk; bellow, roar; lamentation.

screen *n.* **1.** partition, room divider, curtain, lattice. **2.** concealment, protection, cover, coverage, veil, mask, curtain, shroud, cloak, mantle; buffer, safeguard, defense. **3.** motion pictures, movies, cinema, the silver screen, films; the film industry. **4.** screen door, window screen, screening, shutter, Venetian blind, jalousie, lattice. **5.** sieve, strainer, sifter, filter, grate, colander; web, mesh. —*v.* **6.** shield, shelter, protect, defend, secure, safeguard, guard; cover, shroud, shade, veil; keep hidden, conceal, hide from sight; withhold, secrete, keep secret. **7.** examine for suitability, evaluate, size up, rate, grade; eliminate, get rid of, throw away, discard, throw out, eject, weed out; separate, sift, winnow, cull, filter, strain; sort, arrange, order, group, class. **8.** project, show, present; see, view, preview.

screw *n.* **1.** fastener, threaded nail, bolt. **2.** propeller; driver. —*v.* **3.** fasten, bolt, rivet, attach, join, clamp; adjust, tighten; twist, turn. **4.** twist, twist out of shape, contort, distort, pervert, warp; deform, misshape, garble; gnarl, knot. **5.** wring, wrench, wrest, force, exact, extort, twist, squeeze.

screwy *adj.* batty, daft, eccentric, unbalanced, queer, odd, peculiar, funny; *Slang* wacky, dotty, kinky, weird, weirdo, nutty, flaky, kooky, oddball.

scrimp *v.* be sparing, skimp, be frugal, be parsimonious, be stingy, pinch, stint, save, be penurious, pinch pennies, hoard, cut corners, economize; dole out sparingly, use sparingly, begrudge.

script *n.* **1.** handwriting, hand, longhand, cursive; penmanship, calligraphy, chirography. **2.** manuscript, written text; dialogue, lines, book, scenario, libretto, score.

Scripture, Holy Scripture *n.* Often **the Scriptures, the Holy Scriptures** sacred writings, holy writ, inspired writings; the Bible, the Word of God, the Gospels, Old Testament, New Testament, *Informal* The Good Book; *(Judaism)* the Hebrew Scriptures, *(variously)* the Torah, the Law, the Pentateuch, the Septuagint.

scrub[1] *v.* **1.** rub clean, scour, swab. —*n.* **2.** scrubbing, scouring; cleaning by rubbing.

scrub[2] *n.* low trees, brush, brushwood, stunted vegetation.

scrumptious *adj. Informal* delicious, flavorful, tasty, delectable, flavorsome, savory, appetizing, mouth-watering, toothsome, luscious, juicy, succulent, tender; agreeable, enjoyable, pleasant, pleasing, delightful.

scruple *n.* **1.** principle, ethics, moral restraint, compunction, misgiving; conscience, conscientiousness, scrupulousness, concern, care; qualm, anxiety, hesitation, uncertainty, apprehension, doubtfulness, protestation; squeamishness, fearfulness. —*v.* **2.** be ethical, have principles, hesitate, refrain, demur, pause, hang back, blench, balk, halt; waver, fluctuate, falter; have a qualm, feel qualms, be qualmish, have a bad conscience, be timorous, shy, fight shy, take exception.

scrupulous *adj.* having scruples, principled, honest, conscientious, honorable, upright; painstaking, sedulous, deliberate, careful, cautious; exact, exacting, precise, meticulous, fastidious, punctilious; dutiful. —**Syn. Study.** SCRUPULOUS, PUNCTILIOUS imply being very careful to do the right or proper thing. SCRUPULOUS implies conscientious care in attending to details: *The scientist described his observations with scrupulous accuracy.* PUNCTILIOUS suggests strictness and rigidity, esp. in observance of social conventions: *punctilious adherence to the rules of etiquette.* —**Ant.** unscrupulous, dishonest, unprincipled; careless, reckless, inexact, inattentive, sloppy, slipshod.

scrutinize *v.* examine closely, study, observe, look at closely, peruse, scan, regard carefully, *Slang* give the once-over; inspect carefully, survey, look over, take stock of; inquire into, investigate, pry into, peer into; search, explore, probe. **—Ant.** neglect, disregard, overlook; glance at.

scrutiny *n.* examination, attention, study, investigation, inquiry, inspection, perusal, close look, critical regard, watch, surveillance. **—Syn. Study.** See EXAMINATION.

scuffle *v.* **1.** struggle, fight, scrap, tussle, squabble, spar, jostle; come to blows, exchange blows, clash; *Slang* mix it up. *—n.* **2.** struggle, scrap, tussle, row, fight, brawl, imbroglio; melee, donnybrook, free-for-all, fracas; rumpus, commotion.

scum *n.* **1.** surface, film, crust, dross, deposit, slag, refuse. **2.** lowest of the low, trash, rubbish, dregs; riffraff, rabble.

scurrilous *adj.* slanderous, derogatory, disparaging, detracting, derisive, reviling, offensive, contemptuous, insulting; coarsely abusive, coarse, gross, low, churlish, shameless, indecent, indelicate; vulgar, foulmouthed, obscene. **—Ant.** decent, proper, delicate, refined, well-bred, polite.

scurry *v.* **1.** move quickly, run with light steps, scamper, scramble, scuttle, make tracks, rush, speed, hasten, hurry, hie, hustle, scoot, spring, skim, race, tear along. *—n.* **2.** scamper, hasty running; rushing, hurrying, scooting; dispersal, scattering; haste, bustle, confusion.

scurvy *adj.* mean, low, base, shabby, vile; contemptible, despicable, dishonorable, ignoble, worthless. **—Ant.** honorable, dignified, noble.

scuttle *v.* **1.** sink, send to the bottom, send to Davy Jones's locker; sacrifice, abort, discard, dispatch, wreck, scrap, destroy. **2.** scurry, hurry, hasten, scamper, speed, scramble.

scuttlebutt *n.* gossip, rumor, hearsay, talk, tittle-tattle, chitchat, small talk, prattle, scandal.

sea *n.* **1.** ocean, deep, main, waves, waters, the briny deep; large body of water, bay, gulf, bight, lake. **2.** condition of the water's surface. **3.** wave, swell, surge, flood, roller, breaker. **4.** great deal, great quantity, multitude, slew, flood, spate, ton, leap, scads, lots, mass, legion, host, swarm, flock, scores, abundance, profusion. **—Ant.** land, terrain, terra firma.

seacoast *n.* shore, seashore, coast, seaside, seaboard, coastline, waterside, water's edge, shoreline, beach, littoral, lido, riviera, coastland; *French* côte.

seal *n.* **1.** figure, emblem, mark, symbol, distinctive design, insignia, stamp, impression, imprint, brand; signet, imprimatur; hallmark, colophon, trademark. **2.** fastening device, fastener; gummed flap. *—v.* **3.** certify, authenticate, confirm, verify, ratify, validate, endorse; affirm, approve, sanction, accept, OK. **4.** settle, conclude, make final; fix, establish, determine. **5.** close, secure, fasten; shut, shut up, lock; plug, stop, stop up, cork, dam.

seam *n.* **1.** line of stitches, juncture, joining, junction, joint, suture; interface. **2.** wrinkle, incised line, furrow, scar; fissure, chink, crevice, break, breach, rupture, opening, crack, cleft, gap. **3.** layer, stratum, vein, lode. *—v.* **4.** join together in a seam, stitch together; suture. **5.** furrow, wrinkle, mark, line, cut into, incise, notch.

seaman *n.* **—Syn. Study.** See SAILOR.

seamy *adj.* unpleasant, nasty, disagreeable, coarse, sordid, unwholesome, rough, raw, dirty, unclean, dark, squalid. **—Ant.** pleasant, nice, wholesome, agreeable; gentle, tender, sweet.

sear *v.* **1.** burn, scorch, char, singe; cauterize; blast, blister. **2.** harden, caseharden, scar, steel.

search *v.* **1.** examine, scrutinize, explore, scour, scout out, investigate carefully, look over, inspect, overhaul, study, survey, check, check out, probe, sift, comb, drag, look into, pry into, delve into, pore over, ransack, rifle, rummage, turn inside out, turn upside down; snoop, fish; hunt, look, cast about, seek, quest; frisk, shake down. *—n.* **2.** examination, inspection, scrutiny, study, close look, check, investigation, probe, inquiry, exploration; hunt, pursuit, quest; dragnet; tracer.

seasick *adj.* nauseated, sick to one's stomach, queasy, squeamish, qualmish, vomitous; *Slang* barfy, green around the gills; ill, sick, giddy, faint, dizzy, lightheaded, vertiginous; *Slang* woozy, under the weather.

season *n.* **1.** division of the year, (*variously*) spring, summer, the dog days, fall, autumn, Indian summer, winter, quarter; appropriate time, peak time, prime; period, term, stage, spell, stretch, interval, duration. *—v.* **2.** flavor, spice, leaven, lace; enliven, heighten, color, accent, enhance, embellish, ornament. **3.** improve by experience, train, practice, discipline, drill; break in, tame; refine, mellow, soften, temper; accustom, inure, adapt; inform, shape, finish. **4.** age, dry, ripen, temper, mature, prime, cultivate, condition, prepare.

seasoning *n.* **1.** flavoring, spice, condiment, relish, herb; (*variously*) salt, pepper, allspice, basil, thyme, oregano, rosemary, mace, sage, marjoram, clove, parsley, dill, paprika, garlic, onion, cinnamon, nutmeg, ginger; gusto, zest. **2.** training, practice, preparation, orientation, familiarization; ripening, maturation; aging; drying.

seat *n.* **1.** (*variously*) chair, sofa, couch, divan, bench, cushion, place, box. **2.** buttocks, rear end, hindquarters, bottom, haunches, rump, posterior, croup, *French* derrière; *Informal* backside, behind, *Slang* fanny. **3.** center, hub, axis, nucleus; heart, core; capital. **4.** residence, home, house, dwelling, abode, domicile, housing, address, quarters; site, locale, locus, location, habitat; family seat, ancestral hall. **5.** place in a select group, membership; incumbency. —*v.* **6.** show to a seat, provide with a seat; cause to sit, place on a seat; settle, situate.

secede *v.* withdraw, leave, pull out, quit, retire, resign, have done, disaffiliate, break with, forsake. —**Ant.** join, federate.

seclude *v.* place apart, keep apart, separate, dissociate, place in solitude, isolate, shut off, sequester, retire, retire from sight, hide, go into retreat.

secluded *adj.* isolated, sheltered, sequestered, cloistered; unvisited, seldom visited, unfrequented, remote, out-of-the-way, cut off, solitary, lonely, withdrawn, reclusive; shut in, confined; hidden from view, covert, shut away, closeted, private, screened off. —**Ant.** accessible, frequented; sociable; public, open.

seclusion *n.* isolation, solitude, hiding, concealment, retreat, reclusion, withdrawal, sequestration, cloister, retirement, exile, quarantine; secluded place, hiding place, sanctuary, asylum, hermitage, hideaway.

second[1] *adj.* **1.** next after the first; runner-up. **2.** another, one more, additional. **3.** alternate, alternating, other. **4.** inferior, subordinate, second-rate, second fiddle, surpassed, exceeded, outdone. —*n.* **5.** second one; runner-up. **6.** helper, assistant, aid, attendant, lieutenant; agent, representative, deputy, delegate; substitute, alternate, fill-in, stand-in, understudy, pinch hitter, proxy. —*v.* **7.** support, endorse; back, stand by, back up, uphold, stand back of; side with, subscribe to, favor, work for, advocate; promote, encourage, further, advance; help, assist, aid, abet.

second[2] *n.* **1.** sixtieth of a minute. **2.** moment, minute, instant, jiffy, trice, wink, flash; *Informal* bat of an eye, twinkling, shake of a lamb's tail, two shakes.

secondary *adj.* **1.** next after the first, second; following, subsequent, consequent, resultant. **2.** lesser, inferior, smaller, minor, lower; subordinate, ancillary; mediocre, second-rate, middling, second-best, second-string, second fiddle. **3.** other, alternate; subsidiary, auxiliary; not primary, not original; backup. —**Ant. 1–3** primary, first. **1** preceding. **2** superior, larger, bigger, major. **3** sole; original.

second-rate *adj.* inferior, mediocre, second-string, second-best, inadequate, middling, so-so, undistinguished, pedestrian, imperfect, outclassed, fair-to-middling, commonplace, everyday, average; cheap, shabby, low-grade, *Slang* tacky. —**Ant.** first-class, best, prize, A-one, excellent.

secrecy *n.* secretiveness, silence, uncommunicativeness, muteness, confidentiality, closeness; covertness, clandestineness, mystery, stealth, furtiveness, underhandedness, surreptitiousness, dark dealing; private, solitude, concealment, privacy, hiding, sequestration, seclusion.

secret *adj.* **1.** private, confidential, unrevealable, unrevealed, undisclosed, unpublished, hush-hush; hidden, concealed, unseen, invisible, camouflaged, secluded; undercover, disguised; covert, clandestine, surreptitious; unknown, mysterious, mystic, dark, esoteric, arcane, occult. **2.** keeping knowledge to oneself, secretive, close-mouthed, tight-lipped, mum, discreet; mysterious; furtive, stealthy, hugger-mugger. —*n.* **3.** confidential information, confidential matter, confidence. **4.** mystery, enigma, puzzle. **5.** formula, key, recipe, unguessed-at reason, special method. —**Ant. 1, 2** open. **1** public, revealed, disclosed; obvious, evident, apparent, undisguised; well-known, ordinary. **2** candid, frank, straightforward.

secrete *v.* hide, conceal, cache, stash; cloak, curtain, screen, veil, disguise; keep secret, keep under wraps, cover, shroud. —**Syn. Study.** See HIDE. —**Ant.** reveal, show, display, exhibit.

secretive *adj.* unrevealing, uncommunicative, close-mouthed, tight-lipped, silent, mum, mute; reserved, discreet, withdrawn, reticent, private, taciturn, laconic, sparing of words; sly, stealthy, furtive, evasive, surreptitious, underhanded, covert, mysterious, cryptic, enigmatic. —**Ant.** open, communicative, talkative; candid, frank, plain, straightforward, direct.

sect *n.* religious subgroup, denomination, persuasion, school of thought, camp, affiliation, religious creed, religious order, cult; division, faction, splinter group.

section *n.* **1.** part, division, piece, segment, unit, portion; share, installment, increment, allotment, measure, proportion;

chapter, passage. **2.** district, area, side, vicinity, province, sphere, region; sector, department; zone, ward, neighborhood; territory, range, terrain. **3.** slice, cross section, cutting; specimen, sample.

sector *n.* administrative division, zone, district; theater, area, sphere of action.

secular *adj.* worldly, profane, mundane, nonspiritual, nonsacred, nonreligious, temporal, earthly; lay, nonclerical, nonecclesiastical; fleshly, sensual, carnal. **—Ant.** sacred, divine, spiritual, ecclesiastical.

secure *adj.* **1.** free from danger, free from harm, safe, unthreatened, invulnerable, immune, protected, defended, sheltered, out of danger; carefree, reassured, easy, at ease, composed, self-possessed, confident. **2.** unattackable, unassailable, impregnable. **3.** firmly fastened; set, fixed, tight. **4.** sure, certain, assured, guaranteed, definite, positive, absolute; *Slang* in the bag, surefire. **—***v.* **5.** obtain, procure, acquire, get, get hold of, get possession of. **6.** free from harm, make safe, safeguard, defend, protect, shelter, insure. **7.** ensure, guarantee. **8.** make fast, fix firmly, fasten, lash tight, batten down, tie down, bind. **—Syn. Study. 5** See GET. **—Ant. 1–4** insecure. **1** unsafe, endangered, threatened, in danger; unsure, uneasy, anxious. **2** weak, vulnerable. **3** loose, unfixed. **4** unsure, uncertain, unassured, indefinite; unsettled, undetermined; precarious. **5** lose, give up. **6** endanger, imperil, harm, leave unprotected. **8** loose, unloose, untie.

security *n.* **1.** freedom from danger, freedom from harm, protection, safety, safekeeping; preservation, maintenance, support, care, keep. **2.** defense, safeguards, safety measures, protective devices; police, guards, troops. **3.** assurance, guarantee, surety, pledge, bond, warranty; collateral; deposit. **4.** secureness, assurance, confidence, certainty, positiveness, sureness, absoluteness, definiteness, decisiveness; trust, peace of mind, reliance, promise, hope, faith, conviction. **5.** Usu. **securities** stocks, bonds, certificates of title to property.

sedate *adj.* calm, composed, unruffled, collected, levelheaded, self-possessed, self-controlled, cool, coolheaded, imperturbable, impassive, undemonstrative, unexcited; serious, steady, solemn, sober, grave; poised, dignified, decorous, reserved, staid; subdued, quiet, still, serene. **—Ant.** nervous, perturbed, disturbed, impassioned, agitated, excited, noisy, active, restless, unsteady; flighty, frivolous, gay.

sedative *adj.* **1.** soothing, calming, relaxing, comforting, easing, tranquilizing, soporific, narcotic, composing; palliative, calmative, allaying, alleviative, assuasive, lenitive; anodyne, analgesic. **—***n.* **2.** tranquilizer, calmative; analgesic, anodyne, palliative, alleviative, mitigator, lenitive, assuasive; narcotic, opiate.

sedentary *adj.* sitting, seated, inactive, unmoving, unstirring, inert, fixed, stationary; quiescent, resting, still.

sediment *n.* settlings, lees, grounds; dregs, leavings, remains, residue; dross, scum; debris, waste, slag, sludge.

sedition *n.* mutiny, revolt, insurrection, insurgency, rebellion, defiance, subversion, lawlessness, uprising, disloyalty; rebelliousness, disobedience, unruliness, subversiveness. **—Syn. Study.** See TREASON. **—Ant.** allegiance, loyalty, obedience, submission.

seduce *v.* **1.** persuade to do wrong, lure, entice, lead astray; corrupt, defile, debauch, deflower, violate, ravish; deprave, pervert, disgrace, dishonor; abuse, ruin. **2.** attract, turn one's head, win over, conquer, persuade, overcome the resistance to, entice, charm, tempt, lure, allure, captivate. **—Syn. Study. 2** See TEMPT. **—Ant. 1** persuade to do right; save, protect; honor. **2** repel, repulse; disgust; dissuade.

seducer *n.* debaucher, cad, roué, womanizer, woman chaser, skirt-chaser, lady killer, playboy, philanderer, heartbreaker, Don Juan, Casanova, Lothario, Romeo, lover-boy; *Slang* wolf, letch.

seductive *adj.* alluring, enticing, tempting, sexy, provocative, voluptuous, come-hither; attractive, charming, disarming, enchanting, bewitching, beguiling, captivating. **—Ant.** repulsive, repellent; drab, staid, prim.

seductress *n.* siren, temptress, enchantress, Jezebel, adventuress, vamp, mantrap, cocotte, Lorelei, woman of easy virtue.

see *v.* **1.** make out, discern, distinguish, recognize; behold, observe, witness; hold in view, have in sight, notice, look at, regard, spot, catch sight of, sight, glimpse, spy, espy, descry; view, survey, contemplate, take in; eye, set one's eyes on, stare at, gaze at; *Slang* dig, get a load of. **2.** perceive, understand, comprehend, apprehend, appreciate, grasp, take in, fathom, get the drift; know, be cognizant of, realize, be aware of, register, be conscious of. **3.** visualize, envision, picture, conceive, make out; regard, consider. **4.** find out, ascertain, discover, determine; consider, meditate, contemplate, ruminate, give thought to, mull over. **5.** undergo, experience, go through. **6.** make sure, take care, make certain, see to it, watch, mind, observe. **7.** call on, visit; meet, encounter, run into; speak to, consult, confer with; receive, attend to, entertain, listen to, interview. **8.** date, court, woo; keep company with. **9.** escort, accompany, attend. **—Ant. 1** neglect, overlook, disregard, ignore. **2** misunderstand, mistake, be unaware of.

seed *n.* **1.** grain, pit, stone, ovule; seedling. **2.** source, origin, basis, germ, embryo, beginning. **3.** descendants, progeny, issue, offspring, children; heirs, posterity. **—***v.* **4.** sow with seed, plant. **5.** remove the seeds from; pit.

seek *v.* **1.** try to find, search for, look for, track down, look into, dig for, probe for, investigate, explore, examine, scrutinize, inspect; nose out, ferret out, pursue, be after, hunt, fish for, sniff out, scout out, trace. **2.** try to obtain, strive for, aim for, aspire to, pursue; be after, go in for; request, inquire for, petition for, demand, call for; solicit, court, invite. **3.** try, attempt, endeavor, essay, set about, go about, try one's hand at, undertake, venture, *Informal* have a go at. **—Ant. 1** neglect, ignore, abandon; avoid, shun; discard, relinquish, drop.

seem *v.* appear, look, give the impression of being, have the semblance of, look like, look as if, strike one as being. **—Syn. Study.** SEEM, APPEAR, LOOK refer to an outward aspect that may or may not be contrary to reality. SEEM is applied to something that has an aspect of truth and probability: *It seems warmer today.* APPEAR suggests the giving of an impression that may be superficial or illusory: *The house appears to be deserted.* LOOK more vividly suggests the use of the eye (literally or figuratively) or the aspect as perceived by the eye: *She looked frightened.*

seeming *adj.* ostensible, apparent, evident, obvious; presumed, supposed, putative; superficial, surface.

seemly *adj.* suitable, felicitous, proper, appropriate, in good taste, fitting, becoming, befitting, due, acceptable, conventional, correct, prudent, polite, courteous, well-bred, decorous, right, decent, tasteful, refined; *French* comme il faut. **—Ant.** unseemly, unbecoming, improper, rude, impolite, impertinent, pert, forward.

seep *v.* leak, ooze, trickle, dribble, drip; suffuse, diffuse, penetrate, permeate, soak, soak through. **—Ant.** gush, flow, flood.

seer *n.* prophet, sage, oracle, soothsayer, astrologer, stargazer, fortuneteller, psychic, augur, clairvoyant, medium, diviner, necromancer, sorcerer, sorceress, conjurer.

seethe *v.* **1.** boil, bubble, churn, roil; simmer, stew, brew, cook. **2.** be greatly excited, be agitated, be upset, be irate, be livid, be angry, be indignant; rage, rant, rave, boil, storm, breathe fire, fume, smolder, simmer, stew; carry on, foam at the mouth, bluster, raise a rumpus, stamp one's foot, throw a fit, throw a tantrum, blow up, blow one's cool, blow one's top, blow one's stack, *Slang* raise Cain. **—Syn. Study. 2** See BOIL.

segment *n.* **1.** part, piece, section, division, portion; installment, increment; stage, leg. **—***v.* **2.** divide into parts, section, cut up, split up; cleave, separate, disjoin, disunite. **—Ant. 1** whole, entity, entirety. **2** combine, meld, fuse; join, unite.

segregate *v.* separate, isolate, cut off, detach, divide, divorce, disunite, disconnect; keep apart, sequester, set apart, set aside, single out, sort out; seclude, insulate, quarantine. **—Ant.** unite, blend, mix, desegregate, integrate.

seize *v.* **1.** take hold of, take possession of, grab, snatch, pluck, grasp, clutch, embrace, lay hands upon; acquire forcibly, take possession of by force; usurp, arrogate, commandeer; confiscate, impound, appropriate. **2.** grasp, comprehend, apprehend, understand, read, catch, gather, take in, glean. **3.** overwhelm, overpower; possess. **4.** capture, arrest, apprehend, take into custody, take captive; catch, nab, *Informal* bag, collar, pinch. **5.** take advantage of, make use of, utilize, profit from, act upon. **—Ant. 1, 4** let go of, release; relinquish, give up; free, liberate, let go, loose. **5** waste, let pass, pass up.

seizure *n.* **1.** act of seizing, taking, grasping; capture, apprehension, arrest; snatching, usurpation; possession, appropriation, confiscation; commandeering, impressment; abduction, kidnapping. **2.** attack, convulsion, fit, stroke, throe, visitation, paroxysm; onset, access, spell, episode, crisis.

seldom *adv.* rarely, scarcely, not often, not frequently, infrequently; hardly ever, now and then, sporadically, occasionally, once in a great while, uncommonly. **—Ant.** often, frequently, always.

select *v.* **1.** choose, pick, pick out, make one's choice, decide for, elect, single out, opt for, prefer; fix upon, settle upon, put aside, lay aside; *Informal* give the nod to, tap. **—***adj.* **2.** choice, picked, privileged, chosen. **3.** superior, first-rate, first-class, élite; choice, preferred; exclusive, *Informal* top-notch, four-star, A1, posh, fancy. **—Ant. 1** reject, refuse, repudiate, spurn. **2** indiscriminate; random. **3** inferior, second-rate; modest, ordinary, unremarkable, undistinguished.

selection *n.* **1.** choice, choosing, preference, pick, decision, election, option. **2.**

variety, choice, range, option. **3.** selected number, collection, program; medley, miscellany, potpourri.

selective *adj.* choosy, choosing carefully, discerning, discriminating, particular, fastidious, finicky, fussy, meticulous; cautious, careful, *Informal* picky. **—Ant.** unselective, promiscuous, careless, indiscriminate.

self-assured *adj.* confident, self-confident, assured, cocky, cocksure, brash. **—Ant.** self-doubting, insecure, unconfident.

self-centered *adj.* selfish, self-seeking, self-absorbed, self-concerned, wrapped up in oneself, self-important; egotistic, egoistic, egocentric, conceited, narcissistic, vain, swellheaded, immodest.

self-confidence *n.* self-assurance, self-reliance, positive self-image, resolution, mettle, pluck, spirit, nerve; cocksureness, boldness, cockiness, gameness.

self-consciousness *n.* shyness, modesty, timidity, bashfulness, reticence, reserve, diffidence, constraint, hesitancy, fearfulness, apprehension, constraint, abashment, demureness, self-effacement, sheepishness. **—Ant.** assurance, boldness, self-confidence, aggressiveness, self-assertion.

self-control *n.* self-discipline, willpower, self-possession, composure, self-restraint, mental balance, levelheadedness, presence of mind, soberness, firmness, soundness, stability, coolheadedness, sobriety, poise, savoir faire, aplomb, unexcitability, imperturbability, sangfroid; patience, temperance, forbearance.

self-esteem *n.* pride, self-respect, self-regard, confidence, self-confidence, self-assurance, self-sufficiency, self-reliance, independence, pardonable pride. **—Ant.** self-effacement, sheepishness; self-loathing, servility, abjectness.

self-evident *adj.* obvious, plain, evident, manifest, apparent, palpable, glaring, distinct, patent, self-explanatory, incontrovertible, explicit, unarguable, undeniable. **—Ant.** doubtful, questionable, ambiguous, arguable.

selfish *adj.* self-seeking, self-concerned, self-centered, egocentric, egotistic; greedy, rapacious, avaricious, covetous, venal, mercenary, grasping; uncharitable, ungenerous, illiberal, grudging, stingy, parsimonious, miserly, mean, *Informal* tight. **—Ant.** unselfish, selfless, considerate; generous, bighearted, magnanimous, giving; altruistic.

self-love *n.* conceit, narcissism, vanity, haughtiness, amour propre, self-conceit, conceitedness, vainglory, self-satisfaction, complacency, egoism, egotism, self-importance, swellheadedness. **—Ant.** humility, modesty, unpretentiousness, self-deprecation.

self-reliant *adj.* independent, assured, self-confident, self-possessed, self-sufficient, enterprising, spirited, plucky, mettlesome; resolute, hardy.

self-righteous *adj.* sanctimonious, righteous in one's own regard, smug, complacent, pharisaical, hypocritical, insincere, mealymouthed; pompous, pious, moralizing, pretentious, holier-than-thou, pietistic.

self-satisfaction *n.* satisfaction with one's accomplishments, pride, self-pleasure, self-content, complacency, smugness, self-approval, self-admiration, self-righteousness; vanity; flush of success.

self-satisfied *adj.* complacent, smug, self-contented, priggish, overconfident, overproud, cocksure, self-approving, vain, vainglorious, self-righteous, egotistical, narcissistic. **—Ant.** self-critical, humble, modest, self-hating.

sell *v.* **1.** give up for a price, exchange for money; dispose of, dispense, unload, dump. **2.** deal in, trade in, handle; offer for sale, put up for sale, put on sale, effect the sale of; vend, market, barter, peddle, hawk, traffic in. **3.** win the acceptance of, win over, persuade to buy, persuade to accept, convince, prevail upon, enlist. **4.** betray, sell out, deliver up, take a bribe for, play false, deceive.

seller *n.* vendor, dealer, retailer, wholesaler, storekeeper, shopkeeper, tradesman, merchant, salesman, saleswoman, saleslady, salesgirl, salesperson, peddler, middleman, jobber, trader, *British* monger.

semblance *n.* **1.** outward appearance, aspect, likeness, look, show, air, mien, bearing; unreal appearance, pretense, simulacrum. **2.** image, representation, copy, duplicate, replica, reproduction, facsimile, cast, counterpart, likeness.

seminal *adj.* originating, original, primary, germinal, germinative, formative; generative; creative, productive, fruitful.

send *v.* **1.** cause to go, have transported, have transmitted, dispatch, relay, forward, convey. **2.** transmit, project, broadcast, disseminate; give off, emit. **3.** direct, refer, point the way to, indicate the course to, guide, show, lead, head, conduct. **4.** propel, throw, deliver, shoot, hurl, cast, discharge, drive, emit, launch, fling, toss. **—Ant. 1** hold, keep, retain; receive. **2** receive, get.

senile *adj.* doddering, superannuated, doting, foolish, senescent, infirm, decrepit.

senior *adj.* **1.** Often **Senior** older, elder, *French* père. **2.** superior, higher in rank; above, over. **3.** of long tenure, veteran, doyen. —*n.* **4.** one who is older, elder. **5.** person of higher rank, superior, better, higher-up, chief, head. **—Ant. 1–5** junior. **1** younger. **2** subordinate, inferior. **5** subordinate, inferior.

seniority *n.* precedence, longer service, tenure, longevity; superiority in rank; greater age.

sensation *n.* **1.** perception, feeling, sensitivity, sensibility, perceptivity; consciousness, awareness, detection; responsiveness. **2.** impression, sense, perception, feeling. **3.** public excitement, uproar, stir, commotion, to-do, thrill, agitation; cause of excitement, thrilling event; hit; scandal.

sensational *adj.* **1.** outstanding, striking, spectacular, extraordinary, exceptional; exciting, thrilling, electrical, galvanic; dramatic; excellent, superb. **2.** shocking, exaggerated, extravagant, emotional, heartthrobbing; lurid, cheap, meretricious, scandalous. **—Ant. 1** ordinary, common, everyday, routine; mediocre. **2** prosaic, dull, bland.

sense *n.* **1.** faculty, function, feeling, sensation; (*variously*) touch, smell, taste, sight, hearing. **2.** impression, sensation, realization, awareness, recognition, consciousness. **3.** appreciation, understanding, intuition. **4.** mental ability, judgment, reason, mind, understanding, perspicacity, sagacity, wisdom, intelligence, reasonableness. **5.** value, worth, use, good, point, benefit, purpose, practicality, efficacy. **6.** impression, awareness, intuition, premonition, presentiment; aura, atmosphere. **7.** meaning, signification, connotation, denotation, definition; significance, purport. —*v.* **8.** be aware of, perceive, feel; recognize, detect, discern. **9.** grasp, understand, apprehend, comprehend, take in, descry, see, note, perceive, espy, regard, discern, realize. **10.** have a vague impression, feel, suspect, divine, guess. **—Syn. Study. 7** See MEANING. **—Ant. 4** stupidity, folly. **5** nonsense. **9** misunderstand; disregard, ignore, neglect, overlook, miss.

senseless *adj.* **1.** unconscious, without sensation, insensible, insensate; deadened, comatose, numb; knocked out, stunned. **2.** useless, meaningless, purposeless; stupid, witless, brainless, harebrained, foolish, foolhardy, inane, silly, nonsensical, ridiculous, irrational, unreasonable, unwise, ill-advised, irresponsible, *Informal* crazy, dumb, nutty; without reason, illogical, groundless, meaningless, pointless, aimless; idle. **—Ant. 1** conscious. **2** useful, meaningful, worthwhile; sensible, smart, intelligent, clever, wise; rational, reasonable, sound, logical.

sensibility *n.* **1.** ability to perceive, responsiveness, sensitiveness, sensitivity, perception. **2.** artistic responsiveness, esthetic judgment, refined tastes; emotional makeup, temperament. **3.** Often **sensibilities** sensitivity, sensitiveness, susceptibility; thin skin, sore spot, Achilles' heel. **—Ant. 1** insensibility, insensitiveness, insensitivity; deadness, dullness, numbness, unconsciousness.

sensible *adj.* **1.** sound, showing good sense, intelligent, thoughtful, perspicacious; wise, sage, sagacious, farsighted, practical; discerning, discriminating, prudent, discreet, judicious, just; well-advised, well-grounded, logical, rational, reasonable, sane; plausible, credible, possible. **2.** aware, perceiving, perceptive, cognitive, cognizant; conscious, knowing, enlightened, informed, apprised. **3.** perceptible, noticeable, discernible; tangible, palpable, detectable, visible; plain, apparent, evident, obvious. **4.** capable of feeling or perceiving, sensitive, responsive, susceptible. **—Syn. Study. 1** See PRACTICAL. **—Ant. 1** unsound, unintelligent, stupid, unwise, foolish, absurd, senseless, imprudent, indiscreet, injudicious; illogical, irrational, unreasonable. **2** insensible, unaware, ignorant, blind. **3** undetectable, unnoticeable, invisible. **4** insensible, insensitive.

sensitive *adj.* **1.** responsive, perceptive, sentient, sensing. **2.** easily affected emotionally, easily offended or hurt, touchy, thin-skinned; delicate, impressionable, susceptible; perceptive, keen, acute. **3.** detecting slight change, delicate, fine; accurate, precise, exact; faithful. **4.** sore, tender, painful. **—Ant. 2** hard, tough, coarse, thick-skinned, callous, obtuse. **3** rough, coarse, inaccurate, approximate.

sensual *adj.* erotic, carnal, lustful, lewd, licentious, lecherous, sexy, animal; earthy, fleshly, voluptuous, pleasure-seeking, pleasure-loving, hedonistic. **—Syn. Study.** SENSUAL, SENSUOUS both refer to experience through the senses. SENSUAL refers to the enjoyments derived from the senses, esp. to the gratification or indulgence of physical appetites: *sensual pleasures.* SENSUOUS refers to that which is aesthetically pleasing to the senses: *sensuous poetry.* See also CARNAL.

sensuous *adj.* gratifying the senses, strongly appealing, delicious, exquisite, delightful. **—Syn. Study.** See SENSUAL.

sententious *adj.* preachy, didactic, pedantic, holier-than-thou, judgmental, sanctimonious, pietistic, self-righteous, moralistic; pompous, grandiose, high-sounding, high-flown, stilted, orotund.

sentiment *n.* **1.** Often **sentiments** opinion, attitude, view, point of view, viewpoint, feeling, thought, notion, idea. **2.** feeling, emotion, sentimentality, nostalgia, tenderness, heart, softheartedness, emotionalism, romance, romanticism. —**Syn. Study. 1** See OPINION. **2** See FEELING.

sentimental *adj.* **1.** emotional, mawkish, pathetic, weepy, romantic, hearts-and-flowers, melodramatic, romanticized; *Informal* tear-jerking, mushy. **2.** emotional, nostalgic; tearful, maudlin, lachrymose.

sentimentality *n.* emotionalism, mawkishness, sloppiness; sentimentalism, pathos, bathos, mush; emotional nature, heart, temperament, *Slang* kitsch.

sentinel *n.* sentry, guard, lookout, watchman, watch, night watchman, ward, picket, patrol, scout, ranger, guardian, guardsman.

separate *v.* **1.** keep apart, divide, mark off, come between, split, partition; subdivide, cut, sever, detach, break, sunder, bisect, part; disjoin, disunite, disconnect. **2.** set apart, put apart, segregate; sort out, remove, single out, isolate; pick out, cull, sift; distinguish. **3.** go separate ways, go different ways, go apart; divorce, split up; branch out, diverge, part, split, divaricate, bifurcate, fork, ramify, radiate, spread. **4.** come apart, break away, break apart; crack, split, part, crumble. —*adj.* **5.** not joined, not connected, detached, disunited; not shared, single, individual, distinct, discrete; different, diverse, dissimilar. **6.** independent, existing by itself, autonomous. —**Ant. 1** join, attach, link, unite, engage, connect. **2** combine, unite, mix, merge, integrate, consolidate. **3** meet, merge; convene. **4** adhere, cling. **5** joined, connected, united; shared; alike, similar. **6** affiliated, merged, interdependent.

separation *n.* **1.** separating, division, disjunction, disunion, disconnection, disengagement, divorce, severance; detachment, disassociation; sorting, removal, segregation, isolation. **2.** parting, farewell, good-bye, divergence, branching; separate residence, estrangement, divorce; breach, break, split, schism. **3.** partition, boundary, divide, divider, division; branching, fork, bifurcation. **4.** gap, space, opening, distance, interval.

sepulcher *n.* tomb, crypt, vault, ossuary, reliquary, resting place; mausoleum, cenotaph, necropolis, grave, burial place.

sequel *n.* **1.** continuation, follow-up. **2.** subsequent event, aftermath, upshot, offshoot, outgrowth, product; epilogue, postscript, addendum; conclusion, end, finish, denouement, culmination; consequence, result, corollary, outcome.

sequence *n.* **1.** progression, order, succession, arrangement; series, run, course, flow, train, string, chain; consecutiveness, successiveness. **2.** series, cycle, round; procession, parade, cavalcade, course; schedule, routine. —**Syn. Study. 1** See SERIES.

sequester *v.* set apart, sequestrate, seclude, withdraw, isolate, banish, separate, segregate, retire, put aside, confine, lock up, quarantine.

sere *adj.* dry, arid, moistureless, desiccated, droughty, dehumidified, dehydrated, waterless, unwatered, bone-dry, parched, scorched, dried-up, wizened.

serene *adj.* calm, tranquil, peaceful, quiet, still, untroubled, halcyon, unruffled, smooth; sedate, dignified, unperturbed, placid, composed, undisturbed, unexcitable, unimpassioned, poised, cool, nonchalant; clear, fair, bright, unobscured, pellucid, limpid. —**Syn. Study.** See PEACEFUL. —**Ant.** disturbed, troubled, rough, agitated; excitable, anxious, discomposed.

serenity *n.* calmness, placidity, tranquillity, peacefulness, quietude, quiescence, composure, implicit confidence, dignity, equanimity, collectedness, coolness, complacence, nonchalance, *French* sangfroid. —**Ant.** anxiety, uneasiness, alarm, discontent.

serf *n.* slave bound to the land; vassal, villein; bondman, thrall; peasant, cotter. —**Ant.** master, lord.

serial *n.* **1.** story presented in installments. —*adj.* **2.** in installments, in successive parts; continued, continuous, consecutive, sequential, successive; regular, recurring; incremental, piecemeal. **3.** of a series, arranged in a series.

series *n.* sequence, succession, progression, order, procession; set, course, cycle, chain, string, parade; group, number. —**Syn. Study.** SERIES, SEQUENCE, SUCCESSION are terms for an orderly following of things one after another. SERIES is applied to a number of things of the same kind, usu. related to each other, arranged or happening in order: *a series of baseball games.* SEQUENCE stresses the continuity in time, thought, cause and effect, etc.: *The scenes came in a definite sequence.* SUCCESSION implies that one thing is followed by another or others in turn, usu. though not necessarily with a relation or connection between them: *a succession of calamities.*

serious *adj.* **1.** thoughtful, pensive, grave, solemn, frowning, long-faced, saturnine; sober, somber, sedate, staid, grim, rueful; sad, dejected, downcast. **2.** sincere, earnest, not joking, not trifling, determined, decided, resolute, resolved, purposeful. **3.** demanding careful thought, important, consequential, far-reaching, momentous, weighty, heavy, crucial; fateful, portentous. **4.** dangerous, perilous, harmful, critical, severe, alarming, bad; incapacitating, crippling. **—Syn. Study. 2** See EARNEST. **—Ant. 1** thoughtless, careless; joyful, happy, jolly, gay, laughing, frivolous. **2** insincere, joking, trifling; undecided. **3** unimportant, insignificant, trivial. **4** slight, minor.

sermon *n.* **1.** speech containing religious instruction, preaching, preachment, exhortation, homily. **2.** long tedious speech, lecture, harangue, tirade; reproof, admonition, rebuke; dressing-down, tongue-lashing, diatribe.

serpent *n.* **1.** snake, viper, reptile, asp. **2.** traitor, trickster, deceiver, cheat, double-dealer; rogue, snake, snake in the grass; devil, the Devil, Satan.

serpentine *adj.* twisting, winding, snaking, meandering, tortuous, circuitous, coiling, devious, zigzag, roundabout, crooked, mazy, labyrinthine; spiral, convoluted, flexuous, sinuous; undulating.

servant *n.* **1.** employee, attendant, retainer, helper, domestic, factotum; (*variously*) maid, valet, footman, chauffeur, cook, butler, hired man, hired girl, household help, housekeeper; menial, flunky, lackey, slavey, scullion; henchman, underling, minion; man, girl, man Friday, girl Friday; help, hired help. **2.** public employee, public official, server; servitor. **—Ant. 1** master, lord, employer.

serve *v.* **1.** work for, act as a servant to, be in the service of, attend, take care of, wait on. **2.** be of help to, assist, render assistance, minister, tend, supply, provide for, aid, help, promote, further, oblige, attend; give aid or service, be of use. **3.** go through a term of service, work, act, perform, do duty, hold an office, fill a post, officiate; go through, carry out, spend, pass, complete. **4.** wait table, work as a waiter or waitress, *Slang* sling hash. **5.** provide for customers or guests; supply with food, set food on a table. **6.** be enough for, content, satisfy, suit, suffice, do. **7.** act, be of use, be used, be functional, function, be instrumental; answer the purpose, answer the requirements, *Informal* fill the bill. **8.** treat, work for, function for, avail. **9.** deliver, present, hand over. **—Ant. 1** command, order; deceive, betray. **2** obstruct, hinder, thwart, oppose. **6** be insufficient for; dissatisfy. **7** be useless.

service *n.* **1.** Sometimes **services** labor; effort, ministration; attendance, assistance, help, aid; benefit, advantage, usefulness, use, utility, profit, accommodation; support, avail; employment, employ. **2.** use, provision, system, accommodation, facility, utility, convenience. **3.** department, agency, bureau. **4.** armed forces, military. **5.** repair, servicing, maintenance, mechanical work. **6.** attendance, waiting, accommodation, order-filling. **7.** Often **services** professional work, treatment. **8.** ritual, ceremony, ceremonial, rite, celebration, observance. **—*v.*** **9.** repair, maintain, adjust, mend. **10.** supply services to, serve.

serviceable *adj.* usable, useful, utilitarian, functional, effective, operative, workable, practical; durable, lasting, rugged, strong, tough, sturdy.

servile *adj.* **1.** slavish, submissive, abject; unctuous, oily; obsequious, truckling, toadying, cringing, fawning, sycophantic, scraping, groveling, bootlicking. **2.** befitting a slave, menial; in bonds, abject, slavish, subservient, humble. **—Syn. Study. 1** SERVILE, SLAVISH, OBSEQUIOUS describe the submissive or compliant behavior of a slave or an inferior. SERVILE suggests cringing, fawning, and abject submission: *servile responses to questions.* SLAVISH stresses the dependence and laborious toil of one who follows or obeys without question: *slavish attentiveness to orders.* OBSEQUIOUS implies the ostentatious subordination of oneself to the wishes of another, either from fear or from hope of gain: *an obsequious waiter.* **—Ant. 1** masterly, commanding, overbearing, haughty.

servitude *n.* slavery, serfdom, thralldom, enthrallment, bonds, bondage, oppression, subjugation, enslavement, vassalage, fetters, shackles, chains; compulsory service, hard labor, imprisonment. **—Syn. Study.** See SLAVERY. **—Ant.** freedom, independence, emancipation.

session *n.* **1.** meeting, sitting, conference, convention, assembly, synod, conclave. **2.** period, term, semester, quarter; course, round, bout.

set *v.* **1.** put, place, position, move into position, lay, *Informal* plunk, plop; drop. **2.** fix, adjust, regulate, calibrate; prepare, order, arrange, line up, align. **3.** harden, become hard or firm, solidify, consolidate, gel, jellify, congeal, thicken. **4.** sink, pass below the horizon. **5.** place, assign, establish, assess, attach, confer; estimate, rate. **6.** post, station, situate, install, assign. **7.** decide upon, settle, fix, determine, establish, make, create; prescribe, decree, ordain. **8.** put in a setting, locate, represent, suppose to take place. **9.** fix, mount in a frame; imbed; ornament, stud. **10.** fit, arrange, adapt; style. **11.** urge to attack, release, unleash; sic. **—*n.*** **12.** setting, position, carriage, bearing, cut, line, profile; firmness, rigidity. **13.** group, collection, assortment, array, suit, outfit, kit, service.

14. group of persons, crowd, clique, faction, coterie, club, bunch. **15.** apparatus, assembly, machine, complex. **16.** scenery, scene, setting, backdrop; sound stage, studio; locale, location. —*adj.* **17.** definite, fixed, decided, firm, settled, prearranged, agreed upon; anticipated. **18.** established, usual, customary, accustomed; stock, common, commonplace, conventional, everyday, routine, regular, habitual, familiar; banal, trite, hackneyed, stale. **19.** arranged, ready, prepared. **20.** stubborn, obstinate, steadfast, immovable, rigid, inflexible, frozen, hardened, stiff. **—Ant. 1** remove, lift, pick up. **2** disarrange. **3** melt, soften. **4** rise. **7** change, break. **9** remove, extract. **17** undecided, tentative, vague. **18** unexpected, impromptu; unusual, uncommon, irregular. **19** unprepared. **20** flexible, adaptable.

setback *n.* reversal, disappointment, misfortune, mischance, reverse, loss, adversity, defeat, relapse, regression, slump, undoing, failure, rebuff, mishap, *Slang* flop. **—Ant.** progress, advance, gain, advantage.

setting *n.* **—Syn. Study.** See ENVIRONMENT.

settle *v.* **1.** decide, agree, fix, choose, set, determine, establish. **2.** put in order, dispose properly, arrange, bring to order; reconcile, resolve, clear up, straighten out, rectify, put to rest. **3.** pay, discharge, acquit oneself of, dispose of, make good, clear, satisfy. **4.** move to, locate, situate, populate, establish oneself; colonize, put down roots, take root, lodge, inhabit, people, make one's home, set up housekeeping. **5.** calm, bring to rest, soothe, quiet, compose, allay, pacify. **6.** deposit dregs, descend gradually, collect at the bottom, precipitate; clarify, clear. **7.** sink, drop, droop, sag, find one's level. **8.** come to rest; land, alight, light; perch; sit down. **—Ant. 1** disagree. **2** disarrange, upset; confuse. **4** wander; emigrate. **5** agitate, excite, disturb, roil. **7** rise, ascend.

settlement *n.* **1.** adjustment, arrangement, reconciliation, resolution, working out. **2.** colonizing, colonization, peopling; community of settlers, colony, encampment, camp, post, outpost; small community, village, hamlet. **3.** payment, satisfaction, liquidation, discharge, amortization, clearing, clearance, acquittance; adjustment, compensation; bequest, sum, amount.

settler *n.* homesteader, squatter, pioneer, frontiersman; immigrant, colonist, colonizer.

sever *v.* **1.** cut in two, cut off, separate, part, amputate, dismember, disconnect, dissever, lop off, truncate, bisect, cleave, split, slice, saw; rive, rend, tear. **2.** discontinue, dissolve, put an end to, terminate, do away with, disunite, disjoin, split up, break off, rupture. **—Ant. 1** unite, join, bind. **2** continue; keep, maintain.

several *adj.* **1.** more than two, some, a number of, a few, divers. **2.** separate, different, distinct, peculiar; individual, respective, own, particular, certain, specific, exclusive, special, express, private, personal, independent; single, distinctive; diverse, assorted, sundry. —*n.* **3.** several persons or things, a few, a number. **—Ant. 2** joint, combined, communal.

severe *adj.* **1.** strict, harsh, rigorous, taxing, demanding, vigorous, rough, stiff; cruel, brutal, merciless, ruthless, unsparing; drastic, draconian. **2.** serious, stern, dour, strait-laced, grave, sober, grim, saturnine, sedate, somber, austere, forbidding, cold. **3.** restrained, plain, simple, conservative, uniform, unadorned, undecorated; chaste. **4.** intense, violent, extreme, unrelenting, raging, fuming; furious, fierce, savage, wild, brutal; turbulent, tumultuous; bitter, stinging, piercing, biting, cutting. **5.** serious, painful, dangerous, distressing, difficult. **—Syn. Study. 1, 2** See STERN. **—Ant. 1** gentle, lenient, merciful, mild, moderate; easy; kind, considerate. **2** affable, genial, sweet. **3** gay, cheerful; decorative. **4** gentle, mild. **5** tolerable; easy; pleasant, mild.

sex *n.* **1.** gender, sexual classification, sexual identity, reproductive function; masculinity, maleness; femininity, femaleness. **2.** sexuality, generation, reproduction, procreation; sexual urge, sexual instinct, libido, Eros; sexual intercourse, love, lovemaking, coitus, coition, copulation.

sexual *adj.* genital, generative, reproductive, procreative, venereal, copulatory, sex, coital; marital, conjugal, intimate; erotic, sexy, amatory, sensual, libidinous.

sexy *adj.* erotic, lewd, voluptuous, provocative, prurient, flirtatious, coquettish, suggestive, seductive, come-hither, bawdy.

shabby *adj.* **1.** worn, ragged, raggy, threadbare, frayed, torn, ratty, tatty, the worse for wear; neglected, deteriorated, decaying, dilapidated, broken-down, ramshackle, tumbledown, rundown, seedy; impoverished, poverty-stricken. **2.** slovenly, ragged, wearing worn clothes, ill-dressed; dirty, mangy, scruffy, ratty, tatty, sorry; impoverished, down at the heels, down and out. **3.** unfair; mean, wretched, sorry, miserable, contemptible, ignoble, dishonorable, sordid, low, inferior, unworthy; ungenerous, meager, cheap, poor, beggarly, illiberal, tight. —**Ant. 1** pristine, new, neat, well-kept, well-to-do; grand, imposing. **2** well-dressed, fine, splendid; fashionable, chic, dapper. **3** fair, considerate, admirable, honorable; liberal, generous, handsome, lavish.

shackle *n.* **1.** fetter, irons, chains, bonds; handcuffs, cuffs, manacle; hobble. —*v.* **2.** fetter, chain, manacle, handcuff, cuff, secure, bind, tie, tether, pinion. **3.** restrict, thwart, retard, block, hamper, hobble, cramp, hinder, frustrate, foil, limit, impede, curb, check, rein, encumber, inhibit, circumscribe, stall, forestall, balk, bar, prevent, deter, hamstring, hogtie. —**Ant. 2** unshackle, unchain; free, release. **3** aid, help, abet, promote, foster, further.

shade *n.* **1.** shadow, shadows; darkness, semidark. **2.** (*variously*) window shade, blind; drape, curtain, awning, canopy, shutter, shield, screen, hood, veil. **3.** hue, tone, tint, color, cast. **4.** small degree, trace, tinge, touch, bit, whit, jot, iota, particle, scintilla, atom, modicum, soupcon, suggestion, hint. —*v.* **5.** shield from the sun, shield from the light, screen; make shady, darken, dim. —**Ant. 1** sunlight, sunshine, direct light, light, glare, brightness. **4** great amount, full measure, lot, abundance, *Informal* heap, gobs, oodles. **5** light, lighten, illuminate, brighten; expose, uncover.

shadow *n.* **1.** silhouette, reflection; penumbra. **2.** Usu. **shadows** shade, partial darkness; gathering darkness. **3.** trace, shade, bit, slight amount, small degree, touch, tinge; suggestion, whisper, hint, ghost, faint image. **4.** threat, specter, cloud; dark spot, blight, taint, blot, blemish, smirch, smear, smudge, stain. —*v.* **5.** follow, tail, trail, dog the footsteps of, tag after, hound; track, stalk, pursue; keep tabs on.

shady *adj.* **1.** shaded, shadowy. **2.** disreputable, questionable, suspicious, fishy, dubious; unethical, dishonest, crooked, devious, underhanded; untrustworthy. —**Ant. 1** sunny, sunlit, bright, unshaded, exposed. **2** upright, honest, honorable, moral, ethical, proper, aboveboard, straight, reputable, *Slang* square.

shaft *n.* **1.** handle, shank, hilt; spindle, trunk, stalk, stem. **2.** (*variously*) arrow, dart, quill, spear, lance. **3.** sharp remark, barb, cut, gibe, insult, affront, aspersion, *Informal* brickbat. **4.** ray, beam, streak, stream, gleam, patch. **5.** column, tower, obelisk, pillar, pilaster, pylon, monolith, minaret, spire, steeple. **6.** excavation, cavity, pit, chasm, well, abyss; duct, vent, funnel, flue, chimney, conduit.

shaggy *adj.* shagged, hairy, long-haired, hirsute, unshorn, bushy, fuzzy, woolly; downy, tufted, nappy, piled; whiskered, bewhiskered, bearded. —**Ant.** smooth, sleek, short-haired, close-cropped, shorn; flat-woven.

shake *v.* **1.** vibrate, quiver, quake, quaver, totter, wobble, sway, tremble, shudder, shimmy, shiver, flutter, flicker, jiggle, joggle, jostle; agitate, mix. **2.** wave, brandish, flourish, swing. **3.** disturb, distress, unnerve, perturb; jar, jolt, rattle, unsettle, unstring, discompose, disquiet, ruffle, frighten; stun, startle, stagger, move, touch, affect, stir. **4.** escape from, get away from, elude; get rid of, rid oneself of, throw off, slough. —*n.* **5.** jiggle, jog, bounce, jounce, flourish. **6.** trembling, tremble, shaking, shudder, quiver, quivering, quake, quaking, flutter, fluttering, shiver, shivering, flicker, flickering, jerk, twitch. —**Ant. 3** calm, quiet, soothe, reassure, settle, compose, steady. **4** catch, capture, get; keep, retain. **6** steadiness, stillness.

shakeup *n.* reorganization, turnover, cleanup, clean sweep, purge, rearrangement, realignment, restructuring, redistribution, redisposition.

shaky *adj.* **1.** unsteady, trembling, shaking, quivering, wobbly, tremulous, tottering, teetery, teetering, weak, unstable, flimsy, frail, fragile; unsafe, hazardous, insecure, precarious; nervous, jumpy, jittery, fidgety. **2.** wavering, uncertain, unsure, dubious, unreliable, undependable, inconstant, vacillating, faltering, undecided, irresolute, unresolved, half-hearted, halting, hesitant.

shallow *adj.* **1.** shoal, of little depth, (*variously*) ankle-deep, knee-deep, waist-deep. **2.** superficial, insubstantial, frivolous, frothy, trivial, slight, inconsequential, meaningless, unimportant, trifling, surface, skin-deep. —**Ant. 1** deep, bottomless. **2** profound, serious, substantial, important, in-depth, intellectual, thoughtful, perceptive, keen, sharp.

sham *n.* **1.** fraud, fake, pretense, trick; imitation, counterfeit, copy, forgery, phony, put-on. —*adj.* **2.** feigned, fraudulent, fake, pretended, phony, false, make-believe, put-on; counterfeit, bogus, forged, imitation, artificial, synthetic, simulated, spurious. —*v.* **3.** pretend, feign, fake, simulate, put on, act, imitate, affect, assume. —**Syn. Study. 2** See FALSE. —**Ant. 1** original, genuine article, real McCoy, real thing. **2** real, genuine, authentic, true; unfeigned, unpretended, natural.

shame *n.* **1.** guilt, remorse, self-disgust,

self-abomination; embarrassment, humiliation, mortification, chagrin, shamefacedness. **2.** disgrace, dishonor, contempt, ignominy, humiliation, mortification, disrepute, disrespect, degradation, debasement, odium. **3.** disgrace, scandal, stigma. **4.** disappointment, regretful thing, sorrowful happening. *—v.* **5.** embarrass, humiliate, mortify, disgrace, humble. **—Syn. Study. 1** SHAME, EMBARRASSMENT, HUMILIATION, CHAGRIN designate different kinds or degrees of painful feeling caused by injury to one's pride or self-respect. SHAME is a painful feeling caused by the consciousness or exposure of unworthy or indecent conduct or circumstances: *One feels shame at being caught in a lie.* It is similar to guilt in the nature and origin of the feeling. EMBARRASSMENT usu. refers to a less painful feeling, one associated with less serious situations, often of a social nature: *embarrassment over breaking a vase at a party.* HUMILIATION is a feeling of embarrassment at being humbled in the estimation of others: *Being ignored gave him a sense of humiliation.* CHAGRIN is humiliation mingled with vexation or anger: *She felt chagrin at her failure to do well on the test.* **—Ant. 1** shamelessness, pride, self-respect, glory, worthiness. **2** honor, credit, renown, glory, esteem. **5** do credit to, make proud.

shamefaced *adj.* ashamed, embarrassed, chagrined, mortified, humiliated, sheepish, abashed, remorseful, blushing, sorry, humbled, *Slang* put-down, redfaced, crushed, disgraced, shamed. **—Ant.** proud, unashamed, shameless, unabashed.

shameful *adj.* disgraceful, dishonorable, shameless, contemptible, ignoble, ignominious, opprobrious, inglorious, degrading, shocking, outrageous, despicable, deplorable, odious, reprehensible; dastardly, vile, villainous, base, mean, low, unworthy, iniquitous, heinous. **—Ant.** honorable, glorious, noble, worthy, praiseworthy, dignified, decent, virtuous, respectable; admirable, commendable, meritorious.

shameless *adj.* **1.** without shame, disgraceful, dishonorable, degraded, abandoned, dissolute, immodest, wanton, immoral, indecent, indecorous. **2.** brazen, forward, impudent, brash, pert, boldfaced, barefaced, unblushing, saucy, unabashed, unreserved, audacious, flagrant.

shape *n.* **1.** outline, contour, figure, silhouette, profile, conformation, configuration; form, build, physique. **2.** order, array, orderly arrangement, state of neatness. **3.** condition, physical condition, health, fettle, trim. *—v.* **4.** form, mold, model, fashion, frame; make, create, build, construct, develop; guide, determine. **—Ant. 2** disorder, disarray, disarrangement, confusion, chaos. **4** destroy, ruin; warp.

share *n.* **1.** part, portion, allotment, apportionment, allowance, quota, percent, percentage, ration, *Informal* cut. *—v.* **2.** own jointly, use jointly, receive together. **3.** divide and give out, split, cut up, divvy up, apportion, dole, allot, allocate, deal out, measure out, mete out.

sharp *adj.* **1.** keen-edged, fine-edged, fine, not blunt, razor-sharp; pointed, pointy, piked, edged, cutting; serrated, toothed, bristly, thorny, spiny, prickly. **2.** sudden, abrupt, precipitous, rapid; distinct, clear, clearly defined, extreme, acute, fierce, violent, keen, severe, intense, drastic, marked, excessive, immoderate, inordinate; vertical, steep, sheer, angular. **3.** biting, bitter, salty, acid, sour, vinegary, tart, caustic, acrid; piquant, strong; cutting, piercing, nippy, stinging, nipping. **4.** shrill, piercing, harsh, penetrating, raucous, strident; high, high-pitched, high-toned. **5.** keen, acute, intelligent, perceptive, quick; shrewd, astute, clever, penetrating, discerning, alert, awake, wide awake, vigilant. **6.** wily, crafty, cunning, sly, foxy, artful, calculating, conniving, contriving, unscrupulous, unprincipled, unethical, deceptive, tricky. **7.** angry, harsh, scathing, unkind, spiteful, bitter, barbed, cutting, stinging; cruel, severe, vitriolic, rancorous, galling, venomous, acrid; abrupt, gruff, brusque, curt, blunt, crusty, bearish, crabbed. *—adv.* **8.** sharply, keenly, acutely, alertly, quickly, closely, attentively. **9.** suddenly, abruptly, precipitously. **10.** promptly, punctually, on the dot, on the nose, on the button; precisely, exactly, *Spanish* en punto, *French* juste. **—Syn. Study. 5** SHARP, KEEN, INTELLIGENT, QUICK may all be applied to mental qualities and abilities. SHARP means mentally alert or acute; it implies a clever and astute quality: *a sharp mind.* KEEN suggests an incisive, observant, or penetrating nature: *a keen observer.* INTELLIGENT means not only acute, alert, and active, but also able to reason and understand: *an intelligent reader.* QUICK suggests lively and rapid comprehension, prompt response to instruction, and the like: *quick at figures.* **—Ant. 1** dull, blunt; round, rounded, straight, bulbous. **2** slow, gradual; gentle, easy, moderate, indistinct, blurred, unclear. **3** bland, mild, flat, insipid; sweet. **4** soft, mellow, soothing; well-modulated, low. **5** dull, dim, slow; unperceptive, obtuse, uncomprehending, unaware. **6** direct, straightforward, out in the open, aboveboard, ingenuous, guileless, artless; ethical, honest, scrupulous, principled. **7**

sweet, gentle, kind, tender, soothing; polite, courteous, friendly, warm, loving. **8** dully; inattentively, carelessly, distractedly. **9** slowly, gradually, gently. **10** more or less, *Spanish* más o menos, *French* plus ou moins.

sharpen *v.* make sharper, edge, put an edge on; whet, hone, grind, strop.

shatter *v.* **1.** break into pieces, break into smithereens, break into shivers, smash, crash, burst, explode, sunder, rive; splinter, crush, crumble, pulverize; break, crack, fracture, split. **2.** destroy, wreck, ruin, smash, devastate, crush, squash, quash, demolish, scuttle, spoil, upset, topple, overturn. **—Ant. 2** increase, improve, enhance, heighten, better.

shave *v.* **1.** cut off, cut, clip, crop, lop, prune, pare, trim, snip, barber, scissor, shear, fleece; dock; mow. **2.** graze, scrape, glance, brush, skin, touch lightly.

shear *v.* **1.** cut the fleece from, fleece; cut, clip, crop, trim, lop, prune, snip, scissor, shave. **2.** deprive, relieve; take away, remove.

sheath *n.* scabbard; covering, sheathing, wrapper, wrapping, envelope, container, receptacle, jacket, coat, coating, case, slipcase, casing; membrane, skin, capsule, pod.

shed[1] *n.* lean-to; hut, shack, hovel, shanty; toolshed, toolhouse; outbuilding.

shed[2] *v.* **1.** let fall, let flow, spill, pour forth, give forth, emit, radiate, exude, discharge, shower; throw, cast, spread, distribute, scatter, strew, disperse, disseminate, broadcast. **2.** cast off, let fall, drop, discard, slough, doff; lose hair; molt. **—Ant. 1** suppress, repress, withhold, hold back, choke back, stop; gather, collect, amass.

sheen *n.* luster, gloss, shine, glaze, polish, shininess, gleam, shimmer, effulgence, glossiness, glint, glitter, glister, brightness, radiance, burnish, glow, luminousness, refulgence. **—Syn. Study.** See POLISH. **—Ant.** tarnish, filminess, matte, dullness.

sheepish *adj.* **1.** easily led, submissive, passive, docile, tractable, unassertive, obeisant, obedient, servile, subservient, unresisting, yielding. **2.** embarrassed, abashed, shamefaced, ashamed, hangdog, chastened, chagrined, mortified, guilty, blushing; timorous, fearful, bashful, shy, timid, meek, humble, diffident, shrinking. **—Ant. 1** aggressive, strident, overbearing, assertive, masterful, independent; stubborn, obdurate, hardheaded, willful; disobedient, intractable, unyielding. **2** brazen, brash, unabashed, unashamed, unblushing, boldfaced, audacious, bold, immodest, confident, poised.

sheer *adj.* **1.** transparent, thin, fine, diaphanous, gossamer, gauzy, filmy. **2.** unmixed, unadulterated, pure, one-hundred-percent, unalloyed; absolute, utter, total, complete, unlimited, unbounded, unrestrained, consummate, unconditional, unmitigated, unqualified, perfect, utter, out and out. **3.** steep, vertical, perpendicular, plumb, straight up and down, bluff, sharp; abrupt, precipitous. **—Ant. 1** opaque; thick, coarse. **2** mixed, impure, alloyed, adulterated, doctored; partial, fragmentary, incomplete, imperfect, conditional, mitigated, qualified, limited. **3** gradual, gentle, sloping; horizontal.

sheet *n.* **1.** bed sheet; coating, coat, layer, covering, blanket, film, membrane, sheath, overlay, top. **2.** square, rectangle, slab, panel, leaf, piece, plate, pane.

shell *n.* **1.** carapace, case, hull, husk, shuck, pod. **2.** framework, skeleton, hulk, walls and roof. **3.** artillery shell, cartridge shell, cartridge, bullet, round, shot; cannon shell, grenade, bomb, missile, projectile, rocket. **—*v.* 4.** hull, husk, shuck. **5.** fire on, bombard, rain shells on, pound, barrage, pepper.

shelter *n.* **1.** cover, protection, shield, refuge, safety, haven, asylum, sanctuary, security. **2.** housing, lodging, quarters, dwelling place, a roof over one's head. **—*v.* 3.** protect, shield, cover; guard, safeguard, defend; harbor, take in, house, lodge, care for, look after, provide for. **—Ant. 2** exposure. **3** expose, lay bare; expel, turn out, evict; betray.

shelve *v.* lay aside, put aside, set aside, postpone, put off, suspend, defer, table, hold in abeyance, pigeonhole, *Slang* put on ice, put on the back burner. **—Ant.** begin, start, initiate, commence; activate, reactivate, revive; expedite.

shenanigans *n.* hijinks, horseplay, mischief, sport, tomfoolery, antics, capers, sportiveness, deviltry, silliness, nonsense, buffoonery, roguishness, mischievousness.

shepherd *n.* **1.** sheepherder, herder, herdsman. **2.** protector, guardian, shelter, shield, defender, keeper, custodian, safeguard, champion, benefactor, patron, provider. **—*v.* 3.** tend, herd, watch over, protect, guard; guide, lead, pilot, direct, show, escort. **—Ant. 1** rustler. **2** enemy, foe, rival.

sheriff *n.* chief law-enforcement officer of a county, county sheriff, constable.

shield *n.* **1.** (*variously*) buckler, aegis, escutcheon. **2.** badge, emblem, medallion, ensign, insignia; button, star. **3.** protection, protector, guard, safeguard, defense, buffer, cover, screen, shade, fender. —*v.* **4.** protect, guard, safeguard, secure, preserve, keep, keep safe, shelter; house, harbor; screen, cover, shade. —**Ant.** **3** danger, risk, hazard. **4** expose, lay bare, uncover; endanger, imperil, risk, hazard.

shift *v.* **1.** move, transfer; switch, reposition, transpose, change, exchange, interchange, vary; swerve, veer. —*n.* **2.** change, variation, shifting, alteration, modification, deviation, fluctuation, alternating, turning, move, switch, veering, swerve. **3.** work period, stint, assignment, tour of duty, go, hitch. **4.** straight, loose-fitting dress; camisole, chemise, slip.

shiftless *adj.* lazy, idle, inactive, lax, lackadaisical; careless, slothful, indolent, unconscientious; good-for-nothing, ne'er-do-well. —**Ant.** ambitious, willing-to-work, energetic, industrious, assiduous, active; conscientious, painstaking, scrupulous, careful.

shifty *adj.* crafty, foxy, cunning, wily, scheming, contriving, conniving, sneaky, slippery, maneuvering, tricky, deceitful; evasive, unreliable, untrustworthy, treacherous, dishonest. —**Ant.** open, straightforward, direct, artless, guileless; reliable, dependable, trustworthy, loyal.

shilly-shally *v.* waver, vacillate, procrastinate, hesitate, stall, falter, fluctuate, hem and haw, dillydally, dawdle, dither, go back and forth, seesaw, oscillate, straddle the fence, blow hot and cold. —**Ant.** be decisive, act, accomplish, perform, do.

shimmer *v.* **1.** glimmer, twinkle, flicker, flutter, flash, blink, dance, sparkle, glisten, scintillate, coruscate, phosphoresce; gleam, glow, shine, beam. **2.** quiver, quake, shiver, shimmy, waver, vibrate, tremble. —*n.* **3.** twinkle, glimmer, tremulous flickering, blinking, faint glimmering, wavering light.

shindig *n.* party, gala, ball, dance, fête, costume ball, affair, fancy-dress ball, soirée, festivity, revelry, masked ball, masquerade party, dinner dance, tea dance, prom, hop, barn dance, record hop; *Slang* bash, blowout, shindy; *French* thé dansant, bal masqué, bal costumé.

shine *v.* **1.** emit light, shed light, reflect light, gleam, radiate, glow, beam, sparkle, shimmer, glitter, glisten, glister, twinkle, flicker, flash, blink, scintillate, coruscate, irradiate. **2.** polish, gloss, wax; buff, burnish, rub up; brighten. —*n.* **3.** light, illumination, gleam, glow, beam, glare, glint, glitter, glimmer, sparkle, shimmer, twinkle, flicker, flash, blink; luminosity, luminousness, incandescence. **4.** gloss, luster, glow, sheen, brightness, radiance, brilliance, dazzle; polish, polishing, shining, wax, waxing, buffing, burnishing. —**Ant.** **2** dull, darken, dim; tarnish. **3** dark, darkness, blackness; dimness, murkiness. **4** dullness, tarnish.

shiny *adj.* bright, brilliant, shining, gleaming, glistening, shimmering, sparkling, glittering, scintillating; luminous, radiant, lustrous, glowing, glaring, incandescent, effulgent; polished, burnished, glossy.

ship *n.* **1.** large boat, vessel, craft; (*variously*) steamship, steamer, ocean liner, liner, yacht, motorship, sailing ship, freighter, cargo ship, tanker, tramp steamer, tramp, packet, cruiser, battleship, destroyer, carrier, aircraft carrier. **2.** ship's company, crew; ship's passengers. —*v.* **3.** transport, send, dispatch, route, forward.

shirk *v.* get out of doing, avoid, evade, shun, duck, shrink from, sidestep, dodge, escape, elude, ignore, neglect, eschew; malinger, *Slang* goof off, goldbrick. —**Ant.** meet, face, confront; fulfill, perform, undertake, do, honor.

shiver *v.* **1.** shake, tremble, shudder, quiver, quaver, shimmy, quake. —*n.* **2.** tremble, shudder, quiver, quaver. **3.** Often **shivers** bit, piece, fragment, sliver, shard.

shock[1] *n.* **1.** impact, jar, jolt, rock, concussion; blow, collision. **2.** surprise, blow, unexpected blow, disturbance, consternation, trauma, jolt, jar, bolt out of the blue; scare, start, turn. —*v.* **3.** surprise, stun, stagger, shake, daze, stupefy, paralyze, jar, jolt, overwhelm, bowl over, give a turn; perturb, dismay, distress, disturb, upset, unsettle, disquiet, discompose, disconcert, astonish, astound, startle; appall, horrify, disgust, revolt, offend, outrage.

shock[2] *n.* sheaf, stack, bundle, pile; rick, cock.

shock[3] *n.* bush, bushy mass, mass, crop, mop, mane, thatch, mat.

shocking *adj.* **1.** surprising, astounding, astonishing, startling, staggering, stupefying, jarring, jolting, overwhelming; disturbing, perturbing, upsetting, disquieting, unsettling, disconcerting. **2.** scandalous, disgraceful, outrageous, indecent, offensive; appalling; horrifying, horrible, horrid, terrible, awful, disgusting, frightful, monstrous, insufferable, abominable, reprehensible, detestable, abhorrent, repugnant, repellent, odious, foul, wretched, hideous, revolting, ghastly, gruesome, grisly. —**Ant.** **1, 2** unsurprising, expected; gratifying, satisfying, pleasing. **2** acceptable, decent; good, excellent, fine, wonderful, marvelous, glorious, worthy, capital; admirable, honorable, praiseworthy, commendable, laudable; attractive, pleasant, desirable.

shoddy *adj.* **1.** inferior, poor, second-rate, careless, sloppy, negligent, inefficient, haphazard, slipshod, *Informal* tacky. **2.** nasty, mean, shabby, inconsiderate, low, low-down, base, reprehensible, contemptible, dirty; niggardly, miserly, ungenerous, stingy. **—Ant. 1** excellent, first-rate, good, fine; precise, accurate, careful, meticulous, thorough, scrupulous, fastidious. **2** noble, gentlemanly, kind, thoughtful, considerate; sympathetic, compassionate.

shoot *v.* **1.** hit, wing, nick, plug, riddle, pelt, pepper, shell, spray, pump full of lead; kill, pick off, drop, fell, blow one's brains out, *Slang* waste. **2.** fire, open fire, discharge, let fly, hurl, propel, eject, sling, cast, fling, throw, toss, launch, catapult; detonate, explode, go off; bombard, shower, rain, pelt. **3.** move suddenly, charge, spring, dart, bolt, dash, sweep, spurt, jump, leap; race, speed, fly, tear, rush, hurry. **—*n.* 4.** new growth, young branch, twig, sprout, bud; stem, sprig, tendril; offshoot.

shop *n.* **1.** store, retail store, small store, establishment, boutique; emporium, market, mart. **2.** workshop, studio, atelier; factory, plant, works, mill. **—*v.* 3.** seek to purchase, go shopping for, windowshop, look, hunt, browse; buy, purchase, patronize.

shore[1] *n.* **1.** coast, seacoast, seaboard; seashore, seaside, waterside, beach, strand; bank, riverbank; margin, brink. **2.** land, dry land, terra firma.

shore[2] *v.* support, prop, hold, hold up, brace, reinforce, buttress, strengthen, bolster; bulwark, underpin, sustain, mainstay. **—Ant.** weigh down, burden, crush, overwhelm, push over, overturn.

short *adj.* **1.** not long; not tall, stubby, squat, truncated; stunted, runty; small, little, pint-sized, pocket-sized, diminutive, slight, elfin, pygmy, bantam, Lilliputian, dwarfish. **2.** brief, short-lived, quick, fleet, fleeting, momentary, hasty, summary, cursory; concise, terse, succinct, compact; abridged, abbreviated, condensed; curtailed. **3.** curt, brusque, abrupt, gruff, impatient, sharp; cross, snappish, testy; ill-tempered, impolite. **4.** low, scanty, scant, sparse, scarce, meager, skimpy, tight, niggardly, lean, slender, slim, thin; insufficient, deficient, wanting, lacking, limited, not abundant. **—*adv.* 5.** suddenly, abruptly, without warning, precipitously. **6.** unawares, without preparation, by surprise, without warning. **—Syn. Study. 2** SHORT, BRIEF are opposed to *long,* and indicate slight extent or duration. SHORT may imply duration but is also applied to physical distance and certain purely spatial relations: *a short journey.* BRIEF refers esp. to duration of time: *brief intervals.* **—Ant. 1** long; tall, high, reedy, rangy. **2** long, longish, lengthy, protracted, attenuated, elongated, extended; interminable, unending. **3** patient; polite, civil, mannerly; verbose, wordy, long-winded. **4** adequate, sufficient, ample, plenteous, plentiful, abundant, superabundant, copious, well-stocked, inexhaustible, profuse, lavish; overflowing, excessive, overstocked. **5** slowly, gradually, gently.

shortage *n.* lack, want, deficiency, shortfall, insufficiency, inadequacy, scantiness, scant supply, limited amount, scarcity, sparsity, sparseness, dearth, deficit, leanness. **—Ant.** abundance, superabundance, profusion, plenty, copiousness, plethora, sufficiency, adequacy; surplus, excess, overflow, overage.

shortcoming *n.* fault, flaw, defect, blemish, imperfection, failing, weakness, inadequacy, frailty, deficiency, foible; drawback, handicap, failure. **—Ant.** advantage, strength, strong point, virtue, merit.

shorten *v.* make shorter, cut short, cut down, trim, clip, pare, prune, shave, shear; abbreviate, cut, abridge, condense, contract, curtail, reduce, decrease, foreshorten, diminish, lessen. **—Syn. Study.** SHORTEN, ABBREVIATE, ABRIDGE, CURTAIL mean to make shorter or briefer. SHORTEN is a general word meaning to make less in extent or duration: *to shorten a dress; to shorten a prison sentence.* The other three terms suggest methods of shortening. ABBREVIATE usu. means to shorten a word or group of words, as by omission of letters: *to abbreviate a name.* To ABRIDGE is to reduce in length or size by condensing, summarizing, and the like: *to abridge a document.* CURTAIL suggests a lack of completeness due to the omission of some part: *to curtail an explanation.* **—Ant.** lengthen, elongate; extend, protract, expand, increase, enlarge, inflate.

shortly *adv.* soon, in a short time, in a little while, before long, by and by, presently, directly, promptly, anon, in a trice, immediately, forthwith. **—Ant.** later, much later.

shortsighted *adj.* **1.** unable to see far, nearsighted, myopic; amblyopic, weak-eyed, purblind. **2.** lacking foresight, improvident, imprudent, ill-advised, unthinking, injudicious, undiscerning, uncircumspect; careless, heedless, reckless, rash, thoughtless, incautious, foolish. **—Ant. 1, 2** farsighted. **2** foresighted, forehanded, prudent, wise, sagacious, circumspect.

short-tempered *adj.* irritable, cranky, grouchy, hot-tempered, short-fused, ill-humored, irascible, testy, choleric, splenetic, snappish, cantankerous, crusty, sharp, peevish, waspish, *British* shirty, bearish, curt, abrupt. —**Ant.** calm, placid, temperate, sedate, pacific.

shot *n.* **1.** gunfire, report, discharge; volley, salvo, fusillade; detonation, blast, explosion. **2.** ammunition, bullets, slugs, projectiles, balls. **3.** marksman, shooter, rifleman, sharpshooter; archer, bowman. **4.** stroke, throw, toss; play, move; hit, drive. **5.** attempt, try, chance, go; guess, conjecture, surmise, essay; *Informal* crack. **6.** injection; dose.

shoulder *n.* **1.** part of the body between the neck and upper arm; scapula, clavicle. **2.** edge, side, rim, margin, verge, border, brink, bank, skirt; crest, brow. —*v.* **3.** shove, elbow, push, thrust, lunge; jostle, bump. **4.** assume, undertake, take on, bear, carry on one's shoulders, take, carry, uphold, sustain, support. —**Ant. 2** middle, center. **4** shirk, shun, neglect, avoid, evade, eschew, duck, dodge.

shout *v.* **1.** cry out, cry, call out, call, yell, holler, scream, shriek, howl, roar, bellow, bawl, clamor, thunder, exclaim, rend the air; whoop, hoot, yelp, hollo, huzzah. —*n.* **2.** cry, outcry, call, yell, holler, scream, shriek, howl, screech, roar, bellow, yelp; whoop, hoot, hollo, cheer, hurrah, huzzah; clamor, outburst, burst, chorus, hullabaloo, hue and cry.

shove *v.* **1.** push, prod, jostle, elbow, shoulder, crowd, nudge; thrust aside, bump, jolt, joggle, butt; propel, drive, force, impel. —*n.* **2.** push, prod, thrust, boost, nudge; jostle.

show *v.* **1.** be visible, be within view, come into view, appear, peep forth; be noticeable, attract attention. **2.** reveal, disclose, make known, manifest, uncover, bare, lay bare, expose, unveil, bring to light; demonstrate, exhibit, display, prove, evidence, evince, suggest, intimate, hint at, represent, establish, bespeak; argue, testify to, attest, confirm, substantiate, certify, corroborate, bear out, bear witness to. **3.** explain, indicate, make clear, point out, make known to, inform, teach, instruct, coach, school, tutor; demonstrate. **4.** direct, lead, guide, usher, conduct. **5.** grant, give, bestow, endow, tender, proffer, impart, favor, lavish; dispense, distribute. —*n.* **6.** display, demonstration, exhibition, sign, expression, token, mark, evidence, indication, manifestation, revelation, disclosure, testimonial, attestation, confirmation. **7.** exhibit, exhibition, exposition, fair; display, demonstration. **8.** program, production, entertainment, performance; (*variously*) play, drama, comedy, musical, motion picture, picture, movie, opera, operetta, ballet, stage show, vaudeville show, variety show, bill; spectacle, ceremony, pomp. **9.** display, pretext, pretense, pretension, affectation, pose, sham, front, counterfeit; impression, effect, appearance, illusion, delusion; vaunting, flaunting. —**Ant. 1** hide, conceal, secrete, withhold, suppress, be invisible, be unnoticeable. **2** hide, conceal, obscure, veil, screen, mask, cloak, cover; disprove, deny, refute. **5** withhold, keep; withdraw. **6** hiding, concealing; disguise, camouflage.

showdown *n.* confrontation, conflict, climax, crisis, face-off, encounter, clashing, collision; battle, war, combat.

shower *n.* **1.** brief fall of rain, sprinkle, drizzle; downpour, cloudburst, torrent, deluge. **2.** fall, pouring down, rain; deluge, flood, inundation, torrent, stream, rush, surge, profusion, plethora, wealth; salvo, volley, barrage, bombardment. —*v.* **3.** sprinkle, splash, spray, wet; rain, drizzle. **4.** give in abundance, bestow liberally, lavish, rain, deluge, pour, bombard.

showoff *n.* exhibitionist, flaunter, swaggerer, strutter, cock of the walk; egotist, braggart, braggadocio, boaster, fanfaron, windbag.

showpiece *n.* masterpiece, masterwork, prime example, prize, gem, jewel, pearl; classic, paragon, prizewinner, rarity, pride, treasure, wonder; *French* chef d'oeuvre, pièce de résistance. —**Ant.** rubbish, trivia, trash.

showy *adj.* brilliant, splendid, striking, gorgeous, ornate, vivid, florid, magnificent; gaudy, flashy, garish, loud, ostentatious. —**Ant.** dull, drab, lackluster, somber, dreary.

shred *n.* **1.** strip, ribbon, band; fragment, sliver, piece, bit, scrap, snippet, rag, tatter. **2.** bit, particle, speck, grain, morsel, iota, jot, scrap, fragment, trace, atom, molecule, ion, whit, spot, scintilla, hair. —**Ant. 2** mass, pile, heap, heaps, oceans, *Informal* gobs, oodles.

shrew *n.* nag, scold, virago, spitfire, vixen, harridan, hag, harpy, *Slang* battle-ax, fishwife, she-wolf, termagant, Xanthippe; *Yiddish* kvetch, yenta.

shrewd *adj.* **1.** sly, crafty, cunning, foxy, wily, cagey; artful, tricky, shifty, slippery, slick, smooth, disingenuous, contriving, designing, scheming, calculating, self-serving, Machiavellian. **2.** astute, smart, clever, sharp, sharp-witted, acute, keen, knowing, canny, discerning, quick, quick-witted, perceptive, sensible, farseeing, farsighted, probing, piercing, penetrating; wise, intelligent, sagacious, perspicacious, circumspect, prudent, cautious, careful, wary. —**Ant. 1**

straightforward, artless, guileless, ingenuous, candid, open, sincere, fair; innocent, naive, unsophisticated. **2** dull, unknowing, ignorant, undiscerning, slow-witted, slow, nearsighted, shortsighted, imprudent, careless; dumb, stupid.

shriek *n.* **1.** cry, outcry, call, yell, yelp, screech, squeal, squeak, howl, shout, scream, holler, whoop, hoot, peal. —*v.* **2.** cry out, scream, screech, squawk, yell, yelp, squeal, holler, howl.

shrill *adj.* high, high-pitched, screeching, piercing, penetrating, strident, piping, loud, blaring, clamorous, raucous. **—Ant.** soft, mellow, mellifluous, dulcet, silvertoned, velvety, satiny; resonant, deep, low, well-modulated.

shrine *n.* **1.** sacred place, consecrated place, sacred tomb; altar, sanctuary, sanctum, chapel, church, temple. **2.** honored place, consecrated spot, monument.

shrink *v.* **1.** become smaller, make smaller, make less, lessen, shrivel, shorten, draw together, contract, pucker, constrict, deflate, compress, condense; decrease, diminish, decline, curtail, reduce, dwindle, dry up, wane, ebb. **2.** draw back, hang back, recoil, cringe, cower, quail, shudder, shy, blench, flinch, wince, duck, retreat, withdraw, retire; demur, stick, refuse, balk, bridle. **—Syn. Study. 2** See WINCE. **—Ant. 1** stretch, swell, distend, dilate, inflate; increase, enlarge, amplify, grow, expand, mushroom, balloon. **2** welcome, meet head on, confront, stand up to.

shrivel *v.* shrink, dry up, wither, wizen, wrinkle, pucker; parch, scorch; deteriorate, waste away.

shroud *n.* **1.** burial cloth, graveclothes, winding sheet, cerements, cerecloth. **2.** cover, covering, cloak, blanket, sheet, veil, mantle, pall, screen, cloud. —*v.* **3.** wrap, clothe, swathe, cover, envelop, cloak, veil; hide, conceal. **—Ant. 3** uncover, unveil, reveal, expose.

shudder *v.* **1.** tremble, shake, quiver, quaver, quake, shiver; shimmy, twitch, jerk. —*n.* **2.** trembling, tremor, shiver, quiver, quaver, shake, quake, flutter, paroxysm, spasm, pulsation, throb, pang, twitch, jerk, convulsion.

shuffle *v.* **1.** drag, scrape, slide, scuff, walk with clumsy steps, shamble. **2.** jumble, disarrange, rearrange, mix, scramble; exchange the positions of, interchange. —*n.* **3.** dragging gait, sliding gait, clumsy step, scraping movement; limp, gimp. **—Ant. 1** lift. **3** light step, high step.

shun *v.* avoid, evade, elude, dodge, keep away from, keep clear of, steer clear of, shy away from, fight shy of, shrink from, turn away from, circumvent; eschew, refuse, forgo, reject, disdain, boycott, ignore, have nothing to do with, have no part of. **—Ant.** welcome, embrace, encourage, seek, search out, solicit, court.

shut *v.* **1.** close, secure, fasten, snap, clasp, latch, lock; draw to, draw, fold. **2.** enclose, confine, constrain, cloister, closet, cage, coop, fence in, corral, box, lock in; barricade, impound, imprison, intern, incarcerate. —*adj.* **3.** closed, closed up; fastened, secured, latched, locked; drawn, drawn to. **—Ant. 1** open, unshut; unfasten, unlock. **2** free, liberate, release, let out. **3** open, opened; unfastened, unlocked.

shy *adj.* **1.** self-conscious, bashful, shrinking, timid, diffident, timorous, meek, reserved, reticent, demure, modest; fearful, apprehensive, tremulous, nervous, anxious, skittish. **2.** short, under, deficient, lacking, wanting, needing, in need, scant, minus. **3.** wary, leery, suspicious, distrustful, cautious, careful, *Slang* chary. —*v.* **4.** jump back, draw back, recoil from, balk, spring aside, swerve, dodge, shrink, blench, cower, flinch, wince. **—Ant. 1** forward, brash, brazen, brassy; bold, fearless, unfrightened, unapprehensive. **2** over, ahead, above, showing a surplus. **3** rash, reckless, careless, unsuspicious, unsuspecting.

sibyl *n.* oracle, prophetess, seer, augur, predictor, soothsayer, diviner, forecaster, fortune teller, sorceress, Delphic sibyl, prognosticator.

sick *adj.* **1.** ill, unwell, ailing, laid up, indisposed; infirm, sickly, invalid, afflicted, unsound, unhealthy, poorly, frail, delicate, weak; nauseated, throwing up, queasy, under the weather; of a sick person. **2.** deeply upset, greatly affected, stricken, afflicted, suffering, distressed, grieved, wretched, heartbroken, crushed, miserable, troubled, uneasy, disturbed, perturbed, disquieted, discomposed. **3.** fed up with, disgusted with, tired, weary, bored with; adverse to, repelled by, displeased with, revolted by. **—Syn. Study. 1** See ILL. **—Ant. 1** well, fine, tip-top; healthy, hale, hale and hearty, sound, unimpaired, strong, robust, vigorous, blooming, fit as a fiddle. **2** unaffected, untroubled, undisturbed, unperturbed, unconcerned, unworried, easy, tranquil, calm.

sicken *v.* make sick, make ill, nauseate, turn the stomach, disgust, revolt, repel, repulse, horrify, upset, offend, shock; become sick, fall sick, take sick. **—Ant.** cure, make well; please, delight, enchant, gratify.

sickening *adj.* causing sickness, nauseating; disgusting, vile, horrible, nasty, foul, revolting, repugnant, noisome, repulsive, repellent, loathsome, abhorrent, distasteful, unsavory, offensive. **—Ant.** curative; agreeable, mouth-watering, delightful, pleasant, pleasing, heavenly, wonderful, inviting, tempting, attractive, lovely, enchanting, alluring, captivating.

sickly *adj.* **1.** ailing, in poor health, unhealthy, sick, ill, unwell, infirm, invalid, afflicted, unsound, frail, weak, delicate, poorly; pale, wan, ashen, drab, peaked, bloodless, leaden, cadaverous, lackluster. **2.** weak, feeble, flimsy, lame, faint, ineffective, unconvincing, lacking in fervor, insipid, spiritless, flat, uninspired, apathetic, torpid; simpering, smirking, snickering, sneaky, guilty, self-conscious, silly, namby-pamby, wishy-washy.

sickness *n.* **1.** illness, ill health; disease, disorder, infirmity, ailment, malady, complaint, indisposition, affliction; poor health, sickliness, unsoundness, invalidism, frailness, delicate health, debility; disability. **2.** nausea, queasiness, qualmishness; vomiting, throwing up, *Slang* upchucking.

side *n.* **1.** flank; lateral surface, flat surface, surface. **2.** boundary, bound, limit, perimeter, border, edge, periphery, margin, rim, brim, skirt, hem; part, area, segment, section, sector, territory, region, division; half, quarter. **3.** team; group, body, sect, faction, party, clique, coterie, circle; alliance, coalition, association, affiliation, federation. **4.** position, stand, attitude, part, belief, opinion, cause, behalf; viewpoint, point of view, view, standpoint, aspect, angle, slant, light, phase, facet, hand. **5.** part of a family; line of descent, lineage, bloodline, strain, stock, house. *—adj.* **6.** at one side, on one side, lateral, flanking; fringe, border, marginal, skirting. **7.** from the side, toward the side, lateral, postern; sideways, sidewise, sidelong, oblique, indirect, askance. **8.** minor, subordinate, lesser, incidental, secondary, subsidiary, insignificant, unimportant, inconsequential; related, accessory, collateral, contingent, allied. **—Ant. 1** front, back; top, bottom, edge. **2** middle, center, midpoint. **6** front, back, rear; top, bottom; center, central, middle. **7** frontal, direct, headlong; rear. **8** major, main, primary, principal, prime, first, leading, significant.

sideways Also **sideway, sidewise** *adv.* **1.** to the side, toward one side, from one side, sideward; with one side forward, laterally, sidelong, edgeways, edgewise, aslant, obliquely. *—adj.* **2.** sidelong, sidewise, oblique, lateral. **—Ant. 1** forward, backward; head on. **2** direct, headlong.

sift *v.* **1.** sprinkle, scatter; drift, filter. **2.** separate, sort out, sort, discriminate, distinguish, winnow, screen; study, scrutinize, inspect, examine closely, probe, search, investigate, analyze, review.

sigh *v.* **1.** let out one's breath, breathe loudly, moan, groan, sob; say with a sighing sound, whine, hiss. **2.** pine, yearn, long, brood; grieve, weep, lament, mourn, sorrow. *—n.* **3.** deep audible breath; moan, groan, sob, whine; hiss.

sight *n.* **1.** eyesight, vision, visual perception. **2.** range of vision, field of vision, eyeshot, view, ken, scrutiny, gaze, survey. **3.** seeing, vision, appearance, visibility, viewing, glimpse, view. **4.** view, spectacle, display, pageant, exhibit, prospect, scene, vista, image, scenery; place of interest, thing of interest. **5.** peepsight, sighthole, bead; telescopic sight. *—v.* **6.** see, observe, glimpse, spot, catch sight of, spy, espy, perceive, behold, view. **—Ant. 1** blindness.

sign *n.* **1.** symbol, mark, figure, token, evidence, manifestation, emblem, badge, ensign; indication, indicator, omen, portent, prognostic, presage, warning, forewarning, forecast, herald, harbinger, signal, clue, symptom, hint, suggestion, intimation, note, index; characteristic, earmark, trademark, trait, feature, stamp, brand. **2.** signal, motion, gesture; go-ahead, wave, nod. **3.** (*variously*) placard, advertising sign, electric sign, neon sign, signboard, signpost, billboard; road sign, street sign, guidepost; nameplate. *—v.* **4.** write one's signature, set one's hand to, countersign, underwrite, undersign, endorse, sign one's John Hancock; autograph, inscribe. **—Syn. Study. 1** SIGN, OMEN, PORTENT refer to something that gives evidence of a future event. SIGN is a general word for a visible trace or indication of an event, either past, present, or future: *Dark clouds are a sign of rain.* An OMEN is a happening or phenomenon that serves as a warning of things to come; it may foreshadow good or evil: *She believed it was a bad omen if a black cat crossed her path.* PORTENT also refers to an indication of future events, usu. ones that are momentous or of ominous significance: *the portents of war.*

signal *n.* **1.** sign, high sign, indication, indicator, cue, warning, command; gesture, motion, nod; watchword, password. *—adj.* **2.** indicating, direction, directing, guiding, pointing, warning. **3.** singular, unique, exceptional, one-of-a-kind, distinctive, outstanding, extraordinary, remarkable, noteworthy, notable, distinguished, eminent, illustrious, famous, honored, renowned, impressive, important, consequential, significant, momentous, considerable, memorable, unforgettable; conspicuous, striking, arresting, prominent, commanding. *—v.* **4.**

motion, gesture, beckon, give a sign to. —**Ant.** **3** ordinary, commonplace, common, familiar, everyday, run-of-the-mill.

significance *n.* consequence, importance, import, weight, meaning, signification, implication, relevance, moment, portent, gravity, force, influence, authority; concern, interest, note, notability, eminence, priority, prominence, distinction, excellence, value, merit, worth, virtue; sense, drift, purport, intent, intention, aim, object, purpose, direction. —**Syn. Study.** See IMPORTANCE, MEANING.

significant *adj.* **1.** consequential, important, substantial, meaningful, material, principal, great, paramount, major, chief, main, prime, vital, critical, serious, portentous, influential, considerable, momentous, grave, weighty, noteworthy, notable, eminent, prominent, distinct, outstanding, remarkable, impressive, exceptional, signal, eventful. **2.** indicative, expressive, meaningful, suggestive, symbolic, symptomatic, emblematic, representative, demonstrative; eloquent, pregnant, cogent, telling, knowing. —**Ant.** **1** insignificant, inconsequential, trivial, unimportant, insubstantial, meaningless, immaterial.

signify *v.* be a sign of, stand for, mean, import, indicate, represent, connote, convey, express, manifest, evidence, evince, demonstrate, exhibit, show, proclaim, declare, announce, communicate, set forth, designate, disclose, reveal, tell, give notice of; imply, intimate, suggest, hint at, denote, typify, symbolize, bespeak, betoken, import, argue; portend, predict, prognosticate, augur, omen, forebode, foretell, foreshadow, presage, herald, promise.

silence *n.* **1.** quiet, quietness, noiselessness, soundlessness, still, stillness, hush; peace, calm, tranquillity, serenity, placidness, placidity, repose; speechlessness, muteness, dumbness; reserve, reticence, uncommunicativeness, taciturnity, secretiveness, closemouthedness. —*v.* **2.** still, quiet, quieten, hush, calm, strike dumb, tongue-tie; deaden. **3.** gag, muzzle, muffle, choke off, suppress, repress, crush, quell, quash, put down, squelch, squash; stop, halt, stifle, check, curb, vanquish, overcome, defeat, rout, banish, subdue, conquer, extinguish, nullify, allay, quiet, still, put an end to, lay to rest. —**Ant.** **1** sound, noise, noisiness, din, roar, clamor, tumult, turmoil, commotion, agitation, excitement; speech, talking, talkativeness, verbosity, verboseness, loquaciousness, garrulousness, chatter, babel. **2** make noise; arouse, rouse, agitate, incite, inflame, stir up; make louder, amplify. **3** ungag, encourage, support, aid, help, abet, champion, broadcast, publicize.

silent *adj.* **1.** making no sound, having no sound, soundless, noiseless, quiet, still, hushed, muffled, muted, mute; idle, inactive, unstirring, lifeless, inert, quiescent, dormant, calm, peaceful, tranquil, serene, placid. **2.** not speaking, saying nothing, wordless, mum, tongue-tied; speechless, mute, dumb; speaking but little, untalkative, reticent, uncommunicative, closemouthed, close-lipped, tight-lipped, taciturn, reserved; secretive, mysterious, discreet. **3.** not pronounced, unpronounced, not sounded, unsounded, unvocalized, mute. **4.** not taking an active part; tacit, understood, implied, implicit, inferred, intimated, insinuated, suggested, unspoken, unsaid, untalked-of, unmentioned, unexpressed, undeclared, unarticulated; unpublished, unwritten, unrevealed, hidden, covert, concealed. —**Ant.** **1** noisy, clamorous; active, stirring, lively, bustling, tumultuous, agitated, excited. **2** noisy, vocal, vociferous, talkative, talky, garrulous, loquacious, wordy, verbose, chatty, blabbering, babbling. **3** sounded, pronounced, articulated. **4** active; spelled-out, explicit, stated, declared, announced, expressed.

silly *adj.* **1.** lacking judgment, foolhardy, irrational, senseless, unwise, ill-advised, unwary, irresponsible, ridiculous, pointless, unwary; foolish, dumb, stupid, simpleminded, witless, brainless, featherbrained, harebrained, rattlebrained, muddlebrained, empty-headed, muddleheaded; shallow, fatuous, idiotic, absurd, asinine, inane, childish, frivolous, frothy, giddy, mad, insane, crazy. **2.** ridiculous, nonsensical, preposterous, absurd, farcical, ludicrous, laughable; meaningless, purposeless, inconsequential, inappropriate, aimless, unreasonable. —**Ant.** **1** judicious, rational, sensible, wise, reasonable, sane, sound, smart, bright, astute, clever, brainy, intelligent, perceptive, sharp, acute, sage; serious, deep, mature, stable. **2** serious, meaningful, purposeful, consequential, appropriate; sad, sorrowful.

silver *n.* **1.** white shining precious metal, argentine, argent, *Latin* argentum; articles made of silver, silverware, silver jewelry. **2.** change, coins. **3.** grayish white, platinum.

similar *adj.* nearly alike, much the same, kindred, akin, parallel, like, equivalent, comparable, analogous, close, correspondent, corresponding, correlative, agreeing, approximate, resembling, allied, cognate; matching, duplicate, twin. —**Ant.** different, dissimilar, unalike, unlike, disparate, diverse, opposite, opposed, contrary, contradictory, antithetical, disagreeing, alien.

similarity *n.* resemblance, likeness, correspondence, parallelism, kinship, similitude, semblance, sameness, oneness, comparability, equivalence, agreement, congruity, congruence, harmony, concordance, conformance, conformability, affinity, closeness, nearness, reciprocity. **—Ant.** dissimilarity, difference, unlikeness, dissimilitude, disparity, diversity, incongruity, discordance, disagreement.

simmer *v.* **1.** boil gently, stew, seethe; bubble, gurgle, burble. **2.** seethe, fume, foam, boil, sizzle, burn, stew; chafe, smart. **—Syn. Study. 2** See BOIL.

simper *v.* snigger, snicker, smirk, giggle, titter, tee-hee; smile sillily, grin self-consciously.

simple *adj.* **1.** having few parts, not complex, uncomplicated, uninvolved, not elaborate, uncompounded; unsophisticated; basic, elemental, elementary, fundamental, rudimentary; easy, not difficult, manageable, soft. **2.** plain, not fancy, unadorned, undecorated, unembellished, untrimmed, modest, unaffected, unpretentious; unsophisticated, unworldly, natural, common, commonplace, ordinary, workaday; quiet, peaceful, rustic, homey, innocent, naive, guileless, artless, ingenuous. **3.** plain, honest, true, sincere, candid, naked, stark, bare, unadorned, unvarnished, downright, sheer, absolute, straight, unfeigned, open, artless, guileless; blunt, frank, direct, plain-spoken, straightforward, out-and-out. **4.** innocent, naive, artless, guileless, ingenuous, green, callow, unworldly, inexperienced, unsophisticated; dumb; stupid, simple-minded, slow, dense, dull, thick, thick-witted, obtuse, foolish, weak in the upper story. **—Ant. 1** complex, complicated, involved, intricate, elaborate, compound, sophisticated, advanced; difficult, hard, tough. **2** fancy, elaborate, ornate, adorned, decorated, embellished, pretentious, affected, ostentatious, flashy, showy; sophisticated, worldly, cosmopolitan; busy, hectic, bustling, confused, tumultuous. **3** dishonest, insincere, varnished, gilded, indirect, devious, artful, guileful; feigned, pretended, contrived. **4** worldly, sophisticated, knowing, wise, experienced; crafty, sly, cunning, foxy, clever, canny, shrewd, sharp, acute, keen, smart, bright, fast, fast on the uptake.

simpleminded *adj.* foolish, stupid, silly, fatuous, idiotic, dumb, asinine, empty-headed, dull, slow, dull-witted, dim-witted, dense, thick, witless, half-witted, feebleminded. **—Ant.** clear-headed, bright, sharp, sensible, wise.

simpleton *n.* fool, numskull, nincompoop, dunce, blockhead, oaf, ignoramus, dolt, ninny, booby, dumbbell, idiot, dummy, dullard, imbecile, ass, jackass, donkey, dope, goose, *Slang* jerk, stupe; rustic, hick, rube, greenhorn.

simplicity *n.* **1.** lack of complexity; easiness, obviousness, directness, straightforwardness, plainness, clarity, clearness, purity, restraint, cleanliness, lack of adornment, austerity, serenity. **2.** openness, candor, directness, sincerity, honesty, guilelessness, truthfulness, artlessness, naturalness; innocence, naiveté, unworldliness, lack of sophistication. **—Ant. 1** complexity, complicatedness, intricateness, difficulty; elaborateness, fanciness, ornateness, decoration, adornment, embellishment, pretentiousness, affectation, ostentation. **2** sophistication, worldliness; deviousness, insincerity, dishonesty, untruthfulness, guilefulness, guile, craftiness, slyness, cunning, conniving.

simply *adv.* uncomplicatedly, plainly, directly, straightforwardly, explicitly, clearly, lucidly, intelligibly; without adornment, starkly, modestly, unaffectedly, unpretentiously, naturally, ingenuously.

simulate *v.* feign, put on, assume, pretend, dissemble, counterfeit, affect, fabricate, fake, sham; invent; act, play, play-act, pose, make believe, imitate, ape, mimic, copy.

simulated *adj.* imitation, synthetic, artificial, fabricated, manmade, pretend, make-believe, sham; fake, counterfeit, phony, forged. **—Ant.** real, authentic, actual, natural, true, bona fide.

simultaneous *adj.* occurring at the same time, accompanying, concurrent, coincident, synchronous, synchronal, synchronic, concomitant; existing at the same time, coexistent, coexisting, coeval, contemporaneous, contemporary.

sin *n.* **1.** ungodly act, immoral act, irreligious act, sinfulness, iniquity, transgression, trespass; wrong, wrongdoing, evil, evil deed, villainy, vice, misdeed, violation, breach, crime, offense, infraction, error, slip, lapse. **2.** shame, disgrace, scandal. *—v.* **3.** offend against God, offend against morality, transgress, trespass, err, offend, fall, stray, do wrong, do evil, slip, lapse. **—Syn. Study. 1** See CRIME. **—Ant. 1** virtue, goodness, righteousness, sinlessness, godliness, holiness, uprightness; good, honesty, ethics, morality.

sincere *adj.* free from pretense, unfeigned, undeceitful, unaffected, real, honest, natural, genuine, authentic, artless, guileless, ingenuous, candid, frank, straightforward, forthright, truthful; earnest, wholehearted, heartfelt, serious, in good faith. **—Syn. Study.** See EARNEST. **—Ant.** insincere, feigned, pretended, deceitful, contrived, affected, devious, deceptive.

sincerely *adv.* really, genuinely, honestly, truly, truthfully; earnestly, seriously, wholeheartedly. **—Ant.** insincerely, falsely, dishonestly, deceptively, untruthfully, deceitfully.

sincerity *n.* honesty, probity, genuineness, earnestness, seriousness, candor, openness, frankness, straightforwardness, forthrightness, truthfulness, unaffectedness, artlessness, ingenuousness, guilelessness, wholeheartedness, good faith, honor, integrity. **—Syn. Study.** See HONOR.

sinful *adj.* wicked, evil, unrighteous, unholy, impious, ungodly, irreligious, iniquitous, immoral, profligate, miscreant, corrupt, depraved, degenerate; villainous, vile, wrong, bad, heinous, despicable, wayward, errant, criminal, shameful, disgraceful. **—Ant.** sinless, righteous, upright, virtuous, moral, pure, godly; honest, ethical, honorable.

sing *v.* utter musical sounds, intone, chant, croon, lilt, hum, perform a song, tell in song, melodize, tell in verse; warble, chirp, chirrup, trill, tweet, pipe, whistle; carol.

singe *v.* scorch, sear, char, burn, burn slightly, burn superficially, brand.

singer *n.* vocalist, songster, songstress, crooner, diva, chantress, chanteuse; (*variously*) tenor, bass, soprano, contralto, baritone, countertenor, mezzosoprano; minstrel, troubadour, bard; songbird, nightingale, lark.

single *adj.* **1.** one, only one, individual, solitary, lone, sole, singular. **2.** unmarried, unwed, spouseless, wifeless, husbandless, spinster, bachelor, maiden. **—Ant. 1** accompanied; several, some, many, numerous. **2** married, mated, wed, wedded, espoused, *Slang* hitched, hooked-up.

single-minded *adj.* determined, persevering, inflexible, firm, resolved, unswerving, zealous, dogged, staunch, unwavering, devoted, tireless, intense, steadfast, relentless, unflinching, tenacious, dedicated, untiring, persistent. **—Ant.** wavering, irresolute, indecisive, vacillating.

singular *adj.* **1.** unique, rare, unusual, uncommon, exceptional, extraordinary, unequaled, unparalleled, matchless, unprecedented, peerless, surpassing, choice, select, superior; remarkable, noteworthy, wonderful, marvelous, prodigious. **2.** unusual, unnatural, odd, strange, queer, peculiar, curious, freakish, bizarre, fantastic, outlandish, quaint, different, unconventional, eccentric, anomalous, unwonted, uncustomary, atypical, unfamiliar, abnormal, aberrant, unaccountable, out-of-the-ordinary, off the beaten track. **—Ant. 1, 2** common, commonplace, familiar, ordinary, usual, everyday, routine, conventional.

sinister *adj.* **1.** threatening, ominous, menacing, dire, frightening, fearful, alarming, disturbing, disquieting, dismaying; inauspicious, unpropitious, unfavorable, unpromising, adverse, unlucky. **2.** wicked, evil, villainous, vile, foul, treacherous, perfidious, malevolent, malign, malignant, insidious, Machiavellian, rascally, rank, dark, black, blackhearted, reprehensible, despicable, detestable, damnable, accursed, cursed, diabolical, infernal, hellish, devilish. **—Ant. 1** calming, soothing, encouraging, heartening; favorable, auspicious, promising, propitious, opportune, advantageous; beneficial, kindly, benevolent, benign. **2** noble, heroic, honorable, worthy, virtuous, just, high-minded, exemplary, righteous, upright, reputable, principled, ethical.

sink *v.* **1.** descend, go down, lower, drop, fall, plunge; decline, dip, slant, slope, tilt, sag, droop, slump. **2.** descend below the surface, submerse, submerge, go to the bottom, go under, go to Davy Jones's locker; become absorbed, seep, soak; engulf, drown. **3.** put down, set, lay, lower, bury; excavate, dig, bore, drill, drive, gouge, scoop out, hollow out. **4.** lower, decline, fall, lessen, diminish, drop, shrink, subside, go down, reduce, depreciate; deteriorate, degenerate, worsen, regress, retrogress, wane, ebb, slump, slip, languish, give way, droop, sag, go from bad to worse, go downhill, go to pot, go to the dogs. **5.** lower oneself, degrade oneself, debase oneself, stoop, fall, descend; succumb, give way, yield. *—n.* **6.** basin, wash basin, bowl, washbowl, lavatory. **—Ant. 1** rise, ascend, climb, mount, incline. **2** surface, emerge. **3** remove, dig up; fill in. **4** rise, increase, advance, ascend, climb, grow.

sinner *n.* transgressor, evildoer, malefactor, wrongdoer, offender, apostate, backslider, reprobate, misfeasor, miscreant, trespasser, recidivist. **—Ant.** saint, holy person, exemplar.

sinuous *adj.* full of turns, winding, curving, curved, bending, volute, convoluted, folded, serpentine, labyrinthine, mazelike, twisted, twisting, coiling, zigzag, meandering, wandering, circuitous, roundabout, indirect, rambling, tortuous, undulating. **—Ant.** straight, direct, beeline.

sip *v.* **1.** drink, drink bit by bit, drink slowly, lap, sup; sample, taste, savor, nip. *—n.* **2.** small mouthful, small draught, dram, swallow, drop, thimbleful, sup, soupçon, nip, drink, sample, taste. **—Syn. Study. 1** See DRINK. **—Ant. 1** gulp, bolt, swill, swig, quaff, toss off. **2** gulp, swig.

siren *n.* **1.** warning signal; (*variously*) alarm, whistle, horn. **2.** Sometimes **Siren** nymph, sea nymph; seductress, enchantress, witch, temptress, vamp, deceiver; bewitching woman, charmer; *Slang* sexpot.

sit *v.* **1.** be seated, have a seat; squat, sprawl, loll; settle, perch, roost; rest. **2.** be situated, be located, be established, be seated, be placed, stand, rest, lie; remain, stay, endure, reside, abide, linger. **3.** convene, be in session, assemble, meet, gather, deliberate, conduct business; occupy a place, have an official seat, hold an official position; govern, rule, reign, officiate, preside, chair. **4.** baby-sit, watch, watch over, care for, take care of, mind, attend, teach, keep company, chaperon, nurse. **—Ant. 1** stand; lie. **2** move, remove. **3** adjourn, disperse, scatter.

site *n.* spot, place, point, ground, post, position, station; locale, locality, location, locus, whereabouts, territory, region, area, province, section, sector, district, zone, field, scene, setting.

situate *v.* locate, place, position, put, establish, station, set, settle, install, lodge, ensconce, billet, house; plant, post, stand; construct, build. **—Ant.** move, remove.

situation *n.* **1.** state of affairs, state, circumstances, condition, status, case, position, posture; predicament, plight, fix, dilemma, quandary. **2.** position, location, locality, locale, spot, place, site, station, seat. **3.** job, position, post, assignment, place, seat, office, berth, capacity; role, function, duty, work, livelihood.

size *n.* **1.** dimensions, measurement, extent, amplitude, stretch, proportions, area, volume, spread, expanse; magnitude, largeness, greatness, bigness, bulk, mass, scope; content, capacity. **2.** amount, quantity, sum, aggregate, total, totality. **—*v.* 3.** arrange, array, sort, group, grade, classify.

sizzle *v.* **1.** hiss, sputter, splutter, spit, frizzle, crackle; fry. **—*n.* 2.** hissing, hiss, sputtering.

skeleton *n.* bony framework, bones; frame, underlying structure, hulk, shell. **—Ant.** skin; exterior, surface, covering, sheath.

skeptic Also **sceptic** *n.* doubter, doubting Thomas, questioner, scoffer; agnostic, unbeliever, atheist.

skeptical Also **sceptical** *adj.* inclined to question, questioning, dubious, doubting, doubtful, unsure, uncertain, unconvinced, incredulous; disbelieving, unbelieving, scoffing, hypercritical, cynical. **—Syn. Study.** See DOUBTFUL. **—Ant.** convinced, sure, certain, confident, unquestioning, undoubting; believing, credulous, gullible.

sketch *n.* **1.** drawing, preliminary drawing, preliminary painting; rough design, blueprint, graph, chart. **2.** outline, brief description, rough account, summary, abstract, précis, synopsis, digest. **3.** skit, short play, scene, vignette, characterization; lampoon, takeoff, burlesque, satire. **—*v.* 4.** make a quick drawing of, draw; rough out, draft. **5.** set forth briefly, describe quickly, outline, plot, summarize, abstract, map, mark out, picture, depict, delineate, portray, chart, graph, rough out.

sketchy *adj.* incomplete, cursory, rough, vague, bare, essential, outline, brief, short, hazy, slight, skimpy, slender, meager, light, shallow, superficial, undetailed; unfinished, preliminary, provisional, preparatory, unpolished, unrefined, crude, rough-hewn. **—Ant.** complete, full, detailed, lengthy, long, indepth, exact; finished, final, polished.

skid *n.* **1.** slip, sliding motion, slide; glissade. **2.** runner, platform with runners; sled, dray, sledge, drag. **—*v.* 3.** slide, slip, slip sideways, sideslip; glide, glissade, skip, skate, ski, skim, skitter, coast.

skill *n.* **1.** skillfulness, craft, adroitness, adeptness, expertness, deftness, dexterity, handiness, mastery, competence, artistry; acumen, cunning, cleverness, ingenuity, inventiveness. **2.** ability, capacity, prowess, faculty, facility, proficiency, experience, knowhow, expertise, knack; talent, gift. **—Ant. 1** incompetence, ineptness, ineptitude, awkwardness, clumsiness. **2** inability, nonproficiency, inexperience.

skilled *adj.* **—Syn. Study.** See SKILLFUL.

skillful *adj.* skilled, expert, able, competent, capable, proficient, qualified, accomplished, professional, masterful, masterly, experienced, veteran, practiced, trained, well-versed; apt, adept, adroit, dexterous, handy, facile, deft, talented, gifted, ingenious, clever, sharp, keen, cunning, slick. **—Syn. Study.** SKILLFUL, SKILLED, EXPERT refer to ability or competence in an occupation, craft, or art. SKILLFUL suggests adroitness and dexterity: *a skillful watchmaker.* SKILLED implies having had long experience and thus having acquired a high degree of proficiency: *not an amateur but a skilled worker.* EXPERT means having the highest degree of proficiency; it may mean much the same as SKILLFUL or SKILLED, or both: *expert workmanship.* **—Ant.** unskillful, unskilled, inexpert, inept, incompetent, unqualified, unaccomplished, nonprofessional, amateurish, inexperienced, unpracticed, untrained; unqualified; clumsy, awkward, bungling.

skim *v.* **1.** take up from the surface, scrape, ream. **2.** move lightly, glide, sweep, glissade, coast, skate, scud, skid, skip, bounce, float, sail, fly. **3.** read superficially, glance over, scan, flip, thumb through, dip into, leaf through. **—Ant.** **3** examine carefully, peruse.

skimp *v.* **1.** be sparing of, be stingy with, scrimp, stint, slight, hold back, withhold. **2.** be frugal, use economy, economize, be stingy, cut expenses, be parsimonious, be niggardly, pinch, scrimp, stint, scrape along. **—Ant.** **1** lavish, squander, be generous with, be profuse with, pour on, load on. **2** be extravagant, overspend, squander, be thriftless.

skimpy *adj.* **1.** not large enough, small, smallish, scant, scanty, spare, sparse, scrimpy, meager, exiguous, modest, slight; inadequate, insufficient, incomplete, wanting, inconsiderable. **2.** stingy, too thrifty, parsimonious, miserly, niggardly, stinting, penurious, frugal, scrimping, sparing, pennypinching, grudging, illiberal, close, close-fisted, tightfisted, *Informal* tight. **—Ant.** **1** big, too big, large, ample, full; abundant, profuse, copious, generous, lavish, considerable; adequate, sufficient. **2** extravagant, liberal, generous, open-handed.

skin *n.* **1.** epidermis, body covering; complexion; hide, pelt, coat, fur, fleece. **2.** peel, rind, husk, hull, shell, pod, jacket, case, casing, sheath, integument, outer coating. *—v.* **3.** strip the skin from, peel, flay, remove the hide from, lay bare; scrape, bark, abrade.

skinflint *n.* stingy person, miser, hoarder, niggardly person, niggard, penny pincher, pinchpenny, scrooge, *Slang* tightwad. **—Ant.** big spender, spendthrift, sport.

skinny *adj.* thin, slender, lean, scrawny, spindly, emaciated, spare, lank, lanky, wiry, angular, gawky, gangling, scraggy, gaunt, rawboned, skeletal, slight, shrunken. **—Ant.** fat, obese, corpulent, plump, chubby, hefty, husky, rotund, fleshy, robust.

skip *v.* **1.** leap lightly, hop, jump, trip, bob, spring, bounce, bound, flit, prance, gambol, caper, romp; jump lightly over, leap over. **2.** pass over, omit, leave out, overlook, ignore, eschew, neglect, disregard, do without; evade, elude, dodge, shun, miss. **3.** *Informal* leave hurriedly and secretly, slip out of, escape, flee, make off, abscond, skedaddle, disappear, fly the coop; be absent from, be absent from without excuse, play hooky, cut. *—n.* **4.** light jump, leap, bound, spring, hop, bounce; prance, gambol, caper. **—Ant.** **1** shuffle, lumber, drag, trudge, plod, waddle. **2** include, cover, put in, contain, refer to, take into account; confront, meet. **3** stay, remain; be present, attend.

skirmish *n.* **1.** brief fight, encounter, clash, engagement, action, firefight; brush, fray, affray, scrap, tussle, scuffle, fracas, scrimmage, *Slang* set-to, run-in. *—v.* **2.** fight briefly, clash, battle; struggle, scrimmage, brush, scrap, tussle, tilt, joust.

skirt *n.* **1.** (*variously*) overskirt, underskirt, hoop skirt, dirndl, crinoline, kilt; mini, maxi. **2.** outer area, border, fringe, edge, rim, margin, perimeter, boundary, bounds, periphery, verge, hem. *—v.* **3.** pass along the edge of, border, flank, lie along; circle, encircle, circumscribe, enclose, hem in, envelop, gird, girdle, ring. **4.** avoid, evade, shun, fight shy of, keep away from; detour around, go around, circle, circumvent. **—Ant.** **1** pants, slacks, trousers. **2** center, middle, heart, core, hub. **3** diverge from, lead away from. **4** face, confront, meet.

skittish *adj.* **1.** easily startled, easily frightened, fearful, nervous, jumpy, jittery, fidgety, excitable; restless, restive, unsteady, shaky, fitful, impulsive, flighty, mercurial, volatile, unstable. **2.** shy, bashful, timid, demurring; wary, cautious, chary, leery, guarded, distrustful, suspicious, unsure, reluctant. **—Ant.** **1** calm, relaxed, tranquil, serene, sedate, placid, unexcitable, composed, stable, steady, cool as a cucumber, unflappable; phlegmatic.

skulk *v.* **—Syn. Study.** See LURK.

sky *n.* atmosphere; upper atmosphere, the firmament, the heavens, the blue vault of heaven, arch of heaven, space, outer space.

slab *n.* thick flat piece, slice, thick slice; hunk, chunk, wad, block; plank, board, slat; wedge. **—Ant.** bit, fragment, scrap, sliver, splinter, chip, shaving, shred.

slack *adj.* **1.** loose, relaxed, lax, limp, flaccid, not tight, not taut, not firm; pliant, flexible, flabby, baggy; free, untied, unfastened. **2.** unexacting, lax, undemanding, not firm, easy, soft, loose, permissive; careless, slipshod, neglectful, negligent, dilatory, remiss, slapdash, offhand, inattentive, lazy, slothful, indolent, nonchalant, lackadaisical, thoughtless, unthinking, unconcerned, indifferent, heedless, unmindful. **3.** slow, slow-moving, slow-paced, sluggish; not busy, inactive, lethargic, listless, dull; leisurely, lazy, quiet. *—adv.* **4.** limply, loosely, freely, easily; sluggishly, slowly. *—v.* **5.** slacken, loosen, loose, make less taut, untighten, relax, make limp, free, let up on. —**Ant. 1** tight, taut, rigid, stiff, firm, tense, inflexible; tied, fastened. **2** exacting, demanding, meticulous, firm, inflexible, hard; careful, diligent, attentive, sedulous, thoughtful, mindful, concerned, caring, heedful. **3** fast, fast-moving, rapid; busy, active, brisk, quick, bustling; pressing. **4** tight, tightly, taut, tautly, rigidly, stiffly, tensely. **5** tighten, stiffen, pull up, pull in, take up the slack.

slacken *v.* **1.** slack, slack off, slow, slow down, abate, taper off, dwindle, ease, let up, moderate, soften, weaken, mitigate, temper; relax, reduce, lessen, flag, decrease, diminish, curb, check, arrest, restrain, limit, retard, inhibit, keep back. **2.** loosen, loose, relax, untighten, slack, slack up on, let go limp, go limp; free, release, let go, let loose of. —**Ant. 1** quicken, increase, rise, accelerate. **2** tighten, draw tight.

slacker *n.* malingerer, shirker, dodger, laggard, loafer, idler, dawdler, dallier, procrastinator, good-for-nothing, do-nothing, quitter, truant, *Slang* goldbrick, goof-off.

slake *v.* quench, satisfy, sate, satiate, gratify, appease, relieve, mollify, assuage, allay, alleviate, decrease, take the edge off, curb, moderate, modify, ease, temper, mitigate; calm, soothe, compose, still, subdue, quell, hush, quiet, tranquilize, cool. —**Ant.** increase, heighten, intensify, stimulate, aggravate, inflame, fire, pique.

slam *v.* **1.** shut with force and noise, bang. **2.** slap, hit, throw; strike forcefully, smack. **3.** crash, bang; strike with violent impact, collide with, bump, smash. —*n.* **4.** bang, crash; act or sound of slamming.

slander *n.* **1.** defamation, vilification, falsehood; malicious fabrication, false statement, distortion, misrepresentation, calumny; (*loosely*) libel. —*v.* **2.** defame, malign, vilify, revile; smear, sully, soil, besmirch; (*loosely*) libel.

slant *v.* **1.** incline, slope, angle, tilt; lean, list. **2.** color, bias, prejudice, distort, angle, spin. —*n.* **3.** slope, tilt, rake, incline, pitch; slanting direction. **4.** bias, prejudice, angle, spin, view, viewpoint, leaning, attitude. —**Ant. 1** straighten, level off. **3** evenness, level.

slap *n.* **1.** blow, smack, hit, whack, wallop, cuff, clap. **2.** blow, insult, cut, rejection, snub, rebuff. —*v.* **3.** hit, strike, smack, cuff, whack, wallop, swat.

slash *v.* **1.** cut, gash, rip, lacerate, slit, rend, slice. **2.** cut, lower, drop, decrease, reduce, pare. —*n.* **3.** stroke, mark, cut, gash, rip, rent, laceration, slit, tear. **4.** cut, decrease, reduction, drop, lowering.

slate *n.* **1.** dark blue-gray rock. **2.** blackboard, chalkboard, tablet. **3.** ballot, ticket, list of candidates.

slaughter *n.* **1.** killing, butchering. **2.** massacre, bloodbath, mass murder, wholesale killing, pogrom. —*v.* **3.** butcher, kill. **4.** slay, butcher, massacre, destroy, annihilate, exterminate, wipe out. —**Syn. Study. 4** SLAUGHTER, BUTCHER, MASSACRE all imply violent and bloody methods of killing when applied to human beings. SLAUGHTER and BUTCHER emphasize brutal or indiscriminate killing: *to slaughter/butcher enemy soldiers in battle.* MASSACRE indicates a wholesale destruction of helpless or unresisting victims: *to massacre an entire village.*

slave *n.* **1.** serf, vassal, bond servant, bondsman, thrall, chattel. **2.** addict, prey, victim. **3.** drudge, workhorse, menial, toiler, plodder. —*v.* **4.** drudge, toil, work like a slave. —**Ant. 1** master, owner. **3** loafer, idler. **4** loaf, idle.

slavery *n.* **1.** enslavement, bondage, captivity, penal servitude, enthrallment, vassalage, serfdom, subjugation, indentureship, compulsory service, impressment. **2.** drudgery, toil, sweat, travail, labor, struggle, grind, strain, treadmill. —**Syn. Study. 1** SLAVERY, BONDAGE, SERVITUDE refer to involuntary subjection to another or others. SLAVERY emphasizes the idea of complete ownership and control by a master: *to be sold into slavery.* BONDAGE indicates a state of subjugation or captivity often involving burdensome and degrading labor: *in bondage to a cruel master.* SERVITUDE is compulsory service, often such as is required by a legal penalty: *penal servitude.*

slavish *adj.* **1.** servile, subservient, obsequious, slavelike, submissive. **2.** literal, strict, exact; unimaginative, derivative, imitative, unoriginal. —**Syn. Study. 1** See SERVILE. —**Ant. 1** masterful, willful, assertive. **2** original, imaginative, creative, inventive.

slay *v.* kill, slaughter, murder, do in, destroy, execute, annihilate, massacre.

sleazy *adj.* flimsy, shoddy, trashy, insubstantial, shabby; vulgar, cheap, tacky, *Slang* schlock.

sleek *adj.* **1.** glossy, shiny, silky, satiny, velvety, lustrous. **2.** smooth, suave, unctuous, oily, slick, ingratiating, fawning.

sleep *n.* **1.** slumber, snooze, nap, doze. **2.** death, rest, peace. —*v.* **3.** slumber, repose, nap, snooze, doze.

sleepy *adj.* **1.** drowsy, weary, tired, fatigued, exhausted. **2.** quiet, inactive, dull. —**Ant. 1** awake, energetic, spirited, animated, alert. **2** bustling, active, busy, thriving, lively.

slender *adj.* **1.** slight, slim, lean, willowy, skinny, delicate, thin, narrow. **2.** little, small, meager, scant, spare. **3.**

slim, slight, feeble, faint, weak, poor, remote. **—Syn. Study. 1** SLENDER, SLIGHT, SLIM imply a tendency toward thinness. As applied to the human body, SLENDER implies a generally attractive and pleasing thinness: *slender hands.* SLIGHT often adds the idea of frailness to that of thinness: *a slight, almost fragile, figure.* SLIM implies a lithe or delicate thinness: *a slim and athletic figure.* **—Ant. 1** large, fat, thick, stout, bulky, heavy. **2** large, profuse, considerable, appreciable, prolific. **3** strong, considerable, solid.

slice *n.* **1.** piece, portion, section, cut, segment. *—v.* **2.** carve, cut, shave; whittle, pare; divide, separate, cut off, sever, dismember, segment.

slick *adj.* **1.** glossy, sleek, smooth, satiny, shiny. **2.** slippery; oily, greasy, waxy, glassy. **3.** sly, wily, cunning, tricky, foxy, clever, sharp, smooth-talking, fast-talking. *—n.* **4.** film, coating, coat, scum. *—v.* **5.** smooth; make glossy. **—Ant. 1** rough, bumpy, coarse. **2** rough, coarse. **3** honest, open, ingenuous.

slide *v.* **1.** glide, coast. **2.** skid, slip, fall, veer, sideslip, slither. **3.** pass, slip, lapse. *—n.* **4.** coast, glide. **5.** chute, ramp, slope. **6.** small transparency, diapositive, lantern slide, transparent plate.

slight *adj.* **1.** small, little, modest, moderate, limited, restricted, imperceptible, unimportant, inappreciable, negligible, tiny, infinitesimal. **2.** slim, slender, frail, lean, thin, spare, fragile. *—v.* **3.** disregard, neglect, overlook, scamp, shrug off, ignore. **4.** snub, cut, insult, disdain, disregard, rebuff. *—n.* **5.** snub, insult, slap, cut, rebuff, affront; incivility, indignity. **—Syn. Study. 2** See SLENDER. **3** SLIGHT, DISREGARD, NEGLECT, OVERLOOK mean to pay no attention or too little attention to someone or something. To SLIGHT is to ignore or treat as unimportant: *to slight one's responsibilities.* To DISREGARD is to ignore or treat without due respect: *to disregard the rules.* To NEGLECT is to fail in one's duty toward a person or thing: *to neglect one's correspondence.* To OVERLOOK is to fail to notice or consider someone or something, possibly because of carelessness: *to overlook a bill that is due.* **5** See INSULT. **—Ant. 1** considerable, great, big, substantial, appreciable, tangible. **2** husky, muscular, sturdy.

slim *adj.* **1.** slender, thin, lean, svelte, willowy, thready, skinny, slight. **2.** slender, faint, remote, distant, slight, small, meager, negligible. **—Syn. Study. 1** See SLENDER. **—Ant. 1** chubby, fat; broad, broad of beam, wide, huge, elephantine. **2** great, strong, considerable.

slime *n.* mire, muck, ooze, sludge; sticky mud.

slimy *adj.* **1.** mucky, gummy, sticky, viscous, glutinous. **2.** offensive, obnoxious, creepy; nasty, vile, repulsive, foul, putrid, loathsome. **—Ant. 2** pleasant, appealing.

slink *v.* slip, creep, steal, skulk, tiptoe; move in a furtive manner, prowl, sneak.

slip[1] *v.* **1.** slide, glide; put. **2.** skid, slide, lose one's balance. **3.** sneak, steal, go quietly; pass, hand stealthily. **4.** pass quickly, pass imperceptibly. **5.** fail, worsen, decline, sink, fall. **6.** escape; break away, get clear of. **7.** leak, escape, be revealed. *—n.* **8.** skid, slide; fall. **9.** blunder, indiscretion, imprudence, lapse, error, mistake, faux pas, blooper, boner, *Informal* goof, *Slang* boo-boo. **10.** drop, fall, decline. **11.** petticoat, underdress, chemise. **12.** berth, dock. **—Syn. Study. 9** See MISTAKE. **—Ant. 5** improve, rise. **10** rise, improvement, increase.

slip[2] *n.* **1.** cutting, sprig, sprout, shoot, offshoot. **2.** scrap, strip, shred, small piece; receipt, voucher, ticket. **3.** youngster, youngling, sprig, stripling, sapling.

slippery *adj.* **1.** slick, smooth, waxy, greasy, oily, glassy, soapy. **2.** tricky, shifty, deceitful, untrustworthy, unreliable, treacherous, foxy, sneaky, wily, devious, crafty, contriving. **—Ant. 1** rough, coarse; dry. **2** trustworthy, reliable, steady, dependable, responsible.

slipshod *adj.* careless, lax, sloppy; casual, thoughtless, offhand, slovenly, loose, untidy, messy. **—Ant.** careful, correct, meticulous, exact, fastidious; orderly, tidy, neat.

slip-up *n.* mistake, blunder, error, lapse, oversight, miscue, bungle, gaffe, faux pas; *Slang* goof, screw-up, foul-up, boo-boo, clinker, botch, flub, blooper.

slit *n.* **1.** cut, crevice, gash, incision, slash, crack, fissure. *—v.* **2.** cut, slash.

slither *v.* slide, glide; move with a side-to-side motion.

slobber *v.* drivel, slaver, drool, dribble, slop, salivate, water at the mouth, splutter, sputter.

slogan *n.* motto, campaign cry, battle cry, catch phrase; byword, watchword, catchword.

slop *v.* **1.** slosh, splash, splatter, spatter, spill, swash. **2.** feed swill to. *—n.* **3.** slush, sludge, mire, ooze, mud, muck; filth. **4.** swill, garbage; waste, refuse.

slope *v.* **1.** slant, angle, pitch, incline, lean, tip, tilt, bend, bank. *—n.* **2.** slant, incline, downgrade, inclination, descent. **—Ant. 1** flatten, level. **2** plane.

sloppy *adj.* **1.** watery, sloshy, muddy, slushy, wet, sodden, swampy, marshy. **2.** messy, untidy, disorderly, soiled, dirty, unclean. **—Ant. 1** dry. **2** neat, tidy, orderly, clean.

sloth *n.* laziness, lethargy, torpor, indolence, lassitude, listlessness, do-nothingness, shiftlessness, torpidity, languor, phlegm, sluggishness, idleness. **—Ant.** energy, industriousness, diligence, assiduousness, activeness, get-up-and-go.

slothful *adj.* lazy, indolent, do-nothing, otiose, sluggardly, lax, negligent, sluggish, idle, shiftless, inert, torpid, listless, drowsy, supine. **—Syn. Study.** See IDLE. **—Ant.** industrious, energetic, active, lively.

slouch *v.* **1.** droop, slump, stoop, hunch, bend. *—n.* **2.** stoop, droop, slump. **3.** lazybones, laggard, sluggard, loafer, slacker, shirker, idler, *Slang* goldbrick. **—Ant. 1** straighten up. **3** go-getter, eager beaver, ball of fire.

slovenly *adj.* **1.** messy, sloppy, untidy, dirty, unclean, dowdy, frowzy, slatternly, disorderly, unkempt. **2.** slipshod, careless, slapdash, messy; indifferent, unconcerned. **—Ant. 1** neat, tidy, trim, clean, orderly. **2** careful, meticulous, precise, conscientious, methodical, orderly.

slow *adj.* **1.** slow-paced, slow-moving, slow motion, snail-like, tortoise-like. **2.** heavy, sluggish, torpid, lumpish. **3.** long, prolonged, extended, stretched out, drawn out, gradual, protracted, time-consuming, lingering, tarrying, delayed. **4.** late, behind time, overdue, unpunctual, delayed, belated, backward. **5.** dawdling, dilatory, procrastinating, laggard, sluggish. **6.** hesitant, cautious; halfhearted, backward, dragging; indisposed, loath, disinclined, reluctant, averse. **7.** dull, tedious, boring, unexciting, uninteresting; slow-moving, sluggish, ponderous. **8.** leisurely, unhurried, unhasty, deliberate, gradual; inactive, quiet, not busy, not lively, *Informal* off. **9.** slow-witted, dim-witted, dull-witted, slow on the uptake, backward, stupid, obtuse, dense, dumb, dim, dull; impercipient, unperceptive. *—v.* **10.** slow down, reduce speed, decelerate, lose momentum; flag, falter. **11.** slow down, hold up, retard, check, curb, brake; handicap, hinder, obstruct, impede. **—Syn. Study. 8** SLOW, LEISURELY, DELIBERATE, GRADUAL mean unhurried or not happening rapidly. SLOW means acting or moving without haste: *a slow procession of cars.* LEISURELY means moving with the slowness allowed by ample time or the absence of pressure: *a leisurely stroll.* DELIBERATE implies the slowness that marks careful consideration: *a deliberate and calculating manner.* GRADUAL suggests the slowness of something that advances one step at a time: *a gradual improvement.* **—Ant. 1–3, 5** fast, quick, swift, speedy. **1** lightning-like. **4** prompt, punctual, on time. **6** eager, enthusiastic; inclined, disposed. **7** exciting, interesting; fast-moving. **8** hurried, hasty, active, busy, lively. **9** quick-witted, smart, bright, intelligent; perceptive. **10, 11** speed up, accelerate. **10** pick up speed. **11** spur, help, aid, abet.

slowdown *n.* slackening, slowing, slow-up, downturn, falloff, stagnation, decline, retardation, flagging, letup, letdown, ease-up, setback, deceleration, slump. **—Ant.** boom, upswing, upturn, peaking.

slowpoke *n.* laggard, straggler, dawdler, lingerer, dallier, snail, slug, tortoise, stick-in-the-mud, idler, plodder, saunterer, *Slang* foot-dragger, lie-abed, slug-abed.

sludge *n.* mud, mire, dregs, sediment, muck, ooze, slime, slop, slush.

slug *v.* hit, strike, punch, whack, thump, smite, pound, clout, bat, belt, whale, wallop, sock, bash, baste, batter, lambaste, *Slang* clobber.

sluggish *adj.* **1.** lethargic, listless, languid, spiritless, soporific, phlegmatic; lazy, indolent, slothful; inert, inactive, lifeless, torpid. **2.** slow, unhurried, leisurely, protracted. **—Ant. 1** active, energetic, industrious, animated, spirited, lively. **2** rapid, fast, quick, brisk.

slumber *v.* **1.** sleep; doze, snooze, nap. **2.** lie dormant, be inactive; hibernate, vegetate. **—Ant. 1** be awake. **2** erupt; be active.

slump *v.* **1.** collapse, fall, drop, slip, give way, sag, tumble. **2.** dip, plunge, decline; fall off suddenly. *—n.* **3.** slouch, droop, sagging posture. **4.** lapse, decline; falling off, reverse, setback. **—Ant. 2** improve, increase. **4** improvement, rise, upsurge, upturn.

slur *v.* **1.** mumble, mutter, run together, pronounce indistinctly. **2.** overlook, skip, disregard, ignore, gloss over, pass over, slight, let pass; treat with indifference. **3.** blacken, smear, defame, malign, stain, taint, sully. *—n.* **4.** mumbling, muttering, slurred speech, run-on words. **5.** insult, cut, dig, affront. **6.** stain, mark, spot, blemish, taint. **—Ant. 1** enunciate. **2** stress, accentuate. **3** praise, laud, compliment. **4** enunciation. **5** compliment, praise.

slut *n.* slattern, frump, sloven; hussy, jade, wanton, strumpet, trollop, wench, tramp, jezebel; whore, harlot, prostitute; *Slang* doxy, floozy, bimbo.

sly *adj.* **1.** wily, crafty, cunning, tricky, artful, conniving, sneaky, stealthy, foxy, shrewd; mischievous, playful, cunning; dissembling. **2.** secret, furtive, private, covert, confidential. **—Ant. 1, 2** open, direct, straightforward.

smack[1] *v.* **1.** slap, smite, hit, whack,

spank; strike sharply. —*n.* **2.** slap, rap, blow, buffet, whack, spank, hit, cuff, clap. **3.** loud kiss, hearty kiss, buss. —**Ant. 1** pet, caress.

smack[2] *n.* **1.** trace, tinge; hint, suggestion, taste, flavor. **2.** touch, trace, bit, suggestion, dash. —*v.* **3.** taste; smell; savor, suggest, have a flavor.

small *adj.* **1.** little, tiny, petite; diminutive, undersized, slight. **2.** meager, scant, modest, not great. **3.** minor, inconsequential, insignificant, trivial, superficial, unimportant, lesser, trifling; of no account. **4.** mean, petty, ignoble, narrow, opinionated, bigoted; provincial. **5.** feeble, weak, fragile, faint. —**Ant. 1, 2** large, big, great, vast, huge, immense, enormous; appreciable, substantial. **3** major, important, significant, consequential, vital. **4** big, generous, lofty, farsighted, unbiased. **5** strong, powerful, solid, substantial; loud, noisy, heavy.

small talk *n.* chitchat, banter, repartee, bavardage, prattle, chatter, prattling, gossip, idle talk, tittle-tattle, table talk, tea-table talk, light conversation, casual conversation.

smart *adj.* **1.** intelligent, bright, sharp, keen, clever, quick, brainy, astute. **2.** fashionable, chic, modish, elegant, stylish; trim, neat. **3.** witty, clever, shrewd, sharp; smart-aleck, brash, sassy. **4.** energetic, vigorous, brisk, quick. **5.** painful, sharp. —*v.* **6.** hurt, sting, burn; feel pain, be painful. **7.** ache, suffer, wince, flinch, blench. —**Ant. 1** dumb, dull, slow, dense, thick, stupid. **2** sloppy, frowzy; old-fashioned, dowdy; outmoded, passé. **4** crawling, slow.

smart aleck *n.* know-it-all, show-off, smarty, wise guy, smarty-pants, braggart, grandstander, exhibitionist, windbag, wiseacre; blowhard, saucebox, wiseass.

smash *v.* **1.** shatter, break, splinter, disintegrate, demolish. **2.** crash, strike, hit, collide with; crack, break; batter, beat, *Slang* bash, clobber. **3.** destroy, crush, demolish, shatter. —*n.* **4.** blow, bang, clout, forceful hit. **5.** crash, collision, accident, crack-up, smashup. **6.** *Informal* hit, winner, success, sensation, triumph. —**Ant. 6** flop, loser, disaster.

smashing *adj.* *Informal* terrific, sensational, marvelous, wonderful, super, stupendous, magnificent, superb, extraordinary, fabulous, fantastic, great.

smattering *n.* drop, bit, scrap, slight amount, smidgen, snippet, dash, dab, sprinkling.

smear *v.* **1.** spread, rub, daub, coat, cover; lay on. **2.** stain, smudge, besmudge, splotch, soil, smirch, streak. **3.** blur, smudge; obliterate, make indistinct. **4.** soil, stain, tarnish, mar, blacken, besmirch, blemish; malign, slander, denigrate, degrade, injure. —*n.* **5.** blotch, smudge, streak, splotch, stain, smirch; libel, slander, accusation.

smell *v.* **1.** nose, scent, sniff, get wind of, be windward of, get scent of. **2.** have a scent, give out an odor, emit an odor. **3.** reek, stink, have an unpleasant odor, be malodorous. **4.** detect, sense, perceive, feel, suspect. —*n.* **5.** aroma, scent, odor, fragrance; perfume, bouquet, emanation; reek, stink, stench, fetor. —**Syn. Study. 5** See ODOR.

smelly *adj.* stinking, malodorous, odorous, fetid, reeking, noisome, rank, putrid. —**Ant.** fragrant, sweet-smelling, fresh-smelling.

smile *n.* **1.** grin, smirk, simper. —*v.* **2.** grin, beam, show pleasure; simper, smirk. **3.** favor; shine; be benevolent toward.

smirch *v.* **1.** besmirch, soil, smudge, dirty, begrime, besmudge, stain, smear. **2.** besmirch, tarnish, stain, damage, smear, sully, soil, blacken; slander, dishonor, discredit. —*n.* **3.** stain, smudge, blotch, smear, spot. **4.** smear, blemish, stain, taint, blot; mark, stigma; discredit, dishonor.

smirk *n.* **1.** sneer, simper, sarcastic smile, grin, unpleasant grin, leer. —*v.* **2.** sneer; simper; grimace.

smitten *adj.* enamored, bewitched, infatuated, enraptured, stuck (on), gone (on), have a crush (on), soft (on), spoony (over), sweet (on), taken (with); *Slang* nuts (about), crazy (about).

smoke *n.* **1.** sooty vapor; exhalation, fumes. **2.** something smoked; (*variously*) cigar, cigarette, pipe. —*v.* **3.** smolder, fume; give off smoke, billow, reek. **4.** use tobacco; draw, suck, inhale, puff; light up, *Informal* have a drag.

smoky *adj.* **1.** smoldering, fuming; emitting smoke. **2.** smoke-filled, reeking. **3.** sooty, dingy, grimy, smudgy, smoke-darkened.

smolder *v.* **1.** smoke; burn without flame. **2.** seethe, burn inwardly; rage silently, fume.

smooth *adj.* **1.** even, flat, level; silky, velvety, sleek. **2.** without lumps. **3.** even, steady; without abrupt turns, without jerks, without breaks. **4.** orderly, harmonious, well-ordered, well-regulated, methodical, uneventful; easy, calm, even, peaceful. **5.** even, calm, serene, peaceful, placid, easygoing, pleasant, mild, composed, collected, self-possessed. **6.** flattering, ingratiating, glib, facile, suave. **7.** mellow, mild; without sharpness. —*v.* **8.** make even, make level, flatten. **9.** pave, open; prepare; ease; facilitate, help. **10.** refine, cultivate, polish, perfect; soften, mellow, civilize. **11.** calm, soothe, mollify, appease, assuage, allay, mitigate. **—Ant. 1** rough, bumpy, uneven, irregular. **2** lumpy. **3** jerky, uneven, bumpy, rough. **4** disorderly, difficult, turbulent, troublesome. **5** nervous, excitable. **6** rough, unpolished, abrasive. **7** harsh, sharp, pungent. **8** roughen, rough up. **9** hamper, hinder.

smother *v.* **1.** suffocate, asphyxiate, strangle, choke. **2.** extinguish, snuff, deaden, quench. **3.** shower, wrap, surround; envelop in. **4.** hide, suppress, conceal, mask, quash; keep down, choke back.

smudge *n.* **1.** smear, smutch, blot, stain, spot, mark. **2.** heavy smoke, smoky fire, smoke cloud. **—*v.* 3.** smear, stain, spot, dirty, soil. **—Ant. 3** clean, cleanse.

smug *adj.* self-satisfied, complacent, self-righteous, superior, virtuous. **—Ant.** unsure, uncertain, insecure.

smuggler *n.* bootlegger, runner, contrabandist, rumrunner, gunrunner.

smut *n.* **1.** soot, smudge, dirt, grime. **2.** pornography, obscenity, scatology, lewd material, dirt, filth, *Slang* porn.

smutty *adj.* **1.** sooty, dirty, grimy, soiled. **2.** dirty, lewd, obscene, vulgar, indecent; filthy, pornographic. **—Ant. 1** clean, immaculate. **2** clean, pure; puritanical, straitlaced.

snack *n.* **1.** refreshment, light repast, bite, collation, light lunch, pick-me-up, coffee break, tidbit, finger food, lap lunch; *Slang* nosh, munchies, snackies, crunchies, nibblies; *British* tea, elevenses; *French* casse-croûte. **—*v.* 2.** nibble, munch, eat, take tea, *Slang* nosh.

snag *n.* **1.** protrusion, projection; stub, stump; hidden obstruction. **2.** hindrance, obstacle, hitch; difficulty, block, stumbling block, impediment, encumbrance, obstruction, barrier, bar. **—*v.* 3.** tear, rip; catch, grab, fasten upon.

snake *n.* **1.** serpent, viper, ophidian, reptile, reptilian. **2.** sneak, traitor, untrustworthy person.

snap *v.* **1.** crack, click, pop. **2.** latch, catch, lock, secure, clasp; close. **3.** break, crack, fracture. **4.** bite, nip, grab. **5.** jump, click. **6.** snarl, growl, bark, yelp. **—*n.* 7.** crack, click, pop. **8.** catch, clasp, fastener. **9.** nip, bite, grab, snatch. **10.** spell, period. **11.** *Informal* cinch, breeze. **—*adj.* 12.** sudden, hasty, thoughtless, quick, careless, impulsive.

snappish *adj.* peevish, surly, touchy, testy, grouchy, waspish, shirty, querulous, irascible, cross, captious, ill-natured, petulant, hot-tempered, quick-tempered, huffish, edgy, huffy. **—Ant.** affable, amiable, good-humored, pleasant.

snappy *adj.* **1.** classy, smart, tony, swank, ritzy, sharp, swish, stylish, dapper, spiffy, jaunty. **2.** fast, quick, hasty, speedy, swift, rapid, *Slang* lickety-split. **—Ant. 1** dowdy, shabby, tacky. **2** slow, torpid, languid, lazy.

snare *n.* **1.** trap, noose, net. **2.** trap, pitfall, deception, trick, entanglement; lure, bait, decoy, ruse. **—*v.* 3.** capture, ensnare, trap, entrap, hook, catch, seize.

snarl[1] *v.* **1.** growl. **2.** snap, lash out, bark. **—*n.* 3.** growl.

snarl[2] *n.* **1.** tangle, ravel, mat, twist, kink, knot. **2.** tangle, jumble, mess, chaos, confusion, disorder. **—*v.* 3.** tangle, entangle, twist, knot, disorder, jumble, muddle, confuse; hinder, clog, impede. **—Ant. 2** order. **3** unsnarl, untangle, unscramble.

snatch *v.* **1.** grab, seize, grasp; pluck, nab, pull, wrest. **2.** grab, catch, take. **—*n.* 3.** part, snippet, fragment, bit, piece.

sneak *v.* **1.** slip, steal, creep; lurk, skulk, prowl. **2.** slip, spirit, smuggle. **—*n.* 3.** skulker, lurker, slinker; rascal, knave, bounder, rogue, scalawag, scoundrel, rapscallion, scamp, miscreant. **—*adj.* 4.** surprise, secret, secretive, furtive, surreptitious, sly, underhand. **—Syn. Study. 1** See LURK.

sneaky *adj.* underhand, sly, devious, treacherous, traitorous; secretive, furtive; mean, malicious, vicious. **—Ant.** open, aboveboard.

sneer *v.* **1.** scorn, mock, scoff, rebuff, jeer, deride, disdain, ridicule, belittle. **—*n.* 2.** smirk, scoff, leer. **—Syn. Study. 1** See SCOFF.

snicker *v.* giggle, titter, snigger, simper, snort, cackle.

snide *adj.* sarcastic, nasty, malicious, insinuating; mocking, scoffing, contemptuous.

sniff *v.* **1.** snivel, sniffle, snuffle, snuff, snort. **2.** smell, whiff, snuff. **3.** disdain, disparage; mock, scoff, jeer. **—*n.* 4.** sniffle, snuffle, snort. **5.** smell, whiff, odor, aroma.

snip *v.* **1.** clip, cut, crop, lop, trim, prune, shear, bob. **—*n.* 2.** click, clack, snap. **3.** scrap, swatch; bit, fragment, cutting, piece; sample. **4.** *Informal* twerp, brat, shrimp, punk.

snippy *adj.* curt, brusque, rude, impudent, cheeky, saucy, sassy, impertinent, insolent, ill-mannered, smart-alecky, flippant, short, snippety; *Slang* snotty. **—Ant.** polite, respectful, mannerly, deferential.

snob *n.* social climber, elitist, stuck-up person, pretentious person, condescending person.

snobbish *adj.* pretentious, disdainful, condescending, patronizing, overbearing, superior, arrogant, vain, haughty, *Informal* stuck-up, snotty, high-hat, snooty. **—Ant.** unpretentious, humble.

snort *v.* **1.** grunt, pant, puff, blast, blow, huff, gasp; storm, rage. **2.** scoff, jeer, sneer. *—n.* **3.** grunt, gasp, pant, huff.

snub *v.* **1.** ignore, disdain, slight, scorn, rebuff; turn up one's nose at, cut, treat with contempt, give the cold shoulder. **2.** check; stop suddenly. *—n.* **3.** rebuff, slight, cut, repudiation, cold shoulder. *—adj.* **4.** short, blunt, stubby, retroussé.

snuff *v.* **1.** sniff, sniffle, snuffle. **2.** sniff, smell, scent; detect through the nose. *—n.* **3.** sniff, smell, whiff.

snug *adj.* **1.** cozy, comfortable; sheltered, safe, secure; tranquil. **2.** tight, neat, well-organized; close, compact. **3.** tight-fitting, tight, close-fitting; skin-tight. **—Ant. 1** uncomfortable; unprotected. **2** disorganized, disorderly. **3** loose.

snuggle *v.* nestle, nuzzle, lie snug, cuddle, lie closely, curl up, nest, enfold, hug.

soak *v.* **1.** steep, bathe, wet, drench, saturate, immerse. **2.** absorb, take in, take up. **3.** seep, penetrate, permeate, enter, pervade. **4.** penetrate, pervade; sink in, be perceived, be absorbed, come home to.

soar *v.* **1.** wing, glide, float, fly, take wing, go aloft. **2.** climb, rise, mount, increase swiftly; tower, thrust upward. **—Ant. 1** fall, drop. **2** fall, drop, decrease.

sob *v.* **1.** weep, cry, blubber, whimper, wail, snivel, howl, lament. *—n.* **2.** cry, whimper, plaint, wail. **—Ant.** laugh, chortle.

sober *adj.* **1.** solemn, serious, somber, staid, grave, sedate. **2.** grave, grim, sad, serious, solemn, somber, joyless, sorrowful. **3.** drab, subdued, dull, somber, dreary. **4.** realistic, sound, dispassionate, moderate; prudent, judicious; levelheaded, rational, cool, sane, steady. **5.** temperate, dry, abstemious, not drunk. **—Syn. Study. 1** See GRAVE. **—Ant. 1** gay, frivolous, lighthearted, merry. **2** happy, gay, joyous. **3** light, bright, showy, colorful, exciting, lively. **4** frivolous, unrealistic, immoderate, unsound, excessive, passionate, imprudent, injudicious. **5** drunk, intoxicated, inebriated.

sociable *adj.* **1.** gregarious, social, congenial, affable, extroverted, outgoing, gracious, neighborly, companionable, agreeable. **2.** social, friendly, cordial, convivial. **—Ant. 1** unfriendly, withdrawn, forbidding, introverted, unsociable, cold, uncommunicative. **2** stiff, formal, businesslike; cut and dried.

social *adj.* **1.** friendly, sociable. **2.** sociable, gregarious, friendly, neighborly, pleasant, agreeable. **3.** fashionable, smart, stylish, *Informal* in. **4.** gregarious, cooperative, interdependent. **—Ant. 1** business. **2** antisocial, unfriendly, cold. **3** unfashionable. **4** solitary, reclusive, hermit.

society *n.* **1.** humanity, humankind, mankind, the general public. **2.** social order, community. **3.** group, body, club, association, organization, circle, alliance, league. **4.** elite, aristocracy, nobility, gentry, blue bloods, high society, the 400.

sock[1] *n.* short stocking, ankle sock.

sock[2] *v.* **1.** hit, strike, box, punch, slap, wallop, smack, smash; *Slang* belt, clobber. *—n.* **2.** hit, punch, slap, wallop, smack, blow.

sodden *adj.* **1.** drenched, saturated, sopping, soppy, soaked, soggy, wet through, dripping. **2.** mushy, pasty, doughy, lumpy, heavy, soggy. **3.** listless, dull, expressionless, besotted. **—Ant. 1** dry. **2** light, fluffy, crisp.

soft *adj.* **1.** pliable, pliant, supple, malleable; not hard, easily penetrated, easily molded. **2.** smooth, sleek, velvety, satiny, downy, furry, silky, silken. **3.** subdued, faint, muted, hushed, feeble; gentle, pleasantly low. **4.** gentle, mild, subdued, tranquil, restful, quiet; delicate, pale; not sharp, low intensity, shadowed, harmonious, shaded, twilight. **5.** tender, kind, lenient, tolerant, sympathetic, compassionate, pitying; sentimental. **6.** weak; incapable of great endurance; not strong. **7.** not sharp, not hard; having a breathy sound. **8.** *Informal* easy; requiring little effort. **—Ant. 1, 5, 7, 8** hard. **1** unyielding, stiff, inflexible. **2** rough, harsh, coarse, abrasive. **3** loud, strong, noisy. **4** harsh, loud, sharp, glaring, bright. **5** unkind, unsympathetic. **6** strong, tough. **8** difficult, tough, rough.

soften *v.* **1.** lower, subdue, moderate; tone down, make softer, turn down. **2.** make soft. **3.** lessen, temper, ameliorate, mitigate, cushion, palliate, mollify. **—Ant. 1** raise, intensify, increase; louden. **2** harden, freeze, set. **3** heighten.

softhearted *adj.* tender, kindhearted, sympathetic, warmhearted, compassionate, warm, generous, forgiving, humane, considerate, indulgent. **—Ant.** cold, heartless, unforgiving, unfeeling, hardhearted.

softly *adv.* quietly, weakly; gently, easily, mildly. **—Ant.** loud, loudly, blaringly, noisily; roughly; harshly, toughly, unkindly.

soggy *adj.* **1.** soaked, sopping, soppy, saturated, drenched, sodden, dripping. **2.** mushy, pasty, doughy, heavy, sodden. **—Ant. 1** dry. **2** dry, fluffy, light.

soil[1] *n.* **1.** ground, earth, loam, humus. **2.** earth, land, region, country.

soil[2] *v.* **1.** dirty, stain, smudge, grime, smear, spot, muddy, blacken. **2.** blacken, defile, disgrace, tarnish, debase, stain, ruin, sully, foul. **—***n.* **3.** stain, dirt, spot, grime, soot. **—Ant. 1** clean, whiten, cleanse.

sojourn *v.* **1.** abide, visit, vacation; stay in a place temporarily, reside for a time, stay at, stay over. **—***n.* **2.** visit, stay, stopover, layover, pause, vacation, holiday.

solace *n.* **1.** comfort, consolation, reassurance; relief in affliction, help in need. **—***v.* **2.** console, comfort, cheer, calm, assuage, reassure, soothe. **—Ant. 1** pain, distress, discomfort, anxiety, anguish. **2** pain, distress, discomfort, dishearten.

soldier *n.* **1.** military man, enlisted man, serviceman, warrior, G.I., trooper, veteran. **2.** militant leader, zealot, follower, partisan, worker, servant.

sole *adj.* **1.** only, exclusive, lone, solitary, single. **2.** exclusive. **—Ant. 2** shared, divided, joint.

solely *adv.* **1.** exclusively, alone, singly, single-handedly. **2.** exclusively, purely, uniquely, merely.

solemn *adj.* **1.** somber, staid, grave, sedate, sober; quiet in demeanor. **2.** somber, grave, earnest, serious; determined, sincere, steadfast, absolute. **3.** formal, dignified, ceremonious, ceremonial, awe-inspiring. **4.** holy, religious, sacred, spiritual. **5.** dark, gloomy, somber, drab, grim, depressing. **—Syn. Study. 1** See GRAVE. **—Ant. 1** jovial, joyous, bright, lively, gay, happy, merry, spirited. **2** frivolous, halfhearted, insincere. **3** informal. **4** unholy, irreligious, sacrilegious. **5** gay, lively, bright, colorful.

solicit *v.* seek, request, importune, ask, appeal for, entreat, plead, endeavor to obtain.

solicitous *adj.* **1.** concerned, thoughtful, mindful, regardful, anxious, attentive. **2.** eager, zealous, desirous, longing, ardent, intense, keen, avid, enthusiastic, intent. **—Ant. 1** unconcerned, undisturbed. **2** uninterested, unambitious, unenthusiastic.

solicitude *n.* concern, anxiety, worry, care, uneasiness, disquietude, attention, overconcern, inquietude, fearfulness, apprehension. **—Ant.** indifference, heedlessness, neglect, unconcern.

solid *adj.* **1.** real, substantial, concrete, tangible; dense, massy, not hollow. **2.** unbroken, impenetrable, impermeable; constant, continuous, uninterrupted, without breaks. **3.** hard, firm, solidified. **4.** firm, well-constructed, strong, well-built, lasting, tough, sturdy, rugged, durable, substantial. **5.** pure, unmixed, genuine, thorough, one-hundred-percent, real. **6.** real, pure, complete, unalloyed. **7.** sound, stable, steady, reliable, dependable, trustworthy; sober, sensible, levelheaded, rational. **8.** unanimous, undivided. **—Ant. 1** hollow. **2** broken, permeable. **3** liquid, gaseous. **4** flimsy, shaky, unstable, unsteady, unsound. **5** mixed, variegated. **7** unsound, unstable, irresponsible, unreliable. **8** divided, undecided, split.

solidarity *n.* closeness, unity, unification, union; harmony; cooperation; consolidation of interests and responsibilities. **—Ant.** divisiveness, factiousness, discord.

solitary *adj.* **1.** lone, lonely, lonesome, companionless; avoiding the society of others. **2.** lone, isolated, single. **3.** secluded, cloistered, lonely, out-of-the-way, hidden, concealed; desolate, remote, isolated, uninhabited. **—Ant. 1** companionable; gregarious, sociable, social. **3** bustling, busy, well-traveled.

solitude *n.* **1.** isolation, aloneness, loneliness, solitariness, desolation, seclusion, remoteness. **2.** wasteland, wilderness, lonely place.

solution *n.* **1.** solving, resolving, resolution; unraveling. **2.** explanation, answer, key, cipher, resolution. **3.** emulsion, suspension; mixture, blend.

solve *v.* resolve, decipher, unravel, find a solution to, find the answer, find the key, untangle, work out, figure out, decipher, unriddle.

solvent *adj.* **1.** in good financial condition, able to pay debts, financially sound. **2.** dissolvable, dilutable, dissoluble, soluble. **—***n.* **3.** dissolving agent, dissolvent, diluent. **—Ant. 1** bankrupt, broke. **3** hardener.

somber *adj.* **1.** drab, toneless, gloomy, dark, gray, cheerless, dreary, grim. **2.** grim, gloomy, depressing, mournful, funereal, grave, serious, sober, solemn, melancholy. **—Ant. 1** cheerful, gay, colorful, bright, sunny, lively. **2** cheerful, happy, gay, bright.

somnolent *adj.* sleepy, drowsy, dozy, nodding, yawning, half-asleep, half-awake, torpid, slumberous, groggy, heavy-lidded, semiconscious, lethargic, languid, sluggish, dull; *Slang* dopey, out of it. **—Ant.** alert, active, energetic, wide-awake.

song *n.* **1.** ballad, melody, tune, ditty, number. **2.** piping, utterance, call, musical sound. **3.** poem, lyric, verse.

sonorous *adj.* **1.** resonant, full-toned, deep, vibrant, rich, reverberating, resounding, ringing. **2.** eloquent, florid, flamboyant; impressive, grandiose. **—Ant. 1** weak, tinny. **2** plain, weak, unadorned.

soon *adv.* directly, by and by, shortly, anon; instantly, quickly, pronto, right away, presently, forthwith, before long, ere long, betimes, without delay, early on, in a little while, any minute. **—Ant.** never, ne'er, at no time, never in the world.

soothe *v.* **1.** pacify, comfort, calm, tranquilize, console, moderate, placate, mollify, relieve, appease. **2.** lessen, alleviate, relieve, ease, mitigate. **—Syn. Study. 1** See COMFORT. **—Ant. 1** upset, disturb, rouse, excite, disquiet. **2** increase, irritate.

soothsayer *n.* fortune-teller, seer, diviner, prophet, forecaster.

sop *n.* **1.** food for dipping. **2.** tip, gratuity, baksheesh; bribe, payoff, hush money, payola. **—***v.* **3.** dip, dunk, soak, drench, wet, saturate. **4.** soak, absorb; take up. **5.** soak, wet, drench; become wet.

sophisticated *adj.* **1.** seasoned, experienced, worldly, worldly-wise, cosmopolitan. **2.** intellectual, cultured, cultivated, *Informal* highbrow; studied, artificial, precious, mannered. **3.** complicated, complex, difficult, subtle, advanced. **—Ant. 1** unsophisticated, unseasoned, simple, unworldly. **2** unsophisticated, provincial. **3** simple, old-fashioned, uncomplicated.

sophomoric *adj.* juvenile, childish, infantile, adolescent; foolish, puerile, schoolboyish, callow; immature. **—Ant.** adult, mature, sophisticated, grown-up.

soporific *adj.* **1.** hypnotic, somniferous, sleep-inducing, balmy, sluggish, heavy. **2.** sleepy, sluggish, drowsy, somnolent, slumberous; lethargic, lazy. **—***n.* **3.** sedative, hypnotic; sleep-inducer. **—Ant. 1, 2** lively, animated. **3** stimulant.

sopping *adj.* drenched, wet, saturated, soppy, soaked.

sorcery *n.* witchcraft, witchery, wizardry, shamanism, black magic, necromancy, enchantment.

sordid *adj.* **1.** filthy, squalid, unclean, dirty; rank, putrid, rotten. **2.** low, base, depraved, ignoble, vile, wicked, debauched, degraded, vulgar, gross, disreputable, corrupt. **—Ant. 1** clean, pristine. **2** honorable, pure, noble.

sore *adj.* **1.** painful, tender, aching, sensitive, smarting, irritated; hurting, hurt, bruised. **2.** sharp, acute, harsh, painful, wounding; agonizing, distressing, unbearable. **3.** agonized, grieved, distressed, pained. **4.** severe, desperate, critical, grievous, extreme, great. **5.** *Informal* angry, indignant, irritated, irked, upset. **—***n.* **6.** inflammation, wound; sore spot. **—Ant. 1** pain-free, painless. **2** painless. **3** happy, joyous, cheerful. **5** glad, happy, pleased, delighted.

sorely *adv.* badly, severely, greatly, extremely, desperately, critically.

sorrow *n.* **1.** sadness, unhappiness, woe. **2.** misfortune, loss, trial, trouble, hardship, affliction, travail, disaster, catastrophe; bad fortune. **—***v.* **3.** grieve, weep, lament, despair, mourn; be sad. **—Ant. 1** joy, gladness, delight, happiness. **2** good fortune, happiness, joy. **3** rejoice, revel.

sorry *adj.* **1.** regretful, contrite, sorrowful, sad, unhappy; remorseful, repentant. **2.** sad, melancholy, crestfallen, sorrowful; grieved, unhappy, brokenhearted. **3.** miserable, sad, pitiful, pitiable, deplorable, wretched, woeful; pathetic, ridiculous. **—Syn. Study. 3** See MISERABLE. **—Ant. 1** happy, unrepentant. **2** happy, joyous, elated, cheerful. **3** wonderful, uplifting.

sort *n.* **1.** kind, type; make, brand, species, variety, classification. **2.** person, individual. **—***v.* **3.** arrange, group, list, classify, class, divide, organize, systematize, grade, order, catalog, index, categorize; place in a category. **4.** separate, segregate, take from, sift.

so-so *adj.* ordinary, mediocre, fair, modest, passable, average, commonplace, middling, run-of-the-mill, tolerable, adequate, bearable, humdrum, undistinguished, second-rate, indifferent, unexceptional; *Slang* blah, ho-hum.

sot *n.* drunk, drunkard, toper, dipsomaniac, lush, souse, alcoholic, inebriate, soak, rumhound, *Slang* rummy. **—Ant.** teetotaler, abstainer.

soul *n.* **1.** spirit; spiritual part of a person, vital force. **2.** being, spirit; inmost feelings, inner core. **3.** person, creature, individual; a living being. **4.** essence, embodiment, quintessence. **5.** inspiration, force, spirit, vitality.

sound[1] *n.* **1.** noise; that which is heard, sensation produced by hearing. **2.** drift, tone, tenor, suggestion, implication. **3.** range, earshot; hearing distance. **—***v.* **4.** make a noise, produce sound, cause to sound, produce noise. **5.** signal, announce. **6.** seem, convey a certain impression, come off as. **7.** pronounce, articulate, enunciate, voice, utter.

sound[2] *adj.* **1.** robust, sturdy, strong, good, fit, hardy, healthy. **2.** undamaged, intact, unmarred; perfect; substantial, strong, well-built, lasting, sturdy, well-constructed; firm, solid, durable. **3.** solid, strong, stable, solvent. **4.** sensible, solid, reliable, competent, sober, dependable, wise, penetrating, rational, reasonable, responsible. **5.** deep, untroubled. **6.** thorough, thoroughgoing, severe, firm. **—Ant. 1–4** unsound. **1**

poor, ailing, weak. **2** damaged, defective. **3** failing, insolvent, insecure, shaky. **4** unreliable, incompetent, rash, irrational, irresponsible, frivolous. **5** light. **6** halfhearted.

soupçon *n.* trace, dash, suspicion, bit, hint, vestige, suggestion, whiff, taste, tad, shade, drop, clue, taint, tinge, trifle, jot, touch.

sour *adj.* **1.** tart, acid, vinegary, tangy, sharp, keen; acerbic, astringent. **2.** spoiled, turned, fermented, rancid, curdled, bad; clabbered. **3.** offensive, nasty, repugnant, distasteful, unsavory, unpleasant. **4.** disagreeable, nasty, unpleasant, peevish, surly, choleric, bad-tempered, bilious, crabbed, crabby, jaundiced, dour; petulant, uncivil, sullen, ill-humored, ill-tempered, cranky, waspish, tart, testy, acidulous, irritable, grouchy. —*v.* **5.** spoil, become spoiled, ferment, become fermented, curdle, turn. **6.** embitter, ill-dispose, make disagreeable, make unpleasant, jaundice, make bad-tempered; make cynical, make pessimistic, prejudice, alienate, *Slang* turn off. —**Ant. 1** sweet, bland, mild. **2** fresh, unspoiled. **3** sweet, pleasant, agreeable, savory, fresh. **4** sweet, agreeable, pleasant, gracious, amiable, affable, good-natured, good-humored.

source *n.* **1.** origin, derivation, authority, basis; cause, prime mover, antecedent, fountain, fount, spring, wellspring, root, foundation; father, author, begetter. **2.** beginning, rising, headwater, head, wellspring, place of issue, fount, fountain. —**Ant. 1** outcome, result, effect, consequence, end, conclusion. **2** mouth, termination.

sourpuss *n.* grouch, crab, crank, complainer, grumbler, bellyacher, griper, sorehead, grouser, bear, crosspatch, curmudgeon, killjoy, spoilsport, grump.

souse *v.* **1.** wet thoroughly, drench, soak, saturate; douse, inundate, immerse, submerge, duck, dunk, dip. **2.** pickle, steep, soak, marinate. —*n.* **3.** *Slang* drunk, drunkard, alcoholic, inebriate, dipsomaniac, boozer, sot, tippler, lush. —**Ant. 1** dry. **3** teetotaler, abstainer.

souvenir *n.* memento, reminder, remembrance, relic, keepsake, token, emblem, trophy; scar, memory.

sovereign *n.* **1.** supreme ruler, monarch; king, queen, prince, emperor, czar, potentate; crowned head, chief, chieftain, overlord, autocrat, lord. —*adj.* **2.** ruling, supreme, absolute; royal, monarchical, imperial, reigning, regal; powerful, all-powerful, prepotent, potent; kingly, queenly, princely. **3.** principal, chief, foremost, paramount, leading, governing, ruling, supreme, utmost, main, uppermost, highest, dominant, major, prime. **4.** self-governing, free, independent, self-directing, self-ruling, autonomous. —**Ant. 1** subject; peasant, serf. **2** subordinate; limited, partial. **3** minor, secondary, least, lowest.

sovereignty *n.* **1.** power, dominion, authority, supremacy, command, control, ascendancy, sway, jurisdiction, predominance, paramountcy, primacy; kingship, lordship; throne, scepter, crown. **2.** independence, autonomy, self-determination, self-rule, home rule, self-government, freedom.

sow *v.* **1.** plant, seed, scatter, broadcast, disseminate, strew, disperse, cast, implant, sprinkle, set in. **2.** plant, establish, inject, lodge, instill, introduce; spread, scatter, strew.

space *n.* **1.** outer space, the universe, the void, the firmament, the heavens, sky, ether, nothingness, infinity, emptiness. **2.** room, area, sweep, range, territory, expanse, scope, spread, amplitude, swing, field, margin, compass, reach, latitude, breadth, width. **3.** gap, distance, span, chasm, separation, break, hiatus, interruption, interval, interstice, interspace, lacuna, omission, blank. **4.** period, interval, span, duration, term. **5.** seat, place, room, berth, spot, reservation, accommodation. —*v.* **6.** place, arrange, organize, distribute, order, set out, line up, range, rank, mark out; schedule, time. **7.** separate, keep apart, part, spread. —**Ant. 2** confinement, limitation. **3** closure. **7** crowd, bunch.

spacious *adj.* large, ample, wide, broad, sizable, commodious, capacious, roomy; immense, expansive, extensive, vast, enormous; uncrowded. —**Ant.** small, cramped, crowded, close.

span *n.* **1.** distance, breadth, length, dimensions, reach, stretch, proportions, measure, scope, range, sweep, area, territory; extent, term, spell, duration, period, interval. **2.** arch, vault, archway, trestle, wing, extension. —*v.* **3.** bridge, bridge over, cross, extend across, reach over, vault. **4.** cover, reach over, stretch over, reach across; last, endure, survive.

spank *v.* **1.** slap, paddle, whale, hide, tan, wallop; strike, beat, hit, flagellate, strap, belt, thrash, switch, whip, flog, cane, birch, *Slang* whop, lick. —*n.* **2.** slap, strike, hit, blow, wallop, belt, paddling.

spare *v.* **1.** save from death, leave uninjured, refrain from hurting, deal leniently with, forgive, give quarter to, show mercy, be merciful to, have mercy on, show consideration for; exonerate, liberate, release, free; let off, reprieve, pardon, acquit. **2.** safeguard, protect, exempt, guard, shield, shelter, defend; save, relieve. **3.** afford, part with, grant, give, donate, let go of, dispense with, relinquish, forgo, cede. **4.** conserve, withhold, not use, hold back, save, hoard, reserve, husband, lay up, set aside, amass, use frugally, keep. **5.** use frugally, use economically, economize on, be parsimonious with, limit, pinch, conserve, skimp on, stint, be niggardly with. —*adj.* **6.** reserve, extra, auxiliary, supplementary, substitute, supplemental; unnecessary, superfluous, supernumerary, odd, additional, unused, surplus, unconsumed, extraneous, excess, leftover. **7.** fleshless, lean, bony, scrawny, scraggy, thin, emaciated, gaunt, skinny, lank, lanky, skeletal, haggard, weedy, rangy; slight, meager, skimpy, scanty, scant, slender. **—Ant. 1** punish, condemn, destroy, hurt, harm, injure. **2** afflict, expose. **4** squander, use, spend. **5** squander, spend. **7** fat, fleshy, heavy, plump, large.

sparing *adj.* thrifty, economical, frugal, careful, saving; parsimonious, miserly, penurious, near, close-fisted, close, stinting, stingy, ungenerous, niggardly, tightfisted; grudging, meager, scanty, scant. **—Ant.** lavish, profuse, extravagant, generous, openhanded.

spark *n.* **1.** ignited particle, glowing particle, fiery particle; ember, brand. **2.** flash, flicker, sparkle, beam. **3.** bit, iota, trace, jot, glimmer, atom, flicker. **4.** *Informal* vitality, spirit, life, fire, animation, get-up-and-go. —*v.* **5.** sparkle, glitter; gleam, flash. **6.** stimulate, incite, inspire, arouse, excite, pique, provoke, instigate.

sparkle *v.* **1.** shine, glitter, glint, glisten, flicker, twinkle, gleam, shimmer, scintillate, dazzle, flash; coruscate. **2.** bubble, fizzle, effervesce, fizz, pop, foam, froth. **3.** scintillate, shine, be vivacious, be witty, be cheerful, rejoice, be gay, effervesce. —*n.* **4.** glint, glitter, twinkle, flicker, shimmer, scintillation, glimmer, flash; ember, brand. **5.** gleam, radiance, brilliance, glow, dazzle, glimmer, glitter, light, glint, effulgence, luminosity, luminousness. **6.** liveliness, animation, verve, dash, brilliance, élan, pep, vim; vivacity, life, exhilaration, ebullience, exuberance, vitality, spirit; quickness, alertness, briskness; cheerfulness, gaiety, jollity, cheer, effervescence. **—Ant. 1** fade. **5** dullness, flatness. **6** dullness, tedium, cheerlessness, drabness, lethargy.

sparse *adj.* few, few and far between, spotty, thin, thinly distributed, uncrowded, scarce, infrequent; scattered, sporadic, dispersed, spaced-out, diffuse, strewn; meager, scanty, spare, exiguous, scant, skimpy. **—Syn. Study.** See SCANTY. **—Ant.** plentiful, populous, crowded, numerous, dense, thick.

Spartan *adj.* plain, simple, austere, ascetic, frugal, abstemious, stark; disciplined, rigorous, restrained, restricted, stiff, stern, strict, exacting, severe, hard, stringent, inexorable, inflexible, self-denying, self-disciplined. **—Ant.** fancy, self-indulgent, luxurious, lavish, undisciplined, unrestrained, spendthrift, hedonistic, soft, easy, *Slang* cushy; lax.

spasm *n.* **1.** cramp, seizure, crick; twitch, tic, jerk, convulsion, shudder, start, grip, paroxysm; throe, pang. **2.** spell, fit, onset, burst, access, attack, frenzy, storm, flash, spurt, seizure, explosion, tempest, eruption.

spasmodic *adj.* fitful, intermittent, occasional, periodic, fleeting, sporadic, capricious, desultory, flighty, mercurial, erratic, irregular, transient, inconstant, discontinuous. **—Ant.** constant, steady, regular, lasting.

spat *n.* **1.** disagreement, misunderstanding, quarrel, tiff, difference, bicker, dispute, fight, dissent, scrap, set-to, squabble, altercation, wrangle. —*v.* **2.** quarrel, argue, bicker, fight, scrap, differ, contend, disagree, squabble, wrangle, tiff. **—Ant. 1** agreement, concurrence, understanding. **2** agree, concur.

spatter *v.* **1.** splash, plash, bespatter, splatter, sprinkle; spray, swash, slop, spurt; spot, mottle, fleck, stipple, speckle; shower. **2.** spot, stain, soil.

spawn *v.* **1.** deposit eggs, lay eggs. **2.** reproduce, propagate, proliferate, multiply, teem, breed. **3.** engender, generate, give rise to, propagate, give birth to, produce, bring forth, beget, yield. —*n.* **4.** eggs, seed; offspring, brood; product, yield, fruit.

speak *v.* **1.** talk, utter words, articulate, vocalize, sound, give utterance; enunciate, pronounce; mutter, mumble, murmur, whisper; call, shout, cry out; converse, confer, consult, exchange words, chat. **2.** express, say, make known, communicate, tell, state, declare, recite, convey, relate, impart, put into words, voice, give voice to, bespeak; divulge, reveal, disclose, make disclosure, proclaim, announce, advise, air, report; imply, suggest, be expressive, indicate. **3.** give a speech, deliver an address, discourse, lecture; sermonize, preach; expound, orate, declaim, hold forth, harangue, expatiate, dilate. **4.** mention, comment, refer, make reference, remark, treat, discuss, deal. **—Ant. 2** repress, hide, conceal, suppress.

speaker *n.* talker, lecturer, spokesman, spokeswoman, orator, speechmaker; valedictorian; reciter, reader; preacher, sermonizer; rhetorician, declaimer, discourser; monologist; mouthpiece, voice, advocate. **—Ant.** listener, audience.

spear *n.* **1.** javelin, lance, harpoon,

pike, bolt, dart, gaff, spike; shaft. —*v.* **2.** impale, stab, run through, pierce, lance, spike, pike, gore, stick, transfix, spit, penetrate, puncture, prick.

spearhead *n.* **1.** point of a spear, iron. **2.** leader, establisher, pioneer, initiator, creator, spokesman, spokeswoman, begetter, founder, prime mover, instituter, inaugurator, avant-gardist. —*v.* **3.** lead, pioneer, initiate, begin, start, launch, inaugurate, establish, originate, give birth to, institute, found, conceive, develop.

special *adj.* **1.** especial, certain, specific, distinct, specialized, particular; proper. **2.** out of the ordinary, unusual, uncommon, unique, select, distinctive, novel, unconventional, rare, singular, extraordinary, distinct, exceptional, especial, important, momentous, signal, outstanding, distinguished, noteworthy, remarkable. **3.** distinctive, unique, peculiar; personal, individual, typical, endemic, representative. **4.** particular, great, outstanding, especial, exceptional; close, devoted, staunch, fast, steadfast, ardent, good, intimate. —*n.* **5.** specialty, feature, attraction, high point, highlight, headliner, *French* pièce de résistance; extravaganza; bargain, sale item. —**Ant. 1** ordinary, all-purpose, general, standard, unspecialized. **2** common, ordinary, undistinctive, unimportant, routine. **3** ordinary, unexceptional, usual.

specialist *n.* expert, authority, connoisseur, master, maven, skilled hand, past master, adept, *Informal* buff. —**Ant.** amateur, generalist.

specialty *n.* **1.** special field, focus, pursuit, special subject, major; special line of work, profession; hobby; faculty, aptitude, bent, talent, competence, genius, turn, endowment. **2.** special, distinctive product, distinction, particularity, earmark, badge, mark, trademark, stamp, feature, claim to fame, forte.

species *n.* type, sort, kind, class, category, breed, variety, genre, nature, kidney, order, stripe, make, division, form, subdivision, classification, designation.

specific *adj.* **1.** precise, definite, exact, certain, fixed, specified, clearly stated, categorical, clear-cut, concrete, stated, unequivocal; confined, circumscribed, limited, bounded, pinned-down, tied-down, restricted; detailed, minute, determinate, relevant, pertinent, pointed, particular. **2.** especial, peculiar, special, distinctive, individual, unique, singular, particular, intrinsic, endemic, characteristic, typical, personal. —*n.* **3.** Often **specifics** particular, item, fact, relevant point, detail, datum, circumstance. **4.** special remedy, cure, medication, physic. —**Ant. 1** approximate, indefinite, uncertain, vague, hazy; general. **2** common, undistinctive, general.

specification *n.* **1.** itemization, particularization, enumeration; precision; particularity; clarity, detail; concreteness, substance. **2.** requirement, condition, stipulation, qualification.

specify *v.* detail, state in detail, define, indicate, designate, enumerate, name, be specific about, focus on, stipulate, cite, adduce, itemize, denote, particularize, describe, set forth; call for, order.

specimen *n.* sample, model, representative, example, exemplar, instance, case, type, exemplification; prototype.

specious *adj.* deceptive, misleading, fallacious, questionable, casuistic, dubious, false, invalid, faulty, sophistical, unsubstantiated, unsound, unfounded, incorrect, inaccurate, slippery, tricky, untrue, spurious, illogical. —**Ant.** valid, conclusive, undeniable, inescapable.

speck *n.* **1.** particle, grain, mote, bit; dot, spot, mark, speckle, flyspeck, fleck. **2.** drop, trace, trifle, bit, pinch, modicum; whit, particle, mite, scintilla, iota, jot, hair, glimmer, shadow, pin, farthing.

spectacle *n.* **1.** marvel, wonder, phenomenon, curiosity; sight, scene; rarity, rare sight. **2.** exhibition, presentation, extravaganza, demonstration, production, exhibit, exposition, display, pageant, parade.

spectacular *adj.* **1.** magnificent, gorgeous, glorious, striking, elaborate, sumptuous, impressive, showy, eye-filling, splendid, opulent, ceremonious, grand, rich, stately; jeweled, bespangled; theatrical; fabulous, marvelous, astounding, overwhelming. **2.** thrilling, daring, impressive, hair-raising, daredevil, dramatic, sensational. —*n.* **3.** spectacle, elaborate production, ostentatious show, extravaganza, gala. —**Ant. 1** plain, unimpressive, modest, ordinary. **2** simple, easy.

spectator *n.* onlooker, observer, viewer, witness, eyewitness, beholder, sightseer, rubberneck; kibitzer; theatergoer, fan, aficionado; audience, gallery, house; bystander. —**Ant.** performer, entertainer.

specter *n.* ghost, phantom, spook, spirit, wraith, shade, apparition, demon, hobgoblin, sprite, ghoul, banshee, revenant, presence, phantasm; fantasy, vision.

spectral *adj.* ghostly, spooky, phantom, incorporeal; eerie, unearthly, uncanny, weird, creepy, supernatural, otherworldly; gossamer, ethereal, unreal, wraithlike, phantasmal, insubstantial, chimerical, airy, vaporous, shadowy; ghastly. —**Ant.** earthly, homey, tangible.

speculate *v.* **1.** meditate, consider, muse, contemplate, engage in thought, reflect, think, reason, deliberate, ponder, ruminate, study, cogitate, excogitate, wonder, brood; guess, surmise, conjecture, theorize, hazard an opinion, hypothesize, suppose, imagine, fancy, dream. **2.** buy and sell riskily, play the market, wager, take a chance, hazard, trade hazardously, gamble, chance, venture, play a hunch.

speech *n.* **1.** speaking, oral communication, talking, talk, articulation, utterance, voice, vocalization; conversation, dialogue, converse, colloquy, discourse, verbalization, verbal intercourse, parlance, confabulation, oral commerce, discussion; remarks, statement, spoken words, observation, pronouncement, expression, declaration, comment; palaver, prattle, chatter, gossip, chitchat. **2.** address, talk, oration, sermon, lecture, declamation, discourse, recitation, diatribe, tirade, salutation, valedictory, dissertation, appeal, harangue, exhortation, homily; soliloquy, monologue. **3.** style of speaking, manner of speaking, expression, utterance, rhetoric; articulation, pronunciation, enunciation, diction, elocution. **4.** language, dialect, tongue, idiom; jargon, slang, colloquialism, *Informal* lingo. **—Syn. Study. 2** SPEECH, ADDRESS, ORATION, HARANGUE are terms for a communication to an audience. SPEECH is the general word, with no implication of kind or length, or whether planned or not. An ADDRESS is a rather formal, planned speech, appropriate to a particular subject or occasion. An ORATION is a polished, rhetorical address, given usu. on a notable occasion, that employs eloquence and studied methods of delivery. A HARANGUE is an impassioned, vehement speech intended to arouse strong feeling and sometimes to lead to mob action. **—Ant. 1** muteness, dumbness, speechlessness; silence.

speed *n.* **1.** velocity, swiftness, fleetness, rapidness, rapidity, quickness; dispatch, celerity, promptness, alacrity, expedition; briskness, haste, hastiness, dash, hurry, rush, acceleration. **2.** rate, velocity; tempo, momentum. *—v.* **3.** hurry, rush, hasten, make haste, make time, lose no time, tear, tear off, barrel, hurtle, plunge; run, scurry, race, hie, gallop, hustle, dart, dash, bowl along, *Informal* go hell-bent, burn up the road, zip, zoom, hightail. **4.** hurry up, hurry, quicken, hasten, spurt ahead, step up, pick up, speed, put on a burst of speed, put on more speed, expedite, accelerate, *Informal* get a move on, step on it, gun it. **5.** hasten, assist, help, aid, boost, promote, advance, further, favor, give a lift, expedite, propel, impel, push forward, move along, dispatch. **—Syn. Study. 1** SPEED, VELOCITY, CELERITY refer to swift or energetic movement or operation. SPEED may apply to human or nonhuman activity; it emphasizes the rate in time at which something travels or operates: *the speed of an automobile; the speed of thought.* VELOCITY, a more technical term, is commonly used to refer to high rates of speed: *the velocity of a projectile.* CELERITY, a somewhat literary term, usu. refers to human movement or operation, and emphasizes dispatch or economy in an activity: *the celerity of his response.* **—Ant. 1** slowness, delay, sluggishness. **3** creep, crawl, dawdle, drag. **4** slow down. **5** hinder, slow, hamper, inhibit, block, bar.

speedy *adj.* swift, fast, rapid, hurried, hasty, quick, headlong, precipitate, sudden, abrupt, fleet, running, brisk; ready, without delay, early, not delayed, summary, with dispatch, express, quick-fire, rapid-fire, lively. **—Ant.** slow, sluggish, dilatory, laggard, lagging; delayed, late, tardy.

spell[1] *v.* **1.** write the letters of, say the letters of; form a word, make up. **2.** foretell, signify, mean, portend, indicate, typify, promise, forecast, denote, augur, stand for, betoken, suggest, symbolize, purport, bespeak, omen, forebode, imply, presage, herald, represent, amount to, connote.

spell[2] *n.* **1.** charm, enchantment, magic formula, magic, incantation, voodoo, hoodoo, sorcery, witchery, invocation, mumbo jumbo; open-sesame, abracadabra, hex. **2.** enchantment, fascination, rapture, glamour, bewitchment, allure, influence.

spell[3] *n.* **1.** stretch, turn, period, tour, term, bout, time, hitch, course, duration, round, tenure, assignment, stint, trick, go. **2.** while, bit; interval, break, respite, lull, recess, pause. **3.** period, wave, snap, interlude. *—v.* **4.** relieve, take the place of, free, release, take over for, substitute for, cover for, pinch-hit for.

spellbound *adj.* fascinated, transported, enchanted, charmed, enraptured, entranced, enthralled, rapt, bewitched, transfixed, mesmerized, hypnotized, possessed; breathless, speechless, wordless, dumbstruck, tongue-tied, awestruck, agape, openmouthed. **—Ant.** unimpressed, indifferent, disenchanted.

spend *v.* **1.** pay, pay out, expend, disburse, dispense, allocate, dole, outlay, *Informal* give, *Slang* fork out, shell out. **2.** consume, use, employ, expend, devote, invest, squander, waste, dissipate. **3.** burn out, drain, use up, exhaust, destroy, consume, dissipate, deplete, impoverish, wear out, waste; scatter, empty. **4.** occupy, pass, while away, take up, use, fill. **—Ant. 1** earn, make, acquire, get, gain, take in; save, hoard, collect, gather. **2** save, conserve. **3** save, reserve, hoard, conserve, treasure up.

spendthrift *n.* **1.** wastrel, waster, big spender, spend-all, squanderer, prodigal, profligate. *—adj.* **2.** extravagant, wasteful, overgenerous, improvident, wastrel, profligate, prodigal, lavish. **—Ant. 1** tightwad, penny pincher, cheapskate. **2** frugal, penny-pinching, stingy.

spent *adj.* exhausted, weak, weary, wearied, used up, played out, worn out, debilitated, tired out, done, powerless, strengthless, ready to drop, drooping, fatigued, *Slang* bushed, beat; laid low, faint, on one's last legs, prostrate, enfeebled, done in, fagged out. **—Ant.** energetic, lively, strong, robust, vital.

spew *v.* vomit, disgorge, regurgitate, heave, throw out; cast up, spit out, eject, expel.

sphere *n.* **1.** globe, round body, ball, globular mass, spheroid, globule, orb. **2.** orbit, domain, realm, range, area, pale, scope, compass, beat, territory, province, bailiwick; experience.

spice *n.* **1.** seasoning, pungent substance, herb, condiment, flavoring. **2.** zest, tang, flavor, piquancy, relish, excitement, pungency, savor, zip, snap, kick, accent, *Slang* pizzazz. **—Ant. 2** boredom, flatness, dullness.

spicy *adj.* **1.** pungent, hot, piquant, sharp, strong, redolent, peppery, nippy, fiery, tangy, zippy, snappy, aromatic, gingery. **2.** pungent, sharp, keen, piquant, witty, clever, spirited, provocative, pithy; sparkling, scintillating; piercing, trenchant, incisive, acute. **3.** racy, ribald, risqué, scandalous, improper, indelicate, questionable, indecent, bawdy, off-color, suggestive, salty. **—Ant. 1** bland, flat, tasteless, unsavory, insipid. **2** bland, boring, dull, insipid, tedious, spiritless, lifeless. **3** proper, prudish.

spike *n.* **1.** large nail, hobnail, pin, skewer, rivet, peg, stake. **2.** point, prong, barb, tine; thorn, briar, spine, spur, bramble, bristle, spikelet, needle.

spill *v.* **1.** cause to overflow, allow to run over, overturn, slop, slosh, waste; drip, fall, drop, run, flow, overflow, splash. **2.** let flow, shed, pour out. **3.** dump, cause to fall, throw, toss. **4.** *Informal* disclose, reveal, tell, *Slang* blab.

spin *v.* **1.** make by twisting fibers; form into thread or yarn. **2.** twirl, whirl, turn, rotate, revolve, swirl, wheel, pirouette, gyrate. **3.** tell, narrate, render, relate, unfold, recount; invent, concoct, fabricate. *—n.* **4.** turn, spinning, twirl, roll, rotation. **5.** quick drive, rapid ride, turn, fast circle, whirl. **—Syn. Study. 2** See TURN.

spine *n.* **1.** backbone, vertebral column, spinal column, vertebrae. **2.** quill, horn, pointed projection, barb, spike, spur, point, prong, bristle, prickle; bramble, thorn, briar, needle.

spineless *adj.* timid, fearful, faint-hearted, weak, timorous, cowardly, pusillanimous, lily-livered, irresolute, chickenhearted, cowering, spiritless, cringing, vacillating, weak-willed, indecisive, wavering. **—Ant.** fearless, tough, strong, forceful, courageous, resolute.

spinoff *n.* byproduct, outgrowth, offshoot, aftereffect, side effect, issue, adjunct, supplement, descendant, consequence, result, outcome.

spiral *n.* **1.** helix, screw, whorl, whirl, gyre, coil, corkscrew; curl, curlicue, ringlet. *—adj.* **2.** helical, corkscrew, screw-shaped, spiroid, curled, coiled, whorled, winding, twisting.

spire *n.* **1.** steeple, belfry, turret, obelisk, minaret, tower, bell tower, campanile, shaft. **2.** peak, crest, summit, cap, cone, point, pinnacle, apex, vertex, tip.

spirit *n.* **1.** soul, immortal part, vital essence; intellect, mind, psyche. **2.** ghost, shade, spook, apparition, specter, phantom, phantasm, hobgoblin, wraith, banshee, presence; elf, fairy, bugbear, bugaboo, goblin, ghoul, sprite, dybbuk. **3.** will, motivation, resolve, resolution; mind, heart, animus, impulse, urge. **4.** **spirits** mood, feelings, disposition, emotions, attitude, morale, sentiment, temper. **5.** vigor, vim, zest, liveliness, animation, vitality, verve, élan, vivacity, enthusiasm, energy, eagerness; pluck, mettle, enterprise, drive, zeal, avidity; sprightliness, sparkle, ardor, fire, glow, warmth; courage, bravery, doughtiness, audacity, dauntlessness, stoutheartedness, daring, backbone, fortitude, boldness, stoutness, valor, staunchness, fearlessness, spunk, *Informal* sand, guts, grit. **6.** temper, feeling, disposition, frame of mind, vein, stripe, mood, humor, tone, tenor, turn of mind. **7.** allegiance, devotion, loyalty, attachment, bond, fervor, ardor, enthusiasm, feeling. **8.** intention, significance, intent, meaning, essence, purport, substance; sense, gist, effect, purpose, aim. **—Ant. 1, 3** body, flesh, materiality. **5** lifelessness, dullness, spiritlessness, timidity.

spirited *adj.* high-spirited, full of spirit, lively, mettlesome, frisky, fiery; courageous, plucky, nervy, intrepid, fearless, bold. **—Ant.** spiritless, dispirited, timid, sluggish.

spiritual *adj.* **1.** ghostly, supernatural, supernal, psychic, metaphysical, phantom, incorporeal, immaterial, unearthly, otherworldly, spectral, insubstantial, intangible. **2.** of the soul, psychic, psychological, mental, cerebral, inner, innermost; moral, unworldly, unfleshly, platonic. **3.** religious, holy, godly, pious, devotional, divine, ecclesiastical, priestly, Christian, sanctified, churchy, celestial, heavenly; blessed, hallowed, consecrated, sacrosanct. —**Ant. 1** physical, earthly, material, corporeal. **2** fleshly, bodily, physical, carnal, sensuous. **3** earthly, temporal, secular, lay, worldly; atheistic, sacrilegious.

spit[1] *v.* **1.** expectorate, spew, eject; slobber, drool, slaver, froth, foam, dribble. **2.** spew, spatter, throw out, eject, shower, scatter; pop, hiss, sputter. **3.** fling, eject, throw, express violently; hiss, shriek. —*n.* **4.** saliva, sputum, spittle, drool.

spit[2] *n.* **1.** turnspit, rod, skewer, brochette. **2.** long narrow point of land, bar, peninsula, sandbank, headland, promontory, long shoal; atoll, reef.

spite *n.* **1.** malice, gall, hatred, hate, vindictiveness, bitterness, ill will, venom, maliciousness, resentment, malignity, animosity, animus, malevolence, hostility, odium, antipathy, loathing, grudge, enmity, rancor, revengefulness, vengeance, vengefulness, detestation, bad blood; meanness, nastiness. —*v.* **2.** treat maliciously, annoy, humiliate, mortify, pain, injure, misuse, hurt, wound, ill-treat; sting, gall, slap in the face, provoke, irk, vex, harass, nettle, put out, irritate. —**Ant. 1** kindness, kindliness, love, benevolence. **2** please, help, aid, assist, support, serve.

spiteful *adj.* malicious, hateful, vicious, evil, malevolent, wicked, hostile, vindictive, rancorous, antagonistic, vengeful, unforgiving, acrimonious, merciless. —**Ant.** loving, affectionate, altruistic, kind, considerate.

splash *v.* **1.** splatter, spatter, shower, scatter, slosh, dash, fling; spread, strew, bestrew, cast, plash, disperse. **2.** plunge, paddle, wallow, welter, bathe, swash. **3.** bespatter, spatter, splatter, shower, sprinkle, splotch, besmirch, soil, stain, daub, smear, streak, discolor. **4.** wash, dash, hit, buffet, surge, toss, break, strike, smack, batter. **5.** show prominently, blazon, broadcast. —*n.* **6.** flying liquid, spattering, splattering, shower. **7.** stir, commotion, ado, sensation, uproar; impact, effect.

splay *v.* **1.** extend, stretch out, spread out. —*adj.* **2.** spread out, broad, outspread, fan-shaped, fanlike; turned outward. **3.** crooked, awry, askew, irregular, distorted, warped, tilted, aslant, sloping, inclined, slanted, slanting; awkward, clumsy. —**Ant. 1** narrow, compress. **2** narrow; straight. **3** flat, straight, level, even, symmetrical.

spleen *n.* bad temper, rancor, spite, peevishness, spitefulness, venom, bile, gall, acrimony, animosity, animus, malice, malevolence, ill humor, ill will, bitterness, enmity, resentment, hatred, vexation, hostility, irritability, anger. —**Ant.** cheerfulness, happiness, good humor, joy.

splendid *adj.* **1.** beautiful, magnificent, splendorous, splendiferous, flashing, costly, superb, gorgeous, resplendent, dazzling, glittering, effulgent, brilliant; rich, ornate, gleaming; grand, sumptuous, palatial, majestic, elegant, imposing, regal, royal, stately, glorious. **2.** exalted, lofty, high, august, noble, elevated, illustrious, eminent, distinguished, peerless, imposing, glorious, preeminent, brilliant, surpassing. **3.** excellent, exceptional, outstanding, estimable, brilliant, surpassing, transcendent, marvelous, admirable, rare, fine, remarkable, terrific, wonderful. —**Ant. 1** plain, somber, tawdry, poor; beggarly, squalid. **2** inglorious, ignoble, mean, low, sordid, tarnished, ignominious. **3** poor, ordinary, mediocre, unexceptional, unremarkable, unexciting.

splendor *n.* **1.** brilliance, dazzle, luminosity, light, luster, gleam, sheen, fire, glitter, burnish, shine, luminousness, radiance, effulgence, resplendence, irradiance, incandescence, intensity. **2.** pomp, grandeur, gorgeousness, glory, resplendence, brilliance, beauty, magnificence, opulence, stateliness; sublimity, augustness, nobility; preeminence, renown. —**Ant. 1** dullness, paleness, pallidness, drabness. **2** plainness, dullness, drabness.

splice *v.* interweave, braid together, knit, plait, intertwine, dovetail, interlace, interconnect, connect, merge, unite, graft; join together, wed. —**Ant.** cut, break, sever.

splinter *n.* **1.** sliver, fragment, shiver, chip, needle. —*v.* **2.** sliver, split, shiver, shatter, crumble, disintegrate, pulverize, smash, break up; fly apart, fragment; chip, fracture; explode.

split *v.* **1.** divide lengthwise, bisect, halve; cleave, rive, hew; break, crack, snap. **2.** divide, disunite, rupture, part, sever, come between, set at odds, sow dissension, set against, segregate, alienate; disagree, differ, diverge, part company. **3.** tear, tear asunder, become torn; sunder, break, burst, rive, be riven, part, rupture, divide, break apart, dissever; shiver, splinter, fracture, snap, crack, give way. **4.** share, parcel out, divide, divvy up, apportion, disperse, portion, allocate, partition, dispense, dole, deal, distribute, allot, mete, subdivide. —*n.* **5.** tear, rift, rent, breach, cleft, splitting, separation; break, crack, fissure, fracture, opening. **6.** rupture, breach, cleavage, disunion, rift, break, schism, dissension, cleavage, division; quarrel, divorce, disassociation, falling out, difference, divergence, disagreement, alienation, estrangement, parting of the ways. —*adj.* **7.** torn, severed, rent, ripped, riven; broken, segmented, ruptured, dissevered, splintered, fractured, cracked; divided, separated, dual, two-fold; mixed, varied; undecided, ambivalent. —**Ant. 1–3** unite, join. **6** union, merger, junction, agreement, connection. **7** whole, unbroken, sound.

splurge *v.* **1.** indulge oneself, be extravagant, throw caution to the winds, *Informal* live it up, shoot the works. —*n.* **2.** indulgence, self-indulgence, binge, spree, bender; showy display, showing off.

splutter *v.* **1.** sputter, stammer, stutter, mumble, jabber, gibber, hem and haw, stumble; bluster. **2.** spit, hiss, seethe, sputter; spew, burst, spray, spatter, expectorate, slobber.

spoil *v.* **1.** ruin, botch, mess up, foul up, mar, bungle, impair, damage, muddle, blemish, flaw, blight, disrupt, disfigure, mutilate, destroy, harm, injure, deface. **2.** go bad, decay, rot, taint, become tainted, sour, putrefy, decompose, addle, deteriorate, mold, mildew, turn. **3.** indulge, overindulge, pamper, overgratify, coddle, mollycoddle, baby, humor. —**Syn. Study. 3** SPOIL, INDULGE, HUMOR imply attempting to satisfy the wishes or whims of oneself or others. SPOIL implies being so lenient or permissive as to cause harm to a person's character: *to spoil a grandchild.* INDULGE suggests a yielding, though temporary or infrequent, to wishes that perhaps should not be satisfied: *to indulge an irresponsible son.* To HUMOR is to comply with a mood, fancy, or caprice, as in order to satisfy, soothe, or manage: *to humor an invalid.* —**Ant. 1** enhance, improve. **2** preserve, conserve, save. **3** deprive, overtax, discipline.

spoils *n. pl.* benefits, prizes, loot, booty, plunder, swag, pickings, bounty, quarry; profits, take, acquisitions; perquisites, comforts, amenities; patronage; *Slang* haul.

spokesman *n.* spokesperson, spokeswoman, deputy, mouthpiece, delegate, representative, press agent, public relations representative, P.R. man, negotiator, middleman, agent, surrogate, proxy, protagonist.

sponge *v.* **1.** swab, wash, rub, mop, moisten, clean, cleanse; blot, towel, dry. **2.** *Informal* leech, panhandle, obtain free, borrow, bum, cadge, impose on, live on, *Slang* freeload, mooch, scrounge.

sponger *n.* cadger, freeloader, leech, sponge, bloodsucker, barnacle, borrower; *Slang* moocher, scrounger, deadbeat.

sponsor *n.* **1.** promoter, financer, backer, advertiser; patron, angel, protector, guarantor, supporter, defender, advocate, proponent, partisan, champion, upholder, guardian. —*v.* **2.** back, finance, advocate, promote; champion, support, guarantee, warranty, uphold, stand up for, vouch for; set up, start out, underwrite.

spontaneous *adj.* unpremeditated, improvised, impulsive, impetuous, off the cuff, ad lib, extemporaneous; natural, unstudied, uncontrived, ingenuous; extempore, impromptu, unprompted, offhand, unconstrained, voluntary, unplanned, free, gratuitous; unbidden, willing, independent, automatic, unhesitating, instinctive. —**Ant.** premeditated, studied, contrived, forced, planned, calculated, involuntary, constrained.

spoof *n.* **1.** parody, takeoff, burlesque, *British* sendup, satire, travesty, caricature, joke; *Slang* kidding, joshing, ribbing. —*v.* **2.** satirize, lampoon, parody, caricature, take off on, twit; *Slang* kid, josh.

spook *n.* **1.** apparition, ghost, phantom, haunt, specter, bogey, shade, goblin, hobgoblin, spirit, shadow. —*v.* **2.** frighten, alarm, startle, scare, unnerve, terrorize, terrify; unsettle, disquiet, intimidate, disturb. —**Ant. 2** calm, pacify, soothe, relax.

sporadic *adj.* irregular, spotty, scattered, sparse, spasmodic, fitful, widely spaced, now and then, occasional, infrequent, periodic, fragmentary, intermittent, discontinuous, few and far between, meager, few, thin, scarce, rare, isolated, uncommon; haphazard, random. —**Ant.** continuous, regular, steady, constant.

sport *n.* **1.** athletic pastime, physical activity, game, competition, contest, athletics; diversion, recreation, fun, distraction, divertissement, entertainment, amusement, play, relaxation, hobby. **2.** play, jest, jesting, pleasantry, skylarking, trifling, kidding, jollity, gaiety, frolic, mirth, hilarity, antics, lark, fun; joviality, merrymaking, festivity; raillery, ridicule, mockery, scoffing, derision, chaff, badinage, persiflage, depreciation. **3.** laughingstock, monkey, butt, fair game, scapegoat, buffoon, joke, goat. **4.** game person, gambler, daredevil. —*v.* **5.** play, disport, amuse oneself, play games; make merry, dally, caper, gambol, revel, frisk, trip, cavort, frolic, rollick, lark, romp, skylark. **6.** toy, trifle, take advantage of, play, be frivolous, dally, play cat-and-mouse, deal lightly, treat cavalierly, take in, ill-treat, abuse, misuse. **7.** display, exhibit, show off, flourish; carry, bear. —**Ant. 1** business, job, duty, work. 2 cruelty, seriousness, respect, adoration. 4 sissy, coward, stick-in-the-mud. 5 work, toil.

spot *n.* **1.** stain, mark, speck, splotch, smudge, soil, blot, daub, smirch, fleck, patch, speckle, blotch, dot, fly-speck, discoloration, blemish. **2.** disgrace, stain, blemish, brand, taint, blot, defect, discredit, flaw, stigma, slur, imputation, aspersion, reproach. **3.** place, locality, locale, location, point, site, tract, situation, space, seat, locus, premises, position; part, region, district, area, territory, quarter, neighborhood, station, section, sector. **4.** *Informal* bad situation, difficulty, plight, dilemma, fix, bind, predicament. —*v.* **5.** stain, smudge, smirch, soil, sully, blot, dot, discolor, daub, speck, grime, blemish, smear, speckle, sprinkle, spatter, splash. **6.** locate, see, pick out, recognize, discover, light on, espy, spy, discern, detect.

spotless *adj.* **1.** clean, unsoiled, unspotted, immaculate, pristine, unstained, unmarred, flawless, unsullied, untarnished, pure, perfect, unblemished, gleaming, shining, untainted, snowy. **2.** perfect, unflawed, flawless, untarnished, immaculate, unblemished, untainted, unsullied, faultless, pure, clean, stainless, unmarred; impeccable, irreproachable, unexceptionable. —**Ant. 1** filthy, dirty, messy, soiled. **2** tarnished, flawed, marred, blemished, tainted; reprehensible.

spotty *adj.* **1.** mottled, full of spots, dappled, spotted, flecked, freckled, variegated; blotchy, splotchy, pimply, broken out. **2.** uneven, irregular, unmethodical, fitful, erratic, random, unsystematic, disorganized, variable, sporadic, intermittent, episodic, spasmodic, unsteady, capricious, desultory; inconstant, wavering, unreliable, undependable, uncertain. —**Ant. 1** smooth, unmottled; clear. **2** even, regular, methodical, systematic, uniform, constant, dependable.

spout *v.* **1.** spurt, discharge, emit forcibly, squirt, issue, spray, pour out, disgorge, vomit, erupt, spew, eject, expel, gush, jet, stream, flow, surge, shoot, well, exude. **2.** *Informal* speak pompously, carry on, go on, pontificate, harangue, gush, hold forth, rant, bluster. —*n.* **3.** outlet, vent, mouth, pipe, nose, tube, nozzle, lip, conduit, trough, snout, channel, waterspout, beak, sluice. **4.** jet, spurt, shoot, stream, fountain, gush, spray.

sprawl *v.* **1.** spread out, straggle, meander, stretch out, gush out, reach out, wind, extend, branch. **2.** slouch, stretch out, loll, flop, spread-eagle, slump, languish, recline, lean, sit awkwardly, lie awkwardly, lounge.

spray¹ *n.* **1.** droplets, mist, splash, moisture, vapor. **2.** sprayer, nozzle, sprinkler, vaporizer, atomizer, syringe. **3.** barrage, shower, burst, fusillade, volley, discharge. —*v.* **4.** discharge, atomize, scatter, disperse, shower, drizzle, sprinkle, spatter; moisten, dampen; coat, treat.

spray² *n.* sprig, bouquet, nosegay, shoot, switch, twig, bough, posy, blossom.

spread *v.* **1.** stretch out, open, unfold, untwine, unroll, unfurl, extend. **2.** scatter, be scattered, strew, bestrew, sprinkle, overspread, cast, distribute, diffuse, shed, be shed, disperse; extend, stretch, cover. **3.** publish, communicate, circulate, divulge, make known, disseminate, proclaim, broadcast, propagate, make public, air, repeat, report, bruit, blazon, vent, noise abroad, publicize, herald, announce, distribute, issue, ventilate, trumpet, declare, promulgate, whisper about, radiate, diffuse; proliferate, penetrate, pervade, permeate; overrun, suffuse, advance. **4.** apply, coat, lay, smear, besmear, overlay, bedaub, overspread, cover, cloak, pave; spray, spatter; plaster. —*n.* **5.** spreading, increase, expansion, dispersion, enlargement, diffusion, dissemination, advance, circulation, amplification, radiation, pervasion, permeation, suffusion, proliferation. **6.** stretch, reach, extent, extension, span, scope, range, distance, breadth, length, area, field, width, circuit, compass; expanse, open land, sweep, tract. **7.** feast, array of food, table, banquet. **8.** notice, coverage, write-up, report, article, account, story; printed advertisement. —**Ant. 1** fold, roll up, wind, furl. **2** collect, pile up, gather. **3** suppress, conceal, hush; localize, confine; diminish, die, abate. **5** halting, check, abatement, diminishing.

spree *n.* carouse, carousal, revel, revelry, wassail, bacchanal, orgy, debauch; bout, *Informal* binge, bender, drunk; saturnalia, splurge, fling, toot.

sprightly *adj.* animated, lively, alive, lighthearted, playful, vivacious, gay, buoyant, sportive, blithesome, blithe, spry, jolly, chipper, cheery, merry, jovial, active, dashing, jaunty, frolicsome, cheerful, breezy, keen, spirited, dynamic, nimble, brisk, energetic, agile. —**Ant.** glum, lethargic, lifeless, sluggish, phlegmatic.

spring *v.* **1.** leap, bound, rise suddenly, jump, dart, vault, lunge, bounce, start, hop. **2.** release, trigger. **3.** rise, shoot up, arise, appear, mushroom, crop out; sprout, burgeon, pop, loom, start up; pour, issue suddenly, burst forth, stream, flow, well, surge, rush, break forth, gush, jet, spout, spurt, shoot, emanate. **4.** descend, be brought forth, emanate, originate, come forth, be descended, proceed, derive, be derived, come into existence, stem, sprout, start, flow, arise, rise, germinate, begin, commence, issue, come, result, ensue. —*n.* **5.** jump, leap, saltation, vault, bound, hop, caper, bounce, gambol, lunge; entrechat. **6.** springiness, buoyancy, elasticity, kick, bounce, resiliency, elastic force, flexibility, stretchability, reflex, stretch, recoil. **7.** small stream, pool, hot spring, well, waterhole, watering place, fount, fountain, wellspring; baths, spa. —**Ant. 1** crawl, creep; land, alight, drop, fall. **4** end, finish, terminate. **6** inflexibility.

sprinkle *v.* **1.** dust, powder, scatter, dash, strew, spread, bestrew; squirt, spray, water, moisten, spatter, splash, shower, diffuse, splatter. **2.** shower, rain lightly, drizzle.

sprinkling *n.* sprinkle, smattering, modicum, droplet, minimum, dash, drop, soupçon, hint, touch, pinch.

sprint *v.* **1.** run, race, dash, tear, whisk, whiz, shoot, scamper, dart, rush. —*n.* **2.** dash, burst, spurt, kick. —**Ant. 1** stroll, saunter, walk, creep, crawl. **2** walk, stroll.

sprout *v.* **1.** shoot forth, begin to grow, come up, burgeon, spring up, grow, bud, bloom, flower, blossom, put forth; spread, wax, thrive, multiply, germinate. —*n.* **2.** shoot, offshoot, sprig, outgrowth, germinated seed.

spruce *adj.* trim, tidy, neat, smart, sharp, chic, dapper, natty; spick-and-span, shipshape, well-groomed, kempt, elegant, *French* soigné. —**Ant.** sloppy, messy, seedy, shabby, tacky.

spry *adj.* lively, sprightly, animated, frisky, lightfooted, supple, active, nimble, brisk, agile, deft; spirited, jaunty, sportive, full of life, buoyant, vigorous, energetic, playful, chipper, vivacious, hearty, hale, full of spirit, quick. —**Ant.** doddering, slow, inactive, sluggish, lethargic.

spunk *n.* *Informal* guts, pluck, spirit, grit, sand, nerve, courage, boldness, daring, bravery, mettle, fire, pepper, ginger, salt, gumption, heart, backbone, feistiness. —**Ant.** cowardice, timidity, fear, squeamishness.

spur *n.* **1.** boot spike, goad, prod. **2.** stimulus, incitement, inducement, incentive, stimulant, stimulation, goad, excitant, whet, provocation, impetus, prick, instigation, whip, fillip, motive, impulse, encouragement. **3.** branch, arm, wing, leg, fork; tributary, feeder; siding. —*v.* **4.** stimulate, hasten, encourage; goad, prod. —**Ant. 2** discouragement, hindrance, restraint, check, curb, deterrent.

spurious *adj.* not genuine, fake, forged, counterfeit, sham, imitation, unauthentic, bogus, phony, fraudulent; simulated, feigned, mock, make-believe; false, hollow, fallacious, faulty, unsound, specious, illegitimate. —**Ant.** genuine, real, authentic; sound, legitimate, solid.

spurn *v.* reject, turn down, scorn, disdain, refuse, repulse, repudiate, repel, look down upon, treat with contempt, contemn, cast aside, dismiss, decline, sneer at, scoff at, disparage, trample upon, mock, flout, cold-shoulder, rebuff, slight, turn up one's nose at, snub. —**Syn. Study.** See REFUSE. —**Ant.** welcome, embrace, accept, encourage.

spurt *v.* **1.** spout, jet, gush, issue, burst, spring out, stream, flow, pour out, surge, shoot, squirt, spray; emit, disgorge, discharge, vomit forth. **2.** speed, sprint, burst, lunge, tear, scoot, whiz, spring, dart, dash, rush. —*n.* **3.** rush, jet, gush, stream, shoot, spout, sudden flow, squirt, fountain, ejection, spray. **4.** explosion, eruption, burst, outbreak, outburst, flash, outpouring, rush, access, gust. —**Ant. 1** drip, ooze. **2** creep, crawl, dawdle, lag. **3** oozing, drip, dribble, drizzle.

spy *n.* **1.** espionage agent, secret agent, intelligence agent, operative, undercover man, Mata Hari, fifth columnist; saboteur, agent provocateur; informer. —*v.* **2.** watch secretly, keep watch, engage in surveillance, shadow, scout, reconnoiter; snoop, pry, peep. **3.** see, observe, discover, descry, glimpse, spot, catch sight of, sight, make out, detect, recognize, perceive, behold, notice, find, view, discern.

squabble *v.* **1.** wrangle, quarrel, bicker, clash, dispute, differ, spat; have words, argue, bandy words, set to, lock horns, brawl, row, fight, contest, contend, battle, war, tiff. —*n.* **2.** spat, quarrel, tiff, dispute, difference, dissension, fight, disagreement, scrap; contention, words, argument, row, run-in, set-to, altercation, controversy. —**Ant. 1** agree, concur, assent. **2** agreement, concurrence.

squalid *adj.* unclean, foul, dirty, filthy, decayed, slovenly, reeking, nasty, sloppy, disheveled, slatternly, horrid, run-down, tumble-down, deteriorated, dilapidated, ramshackle; degraded, wretched, sordid, rotten, miserable, poverty-stricken, abject, mean, shabby, battered, broken-down. —**Ant.** clean, attractive, well-kept, tidy.

squalor *n.* wretchedness, foulness, filth, squalidness, uncleanness, dirtiness, dirt, nastiness, uncleanliness; ugliness, degraded condition, sordidness, meanness, grubbiness, abjectness, poverty, seediness, dinginess, misery, neglect. —**Ant.** cleanliness, beauty, fineness, splendor, luxury, nobility.

squander *v.* waste, throw away, misspend, dissipate, fritter away, misuse, *Slang* blow; lavish, run through, exhaust, be prodigal with, spend, spend like water; consume, deplete. —**Ant.** save, conserve, hoard.

square *n.* **1.** quadrangle, quadrate, quadrilateral, box. **2.** plaza, place, large intersection, *British* circus; block; park; marketplace; green, common. **3.** *Slang* dull person, conservative, stick-in-the-mud, fogy; prig, prude; jerk, cornball, hick, apple knocker, clodhopper. —*v.* **4.** reduce to square form, block out, quadrate, set at right angles; form into right angles. **5.** even, make even, even up, balance; pay off, settle up, close, discharge, liquidate. **6.** align, make straight, straighten, even out, make level, make even; flatten, plane, smooth. **7.** agree, tally, harmonize, blend, accord, fit, conform, match, correspond, jibe, be in unison, cohere, be congruous, concur, fall in, equal. **8.** settle, resolve, reconcile, heal, rectify, adjust, set right, reach agreement on, compose, arbitrate, patch up, arrange, mend, straighten out, mediate, clear up. —*adj.* **9.** honest, just, equitable; truthful, candid, straightforward. —**Ant. 3** hippie, hipster, mod, sophisticate. **6** make crooked, distort. **7** disagree, contrast, contradict. **8** entangle, prolong, worsen.

squash *v.* **1.** smash, crush, flatten, press flat, compress, pulp, mash, ram down, squish; squeeze, jam, cram, crowd; compact, concentrate. **2.** put down, quell, quash, prostrate, crush, suppress, repress, dispel, squelch, dissipate, trample, upset, flatten, level, undermine, overthrow; destroy, annihilate, obliterate. —**Ant. 2** aid, promote, enhance, support.

squat *v.* **1.** crouch, bend the knees, sit on the heels; kneel, *Informal* hunker; cringe, cower, lie low, shrink. **2.** settle without title, dwell, establish oneself, set up housekeeping, move in, make a home, take up residence, encamp, locate. —*adj.* **3.** dumpy, stumpy, stocky, chunky, stubby, pudgy, thickset, square. —**Ant. 3** lanky, tall, slim, reedy, willowy.

squawk *v.* **1.** scream, squall, blare, screech, croak. **2.** *Slang* complain, protest, grumble, gripe.

squeak *v.* screech, squeal, shriek, grate, creak; cheep, peep, cry, shrill, chirp, yelp.

squeal *v.* **1.** wail, yelp, cry, whine, shrill, screech, shriek, peep, cheep, scream, yell, bawl, squeak. **2.** *Slang* inform, turn informer, betray accomplices, *Slang* blab, sing, fink.

squeamish *adj.* **1.** priggish, puritanical, prudish, modest, prim, proper, easily shocked, demure, fastidious, straitlaced, coy, sanctimonious, mincing, finicky, finicking, finical, fussy. **2.** easily nauseated, qualmish, easily disgusted, weak-stomached, delicate, sick, sickish, queasy, nauseous. —**Ant. 1** bold, immodest, brazen, brash. **2** coarse, tough, strong-stomached.

squeeze *v.* **1.** press, compress, clutch. **2.** extract, press out, force out; elicit, wring, wrest, wrench; pry, pull out, tear out, draw out, withdraw, extricate; extort, compel, coerce. **3.** crowd, cram, pack, jam, stuff, thrust, cramp, wedge; concentrate, compact, consolidate. **4.** hug, embrace, clasp, hold. **5.** press, push, force one's way, wedge, elbow, crowd, shove, shoulder, ram, drive, jostle, butt, edge. —*n.* **6.** clasp, grasp, grip, hold, embrace, hug, clutch; pressure, crushing, compression, pinching, constriction; narrowing, crowding, stricture, wedge; bottleneck; passage, defile.

squelch *v.* **1.** crush, put down, squash, quash, smash, trample on, abort, suppress; quell, silence, hush, quiet. —*n.* **2.** retort, riposte, crushing reply, put-down, silencer. —**Ant. 1** incite, encourage, provoke.

squire *n.* **1.** country gentleman, landowner, rich farmer, planter; member of the gentry, lord of the manor. **2.** escort, consort, attendant; gallant, cavalier, date, companion, *Informal* boyfriend. —*v.* **3.** escort, attend, court, accompany, take, date; chaperon, chauffeur.

squirm *v.* **1.** turn, twist, contort, wriggle, writhe, wiggle, jerk, bend, twitch, pitch, toss. **2.** show discomfort, be restless, fidget, writhe, shift, shrink, blench, be upset, smart, flinch, wince, sweat, agonize; flounder.

squirt *v.* **1.** spray, spurt, shoot, gush, spout, splash, discharge. **2.** spray, shower, spatter, sprinkle, splash, dash, besprinkle; shoot, discharge. —*n.* **3.** spray, jet, spurt, stream. **4.** *Slang* insignificant person, punk, piker, runt.

stab *v.* **1.** jab, pierce, stick, spear, bayonet, impale, gore, wound, gash, cut, spike, lance, run through, thrust through, knife, transfix, lacerate, prick, spit, gouge, slash, cleave. **2.** wound, hurt, injure the feelings of, pierce, cut, pain. —*n.* **3.** jab, thrust, lunge, dagger, stroke, cut, prick, slash, wound, laceration, gash. **4.** pang, prick, painful sensation, ache, sting, twinge, bite, shiver, thrill, qualm. **5.** *Informal* try, attempt, effort, pass; trial, essay, endeavor; shot, go. —**Ant. 2** soothe, assuage, ease, comfort, please, delight.

stability *n.* **1.** steadiness, constancy, solidness, soundness, poise, aplomb, balance, equilibrium, evenness, reliability, stableness, steadfastness. **2.** solidity, soundness, firmness, steadiness, solidness, sturdiness, security, fixedness. **3.** permanence, fixity, firmness, unchangeableness, abidingness, durability, changelessness, continuity. **—Ant. 1** instability, inconstancy, weakness, unsteadiness, unreliability, irresolution. **2** frailty, instability, fragility, unsteadiness, weakness. **3** instability, impermanence, changeableness.

stable *adj.* **1.** established, reliable, durable, sound, secure, well-grounded, indissoluble, solid. **2.** sound, sturdy, solid, steady, fixed, stationary, firm, safe, secure, immovable, anchored, moored. **3.** fixed, unchangeable, firm, unchanging, steady, abiding, persisting, enduring, constant, uniform, even. **4.** reliable, steady, steadfast, resolute, true, staunch, loyal, stalwart, dependable, unwavering, firm, constant, faithful, unfaltering. **—Ant. 1–4** unstable. **1** impermanent, shaky, unsound, unsteady. **2** frail, shaky, unsteady, unsubstantial, unsound. **3** changeable, alterable, variable, shaky, wavering. **4** unreliable, unsteady, mercurial, volatile, erratic.

stack *n.* **1.** pile, heap, bank, sheaf, mass, rick, clump, mound, mountain, bunch, load; accumulation, aggregation, amassment, batch, bundle. **2.** smokestack, chimney, flue, funnel. *—v.* **3.** heap, pile, arrange vertically, mound, bank; gather, bunch, lump, amass, assemble, batch, hoard, accumulate.

stadium *n.* arena, bowl, coliseum, amphitheater, circus, ballpark, field, park, palaestra, hippodrome, stade.

staff *n.* **1.** cane, stick, walking stick, rod, crutch, pole, alpenstock; cudgel, wand, stave, bludgeon, billy club, bat, shillelagh; scepter. **2.** pole, flagpole, flagstaff, support. **3.** force, crew, personnel, help, employees, group, cadre, team; assistants, advisors, retinue. *—v.* **4.** make up the staff of, man, work, tend, manage, service.

stage *n.* **1.** period, phase, level, step, grade. **2.** raised platform, raised floor, *Slang* the boards; rostrum, pulpit, podium, dais, soapbox, scaffold, stump. **3.** dramatic profession, show business, theater, stage playing, acting, drama, the footlights, *Slang* the boards, show biz. **4.** spot, surroundings, scene of action, setting, locale, locality, arena, whereabouts, position, theater, location, sight, bearings. *—v.* **5.** produce, put on the stage, present, put on; act, perform, dramatize, play.

stagger *v.* **1.** stumble, sway, wobble, reel, hobble, totter, lurch, shamble, blunder, waver, flounder. **2.** cause to sway, cause to reel, make unsteady, stun, knock silly, totter, throw off balance. **3.** stun, jolt, shock, nonplus, astound, astonish, shake, amaze, dumbfound, unsettle, disconcert, jar, bowl over, overwhelm, strike dumb, take away the breath of, stupefy, startle, flabbergast, bewilder, confound, give a turn, consternate. **4.** spread out, arrange in a zigzag order; alternate, overlap, take in turns. **—Ant. 2** steady. **3** steady, stabilize; strengthen.

stagnant *adj.* **1.** still, not running, not flowing, motionless, inert, lifeless, close, standing, stationary, unstirring, dead, quiet, quiescent, inactive, uncirculating; filthy, polluted, foul, tainted, putrid, putrefied, slimy, stale. **2.** lifeless, inactive, dull, listless, dormant, dead, sluggish, inert, static, languid, torpid, slow, leaden, lethargic; vegetative, lazy, supine, ponderous, dronish, monotonous. **—Ant. 1** running, flowing, moving, circulating; clean, pure, fresh, unpolluted. **2** lively, active, busy, thriving.

stagnate *v.* remain motionless, cease to flow, lie still, be stagnant, not stir, stand still; putrefy, become foul, become contaminated, become polluted; become sluggish, vegetate, become dull, stop developing, stop growing, go to seed, deteriorate, go to pot; become inactive, lie idle. **—Ant.** flow, circulate; grow, bustle.

staid *adj.* sedate, sober, settled, somber, subdued, serious, dignified, reserved, undemonstrative, solemn, stiff, quiet, earnest, demure, grave, complacent, priggish, prudish; decent, decorous, seemly, proper. **—Ant.** exuberant, jaunty, wild, indecorous, flighty, frivolous, demonstrative, playful, capricious, loose.

stain *n.* **1.** spot, discoloration, blemish, tarnish, blot, smudge, soil, smear, blotch, splotch, speck, mark, taint, daub, patch, smirch. **2.** blot, spot, brand, stigma, blemish, taint, tarnish, flaw, imputation, soil, smudge, shame, disgrace, slur, dishonor. **3.** tint, dye, coloring, dye-stuff, tincture. *—v.* **4.** spot, discolor, blemish, smirch, tarnish, blotch, sully, soil, dirty, smear, smudge, mar, spoil, grime, daub, mark, splotch, blot. **5.** dye, color, tint, pigment. **6.** blemish, taint, disgrace, bring reproach upon, tarnish, defile, blot, blacken, impair, besmirch, foul, debase, stigmatize, dishonor, befoul, sully, drag in the mud, spoil, subvert, ruin, undermine, detract from; vilify, slander, libel, malign, discredit, denigrate, disparage. **—Ant. 2** honor, credit, accolade. **4** clean. **6** clear, honor, enhance.

stake *n.* **1.** post, picket, pale, pole, peg,

spike, stick, pile, rod, bar; column, pillar, marker, standard. **2.** money risked, hazard, bet, ante, wager, play; prize, pot, kitty, jackpot, reward, spoils, take, haul, booty, winnings, purse, grab, pickings, loot, returns. **3.** share, investment, risk, interest, speculation, venture, hazard. **4.** personal concern, interest, involvement. —*v.* **5.** mark off, delineate, mark out, outline, demarcate, define, delimit. **6.** brace, support, hold up, prop, stay; tie to a stake, hitch, secure, fasten, tether, trammel, moor, make fast, fetter, lash, peg down. **7.** bet, wager, hazard, risk, chance, jeopardize, pawn, speculate, venture. **8.** *Informal* stand, treat; back, finance, underwrite, sponsor, subsidize.

stale *adj.* **1.** flat, not fresh, vapid, tasteless, savorless; fusty, musty, close, stagnant. **2.** trite, banal, hackneyed, insipid, flat, vapid, dull, common, commonplace, ordinary, mediocre, humdrum, unvaried, tedious, worn-out, threadbare, prosaic, pedestrian, unimaginative, monotonous, uninteresting. —**Ant. 1** fresh, crisp. **2** original, imaginative, varied.

stalemate *n.* deadlock, impasse, tie, standoff, dead heat, draw; halt, blockage, standstill; dead end, cul-de-sac. —**Ant.** decision.

stalk[1] *n.* stem, shaft, column, trunk, spire, pedicel.

stalk[2] *v.* **1.** approach stealthily, pursue quietly, creep up on, sneak up on, track, hunt; steal, lurk, prowl; threaten, menace. **2.** march, strut, swagger, walk stiffly, stamp, stomp, tramp, stride. **3.** haunt, go through, hang over, pervade.

stall *n.* **1.** booth, cubicle, cell, compartment, coop, pen, confine, shed. **2.** booth, stand, arcade, shop, kiosk. **3.** enclosed seat, box, *British* orchestra seat. —*v.* **4.** confine, pen, put in a stall; bed down. **5.** stop, halt, bring to a standstill, be brought to a standstill, arrest, impede, check, paralyze, incapacitate, pull up, stop short, stop running, trammel, block, interrupt, obstruct, disable, hobble; delay, put off, postpone. **6.** delay, play for time, temporize; be evasive, equivocate.

stalwart *adj.* **1.** sturdy, robust, sound, strong, muscular, strapping, hardy, brawny, powerful, vigorous, rugged, hefty, ablebodied, hale, mighty, beefy, husky. **2.** valiant, bold, heroic, intrepid, courageous, stouthearted, lionhearted, indomitable, gallant, brave, valorous, manly, strong-willed, unflinching, spunky, plucky, staunch, gritty. **3.** unwavering, steadfast, staunch, stable, firm, unshakable, resolute, constant, unswerving, unflagging, unbending, intransigent, uncompromising, indomitable, unfaltering, unflinching, undeviating, persistent, unyielding, undaunted, unshrinking. —**Ant. 1** weak, feeble, frail, infirm, puny, unsteady, shaky. **2** cowardly, fearful, timorous, faint-hearted, weak. **3** faithless, weak, shaky, flagging, deviating, halfhearted, uncertain, fragile, feeble, frail.

stamina *n.* endurance, strength of constitution, vigor, sturdiness, hardiness, staying power, vitality, stoutness, ruggedness, pith, energy, perseverance.

stammer *v.* speak with breaks and pauses, speak hesitantly, falter, stutter, stumble; sputter, hem and haw, fumble, mumble, splutter.

stamp *v.* **1.** step on, stomp, thump, pound; crush, smash, trample. **2.** Usu. **stamp out** extinguish, put out, crush, put down, squelch, suppress. **3.** tramp, stomp, clump, trudge, stalk, stride, strut, march. **4.** print, mark, imprint, brand, impress, engrave, seal, inscribe, label. **5.** mark, characterize, brand, tag, identify; reveal, demonstrate, betray, exhibit, distinguish, manifest, display, expose, personify; stigmatize; typecast. —*n.* **6.** engraved block, seal, die, mold, matrix, mint, intaglio, signet, punch. **7.** mark, engraving, character, seal, brand, hallmark, imprint, identification, signature, official mark, trademark, authentication, emblem, label; ratification, endorsement, imprimatur, attestation, certificate, certification, voucher, validation, *Informal* OK. **8.** mark, characteristic; type, variety, character, sort, kind, nature, order, make, strain, genre, cast, breed, brand.

stampede *n.* **1.** frenzied rush, headlong flight, retreat, rout, sudden scattering, panic; chaos, pandemonium. **2.** race, rush, dash. —*v.* **3.** take flight, flee, beat a retreat, scatter, race, bolt, rush, panic, take to one's heels; crowd around, overrun, flood, inundate, engulf.

stand *v.* **1.** be upright, be erect, hold oneself erect, be on one's feet; rise, rise to one's feet, get up. **2.** put, place, be placed, set, set upright, be set upright, rear, raise, rest, put up, stick up, set on its feet, hoist, erect, mount. **3.** step, move, remove, take a position, shift, draw. **4.** support, uphold, defend a cause, argue, champion, be in favor of, declare oneself for, commend, sanction, speak well or highly of, plead for, endorse, countenance, honor, advocate. **5.** be present, be located, be situated, rest, remain, exist, have its seat, stay, continue, be permanent; persist, prevail, remain in force, remain valid, hold. **6.** endure, last, remain intact, abide, remain erect or whole, persist, sustain, survive, resist destruction, resist decay or change, prove good, hold, be indestructible, obtain, hold out, remain steadfast, remain firm, bear up, keep one's position, carry on; withstand, tolerate, take, suffer, endure, bear, submit to, undergo, brook, put up with, face, weather, stomach; stand one's ground, persevere, stand pat. **7.** be, rank, place. **8.** pay for, undertake, provide, finance; treat. —*n.* **9.** standing, wait without a seat; stance. **10.** defense, resistance, effort, hold. **11.** position, point of view, policy, opinion, viewpoint, sentiment, standpoint, stance, posture, disposition. **12.** booth, stall, counter, kiosk; tent, pavilion. —**Syn. Study. 6** See BEAR. —**Ant. 1** sit, lie, lay, recline. **6** collapse, succumb, falter, waver, yield, give way. **9** repose, sit, sitting. **10** retreat, collapse, withdrawal.

standard *n.* **1.** requirement, specification; criterion, guideline, principle; prototype, model, measure, gauge, yardstick, benchmark, touchstone, ideal, guide, canon. **2.** flag, pennant, banner, streamer, ensign, jack. **3.** pillar, support, stanchion, upright, post, column; leg, foot; base, foundation. —*adj.* **4.** normal, basic, usual, customary, universal, accepted, common, ordinary, typical, regular, stock. —**Syn. Study. 1** STANDARD, CRITERION refer to the basis for making a judgment. A STANDARD is an authoritative principle or rule that usu. implies a model or pattern for guidance, by comparison with which the quantity, excellence, correctness, etc., of other things may be determined: *She could serve as the standard of good breeding.* A CRITERION is a rule or principle used to judge the value, suitability, probability, etc., of something, without necessarily implying any comparison: *Wealth is no criterion of a person's worth.* —**Ant. 4** abnormal, exceptional, irregular, unusual.

stand-in *n.* substitute, sub, fill-in, surrogate, agent, proxy, deputy, alternate, pinch hitter, replacement, understudy, assistant, second, double, backup.

standing *n.* **1.** rank, order, position, place, footing, station, grade, status, importance, reputation. **2.** duration, length of existence, continuance, age, tenure, time, term, life. —*adj.* **3.** stand-up, vertical, upright, perpendicular, upended, erect. **4.** motionless, still, stationary, inactive, not flowing, inert, static, dormant, unstirring, stagnant, at rest, quiescent. **5.** fixed, continuing, immovable, permanent, perpetual, lasting, renewable. —**Ant. 3** sitting, reclining, recumbent, lying. **4** flowing, moving, running.

standoffish *adj.* unsociable, distant, cool, aloof, reserved, detached, withdrawn, remote, uncompanionable, unfriendly, reclusive, solitary, misanthropic, antisocial, uncommunicative, taciturn. —**Ant.** friendly, gregarious, affable, extroverted.

standstill *n.* stop, halt, cessation, pause, end, termination, full stop, impasse, dead stop, stalemate, discontinuance, abeyance, suspension, breakdown, hiatus, dead end, deadlock. —**Ant.** continuation, resumption, growth, progress.

staple *n.* **1.** basic item, feature, leader, fundamental component, article of merchandise, resource, commodity, raw material, product, vendible. —*adj.* **2.** chief, primary, basic, fundamental, main, essential, key, major, prime, necessary, vital, indispensable.

star *n.* **1.** sun; (*loosely*) heavenly body, celestial body, planet, satellite, asteroid, meteoroid, meteor, comet; constellation, galaxy, Milky Way, nebula. **2. stars** fortune, fate, destiny, predestination, the future, signs of the future, portents, omens; astrological chart. **3.** principal actor, principal, lead; hero, heroine, protagonist; well-known actor, popular entertainer, main attraction, headliner, drawing card, top draw, top banana, starlet; superior performer, superstar, All-American, great, giant, idol, immortal, god, goddess; (*variously*) prima donna, diva, prima ballerina, virtuoso, soloist; prominent figure, famous person, celebrity, name, luminary, eminence, notable, lion, mainstay, cynosure, VIP, bigwig. —*v.* **4.** present in a leading role, feature, showcase, be a vehicle for; play the lead, take the lead role, head the cast, top the bill. **5.** do well, excel, shine, succeed, gain approval, stand out, attract attention, be conspicuous.

stare *v.* **1.** gaze intently, fix one's gaze, look intently, gape, gawk, ogle, peep, *Slang* rubberneck; goggle; glare, lower, peer, eye, watch; glower. —*n.* **2.** glare, fixed look, long glance, glower, staring, gaze, gape, gaping, ogling; scrutiny, regard, inspection; once-over.

stark *adj.* **1.** downright, bare, utter, plain, sheer, simple, pure, bold, patent, obvious, flagrant, absolute, complete, unmistakable, glaring, unmitigated, outright, palpable, arrant, evident, blunt, staring, conspicuous, gross, total, out-and-out, unalloyed, veritable, consummate. **2.** bare, severe, naked, plain, unadorned, barren, chaste, austere, empty; cold, forsaken, harsh, grim, bleak, desolate, abandoned, deserted, vacant, forlorn. —*adv.* **3.** absolutely, fully, utterly, wholly, quite, downright, completely, altogether, entirely, clean, plain, out-and-out, plumb, to the nth degree, through and through. —**Ant. 2** fancy, adorned, embellished; gay, bright; cozy, warm, inviting; cultivated.

start *v.* **1.** commence, get going, begin to move, make off, set out, leave, set off, take off, venture out, sally forth, hit the trail, depart, set sail, push off, embark. **2.** set in operation, put in motion, set going, set in action; touch off, ignite, kindle, propel. **3.** begin, commence, undertake, set about, embark on, enter upon, venture on, break ground, put in execution, take the first step, fall to, initiate, take up, plunge into, broach, turn one's hand to, make a beginning, buckle down. **4.** initiate, be initiated, originate, be originated, institute, found, be founded, establish, launch, set up, organize, set moving, begin, inaugurate, create, give birth to, form, give rise to, introduce, lay the foundation of, touch off, usher in, fabricate, bring about, forge, propagate, engender, generate, beget, father, be the cause of. **5.** spring, move suddenly, bound, jump, rise suddenly, burst forth, leap; rush, issue suddenly, spurt, gush, erupt, break forth, issue, shoot, emerge; pop out. **6.** flush, rouse, disturb, scatter; eject, displace, turn out, evict. **7.** jump, twitch, jerk involuntarily, recoil, wince, blink, blench, shy, flinch. —*n.* **8.** beginning, outset, commencement, first step, opening, onset, setting in motion; inauguration, inception, birth, creation, origin, genesis, dawn, initiation. **9.** jump, spasm, jolt, jerk, wince, twitch, turn. **10.** lead, advantage, head start, inside track, edge, advance, odds, drop, jump, priority, leg up. **11.** opening, chance, introduction, opportunity; support, aid, assistance, backing, advocacy. **—Syn. Study. 3** See BEGIN. **—Ant. 1** delay. **2** stall, turn off. **3, 4** end, finish, terminate, stop, cease. **8** end, finish, finale, termination; windup. **10** disadvantage, handicap.

startle *v.* frighten, surprise, shock, disturb suddenly, cause to start, cause to jump, scare, alarm, unnerve, disquiet, disconcert, shake, faze, perturb, intimidate, discompose, upset, give a turn, jar, unsettle, take off one's guard. **—Ant.** calm, soothe, reassure, compose, settle.

starve *v.* **1.** perish from hunger, die from hunger; go hungry, suffer from lack of food, famish, hunger, fast. **2.** cut off from food, weaken by lack of food, undernourish, underfeed; force by underfeeding. **3.** hunger, yearn, long, be hungry, pine, crave, desire earnestly, thirst, lust, burn, languish, gasp, yen, raven, aspire; deprive, make eager, make desperate, deny, refuse, cut off. **—Ant. 1** glut, overeat, gorge. **2** feed, overfeed, surfeit, glut.

state *n.* **1.** condition, position, constitution, form, mode, guise, shape, stage, phase, structure, aspect; circumstances, status, situation, posture; predicament, plight, pass. **2.** high style, luxury, comfort; pomp, full dress, ceremony, ritual, formality. **3.** condition, attitude, mind, frame of mind, mood, state of mind, spirits, morale. **4.** nation, republic, commonwealth, country, monarchy, dominion, kingdom, realm, land, principality; body politic, people, government. —*adj.* **5.** ceremonial, official, governmental. —*v.* **6.** declare, express, propound, recite, recount, narrate, set forth, offer, present, put, explain; report, relate, describe, expound, elucidate. **—Ant. 6** repudiate, deny, contradict, refute; disclaim.

stately *adj.* **1.** impressive, majestic, awesome, imposing, grand, regal, glorious, lofty, lordly, proud, magnificent, august, noble, royal, imperial. **2.** formal, ceremonial, dignified, eminent, elegant, grandiose. **—Ant. 1** unimpressive, humble, modest, poor. **2** ordinary, common.

statement *n.* **1.** utterance, avowal, pronouncement, speech, assertion, declaration, allegation, profession, claim, explanation, testimony, mention, comment, remark, observation, sentence. **2.** report, record, account, announcement, specification, delineation; relation, exposition, recitation, recital; bill, invoice, account, tally, check, charge, reckoning, tab; balance sheet, count, accounting, valuation; communiqué, manifesto.

statesman *n.* **—Syn. Study.** See POLITICIAN.

static *adj.* **1.** inactive, motionless, stagnant, unmoving, inert, still, suspended, immobile, stationary, fixed, changeless, unchanging. —*n.* **2.** crackling, interference. **—Ant. 1** moving, mobile, dynamic, kinetic; lively, spirited, vigorous, brisk, active.

station *n.* **1.** assigned place, position, post, location, placement, emplacement, spot, site. **2.** terminal, terminus, depot, stop, whistle-stop. **3.** station house; (*variously*) headquarters, precinct station, guardhouse, firehouse. **4.** facility, dispensary. **5.** social standing, rank, position, status, place, footing, grade, condition, level, class, sphere, degree, importance, prestige, caste. —*v.* **6.** assign, post; locate, place, install, ensconce.

stationary *adj.* **1.** immovable, motionless, standing still, standing, immobile; fixed, riveted, firm, moored; inert, transfixed, stable, stock-still, dead-still. **2.** constant, unchanged, not changing, steady, stable, fixed, even, intact, undeviating, firm, uniform, unvarying, unchangeable, immutable. **—Ant. 1** moving, mobile. **2** varying, changing, unstable, volatile, irregular; changeable.

stature *n.* **1.** height, tallness, size. **2.** rank, standing, place, position, high station, eminence, prestige, distinction, regard, elevation, prominence, importance, reputation. **—Ant. 2** low rank, inferiority, lowliness.

status *n.* **1.** position, rank, grade, degree, caliber, standing, footing, condition, estimation, station, caste, class, place; eminence, distinction, prestige, social superiority. **2.** situation, state, condition.

staunch Also **stanch** *adj.* **1.** firm, steadfast, true, steady, constant, zealous, strong, stout, solid, loyal, faithful, resolute, stalwart. **2.** substantial, solid, sturdy, stout, rugged, well-built, well-constructed, sound. **3.** watertight, sound. *—v.* **4.** stop the flow of, check, dam, hold back, obstruct, stem, impede, contain. **—Ant. 1** inconstant, unfaithful, fickle, capricious, lukewarm. **2** weak, shoddy, jerry-built, flimsy. **3** leaky.

stay[1] *v.* **1.** remain, tarry, visit, hang around, linger. **2.** remain, reside, dwell, abide, sojourn, take up quarters, lodge, room, bunk, live. **3.** keep oneself, endure, continue to be, remain, go on being. **4.** remain, continue, persist, persevere, hold out, carry on, stick; last out, see through. **5.** restrain, hold back, suppress, rein in, postpone, withhold, curb, check, keep in, stifle, quell. **6.** block, foil, frustrate, thwart, ward off, stem. *—n.* **7.** sojourn, stop, stopover, temporary residence, halt, visit, vacation, holiday. **8.** postponement, suspension, delay, deferment, abeyance; reprieve. **—Ant. 1** leave, go, depart. **4** quit, give up, succumb. **5** loose, free, release, express. **6** fall to; surrender to.

stay[2] *n.* support; (*variously*) brace, prop, buttress, reinforcement, stanchion, standard, rest, rod, pole, guy, splint, shore, aim, rib, mainstay, block.

steadfast *adj.* **1.** steady, fixed, undeviating, direct; unwavering, attentive, undistracted, unflinching, rapt, intent, keen, persevering, unfaltering, unflagging. **2.** resolute, indomitable, undaunted, staunch; intransigent, obstinate, tenacious, inflexible, unyielding, uncompromising; unchangeable, unchanging, unalterable, deep-rooted, deep-seated, single-minded. **—Syn. Study. 1, 2** STEADFAST, STEADY, STAUNCH imply a sureness and continuousness that may be depended upon. STEADFAST literally means fixed in place, but is chiefly used figuratively to indicate undeviating constancy or resolution: *steadfast in one's faith.* Literally, STEADY is applied to that which is relatively firm in position or continuous in movement or duration: *a steady flow;* figuratively, it implies sober regularity or persistence: *a steady worker.* STAUNCH literally means watertight, as of a vessel, and therefore strong and firm; figuratively, it is used of loyal support that will endure strain: *a staunch advocate of free trade.* **—Ant. 1** deviating, wavering, flagging, faltering; fragile, unstable. **2** unreliable, irresolute, wavering, vacillating, capricious, half-hearted, changeable, fickle.

steady *adj.* **1.** stable, firm, substantial, immovable. **2.** constant, unremitting, continuous, continuing, persistent, incessant, unending, unceasing, ceaseless; regular, even. **3.** habitual, constant, frequent, regular, faithful, devoted, confirmed. **4.** steadfast, constant, undeviating, unwavering, firm, resolute, staunch, untiring, unfaltering, unflagging, persevering, tenacious, dedicated, devoted, unremitting, resolute, single-minded. **5.** reliable, dependable, careful, serious, sober, deliberate, conscientious, methodical, stable; levelheaded, coolheaded, sure. *—v.* **6.** stabilize, balance, hold fast, secure. **—Syn. Study. 4** See STEADFAST. **—Ant. 1** unsteady, shaky, unstable, insecure. **2** sporadic, intermittent, uneven, irregular, syncopated, broken, varying. **3** infrequent, irregular, rare, sporadic, sometime. **4** irregular; on-again, off-again, erratic; undependable, unreliable; ambivalent, of two minds, vacillating, irresolute, faltering, uncertain. **5** unsteady, unreliable, careless, frivolous; unsteady, shaky. **6** shake, rock, tip, tilt.

steal *v.* **1.** take, burglarize, purloin, filch, pilfer, lift, snatch; make off with, abscond with, swindle, embezzle, extort, usurp, misappropriate; defraud; thieve, copy, crib, plagiarize; abstract, borrow, appropriate, imitate, help oneself to; pocket, *Slang* rip off, liberate, pinch, snitch, swipe, cop. **2.** take secretly, sneak. **3.** slip, slide, sneak, creep, pass stealthily, slink, skulk, pass unobserved. **4.** slip, pass gradually, creep, slide, drift, elapse, escape, glide, happen gently, diffuse, flow, filter, flit.

stealth *n.* covertness, secrecy, clandestine procedure, secretiveness, furtiveness, sneakiness, stealthiness, slyness, subterfuge, surreptitiousness, unobtrusiveness. **—Ant.** openness, candidness.

stealthy *adj.* surreptitious, covert, underhand, underhanded, sneaky, shady, furtive, sly, sneaking, clandestine, devious, secretive, hugger-mugger, slippery, shifty. **—Ant.** open, aboveboard, direct, obvious, forthright.

steel *n.* **1.** tempered iron, steel articles. **2.** blade, bayonet, sword, knife, saber, foil, cutlass, dagger, dirk, rapier, machete, scimitar, falchion, broadsword. *—v.* **3.** brace, fortify, gird, nerve.

steep[1] *adj.* close to vertical, sheer, precipitous, abrupt, sharp. **—Ant.** flat, gentle, gradual.

steep[2] *v.* **1.** soak, be soaked, immerse,

be immersed, saturate, brew, souse, impregnate, suffuse, marinate. **2.** immerse, plunge, bury, saturate, engulf, drench, imbue, submerge, infuse, fill, pervade. **—Ant. 1** drain.

steer *v.* **1.** sail, navigate, direct, guide, pilot, run, conduct, govern, supervise, manage, lead, head, coach. **2.** proceed, head, sail, make, lay, lay a course, take a course, aim, bear, run, be bound, make a beeline.

stem[1] *n.* **1.** main stalk; (*variously*) trunk, spear, shoot, cane, stalk, leafstalk, stock, spire, peduncle, pedicel, petiole, tendril. **2.** shank. **—*v.* 3.** come, derive, issue, result, proceed, arise, rise, originate, spring, ensue, grow.

stem[2] *v.* stop, hold back, curb, stay, restrain, check, quell, arrest, prevent, impede, obstruct, dam, withstand, oppose, hold one's own against, resist, stanch, thwart, stall, halt, block, surmount, hinder, bring to a standstill, buck, retard, deter, counter. **—Ant.** further, promote, encourage, stimulate, incite, excite, unleash.

stench *n.* stink, bad smell, offensive odor, fetidness, fetor, reek. **—Syn. Study.** See ODOR. **—Ant.** fragrance, aroma, perfume, redolence.

step *n.* **1.** footstep, pace, stride, gait; (*variously*) strut, hobble, shuffle, shamble, swagger, clip. **2.** footfall, tread, stepping sound. **3.** footprint, track. **4.** stage, phase, move, process, measure, maneuver, proceeding, act, action, procedure. **5.** grade level, stage, rank, rung, degree, point, gradation, notch, period, span, remove. **6.** stair, foothold, tread, riser, rung, footing, purchase. **—*v.* 7.** move, walk, pace, tread, stride. **8.** tread, tramp, trample.

stereotype *n.* **1.** conventional image, received idea, popular preconception, cliché, formula. **—*v.* 2.** pigeonhole, typecast, type, categorize, crudely identify.

sterile *adj.* **1.** sterilized, disinfected, free from germs, pure, uncontaminated, sanitary, uninfected, aseptic, antiseptic. **2.** barren, infertile, childless; unfruitful, infecund, fallow, bare, empty. **3.** unproductive, unprofitable, worthless, fruitless, ineffective, profitless, unrewarding, ineffectual, bootless, impotent, abortive, futile, vain, useless, unavailing. **—Ant. 1** unsterile, infected, germ-ridden, unsanitary. **2** fertile, prolific, productive; fecund, fruitful. **3** productive, profitable, fruitful, effective.

sterling *adj.* noble, high-principled, estimable, meritorious, honorable, worthy, true, superb, admirable, superior, first-rate, invaluable, superlative; genuine, pure, perfect, flawless. **—Ant.** inferior, shoddy, shabby, tacky.

stern *adj.* **1.** severe, strict, hard, unfeeling, unreasonable, despotic, ironhanded, ironfisted, unmerciful, stringent, cruel, tyrannical, sharp, pitiless, harsh, coercive, cold-blooded, ruthless, austere, grim, brutal, ungentle, rigorous. **2.** grim, austere, forbidding, hard, unkind, severe, serious, somber, gloomy, cold, unapproachable, unsympathetic, sharp, rigid, grave, implacable, harsh, stiff, frowning, reproachful, reproving, admonishing. **—Syn. Study. 1, 2** STERN, SEVERE, HARSH mean strict or firm and can be applied to methods, aspects, manners, or facial expressions. STERN implies uncompromising, inflexible firmness, and sometimes a forbidding aspect or nature: *a stern parent.* SEVERE implies strictness, lack of sympathy, and a tendency to discipline others: *a severe judge.* HARSH suggests a great severity and roughness, and cruel, unfeeling treatment of others: *a harsh critic.* **—Ant. 1** permissive, soft, lenient, flexible, gentle, benign, merciful, kind. **2** friendly, approachable, kind, smiling, amused, relaxed, warm, sympathetic.

stew *v.* **1.** boil slowly, cook in water, simmer, seethe, steep. **2.** become irritated, get angry; fuss, fume, chafe, worry, agonize, fret, seethe, simmer, boil; grumble, gripe, grouse. **—*n.* 3.** stewed food, ragout; mixture, miscellany. **4.** state of worry, mental agitation, fuss, fret, flutter, tizzy, fluster. **—Syn. Study. 2** See BOIL.

steward *n.* **1.** manager, financial manager, administrator, supervisor; overseer, bailiff, agent, factor, executor, trustee, deputy, comptroller, controller, representative, proxy. **2.** (*variously*) ship's attendant, airplane attendant, (*fem.*) stewardess; waiter.

stick[1] *n.* **1.** branch, switch, twig, fagot. **2.** cane, staff; baton, swagger stick, wand, rod; bat, club, cudgel, shillelagh, billy, truncheon, bludgeon; cue; pole, shaft, stave, stake, bar, skewer; scepter, staff, caduceus, crosier.

stick[2] *v.* **1.** puncture, pierce, stab, jab, prick, poke, pink, spear, spike, perforate, punch. **2.** jab, thrust, dig, poke, insert, punch. **3.** fix, put, place, set, plant, fasten, tack, pin, affix, nail, attach. **4.** join; (*variously*) glue, fasten, paste, seal, adhere, cement, fuse, attach, affix, pin, staple, weld, bind; cohere. **5.** lodge, become fastened, catch, snag, be embedded. **6.** stall, mire, be unable to proceed, be tangled, hinder, check, block, immobilize, bind, trammel, hold, obstruct, curb, snarl, impede, hog-tie, constrain, shackle, scotch, thwart, hamper, balk, detain, inhibit, bar, back up, checkmate, stop. **7.** be true, keep steadily at, hold, be faithful, be constant. **8.**

endure, abide, stand, bear up under, last, continue, not give up on, carry on. **9.** stymie, balk, stump, bewilder, boggle, puzzle, perplex, confuse. **10.** impose on, leave, burden, make responsible, victimize. **—Syn. Study. 4** STICK, ADHERE, COHERE mean to be fastened or attached to something. STICK is the general term; it means to be fastened with glue, pins, nails, etc.: *A gummed label will stick to a package.* Used figuratively, STICK means to hold faithfully or keep steadily to something: *to stick to a promise.* ADHERE is a more formal term meaning to cling or to stay firmly attached: *Wallpaper will not adhere to a rough surface.* Used figuratively, ADHERE means to be attached as a follower: *to adhere to religious beliefs.* COHERE means to hold fast to something similar to itself: *The particles of sealing wax cohered into a ball.* Used figuratively, COHERE means to be logically connected or attached: *The pieces of evidence did not cohere.* **—Ant. 3** remove, dislodge, unfasten, untack, unpin, unscrew. **4** separate, detach, disengage. **6** release, free, unblock, untangle, unfasten. **10** relieve, free.

stickler *n.* **1.** purist, fanatic, martinet; devotee, enthusiast, *Slang* nut, bug, crank; monomaniac, zealot. **2.** knotty point, tough proposition, mystery, enigma, hard nut to crack, poser, riddle, puzzle, dilemma, Gordian knot, *Informal* stumper. **—Ant. 2** cinch.

sticky *adj.* **1.** gummy, sticking, adhesive, tenacious, adherent, gluey, tacky, viscid, viscous, clinging, clingy, pasty, gooey, glutinous, cohesive, gelatinous, mucilaginous. **2.** clammy, humid, muggy, sultry, damp, moist, wet, steamy, dank. **—Ant. 1** slick, slippery. **2** dry, crisp.

stiff *adj.* **1.** starchy, rigid, crisp, inelastic. **2.** unyielding, tight, resistant, hard to move; unlimber, inflexible, tense, taut, rigid. **3.** vigorous, strong, intense, forceful, pounding, persistent, gusty, powerful, raging, violent, keen, brisk, smart, spanking. **4.** stubborn, tenacious, firm, steadfast, decided, determined, strong, indomitable, fixed, staunch, unfaltering, unflinching, iron, steely, steeled, dogged, steady, unswerving, grim, obstinate, persistent, strong-willed, uncompromising, stern, constant, settled, resolute, resolved, intense; valiant, brave, unshaken, courageous. **5.** cold, austere, formal, precise, stately, aloof, ceremonious, prim, wooden, stilted, starchy, cool, chilly, constrained, strait-laced, distant, *Slang* uptight. **6.** wooden, graceless, awkward, uneasy, forced, clumsy, stilted, ungainly, inelegant, labored, cold, unnatural, affected, mannered, artificial. **7.** difficult, exacting, laborious, heavy, tough, hard, stringent, rigorous, formidable. **8.** steep, high, excessive, heavy, exorbitant, undue, inordinate, immoderate, unwarranted, extravagant. **9.** harsh, stern, severe, stringent, cruel, sharp, brutal, drastic, violent, fearful, austere, unreasonable, sore, awful, bitter, uncompromising, extreme, merciless, draconian, pitiless, ruthless, grievous. **10.** thick, firm, solid, solidified, heavy, dense, viscid, viscous, jellied, gelatinous, clotted. **—Ant. 1** soft, loose, yielding, bendable, supple, flexible, pliant, pliable, elastic, malleable. **2** supple, loose, limber, relaxed. **3** gentle, easy, soft. **4** halfhearted, undecided, faltering, irresolute, shaky. **5** casual, informal, cozy, relaxed, unceremonious, warm. **6** smooth, graceful, easy, unforced, natural, unaffected. **7** easy, soft, cushy, cinchy. **8** easy, simple, soft, moderate. **9** mild, moderate, permissive, soft, sparing, merciful. **10** thin, soft, mushy, liquid.

stiff-necked *adj.* stubborn, obstinate, mulish, intractable, intransigent, pigheaded, willful, unyielding, pertinacious, refractory, bullheaded, obdurate, unbending, contrary, self-willed, unshakable. **—Ant.** indecisive, vacillating; reasonable, flexible.

stifle *v.* **1.** asphyxiate, smother, choke, suffocate, strangle, throttle, garrote; gasp for air, swelter, gag. **2.** suppress, repress, curb, subdue, restrain, keep back, smother, muffle, squelch, check, inhibit. **—Ant. 2** release, express; encourage, further, foster.

stigma *n.* disgrace, shame, odium, dishonor; blot, blemish, brand, flaw, mark of shame, smirch, smudge, besmirchment, taint, tarnish. **—Ant.** glory, honor, distinction, credit, approval.

still *adj.* **1.** motionless, without movement, inert, stationary, at rest, unstirring, unmoving, immobile. **2.** silent, hushed, quiet, noiseless, soundless. *—v.* **3.** calm, quiet; hush, silence, turn off. **4.** restrain, overcome, repress, suppress. **5.** assuage, appease, gratify, pacify. **6.** put an end to, restore to order, put down, settle. **—Ant. 1** active, moving, disturbed, agitated, restless, turbulent. **2** noisy, loud.

stilted *adj.* stiff, wooden, awkward, graceless, labored, unnatural, pompous, starched, starchy, stuffy, cold, mannered, studied, ceremonious, formal, rigid, prim, priggish, forced, artificial, constrained, *Slang* uptight. **—Ant.** relaxed, easy, graceful, informal, spontaneous, natural, unforced.

stimulant *n.* energizer, tonic, bracer, excitant, *Slang* upper. **—Ant.** anesthetic, narcotic, depressant, tranquilizer, *Slang* downer.

stimulate *v.* incite, arouse, excite, awaken, enkindle, fan, rouse, spur, actuate, prompt, stir, alert, animate, quicken, activate, initiate, wake, inflame, vivify, inspire, inspirit, sharpen. **—Ant.** deaden; discourage, dull; calm, soothe, assuage.

stimulus *n.* **1.** (*loosely*) stimulant, tonic, bracer, activator, energizer, excitant. **2.** incentive, spur, incitement, inducement, goad, impetus, provocation, encouragement, fillip, quickener, motive, whet. **—Ant. 1** repressant, depressant, suppressant. **2** discouragement, damper, deadener, obstacle, handicap.

sting *v.* **1.** prick, wound, stab, pierce, nettle, penetrate. **2.** burn, pain sharply, chafe, hurt, cause to wince, irritate, prick, wound; anger, rack, pique, rasp, agonize, grate, offend, disturb, insult, provoke, inflame, rile, grip, gnaw, vex, nettle, incense, madden, torment, harrow, torture, infuriate, gall. **3.** burn, feel sharp pain, smart, prick, wince, itch, twinge, tingle. **4.** impel, incite, provoke, irritate, goad, prod, kindle, fire, excite, stir up, nettle, whip, egg on, shake, arouse, instigate, spur, actuate, quicken, lash, awaken, propel, motivate, pierce, prompt, move. **—*n.* 5.** stinging organ, prick, stinger, barb. **6.** bite, wound, sore, burn, pinch, nip; pain, hurt, tingle, prickle, irritation. **7.** wound, pain, hurt, ache, blow, affliction, bite, irritation, gall, scourge, rub, venom, cut, vexation, bitter pill, bitter cup, bitter draft, cross, shock. **—Ant. 2** soothe, caress; mollify, assuage, calm. **4** delay, hinder, obstruct, halt, thwart, deaden, paralyze. **7** balm, caress.

stingy *adj.* **1.** parsimonious, miserly, tight, tight-fisted, close, penurious, close-fisted, niggardly, ungenerous, penny-pinching, mean, sparing, illiberal, cheap, near, stinting, cheeseparing. **2.** meager, slender, scanty, scant, sparse, lean, scrimpy, skimpy, small, modest, insufficient, thin, paltry, piddling, niggardly, inadequate. **—Syn. Study. 1** STINGY, PARSIMONIOUS, MISERLY mean reluctant to part with money, possessions, or other things. STINGY means unwilling to give, share, or spend anything of value: *a stingy employer; an expert stingy with advice.* PARSIMONIOUS describes a stinginess arising from excessive frugality or unwillingness to spend money: *a parsimonious family.* MISERLY implies a pathological pleasure in acquiring and hoarding money: *a miserly neighbor.* **—Ant. 1** generous, liberal, open-handed, bountiful, munificent; prodigal, extravagant, lavish, charitable. **2** large, lavish, huge, handsome, profuse, ample, abundant, bountiful.

stink *v.* **1.** reek, emit a bad odor, smell to high heaven, be malodorous, offend the nostrils, give a bad odor. **2.** *Slang* be rotten, be boring, be worthless, be no good. **—*n.* 3.** stench, bad smell, unpleasant odor, reek, fetor. **—Ant. 3** perfume, aroma, fragrance, sweetness, redolence.

stint *v.* **1.** restrict, set limits to, give in small amounts, limit, cut down on, reduce, be sparing with, restrain, constrain, circumscribe, check, curb. **2.** be sparing, hold back, scrimp, be frugal, save, deny oneself, economize, pinch pennies, withhold, be parsimonious. **—*n.* 3.** job, chore, task, duty, work period, term, assignment, part, turn, shift, quota; engagement.

stipend *n.* income, allowance, fixed pay, salary, compensation, wages, pension, emolument, remuneration, recompense; grant, scholarship.

stipulate *v.* specify, set forth, insist upon, state, designate, indicate, name, cite, make a point of, make provision; promise, pledge, guarantee, insure, grant, provide, allow, assure, agree, warrant.

stir *v.* **1.** move, rustle, shake, shiver, twitch, flutter, quiver. **2.** move, mix, scramble, agitate, beat, whip, set in motion, commix, blend, mingle, intermix, commingle. **3.** act, move; (*variously*) exert oneself, make an effort, bestir oneself, hustle, get moving, get a move on, scramble, bustle, be active, step lively, rush, scamper, hasten. **4.** rouse, arouse, inspire, excite, animate, awaken, inspirit, energize, electrify, kindle, quicken, vivify, work up, stimulate, fire, enflame, jolt, goad, provoke, start, spur, prod. **—*n.* 5.** stirring, moving, movement, rustle, rustling, sough. **6.** stirring, mixing, prodding, agitation, mingling. **7.** commotion, tumult, flurry, pother, uproar, to-do. **—Ant. 3** relax, settle down. **4** calm, pacify; lull, deaden. **5** stillness, immobility, quiet, silence.

stitch *n.* **1.** loop of thread; suture. **2.** bit of clothing, piece, garment, particle, shred, article, scrap. **3.** bit, slightest amount, particle, shred, scrap, jot, iota. **4.** pain, kink, pang, crick, twinge, twitch, tingle, ache, shoot; cramp, charley horse. **—*v.* 5.** sew, fasten with thread, mend, baste, seam, tack; embroider; suture.

stock *n.* **1.** supply, store, inventory, array, quantity, selection, assortment; cache, accumulation, stockpile, fund, reserve, hoard, provision, reservoir; wares, merchandise, goods. **2.** ownership, shares, capital, capital shares; investment. **3.** livestock, cattle, domestic animals, herd. **4.** descent, lineage, ancestry, strain, line, breed, parentage, family, heredity, birth, root, extraction, blood, race, house, tribe, progeniture, nationality, pedigree, caste, people, genealogy, family tree, clan, dynasty, origin, source, forebears, background. **5.** breed, type, kind. **6.** handle, haft, grasp, shaft, butt, pull, hold. **7.** broth; bouillon. *—adj.* **8.** standard, basic, regular, staple. **9.** routine, standard, formal, form, pro forma. *—v.* **10.** supply, furnish, appoint, equip, store, provide, fit out, accoutre, provision. **11.** handle, keep in stock, offer. **—Ant. 10** empty, drain, deplete.

stocky *adj.* thickset, short and heavy, husky, solid, sturdy, stumpy, chunky, squat, blocky, stout, stubby, dumpy, pudgy. **—Ant.** slim, slender, lanky.

stodgy *adj.* **1.** dull, stuffy, humdrum, boring, uninteresting, tiresome, dreary, wearisome, tedious, monotonous, lifeless; flat, prosaic, pompous, lumbering, prolix, clumsy, laborious, pedantic. **2.** indigestible, starchy, heavy, thick, lumpy. **3.** old-fashioned, antiquated, dated, passé, narrow, inflexible; staid, serious, stuffy. **—Ant. 1** exciting, lively, sprightly, interesting, vital, vivacious, animated. **2** light, fluffy, airy. **3** new, modern, up-to-date, flexible, *Slang* with-it.

stoic *n.* **1.** fatalist, quietist; man of stone, man of iron. *—adj.* **2.** stoical, detached, philosophic, impassive, unruffled, unimpassioned, imperturbable, calm, tranquil, dispassionate. **—Ant. 2** uncontrolled, undisciplined, excitable, volatile, emotional, passionate, disturbed.

stoicism *n.* impassivity, imperturbability, tranquillity, fortitude, philosophical attitude, fatalism. **—Ant.** emotionalism, excitability, hysteria.

stolid *adj.* impassive, unemotional, apathetic, sluggish, lethargic, phlegmatic, dull, obtuse, lumpish, bovine, dense; insensitive. **—Ant.** excitable, emotional, passionate, energetic, lively, active, animated, acute.

stomach *n.* **1.** belly, abdomen, tummy; craw, crop, gizzard, maw; paunch, midsection, midriff, middle, *Slang* guts, pot, potbelly, breadbasket. **2.** hunger, appetite, taste, thirst, keenness, relish. **3.** liking, taste, appetite, disposition, keenness, desire, fancy, inclination, hunger, pleasure, affinity, leaning, attraction, proclivity, predilection, relish, partiality, mind, bent, temper, bias, sympathy, propensity, humor. *—v.* **4.** keep down, hold in the stomach, retain. **5.** stand, bear, swallow, put up with, take, endure, suffer, bear with, tolerate, countenance, brook, abide, submit to, resign oneself to, reconcile oneself to, let pass, close the eyes to, overlook, make allowance for, pass over, be patient with. **—Ant. 2** distaste, disrelish. **3** dislike, distaste, disinclination, abhorrence, aversion, displeasure. **4** regurgitate, vomit, throw up. **5** reject, condemn, discountenance.

stone *n.* **1.** rock, pebble. **2.** gem, precious stone, jewel, brilliant, birthstone, bijou, *Slang* rock. **3.** pit, kernel, seed, nut. *—v.* **4.** throw rocks at, pelt with stones.

stony *adj.* **1.** full of rocks, rocky, pebbly, bumpy, gravelly, craggy, jagged, uneven, coarse, rough, rugged. **2.** stonelike, rocklike, rocky; (*variously*) adamantine, flinty, ossified, concrete, lithoid, marble, granite, fossilized, petrified, crystallized. **3.** unfeeling, insensible, unsympathetic, cold, hard-hearted, coldhearted, merciless, austere, severe, soulless, unresponsive, icy, heartless, callous, obdurate, frigid, stern, stolid, passionless, unemotional, indifferent, flinty, hardened, blank, expressionless, coldblooded, stoical, unyielding, inexorable, pitiless, chill, forbidding, indurate, steely, deadened, untouched, unaffected, uncaring, *Informal* hard-boiled; bloodless. **—Ant. 1** smooth, even. **2** soft, flexible, yielding. **3** feeling, sensitive, sympathetic, warm, responsive, softhearted, tenderhearted, tender, compassionate, merciful, soft, mellow, kind, friendly.

stoop[1] *v.* **1.** bend down, lean over. **2.** slouch, slump, be round-shouldered, be bowed, be doubled over, lean forward. **3.** lower oneself, degrade oneself, sink, descend, fall, deign, bow, condescend, resort, succumb, bend, prostrate oneself; acquiesce, concede, yield, submit. *—n.* **4.** stooping posture, stooping carriage, slump, slouch, round-shoulderedness, bend, droop, sag. **—Ant. 1** stand erect. **3** rise, ascend. **4** straightness, erectness.

stoop[2] *n.* entrance staircase, entranceway, doorstep, steps; porch, small veranda.

stop *v.* **1.** halt, stay, stand fast, hold; discontinue, suspend, put an end to, cut short, bring to a standstill, postpone; arrest, check, suppress, block, stem, stall, interrupt the flow of, stanch, cut off; curb, rein in. **2.** restrain, hinder, hold back, prevent, bar, obstruct, preclude, deter, thwart, hamper, frustrate. **3.** plug, caulk, close, block, fill, stop up, fill the holes in, close up, occlude, stanch, seal. **4.** come to an end, cease, come to a halt, discontinue, conclude, finish, be over, desist, leave off, break off, terminate, run its course, run out, wind down, peter out, quit, hold, reach completion, come to a standstill, pause, intermit, lapse, pass away, draw to a close, expire, surcease; draw up, brake, stall, pull up, alight, become inactive, idle, falter, rest, stand; drop anchor. **5.** sojourn, stay, rest, dwell, lodge, stop over, put up, abide, take up quarters, visit, tarry, repose, suspend one's journey. —*n.* **6.** cessation, termination, halt, halting, stoppage, suspension, arrest, break, discontinuation, desistance, leaving off, pause, rest, respite, lapse, spell, interruption, intermission, abeyance, wait, interlude, recess, interval, hiatus, breathing spell; end, standstill, ban, curb, block, prohibition. **7.** visit, stay, stopover, sojourn, rest, respite, layover, pause. **8.** stop-off; depot, station, terminus, terminal; destination. **—Syn. Study. 1** STOP, HALT, ARREST, CHECK imply causing a cessation of movement or progress (literal or figurative). STOP is the general term for the idea: *to stop a clock.* To HALT means to make, or cause to make, a temporary stop, esp. as the result of a command: *to halt a company of soldiers.* ARREST usu. refers to stopping by imposing a sudden and complete restraint: *to arrest development.* CHECK implies bringing about an abrupt, partial, or temporary stop: *to check a trotting horse.* See also CHECK. **—Ant. 1** start, begin, commence, initiate, continue, set going, institute, originate, inaugurate. **2** speed, assist, expedite, facilitate, further, encourage, incite. **3** unplug, open, uncork, unseal. **4** start, begin, commence, continue, proceed, progress, advance. **6** start, commencement, beginning; resumption.

stopgap *adj.* provisional, makeshift, improvised, temporary, substitute, emergency, impromptu, stand-by, tentative, contrived; *Latin* pro tem, ad hoc. **—Ant.** permanent, well-established, unalterable.

stoppage *n.* blockage, obstruction, obstacle, barrier, stricture, impediment, hindrance, interruption, disruption, curtailment, tieup, gridlock, check, checkmate.

store *n.* **1.** shop, market, mart, supermarket, department store, anchor, emporium, superstore, establishment. **2.** supply, provision, stock, pile, stockpile, hoard, accumulation, inventory, stock in trade, reserve, wares, effects, fund, reservoir, quantity, cache. **3.** faith, confidence, regard, value, credit, trust, reliance, dependence, estimation, esteem. **4.** abundance, multitude, plethora, full measure, wealth, overflow, plenty, large quantity, legion, luxuriance, fund, richness, satiety, array, lot, volume, pack, host, profusion, copiousness, plenteousness, hoard, scores, riches, prodigality, multiplicity, exuberance, cornucopia. —*v.* **5.** save, stow away, keep, lay aside, put away, deposit, salt away, sock away, hoard, amass, stockpile, reserve, lay up or by, husband, lay in, accumulate, gather, hold, heap up, store up, cache, put in storage, put in mothballs, *Informal* stash. **—Ant. 3** disbelief, distrust, skepticism, doubt, suspicion. **4** paucity, lack, poverty, dearth, skimpiness. **5** waste, spend, squander.

storehouse *n.* repository, warehouse, depot, depository, store, magazine, arsenal; silo, elevator, granary; stockroom, storeroom; bank, treasury, vault.

storm *n.* **1.** torrent, deluge, rainstorm, cloudburst, downpour; snowstorm, blizzard; windstorm, tempest, gale, squall, blow, hurricane, typhoon, cyclone; tornado, twister. **2.** outburst, eruption, outbreak, burst, explosion, roar, tumult, disturbance, agitation, commotion, clamor, hubbub, turmoil, furor, flurry, uproar, row, stir, ruckus, upheaval, pother, to-do, ado, hullabaloo, brouhaha, fuss, tempest. **3.** sudden attack, violent assault, frontal attack, overwhelming onslaught. —*v.* **4.** rain heavily, snow heavily, blow violently. **5.** rage, rant, rave, lose one's temper, complain furiously, bluster, carry on, rampage, raise hell, vent one's rage, fly into a rage, snarl, raise the devil, fume, fulminate, *Slang* blow one's top, blow one's cool, fly off the handle. **6.** rush, stamp, stomp, rage, tear, tramp, stalk. **7.** charge, attack, assail, strike, rush, assault, make an onslaught, fall upon, besiege. **—Ant. 1** calm, fair weather. **2** calm, peace, hush, tranquillity. **5** whisper, reason, cajole. **6** amble, saunter.

stormy *adj.* rainy; snowy; windy; turbulent, rough, blustering, tempestuous, inclement, blustery, raging, violent, squally, roaring, rugged, howling, wild, foul. **—Ant.** mild, calm, fair.

story *n.* **1.** report, account, allegation, version, statement, word, testimony, tidings, article, news, information, dispatch, news item, piece. **2.** tale, narrative, romance, fable, yarn, sketch, allegory, anecdote, parable; plot, argument, legend. **3.** lie, white lie, falsehood, fib, fabrication, prevarication; excuse, alibi.

stout *adj.* **1.** fat, corpulent, large, thickset, portly, rotund, plump, obese, big, round, heavy, tubby, pudgy, fleshy, bulky, chubby, stocky. **2.** brave, stouthearted, courageous, heroic, dauntless, lionhearted, valorous, valiant, intrepid, bold, daring, unshrinking, unflinching, stalwart, gallant, resolute, indomitable, plucky, doughty, fearless, confident, *Informal* spunky; steadfast, determined, staunch, resolved, firm, faithful, unwavering, true, unfaltering, steady, constant, inflexible, untiring, unshakable, unswerving, enduring. **3.** sturdy, strapping, strong, husky, stalwart, hardy, robust, muscular, tough, vigorous, rugged, able-bodied, athletic, brawny, mighty, burly, fit, staunch, able, leathery, hefty, solid. **—Ant. 1** lean, lanky, spare, skinny, slim, slender, thin. **2** cowardly, timid, irresolute, fearful, shrinking, apprehensive. **3** weak, frail, delicate, puny, feeble, fragile, unfit, unsound, flimsy, jerry-built, unsubstantial.

stouthearted *adj.* brave, fearless, bold, heroic, valiant, courageous, dauntless, hardy, lionhearted, spirited, unflinching, intrepid, undaunted, resolute, unblenching; *Slang* spunky, gutsy. **—Ant.** timid, fearful, afraid, cowardly.

stow *v.* store, put, place, set, pack, ensconce, cache, tuck, stuff, squeeze, jam, load, cram, crowd, wedge, salt away, deposit, *Informal* stash.

straight *adj.* **1.** direct, unbent, unswerving, undeviating, not curved. **2.** square, even, adjusted, aligned. **3.** straightforward, honest, candid, forthright, true, truthful, reliable, veracious, square, frank, clear, aboveboard, accurate, four-square, right, sound, trustworthy. **4.** direct, unwavering, unswerving, undeviating. **5.** unbroken, solid, uninterrupted, continuous, successive, consecutive, incessant, sustained, ceaseless, persistent, unrelieved. **6.** orderly, tidy, in order, neat, shipshape; coordinated, sorted out, arranged, methodical. *—adv.* **7.** directly, immediately, instantly, forthwith; in a straight line, without wandering. **8.** straightly, erectly, upright; evenly, on a level, squarely. **—Ant. 1** curved, crooked, indirect, winding, bent, zigzag. **2** crooked, uneven, awry. **3** unreliable, confused, false, ambiguous, qualified, evasive, equivocal. **4** indirect, wavering, deviating, uncertain. **5** broken, interrupted, discontinuous, nonconsecutive. **6** messy, disorderly, untidy, mussed, disarranged, confused, disarrayed, in error. **7** eventually, later, afterward. **8** crookedly, unevenly, askew, awry.

straightforward *adj.* **1.** direct, straight. **2.** open, candid, frank, honest, guileless, plainspoken, blunt, aboveboard, direct, forthright; trustworthy, square, upright, honorable, straight, ethical, scrupulous, creditable. **—Ant. 1** indirect, roundabout, circuitous. **2** devious, sharp, guileful, unethical, deceitful, unscrupulous, shady.

strain[1] *v.* **1.** draw tight, stretch, put under tension, pull, tug, make tense or taut, tighten; stretch, elongate, protract, distend, extend. **2.** struggle, heave, exert one's strength, labor, toil, make a supreme effort, huff and puff. **3.** drive oneself, exert oneself, press, struggle, overwork, push to the utmost, work day and night, grind, overexert, tax, overtax, fatigue, wear out, exhaust, burden, overburden, drudge, burn the midnight oil, work one's fingers to the bone, work like a slave, work like a horse, burn the candle at both ends, overdo, do double duty; try hard, bear down, buckle down. **4.** pull, sprain, impair by stretching, injure, wrench, weaken, twist, hurt by overexertion. **5.** sieve, filter, screen, sift, winnow, purify, drain, refine. *—n.* **6.** stress, pressure, force, tension. **7.** effort, exertion, struggle. **8.** sprain, pull, injury, wrench, twist. **9.** tension, pressure, stress, hardship. **10.** tune, song, melody, air. **—Ant. 1** relax, loosen, slacken. **2** relax, yield. **3** idle; pamper, coddle. **7** effortlessness. **9** relaxation.

strain[2] *n.* **1.** parentage, ancestry, lineage, descent, stock, derivation, family, people, extraction, breed, heredity, line, species, blood. **2.** type, breed, variety, kind, sort, group. **3.** streak, hereditary character, vein, natural capacity, tendency, trait, predisposition, grain, genius, inclination, disposition.

strait *n.* **1.** narrow passage of water, narrows; channel. **2.** Often **straits** predicament, difficulty, plight, distress, embarrassment, extremity, fix, pickle, hole. **—Ant. 2** ease, comfort, luxury.

straitened *adj.* distressed, pinched, restricted, needy, hard-up, strapped, penniless, embarrassed, poverty-stricken, destitute, bankrupt, broke, impoverished, penurious, indigent, pauperized, wiped-out. **—Ant.** comfortable, well-off, affluent, flush.

straitlaced *adj.* puritanical, proper, strict, prudish, prim, rigid, overscrupulous, narrow; formal, reserved, inhibited, undemonstrative, stiff, austere, severe, *Slang* uptight. **—Ant.** loose, immoral; relaxed, uninhibited, broad-minded.

strand[1] *v.* **1.** run aground, go aground, beach, drive ashore, leave ashore, ground; shipwreck. **2.** leave, leave high and dry, leave in the lurch, maroon, desert. *—n.* **3.** shore, coast, seashore, beach, seacoast, bank, riverside.

strand[2] *n.* **1.** filament, fiber, thread; cord, rope, string, tress, lock, braid, twist; ingredient, component. **2.** string, necklace.

strange *adj.* **1.** peculiar, odd, unusual, queer, extraordinary, abnormal, curious, singular, uncommon, eccentric, irregular, outlandish, unnatural, unconventional, bizarre, unaccountable, freakish, erratic, out-of-the-way, unaccustomed, fantastic, aberrant, anomalous, farfetched. **2.** out of place, uncomfortable, ill at ease, uneasy, awkward, disoriented, estranged, lost, discomposed, bewildered, foreign, alien, alienated. **3.** unknown, unfamiliar, foreign, alien, unaccustomed, unexplored, undiscovered. **4.** unfamiliar, unaccustomed, unused, new; unhabituated. **—Ant. 1** regular, conventional, normal, commonplace, run-of-the-mill, usual, common, accustomed, ordinary. **2** at home, comfortable, at ease, easy. **3** known, familiar. **4** familiar, acquainted, experienced, used.

stranger *n.* **1.** unknown person. **2.** outsider, newcomer, alien, foreigner, auslander, immigrant, outlander. **—Syn. Study. 2** STRANGER, ALIEN, FOREIGNER all refer to someone regarded as outside of or distinct from a particular group. STRANGER may apply to one who does not belong to some group--social, professional, national, etc.--or it may apply to a person with whom one is not acquainted. ALIEN emphasizes a difference in political allegiance and citizenship from that of the country in which one is living. FOREIGNER emphasizes a difference in language, customs, and background. **—Ant. 1** friend, acquaintance, buddy, chum. **2** native, insider, resident, habitué.

strangle *v.* **1.** choke, suffocate, stifle, smother, asphyxiate, throttle, garrote; *British* burke. **2.** stop, suppress, repress, stifle, throttle, choke off, squelch, quell, put a stop to, check, crush, put down, snuff out, extinguish, muzzle, gag, smother. **—Ant. 2** assist, further, encourage, promote, forward, abet, aid, help.

strap *n.* **1.** fastening strip, thong, band, tie, cord, belt. *—v.* **2.** lash, tie, bind, truss, leash, tether. **3.** whip, thrash, beat, flog, belt, lash, flail, scourge.

strapping *adj.* robust, sturdy, strongly built, husky, stalwart, hardy, burly, muscular, brawny, powerful, stout, strong. **—Ant.** frail, weak, fragile, puny.

stratagem *n.* maneuver, scheme, plan, plot, trick, intrigue, ruse, artifice, tactic, trickery, device, contrivance, machination, game, deception, subterfuge, deceit, ploy, dodge, feint, blind, wile. **—Syn. Study.** See TRICK.

strategic *adj.* **1.** tactical, military; calculated; politic, diplomatic; planned, well thought-out, deliberate, clever, cunning, cautious, careful, guarded, prudent, precautionary, vigilant, wary. **2.** crucial, important, decisive, critical, vital, significant, momentous, key, principal, consequential, turning. **—Ant. 1** nonstrategic; unplanned. **2** unimportant, inconsequential, trifling.

strategy *n.* **1.** military plan, overall plan, grand design, scheme; tactics, maneuvering, devices, game, artifice, policy, machination, plotting. **2.** military science, war planning, war policy, art of war. **3.** artfulness, craft, cunning, craftiness, wiles, artifice, game plan, tactics.

straw *n.* **1.** stem of grain; hay, chaff. **2.** tube for sucking liquid; pipette.

stray *v.* **1.** go astray, roam, wander, drift, rove, straggle, lose one's way. **2.** wander, drift, digress. *—n.* **3.** homeless person or creature, waif, lost person, lost animal, itinerant, vagabond, wanderer, drifter, straggler. *—adj.* **4.** straying, lost, misplaced. **5.** scattered, set apart, separate, random.

streak *n.* **1.** long smear, line, stripe, strip, bar, band; (*loosely*) smudge, blotch, splotch, smirch, blur, daub, blot. **2.** layer, portion, vein, lode, bed, seam; level, stratum, plane. **3.** vein, cast, strain, touch. *—v.* **4.** race, speed, rush, hurtle; whiz, tear, zoom, dart, dash, fly. **—Ant. 4** creep, crawl, go at a snail's pace.

stream *n.* **1.** narrow river, streamlet, brook, creek, rivulet, rill, branch, run, watercourse, tributary, feeder, freshet. **2.** flow, torrent, run, course, rush, race, current, spout, sluice, river, gush, onrush, jet, flux, surge, deluge, flood, tide; effusion, spate, profusion. *—v.* **3.** flow, pour, run, issue, course, rush, surge, burst, spill, gush, spout, spurt, flood, fountain, shoot; move continuously, file, go on endlessly. **4.** teem, abound, flow, overflow. **5.** wave, float, flutter, blow, waft, stretch out, extend.

street *n.* road; (*variously*) thoroughfare, roadway, route, highway, turnpike, expressway, thruway, way, avenue, boulevard, lane, alley, mews, terrace; block.

strength *n.* **1.** power, vigor, might, muscles, hardiness, force, brawn, *Slang* beef; robustness, puissance, potency, sturdiness, stoutness, sinew, lustiness, stamina, endurance, viability, vitality, pith, backbone; firmness, fortitude, toughness, solidity, vitality, spirit; tenacity, pluck, grit, mettle, bravery, stoutheartedness, spice, *Slang* sand. **2.** force, number, size. **3.** potency, power, force, effectiveness, efficacy, kick, *Archaic* virtue. **4.** intensity, concentration, purity, vitality. **5.** source of power, support, security, anchor, mainstay, buttress, sustenance, succor; forte, strong point. **—Ant. 1** weakness, frailness, powerlessness, impotence, spiritlessness, feebleness. **3** ineffectiveness, inefficacy, unsoundness. **4** flatness, dilution, adulteration. **5** frailty, flaw.

strengthen *v.* make stronger, become stronger, give strength to, gain strength, grow stronger, reinforce; fortify, build up, buttress, support, brace, prop, shore up, sustain; harden, steel, restore, renew, enhance, improve. **—Ant.** weaken, debilitate, crush, enervate, destroy, devitalize.

strenuous *adj.* **1.** laborious, taxing, exhausting, physically demanding, arduous, difficult, punishing; intense, vigorous, hard, uphill. **2.** energetic, dynamic, vigorous, zealous, active, industrious, intense, earnest, ardent, eager, enterprising, animated, spirited, assiduous, sedulous, diligent, hardworking, dogged, on one's toes, painstaking, indefatigable, untiring. **—Ant. 1** easy, light, effortless. **2** lazy, indolent.

stress *n.* **1.** emphasis, importance, weight, consequence, significance, meaning, gravity, value, seriousness, prominence, worth, urgency, necessity, concern, consideration, moment. **2.** accent, accentuation, emphasis, beat. **3.** strain, tension, anxiety, force, burden, pressure, oppression. *—v.* **4.** emphasize, lay emphasis on, accentuate, accent, underscore, underline, mark, assert positively, insist upon, feature, repeat, affirm, assert. **5.** accent, emphasize, accentuate. **—Ant. 1** unimportance, insignificance, de-emphasis. **5** de-emphasize, underplay, understate; ignore, neglect, pass over.

stretch *v.* **1.** distend, extend, draw out, pull out, widen, lengthen, deepen, protract, expand, be expandable, elongate; strain, make tense or tight, draw tight, draw taut, put under tension, be elastic, be extendable, bear extension. **2.** extend, put forth, reach, reach out. **3.** lie over, cover, extend, reach, spread, span, traverse. **4.** lie at full length; sprawl. **5.** strain the body, draw out the muscles. **6.** exaggerate, strain, push to the limit, carry too far, push too far, run into the ground; overtax, overstrain, overwork, overburden, burden, overcharge, overtask, fatigue, tire, overexert. *—n.* **7.** spell, term, duration, period, interval, stint, while. **8.** expanse, spread, tract, distance. **9.** elasticity, elastic quality, resiliency, tautness, spring. **—Ant. 1** shrink, loosen, relax, slacken, tighten, tauten, contract, condense, compress, narrow, shorten. **2** withdraw, retract.

stricken *adj.* afflicted, smitten; (*variously*) ill, sick, taken sick, diseased, blighted, incapacitated, wounded, injured, hurt.

strict *adj.* **1.** stern, rigid, severe, authoritarian, rigorous, uncompromising, austere, stringent, unyielding, exacting, inflexible. **2.** perfect, absolute, complete, unerring, conscientious, fastidious, exact, meticulous, scrupulous, nice. **—Syn. Study. 1** STRICT, RIGID, RIGOROUS, STRINGENT imply inflexibility, severity, and an exacting quality. STRICT suggests close conformity to rules, requirements, obligations, or principles: *to maintain strict discipline.* RIGID suggests an inflexible, uncompromising, or unyielding nature or character: *a rigid parent.* RIGOROUS suggests that which is harsh or severe, esp. in action or application: *rigorous self-denial.* STRINGENT refers to something that is vigorously exacting, or absolutely binding: *stringent measures to suppress disorder.* **—Ant. 1** lax, lenient, indulgent, permissive; loose, flexible; broad, approximate. **2** loose, inattentive, careless.

stride *v.* **1.** march, walk with long steps, take long steps, stalk, lope, step. *—n.* **2.** pace, long step. **3.** gait, step. **4.** step, advance, advancement, progress, headway, improvement.

strident *adj.* grating, harsh, piercing, jangling, jarring, raucous, discordant, rasping, grinding, shrill, high-pitched, screeching, dissonant, clashing, cacophonous, twanging. **—Ant.** soft, mellow, dulcet, mellifluous, soothing.

strife *n.* conflict, discord, dissension, turmoil, upheaval, fighting, trouble, unrest, disharmony, contention, altercation, disturbance, disquiet, convulsion, struggle, violence, warfare. **—Ant.** peace, accord, calm, agreement, harmony.

strike *v.* **1.** hit, slug, deal a blow to, bang, box, cuff, slap, club, thump, smash, pound, knock, tap, clap, bump, beat, cudgel, clout, slam, bat, sock, punch, wallop, pommel, pelt, smite, whack, buffet, hammer, clip, drub, belt; thrash, flog, batter, lash, whip, whale, lambaste, scourge, flail, flagellate. **2.** attack, assail, hit, assault, charge. **3.** hit, dash against, meet head-on, run into, hurtle against, knock into, bump into, beat against, ram into, run or fall foul of, collide with. **4.** reach, fall upon, hit; burst upon. **5.** occur to, come to the mind of, dawn upon, reach. **6.** impress, affect, appear to, seem to. **7.** hit, come, arrive, run, light, chance, meet, stumble, find, encounter, come upon, come across, reach, unearth, discover. **8.** reach, achieve, make, effect, arrange. **9.** take down, pull down, put away, fold up, take apart. **10.** remove, cancel, eliminate, erase, eradicate, delete, wipe, cross out, scratch. **11.** sound, ring, chime, knell, toll. **12.** hit, afflict suddenly, assault, assail, affect severely, deal a blow to, devastate, smite. **13.** go on strike, walk out. *—n.* **14.** walkout, work stoppage, tie-up, labor dispute; protest, boycott. **—Syn. Study. 1** See BEAT.

striking *adj.* remarkable, noteworthy, noticeable, notable, conspicuous, prominent, marked, outstanding, impressive; astounding, extraordinary, surprising.

string *n.* **1.** cord, thread, twine, strand, line, binding. **2.** strand, rope, necklace. **3.** procession, file, parade; row, chain, train, succession, column, line, sequence, series, queue. —*v.* **4.** thread, put on a string. **5.** stretch, extend, spread.

stringent *adj.* **1.** strict, stiff, demanding, rigorous, exacting, compelling obedience, inflexible, rigid, unbending, uncompromising, unyielding, harsh, severe, stern. **2.** forceful, cogent, effectual, severe, rigorous. **3.** tight, close, sparing, spare, frugal. **—Syn. Study. 1** See STRICT. **—Ant. 1** flexible, loose; ineffective, relaxed. **2** ineffective, unconvincing, equivocal, unsound, inconclusive. **3** lavish, ample, generous.

strip[1] *v.* **1.** unclothe, undress, remove one's clothes, disrobe, divest of clothing, undrape; lay bare, unwrap, uncover, disencumber. **2.** remove, shave, peel, flay, flake, draw off, pull off, tear, lay bare, skin, denude. **3.** deprive, rob, divest. **4.** plunder, ravage, sack, rob, despoil, loot, ransack, desolate, spoliate, lay waste, raid, steal from, rifle. **—Ant. 1** dress, clothe; cover. **2** apply, put on. **3** invest, furnish.

strip[2] *n.* **1.** long narrow piece, length, slip, ribbon, band, stripe; measure. **2.** airstrip, field.

stripe *n.* **1.** band, streak, line, swath, strip, bar, striation. **2.** strip of material, tape, braid, ribbon; emblem of rank, insignia, chevron, bar.

strive *v.* **1.** struggle, try, try hard, attempt earnestly, exert oneself, apply oneself, make efforts, labor, do all one can, push, take pains, do one's utmost, strain; leave no stone unturned, do one's best, spare no pains, work like a Trojan, move heaven and earth, break one's back; essay, undertake, endeavor. **2.** fight, contend, vie, struggle, battle. **—Syn. Study. 1** See TRY. **—Ant. 1** take it easy, *Informal* goof off, *Slang* goldbrick.

stroke *n.* **1.** blow, punch, chop, whack, swat, sock, wallop. **2.** brush, massage, light touch, caress. **3.** striking, tolling, sounding, chime, ringing. **4.** paralytic stroke, brain hemorrhage, apoplectic fit, apoplexy, seizure. **5.** movement, flourish. **6.** hit, achievement, blow, feat, deed, transaction, coup; piece of luck, chance, fluke, coincidence, accident. —*v.* **7.** hit lightly, tap, punch, slap, bat, swat, poke. **8.** caress, pat, pet.

stroll *v.* **1.** walk slowly, amble, saunter, promenade, wander, dawdle along, ramble, meander, poke along, *Slang* mosey. —*n.* **2.** walk, amble, promenade, ramble, saunter, turn, tour, constitutional. **—Ant. 1** run, race, hurry, dash, scurry.

strong *adj.* **1.** powerful, having great strength, forceful, mighty, potent, puissant; muscular, sinewy, stalwart, stout, herculean, burly, hardy, brawny, robust, healthy, hearty, tough, athletic, vigorous, energetic; severe, intense, violent. **2.** able, competent, capable, skilled, well-qualified, well-endowed, proficient, advantageous. **3.** firm in spirit, resourceful, plucky, gritty, stalwart, stout, courageous, sturdy, sound, tough, tenacious, persistent, persevering; resilient, buoyant; tireless, indefatigable. **4.** convincing, compelling, forceful, powerful, moving, potent, effective, solid, sound, cogent. **5.** close, clear, distinct, definite, emphatic, unmistakable. **6.** bright, bold, vivid, intense, fiery. **7.** keen, fervent, intense, deep, deep-seated, zealous, ardent, vehement, earnest, impassioned, fervid, fierce, confirmed, assiduous, faithful, devoted, sedulous, diligent, high-spirited, animated, spirited. **8.** highly flavored, tangy, sharp, potent, concentrated, undiluted; highly seasoned, pungent, nippy, highly spiced, piquant, savory, tart, biting, hot. **—Ant. 1** weak, frail, feeble, powerless, soft. **2** unqualified. **3** passive, spiritless, submissive. **4** unconvincing, ineffectual, unsound; meek, mild, conciliatory. **5** slight, vague. **6** faint, dull, colorless. **7** shallow, spiritless, apathetic, lethargic, halfhearted, faint, wavering, insecure, unfaithful. **8** diluted, watery; faint, subtle; bland, tasteless, insipid; soothing, balmy; odorless.

stronghold *n.* **1.** fortified place, fortress, fortification, fort, bulwark, battlement, citadel, bastion, fastness, stockade, bunker, blockhouse, rampart, keep, safehold, hold, redoubt. **2.** center, refuge, home, locale; bulwark, bastion, citadel, rampart.

structure *n.* **1.** building, construction, edifice. **2.** arrangement, plan, form, makeup, organization, composition, interrelation of parts, configuration, conformation, formation, design, pattern. —*v.* **3.** put together, construct, organize, conceive, arrange, design, assemble.

struggle *v.* **1.** battle, fight, join issue, combat, contend, compete, vie, tussle, scuffle, skirmish, joust, tilt, brush, duel, engage, match, exchange blows, spar, cross swords, lock horns, brawl, jostle, grapple, scrap; clash, argue, oppose, resist, differ, feud, quarrel. **2.** strain, push, work hard, do all one can, exert oneself, labor, strive, take pains, endeavor, spare no pains, move heaven and earth, do one's utmost, leave no stone unturned, work like a Trojan. —*n.* **3.** fight, conflict, battle, combat, war, engagement, encounter, altercation, action, strife, contest. **4.** strain, grind, trial, labor, long haul, exertion, effort, push, pull, endeavor, stress. **—Ant. 1** surrender, give in, yield, succumb. **4** cinch, sure thing.

strut *v.* swagger, walk pompously, parade, sail, sashay, peacock, promenade. **—Syn. Study.** STRUT and SWAGGER refer esp. to carriage in walking. STRUT implies swelling pride or pompousness; it means to walk with a stiff, seemingly affected or self-conscious gait: *a turkey strutting about the barnyard.* SWAGGER implies a domineering, sometimes jaunty superiority or challenge and a self-important manner: *to swagger down the street.* **—Ant.** cringe, cower, slink, sneak.

stub *n.* **1.** stump, dock, butt, end, fag end, broken remnant, remains; tail. **2.** torn ticket, cancelled ticket, counterfoil; payment voucher, receipt. **—***v.* **3.** strike accidentally, scrape, bump, knock. **4.** snuff, crush, tamp out, extinguish.

stubborn *adj.* **1.** obstinate, unmovable, immovable, unyielding, obdurate, tenacious, opinionated, indomitable, unbending, intractable, perverse, refractory, recalcitrant, headstrong, self-willed, willful, uncompliant, inflexible, ungovernable, mulish, pigheaded, bullheaded, dogged. **2.** purposeful, persistent, resolute, sturdy, strong, forceful, concerted, wholehearted. **3.** hard to handle or manage; unshakable, tenacious, resistant. **—Syn. Study. 1, 2** STUBBORN, OBSTINATE, DOGGED, PERSISTENT imply fixity of purpose or condition and resistance to change. STUBBORN and OBSTINATE both imply resistance to advice, entreaty, protest, or force; but STUBBORN implies an innate characteristic and is the term usu. used when referring to inanimate things: *a stubborn child; a stubborn lock; an obstinate customer.* DOGGED implies willfulness and tenacity, esp. in the face of obstacles: *dogged determination.* PERSISTENT implies having staying or lasting qualities, resoluteness, and perseverance: *persistent questioning.* **—Ant. 1** pliable, adaptable, tractable, flexible; irresolute, yielding, docile, manageable; vacillating, wavering, undecided. **2** weak, feeble, frail, halfhearted. **3** manageable.

stubby *adj.* short and thick, stumpy, pudgy, squab, squat, squatty, dumpy, thickset, chubby, tubby, stodgy, stocky, chunky. **—Ant.** slim, lean, long, slender.

stuck-up *adj.* conceited, vain, arrogant, high-hat, snobbish, uppish, haughty, snooty, self-important, hoity-toity, uppity, swellheaded, egocentric, disdainful, bigheaded, self-satisfied, cocky, overbearing. **—Ant.** modest, humble, unassuming, unpretentious.

student *n.* **1.** pupil, learner, scholar, matriculant; collegian, undergraduate, schoolgirl, schoolboy, *Informal* coed; disciple, follower. **2.** observer, examiner, spectator, reviewer, watcher, interpreter, analyst, commentator, reader. **—Ant. 1** teacher, professor, mentor, instructor.

studied *adj.* calculated, deliberate, measured, purposeful, intentional, premeditated. **—Ant.** spontaneous, impulsive, unplanned, instinctive.

studious *adj.* **1.** devoted to study, scholarly, academic, intellectual, erudite, brainy, cerebral, bookish, scholastic; well-read, literate. **2.** earnest, diligent, painstaking, purposeful, laborious, determined, intent. **—Ant. 1** fun-loving, frivolous; unscholarly. **2** idle, indulgent, careless, inattentive, thoughtless, negligent, indifferent.

study *n.* **1.** pursuit of knowledge, learning, education, work at school, academic work, scholarship, instruction, mental cultivation, reading. **2.** investigation, inquiry, survey, research, examination, search, consideration, analysis, scrutiny, inspection, exploration, probe. **3.** library, studio, reading room, office, den. **—***v.* **4.** work at learning, educate oneself, school oneself, pursue knowledge, *Informal* cram, grind, read, hit the books. **5.** plunge into, read up on, delve into, investigate, examine, inquire into, explore, observe, probe, survey, search through, research; consider, reflect on, weigh, ponder. **6.** examine, read closely, look at carefully, pore over, survey, review, glance over, peruse, scrutinize. **—Syn. Study. 5** STUDY, CONSIDER, REFLECT, WEIGH imply fixing the mind upon something, generally doing so with a view to some decision or action. STUDY implies an attempt to obtain a grasp of something by methodical or exhaustive thought: *to study a problem.* CONSIDER implies fixing the mind on something and giving it close attention before making a decision or taking action: *to consider the alternatives.* REFLECT implies looking back quietly over past experience and giving it consideration: *to reflect on similar cases in the past.* WEIGH implies a deliberate and judicial estimate, as by a balance: *to weigh a decision.*

stuff *n.* **1.** raw material, material, staple; matter, substance, component, constituent, ingredient; essence, inmost substance, quintessence. **2.** things, effects, gear, belongings, possessions, paraphernalia, tackle. **3.** nonsense, stuff and nonsense, spinach, bunk, empty talk, humbug, balderdash, rubbish, foolishness, trash, bosh, hooey, hokum, hogwash, falderal, twaddle. **4.** best, utmost, darndest; thing, bit, tricks, act, performance. **—***v.* **5.** pile, fill, fill up, jam, cram, load, pack, wad, heap, burden. **6.** fill with stuffing, fill, pad. **7.** gorge, cram, overeat, feed gluttonously, gluttonize, overindulge, satiate, sate, make a pig of. **8.** load, pack, thrust, jam, cram, crowd, stash, cache, wedge, store, stow. **—Syn. Study. 1** See MATTER. **—Ant. 3** facts, truth. **5** empty, unpack. **8** take out, remove.

stuffing *n.* **1.** filling, padding, wadding, packing. **2.** dressing, filling, forcemeat, farce.

stuffy *adj.* **1.** close, unventilated, ill-ventilated, fusty, suffocating, stagnant, heavy, stifling, muggy, musty, sultry, sweltering, stale-smelling, oppressive, airless. **2.** congested, stopped-up, stuffed-up, clogged-up. **3.** smug, pompous, pretentious, high-flown, self-satisfied, supercilious, cold, reserved, straitlaced; stodgy, old-fogyish, staid. **—Ant. 1** airy, well-ventilated, cool. **2** unclogged. **3** natural, modest, unpretentious.

stultify *v.* vitiate, make useless, cripple, hamstring, impair, impede, nullify, frustrate, suppress, thwart, hinder, inhibit, balk. **—Ant.** arouse, encourage, spark, enliven, animate, spur, inspire.

stumble *v.* **1.** trip, stagger, pitch forward; fall, take a spill, sprawl, lurch, topple. **2.** stagger, reel, walk unsteadily, totter, sway, flounder, hobble, shamble, pitch, roll. **3.** blunder, slip up, make mistakes, falter; hash up, botch, mess up, bungle. **4.** happen, fall, blunder, hit, come by chance. *—n.* **5.** trip, stagger, misstep, spill, fall, topple, pitch.

stumbling block *n.* obstacle, obstruction, hindrance, barrier, hamper, impediment, hurdle, interference, snag, block, bar, difficulty, hitch, drawback, catch, rub. **—Ant.** aid, support, encouragement, assistance.

stump *n.* **1.** tree stump, stub. **2.** stub, nubbin, butt, end. **3.** tramping, stomping, footfall, clunk, thud. *—v.* **4.** mystify, baffle, dumbfound, perplex, foil, bewilder, confound, stymie, befog, confuse, nonplus, *Informal* bamboozle. **5.** stomp, stamp, tramp, thud, clonk, clump, clomp, walk heavily.

stun *v.* **1.** daze, stagger, stupefy, numb. **2.** shock, dumbfound, stupefy, startle, amaze, astonish, stagger, astound, flabbergast.

stunning *adj.* **1.** dazing, stupefying, numbing; dumbfounding, amazing, astounding, shocking, startling, flabbergasting, astonishing, staggering. **2.** striking, strikingly attractive, beautiful, lovely, exquisite, electrifying, to die for. **—Ant. 1** mild, harmless; expected, commonplace, ordinary. **2** plain, ordinary, run-of-the-mill, unimpressive, unremarkable.

stunt¹ *v.* check, curtail, dwarf, curb, impede, stint, limit, delimit, restrain, restrict, cramp, stifle, suppress, abort. **—Ant.** increase, stimulate.

stunt² *n.* trick, act, feat, number.

stupefy *v.* **1.** daze, stun, shock, make punch-drunk, make one feel punchy. **2.** daze, flabbergast, stagger, amaze, astound, dumbfound, astonish, confound, surprise, overwhelm, nonplus.

stupendous *adj.* **1.** remarkable, astounding, extraordinary, wonderful, astonishing, marvelous, terrific, great, fabulous, unusual, prodigious, incredible, stunning, amazing, surprising, unexpected. **2.** gigantic, huge, mammoth, vast, enormous, prodigious, phenomenal, tremendous, immense, massive, giant, colossal, very large, imposing, monumental, big, titanic, jumbo, very great, mighty, herculean, cyclopean, monstrous, gargantuan, elephantine. **—Ant. 1** ordinary, unsurprising. **2** small, little, minuscule, modest, diminutive, Lilliputian, wee, tiny.

stupid *adj.* **1.** dull, dumb, brainless, witless, unintelligent, dense, simple-minded, simple, slow-learning, backward, weak-minded, doltish, rattle-brained, empty-headed; muddleheaded, dimwitted, duncelike, obtuse, oafish; idiotic, half-witted, imbecilic, moronic, cretinous, *Slang* brain-dead. **2.** foolish, irresponsible, unwise, reckless, indiscriminating, imprudent, ill-advised, ill-considered, ill-judged, mistaken, absent-minded, heedless, foolhardy, thoughtless, unintelligent, idiotic, silly, childish, inane, senseless, nonsensical, unreasonable, inappropriate, fatuous, asinine; tactless, indiscreet, boorish. **3.** senseless, meaningless, absurd, silly, nonsensical, pointless, irrelevant, inept, inconsequential, preposterous, aimless, purposeless, asinine. **—Ant.** intelligent. **1** bright, clever, shrewd, quick, sharp, responsive, *Slang* hip. **2** smart, sensible, wise, thoughtful, tactful, prudent, well-advised, adult, mature, reasonable, canny, appropriate. **3** meaningful, interesting, deep, relevant, consequential, purposeful, sensible.

stupor *n.* **1.** stunned condition, near-unconsciousness, insensibility, stupefaction, numbness, somnolence; blackout, faint. **2.** torpor, apathy, inertness, inertia, lethargy, daze.

sturdy *adj.* **1.** strong, mighty, muscular, rugged, powerful, robust, tough, burly, vigorous, stout, stalwart, forceful, sinewy, strapping, hardy, able. **2.** solid, substantial, sound, strong, heavy, secure, tough, rugged, lasting, durable, well-constructed, well-made, well-built. **3.** brave, courageous, gallant, resolute, stouthearted, intrepid, plucky, valiant, unshrinking, spirited, stout, indomitable, undaunted, dauntless, heroic, firm, daring, invincible, doughty, dogged, high-spirited, fearless, unabashed, gritty, determined, stubborn, enduring, defiant, *Informal* spunky, gutsy. **—Ant.** weak. **1** frail, feeble, powerless. **2** fragile, unsubstantial, light, flimsy. **3** cowardly, fearful, irresolute, shrinking.

stygian *adj.* infernal, hellish; dreary, somber, murky, dark, funereal, gloomy, dim, black, starless, tenebrous, unlighted. **—Ant.** bright, light, cheerful, sunny, lighted.

style *n.* **1.** typical mode of expression, manner, characteristic tone. **2.** luxury, elegance, pomp, comfort, affluence. **3.** grace, smoothness, polish, class, savoir faire, charm, taste, flair, *French* élan. **4.** fashion, vogue, currency, favor; trend, taste, craze, fad, mode, rage. **5.** type, kind, sort, pattern, model. **—***v.* **6.** design, arrange, give style to. **7.** call, name, designate. **—Ant. 1** substance, content, essence. **2** squalor, drabness. **3** awkwardness, tastelessness.

stylish *adj.* fashionable, chic, voguish, in vogue, modish, up-to-date, up-to-the-minute, latest, in fashion, à la mode, new, modern, smart, elegant, sophisticated, *Slang* hip, with-it, jiggy; dapper, natty, swank. **—Ant.** unstylish, unfashionable, passé, out-of-date, outmoded, dowdy, old-fashioned.

stymie *v.* stump, mystify, confound, puzzle, baffle, confuse; block, balk, check, thwart, hinder, frustrate, obstruct.

suave *adj.* urbane, smooth, silken, polished, gracious, politic, diplomatic, charming, affable, mannerly, civilized, elegant; flattering, smooth-tongued, unctuous, diplomatic, ingratiating.

subconscious *adj.* subliminal, half-conscious, intuitive, instinctive, dim, dawning. **—Ant.** conscious, explicit, expressed, clear.

subdue *v.* **1.** overcome, crush, master, quell, put down, overpower, down, still, smash, subject, subjugate, oppress, defeat, foil, overwhelm, thrash, drub, whip, trim, rout, triumph over, conquer, vanquish, get the upper hand over, trample, floor, overrun, surmount, break, bow, reduce, get the better of. **2.** calm, reduce, curb, check, moderate, palliate, mellow, soften, temper, assuage, ease, allay, salve, soothe, tranquillize, slacken, mollify, relieve, appease, deaden, mitigate, ameliorate, meliorate. **3.** tone down, moderate, quiet down, mute, muffle, soften, soft-pedal. **—Syn. Study. 1** See DEFEAT. **—Ant. 2** awaken, quicken, arouse, provoke, inflame, agitate, irritate. **3** vent, unleash.

subject *n.* **1.** topic, matter, subject matter, matter in hand, theme, substance, issue, motif, point at issue, question, point in question; concern, case, affair, business; thesis, text; gist, pith. **2.** branch of knowledge, field, study, discipline. **3.** follower, dependent, subordinate; liege, vassal; citizen. **—***adj.* **4.** bound by, owing allegiance, owing obedience; subservient, subordinate, at another's command, answerable, subjected, obedient. **5.** dependent upon, conditional upon, contingent on, stipulatory. **6.** susceptible, vulnerable, open, liable, prone, disposed, exposed, at the mercy of, in danger of. **—***v.* **7.** expose, put through, cause to undergo or experience, submit. **8.** make liable, lay open, bare, expose. **—Syn. Study. 1** SUBJECT, TOPIC, THEME refer to the central idea or matter considered in speech or writing. SUBJECT refers to the broad or general matter treated in a discussion, literary work, etc.: *The subject of the novel was a poor Southern family.* TOPIC often applies to one specific part of a general subject; it may also apply to a limited and well-defined subject: *We covered many topics at the meeting. The topic of the news story was an escaped prisoner.* THEME usu. refers to the underlying idea of a discourse or composition, perhaps not clearly stated but easily recognizable: *The theme of social reform runs throughout her work.* **—Ant. 3** sovereign, ruler. **5** independent, unrelated. **6** invulnerable, unsusceptible, undisposed. **8** exempt, protect.

subjective *adj.* personal, individual, emotional, inner, individual, partial, partisan, biased, prejudiced, nonobjective. **—Ant.** objective, impersonal; external, concrete, tangible; impartial, unbiased.

subjugate *adj.* conquer, subdue, make subservient, vanquish, overmaster, reduce to submission, lay one's yoke upon, suppress, bring under the yoke, dominate, quell, tame, crush, put down. **—Ant.** release, free, liberate.

sublimate *v.* redirect, divert, channel, shift, turn, transfer; convert, transform, transmute; spiritualize, purify, elevate, exalt, ennoble.

sublime *adj.* **1.** lofty, exalted, imposing, elevated, noble, majestic, grand, stately, high, high-wrought, awe-inspiring. **2.** excellent, splendid, superb, very good, marvelous; estimable, praiseworthy; wonderful, great, terrific. **—Ant. 1** low, ordinary, everyday, commonplace. **2** poor, bad, ordinary, mediocre.

submerge *v.* **1.** plunge, put or go under water, immerse, submerse, sink, souse, douse, go under, dive, go down. **2.** inundate, cover with water, flood, engulf, cover completely, stream over, submerse, deluge, pour over, drown. —Ant. 1 surface, emerge. 2 uncover.

submission *n.* 1. submitting, yielding, giving in, surrender, capitulation; submissiveness, obedience, compliance, nonresistance, acquiescence, passivity, passiveness, meekness, tractability, subservience, tameness. 2. handing in, presentation, remittance, submitting, tendering. —Ant. 1 resistance, rebellion, mutiny; rebelliousness, disobedience, defiance.

submissive *adj.* obedient, yielding, meek, humble, mild, nonresisting, deferential, pliant, docile, compliant, complaisant, acquiescent, malleable, passive, capitulating, dutiful, unassertive, tractable, accommodating; truckling, toadying, obsequious, slavish, servile, fawning, ingratiating, subservient, crawling, bootlicking. —Ant. rebellious, disobedient, haughty, proud, arrogant, unyielding, defiant, refractory, resistant, assertive, masterful.

submit *v.* 1. give in, give up, surrender, yield, succumb, accede, bow, resign oneself, capitulate, cede, bend, back down, knuckle under, acquiesce, acknowledge defeat, kneel, stoop, lay down one's arms, defer, prostrate oneself, humble oneself, comply, hoist the white flag, throw in the towel, cry uncle, say uncle. 2. subject oneself, expose oneself, acquiesce, agree; resort. 3. present, tender, put forward, put forth, commit, suggest, propose, hold out, volunteer, offer, proffer. 4. claim, contend, assert, propose, argue. —Syn. Study. 1 See YIELD. —Ant. 1, 2 resist, withstand, fight, defy. 3 withdraw.

subnormal *adj.* substandard, mediocre, inferior, second-rate, subpar, deficient, inadequate, insufficient; sorry, bad, wretched, abysmal, dismal; *Slang* shabby, seedy, sleazy, crummy.

subordinate *adj.* 1. lower in rank, of low rank, outranked, inferior, junior, subaltern; subservient, subject, ancillary, auxiliary, subsidiary, secondary; lesser, lower. —*n.* 2. person of lower rank, inferior, assistant, junior, help, worker, dependent, attendant; servant, underling, hireling, lackey, menial. —Ant. 1, 2 superior, senior. 1 higher, primary; leading, prominent. 2 chief, master, leader, supervisor, boss.

sub rosa *adv.* confidentially, secretly, in secret, privately, in private, covertly, behind closed doors, behind-the-scenes, off-the-record, *Informal* on the sly. —Ant. openly, publicly.

subscribe *v.* 1. pledge money, promise to give, contribute, donate, open one's purse strings, lend one's aid, help, *Informal* chip in. 2. sign, undersign, set one's name to, affix one's signature to. 3. have a subscription, receive a periodical by mail. 4. lend approval, assent, consent; go along with, hold with, support, endorse. —Ant. 4 be opposed, dissent.

subsequent *adj.* ensuing, consequent, succeeding, following, proximate, next, successive. —Ant. previous, preceding.

subservient *adj.* 1. excessively submissive, fawning, obsequious, toadying, servile, slavish, ingratiating, sycophantic, bootlicking, menial, cringing, docile, truckling, prostrate. 2. subordinate, subsidiary, subject, auxiliary, contributory, accessory, ancillary. —Ant. 1 domineering, overbearing, assertive, masterful; disobedient, rebellious. 2 superior.

subside *v.* 1. settle, sink; drop, cave in, sag, descend. 2. diminish, lessen, abate, decrease, wane, moderate, level off, ebb, calm, recede, melt away, let up, ease, shrink, dwindle. —Ant. 1, 2 rise; increase, swell. 2 grow, heighten, intensify.

subsidiary *adj.* 1. supplementary, supplemental, additional, extra. 2. secondary, junior, subordinate, lower, lesser, minor, inferior. —*n.* 3. auxiliary, addition, supplement, adjunct, accessory. 4. subsidiary company, affiliate, division, branch. —Ant. 1, 2 primary, principal, main, chief, major, most important. 2 senior, leading, superior. 4 parent company, main office.

subsidy *n.* grant, aid, appropriation, provision, backing, subvention, sponsorship, allotment, honorarium, award, gift, support, subsidization; scholarship, fellowship, grant-in-aid, assistantship.

subsist *v.* live, survive, exist, stay alive, sustain oneself, nourish oneself, support life, feed oneself; eke out a living, keep body and soul together, make ends meet. —Ant. die, perish, starve.

subsistence *n.* survival, continued existence, maintenance, nourishment, sustenance, support, upkeep; livelihood, living.

substance *n.* 1. material, matter, stuff; ingredient, constituent, element. 2. corporality, substantiality, corporeality, corporealness, reality, actuality; solidity, body, real content. 3. burden, core, thrust, main point, essence, import, germ, soul, keynote, connotation, gist, basic idea, purport; intent, pith, marrow, heart; sum and substance, quintessence, backbone, sense, force. 4. affluence, property, money, means, wealth, riches. —Syn. Study. 1 See MATTER.

substantial *adj.* 1. sizable, considerable, plentiful, plenteous, large, ample, big, full, abundant. 2. firm, solid, sound. 3. big, bulky, monumental, massive, massy. —Ant. 1 unsubstantial, poor, meager, small, paltry, inconsiderable, scanty. **2** slight, weak, unsound, feeble. **3** small, tacky; lightweight, slender.

substantiate *v.* verify, corroborate, prove, demonstrate, show to be true, confirm, authenticate, sustain, support. **—Ant.** disprove, refute, discredit, undermine, tear to shreds, explode.

substitute *n.* **1.** alternate, replacement, fill-in, surrogate, makeshift, stopgap, temporary, standby, understudy, backup, ersatz, pinch hitter. *—v.* **2.** exchange, change, switch. **3.** fill in, take over, stand in, pinch-hit, act, deputize. *—adj.* **4.** surrogate, alternate, alternative, stand-in, replacement, temporary.

subterfuge *n.* scheme, artifice, trick, stratagem, dodge, deception, evasion, shift, smoke screen, ruse, blind, machination, wile, imposture; sham, chicanery, deviousness, sneakiness, gameplaying, intrigue, scheming, guile, duplicity, pretense, evasiveness, camouflage, sophistry, casuistry, make-believe. **—Ant.** straightforwardness, openness, honesty.

subtle Also **subtile** *adj.* **1.** understated, indirect, delicate, elusive, light, refined, fine. **2.** fine, keen, sharp, astute, skillful, masterly, discriminating, discerning, sophisticated, perspicacious, clever, ingenious, deft, expert, quick. **3.** sly, tricky, crafty, wily, foxy, cagy, cunning, shrewd, artful, slick, designing, devious, deceptive, shifty, underhand. **—Ant. 1** heavy-handed, blunt, obvious, direct. **2** unskillful, undiscerning, undiscriminating, unsophisticated. **3** obvious, artless.

subversive *adj.* **1.** seditious, traitorous, treasonous, insurrectionary, revolutionary, incendiary, insurgent. *—n.* **2.** traitor, quisling, collaborator, seditionary, fifth columnist, insurrectionary, insurgent, collaborationist, revolutionary, incendiary.

subvert *v.* overthrow, upset, disrupt, wreck, ruin, undermine, undo, overturn, destroy, spoil, devastate, demolish, shatter, smash; poison, contaminate, despoil, defile, mar, ravage. **—Ant.** support, endorse, back, encourage, promote.

succeed *v.* **1.** be fruitful, turn out successfully, be effective, be efficacious, do well, make a hit, bear fruit, click, hit, catch, strike oil, attain a goal, achieve one's aim, triumph, prevail, gain one's end, avail, win, hit the jackpot. **2.** attain fame, attain wealth, come into one's own, make good, make a hit, triumph, gain one's end, strike oil; prosper, flourish, thrive, find fulfillment. **3.** accede, move up, come next in order, become heir; assume the office of, take over, supplant, replace, come into possession of, inherit; follow, come afterward, be subsequent to, take the place of, replace. **—Syn. Study. 2** SUCCEED, PROSPER, FLOURISH, THRIVE mean to do well. To SUCCEED is to turn out well or do well; it may also mean to attain a goal: *The strategy succeeded. She succeeded in school.* To PROSPER is to do well, esp. materially or financially: *They worked hard and prospered.* To FLOURISH is to grow well or fare well: *The plants flourished in the sun. The business flourished under new management.* To THRIVE is to do well, esp. to achieve wealth; it may also mean to grow or develop vigorously: *The shopping center thrived. The dog thrived on the new diet.* **3** See FOLLOW. **—Ant. 1, 2** fail, flop, fall short, miss. **3** precede.

succeeding *adj.* subsequent, ensuing, consequent, successive, later, following, future, impending, coming, oncoming, posterior. **—Ant.** preceding, foregoing, earlier, previous, prior, former.

success *n.* **1.** happy outcome, triumph, fulfillment. **2.** attainment, prosperity, good fortune, achievement, advancement, fame, conquest, triumph, ascendancy, affluence. **3.** well-received venture, hit, triumph, victory, *Informal* smash. **—Ant. 1–3** failure, disaster, downfall, collapse.

successful *adj.* **1.** triumphant, effective, efficacious, accomplished, achieved, complete, fruitful, perfect. **2.** prosperous, flourishing, thriving, rich, well-off, affluent, wealthy; proven, acknowledged. **—Ant. 1, 2** unsuccessful. **1** defeated. **2** unprosperous.

succession *n.* **1.** series, procession, progression, sequence, chain, round, cycle, course, run, train. **2.** taking over, assumption, accession, inheritance, stepping-up. **—Syn. Study. 1** See SERIES.

successive *adj.* succeeding, ensuing, following one after another, consecutive, continuous.

successor *n.* follower, replacement, substitute; beneficiary, legatee; heir, heir apparent, heiress, heritor, heritress, joint heir; *Law* devisee, donee, reversioner, coparcener, parcener.

succinct *adj.* to the point, terse, expressed in few words, brief, direct, clipped, concise, neat, condensed, compact, sparing of words, epigrammatic, short, tight, summary, crisp, pithy, gnomic, aphoristic. **—Syn. Study.** See CONCISE. **—Ant.** discursive, rambling, maundering, circuitous, prolix, wordy, verbose, long-winded.

succor *n.* **1.** help, sustenance, relief, aid, accommodation, helping hand, comfort, assistance, support, maintenance. *—v.* **2.** aid, assist, comfort, lend a hand to, help, relieve, support, sustain, nurture, wait on, minister to, nurse, take care of, render assistance to, back up, give a lift to, protect, shield, befriend. —**Syn. Study. 2** See HELP.

succumb *v.* **1.** die, pass away, expire, go under. **2.** give in, yield, give way, submit, comply with, accede, defer to, capitulate, surrender; fall victim to. —**Ant. 1** live, survive. **2** resist, fight, hold firm.

sucker *n.* dupe, chump, fool, gull, mark, sap, boob, pushover, victim, easy mark, pigeon, sitting duck, cat's-paw, fair game, patsy, butt, fall guy, soft touch, goat, schlemiel, jerk.

sudden *adj.* abrupt, quick, speedy, rapid, immediate, instant, instantaneous; hasty, impetuous, precipitate, rash; unlooked-for, unexpected, unanticipated, unforeseen, unforeseeable, surprising. —**Ant.** slow, gradual; extended, prolonged; deliberate; foreseen, anticipated, expected.

suddenly *adv.* abruptly, all of a sudden, without warning, all at once, unexpectedly, at short notice, on the spur of the moment, in an instant, quickly, instantly, before one knows it, on the spot, in the twinkling of an eye, in no time. —**Ant.** gradually, slowly, deliberately, not unexpectedly.

sue *v.* **1.** bring a civil action against, litigate against, institute process in law against, prefer a claim against, start a lawsuit against. **2.** beg, plead, beseech, entreat, appeal, make appeal to, importune, implore, supplicate, petition, pray.

suffer *v.* **1.** feel distress, lament, despair, go through a lot, bear the cross, pine, grieve; feel pain, agonize, ache, hurt. **2.** deteriorate, fall off, be impaired, drop off. **3.** endure, bear, sustain, go through, undergo, tolerate, bear with, withstand, stand, stomach, put up with.

suffering *n.* **1.** sorrow, distress, travail, heartache, heavy heart, grief, misery, dolor, woe, tribulation, care, anxiety, anguish, trial. **2.** ache, pain, hurt, soreness, irritation, torture, affliction, agony, discomfort, pang, misery, twinge, distress, throe, torment. —**Ant. 1** pleasure, joy, happiness.

sufficient *adj.* enough, adequate, ample, plenty, abundant, copious, satisfactory, minimal, up to the mark, plentiful, plenteous. —**Ant.** insufficient, deficient, inadequate, wanting, meager, scant.

suffocate *v.* choke, gag, smother, asphyxiate, stifle; strangle, throttle, garrote; extinguish, quench, snuff out.

suffuse *v.* cover, overspread, saturate, fill, overflow, pervade, diffuse, permeate, soak, transfuse, steep, impregnate, infiltrate, infuse, overrun.

sugary *adj.* sweet, honeyed, saccharine, syrupy, cloying; flattering, cajoling, blandishing, mushy, gushing, mawkish, fulsome, unctuous. —**Ant.** acid, tart, crusty, sarcastic, venomous.

suggest *v.* **1.** recommend, advocate, move, urge, advise, propose, bid, counsel, posit, submit, propound, advance. **2.** intimate, hint at, imply, insinuate, lead one to believe, indicate, give a clue. —**Syn. Study. 2** See HINT.

suggestion *n.* **1.** advice, prompting, counsel, urging, recommendation, exhortation; pointer, tip. **2.** suspicion, shade, hint, trace, touch, dash, grain, taste, tinge, tint, soupçon, dab, sprinkling, feeling, intimation.

suggestive *adj.* **1.** reminiscent, evocative, expressive, allusive, remindful. **2.** improper, indelicate, unseemly, off-color; indecent, loose, shameless, lewd, wanton, seductive, sexual, licentious, risqué, racy, bawdy; stimulating, prurient, provocative. —**Ant. 2** decent, delicate, decorous, chaste, clean.

suit *n.* **1.** set of garments, outfit; jacket and pants, jacket and skirt; clothing, garb, costume, clothes, apparel, habit, habiliment, raiment, trappings, duds, getup, attire, accoutrements, togs; livery, uniform. **2.** courtship, court, wooing, blandishment, addresses, lovemaking, attentions, overtures. **3.** plea, appeal, solicitation, entreaty, begging, supplication, prayer, petition. —*v.* **4.** conform to, match, follow, befit, fit, beseem, correspond to, be proper for, harmonize with, fall in with, agree with, square with, go along with, be appropriate to, jell with, tally with, accord with, comply with, dovetail with, comport with. **5.** become, be appropriate for, befit, be suitable for, be becoming to, do one good. **6.** be acceptable to, be convenient to, accommodate, content, oblige, be agreeable to, seem good to; make glad, gratify, satisfy, please, gladden, delight. —**Ant. 4** disagree with, not go with, be inappropriate to. **6** inconvenience, displease, discommode.

suitable *adj.* proper, appropriate, meet, fitting, fit, befitting, seemly, right, adequate, apt, qualified, cut out for, becoming, worthy, apropos, applicable, congruous, seasonable, relevant, pertinent, germane, commensurate. —**Ant.** unsuitable, inappropriate, unbecoming, improper, incompatible, dissonant, inconsistent, unfit, unseemly.

suitcase *n.* bag; (*variously*) valise, grip, satchel, traveling bag, overnight bag, two-suiter, gladstone, portmanteau; duffel bag, rucksack, knapsack.

suitor *n.* beau, boyfriend, young man, lover, admirer, love, flame, fellow, gallant, wooer, swain, sweetheart.

sulk *v.* pout, be sullen, wear a long face,

mope, brood, show ill temper, be in a huff, be disgruntled, be resentful, be in a pet, grumble, grump, fret, be out of humor, be miffed, fume, be put out, chafe, crab, grouch, scowl, frown, glower, look glum.

sullen *adj.* **1.** ill-tempered, gloomy, ill-humored, brooding, grumpy, out of humor, out of sorts, surly, glowering, sulky, crabbed, resentful, grouchy, sour, morose, scowling, peevish, petulant, splenetic, sore, grim, ill-natured, temperamental, glum, saturnine, moody, unsociable, crabby, unamiable, cross, touchy. **2.** gloomy, grim, dismal, somber, funereal, mournful, dolorous, depressing, melancholy, dark, blue, doleful, foreboding, dreary, heavy, cheerless, desolate, forlorn. **—Syn. Study. 2** See GLUM. **—Ant. 1** cheerful, happy, gay, smiling, sociable, merry, amiable. **2** bright, cheerful, sunny.

sully *v.* soil, dirty, besmear, stain, spot, befoul, smudge, begrime, blemish, spoil, ruin; contaminate, defile, corrupt, adulterate; disgrace, dishonor, defame. **—Ant.** cleanse, purify, tidy, decontaminate; honor, glorify.

sultry *adj.* **1.** sweltering, suffocating, stifling, oppressive, close, stuffy, warm and damp, humid, hot and moist, muggy, sweaty. **2.** erotic, hot, voluptuous, sexy, sensual, provocative.

sum *n.* **1.** amount, quantity, sum total, measure, entire amount, entirety, totality, summation, aggregate, whole, tally, score. **2.** amount of money, cash, funds, currency, coin; *Slang* dough, bread, bucks, lettuce, jack, moolah.

summarily *adv.* at short notice, unhesitatingly, on the spur of the moment, precipitately, arbitrarily, without delay, on the spot, promptly, with dispatch, immediately, straightaway, straightway, directly, at once, quickly, speedily, forthwith.

summarize *v.* condense, capsulize, abstract, abridge, compress, digest, sum up, recapitulate, epitomize, concentrate, synopsize, outline. **—Ant.** expand, flesh out, enlarge on, embroider.

summary *n.* **1.** concise statement, short version, brief, abstract, résumé, detailed outline, précis, survey, digest, *Informal* rundown; abridgment, recapitulation, condensation, breakdown, epitome, syllabus, synopsis, sketch, abbreviation, sum and substance, analysis, aperçu. —*adj.* **2.** short, brief, hasty, concise, abridged, succinct, condensed, terse, curt, hurried; perfunctory, token, cursory. **3.** unceremoniously fast, rapid, done without consideration, peremptory, conducted without delay, hasty, quickly performed, instantaneous, sudden. **—Syn. Study. 1** SUMMARY, BRIEF, DIGEST, SYNOPSIS are terms for a short version of a longer work. A SUMMARY is a brief statement or restatement of main points, esp. as a conclusion to a work: *a summary of a chapter.* A BRIEF is a concise statement, usu. of the main points of a legal case: *The attorney filed a brief.* A DIGEST is a condensed and systematically arranged collection of literary, legal, or scientific matter: *a digest of Roman law.* A SYNOPSIS is a condensed statement giving a general overview of a subject or a brief summary of a plot: *a synopsis of a play.* **—Ant. 2** complete, full, detailed, lengthy. **3** deliberate, considered, slow.

summery *adj.* summerlike, vernal, aestival, sunny, sunshiny; hot, muggy, humid, close, oppressive, sultry, stifling, stuffy, torrid, scorching, roasting. **—Ant.** cold, wintry, raw, blustery, freezing.

summit *n.* peak, crest, crown, highest point, apex, vertex, tip, height, top, pinnacle, zenith, apogee; acme, crowning point, culminating point, culmination, climax. **—Ant.** base, bottom, depth, nadir, all-time low.

summon *v.* **1.** call for, beckon, send for, rouse; call together, muster, activate, call into action, gather, call out. **2.** call, command to appear, subpoena, serve with a writ. **3.** call forth, call on, invoke, command, muster, call into action, gather, draw on, strain. **—Ant. 1** dismiss, discharge.

sumptuous *adj.* splendid, luxurious, magnificent, grand, regal, spectacular, elaborate, lavish, munificent, elegant, superb; dear, costly, expensive, exorbitant, plush, rich, deluxe, extravagant, posh. **—Ant.** plain, ordinary, cheap.

sundry *adj.* various, divers, several, manifold, many, numerous, myriad, diverse, varied, motley, assorted, miscellaneous, heterogeneous, multifarious, dissimilar, different. **—Ant.** uniform, unvarying, same, regular.

sunny *adj.* **1.** sunshiny, bright, sunlit; cloudless, shining, clear, brilliant, unclouded, fair, fine. **2.** amiable, affable, happy, smiling, cheerful, cheery, joyful, blithe, jolly, joyous, lighthearted, genial, sparkling, buoyant, optimistic, breezy, jovial, merry. **—Ant. 1** shaded, dark, cloudy, overcast, dim, gloomy, gray, murky, somber, wintry. **2** glum, gloomy, dour, unhappy, morbid, unsmiling, uncheerful.

sunrise *n.* dawn, sunup, dawning, daybreak, daylight, aurora, break of day, cockcrow, dawn's early light, rosy-fingered day, newborn day.

sunset *n.* dusk, twilight, sundown, nightfall, eventide, gloaming, crepuscule, blue hour, close of day.

super *adj.* outstanding, matchless, great, extraordinary, superlative, peerless, superior, incomparable, prime, prize, excellent, world-class, unexcelled, nonpareil. **—Ant.** commonplace, ordinary, mediocre, run-of-the-mill.

superabundance *n.* overabundance, overflow, glut, surplus, excess, plethora, superfluity, oversupply, redundance, pleonasm, surfeit, deluge, flood, spate, avalanche, riot, extravagance, overdose, inundation, *French* embarras de richesses. **—Ant.** scarcity, lack, shortage, paucity.

superb *adj.* **1.** very fine, first-rate, excellent, magnificent, admirable, laudable, praiseworthy, Al, first-class, top-notch, top-drawer, of the first water, tiptop, *Slang* crackerjack. **2.** sumptuous, splendid, grand, magnificent, marvelous, luxurious, deluxe, gorgeous, exquisite, costly, rich, expensive, priceless, precious, elegant, choice, select, golden, elect, matchless, rare; majestic, breathtaking, imposing, peerless, regal, princely, stately, lordly. **—Ant. 1** bad, awful, terrible, second-rate, inferior. **2** tawdry, ordinary, plain, mean.

supercilious *adj.* haughty, self-important, lordly, pompous, disdainful, condescending, patronizing, arrogant, high-and-mighty, proud, overbearing, vainglorious, egotistical, magisterial, *Informal* snooty, *Slang* stuck-up; uppity, snobbish, prideful.

superficial *adj.* **1.** on the surface, outer, surface, exterior, skin-deep. **2.** shallow, skin-deep, summary, incomplete, slight, faint, slim, flimsy, cursory, perfunctory, passing, partial, minimal, surface, nodding, desultory. **3.** frivolous, shallow, hollow, empty-headed, narrow-minded, lacking depth, mindless, silly, myopic, shortsighted, trite. **—Ant. 1–3** deep, in-depth, profound. **1** substantial, pervasive. **2** thorough, complete, total. **3** serious, intent, earnest, farsighted.

superfluous *adj.* unnecessary, excessive, redundant, overgenerous, needless, nonessential, inessential; excess, surplus, extra, superabundant, supererogatory, pleonastic, supernumerary, extraneous, spare, gratuitous. **—Ant.** essential, vital, indispensable, required, necessary.

superhuman *adj.* superior, supreme, transcendent, supernatural, godlike, herculean, omnipotent, unearthly, miraculous, supermundane, supranatural, preternatural, otherworldly, divine. **—Ant.** mundane, earthly, normal, natural, terrestrial.

superintendent *n.* supervisor, chief administrator; director, head, overseer, proctor, chief, custodian, guardian, foreman, boss, manager, warden, steward, headman.

superior *adj.* **1.** excellent, exceptional, fine, notable, incomparable, distinguished, preeminent, noteworthy, nonpareil, unrivaled, foremost, first-rate, illustrious, peerless, inimitable, matchless; deluxe, choice. **2.** greater, better, more extensive, more advanced. **3.** haughty, lordly, imperious, condescending, patronizing, snobbish, arrogant, high-and-mighty, vainglorious. *—n.* **4.** senior, boss, chief, supervisor; leader, higher-up, better, commander. **—Ant. 1** inferior, lower, worse, poorer, unexceptional, undistinguished, lesser, mediocre, ordinary, average, second-rate, common, unremarkable; inconspicuous, obscure. **2** inferior, less worthy. **4** inferior, subordinate, employee; underling, minion.

superlative *adj.* most excellent, of the highest order, greatest, of the first water, superior, surpassing, best, supreme, magnificent, preeminent, foremost, transcendent, unsurpassed, expert, prime, surpassing all others, paramount, crack, exquisite, consummate, first-rate; matchless, incomparable, unrivaled, peerless, unequaled, unmatched, unparalleled, nonpareil. **—Ant.** inferior, poor, unexceptional, undistinguished.

supernatural *adj.* preternatural, otherworldly, occult, mystic, transcendental, unearthly, spiritual, psychic, paranormal, miraculous, superphysical, supranatural. **—Syn. Study.** See MIRACULOUS. **—Ant.** natural, explainable, worldly.

supersede *v.* supplant, replace, take the place of, substitute for, displace, succeed; discard, set aside. **—Syn. Study.** See REPLACE.

supervise *v.* superintend, watch over, oversee, look after, preside over, manage, regulate, direct, govern, survey, control, guide, conduct, have charge of, administer, head, boss, handle.

supervision *n.* direction, guidance, regulation, control, superintendence, governance, government, surveillance, orders, management.

supervisor *n.* overseer, manager, administrator, director, superintendent, foreman, boss, head, chief, steward, commander, man at the wheel.

supplant *v.* supersede, replace, take the place of, usurp the place of, displace, depose. **—Syn. Study.** See REPLACE.

supple *adj.* **1.** pliant, flexible, plastic, tractable, bendable, pliable, elastic. **2.** lithe, limber, lissome, coordinated, graceful. **3.** adaptable, flexible, amenable, tractable, compliant, complaisant, yielding, acquiescent, submissive, malleable. **—Ant. 1** stiff, rigid, firm, inflexible. **2** stiff, awkward, graceless.

supplement *n.* **1.** complement, annex,

addition, augmentation, corollary, extra, extension, addendum, adjunct. **2.** section, insert, attachment; appendix, addendum, rider, postscript, codicil, added part. —*v.* **3.** add to, extend, increase, augment, complement. —**Syn. Study.** See COMPLEMENT.

suppliant *n.* supplicant, petitioner, beseecher, beggar, entreater, seeker, suitor, supplicator, asker, claimant, appellant; mendicant, cadger, almsman, almswoman.

supplication *n.* entreaty, petition, plea, appeal, beseechment, solicitation, application, request, invocation, prayer, orison, suit, cry, imprecation, imploration; cadging, panhandling; *Slang* bumming, mooching.

supply *v.* **1.** provide, furnish, outfit, turn over to, stock, equip; present, give, contribute, bestow, yield, deal out, come up with, deliver, render, grant, provision. —*n.* **2.** provisioning, providing, furnishing, allocation; stock, reservoir, reserve, store, quota, provision, cache, fund. **3.** Often **supplies** equipment, needed items, goods, material, items, provisions; gear, trappings, accoutrements; foodstuff.

support *v.* **1.** bear up, hold up; prop, bolster, uphold, brace, sustain, buttress, stay, shore up. **2.** sustain, bear, hold. **3.** maintain, provide for, subsidize, keep, finance, pay for, underwrite, back financially, foster. **4.** help, sustain, succor, comfort, give hope to, aid, carry, be a source of strength, strengthen. **5.** defend, back up, champion, uphold, stand up for, stick up for, second, advocate, go along with, say yes to, reinforce, espouse, sanction, favor, countenance; aid, boost, assist, further, patronize, bolster. **6.** verify, confirm, make good, establish, substantiate, corroborate, accord with, bear out, vouch for, accredit, clinch, warrant, attest to, endorse, bolster, guarantee, ratify. **7.** endure, tolerate, put up with, suffer, abide, bear, brook, stand. —*n.* **8.** holding up, buttressing; supporter, brace, prop, underpinning, post, buttress, abutment, shore, pile, pedestal, stanchion, bolster, pillar, column, pilaster, base. **9.** sustenance, maintenance, upkeep, livelihood, means, subsistence, keeping, nurture; comfort, succor, aid, help, strength, boost, encouragement, consolation, lift. **10.** backing, patronage, aid, help, assistance, espousal, defense, advocacy, boost, promotion, furtherance, involvement.

supporter *n.* backer, upholder, defender, champion, patron, adherent, benefactor, disciple, wellwisher, partisan, advocate, ally, helper, follower, sympathizer. —**Ant.** adversary, antagonist, opponent.

suppose *v.* **1.** assume, hypothesize, presume, predicate, posit, consider. **2.** guess, imagine, believe, reckon, take for granted, presume, assume, gather, judge, fancy, conceive, suspect, divine, surmise.

supposition *n.* presumption, assumption, conjecture, opinion, predication, surmise, guess, guesswork, suspicion, belief, theory, thesis, notion, view, speculation, hypothesis, proposition, postulate, idea, given. —**Ant.** certainty, surety, fact, knowledge.

suppress *v.* **1.** put down, overpower, crush, subdue, put an end to, quash, overcome, snuff out, squash, quench, quell, extinguish. **2.** repress, withhold, stifle, squelch, keep back, check, control, smother, restrict, restrain, muffle, still, hold back, put a damper on, hold in leash, inhibit, keep in, curb. **3.** keep secret, keep private, cover up, conceal, hide, put under wraps, bury, silence. —**Ant. 2** express, let out, unleash, unloose, pour forth. **3** reveal, uncover, expose, broadcast.

supremacy *n.* preeminence, superiority, primacy, paramountcy, precedence, transcendency; domination, power, sovereignty, mastery, absolute authority, ascendancy, power to command, absolute rule, supreme leadership, omnipotence.

supreme *adj.* **1.** sovereign, dominant, uppermost, front-ranking, first, highest, chief, principal, paramount, foremost, peerless, all-powerful, topmost, leading, ruling; commanding, prime, unqualified, absolute, unconditional, unlimited. **2.** perfect, consummate, nonpareil, peerless, superlative, matchless, unexcelled, incomparable, unsurpassed, unequaled, unparalleled, second to none, unmatched, tops, unrivaled; extreme, immeasurable.

sure *adj.* **1.** confident, assured, fully persuaded, convinced, positive, certain, undoubting. **2.** trustworthy, never-failing, reliable, worthy of confidence, unfailing, dependable, firm, steady, fast, solid, true, faithful; surefire, fail-safe, infallible. **3.** unerring, certain, accurate, unfailing, flawless, infallible, dependable, reliable, sound, steady, stable, firm. —**Ant. 1, 3** unsure. **1–3** uncertain. **1** insecure, unassured, unconvinced, doubtful, distrustful. **2** fallible, unsteady, inconstant, wavering, unworthy, faithless, undependable, untrue, unreliable. **3** erring, inaccurate, unreliable, unsteady, unstable.

surely *adv.* for certain, assuredly, without doubt, undoubtedly, certainly, doubtless, unquestionably, definitely, positively, indubitably, emphatically, by all means, come what may, without fail, no doubt, to be sure, infallibly, of course.

surface *n.* outside, superficies, face, facade, outer face, exterior; (*variously*) covering, shell, coat, finish, coating, veneer, crust, skin, top.

surfeit *n.* glut, surplus, excess, overabundance, superfluity, plethora, extravagance, oversupply, exorbitance, surplusage, overmuch, profusion, prodigality, supersaturation. **—Ant.** shortage, dearth, lack, paucity, shortfall.

surge *n.* wave, swell, torrent, flood, rush.

surly *adj.* sullen, rude, snarling, irascible, grouchy, discourteous, ill-humored, bad-tempered, testy, crabbed, ill-natured, abrupt, cross, crusty, uncivil, grumpy, touchy, waspish, snappish, peevish, churlish, unfriendly, gruff, petulant, sour, harsh, hostile, unamiable, splenetic, bearish, choleric, insolent. **—Ant.** amiable, gracious, cordial, affable, genial, nice, pleasant, courteous, friendly, civil.

surmise *v.* **1.** conjecture, imagine, guess, suppose, presuppose, think, presume, opine, judge, suspect, consider, theorize, believe, deem, infer, hypothesize, posit, conclude. *—n.* **2.** guess, supposition, notion, idea, conjecture, opinion, speculation, assumption, hypothesis, *Informal* shot in the dark; presumption, belief, suspicion, thought. **—Syn. Study. 1** See GUESS.

surmount *v.* **1.** get over, scale, climb, top, clear. **2.** conquer, defeat, master, overcome, prevail over, vanquish, best, get the better of, worst, triumph over.

surpass *v.* **1.** exceed, go beyond, outdo, top, best, outstrip, beat, outdistance, leave behind, triumph over, go one better, outrun, transcend. **2.** excel, outdo, be superior to, rise above, outshine, eclipse, overshadow, override, outclass, take precedence over, be better than, have it all over.

surplus *n.* **1.** oversupply, surfeit, superfluity, overage, surplusage, excess, overflow, plethora, overproduction, glut. *—adj.* **2.** excess, extra, superfluous, leftover, residual. **—Ant. 1** deficiency, shortage, insufficiency, inadequacy, dearth, paucity, lack.

surprise *v.* **1.** astonish, astound, nonplus, startle, amaze, flabbergast, take aback, strike with wonder, shock, stun, dumbfound, stagger, strike with awe, defy belief, leave open-mouthed, stupefy, confound, boggle the mind. **2.** catch in the act of, come upon unexpectedly, take unawares, discover, catch off one's guard, burst in on. **3.** ambush, assail suddenly, set upon, make a sneak attack on, take by surprise, fall upon, pounce upon, take unawares. *—n.* **4.** something unexpected, bolt out of the blue, bombshell, revelation. **5.** amazement, wonder, astonishment, wonderment, incredulity, shock.

surrender *v.* **1.** give up, yield, submit, capitulate, concede, lay down arms, show the white flag, throw in the towel, cry uncle, say uncle. **2.** give up, let go, abandon, relinquish, renounce, give over, yield, forgo, part with, forsake, vacate, waive, turn over, hand over, render, accede, cede, deliver up. *—n.* **3.** yielding, capitulation, submission; relinquishment, giving up, delivery; forgoing, renunciation. **—Syn. Study. 1** See YIELD. **—Ant. 1** resist, withstand, oppose. **2** retain, keep, hold on to.

surreptitious *adj.* secret, secretive, stealthy, undercover, furtive, clandestine, hidden, covert, *Informal* hush-hush; concealed, veiled. **—Ant.** open, aboveboard, candid, direct, straightforward.

surround *v.* encircle, circle, enclose, ring, encompass, girdle, engird, enfold, belt, compass, circumscribe, envelop, hedge, hedge in, shut in, close in, hem in, fence in.

surroundings *n. pl.* circumstances, environs, conditions; environment, habitat, milieu, setting, scene, ambience, atmosphere.

surveillance *n.* watch, observation, vigil, scrutiny; eavesdropping, trailing.

survey *v.* **1.** review, look over, view generally, pass in review, consider, contemplate, scan, examine, inspect, study, scrutinize. **2.** measure, determine the extent of, verify the boundaries of, delimit, plot, graph, gauge, block out; fathom, plumb; reconnoiter, observe, scout. *—n.* **3.** review, study, comprehensive view, overview, investigation, probe, poll, canvass, analysis.

survival *n.* **1.** living, keeping alive, subsistence. **2.** carry-over, relic, vestige, hangover, continuation, atavism, throwback. **—Ant. 1** death, extermination, extinction, eradication.

survive *v.* **1.** keep alive, continue to live, subsist, last, hang on, hold out; live on, persist, endure, prevail, continue, abide, subsist, be extant, exist. **2.** live through, come through alive. **3.** outlive, outlast, live longer than. **—Syn. Study. 2, 3** SURVIVE, OUTLIVE refer to remaining alive longer than someone else or after some event. SURVIVE usu. means to succeed in staying alive against odds, to live after some event that has threatened one: *to survive an automobile accident.* It is also used of living longer than another person (usu. a relative), but today mainly in the passive, as in the fixed expression *The deceased is survived by his* *wife and children.* OUTLIVE stresses capacity for endurance, the time element, and sometimes a sense of competition: *She outlived all her enemies.* It is also used, however, of a person or thing that has lived or lasted beyond a certain point: *The machine has outlived its usefulness.* **—Ant. 1** perish, disappear. **2** succumb to. **3** predecease.

susceptible *adj.* **1.** open, prone, subject, vulnerable, receptive to, capable of being affected by, sensitive to, disposed to, conducive to, liable to. **2.** sensitive, alive to, responsive, easily moved by, vulnerable, readily impressed by, easily touched by, sympathetic, sensible. **—Ant. 1, 2** unsusceptible. **1** immune, invulnerable. **2** insensitive, unresponsive, unmoved, invulnerable, insensible, resistant.

suspect *v.* **1.** mistrust, doubt, distrust, question, have no confidence in, have one's doubts about, harbor suspicions about, wonder about, misdoubt, be suspicious of, believe guilty. **2.** guess, imagine, conjecture, surmise, opine, fancy, hypothesize, believe, posit, theorize, judge, presume, speculate, suppose, think. *—n.* **3.** suspected person, alleged culprit. **—Ant. 1** trust, believe. **2** know, know for sure, be sure, be certain.

suspend *v.* **1.** hang, dangle, swing, append, sling. **2.** put off, postpone, delay, defer, table, reserve, shelve, stay, withhold. **3.** discontinue, cease, stop, halt, arrest, interrupt, leave off, break off, bring to a stop, bring to a standstill, stop short, check, cut short, put an end to, quit.

suspense *n.* uncertainty, incertitude, indecision, unresolved situation, indetermination, expectation, anticipation, tension, anxiety, being on pins and needles, edginess, curiosity. **—Ant.** certainty, certitude, resolution.

suspicion *n.* **1.** distrust, mistrust, jealous apprehension. **2.** conjecture, feeling, idea, surmise, guess, supposition, hunch, hypothesis, notion. **—Syn. Study. 1** SUSPICION, DISTRUST are terms for a feeling that appearances are not reliable. SUSPICION is the positive tendency to doubt the trustworthiness of appearances and therefore to believe that one has detected possibilities of something unreliable, unfavorable, menacing, or the like: *to feel suspicion about the honesty of a prominent man.* DISTRUST may be a passive want of trust, faith, or reliance in a person or thing: *to feel distrust of one's own ability.* **—Ant. 1** trust, trustfulness, credulity, belief, confidence.

suspicious *adj.* **1.** open to doubt, questionable, dubious, suspect, doubtful, slippery, ambiguous, untrustworthy, shady. **2.** inclined to suspect, mistrustful, distrustful, untrusting, wary, doubting, incredulous, disbelieving, jealously unbelieving. **—Ant. 1, 2** unsuspicious. **1** open, aboveboard, clear, unambiguous. **2** trusting, confident, credulous.

sustain *v.* **1.** support, bear up, uphold, hold up, underpin, prop. **2.** bear, brook, endure, carry on under, hold out against, abide, stand, withstand, brave, tolerate. **3.** suffer, undergo, experience. **4.** maintain, keep up, prolong, protract. **5.** nourish, maintain; nurture, feed, keep alive.

svelte *adj.* slender, slim, thin, lissome, lithe, lean, willowy, spare, sylphlike; shapely, trim, neat, graceful, elegant, fine. **—Ant.** plump, stocky, pudgy; dumpy, squat, obese.

swagger *v.* strut, stride, stride insolently, sashay, swashbuckle, sweep, parade, saunter. **—Syn. Study.** See STRUT. **—Ant.** slink, sneak, creep.

swallow *v.* **1.** ingest; gulp, gobble, devour, gulp down; imbibe, guzzle, swig, down, swill, tipple, quaff. **2.** repress, hold in, suppress, keep back, withhold, hold back. *—n.* **3.** mouthful, drink, gulp, nip, sip, taste, bit.

swamp *n.* **1.** marsh, bog, morass, quagmire, mire, bottoms, quag, fen, bayou, everglade, marshland, swampland, slough, slew, slue, moor, ooze, swale. *—v.* **2.** sink, submerge, fill; engulf, flood, wash over, inundate, envelop, deluge, swallow up. **3.** overwhelm, flood, besiege, engulf, beset, snow under.

swanky *adj.* smart, stylish, chic, elegant, fashionable, showy, fancy, dashing, sporty, swank, flashy, splashy, sumptuous, rich, grand; *Slang* ritzy, sharp, jazzy, plush, posh, snazzy, spiffy. **—Ant.** restrained, subdued, conservative, austere.

swap *v.* trade, dicker, exchange, switch, bargain, barter, give and take.

swarm *n.* **1.** multitude; drove, throng, horde, cloud, mass, herd, press, great number, legion, stampede, host, crowd, myriad. *—v.* **2.** flock, surge, throng, crowd, herd, overrun, cluster, rush, mass, stream. **3.** abound, teem. **—Syn. Study. 1** See CROWD.

swarthy *adj.* dark-complexioned, dark-skinned, brunet, dusky, tawny, swart, brown-skinned, brown-colored, olive-skinned. **—Ant.** pale, light, fair, light-complexioned, fair-skinned.

swat *v.* hit, smack, knock, tap, strike, smite, wallop, belt, clout, buffet, clobber, sock, slam, bash, whack, slug.

sway *v.* **1.** rock, list, move to and fro, swing, roll, oscillate, wave, undulate, pendulate, fluctuate, waver; reel, totter, wobble, stagger. **2.** move, influence, prompt, persuade, motivate, rouse, lead, induce, bend the will of, stimulate, predispose, dispose, incite, encourage, spur, impel, prevail on, bring round. **3.** fluctuate, vacillate, change, shift, vary, hesitate, alter, swerve, bend. —*n.* **4.** swaying, swinging, waving, pulsation, oscillation, undulation, fluctuation, back and forth, to-and-fro. **5.** control, authority, rule, domination, command, mastery, power, domain, jurisdiction, government, iron hand, dictatorship, reign, grip, suzerainty, hold. **6.** influence, control, domination, hold, command, grip, direction, power, manipulation, *Slang* clout.

swear *v.* **1.** state under oath, take an oath, vow, vouch, avow, bind oneself by oath, certify, warrant, bear witness, attest, adjure, pledge oneself, aver, assert, promise. **2.** cause to promise, bind by an oath, pledge. **3.** curse, cuss, use profanity, utter oaths, blaspheme.

sweep *v.* **1.** whisk, gather. **2.** race, dash, rush, dart, scurry, hurry, charge, scud, fly, zoom, swoop, tear. —*n.* **3.** stretch, distance, spell. **4.** swing, arc, stroke, swish, swoop.

sweeping *adj.* extensive, far-reaching, widespread, wide-ranging, broad, wholesale, radical, exhaustive, blanket, comprehensive, all-inclusive, large-scale, thoroughgoing, out-and-out. —**Ant.** small, modest, trifling, trivial, limited, superficial, narrow, slight.

sweet *adj.* **1.** sweet-tasting, sugary; saccharine, cloying. **2.** not salt, not salty, nonsalt; fresh, nonfermented, wholesome, not spoiled, not rancid. **3.** melodious, dulcet, pleasing, mellifluous, tuneful, silver-toned, mellow, euphonious, smooth. **4.** fragrant, fresh. **5.** attractive, sympathetic, agreeable, nice, pleasant, good-natured, dear, kind, lovable, amiable, darling. —*n.* **6.** candy, piece of candy, confection, sweetmeat, *British* dessert. —**Ant. 1** sour, acid, acerbic, bitter, nasty. **2** saltwater, salt, salty, salted; stale, rancid, sour, decaying, tainted, turned. **3** harsh, shrill; raucous, discordant, unmelodious, displeasing, unmusical, inharmonious, dissonant, strident. **4** stale, bad-smelling, rank. **5** disagreeable, unpleasant, unattractive, nasty, ill-natured, unlovable, unamiable; dreadful, awful.

sweetheart *n.* love, beloved, true love, dear, darling, flame, steady, girlfriend, lover; mistress, ladylove, lady friend, valentine, inamorata; boyfriend, beau, swain, suitor, gentleman friend; fiancé, (*fem.*) fiancée, *Slang* honey, old lady, old man.

swell *v.* **1.** distend, puff, puff up, grow, blow up, fatten, bulge, inflate, extend, bloat, thicken; expand, increase, lengthen, stretch, widen, spread out, burgeon, rise. **2.** intensify, amplify, heighten, rise, mount, throb; billow, surge, wax, heave. —*adj.* **3.** *Informal* fine, first-rate, good, excellent, super, marvelous, terrific, great, delightful, splendid, pleasurable, first-class, okay, dandy, A1, fabulous, tremendous. —*n.* **4.** wave, billow; breaker, comber; undulation. **5.** fashion plate, smart dresser, dandy, fop, clotheshorse. —**Ant. 1** shrink, contract, condense, compress, constrict. **2** decrease, diminish, lessen, fall, wane, lower, ebb away. **3** horrible, awful, dreadful, lousy, bad, disgusting.

swelling *n.* swell, puffiness, distension, dilation, bulge, bump, lump, swell, protuberance, enlargement.

swelter *v.* be oppressed with heat, be hot, sweat, perspire, languish, *Informal* cook, fry, boil, broil. —**Ant.** freeze, shiver.

sweltry *adj.* hot, sizzling, roasting, baking, broiling, boiling, torrid, scorching, blistering, sweltering, stifling, suffocating, humid, sultry, clammy, sticky, muggy, dank, steamy. —**Ant.** cold, blustery, raw, nippy.

swift *adj.* fast, rapid, fleet, quick, speedy, brisk, prompt, immediate, expeditious; precipitate, headlong, hasty, abrupt, flying. —**Syn. Study.** See QUICK. —**Ant.** slow, sluggish, inexpeditious, late, tardy.

swill *v.* **1.** guzzle, drink greedily, gulp down, swallow noisily, quaff, soak up, swig, tipple, drain the cup, chugalug. —*n.* **2.** slop, liquid food, mash; garbage, refuse, scraps, leavings, waste.

swindle *v.* **1.** cheat, defraud, gyp, hoax, trick, fleece, cozen, bilk, do, gull, hoodwink, bamboozle, con, dupe, deceive, delude, rook. **2.** embezzle, mulct, steal, defalcate, *Slang* rip off. —*n.* **3.** fraud, hoax, cheat, steal, gyp, embezzlement, trick, confidence game, con game, racket, *Slang* rip-off.

swindler *n.* embezzler; con man; crook, charlatan, mountebank, gyp, fraud, sharper, cheat, faker, deceiver, *Slang* rip-off artist, chiseler.

swing *v.* **1.** move to and fro, oscillate, sway, rock, undulate, seesaw, move back and forth. **2.** hang, dangle, suspend, be suspended, drop, loop. **3.** *Informal* manage, manipulate, handle, accomplish, maneuver, pull off, wangle, inveigh, extract. **4.** pivot, rotate, turn, whirl. **5.** influence, sway, decide, determine, rally, move, manipulate. —*n.* **6.** swaying, rocking, listing, pitching, rolling, oscillation. **7.** sweep, sweeping blow, stroke. **8.** liberty, license, freedom; scope, sweep, compass, rein.

swirl *v.* **1.** whirl, spin, twist, revolve,

wheel, turn, roll, twirl; rotate, eddy, churn, gyrate, bowl. **2.** be dizzy, reel, spin, swim.

switch *n.* **1.** rod, small branch, stick. **2.** actuator device, box, lever, handle, button. **3.** shunting device, shunt, train switch; railroad sidetrack. **4.** change, alternation, trade, shift. —*v.* **5.** whip, birch, lash, cane, tan. **6.** whisk, jerk, move, swing, lash. **7.** exchange, change, trade; alternate, shift.

swollen *adj.* puffed-up, puffy, swelled, distended, bloated, inflated, bulging. —**Ant.** shrunken, contracted.

swoop *v.* **1.** descend, pitch, drop, plunge, sweep down, plummet, nosedive, dive; spring, pounce, rush headlong. —*n.* **2.** dive, swooping, plunge, sweep, drop; pounce, rush.

sword *n.* blade, steel; (*variously*) saber, rapier, cutlass, foil, scimitar, épée, broadsword.

sybaritic *adj.* hedonistic, self-indulgent, pleasure-loving, pleasure-seeking, voluptuous, luxury-loving, sensual, epicurean, dissolute, dissipated, pleasure-bent. —**Ant.** austere, ascetic, self-denying, abstinent.

sycophant *n.* parasite, toady, flatterer, bootlicker, lickspittle, fawner, flunky, stooge, hanger-on, yes-man, truckler, rubber stamp, slave, lackey, cat's-paw, tool, jackal, puppet, *Informal* apple-polisher.

sylvan *adj.* woody, forestlike, woodland, arcadian, wooded, woodsy, timbered, forested, thicket-grown, forest-clad, overgrown, luxuriant, bushy, leafy, moss-carpeted.

symbol *n.* **1.** sign, mark, figure, indication. **2.** emblem, token, badge, mark, representation, exemplification, sign, signal, figure.

symbolize *v.* stand for, mean, emblemize, represent, express, personify, connote, denote, emblematize, signify, betoken, symbol, signalize, imply, allegorize, shadow forth, embody, exemplify.

symmetrical *adj.* balanced, well-balanced, orderly, regular, congruent, well-proportioned. —**Ant.** asymmetrical, unbalanced, irregular, uneven, unequal, disorderly.

symmetry *n.* correspondence of parts, regularity, conformity, balance, congruity, proportion, proportionality, equilibrium, order, parallelism, orderliness, harmony; beauty of form, form, shapeliness. —**Syn. Study.** SYMMETRY, BALANCE, PROPORTION, HARMONY all denote qualities based on a correspondence or agreement, usu. pleasing, among the parts of a whole. SYMMETRY implies a regularity in form and arrangement of corresponding parts: *the perfect symmetry of pairs of matched columns.* BALANCE implies equilibrium of dissimilar parts, often as a means of emphasis: *a balance of humor and seriousness.* PROPORTION implies a proper relation among parts: *His long arms were not in proportion to his body.* HARMONY suggests a consistent, pleasing, or orderly combination of parts: *harmony of color.* —**Ant.** disproportion, disharmony, irregularity, disagreement, disparity, malformation, imbalance, lopsidedness.

sympathetic *adj.* **1.** sympathizing, compassionate, understanding, sensitive, tenderhearted, commiserative, warmhearted, softhearted, pitying, comforting, humane, kindly, merciful, benevolent, benign, benignant, feeling. **2.** favorably disposed, well-disposed, agreeable, approving, friendly. —**Ant. 1, 2** unsympathetic. **1** uncompassionate, coldhearted, inhumane, insensitive, pitiless, unpitying, unfeeling, unmerciful.

sympathize *v.* **1.** agree, be in accord, side, go along; understand, appreciate, approve, sanction, regard with favor, favor, back, support; bear goodwill toward, stand behind, take an interest in. **2.** feel compassion for, be sorry for, feel for, have pity for, pity, empathize, feel sympathy for; identify with, grieve with, share the sorrow of, commiserate with, lament with, condole with, mourn with. —**Ant. 1** disagree, oppose, fail to understand, misunderstand, disallow, reject.

sympathy *n.* **1.** concord, accord, harmony, congeniality, understanding, agreement, rapport, affinity, consanguinity, communion, consonance, unanimity, concert, regard, amity, fellow feeling, fellowship, friendship. **2.** concern, compassion, feeling, commiseration, pity, tenderness, empathy, grief, sorrow. **3.** support, favor, sanction, approval, agreement, advocacy, well-wishing, partisanship, patronage. —**Syn. Study. 2** SYMPATHY, COMPASSION, PITY, EMPATHY denote the tendency or capacity to share the feelings of others. SYMPATHY signifies a general kinship with another's feelings, no matter of what kind: *sympathy with their yearning for freedom; sympathy for the bereaved.* COMPASSION implies a deep sympathy for the sorrows or troubles of another, and a powerful urge to alleviate distress: *compassion for homeless refugees.* PITY suggests a kindly, but sometimes condescending, sorrow aroused by the suffering or misfortune of others: *Mere pity for the flood victims is no help.* EMPATHY refers to a vicarious participation in the emotions of another, or to the ability to imagine oneself in someone else's predicament: *to feel empathy* *with a character in a play.* **—Ant. 1** antipathy, hostility, misunderstanding, antagonism. **2** coldness, mercilessness, pitilessness, insensibility, indifference, unconcern. **3** disfavor, disapproval, opposition.

symposium *n.* conference, parley, discussion, panel discussion, forum, round table, colloquy, congress, meeting, deliberation, synod, debate, *Slang,* powwow.

symptom *n.* signal, sign, indication, evidence, token, warning, prognostication, mark, earmark, giveaway.

syndicate *n.* combine, coalition, alliance, league, federation, union, merger, association, group, trust, cartel, consortium.

synonym *n.* equivalent word, parallel word, analogue, equivalent; another name. **—Ant.** antonym, opposite.

synonymous *adj.* equivalent, similar in meaning, alike, like, same, equal, coequal. **—Ant.** antonymous, opposite in meaning.

synopsis *n.* outline, summary, précis, epitome, digest, brief, argument, abstract, abridgement, *Informal* rundown; aperçu, résumé. **—Syn. Study.** See SUMMARY.

synthetic *adj.* artificial, unnatural, man-made, manufactured, ersatz; fake, phony, counterfeit, sham. **—Ant.** real, authentic, genuine, natural, organic.

system *n.* **1.** combination of parts, organization, organized entity, overall unit, unit, structure, setup. **2.** constitution, body, organism. **3.** theory, theoretical base, hypothesis, frame of reference. **4.** method, procedure, arrangement, scheme, program, mode of operation, modus operandi, regimen, routine.

systematic *adj.* **1.** planned, organized, systematized, orderly, ordered. **2.** methodical, precise, orderly, well-organized, businesslike, tidy, neat, well-regulated, constant, regular. **—Syn. Study. 2** See ORDERLY. **—Ant. 1, 2** unsystematic. **1** arbitrary, haphazard, random. **2** unmethodical, disorderly, disorganized, unbusinesslike, messy, sloppy.

tab *n.* **1.** short strip, loop, eyehole, flap, projection, lip, tongue. **2.** *Informal* bill, check, cost, price, tally.

table *n.* **1.** (*variously*) eating table, dining room table, kitchen table, breakfast table; stand, end table, coffee table, bedside table, display table. **2.** board, spread, fare. **3.** list, chart, tabular arrangement, tabulation, schedule, record, inventory, catalog, register, roll, roster; synopsis, index, syllabus. —*v.* **4.** lay aside, put aside, postpone, shelve. —**Ant. 4** act on, vote on, activate, begin, start, initiate; continue.

tableau *n.* scene, spectacle, still life, grouping, picture, illustration, stage picture, view, setting, arrangement, pageant, picturization, delineation, depiction, *French* tableau vivant.

tablet *n.* **1.** pad of paper, writing pad, pad, memo pad. **2.** plaque, panel, tablature; thin slab, surface, sheet, leaf. **3.** flat cake, lozenge, troche, wafer, pellet, bolus.

taboo Also **tabu** *adj.* **1.** forbidden, banned, prohibited, proscribed, outlawed, anathema, unacceptable, disapproved, unthinkable, unmentionable, *German* verboten. —*n.* **2.** religious ban, social ban, ban, prohibition, proscription, interdiction, *Slang* no-no. —**Ant.** allowed, permitted, permissible; approved, sanctioned, encouraged.

tabulate *v.* arrange, order, systematize, file, index, classify, rank, list, group, rate, organize, sort, grade, range, categorize, codify, catalog, sort out. —**Ant.** mix, confuse, jumble, tangle, muddle.

tacit *adj.* unexpressed, understood, assumed, implied, inferred, implicit, wordless, undeclared, unspoken, unstated, taken for granted.

taciturn *adj.* reserved, aloof, reticent, sparing of words, uncommunicative, close-mouthed, tight-lipped, laconic, silent, quiet, secretive. —**Ant.** talkative, loquacious, voluble, garrulous, chatty, open, unreserved, wordy, verbose.

tack *n.* **1.** short nail; (*variously*) thumbtack, carpet tack; thole, tholepin, peg, spike. **2.** zigzag, change, swerve, shift, switch. **3.** course of action, approach, method, way. —*v.* **4.** nail, pin; attach, fasten, affix. **5.** add, attach, affix, append, *Slang* slap, clap. **6.** change course, go about, veer, sheer, swerve, zigzag. —**Ant. 4** untack, unnail, unpin; loose, take off, take down. **5** subtract, deduct, separate, detach, delete, cut.

tackle *n.* **1.** equipment, gear, paraphernalia, apparatus, trappings, rigging, accoutrements, appointments, implements; tools, instruments, material, appliances. **2.** system of ropes and pulleys; (*variously*) hoist, lift, crane, derrick, winch, windlass, capstan, halyard, jenny. **3.** throw, pinioning of the legs. —*v.* **4.** undertake, attempt, try, assay, endeavor, attack, take on, take up, accept, embrace, assume, devote oneself to, turn one's hand to, embark upon, engage in, set about, go about, enter upon, begin. **5.** seize and throw down, throw, wrestle to the ground. —**Ant. 4** reject, spurn, shun, evade, forgo, forswear, eschew; postpone, set aside, shelve.

tacky *adj.* **1.** slovenly, messy, sloppy, disordered, untidy, unkempt, slipshod, shabby, shoddy, tatty, ratty, frazzled, dowdy, seedy, grubby. **2.** sticky, gluey, gummy, adhesive, viscous, stringy, viscid; *Slang* gooey, gucky. —**Ant. 1** neat, orderly, tidy, immaculate.

tact *n.* diplomacy, circumspection, delicacy, savoir faire, suavity, suaveness, finesse, discretion, consideration, sensibility. —**Ant.** tactlessness, crudeness, clumsiness, awkwardness, heavy-handedness, indiscretion, indelicacy, insensitivity.

tactful *adj.* socially adroit, diplomatic, politic, smooth, suave, decorous, subtle, discreet, delicate, considerate, thoughtful; mannerly, sensitive, polite. —**Syn. Study.** See DIPLOMATIC. —**Ant.** tactless, undiplomatic, unpolitic, unsubtle, indecorous, indiscreet; indelicate, tasteless, clumsy, untoward, awkward, gauche.

tactic *n.* **1.** course of action, plan, stratagem, way, tack, method, scheme, policy, approach, line, means of getting one's way. **2.** Usu. **tactics** maneuvers, battle arrangements, military operations.

tactless *adj.* rude, thoughtless, undiplomatic, inconsiderate, insensitive, ill-considered, clumsy, ham-handed, untactful, brash, stupid, boorish, impolitic, imprudent, indiscreet, gauche, blundering, impolite. —**Ant.** tactful, polite, diplomatic, considerate, discreet.

tag *n.* **1.** label, tab, ticket, slip, card, stub, mark, marker; pendant, appendage, attachment. —*v.* **2.** attach a tag to, label, ticket, tab, earmark, mark, identify; term, title, name. **3.** add, add on, tack on, attach, append, annex, affix; fasten, join to. **4.** *Informal* accompany, attend, follow, shadow, trail, tail, dog, heel, hound, hang on the skirts of.

tailor *n.* **1.** garment maker, dressmaker,

seamstress, costumer, clothier, *French* couturier; alteration man, alteration lady. —*v.* **2.** fashion, make, create, design, devise, shape, construct, build, produce, fabricate; alter, adapt, convert, change, fit, modify, transform, redo; sew. —**Ant. 2** destroy, tear up; leave alone, let be.

taint *n.* **1.** stain, spot, blemish, blot, stigma, tarnish, smudge, flaw, defect, fault, imperfection. —*v.* **2.** spoil, damage, ruin, sully, defile, debase, stain, spot, soil, tarnish, blemish, besmirch, dirty, smudge, smear, mar; become spoiled, go bad, putrefy, rot, turn. —**Ant. 2** enhance, elevate, exalt, strengthen, reinforce, boost.

take *v.* **1.** get, have, obtain, acquire, secure, avail oneself of, help oneself to; grip, grasp, clutch, clasp, hold, lay hold of, get hold of, lay hands on, seize, grab, snatch, nab. **2.** seize, grab, usurp, appropriate, misappropriate, capture, commandeer, confiscate, deprive of, divest; steal, purloin, filch, pocket, pilfer, cheat, bilk, fleece; loot, plunder, sack, pillage. **3.** deliver, carry, bring, bear, tote, lug, convey, transport, move, transfer; conduct, guide, lead, escort, usher. **4.** buy, purchase; rent, lease, hire, obtain, acquire, get, use, employ; catch. **5.** subtract, deduct, take away, remove, eliminate. **6.** interpret, understand, regard, respond to, receive, look on, see, perceive, deem, suppose, believe, comprehend, hold, consider, conceive, conclude, deduce, ascertain, infer, make out, *Slang* read. **7.** accept, comply with, accede to, agree to, consent to, assent to, heed, follow, mind, obey, mark, listen to, observe, respect, be ruled by, resign oneself to, go along with. **8.** require, necessitate, need, demand, call for; use, use up, employ, consume, claim. **9.** endure, bear, stand, tolerate, suffer, stomach, brook, submit to, undergo, put up with. **10.** feel, have, experience, know; derive, gain, attain, get, draw. **11.** accept, assume, undertake, shoulder, draw. **12.** take effect, begin to work; work, succeed. —*n.* **13.** catch, haul. **14.** proceeds, net; profit, gross. —**Ant. 1** give, put; let go, put down. **2** surrender, give up, yield, let go; return, restore, give back. **5** add, tack on. **7** reject, refuse, spurn, decline, veto, turn down, dismiss, renounce, repudiate, scorn. **11** forgo, forswear, avoid, evade, eschew. **12** fail, flop. **14** loss.

tale *n.* **1.** story, narrative, narration, recital, account, report, yarn, anecdote; (*variously*) novel, short story, romance, fable, legend, myth, epic, saga. **2.** fib, lie, falsehood, untruth, fabrication, fiction, falsification, tall story, cock-and-bull story, fish story; piece of gossip, scandal, rumor, hearsay, tittle-tattle, *Slang* scuttlebutt.

talent *n.* ability, special ability, natural gift, gift, faculty, facility, endowment, genius, aptitude, capacity, capability, proficiency, skill, knack, bent, flair, turn, forte, strength. —**Syn. Study.** See ABILITY.

talented *adj.* gifted, artistic, accomplished, well-endowed, polished, brilliant, expert, proficient, competent, adept, capable, born for, cut out for, made for.

talk *v.* **1.** utter words, speak, speak about; (*variously*) converse, exchange words, bandy words, communicate orally, discuss, chat, chatter, gab, gossip, palaver, prattle, prate, babble, rap, jaw, rattle on. **2.** confer, consult, speak, take up; negotiate, parley. **3.** utter, speak, say, express, intone, enunciate, state, proclaim, pronounce, deliver, declare; preach, pontificate. —*n.* **4.** conversation, chat, tête-à-tête, chitchat, colloquy, confabulation; discussion, conference, consultation, parley, dialogue, *Slang* powwow, palaver, confab, rap session. **5.** address, lecture, speech, oration, discourse, sermon; harangue, tirade, exhortation; declamation, recitation, utterance. **6.** gossip, rumor, hearsay, noise, report, word, *Slang* tittle-tattle, scuttlebutt, watercooler talk; empty speech, hot air, empty words, blarney, verbiage, bunkum, prattle, chatter, chat, twaddle, blather, blatherskite, gab. **7.** idiom, language, lingo, dialect, patois, slang, cant, jargon, argot. —**Ant. 1** be silent, be mute; listen.

talkative *adj.* loquacious, voluble, effusive, garrulous, talky, chatty, gabby, gossipy, babbly, prolix, long-winded, windy, wordy, verbose. —**Syn. Study.** TALKATIVE, LOQUACIOUS, GARRULOUS characterize a person who talks a great deal. TALKATIVE is a neutral or mildly unfavorable word for a person who is much inclined to talk, sometimes without significance: *a talkative child.* A LOQUACIOUS person, intending to be sociable, talks continuously and at length: *a loquacious host.* The GARRULOUS person talks with wearisome persistence, usu. about trivial things: *a garrulous cab driver.* —**Ant.** silent, mute, mum, speechless; reticent, reserved, taciturn, uncommunicative, secretive, close-mouthed, tight-lipped.

talker *n.* **1.** conversationalist, converser; speaker, lecturer, orator, speechmaker, speechifier; spokesperson, *Slang* mouthpiece. **2.** loquacious person, voluble person, garrulous person, chatterbox, chatterer, windbag, gabber, prattler, babbler, blatherskite; magpie, gossip, rumormonger, scandalmonger.

tall *adj.* **1.** high, in height. **2.** of more

than average height, long-limbed, big, lanky, rangy, gangling, stringy; high, lofty, towering, soaring, elevated. **3.** *Informal* hard to believe, implausible, incredible, unbelievable, preposterous, absurd, hard to swallow, exaggerated, embellished. **—Ant. 1** wide, broad, long, deep. **2** short, squat, low, stubby, dwarflike; tiny, small, diminutive. **3** believable, credible, plausible, reasonable, unexaggerated, unembellished, unadorned; true, real, authentic.

tally *n.* **1.** scorecard, scorepad. **2.** count, reckoning, mark, score; total, sum, enumeration, muster, census, poll. *—v.* **3.** record, mark down, register, list, catalog, post; count, add, sum up, total, compute, calculate, tabulate, reckon. **4.** match, jibe, square, correspond, agree, conform, coincide, accord, concur, harmonize.

tame *adj.* **1.** domesticated, domestic, broken; docile, gentle, mild, tractable, unresisting, submissive, subdued, pliable, pliant, complaisant, amenable, meek, timorous, timid. **2.** unexciting, uninteresting, dull, boring, tedious, prosaic, flat, lifeless; quiet, placid, serene, tranquil. *—v.* **3.** break, make docile, domesticate, subdue, train; control, conquer, overcome, master, dominate, govern, manage, restrain, repress, suppress, curb, bridle, rein, check, regulate, damp. **—Ant. 1** wild, untamed, undomesticated, intractable, unsubmissive, stubborn, obdurate, strong-willed. **2** exciting, interesting, stimulating, spirited, lively, wild, frenzied, tumultuous.

tamper *v.* **1.** meddle, interfere, intrude, obtrude, intervene, horn in, butt in, mix, poke one's nose in. **2.** tinker, fool around, fiddle, *Informal* mess around, monkey around, *British* muck.

tan *v.* **1.** convert to leather, treat with tanning solution. **2.** suntan; brown, bronze. *—adj.* **3.** suntanned, bronzed; sunburned, sunburnt. **4.** light brown, brownish, yellow-brown, beige, tawny, sandy, cinnamon, roan, sorrel, khaki. **—Ant. 2** fade; peel. **3** white, pale, light. **4** dark brown, mahogany, nut-brown.

tang *n.* **1.** strong taste, flavor, savor, pungency, bite, punch, sharpness, sting, piquancy, spiciness, tartness, acridness, acridity; odor, smell, reek, aroma, scent. **2.** trace, tinge, hint, touch, suggestion, bit, smack.

tangible *adj.* **1.** palpable, touchable, material, solid, physical, corporeal, substantial. **2.** concrete, real, actual, material, verifiable, indubitable, positive, clear-cut, obvious, manifest. **—Ant. 1** intangible, untouchable, impalpable; immaterial, ethereal, spiritual, incorporeal, disembodied.

tangle *v.* **1.** twist, snarl, entangle, ravel, knot; disarrange, dishevel, muss, tousle, jumble, disorder, rumple, ruffle. *—n.* **2.** snarl, knot, tanglement, entanglement, web, net, network, mesh, skein, jungle, labyrinth, maze; fix, impasse. **—Ant. 1** untangle, unsnarl, unknot, unravel, loose, loosen, untwist; arrange, order, array, organize, straighten, disentangle.

tank *n.* **1.** storage tank, vat, container, receptacle; reservoir, cistern, boiler; fish tank, aquarium. **2.** armored vehicle on caterpillar treads; armored car.

tantalize *v.* torment with unobtainable prospects, tease, provoke, taunt, torment, make one's mouth water, whet the appetite, tempt, bait, titillate, lead on, intrigue; fascinate, bewitch, charm, captivate, entice. **—Ant.** satisfy, gratify, fulfill, appease.

tantrum *n.* burst of temper, rampage, fit of passion, flare-up, storm, conniption fit, outburst, fit, paroxysm, explosion, *Slang* hissy, hissy fit.

tap[1] *v.* **1.** strike lightly, touch lightly, rap, pat, beat softly, drum, peck, thud, hammer. *—n.* **2.** light strike, gentle blow, touch, stroke, pat, rap, peck.

tap[2] *n.* **1.** faucet, spigot, stopcock, cock, valve, spout. *—v.* **2.** put a tap in, unplug, unstopper, remove the stopple, uncork; open the stopcock of; draw liquid from, draw off, broach. **3.** draw upon, use, utilize, exploit, employ, put to work.

tardy *adj.* **1.** late, not on time, unpunctual, behind time, behindhand, belated; overdue, remiss, dilatory. **2.** slow, slow-paced, sluggish, slack, creeping, crawling, leisurely, languid, snail-like, slowpoke, slow as molasses; procrastinating, reluctant. **—Ant. 1** punctual, on time, prompt; undelayed; early, premature. **2** fast, fast-moving, speedy, quick, rapid; industrious, eager, zealous.

target *n.* **1.** mark, object aimed at; objective, object, goal, aim, end, purpose, ambition; design, plan, intent, intention. **2.** butt, goat, victim, prey, dupe, gull, patsy, pigeon, laughingstock.

tariff *n.* **1.** duty, input tax, export tax, excise tax, excise, assessment, impost, levy; list of import-export taxes, customs list, trade controls. **2.** fare, freightage; (*loosely*) charge, rate, fee, price, cost, expense, rent, commission.

tarnish *v.* **1.** oxidize, corrode, discolor, blacken, dull, dim, darken, lose luster. **2.** discredit, degrade, defile, defame, vilify, stigmatize, denigrate, disgrace, dishonor, taint, stain, sully, spot, blemish, blacken, foul, befoul, smirch, besmirch, soil, blot, erode, dirty, dull, dim, darken, drag through the mud. **—Ant. 1** shine, gleam, polish, burnish, clean; brighten. **2** enhance, glorify, credit, exalt.

tarry *v.* **1.** linger, dally, remain, stay, bide, abide, rest, pause, *Informal* hang around, cool one's heels. **2.** dawdle, delay, wait, take time, be tardy, lag, procrastinate, put off, postpone, stave off, temporize, stall, hang back. **—Ant. 1** leave, go, depart, be off, run, run along, move on, get moving. **2** rush, hurry, hasten, quicken, hustle, expedite, precipitate, spur.

tart[1] *adj.* **1.** sour, sourish, sharp, astringent, acid, acrid, acetic, vinegary; piquant, spicy, tangy, pungent, bitter. **2.** sharp, caustic, cutting, barbed, biting, acerb, acrid, crusty. **—Ant. 1** sweet, sugary, saccharine, cloying; mild, bland, mellow, flat. **2** sweet, kind, kindly, gentle, mild, pleasant, agreeable, benign, genial, polite, gracious, friendly, amiable, good-natured.

tart[2] *n.* individual pie, small fruit pie, small open-faced pie; pastry shell.

task *n.* chore, duty, work, labor, stint, mission, assignment, job, charge, responsibility, errand, business, undertaking. **—Syn. Study.** TASK, CHORE, ASSIGNMENT, JOB refer to a specific instance or act of work. TASK refers to a clearly defined piece of work, usu. of short or limited duration, assigned to or expected of a person: *the task of collecting dues.* A CHORE is a minor, usu. routine task, often more tedious than difficult: *the chore of taking out the garbage.* ASSIGNMENT usu. refers to a specific task assigned by someone in authority: *a homework assignment.* JOB is the most general of these terms, referring to almost any work or duty, including one's livelihood: *the job of washing the windows; a well-paid job in advertising.*

taskmaster *n.* martinet, slave driver, tyrant, disciplinarian, despot, Simon Legree, stickler; master, boss, supervisor, superintendent, overseer, foreman, director, headman, manager.

taste *v.* **1.** experience the flavor of; savor, discern; have a flavor of, savor of, smack of. **2.** sample, eat a little of, take a bite of, try, test; drink a little of, take a sip of. **3.** experience, partake of, encounter, meet, undergo, feel, enjoy, relish, savor, have a foretaste of. *—n.* **4.** flavor, savor, relish, smack, tang, piquancy. **5.** mouthful, bite, morsel, bit, crumb, sample, forkful, spoonful; sip, swallow, nip. **6.** liking, predilection, propensity, leaning, inclination, penchant, bent, partiality, disposition, fondness, craving, hankering, longing, desire, fancy, yearning, yen, whim, relish, appetite, thirst, hunger. **7.** esthetic judgment, sense of beauty, discernment, artistic appreciation; sense of propriety, propriety, correctness, judgment, discrimination, insight, delicacy, decorum. **—Ant. 3** miss. **6** distaste, dislike, disinclination, disrelish; hatred, abhorrence, loathing. **7** tastelessness; impropriety, indelicacy, coarseness, crudeness.

tasteful *adj.* showing good taste, esthetic, artistic, attractive, elegant, exquisite, refined, cultured, well-chosen, handsome, beautiful, suitable, becoming. **—Ant.** tasteless, unesthetic, inelegant, ugly, loud, flashy, garish, tawdry, gaudy, unrefined, uncultured.

tasteless *adj.* **1.** having no taste, flavorless, unflavored, without savor, bland, insipid, weak, flat, mild, watery. **2.** lacking good taste, cheap, common, crude, rude, coarse, crass, gross, uncouth, improper, inappropriate, unseemly, unsuitable, insensitive, indelicate, indecent, indecorous, low, ribald, disgusting, distasteful, offensive, gaudy, flashy, garish, inelegant, unrefined, uncultured, unesthetic.

tasty *adj.* good-tasting, delicious, delectable, luscious, toothsome, scrumptious, yummy; flavorful, flavorsome, full-flavored, appetizing, savory; piquant, spicy, well-seasoned, hot, zestful, tangy; palatable. **—Syn. Study.** TASTY, APPETIZING, SAVORY, PALATABLE refer to tastes or aromas pleasing to the palate, and sometimes to the senses of sight and smell. TASTY refers to food that has an appealing taste: *a tasty sausage.* APPETIZING suggests stimulation of the appetite by the smell, taste, or sight of food: *an appetizing display of meats and cheeses.* SAVORY refers most often to well or highly seasoned food that is pleasing to the taste or smell: *a savory stew.* PALATABLE usu. refers to food that is merely acceptable: *a barely palatable plate of vegetables.*

tatters *n. pl.* shreds, rags; ragged clothing, torn clothes, cast-off clothes; patches.

tattle *v.* **1.** tell on, inform on, divulge secrets, blab, gossip; *Slang* snitch, rat, squeal; babble, prattle, gabble, prate, blurt out confidences, blather. *—n.* **2.** gossip, prattle, blather, chatter, babble, rumormongering, tittle-tattle, twaddle, tongue-wagging, hearsay, mudslinging, loose talk.

tattletale *n.* tattler, talebearer, rumormonger, newsmonger, gossip, telltale, busybody, informer, betrayer, troublemaker, scandalmonger, blabbermouth; *Slang* snitch, squealer, fink, rat, stool pigeon, stoolie, ratfink, *Brit.* sneak.

taunt *v.* **1.** jeer at, jeer, mock, insult, tease, rag, jive, gibe, twit, guy; ridicule, deride, snigger at, sneer at, make fun of, poke fun at, make game of; torment, provoke, harass. *—n.* **2.** jeer, mockery, insult, teasing remark, ragging, chaffing, gibe, derision, sneer, scoff, snigger, ridicule, sarcastic remark, scornful remark, slur, verbal abuse; tormenting, provocation, harassment. —**Syn. Study. 1** See RIDICULE. —**Ant. 1** humor, flatter, jolly, coddle, court, pander to, truckle to, curry favor with, butter up; praise, compliment. **2** humoring, flattering, coddling, pandering, truckling, currying favor, buttering up, praise, compliment.

taut *adj.* **1.** drawn tight, tight, stretched out full, tense, not slack, not loose, rigid, unbending, inflexible, under strain, unrelaxed. **2.** well-regulated, orderly, businesslike, well-disciplined, tight, neat, tidy, trim, trig, spruce, smart, shipshape, snug, no-nonsense. —**Ant. 1** slack, loose, relaxed, flexible. **2** sloppy, slovenly, undisciplined, messy, untidy.

tavern *n.* saloon, barroom, taproom, bar, alehouse, restaurant, brasserie, bistro, cocktail lounge; *Brit.* pub, public house; *Slang* watering hole, grogshop, drinkery, gin mill, beer joint, honkytonk, dive.

tawdry *adj.* showy, flashy, raffish, flamboyant, garish, meretricious, gaudy, loud, tasteless, inelegant, vulgar, crass, tacky, cheap, tinsel, gimcrack, pretentious, ostentatious, conspicuous, obtrusive. —**Ant.** tasteful, elegant, refined, *Informal* classy, high-class; simple, plain, quiet, reserved, understated.

tawny *adj.* tan, bronze, yellowish-brown, light brown, brownish, beige, fawn, sandy; dusky, swarthy, olive.

tax *n.* **1.** payment of money to support a government and its services; *(variously)* income tax, property tax, sales tax, excise tax, luxury tax, inheritance tax, excess profit tax, state tax, county tax, city tax; impost, assessment, excise, levy, tariff, duty, custom, toll. **2.** burden, strain, strenuous demand, load, exertion, drain; charge, obligation, duty. —*v.* **3.** impose a tax on, assess, levy, exact a duty from. **4.** burden, overburden, weigh, weight, lade, load, saddle, strain, overwork, tire, stretch, try; drain, exhaust, sap, wear out, deplete. —**Ant. 1** deduction, nontaxable income.

teach *v.* give instruction in, conduct classes in, give lessons in, be employed as a teacher; give instruction to, conduct class for, give lessons to, instruct, educate, school, tutor, train, coach, drill, exercise, discipline, prepare, prime; inform, enlighten, edify, indoctrinate, inculcate, implant. —**Syn. Study.** TEACH, INSTRUCT, EDUCATE, TRAIN share the meaning of imparting information, understanding, or skill. TEACH is the most general of these terms, referring to any practice that furnishes a person with skill or knowledge: *to teach children to write.* INSTRUCT usu. implies a systematic, structured method of teaching: *to instruct paramedics in first aid.* EDUCATE stresses the development of reasoning and judgment; it often involves preparing a person for an occupation or for mature life: *to educate the young.* TRAIN stresses the development of a desired proficiency or behavior through practice, discipline, and instruction: *to train military recruits.* —**Ant.** learn, study, attend school, be educated.

teacher *n.* *(variously)* schoolteacher, schoolmaster, master, schoolmistress, schoolmarm, instructor, professor, don, tutor, maestro, educator, preceptor, trainer, mentor, coach.

teaching *n.* **1.** instruction, instructing, schooling, tutoring, tutelage, training, preparation; the teaching profession, education, pedagogy; indoctrination, inculcation, nurture. **2.** precept, doctrine, dogma, principle, tenet.

team *n.* **1.** harnessed pair, yoked group; pair, set, yoke, tandem. **2.** sports team, side; *(football)* eleven, *(baseball)* nine, *(basketball)* five. **3.** group, unit, staff, crew, band, gang, company, squad, association, alliance, league, confederation, federation, coalition, combine, party, force, faction, circle, clique, coterie. —*v.* **4.** yoke, join, couple, rig; combine, unite, join together, band together, get together, ally, form an alliance, merge, incorporate, federate, unify, consolidate, amalgamate; cooperate, pool one's efforts. —**Ant. 4** unjoin, unyoke, unhook, uncouple; separate, divide, part, go one's separate way.

tear[1] *n.* **1.** teardrop. —*v.* **2.** fill with tears, shed tears, swim, mist.

tear[2] *v.* **1.** rip, rend, rive, split, slit, cleave, sever, sunder, shred, pull apart, come apart, pull to pieces, run, snag. **2.** pull, grab, seize, wrench, pluck, snatch, yank. **3.** divide, disunite, split, splinter, rend, disrupt. **4.** speed, race, rush, hasten, run, bolt, dash, dart, sprint, spurt, shoot, fly, hie, scurry, scuttle, scoot, scud, whiz, gallop, sweep, whisk, plunge, scamper, scramble, skedaddle, hustle, hotfoot it, make tracks. —*n.* **5.** damage, destruction, ravage, hard treatment, abuse, hard use; impairment, injury. **6.** rip, rent, slit, split, hole; gap, break, breach, crack, rift, fissure, fault, rupture, opening. —**Ant. 1** mend, repair, sew, stitch up. **3** unite, reunite, bind, solidify, join, strengthen. **4** creep, crawl, amble, stroll, saunter. **6** patch, mend.

tearful *adj.* weeping, teary, crying, lachrymose, mournful, lamenting; weepy, wailing, bawling, sobbing, blubbering, whimpering, sniveling; heartbroken, inconsolable, crushed, brokenhearted.

tease *v.* **1.** taunt, gibe, ridicule, mock, chafe, vex, rag, needle, haze, make fun of, josh, laugh at, twit, guy, bait, goad, heckle, mimic, tantalize, bedevil, torment; pester, plague, worry, provoke, annoy, irritate, bother, aggravate; harry, badger, irk, persecute, harass, hector, rile, gall, pique, nag. —*n.* **2.** taunt, jeer, gibe, twit, ridicule, mocking remark, scornful remark, chafing, razzing, hazing, needling, derision, sneer, scoff, snigger, heckling, mimicking, harassment, persecution. **3.** teaser, taunter, mocker, needler, tantalizer, tormentor; pest, nag, worrier. **—Ant. 1** praise, laud, compliment; humor, flatter; comfort, console, soothe, placate. **2** praise, compliment; comforting, consoling, soothing, placating.

technique *n.* **1.** technical skill, form, style, skillfulness, craft, expertness, proficiency, facility, art, adroitness, knowhow, knack. **2.** procedure, method, way, technology, formula, approach, manner, system.

tedious *adj.* **1.** time-consuming, drawn-out, slow, long; tiring, wearying, fatiguing, exhausting, irksome, burdensome, onerous, oppressive, laborious, dreary, dismal. **2.** dull, boring, monotonous, unexciting, uninteresting, unimaginative, prosaic, humdrum, insipid, vapid, drab, dreary, dismal, dry, lifeless, tiresome, wearisome, jejune. **—Ant. 1, 2** exhilarating, exciting, interesting, amusing, enthralling, stimulating. **1** quick, fast, short. **2** imaginative, stirring, lively, provocative, inspiring.

tedium *n.* monotony, dullness, tediousness, sameness, routineness, boredom, rut, ennui, tiresomeness, drabness, dreariness. **—Ant.** excitement, interest, amusement, fascination, stimulation, liveliness, exhilaration; inspiration, challenge.

teem *v.* swarm, be overrun, overflow, abound, be full of, be inundated, brim, gush, bristle with, be well-stocked, burst at the seams. **—Ant.** be empty of, have a scarcity of.

teeter *v.* wobble, totter, sway, seesaw, stagger, lurch, reel; waver, hesitate, vacillate.

teetotaler *n.* nondrinker, abstainer, prohibitionist, dry. **—Ant.** drunk, drunkard, alcoholic, dipsomaniac, sot, *Slang* boozehound, boozer, wino.

telepathy *n.* thought transference, sixth sense, second sight, extrasensory perception, ESP; clairvoyance, spirit communication.

tell *v.* **1.** narrate, declare, relate, recount, give an account of, report, set forth, recite, speak, utter, express, state, say, pronounce, mention, enunciate, advise, acquaint, apprise, communicate, make known, impart, reveal, divulge, disclose, unfold, let fall, spout, publish, broadcast, spread abroad, bruit, blab, blazon, babble, inform, betray, breathe a word about, describe, chronicle, write, detail, depict, portray, sketch, paint a picture; confess, own. **2.** tell apart, distinguish, discriminate, discern, identify, make out, recognize, perceive, ascertain, find out, figure, calculate, reckon, apprehend, see; predict, forecast, foretell. **3.** direct, instruct, order, command, bid, ask, request. **4.** count, count off, number, enumerate; compute, calculate, reckon, estimate. **5.** take effect, influence, have force, weigh, carry weight, take a toll on, be potent, register, be of account. **—Ant. 1** keep quiet, keep mum, be mute, keep secret, hide, conceal; listen. **2** confuse, mix up.

telling *adj.* effective, effectual, efficacious, powerful, forceful, striking, potent, weighty, momentous, trenchant, significant, influential, cogent, material, definite, definitive, decisive, decided, positive, conclusive, valid, solid, important, impressive, consequential. **—Ant.** ineffective, unimportant, immaterial, insignificant, unmeaningful, trivial, inconsequential, indefinite, indecisive.

telltale *n.* **1.** talebearer; tattletale, tattler, blabbermouth, gossip, busybody, scandalmonger, newsbearer; informer, squealer. —*adj.* **2.** revealing, giveaway, tattletale, betraying, divulging, disclosing, informative, enlightening; confirming, verifying, affirming.

temerity *n.* audacity, insolence, gall, brazenness, brashness, nerve, cheek, brass, impudence, effrontery, forwardness, sauciness, freshness, impertinence, intrusiveness, pushiness, indiscretion, *Yiddish* chutzpah; foolhardiness, rashness, boldness. **—Ant.** reserve, reticence, politeness, tact, discretion, meekness; bashfulness, shyness; timidity, cowardice, caution, wariness.

temper *n.* **1.** frame of mind, mood, disposition, humor. **2.** anger, rage, fury, wrath, ire, irritation, irritability, annoyance, vexation, bad humor, pique, peevishness, acrimony, choler, spleen, gall, bile, animus, dander, huffiness, irascibility, churlishness, dudgeon, indignation, displeasure, umbrage, passion, emotion, ferment. **3.** good humor, kindly disposition; calmness, composure, equilibrium, balance. —*v.* **4.** strengthen, harden, toughen, anneal. **5.** soften, moderate, allay, appease, pacify, tranquilize, mitigate, palliate, calm, compose, quiet, soothe, still. **—Ant. 2** goodwill, good humor, calmness, composure. **3** bad humor, bad disposition, anger, rage, fury, indignation, wrath, ire, irritation, vexation, pique, peevishness; fit of emotion, ferment. **4** soften, weaken. **5** intensify, heighten, aggravate, excite, increase, stir, rouse, arouse, pique.

temperament *n.* disposition, nature, mood, frame of mind; temper, makeup, character, personality, spirit, soul; humor, tone, cast, quality, tenor, complexion, leaning, tendency, bent.

temperamental *adj.* high-strung, excitable, moody, thin-skinned, sensitive, explosive, mercurial, volatile, passionate, emotional, hotheaded, fiery, tempestuous, peppery, mettlesome, turbulent, hysterical; unpredictable, capricious, erratic, fickle, unreliable, undependable, unstable; willful, headstrong. **—Ant.** eventempered, easygoing, cool, coolheaded, calm, unexcitable, *Slang* unflappable; reliable, dependable, predictable, steady.

temperance *n.* **1.** moderation, forbearance, self-control, self-discipline, restraint, discretion, prudence; abstention, self-denial. **2.** teetotalism, abstinence, abstemiousness, sobriety, prohibition. **—Ant. 1, 2** intemperance, immoderation. **1** unrestraint, abandon, wantonness, indulgence, extravagance. **2** drinking, imbibing; alcoholism, dipsomania, boozing.

temperate *adj.* **1.** self-restrained, self-controlled, moderate, unextravagant, sparing, sedate, sober, sane, rational, reasonable; calm, even, cool, coolheaded, levelheaded, composed, collected, unruffled, steady, tranquil, easygoing, self-possessed, patient, dispassionate, unimpassioned. **2.** mild, gentle, soft, moderate, clement, pleasant, mellow; balmy, sunny, warm. **—Syn. Study. 1** See MODERATE. **—Ant. 1, 2** intemperate, immoderate. **1** unrestrained, uncontrolled, abandoned, inordinate, extreme, excessive, extravagant, unreasonable, irrational; temperamental, excitable, passionate, impassioned, explosive, volatile, hotheaded, hysterical, frenzied, wild. **2** inclement, harsh, severe, unpleasant.

tempest *n.* storm, uproar, commotion, furor, upheaval, disturbance, tumult, cataclysm, outbreak, turbulence, hurly-burly, chaos, agitation, hubbub, *Slang* brouhaha. **—Ant.** calm, serenity, peace, tranquillity.

tempestuous *adj.* stormy, turbulent, raging, violent, furious, agitated, tumultuous; passionate, impassioned, emotional, frenzied, overwrought, wrought-up, hysterical, frantic, excited, fiery, hot, explosive, feverish. **—Ant.** calm, placid, peaceful; relaxed, unagitated, easy, serene, tranquil, quiet, coolheaded, unemotional, disinterested.

tempo *n.* speed, pace, time, meter, momentum, rate, velocity, gait, stride, pacing, timing, *Slang* clip.

temporal *adj.* **1.** civil, lay, secular, nonspiritual, nonclerical, nonecclesiastical, profane. **2.** noneternal, temporary, transient, fleeting, passing, ephemeral, evanescent, day-to-day, fugitive, impermanent, worldly, mundane, mortal. **—Ant. 1** ecclesiastical, clerical; spiritual, sacred, religious. **2** eternal, everlasting, otherworldly, unearthly.

temporary *adj.* momentary, brief, impermanent, passing, fleeting, fleet, transient, transitory, fugitive, short-lived, ephemeral, evanescent, flash-in-the-pan; stopgap, provisional, provisory, interim. **—Syn. Study.** TEMPORARY, TRANSIENT, TRANSITORY agree in referring to that which is not lasting or permanent. TEMPORARY implies an arrangement established with no thought of continuance but with the idea of being changed soon: *a temporary structure.* TRANSIENT describes that which is in the process of passing by, and which will therefore last or stay only a short time: *a transient condition.* TRANSITORY describes an innate characteristic by which a thing, by its very nature, lasts only a short time: *Life is transitory.* **—Ant.** lasting, everlasting, eternal, permanent, durable, enduring, long-lived, persisting, protracted.

temporize *v.* delay, hedge, stall, equivocate, tergiversate, tarry, hem and haw, maneuver, drag one's feet, play for time, waver, vacillate, procrastinate, hang back. **—Ant.** act, decide, execute, proceed.

tempt *v.* **1.** seduce, entice, inveigle, lure, allure, woo, bait, decoy; appeal to, attract, pull, invite, take one's fancy, whet the appetite, draw, intrigue, tantalize; captivate, bewitch, charm. **2.** put to the test, fly in the face of, try, risk, provoke, incite, goad, rouse, arouse, prick. **—Syn. Study. 1** TEMPT, SEDUCE both mean to allure or entice someone into an unwise, wrong, or wicked action. To TEMPT is to attract by holding out the probability of gratification or advantage, often in regard to what is wrong or unwise: *to tempt a high official with a bribe.* To SEDUCE is to lead astray, as from duty or principles, but more often from moral rectitude, chastity, etc.: *to seduce a soldier from loyalty.* **—Ant. 1** discourage, repel, repulse, disgust.

temptation *n.* tempting, allurement, snare, lure, enticement, attraction, seduction, pull, urge, draw, bait, inducement, incentive, incitement, provocation, stimulus, fascination, captivation, charm, spell.

temptress *n.* seductress, siren, enchantress, femme fatale, sorceress, Circe, Lorelei, vamp, vampire, flirt, coquette, charmer, odalisque, Jezebel, Delilah.

tenable *adj.* defendable, defensible,

warrantable, condonable, workable, viable, justifiable, excusable, vindicable, maintainable, arguable, rational, sensible. **—Ant.** unjustifiable, untenable, indefensible, irrational.

tenacious *adj.* fast, firm, clinging, iron, hard, set; persevering, persistent, determined, resolute, obstinate, stubborn, obdurate, inflexible, uncompromising, immovable, unchangeable, unbending, unyielding, adamant, intransigent, inexorable, unwavering, unfaltering, unswerving, undeviating, steadfast, staunch, unremitting, stalwart, constant, relentless, mulish, pigheaded, dogged. **—Ant.** loose, lax, limp, slack; unpersevering, undetermined, irresolute, flexible.

tenacity *n.* perseverance, persistence, pertinacity, determination, steadfastness, stalwartness, constancy; relentlessness, doggedness, obstinacy, stubbornness, mulishness, pigheadedness. **—Syn. Study.** TENACITY, PERSEVERANCE, PERSISTENCE imply determined continuance in a state or in a course of action. TENACITY is a dogged and determined holding on: *the stubborn tenacity of a salesman.* PERSEVERANCE suggests effort maintained in spite of difficulties or long-continued application; it is used in a favorable sense: *The scientist's perseverance finally paid off in an important discovery.* PERSISTENCE, which may be used in a favorable or unfavorable sense, implies steadfast, unremitting continuance in spite of opposition or protest: *an annoying persistence in a belief.*

tenant *n.* renter, lessee, leaseholder; lodger, paying guest, roomer, boarder; occupant, inhabitant, resident, householder, dweller, denizen. **—Ant.** landlord, lessor, leaser.

tend[1] *v.* **1.** be inclined, be disposed, have a tendency, be apt, be likely, be liable, have an inclination, lean, have a leaning, predispose, bid fair to. **2.** lead, bear, extend, point, head, aim, be bound for, gravitate, move.

tend[2] *v.* attend to, care for, take care of, look after, keep an eye on, mind, watch over, watch; nurse, nurture, foster, wait on, minister to; supervise, manage, guide. **—Ant.** neglect, ignore.

tendency *n.* inclination, disposition, proclivity, proneness, propensity, trend, predisposition, readiness, penchant, bent, leaning, impulse, habit, set, drive, trend, turning, drift, direction, course, gravitation, heading, aim. **—Ant.** disinclination, indisposition, aversion, reluctance, unreadiness, hesitancy.

tender[1] *adj.* **1.** soft, gentle, delicate, dainty; kind, good, compassionate, sympathetic, considerate, understanding, thoughtful, caring, softhearted, warm-hearted, loving, affectionate, fond, sentimental, merciful, benevolent, benign, generous. **2.** weak, weakly, fragile, frail, feeble, delicate, vulnerable. **3.** young, youthful, juvenile, underage, immature, inexperienced, unsophisticated, impressionable, callow, green. **4.** sensitive, painful, requiring delicacy; sore, aching, raw, swollen, inflamed. **—Ant. 1** tough, hard; mean, cruel, brutal, inhuman, sadistic, vicious, unsympathetic, unkind, inconsiderate, uncaring, hard-hearted, cold-hearted, hateful, merciless, pitiless, ruthless. **2** hardy, strong, robust, sturdy, rugged, vigorous, hale, flourishing, thriving. **3** old, elderly, advanced; full-grown, grown-up, mature, experienced, seasoned, practiced, worldly, worldly-wise, sophisticated. **4** insensitive.

tender[2] *v.* present, present formally, make formal offer of, offer, proffer, prefer, submit, put forward, lay before, place, volunteer, give, hold out, advance, propound, propose, extend, suggest, hand in. **—Syn. Study.** See OFFER. **—Ant.** withhold; withdraw, retract.

tenderhearted *adj.* sympathetic, compassionate; softhearted, kindhearted, warm-hearted, considerate, understanding, thoughtful, responsive, gentle, mild, humane, benevolent, benign, merciful, generous, altruistic. **—Ant.** hard-hearted, coldhearted, mean, cruel, brutal, sadistic, inhuman, vicious, merciless, pitiless, callous, unsympathetic, inconsiderate.

tenderness *n.* **1.** softness, gentleness, delicacy, mildness; kindness, kindliness, loving-kindness, compassion, sympathy, goodness, benevolence, beneficence, humanity, humaneness, mercifulness; fondness, warmth, affection, lovingness, love. **2.** sensitivity, soreness, painfulness, aching, rawness, smarting. **—Ant. 1** hardness, toughness; cruelty, meanness, brutality, viciousness, unkindness, hardheartedness, coldheartedness, coldness, harshness, severity, mercilessness. **2** insensitivity.

tenet *n.* belief, doctrine, dogma, way of thinking, creed, credo, canon, teaching, conviction, position, persuasion, principle, maxim, rule, thesis, view, opinion, ideology.

tenor *n.* meaning, sense, import, argument, significance, essence, content, substance, gist, drift, course, nature, implication, connotation; intent, intention, object, purport, purpose, trend, direction, tendency.

tense *adj.* **1.** stretched tight, tight, taut, drawn, rigid, braced, stiff; inflexible, unyielding. **2.** nervous, strained, taut, drawn, wrought-up, high-strung, tremulous, uneasy, restless, restive, fidgety, jittery, on edge, excited, agitated, shaky, fearful, apprehensive, anxious, timorous, *Slang* uptight. —*v.* **3.** tighten up, draw up, make taut, stiffen, brace. —**Ant. 1** relaxed, slack, loose, limp, flaccid; pliant, flexible. **2** relaxed, loose, calm, cool, collected, self-possessed. **3** relax, loosen.

tension *n.* **1.** stretching, straining, stress, tugging, traction, pressure, pulling, exertion; spring, elastic force; tightness, tautness, rigidity, stiffness. **2.** strain, stress, anxiety, apprehension, dread, nervousness, restiveness, trepidation, misgiving, fearfulness, perturbation, hostility, combativeness, suppressed anger, *Slang* bad vibrations, bad vibes. —**Ant. 1** slack, looseness, laxness. **2** relief, relaxation, ease, calmness, serenity, tranquillity.

tentative *adj.* unconfirmed, not settled, unsettled, not final, under consideration, open to consideration, subject to change, provisional, conditional, speculative, contingent, not definite, indefinite, undecided, *Informal* iffy; experimental, trial, temporary, not permanent, ad interim, acting, probational, probationary, proposed. —**Ant.** confirmed, settled, final, set, firm, conclusive, definite, decided, closed, unchangeable.

tenuous *adj.* weak, flimsy, shaky, unsubstantial, unsupported, slight, slim, thin, slender, frail, fragile, delicate, gossamer, shallow, paltry, unconvincing, halfhearted, uncertain, indefinite. —**Ant.** strong, solid, valid, substantial.

tenure *n.* **1.** term, incumbency, rule, tenancy, occupancy, time, administration, possession, reign, retention, occupation. **2.** permanent status, job security, employment guarantee, entitlement, permanency.

tepid *adj.* lukewarm, temperate, warmish; moderate, mild, unemotional, halfhearted, indifferent, cool, impassive, phlegmatic, languid, apathetic, nonchalant, lackadaisical, unenthusiastic.

term *n.* **1.** word, phrase, expression, idiom, technical word, technical expression; name, designation, appellation. **2.** span of time, span, period, time, duration, course, spell, while, interval, stage, cycle; age, era, epoch, reign, administration, dynasty. **3.** stipulation, condition, provision, proviso, clause, item, detail, requirement, prerequisite, requisite, *Slang* catch, string. **4. terms** relations, standing, footing, status, state, position, circumstance. —*v.* **5.** call, name, designate, dub, tag, style, characterize, cite.

termagant *n.* shrew, scold, nag, virago, harridan, fury, vixen, fishwife, hellion, spitfire, Xanthippe, she-wolf, ogress, tigress, hellcat, battle-ax.

terminal *adj.* **1.** last, final, concluding, end. **2.** causing death, mortal, fatal, deadly, lethal. —*n.* **3.** station, depot, terminus, stand. —**Ant. 1** first, initial; beginning, opening. **2** nonfatal; temporary, passing.

terminate *v.* bring to an end, come to an end, end, conclude, finish, stop, cease, close, wind up, complete, discontinue, expire, lapse, run out. —**Ant.** begin, start, commence, initiate, open; continue, pursue, extend.

termination *n.* end, ending, close, closing, conclusion, concluding, finish, windup, completion, cessation, discontinuation, finis, finale, expiration, lapse, halt, stoppage. —**Ant.** beginning, start, commencement, initiation, opening, inception.

terminus *n.* end, conclusion, stop, ending, furthermost part, last stop, boundary, extreme, limit, terminal, extremity.

terrain *n.* topography, ground, area, region, territory, tract, countryside; surroundings, environment, milieu, setting, zone, district.

terrestrial *adj.* **1.** land, ground, earthbound; riparian. **2.** earth's, earthly, worldly, global, mundane. —**Syn. Study. 2** See EARTHLY. —**Ant. 1** marine, aquatic, sea, water. **2** celestial, astral, lunar, cosmic, space.

terrible *adj.* **1.** severe, fierce, intense, strong, harsh, brutal, rough; great, huge, tremendous, immoderate, extreme, excessive, inordinate, monstrous, enormous, terrific. **2.** extremely bad, horrible, horrid, awful, hideous, repulsive, revolting, obnoxious, offensive, odious, distasteful, unpleasant, objectionable, intolerable, insufferable, appalling, hateful, bad, heinous, dire, ghastly, shocking, beastly. **3.** alarming, frightening, terrifying, fearful, fearsome, scary, harrowing, awful, dreadful, horrifying, formidable, distressing, upsetting, disturbing. —**Ant. 1** mild, moderate, harmless, gentle; small, insignificant, paltry. **2** wonderful, excellent, fine, good, great, pleasing, pleasant, delightful, admirable, nice; worthy, praiseworthy, laudable, commendable. **3** comforting, reassuring, encouraging, settling, soothing, calming, easing.

terrific *adj.* **1.** severe, intense, fierce, harsh, terrible, extreme, excessive, monstrous, great, enormous, huge, inordinate, immoderate, tremendous; frightening, terrifying, fearful, fearsome, alarming, scary, harrowing, distressing, awful, dreadful, horrifying, upsetting, disturbing. **2.** great, fine, good, wonderful, superb, excellent, splendid, marvelous, sensational, fabulous, fantastic, stupendous, smashing, super, superduper, extraordinary, remarkable, exceptional, *Slang* bang-up, marvy, fab, sensash, out of this world. **—Ant. 1** mild, moderate, harmless, gentle, slight, insignificant, paltry; comforting, reassuring, encouraging, settling, soothing, calming, easing. **2** bad, terrible, awful, lousy, stinking, horrible, dreadful, hideous, revolting, unpleasant, appalling, distasteful.

terrify *v.* fill with terror, frighten, scare, alarm, horrify, panic, petrify, unman, abash, daunt, cow, intimidate, overawe, make one's hair stand on end, make one's blood run cold, make one's skin crawl; upset, disturb, appall, dismay, agitate, disquiet. **—Ant.** comfort, reassure, encourage, hearten, soothe, calm, ease, please, delight.

territory *n.* **1.** terrain, region, land, acreage, area, zone, district, sector, clime, tract, countryside, locale. **2.** domain, realm, province, sphere of influence, dominion, commonwealth, state, nation, principality, kingdom, empire; protectorate, dependency, mandate, colony; bailiwick, pale, limits, confines, bounds.

terror *n.* fear, fear and trembling, fright, affright, horror, panic, alarm, dread; dismay, trepidation, perturbation, consternation, apprehension, awe, anxiety, agitation, disquiet, disquietude. **—Ant.** security, reassurance, encouragement, comfort, calm, quiet, tranquillity.

terse *adj.* brief and to the point, concise, pithy, succinct, crisp, clipped, incisive, pointed, neat, compact, condensed, compressed, clear, clearcut, unambiguous, summary, trenchant, laconic, epigrammatic, axiomatic; brief, short, abrupt, curt. **—Syn. Study.** See CONCISE. **—Ant.** rambling, circuitous, roundabout, diffuse, discursive, verbose, wordy, lengthy, long, long-winded; vague, confused, ambiguous.

test *n.* **1.** analysis, investigation; trial, tryout, dry run, probe, check, feeler, flyer; proof, verification, confirmation, corroboration. **2.** examination, exam, quiz; (*variously*) final, comprehensive, midterm; questioning, questionnaire, catechism. *—v.* **3.** quiz, examine; analyze, investigate, probe, experiment with; try out, put to the proof, prove, verify, confirm, corroborate, substantiate, validate, send up a trial balloon, throw out a feeler.

testament *n.* **1.** final written will; bequest, legacy, settlement. **2. Testament** Old Testament, New Testament; Bible, Scriptures, the Book.

testify *v.* bear witness, give evidence, state as fact, declare, affirm, swear; attest, show, indicate, signify, demonstrate, evidence, evince, manifest, prove.

testimonial *n.* **1.** recommendation, reference, commendation, endorsement, citation; certificate, affidavit, deposition. **2.** testimonial dinner, banquet in someone's honor; memorial, monument, tribute; medal, ribbon, trophy.

testimony *n.* **1.** declaration under oath, statement, attestation, avowal, averment, profession, acknowledgment, deposition, affidavit, evidence. **2.** evidence, witness, indication, demonstration, manifestation, proof, verification, corroboration, confirmation, affirmation, certification, endorsement, documentation. **—Ant. 2** denial, disavowal, refutation, disproof, contradiction, rebuttal.

testy *adj.* irritable, ill-humored, quick-tempered, irascible, cross, cranky, grumpy, crabby, snappish, snappy, fretful, peevish, petulant, sullen, waspish, churlish, splenetic, choleric, snarling, cantankerous, contentious, touchy, temperamental, impatient, crusty, fractious, captious, caviling, faultfinding, sharp-tongued, perverse, acrimonious, moody, *Informal* filthy. **—Syn. Study.** See IRRITABLE. **—Ant.** good-natured, good-humored, even-tempered, sweet, pleasant, amiable, genial, friendly, agreeable, kind, generous, patient, smiling, sunny, *Informal* smiley.

tête-à-tête *n.* private conversation, intimate conversation, confidential talk, private interview; chat, talk, parley, confabulation.

tether *n.* **1.** leash, rein, halter; rope, chain, cord. *—v.* **2.** put on a leash, tie with a rope, tie, chain, fasten, secure; hobble. **—Ant. 2** untether, unleash, untie, unchain, unfasten; release, free, loose, loosen.

text *n.* **1.** main body of writing, words, wording, content; textbook, schoolbook, primer; manual, workbook. **2.** sermon, subject, subject matter, theme, motif, topic, thesis, argument; passage, quotation, verse, paragraph, sentence. **—Ant. 1** illustration; notes, index, glossary; prologue, introduction, epilogue.

textile *n.* woven material, fabric, cloth, piece goods, yard goods; fiber, yarn, filament.

texture *n.* weave, composition, structure, character, quality, makeup, surface, nap, grain, feel, touch, look; fineness, coarseness.

thank *v.* **1.** express gratitude to, express appreciation to, make acknowledgment to, tender thanks to, be grateful to, bless. *—n.* **2. thanks** gratitude, gratefulness, appreciation, thankfulness; benediction, blessing, grace. **—Ant. 2** ingratitude, ungratefulness.

thankful *adj.* full of thanks, grateful, appreciative, feeling gratitude, expressing appreciation; obliged, beholden, indebted to.

thankless *adj.* **1.** not likely to be appreciated, unappreciated, unacknowledged, unrewarded; unrewarding, fruitless, useless, profitless, vain, bootless; undesirable, unwelcome, uninviting, unpleasant, disagreeable, distasteful. **2.** ungrateful, ingrate, unappreciative, unthankful, thoughtless, inconsiderate, heedless, unmindful, ungracious; critical, faultfinding, caviling. **—Ant. 1** appreciated, acknowledged, rewarded; rewarding, fruitful, useful, desirable, pleasant, agreeable. **2** appreciative, grateful, thankful.

thaw *v.* **1.** melt, dissolve, liquefy, soften; warm, warm up. **2.** melt, warm, make friendly, make sympathetic, make affectionate, make forgiving; become genial, relax, unbend, break the ice, shed one's reserve. —*n.* **3.** thawing, melting; period of above-freezing winter weather, first warm weather of spring. **—Ant. 1** freeze, freeze solid, solidify, congeal, harden; cool, chill. **3** freeze, frost.

theater *n.* **1.** (*variously*) playhouse; movie theater, movie, cinema, movie house, megaplex, multiplex, music hall, amphitheater, colosseum, arena, lecture hall, auditorium, lyceum, odeum. **2.** drama, stage entertainment, theatricals, show business; theatricality, histrionics. **3.** audience, spectators, house, auditorium, assemblage, assembly, gallery. **4.** field of operations, site, arena, stage, setting, scene, place.

theatrical *adj.* **1.** of the theater, stage, movie, film, entertainment, show-business, *Slang* show-biz; dramatic, thespian, histrionic. **2.** exaggerated, stilted, affected, artificial, stagy, unnatural, mannered; pretentious, ostentatious, extravagant, showy, flashy, grandiloquent, grandiose, magniloquent, fustian, *Slang* hammy.

theft *n.* stealing; (*variously*) robbery, burglary, thievery, larceny, filching, pilfering, purloining, shoplifting, hijacking, fraud, swindling, embezzlement, rustling, looting.

theme *n.* **1.** subject, subject matter, topic, text, motif, thesis, general idea, focus, keynote, point, question, argument, proposition, premise. **2.** essay, composition, treatise, discourse, tract, monograph, report, critique, commentary, review, thesis, dissertation. **3.** melody, strain, tune, air, song, motif, leitmotif; theme song. **—Syn. Study. 1** See SUBJECT.

theological *adj.* religious, spiritual, holy, sacred; ecclesiastical, apostolic, canonical, doctrinal, dogmatic; Biblical, scriptural.

theology *n.* divinity; (*variously*) science of divine things, religion, dogma, doctrine, system of belief.

theoretical *adj.* consisting in theory, concerning theory, theoretic, conjectural, hypothetical, speculative, suppositional, postulatory, putative; abstract, academic, nonpractical. **—Ant.** proven, known, verified, corroborated, demonstrated, substantial, established; practical, applied.

theorize *v.* speculate, hypothesize, conjecture, posit, propose, imagine, think, suppose, assume, infer, presume, propound, formulate, hypothecate, predicate.

theory *n.* **1.** principle, law; science, doctrine, philosophy, ideology. **2.** idea, notion, concept, hypothesis, postulate, conjecture, thesis, speculation, surmise, supposition, guess, thought, opinion, persuasion, belief, presumption, judgment, conclusion, deduction, view. **—Syn. Study. 1, 2** THEORY, HYPOTHESIS are used in nontechnical contexts to mean an untested idea or opinion. A THEORY in technical use is a more or less verified or established explanation accounting for known facts or phenomena: *Einstein's theory of relativity.* A HYPOTHESIS is a conjecture put forth as a possible explanation of phenomena or relations, which serves as a basis of argument or experimentation to reach the truth: *This idea is only a hypothesis.* **—Ant. 2** practice, application; proof, verification, corroboration, substantiation, demonstration, exhibit, example.

therapeutic Also **therapeutical** *adj.* healing, sanative, salutary, curative, remedial, ameliorative, restorative.

therapy *n.* treatment, remedial procedure, healing, rehabilitation.

thereafter *adv.* after that, afterward, afterwards, subsequently, later, from that time on, from then on, thenceforth. **—Ant.** before, previously.

therefore *adv.* in consequence, consequently, so, accordingly, hence, thus, ergo, for that reason, for which reason, on that account, on that ground.

thereupon *adv.* then, thereon, forthwith, straightaway, directly, immediately, suddenly, upon that, upon which, at once, without delay, in a moment, in the twinkling of an eye.

thesaurus *n.* synonym dictionary, synonymy, dictionary of synonyms and antonyms, synonym finder, word finder, word treasury, conceptual dictionary, semantic dictionary, synonymicon.

thesis *n.* **1.** proposition, proposal, argument; theory, hypothesis, postulate, concept, notion, conjecture, speculation, surmise, supposition. **2.** dissertation, long essay, research paper, term paper,

paper, treatise, disquisition, discourse, formal composition, article, monograph, tract; critique, commentary; master's thesis.

thespian *n.* actor, actress, trouper, performer, player, stage performer, stage player, *Slang* ham; star, guest star, co-star, leading man, leading lady, juvenile, ingenue, character man, character woman, bit player, walk-on, extra, supernumerary.

thick *adj.* **1.** fat, deep, wide, broad, big, bulky; generous, lavish, unstinted, munificent, liberal. **2.** dense, heavy, impenetrable; viscous, viscid, gelatinous, glutinous, concentrated, condensed, compact, solid, coagulated, clotted. **3.** strong, decided, pronounced, extreme, great, heavy, intense, deep, profound. **4.** inarticulate, indistinct, muffled, fuzzy, blurred; hoarse, husky, guttural, throaty. **5.** stupid, dumb, dense, obtuse, slow, slow-witted, dull, dull-witted, doltish, *Informal* wooden, fatheaded. **6.** close, intimate, chummy, familiar, friendly, inseparable, devoted; brotherly, sisterly. **7.** swarming, teeming, dense, profuse, overflowing, packed, crowded; abundant, copious, plenteous, heaped, piled. **—Ant. 1, 2** thin. **1** slim, narrow, shallow, slight, lean, spare, small. **2** light, watery, runny, diluted. **3** slight, faint, weak, vague. **4** articulate, distinct, clear; shrill, shrieking. **5** smart, clever, intelligent, keen, sharp, quick, quick-witted. **6** distant, unfriendly, hostile, estranged. **7** bare, barren, bereft, empty.

thicken *v.* **1.** make thick, become thicker, make dense; set, compact, clot, cake, congeal, coagulate, condense, gelatinize, jell, jellify. **2.** become more complicated, intensify, deepen, darken, muddy, muddle. **—Ant. 1** thin, dilute, thaw. **2** solve, resolve.

thicket *n.* thick bushes, bush, undergrowth, underbrush, brush, covert, shrubs, shrubbery; growth of small trees, brake, bracken, grove, copse, scrub, forest, wood.

thickheaded *adj.* stupid, dumb, dimwitted, blank, dull-witted, half-witted, obtuse, thick, chuckleheaded, blockheaded, thick-witted, slow-witted, fatheaded, knuckleheaded, boneheaded, *Slang* dopey. **—Ant.** bright, clever, smart, intelligent.

thickset *adj.* **1.** close-planted, close-set, dense, packed, solid, close. **2.** stocky, husky, sturdy, chunky, bulky, heavyset, stout; squat, stubby, stumpy, tubby, dumpy, roly-poly. **—Ant. 1** scattered, dispersed, sparse. **2** slim, slender; tall, rangy, reedy, gangling, lanky.

thickskinned *adj.* **1.** having a thick skin, pachydermatous. **2.** insensitive, insensible, unfeeling, unsusceptible, imperturbable, unmovable, unconcerned, impervious, callous, hardened, inured. **—Ant. 1, 2** thinskinned. **2** sensitive, feeling; concerned, caring, passionate, emotional; vulnerable, soft, fragile.

thief *n.* robber, burglar, bandit, crook; (*variously*) purloiner, holdup man, filcher, pilferer, purse-snatcher, mugger, shoplifter, pickpocket, sneak thief, kleptomaniac, housebreaker, second-story man, highwayman, hijacker, rustler; swindler, confidence man, racketeer, larcenist, embezzler, defrauder. **—Syn. Study.** THIEF, ROBBER refer to one who steals. A THIEF takes the goods or property of another by stealth without the latter's knowledge: *like a thief in the night.* A ROBBER trespasses upon the house, property, or person of another, and makes away with things of value, even at the cost of violence: *An armed robber held up the jewelry store.*

thievish *adj.* **1.** thieving, given to stealing, larcenous, light-fingered, sticky-fingered, dishonest. **2.** thieflike, stealthy, furtive, sneaky, surreptitious, secretive, sly. **—Ant. 1** honest. **2** open, frank, direct, aboveboard, straightforward.

thin *adj.* **1.** lean, not fat, slender, slim, skinny, slight, scrawny, emaciated, gaunt, lanky, lank, spindly, fine, finespun, narrow, threadlike, delicate; fragile, sheer, transparent. **2.** watery, runny, diluted. **3.** weak, unsubstantial, feeble, faint, inadequate, insufficient; scant, sparse, spare. *—v.* **4.** make thin, thin out, prune, reduce, diminish, grow thin, curtail. **5.** dilute, water, water down. **—Ant. 1–3** thick. **1** fat, obese, corpulent, chubby, rotund, plump, overweight. **2** viscous, concentrated. **3** strong, substantial, solid, forceful, adequate, sufficient; full, abundant, dense, plentiful. **4, 5** thicken. **4** increase, grow, heighten.

thing *n.* **1.** object, article, gadget, *Slang* thingamajig, thingamabob, gizmo, doohickey, dingus. **2.** creature, living being, person, human being, entity. **3.** deed, act, feat, action; event, occurrence, eventuality, proceeding, happening, matter, affair, transaction, business, concern, circumstance. **4.** statement, thought; detail, particular, item, feature, point, aspect. **5.** Often **things** article of clothing, suitable outfit; clothing, clothes, possessions, belongings, effects, goods, movables, equipment, gear, paraphernalia.

think *v.* **1.** use one's mind, apply the mind, reason, reflect, cogitate, deliberate, turn over in the mind, mull over, ponder, contemplate, meditate, ruminate, have in mind, make the subject of one's thought, dwell on, brood, keep in mind, remember, recall, recollect, use one's wits, rack one's brain. **2.** believe, have an opinion, deem, judge, surmise, presume, anticipate, conclude, guess, suppose, reckon, expect, speculate; imagine, conceive, fancy; intend, purpose, propose, plan, mean, design, contrive. **—Ant. 1** be thoughtless, act rashly, act unreasonably; forget, slip one's mind.

thinker *n.* man of thought, woman of thought, intellect, sage, savant, mastermind, wizard, mental giant, smart person, bright person, scholar, philosopher, metaphysician, intellectual, *Informal* egghead. **—Ant.** man of action, woman of action; dunce, dumbbell, dummy, ninny, nincompoop, dope, idiot, imbecile, moron, dunderhead, noodlehead.

thinking *adj.* **1.** rational, reasoning, reflective, thoughtful, contemplative, meditative, philosophical; intelligent, smart, bright, studious, educated, cultured, cultivated, sophisticated. *—n.* **2.** using one's head, thought, brainwork, judgment, deduction; conclusion, belief, inference; view, concept, position, stand, impression, surmise; contemplation, meditation, reflection, consideration, rumination, study, deliberation, speculation, mental absorption. **3.** paying attention, using one's head, being heedful.

thinskinned *adj.* **1.** having a thin skin. **2.** easily offended, sensitive, hypersensitive, oversensitive, touchy, susceptible, squeamish; irritable, petulant, ill-tempered, snappish, peevish, irascible, testy, huffy, sullen, sulky, quarrelsome, cross, cantankerous, crabbed, grumpy. **—Ant. 1, 2** thickskinned. **2** insensitive, callous, hardened; even-tempered, sweet-tempered, good-natured, sweet, kind, happy, content.

thirst *n.* **1.** need of liquid, dryness in the mouth, thirstiness. **2.** desire, keenness, craving, hankering, yearning, yen, hunger, appetite, voracity, stomach, lust, passion, itch, relish, fervor, ardor. *—v.* **3.** be thirsty for, desire to drink, be thirsty, be parched. **4.** desire, covet, crave, hanker for, yearn, yen, lust, itch, hunger, pant. **—Ant. 2** disinterest, apathy; dislike, distaste, hate, abhorrence, aversion, revulsion, repulsion. **4** scorn, disdain, be disinterested in, be apathetic toward; dislike, hate, detest, abhor.

thorn *n.* **1.** sharp spine, spike, barb, spur, prickle. **2.** bane, curse, torment, affliction, infliction, care, woe, trouble, plague, scourge, sting, gall, bitter pill, nuisance, annoyance, irritation, vexation, crown of thorns, cross, sore point.

thorny *adj.* **1.** full of thorns, overgrown with thorns; prickly, spiny, brambly, barbed, spiked, bristling. **2.** difficult, full of difficulties, full of dilemmas, hard, tough, arduous, troublesome, dangerous, dire, formidable, sticky, ticklish, critical, crucial; complex, perplexing, involved, complicated, annoying, trying, vexatious, nettlesome, irksome. **—Ant. 2** easy, simple, untroublesome, uncomplicated.

thorough *adj.* **1.** complete, thoroughgoing, careful, full, painstaking, meticulous, exhaustive, all-inclusive, all-embracing, definitive. **2.** perfect, pure, utter, sheer, total, entire, absolute, unmitigated, unqualified, downright, out-and-out; uniform, consistent, of a piece. **—Ant. 1, 2** partial, incomplete. **1** careless, slipshod, sloppy, lackadaisical. **2** marred, mitigated, qualified, imperfect, with reservation.

thoroughbred *adj.* **1.** purebred, pure-blooded, full-blooded, unmixed, pedigreed. *—n.* **2.** purebred animal, pure-blooded animal. **3.** Sometimes **Thoroughbred** horse of the Thoroughbred breed, racehorse. **4.** *Informal* aristocrat, blueblood, silkstocking, high-class person.

thoroughfare *n.* through street, street, main road, road, avenue, boulevard, concourse, parkway; highway, thruway, expressway, turnpike, roadway, freeway, interstate, superhighway. **—Ant.** dead-end street, cul-de-sac; alley, lane, backstreet, sidestreet.

thoroughly *adv.* **1.** completely, fully, exhaustively, inclusively, from top to bottom, through and through, carefully, meticulously. **2.** perfectly, in all respects, utterly, entirely, totally, completely, absolutely, downright, out-and-out; uniformly, consistently, from beginning to end, throughout. **—Ant. 1, 2** partially, incompletely. **1** carelessly, sloppily, inconclusively, lackadaisically. **2** imperfectly, somewhat, in part; slightly.

thought *n.* **1.** thinking, mental activity, deliberation, cogitation, consideration, reflection; introspection, meditation, contemplation, rumination, musing, reverie, thoughtfulness, brown study. **2.** idea, notion; opinion, conclusion, judgment, belief, view, speculation, supposition, surmise, sentiment, fancy, imagination, concept, conception; doctrine, credo, tenet, dogma. **3.** thoughtfulness, consideration, concern, caring, attention, kindness, kindheartedness, regard; intent, intention, purpose, design, aim, plan, scheme, goal, object, objective, end, anticipation, expectation. **—Syn. Study. 2** See IDEA.

thoughtful *adj.* **1.** full of thought, serious, thinking, probing; contemplative, reflective, meditative, musing, introspective, pensive, wistful. **2.** considerate, kind, kindhearted, neighborly, solicitous, attentive, caring, loving. **—Ant. 1, 2**

thoughtless. **1** shallow, facetious, unthinking, heedless, rash, reckless, irresponsible, remiss. **2** inconsiderate, insensitive, unkind, mean, cruel, coldhearted; rude, impolite, neglectful.

thoughtfulness *n.* **1.** thought, thinking, contemplation, meditation, reflection, consideration, probing, questioning. **2.** consideration, kindness, kindheartedness, solicitousness, attentiveness.

thoughtless *adj.* **1.** unthinking, careless, heedless, inattentive, imprudent, improvident, ill-considered, ill-advised, neglectful; stupid, dumb, silly, foolish, scatterbrained, rattlebrained, harebrained, absent-minded. **2.** inconsiderate, insensitive, rude, impolite, unkind, indiscreet, inadvertent, rash, reckless, unreflecting. **—Ant. 1, 2** thoughtful. **1** intelligent, smart, wise, sage, prudent, provident, well-advised, thinking, careful, alert. **2** considerate, sensitive, diplomatic, kindhearted, solicitous, polite, courteous, discreet.

thoughtlessness *n.* **1.** carelessness, inattention, inattentiveness, heedlessness, neglect, negligence, oversight, absentmindedness, rashness, recklessness, imprudence. **2.** lack of consideration, unconcern, insensitivity, unkindness, rudeness, impoliteness.

thrash *v.* **1.** whip, spank, cane, switch, birch, strap; lash, beat, flog, flail, scourge, flagellate; pommel, lambaste, trounce, maul, drub, pound, strike, hit. **2.** toss, plunge, wiggle, squirm, writhe, flounce, tumble, joggle, jiggle, heave, jerk. **3.** separate the grains of, flail, separate the wheat from the chaff. **4.** thresh out, resolve, argue out, solve, conclude by discussion. **—Syn. Study. 1** See BEAT.

threadbare *adj.* **1.** worn, worn-out, frayed, raveled, shabby, ragged, tacky, napless, pileworn, worn to a thread, the worse for wear. **2.** hackneyed, banal, trite, clichéd, bromidic, stereotyped, stock, overfamiliar, stale, well-known, commonplace, routine, everyday, conventional, prosaic, boring, dull, humdrum, jejune. **—Ant. 1, 2** new, brand-new. **1** unused, unworn, good as new. **2** novel, fresh, unique, singular, exciting, surprising, different, unusual.

threat *n.* **1.** menacing statement, terrorizing statement, intimidation; ill omen, portent, warning sign, premonition, foreboding, handwriting on the wall. **2.** menace, danger, risk, hazard, peril, jeopardy. **—Ant. 1, 2** promise. **1** bribe, enticement, reward.

threaten *v.* **1.** promise injury, promise harm; menace, intimidate, cow, terrorize; warn, forewarn. **2.** menace, endanger, imperil, jeopardize; be imminent, impend, hang over. **—Ant. 1, 2** protect, defend, safeguard, guard.

threatening *adj.* **1.** menacing, terrorizing, sinister, intimidating; warning, forewarning. **2.** ominous, menacing, sinister, baleful, grim, alarming, ill-omened, foreboding, forbidding, inauspicious, unpropitious; imminent, impending, approaching; portentous, fateful. **—Syn. Study. 2** See OMINOUS.

threshold *n.* **1.** doorsill, sill, groundsel, limen; entranceway, entrance, doorway, door, gateway, portal. **2.** brink, verge, edge; beginning, onset, start, commencement, starting point, inception, opening, dawn, prelude. **—Ant. 2** end, termination, conclusion, finish; destruction, disappearance.

thrift *n.* economy, prudence, frugality, thriftiness, husbandry, parsimony, parsimoniousness, sparingness, closefistedness; moderation, reasonableness. **—Ant.** extravagance, prodigality, thriftlessness, wastefulness; excess, immoderation, unreasonableness.

thrifty *adj.* economical, frugal, parsimonious, economizing, sparing, saving, closefisted, tightfisted, penny-pinching, penny-wise, niggardly, stingy. **—Syn. Study.** See ECONOMICAL. **—Ant.** extravagant, free-spending, prodigal, spendthrift, uneconomical, wasteful, improvident; openhanded, generous.

thrill *n.* **1.** rush of excitement, tingle, quiver, throb, tremble, tremor, glow, flush. **2.** thrilling event, adventure, satisfaction, kick; thrilling story, exciting thing. —*v.* **3.** electrify, galvanize, stir, rouse, arouse, stimulate, excite, inspire, fire; delight, enrapture, transport, impress, tickle. **—Ant. 2, 3** bore, weary; irk, annoy.

thrilling *adj.* exciting, stirring, awesome, sensational, electrifying, riveting, engaging, fascinating, absorbing, provocative, tantalizing, titillating; delightful, pleasurable, exquisite. **—Ant.** boring, dull, uninteresting, tedious, monotonous.

thrive *v.* **1.** grow vigorously, flourish, wax, bloom, burgeon, fatten. **2.** prosper, succeed, get ahead, get on, grow rich, boom, flourish; be successful, be fortunate, turn out well. **—Syn. Study. 2** See SUCCEED. **—Ant. 1** languish, die, wither, fade. **2** fail, go bankrupt; be unsuccessful, be unfortunate.

thriving *adj.* **1.** growing fast; blooming, blossoming, flowering, luxuriant, rank, lush. **2.** flourishing, prospering, prosperous, successful, succeeding, busy, vigorous; wealthy, rich, well-to-do, well-off, *Slang* on Easy Street, in clover. **—Ant. 1** languishing, dying, withering, fading. **2** failing, bankrupt, unsuccessful; poor, moneyless, penniless, destitute, poverty-stricken, impoverished, badly off, indigent, broke.

throaty *adj.* husky, deep, low, base, full-toned, sonorous, resonant; guttural, thick, gruff, hoarse, grating, rasping, croaking, cracked, dry. **—Ant.** high, thin, shrill, squeaky.

throb *v.* **1.** beat, beat abnormally fast, pulsate, palpitate, vibrate, flutter, quiver, tremble, shake, twitch, heave, pant. *—n.* **2.** throbbing, beat, beating, pulsation, pulse, palpitation, vibration, oscillation, reverberation; flutter, fluttering, quiver, quivering, shake, shaking, tremble, trembling, twitch, jerk, tremor.

throes *n. pl.* **1.** upheaval, disorder, confusion, chaos, tumult, turmoil, disruption. **2.** pangs, spasms, paroxysms; ordeal, anguish. **3.** paroxysm, convulsion, agony.

throng *n.* **1.** great number, multitude, assemblage, crowd, horde, host, army, mass, swarm, flock, pack, jam, rush, crush, flood, deluge. *—v.* **2.** crowd, jam, cram, pack, swarm, mass, bunch, flock, press, surge, stream, herd, huddle, mill; gather, congregate, assemble, collect, cluster, converge. **—Syn. Study. 1** See CROWD. **—Ant. 1** smattering, sprinkling, few. **2** disperse, scatter, disband.

throttle *v.* **1.** choke, strangle, strangulate, garrote, burke; choke off, block, check, smother, stifle, silence, gag, seal off, shut off, stop. **2.** work a fuel lever, feed the flow of fuel to an engine; (*variously*) change speed, reduce speed, increase speed. *—n.* **3.** fuel valve, fuel lever; gas pedal, gas. **—Ant. 1** breathe, breathe easily; announce, proclaim, broadcast, reveal, disclose. **3** brake.

through Informal **thru** *adj.* **1.** finished, done, completed, concluded, ended, terminated, past. **2.** direct, long-distance; express. *—adv.* **3.** in one side and out the other, from one end to the other; from beginning to end, from first to last, from A to Z, all the way, to the end. **—Ant. 1** begun, started, initiated. **2** local.

throughout *adv.* all over, in every part, everywhere; all the time, from beginning to end, all the way through. **—Ant.** here and there, in some places, in some parts; now and then, some of the time.

throw *v.* **1.** fling, hurl, toss, cast, pitch, heave, sling, let fly, lob, chuck, shy; propel, impel, launch, project, hurtle; put, place, put in, put on, put around. **2.** throw off, throw down, cause to fall to the ground, unseat; knock down, floor. *—n.* **3.** toss, hurl, fling, cast, pitch, heave, sling, chuck, lob, delivery, shot. **4.** act of causing someone to fall to the ground; act of throwing off. **—Ant. 1, 3** catch. **1** receive; give, hand.

thrust *v.* **1.** shove, push, poke, prod, butt, drive, press, force, ram, jam, impel, propel. **2.** wield a sword, place a sword; stab, pierce, plunge, jab, lunge. *—n.* **3.** shove, push, poke, prod, boost, impulse; propelling force, propulsion force, impetus, momentum. **4.** sword thrust, stab, stroke, lunge, plunge, pass, riposte, swipe. **5.** military advance, assault, attack, charge, drive, sally, raid, foray, sortie, incursion, aggression, strike. **—Ant. 1, 3** pull, draw, drag. **2, 4** parry. **5** retreat, withdrawal.

thud *n.* dull sound, thump, clunk, bang, knock, smack.

thug *n.* ruffian, hoodlum, hood; (*variously*) gangster, gunman, mobster, robber, bandit, killer, hit man, murderer, assassin, mugger, cutthroat.

thumb *n.* **1.** inside finger, short finger next to the forefinger. *—v.* **2.** flip through, leaf through, glance through, run one's eye through; handle, finger. **3.** *Informal* hitchhike, hitch, hitch a ride, catch a ride.

thump *v.* **1.** strike, beat, hit, pound, knock, whack, thwack, bang, punch, buffet, batter, pommel, lambaste, slap, cuff, clip, jab, poke. **2.** fall heavily, collapse, bounce, sit down heavily. *—n.* **3.** clunk, thud, bang; heavy blow, heavy fall, knock, rap, slam, smack, clout, swat, whack, hit.

thunder *n.* **1.** loud rumbling noise accompanying lightning discharge, thunderbolt, thunderclap; rumbling, clap, explosion, discharge, roar, boom, crash, crack. *—v.* **2.** give forth thunder, discharge thunder; rumble, reverberate, echo, resound, roll, peal, explode, boom.

thunderstruck *adj.* astounded, astonished, dumbfounded, flabbergasted, aghast, agog, agape, awed, awestruck, overcome, amazed, surprised, bewildered, confused, perplexed. **—Ant.** unmoved, unexcited, indifferent, apathetic, calm.

thus *adv.* **1.** in this way, in this manner, like this, like so, so; as follows. **2.** therefore, so, hence, wherefore, consequently, accordingly, for this reason, ergo. **—Ant. 1** the other way, the reverse way. **2** but, however, nevertheless, nonetheless, even so, in spite of this.

thwack *n.* **1.** blow, whack, rap, smack, wallop, thump, knock, slap, clout, slam. *—v.* **2.** whack, paddle, rap, strike, hit, bang, baste, smack, wallop, thump, slap.

thwart *v.* stop, frustrate, foil, balk, check, hinder, obstruct, baffle, inhibit, prevent, bar, ward off, stave off; contravene, cross, oppose. **—Ant.** encourage, help, aid, support, abet; hasten, increase, aggravate, multiply, magnify.

tic *n.* involuntary twitch, facial twitch, twitch, *Medical* trigeminal neuralgia, tic douloureux.

tick *v.* **1.** make a slight, sharp sound; click, clack, tap; make a sharp sound over and over, ticktock, beat, vibrate, oscillate, swing. **2.** check, mark; record, note, mark down, list, enter, register, chronicle. *—n.* **3.** ticking noise; slight, sharp repeated sound; ticktock, click, clack, tap; vibration, oscillation, throb, pulsation. **4.** checkmark, check, mark, stroke, line, dot; scratch, notch, nick, blaze.

ticket *n.* **1.** ticket of admission, trip ticket, voucher, coupon, pass; stub. **2.** traffic ticket, traffic summons; parking ticket. **3.** tag, label, slip, marker, card, sticker. **4.** list of political candidates, list of nominees, slate, roster; ballot. *—v.* **5.** provide with a ticket, hold a ticket, buy a ticket, sell a ticket; put a ticket on, tag, label, mark. **6.** attach a traffic summons to, serve a traffic summons to, give a traffic ticket to, attach a parking ticket to.

tickle *v.* **1.** stroke with the fingertips, stroke lightly, rub lightly, stroke, titillate. **2.** tingle, twitch, itch, prickle, sting, prick, throb. **3.** amuse, regale, divert, enliven, gladden, cheer, delight, please, fascinate, enchant, captivate, enthrall, entrance, excite agreeably, thrill, rejoice, gratify, do one's heart good. *—n.* **4.** teasing stroke, tingling rub. **5.** tickling sensation, tingle, twitching sensation, itch, scratchiness, prickle, sting.

ticklish *adj.* **1.** sensitive to tickling, easily tickled, tickly; tingling, itchy, scratchy, prickly. **2.** delicate, awkward, requiring tact, touchy, sensitive, uncertain, critical; difficult, complicated, intricate, tricky, tough, hard, knotty, thorny. **—Ant. 2** easy, simple.

tidbit *n.* delicate bit, morsel, mouthful, delicacy, treat, choice bit, bit, item.

tide *n.* **1.** twice daily rise and fall of the oceans; (*variously*) high tide, ebb tide, neap tide, flood tide, low tide, riptide, undertow; tidal water, tidewater, wave, current, flow. **2.** rise and fall, ebb and flow, wax and wane; drift, current, tendency, movement, direction, state.

tidings *n.* news, information, word, advice, intelligence, report, announcement, declaration, good word, notification.

tidy *adj.* **1.** neat, orderly, trim, shipshape, trig, in apple-pie order; methodical, systematic, organized, meticulous, precise, careful, regular, regulated, businesslike; clean, immaculate, spotless. **2.** considerable, fairly large, substantial, sizable, goodly, ample. *—v.* **3.** tidy up, neaten, neaten up, put in order, straighten, straighten up, clean up, spruce up, arrange, array. **—Ant. 1** messy, sloppy, untidy, slovenly, unkempt, disordered, disorderly, unmethodical, unsystematic, unbusinesslike, careless, slipshod; filthy, dirty. **2** inconsiderable, unsubstantial, small, little, tiny. **3** mess, mess up, disarrange, disorder; dirty.

tie *v.* **1.** bind, fasten, make fast, attach, secure, engage, tether, clinch, truss, lash; draw together and knot, knot, make a bow. **2.** bind, fasten, attach, join, unite, connect, link, yoke, ally, couple, marry. **3.** limit, confine, constrain, restrain, restrict, hinder, hamper. **4.** make the same score, have the same record of wins and losses, draw, come out even, match, divide the honors. *—n.* **5.** fastener for tying, cord, rope, string, line, cable, fastening, belt, band, ribbon, cinch, girdle, cincture, sash, cummerbund. **6.** necktie, cravat; bow tie. **7.** bond, link, affinity, connection, relation, relationship, kinship, affiliation, shared interest, mutual interest, allegiance; duty, obligation. **8.** tied score, tied record, tied vote; draw, dead heat. **9.** brace, support, beam, rod, connecting rod; crossbeam. **—Ant. 1** untie, unbind, unfasten, loose, loosen, disengage, unknot. **2** detach, separate, divorce, disunite.

tier *n.* row, rank, line, file, step, level, range, bank; layer, story, stratum, stratification.

tie-up *n.* snag, jam, block, hitch, bottleneck, snarl, stoppage, blockage, gridlock, failure, malfunction, breakdown, disruption, slow-up, *French* embouteillage.

tiff *n.* **1.** minor quarrel, petty quarrel, clash, scrap, run-in, spat, words, squabble, argument, dispute, wrangle, altercation, disagreement, difference, misunderstanding; *Slang* hassle, rhubarb. **2.** slight fit of anger, annoyed mood, huff, snit, tizzy, miff, rage, ill humor, bad mood.

tight *adv.* Also **tightly. 1.** firmly, securely, solidly, closely. **2.** taut, tense, stretched out, stretched as far as possible, rigidly, stiffly, drawn tight. **3.** too closely, fitting closely, fitting too closely, close-fitting, snug, skintight, not big enough, too small, uncomfortably small, constricted. **4.** full, crammed, jammed, jam-packed, stuffed, gorged; crowded, busy. *—adj.* **5.** firm, secure, solid. **6.** taut, tense, stretched out, stretched as far as possible, rigid, stiff, drawn tight. **7.** close-fitting, snug, skintight, not big enough, too small, uncomfortably small, constricted. **8.** full, crammed, jammed, jam-packed, stuffed, gorged; crowded, busy. **9.** closely constructed, closely fitted, close, dense, compact, set closely together, solid, compressed, impermeable, impenetrable, impassable. **10.** strict, firm, stern, rigid, rigorous, severe, exact, stringent, austere, stiff, inflexible, unyielding, uncompromising, tyrannical, dictatorial, harsh. **11.** difficult, worrisome, troublesome, hard, hard-up, tough, onerous, burdensome, trying. **12.** scarce, difficult to obtain, scant, sparing, skimpy; insufficient, inadequate, deficient. **13.** nearly even, nearly equal, nearly tied, close, well-matched, nip-and-tuck, nose-to-nose. **14.** stingy, miserly, tightfisted, close, closefisted, parsimonious, frugal, niggardly, penurious, illiberal, ungenerous, sparing, grudging. **15.** drunk, drunken, intoxicated, inebriated, tipsy, happy, plastered, blind, smashed, soused, loaded, pickled, stewed, pie-eyed, glassy-eyed, juiced, sloppy, stiff, stoned, zonked, high, in one's cups, three sheets to the wind, feeling no pain, lit-up. **—Ant. 1–3, 9, 10** loose. **1–3** loosely. **1** insecure, insecurely. **2** slack, relaxed, limp, free, flexible. **3** big, too big, loose-fitting. **4** empty; sparse. **9** open, porous, airy, lacy. **10–13** easy. **10** lenient, indulgent, soft, relaxed, undemanding, permissive, unexacting, slack, lax, mild, informal, flexible, yielding, easygoing, free-and-easy. **11** comfortable, enviable. **12** abundant, plentiful, profuse, rife, ready, ample, sufficient. **13** uneven, runaway, landslide. **14** extravagant, spendthrift, thriftless, prodigal, squandering, wasteful, lavish; generous, openhanded, liberal, munificent, charitable. **15** sober, sober as a judge.

tighten *v.* make tight, make tighter, fix firmly, fasten, anchor, make fast, secure; draw tight, make taut, make tense, take up the slack; narrow, squeeze, contract, constrict, pinch. **—Ant.** loosen, loose, slacken, slack off, relax, ease, ease off; free, release, untie, open.

tightfisted *adj.* stingy, parsimonious, niggardly, penny-pinching, tight, penurious, miserly, cheap, illiberal, mingy, closefisted, greedy, avaricious, cheeseparing. **—Ant.** openhanded, generous, liberal, unstinting.

tight-laced *adj.* prim, prudish, priggish, straitlaced, prissy, stuffy, Victorian, puritanical, self-righteous, standoffish, repressed, inhibited. **—Ant.** uninhibited, free, fast, promiscuous.

tight-lipped *adj.* close-mouthed, reticent, discreet, reserved, taciturn, quiet, mum, uncommunicative, terse, brief, untalkative, unsociable, curt, short. **—Ant.** talkative, unreserved, indiscreet, reckless.

tightwad *n. Informal* stingy person, skinflint, miser, niggard, moneygrubber, pinchpenny, cheapskate, piker, lickpenny, Scrooge. **—Ant.** spendthrift, prodigal, squanderer, wastrel, big spender, big-time spender; philanthropist, good Samaritan.

tilt *v.* **1.** slant, incline, lean, slope, tip, list, cant. **2.** joust, fight on horseback with a lance; fight, oppose, contend against, battle, contest; fence, spar, skirmish. *—n.* **3.** slope, slant, incline, cant, rake, pitch, grade. **4.** joust, jousting match, tournament; fight, contest, combat, battle, skirmish, encounter, affray; dispute, argument, quarrel, altercation, squabble, row, brawl, tiff. **—Ant. 1** be even, be flat, be plumb. **3** evenness, flatness.

timber *n.* **1.** wood, wood for building, lumber, boards, logs. **2.** timberland, wooded land; forest, woods, trees, bush, thicket, copse. **—Ant. 1** firewood, kindling. **2** clearing, field, pasture, grassland, meadow, prairie, savanna.

timbre *n.* tone, sound quality, pitch, resonance.

time *n.* **1.** the passage of time, duration, continuation of all existence; period, interval, span of time, elapsed time, spell, term, while, stretch. **2.** Usu. **times** epoch, era, period, age, eon; stage, season, cycle, day. **3.** particular point in time, appointed time, proper moment, appropriate period, high time; (*variously*) instant, moment, hour, part of the hour, day, part of the day, week, part of the week, month, part of the month, year, part of the year, season, term, decade, century, period. **4.** lifetime, years, days, period, phase, season, generation. **5.** leisure time, spare time, free time, liberty, opportunity, chance, freedom. **6.** experience, occasion, period, event, episode, incident. **7.** tempo; rhythm, beat, measure. *—v.* **8.** measure the speed of, clock; measure the duration of; choose the time of. **9.** synchronize, keep time, set to the rhythm of, adjust, match.

timeless *adj.* without beginning or end, eternal, infinite, never-stopping, never-ending, unending, endless, everlasting, interminable, perpetual, ceaseless, incessant, boundless, continuous; enduring; lasting, persistent, durable, permanent, abiding, unchangeable, immutable, indestructible, immortal, undying, deathless. **—Ant.** brief, quick, short, short-lived, temporary, passing, fleeting, unenduring, evanescent, ephemeral, transient, transitory, impermanent, changing.

timely *adj.* occurring at the right time, well-timed, opportune, felicitous, convenient, seasonable, prompt, punctual, providential. **—Ant.** untimely, inopportune, inconvenient, ill-timed, unseasonable, late, tardy.

timeworn *adj.* **1.** aged, ancient, antique, old, age-old, worn, venerable, hoary, antediluvian, ravaged with age, the worse for wear, battered, dog-eared, shabby, weathered, *Slang* beat-up. **2.** passé, antiquated, dated, obsolete, out of date; hackneyed, stale, trite, overused, *Slang* old-hat. —**Ant. 1** new, brand-new, in mint condition. **2** fresh, novel, original.

timid *adj.* lacking self-assurance, fainthearted, fearful, afraid, scared, timorous, apprehensive, cowardly, spineless, pusillanimous, weak-kneed; shy, bashful, coy, diffident, modest, overly modest, humble, sheepish, retiring, shrinking, unassuming. —**Ant.** self-assured, confident, daring, audacious, stouthearted, fearless, brave, bold, intrepid, courageous, adventuresome; brash, brazen, forward, impertinent, impudent, presumptuous, insolent, fresh, saucy, immodest, unabashed, shameless, cheeky.

timidity *n.* timidness, timorousness, shyness, lack of self-assurance, faintheartedness, fearfulness, trepidation, cowardice, spinelessness; bashfulness, diffidence, modesty, humility, sheepishness, *Slang* cold feet. —**Ant.** self-assurance, self-confidence, daring, audacity, fearlessness, bravery, boldness, courage; brashness, brazenness, forwardness, impertinence, impudence, presumption, insolence, immodesty, cheek.

tinge *v.* **1.** color slightly, color, tint, dye, stain; touch, infuse, imbue, instill, lace, season, flavor. —*n.* **2.** slight coloration, tint, shade, cast, stain; tone, touch, trace, hint, dash, vein, nuance, suspicion, flavor, taste, smack, soupçon.

tingle *v.* **1.** have a prickling sensation, sting, prickle, tickle. —*n.* **2.** prickling, thrill, tremor, flutter, throb, palpitation, pulsation.

tinkle *v.* **1.** ring lightly, jingle, clink, chink, clank, chime, ping, plink, peal, ding. —*n.* **2.** light ring, jingle, clink, chink, clank, chime, peal, ding, ting-a-ling. —**Ant. 1, 2** boom, roar, bang, thunder.

tinsel *n.* **1.** decorative foil, shiny metal strip, spangle, sequin, glitter. **2.** show, decoration, gaudiness, ostentation; sham, pretense, masquerade, camouflage, gloss, false colors, affectation, make-believe, showy thing, gaudy thing.

tint *n.* **1.** shade, hue, tone, nuance, tincture. **2.** tinge, trace, hint, suggestion, touch. **3.** dye, stain, coloring, pigment. —*v.* **4.** color slightly, color, dye, stain, tone, wash; tinge, frost.

tiny *adj.* small, little, minute, miniature, diminutive, minuscule, microscopic, wee, *Informal* teeny, teeny-weeny, teensy-weensy, itsy-bitsy; undersized, pocket-sized, pint-sized, midget, pygmy, dwarfish, runty, Lilliputian, bantam, petite. —**Ant.** large, big, huge, enormous, immense, mammoth, oversized, giant, gigantic, monstrous, colossal, gargantuan, titanic.

tip¹ *v.* **1.** tilt, slant, incline, lean, list, slope, cant. **2.** Often **tip over** overturn, topple over, tumble over, upset, upturn, capsize, upend, turn turtle. —*n.* **3.** tipping, tilting, leaning, slanting; slant, incline, tilt, slope, list, pitch, rake, cant. —**Ant. 1** be even, be flat, be plumb. **2** upright. **3** flatness, evenness.

tip² *n.* **1.** pointed end, tapering end, small end; point, head, prong, spike. **2.** top, peak, apex, vertex, acme, zenith, summit, crown, crest, pinnacle, cap; upper part, brow. —*v.* **3.** furnish with a slender end, serve as a pointed end, top, cap, crown; sharpen, barb, hook, point.

tip³ *n.* **1.** gratuity, small gift of money for services rendered, small reward, lagniappe, baksheesh, small bones, *French* pourboire; perquisite. **2.** hint, suggestion, pointer, clue, advice, word to the wise, warning, forewarning, admonition; secret information, inside information, inside dope, tip-off, lowdown. **3.** tap, light blow, weak blow, stroke, pat. —*v.* **4.** give a gratuity, give a small gift of money for services rendered, reward. **5.** tap, hit lightly, strike weakly, stroke, pat.

tippler *n.* heavy drinker, habitual drinker, hard drinker, sot, toper, boozer, booze hound, guzzler, swiller, imbiber, sponge, bibber, soak, tosspot; drunk, drunkard, alcoholic, inebriate, dipsomaniac, lush, souse, wino, rummy. —**Ant.** teetotaler, abstainer, nondrinker; moderate drinker, social drinker.

tipsy *adj.* mildly drunk, slightly intoxicated, *Slang* high; drunk, drunken, intoxicated, inebriate, inebriated, tight, happy, plastered, blind, smashed, soused, loaded, pickled, stewed, pie-eyed, glassy-eyed, juiced, sloppy, stiff, stoned, sodden, awash, in one's cups, three sheets to the wind, half seas over, feeling no pain, lit-up. —**Ant.** sober, sober as a judge.

tirade *n.* long angry speech, harangue, diatribe, jeremiad, lecture, reprimand, scolding, dressing-down, screed, fulmination; denunciation, condemnation, castigation, vilification, invective, vituperation, curse. —**Ant.** good word, short eulogy, panegyric, complimentary speech, praising speech, laudation, commendation, homage, paean.

tire *v.* **1.** weary, wear out, fatigue, exhaust, fag, tucker; make sleepy. **2.** bore, exhaust the patience of, be fed up with, be sick of, lose patience, lose interest, irk, annoy, bother, disgust. —**Ant. 1**

refresh, stimulate; wake up. **2** delight, interest, excite, enchant, fascinate, please, soothe.

tired *adj.* weary, wearied, fatigued, exhausted, enervated, worn out, all in, dog-tired, tuckered, fagged, played out, *Slang* beat, pooped, bushed; sleepy, drowsy. **—Ant.** energetic, full of pep, peppy, fresh, refreshed; raring to go; wide-awake.

tireless *adj.* untiring, never-tiring, unwearied; industrious, hard-working, unflagging, unfaltering, unswerving, unremitting, indefatigable, devoted, unceasing, steadfast, resolute, determined, staunch, steady, constant, persevering, determined, faithful. **—Ant.** halfhearted, lackadaisical, sporadic, random; flagging, faltering, wavering, irresolute.

tiresome *adj.* **1.** fatiguing, wearying, wearing, tiring, exhausting, fagging; arduous, laborious, tedious, hard, difficult. **2.** boring, monotonous, uninteresting, dull, drab, dismal, wearisome, deadly, humdrum, tedious; annoying, bothersome, irksome, vexing, trying. **—Ant.** **1** refreshing; easy. **2** delightful, interesting, exciting, stimulating, fascinating, enchanting, pleasing, soothing.

titanic *adj.* gigantic, huge, enormous, immense, vast, colossal, giant, mammoth, monumental, monstrous, gargantuan; great, strong, stout, prodigious, mighty, herculean; *Slang* humongous, whopping. **—Ant.** small, little, tiny, minute, diminutive, minuscule, wee, teeny, teeny-weeny, itsy-bitsy, pocket-sized, pint-sized, midget, pygmy, dwarfish, Lilliputian, bantam; weak, feeble.

titillate *v.* excite, tickle, tease, provoke, stimulate, rouse, arouse, turn on, allure, tempt, seduce, entrance, captivate, attract, fascinate, charm, whet the appetite. **—Ant.** allay, quiet, quench, quell, still, dull, slake, blunt, satisfy, sate, satiate.

titillating *adj.* provocative, exciting, alluring, tempting, suggestive, seductive.

title *n.* **1.** name, designation, appellation, epithet. **2.** rank, occupational rank, position, status, station, condition, grade, place; title of nobility, lordly rank, nobility, noble birth. **3.** legal right, legal possession, right, possession, ownership, tenure, deed, claim. **4.** championship, crown. *—v.* **5.** entitle, name, designate, term, dub, label, christen.

titter *v.* **1.** laugh self-consciously, laugh nervously, giggle, laugh softly, chuckle, cackle, snigger, snicker, simper, smirk, chirp. *—n.* **2.** self-conscious laugh, nervous laugh, giggle, snigger, snicker, simper, smirk, chuckle, soft laugh, teehee. **—Ant.** **1, 2** roar, guffaw. **1** split one's sides, die laughing, roll in the aisles. **2** burst of laughter, horselaugh.

titular *adj.* in name only, in title only, so-called, ostensible, nominal, known as. **—Ant.** actually, really, in fact, for all practical purposes.

toady *v.* **1.** flatter to gain favor, curry favor, fawn, grovel before, kowtow to, *Slang* apple-polish. *—n.* **2.** sycophant, flatterer, fawner, lickspittle, truckler, backscratcher, yes-man, *Slang* apple-polisher, bootlicker; servile follower, flunky, stooge, hanger-on, parasite. **—Ant.** **1** defy, confront, be hostile to, stand up to, oppose, resist, scorn, disdain, mock, taunt, twist the lion's tail. **2** defiant person, hostile person, opponent, enemy, foe, antagonist.

toast *v.* **1.** warm, warm up, heat; dry. **2.** heat until crisp, brown; grill, cook over an open fire. **3.** drink in honor of, salute with a drink, drink one's health, clink glasses; honor, celebrate, compliment, commemorate. *—n.* **4.** toasted bread, browned bread; a slice of browned, crisp bread. **5.** drink in honor of, drink to compliment, drink to commemorate. **—Ant.** **1** cool, cool off, chill.

today *n.* **1.** the present day, this day; the present age, the present, this epoch, this era, this time, modern times. *—adv.* **2.** on this day; nowadays, now, in this day and age, in modern times, during the present age, in this epoch, in this era. **—Ant.** **1, 2** yesterday; tomorrow.

toddle *v.* take short, unsteady steps; walk unsteadily, wobble, waddle. **—Ant.** stride; run, skip, prance.

to-do *n.* fuss, commotion, hurly-burly, stir, disturbance, flurry, ado, turmoil, bustle, tumult, uproar, excitement, noise, racket, furor, hubbub, rumpus, ruckus. **—Ant.** peace, calm, serenity, tranquillity.

togs *n. pl.* clothes, clothing, outfit, apparel, attire, duds, *Slang* threads.

toil *n.* **1.** hard work, work, labor, effort, exertion, application, industry, pains, drudgery, grind, struggle, sweat, elbow grease; hardship, travail. *—v.* **2.** work hard, labor, drudge, slave, moil, grub, sweat, exert oneself, apply oneself, work like a horse. **—Syn. Study.** **1** See WORK. **—Ant.** **1, 2** play. **1** amusement, entertainment, recreation, indolence, idleness, cavorting, ease; *Informal* goofing off, *Slang* goldbricking. **2** take one's ease, relax, enjoy oneself, amuse oneself, take one's pleasure, *Informal* goof off, *Slang* goldbrick.

toiler *n.* worker, laborer, wage earner, drudge, peon, field hand, hired hand, menial, servant, workhorse, slave, serf, slavey, galley slave; *Slang* prole, flunky, slogger; *Brit.* navvy, swot.

toilet *n.* water closet, W.C., flush toilet; latrine, lavatory, washroom, rest room, men's room, ladies' room; privy, outhouse; convenience, facility, commode; *Slang* john, can, *Brit.* loo.

toilsome *adj.* laborious, wearisome, difficult, hard, arduous, strenuous, tough, tedious, tiring, wearying, fatiguing, burdensome, effortful, uphill, backbreaking, herculean. **—Ant.** easy, simple, light, soft.

token *n.* **1.** symbol, sign, expression, indication, proof, mark, index, evidence, manifestation; reminder, memento, keepsake, souvenir, remembrance, testimonial. **2.** coinlike metal piece, *French* jeton. *—adj.* **3.** superficial, passing, nodding, of no real value, perfunctory, symbolic, nominal, for show; minimal, serving as a sample, vestigial. **—Ant. 3** real, actual, valuable, worthwhile, serious, equitable, deep.

tolerable *adj.* **1.** able to be tolerated, bearable, endurable, sufferable, abidable; acceptable, allowable, permissible. **2.** fairly good, fair, passable, acceptable, adequate, innocuous, mediocre, average, ordinary, commonplace, indifferent, run-of-the-mill, so-so, middling, fair-to-middling, betwixt and between. **—Ant. 1** intolerable, unbearable, unendurable, insufferable; unacceptable. **2** excellent, outstanding, wonderful, terrific, superior, great, choice, exemplary, noteworthy, memorable; awful, dreadful, terrible, lousy, bad.

tolerance *n.* **1.** ability to tolerate, capacity to resist, power to endure, endurance. **2.** an understanding attitude, fair treatment, fairness, lack of prejudice, freedom from bigotry, democratic spirit, goodwill, brotherly love, fellow feeling, live-and-let-live attitude; forbearance, patience, sufferance, compassion, sympathy, charity. **—Ant. 1** sensitivity. **2** prejudice, bigotry, bias, predisposition, ill will, unfairness, discrimination; irritability, anger, irascibility.

tolerant *adj.* **1.** understanding, unprejudiced, unbigoted, fair, having goodwill, having brotherly love, liberal, broad-minded, moderate; forbearing, patient, compassionate, sympathetic, charitable. **2.** lenient, permissive, indulgent, soft, easy, easygoing, forbearing, forgiving, uncomplaining, kindhearted, soft-hearted, sparing. **—Ant. 1** intolerant, prejudiced, bigoted, biased, unfair, illiberal, narrow-minded, closed-minded. **2** strict, rigid, harsh, stiff, severe, stern, exacting, uncompromising, unyielding, unbending, authoritarian, tyrannical, dictatorial, despotic.

tolerate *v.* **1.** bear, endure, put up with, stand, take, suffer, abide, brook, stomach, submit to, undergo. **2.** allow, permit, let, sanction, consent to, admit, recognize, vouchsafe, indulge, be soft on, be easy on, be sparing of, show mercy toward, wink at. **—Ant. 2** forbid, prohibit, disallow, outlaw, proscribe, ban, prevent, oppose.

toll *n.* **1.** fee, charge, payment, levy, duty, exaction, impost, assessment, tax, tariff, tribute. **2.** loss, amount of loss, extent of damage, destruction, extermination, extinction, annihilation, sacrifice, penalty; undoing, disruption, depletion.

tomb *n.* burial chamber, mausoleum, vault, sepulcher, crypt, monument to the dead; resting place, burial place, grave.

tomfoolery *n.* foolishness, silliness, prankishness, play, horseplay, drollery, high jinks, antics, monkeyshines, skylarking, nonsense, playing around, fooling around, messing around, goofing off, lollygagging.

tommyrot *n.* nonsense, balderdash, tomfoolery, bosh, rot, rubbish, bilge, stuff and nonsense, twaddle, humbug, fiddle-faddle; *Slang* hogwash, hooey, crap, poppycock, malarkey, bunk, *Brit.* tosh.

tomorrow *n.* **1.** the day after today, the morrow, *Spanish* mañana; the future, the next generation. *—adv.* **2.** on the day after today; in the future, in days to come. **—Ant. 1, 2** yesterday; today.

tone *n.* **1.** pitch, sound quality, sound, quality, tonality; note, musical interval of two semitones, overtone, harmonic; intonation, modulation, accent, stress, inflection, cadence, lilt. **2.** attitude, mood, spirit, style, manner, means of expression, note, tenor, quality, temper. **3.** shade, tint, hue, tinge, cast, color, chroma. *—v.* **4.** pitch, sound, subdue, moderate, temper, modulate, soften; shade, tint. **5.** make firm, firm up, make supple, make more elastic.

tongue *n.* **1.** organ of speech, lingua, lingula. **2.** language, speech, dialect, vernacular, patois, vocabulary; style of speech; power of speech. **3.** flap, overhanging strip. **4.** point, spit, promontory. **5.** shaft, harnessing pole. *—v.* **6.** touch with the tongue, move the tongue against; lick, lap.

tonic *n.* **1.** strengthening medicine, restorative, stimulant, invigorant, analeptic, bracer, refresher, pickup, pick-me-up. **2.** keynote; primary note of a diatonic scale.

tool *n.* **1.** implement, handheld instrument, instrument, device, utensil, contrivance, apparatus, appliance, machine, mechanism. **2.** agent, means, instrumentality, medium, vehicle, intermediary, wherewithal. **3.** person used by another, instrument, tool, pawn, puppet, dupe, hireling, stooge, cat's-paw. **—Syn. Study. 1, 3** TOOL, IMPLEMENT, INSTRUMENT, UTENSIL refer to contrivances for doing work. A TOOL is a contrivance held in and worked by the hand and used for cutting, digging, etc.: *a carpenter's tools.* An IMPLEMENT is any tool or contrivance designed or used for a particular purpose: *agricultural implements.* An INSTRUMENT is anything used in doing certain work or producing a certain result, esp. such as requires delicacy, accuracy, or precision: *surgical or musical instruments.* A UTENSIL is usu. an article for domestic use: *kitchen utensils.* When used figuratively of human agency, TOOL is generally used in a contemptuous sense; INSTRUMENT, in a neutral or good sense: *a tool of unscrupulous men; an instrument of Providence.*

tooth *n.* **1.** hard bony part growing from the jaw; (*variously*) incisor, molar, grinder, cuspid, canine, bicuspid, wisdom tooth; fang, tusk. **2.** serration; (*variously*) point, spike, tine, tang, spur, barb, thorn, cusp, nib, cog, sprocket.

top *n.* **1.** highest point, summit, peak, apex, vertex, pinnacle, acme, zenith, tiptop; crest, crown, brow; upper surface, upper part. **2.** lid, cap, cover; cork, stopper. **3.** highest rank, highest position, head, lead, first place, fore, van, front, place of honor. *—adj.* **4.** topmost, highest, uppermost, upper; greatest, best. **5.** highest-ranking, foremost, best, chief, principal, paramount, eminent, preeminent, renowned, noted, notable, celebrated, famous, greatest. *—v.* **6.** put a topping on, put a top on, put over, crown, cap, cover; complete, add a finishing touch to. **7.** be at the top of, be greater than, surpass, exceed, transcend, better, best, excel, outdo, eclipse, outshine, overshadow, outstrip. **—Ant. 1–4** bottom. **1** base, foot, lowest point; underside, underneath. **3** foot, end, tail end, last place, rear. **4** lowest, lower; least, worst. **5** inferior, second-rate, inept, incompetent; unknown, anonymous. **7** trail, be at the bottom, be less than.

topic *n.* subject, subject matter, theme, keynote, matter at hand; text, thesis. **—Syn. Study.** See SUBJECT.

topical *adj.* about current matters, current, contemporary; local, localized, parochial, limited, restricted, particular. **—Ant.** historical, traditional; general, universal, comprehensive, all-inclusive.

topmost *adj.* top, highest, uppermost; supreme, chief, head, preeminent, leading, foremost, principal, paramount.

topnotch *adj.* first-rate, outstanding, finest, supreme, prime, choice, nonpareil, superior, incomparable, tip-top, ace, unparalleled, preeminent. **—Ant.** so-so, ordinary, run-of-the-mill, commonplace.

topple *v.* **1.** tip over, overturn, turn over, upset, fall over; fall, tumble, pitch forward, sprawl. **2.** overthrow, bring down, abolish; defeat, vanquish, overcome, overpower, crush, smash, shatter, quash, quell.

topsy-turvy *adv.* **1.** upside down, inside out, into a confused state, in a disorderly state. *—adj.* **2.** confused, confusing, disorderly, disarranged, disorganized, untidy, messy, chaotic; upside-down, wrong side up, inverted, reversed. **—Ant. 1, 2** right side up. **1** straight, into a state of order. **2** orderly, well-arranged, organized, systematic, tidy, neat, trim.

torch *n.* **1.** burning brand, brand, firebrand, cresset, flambeau. **2.** portable device for producing a hot flame; welder's torch.

torment *v.* **1.** cause to suffer, afflict, torture, rack, distress, pain; plague, worry, trouble, annoy, agonize, persecute, harass, harrow, vex, nag, irritate, pester. *—n.* **2.** suffering, agony, torture, anguish, pain, distress, misery, worry, annoyance, irritation, despair; cause of suffering, source of agony, scourge, bane, curse. **—Ant. 1, 2** delight, comfort, ease. **1** please, make happy; soothe, mitigate, allay, alleviate, assuage. **2** pleasure, happiness, joy.

torn *adj.* ripped, rent, split, slit, ruptured; ragged, shredded, unraveled.

torpid *adj.* slow-moving, sluggish, inactive, inert, lethargic, lazy, listless, spiritless, indolent, languid, languorous, apathetic, lackadaisical, passive, slow-thinking, dull; half asleep, sleepy, drowsy, somnolent; dormant. **—Syn. Study.** See INACTIVE. **—Ant.** quick-moving, active, energetic, vigorous, peppy, full of pep, animated, lively, spirited, alert, *Slang* sharp, on, bright-eyed; wide-awake.

torpor Also **torpidity** *n.* sluggishness, slow movement, inertia, lethargy, laziness, languidness, listlessness, lassitude, indolence, languor, apathy, passiveness, dullness; sleepiness, drowsiness, somnolence; inactivity, inertia. **—Ant.** energy, vigor, vim, pep, animation, liveliness, alertness; wide-awakeness.

torrent *n.* **1.** heavy rain, downpour, deluge, cloudburst, torrential rain, cascade, waterfall, cataract, Niagara; fast-flowing stream, rapids, violent stream of water, white water, strong current. **2.** stream, rapid flow, outburst, outpouring, discharge, effusion, rain, deluge, flood, volley, barrage, salvo, burst, eruption, gush, rush. **—Ant. 1** shower, sprinkle, drizzle.

torrid *adj.* **1.** hot and dry, scorching, parching, sweltering, boiling, burning, broiling, sizzling, fiery, sultry, tropical. **2.** passionate, impassioned, ardent, fervent, fervid, vehement, spirited, excited, hot, hot and heavy, heated, intense; amorous, desirous, erotic, sexy, sexual, lustful. **—Ant. 1** cold, cool, chilly; mild, gentle. **2** dispassionate, unimpassioned, spiritless; serene, moderate, mild, cool, apathetic, lethargic.

tortuous *adj.* winding, twisting, full of curves, circuitous, sinuous, serpentine, zigzag, meandering, crooked; labyrinthine, convoluted, complicated, involved; indirect, roundabout, devious, ambiguous, hard to follow. **—Ant.** straight, straight as an arrow, beeline, direct; straightforward, simple.

torture *v.* **1.** subject to severe pain, put to the rack; mistreat, maltreat, abuse. **2.** have anxiety, torment, distress, cause anguish; rack, harrow, wring, prick, smite. *—n.* **3.** punishment by causing pain, extorting information by subjecting to pain, cause of severe pain, brutality. **4.** torment, agony, anguish, suffering, distress, pain, ordeal, trial, tribulation, infliction, cruelty. **—Ant. 1** persuade, coax, cajole, wheedle, entice, flatter, charm. **2** set at ease, disburden, calm, quiet, relax; cheer, comfort, solace. **3** pleasure, enjoyment, comfort, contentment, well-being, happiness, mirth, gaiety, cheer. **4** joy, delight, ecstasy, rapture, happiness, enjoyment, gratification.

torturous *adj.* torturing, painful, agonizing, racking, cruel, anguishing, tormenting, distressing, distressful, excruciating, miserable, harrowing, anguished, tormented, distressed, annoying, irksome, unpleasant, galling, disagreeable. **—Ant.** painless, pleasant, pleasing, delightful, enjoyable, agreeable, welcome, comforting; gratifying; contented, cheerful, joyous, happy.

toss *v.* **1.** throw, throw carelessly, pitch, flip, fling, sling, heave, hurl, cast, lob, let fly, propel. **2.** pitch, jerk, sway, rock, shake, agitate, roll, joggle, churn, tumble about, wiggle, wriggle, writhe, flounce, undulate, oscillate. *—n.* **3.** pitch, throw, heave, fling, sling, hurl, cast, lob, flip. **4.** sudden upward raise, flounce, jerk, shake, flourish. **—Ant. 1, 3** catch, grasp. **1** seize, snatch, clutch, take; hold, keep, retain.

total *n.* **1.** sum, sum total, full amount, whole amount, whole, aggregate, totality, entirety; gross. *—adj.* **2.** entire, whole, complete, combined, full, gross, integral. **3.** absolute, complete, utter, perfect, thorough, unconditional, unqualified, unlimited, unmodified, undisputed, sheer, sweeping, comprehensive, downright, outright, out-and-out, *Slang* solid, wholesale. *—v.* **4.** total up, tote up, add up, add, sum up, reckon, compute, calculate, figure up, figure, find the sum; add up to. **—Ant. 1** subtotal, partial amount, part. **2, 3** partial, limited, incomplete. **2** fractional. **3** slight, meager, hollow, fragmentary; conditional, qualified, mixed, uneven, halfway; marred, defective, wanting. **4** subtract, deduct.

totalitarian *adj.* strictly controlled, undemocratic, unrepresentative, fascistic, fascist, autocratic, dictatorial, despotic, tyrannous, tyrannical. **—Ant.** anarchistic; democratic, republican, representative, popular.

totally *adv.* completely, utterly, entirely, from beginning to end, throughout, thoroughly, absolutely, unconditionally, without qualification, perfectly, downright, out-and-out, *Slang* solidly. **—Ant.** partially, in part, incompletely, slightly, somewhat, halfway, conditionally, with qualifications.

tote *v.* carry, carry around, lug, cart, drag, pull, haul, move, fetch, convey, transport; carry on one's person, bear, pack, *Slang* schlepp.

totter *v.* walk unsteadily, shuffle, waddle, stagger, stumble, reel, lurch, falter; wobble, sway, waver, teeter, shake, rock, oscillate, vacillate.

touch *v.* **1.** put a hand against, put a finger against, handle, finger, paw, thumb, feel, stroke, rub, manipulate, caress, fondle, pet. **2.** be in contact, meet, join, unite, be contiguous, abut, adjoin, border, converge, come together, bring into contact. **3.** use, utilize; consume; avail oneself of, resort to, have recourse to, have to do with, be associated with, deal with. **4.** affect, move, impress, work, soften, melt, sadden; influence, sway, strike, inspire, thrill, excite, arouse, rouse, stir, fire, inflame, inspirit, electrify. **5.** mention, discuss briefly, deal with in passing, allude to, refer to, broach, hint at, bear upon, concern, pertain to; note, cite. **6.** compare with, equal, match, rival, come up to, come near, keep pace with. *—n.* **7.** the sense of touch; feel, feeling; touching, stroke, handling, fingering, pawing, thumbing, manipulation, palpation; caress, fondling. **8.** feel, texture, fineness, surface, quality. **9.** communication, contact; awareness, familiarity, acquaintance, realization, understanding, comprehension, perception. **10.** trace, tinge, tint, bit, pinch, dash, sprinkling, soupçon, smack, taste, speck, hint, suggestion, suspicion, intimation. **11.** technique, deftness, adroitness, hand, style, manner, method, skill, art, artistry, form, mastery, finesse, flair, gift, finish, polish, virtuosity; guiding hand, influence, direction. **—Ant. 2** separate, diverge. **4**

leave one unaffected, leave unmoved, leave one cold; bore. **5** ignore, disregard, overlook, pass over, skip, omit, leave out, reject, slight.

touching *adj.* moving, affecting, stirring; emotional, dramatic, sentimental; saddening, sad, heartfelt, heartbreaking, heartrending, distressing, pitiful, poignant, tender, pathetic, sorrowful. **—Ant.** unmoving, unaffecting, unemotional.

touchstone *n.* standard, yardstick, measure, criterion, gauge, model, example, guide, rule, pattern, guideline, norm, principle, proof, benchmark.

touchy *adj.* **1.** sensitive, easily offended, easily hurt, thinskinned, concerned, resentful, bitter; irritable, huffy, grumpy, grouchy, cross, testy, crabby, peevish, snappish, petulant, surly, quick-tempered, irascible, cantankerous, querulous, captious, waspish. **2.** delicate, requiring diplomacy, requiring tact, sensitive, ticklish, awkward, critical, requiring caution, precarious, difficult, fragile. **—Syn. Study. 1** See IRRITABLE. **—Ant. 1** insensitive, thickskinned, callous, hardened, inured, impervious, indifferent, unconcerned, nonchalant; sweet, good-humored, happy, pleasant, cheerful, cheery, smiling, blithe, jaunty, friendly, even-tempered, in good spirits, lighthearted, sunny. **2** noncritical, easy, easily handled, stable.

tough *adj.* **1.** strong, durable, lasting, enduring, hardy, sturdy, firm, resistant, rugged, solid, impenetrable, infrangible, heavy-duty; leathery. **2.** difficult, hard, laborious, arduous, strenuous, toilsome, exhausting, onerous, formidable, exacting, troublesome, trying, grievous, irksome, hard-to-solve, baffling, bewildering, puzzling, perplexing, confusing, complicated, intricate, complex, involved, thorny, knotty, ticklish, enigmatic. **3.** hard, stern, strict, firm, rigid, exacting, unyielding, uncompromising, inflexible, unbending; stubborn, obstinate, obdurate, perverse, adamant, hardheaded, dogged, mulish, bullheaded, pigheaded; wily, crafty, canny, cagey, calculating, cold. **4.** rough, vicious, bloodthirsty, ruthless, mean, cruel, brutal, savage, barbaric, inhuman, cold-blooded, heartless, hardhearted, hard, unfeeling, insensitive, unsympathetic, pitiless, callous. **—Ant. 1, 2** soft. **1** weak, delicate, frail, fragile, flimsy, brittle, frangible, susceptible; tender. **2, 3** easy. **2** simple, effortless, slight. **3** lenient, indulgent, permissive, unexacting; accommodating, amenable, acquiescent, complaisant, compliant, compromising, flexible. **4** sweet, kind, humane, benign, gentle, mild, softhearted, sympathetic, compassionate, considerate, loving, merciful.

toughen *v.* strengthen, harden, firm, firm up, fortify, inure, stiffen, temper, steel, discipline; accustom, acclimate, acclimatize, habituate, season. **—Ant.** weaken, exhaust, enfeeble, enervate.

toupee *n.* small wig, hairpiece, wig, periwig, peruke; *Slang* carpet, rug.

tour *n.* **1.** (*variously*) circular journey, sightseeing trip, jaunt, excursion, junket, peregrination, voyage, trek, safari; itinerary. **—*v.* 2.** visit, travel around, travel through, sightsee in, vacation through, travel and perform at, travel and work at, inspect.

tourist *n.* sightseer, journeyer, traveler, voyager, excursionist, globetrotter, world traveler; wayfarer, wanderer, pilgrim, vagabond; *Slang* rubberneck, *Brit.* tripper.

tousled *adj.* uncombed, mussed, mussed-up, disheveled, unkempt, disordered, rumpled, messy, untidy, tangled. **—Ant.** combed, combed and brushed; unmussed, well-kempt, neat, tidy.

tout *v.* praise, publicize, advertise, vaunt, brag about, ballyhoo, promote, celebrate, extol, exalt, glorify, acclaim, aggrandize; *Slang* plug, talk up. **—Ant.** belittle, deprecate; *Slang* slam, run down.

tow *v.* **1.** haul, drag, drag along, draw, pull, lug, trail; hoist, lift. **—*n.* 2.** act of towing, towing. **—Ant. 1, 2** push, shove.

tower *n.* **1.** tall structure; (*variously*) water tower, clock tower, bell tower, belfry, prison tower, guard tower, lookout tower; steeple, spire, turret, minaret, skyscraper, column, obelisk; castle, keep. **2.** pillar, mainstay, bulwark, stronghold, rock, foundation, wellspring, fountainhead, refuge. **—*v.* 3.** rise high, rise above, ascend, soar, mount, shoot up, loom, surge, extend above, overhang, overtop, overshadow, eclipse; surpass, exceed, outshine, transcend, outdo, outclass, leave behind. **—Ant. 3** fall, sink, descend, drop.

towering *adj.* **1.** high, tall, lofty, ascending, soaring, mounting, overhanging, alpine, cloud-swept, cloud-capped, snowclad. **2.** surpassing, supreme, transcendent, preeminent, paramount, foremost, principal, dominant, sublime, superior, extraordinary, incomparable, peerless, unexcelled, unequaled, unrivaled, unparalleled, without parallel, unmatched, matchless, second to none. **—Ant. 1** low, low-lying, short, squat, dumpy, stubby, truncated; flat, deep, submerged. **2** lowly, lesser, inferior, sorry, poor, paltry, inconsequential, insignificant; ordinary, commonplace, common, average, mediocre, run-of-the-mill, everyday.

town *n.* **1.** small town, large village, small city; (*loosely*) village, hamlet, burg, settlement. **2.** self-governing populated place, municipality, borough, township, parish; city, urban area, population center, metropolis, cosmopolis. **3.** townspeople, inhabitants, citizenry, residents. **4.** main business district, business district, shopping district, downtown, city center, central city, inner city.

toxic *adj.* poisonous, venomous, poisoned, deadly, fatal, mortal, lethal; pernicious, noxious, unhealthy. **—Ant.** nontoxic, nonpoisonous, nonlethal; healthy, salubrious, refreshing, invigorating.

toxin *n.* **—Syn. Study.** See POISON.

toy *n.* **1.** plaything; bauble, trinket, gadget, gewgaw, gimcrack, trifle. *—adj.* **2.** for play, for amusement. **3.** miniature, diminutive, small-scale, small-sized, bantam, midget, pygmy, stunted, dwarfed; little, tiny, Lilliputian. *—v.* **4.** play, trifle, dally, sport, fiddle, amuse oneself with. **—Ant. 1** necessity; tool, instrument, utensil. **2** real, actual. **3** full-sized; oversize, giant, large, big, huge, enormous, immense, colossal, gigantic, mammoth, gargantuan.

trace *n.* **1.** sign left behind, sign, mark, indication, evidence, relic, vestige, token, remains; trail, track, footprint. **2.** tinge, touch, hint, suspicion, suggestion, shade, flavor; small amount, little bit, bit, trifle, jot, iota, drop. *—v.* **3.** follow the trail of, track, track down, hunt for, hunt, nose out, ferret out, search for, look for, seek; find, discover, come across, light upon, unearth, dig up, uncover. **4.** map, diagram, draw, outline, delineate, describe, depict, mark out. **5.** copy by drawing over, draw over, follow the outline of. **—Syn. Study. 1** TRACE, VESTIGE agree in denoting marks or signs of something, usu. of the past. TRACE, the broader term, denotes any mark or slight indication of something past or present: *a trace of ammonia in water.* VESTIGE is more limited and refers to some slight, though actual, remains of something that no longer exists: *vestiges of one's former wealth.*

track *n.* **1.** rail, guide rail, parallel rails; (*variously*) train track, streetcar track. **2.** footprint, mark, sign, spoor; trail, path, scent. **3.** course, path, route, trail, tack, way. **4.** racetrack, running track; sports performed on a track. *—v.* **5.** follow the track, follow the path, trail, follow, trace. **6.** leave footprints on, mark, dirty.

tract[1] *n.* stretch, expanse, region, zone, area, quarter, district, territory; plot, lot, parcel.

tract[2] *n.* **1.** pamphlet, leaflet, brochure, booklet, monograph. **2.** treatise, essay, disquisition.

tractable *adj.* amenable, easy to manage, manageable, easy to control, controllable, governable, obedient, trainable, teachable, docile, tame, submissive, compliant, yielding. **—Ant.** intractable, unmanageable, uncontrollable, ungovernable, disobedient, wild, unruly, refractory, recalcitrant, headstrong, willful, stubborn, obstinate.

trade *n.* **1.** commerce, buying and selling, business, mercantile business, business dealings, transactions, merchandising. **2.** manual occupation, skilled occupation, skilled labor, occupational skill, manual skill, craft, handicraft; occupation, profession, calling, vocation, line of work, line, business, pursuit, employment. **3.** exchange, swap. **4.** clientele, customers, patrons, buyers, shoppers. *—v.* **5.** exchange, swap, barter. **6.** carry on commerce, do business, buy and sell, deal. **7.** shop, be a customer, be a client, patronize, buy, deal.

trader *n.* merchant, dealer, seller, businessperson, merchandiser, trafficker, tradesperson, salesperson, wholesaler, shopkeeper, retailer, storekeeper; *Slang* drummer, *Brit.* monger.

tradition *n.* **1.** handed-down belief, custom, habit, typical way, practice, convention, usage, unwritten law, order of the day. **2.** legend, myth, folk story, tale, saga; folklore, lore, superstition. **—Ant. 1** novelty, innovation, new wrinkle, new idea, the latest thing; law, decree, dogma. **2** true story, biography, autobiography; fact.

traditional *adj.* handed down from generation to generation, customary, typical, conventional, usual, habitual, accustomed, fixed, inveterate, established, acknowledged; old, ancestral, historic. **—Ant.** new, modern, unusual, novel, original, innovative, unusual, unconventional.

traduce *v.* slander, malign, defame, libel, disparage, vilify, abuse, calumniate, deprecate, smear, backbite, sully, besmirch; *Slang* bad-mouth, run down. **—Ant.** honor, praise, extol, defend.

traffic *n.* **1.** vehicular movement; (*variously*) cars, trucks, buses, trains, planes, ships; pedestrian movement, pedestrians. **2.** passengers, travelers, voyagers; (*variously*) riders, tourists, vacationists, excursionists, commuters; freight. **3.** transportation of goods, trade, dealings, business, enterprise, commerce, buying and selling, barter, exchange, transactions; smuggling, bootlegging. **4.** dealings, relations, doings, contact, proceedings, intercourse. *—v.* **5.** trade, deal, buy and sell, carry on commerce; smuggle, bootleg.

tragedy *n.* **1.** dreadful happening, sad

thing, unfortunate affair, shocking misfortune, pathetic occurrence, setback, reversal, affliction; misery, anguish, sorrow, grief, woe, heartache, unhappiness, heartbreak, blow, grievous day; accident, disaster, catastrophe, calamity. **2.** play with a disastrous ending, play about the downfall of a great man or woman. **—Ant. 1** blessing, boon, kindness, wonderful thing, good fortune; happiness, joy, pleasure, satisfaction, gratification, bliss, contentment. **2** comedy.

tragic *adj.* **1.** dreadful, unfortunate, appalling, heartbreaking, sad, lamentable, pathetic, piteous, pitiful, pitiable, deplorable, mournful, grievous, dreary, woeful, unhappy, dire, shocking, awful, frightful, terrible, horrible; disastrous, calamitous, catastrophic, fatal, deadly; ruinous, devastating, destructive. **2.** of dramatic tragedy; serious, dramatic. **—Ant. 1** fortunate, happy, felicitous, pleasant, satisfying, gratifying, agreeable, joyful, worthwhile, wonderful, lucky. **2** comic.

trail *v.* **1.** drag, drag along, drag behind, tow, draw; dangle, hand down, float, stream, flow. **2.** follow, lag behind, be behind, tread on the heels of, follow in the wake of, bring up the rear; move slowly, dawdle, poke; be losing, be down. **3.** track, trace, follow, tail, hunt, hound, dog. **4.** diminish, dwindle, shrink, subside, fall, grow faint, grow weak, grow small, lessen, decrease, taper off, peter out. *—n.* **5.** track, course, footprints, scent, spoor; sign, mark, trace, path. **6.** path, footpath, pathway, beaten track, way; bridle path. **—Ant. 1** push, shove. **2** lead, go before, be winning. **3** flee, run away. **4** increase, rise, swell, grow, intensify, strengthen.

train *n.* **1.** railroad train; subway train, subway, elevated, el; caravan, procession, column. **2.** series, succession, sequence, progression, chain, line, set. **3.** trailing part, trail, queue, appendage, continuation, afterpart. **4.** retinue, attendants, escort, followers, entourage, cortege. *—v.* **5.** teach good behavior, teach a habit, discipline, domesticate, break; instruct, teach, drill, tutor, educate, school, prepare. **6.** exercise, get in shape, work out, pump iron; prepare, practice, rehearse. **7.** aim, point, direct, level, sight, focus, bring to bear. **—Syn. Study. 5** See TEACH.

trait *n.* characteristic, quality, mark, distinguishing mark, hallmark, earmark, attribute, feature; peculiarity, idiosyncracy, quirk, mannerism.

traitor *n.* one who betrays his country, one who commits treason, turncoat, renegade, serpent, snake in the grass, wolf in sheep's clothing; (*variously*) deserter, mutineer, revolutionary, rebel; betrayer, double-crosser, double-dealer, deceiver, hypocrite, false friend, Judas, apostate, quisling, fifth columnist, *Slang* rat, ratter, ratfink. **—Ant.** patriot, loyalist; defender, supporter, true friend.

tramp *v.* **1.** trek, hike, march, trudge, walk, traipse, slog; (*loosely*) wander, ramble, roam, rove, meander, perambulate, gallivant, peregrinate, prowl. **2.** stamp, stomp, walk noisily, tread heavily, trample. *—n.* **3.** hobo, wandering beggar, panhandler, bum, vagrant, derelict, floater, knight-of-the-road, itinerant.

trample *v.* grind under foot, run over, crush, flatten, squash; step heavily upon, stamp, stomp.

trance *n.* spell, daze, dazed condition, half-conscious state, hypnosis, hypnotic state, sleepwalking, coma, stupor; vision, daydream, reverie, dream, pipe dream; absorption, concentration, abstraction, brown study, preoccupation, woolgathering.

tranquil *adj.* peaceful, calm, unperturbed, serene, restful, placid, still, halcyon, quiet, unruffled, unexcited, composed, self-possessed, cool, undisturbed, mild, gentle. **—Syn. Study.** See PEACEFUL. **—Ant.** agitated, disturbed, confused, busy, restless; excited, rattled, distracted.

tranquillity or **tranquility** *n.* peace, calm, quiet, serenity, peacefulness, repose, hush, placidity, stillness, restfulness, quietude, harmony, concord, composure. **—Ant.** uproar, tumult, commotion, disorder.

transact *v.* carry on, carry out, carry through, conduct, exact, perform, do, exercise, execute, handle, accomplish, manage, discharge, achieve, settle, take care of.

transaction *n.* business dealing, dealing, deal, bargain, piece of business, venture, enterprise, affair, operation, exchange, settlement, negotiation.

transcend *v.* **1.** exceed, go beyond, rise above, outdo, surmount, surpass, overstep, overleap. **2.** surpass, be greater than, be superior to, exceed, excel, outdo, outstrip, overshadow, outshine, eclipse, outrival, outdistance, outrank.

transcendental *adj.* **1.** metaphysical, transcending experience, spiritual, mental, intuitive. **2.** extraordinary, unusual, uncommon, superior, unrivaled, peerless, matchless, incomparable, unequaled, unsurpassed, supreme, great, exceeding, surpassing, elevated. **—Ant. 1** physical, empirical. **2** ordinary, common, commonplace, usual, average; inferior, little.

transfer *v.* **1.** move, remove, shift, relocate, change, convey, carry, bring, send, transport, transmit; consign, turn over, hand over, relegate, make over, deed, cede. —*n.* **2.** transferring, transferal, transference, moving, removal, shifting, shift, relocation, relocating, conveying, carrying, bringing, sending, transportation, transporting, transmittal, shipment; consignment, delivering, relegation, deeding. —**Ant. 1** keep, retain; leave. **2** keeping, retention.

transfix *v.* **1.** impale, skewer, spear, run through, fix fast, pin, stick, stab, spike, pierce, penetrate. **2.** rivet the attention of, rivet, hold rapt, engross, hold, absorb, fascinate, spellbind, mesmerize, hypnotize, bewitch, captivate, intrigue, enchant; stun, astound, astonish; terrify.

transform *v.* change, turn, convert, transfigure, transmute, alter, make over, transmogrify, metamorphose; remodel, reconstruct, remold, recast, refurbish. —**Syn. Study.** TRANSFORM, CONVERT mean to change one thing into another. TRANSFORM means to radically change the outward form or inner character: *a frog transformed into a prince; delinquents transformed into responsible citizens.* CONVERT usu. means to modify or adapt so as to serve a new or different use or function: *to convert a barn into a house.*

transgression *n.* offense, sin, misdeed, evil deed, trespass, lapse, iniquity, wrongdoing, wrong, immorality, error; infraction, infringement, breach, encroachment, contravention, overstepping; violation, infraction, crime, lawbreaking. —**Ant.** virtue, morality, probity, righteousness, grace, good deed, merit; observance, compliance, adherence.

transgressor *n.* sinner, evildoer, trespasser, offender; lawbreaker, violator, wrongdoer, culprit, malefactor, miscreant, felon, criminal. —**Ant.** innocent, exemplar; law-abider.

transient *adj.* **1.** temporary, transitory, fleeting, brief, momentary, ephemeral, evanescent, impermanent, unenduring, not lasting, perishable, short-lived, temporal, soon past, passing, here today and gone tomorrow. **2.** temporary, staying a short time, short-term, passing through. —**Syn. Study. 1** See TEMPORARY. —**Ant. 1, 2** permanent. **1** lasting, long-lasting, undying, unfading, imperishable, perpetual, persistent, durable, abiding.

transition *n.* change, changeover, alteration, passing, passage, shifting, jump, leap, conversion, variation, transformation, transmutation; progression, gradation, graduation.

transitory *adj.* temporary, transient, fleeting, brief, short-lived, passing, impermanent, fugitive, not lasting, unenduring, evanescent, ephemeral, here today and gone tomorrow. —**Syn. Study.** See TEMPORARY. —**Ant.** long, long-lived, lasting, persistent, durable, enduring, permanent, undying, imperishable, abiding, everlasting, perpetual, eternal.

translate *v.* **1.** render, convert; decode, decipher. **2.** change, turn, transform, apply, convert, transmute; recast, alter. **3.** explain, interpret, simplify, elucidate, clarify, make clear, spell out; paraphrase, rephrase, reword, express differently.

translucent *adj.* semitransparent, semiopaque, pellucid, translucid. —**Syn. Study.** See TRANSPARENT. —**Ant.** opaque.

transmission *n.* **1.** transmitting, transfer, transferring, transference, passage, passing, handing over, changing of hands, transmittal, transmittance, sending, conveyance, dispatch, forwarding, transportation, delivery, remittance. **2.** message, dispatch, communication, delivery, note, broadcast.

transmit *v.* **1.** send, convey, deliver, relay, transfer, dispatch, issue, forward, ship, remit, pass on, carry, spread, disseminate, communicate. **2.** broadcast, televise, send, relay a signal.

transparent *adj.* **1.** clear, crystal-clear, lucid, limpid, pellucid, glassy. **2.** see-through, thin, sheer, gauzy, translucent, diaphanous, peekaboo. **3.** evident, self-evident, plain, obvious, apparent, perceptible, palpable, manifest, visible, patent; explicit, distinct, clear-cut, unmistakable, unambiguous, unequivocal. —**Syn. Study. 1, 2** TRANSPARENT, TRANSLUCENT agree in describing material that light rays can pass through. That which is TRANSPARENT allows objects to be seen clearly through it: *Clear water is transparent.* That which is TRANSLUCENT allows light to pass through, diffusing it, however, so that objects beyond are not distinctly seen: *Ground glass is translucent.* —**Ant. 1, 2** opaque. **1** muddy, roiled, murky. **2** thick. **3** imperceptible, unapparent, hidden, concealed, unrevealed, invisible, undetectable; indistinct, confused, vague, mysterious, mystifying.

transpire *v.* **1.** become known, be discovered, be revealed, be disclosed, come to light, come out, make public, become public knowledge, get abroad, show its face, leak out. **2.** occur, happen, come to pass, evolve, take place, eventuate, be met with; befall, arise, present itself, chance, appear, turn up, crop up.

transport *v.* **1.** transfer, move, remove, convey, carry, transmit, take, bring, send, deliver, dispatch, fetch, bear, cart, tote, lug; ship, truck, freight. **2.** carry away, move, thrill, enrapture, enchant, lift, enthrall, entrance, overpower, make ecstatic, electrify, captivate, delight, charm, bewitch, *Slang* send. —*n.* **3.**

transporting, transportation, shipment, shipping, conveying, conveyance, moving, transfer, removal, carrying, sending, delivery, dispatch, bearing, carting, trucking. **4.** vehicle, conveyance; (*variously*) ship, freighter, cargo ship, train, freight train, airplane, cargo plane, truck, bus. **5.** ecstasy, exaltation, joy, delight, thrill, bliss, rapture, elation. **—Syn. Study. 5** See RAPTURE.

transportation *n.* conveyance, transference, transferal, transport, shipment, transmission, delivery, dispatch, removal, movement, haulage, cartage, portage, transit, transmittance.

trap *n.* **1.** (*variously*) snare, springe, net, pit, pitfall. **2.** ruse, trick, artifice, stratagem, wile, feint, ploy, device, machination, maneuver; ambush, booby trap. *—v.* **3.** entrap, catch, snare, ensnare, enmesh, hunt down, lure, entangle. **4.** seal, stop, lock in, hold back, compartmentalize.

trappings *n. pl.* dress, garb, costume, raiment, attire, clothing, clothes, apparel, vesture, investment, outfit, habiliment; gear, accoutrements, paraphernalia, trimmings, effects, array, things, fittings, ornaments, adornments, decorations, embellishments, adjuncts.

trash *n.* **1.** litter, rubbish, junk, rubble, refuse, garbage, waste matter, residue, sweepings, dregs, leavings, dross, debris; worthless stuff, odds and ends, castoffs. **2.** worthless writing, worthless talk, junk, drivel, rot, hogwash, balderdash, twaddle; *Slang* tripe, crap, poppycock; nonsense, foolishness. **3.** disreputable persons, bums, unsavory element, shady types, scum, riffraff, good-for-nothings, tramps, ne'er-do-wells, idlers, loafers. **—Ant. 1** valuables, treasure. **3** elite, worthies.

travail *n.* **1.** toil, drudgery, hard work, backbreaking work, burdensome work, exertion. **2.** anguish, suffering, strain, stress, hardship, worry, distress, pain. **3.** labor, labor pains, birth pains; childbirth, delivery, parturition, accouchement. **—Ant. 1** ease, relaxation, rest, loafing. **2** comfort, pleasure.

travel *v.* **1.** move, proceed, progress, go, wend, press onward. **2.** take a trip, journey, tour, sightsee, visit; pass over, traverse, cross, be on, pass through; roam, rove, wander, junket, trek, globetrot, range; (*variously*) voyage, cruise, sail, drive, hitchhike. **—Ant. 2** stay, remain, settle, remain stationary.

traveler *n.* **1.** one who travels; (*variously*) tourist, journeyer, vacationer, wayfarer, voyager, excursionist, tripper, trekker, sightseer, globetrotter, wanderer, itinerant, rover, vagabond, nomad, migrant, gypsy, pilgrim. **2.** traveling salesperson, commercial traveler, *Slang* road warrior; representative, drummer.

traverse *v.* **1.** cross, go across, move over, move along, travel over, travel, cut across; move through, negotiate, pass through. **2.** cross, cross over, span, reach across, go across, extend over, reach over, overpass, bridge, intersect, run through.

travesty *n.* **1.** ludicrous imitation, burlesque, spoof, takeoff, parody, caricature, lampoon, mockery, broad satire, farce. **2.** mockery, perversion, shameful imitation, shameful example, misrepresentation, distortion, sham, disgrace. **—Syn. Study. 1** See BURLESQUE.

treacherous *adj.* **1.** traitorous, treasonous, untrustworthy, faithless, falsehearted, unfaithful, disloyal, untrue, deceitful, deceptive, false, perfidious, tricky, misleading, devious, twofaced. **2.** dangerous, hazardous, unsafe, perilous, precarious, risky. **—Ant. 1** loyal, true, true-blue, faithful, trusty, trustworthy, dependable, reliable. **2** safe, reliable.

treachery *n.* disloyalty, treason, betrayal, faithlessness, untrustworthiness, falseness, deceit, deceitfulness, deception, perfidy, violation of faith, breach of faith, underhandedness, duplicity, trickery, guile, double-dealing, double cross, infidelity, apostasy.

tread *v.* **1.** walk, walk along, walk on, step, step on, trudge along, tramp, hike, stroll; roam, rove, range, prowl. **2.** trample, stomp, stamp, crush under foot. *—n.* **3.** step, sound of footsteps, footstep, footfall; walk; manner of walking, gait, pace, stride.

treason *n.* betrayal of one's country, aiding an enemy; subversion, conspiracy, rebellion, revolt, revolution, insurgence, insurrection, mutiny; disloyalty, treachery, perfidy, duplicity, apostasy. **—Syn. Study.** TREASON, SEDITION mean disloyalty or treachery to one's country or its government. TREASON is any attempt to overthrow the government or impair the well-being of a state to which one owes allegiance. According to the U.S. Constitution, it is the crime of levying war against the U.S. or giving aid and comfort to its enemies. SEDITION is any act, writing, speech, etc., directed unlawfully against state authority, the government, or the constitution, or calculated to bring it into contempt or to incite others to hostility or disaffection; it does not amount to treason and therefore is not a capital offense. **—Ant.** loyalty, allegiance, patriotism; faithfulness, fidelity.

treasure *n.* **1.** stored wealth, riches, hoard, store, deposit, *Slang* gold mine; (*variously*) precious gems, jewels, gold, silver. **2.** gem, jewel, paragon, pride and joy, apple of one's eye, pearl of great price. —*v.* **3.** value, cherish, revere, esteem, prize, hold dear, count precious, regard, dote upon, care greatly for, bank upon. —**Ant. 3** disclaim, scorn, disregard, hold for naught, take lightly.

treasurer *n.* controller, auditor, bursar, cash-keeper, purser; secretary of the treasury, minister of finance, *Brit.* Chancellor of the Exchequer; teller, cashier; financier, banker, financial officer; bookkeeper, accountant.

treasury *n.* **1.** place where funds are kept, exchequer, repository, depository, storehouse, bank; vault, till, coffer, safe, strongbox, money box. **2.** amount on hand, purse, funds, bank account. **3.** collection, anthology, compendium, compilation, thesaurus.

treat *v.* **1.** act toward, behave toward, deal with, relate to, consider, look upon; manage, handle. **2.** try to cure, try to heal, doctor, attend, minister to, prescribe for, remedy, medicate, patch up. **3.** discuss, have as a subject matter, write about, expatiate on, address oneself to, speak about. **4.** apply, cover, coat, imbue, impregnate. **5.** entertain as a guest, take out, give, *Slang* stand, blow, spring; favor, grant; divert. —*n.* **6.** pleasure, satisfaction, gratification, comfort, delight, joy, thrill. **7.** small gift of food, small gift; favor, grant; entertainment paid for by another.

treatise *n.* systematic work, detailed article, discourse, essay, thesis, dissertation, study, monograph, exhaustive paper, extensive piece, tract, tractate, manual, report, memoir, textbook, text.

treatment *n.* **1.** manner of dealing, handling, management, treating, manipulation, operation, conduct, approach, process, procedure, way, course. **2.** medical care, cure, remedy, therapy, doctoring; regimen; application, medication, antidote.

treaty *n.* international agreement, formal agreement, accord, bargain, deal, pact, compact, covenant, concordat, entente, understanding.

trek *n.* **1.** trip, journey; tramp, hike, outing, march; jaunt, junket, voyage, sail, excursion, odyssey, expedition, peregrination, pilgrimage; passage, migration. —*v.* **2.** tramp, hike, rove, roam, march, trudge, range, wander, plod, *Slang* slog; travel, traverse, journey, peregrinate.

tremble *v.* shake, quiver, shiver, shudder, quake, quail, quaver, waver, flutter, pulsate, palpitate.

tremendous *adj.* **1.** huge, gigantic, immense, colossal, enormous, extremely large, great, mammoth, giant, monstrous, gargantuan, elephantine, titanic, vast, towering, *Slang* humongous; formidable, awesome, major, considerable, sizable; important, consequential. **2.** wonderful, excellent, exceptional, unusual, uncommon, extraordinary, marvelous, fantastic, incredible, amazing, first-rate, noteworthy, great, fabulous, fine, terrific, stupendous. —**Syn. Study. 1** See HUGE. —**Ant. 1** small, little, tiny, diminutive, wee, undersized, miniature, dwarfed, stunted, pygmy; easy, simple, minor, unimportant. **2** ordinary, fair, average, mediocre, unexceptional, unremarkable, run-of-the-mill; bad, poor, awful, terrible, lousy, second-rate.

tremor *n.* shaking, shake, trembling, tremble, quiver, quivering, shiver, shivering, shudder, waver, flutter, quavering, pulsation, throb, spasm, paroxysm, convulsion, palpitation, vibration; quake, jolt, shock, jar. —**Ant.** steadiness.

tremulous *adj.* **1.** hesitant, faltering, timid, irresolute, uncertain, fearful, wavering; jittery, wobbly, shaky, nervous, trembling, jumpy, quivering, quaking; panicky, panic-stricken. **2.** excited, aflutter, keyed-up, atremble, worked-up, aquiver, restless, stimulated, agitated, impatient, on tenterhooks. —**Ant.** calm, collected, composed, relaxed, cool, unperturbed.

trenchant *adj.* **1.** clear-cut, incisive, keen, penetrating, distinct, well-defined, probing, crisp, concise, razor-sharp. **2.** caustic, bitter, sarcastic, tart, acid, acrimonious, mordant, acerbic, scathing, scorching. —**Ant. 1** vague, rambling, disorganized. **2** flattering, kind, soothing, complimentary.

trend *n.* fashion, mode, style; drift, direction, movement, flow, bent, tendency, leaning, inclination, propensity, proclivity, impulse.

trendy *adj.* stylish, fashionable, faddish, modish, voguish, current, popular, swank, tony, all the rage; *Slang* in, with-it; up-to-the-minute. —**Ant.** classic, dated, old-fashioned, passé, outmoded, *Slang* old hat.

trepidation *n.* apprehension, disquiet, uneasiness, anxiety, dread, alarm, panic, jitters, fear, consternation, worry, disquietude, nervousness, jitteriness, *Informal* cold feet, butterflies. —**Ant.** confidence, sureness, fearlessness, quietude, steadiness, poise, composure, calm, cool.

trespass *v.* **1.** enter unlawfully, intrude, invade, encroach, infringe, impinge. —*n.* **2.** wrongful entry, unlawful entry, encroachment, intrusion, infringement, invasion. **3.** sin, wrongdoing, evildoing, immorality, iniquity, transgression, error, misdeed, violation, wrong, offense; misconduct, misbehavior, infraction, overstepping, delinquency. —**Syn. Study. 1**

TRESPASS, ENCROACH, INFRINGE imply overstepping boundaries or violating the rights of others. To TRESPASS is to invade the property or rights of another, esp. to pass unlawfully within the boundaries of private land: *The hunters trespassed on the farmer's fields.* To ENCROACH is to intrude, gradually and often stealthily, on the territory, rights, or privileges of another, so that a footing is imperceptibly established: *The sea slowly encroached on the land.* To INFRINGE is to break in upon or invade another's rights, customs, or the like, by violating or disregarding them: *to infringe on a patent.* **—Ant. 3** good deed, virtue.

trial *n.* **1.** court case, litigation, judicial contest, hearing. **2.** test, testing, test run, tryout, trying, putting to the proof; try, attempt, essay, venture, go, shot, endeavor, effort, *Informal* flyer, whirl. **3.** hardship, misfortune, trouble, distress, affliction, woe, misery, pain, adversity, burden, ordeal, vexation, suffering, wretchedness, agony, anguish, torment, care, worry, heartache, misadventure, accident, bad luck, cross to bear. **—Ant. 3** ease, comfort, happiness, joy, delight, good fortune, good luck.

tribulation *n.* affliction, trouble, ordeal, suffering, wretchedness, misfortune, worry, care, hardship, heartache, agony, anguish, torment, pain, adversity, trial; woe, misery, distress, grief, vexation, sorrow, unhappiness; ill fortune, bad luck. **—Ant.** happiness, joy, delight, ease, comfort; good fortune, good luck.

tribunal *n.* court, bar, bench, forum, seat of judgment, authority, judiciary, judges, ruling body; judge's bench, judge's chair.

tribute *n.* **1.** honor, respect, esteem, gratitude, acknowledgment, recognition; praise, compliment, accolade, kudos, commendation, laudation, eulogy, panegyric, extolling, encomium; testimonial, memorial. **2.** payment, settlement, ransom, bribe, peace offering, levy, excise, impost, assessment, tax, duty, toll, consideration, payoff, blood money, pound of flesh. **—Ant. 1** dishonor, disrespect, ingratitude, disdain, scorn; blame, insult, condemnation, slur, slap in the face.

trice *n.* instant, second, minute, moment, split second, shake, wink, flash, blink, twinkling, jiffy, *French* coup d'oeil; *Slang* jiff, sec.

trick *n.* **1.** artifice, ruse, device, deception, deceit, stratagem, machination, wile, feint, blind, maneuver, ploy, gimmick, resort, hoax; underhanded act, chicanery, sophistry, trap, fraud, imposture, subterfuge, contrivance, dodge, hocus-pocus. **2.** prank, joke, gag, antic, bluff, put-on, practical joke, caper. **3.** clever act, skilled act, stunt, feat, antic, number; magic demonstration, sleight of hand, prestidigitation, piece of legerdemain. **4.** knack, art, know-how, skill, deftness, gift, dexterity, adroitness, technique, secret. **—*v.*** **5.** deceive, take in, trap, hoax, gull, dupe, bait, outmaneuver, hoodwink, mislead, have, outwit, bamboozle, outfox, bluff; cheat, swindle, manipulate, flimflam; victimize. **—Syn. Study. 1** TRICK, ARTIFICE, RUSE, STRATAGEM are terms for crafty or cunning devices intended to deceive. TRICK, the general term, refers usu. to an underhanded act designed to cheat someone, but it sometimes refers merely to a pleasurable deceiving of the senses: *to win by a trick.* Like TRICK, but to a greater degree, ARTIFICE emphasizes the cleverness or cunning with which the proceeding is devised: *an artifice of diabolical ingenuity.* RUSE and STRATAGEM emphasize the purpose for which the trick is designed; RUSE is the more general term, and STRATAGEM sometimes implies a more elaborate procedure or a military application: *We gained entrance by a ruse. His stratagem gave the army command of the hill.* **5** See CHEAT. **—Ant. 1** honesty, truth, sincerity, candor, frankness, openness, straightforwardness, guilelessness. **4** luck.

trickery *n.* deceitfulness, deceit, guile, chicanery, charlatanism, duplicity, deviousness, skullduggery, stratagem, wiliness, craftiness, artfulness, slipperiness, quackery, rascality, pretense, hocus-pocus, imposture, crookedness, deception, bunkum, flimflam, artifice, shiftiness. **—Ant.** honesty, straightforwardness, artlessness, candidness, candor, frankness, openness, truth, uprightness.

trickle *v.* **1.** drip, dribble, seep, leak, exude, ooze, percolate; move slowly, pass bit by bit, go gradually. **—*n.*** **2.** dribble, drip, seepage, slow stream; little bit, small amount, small quantity. **—Ant. 1** splash, gush, stream, course, pour, spurt, surge. **2** stream, gush, flood, cascade, surge, spurt; lot, lots, much, many.

tricky *adj.* **1.** crafty, sly, cunning, foxy, slippery, wily, rascally, artful, deceptive, underhanded, shifty, devious. **2.** difficult, complicated, hard to handle, touch-and-go, temperamental. **3.** unreliable, unstable, undependable, unpredictable, hazardous, unsafe, dangerous, risky. **—Ant. 1** candid, straightforward, open, frank, artless, ingenuous, guileless, honest, truthful. **2** simple, easy. **3** reliable, dependable, stable.

trifle *n.* **1.** trinket, bauble, gimcrack, knickknack, bagatelle, gewgaw, plaything, toy; triviality, thing of no importance, small matter, unimportant matter, nothing. **2.** small quantity, little, morsel, bit, mite, dash, dab, drop, nip, pinch, speck, scrap, sliver, crumb, fragment, trace, iota, jot, modicum, sprinkling, tinge, touch. —*v.* **3.** treat lightly, deal lightly, amuse oneself, toy, play. **4.** dally, dawdle, linger, idle, dillydally, pass the time of day, kill time, waste time. **—Ant. 2** lot, lots, gobs, oodles.

trifling *adj.* insignificant, unimportant, inconsequential, trivial, negligible, small, slight, petty, puny, piddling, nugatory, picayune, inconsiderable, niggling, nominal, token, inappreciable, beneath notice, not worthy of mention, worthless, paltry, sorry, beggarly. **—Syn. Study.** See PETTY. **—Ant.** important, significant, consequential, major, worthwhile, considerable, appreciable, large.

trim *v.* **1.** prune, clip, crop, pare, lop, shave, shear, cut. **2.** decorate, ornament, adorn, deck, bedeck, array, garnish, embellish, furbish, trick out, beautify, bedizen, embroider. **3.** balance, distribute, arrange, adjust, equalize; change, shift, adjust to the direction of the wind. —*n.* **4.** shape, condition, fitness, state, form, fettle, kilter. **5.** trimming, adornment, embellishment, decoration, garnish, ornamentation, border, piping. **6.** trimming, cutting, evening-off, clipping, shearing, cropping, pruning, paring. —*adj.* **7.** lean, slim, sleek, slender, svelte, shapely, streamlined, willowy, well-proportioned, thin, lissome, shipshape, compact; fit, limber, supple, lithe, athletic.

trinket *n.* trifle, bauble, charm, small ornament, bijou, bit of jewelry, bagatelle, gewgaw, gimcrack, knickknack, odds and ends, notion, toy, plaything.

trip *n.* **1.** journey, excursion, outing, tour, jaunt, cruise, voyage, expedition, foray, junket, trek, safari, pilgrimage; commute. —*v.* **2.** stumble, fall over, miss one's footing, misstep, slip, cause to fall, throw off balance, lose one's balance, upset. **3.** make a mistake, err, blunder, slip up, bungle, flounder, fluff, flub, muff; cause to make a mistake, cause to err, throw off, disconcert, confuse, fool, catch, catch off guard, outdo, hoodwink, outfox. **4.** skip, step lightly, tread gracefully, flounce, caper, prance, dance, gambol, bob, scamper, frolic. **5.** release, undo, pull, flip, throw, activate, set off. **—Syn. Study. 1** TRIP, JOURNEY, VOYAGE, EXPEDITION, PILGRIMAGE are terms for a course of travel made to a particular place, usu. for some specific purpose. TRIP is the general word, indicating going any distance and returning, for either business or pleasure, and in either a hurried or a leisurely manner: *a trip to Europe; a bus trip.* JOURNEY indicates a trip of considerable length, mainly by land, and is usu. applied to travel that is more fatiguing than a trip: *an arduous journey to Tibet.* A VOYAGE usu. indicates leisurely travel by water to a distant place: *a voyage around the world.* An EXPEDITION, made often by an organized group, is designed for a specific purpose: *an archaeological expedition.* A PILGRIMAGE is made as to a shrine, from motives of piety or veneration: *a pilgrimage to Lourdes.*

trite *adj.* banal, stale, hackneyed, pedestrian, worn-out, shopworn, stereotyped, clichéd, bromidic, overdone, commonplace, routine, run-of-the-mill, platitudinous, oft-repeated, threadbare, everyday, common, humdrum, ordinary; silly, frivolous, shallow, unimportant. **—Syn. Study.** See COMMONPLACE. **—Ant.** original, fresh, unusual, new, novel, exciting.

triumph *n.* **1.** victory, win, success, conquest, mastery, ascendancy, superiority, accomplishment, attainment, achievement, hit, coup, *Informal* smash hit, smash. —*v.* **2.** be victorious, succeed, be successful, win, prevail, come out on top, get the better of, best, subdue, conquer, overwhelm, vanquish, overcome, surpass, gain the day, take the prize, have the best of it. **—Syn. Study. 1** See VICTORY. **—Ant. 1** defeat, loss; failure. **2** lose; fail; succumb.

triumphal *adj.* victorious, successful, ascendant, fulfilling, rewarding, gratifying; joyous, exultant; spectacular, proud, marking a triumph, triumphant.

triumphant *adj.* **1.** victorious, winning, successful, conquering, trophy-winning, prizewinning, laurel-wreathed, first-place. **2.** rejoicing, celebrating, exultant, jubilant, elated, joyful. **—Ant. 1** defeated, beaten, unsuccessful. **2** despairing, disappointed.

trivial *adj.* trifling, unimportant, inconsequential, petty, slight, piddling, paltry, picayune, insignificant, meaningless, unessential, flimsy, nugatory, inconsiderable, small, little, slim, meager, puny, niggling, beggarly, worthless, idle, foolish, inappreciable, of little value, incidental, *Informal* two-bit, *Slang* rinky-dink; everyday, ordinary, common, commonplace, pedestrian, trite, banal. **—Syn. Study.** See PETTY. **—Ant.** weighty, important, consequential, significant, essential, worthwhile, momentous, material, considerable, large, appreciable, substantial; unusual, extraordinary, uncommon, exceptional.

troop *n.* **1.** band, unit, company; throng, horde, drove, crowd, swarm, herd, flock, gathering, assemblage, aggregate, congregation, collection, crush, press, army, bunch, gang. **2. troops** soldiers, soldiery, army, armed force, military force, infantry, fighting men, militia;

cavalry, cavalry unit; uniformed men, police force, troopers. —*v.* **3.** march, file, parade; walk briskly, stride, step, trudge, tramp.

trophy *n.* (*variously*) loving cup, award, medal, blue ribbon, prize, citation, honor, kudos, wreath, laurels, palm; testimonial, souvenir, relic, memento; spoil, booty.

tropical *adj.* in the tropics, of the tropics; hot and humid, torrid, sultry, stifling, sweltering, muggy. —**Ant.** arctic; cold, wintry, icy, frosty, frigid, chilly, cool.

trot *v.* go at a gait between a walk and a gallop; jog, go briskly, walk smartly, step quickly. —**Ant.** gallop, run; plod, creep, crawl.

trouble *v.* **1.** distress, worry, upset, dismay, grieve, disquiet, make uneasy, agitate, perturb, concern, discompose, disconcert, unsettle, oppress, torment, plague, harry, depress; bother, disturb, inconvenience, annoy, pester, badger, harass, discommode, put out. **2.** exert oneself, take time, make the effort, attempt, think, attend, heed. **3.** bother, afflict, affect, pain, annoy, vex, plague. —*n.* **4.** difficulty, bother, pains, inconvenience, annoyance, irritation, vexation, pother, fuss, strain, stress, struggle; effort, care, attention, exertion, work, labor. **5.** difficulty, predicament, dilemma, quandary, entanglement, pass, pinch, strait, crisis, *Informal* scrape, mess, pickle, fix, hot water, deep water; challenge, competition, opposition. **6.** woe, misery, distress, pain, suffering, affliction, agony, tribulation, ordeal, hardship, trial, misfortune, adversity, disaster, burden, difficulty, reverse, setback, grief, sorrow, worry, blow, hard times, ill wind, rainy day. **7.** unrest, instability, disorder, agitation, dissension, commotion, discord, row, disunity, disturbance, ferment, convulsion, embroilment; dissatisfaction, discontentment, discontent, strife. **8.** ailment, disability, defect, disorder, difficulty; breakdown, malfunction, snag. —**Ant. 1, 3** relieve, ease. **1** calm, soothe, compose, please, delight. **3** assuage, mollify. **4** convenience, facility. **6** pleasure, delight, happiness, joy, ease, comfort; success, good fortune. **7** peace, peacefulness, calm, tranquillity, content, contentment; unity, accord, concord, harmony.

troublemaker *n.* agitator, *French* agent provocateur, mischief-maker, provoker, instigator, incendiary, fomenter, inciter, rabble-rouser, miscreant; gossip, rumormonger, scandalmonger, scaremonger. —**Ant.** peacemaker, peace-lover, arbiter, pacifier.

troublesome *adj.* **1.** distressing, worrisome, bothersome, demanding, trying, taxing, disturbing, annoying, vexing, irksome, irritating, exasperating, tormenting, harassing, pesky, inconvenient, difficult, tough, cursed; disobedient, undisciplined, uncontrolled. **2.** laborious, difficult, arduous, herculean, onerous, oppressive, burdensome, cumbersome, unwieldy, unpleasant, disagreeable, fatiguing, tiresome, tiring, tedious, wearisome, hard, tough, heavy, knotty, thorny. —**Ant. 1, 2** easy, simple, undemanding; pleasant, pleasing, delightful. **1** soothing, calming; obedient, disciplined, accommodating, congenial.

trough *n.* **1.** boxlike receptacle, drinking box; tray. **2.** depression, hollow, channel, watercourse, canal, flume, aqueduct, duct, furrow, trench, gully, gorge, ravine; moat, ditch, race.

trounce *v.* defeat decisively, win easily over, overwhelm, overpower, vanquish, beat, whip, drub, clobber, lick, trim, humble, carry the day, take care of, get the better of; *Slang* cream, skunk.

truant *n.* absentee, vagrant, hookyplayer, delinquent, loafer, idler, shirker, evader, deserter, layabout, drifter, malingerer, dodger, slacker; *Slang* goldbrick, goof-off, boondoggler.

truce *n.* temporary halt in fighting, cease-fire, suspension of hostilities, armistice; respite, lull, pause, rest, stay, break, interruption, breathing spell, discontinuance, stop, halt. —**Ant.** war, warfare, hostilities, fighting.

truck *n.* (*variously*) delivery truck, van; pickup truck, panel truck, rig, eighteen-wheeler, trailer truck, *British* lorry.

truckle *v.* ingratiate oneself, fawn, flatter, submit, bow, yield, knuckle under, defer, take orders, pander, grovel, bootlick, curry favor, court; *Slang* suck up to, fall all over, apple-polish, shine up to, butter up. —**Ant.** resist, stand up to, oppose, disagree with.

truculent *adj.* belligerent, bellicose, aggressive, pugnacious, hostile, defiant, fierce, ferocious, nasty, ill-tempered, bad-tempered, ill-humored, ill-natured, snarling; surly, cross, touchy, peevish, snappish, petulant, sour, ungracious, churlish, sulky, insolent, rude. —**Syn. Study.** See FIERCE. —**Ant.** peaceful, gentle, kind, diffident, accommodating, friendly, gracious, amiable, affable.

trudge *v.* plod, walk wearily, hobble, drag, lumber, clump, limp, shamble, march, tramp, pace. —**Syn. Study.** See PACE. —**Ant.** bound, skip, prance, scamper, trot.

true *adj.* **1.** in accordance with the facts, accurate, correct, right, exact, precise; factual, truthful, trustworthy, literal, strict, faithful. **2.** genuine, authentic, real, valid, bona fide, legitimate, actual;

positive, absolute, in the true sense of the term, unquestionable, true-blue, pure, simon-pure. **3.** faithful, loyal, steadfast, trusty, devoted, firm, staunch, constant, dependable, reliable, unwavering, unswerving, steady. **4.** rightful, lawful, legitimate, legal, official, proper, just, bona fide, real. **5.** normal, regular, even, typical, usual, real, full. **—Ant. 1–5** false. **1, 3** untrue. **1** inaccurate, incorrect, wrong, fallacious, inexact; nonfactual, fictitious, imaginary, figurative. **2** fake, phony, counterfeit, bogus, spurious, imitation, artificial, synthetic. **3** faithless, disloyal, treacherous, deceitful, untrustworthy, unreliable, inconstant, undependable. **4** illegal, unofficial, unlawful, illegitimate. **5** abnormal, atypical.

truly *adv.* **1.** unquestionably, beyond question, beyond doubt, indubitably, no doubt, unequivocally, assuredly, verily, certainly, incontestably, without question, indisputably, absolutely, indeed, really, in truth, in actuality, in fact, surely, positively, definitely, to be sure. **2.** accurately, correctly, exactly, precisely, literally, actually, factually. **3.** sincerely, truthfully, honestly, really, genuinely, faithfully, upon my word, so help me God, all kidding aside. **—Ant. 1** questionably, dubiously, uncertainly. **2** inaccurately, incorrectly, inexactly, imprecisely. **3** insincerely, untruthfully, unfaithfully.

truncate *v.* shorten, abbreviate, abridge, cut short, bob, prune, snub, trim, nip, lop, dock, crop, curtail, clip, amputate, condense. **—Ant.** lengthen, elongate, extend, protract.

truss *v.* **1.** tie, secure, strap, bind, fasten, make fast, hitch; tie up, bind up, pinion, constrict, confine. *—n.* **2.** braced framework, brace, support, prop, underpinning, stay, shore, stanchion, beam, girder. **—Ant. 1** untie, loosen, unbind, unfasten, unhitch.

trust *n.* **1.** confidence, faith, belief, credence, assuredness, reliance, certitude, certainty, sureness, conviction. **2.** care, custody, guardianship, safekeeping, protection, keeping, charge, hands. **3.** responsibility, charge, obligation, duty. *—v.* **4.** have faith in, put confidence in, believe, rely on, depend upon, count upon, look to, place oneself in the hands of, swear by, pin one's faith upon; credit, accept, take on faith, give credence to, subscribe to, take stock in. **5.** presume, assume, expect, hope, be confident, anticipate, feel sure, contemplate, reckon upon, count on, take for granted. **—Ant. 1, 4** mistrust, distrust, doubt. **1** disbelief, incredulity, suspicion, uncertainty, misgiving, skepticism. **4** disbelieve, discredit, question.

trusting *adj.* trustful, believing, unsuspicious; credulous, gullible. **—Ant.** distrustful, doubting, suspicious, skeptical.

trustworthy *adj.* responsible, dependable, reliable, trusted; faithful, loyal, true, true-blue, tried and true, steadfast, honorable, high-principled, honest, ethical, aboveboard, upright, incorruptible, scrupulous, unimpeachable. **—Ant.** untrustworthy, irresponsible, undependable, unreliable, disreputable; unfaithful, disloyal, treacherous, dishonorable, dishonest, shady, slippery, crooked, corrupt, unscrupulous.

truth *n.* **1.** facts, reality; truthfulness, trueness, veracity, verity, reliability, authenticity, actuality, trustworthiness, fidelity, integrity, faithfulness, accuracy, exactness. **2.** fact, proven principle, verity, reality, law. **—Ant. 1, 2** untruth. **1** untruthfulness, falseness, falsity, mendacity, deceit, deception, dishonesty, inaccuracy. **2** fiction, fabrication, delusion, fallacy, error.

truthful *adj.* **1.** honest, veracious, trustworthy, sincere, guileless, artless, undeceitful, candid, frank, open, straightforward, aboveboard. **2.** factual, in accordance with fact, true, honest, correct, accurate, reliable, authentic, trustworthy, faithful, scrupulous, precise, exact, meticulous, unvarnished, unadulterated. **—Ant. 1, 2** untruthful. **1** lying, deceitful, deceptive, dishonest, insincere. **2** false, untrue, dishonest, inaccurate, fictitious, fabricated, fallacious, incorrect.

try *v.* **1.** attempt, endeavor, strive, make an effort, set one's sights on, essay, aim, seek, undertake. **2.** test, put to a test, prove, make trial of, tackle, have a fling at, have a go at, take a crack at; sample, use, partake of, avail oneself of. **3.** risk, venture, take a chance on, undertake. **4.** hear and decide, adjudicate, adjudge, sit in judgment, deliberate. **5.** strain, tax to the limit, put to a severe test. *—n.* **6.** attempt, effort, endeavor, opportunity, turn, *Informal* shot, go, crack, fling, whack. **7.** trial, test. **—Syn. Study. 1** TRY, ATTEMPT, ENDEAVOR, STRIVE all mean to put forth an effort toward a specific end. TRY is the most often used and most general term: *to try to decipher a message; to try hard to succeed.* ATTEMPT, often interchangeable with TRY, sometimes suggests the possibility of failure and is often used in reference to more serious or important matters: *to attempt to formulate a new theory of motion.* ENDEAVOR emphasizes serious and continued exertion of effort, sometimes aimed at dutiful or socially appropriate behavior: *to endeavor to fulfill one's obligations.* STRIVE stresses persistent, vigorous, even strenuous effort, often in the face of obstacles: *to strive to overcome a handicap.*

trying *adj.* difficult, tough, hard, arduous, taxing, irksome, bothersome, troublesome, onerous, burdensome, distressing, irritating, vexing, pesky, exasperating, aggravating, harrowing, tiresome, wearisome, tedious, fatiguing, exhausting.

tryst *n.* appointment, engagement, rendezvous, date, assignation, meeting, vis-à-vis, tête-à-tête, secret meeting.

tube *n.* pipe, cylinder, conduit, duct, hose; cylindered container.

tuck *v.* **1.** stick, insert, thrust, stuff, shove, cram, put; gather, gather in, roll up. **2.** wrap snugly, cover snugly, enwrap, swaddle, swathe, shroud. —*n.* **3.** gather, pleat, pucker; ruffle, crinkle.

tuft *n.* cluster, bunch, wisp, bundle, batch, sheaf, tassel, brush, clump; topknot, crest, plume.

tug *v.* **1.** pull, yank, jerk, draw, wrench, wrestle; haul, drag, tow, lug. —*n.* **2.** pull, yank, jerk. **—Ant. 1, 2** push, shove, poke.

tumble *v.* **1.** fall end over end, fall, roll, topple, go sprawling, stumble. **2.** do forward rolls, somersault, cartwheel, flip, do acrobatics, bounce. **3.** toss, whirl, mix, shuffle, stir up, jumble. **4.** drop, fall, plunge, dive, descend. **—Ant. 4** rise, ascend, soar, increase.

tumbledown *adj.* dilapidated, decrepit, rickety, unstable, ramshackle, broken-down, falling-down, disintegrating, tottering, shaky, jerry-built, crumbling, rundown. **—Ant.** solid, substantial, sturdy, strong, invulnerable.

tumid *adj.* swollen, puffy, enlarged, bloated, edematous, tumescent, dilated, expanded, inflated, distended, protuberant. **—Ant.** deflated, shrunken, detumescent, withered, shriveled.

tumult *n.* uproar, commotion, hullabaloo, din, disorder, bedlam, pandemonium, clamor, racket, hubbub; disturbance, turmoil, upheaval, confusion, bustle, agitation, excitement, ado. **—Ant.** peace, quiet, stillness, calm, serenity, tranquillity.

tumultuous *adj.* boisterous, raucous, noisy, rowdy, turbulent, disorderly, unruly, tempestuous, stormy, riotous, chaotic, clamorous, uproarious. **—Ant.** quiet, restrained; cool, lukewarm, indifferent.

tune *n.* **1.** melody, theme, motif; aria, song, air, strain, ditty, number. **2.** pitch; agreement, harmony, accord, concord, unison, concert, conformity, *Slang* step, line. —*v.* **3.** adjust to the correct pitch, pitch; adjust for proper functioning; adjust for proper reception, adjust the tone, adjust.

turbid *adj.* unclear, opaque, murky, clouded, cloudy, stirred up, full of sediment, roiled, muddy; disturbed, agitated, unsettled. **—Ant.** clear, crystal-clear, limpid, clean; calm, placid, smooth.

turbulent *adj.* disturbed, agitated, tumultuous, tempestuous, blustering, violent, raging, fierce, stormy, furious; restless, chaotic, disorderly, uproarious, clamorous, unruly, boisterous, rowdy, riotous. **—Ant.** calm, smooth, placid, quiet, orderly.

turgid *adj.* **1.** swollen, puffed up, puffy. **2.** pompous, bombastic, grandiose, overblown, inflated, pretentious, hyperbolic, grandiloquent; ostentatious, showy, florid, flowery, ornate. **—Ant. 1** shrunken, puckered. **2** simple, modest, restrained, reserved; concise, succinct, pithy, terse, plain-spoken.

turmoil *n.* state of confusion, confusion, disturbance, chaos, disorder, mess; tumult, commotion, uproar, pandemonium, ferment, agitation, convulsion. **—Ant.** order, peace, peacefulness, state of calm.

turn *v.* **1.** revolve, rotate, move in a circle, spin, whirl, wheel, roll, swivel, gyrate, pivot; move around, pass around, shift, swerve, veer, wing, twist, curve, bend, flex; roll over, overturn, invert, reverse, upend. **2.** change, change to, become; transform, metamorphose, convert, alter, make. **3.** be contingent on, be decided by, depend, hang, hinge, pivot, rest, reside, lie. **4.** direct, apply, put; look, go, come. **5.** make skillfully, perform, execute, deliver, accomplish; carry out, do. **6.** wrench, twist, sprain. **7.** send, cause to go, discharge; eject, throw, drive. **8.** sour, spoil, curdle, ferment, acidify. **9.** make round, cut into a round form, grind into a cylinder. —*n.* **10.** rotation, revolution, spin, swing, twirl, whirl, roll, swivel, pivot, gyration, twist; change of direction. **11.** change, shift, fluctuation, deviation, alteration. **12.** curve, bend, twist, zigzag, winding, arc; loop, coil. **13.** opportunity, chance, go, crack, shot, whack, round, fling, attempt, effort; time, stint, shift, spell, period. **14.** deed, act, action, service. **15.** short walk, walk, stroll, constitutional; short drive, ride. **16.** shock, start, surprise, scare, fright, upset. **—Syn. Study. 1** TURN, REVOLVE, ROTATE, SPIN indicate moving in a more or less rotary, circular fashion. TURN is the general and popular word for motion on an axis or around a center, but it is used also of motion that is less than a complete circle: *A gate turns on its hinges.* REVOLVE refers esp. to movement in an orbit around a center, but is sometimes exchangeable with ROTATE, which refers only to the motion of a body around its own center or axis: *The moon revolves about the earth. The earth rotates on its* *axis.* To SPIN is to rotate very rapidly: *A top spins.* —**Ant. 2** remain, stay, continue to be. **7** keep, retain, hold; capture, catch, secure.

turncoat *n.* traitor, renegade, betrayer, double-dealer, quisling, apostate, Judas; deserter, defector, bolter. —**Ant.** patriot, loyalist.

turnout *n.* **1.** gathering, crowd, throng, assemblage, assembly, audience. **2.** output, production.

turpitude *n.* wickedness, depravity, immorality, vice, vileness, corruption, baseness, lewdness, degeneracy, wrongdoing, perversion, defilement, evil, sinfulness, debauchery, dissoluteness, licentiousness.

tussle *v.* **1.** scuffle, grapple, fight, brawl, wrestle, struggle, battle. —*n.* **2.** fight, scuffle, scrap, brawl, fracas, fray, melee, altercation, conflict, donnybrook, set-to, free-for-all; struggle, battle.

tutelage *n.* supervision, guidance, direction; instruction, training, teaching, coaching, schooling, education, tutoring, inculcation, discipline, indoctrination.

tutor *n.* **1.** coach, private teacher, instructor, master, teacher, mentor, coach, guru. —*v.* **2.** teach privately, coach, instruct, give lessons in, teach, school, drill, prepare. —**Ant. 1** pupil, student, disciple. **2** study, learn.

twaddle *n.* idle talk, silly talk, drivel, prattle, tripe, nonsense, tommyrot, rubbish, babble, chatter.

twang *n.* **1.** sharp vibrating sound, vibration, resonance, reverberation. **2.** nasal sound, nasal resonance.

twilight *n.* **1.** dusk, gloaming, half-light, edge of darkness; nightfall, evening, eve, sundown, sunset, moonrise, eventide. **2.** decline, last phase, ebb. —**Ant. 1** dawn, sunrise, daybreak. **2** advent, beginning, unfolding; peak, height, crowning point, climax.

twin *adj.* **1.** born as one of a pair, forming a pair. **2.** paired, matched, identical, duplicate, like, alike. **3.** double, dual, twofold.

twine *n.* **1.** string, cord, two-strand string, twisted thread; binding; rope, cable. —*v.* **2.** intertwine, interlace, weave, entwine, twist, plait, braid; wind, coil.

twinge *n.* **1.** sudden sharp pain, pain, cramp, spasm, stab, pang, stitch; throb, tingle, twitch. **2.** pang, stab.

twinkle *v.* **1.** glimmer, shimmer, shine, flicker, flash, sparkle, gleam, glisten, glow, scintillate, blaze, flare. —*n.* **2.** glimmer, shimmer, flicker, sparkle, gleam, glow, flare, flash.

twirl *v.* spin, whirl, rotate, revolve, gyrate, wheel, pivot, twine, pirouette.

twist *v.* **1.** wind, twine, intertwine, entwine, interlace, tangle, knot, ravel; coil, curl, roll, wrap; rotate, turn, swivel, pivot, whirl, spin. **2.** bend, curve, wind, arc, swing, swerve, veer, curl, snake, zigzag, meander. **3.** wrench, turn, sprain; wrest, yank, pull. **4.** distort, contort, wrench out of shape. —*n.* **5.** curl, coil, roll, corkscrew, spiral; tangle, knot, kink. **6.** turn, rotation, spin, whirl, wrench. **7.** bend, zigzag, winding curve, corkscrew curve, convolution, involution. **8.** change, development, surprise, turn; notion, idea, approach, slant, treatment, way, system, method. —**Ant. 1** untwist, unwind; straighten, uncoil, unroll, unwrap; untangle, disentangle, unknot, unravel.

twitch *v.* **1.** jerk, quiver, quaver, throb, shake, tremble; wiggle, squirm, writhe. —*n.* **2.** tic, involuntary movement, jerk, spasm, quiver, quaver, throb, shake, tremor; paroxysm, convulsion.

twitter *v.* **1.** chirp, chirrup, cheep, tweet, chatter, peep, warble. —*n.* **2.** twittering, chirp, chirping, chirrup, chirruping, cheep, peep. **3.** flutter, tizzy, flurry, fluster, whirl, bustle, ferment, stew, fuss, pother, uproar, turbulence.

twofaced *adj.* hypocritical, duplicitous, perfidious, double-dealing, double-faced, deceitful, disingenuous, devious, treacherous, dishonest, insincere, false, dissembling, fork-tongued, underhanded, slippery, deceptive, untrustworthy. —**Ant.** honest, straightforward, open, candid, frank, sincere, aboveboard.

tycoon *n.* powerful businessperson, wealthy businessperson, magnate, mogul, nabob, potentate, captain of industry, entrepreneur, industrialist, *Slang* big shot, bigwig, big gun, big wheel, boss.

tyke *n.* tot, child, little one, tad, wee one, kid, squirt, shaver.

type *n.* **1.** class, kind, sort, variety, category, order, species, genus, race, family, phylum, group, division, brand. **2.** typical person, typical thing, individual example, specimen, model, sample; prototype, archetype. **3.** typeface, printed letters, design, pattern, print, printing character, typography, font.

typical *adj.* **1.** representative, standard, normal, average, stock, regular, usual, ordinary; true-to-type, conventional; orthodox; prototypal, model, exemplary. **2.** characteristic, in character, to be expected, in keeping, true to type; distinctive, individual. —**Ant. 1** atypical, abnormal, unrepresentative, irregular, unusual, uncommon, unique, singular, unconventional, strange, weird. **2** uncharacteristic, out of keeping, unexpected.

typify *v.* personify, represent, exemplify, characterize, embody, sum up, epitomize, stand for, betoken, incarnate, pass for, instance, connote.

tyranny *n.* despotism, cruel authority, unjust rule, cruelty, harshness, severity, domination, oppression, repression, persecution, coercion; absolute rule, iron rule, iron fist, iron hand, reign of terror, dictatorship, fascism, totalitarianism. **—Ant.** humanity, kindness, benevolence, fairness; democracy, freedom.

tyrant *n.* cruel and unjust ruler, despot, cruel master, uncompromising superior, slave driver, taskmaster, martinet, bully, persecutor; absolute ruler, dictator.

tyro *n.* beginner, novice, neophyte, tenderfoot, greenhorn, newcomer, rookie, initiate, recruit, apprentice, learner, trainee, intern. **—Ant.** veteran, master, expert, professional.

ubiquitous *adj.* omnipresent, pervading, pervasive, prevalent, widespread, worldwide, universal, allover, everpresent, all-pervading, everywhere.

ugly *adj.* **1.** homely, unattractive, unsightly, unseemly, unbecoming, ill-favored, repulsive, hideous, frightful, grotesque, monstrous; evil-looking. **2.** nasty, quarrelsome, cantankerous, unpleasant, mean, hostile, belligerent, difficult; disagreeable, obnoxious, repulsive, offensive, dreadful, unbearable, disgusting, foul, odious, vile, abominable, abhorrent, sickening, horrid, horrible, repellent, repugnant. **3.** forbidding, ominous, portentous, threatening, menacing, inauspicious, dangerous, troublesome. **—Ant. 1** beautiful, pretty, handsome, fair, lovely, comely, attractive. **2** pleasant, agreeable, personable, good-natured, likable, friendly; good, nice, sweet, attractive. **3** promising, auspicious, fortuitous.

ukase *n.* edict, directive, ruling, decree, order, proclamation, fiat, mandate, manifesto, pronouncement, statute, ordinance, pronunciamento, dictum.

ulterior *adj.* hidden, covert, concealed, secret, unrevealed, unexpressed, undisclosed, undivulged; selfish, self-serving, opportunistic. **—Ant.** obvious, manifest, evident, self-evident, plain; altruistic, public-spirited.

ultimate *adj.* **1.** final, last, resulting, terminal, definitive, conclusive, crowning, end, eventual, long-range. **2.** greatest, utmost, highest possible, supreme, maximum, extreme, crowning, at the peak. **—***n.* **3.** height, final point, utmost, peak, apex, acme, high point, extreme, last straw. **—Ant. 1** initial, first, beginning. **2** least, lowest, minimum.

umpire *n.* **1.** referee, judge; arbiter, arbitrator, mediator, intercessor, negotiator, moderator, adjudicator, go-between. **—***v.* **2.** referee; judge, arbitrate, mediate, adjudicate, moderate. **—Syn. Study. 1** See JUDGE.

unabbreviated *adj.* unshortened, unabridged, complete, uncondensed, uncompressed, uncurtailed, untrimmed, unsnipped, unpruned, uncropped, uncut, undocked, unexpurgated, unreduced. **—Ant.** abridged, incomplete, condensed, expurgated.

unabridged *adj.* not abridged, not shortened, full-length, entire, complete, uncut, intact, uncondensed. **—Ant.** abridged, shortened, condensed.

unacceptable *adj.* not acceptable, not allowable, unsatisfactory, unsuitable, unseemly, improper, displeasing, unwelcome, insupportable, not up to snuff.

unaccompanied *adj.* solo, lone, unattended, solitary, single; unescorted, apart, separate, companionless, lonesome, all by oneself, alone, isolated, *Music* a cappella. **—Ant.** escorted, accompanied, squired, chaperoned.

unaccountable *adj.* **1.** unexplained, inexplicable, baffling, strange, odd, queer, weird, peculiar, curious, bizarre, incomprehensible, unfathomable, mysterious; unusual, intriguing, extraordinary, astonishing, surprising, unheard-of. **2.** not responsible, not answerable, not accountable, not liable, blameless, innocent, inculpable, free, clear, excused; exempt, immune. **—Ant. 1** explainable, explicable, comprehensible; usual, ordinary, normal, natural. **2** accountable, responsible, answerable, liable, culpable, guilty, blamable, blameworthy.

unaccustomed *adj.* **1.** unusual, unfamiliar, uncommon, out of the ordinary, extraordinary, strange, foreign, quaint, unique, singular, curious, peculiar, odd, queer, bizarre, surprising, astonishing, unimaginable, startling, out-of-the-way, unheard-of, amazing, remarkable, fantastic, *Slang* wild; new, novel, original, rare. **2.** not used to, unused, not accustomed, unhabituated, strange, unacquainted, ungiven to; inexperienced, unpracticed, untried, green, a novice at, unfamiliar with, unversed in, new to. **—Ant. 1, 2** accustomed, familiar. **1** ordinary, common, regular, run-of-the-mill. **2** used to, well-acquainted, given to; experienced, practiced, well-versed, seasoned.

unaffected *adj.* **1.** not affected, not influenced, untouched, unbothered, undisturbed; unmoved, unstirred, unresponsive to, indifferent to, insensitive to, unconcerned, unfeeling, impervious to, unsympathetic to. **2.** natural, sincere, genuine, simple, wholesome, plain, open, honest, frank, candid, direct, straightforward, plain-spoken, unreserved, open-hearted, undesigning, guileless, ingenuous; naive, innocent, childlike, unsophisticated, unworldly. **—Ant. 1, 2** affected. **1** influenced, touched, changed, disturbed; moved, stirred, responsive, interested, concerned, sympathetic. **2** unnatural, artificial, insincere, pretentious, assumed, *Informal* put-on, phony; indirect, devious, scheming, designing, Machiavellian; sophisticated, worldly.

unanimous *adj.* showing complete agreement, in complete accord, with no dissent; united, allied, harmonious, like-minded, accordant, consonant, of one mind, of the same mind. **—Ant.** not agreed, dissenting, discordant, disagreeing, unharmonious, inharmonious.

unapproachable *adj.* **1.** inaccessible, unreachable, beyond reach, unattainable; remote, aloof, distant, austere, stand-offish, cold, cool, forbidding, intimidating, awesome. **2.** unequaled, unrivaled, matchless, unparalleled, peerless, incomparable, beyond compare, inimitable, unique, nonpareil; supreme, preeminent, superior, foremost, second to none.

unasked *adj.* unsolicited, uninvited, unsought, unbidden, unrequested; unwanted, unwelcome, undesirable; unasked-for, gratuitous, uncalled-for, wanton. **—Ant.** wanted, invited, welcome, sought.

unassuming *adj.* modest, unpretentious, not vain, without airs, easygoing, unostentatious, natural, simple, plain, homely, unobtrusive, unassertive, muted.

unauthorized *adj.* unofficial, unsanctioned, unapproved, uncertified, prohibited; unlawful, banned, outlawed, unwarranted, unpermitted, unallowed; covert, concealed, furtive, clandestine, underhand, under-the-table. **—Ant.** official, certified, sanctioned, permitted.

unavailing *adj.* futile, unproductive, useless, idle, ineffective, inept, weak, empty, ineffectual, fruitless, vain, bootless, unsuccessful; impotent, worthless, invalid. **—Ant.** effective, valid, useful, productive.

unavoidable *adj.* inevitable, inescapable, unpreventable, uncontrollable, fated, sure, certain; necessary, requisite, compulsory, obligatory, imperative, fixed.

unaware *adj.* unsuspecting, ignorant, unenlightened, unknowing, unconscious, unapprised, unacquainted, incognizant; unwarned, unalerted, heedless, in the dark about, off one's guard, unmindful. **—Ant.** aware, cognizant, knowing, conscious, acquainted, heedful, mindful, enlightened, suspicious, wary, on one's guard, *Slang* hip.

unawares *adv.* **1.** unknowingly, unwittingly, inadvertently, unintentionally, unconsciously, unthinkingly, accidentally, by accident, mistakenly, by mistake, involuntarily, by chance. **2.** unexpectedly, abruptly, without warning, suddenly, by surprise, like a bolt from the blue, like a thunderbolt, like a thief in the night, out of nowhere. **—Ant. 1** knowingly, wittingly, intentionally, purposely, on purpose, consciously, voluntarily. **2** prepared, forewarned.

unbalanced *adj.* **1.** not balanced, unequal, uneven, unpoised, out of equilibrium, unadjusted, lopsided, leaning, unsteady, unstable. **2.** mentally disturbed, unsound, deranged, demented, mad, irrational, illogical, unsettled, unhinged, unstable, crazed, psychotic, psychopathic, warped, *Informal* cracked, daft, wacky, nutty, unglued, batty, not all there, loco, bonkers.

unbearable *adj.* intolerable, insufferable, unendurable, unacceptable, insupportable, inadmissible, unthinkable.

unbecoming *adj.* **1.** unattractive, unappealing, ugly, tasteless, homely, unsightly. **2.** unsuitable, improper, unsuited, inappropriate, unfitted, unbefitting, indecorous, unseemly; tasteless, offensive, vulgar. **—Syn. Study. 2** See IMPROPER.

unbelieving *adj.* doubting, nonbelieving, skeptical, disbelieving, questioning, quizzical, incredulous, distrustful, suspicious, dubious, unconvinced. **—Ant.** trusting, believing, gullible, credulous.

unbending *adj.* rigid, stiff, inflexible, unyielding, severe, firm, strict, tough, obstinate, stubborn, uncompromising, *Informal* hard as nails, stone-faced. **—Ant.** soft, easy, flexible, compromising, pliant, adaptable; wishy-washy.

unbiased *adj.* unprejudiced, impartial, neutral, disinterested, dispassionate, detached, open-minded, just, fair, uninfluenced, neutral, liberal, broad-minded, tolerant, unbigoted, undogmatic, fair-minded.

unblemished *adj.* flawless, perfect, unvitiated, immaculate, spotless, pure, uncontaminated, unadulterated, unsoiled, unmarred, unsullied, white as snow, clean as a whistle.

unbounded *adj.* boundless, unlimited, unrestrained, unconditional, unrestricted, absolute, unconstrained, uncontrolled, unbridled.

unbroken *adj.* **1.** (*variously*) uncracked, unshattered, unsmashed, unruptured; whole, intact, complete, entire, undivided, undiminished. **2.** continuous, uninterrupted, successive, consecutive; ceaseless, endless, incessant, continual, unremitting; progressive, sequential. **—Ant. 1** broken, cracked, shattered, smashed, ruptured, damaged, incomplete. **2** intermittent, interrupted, occasional, irregular, fitful, uneven, disconnected.

unburden *v.* relieve, disburden, free, unencumber, disencumber; disclose, confess, reveal, confide, *Slang* get off one's chest, get out of one's system; unbosom.

uncalled-for *adj.* unnecessary, needless, unneeded, redundant, nonessential, unwanted; unsought, unsolicited, unprompted, uninvited, unasked; unjustified, gratuitous, supererogatory, wanton. **—Ant.** justified, needed, necessary, essential.

uncanny *adj.* **1.** extraordinary, unimaginable, remarkable, unexampled, exceptional, astonishing, unbelievable, incredible, marvelous, fantastic, inspired, prodigious, unheard-of; intuitive. **2.** curious, mysterious, strange, uncomfortable, unnatural, eerie, weird, unearthly, spooky. **—Syn. Study. 2** See WEIRD. **—Ant. 1** average, normal, common, usual, unexceptional, unnoteworthy, unremarkable, mediocre, run-of-the-mill. **2** natural, obvious.

uncertain *adj.* **1.** not certain, not sure, unsure, not confident, doubtful, dubious; not definite, indefinite, speculative, unconfirmed, undecided, up in the air. **2.** indeterminate, unpredictable, not known exactly, undetermined, indefinite, indistinct, unclear, hazy, obscure, nebulous, doubtful, not fixed, unsettled, in question, debatable, disputable, questionable, conjectural. **3.** wavering, variable, vacillating, fluctuating, erratic, fitful, unresolved, irresolute, unsure, hesitant. **—Ant. 1–3** certain, definite. **1** sure, assured, confirmed, decided, positive. **2** predictable, known, determined, clear, settled, indisputable, unquestionable. **3** firm, resolute, certain, staunch, unvarying, unwavering, unhesitating.

uncertainty *n.* **1.** hesitancy, hesitation, indefiniteness, irresolution, unsureness, vagueness, indecision, doubt, ambiguity, vacillation, equivocation, ambivalence, confusion, perplexity, quandary, *Informal* shilly-shally. **2.** something uncertain, chance, gamble, odds, risk.

uncharitable *adj.* ungenerous, stingy, tight, niggardly, miserly, illiberal, parsimonious, tightfisted, closefisted; ungracious, unkind, unfriendly, unfeeling, uncompassionate, insensitive, unsympathetic.

uncivilized *adj.* **1.** savage, barbaric, barbarous, untamed. **2.** uncouth, brutish, churlish, rude, boorish, uncultured, unpolished, obnoxious, ill-bred, ungenteel, vulgar, uncultivated.

unclad *adj.* unclothed, undressed, unrobed, disrobed, uncovered; nude, naked, bare, stripped, stark-naked, *Brit.* starkers, in the raw, in the altogether, exposed. **—Ant.** dressed, clad, clothed, covered.

uncomfortable *adj.* **1.** causing discomfort, causing distress, painful, bothersome, irritating, distressful. **2.** uneasy, ill at ease, awkward, out of place, discomposed, edgy, nervous, disquieted, tense, keyed up, on tenterhooks, discomfited, troubled, on edge, strained, confused, upset.

uncommon *adj.* **1.** unusual, rare, infrequent, unfamiliar, unique, scarce, extraordinary, exceptional, unconventional, few and far between, novel, peculiar, curious, bizarre, *Informal* once in a lifetime. **2.** exceptional, remarkable, outstanding, incomparable, unusual, unparalleled, notable, extraordinary; superior, superlative, matchless, peerless, unmatched, unexcelled, supreme.

uncommunicative *adj.* unsociable, reticent, taciturn, close-mouthed, withdrawn, retiring, shy, reserved; speechless, inexpressive, mute, mum, silent, quiet, tongue-tied, dumb, secretive. **—Ant.** talkative, voluble, loquacious, garrulous, gregarious, sociable, communicative, open, extroverted, outgoing, expressive.

uncomplimentary *adj.* disapproving, disparaging, unadmiring, unflattering, insulting, critical, negative, derisive.

uncompromising *adj.* firm, strict, rigid, scrupulous; stiff, unrelenting, exacting, inflexible, unvarying, immovable, unbending, unyielding, hardline, obdurate, inexorable.

unconcerned *adj.* indifferent, oblivious, apathetic, insensitive, uninvolved, unaware, nonchalant, uncaring, unsympathetic, unfeeling, unmoved, unresponsive; aloof, distant, passionless, cold; serene, untroubled, unperturbed, unmindful, composed, impervious. **—Ant.** concerned, aware, mindful, involved, caring, interested, sympathetic, compassionate; anxious, worried, perturbed, troubled.

unconditional *adj.* unlimited, unqualified, unrestricted, absolute, categorical, thoroughgoing, complete, entire, utter, conclusive; downright, outright. **—Ant.** conditional, provisional, restricted, qualified, limited; partial, incomplete, inconclusive.

unconquerable *adj.* invincible, undefeatable, unvanquishable, unable to be overcome, insurmountable, unbeatable, invulnerable, impenetrable; inveterate, ingrained, innate.

unconscionable *adj.* excessive, extreme, unreasonable, immoderate, unwarranted, unjustifiable, unjustified, inordinate; outrageous, preposterous, unpardonable, unforgivable, inexcusable, indefensible. **—Ant.** moderate, reasonable, judicious, sensible.

unconscious *adj.* **1.** without consciousness, senseless, insensate, without awareness, in a faint, in a coma, comatose, *Informal* out, out cold, dead to the world. **2.** unrealized, incognizant, unsuspecting, unknowing, unmindful, latent, suppressed. **—Ant. 1, 2** conscious, aware. **2** cognizant, knowing, active.

unconventional *adj.* uncommon, unusual, extraordinary, exceptional, unaccustomed, atypical, rare, original, unique, singular, irregular, quaint, newfangled, fantastic, strange, peculiar, odd, curious, queer, outlandish, bizarre; nonconformist, nonconforming, unorthodox, different, eccentric, individualistic, idiosyncratic, bohemian, freakish, weird, off the beaten path, aberrant, offbeat, *Slang* wacky, nutty, crazy, kinky, far-out.

uncouth *adj.* crude, rude, boorish, churlish, crass, coarse, rough, gross, uncivil, callow, indelicate, loutish, brutish, impolite, ill-bred, ill-mannered, unmannerly, unrefined, uncultured, uncivilized, barbaric; uncultivated. **—Ant.** refined, polite, genteel, cultivated, well-mannered, delicate, gentlemanly.

uncover *v.* **1.** remove the cover from, unwrap, undo, unsheathe; undress, disrobe, bare, uncloak, undrape, strip, unclothe, denude. **2.** bring to light, disclose, expose, reveal, lay bare, make known, unmask, unveil, make visible, dig up, dig out, unearth. **—Ant. 1** cover, wrap, sheathe; dress, clothe, drape. **2** hide, conceal, cloak, veil, suppress.

uncritical *adj.* undiscriminating, unthinking, unreflecting; shallow, perfunctory, superficial, casual, offhand; inexact, imprecise, inaccurate; careless, slipshod; uneducated, unschooled, untutored; dumb, ignorant, stupid; dull, obtuse. **—Ant.** perceptive, discerning, thoughtful, penetrating.

unctuous *adj.* too smooth, too suave, smug, ingratiating, flattering, sycophantic, obsequious, sanctimonious, oily, slippery, smarmy, honeyed, honey-tongued, fawning, servile, self-righteous, pietistic. **—Ant.** blunt, brusque, open, frank, candid, straightforward.

uncustomary *adj.* rare, unaccustomed, uncommon, singular, unwonted, exceptional, unique, unusual, extraordinary, unexpected, unanticipated; unheard-of, amazing, unbelievable, astonishing, incredible. **—Ant.** standard, normal, customary, usual.

undaunted *adj.* not discouraged, unperturbed, undismayed, not put off, unfazed; resolute, courageous, unshrinking, valiant, valorous, stalwart, intrepid, unflinching, stouthearted, heroic, brave, fearless, indomitable, *Informal* plucky, gritty. **—Ant.** daunted, discouraged, perturbed, dismayed, disconcerted, fazed; irresolute, vacillating, meek, cowardly, fearful.

undecided *adj.* **1.** not decided, undetermined, uncertain, unsure, indefinite, unsettled, unresolved, not final, pending, open, tentative, in abeyance, unformulated, vague, *Informal* up in the air. **2.** unsure, irresolute, indecisive, of two minds, open-minded, fluctuating, wavering, vacillating, dubious, in a dilemma, *Informal* going around in circles, blowing hot and cold, hemming and hawing. **—Ant. 1, 2** sure, resolved. **1** decided, determined, certain, definite, settled, final, firm. **2** resolute, decisive, closed-minded, steadfast, unwavering, certain.

undemonstrative *adj.* reserved, shy, inexpressive, not affectionate, not displaying emotions, unemotional, unresponsive, distant, cold, aloof, impassive; stoical, self-controlled. **—Ant.** demonstrative, affectionate, emotional, responsive, unreserved, expressive, warm, outgoing.

undeniable *adj.* unquestionable, indisputable, incontestable, irrefutable, indubitable, beyond a doubt, incontrovertible, sure, certain, established, demonstrable, proven, decisive, conclusive, obvious, manifest, patent. **—Ant.** questionable, debatable, dubious, disputable, refutable, uncertain, indecisive, inconclusive, up in the air.

undependable *adj.* not to be depended on, unreliable, untrustworthy, irresponsible, unpredictable, erratic, inconstant; variable, wavering, changeable, fickle, unstable, flighty, capricious. **—Ant.** dependable, reliable, responsible, trustworthy, predictable, exact, unchanging.

undercover *adj.* secret, hush-hush, covert, concealed, clandestine, unrevealed, surreptitious, disguised, hidden, sub rosa, confidential, undisclosed; sly, stealthy, furtive. **—Ant.** open, undisguised, unconcealed, aboveboard.

undercurrent *n.* **1.** undertow, riptide, crosscurrent. **2.** underlying attitude, hidden feeling, undertone, mood, atmosphere, aura, quality, intimation, suggestion, hint, sense, tinge, vibrations, *Informal* vibes.

underestimate *v.* rate too low, undervalue, underrate, misjudge, miscalculate, undersell, sell short; disregard, dismiss, minimize, discredit, detract from, belittle, depreciate, disparage, deprecate, *Slang* put down. **—Ant.** overestimate, overvalue, overrate, overstate, exaggerate.

undergo *v.* go through, submit to, experience; withstand, stand, encounter, endure, sustain, weather, suffer, brave. **—Ant.** evade, shun, avoid, escape, forgo, sidestep, circumvent, steer clear of.

underground *adj.* **1.** buried, belowground, below the surface, subterranean. **2.** secret, covert, undercover, clandestine, surreptitious, sub rosa.

underhand Also **underhanded** *adj.* unethical, unscrupulous, unprincipled, devious, tricky, sneaking, sneaky, surreptitious, stealthy, covert, evasive, furtive, conniving, cunning, crafty; illegal, dishonest, crooked, fraudulent, corrupt. **—Ant.** open, aboveboard, ethical, scrupulous, principled; legal, honest.

underling *n.* menial, flunky, hireling, servant, subordinate, lackey, minion, inferior, minor employee, domestic employee, hired hand; subject, vassal, serf, thrall, attendant. **—Ant.** executive, supervisor, boss, employer, chief.

undermine *v.* **1.** excavate under, tunnel under, burrow under; eat away at, erode, wear away the base of, riddle. **2.** subvert, weaken, injure, cripple, ruin, destroy, *Informal* torpedo; render powerless, thwart, foil, scotch, frustrate, neutralize, hamstring, sabotage, cut the ground from under. **—Ant. 2** reinforce, strengthen, buttress, encourage, support, forward, help, aid, abet.

underprivileged *adj.* disadvantaged, deprived, badly-off, unfortunate, hapless, ill-starred, ill-fated, unlucky, in adverse circumstances; poor, indigent, impoverished, needy, in need, pauperized, penurious, penniless, destitute. **—Ant.** advantaged, privileged, affluent, well-off.

underscore *v.* underline, draw a line under; stress, emphasize, accentuate, press home, accent, point up, mark, bring out forcibly, feature, intensify, play up, draw attention to, heighten, deepen. **—Ant.** de-emphasize, moderate, skip over.

understand *v.* **1.** grasp the meaning of, comprehend, absorb, make out, fathom, get, *Slang* dig; know, recognize, appreciate, see, be aware, perceive, discern, apprehend, realize, grasp. **2.** interpret, see, read, take, take to mean. **3.** gather, hear, learn, presume, take for granted, take it, conclude, assume. **4.** sympathize with, appreciate, can see, see the reasons for, accept. **—Syn. Study. 1** See KNOW.

understanding *n.* **1.** knowledge, grasp, comprehension, appreciation, cognizance, perception, awareness, apprehension. **2.** sympathy, compassion, appreciation, empathy, sensitivity, insight, perception, intuition. **3.** agreement, meeting of the minds, pact, concordance, compromise. *—adj.* **4.** sympathetic, compassionate, appreciative, responsive, sensitive, tolerant, perceptive, discerning, knowing. **—Ant. 1** misunderstanding, incomprehension, ignorance. **2** insensitivity, lack of insight, obtuseness, aloofness. **4** unsympathetic, uncompassionate, unresponsive, unfeeling, insensitive; intolerant, strict, stiff, rigid.

understudy *n.* stand-by, alternate, replacement, substitute, surrogate, double, backup, pinch hitter, fill-in, stand-in, relief; *Slang* sub.

undertake *v.* set about, take on, assume, enter upon, embark on, tackle, shoulder, agree to do, promise to do, obligate oneself to, commit oneself to, get involved in, attempt, strive, endeavor, essay, try; commence, begin, start, set about. **—Ant.** abandon, drop, desist, decline, forswear, eschew, avoid; discontinue, stop.

undertaking *n.* endeavor, enterprise, project, task, job, effort, commitment, venture, pursuit, concern.

undertone *n.* **1.** low tone, subdued voice, whisper, murmur, mumble. **2.** undercurrent, feeling, sense, quality, mood, coloring, implication, intimation, atmosphere, aura, nuance, inkling, suggestion, hint, trace, tinge, scent, flavor; connotation.

underweight *adj.* gaunt, skinny, skin-and-bones, scrawny, lanky, bony, undernourished, spindly, underfed, lank; emaciated, skeletal, hollow-cheeked, spindle-shanked. **—Ant.** overweight, obese, flabby, *Slang* gross.

underworld *n.* **1.** criminal element, criminals, organized crime, gangsters, mobsters, *Informal* the mob; (*loosely*) the syndicate, the Mafia, the Cosa Nostra. **2.** Hell, Hades, purgatory, limbo, abode of the damned, bottomless pit, infernal regions, lake of fire and brimstone, place of departed spirits, shades below.

underwrite *v.* subsidize, sponsor, back, support, guarantee, aid; approve, validate, sanction; endorse, countersign. **—Ant.** reject, veto, refuse, cancel, *Slang* nix.

undesirable *adj.* unsavory, offensive, unworthy, unattractive, objectionable, distasteful, disagreeable, unwelcomed, uninviting, unseemly, unsatisfactory; unacceptable, unsuitable, inadmissible, unwished-for, unwanted, unbidden, unpopular, disliked; inappropriate, unbefitting, unfit, improper, unbecoming.

undignified *adj.* lacking dignity, indecorous, inappropriate, unbecoming, unsuitable, unseemly, inelegant, boorish, unladylike, ungentlemanly, unrefined, improper, unbefitting, tasteless, indelicate, in bad taste; low, discreditable, unworthy, degrading, shameful, beneath one, beneath one's dignity, *Latin* infra dignitatem, *Informal* infra dig.

undisciplined *adj.* unrestrained, wayward, willful, obstreperous, wild, uncontrolled; undependable, unreliable, fitful, erratic, capricious, fickle, changeable, mercurial, unsteady, inconstant, unpredictable; untrained, untaught, unschooled, uneducated, untutored, unpracticed, unfinished.

undisguised *adj.* open, unconcealed, unhidden, obvious, evident, unmistakable, manifest, evident, distinct, pronounced, clear; unreserved, wholehearted, utter, out-and-out, complete, thoroughgoing, plain as the nose on one's face, plain as day.

undismayed *adj.* undiscouraged, not disheartened, still confident, undaunted, not disconcerted, unabashed; unalarmed, not apprehensive, unfrightened, unafraid, unintimidated, not cowed, not put off.

undisputed *adj.* uncontested, not disputed, unchallenged, unquestioned, accepted; indisputable, incontestable, undeniable, freely admitted, granted, undoubted, beyond doubt, past dispute, irrefutable, without question, beyond question, incontrovertible, a matter of fact, acknowledged, unquestionable, indubitable, conclusive, certain, sure.

undistinguished *adj.* ordinary, common, commonplace, mediocre, unexceptional, unremarkable, usual, plain, prosaic, nothing to rave about, unexciting, pedestrian, run-of-the-mill, everyday.

undisturbed *adj.* **1.** unruffled, unperturbed, unagitated, unexcited, untroubled, unbothered; composed, placid, serene, peaceful, tranquil, equable, self-possessed, calm, cool, collected, steady. **2.** uninterrupted, without interruption, quiet, of solitude; untouched, unmoved, not meddled with, left in order. **—Ant. 1, 2** disturbed. **1** upset, perturbed, agitated, troubled, excited, nervous, ruffled. **2** interrupted, confused, busy; moved, meddled with, disordered.

undivided *adj.* not divided, solid, whole, entire, complete, unstinting, wholehearted; unanimous, united, unified, unsplit, of one mind.

undo *v.* **1.** offset, reverse, cancel, nullify, erase, annul, wipe out, neutralize, void, repair, counterbalance, counteract; compensate for, make up for, rectify. **2.** open, free, unfasten, loose, loosen; (*variously*) disentangle, unknot, unravel, unwrap, unfold, untie, unbind, unlace, disengage, unbutton, unchain, unlock, unhook. **3.** ruin, destroy, subvert, undermine, end, eliminate, demolish, wipe out, defeat, overturn, invalidate, quash. **—Ant. 1** do, accomplish, effect, realize, produce, commit, manage. **2** fasten, close, tie, knot, tangle, button, lock, hook, close. **3** enhance, help, aid, abet, further.

undoing *n.* **1.** reversal, cancellation, wiping out, erasure, negation, annulment, nullification, neutralization, invalidation, thwarting, counteraction, upset. **2.** ruin, ruination, collapse, downfall, destruction, doom, defeat, breakdown, overthrow. **3.** cause of ruin, nemesis, downfall, weakness, jinx, Achilles' heel. **—Ant. 1** realization, accomplishment, establishment, furtherance. **2** victory, success, triumph. **3** strength, strong point, specialty.

undoubtedly *adv.* doubtless, unquestionably, beyond question, without doubt, beyond a doubt, undeniably, indubitably; certainly, definitely, assuredly, decidedly, positively, absolutely.

undress *v.* **1.** take off one's clothes, disrobe, unclothe, strip, uncover, undrape. *—n.* **2.** nakedness, nudity; disarray, carelessness of attire, dishabille. **—Ant. 1** dress, clothe, robe, drape, cover.

undue *adj.* excessive, too great, inordinate, uncalled-for, unwarranted, unnecessary, overmuch, unjustified, needless, superfluous; improper, unsuitable, inappropriate, not fitting, ill-advised, unseemly, tasteless, unmeet, indiscreet, unworthy, unbecoming, objectionable, impolite, in bad taste. **—Ant.** due, proper, necessary, needed, justified; suitable, appropriate, fitting, seemly, meet, well-taken.

undying *adj.* eternal, never-ending, unending, unceasing, unfading, perpetual, endless, everlasting, lasting, enduring, abiding, imperishable, perennial, perpetual, incessant, permanent, constant, continual, continuing, unremitting, unrelenting, indestructible, unfaltering, neverfailing, untiring, undiminished, uninterrupted, steady; deathless, immortal. **—Ant.** temporary, unlasting, impermanent, passing, ephemeral, transitory, transient, fleeting, temporal, brief, momentary; mortal, dying.

unearth *v.* **1.** dig up, dig out, dredge up, excavate; exhume, disentomb, disinter. **2.** discover, uncover, find, come across, dig up, ferret out, bring to light, root out, come up with; divulge, disclose, reveal, expose, show, display, exhibit. **—Ant. 1, 2** bury. **2** cover up, conceal, hide.

unearthly *adj.* **1.** not of this earth, not of this world, supernatural, extramundane, ethereal, spectral, ghostly, phantom; incorporeal, disembodied, preternatural, weird, eerie, uncanny. **2.** strange, abnormal, unusual, absurd, extraordinary, extreme; terrible, horrendous, disagreeable, unspeakable, awful, unpleasant, ungodly. **—Ant. 1** earthly, natural, mundane. **2** normal, usual, common, ordinary, typical; pleasant, agreeable.

uneasy *adj.* **1.** worried, disturbed, upset, apprehensive, troubled, perturbed. **2.** ill at ease, awkward, uncomfortable, strained, nervous, nervy, edgy, on edge, unsure, tense, constrained, disquieted, *Slang* uptight. **3.** upsetting, queasy, bothersome, unpleasant, disturbing, uncomfortable, worrying, irksome, disquieting.

uneducated *adj.* **—Syn. Study.** See IGNORANT.

unemotional *adj.* unfeeling, passionless, apathetic, impassive, indifferent, unconcerned, unresponsive, undemonstrative, cold, cool, lukewarm, remote, distant, reserved, formal.

unemployed *adj.* jobless, laid-off, out of work, workless, idle, at leisure, at liberty, unoccupied; fired, discharged, dismissed; *Slang* axed, sacked, booted-out, canned, bounced, pink-slipped. **—Ant.** working, employed, engaged, busy.

unending *adj.* incessant, unceasing, never-ending, perpetual, constant, endless, eternal, permanent, perennial, enduring, lasting, everlasting, unremitting, steady, undiminished, unwavering, continual, continuous, uninterrupted. **—Ant.** brief, short, fleeting, momentary, transitory, transient, temporary, passing; sporadic, intermittent, unsteady, interrupted.

unenlightened *adj.* uninformed, unknowledgeable, ignorant, unfamiliar with, unlearned, uninitiated, uninstructed, uneducated, in the dark. **—Ant.** enlightened, well-informed, knowledgeable, knowing, familiar, learned.

unequal *adj.* **1.** not equal, uneven, different, unmatched, unlike, dissimilar, not uniform, disparate. **2.** unfair, unjust, not equitable, prejudiced, biased, partial, bigoted. **—Ant. 1, 2** equal. **1** even, matched, uniform, similar, like, alike. **2** fair, just, right, unprejudiced, unbiased, unbigoted.

unequaled *adj.* unsurpassed, unmatched, unparalleled, matchless, beyond compare, incomparable, unrivaled, second to none, unapproached, beyond comparison, unexcelled, supreme, paramount, peerless, consummate, *Latin* ne plus ultra.

unequivocal *adj.* decisive, unambiguous, clear, clear-cut, absolute, definite, final, certain, incontestable, indisputable, incontrovertible, emphatic. **—Ant.** equivocal, ambiguous, indecisive, vague, doubtful, indefinite.

unerring *adj.* infallible, unfailing, faultless, certain, sure, precise, reliable, faithful, unchanging, constant.

unethical *adj.* unprincipled, dishonorable, disreputable, shoddy, shady, underhand, devious, *Informal* dirty; unfair, wrong, unconscionable, dishonest, questionable, unworthy, ungentlemanly, unladylike. **—Ant.** ethical, principled, honorable, reputable, honest, clean, fair, aboveboard, conscionable.

uneven *adj.* **1.** not even, not level, not flat, not plumb, slanted, angled, awry, sloping, tilted, bent, crooked, curved; unsmooth, bumpy, lumpy, craggy, jagged, rough, coarse. **2.** unequal, one-sided, unbalanced, lopsided, ill-matched, unfair, unjust; disparate, dissimilar, different, unlike. **—Ant. 1, 2** even. **1** level, flat, straight, plane, smooth, uniform. **2** equal, well-matched, well-balanced, fair, just; similar, alike, like.

uneventful *adj.* not eventful, quiet, unexceptional, routine, ordinary, commonplace, average, usual, standard, conventional, insignificant; dull, tedious, boring, humdrum, prosaic, tiresome, monotonous, uninteresting.

unexcelled *adj.* unsurpassed, unbeaten, supreme, peerless, transcendent, superior, consummate, flawless, faultless; unequaled, unrivaled, matchless, unmatched, incomparable, beyond compare, unparalleled, unapproached, second to none.

unexpected *adj.* unanticipated, unlooked-for, unforeseen, unpredicted, startling, astonishing, surprising, out of the blue; undesigned, unplanned, sudden, accidental, unintentional, unintended.

unfailing *adj.* inexhaustible, endless, continual, continuous, constant, dependable, reliable, never-failing, faithful, unchanging, true, loyal, unwavering, steady, infallible, enduring. **—Ant.** undependable, unreliable, unfaithful, treacherous, disloyal, untrue, inconstant, wavering, unsteady, faulty, fallible.

unfair *adj.* not fair, unjust, not right, inequitable, unreasonable, *Slang* not cricket; partial, biased, prejudiced, partisan, unequal, one-sided, dishonorable, unconscionable, unscrupulous, unprincipled, unethical, underhand, dishonest, corrupt, dirty, foul, crooked.

unfaithful *adj.* **1.** disloyal, treacherous, perfidious, untrustworthy, faithless, false, falsehearted, deceitful; adulterous, inconstant, untrue, unchaste. **2.** not accurate, inaccurate, erroneous, untrue, false, inexact, imperfect, faulty, distorted. **—Ant. 1, 2** faithful, true. **1** loyal, trustworthy, steadfast, true-blue; constant, chaste. **2** accurate, correct, exact, perfect.

unfaltering *adj.* firm, steady, resolute, unwavering, wholehearted, unfailing, steadfast, unswerving, enduring, unflagging, undeviating, never-failing, sure, dependable; persistent, obstinate, persevering. **—Ant.** irresolute, undependable, fickle, vacillating.

unfamiliar *adj.* **1.** unacquainted, not acquainted, unconversant, unaccustomed to, a stranger to, unexposed to, unversed in, unenlightened about, ignorant of, uninformed about, inexperienced in, unpracticed in, unskilled in, uninitiated. **2.** unknown, unusual, strange, curious, unique, different, new, novel, out-of-the-way, exotic, foreign; not well-known, little known. **—Ant. 1, 2** familiar. **1** acquainted, conversant, accustomed, well-versed, versed, knowledgeable, experienced, practical. **2** common, commonplace, normal, everyday, average, run-of-the-mill; well-known, known, recognized.

unfavorable *adj.* not favorable, adverse, poor, unsuited, ill-suited, unpropitious, inauspicious, regrettable, unhappy, infelicitous, bad, disadvantageous, untimely, inconvenient, inopportune, unseasonable, unpromising, ill-favored, unfortunate.

unfinished *adj.* **1.** not finished, uncompleted, incomplete, undone, unexecuted, unfulfilled; imperfect, immature, deficient, lacking, wanting. **2.** rough, sketchy, crude, deficient, wanting, unpolished, unrefined; unnatural, (*variously*) unpainted, unvarnished, unstained, unlacquered.

unfit *adj.* **1.** not fit, unsuited, unsuitable, not suited, inappropriate, inadequate, not designed, ill-contrived, ineffective, inefficient, not equal to, useless. **2.** unqualified, inadequate, incompetent, unprepared, untrained, unskilled, unequipped, ill-equipped, incapable, unready, unequal, unsuited, not equal to, not up to, not cut out for, ineligible. **3.** unsound, unhealthy, debilitated, sick, sickly, frail, weak, infirm, incapacitated, delicate, disabled. **—Ant. 1–3** fit. **1** suitable, adequate, useful, adaptable. **2** suited, qualified, competent, capable, able, equipped, prepared, ready, eligible. **3** healthy, sound, hale, in good health, strong, sturdy.

unflagging *adj.* unfaltering, untiring, tireless, indefatigable, undrooping, unremitting, unswerving, steady, steadfast, firm, resolute, undeviating, unwavering, unshaken, unyielding, indomitable, relentless, uncompromising, persevering, constant, fixed, firm, staunch, determined, undaunted, enduring, tenacious, persistent. **—Ant.** faltering, wavering, flagging, drooping, irresolute, relenting, compromising, half-hearted.

unflinching *adj.* steady, unshaken, unshrinking, steadfast, unabashed, plucky, unfaltering, tenacious, persistent, strong, gritty, game, fearless, firm, indomitable, unhesitating, unwavering, unswerving, staunch, stalwart, undaunted, unyielding, resolute. **—Ant.** shaken, hesitant, faltering, weak, wavering, irresolute.

unfold *v.* **1.** spread out, open up, open out, stretch out, unwrap, unroll, unfurl. **2.** reveal, make known, disclose, divulge, unveil, uncover, show, bare, lay open, set forth, present, tell, explain, expound, explicate, describe, recount, elucidate. **—Ant. 1** fold, close, roll up, furl. **2** conceal, hide, cloak, veil; keep secret, keep mum about.

unforeseen *adj.* unexpected, unpredicted, surprise, unanticipated, unlooked-for, sudden, abrupt, out of the blue; unplanned, unintended, accidental, surprising. **—Ant.** foreseen, expected, anticipated, looked-for, predicted; planned, intended.

unfortunate *adj.* unlucky, luckless, ill-starred, hapless, unhappy, ill-fated, infelicitous, cursed, unsuccessful, unblest, jinxed, unprosperous; regrettable, wretched, sorry, disastrous, woeful, ill-advised, unfavorable, unpropitious, inopportune, untimely, ill-timed, inauspicious. **—Ant.** fortunate, lucky, happy, felicitous, successful, propitious, opportune, timely, auspicious.

unfounded *adj.* baseless, groundless, without foundation, without substance, idle; false, untrue, erroneous, fabricated, spurious.

unfriendly *adj.* antagonistic, hostile, warlike; disagreeable, unsociable, chilly, cold, unsympathetic, distant, inhospitable, ungracious, uncongenial; withdrawn, reclusive; snobbish, haughty, aloof. **—Ant.** warm, hospitable, agreeable, congenial, friendly.

unfruitful *adj.* fruitless, unproductive, unprofitable, unrewarding, unremunerative; unavailing, useless, futile, vain, purposeless; barren, infecund, impoverished, worn-out, fallow. **—Ant.** fruitful, productive, useful, rewarding, profitable.

ungainly *adj.* ungraceful, clumsy, awkward, maladroit, uncoordinated, stiff, lumbering, *Slang* klutzy. **—Ant.** graceful, lithe, willowy, limber, supple, sylphlike.

ungodly *adj.* **1.** not religious, godless; impious, blasphemous; wicked, sinful, immoral, heinous, iniquitous, depraved, degenerate, dissolute, dishonorable, corrupt, villainous, rotten, base, vile. **2.** dreadful, awful, horrendous, outrageous, terrible, ghastly, unreasonable. **—Ant. 1** godly, religious, pious, moral, good, virtuous, wholesome, honorable. **2** agreeable, pleasant, acceptable, reasonable.

ungracious *adj.* discourteous, rude, unmannerly, ill-mannered, uncouth, uncivil, churlish, impolite, disrespectful, impertinent, bad-mannered, boorish, ungentlemanly, unladylike; loutish, coarse, vulgar. **—Ant.** polite, courteous, well-bred, urbane, gracious.

unguarded *adj.* **1.** indiscreet, imprudent, ill-considered, tactless, undiplomatic, uncircumspect, careless, unmindful, incautious, unwary; unrestrained, overly candid, too frank. **2.** unprotected, unpatrolled, unwatched, defenseless, undefended. **—Ant. 1, 2** guarded. **1** discreet, circumspect, cautious, wary, careful. **2** protected, patrolled, watched, defended.

unhandy *adj.* clumsy, awkward, hamhanded, all thumbs, maladroit, fumbling, inept, bumbling, gauche, unskillful, inexpert; *Slang* butterfingered, klutzy. **—Ant.** adroit, expert, deft, skilled, handy.

unhappy *adj.* **1.** not happy, sad, sorrowful, despondent, depressed, dejected, downcast, heavyhearted, doleful, gloomy, forlorn, melancholy, dispirited, joyless, crestfallen, woebegone, somber, blue, long-faced, down in the mouth. **2.** unfortunate, hapless, unsuccessful, unwise, imprudent, foolish, injudicious, ill-advised, regrettable, sorry, infelicitous, adverse, poor, bad, unlucky, luckless, inappropriate, inapt, unsuitable, awkward, unseemly, unbecoming, unbefitting. **—Ant. 1, 2** happy. **1** gay, cheerful, joyful, joyous, lighthearted, sunny, smiling, exuberant, effervescent, enthusiastic. **2** fortunate, successful, wise, prudent, smart, shrewd, good, fine, wonderful, lucky, blessed, favorable; appropriate, apt, suitable, seemly, becoming, correct, befitting.

unhealthy *adj.* **1.** sickly, sick, infirm, ailing, not well, unwell, in poor health, indisposed, poorly, feeble, weak, unsound; invalid, diseased. **2.** unhealthful, harmful to health, noxious, hurtful, detrimental, unwholesome, insalubrious. **3.** demoralizing, harmful, morally bad, undesirable, destructive, corrupting, contaminating, degrading, depraved, morbid, negative, bad; hazardous, dangerous, perilous. **—Ant. 1–3** healthy. **1** well, sound, strong, robust. **2** healthful, salubrious, salutary, wholesome, beneficial. **3** moral, positive, constructive, desirable, good.

unheard-of *adj.* outrageous, preposterous, outlandish, unbelievable, unreasonable, inconceivable; unique, unprecedented, unusual, original, exceptional, unparalleled, incomparable, matchless. **—Ant.** reasonable, expected, believable, usual, ordinary.

unheralded *adj.* unannounced, unexpected, unanticipated, unforeseen, unlooked-for; unsung, unacclaimed, unproclaimed, unrecognized, unpublicized.

unhesitating *adj.* **1.** immediate, quick, instantaneous, prompt, without hesitation, without delay, ready, direct. **2.** unreserved, wholehearted, unflinching, eager, without reservation.

unholy *adj.* **1.** wicked, evil, ungodly, sinful, depraved, immoral, wicked, heinous, iniquitous, corrupt, villainous, dishonest, dishonorable; rotten, base, vile. **2.** dreadful, shocking, awful, ungodly, horrendous, outrageous, unreasonable. **—Ant. 1** moral, good, virtuous, honest, honorable, wholesome; godly, religious, pious. **2** agreeable, pleasant, acceptable, reasonable.

unidentified *adj.* unknown, nameless, anonymous, vague, unrecognized; unnamed, unspecified, undesignated, unlabeled. **—Ant.** known, named, recognized; specified, designated, labeled.

unification *n.* uniting, union, consolidation, consolidating, unity, junction, alliance, merger, combining, combination, confederation, confederacy, coalition, coalescence, incorporation, amalgamation, fusion. **—Ant.** separation, division, splitting, disunion, disunity.

uniform *n.* **1.** dress, apparel, attire, costume, garb, array; (*variously*) vestment, habit, livery, regalia, regimentals. *—adj.* **2.** alike, equal, identical, similar, consistent, consonant, of a piece, harmonious, agreeing, of one mind, conforming, at one, in accord, in step, in line. **3.** the same, even, equal, unvarying, unvaried, undeviating, unchanging, unaltered, constant, regular, consistent. **—Ant. 2, 3** different. **2** unalike, unlike, dissimilar, nonstandard, multiform, mixed; disagreeing, discordant, individual. **3** uneven, unequal, mixed, variable, inconsistent, irregular, erratic, deviating, changed, altered.

unify *v.* unite, combine, form into one, join, consolidate, bring together, confederate, federate, incorporate, ally, coalesce, amalgamate, fuse, merge; link up, couple, wed, blend, lump together. **—Ant.** disunite, separate, divide, part, split, cleave, sever, disband.

unimaginative *adj.* uninspired, unoriginal, routine, uncreative, ordinary, prosaic, mediocre, trite, commonplace, clichéd, run-of-the-mill, stock, pedestrian, everyday, stale, hackneyed, usual, predictable, unromantic, dull, unexciting, tedious, uninteresting, vapid, humdrum, dreary, unremarkable. **—Ant.** imaginative, original, creative, inspired, extraordinary, unusual, different, fanciful, exciting, interesting, fresh, novel, new.

unimpeachable *adj.* totally honest, beyond criticism, impeccable, irreproachable, above reproach, unassailable, beyond question, blameless, inculpable, faultless, perfect, unmarred, unblemished, spotless, stainless, untainted, clean, undefiled, inviolate, pure, immaculate; reliable, trustworthy, unquestionable, solid, unchallengeable, infallible. **—Ant.** questionable, dubious, debatable, controversial, suspect, faulty, imperfect, tainted, untrustworthy, unreliable.

unimportant *adj.* not important, inconsequential, of no consequence, insignificant, of no moment, immaterial, irrelevant, nugatory, nonessential, not vital; inconsiderable, negligible, minor, lesser, subordinate, inferior, trivial, trifling, paltry, meager, slight, piddling, low-ranking, second-rate, mediocre. **—Ant.** important, consequential, significant.

uninformed *adj.* ignorant, unread, unaware, uninstructed, unknowing, unlearned, unenlightened, unschooled, uneducated, unconversant, unadvised; *Slang* not with it, in the dark. **—Ant.** informed, enlightened; *Slang* with it.

uninhabited *adj.* unoccupied, unlived in, vacant, empty, untenanted; unpopulated, unpeopled, unsettled, deserted, abandoned, forsaken. **—Ant.** inhabited, occupied, lived in; populated, peopled, settled.

uninhibited *adj.* **1.** unself-conscious, not shy, open; spontaneous, impulsive, impetuous, rash, instinctive, *Informal* fast; heedless, unwary, unguarded, incautious, careless, indiscreet; outspoken, candid, frank, unreserved, plainspoken, straightforward, forthright; reckless, madcap, capricious, headstrong, abandoned, free, free-spirited, daring, flamboyant, immodest. **2.** free, unrestrained, unconstrained, uncontrolled, unrestricted, unchecked, unobstructed, unhampered, unstopped, unimpeded, unhindered, uncurbed, unbridled, unreined. **—Ant. 1, 2** inhibited. **1** self-conscious, shy, bashful, retiring, sheepish, modest, demure; wary, guarded, cautious, careful, discreet, self-controlled; stiff, rigid, *Slang* uptight. **2** restrained, constrained, controlled, restricted, checked, hampered, hindered, curbed, bridled.

uninspired *adj.* **1.** unmoved, unstirred, unimpressed, unexcited, unaffected, untouched, unemotional, unstimulated, uninfluenced. **2.** unimaginative, unoriginal, ordinary, prosaic, trite, commonplace, clichéd, run-of-the-mill, stock, pedestrian, stale, hackneyed, predictable, dull, unexciting, indifferent, uninteresting, vapid, humdrum. **—Ant. 1, 2** inspired. **1** moved, stirred, impressed, excited, affected, touched, influenced, stimulated. **2** imaginative, creative, original, fresh, novel, new, extraordinary, unusual, different, exciting, interesting.

unintelligent *adj.* stupid, dumb, obtuse, asinine, simpleminded, blockheaded, thickheaded, half-witted, slow-witted, dull, dense, dull-witted, thick, slow, doltish, blank, *Slang* dopey. **—Ant.** intelligent, smart, brainy, sharp, brilliant.

unintelligible *adj.* impossible to understand, incoherent, inarticulate, incomprehensible, illegible, incapable of being understood, meaningless, unfathomable, baffling, confusing, puzzling, perplexing; undecipherable, impenetrable, insoluble. **—Ant.** intelligible, understandable, coherent, articulate, legible; comprehensible, clear, decipherable, soluble.

unintentional *adj.* accidental, fortuitous, unpremeditated, unintended, undesigned, unplanned, not done purposely, unconscious, inadvertent, unthinking, unwitting, involuntary.

uninterested *adj.* unconcerned, heedless, indifferent, incurious, apathetic, unmindful, listless, blasé, uninvolved, *Slang* above it all; remote, aloof; uncaring, unimpressible. **—Ant.** concerned, interested, involved, curious, alive.

uninteresting *adj.* boring, tiresome, dreary, dull, tedious, uneventful, monotonous, drab, wearisome, prosaic, dry, jejune, trite, insipid, humdrum, pedestrian, vapid, uninspiring, unmoving, insignificant, ordinary, lifeless, colorless, unsatisfying.

uninviting *adj.* unappealing, unwelcoming, unalluring, untempting, unattractive, unpleasant, displeasing, undesirable, disagreeable, distasteful, offensive, unappetizing, annoying.

union *n.* **1.** combination, mixture, amalgam, amalgamation, consolidation, joining, blend, merger, unity, uniting, oneness, marriage, wedding; fusion, synthesis, unifying, unification, unity. **2.** federation, confederation, association, affiliation, alliance, league, partnership, corporation, fraternity. **3.** (*variously*) labor union, trade union, craft union, workers' association, guild. **—Syn. Study. 2** See ALLIANCE. **—Ant. 1** separation, division, disunion, schism.

unique *adj.* singular, distinctive, one of a kind, by itself, incomparable, unrivaled, unparalleled, unequaled, matchless, unmatched, unexcelled, unsurpassed, peerless, unapproached, unexampled, inimitable, nonpareil, surpassing. **—Ant.** commonplace, common, usual, everyday, ordinary, average, routine, typical, run-of-the-mill.

unit *n.* **1.** part, element, segment, section, component, constituent, member, division; entity, whole, quantity, group, package, detachment. **2.** measure, measurement, quantity, category, denomination, entity.

unite *v.* **1.** unify, combine, join, consolidate, confederate, federate, incorporate, ally, coalesce, amalgamate, fuse, merge, couple, connect, blend, homogenize, pool, lump together. **2.** join together, join forces, lock arms, stand together, organize, become one voice. **—Syn. Study. 1** See JOIN. **—Ant. 1** divide, separate, disunite, split, part, sever, disjoin, detach, disengage.

united *adj.* **1.** unified, combined, consolidated, incorporated, amalgamated, fused, merged, joined, coupled, blended, allied, collective, pooled, lumped together; federated, leagued. **2.** joined together, one, of the same opinion, unanimous, of one mind, in agreement. **—Ant. 1, 2** divided. **2** split, on opposite sides of the fence, at odds.

unity *n.* **1.** oneness, wholeness, entity, unification, consolidation, amalgamation, fusion, synthesis, merger, joining, association, federation, confederation, affiliation, league, alliance, union, partnership. **2.** accord, concord, peace, harmony, cooperation, friendship, amicableness, unanimity, understanding, goodwill, fellowship, compatibility, likemindedness, rapport. **—Ant. 1, 2** disunity. **1** independence, individuality, heterogeneity, isolation, division, separateness, separation, severance. **2** disagreement, discord, disharmony, enmity, ill will.

universal *adj.* concerning everyone, affecting all, worldwide, international, omnipresent, widespread, ubiquitous, existing everywhere, common; general, all-embracing, all-inclusive. **—Syn. Study.** See GENERAL. **—Ant.** individual, personal, private, local, localized, parochial, limited, restricted, exclusive, confined, special, specific.

unjust *adj.* unfair, wrongful, unjustified, unwarranted, undeserved, unmerited, inequitable; prejudiced, biased, partisan, warped, one-sided, unbalanced. **—Ant.** just, impartial, fair, justified, deserved.

unkempt *adj.* uncombed, tousled, disheveled, ungroomed, untidy, messy, sloppy, rumpled, disarranged, disordered, mussed-up, slovenly. **—Ant.** combed, well-groomed, neat, tidy, orderly.

unkind *adj.* inconsiderate, thoughtless, unfeeling, unsympathetic, insensitive, uncaring, unfriendly, ungracious, inhospitable, uncharitable, ungenerous; mean, nasty, malicious, abusive.

unknown *adj.* anonymous, unidentified, undiscovered, unnamed, nameless, undesignated, undetermined; obscure, unrenowned, unheard-of, uncelebrated. **—Ant.** well-known, celebrated, famous, renowned.

unlawful *adj.* illegal, prohibited, unauthorized, forbidden, illicit, unconstitutional, unofficial, unlicensed, against the law, lawless, criminal, *Informal* illegit. **—Syn. Study.** See ILLEGAL. **—Ant.** legal, lawful, licit, official, authorized, permissible.

unlike *adj.* different, unalike, diverse, dissimilar, disparate, different as night and day, separate and distinct, not comparable, like apples and oranges. **—Ant.** like, similar, alike as two peas, identical.

unlikely *adj.* **1.** not likely, improbable, questionable, unbelievable, scarcely conceivable. **2.** unpromising, unpropitious, hopeless. **—Ant. 1** likely, probable, unquestionable, sure, certain. **2** promising, propitious, encouraging.

unlimited *adj.* **1.** limitless, unrestricted, unrestrained, unchecked, uncontrolled, absolute, total, totalitarian, complete, unconstrained, unqualified, all-encompassing, comprehensive. **2.** endless, limitless, boundless, unbounded, infinite, inexhaustible, vast, immense, huge, immeasurable. **—Ant. 1** limited, restricted, controlled, confined, checked, constrained; partial. **2** finite, limited, bounded, small, little, minute.

unlucky *adj.* ill-fated, hapless, ill-omened, inauspicious, ill-starred, unfortunate, unhappy, star-crossed, jinxed, cursed, luckless, untoward, misfortunate. **—Ant.** happy, providential, auspicious, fortunate.

unmanly *adj.* **1.** faint-hearted, weak-kneed, lily-livered, weakhearted, chickenhearted, cowardly, timid, pusillanimous, *Slang* yellow. **2.** effeminate, womanish, sissyish, sissified. **—Ant. 1** courageous, brave, valiant, lionhearted, stouthearted; brash, bold, reckless. **2** masculine, manly, virile.

unmannerly *adj.* badly behaved, ill-mannered, ill-bred, ungracious, ungentlemanly, unladylike; discourteous, impolite, crude, gross, uncouth, coarse, boorish, loutish, uncivil, surly. **—Ant.** well-behaved, courteous, polite, gracious, well-bred, mannerly; gentlemanly, ladylike, refined, cultured.

unmarried *adj.* single, unwed, spouseless, free, available, footloose and fancy-free; husbandless, wifeless, maiden, spinster, old maid, bachelor; divorced, widowed. **—Ant.** married, wed, mated; *Slang* hitched, yoked.

unmask *v.* **1.** remove a mask; take off one's disguise. **2.** reveal, expose, show, disclose, uncover, discover, unveil, bare, lay open, bring to light, betray.

unmatched *adj.* **1.** not matched, unmatching, not paired, unlike, differing, not uniform, unequal, dissimilar, disparate, diverse, variable. **2.** matchless, unequaled, unparalleled, peerless, supreme, second to none, beyond compare. **—Ant. 1** matched, matching, paired, like, uniform, equal, similar.

unmindful *adj.* negligent, derelict, lax, remiss, heedless, unheeding, thoughtless, careless, oblivious, unaware, unconscious, forgetful. **—Ant.** careful, heedful, aware, unremiss.

unmistakable *adj.* clear, obvious, evident, manifest, plain, apparent, distinct, patent, palpable, pronounced, prominent, glaring, conspicuous; undeniable, indisputable, unequivocal, unquestionable. **—Ant.** vague, indistinct, dim, faint, unrecognizable, unclear; hidden, concealed.

unmitigated *adj.* **1.** unrelieved, unalleviated, unabated, unbroken, persistent, uninterrupted. **2.** downright, out-and-out, absolute, unqualified, arrant. **—Ant. 1** mitigated, relieved, alleviated, abated, eased, lessened, softened, mild, soft; sporadic, intermittent, random, occasional. **2** partial, incomplete, qualified, limited, redeemed, regenerate.

unmoved *adj.* **1.** not moved, not shifted, left in place, not transplanted. **2.** firm, steadfast, unwavering, unswerving, unshaken, unfaltering, inflexible, undeviating; staunch, determined, resolute, resolved, persistent, obstinate, dogged, uncompromising, relentless; devoted, dedicated. **3.** unaffected, untouched, calm, unstirred, indifferent, uninterested, undisturbed, unresponsive, unconcerned, uncaring; cold, stonyhearted, aloof, unpitying, unfeeling. **—Ant. 1** moved, transferred, shifted. **2** wavering, vacillating, shaken; compliant, flexible, yielding, adaptable, submissive. **3** moved, touched, stirred, affected, concerned, responsive, sympathetic.

unnamed *adj.* anonymous, nameless, undisclosed, unrevealed, unidentified, uncredited, unacknowledged, pseudonymous, unsigned, incognito, undesignated, unspecified, undiscovered, unreported. **—Ant.** known, identified, disclosed, credited, signed.

unnatural *adj.* **1.** not natural, abnormal, aberrant, peculiar, freakish, unusual, anomalous. **2.** artificial, affected, mannered, stilted, studied, forced, assumed, contrived, phony, fake, put-on, self-conscious; theatrical. **—Ant. 1, 2** natural, normal. **1** common, ordinary, typical. **2** unaffected, unpretentious, sincere, genuine, honest.

unnecessary *adj.* not necessary, needless, uncalled-for, dispensable, unessential, unrequired, expendable, gratuitous; overmuch, excessive, extra, surplus, excess, superfluous, supplementary, auxiliary.

unnerve *v.* upset, unsettle, unhinge, agitate, daunt, intimidate, frighten, scare. **—Ant.** encourage, reassure; nerve, steel.

unnoticeable *adj.* inconspicuous, unemphatic, obscure, unobtrusive, undiscernible, indistinct, unobserved, unassuming, faint, dim, unostentatious, insignificant. **—Ant.** clear, distinct, noticeable, visible, obvious.

unnoticed *adj.* **1.** unseen, unobserved, undiscovered, unperceived; (*variously*) unheard, untasted, not smelled, unfelt. **2.** overlooked, disregarded, unnoted, unheeded. **—Ant. 1, 2** noticed. **1** seen, observed, witnessed, discovered, perceived; heard, tasted, smelled, felt. **2** noted, heeded, marked.

unobtrusive *adj.* inconspicuous, unpretentious, modest, humble, unostentatious; unassuming, diffident, bashful, reserved, unassertive, reticent, retiring, shy. **—Ant.** conspicuous, prominent, eye-catching, glaring, noticeable; ostentatious, pretentious, assuming, bold, brash, brazen, assertive.

unorganized *adj.* unordered, orderless, unsystematized, unsystematic, unarranged, random, casual, haphazard, confused, loose, helter-skelter, harum-scarum, chaotic, unclassified, aimless, disjointed, undirected. **—Ant.** organized, ordered, systematized, systematic, arranged, classified.

unperturbed *adj.* calm, tranquil, cool, collected, composed, poised, unruffled, unexcited, unagitated, undisturbed, untroubled, undismayed, levelheaded, coolheaded, unimpassioned, nonchalant. **—Ant.** perturbed, excited, discomposed, upset, disturbed, troubled, dismayed, impassioned.

unpleasant *adj.* disagreeable, displeasing, nasty, distasteful, offensive, repulsive, repugnant, obnoxious, objectionable, unlikable, unattractive, irksome, annoying, vexatious, noisome, pesky; ill-natured, churlish, ill-humored. **—Ant.** pleasant, pleasing, agreeable, attractive, likable; congenial, good-natured.

unpopular *adj.* disliked, unaccepted, disdained, unwanted, unacceptable, unwelcome, snubbed, slighted, rebuffed, neglected, disapproved, looked down on, undesirable, rejected. **—Ant.** loved, wanted, courted, sought-after.

unprecedented *adj.* hitherto unknown, unheard-of, unexampled, unparalleled, unique, extraordinary, exceptional, novel. **—Ant.** familiar, usual, regular, normal, routine.

unpredictable *adj.* not predictable, not

foreseeable, erratic, unstable, fitful, variable, uncertain, eccentric, inconstant, arbitrary, changeable, mercurial, impulsive, capricious, whimsical, fanciful. —**Ant.** predictable, stable, constant, undeviating, reasonable.

unprejudiced *adj.* without prejudice, impartial, objective, unbiased, unbigoted, fair, fair-minded, just, even-handed, uninfluenced, unswayed, undogmatic, disinterested, open-minded, broad-minded. —**Ant.** prejudiced, partial, biased, bigoted, unjust, unfair, closed-minded, narrow-minded.

unpretentious *adj.* unassuming, simple, plain, modest, unostentatious, unelaborate, unimposing, unobtrusive, humble, homely.

unprincipled *adj.* without principles, unscrupulous, unconscionable, amoral, conscienceless. —**Syn. Study.** See UNSCRUPULOUS.

unprofessional *adj.* amateurish, amateur, unbusinesslike, unworkmanlike, undisciplined, inexperienced, unpracticed, inefficient; incompetent, careless, sloppy, bungling, shoddy; unethical, negligent, unprincipled. —**Ant.** efficient, meticulous, businesslike, workmanlike.

unqualified *adj.* **1.** lacking the qualifications, untrained, unschooled, uneducated, unskilled, inexpert, inexperienced, unprepared, ill-equipped; unfit, unsuited, incompetent. **2.** absolute, total, complete, positive, consummate, utter, downright, thorough, through and through, out-and-out, unconditional, undisputed.

unquestionable *adj.* beyond doubt, undeniable, indisputable, uncontestable, irrefutable, proven, unequivocal, unimpeachable, definite, certain, sure, clear, plain, obvious, self-evident, evident, perfect, flawless, faultless, impeccable, errorless, blameless, irreproachable, uncensurable.

unreal *adj.* not real, nonexistent, imaginary, imagined, illusory, illusive, chimerical, insubstantial, fictitious, legendary, fantastic; ghostly, shadowy, spectral, intangible, phantasmagorical, phantom, ethereal, dreamlike, dreamy, dream, airy, idealistic.

unrealistic *adj.* impractical, unreasonable, illogical, idealistic, improbable, infeasible; delusory, fanciful, starry-eyed, wild, silly, crazy, foolish, crackpot, asinine, absurd. —**Ant.** realistic, sound, sensible, reasonable, practical.

unreasonable *adj.* **1.** contrary to reason, senseless, irrational, illogical, absurd, far-fetched, preposterous, nonsensical. **2.** obstinate, headstrong, stubborn, inflexible, unyielding, unbending, obdurate, mulish, bullheaded, pigheaded, unmanageable, hard to deal with, ungovernable, intractable; opinionated, closed-minded, bigoted, biased, prejudiced, fanatical. **3.** excessive, too great, exorbitant, extravagant, inordinate, immoderate, unfair, unwarranted, unjustifiable, undue, uncalled-for. —**Ant. 1–3** reasonable. **1** sensible, logical, plausible, rational, sober, wise, prudent. **2** complaisant, agreeable, flexible, tractable, open-minded. **3** moderate, temperate, restrained, equitable, fair, justified, warranted.

unrehearsed *adj.* spontaneous, improvised, extemporaneous, impromptu, informal, off-the-cuff, offhand, spur-of-the-moment, unplanned, unpremeditated, unstudied, improvisational, unprepared, impulsive. —**Ant.** planned, contrived, rehearsed, prepared, studied.

unrelated *adj.* **1.** not related, not kin, not kindred; dissimilar, unlike. **2.** extraneous, irrelevant, unconnected, nongermane, foreign, unassociated, unallied, inappropriate, inapplicable, incompatible. —**Ant. 1, 2** related. **1** kin, akin; similar, like, equal. **2** relevant, pertinent, germane, connected, applicable, appropriate, associated.

unrelenting *adj.* relentless, unremitting, unrelieved, incessant, ceaseless, unbroken, endless, unabated, unwavering; steady, constant, unswerving, undeviating, unyielding, inflexible, unbending, rigid, adamant, tenacious, uncompromising, implacable, inexorable.

unreliable *adj.* **1.** undependable, not to be trusted; questionable, uncertain, fallible, undependable; phony, fake, false, inaccurate, mistaken, erroneous. **2.** undependable, irresponsible, not conscientious, untrustworthy, deceitful; unstable, changeable, fickle, inconstant, capricious. —**Ant. 1, 2** reliable, dependable. **1** certain, sure, unquestionable, infallible; real, genuine, authentic, correct, accurate, true, right. **2** responsible, conscientious, trustworthy.

unrepentant *adj.* without repenting, not contrite, uncontrite, not penitent, unexpiated, unatoned; unregenerate, remorseless, unashamed; hardened, incorrigible, obdurate, callous. —**Ant.** repentant, penitent, expiated, atoned; contrite, regenerate, remorseful, ashamed.

unresolved *adj.* undetermined, unsettled, undecided, unanswered, unsolved, unascertained, pending, tentative; doubtful, vague, uncertain, questionable, moot, problematical, speculative; disputable, contestable.

unrest *n.* restlessness, turmoil, disquiet, ferment, tumult, turbulence, upheaval;

discontent, discord, agitation, dissatisfaction, protest, rebellion; anarchy, disorder, chaos. **—Ant.** peace, quiet, calm, tranquillity, serenity.

unrestrained *adj.* uncontrolled, unrestricted, unchecked, uninhibited, irrepressible, unrepressed, unreserved, unsuppressed, uncurbed, unbridled, unhampered, unfettered, unchecked, ungoverned, unhindered; unlimited, boundless, excessive, extravagant, inordinate, immoderate, intemperate, abandoned.

unruly *adj.* disobedient, obstreperous, wild, willful, unmanageable, ungovernable, undisciplined, uncontrollable, intractable, wayward, headstrong, perverse, recalcitrant, refractory, fractious, contrary, unbridled, restive, rowdy, disorderly, boisterous. **—Syn. Study.** UNRULY, INTRACTABLE, RECALCITRANT, REFRACTORY describe persons or things that resist management or control. UNRULY suggests constant disorderly behavior or character: *an unruly child; unruly hair.* INTRACTABLE suggests in persons a determined resistance to all attempts to guide or direct them, and in things a resistance to attempts to shape, improve, or modify them: *an intractable social rebel; an intractable problem.* RECALCITRANT implies a stubborn rebellion against authority or direction: *a recalcitrant prisoner.* REFRACTORY also implies a mulish disobedience, but leaves open the possibility of eventual compliance: *The refractory youth needs more understanding.* **—Ant.** obedient, well-behaved, well-mannered, manageable, controllable, docile, tractable, submissive, compliant, sweet-tempered, agreeable; calm, reserved.

unsafe *adj.* dangerous, not safe, hazardous, perilous, risky; treacherous, untrustworthy, unreliable, unprotected, vulnerable, defenseless, exposed, undefended, unguarded, insecure. **—Ant.** safe, secure, immune from danger, reliable, trustworthy, guaranteed; protected, guarded, defended.

unsatisfactory *adj.* not satisfactory, unacceptable, unworthy, inept; inadequate, deficient, below par, inferior, poor, unsuitable, inappropriate, unfit, inadmissible, ineligible.

unsavory *adj.* **1.** flat, insipid, tasteless, without savor. **2.** distasteful, unpleasant, bad-tasting, unappetizing, unpalatable, nasty, foul, nauseating, disagreeable. **3.** morally objectionable, unpleasant, bad, tainted. **—Ant. 1, 2** savory, appetizing, tasty, agreeable, pleasing. **3** virtuous, good, moral.

unscathed *adj.* unhurt, uninjured, unharmed, unscratched, untouched, unimpaired, whole, entire, perfect, sound, intact, all in one piece. **—Ant.** hurt, injured, harmed, damaged.

unscrupulous *adj.* unprincipled, dishonorable, devious, unethical, immoral, amoral, sharp, crooked. **—Syn. Study.** UNSCRUPULOUS, UNPRINCIPLED refer to a lack of moral or ethical standards. UNSCRUPULOUS means not controlled by one's conscience and contemptuous of what one knows to be right or honorable: *an unscrupulous landlord.* UNPRINCIPLED means lacking or not aware of moral standards that should restrain one's actions: *an unprincipled rogue.* **—Ant.** scrupulous, principled, moral, ethical, honorable, honest, just, fair, trustworthy.

unseemly *adj.* improper, inappropriate, unbefitting, unbecoming, indecorous, ungentlemanly, unladylike, unsuitable, out of character, out of place, discreditable, undignified, unworthy, disreputable, reprehensible, tasteless, offensive, distasteful, vulgar, indelicate, incorrect, indecent, gross, crude, coarse, rude, discourteous, ill-mannered, boorish, churlish, loutish. **—Syn. Study.** See IMPROPER. **—Ant.** seemly, proper, appropriate, fit, befitting, becoming, suitable, dignified, tasteful, cultivated, polite, courteous, mannerly, genteel, gentlemanly, ladylike.

unselfish *adj.* selfless, altruistic, generous, munificent, considerate, bighearted, liberal, open-handed, self-sacrificing, handsome, princely, charitable, philanthropic, benevolent, humanitarian, magnanimous.

unsettle *v.* make unstable, unbalance, disturb, perturb, upset, disorder; disconcert, confuse, bewilder, fluster, confound, ruffle, bother, trouble, agitate, unhinge, throw off one's guard, *Slang* rattle.

unshaken *adj.* **1.** undaunted, unaffected, undisturbed, undeviating, unwavering, unfaltering, unswerving, unflinching, steadfast, determined, resolved, staunch, constant, stable, inflexible, uncompromising, tenacious, relentless. **2.** cool, calm, composed, controlled, poised, self-possessed, levelheaded, serene, unperturbed, untroubled, unmoved, unruffled, unemotional, unexcited. **—Ant. 1, 2** shaken. **1** wavering, faltering; destroyed, ruined, demolished, smashed, shattered, undone. **2** disconcerted, upset, emotional, excited, uncontrolled, moved, perturbed, troubled, dismayed, ruffled.

unsightly *adj.* ugly, unattractive, hideous, obnoxious, offensive, distasteful, repellent, repulsive, revolting, odious, horrid, revolting, sickening. **—Ant.** attractive, lovely, beautiful, appealing.

unsolicited *adj.* unasked for, unrequested, unsought, uninvited, gratuitous, volunteered; unwanted, unwelcome, unwished for, undesired, unnecessary; voluntary, unforced, free, spontaneous. —**Ant.** requested, sought, invited, solicited, desired, welcomed; enticed, courted.

unsophisticated *adj.* natural, ingenuous, artless, unworldly, unpretentious, unaffected, unassuming, open, candid, straightforward, homespun, unstudied, uncontrived, undissembling; naive, green, innocent, trusting.

unsound *adj.* **1.** unhealthy, sickly, diseased, crippled, defective, ailing, in poor health, infirm, unfit, invalid; feeble, weak, decrepit, drooping, languishing; mentally ill, deranged, insane, mad, unbalanced, unhinged, unsettled, disordered, confused, *Slang* off, off one's rocker. **2.** not solid, shaky, unsteady, weak, unstable, unsubstantial, rickety, tottery; unsafe, hazardous, dangerous, precarious, risky, perilous, unreliable, uncertain, insecure. **3.** not valid, unfounded, groundless, weak, shaky, untenable, fallacious, faulty, incorrect, wrong, erroneous, illogical, defective, spurious, specious, marred, blemished, impaired, imperfect, flawed; senseless, irrational, foolish, absurd. —**Ant. 1–3** sound, strong. **1** healthy, whole, well, fit, in good health, of strong constitution, vigorous, robust, hardy, hale and hearty, in the pink; sane, rational, reasonable, stable, clearheaded. **2** solid, sturdy, firm, safe, secure, durable, lasting. **3** valid, well-founded, convincing, cogent, correct, accurate, true, judicious, sensible, meaningful, reliable, authoritative.

unsparing *adj.* ungrudging, unstinting, generous, giving, bountiful, munificent, magnanimous, liberal, big-hearted, lavish, profuse, plenteous, abundant, extravagant, copious, plentiful, full; unconditional, unqualified, unlimited.

unspeakable *adj.* **1.** inexpressible, too wonderful to describe, undescribable, unutterable, inconceivable, unimaginable, incredible, overwhelming, astonishing, extraordinary, immense, huge, vast, enormous, great, prodigious. **2.** too horrible to talk about, awful, shocking, frightful, fearful, unheard of, repulsive, repellent, disgusting, odious, loathsome, abhorrent, nauseating, sickening, revolting, abominable, monstrous.

unspecified *adj.* unnamed, unmentioned, unannounced, unpublicized, undetermined, undefined, undesignated, unindicated, unstipulated, unsettled; vague, general, indefinite.

unspoiled *adj.* **1.** unpampered, not coddled; natural, artless, unaffected, unassuming, unpretentious, open, unstudied, unself-conscious, unsophisticated, unworldly, uncorrupted, trusting. **2.** preserved, undamaged, unharmed, unimpaired, pristine, perfect; spotless, unspotted, unmarred, unblemished, unscarred.

unstable *adj.* **1.** unsteady, unsubstantial, shaky, insecure, tippy, wobbly, tottering; flimsy, rickety, fragile, frail, weak. **2.** fluctuating, not constant, changing, changeable, vacillating, shifting, unsteady; erratic, volatile, emotional, mercurial, unpredictable, irrational, fitful, inconsistent, insecure, irresponsible, fickle, capricious, fly-by-night.

unsuccessful *adj.* **1.** without success, futile, vain, useless, unavailing, unfruitful, fruitless, abortive, unproductive, ineffectual. **2.** unlucky, hapless, unfortunate, ill-starred, luckless, unprosperous; thwarted, foiled, baffled; poor, moneyless, penniless, strapped, hard up, badly off; profitless, unprofitable, unremunerative. —**Ant. 1, 2** successful. **1** victorious, winning, triumphant, unbeaten; useful, fruitful, productive, effective, worthwhile. **2** lucky, fortunate; prosperous, thriving, flourishing, rich, wealthy, well-to-do, well-off, affluent; profitable, remunerative.

unsuitable *adj.* inappropriate, inapt, unbefitting, unfit, unfitting, improper, unsuitable, unbecoming, unseemly, out of place, out of keeping, out of character, unhappy, infelicitous, indecorous, incongruous, inconsistent, incompatible; unacceptable, inadmissible, inadequate, worthless, useless.

unsullied *adj.* unsoiled, clean, spotless, untainted, untarnished, unblemished, unblackened, uncorrupted, uninjured, uncontaminated, unpolluted, undefiled.

unsure *adj.* undecided, hesitant, unconvinced, uncertain, in a quandary, unassured, insecure, unconfident, self-doubting, self-distrustful; bashful, shy, timid, reserved. —**Ant.** self-confident, secure, unhesitating, decisive.

unsurpassed *adj.* supreme, consummate, superior, best, paramount, peerless, nonpareil, highest, greatest, transcendent, exceptional, unexcelled, incomparable, unparalleled, matchless, unmatched, unequaled, unrivaled.

unsuspecting *adj.* unsuspicious, unaware, off one's guard; credulous, trusting, believing; overtrustful, gullible, unwary, naive, overcredulous. —**Ant.** knowing, heedful, aware, alert; suspicious, cautious, wary.

unswerving *adj.* dedicated, faithful, devoted, steadfast, unwavering, undeviating, unflinching, unyielding, unfaltering, untiring, unflagging, inflexible, uncompromising, resolute, resolved, determined, single-minded, staunch, strong, firm, steady, unremitting, unshaken, undaunted. —**Ant.** wavering, faltering, flagging, irresolute, weak, faint, halfhearted.

unsympathetic *adj.* **1.** unfeeling, indifferent, coldhearted, hardhearted, hardboiled, heartless, uncompassionate, callous, pitiless, unmerciful, uncaring. **2.** uncongenial, antipathetic, repellent, repugnant, unlikable, displeasing, unattractive, unpleasant. —**Ant. 1** sympathetic, warmhearted, understanding. **2** congenial, attractive, pleasing.

untangle *v.* unsnarl, unravel, disentangle, untwist; straighten out, clear up, solve, extricate. —**Ant.** tangle, entangle, snarl, twist.

untarnished *adj.* **1.** unoxidized, unblackened, shining, bright, polished. **2.** spotless, unsoiled, unstained, untainted, unsullied, unblemished, unbesmirched, undefiled, unimpeachable, undisputed, faultless, flawless, immaculate, impeccable, perfect. —**Ant. 1, 2** tarnished. **1** oxidized, blackened, dull. **2** tainted, sullied, soiled, blemished, stained, besmirched, defiled, questionable, damaged, marred, discredited.

untenable *adj.* indefensible, unmaintainable, unsustainable, unjustifiable, insupportable, baseless, groundless, unsound, invalid, illogical, erroneous, fallacious, faulty, flawed, weak, spurious, specious, unreliable; questionable, debatable, contestable. —**Ant.** justified, sustained, supported, well-grounded; valid, reasonable, sound, logical; unquestionable, uncontestable.

unthinkable *adj.* out of the question, not to be considered, inconceivable, unimaginable, incomprehensible, insupportable, unjustifiable, unwarranted.

unthinking *adj.* thoughtless, inconsiderate, heedless, careless, inadvertent, tactless, insensitive, undiplomatic, uncircumspect; senseless, mindless, witless, imprudent, negligent.

untidy *adj.* messy, disorderly, littered, cluttered, unkempt, chaotic, disarrayed, confused, helter-skelter, topsy-turvy; slovenly, sloppy, slatternly, disheveled, mussed, mussed up, dowdy, frowsy, rumpled, tousled, bedraggled; careless, slipshod, unmethodical.

untimely *adj.* ill-timed, mistimed, inconvenient, inopportune, unexpected, premature; inappropriate, inapt, unsuitable, unfitting, unseemly, unbecoming, unbefitting, imprudent, out of place, unhappy, malapropos, infelicitous, unfortunate, ill-advised.

untiring *adj.* **1.** not becoming tired, tireless, never tiring, unwearied, fresh. **2.** unflagging, indefatigable, unfaltering, constant, unremitting, unceasing, wholehearted, determined, staunch, steadfast, resolute, steady, patient, persevering, persistent, tenacious, relentless, diligent, sedulous, assiduous; devoted, dedicated, zealous, earnest. —**Ant. 1** tiring, tired, weary, exhausted, fatigued, spent, *Slang* dog tired, played out, bushed, beat. **2** flagging, faltering, wavering, irresolute, fainthearted, lukewarm, indifferent, perfunctory, sporadic.

untold *adj.* **1.** unrevealed, secret, private, concealed, unknown, suppressed, withheld, hushed up; unrelated, unpublished, unreported, undisclosed, unsaid, unspoken, unexpressed. **2.** innumerable, countless, uncounted, numerous, myriad, undetermined, numberless, unnumbered; incalculable, immeasurable, limitless, unbounded, endless, infinite.

untroubled *adj.* calm, placid, serene, peaceful, tranquil, carefree, halcyon, undisturbed, unperturbed, easygoing, unbothered, relaxed. —**Ant.** troubled, agitated, disturbed, roiled.

untrue *adj.* **1.** not true, untruthful, false, fallacious, falsified, groundless, unfounded, made up, fictitious, spurious, meretricious, fake, sham, fraudulent; incorrect, erroneous, inaccurate. **2.** unfaithful, faithless, inconstant, adulterous, unchaste, promiscuous, false, perfidious; disloyal, dishonest, treacherous, double-dealing. —**Ant. 1, 2** true. **1** right, correct, accurate, authentic, genuine, real, valid, legitimate, *Slang* straight. **2** faithful, constant, chaste, pure, virtuous; loyal, honest, trustworthy, incorruptible, dependable, honorable, righteous, truthful.

untrustworthy *adj.* unreliable, undependable, unauthenticated, questionable, fallible, uncertain; unfaithful, disloyal, faithless, dishonest, false, insincere, untruthful, untrue, unprincipled, devious, deceitful, unscrupulous, disreputable, corrupted, treacherous, inconstant, two-faced, perfidious, irresponsible, shifty, slippery, capricious, fickle.

untruth *n.* lie, falsehood, fib, story, tale, canard, prevarication, fabrication, falsification, misrepresentation, invention, yarn, cock-and-bull story, deception, humbug, *Slang* flimflam.

untypical *adj.* atypical, abnormal, anomalous, aberrant, unrepresentative, deviant; odd, bizarre, unusual, rare, irregular, unnatural, strange, uncommon, alien, unfamiliar. —**Ant.** typical, common, usual, normal, ordinary.

unusual *adj.* singular, rare, exceptional, extraordinary, remarkable, noteworthy, atypical, untypical, novel, phenomenal, unique, uncommon, unfamiliar, surprising; strange, curious, peculiar; unparalleled, unequaled, unprecedented, unmatched, incomparable, unheard-of, out of the ordinary, one of a kind, offbeat. **—Ant.** usual, common, commonplace, ordinary, unremarkable, unexceptional, average, typical, familiar, routine, normal, natural, traditional, conventional, orthodox, stock.

unvarnished *adj.* plain, frank, bare, naked, candid, direct, honest, sincere, straightforward, straight, straight-from-the-shoulder; unembellished, unadorned. **—Ant.** embellished, exaggerated; hypocritical, evasive, insincere, dishonest.

unveil *v.* **1.** uncover, unsheathe, uncloak. **2.** disclose, reveal, divulge, bare, make known, announce, broadcast, publish, bring to light. **—Ant. 1, 2** veil. **1** cover. **2** conceal, hide, disguise, camouflage.

unwarranted *adj.* unjustified, uncalled-for, indefensible, unreasonable, inexcusable, unfounded, groundless, arbitrary; unauthorized, unsanctioned, unapproved, culpable, censurable, unlawful, illegal.

unwary *adj.* unwatchful, incautious, unalert, heedless, reckless, hasty, uncircumspect, imprudent, rash, precipitate, indiscreet, careless, headlong, unguarded, disregardful. **—Ant.** wary, cautious, discreet, guarded, circumspect.

unwavering *adj.* unswerving, unfaltering, untiring, unflagging, dedicated, single-minded, faithful, undeviating, unflinching, resolute, determined, steadfast, staunch, strong, firm, steady, persevering, unremitting, persistent, tenacious, uncompromising, unshaken.

unwelcome *adj.* **1.** unwanted, unwished for, uninvited, undesirable, unacceptable, rejected, excluded, unpopular, outcast, uncared for; unnecessary, unessential, unrequired. **2.** disagreeable, unpleasant, displeasing, distasteful, undesirable, thankless.

unwell *adj.* ailing, low, indisposed, poorly, infirm, sickly, queasy, qualmish, ill, sick, run-down, laid up, having a malaise, frail, delicate; *Slang* under the weather, off one's feed, not feeling oneself. **—Ant.** well, fit, tiptop; *Slang* perky, chipper.

unwholesome *adj.* **1.** unhealthful, unhealthy, insalubrious, deleterious, harmful, hurtful, detrimental; unnourishing, noxious, pernicious, poisonous, venomous, baneful, deadly, toxic. **2.** morally harmful, immoral, corrupting, evil, sinful, wicked, bad, depraved, dishonorable, degrading, ruinous, corrupted, demoralizing, undesirable; dangerous, polluting, contaminating, filthy, foul. **—Ant. 1, 2** wholesome. **1** healthful, healthy, salubrious; nutritious, hygienic, sanitary. **2** moral, uplifting, edifying, inspiring.

unwieldy *adj.* hard to handle, not handy, awkward, clumsy, inconvenient, uncomfortable, incommodious, cumbersome, bulky, heavy, burdensome, weighty. **—Ant.** handy, convenient, comfortable.

unwilling *adj.* reluctant, loath, disinclined, unfavorably disposed, indisposed, undesirous, averse, against, opposed, resistant, recalcitrant, dissenting, demurring, unenthusiastic, not in the mood.

unwise *adj.* imprudent, improvident, ill-advised, inadvisable, injudicious, unsound, unreasonable, short-sighted, foolish, senseless, unintelligent, reckless, foolhardy, irresponsible, silly, dumb, stupid, *Slang* crazy.

unwitting *adj.* unknowing, unaware, unintentional, inadvertent, unthinking, unmeant, accidental, unpremeditated, undesigned, unplanned, unexpected; involuntary, unconsenting. **—Ant.** witting, knowing, premeditated, voluntary, intentional.

unwonted *adj.* unaccustomed, atypical, unusual, unfamiliar, unexpected, rare, infrequent, uncommon, exceptional, extraordinary, remarkable. **—Ant.** accustomed, customary, habitual, typical, routine, usual, normal, standard, predictable.

unworldly *adj.* **1.** unsophisticated, naive, innocent, inexperienced, provincial, overtrusting, trusting, idealistic, callow, green. **2.** spiritual, holy, sacred, divine, pious, religious, devout, godly, solemn, pure, celestial, heavenly, transcendental, ethereal, unearthly, immaterial; aesthetic, metaphysical, intellectual, moral, ethical, philosophical.

unworthy *adj.* inappropriate, unbefitting, unfit, improper, unbecoming, unseemly, unsuitable, unacceptable; ignoble, dishonorable, unethical, shameful, discreditable, disreputable, degrading, objectionable. **—Ant.** worthy, honorable, noble, commendable, admirable, praiseworthy; appropriate, fitting, befitting, proper, becoming.

unwritten *adj.* **1.** not written down, not reduced to writing, unrecorded, unregistered; spoken only, oral, vocal, by word of mouth. **2.** unformulated, unstated, unexpressed, implied, implicit, understood, inferred, tacit, assumed; traditional, customary.

unyielding *adj.* **1.** stiff, hard, rigid, unbending, inflexible, unpliable, stony, wooden, rocklike, tough. **2.** unbending, inflexible, unwavering, firm, steadfast, resolute, determined, uncompromising, unswerving, undeviating, inexorable; persistent, stubborn, obstinate.

upbraid *v.* reproach, scold, rebuke, reprove, reprimand, censure, chastise, admonish, find fault with; berate, castigate, revile, denounce, tongue-lash, dress down; *Informal* bawl out, *Slang* chew out. **—Syn. Study.** See REPRIMAND. **—Ant.** praise, laud, compliment, commend, applaud, eulogize.

upcoming *adj.* approaching, coming, forthcoming, nearing, pending, prospective, imminent, drawing nigh, nearby, impending, momentary, looming, in the offing. **—Ant.** distant, remote, far-off, postponed, delayed.

update *v.* revise, renew, bring up to date, emend, overhaul, revamp, rework, refurbish, renovate, restore, rejuvenate, streamline, recast, reorganize, touch up, upgrade.

upheaval *n.* **1.** (*variously*) upthrust, volcanic eruption, explosion, blowup, earthquake, quake, flood, tidal wave; cataclysm, catastrophe. **2.** drastic change, disruption, disorder, revolution, disturbance, tumult, turmoil.

uphill *adv.* **1.** up the slope of a hill, upward. *—adj.* **2.** going upward on a hill, ascending, rising, upward. **3.** difficult, arduous, strenuous, hard, tough, exhausting, taxing, toilsome, enervating, tiring, fatiguing, wearisome, wearying, backbreaking, burdensome, onerous.

uphold *v.* **1.** hold up, carry the weight of, support, bear, carry, prop, prop up, sustain, brace, shore, shore up, buttress, bolster, underbrace, underpin, elevate, raise. **2.** support, maintain, sustain, preserve, protect, defend, champion, advocate, stand up for; approve, endorse, confirm, acknowledge, corroborate, encourage.

upkeep *n.* maintenance, operating costs, running expenses, overhead; preservation, sustenance, keep, subsistence, living, support, management.

uplift *v.* **1.** raise, elevate, advance, better, improve, refine, upgrade, cultivate, civilize, edify, inspire. *—n.* **2.** support, lifting, propping, bracing, shoring, buttressing, bolstering, underpinning. **3.** betterment, elevation, advancement, improvement, enhancement, refinement, enrichment, edification, cultivation. **—Ant. 1** degrade, debase; depress, demoralize. **3** degradation, debasement, lowering; dishonor, disgrace, discredit, ignominy.

upper *adj.* **1.** top, topmost, high, higher; superior, greater. **2.** top, elevated, high, superior, eminent, major, important. **3.** northern, more northerly; inland, further from the sea.

uppermost Also **upmost** *adj.* **1.** highest, top, topmost, closest to the top, loftiest, crowning. **2.** most important, greatest, chief, foremost, major, main, principal, predominant, supreme, leading, prime, primary, first, essential, paramount, transcendent, preeminent, highest, dominant. **—Ant. 1** lowermost, lowest, bottom. **2** least, last, lowliest, minor, slightest, unessential, insignificant.

upright *adj.* **1.** erect, vertical, perpendicular, standing-up; upended. **2.** honest, ethical, honorable, moral, principled, trustworthy, upstanding, righteous, reliable, high-minded, good, fair, just, aboveboard, *Slang* on the up-and-up. *—n.* **3.** post, pillar, column, shaft, support, prop, pier, pile, stanchion, standard, strut, rib; stake, picket, pale, pole. **—Ant. 1** horizontal, prone, lying down. **2** dishonest, crooked, unethical, dishonorable, unprincipled, untrustworthy, unreliable, unscrupulous, shady. **3** beam, lintel, transverse.

uprising *n.* rebellion, revolution, revolt, insurrection, insurgence, mutiny; riot, outbreak.

uproar *n.* state of confusion, clamor, agitation, ado, commotion, furor, stir, tumult, turmoil, disturbance, burst of excitement, to-do, pandemonium.

uproarious *adj.* **1.** full of commotion, tumultuous, turbulent, riotous, disorderly, tempestuous, raging, stormy, intense, wild, furious; boisterous, noisy, clamorous, loud. **2.** very funny, hilarious, hysterical, sidesplitting. **—Ant. 1** quiet, calm, peaceful, serene, tranquil, placid. **2** sad, tragic, melancholy, tearful, doleful, gloomy; solemn, grave.

uproot *v.* **1.** pull up by the roots, extirpate, root out; do away with, cast out, banish, destroy, eliminate, abolish, exterminate, annihilate, wipe out. **2.** force to move, force out, displace, dislodge. **—Ant. 1** plant; establish, institute, found, create, form, build; encourage, further, aid, abet.

upset *v.* **1.** overturn, turn over, upend, invert; tip over, topple over, turn topsy-turvy, capsize. **2.** disturb, distress, trouble, grieve, make miserable, annoy, bother, worry, perturb, unnerve, discompose, disconcert, discomfit, agitate, fluster, rattle; anger, enrage, incense, ire, irk, infuriate, pique, vex. **3.** cancel, reverse, change; disorganize, disorder, confuse, muddle, jumble, mix up, turn topsy-turvy. **4.** defeat a favorite, win against the odds; (*loosely*) defeat, beat, be victorious over, overthrow, vanquish, overcome, overwhelm, overpower, conquer, crush, quash, thrash, trounce, demolish, smash. *—adj.* **5.** overturned, turned over, upside-down, upended, inverted, upturned, wrong side up, tipped over, capsized. **6.** disorganized, disordered, disorderly, disarranged, chaotic, confused, jumbled, mixed-up; mussed, messy, disheveled, untidy, slovenly, topsy-turvy. **7.** perturbed, disturbed, distressed, bothered, annoyed, worried, agitated, troubled, grieved, disquieted, unnerved, overwrought, hysterical, angered, enraged, furious, incensed, mad, irked, vexed. **—Ant. 1** right. **2** calm, quiet, pacify, put at ease, comfort. **3** settle, steady, stabilize; organize, order, arrange, straighten. **4** be defeated, lose. **5** right side up. **6** organized, ordered, orderly, well-arranged, neat, tidy, straightened. **7** calmed, quieted, pacified, eased, comforted, composed, placated.

upshot *n.* outcome, result, effect, conclusion, culmination, end, final development, eventuality, consequence; sequel, aftermath, outgrowth, aftereffect, offshoot, *Slang* payoff.

upstanding *adj.* **1.** tall, erect; upright, straight, perpendicular, on end, vertical. **2.** upright, honorable, trustworthy, high principled, virtuous, incorruptible, righteous, good, honest, ethical, moral, truthful, true.

up-to-date *adj.* modern, current, au courant, up-to-the-minute, contemporary, timely, modish, stylish, abreast of the times; *Slang* trendy, today, in. **—Ant.** old-fashioned, out-of-date, passé, dated.

urban *adj.* city, town, metropolitan, municipal, civic, heavily populated; citified, cosmopolitan, sophisticated, worldly-wise.

urbane *adj.* suave, elegant, polished, debonair, smooth, sophisticated, cosmopolitan, civilized, refined, cultivated, gracious, courtly, gallant, genteel, chivalrous, gentlemanly, diplomatic, tactful, politic, courteous, polite, mannerly, civil, well-mannered, well-bred. **—Ant.** crude, coarse, rough, rude, boorish, unrefined, unpolished, uncultivated, unsophisticated, tactless, discourteous, impolite; rustic, cloddish, countrified, provincial.

urchin *n.* young rogue, mischievous boy, whippersnapper, imp, gamin, (*fem.*
) gamine, brat; homeless boy, waif, stray, street youth, young hooligan, young tough, young punk, juvenile delinquent, Slang guttersnipe; boy, lad, laddie, youth, youngster, stripling, young fellow, whelp, young pup. **—Ant.** young gentleman, goody-goody, little Lord Fauntleroy, sissy.

urge *v.* **1.** drive, goad, prod, spur, push, force, press, poke, prick, *Slang* egg on; hasten, speed, accelerate, quicken. **2.** beseech, implore, plead with, exhort, petition, entreat, request, appeal to, supplicate, importune, press, prevail upon, solicit; coax, persuade, convince, sway. **3.** argue for, advocate, recommend, advise, counsel, prescribe, suggest, push for, champion, support strongly, back. **—*n.*** **4.** impulse, desire, yearning, longing, craving, hankering, itch, yen, wish, fancy, hunger, thirst, passion; motive, motivation, reason, incentive, stimulus, drive, provocation, dictate, inducement, prompting, pressure. **—Ant. 1** hinder, hold back, deter, prevent, restrain. **2** order, demand, command, require, force, coerce; discourage. **3** oppose, object to.

urgent *adj.* **1.** pressing, important, serious, requiring immediate attention, compelling, essential, grave, crucial, critical, momentous, weighty; imperative, obligatory, compulsory, necessary, required, indispensable. **2.** earnest, intense, ardent, heartfelt, wholehearted, demanding, insistent, zealous, fervent, passionate, spirited, pleading, beseeching. **—Ant. 1** unnecessary, unimportant, trivial, paltry, insignificant, inconsequential, trifling, facetious. **2** weak, feeble, halfhearted, lukewarm, indifferent, perfunctory, spiritless, laconic, apathetic, impassive, nonchalant, lackadaisical.

usage *n.* **1.** custom, tradition, convention, etiquette, practice, good form, normal procedure, habit, habitude; system, method, mode, manner. **2.** way of using words. **3.** use, treatment, care, handling, operation, employment, manipulation; management, control.

use *v.* **1.** make use of, put to use, operate, employ, work, manipulate, handle, ply, wield; utilize, apply, exercise, exert, resort to, have recourse to, avail oneself of, take advantage of, profit by, capitalize on, make the most of, exploit. **2.** consume, expend, spend; deplete, drain, exhaust, run through, devour, swallow up, sap; squander, waste, dissipate, fritter away, throw away. **3.** treat, behave toward, act toward, deal with; handle, manipulate. **—*n.*** **4.** service, serviceability, operation, usage, usefulness, employment, work, function, enjoyment; application, utilization, handling, exercise. **5.** good, value, worth, profit, benefit, advantage, avail; usefulness, service, help, aid, convenience. **—Syn. Study. 1** USE, UTILIZE mean to put something into action or service. USE is a general word referring to the application of something to a given purpose: *to use a telephone.* USE may also imply that the thing is consumed or diminished in the process: *I used all the butter.* When applied to persons, USE implies a selfish or sinister purpose: *He used his friend to advance himself.* UTILIZE, a more formal word, implies practical, profitable, or creative use: *to utilize solar energy to* *run a machine.* **—Ant. 2** save, conserve, preserve. **4** disuse, unemployment. **5** bad, detriment, disadvantage, loss, drawback, obstacle, hindrance, futility.

useful *adj.* practical, serviceable, functional, utilitarian; helpful, beneficial, advantageous, worthwhile, rewarding, valuable, profitable; effective, convenient, handy, time-saving.

useless *adj.* of no use, unusable, worthless, unserviceable, nonfunctional, unhelpful, ineffectual, impracticable, inadequate, inefficient, incompetent, futile, vain, inefficacious, fruitless, unavailing, unproductive, profitless, bootless. **—Syn. Study.** USELESS, FUTILE, VAIN refer to something that is of no use, value, profit, or advantage. USELESS refers to something of no avail because of the circumstances or because of some inherent defect: *It is useless to reason with him.* FUTILE suggests wasted or ill-advised effort and complete failure to achieve a desired end: *Their attempts to save the business were futile.* VAIN describes something that is fruitless or unsuccessful in spite of all possible effort: *It is vain to keep on hoping.*

usher *n.* **1.** person who escorts people to seats, escort; guide, conductor, leader, director; porter; doorkeeper, gatekeeper. *—v.* **2.** escort, guide, show, conduct, convoy, attend, direct, steer, lead, squire. **3.** herald, introduce, announce, proclaim; precede, preface, inaugurate, launch, *Slang* ring in.

usual *adj.* customary, accustomed, expected, familiar, habitual, normal, wonted, established, well-established; typical, ordinary, routine, common, commonplace, regular, standard, stock, traditional, conventional, orthodox, prescribed, oft-repeated, popular; run-of-the-mill, trite, hackneyed, threadbare. **—Syn. Study.** USUAL, CUSTOMARY, HABITUAL refer to something that is familiar because it is commonly met with or observed. USUAL indicates something that is to be expected by reason of previous experience, which shows it to occur more often than not: *There were the usual crowds at the monument.* CUSTOMARY refers to something that accords with prevailing usage or individual practice: *customary courtesies; a customary afternoon nap.* HABITUAL refers to a practice that has become fixed by regular repetition: *a clerk's habitual sales pitch.* **—Ant.** unusual, uncommon, exceptional, unique, singular, individual, rare, extraordinary, unconventional, unorthodox, novel, new, fresh, one of a kind, out-of-the-way, offbeat, *Slang* far-out.

usually *adv.* **—Syn. Study.** See OFTEN.

usurp *v.* seize illegally, take unlawfully, steal, grab; take for oneself, appropriate, commandeer, preempt, arrogate, encroach upon, infringe upon. **—Ant.** give up, surrender, yield, relinquish, renounce.

utensil *n.* **—Syn. Study.** See TOOL.

utilitarian *adj.* useful, practical, serviceable, functional, pragmatic, sensible; efficient, workable, effective; convenient, handy, usable, beneficial, advantageous, valuable, profitable.

utility *n.* **1.** usefulness, serviceability, use, service, availability, function; benefit, advantage, aid, help, avail, convenience. **2.** public service; (*variously*) gas, electricity, telephone, public transportation. *—adj.* **3.** alternate, substitute, surrogate, secondary; extra, accessory, reserve, additional, backup, supplemental, auxiliary. **—Ant. 1** uselessness, worthlessness, futility, folly; disadvantage, inconvenience, drawback. **3** main, primary, prime, first, first-string, original, basic, essential.

utilize *v.* use, make use of, put to use, employ, take advantage of, turn to account, make the most of, capitalize on, exploit, put into service, bring into play; avail oneself of, profit by, resort to, have recourse to. **—Syn. Study.** See USE.

utmost Also **uttermost** *adj.* **1.** greatest, maximum, highest; foremost, chief, major, main, principal, predominant, paramount, prime, primary, first, leading, sovereign, supreme, preeminent, cardinal, capital. *—n.* **2.** ultimate, last word, best, acme, zenith, peak, tiptop, *Slang* tops, the most.

utopia *n.* ideal life, perfect bliss, supreme happiness; perfect place, heaven, seventh heaven, Erewhon, paradise, Eden, Shangri-la. **—Ant.** hell, hell on earth.

utopian *adj.* idealistic, visionary, impracticable, unrealistic, unfeasible, otherworldly, insubstantial, unrealizable, unworkable, unattainable, unfulfillable. **—Ant.** worldly, realistic, feasible, practicable.

utter[1] *adj.* complete, total, absolute, thorough, downright, outright, out-and-out, sheer, entire, perfect, pure, unrelieved, unqualified, unequivocal, categorical, unmodified, unmitigated, unchecked. **—Ant.** partial, moderate, slight, relative, reasonable, limited, qualified, passable, tolerable.

utter[2] *v.* speak, say, voice, pronounce, articulate, enunciate, vocalize, talk, express, emit, deliver; disclose, reveal, divulge, tell, state, proclaim, declare; mutter, whisper; shout, exclaim, yell.

—**Ant.** be mute, remain silent, keep quiet, keep mum; keep secret, keep confidential, conceal.

utterance *n.* **1.** expression, speech, vocalization, articulation, talk, verbalization, declaration, pronouncement, proclamation. **2.** statement, discourse, talk, word, remark, answer, exclamation, opinion, expression.

utterly *adv.* thoroughly, entirely, fully, completely, totally, wholly, absolutely, perfectly, downright, outright, extremely, just, to the nth degree. —**Ant.** partly, partially, somewhat, moderately, a little, rather, reasonably, passably, tolerably.

uttermost *adj.* **1.** outermost. **2.** utmost, extreme, maximum, sovereign, supreme. —*n.* **3.** utmost, extreme limit, maximum.

vacancy *n.* **1.** empty space, void, gap, opening, hole, hollow, cavity, breach, fissure, crevice. **2.** emptiness, vacantness. **3.** unoccupied place, vacant quarters, room for rent, apartment for rent, house for rent, office for rent, suite for rent; housing, lodging, abode. **4.** unfilled position, available job, opening, situation, place. **—Ant. 2** occupation, occupancy.

vacant *adj.* **1.** unoccupied, empty, unfilled, unused, not in use, for rent, for lease, untenanted, tenantless; deserted, uninhabited, abandoned, forsaken; unfurnished, clear, open. **2.** leisure, unoccupied, free, idle, unemployed, unengaged, unencumbered. **3.** blank, expressionless, uncomprehending, empty, vacuous, vapid, wooden, dull, deadpan, poker-face; incurious, indifferent, unconcerned, oblivious, apathetic, aloof, detached, blasé. **—Ant. 1, 2** occupied, filled, taken, engaged, full, booked-up, crowded, packed. **1** rented, leased, in use, inhabited; crammed, jammed. **2** busy, employed. **3** expressive, comprehending, meaningful, thoughtful, reflective; animated, alert, lively; interested, concerned, engrossed, rapt.

vacate *v.* give up possession of, give up, quit, leave, withdraw from, depart from, evacuate, empty; relinquish, surrender, hand over, resign, abdicate. **—Ant.** occupy, move into, take possession of, fill, possess, employ, retain, keep, hold, hang on to.

vacation *n.* **1.** leave, rest, holidays, intermission; academic intermission, judicial intermission, recess; furlough, *U.S. Military* rest-and-recreation, *Informal* R&R; leave, leave of absence, sabbatical, *French* vacances. *—v.* **2.** take a vacation, be on vacation, pass one's vacation. **—Ant. 1** work time, work; academic year, semester, study time, scholarship, teaching; court session; active duty. **2** work.

vacillate *v.* **1.** waver, be irresolute, hesitate, be unsettled, be doubtful, be changeable, fluctuate, falter, not know one's own mind, shilly-shally, hem and haw, blow hot and cold. **2.** sway, move to and fro, rock, roll, toss, pitch, shift, waver, totter, teeter, reel, oscillate, wobble, flutter, vibrate. **—Syn. Study. 1** See WAVER. **—Ant. 1** be determined, be resolute, be steadfast, be certain, be settled.

vagabond *n.* **1.** wanderer, roamer, rover, rambler, wayfarer, itinerant, floater, drifter, nomad, gypsy, migrant; vagrant, tramp, hobo, beachcomber. *—adj.* **2.** wandering, roaming, roving, rambling, wayfaring, footloose, itinerant, nomadic, journeying, traveling, transient, vagrant, homeless; carefree, bohemian. **—Ant. 1** householder, homebody; worker, businessman. **2** nontraveling, settled, rooted, ensconced, resident.

vagary *n.* whim, caprice, notion, whimsy, fancy, crotchet, impulse, fantasy, daydream, quirk, kink, humor, passing fancy, idiosyncrasy, eccentricity, *Slang* brainstorm.

vagrant *n.* **1.** person with no permanent address, homeless person, bag lady; person with no means of support; itinerant, floater, wanderer, roamer, rover, vagabond, knight-of-the-road, nomad, migrant; tramp, hobo; beggar, panhandler, loafer, bum. *—adj.* **2.** roaming, roving, rambling, wandering, itinerant, peripatetic, nomadic, vagabond; homeless, transient.

vague *adj.* not definite, indefinite, inexplicit, unclear, imprecise, ill-defined, undetailed, uncertain, unsettled, undetermined, confused, unsure, fuzzy, hazy, nebulous, unspecific, unspecified, loose, general, random, casual. **—Ant.** definite, explicit, clear, clear-cut, precise, specific, distinct, well-defined, detailed, express, settled, determined, fixed.

vain *adj.* **1.** proud, too concerned, self-satisfied, self-admiring, conceited, arrogant, puffed-up, vainglorious, pompous, self-important, *Slang* stuck-up; egotistical, boastful, disdainful, cocky, swaggering, dandyish. **2.** unsuccessful, unavailing, useless, futile, fruitless, bootless, ineffectual, ineffective, unprofitable, profitless; nugatory, worthless, trifling, pointless, time-wasting, without merit, idle, foolish, silly, supercilious, superficial. **—Syn. Study. 2** See USELESS. **—Ant. 1** modest, humble, unconcerned, unsatisfied; meek, unsure, shy, bashful. **2** successful, victorious, useful, fruitful, effective, expedient, serviceable; profitable, beneficial, beneficient, worthwhile; serious, substantial, valid, worthy.

vainglorious *adj.* conceited, stuck-up, narcissistic, haughty, affected, egotistical, cocky, swell-headed, boastful, bragging, supercilious, insolent. **—Ant.** humble, shy, reserved, modest, self-effacing.

valedictory *adj.* **1.** farewell, parting,

leave-taking, departing; final, last, terminal, ultimate, conclusive. —*n.* **2.** farewell speech; oration for a graduating class, commencement address.

valiant *adj.* courageous, brave, dauntless, undaunted, intrepid, valorous, heroic, bold, bold-spirited, fearless, unafraid, daring, audacious, unflinching, lionhearted, great-hearted, stout-hearted, stalwart, resolute; chivalrous, gallant, knightly, noble. **—Syn. Study.** See BRAVE. **—Ant.** cowardly, craven, fearful, timorous, timid, afraid, fainthearted.

valid *adj.* **1.** acceptable, suitable, proper, fitting, applicable, effective, accurate, truthful, genuine, sound, well-grounded, well-founded, substantial, realistic, logical, good, convincing, forceful, compelling, decisive, weighty, strong, powerful. **2.** legally binding, having legal force, legal, legalized, lawful, licit, being in effect, official, legitimate, authoritative, authentic, constitutional. **—Ant. 1** unacceptable, unsuitable, improper, unfitting, inapplicable, ineffective, false, inaccurate, untrue, *Informal* phony; bogus, sham, unfounded, baseless, insubstantial, illogical, unrealistic, unforceful, weak. **2** invalid, void, null, inoperative, illegal, unlawful, illicit, unofficial, illegitimate.

validate *v.* make valid, make legally binding, make legal, legalize, make lawful, make official, authorize, certify, stamp, ratify, confirm, countersign, witness, authenticate, verify, corroborate, substantiate, prove, sustain, sanction, warrant; enact, put into effect. **—Ant.** invalidate, cancel, void, annul, terminate.

validity *n.* **1.** soundness, grounds, factual foundation, substance, logic, convincingness, force, weight, strength, power, potency, accuracy, truthfulness, authenticity, conclusiveness; acceptability, suitability, applicability, effectiveness. **2.** legality, legal force, power; authority, authenticity, legitimacy, right, properness. **—Ant. 1** unsoundness, weakness, flaws, lies, falsity, inaccuracy, ineffectiveness. **2** illegality, illegitimacy.

valley *n.* flat region between mountains, river valley, river basin, basin; dell, dale, glade, glen, vale, hollow, bottom, dip, ravine, gully, gulch, gorge, canyon, divide, chasm, water gap, gap, cut. **—Ant.** mountain, mount, peak, cliff, bluff, butte, ridge, hill, hillock, hummock, knoll, rise, height.

valor *n.* bravery, courage, dauntlessness, intrepidity, fearlessness, heroism, boldness, daring, fortitude; mettle, grit, spunk, nerve, guts; pluck, gallantry, chivalry. **—Ant.** cowardice, fear, fearfulness, timidity, pusillanimity, baseness, ignobility.

valuable *adj.* **1.** invaluable, worthwhile, precious, important, significant, priceless, treasured, prized, valued, esteemed, admired, respected; useful, beneficial, helpful, advantageous, profitable, good, fruitful, serviceable, utilitarian. **2.** of great monetary value, costly, expensive, high-priced, dear, precious, priceless. **—Ant. 1** worthless, valueless, unimportant, insignificant, trivial, unesteemed, disliked; useless, pointless, fruitless, unprofitable, silly, trifling. **2** cheap, inexpensive, worthless.

value *n.* **1.** merit, worth, importance, significance, esteem, respect, admiration; prestige, greatness, excellence, superiority; use, usefulness, benefit, help, advantage, profit, service, utility. **2.** worth, monetary worth, face value, market price; amount, cost, charge, rate, appraisal, assessment, estimation. **3. values** ideals, standards, moral code, code of ethics; institutions, customs, rules, beliefs, practices, conventions. —*v.* **4.** assess, assay, appraise, evaluate, set a value on; fix the price of, price, compute; count, weigh, judge, size up, reckon, rate. **5.** regard highly, prize, respect, treasure, esteem, hold in high esteem, cherish, revere, set store by, admire, appreciate. **—Syn. Study. 1** VALUE, WORTH both imply excellence and merit. VALUE is excellence based on desirability, usefulness, or importance; it may be measured in terms of its equivalent in money, goods, or services: *the value of sunlight; the value of a painting.* WORTH usu. implies inherent excellence based on spiritual and moral qualities that command esteem: *Few knew her true worth.* **5** See APPRECIATE. **—Ant. 1** unimportance, insignificance, inferiority; disadvantage, worthlessness, uselessness. **5** disregard, disesteem, misprize, be contemptuous of; undervalue, underestimate.

valued *adj.* highly regarded, esteemed, prized, treasured, respected, cherished, revered, appreciated.

van[1] *n.* large truck, covered truck, truck, wagon, minivan, cart, dray, trailer, *British* lorry; camper, trailer.

van[2] *n.* vanguard, advance guard, avant-garde, forefront, front rank, first line, foremost division, head; front of an army, scout, sentinel, picket.

vandal *n.* willful destroyer, despoiler, saboteur, wrecker, demolisher, barbarian, looter, plunderer, pillager, ravager, raider, marauder.

vanguard *n.* **1.** advance guard, avant-garde, van, front rank, front line, forward troops, foremost division, first line, spearhead, forerank. **2.** avant-garde, forefront, tastemakers, trendsetters, pacesetters, modernists, leaders, leadership, trailblazers, innovators.

vanish *v.* **1.** disappear, become invisible, be lost to sight, dematerialize. **2.** disappear, cease, expire, perish, end, terminate, die, die away, die out, fade, fade away, evaporate, melt away, pass away, dissolve. **—Syn. Study. 1, 2** See DISAPPEAR. **—Ant. 1** appear, loom, come into view; materialize. **2** arrive, commence, begin, start.

vanity *n.* **1.** pride, conceit, self-conceit, self-love, self-admiration, self-praise, narcissism, egotism, vainglory. **2.** lack of real value, worthlessness, uselessness, emptiness, hollowness, inanity, folly, idleness, futility, fruitlessness, unsubstantialness, superficiality, sham, falsity; mirage, delusion. **3.** dressing table, mirror table, makeup table. **4.** compact, vanity case, powder box, vanity bag. **—Syn. Study. 1** See PRIDE. **—Ant. 1** self-hate, self-abasement, masochism; humility, modesty, meekness. **2** value, worth, usefulness, meaningfulness.

vanquish *v.* defeat, conquer, overcome, overpower, crush, overwhelm, triumph over, beat, thrash, best, drub, lick, rout, master, subdue, subjugate, overthrow, get the upper hand over. **—Ant.** be defeated, lose, surrender, capitulate, give up, yield, submit, succumb, bow down, knuckle under.

vapid *adj.* lifeless, dull, flat, insipid, bland, flavorless, empty; tame, uninspiring, unsatisfying, colorless, lame, stale, characterless, wishy-washy, pointless, meaningless. **—Ant.** lively, exciting, inspiring, satisfying, colorful.

vapor *n.* moisture, mist, dew, haze, fog, miasma, steam; smoke, smog; fumes.

variable *adj.* **1.** changeable, changing, shifting, fluctuating, unstable, fitful, spasmodic, fickle, capricious, wavering, inconstant. **2.** indefinite, unsettled, diverse, different, uneven, unlike; alterable, mutable. *—n.* **3.** changeable factor. **—Ant. 1** constant, unchanging, stable, steady. **2** invariable, firm, settled, unalterable, immutable, alike. **3** constant.

variant *adj.* **1.** derived, different, modified, altered, transformed, divergent. *—n.* **2.** variation, different form, modification, alteration, transformation, departure, takeoff. **—Ant. 1, 2** original. **1** basic, fundamental, root, earliest, underived, intrinsic, prime, primary, first, preferred. **2** archetype, prototype, pattern, model, source.

variation *n.* variance, variety, change, difference, diversity, innovation, modification, transformation, alteration, departure, variant, aberration, mutation, metamorphosis; disagreement, discrepancy, divergency, deviation; rate of change, amount of change. **—Ant.** uniformity, sameness, regularity, consistency, permanence.

varicolored *adj.* multicolored, multihued, polychromatic, technicolor, motley, variegated, dappled, mottled, opalescent, iridescent, parti-colored, flecked, marbled, rainbowlike, tartan, piebald, calico. **—Ant.** solid, plain, uniform, monochromatic.

varied *adj.* diversified; diverse, various; assorted, different, miscellaneous, mixed, heterogeneous, sundry, motley, variegated. **—Ant.** uniform, standardized, homogeneous.

variety *n.* **1.** change, diversity, diversification, difference, variation, dissimilarity, nonuniformity, unconformity, innovation. **2.** assortment, medley, miscellany, mixture, collection, mélange, pastiche, motley, multiplicity, heterogeneity, hodgepodge, jumble, hash, patchwork, omnium-gatherum. **3.** kind, type, sort, classification; class, category, breed, strain, stock, species, subspecies, genus, genre, brand, group, division, subdivision, denomination; race, tribe, family. **—Ant. 1, 2** sameness, uniformity, homogeneity, standardization, conformity; similarity, likeness.

various *adj.* **1.** diverse, different, sundry, varied, divers, assorted, distinct, dissimilar, miscellaneous, other. **2.** numerous, many, countless, innumerable, myriad, manifold, multitudinous, multifarious; several, some, few. **—Syn. Study. 1** VARIOUS, DIVERSE, DIFFERENT, DISTINCT describe things that are not identical. VARIOUS stresses the multiplicity and variety of sorts or instances of a thing or class of things: *various kinds of seaweed.* DIVERSE suggests an even wider variety or disparity: *diverse opinions.* DIFFERENT points to a separate identity, or a dissimilarity in quality or character: *two different versions of the same story.* DISTINCT implies a uniqueness and lack of connection between things that may possibly be alike: *plans similar in objective but distinct in method.* **—Ant. 1** same, like, alike, identical, uniform.

varnish *n.* **1.** resin solution; stain, lacquer, gloss. *—v.* **2.** stain, lacquer, gloss. **3.** gilt, embellish, adorn, disguise; mitigate, soften, make allowance for, gloss over, excuse, smooth over; cover, conceal. **—Ant. 3** be frank, be candid, be open; bare.

vary *v.* **1.** change, alter, diversify, modify, shift. **2.** differ, be unlike, contrast, fluctuate, alternate; deviate, diverge, depart, veer; disagree, disaccord, dissent. **—Ant. 1** keep unchanged, keep uniform, regulate, standardize. **2** conform, be uniform, be similar, be alike, be constant, be stable, correspond, harmonize;

agree, comply with, reconcile with, fall in with, go along with.

vast *adj.* extensive, wide, widespread, far-flung, far-reaching, boundless, unbounded, infinite, measureless, immeasurable, unlimited, limitless, endless, interminable, great, immense, huge, enormous, prodigious, tremendous, stupendous, gigantic, colossal, titanic, jumbo, monumental, very large, very big, substantial, significant, monstrous; spacious, capacious, voluminous. **—Ant.** limited, narrow; small, little, tiny; moderate-sized, modest.

vault¹ *n.* **1.** dome, arched roof, arched ceiling, arch; arcade, cupola. **2.** strongroom; wall safe, safe, strongbox. **3.** burial chamber, mausoleum, crypt, sepulcher, tomb; ossuary, catacomb.

vault² *v.* **1.** hurdle, jump, jump over, leap over, spring over, leapfrog, bound, clear; pole-vault. *—n.* **2.** jump, leap, spring, bound, hurdle. **—Ant. 1** crawl under, creep beneath.

vaunt *v.* boast about, brag of, crow about, gloat over, exult in, talk big about, give oneself airs about, blow one's own horn, gasconade; flaunt, swagger, show off, make a display of, strut. **—Ant.** decry, disparage, detract; conceal, repress, suppress, keep quiet about.

veer *v.* change direction, swerve, wheel, turn, zigzag, turn aside, shift, dodge, curve, drift, *Nautical* go about, come round, tack, yaw, jibe. **—Ant.** go straight, go in a straight line, make a beeline for; hold course.

vegetable *n.* edible herbaceous plant; legume, produce, greens.

vegetation *n.* **1.** plant life, plants, flora, shrubbery, foliage, herbage, verdure, flowerage, leaves; grass, weeds, vegetable growth. **2.** inactivity, idleness, loafing, sloth, torpor, lethargy, sluggishness, languor, languidness, indolence, inert existence; dormancy, hibernation, rustication.

vehement *adj.* ardent, fervent, fervid, intense, fierce, passionate, impassioned, emotional, excited, violent, forceful, furious, heated, hot, hotheaded, fiery, frenzied, agitated, stormy, tempestuous; enthusiastic, zealous, vigorous, fanatic, fanatical, rabid, wild, eager, earnest. **—Ant.** indifferent, unconcerned, mild, weak, feeble, lukewarm, halfhearted, dispassionate, apathetic, impassive, subdued, calm, cool, quiet, placid, serene.

vehemently *adv.* ardently, fervently, intensely, passionately, excitedly, violently, furiously, fiercely, hotly, strongly, tempestuously, emotionally; enthusiastically, zealously, vigorously, fanatically, wildly, eagerly, earnestly. **—Ant.** indifferently, mildly, feebly, halfheartedly, impassively, calmly, coolly, quietly.

vehicle *n.* **1.** conveyance, means of transport, transportation; (*variously*) motor vehicle, car, truck, sedan, van, minivan, convertible, sports car, SUV, sport-utility vehicle; bus, train, plane, space vehicle, rocket ship, motorcycle, bicycle, scooter. **2.** medium, means, agent, agency, instrument, tool, device, mechanism, intermediary, organ.

veil *n.* **1.** cloth facial covering; cover, covering, blanket, curtain, cloak, screen, cloud, mantle, shroud. *—v.* **2.** hide, conceal, cover, cloak, mask, screen, shroud, enwrap, envelop; dim, obscure, camouflage. **—Ant. 2** expose, disclose, reveal, show, divulge; unveil, uncover, unwrap, strip, denude.

vein *n.* **1.** blood vessel, capillary. **2.** stratum, stria, layer, seam, lode; streak, line, stripe, thread, rib. **3.** mood, tone, manner, style; nature, character, disposition, complexion, temper, temperament, tendency, inclination, bent, predisposition, propensity, predilection; strain, streak, touch, hint. *—v.* **4.** line, streak, mark, marble, stripe, furrow, rib, web, fleck.

velocity *n.* **1.** rapidity, swiftness, speed, fleetness. **2.** speed, haste, pace, quickness, speediness, celerity, alacrity, fleetness, expedition. **—Syn. Study. 2** See SPEED.

venal *adj.* willing to be bribed, bribable, corruptible, corrupt, unprincipled, unscrupulous, dishonest; greedy, rapacious, avaricious, covetous, grasping, mercenary, money-grubbing, selfish, *Slang* shady, crooked. **—Ant.** unbribable, incorruptible, honest; public-spirited, selfless, altruistic.

vend *v.* peddle, hawk, huckster, sell; retail, merchandise, deal in, trade in, market; auction, trade, barter.

vendor Also **vender** *n.* seller, hawker, peddler, street peddler, huckster, monger, salesman, trader; retailer, wholesaler, dealer, merchandiser, supplier, purveyor; merchant, tradesman. **—Ant.** buyer, purchaser, customer.

veneer *n.* **1.** facing, façade, outer layer, layer, covering, coat, coating, overlay, wrapper, sheath, envelope, casing, jacket. **2.** outward appearance, façade, front, show, mask, pretense.

venerable *adj.* worthy of respect, respected, venerated, revered, august, esteemed, honored, admired; deserving respect because of age, elderly, aged, old, patriarchal, ancient, hoary, white-haired. **—Ant.** dishonorable, disreputable, shameful, ignominious, inglorious, infamous, dishonored, discredited, disgraced; young, youthful, inexperienced, green, callow.

venerate *v.* revere, esteem, respect, honor, admire, idolize, adore, cherish, extol, glorify, look up to, treat with deference, pay homage to, reverence, worship, hallow. **—Ant.** scorn, disdain, contemn, despise, detest, hate, execrate, dishonor; disregard, slight, spurn.

veneration *n.* **—Syn. Study.** See RESPECT.

vengeance *n.* revenge, reprisal, retaliation, avenging, retribution, requital, revengefulness, a tooth for a tooth, an eye for an eye; vindictiveness, malevolence, implacability, ruthlessness.

venial *adj.* forgivable, pardonable, excusable; justifiable, warrantable, allowable, defensible; slight, minor, trivial, unimportant, not serious. **—Ant.** mortal; unpardonable, unforgivable, inexpiable; inexcusable, unwarrantable, unjustifiable, indefensible; flagrant, infamous.

venom *n.* **1.** poisonous fluid; toxin, poison. **2.** hate, hatred, bitterness, ill will, malevolence, maliciousness, malice, animosity, resentment, rancor, rancorousness, spite, spitefulness, acrimony, hostility, enmity, grudge, anger, ire, choler, spleen, gall; savagery, barbarity, brutality. **—Syn. Study. 1** See POISON. **—Ant. 1** antidote, antitoxin. **2** love, affection, friendliness, kindness, sweetness, goodwill, good feeling, amity, brotherly love, benevolence, humanitarianism, charity.

venomous *adj.* **1.** poisonous, noxious, toxic; lethal, deadly, fatal, virulent. **2.** spiteful, malicious, malevolent, resentful, rancorous, hostile, ill-disposed, abusive, malign, malignant; caustic, bitter, vicious, cruel, brutal, savage, bloodthirsty. **—Ant. 1** nonpoisonous, nontoxic. **2** loving, affectionate, friendly, kind, kindly, sweet, genial, benevolent, compassionate, charitable, magnanimous, forgiving.

vent *n.* **1.** opening, outlet, aperture, vent-hole, hole, orifice, air hole; (*variously*) ventilator, chimney, flue, smokestack, spout, pipe; faucet, tap, spigot. **2.** outlet, means of escape, means of exit. **3.** expression, utterance, voice; declaration, disclosure, revelation, exposure. **—*v.* 4.** let out, let escape, serve as an exit for; emit, discharge, release, debouch, escape, pour forth, gush, spout, exude, effuse, drip, ooze. **5.** express, communicate, voice, utter, declare; disclose, reveal, divulge, bare, air. **—Ant. 1** obstruction, closure, stoppage, impediment, check. **4** block, stop, obstruct. **5** suppress, repress, withhold, restrain, inhibit, check, curb, bridle; hide, conceal.

ventilate *v.* **1.** provide with fresh air, circulate fresh air, air, air out; aerate, oxygenate. **2.** make widely known, broadcast, publicize, report, circulate, voice, declare, divulge, disseminate, spread abroad, spread, air, sow, bandy about, noise abroad; discuss, talk about, express, comment on, review, analyze, examine, criticize, dissent.

venture *n.* **1.** endeavor, undertaking, enterprise, project; gamble, risk, adventure, chance, uncertainty, speculation, flyer, plunge. **—*v.* 2.** risk, hazard, dare, chance, gamble, wager, bet, undertake, endeavor, attempt, strive for, try. **3.** advance, put forward, offer, proffer, tender, volunteer, submit, hold out; presume, take the liberty, make free with, make bold. **4.** travel, go, risk going, plunge, take a flyer. **—Ant. 1** certainty, surety, security, stability, reliability; caution, safety, protection. **2** assure, secure, guarantee; save, safeguard, conserve, protect.

venturesome Also **adventuresome** *adj.* **1.** adventurous, ready to take risks, daring, bold, daredevil, audacious, rash, impulsive, impetuous, reckless, foolhardy; enterprising, ambitious, energetic, aggressive. **2.** dangerous, hazardous, risky, perilous, precarious, unsafe; uncertain, insecure, unsure, speculative, doubtful, dubious, questionable, ticklish, tricky. **—Ant. 1** cautious, wary, timid, timorous, apprehensive, fearful, afraid, fearsome; reluctant, adverse, loath, unwilling. **2** safe, protected, guarded; certain, sure, secure, reliable, sound, dependable, stable, trustworthy, infallible.

veracity *n.* truthfulness, adherence to truth, honesty, integrity, probity, candor, frankness, openness, sincerity, guilelessness, ingenuousness; truth, accuracy, correctness, exactness, verity, verisimilitude, exactitude. **—Ant.** untruthfulness, deception, deceit, duplicity, guile, mendacity; lie, falsehood, fiction, fabrication, error.

verbal *adj.* **1.** of words, in words, expressed in words; (*loosely*) oral, spoken, said, voiced, vocal, unwritten, expressed, uttered. **2.** of verbs; derived from a verb.

verbatim *adv., adj.* word for word, exactly, in exactly the same words, letter for letter, chapter and verse; to the letter, literatim; literal, literally, exact, exactly, accurate, accurately, faithful, faithfully, precise, precisely.

verbiage *n.* wordiness, long-windedness, verbosity, verboseness, circumlocution, logorrhea, volubility, grandiloquence, effusiveness, loquacity, prolixity.

verbose *adj.* wordy, long-winded, voluble, circumlocutory, effusive, grandiloquent, prolix, talkative, garrulous, gabby, loquacious; redundant. **—Syn. Study.** See WORDY. **—Ant.** terse, concise, succinct, pithy; reticent, curt, brusque.

verdant *adj.* green, grassy, leafy, shady, turfy, meadowy; lush, luxuriant, blooming, burgeoning, flourishing, thriving; springlike. **—Ant.** fading, waning, dying, withering; autumnal.

verdict *n.* decision, judgment, finding, opinion, determination, ruling, decree, sentence, assessment, estimation, valuation, answer; adjudication, arbitration, arbitrament.

verge *n.* **1.** edge, border, brink, margin, rim, brim, hem, skirt, fringe, lip, ledge, flange; limit, threshold, bound, boundary, frontier, extreme, confine, end, terminus. *—v.* **2.** border, be on the brink, fringe, skirt, edge; be near, approach, approximate. **—Ant. 1** center, middle, midst, heart, depth.

verify *v.* confirm, corroborate, substantiate, attest to, prove, establish, support, sustain; certify, guarantee, validate, authenticate, witness, document, testify to, vouch for, accredit. **—Ant.** disprove, deny, refute, dispute, confute, contradict, controvert, gainsay, discredit; invalidate, subvert, falsify, misrepresent.

veritable *adj.* true, real, genuine, actual, bona fide, valid, authentic, absolute, complete, utter, through-and-through, positive, literal, unquestionable, incontestable, unimpeachable, true-blue. **—Ant.** sham, spurious, feigned, false, deceptive, supposed, questionable, so-called, figurative.

vermin *n. pl.* **1.** noxious animals and birds, varmints, pests; (*loosely*) mice, rats, snakes, wolves, foxes, coyotes, weasels, owls, birds of prey, crows, etc. **2.** pestiferous insects, (*variously*) roaches, lice, fleas, bedbugs, silverfish, centipedes, termites, water bugs, spiders, ants.

vernacular *n.* **1.** common speech, everyday language, slang, natural speech, colloquial speech, informal speech; native language, native tongue, the vulgar. **2.** jargon, lingo, parlance, slang, cant, idiom, dialect, patois, shoptalk. **—Syn. Study. 1, 2** See LANGUAGE. **—Ant. 1** formal speech, educated speech, literary language; foreign language, second language. **2** standard speech, received speech.

vernal *adj.* spring; springlike, fresh, new, green, youthful.

versatile *adj.* **1.** having many abilities, many-sided, all-around, multifaceted, many-skilled, handy, adaptable, resourceful, protean; gifted, talented, accomplished, ingenious, proficient, clever, adroit, apt, able, expert. **2.** having many uses, having many applications. **—Ant. 1, 2** specialized, limited.

verse *n.* **1.** poetry, measure, meter. **2.** little poem, rhyme, jingle. **3.** stanza, stave, strophe; jingle. **4.** Biblical chapter division, passage of Scripture, line of Scripture.

versed *adj.* experienced, practiced, familiar with, having an intimate knowledge of, acquainted with, conversant with, at home with, skilled, skillful, expert, proficient, accomplished, competent, able, adept; schooled, taught, instructed, tutored, well-informed, well-read, enlightened, lettered, learned, scholarly, erudite. **—Ant.** inexperienced, unpracticed, unfamiliar, unacquainted, green, raw, unfledged, callow, unskilled, unaccomplished, incompetent, inept; ignorant, untaught, unschooled.

versifier *n.* rhymer, poetaster, rhymester, versemonger, balladmonger, versemaker, poetling, versesmith, rhymesmith.

version *n.* **1.** account, story, report, description, depiction, interpretation, side. **2.** rendering, adaptation, restatement. **3.** translation, rendering, paraphrase, recreation.

vertical *adj.* **1.** perpendicular, straight up and down, upright, 90-degree, sheer, plumb. *—n.* **2.** perpendicular, upright position, upright. **—Ant. 1, 2** horizontal. **1** level with the ground; prostrate, flat, prone, supine; slanting, sloping, inclined.

vertigo *n.* dizziness, lightheadedness, swimming of the head, giddiness, reeling, unsteadiness, loss of equilibrium; fainting.

verve *n.* liveliness, animation, spirit, vivacity, vitality, sparkle, dash, vigor, energy, vim, élan, zip, gusto, zeal, relish, enthusiasm, eagerness, ardor, fervor, passion, fire, abandon, rapture, feeling, warmth, vehemence, force, drive, punch. **—Ant.** apathy, lethargy, languor, torpor, sluggishness, indolence, indifference, spiritlessness, calmness, halfheartedness, reluctance, dislike, disdain, scorn.

very *adv.* **1.** extremely, exceedingly, especially, unusually, exceptionally, uncommonly, abnormally, terribly, awfully; intensely, deeply, profoundly; definitely, certainly, assuredly, decidedly, unquestionably, emphatically, perfectly, absolutely; really, truly, obviously, undeniably, veritably; remarkably, notably, strikingly, markedly, significantly, eminently; greatly, vastly, hugely, immensely, tremendously, highly, most, much, mighty, quite, extra; completely, totally, entirely, thoroughly, abundantly, excessively, surpassingly, *Informal* real, *Slang* way, *Archaic* passing. **2.** exactly, precisely, actually, really. **—*adj.*** **3.** mere, sheer, bare, plain, simple, pure. **4.** precise, exact, specific, particular; perfect, appropriate, suitable, fitting; necessary, essential.

vessel *n.* **1.** ship, boat, craft; (*variously*) liner, steamship, steamboat, ocean liner, packet, freighter, tanker, collier, tugboat, barge, scow, houseboat, ferryboat, trawler, whaler, sailboat, cruiser, yacht, *French* paquebot. **2.** utensil, receptacle, container; (*variously*) pot, bowl, jug, crock, jar, vase, tub, vat, barrel, keg, cask, butt, caldron; glass, tumbler, cup, mug, carafe, flagon, goblet, beaker, tankard, decanter, flask; platter, dish, plate. **3.** blood vessel, vein, artery, capillary; duct, tube.

vest *n.* **1.** waistcoat, jacket, *Historical* jerkin, doublet. **—*v.*** **2.** dress, robe, attire, clothe, garb, accouter, apparel, array, deck out, fit out, rig; drape, enwrap, envelop. **3.** place in control of, put into the hands of, put in the possession of. **—Ant. 2** divest, strip, unfrock, disrobe, unclothe; uncover, expose, lay bare; dismantle.

vestal *adj.* **1.** chaste, pure, virtuous, virginal; simple, unsophisticated, unworldly; undefiled, immaculate; maidenly, virgin, unmarried. **—*n.*** **2.** virgin, maiden, chaste woman, pure woman.

vested *adj.* permanent, complete, established, fixed, settled, guaranteed, inalienable, indisputable, unquestionable, absolute.

vestibule *n.* entrance hall, entrance way, foyer, entry, lobby, antechamber, anteroom, waiting room, lounge; hall, hallway, corridor, passage, passageway.

vestige *n.* trace, remnant, sign, token, evidence, relic; record, memento, souvenir. **—Syn. Study.** See TRACE.

vestments *n. pl.* ritual garments, official attire, raiment, apparel, dress, garb, costume, outfit, regalia, clothing, clothes, livery, uniform, gear, trappings, accoutrements.

veteran *n.* **1.** expert, master, campaigner, *Informal* old hand, old-timer, vet. **2.** war veteran, ex-serviceman, ex-soldier, old soldier, *Informal* vet. **—*adj.*** **3.** experienced, seasoned, long-practiced. **—Ant. 1, 3** beginner, apprentice, novice, neophyte, tyro, greenhorn, tenderfoot. **2** recruit, raw recruit.

veto *v.* **1.** reject, turn down, turn thumbs down on, deny, negate, nullify, void, enjoin, prevent, forbid, disallow, prohibit. **—*n.*** **2.** rejection, refusal, denial, disallowing, disallowance, prevention, prohibition. **—Ant. 1** ratify, sign into law, approve, endorse, sanction. **2** ratification, signing, approval, endorsement, sanction.

vex *v.* annoy, irritate, nettle, pique, exasperate, anger, irk, chagrin, provoke, rile, miff, ruffle, chafe, fret, ruffle one's feathers, displease, pester, bother, torment, gall, harass, plague, harry, badger; trouble, distress, worry, disturb, upset, grieve, pain, *Slang* hassle, bug. **—Ant.** please, delight, gratify, satisfy; calm, quiet, soothe, placate, pacify, appease, mollify, conciliate.

vexatious *adj.* bothersome, troublesome, pesky, harassing, pestiferous, thorny, troubling, hectoring, badgering, worrisome, annoying, irritating, nettling, provoking, vexing, disquieting. **—Ant.** soothing, calming, pacifying, relaxing.

viable *adj.* **1.** capable of independent life, able to live, able to develop, able to thrive, capable of growing. **2.** workable, practical, practicable, feasible, usable, applicable, adaptable. **—Ant. 1, 2** nonviable. **2** unviable, impractical, useless, unworkable, unusable.

viaduct *n.* overpass, span, ramp.

vial *n.* small medicine bottle, phial; (*loosely*) ampul, ampoule, flask.

vibrant *adj.* **1.** fluttering, vibrating, quivering, pulsing. **2.** bright, brilliant, vivid, colorful, intense, deep, florid, loud, glowing, shimmering, glittering, luminous, lustrous, radiant, resplendent. **3.** resonant, reverberant, resounding, sonorous, deep-toned, orotund, throbbing; bell-like, quivering, pealing, ringing. **4.** vivacious, lively, alive, vital, animated, spirited, electrifying, thrilling, full of vigor, energetic, forceful, vehement, eager, enthusiastic, ardent, fervent. **—Ant. 1** still. **2** dull, drab, grayish; pale, soft, pastel. **3** shrill, piercing, screeching. **4** listless, sluggish, phlegmatic, spiritless, boring, dull.

vibrate *v.* reverberate, quiver, quaver, quake, tremble, flutter, wobble; sway, waver, swing, oscillate, undulate, pendulate; palpitate, throb, pulsate, beat, ripple.

vibration *n.* tremor, quiver, quivering, quake, quaking, trembling, throbbing.

vicarious *adj.* secondhand, indirect, surrogate, sympathetic, at one remove, empathetic, imagined, imaginary, fantasized, mental, by proxy. **—Ant.** firsthand, direct, personal, on-the-spot.

vice *n.* **1.** sexual immorality, debauchery, depravity, corruption, iniquity, wickedness, wantonness, profligacy, degeneracy, licentiousness. **2.** fault, shortcoming, failing, flaw, imperfection, blemish, defect, frailty, foible, weakness, weak point. **—Syn. Study. 2** See FAULT.

—**Ant. 1** virtue, good morals, morality. **2** good point, accomplishment, attainment, strong point, gift, talent, facility, forte.

vice versa *adv.* the other way round, in reverse, in the opposite order, contrariwise, conversely.

vicinity *n.* proximity, neighborhood, region, area, environs, surroundings, precincts, adjoining region, vicinage, propinquity.

vicious *adj.* **1.** ferocious, savage, fierce, violent, dangerous, untamed, wild, predatory, bloodthirsty; cruel, brutal, barbarous, treacherous, ill-humored, ill-tempered, ill-natured, sullen, surly, churlish. **2.** wicked, evil, atrocious, heinous, monstrous, villainous, fiendish, inhuman, foul, gross, base, vile, terrible, awful, bad, nasty, depraved, nefarious, immoral, abominable, offensive, abhorrent, horrid, shocking, diabolical, hellish. **3.** spiteful, malicious, rancorous, mean, nasty, malevolent, venomous, acrimonious, invidious, vindictive, pernicious, hateful, defamatory, libelous, slanderous. —**Ant. 1** tame, friendly, playful, good-humored, good-natured, sweet-tempered. **2** moral, virtuous, righteous, upright, good, noble. **3** sweet, genial, kind, kindly, complimentary, laudatory.

victim *n.* **1.** fatality, dead; casualty, injured, wounded. **2.** quarry, prey, target, dupe, gull, patsy, innocent, sucker, *Slang* mark, pigeon; butt, scapegoat, tool, pawn. —**Ant. 2** offender, culprit, guilty party, crook.

victor *n.* winner, champion, medalist, prizewinner; conqueror, vanquisher.

Victorian *adj.* proper, puritanical, stuffy, straitlaced, prudish, smug, priggish, prim, sanctimonious, narrow, pietistic, insular, hypocritical, conventional, stuffy, tight-laced. —**Ant.** broad-minded, liberal, relaxed, *Slang* laid-back.

victorious *adj.* conquering, winning, triumphant, successful, champion, championship, prizewinning, vanquishing. —**Ant.** defeated, beaten, bested, worsted; conquered, vanquished, overcome, repulsed.

victory *n.* triumph, conquest, success, superiority, supremacy, ascendancy, win; the prize, laurels, the palm. —**Syn. Study.** VICTORY, TRIUMPH, CONQUEST refer to a successful outcome of a struggle. VICTORY suggests the decisive defeat of an opponent in a contest of any kind: *victory in battle; a football victory.* TRIUMPH implies a particularly outstanding victory: *the triumph of a righteous cause; the triumph of justice.* CONQUEST implies the taking over of control by the victor, and the obedience of the conquered: *a war of conquest; the conquest of Peru.* —**Ant.** defeat, loss, failure, overthrow; retreat.

victuals *n.* **1.** food, meals, repast, cooking, cuisine, edibles, comestibles, nourishment, fare, diet, viands, meat, refreshment; *Slang* eats, grub, vittles, chow, feed. **2.** supplies, stores, provisions, groceries, provender, rations, foodstuffs; fodder, forage.

vie *v.* compete, contest, contend, struggle, strive, challenge, fight, be a rival, tilt with. —**Ant.** cooperate, share; negotiate.

view *n.* **1.** look, glimpse, peep, glance, peek, gaze, sight. **2.** range of vision, vision, sight, ken. **3.** prospect, scene, vista, outlook, scenery, panorama, spectacle, perspective, bird's-eye view, landscape, picture, diorama. **4.** opinion, notion, feeling, sentiment, attitude, belief, conviction, conception, thought, theory, judgment. —*v.* **5.** watch, see, look at, witness, observe, behold, eye, take in, scan, glance at, glimpse, note; gaze at, survey, inspect, examine, scrutinize, explore, study, contemplate, pore over. **6.** think about, regard, consider, perceive, judge. —**Syn. Study. 3** VIEW, PROSPECT, SCENE, VISTA refer to whatever lies open to sight. VIEW is the general word: *a fine view of the surrounding countryside.* PROSPECT suggests a sweeping and often distant view, as from a vantage point: *The prospect from the mountaintop was breathtaking.* SCENE suggests an organic unity in the details, as is found in a picture: *a woodland scene.* VISTA suggests a long narrow view, as along an avenue between rows of trees: *a pleasant vista.* **4** See OPINION.

viewpoint *n.* perspective, standpoint, attitude, position, point of view, angle, slant, vantage point, frame of reference, orientation, opinion, bias, conviction, belief, sentiment, feeling.

vigilance *n.* watchfulness, alertness, attention, heedfulness, heed, care, concern, guardedness, carefulness; caution, cautiousness, precaution, prudence, circumspection, forethought. —**Ant.** negligence, neglect, laxity, carelessness, unwariness, inattention, lackadaisicalness.

vigilant *adj.* alert, on the alert, watchful, wide-awake, attentive, heedful, observant, on the lookout; careful, cautious, prudent, guarded, circumspect, wary, chary, on guard, on one's guard, on one's toes, on the qui vive. —**Ant.** negligent, neglectful, lax, slack, remiss, careless, heedless, inattentive, unmindful.

vigor *n.* **1.** energy, vitality, drive, verve, spirit, dash, vim, pep, zip; strength, force, might, power, robustness, hardiness; haleness, stamina. **2.** forcefulness, animation, enthusiasm, verve, vim, spirit, élan, liveliness, vivacity; ardor, fervor, zeal, fire, vehemence, intensity, earnestness, passion. **—Ant. 1, 2** lethargy, apathy, torpor; weakness, feebleness. **1** frailty. **2** calmness, serenity, tranquillity.

vigorous *adj.* energetic, active, dynamic, intense, forceful, vibrant, vital, spirited, ardent, strong, powerful, mighty, sturdy, muscular, brawny, virile, robust, hale, hardy; lusty, bold, aggressive, assertive, lively. **—Ant.** inactive, lethargic, languorous, indolent, apathetic, torpid, spiritless; weak, feeble, frail, effete, enervated.

vile *adj.* **1.** disgusting, offensive, revolting, repugnant, repulsive, repellent, nasty, obnoxious, odious, foul, objectionable, abhorrent, loathsome, unpleasant, bad, awful. **2.** vicious, sordid, gross, base, low, mean, ignoble, nefarious, wretched; wicked, evil, sinful, iniquitous, heinous, abominable, loathsome, ugly, shocking, invidious, contemptible, despicable, shameful, beastly, villainous, hateful, detestable, execrable; immoral, depraved, degenerate, perverted, disgraceful, degrading, humiliating. **3.** vulgar, gross, coarse, filthy, smutty, lewd, obscene, foulmouthed, salacious. **—Ant. 1** pleasant, agreeable, attractive, appealing, appetizing, good, wonderful. **2** honorable, noble, elevated, exalted, sublime, admirable, worthy; moral, upright, righteous, sinless. **3** refined, polite, cultured; delicate, chaste.

village *n.* small town, suburb, municipality, hamlet, burg, farming village, rural community, *Slang* hick town, burg, whistle stop, wide place in the road. **—Ant.** city, big city, metropolis, megalopolis, urban center, metropolitan area.

villain *n.* wicked person, scoundrel, rascal, rogue, knave, rapscallion, varlet, rotter, cad, blackguard, cur, scalawag, snake in the grass, caitiff; evildoer, malefactor, miscreant, transgressor; *Slang* louse, stinker, rat. **—Ant.** hero, protagonist, leading man; gentleman, worthy, champion.

vim *n.* **1.** pep, vigor, energy, vitality, zip, snap, dash, animation, liveliness, vivacity, verve, *Slang* go. **2.** enthusiasm, spirit, zeal, fervor, ardor, intensity, fire, passion, vehemence; drive, power, punch, force; strength, might, potency. **—Ant. 1, 2** lethargy, apathy, torpor.

vindicate *v.* **1.** exonerate, clear, absolve, acquit, discharge, free, excuse, exculpate. **2.** uphold, support, defend, champion, advocate, maintain, assert; justify, bear out, corroborate, substantiate, bolster. **—Ant. 1** blame, accuse, charge; convict. **2** counter, contradict, oppose, refute.

vindictive *adj.* vengeful, revengeful, avenging, punitive, retaliative, retaliatory, unforgiving, spiteful, bitter, malicious, malign, malevolent. **—Ant.** forgiving, relenting, generous, magnanimous.

vintage *n.* **1.** wine of a particular year, grape harvest for a particular year. **2.** date, period, era, epoch. *—adj.* **3.** choice, prime, rare, outstanding, wonderful, fine, superior, excellent, great, sterling, prize. **4.** antique, ancient, old, aged, old-fashioned, out-of-date. **—Ant. 3** bad, inferior, awful, terrible, *Informal* lousy. **4** new, brand-new, modern, up-to-date.

violate *v.* **1.** break, disobey, infringe, contravene, act contrary to, transgress, disregard; trespass, encroach upon, trample on, invade. **2.** profane, desecrate, defile, commit sacrilege, blaspheme, dishonor; abuse, outrage, rape, ravish. **—Ant. 1, 2** respect, honor. **1** obey, uphold. **2** revere; protect, defend.

violation *n.* breach, infringement, infraction, transgression, trespass, encroachment; contravention, nonobservance, abuse; dishonoring, defilement, desecration, sacrilege. **—Syn. Study.** See BREACH. **—Ant.** obedience, compliance, honoring, revering, upholding.

violence *n.* **1.** force, might, power, impact, onslaught; fury, ferocity, rage, fierceness, severity, intensity. **2.** physical force, brutality, bestiality, bloodthirstiness, ferocity, ferociousness, savagery; desecration, profanation, outrage. **—Ant. 1** mildness, weakness, feebleness; calmness. **2** gentleness, tenderness, humaneness.

violent *adj.* **1.** full of force, strong, intense, severe, furious, fierce, raging. **2.** tempestuous, vehement, strong, fierce, furious, ferocious, fiery, hot, passionate, hotheaded, raging, explosive, uncontrollable, ungovernable, unbridled, unruly, intractable, savage, murderous; wild, insane, maniacal, berserk, rampant. **3.** resulting from the use of force, cruel, brutal. **—Ant. 1** mild, weak, feeble. **2** gentle, calm, composed, collected, cool, quiet, serene, tranquil, unruffled, pacific; sane, rational. **3** peaceful.

virago *n.* shrew, scold, nag, termagant, Xanthippe, harpy, vixen, fury, harridan, dragon, gorgon, she-wolf; fishwife, *Slang* battle-ax.

virgin *n.* **1.** maiden, maid, damsel, lass, girl. *—adj.* **2.** unused, untouched, unpolluted, unsullied, uncontaminated; pure, pristine, unadulterated, undefiled, unalloyed, unmixed; chaste.

virile *adj.* male, manly, masculine, manful; vigorous, forceful, masterful, strong, powerful, muscular, robust, mighty, hardy, husky, strapping, brawny; courageous, brave, stouthearted, bold, fearless, undaunted, resolute, stalwart, valiant, heroic, audacious, lusty; potent, capable of fathering children. **—Syn. Study.** See MALE. **—Ant.** effeminate, sissified, unmanly, womanish, emasculate, weak, *Informal* wimpy; impotent, sterile.

virtual *adj.* tacit, implied, indirect, implicit; essential, practical, substantial. **—Ant.** explicit, direct, stated, expressed, definite, emphatic.

virtually *adv.* substantially, practically, in essence, essentially, in effect, to all intents and purposes, in substance, for the most part, for all practical purposes.

virtue *n.* **1.** moral goodness, morality, goodness, righteousness, uprightness, honor, honesty, integrity, probity, high-mindedness, rectitude. **2.** moral quality, moral principle, strength, principle; benefit, advantage, value, reward, strong point, good point, favorable point. **3.** chastity, purity, virginity, innocence, modesty; good behavior, decency. **—Syn. Study. 1** See GOODNESS. **—Ant. 1** vice, wickedness, evil, sinfulness, immorality, badness, dishonor, dishonesty, corruption. **2** weakness, weak point, frailty, failing, defect, deficiency, fault; disadvantage, drawback. **3** unchastity, promiscuousness, promiscuity, immodesty.

virtuoso *n.* expert, master, master hand, genius, artiste, prodigy, *Slang* wizard, whiz.

virtuous *adj.* **1.** morally good, moral, good, righteous, upright, honorable, high-principled; ethical, just; meritorious, praiseworthy, commendable, laudable, exemplary. **2.** chaste, pure, virginal, innocent, continent, unsullied, modest, decent. **—Ant. 1** wicked, evil, sinful, immoral, bad, dishonorable, dishonest, corrupt. **2** unchaste, promiscuous, loose, impure, immodest.

virulent *adj.* **1.** dangerously infectious, deadly, lethal, poisonous, toxic, noxious, venomous, pernicious; hurtful, harmful, deleterious, injurious, unhealthy. **2.** malicious, spiteful, malevolent, rancorous, hostile, vicious, malign, bitter, resentful, acrimonious. **—Ant. 1** harmless, nonpoisonous, nontoxic, innocuous. **2** benign, kind, gentle, sweet, good, friendly, amiable; charitable, sympathetic, compassionate, merciful.

virus *n.* microorganism smaller than a bacterium; (*loosely*) germ, microbe, *Slang* bug.

visage *n.* face, features, countenance; appearance, look, aspect, semblance, image, mien, demeanor, air; profile, physiognomy. **—Syn. Study.** See FACE.

vis-à-vis *adv., adj.* **1.** face-to-face, tête-à-tête, eye to eye, side by side; together, in company; confidentially, privately. *—prep.* **2.** as compared with, in contrast to, as distinguished from, as opposed to.

viscera *n. pl.* intestines, bowels, insides, guts, entrails, *Slang* innards.

viscous *adj.* thick, viscid, sticky, gluey, syrupy, tacky, slimy, gummy, glutinous, *Informal* gooey.

visibility *n.* **1.** capability of being seen, conspicuousness, prominence, discernibleness, clarity, perceptibility, distinctness, definition. **2.** field of observation, range of view, reach of sight; ceiling; horizon.

visible *adj.* **1.** capable of being seen, observable, perceivable, perceptible, discernible, seeable, in sight, in view; clear, distinct, prominent, well-defined, in focus. **2.** plain, manifest, open, unmistakable, inescapable, revealed, salient, glaring, patent, conspicuous, marked, pointed, pronounced, blatant; obvious, noticeable, evident, apparent, palpable. **—Ant. 1, 2** invisible, imperceptible, indiscernible, unapparent; hidden, concealed, obscured, buried.

vision *n.* **1.** eyesight, sight; perception, discernment. **2.** foresight, ability to plan ahead, ability to foresee, imagination. **3.** mental image, concept, conception, idea, notion; dream, daydream, fancy, fantasy, illusion. **4.** apparition, supernatural appearance, materialization, revelation; ghost, phantom, specter. **—Ant. 1** blindness. **2** hindsight; shortsightedness. **3** reality, fact, actuality.

visionary *adj.* **1.** impractical, idealistic, utopian, starry-eyed, dreamy; unreal, imaginative, imaginary, insubstantial, illusory, fanciful, fancied, unfounded, chimerical, delusive. *—n.* **2.** person who has visions, seer. **3.** imaginative thinker, theorist, speculative thinker; dreamer, daydreamer, idealist, romantic, utopian; fanatic, zealot. **—Ant. 1** practical, pragmatic, realistic, hardheaded; substantial, material, real, true, actual, authentic.

visit *v.* **1.** pay a visit to, call on, drop in on, look in on; be a guest of, sojourn at, stay with, go to see. **2.** afflict, affect, befall, happen to, assail, assault, attack, smite, punish, frequent, haunt. *—n.* **3.** stay, call; sojourn.

visitor *n.* caller, guest, house guest, company; sojourner, transient; tourist, vacationer, voyager, sightseer, traveler, journeyer, tripper.

vista *n.* **1.** view, scene, picture, perspective, prospect, outlook; scenery, landscape, panorama. **2.** mental picture, prospect, outlook, vision, view. **—Syn. Study. 1** See VIEW.

visual *adj.* conveying visible information, relating to sight, for the eye, optical, optic, ophthalmic, ocular; visible, noticeable, seeable, observable, perceptible.

visualize *v.* envision, imagine, see in the mind's eye, picture, conceive of; foresee, image, fancy, daydream of, dream of.

vital *adj.* **1.** life, living, animate, vivifying; alive, live, existing, breathing, viable, quick. **2.** lively, energetic, animated, vibrant, dynamic, vigorous, spirited, forceful. **3.** important, significant, critical, crucial, urgent, pressing; serious, essential, necessary, indispensable, requisite, material, chief, basic, fundamental, paramount, cardinal, foremost, primary. **—Ant. 1** dying, dead, inanimate. **2** lethargic, apathetic, torpid, listless, phlegmatic, uninvolved. **3** unimportant, insignificant, trivial, trifling, negligible, nonessential, unnecessary, dispensable, subordinate.

vitality *n.* strength, life force, vital power, dynamism, the vital spark, animal spirits, energy, vigor, *Informal* pep, vim, zip; animation, enthusiasm, vivacity, liveliness, exuberance, ebullience, zest, zeal, verve. **—Ant.** lifelessness, lethargy, torpor, sluggishness, listlessness, apathy.

vitiate *v.* weaken, dilute, thin; pollute, taint, contaminate, adulterate, depreciate, impair; undermine, corrupt, debase, spoil, mar, invalidate, undo; sabotage, injure, obliterate; poison, blight, infect. **—Ant.** strengthen, reinforce, fortify, enhance.

vitriolic *adj.* caustic, acid, acrimonious, acerbic, acerb, cutting, sharp, biting, scathing, withering, hypercritical, abusive, nasty, sarcastic, sardonic, satirical. **—Ant.** kind, sweet, friendly, affable, amiable, sympathetic, compassionate; mild, bland.

vituperation *n.* abuse, faultfinding, invective, scolding, denunciation, censure, blame, tongue-lashing, revilement, obloquy, scurrility, castigation, tirade, calumniation. **—Ant.** praise, acclaim, adulation, flattery.

vivacious *adj.* lively, buoyant, full of life, vital, animated, effervescent, sparkling, bubbling, bubbly, ebullient, sprightly, spirited, active; merry, gay, lighthearted, cheerful, cheery, sunny, bright, genial, convivial, jolly, frolicsome. **—Ant.** lifeless, languid, spiritless, lethargic, listless, impassive, stolid; somber, melancholy, sad.

vivid *adj.* **1.** bright, intense, brilliant, strong, rich, deep, distinct, conspicuous, garish, showy, loud, florid, gay, colorful; shining, shiny, radiant, luminous, luminescent, glowing, lustrous, effulgent, resplendent. **2.** lifelike, true-life, realistic, graphic, descriptive, dramatic, expressive, pictorial, picturesque, moving, stirring; lively, energetic, vigorous. **3.** striking, strong, powerful, remarkable, impressive, astounding, astonishing, marvelous, extraordinary, memorable; clear, distinct, definite, unmistakable, inescapable, forceful, emphatic. **—Ant. 1–3** dull, colorless, pale, drab, vague, indistinct, indefinite, nondescript; weak, faint, dim. **1** pastel; somber. **3** average, usual, unremarkable, everyday, routine, run-of-the-mill.

vixen *n.* **1.** female fox. **2.** ill-tempered woman, quarrelsome woman, fishwife, harridan, shrew, scold, virago, termagant, witch, fury; spirited woman, spitfire.

vocabulary *n.* **1.** word stock, lexicon. **2.** speech, language, vernacular, lingo, tongue, jargon, argot, cant, slang, dialect, patois, phraseology, phrasing, terminology, style, idiom.

vocal *adj.* **1.** of the voice, oral, spoken, voiced, vocalized, uttered, articulated. **2.** sung, for singing; lyric, choral, operatic. **3.** outspoken, plainspoken, blunt, open, frank, forthright, candid, direct, voluble. **—Ant. 1** written; unvoiced, unspoken, unsaid. **2** instrumental. **3** reserved, reticent.

vocalize *v.* **1.** put into words, utter, speak, say, express, articulate, air, vent, ventilate. **2.** sing without words. **—Ant. 1** suppress, pass over in silence, say nothing of, leave unsaid, reduce to silence, hush, hold one's tongue about, keep secret. **2** sing words.

vocation *n.* calling, profession, métier, field, career, line, pursuit, lifework; line of work, occupation, business, trade, job, employment, situation, assignment, task, stint, post, berth; role, station, estate. **—Ant.** avocation, hobby, distraction, diversion, leisure pursuit.

vociferous *adj.* **1.** crying loudly, loud, shouting, loud-voiced, clamorous, noisy, boisterous, uproarious; shrill, piercing. **2.** demanding to be heard, strident, blatant; importunate, vehement; vocal, outspoken. **—Ant. 1** quiet. **2** reticent, soft-spoken, subdued, calm.

vogue *n.* **1.** fashion, style, mode, prevailing taste; rage, fad, trend, craze, the latest thing, the last word, the thing; custom, practice. **2.** popularity, acceptance, popular favor, currency.

voice *n.* **1.** vocal sound, speech, power of speech; mode of speaking, tone, delivery, intonation, modulation, articulation. **2.** right to express an opinion, vote, say, role, part, participation, representation;

will, desire, wish, opinion, choice, preference, option. **3.** singer; (*variously*) tenor, soprano, alto, baritone, mezzo-soprano, contralto, bass; singers. —*v.* **4.** pronounce, articulate, enunciate, vocalize, utter, speak. **5.** state, express, declare, proclaim, announce, communicate, utter, say, air, ventilate, vent, vocalize, divulge, disclose, reveal. —**Ant. 1** dumbness, muteness, speechlessness, voicelessness. **5** keep silent, keep to oneself, keep one's own counsel, be quiet; stifle, suppress.

void *adj.* **1.** devoid, empty, barren, blank, lacking, wanting; vacant, bare, destitute, clear, free; drained, depleted, exhausted, emptied. **2.** invalid, not legally binding, not legally enforceable, not in force, inoperative, null, nugatory. —*n.* **3.** empty space, emptiness, vacuum, vacuity, blank. —*v.* **4.** discharge, evacuate, empty, emit, eject, purge, pass, drain, exhaust, throw out, pour out. **5.** invalidate, revoke, cancel, nullify, annul, abolish, repeal, repudiate, renounce, recant, reverse, countermand, rescind. —**Ant. 1** full, filled, fraught; occupied, cluttered, jammed, mobbed, packed. **2** valid, in effect, binding, enforceable, operative. **4** take in, fill, replenish. **5** validate, enforce; reiterate, strengthen.

volatile *adj.* **1.** evaporating quickly, evaporable, vaporizing, vaporous; gaseous. **2.** explosive, eruptive; unstable, unsettled. **3.** changeable, erratic, unstable, variable, unsteady, irresolute, fitful, spasmodic, unpredictable, undependable, inconstant, capricious, mercurial, temperamental, moody, fickle, flighty, giddy, frivolous; brash, reckless, wild, rash. —**Ant. 1–3** stable. **2** calm, peaceful. **3** constant, consistent, steady, even-tempered, dependable, resolute, determined, coolheaded, self-controlled, serious, sober.

volition *n.* free will, will, choosing, conscious choice, choice, decision, resolution, discretion, option, determination. —**Ant.** coercion, compulsion, duress, force, necessity, unavoidability.

volley *n.* salvo, fusillade, barrage, discharge, broadside, curtain of fire; outburst, burst, outbreak, shower, outpouring.

voluble *adj.* —**Syn. Study.** See FACILE.

volume *n.* **1.** cubic content, space occupied, capacity; measure, size, dimensions, bulk, magnitude, extent, vastness. **2.** quantity, mass, amount, aggregate, heap, abundance. **3.** book, treatise, tract, monograph, quarto, folio; tome, one book of a series. **4.** loudness, sound, amplification.

voluminous *adj.* of great volume, large, extensive, abundant, copious, ample, sizable, massive. —**Ant.** small, minimal, slight, sparse, scant, skimpy, restricted.

voluntary *adj.* **1.** free-will, optional, volunteered, discretionary, noncompulsory, unforced. **2.** deliberate, done consciously, intentional, intended, willed. —**Syn. Study. 2** See DELIBERATE. —**Ant. 1** forced, compelled, compulsory. **2** involuntary, instinctive, unconscious, automatic; unintentional, unpremeditated.

volunteer *n.* **1.** charity worker, unpaid worker, nonprofessional. **2.** enlistee, recruit. —*adj.* **3.** of volunteers, by volunteers; voluntary; unpaid, nonprofessional. —*v.* **4.** offer willingly, offer, express willingness, step forward; take on a task willingly; place at one's disposal; be at one's service. **5.** tell voluntarily, offer willingly, proffer, tender, present, extend, advance, put forward. —**Ant. 1** forced laborer, appointed agent. **2** draftee, conscript. **3** paid, professional; commercial. **4** draft, force, coerce, compel, constrain, necessitate; requisition, levy, confiscate.

voluptuary *n.* sensualist, hedonist, pleasure seeker, seeker of sensual pleasures; high liver, bon vivant, epicure, gourmet, gourmand, gastronome; libertine, debauchee, sybarite, rake, roué, womanizer, seducer. —**Ant.** ascetic, aesthete; self-denier, abstainer.

voluptuous *adj.* **1.** pleasing to the senses, sensuous, sensual; luxurious, soft, smooth. **2.** sensual, pleasure-seeking, pleasure-loving, self-indulgent, hedonistic, sybaritic; erotic, sexual, wanton, fleshly, carnal, licentious, lascivious, lustful, profligate, dissolute, debauched, dissipated. —**Ant. 1** rough, coarse, unpleasant. **2** ascetic, abstinent, abstemious, self-denying, austere, puritanical.

vomit *v.* **1.** throw up, regurgitate, retch, bring up, disgorge, *Informal* puke, *Slang* upchuck, barf, heave, toss one's cookies. **2.** spew forth, eject, emit, expel, belch forth, discharge, disgorge.

voracious *adj.* ravenous, ravenously hungry, edacious, gluttonous; insatiable, greedy, hoggish, omnivorous. —**Ant.** satisfied, satiated, sated, replete; apathetic, indifferent; delicate, dainty, fastidious.

vortex *n.* whirlpool, eddy, maelstrom; whirling mass, whirlwind, cyclone, twister.

votary *n.* devotee, enthusiast, admirer, aficionado, partisan, buff, fan, fanatic, champion, zealot; disciple, follower, adherent, habitué.

vote *n.* **1.** election choice, ballot, selection; expression of opinion, choice, selection, preference, option, decision, determination, judgment, approval, voice, say; ballot, ticket. **2.** election, plebiscite, referendum, poll. **3.** right to vote, suffrage, franchise. **—***v.* **4.** cast a vote, cast a ballot; support by one's vote.

vouch *v.* swear to, attest to, affirm, confirm, guarantee, warrant, endorse, corroborate, verify, certify, witness, attest, authenticate; support, uphold, maintain, sustain, back, back up. **—Ant.** refute, repudiate, deny, abjure, denounce.

vow *n.* **1.** solemn promise, pledge, parole, oath, plight, troth, word, word of honor; solemn promise to God, religious pledge. **—***v.* **2.** promise, pledge, pledge one's word, swear, resolve, contract; declare, assert, affirm, vouch, assure, emphasize, stress.

voyage *n.* **1.** sea journey, cruise, passage, ocean trip, crossing, sail; trip, expedition, pilgrimage. **—***v.* **2.** cruise, sail, navigate, journey by water, travel by water. **—Syn. Study. 1** See TRIP.

voyager *n.* traveler, cruiser, wayfarer, rambler, rover, pilgrim, peregrinator, adventurer, journeyer, tourist, sightseer, excursionist, world traveler, jet-setter; *Slang* globe-trotter. **—Ant.** stay-at-home, recluse, hermit, shut-in.

vulgar *adj.* **1.** lacking good taste, tasteless, coarse, rude, rough, crude, gross, uncouth, low, base; ill-mannered, impolite, boorish, ill-bred, unrefined, uncultivated; indecent, offensive, obscene, pornographic, smutty, dirty, filthy, ribald, off-color, suggestive, risqué. **2.** common, plebeian, proletarian, lowbrow, ordinary. **—Syn. Study. 2** See COMMON. **—Ant. 1** elegant, refined, cultivated, tasteful, polite, mannerly, delicate. **2** aristocratic, noble, highborn, patrician; educated, cultured, highbrow.

vulgarity *n.* **1.** bad taste, tastelessness, coarseness, crudeness, grossness, indecorum, indelicacy; indecency, smuttiness, obscenity, pornography. **2.** ill manners, rudeness, impoliteness, boorishness, lack of refinement. **—Ant. 1** good taste, tastefulness, decorum, delicacy, decency. **2** good manners, politeness, refinement, cultivation, good breeding, sensitivity.

vulnerable *adj.* open to attack, defenseless, unprotected, insecure, undefended, unguarded, exposed, exposed to harm, liable to harm, susceptible; easily hurt, easily wounded, weak, sensitive, thin-skinned. **—Ant.** well defended, protected, guarded, unexposed, invincible, unassailable; impervious, insensitive, thick-skinned.

waddle *v.* wobble, totter, toddle, hobble, sway, wag.

wade *v.* **1.** walk in the water, walk in mud, ford. **2.** trudge, trek, labor, toil, plod, drudge, plow.

waft *v.* float, drift, blow, puff.

wag¹ *v.* **1.** move from side to side, move up and down repeatedly, oscillate, move, stir, wave, shake, waggle, wiggle, jiggle, bob, switch, flutter, flicker, flick, twitch, wigwag. **—***n.* **2.** switch, wave, shake, waggle, wiggle, jiggle, bob, flutter, flick, flicker, twitch, wigwag.

wag² *n.* joker, jokester, jester, clown, comedian, buffoon, life of the party, wit, humorist, farceur, wisecracker, droll, *Slang* card.

wage *n.* **1.** salary, payment, remuneration, compensation, recompense, stipend, emolument, earnings, income, fee, pay, revenue. **—***v.* **2.** carry on, conduct, maintain, undertake, engage in, practice.

wager *n.* **1.** bet; gamble, hazard, speculation; stake, venture, ante; pool, pot, jackpot. **—***v.* **2.** bet, make a bet, venture, hazard, risk, stake; gamble, speculate, take a flyer, tempt fortune, try one's luck. **3.** speculate, guess, hazard an opinion, assume, suppose, presume, imagine, fancy, conjecture, surmise, theorize.

waif *n.* homeless child, foundling, stray, urchin, ragamuffin, gamin, (*fem.*) gamine, guttersnipe, street arab, tatterdemalion, mud-lark.

wail *v.* **1.** utter a long mournful cry, cry, weep, keen, bemoan, moan, groan, lament, bewail; cry out, howl, roar, yell, bellow, bawl, shout, caterwaul, rend the air, whine. **—***n.* **2.** mournful cry, plaint, loud weeping, wailing, keening, moaning, moan, lament, lamentation, groan; outcry, howl, roar, shout, yell, bellow, caterwaul, whine. **—Ant. 1, 2** laugh. **1** be jubilant, be happy, rejoice, celebrate; whisper, murmur. **2** laughter; shout of joy; whisper, murmur.

waist *n.* **1.** middle part, middle, midsection, midriff, mid-region. **2.** waistline, waistband; shirtwaist, blouse, shirt, top, bodice.

wait *v.* **1.** bide one's time, remain inactive, *Informal* take it easy, cool one's heel's, hold one's horses; linger, tarry, dally, remain ready, rest in expectation. **2.** be postponed, be put off, be delayed, be tabled, be shelved, linger, hang fire; delay, stay, postpone, put off, suspend. **—***n.* **3.** delay, suspension, stay, pause, halt, stop, stopover, postponement, deferment, *Law* continuance.

waive *v.* **1.** relinquish a legal right, surrender, give up, give up claim to, forbear, to insist on, yield, forgo, forswear, renounce, disclaim, let go, not use, dispense with. **2.** postpone, defer, put off, put aside, lay over, shelve, table, stay. **—Ant. 1** claim, demand, press, insist on, exact, assert, pursue, maintain, defend. **2** hasten, hurry, speed up.

waiver *n.* relinquishment, disclaimer, renunciation, abdication, abandonment, dismissal.

wake¹ *v.* **1.** awake, awaken, waken, wake up, rouse from sleep. **2.** arouse, rouse, awaken, waken, stimulate, provoke, kindle, fire, stir, excite, enliven, quicken, galvanize, rally; revive, resuscitate. **—***n.* **3.** all-night vigil over corpse before burial, all-night watch over the dead. **—Ant. 1** put to sleep, go to sleep; soothe, quiet, hush. **2** allay, quell, appease, calm; sate.

wake² *n.* wash, track of a vessel, backwash; trail, path, course, train.

wakeful *adj.* **1.** unable to sleep, sleepless, unsleeping, awake, wide-awake, insomniac; restless, astir. **2.** alert, vigilant, watchful, wary, careful, heedful, observant; cautious, circumspect. **—Ant. 1** sleepy, somnolent, drowsy; asleep, sleeping, restful. **2** off-guard, unalert, unvigilant, heedless, unwary.

walk *v.* **1.** proceed by steps, go on foot, travel on foot; stroll, saunter, amble, perambulate, promenade, march, tramp, traipse, trek, trudge, take a turn, *Informal* foot it, go by shank's mare. **—***n.* **2.** stroll, saunter, constitutional, promenade, perambulation, march, trek, hike, journey by foot. **3.** way of walking, gait, step, stride. **4.** place for walking; (*variously*) sidewalk, path, pathway, trail, road, way, lane, promenade, route, passage.

wall *n.* side of a room, partition, divider; side of a building; fence, barrier, confine, barricade, rampart, stockade, parapet, battlement, breastwork, fortification, bastion.

wallop *v.* **1.** hit hard, strike hard, lambaste, clobber, belt, punch, smack, slap, swat, cuff; beat, thrash, pummel, spank, buffet; whip, strap, switch, lash. **2.** beat badly, defeat, trounce, rout, crush, clobber, best, worst, *Slang* lick, trim. **—***n.* **3.** hard blow, punch, hit, smack, whack, cuff, belt, slap, swat.

wallow *v.* **1.** roll in mud, lie in mud. **2.**

luxuriate, indulge, revel, enjoy selfishly, live self-indulgently; bask in, swim in, riot in, feast on, relish.

wan *adj.* **1.** pale, sickly pale, pallid, white, pasty, colorless, livid, sallow, anemic, ashen; cadaverous, ghostly, ghastly. **2.** weak, feeble, sickly, sad, halfhearted, forced, unconvincing, spiritless, vapid, lame, limp, ineffective, ineffectual, unavailing. **—Syn. Study. 1** See PALE. **—Ant. 1** ruddy, rosy, rosy-cheeked, pink-cheeked, florid, flushed. **2** strong, forceful, spirited, convincing, wholehearted, effective.

wand *n.* rod, stick, staff, baton, mace, scepter.

wander *v.* **1.** walk aimlessly, move about aimlessly, roam, ramble, meander, rove, range, prowl; travel, journey, trek, jaunt, *Slang* knock about. **2.** meander, curve, twist, zigzag; swerve, veer, alter course. **3.** stray away, become lost. **—Ant. 1** stay, remain, settle; rest, pause, stop, halt. **2** go straight as an arrow, make a beeline. **3** be found; come home, return.

wanderer *n.* roamer, rover, rambler, nomad, itinerant, vagrant, vagabond, beachcomber, gypsy, hobo, knight of the road; wayfarer, journeyer, traveler, voyager, globe-trotter, gadabout. **—Ant.** homebody, stay-at-home, stick-in-the-mud.

wane *v.* **1.** fade away, fade, decline, dwindle, weaken, decrease, diminish, subside, abate, ebb, lessen; wither, waste, droop, sink. *—n.* **2.** fading away, fading, decline, decrease, dwindling, subsiding, abating, ebbing, lessening, recession, weakening, withering, wasting away. **—Ant. 1** appear, rise, increase, expand, advance, strengthen, grow, develop, wax, improve, flourish, thrive, soar, blossom, brighten. **2** rise, increase, expansion, advancement, strengthening, growth, development, waxing.

wangle *v.* maneuver, finagle, engineer, machinate, manipulate, wheedle, scheme, worm, angle, jockey, trick, intrigue.

want *v.* **1.** desire, wish for, crave, fancy, hope for, long for, yearn for, pine for, covet, hanker for, hunger for, thirst for, hunger after. **2.** seek, search for, hunt; have a warrant for. **3.** need, require, lack, be without; be deficient in, be destitute of, fall short in, come short of. **4.** be needy, have a shortage of, be without, lack. *—n.* **5.** need, necessity, requirement, desire, yearning, craving, wish, requisite, demand. **6.** deficiency, lack, scarcity, shortage, dearth, insufficiency, paucity, need; privation, hunger, hard times; poverty, destitution, impoverishment, pauperism, indigence, penury, pennilessness, impecuniosity, insolvency, straitened circumstances. **—Syn. Study. 3** See LACK. **—Ant. 1** be sated, be satisfied; have, own, possess, enjoy; refuse, reject, decline, repudiate, spurn, relinquish, give up, give away, surrender; loathe, hate, dislike. **6** plenty, abundance, copiousness; sufficiency, adequacy; wealth, opulence, affluence, luxury.

wanting *adj.* deficient, inadequate, substandard, lacking, insufficient; imperfect, defective, short; missing, absent. **—Ant.** adequate, sufficient, passable; perfect, complete, full.

wanton *adj.* **1.** deliberate, willful, malicious, malevolent, unjustified, unprovoked, needless, uncalled-for, groundless, senseless, inconsiderate, heedless, careless, mindless, irresponsible. **2.** loose, of loose morals, immoral, dissolute, fast, debauched, abandoned, promiscuous, unchaste, lewd, lecherous, lustful, libertine, licentious; gross, obscene, bestial. *—n.* **3.** immoral person, dissolute person, lewd person, debauchee, libertine, profligate, voluptuary, sensualist, sybarite; (*of a man*) lecher, seducer, adulterer, fornicator, womanizer, rake, satyr, roué, whoremaster; (*of a woman*) hussy, trollop, slut, strumpet, whore, prostitute, harlot, tart, bawd, chippy, jade, concubine, fornicatrix.

war *n.* **1.** state of armed conflict, armed conflict, warfare, hostilities, military operations, clash of arms; fighting, battle, combat. **2.** fight, struggle, attack, battle, combat, opposition, conflict. *—v.* **3.** wage war, make war, be at war, carry on hostilities, battle with, fight, combat, contend, struggle, clash, exchange shots, declare war, go to war, take up arms, attack, invade, march against. **—Ant. 1** peace, peacetime; neutrality; treaty, armistice, truce, cease-fire. **2** acceptance, approval, assent, compliance, sanction, agreement. **3** make peace, call a truce.

ward *n.* **1.** administrative district, voting district; municipal district, precinct, quarter, zone. **2.** section of a hospital, pavilion; section of a prison. **3.** charge, dependent; protégé. *—v.* **4.** turn aside, turn away, fend off, stave off, keep at bay, block, repel, beat off, defend against, guard against; avert, prevent, thwart, forestall, hold at arm's length.

warden *n.* **1.** chief prison officer, prison superintendent. **2.** keeper, ranger, guard, sentry, watchman, protector, guardian, manager, superintendent, warder, curator.

wardrobe *n.* **1.** collection of clothes, supply of clothing; apparel, clothing, wearing apparel, outfit, attire, togs, garments, habiliments. **2.** clothes closet, clothes cabinet, clothespress, closet; bureau, chest, cedar chest, commode, chiffonier, armoire.

wares *n. pl.* articles for sale, goods for sale, line, merchandise, stock-in-trade, stock, inventory, supplies, staples, commodities.

warfare *n.* state of war, war, armed conflict, hostilities, military operation, clash of arms, fighting, fight, battle, combat, conflict.

warm *adj.* **1.** moderately hot, somewhat hot, lukewarm, tepid, heated, not cold; hot. **2.** providing warmth, warming, keeping in the body's heat. **3.** bright, sunny, vivid, brilliant, glowing. **4.** loving, warmhearted, affectionate, kind, kindly, kindhearted, tender, tenderhearted, sympathetic, compassionate, friendly, outgoing, cheerful, joyful, joyous, pleasant, cordial, happy, affable, gracious. **5.** lively, vigorous, animated, fervent, earnest, passionate, heated, enthusiastic, spirited, intense, vehement. —*v.* **6.** heat, heat up, warm up, warm over, make hot; cook, simmer. **7.** cheer, make joyful, make happy; arouse affection in, arouse sympathy in, thaw, melt. **—Ant. 1–4, 6, 7** cool. **1, 3, 4** cold. **1** chilly, frigid, icy, ice-cold. **3** dull, drab, austere. **4** unfriendly, frigid, remote, standoffish, aloof, haughty; cruel, hardhearted, coldhearted, unsympathetic, uncaring. **5** lethargic, apathetic, torpid, dull, boring. **6, 7** cool off, chill, freeze. **7** alienate; depress, sadden.

warmhearted *adj.* kind, kindly, kindhearted, tenderhearted, sympathetic, compassionate, affectionate, loving, cordial, genial, warm, solicitous. **—Ant.** unkind, coldhearted, hardhearted.

warmth *n.* **1.** warmness, heat, hotness; feeling of being warm, warm sensation. **2.** lovingness, warmheartedness, kindliness, kindness, kindheartedness, tenderness, tenderheartedness, sympathy, compassion, cheerfulness, cheer, joy, joyfulness, cordiality, affability, graciousness, happiness, friendliness. **3.** heat, passion, fire, excitement, spirit, enthusiasm, vehemence, vigor, intensity, animation, earnestness, zeal, fervor, liveliness, verve, ardor. **—Ant. 1, 2** chill, coolness, coldness, iciness. **2** sternness, austerity, severity; frigidity, remoteness, aloofness, unfriendliness. **3** lethargy, apathy, torpor, indifference; insincerity.

warn *v.* alert, forewarn, give warning of danger, alert to danger, put on one's guard, caution, notify, make aware, apprise, signal, inform; advise, counsel, admonish. **—Syn. Study.** WARN, CAUTION, ADMONISH imply attempting to prevent someone from running into danger or unpleasant circumstances. To WARN is to inform plainly and strongly of possible or imminent trouble, or to advise that doing or not doing something will have dangerous consequences: *The scout warned the fort of the attack. I warned them not to travel to that country.* To CAUTION is to advise to be careful and to take necessary precautions: *Tourists were cautioned to watch their belongings.* To ADMONISH is to advise of negligence or a fault in an earnest, authoritative, but friendly way, so that corrective action can be taken: *to admonish a student for constant lateness.*

warning *n.* warning signal, warning sign, alarm, signal, heads-up, forewarning, notice: notification, intimation, hint, sign, token, omen, portent, foretoken, presage; apprisal, advice.

warp *v.* **1.** bend, twist, contort, distort, misshape, deform. **2.** pervert, twist, distort, corrupt, pervert, lead astray, debase, infect; misguide, bias, prejudice, mislead. —*n.* **3.** bend, twist, distortion, contortion, deformation. **4.** quirk, twist, bent, leaning, tendency, disposition, inclination, proneness, propensity, proclivity, predisposition, one-sidedness, partiality. **—Ant. 1** straighten, straighten out, unbend.

warrant *n.* **1.** authorization, permission, permit; license. —*v.* **2.** justify, provide grounds for, give sufficient reason for; permit, authorize, license. **3.** guarantee, certify, vouch for, pledge, swear, attest, affirm, promise, vow, avow, assure, assert, declare, asseverate, aver.

warranty *n.* written guarantee; pledge, agreement, certificate.

warrior *n.* soldier, legionnaire, fighting man, man-at-arms, military man, fighter, combatant; veteran, campaigner.

wary *adj.* cautious, careful, guarded, suspicious, chary, heedful, mindful, watchful, vigilant, on one's guard, alert, wakeful, wide-awake; discreet, circumspect, close-mouthed, prudent. **—Syn. Study.** See CAREFUL. **—Ant.** unwary, unsuspecting, unguarded, rash, reckless, foolhardy, careless, heedless, incautious; negligent, remiss.

wash *v.* **1.** clean with soap and water, clean, cleanse; (*variously*) launder, rinse, scrub, mop, swab, scour, sponge, wipe, rub, bathe, shampoo, lave. **2.** wet, moisten, drench, soak, irrigate, immerse, flood, inundate. **3.** float, be carried by the tide; move by the flow of water, move in waves. —*n.* **4.** washing, cleaning, cleansing: (*variously*) laundering, mopping, scouring, bath, shower, shampoo, ablution, lavation. **5.** laundry, clothes washing; group of things laundered.

waspish *adj.* testy, huffy, fretful, pettish, peevish, irritable, petulant, snappish, fractious, querulous, cantankerous, cranky, crotchety, bearish, ornery, *Brit.* shirty. **—Ant.** good-natured, agreeable, cheerful, genial.

waste *v.* **1.** squander, dissipate, throw away, fritter away, expend needlessly, consume extravagantly, use up fruitlessly, devour, burn up, run through, deplete, empty, drain, exhaust; misuse, use unwisely, misspend, misapply, misemploy. **2.** lay waste, destroy, ruin, devastate, spoil, wreck, demolish, crush, smash, shatter, raze; despoil, ravage, pillage, plunder, loot, sack, strip, rob, prey upon. **3.** fade, dwindle, decline, weaken, decrease, diminish, subside, abate, ebb, wane, wither, crumble, decay; droop, sink, die; disappear, evaporate, melt. *—n.* **4.** waste material, refuse, garbage, trash, rubbish, debris, litter, sweepings, dregs; excrement; offal. **5.** remnants, leftovers, remainders, scraps, leavings. **6.** wastefulness, squandering, extravagance, needless expenditure, prodigality, useless consumption, needless loss; misuse, misapplication, dissipation. **7.** wasteland, barren expanse, emptiness, void; (*variously*) barren, wilderness, desert region, arid region, tundra, steppe, badlands. **8.** destruction, ruin, ruination, devastation, wreck, wrecking, demolition, razing; ravage, despoliation, pillage, plundering, looting, sack, rape. **—Ant. 1** save, conserve, husband, economize; spend wisely, use well. **2** build, rebuild, restore; protect, defend, guard. **3** strengthen, develop, grow, improve, rally, increase, advance. **6** saving, economy, thrift, frugality, conservation.

wasteful *adj.* squandering, prodigal; extravagant, uneconomical, thriftless, unthrifty, spendthrift, improvident. **—Ant.** economical, thrifty, frugal, prudent, unwasteful.

watch *v.* **1.** look, look on, look at, stare, stare at, gaze at, see, eye, keep an eye on, peep at, peer at, ogle; observe, notice, note, pay attention to, attend, mark, regard, rivet one's eyes on, examine, scrutinize, survey, contemplate, pore over. **2.** look out for, be on the lookout, be on the alert, keep an eye out for. **3.** pay attention, be careful, be cautious, be on guard, be wary, take heed, be chary. **4.** look after, look out for, keep an eye on, tend, tend to, care for, take care of, mind, oversee, superintend; save, preserve, protect, guard. *—n.* **5.** eye, surveillance, observance, observation, watchfulness, supervision, superintendence, attention, notice, heed, vigilance; lookout, alert, guard, survey. **6.** watchman, guard, guards, sentry, sentries, sentinel, patrol, foot patrol, patrolman, picket, scout; period of time for standing guard, period of time for being on duty. **7.** wristwatch; pocket watch. **—Ant. 2** overlook, ignore, disregard. **3** be rash, be reckless, be careless. **4** neglect. **5** inattention, disregard, heedlessness.

watchful *adj.* **1.** alert, observant, vigilant, on the lookout, attentive, heedful, aware, mindful, open-eyed, wide-awake. **2.** careful, prudent, cautious, circumspect, wary, guarded, on one's guard, chary, canny, shrewd. **—Ant. 1, 2** careless, inattentive, heedless, unaware, unmindful. **1** unobservant. **2** rash, reckless, unguarded, unwary, thoughtless.

watchman *n.* guard, sentry, sentinel, watch, patrol, foot patrol, patrolman; picket, scout, lookout.

water *n.* **1.** H_2O; drinking water. **2.** body of water; (*variously*) sea, ocean, lake, pond, pool, lagoon, river, stream. *—v.* **3.** supply water to; (*variously*) sprinkle, wet, moisten, damp, dampen, souse, soak, drench, douse, dip, submerge, immerse, splash, irrigate, flood, inundate, deluge. **4.** give water to drink. **5.** add water to, dilute, thin, adulterate, cut. **6.** tear, fill with tears. **—Ant. 2** land, dry land, terra firma. **3** dry, dry up; parch, dehydrate, desiccate; wipe up, sponge, blot, swab.

watery *adj.* **1.** of water, like water, wet, moist, damp, liquid, fluid, aqueous. **2.** thin, diluted, watered, wishy-washy, weak, adulterated. **3.** teary, tearing, tearful, rheumy.

wave *n.* **1.** swell, billow, breaker, comber, whitecap, roller; ripple, undulation. **2.** pulse, pulsation, vibration. **3.** moving row, advancing rank, file, line, string, train, column, tier. **4.** curve, series of curves, curl; coil, winding, spiral, roll, twirl. **5.** salutation, to-and-fro hand gesture of greeting; gesture, gesticulation, hand signal, motion, flourish. **6.** surge, rush, deluge, flood; rise, increase, heightening. *—v.* **7.** move to and fro, flutter, flap, swing, sway, shake, waver, tremble, quiver; oscillate, vibrate, undulate, pulsate; brandish, flourish, wield. **8.** signal, gesture, gesticulate.

waver *v.* **1.** wave, move to and fro, sway, swing, shake, flutter, flap; tremble, quiver, undulate. **2.** totter, reel, stagger, wobble, sway, weave, careen, falter, begin to give way. **3.** falter, be irresolute, be undecided, be undetermined, be doubtful, vacillate, shilly-shally, dilly-dally, hesitate, pause, change, vary, fluctuate, sway. **—Syn. Study. 3** WAVER, VACILLATE refer to an inability to decide or to stick to a decision. WAVER usu. implies a state of doubt, uncertainty, or fear that prevents one from pursuing a chosen course: *He made plans to move but wavered at the last* *minute.* VACILLATE means to go back and forth between choices without reaching a decision, or to make up one's mind and change it again suddenly: *Stop vacillating and set a day.* **—Ant. 3** be resolute, be steadfast, be certain, be determined, be decisive, stand firm.

wavy *adj.* rippling, curved, sinuous, rolling, winding, curvilinear, serpentine, curly, coiled, undulating; tortuous, labyrinthine, meandering, mazelike. **—Ant.** straight, uncurved, unbending, rigid.

wax *v.* grow, become; become larger, enlarge, increase, expand, develop, thrive, extend, widen, become fuller, fill out, swell, dilate, spread out, inflate, puff out, blow up, balloon. **—Ant.** wane, become smaller, diminish, decrease, contract, narrow, deflate.

way *n.* **1.** custom, practice, manner, habit, usage, form; behavior, conduct, nature, wont. **2.** method, means, process, procedure, manner, mode, system, technique, course of action. **3.** direction; neighborhood, vicinity, area, region. **4.** route, course, road, path, pathway, trail, lane, pass, passage; distance. **5.** space, room, room to advance. *—adv.* **6.** away, from this place, off. **7.** far, far off, remotely. **—Syn. Study. 2** See METHOD.

waylay *v.* ambush, fall upon from ambush, lie in wait for, lay a trap for; set upon, assail, assault, attack; lure, entrap, ensnare, decoy, inveigle.

wayward *adj.* **1.** disobedient, unmanageable, ungovernable, incorrigible, intractable, unruly, insubordinate, rebellious, refractory, troublesome; headstrong, self-willed, willful, contrary, perverse, obstinate, stubborn, recalcitrant, balky, mulish. **2.** fitful, erratic, changeable, undependable, inconsistent, inconstant, variable, fluctuating; fickle, restive, mercurial, capricious, whimsical. **—Syn. Study. 1** See WILLFUL. **—Ant. 1** obedient, manageable, docile, malleable, tractable, compliant. **2** steady, fixed, constant, regular, consistent, dependable.

weak *adj.* **1.** lacking strength, weakened, feeble, faint, frail, debilitated; exhausted, spent, wasted, enervated; shaky, unsteady, helpless. **2.** frail, flimsy, unsubstantial, puny, shaky, unsteady, fragile, breakable, brittle, frangible, delicate. **3.** powerless, spineless, cowardly, soft, timorous, irresolute, unmanly, effeminate, namby-pamby, wishy-washy; ineffective, ineffectual, inefficacious, inefficient, unsatisfactory, poor, lame. **4.** vulnerable, exposed, defenseless, assailable, unprotected, unguarded, unsafe, wide open; untenable, unsupported, unconvincing, untrustworthy, lacking. **5.** watery, thin, diluted, adulterated; tasteless, insipid. **—Ant. 1–5** strong. **2–4** strengthened, sturdy, powerful. **1–3** steady. **1** vigorous, hardy, hearty, hale. **2** substantial, sound, solid, hefty; unbreakable; vivid, beaming, radiant, brilliant; ardent, eager. **3** forceful, aggressive, vigorous, energetic; firm, hard, tough, brave, bold, stalwart, staunch, manly; able, capable, potent, effective. **4** solid, sound, substantial, forceful, convincing, trustworthy, valid, good, satisfactory, effective; impregnable, invulnerable, unassailable, well-guarded, protected, safe, secure. **5** potent.

weaken *v.* make weak, impair, undermine, cripple, emasculate, unman, soften, soften up, expose; diminish, lessen, lower, sap, mitigate, moderate, exhaust, waste, devitalize, enervate, dilute, water down, thin, thin out; fail, flag, droop, dwindle, wane, fade, abate. **—Ant.** strengthen, increase, grow, develop, rise, improve, enhance, better; invigorate, energize, revitalize.

weakling *n.* **1.** physically weak person, frail person, feeble person, physical wreck. **2.** weak-willed person, weak sister, coward, sissy, namby-pamby, milksop, pantywaist, jellyfish, mouse, chicken, cream puff, mollycoddle, milquetoast, *Slang* wimp, twit, wuss.

weakness *n.* **1.** feebleness, lack of strength, frailty, debility, debilitation; shakiness, unsteadiness. **2.** fault, defect, deficiency, imperfection, unsubstantiality, lack of force, ineffectiveness, lameness, flimsiness; failing, frailty, foible, vice; vulnerability, susceptibility, unconvincingness, untrustworthiness. **3.** passion, fondness, intense liking, penchant, propensity, proclivity, tendency, inclination, proneness, leaning, prejudice, bias, bent, hunger, thirst, appetite, *Informal* soft spot in one's heart. **—Syn. Study. 2** See FAULT. **—Ant. 1, 2** strength. **1** vigor, vitality, stamina; health, hardiness, soundness, sturdiness; power. **2** force, effectiveness, potency; validity, perfection, soundness, unassailability, impregnability, trustworthiness. **3** dislike, hatred, loathing, aversion, disgust, horror.

wealth *n.* **1.** money, quantity of money, riches, fortune, assets, resources, means, capital, estate, property, goods, chattels. **2.** affluence, prosperity; luxury, luxuriousness, opulence, independence, easy circumstances, easy street. **3.** abundance, profusion, richness, copiousness, plenitude, amplitude, fullness, bounty, fund, store, mine. **—Ant. 2** poverty, penury, pauperism, destitution, indigence, privation, straitened circumstances, want, need, wretchedness. **3** want, lack, dearth, paucity, scarcity, shortage, scantiness, deficiency.

wealthy *adj.* rich, prosperous, affluent, moneyed, well-to-do, well-off, well-heeled, well-fixed, flush, loaded. **—Ant.** poor, impoverished, poverty-stricken, destitute, indigent, needy, down-and-out.

weapon *n.* **1.** arm, armament, instrument of war, lethal instrument, deadly weapon. **2.** defense, protection, guard, countermeasure, safeguard, security, bulwark; offense, offensive, attack; means, measure, resort, resource.

wear *v.* **1.** dress in, clothe oneself in, carry on the person, put on, don, slip on, attire oneself with, fit oneself with, costume oneself, garb oneself, array oneself, wrap, swathe, shroud, swaddle. **2.** wear away, wear out; abrade, rub away, fray, frazzle, shred; erode, wash away; corrode, eat away. **3.** resist abrasion, stand up to wear and tear; last, endure. **4.** exhaust, tire, fatigue, weary, drain; overwork, overburden, tax. *—n.* **5.** wearability, use, service; utility, utilization, employment, application, consumption. **6.** clothing, clothes, apparel, wearing apparel, attire, garments, costumes, togs, duds. **7.** worn place, rubbed place, deterioration, disintegration, disrepair, wear and tear; damage, injury, dilapidation.

wearisome *adj.* tedious, irksome, tiresome, vexatious, annoying, trying, irritating, bothersome, oppressive, burdensome; dreary, boring, dull, monotonous; tiring, exhausting, fatiguing. **—Ant.** agreeable, pleasant, enjoyable, pleasurable.

weary *adj.* **1.** tired, exhausted, fatigued, wearied, spent, worn-out, drained, done in, tuckered out, fagged out, played out, all in, dog tired, ready to drop, *Slang* beat, pooped, bushed; sleepy, drowsy. **2.** tiring, fatiguing, wearying, wearing, tedious, exhausting; boring, monotonous, tiresome, wearisome, humdrum, dull, routine; soporific, somniferous. **3.** tired, sick and tired, impatient, annoyed, dissatisfied; dispirited, discontented, disgusted; bored, blasé, jaded, fed up. *—v.* **4.** tire, tire out, fatigue, exhaust, wear out, play out, fag, tucker; overtax, overwork, overburden. **—Ant. 1** refreshed, revivified, invigorated; energetic, full of pep. **2** easy; refreshing, invigorating; interesting, exciting, amusing, delightful. **3** invigorated, refreshed; delighted, pleased, interested; patient, forbearing. **4** refresh, invigorate, revive; energize, enliven.

weather *n.* **1.** atmospheric conditions; (*loosely*) climate, temperature, clime. *—v.* **2.** expose to weather, dry, season, toughen; bleach, tan; rust, oxidize. **3.** harm by exposure to the weather. **4.** pass through safely, withstand, stand; brave, face, confront. *—adj.* **5.** windward, facing the wind.

weave *v.* **1.** loom, interlace, intertwine, interweave, twist, knit, entwine, braid, lace, plait, crisscross. **2.** interweave, combine, meld, blend, fuse, mingle, incorporate, unify, unite, join, link. **3.** zigzag, wind, curve, meander, writhe, snake, twist and turn. *—n.* **4.** woven pattern; texture. **—Ant. 1** unravel, untwist, disentangle. **2** isolate, segregate; separate, divorce, divide. **3** go straight as an arrow, make a beeline.

web *n.* **1.** spiderweb; cobweb; snare, trap. **2.** webbing, net, netting, mesh, screening, screen, gossamer. **3.** network, tissue, complex, tangle; maze, labyrinth.

wed *v.* **1.** marry, join in marriage, unite in holy wedlock, mate, make one, couple, hitch, tie the knot, splice; take for husband, take for wife, espouse, take for better or worse, lead to the altar. **2.** bind, attach, marry, commit, dedicate, devote, pledge; enamor of, captivate by, fascinate by, win over. **3.** blend, combine, unite, meld, weave, link, fuse, merge, incorporate, unify, tie. **—Ant. 1, 3** divorce, separate. **3** isolate, segregate; unravel, disentangle.

wedded *adj.* **1.** married, united in marriage, marital. **2.** united, joined, bound, tied, connected, linked; fused, merged, unified, incorporated, blended, melded. **3.** devoted, committed, bound, deeply attached, married, pledged. **—Ant. 1, 2** separated, divorced. **1** single, solitary, unwed, unmarried; bachelor, spinster.

wedding *n.* **1.** wedding ceremony, marriage ceremony, marriage, nuptials, nuptial rite. **2.** wedding anniversary; wedding day, marriage day, the big day. **—Ant. 1** separation, divorce.

wedge *n.* **1.** V-shaped block, chock; pie-shaped piece, chunk. *—v.* **2.** split, cleave, rend, rive, force; chock. **3.** cram, jam, stuff, crowd, ram, squeeze, pack, press.

wedlock *n.* marriage, matrimony, holy matrimony, nuptial state.

wee *adj.* tiny, very small, little, minute, minuscule, scant, scanty, *Informal* teeny, teeny-weeny, itty-bitty; diminutive, miniature, microscopic, pocket-size, petite; undersized, dwarf, Lilliputian. **—Ant.** big, large, huge, immense, enormous, gigantic, titanic.

weigh *v.* **—Syn. Study.** See STUDY.

weight *n.* **1.** heaviness, poundage, tonnage, mass, heft, ponderousness; relative density. **2.** load, burden, stress, strain, pressure. **3.** importance, influence, import, magnitude, significance, consequence, value, consideration, emphasis, urgency, concern. *—v.* **4.** add weight to, weigh down, make heavy, make heavier;

ballast. **5.** weigh, weigh down, burden, oppress, encumber, saddle, tax, load. —**Ant. 1** weightlessness. **3** unimportance, insignificance. **4** lighten. **5** buoy, lift up.

weighty *adj.* **1.** heavy, massive, hefty; ponderous, cumbrous, cumbersome, burdensome. **2.** burdensome, onerous, oppressive, crushing, trying, taxing, difficult, arduous, troublesome. **3.** important, significant, consequential, serious, grave, earnest, solemn; substantial, considerable; urgent, crucial, critical, pressing, vital, essential. —**Ant. 1–3** light, lightweight. **2** easy, easy to bear. **3** unimportant, insignificant, inconsequential, trivial, trifling, paltry, slight, frivolous.

weird *adj.* **1.** eerie, mysterious, strange, uncanny, unearthly, spooky, supernatural, ghostly, phantasmal; mystic, magical. **2.** odd, queer, eccentric, bizarre, freakish, grotesque, abnormal, unconventional, unnatural, unorthodox, strange, curious, peculiar, unusual, outlandish, irregular, crazy, wild, *Slang* nutty, kooky, far-out. —**Syn. Study. 1** WEIRD, EERIE, UNCANNY refer to that which is mysterious and apparently outside natural law. WEIRD suggests the intervention of supernatural influences in human affairs: *weird doings in the haunted house; a weird coincidence.* EERIE refers to something ghostly that makes one's flesh creep: *eerie moans from a deserted house.* UNCANNY refers to an extraordinary or remarkable thing that seems to defy the laws established by experience: *an uncanny ability to recall numbers.* —**Ant. 1, 2** natural, normal. **2** usual, everyday, customary, routine, regular, common, familiar, conventional, orthodox, run-of-the-mill, *Slang* square.

welcome *n.* **1.** greeting, salutation, salute; reception. —*v.* **2.** greet, receive, bid welcome, meet; admit, usher in, treat hospitably, offer hospitality to, entertain, do the honors, embrace, hold out the hand to, shake hands with, roll out the welcome mat; receive with open arms, accept eagerly. —*adj.* **3.** gladly received, wanted, accepted, at home, comfortable, hospitably entertained; agreeable, delightful, pleasant, pleasing, gratifying, inviting, engaging, winning, enticing, charming. **4.** given full right to, free to enjoy, admitted; under no obligation. —**Ant. 1** snub, rebuff, cold shoulder, brush-off. **3** unwelcome, unwanted, cold-shouldered, excluded.

welfare *n.* **1.** well-being, happiness, good, good fortune, success, good circumstances, advantage, benefit, profit; health. **2.** relief, public assistance, the dole.

well[1] *n.* **1.** hole drilled in the ground to obtain water, oil, etc. **2.** spring, pool, fountain. **3.** shaft. **4.** store, fund, mine, treasure chest; source, fount, wellspring. —*v.* **5.** pour, flow, stream, surge, issue, run, rise, gush, spurt, spout, spring, jet, ooze.

well[2] *adv.* **1.** [fairly well] satisfactorily, nicely, adequately, acceptably, properly, agreeably; [quite well] successfully, commendably, laudably, advantageously, splendidly, famously, capitally, first-rate; auspiciously, favorably, propitiously. **2.** thoroughly, fully, completely, carefully. **3.** properly, rightly, justly, fairly, correctly, suitably; readily, easily. **4.** favorably, kindly, approvingly, warmly, sympathetically, enthusiastically. **5.** considerably, substantially, amply, abundantly, sufficiently, very much. **6.** intimately, familiarly, personally. —*adj.* **7.** in good health, healthy, strong, robust, vigorous, sound, hale, hearty, in fine fettle, chipper; rosy-cheeked. **8.** good, right, proper, fitting; fortunate. **9.** satisfactory, good, going well, faring well, happy, successful, prosperous, auspicious, felicitous; advantageous, favorable, promising, lucky. —**Ant. 1, 2, 4** badly, poorly. **8, 9** bad. **1** unsatisfactorily, inadequately, imperfectly, unacceptably, unsuccessfully. **2** carelessly, indifferently, sloppily, incompletely. **3** unjustly, unfairly, incorrectly, improperly. **4** unfavorably, unkindly, disapprovingly, unsympathetically; unenthusiastically, mildly, coolly. **5** somewhat, not much, scarcely. **7** sick, sickly, ill, unwell, infirm, diseased, ailing; poorly; weak, feeble, frail. **8** wrong, improper, unfitting, unfortunate. **9** unsatisfactory, going badly, unsuccessful; inauspicious, unfavorable.

well-being *n.* welfare, weal, happiness, felicity, good; success, profit, advantage, benefit, luck, good luck, fortune, affluence, prosperity, ease, comfort; health, wellness.

well-bred *adj.* cultivated, refined, genteel, polite, cultured, polished, urbane, civilized, well-mannered, well-brought-up, gentlemanly, ladylike, gallant, suave, sophisticated. —**Ant.** ill-bred, coarse, vulgar, uncouth.

well-known *adj.* prominent, famous, noted, popular, leading, outstanding, important, famed, celebrated, talked-about, big-time, eminent, illustrious; notorious, infamous, scandalous. —**Ant.** unknown, obscure, nameless, unheard-of.

well-off *adj.* prosperous, moneyed, wealthy, rich, affluent, comfortable, flush, well-fixed, well-to-do, well-heeled, *Slang* loaded. —**Ant.** broke, needy, penniless, indigent, poor.

welt *n.* raised ridge on the skin, wale,

weal, swelling, stripe, streak; lump, bump, mark, bruise, contusion.

welter *v.* **1.** roll, toss, heave, writhe; wallow, grovel, tumble about. —*n.* **2.** jumble, mass, heap, mess, pile, hodgepodge. **3.** confusion, tumult, commotion, turmoil, hubbub, racket, bustle; turbulence, storm, tempest.

wend *v.* direct one's path, proceed on, move along toward, betake oneself, hie to, steer toward, make.

wet *adj.* **1.** wringing wet, soaked, soaking, drenched, dripping, sodden, sopping, waterlogged, watery, soggy, squishy, moist, damp, dampened; dank, humid, clammy. **2.** rainy, showery, stormy. **3.** liquid, liquified, not dry, not dried; not set, not hardened. —*n.* **4.** wetness, moisture, moistness, dampness, dankness, clamminess, condensation, exudation. **5.** rain, rainy weather, rainstorm, storm, bad weather, shower; precipitation, water. —*v.* **6.** moisten, dampen, damp, sprinkle, splash, soak, drench, immerse, submerge, dip, steep; water, irrigate, inundate. **—Ant. 1–3, 6** dry. **1** bone-dry, parched. **3** dried; set, hardened; nonliquid, solid. **4** dryness. **5** dry weather, fair weather, good weather. **6** parch, desiccate, dehydrate, evaporate.

whack *v.* **1.** strike, smack, clout, hit, belt, slug, sock, wallop, slam, smite, pound, baste, slap, cuff, box. —*n.* **2.** hit, blow, smack, clout, knock, belt, sock, wallop, thump, rap, bang; punch, slap, cuff, box. **3.** try, go, attempt, trial, turn, *Slang* crack, stab; endeavor, venture.

wharf *n.* pier, dock, quay, marina, landing, landing dock, slip, jetty, breakwater.

wheedle *v.* coax, cajole, flatter, inveigle, charm, beguile, lure, entice, persuade, induce, *Slang* softsoap, butter up. **—Ant.** force, coerce, bully, browbeat, cow, intimidate, dragoon, bulldoze.

wheel *n.* **1.** disk mounted on an axle; roller, caster, drum. **2.** ring, circle, hoop, round, disk. —*v.* **3.** turn quickly, turn round, pivot, rotate, revolve, spin, swivel, whirl; circle, gyrate, swirl, twirl, pirouette. **4.** roll, push along on wheels.

wheeze *v.* **1.** breathe audibly, breathe with a whistling sound; breathe hard, gasp, puff, huff and puff, pant; hiss, whistle. —*n.* **2.** audible breath, whistling breath, gasp, puff, huffing and puffing, panting; whistle, hiss.

whelp *n.* **1.** pup, puppy; cub. **2.** whippersnapper, cub, urchin, brat, mischievous boy; youngster, lad, youth, stripling, child, kid, boy.

whet *v.* **1.** hone, grind, strop, sharpen, edge, put an edge on. **2.** arouse, excite, stir, awaken, kindle, stimulate, animate, quicken, pique, provoke, induce, tempt, allure, entice, make eager, make avid, make keen. **—Ant. 1** dull, blunt. **2** quench, satisfy, sate, satiate, extinguish, deaden; slake, stifle, damp, dampen, cool.

whiff *n.* **1.** breath, puff, slight gust, draft; zephyr, breeze. **2.** faint smell, scent, odor, aroma, bouquet; sniff, smell, breath; hint, trace, soupçon.

whim *n.* fancy, fanciful notion, notion, quirk, whimsy, caprice, conceit, eccentricity, crotchet; sudden notion, urge, impulse, inspiration, vagary.

whimper *v.* **1.** cry softly, sob brokenly, blubber; whine plaintively, snivel, sniffle, pule. —*n.* **2.** sniveling, whine, sobbing, sob. **—Ant. 1** howl, bawl. **2** howl.

whimsical *adj.* **1.** fanciful, capricious, notional, eccentric, quixotic; fickle, fitful, inconsistent, erratic, changeable, chimerical. **2.** droll, amusing, waggish, fanciful, quaint. **—Ant. 1** staid, serious, sedate, sober, practical, down-to-earth, pragmatic, matter-of-fact; steady, consistent.

whine *v.* **1.** cry plaintively, whimper, snivel, mewl. **2.** complain, grumble, fret, grouse, gripe meekly. —*n.* **3.** whimper, plaintive cry, snivel; wail, moan, cry, sob; murmur, complaint, mutter, grumble. **—Syn. Study. 2** See COMPLAIN.

whip *n.* **1.** horsewhip, rawhide, cowhide, thong, lash, strap, scourge, blacksnake, cat-o'-nine-tails, switch, birch rod, rod, rattan. —*v.* **2.** horsewhip, flog, strap, scourge, lash, switch, birch, cane; flagellate; beat, spank. **3.** trounce, drub, maul, beat decisively, defeat soundly, vanquish, rout, *Slang* lick. **4.** lash, flick, flap; move violently, toss about. **5.** snatch, jerk, whisk, jolt. **6.** beat, beat into a froth, whisk.

whir *v.* **1.** run with a humming sound; drone, hum, buzz, whisper, purr. —*n.* **2.** drone, hum, buzz, whisper.

whirl *v.* **1.** turn, turn round, spin, rotate, revolve; twirl, pivot, gyrate, pirouette, wheel, circle, swirl. **2.** spin, reel; feel dizzy, feel giddy. —*n.* **3.** turning, turn, spin, spinning, rotation, revolving, revolution, twirl, twirling, pivoting, pivot, gyration, pirouette, wheeling, circle, circling, swirling. **4.** rapid round, dizzy round, dizzying succession, flurry, merry-go-round; dither, state of excitement. **5.** try, go, attempt, trial, whack, turn, fling, *Slang* crack, stab.

whirlpool *n.* whirling current, maelstrom, vortex, whirl, swirl, eddy.

whirlwind *n.* **1.** funnel-shaped column of rapidly rotating air; dust spout, waterspout; cyclone, twister. —*adj.* **2.** impetuous, headlong, breakneck, rash, impulsive, short, quick, rapid, swift, hasty.

—**Ant.** **2** long, lengthy, plodding, leisurely; careful, thoughtful, well-considered.

whisk *v.* **1.** brush, sweep lightly, flick. **2.** rush, speed, hasten, move quickly; race, spurt, shoot, tear, fly, whiz, sweep, zip, hurry, scurry, sprint, scoot, dash, bolt, dart, spring, bound, bowl along. **3.** beat, whip. —*n.* **4.** sweep, brush, flick. **5.** wire whisk, omelette whisk, French whisk. —**Ant.** **1** rub, scrape. **2** move slowly, crawl, creep, drag, inch.

whiskey Also **whisky** *n.* **1.** alcohol, liquor, hard liquor, spirits, moonshine, firewater, John Barleycorn, booze; *Slang* sneaky pete, redeye, mountain dew, juice, hooch, rotgut, white lightning, (*variously*) rye, Scotch, Irish, unblended, blended, bourbon, corn, vodka, gin, rum, *Irish & Scottish* usquebaugh, (*loosely*) aqua vitae, aquavit, eau-de-vie. **2.** shot of whiskey, *Informal* shot, *Slang* belt.

whisper *v.* **1.** speak softly, utter under the breath; murmur, mutter, sigh, breathe; confide, speak confidentially. **2.** gossip, make an insinuation, spread rumor, rumor, intimate, hint; reveal, divulge, disclose, tell, blurt, blab, bruit. **3.** rustle, murmur, sigh; drone, hum, buzz. —*n.* **4.** undertone, murmur, mutter; indistinct utterance. **5.** insinuation, innuendo, rumor, piece of gossip, gossip; hint, suggestion, inkling. **6.** rustling sound, rustle, murmur, sigh; drone, hum, purr, buzz. —**Ant.** **1, 4** shout, scream, roar, bellow, yell, cry, whoop. **2** speak out; keep secret, keep confidential, keep under one's hat. **3, 6** roar.

whit *n.* least bit, little bit, speck, mite; dab, drop, dash, pinch, morsel, grain, smidgen, trifle, jot, tittle, dot, iota, modicum, scintilla; fragment, particle, crumb, snip, splinter, chip. —**Ant.** great deal, large amount, lot, heap, scads.

white *adj.* **1.** ivory, ivory-colored, pearl, pearly, snow-white, snowy, alabaster, milk white, cream-colored. **2.** colorless, pale, pallid, blanched, bleached, wan, ashen, ashy, pasty, ghostly, cadaverous, bloodless, sallow, gray, leaden. **3.** gray, silver, silvery, hoary, frosty, snowy, grizzled; cloudy, smoky, filmy, translucent, chalky, milky, off-white. **4.** Caucasian, light-skinned; fair, blond. **5.** harmless, unmalicious, benign, innocent. **6.** pure, spotless, unblemished, unsullied, unstained, unspotted, stainless, clean, immaculate; chaste, innocent, undefiled, virtuous. —**Ant.** **1** black, jet black, jet, coal black, ebony, raven, inky. **2** ruddy, flushed, rosy, rosy-cheeked, red, pink, florid, high-colored. **3** clear, colorless, transparent. **4** black, Negro; red, Indian; yellow, Oriental. **5** harmful, corrupting, sinister, malicious, vicious, venomous, malevolent, malign, pernicious, destructive. **6** evil, wicked, bad, nefarious, notorious; black, blemished, impure, sullied, stained, spotted, tarnished, besmirched.

whiten *v.* **1.** make white, make whiter, color white, frost, silver; clean, bleach, blanch, lighten. **2.** pale, blanch, turn pallid, turn ashen, turn white. —**Ant.** **1** blacken; darken, dull. **2** flush, blush, color.

whitewash *v.* **1.** paint with a mixture of lime and water, calcimine. **2.** excuse, justify, vindicate, absolve, exonerate; play down, downplay, minimize, soft-pedal, cover up, gloss over, glaze over, make allowance for.

whittle *v.* **1.** cut away bit by bit, carve roughly, carve, pare, shave, chip away at. **2.** reduce gradually, lessen the amount of, pare, cut, shave, slash, decrease, shorten, curtail, clip.

whiz *v.* **1.** whistle, swish, sizzle, whir, whine, hiss, buzz, hum, drone. **2.** speed, race, shoot, tear, fly, spurt, zoom, zip, sweep, whisk, scoot, rush, hasten, scurry, scud, scuttle, dash, dart, sprint, bolt, bowl along, make time, make tracks. —*n.* **3.** swish, whistle, whir, whine, hiss, buzz, hum, drone. **4.** *Informal* expert, adept, prodigy, wizard, crackerjack, shark, genius; master, masterhand, skilled hand.

whole *adj.* **1.** entire, complete, full, total, unabridged. **2.** in one piece, entire, undivided, uncut, unbroken; complete, intact, undiminished. **3.** sound, well, healthy, in good health, hale, robust, vigorous; unharmed, uninjured, unbroken, undiminished, perfect. —*n.* **4.** entire amount, total, sum total, aggregate, *Chiefly Brit. Slang* the full monty; bulk, major part, main part, body, essence, quintessence. **5.** totality, entirety, ensemble, unit, system, assemblage, completeness. —**Ant.** **1** partial, incomplete. **2** divided, cut up, cut, broken, fractional. **3** sick, sickly, ill, ailing, unwell, diseased, feeble, faint, frail; injured, hurt, broken, flawed, imperfect. **4, 5** part, piece, segment, division, portion. **5** component, element, constituent; particular, detail, item.

wholehearted *adj.* sincere, unfeigned, true, heartfelt, deeply felt, complete, unreserved, unstinting, earnest, serious, enthusiastic, zealous, emphatic. —**Ant.** halfhearted, lukewarm, faint, indifferent, perfunctory, unenthusiastic.

wholesome *adj.* **1.** healthful, healthy, nutritious, nourishing, health-giving, strengthening, invigorating; sanitary, hygienic. **2.** healthy, hale, sound, well, hardy, vigorous; blooming, rosy-cheeked, clear-complexioned, fresh, chipper, bright-eyed, bright-eyed and bushy-tailed. **3.** morally healthy, moral, honorable, right-minded, responsible, virtuous, upright, nice, decent, pure, clean-minded, clean, innocent, uplifting, worthy, meritorious, exemplary, ethical, honest, principled, dutiful. **—Syn. Study. 1** See HEALTHY. **—Ant. 1–3** unwholesome. **1** unhealthful, unhealthy, pernicious, harmful, detrimental, deleterious, noxious; unsanitary, unhygienic. **2** unhealthy, pale, wan, pallid, ashen, gray; sickly, ailing, diseased, feeble, frail, weak, exhausted, tired. **3** immoral, dishonorable, evil, evil-minded, wicked, sinful, bad, indecent, impure, dirty-minded, filthy, lewd, degrading, unworthy, unethical, dishonest, crooked, unprincipled.

wholly *adv.* entirely, completely, fully, totally, *Latin* in toto; utterly, quite, perfectly, thoroughly, altogether, as a whole, in every respect, from beginning to end. **—Ant.** partially, incompletely, in part, somewhat, imperfectly, in some respects.

whoop *n.* **1.** shout, yell, scream, cry, holler, shriek, roar, bellow, howl, screech, hollo, out-cry, hue and cry; cheer, hurrah. *—v.* **2.** shout, yell, cry, cry out, holler, shriek, screech, scream, howl, roar, bellow, hoot, rend the air; cheer, hurrah; hollo.

whore *n.* prostitute, hooker, woman of ill fame, woman of ill repute, fallen woman, harlot, bawd, hustler, strumpet, trollop, jade, doxy, woman of easy virtue, demimondaine, demirep, lady of the night, fancy woman, painted lady, tart, streetwalker, chippy, call girl, *Slang* pro, prosty; mistress, kept woman, courtesan, concubine; hussy, slut, wanton, tramp. **—Ant.** nice girl, good girl, honest woman, respectable woman, lady.

whorl *n.* spiral arrangement, circular arrangement, spiral, circle, coil, convolution, curl, roll, corkscrew, helix.

wicked *adj.* **1.** evil, sinful, immoral, bad, iniquitous, reprehensible, vile, foul, base, gross, low, heinous, abominable, atrocious, hellish, fiendish, devilish, Satanic, nefarious, cursed, villainous, blackhearted, infamous, vicious, malicious, malevolent, evil-minded, shameful, scandalous, dishonorable, disgraceful, corrupt, depraved, degenerate, monstrous. **2.** naughty, mischievous, rowdy, impish, knavish, rascally, ill-behaved, incorrigible. **3.** intense, severe, serious, acute, fierce, extreme, bad, raging, rampant, awful, dreadful, fearful, painful, bothersome, troublesome, galling. **—Ant. 1** moral, wholesome, upright, righteous, honorable, good, noble, ethical, honest, principled, benevolent, worthy, exemplary. **2** well-behaved, well-mannered, obedient.

wide *adj.* **1.** broad, spacious, large. **2.** broad, extensive, vast, spacious, immense, great, boundless, far-flung, far-reaching, far-ranging, widespread. **3.** large from side to side, ample, roomy, commodious, capacious. **4.** wide open, fully open; expanded, dilated; extended, distended; outstretched, outspread. *—adv.* **5.** fully, completely, as far as possible. **—Ant. 1–4** narrow. **1** long; deep. **2** restricted, constricted, limited, small. **3** tight, cramped, confined. **4** shut, closed, contracted. **5** barely, narrowly; partially.

widen *v.* make wider, broaden, spread, spread out, stretch; enlarge, expand, extend. **—Ant.** narrow, close, take in; reduce, decrease, contract.

widespread *adj.* **1.** affecting a large area, extending far and wide, far-flung, pervasive, far-reaching, extensive, broad; nationwide, worldwide. **2.** wide open, fully extended, outspread. **—Ant. 1** localized, narrow, restricted, confined, limited, small. **2** closed.

wield *v.* **1.** handle, ply, manage, use, utilize, manipulate; brandish, flourish, wave, swing. **2.** exert, exercise, employ, apply, display, put to use, have and use.

wife *n.* spouse, consort, companion, marriage partner; better half, helpmate, mate, helpmeet, rib, squaw, *Dialectal* woman, *Slang* missus, old lady; bride; married woman. **—Ant.** single woman, miss, spinster, old maid.

wig *n.* toupee, hairpiece; *Slang* carpet, rug, topper; fall, switch, wiglet, *Archaic* periwig, peruke.

wiggle *v.* **1.** wag, waggle, shake, twitch, jerk, flutter, quiver; twist, squirm, writhe, wriggle. *—n.* **2.** jerk, twitch, wag, waggle, flutter, shake; squirming, wriggling, writhing.

wild *adj., adv.* **1.** living in a natural state, untamed, undomesticated, unbroken; feral, savage. **2.** uncultivated; without cultivation, naturally, by themselves. **3.** untouched by man, uninhabited, uncultivated, natural; rugged, waste, bleak, desolate, abandoned; wooded, forested, overgrown. **4.** uncivilized, primitive, savage, barbaric; ferocious, fierce; in an uncivilized state, in a primitive state. **5.** violent, furious, tempestuous, blustery, howling; rough, choppy, turbulent; wildly, violently, furiously. **6.** unrestrained, disorderly, undisciplined, ungovernable, lawless, unruly, violent; frantic, frenzied, fanatical, rabid, raging, raving, berserk, crazed, insane, maniacal, mad, demented, unhinged; wildly, without restraint, lawlessly, violently, rampantly, insanely, maniacally, madly. **7.** reckless, rash, uninformed, ill-advised, illogical; impractical, fantastic, bizarre, giddy, flighty, fanciful, madcap, harebrained, rattlebrained, *Slang* nutty, screwball; wide of the mark. —*n.* **8. the wild** or **wilds** wilderness, bush; barren area, wasteland. —**Ant. 1** domesticated, tame, broken. **2** cultivated, planted. **3** populated, inhabited, cultivated; bare, barren. **4** civilized, advanced; friendly. **5, 6** calm, mild, gentle, quiet; calmly, mildly, gently, quietly. **6** well-behaved, orderly, law-abiding, lawful, peaceful; serene, tranquil; rational, sane; politely, peacefully, serenely. **7** careful, thoughtful, well-advised; realistic, practical, logical, intelligent.

wilderness *n.* wild, wilds, bush, unsettled area, remote area; wasteland, waste, barrens, badlands, desert, tundra, desolate tract.

wile *n.* Often **wiles 1.** sly trick, trickery, artifice, ruse, subterfuge, contrivance, machination, chicanery, stratagem, maneuver, ploy, expedient, gambit, trap; cunning, artfulness, craftiness, guile, subtlety. —*v.* **2.** lure, entice, seduce, charm; coax, cajole, persuade. —**Ant. 1** frankness, openness, artlessness, simplicity, candor, straightforwardness, ingenuousness.

will *n.* **1.** willpower, force of will, moral courage, self-discipline, strength of purpose, conviction; determination, resolution, resoluteness; desire, wish. **2.** desire, wish, preference, inclination, pleasure; longing, yearning, craving, hankering. **3.** feeling, personal feeling, disposition, attitude. **4.** last will and testament, testament. —*v.* **5.** be resolved for, resolve, desire, want, wish for, determine upon. **6.** bequeath, endow, bestow, leave as an inheritance, confer, convey at death. —**Ant. 1** irresolution, indecision, vacillation, wishy-washiness, indifference. **2** dislike, hatred, disinclination; loathing, detestation. **5** be irresolute, be indecisive, vacillate.

willful *adj.* **1.** deliberate, purposeful, intentional, intended, planned, premeditated, studied, designed, contemplated. **2.** stubborn, obstinate, unyielding, uncompromising, inflexible, persistent, determined, headstrong, perverse, self-willed, intractable, obdurate, closed-minded, mulish, pigheaded, bullheaded; unruly, ungovernable, undisciplined, wayward. —**Syn. Study. 2** WILLFUL, HEADSTRONG, PERVERSE, WAYWARD refer to a person who stubbornly persists in doing as he or she pleases. WILLFUL implies opposition to those whose wishes, suggestions, or commands ought to be respected or obeyed: *a willful son who ignored his parents' advice.* HEADSTRONG is used in a similar way, but implies foolish and sometimes reckless behavior: *headstrong teens who could not be restrained.* PERVERSE implies stubborn persistence in opposing what is right or acceptable, often with the express intention of being contrary or disagreeable: *taking a perverse delight in arguing with others.* WAYWARD suggests stubborn disobedience that gets one into trouble: *a reform school for wayward youths.* —**Ant. 1** unintentional, unintended, accidental, involuntary, unpremeditated, unplanned. **2** compliant, acquiescent, manageable, submissive, amenable, agreeable; obedient, tractable, docile.

willing *adj.* favorably inclined, content, favorably disposed, amenable, agreeable, responsive, compliant, not averse, game; ready. —**Ant.** unwilling, disinclined, reluctant, loath, averse.

willowy *adj.* gracefully slender, svelte, sylphlike, long-legged, lithe, lissome, supple, limber, pliant, flexible.

willy-nilly *adv.* whether or no, perforce, inevitably, unavoidably, inescapably, compulsively, irresistibly, helplessly, uncontrollably, come what may. —**Ant.** voluntarily, by design, intentionally, deliberately.

wilt *v.* **1.** wither, droop, become limp; shrivel, die. **2.** wither, fade, wane, ebb, recede, subside, sink, dwindle, diminish, languish, decline, weaken, decrease, deteriorate, degenerate, flag, sag.

wily *adj.* devious, sly, cunning, crafty, foxy, tricky, scheming, calculating, designing, intriguing, artful, deceptive, underhand, treacherous, deceitful, guileful, shifty, crooked; shrewd, sharp, alert. —**Ant.** open, candid, frank, sincere, honest, straightforward, aboveboard; innocent, simple, artless, guileless.

win *v.* **1.** be victorious, triumph, prevail, conquer, vanquish, overcome, master, carry all before one, win the day. **2.** earn, gain, attain, achieve, accomplish, realize, acquire, obtain, secure, get, procure, receive, collect, pick up; *Informal* bag, net. **3.** convince, persuade, influence, convert, induce, sway, prevail on, bring round. —*n.* **4.** victory, triumph, success, conquest; winning game, winning contest. —**Syn. Study. 2** See GAIN. —**Ant. 1–3** lose. **1** be defeated, be beaten, fail, miss. **3** alienate, estrange. **4** loss, defeat.

wince *v.* **1.** grimace, make a face, flinch, shudder, draw back, recoil, shrink, quail, cower, cringe. —*n.* **2.** grimace, flinch, shudder, recoil, shrinking, quailing, cowering, cringing. —**Syn. Study. 1** WINCE, RECOIL, SHRINK, QUAIL all mean to draw back from what is dangerous, fearsome, difficult, or unpleasant. WINCE suggests an involuntary contraction of the facial features triggered by pain, embarrassment, or revulsion: *to wince as a needle pierces the skin; to wince at coarse language.* RECOIL denotes a physical movement away from something disgusting or shocking, or a similar psychological shutting out or avoidance: *to recoil at the sight of a dead body; to recoil from the idea of retiring.* SHRINK may imply a fastidious and scrupulous avoidance of the distasteful, or a cowardly withdrawal from what is feared: *to shrink from mentioning a shameful act; to shrink from asking for a raise.* QUAIL often suggests trembling or other physical manifestations of fear: *to quail before an angry mob.*

wind[1] *n.* **1.** air current, breeze, zephyr, draft, gust, blast, whiff, puff, *Regional* air. **2.** heavy wind, windstorm, gale, blow; (*variously*) tornado, twister, cyclone, hurricane, tempest, typhoon, whirlwind. **3. winds** wind instrument, aerophone. **4.** breath, air. **5.** scent, smell; hint, suggestion, inkling, intimation, clue, whisper, information, intelligence, news, knowledge, tidings, report. **6.** empty talk, idle talk, boasting, bombast, bluster, mere words, bluff, braggadocio, fanfaronade, twaddle, *Informal* hot air. **—Syn. Study. 1** WIND, BREEZE, ZEPHYR, GUST, BLAST refer to a current of air set in motion naturally. WIND applies to air in motion, blowing with any degree of gentleness or violence: *a strong wind; a westerly wind.* A BREEZE is usu. a cool, light wind; technically, it is a wind of 4-31 mph: *a refreshing breeze.* ZEPHYR, a literary word, refers to a soft, mild breeze: *a zephyr whispering through palm trees.* A GUST is a sudden, brief rush of air: *A gust of wind scattered the leaves.* A BLAST is a brief but more violent rush of air, usu. a cold one: *a wintry blast.* **—Ant. 1** calm, dead calm, calmness, stillness. **3** brass; percussions.

wind[2] *v.* **1.** curve, bend, snake, wend, sinuate, twist, zigzag, ramble, wander, meander. **2.** coil, twist, curl, loop, twine, entwine, lap, fold; roll, twirl. **—Ant. 1** go straight as an arrow, make a beeline.

window *n.* opening to admit air or light; aperture, orifice, opening; (*variously*) dormer, bay, oriel, casement, transom, skylight, porthole.

windy *adj.* **1.** breezy, blowy, gusty, blustery; windswept. **2.** long-winded, wordy, rambling, meandering, verbose, garrulous, talkative, loquacious, gabby; empty, bombastic, grandiloquent, rhetorical. **—Ant. 1** windless; calm, still. **2** terse, concise, pithy, succinct, pointed, trenchant.

wing *n.* **1.** pinion, pennon, ala; supporting surface, flap, aileron. **2.** section; annex, addition, extension, appendage, adjunct. **3.** side part of a stage, coulisse. **4.** faction, segment, fraternity, group, band, knot, clique, circle, set, coterie. *—v.* **5.** fly, soar, zoom; take wing, take to the air. **6.** hit in the arm, hit in the wing; wound slightly, graze, nick, clip.

winner *n.* victor, champion, master, vanquisher, conqueror, *Slang* champ.

winsome *adj.* charming, engaging, winning, pleasing, attractive, agreeable, likable, amiable, sweet, appealing, comely, endearing, delightful, bewitching, lovable. **—Ant.** dull, boring; disagreeable, unpleasant; ugly, repulsive.

wintry *adj.* cold, frosty, snowy, glacial, icy, chilly, frozen, arctic, polar, Siberian, ice-cold, ice-bound; stormy, bleak, harsh, cheerless, stark, dreary, gloomy. **—Ant.** summery, sunny, bright, warm, balmy.

wipe *v.* **1.** rub lightly; (*variously*) clean, swab, sponge, mop, scrub, scour, rub off; dry, towel; remove, take off, clean off; rub on, apply. **2.** remove, take away from, banish, get rid of, erase, eradicate. *—n.* **3.** swipe, rub, swab, stroke, brush.

wire *n.* **1.** metal thread, metal strand; electric wire, electric cable, filament. **2.** telegraph, cable, radiotelegraph; telegram, cablegram. *—v.* **3.** attach by a wire, fasten with wires, bind with wires; equip with wiring, install wires in. **4.** telegraph, send by telegraph, cable.

wiry *adj.* **1.** resembling wire, wire-like; stiff, brittle, kinky. **2.** sinewy, lean, spare, lanky; strong and supple, agile, limber, pliant.

wisdom *n.* **1.** good judgment, sagacity, understanding, profundity, judiciousness, discernment, comprehension, penetration, apperception, intelligence, brains. **2.** philosophy, teachings, principles. **—Ant. 1** folly, foolishness, stupidity, nonsense, absurdity, senselessness, silliness.

wise[1] *adj.* having good judgment, sagacious, sage, sapient, understanding, profound, judicious, discerning, perceptive, perspicacious, intelligent, knowing, knowledgeable. **—Ant.** foolish, stupid, silly, injudicious, unwise.

wise[2] *n.* way, manner, respect.

wish *v.* **1.** want, desire, hope, long, crave, yearn, pine, hunger, thirst, yen, aspire, set one's heart upon; desire one to have, want to come about. *—n.* **2.** want, desire, hope, longing, craving, yearning, yen, aspiration, ambition; hunger, thirst, appetite, whim, fondness, love, penchant, inclination, leaning, partiality, predilection. **3.** request, command, will, desire, want. **4.** Usu. **wishes** good wishes, best wishes, felicitations, congratulations, compliments.

wishful *adj.* **1.** hopeful, desirous, wanting, keen on, eager, bent upon, anxious, avid, ambitious, expectant, aspiring;

longing, hankering after, craving, yearning, pining, hungering after, thirsting after. **2.** wistful, fanciful, dreamy-eyed, overoptimistic.

wishy-washy *adj.* indecisive, irresolute, shilly-shallying, vacillating, tergiversating, equivocating, wavering, noncommittal, blowing hot and cold, straddling the fence; weak, ineffectual, ineffective. **—Ant.** decisive, resolute, unwavering.

wistful *adj.* **1.** desirous, yearning, longing, craving, hankering, pining. **2.** pensive, sadly thoughtful, reflective, musing, contemplative, meditative, introspective; melancholy, forlorn, sad, sorrowful, woebegone, doleful, mournful, disconsolate.

wit *n.* **1.** cleverness, sense of humor, humor, drollery, levity, jocularity, funniness, waggery, quickness at repartee; brightness, sparkle, vivacity. **2.** raillery, badinage, persiflage, banter, joking, witty sayings, witticisms, quips, jokes, gags. **3.** witty person, humorist, joker, jokester, wag, gagster, comedian, comic, wisecracker, jester, funster, epigrammatist, punster; satirist. **4.** intelligence, understanding, perception, comprehension, judgment, sense, good sense, common sense, wisdom, insight, penetration, perspicacity, acumen, sagaciousness, sagacity, discernment, astuteness, cleverness, shrewdness, cunning, intellect, *Informal* brains. **5. wits** mind, sanity, composure, mental balance, coolheadedness; mental alertness. **—Syn. Study. 1** See HUMOR. **—Ant. 1** seriousness, gravity, solemnity, sobriety, dullness. **4** foolishness, stupidity, silliness, folly, dumbness, obtuseness.

witch *n.* **1.** devil's consort, sorceress, female magician; (*loosely*) seeress, prophetess, enchantress, temptress. **2.** hag, crone, harridan, ugly old woman, battle-ax, beldam, ogress; mean woman, shrew, virago, termagant, scold, fury, vixen.

witchcraft *n.* worship of the Devil, diabolism, the cult of Satan; sorcery, wizardry, necromancy, black magic, black art, witchery, voodoo, voodooism, hoodoo, conjuration, casting of spells, divination, enchantment, fetishism.

withdraw *v.* **1.** remove, take away, take off; extract, unsheathe. **2.** retire, retreat, go away, go, move away, leave, depart, disappear, absent oneself, make oneself scarce, *Slang* vamoose, split. **3.** retract, take back, recant; rescind, recall. **—Ant. 1** put on; put in; sheathe. **2** arrive, come, come near, appear. **3** introduce, propose, advance, offer; repeat, reiterate.

withdrawn *adj.* retiring, reserved, uncommunicative, shy, reclusive, quiet, introverted, unsocial, unfriendly. **—Ant.** boisterous, extroverted, open, outgoing, sociable, friendly, gregarious, warm.

wither *v.* **1.** wilt, droop, shrivel, dry up, fade, dehydrate, desiccate, blast. **2.** shame, cut down, humiliate, blast, abash, mortify. **—Ant. 1** bloom, flower, blossom; flourish, thrive. **2** praise, compliment.

withhold *v.* **1.** hold, hold back, keep back, keep, retain, reserve. **2.** conceal, hold back, keep back, hide, refrain from disclosing, suppress, keep secret, cover up, hush up. **—Syn. Study. 1, 2** See KEEP. **—Ant. 1, 2** give, provide, furnish. **1** grant, bestow, confer, yield, let go; let loose, free, promote, advance, encourage. **2** reveal, disclose, divulge, expose, lay bare.

withstand *v.* stand up to, confront, defy, oppose, resist; endure, bear, suffer, tolerate, weather, brave; grapple with, cope with. **—Syn. Study.** See OPPOSE.

witness *v.* **1.** see firsthand, see, observe, view, behold, look on; note, mark, notice, perceive; attend, be present at. **2.** verify, certify, corroborate, authenticate, substantiate, document, validate, endorse, sign, countersign, initial; attest to, confirm, vouch for, testify to, give testimony of, evidence, establish, bear out. **—*n.* 3.** eyewitness, onlooker, observer, spectator, looker-on, beholder. **4.** person who gives testimony, person who gives evidence, testifier, attester, deponent. **5.** evidence, testimony, proof, confirmation, corroboration, verification, authentication, substantiation, documentation, validation.

witty *adj.* amusing, clever, funny, humorous, quick-witted, comic, jocular, jocose, mirthful, waggish, droll, whimsical; sparkling, bright, scintillating, brilliant. **—Ant.** serious, somber; sententious, dull, dry; sad, melancholy.

wizard *n.* **1.** sorcerer, magician, conjurer, enchanter, medicine man; oracle, seer, soothsayer; necromancer, diviner, clairvoyant. **2.** *Informal* genius, prodigy, expert, adept, virtuoso, *Slang* whiz, shark; sage; wise man.

wobble *v.* **1.** sway, teeter, totter, be unsteady, reel, stagger, waver, shake, quake, shimmy. **—*n.* 2.** sway, swaying, teetering, tottering, unsteadiness, wavering, shake, shaking, shimmy, shimmying, quaking.

woe *n.* suffering, distress, affliction, trouble, misfortune, calamity, adversity, misery, trial, tribulation, wretchedness, torment, agony, torture, sorrow, grief, heartache, anguish, dejection, gloom, anxiety, worry, melancholy, depression, despair. **—Ant.** joy, delight, pleasure, good fortune, happiness, bliss, satisfaction.

woebegone *adj.* woeful, suffering, distressed, troubled, miserable, wretched, agonizing, tortured, sorrowful, doleful, mournful, forlorn, grief-stricken, sad, anguished, dejected, gloomy, funereal, glum. **—Ant.** happy, cheerful, elated, smiling, joyful.

woeful *adj.* **1.** distressing, unhappy, tragic, wretched, agonizing, painful, cruel, sorrowful, doleful, grievous, sad, heartrending, heartbreaking, depressing, crushing, disheartening, lamentable, deplorable, calamitous, disastrous, dreadful, catastrophic. **2.** of very poor quality, unpromising, unlikely, awful, hopeless, terrible, bad, dreadful, horrible, miserable, appalling. **—Ant. 1** happy, joyous, joyful, delightful, glad, heartening, cheering, cheerful, ecstatic. **2** promising, likely, excellent, wonderful, fine.

woman *n.* **1.** adult female, lady; (*variously*) dowager, matron; damsel, maiden, maid. **2.** womankind, women, females, the female sex, the fair sex, the weaker sex. **3.** handmaiden, chambermaid, female attendant, lady-in-waiting, maid, maidservant, housekeeper, cleaning woman, charwoman. **4.** paramour, lover, mistress, concubine, kept woman; sweetheart, ladylove, beloved, darling, inamorata, girl, girlfriend, sweetie, sweetie pie, flame; wife, fiancée, steady girl. **—Syn. Study. 1** WOMAN, FEMALE, LADY are nouns referring to adult human beings who are biologically capable of bearing offspring. WOMAN is the general, neutral term: *a wealthy woman.* In scientific, statistical, and other objective use FEMALE is the neutral contrastive term to MALE: *104 females to every 100 males.* FEMALE is sometimes used disparagingly: *a gossipy female.* LADY in the sense "polite, refined woman" is a term of approval: *We know you will always behave like a lady.* **—Ant. 1–4** man. **1** girl. **3** butler, valet. **4** beau, boyfriend, *Slang* John; husband, fiancé.

womanish *adj.* **—Syn. Study.** See WOMANLY.

womanlike *adj.* **—Syn. Study.** See WOMANLY.

womanly *adj.* feminine, female; mature, adult, fully developed; alluring, sexy, attractive, seductive. **—Syn. Study.** WOMANLY, WOMANLIKE, WOMANISH mean having traits or qualities considered typical of or appropriate to adult human females. WOMANLY, a term of approval, suggests such admirable traits as self-possession, modesty, and motherliness: *a womanly consideration for others.* It also suggests the full expression of sexual maturity in a female, either in appearance or in behavior, esp. when the behavior is taken to be the natural outcome of sexual ripeness: *a tall, womanly figure; practicing her womanly wiles.* WOMANLIKE may be a neutral synonym for WOMANLY, or it may convey mild disapproval: *womanlike tears and reproaches.* WOMANISH is usu. disparaging. Applied to women, it suggests traits not socially approved: *a womanish petulance;* applied to men, it suggests traits not culturally acceptable for men but (in what is rejected as a sexist notion) typical of women: *a womanish shrillness in his speech.* See also FEMALE.

wonder *v.* **1.** be curious about, be inquisitive; speculate, conjecture, question, be doubtful, be uncertain; meditate, ponder, cogitate. **2.** marvel, be wonderstruck, stand agog, be awed, be amazed, be dazed, be stunned, be stupefied, be dumbstruck, be surprised, be flabbergasted, gape, stare. **—*n.*** **3.** phenomenon, marvel, miracle, wonderwork, rarity, spectacle, sight. **4.** amazement, astonishment, wonderment, awe, fascination, stupefaction. **—Ant. 1** know, be sure, be certain, comprehend, understand, perceive, see, fathom, figure out; ignore, not care, be uninterested. **2** be unfazed, be unmoved, accept matter-of-factly. **3** common occurrence, commonplace, cliché. **4** apathy, unconcern, indifference; boredom.

wonderful *adj.* **1.** causing wonder, awe-inspiring, miraculous, amazing, incredible, phenomenal, fabulous, fantastic, unique, singular, extraordinary, astonishing, astounding, staggering, fascinating, striking, surprising, spectacular. **2.** excellent, admirable, marvelous, magnificent, good, fine, great, terrific, first-rate, capital, tiptop, smashing, super, sensational, fabulous, fantastic, superb, divine, *Informal* crackerjack, *Slang* def, phat, jiggy. **—Ant. 1** ordinary, common, usual, mediocre, average, modest, paltry, indifferent, uninteresting. **2** awful, terrible, bad, dreadful, abominable, miserable, appalling, horrid, unpleasant, unpleasing, *Slang* lousy, godawful.

woo *v.* **1.** court, pay court to, seek the love of, seek the favors of, pay one's addresses to, pursue, chase, set one's cap for. **2.** try to persuade, solicit, petition, solicit the approval of, court, appeal to, pursue, address, sue, cajole, importune, entreat, curry favor with, *Slang* butter up.

wood *n.* **1.** lumber, timber, boards, planks, siding, wallboard, clapboard; log, firewood, kindling. **2.** *Usu.* **woods** forest, timberland, woodland, wildwood, bush, brush, grove, copse, thicket, brake. —**Ant. 2** prairie, grasslands, savanna, tundra, meadow, moor, mesa, desert, clearing.

wooden *adj.* **1.** made of wood, wood, frame. **2.** stiff, rigid, unbending, inflexible, awkward, clumsy, ungainly, ungraceful. **3.** expressionless, dull, vacant, lifeless, unemotional, impassive, deadpan, poker-faced, glassy-eyed. —**Ant. 2** lissome, supple, limber, lithe, pliant, pliable, flexible, graceful. **3** expressive, animated, lively, spirited, emotional, passionate, fervent.

woozy *adj.* giddy, befuddled, lightheaded, muddled, faint, dizzy, fuzzy, hazy, foggy, shaky, punch-drunk, punchy. —**Ant.** clearheaded.

word *n.* **1.** meaningful combination of letters, articulate sounds, unit of discourse; term, expression, locution, appellation, designation, sobriquet. **2.** brief statement, remark, comment, utterance, phrase, pronouncement. **3.** short talk, chat, brief conversation, discussion, conference, consultation, audience, interview, tête-à-tête, chitchat, dialogue, discourse, colloquy. **4. words** angry words, argument, quarrel, dispute, bickering, wrangling, altercation, contention, *Informal* set-to. **5.** message, communication, news, information, report, advice, tidings, intelligence; dispatch, bulletin, communiqué, letter, telegram, telephone call; rumor, gossip, hearsay, *Slang* scuttlebutt, tittle-tattle, poop, dirt, lowdown. **6.** assurance, promise, word of honor, pledge, vow, avowal, assertion, declaration. **7.** command, order, direction, decree, notice, summons, dictate, edict, mandate; decision, ruling, ultimatum; signal. —*v.* **8.** phrase, put into words, find words for, express, articulate, voice, describe, explain.

wording *n.* phrasing, phraseology, manner of expression, choice of words, language.

wordy *adj.* verbose, long-winded, windy, loquacious, garrulous, talkative, discursive, mumbling, roundabout, prolix, redundant, tautological; grandiloquent, bombastic, turgid, fustian, gushing, effusive, rhetorical. —**Syn. Study.** WORDY, VERBOSE, PROLIX, REDUNDANT all mean using more words than necessary to convey the desired meaning. WORDY, the broadest of these terms, may merely refer to the use of many words but usu. implies that the speech or writing is wearisome or ineffectual: *a wordy review that obscured the main point.* VERBOSE expresses the idea of pompous or bombastic speech or writing that has little substance: *a verbose speech that put everyone to sleep.* PROLIX refers to speech or writing extended to tedious length by the inclusion of inconsequential details: *a prolix style that robs the story of all its excitement.* REDUNDANT refers to unnecessary repetition by using different words or expressions to convey the same idea: *The editor cut four redundant paragraphs from the article.* —**Ant.** concise, terse, succinct, pithy.

work *n.* **1.** labor, effort, industry, exertion, toil, endeavor, drudgery, trouble, manual labor, elbow grease, sweat. **2.** piece of work, job, task, chore, employment, pursuit, assignment. **3.** employment, job, paying job; line of work, occupation, profession, business, vocation, line, métier, trade, craft, calling, pursuit; function, duty, office. **4.** work of art, creation, composition, achievement, performance, handiwork, piece, product, production, endeavor, structure, output; (*variously*) painting, drawing, sculpture, book, opus, symphony, opera, concerto, song, building. **5.** deed, act, achievement, feat; exploit, enterprise, transaction. **6. works** plant, factory, mill, foundry, yard, shop, workshop. **7. works** internal mechanism, moving parts, contents, insides, *Slang* innards. —*v.* **8.** be employed, have a job, be occupied, do business, pursue a vocation; labor, toil, be industrious, exert oneself, apply oneself, endeavor, perform, drudge, slave, sweat, *Informal* use elbow grease, put one's shoulder to the wheel. **9.** operate, function, perform, run, go, act; take effect, be effective, succeed; do, solve, execute, enact, transmit, achieve. **10.** shape, form, fashion, mold, make, manipulate. **11.** make one's way, progress, move, maneuver, win, achieve, gain. **12.** bring about, produce, cause, effect; originate, engender, beget. —*adj.* **13.** for working, of working. —**Syn. Study. 1** WORK, LABOR, TOIL, DRUDGERY refer to exertion of body or mind in performing or accomplishing something. WORK is a general word that refers to exertion that is either easy or hard: *pleasurable work; backbreaking work.* LABOR denotes hard manual work, esp. for wages: *Repairing the bridge will require months of labor.* TOIL suggests wearying or exhausting labor: *The farmer's health was failing from constant toil.* DRUDGERY suggests continuous, dreary, and dispiriting work, esp. of a menial or servile kind: *Cleaning these blinds is sheer drudgery.* —**Ant. 1, 2, 8** play. **1** child's play; ease, leisure. **2** recreation, entertainment, fun; rest, relaxation. **3** unemployment; vacation, leave, retirement; avocation, hobby, leisure-time activity. **8** entertain oneself, have fun, relax, take it easy, vacation. **11** remain, stay put, mark time. **12** nullify, counteract, reverse. **13** leisure, play.

worked *adj.* **—Syn. Study.** See WROUGHT.

worker *n.* workingman, workingwoman, workman, laborer, toiler, laboring man, laboring woman, proletarian; hired hand, hand; employee, job holder, artisan, craftsman, wage earner, breadwinner; doer, performer, producer, achiever, *Slang* hustler, eager beaver; drudge, plodder, grind; workaholic. **—Ant.** employer; unemployed person, retiree; idler, loafer, good-for-nothing, do-nothing, *Slang* goldbrick, deadbeat, bum.

working *n.* **1.** labor, laboring, toil, industry, exertion, drudgery; employment, job, tasks, chores, assignments, business, profession, occupation, duty. **2.** operation, action, functioning, performance. *—adj.* **3.** employed, holding down a job, laboring. **4.** usable, useful, practical, effective, operative, functioning, fluent. **—Ant. 1** play, playing, recreation, fun, entertainment; rest, relaxation, leisure. **3** nonworking, unemployed, jobless; retired, vacationing.

workmanship *n.* craftsmanship, handiwork, manual skill, handicraft, handcraft; construction, manufacture, technique.

world *n.* **1.** the planet Earth, globe, Earth, wide world; planet, orb, heavenly body, celestial object, star. **2.** creation, universe, cosmos, macrocosm; nature. **3.** mankind, humanity, men and women, the human race, humankind, people; the public, everyone, everybody. **4.** group, class, division, system, sphere, domain, realm; profession, industry. **5.** human affairs, society, social intercourse, day-to-day living; material matters, secular things, mundane interests, worldly things. **6.** era, period, epoch, age, times, duration. **7.** a great deal, large amount, *Informal* lots, oodles, gobs, heaps. **—Ant. 5** spiritual matters, aesthetic matters. **7** a little bit.

worldly *adj.* **1.** earthly, terrestrial, mundane, temporal, secular, profane; material, mercenary; physical, corporeal, fleshly. **2.** sophisticated, cosmopolitan, urbane, worldly-wise, blasé, knowing, shrewd, astute, experienced, callous, hard-boiled. **—Syn. Study. 1** See EARTHLY. **—Ant. 1** spiritual, heavenly, celestial, divine, holy, sacred; ethereal, ephemeral, transcendental, nonmaterial. **2** innocent, naive, unsophisticated, artless, ingenuous.

worm *n.* **1.** small legless elongated animal; (*variously*) earthworm, angleworm, inchworm, tapeworm, intestinal worm. *—v.* **2.** creep, crawl, wriggle, writhe, inch, edge, steal, infiltrate, penetrate, advance stealthily. **—Ant. 2** run, dart, sprint, dash.

worn *adj.* **1.** worn through, worn-down, worn-out, frayed, abraded, threadbare, worn to a thread, worse for wear; decrepit, dilapidated, shabby, weather-beaten, battered, tumbledown, rickety, seedy, timeworn; faded, dingy. **2.** exhausted, fatigued, worn-out, weary, wearied, spent, tired, dog-tired, haggard, played out, ready to drop, drooping; weak, enfeebled, wasted, debilitated; pinched, drawn. **—Ant. 1** new, brand-new, spanking new, none the worse for wear. **2** energetic, vigorous, peppy, alive, dynamic, refreshed, restored, rejuvenated.

worrisome *adj.* **1.** causing worry, troublesome, aggravating, annoying, irritating, tormenting, vexing, trying, irksome, bothersome, disturbing, pesky. **2.** tending to worry, anxious, apprehensive, uneasy, despairing, fretful, fussy. **—Ant. 1** soothing, calming, nonirritating. **2** confident, secure; carefree, nonchalant, devil-may-care, lackadaisical.

worry *v.* **1.** be anxious, feel uneasy, be apprehensive, be disturbed, be troubled, be distressed, agonize, fret, despair, lose heart, be downhearted, be heavyhearted, be afraid, dread, brood over, stew. **2.** make anxious, make uneasy, disturb, upset, perturb, agitate, trouble, distress, harass, harry, badger, hector, bother, pester, vex, beset, plague, torment, persecute. *—n.* **3.** anxiety, uneasiness, apprehension, concern, misgiving, consternation, dismay, trouble, distress, bother, grief, anguish, torment, agony, misery, woe, difficulty, care, vexation. **4.** concern, care, problem, dread, bugaboo. **—Syn. Study. 4** See CONCERN. **—Ant. 2** comfort, solace, console, soothe, calm, allay. **3** certainty, assurance, security, trust, certitude; calm, composure, equanimity, serenity, tranquillity, placidity, quiet, peace of mind; comfort, solace.

worsen *v.* decline, deteriorate, slip, go downhill, slide, take a turn for the worse, degenerate, lapse, fail, retrogress, erode, disintegrate, go to pieces. **—Ant.** improve, better, get better, ameliorate.

worship *n.* **1.** adoration, veneration, exaltation, reverence. **2.** divine service, religious service, devotionals. *—v.* **3.** pray to, adore, revere, venerate, reverence; glorify, exalt, praise, extol. **4.** idolize, adore, revere, esteem, admire, adulate, dote upon, lionize, put on a pedestal. **—Ant. 4** hate, detest, loathe, despise, scorn, disdain.

worth *n.* **1.** use, usefulness, utility, benefit, value, good, merit, worthiness, importance, consequence, justification. **2.** value, price, cost, selling price, market price, current price, going price; valuation, appraisal. **3.** assets, wealth, resources, holdings, real property, possessions, effects, estate. **—Syn. Study. 1, 2** See VALUE. **—Ant. 1** uselessness, fruitlessness, futility, worthlessness, inutility; drawback, handicap. **3** debts.

worthless *adj.* without value, useless, unusable, unavailing, unproductive, ineffectual, pointless, fruitless, bootless, futile, meritless, meretricious; unimportant, inconsequential, insignificant, trivial, paltry, piddling, undeserving, of no account, good-for-nothing, not worth a straw. **—Ant.** worthwhile, worthy, valuable, precious, profitable, useful, usable, utilitarian, productive, effective, fruitful; important, consequential, significant.

worthwhile *adj.* valuable, worthy, profitable, rewarding, useful, usable, beneficial, good; worth one's time, worth the effort. **—Ant.** worthless, unworthy, useless, pointless, valueless, time-consuming, unimportant, inconsequential, trivial, of no account.

worthy *adj.* **1.** worthwhile, deserving, praiseworthy, laudable, commendable, admirable, estimable, excellent, good, meritorious, suitable, fit, fitting, befitting, appropriate, proper, creditable, honorable, virtuous, moral, ethical, reputable, upright, decent, respectable, noble, honest, reliable, trustworthy. *—n.* **2.** notable, dignitary, leader, official, person of distinction, great man, great woman, personage, name, immortal, luminary, a somebody, pillar of society, *Slang* VIP, bigwig, big shot, big wheel. **—Ant. 1** unworthy, worthless, undeserving, useless, unproductive, ineffectual; dishonorable, disreputable, ignoble, dishonest, unethical, unreliable, untrustworthy, *Slang* no-account. **2** member of the rank and file, nobody, anonym, anonymity, one of the little people, obscure person, obscurity; everyman; Tom, Dick, and Harry, *Slang* Joe Blow.

wound *n.* **1.** laceration, gash, cut, slit, lesion; contusion, bruise. **2.** hurt feelings, trauma, provocation, irritation, vexation, pain, sting, distress, affliction, anguish, torment; hurt, injury, damage. *—v.* **3.** lacerate, gash, cut, slash, tear, pierce, bruise; hurt, injure. **4.** hurt the feelings of, offend, pain, sting, distress, grieve, mortify, torment; harm, damage, hurt, injure. **—Ant. 3, 4** heal. **4** appease, assuage, calm, soothe, comfort.

wraith *n.* ghost, spirit, shade, specter, apparition, doppelganger, phantom, phantasm, banshee, spook, materialization, revenant.

wrap *v.* **1.** wrap up, enclose, enwrap, bundle, encase; bind, wind, fold. **2.** clothe, cover, envelop, enclose, swathe, enfold, surround, girdle, gird, shroud, cloak, veil, mask, hide, conceal. *—n.* **3.** (*variously*) shawl, cloak, cape, stole, mantle, wrapper, scarf; sweater, jacket, coat. **—Ant. 1** unwrap, unbundle; unbind, unwind, undo. **2** uncover, expose, reveal, open.

wrapper Also **wrapping** *n.* paper wrapping, envelope; covering, case, slipcase, casing, sheath, jacket, container.

wrath *n.* anger, rage, fury, vexation, irritableness; ire, indignation, rancor, resentment, hostility, animosity, animus, irritation, displeasure, spleen, choler, gall, bile. **—Ant.** appeasement, calm; kindness, friendship, geniality, affability, tenderness, forgiveness.

wreak *v.* inflict, visit, work, execute; retaliate with, vent, indulge, give full rein to, unleash.

wreath *n.* garland, laurel, lei, festoon; coronet, crown, chaplet, diadem.

wreck *v.* **1.** ruin, destroy, demolish, level, raze, smash, shatter, break, break to pieces, devastate, ravage, *Slang* total. *—n.* **2.** dilapidated structure, ruin, mess; sick person, ailing person, debilitated person; derelict, wretch. **3.** shipwrecked vessel, stranded ship, derelict, damaged remains, ruins. **4.** ruin, destruction, devastation, undoing, dissolution, disruption, overthrow, upset, breakup, crash, crack-up; end, death, finish, annihilation. **—Ant. 1** build, create, construct; save, salvage, preserve, conserve, protect. **4** formation, formulation, creation; preservation, salvage, saving, conservation, protection.

wrench *v.* **1.** twist, wrest, wring, force, pull, jerk, tear, rip. **2.** twist painfully, sprain, strain. **3.** distort, twist, warp, put in a false light, pervert, misrepresent. *—n.* **4.** (*variously*) monkey wrench, socket wrench, *British* spanner. **5.** twist, wring, jerk, pull; tear, rip. **6.** sprain, strain, painful twist.

wrest *v.* **1.** wrench, twist, wring, take, grab, pull, jerk, tear, rip, force. **2.** obtain, get, gain, attain, achieve, secure, earn, make, glean, extract, squeeze. **—Ant. 2** yield, give, furnish, supply.

wrestle *v.* **1.** engage in wrestling; tussle, scuffle, grapple. **2.** grapple, strive, contend, struggle, tussle, labor, toil, battle, attempt to find a solution.

wretch *n.* **1.** unfortunate, miserable being, unhappy person, sufferer; outcast, castoff, misfit, homeless person, vagabond, hobo, tramp, derelict, waif. **2.** contemptible person, vile fellow, villain, scoundrel, rotter, worm, blackguard, rascal, rogue, knave, scalawag, varlet, swine, pig, cur; *Slang* louse, rat, stinker.

wretched *adj.* **1.** pitiable, pitiful, unfortunate; pathetic, miserable, unhappy, hapless, woebegone, forlorn, downcast, doleful, cheerless, crestfallen, despondent, disheartened, depressed, dejected, abject, brokenhearted, inconsolable, disconsolate, crushed, melancholy, sorrowful, gloomy, worried, low-spirited, despairing, hopeless, sick at heart. **2.** contemptible, despicable, mean, miserable, vile, low, base, niggardly; inferior, worthless, sorry, awful, terrible, dreadful, rotten, abominable, shabby, sleazy, *Informal* lousy. **—Syn. Study. 1, 2** See MISERABLE. **—Ant. 1** fortunate, enviable, prosperous, flourishing, successful, thriving; happy, cheerful, gay, carefree, lighthearted, jovial. **2** noble, admirable, excellent, good, wonderful, fine, great, worthy.

wring *v.* **1.** twist, force by twisting; squeeze, press, compress, choke. **2.** force, coerce, wrest, wrench, extract. **3.** affect sorrowfully, sadden, grieve, distress, agonize, rend, pain, hurt, torture, pierce, stab. **—Ant. 2** coax, wheedle, cajole, entice, beguile, inveigle, charm. **3** gladden, fill with joy, cheer, uplift.

wrinkle[1] *n.* **1.** crease, rimple, crinkle, crimp, pucker, furrow, crumple, corrugation, fold, gather, pleat; crow's-feet. *—v.* **2.** crease, rumple, crinkle, crumple, pucker, crimp, furrow, fold, gather, pleat.

wrinkle[2] *n.* trick, device, gimmick; idea, notion, fancy; viewpoint, point of view, slant.

writ *n.* court order, mandatory order, sealed order.

write *v.* **1.** be literate; set down, write down, jot down, record, put on paper, put in writing, put in black and white, scribble, scrawl, take pen in hand; transcribe, copy; inscribe. **2.** compose, produce, turn out, dash off, *Informal* author, pen. **3.** draw up, draft, make out. **4.** be evident, be manifest, be conspicuous, be apparent, be patient, show, stand out, be visible. **—Ant. 1** be illiterate; say, speak, tell. **4** hide, conceal, mask, cloak, veil.

writer *n.* **1.** letter writer; penman, calligrapher, scribe, copyist, scribbler, scrawler. **2.** author, professional writer; (*variously*) novelist, playwright, dramatist, poet, essayist, littérateur, reporter, journalist, newspaperman, newspaperwoman, correspondent, reviewer, critic, columnist, scriptwriter, screenwriter, television writer, songwriter, librettist, *Informal* hack, penny-a-liner. **—Ant. 2** reader; viewer; listener.

writhe *v.* twist about, flail, thresh, thrash, jerk, contort, toss about, squirm, wiggle, wriggle.

writing *n.* **1.** writing down, jotting down, putting on paper, composing, drafting, turning out, dashing off, *Informal* authoring, penning; transcribing, recording, copying, inscribing. **2.** written form, print, handwriting, penmanship, longhand, calligraphy. **3.** (*variously*) document, letter, diary, journal, composition, publication, book, work, volume, tome, opus, novel, play, story, poem, essay, article, report, editorial, column, critique, manuscript, script, libretto. **—Ant. 1, 3** reading; speech, talk, address.

wrong *adj.* **1.** immoral, evil, wicked, sinful, bad, iniquitous, wrongful, dishonest, unethical, dishonorable; unlawful, illegal, illicit, felonious, crooked, criminal, unfair, unjust; unwarranted, unjustifiable, inexcusable, blameworthy, reprehensible. **2.** incorrect, erroneous, untrue, false, inaccurate, mistaken, faulty, fallacious, inexact, wide of the mark; illogical, unsound. **3.** improper, incorrect, unsuitable, inappropriate, undesirable, unbecoming, unseemly, unfitting, unfit, unbefitting, indecorous, inapt, unhappy, infelicitous, incongruous, malapropos; indelicate, immodest. **4.** faulty, amiss, out of order, in bad condition, out of kilter, out of gear, awry; ruined, *Slang* kaput. **5.** inverse, reverse, opposite. *—n.* **6.** immorality, evil, wickedness, sinfulness, iniquity, unrighteousness, dishonesty, unlawfulness, illegality, unfairness, injustice; immoral act, evil deed, sin, vice, offense, crime, misdeed, wrongdoing, injury, villainy, transgression, trespass. *—adv.* **7.** incorrectly, erroneously, inaccurately, mistakenly. *—v.* **8.** ill-treat, mistreat, maltreat, treat unjustly, treat unfairly, abuse, dishonor, harm, injure, hurt, ruin; cheat, defraud, bilk, swindle, fleece; impose upon, encroach upon. **—Ant. 1–3, 5–7** right. **1** moral, virtuous, righteous, rightful, godly, good, honest, ethical, highminded, honorable, lawful, legal, just, fair; admirable, commendable, praiseworthy, worthy, meritorious, laudable. **2** correct, true, accurate, exact, precise, perfect; logical, sound, sensible. **3** proper, correct, suitable, appropriate, becoming, seemly, fit, fitting, befitting, meet, happy, felicitous. **6** morality, righteousness, goodness, godliness, honesty, highmindedness, lawfulness, legality, justice, fairness; virtue, good deed. **7** correctly, accurately, truly, exactly, precisely.

wrongdoer *n.* malefactor, perpetrator,

miscreant, knave, evildoer, villain, culprit, felon, lawbreaker, transgressor, sinner, scoundrel, blackguard, trespasser, offender, rogue, rascal.

wrought *adj.* **1.** worked, formed, made, fashioned, crafted, handcrafted, constructed. **2.** hammered, beaten. **—Syn. Study. 1** WROUGHT, WORKED both apply to something on which effort has been applied. WROUGHT implies fashioning, molding, or making, esp. of metals: *wrought iron.* WORKED implies expended effort of almost any kind: *a worked silver mine.*

wry *adj.* **1.** twisted, crooked, contorted, distorted, askew, awry, warped. **2.** ironic, cynical, sarcastic, caustic, sardonic, satiric, bitter, perverse; amusing, droll, dry. **—Ant. 1** straight, direct, symmetrical.

x-ray *n.* roentgenogram, roentgenograph, radiogram, radiograph; picture.

yank *v.* **1.** pull suddenly, jerk, wrest, tug, snatch, wrench; pull out, pluck, extract, draw out. **—***n.* **2.** pull, jerk, tug, wrench. **—Ant. 1, 2** push, shove.

Yankee, Yank *n.* **1.** New Englander. **2.** Northerner, damn Yankee, *Historical* Union soldier. **3.** US citizen, US serviceman, *Historical* doughboy, teddy, GI, American, *Spanish* yanqui; (*disparagingly*) gringo.

yap *v.* **1.** bark shrilly, yelp, yip, yawp. **2.** talk incessantly, talk foolishly, chatter, jabber, gabble, babble, blather, prattle, rave, rave on, gush, blab, gossip, tattle; talk, lecture, scold, complain; converse, palaver. **—***n.* **3.** shrill bark, yelp, yip, yawp.

yard[1] *n.* ground surrounding a building, grounds; enclosure, compound, confine, close; courtyard, court; garden, lawn, pasture.

yard[2] *n.* **1.** three feet, 36 inches, .914 meter; *Abbreviation* yd. **2.** yardarm, horizontal spar.

yarn *n.* **1.** spun thread, knitting thread, weaving thread. **2.** tale, story, anecdote, adventure story, narrative, account, adventure, experience.

year *n.* **1.** period of 365 days (or in leap year 366 days), 12-month period, 52-week period, period of Earth's revolution around the sun. **2.** period of planet's revolution around the sun. **3. years** age, time of life. **4. years** period, time, era, epoch, cycle.

yearn *v.* crave, have a strong desire, want, long, hanker, ache, hunger, thirst, wish, covet; languish, pine, sigh, have a fancy for, set one's heart upon, be bent upon, have a passion for, have a yen for. **—Syn. Study.** YEARN, LONG, HANKER, PINE all mean to feel a strong desire for something. YEARN stresses the depth and power of the desire: *to yearn to begin a new life.* LONG implies a wholehearted desire for something that is or seems unattainable: *to long to relive one's childhood.* HANKER suggests a restless or incessant craving: *to hanker after fame and fortune.* PINE adds the notion of physical or emotional suffering due to the real or apparent hopelessness of one's desire: *to pine for a lost love.* **—Ant.** detest, despise, hate, loathe, abhor, abominate, be repelled by, recoil from, be revolted by, shudder at.

yearning *n.* craving, longing, hankering, yen, hunger, thirst, ache, strong desire, fancy, wish, want, desire, passion, aspiration, inclination. **—Syn. Study.** See DESIRE.

yell *v.* **1.** cry out, shout, holler, scream, bellow, roar, howl, shriek, bawl, whoop, yowl, hollo, hoot, screech, squall, yelp, clamor, rend the air, raise one's voice; cheer, hurrah, huzzah; boo. **—***n.* **2.** cry, outcry, shout, holler, scream, bellow, roar, howl, shriek, whoop, hoot, screech, squeal, yelp, hollo, clamor; cheer, hurrah, huzzah; boo.

yellow *adj.* **1.** yellow-colored, lemon, canary, gold, ocher, mustard-yellow, saffron, yellow-orange, flaxen, straw-colored, blond. **2.** cowardly, timorous, pusillanimous, craven, fainthearted, afraid, fearful, apprehensive, frightened, *Slang* chicken, lily-livered, chicken-hearted. **—***v.* **3.** turn yellow; make yellow. **—Ant. 2** brave, courageous, fearless, bold, daring, audacious, venturesome, unafraid, stouthearted, lionhearted, *Slang* game. **3** bleach, whiten, brighten.

yelp *n.* **1.** sharp cry, yap, howl, yip, bark, squeal. **—***v.* **2.** cry shrilly, scream, shriek, screech, bark, squeal, clamor, holler, shout; yap, yip, howl.

yen *n.* **1.** craving, longing, hankering, yearning, hunger, thirst, appetite, aching, desire, fancy, wish, want, passion, aspiration, inclination, relish. **—***v.* **2.** crave, long, hanker, yearn, ache, hunger, thirst, wish, pine, sigh, languish, desire, fancy, wish, want, set one's heart upon, be bent upon, have a passion for. **—Ant. 1** hatred, loathing, abhorrence, revulsion. **2** detest, despise, hate, loathe, abhor, abominate, be repelled by, recoil from, be revolted by, shudder at.

yes *adv.* **1.** aye, yea, it is so, just so, true, granted, of course, surely, really, truly, verily, to be sure, assuredly, certainly, indeed, emphatically, no doubt, undoubtedly, doubtless, positively, precisely, exactly, so be it, amen; affirmatively, in the affirmative. **—***n.* **2.** affirmative reply, affirmative vote, affirmation, consent, assent, okay, acquiescence, acceptance, agreement, authorization, approval. **—Ant. 1, 2** no, nay. **1** not so, untrue, wrong, false, of course not, no indeed, doubtfully, negatively, in the negative. **2** refusal, rejection, veto, disapproval.

yesterday *adv.* **1.** on the day preceding today. **—***n.* **2.** the day before today; yestermorn, yestereve. **3.** the recent past, bygone days, former times, the past, yesteryear, the good old days, days of yore, time gone by, olden times. **—Ant. 1, 2** tomorrow.

yield *v.* **1.** bear, bring forth, produce, give forth, put forth; give birth to, beget, spawn, procreate, generate. **2.** earn, return, generate, pay, provide, furnish, supply, render, give. **3.** submit, surrender, give up, give in, give way, capitulate, succumb, accede, acquiesce, resign oneself, truckle, bow down, kowtow, cave in, cry uncle, say uncle. **4.** relinquish, grant, concede, give up, give, give away, defer, forgo, waive, renounce, forbear. **5.** give way, sag, droop, cave in, collapse, break, split, burst. **—***n.* **6.** harvest, crop, gleanings; produce, product. **7.** interest, return, earnings, proceeds, gain, payment, revenue, premium. **—Syn. Study. 3** YIELD, SUBMIT, SURRENDER mean to give way or give up to a person or thing. To YIELD is to relinquish or concede under some degree of pressure, either from a position of weakness or from one of advantage: *to yield ground to an enemy; to yield the right of way.* To SUBMIT is to give up more completely to authority or superior force and to cease opposition, usu. with reluctance: *The mutineers finally submitted to the captain's orders.* To SURRENDER is to give up complete possession of and claim to, usu. after resistance: *to surrender a fortress; to surrender one's rights.* **—Ant. 3** resist, oppose, combat, counterattack, attack; repulse, repel. **4** keep, retain, maintain, reserve, hold on to; appropriate, take, seize, grab, arrogate, claim.

yoke *n.* **1.** double harness, coupler, collar, bond, clasp. **2.** pair, team, brace, couple, span. **3.** bondage, slavery, enslavement, servitude; serfdom, vassalage, thralldom. **4.** burden, weight, oppression, load, strain, pressure, tax, troubles, distress, trial, tribulation. **—***v.* **5.** couple, double harness; hitch, harness. **6.** join, unite, couple, link, attach, fasten. **—Ant. 3** freedom, liberty, independence. **4** joy, pleasure, delight, enjoyment, comfort, satisfaction. **5** unyoke, uncouple, unhitch, unharness. **6** separate, divide, divorce.

yokel *n.* bumpkin, country bumpkin, naive rustic, rube, provincial, clod, clodhopper, hayseed, peasant, plowboy, hick, country boy.

yolk *n.* egg yolk, yellow. **—Ant.** white, albumen.

yonder *adj.* **1.** more distant, farther, thither, yon, far-off. **—***adv.* **2.** faraway, far-off, over the hills and faraway, over the horizon; over there, there, thither. **—Ant. 1** near, nearer, closer; nearby, close, at hand. **2** nearby, near here, close-by; over here, here.

young *adj.* **1.** youthful, not old; younger, junior, juvenile, infantile, underage, minor, childish, boyish, girlish, puerile, adolescent, beardless, teenage; immature, wet behind the ears, inexperienced, undeveloped, callow, sophomoric; growing, budding. **—***n.* **2.** young persons, young people, children, juveniles, youngsters, kids, youths, teenagers, adolescents. **3.** baby, child, cub, pup, whelp, kitten; offspring, issue, progeny, descendant. **—Ant. 1, 2** old, aged. **1** elderly, older, elder, senior, gray, hoary, old-mannish, old-womanish, ancient, venerable; adult, mature, grown-up, experienced, ripe, fully developed, full-grown. **2** the old, senior citizens, oldsters, old-timers; adults, grown-ups. **3** parent, progenitor.

youngster *n.* child, boy, girl, youth, kid, young person, fledgling, minor, adolescent, juvenile, teenager; offspring, progeny, tot, baby. **—Ant.** oldster, old-timer, senior citizen; adult, grownup.

youth *n.* **1.** early life, childhood, boyhood, girlhood, adolescence, growing years, teens, pubescence, juvenile period, minority, school days, salad days, younger days, springtime of life, prime, bloom, heyday; youthful condition, youthful appearance. **2.** boy, schoolboy, lad, youngster, child, kid, juvenile, minor, teenager, adolescent, young man, stripling, young shaver, fledgling. **3.** young persons, young people, the young, children, boys and girls, youngsters, kids, juveniles, teenagers, adolescents, the rising generation, young men and women. **—Ant. 1** old age, later life; adulthood, maturity. **2** man, old man, old coot, codger; adult. **3** senior citizens, oldsters, old-timers; adults, grownups.

youthful *adj.* young, juvenile, adolescent, teenage; childish, boyish, girlish, puerile, immature, inexperienced, callow, sophomoric; of the young, for the young; young-looking, enthusiastic, fresh, lighthearted, bright-eyed, starry-eyed, having young attitudes, young at heart. **—Ant.** old, aged, elderly, older, senior, hoary; adult, mature, grown-up, full-grown, experienced; old-mannish, old-womanish, old-looking, old-fashioned; senile, decrepit.

yowl *v.* **1.** howl, bay, caterwaul, yelp, scream, shriek, screech, squeal, bawl, whine. **—***n.* **2.** howl, wail, yelp, cry, shout, holler, bellow, roar, scream, shriek, screech, squeal, whine, bawl, caterwaul.

yule *n.* Christmas season, Christmas, Christmastide, Noel, yuletide; the feast of Christmas.

zany *adj.* **1.** clownish, outlandish, foolishly comical, silly, inane, nonsensical, ludicrous, slapstick, daffy, dizzy, crazy, wild; *Slang* nutty, goofy, wacky, screwy, batty, balmy. —*n.* **2.** clown, buffoon, jester, comic, cutup; harlequin, buffo, pantaloon, farceur. **3.** daffy person, dizzy person, eccentric, lunatic, *Slang* nut, crazy, weirdo; nitwit, half-wit, imbecile, noodlehead, blockhead, bonehead, nincompoop, numskull, simpleton, booby, lunkhead. **—Ant. 1** droll, ironic, sarcastic, wry, dry.

zeal *n.* zest, gusto, relish, eagerness, fervor, ardor, industry, enthusiasm, animation, vigor, verve, fierceness, intensity, earnestness, intentness, vehemence, fire, passion, devotion, fanaticism. **—Ant.** apathy, indifference, impassivity, nonchalance, coolness, torpor, languor, listlessness.

zealot *n.* **1.** believer, enthusiast, partisan, champion, devotee, fan, buff; go-getter, pusher, hustler, live wire, eager beaver. **2.** fanatic, true believer, obsessed person, bigot, extremist, crank, crackpot, *Slang* nut, freak. **—Syn. Study. 1, 2** See FANATIC.

zealous *adj.* full of zeal, eager, fervent, fervid, vigorous, ardent, earnest, enthusiastic, gung ho, animated, intense, fierce, vehement, passionate, impassioned, devoted, industrious; fanatic, rabid, raging, raving. **—Ant.** apathetic, languorous, torpid, listless, unenthusiastic, dispassionate, passionless, indifferent, lackluster, lackadaisical, nonchalant, dull, calm, cool, quiet, low-key.

zenith *n.* **1.** point in the sky directly overhead; twelve o'clock high. **2.** peak, highest point, high point, crowning point, pinnacle, acme, summit, apex, vertex, apogee, maximum, best, culmination, culminating point, climax. **—Ant. 1, 2** nadir. **2** lowest point, low point, depth, minimum, worst.

zephyr *n.* light breeze, gentle wind, breath of air, puff of air; west wind. **—Syn. Study.** See WIND. **—Ant.** gust, blast, gale, squall, blow, windstorm, tornado; east wind.

zero *n.* **1.** nothing, nothingness, naught, aught, cipher, *Slang* goose egg, zilch, zip; *symbol* 0. **2.** the lowest positive point on a scale, zero degrees; lowest point, nadir. —*adj.* **3.** amounting to zero, nil, nonexistent, no, naught, aught, *Slang* zilch, zip. **—Ant. 1** infinity; something, everything. **2** zenith, highest point. **3** perfect, excellent.

zest *n.* **1.** keen enjoyment, gusto, relish, appetite, zeal, eagerness, enthusiasm, verve, passion; exhilaration, excitement, thrill, delight, joy, pleasure, satisfaction. **2.** flavoring, flavor, savor, taste, tang, zing, zip, piquancy, seasoning; spice, salt. **—Ant. 1** apathy, weariness, dullness, distaste, disrelish, displeasure, aversion, abhorrence, repugnance, loathing.

Zion *n.* **1.** City of David, hill in Jerusalem on which the Temple was built; ancient Israel; the Jewish people. **2.** community under God's protection, godly community, city of God, utopia.

zip *n.* **1.** hiss, whine, whistle, buzz. **2.** energy, vim, vigor, pep, dash, verve, animation, vivacity, liveliness, life, vitality, spirit, effervescence, exuberance, zest, gusto, enthusiasm; power, drive, force, strength, intensity, punch, impact. —*v.* **3.** run, go quickly, dash, dart, streak, rush, hurry, speed, fly. **4.** zip up, zipper, fasten with a zipper, close. **—Ant. 2** lethargy, torpor, languor, sluggishness, lassitude, apathy, listlessness, coolness; dullness, weakness. **3** creep, crawl, inch. **4** unzip.

zone *n.* **1.** region, territory, area, terrain, belt; district, quarter, precinct, ward, sector, section, locality, location, tract. —*v.* **2.** divide into zones, designate as a zone.

zoo *n.* zoological garden, zoological park, animal farm; menagerie, vivarium.

zoom *v.* **1.** speed, race, streak, flash, buzz, zip, shoot, fly. **2.** rise, climb, soar, advance, skyrocket, rocket, ascend, take off.